Occupational Outlook Handbook

2014–2015

U.S Department of Labor
Thomas E. Perez, Secretary

Bureau of Labor Statistics
Erica L. Groshen, Commissioner

Bulletin 2700

The following bonus chapters are exclusive to JIST Publishing's *OOH*

Introduction

The *Occupational Outlook Handbook (OOH)* is a nationally recognized source of career information, designed to provide valuable assistance to individuals making decisions about their future work lives. Revised every two years, the *OOH* describes what workers do on the job, working conditions, the training and education needed, earnings, and expected job prospects in a wide range of occupations.

Employment in the hundreds of occupations discussed in detail in the 2014–2015 *OOH* accounts for nine of every ten jobs in the economy. Combined with the updated special features of the *OOH*, the occupational information presented in this new edition provides invaluable assistance to individuals making decisions about their future work lives.

3 1336 09439 1472

JIST
PUBLISHING

St. Paul

Director of Editorial: Christine Hurney
Director of Production: Timothy W. Larson
Senior Production Editor: Lori Michelle Ryan
Cover Designer: Sara Schmidt Boldon
Senior Design and Production Specialist: Jack Ross
Design and Production Specialist: Tammy Norstrem
Copy Editor/Proofreader: Nancy Reinhardt
Product Manager: Becky Wagner
Contributing Editor: Laurence Shatkin, Ph.D.

JIST Publishing's materials encourage people to be self-directed and to take control of their destinies. We work hard to provide excellent content, solid advice, current labor market information, and techniques that get results. Visit www.jist.com for free job search information, tables of contents, sample pages, and ordering information on our many products.

Minor differences exist between this edition and the Web-based *Occupational Outlook Handbook (OOH)*, as released by the U.S. Department of Labor in January 2014. Most of these differences occur in the photographic images. JIST Publishing has also added useful bonus content to this edition.

Photo Credits: 85 © William C. Haneberg, Ph.D., courtesy of GeoTek Solutions; *178* © Dawn Arlotta, courtesy of the Centers for Disease Control and Prevention; *203* © Maggie Bartlett, courtesy of the National Human Genome Research Institute (www.genome.gov); *222* Courtesy of the Centers for Disease Control and Prevention; *388* Courtesy of the Centers for Disease Control and Prevention; *409* Courtesy of the Department of Nurse Anesthesia Education, University of Kansas; *412* © Rhoda Baer, courtesy of the National Cancer Institute (www.cancer.gov); *422* © Amanda Mills, courtesy of the Centers for Disease Control and Prevention; *439* Courtesy of the U.S. Department of Veterans Affairs; *454* © Mathews Media Group, courtesy of the National Cancer Institute (www.cancer.gov); *513* Courtesy of Ardus Medical, Inc.; *544* Courtesy of the Kentucky Archaeological Survey; *567* © Ron Nichols, courtesy of the USDA Natural Resources Conservation Service; *576* © Airman 1st Class Melissa Rodrigues, courtesy of the United States Air Force Office of Special Investigations; *593* © Scott Bauer, courtesy of the U.S. Department of Agriculture, Agricultural Research Service; *596* Courtesy of the Centers for Disease Control and Prevention; *619* Courtesy of the National Parks Service; *641* © Jocelyn Augustino, courtesy of the Federal Emergency Management Administration; *715* © Jocelyn Augustino, courtesy of the Federal Emergency Management Administration; *792* © Mo Riza, www.flickr.com/photos/moriza/62054214/sizes/l.

Important Note

Many trade associations, professional societies, unions, industrial organizations, and government agencies provide career information that is valuable to counselors and job seekers. For the convenience of *OOH* users, some of these organizations and, in many cases, their Internet addresses are listed at the end of each occupational statement. Although these references were carefully compiled, the Bureau of Labor Statistics has neither authority nor facilities for investigating the organizations or the information or publications that may be sent in response to a request and cannot guarantee the accuracy of such information. The listing of an organization, therefore, does not constitute in any way an endorsement or recommendation by the Bureau either of the organization and its activities or of the information it may supply. Each organization has sole responsibility for whatever information it may issue.

The *OOH* describes the job outlook over a projected ten-year period for occupations across the nation; consequently, short-term labor market fluctuations and regional differences in job outlook generally are not discussed. Similarly, the *OOH* provides a general, composite description of jobs and cannot be expected to reflect work situations in specific establishments or localities. Therefore, the *OOH* is not intended and should never be used for any legal purpose. For example, the *OOH* should not be used as a guide for determining wages, hours of work, the right of a particular union to represent workers, appropriate bargaining units, or formal job evaluation systems. Nor should earnings data in the *OOH* be used to compute future loss of earnings in adjudication proceedings involving work injuries or accidental deaths.

Except for the three exclusive chapters by JIST Publishing and some of the photographs (as noted above), material in this publication is in the public domain and, with appropriate credit, may be reproduced without permission. Comments about the contents of this publication and suggestions for improving it are welcome. Please address them to Chief, Division of Occupational Outlook, Office of Occupational Statistics and Employment Projections, Bureau of Labor Statistics, U.S. Department of Labor, 2 Massachusetts Ave. NE, Room 2135, Washington, DC 20212. Phone: (202) 691-5700. Fax: (202) 691-5745. Email: oohinfo@bls.gov. Information in the *OOH* is available to sensory-impaired individuals upon request. Voice phone: (202) 691-5200; Federal Relay Service: (800) 877-8339.

ISBN 978-1-59357-988-3 (softcover)
ISBN 978-1-59357-987-6 (hardcover)

© 2015 by JIST Publishing, Inc.
875 Montreal Way
St. Paul, MN 55102
Email: info@jist.com
Website: www.jist.com

Printed in the United States of America

23 22 21 20 19 18 17 16 15 14   1 2 3 4 5 6 7 8 9 10

Contents

The Personality-Career Quiz: Match Your Personality to Jobs

With so many occupations to choose from, you might appreciate some help narrowing down your options. That's what this chapter is for. In the following pages, you'll gain some insights into the work-related aspects of your personality and learn which careers in the *Occupational Outlook Handbook (OOH)* best suit your personality. Of course, personality is not the only factor you should consider when you make a career choice, but it's a good place to start because it provides a big-picture view of the world of work.

In the early 1950s, John L. Holland developed the most widely used personality theory about careers. The theory says that people tend to be happier and more successful in jobs in which they feel comfortable with the work tasks, the physical environment, and their coworkers. Holland identified six personality types that describe basic aspects of work situations:

- Realistic
- Investigative
- Artistic
- Social
- Enterprising
- Conventional

The initials spell RIASEC, so that acronym is often used to refer to the personality types.

Holland argued that most people can be described by one of the RIASEC personality types—and that likewise each of the various occupations that make up our economy can be described as having work situations and settings compatible with one of these personality types. Therefore, if you understand your dominant personality type, jobs consistent with that type will suit you best.

Holland recognized that many people and jobs also tend toward a second or third personality type—for example, someone might be described primarily as Social and secondarily as Enterprising. That person would fit best in a job with the "SE" code, such as Health Educators. People like this should also consider jobs coded "ES," and they might find satisfaction in many jobs with a variety of Holland codes beginning with either S or E.

This exercise helps you clarify your main personality type or types. Keep in mind that personality measurement is not an exact science and this checklist is not scientific. Use common sense to combine your results with other information about yourself and your work options.

The exercise is easy—just follow the directions. This is not a test, so there are no right or wrong answers and no time limit.

If someone else will be using this book, write your responses on a separate sheet of paper.

Step 1: Respond to the Statements

Carefully read each work activity (items 1 through 120). If you think you would LIKE to do the activity, circle the number of the activity. Don't consider whether you have the education or training needed for it or how much money you might earn if it were part of your job. Simply decide whether you would *like* the activity. If you know you would dislike the activity or you're not sure, leave the number unmarked.

After you respond to all 120 activities, score your responses in Step 2.

Circle the numbers of the activities you would LIKE to do.

1. Build kitchen cabinets

2. Guard money in an armored car

3. Operate a dairy farm

4. Lay brick or tile

5. Monitor a machine on an assembly line

6. Repair household appliances

7. Drive a taxicab

8. Assemble electronic parts

9. Drive a truck to deliver packages to offices and homes

10. Paint houses

11. Enforce fish and game laws

12. Work on an offshore oil-drilling rig

13. Perform lawn care services

14. Catch fish as a member of a fishing crew

15. Refinish furniture

16. Fix a broken faucet

17. Do cleaning or maintenance work

18. Test the quality of parts before shipment

19. Operate a motorboat to carry passengers

20. Put out forest fires

_____ **Total Score for R**

Circle the numbers of the activities you would LIKE to do.

1. Study the history of past civilizations
2. Study animal behavior
3. Develop a new medicine
4. Study ways to reduce water pollution
5. Determine the infection rate of a new disease
6. Study rocks and minerals
7. Diagnose and treat sick animals
8. Study the personalities of world leaders
9. Study whales and other types of marine life
10. Investigate crimes
11. Study the movement of planets
12. Examine blood samples by using a microscope
13. Investigate the cause of a fire
14. Develop psychological profiles of criminals
15. Invent a replacement for sugar
16. Study genetics
17. Study the governments of different countries
18. Do research on plants or animals
19. Do laboratory tests to identify diseases
20. Study weather conditions

_____ **Total Score for I**

1. Direct a play
2. Create dance routines for a show
3. Write books or plays
4. Play a musical instrument
5. Write reviews of books or plays
6. Compose or arrange music
7. Act in a movie
8. Dance in a Broadway show
9. Draw pictures
10. Create special effects for movies
11. Conduct a musical choir
12. Audition singers and musicians for a musical show
13. Design sets for plays
14. Announce a radio show
15. Write a song
16. Perform jazz or tap dance
17. Direct a movie
18. Sing in a band
19. Design artwork for magazines
20. Pose for a photographer

_____ **Total Score for A**

Circle the numbers of the activities you would LIKE to do.

1. Perform nursing duties in a hospital
2. Give CPR to someone who has stopped breathing
3. Help people with personal or emotional problems
4. Teach children how to read
5. Work with children with developmental disabilities
6. Teach an elementary school class
7. Give career guidance to people
8. Supervise the activities of children at a camp
9. Help people with family-related problems
10. Perform rehabilitation therapy
11. Help elderly people with their daily activities
12. Teach children how to play sports
13. Teach sign language to people with hearing disabilities
14. Help people who have problems with drugs or alcohol
15. Help families care for ill relatives
16. Provide massage therapy to people
17. Plan exercises for disabled students
18. Organize activities at a recreational facility
19. Take care of children at a day-care center
20. Teach a high school class

_____ **Total Score for S**

1. Buy and sell stocks and bonds
2. Manage a retail store
3. Operate a beauty salon or barbershop
4. Sell merchandise over the telephone
5. Run a stand that sells newspapers and magazines
6. Give a presentation about a product you are selling
7. Sell furniture at a home furnishings store
8. Manage the operations of a hotel
9. Sell houses
10. Manage a supermarket
11. Sell a soft drink product line to stores and restaurants
12. Sell refreshments at a movie theater
13. Sell hair-care products to stores and salons
14. Start your own business
15. Negotiate business contracts
16. Represent a client in a lawsuit
17. Negotiate contracts for professional athletes
18. Market a new line of clothing
19. Sell automobiles
20. Sell computer equipment in a store

_____ **Total Score for E**

Circle the numbers of the activities you would LIKE to do.

1. Develop a spreadsheet using computer software

2. Proofread records or forms

3. Use a computer program to generate customer bills

4. Schedule conferences for an organization

5. Keep accounts payable/receivable for an office

6. Load computer software into a large computer network

7. Organize and schedule office meetings

8. Use a word processor to edit and format documents

9. Direct or transfer phone calls for a large organization

10. Perform office filing tasks

11. Compute and record statistical and other numerical data

12. Take notes during a meeting

13. Calculate the wages of employees

14. Assist senior-level accountants in performing bookkeeping tasks

15. Inventory supplies by using a hand-held computer

16. Keep records of financial transactions for an organization

17. Record information from customers applying for charge accounts

18. Photocopy letters and reports

19. Stamp, sort, and distribute mail for an organization

20. Handle customers' bank transactions

_____ **Total Score for C**

Step 2: Score Your Responses

Here's how to score your responses:

1. **Score the responses in each column.** In each column of responses, go from top to bottom and count how many numbers are circled. Then write that total on the "Total Score" line at the bottom of the column. Calculate the totals for each of the remaining columns.

2. **Determine your primary interest area.** Which Total Score is your highest: R, I, A, S, E, or C? Enter the letter for that personality type on the following line.

My Primary Personality Type: _____

You will use your Primary Personality Type *first* to explore careers. (If two Total Scores are tied for the highest score or are within 4 points of each other, use both of them for your Primary Personality Type. You are equally divided between two types.)

R = Realistic. Realistic personalities like work activities that include practical, hands-on problems and solutions. They enjoy dealing with plants and animals and real-world materials such as wood, tools, and machinery. They enjoy outside work. Often they do not like occupations that mainly involve doing paperwork or working closely with others.

I = Investigative. Investigative personalities like work activities that have to do with ideas and thinking more than with physical activity. They like to search for facts and figure out problems mentally rather than persuade or lead people.

A = Artistic. Artistic personalities like work activities that deal with the artistic side of things, such as forms, designs, and patterns. They like self-expression in their work. They prefer settings in which work can be done without following a clear set of rules.

S = Social. Social personalities like work activities that assist others and promote learning and personal development. They prefer to communicate more than to work with objects, machines, or data. They like to teach, give advice, help, or otherwise be of service to people.

E = Enterprising. Enterprising personalities like work activities involving starting up and carrying out projects, especially business ventures. They like persuading and leading people and making decisions. They like taking risks for profit. These personalities prefer action rather than thought.

C = Conventional. Conventional personalities like work activities that follow set procedures and routines. They prefer working with data and details rather than with ideas. They prefer work in which there are precise standards rather than work in which they have to judge things by themselves. These personalities like working where the lines of authority are clear.

3. **Determine your secondary interest areas.** Which Total Score is the next highest? Which is your third-highest score? Enter the letters for those areas on the following lines.

My Secondary Personality Types: _____ _____

(If you do not find many occupations that you like by using your Primary Personality Type, you can use your Secondary Personality Types to look at more career options.)

Step 3: Find Jobs That Suit Your Personality Type

Find jobs that match your Primary Personality Type in the following table, which is organized according to the six personality types (RIASEC). When you find a job that interests you, turn to the index to find the page where the job is described.

Don't rule out a job just because the title is not familiar to you. If you want to find jobs that combine your Primary Personality Type and a Secondary Personality Type, look in the following table for RIASEC codes that match the two codes. For example, if your Primary Personality Type is Investigative and your Secondary Personality Type is Realistic, you would look for jobs in the table coded IR—and you'd find 15, such as Microbiologists. You will also find jobs coded with three letters, IR_, such as Dentists (coded IRS) and Environmental Scientists and Specialists (coded IRC). If you look further you'll find still more jobs coded I_R, such as Software Developers (coded ICR). All of these jobs are worth considering. Finally, to cast an even wider net, you may want to consider reversing the codes you're looking for. In the current example, you might look for jobs coded RI or RI_, such as Dental Laboratory Technicians (coded RIC) or Conservation Scientists and Foresters (coded RIE). But keep in mind that these jobs may not be quite as satisfying because your Primary Personality Type, although represented, does not dominate.

The following table omits Military Careers and Nursing Aides, Orderlies, and Attendants. The Department of Labor does not provide personality-type information for these jobs, but that does not mean you should rule them out.

Occupation Names	RIASEC Codes
Agricultural Workers	R
Automotive Body and Glass Repairers	R
Fishers and Related Fishing Workers	R
Sheet Metal Workers	R
Automotive Service Technicians and Mechanics	RI
Mechanical Engineers	RI
Veterinary Technologists and Technicians	RI
Conservation Scientists and Foresters	RIE
Aerospace Engineering and Operations Technicians	RIC
Agricultural and Food Science Technicians	RIC
Biological Technicians	RIC
Civil Engineers	RIC
Dental and Ophthalmic Laboratory Technicians and Medical Appliance Technicians	RIC
Electrical and Electronics Engineering Technicians	RIC
Electrical and Electronics Installers and Repairers	RIC
Electro-mechanical Technicians	RIC
Elevator Installers and Repairers	RIC
Environmental Engineering Technicians	RIC
Geological and Petroleum Technicians	RIC
Mechanical Engineering Technicians	RIC
Medical Equipment Repairers	RIC
Stationary Engineers and Boiler Operators	RIC
Telecommunications Equipment Installers and Repairers, Except Line Installers	RIC
Jewelers and Precious Stone and Metal Workers	RA
Firefighters	RS
Radiologic and MRI Technologists	RS
Veterinary Assistants and Laboratory Animal Caretakers	RSI
Surgical Technologists	RSC

Occupation Names	RIASEC Codes
Athletes and Sports Competitors	RE
Cement Masons and Terrazzo Workers	RE
Taxi Drivers and Chauffeurs	RE
Forest and Conservation Technicians	REI
Correctional Officers	REC
Manicurists and Pedicurists	REC
Animal Care and Service Workers	RC
Bakers	RC
Boilermakers	RC
Bus Drivers	RC
Construction Equipment Operators	RC
Construction Laborers and Helpers	RC
Diesel Service Technicians and Mechanics	RC
Drywall and Ceiling Tile Installers, and Tapers	RC
Food and Tobacco Processing Workers	RC
Food Preparation Workers	RC
Glaziers	RC
Grounds Maintenance Workers	RC
Hand Laborers and Material Movers	RC
Hazardous Materials Removal Workers	RC
Heating, Air Conditioning, and Refrigeration Mechanics and Installers	RC
Heavy and Tractor-trailer Truck Drivers	RC
Insulation Workers	RC
Janitors and Building Cleaners	RC
Laundry and Dry-cleaning Workers	RC
Line Installers and Repairers	RC
Maids and Housekeeping Cleaners	RC
Material Moving Machine Operators	RC
Metal and Plastic Machine Workers	RC
Painters, Construction and Maintenance	RC
Painting and Coating Workers	RC
Pest Control Workers	RC
Plumbers, Pipefitters, and Steamfitters	RC
Power Plant Operators, Distributors, and Dispatchers	RC
Printing Workers	RC
Roofers	RC
Slaughterers, Meat Packers, and Meat, Poultry, and Fish Cutters and Trimmers	RC
Small Engine Mechanics	RC
Solar Photovoltaic Installers	RC
Water and Wastewater Treatment Plant and System Operators	RC
Welders, Cutters, Solderers, and Brazers	RC
Wind Turbine Technicians	RC
Woodworkers	RC
Aircraft and Avionics Equipment Mechanics and Technicians	RCI
Airline and Commercial Pilots	RCI
Brickmasons, Blockmasons, and Stonemasons	RCI
Broadcast and Sound Engineering Technicians	RCI
Carpenters	RCI
Cartographers and Photogrammetrists	RCI
Civil Engineering Technicians	RCI
Computer Support Specialists	RCI
Computer, ATM, and Office Machine Repairers	RCI
Construction and Building Inspectors	RCI
Drafters	RCI
Electricians	RCI
Fire Inspectors and Investigators	RCI
Forest and Conservation Workers	RCI
General Maintenance and Repair Workers	RCI
Heavy Vehicle and Mobile Equipment Service Technicians	RCI

Occupation Names	RIASEC Codes
Mental Health Counselors and Marriage and Family Therapists	SIA
Postsecondary Teachers	SIA
Speech-Language Pathologists	SIA
Childcare Workers	SA
Middle School Teachers	SA
Preschool Teachers	SA
Special Education Teachers	SA
Recreational Therapists	SAI
Substance Abuse and Behavioral Disorder Counselors	SAI
Adult Literacy and High School Equivalency Diploma Teachers	SAE
High School Teachers	SAE
Kindergarten and Elementary School Teachers	SAC
Training and Development Specialists	SAC
Arbitrators, Mediators, and Conciliators	SE
Emergency Management Directors	SE
Health Educators and Community Health Workers	SE
Coaches and Scouts	SER
Instructional Coordinators	SEI
Recreation Workers	SEA
Customer Service Representatives	SEC
Probation Officers and Correctional Treatment Specialists	SEC
Waiters and Waitresses	SEC
Teacher Assistants	SC
Nursing Assistants and Orderlies	SCR
Sales Engineers	ERI
Chefs and Head Cooks	ERA
Police and Detectives	ERS
Skincare Specialists	ERS
Computer Network Architects	ERC
Construction Managers	ERC
Farmers, Ranchers, and Other Agricultural Managers	ERC
Umpires, Referees, and Other Sports Officials	ERC
Architectural and Engineering Managers	EI
Lawyers	EI
Natural Sciences Managers	EIC
Public Relations and Fundraising Managers	EA
Announcers	EAS
Public Relations Specialists	EAS
Producers and Directors	EAC
Social and Community Service Managers	ES
Training and Development Managers	ES
Judges and Hearing Officers	ESI
Elementary, Middle, and High School Principals	ESC
Flight Attendants	ESC
Funeral Service Occupations	ESC
Human Resources Managers	ESC
Preschool and Childcare Center Directors	ESC
Administrative Services Managers	EC
Air Traffic Controllers	EC
Financial Examiners	EC
Financial Managers	EC
Private Detectives and Investigators	EC
Property, Real Estate, and Community Association Managers	EC
Purchasing Managers, Buyers, and Purchasing Agents	EC
Real Estate Brokers and Sales Agents	EC
Retail Sales Workers	EC
Sales Managers	EC
Securities, Commodities, and Financial Services Sales Agents	EC
Travel Agents	EC
Wholesale and Manufacturing Sales Representatives	EC

Occupation Names	RIASEC Codes
Food Service Managers	ECR
Industrial Production Managers	ECR
Opticians, Dispensing	ECR
Computer and Information Systems Managers	ECI
Advertising Sales Agents	ECA
Advertising, Promotions, and Marketing Managers	ECA
Fundraisers	ECA
Compensation and Benefits Managers	ECS
Human Resources Specialists and Labor Relations Specialists	ECS
Insurance Sales Agents	ECS
Lodging Managers	ECS
Medical and Health Services Managers	ECS
Meeting, Convention, and Event Planners	ECS
Personal Financial Advisors	ECS
Postsecondary Education Administrators	ECS
Top Executives	ECS
Medical Transcriptionists	CR
Occupational Health and Safety Technicians	CR
Pharmacy Technicians	CR
Postal Service Workers	CR
Quality Control Inspectors	CR
Surveying and Mapping Technicians	CR
Archivists, Curators, and Museum Workers	CRI
Phlebotomists	CRI
Dental Assistants	CRS
Food and Beverage Serving and Related Workers	CRE
Material Recording Clerks	CRE
Police, Fire, and Ambulance Dispatchers	CRE
Database Administrators	CI
Statisticians	CI
Information Security Analysts	CIR
Web Developers	CIR
Actuaries	CIE
Financial Analysts	CIE
Paralegals and Legal Assistants	CIE
Library Technicians and Assistants	CSR
Medical Assistants	CSR
Librarians	CSE
Social and Human Service Assistants	CSE
Appraisers and Assessors of Real Estate	CE
Bill and Account Collectors	CE
Bookkeeping, Accounting, and Auditing Clerks	CE
Cashiers	CE
Claims Adjusters, Appraisers, Examiners, and Investigators	CE
Compensation, Benefits, and Job Analysis Specialists	CE
Cost Estimators	CE
Court Reporters	CE
Financial Clerks	CE
Medical Records and Health Information Technicians	CE
Secretaries and Administrative Assistants	CE
Tax Examiners and Collectors, and Revenue Agents	CE
Tellers	CE
Bartenders	CER
Gaming Services Occupations	CER
General Office Clerks	CER
Accountants and Auditors	CEI
Budget Analysts	CEI
Insurance Underwriters	CEI
Logisticians	CEI
Information Clerks	CES
Loan Officers	CES
Receptionists	CES

How Educators, Counselors, Librarians, and Business Professionals Can Best Use the *OOH*

Note: If you are a job seeker or career explorer, turn to the chapter titled "Occupational Information Included in the **OOH***" for guidance on using this book.*

The *Occupational Outlook Handbook (OOH)* is the best-selling career information resource of all time. It is so popular because it has such a wide range of information and is designed to appeal to many kinds of career explorers. One drawback of this format, however, is that people who are in the early stages of career exploration may not know where in this thick volume to get started. On the other hand, people with highly specific career information needs may require help to apply the general statements in the *OOH* to their particular situations.

If you are a professional who works with career decision makers, this chapter suggests ways to help your clients get the most out of the *OOH*. It also has suggestions for how to use the *OOH* in classroom activities for academic subjects.

Identifying Occupations to Consider

Many of your clients may want to use the *OOH* to discover interesting occupations they previously had not thought about. Some may enjoy browsing randomly through the pages and looking at the photos, summary tables, and graphs to identify occupations that seem promising. You may save these clients time, however, by showing them the table of contents and encouraging them to focus their browsing on the major occupational group or groups that are of greatest interest to them. The table of contents can be especially useful for these kinds of clients:

- People who are transitioning from one occupation to another and want to find work in a similar field

- Students who want to identify occupations related to their programs of study

- Career explorers who have a rough idea of their interests

Note that, with a few exceptions, the table of contents uses three-tiered organization to help clients zoom in from major occupational groups to specific occupations. For example, the section on Service Occupations is divided into a second tier of occupational families such as Building and Grounds Cleaning and Maintenance Occupations, Food Preparation and Serving-Related Occupations, Health-Care Support Occupations, and so on. Each of these families contains specific occupations; for example, Health-Care Support Occupations includes Dental Assistants, Medical Assistants, Medical Transcriptionists, and so on. This organization helps clients narrow down their options.

Alternatively, you may recommend that career explorers start with the introductory chapter called "Overview of the 2012–2022 Projections," which highlights the parts of the U.S. economy that will create the most opportunities for workers. Because the text of this chapter can be burdensome, encourage clients to look at the charts and tables for a quick way to identify promising occupations. For example, one table shows—for each level of education

or training—the occupations that are expected to grow the fastest and those that are expected to produce the most job openings. At the same time, keep in mind that job opportunity is not the only factor your clients should consider when choosing an occupation. They should also think about their interests and other pursuits.

Looking for a Specific Occupation

If a client already has a specific occupation in mind, you can find the page number quickly in the index. The index also includes alternative titles so that, for example, a client who looks for CAD Operators is directed to look under Drafters, which is the name of the *OOH* article. (*OOH* refers to these articles as "profiles.") If a client is unable to make clear to you what occupation he or she is trying to find or you cannot find a good match in the index, use the table of contents, where the general-to-specific structure can help you locate the occupation that the client has in mind or one reasonably close to it.

Occasionally, a client may be looking for an occupation that is so specialized that the *OOH* does not cover it. In such cases, you can often locate information about the specialized occupation by finding the most closely related *OOH* occupation and consulting resources identified in the "Contacts for More Information" section. For example, the occupation Underwater Welders does not appear in the index or table of contents and is not referred to in the *OOH* article about Welding, Cutters, Solderers, and Brazers. Nevertheless, this article refers to the website of the American Welding Society, which has information about Underwater Welders.

Getting the Most from an *OOH* Article

You can easily locate the information you want in the *OOH* because every article is organized in the same format.

Quick Facts

The bulleted items under the "Quick Facts" heading highlight key topics of information for each occupation: the earnings; requirements for education, experience, and on-the-job training; the size of the workforce in 2012; the projected growth of the workforce for the 2012–2022 period; and the projected job openings over that same time period. These facts are presented here because they are important, but if you think the occupation may be one the client should consider, warn the client not to make a snap judgment against the occupation based solely on these points.

What People in the Occupation Do

This section discusses what workers do on the job, what tools and equipment they use, and how closely they are supervised. You should point out to your clients that this is an overview of a diverse collection of workers and that in fact, few workers perform the full set of tasks itemized here. The duties for an individual worker often vary by industry or employer, and beginning workers often perform a limited number of routine tasks under close supervision until they are trained for more varied tasks and can take greater responsibility.

In many cases, the workforce covered by the article is so diverse that it actually divides into several occupational specializations. For example, the article on Accountants and Auditors discusses a few specializations, such as public accountants, management accountants, and internal auditors. Although the skills and knowledge required for the occupation usually are discussed in a later section, this section sometimes mentions them, particularly the unique requirements of occupational specializations. For example, the article on Secretaries and Administrative Assistants notes, "*Legal secretaries* do specialized work requiring knowledge of legal terminology and procedures." Specializations and alternative occupational titles are in italicized text. Some articles—such as the one for Advertising, Promotions, and Marketing Managers—discuss titles or specializations for which separate articles are available elsewhere in the *OOH:* "For more information on sales or public relations, see the profiles on sales managers, public relations managers and specialists, and market research analysts."

Your clients will find this section useful for a couple of reasons:

- If you have discussed or assessed your clients' interests, this section gives your clients an idea of what kinds of problems, materials, and tools they will encounter on the job so they can decide whether it is a good match for their interests. Remind them to make these comparisons.

- Clients who want to change careers may want to read this section of the article about their *current* occupations. The description of tasks and tools may suggest experiences that they can mention in their resumes. It can also provide fodder for a discussion about what aspects of the current job are interesting and rewarding—or uninteresting and discouraging. Some clients may find occupational specializations that are promising alternatives to what they are doing now.

Work Environment

This section identifies the workplace environment (both physical and psychological), physical activities and susceptibility to injury, special equipment, travel required, typical hours worked, and the percentage of self-employed workers. If conditions vary between the occupational specializations, that is mentioned here.

Here are some of the ways this section may be valuable to your clients:

- Clients with disabilities will want to take note of the physical requirements mentioned here and consider whether they can meet these requirements with or without suitable accommodations.

- Clients who are sensitive to conditions such as heights, stress, or a cramped workspace should pay attention to this section.

- As with the first section, you may want to have your clients read this section of the article about their current occupations. Encourage them to discuss which aspects of their present working conditions please and displease them.

- If the work environment of an otherwise promising occupation has a condition that a client wants to avoid, check the wording of the section to see whether this is an inevitable attribute of the occupation or whether it only *may* apply. Even if the wording implies that the condition is typical of the occupation, encourage the client to explore the occupation using other sources, especially personal contacts with workers or educators, to learn whether it is possible to carve out a niche in this occupation that avoids the unappealing working condition.

How to Become One

This is the section in which your clients can learn how to prepare for the occupation:

- It identifies the entry routes that are most popular and that are preferred by employers. These entry routes may be informal methods such as hobbies or work experience; they may be formal training programs such as apprenticeship, military, and on-the-job programs; or they may be educational programs such as vocational school, a postsecondary certification program, a college major, or an advanced degree.

- The "Important Qualities" subsection identifies the particular skills, aptitudes, and work habits that employers value. Note that these are not selected from a consistent taxonomy.

- Other subsections are usually included, but the topics vary among occupations. If licensure or certification is necessary for career entry, the subsection titled "Licenses," "Certification," or "Licenses and Certification" mentions this requirement and how to qualify for it. A "Work Experience" subsection may also be included. Finally, an "Advancement" subsection may identify common career ladders within the occupation and to related occupations.

Your clients may benefit from this section in several ways:

- Clients who are considering entering an occupation can learn what hurdles they must overcome to enter it. You can help them by comparing the requirements to their backgrounds and to the educational and training opportunities that are available to them. Be sure to consider nontraditional and informal entry routes as well as the formal routes.

- Suggest that clients try to leverage their previous education, training, and work experience rather than abandon it. As they read the educational and skill requirements in this section, they should look for specifics already on their resumes—educational accomplishments, skills, work habits—that will meet employers' expectations and thus make a career transition easier. These considerations should be part of the career decision.

- Clients who are decided on an occupation and ready to apply for a job in it should be encouraged to pay attention to what the "Important Qualities" subsection says about relevant skills and personal attributes. This information can help these clients slant their resumes and focus their interview statements in ways that make them stronger job candidates.

- Clients may also find it useful to read what this section says about their current occupations. It may suggest skills they can try to improve for the sake of career advancement. Alternatively, it may suggest transferable skills that should be included in clients' resumes if they want to make a career shift to a different occupation. In addition, the "Advancement" subsection, if one is present, may suggest a career move that is a frequent option for people within this occupation.

- If the "Certification" or "Licenses" subsection mentions that certification with a professional organization is required or recommended, contact information for the organization is usually listed at the end of the article among the "Contacts for More Information," so your clients can easily find where to learn the details about certification prerequisites and procedures.

Pay

This section discusses average earnings for the occupation and identifies the most common ways workers are compensated—for example, with an hourly wage, a commission, tips, and so on. Standard benefits usually are not mentioned, but uncommon benefits such as summers off or discounted merchandise may be mentioned. A graph shows how the median wage for the occupation compares to wages in the family of similar occupations and in the whole world of work.

The wage figures are derived from the Occupational Employment Statistics survey from the Bureau of Labor Statistics (BLS).

Your clients are likely to be interested in this section. Here are some suggestions on how to help them use this information:

- Remind your clients that the wage figures are national averages. This is particularly important for clients to understand if they look at the wages that the *OOH* lists for their current occupations. If actual wages in your geographic region are considerably higher or lower, tell your clients what the trend is. Be sure the clients note not only the median but also the highest and lowest 10 percent, so they understand some of the variation in wages.

- Your clients may find that the information in this section helps them choose an occupation that meets or exceeds their wage aspirations. However, you can help your clients by getting a sense of whether they have considered *other* potential job satisfactions and work conditions and are putting the wages into a realistic context. Be sure they are making a choice based on the whole occupation, not just the paycheck.

- If your clients are young or do not have much work experience, they may not have a realistic understanding of the relationship between wages and lifestyles. That is, the wage figures given in this section may not have concrete meaning for them in terms of what kind of neighborhood they might live in, what kind of car they might drive, and so on. You can help them by preparing descriptions of fictional people (perhaps familiar characters on television) in various lifestyles, together with the wage levels that would correspond.

Job Outlook

This section gives the *OOH* its name. The opening paragraphs describe the economic forces that will affect future employment in the occupation: the growth or decline of industries that employ workers; factors such as technology, business practices, or changes in the law that affect demand for workers; and demographic issues such as the impending retirement of large numbers of workers. A table shows the workforce size in 2012, the size projected for 2022, and the percent and numeric change that this amounts to. A bar graph compares the projected workforce growth to the growth of related occupations and all occupations. The subsection titled "Job prospects" indicates how the supply of workers compares to the demand for workers. It mentions what kinds of workers have the best chances for employment.

Here are some of the ways you can use this section to your clients' advantage:

- The information in this section can help your clients identify occupations with a good job outlook so that they have better-than-average chances of finding work. You should tell them to be alert for any mention of an advantage that they may have over other job seekers (for example, a college degree) or any other factor, such as geographic location or type of employer, that can improve job opportunities or might lead to competition.

- The table indicates whether the occupation has a large or small workforce. You may want to point out to your clients that a large occupation can provide many job openings—even if it is

shrinking in size—because of job turnover. Conversely, a small occupation may provide few job openings even though it is growing rapidly.

- In many cases, this table consists of more than one row because the article covers a family of occupations for which the Bureau of Labor makes separate projections. In such cases, clients can see which specializations within the family of occupations have the largest workforces and which have the most promising projections for employment growth. For example, the table for Craft and Fine Artists has four rows and indicates that one specialization employs more than 25,000 workers and is projected to grow by 8 percent, whereas another specialization employs about 19,000 workers and is projected to grow by only 1 percent. Show clients how they can use this knowledge to direct their planning toward specializations that offer the greatest job opportunities.

- If a client is highly motivated and highly qualified for a particular occupation, do not let a bad employment outlook discourage the client. Job openings occur even in shrinking or overcrowded occupations, and people with, for example, exceptional talent or good personal connections may go on to great success.

- Keep in mind that, although these projections are the most definitive ones available, they are not foolproof and apply only to a 10-year time span. Help your clients understand that, no matter what occupation they choose, they will need to be flexible and adapt to future changes in the economy.

- Clients should consult this section of the article about their present occupation. If the outlook is not good, the information may convince them to consider preparing for work in another field. Alternatively, with knowledge of the forces that are threatening the occupation, they may be able to devise a counterstrategy—for example, moving into a specialization where jobs will remain plentiful. If the outlook is good, they may learn how to take advantage of the best opportunities.

Similar Occupations

This section identifies occupations that are similar to the occupation that is featured in the article in terms of work tasks, interests, skills, education, or training. Your clients may find the information useful in the following ways:

- If a client is interested in an occupation but is not strongly committed to pursuing it, this section may suggest another occupation with similar rewards or tasks that may turn out to be a better fit. Advise the client to read the *OOH* articles on the related occupations. If you know some specific shortcomings the client perceives in the occupation at hand (for example, a lot of weekend work), you may know which related occupations are most likely to be more satisfying.

- You may be able to use occupations listed here to inspire clients whose aspirations fall short of their full potential. For example, you could point out that only a little more education in the same field would open the door to certain highly rewarding occupations. Note that one column of the table identifies the usual educational requirement for each occupation.

- Conversely, you may use this section to suggest realistic alternatives to a client whose aspirations seem unrealistic. Try to do so in a manner that does not disrespect the client's dreams—encourage the client to select one of these alternative occupational choices as an achievable plan-B goal if the original goal should turn out to be unattainable. For example, if a client is unlikely to be able to get into or complete law school, you could point to Paralegals and Legal Assistants as an occupation in the same field that requires less education.

Contacts for More Information

Although information-packed, the *OOH* has limited space to describe the occupations it includes. This section lists several sources and resources your clients can turn to for more information about the occupation. Here are some suggestions for advising your clients about using these references:

- Encourage your clients to consult these sources. The *OOH* should be only the beginning of their career decision-making process. They need more detailed information from several viewpoints to make an informed decision. Ask some probing questions to be sure that your clients know how to locate the additional resources. Although only Web-based resources are listed here, you may help your clients' further research efforts by providing printed aids such as a college directory or a local business directory.

- Many people, especially young people, regard the Internet as the font of all knowledge and may not explore beyond the websites listed here. Remind your clients that all jobs are local. Your clients need to talk to and observe individual workers to learn what the workdays are like, what the workers enjoy and dislike about the job, how they got hired, and what effects the job has had on other aspects of their lives. Your clients may make contact with local workers through the local chapter of an organization listed here.

- If licensure or certification is mentioned as a requirement in the "Education/Training" section, one of the sources listed here should have detailed information about the procedures that apply to your clients' jurisdictions. Be sure your clients investigate these matters so they understand all the hurdles that stand between them and job entry and can plan an appropriate course of action.

- Remind your clients that these sources may provide detailed information about occupational specializations that are not described, or that are described only briefly, in the *OOH* article. If a client perceives certain minor drawbacks in an otherwise appealing occupation, these sources may point out niche jobs that avoid these problems—for example, the high-paying specializations in an occupation that generally pays a moderate salary.

- One of these sources may provide information that contradicts what the *OOH* says. Such situations are rare but might occur because the information in the *OOH* has become out-of-date or because local conditions are different from national norms. Try to help your client identify the reason for the inconsistency in light of what will be most helpful in making a career decision. For example, if local job conditions are unique but the client intends to relocate elsewhere, advise the client to base the career decision on the national averages reported in the *OOH*.

Using the *OOH* for Class Assignments

The preceding paragraphs explain how to use the *OOH* to help people make career decisions and plans. The *OOH* is also useful as the focus of many kinds of class activities that can teach important academic skills and concepts while simultaneously making young people better informed about careers. Here are some examples:

For a Mathematics Class

- The "Job Outlook" section of some articles about diverse occupations (e.g., Food and Beverage Serving and Related Workers) includes a table that lists the employment of workers in specialized occupations. Have students use such a table to create a pie chart.

- The "Job Outlook" section of each article includes a bar chart that shows the projected employment growth of the occupation compared to the growth for related occupations and all occupations. Have students use the data to create bar charts comparing the projected growth of several occupations across articles or specialized occupations within an article.

- The "Pay" section of each article includes a bar chart that shows the earnings of the occupation compared to the earnings of a family of occupations and of all occupations. Have students use the data to create bar charts comparing the earnings of several occupations across articles.

- The "Pay" section of each article identifies the median earnings of all workers in the occupation, plus the earnings of the highest and lowest 10 percent of workers. Have students make a graph on which the x axis shows dollar figures in increments of \$5,000 or \$10,000 (or 50 cents if hourly earnings are shown). Have them mark the locations of the three data points mentioned in the section and then superimpose a normal curve over the graph with the highest point above the median figure. Ask students to comment on whether the curve accurately describes the distribution of earnings. For example, are the high and low 10 percent figures equidistant from the median? For a particularly lopsided distribution, choose the article on Real Estate Brokers and Sales Agents.

For an English Class

- Have students write an essay comparing and contrasting two occupations. (It may be useful to ask the students to choose two from the same occupational group or that list each other as "Similar Occupations.")

- Have students write an essay comparing and contrasting the work experiences of a contemporary fictional character with the facts reported in the *OOH* article on the equivalent occupation. The thesis of the essay might be a judgment of how realistic the fictional portrayal is.

- Have students write an article in the *OOH* format describing the occupation of a fictional character from a work they have read. Tell them that every fact must be based on evidence from the fictional work (you may even require them to cite page numbers) rather than on facts from the *OOH* itself.

For a Social Studies Class

- The "Job Outlook" section of many articles mentions economic forces that are causing the occupation to grow or shrink. Have students look at several such statements and identify one economic trend that is affecting several occupations (examples: aging baby boomers, increased use of automation, increased interest in energy conservation). Have them research the trend by using other current resources and prepare a poster that identifies the trend, defines it briefly, and lists some occupations that are affected.

- Have students write an article in the *OOH* format describing an occupation that no longer exists (or is held by only a few crafts workers), such as scrivener, bowmaker, hand weaver, blacksmith, squire, saddler, alchemist, or wheelwright.

Best 100 Jobs in the *OOH*

The *Occupational Outlook Handbook (OOH)* covers so many jobs that you may be looking for a quick way to narrow down your choices. The Personality-Career Quiz on page 1 is one way to do this, and this chapter offers another—it identifies the 100 jobs with the best economic rewards.

The procedure used to create this chapter is the same one used in many popular JIST books, such as *Best Jobs for the 21st Century, Sixth Edition, 50 Best Jobs for Your Personality, Third Edition,* and *150 Best Jobs for Your Skills, Second Edition.* We determined the best 100 jobs in the *OOH* by focusing on three economic criteria: earnings, projected job growth, and projected job openings.

Why these three criteria? Everybody agrees that these three are important. Many other characteristics of jobs are matters of individual preference. One person may be looking for a job that offers opportunities for leadership; somebody else may be looking for a great variety of work tasks; still another person may be looking for work that contributes to society. But everybody wants to get paid, and almost everybody agrees that more pay is better.

It's also important for you to get hired. After all, if you're not hired, you won't get any of the satisfactions of work. So job growth and job openings are both important. Understand that these are not two ways of saying the same thing. You need to know both. Consider the occupation Biomedical Engineers, which is projected to grow at the impressive rate of 27 percent. There should be lots of opportunities in such a fast-growing job, right? Not exactly. This is a small occupation, with only about 19,000 people currently employed. So, even though the workforce is growing rapidly, the occupation will not create many new jobs (about 1,000 per year). Now consider Elementary, Middle, and High School Principals. This occupation is projected to grow only slightly, by 6 percent. Nevertheless, this is a large occupation that employs more than 200,000 workers. So, even though the workforce size will not grow at a rapid pace, the occupation is expected to take on 7,470 new workers each year, many through job turnover. That's why we base our selection of the best jobs on both of these economic indicators

and why you should pay attention to both when you scan the list of the 100 best jobs.

Another important reason we use these three criteria is that accurate and objective information about them is available. People might disagree about which occupations offer the most opportunities for creativity or freedom from stress. But the U.S. Department of Labor gets universal respect for the figures it publishes on earnings, projected job growth, and projected job openings. These concepts are numerical and therefore are easy to compare objectively.

Here's how we made the comparisons: We started with the 333 civilian occupations that the *OOH* describes with full profiles and eliminated three occupations because annual earnings data was not available either for the occupation as a whole (as was the case with Actors and with Musicians and Singers) or for a component occupation (as was the case with Dancers as a component of Dancers and Choreographers). We sorted the remaining 330 occupations three times, from highest to lowest, in terms of earnings, growth rate through 2022, and average number of annual openings. Each time, we assigned a number to their relative position on the list. We then combined the job-position numbers of the three lists, putting the job with the best total score at the top, followed by the job with next-best total score, on down the list.

Some jobs have the same scores for one or more data elements.

In those cases, we ordered the jobs alphabetically, and their order in relation to each other has no other significance. Avoiding these ties was impossible, so understand that the difference of several positions on a list may not mean as much as it seems.

We're not suggesting that these 100 jobs are all good ones for you to consider—some will not be. Read the job descriptions, and use some of the resources listed there for additional information. As you narrow down your choices, talk to people in the career and in the educational or training programs. Do some on-site career exploration. If you do your homework, you probably can identify a career that has good economic rewards and many other features that will suit you.

Job	Annual Earnings	Percent Growth	Annual Openings
1. Software Developers	$93,640	22%	35,320
2. Physicians and Surgeons	$182,294	18%	29,630
3. Physical Therapists	$79,860	36%	12,370
4. Computer Systems Analysts	$79,680	25%	20,960
5. Nurse Anesthetists, Nurse Midwives, and Nurse Practitioners	$103,602	31%	7,700
6. Medical and Health Services Managers	$88,580	23%	14,990
7. Registered Nurses	$65,470	19%	105,260
8. Management Analysts	$78,600	19%	24,520
9. Dental Hygienists	$70,210	33%	11,350
10. Postsecondary Teachers	$70,380	19%	42,690
11. Market Research Analysts	$60,300	32%	18,850
12. Physician Assistants	$90,930	38%	4,890
13. Top Executives	$104,073	11%	70,090
14. Civil Engineers	$79,340	20%	12,010
15. Computer and Information Systems Managers	$120,950	15%	9,710

Job	Annual Earnings	Percent Growth	Annual Openings
16. Construction Managers	$82,790	16%	15,460
17. Pharmacists	$116,670	14%	10,980
18. Personal Financial Advisors	$67,520	27%	9,640
19. Information Security Analysts	$86,170	36%	3,920
20. Dentists	$149,795	16%	5,910
21. Occupational Therapists	$75,400	29%	4,820
22. Cost Estimators	$58,860	26%	11,800
23. Lawyers	$113,530	10%	19,650
24. Accountants and Auditors	$63,550	13%	54,420
25. Financial Analysts	$76,950	16%	10,090
26. Diagnostic Medical Sonographers and Cardiovascular Technologists and Technicians, Including Vascular Technologists	$59,422	39%	5,830
27. Petroleum Engineers	$130,280	26%	1,960
28. Postsecondary Education Administrators	$86,490	15%	6,650
29. Financial Managers	$109,740	9%	14,690
30. Advertising, Promotions, and Marketing Managers	$115,087	12%	7,510
31. Operations Research Analysts	$72,100	27%	3,600
32. Electricians	$49,840	20%	22,460
33. Licensed Practical and Licensed Vocational Nurses	$41,540	25%	36,310
34. Logisticians	$72,780	22%	4,220
35. Medical and Clinical Laboratory Technologists and Technicians	$47,499	22%	15,600
36. Computer Network Architects	$91,000	15%	4,350
37. Carpenters	$39,940	24%	32,920
38. Optometrists	$97,820	24%	1,770
39. Plumbers, Pipefitters, and Steamfitters	$49,140	21%	13,050
40. Radiologic and MRI Technologists	$56,035	21%	8,090
41. Computer Support Specialists	$49,488	17%	23,650
42. Social and Community Service Managers	$59,970	21%	5,510
43. Administrative Services Managers	$81,080	12%	7,990
44. Speech-Language Pathologists	$69,870	19%	4,620
45. Web Developers	$62,500	20%	5,070
46. Sales Managers	$105,260	8%	10,690
47. Actuaries	$93,680	26%	1,320
48. Human Resources Managers	$99,720	13%	4,060
49. Kindergarten and Elementary School Teachers	$53,060	12%	53,250
50. Social Workers	$44,541	19%	24,280
51. Architects	$73,090	17%	4,410
52. Network and Computer Systems Administrators	$72,560	12%	10,050
53. Securities, Commodities, and Financial Services Sales Agents	$71,720	11%	12,260
54. Database Administrators	$77,080	15%	4,030
55. Personal Care Aides	$19,910	49%	66,600
56. Construction Laborers and Helpers	$29,277	25%	58,790
57. Home Health Aides	$20,820	48%	59,070
58. Industrial Machinery Mechanics and Maintenance Workers and Millwrights	$45,848	17%	18,700
59. Wholesale and Manufacturing Sales Representatives	$58,484	9%	53,250
60. Heating, Air Conditioning, and Refrigeration Mechanics and Installers	$43,640	21%	12,370
61. Biomedical Engineers	$86,960	27%	1,010
62. Medical Assistants	$29,370	29%	26,990
63. Physical Therapist Assistants and Aides	$40,539	41%	7,630

Job	Annual Earnings	Percent Growth	Annual Openings
64. Statisticians	$75,560	26%	1,610
65. Mental Health Counselors and Marriage and Family Therapists	$41,592	29%	8,360
66. Middle School Teachers	$53,430	12%	21,120
67. Architectural and Engineering Managers	$124,870	7%	6,060
68. Training and Development Specialists	$55,930	15%	7,720
69. Construction Equipment Operators	$41,099	19%	16,480
70. Meeting, Convention, and Event Planners	$45,810	33%	4,420
71. Dental Assistants	$34,500	25%	13,720
72. Psychologists	$69,807	12%	6,230
73. Podiatrists	$116,440	22%	460
74. Interpreters and Translators	$45,430	46%	3,810
75. Computer Programmers	$74,280	8%	11,810
76. Environmental Scientists and Specialists	$63,570	15%	3,970
77. Medical Scientists	$76,980	13%	3,550
78. Geoscientists	$90,890	16%	1,730
79. Paralegals and Legal Assistants	$46,990	17%	9,120
80. Nursing Assistants and Orderlies	$24,404	21%	61,300
81. Respiratory Therapists	$55,870	19%	4,010
82. Radiation Therapists	$77,560	24%	840
83. Public Relations and Fundraising Managers	$95,450	13%	2,130
84. Brickmasons, Blockmasons, and Stonemasons	$44,935	34%	3,840
85. Environmental Engineers	$80,890	15%	2,110
86. Occupational Therapy Assistants and Aides	$47,638	41%	2,560
87. Biochemists and Biophysicists	$81,480	18%	1,370
88. Elevator Installers and Repairers	$76,650	24%	800
89. Veterinarians	$84,460	12%	3,100
90. Audiologists	$69,720	33%	700
91. Mathematicians	$101,360	23%	170
92. Social and Human Service Assistants	$28,850	22%	17,870
93. Secretaries and Administrative Assistants	$36,198	12%	97,210
94. Substance Abuse and Behavioral Disorder Counselors	$38,520	31%	4,720
95. Political Scientists	$102,000	21%	250
96. Property, Real Estate, and Community Association Managers	$52,610	12%	10,210
97. Computer and Information Research Scientists	$102,190	15%	830
98. Elementary, Middle, and High School Principals	$87,760	6%	7,470
99. Cement Masons and Terrazzo Workers	$35,856	29%	5,830
100. EMTs and Paramedics	$31,020	23%	12,060

Overview of the 2012–2022 Projections

Occupations and industries related to healthcare and construction are projected to experience the fastest job growth over the coming decade, as an aging population and expanding health insurance coverage change the preferences of consumers and a resurging housing market spurs long-awaited recovery in construction.

In the two years that have elapsed since the last set of BLS projections, economic recovery has taken hold. As the economy continues to improve in the wake of the Great Recession, the long-term patterns of growth and industry activity can be more readily observed. Because the projections cover a 10-year period, BLS does not attempt to predict fluctuations in the business cycle and assumes that the economy will have reached full employment by 2022, the target year for the projections. In a full-employment economy, any existing unemployment is frictional, that is, attributable to the usual churn of workers who are transitioning between jobs, rather than a cyclical lack of demand for final goods and services.

In the coming decade, demographic changes are expected to have pervasive effects on the nation's economic outlook. As individuals age, their consumption patterns change and their demand for healthcare and related services rises. These trends are expected to play an important role in sectoral growth of output and employment. In addition, by expanding insurance coverage to millions of Americans, the Patient Protection and Affordable Care Act will place even greater demands on the healthcare system. Four articles detailing BLS projections for the U.S. labor force, macroeconomy, industry output and employment, and occupational employment explore how the nation's economy may shift in response to the changing needs of aging citizens and the provisions of the new healthcare legislation.

Highlights of the 2012–2022 projections include the following:

- Labor force growth will slow to 0.5 percent annually as participation rates decrease among younger and prime-age workers and as more baby boomers leave the labor force.

- Slow gains in the labor force will limit the potential growth in gross domestic product (GDP); GDP is projected to increase at an annual rate of 2.6 percent.

- Total employment is expected to grow by 1.0 percent annually, with the fastest job gains occurring in the construction sector and the health care and social assistance sector.

- Occupations related to healthcare, healthcare support, construction, and personal care services are projected to add a combined 5.3 million jobs, an increase representing approximately one-third of all employment gains over the coming decade.

- The number of jobs in occupations requiring a master's degree for entry is projected to grow by 18.4 percent, which is faster than the growth rate of any other educational category. Occupations requiring a high school diploma are expected to add the greatest number of new jobs, accounting for nearly 30 percent of all employment gains over the projection period.

Between 2012 and 2022, the influence of changing demographics is expected to be felt across all facets of the economy examined in the BLS projections. The dominant pattern of declining labor force participation is projected to continue, largely because of the substantial number of baby boomers moving into older age cohorts, in which participation is lower. Declining participation leads to slower labor force growth, which, in turn, constrains output growth in the entire economy. As demand for medical services increases as a result of population aging and expanding medical insurance coverage, the health care sector and its associated occupations are expected to see sizable gains in employment and output. The construction industry, as well as the occupations that support it, also will experience rapid growth in employment and output. Employment in the construction sector is expected to return to its long-term trend of increase, a rebound consistent with expectations about future population growth and the need to replace older structures. Although the projected growth in this sector appears rapid because of a low starting point occasioned by the Great Recession (the recession left the sector well below trend growth in 2011), construction employment and output are not expected to reach their prerecession levels.

Finding and Applying for Jobs and Evaluating Offers

Job Search Methods

Finding a job can take months of time and effort. But you can speed the process by using many methods to find job openings. Data from the Bureau of Labor Statistics suggest that people who use many job search methods find jobs faster than people who use only one or two.

Personal Contacts

Most jobs are never advertised, or they are filled before they are advertised. People get them by talking to friends, family, neighbors, acquaintances, teachers, former coworkers, and others who know of an opening. Be sure to tell people that you are looking for a job because the people you know may be some of the most effective resources for your search. To develop new contacts, join student, community, or professional organizations.

School Career Planning and Placement Offices

High school and college placement services help their students and alumni find jobs. Some invite recruiters to use their facilities for interviews or career fairs. They also may have lists of open jobs. Most also offer career counseling, career testing, and job search advice. Some have career resource libraries; host workshops on job search strategy, resume writing, letter writing, and effective interviewing; critique drafts of resumes; conduct mock interviews; and sponsor job fairs.

Employers

Directly contacting employers is one of the most successful means of job hunting. Through library and Internet research, develop a list of potential employers in your desired career field. Then call these employers and check their websites for job openings. Websites and business directories can tell you how to apply for a position or whom to contact. Even if no open positions are posted, do not

hesitate to contact the employer: You never know when a job might become available. Consider asking for an informational interview with people working in the career you want to learn more about. Ask them how they got started, what they like and dislike about the work, what type of qualifications are necessary for the job, and what type of personality succeeds in that position. In addition to giving you career information, they may be able to put you in contact with other employers who may be hiring, and they can keep you in mind if a position opens up.

Classified Ads

The "Help Wanted" ads in newspapers and the Internet list numerous jobs, and many people find work by responding to these ads. But when using classified ads, keep the following in mind:

- Follow all leads to find a job; do not rely solely on the classifieds.
- Answer ads promptly, because openings may be filled quickly, even before the ad stops appearing in the paper.
- Read the ads every day, particularly the Sunday edition, which usually includes the most listings.
- Keep a record of all ads to which you have responded, including the specific skills, educational background, and personal qualifications required for the position. You may want to follow up on your initial inquiry.

Internet Resources

The Internet includes many job hunting websites with job listings. Some job boards provide national listings of all kinds; others are local. Some relate to a specific type of work; others are general. To find good prospects, begin with an Internet search using keywords related to the job you want. Also look for the websites of related professional associations.

In online job databases, remember that job listings may be posted by field or discipline, so begin your search using keywords. Many websites allow job seekers to post their resumes online for free.

Consider checking Internet forums, also called message boards. These are online discussion groups where anyone may post and read messages. Use forums specific to your profession or to career-related topics to post questions or messages and to read about the job searches or career experiences of other people. Although these message boards may seem helpful, carefully evaluate all advice before acting; it can be difficult to determine the reliability of information posted on message boards.

Social media such as Facebook (www.facebook.com), Twitter (www.twitter.com), and especially LinkedIn (www.linkedin.com) can be very helpful in learning about job openings and making contact with people who may know about job openings.

Professional Associations

Many professions have associations that offer employment information, including career planning, educational programs, job listings, and job placement. Information can be obtained directly from most professional associations through the Internet, by telephone, or by mail. Associations usually require that you be a member to use these services.

Labor Unions

Labor unions provide various employment services to members and potential members, including apprenticeship programs that teach a specific trade or skill. Contact the appropriate labor union or state apprenticeship council for more information.

State Employment Service Offices

The state employment service, sometimes called the Job Service, operates in coordination with the U.S. Department of Labor's Employment and Training Administration. Local offices, found nationwide, help job seekers to find jobs and help employers to find qualified workers at no cost to either. To find the office nearest you, follow the links at www.statelocalgov.net/50states-jobs.cfm or look in the state government telephone listings under "Job Service" or "Employment."

Job matching and referral. At the state employment service office, an interviewer will determine if you are "job ready" or if you need help from counseling and testing services to assess your occupational aptitudes and interests and to help you choose and prepare for a career. After you are job ready, you may examine available job listings and select openings that interest you. A staff member can then describe the job openings in detail and arrange for interviews with prospective employers.

Services for special groups. By law, veterans are entitled to priority job placement at state employment service centers. If you are a veteran, a veterans' employment representative can inform you of available assistance and help you to deal with problems.

State employment service offices also refer people to opportunities available under the Workforce Investment Act (WIA) of 1998. Educational and career services and referrals are provided to employers and job seekers, including adults, dislocated workers, and youth. These programs help to prepare people to participate in the state's workforce, increase their employment and earnings potential, improve their educational and occupational skills, and reduce their dependency on welfare.

Federal Government

Information on obtaining a position with the federal government is available from the U.S. Office of Personnel Management (OPM) through USAJOBS, the federal government's official employment information system. This resource for locating and applying for job opportunities can be accessed through the Internet at www.usajobs. gov or through an interactive voice response telephone system at 1 (703) 724-1850, (866) 204-2858, or TDD 1 (978) 461-8404. These numbers are not all toll free, and telephone charges may result.

Community Agencies

Many nonprofit organizations, including religious institutions and vocational rehabilitation agencies, offer counseling, career development, and job placement services, generally targeted to a particular group, such as women, youths, minorities, ex-offenders, or older workers.

Private Employment Agencies and Career Consultants

Private agencies can save you time, and they will contact employers who otherwise might be difficult to locate. Such agencies may be called recruiters, head hunters, or employment placement agencies. These agencies may charge for their services. Most operate on a commission basis, charging a percentage of the first-year salary paid to a successful applicant. You or the hiring company will pay the fee. Find out the exact cost and who is responsible for paying

associated fees before using the service. When determining if the service is worth the cost, consider any guarantees that the agency offers. If you use a private employment agency, ask for interviews with the employers who agree to pay the agency's fee. Do not sign an exclusive agreement or be pressured into accepting a job.

Internships. Many people find jobs with business and organizations where they have interned or volunteered. Look for internships and volunteer opportunities on job boards, school career centers, and company and association websites, but also check community service organizations and volunteer opportunity databases. Some internships and long-term volunteer positions come with stipends and all provide experience and the chance to meet employers and other good networking contacts.

Applying for a Job

After you have found some jobs that interest you, the next step is to apply for them. Many potential employers require complete resumes or application forms and cover letters. Later, you will probably need to go on interviews to meet with employers face to face.

Resumes and Application Forms

Resumes and application forms give employers written evidence of your qualifications and skills. Your goal with these documents is to prove—as clearly and directly as possible—how your qualifications match the job's requirements. Do this by highlighting the experience, accomplishments, education, and skills that most closely fit the job you want.

Gathering information. Resumes and application forms both include the same information. As a first step, gather the following facts:

- Contact information, including your name, mailing address, e-mail address (if you have one you check often), and telephone number.

- Type of work or specific job you are seeking or a qualifications summary that describes your best skills and experience in just a few lines.

- Education, including school name and its city and state, months and years of attendance, highest grade completed or diploma or degree awarded, and major subject or subjects studied. Also consider listing courses and awards that might be relevant to the position. Include a grade point average if you think it would help in getting the job.

- Experience, paid and volunteer. For each job, include the job title, name and location of employer, and dates of employment. Briefly describe your job duties and major accomplishments. In a resume, use phrases instead of sentences to describe your work; write, for example, "Supervised 10 children" instead of writing "I supervised 10 children."

- Special skills. You might list computer skills, proficiency in foreign languages, achievements, or membership in organizations in a separate section.

- References. Leave these off your resume, but be ready to provide references if requested. Good references could be former employers, coworkers, or teachers or anyone else who can describe your abilities and job-related traits. You will be asked to provide contact information for the people you choose.

Throughout the application or resume, focus on accomplishments that relate most closely to the job you want. You can even use the job announcement as a guide, using some of the same words and phrases to describe your work and education.

Look for concrete examples that show your skills. When describing your work experience, for instance, you might say that you increased sales by 10 percent, finished a task in half the usual time, or received three letters of appreciation from customers.

Choosing a Format

After gathering the information you want to present, the next step is to put it in the proper format. In an application form, the format is set. Just fill in the blanks. But make sure you fill it out completely and follow all instructions. Do not omit any requested information. (One exception is salary expectations; the best strategy is to write "Negotiable.") Consider making a copy of the form before filling it out, in case you make a mistake and have to start over. If possible, have someone else look over the form before submitting it.

In a resume, there are several acceptable ways of organizing the information you want to include. It is common to place the most important information first. One format is to list the applicant's past jobs in reverse chronological order, describing the most recent employment first and working backward. But some applicants use a functional format, organizing their work experience under headings that describe their major skills. They then include a brief work history section that lists only job titles, employers, and dates of employment. Still other applicants choose a format that combines these two approaches in some way. Choose the style that best showcases your skills and experience. Examples of resume formats can be found on the websites of career centers, job boards, and state employment services.

Whatever format you choose, keep your resume short. Many experts recommend that new workers use a one-page resume. Avoid long blocks of text and italicized material. Consider using bullets to highlight duties or key accomplishments.

Before submitting your resume, make sure that it is easy to read. Are the headings clear and consistently formatted with bold or some other style of type? Is the typeface large enough? Much like application forms, it is useful to ask someone to proofread your resume for spelling and other errors. In addition, use your computer's spell checker.

Keep in mind that some employers scan resumes into databases, which they then search for specific keywords or phrases. The keywords are usually nouns referring to experience, education, personal characteristics, or industry buzz words. Identify keywords by reading the job description and qualifications in the job ad; use these same words in your resume. For example, if the job description includes customer service tasks, use the words "customer service" on your resume. Scanners sometimes misread paper resumes, which could mean some of your keywords don't get into the database. Therefore, if you know that your resume will be scanned, and you have the option, e-mail an electronic version. If you must submit a paper resume, make it scannable by using a simple font and avoiding underlines, italics, and graphics. It is also a good idea to send a traditionally formatted resume along with your scannable resume, with a note on each marking its purpose.

Cover Letters

When sending a resume, most people include a cover letter to introduce themselves to the prospective employer. Most cover letters are no more than three short paragraphs. Your cover letter should capture the employer's attention, follow a business letter format, and usually should include the following information:

- Name and address of the specific person to whom the letter is addressed.
- Reason for your interest in the company or position.
- Your main qualifications for the position.
- Request for an interview.
- Your home and work telephone numbers.

If you send a scannable resume, you should also include a scannable cover letter, which avoids graphics, fancy fonts, italics, and underlines.

As with your resume, it may be helpful to look for examples and common formats of cover letters on the Internet or in books at your local library or bookstore, but do not copy letters directly from other sources.

Job Interview Tips

An interview gives you the opportunity to showcase your qualifications to an employer, so it pays to be well prepared. The following information provides some helpful hints.

Preparation
Learn about the organization.
Have a specific job or jobs in mind.
Review your qualifications for the job.
Be ready to briefly describe your experience, showing how it relates it the job.
Be ready to answer broad questions, such as

- "Why should I hire you?"
- "Why do you want this job?"
- "What are your strengths and weaknesses?"

Practice an interview with a friend or relative.

Personal Appearance
Be well groomed.
Dress appropriately.
Do not chew gum or smoke.

The Interview
Be early.
Learn the name of your interviewer and greet him or her with a firm handshake.
Use good manners with everyone you meet. This includes having your cell phone turned off.
Relax and answer each question concisely.
Use proper English—avoid slang.
Be cooperative and enthusiastic.
Use body language to show interest—use eye contact and don't slouch.
Ask questions about the position and the organization, but avoid questions whose answers can easily be found on the company website.
Also avoid asking questions about salary and benefits unless a job offer is made.
Thank the interviewer when you leave and shake hands.
Send a short thank-you note following the interview.

Information to Bring to an Interview
Social Security card.
Government-issued identification (driver's license).
Resume or application. Although not all employers require a resume, you should be able to furnish the interviewer information about your education, training, and previous employment.
References. Employers typically require three references. Get permission before using anyone as a reference. Make sure that they will give you a good reference. Try to avoid using relatives as references.

Transcripts. Employers may require an official copy of transcripts to verify grades, coursework, dates of attendance, and highest grade completed or degree awarded.

Evaluating a Job Offer

Once you receive a job offer, you must decide whether you want the job. Fortunately, most organizations will give you a few days to accept or reject an offer.

There are many issues to consider when assessing a job offer. Will the organization be a good place to work? Will the job be interesting? Are there opportunities for advancement? Is the salary fair? Does the employer offer good benefits? Now is the time to ask the potential employer about these issues—and to do some checking on your own.

The Organization

Background information on an organization can help you to decide whether it is a good place for you to work. Factors to consider include the organization's business or activity, financial condition, age, size, and location.

You generally can get background information on an organization, particularly a large organization, on its website or by telephoning its public relations office. A public company's annual report to the stockholders tells about its corporate philosophy, history, products or services, goals, and financial status. Most government agencies can furnish reports that describe their programs and missions. Press releases, company newsletters or magazines, and recruitment brochures also can be useful. Ask the organization for any other items that might interest a prospective employee. If possible, speak to current or former employees of the organization.

Background information on the organization may be available at your public or school library. If you cannot get an annual report, check the library for reference directories that may provide basic facts about the company, such as earnings, products and services, and number of employees. Some directories widely available in libraries either in print or as online databases include:

- *Dun & Bradstreet's Million Dollar Directory*
- *Standard and Poor's Register of Corporations*
- *Mergent's Industry Review (formerly Moody's Industrial Manual)*
- *Thomas Register of American Manufacturers*
- *Ward's Business Directory*

Stories about an organization in magazines and newspapers can reveal a great deal about its successes, failures, and plans for the future. You can identify articles on a company by looking under its name in periodical or computerized indexes in libraries, or by using one of the Internet's search engines. However, it probably will not be useful to look back more than two or three years.

The library also may have government publications that present projections of growth for the industry in which the organization is classified. Long-term projections of employment and output for detailed industries, covering the entire U.S. economy, are developed by the Bureau of Labor Statistics and revised every 2 years. (See www.bls.gov/emp/ep_table_201.htm.) Trade magazines also may include articles on the trends for specific industries.

Career centers at colleges and universities often have information on employers that is not available in libraries. Ask a career center representative how to find out about a particular organization.

During your research consider the following questions:

Does the organization's business or activity match your own interests and beliefs? It is easier to apply yourself to the work if you are enthusiastic about what the organization does.

How will the size of the organization affect you? Large firms generally offer a greater variety of training programs and career paths, more managerial levels for advancement, and better employee benefits than do small firms. Large employers also may have more advanced technologies. However, many jobs in large firms tend to be highly specialized. Jobs in small firms may offer broader authority and responsibility, a closer working relationship with top management, and a chance to clearly see your contribution to the success of the organization.

Should you work for a relatively new organization or one that is well established? New businesses have a high failure rate, but for many people, the excitement of helping to create a company and the potential for sharing in its success more than offset the risk of job loss. However, it may be just as exciting and rewarding to work for a young firm that already has a foothold on success.

The Job

Even if everything else about the job is attractive, you will be unhappy if you dislike the day-to-day work. Determining in advance whether you will like the work may be difficult. However, the more you find out about the job before accepting or rejecting the offer, the more likely you are to make the right choice. Consider the following questions:

Where is the job located? If the job is in another section of the country, you need to consider the cost of living, the availability of housing and transportation, and the quality of educational and recreational facilities in that section of the country. Even if the job location is in your area, you should consider the time and expense of commuting.

Does the work match your interests and make good use of your skills? The duties and responsibilities of the job should be explained in enough detail to answer this question.

How important is the job to the company or organization? An explanation of where you fit in the organization and how you are supposed to contribute to its overall goals should give you an idea of the job's importance.

What will the hours be? Most jobs involve regular hours—for example, 40 hours a week, during the day, Monday through Friday. Other jobs require night, weekend, or holiday work. In addition, some jobs routinely require overtime to meet deadlines or sales or production goals, or to better serve customers. Consider the effect that the work hours will have on your personal life.

How long do most people who enter this job stay with the company? High turnover can mean dissatisfaction with the nature of the work or something else about the job.

Opportunities Offered by Employers

A good job offers you opportunities to learn new skills, increase your earnings, and rise to positions of greater authority, responsibility, and prestige. A lack of opportunities can dampen interest in the work and result in frustration and boredom.

Some companies develop training plans for their employees. What valuable new skills does the company plan to teach you?

The employer should give you some idea of promotion possibilities within the organization. What is the next step on the career ladder? If you have to wait for a job to become vacant before you can be promoted, how long does this usually take? When opportunities for advancement do arise, will you compete with applicants from outside the company? Can you apply for jobs for which you qualify elsewhere within the organization, or is mobility within the firm limited?

Salaries and Benefits

When an employer makes a job offer, information about earnings and benefits are usually included. You will want to research to determine if the offer is fair. If you choose to negotiate for higher pay and better benefits, objective research will help you strengthen your case.

You may have to go to several sources for information. One of the best places to start is the information from the Bureau of Labor Statistics. Data on earnings by detailed occupation from the Occupational Employment Statistics (OES) Survey are available from the Bureau of Labor Statistics, Office of Occupational Statistics and Employment Projections, 2 Massachusetts Ave. NE., Room 2135, Washington, DC 20212-0001. (202) 691-6569. www.bls.gov/OES.

Data from the Bureau's National Compensation Survey are available from the Bureau of Labor Statistics, Office of Compensation Levels and Trends, 2 Massachusetts Ave. NE., Room 4175, Washington, DC 20212-0001. (202) 691-6199. www.bls.gov/eci.

You should also look for additional information, specifically tailored to your job offer and circumstances. Try to find family, friends, or acquaintances who recently were hired in similar jobs. Ask your teachers and the staff in placement offices about starting pay for graduates with your qualifications. Help-wanted ads in newspapers sometimes give salary ranges for similar positions. Check the library or your school's career center for salary surveys such as those conducted by the National Association of Colleges and Employers or various professional associations.

If you are considering the salary and benefits for a job in another geographic area, make allowances for differences in the cost of living, which may be significantly higher in a large metropolitan area than in a smaller city, town, or rural area.

You also should learn the organization's policy regarding overtime. Depending on the job, you may or may not be exempt from laws requiring the employer to compensate you for overtime. Find out how many hours you will be expected to work each week and whether you receive overtime pay or compensatory time off for working more than the specified number of hours in a week.

Also take into account that the starting salary is just that—the start. Your salary should be reviewed on a regular basis; many organizations do it every year. How much can you expect to earn after one, two, or three or more years? An employer may be unable to be specific about the amount of pay if it includes commissions and bonuses.

Benefits also can add a lot to your base pay, but they vary widely. Find out exactly what the benefit package includes and how much of the cost you must bear.

For More Information

To learn more about finding and applying for jobs, visit your local library and career center. You can find career centers that are part of the U.S. Department of Labor One-Stop Career system by calling toll free (877) 348-0502 or visiting its website at www. careeronestop.org.

The *Occupational Outlook Quarterly*, a career magazine published by the Bureau of Labor Statistics, is one of the resources available at many libraries and career centers. The magazine includes many articles about finding, applying for, and choosing jobs. See, for example:

- "Focused jobseeking: A measured approach to looking for work," online at www.bls.gov/opub/ooq/2011/spring/art01.pdf

- "Informational interviewing: Get the inside scoop on careers," online at www.bls.gov/opub/ooq/2010/summer/art03.pdf.

- "Job search in the age of the Internet: Six job seekers in search of employers," online at www.bls.gov/opub/ooq/2003/summer/art01.pdf

- "Internships: Previewing a profession," online at www.bls.gov/opub/ooq/2006/summer/art02.pdf

- "Resumes, applications, and cover letters," online at www.bls.gov/opub/ooq/2009/summer/art03.pdf

Occupational Information Included in the *OOH*

The *Occupational Outlook Handbook (OOH)* is a career resource offering information on the hundreds of occupations that provide the overwhelming majority of jobs in the United States. Each occupational profile describes the duties required by the occupation, the work environment of that occupation, the typical education and training needed to enter the occupation, the median pay for workers in the occupation, and the job outlook into the next ten years for that occupation. Each profile is in a standard format that makes it easy to compare occupations.

Sections of the Occupational Profiles

Each occupational profile contains the following content:

- Summary
- What They Do
- Work Environment
- How to Become One
- Pay
- Job Outlook
- Similar Occupations
- Contacts for More Information

Summary

Below the job heading, all profiles have a "Quick Facts" table that gives information on the following topics:

- **2012 Median Pay.** The wage at which half of the workers in the occupation earned more than that amount and half earned less. Median wage data are from the Bureau of Labor Statistics (BLS) Occupational Employment Statistics (OES) survey. In May 2012, the median annual wage for all workers was $34,750.
- **Entry-Level Education.** Typical level of education that most workers need to enter the occupation.
- **Work Experience in a Related Occupation.** Work experience that is commonly considered necessary by employers or is a commonly accepted substitute for more formal types of training or education.
- **On-the-job Training.** Postemployment training necessary to attain competency in the skills needed in the occupation.
- **Number of Jobs 2012.** The employment, or size, of the occupation in 2012, the base year of the 2012–22 employment projections.
- **Job Outlook, 2012-22.** The projected percent change in employment from 2012 to 2022. The average growth rate for all occupations is 11 percent.
- **Employment Change, 2012-22.** The projected numeric change in employment from 2012 to 2022.

What They Do

This section describes the main work of people in the occupation.

All occupations have a list of duties or typical tasks performed by these workers. The list includes daily responsibilities, such as answering phone calls or taking a patient's medical history.

This section also may describe the equipment, tools, software, or other items that people in the occupation typically use. For exam-ple, medical records and health information technicians frequently use electronic health records to document a patient's medical information. The section also may describe those with whom workers in the occupation interact, such as clients, patients, and coworkers.

Some profiles discuss specific specialties, job titles, or types of occupations within a given occupation. This subsection includes a brief explanation of each specialty's job duties and how specialties differ from one another. For example, the profile on dentists includes several specialties, such as orthodontists, oral and maxillofacial surgeons, and pediatric dentists.

Work Environment

This section describes an occupation's working conditions, including the workplace, expected level of physical activity, and typical hours.

The section typically begins by noting the employment size of the occupation in 2012 and often includes a table of the industries or settings that employed the most workers in the occupation that year. The section also notes whether employees sometimes need to travel, and if so, how frequently. The section describes the workplace and discusses whether employees work in a safe work environment (such as an office) or a potentially hazardous one (such as a commercial fishing boat). If the workplace is hazardous, the section lists the type of equipment an employee must wear, such as a hardhat or protective goggles, to guard against accidents or exposure to harmful conditions. A subsection on Injuries and Illnesses may appear if this information is notable.

Work Schedules

This subsection includes information on the typical schedule for workers in an occupation, noting whether the majority of workers are employed full time or part time. Full-time workers typically work 35 or more hours in a week, whereas part-time employees work less than 35 hours. For some occupations, the profile also might also include the time of day an employee is expected to begin work and for how long. Registered nurses, for example, may work all hours of the day and on weekends because medical facilities are open around the clock. A discussion of work schedules for occupations in which work may be seasonal, such as farmers, ranchers, and other agricultural managers, also is in this section.

How to Become One

This section describes the typical paths for entry into, and advancement in, an occupation. All profiles have subsections on education and important qualities of workers in the occupation. Optional subsections include information on work experience; training; other experience, such as volunteering or internships; licenses, certifications, and registrations; and advancement.

Education

This subsection describes the education that most workers typically need to enter an occupation. Some occupations require no formal education, whereas others may require, for example, a doctoral or professional degree. In some occupations, such as computer support specialists, workers can enter with different educational backgrounds. In these cases, the profile discusses all of the typical paths for entry into the occupation.

This subsection also may include information on the college majors and subjects that people study in preparation for the occupation, as well as a list of typical courses that may aid a high school student in preparing for an occupation. For example, high school students interested in applying to respiratory therapy programs should take courses in health, biology, mathematics, chemistry, and physics.

Work Experience in a Related Occupation

This subsection describes whether employers require work experience in a related occupation. Many managerial occupations rely on work experience in a related occupation. For example, architectural and engineering managers typically have previous work experience as an architect or engineer.

Training

This subsection describes the typical on-the-job training necessary to attain competency in an occupation, including both practical and classroom training that workers receive after being hired. For example, firefighters must complete training at a fire academy or at an institution with a similar program before they are considered prepared to combat fires.

Apprenticeships, internships, and residency programs are also discussed this subsection. For example, the profile on physicians and surgeons includes information on residency programs and the architects profile has information on internships that architects complete as part of a training program to become licensed.

Other Experience

This subsection describes other types of experience that would be helpful or essential in getting a job in the occupation, such as experience gained through volunteering or student internships completed while one is in school.

Licenses, Certifications, and Registrations

This subsection describes whether credentials such as licenses, certifications, and registrations typically are needed for an occupation and, if so, how workers can earn the credentials.

States issue licenses to workers to signify that they have met specific legal requirements to practice in certain occupations. To become licensed, workers usually need to pass an examination and comply with eligibility requirements, such as possessing a minimum level of education, work experience, or training; or completing an internship, a residency, or a formal apprenticeship. States have their own regulatory boards that set standards for practicing a licensed occupation, so rules and eligibility criteria may vary from state to state, even for the same occupation.

Some occupations have certifications available that typically are voluntary. For example, fitness trainers and instructors are encouraged, but not required, to become certified before entering the occupation. Some employers will allow a trainer or instructor to become certified after being hired.

Certification requires demonstrated competency in a skill or a set of skills and commonly requires passing an examination or having a certain amount and type of work experience or training. For some certification programs, the candidate must have a certain level of education before becoming eligible for certification.

This subsection explains any prerequisites for certification, licensure, or registration, as well as how a person would complete them—such as by passing an exam, performing a certain type of work, or receiving certain training or education. If states require workers to be certified before they can be licensed, this section also notes that information.

Certification should not be confused with certificates from an educational institution. A certificate awarded by a postsecondary educational institution is a postsecondary non-degree award and is discussed in the subsection on education.

Registrations typically are required and issued by state or local governments. Workers seeking registration may need to be licensed or certified. In most cases, workers must pay fees to receive or maintain their registration.

Important Qualities

This subsection describes important characteristics of workers in the occupation and includes an explanation of why those characteristics are useful.

The qualities include areas of skills, aptitudes, and personal characteristics. For example, an emergency medical technician must be physically strong, and a web developer needs creativity and customer-service skills.

Advancement

This subsection describes the advancement opportunities for workers in the occupation.

Opportunities for advancement can come from within the occupation, such as a promotion to a supervisory or managerial level; from advancement into another occupation, such as moving from a computer support specialist to a network and computer systems administrator; or by becoming self-employed, such as a dentist opening up his or her own practice.

The subsection often explains the requirements for advancement, such as certification or additional formal education.

Pay

This section discusses the wages of workers in the occupation.

Almost all occupational profiles in the *OOH* show median wage data for wage and salary workers in the occupation. The data are from the Bureau of Labor Statistics (BLS) Occupational Employment Statistics (OES) survey. The median wage is the wage at which half of the workers in an occupation earned more and half earned less. A chart that compares the median wage of workers in the occupation to the median wage of workers across all occupations accompanies the wage data.

Profiles typically include median wages and the wages earned by the top 10 percent and bottom 10 percent of workers in the occupation. Many also include wages earned by workers in selected industries—those in which most of an occupation's workers are employed. The wage data by industry are also from the OES survey.

Some occupational profiles may cite wage data from sources other than the BLS. For example, the Academy of Nutrition and Dietetics provides wage data on dietitians and nutritionists. Unless otherwise noted, the source of pay data for occupations in the *OOH* is the OES survey.

The "Pay" section provides work schedule information, also found in the "Work Environment" section. The section also might include, when noteworthy, information about union membership.

Job Outlook

This section describes how employment is projected to grow or decline between 2012 and 2022. In addition to presenting these projections, the section discusses the major factors expected to affect the outlook for employment in the occupation. Some of the factors are changes in technology, in business practices, and in demographics.

The outlook section sometimes includes a "Job Prospects" subsection, which provides a qualitative discussion of the relative ease or difficulty experienced by those who seek to enter the occupation.

Similar Occupations

This section identifies other occupational profiles with similar job duties or similar required skills.

Contacts for More Information

This section identifies associations, organizations, and other institutions that provide readers with additional information. The section also includes references to the Occupational Information Network (O*NET) system for the occupation or occupations included in the profile. State employment service offices use O*NET to classify applicants and job openings. For each occupation, O*NET lists a number of descriptors, including common tasks, necessary knowledge and skills, and frequently used technology.

Key Phrases in the OOH

The following list explains how to interpret the key phrases used to describe projected changes in employment:

If the statement reads:	*Employment is projected to:*
Grow much faster than average	increase 22 percent or more
Grow faster than average	increase 15 to 21 percent
Grow about as fast as average	increase 8 to 14 percent
Grow more slowly than average	increase 3 to 7 percent
Little or no change	decrease 2 percent to increase 2 percent
Decline	decrease 3 percent or more

Architecture and Engineering

Aerospace Engineering and Operations Technicians

- **2012 Median Pay** .... $61,530 per year
  $29.58 per hour
- **Entry-Level Education** .... Associate's degree
- **Work Experience in a Related Occupation** .... None
- **On-the-Job Training** .... None
- **Number of Jobs 2012** 9,900
- **Job Outlook, 2012–22** .... 0% (Little or no change)
- **Employment Change, 2012–22** 0

What Aerospace Engineering and Operations Technicians Do

Aerospace engineering and operations technicians operate and maintain equipment used in testing new aircraft and spacecraft. Increasingly, these workers are being required to program and run computer simulations that test new designs. Their work is critical in preventing the failure of key parts of new aircraft, spacecraft, or missiles. They also help in quality assurance, testing, and operation of advanced technology equipment used in producing aircraft and the systems that go into the aircraft.

Duties. Aerospace engineering and operations technicians typically do the following:

- Meet with aerospace engineers to discuss details and implications of test procedures
- Build and maintain test facilities for aircraft systems
- Make and install parts and systems to be tested in test equipment
- Operate and calibrate computer systems so that they comply with test requirements
- Ensure that test procedures are performed smoothly and safely
- Record data from test parts and assemblies
- Install instruments in aircraft and spacecraft
- Monitor and ensure quality in producing systems that go into the aircraft

Aerospace engineering and operations technicians maintain and operate equipment used in testing new aircraft.

New aircraft designs undergo years of testing before they are put into service, because the failure of key parts during flight can be fatal. As part of the job, technicians often calibrate test equipment, such as wind tunnels, and determine the causes of equipment malfunctions. They also may program and run computer simulations that test the new designs.

Work of aerospace engineering and operations technicians involves additive manufacturing, also known as 3D printing, which some workers in this occupation are beginning to specialize in.

Work Environment

Aerospace engineering and operations technicians held about 9,900 jobs in 2012. They usually work full time in laboratories, offices, and manufacturing or industrial plants. Many are exposed to hazards from equipment or from toxic materials, but incidents are rare as long as proper procedures are followed.

The industries that employed the most aerospace engineering and operations technicians in 2012 were as follows:

Aerospace product and parts manufacturing 37%
Navigational, measuring, electromedical, and
  control instruments manufacturing 18
Architectural, engineering, and related services 14

Median Annual Wages, May 2012

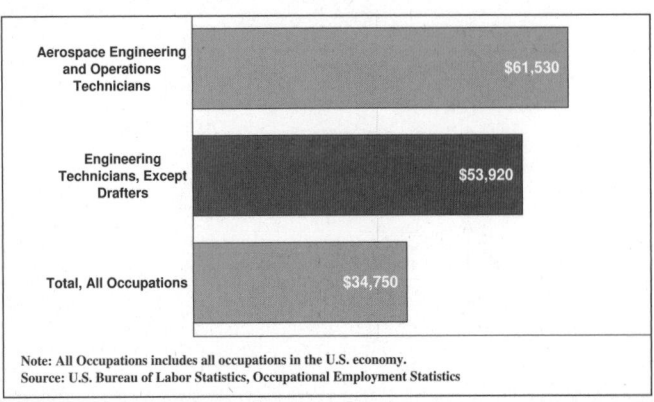

Aerospace Engineering and Operations Technicians — $61,530

Engineering Technicians, Except Drafters — $53,920

Total, All Occupations — $34,750

Note: All Occupations includes all occupations in the U.S. economy.
Source: U.S. Bureau of Labor Statistics, Occupational Employment Statistics

Percent Change in Employment, Projected 2012–2022

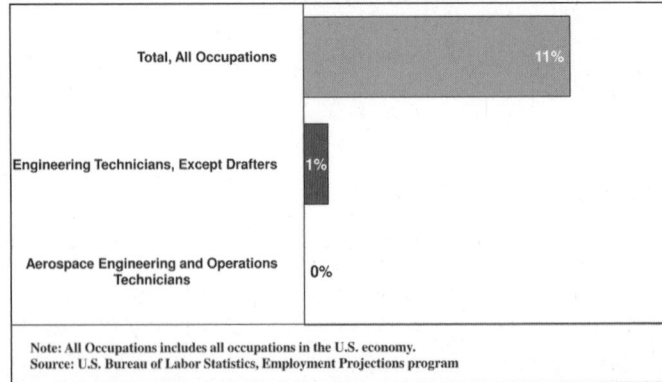

Total, All Occupations — 11%

Engineering Technicians, Except Drafters — 1%

Aerospace Engineering and Operations Technicians — 0%

Note: All Occupations includes all occupations in the U.S. economy.
Source: U.S. Bureau of Labor Statistics, Employment Projections program

Employment Projections Data for Aerospace Engineering and Operations Technicians

Occupational title	SOC Code	Employment, 2012	Projected Employment, 2022	Change, 2012–2022	
				Percent	Numeric
Aerospace engineering and operations technicians................. 17-3021		9,900	9,900	0	0

Source: U.S. Bureau of Labor Statistics, Employment Projections Program

Note: Data are rounded. Go to Occupational Information Included in the OOH *for a discussion of the data in this table.*

Communications equipment manufacturing............................. 6
Scheduled air transportation.. 4

Aerospace engineering and operations technicians are physically active in constructing the designs that aerospace engineers develop. Consequently, these technicians often work directly in manufacturing or industrial plants, where they help to assemble aircraft, missiles, and spacecraft away from an office environment.

Work Schedules. Aerospace engineering and operations technicians have opportunities for employment throughout the private sector, with large and small manufacturing organizations, as well as with engineering services firms. Schedules worked tend to parallel those of the engineering and operations staff members.

How to Become One

Aerospace engineering and operations technicians with an associate's degree in engineering technology are increasingly being preferred by employers because of the advanced technologies being used in design, test, and production. Prospective technicians also may earn certificates or diplomas offered by vocational or technical schools. Some aerospace engineering and operations technicians must have security clearances to work on projects related to national defense. U.S. citizenship may be required for certain types and levels of clearances.

Education. High school students interested in becoming aerospace engineering and operations technicians should take classes in math, science, and, if available, drafting and computer skills. Courses that help students develop skills working with their hands also are valuable, because these technicians build what aerospace engineers design. In addition, technicians should have a basic understanding of computers and programs in order to model or simulate products.

Vocational–technical schools include postsecondary public institutions that emphasize training needed by local employers. Students who complete these programs typically receive a diploma or certificate. Community colleges offer programs similar to those in technical institutes but include more theory-based and liberal arts coursework and programs. Community colleges typically award an associate's degree.

The Engineering Technology Accreditation Commission of ABET accredits programs that include at least college algebra, trigonometry, and basic science courses.

Many vocational and community college programs offer cooperative programs with work experience built into the curriculum.

Important Qualities

Communication skills. Aerospace engineering and operations technicians receive instructions from aerospace engineers. This means they must be able to understand and follow the instructions, as well as communicate any problems to their supervisors.

Critical-thinking skills. Aerospace engineering and operations technicians must be able to help aerospace engineers troubleshoot particular design issues. They must be able to help evaluate system capabilities, identify problems, formulate the right question, and then find the right answer.

Detail oriented. Aerospace engineering and operations technicians make and keep precise measurements needed by aerospace engineers. Consequently, they must make correct measurements and keep accurate records.

Interpersonal skills. Aerospace engineering and operations technicians must be able to take instructions and offer advice. The ability to work well with supervising engineers, other technicians, and mechanics is essential because technicians interact with people from other divisions, businesses, and governments.

Math skills. Aerospace engineering and operations technicians use the principles of mathematics for analysis, design, and troubleshooting tasks in their work.

Mechanical skills. Aerospace engineering and operations technicians must be able to assist aerospace engineers by building what the engineers design. Mechanical skills are needed to help with the processes and directions required to move from design to production.

Licenses, Certifications, and Registrations. Though not required for the job, certification is offered by the Federal Aviation Administration (FAA). Certification may be beneficial because it shows employers that a technician can carry out the theoretical designs of aerospace engineers.

Both companies and the FAA seek to ensure the highest standards for the safety of the aircraft SpaceTEC coordinates a nation-

Similar Occupations   This table shows a list of occupations with job duties that are similar to those of aerospace engineering and operations technicians.

Occupations	Entry-level Education	2012 Pay	Projected Job Growth	Average Annual Openings
Aerospace Engineers	Bachelor's degree	$103,720	7%	2,540
Drafters	Associate's degree	$49,726	1%	3,220
Electro-mechanical Technicians	Associate's degree	$51,820	4%	430
Industrial Engineering Technicians	Associate's degree	$50,980	-3%	1,410
Mechanical Engineering Technicians	Associate's degree	$51,980	5%	1,210

wide program through community and technical colleges to help students prepare for certification.

Pay

The median annual wage for aerospace engineering and operations technicians was $61,530 in May 2012. The median wage is the wage at which half the workers in an occupation earned more than that amount and half earned less. The lowest 10 percent earned less than $40,020, and the top 10 percent earned more than $87,370.

In May 2012, the median annual wage for aerospace engineering and operations technicians in the top five industries in which these technicians worked were as follows:

Scheduled air transportation	$67,870
Aerospace product and parts manufacturing	66,380
Navigational, measuring, electromedical, and control instruments manufacturing	59,960
Architectural, engineering, and related services	56,330
Communications equipment manufacturing	55,870

Aerospace engineering and operations technicians have opportunities for employment throughout the private sector, with large and small manufacturing organizations, as well as with engineering services firms. Schedules worked tend to parallel those of the engineering and operations staff members.

Job Outlook

Employment of aerospace engineering and operations technicians is projected to show little or no change from 2012 to 2022. Aerospace engineering and operations technicians work on many projects related to national defense and therefore require security clearances. This restriction will help to keep jobs in the United States. In addition, aircraft are being redesigned to cut down on noise pollution and to raise fuel efficiency, increasing demand for research and development particularly in support of air transportation.

Aerospace engineering and operations technicians work mainly in national defense–related projects or in designing civilian aircraft. Research and development projects, ranging from more efficient propulsion systems to new air transport concepts, will create demand for these workers.

Those who work on engines or propulsion will be increasingly needed as design and production emphasis shifts to rebuilding existing aircraft so that they give off less noise while using less fuel. Domestically, as space flight shifts to the civilian market from government agencies, there will be a move toward hiring by emerging civilian space companies.

However, aerospace engineering and operations technicians also are working to improve productivity through the use of automation and robotics, and the increased productivity will likely reduce low-end production employment in this occupation. Another factor that may slow growth in the occupation is the continuing adoption of computational fluid dynamics (CFD) software. This technology has lowered testing costs and has replaced more traditional testing. As a result, these technicians will see a shift toward more high-end technology tasks.

Job Prospects. Job openings should be available for aerospace engineering and operations technicians. These workers usually retire at a younger age than aerospace engineers, and indications are that the proportion of those eligible to retire will be rising substantially over the next few years.

O*NET

➤ Aerospace Engineering and Operations Technicians (17-3021.00)

Contacts for More Information

For more information about accredited programs, visit
➤ ABET (www.abet.org/)
  For more information about careers in engineering, visit
➤ Technology Student Association (www.tsaweb.org/)
  For more information about certification, visit
➤ SpaceTEC (http://spacetec.us/wordpress11/)

Aerospace Engineers

- **2012 Median Pay** .... $103,720 per year
  $49.87 per hour
- **Entry-Level Education** ....Bachelor's degree
- **Work Experience in a Related Occupation**............... None
- **On-the-Job Training** .... None
- **Number of Jobs 2012** 83,000
- **Job Outlook, 2012–22** .... 7% (Slower than average)
- **Employment Change, 2012–22** 6,100

What Aerospace Engineers Do

Aerospace engineers design aircraft, spacecraft, satellites, and missiles. In addition, they test prototypes to make sure that they function according to design.

Duties. Aerospace engineers typically do the following:

- Direct and coordinate the design, manufacture, and testing of aircraft and aerospace products
- Assess proposals for projects to determine if they are technically and financially feasible
- Determine if proposed projects will result in safe aircraft and parts
- Evaluate designs to see that the products meet engineering principles, customer requirements, and environmental challenges
- Develop acceptance criteria for design methods, quality standards, sustainment after delivery, and completion dates
- Ensure that projects meet quality standards
- Inspect malfunctioning or damaged products to identify sources of problems and possible solutions

Aerospace engineers study the necessary physics for designing aircraft that will fly.

Median Annual Wages, May 2012

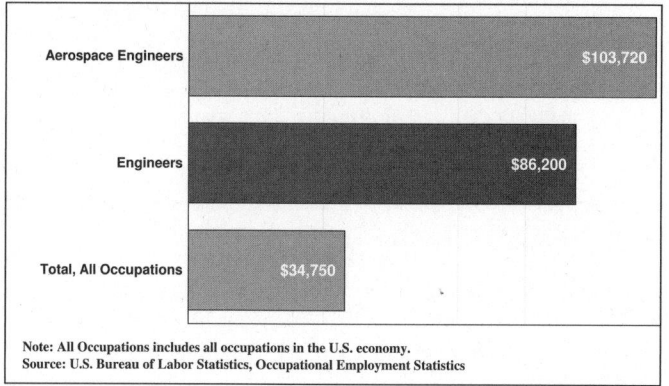

Note: All Occupations includes all occupations in the U.S. economy.
Source: U.S. Bureau of Labor Statistics, Occupational Employment Statistics

Percent Change in Employment, Projected 2012–2022

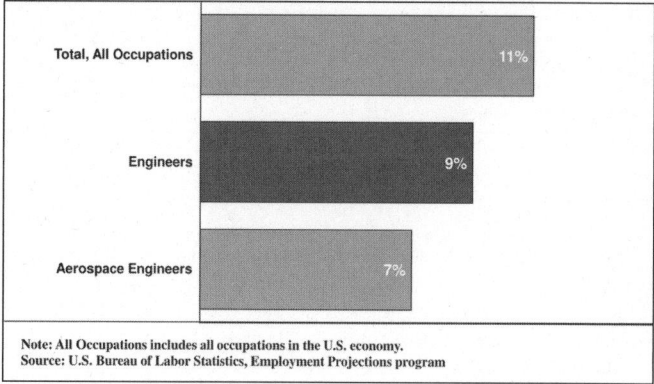

Note: All Occupations includes all occupations in the U.S. economy.
Source: U.S. Bureau of Labor Statistics, Employment Projections program

Aerospace engineers may develop new technologies for use in aviation, defense systems, and spacecraft. They often specialize in areas such as aerodynamic fluid flow; structural design; guidance, navigation, and control; instrumentation and communication; robotics; and propulsion and combustion.

Aerospace engineers can specialize in designing different types of aerospace products, such as commercial and military airplanes and helicopters; remotely piloted aircraft and rotorcraft; spacecraft, including launch vehicles and satellites; and military missiles and rockets.

Aerospace engineers often become experts in one or more related fields: aerodynamics, thermodynamics, celestial mechanics, flight mechanics, propulsion, acoustics, and guidance and control systems.

Aerospace engineers typically specialize in one of two types of engineering: aeronautical or astronautical.

Aeronautical engineers work with aircraft. They are involved primarily in designing aircraft and propulsion systems and in studying the aerodynamic performance of aircraft and construction materials. They work with the theory, technology, and practice of flight within Earth's atmosphere.

Astronautical engineers work with the science and technology of spacecraft and how they perform inside and outside Earth's atmosphere.

Aeronautical and astronautical engineers face different environmental and operational issues in designing aircraft and spacecraft. However, the two fields overlap a great deal because they both depend on the basic principles of physics.

Work Environment

Aerospace engineers held about 83,000 jobs in 2012. They are employed in industries where workers design or build aircraft, missiles, systems for national defense, or spacecraft. Aerospace engineers work primarily for firms that engage in analysis and design, manufacturing, research and development, and for the federal government.

The industries that employed the most aerospace engineers in 2012 were as follows:

Aerospace product and parts manufacturing 38%
Scientific research and development services 16
Architectural, engineering, and related services 12
Federal government 12
Navigational, measuring, electromedical, and
    control instruments manufacturing 6

Aerospace engineers now spend more of their time in an office environment than they have in the past, because modern aircraft design requires the use of sophisticated computer equipment and software design tools, modeling, and simulations for tests, evaluation, and training.

Aerospace engineers work with other professionals involved in designing and building aircraft, spacecraft, and their components. Therefore, they must be able to communicate well, divide work into manageable tasks, and work with others toward a common goal.

Work Schedules. Aerospace engineers typically work full time. Engineers who direct projects must often work extra hours to monitor progress, to ensure that the design meets requirements, to determine how to measure aircraft performance, to see that production meets design standards, and to ensure that deadlines are met.

How to Become One

Aerospace engineers must have a bachelor's degree in aerospace engineering or some other field of engineering or science related to aerospace systems. Some aerospace engineers work on projects that are related to national defense and thus require security clearances. U.S. citizenship may be required for certain types and levels of clearances.

Education. Entry-level aerospace engineers usually need a bachelor's degree. High school students interested in studying aerospace engineering should take courses in chemistry, physics, and math, including algebra, trigonometry, and calculus.

Bachelor's degree programs include classroom, laboratory, and field studies in subjects such as general engineering principles, propulsion, stability and control, structures, mechanics, and aerodynamics, which is the study of how air interacts with moving objects.

Some colleges and universities offer cooperative programs, in partnership with industry, that give students practical experience while they complete their education. Cooperative programs and internships enable students to gain valuable experience and to finance part of their education.

At some universities, a student can enroll in a 5-year program that leads to both a bachelor's degree and a master's degree upon completion. A graduate degree will allow an engineer to work as an instructor at a university or to do research and development. Programs in aerospace engineering are accredited by ABET.

Important Qualities

Analytical skills. Aerospace engineers must be able to identify design elements that may not meet requirements and then must formulate alternatives to improve their performance.

Business skills. Much of the work done by aerospace engineers involves meeting federal government standards. Meeting these standards often requires knowledge of standard business practices, as well as knowledge of commercial law.

Employment Projections Data for Aerospace Engineers

Occupational title	SOC Code	Employment, 2012	Projected Employment, 2022	Change, 2012–2022	
				Percent	Numeric
Aerospace engineers...	17-2011	83,000	89,100	7	6,100

Source: *U.S. Bureau of Labor Statistics, Employment Projections Program*

Note: *Data are rounded. Go to* Occupational Information Included in the OOH *for a discussion of the data in this table.*

Critical-thinking skills. Aerospace engineers must be able to translate a set of issues into requirements and to figure out why a particular design does not work. They must be able to ask the right question, then find an acceptable answer.

Math skills. Aerospace engineers use the principles of calculus, trigonometry, and other advanced topics in math for analysis, design, and troubleshooting in their work.

Writing skills. Aerospace engineers must be able to write papers that explain their designs clearly and create documentation for future reference.

Licenses, Certifications, and Registrations. Aerospace engineers are not required to be licensed at the entry level. More experienced aerospace engineers, who assume more responsibility, usually earn the Professional Engineer (PE) license. Licensure generally requires the following:

- A degree from an engineering program accredited by ABET
- A passing score on the Fundamentals of Engineering (FE) exam
- Relevant work experience
- A passing score on the Professional Engineering exam

The initial Fundamentals of Engineering (FE) exam can be taken right after graduating with a bachelor's degree. Engineers who pass this exam commonly are called engineers in training (EITs) or engineer interns (EIs). After acquiring suitable work experience, EITs can take the second exam, called the Principles and Practice of Engineering (PE) exam.

Several states require engineers to take continuing education courses to keep their licenses. Most states recognize licenses from other states, as long as the other states' licensing requirements meet or exceed their own licensing requirements.

Advancement. Eventually, aerospace engineers may advance to become technical specialists or to supervise a team of engineers and technicians. Some may even become engineering managers or move into executive positions, such as program managers. However, preparation for assuming a managerial position usually requires serving an apprenticeship under a more experienced aerospace engineer.

Pay

The median annual wage for aerospace engineers was $103,720 in May 2012. The median wage is the wage at which half of the workers in an occupation earned more than that amount and half earned less. The lowest 10 percent earned less than $65,450, and the top 10 percent earned more than $149,120.

In May 2012, the median annual wages for aerospace engineers in the top five industries in which these engineers worked were as follows:

Federal government	$110,860
Scientific research and development services	109,740
Navigational, measuring, electromedical, and control instruments manufacturing	107,510
Architectural, engineering, and related services	102,720
Aerospace product and parts manufacturing	97,560

A compensation study published by *Aviation Week* in 2012 found that average annual pay among aerospace engineers was $71,859 at the entry level.

Union Membership. Compared with workers in all occupations, aerospace engineers had a higher percentage of workers who belonged to a union in 2012.

Job Outlook

Employment of aerospace engineers is projected to grow 7 percent from 2012 to 2022 slower than the average for all occupations. Some aerospace engineers work on projects that are related to national defense and thus require security clearances. This requirement will help to keep jobs in the United States. In addition, aircraft are being redesigned to cut down on noise pollution and to raise fuel efficiency, which will help spur demand for research and development. However, growth will be tempered because many of these engineers are employed in manufacturing industries that are projected to grow slowly or even decline.

Most of the work of aerospace engineers involves national defense–related projects or the design of civilian aircraft. Research

Similar Occupations   This table shows a list of occupations with job duties that are similar to those of aerospace engineers.

Occupations	Entry-level Education	2012 Pay	Projected Job Growth	Average Annual Openings
Aerospace Engineering and Operations Technicians	Associate's degree	$61,530	0%	210
Architectural and Engineering Managers	Bachelor's degree	$124,870	7%	6,060
Computer Hardware Engineers	Bachelor's degree	$100,920	7%	2,410
Electrical and Electronics Engineering Technicians	Associate's degree	$57,850	0%	3,040
Electrical and Electronics Engineers	Bachelor's degree	$89,701	4%	7,940
Industrial Engineers	Bachelor's degree	$78,860	5%	7,540
Materials Engineers	Bachelor's degree	$85,150	1%	750
Mechanical Engineers	Bachelor's degree	$80,580	4%	9,970

and development projects, such as those related to improving the safety, efficiency, and environmental soundness of aircraft, should create demand for workers in this occupation.

Aerospace engineers who work on engines or propulsion will be needed as the emphasis in design and production shifts to rebuilding existing aircraft so that they are less noisy and more fuel efficient.

In addition, as governments refocus their space efforts, new companies are emerging to provide access to space outside of standard space agencies. The efforts of these companies will include low-orbit and beyond-earth-orbit capabilities for human and robotic space travel.

Job Prospects. Aerospace engineers who know how to use collaborative engineering tools and processes and are familiar with modeling, simulation, and robotics should have good opportunities. Employment opportunities also should be favorable for those trained in computational fluid dynamics software, which has enabled companies to test designs in a digital environment, thereby lowering testing costs. The aging of workers in this occupation also should help to create openings in the occupation over the next decade.

O*NET

➤ Aerospace Engineers (17-2011.00)

Contacts for More Information

For information about general engineering education and career resources, visit
➤ American Society for Engineering Education (www.asee.org/)
➤ Technology Student Association (www.tsaweb.org/)
    For more information about licensure as an aerospace engineer, visit
➤ National Council of Examiners for Engineering and Surveying (www.ncees.org/)
➤ National Society of Professional Engineers (www.nspe.org/index.html)
    For information about accredited engineering programs, visit
➤ ABET (www.abet.org/)
    For information about licensure and current developments in aeronautics, visit
➤ American Institute of Aeronautics and Astronautics (www.aiaa.org/)

Agricultural Engineers

- **2012 Median Pay** .... $74,000 per year
                                                  $35.58 per hour
- **Entry-Level Education** ....Bachelor's degree
- **Work Experience in a Related Occupation**............... None
- **On-the-Job Training** .... None
- **Number of Jobs 2012** 2,600
- **Job Outlook, 2012–22** .... 5% (Slower than average)
- **Employment Change, 2012–22** 100

What Agricultural Engineers Do

Agricultural engineers–also known as biological and agricultural engineers–work on a variety of activities. These activities range from aquaculture (raising food, such as fish, that thrive in water) to land farming to forestry; from developing biofuels to improving conservation; from planning animal environments to finding better ways to process food.

Agricultural engineering includes designing farming equipment and processes.

Duties. Agricultural engineers typically do the following:

- Design agricultural machinery components and equipment, using computer-aided design (CAD) technology
- Test agricultural machinery and equipment to ensure that they perform properly
- Design food-processing plants and supervise manufacturing operations
- Plan and direct construction of rural electric-power distribution systems
- Design structures to store and process crops
- Design housing and environments to maximize animals' comfort, health, and productivity
- Provide advice on water quality and issues related to managing pollution, controlling rivers, and protecting and using other water resources
- Design and supervise environmental and land reclamation projects in agriculture and related industries
- Discuss plans with clients, contractors, consultants, and other engineers so that the plans can be evaluated and any necessary changes made

Agricultural engineers apply technological advances to farming. For example, they design farming equipment that uses GPS systems (Global Positioning Systems). They help agricultural and food scientists create biological applications for developing crops with new, sturdier traits. They also help with pollution control at larger farms and with water resource matters. These engineers are also heavily involved in efforts to produce new forms of biomass, including algae, for power generation.

Some engineers specialize in areas such as power systems and machinery design, structural and environmental engineering, and food and bioprocess engineering. Agricultural engineers often work in research and development, production, or sales.

Work Environment

Agricultural engineers held about 2,600 jobs in 2012.

The industries that employed the most agricultural engineers in 2012 were as follows:

Architectural, engineering, and related services 17%
Federal government, excluding postal service 16

Median Annual Wages, May 2012

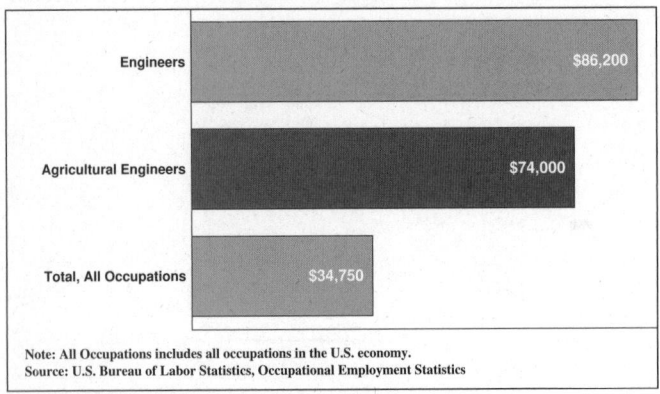

Note: All Occupations includes all occupations in the U.S. economy.
Source: U.S. Bureau of Labor Statistics, Occupational Employment Statistics

Percent Change in Employment, Projected 2012–2022

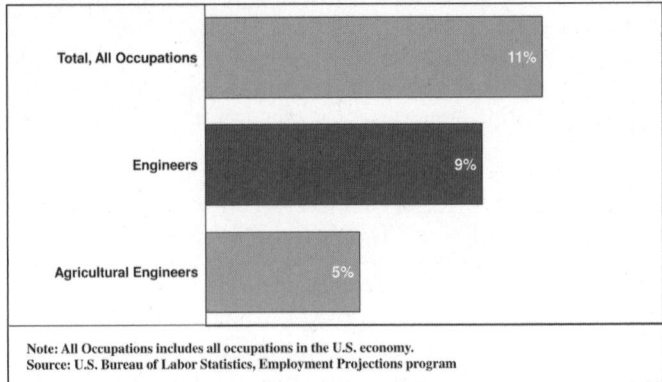

Note: All Occupations includes all occupations in the U.S. economy.
Source: U.S. Bureau of Labor Statistics, Employment Projections program

Food manufacturing 14
Agriculture, construction, and mining machinery
    manufacturing.. 13
Educational services; state, local, and private 6

Agricultural engineers spend time at a variety of worksites, both indoors and outdoors, traveling to agricultural settings to see that equipment and machinery are functioning according to both the manufacturers' instructions and federal and state regulations. They may work onsite when they supervise environmental reclamation or water resource management projects. Other worksites where they are employed include research and development laboratories, classrooms, and offices.

Agricultural engineers work with others in designing solutions to problems or applying technological advances. Thus, they must be able to work with, and accept feedback from, people from a variety of backgrounds such as agronomy, animal sciences, genetics, and horticulture.

Work Schedules. Agricultural engineers typically work full time. They must sometimes work overtime because of the nature of agricultural projects.

In addition, agricultural engineers often must be available to address problems that may come up in manufacturing operations or rural construction projects.

Weather also has a role in their work schedules. Some outdoor projects for environmental reclamation or pollution management need favorable weather; and, therefore, agricultural engineers may work long hours to take advantage of good weather.

How to Become One

Agricultural engineers must have a bachelor's degree, preferably in agricultural engineering or biological engineering. Employers also value practical experience, so cooperative-education engineering programs at universities are valuable as well.

Education. Students who are interested in studying agricultural engineering will benefit from taking high school courses in mathematics, such as algebra, trigonometry, and calculus; and science, such as biology, chemistry, and physics.

Entry-level jobs in agricultural engineering require a bachelor's degree. Bachelor's degree programs typically are 4-year programs that include classroom, laboratory, and field studies in areas such as science, mathematics, and engineering principles. Most colleges and universities offer cooperative programs that allow students to gain practical experience while completing their education.

ABET accredits programs in agricultural engineering.

Important Qualities

Analytical skills. Because agricultural engineers sometimes design systems that are part of a larger agricultural or environmental system, they must be able to propose solutions that interact well with other workers, machinery and equipment, and the environment.

Listening skills. Agricultural engineers must listen to and seek out information from clients, workers, and other professionals working on a project. Furthermore, they must be able to address the concerns of those who will be using the systems and solutions they design.

Math skills. Agricultural engineers use the principals of calculus, trigonometry, and other advanced topics in math for analysis, design, and troubleshooting in their work.

Problem-solving skills. Agricultural engineers work on problems affecting many different aspects of agricultural production, from designing safer equipment for food processing to water erosion. To solve these problems, agricultural engineers must be able to apply general principles of engineering to new circumstances.

Licenses, Certifications, and Registrations. Agricultural engineers who offer their services directly to the public must have a license. Licensed engineers are called professional engineers (PEs). Licensure generally requires

• A degree from an ABET-accredited engineering program

• A passing score on the Fundamentals of Engineering (FE) exam

• Relevant work experience, typically at least 4 years

• A passing score on the Professional Engineering (PE) exam

The initial Fundamentals of Engineering (FE) exam can be taken after earning a bachelor's degree. Engineers who pass this exam

Employment Projections Data for Agricultural Engineers

Occupational title	SOC Code	Employment, 2012	Projected Employment, 2022	Change, 2012–2022	
				Percent	Numeric
Agricultural engineers..	17-2021	2,600	2,700	5	100

Source: U.S. Bureau of Labor Statistics, Employment Projections Program

Note: Data are rounded. Go to **Occupational Information Included in the OOH** *for a discussion of the data in this table.*

Similar Occupations   This table shows a list of occupations with job duties that are similar to those of agricultural engineers.

Occupations	Entry-level Education	2012 Pay	Projected Job Growth	Average Annual Openings
Agricultural and Food Science Technicians	Associate's degree	$34,070	3%	1,010
Agricultural and Food Scientists	See "How to Become One"	$58,636	10%	1,640
Biological Technicians	Bachelor's degree	$39,750	10%	3,210
Civil Engineers	Bachelor's degree	$79,340	20%	12,010
Environmental Engineers	Bachelor's degree	$80,890	15%	2,110
Farmers, Ranchers, and Other Agricultural Managers	High school diploma or equivalent	$69,300	-19%	15,020
Hydrologists	Master's degree	$75,530	9%	290
Industrial Engineers	Bachelor's degree	$78,860	5%	7,540
Mechanical Engineers	Bachelor's degree	$80,580	4%	9,970

commonly are called engineers in training (EITs) or engineer interns (EIs). After getting suitable work experience, EITs and EIs can take the second exam, called the Principles and Practice of Engineering.

Several states require continuing education for engineers to keep their license. Most states recognize licensure from other states, as long as the licensing state's requirements meet or exceed their own licensure requirements.

Advancement. Beginning engineers usually work under the supervision of experienced engineers. As they gain knowledge and experience, beginning engineers move to more difficult projects with greater independence to develop designs, solve problems, and make decisions.

Eventually, agricultural engineers may advance to supervise a team of engineers and technicians. Some advance to become engineering managers. Agricultural engineers who go into sales use their engineering background to discuss a product's technical aspects with potential buyers and help in product planning, installation, and use. For more information, see the profiles on architectural and engineering managers and sales engineers.

Pay

The median annual wage for agricultural engineers was $74,000 in May 2012. The median wage is the wage at which half the workers in an occupation earned more than that amount and half earned less. The lowest 10 percent earned less than $44,750, and the top 10 percent earned more than $115,680.

In May 2012, median annual wages for agricultural engineers in the top five industries in which these engineers worked were as follows:

Architectural, engineering, and related services $82,090
Federal government, excluding postal service 77,030
Food manufacturing 73,380
Agriculture, construction, and mining machinery
    manufacturing.. 67,690
Educational services; state, local, and private 50,100

Job Outlook

Employment of agricultural engineers is projected to grow 5 percent from 2012 to 2022, slower than the average for all occupations.

Agricultural engineers are pursuing new areas related to agriculture, such as high-tech applications to agricultural products, water resource management, and alternative energies. However, activity related to designing new machinery and equipment in agriculture also is expected to continue to create some employment opportunities.

These engineers are also involved with designing and building machinery and equipment needed to implement findings from research on genetically modified plants and seeds. Consequently, demand is also expected to come from U.S. firms that market their farm technology products to farmers internationally.

O*NET

➤ Agricultural Engineers (17-2021.00)

Contacts for More Information

For more information about agricultural engineers, visit
➤ American Society of Agricultural and Biological Engineers (www.asabe.org/)

For information about general engineering education and career resources, visit
➤ American Society for Engineering Education (www.asee.org/)
➤ Technology Student Association (www.tsaweb.org/)

For more information about licensure for agricultural engineers, visit
➤ National Council of Examiners for Engineering and Surveying (http://ncees.org/)
➤ National Society of Professional Engineers (www.nspe.org/index.html)

For information about accredited engineering programs, visit
➤ ABET (www.abet.org/)

Architects

- **2012 Median Pay** .... $73,090 per year
  $35.14 per hour
- **Entry-Level Education** ....Bachelor's degree
- **Work Experience in a Related Occupation**.............. None
- **On-the-Job Training** .... Internship/residency
- **Number of Jobs 2012** 107,400
- **Job Outlook, 2012–22**............. 17% (Faster than average)
- **Employment Change, 2012–22** 18,600

What Architects Do

Architects plan and design houses, office buildings, and other structures.

Duties. Architects typically do the following:

- Meet with clients to determine objectives and requirements for structures

It takes many years of education and experience to become a licensed architect.

- Estimate the amount of required materials, equipment, and construction time
- Prepare structure specifications
- Direct workers who prepare drawings and documents
- Prepare scaled drawings with computer software and by hand
- Prepare contract documents for building contractors
- Manage construction contracts
- Visit worksites to ensure that construction adheres to architectural plans
- Seek new work by marketing and giving presentations

People need places to live, work, play, learn, shop, and eat. Architects are responsible for designing these places. They work on public or private projects and design both indoor and outdoor spaces. Architects can be commissioned to design anything from a single room to an entire complex of buildings.

Architects discuss the objectives, requirements, and budget of a project with clients. In some cases, architects provide various predesign services, such as feasibility and environmental impact studies, site selection, cost analyses, and design requirements.

After discussing and agreeing on the initial proposal with clients, architects develop final construction plans that show the building's appearance and details for its construction. Accompanying these plans are drawings of the structural system; air-conditioning, heating, and ventilating systems; electrical systems; communications systems; plumbing; and, possibly, site and landscape plans. In developing designs, architects must follow state and local building codes, zoning laws, fire regulations, and other ordinances, such as those requiring easy building access for people who are disabled.

Computer-aided design and drafting (CADD) and building information modeling (BIM) have replaced traditional drafting paper and pencil as the most common methods for creating designs and construction drawings. However, hand-drawing skills are still used, especially during the conceptual stages of a project.

As construction proceeds, architects may visit building sites to ensure that contractors follow the design, keep to the schedule, use the specified materials, and meet work-quality standards. The job is not complete until all construction is finished, required tests are conducted, and construction costs are paid.

Architects also may help clients get construction bids, select contractors, and negotiate construction contracts.

Architects often collaborate with workers in related occupations, such as civil engineers, urban and regional planners, interior designers, and landscape architects.

Work Environment

Architects held about 107,400 jobs in 2012, with two-thirds employed in the architectural, engineering, and related services industry. About 1 in 5 were self-employed.

Architects spend much of their time in offices, where they meet with clients, develop reports and drawings, and work with other architects and engineers. They also visit construction sites to ensure the client's objectives are met and to review the progress of projects. Some architects work from home offices.

Work Schedules. Although most architects work full time, many work long hours, especially when facing deadlines. Self-employed architects may have to work long hours, too, but they have more flexible work schedules.

How to Become One

There are typically three main steps to becoming a licensed architect: completing a professional degree in architecture, gaining relevant experience through a paid internship, and passing the Architect Registration Exam.

Education. Earning a professional degree in architecture is the typical path to becoming an architect in all states. Most architects earn their professional degree through a 5-year Bachelor of Architecture degree program, intended for students with no previous architectural training. Many earn a master's degree in architecture, which can take 1 to 5 years to complete, depending on the extent of the student's previous training in architecture.

Median Annual Wages, May 2012

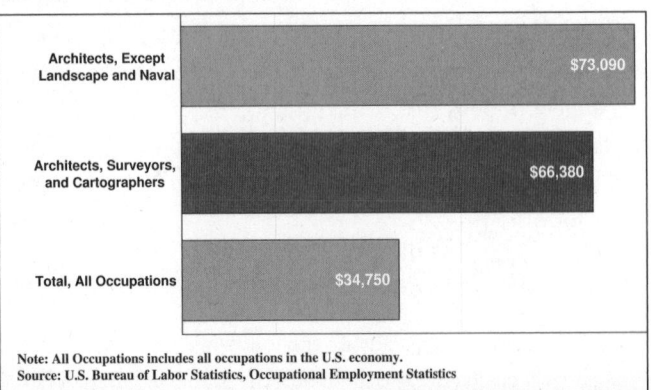

Note: All Occupations includes all occupations in the U.S. economy.
Source: U.S. Bureau of Labor Statistics, Occupational Employment Statistics

Percent Change in Employment, Projected 2012–2022

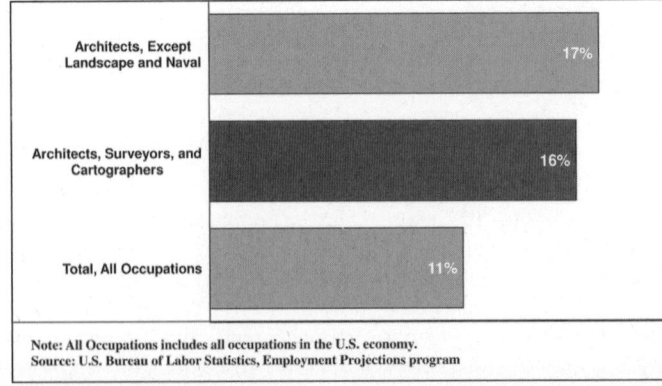

Note: All Occupations includes all occupations in the U.S. economy.
Source: U.S. Bureau of Labor Statistics, Employment Projections program

Employment Projections Data for Architects

Occupational title	SOC Code	Employment, 2012	Projected Employment, 2022	Change, 2012–2022 Percent	Change, 2012–2022 Numeric
Architects, except landscape and naval.................................. 17-1011		107,400	126,000	17	18,600

Source: U.S. Bureau of Labor Statistics, Employment Projections Program

Note: Data are rounded. Go to **Occupational Information Included in the OOH** *for a discussion of the data in this table.*

A typical program includes courses in architectural history and theory, building design with an emphasis on computer-aided design and drafting (CADD), structures, technology, construction methods, professional practices, math, physical sciences, and liberal arts. Central to most architectural programs is the design studio, where students apply the skills and concepts learned in the classroom to create drawings and three-dimensional models of their designs.

Currently, 35 states require that architects hold a professional degree in architecture from one of the 123 schools of architecture accredited by the National Architectural Accrediting Board (NAAB). State licensing requirements can be found at the National Council of Architectural Registration Boards.

Training. All state architectural registration boards require architecture graduates to complete a lengthy paid internship–most require at least 3 years of experience–before they may sit for the Architect Registration Exam. Most new graduates complete their training period by working at architectural firms through the Intern Development Program (IDP). Some states allow a portion of the training to occur in the offices of related careers, such as engineers and general contractors. Architecture students who complete internships while still in school can count some of that time toward the 3-year training period.

Interns in architectural firms may help design part of a project. They may help prepare architectural documents and drawings, build models, and prepare construction drawings on CADD. Interns may also research building codes and write specifications for building materials, installation criteria, the quality of finishes, and other related details.

Licenses, Certifications, and Registrations. All states and the District of Columbia require architects to be licensed. Licensing requirements typically include completing a professional degree in architecture, gaining relevant experience through a paid internship, and passing the Architect Registration Exam.

Most states also require some form of continuing education to keep a license, and some additional states are expected to adopt mandatory continuing education. Requirements vary by state but usually involve additional education through workshops, university classes, conferences, self-study courses, or other sources.

A growing number of architects voluntarily seek certification from the National Council of Architectural Registration Boards (NCARB). Certification makes it easier to become licensed across states. In fact, it is the primary requirement for reciprocity of licensing among state boards that are NCARB members. In 2012, approximately one-third of all licensed architects had this certification.

Important Qualities

Analytical skills. Architects must understand the content of designs and the context in which they were created. For example, architects must understand the locations of mechanical systems and how those systems affect building operations.

Communication skills. Architects share their ideas, both in oral presentations and in writing, with clients, other architects, and workers who help prepare drawings. Many also give presentations to explain their designs.

Creativity. Architects design the overall look of houses, buildings, and other structures. Therefore, the final product should be attractive and functional.

Organizational skills. Architects often manage contracts. Therefore, they must keep records related to the details of a project, including total cost, materials used, and progress.

Technical skills. Architects use computer-aided design and drafting (CADD) technology to create plans as part of integrated building information modeling (BIM).

Visualization skills. Architects must be able to see how the parts of a structure relate to each other. They also must be able to visualize how the overall building will look once completed.

Pay

The median annual wage for architects was $73,090 in May 2012. The median wage is the wage at which half the workers in an occupation earned more than that amount and half earned less. The lowest 10 percent earned less than $44,600, and the top 10 percent earned more than $118,230.

Some firms pay tuition and fees toward continuing education requirements for their employees.

Similar Occupations   This table shows a list of occupations with job duties that are similar to those of architects.

Occupations	Entry-level Education	2012 Pay	Projected Job Growth	Average Annual Openings
Civil Engineers	Bachelor's degree	$79,340	20%	12,010
Construction Managers	Bachelor's degree	$82,790	16%	15,460
Graphic Designers	Bachelor's degree	$44,150	7%	8,600
Industrial Designers	Bachelor's degree	$59,610	4%	1,210
Interior Designers	Bachelor's degree	$47,600	13%	2,150
Landscape Architects	Bachelor's degree	$64,180	14%	760
Urban and Regional Planners	Master's degree	$65,230	10%	2,140

Job Outlook

Employment of architects is projected to grow 17 percent from 2012 to 2022, faster than the average for all occupations.

Architects will be needed to make plans and designs for the construction and renovation of homes, offices, retail stores, and other structures. As campus buildings age, many school districts and universities are expected to build new facilities or renovate existing ones. Demand is expected for more healthcare facilities as the baby-boomer population ages and as more individuals use healthcare services.

Demand is projected for architects with knowledge of green design, also called sustainable design. Sustainable design emphasizes the efficient use of resources, such as energy and water conservation; waste and pollution reduction; and environmentally friendly design, specifications, and materials. Rising energy costs and increased concern about the environment have led to many new buildings being built with more sustainable designs.

Job Prospects. With a growing number of students graduating with architectural degrees, strong competition for internships and jobs in the field is expected. Competition for jobs will be especially strong at the most prestigious architectural firms. Those with up-to-date technical skills and training in sustainable design could have an advantage.

Employment of architects is strongly tied to the activity of the construction industry. Therefore, these workers may experience periods of unemployment when there is a slowdown in requests for new projects or when the overall level of construction falls.

O*NET

➤ Architects, Except Landscape and Naval (17-1011.00)

Contacts for More Information

For information about careers in architecture, visit
➤ American Institute of Architects (www.aia.org/)
➤ ARCHcareers (www.archcareers.org)
➤ National Architectural Accrediting Board (www.naab.org/)
➤ National Council of Architectural Registration Boards (www.ncarb. org/)

Biomedical Engineers

- **2012 Median Pay** .... $86,960 per year
  $41.81 per hour
- **Entry-Level Education** .... Bachelor's degree
- **Work Experience in a Related Occupation** .... None
- **On-the-Job Training** .... None
- **Number of Jobs 2012** 19,400
- **Job Outlook, 2012–22** .... 27% (Much faster than average)
- **Employment Change, 2012–22** 5,200

What Biomedical Engineers Do

Biomedical engineers analyze and design solutions to problems in biology and medicine, with the goal of improving the quality and effectiveness of patient care.

Duties. Biomedical engineers typically do the following:

- Design systems and products, such as artificial internal organs, artificial devices that replace body parts, and machines for diagnosing medical problems

Biomedical engineers combine the work of science and engineering to build new replacement parts for the human body.

- Install, adjust, maintain, repair, or provide technical support for biomedical equipment
- Evaluate the safety, efficiency, and effectiveness of biomedical equipment
- Train clinicians and other personnel on the proper use of equipment
- Work with life scientists, chemists, and medical scientists to research the engineering aspects of biological systems of humans and animals

Biomedical engineers may design instruments, devices, and software; bring together knowledge from many technical sources to develop new procedures; or conduct research needed to solve clinical problems.

They often serve a coordinating function, using their background in both engineering and medicine. For example, in industry, they may create products for which an in-depth understanding of living systems and technology is essential. Also, they frequently work in research and development or in quality assurance.

Biomedical engineers design electrical circuits, software to run medical equipment, or computer simulations to test new drug therapies. They also design and build artificial body parts such as hip and knee joints. In some cases, they develop the materials needed to make the replacement body parts. They also design rehabilitative exercise equipment.

The work of these engineers spans many professional fields. For example, although their expertise is based in engineering and biology, they often design computer software to run complicated instruments, such as three-dimensional X-ray machines. Alternatively, many of these engineers use their knowledge of chemistry and biology to develop new drug therapies. Others draw heavily on mathematics and statistics to build models to understand the signals transmitted by the brain or heart.

Some specialty areas within biomedical engineering include bioinstrumentation; biomaterials; biomechanics; cellular, tissue, and genetic engineering; clinical engineering; medical imaging; orthopedic surgery; rehabilitation engineering; and systems physiology.

Some people with training in biomedical engineering become professors. For more information, see the profile on postsecondary teachers.

Median Annual Wages, May 2012

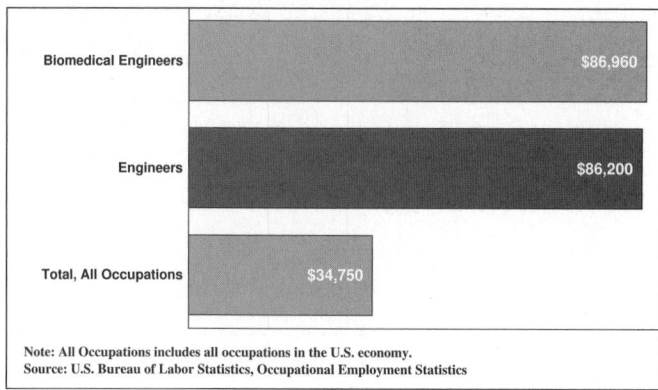

Biomedical Engineers $86,960

Engineers $86,200

Total, All Occupations $34,750

Note: All Occupations includes all occupations in the U.S. economy.
Source: U.S. Bureau of Labor Statistics, Occupational Employment Statistics

Percent Change in Employment, Projected 2012–2022

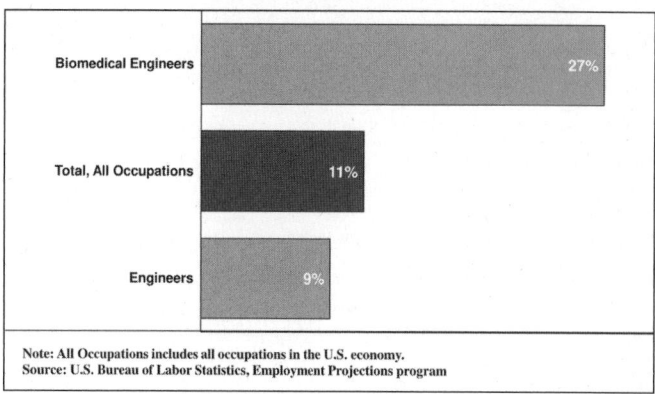

Biomedical Engineers 27%

Total, All Occupations 11%

Engineers 9%

Note: All Occupations includes all occupations in the U.S. economy.
Source: U.S. Bureau of Labor Statistics, Employment Projections program

Work Environment

Biomedical engineers held about 19,400 jobs in 2012. Biomedical engineers work in a variety of settings, depending on what they do. Some work in hospitals where therapy occurs and others work in laboratories doing research. Still others work in manufacturing settings where they design biomedical engineering products. In addition, some biomedical engineers also work in commercial offices where they make or support business decisions.

The industries that employed the most biomedical engineers in 2012 were as follows:

Medical equipment and supplies manufacturing	25%
Scientific research and development services	18
Pharmaceutical and medicine manufacturing	15
Colleges, universities, and professional schools; state, local, and private	9
General medical and surgical hospitals; state, local, and private	7

Biomedical engineers work in teams with scientists, healthcare workers, or other engineers. Thus, where and how they work is often determined by others' specific needs. For example, a biomedical engineer who has developed a new device designed to help a person with a disability to walk again might have to spend hours in a hospital to determine whether the device works as planned. If the engineer finds a way to improve the device, the engineer might have to return to the manufacturer to help alter the manufacturing process to improve the design.

Work Schedules. Biomedical engineers usually work full time on a normal schedule. However, as with employees in almost any engineering occupation, biomedical engineers may occasionally have to work additional hours to meet the needs of patients, managers, colleagues, and clients.

How to Become One

Biomedical engineers typically need a bachelor's degree in biomedical engineering from an accredited program to enter the occupation. Alternatively, they can get a bachelor's degree in a different field

of engineering and then either get a graduate degree in biomedical engineering or get on-the-job training in biomedical engineering.

Education. Prospective biomedical engineering students should take high school science courses, such as chemistry, physics, and biology. They should also take math courses, including calculus. Courses in drafting or mechanical drawing and computer programming are also useful.

Bachelor's degree programs in biomedical engineering focus on engineering and biological sciences. Programs include laboratory-based courses in addition to classroom-based courses in subjects such as fluid and solid mechanics, computer programming, circuit design, and biomaterials. Other required courses may include biological sciences, such as physiology.

Accredited programs also include substantial training in engineering design. Many programs include co-ops or internships, often with hospitals, to provide students with practical applications as part of their study. Biomedical engineering programs are accredited by ABET.

Important Qualities

Analytical skills. Biomedical engineers must be able to analyze the needs of patients and customers to design appropriate solutions.

Communication skills. Because biomedical engineers sometimes work with patients and frequently work with medical scientists or other engineers, they must be able to express themselves clearly.

Listening skills. Biomedical engineers often work in teams and gather input from patients, therapists, physicians, and business professionals. They must seek others' ideas and incorporate them into the problem-solving process.

Math skills. Biomedical engineers use the principals of calculus and other advanced topics in mathematics for analysis, design, and troubleshooting in their work.

Problem-solving skills. Biomedical engineers typically deal with and solve problems in complex biological systems.

Advancement. To lead a research team, a biomedical engineer typically needs a graduate degree. Some biomedical engineers

Employment Projections Data for Biomedical Engineers

Occupational title	SOC Code	Employment, 2012	Projected Employment, 2022	Change, 2012–2022	
				Percent	Numeric
Biomedical engineers	17-2031	19,400	24,600	27	5,200

Source: U.S. Bureau of Labor Statistics, Employment Projections Program

Note: Data are rounded. Go to **Occupational Information Included in the OOH** *for a discussion of the data in this table.*

Similar Occupations This table shows a list of occupations with job duties that are similar to those of biomedical engineers.

Occupations	Entry-level Education	2012 Pay	Projected Job Growth	Average Annual Openings
Architectural and Engineering Managers	Bachelor's degree	$124,870	7%	6,060
Biochemists and Biophysicists	Doctoral or professional degree	$81,480	18%	1,370
Chemical Engineers	Bachelor's degree	$94,350	5%	920
Electrical and Electronics Engineers	Bachelor's degree	$89,701	4%	7,940
Mechanical Engineers	Bachelor's degree	$80,580	4%	9,970
Physicians and Surgeons	Doctoral or professional degree	$182,294	18%	29,630
Sales Engineers	Bachelor's degree	$91,830	9%	1,740

attend dental or medical school to specialize in applications at the forefront of patient care, such as using electric impulses in new ways to get muscles moving again. Some earn law degrees and work as patent attorneys.

Pay

The median annual wage for biomedical engineers was $86,960 in May 2012. The median wage is the wage at which half the workers in an occupation earned more than that amount and half earned less. The lowest 10 percent earned less than $52,600, and the top 10 percent earned more than $139,450.

In May 2012, the median annual wages in the top five industries in which these engineers worked were as follows:

Scientific research and development services	$94,150
Medical equipment and supplies manufacturing	88,850
Pharmaceutical and medicine manufacturing	87,340
General medical and surgical hospitals; state, local, and private	69,910
Colleges, universities, and professional schools; state, local, and private	63,440

Job Outlook

Employment of biomedical engineers is projected to grow 27 percent from 2012 to 2022, much faster than the average for all occupations. However, because it is a small occupation, the fast growth will result in only about 5,200 new jobs over the 10-year period.

Biomedical engineers will likely see more demand for their services because of the breadth of activities they engage in, made possible by the diverse nature of their training.

As the aging baby-boom generation lives longer and stays active, they are expected to increase the demand for biomedical devices and procedures, such as hip and knee replacements. In addition, as the public has become aware of medical advances, increasing numbers of people are seeking biomedical solutions to health problems for themselves from their physicians.

Biomedical engineers work with medical scientists, other medical researchers, and manufacturers to address a wide range of injuries and physical disabilities. Their ability to work in different activities with other professionals is enlarging the range of applications for biomedical engineering products and services, particularly in healthcare.

Job Prospects. Rapid advances in technology will continue to change what biomedical engineers do and continue to create new areas for them to work in. Thus, the expanding range of activities in which biomedical engineers are engaged should translate into very favorable job prospects. In addition, the aging and retirement of a substantial percentage of biomedical engineers are likely to help create job openings between 2012 and 2022.

O*NET

➤ Biomedical Engineers (17-2031.00)

Contacts for More Information

For information about general engineering education and career resources, visit
➤ American Society for Engineering Education (www.asee.org/)
➤ Technology Student Association (www.tsaweb.org/)
  For information about accredited engineering programs, visit
➤ ABET (www.abet.org/)
  For more information about careers in biomedical engineering, visit
➤ Biomedical Engineering Society (http://bmes.org/)
➤ IEEE Engineering in Medicine and Biology Society (http://embs.org/)

Cartographers and Photogrammetrists

- **2012 Median Pay** .... $57,440 per year
  $27.62 per hour
- **Entry-Level Education** .... Bachelor's degree
- **Work Experience in a Related Occupation** .... None
- **On-the-Job Training** .... None
- **Number of Jobs 2012** 12,100
- **Job Outlook, 2012–22** .... 20% (Faster than average)
- **Employment Change, 2012–22** 2,400

What Cartographers and Photogrammetrists Do

Cartographers and photogrammetrists collect, measure, and interpret geographic information to create maps and charts for political, educational, and other purposes.

Cartographers are mapmakers who use principles of cartographic design to make user-friendly maps. Photogrammetrists are specialized mapmakers who use aerial photographs, satellite images, and light-imaging detection and ranging technology (LIDAR) to build models of Earth's surface and its features for purposes of creating maps.

Duties. Cartographers typically do the following:

- Collect and create visual representations of geographic data, such as annual precipitation patterns

- Examine and compile data from ground surveys, reports, aerial photographs, and satellite images

- Prepare thematic maps in digital or graphic form for environmental and educational purposes

Cartographers and photogrammetrists are employed at firms in architectural and engineering services, and also in local and federal government agencies.

- Update and revise existing maps and charts

  Photogrammetrists typically do the following:

- Plan aerial and satellite surveys to ensure complete coverage of the area in question

- Collect and analyze spatial data, such as elevation and distance

- Develop base maps that allow geographic information system (GIS) data to be layered on top

Cartographers and photogrammetrists use information from geodetic surveys and remote sensing systems, including aerial cameras and satellites. Some also use light-imaging detection and ranging (LIDAR) technology. LIDAR systems use lasers attached to planes or cars to digitally map the topography of Earth. Because LIDAR is often more accurate than traditional surveying methods, it can also be used to collect other forms of data, such as the location and density of forest canopies.

Cartographers and photogrammetrists increasingly work on online and mobile maps. Interactive maps are growing in popularity, and cartographers and photogrammetrists collect data and design these maps for mobile phones and navigation systems.

Cartographers and photogrammetrists also create maps and perform aerial surveys for local governments to aid in urban and regional planning. Such maps may include information on population density and demographic characteristics. Some help build maps for federal agencies for work involving national security.

A cartographer who creates maps using geographic information system (GIS) technology is often known as a *geographic information specialist*. GIS technology is typically used to assemble, integrate, analyze, and display spatial information in a digital format. Maps created with GIS technology combine spatial graphic features with nongraphic information. These maps are useful for providing support for decisions involving environmental studies, geology, engineering, land-use planning, and business marketing.

Work Environment

Cartographers and photogrammetrists held about 12,100 jobs in 2012.

The industries that employed the most cartographers and photogrammetrists in 2012 were as follows:

Architectural, engineering, and related services 33%
Local government, excluding education and hospitals 23
Management, scientific, and technical consulting services 11
Federal government, excluding postal service 6
State government, excluding education and hospitals 4

Although cartographers and photogrammetrists spend much of their time in offices, certain jobs require extensive fieldwork to acquire data and verify results. For example, cartographers may travel to the physical locations that they are mapping to better understand the topography. Similarly, photogrammetrists may do fieldwork to plan ground control for an aerial survey and to validate interpretations. Some photogrammetrists may fly in special aircrafts to calibrate cameras and equipment that take aerial photographs.

Work Schedules. Most cartographers and photogrammetrists work full time. Those who do fieldwork often have longer workdays.

How to Become One

A bachelor's degree in cartography, geography, geomatics, civil engineering, or a related field is the most common path of entry into this occupation. Some states require cartographers and photogrammetrists to be licensed as surveyors, and some states have specific licenses for photogrammetrists.

Education. Cartographers and photogrammetrists usually have a bachelor's degree in cartography, geography, geomatics, or surveying. (Geomatics combines the science, engineering, mathematics, and art of collecting and managing geographically referenced information.) Although it is not as common, some have a bachelor's degree in engineering, forestry, or computer science. Some people enter this occupation after working as surveying and mapping technicians.

Growing use of GIS (geographic information system) technology has resulted in cartographers and photogrammetrists needing

Median Annual Wages, May 2012

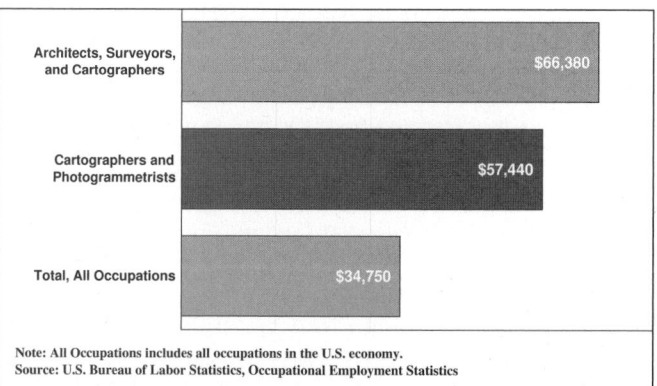

Architects, Surveyors, and Cartographers — $66,380
Cartographers and Photogrammetrists — $57,440
Total, All Occupations — $34,750

Note: All Occupations includes all occupations in the U.S. economy.
Source: U.S. Bureau of Labor Statistics, Occupational Employment Statistics

Percent Change in Employment, Projected 2012–2022

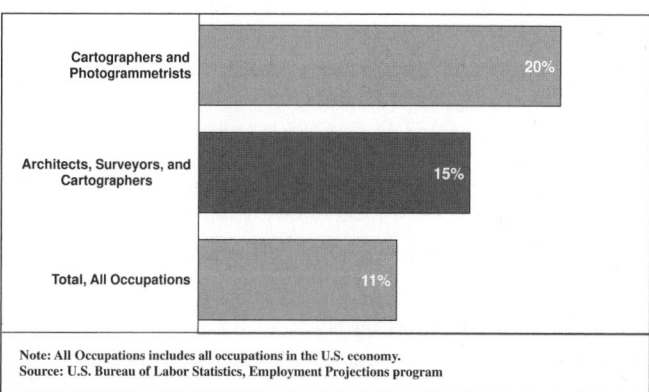

Cartographers and Photogrammetrists — 20%
Architects, Surveyors, and Cartographers — 15%
Total, All Occupations — 11%

Note: All Occupations includes all occupations in the U.S. economy.
Source: U.S. Bureau of Labor Statistics, Employment Projections program

Employment Projections Data for Cartographers and Photogrammetrists

Occupational title	SOC Code	Employment, 2012	Projected Employment, 2022	Change, 2012–2022	
				Percent	Numeric
Cartographers and photogrammetrists	17-1021	12,100	14,500	20	2,400

Source: U.S. Bureau of Labor Statistics, Employment Projections Program

Note: Data are rounded. Go to Occupational Information Included in the OOH *for a discussion of the data in this table.*

more education and stronger technical skills–including more experience with computers–than in the past. Taking courses in computer programming, engineering, mathematics, GIS technology, surveying, and geography usually are required for those looking to become a cartographer or photogrammetrist.

Cartographers must also be familiar with Web-based mapping technologies, including newer modes of compiling data that incorporate the positioning capabilities of mobile phones and in-car navigation systems.

Photogrammetrists must be familiar with remote sensing, image processing, light-imaging detection and ranging (LIDAR), and they must be knowledgeable about using the software necessary for these tools.

High school students interested in becoming a cartographer or photogrammetrist should take courses in algebra, geometry, trigonometry, drafting, and computer science.

Licenses, Certifications, and Registrations. Licensing requirements for cartographers and photogrammetrists vary by state. A number of states require cartographers and photogrammetrists to be licensed as surveyors, and some states have specific licenses for photogrammetrists. Although licensing requirements vary by state, candidates must have a minimum of a high school diploma and pass a test.

Cartographers and photogrammetrists may also receive certification from the American Society for Photogrammetry and Remote Sensing (ASPRS). Candidates must meet experience and education requirements, and pass an exam. Although certification is not required, it can demonstrate competence and may help candidates get a job.

Other Experience. Many aspiring cartographers and photogrammetrists benefit from internships while in school. Internships offer an opportunity for students to learn practical skills, thus reducing time in training by employers.

Important Qualities

Computer skills. Both cartographers and photogrammetrists must have experience working with computer datasets and coding. Because maps are created digitally, knowing how to edit them on a computer is essential.

Critical-thinking skills. Cartographers work from existing maps, surveys, and other records. To do so, they must be able to determine the thematic and positional accuracy of each feature being mapped.

Decision-making skills. Both cartographers and photogrammetrists must make decisions about the accuracy and readability of a map. They must decide what information they need in order to meet the client's needs.

Detail oriented. Cartographers must focus on details when conceiving a map and deciding on the features needed on a final map. Photogrammetrists must pay close attention to detail when interpreting aerial photographs and remotely sensed data.

Problem-solving skills. Cartographers and photogrammetrists must be able to identify and resolve issues with the tools available to them.

Pay

The median annual wage for cartographers and photogrammetrists was $57,440 in May 2012. The median wage is the wage at which half the workers in an occupation earned more than that amount and half earned less. The lowest 10 percent earned less than $34,850, and the top 10 percent earned more than $94,980.

In May 2012, the median annual wages for cartographers and photogrammetrists in the top five industries in which these specialists worked were as follows:

Federal government, excluding postal service $84,850
Local government, excluding education and hospitals......... 57,780
Management, scientific, and technical consulting services... 57,180
Architectural, engineering, and related services 55,260
State government, excluding education and hospitals.......... 51,910

Job Outlook

Employment of cartographers and photogrammetrists is projected to grow 20 percent from 2012 to 2022, faster than the average for all occupations. However, because it is a small occupation, the fast employment growth will result in only about 2,400 new jobs over the 10-year period.

Similar Occupations   This table shows a list of occupations with job duties that are similar to those of cartographers and photogrammetrists.

Occupations	Entry-level Education	2012 Pay	Projected Job Growth	Average Annual Openings
Civil Engineers	Bachelor's degree	$79,340	20%	12,010
Environmental Scientists and Specialists	Bachelor's degree	$63,570	15%	3,970
Geographers	Bachelor's degree	$74,760	29%	80
Landscape Architects	Bachelor's degree	$64,180	14%	760
Surveying and Mapping Technicians	High school diploma or equivalent	$39,670	14%	1,700
Surveyors	Bachelor's degree	$56,230	10%	1,340
Urban and Regional Planners	Master's degree	$65,230	10%	2,140

Overall, cartographers and photogrammetrists are likely to be in demand to ensure the reliability and accuracy of maps produced and updated.

In addition, increasing use of maps for national security and local government planning should fuel employment growth. The growing number of mobile and Web-based map products also should result in new jobs for cartographers and photogrammetrists.

Photogrammetrists, in particular, will be needed to manage the aerial, satellite, and light-imaging detection and ranging (LIDAR) images that are now common.

Cartographers will also be needed to visualize spatial information and design the final presentation of information for clients. Their design skills help data become more accessible to users.

Job Prospects. Photogrammetrists are expected to have excellent job opportunities. There has been a large increase in the amount of mapping data available and photogrammetrists will be needed to interpret and refine this data. These workers will also be needed to calibrate cameras and other tools when collecting this data.

O*NET

➤ Cartographers and Photogrammetrists (17-1021.00)

Contacts for More Information

For more information about cartographers and photogrammetrists, visit

➤ Cartography and Geographic Information Society (www.cartogis.org/)

For career information about photogrammetrists, photogrammetric technicians, remote sensing scientists, image-based cartographers, or geographic information system specialists, visit

➤ American Society for Photogrammetry and Remote Sensing (www.asprs.org/)

For information about careers in remote sensing, photogrammetry, surveying, GIS analysis, and other geography-related disciplines, visit

➤ Association of American Geographers (www.aag.org/)

Chemical Engineers

- **2012 Median Pay** .... $94,350 per year
  $45.36 per hour
- **Entry-Level Education** .... Bachelor's degree
- **Work Experience in a Related Occupation** .... None
- **On-the-Job Training** .... None
- **Number of Jobs 2012** 33,300
- **Job Outlook, 2012–22** .... 4% (Slower than average)
- **Employment Change, 2012–22** 1,500

What Chemical Engineers Do

Chemical engineers apply the principles of chemistry, biology, physics, and mathematics to solve problems that involve the production or use of chemicals, fuel, drugs, food, and many other products. They design processes and equipment for large-scale manufacturing, plan and test methods of manufacturing products and treating byproducts, and supervise production.

Duties. Chemical engineers typically do the following:

- Conduct research to develop new and improved manufacturing processes
- Develop safety procedures for those working with potentially dangerous chemicals

Chemical engineers generally work in a laboratory setting, although sometimes they must work in an industrial setting to oversee production.

- Develop processes to separate components of liquids and gases or to generate electrical currents using controlled chemical processes
- Design and plan the layout of equipment
- Do tests and monitor performance of processes throughout production
- Troubleshoot problems with manufacturing processes
- Evaluate equipment and processes to ensure compliance with safety and environmental regulations
- Estimate production costs for management

Some chemical engineers specialize in a particular process, such as oxidation (a reaction of oxygen with chemicals to make other chemicals) or polymerization (making plastics and resins). Others specialize in a particular field, such as nanomaterials (making extremely small substances), biological engineering, or in developing specific products.

Chemical engineers also work in producing energy, electronics, food, clothing, and paper. They work in research in life sciences, biotechnology, and business services.

Chemical engineers must be aware of all aspects in the manufacturing of chemicals, drugs, or other products. They must also understand how the manufacturing process affects the environment and the safety of workers and consumers.

Work Environment

Chemical engineers held about 33,300 jobs in 2012.

Chemical engineers work mostly in offices or laboratories. They may spend time at industrial plants, refineries, and other locations, where they monitor or direct operations or solve onsite problems. Chemical engineers must be able to work with professionals who design other systems and with the technicians and mechanics who put the designs into practice.

Some engineers travel extensively to plants or worksites both domestically and abroad.

The industries that employed the most chemical engineers in 2012 were as follows:

Architectural, engineering, and related services 17%
Basic chemical manufacturing 13
Scientific research and development services 10

Median Annual Wages, May 2012

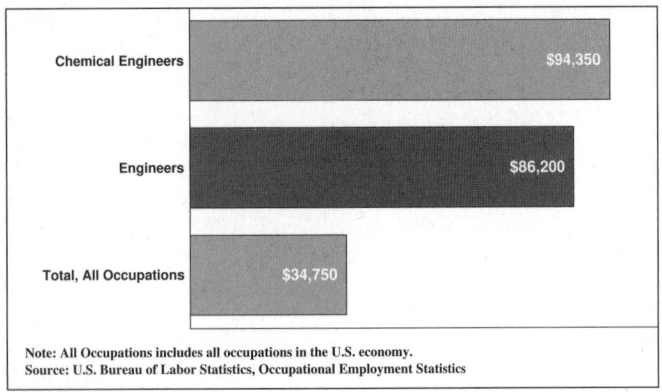

Note: All Occupations includes all occupations in the U.S. economy.
Source: U.S. Bureau of Labor Statistics, Occupational Employment Statistics

Percent Change in Employment, Projected 2012–2022

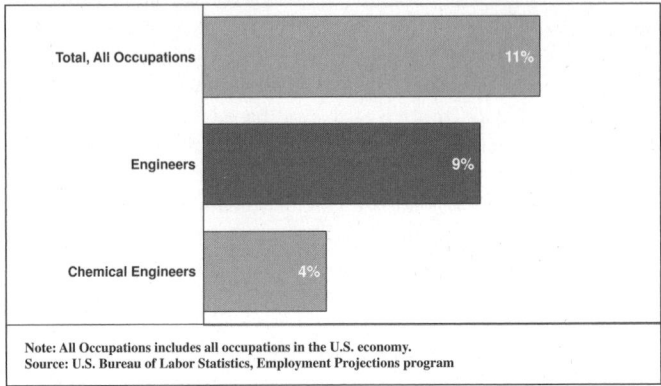

Note: All Occupations includes all occupations in the U.S. economy.
Source: U.S. Bureau of Labor Statistics, Employment Projections program

Resin, synthetic rubber, and artificial synthetic fibers and
    filaments manufacturing 6
Petroleum and coal products manufacturing 6

Work Schedules. Nearly all chemical engineers work full time.

How to Become One

Chemical engineers must have a bachelor's degree in chemical engineering. Employers also value practical experience, so cooperative engineering programs, in which students earn college credit for structured job experience, are valuable as well.

Education. Chemical engineers must have a bachelor's degree in chemical engineering. Programs usually take 4 years to complete and include classroom, laboratory, and field studies. High school students interested in studying chemical engineering will benefit from taking science courses, such as chemistry, physics, and biology. They also should take math courses, including algebra, trigonometry, and calculus.

At some universities, a student can opt to enroll in a 5-year program that leads to both a bachelor's degree and a master's degree. A graduate degree, which may include a degree up to the Ph.D. level, allows an engineer to work in research and development or as a postsecondary teacher.

Some colleges and universities offer cooperative programs where students gain practical experience while completing their education. Cooperative programs combine classroom study with practical work, permitting students to gain valuable experience and to finance part of their education.

Engineering programs should be accredited by ABET. ABET-accredited programs in chemical engineering include courses in chemistry, physics, and biology. These programs also include applying the sciences to the design, analysis, and control of chemical, physical, and biological processes.

Important Qualities

Analytical skills. Chemical engineers must be able to figure out why a particular design does not work as planned. They must be able to ask the right questions and then find answers that work.

Creativity. Chemical engineers must be able to explore new ways of applying engineering principles. They work to invent new materials, advanced manufacturing techniques, and new applications in chemical and biomedical engineering.

Ingenuity. Chemical engineers learn the broad concepts of chemical engineering, but their work requires them to apply those concepts to specific production problems.

Interpersonal skills. Chemical engineers must develop good working relationships with people in production because their role is to put scientific principles into practice in manufacturing industries.

Math skills. Chemical engineers use the principals of calculus and other advanced topics in mathematics for analysis, design, and troubleshooting in their work.

Problem-solving skills. In designing equipment and processes for manufacturing, these engineers strive to solve several problems at once, including such issues as workers' safety and problems related to manufacturing and environmental protection. They must also be able to anticipate and identify problems to prevent losses for their employers, safeguard workers' health, and prevent environmental damage.

Licenses, Certifications, and Registrations. Licensure for chemical engineers is not as common as it is for other engineering occupations, but it is encouraged for professional advancement. Chemical engineers who become licensed carry the designation of professional engineers (PEs). Licensure generally requires the following:

• A degree from an engineering program accredited by ABET

• A passing score on the Fundamentals of Engineering (FE) exam

• Relevant work experience

• A passing score on the Professional Engineering (PE) exam

The initial Fundamentals of Engineering (FE) exam can be taken right after graduation. Engineers who pass this exam commonly are called engineers in training (EITs) or engineer interns (EIs). After they get work experience, EITs can take the second exam, called the Principles and Practice of Engineering exam.

Employment Projections Data for Chemical Engineers

Occupational title	SOC Code	Employment, 2012	Projected Employment, 2022	Change, 2012–2022	
				Percent	Numeric
Chemical engineers..	17-2041	33,300	34,800	4	1,500

Source: U.S. Bureau of Labor Statistics, Employment Projections Program

Note: Data are rounded. Go to **Occupational Information Included in the OOH** *for a discussion of the data in this table.*

Similar Occupations   This table shows a list of occupations with job duties that are similar to those of chemical engineers.

Occupations	Entry-level Education	2012 Pay	Projected Job Growth	Average Annual Openings
Architectural and Engineering Managers	Bachelor's degree	$124,870	7%	6,060
Biomedical Engineers	Bachelor's degree	$86,960	27%	1,010
Chemical Technicians	Associate's degree	$42,920	9%	2,160
Chemists and Materials Scientists	Bachelor's degree	$73,247	6%	3,040
Nuclear Engineers	Bachelor's degree	$104,270	9%	710
Occupational Health and Safety Specialists	Bachelor's degree	$66,790	7%	2,130

Several states require engineers to take continuing education to keep their license. Most states recognize licensure from other states, if the licensing state's requirements meet or exceed their own licensure requirements.

Advancement. Entry-level engineers usually work under the supervision of experienced engineers. In large companies, new engineers may also receive formal training in classrooms or seminars. As beginning engineers gain knowledge and experience, they move to more difficult projects with greater independence to develop designs, solve problems, and make decisions.

Eventually, chemical engineers may advance to supervise a team of engineers and technicians. Some may become architectural and engineering managers. However, preparing for management positions usually requires working under the guidance of a more experienced chemical engineer.

An engineering background enables chemical engineers to discuss a product's technical aspects and assist in product planning and use. For more information, see the profile on sales engineers.

Pay

The median annual wage for chemical engineers was $94,350 in May 2012. The median wage is the wage at which half the workers in an occupation earned more than that amount and half earned less. The lowest 10 percent earned less than $58,830, and the top 10 percent earned more than $154,840.

In May 2012, the median annual wages for chemical engineers in the top five industries employing these engineers were as follows:

Petroleum and coal products manufacturing $105,310
Basic chemical manufacturing 99,510
Scientific research and development services 97,880
Resin, synthetic rubber, and artificial synthetic fibers and
    filaments manufacturing 94,810
Architectural, engineering, and related services 93,390

A June 2013 salary survey by the American Institute of Chemical Engineers of their members reported that graduates of bachelor's degree programs in 2011 had a median yearly salary of $67,800. The survey also noted that many chemical engineers receive benefits such as stock options or profit-sharing awards.

Job Outlook

Employment of chemical engineers is projected to grow 4 percent from 2012 to 2022, slower than the average for all occupations. Demand for chemical engineers' services depends largely on demand for the products of various manufacturing industries. Employment growth will be sustained by the ability of these engineers to stay on the forefront of new, emerging technologies.

Many chemical engineers work in industries that have output sought by many manufacturing firms. For instance, they work for firms that manufacture plastic resins, used to increase fuel efficiency in automobiles. Increased availability of domestically produced natural gas should increase manufacturing potential in the industries employing these engineers.

In addition, chemical engineering is also migrating into new fields, such as nanotechnology, alternative energies, and biotechnology, which will help to sustain demand for engineering services in many manufacturing industries.

However, overall growth of employment will be tempered by a decline in employment in manufacturing sectors, including chemical manufacturing.

Job Prospects. Chemical engineers should have favorable job prospects as many workers in the occupation reach retirement age from 2012 to 2022.

O*NET

➤ Chemical Engineers (17-2041.00)

Contacts for More Information

For more information on becoming a chemical engineer, visit
➤ American Institute of Chemical Engineers (www.aiche.org/)
    For information about general engineering education and career resources, visit
➤ American Society for Engineering Education (www.asee.org/)
➤ Technology Student Association (www.tsaweb.org/)
    For more information about licensure as a professional engineer, visit
➤ National Council of Examiners for Engineering and Surveying (www.ncees.org/)
➤ National Society of Professional Engineers (www.nspe.org/index.html)
    For information about accredited engineering programs, visit
➤ ABET (www.abet.org/)

Civil Engineering Technicians

- **2012 Median Pay** .... $47,560 per year
                                                    $22.87 per hour
- **Entry-Level Education** .... Associate's degree
- **Work Experience in a Related Occupation** .... None
- **On-the-Job Training** .... None
- **Number of Jobs 2012** 73,100
- **Job Outlook, 2012–22** .... 1% (Little or no change)
- **Employment Change, 2012–22** 400

Civil engineering technicians read and review project blueprints to determine dimensions of structures.

What Civil Engineering Technicians Do

Civil engineering technicians help civil engineers plan and design the construction of highways, bridges, utilities, and other major infrastructure projects. They also help with commercial, residential, and land development.

Duties. Civil engineering technicians typically do the following:

• Read and review project blueprints to determine dimensions of structures

• Confer with their supervisors about preparing plans and evaluating field conditions

• Inspect project sites and evaluate contractors' work in order to detect problems with a design

• Test construction materials–especially concrete–and soil samples in laboratories

• Help to ensure that projects conform to design specifications and applicable codes

• Develop plans and estimate costs for installing systems and operating facilities

• Prepare reports and document project activities and data

Civil engineering technicians must work under the direction of licensed civil engineers. These technicians generally help civil engineers, often doing many of the same tasks as the engineers. However, because they are not licensed, civil engineering technicians cannot approve designs or supervise the overall project.

Civil engineering technicians sometimes estimate construction costs and specify materials to be used. Other times, they prepare drawings or survey land. They also may set up and monitor various instruments for traffic studies.

Work Environment

Civil engineering technicians held about 73,100 jobs in 2012.

Civil engineering technicians work in offices, where they help civil engineers plan and design projects. The industries that employed the most civil engineering technicians in 2012 were as follows:

Architectural, engineering, and related services......................44%
State government, excluding education and hospitals............. 29
Local government, excluding education and hospitals............ 18

Civil engineering technicians sometimes visit the jobsite where a construction project is taking place, in order to test materials or inspect the project. They do this to help ensure that the designs approved by licensed civil engineers are being carried out correctly.

Work Schedules. Civil engineering technicians keep schedules that closely resemble those of construction workers. Thus, weather might determine a schedule on a given day. In addition, schedules vary with the length and completion of construction projects. Those who work primarily in laboratories to test construction materials have more stable work schedules.

How to Become One

Although not always required, an associate's degree in civil engineering technology is preferred for civil engineering technicians. It is best to seek programs that are accredited by ABET.

Education. To prepare for programs in engineering technology after high school, prospective civil engineering technicians should take science and math courses, such as chemistry and calculus.

Employers generally prefer engineering technicians to have an associate's degree from an ABET-accredited program, although a degree is not always required. Engineering technology programs are also available at technical or vocational schools that award a postgraduate certificate or diploma.

Courses at technical or vocational schools may include engineering, design, and computer software. To complete an associate's degree in civil engineering technology, students also usually need to take other courses in liberal arts and the sciences.

Important Qualities

Critical-thinking skills. As assistants to civil engineers, civil engineering technicians must help the engineers identify problems to avoid wasting time, effort, and funds.

Median Annual Wages, May 2012

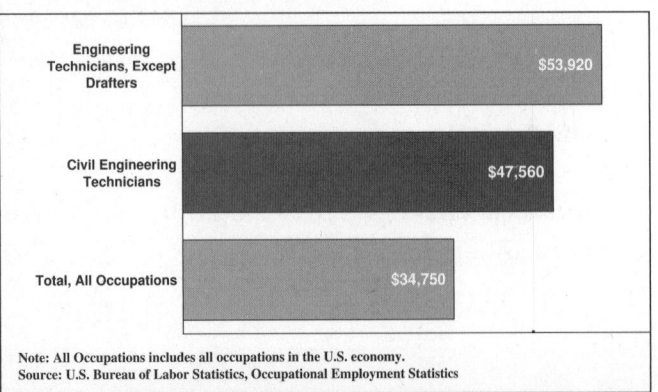

Note: All Occupations includes all occupations in the U.S. economy.
Source: U.S. Bureau of Labor Statistics, Occupational Employment Statistics

Percent Change in Employment, Projected 2012–2022

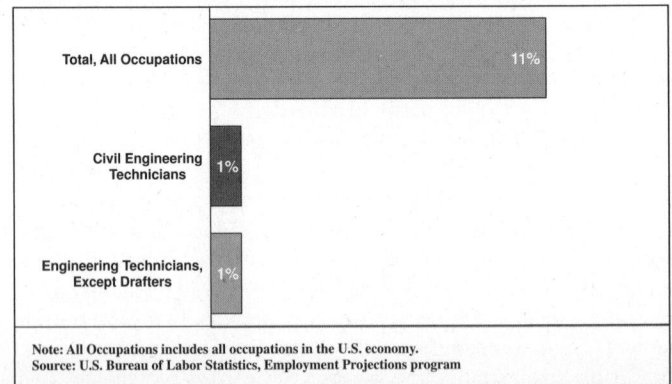

Note: All Occupations includes all occupations in the U.S. economy.
Source: U.S. Bureau of Labor Statistics, Employment Projections program

Employment Projections Data for Civil Engineering Technicians

Occupational title	SOC Code	Employment, 2012	Projected Employment, 2022	Change, 2012–2022	
				Percent	Numeric
Civil engineering technicians...	17-3022	73,100	73,600	1	400

Source: U.S. Bureau of Labor Statistics, Employment Projections Program

Note: Data are rounded. Go to Occupational Information Included in the OOH *for a discussion of the data in this table.*

Decision-making skills. Pressures from deadlines mean that technicians must quickly see which types of information are most important and which plan of action will help keep the project on schedule.

Math skills. Civil engineering technicians use math for analysis, design, and troubleshooting in their work.

Observational skills. Civil engineering technicians sometimes have to go to jobsites and assess a project for the engineer. Therefore, they must know what to look for and how best to report back to the engineer who is overseeing the project.

Problem-solving skills. Like civil engineers, civil engineering technicians help design projects to solve a particular problem. Technicians must be able to understand and work with all the related systems involved in building a project.

Reading skills. Civil engineering technicians carry out plans and designs for projects that a civil engineer has approved. They must be able to understand all the reports describing these designs.

Writing skills. Civil engineering technicians often are asked to relay their findings in writing. The reports must be well organized and clearly written.

Work Experience

Although an associate's degree is preferred by most employers, prospective civil engineering technicians may enter the occupation after gaining work experience in a related occupation, particularly as a drafter. A worker who begins as a drafter for an engineering firm may advance to a civil engineering technician position as his or her knowledge of design improves.

Licenses, Certifications, and Registrations. Certification is not needed to enter this occupation, but it can help technicians advance their careers. The National Institute for Certification in Engineering Technologies (NICET) is one of the primary organizations overseeing certification for civil engineering technicians.

Certification as a technician requires passing an exam and providing documentation, including a work history, recommendations, and, for most programs, supervisor verification of specific experience. NICET requires technicians to update their skills and knowledge through a recertification process that encourages continuing professional development.

Advancement. Civil engineering technicians can advance in their careers by learning to design systems for a variety of projects, such as storm sewers and sanitary systems. It is also useful for civil

engineering technicians to become proficient at reading profiles–graphical plans of proposed utility projects.

Pay

The median annual wage for civil engineering technicians was $47,560 in May 2012. The median wage is the wage at which half the workers in an occupation earned more than that amount and half earned less. The lowest 10 percent earned less than $30,430, and the top 10 percent earned more than $71,800.

In May 2012, median annual wages for civil engineering technicians in the top three industries in which most of these technicians were employed were as follows:

Local government, excluding education and hospitals.......	$53,600
Architectural, engineering, and related services...................	46,900
State government, excluding education and hospitals..........	43,770

Civil engineering technicians keep schedules that closely resemble those of construction workers. Thus, weather might determine a schedule on a given day. Those who work primarily in laboratories to test construction materials have more stable work schedules.

Job Outlook

Employment of civil engineering technicians is projected to show little or no change from 2012 to 2022.

The need to maintain and repair the country's infrastructure continues to increase. Bridges need rebuilding, roads need maintaining, and levees and dams need upgrading. Moreover, a growing population means that water systems must be maintained to reduce or eliminate loss of drinkable water. In addition, more waste treatment plants will be needed to help clean the nation's waterways. Civil engineers must plan, design, and oversee this work, and civil engineering technicians will be needed to assist the engineers in these projects.

Civil engineering technicians also will find work assisting civil engineers with renewable-energy projects. With regard to wind energy, these engineering technicians may assist in the development of a wind farm to minimize costs while also accommodating the unique dimensions and weight of wind turbines. For installation of solar power, these engineering technicians make sure that civil engineers' designs for foundations to hold up solar arrays are implemented correctly.

States, however, continue to face financial challenges and may have difficulty funding all the projects that need attention.

Similar Occupations   This table shows a list of occupations with job duties that are similar to those of civil engineering technicians.

Occupations	Entry-level Education	2012 Pay	Projected Job Growth	Average Annual Openings
Civil Engineers	Bachelor's degree	$79,340	20%	12,010
Drafters	Associate's degree	$49,726	1%	3,220
Surveying and Mapping Technicians	High school diploma or equivalent	$39,670	14%	1,700
Surveyors	Bachelor's degree	$56,230	10%	1,340

Job Prospects. Civil engineering technicians learn to use design software that civil engineers might not learn in their college curriculum. Thus, those civil engineering technicians who master that software, keep their skills current, and stay abreast of new software will improve their chances for employment.

O*NET

➤ Civil Engineering Technicians (17-3022.00)

Contacts for More Information

For more information about summer apprenticeships in civil engineering, visit
➤ Pathways to Science (www.pathwaystoscience.org/)
    For more information about accredited programs, visit
➤ ABET (www.abet.org/)
    For more information about certification, visit
➤ American Society of Certified Engineering Technicians (www.ascet.org/)
➤ National Institute for Certification in Engineering Technologies (www.nicet.org/become-certified/what-certifications-are-available/)

Civil Engineers

- **2012 Median Pay** .... $79,340 per year
    $38.14 per hour
- **Entry-Level Education** ....Bachelor's degree
- **Work Experience in a Related Occupation**............... None
- **On-the-Job Training** .... None
- **Number of Jobs 2012** 272,900
- **Job Outlook, 2012–22**............. 20% (Faster than average)
- **Employment Change, 2012–22** 53,700

What Civil Engineers Do

Civil engineers design, construct, supervise, operate, and maintain large construction projects and systems, including roads, buildings, airports, tunnels, dams, bridges, and systems for water supply and sewage treatment. Many civil engineers work in design, construction, research, and education.

Duties. Civil engineers typically do the following:

- Analyze survey reports, maps, and other data to plan projects
- Consider construction costs, government regulations, potential environmental hazards, and other factors in planning stages and risk analysis
- Compile and submit permit applications to local, state, and federal agencies verifying that projects comply with various regulations
- Perform or oversee soil testing to determine the adequacy and strength of foundations
- Test building materials, such as concrete, asphalt, or steel, for use in particular projects
- Provide cost estimates for materials, equipment, or labor to determine a project's economic feasibility
- Use design software to plan and design transportation systems, hydraulic systems, and structures in line with industry and government standards
- Perform or oversee, surveying operations to establish reference points, grades, and elevations to guide construction

Civil engineers design major transportation projects.

- Present their findings to the public on topics such as bid proposals, environmental impact statements, or property descriptions
- Manage the repair, maintenance, and replacement of public and private infrastructure

Many civil engineers hold supervisory or administrative positions ranging from supervisor of a construction site to city engineer. Others work in design, construction, research, and teaching. Civil engineers work with others on projects and may be assisted by civil engineering technicians.

The federal government employs civil engineers to do many of the same things done in private industry, except that the federally employed civil engineers may also inspect projects to be sure that they comply with regulations.

Civil engineers work on complex projects, so they usually specialize in one of several areas.

Construction engineers manage construction projects, ensuring that they are scheduled and built in accordance with the plans and specifications. They are typically responsible for design and safety of temporary structures used during construction.

Geotechnical engineers work to make sure that foundations are solid. They focus on how structures built by civil engineers, such as buildings and tunnels, interact with the earth (including soil and rock). In addition, they design and plan for slopes, retaining walls, and tunnels.

Structural engineers design and assess major projects, such as buildings, bridges, or dams, to ensure their strength and durability.

Transportation engineers plan, design, operate, and maintain everyday systems, such as streets and highways, but they also plan larger projects, such as airports, ports, mass transit systems, and harbors.

Work Environment

Civil engineers held about 272,900 jobs in 2012. Civil engineers generally work indoors in offices. However, they sometimes spend time outdoors at construction sites so they can monitor operations or solve problems at the site. Occasionally, civil engineers travel abroad to work on large engineering projects in other countries.

The industries that employed the most civil engineers in 2012 were:

Architectural, engineering, and related services 50%
State government, excluding education and hospitals............. 13
Local government, excluding education and hospitals............ 11

Median Annual Wages, May 2012

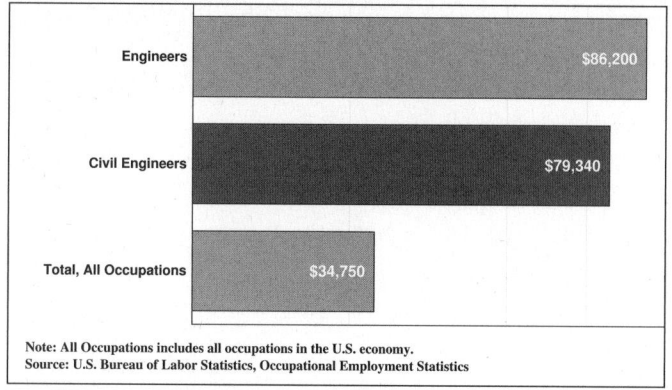

Note: All Occupations includes all occupations in the U.S. economy.
Source: U.S. Bureau of Labor Statistics, Occupational Employment Statistics

Percent Change in Employment, Projected 2012–2022

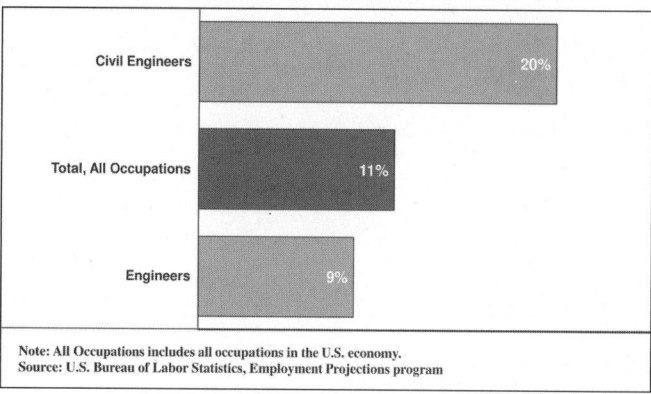

Note: All Occupations includes all occupations in the U.S. economy.
Source: U.S. Bureau of Labor Statistics, Employment Projections program

Nonresidential building construction...5
Federal government, excluding postal service 4

Work Schedules. Civil engineers typically work full time, and about 1 in 4 worked more than 40 hours per week in 2012. Engineers who direct projects may need to work extra hours to monitor progress of the overall projects, to ensure that the design meets requirements, and to ensure that deadlines are met.

How to Become One

Civil engineers need a bachelor's degree. They typically need a graduate degree and licensure for promotion to senior positions. Though licensure requirements vary within the U.S., civil engineers must usually be licensed in the locations where they provide services publicly.

Education. Civil engineers must first complete a bachelor's degree in civil engineering or one of its specialties. A program accredited by ABET is needed in order to gain licensure, which is required to work as a professional engineer (PE). In many states, a bachelor's degree in civil engineering technology will also suffice as an academic requirement for obtaining a license.

Bachelor's degree programs in civil engineering or civil engineering technology include coursework in math, statistics, engineering mechanics and systems, and fluid dynamics, among other courses, depending on the specialty. Courses include a mix of traditional classroom learning, work in a laboratory, and fieldwork.

More than one of every five civil engineers has a master's degree. Further education after the bachelor's degree is helpful in getting a job as a manager, along with the PE license and previous experience. For more information on engineering managers, see the profile on architectural and engineering managers.

Important Qualities

Decision-making skills. Civil engineers often balance multiple and frequently conflicting objectives, such as determining the feasibility of plans with regard to financial costs and safety concerns. Urban and regional planners often look to civil engineers for advice on these issues.

Leadership skills. Civil engineers take ultimate responsibility for the projects or research that they perform. Therefore, they must be able to lead surveyors, construction managers, civil engineering technicians, and others to implement their project plan.

Math skills. Civil engineers use the principals of calculus, trigonometry, and other advanced topics in mathematics for analysis, design, and troubleshooting in their work.

Organizational skills. Only licensed civil engineers can sign the design documents for infrastructure projects. This makes it imperative that civil engineers be able to monitor and evaluate the work at the job site as a project progresses to assure compliance with design documents.

Problem-solving skills. Civil engineers work at the highest level of planning, design, construction, and operation of multi-faceted projects or research with many variables that require the ability to evaluate and resolve complex problems.

Writing skills. Civil engineers must be able to communicate with other professionals, such as architects, landscape architects, and urban and regional planners. This means that civil engineers must be able to write reports clearly so that people without an engineering background can follow.

Licenses, Certifications, and Registrations. Civil engineers who sell their own services publicly must be licensed in all states and the District of Columbia. A license is required to exercise direct control of a project and to supervise other civil engineers and civil engineering technicians. A degree from an ABET-accredited program in civil engineering or civil engineering technology is generally required to obtain a license.

Early in the licensing process, a civil engineer must take and pass the Fundamentals of Engineering (FE) Examination. After passing this exam and meeting a particular state's requirements, an engineer then becomes a Civil Engineering (CE) Intern or an Engineer-in-Training (EIT). Afterward, depending on the state, civil engineers must have a minimum of experience, pass more exams, and satisfy other requirements to qualify as a CE Professional. Each state's licensure board for professional engineers, which can be found through these state societies of professional engineers, can give further details.

Employment Projections Data for Civil Engineers

Occupational title	SOC Code	Employment, 2012	Projected Employment, 2022	Change, 2012–2022	
				Percent	Numeric
Civil engineers	17-2051	272,900	326,600	20	53,700

Source: U.S. Bureau of Labor Statistics, Employment Projections Program

Note: Data are rounded. Go to **Occupational Information Included in the OOH** *for a discussion of the data in this table.*

Similar Occupations   This table shows a list of occupations with job duties that are similar to those of civil engineers.

Occupations	Entry-level Education	2012 Pay	Projected Job Growth	Average Annual Openings
Architects	Bachelor's degree	$73,090	17%	4,410
Civil Engineering Technicians	Associate's degree	$47,560	1%	1,560
Construction Managers	Bachelor's degree	$82,790	16%	15,460
Environmental Engineers	Bachelor's degree	$80,890	15%	2,110
Landscape Architects	Bachelor's degree	$64,180	14%	760
Mechanical Engineers	Bachelor's degree	$80,580	4%	9,970
Surveyors	Bachelor's degree	$56,230	10%	1,340
Urban and Regional Planners	Master's degree	$65,230	10%	2,140

Advancement. Civil engineers with ample experience may move into senior positions, such as project managers or functional managers of design, construction, operation, or maintenance. However, they would first need to obtain the Professional Engineering (PE) license, because only licensed engineers can assume responsibilities for public projects.

After gaining licensure, credentialing that attests to a Professional Engineer's expertise in a civil engineering specialty may be of help for advancement to senior technical or even managerial positions.

Pay

The median annual wage for civil engineers was $79,340 in May 2012. The median wage is the wage at which half of the workers in an occupation earned more than that amount and half earned less. The lowest 10 percent earned less than $51,280, and the top 10 percent earned more than $122,020.

In May 2012, the median annual wages for civil engineers in the top five industries in which these engineers worked were as follows:

Federal government, excluding postal service $89,440
Local government, excluding education and hospitals 83,670
Architectural, engineering, and related services 79,470
State government, excluding education and hospitals 74,180
Nonresidential building construction 73,740

Job Outlook

Employment of civil engineers is projected to grow 20 percent from 2012 to 2022, faster than the average for all occupations. As infrastructure continues to age, civil engineers will be needed to manage projects to rebuild bridges, repair roads, and upgrade levees and dams.

Moreover, a growing population means that new water systems will be required while the aging, existing water systems must be maintained to reduce or eliminate leaks of drinkable water. In addition, more waste treatment plants will be needed to help clean the nation's waterways. Civil engineers play a key part in all of this work.

The work of civil engineers will be needed for renewable energy projects. Civil engineers prepare the permit documents for these types of projects, verifying that the project will comply with federal, state, and local requirements. With regard to solar energy, these engineers conduct structural analyses for large-scale photovoltaic projects. They also evaluate the ability of solar array support structures and buildings to tolerate stresses from wind, seismic activity, and other sources. For large-scale wind projects, civil engineers often prepare road beds to handle large trucks that haul in the turbines. In addition, they prepare the sites on shore or offshore to make sure that the foundations for the turbines will safely keep the turbines upright in expected environmental conditions.

Although states continue to face financial challenges and may have difficulty funding all the projects that need attention, some of the projects that have been delayed will ultimately have to be completed in order to build and maintain critical infrastructure.

Job Prospects. Although a bachelor's degree is the typical requirement for entry, applicants who gain experience by participating in a co-op program while in college will have the best opportunities.

O*NET

➤ Civil Engineers (17-2051.00)
➤ Transportation Engineers (17-2051.01)

Contacts for More Information

For information about general engineering education and career resources, visit
➤ American Society for Engineering Education (www.asee.org/)
➤ Technology Student Association (www.tsaweb.org/)
   For more information about licensure, visit
➤ National Council of Examiners for Engineering and Surveying (http://ncees.org/)
➤ National Society of Professional Engineers (www.nspe.org/index.html)
   For information about accredited programs in civil engineering and civil engineering technology, visit
➤ ABET (www.abet.org/)
   For more information about civil engineers, visit
➤ American Society of Civil Engineers (www.asce.org/)

Computer Hardware Engineers

- **2012 Median Pay** .... $100,920 per year
  $48.52 per hour
- **Entry-Level Education** ....Bachelor's degree
- **Work Experience in a Related Occupation**............... None
- **On-the-Job Training** .... None
- **Number of Jobs 2012** 83,300
- **Job Outlook, 2012–22** .... 7% (Slower than average)
- **Employment Change, 2012–22** 6,200

What Computer Hardware Engineers Do

Computer hardware engineers research, design, develop, and test computer systems and components such as processors, circuit boards, memory devices, networks, and routers. By creating new

Computer hardware engineers solve problems that arise in complex computer systems.

directions in computer hardware, these engineers create rapid advances in computer technology.

Duties. Computer hardware engineers typically do the following:

- Design new computer hardware, creating blueprints of computer equipment to be built
- Test the completed models of the computer hardware they design
- Analyze the test results and modify the design as needed
- Update existing computer equipment so that it will work with new software
- Oversee the manufacturing process for computer hardware
- Maintain knowledge of computer engineering trends and new technology

Many hardware engineers design noncomputer devices that incorporate processors and other computer components and connect to the Internet. For example, there are many car parts with computer systems embedded in them. A growing number of medical devices are also designed by computer hardware engineers with a computer system and the ability to connect to the Internet.

Computer hardware engineers ensure that computer hardware components work together with the latest software developments. Therefore, hardware engineers sometimes work with software developers. For example, the hardware and software for a mobile phone are often jointly developed. Hardware engineers may also perform some basic computer programming and test computer code.

Work Environment

Computer hardware engineers held about 83,300 jobs in 2012. The industries that employed the largest number of computer hardware engineers in 2012 were as follows:

Computer systems design and related services 20%
Semiconductor and other electronic component
    manufacturing 17
Computer and peripheral equipment manufacturing 12
Research and development in the physical, engineering,
    and life sciences 12
Navigational, measuring, electromedical, and
    control instruments manufacturing 7

Computer hardware engineers usually work in research laboratories that build and test various types of computer models. Most work in high-tech manufacturing firms.

Work Schedules. Most computer hardware engineers work full time. About 1 in 3 worked more than 40 hours per week in 2012.

How to Become One

Most computer hardware engineers need a bachelor's degree from an accredited computer engineering program.

Education. Most entry-level computer hardware engineers have a bachelor's degree in computer engineering, although a degree in electrical engineering or computer science generally is acceptable. A computer engineering major is similar to electrical engineering but with a heavy emphasis on computer science curriculum.

Many engineering programs are accredited by ABET (formerly the Accreditation Board for Engineering and Technology). Employers may prefer students from an accredited program. To prepare for a major in computer or electrical engineering, students should have a solid background in math and science.

Because hardware engineers commonly work with computer software systems, a familiarity with computer programming is usually expected. This background may be obtained through computer science courses.

Some large firms or specialized jobs require a master's degree in computer engineering. Some experienced engineers obtain a master's degree in business administration (MBA). All engineers must continue their learning over the course of their careers to keep up with rapid advances in technology.

Other Experience. Some students participate in internships while in school to gain practical experience.

Advancement. Some computer hardware engineers can advance to become computer and information systems managers.

Median Annual Wages, May 2012

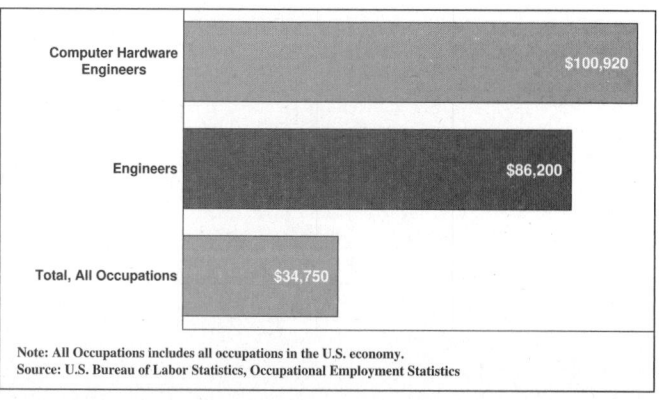

Note: All Occupations includes all occupations in the U.S. economy.
Source: U.S. Bureau of Labor Statistics, Occupational Employment Statistics

Percent Change in Employment, Projected 2012–2022

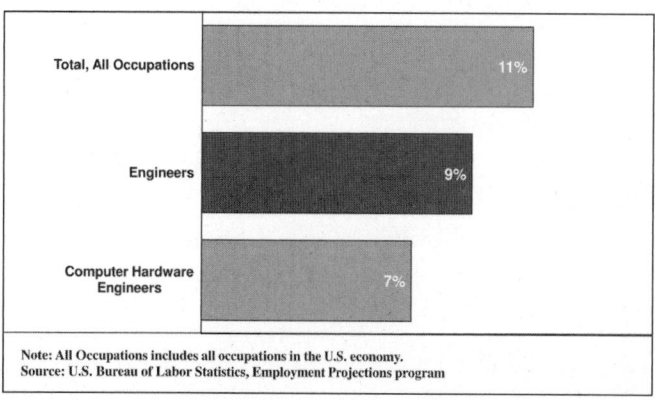

Note: All Occupations includes all occupations in the U.S. economy.
Source: U.S. Bureau of Labor Statistics, Employment Projections program

Employment Projections Data for Computer Hardware Engineers

Occupational title	SOC Code	Employment, 2012	Projected Employment, 2022	Change, 2012–2022	
				Percent	Numeric
Computer hardware engineers................................	17-2061	83,300	89,400	7	6,200

Source: U.S. Bureau of Labor Statistics, Employment Projections Program

Note: Data are rounded. Go to **Occupational Information Included in the OOH** *for a discussion of the data in this table.*

Important Qualities

Analytical skills. Computer hardware engineers analyze complex equipment to determine the best way to improve it.

Creativity. Computer hardware engineers design new types of information technology devices.

Critical-thinking skills. These engineers use logic and reasoning to clarify goals, examine assumptions, and identify the strengths and weaknesses of alternative solutions to problems.

Problem-solving skills. Computer hardware engineers identify complex problems in computer hardware, develop and evaluate possible solutions, and figure out the best way to implement them.

Speaking skills. Engineers often work on teams and must be able to communicate with other types of engineers as well as with nontechnical team members.

Pay

The median annual wage for computer hardware engineers was $100,920 in May 2012. The median wage is the wage at which half the workers in an occupation earned more than that amount and half earned less. The lowest 10 percent earned less than $63,970, and the top 10 percent earned more than $150,130.

In May 2012, the median annual wages for computer hardware engineers in the top five industries in which these engineers worked were as follows:

Computer and peripheral equipment manufacturing......	$109,860
Semiconductor and other electronic component manufacturing...	101,680
Computer systems design and related services...................	101,510
Navigational, measuring, electromedical, and control instruments manufacturing...................................	97,970
Scientific research and development services	95,710

Job Outlook

Employment of computer hardware engineers is projected to grow 7 percent from 2012 to 2022, slower than the average for all occupations. A limited number of engineers will be needed to meet the demand for new computer hardware because more innovation takes place with software than with hardware. Although declining employment in the manufacturing industries that employ many of these workers will negatively affect the growth of this occupation, computer hardware engineers should be less affected than production occupations because firms are less likely to outsource their type of work.

An increase in hardware startup firms and the increase in devices with computer chips embedded in them such as household appliances, medical devices, or automobiles may lead to some job growth for computer hardware engineers.

Job Prospects. Engineers who have a higher-level degree and knowledge or experience with computer software will have the best job prospects. Job applicants with a computer engineering degree from an ABET-accredited program will have better chances of landing a job.

O*NET

➤ Computer Hardware Engineers (17-2061.00)

Contacts for More Information

For more information about computer hardware engineers, visit
➤ Association for Computing Machinery (www.acm.org/)
➤ IEEE (www.computer.org/)

For more information about ABET-accredited college and university programs in applied science, computing, engineering, and technology, visit
➤ ABET (www.abet.org)

Similar Occupations   This table shows a list of occupations with job duties that are similar to those of computer hardware engineers.

Occupations	Entry-level Education	2012 Pay	Projected Job Growth	Average Annual Openings
Aerospace Engineers	Bachelor's degree	$103,720	7%	2,540
Computer and Information Research Scientists	Doctoral or professional degree	$102,190	15%	830
Computer and Information Systems Managers	Bachelor's degree	$120,950	15%	9,710
Computer Network Architects	Bachelor's degree	$91,000	15%	4,350
Computer Programmers	Bachelor's degree	$74,280	8%	11,810
Electrical and Electronics Engineers	Bachelor's degree	$89,701	4%	7,940
Information Security Analysts	Bachelor's degree	$86,170	36%	3,920
Mathematicians	Master's degree	$101,360	23%	170
Mechanical Engineers	Bachelor's degree	$80,580	4%	9,970
Software Developers	Bachelor's degree	$93,640	22%	35,320

Drafters

- **2012 Median Pay** .... $49,630 per year
  $23.86 per hour
- **Entry-Level Education** .... Associate's degree
- **Work Experience in a Related Occupation**.............. None
- **On-the-Job Training** .... None
- **Number of Jobs 2012** 199,800
- **Job Outlook, 2012–22** .... 1% (Little or no change)
- **Employment Change, 2012–22** 2,200

What Drafters Do

Drafters use software to convert the designs of architects and engineers into technical drawings and plans. Workers specialize in architectural, civil, electrical, or mechanical drafting and use technical drawings to help design everything from microchips to skyscrapers.

Duties. Drafters typically do the following:

- Design plans using computer-aided design and drafting (CADD) software
- Work from rough sketches and specifications created by engineers and architects
- Help design products with engineering and manufacturing techniques
- Add details to architectural plans from their knowledge of building techniques
- Prepare multiple versions of designs for review by engineers and architects
- Specify dimensions, materials, and procedures for new products
- Work under the supervision of engineers or architects

Many drafters are referred to as *CADD operators*. Using CADD systems, drafters create and store technical drawings electronically. These drawings contain information on how to build a structure or machine, the dimensions of the project, and what materials are needed to produce the project.

Drafters work with CADD so they can create schematics that can be viewed, printed, or programmed directly into building information modeling (BIM) systems and product data management (PDM) systems. These systems allow drafters, architects, construction managers, and engineers to create and collaborate on digital models of physical buildings and machines. Through three-dimensional rendering, BIM software allows designers and engineers to see how different elements in their projects work together. PDM software helps workers track and control data, such as technical specifications, related to projects.

Just as BIM is changing the work of architectural drafters, PDM is changing the work of mechanical drafters. These software systems allow drafting and design work to be done simultaneously with the work done by other professionals involved in the project.

The following are examples of types of drafters:

Aeronautical drafters prepare engineering drawings that show detailed plans and specifications used in manufacturing aircraft, missiles, and related parts.

Architectural drafters draw architectural and structural features of buildings for construction projects. These workers may specialize in a type of building, such as residential or commercial. They

Most drafters use computer-aided design and drafting software.

may also specialize by the materials used, such as steel, wood, or reinforced concrete.

Civil drafters prepare topographical maps used in major construction or civil engineering projects, such as highways, bridges, and flood-control projects.

Electrical drafters prepare wiring diagrams that other construction workers use to install and repair electrical equipment and wiring in power plants, electrical distribution systems, and residential and commercial buildings.

Electronics drafters produce wiring diagrams, assembly diagrams for circuit boards, and layout drawings used in manufacturing and in installing and repairing electronic devices and components.

Mechanical drafters prepare layouts that show the details for a wide variety of machinery and mechanical tools and devices, such as medical equipment. These layouts indicate dimensions, fastening methods, and other requirements needed for assembly. Workers sometimes create production molds.

Process piping or pipeline drafters prepare plans used in the layout, construction, and operation of oil and gas fields, refineries, chemical plants, and process piping systems.

Work Environment

Drafters held about 199,800 jobs in 2012. The industries that employed the most drafters in 2012 were as follows:

Architectural, engineering, and related services 47%
Manufacturing.. 28
Construction... 7

Work Schedules. Although drafters usually work with computers in an office, some projects require visits to a job site in order to collaborate with architects and engineers.

Most drafters work full time.

Median Annual Wages, May 2012

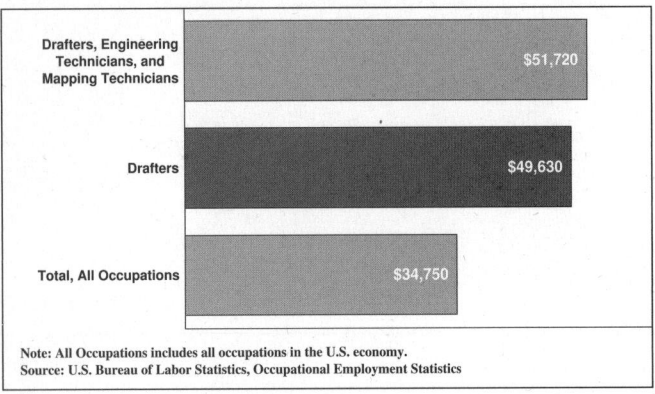

Note: All Occupations includes all occupations in the U.S. economy.
Source: U.S. Bureau of Labor Statistics, Occupational Employment Statistics

Percent Change in Employment, Projected 2012–2022

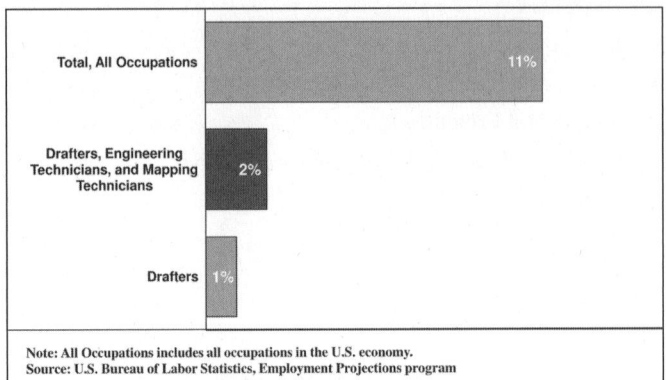

Note: All Occupations includes all occupations in the U.S. economy.
Source: U.S. Bureau of Labor Statistics, Employment Projections program

How to Become One

Drafters typically need specialized training, which can be accomplished through a technical program that leads to a certificate or an associate's degree in drafting.

Education. Employers generally prefer applicants who have completed postsecondary education in drafting, typically a 2-year associate's degree from a technical institute or community college.

Technical institutes offer instruction in design fundamentals, sketching, and CADD (computer-aided design and drafting) software. They award certificates or diplomas, and programs vary considerably in length and in the types of courses offered. Some institutions may only specialize in one type of drafting, such as mechanical or electrical drafting.

Community colleges offer programs similar to those in technical institutes but typically include more classes in drafting theory and often require general education classes. After completing an associate's degree program, graduates may get jobs as drafters or continue their education in a related field at a 4-year college. Most 4-year colleges do not offer training in drafting, but they do offer classes in engineering, architecture, and mathematics. Courses taken at community colleges are more likely to be accepted for credit at colleges or universities.

To prepare for postsecondary education, high school students who take courses in mathematics, science, computer technology, design, computer graphics, and where available, drafting, may find such classes useful.

Licenses, Certifications, and Registrations. The American Design Drafting Association (ADDA) offers certification for drafters. Although not mandatory, certification demonstrates competence and knowledge of nationally recognized practices. Certifications are offered for several specialties, including architectural, civil, and mechanical drafting.

Important Qualities

Critical-thinking skills. Drafters help the architects and engineers they work for by spotting problems with plans and designs.

Detail oriented. Drafters must pay close attention to details so that the plans they are helping to build are technically accurate to the outlined specifications.

Interpersonal skills. Drafters work closely with architects, engineers, and other designers to make sure that final plans are accurate. This requires the ability to take advice and constructive criticism, as well as to offer it.

Math skills. Drafters work with technical drawings that may require solving mathematical calculations involving angles, weights, and costs.

Technical skills. Drafters in all specialties must be able to use computer software, such as CADD, and work with database tools, such as BIM (building information modeling).

Time-management skills. Drafters often work under strict deadlines. As a result, they must work efficiently in order to produce the required output according to set schedules.

Pay

The median annual wage for drafters was $49,630 in May 2012. The median wage is the wage at which half the workers in an occupation earned more than that amount and half earned less. The lowest 10 percent earned less than $32,190, and the top 10 percent earned more than $77,770.

The median wages for detailed drafting occupations in May 2012 were as follows:

$55,700 for electrical and electronics drafters
$50,360 for mechanical drafters
$47,870 for architectural and civil drafters
$46,110 for drafters, all other

Employment Projections Data for Drafters

Occupational title	SOC Code	Employment, 2012	Projected Employment, 2022	Change, 2012–2022	
				Percent	Numeric
Drafters............	17-3010	199,800	202,000	1	2,200
Architectural and civil drafters............	17-3011	87,900	88,500	1	700
Electrical and electronics drafters............	17-3012	29,600	32,500	10	2,900
Mechanical drafters............	17-3013	66,700	63,400	-5	-3,300
Drafters, all other............	17-3019	15,600	17,600	13	2,000

Source: U.S. Bureau of Labor Statistics, Employment Projections Program

Note: Data are rounded. Go to **Occupational Information Included in the OOH** *for a discussion of the data in this table.*

Similar Occupations   This table shows a list of occupations with job duties that are similar to those of drafters.

Occupations	Entry-level Education	2012 Pay	Projected Job Growth	Average Annual Openings
Architects	Bachelor's degree	$73,090	17%	4,410
Civil Engineering Technicians	Associate's degree	$47,560	1%	1,560
Electrical and Electronics Engineering Technicians	Associate's degree	$57,850	0%	3,040
Electrical and Electronics Engineers	Bachelor's degree	$89,701	4%	7,940
Electrical and Electronics Installers and Repairers	Postsecondary non-degree award	$51,081	1%	2,980
Electro-mechanical Technicians	Associate's degree	$51,820	4%	430
Industrial Designers	Bachelor's degree	$59,610	4%	1,210
Landscape Architects	Bachelor's degree	$64,180	14%	760
Mechanical Engineering Technicians	Associate's degree	$51,980	5%	1,210
Mechanical Engineers	Bachelor's degree	$80,580	4%	9,970
Surveying and Mapping Technicians	High school diploma or equivalent	$39,670	14%	1,700
Surveyors	Bachelor's degree	$56,230	10%	1,340

Although drafters usually work with computers in an office, some projects require visits to a job site in order to collaborate with architects and engineers.

Job Outlook

Overall employment of drafters is projected to show little or no change from 2012 to 2022. Employment growth will vary by specialty.

Employment of architectural and civil drafters is projected to show little or no change from 2012 to 2022. Although construction projects will likely result in some demand for architectural and civil drafters, efficiencies gained from computer-aided design and drafting (CADD) and building information modeling (BIM) will continue to reduce the need for these specialists.

Employment of electrical and electronics drafters is projected to grow 10 percent from 2012 to 2022, about as fast as the average for all occupations. Electrical and electronics drafters will continue to be needed to work on the electrical system designs in buildings, cars, and devices that have electrical systems. However, employment growth might be tempered as computer software and database tools continue to make workers more efficient.

Employment of mechanical drafters is projected to decline 5 percent from 2012 to 2022. Although some mechanical drafters will to be needed to aid in designing machines, vehicles, and medical equipment, most of these workers are employed in declining or slow-growing manufacturing industries, offering few opportunities for growth from industry expansion.

CADD systems that are more user friendly and more powerful than current systems will allow other technical professionals, such as engineering technicians and engineers, to perform many tasks previously done by drafters. This development may curb demand for all specialty drafters. In addition, some drafting work may be outsourced to other countries at lower wages, further reducing the need for these workers.

Still, software such as PDM (product data management) and BIM (building information modeling) will require drafters to collaborate with other design workers, such as architects and engineers, on projects, whether constructing a new building or manufacturing a new product. This software requires that someone build and maintain large databases. Skilled drafters with knowledge of these systems will be needed to oversee these databases.

Job Prospects. Overall competition for jobs should be strong.

Specifically, architectural and civil drafters may experience more competition for jobs than mechanical or electrical drafters due to the number of students graduating in those drafting specialties. Typically, the number of graduates in architectural and civil programs greatly exceeds the number of available positions.

Demand for particular drafting specialties varies across the country because jobs depend on the needs of local industries. Job prospects for mechanical drafters should be best in large manufacturing hubs.

Because many drafting jobs are in construction and manufacturing, job opportunities for drafters will be sensitive to fluctuations in the overall economy.

Candidates proficient in BIM and PDM are likely to have better job opportunities.

O*NET

➤ Architectural and Civil Drafters (17-3011.00)
➤ Architectural Drafters (17-3011.01)
➤ Civil Drafters (17-3011.02)
➤ Electrical and Electronics Drafters (17-3012.00)
➤ Electronic Drafters (17-3012.01)
➤ Electrical Drafters (17-3012.02)
➤ Mechanical Drafters (17-3013.00)
➤ Drafters, All Other (17-3019.00)

Contacts for More Information

For more information on schools offering programs in drafting and related fields, visit

➤ Accrediting Commission of Career Schools and Colleges (www.accsc.org)

For more information on certification, visit

➤ American Design Drafting Association (www.adda.org)

Electrical and Electronics Engineering Technicians

- **2012 Median Pay** .... $57,850 per year
  $27.81 per hour
- **Entry-Level Education** ....Associate's degree
- **Work Experience in a Related Occupation**............... None
- **On-the-Job Training** .... None
- **Number of Jobs 2012** 146,500
- **Job Outlook, 2012–22** ....0% (Little or no change)
- **Employment Change, 2012–22** 0

Engineering technicians assist engineers in designing and testing new products.

What Electrical and Electronics Engineering Technicians Do

Electrical and electronics engineering technicians help engineers design and develop computers, communications equipment, medical monitoring devices, navigational equipment, and other electrical and electronic equipment. They often work in product evaluation and testing, using measuring and diagnostic devices to adjust, test, and repair equipment.

Duties. Electrical engineering technicians typically do the following:

- Put together electrical and electronic systems and prototypes
- Build, calibrate, and repair electrical instruments or testing equipment
- Visit construction sites to observe conditions affecting design
- Identify solutions to technical design problems that arise during construction of electrical systems
- Inspect designs for quality control, report findings, and make recommendations
- Draw diagrams and write specifications to clarify design details of experimental electronics units

Electrical engineering technicians install and maintain electrical control systems and equipment and modify electrical prototypes, parts, and assemblies to correct problems. When testing systems they set up test equipment and evaluate the performance of developmental parts, assemblies, or systems under simulated conditions. They then analyze test information to resolve design-related problems.

Electronics engineering technicians typically do the following:

- Design basic circuitry and draft sketches to clarify details of design documentation, under engineers' direction
- Build prototypes from rough sketches or plans
- Assemble, test, and maintain circuitry or electronic components according to engineering instructions, technical manuals, and knowledge of electronics
- Adjust and replace defective circuitry and electronics components
- Make parts, such as coils and terminal boards, by using bench lathes, drills, or other machine tools

Electronics engineering technicians identify and resolve equipment malfunctions, working with manufacturers to get replacement parts. They also calibrate and perform preventative maintenance on equipment and systems.

These technicians often need to read blueprints, schematic drawings, and engineering instructions for putting together electronics units, as well as write reports and record data on testing techniques, laboratory equipment, and specifications.

Work Environment

Electrical and electronics engineering technicians held about 146,500 jobs in 2012. The industries that employed the most electrical and electronic engineering technicians in 2012 were as follows:

Architectural, engineering, and related services 13%
Semiconductor and other electronic component
    manufacturing.. 12
Navigational, measuring, electromedical, and control
    instruments manufacturing 8

Median Annual Wages, May 2012

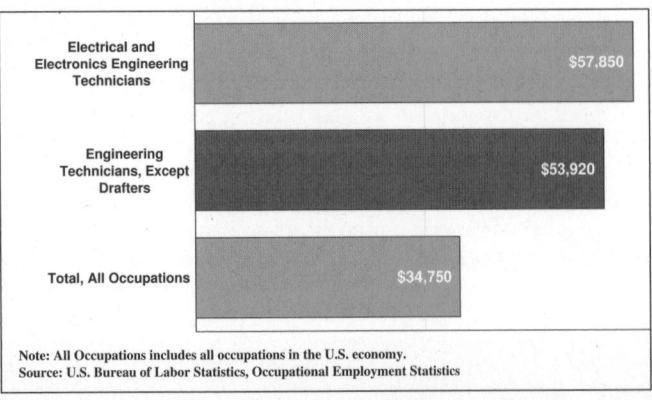

Electrical and Electronics Engineering Technicians — $57,850
Engineering Technicians, Except Drafters — $53,920
Total, All Occupations — $34,750

Note: All Occupations includes all occupations in the U.S. economy.
Source: U.S. Bureau of Labor Statistics, Occupational Employment Statistics

Percent Change in Employment, Projected 2012–2022

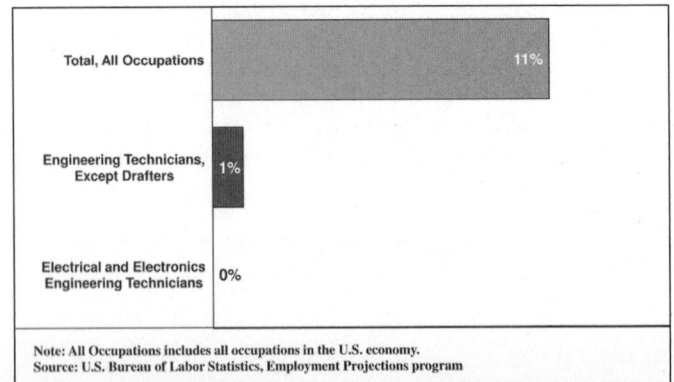

Total, All Occupations — 11%
Engineering Technicians, Except Drafters — 1%
Electrical and Electronics Engineering Technicians — 0%

Note: All Occupations includes all occupations in the U.S. economy.
Source: U.S. Bureau of Labor Statistics, Employment Projections program

Employment Projections Data for Electrical and Electronics Engineering Technicians

Occupational title	SOC Code	Employment, 2012	Projected Employment, 2022	Change, 2012–2022	
				Percent	Numeric
Electrical and electronics engineering technicians.................. 17-3023		146,500	146,500	0	0

Source: U.S. Bureau of Labor Statistics, Employment Projections Program

Note: Data are rounded. Go to Occupational Information Included in the OOH for a discussion of the data in this table.

Federal government, excluding postal service 6
Postal service 5

Electrical and electronics engineering technicians work closely with electrical and electronics engineers. For this reason, teamwork is an important part of the job. They work in offices, laboratories, and factories because their job tasks involve both engineering theory and assembly-line production.

Electrical and electronics engineering technicians may be exposed to hazards from equipment or toxic materials, but incidents are rare if proper procedures are followed.

Work Schedules. Electrical and electronics engineering technicians work schedules common to production workers in the industries in which they are employed. In the federal government, their schedules tend to follow a standard workweek. In manufacturing industries and laboratories, these technicians most commonly work a standard workweek, except for particular periods when overtime might be required.

How to Become One

Electrical and electronics engineering technicians typically need an associate's degree.

Education. Programs for electrical and electronics engineering technicians usually lead to an associate's degree in electrical or electronics engineering technology. Vocational–technical schools include postsecondary institutions that serve local students and emphasize training needed by local employers. Community colleges offer programs similar to those in technical institutes but include more theory-based and liberal arts coursework.

Prospective electrical and electronics engineering technicians usually take courses in C++ programming, physics, microprocessors, and circuitry. The Technology Accreditation Commission of ABET accredits programs that include at least college algebra, trigonometry, and basic science courses.

Important Qualities

Logical-thinking skills. Electrical and electronics engineering technicians must isolate and then identify problems for the engineering staff to work on. They need good reasoning skills to identify and fix problems. Technicians must also be able to follow a logical sequence or specific set of rules to carry out engineers' designs, inspect designs for quality control, and put together prototypes.

Math skills. Electrical and electronics engineering technicians use math for analysis, design, and troubleshooting in their work.

Mechanical skills. Electronics engineering technicians in particular must be able to use handtools and soldering irons on small circuitry and electronic parts to create detailed electronic components by hand.

Observational skills. Electrical engineering technicians sometimes visit a construction site to make sure that electrical engineers' designs are being carried out correctly. They are responsible for evaluating the project onsite and reporting problems to the engineer.

Problem-solving skills. Electrical and electronics engineering technicians create what engineers have designed and often test the designs to make sure that they work. Technicians help to resolve any problems that come up in carrying out the engineers' designs.

Writing skills. These technicians must write reports on onsite construction, the results of testing, or problems they find when carrying out designs. Their writing must be clear and well organized so that the engineers they work with can understand the reports.

Licenses, Certifications, and Registrations. The National Institute for Certification in Engineering Technologies (NICET) offers certification in Electrical Power testing. This certification would benefit those technicians working in the electric power generation, transmission, and distribution industry.

Pay

The median annual wage for electrical and electronics engineering technicians was $57,850 in May 2012. The median wage is the wage at which half the workers in an occupation earned more than that amount and half earned less. The lowest 10 percent earned less than $34,560, and the top 10 percent earned more than $83,120.

In May 2012, the median annual wages for electrical and electronics engineering technicians in the top five industries in which these technicians worked were as follows:

Federal government, excluding postal service $75,690
Postal service 62,180
Architectural, engineering, and related services 56,610
Navigational, measuring, electromedical, and control
  instruments manufacturing 52,130
Semiconductor and other electronic component
  manufacturing.. 52,050

Similar Occupations   This table shows a list of occupations with job duties that are similar to those of electrical and electronics engineering technicians.

Occupations	Entry-level Education	2012 Pay	Projected Job Growth	Average Annual Openings
Electrical and Electronics Engineers	Bachelor's degree	$89,701	4%	7,940
Electrical and Electronics Installers and Repairers	Postsecondary non-degree award	$51,081	1%	2,980
Electro-mechanical Technicians	Associate's degree	$51,820	4%	430
Mechanical Engineering Technicians	Associate's degree	$51,980	5%	1,210

Electrical and electronics engineering technicians work schedules common to production workers in the industries in which they are employed. In the federal government, their schedules tend to follow a standard workweek.

Job Outlook

Employment of electrical and electronics engineering technicians is projected to show little or no change from 2012 to 2022.

Some of these technicians work in traditional manufacturing industries, many of which are declining or growing slowly. However, employment growth for electrical and electronics engineering technicians will likely occur in engineering services firms as companies seek to contract out these services as a way to lower costs.

They also work closely with electrical and electronics engineers and computer hardware engineers in the computer systems design services industry. Demand is expected to be high for technicians in this industry as computer and electronics systems become more integrated. For example, computer, cellular phone, and global positioning systems (GPS) technologies are being included in automobiles and various portable and household electronics systems.

O*NET

➤ Electrical and Electronic Engineering Technicians (17-3023.00)
➤ Electronics Engineering Technicians (17-3023.01)
➤ Electrical Engineering Technicians (17-3023.03)

Contacts for More Information

For information about general engineering education and career resources, visit
➤ American Society for Engineering Education (www.asee.org/)
➤ Technology Student Association (www.tsaweb.org/)
    For information about accredited programs, visit
➤ ABET (www.abet.org/)
    For information about certification, visit
➤ National Institute for Certification in Engineering Technologies (www.nicet.org/become-certified/how-do-i-get-certified/technician-certification-programs/electrical-and-mechanical-systems/electrical-power-testing/)

Electrical and Electronics Engineers

- **2012 Median Pay** .... $89,630 per year
  $43.09 per hour
- **Entry-Level Education** .... Bachelor's degree
- **Work Experience in a Related Occupation** .... None
- **On-the-Job Training** .... None
- **Number of Jobs 2012** 306,100
- **Job Outlook, 2012–22** .... 4% (Slower than average)
- **Employment Change, 2012–22** 12,600

What Electrical and Electronics Engineers Do

Electrical engineers design, develop, test, and supervise the manufacturing of electrical equipment, such as electric motors, radar and navigation systems, communications systems, or power generation equipment. Electrical engineers also design the electrical systems of automobiles and aircraft.

Electronics engineers design and develop electronic equipment, such as broadcast and communications systems, from portable music players to global positioning systems (GPS). Many also work in areas closely related to computer hardware.

Duties. Electrical engineers typically do the following:

- Design new ways to use electrical power to develop or improve products
- Do detailed calculations to develop manufacturing, construction, and installation standards and specifications
- Direct manufacturing, installing, and testing of electrical equipment to ensure that products meet specifications and codes
- Investigate complaints from customers or the public, evaluate problems, and recommend solutions
- Work with project managers on production efforts to ensure that projects are completed satisfactorily, on time, and within budget

Electronics engineers typically do the following:

- Design electronic components, software, products, or systems for commercial, industrial, medical, military, or scientific applications
- Analyze customer needs and determine electrical system requirements, capacity, and cost to develop a system plan
- Develop maintenance and testing procedures for electronic components and equipment
- Evaluate systems and recommend design modifications or equipment repair
- Inspect electronic equipment, instruments, and systems to make sure they meet safety standards and applicable regulations
- Plan and develop applications and modifications for electronic properties used in parts and systems to improve technical performance

Electronics engineers who work for the federal government research, develop, and evaluate electronic devices used in a variety of areas, such as aviation, computing, transportation, and manufacturing. They work on federal electronic devices and systems, including satellites, flight systems, radar and sonar systems, and communications systems.

The work of electrical engineers and electronics engineers is often similar. Both use engineering and design software and equipment to do engineering tasks. Both types of engineers also must work with other engineers to discuss existing products and possibilities for engineering projects.

Engineers whose work is related exclusively to computer hardware are considered computer hardware engineers.

Electrical engineers design tests for new products.

Median Annual Wages, May 2012

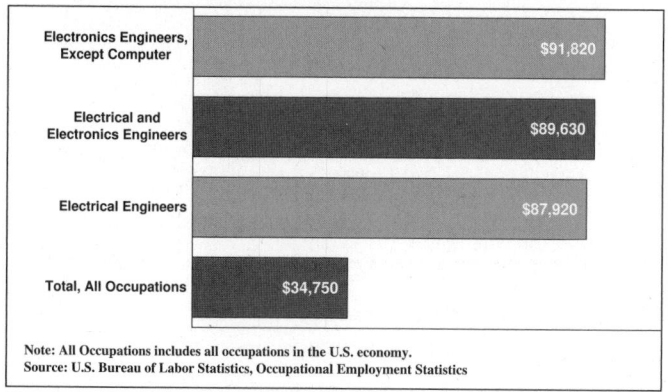

Note: All Occupations includes all occupations in the U.S. economy.
Source: U.S. Bureau of Labor Statistics, Occupational Employment Statistics

Percent Change in Employment, Projected 2012–2022

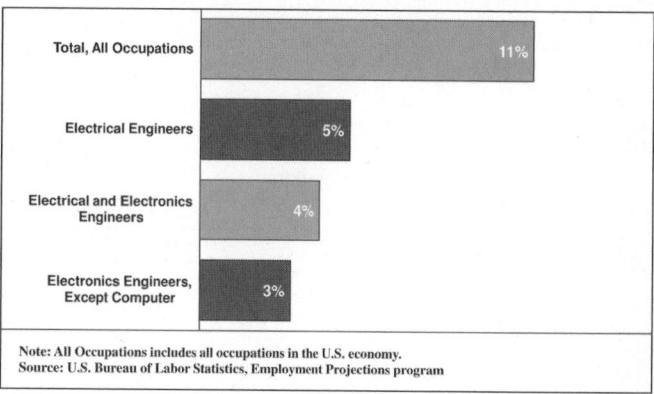

Note: All Occupations includes all occupations in the U.S. economy.
Source: U.S. Bureau of Labor Statistics, Employment Projections program

Work Environment

Electrical and electronics engineers held about 306,100 jobs in 2012. The industries that employed the most electrical engineers in 2012 were as follows:

Engineering services.. 20%
Electric power generation, transmission and distribution 9
Navigational, measuring, electromedical, and control
  instruments manufacturing 9
Semiconductor and other electronic component
  manufacturing... 8
Machinery manufacturing 5

The industries that employed the most electronics engineers in 2012 were as follows:

Telecommunications 18%
Federal government, excluding postal service 13
Architectural, engineering, and related services 12
Semiconductor and other electronic component
  manufacturing... 9
Navigational, measuring, electromedical, and control
  instruments manufacturing 6

Electrical and electronics engineers generally work indoors in offices. However, they may visit sites to observe a problem or a piece of complex equipment.

Work Schedules. Electrical and electronics engineers typically work a standard, full-time schedule, although overtime work is sometimes required to meet deadlines.

How to Become One

Electrical and electronics engineers must have a bachelor's degree. Employers also value practical experience, so participation in cooperative engineering programs, in which students earn academic credit for structured work experience, is valuable as well. Having a Professional Engineer (PE) license may improve an engineer's chances of finding employment.

Education. High school students interested in studying electrical or electronics engineering benefit from taking courses in physics and mathematics, including algebra, trigonometry, and calculus. Courses in drafting are also helpful, because electrical and electronics engineers are often required to prepare technical drawings.

Entry-level jobs in electrical or electronics engineering generally require a bachelor's degree in electrical engineering, electronics engineering, or electrical engineering technology. Programs include classroom, laboratory, and field studies. Courses include digital systems design, differential equations, and electrical circuit theory. Programs in electrical engineering should be accredited by ABET.

Some colleges and universities offer cooperative programs in which students gain practical experience while completing their education. Cooperative programs combine classroom study with practical work.

At some universities, students can enroll in a 5-year program that leads to both a bachelor's degree and a master's degree. A graduate degree allows an engineer to work as an instructor at some universities, or in research and development.

Important Qualities

Concentration. Electrical and electronics engineers design and develop complex electrical systems and electronic components and products. They must be able to keep track of multiple design elements and technical characteristics when performing these tasks.

Initiative. Electrical and electronics engineers must be able to apply their academic knowledge to new tasks in every project they undertake. In addition, they must engage in continuing education to keep up with changes in technology.

Interpersonal skills. Electrical and electronics engineers must be able to work with others during the manufacturing process to ensure that their plans are implemented correctly. This collaboration includes monitoring technicians and devising remedies to problems as they arise.

Math skills. Electrical and electronics engineers must be able to use the principles of calculus and other advanced topics in math in order to analyze, design, and troubleshoot equipment.

Speaking skills. Electrical and electronics engineers work closely with other engineers and technicians. They must be able to explain their designs and reasoning clearly and to relay instructions during product development and production. They may also need to explain complex issues to customers who have little or no technical expertise.

Licenses, Certifications, and Registrations. Licensure for electrical and electronics engineers is not as common as it is for other engineering occupations; however, it is encouraged for those working in companies that have contracts with federal, state, and local government. Engineers who become licensed are designated Professional Engineers (PEs). Licensure generally requires the following:

• A degree from an ABET-accredited engineering program

• A passing score on the Fundamentals of Engineering (FE) exam

• Relevant work experience

• A passing score on the Professional Engineering (PE) exam

The initial Fundamentals of Engineering (FE) exam can be taken right after graduation from a college or university. Engineers who pass this exam commonly are called engineers in training (EITs) or engineer interns (EIs). After getting work experience,

Employment Projections Data for Electrical and Electronics Engineers

Occupational title	SOC Code	Employment, 2012	Projected Employment, 2022	Change, 2012–2022	
				Percent	Numeric
Electrical and electronics engineers.......................................	17-2070	306,100	318,700	4	12,600
Electrical engineers	17-2071	166,100	174,000	5	7,900
Electronics engineers, except computer	17-2072	140,000	144,800	3	4,800

Source: U.S. Bureau of Labor Statistics, Employment Projections Program

Note: Data are rounded. Go to **Occupational Information Included in the OOH** *for a discussion of the data in this table.*

EITs can take the second exam, called the Principles and Practice of Engineering exam.

Several states require engineers to take continuing education courses to keep their license. Most states recognize licensure from other states if the licensing state's requirements meet or exceed their own licensure requirements.

Advancement. Electrical and electronic engineers may advance to supervisory positions that require leading a team of engineers and technicians. Some may move to management positions, working as engineering or program managers. Preparation for managerial positions usually requires working under the guidance of a more experienced engineer. For more information, see the profile on architectural and engineering managers.

For sales work, an engineering background enables engineers to discuss a product's technical aspects and assist in product planning and use. For more information, see the profile on sales engineers.

Pay

The median annual wage for electrical engineers was $87,920 in May 2012. The median wage is the wage at which half the workers in an occupation earned more than that amount and half earned less. The lowest 10 percent earned less than $56,490, and the top 10 percent earned more than $136,690.

The median annual wage for electronics engineers was $91,820 in May 2012. The lowest 10 percent earned less than $58,470, and the top 10 percent earned more than $141,190.

In May 2012, the median annual wages for electrical engineers in the top five industries employing these engineers were as follows:

Semiconductor and other electronic component
   manufacturing.. $94,990

Navigational, measuring, electromedical, and control
   instruments manufacturing 91,810
Engineering services.. 87,640
Electric power generation, transmission and distribution 85,350
Machinery manufacturing 79,480

In May 2012, the median annual wages for electronics engineers in the top five industries employing these engineers were as follows:

Federal government, excluding postal service $103,270
Semiconductor and other electronic component
   manufacturing.. 96,140
Architectural, engineering, and related services 96,110
Navigational, measuring, electromedical, and control
   instruments manufacturing 90,440
Telecommunications 83,020

Electrical and electronics engineers typically work a standard, full-time schedule, although overtime work is sometimes required to meet deadlines.

Job Outlook

Employment of electrical and electronics engineers is projected to grow 4 percent from 2012 to 2022, slower than the average for all occupations. Job growth is expected because of electrical and electronics engineers' versatility in developing and applying emerging technologies. On the other hand, employment growth could be tempered by slow growth or decline in most manufacturing sectors in which electrical and electronics engineers are employed.

Job growth for electrical and electronics engineers will largely occur in engineering services firms, because more companies are expected to cut costs by contracting engineering services rather than directly employing engineers. These engineers will also experience

Similar Occupations   This table shows a list of occupations with job duties that are similar to those of electrical and electronics engineers.

Occupations	Entry-level Education	2012 Pay	Projected Job Growth	Average Annual Openings
Aerospace Engineers	Bachelor's degree	$103,720	7%	2,540
Architectural and Engineering Managers	Bachelor's degree	$124,870	7%	6,060
Biomedical Engineers	Bachelor's degree	$86,960	27%	1,010
Computer Hardware Engineers	Bachelor's degree	$100,920	7%	2,410
Electrical and Electronics Engineering Technicians	Associate's degree	$57,850	0%	3,040
Electrical and Electronics Installers and Repairers	Postsecondary non-degree award	$51,081	1%	2,980
Electricians	High school diploma or equivalent	$49,840	20%	22,460
Electro-mechanical Technicians	Associate's degree	$51,820	4%	430
Sales Engineers	Bachelor's degree	$91,830	9%	1,740

job growth in computer systems design, as these industries continue to implement more powerful portable computing devices.

The rapid pace of technological innovation and development will likely drive demand for electrical and electronics engineers in research and development, an area in which engineering expertise will be needed to develop distribution systems related to new technologies.

O*NET

➤ Electrical Engineers (17-2071.00)
➤ Electronics Engineers, Except Computer (17-2072.00)
➤ Radio Frequency Identification Device Specialists (17-2072.01)

Contacts for More Information

For information about general engineering education and career resources, visit

➤ American Society for Engineering Education (www.asee.org/)
➤ Technology Student Association (www.tsaweb.org/)

For more information about licensure as an electrical or electronics engineer, visit

➤ National Council of Examiners for Engineering and Surveying (http://ncees.org/)
➤ National Society of Professional Engineers (www.nspe.org/index.html)

For information about accredited engineering programs, visit

➤ ABET (www.abet.org/)

Electro-mechanical Technicians

- **2012 Median Pay** .... $51,820 per year
  $24.91 per hour

- **Entry-Level Education** .... Associate's degree

- **Work Experience in a Related Occupation** .... None

- **On-the-Job Training** .... None

- **Number of Jobs 2012** 17,300

- **Job Outlook, 2012–22** .... 4% (Slower than average)

- **Employment Change, 2012–22** 700

What Electro-mechanical Technicians Do

Electro-mechanical technicians combine knowledge of mechanical technology with knowledge of electrical and electronic circuits. They install, troubleshoot, repair, and upgrade electronic and computer-controlled mechanical systems, such as robotic assembly machines.

Duties. Electro-mechanical technicians typically do the following:

- Read blueprints, schematics, and diagrams to determine the method and sequence of assembly of a part, machine, or piece of equipment

- Verify dimensions of parts, using precision measuring instruments, to ensure that specifications are met

- Operate metalworking machines to make housings, fittings, and fixtures

- Repair and calibrate hydraulic and pneumatic assemblies

- Test the performance of electro-mechanical assemblies, using test instruments

- Install electronic parts and hardware, using soldering equipment and hand tools

Electro-mechanical technicians sometimes test and operate machines in factories and other worksites. They also analyze and record test results, and prepare written documentation to describe the tests they did and what the test results were.

Work Environment

Electro-mechanical technicians held about 17,300 jobs in 2012.

Electro-mechanical technicians work closely with electrical and mechanical engineers. They work primarily in manufacturing, engineering services, and research and development. Their job tasks involve both engineering theory and assembly line production work. Consequently, they often work both at production sites and in offices.

The industries that employed the most electro-mechanical technicians in 2012 were as follows:

Architectural, engineering, and related services	13%
Navigational, measuring, electromedical, and control instruments manufacturing	11
Semiconductor and other electronic component manufacturing	10
Scientific research and development services	8
Support activities for mining	7

Because their job involves manual work with many machines and types of equipment, electro-mechanical technicians are sometimes exposed to hazards from equipment or toxic materials. However, incidents are rare as long as they follow proper safety procedures.

Work Schedules. Electro-mechanical technicians often work for larger companies in manufacturing or for engineering firms. Like others at these firms, these technicians tend to work a regular shift. However, sometimes they must work longer hours to make repairs so that manufacturing operations can continue.

How to Become One

Electro-mechanical technicians typically need either an associate's degree or a postsecondary certificate.

Education. Associate's degree programs and postsecondary certificates for electro-mechanical technicians are offered at vocational–technical schools and community colleges. Vocational–technical schools include postsecondary public institutions that serve local students and emphasize teaching the skills needed by local employers. Community colleges offer programs similar to those in

Electro-mechanical technicians install, repair, upgrade, and test electronic and computer-controlled mechanical systems.

Median Annual Wages, May 2012

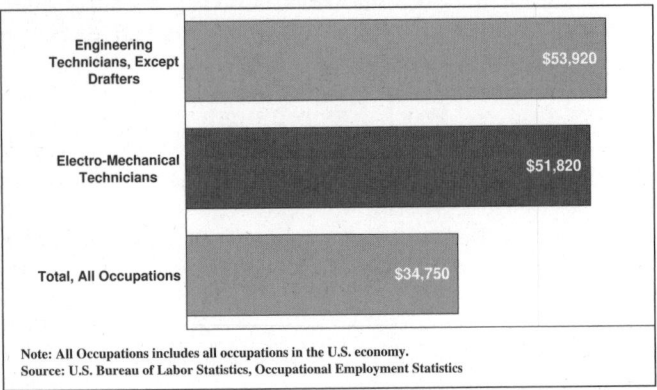

Note: All Occupations includes all occupations in the U.S. economy.
Source: U.S. Bureau of Labor Statistics, Occupational Employment Statistics

Percent Change in Employment, Projected 2012–2022

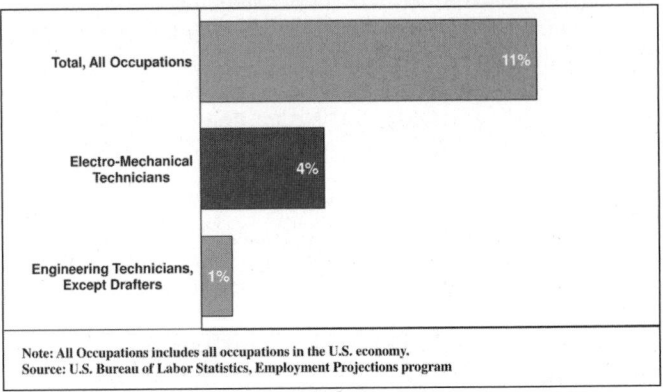

Note: All Occupations includes all occupations in the U.S. economy.
Source: U.S. Bureau of Labor Statistics, Employment Projections program

technical institutes, but they may include more theory-based and liberal arts coursework.

ABET accredits associate's and higher degree programs. Most associate's degree programs that are accredited by ABET include at least college algebra and trigonometry, as well as basic science courses.

ABET-accredited programs offer training in engineering technology specialties. In community college programs, prospective electro-mechanical technicians can concentrate in fields such as the following:

- Electro-mechanics
- Industrial maintenance
- Computer-integrated manufacturing
- Mechatronics

Earning an associate's degree in electronic or mechanical technology eases entry into a bachelor's degree programs in electrical engineering and mechanical engineering. For more information, see the profiles on electrical and electronics engineers and mechanical engineers.

Important Qualities

Detail oriented. Electro-mechanical technicians must make and keep the precise, accurate measurements that mechanical engineers need.

Dexterity. Electro-mechanical engineering technicians in particular must be able to use hand tools and soldering irons on small circuitry and electronic parts to create detailed electronic components by hand.

Interpersonal skills. Electro-mechanical technicians must be able to take instruction and offer advice when needed. In addition, they often need to coordinate their work with that of others.

Logical-thinking skills. To carry out engineers' designs, inspect designs for quality control, and assemble prototypes, electro-mechanical technicians must be able to read instructions and follow a logical sequence or a specific set of rules.

Math skills. Electro-mechanical engineering technicians use mathematics for analysis, design, and troubleshooting in their work.

Mechanical skills. Electro-mechanical technicians must be able to apply the theory and instructions of engineers by creating or building new components for industrial machinery or equipment. They must be adept at operating machinery, including drill presses, grinders, and engine lathes.

Writing skills. Electro-mechanical technicians must write reports on onsite construction, the results of testing, or problems they find when carrying out designs. Their writing must be clear and well organized so that the engineers they work with can understand the reports.

Licenses, Certifications, and Registrations. Electro-mechanical technicians can gain certification as a way to demonstrate professional competence.

The International Society of Automation offers certification as a Certified Control Systems Technician. This requires, at a minimum, 5 years of experience on the job, or only 3 years if the technician has completed 2 years of postsecondary education.

The National Institute for Certification in Engineering Technologies (NICET) offers certification in electrical power testing and other specialties.

Pay

The median annual wage for electro-mechanical technicians was $51,820 in May 2012. The median wage is the wage at which half the workers in an occupation earned more than that amount and half earned less. The lowest 10 percent earned less than $33,360, and the top 10 percent earned more than $76,590.

In May 2012, the median annual wages for electro-mechanical technicians in the top five industries in which these technicians worked were as follows:

Scientific research and development services $60,750
Architectural, engineering, and related services 52,620
Navigational, measuring, electromedical, and control
   instruments manufacturing 49,950

Employment Projections Data for Electro-mechanical Technicians

Occupational title	SOC Code	Employment, 2012	Projected Employment, 2022	Change, 2012–2022	
				Percent	Numeric
Electro-mechanical technicians	17-3024	17,300	18,000	4	700

Source: U.S. Bureau of Labor Statistics, Employment Projections Program

Note: Data are rounded. Go to **Occupational Information Included in the OOH** *for a discussion of the data in this table.*

Similar Occupations This table shows a list of occupations with job duties that are similar to those of electro-mechanical technicians.

Occupations	Entry-level Education	2012 Pay	Projected Job Growth	Average Annual Openings
Drafters	Associate's degree	$49,726	1%	3,220
Electrical and Electronics Engineering Technicians	Associate's degree	$57,850	0%	3,040
Electrical and Electronics Engineers	Bachelor's degree	$89,701	4%	7,940
Electrical and Electronics Installers and Repairers	Postsecondary non-degree award	$51,081	1%	2,980
Machinists and Tool and Die Makers	High school diploma or equivalent	$40,733	7%	13,060
Mechanical Engineering Technicians	Associate's degree	$51,980	5%	1,210
Mechanical Engineers	Bachelor's degree	$80,580	4%	9,970

Semiconductor and other electronic component
  manufacturing...46,840
Support activities for mining 42,480

Job Outlook

Employment of electro-mechanical technicians is projected to grow 4 percent from 2012 to 2022, slower than the average for all occupations. Many of these technicians are employed in manufacturing industries that are projected to experience employment declines.

Electro-mechanical technicians are generalists in technology, and their broad skill set will help sustain employment. This is especially the case as their skills working with machines wired to computer control systems grow in importance in the manufacturing sector.

As demand increases for engineers to design and build new equipment in various fields, employment of electro-mechanical technicians should also increase. This will be seen in new applications designed by engineers to automate more processes within manufacturing and other sectors.

Job Prospects. Job prospects are likely to be best for electro-mechanical technicians who train in a field known as mechatronics, which provides an understanding of four key systems:

• Mechanical systems

• Electronic systems

• Control systems

• Computer systems

Training in mechatronics has two advantages for electro-mechanical technicians. First, it is multidisciplinary, which gives technicians more versatile training that is applicable across a broad range of fields. Second, it allows a technician to contribute to a product in its entirety, from concept and design to delivery.

O*NET

➤ Electro-Mechanical Technicians (17-3024.00)
➤ Robotics Technicians (17-3024.01)

Contacts for More Information

For information about general engineering education and career resources, visit
➤ American Society for Engineering Education (www.asee.org/)
➤ IEEE (www.ieee.org/index.html)
➤ Technology Student Association (www.tsaweb.org/)
  For information on accredited programs, visit

➤ ABET (www.abet.org/)
  For more information about certification, visit
➤ International Society of Automation (www.isa.org/Content/NavigationMenu/Products_and_Services/Certification3/Certified_Control_Systems_Technician/Certified_Control_Systems_Technician.htm)
➤ National Institute for Certification in Engineering Technologies (www.nicet.org/)
  For information about working in automation, visit
➤ Automation Federation (www.automationfederation.org/AFTemplate.cfm?Section=Automation_Mentor_Program&Template=/customsource/af/mentorprogram/index.cfm)

Environmental Engineering Technicians

• **2012 Median Pay** ....$45,350 per year
                                        $21.80 per hour

• **Entry-Level Education** ....Associate's degree

• **Work Experience in a Related Occupation**............... None

• **On-the-Job Training** .... None

• **Number of Jobs 2012** 19,000

• **Job Outlook, 2012–22** .... 18% (Faster than average)

• **Employment Change, 2012–22** 3,500

What Environmental Engineering Technicians Do

Environmental engineering technicians carry out the plans that environmental engineers develop.

Duties. Environmental engineering technicians typically do the following:

• Set up, test, operate, and modify equipment used to prevent or clean up environmental pollution

• Maintain project records and computer program files

• Conduct pollution surveys, for which they collect and analyze samples such as air and ground water

• Perform indoor and outdoor work on environmental quality

• Work to mitigate sources of environmental pollution

• Review technical documents to ensure their completeness and conformance to requirements

• Review work plans to schedule activities

• Arrange for the disposal of lead, asbestos, and other hazardous materials

Environmental engineering technicians spend some time working outdoors and often must wear protective gear.

Environmental engineering technicians work under the direction of engineers and as part of a team with other technicians. They must be able to communicate and work well with both supervisors and peers.

In laboratories, environmental engineering technicians record observations, test results, and document photographs. To keep the laboratory supplied, they also may get product information, identify vendors and suppliers, and order materials and equipment.

Environmental engineering technicians help environmental engineers develop devices used to clean up environmental pollution. They also inspect facilities for compliance with the regulations that govern substances such as asbestos, lead, and wastewater.

Work Environment

Environment engineering technicians held about 19,000 jobs in 2012. The industries that employed the most environmental engineering technicians in 2012 were as follows:

Engineering services	22%
Management, scientific, and technical consulting services	20
Local government, excluding education and hospitals	11
Waste management and remediation services	9
Testing laboratories	8

Environment engineering technicians typically work indoors, usually in laboratories, and often have regular working hours. They also work outdoors, sometimes in remote locations.

Because environmental engineering technicians help out in environmental cleanup, they can be exposed to hazards from equipment, chemicals, or other toxic materials. For this reason, they must follow proper safety procedures, such as wearing hazmat suits and sometimes respirators, even in warm weather. When they work in wet areas, environmental engineering technicians wear heavy rubber boots to keep their legs and feet dry.

Work Schedules. Most environmental engineering technicians work full time and typically have regular hours. However, they must sometimes work irregular hours in order to monitor operations.

How to Become One

Environmental engineering technicians typically have an associate's degree in environmental engineering technology or a related field.

Education. Prospective engineering technicians should take as many high school science and math courses as possible to prepare for programs in engineering technology after high school.

Environmental engineering technicians typically have an associate's degree in environmental engineering technology or a related field. Programs can be found in vocational-technical schools and community colleges. Vocational-technical schools include postsecondary public institutions that serve local students and emphasize training needed by local employers. Community colleges offer programs similar to those in technical institutes but include more theory-based and liberal arts coursework. Associate's degree programs generally include courses in mathematics, chemistry, solid and hazardous waste, and environmental biology, among others.

ABET accredits programs at the associate's level and above. Some environmental engineering technicians enter the occupation with a bachelor's degree in a natural science, such as biology or chemistry.

Important Qualities

Critical-thinking skills. Environmental engineers rely on environmental engineering technicians to help identify problems and their solutions and to implement the engineers' plans. To do these tasks, technicians must be able to think critically and logically.

Listening skills. Environmental engineering technicians must be able to listen carefully to the instructions that engineers give them.

Observational skills. Environmental engineering technicians are the eyes and ears of environmental engineers and must assume responsibility for properly evaluating situations onsite. These technicians must be able to recognize problems so that the environmental engineers are informed as quickly as possible.

Reading skills. Environmental engineering technicians must be able to read and understand legal and technical documents to ensure that regulatory requirements are being met.

Median Annual Wages, May 2012

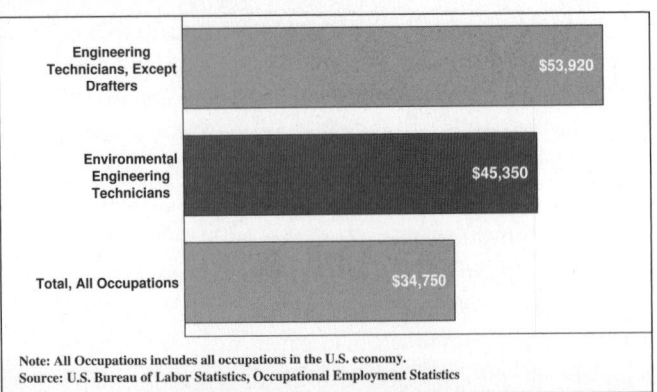

Note: All Occupations includes all occupations in the U.S. economy.
Source: U.S. Bureau of Labor Statistics, Occupational Employment Statistics

Percent Change in Employment, Projected 2012–2022

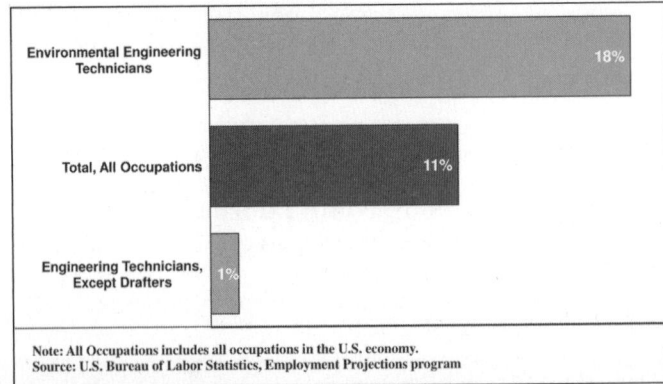

Note: All Occupations includes all occupations in the U.S. economy.
Source: U.S. Bureau of Labor Statistics, Employment Projections program

Employment Projections Data for Environmental Engineering Technicians

Occupational title	SOC Code	Employment, 2012	Projected Employment, 2022	Change, 2012–2022	
				Percent	Numeric
Environmental engineering technicians..................................	17-3025	19,000	22,500	18	3,500

Source: U.S. Bureau of Labor Statistics, Employment Projections Program

Note: Data are rounded. Go to Occupational Information Included in the OOH *for a discussion of the data in this table.*

Similar Occupations   This table shows a list of occupations with job duties that are similar to those of environmental engineering technicians.

Occupations	Entry-level Education	2012 Pay	Projected Job Growth	Average Annual Openings
Environmental Engineers	Bachelor's degree	$80,890	15%	2,110
Environmental Science and Protection Technicians	Associate's degree	$41,240	19%	1,900
Environmental Scientists and Specialists	Bachelor's degree	$63,570	15%	3,970
Hazardous Materials Removal Workers	High school diploma or equivalent	$37,590	14%	1,340

Advancement. Environmental engineering technicians usually begin work as trainees in entry-level positions supervised by an environmental engineer or a more experienced technician. As they gain experience, technicians take on more responsibility and carry out assignments under general supervision. Some eventually become supervisors.

Technicians who have a bachelor's degree often are able to advance to engineering positions.

Pay

The median annual wage for environmental engineering technicians was $45,350 in May 2012. The median wage is the wage at which half the workers in an occupation earned more than that amount and half earned less. The lowest 10 percent earned less than $28,680, and the top 10 percent earned more than $76,560.

In May 2012, the median annual wages for environmental engineering technicians in the top five industries in which these technicians worked were as follows:

Local government, excluding education and hospitals.......	$53,170
Engineering services..	44,660
Waste management and remediation services	43,100
Management, scientific, and technical consulting services...	40,280
Testing laboratories...	36,030

Job Outlook

Employment of environmental engineering technicians is projected to grow 18 percent from 2012 to 2022, faster than the average for all occupations. However, because it is a small occupation, the fast growth will result in only about 3,500 new jobs over the 10-year period.

Employment in this occupation is typically tied to projects created by environmental engineers. Over the next ten years, state and local governments are expected to focus their efforts and resources on efficient water use and wastewater treatment, and thus to increase demand for environmental engineering technicians.

The increasing call to clean up contaminated sites, as mandated by Congress and directed by the Environmental Protection Agency, is expected to help sustain demand for environmental engineering technicians' services. In addition, wastewater treatment is becoming a larger concern in areas of the country where new methods of drilling for shale gas require the use and disposal of large volumes of water. Environmental engineering technicians will continue to be needed to help utilities and water treatment plants comply with new federal or state environmental regulations.

O*NET

➤ Electro-Mechanical Technicians (17-3024.00)
➤ Robotics Technicians (17-3024.01)

Contacts for More Information

For more information about accredited programs, visit
➤ ABET (www.abet.org/)

For more information about general engineering education and career resources, visit
➤ Technology Student Association (www.tsaweb.org/)

Environmental Engineers

- **2012 Median Pay** .... $80,890 per year
  $38.89 per hour
- **Entry-Level Education** ....Bachelor's degree
- **Work Experience in a Related Occupation**.............. None
- **On-the-Job Training** .... None
- **Number of Jobs 2012** 53,200
- **Job Outlook, 2012–22**............. 15% (Faster than average)
- **Employment Change, 2012–22** 8,100

What Environmental Engineers Technicians Do

Environmental engineers use the principles of engineering, soil science, biology, and chemistry to develop solutions to environmental problems. They are involved in efforts to improve recycling, waste disposal, public health, and water and air pollution control. They also address global issues, such as unsafe drinking water, climate change, and environmental sustainability.

Duties. Environmental engineers typically do the following:

- Prepare, review, and update environmental investigation reports
- Design projects leading to environmental protection, such as water reclamation facilities, air pollution control systems, and operations that convert waste to energy

Environmental engineers design systems for managing and cleaning municipal water supplies.

- Obtain, update, and maintain plans, permits, and standard operating procedures
- Provide technical support for environmental remediation projects and for legal actions
- Analyze scientific data and do quality-control checks
- Monitor the progress of environmental improvement programs
- Inspect industrial and municipal facilities and programs to ensure compliance with environmental regulations
- Advise corporations and government agencies about procedures for cleaning up contaminated sites

Environmental engineers conduct hazardous-waste management studies in which they evaluate the significance of the hazard and advise on treating and containing it. They also design systems for municipal and industrial water supplies and industrial wastewater treatment, and research the environmental impact of proposed construction projects. Environmental engineers in government develop regulations to prevent mishaps.

Some environmental engineers study ways to minimize the effects of acid rain, global warming, automobile emissions, and ozone depletion. They also collaborate with environmental scientists, planners, hazardous waste technicians, engineers, and other specialists, such as experts in law and business, to address environmental problems and environmental sustainability. For more information, see the job profiles on environmental scientists and specialists, hazardous materials removal workers, lawyers, and urban and regional planners.

Work Environment

Environmental engineers held about 53,200 jobs in 2012. They work in a variety of settings because of the nature of the tasks they do:

- When they are working with other engineers and urban and regional planners, environmental engineers are likely to be in offices.
- When they are working with business people and lawyers, environmental engineers are likely to be at seminars, where they present information and answer questions.
- When they are working with hazardous waste technicians and environmental scientists, environmental engineers work at specific sites outdoors.

The industries that employed the most environmental engineers in 2012 were as follows:

Architectural, engineering, and related services 28%
Management, scientific, and technical consulting services......21
State government, excluding education and hospitals.............13
Federal government, excluding postal service 7
Local government, excluding education and hospitals..............6

Work Schedules. Most environmental engineers work full time. Those who manage projects often work overtime to monitor the project's progress and recommend corrective action when needed. Overtime work frequently is necessary to make sure that deadlines are met and that the project is built according to specifications.

How to Become One

Environmental engineers must have a bachelor's degree in environmental engineering or a related field, such as civil, chemical, or general engineering. Employers also value practical experience. Therefore, cooperative engineering programs, in which college credit is awarded for structured job experience, are valuable as well. Getting a license improves the chances for employment.

Education. Students interested in becoming an environmental engineer should take high school courses in chemistry, biology, physics, and math, including algebra, trigonometry, and calculus.

Entry-level environmental engineering jobs require a bachelor's degree. Programs typically last 4 years and include classroom, laboratory, and field studies. Some colleges and universities offer cooperative programs in which students gain practical experience while completing their education.

Median Annual Wages, May 2012

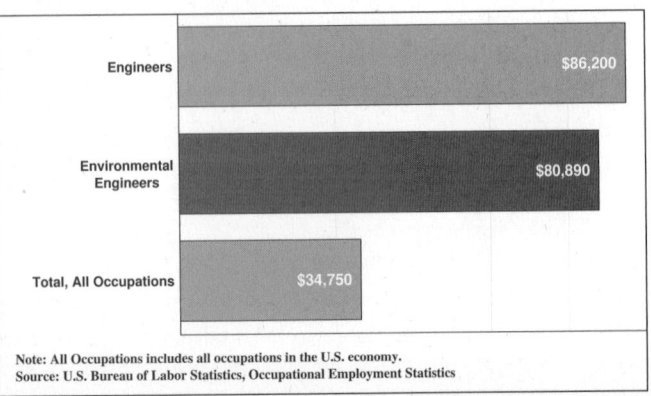

Note: All Occupations includes all occupations in the U.S. economy.
Source: U.S. Bureau of Labor Statistics, Occupational Employment Statistics

Percent Change in Employment, Projected 2012–2022

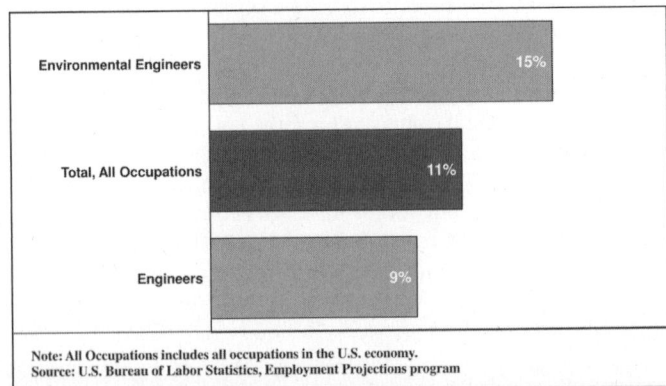

Note: All Occupations includes all occupations in the U.S. economy.
Source: U.S. Bureau of Labor Statistics, Employment Projections program

Employment Projections Data for Environmental Engineers

Occupational title	SOC Code	Employment, 2012	Projected Employment, 2022	Change, 2012–2022	
				Percent	Numeric
Environmental engineers	17-2081	53,200	61,400	15	8,100

Source: U.S. Bureau of Labor Statistics, Employment Projections Program

Note: Data are rounded. Go to Occupational Information Included in the OOH *for a discussion of the data in this table.*

At some colleges and universities, a student can enroll in a 5-year program that leads to both a bachelor's and a master's degree. A graduate degree allows an engineer to work as an instructor at some colleges and universities or to do research and development.

Many engineering programs are accredited by ABET. Some employers prefer to hire candidates who have graduated from an accredited program. A degree from an ABET-accredited program is usually necessary to become a licensed professional engineer.

Important Qualities

Detail oriented. Electro-mechanical technicians must make and keep the precise, accurate measurements that mechanical engineers need.

Imagination. Environmental engineers sometimes have to design systems that will be part of larger ones. They must be able to foresee how the proposed designs will interact with other components of the larger system, including the workers, machinery, and equipment, as well as the environment.

Interpersonal skills. Environmental engineers must be able to work with others toward a common goal. They usually work with engineers and scientists who design other systems and with the technicians and mechanics who put the designs into practice.

Problem-solving skills. When designing facilities and processes, environmental engineers strive to solve several issues at once, from workers' safety to environmental protection. They must be able to identify and anticipate problems in order to prevent losses for their employers, safeguard workers' health, and mitigate environmental damage.

Reading skills. Environmental engineers often work with business people, lawyers, and other professionals outside their field. They frequently are required to read and understand documents with topics outside their scope of training.

Writing skills. Environmental engineers must be able to write clearly so that others without their specific training can understand their plans, proposals, specifications, findings, and other documents.

Licenses, Certifications, and Registrations. Environmental engineers are encouraged to become licensed as a professional engineer (PE). Licensure generally requires the following:

• A degree from an engineering program accredited by ABET

• A passing score on the Fundamentals of Engineering (FE) exam

• Relevant work experience

• A passing score on the Professional Engineering (PE) exam

The initial FE exam can be taken after graduation. Engineers who pass this exam are commonly called engineers in training (EITs) or engineer interns (EIs). After getting suitable work experience, EITs can take the second exam, called the Principles and Practice of Engineering.

Several states require continuing education for engineers to keep their licenses. Most states recognize licensure from other states if the licensing state's requirements meet or exceed their own requirements.

After licensing, environmental engineers can earn board certification from the American Academy of Environmental Engineers and Scientists. This certification shows that an environmental engineer has expertise in one or more areas of specialization.

Advancement. As beginning engineers gain knowledge and experience, they move on to more difficult projects and they have greater independence to develop designs, solve problems, and make decisions. Eventually, environmental engineers may advance to become technical specialists or to supervise a team of engineers and technicians.

Some may even become engineering managers or move into executive positions, such as program managers. However, before assuming a managerial position, an engineer most often works under the supervision of a more experienced engineer. Advancement into a managerial position usually requires a master's degree.

Pay

The median annual wage for environmental engineers was $80,890 in May 2012. The median wage is the wage at which half the workers in an occupation earned more than that amount and half earned less. The lowest 10 percent earned less than $49,510, and the top 10 percent earned more than $122,290.

In May 2012, the median annual wages for environmental engineers in the top five industries employing these engineers were as follows:

Federal government, excluding postal service $98,890
Architectural, engineering, and related services 81,900

Similar Occupations   This table shows a list of occupations with job duties that are similar to those of environmental engineers.

Occupations	Entry-level Education	2012 Pay	Projected Job Growth	Average Annual Openings
Chemical Engineers	Bachelor's degree	$94,350	5%	920
Civil Engineers	Bachelor's degree	$79,340	20%	12,010
Environmental Engineering Technicians	Associate's degree	$45,350	18%	740
Environmental Scientists and Specialists	Bachelor's degree	$63,570	15%	3,970
Hydrologists	Master's degree	$75,530	9%	290
Natural Sciences Managers	Bachelor's degree	$115,730	6%	1,370

Management, scientific, and technical consulting services... 77,000
Local government, excluding education and hospitals......... 75,350
State government, excluding education and hospitals.......... 69,570

Union Membership. Compared with workers in all occupations, environmental engineers had a higher percentage of workers who belonged to a union in 2012.

Job Outlook

Employment of environmental engineers is projected to grow 15 percent from 2012 to 2022, faster than the average for all occupations.

State and local governments' concerns about water are leading to efforts to increase the efficiency of water use. This focus differs from that of wastewater treatment, for which this occupation is traditionally known.

The requirement by the federal government to clean up contaminated sites is expected to help sustain demand for these engineers' services, particularly those who work for the government sector. In addition, wastewater treatment is becoming a larger concern in areas of the country where new methods of drilling for shale gas require the use and disposal of massive volumes of water. Environmental engineers will continue to be needed to help utilities and water treatment plants comply with any new federal or state environmental regulations.

Job Prospects. Job prospects should be favorable because this occupation may experience a wave of retirements. A person can also improve his or her job prospects by obtaining a master's degree in environmental engineering, an advanced degree that many employers prefer.

O*NET

➤ Environmental Engineers (17-2081.00)
➤ Water/Wastewater Engineers (17-2081.01)

Contacts for More Information

For more information about environmental engineers, visit
➤ American Academy of Environmental Engineers and Scientists (www.aaees.org/)
  For more information about education for engineers, visit
➤ American Society for Engineering Education (www.asee.org/)
  For more information about accredited engineering programs, visit
➤ ABET (www.abet.org/)
  For more information about becoming licensed as a professional engineer, visit
➤ National Council of Examiners for Engineering and Surveying (http://ncees.org/)
➤ National Society of Professional Engineers (www.nspe.org/index.html)

Health and Safety Engineers

- **2012 Median Pay** .... $76,830 per year
                                                          $36.94 per hour
- **Entry-Level Education** ....Bachelor's degree
- **Work Experience in a Related Occupation**............... None
- **On-the-Job Training** .... None
- **Number of Jobs 2012** 24,100
- **Job Outlook, 2012–22**.................. 4% (As fast as average)
- **Employment Change, 2012–22** 2,600

What Health and Safety Engineers Do

Health and safety engineers develop procedures and design systems to prevent people from getting sick or injured and to keep property from being damaged. They combine knowledge of systems engineering and of health or safety to make sure that chemicals, machinery, software, furniture, and consumer products will not cause harm to people or buildings.

Duties. Health and safety engineers typically do the following:

- Review plans and specifications for new machinery and equipment to make sure they meet safety requirements
- Identify and correct potential hazards by inspecting facilities, machinery, and safety equipment
- Evaluate the effectiveness of various industrial control mechanisms
- Ensure that a building or product complies with health and safety regulations, especially after an inspection that required changes
- Install safety devices on machinery or direct the installation of these devices
- Review employee safety programs and recommend improvements
- Maintain and apply knowledge of current policies, regulations, and industrial processes

Health and safety engineers also investigate industrial accidents, injuries, or occupational diseases to determine their causes and to determine whether the incidents could have been or can be prevented. They interview employers and employees to learn about work environments and incidents that lead to accidents or injuries. They also evaluate the corrections that were made to remedy violations found during health inspections.

Health and safety engineers are also active in two related fields: industrial hygiene and occupational hygiene. In industrial hygiene, they focus on the effects of chemical, physical, and biological agents. They recognize, evaluate, and control these agents to keep people from becoming sick or injured. For example, they might anticipate that a particular manufacturing process will give off a potentially harmful chemical and recommend either a change to the process or a way to contain and control the chemical.

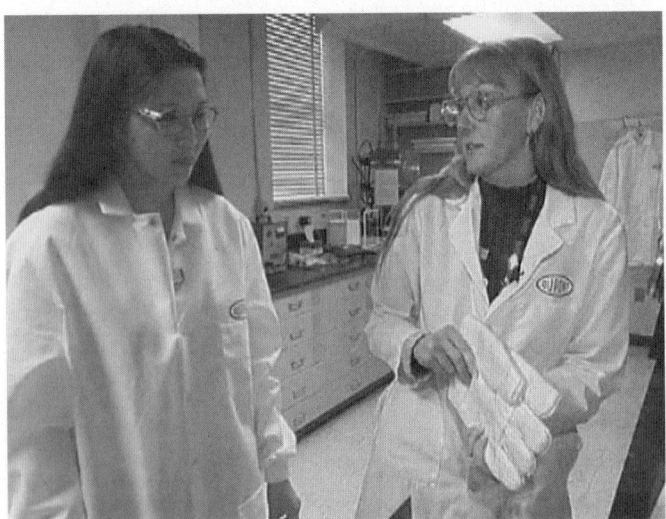

Health and safety engineers apply their knowledge of the sciences, such as chemistry, to promote safety on the job.

Median Annual Wages, May 2012

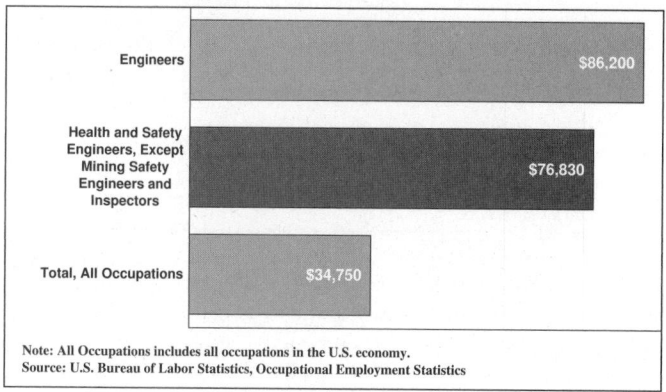

Note: All Occupations includes all occupations in the U.S. economy.
Source: U.S. Bureau of Labor Statistics, Occupational Employment Statistics

Percent Change in Employment, Projected 2012–2022

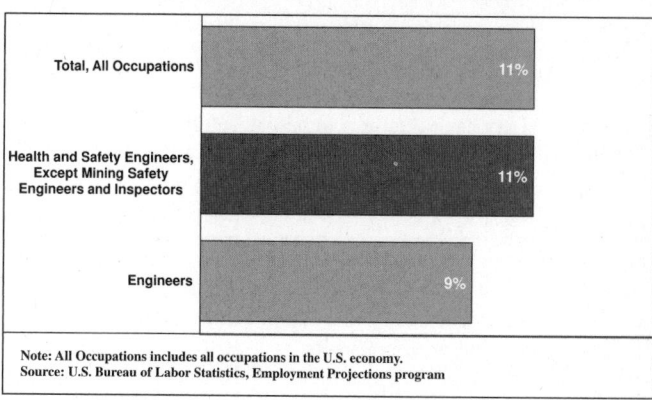

Note: All Occupations includes all occupations in the U.S. economy.
Source: U.S. Bureau of Labor Statistics, Employment Projections program

In occupational hygiene, health and safety engineers investigate the environment in which people work and use science and engineering to recommend changes to keep workers from being exposed to sickness or injuries. They help employers and employees understand the risks, and improve working conditions and working practices. For example, they might observe that the noise level in a factory is likely to cause harm to workers' hearing and recommend ways to reduce the noise level through changes to the building, reducing exposure time, or by having workers wear proper hearing protection.

Health and safety engineering is a broad field covering many activities. The following are examples of types of health and safety engineers:

Aerospace safety engineers work on missiles, radars, and satellites to make sure that they function safely as designed.

Fire prevention and protection engineers design fire prevention systems for all kinds of buildings. They often work for architects during the design phase of new buildings or renovations. They must be licensed, and they must keep up with changes in fire codes and regulations.

Product safety engineers investigate the causes of accidents or injuries that might have resulted from the use or misuse of a product. They propose solutions to reduce or eliminate any safety issues associated with products. They also participate in the design phase of new products to prevent injuries, illnesses, or property damage that could occur with the use of the product.

Systems safety engineers work in many fields, including aerospace, and are moving into new fields, such as software safety, medical safety, and environmental safety. These engineers take a systemic approach to identify hazards so that accidents and injuries can be avoided.

For information on health and safety engineers who work in mines, see the profile on mining and geological engineers.

Work Environment

Health and safety engineers held about 24,100 jobs in 2012.

Health and safety engineers typically work in offices. However, they also must spend time at worksites when necessary, which sometimes requires travel.

The industries that employed the most health and safety engineers in 2012 were as follows:

Professional, scientific, and technical services...........................18%
Construction of buildings...10
State and local government, excluding education
    and hospitals..10
Heavy and civil engineering construction 8

Work Schedules. Most health and safety engineers work full time.

How to Become One

Health and safety engineers must have a bachelor's degree, typically in an engineering discipline such as electrical, chemical, mechanical, industrial, or systems engineering. Another acceptable field of study is occupational or industrial hygiene. Employers value practical experience, so cooperative-education engineering programs at universities are valuable as well.

Education. High school students interested in becoming health and safety engineers will benefit from taking high school courses in math, such as algebra, trigonometry, and calculus; and science, such as biology, chemistry, and physics.

Entry-level jobs as a health and safety engineer require a bachelor's degree. Bachelor's degree programs typically are 4-year programs and include classroom, laboratory, and field studies in applied engineering. In addition to programs in mechanical, electrical, and industrial engineering, programs in systems engineering and fire protection engineering are offered at some colleges and universities. Students interested in becoming a health and safety engineer should seek out coursework in occupational safety and health, industrial hygiene, ergonomics, or environmental safety.

Students interested in entering the relatively new field of software safety engineering may pursue a degree in computer science.

Many colleges and universities offer cooperative programs, which allow students to gain practical experience while completing their education.

A few colleges and universities offer 5-year accelerated programs that lead to both a bachelor's and a master's degree. A master's degree allows engineers to enter the occupation at a higher level, where they can develop and implement safety systems.

ABET accredits programs in engineering.

Important Qualities

Creativity. Health and safety engineers are asked to produce designs showing potential problems and remedies for them. They must be creative to work with unique situations during each project.

Critical-thinking skills. Health and safety engineers must identify potential hazards and problems before they cause material damage or become a health threat. Thus, these engineers must be able to sense hazards to humans and property wherever they may arise in the workplace or in the home.

Observational skills. Health and safety engineers must observe and learn how operations function so that they can identify risks to people and property. This type of observation and learning

Employment Projections Data for Health and Safety Engineers

Occupational title	SOC Code	Employment, 2012	Projected Employment, 2022	Change, 2012–2022	
				Percent	Numeric
Health and safety engineers, except mining safety engineers and inspectors..................................	17-2111	24,100	26,700	11	2,600

Source: U.S. Bureau of Labor Statistics, Employment Projections Program

Note: **Data are rounded.** Go to **Occupational Information Included in the OOH** *for a discussion of the data in this table.*

requires the ability to think in terms of overall processes within an organization. Health and safety engineers can then recommend systemic changes to minimize risks.

Problem-solving skills. In designing solutions for entire organizational operations, health and safety engineers must take into account processes from more than one system at the same time. In addition, they must try to anticipate a range of human reactions to the changes they recommend.

Reading skills. Health and safety engineers must be able to interpret federal and state regulations and understand the goals of those regulations so that they can propose proper designs for specific work environments.

Licenses, Certifications, and Registrations. Only a few states require health and safety engineers to be licensed. Licensure is generally advised for those opting for a career in systems safety engineering.

Licensed engineers are called professional engineers (PEs). Licensure generally requires the following:

- A degree from an ABET-accredited engineering program
- A passing score on the Fundamentals of Engineering (FE) exam
- Relevant work experience, typically at least 4 years
- A passing score on the Professional Engineering (PE) exam

The initial Fundamentals of Engineering (FE) exam can be taken after graduation from college. Engineers who pass this exam are commonly called engineers in training (EITs) or engineer interns (EIs). After getting suitable work experience, EITs and EIs can take the second exam, called the Principles and Practice of Engineering.

States requiring licensure usually require continuing education for engineers in order to keep their license. Most states recognize licensure from other states, if the licensing state's requirements meet or exceed their own licensure requirements.

Health and safety engineers typically have professional certification. Most earn either the Certified Safety Professional (CSP) certification, awarded by the Board of Certified Safety Professionals, or the Certified Industrial Hygienist (CIH) certification, awarded

by the American Board of Industrial Hygiene. Certification is generally needed to advance into management positions.

Advancement. New health and safety engineers usually work under the supervision of experienced engineers. To move to more difficult projects with greater independence, a graduate degree is generally required, such as a master's degree in engineering or a Master of Public Health (MPH) degree.

This advanced degree allows an engineer to develop and implement safety programs. Certification as a safety professional or as an industrial hygienist is generally required for entry into management positions.

Pay

The median annual wage for health and safety engineers was $76,830 in May 2012. The median wage is the wage at which half the workers in an occupation earned more than that amount and half earned less. The lowest 10 percent earned less than $45,370, and the top 10 percent earned more than $118,750.

In May 2012, the median annual wages for health and safety engineers in the top four industries in which these engineers worked were as follows:

Professional, scientific, and technical services....................	$75,870
State and local government, excluding education and hospitals..	75,180
Construction of buildings..	70,420
Heavy and civil engineering construction	69,910

Job Outlook

Employment of health and safety engineers is projected to grow 11 percent from 2012 to 2022, about as fast as the average for all occupations.

Health and safety engineers have long been employed in manufacturing industries to cut costs, save lives, and produce safe consumer products. The same principles are being applied in new areas, such as health care. Recent studies have documented the high costs of accidents in hospitals. Health and safety engineers can help prevent accidents as biomedical engineers develop

Similar Occupations   This table shows a list of occupations with job duties that are similar to those of health and safety engineers.

Occupations	Entry-level Education	2012 Pay	Projected Job Growth	Average Annual Openings
Construction and Building Inspectors	High school diploma or equivalent	$53,450	12%	3,670
Fire Inspectors and Investigators	High school diploma or equivalent	$53,990	7%	440
Industrial Engineers	Bachelor's degree	$78,860	5%	7,540
Mining and Geological Engineers	Bachelor's degree	$84,320	13%	300
Occupational Health and Safety Specialists	Bachelor's degree	$66,790	7%	2,130
Occupational Health and Safety Technicians	High school diploma or equivalent	$47,440	10%	480

advances in their field. Accident prevention, particularly with regard to radiation safety, is likely to become increasingly important for the healthcare industry as a way of cutting costs.

Another major factor likely to drive employment is the emerging field of software safety engineering. Software must work exactly as intended, especially when it controls, for example, elevators or automobiles, where a glitch in the software could cause serious injury to people and damage to equipment. The number of machines and mechanical devices controlled by software is expected to continue to grow, and the need to apply the principles of systems safety engineering to this software is expected to grow as well.

O*NET

➤ Industrial Safety and Health Engineers (17-2111.01)
➤ Fire-Prevention and Protection Engineers (17-2111.02)
➤ Product Safety Engineers (17-2111.03)

Contacts for More Information

For information about general engineering education and career resources, visit
➤ American Society for Engineering Education (www.asee.org/)
➤ Technology Student Association (www.tsaweb.org/)
For information about accredited engineering programs, visit
➤ ABET (www.abet.org/)
➤ American Society of Safety Engineers (www.asse.org/)
For more information about the Professional Engineer license, visit
➤ National Council of Examiners for Engineering and Surveying (http://ncees.org/)
➤ National Society of Professional Engineers (www.nspe.org/index.html)
For information about protecting worker health, visit
➤ American Industrial Hygiene Association (www.aiha.org/Pages/default.aspx)
For more information about certification, visit
➤ American Board of Industrial Hygiene (www.abih.org/)
➤ Board of Certified Safety Professionals (www.bcsp.org/)

Industrial Engineering Technicians

- **2012 Median Pay** .... $50,980 per year
  $24.51 per hour
- **Entry-Level Education** ....Associate's degree
- **Work Experience in a Related Occupation**............... None
- **On-the-Job Training** .... None
- **Number of Jobs 2012** 68,000
- **Job Outlook, 2012–22** .... -3% (Decline)
- **Employment Change, 2012–22** .... -2,200

What Industrial Engineering Technicians Do

Industrial engineering technicians help industrial engineers implement designs to effectively use personnel, materials, and machines in factories, stores, healthcare organizations, repair shops, and offices. They prepare machinery and equipment layouts, plan workflows, conduct statistical production studies, and analyze production costs.

Duties. Industrial engineering technicians typically do the following:

- Suggest revisions for methods of operation, material handling, or equipment layout

- Interpret engineering drawings, schematic diagrams, and formulas
- Confer with management or engineering staff to determine quality and reliability standards
- Recommend changes to production standards for achieving the best quality within the limits of equipment capacity
- Help plan work assignments, taking into account workers' performance, machine capacity, and production schedules
- Prepare charts, graphs, and diagrams to illustrate workflow, routing, floor layouts, how materials are handled and how machines are used
- Collect data to assist in process improvement activities

Industrial engineering technicians study the time and steps workers take to do a task (time and motion studies). To set reasonable production rates, they consider how workers are doing operations such as maintenance, production, and service.

They also observe workers to make sure that equipment is being used and maintained according to quality assurance standards. They then evaluate the resulting data to recommend or justify changes to the operations or to the standards for improving quality and efficiency.

Industrial engineering technicians' versatility allows them to be useful to a variety of businesses, governments, and nonprofits. For example, they work in supply chain management to help businesses minimize inventory costs, in quality assurance to help businesses keep their customers satisfied, and in the growing field of project management to control costs and maximize efficiencies.

Industrial engineering technicians generally work in teams under the supervision of industrial engineers.

Work Environment

Industrial engineering technicians held about 68,000 jobs in 2012. They work in various industries and businesses to coordinate activities that ensure the quality of final products or services.

The industries that employed the most industrial engineering technicians in 2012 were as follows:

Semiconductor and other electronic component manufacturing	14%
Aerospace product and parts manufacturing	9
Plastics and rubber products manufacturing	7
Motor vehicle parts manufacturing	6

Industrial engineering technicians help develop plans for use of machinery and for efficient workflow.

Median Annual Wages, May 2012

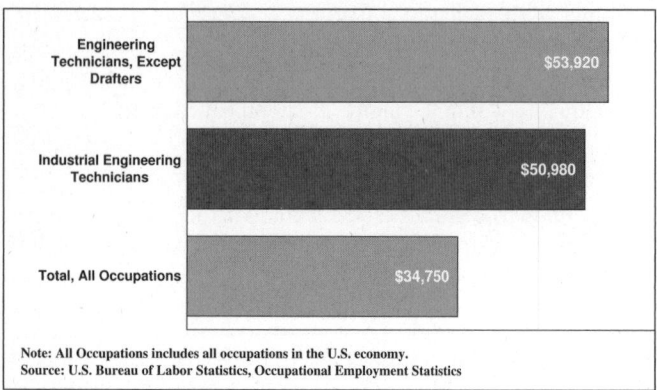

Note: All Occupations includes all occupations in the U.S. economy.
Source: U.S. Bureau of Labor Statistics, Occupational Employment Statistics

Percent Change in Employment, Projected 2012–2022

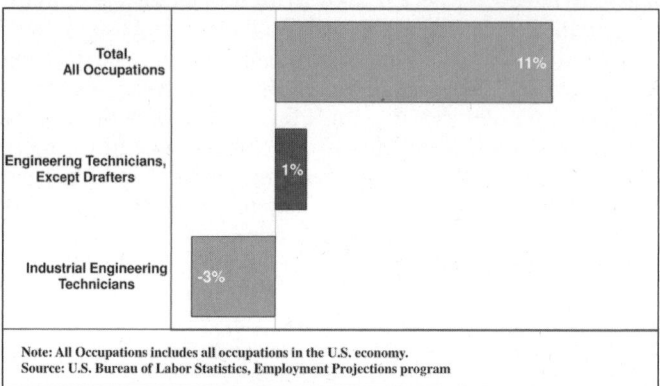

Note: All Occupations includes all occupations in the U.S. economy.
Source: U.S. Bureau of Labor Statistics, Employment Projections program

Navigational, measuring, electromedical, and control
instruments manufacturing 5

Industrial engineers usually ask industrial engineering technicians to help carry out certain studies and make specific observations. Consequently, these technicians typically work at the
location where products are manufactured or where services are
delivered.

Work Schedules. Industrial engineering technicians usually work
standard schedules. Most work full time.

How to Become One

High school students interested in becoming industrial engineering technicians should take courses in math, science, and drafting,
where available. Courses that help students develop computer skills
are helpful when they later need to learn computer-aided design/
computer-aided manufacturing software, known as CAD/CAM.

Education. After high school, students interested in becoming
industrial engineering technicians can continue at a vocational-
technical school, community college, or technical institute.

Vocational-technical schools include postsecondary public institutions that serve local students and emphasize training needed
by local employers. These programs generally award a certificate.

Community colleges offer programs similar to those in technical
institutes, but usually include more theory-based and liberal arts
courses. Students who complete these programs earn associate's
degrees.

ABET accredits engineering and engineering technology programs.

Generally, prospective industrial engineering technicians should
major in applied science, industrial technology, or industrial engineering technology.

Important Qualities

Analytical skills. Industrial engineering technicians must be able
to help industrial engineers figure out how a system should work
and how changes in conditions, operations, and the environment
will affect outcomes.

Communication skills. Industrial engineering technicians receive
instructions from industrial engineers. They must be able to clearly
understand and follow instructions and communicate problems to
their supervisors.

Critical-thinking skills. Industrial engineering technicians must
be able to help industrial engineers figure out why a certain process
or operation is not working as well as it might. They must ask the
right questions to identify and correct weaknesses.

Employment Projections Data for Industrial Engineering Technicians

Occupational title	SOC Code	Employment, 2012	Projected Employment, 2022	Change, 2012–2022	
				Percent	Numeric
Industrial engineering technicians	17-3026	68,000	65,800	-3	-2,200

Source: U.S. Bureau of Labor Statistics, Employment Projections Program

Note: Data are rounded. Go to Occupational Information Included in the OOH *for a discussion of the data in this table.*

Similar Occupations   This table shows a list of occupations with job duties that are similar to those of industrial
engineering technicians.

Occupations	Entry-level Education	2012 Pay	Projected Job Growth	Average Annual Openings
Cost Estimators	Bachelor's degree	$58,860	26%	11,800
Health and Safety Engineers	Bachelor's degree	$76,830	11%	970
Industrial Engineers	Bachelor's degree	$78,860	5%	7,540
Logisticians	Bachelor's degree	$72,780	22%	4,220
Quality Control Inspectors	High school diploma or equivalent	$34,460	6%	12,770

Detail oriented. Industrial engineering technicians must gather and record measurements and observations needed by industrial engineers.

Math skills. Industrial engineering technicians use the principles of mathematics for analysis, design, and troubleshooting in their work.

Observational skills. These technicians spend much of their time evaluating the performance of other people or organizations to make suggestions for improvements or corrective action. They must gather and record information without interfering with workers in their environments.

Pay

The median annual wage for industrial engineering technicians was $50,980 in May 2012. The median wage is the wage at which half the workers in an occupation earned more than that amount and half earned less. The lowest 10 percent earned less than $33,100, and the top 10 percent earned more than $76,020.

In May 2012, the median annual wages for industrial engineering technicians in the top five industries in which these technicians worked were as follows:

Aerospace product and parts manufacturing $63,170
Semiconductor and other electronic component manufacturing.... 52,320
Navigational, measuring, electromedical, and control
   instruments manufacturing 51,190
Plastics and rubber products manufacturing........................ 47,890
Motor vehicle parts manufacturing 46,130

Job Outlook

Employment of industrial engineering technicians is projected to decline 3 percent from 2012 to 2022.

Industrial engineering is versatile because of its wide applicability in many industries. The growing emphasis on cost control through increasing efficiency is expected to sustain demand for industrial engineering technicians' services in most industries, including nonprofits.

However, this occupation's employment is expected to decrease overall in large part because of the expected employment declines in manufacturing industries, such as computer and electronic products, transportation equipment, and machinery manufacturing.

O*NET

➤ Industrial Engineering Technicians (17-3026.00)

Contacts for More Information

For more information about industrial engineering, visit
➤ Institute of Industrial Engineers (www.iienet2.org/Default.aspx)
   For information on general engineering education and career resources, visit
➤ American Society for Engineering Education (www.asee.org/)
➤ Technology Student Association (www.tsaweb.org/)
   For more information about accredited programs, visit
➤ ABET (www.abet.org/)

Industrial Engineers

- **2012 Median Pay** .... $78,860 per year
  $37.92 per hour
- **Entry-Level Education** ....Bachelor's degree
- **Work Experience in a Related Occupation**............... None
- **On-the-Job Training** .... None
- **Number of Jobs 2012** 223,300
- **Job Outlook, 2012–22** .... 5% (Slower than average)
- **Employment Change, 2012–22** 10,100

What Industrial Engineers Do

Industrial engineers find ways to eliminate wastefulness in production processes. They devise efficient ways to use workers, machines, materials, information, and energy to make a product or provide a service.

Duties. Industrial engineers typically do the following:

- Review production schedules, engineering specifications, process flows, and other information to understand methods and activities in manufacturing and services
- Figure out how to manufacture parts or products, or deliver services, with maximum efficiency
- Develop management control systems to make financial planning and cost analysis more efficient
- Enact quality control procedures to resolve production problems or minimize costs
- Work with customers and management to develop standards for design and production
- Design control systems to coordinate activities and production planning to ensure that products meet quality standards
- Confer with clients about product specifications, vendors about purchases, management personnel about manufacturing capabilities, and staff about the status of projects

Industrial engineers apply their skills to many different situations from manufacturing to business administration. For example, they design systems for

- Moving heavy parts within manufacturing plants
- Getting goods from a company to customers, including finding the most profitable places to locate manufacturing or processing plants

Industrial engineers devise ways to most effectively use all resources in a production process.

Median Annual Wages, May 2012

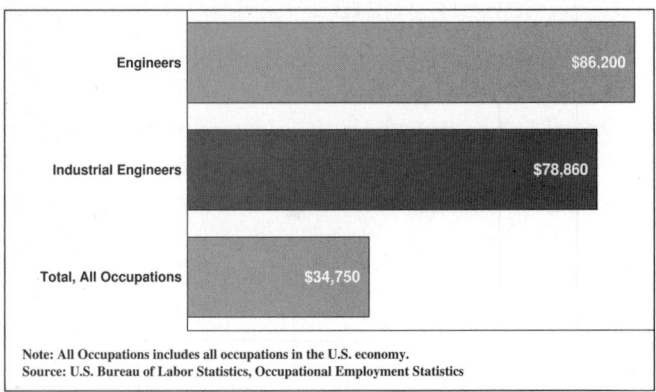

Note: All Occupations includes all occupations in the U.S. economy.
Source: U.S. Bureau of Labor Statistics, Occupational Employment Statistics

Percent Change in Employment, Projected 2012–2022

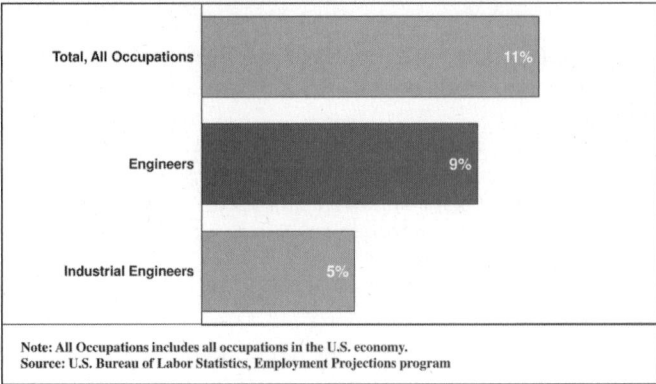

Note: All Occupations includes all occupations in the U.S. economy.
Source: U.S. Bureau of Labor Statistics, Employment Projections program

- Evaluating how well people do their jobs
- Paying workers

Industrial engineers focus on how to get the work done most efficiently, balancing many factors–such as time, number of workers needed, available technology, actions workers need to take, achieving the end product with no errors, workers' safety, environmental concerns, and cost.

To find ways to reduce waste and improve performance, industrial engineers first study product requirements carefully. Then they use mathematical methods and models to design manufacturing and information systems to meet those requirements most efficiently.

Their versatility allows industrial engineers to engage in activities that are useful to a variety of businesses, governments, and nonprofits. For example, industrial engineers engage in supply chain management to help businesses minimize inventory costs, conduct quality assurance activities to help businesses keep their customer bases satisfied, and work in the growing field of project management as industries across the economy seek to control costs and maximize efficiencies.

Work Environment

Industrial engineers held about 223,300 jobs in 2012. Depending on their tasks, industrial engineers work both in offices and in the settings they are trying to improve. For example, when observing problems, they may watch workers assembling parts in a factory or staff carrying out their tasks in a hospital. When solving problems, industrial engineers may be in an office at a computer looking at data that they or others have collected.

Industrial engineers may need to travel to observe processes and make assessments in various work settings.

The industries that employed the most industrial engineers in 2012 were as follows:

Aerospace product and parts manufacturing 8%
Machinery manufacturing 8
Architectural, engineering, and related services 6
Motor vehicle parts manufacturing 6
Management of companies and enterprises 6

Industrial engineers must be able to work with other professionals to serve as a bridge between the technical and business sides of an organization. This requires being able to work with people from a wide variety of backgrounds.

Work Schedules. Most industrial engineers work full time. Hours may vary, however, depending upon the projects in which

these engineers are engaged, and upon the industries in which the projects are taking place.

How to Become One

Industrial engineers must have a bachelor's degree. Employers also value experience, so cooperative education engineering programs at universities are also valuable.

Education. Industrial engineers need a bachelor's degree, typically in industrial engineering. However, many industrial engineers have degrees in mechanical engineering, manufacturing engineering, industrial engineering technology, or general engineering. Students interested in studying industrial engineering should take high school courses in mathematics, such as algebra, trigonometry, and calculus; computer science; and sciences such as chemistry and physics.

Bachelor's degree programs include lectures in classrooms and practice in laboratories. Courses include statistics, production systems planning, and manufacturing systems design, among others. Many colleges and universities offer cooperative education programs in which students gain practical experience while completing their education.

A few colleges and universities offer 5-year degree programs in industrial engineering that lead to a bachelor's and master's degree upon completion, and several more offer similar programs in mechanical engineering. A graduate degree allows an engineer to work as a professor at a college or university or to engage in research and development. Some 5-year or even 6-year cooperative education plans combine classroom study with practical work, permitting students to gain experience and to finance part of their education.

Programs in industrial engineering are accredited by ABET.

Important Qualities

Creativity. Industrial engineers use creativity and ingenuity to design new production processes in many kinds of settings to reduce use of material resources, time, or labor while accomplishing the same goal.

Critical-thinking skills. Industrial engineers create new systems to solve problems related to waste and inefficiency. Solving these problems requires logic and reasoning to identify strengths and weaknesses of alternative solutions, conclusions, or approaches to the problems.

Listening skills. These engineers often operate in teams, but they must also solicit feedback from customers, vendors, and production staff. They must listen to customers and clients to fully grasp ideas and problems the first time.

Employment Projections Data for Industrial Engineers

Occupational title	SOC Code	Employment, 2012	Projected Employment, 2022	Change, 2012–2022	
				Percent	Numeric
Industrial engineers	17-2112	223,300	233,400	5	10,100

Source: *U.S. Bureau of Labor Statistics, Employment Projections Program*

Note: **Data are rounded. Go to Occupational Information Included in the OOH** *for a discussion of the data in this table.*

Math skills. Industrial engineers use the principles of calculus, trigonometry, and other advanced topics in mathematics for analysis, design, and troubleshooting in their work.

Problem-solving skills. In designing facilities for manufacturing and processes for providing services, these engineers deal with several issues at once, from workers' safety to quality assurance.

Speaking skills. Industrial engineers sometimes have to explain their instructions to production staff or technicians before they can make written instructions available. Being able to explain concepts clearly and quickly is crucial to preventing costly mistakes and loss of time.

Writing skills. Industrial engineers must create documentation for other professionals or for future reference. The documentation must be coherent and explain their thinking clearly so that others can understand the information.

Licenses, Certifications, and Registrations. Licensure for industrial engineers is not as common as it is for other engineering occupations, but it is encouraged for those working in companies that have government contracts. Industrial engineers who become licensed carry the designation of professional engineer (PE). Licensure generally requires the following:

- A degree from an engineering program accredited by ABET
- A passing score on the Fundamentals of Engineering (FE) exam
- Relevant work experience
- A passing score on the Professional Engineering (PE) exam

The initial FE exam can be taken right after graduating. Engineers who pass this exam commonly are called engineers in training (EITs) or engineer interns (EIs). After getting suitable work experience, EITs can take the second exam, called the Principles and Practice of Engineering exam.

Several states require engineers to take continuing education to keep their licenses. Most states recognize licenses from other states, as long as the other state's licensing requirements meet or exceed their own licensing requirements.

Advancement. Beginning industrial engineers usually work under the supervision of experienced engineers. In large companies, new engineers also may receive formal training in classes or seminars. As beginning engineers gain knowledge and experience, they move to more difficult projects with greater independence to develop designs, solve problems, and make decisions.

Eventually, industrial engineers may advance to become technical specialists, such as quality engineers or facility planners. In that role, they supervise a team of engineers and technicians. Many industrial engineers move into management positions because the work they do is closely related to the work of managers. For more information, see the profile on architectural and engineering managers.

Pay

The median annual wage for industrial engineers was $78,860 in May 2012. The median wage is the wage at which half of the workers in an occupation earned more than that amount and half earned less. The lowest 10 percent earned less than $51,180, and the top 10 percent earned more than $118,300.

In May 2012, the median annual wages for industrial engineers in the top five industries employing these engineers were as follows:

Aerospace product and parts manufacturing	$84,600
Management of companies and enterprises	82,290
Architectural, engineering, and related services	81,240
Machinery manufacturing	72,920
Motor vehicle parts manufacturing	71,580

Job Outlook

Employment of industrial engineers is projected to grow 5 percent from 2012 to 2022, slower than the average for all occupations. This occupation is versatile both in the nature of the work it does and in the industries in which its expertise can be put to use. In

Similar Occupations   This table shows a list of occupations with job duties that are similar to those of industrial engineers.

Occupations	Entry-level Education	2012 Pay	Projected Job Growth	Average Annual Openings
Architectural and Engineering Managers	Bachelor's degree	$124,870	7%	6,060
Cost Estimators	Bachelor's degree	$58,860	26%	11,800
Health and Safety Engineers	Bachelor's degree	$76,830	11%	970
Industrial Engineering Technicians	Associate's degree	$50,980	-3%	1,410
Industrial Production Managers	Bachelor's degree	$89,190	-2%	3,140
Logisticians	Bachelor's degree	$72,780	22%	4,220
Management Analysts	Bachelor's degree	$78,600	19%	24,520
Materials Engineers	Bachelor's degree	$85,150	1%	750
Occupational Health and Safety Specialists	Bachelor's degree	$66,790	7%	2,130
Quality Control Inspectors	High school diploma or equivalent	$34,460	6%	12,770

addition, because industrial engineers' work can help with cost control by increasing efficiency, these engineers are attractive to employers in most industries, including nonprofits.

Because they are not as specialized as other engineers, industrial engineers are employed in a wide range of industries, including major manufacturing industries, hospitals, consulting and engineering services, and research and development firms. This versatility arises from the fact that these engineers' expertise focuses on reducing internal costs, making their work valuable for many industries. For example, their work is important for manufacturing industries considering relocation to domestic sites. In addition, growth in healthcare and changes in how care is delivered will create demand for industrial engineers. Firms in a variety of industries are seeking new ways to contain costs and improve efficiency, leading to more demand for these workers.

O*NET

➤ Industrial Engineers (17-2112.00)
➤ Human Factors Engineers and Ergonomists (17-2112.01)

Contacts for More Information

For more information about industrial engineers, visit
➤ Institute of Industrial Engineers (www.iienet2.org/Default.aspx)

For information about general engineering education and career resources, visit
➤ American Society for Engineering Education (www.asee.org/)
➤ Technology Student Association (www.tsaweb.org/)

For more information about licensure as an industrial engineer, visit
➤ National Council of Examiners for Engineering and Surveying (http://ncees.org/)
➤ National Society of Professional Engineers (www.nspe.org/index.html)

For information about accredited engineering programs, visit
➤ ABET (www.abet.org/)

Landscape Architects

- **2012 Median Pay** .... $64,180 per year
  $30.86 per hour
- **Entry-Level Education** ....Bachelor's degree
- **Work Experience in a Related Occupation**............... None
- **On-the-Job Training** .... Internship/residency
- **Number of Jobs 2012** 20,100
- **Job Outlook, 2012–22**................ 14% (As fast as average)
- **Employment Change, 2012–22** 2,900

What Landscape Architects Do

Landscape architects plan and design land areas for parks, recreational facilities, private homes, campuses, and other open spaces.
Duties. Landscape architects typically do the following:

- Confer with clients, engineers, and building architects to understand a project
- Prepare site plans, specifications, and cost estimates
- Coordinate the arrangement of existing and proposed land features and structures
- Prepare graphic representations of proposed plans using computer-aided design and drafting (CADD) software
- Select appropriate materials for use in landscape designs

- Analyze environmental reports on land conditions, such as drainage and energy usage
- Inspect landscape work to ensure that it adheres to original plans
- Seek new work through marketing or by giving presentations

People enjoy attractively designed gardens, public parks, playgrounds, residential areas, college campuses, and public spaces. Landscape architects design these areas so that they are not only functional but also beautiful and harmonious with the natural environment. Landscape architects also plan the locations of buildings, roads, walkways, flowers, shrubs, and trees within these environments.

Landscape architects use several different technologies in their work. For example, through the use of computer-aided design and drafting (CADD) software, landscape architects prepare models of their proposed work. They then present these models to clients for feedback to demonstrate the final look of the project. Many landscape architects also use geographic information systems (GIS), which allow them to present data visually as maps, reports, and charts.

Landscape architects undertake projects that seek to enhance the natural beauty of a space and provide environmental benefits. They may plan the restoration of natural places disturbed by humans, such as wetlands, streams, and mined areas. They may also design "green roofs" or rooftop gardens that can retain storm water, absorb air pollution, and cool buildings while also providing pleasant scenery. Managing storm water runoff is another important part of many landscape architectural plans because it protects clean water sources and natural ecosystems from pollutants. Landscape architects also play a role in preserving and restoring historic landscapes.

Landscape architects who work for government agencies design sites and landscapes for government buildings, parks, and other public lands, as well as plan for landscapes and recreation areas in national parks and forests. In addition, they prepare environmental impact assessments based on proposed construction.

Landscape architects are involved in a wide variety of construction projects.

Median Annual Wages, May 2012

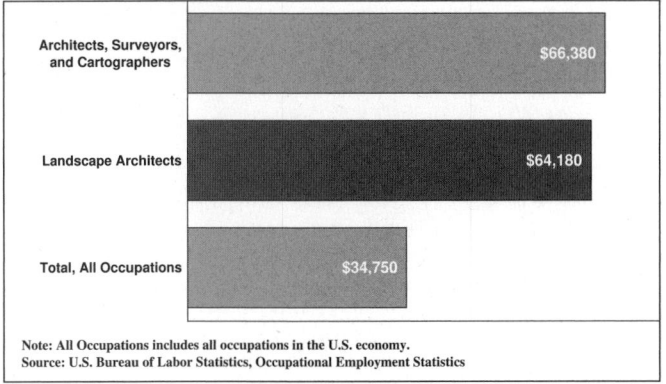

Architects, Surveyors, and Cartographers — $66,380

Landscape Architects — $64,180

Total, All Occupations — $34,750

Note: All Occupations includes all occupations in the U.S. economy.
Source: U.S. Bureau of Labor Statistics, Occupational Employment Statistics

Percent Change in Employment, Projected 2012–2022

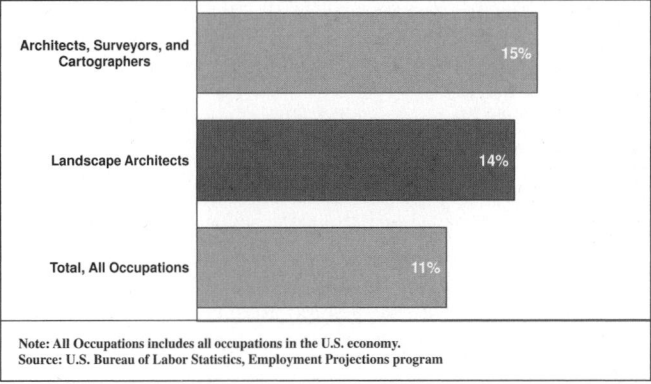

Architects, Surveyors, and Cartographers — 15%

Landscape Architects — 14%

Total, All Occupations — 11%

Note: All Occupations includes all occupations in the U.S. economy.
Source: U.S. Bureau of Labor Statistics, Employment Projections program

Work Environment

Landscape architects held about 20,100 jobs in 2012, of which 46 percent were employed in the architectural, engineering, and related services industry. Another 15 percent were employed in the landscaping services industry. About 1 in 5 were self-employed.

Landscape architects spend much of their time in offices, creating plans and designs, preparing models and cost estimates, doing research, and attending meetings with clients and workers involved in designing or planning a project. They spend the rest of their worktime at jobsites.

Work Schedules. Most landscape architects work full time. Many work long hours, especially when facing deadlines.

How to Become One

All states require landscape architects to be licensed, except for Illinois, Massachusetts, Maine, and the District of Columbia. In addition, all 50 states (but not the District of Columbia) require applicants to be licensed before they can use the title "landscape architect" and start soliciting business. Licensing requirements vary among states, but usually include a degree in landscape architecture from an accredited school, internship experience, and a passing score on the Landscape Architect Registration Exam.

Education. A bachelor's or master's degree in landscape architecture usually is necessary for entry into the profession. There are two undergraduate landscape architect professional degrees: a Bachelor of Landscape Architecture (BLA) and a Bachelor of Science in Landscape Architecture (BSLA). These programs usually require 4 years of study.

Accredited programs are approved by the Landscape Architectural Accreditation Board (LAAB). Those with an undergraduate degree in a field other than landscape architecture can enroll in a Master of Landscape Architecture (MLA) graduate degree program, which typically takes 3 years of full-time study.

Courses typically include surveying, landscape design and construction, landscape ecology, site design, and urban and regional planning. Other courses include history of landscape architecture, plant and soil science, geology, professional practice, and general management.

The design studio is a key component of any curriculum. Whenever possible, students are assigned real projects, providing them with valuable hands-on experience. While working on these projects, students become proficient in the use of computer-aided design and drafting (CADD), model building, and other design software.

Training. In order to become licensed, candidates must meet experience requirements determined by each state. A list of

training requirements can be found at the Council of Landscape Architectural Registration Boards.

New hires are called apprentices or intern landscape architects until they become licensed. Although duties vary with the type and size of the employing firm, all interns must work under the supervision of a licensed landscape architect for the experience to count towards licensure. In addition, all drawings and specifications must be signed and sealed by the licensed landscape architect.

Some employers recommend that prospective landscape architects complete an internship with a landscape architecture firm during their educational studies. Interns can improve their technical skills and gain an understanding of the day-to-day operations of the business, including how to win clients, generate fees, and work within a budget.

Licenses, Certifications, and Registrations. All states require landscape architects to be licensed in order to practice except for Illinois, Massachusetts, Maine, and the District of Columbia. In addition, all 50 states (but not the District of Columbia) require applicants to be licensed before they can use the title "landscape architect" and start soliciting business. Licensing is based on the Landscape Architect Registration Examination (L.A.R.E.), which is sponsored by the Council of Landscape Architectural Registration Boards. Candidates can take the L.A.R.E. at different times of the year.

Those interested in taking the exam usually need a degree from an accredited school and 1 to 4 years of work experience under the supervision of a licensed landscape architect, although standards vary by state. For those without an accredited landscape architecture degree, many states provide alternative paths to qualify to take the L.A.R.E., usually requiring more work experience.

Currently, 13 states require landscape architects to pass a state exam, in addition to the L.A.R.E., to satisfy registration requirements. State exams focus on laws, environmental regulations, plants, soils, climate, and other characteristics unique to the state.

Because requirements for licensure vary, landscape architects may find it difficult to transfer their registration from one state to another. Common requirements include graduating from an accredited program, completing 3 years of an internship under the supervision of a registered landscape architect, and passing the L.A.R.E. By meeting national requirements, a landscape architect can also obtain certification from the Council of Landscape Architectural Registration Boards. That certification can be useful in getting a license in another state.

Important Qualities

Analytical skills. Landscape architects need to understand the content of designs. When designing a building's drainage system,

Employment Projections Data for Landscape Architects

Occupational title	SOC Code	Employment, 2012	Projected Employment, 2022	Change, 2012–2022	
				Percent	Numeric
Landscape architects	17-1012	20,100	22,900	14	2,900

Source: U.S. Bureau of Labor Statistics, Employment Projections Program

Note: Data are rounded. Go to **Occupational Information Included in the OOH** *for a discussion of the data in this table.*

for example, landscape architects need to understand how the building's location and surrounding land affect each other.

Communication skills. Landscape architects share their ideas, both orally and in writing, with clients, other architects, and workers who help prepare drawings. Many landscape architects also give presentations to explain their designs.

Creativity. Landscape architects create the overall look of gardens, parks, and other outdoor areas. Designs should be both pleasing to the eye and functional.

Problem-solving skills. When designing outdoor spaces, landscape architects must be able to provide solutions to unanticipated challenges. These solutions often involve looking at the challenge from many perspectives.

Technical skills. Landscape architects use computer-aided design and drafting (CADD) programs to create representations of their projects. Some also must use geographic information systems (GIS) for their designs.

Visualization skills. Landscape architects must be able to imagine how an overall outdoor space will look once complete.

Pay

The median annual wage for landscape architects was $64,180 in May 2012. The median wage is the wage at which half the workers in an occupation earned more than that amount and half earned less. The lowest 10 percent earned less than $38,450, and the top 10 percent earned more than $101,850.

Job Outlook

Employment of landscape architects is projected to grow 14 percent from 2012 to 2022, about as fast as the average for all occupations.

Planning and development of new and existing commercial, industrial, and residential construction projects' landscapes will drive employment growth. The public's desire for beautiful and functional spaces will continue to require good site planning and landscape design.

In addition, environmental concerns and increased demand for sustainably designed buildings and open spaces will spur demand for the services of landscape architects. For example, landscape architects are involved in the design of green roofs, which are covered with some form of vegetation and can reduce air and water pollution and reduce the costs of heating and cooling a building. Landscape architects also will be needed to design plans to manage storm-water runoff in order to conserve water resources and avoid polluting waterways.

Job Prospects. Good job opportunities are expected overall. However, competition for jobs in the largest and most prestigious landscape architecture firms is expected to be strong.

Many employers prefer to hire entry-level landscape architects who already have internship experience. Having experience significantly reduces the amount of on-the-job training required.

Job opportunities will be best for landscape architects who have strong technical and communication skills and an in-depth knowledge of environmental codes and regulations.

O*NET

➤ Landscape Architects (17-1012.00)

Contacts for More Information

For additional information, including a list of colleges and universities offering accredited programs in landscape architecture, visit
➤ American Society of Landscape Architects (www.asla.org/)

For general information on registration or licensing requirements, visit
➤ Council of Landscape Architectural Registration Boards (www.clarb.org/)

Similar Occupations   This table shows a list of occupations with job duties that are similar to those of landscape architects.

Occupations	Entry-level Education	2012 Pay	Projected Job Growth	Average Annual Openings
Architects	Bachelor's degree	$73,090	17%	4,410
Cartographers and Photogrammetrists	Bachelor's degree	$57,440	20%	490
Civil Engineers	Bachelor's degree	$79,340	20%	12,010
Construction Managers	Bachelor's degree	$82,790	16%	15,460
Environmental Scientists and Specialists	Bachelor's degree	$63,570	15%	3,970
Geoscientists	Bachelor's degree	$90,890	16%	1,730
Hydrologists	Master's degree	$75,530	9%	290
Surveying and Mapping Technicians	High school diploma or equivalent	$39,670	14%	1,700
Surveyors	Bachelor's degree	$56,230	10%	1,340
Urban and Regional Planners	Master's degree	$65,230	10%	2,140

Marine Engineers and Naval Architects

- **2012 Median Pay** .... $88,100 per year
  $42.36 per hour
- **Entry-Level Education** .... Bachelor's degree
- **Work Experience in a Related Occupation**............... None
- **On-the-Job Training** .... None
- **Number of Jobs 2012** 7,300
- **Job Outlook, 2012–22** .... 10% (As fast as average)
- **Employment Change, 2012–22** 800

Marine engineers and naval architects design and supervise the construction of ships.

What Marine Engineers and Naval Architects Do

Marine engineers and naval architects design, build, and maintain ships from aircraft carriers to submarines, from sailboats to tankers. Marine engineers work on the mechanical systems, such as propulsion and steering. Naval architects work on the basic design, including the form and stability of hulls.

Duties. Marine engineers typically do the following:

- Prepare system layouts and detailed drawings and schematics
- Inspect marine equipment and machinery, and draw up work requests and job specifications
- Conduct environmental, operational, or performance tests on marine machinery and equipment
- Design and oversee testing, installation, and repair of marine equipment
- Investigate and observe tests on machinery and equipment for compliance with standards
- Coordinate activities with regulatory bodies to ensure that repairs and alterations are done safely and at minimal cost
- Prepare technical reports for use by engineers, managers, or sales personnel
- Prepare cost estimates, contract specifications, and design and construction schedules
- Maintain contact with contractors to be sure the work is being done correctly, on schedule, and within budget

Naval architects typically do the following:

- Study design proposals and specifications to establish basic characteristics of a ship, such as size, weight, and speed

- Develop sectional and waterline curves of the hull to establish the center of gravity, ideal hull form, and data on buoyancy and stability
- Design entire ship hulls and superstructures, following safety standards
- Design the layout of ships' interiors, including passenger compartments, cargo space, ladder wells, and elevators
- Confer with marine engineers to design the layout of boiler room equipment, heating and ventilation systems, refrigeration equipment, and propulsion machinery
- Lead teams from a variety of specialties to oversee building and testing prototypes
- Evaluate how ships perform during trials, both at dock and at sea, and change designs as needed to make sure national and international standards are met

Marine engineers and naval architects apply knowledge from a range of engineering fields to the entire water vehicles design and production processes. Marine engineers also design and maintain offshore oil rigs and may work on alternative energy projects, such as wind turbines located offshore or tidal power.

Marine engineers and naval architects working for ship and boat building firms design large ships such as passenger ships and cargo ships, as well as small craft such as inflatable boats and rowboats. Those who work in the federal government may design or test the designs of ships or systems for the Navy or Coast Guard.

Median Annual Wages, May 2012

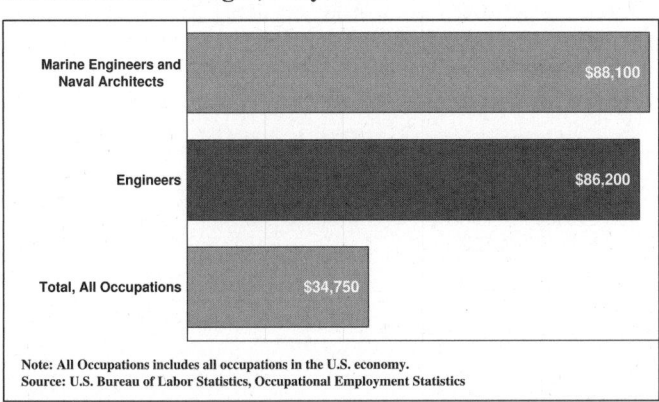

Marine Engineers and Naval Architects	$88,100
Engineers	$86,200
Total, All Occupations	$34,750

Note: All Occupations includes all occupations in the U.S. economy.
Source: U.S. Bureau of Labor Statistics, Occupational Employment Statistics

Percent Change in Employment, Projected 2012–2022

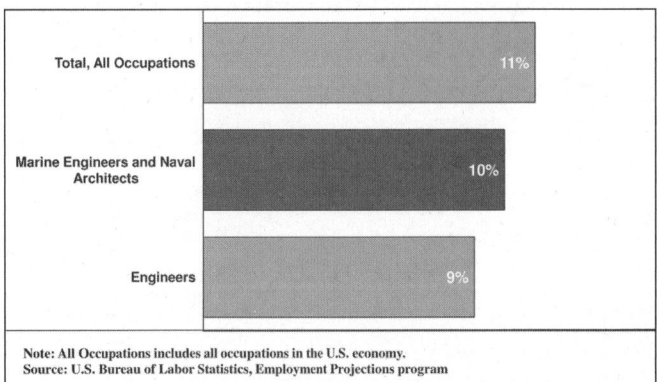

Total, All Occupations	11%
Marine Engineers and Naval Architects	10%
Engineers	9%

Note: All Occupations includes all occupations in the U.S. economy.
Source: U.S. Bureau of Labor Statistics, Employment Projections program

Employment Projections Data for Marine Engineers and Naval Architects

Occupational title	SOC Code	Employment, 2012	Projected Employment, 2022	Change, 2012–2022	
				Percent	Numeric
Marine engineers and naval architects..................................	17-2121	7,300	8,100	10	800

Source: U.S. Bureau of Labor Statistics, Employment Projections Program

Note: Data are rounded. Go to **Occupational Information Included in the OOH** *for a discussion of the data in this table.*

Ship engineers, who are sometimes called marine engineers, operate or supervise the operation of the machinery on a ship. Their work differs from that of the marine engineers discussed in this profile. For more information on ship engineers, see the profile on water transportation occupations.

Work Environment

Marine engineers and naval architects held about 7,300 jobs in 2012. They typically work in offices, where they have access to computer software and other tools necessary for analyzing projects and designing solutions. Sometimes, they must go to sea on ships for testing or maintenance.

Those working on power generation projects, such as offshore wind turbines or tidal power, work along the coast–both offshore and on land. They also sometimes work on oil rigs where they oversee repair or maintenance of systems that they may have designed.

The industries that employed the most marine engineers and naval architects in 2012 were as follows:

Architectural, engineering, and related services 40%
Federal government, excluding postal service 14
Ship and boat building... 14
Other professional, scientific, and technical services................. 6
Deep sea, coastal, and great lakes water transportation 5

Naval architects often lead teams of diverse professionals to create feasible designs, and they must effectively use the skills that each person brings to the design process.

Work Schedules. Marine engineers who work at sea will work a schedule tied to the operations of their particular ship. Those who work on shore will have somewhat more regular work schedules. Naval architects, as they are primarily designers, are much more likely to work a regular schedule in an office environment or at a shipyard.

How to Become One

Marine engineers and naval architects must have a bachelor's degree in marine engineering, naval architecture, marine systems engineering, or marine engineering technology. Employers also value practical experience, so cooperative education programs,

which provide college credit for structured job experience, are valuable.

Education. Entry-level jobs in marine engineering and naval architecture require a bachelor's degree in marine engineering, naval architecture, marine systems engineering, or marine engineering technology. Programs typically include courses in calculus, physics, and computer-aided design. Courses specific to marine engineering and naval architecture include fluid mechanics, ship hull strength, and mechanics of materials. Some marine engineers have bachelor's degrees in mechanical or electrical engineering. Programs in marine engineering, naval architecture, marine systems engineering, and marine engineering technology are accredited by ABET.

Students interested in preparing for this occupation benefit from taking high school courses in math, such as algebra, trigonometry, and calculus; and science, such as chemistry and physics. For aspiring naval architects, drafting courses are helpful.

Important Qualities

Communication skills. Marine engineers and naval architects must be able to give clear instructions and explain complex concepts when leading teams of professionals on projects.

Ingenuity. Marine engineers and naval architects must employ operations analysis to create a design that will most likely perform the ship's functions, and then employ skills of critical thinking to anticipate and correct any deficiencies before the ship is built or set to sea.

Interpersonal skills. Marine engineers and naval architects meet with clients to analyze their needs for ship systems. Engineers must be able to discuss progress with clients to keep redesign options open before the project is too far along.

Math skills. Marine engineers and naval architects use the principles of calculus, trigonometry, and other advanced topics in math for analysis, design, and troubleshooting in their work.

Problem-solving skills. Marine engineers must design several systems for ships that work well together. Naval architects and marine engineers are expected to solve problems for their clients. They must draw on their knowledge and experience to make effective decisions.

Licenses, Certifications, and Registrations. Along with earning a bachelor's degree, marine engineers and naval architects usually

Similar Occupations   This table shows a list of occupations with job duties that are similar to those of marine engineers and naval architects.

Occupations	Entry-level Education	2012 Pay	Projected Job Growth	Average Annual Openings
Aerospace Engineers	Bachelor's degree	$103,720	7%	2,540
Drafters	Associate's degree	$49,726	1%	3,220
Electrical and Electronics Engineers	Bachelor's degree	$89,701	4%	7,940
Mechanical Engineers	Bachelor's degree	$80,580	4%	9,970
Petroleum Engineers	Bachelor's degree	$130,280	26%	1,960

take an exam for a mariner's license from the U.S. Coast Guard. The first stage of the license is known as the 3rd Assistant License. With experience and further testing, a marine engineer may get a 2nd and then a 1st Assistant License. The highest level of licensure is known as Chief Assistant. Higher grades of licensing are usually accompanied by higher pay and more responsibilities.

Advancement. Beginning marine engineers usually work under the supervision of experienced engineers. In larger companies, new engineers also may receive formal training in classrooms or seminars. As beginning engineers gain knowledge and experience, they move on to more difficult projects where they have greater independence to develop designs, solve problems, and make decisions.

Eventually, marine engineers may advance to become technical specialists or to supervise a team of engineers and technicians. Some may even become engineering managers or move into other managerial positions or sales work. In sales, an engineering background enables them to discuss technical aspects of certain kinds of engineering projects. Such knowledge is also useful in assisting clients in project planning, installation, and use.

Pay

The median annual wage for marine engineers and naval architects was $88,100 in May 2012. The median wage is the wage at which half of the workers in an occupation earned more than that amount and half earned less. The lowest 10 percent earned less than $54,260, and the top 10 percent earned more than $150,560.

In May 2012, the median annual wages for marine engineers and naval architects in the top five industries employing these engineers were as follows:

Federal government, excluding postal service	$97,550
Architectural, engineering, and related services	92,010
Deep sea, coastal, and great lakes water transportation	89,220
Ship and boat building	82,510
Other professional, scientific, and technical services	71,220

Marine engineers who work at sea will work a schedule tied to the operations of their particular ship. Naval architects, as they are primarily designers, are much more likely to work a regular schedule in an office environment or at a shipyard.

Union Membership. Compared with workers in all occupations, marine engineers and naval architects had a higher percentage of workers who belonged to a union in 2012.

Job Outlook

Employment of marine engineers and naval architects is projected to grow 10 percent from 2012 to 2022, about as fast as the average for all occupations. The need to design ships and systems to transport energy products, such as liquefied natural gas, across the globe will help to spur employment growth for this occupation. Employment of marine engineers and naval architects also will be supported by the need to modify existing ships and their systems because of new emissions and pollution regulations on cargo shipping.

Marine engineers who design and maintain offshore oil rigs are expected to be in demand as more companies seek and drill for oil and gas deposits in the ocean floor.

In addition, the increase in international overseas transportation of liquefied natural gas is expected to lead to demand for marine engineers to work on ship crews, though sometimes on ships sailing under foreign flags.

For the immediate future, demand for naval architects will come from the need to update fleets to meet new federal requirements for double-hulled ships for transporting oil and gas.

Demand for marine engineers and naval architects will also come from the desire to have cargo ships that pollute less. The technology to do this is becoming more cost-effective and the United States and other countries are focusing more on reducing pollution. This will also include the adoption of new and alternative energy sources, such as offshore wind turbines and tidal power generators.

O*NET

➤ Marine Engineers and Naval Architects (17-2121.00)
➤ Marine Engineers (17-2121.01)
➤ Marine Architects (17-2121.02)

Contacts for More Information

For more information about the occupation, visit
➤ Marine Engineers' Beneficial Association (http://mebaunion.org/MEBA/)

For more information about general engineering education and career resources, visit
➤ American Society for Engineering Education (www.asee.org/)
➤ Technology Student Association (www.tsaweb.org/)

For more information about accredited engineering programs, visit
➤ ABET (www.abet.org/)

Materials Engineers

- **2012 Median Pay** .... $85,150 per year
  $40.94 per hour
- **Entry-Level Education** ....Bachelor's degree
- **Work Experience in a Related Occupation**.............. None
- **On-the-Job Training** .... None
- **Number of Jobs 2012** 23,200
- **Job Outlook, 2012–22** ....1% (Little or no change)
- **Employment Change, 2012–22** 200

What Materials Engineers Do

Materials engineers develop, process, and test materials used to create a range of products, from computer chips and aircraft wings to golf clubs and snow skis. They work with metals, ceramics, plas-

Materials engineers develop, process, and test a wide variety of materials used in all kinds of products.

Median Annual Wages, May 2012

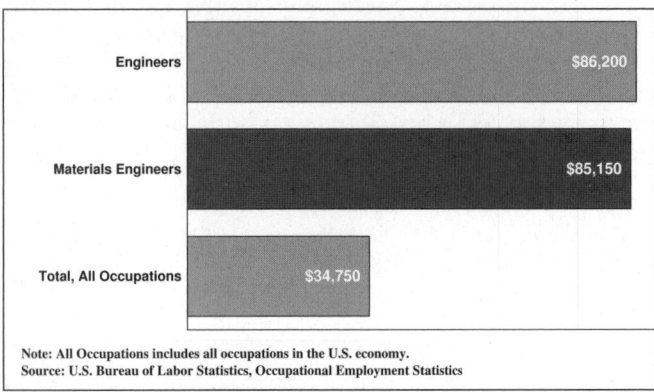

Note: All Occupations includes all occupations in the U.S. economy.
Source: U.S. Bureau of Labor Statistics, Occupational Employment Statistics

Percent Change in Employment, Projected 2012–2022

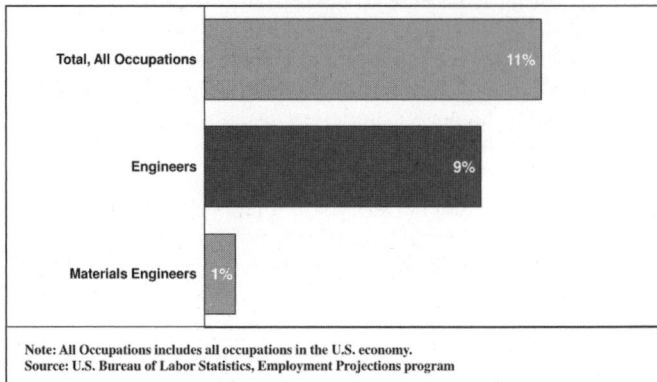

Note: All Occupations includes all occupations in the U.S. economy.
Source: U.S. Bureau of Labor Statistics, Employment Projections program

tics, composites, and other substances to create new materials that meet certain mechanical, electrical, and chemical requirements. They also help select materials for specific products, develop new ways to use materials, and develop new materials.

Duties. Materials engineers typically do the following:

- Plan and evaluate new projects, consulting with others as necessary

- Prepare proposals and budgets, analyze labor costs, write reports, and perform other managerial tasks

- Supervise the work of technologists, technicians, and other engineers and scientists

- Design and direct the testing of processing procedures

- Monitor how materials perform and evaluate how they deteriorate

- Determine causes of product failure and develop solutions

- Evaluate technical specifications and economic factors relating to the design objectives of processes or products

Materials engineers create and study materials at an atomic level. They use computers to replicate the characteristics of materials and their components. They solve problems in a number of engineering fields, such as mechanical, chemical, electrical, civil, nuclear, and aerospace.

Materials engineers may specialize in understanding specific types of materials. The following are examples of types of materials engineers:

Ceramic engineers develop ceramic materials and the processes for making them into useful products, from high-temperature rocket nozzles to glass for LCD flat-panel displays.

Composites engineers work in developing materials with special, engineered properties for applications in aircraft, automobiles, and related products.

Metallurgical engineers specialize in metals, such as steel and aluminum, usually in alloyed form with additions of other elements to provide specific properties.

Plastics engineers work in developing and testing new plastics, known as polymers, for new applications.

Semiconductor processing engineers apply materials science and engineering principles to develop new microelectronic materials for computing, sensing, and related applications.

Work Environment

Materials engineers held about 23,200 jobs in 2012. They often work in offices where they have access to computers and design equipment. Others work in supervisory roles either in a factory or in research and development laboratories. Materials engineers

may work in teams with scientists and engineers from other backgrounds.

The industries that employed the most materials engineers in 2012 were as follows:

Aerospace product and parts manufacturing 19%
Architectural, engineering, and related services 10
Scientific research and development services 7
Semiconductor and other electronic component
   manufacturing 6
Federal government, excluding postal service 6

Work Schedules. Materials engineers generally work full time. However, these engineers occasionally have to work overtime.

How to Become One

Materials engineers typically have a bachelor's degree in materials science or engineering, or a related field. Employers also value practical experience. Therefore, cooperative engineering programs, which provide college credit for structured job experience, are valuable as well.

Education. Students interested in studying materials engineering should take high school courses in mathematics, such as algebra, trigonometry, and calculus; and in science, such as biology, chemistry, and physics.

Entry-level jobs as a materials engineer require a bachelor's degree. Bachelor's degree programs include classroom and laboratory work focusing on engineering principles. Many colleges and universities offer cooperative programs in which students gain practical experience while earning college credits.

Some colleges and universities offer a 5-year program leading to both a bachelor's and master's degree. A graduate degree allows an engineer to work as an instructor at some colleges and universities or to do research and development. Some 5- or 6-year cooperative plans combine classroom study with practical work, allowing students to gain experience and to finance part of their education.

Many engineering programs are accredited by ABET. Some employers prefer to hire candidates who have graduated from an accredited program. A degree from an ABET-accredited program is usually necessary to become a licensed professional engineer.

Important Qualities

Analytical skills. Materials engineers often work on projects related to other fields of engineering. They must be able to determine how materials will be used in a wide variety of conditions and how the materials must be structured to withstand the requirements of those conditions.

Employment Projections Data for Materials Engineers

Occupational title	SOC Code	Employment, 2012	Projected Employment, 2022	Change, 2012–2022	
				Percent	Numeric
Materials engineers	17-2131	23,200	23,400	1	200

Source: U.S. Bureau of Labor Statistics, Employment Projections Program

Note: Data are rounded. Go to **Occupational Information Included in the OOH** *for a discussion of the data in this table.*

Math skills. Materials engineers use the principals of calculus and other advanced topics in math for analysis, design, and troubleshooting in their work.

Problem-solving skills. Materials engineers must understand the relationship between the structure of materials and their properties and means of processing, and how these factors affect the product. They must also figure out why a product might have failed, design a solution, and then conduct tests to make sure the product does not fail again. This involves being able to identify root causes when many factors could be at fault.

Speaking skills. In supervising technicians, technologists, and other engineers, materials engineers must be able to state concepts and directions clearly. When speaking with managers at high-level meetings, these engineers must also be able to communicate engineering concepts to people who do not have an engineering background.

Writing skills. Materials engineers must write plans and reports clearly so that people without a materials engineering background can understand the concepts.

Licenses, Certifications, and Registrations. Though licensure is not required to enter the occupation, some states license materials engineers; requirements vary by state. Licensed engineers are called professional engineers (PEs), and licensure generally has the following requirements:

- A degree from an ABET-accredited engineering program
- A passing score on the Fundamentals of Engineering (FE) exam
- Relevant work experience
- A passing score on the Professional Engineering (PE) exam

The initial Fundamentals of Engineering (FE) exam can be taken after graduation from college. Engineers who pass this exam are commonly called engineers in training (EITs) or engineer interns (EIs). After acquiring suitable work experience, EITs and EIs can take the second exam, called the Principles and Practice of Engineering.

Several states require continuing education for engineers to keep their license. Most states recognize licensure from other states, if the licensing state's requirements meet or exceed their own requirements.

Certification in the field of metallography, the science and art of dealing with the structure of metals and alloys, is available through ASM International and other materials organizations.

Additional training in fields directly related to metallurgy and materials' properties, such as corrosion or failure analysis, is available through ASM International.

Advancement. Beginning materials engineers usually work under the supervision of experienced engineers. In large companies, new engineers may receive formal training in classrooms or seminars. As engineers gain knowledge and experience, they move on to more difficult projects where they have greater independence to develop designs, solve problems, and make decisions.

Eventually, materials engineers may advance to become technical specialists or to supervise a team of engineers and technicians. Many become engineering managers or move into other managerial positions or sales work. An engineering background is useful in sales because it enables sales engineers to discuss a product's technical aspects and assist in product planning, installation, and use.

Pay

The median annual wage for materials engineers was $85,150 in May 2012. The median wage is the wage at which half the workers in an occupation earned more than that amount and half earned less. The lowest 10 percent earned less than $52,900, and the top 10 percent earned more than $130,020.

In May 2012, the median annual wages in the top five industries employing these engineers were as follows:

Federal government, excluding postal service	$109,810
Aerospace product and parts manufacturing	97,160
Scientific research and development services	86,250
Semiconductor and other electronic component manufacturing	84,090
Architectural, engineering, and related services	80,080

Similar Occupations   This table shows a list of occupations with job duties that are similar to those of materials engineers.

Occupations	Entry-level Education	2012 Pay	Projected Job Growth	Average Annual Openings
Aerospace Engineers	Bachelor's degree	$103,720	7%	2,540
Architectural and Engineering Managers	Bachelor's degree	$124,870	7%	6,060
Biomedical Engineers	Bachelor's degree	$86,960	27%	1,010
Chemical Engineers	Bachelor's degree	$94,350	5%	920
Chemists and Materials Scientists	Bachelor's degree	$73,247	6%	3,040
Electrical and Electronics Engineers	Bachelor's degree	$89,701	4%	7,940
Mechanical Engineers	Bachelor's degree	$80,580	4%	9,970
Physicists and Astronomers	Doctoral or professional degree	$105,722	10%	810
Sales Engineers	Bachelor's degree	$91,830	9%	1,740

Job Outlook

Employment of materials engineers is projected to show little or no change from 2012 to 2022.

Materials engineers will be needed to design uses for new materials both in traditional industries, such as aerospace manufacturing, and in industries focused on new medical or scientific products.

Materials engineers are in demand in growing fields such as biomedical engineering. Their expertise is crucial in helping biomedical engineers develop new materials for medical implants. Research and development firms will continue to employ materials engineers as they explore new uses for materials technology in consumer products, industrial processes, and medicine.

However, most material engineers work in manufacturing industries which are expected to experience employment declines.

Job Prospects. Despite a projected slow growth rate for this occupation, job prospects should be favorable as materials engineers will be needed to fill positions as more experienced materials engineers are promoted or retire. Prospects should also be favorable for those who train in traditional fields of materials engineering, such as metallurgy.

O*NET

➤ Materials Engineers (17-2131.00)

Contacts for More Information

For information about general engineering education and career resources, visit

➤ American Society for Engineering Education (www.asee.org/)
➤ Technology Student Association (www.tsaweb.org/)

For more information about licensure as a professional engineer, visit

➤ National Council of Examiners for Engineering and Surveying (www.ncees.org/)
➤ National Society of Professional Engineers (www.nspe.org/index.html)

For information about accredited engineering programs, visit

➤ ABET (www.abet.org/)

For more information about certification, visit

➤ ASM International (www.asminternational.org/portal/site/www/)

Mechanical Engineering Technicians

- **2012 Median Pay** ....$51,980 per year
  $24.99 per hour
- **Entry-Level Education** ....Associate's degree
- **Work Experience in a Related Occupation**...............None
- **On-the-Job Training** ....None
- **Number of Jobs 2012** 47,500
- **Job Outlook, 2012–22** ....5% (Slower than average)
- **Employment Change, 2012–22** 2,200

What Mechanical Engineering Technicians Do

Mechanical engineering technicians help mechanical engineers design, develop, test, and manufacture mechanical devices, including tools, engines, and machines. They may make sketches and rough layouts, record and analyze data, make calculations and estimates, and report their findings.

Duties. Mechanical engineering technicians typically do the following:

- Evaluate design drawings for new or changed tools by measuring dimensions on the drawings and comparing them with the original specifications
- Prepare layouts and drawings of parts to be made and of the process for putting them together
- Discuss changes with coworkers–for example, in the design of the part, in the way it will be made and put together, and in the techniques and process they will use
- Review instructions and blueprints for the project to ensure the test specifications and procedures are followed and objectives are met
- Plan, produce, and assemble new or changed mechanical parts for products, such as industrial machinery or equipment
- Set up and conduct tests of complete units and of parts as they would actually be used, as a way to investigate proposals for improving equipment performance
- Record test procedures and results, numerical and graphical data, and recommendations for changes in products or test methods
- Compare test results to design specifications and test objectives

Mechanical engineering technicians also estimate labor costs, equipment life, and plant space. Some test and inspect machines and equipment or work with engineers to eliminate production problems. They may assist in testing products by, for example, setting up instrumentation for vehicle crash tests.

Work Environment

Mechanical engineering technicians held about 47,500 jobs in 2012. They work closely with mechanical engineers and are employed primarily in traditional manufacturing settings and in research and development laboratories.

The industries employing the most mechanical engineering technicians in 2012 were as follows:

Engineering services.. 19%
Research and development in the physical, engineering,
  and life sciences.. 7
Motor vehicle parts manufacturing 6
Testing laboratories.. 5
Navigational, measuring, electromedical, and control
  instruments manufacturing 5

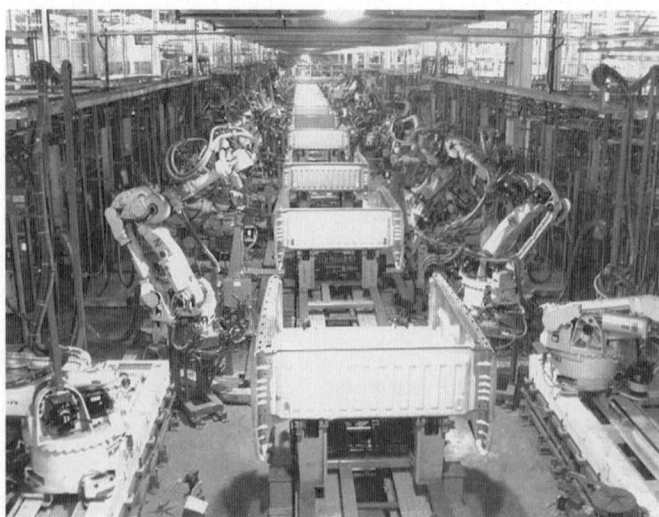

Mechanical engineering technicians plan the assembly process to be used in industrial settings.

Median Annual Wages, May 2012

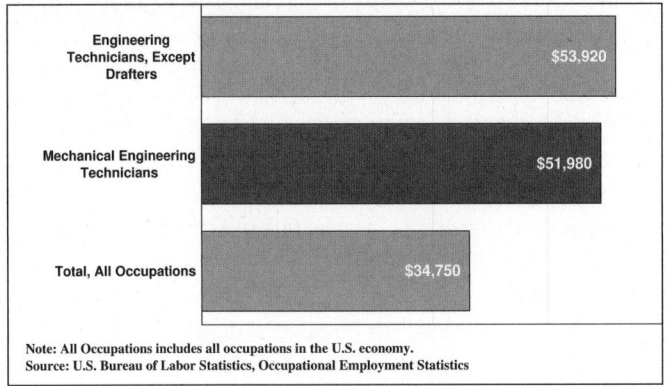

Note: All Occupations includes all occupations in the U.S. economy.
Source: U.S. Bureau of Labor Statistics, Occupational Employment Statistics

Percent Change in Employment, Projected 2012–2022

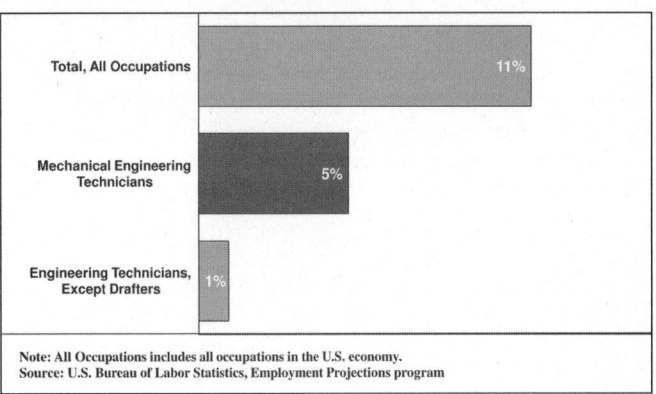

Note: All Occupations includes all occupations in the U.S. economy.
Source: U.S. Bureau of Labor Statistics, Employment Projections program

Some mechanical engineering technicians may be exposed to hazards from equipment, chemicals, or toxic materials, but injuries are rare as long as proper procedures are followed.

Work Schedules. Most mechanical engineering technicians work full time.

How to Become One

Most employers prefer to hire candidates with associate's degrees or other postsecondary training in mechanical engineering technology. Prospective engineering technicians should take as many science and math courses as possible while in high school.

Education. Prospective mechanical engineering technicians usually take courses in fluid mechanics, thermodynamics, and mechanical design in a program leading to an associate's degree. ABET accredits programs that include at least college algebra, trigonometry, and basic science courses. Associate's degree programs are found in the following types of institutions:

- Vocational–technical schools, which include postsecondary public institutions that serve local students and emphasize training needed by local employers

- Community colleges, which offer programs similar to those in technical institutes but include more theory-based and liberal arts coursework

Completing an associate's degree in mechanical engineering technology opens the way to studying for a bachelor's degree.

Important Qualities

Communication skills. Mechanical engineering technicians must be able to clearly understand and follow instructions or, if they do not understand, ask their supervisors to explain. They must be able to clearly explain the need for changes in designs or test procedures both verbally and in writing.

Creativity. Mechanical engineering technicians help mechanical engineers bring their plans and designs to life. This often requires helping the engineer to overcome problems that might not have been anticipated.

Detail oriented. Mechanical engineering technicians must make precise measurements and keep accurate records for mechanical engineers.

Interpersonal skills. Mechanical engineering technicians must be able to take instructions and offer advice when it is needed.

Math skills. Mechanical engineering technicians use mathematics for analysis, design, and troubleshooting in their work.

Mechanical skills. Mechanical engineering technicians must apply theory and instructions from engineers by making new components for industrial machinery or equipment. They may need to be able to operate machinery such as drill presses, grinders, and engine lathes.

Employment Projections Data for Mechanical Engineering Technicians

Occupational title	SOC Code	Employment, 2012	Projected Employment, 2022	Change, 2012–2022	
				Percent	Numeric
Mechanical engineering technicians	17-3027	47,500	49,700	5	2,200

Source: U.S. Bureau of Labor Statistics, Employment Projections Program

Note: Data are rounded. Go to Occupational Information Included in the OOH for a discussion of the data in this table.

Similar Occupations   This table shows a list of occupations with job duties that are similar to those of mechanical engineering technicians.

Occupations	Entry-level Education	2012 Pay	Projected Job Growth	Average Annual Openings
Drafters	Associate's degree	$49,726	1%	3,220
Environmental Engineering Technicians	Associate's degree	$45,350	18%	740
Industrial Engineering Technicians	Associate's degree	$50,980	-3%	1,410
Machinists and Tool and Die Makers	High school diploma or equivalent	$40,733	7%	13,060
Semiconductor Processors	Associate's degree	$33,020	-27%	500

Pay

The median annual wage for mechanical engineering technicians was $51,980 in May 2012. The median wage is the wage at which half of the workers in an occupation earned more than that amount and half earned less. The lowest 10 percent earned less than $33,370, and the top 10 percent earned more than $76,660.

In May 2012, the median annual wages in the top five industries in which these technicians worked were as follows:

Navigational, measuring, electromedical, and control
   instruments manufacturing $54,030
Research and development in the physical, engineering,
   and life sciences... 53,230
Engineering services.. 51,920
Motor vehicle parts manufacturing 51,610
Testing laboratories.. 48,290

Job Outlook

Employment of mechanical engineering technicians is projected to grow 5 percent from 2012 to 2022, slower than the average for all occupations. Employment in this occupation depends on the overall state of manufacturing.

Mechanical engineering technicians also work for firms in engineering services and in research and development, both of which provide contract services to manufacturing and other industries. Contracting for this work allows firms to hire these services at a lower cost than employing in-house technicians. Employment growth of mechanical engineering technicians will vary by industry.

Mechanical engineering technicians will find work in emerging fields, such as automation, remanufacturing, 3-D printing, and alternative energies.

Job Prospects. Mastering new technology and software will likely become more important for workers in this occupation. Those who gain skills to help deploy the latest technological developments should have the best job prospects.

O*NET

➤ Mechanical Engineering Technicians (17-3027.00)
➤ Automotive Engineering Technicians (17-3027.01)

Contacts for More Information

For more information about general engineering education and career resources, visit
➤ American Society for Engineering Education (www.asee.org/)
➤ Technology Student Association (www.tsaweb.org/)
   For information about accredited programs, visit
➤ ABET (www.abet.org/)

Mechanical Engineers

- **2012 Median Pay** .... $80,580 per year
  $38.74 per hour
- **Entry-Level Education** ....Bachelor's degree
- **Work Experience in a Related Occupation**............... None
- **On-the-Job Training** .... None
- **Number of Jobs 2012** 258,100
- **Job Outlook, 2012–22** .... 5% (Slower than average)
- **Employment Change, 2012–22** 11,600

What Mechanical Engineers Do

Mechanical engineering is one of the broadest engineering disciplines. Mechanical engineers research, design, develop, build, and test mechanical and thermal devices, including tools, engines, and machines.

Duties. Mechanical engineers typically do the following:

- Analyze problems to see how mechanical and thermal devices might help solve the problem
- Design or redesign mechanical and thermal devices using analysis and computer-aided design
- Develop and test prototypes of devices they design
- Analyze the test results and change the design as needed
- Oversee the manufacturing process for the device

Mechanical engineers design and oversee the manufacturing of many products ranging from medical devices to new batteries.

Mechanical engineers design power-producing machines such as electric generators, internal combustion engines, and steam and gas turbines as well as power-using machines, such as refrigeration and air-conditioning systems.

Mechanical engineers design other machines inside buildings, such as elevators and escalators. They also design material-handling systems, such as conveyor systems and automated transfer stations.

Like other engineers, mechanical engineers use computers extensively. Computers help mechanical engineers create and analyze designs, run simulations and test how a machine is likely to work, and generate specifications for parts.

Work Environment

Mechanical engineers held about 258,100 jobs in 2012. They work mostly in manufacturing industries, architectural and engineering services, and research and development.

The industries employing the most mechanical engineers in 2012 were as follows:

Architectural, engineering, and related services 22%
Machinery manufacturing 14
Transportation equipment manufacturing 13
Computer and electronic product manufacturing.................... 8
Fabricated metal product manufacturing................................. 6

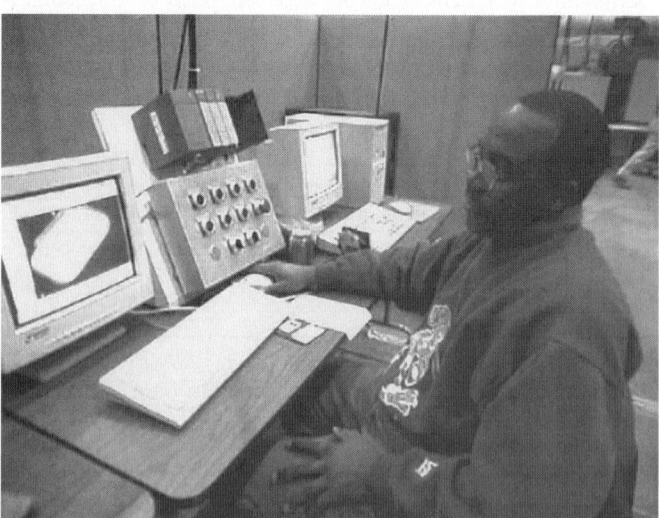

Mechanical engineers develop and build mechanical devices for use in industrial processes.

Median Annual Wages, May 2012

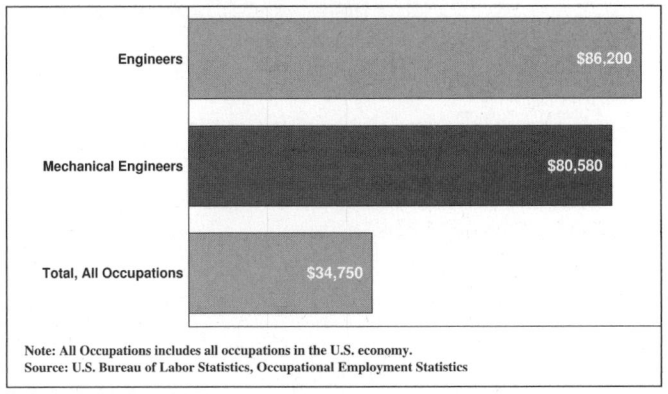

Note: All Occupations includes all occupations in the U.S. economy.
Source: U.S. Bureau of Labor Statistics, Occupational Employment Statistics

Percent Change in Employment, Projected 2012–2022

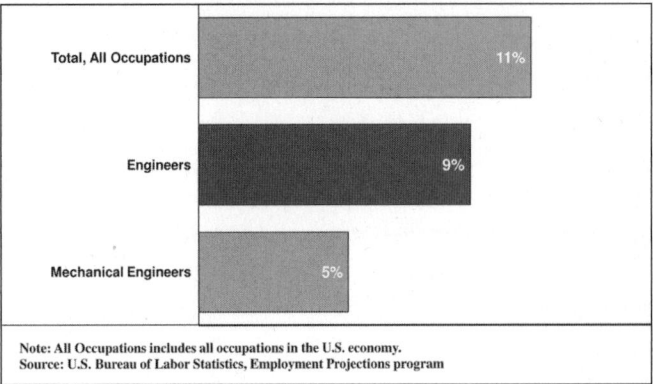

Note: All Occupations includes all occupations in the U.S. economy.
Source: U.S. Bureau of Labor Statistics, Employment Projections program

The rest are employed in general-purpose machinery manufacturing, automotive parts manufacturing, and testing laboratories.

Mechanical engineers generally work in professional office settings. They may occasionally visit worksites where a problem or piece of equipment needs their personal attention. In most settings, they work with other engineers, engineering technicians, and other professionals as part of a team.

Work Schedules. Most mechanical engineers work full time, and about one-third worked more than 40 hours a week in 2012.

How to Become One

Mechanical engineers need a bachelor's degree. A graduate degree is typically needed to conduct research. Mechanical engineers who sell services publicly must be licensed in all states and the District of Columbia.

Education. Nearly all entry-level mechanical engineering jobs require a bachelor's degree in mechanical engineering or mechanical engineering technology.

Mechanical engineering degree programs usually include courses in mathematics and life and physical sciences, as well as engineering and design courses. Mechanical engineering technology programs focus less on theory and more on the practical application of engineering principles. Programs typically last 4 years, but many students take between 4 and 5 years to earn a degree. Mechanical engineering degree programs may emphasize internships and co-ops to prepare students for work in industry.

Some colleges and universities offer 5-year programs that allow students to obtain both a bachelor's and a master's degree. Some 5-year or even 6-year cooperative plans combine classroom study with practical work, enabling students to gain valuable experience and earn money to finance part of their education.

ABET accredits programs in mechanical engineering and mechanical engineering technology. Most employers prefer to hire students from an accredited program. A degree from an ABET-accredited program is usually necessary to become a licensed professional engineer.

Important Qualities

Creativity. Mechanical engineers design and build complex pieces of equipment and machinery. A creative mind is essential for this kind of work.

Listening skills. Mechanical engineers often work on projects with other engineers and professionals, such as architects. They must listen to and analyze different approaches to the task at hand.

Math skills. Mechanical engineers use the principles of calculus, trigonometry, and other advanced topics in math for analysis, design, and troubleshooting in their work.

Mechanical skills. Mechanical skills allow engineers to apply basic engineering concepts and mechanical processes to the design of new devices.

Problem-solving skills. Mechanical engineers take scientific discoveries and seek to make them into products that would be useful to people, companies, and governments. Experience gained through laboratory courses at university or a cooperative education program in college helps mechanical engineers develop skills that are useful in solving real-world problems.

Licenses, Certifications, and Registrations. All 50 states and the District of Columbia require licensure for engineers who offer their services directly to the public. Licensed mechanical engineers are designated as professional engineers (PEs). The PE license generally requires a degree from an ABET-accredited engineering program, 4 years of relevant work experience, and passing a state exam.

Recent graduates can start the licensing process by taking the exam in two stages. They can take the Fundamentals of Engineering (FE) exam prior to or right after graduation. Engineers who pass this exam commonly are called engineers in training (EITs) or engineer interns (EIs). After gaining experience, EITs can take a second exam, called the Principles and Practice of Engineering exam, for full licensure as a PE.

Several states require engineers to take continuing education to renew their licenses every year. Most states recognize licensure from other states, as long as the other state's licensing requirements meet or exceed their own licensing requirements.

Employment Projections Data for Mechanical Engineers

Occupational title	SOC Code	Employment, 2012	Projected Employment, 2022	Change, 2012–2022 Percent	Numeric
Mechanical engineers	17-2141	258,100	269,700	5	11,600

Source: U.S. Bureau of Labor Statistics, Employment Projections Program

Note: Data are rounded. Go to Occupational Information Included in the OOH for a discussion of the data in this table.

Similar Occupations   This table shows a list of occupations with job duties that are similar to those of mechanical engineers.

Occupations	Entry-level Education	2012 Pay	Projected Job Growth	Average Annual Openings
Architectural and Engineering Managers	Bachelor's degree	$124,870	7%	6,060
Drafters	Associate's degree	$49,726	1%	3,220
Materials Engineers	Bachelor's degree	$85,150	1%	750
Mathematicians	Master's degree	$101,360	23%	170
Mechanical Engineering Technicians	Associate's degree	$51,980	5%	1,210
Natural Sciences Managers	Bachelor's degree	$115,730	6%	1,370
Petroleum Engineers	Bachelor's degree	$130,280	26%	1,960
Physicists and Astronomers	Doctoral or professional degree	$105,722	10%	810
Sales Engineers	Bachelor's degree	$91,830	9%	1,740

Professional organizations, such as the American Society of Mechanical Engineers, offer a variety of certification programs for engineers to demonstrate competency in specific fields of mechanical engineering.

Advancement. Graduate education is essential for engineering faculty positions in higher education, as well as for some research and development programs. Many experienced mechanical engineers earn graduate degrees in engineering or business administration to learn new technology and broaden their education and enhance their project management skills. Many become administrators or managers after obtaining a graduate degree.

Pay

The median annual wage for mechanical engineers was $80,580 in May 2012. The median wage is the wage at which half the workers in an occupation earned more than that amount and half earned less. The lowest 10 percent earned less than $52,030, and the top 10 percent earned more than $121,530.

In May 2012, the median annual wages for mechanical engineers in the top five industries employing these engineers were as follows:

Computer and electronic product manufacturing $84,860
Architectural, engineering, and related services 84,030
Transportation equipment manufacturing 83,540
Machinery manufacturing 72,270
Fabricated metal product manufacturing 69,890

Job Outlook

Employment of mechanical engineers is projected to grow 5 percent from 2012 to 2022, slower than the average for all occupations. Job prospects may be best for those who stay informed regarding the most recent advances in technology. Mechanical engineers can work in many industries and on many types of projects. As a result, their growth rate will differ by the industries that employ them.

Mechanical engineers should experience faster than average growth in architectural, engineering, and related services as companies continue to contract work from these firms. Mechanical engineers will also remain involved in various manufacturing industries–specifically, transportation equipment and machinery manufacturing. They will be needed to design the next generation of vehicles and vehicle systems, such as hybrid-electric cars and clean diesel automobiles. Machinery will continue to be in demand as machines replace more expensive human labor in various industries. This phenomenon in turn should drive demand for mechanical engineers who design industrial machinery.

Mechanical engineers are projected to experience faster than average growth in oil and gas extraction because of their knowledge and skills regarding thermal energy.

Mechanical engineers often work on the newest industrial pursuits. The fields of alternative energies, remanufacturing, and nanotechnology may offer new opportunities for occupational growth. Remanufacturing–rebuilding goods for use in a second life–holds promise because it reduces the cost of waste disposal. Training in remanufacturing may become common in mechanical engineering programs at colleges and universities.

Nanotechnology, which involves manipulating matter at the tiniest levels, may affect employment for mechanical engineers because they will be needed to design production projects based on this technology. Nanotechnology will be useful in areas such as designing more powerful computer chips and in healthcare.

Job Prospects. Although prospects for mechanical engineers overall are expected to be good, they will be best for those with training in the latest software tools, particularly for computational design and simulation. Such tools allow engineers and designers to take a project from the conceptual phase directly to a finished product, eliminating the need for prototypes. Along those lines, students who can take courses in 3-D printing will also improve their job prospects.

O*NET

➤ Mechanical Engineers (17-2141.00)
➤ Fuel Cell Engineers (17-2141.01)
➤ Automotive Engineers (17-2141.02)

Contacts for More Information

For more information about general engineering education and mechanical engineering career resources, visit
➤ American Society of Mechanical Engineers (www.asme.org/)
➤ American Society for Engineering Education (www.asee.org/)
➤ Technology Student Association (www.tsaweb.org/)
   For more information about accredited engineering programs, visit
➤ ABET (www.abet.org/)
   For more information about licensure as a mechanical engineer, visit
➤ National Council of Examiners for Engineering and Surveying (http://ncees.org/)
➤ National Society of Professional Engineers (www.nspe.org/index.html)

Mining and Geological Engineers

- **2012 Median Pay** .... $84,320 per year
  $40.54 per hour
- **Entry-Level Education** ....Bachelor's degree
- **Work Experience in a Related Occupation**.............. None
- **On-the-Job Training** .... None
- **Number of Jobs 2012** 7,900
- **Job Outlook, 2012–22** .... 12% (As fast as average)
- **Employment Change, 2012–22** 1,000

What Mining and Geological Engineers Do

Mining and geological engineers design mines for the safe and efficient removal of minerals such as coal and metals for manufacturing and utilities.

Duties. Mining and geological engineers typically do the following:

- Design open-pit and underground mines
- Supervise the construction of mine shafts and tunnels in underground operations
- Devise methods for transporting minerals to processing plants
- Prepare technical reports for miners, engineers, and managers
- Monitor production to assess the effectiveness of operations
- Provide solutions to problems related to land reclamation, water and air pollution, and sustainability
- Ensure that mines are operated in safe and environmentally sound ways

Geological engineers use their knowledge of geology to search for mineral deposits and evaluate possible sites. Once a site is identified, they plan how the metals or minerals will be extracted in efficient and environmentally sound ways.

Mining engineers often specialize in one particular mineral or metal, such as coal or gold. They typically design and develop mines and determine the best way to extract metal or minerals to get the most out of deposits.

Some mining engineers work with geologists and metallurgical engineers to find and evaluate new ore deposits. Other mining engineers develop new equipment or direct mineral-processing operations to separate minerals from dirt, rock, and other materials.

Mining safety engineers use their knowledge of mine design and best practices to ensure workers' safety and to ensure compliance

Mining and geological engineers often work outdoors to collect samples and take measurements.

with state and federal safety regulations. They inspect mines' walls and roofs, monitor the air quality, and examine mining equipment for possible hazards.

Engineers who hold a master's or a doctoral degree frequently teach engineering at colleges and universities. For more information, see the profile on postsecondary teachers.

Work Environment

Mining and geological engineers held about 7,900 jobs in 2012. They work at mining operations in remote locations. However, some work in sand-and-gravel operations that are located near large cities. More experienced engineers can get jobs in offices of mining firms or consulting companies, which are generally in large urban areas.

Median Annual Wages, May 2012

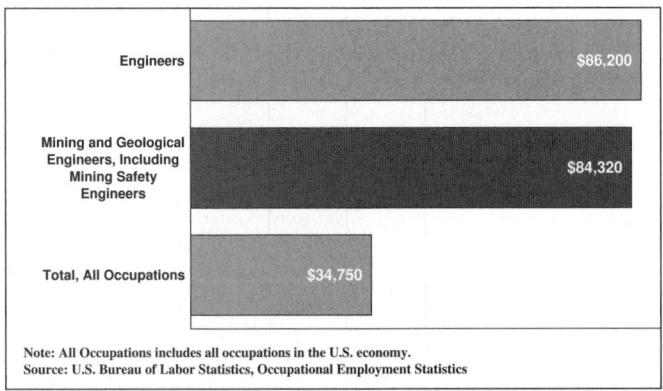

Engineers	$86,200
Mining and Geological Engineers, Including Mining Safety Engineers	$84,320
Total, All Occupations	$34,750

Note: All Occupations includes all occupations in the U.S. economy.
Source: U.S. Bureau of Labor Statistics, Occupational Employment Statistics

Percent Change in Employment, Projected 2012–2022

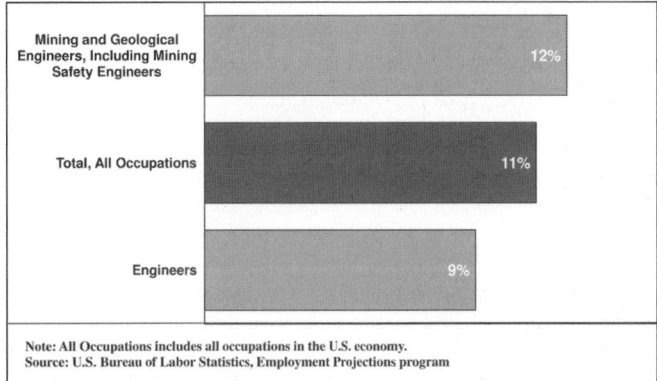

Mining and Geological Engineers, Including Mining Safety Engineers	12%
Total, All Occupations	11%
Engineers	9%

Note: All Occupations includes all occupations in the U.S. economy.
Source: U.S. Bureau of Labor Statistics, Employment Projections program

Employment Projections Data for Mining and Geological Engineers

Occupational title	SOC Code	Employment, 2012	Projected Employment, 2022	Change, 2012–2022	
				Percent	Numeric
Mining and geological engineers, including mining safety engineers	17-2151	7,900	8,900	12	1,000

Source: U.S. Bureau of Labor Statistics, Employment Projections Program

Note: Data are rounded. Go to Occupational Information Included in the OOH for a discussion of the data in this table.

The industries that employed the most mining and geological engineers in 2012 were as follows:

Architectural, engineering, and related services	30%
Metal ore mining	17
Coal mining	10
Management of companies and enterprises	8
Support activities for mining	6

Work Schedules. Most mining and geological engineers work full time. The remoteness of some of the locations gives rise to working variable schedules and longer-than-normal workweeks.

How to Become One

A bachelor's degree from an accredited engineering program is required, to become a mining or geological engineer, including a mining safety engineer. However, to work as a credentialed professional engineer requires licensure. Requirements for licensure vary by state but generally require passing two exams.

Education. High school students interested in entering mining engineering programs should take courses in mathematics and science in high school.

Relatively few schools offer mining engineering programs. Typical bachelor's degree programs in mining engineering include courses in geology, physics, thermodynamics, mine design and safety, and mathematics. Programs also include laboratory and field work, as well as traditional classroom study.

Programs in mining and geological engineering are accredited by ABET. ABET accreditation is based on a program's faculty, curriculum, facilities, and other factors.

Master's degree programs in mining and geological engineering typically are 2-year programs and include coursework in specialized subjects, such as mineral resource development and mining regulations. Some programs require a written thesis for graduation.

Important Qualities

Analytical skills. Mining and geological engineers must consider the wider implications of their immediate work to plan for environmental reclamation. They must be able to consider several competing, but interconnected, issues at the same time.

Decision-making skills. These engineers perform work that can affect not only companies' profits but also miners' lives. The ability to anticipate problems and deal with them immediately is crucial.

Logical-thinking skills. In planning mines' operations, mineral processing, and environmental reclamation, these engineers have to be able to put work plans into a coherent, logical sequence.

Math skills. Mining and geological engineers use the principals of calculus, trigonometry, and other advanced topics in math for analysis, design, and troubleshooting in their work.

Problem-solving skills. Mining and geological engineers must explore for mines, plan the operations of mines, work out the mineral processing, and design environmental reclamation projects. These are all complex projects requiring an ability to identify and work toward goals, while solving problems along the way.

Writing skills. Mining and geological engineers must prepare reports and instructions for other workers. Therefore, they must be able to write clearly so that others can easily understand their thoughts and plans.

Licenses, Certifications, and Registrations. In every state, engineers who offer their services directly to the public must be licensed in that state. The National Council of Examiners for Engineering and Surveying (NCEES) administers two exams for licensure for this occupation. The first covers the fundamentals of engineering (FE), the second the principles and practices of engineering (PPE). The FE exam can be taken upon graduation. Engineers who pass this exam are commonly called engineers in training (EITs) or engineer interns (EIs). After 4 years of relevant work experience, EITs and EIs can take the PPE exam.

Similar Occupations   This table shows a list of occupations with job duties that are similar to those of mining and geological engineers.

Occupations	Entry-level Education	2012 Pay	Projected Job Growth	Average Annual Openings
Architectural and Engineering Managers	Bachelor's degree	$124,870	7%	6,060
Civil Engineers	Bachelor's degree	$79,340	20%	12,010
Environmental Scientists and Specialists	Bachelor's degree	$63,570	15%	3,970
Geological and Petroleum Technicians	Associate's degree	$52,700	15%	810
Geoscientists	Bachelor's degree	$90,890	16%	1,730
Hydrologists	Master's degree	$75,530	9%	290
Mechanical Engineers	Bachelor's degree	$80,580	4%	9,970
Natural Sciences Managers	Bachelor's degree	$115,730	6%	1,370
Petroleum Engineers	Bachelor's degree	$130,280	26%	1,960
Sales Engineers	Bachelor's degree	$91,830	9%	1,740

Licensed engineers are called professional engineers (PEs). Generally, licensure requires the following:

- A degree from an ABET-accredited engineering program
- 4 years of relevant work experience
- Successful completion of a state examination

In several states, engineers must take continuing education credits to keep their licenses. Most states recognize licenses from other states, provided that licensure requirements in the other states meet or exceed the first state's own requirements.

Advancement. Beginning engineering graduates usually work under the supervision of experienced engineers. In large companies, engineers starting out also may receive formal classroom or seminar-type training. As new engineers gain knowledge and experience, they are assigned more difficult projects with greater independence to develop designs, solve problems, and make decisions.

Engineers may advance to become technical specialists or to supervise a staff or team of engineers and technicians. Some eventually become engineering managers or enter other managerial or sales jobs. In sales, an engineering background enables them to discuss a product's technical aspects and to assist in product planning, installation, and use. For more information, see the job profile on sales engineers.

Pay

The median annual wage for mining and geological engineers, including mining safety engineers, was $84,320 in May 2012. The median wage is the wage at which half the workers in an occupation earned more than that amount and half earned less. The lowest 10 percent earned less than $49,680, and the top 10 percent earned more than $140,130.

In May 2012, the median annual wages for mining and geological engineers in the top five industries in which these engineers worked were as follows:

Management of companies and enterprises	$92,030
Support activities for mining	84,030
Metal ore mining	83,280
Coal mining	80,980
Architectural, engineering, and related services	79,580

Job Outlook

Employment of mining and geological engineers is projected to grow 12 percent from 2012 to 2022, about as fast as the average for all occupations.

Employment growth for mining and geological engineers will be driven by demand for mining operations. Some growth may come from recent changes in federal policy concerning access to coal deposits on federal lands in some western states. Because this coal is low in sulfur content, it is in demand globally. The feasibility studies and proposals needed to gain access to these and other mineral deposits will spur demand for these engineers.

Additionally, other countries may restrict exports of certain minerals known as "rare earths," which are used in the manufacture of many high-tech products. This should help spur exploration and further development of mines in the United States that yield these minerals.

Employment growth also will be driven by demand for engineering services. As companies look for ways to cut costs, they are expected to contract more engineering services with these firms, rather than employ engineers directly.

Job Prospects. Job prospects should be favorable for those entering the occupation, because many of these engineers will be reaching retirement age by 2022. In addition, the education and licensing required to enter this occupation will limit the supply of engineers competing for these positions. Lastly, mining and extraction companies are expected to increasingly seek the skills of mining safety engineers. Engineers who specialize in this area should enjoy favorable prospects.

O*NET

➤ Mining and Geological Engineers, Including Mining Safety Engineers (17-2151.00)

Contacts for More Information

For more information about mining and geological engineers, visit
➤ Society for Mining, Metallurgy, and Exploration (www.smenet.org/index.cfm)

For information about general engineering education and career resources, visit
➤ American Society for Engineering Education (www.asee.org/)
➤ Technology Student Association (www.tsaweb.org/)

For more information about licensure as a mining or geological engineer, visit
➤ National Council of Examiners for Engineering and Surveying (http://ncees.org/)
➤ National Society of Professional Engineers (www.nspe.org/index.html)

For information about accredited engineering programs, visit
➤ ABET (www.abet.org/)

Nuclear Engineers

2012 Median Pay	$104,270 per year $50.13 per hour
Entry-Level Education	Bachelor's degree
Work Experience in a Related Occupation	None
On-the-Job Training	None
Number of Jobs 2012	20,400
Job Outlook, 2012–22	9% (As fast as average)
Employment Change, 2012–22	1,900

A principal job of nuclear engineers is to design and operate nuclear power plants.

Median Annual Wages, May 2012

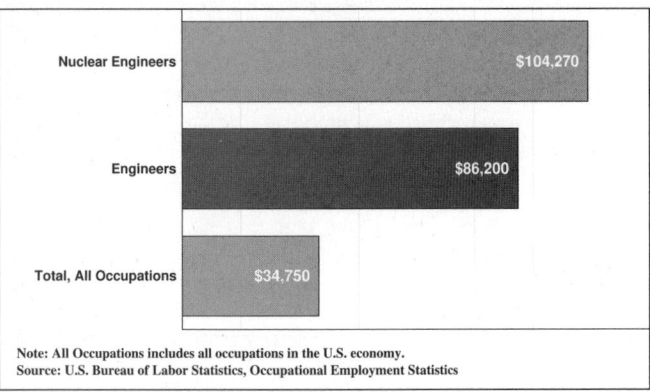

Note: All Occupations includes all occupations in the U.S. economy.
Source: U.S. Bureau of Labor Statistics, Occupational Employment Statistics

Percent Change in Employment, Projected 2012–2022

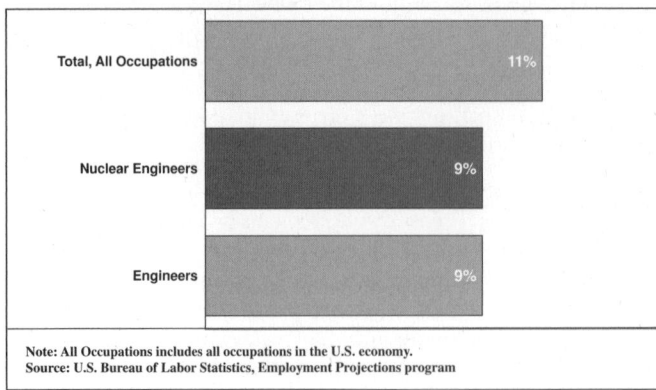

Note: All Occupations includes all occupations in the U.S. economy.
Source: U.S. Bureau of Labor Statistics, Employment Projections program

What Nuclear Engineers Do

Nuclear engineers research and develop the processes, instruments, and systems used to derive benefits from nuclear energy and radiation. Many of these engineers find industrial and medical uses for radioactive materials–for example, in equipment used in medical diagnosis and treatment. Many others specialize in the development of nuclear power sources for ships or spacecraft.

Duties. Nuclear engineers typically do the following:

- Design or develop nuclear equipment, such as reactor cores, radiation shielding, and associated instrumentation

- Direct operating or maintenance activities of operational nuclear powerplants to ensure that they meet safety standards

- Write operational instructions to be used in nuclear plant operation or in handling and disposing of nuclear waste

- Monitor nuclear facility operations to identify any design, construction, or operation practices that violate safety regulations and laws

- Perform experiments to test whether methods of using nuclear material, reclaiming nuclear fuel, or disposing of nuclear waste are acceptable

- Take corrective actions or order plant shutdowns in emergencies

- Examine nuclear accidents and gather data that can be used to design preventive measures

Nuclear engineers are also at the forefront of developing uses of nuclear material for medical imaging devices, such as positron emission tomography (PET) scanners. They also may develop or design cyclotrons, which produce a high-energy beam that the healthcare industry uses to treat cancerous tumors.

Work Environment

Nuclear engineers held about 20,400 jobs in 2012. They typically work in offices. However, their work setting varies with the industry in which they are employed. For example, those employed in power generation and supply work in powerplants. Many also work in National Laboratories operated by the Department of Energy, and in consulting firms.

The industries that employed the most nuclear engineers in 2012 were as follows:

Electric power generation, transmission and distribution 32%
Federal government, excluding postal service 14
Scientific research and development services 11
Architectural, engineering, and related services 9

Nuclear engineers work with others, including mechanical engineers and electrical engineers, and they must be able to incorporate systems designed by these engineers into their own designs.

Work Schedules. The majority of nuclear engineers work full time, and some work overtime. These schedules may vary according to the industries in which they work.

How to Become One

Nuclear engineers must have a bachelor's degree in nuclear engineering. Employers also value experience, so cooperative-education engineering programs at universities are also valuable.

Education. Entry-level nuclear engineering jobs require a bachelor's degree. Students interested in studying nuclear engineering should take high school courses in mathematics, such as algebra, trigonometry, and calculus; and science, such as biology, chemistry, and physics.

Bachelor's degree programs typically are 4-year programs and include classroom, laboratory, and field studies in areas that include mathematics and engineering principles. Most colleges and universities offer cooperative-education programs in which students gain experience while completing their education.

Some universities offer 5-year programs leading to both a bachelor's and a master's degree. A graduate degree allows an engineer to work as an instructor at a university or engage in research and development. Some 5-year or even 6-year cooperative-education plans combine classroom study with work, permitting students to gain experience and to finance part of their education.

Programs in nuclear engineering are accredited by ABET.

Important Qualities

Analytical skills. Nuclear engineers must be able to identify design elements to help build facilities and equipment that produce material needed by various industries.

Communication skills. Nuclear engineers' work depends heavily on their ability to work with other professional engineers and technicians. They need to be able to communicate effectively, both in writing and face to face, with technicians and engineers from other fields.

Detail oriented. Nuclear engineers supervise the operation of nuclear facilities. They must pay close attention to what is happening at all times, and ensure that operations comply with all regulations and laws pertaining to the safety of workers and the environment.

Logical-thinking skills. Nuclear engineers design complex systems. Therefore, they must be able to order information logically and clearly so that others can follow their written information and instructions.

Employment Projections Data for Nuclear Engineers

Occupational title	SOC Code	Employment, 2012	Projected Employment, 2022	Change, 2012–2022	
				Percent	Numeric
Nuclear engineers	17-2161	20,400	22,300	9	1,900

Source: U.S. Bureau of Labor Statistics, Employment Projections Program

Note: **Data are rounded. Go to Occupational Information Included in the OOH** *for a discussion of the data in this table.*

Math skills. Nuclear engineers use the principles of calculus, trigonometry, and other advanced topics in math for analysis, design, and troubleshooting in their work.

Problem-solving skills. Because of the potential hazard posed by nuclear materials and by accidents at facilities, nuclear engineers must be able to anticipate problems before they occur and suggest remedies.

Training. A newly hired nuclear engineer at a nuclear power plant must usually complete as many as 8 months of training on site, in such areas as safety procedures, safety practices, and regulations, before being allowed to work independently. In addition, these engineers must undergo continuous training every year to keep their knowledge, skills, and abilities current with laws, regulations, and safety procedures.

Licenses, Certifications, and Registrations. Nuclear engineers who work for nuclear powerplants are not required to be licensed. However, they are eligible to seek licensure as professional engineers. Those who become licensed carry the designation of professional engineer (PE). Licensure is recommended and generally requires the following:

- A degree from an engineering program accredited by ABET
- A passing score on the Fundamentals of Engineering (FE) exam
- Relevant work experience
- A passing score on the Professional Engineering (PE) exam

The initial Fundamentals of Engineering (FE) exam can be taken right after graduating. Engineers who pass this exam commonly are called engineers in training (EITs) or engineer interns (EIs). After gaining work experience, EITs or EIs can take the second exam, called the Principles and Practice of Engineering exam.

Several states require engineers to take continuing education to keep their license. Most states recognize licenses from other states, as long as the other state's licensing requirements meet or exceed their own licensing requirements.

Nuclear engineers can obtain the Senior Reactor Operator Class certification, which is granted after an intensive, 2-year, site-specific program. The credential, granted by the Nuclear Regulatory Commission, proves that the engineer can operate a nuclear power plant within federal government requirements.

Advancement. Beginning engineering graduates usually work under the supervision of experienced engineers. In large companies, new engineers may receive formal training in classrooms or seminars. As beginning engineers gain knowledge and experience, they move to more difficult projects with greater independence to develop designs, solve problems, and make decisions.

Eventually, nuclear engineers may advance to become technical specialists or to supervise a team of engineers and technicians. Some may become engineering managers or move into sales work. For more information, see the profiles on architectural and engineering managers and sales engineers.

Nuclear engineers can also become medical physicists. A master's degree in medical or health physics or a related field is necessary to enter this field.

Pay

The median annual wage for nuclear engineers was $104,270 in May 2012. The median wage is the wage at which half the workers in an occupation earned more than that amount and half earned less. The lowest 10 percent earned less than $68,940, and the top 10 percent earned more than $149,940.

In May 2012, the median annual wages for nuclear engineers in the top four industries employing these engineers were as follows:

Scientific research and development services	$112,560
Architectural, engineering, and related services	108,340
Electric power generation, transmission and distribution	99,050
Federal government, excluding postal service	90,310

Union Membership. Compared with workers in all occupations, nuclear engineers had a higher percentage of workers who belonged to a union in 2012.

Job Outlook

Employment of nuclear engineers is projected to grow 9 percent from 2012 to 2022, about as fast as the average for all occupations. Employment trends in power generation may be favorable because of the likely need to upgrade safety systems at powerplants. These

Similar Occupations   This table shows a list of occupations with job duties that are similar to those of nuclear engineers.

Occupations	Entry-level Education	2012 Pay	Projected Job Growth	Average Annual Openings
Civil Engineers	Bachelor's degree	$79,340	20%	12,010
Electrical and Electronics Engineering Technicians	Associate's degree	$57,850	0%	3,040
Electrical and Electronics Engineers	Bachelor's degree	$89,701	4%	7,940
Health and Safety Engineers	Bachelor's degree	$76,830	11%	970
Mechanical Engineers	Bachelor's degree	$80,580	4%	9,970
Physicists and Astronomers	Doctoral or professional degree	$105,722	10%	810

engineers also will find work in creating designs for powerplants to be built abroad and in the growing field of nuclear medicine.

Utilities that own or build nuclear powerplants have traditionally employed the greatest number of nuclear engineers. Recent events might cause the Nuclear Regulatory Commission (NRC) to issue guidelines for upgrading safety protocols at nuclear utility plants. Those upgrades may spur employment. However, the upgrades also could raise the cost of building new nuclear powerplants, and that might limit new plant construction. Nuclear engineers will be in demand to design and help build nuclear power plants outside the United States.

Developments in nuclear medicine and diagnostic imaging will also drive demand for nuclear engineers. These engineers will be needed to develop new methods of radiologic imaging. In addition, these engineers will be called upon to help build and operate cyclotrons, which produce a high-energy beam that the healthcare industry uses to treat cancerous tumors.

Job Prospects. Job prospects are expected to be relatively favorable in this occupation because many older engineers will retire over the next decade. Training in developing fields, such as nuclear medicine, should help to improve a person's chances of finding a job.

O*NET

➤ Nuclear Engineers (17-2161.00)

Contacts for More Information

For more information about general engineering education and career resources, visit

➤ American Society for Engineering Education (www.asee.org/)
➤ Technology Student Association (www.tsaweb.org/)

For more information about licensure as a nuclear engineer, visit

➤ National Council of Examiners for Engineering and Surveying (http://ncees.org/)
➤ National Society of Professional Engineers (www.nspe.org/index.html)

For more information about accredited engineering programs, visit

➤ ABET (www.abet.org/)

For more information about federal government education requirements for nuclear engineer positions, visit

➤ U.S. Office of Personnel Management (www.opm.gov/policy-data-oversight/classification-qualifications/general-schedule-qualification-standards/0800/nuclear-engineering-series-0840/)

Petroleum Engineers

- **2012 Median Pay** .... $130,280 per year
  $62.64 per hour
- **Entry-Level Education** ....Bachelor's degree
- **Work Experience in a Related Occupation**............... None
- **On-the-Job Training** .... None
- **Number of Jobs 2012** 38,500
- **Job Outlook, 2012–22** .... 26% (Much faster than average)
- **Employment Change, 2012–22** 9,800

What Petroleum Engineers Do

Petroleum engineers design and develop methods for extracting oil and gas from deposits below Earth's surface. Petroleum engineers also find new ways to extract oil and gas from older wells.

Duties. Petroleum engineers typically do the following:

- Design equipment to extract oil and gas in the most profitable way
- Develop ways to inject water, chemicals, gases, or steam into an oil reserve to force out more of the oil
- Develop plans to drill in oil and gas fields, and then to recover the oil and gas
- Make sure that wells, well testing, and well surveys are completed and evaluated
- Use computer-controlled drilling or fracturing to connect a larger area of an oil and gas deposit to a single well
- Make sure that oil field equipment is installed, operated, and maintained properly

Oil and gas deposits, or reservoirs, are located deep in rock formations underground. These reservoirs can only be accessed by drilling wells, either on land or at sea from offshore oil rigs.

Once oil and gas are discovered, petroleum engineers work with geologists and other specialists to understand the geologic formation of the rock containing the reservoir. They then determine drilling methods, design and implement the drilling equipment, and monitor operations.

The best techniques currently being used recover only a portion of the oil and gas in a reservoir, so petroleum engineers also research and develop new ways to recover the oil and gas. This helps to lower the cost of drilling and production.

The following are examples of types of petroleum engineers:

Completions engineers decide the optimal way to finish building a well so that the oil or gas will flow up from underground. They oversee well-completions work, which might involve the use of tubing, hydraulic fracturing, or pressure-control techniques.

Drilling engineers determine the best way to drill an oil or gas well, taking into account a number of factors, including cost. They also ensure that the drilling process is safe, efficient, and minimally disruptive to the environment.

Production engineers take over after a well is completed. They typically monitor the well's oil and gas production. If a well is not producing as much as it was expected to, production engineers figure out ways to increase the amount being extracted.

Reservoir engineers estimate how much oil or gas can be recovered from underground deposits, known as reservoirs. They study

Petroleum engineers often travel to the oil rigs and pumping stations to oversee operations first-hand.

Median Annual Wages, May 2012

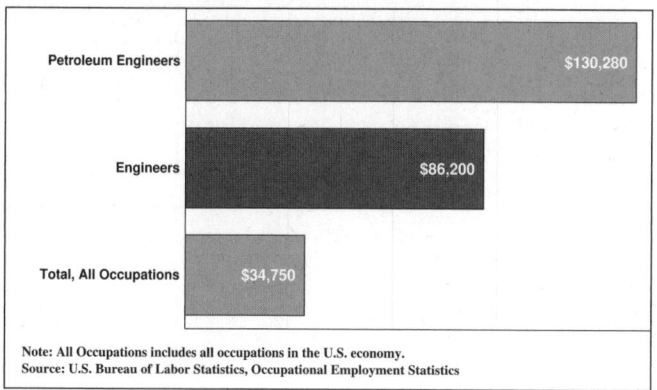

Petroleum Engineers $130,280

Engineers $86,200

Total, All Occupations $34,750

Note: All Occupations includes all occupations in the U.S. economy.
Source: U.S. Bureau of Labor Statistics, Occupational Employment Statistics

Percent Change in Employment, Projected 2012–2022

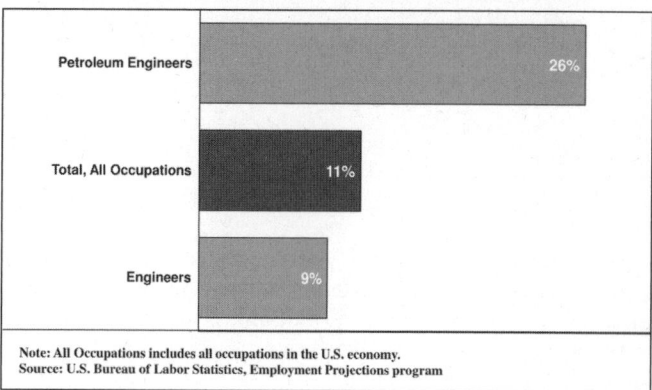

Petroleum Engineers   26%

Total, All Occupations   11%

Engineers   9%

Note: All Occupations includes all occupations in the U.S. economy.
Source: U.S. Bureau of Labor Statistics, Employment Projections program

a reservoir's characteristics and determine which methods will get the most oil or gas out of the reservoir. They also monitor operations to ensure that the optimal levels of these resources are being recovered.

Work Environment

Petroleum engineers held about 38,500 jobs in 2012.

Petroleum engineers generally work in offices or in research laboratories. However, they also must spend time at drilling sites, often for long periods of time. This means they must travel, sometimes with little notice.

The industries that employed the most petroleum engineers in 2012 were as follows:

Oil and gas extraction 53%
Support activities for mining 14
Architectural, engineering, and related services 7
Petroleum and coal products manufacturing 6
Management of companies and enterprises 6

Petroleum engineers work around the world; in fact, the best employment opportunities may include some work in other countries. Petroleum engineers also must be able to work with people from a wide variety of backgrounds, including other oil and gas workers who will carry out the engineers' drilling plans.

Work Schedules. Petroleum engineers typically work regular full-time schedules. However, some work as many as 50 or 60 hours per week when traveling to and from drilling sites to help in their operation or respond to problems when they arise. When they are at a drilling site, it is common for these engineers to work in a rotation: on duty for 84 hours and then off duty for 84 hours.

How to Become One

Petroleum engineers must have a bachelor's degree in engineering, preferably in petroleum engineering. However, a bachelor's degree in mechanical or chemical engineering may also suffice. Employers also value work experience, so cooperative education programs, in which students earn academic credit for structured job experience, are valuable as well.

Education. Students interested in studying petroleum engineering will benefit from taking high school courses in math, such as algebra, trigonometry, and calculus; and in science, such as biology, chemistry, and physics.

Entry-level petroleum engineering jobs require a bachelor's degree. Bachelor's degree programs typically take 4 years and include classroom, laboratory, and field studies in areas such as engineering principles, geology, and thermodynamics. Most col-

leges and universities offer cooperative programs in which students gain practical experience while completing their education.

Some colleges and universities offer a 5-year program in chemical or mechanical engineering that leads to both a bachelor's degree and a master's degree. Some employers may prefer applicants who have earned a graduate degree. A graduate degree also allows an engineer to work as an instructor at some universities or in research and development.

ABET accredits programs in petroleum engineering.

Important Qualities

Analytical skills. Petroleum engineers must be able to assess complex plans for drilling and anticipate possible flaws or complications before the company commits money and people to a project.

Creativity. Petroleum engineers must come up with new ways to extract oil and gas because each new drill site presents challenges. They must know how to ask the necessary questions to find possible deposits of oil and gas.

Math skills. Petroleum engineers use the principals of calculus and other advanced topics in math for analysis, design, and troubleshooting in their work.

Problem-solving skills. Identifying problems in drilling plans is critical for petroleum engineers because drilling operations can be costly. They must be careful not to overlook any potential issues and quickly address those that do occur.

Licenses, Certifications, and Registrations. All 50 states and the District of Columbia require petroleum engineers to have a license if they offer their services directly to the public. Licensed engineers are called professional engineers (PEs). Licensure generally has the following requirements:

• A degree from an ABET-accredited engineering program

• A passing score on the Fundamentals of Engineering (FE) exam

• A minimum of 4 years of relevant work experience

• A passing score on the Professional Engineering (PE) exam

The initial Fundamentals of Engineering (FE) exam can be taken after earning a bachelor's degree. Engineers who pass this exam commonly are called engineers in training (EITs) or engineer interns (EIs). After gaining suitable work experience, EITs and EIs can take the second exam, called the Principles and Practice of Engineering.

Several states require continuing education for engineers to keep their license. Most states recognize licensure from other states if the licensing state's requirements meet or exceed their own licensure requirements.

Employment Projections Data for Petroleum Engineers

Occupational title	SOC Code	Employment, 2012	Projected Employment, 2022	Change, 2012–2022	
				Percent	Numeric
Petroleum engineers..	17-2171	38,500	48,400	26	9,800

Source: U.S. Bureau of Labor Statistics, Employment Projections Program

Note: Data are rounded. Go to **Occupational Information Included in the OOH** *for a discussion of the data in this table.*

The Society of Petroleum Engineers offers certification. To be certified, petroleum engineers must be members of the Society, pass an exam, and meet other qualifications.

Advancement. Entry-level engineers usually work under the supervision of experienced engineers. In large companies, new engineers also may receive formal training. As beginning engineers gain knowledge and experience, they move to more difficult projects with greater independence to develop designs, solve problems, and make decisions.

Eventually, petroleum engineers may advance to supervise a team of engineers and technicians. Some become engineering managers or move into other managerial positions. For more information, see the profile on architectural and engineering managers.

Petroleum engineers who go into sales use their engineering background to discuss a product's technical aspects with potential buyers and help in product planning, installation, and use. For more information, see the profile on sales engineers.

Pay

The median annual wage for petroleum engineers was $130,280 in May 2012. The median wage is the wage at which half the workers in an occupation earned more than that amount and half earned less. The lowest 10 percent earned less than $75,030, and the top 10 percent earned more than $187,200.

In May 2012, the median annual wages for petroleum engineers in the top five industries employing these engineers were as follows:

Oil and gas extraction......................................	$144,810
Management of companies and enterprises.......................	143,240
Architectural, engineering, and related services.................	121,790
Petroleum and coal products manufacturing.....................	120,440
Support activities for mining	101,800

The Society of Petroleum Engineers reports that the median base pay among its members in 2012 varied by type of petroleum engineer:

Engineers – Drilling.......................................	$212,123
Engineers – Completions	197,739
Engineers – Production..................................	194,481
Engineers – Reservoir	187,780

Job Outlook

Employment of petroleum engineers is projected to grow 26 percent from 2012 to 2022, much faster than the average for all occupations. Oil prices will be a major determinant of employment growth, as higher prices lead to increasing complexity of oil companies' operations. Additionally, job prospects should be highly favorable because many engineers are expected to retire.

Because oil and gas extraction is the largest industry employing petroleum engineers, any effects of rising oil prices will likely be noticed here first. Higher prices can cause oil and gas companies to drill in deeper waters and in less hospitable places and return to existing wells to try new extraction methods. This means that oil drilling operations will likely become more complex and will require more engineers to work on each drilling operation. In addition, more petroleum engineers will be needed to help companies comply with new regulations for drilling in deep water.

Demand for petroleum engineers in support activities for mining should also be strong, as oil and gas companies find it convenient and cost-effective to seek their services on an as-needed basis. This is partly because petroleum engineering is one of the higher paying occupations in the economy. Experienced petroleum engineers also may start their own companies and provide services to larger oil and gas companies.

Job Prospects. Job prospects are expected to be highly favorable because of projected growth and because many petroleum engineers may retire or leave the occupation for other reasons over the next decade.

O*NET

➤ Petroleum Engineers (17-2171.00)

Similar Occupations   This table shows a list of occupations with job duties that are similar to those of petroleum engineers.

Occupations	Entry-level Education	2012 Pay	Projected Job Growth	Average Annual Openings
Aerospace Engineers	Bachelor's degree	$103,720	7%	2,540
Architectural and Engineering Managers	Bachelor's degree	$124,870	7%	6,060
Chemists and Materials Scientists	Bachelor's degree	$73,247	6%	3,040
Geoscientists	Bachelor's degree	$90,890	16%	1,730
Industrial Engineering Technicians	Associate's degree	$50,980	-3%	1,410
Industrial Engineers	Bachelor's degree	$78,860	5%	7,540
Materials Engineers	Bachelor's degree	$85,150	1%	750
Mechanical Engineering Technicians	Associate's degree	$51,980	5%	1,210
Mechanical Engineers	Bachelor's degree	$80,580	4%	9,970
Sales Engineers	Bachelor's degree	$91,830	9%	1,740

Contacts for More Information

For information about general engineering education and career resources, visit

➤ American Society for Engineering Education (www.asee.org/)
➤ Technology Student Association (www.tsaweb.org/)

For information about the Professional Engineer license, visit

➤ National Council of Examiners for Engineering and Surveying (http://ncees.org/)
➤ National Society of Professional Engineers (www.nspe.org/index.html)

For information about accredited engineering programs, visit

➤ ABET (www.abet.org/)

For information about certification, visit

➤ Society of Petroleum Engineers (www.spe.org/index.php)

Surveying and Mapping Technicians

- **2012 Median Pay** .... $39,670 per year
  $19.07 per hour
- **Entry-Level Education** ... High school diploma or equivalent
- **Work Experience in a Related Occupation** .... None
- **On-the-Job Training** .... Moderate-term on-the-job training
- **Number of Jobs 2012** 54,000
- **Job Outlook, 2012–22** .... 14% (As fast as average)
- **Employment Change, 2012–22** 7,300

What Surveying and Mapping Technicians Do

Surveying and mapping technicians assist surveyors, cartographers, and photogrammetrists. Together, they collect data and make maps of Earth's surface. Surveying technicians visit sites to take measurements of the land. Mapping technicians use geographic data to create maps.

Duties. Surveying technicians typically do the following:

- Visit sites to record survey measurements and other descriptive data
- Operate surveying instruments, such as electronic distance-measuring equipment, to collect data on a location
- Set out stakes and marks to conduct the survey, and then retrieve them
- Search for previous survey points, such as old stone markers
- Enter the data from surveying instruments into computers, either in the field or in an office

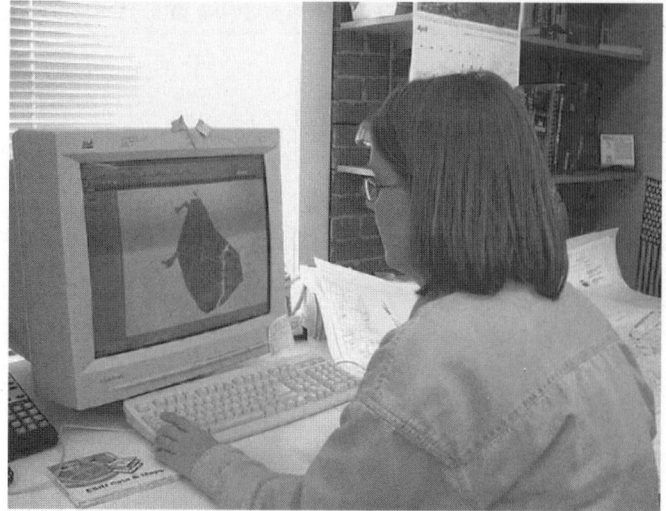

Surveying and mapping technicians do field work but also represent measurements in graphic form.

Surveying technicians help surveyors in the field on teams, known as survey parties. A typical survey party has a party chief and one or more surveying technicians and assistants. The party chief, either a surveyor or a senior surveying technician, leads day-to-day work activities. After data are collected by the survey party, surveying technicians help to process the data by entering the data into computers.

Mapping technicians typically do the following:

- Select needed information from relevant databases to create maps
- Produce maps showing boundaries, water locations, elevation, and other features of the terrain
- Update maps to ensure accuracy
- Assist photogrammetrists by laying out aerial photographs in sequence to identify areas not captured by aerial photography

Mapping technicians help cartographers and photogrammetrists produce and upgrade maps. They do this work on computers, combining data from different sources.

Geographic information systems (GIS) technicians use geographic information system (GIS) technology to assemble, integrate, and display data about a particular location in a digital format. They also use GIS technology to compile information from a variety of sources. GIS technicians also maintain and update databases for GIS devices.

Median Annual Wages, May 2012

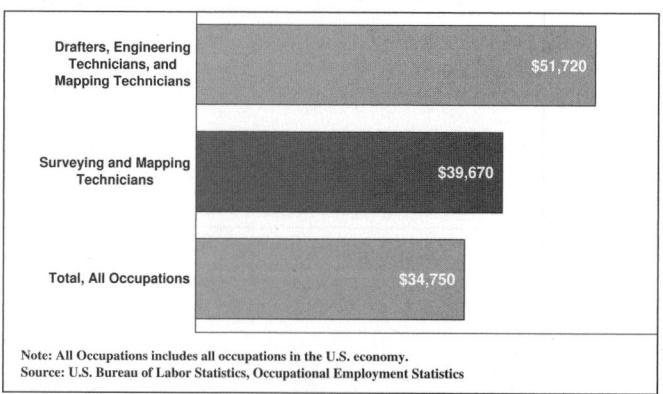

Drafters, Engineering Technicians, and Mapping Technicians	$51,720
Surveying and Mapping Technicians	$39,670
Total, All Occupations	$34,750

Note: All Occupations includes all occupations in the U.S. economy.
Source: U.S. Bureau of Labor Statistics, Occupational Employment Statistics

Percent Change in Employment, Projected 2012–2022

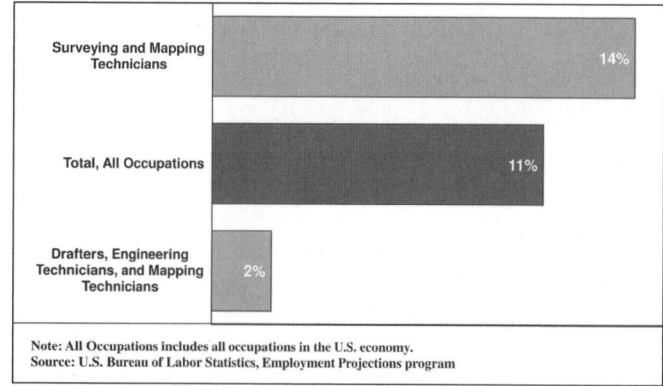

Surveying and Mapping Technicians	14%
Total, All Occupations	11%
Drafters, Engineering Technicians, and Mapping Technicians	2%

Note: All Occupations includes all occupations in the U.S. economy.
Source: U.S. Bureau of Labor Statistics, Employment Projections program

Employment Projections Data for Surveying and Mapping Technicians

Occupational title	SOC Code	Employment, 2012	Projected Employment, 2022	Change, 2012–2022	
				Percent	Numeric
Surveying and mapping technicians	17-3031	54,000	61,300	14	7,300

Source: U.S. Bureau of Labor Statistics, Employment Projections Program

Note: Data are rounded. Go to Occupational Information Included in the OOH *for a discussion of the data in this table.*

Work Environment

Surveying and mapping technicians held about 54,000 jobs in 2012. Most surveying and mapping technicians work for firms that provide engineering, surveying, and mapping services on a contract basis. State and local governments also employ these workers in highway and planning departments.

Surveying technicians work outside extensively and can be exposed to all types of weather. They often stand for long periods, walk considerable distances, and may have to climb hills with heavy packs of instruments and other equipment. Traveling is sometimes part of the job, and surveying technicians may commute long distances, stay away from home overnight, or temporarily relocate near a survey site.

Mapping technicians work primarily on computers in office environments. However, mapping technicians must sometimes conduct research by using resources such as survey maps and legal documents to verify property lines and to obtain information needed for mapping. This task may require traveling to storage sites housing these legal documents, such as county courthouses or lawyers' offices.

About 11 percent of surveying and mapping technicians were self-employed in 2012.

Work Schedules. Surveying and mapping technicians typically work full time but may have longer hours during the summer, when weather and light conditions are most suitable for fieldwork. Construction-related work may be limited during times of harsh weather.

Mapping technicians who develop and maintain geographic information systems (GIS) databases generally work normal business hours.

How to Become One

Surveying technicians usually need only a high school diploma. However, mapping technicians often need formal education after high school to study advances in technology such as geographic information systems (GIS).

Education. Surveying technicians generally need a high school diploma, but some have postsecondary training in survey technology. Postsecondary training is more common among mapping technicians. An associate's degree or bachelor's degree in a relevant field, such as geomatics, is beneficial for these workers.

High school students interested in working as a surveying or mapping technician should take courses in algebra, geometry, trigonometry, drafting, mechanical drawing, and computer science. Knowledge of these subjects will help in finding a job and in advancing.

Important Qualities

Concentration. Surveying and mapping technicians need to operate specialized equipment. They must be precise and accurate in their work.

Decision-making skills. As assistants to surveyors and cartographers, surveying technicians must be able to exercise some independent judgment in the field because they may be working away from team members and need to meet tight deadlines.

Listening skills. Surveying technicians work outdoors and must communicate with party chiefs and other team members across distances. Following spoken instructions from the party chief is crucial for saving time and preventing errors.

Physical stamina. Surveying technicians usually work outdoors, often in rugged terrain. Physical fitness is necessary to carry equipment and to stand most of the day.

Problem-solving skills. Surveying and mapping technicians must be able to identify and fix problems with their equipment. Also, because party chiefs rely on them, they must note potential problems with the day's work plan.

Training. Surveying technicians learn their job duties under the supervision of a surveyor or a surveying party chief. Initially, surveying technicians handle simple tasks, such as placing markers on land and entering data into computers. With experience, they help to decide where and how to measure the land. Eventually, technicians can get an apprenticeship or an associate's degree so that they can develop skills based on math, drafting, and technical drawing.

Licenses, Certifications, and Registrations. The growing need to make sure that data are useful to other professionals has caused certification to become more common. The American Society for Photogrammetry and Remote Sensing (ASPRS) offers certification for photogrammetric technologists, remote-sensing technologists, and geographic information system/land information system (GIS/LIS) technologists. The National Society of Professional Surveyors offers the Certified Survey Technician credential.

The GIS Certification Institute offers a certification program for people who wish to concentrate on database management of surveying and mapping data.

Advancement. With experience and formal training in surveying, surveying technicians may advance to senior survey technician,

Similar Occupations   This table shows a list of occupations with job duties that are similar to those of surveying and mapping technicians.

Occupations	Entry-level Education	2012 Pay	Projected Job Growth	Average Annual Openings
Cartographers and Photogrammetrists	Bachelor's degree	$57,440	20%	490
Drafters	Associate's degree	$49,726	1%	3,220
Surveyors	Bachelor's degree	$56,230	10%	1,340

then to party chief. Depending on state licensing requirements, they can become licensed surveyors.

Pay

The median annual wage for surveying and mapping technicians was $39,670 in May 2012. The median wage is the wage at which half the workers in an occupation earned more than that amount and half earned less. The lowest 10 percent earned less than $24,180, and the top 10 percent earned more than $65,870.

Union Membership. Compared with workers in all occupations, surveying and mapping technicians had a higher percentage of workers who belonged to a union in 2012.

Job Outlook

Employment of surveying and mapping technicians is projected to grow 14 percent from 2012 to 2022, about as fast as the average for all occupations. Recent advancements in mapping technology have led to new uses for maps and a need for more of the data used to build maps. As a result, surveying and mapping technicians are likely to have more work.

The digital revolution in mapmaking has created a need to harmonize property maps made the traditional way by making maps based on data fed into a geographic information system (GIS). Owners of private property will need to hire surveyors and surveying technicians to gather data in the field.

Cities, towns, and counties are finding that the data gathered by surveying and mapping technicians are crucial in implementing systems integration, which is the process of putting onto one map all the information about wires, pipes, and other underground infrastructure. That way, a city, town, or county can upgrade the entire infrastructure under a street at the same time, and thus have all needed construction done as one project. This coordination of all such construction projects results in savings for the local government.

Job Prospects. Retirements of older workers may open up prospects for surveying and mapping technicians, although competition will remain keen. However, prospects will be best for those who are trained in geographic information systems (GIS).

O*NET

➤ Surveying and Mapping Technicians (17-3031.00)
➤ Surveying Technicians (17-3031.01)
➤ Mapping Technicians (17-3031.02)

Contacts for More Information

For more information on certification in GIS, visit
➤ GIS Certification Institute (www.gisci.org/)

For information about career opportunities and the surveying technician certification program, visit
➤ National Society of Professional Surveyors (www.acsm.net/)

For more information about photogrammetric technicians and geographic information system specialists, visit
➤ ASPRS: The Imaging & Geospatial Information Society (www.asprs.org/)

Surveyors

- **2012 Median Pay** .... $56,230 per year
  $27.04 per hour
- **Entry-Level Education** .... Bachelor's degree
- **Work Experience in a Related Occupation** .... Less than
  .... 5 years
- **On-the-Job Training** .... None
- **Number of Jobs 2012** 42,400
- **Job Outlook, 2012–22** .... 10% (As fast as average)
- **Employment Change, 2012–22** 4,400

What Surveyors Do

Surveyors make precise measurements to determine property boundaries. They provide data relevant to the shape and contour of Earth's surface for engineering, mapmaking, and construction projects.

Duties. Surveyors typically do the following:

- Measure distances and angles between points on, above, and below Earth's surface
- Travel to locations and select known reference points to determine the exact location of important features
- Establish stake sites and official land and water boundaries
- Research land records, survey records, and land titles
- Look for evidence of previous boundaries to determine where boundary lines are located
- Record the results of surveying and verify the accuracy of data
- Prepare plots, maps, and reports
- Present findings to clients, government agencies, and others

Land surveyors frequently take measurements in the field.

Median Annual Wages, May 2012

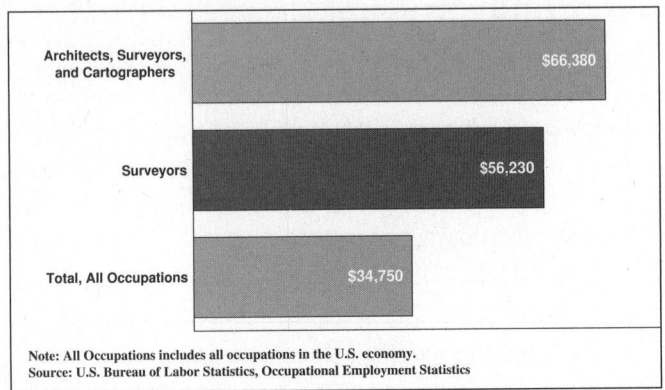

Architects, Surveyors, and Cartographers $66,380

Surveyors $56,230

Total, All Occupations $34,750

Note: All Occupations includes all occupations in the U.S. economy.
Source: U.S. Bureau of Labor Statistics, Occupational Employment Statistics

Percent Change in Employment, Projected 2012–2022

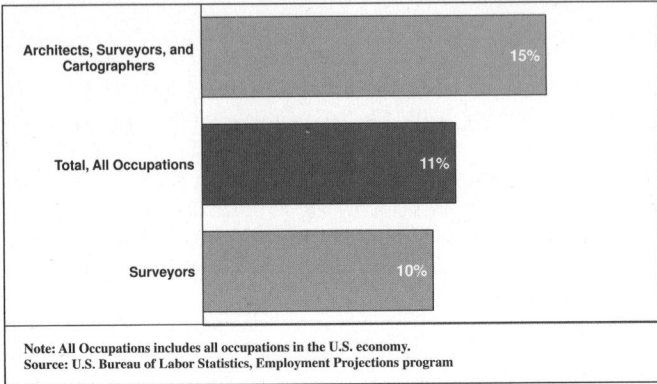

Architects, Surveyors, and Cartographers   15%

Total, All Occupations   11%

Surveyors   10%

Note: All Occupations includes all occupations in the U.S. economy.
Source: U.S. Bureau of Labor Statistics, Employment Projections program

- Take notes of land for deeds, leases, and other legal documents
- Provide expert testimony in court regarding survey work

Surveyors provide documentation of legal property lines and help determine the exact locations of real estate and construction projects. For example, when property, such as a house or commercial building, is bought or sold, it may need to be surveyed to prevent boundary disputes. During construction, surveyors determine the precise location of roads or buildings and proper depths for building foundations. The survey also shows changes to the property line and indicates potential restrictions on the property as far as what can be built on it.

In their work, surveyors use Global Positioning System (GPS), a system of satellites that locates reference points with a high degree of precision. Surveyors interpret and verify GPS results.

Surveyors also use Geographic Information System (GIS)–a technology that allows surveyors to present data visually as maps, reports, and charts. For example, a surveyor can overlay aerial or satellite images with GIS data, such as tree density in a given region, and create computerized maps. They then use the results to advise governments and businesses on where to plan homes, roads, and landfills.

Surveyors take measurements in the field with a crew, a group that typically consists of a licensed surveyor and trained survey technicians. The person in charge of the crew (called the party chief) may be either a surveyor or a senior surveying technician. The party chief leads day-to-day work activities.

Surveyors may be involved in settling boundary disputes. When property is sold or new construction takes place, such as the building of a fence, issues may arise due to lack of up-to-date records or the misinterpretation of available records. A surveyor would be called in to settle the dispute, and may even have to provide testimony in court if the involved parties do not come to an agreement.

Surveyors also work with civil engineers, landscape architects, and urban and regional planners to develop comprehensive design documents.

Some surveyors work in specialty fields to survey particular characteristics of Earth.

The following are examples of types of surveyors:

Geodetic surveyors use high-accuracy technology, including aerial and satellite observations, to measure large areas of Earth's surface.

Geophysical prospecting surveyors mark sites for subsurface exploration, usually to look for petroleum or natural gas fields.

Marine or hydrographic surveyors survey harbors, rivers, and other bodies of water to determine shorelines, the topography of the bottom, water depth, and other features.

Work Environment

Surveyors held about 42,400 jobs in 2012. Although most worked for private surveying or engineering firms, some worked for state and local governments.

The industries that employed the most surveyors in 2012 were as follows:

Architectural, engineering, and related services	69%
Local government, excluding education and hospitals	6
Heavy and civil engineering construction	5
State government, excluding education and hospitals	4
Mining, quarrying, and oil and gas extraction	3

Depending on the specific job duties, surveying involves both field work and office work. Field work involves working outdoors, standing for long periods, and often walking long distances. Surveyors sometimes climb hills with heavy packs of surveying instruments and other equipment. When working near hazards such as traffic, surveyors generally wear brightly colored vests or reflective material so they may be seen more easily. When working outside, they are exposed to all types of weather.

Traveling is often part of the job, and surveyors may commute long distances or stay at a project location for an extended period of time. Those who work on resource extraction projects may spend long periods away from home, as they must work in remote areas.

Work Schedules. Surveyors usually work full time. They may work more when construction activity is high.

How to Become One

Surveyors typically need a bachelor's degree. They must be licensed before they can certify legal documents and provide surveying services to the public.

Education. Surveyors typically need a bachelor's degree due to greater use of sophisticated technology and mathematics. Some colleges and universities offer bachelor's degree programs specifically designed to prepare students to become licensed surveyors. Many states require that a bachelor's degree come from a school accredited by ABET (formerly the Accreditation Board for Engineering and Technology). A bachelor's degree in a closely related field, such as civil engineering or forestry, is sometimes acceptable as well.

Many states require individuals who want to become licensed surveyors to have a bachelor's degree from a school accredited by ABET and about 2 years of work experience under a licensed surveyor. In other states, an associate's degree in surveying, coupled with several years of work experience under a licensed surveyor may be sufficient. The amount of work experience required varies by state. Most states also have continuing education requirements.

Employment Projections Data for Surveyors

Occupational title	SOC Code	Employment, 2012	Projected Employment, 2022	Change, 2012–2022	
				Percent	Numeric
Surveyors...	17-1022	42,400	46,800	10	4,400

Source: U.S. Bureau of Labor Statistics, Employment Projections Program

Note: Data are rounded. Go to Occupational Information Included in the OOH *for a discussion of the data in this table.*

Work Experience in a Related Occupation. Many states allow candidates with significant work experience to become licensed surveyors. To receive credit for this experience, candidates must work under a licensed surveyor. Many surveying technicians become licensed surveyors after working for as much as 10 years in the field of surveying.

Licenses, Certifications, and Registrations. All 50 states and the District of Columbia require surveyors to be licensed before they can certify legal documents that show property lines or determine proper markings on construction projects. Candidates with a bachelor's degree must usually work for about 2 years under the direction of a licensed surveyor in order to qualify for licensure.

Although the process of obtaining a license varies by state, the National Council of Examiners for Engineering and Surveying has a generalized process of four steps:

• Complete the level of education required in your state

• Pass the Fundamentals of Surveying (FS) exam

• Gain sufficient work experience under a licensed surveyor

• Pass the Principles and Practice of Surveying (PS) exam

Important Qualities

Communication skills. Surveyors must provide clear instructions to team members. They must also be able to receive instructions from architects and construction managers, and explain the job's progress to developers, lawyers, financiers, and government authorities.

Detail oriented. Surveyors must work with precision and accuracy due to the legal nature of the documents they produce.

Physical stamina. Surveyors traditionally work outdoors, often in rugged terrain. Therefore, they must be able to walk long distances for several hours.

Problem-solving skills. Surveyors must figure out discrepancies between documents showing property lines and current conditions on the land. If there were changes in previous years, they must figure out the reason for the changes so that property lines can be reestablished.

Technical skills. Surveyors use sophisticated technologies such as distance- and slope-measuring "total stations" and GPS devices to collect land survey data.

Time-management skills. Surveyors must be able to plan their time and their team members' time on the job. This is critical when pressing deadlines exist or while working outside during winter months when daylight hours are short.

Visualization skills. Surveyors must be able to envision new buildings and distances.

Pay

The median annual wage for surveyors was $56,230 in May 2012. The median wage is the wage at which half the workers in an occupation earned more than that amount and half earned less. The lowest 10 percent earned less than $32,190, and the top 10 percent earned more than $90,920.

In May 2012, the median annual wages for surveyors in the top five industries in which these workers worked were as follows:

State government, excluding education and hospitals	$68,590
Local government, excluding education and hospitals	61,880
Heavy and civil engineering construction	57,250
Mining, quarrying, and oil and gas extraction	55,260
Architectural, engineering, and related services	54,430

Job Outlook

Employment of surveyors is projected to grow 10 percent from 2012 to 2022, about as fast as the average for all occupations. Employment growth will result from increased construction related to improving the nation's infrastructure.

An increasing number of firms are interested in geographic information and its applications. For example, Geographic Information Systems (GIS) can be used to create maps and information for emergency planning, security, urban planning, natural resource exploration, construction, and other applications. will also be needed for legal reasons to verify the accuracy of the data and information gathered for input into a GIS.

Surveyors will continue to be needed for construction and resource extraction projects. States rich in oil and gas may continue to see higher demand for surveyors due to growth in extraction projects in those areas. In addition, some will also be hired by county and state governments for land boundary clarification.

Job Prospects. Job opportunities for those with a bachelor's degree in surveying or a related field are expected to be excellent.

Similar Occupations   This table shows a list of occupations with job duties that are similar to those of surveyors.

Occupations	Entry-level Education	2012 Pay	Projected Job Growth	Average Annual Openings
Architects	Bachelor's degree	$73,090	17%	4,410
Cartographers and Photogrammetrists	Bachelor's degree	$57,440	20%	490
Civil Engineers	Bachelor's degree	$79,340	20%	12,010
Landscape Architects	Bachelor's degree	$64,180	14%	760
Surveying and Mapping Technicians	High school diploma or equivalent	$39,670	14%	1,700
Urban and Regional Planners	Master's degree	$65,230	10%	2,140

Increased use of sophisticated technology and mathematics has resulted in higher education requirements. As a result, those with the right combination of skills and a bachelor's degree from a school accredited by ABET will have the best job opportunities.

Demand for traditional surveying services is closely tied to construction activity and job opportunities will vary by geographic region, often depending on local economic conditions. When real estate sales and construction activity slows down, surveyors may face greater competition for jobs. However, because surveyors can work on many different types of projects, they may have steadier work than others when construction slows.

Job prospects should be particularly excellent in fast growing industries, such as oil and gas mining.

O*NET

➤ Surveyors (17-1022.00)
➤ Geodetic Surveyors (17-1022.01)

Contacts for More Information

For information about surveying, career opportunities, and licensure requirements, visit
➤ National Society of Professional Surveyors (www.nspsmo.org)
➤ National Council of Examiners for Engineering and Surveying (www.ncees.org)

For information about a career as a geodetic surveyor, visit
➤ American Association for Geodetic Surveying (www.aagsmo.org)

Arts and Design

Art Directors

- **2012 Median Pay** .... $80,880 per year
  $38.88 per hour
- **Entry-Level Education** ....Bachelor's degree
- **Work Experience in a Related
  Occupation** ....5 years or more
- **On-the-Job Training** .... None
- **Number of Jobs 2012** 74,800
- **Job Outlook, 2012–22**.............. 3% (Slower than average)
- **Employment Change, 2012–22** 2,200

What Art Directors Do

Art directors are responsible for the visual style and images in magazines, newspapers, product packaging, and movie and television productions. They create the overall design and direct others who develop artwork or layouts.

Duties. Art directors typically do the following:

- Determine how best to represent a concept visually
- Determine which photographs, art, or other design elements to use
- Develop the overall look or style of a publication, an advertising campaign, or a theater, television, or film set
- Supervise design staff
- Review and approve designs, artwork, photography, and graphics developed by other staff members
- Talk to clients to develop an artistic approach and style
- Coordinate activities with other artistic and creative departments
- Develop detailed budgets and timelines
- Present designs to clients for approval

Art directors typically oversee the work of other designers and artists who produce images for television, film, live performances, advertisements, or video games. They determine the overall style or tone, desired for each project and articulate their vision to artists. The artists then create images, such as illustrations, graphics,

Art directors determine which photographs, art, or other design elements to use.

photographs, or charts and graphs, or design stage and movie sets, according to the art director's vision.

Art directors work with art and design staffs in advertising agencies, public relations firms, and book, magazine, or newspaper publishers to create designs and layouts. They also work with producers and directors of theater, television, or movie productions to oversee set designs. Their work requires them to understand the design elements of projects, inspire other creative workers, and keep projects on budget and on time. Sometimes they are responsible for developing budgets and timelines.

Art directors work in a variety of industries, and the type of work they do varies by industry. However, almost all art directors set the overall artistic style and visual image to be created for each project, and oversee a staff of designers, artists, photographers, writers, or editors who are responsible for creating the individual works that collectively make up a completed product.

The following are some specifics of what art directors do in different industries:

In publishing, art directors typically oversee the page layout of catalogs, newspapers, or magazines. They also choose the cover art for books and periodicals. Often, this work includes publications

Median Annual Wages, May 2012

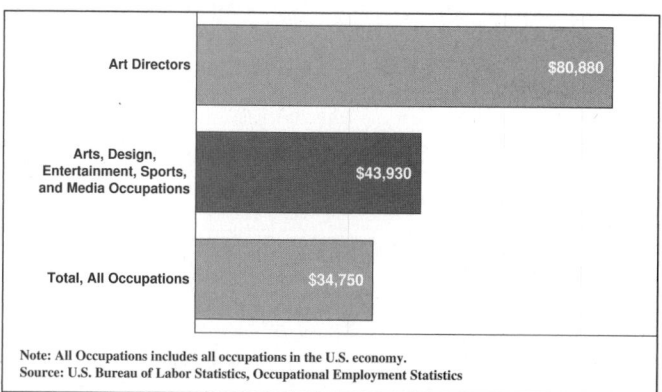

Art Directors	$80,880
Arts, Design, Entertainment, Sports, and Media Occupations	$43,930
Total, All Occupations	$34,750

Note: All Occupations includes all occupations in the U.S. economy.
Source: U.S. Bureau of Labor Statistics, Occupational Employment Statistics

Percent Change in Employment, Projected 2012–2022

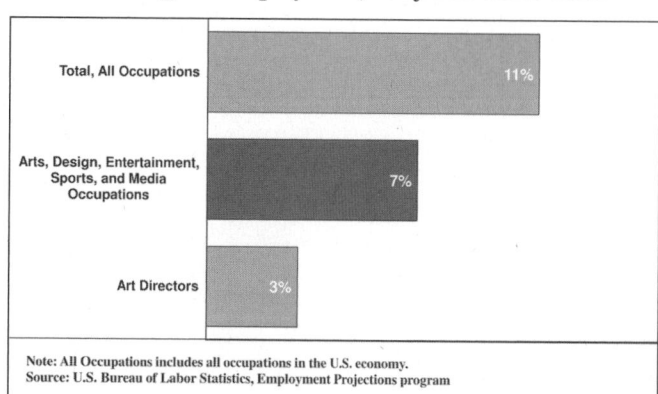

Total, All Occupations	11%
Arts, Design, Entertainment, Sports, and Media Occupations	7%
Art Directors	3%

Note: All Occupations includes all occupations in the U.S. economy.
Source: U.S. Bureau of Labor Statistics, Employment Projections program

Employment Projections Data for Art Directors

Occupational title	SOC Code	Employment, 2012	Projected Employment, 2022	Change, 2012–2022 Percent	Change, 2012–2022 Numeric
Art directors	27-1011	74,800	77,000	3	2,200

Source: U.S. Bureau of Labor Statistics, Employment Projections Program

Note: Data are rounded. Go to **Occupational Information Included in the OOH** *for a discussion of the data in this table.*

for the Internet, so art directors oversee production of the websites used for publication.

In advertising and public relations, art directors ensure that their clients' desired message and image is conveyed to consumers. Art directors are responsible for the overall visual aspects of an advertising or media campaign and coordinate the work of other artistic or design staff, such as graphic designers.

In movie production, art directors collaborate with directors to determine what sets will be needed for the film and what style or look the sets should have. They hire and supervise a staff of assistant art directors or set designers to complete designs.

Work Environment

Art directors held about 74,800 jobs in 2012. About 15 percent of art directors worked for advertising and public relations firms. Others worked for newspaper and magazine publishers, specialized design services firms, and motion picture and video industries.

The industries that employed the most art directors in 2012 were as follows:

Advertising, public relations, and related services 15%
Newspaper, periodical, book, and directory publishers 5
Specialized design services 4
Motion picture and video industries 3
Manufacturing 2

About 57 percent of art directors were self-employed in 2012. Even though the majority of art directors are self-employed, they must still collaborate with designers or other staff on visual effects or marketing teams. Art directors usually work in a fast-paced office environment, and they often work under pressure to meet strict deadlines.

Work Schedules. Most art directors worked full time in 2012.

How to Become One

Art directors need at least a bachelor's degree in an art or design subject and previous work experience. Depending on the industry, they may have worked as graphic designers, fine artists, editors, or photographers, or in another art or design occupation before becoming art directors.

Education. Many art directors start out as graphic, industrial, or set designers in another art-related occupation, such as fine artists or photographers. They gain the appropriate education for that occupation, usually by earning a Bachelor of Arts or Bachelor of Fine Arts degree.

To supplement their work experience in those occupations and show their ability to take on a more creative or a more managerial role, some complete a Master of Fine Arts (MFA) degree.

Work Experience in a Related Occupation. Most art directors work 5 years or more in another occupation before being selected for positions as art directors. Depending upon the industry, they may work as graphic designers, fine artists, editors, photographers, or in another art or design occupation before becoming art directors.

For many artists, including art directors, developing a portfolio–a collection of an artist's work that demonstrates his or her styles and abilities–is essential. Managers, clients, and others look at artists' portfolios when they are deciding whether to hire an employee or contract for an art project.

Important Qualities

Communication skills. Art directors must be able to listen to and speak with staff and clients to ensure that they understand employees' ideas and clients' desires for advertisements, publications, or movie sets.

Creativity. Art directors must be able to come up with interesting and innovative ideas to develop advertising campaigns, set designs, or layout options.

Leadership skills. Art directors must be able to organize, direct, and motivate other artists. They need to articulate their visions to artists and oversee production.

Time-management skills. Balancing competing priorities and multiple projects while meeting strict deadlines is critical for art directors.

Pay

The median annual wage for art directors was $80,880 in May 2012. The median wage is the wage at which half the workers in an occupation earned more than that amount and half earned

Similar Occupations   This table shows a list of occupations with job duties that are similar to those of art directors.

Occupations	Entry-level Education	2012 Pay	Projected Job Growth	Average Annual Openings
Craft and Fine Artists	High school diploma or equivalent	$46,065	3%	1,360
Fashion Designers	Bachelor's degree	$62,860	-3%	590
Graphic Designers	Bachelor's degree	$44,150	7%	8,600
Industrial Designers	Bachelor's degree	$59,610	4%	1,210
Multimedia Artists and Animators	Bachelor's degree	$61,370	6%	2,060
Photographers	High school diploma or equivalent	$28,490	4%	2,030
Writers and Authors	Bachelor's degree	$55,940	3%	3,180

less. The lowest 10 percent earned less than $43,870, and the top 10 percent earned more than $162,800.

In May 2012, the median annual wages for art directors in the top five industries in which these art directors worked were as follows:

Motion picture and video industries	$104,630
Specialized design services	90,210
Advertising, public relations, and related services	85,390
Manufacturing	68,210
Newspaper, periodical, book, and directory publishers	67,170

Job Outlook

Employment of art directors is projected to grow 3 percent from 2012 to 2022, slower than the average for all occupations. Art directors will continue to be needed to oversee the work of graphic designers, illustrators, photographers, and others engaged in artwork or layout design.

Employment of art directors is projected to decline in the publishing industry from 2012 to 2022. Although job opportunities may decline as traditional print publications lose ground to other media forms, new opportunities are expected to arise, as the number of electronic magazines and Internet-based publications grows. Rather than focusing on the print layout of images and text, art directors for newspapers and magazines will design Web pages that incorporate a variety of photographs, illustrations, infographics, graphic designs, and text images.

Job Prospects. Strong competition for jobs is expected as many talented designers and artists seek to move into art director positions. Workers with a good portfolio, which demonstrates strong visual design and conceptual work across all multimedia platforms, will have the best prospects.

O*NET

➤ Art Directors (27-1011.00)

Contacts for More Information

For more information about art directors in advertising, public relations, or publishing, visit
➤ Art Directors Club (www.adcglobal.org/)

For more information about art directors in film and television, visit
➤ Art Directors Guild (www.adg.org/)

Craft and Fine Artists

- **2012 Median Pay** .... $44,380 per year
  $21.34 per hour
- **Entry-Level Education** ... High school diploma or equivalent
- **Work Experience in a Related Occupation** .... None
- **On-the-Job Training** .... Long-term on-the-job training
- **Number of Jobs 2012** 51,400
- **Job Outlook, 2012–22** .... 3% (Slower than average)
- **Employment Change, 2012–22** 1,300

What Craft and Fine Artists Do

Craft and fine artists use a variety of materials and techniques to create art for sale and exhibition. Craft artists create handmade objects, such as pottery, glassware, textiles or other objects that are designed to be functional. Fine artists, including painters, sculptors, and illustrators, create original works of art for their aesthetic value, rather than for a functional one.

Duties. Craft and fine artists typically do the following:

- Use techniques, such as knitting, weaving, glass blowing, painting, drawing, or sculpting
- Develop creative ideas or new methods for making art
- Create sketches, templates, or models to guide their work
- Select which materials to use on the basis of color, texture, strength, and other qualities
- Process materials, often by shaping, joining, or cutting
- Use visual elements, such as composition, color, space, and perspective, to produce desired artistic effects
- Develop portfolios highlighting their artistic styles and abilities to show to gallery owners and others interested in their work
- Display their work at auctions, galleries, museums and online marketplaces

Artists create objects that are beautiful, thought-provoking, and sometimes shocking. They often strive to communicate ideas or feelings through their art.

Craft artists work with many different materials, including ceramics, glass, textiles, wood, metal, and paper, to create unique pieces of art, such as pottery, quilts, stained glass, furniture, jewelry, and clothing. Many craft artists also use fine-art techniques–for example, painting, sketching, and printing–to add finishing touches to their products.

Fine artists typically display their work in museums, commercial or non-profit art galleries, corporate collections, on the Internet, and in private homes. Some of their artwork may be commissioned

Many artists receive formal training in their specialty.

Median Annual Wages, May 2012

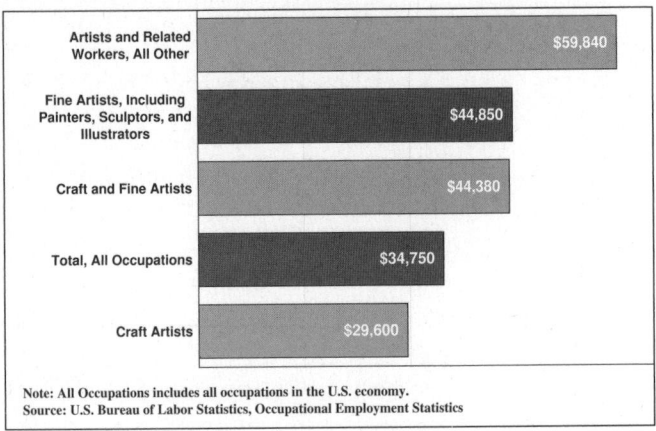

Note: All Occupations includes all occupations in the U.S. economy.
Source: U.S. Bureau of Labor Statistics, Occupational Employment Statistics

Percent Change in Employment, Projected 2012–2022

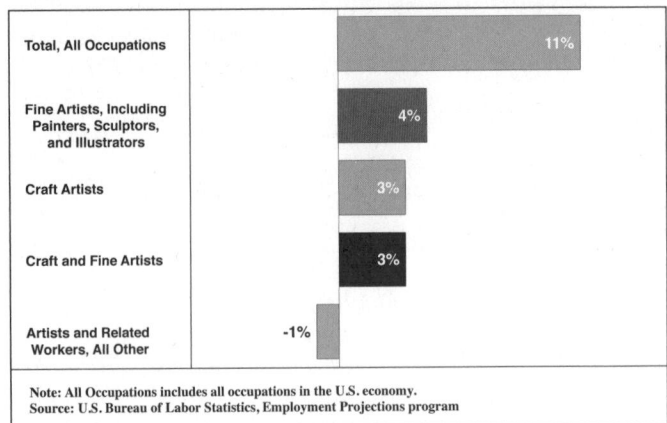

Note: All Occupations includes all occupations in the U.S. economy.
Source: U.S. Bureau of Labor Statistics, Employment Projections program

(requested by a client), but most is sold by the artist or through private art galleries or dealers. The gallery and the artist decide in advance how much of the sale proceeds each will keep.

Most craft and fine artists spend their time and effort selling their artwork to potential customers and building a reputation. However, only the most successful artists are able to support themselves solely through the sale of their works. Many artists have at least one other job to support their craft or art careers.

Some artists work in museums or art galleries as art directors or as archivists, curators, or museum workers, planning and setting up exhibits. Others teach craft or art classes or conduct workshops in schools or in their own studios. For more information on workers who teach art classes, see the profiles on kindergarten and elementary school teachers, middle school teachers, high school teachers, and postsecondary teachers.

Craft and fine artists specialize in one or more types of art. The following are examples of types of craft and fine artists:

Cartoonists draw political, advertising, comic, and sports cartoons. Some cartoonists work with others who create the idea or story and write captions. Some create plots and write captions themselves. Most cartoonists have comic, critical, or dramatic talents, in addition to drawing skills.

Ceramic artists shape, form, and mold artworks out of clay, often using a potter's wheel and other tools. They glaze and fire pieces in kilns, which are special furnaces that dry and harden the clay.

Fiber artists use fabric, yarn, or other natural and synthetic fibers to weave, knit, crochet, or sew textile art. They may use a loom to weave fabric, needles to knit or crochet yarn, or a sewing machine to join pieces of fabric for quilts or other handicrafts.

Fine art painters paint landscapes, portraits, and other subjects in a variety of styles, ranging from realistic to abstract. They may use one or more media, such as watercolors, oil paints, or acrylics.

Furniture makers cut, sand, join, and finish wood and other materials to make handcrafted furniture. For more information about other workers who assemble wood furniture, see the profile on woodworkers.

Glass artists process glass in a variety of ways–such as by blowing, shaping, or joining it–to create artistic pieces. Specific processes used include glassblowing, lampworking, and stained glass. These workers also decorate glass objects, such as by etching or painting.

Illustrators create pictures for books, magazines, and other publications, and for commercial products, such as textiles, wrapping paper, stationery, greeting cards, and calendars. Increasingly, illustrators use computers in their work. They might draw in pen and pencil and then scan the image into a computer to be colored in, or use a special pen to draw images directly onto the computer.

Jewelry artists use metals, stones, beads, and other materials to make objects for personal adornment, such as earrings or necklaces. For more information about other workers who create jewelry, see the profile on jewelers and precious stone and metal workers.

Medical and scientific illustrators combine drawing skills with knowledge of biology or other sciences. Medical illustrators work with computers or with pen and paper to create images of human anatomy and surgical procedures, as well as three-dimensional models and animations. Scientific illustrators draw animal and plant life, atomic and molecular structures, and geologic and planetary formations. These illustrations are used in medical and scientific publications and in audiovisual presentations for teaching purposes. Some medical and scientific illustrators work for lawyers, producing exhibits for court cases.

Printmakers create images on a silk screen, woodblock, lithography stone, metal etching plate, or other types of matrices. The matrix is then inked and transferred to a piece of paper, using a printing press or hand press to create the final work of art. Workers who do photoengraving are called printing workers.

Sculptors design and shape three-dimensional works of art, either by molding and joining materials such as clay, glass, plastic, or metal, or by cutting and carving forms from a block of plaster, wood, or stone. Some sculptors combine various materials to create mixed-media installations. For example, some incorporate light, sound, and motion into their works.

Sketch artists, a particular type of illustrator, often create likenesses of subjects with pencil, charcoal, or pastels. Sketches are used by law enforcement agencies to help identify suspects, by the news media to show courtroom scenes, and by individual customers for their own enjoyment.

Video artists shoot and record experimental video that is typically shown on a loop in art galleries, museums, or performance spaces. These artists sometimes use multiple monitors or create unusual spaces for the video to be shown.

Work Environment

Craft and fine artists held about 51,400 jobs in 2012.

About half of craft and fine artists are self-employed; others are employed in various private sector industries or in government.

Craft artists, for example, might work for companies that manufacture glass or clay products, or for museums, historical sites, or similar institutions. Fine artists are often employed by newspaper, periodical, book, and directory publishers. They also are employed by colleges and universities. Other types of artists

Employment Projections Data for Craft and Fine Artists

Occupational title	SOC Code	Employment, 2012	Projected Employment, 2022	Change, 2012–2022	
				Percent	Numeric
Craft and fine artists	—	51,400	52,700	3	1,300
Fraft artists...	27-1012	11,200	11,600	3	400
Fine artists, including painters, sculptors, and illustrators....	27-1013	28,800	29,900	4	1,100
Artists and related workers, all other	27-1019	11,400	11,200	-1	-200

Source: U.S. Bureau of Labor Statistics, Employment Projections Program

Note: Data are rounded. Go to **Occupational Information Included in the OOH** *for a discussion of the data in this table.*

and related workers work for the federal government, motion picture and video production companies, and advertising and public relations firms.

Many artists work in fine art or commercial art studios located in office buildings, warehouses, or lofts. Others work in private studios in their homes. Some artists share studio space, where they also may exhibit their work.

Studios are usually well-lighted and ventilated. However, artists may be exposed to fumes from glue, paint, ink, and other materials. They may also have to deal with dust or other residue from filings, splattered paint, or spilled cleaners and other fluids.

Work Schedules. Part-time and variable work schedules are common for artists. Many hold another job, in addition to their work as an artist. During busy periods, artists may work overtime to meet deadlines. Self-employed artists can set their own hours.

How to Become One

Formal schooling is not required for craft and fine artists. However, many artists take classes or earn a bachelor's or master's degree in fine arts, which can improve their skills and job prospects.

Education. Formal schooling beyond a high school diploma is rarely required for craft and fine artists. However, it is difficult to gain adequate artistic skills, without some formal education in the fine arts.

Most craft and fine artists have at least a high school diploma. High school classes like art, shop, and home economics can teach prospective artists some of the basic skills they will need, such as drawing, woodworking, or sewing.

Many artists pursue postsecondary education and take classes or earn degrees that can improve their skills and job prospects. Many colleges and universities offer bachelor's and master's degrees in fine arts. In addition to studio art and art history, programs may include core subjects, such as English, social science, and natural science.

Independent schools of art and design also offer postsecondary training, which can lead to a certificate in an art-related specialty or to an associate's, bachelor's, or master's degree in fine arts.

In 2013, the National Association of Schools of Art and Design (NASAD) accredited approximately 330 postsecondary institutions with programs in art and design. Most of these schools award a degree in art.

Medical illustrators must have a demonstrated artistic ability and a detailed knowledge of human and animal anatomy, living organisms, and surgical and medical procedures. They usually need a bachelor's degree combining art and premedical courses. Most medical illustrators, however, choose to get a master's degree in medical illustration. Four accredited schools offer this degree in the United States.

Education gives artists an opportunity to develop their portfolio, which is a collection of an artist's work that demonstrates his or her styles and abilities. Portfolios are essential, because art direc-

tors, clients, and others look at them when deciding whether to hire the artist or to buy their work.

Those who want to teach fine arts at public elementary or secondary schools usually must have a teaching certificate in addition to a bachelor's degree. Advanced degrees in fine arts or arts administration are usually necessary for management or administrative positions in government, management positions in private foundations, and teaching positions in colleges and universities. For more information on workers who teach art classes, see the profiles on kindergarten and elementary school teachers, middle school teachers, high school teachers, and postsecondary teachers.

Important Qualities

Artistic ability. Craft and fine artists create artwork and other objects that are visually appealing or thought-provoking. This usually requires significant skill in one or more art forms.

Business skills. Craft and fine artists must promote themselves and their art to build a reputation and to sell their art. They often study the market for their crafts or artwork to increase their understanding of what potential customers might want. Many craft and fine artists sell their work on the Internet, so developing an online presence is an important part of their art sales.

Creativity. Artists must have active imaginations to develop new and original ideas for their work.

Customer-service skills. Craft and fine artists, especially those who sell their work themselves, must be good at dealing with customers and potential buyers.

Dexterity. Most artists work with their hands and must be good at manipulating tools and materials to create their art.

Interpersonal skills. Artists often must interact with many people, including co-workers, gallery owners, and the public.

Training. Craft and fine artists improve their skills through practice and repetition. They can train in several ways other than–or in addition to–formal schooling. Craft and fine artists can train with simpler projects before attempting something more ambitious.

Some craft and fine artists learn on the job from more experienced artists. Others attend noncredit classes or workshops or take private lessons, which may be offered in artists' studios or at community colleges, art centers, galleries, museums, or other art-related institutions.

Still other craft and fine artists work closely with another artist on either a formal or informal basis. Formal arrangements may include internships or apprenticeship programs. Artists hired by firms often start with relatively routine work. While doing this work, however, they may observe other artists and practice their own skills.

Advancement. Craft and fine artists advance professionally as their work circulates and as they establish a reputation for their particular style. Many of the most successful artists continually develop new ideas, and their work often evolves over time.

Similar Occupations   This table shows a list of occupations with job duties that are similar to those of craft and fine artists.

Occupations	Entry-level Education	2012 Pay	Projected Job Growth	Average Annual Openings
Archivists, Curators, and Museum Workers	See "How to Become One"	$44,625	12%	970
Art Directors	Bachelor's degree	$80,880	3%	2,000
Fashion Designers	Bachelor's degree	$62,860	-3%	590
Graphic Designers	Bachelor's degree	$44,150	7%	8,600
Industrial Designers	Bachelor's degree	$59,610	4%	1,210
Jewelers and Precious Stone and Metal Workers	High school diploma or equivalent	$35,350	-10%	670
Multimedia Artists and Animators	Bachelor's degree	$61,370	6%	2,060
Photographers	High school diploma or equivalent	$28,490	4%	2,030
Woodworkers	High school diploma or equivalent	$28,576	8%	3,940

Many artists do freelance work while continuing to hold a full-time job until they are established as professional artists. Others freelance part time while still in school, to develop experience and to build a portfolio of published work.

Freelance artists try to develop a set of clients who regularly contract for work. Some freelance artists are widely recognized for their skill in specialties like cartooning or children's book illustrations. These artists may earn high incomes and can choose the type of work they do.

Pay

The median annual wage for craft and fine artists was $44,380 in May 2012. The median wage is the wage at which half the workers in an occupation earned more than that amount and half earned less. The lowest 10 percent earned less than $19,200, and the top 10 percent earned more than $93,220.

The median annual wages for craft and fine artist occupations in May 2012 were as follows:

Fine artists, including painters, sculptors,
    and illustrators $44,850
Craft artists 29,600
All other artists and related workers 59,840

Earnings for self-employed artists vary widely. Some charge only a nominal fee, while they gain experience and build a reputation for their work. Others, such as well-established freelance fine artists and illustrators, can earn more than salaried artists. Many, however, find it difficult to rely solely on income earned from selling paintings or other works of art.

Job Outlook

Employment of craft and fine artists is projected to grow 3 percent from 2012 to 2022, slower than the average for all occupations.

Employment growth of artists depends in large part on the overall state of the economy, because purchases of art usually are optional. During good economic times, more people and businesses are interested in buying artwork; during economic downturns, they generally buy less.

Although there is always a demand for art by collectors and museums, the employment of artists can be affected by the level of charitable giving to the arts, which has been decreasing somewhat in recent years.

In addition, job growth for craft artists may be limited by the sale of inexpensive, mass-produced items designed to look like handmade American crafts. However, continued interest in locally made products and craft goods sold online will likely offset some of these employment losses.

Demand for illustrators who work on a computer will increase, as media companies use more detailed images and backgrounds in their designs. Illustrators and cartoonists who work in publishing may see job opportunities decline, as traditional print publications lose ground to other media forms. However, new opportunities are expected to arise, as the number of electronic magazines, Internet-based publications, and video games grows.

Job Prospects. Competition for jobs as craft and fine artists is expected to be strong, because there are more qualified candidates than available jobs. Only the most successful craft and fine artists receive major commissions for their work.

Despite the competition, studios, galleries, and individual clients are always on the lookout for artists who display outstanding talent, creativity, and style. Talented individuals who have developed a mastery of artistic techniques and marketing skills will have the best job prospects.

Competition among artists for the privilege of being shown in galleries is expected to remain intense, as will competition for grants from funders, such as private foundations, state and local arts councils, and the National Endowment for the Arts. Because of their reliance on grants, and because the demand for artwork is dependent on consumers having extra income to spend, many of these artists will find that their income changes with the overall economy and the federal budget.

O*NET

➤ Craft Artists (27-1012.00)
➤ Fine Artists, Including Painters, Sculptors, and Illustrators (27-1013.00)
➤ Artists and Related Workers, All Other (27-1019.00)

Contacts for More Information

For more about art and design and a list of accredited college-level programs, visit
➤ National Association of Schools of Art and Design (http://nasad.arts-accredit.org/)

For more information on careers in the craft arts and for a list of schools and workshops, visit
➤ American Craft Council (www.craftcouncil.org)

For more information on careers in the arts, visit
➤ New York Foundation for the Arts (www.nyfa.org/level2.asp?id=51&fid=1&sid=205)

For more information on careers in illustration, visit
➤ Society of Illustrators (www.societyillustrators.org)

For more information on careers in medical illustration, visit
➤ The Association of Medical Illustrators (www.ami.org)

For information on grant-funding programs and other local resources for artists, contact your state arts agency. A list of these agencies is available from the National Assembly of State Arts Agencies (www.nasaa-arts.org/)

For more information on how the federal government awards grants for art, visit
➤ National Endowment for the Arts (http://arts.gov/)

Fashion Designers

- **2012 Median Pay** .... $62,860 per year
  $30.22 per hour
- **Entry-Level Education** ....Bachelor's degree
- **Work Experience in a Related Occupation**.............. None
- **On-the-Job Training** .... None
- **Number of Jobs 2012** 22,300
- **Job Outlook, 2012–22** .... -3% (Decline)
- **Employment Change, 2012–22** .... -700

What Fashion Designers Do

Fashion designers create original clothing, accessories, and footwear. They sketch designs, select fabrics and patterns, and give instructions on how to make the products they designed.

Duties. Fashion designers typically do the following:

- Study fashion trends and anticipate designs that will appeal to consumers
- Decide on a theme for a collection
- Use computer-aided design programs (CAD) to create designs
- Visit manufacturers or trade shows to get fabric samples
- Select fabrics, embellishments, colors, or style for each garment or accessory
- Work with other designers or team members to create a prototype design
- Present design ideas to the creative director or showcase them in fashion or trade shows
- Market designs to clothing retailers or directly to consumers
- Oversee the final production of their designs

Larger apparel companies typically employ a team of designers headed by a creative designer. Some fashion designers specialize in

Fashion designers study trends and design clothing and accessories for consumers.

clothing, footwear, or accessory design, but others create designs in all three fashion categories.

For some fashion designers, the first step in creating a new design is researching current fashion and making predictions of future trends, using trend reports published by fashion industry trade groups. Other fashion designers create collections from inspirations they get from their regular surroundings, from the cultures they have experienced and places they have visited, or from various art media that inspire them.

After they have an initial idea, fashion designers try out various fabrics and produce a prototype, often with less expensive material than will be used in the final product. They work with models to see how the design will look and adjust the designs as needed.

Although most designers first sketch their designs by hand, many now also sketch their ideas digitally with computer-aided design (CAD) programs. CAD allows designers to see their work on virtual models. They can try out different colors, design, and shapes while making adjustments more easily than they can when working with real fabric on real people.

The designers produce samples with the actual materials that will be used in manufacturing. Samples that get good responses from editors or trade and fashion shows are then manufactured and sold to consumers.

Although the design process may vary by specialty, in general it takes 6 months from initial design concept to final production, when either the spring or fall collection is released. Some com-

Median Annual Wages, May 2012

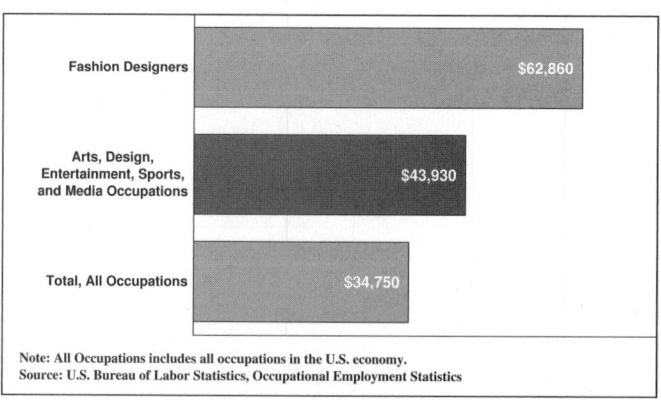

Fashion Designers: $62,860
Arts, Design, Entertainment, Sports, and Media Occupations: $43,930
Total, All Occupations: $34,750

Note: All Occupations includes all occupations in the U.S. economy.
Source: U.S. Bureau of Labor Statistics, Occupational Employment Statistics

Percent Change in Employment, Projected 2012–2022

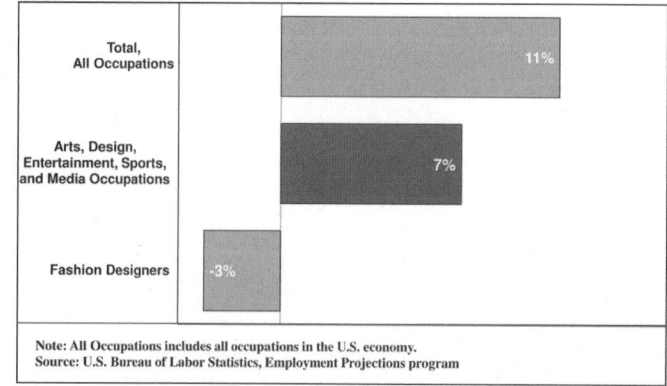

Total, All Occupations: 11%
Arts, Design, Entertainment, Sports, and Media Occupations: 7%
Fashion Designers: -3%

Note: All Occupations includes all occupations in the U.S. economy.
Source: U.S. Bureau of Labor Statistics, Employment Projections program

Employment Projections Data for Fashion Designers

Occupational title	SOC Code	Employment, 2012	Projected Employment, 2022	Change, 2012–2022	
				Percent	Numeric
Fashion designers..	27-1022	22,300	21,700	-3	-700

Source: U.S. Bureau of Labor Statistics, Employment Projections Program

Note: Data are rounded. Go to **Occupational Information Included in the OOH** *for a discussion of the data in this table.*

panies may release new designs as frequently as every month, in addition to releases during the spring and fall.

The Internet and e-commerce allow fashion designers to offer their products outside of the traditional brick-and-mortar stores. Instead they can ship directly to the consumer, without having to invest in a physical shop to showcase their products lines.

The following are examples of types of fashion designers:

Clothing designers create and help produce men's, women's, and children's apparel, including casual wear, suits, sportswear, evening wear, outerwear, maternity, and intimate apparel.

Footwear designers create and help produce different styles of shoes and boots. As new materials become available, such as lightweight synthetic materials used in shoe soles, footwear designers produce new designs that combine comfort, form, and function.

Accessory designers design and produce items such as handbags, suitcases, belts, scarves, hats, hosiery, and eyewear.

Costume designers design costumes for the performing arts and for motion picture and television productions. They research the styles worn during the period in which the performance takes place, or they work with directors to select and create appropriate attire. They also must stay within the costume budget for the particular production.

Work Environment

Fashion designers held about 22,300 jobs in 2012. Fashion designers work in wholesale or manufacturing establishments, apparel companies, retailers, theater or dance companies, and design firms.

More fashion designers work for wholesalers or manufacturers than for any other industry. The lines of apparel and accessories of these wholesalers and manufacturers are sold to retailers or other marketers for distribution to individual stores, catalog companies, or online retailers. In many cases, these designers are "in-house designers." Although the brands may be familiar to many consumers, the individual designers are largely unknown.

About 25 percent of fashion designers were self-employed in 2012. They typically design high-fashion garments and one-of-a-kind apparel on an individualized or custom basis. Self-employed

fashion designers who are able to set up their own independent clothing lines often already have experience and a strong understanding of the industry. In some cases, a self-employed fashion designer may have a clothing line that bears their name.

The industries that employed the most fashion designers in 2012 were as follows:

Apparel, piece goods, and notions merchant wholesalers 28%
Apparel manufacturing... 17
Management of companies and enterprises............................. 12
Specialized design services 5
Wholesale electronic markets and agents and brokers 2

Most designers travel several times a year to trade and fashion shows to learn about the latest fashion trends. Designers also sometimes travel to other countries to meet suppliers of materials and manufacturers who produce the final products.

Most fashion designers work in New York and California.

Work Schedules. Most fashion designers work full time; however, some work part time. Occasionally, fashion designers work long hours to meet production deadlines or prepare for fashion shows. Designers who freelance generally work under a contract and tend to work longer hours and adjust their workday to their clients' schedules and deadlines.

How to Become One

Most fashion designers have a bachelor's degree in a related field, such as fashion design or fashion merchandising. Employers usually seek applicants with creativity, as well as a good technical understanding of the production process for clothing, accessories, or footwear.

Education. Most fashion designers have a bachelor's degree in fashion design or fashion merchandising. In these programs they learn about textiles and fabrics and how to use computer-aided design (CAD) technology. They are also able to work on designs that can be added to their portfolio.

For many artists, including fashion designers, developing a portfolio–a collection of design ideas that demonstrates their styles and abilities–is essential because employers rely heavily on

Similar Occupations   This table shows a list of occupations with job duties that are similar to those of fashion designers.

Occupations	Entry-level Education	2012 Pay	Projected Job Growth	Average Annual Openings
Art Directors	Bachelor's degree	$80,880	3%	2,000
Floral Designers	High school diploma or equivalent	$23,810	-8%	1,650
Graphic Designers	Bachelor's degree	$44,150	7%	8,600
Industrial Designers	Bachelor's degree	$59,610	4%	1,210
Jewelers and Precious Stone and Metal Workers	High school diploma or equivalent	$35,350	-10%	670
Models	Less than high school	$18,750	15%	210
Purchasing Managers, Buyers, and Purchasing Agents	See "How to Become One"	$63,128	4%	12,230

a designer's portfolio in deciding whether to hire the individual. For employers, it is an opportunity to gauge talent and creativity. Students studying fashion design often have opportunities to enter their designs in student or amateur contests, helping them to develop their portfolios.

The National Association of Schools of Art and Design accredits approximately 300 postsecondary institutions with programs in art and design, and many of these schools award degrees in fashion design. Many schools require students to have completed basic art and design courses before they enter a program. Applicants usually have to submit sketches and other examples of their artistic ability.

Other Experience. Fashion designers often gain their initial experience in the fashion industry through internships or by working as an assistant designer. Internships provide aspiring fashion designers an opportunity to experience the design process, building their knowledge of textiles, colors, and how the industry works.

Advancement. Experienced designers may advance to chief designer, design department head, creative director, or another supervisory position in which they oversee certain fashion lines or brands by a company.

Some experienced designers may start their own design company or sell their designs in their own retail stores. A few of the most successful designers work for high-fashion design houses that offer personalized design services to their clients.

Important Qualities

Artistic ability. Fashion designers sketch their initial design ideas, which are used later to create prototypes. Consequently, designers must be able to express their vision for the design through illustration.

Communication skills. Fashion designers often work in teams throughout the design process and therefore must be effective in communicating with their team members. For example, they may need to give instructions to sewers regarding how the garment should be constructed.

Computer skills. Fashion designers use technology to design. They must be able to use computer-aided design (CAD) programs and be familiar with graphics editing software.

Creativity. Fashion designers work with a variety of fabrics, shapes, and colors. Their ideas must be unique, functional, and stylish.

Decision-making skills. Because they often work in teams, fashion designers are exposed to many ideas. They must be able to decide which ideas to incorporate into their designs.

Detail oriented. Fashion designers must have a good eye for small differences in color and other details that can make a design successful.

Pay

The median annual wage for fashion designers was $62,860 in May 2012. The median wage is the wage at which half the workers in an occupation earned more than that amount and half earned less. The lowest 10 percent earned less than $34,110, and the top 10 percent earned more than $126,290.

Earnings in this occupation can vary widely based on experience, employer, and reputation. Starting salaries in fashion design tend to be very low. Salaried fashion designers usually earn higher and more stable incomes than self-employed, freelance designers. However, a few of the most successful self-employed fashion designers earn many times the salary of the highest paid salaried designers.

In May 2012, the median annual wages for fashion designers in the top five industries in which these designers worked were as follows:

Management of companies and enterprises	$78,590
Specialized design services	62,560
Apparel manufacturing	62,390
Apparel, piece goods, and notions merchant wholesalers	60,590
Wholesale electronic markets and agents and brokers	57,950

Job Outlook

Employment of fashion designers is projected to decline 3 percent from 2012 to 2022.

Most apparel continues to be produced internationally. As a result, employment of fashion designers in the apparel manufacturing industry is projected to decline 51 percent during the projection period. Declining employment in the apparel manufacturing industry is preventing overall employment of fashion designers from increasing.

However, designers will still be needed to design clothing and accessories for the mass market and everyday wear. In addition, as new clothing technology is developed, fashion designers will be needed to create garments using new fabrics, such as moisture-wicking fabrics.

Job Prospects. Those with formal education in fashion design, with excellent portfolios, and with industry experience will have the best job prospects. However, strong competition for jobs is expected because of the large number of people who seek employment as fashion designers and the relatively few positions available.

In addition, it may be necessary for some fashion designers to relocate. Employment opportunities for fashion designers are highly concentrated in New York and California.

O*NET

➤ Fashion Designers (27-1022.00)

Contacts for More Information

For more information about careers in fashion design, visit
➤ Council of Fashion Designers of America (www.cfda.com/)

For more information about educational programs in fashion design, visit
➤ National Association of Schools of Art and Design (http://nasad.arts-accredit.org/)

Floral Designers

- **2012 Median Pay** .... $23,810 per year / $11.45 per hour
- **Entry-Level Education** ... High school diploma or equivalent
- **Work Experience in a Related Occupation** .... None
- **On-the-Job Training** .... Moderate-term on-the-job training
- **Number of Jobs 2012** 62,400
- **Job Outlook, 2012–22** .... -8% (Decline)
- **Employment Change, 2012–22** .... -5,000

What Floral Designers Do

Floral designers, also called florists, cut and arrange live, dried, and silk flowers and greenery to make decorative displays. They also help customers select flowers, containers, ribbons, and other accessories.

Duties. Floral designers typically do the following:

- Grow or order flowers from wholesalers, to ensure an adequate supply to meet customers' needs
- Determine the type of arrangement desired, the occasion, and the date, time, and location for each arrangement needed

Most floral designers work in small independent floral shops.

- Recommend flowers and greenery for each arrangement
- Consider the customer's budget when making recommendations
- Design floral displays that evoke a particular sentiment or style
- Answer telephones, take orders, wrap arrangements

Floral designers may create a single arrangement for a special occasion or design floral displays for rooms and open spaces for large scale functions, such as weddings, funerals, and banquets. They use their sense of artistry and knowledge of different types of flowers to choose the appropriate flowers for each occasion. They need to know what flowers are in season and when they will be available.

Floral designers must know the color varieties of each flower and the average size of each type of flower. They may calculate the number of flowers that will fit into a particular vase, or how many rose petals are needed to cover a carpet.

Floral designers also need to know the properties of each flower. Some flowers, like carnations, can last for many hours outside of water. Other flowers are more delicate and wilt more quickly. Some plants are poisonous for certain types of animals. For example, lilies are toxic for cats.

Floral designers use their knowledge to recommend flowers and designs to customers. After the customer selects the flowers, the designer arranges them in a visually appealing display.

Although more complex displays must be ordered in advance, designers will often create small bouquets or arrangements while customers wait. When they are responsible for floral arrangements for a special occasion, such as a wedding or banquet, floral designers usually set up the floral decorations just before the event, then tear down the floral decorations afterwards. Some work with event planners on a contract basis when creating arrangements for events such as weddings.

Floral designers also give customers instructions on how to care for flowers, including the ideal temperature and how often the water should be changed. For cut flowers, floral designers will often provide flower food to the customer.

When not serving customers, floral designers order new flowers from suppliers. They process newly arrived flowers by stripping leaves that would be below the waterline. They cut new flowers, mix flower food solutions, fill floral containers with the food solutions, and sanitize workspaces. They keep most flowers in cool display cases, so the flowers stay fresh and live longer.

Some designers have long-term agreements with hotels and restaurants or the owners of office buildings and private homes to replace old flowers with new flower arrangements on a recurring schedule–usually daily, weekly, or monthly–to keep areas looking fresh and appealing. Some work with interior designers in creating displays.

Floral designers who are self-employed or own their shop also must do business tasks. Some hire and supervise staff. They must keep track of income, expenses, and taxes–or hire others to help with those tasks.

Work Environment

Floral designers held about 62,400 jobs in 2012. Most floral designers work in retail businesses: about 49 percent worked in florist shops and 12 percent worked in grocery stores in 2012. Floral designers in retail businesses can expect walk-in customers, as well as customer orders placed over the telephone, over the Internet, and transmitted electronically by other florists. Some floral designers who work on a contract basis when creating arrangements for events, such as weddings, have to travel to the various locations of the events.

The industries that employed the most floral designers in 2012 were as follows:

Florists	49%
Grocery stores	12
Merchant wholesalers, nondurable goods	2
Sporting goods, hobby, book, and music stores	2
Lawn and garden equipment and supplies stores	2

About 26 percent of floral designers were self-employed in 2012.

Although designers often work in well-lighted, comfortable surroundings, room temperatures tend to be a little cooler than office or retail spaces, because temperatures are set low to help keep the flowers fresh.

Work Schedules. Most floral designers work full time, although their hours may differ, depending on the location of a particular store.

Median Annual Wages, May 2012

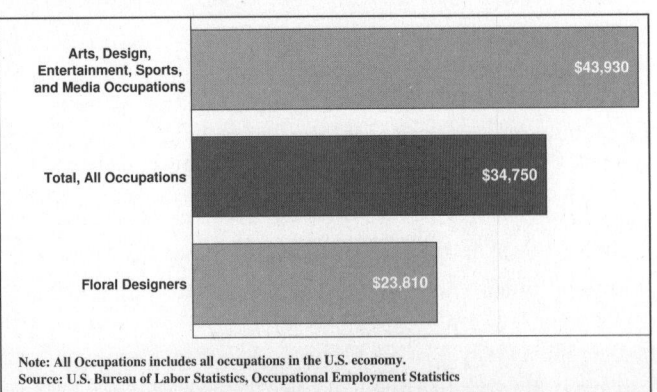

Note: All Occupations includes all occupations in the U.S. economy.
Source: U.S. Bureau of Labor Statistics, Occupational Employment Statistics

Percent Change in Employment, Projected 2012–2022

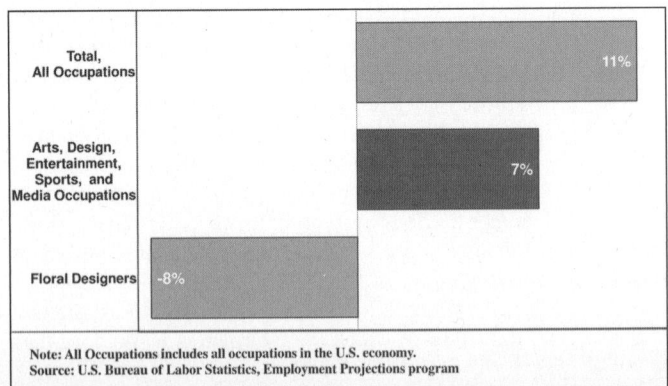

Note: All Occupations includes all occupations in the U.S. economy.
Source: U.S. Bureau of Labor Statistics, Employment Projections program

Employment Projections Data for Floral Designers

Occupational title	SOC Code	Employment, 2012	Projected Employment, 2022	Change, 2012–2022	
				Percent	Numeric
Floral designers 27-1023		62,400	57,300	-8	-5,000

Source: U.S. Bureau of Labor Statistics, Employment Projections Program

Note: Data are rounded. Go to Occupational Information Included in the OOH for a discussion of the data in this table.

Independent shops in downtown areas or business districts are typically open during business hours. Floral departments inside grocery stores or other stores in suburban locations and shopping malls may remain open longer.

During certain times of the year, such as holidays, floral designers are predictably busier than at other times. Because freshly cut flowers are perishable, most orders cannot be completed too far in advance. Therefore, designers often work long hours just before and during holidays. In addition, many part-time and seasonal opportunities can be found around certain holidays, such as Christmas, Valentine's Day, and Mother's Day.

How to Become One

Most floral designers have a high school diploma or the equivalent and learn their skills on the job over the course of a few months.

Education. Most floral designers have a high school diploma or the equivalent. There are postsecondary programs that are useful for florists who want to start their own businesses. Programs in design and caring techniques for flowers are available through private floral schools, vocational schools, and community colleges. Most offer a certificate or diploma. Classes in flower and plant identification, floral design concepts, advertising and other business courses, plus experience working in a greenhouse are part of many certificate and diploma programs.

Some community colleges and universities offer an associate's or bachelor's degree in floral design.

Training. New floral designers typically get hands-on experience working with an experienced floral designer. They may start by preparing simple flower arrangements and practicing the basics of tying bows and ribbons, cutting stems to appropriate lengths, and learning about the proper handling and care of flowers. They also learn about the different types of flowers, their growing properties, and how to use them in more complex floral designs.

Many floral designers gain initial experience working as cashiers or delivery people for retail floral stores.

Licenses, Certifications, and Registrations. The American Institute of Floral Designers offers a Certified Floral Designer certification. Although certification in floral design is voluntary, it indicates a measure of achievement and expertise. To become certified, a floral designer must demonstrate a grasp of floral design knowledge gained through work experience or education.

Advancement. Taking formal design training can help people who are interested in opening their own business or in becoming a chief floral designer or supervisor.

Important Qualities

Artistic ability. Designers use their sense of style to develop aesthetically pleasing designs.

Creativity. Floral designers use their artistic abilities and knowledge of design to develop appropriate designs for different occasions. They also must be open to new ideas, as trends in floral design change quickly.

Customer-service skills. Floral designers spend a substantial part of their day interacting with customers and suppliers. They must be able to understand what a customer is looking for, to explain options, and to ensure high-quality flowers and service.

Organizational skills. Floral designers need to be well organized, to keep the business operating smoothly and to ensure that orders are completed on time.

Pay

The median annual wage for floral designers was $23,810 in May 2012. The median wage is the wage at which half the workers in an occupation earned more than that amount, and half earned less. The lowest 10 percent earned less than $17,480, and the top 10 percent earned more than $36,580.

In May 2012, the median annual wages for floral designers in the top five industries in which these designers worked were as follows:

Lawn and garden equipment and supplies stores	$25,400
Grocery stores...	24,770
Sporting goods, hobby, book, and music stores	24,540
Florists..	23,560
Merchant wholesalers, nondurable goods	22,760

Job Outlook

Employment of floral designers is projected to decline 8 percent from 2012 to 2022. The need for floral designers is expected to decrease as people buy fewer elaborate floral decorations.

Floral designers are largely concentrated in florist shops, where overall employment is projected to decline over the projection period. Customers are purchasing fewer elaborate floral decorations from such shops and are increasingly buying loose cut fresh flowers from grocery stores and general merchandise stores. As a

Similar Occupations   This table shows a list of occupations with job duties that are similar to those of floral designers.

Occupations	Entry-level Education	2012 Pay	Projected Job Growth	Average Annual Openings
Craft and Fine Artists	High school diploma or equivalent	$46,065	3%	1,360
Fashion Designers	Bachelor's degree	$62,860	-3%	590
Graphic Designers	Bachelor's degree	$44,150	7%	8,600
Interior Designers	Bachelor's degree	$47,600	13%	2,150
Meeting, Convention, and Event Planners	Bachelor's degree	$45,810	33%	4,420

result, employment of floral designers is projected to decline 22 percent in florist shops and grow 7 percent in grocery stores.

O*NET

➤ Floral Designers (27-1023.00)

Contacts for More Information

For more information about becoming a Certified Floral Designer, visit

➤ American Institute of Floral Designers (www.aifd.org/)

For more information about careers in floral design, visit

➤ Society of American Florists (www.safnow.org/)

Graphic Designers

Graphic designers must be familiar with computer graphics and design software.

- **2012 Median Pay** .... $44,150 per year
$21.22 per hour
- **Entry-Level Education** ....Bachelor's degree
- **Work Experience in a Related Occupation**............... None
- **On-the-Job Training** .... None
- **Number of Jobs 2012** 259,500
- **Job Outlook, 2012–22** .... 7% (Slower than average)
- **Employment Change, 2012–22** 17,400

What Graphic Designers Do

Graphic designers create visual concepts, by hand or using computer software, to communicate ideas that inspire, inform, or captivate consumers. They develop the overall layout and production design for advertisements, brochures, magazines, and corporate reports.

Duties. Graphic designers typically do the following:

- Meet with clients or the art director to determine the scope of a project
- Advise clients on strategies to reach a particular audience
- Determine the message the design should portray
- Create images that identify a product or convey a message
- Develop graphics for product illustrations, logos, and websites
- Select colors, images, text style, and layout
- Present the design to clients or the art director
- Incorporate changes recommended by the clients into the final design
- Review designs for errors before printing or publishing them

Graphic designers combine art and technology to communicate ideas through images and the layout of websites and printed pages. They may use a variety of design elements to achieve artistic or decorative effects.

Graphic designers work with both text and images. They often select the type, font, size, color, and line length of headlines, headings, and text. Graphic designers also decide how images and text will go together on a print or webpage, including how much space each will have. When using text in layouts, graphic designers collaborate closely with writers who choose the words and decide whether the words will be put into paragraphs, lists, or tables. Through the use of images, text, and color, graphic designers can transform statistical data into visual graphics and diagrams, which can make complex ideas more accessible.

Graphic design is important in the sales and marketing of products, and is a critical component of brochures and logos. Therefore, graphic designers, also referred to as graphic artists or communication designers, often work closely with people in advertising and promotions, public relations, and marketing.

Frequently, designers specialize in a particular category or type of client. For example, some create the graphics used in packaging for various types of retail products, while others may work on the visual design used on a book jacket.

Graphic designers also need to keep up to date with the latest software and computer technologies to remain competitive.

Some individuals with a background in graphic design teach in design schools, colleges, and universities. For more information, see the profile on postsecondary teachers.

Median Annual Wages, May 2012

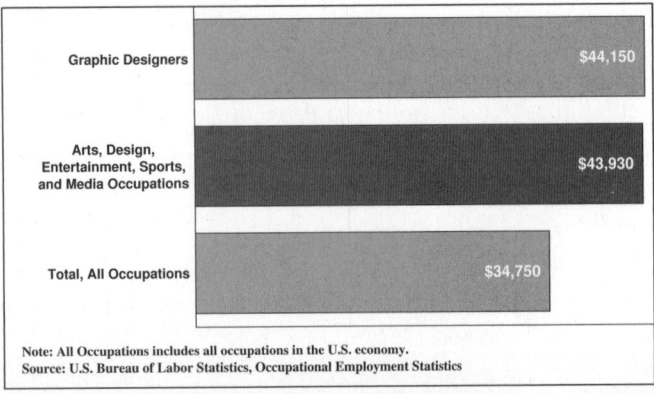

Graphic Designers	$44,150
Arts, Design, Entertainment, Sports, and Media Occupations	$43,930
Total, All Occupations	$34,750

Note: All Occupations includes all occupations in the U.S. economy.
Source: U.S. Bureau of Labor Statistics, Occupational Employment Statistics

Percent Change in Employment, Projected 2012–2022

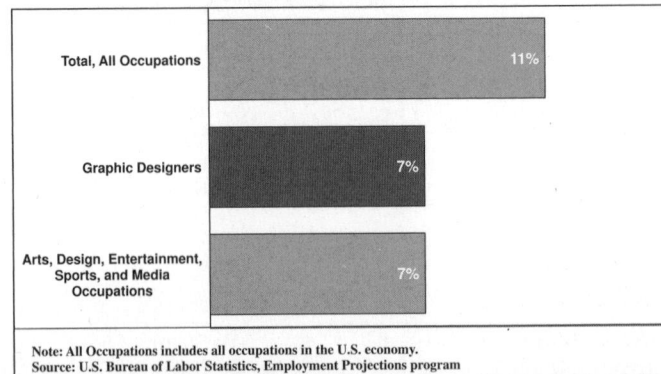

Total, All Occupations	11%
Graphic Designers	7%
Arts, Design, Entertainment, Sports, and Media Occupations	7%

Note: All Occupations includes all occupations in the U.S. economy.
Source: U.S. Bureau of Labor Statistics, Employment Projections program

Employment Projections Data for Graphic Designers

Occupational title	SOC Code	Employment, 2012	Projected Employment, 2022	Change, 2012–2022	
				Percent	Numeric
Graphic designers	27-1024	259,500	276,900	7	17,400

Source: U.S. Bureau of Labor Statistics, Employment Projections Program

Note: Data are rounded. Go to **Occupational Information Included in the OOH** *for a discussion of the data in this table.*

Work Environment

Graphic designers held about 259,500 jobs in 2012.

The industries that employed the most graphic designers in 2012 were as follows:

Manufacturing...	14%
Specialized design services	10
Newspaper, periodical, book, and directory publishers	9
Advertising, public relations, and related services.....................	8
Wholesale trade	5

Graphic designers generally work in studios where they have access to drafting tables, computers, and the software necessary to create their designs. Although many graphic designers work independently, those who work for specialized graphic design firms often work as part of a design team. Some designers telecommute. Many graphic designers collaborate with colleagues on projects or work with clients located around the world.

Work Schedules. Most graphic designers work full time, but schedules can vary depending on workload and deadlines.

In 2012, about 24 percent of graphic designers were self-employed. Graphic designers who are self-employed may need to adjust their workday to meet with clients in the evenings or on weekends. In addition, they may spend some of their time looking for new projects or competing with other designers for contracts.

How to Become One

Graphic designers usually need a bachelor's degree in graphic design or a related field. Candidates for graphic design positions should demonstrate their creativity and originality through a professional portfolio that features their best designs.

Education. A bachelor's degree in graphic design or a related field is usually required. However, those with a bachelor's degree in another field may pursue technical training in graphic design to meet most hiring qualifications.

The National Association of Schools of Art and Design accredits about 300 postsecondary colleges, universities, and independent institutes with programs in art and design. Most schools include studio art, principles of design, computerized design, commercial graphics production, printing techniques, and website design. In addition, students should consider courses in writing, marketing, and business, all of which are useful in helping designers work effectively on project teams.

Many programs provide students with the opportunity to build a professional portfolio of their designs. This means collecting examples of their designs from classroom projects, internships, or other experiences. Students can use these examples of their work to demonstrate their design skills when applying for jobs and bidding on projects. A good portfolio often is the deciding factor in getting a job.

Students interested in graphic design programs should take basic art and design courses in high school, if the courses are available. Many bachelor's degree programs require students to complete a year of basic art and design courses before being admitted to a formal degree program. Some schools require applicants to submit sketches and other examples of their artistic ability.

Graphic designers must keep up with new and updated computer graphics and design software, either on their own or through formal software training programs. Professional associations that specialize in graphic design, such as AIGA and the Graphic Artists Guild, offer courses intended to keep the skills of their members up to date.

Licenses, Certifications, and Registrations. Certification programs are generally available through software product vendors. Certification in graphic design software can demonstrate a level of competence and may provide a jobseeker with a competitive advantage.

Advancement. Beginning graphic designers usually need 1 to 3 years of work experience before they can advance to higher positions. Experienced graphic designers may advance to chief designer, art or creative director, or other supervisory positions.

Similar Occupations   This table shows a list of occupations with job duties that are similar to those of graphic designers.

Occupations	Entry-level Education	2012 Pay	Projected Job Growth	Average Annual Openings
Advertising, Promotions, and Marketing Managers	Bachelor's degree	$115,087	12%	7,510
Art Directors	Bachelor's degree	$80,880	3%	2,000
Craft and Fine Artists	High school diploma or equivalent	$46,065	3%	1,360
Desktop Publishers	Associate's degree	$37,040	-5%	300
Drafters	Associate's degree	$49,726	1%	3,220
Industrial Designers	Bachelor's degree	$59,610	4%	1,210
Multimedia Artists and Animators	Bachelor's degree	$61,370	6%	2,060
Printing Workers	See "How to Become One"	$34,110	-5%	5,190
Technical Writers	Bachelor's degree	$65,500	15%	2,260
Web Developers	Associate's degree	$62,500	20%	5,070

Important Qualities

Analytical skills. Graphic designers must be able to look at their work from the point of view of their consumers and examine how the designs they develop will be perceived by the consumer to ensure they convey the client's desired message.

Artistic ability. Graphic designers must be able to create designs that are artistically interesting and appealing to clients and consumers. They produce rough illustrations of design ideas, either by hand sketching or by using a computer program.

Communication skills. Graphic designers must communicate with clients, customers, and other designers to ensure that their designs accurately reflect the desired message and effectively express information.

Computer skills. Most graphic designers use specialized graphic design software to prepare their designs.

Creativity. Graphic designers must be able to think of new approaches to communicating ideas to consumers. They develop unique designs that convey a recognizable meaning on behalf of their clients.

Time-management skills. Graphic designers often work on multiple projects at the same time, each with a different deadline.

Pay

The median annual wage for graphic designers was $44,150 in May 2012. The median wage is the wage at which half the workers in an occupation earned more than that amount and half earned less. The lowest 10 percent earned less than $26,250, and the top 10 percent earned more than $77,490.

Job Outlook

Employment of graphic designers is projected to grow 7 percent from 2012 to 2022, slower than the average for all occupations. Graphic designers will continue to play important roles in the marketing of products.

The change in employment of graphic designers from 2012 to 2022 is projected to vary by industry. Employment of graphic designers in newspaper, periodical, book, and directory publishers is projected to decline 16 percent from 2012 to 2022. However, employment of graphic designers in computer systems design and related services is projected to grow 35 percent over the same period. With the increased use of the Internet, graphic designers will be needed to create designs and images for portable devices, websites, electronic publications, and video entertainment media.

Job Prospects. Graphic designers are expected to face strong competition for available positions. Many talented individuals are attracted to careers as graphic designers. Prospects will be better for job applicants who work with various types of media, such as websites and print publications.

O*NET

➤ Graphic Designers (27-1024.00)

Contacts for More Information

For more information about graphic design, visit
➤ AIGA (www.aiga.org/)
➤ Graphic Artists Guild (www.graphicartistsguild.org/)
For more information about art and design and a list of accredited college-level programs, visit
➤ National Association of Schools of Art and Design (http://nasad.arts-accredit.org/)

Industrial Designers

- **2012 Median Pay** .... $59,610 per year
  $28.66 per hour
- **Entry-Level Education** ....Bachelor's degree
- **Work Experience in a Related Occupation**............... None
- **On-the-Job Training** .... None
- **Number of Jobs 2012** 39,200
- **Job Outlook, 2012–22** .... 4% (Slower than average)
- **Employment Change, 2012–22** 1,700

What Industrial Designers Do

Industrial designers develop the concepts for manufactured products, such as cars, home appliances, and toys. They combine art, business, and engineering to make products that people use every day. Industrial designers focus on the user experience in creating style and function for a particular gadget or appliance.

Duties. Industrial designers typically do the following:

- Consult with clients to determine requirements for designs
- Research who will use a particular product, and the various ways it might be used
- Sketch out ideas or create renderings, which are images on paper or on a computer that provide a better visual of design ideas
- Use computer software to develop virtual models of different designs
- Create physical prototypes of their designs
- Examine materials and production costs to determine manufacturing requirements
- Work with other specialists such as mechanical engineers or manufacturers to evaluate whether their design concepts will fill a need at a reasonable cost

Many commercial and industrial designers use computer-aided design software to create new products.

Median Annual Wages, May 2012

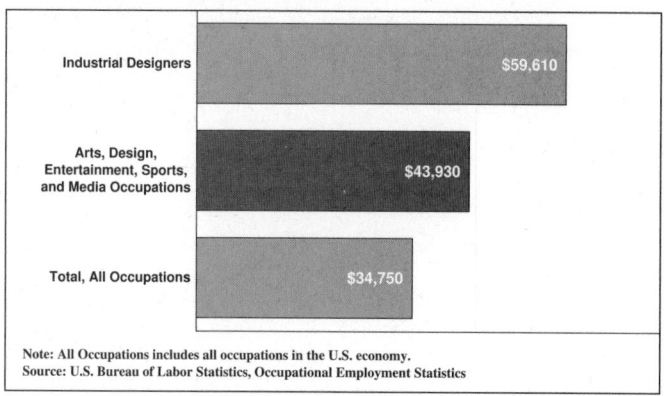

Note: All Occupations includes all occupations in the U.S. economy.
Source: U.S. Bureau of Labor Statistics, Occupational Employment Statistics

Percent Change in Employment, Projected 2012–2022

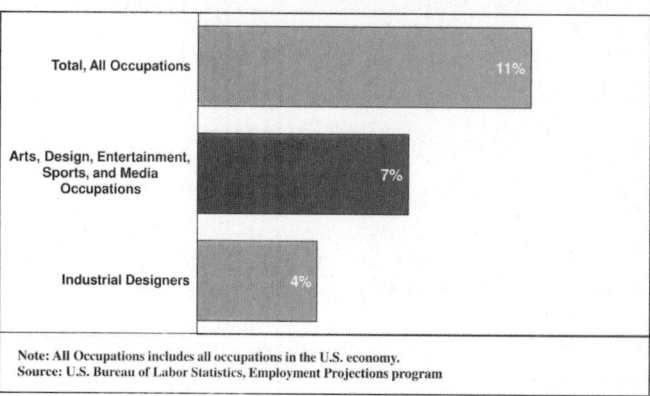

Note: All Occupations includes all occupations in the U.S. economy.
Source: U.S. Bureau of Labor Statistics, Employment Projections program

- Evaluate product safety, appearance, and function to determine if a design is practical

- Present designs and demonstrate prototypes to clients for approval

Some industrial designers focus on a particular product category. For example, some design medical equipment, or work on consumer electronics products, such as computers or smart phones. Other designers develop ideas for new bicycles, furniture, housewares, or snowboards. Self-employed designers have more flexibility in the product categories they work on. Designers who work for manufacturers help create the look and feel of a brand through their designs.

Industrial designers imagine how consumers might use a product and test different designs with consumers to see how each design looks and works. Industrial designers often work with engineers, production experts, and market research analysts to find out if their designs are feasible. They apply the input from their colleagues' professional expertise to further develop their designs. For example, industrial designers may work with market research analysts to develop plans to market new product designs to consumers.

Computers are a major tool for industrial designers. They use two-dimensional computer-aided design (CAD) software to sketch ideas, because computers make it easy to make changes and show alternatives. Three-dimensional CAD software is increasingly being used by industrial designers as a tool to transform their two-dimensional designs into models with the help of three-dimensional printers. If they work for manufacturers, they also may use computer-aided industrial design (CAID) software to create specific machine-readable instructions that tell other machines exactly how to build the product.

Work Environment

Industrial designers held about 39,200 jobs in 2012. Work spaces for industrial designers often include drafting tables for sketching designs, meeting rooms with whiteboards for brainstorming with colleagues, and computers and other office equipment for preparing designs and communicating with clients. Although industrial designers work primarily in offices, they may travel to testing facilities, design centers, clients' exhibit sites, users' homes or workplaces, and places where the product is manufactured. About 25 percent were self-employed in 2012.

The industries that employed the most industrial designers in 2012 were as follows:

Manufacturing 30%
Specialized design services 10

Wholesale trade 9
Architectural, engineering, and related services 7

Work Schedules. Most industrial designers work full time.

Industrial designers who are self-employed or work for firms that hire them out to other organizations may need to frequently adjust their workdays to meet with clients in the evenings or on weekends. In addition, they may spend some of their time looking for new projects or competing with other designers for contracts.

How to Become One

A bachelor's degree is usually required for most entry-level industrial design jobs. It is also important for industrial designers to have an electronic portfolio with examples of their best design projects.

Education. A bachelor's degree in industrial design, architecture, or engineering is usually required for entry-level industrial design jobs. Most design programs include the courses that industrial designers need in design: sketching, computer-aided design and drafting (CADD), industrial materials and processes, and manufacturing methods.

The National Association of Schools of Art and Design accredits approximately 300 postsecondary colleges, universities, and independent institutes with programs in art and design. Many schools require successful completion of some basic art and design courses before entry into a bachelor's degree program. Applicants also may need to submit sketches and other examples of their artistic ability.

Many programs provide students with the opportunity to build a professional portfolio of their designs by collecting examples of their designs from classroom projects, internships, or other experiences. Students can use these examples of their work to demonstrate their design skills when applying for jobs and bidding on contracts for work.

An increasing number of designers are getting a Master's of Business Administration (MBA) to gain business skills. Business skills help designers understand how to fit their designs to meet the cost limitations a firm may have for the production of a given product.

Important Qualities

Analytical skills. Industrial designers use logic or reasoning skills to study consumers and recognize the need for new products.

Artistic ability. Industrial designers sketch their initial design ideas, which are used later to create prototypes. As such, designers must be able to express their design through illustration.

Computer skills. Industrial designers use computer-aided design software to develop their designs and create prototypes.

Employment Projections Data for Industrial Designers

Occupational title	SOC Code	Employment, 2012	Projected Employment, 2022	Change, 2012–2022	
				Percent	Numeric
Commercial and industrial designers......................................	27-1021	39,200	40,900	4	1,700

Source: U.S. Bureau of Labor Statistics, Employment Projections Program

Note: *Data are rounded. Go to* **Occupational Information Included in the OOH** *for a discussion of the data in this table.*

Creativity. Industrial designers must be innovative in their designs and the ways in which they integrate existing technologies into their new product.

Interpersonal skills. Industrial designers must develop cooperative working relationships with clients and colleagues who specialize in related disciplines.

Mechanical skills. Industrial designers must understand how products are engineered, at least for the types of products that they design.

Problem-solving skills. Industrial designers identify complex design problems such as the need, size, and cost of a product, anticipate production issues, develop alternatives, evaluate options, and implement solutions.

Advancement. Experienced designers in large firms may advance to chief designer, design department head, or other supervisory positions. Some designers become teachers in design schools or in colleges and universities. For more information, see the profile on postsecondary teachers. Many teachers continue to consult privately or operate small design studios in addition to teaching. Some experienced designers open their own design firms.

Pay

The median annual wage for industrial designers was $59,610 in May 2012. The median wage is the wage at which half the workers in an occupation earned more than that amount and half earned less. The lowest 10 percent earned less than $34,610, and the top 10 percent earned more than $94,250.

As shown in the tabulation below, the median annual wage for industrial designers in the manufacturing industry was $56,880 in May 2012, lower than the median annual wage for the occupation in general. In May 2012, the median annual wages for industrial designers in the top four industries in which these designers worked were as follows:

Architectural, engineering, and related services $69,250
Specialized design services 58,530
Manufacturing.. 56,880
Wholesale trade 51,770

Job Outlook

Employment of industrial designers is projected to grow 4 percent from 2012 to 2022, slower than the average for all occupations. Consumer demand for new products and new product styles should sustain the demand for industrial designers. Employment in the manufacturing industry is projected to experience a slight decline over the projection period contributing to the slower than the average growth for industrial designers.

Employment of industrial designers who design precision instruments and medical equipment is likely to grow more rapidly. Both areas require a high degree of technical ability and design sophistication. Products in these areas also require detailed specifications and precise equipment manufacturing because of the delicate uses of the finished product.

Job Prospects. Prospects are best for job applicants with a strong background in two- and three-dimensional computer-aided design (CAD) and computer-aided industrial design (CAID). The increasing trend toward the use of sustainable resources is likely to improve prospects for applicants with the knowledge to work with sustainable resources.

O*NET

➤ Commercial and Industrial Designers (27-1021.00)

Contacts for More Information

For more information about industrial designers, visit
➤ Industrial Designers Society of America (www.idsa.org/)
For more information about accredited college-level programs in art and design, visit
➤ National Association of Schools of Art and Design (http://nasad. arts-accredit.org/)

Similar Occupations   This table shows a list of occupations with job duties that are similar to those of industrial designers.

Occupations	Entry-level Education	2012 Pay	Projected Job Growth	Average Annual Openings
Architects	Bachelor's degree	$73,090	17%	4,410
Art Directors	Bachelor's degree	$80,880	3%	2,000
Desktop Publishers	Associate's degree	$37,040	-5%	300
Drafters	Associate's degree	$49,726	1%	3,220
Fashion Designers	Bachelor's degree	$62,860	-3%	590
Graphic Designers	Bachelor's degree	$44,150	7%	8,600
Industrial Engineers	Bachelor's degree	$78,860	5%	7,540
Interior Designers	Bachelor's degree	$47,600	13%	2,150
Software Developers	Bachelor's degree	$93,640	22%	35,320

Interior Designers

- **2012 Median Pay** .... $47,600 per year
  $22.89 per hour
- **Entry-Level Education** ....Bachelor's degree
- **Work Experience in a Related Occupation**............... None
- **On-the-Job Training** .... None
- **Number of Jobs 2012** 54,900
- **Job Outlook, 2012–22** .... 13% (As fast as average)
- **Employment Change, 2012–22** 7,000

What Interior Designers Do

Interior designers make interior spaces functional, safe, and beautiful by determining space requirements and selecting decorative items, such as colors, lighting, and materials. They read blueprints and must be aware of building codes and inspection regulations.

Duties. Interior designers typically do the following:

- Search for and bid on new projects
- Determine the client's goals and requirements of the project
- Consider how the space will be used and how people will move through the space
- Sketch preliminary design plans, including electrical layouts
- Specify materials and furnishings, such as lighting, furniture, wall finishes, flooring, and plumbing fixtures
- Prepare final plans, using computer applications
- Create a timeline for the interior design project and estimate project costs
- Place orders for materials and oversee installing the design elements
- Visit after the project to ensure that the client is satisfied

Interior designers work closely with architects, structural engineers, mechanical engineers, and builders, to determine how interior spaces will function, look, and be furnished. Interior designers read blueprints and must be aware of building codes and inspection regulations.

An increasing number of interior designers are involved with architectural detailing.

Although some sketches or drawings may be freehand, most interior designers use computer-aided design (CAD) software for the majority of their drawings.

Many designers specialize in a particular type of building (home, hospital, or hotel), a specific room (bathroom or kitchen), or a specific style. Some designers work for home furnishings stores, providing design services to help customers choose materials and furnishings.

Some interior designers produce designs, plans, and drawings for construction and installation. This may include floor plans, electrical layouts, and plans needed for building permits. Interior designers may draft the preliminary design into documents that could be as simple as sketches or as inclusive as construction documents, with schedules and attachments.

The following are examples of types of interior designers:

Sustainable designers use strategies to improve energy and water efficiencies and indoor air quality, and they specify environmentally preferable products, such as bamboo and cork for floors. They may obtain certification in Leadership in Energy and Environmental Design (LEED) from the U.S. Green Building Council. Such certification indicates that a building and its interior space was designed with the use of sustainable concepts.

Universal designers renovate spaces, to make them more accessible. Often, these designs are used to renovate spaces for elderly people and people with special needs; however, universal designs can benefit anyone. For example, an entry without steps may be necessary for someone in a wheelchair, but it is also helpful for someone pushing a baby stroller.

Kitchen and bath designers specialize in kitchens and bathrooms and have expert knowledge of the variety of cabinets, fixtures, appliances, plumbing, and electrical solutions for these rooms.

Lighting designers focus on the effect of lighting for home, office, and public spaces. For example, lighting designers may work on stage productions, in gallery and museum spaces, and in healthcare facilities, to find appropriate light fixtures and lighting effects for each space.

Work Environment

Interior designers held about 54,900 jobs in 2012. Most interior designers work in clean, comfortable offices. About 25 percent of interior designers were self-employed in 2012. Technology has changed the way many designers work. For example, rather than using drafting tables, interior designers now use complex software to create 2-D or 3-D images.

The industries that employed the most interior designers in 2012 were as follows:

Specialized design services 30%
Architectural, engineering, and related services 16
Furniture stores 6
Merchant wholesalers, durable goods 5
Construction.. 4

Work Schedules. Most interior designers work full time. They may need to adjust their workday to suit their clients' schedules and deadlines, meeting with clients during evening and weekend hours, when necessary. Interior designers also travel to the clients' design sites.

How to Become One

Interior designers usually need a bachelor's degree with a focus on interior design.

Education. A bachelor's degree is usually required, as are classes in interior design, drawing, and computer-aided design (CAD). A bach-

Median Annual Wages, May 2012

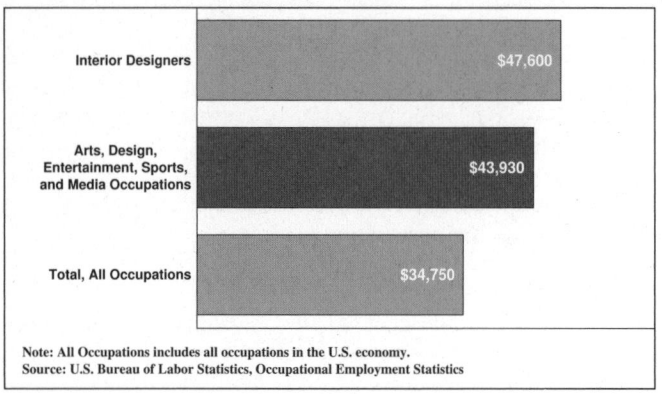

Note: All Occupations includes all occupations in the U.S. economy.
Source: U.S. Bureau of Labor Statistics, Occupational Employment Statistics

Percent Change in Employment, Projected 2012–2022

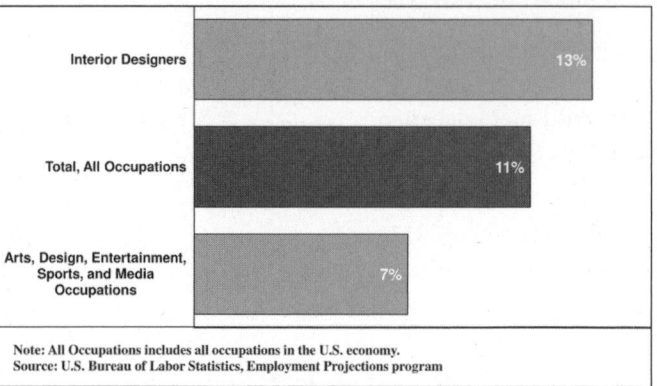

Note: All Occupations includes all occupations in the U.S. economy.
Source: U.S. Bureau of Labor Statistics, Employment Projections program

elor's degree in any field is acceptable, and interior design programs are available at the associate's-, bachelor's-, and master's-degree levels.

The National Association of Schools of Art and Design accredits about 300 postsecondary colleges, universities, and independent institutes with programs in art and design. The Council for Interior Design Accreditation accredits more than 150 professional-level (bachelor's or master's degrees) interior design programs.

The National Kitchen & Bath Association accredits kitchen and bath design specialty programs (certificate, associate's, and bachelor's degree level) in 45 colleges and universities.

Applicants may be required to submit sketches and other examples of their artistic ability, for admission to interior design programs.

Licenses, Certifications, and Registrations. Licensure requirements vary by state. In some states, only licensed designers may do interior design work. In other states, both licensed and unlicensed designers may do interior design work, however only licensed designers may use the title interior designer. Yet in other states, both licensed and unlicensed designers may call themselves interior designers and do interior design work.

In states where laws restrict the use of the title "interior designer," only those who pass their state-approved exam, most commonly the National Council for Interior Design Qualification (NCIDQ) exam, may call themselves registered interior designers. Qualifications to take the NCIDQ exam include a combination of education and experience. Typically, applicants have at least a bachelor's degree in interior design, plus 2 years of experience.

California requires a different exam, administered by the California Council for Interior Design Certification (CCIDC). Qualifications to take the CCIDC exam include a combination of education and experience.

Voluntary certification in an interior design specialty, such as kitchens and baths, allows interior designers to demonstrate expertise in a particular area of interior design. Interior designers often specialize, to distinguish the type of design work they do and to promote their expertise. Certifications usually are available through professional and trade associations and are independent from the NCIDQ licensing examination.

Important Qualities

Artistic ability. Interior designers use their sense of style, to develop designs that look great and are aesthetically pleasing.

Creativity. Interior designers need to be imaginative in selecting furnishings and fabrics and in creating spaces that serve the client's needs and fit the client's lifestyle.

Detail oriented. Interior designers need to be precise in measuring interior spaces and making drawings, so that furniture and furnishings will fit correctly and create the appropriate environment.

Interpersonal skills. Interior designers need to be able to communicate effectively with clients and others. Much of their time is spent soliciting new clients and new work and collaborating with other designers, engineers, and general building contractors on ongoing projects.

Problem-solving skills. Interior designers must address challenges, such as construction delays and the high cost or sudden unavailability of selected materials, while keeping the project on time and within budget.

Visualization. Interior designers need a strong sense of proportion and visual awareness, to understand how pieces of a design will fit together to create the intended interior environment.

Pay

The median annual wage for interior designers was $47,600 in May 2012. The median wage is the wage at which half the workers in an occupation earned more than that amount and half earned less. The lowest 10 percent earned less than $25,670, and the top 10 percent earned more than $86,900.

In May 2012, the median annual wages for interior designers in the top five industries in which these designers worked were as follows:

Architectural, engineering, and related services $54,360
Merchant wholesalers, durable goods 48,550
Specialized design services 47,090
Construction 44,320
Furniture stores 39,930

Employment Projections Data for Interior Designers

Occupational title	SOC Code	Employment, 2012	Projected Employment, 2022	Change, 2012–2022	
				Percent	Numeric
Interior designers...	27-1025	54,900	61,900	13	7,000

Source: U.S. Bureau of Labor Statistics, Employment Projections Program

Note: Data are rounded. Go to **Occupational Information Included in the OOH** *for a discussion of the data in this table.*

Similar Occupations   This table shows a list of occupations with job duties that are similar to those of interior designers.

Occupations	Entry-level Education	2012 Pay	Projected Job Growth	Average Annual Openings
Architects	Bachelor's degree	$73,090	17%	4,410
Art Directors	Bachelor's degree	$80,880	3%	2,000
Craft and Fine Artists	High school diploma or equivalent	$46,065	3%	1,360
Fashion Designers	Bachelor's degree	$62,860	-3%	590
Floral Designers	High school diploma or equivalent	$23,810	-8%	1,650
Graphic Designers	Bachelor's degree	$44,150	7%	8,600
Industrial Designers	Bachelor's degree	$59,610	4%	1,210
Landscape Architects	Bachelor's degree	$64,180	14%	760

Job Outlook

Employment of interior designers is projected to grow 13 percent from 2012 to 2022, about as fast as the average for all occupations. Designers will be needed to respond to consumer expectations that the interiors of homes and offices meet certain conditions, such as being environmentally friendly and more easily accessible.

Although only about 4 percent of interior designers are directly employed in the construction industry, many interior designers are heavily dependent on the construction industry to generate new construction and renovation projects for them to work on. Overall employment in the construction industry is projected to grow over the projection period.

Remodeling of large public spaces and facilities, such as hospitals, hotels, and schools, is often funded as part of a long-term project. Companies typically budget money over many years, so that they can afford remodeling efforts when necessary, regardless of economic conditions. In addition, as part of creating their corporate image, more companies are expected to take advantage of opportunities to use new furnishing and design concepts, to make their interior space easily identifiable.

Employment of interior designers in specialized design services firms is projected to grow 20 percent from 2012 to 2022. As interior designers focus on increasingly specialized design areas, there will be a greater need for them to collaborate with other designers and in other design-related fields.

Job Prospects. Job prospects should be better in high-income areas, because wealthy clients are more likely than others to engage in remodeling and renovating their homes.

Interior designers who specialize, such as those who design kitchens, may benefit by becoming an expert in their particular area. By specializing in a unique area of design, interior designers can use their knowledge of products to better fulfill customer requests.

O*NET

➤ Interior Designers (27-1025.00)

Contacts for More Information

For more information about interior designers, visit
➤ American Society of Interior Designers (www.asid.org)
➤ International Interior Design Association (www.iida.org/)
   For more information on accredited college degree programs in interior design, visit
➤ National Association of Schools of Art and Design (http://nasad.arts-accredit.org)
➤ Council for Interior Design Accreditation (www.accredit-id.org)

For more information on the national licensure qualifying exam, visit
➤ National Council for Interior Design Qualification (www.ncidq.org)
   For more information on accredited kitchen and bath specialty programs in colleges and universities and voluntary certification programs in residential kitchen and bath design, visit
➤ National Kitchen & Bath Association (www.nkba.org/)

Multimedia Artists and Animators

- **2012 Median Pay** .... $61,370 per year
  $29.50 per hour
- **Entry-Level Education** .... Bachelor's degree
- **Work Experience in a Related Occupation** .... None
- **On-the-Job Training** .... Moderate-term on-the-job training
- **Number of Jobs 2012** 68,900
- **Job Outlook, 2012–22** .... 6% (Slower than average)
- **Employment Change, 2012–22** 4,300

What Multimedia Artists and Animators Do

Multimedia artists and animators create animation and visual effects for television, movies, video games, and other forms of media. They create two- and three-dimensional models and animation.

Multimedia artists and animators often work in a specific form of media, such as animated movies, video games, or visual effects.

Median Annual Wages, May 2012

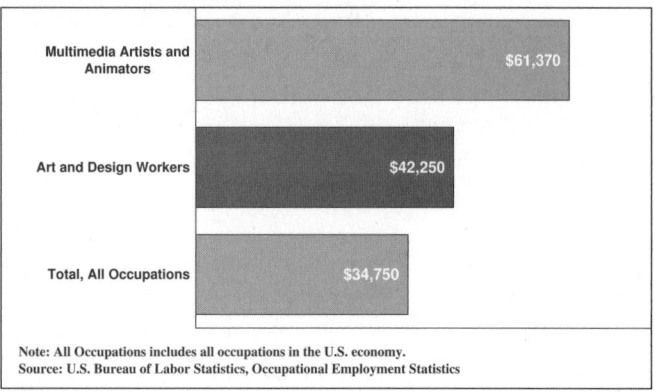

Note: All Occupations includes all occupations in the U.S. economy.
Source: U.S. Bureau of Labor Statistics, Occupational Employment Statistics

Percent Change in Employment, Projected 2012–2022

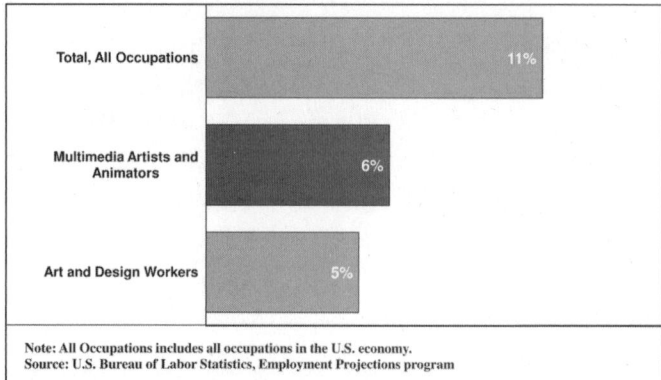

Note: All Occupations includes all occupations in the U.S. economy.
Source: U.S. Bureau of Labor Statistics, Employment Projections program

Duties. Multimedia artists and animators typically do the following:

• Create graphics and animation using computer programs and illustrations

• Work with a team of animators and artists to create a movie, game, or visual effect

• Research upcoming projects to help create realistic designs or animations

• Develop storyboards that map out key scenes in animations

• Edit animations and effects on the basis of feedback from directors, other animators, game designers, or clients

• Meet with clients, other animators, games designers, directors, and other staff (which may include actors) to review deadlines and development timelines

Multimedia artists and animators often work in a specific medium. Some focus on creating animated movies or video games. Others create visual effects for movies and television shows. Creating computer-generated images (known as CGI) may include taking images of an actor's movements, which are then animated into three-dimensional characters. Other animators design scenery or backgrounds for locations.

Artists and animators can further specialize within these fields. Within animated movies and video games, artists often specialize in characters or in scenery and background design. Video game artists may focus on level design: creating the look, feel, and layout for the levels of a video game.

Animators work in teams to develop a movie, a visual effect, or an electronic game. Each animator works on a portion of the project, and then all the animators put the pieces together to create one cohesive animation.

Some multimedia artists and animators create their work primarily by using computer software or by writing their own computer code. Many animation companies have their own computer animation software that artists must learn to use. Video game designers also work in a wide variety of platforms, including mobile gaming and online social networks.

Other artists and animators prefer to work by drawing and painting by hand and then translating the resulting images into computer programs. Some multimedia artists use storyboards or "animatics," which look like a comic strip, to help visualize the final product during the design process.

Many multimedia artists and animators put their creative work on the Internet. If the images become popular, these artists can gain more recognition, which can lead to future employment or freelance work.

Work Environment

Multimedia artists and animators held about 68,900 jobs in 2012. In 2012, about 57 percent of workers were self-employed. Artists and animators, not just those who are self-employed, often work from home. Some work for motion picture or video game studios and frequently work in offices.

The industries that employed the most multimedia artists and animators in 2012 were as follows:

Motion picture and video industries 13%
Computer systems design and related services 6
Software publishers 5
Advertising, public relations, and related services 4

Work Schedules. Most multimedia artists and animators work a regular work schedule, although it is not unusual for them to work 50-hour weeks. When deadlines are approaching, they may work nights and weekends.

How to Become One

Most multimedia artists and animators need a bachelor's degree in computer graphics, art, or a related field to develop a strong portfolio of work and learn the strong technical skills that many employers prefer.

Education. Employers typically require a bachelor's degree, and they look for workers who have a good portfolio of work

Employment Projections Data for Multimedia Artists and Animators

Occupational title	SOC Code	Employment, 2012	Projected Employment, 2022	Change, 2012–2022	
				Percent	Numeric
Multimedia artists and animators	27-1014	68,900	73,200	6	4,300

Source: U.S. Bureau of Labor Statistics, Employment Projections Program

Note: Data are rounded. Go to Occupational Information Included in the OOH for a discussion of the data in this table.

Similar Occupations   This table shows a list of occupations with job duties that are similar to those of multimedia artists and animators.

Occupations	Entry-level Education	2012 Pay	Projected Job Growth	Average Annual Openings
Art Directors	Bachelor's degree	$80,880	3%	2,000
Computer Network Architects	Bachelor's degree	$91,000	15%	4,350
Computer Programmers	Bachelor's degree	$74,280	8%	11,810
Craft and Fine Artists	High school diploma or equivalent	$46,065	3%	1,360
Graphic Designers	Bachelor's degree	$44,150	7%	8,600
Web Developers	Associate's degree	$62,500	20%	5,070

and strong technical skills. Multimedia artists and animators typically have a bachelor's degree in fine art, computer graphics, animation, or a related field. Programs in computer graphics often include courses in computer science, such as programming, and in graphics.

Bachelor's degree programs in art include courses in painting, drawing, and sculpture. Degrees in animation often require classes in drawing, animation, and film. Many schools have specialized degrees in topics such as interactive media or game design.

Important Qualities

Artistic talent. Animators and artists should have artistic ability and a good understanding of color, texture, and light. However, they may be able to compensate for artistic shortcomings with better technical skills.

Communication skills. Multimedia artists and animators need to work as part of a complex team and respond well to criticism and feedback.

Computer skills. Many multimedia artists and animators use computer programs or write programming code to do most of their work. Those with artistic talent, however, may be able to find work that does not require strong computer skills.

Creativity. Artists and animators must be able to think creatively to develop original ideas and make them come to life.

Time-management skills. The hours required by most studio and game design companies are long, particularly when there are tight deadlines. Artists and animators need to be able manage their time when a deadline approaches.

Training. Some animation studios have their own software and computer applications that they use to create films. They give workers on-the-job training to use this software. Animators may be hired for a probationary period while they prove that they have the skills and talent to become a permanent employee.

Pay

The median annual wage for multimedia artists and animators was $61,370 in May 2012. The median wage is the wage at which half the workers in an occupation earned more than that amount and half earned less. The lowest 10 percent earned less than $34,860, and the top 10 percent earned more than $113,470.

In May 2012, the median annual wages for multimedia artists and animators in the top four industries in which these artists and animators worked were as follows:

Motion picture and video industries	$72,680
Software publishers	62,310
Advertising, public relations, and related services	60,220
Computer systems design and related services	58,950

Job Outlook

Employment of multimedia artists and animators is projected to grow 6 percent from 2012 to 2022, slower than the average for all occupations. Projected growth will be due to increased demand for animation and visual effects in video games, movies, and television. Job growth will be slowed, however, by companies hiring animators and artists who work overseas. Studios often save money on animation by using lower paid workers outside of the United States.

Consumers will continue to demand more realistic video games, movie and television special effects, and three-dimensional movies. They will also demand newer computer hardware, which adds to the complexity of the games themselves. Video game studios will require additional multimedia artists and animators to meet this increased demand. Some of the additional work may be sent overseas.

In addition, an increased demand for computer graphics for mobile devices, such as smart phones, could lead to more job opportunities. Multimedia artists will be needed to create animation for games and applications for mobile devices.

Job Prospects. Despite modest job growth, there will be competition for job openings because many recent graduates are interested in entering the occupation. Opportunities should be best for those who have a wide range of skills or who specialize in a highly specific type of animation or effect.

O*NET

➤ Multimedia Artists and Animators (27-1014.00)

Contacts for More Information

For more information about careers in video game design, read the *Occupational Outlook Quarterly* article titled "Work for Play: Careers in Video Game Development" (www.bls.gov/opub/ooq/2011/fall/art01.pdf).

For information on accredited schools of art and design, visit
➤ National Association of Schools of Art and Design (http://nasad.arts-accredit.org/)

For additional information about careers in video game design, visit
➤ Game Career Guide (www.gamecareerguide.com/)

Building and Grounds Cleaning

Grounds Maintenance Workers

- **2012 Median Pay** .... $23,970 per year
  $11.53 per hour
- **Entry-Level Education** ....See "How to Become One"
- **Work Experience in a Related Occupation**............... None
- **On-the-Job Training** ....See "How to Become One"
- **Number of Jobs 2012** 1,227,100
- **Job Outlook, 2012–22** .... 13% (As fast as average)
- **Employment Change, 2012–22** 154,200

What Grounds Maintenance Workers Do

Grounds maintenance workers provide a pleasant outdoor environment by ensuring that the grounds of houses, businesses, and parks are attractive, orderly, and healthy.

Duties. Grounds maintenance workers typically do the following:

- Mow, edge, and fertilize lawns
- Weed and mulch landscapes
- Trim hedges, shrubs, and small trees
- Remove dead, damaged, or unwanted trees
- Plant flowers, trees, and shrubs
- Water lawns, landscapes, and gardens

Grounds maintenance workers mow lawns and trim hedges and trees.

Grounds maintenance workers perform a variety of tasks to achieve a pleasant and functional outdoor environment. They also care for indoor gardens and plantings in commercial and public facilities, such as malls, hotels, and botanical gardens.

The following are examples of types of grounds maintenance workers:

Landscaping workers create new outdoor spaces or upgrade existing ones by planting trees, flowers, and shrubs. They also trim, fertilize, mulch, and water plants. Some grade and install lawns or construct hardscapes such as walkways, patios, and decks. Others help install lighting or sprinkler systems. Landscaping workers are employed in a variety of residential and commercial settings, such as homes, apartment buildings, office buildings, shopping malls, and hotels and motels.

Groundskeeping workers, also called *groundskeepers*, maintain existing grounds. They care for plants and trees, rake and mulch leaves, and clear snow from walkways. They work on athletic fields, golf courses, cemeteries, university campuses, and parks, as well as in many of the same settings as landscaping workers. They also see to the proper upkeep of sidewalks, parking lots, groundskeeping equipment, fountains, fences, planters, and benches.

Groundskeeping workers who care for athletic fields keep natural and artificial turf in top condition, mark out boundaries, and paint turf with team logos and names before events. They mow, water, fertilize, and aerate the fields regularly. They must ensure that the underlying soil on fields with natural turf has the required composition to allow proper drainage and to support the grass used on the field. In sports venues, they vacuum and disinfect synthetic turf to prevent the growth of harmful bacteria, and they remove the turf and replace the cushioning pad periodically.

Groundskeepers in parks and recreation facilities care for lawns, trees, and shrubs; maintain playgrounds; clean buildings; and keep parking lots, picnic areas, and other public spaces free of litter. They also may erect and dismantle snow fences, and maintain swimming pools. These workers inspect buildings and equipment, make needed repairs, and keep everything freshly painted.

Some groundskeepers specialize in caring for cemeteries and memorial gardens. They dig graves to specified depths, generally using a backhoe. They mow grass regularly, apply fertilizers and other chemicals, prune shrubs and trees, plant flowers, and remove debris from graves.

Greenskeepers maintain golf courses. Their work is similar to that of groundskeepers, but they also periodically relocate holes on putting greens and maintain benches and tee markers along the course. In addition, greenskeepers keep canopies, benches, and tee markers repaired and freshly painted.

Pesticide handlers, sprayers, and applicators apply herbicides, fungicides, or insecticides on plants or the soil to prevent or control weeds, insects, and diseases. Those who work for chemical lawn or tree service firms are more specialized, inspecting lawns for problems and applying fertilizers, pesticides, and other chemicals to stimulate growth and prevent or control weeds, diseases, or insect infestations.

Arborists, also called *tree trimmers and pruners*, cut away dead or excess branches from trees or shrubs to clear utility lines, roads, and sidewalks. Although many workers strive to improve the appearance and health of trees and plants, some specialize in diagnosing and treating tree diseases. Others specialize in pruning,

Median Hourly Wages, May 2012

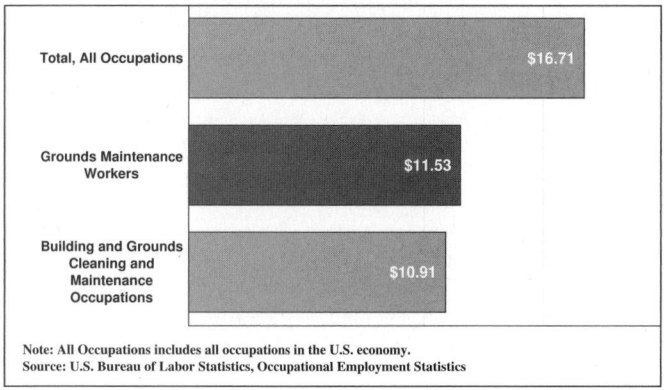

Note: All Occupations includes all occupations in the U.S. economy.
Source: U.S. Bureau of Labor Statistics, Occupational Employment Statistics

Percent Change in Employment, Projected 2012–2022

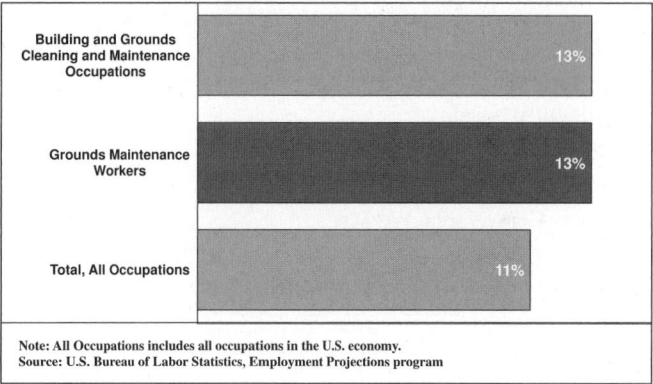

Note: All Occupations includes all occupations in the U.S. economy.
Source: U.S. Bureau of Labor Statistics, Employment Projections program

trimming, and shaping ornamental trees and shrubs. Tree trimmers and pruners use chain saws, chippers, and stump grinders while on the job. When trimming near power lines, they usually work on truck-mounted lifts and use power pruners.

Work Environment

Grounds maintenance workers held about 1.2 million jobs in 2012.

Employment in the detailed occupations that make up grounds maintenance workers was distributed as follows:

Landscaping and groundskeeping workers 1,124,900
Tree trimmers and pruners.. 53,200
Pesticide handlers, sprayers, and applicators, vegetation...... 29,600
Grounds maintenance workers, all other 19,300

The industries that employed the most grounds maintenance workers in 2012 were as follows:

Services to buildings and dwellings... 40%
Arts, entertainment, and recreation 8
Government.. 8
Other services (except public administration) 4
Educational services; state, local, and private 4

Grounds maintenance work is done outdoors in all kinds of weather. The work can be repetitive and physically demanding, requiring frequent bending, lifting, and shoveling.

Injuries and Illnesses. Grounds maintenance workers have a rate of injuries and illnesses that is higher than the national average. Workers who use dangerous equipment such as lawn mowers and chain saws must wear protective eyewear and earplugs. Those who apply chemicals such as pesticides or fertilizers or work at great heights also must take precautions.

In addition, arborists must wear hard hats for most activities, as well as special protective apparel when using chainsaws.

Work Schedules. Many grounds maintenance jobs are seasonal. Jobs are most common in the spring, summer, and fall, when planting, mowing, and trimming are most frequent.

How to Become One

Most grounds maintenance workers need no formal education and are trained on the job. Most states require licensing for workers who apply pesticides.

Education. Although most grounds maintenance jobs have no education requirements, some employers may require formal education or certification in areas such as landscape design, horticulture, or arboriculture.

Licenses, Certifications, and Registrations. Most states require workers who apply pesticides to be licensed. Obtaining a license usually involves passing a test on the proper use and disposal of insecticides, herbicides, and fungicides.

The Professional Landcare Network offers seven certifications in landscaping and grounds maintenance for workers at various experience levels.

The Tree Care Industry Association offers certification for tree care safety professionals.

The International Society of Arboriculture offers six certifications for workers at various experience levels.

The Professional Grounds Management Society offers certification for workers at various experience levels.

Training. A short period of on-the-job training is usually enough to teach new hires the skills they need, which often includes how to plant and maintain areas and how to use mowers, trimmers, leaf blowers, small tractors, and other equipment. Large institutional employers such as golf courses, university campuses, or municipalities may supplement on-the-job training with coursework in horticulture or small-engine repair.

Advancement. Grounds maintenance workers who have good communication skills may become crew leaders or advance into

Employment Projections Data for Grounds Maintenance Workers

Occupational title	SOC Code	Employment, 2012	Projected Employment, 2022	Change, 2012–2022 Percent	Change, 2012–2022 Numeric
Grounds maintenance workers	37-3000	1,227,100	1,381,300	13	154,200
Landscaping and groundskeeping workers.........................	37-3011	1,124,900	1,264,000	12	139,200
Pesticide handlers, sprayers, and applicators, vegetation ...	37-3012	29,600	33,000	11	3,300
Tree trimmers and pruners...	37-3013	53,200	63,000	18	9,800
Grounds maintenance workers, all other	37-3019	19,300	21,300	10	1,900

Source: U.S. Bureau of Labor Statistics, Employment Projections Program

Note: Data are rounded. Go to **Occupational Information Included in the OOH** *for a discussion of the data in this table.*

Similar Occupations   This table shows a list of occupations with job duties that are similar to those of grounds maintenance workers.

Occupations	Entry-level Education	2012 Pay	Projected Job Growth	Average Annual Openings
Agricultural Workers	See "How to Become One"	$19,703	-3%	23,190
Farmers, Ranchers, and Other Agricultural Managers	High school diploma or equivalent	$69,300	-19%	15,020
Forest and Conservation Workers	High school diploma or equivalent	$24,340	5%	230
Landscape Architects	Bachelor's degree	$64,180	14%	760
Logging Workers	High school diploma or equivalent	$33,697	-8%	730

other supervisory positions. Becoming a manager or a landscape contractor may require some formal education and several years of related work experience. Some workers use their experience to start their own landscaping company.

Important Qualities

Physical stamina. Grounds maintenance workers must be capable of doing physically strenuous labor for long hours, occasionally in extreme heat or cold.

Self-motivated. Because they often work with little supervision, grounds maintenance workers must be able to do their job independently.

Pay

The median hourly wage for grounds maintenance workers was $11.53 in May 2012. The median wage is the wage at which half the workers in an occupation earned more than that amount and half earned less. The lowest 10 percent earned less than $8.38, and the top 10 percent earned more than $18.67.

Median hourly wages for grounds maintenance occupations in May 2012 were as follows:

Tree trimmers and pruners...$15.54
Pesticide handlers, sprayers, and applicators, vegetation........14.55
Grounds maintenance workers, all other 12.86
Landscaping and groundskeeping workers 11.33

Job Outlook

Overall employment of grounds maintenance workers is projected to grow 13 percent from 2012 to 2022, about as fast as the average for all occupations. Employment growth will vary by specialty.

Employment of landscaping and groundskeeping workers–the largest specialty–is projected to grow 12 percent from 2012 to 2022, about as fast as the average for all occupations. More workers will be needed to keep up with increasing demand for lawn care and landscaping services from large institutions, including universities and corporate campuses. Many aging or busy homeowners also will require lawn care services to help maintain their yards.

Employment of tree trimmers and pruners is projected to grow 18 percent, faster than the average for all occupations. Many municipalities are planting more trees in urban areas, likely increasing the demand for these workers.

Job Prospects. Overall job opportunities are expected to be very good. Job opportunities will stem from employment growth and from the need to replace workers who leave the occupation each year.

Job opportunities should be best in areas with temperate climates, where landscaping services are required year round.

O*NET

➤ Landscaping and Groundskeeping Workers (37-3011.00)

➤ Pesticide Handlers, Sprayers, and Applicators, Vegetation (37-3012.00)
➤ Tree Trimmers and Pruners (37-3013.00)
➤ Grounds Maintenance Workers, All Other (37-3019.00)

Contacts for More Information

For more information about tree trimmers and pruners, including certification, visit
➤ International Society of Arboriculture (www.isa-arbor.com/)
➤ Tree Care Industry Association (www.tcia.org/)
    For information about landscaping and groundskeeping workers, visit
➤ Professional Grounds Management Society (http://pgms.org/)
➤ Professional Landcare Network (www.landcarenetwork.org/index.cfm)
    For information about becoming a licensed pesticide applicator, contact your state's licensing official.

Janitors and Building Cleaners

- **2012 Median Pay** ....$22,320 per year
                                                              $10.73 per hour
- **Entry-Level Education** ....Less than high school
- **Work Experience in a Related Occupation**............... None
- **On-the-Job Training** ....Short-term on-the-job training
- **Number of Jobs 2012** 2,324,000
- **Job Outlook, 2012–22**................ 12% (As fast as average)
- **Employment Change, 2012–22** 280,000

Building cleaning workers are employed in hospitals, office buildings, and other settings.

Median Hourly Wages, May 2012

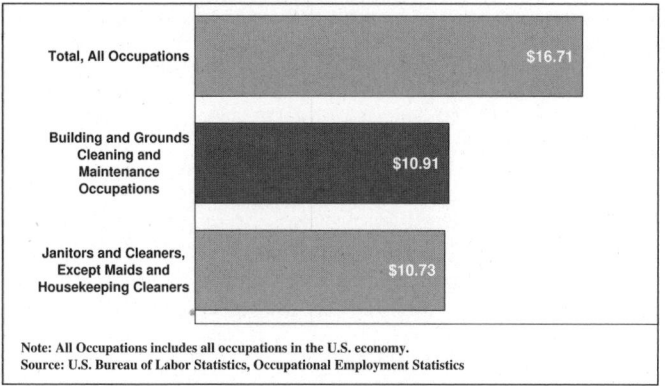

Note: All Occupations includes all occupations in the U.S. economy.
Source: U.S. Bureau of Labor Statistics, Occupational Employment Statistics

Percent Change in Employment, Projected 2012–2022

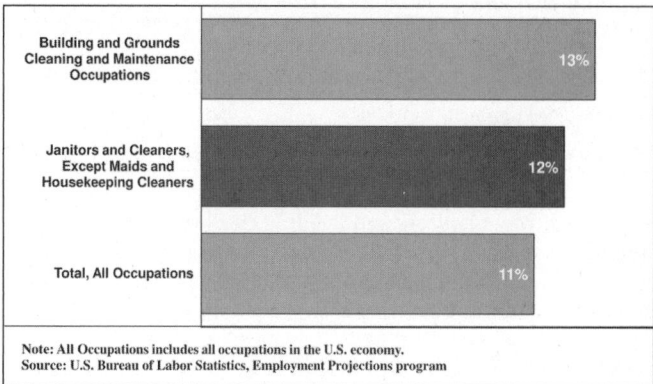

Note: All Occupations includes all occupations in the U.S. economy.
Source: U.S. Bureau of Labor Statistics, Employment Projections program

What Janitors and Building Cleaners Do

Janitors and building cleaners keep many types of buildings clean, orderly, and in good condition.

Duties

Janitors and building cleaners typically do the following:

- Gather and empty trash and trash bins
- Clean building floors by sweeping, mopping, or vacuuming them
- Clean restrooms and stock them with supplies
- Keep buildings secure by locking doors
- Clean spills and other hazards with appropriate equipment
- Wash windows, walls, and glass
- Order cleaning supplies
- Make minor repairs in buildings, such as changing light bulbs
- Notify managers when a building needs major repairs

Janitors and building cleaners keep office buildings, schools, hospitals, retail stores, hotels, and other places clean, sanitary, and in good condition. Some only clean, while others have a wide range of duties.

In addition to keeping the inside of buildings clean and orderly, some janitors and building cleaners work outdoors, mowing lawns, sweeping walkways, and shoveling snow. Some workers also monitor the heating and cooling system, ensuring that it functions properly.

Janitors and building cleaners use many tools and equipment. Simple cleaning tools may include mops, brooms, rakes, and shovels. Other tools may include snow blowers, floor buffers, and carpet extraction equipment.

Some janitors may be responsible for repairing minor electric or plumbing problems, such as leaky faucets.

The following are examples of types of janitors and building cleaners:

Building superintendents are responsible for maintaining residential buildings, such as apartments and condominiums. Although their duties are similar to those of other janitors, some building superintendents also help collect rent and show vacancies to potential tenants.

Custodians are janitors or cleaning workers that typically maintain institutional facilities, such as public schools and hospitals.

Work Environment

Janitors and building cleaners held about 2.3 million jobs in 2012. About 34 percent were employed in the services to buildings and dwellings industry, and another 14 percent were employed in elementary and secondary schools. The remainder was employed throughout all other industries.

Most janitors and building cleaners work indoors, but some work outdoors part of the time, sweeping walkways, mowing lawns, and shoveling snow. They spend most of the day walking, standing, or bending while cleaning; and sometimes they must move or lift heavy supplies and equipment. As a result, the work may be strenuous on the back, arms, and legs. Some tasks, such as cleaning restrooms and trash areas, can be dirty and unpleasant.

Injuries and Illnesses. Janitors and building cleaners have one of the highest rates of injuries and illnesses of all occupations. Workers suffer minor cuts, bruises, and burns from machines, tools, and chemicals. As a result, workers are increasingly required to take safety training and ergonomics instruction.

Work Schedules. Most janitors and building cleaners work full time, but a significant number work part time. Because office buildings are often cleaned while they are empty, many cleaners work evening hours. Janitors in schools, however, usually work during the day.

When there is a need for 24-hour maintenance, janitors work in shifts. This is particularly true of hospitals and hotels.

How to Become One

Most janitors and building cleaners learn on the job. Formal education is not required.

Education. Janitors and building cleaners do not need formal education. However, high school courses in shop can be helpful for jobs involving repair work. Workers should also know basic math.

Employment Projections Data for Janitors and Building Cleaners

Occupational title	SOC Code	Employment, 2012	Projected Employment, 2022	Change, 2012–2022 Percent	Change, 2012–2022 Numeric
Janitors and cleaners, except maids and housekeeping cleaners	37-2011	2,324,000	2,604,000	12	280,000

Source: U.S. Bureau of Labor Statistics, Employment Projections Program

Note: Data are rounded. Go to **Occupational Information Included in the OOH** *for a discussion of the data in this table.*

Similar Occupations   This table shows a list of occupations with job duties that are similar to those of janitors and building cleaners.

Occupations	Entry-level Education	2012 Pay	Projected Job Growth	Average Annual Openings
Grounds Maintenance Workers	See "How to Become One"	$24,180	13%	46,350
Maids and Housekeeping Cleaners	Less than high school	$19,570	13%	46,770

Training. Most janitors and building cleaners learn on the job. Beginners typically work with a more experienced janitor, learning how to use and maintain equipment such as wet-and-dry vacuums and floor buffers and polishers. On the job they also learn how to repair minor electrical and plumbing problems.

Licenses, Certifications, and Registrations. Although not required, certification is available through the Building Service Contractors Association International, the IEHA, and the ISSA-The Worldwide Cleaning Industry Association. Certification can demonstrate competence and may make applicants more appealing to employers.

Important Qualities

Interpersonal skills. Janitors and building cleaners should get along well with other cleaners, the people who live or work in the buildings they clean, and their supervisors.

Mechanical skills. Janitors and building cleaners should understand general building operations. They should be able to make routine repairs, such as repairing leaky faucets.

Physical stamina. Janitors and building cleaners spend most of the work day on their feet–operating cleaning equipment and lifting and moving supplies or tools. As a result, they should have good physical stamina.

Physical strength. Janitors and building cleaners often must lift and move cleaning materials and heavy equipment. Cases of liquid cleaner and trash receptacles, for example, can be very heavy, so workers should be strong enough to lift them without injuring their back.

Time-management skills. Janitors and building cleaners should be able to plan and complete tasks in a timely manner.

Pay

The median hourly wage for janitors and building cleaners was $10.73 in May 2012. The median wage is the wage at which half the workers in an occupation earned more than the amount and half earned less. The lowest 10 percent earned less than $8.08 per hour, and the top 10 percent earned more than $18.17 per hour.

In May 2012, the median hourly wages for janitors and building cleaners in the top five industries in which these cleaners worked were as follows:

Government	$14.20
Elementary and secondary schools; state, local, and private	13.05
Health care and social assistance	11.06
Religious, grantmaking, civic, professional, and similar organizations	10.35
Services to buildings and dwellings	9.49

Job Outlook

Employment of janitors and building cleaners is projected to grow 12 percent from 2012 to 2022, about as fast as the average for all occupations. Many new jobs are expected in facilities related to health care, as this industry is expected to grow rapidly.

In addition, as more companies outsource their cleaning services, cleaning or janitorial contractors are likely to benefit and experience employment growth.

Job Prospects. Overall job prospects are expected to be favorable. Those with related work experience and training should have the best job opportunities. Most job openings will come from the need to replace the many workers who leave or retire from this very large occupation.

O*NET

➤ Janitors and Cleaners, Except Maids and Housekeeping Cleaners (37-2011.00)

Contacts for More Information

For more information about janitors and building cleaners, visit

➤ Association of Residential Cleaning Services International (www.arcsi.org/)

➤ Building Service Contractors Association International (www.bscai.org/)

   IEHA (formerly International Executive Housekeepers Association) (www.ieha.org/)

➤ ISSA-The Worldwide Cleaning Industry Association (www.issa.com/)

   Information about janitorial and building cleaning jobs is available from state employment service offices.

Maids and Housekeeping Cleaners

- **2012 Median Pay** .... $19,570 per year
  $9.41 per hour

- **Entry-Level Education** .... Less than high school

- **Work Experience in a Related Occupation** .... None

- **On-the-Job Training** .... Short-term on-the-job training

- **Number of Jobs 2012** 1,434,600

- **Job Outlook, 2012–22** .... 13% (As fast as average)

- **Employment Change, 2012–22** 183,400

Housekeeping cleaners usually follow a set of procedures to give a room the desired look.

Median Annual Wages, May 2012

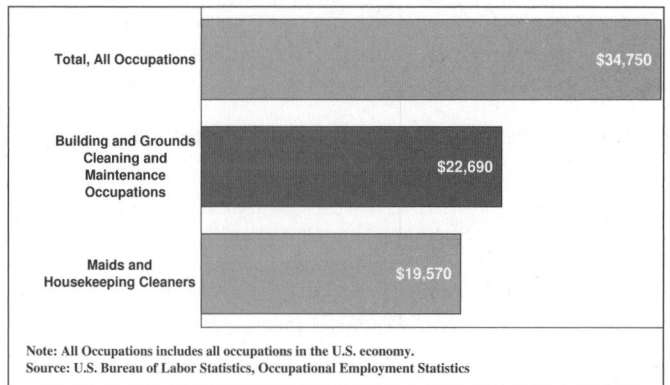

Note: All Occupations includes all occupations in the U.S. economy.
Source: U.S. Bureau of Labor Statistics, Occupational Employment Statistics

Percent Change in Employment, Projected 2012–2022

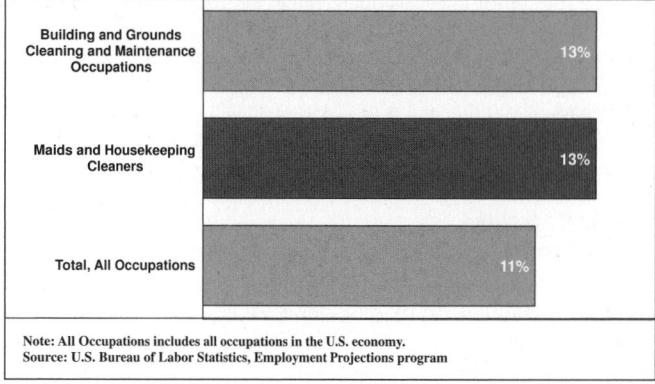

Note: All Occupations includes all occupations in the U.S. economy.
Source: U.S. Bureau of Labor Statistics, Employment Projections program

What Maids and Housekeeping Cleaners Do

Maids and housekeeping cleaners perform general cleaning tasks, including making beds and vacuuming halls, in private homes and commercial establishments.

Duties. Maids and housekeeping cleaners typically do the following:

- Clean rooms, hallways, and other living or work areas
- Change sheets and towels; make beds; and wash, fold, and iron clothes
- Empty wastebaskets and take trash to disposal areas
- Replenish supplies, such as soap and toilet paper
- Dust and polish furniture and equipment
- Sweep, wax, or polish floors, using brooms, mops, and other floor-cleaning equipment
- Vacuum rugs, carpets, and upholstered furniture
- Clean and polish windows, walls, and woodwork
- Lift and move lightweight objects and equipment

Maids and housekeeping cleaners do light cleaning tasks in homes and commercial establishments, such as hotels, restaurants, hospitals, and nursing facilities.

In addition to keeping places clean and neat, maids who work in private homes also may prepare meals, polish silver, and clean ovens, refrigerators, and sometimes windows. Some also shop for groceries, pick up and drop off drycleaning, and run other errands.

Those who work in hotels, hospitals, and other commercial establishments are responsible for cleaning and maintaining the premises. They also may share other duties. For example, house-keeping cleaners who work in hotels may deliver ironing boards, cribs, and roll-away beds to guests' rooms. In hospitals, workers may have to wash bedframes and disinfect and sanitize other equipment with germicides.

Work Environment

Maids and housekeeping cleaners held about 1.4 million jobs in 2012. About 12 percent were self-employed.

Although most cleaners work indoors in a hotel, restaurant, hospital, or nursing home, many maids who work for individuals or families may have to run errands outside the home. The work can be physically demanding.

The industries that employed the most maids and housekeeping cleaners in 2012 were as follows:

Traveler accommodation	30%
Nursing and residential care facilities	9
Hospitals; state, local, and private	8
Services to buildings and dwellings	7

Work Schedules. Most maids and housekeeping cleaners work full time. Part-time maids and cleaners–particularly those who work at hotels and hospitals–often work evenings and weekends.

Injuries and Illnesses. Maids and housekeeping cleaners spend most of their day on their feet, sometimes lifting or pushing heavy furniture. Many tasks, such as dusting or sweeping, require frequent bending, stooping, and stretching. Lifting mattresses to change the linens can cause back injuries and sprains. Because of these hazards, maids and housekeeping cleaners have a rate of injuries and illnesses that is much higher than the national average.

Employment Projections Data for Maids and Housekeeping Cleaners

Occupational title	SOC Code	Employment, 2012	Projected Employment, 2022	Change, 2012–2022 Percent	Change, 2012–2022 Numeric
Maids and housekeeping cleaners	37-2012	1,434,600	1,618,000	13	183,400

Source: U.S. Bureau of Labor Statistics, Employment Projections Program

Note: Data are rounded. Go to **Occupational Information Included in the OOH** *for a discussion of the data in this table.*

Similar Occupations   This table shows a list of occupations with job duties that are similar to those of maids and housekeeping cleaners.

Occupations	Entry-level Education	2012 Pay	Projected Job Growth	Average Annual Openings
Janitors and Building Cleaners	Less than high school	$22,320	12%	71,730

How to Become One

Most maids and housekeeping cleaners are trained on the job. No formal education is required.

Education. Formal education is not required. Most maids and housekeeping cleaners are trained on the job.

Training. Entry-level maids and housekeeping cleaners typically work alongside a more experienced cleaner and gain more responsibilities and more difficult work as they become experienced.

Important Qualities

Detail oriented. Because maids and housekeeping cleaners are responsible for cleaning rooms, they must pay close attention to detail. For example, household maids need to be thorough when polishing silver.

Interpersonal skills. Maids and housekeeping cleaners who work in private homes must get along well with the people they provide services for. Those who work in hotels, hospitals, office buildings, and other places also often come into contact with people whose spaces they are cleaning. They must be polite and friendly.

Physical stamina. Maids and housekeeping cleaners spend many hours on their feet, scrubbing, bending, and stretching. As a result, they should have good physical stamina.

Pay

The median annual wage for maids and housekeeping cleaners was $19,570 in May 2012. The median wage is the wage at which half the workers in an occupation earned more than that amount and half earned less. The lowest 10 percent earned less than $16,430, and the top 10 percent earned more than $30,980.

In May 2012, the median annual wages in the top four industries employing the largest numbers of maids and housekeeping cleaners were as follows:

Hospitals; state, local, and private	$22,840
Nursing and residential care facilities	19,910
Administrative and support services	19,140
Accommodation and food services	19,010

Job Outlook

Employment of maids and housekeeping cleaners is projected to grow 13 percent from 2012 to 2022, about as fast as the average for all occupations.

Most new jobs are expected in health care, as this industry is expected to grow rapidly. In addition, many jobs will continue to be at hotels–the largest employing industry–as demand for accommodations increases.

Companies that supply cleaning services on a contract basis also will experience employment growth as more of this work is being contracted out.

Job Prospects. Job opportunities are expected to be good overall and more favorable for those who have related work experience. Many job openings will result from the need to replace workers who leave the occupation each year.

O*NET

➤ Maids and Housekeeping Cleaners (37-2012.00)

Contacts for More Information

For more information about certification for maids and housekeeping cleaners, visit:

➤ Building Service Contractors Association International (www.bscai.org/)

➤ IEHA (formerly International Executive Housekeepers Association) (www.ieha.org/)

For information about the home cleaning industry, visit

➤ Association of Residential Cleaning Services International (www.arcsi.org/)

For more information about cleaning and housekeeping, visit

➤ The Housekeeping Channel (www.housekeepingchannel.com/)

Pest Control Workers

- **2012 Median Pay** .... $30,060 per year
  $14.45 per hour

- **Entry-Level Education** ... High school diploma or equivalent

- **Work Experience in a Related Occupation**............... None

- **On-the-Job Training** ...Moderate-term on-the-job training

- **Number of Jobs 2012** 65,400

- **Job Outlook, 2012–22** .... 20% (Faster than average)

- **Employment Change, 2012–22** 12,800

What Pest Control Workers Do

Pest control workers remove unwanted creatures, such as roaches, rats, ants, bedbugs, and termites that infest buildings and surrounding areas.

Duties. Pest control workers typically do the following:

- Inspect buildings and premises for signs of pests or infestation
- Determine the type of treatment needed to eliminate pests
- Measure the dimensions of the area needing treatment

Pest control workers help to keep buildings free of insects, rodents, and other animals.

Median Annual Wages, May 2012

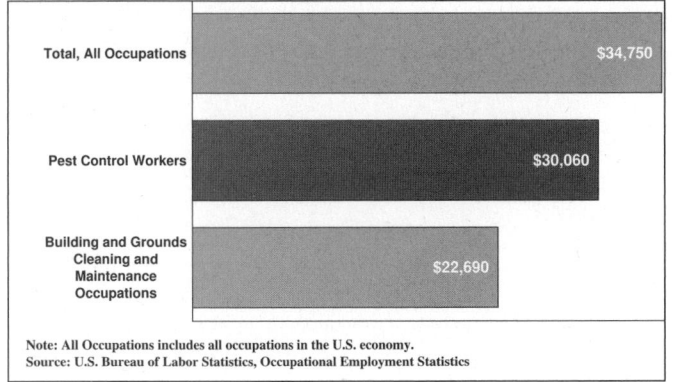

Total, All Occupations — $34,750
Pest Control Workers — $30,060
Building and Grounds Cleaning and Maintenance Occupations — $22,690

Note: All Occupations includes all occupations in the U.S. economy.
Source: U.S. Bureau of Labor Statistics, Occupational Employment Statistics

Percent Change in Employment, Projected 2012–2022

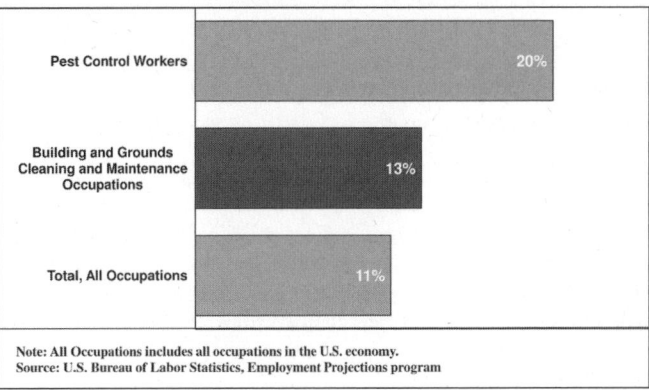

Pest Control Workers — 20%
Building and Grounds Cleaning and Maintenance Occupations — 13%
Total, All Occupations — 11%

Note: All Occupations includes all occupations in the U.S. economy.
Source: U.S. Bureau of Labor Statistics, Employment Projections program

- Estimate the cost of their services
- Use baits and set traps to remove or kill pests
- Apply pesticides in and around buildings and other structures
- Design and carry out pest management plans
- Drive trucks equipped with power spraying equipment
- Create barriers to prevent pests from entering a building

Unwanted pests that infest buildings and surrounding areas can pose serious risks to the health and safety of occupants. Pest control workers control, manage, and remove these creatures from homes, apartments, offices, and other structures to protect people and to maintain buildings' structural integrity.

To design and carry out integrated pest management plans, pest control workers must know the identity and biology of a wide range of pests. They must also know the best ways to control and remove the pests.

Although roaches, rats, ants, bedbugs, and termites are the most common pests, some pest control workers also remove irritant birds and wildlife.

Pest control workers' position titles and job duties often vary by state.

The following are examples of types of pest control workers:

Pest control technicians identify potential and actual pest problems, conduct inspections, and design control strategies. They work directly with customers and, as entry-level workers, use only a limited range of pesticides.

Applicators use a wide range of pesticides and may specialize in a particular area of pest control:

- *Termite control technicians* use chemicals and modify structures to eliminate termites and prevent future infestations. Some also repair structural damage caused by termites and build barriers to separate pests from their food source.
- *Fumigators* use gases, called fumigants, to treat specific kinds of pests or large-scale infestations. Fumigators seal infested buildings before using hoses to fill the structure with fumigants.

Warning signs are posted to keep people from going into fumigated buildings, and fumigators monitor buildings closely to detect and stop leaks.

Work Environment

Pest control workers held about 65,400 jobs in 2012. About 88 percent worked in the services to buildings and dwellings industry.

Pest control workers must travel to clients' sites. They work both indoors and outdoors, in all types of weather. To inspect sites and treat them, workers must often kneel, bend, and crawl in tight spaces.

When working with pesticides, pest control workers must wear protective gear, including gloves, goggles, and when required, respirators.

Work Schedules. Most pest control workers are employed full time. Working evenings and weekends is common.

Injuries and Illnesses. Pest control chemicals are toxic and can be harmful to humans, so care should be taken to use such chemicals properly. Although workers are trained and licensed for pesticide usage and wear protective equipment, some injuries and illnesses from pesticide exposure may still occur.

How to Become One

State laws require pest control workers to be licensed. Most workers need a high school diploma and receive on-the-job training, usually lasting less than 3 months.

Many pest control companies require that employees have good driving records.

Education. A high school diploma or equivalent is the minimum qualification for most pest control jobs.

Training. Most pest control workers begin as technicians, receiving both formal technical instruction and moderate-term on-the-job training from employers. They often study specialties such as rodent control, termite control, and fumigation. Technicians also must complete general training in pesticide use and safety. Pest control training can usually be completed in less than 3 months.

Employment Projections Data for Pest Control Workers

Occupational title	SOC Code	Employment, 2012	Projected Employment, 2022	Change, 2012–2022	
				Percent	Numeric
Pest control workers	37-2021	65,400	78,200	20	12,800

Source: U.S. Bureau of Labor Statistics, Employment Projections Program

*Note: Data are rounded. Go to **Occupational Information Included in the OOH** for a discussion of the data in this table.*

Similar Occupations   This table shows a list of occupations with job duties that are similar to those of pest control workers.

Occupations	Entry-level Education	2012 Pay	Projected Job Growth	Average Annual Openings
Construction Laborers and Helpers	See "How to Become One"	$29,277	25%	58,790
Grounds Maintenance Workers	See "How to Become One"	$24,180	13%	46,350
Janitors and Building Cleaners	Less than high school	$22,320	12%	71,730

After completing the required training, workers are qualified to provide pest control services. Because pest control methods change, workers often attend continuing education classes.

Licenses, Certifications, and Registrations. Pest control workers must be licensed. Licensure requirements vary by state, but workers usually must complete training and pass an exam. Some states have additional requirements, such as having a high school diploma or GED, completing an apprenticeship, and passing a background check. States may have yet more requirements for applicators.

Advancement. Pest control workers typically advance as they gain experience. Applicators with several years of experience often become supervisors. Some experienced workers start their own pest management company.

Important Qualities

Bookkeeping skills. Pest control workers must keep accurate records of the hours they work, chemicals they use, and payments they collect. Self-employed workers, in particular, need these skills to run their business.

Customer-service skills. Pest control workers should be friendly and polite when they interact with customers at their homes or businesses.

Detail oriented. Because pest control workers apply pesticides, they need to be able to follow instructions carefully in order to prevent harm to residents, pets, the environment, and themselves.

Physical stamina. Pest control workers may spend hours on their feet, often crouching, kneeling, and crawling. They also must be able to withstand uncomfortable conditions, such as heat when they climb into attics in the summertime and cold when they slide into crawl spaces during winter.

Pay

The median annual wage for pest control workers was $30,060 in May 2012. The median wage is the wage at which half the workers in an occupation earned more than that amount and half earned less. The lowest 10 percent earned less than $19,540, and the top 10 percent earned more than $47,770.

Job Outlook

Employment of pest control workers is projected to grow 20 percent from 2012 to 2022, faster than the average for all occupations.

Employment is projected to increase as more people use professional pest control services rather than trying to control pests themselves. Environmental and health concerns also will result in more people hiring professionals.

Population growth, particularly in the South, where pests are more common, will result in the construction of more buildings, requiring additional pest management.

Job Prospects. Job opportunities are expected to be very good. The limited number of people seeking work in pest control, expected employment growth, and the need to replace workers who leave this occupation should result in many job openings.

O*NET

➤ Pest Control Workers (37-2021.00)

Contacts for More Information

For information about state licensing requirements, contact state licensing officials.

For information on pest control officials, visit
➤ Association of Structural Pest Control Regulatory Officials (www.aspcro.org/?q=control-officials)

For more information on pest control careers, visit
➤ National Pest Management Association (www.pestworld.org/)

Business and Financial

Accountants and Auditors

- **2012 Median Pay** .... $63,550 per year
  $30.55 per hour
- **Entry-Level Education** .... Bachelor's degree
- **Work Experience in a Related Occupation** .... None
- **On-the-Job Training** .... None
- **Number of Jobs 2012** 1,275,400
- **Job Outlook, 2012–22** .... 13% (As fast as average)
- **Employment Change, 2012–22** 166,700

What Accountants and Auditors Do

Accountants and auditors prepare and examine financial records. They ensure that financial records are accurate and that taxes are paid properly and on time. Accountants and auditors assess financial operations and work to help ensure that organizations run efficiently.

Duties. Accountants and auditors typically do the following:

- Examine financial statements to ensure that they are accurate and comply with laws and regulations
- Compute taxes owed, prepare tax returns, and ensure that taxes are paid properly and on time
- Inspect account books and accounting systems for efficiency and use of accepted accounting procedures

Accountants and auditors analyze and interpret financial information.

- Organize and maintain financial records
- Assess financial operations and make best-practices recommendations to management
- Suggest ways to reduce costs, enhance revenues, and improve profits

In addition to examining and preparing financial documentation, accountants and auditors must explain their findings. This includes face-to-face meetings with organization managers and individual clients, and preparing written reports.

Many accountants and auditors specialize, depending on the particular organization that they work for. Some organizations specialize in assurance services (improving the quality or context of information for decisionmakers) or risk management (determining the probability of a misstatement on financial documentation). Other organizations specialize in specific industries, such as healthcare.

Some workers with a background in accounting and auditing teach in colleges and universities. For more information, see the profile on postsecondary teachers.

The following are examples of types of accountants and auditors:

Public accountants perform a broad range of accounting, auditing, tax, and consulting tasks. Their clients include corporations, governments, and individuals.

They work with financial documents that clients are required by law to disclose. These include tax forms and balance sheet statements that corporations must provide potential investors. For example, some public accountants concentrate on tax matters, advising corporations about the tax advantages of certain business decisions, or preparing individual income tax returns.

Public accountants, many of whom are Certified Public Accountants (CPAs), generally have their own businesses or work for public accounting firms. Publicly traded companies are required to have CPAs sign documents they submit to the Securities and Exchange Commission (SEC), including annual and quarterly reports.

External auditors review clients' financial statements and inform investors and authorities that the statements have been correctly prepared and reported.

Some public accountants specialize in forensic accounting, investigating financial crimes such as securities fraud and embezzlement, bankruptcies and contract disputes, and other complex and possibly criminal financial transactions. Forensic accountants combine their knowledge of accounting and finance with law and investigative techniques to determine if an activity is illegal. Many forensic accountants work closely with law enforcement personnel and lawyers during investigations and often appear as expert witnesses during trials.

Management accountants, also called *cost, managerial, industrial, corporate,* or *private accountants,* record and analyze the financial information of the organizations for which they work. The information that management accountants prepare is intended for internal use by business managers, not by the general public.

They often work on budgeting and performance evaluation. They also may help organizations plan the cost of doing business. Some may work with financial managers on asset management,

Median Annual Wages, May 2012

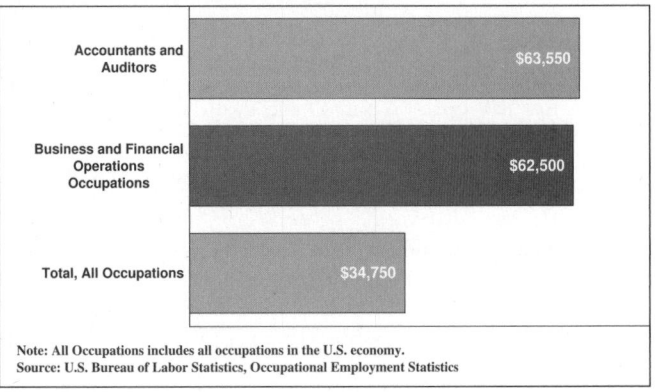

Note: All Occupations includes all occupations in the U.S. economy.
Source: U.S. Bureau of Labor Statistics, Occupational Employment Statistics

Percent Change in Employment, Projected 2012–2022

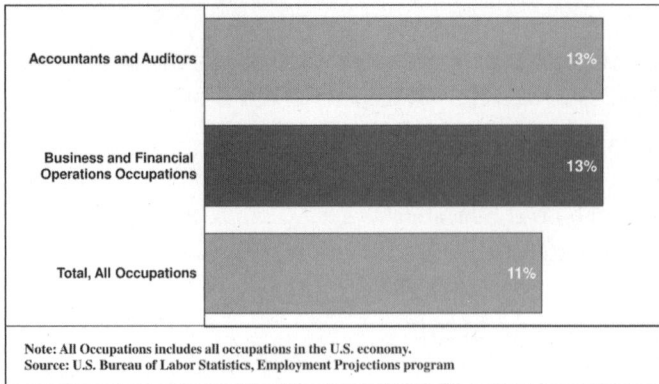

Note: All Occupations includes all occupations in the U.S. economy.
Source: U.S. Bureau of Labor Statistics, Employment Projections program

which involves planning and selecting financial investments such as stocks, bonds, and real estate.

Government accountants maintain and examine the records of government agencies and audit private businesses and individuals whose activities are subject to government regulations or taxation. Accountants employed by federal, state, and local governments ensure that revenues are received and spent in accordance with laws and regulations.

Internal auditors check for mismanagement of an organization's funds. They identify ways to improve the processes for finding and eliminating waste and fraud. The practice of internal auditing is not regulated, but The Institute of Internal Auditors (IIA) provides generally accepted standards.

Information technology auditors are internal auditors who review controls for their organization's computer systems, to ensure that the financial data comes from a reliable source.

Work Environment

Accountants and auditors held about 1.3 million jobs in 2012.

Most accountants and auditors work in offices, although some work from home. The work tends to be fast-paced and can be stressful. Although they complete much of their work alone, they sometimes work in teams with other accountants and auditors. Accountants and auditors may travel to their clients' places of business.

The industries that employed the most accountants and auditors in 2012 were as follows:

Accounting, tax preparation, bookkeeping, and payroll services	25%
Government	8
Finance and insurance	8
Management of companies and enterprises	7
Manufacturing	6

Work Schedules. Most accountants and auditors work full time. In 2012, about 1 in 5 worked more than 40 hours per week. Longer hours are typical at certain times of the year, such as at the end of the budget year or during tax season.

How to Become One

Most accountants and auditors need at least a bachelor's degree in accounting or a related field. Certification within a specific field of accounting improves job prospects. For example, many accountants become Certified Public Accountants (CPAs).

Education. Most accountant and auditor positions require at least a bachelor's degree in accounting or a related field. Some employers prefer to hire applicants who have a master's degree, either in accounting or in business administration with a concentration in accounting.

A few universities and colleges offer specialized programs, such as a bachelor's degree in internal auditing. In some cases, those with associate's degrees, as well as bookkeepers and accounting clerks who meet the education and experience requirements set by their employers, get junior accounting positions and advance to accountant positions by showing their accounting skills on the job.

Many colleges help students gain practical experience through summer or part-time internships with public accounting or business firms.

Licenses, Certifications, and Registrations. Every accountant filing a report with the Securities and Exchange Commission (SEC) is required by law to be a Certified Public Accountant (CPA). Many other accountants choose to become a CPA to enhance their job prospects or to gain clients. Many employers will often pay the costs associated with the CPA exam.

CPAs are licensed by their state's Board of Accountancy. Becoming a CPA requires passing a national exam and meeting other state requirements. Almost all states require CPA candidates to complete 150 semester hours of college coursework to be certified, which is 30 hours more than the usual 4-year bachelor's degree. Many schools offer a 5-year combined bachelor's and master's degree to meet the 150-hour requirement, but a master's degree is not required.

A few states allow a number of years of public accounting experience to substitute for a college degree.

All states use the four-part Uniform CPA Examination from the American Institute of Certified Public Accountants (AICPA). Candidates do not have to pass all four parts at once, but most states require that they pass all four parts within 18 months of passing their first part.

Almost all states require CPAs to take continuing education to keep their license.

Certification provides an advantage in the job market because it shows professional competence in a specialized field of accounting and auditing. Accountants and auditors seek certifications from a variety of professional societies. Some of the most common certifications are listed below:

The Institute of Management Accountants offers the Certified Management Accountant (CMA) to applicants who complete a bachelor's degree. Applicants must have worked at least 2 years in management accounting, pass a two-part exam, agree to meet continuing education requirements, and comply with standards of professional conduct. The exam covers areas such as financial statement analysis, working-capital policy, capital structure, valuation issues, and risk management.

Employment Projections Data for Accountants and Auditors

Occupational title	SOC Code	Employment, 2012	Projected Employment, 2022	Change, 2012–2022	
				Percent	Numeric
Accountants and auditors...	13-2011	1,275,400	1,442,200	13	166,700

Source: U.S. Bureau of Labor Statistics, Employment Projections Program

Note: Data are rounded. Go to Occupational Information Included in the OOH for a discussion of the data in this table.

The Institute of Internal Auditors (IIA) offers the Certified Internal Auditor (CIA) to graduates from accredited colleges and universities who have worked for 2 years as internal auditors and have passed a four-part exam. The IIA also offers the Certified in Control Self-Assessment (CCSA), Certified Government Auditing Professional (CGAP), and Certified Financial Services Auditor (CFSA) to those who pass the exams and meet educational and experience requirements.

ISACA offers the Certified Information Systems Auditor (CISA) to candidates who pass an exam and have 5 years of experience auditing information systems. Information systems experience, financial or operational auditing experience, or related college credit hours can be substituted for up to 2 years of experience in information systems auditing, control, or security.

For accountants with a CPA, the AICPA offers the option to receive any or all of the Accredited in Business Valuation (ABV), Certified Information Technology Professional (CITP), or Personal Financial Specialist (PFS) certifications. The ABV requires a written exam and completion of at least six business valuation projects that demonstrate a candidate's experience and competence. The CITP requires 1,000 hours of business technology experience and 75 hours of continuing education. Candidates for the PFS also must complete a certain amount work experience and education, and pass a written exam.

Advancement. Some top executives and financial managers have a background in accounting, internal auditing, or finance.

Beginning public accountants often advance to positions with more responsibility in 1 or 2 years and to senior positions within another few years. Those who excel may become supervisors, managers, or partners; open their own public accounting firm; or transfer to executive positions in management accounting or internal auditing in private firms.

Management accountants often start as cost accountants, junior internal auditors, or trainees for other accounting positions. As they rise through the organization, they may advance to accounting manager, chief cost accountant, budget director, or manager of internal auditing. Some become controllers, treasurers, financial vice presidents, chief financial officers, or corporation presidents.

Public accountants, management accountants, and internal auditors can move from one aspect of accounting and auditing to another. Public accountants often move into management accounting or internal auditing. Management accountants may become internal auditors, and internal auditors may become management accountants. However, it is less common for management accountants or internal auditors to move into public accounting.

Important Qualities

Analytical skills. Accountants and auditors must be able to identify issues in documentation and suggest solutions. For example, public accountants use analytical skills in their work to minimize tax liability, and internal auditors do so when identifying fraudulent use of funds.

Communication skills. Accountants and auditors must be able to listen carefully to facts and concerns from clients, managers, and others. They must also be able to discuss the results of their work in both meetings and written reports.

Detail oriented. Accountants and auditors must pay attention to detail when compiling and examining documentation.

Math skills. Accountants and auditors must be able to analyze, compare, and interpret facts and figures, although complex math skills are not necessary.

Organizational skills. Strong organizational skills are important for accountants and auditors who often work with a range of financial documents for a variety of clients.

Similar Occupations
This table shows a list of occupations with job duties that are similar to those of accountants and auditors.

Occupations	Entry-level Education	2012 Pay	Projected Job Growth	Average Annual Openings
Bookkeeping, Accounting, and Auditing Clerks	High school diploma or equivalent	$35,170	11%	37,000
Budget Analysts	Bachelor's degree	$69,280	6%	2,850
Cost Estimators	Bachelor's degree	$58,860	26%	11,800
Financial Analysts	Bachelor's degree	$76,950	16%	10,090
Financial Managers	Bachelor's degree	$109,740	9%	14,690
Management Analysts	Bachelor's degree	$78,600	19%	24,520
Personal Financial Advisors	Bachelor's degree	$67,520	27%	9,640
Postsecondary Teachers	See "How to Become One"	$70,380	19%	42,690
Tax Examiners and Collectors, and Revenue Agents	Bachelor's degree	$50,440	-4%	2,390
Top Executives	Bachelor's degree	$104,073	11%	70,090

Pay

The median annual wage for accountants and auditors was $63,550 in May 2012. The median wage is the wage at which half the workers in an occupation earned more than that amount and half earned less. The lowest 10 percent earned less than $39,930, and the top 10 percent earned more than $111,510.

In May 2012, the median annual wages for accountants and auditors in the top five industries in which they worked were as follows:

Finance and insurance	$66,530
Manufacturing	65,300
Management of companies and enterprises	64,670
Accounting, tax preparation, bookkeeping, and payroll services	63,910
Government	61,490

Job Outlook

Employment of accountants and auditors is projected to grow 13 percent from 2012 to 2022, about as fast as the average for all occupations. In general, employment growth of accountants and auditors is expected to be closely tied to the health of the overall economy. As the economy grows, these workers will continue to be needed to prepare and examine financial records.

There has been an increased focus on accounting in response to corporate scandals and recent financial crises. Stricter laws and regulations, particularly in the financial sector, will likely increase the demand for accounting services as organizations seek to comply with new standards. In addition, tighter lending standards are expected to increase the importance of audits, as this is a key way for organizations to demonstrate their creditworthiness.

The continued globalization of business should lead to increased demand for accounting expertise and services related to international trade and international mergers and acquisitions.

Job Prospects. Accountants and auditors who have earned professional recognition, especially as Certified Public Accountants (CPAs), should have the best prospects. Job applicants who have a master's degree in accounting or a master's degree in business with a concentration in accounting also may have an advantage.

However, competition should be strong for jobs with the most prestigious accounting and business firms.

O*NET

➤ Accountants and Auditors (13-2011.00)
➤ Accountants (13-2011.01)
➤ Auditors (13-2011.02)

Contacts for More Information

For more information about accredited accounting programs, visit
➤ AACSB International Association to Advance Collegiate Schools of Business (www.aacsb.edu)

For more information about the Certified Public Accountant (CPA) designation, visit
➤ American Institute of Certified Public Accountants (AICPA) (www.aicpa.org/)

For more information about management accounting and the Certified Management Accountant (CMA) designation, visit
➤ Institute of Management Accountants (www.imanet.org/)

For more information about internal auditing and the Certified Internal Auditor (CIA) designation, visit
➤ The Institute of Internal Auditors (https://na.theiia.org/Pages/IIA-Home.aspx)

For more information about information systems auditing and the Certified Information Systems Auditor (CISA) designation, visit
➤ ISACA (www.isaca.org/)

Appraisers and Assessors of Real Estate

- **2012 Median Pay** .... $49,540 per year
  $23.82 per hour
- **Entry-Level Education** .... Bachelor's degree
- **Work Experience in a Related Occupation** .... None
- **On-the-Job Training** .... Long-term on-the-job training
- **Number of Jobs 2012** 83,700
- **Job Outlook, 2012–22** .... 6% (Slower than average)
- **Employment Change, 2012–22** 4,700

What Appraisers and Assessors of Real Estate Do

Appraisers and assessors of real estate estimate the value of land and the buildings on the land usually before it is sold, mortgaged, taxed, insured, or developed.

Duties. Appraisers and assessors of real estate typically do the following:

- Verify legal descriptions of real estate properties in public records
- Inspect new and existing properties, noting unique characteristics
- Photograph the interior and exterior of properties
- Use "comparables," or similar nearby properties, to help determine value
- Prepare written reports on the property value
- Prepare and maintain current data on each real estate property

Appraisers and assessors work in localities that they are familiar with so that they know any environmental or other concerns that may affect the property's value.

Appraisers typically value one property at a time, and they often specialize in a certain type of real estate:

- *Commercial appraisers* specialize in property used commercially, such as office buildings, stores, and hotels.

Appraisers play an important role in the purchasing and selling of real estate.

Median Annual Wages, May 2012

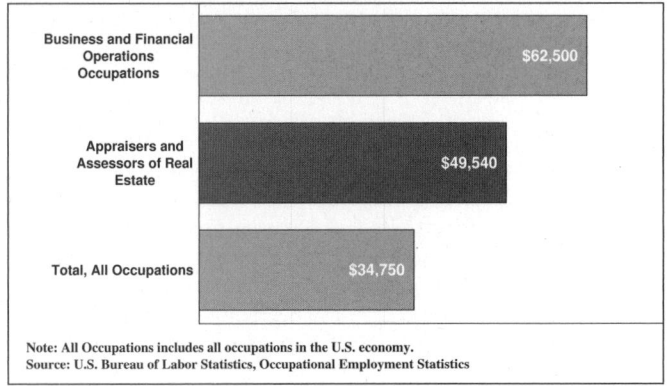

Note: All Occupations includes all occupations in the U.S. economy.
Source: U.S. Bureau of Labor Statistics, Occupational Employment Statistics

Percent Change in Employment, Projected 2012–2022

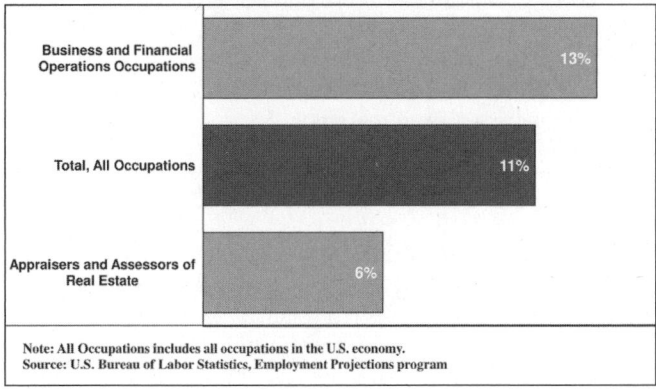

Note: All Occupations includes all occupations in the U.S. economy.
Source: U.S. Bureau of Labor Statistics, Employment Projections program

- *Residential appraisers* focus on appraising property in which people live, such as single family homes and condominiums, and appraise only those properties that house one to four families.

When estimating a property's value, appraisers note unique characteristics of the property and surrounding area, such as a noisy highway or airport nearby. They also consider the condition of a building's foundation and roof or any renovations that may have been done. In addition to photographing the outside of the building to document its condition, appraisers might also photograph a certain room or feature. After visiting the property, the appraiser estimates the value of the property by considering comparable home sales, lease records, location, view, previous appraisals, and income potential. During the entire process, appraisers record their research, observations, and methods used in calculating the property's value.

Assessors mostly work for local governments and value properties for property tax assessments. Unlike appraisers, who generally focus on one property at a time, assessors often value an entire neighborhood of homes at once by using mass appraisal techniques and computer-assisted mass appraisal systems.

Assessors must be up to date on tax assessment procedures. Taxpayers sometimes challenge the assessed value because they feel they are being charged too much for property tax. Assessors must be able to defend the accuracy of their property assessments, either to the owner directly or at a public hearing.

Assessors also keep a database of every property in their jurisdiction, identifying the property owner, assessment history, and size of the property, as well as property maps detailing the property distribution of the jurisdiction.

Work Environment

Appraisers and assessors of real estate held about 83,700 jobs in 2012. About 27 percent were self-employed. The industries that employed the most appraisers and assessors of real estate in 2012 were as follows:

Activities related to real estate 30%
Local government, excluding education and hospitals 29
Credit intermediation and related activities 4
State government, excluding education and hospitals 3
Offices of real estate agents and brokers 1

Although appraisers and assessors of real estate work in offices, they spend a large part of their day conducting site visits. Time spent on site versus in the office depends on the specialty. For example, residential appraisers tend to spend less time on office work than commercial appraisers, who might spend up to several weeks analyzing information and writing reports on one property. Appraisers who work for banks and mortgage companies generally spend most of their time inside the office, making site visits only when necessary.

Work Schedules. Appraisers and assessors of real estate typically work full time during regular business hours. However, self-employed appraisers, often called *independent fee appraisers*, usually work more than a standard 40-hour workweek, because they must often write reports during evenings and on weekends.

How to Become One

The requirements to become a fully qualified appraiser or assessor of real estate are complex and vary by state and, sometimes, by the value or type of property. Currently, most appraisers of residential real property must have at least an associate's degree to obtain the entry-level state license category. Appraisers of more complex residential and commercial real property must have at least a bachelor's degree to obtain licensure. In some localities, appraisers may qualify with a high school diploma. Employers generally require these candidates to take basic appraisal courses, complete on-the-job training through an apprenticeship, and work enough hours to meet the requirements for appraisal licenses or certificates. Beginning January 1, 2015, all certified appraisers will be required to have a bachelor's degree prior to obtaining their appraisal license.

In addition, all assessors must be licensed or certified, but requirements vary by state. Check with your state's licensing board for specific requirements for both assessors and appraisers.

Education. Although requirements vary by state, appraisers of residential real property usually must have at least an associate's degree, and appraisers of more complex residential or commercial property usually must have at least a bachelor's degree. In practice, however, most have a bachelor's degree.

Courses in subjects such as economics, finance, mathematics, computer science, English, and business or real estate law can be useful for prospective appraisers and assessors.

For assessors, most states set education and experience requirements that an assessor must meet in order to practice. A few states have no statewide requirements; instead, each locality sets the standards. In some localities, candidates may qualify with a high school diploma.

Training. Employers generally require candidates to take basic appraisal courses, complete on-the-job training through long-term on-the-job training, and work enough hours to meet the requirements for licenses or certificates.

Licenses, Certifications, and Registrations. Federal law requires that most appraisers performing appraisals in federally related transactions (federally insured banks and financial institutions) have a state license or certification. There is no such federal requirement for assessors, although some states require certification.

Employment Projections Data for Appraisers and Assessors of Real Estate

Occupational title	SOC Code	Employment, 2012	Projected Employment, 2022	Change, 2012–2022	
				Percent	Numeric
Appraisers and assessors of real estate................................ 13-2021		83,700	88,400	6	4,700

Source: U.S. Bureau of Labor Statistics, Employment Projections Program

Note: **Data are rounded. Go to Occupational Information Included in the OOH** *for a discussion of the data in this table.*

Real property appraisers usually value one property at a time, while assessors value many at once, but both occupations use similar methods and techniques. As a result, assessors and appraisers tend to take the same courses for certification. In addition to passing a statewide examination, candidates must usually complete a set number of on-the-job hours.

The level of certification determines what type of property a person may appraise. The two federally required certifications are:

• Certified Residential Real Property Appraiser

• Certified General Real Property Appraiser

Being a Certified Residential Real Property Appraiser is the minimum requirement to appraise a residential property with a loan amount over $250,000 or any other type of property even if the loan amount is less than $250,000. Obtaining this certification requires:

• Associate's degree or 21 units of continuing education (as of 2015, a bachelor's degree)

• 200 hours of appraiser-specific classroom training

• 2,500 hours of work experience over at least 2 years

Being a Certified General Real Property Appraiser permits a person to appraise any property of any type and any value. Obtaining this certification requires:

• Bachelor's degree or 30 units of specific college-level education

• 300 hours of appraiser-specific classroom training

• 3,000 hours of work experience over at least 2A« years

Most states offer a third certification: the Licensed Residential Real Property Appraiser. With this certification, appraisers may appraise noncomplex one-to-four unit residences with a value of less than $1,000,000 and complex one-to-four unit residences with a value of less than $250,000. Obtaining this certification requires:

• 150 qualifying education hours (as of January 2015, 30 semester hours of college-level education)

• 2,000 hours of on-the-job training over at least 1 year

For all of these certifications, candidates must:

• Have 15 hours of classroom instruction on the Uniform Standards of Professional Appraisal Practice

• Pass an exam

In most states, candidates working toward licensure or certification as an appraiser are considered to be trainees. Training programs vary by state, but they usually require candidates to take at least 75 hours of specified appraiser education before applying for a job as a trainee.

Unlike appraisers, assessors have no federal requirement for certification. In states that mandate certification for assessors, the requirements are usually similar to those for appraisers. Some states also have more than one level of certification. For example, the International Association of Assessing Officers (IAAO) offers the Certified Assessment Evaluator (CAE). This designation covers topics that include property valuation for tax purposes, property tax administration, and property tax policy. As of January 1, 2014, applicants are required to have a bachelor's degree prior to obtaining the designation.

For those states that do not require certification for assessors, the hiring office usually requires the candidate to take basic appraisal courses, complete on-the-job training, and work enough hours to meet the requirements for appraisal licenses or certificates. Many assessors also have a state appraisal license.

Assessors tend to start working in an assessor's office that provides on-the-job training; smaller municipalities are often unable to provide this work experience. An alternate source of experience for aspiring assessors is through a revaluation firm.

Both appraisers and assessors must take continuing education courses to keep the license or certification. Requirements vary by state.

Important Qualities

Analytical skills. Appraisers and assessors of real estate use many sources of data when valuing a property. As a result, they must carefully research and analyze all data before estimating a value and producing a final written report.

Customer-service skills. Because appraisers must regularly interact with clients, being polite and friendly is important. In addition, these characteristics may help expand future business opportunities.

Math skills. Accurately analyzing real estate data, such as calculating square footage of land and building space, requires workers to have good math skills.

Organizational skills. To successfully accomplish all the tasks related to appraising and assessing a property, appraisers and assessors of real estate need good organizational skills.

Similar Occupations   This table shows a list of occupations with job duties that are similar to those of appraisers and assessors of real estate.

Occupations	Entry-level Education	2012 Pay	Projected Job Growth	Average Annual Openings
Claims Adjusters, Appraisers, Examiners, and Investigators	See "How to Become One"	$59,902	3%	8,340
Construction and Building Inspectors	High school diploma or equivalent	$53,450	12%	3,670
Real Estate Brokers and Sales Agents	High school diploma or equivalent	$42,723	11%	8,630

Problem-solving skills. Appraisers and assessors of real estate may encounter unexpected problems when appraising or assessing a property's value. The ability to develop and apply an alternative solution is crucial to successfully completing the appraisal and report on time.

Time-management skills. Appraisers and assessors of real estate often work under time constraints, sometimes appraising many properties in a single day. As a result, managing time and meeting deadlines are important.

Pay

The median annual wage for appraisers and assessors of real estate was $49,540 in May 2012. The median wage is the wage at which half the workers in an occupation earned more than that amount and half earned less. The lowest 10 percent earned less than $25,850, and the top 10 percent earned more than $91,700.

In May 2012, the median annual wages in the top five industries in which appraisers and assessors worked were as follows:

Credit intermediation and related activities	$65,830
State government, excluding schools and hospitals	52,960
Activities related to real estate	49,810
Local government, excluding schools and hospitals	46,320
Offices of real estate agents and brokers	37,070

Earnings for independent fee appraisers can vary significantly because they are paid fees on the basis of each appraisal.

Job Outlook

Employment of appraisers and assessors of real estate is projected to grow 6 percent from 2012 to 2022, slower than the average for all occupations.

Demand for appraisal services is linked to the real estate market, which can fluctuate in the short term. Over the long term, employment growth will be driven by economic expansion and population increases–factors that generate demand for real property.

Although economic expansion and population increases are expected over the coming decade, employment is projected to slow down due to productivity increases brought about by greater use of mobile technologies, which allow workers to appraise and assess properties more efficiently. In addition, the increased use of automated valuation models to aid in the appraisal of property for mortgages might also increase appraisers' productivity, reducing demand for additional appraisers for traditional lending practices.

Job Prospects. Overall job opportunities are expected to be highly competitive. Job opportunities should be best in areas with active real estate markets. Although job opportunities for established certified appraisers are expected to be available in these areas, the cyclical nature of the real estate market will directly affect demand for appraisers, especially those who appraise residential properties. In times of recession, fewer people buy or sell real estate, decreasing the demand for appraisals. As a result, job opportunities should be best for those who are able to switch specialties and appraise different types of properties.

O*NET

➤ Appraisers and Assessors of Real Estate (13-2021.00)
➤ Assessors (13-2021.01)
➤ Appraisers, Real Estate (13-2021.02)

Contacts for More Information

For more information about appraisers of real estate, visit
➤ American Society of Appraisers (www.appraisers.org)
➤ Appraisal Institute (www.appraisalinstitute.org/)

For more information about assessors of real estate, visit
➤ International Association of Assessing Officers (www.iaao.org/)
For more information about licensure requirements for appraisers and assessors of real estate, visit
➤ The Appraisal Foundation (www.appraisalfoundation.org/)

Budget Analysts

- **2012 Median Pay** .... $69,280 per year
  $33.31 per hour
- **Entry-Level Education** ....Bachelor's degree
- **Work Experience in a Related Occupation**.............. None
- **On-the-Job Training** .... None
- **Number of Jobs 2012** 61,700
- **Job Outlook, 2012–22** .... 6% (Slower than average)
- **Employment Change, 2012–22** 3,800

What Budget Analysts Do

Budget analysts help public and private institutions organize their finances. They prepare budget reports and monitor institutional spending.

Duties. Budget analysts typically do the following:

- Work with program and project managers to develop the organization's budget
- Review managers' budget proposals for completeness, accuracy, and compliance with laws and other regulations
- Combine all the program and department budgets together into a consolidated organizational budget and review all funding requests for merit
- Explain their recommendations for funding requests to others in the organization, legislators, and the public

Budget analysts help organizations determine the best use of financial resources.

Median Annual Wages, May 2012

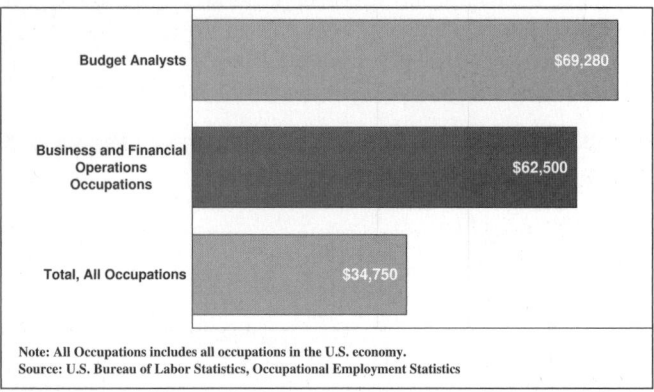

Note: All Occupations includes all occupations in the U.S. economy.
Source: U.S. Bureau of Labor Statistics, Occupational Employment Statistics

Percent Change in Employment, Projected 2012–2022

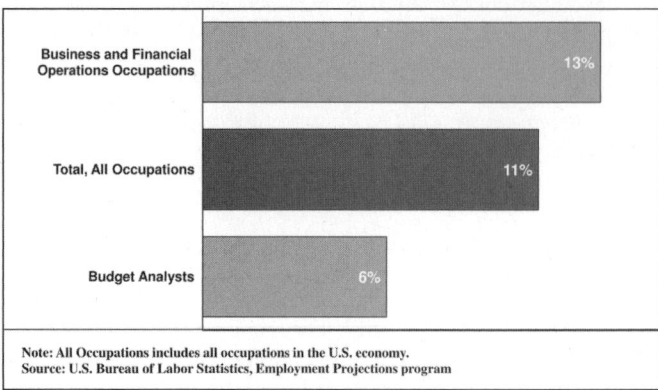

Note: All Occupations includes all occupations in the U.S. economy.
Source: U.S. Bureau of Labor Statistics, Employment Projections program

- Help the chief operations officer, agency head, or other top managers analyze proposed plans and find alternatives if the projected results are unsatisfactory

- Monitor organizational spending to ensure that it is within budget

- Inform program managers of the status and availability of funds

- Estimate future financial needs

Budget analysts advise various institutions–including governments, universities, and businesses–on how to organize their finances. They prepare annual and special reports and evaluate budget proposals. They analyze data to determine the costs and benefits of various programs and recommend funding levels based on their findings. Although elected officials (in government) or top executives (in a private company) usually make the final decision on an organization's budget, they rely on the work of budget analysts to prepare the information for that decision.

Sometimes, budget analysts use cost-benefit analyses to review financial requests, assess program tradeoffs, and explore alternative funding methods. Budget analysts also may examine past budgets and research economic and financial developments that affect the organization's income and expenditures. Budget analysts may recommend program spending cuts or redistributing extra funds.

Throughout the year, budget analysts oversee spending to ensure compliance with the budget and determine whether changes to funding levels are needed for certain programs. Analysts also evaluate programs to determine whether they are producing the desired results.

In addition to providing technical analysis, budget analysts must effectively communicate their recommendations to officials within the organization. For example, if there is a difference between the approved budget and actual spending, budget analysts may write a report explaining the variations and recommend changes to reconcile the differences.

Budget analysts working in government attend committee hearings to explain their recommendations to legislators. Occasionally,

budget analysts may evaluate how well a program is doing, provide policy analysis, and draft budget-related legislation.

Work Environment

Budget analysts held about 61,700 jobs in 2012. They worked in a variety of settings, including government agencies, universities, and companies. Although budget analysts usually work in offices, some may travel to get budget details firsthand or to verify funding allocations. The industries that employed the most budget analysts in 2012 were as follows:

Federal government, excluding postal service 20%
Educational services; state, local, and private 14
State government, excluding education and hospitals 12
Manufacturing 10
Professional, scientific, and technical services 10

Budget analysts spend most of their time analyzing data and preparing budget proposals. In nonprofit and government organizations, analysts try to find the most efficient way to distribute funds and other resources among various departments and programs. In private firms, a budget analyst's main responsibility is to review the budget and seek new ways to improve efficiency and increase profits.

Work Schedules. Most budget analysts work full time, and overtime is sometimes required during final reviews of budgets. The pressures of deadlines and tight work schedules can be stressful.

How to Become One

A bachelor's degree is typically required to become a budget analyst, although some employers prefer candidates with a master's degree.

Education. Employers generally require budget analysts to have at least a bachelor's degree. However, some employers may require candidates to have a master's degree. Because developing a budget requires strong numerical and analytical skills, courses in statistics or accounting are helpful. For the federal government, a bachelor's degree in any field is enough for an entry-level budget analyst position. State and local governments have varying requirements but

Employment Projections Data for Budget Analysts

Occupational title	SOC Code	Employment, 2012	Projected Employment, 2022	Change, 2012–2022	
				Percent	Numeric
Budget analysts	13-2031	61,700	65,500	6	3,800

Source: U.S. Bureau of Labor Statistics, Employment Projections Program

Note: Data are rounded. Go to **Occupational Information Included in the OOH** *for a discussion of the data in this table.*

Similar Occupations   This table shows a list of occupations with job duties that are similar to those of budget analysts.

Occupations	Entry-level Education	2012 Pay	Projected Job Growth	Average Annual Openings
Accountants and Auditors	Bachelor's degree	$63,550	13%	54,420
Cost Estimators	Bachelor's degree	$58,860	26%	11,800
Economists	Master's degree	$91,860	14%	740
Financial Analysts	Bachelor's degree	$76,950	16%	10,090
Financial Managers	Bachelor's degree	$109,740	9%	14,690
Management Analysts	Bachelor's degree	$78,600	19%	24,520
Tax Examiners and Collectors, and Revenue Agents	Bachelor's degree	$50,440	-4%	2,390

usually require a bachelor's degree in one of many areas, such as accounting, finance, business, public administration, economics, statistics, political science, or sociology.

Sometimes, budget-related or finance-related work experience can be substituted for formal education.

Licenses, Certifications, and Registrations. Government budget analysts may earn the Certified Government Financial Manager credential from the Association of Government Accountants. To earn this certification, candidates must have a minimum of a bachelor's degree, 24 credit hours of study in financial management, 2 years of professional-level experience in governmental financial management, and they must pass a series of exams. To keep the certification, budget analysts must take 80 hours of continuing education every 2 years.

Advancement. Entry-level budget analysts begin with limited responsibilities, but advancement is common. As analysts gain experience, they have the opportunity to advance to intermediate and senior budget analyst positions.

Important Qualities

Analytical skills. Budget analysts must be able to process a variety of information, evaluate costs and benefits, and solve complex problems.

Communication skills. Budget analysts need strong communication skills because they often have to explain and defend their analyses and recommendations in meetings and legislative committee hearings.

Detail oriented. Creating an efficient budget requires careful analysis of each budget item.

Math skills. Most budget analysts need math skills and should be able to use certain software, including spreadsheets, database functions, and financial analysis programs.

Writing skills. Budget analysts must present technical information in writing that is understandable for the intended audience.

Pay

The median annual wage for budget analysts was $69,280 in May 2012. The median wage is the wage at which half the workers in an occupation earned more than that amount and half earned less. The lowest 10 percent earned less than $45,720, and the top 10 percent earned more than $103,590.

Job Outlook

Employment of budget analysts is projected to grow 6 percent from 2012 to 2022, slower than the average for all occupations. Budget analysis is getting more complex as more types of data and statistical techniques become available. The greater complexity of

the job and its expanding job duties are expected to create a need for more budget analysts.

Efficient use of public funds is increasingly expected. During periods of budget cutbacks, the expertise of budget analysts remains in high demand, meaning employment remains more stable in comparison with other public employees. Therefore, some employment growth from 2012 to 2022 is likely, but it also may be tempered by limited government spending.

Job Prospects. This occupation has fairly steady turnover, as budget analysts often leave the occupation to pursue opportunities to work in similar areas. These opportunities include positions as higher-level budget analysts at other organizations and positions in related business and financial occupations, such as financial analysts. For this reason, job prospects are expected to be good for entry-level budget analysts.

O*NET

➤ Budget Analysts (13-2031.00)

Contacts for More Information

For information about becoming a state budget analyst, visit
➤ National Association of State Budget Officers (www.nasbo.org/)

For information about the Government Financial Manager certification, visit
➤ Association of Government Accountants (www.agacgfm.org)

Claims Adjusters, Appraisers, Examiners, and Investigators

- **2012 Median Pay** .... $59,850 per year
  $28.78 per hour
- **Entry-Level Education** ....See "How to Become One"
- **Work Experience in a Related Occupation**............... None
- **On-the-Job Training** ....See "How to Become One"
- **Number of Jobs 2012** 311,100
- **Job Outlook, 2012–22**.............. 3% (Slower than average)
- **Employment Change, 2012–22** 10,800

What Claims Adjusters, Appraisers, Examiners, and Investigators Do

Claims adjusters, appraisers, examiners, and investigators evaluate insurance claims. They decide whether an insurance company must pay a claim, and if so, how much.

Duties. Claims adjusters, appraisers, examiners, and investigators typically do the following:

- Investigate, evaluate, and settle insurance claims
- Determine whether the insurance policy covers the loss claimed
- Decide the appropriate amount the insurance company should pay
- Ensure that claims are not fraudulent
- Contact claimants' doctors or employers to get additional information on questionable claims
- Confer with legal counsel on claims when needed
- Negotiate settlements
- Authorize payments

What claims adjusters, appraisers, examiners, and investigators do varies by the type of insurance company they work for. They must know a lot about what their company insures. For example, workers in property and casualty insurance must know housing and construction costs to properly evaluate damage from floods or fires. Workers in health insurance must be able to determine which types of treatments are medically necessary and which are questionable.

Adjusters inspect property damage to determine how much the insurance company should pay for the loss. The property they inspect could be a home, a business, or an automobile.

They interview the claimant and witnesses, inspect the property, and do additional research, such as look at police reports. Adjusters may consult with other workers, such as accountants, architects, construction workers, engineers, lawyers, and physicians, who can offer a more expert evaluation of a claim.

They gather information–including photographs and statements, either written or recorded audio or video–and put it in a report that claims examiners use to evaluate the claim. When the examiner approves the policyholder's claim, the claims adjuster negotiates with the claimant and settles the claim.

If the claimant contests the outcome of the claim or the settlement, adjusters work with attorneys and expert witnesses to defend the insurer's position.

Some claims adjusters work as self-employed *public adjusters.* Often, they are hired by claimants who prefer not to rely on the insurance company's adjuster. The goal of adjusters working for insurance companies is to save as much money for the company as possible. The goal of a public adjuster working for a claimant is to get the highest possible amount paid to the claimant. They are paid a percentage of the settled claim.

Claims adjusters evaluate insurance claims, report their findings, and make recommendations.

Sometimes, self-employed adjusters are hired by insurance companies in place of hiring adjusters as regular employees. In this case, the self-employed adjusters work in the interest of the insurance company.

Appraisers estimate the cost or value of an insured item. Most appraisers who work for insurance companies and independent adjusting firms are *auto damage appraisers.* They inspect damaged vehicles after an accident and estimate the cost of repairs. This information then goes to the adjuster, who puts the estimated cost of repairs into the settlement.

Claims examiners review claims after they are submitted to ensure that proper guidelines have been followed by claimants and adjusters. They may assist adjusters with complicated claims or when, for example, a natural disaster occurs and the volume of claims increases.

Most claims examiners work for life or health insurance companies. Examiners who work for health insurance companies review health-related claims to see whether the costs are reasonable, given the diagnosis. After they review the claim, they authorize appropriate payment, deny the claim, or refer the claim to an investigator.

Examiners who work for life insurance companies review the causes of death and pay particular attention to accidents, because most life insurance companies pay additional benefits if a death is accidental. Examiners also may review new applications for life insurance policies to make sure the applicants have no serious illnesses that would make them a high risk to insure.

Insurance investigators handle claims in which the company suspects fraudulent or criminal activity such as arson, staged accidents, or unnecessary medical treatments. The severity of insur-

Median Annual Wages, May 2012

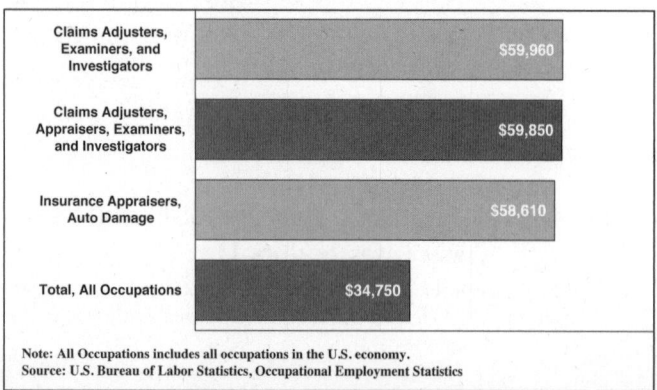

Claims Adjusters, Examiners, and Investigators	$59,960
Claims Adjusters, Appraisers, Examiners, and Investigators	$59,850
Insurance Appraisers, Auto Damage	$58,610
Total, All Occupations	$34,750

Note: All Occupations includes all occupations in the U.S. economy.
Source: U.S. Bureau of Labor Statistics, Occupational Employment Statistics

Percent Change in Employment, Projected 2012–2022

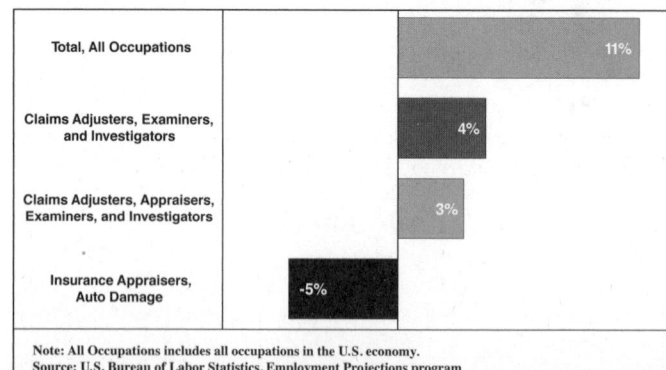

Total, All Occupations	11%
Claims Adjusters, Examiners, and Investigators	4%
Claims Adjusters, Appraisers, Examiners, and Investigators	3%
Insurance Appraisers, Auto Damage	-5%

Note: All Occupations includes all occupations in the U.S. economy.
Source: U.S. Bureau of Labor Statistics, Employment Projections program

Employment Projections Data for Claims Adjusters, Appraisers, Examiners, and Investigators

Occupational title	SOC Code	Employment, 2012	Projected Employment, 2022	Change, 2012–2022	
				Percent	Numeric
Claims adjusters, appraisers, examiners, and investigators	13-1030	311,100	321,900	3	10,800
Claims adjusters, examiners, and investigators.................	13-1031	297,600	309,100	4	11,500
Insurance appraisers, auto damage	13-1032	13,500	12,800	-5	-700

Source: U.S. Bureau of Labor Statistics, Employment Projections Program

Note: Data are rounded. Go to **Occupational Information Included in the OOH** *for a discussion of the data in this table.*

ance fraud cases varies, from claimants overstating vehicle damage to complicated fraud rings. Investigators often do surveillance work. For example, in the case of a fraudulent workers' compensation claim, an investigator may covertly watch the claimant to see if he or she does activities that would be ruled out by injuries stated in the claim.

Work Environment

Claims adjusters, appraisers, examiners, and investigators held about 311,100 jobs in 2012. Their work environments vary. Claims adjusters and examiners spend time in offices reviewing documents and conducting research, in addition to working outside when examining damaged property. Appraisers and investigators work outside more often, inspecting damaged buildings and automobiles and conducting surveillance. Auto damage appraisers spend much of their time at automotive body shops estimating vehicle damage costs.

Workers who inspect damaged buildings must be wary of potential hazards, such as collapsed roofs and floors, as well as weakened structures.

The industries that employed the most claims adjusters, appraisers, examiners, and investigators in 2012 were as follows:

Insurance carriers 49%
Agencies, brokerages, and other insurance related activities ... 22
Federal government, excluding postal service 15
State and local government, excluding education
   and hospitals.. 4
Management of companies and enterprises.............................. 2

Work Schedules. Most claims adjusters, appraisers, examiners, and investigators work full time. However, their work schedules vary.

Adjusters often must arrange their work schedules to accommodate evening and weekend appointments with clients. This sometimes results in adjusters working irregular schedules, especially when they have a lot of claims to review.

In contrast, auto damage appraisers typically work regular hours and rarely work on the weekends, although they often spend much of their time at automotive body shops estimating vehicle damage costs.

Insurance investigators often work irregular schedules because of the need to conduct surveillance and contact people who are not available during normal working hours. Early morning, evening, and weekend work is common.

How to Become One

A high school diploma or equivalent is typically required by employers who hire workers as entry-level claims adjusters, examiners, or investigators. Higher positions may require a bachelor's degree or some insurance-related work experience. Auto damage appraisers typically have a postsecondary non-degree award or work experience in identifying and estimating the cost of automotive repair.

Education. A high school diploma or equivalent is typically required to work as an entry-level claims adjuster, examiner, or investigator. However, employers sometimes prefer to hire applicants who have a bachelor's degree or some insurance-related work experience or vocational training. Auto damage appraisers typically have a postsecondary non-degree award or experience working in an auto repair shop, identifying and estimating the cost of automotive repair.

Different backgrounds or college coursework are best for different types of work in these occupations. For example, a business or an accounting background might be best for someone to specialize in claims of financial loss due to strikes, equipment breakdowns, or merchandise damage. College training in architecture or engineering is helpful for adjusting industrial claims, such as those involving damage from fires or other accidents. A legal background is beneficial to someone handling workers' compensation and product liability cases. A medical background is useful for examiners working on medical and life insurance claims.

Although auto damage appraisers are not required to have a college education, most companies prefer to hire people who have

Similar Occupations   This table shows a list of occupations with job duties that are similar to those of claims adjusters, appraisers, examiners, and investigators.

Occupations	Entry-level Education	2012 Pay	Projected Job Growth	Average Annual Openings
Appraisers and Assessors of Real Estate	Bachelor's degree	$49,540	6%	1,210
Automotive Body and Glass Repairers	High school diploma or equivalent	$37,817	13%	5,700
Automotive Service Technicians and Mechanics	High school diploma or equivalent	$36,610	9%	23,760
Construction and Building Inspectors	High school diploma or equivalent	$53,450	12%	3,670
Cost Estimators	Bachelor's degree	$58,860	26%	11,800
Fire Inspectors and Investigators	High school diploma or equivalent	$53,990	7%	440

formal training, experience, or knowledge and technical skills to identify and estimate the cost of automotive repair. Many vocational schools and some community colleges offer programs in auto body repair and teach students how to estimate the costs to repair damaged vehicles.

For investigator jobs, a high school diploma or equivalent is the typical education requirement. Most insurance companies prefer to hire people trained as law enforcement officers, private investigators, claims adjusters, or examiners because these workers have good interviewing and interrogation skills.

Training. At the beginning of their careers, claims adjusters, examiners, and investigators work on small claims, under the supervision of an experienced worker. As they learn more about claims investigation and settlement, they are assigned larger, more complex claims.

Auto damage appraisers typically get on-the-job training, which may last several months. This training usually involves working under supervision of a more experienced appraiser while estimating damage costs until the employer decides the trainee is ready to do estimates on his or her own.

Licenses, Certifications, and Registrations. Licensing requirements for claims adjusters, appraisers, examiners, and investigators vary by state. Some states have few requirements, and others require either completing pre-licensing education, a satisfactory score on a licensing exam, or both.

In some states, claims adjusters employed by insurance companies can work under the company license and need not become licensed themselves.

Public adjusters may need to meet separate or additional requirements.

Some states that require licensing also require a certain number of continuing education credits per year to renew the license. Federal and state laws and court decisions affect how claims must be handled and what insurance policies can and must cover. Examiners working on life and health claims must stay up to date on new medical procedures and prescription drugs. Examiners working on auto claims must be familiar with new car models and repair techniques. Workers can fulfill their continuing education requirements by attending classes or workshops, by writing articles for claims publications, or by giving lectures and presentations.

Important Qualities

Analytical skills. Adjusters and examiners must evaluate whether the insurance company is obligated to pay a claim and determine the amount to pay. Adjusters must carefully consider various pieces of information to reach a decision.

Communication skills. Claims adjusters and investigators must get information from a wide range of people, including claimants, witnesses, and medical experts. They must know the right questions to ask in order to gather the information they need.

Interpersonal skills. Adjusters, examiners, and investigators often meet with claimants and others who may be upset by the situation that requires a claim or by the settlement the company is offering. These workers must be understanding yet firm with their company's policies.

Math skills. Appraisers must be able to calculate property damage.

Pay

The median annual wage for claims adjusters, examiners, and investigators was $59,960 in May 2012. The median wage is the wage at which half of the workers in an occupation earned more than that amount and half earned less. The lowest 10 percent earned less than $36,950, and the top 10 percent earned more than $89,810.

The median annual wage for insurance appraisers of auto damage was $58,610 in May 2012. The lowest 10 percent earned less than $42,260, and the top 10 percent earned more than $82,540.

Job Outlook

Employment of claims adjusters, appraisers, examiners, and investigators is projected to grow 3 percent from 2012 to 2022, slower than the average for all occupations.

Employment of claims adjusters, examiners, and investigators is projected to grow 4 percent from 2012 to 2022, slower than the average for all occupations. Employment growth should stem primarily from the growth of the health insurance industry. Federal legislation mandating individual coverage may increase the number of health insurance customers, including high-risk individuals who are more likely to file claims. This is expected to increase the demand for claims adjusters to determine which treatments are approved and how much the company will pay.

In addition, rising medical costs may result in a greater need for claims examiners to carefully review a growing number of medical claims. An increase in the number of claims being made by a growing elderly population should also spur demand for health insurance claims adjusters and examiners.

Demand for claims adjusters in property and casualty insurance is influenced by the number of natural disasters, such as floods and fires. According to data from the Federal Emergency Management Agency, the number of natural disasters has increased in recent years. If this trend continues, claims adjusters in this field may see strong employment growth.

These factors will be somewhat offset by automation. Technology allows less complex claims to be processed automatically, which frees adjusters to work on more complex claims. This means that fewer adjusters are needed per claim, reducing the needed number of adjusters on staff.

Employment of auto damage appraisers is projected to decline 5 percent from 2012 to 2022. In recent years, the number of automobile accidents relative to the population has declined. As automobiles become safer, the number of traffic accidents is expected to decline. This will result in decreased demand for the services of auto damage appraisers.

Job Prospects. Job opportunities for claims adjusters and examiners should be best in the health insurance industry as the number of health insurance customers expands. In addition, prospects for claims adjusters in property and casualty insurance will likely be best in areas susceptible to natural disasters. These areas include the Gulf Coast, which can have a large number of hurricanes, and the West Coast, which is vulnerable to wildfires.

O*NET

➤ Claims Adjusters, Examiners, and Investigators (13-1031.00)
➤ Claims Examiners, Property and Casualty Insurance (13-1031.01)
➤ Insurance Adjusters, Examiners, and Investigators (13-1031.02)
➤ Insurance Appraisers, Auto Damage (13-1032.00)

Contacts for More Information

For more information about insurance, visit
➤ The Institutes (www.aicpcu.org/)
➤ International Claim Association (www.claim.org/)
➤ National Association of Public Insurance Adjusters (www.napia.com/)

Compensation, Benefits, and Job Analysis Specialists

- **2012 Median Pay** .... $59,090 per year
  $28.41 per hour
- **Entry-Level Education** ....Bachelor's degree
- **Work Experience in a Related Occupation**............... None
- **On-the-Job Training** .... None
- **Number of Jobs 2012** 91,700
- **Job Outlook, 2012–22** .... 6% (Slower than average)
- **Employment Change, 2012–22** 5,300

What Compensation, Benefits, and Job Analysis Specialists Do

Compensation, benefits, and job analysis specialists conduct an organization's compensation and benefits programs. They also evaluate job positions to determine details such as classification and salary.

Duties. Compensation, benefits, and job analysis specialists typically do the following:

- Research compensation and benefits policies and plans to ensure the organization's offerings are up-to-date, cost effective, and competitive
- Monitor important compensation and benefits trends
- Compare benefits plans, job classifications, or salaries through data and cost analyses
- Prepare job descriptions, salary scales, and occupational classifications
- Evaluate job positions to determine classification and salary
- Ensure company compliance by adhering to federal and state laws
- Collaborate with outside partners such as benefits vendors and investment brokers
- Design and prepare reports summarizing the research and analysis
- Present recommendations to compensation, benefits, human resources, or other managers

Some specialists perform tasks within all areas of compensation, benefits, and job analysis. Others specialize in a specific area.

Compensation, benefits, and job analysis specialists analyze employees' pay, fringe benefits, and other forms of compensation.

Compensation specialists assess the organization's pay structure. They research compensation trends and review compensation surveys to see how their organization's pay compares with that in other organizations. To evaluate compensation policies, they often perform complex data or cost analyses. For example, they may research and analyze the cost of different pay-for-performance strategies, which offer rewards such as bonuses, paid leave, or other incentives.

Compensation specialists also must ensure that the organization's pay practices comply with federal and state laws and regulations, such as workers' compensation or minimum wage laws.

Benefits specialists administer the organization's benefits programs, which include retirement plans, leave policies, wellness programs, and insurance policies, such as health, life, and disability. They research and analyze benefits plans, policies, and programs, and make recommendations based on their analysis. They must frequently monitor government regulations, legislation, and benefits trends to ensure that their programs are legal, current, and competitive.

Benefits specialists also work closely with insurance brokers and benefits carriers and manage the enrollment, renewal, and distribution processes for an organization's employees.

Job analysis specialists, also known as *position classifiers*, evaluate job positions by writing or assigning job descriptions, determining position classifications, and preparing salary scales. When an organization introduces a new job or reviews existing jobs, specialists must research and make recommendations to managers on the status, description, classification, and salary of those jobs.

Median Annual Wages, May 2012

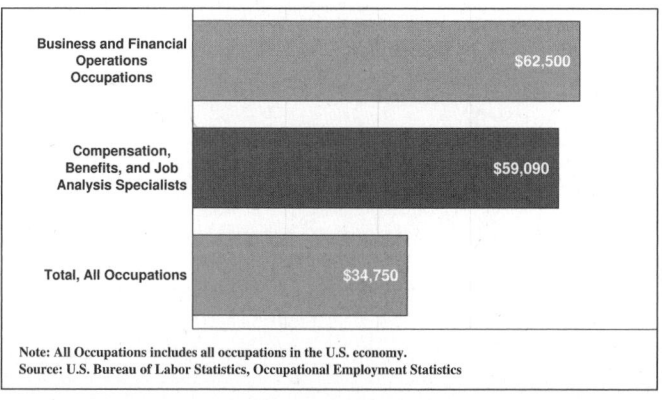

Note: All Occupations includes all occupations in the U.S. economy.
Source: U.S. Bureau of Labor Statistics, Occupational Employment Statistics

Percent Change in Employment, Projected 2012–2022

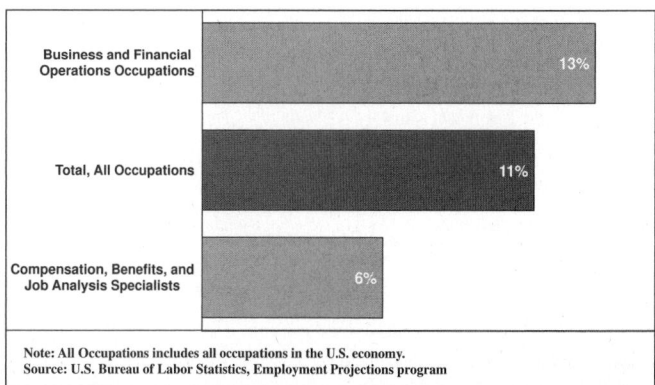

Note: All Occupations includes all occupations in the U.S. economy.
Source: U.S. Bureau of Labor Statistics, Employment Projections program

Employment Projections Data for Compensation, Benefits, and Job Analysis Specialists

Occupational title	SOC Code	Employment, 2012	Projected Employment, 2022	Change, 2012–2022	
				Percent	Numeric
Compensation, benefits, and job analysis specialists...............	13-1141	91,700	97,000	6	5,300

Source: U.S. Bureau of Labor Statistics, Employment Projections Program

Note: Data are rounded. Go to **Occupational Information Included in the OOH** *for a discussion of the data in this table.*

Work Environment

Compensation, benefits, and job analysis specialists held about 91,700 jobs in 2012 and worked in nearly every industry. Many specialists work for large firms, such as those found in the finance and insurance and healthcare industries. Many also work for government or educational institutions.

Compensation, benefits, and job analysis specialists typically work in offices.

Work Schedules. Most compensation, benefits, and job analysis specialists work full time during regular business hours.

How to Become One

Compensation, benefits, and job analysis specialists need a bachelor's degree, and some specialists need related work experience.

Education. Compensation, benefits, and job analysis specialists need a bachelor's degree. Many have a degree in human resources, business administration, finance, or a related field. Not all colleges and universities offer an undergraduate degree in human resources, but many offer courses in human resources management, compensation analysis, and benefits administration.

Students with a background in other disciplines, such as psychology or sociology, would also benefit from taking courses in business, management, finance, and accounting.

Work Experience in a Related Occupation. For many jobs, compensation, benefits, and job analysis specialists must have previous work experience. Employers commonly require that the previous experience includes performing compensation analysis, benefits administration, or general human resources work. Experience in related fields such as finance, insurance, or business administration can also be beneficial.

Jobseekers without a degree in human resources must have relevant work experience. Some workers may gain this experience through internships. However, most gain experience working in human resources.

Licenses, Certifications, and Registrations. Many professional associations for human resources professionals offer classes to enhance the skills and credibility of their members. Some associations, including the International Foundation of Employee Benefit Plans and WorldatWork, offer certification programs that specialize in compensation and benefits. Others, including the HR Certification Institute, offer general human resources credentials.

Although not required, certification can show professional expertise and credibility. In fact, many employers prefer to hire certified candidates, and some positions may require certification. Certification programs for management positions often require several years of related work experience to qualify for the credential.

Advancement. Compensation, benefits, and job analysis specialists may advance to compensation and benefits manager or human resources manager positions. Workers typically need several years of experience to advance.

Important Qualities

Analytical skills. Many compensation, benefits, and job analysis specialists perform data or cost analyses to form logical conclusions. For example, they may analyze the cost of choosing a particular salary scale for a class of workers.

Business acumen. Compensation, benefits, and job analysis specialists must understand basic finance and accounting.

Communication skills. Compensation, benefits, and job analysis specialists often work with employees throughout their organization to provide information on compensation and benefits. They may give presentations or advise managers or employees about compensation policies or benefit plans.

Critical-thinking skills. Compensation, benefits, and job analysis specialists must think critically when evaluating job positions, salary scales, promotion practices, and other compensation and benefits policies.

Detail oriented. Compensation, benefits, and job analysis specialists must pay attention to detail, especially when ensuring that the organization is compliant with federal and state laws.

Similar Occupations　This table shows a list of occupations with job duties that are similar to those of compensation, benefits, and job analysis specialists.

Occupations	Entry-level Education	2012 Pay	Projected Job Growth	Average Annual Openings
Compensation and Benefits Managers	Bachelor's degree	$95,250	3%	610
Human Resources Managers	Bachelor's degree	$99,720	13%	4,060
Human Resources Specialists and Labor Relations Specialists	Bachelor's degree	$55,616	7%	12,370
Insurance Sales Agents	High school diploma or equivalent	$48,150	10%	15,020
Purchasing Managers, Buyers, and Purchasing Agents	See "How to Become One"	$63,128	4%	12,230
Training and Development Managers	Bachelor's degree	$95,400	11%	1,070
Training and Development Specialists	Bachelor's degree	$55,930	15%	7,720

Pay

The median annual wage for compensation, benefits, and job analysis specialists was $59,090 in May 2012. The median wage is the wage at which half the workers in an occupation earned more than that amount and half earned less. The lowest 10 percent earned less than $37,570, and the top 10 percent earned more than $92,520.

Job Outlook

Employment of compensation, benefits, and job analysis specialists is projected to grow 6 percent from 2012 to 2022, slower than the average for all occupations. As compensation and benefits plans become increasingly complex and costly, companies will need specialists to analyze and administer these plans and programs.

Due to healthcare reform and rising healthcare costs, organizations will need benefits specialists to analyze, choose, and update their benefits policies. Employee wellness programs are also becoming increasingly popular as a way to reduce healthcare costs. Organizations will need benefits specialists to design, analyze, or administer these programs.

To attract and keep highly qualified workers, organizations offer competitive compensation packages. To allocate their limited compensation funds effectively, many organizations are using strategies such as pay-for-performance plans, which may include bonuses, paid leave, or other incentives as part of the compensation package. Organizations will need specialists to analyze these compensation policies and plans and ensure they are both competitive and cost effective.

However, employment growth will likely be tempered as companies increasingly outsource a portion of their compensation and benefits functions to human resources consulting firms to reduce costs and gain access to technical expertise. For example, to reduce administrative costs, organizations commonly use an outside vendor for processing payroll and insurance claims. These consulting firms are able to automate tasks and operate overseas call centers, reducing the need for specialists.

Job Prospects. Job prospects should be best for those with several years of experience performing compensation analysis, benefits administration, or related human resources work.

O*NET

➤ Compensation, Benefits, and Job Analysis Specialists (13-1141.00)

Contacts for More Information

For more information about compensation, benefits, and job analysis specialists, including certification, visit
➤ International Foundation of Employee Benefit Plans (www.ifebp.org)
➤ WorldatWork (www.worldatwork.org)
For information about human resources careers, visit
➤ Society for Human Resource Management (www.shrm.org)
For more information about human resources certifications, visit
➤ HR Certification Institute (www.hrci.org/)

Cost Estimators

- **2012 Median Pay** .... $58,860 per year
  $28.30 per hour
- **Entry-Level Education** .... Bachelor's degree
- **Work Experience in a Related Occupation** .... None
- **On-the-Job Training** .... None
- **Number of Jobs 2012** 202,200
- **Job Outlook, 2012–22** .... 26% (Much faster than average)
- **Employment Change, 2012–22** 53,000

What Cost Estimators Do

Cost estimators collect and analyze data in order to estimate the time, money, materials, and labor required to manufacture a product, construct a building, or provide a service. They generally specialize in a particular industry or type of product.

Duties. Cost estimators typically do the following:

- Identify and quantify cost factors, such as production time, materials, and labor expenses
- Travel to jobsites to gather information on materials needed, labor required, and other factors
- Read blueprints and technical documents in order to prepare estimates
- Collaborate with engineers, architects, clients, and contractors on estimates
- Consult with industry experts to discuss estimates and resolve issues
- Use computer software to calculate estimates
- Evaluate a product's cost-effectiveness or profitability
- Recommend ways to make a product more cost effective or profitable
- Work with sales teams to prepare estimates and bids for clients
- Develop project plans for the duration of the project

Accurately predicting the cost, size, and duration of future construction and manufacturing projects is vital to the survival of businesses. Cost estimators' calculations give managers or investors this information.

Cost estimators develop information that business owners and managers need to determine the potential profitability of a new project or product.

Median Annual Wages, May 2012

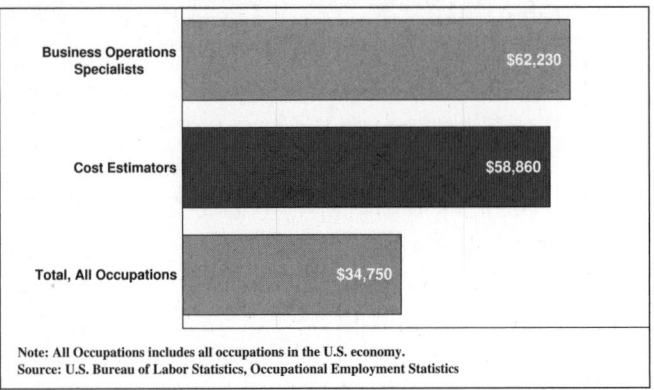

Note: All Occupations includes all occupations in the U.S. economy.
Source: U.S. Bureau of Labor Statistics, Occupational Employment Statistics

Percent Change in Employment, Projected 2012–2022

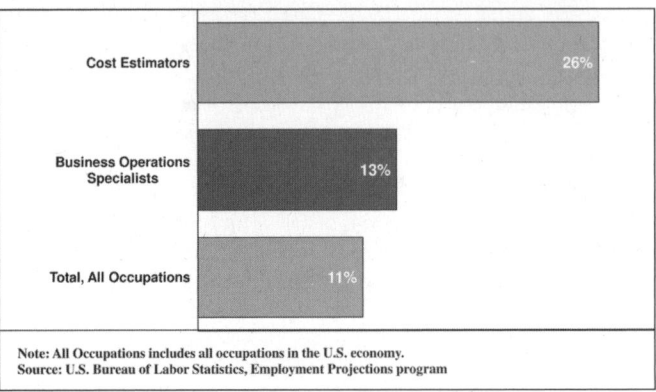

Note: All Occupations includes all occupations in the U.S. economy.
Source: U.S. Bureau of Labor Statistics, Employment Projections program

When making calculations, estimators analyze many inputs in order to determine how much time, money, and labor a project needs and how profitable it will be. These estimates have to take many factors into account, including allowances for wasted material, bad weather, shipping delays, and other factors that can increase costs and lower profitability.

Cost estimators use computer software, including databases, to simulate building construction. Cost estimators often use a computer database with information on the costs of other, similar projects.

General contractors usually hire cost estimators for specific parts of a large construction project, such as estimating the cost of the electrical work or the excavation phase. In such cases, the estimator calculates the cost of the construction phase for which the contractor is responsible, rather than calculating the cost of the entire project. Construction companies will hire cost estimators that calculate the total project cost by analyzing the bids that the subcontractors' cost estimators prepared.

Some estimators are hired by manufacturers to analyze certain products or processes.

The following are examples of types of cost estimators:

Construction cost estimators estimate the cost of construction work. They may, for example, estimate the total cost of building a bridge or commercial shopping center. They may identify direct costs, such as the cost of raw materials and the cost of labor, and set a timeline for how long the project will take. Although many work directly for construction firms, some work for contractors, architects, and engineering firms.

Manufacturing cost estimators calculate the costs of developing, producing, or redesigning a company's goods or services. For example, a cost estimator working for a home appliance manufacturer may determine whether a new type of dishwasher will be profitable to manufacture.

Some manufacturing cost estimators work in software development. Many high-technology products require a considerable amount of computer programming, and calculating the costs of software development requires great expertise.

Two other groups also estimate costs in their jobs: operations research analysts and construction managers may do significant amounts of cost estimating in the course of their usual duties.

Work Environment

Cost estimators held about 202,200 jobs in 2012. The industries that employed the most cost estimators in 2012 were as follows:

Construction of buildings	16%
Building equipment contractors	16
Manufacturing	14
Foundation, structure, and building exterior contractors	8

Although cost estimators work mostly in offices, they often visit construction sites and factory floors. Depending on the industry, these visits may involve frequent travel.

Cost estimators need to meet deadlines in order to prepare bids. Inaccurate estimates can cause a firm to lose a bid or to lose money on a job that otherwise could have been profitable.

Work Schedules. Cost estimators usually work full time. Some, however, are required to work overtime in order to meet deadlines.

How to Become One

A bachelor's degree is generally required for someone to become a cost estimator. However, a few highly experienced construction workers may qualify without a bachelor's degree.

Education. Increasingly, employers prefer candidates who have a bachelor's degree. A strong background in mathematics is essential.

Construction cost estimators generally need a bachelor's degree in an industry-related field, such as construction management, building science, or engineering. Those interested in estimating manufacturing costs typically need a bachelor's degree in engineering, physical sciences, mathematics, or statistics. Some employers accept candidates with backgrounds in business-related disciplines, such as accounting, finance, and business.

Training. Newly hired cost estimators may receive some on-the-job training based on their prior experience. Training often

Employment Projections Data for Cost Estimators

Occupational title	SOC Code	Employment, 2012	Projected Employment, 2022	Change, 2012–2022	
				Percent	Numeric
Cost estimators	13-1051	202,200	255,200	26	53,000

Source: U.S. Bureau of Labor Statistics, Employment Projections Program

Note: Data are rounded. Go to **Occupational Information Included in the OOH** *for a discussion of the data in this table.*

Similar Occupations   This table shows a list of occupations with job duties that are similar to those of cost estimators.

Occupations	Entry-level Education	2012 Pay	Projected Job Growth	Average Annual Openings
Accountants and Auditors	Bachelor's degree	$63,550	13%	54,420
Budget Analysts	Bachelor's degree	$69,280	6%	2,850
Claims Adjusters, Appraisers, Examiners, and Investigators	See "How to Become One"	$59,902	3%	8,340
Construction Managers	Bachelor's degree	$82,790	16%	15,460
Financial Analysts	Bachelor's degree	$76,950	16%	10,090
Financial Managers	Bachelor's degree	$109,740	9%	14,690
Industrial Production Managers	Bachelor's degree	$89,190	-2%	3,140

includes learning a company's cost-estimating software and techniques.

Work Experience in a Related Occupation. Increasingly, employers prefer that cost estimators–particularly those without a bachelor's degree–have previous work experience in the construction industry. For example, experienced electricians and plumbers can become construction cost estimators if they have the necessary construction knowledge and math skills.

Candidates interested in becoming cost estimators also can gain experience through internships and cooperative education programs.

Licenses, Certifications, and Registrations. Voluntary certification can show competence and experience in the field. In some instances, employers may require professional certification before hiring. The American Society of Professional Estimators, the Association for the Advancement of Cost Estimating International (also known as AACE International), and the International Cost Estimating and Analysis Association each offer a variety of certifications.

To become certified, estimators generally must have at least 2 years of estimating experience and must pass a written exam.

Important Qualities

Analytical skills. Accurately evaluating detailed specifications is crucial to a cost estimator's success. For example, a cost estimator must determine how to minimize costs without sacrificing quality.

Detail oriented. Cost estimators must pay attention to small details because such details may have a large impact on a product's overall cost.

Technical skills. Detailed knowledge of industry processes, materials, and costs are vital to estimators. In addition, they should be able to use specialized computer programs to calculate equations and handle large databases.

Time-management skills. Because cost estimators often work on fixed deadlines, they must plan their work in advance and work efficiently and accurately.

Writing skills. Cost estimators must be able to write detailed reports. Often, these reports determine whether or not contracts are awarded or products are manufactured.

Pay

The median annual wage for cost estimators was $58,860 in May 2012. The median wage is the wage at which half the workers in an occupation earned more than that amount and half earned less. The lowest 10 percent earned less than $34,520, and the top 10 percent earned more than $96,670.

Job Outlook

Employment of cost estimators is projected to grow 26 percent from 2012 to 2022, much faster than the average for all occupations.

Demand for cost estimators is expected to be strong because companies need accurate cost projections to ensure that their products and services are profitable. For this reason, cost estimators are essential to companies.

Growth in the construction industry will create the majority of new jobs. In particular, the construction and repair of infrastructure, including roads, bridges, airports, and subway systems, will drive demand for qualified estimators.

Job Prospects. Rapid employment growth should result in good job prospects overall. Those with a bachelor's degree and excellent math skills will have the best job opportunities.

In manufacturing, those who have a strong background in mathematics, statistics, or engineering and previous experience with cost estimation software should have the best job prospects.

In construction, those with knowledge of building information modeling software are likely to have the best job prospects. Jobs of cost estimators working in construction, like those of workers in many other trades in the construction industry, are sensitive to changing economic conditions.

O*NET

➤ Cost Estimators (13-1051.00)

Contacts for More Information

For more information about cost estimators, visit
➤ Association for the Advancement of Cost Engineering International (www.aacei.org/)
➤ American Society of Professional Estimators (www.aspenational.org/)
➤ International Cost Estimating and Analysis Association (www.iceaaonline.org/)

Financial Analysts

- **2012 Median Pay** .... $76,950 per year
  $37.00 per hour
- **Entry-Level Education** ....Bachelor's degree
- **Work Experience in a Related Occupation**............... None
- **On-the-Job Training** .... None
- **Number of Jobs 2012** 253,000
- **Job Outlook, 2012–22** .... 16% (Faster than average)
- **Employment Change, 2012–22** 39,300

What Financial Analysts Do

Financial analysts provide guidance to businesses and individuals making investment decisions. They assess the performance of stocks, bonds, and other types of investments.

Duties. Financial analysts typically do the following:

- Recommend individual investments and collections of investments, which are known as portfolios
- Evaluate current and historical data
- Study economic and business trends
- Study a company's financial statements to determine its value
- Meet with company officials to gain better insight into the company's prospects and management
- Prepare written reports
- Meet with investors to explain recommendations

Financial analysts evaluate investment opportunities. They work in banks, pension funds, mutual funds, securities firms, insurance companies, and other businesses. They are also called securities analysts and investment analysts.

Financial analysts can be divided into two categories: buy-side analysts and sell-side analysts.

- Buy-side analysts develop investment strategies for companies that have a lot of money to invest. These companies, called institutional investors, include mutual funds, hedge funds, insurance companies, independent money managers, and nonprofit organizations with large endowments, such as some universities.
- Sell-side analysts advise financial services sales agents who sell stocks, bonds, and other investments.

Some analysts work for the business media and belong to neither the buy side nor the sell side.

Financial analysts generally focus on trends affecting a specific industry, geographical region, or type of product. For example, an analyst may focus on a subject area such as the energy industry, a world region such as Eastern Europe, or the foreign exchange market. They must understand how new regulations, policies, and political and economic trends may affect investments.

Investing is becoming more global, and some financial analysts specialize in a particular country or region. Companies want those financial analysts to understand the language, culture, business environment, and political conditions in the country or region that they cover.

The following are examples of types of financial analysts:

Portfolio managers supervise a team of analysts and select the mix of products, industries, and regions for their company's

Financial analysts research and analyze financial data, helping managers make sound decisions.

investment portfolio. These managers not only are responsible for the overall portfolio, but also are expected to explain investment decisions and strategies in meetings with investors.

Fund managers work exclusively with hedge funds or mutual funds. Both fund and portfolio managers frequently make split-second buy or sell decisions in reaction to quickly changing market conditions.

Ratings analysts evaluate the ability of companies or governments to pay their debts, including bonds. On the basis of their evaluation, a management team rates the risk of a company or government not being able to repay its bonds.

Risk analysts evaluate the risk in investment decisions and determine how to manage unpredictability and limit potential losses. This job is carried out by making investment decisions such as selecting dissimilar stocks or having a combination of stocks, bonds, and mutual funds in a portfolio.

Median Annual Wages, May 2012

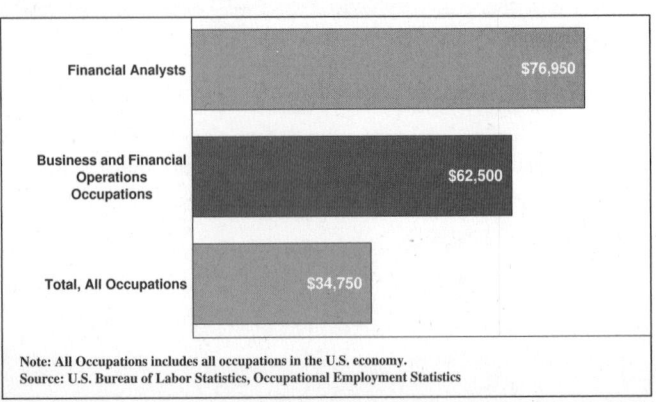

Financial Analysts	$76,950
Business and Financial Operations Occupations	$62,500
Total, All Occupations	$34,750

Note: All Occupations includes all occupations in the U.S. economy.
Source: U.S. Bureau of Labor Statistics, Occupational Employment Statistics

Percent Change in Employment, Projected 2012–2022

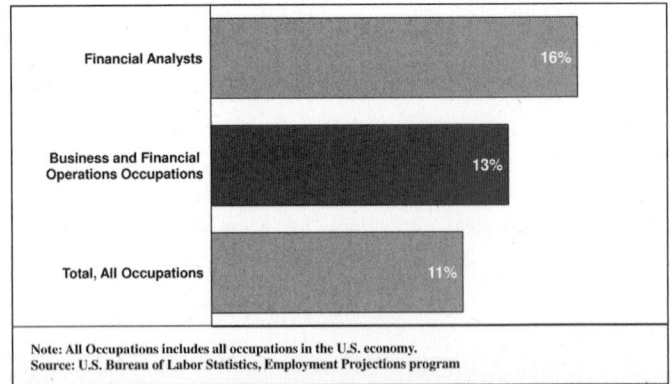

Financial Analysts	16%
Business and Financial Operations Occupations	13%
Total, All Occupations	11%

Note: All Occupations includes all occupations in the U.S. economy.
Source: U.S. Bureau of Labor Statistics, Employment Projections program

Employment Projections Data for Financial Analysts

Occupational title	SOC Code	Employment, 2012	Projected Employment, 2022	Change, 2012–2022	
				Percent	Numeric
Financial analysts..	13-2051	253,000	292,400	16	39,300

Source: U.S. Bureau of Labor Statistics, Employment Projections Program

Note: Data are rounded. Go to **Occupational Information Included in the OOH** *for a discussion of the data in this table.*

Work Environment

Financial analysts held about 253,000 jobs in 2012. They work primarily in offices, but travel frequently to visit companies or potential investors.

Many financial analysts work at large financial institutions based in New York City or other major financial centers. In 2012, about 45 percent of financial analysts worked in finance and insurance industries. They worked primarily for security and commodity brokerages, banks and credit institutions, and insurance carriers. Others worked throughout private industry and for government.

The industries that employed the most financial analysts in 2012 were as follows:

Securities, commodity contracts, and other financial
    investments and related activities 21%
Credit intermediation and related activities 13
Professional, scientific, and technical services......................... 13
Management of companies and enterprises............................. 12
Insurance carriers and related activities................................... 8

Work Schedules. Most financial analysts work full time, and about one-third of financial analysts worked more than 40 hours per week in 2012. Much of their research must be done after office hours because their days are filled with telephone calls and meetings.

How to Become One

Financial analysts typically must have a bachelor's degree, but a master's degree is often required for advanced positions.

Education. Most positions require a bachelor's degree. A number of fields of study provide appropriate preparation, including accounting, economics, finance, statistics, mathematics, and engineering. For advanced positions, employers often require a master's in business administration (MBA) or a master's degree in finance. Knowledge of options pricing, bond valuation, and risk management are important.

Licenses, Certifications, and Registrations. The Financial Industry Regulatory Authority (FINRA) is the main licensing organization for the securities industry. It requires licenses for many financial analyst positions. Most of the licenses require sponsorship by an employer, so companies do not expect individuals to have these licenses before starting a job.

Certification is often recommended by employers and can improve the chances for advancement. An example is the Chartered Financial Analyst (CFA) certification from the CFA Institute, which financial analysts can get if they have a bachelor's degree, 4 years of experience, and pass three exams. Financial analysts can also become certified in their field of specialty.

Advancement. Financial analysts typically start by specializing in a specific investment field. As they gain experience, they can become portfolio managers, who supervise a team of analysts and select the mix of investments for the company's portfolio. They can also become fund managers, who manage large investment portfolios for individual investors. A master's degree in finance or business administration can improve an analyst's chances of advancing to one of these positions.

Important Qualities

Analytical skills. Financial analysts must process a range of information in finding profitable investments.

Communication skills. Financial analysts must explain their recommendations to clients in clear language that clients can easily understand.

Computer skills. Financial analysts must be adept at using software packages to analyze financial data, see trends, create portfolios, and make forecasts.

Decision making skills. Financial analysts must provide a recommendation to buy, hold, or sell a security. Fund managers must make split-second trading decisions.

Detail oriented. Financial analysts must pay attention to details when reviewing possible investments, as small issues may have large implications for the health of an investment.

Math skills. Financial analysts use mathematical skills when estimating the value of financial securities.

To be successful, financial analysts must be motivated to seek out obscure information that may be important to the investment. Many work independently and must have self-confidence in their judgment.

Pay

The median annual wage for financial analysts was $76,950 in May 2012. The median wage is the wage at which half the workers in an occupation earned more than that amount and half earned less. The lowest 10 percent earned less than $47,130 and the top 10 percent earned more than $148,430.

Similar Occupations   This table shows a list of occupations with job duties that are similar to those of financial analysts.

Occupations	Entry-level Education	2012 Pay	Projected Job Growth	Average Annual Openings
Budget Analysts	Bachelor's degree	$69,280	6%	2,850
Financial Managers	Bachelor's degree	$109,740	9%	14,690
Insurance Underwriters	Bachelor's degree	$62,870	-6%	2,890
Personal Financial Advisors	Bachelor's degree	$67,520	27%	9,640
Securities, Commodities, and Financial Services Sales Agents	Bachelor's degree	$71,720	11%	12,260

In May 2012, the median annual wages for financial analysts in the top five industries in which these analysts worked were as follows:

Securities, commodity contracts, and other financial investments and related activities	$90,560
Professional, scientific, and technical services	75,920
Credit intermediation and related activities	75,300
Management of companies and enterprises	75,200
Insurance carriers and related activities	72,270

Job Outlook

Employment of financial analysts is projected to grow 16 percent from 2012 to 2022, faster than the average for all occupations. A growing range of financial products and the need for in-depth knowledge of geographic regions are expected to lead to strong employment growth.

Investment portfolios are becoming more complex, and there are more financial products available for trade. In addition, emerging markets throughout the world are providing new investment opportunities, which require expertise in geographic regions where those markets are located.

The continued implementation of financial regulatory reform could constrict growth in the industry, as rule-making bodies place a greater emphasis on stability. Restrictions on trading by banks may shift employment of financial analysts from investment banks to hedge funds and private equity groups.

Job Prospects. Despite employment growth, strong competition is expected for these high-paying jobs. Growth in financial services should create new positions, but there are still far more people who would like to enter the occupation than there are jobs in the occupation. Having certifications and a graduate degree can significantly improve an applicant's prospects.

O*NET

➤ Financial Analysts (13-2051.00)

Contacts for More Information

For more information about licensure for financial analysts, visit
➤ Financial Industry Regulatory Authority (FINRA) (www.finra.org/)
➤ Securities Industry and Financial Markets Association (SIFMA) (www.sifma.org/)
For more information about training and certification, visit
➤ American Academy of Financial Management (www.aafm.us/)
➤ CFA Institute (www.cfainstitute.org/)

Financial Examiners

- **2012 Median Pay** .... $75,800 per year
  $36.44 per hour
- **Entry-Level Education** ....Bachelor's degree
- **Work Experience in a Related Occupation**............... None
- **On-the-Job Training** .... Moderate-term on-the-job training
- **Number of Jobs 2012** 29,200
- **Job Outlook, 2012–22** .... 6% (Slower than average)
- **Employment Change, 2012–22** 1,800

What Financial Examiners Do

Financial examiners ensure compliance with laws governing financial institutions and transactions. They review balance sheets, evaluate the risk level of loans, and assess bank management.

Duties. Financial examiners typically do the following:

- Monitor the financial condition of banks and other financial institutions
- Review balance sheets, operating income and expense accounts, and loan documentation to confirm institution assets and liabilities
- Prepare reports that detail an institution's safety and soundness
- Examine the minutes of meetings of managers and directors
- Train other examiners in the financial examination process
- Review and analyze new regulations and policies to determine their impact on the organization
- Establish guidelines for procedures and policies that comply with new and revised regulations

Financial examiners typically work in one of two main areas: risk scoping or consumer compliance.

Those working in risk scoping evaluate the health of financial institutions. Their role is to ensure that banks and other financial institutions offer safe loans and that they have enough cash on hand to handle unexpected losses. These procedures help ensure that the financial system as a whole remains stable. These examiners also evaluate the performance of bank managers.

Financial examiners working in consumer compliance monitor lending activity to ensure that borrowers are treated fairly. They ensure that banks extend loans that borrowers are likely to be able to pay back. They help borrowers avoid "predatory loans"–loans that may generate profit for banks through high interest payments but may be costly to borrowers and damage their credit scores. Examiners also ensure that banks do not discriminate against borrowers based on ethnicity or other characteristics.

Work Environment

Financial examiners held about 29,200 jobs in 2012. The industries that employed the most financial examiners in 2012 were as follows:

Federal government, excluding postal service	24%
Depository credit intermediation	14
State government, excluding education and hospitals	12
Other financial investment activities	9

Financial examiners typically work in offices. They frequently have to travel to inspect a bank onsite.

Financial examiners review balance sheets, evaluate the risk level of loans, and assess bank management.

Median Annual Wages, May 2012

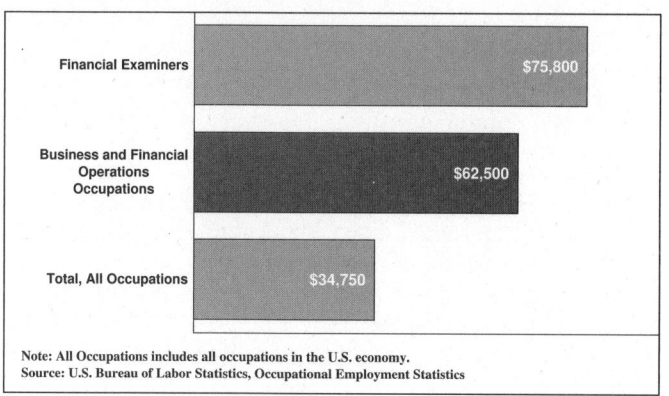

Note: All Occupations includes all occupations in the U.S. economy.
Source: U.S. Bureau of Labor Statistics, Occupational Employment Statistics

Percent Change in Employment, Projected 2012–2022

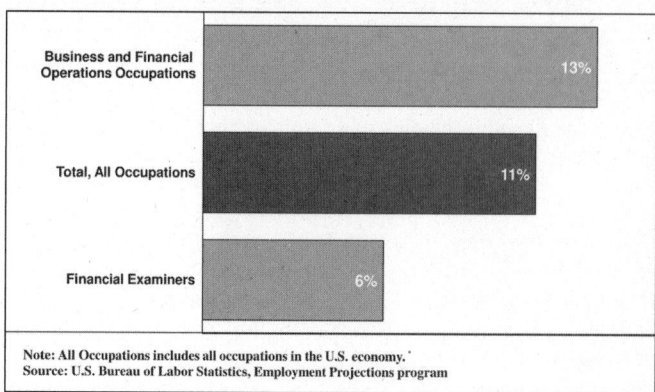

Note: All Occupations includes all occupations in the U.S. economy.
Source: U.S. Bureau of Labor Statistics, Employment Projections program

Work Schedules. Most financial examiners worked full time in 2012.

How to Become One

Financial examiners typically need a bachelor's degree that includes some coursework in accounting. Entry-level examiners are trained on the job by senior examiners.

Education. Specific requirements for financial examiners vary between federal and state governments. However, all financial examiners typically need a bachelor's degree that includes some coursework in accounting, finance, economics, or a related field. Examiners working for the Federal Deposit Insurance Corporation (FDIC) must have at least 6 semester hours in accounting.

Training. Once hired, financial examiners receive on-the-job training. Entry-level workers begin under the supervision of senior examiners, as they learn their job duties.

Advancement. After a few years of experience, financial examiners can advance to a senior examiner position. Requirements for these positions vary by employer but often require a master's degree in either accounting or business or becoming a Certified Public Accountant (CPA).

Important Qualities

Analytical skills. Financial examiners need strong analytical skills to evaluate how well the managers of financial institutions are handling risk and whether the individual loans the institution makes are safe.

Detail oriented. Financial examiners must pay close attention to details when reviewing balance sheets to identify risky assets.

Math skills. Financial examiners need good basic math skills to monitor balance sheets and see if the bank's or other financial institution's available cash is dangerously low.

Writing skills. Financial examiners regularly write reports on the safety and soundness of financial institutions. They must be able to explain technical information clearly.

Pay

The median annual wage for financial examiners was $75,800 in May 2012. The median wage is the wage at which half the workers in an occupation earned more than that amount and half earned less. The lowest 10 percent earned less than $43,240, and the top 10 percent earned more than $140,580.

Employment Projections Data for Financial Examiners

Occupational title	SOC Code	Employment, 2012	Projected Employment, 2022	Change, 2012–2022	
				Percent	Numeric
Financial examiners..	13-2061	29,200	31,100	6	1,800

Source: U.S. Bureau of Labor Statistics, Employment Projections Program

Note: Data are rounded. Go to **Occupational Information Included in the OOH** *for a discussion of the data in this table.*

Similar Occupations   This table shows a list of occupations with job duties that are similar to those of financial examiners.

Occupations	Entry-level Education	2012 Pay	Projected Job Growth	Average Annual Openings
Accountants and Auditors	Bachelor's degree	$63,550	13%	54,420
Budget Analysts	Bachelor's degree	$69,280	6%	2,850
Financial Analysts	Bachelor's degree	$76,950	16%	10,090
Loan Officers	Bachelor's degree	$59,820	8%	7,720
Management Analysts	Bachelor's degree	$78,600	19%	24,520
Personal Financial Advisors	Bachelor's degree	$67,520	27%	9,640
Tax Examiners and Collectors, and Revenue Agents	Bachelor's degree	$50,440	-4%	2,390

In May 2012, the median annual wages for financial examiners in the top four industries in which these examiners worked were as follows:

Federal government, excluding postal service	$109,380
Other financial investment activities	78,030
State government, excluding education and hospitals	65,640
Depository credit intermediation	64,490

Job Outlook

Employment of financial examiners is projected to grow 6 percent from 2012 to 2022, slower than the average for all occupations. Implementation of new financial regulations is expected to create a need for more examiners, though declining employment in federal government will slow growth for these workers.

Employment growth for financial examiners will vary by industry group. Financial examiners' employment is projected to grow 11 percent from 2012 to 2022 in the finance and insurance industry. Employment of financial examiners in the federal government is projected to decline 3 percent from 2012 to 2022.

Employment of financial examiners tends to increase during periods of financial instability. As bank losses and failures become more prevalent, more examiners are needed to enforce regulation. However, during normal economic times, employment tends to be steady.

Some large financial institutions that were not previously subject to Federal Deposit Insurance Corporation (FDIC) regulation have now been placed under that agency's supervision. More examiners will be needed to monitor these institutions' available cash levels and any potentially risky trading activity.

O*NET

➤ Financial Examiners (13-2061.00)

Contacts for More Information

For more information about financial examiners, visit
➤ Federal Deposit Insurance Corporation (www.fdic.gov)

Fundraisers

- **2012 Median Pay** .... $50,680 per year
  $24.37 per hour
- **Entry-Level Education** ....Bachelor's degree
- **Work Experience in a Related Occupation** .... None
- **On-the-Job Training** .... None
- **Number of Jobs 2012** 65,700
- **Job Outlook, 2012–22** .... 17% (Faster than average)
- **Employment Change, 2012–22** 11,400

What Fundraisers Do

Fundraisers organize events and campaigns to raise money and other donations for an organization. They may design promotional materials and increase awareness of an organization's work, goals, and financial needs.

Duties. Fundraisers typically do the following:

- Research prospective donors
- Create a strong fundraising message that appeals to potential donors
- Conduct fundraising strategies for an organization
- Identify and contact potential donors
- Organize a campaign or event that will lead to soliciting donations
- Maintain records of donor information for future use
- Evaluate the success of previous fundraising events
- Train volunteers in fundraising procedures and practices
- Ensure that all legal reporting requirements are satisfied

Fundraisers are responsible for raising money and other kinds of donations for an organization. To accomplish these goals, fundraisers generally plan and oversee campaigns and events. They ensure that campaigns are effective by researching potential donors ahead of time and examining records of those who have given in the past. Many of the organizations that employ fundraisers rely heavily on donations in order to run their operations.

Many states require what they call "charitable soliciting organizations" to register with a state agency. The National Association of State Charity Officials provides advice to charities, as well as links to each state's charity office. Professional fundraisers who work as private consultants will need to register with the state in which they do business. Fundraisers who work for an organization that engages in fundraising activity will not have to register individually as long as their organization is already registered.

Fundraisers who work for political campaigns must be knowledgeable about campaign finance laws, such as the contribution limits of an individual giving to a specific candidate. More information on federal campaign finance laws can be found at the Federal Election Commission. State laws can be found at the National Conference of State Legislatures.

The following are examples of types of fundraisers:

Major gifts fundraisers specialize in face-to-face interaction with donors who can give large amounts.

Planned-giving fundraisers solicit donations from those who are looking to pledge money at a future date or in installments over time. These fundraisers must have specialized training in taxes regarding gifts of stocks, bonds, charitable annuities, and real estate bequests in a will.

Direct-mailing fundraisers send out requests for donations to large numbers of people through the mail, over the phone, and online.

Events fundraisers obtain donations through charity events, including dinners, auctions, galas, and charity races such as 10Ks.

Fundraisers identify and contact potential donors and apply for grants.

Median Annual Wages, May 2012

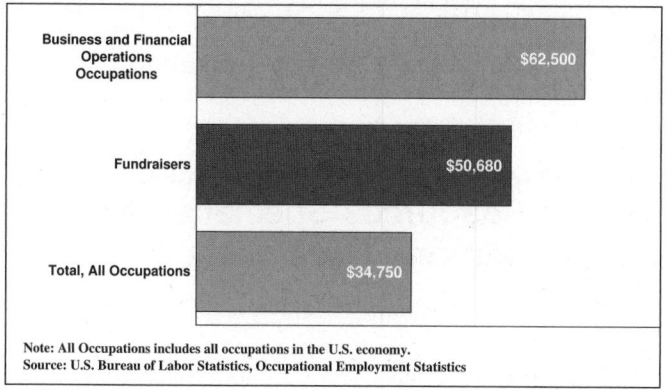

Note: All Occupations includes all occupations in the U.S. economy.
Source: U.S. Bureau of Labor Statistics, Occupational Employment Statistics

Percent Change in Employment, Projected 2012–2022

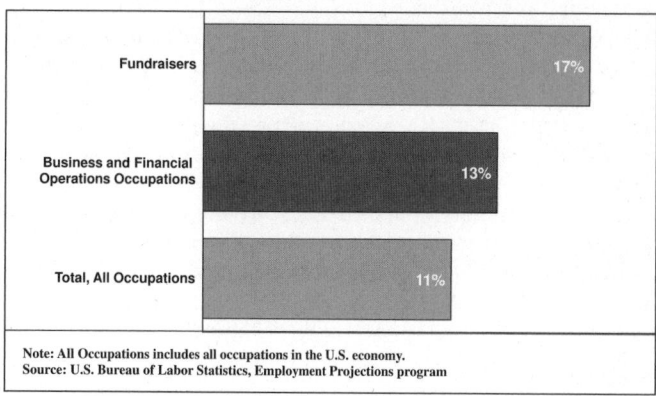

Note: All Occupations includes all occupations in the U.S. economy.
Source: U.S. Bureau of Labor Statistics, Employment Projections program

Annual campaign fundraisers solicit donations once a year for their organization. Many nonprofit organizations have annual giving campaigns.

Capital campaign fundraisers raise money for a specific project such as the construction of a new building at a university. Capital campaigns also raise money for renovations and the creation or expansion of an endowment.

Work Environment

Fundraisers held about 65,700 jobs in 2012. The industries that employed the most fundraisers in 2012 were as follows:

Religious, grantmaking, civic, professional, and similar
organizations... 55%
Educational services; state, local, and private 18
Health care and social assistance 14

Fundraisers work primarily for nonprofit charitable organizations, including educational institutions, religious organizations, healthcare foundations, and political campaigns.

Most fundraisers are employed by the organization they raise funds for. Some fundraisers work for consulting firms that work for many clients.

Fundraisers spend much of their time communicating with other employees and potential donors, either in person, on the phone, or through email.

Some fundraisers may need to travel to locations where fundraising events are held. Events may include charity runs, walks, galas, and dinners.

Work Schedules. Fundraisers generally work full time during regular business hours. Some, however, work under pressure of deadlines and tight schedules, possibly requiring additional hours. About 1 in 5 worked part time in 2012.

How to Become One

Fundraisers typically need a bachelor's degree and strong communication and organizational skills. Employers generally prefer candidates who have studied public relations, journalism, communications, English, or business.

Education. Fundraisers often have a variety of academic backgrounds. However, some employers prefer candidates with degrees in business or communications, but bachelor's degrees in other subjects are usually acceptable.

Several schools offer master's degree programs in philanthropic studies or fundraising. Requirements to enter such programs are generally based on work or volunteer experience at a nonprofit or grantmaking foundation. Students may take courses in annual campaigns, planned giving, major gifts, grant proposals, and marketing.

In addition to taking relevant coursework, students can gain experience by volunteering at local charities or participating in student-led organizations.

Other Experience. Internships and previous work experience are important in obtaining a paid position as a fundraiser. Many fundraising campaigns rely on volunteers having face-to-face or over-the-phone interaction with potential donors, so it is impor-

Employment Projections Data for Fundraisers

Occupational title	SOC Code	Employment, 2012	Projected Employment, 2022	Change, 2012–2022	
				Percent	Numeric
Fundraisers.. 13-1131		65,700	77,100	17	11,400

Source: U.S. Bureau of Labor Statistics, Employment Projections Program

Note: Data are rounded. Go to **Occupational Information Included in the OOH** *for a discussion of the data in this table.*

Similar Occupations   This table shows a list of occupations with job duties that are similar to those of fundraisers.

Occupations	Entry-level Education	2012 Pay	Projected Job Growth	Average Annual Openings
Meeting, Convention, and Event Planners	Bachelor's degree	$45,810	33%	4,420
Public Relations and Fundraising Managers	Bachelor's degree	$95,450	13%	2,130
Public Relations Specialists	Bachelor's degree	$54,170	12%	5,880

tant that the fundraiser who organizes the campaign has experience with this type of work.

Licenses, Certifications, and Registrations. CFRE International offers the Certified Fund Raising Executive designation for fundraisers. Certification is voluntary, but fundraisers may obtain it to demonstrate a level of professional competency. Candidates are required to have 5 years of work experience in fundraising, as well as 80 hours of continuing education through both attendance at conferences and classroom instruction. To keep their certification valid, fundraisers must apply for renewal every 3 years.

Advancement. Fundraisers can advance to fundraising manager positions. However, some manager positions may require a master's degree, in addition to years of work experience as a fundraiser.

Important Qualities

Communication skills. Fundraisers need impeccable communication skills in order to communicate the message of their organization so that people will make donations.

Detail oriented. Fundraisers must be detail oriented because they deal with large volumes of data, including lists of people's names and phone numbers, and must comply with state and federal regulations. Failing to do so may result in penalties.

Leadership. Many fundraisers manage large teams of volunteers and must be able to lead them without having the usual incentive of pay at their disposal.

Organizational skills. Fundraisers manage large campaigns and events that require planning and organizational skills to succeed.

Pay

The median annual wage for fundraisers was $50,680 in May 2012. The median wage is the wage at which half the workers in an occupation earned more than that amount and half earned less. The lowest 10 percent earned less than $30,050, and the top 10 percent earned more than $88,010.

In May 2012, the median annual wages for fundraisers in the top three industries in which these workers worked were as follows:
Educational services; state, local, and private $55,940
Religious, grantmaking, civic, professional, and similar
   organizations 51,100
Health care and social assistance 46,750

Job Outlook

Employment of fundraisers is projected to grow 17 percent from 2012 to 2022, faster than the average for all occupations. Employment growth will be driven by the continued need of nonprofit organizations to collect donations in order to run their operations.

Organizations that will receive less financial support than in the past, such as colleges and universities, will need fundraisers to solicit donations to make up for shortfalls. Political campaigns also will continue to hire fundraisers.

More nonprofit organizations are focusing on cultivating an online presence and are increasingly using social media for fundraising activities. As a result, social media have created a new avenue for fundraisers to connect with potential donors and to spread their organization's message.

Job Prospects. Job prospects for fundraisers are expected to be good because organizations are always looking to raise more donations. Although candidates with different backgrounds are often eligible to become a fundraiser, those with experience in nonprofit and grant making industries will have better job opportunities.

O*NET

➤ Fundraisers (13-1131.00)

Contacts for More Information

For more information about fundraising certification, visit
➤ CFRE International (http://cfre.org/)

Human Resources Specialists and Labor Relations Specialists

- **2012 Median Pay** .... $55,640 per year
  $26.75 per hour
- **Entry-Level Education** .... Bachelor's degree
- **Work Experience in a Related Occupation** .... None
- **On-the-Job Training** .... None
- **Number of Jobs 2012** 495,500
- **Job Outlook, 2012–22** .... 7% (Slower than average)
- **Employment Change, 2012–22** 32,500

What Human Resources Specialists and Labor Relations Specialists Do

Human resources specialists recruit, screen, interview, and place workers. They often handle other human resources work, such as those related to employee relations, payroll and benefits, and training. Labor relations specialists interpret and administer labor contracts regarding issues such as wages and salaries, employee welfare, healthcare, pensions, and union and management practices.

Duties. Human resources specialists typically do the following:

- Consult with employers to identify employment needs
- Interview applicants about their experience, education, and skills
- Contact references and perform background checks on job applicants
- Inform applicants about job details, such as duties, benefits, and working conditions
- Hire or refer qualified candidates for employers
- Conduct or help with new employee orientation
- Keep employment records and process paperwork

Human resources specialists consult with managers to identify employment needs and preferred qualifications.

Median Annual Wages, May 2012

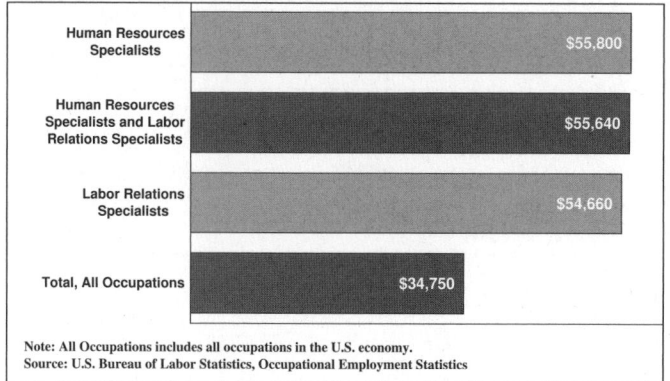

Human Resources Specialists	$55,800
Human Resources Specialists and Labor Relations Specialists	$55,640
Labor Relations Specialists	$54,660
Total, All Occupations	$34,750

Note: All Occupations includes all occupations in the U.S. economy.
Source: U.S. Bureau of Labor Statistics, Occupational Employment Statistics

Percent Change in Employment, Projected 2012–2022

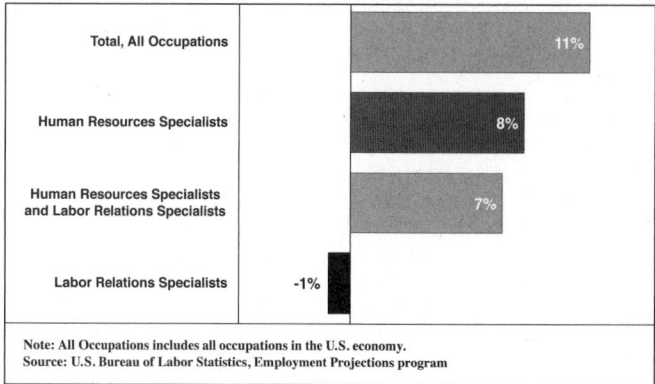

Total, All Occupations	11%
Human Resources Specialists	8%
Human Resources Specialists and Labor Relations Specialists	7%
Labor Relations Specialists	-1%

Note: All Occupations includes all occupations in the U.S. economy.
Source: U.S. Bureau of Labor Statistics, Employment Projections program

Labor relations specialists typically do the following:

- Advise management on contracts, worker grievances, and disciplinary procedures

- Lead meetings between management and labor

- Draft proposals and rules or regulations in order to help facilitate collective bargaining

- Interpret formal communications between management and labor

- Investigate validity of labor grievances

- Train management on labor relations

Human resources specialists are often trained in all human resources disciplines and perform tasks throughout all areas of the department. In addition to recruiting and placing workers, human resources specialists help guide employees through all human resources procedures and answer questions about policies. They often administer benefits, process payroll, and handle any associated questions or problems. They also ensure that all human resources functions comply with federal, state, and local regulations.

The following are examples of types of human resources specialists:

Employment interviewers work in an employment office and interview potential applicants for job openings. They refer suitable candidates to employers for consideration.

Human resources generalists handle all aspects of human resources work. They may have duties in all areas of human resources including recruitment, employee relations, payroll, benefits, training, as well as the administration of human resources policies, procedures, and programs.

Placement specialists match employers with qualified jobseekers. They search for candidates who have the skills, education, and work experience needed for jobs, and they try to place those candidates with employers. They also may help set up interviews.

Recruitment specialists, sometimes known as *personnel recruiters*, find, screen, and interview applicants for job openings in an organization. They search for applicants by posting listings, attending job fairs, and visiting college campuses. They also may test applicants, contact references, and extend job offers.

Labor relations specialists work with a labor union and a company's management. In addition to leading meetings between the two groups, these specialists draft formal language as part of the collective bargaining process. They often address specific grievances a worker might have, and ensure that all labor and management solutions comply within the relevant collective bargaining agreement.

Work Environment

Human resources specialists and labor relations specialists held about 495,500 jobs in 2012. Of this total, about 418,000 were human resources specialists, and 77,600 were labor relations specialists.

About 15 percent of human resources specialists worked in the employment services industry, which includes employment placement agencies, temporary help services, and professional employer organizations.

Because hiring needs may vary throughout the year, many organizations contract recruitment and placement work to outside human resources firms rather than keep permanent human resources specialists on staff.

About 73 percent of labor relations specialists worked in labor unions and similar labor organizations in 2012.

Work Schedules. Human resources specialists and labor relations specialists generally work in offices. Some, particularly recruitment specialists, travel extensively to attend job fairs, visit college campuses, and meet with applicants.

Most specialists work full time during regular business hours.

How to Become One

Applicants must usually have a bachelor's degree. However, the level of education and experience required to become a human resources specialist or labor relations specialist varies by position and employer.

Education. Applicants seeking positions as human resources specialists or labor relations specialists must usually have a bachelor's degree in human resources, business, or a related field.

Coursework should include business, professional writing, human resource management, and accounting.

Work Experience in a Related Occupation. Although candidates with a high school diploma may qualify for some interviewing and recruiting positions, employers usually require several years of related work experience as a substitute for education.

Some positions, particularly human resources generalists, may require previous work experience. Candidates can gain experience as human resources assistants, in customer service positions, or in other related jobs.

Licenses, Certifications, and Registrations. Many professional associations that specialize in human resources offer courses intended to enhance the skills of their members, and some offer certification programs.

Although certification is usually voluntary, some employers may prefer or require it. Human resources generalists, in particular, can benefit from certification because it shows knowledge and professional competence across all human resources areas.

Employment Projections Data for Human Resources Specialists and Labor Relations Specialists

Occupational title	SOC Code	Employment, 2012	Projected Employment, 2022	Change, 2012–2022	
				Percent	Numeric
Human resources specialists and labor relations specialists....	—	495,500	528,100	7	32,500
Human resources specialists..	13-1071	418,000	451,100	8	33,200
Labor relations specialists	13-1075	77,600	76,900	-1	-600

Source: U.S. Bureau of Labor Statistics, Employment Projections Program

Note: Data are rounded. Go to **Occupational Information Included in the OOH** *for a discussion of the data in this table.*

Some colleges and universities offer labor relations certificates to specialists who prefer greater specialization in mediation.

Important Qualities

Decision-making skills. Human resources specialists and labor relations specialists use decision-making skills when reviewing candidates' qualifications or when working to resolve labor disputes.

Detail oriented. Specialists must be detail oriented when evaluating applicants' qualifications, performing background checks, and maintaining records of an employee grievance.

Interpersonal skills. Interpersonal skills are essential for human resources specialists and labor relations specialists. When recruiting candidates and mediating between labor and management, specialists continually interact with new people and must be able to converse and connect with people from different backgrounds.

Listening skills. Listening skills are essential for human resources specialists and labor relations specialists. When interviewing job applicants, for example, they must pay careful attention to candidates' responses, understand the points they are making, and ask relevant followup questions.

Speaking skills. All specialists need strong speaking skills to be effective at their job. They often give presentations and must be able to convey information about their organizations and jobs within them.

Pay

The median annual wage for human resources specialists was $55,800 in May 2012. The median wage is the wage at which half the workers in an occupation earned more than that amount, and half earned less. The lowest 10 percent earned less than $32,770, and the top 10 percent earned more than $95,380.

The median annual wage for labor relations specialists was $54,660 in May 2012. The lowest 10 percent earned less than $17,690, and the top 10 percent earned more than $99,030.

Job Outlook

Employment of human resources specialists and labor relations specialists is projected to grow 7 percent from 2012 to 2022, slower than the average for all occupations. Employment growth will vary by specialty.

Employment of human resources specialists is projected to grow 8 percent, about as fast as the average for all occupations. About 15 percent of human resources specialists work in the employment services industry, which includes employment placement agencies, temporary help services, and professional employer organizations. Employment growth in employment services is projected to be much faster than the average as organizations continue to outsource human resources functions to professional employer organizations–companies that provide human resources services to client businesses.

In addition, rather than having recruiters and interviewers on staff, these businesses will contract preliminary staffing work to employment placement and temporary staffing agencies as needed.

Companies will also need human resources specialists to find replacements for workers leaving the workforce. Organizations will likely need more human resources generalists to handle increasingly complex employment laws and healthcare coverage options.

However, employment of human resources specialists will be tempered as companies make better use of available technologies. Rather than sending recruiters to colleges and job fairs, for example, some employers are increasingly conducting their entire recruiting and application process online. In addition, some of the tasks of generalists can be automated or made more efficient using Human Resources Information Systems–software that allows workers to quickly manage, process, or update human resources information.

Employment of labor relations specialists is projected to show little or no change from 2012 to 2022. Union membership has been

Similar Occupations   This table shows a list of occupations with job duties that are similar to those of human resources specialists and labor relations specialists.

Occupations	Entry-level Education	2012 Pay	Projected Job Growth	Average Annual Openings
Compensation and Benefits Managers	Bachelor's degree	$95,250	3%	610
Customer Service Representatives	High school diploma or equivalent	$30,580	13%	94,160
Human Resources Managers	Bachelor's degree	$99,720	13%	4,060
Insurance Sales Agents	High school diploma or equivalent	$48,150	10%	15,020
Public Relations Specialists	Bachelor's degree	$54,170	12%	5,880
Social and Human Service Assistants	High school diploma or equivalent	$28,850	22%	17,870
Tax Examiners and Collectors, and Revenue Agents	Bachelor's degree	$50,440	-4%	2,390
Training and Development Managers	Bachelor's degree	$95,400	11%	1,070

on a downward trend, resulting in less demand for the services of labor relations specialists.

Job Prospects. Job prospects for human resources specialists are expected to be favorable. Specifically, job opportunities should be best in the employment services industry, as companies continue to outsource portions of their human resources functions to other firms.

Human resources generalists, in particular may benefit from having knowledge of human resources programs, employment laws, collective bargaining, and human resources information systems.

Job prospects for labor relations specialists, however, are expected to be less favorable. Union membership has been declining, which means there are fewer opportunities for these specialists to negotiate with management.

Overall, candidates with a bachelor's degree and related work experience should have the best job prospects.

O*NET

➤ Human Resources Specialists (13-1071.00)
➤ Labor Relations Specialists (13-1075.00)

Contacts for More Information

For more information about human resources careers and certification, visit

➤ Society for Human Resource Management (www.shrm.org)

Insurance Underwriters

- **2012 Median Pay** .... $62,870 per year
  $30.22 per hour
- **Entry-Level Education** ....Bachelor's degree
- **Work Experience in a Related Occupation**.............. None
- **On-the-Job Training**.... Moderate-term on-the-job training
- **Number of Jobs 2012** 106,300
- **Job Outlook, 2012–22** .... -6% (Decline)
- **Employment Change, 2012–22** .... -6,500

What Insurance Underwriters Do

Insurance underwriters decide whether to provide insurance and under what terms. They evaluate insurance applications and determine coverage amounts and premiums.

Duties. Insurance underwriters typically do the following:

- Analyze information in insurance applications
- Determine the risk of insuring a client
- Screen applicants on the basis of set criteria
- Evaluate recommendations from underwriting software
- Contact field representatives, medical personnel, and others to obtain further information
- Decide whether to offer insurance
- Determine appropriate premiums and amounts of coverage

Underwriters are the main link between an insurance company and an insurance agent. Insurance underwriters use computer software programs to determine whether to approve an applicant. They take specific information about a client and enter it into a program. The program then provides recommendations on coverage and premiums. Underwriters evaluate these recommendations and decide whether to approve or reject the application. If a

decision is difficult, they may consult additional sources, such as medical documents and credit scores.

Underwriters analyze the risk factors on an application. For instance, if an applicant reports a previous bankruptcy, the underwriter must determine whether this is relevant for the current policy. They would consider how far in the past this occurred, and how the applicant's financial situation has changed since the applicant filed for bankruptcy.

Insurance underwriters must achieve a balance between risky and cautious decisions. If underwriters allow too much risk, the insurance company will pay out too many claims. But if they don't approve enough applications, the company will not make enough money from premiums.

Most insurance underwriters specialize in one of three broad fields: life, health, and property and casualty. Although job duties are similar, the criteria that underwriters use vary. For example, for someone seeking life insurance, underwriters consider age and financial history. For someone applying for car insurance (a form of property and casualty insurance), underwriters consider the person's driving record.

Within the broad field of property and casualty, underwriters may specialize even further into commercial (business insurance) or personal insurance. They may also specialize by the type of policy, such as insuring automobiles, boats (marine insurance), or homes (homeowners' insurance).

Work Environment

Insurance underwriters held about 106,300 jobs in 2012. They work indoors in offices. Some property and casualty underwriters may visit properties to assess them in person. The following industries employed the most insurance underwriters in 2012:

Insurance underwriters review insurance applications and determine the appropriate premium to charge a customer.

Median Annual Wages, May 2012

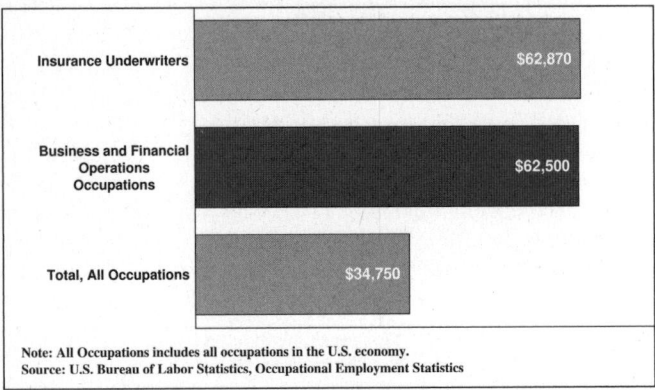

Note: All Occupations includes all occupations in the U.S. economy.
Source: U.S. Bureau of Labor Statistics, Occupational Employment Statistics

Percent Change in Employment, Projected 2012–2022

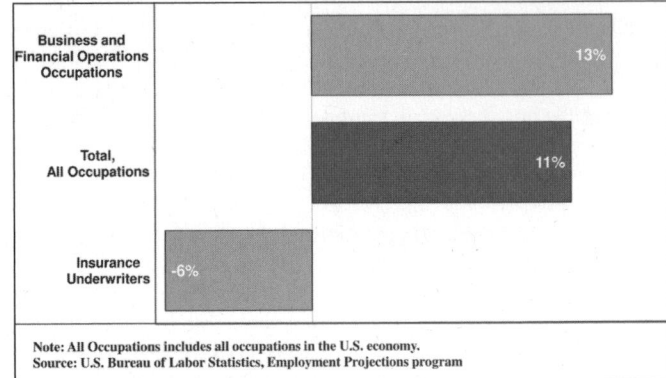

Note: All Occupations includes all occupations in the U.S. economy.
Source: U.S. Bureau of Labor Statistics, Employment Projections program

Insurance carriers 72%
Agencies, brokerages, and other insurance related activities ... 18
Credit intermediation and related activities 3
Management of companies and enterprises............................... 2

Work Schedules. Most underwriters work full time.

How to Become One

Employers prefer to hire candidates who have a bachelor's degree. However, insurance-related work experience and strong computer skills may be enough. Certification is necessary for advancement to senior underwriter and underwriter manager positions.

Education. Most firms prefer to hire applicants who have a bachelor's degree. Courses in business, finance, economics, and mathematics are particularly helpful.

Training. Beginning underwriters usually work as trainees under the supervision of senior underwriters. Trainees work on basic applications and learn the most common risk factors. As they gain experience, they become responsible for more complex applications and work independently.

Licenses, Certifications, and Registrations. Employers often expect underwriters to get certification through coursework. These courses are important for keeping current with new insur-

ance policies and adjusting to new technology and changes in state and federal regulations. Certification is often necessary for advancement to senior underwriter and underwriter management positions. Many certification options are available.

For underwriters with at least 3 years of insurance experience, The Institutes offers the Chartered Property and Casualty Underwriter (CPCU) designation.

For beginning underwriters, The Institutes offers a training program. The Institutes also offers two special designations, an Associate in Commercial Underwriting (AU) and an Associate in Personal Insurance (API). To earn either the AU or API designation, underwriters complete a series of courses and exams that generally take 1 to 2 years.

The American College of Financial Services also offers an introductory course in basic insurance concepts: The Life Underwriter Training Council Fellow (LUTCF). They also offer a Chartered Life Underwriter (CLU) and Registered Health Underwriter (RHU) designation.

Important Qualities

Analytical skills. Underwriters must be able to evaluate information from a variety of sources and solve complex problems.

Employment Projections Data for Insurance Underwriters

Occupational title	SOC Code	Employment, 2012	Projected Employment, 2022	Change, 2012–2022	
				Percent	Numeric
Insurance underwriters.. 13-2053		106,300	99,800	-6	-6,500

Source: U.S. Bureau of Labor Statistics, Employment Projections Program

Note: Data are rounded. Go to **Occupational Information Included in the OOH** *for a discussion of the data in this table.*

Similar Occupations This table shows a list of occupations with job duties that are similar to those of insurance underwriters.

Occupations	Entry-level Education	2012 Pay	Projected Job Growth	Average Annual Openings
Actuaries	Bachelor's degree	$93,680	26%	1,320
Budget Analysts	Bachelor's degree	$69,280	6%	2,850
Claims Adjusters, Appraisers, Examiners, and Investigators	See "How to Become One"	$59,902	3%	8,340
Cost Estimators	Bachelor's degree	$58,860	26%	11,800
Insurance Sales Agents	High school diploma or equivalent	$48,150	10%	15,020
Loan Officers	Bachelor's degree	$59,820	8%	7,720

Decision-making skills. Underwriters must consider the costs and benefits of various decisions and choose the appropriate one.

Detail oriented. Underwriters must pay attention to detail, because each individual item on an insurance application can affect the coverage decision.

Interpersonal skills. Underwriters need good communication and interpersonal skills because much of their work involves dealing with other people, such as insurance agents.

Math skills. Determining the probability of losses on an insurance policy and calculating appropriate premiums require mathematical ability.

Pay

The median annual wage for insurance underwriters was $62,870 in May 2012. The median wage is the wage at which half the workers in an occupation earned more than that amount and half earned less. The lowest 10 percent earned less than $39,050, and the top 10 percent earned more than $109,900.

In May 2012, the median annual wages for insurance underwriters in the top four industries in which they worked were as follows:

Credit intermediation and related activities $66,260
Insurance carriers 63,820
Management of companies and enterprises........................ 61,680
Agencies, brokerages, and other insurance
    related activities 59,340

Job Outlook

Employment of insurance underwriters is projected to decline 6 percent from 2012 to 2022. Automated underwriting software allows workers to process applications more quickly than before, reducing the need for underwriters. However, there still will be a need for underwriters to evaluate automated recommendations.

Job Prospects. The need to replace workers who retire or transfer to another occupation will likely create many additional job openings. Job opportunities should be best for those with a background in finance, and strong computer and communication skills.

O*NET

➤ Insurance Underwriters (13-2053.00)

Contacts for More Information

For more information about property and casualty insurance, visit
➤ Insurance Information Institute (www.iii.org/)

For more information about certifications, visit
➤ The Institutes (www.theinstitutes.org/)
➤ CPCU Society (www.cpcusociety.org/)
➤ The American College of Financial Services (www.theamericancollege.edu/)

Loan Officers

- **2012 Median Pay** .... $59,820 per year
                                            $28.76 per hour
- **Entry-Level Education** ....Bachelor's degree
- **Work Experience in a Related Occupation**.............. None
- **On-the-Job Training** .... Moderate-term on-the-job training
- **Number of Jobs 2012** 296,900
- **Job Outlook, 2012–22** .... 8% (As fast as average)
- **Employment Change, 2012–22** 22,900

What Loan Officers Do

Loan officers evaluate, authorize, or recommend approval of loan applications for people and businesses.

Duties. Loan officers typically do the following:

- Contact companies or people to ask if they need a loan
- Meet with loan applicants to gather personal information and answer questions
- Explain different types of loans and the terms of each one to applicants
- Obtain and verify financial information, such as the applicant's credit rating and income level
- Analyze and evaluate the applicant's finances to decide if the applicant should get the loan
- Approve loan applications or refer them to management for a decision

Loan officers use a process called underwriting to assess whether applicants qualify for loans. After collecting and verifying all the required financial documents, the loan officer evaluates this information to determine the applicant's loan needs and ability to pay back the loan. Some firms underwrite loans manually, calculating the applicant's financial status by following a certain formula or set of guidelines. Other firms use underwriting software, which analyzes applications almost instantly. More often, firms use underwriting software to produce a recommendation, while relying on loan officers to consider any additional information to make a final decision.

The work of loan officers has sizeable customer-service and sales components. Loan officers often answer questions and guide customers through the application process. In addition, many loan officers must market the products and services of their lending institution and actively solicit new business.

The following are common types of loan officers:

Commercial loan officers specialize in loans to businesses. Businesses often use loans to buy supplies and upgrade or expand operations. Commercial loans are often larger and more complicated than other types of loans. Because companies have such complex financial situations and statements, commercial loans usually

Loan officers guide clients through the loan application process.

Median Annual Wages, May 2012

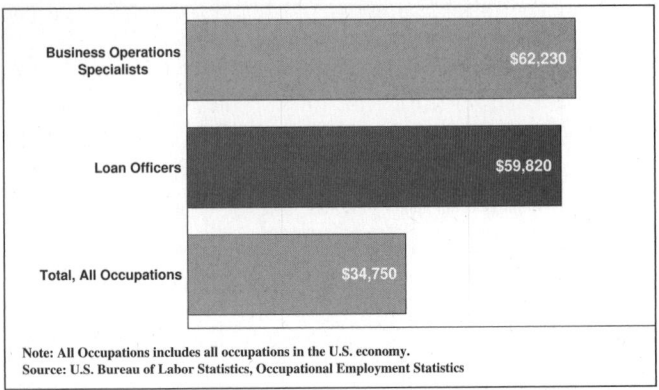

Note: All Occupations includes all occupations in the U.S. economy.
Source: U.S. Bureau of Labor Statistics, Occupational Employment Statistics

Percent Change in Employment, Projected 2012–2022

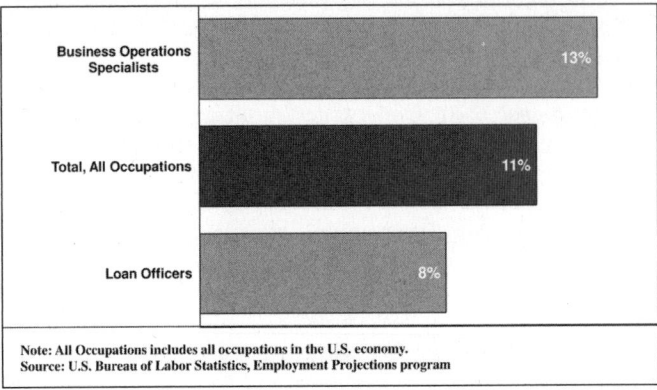

Note: All Occupations includes all occupations in the U.S. economy.
Source: U.S. Bureau of Labor Statistics, Employment Projections program

require human judgment in addition to the analysis by underwriting software. Furthermore, some commercial loans are so large that a single bank will not provide the entire amount requested. In such cases, loan officers may have to work with multiple banks to put together a package of loans.

Consumer loan officers specialize in loans to people. Consumers take out loans for many reasons, such as buying a car or paying for college tuition. For some simple consumer loans, the underwriting process is fully automated. However, the loan officer is still needed to guide applicants through the process and to handle cases with unusual circumstances. Some institutions–usually small banks and credit unions–do not use underwriting software and instead rely on loan officers to complete the underwriting process manually.

Mortgage loan officers specialize in loans used to buy real estate (property and buildings), which are called mortgage loans. Mortgage loan officers work on loans for both residential and commercial properties. Often, mortgage loan officers must seek out clients, which requires developing relationships with real estate companies and other sources that can refer prospective applicants.

Within these three fields, some loan officers specialize in a particular part of the loan process:

Loan collection officers contact borrowers who fail to make their loan payments on time. They work with borrowers to help them find a way to keep paying off the loan. If the borrower continues to miss payments, loan officers start the process of taking away what the borrower used to secure the loan (called "collateral")–often a home or car–and selling it to repay the loan.

Loan underwriters specialize in evaluating whether a client is credit worthy. They do this by collecting, verifying, and evaluating the client's financial information provided on their loan applications. They may use loan underwriting software, or they may perform the process manually.

Work Environment

Loan officers held about 296,900 jobs in 2012, of which 84 percent were in the credit intermediation and related activities industry. This includes commercial banks, credit unions, mortgage companies, and other financial institutions.

Loan officers who specialize in consumer loans usually work in offices. Mortgage and commercial loan officers often work outside the office and meet with clients at their homes or businesses.

Work Schedules. Most loan officers work full time.

How to Become One

Most loan officers need a bachelor's degree and receive on-the-job training. Mortgage loan officers must be licensed.

Education. Loan officers typically need a bachelor's degree, usually in a field such as business or finance. Because commercial loan officers analyze the finances of businesses applying for credit, they need to understand general business accounting, including how to read financial statements.

Some loan officers may be able to enter the occupation without a bachelor's degree if they have related work experience, such as in sales, customer service, or banking.

Training. Once hired, loan officers usually receive some on-the-job training. This may be a combination of formal, company-sponsored training and informal training during the first few months on the job. Those who use underwriting software often take classes to learn the company's software programs.

Licenses, Certifications, and Registrations. Mortgage loan officers must have a Mortgage Loan Originator (MLO) license. To become licensed, mortgage loan officers must complete at least 20 hours of coursework, pass an exam, and submit to background and credit checks. Licenses must be renewed annually, and individual states may have additional requirements.

Several banking associations and schools offer courses or certifications for loan officers. The American Bankers Association and the Mortgage Bankers Association both offer certification and training programs for loan officers. Although not required, certification shows dedication and expertise and thus may enhance a candidate's employment opportunities.

Other Experience. Employers may prefer candidates who have work experience in lending, banking, sales, or customer service. For those without a bachelor's degree, work experience in a related field can be particularly useful.

Employment Projections Data for Loan Officers

Occupational title	SOC Code	Employment, 2012	Projected Employment, 2022	Change, 2012–2022	
				Percent	Numeric
Loan officers	13-2072	296,900	319,800	8	22,900

Source: U.S. Bureau of Labor Statistics, Employment Projections Program

Note: Data are rounded. Go to **Occupational Information Included in the OOH** *for a discussion of the data in this table.*

Similar Occupations This table shows a list of occupations with job duties that are similar to those of loan officers.

Occupations	Entry-level Education	2012 Pay	Projected Job Growth	Average Annual Openings
Financial Analysts	Bachelor's degree	$76,950	16%	10,090
Financial Examiners	Bachelor's degree	$75,800	7%	920
Financial Managers	Bachelor's degree	$109,740	9%	14,690
Insurance Sales Agents	High school diploma or equivalent	$48,150	10%	15,020
Insurance Underwriters	Bachelor's degree	$62,870	-6%	2,890
Personal Financial Advisors	Bachelor's degree	$67,520	27%	9,640
Real Estate Brokers and Sales Agents	High school diploma or equivalent	$42,723	11%	8,630
Securities, Commodities, and Financial Services Sales Agents	Bachelor's degree	$71,720	11%	12,260
Tax Examiners and Collectors, and Revenue Agents	Bachelor's degree	$50,440	-4%	2,390
Tellers	High school diploma or equivalent	$24,940	1%	25,980

Important Qualities

Decision-making skills. Decision-making skills are important for loan officers, who must assess an applicant's financial information and decide whether to award a loan.

Initiative. Loan officers need to have initiative when seeking out clients. They often act as salespeople, promoting their lending institution and contacting firms to determine their loan needs.

Interpersonal skills. Because loan officers work with people, they must be able to guide customers through the application process and answer their questions.

Pay

The median annual wage for loan officers was $59,820 in May 2012. The median wage is the wage at which half the workers in an occupation earned more than that amount and half earned less. The lowest 10 percent earned less than $32,600, and the top 10 percent earned more than $119,710.

The form of compensation varies widely by employer. Some loan officers are paid a flat salary; others are paid on commission. Those on commission usually are paid a base salary plus a commission for the loans they originate. Loan officers also may receive extra commission or bonuses based on the number of loans they originate or how well the loans do.

Job Outlook

Employment of loan officers is projected to grow 8 percent from 2012 to 2022, about as fast as the average for all occupations. The need for loan officers fluctuates with the economy, generally increasing in times of economic growth, low interest rates, and population growth–all of which create demand for loans.

After a period of decreased lending resulting from the recent recession, banks and other lending institutions are granting an increasing number of loans to people and businesses. Because lending activity is sensitive to fluctuations in the economy, consumer and mortgage loans are expected to increase as the economy recovers. Similarly, many businesses postponed borrowing funds for maintenance, improvement, and expansion during the recession, so commercial loans should increase as businesses are more willing to borrow and banks are more willing to lend.

However, growth in the number of jobs is expected to be tempered by the expanded use of loan underwriting software, which has made the loan application process much faster than in the past. Some loan applications can be completed online and underwritten automatically, allowing loan officers to process more applications in a much shorter period of time. This factor may limit the number of new loan officers needed in the future, despite an increasing number of loan applications.

Job Prospects. Prospects for loan officers should improve over the coming decade as lending activity rebounds from the recent recession. Job opportunities should be good for those with lending, banking, or sales experience. In addition, some firms require loan officers to find their own clients, so candidates with established contacts and a referral network should have the best job opportunities.

O*NET

➤ Loan Officers (13-2072.00)

Contacts for More Information

For more information about certification and training for loan officers, visit

➤ American Bankers Association (www.aba.com)

For more information about a career as a mortgage loan officer, visit

➤ Mortgage Bankers Association (www.mortgagebankers.org/)

For more information about licensing for mortgage loan officers, visit

➤ Nationwide Mortgage Licensing System & Registry Resource Center (http://mortgage.nationwidelicensingsystem.org)

State bankers associations have specific information about job opportunities in their state. Also, individual banks can supply information about job openings and the activities, responsibilities, and preferred qualifications of their loan officers.

Logisticians

- **2012 Median Pay** .... $72,780 per year
  $34.99 per hour
- **Entry-Level Education** ....Bachelor's degree
- **Work Experience in a Related Occupation**.............. None
- **On-the-Job Training** .... None
- **Number of Jobs 2012** 125,900
- **Job Outlook, 2012–22** .... 22% (Much faster than average)
- **Employment Change, 2012–22** 27,600

What Logisticians Do

Logisticians analyze and coordinate an organization's supply chain–the system that moves a product from supplier to consumer. They manage the entire life cycle of a product, which includes how a product is acquired, distributed, allocated, and delivered.

Duties. Logisticians typically do the following:

- Direct the allocation of materials, supplies, and finished products

- Develop business relationships with suppliers and customers

- Work to understand customers' needs and how to meet them

- Design strategies to minimize the cost or time required to move goods

- Review the success of logistical functions and identify areas for improvement

- Propose improvements to management and customers

Logisticians oversee activities that include purchasing, transportation, inventory, and warehousing. They may direct the movement of a range of goods, people, or supplies, from common consumer goods to military supplies and personnel.

Logisticians use sophisticated software systems to plan and track the movement of goods. They operate software programs tailored specifically to manage logistical functions, such as procurement, inventory management, and other supply chain planning and management systems.

Work Environment

Logisticians held about 125,900 jobs in 2012.

Although logisticians work in nearly every industry, the majority is concentrated in manufacturing and the federal government. About 25 percent of logisticians worked in manufacturing, and about 23 percent worked in the federal government, many of whom were civilians doing logistical work for the military.

Some logisticians work in the logistical department of a company, and others work for firms that specialize in logistical work, such as a freight-shipping company. The industries that employed the most logisticians in 2012 were as follows:

Manufacturing	25%
Federal government, excluding postal service	23
Professional, scientific, and technical services	17
Transportation equipment manufacturing	11
Aerospace product and parts manufacturing	8

The job can be stressful because logistical work is fast paced. Logisticians must ensure that operations stay on schedule, and they

When problems arise, logisticians must respond quickly and devise solutions.

must work quickly to solve any problems that arise. Some logisticians travel to visit manufacturing plants or distribution centers.

Work Schedules. Most logisticians work full time during regular business hours. When dealing with delivery problems or other logistical issues, they may work overtime to ensure that operations stay on schedule.

How to Become One

Although an associate's degree may be sufficient for some logistician jobs, a bachelor's degree is typically required for most positions. Work experience in a related field is helpful for jobseekers.

Education. Logisticians may qualify for positions with an associate's degree. However, as logistics becomes increasingly complex, more companies prefer to hire workers who have at least a bachelor's degree. Many logisticians have a bachelor's degree in business, industrial engineering, process engineering, or supply chain management.

Bachelor's degree programs often include coursework in operations and database management, decisionmaking, and system dynamics. In addition, most programs offer courses that train students on software and technologies commonly used by logisticians, such as radio-frequency identification (RFID).

Licenses, Certifications, and Registrations. Logisticians can obtain certification through the American Society of Transportation and Logistics (ASTL) or the International Society of Logistics (SOLE). The certification offered by each of these organizations typically requires a combination of education, experience, and

Median Annual Wages, May 2012

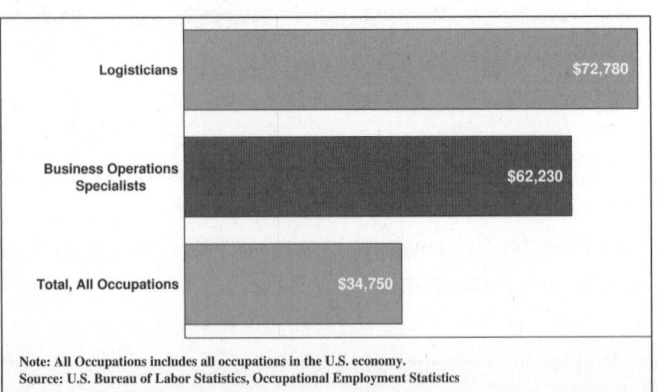

Logisticians	$72,780
Business Operations Specialists	$62,230
Total, All Occupations	$34,750

Note: All Occupations includes all occupations in the U.S. economy.
Source: U.S. Bureau of Labor Statistics, Occupational Employment Statistics

Percent Change in Employment, Projected 2012–2022

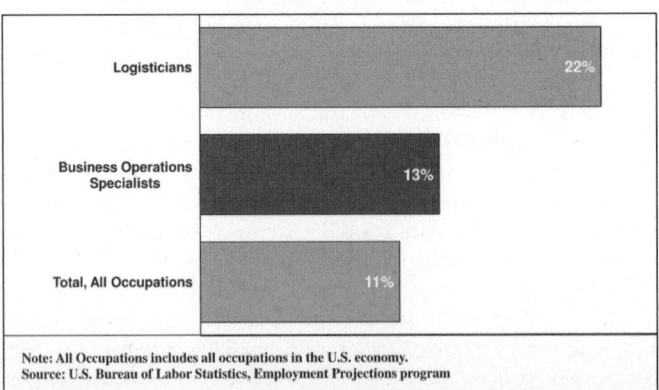

Logisticians	22%
Business Operations Specialists	13%
Total, All Occupations	11%

Note: All Occupations includes all occupations in the U.S. economy.
Source: U.S. Bureau of Labor Statistics, Employment Projections program

Employment Projections Data for Logisticians

Occupational title	SOC Code	Employment, 2012	Projected Employment, 2022	Change, 2012–2022	
				Percent	Numeric
Logisticians 13-1081		125,900	153,600	22	27,600

Source: U.S. Bureau of Labor Statistics, Employment Projections Program

Note: Data are rounded. Go to Occupational Information Included in the OOH *for a discussion of the data in this table.*

passing an exam. Although not required, certification can demonstrate professional competence and a broad knowledge of logistics.

Other Experience. Prospective logisticians can benefit from previous work experience in a field related to logistics or business. Because military operations require a large amount of logistics, some logisticians gain work experience while serving in the military. Some firms allow applicants to substitute several years of work experience for a degree.

Important Qualities

Communication skills. Logisticians need strong communication skills in order to collaborate with colleagues and do business with suppliers and customers.

Critical-thinking skills. Logisticians must develop, adjust, and successfully carry out logistical plans, and they often must find ways to cut costs and improve efficiency.

Organizational skills. Logisticians must be able to perform several tasks at one time, keep detailed records, and simultaneously manage several projects in a fast-paced environment.

Problem-solving skills. Logisticians must handle unforeseen issues, such as delivery problems, and adjust plans as needed to resolve the issues.

Pay

The median annual wage for logisticians was $72,780 in May 2012. The median wage is the wage at which half the workers in an occupation earned more than that amount and half earned less. The lowest 10 percent earned less than $45,190, and the top 10 percent earned more than $112,100.

In May 2012, the median annual wages for logisticians in the top five industries employing logisticians were as follows:

Federal government, excluding postal service	$78,000
Aerospace product and parts manufacturing	75,230
Transportation equipment manufacturing	74,210
Manufacturing	71,940
Professional, scientific, and technical services	71,510

Job Outlook

Employment of logisticians is projected to grow 22 percent from 2012 to 2022, much faster than the average for all occupations. Employment growth will be driven by the vital role logistics plays in the transportation of goods in a global economy.

Companies rely on logisticians to manage the movement of their products and supplies. Managing their operations in this way allows the companies to compete in a highly globalized market. The performance of the logistical and supply chain process is an important factor in a company's profitability. Supply and distribution systems have become increasingly complex, with the aim of maximizing efficiency while minimizing cost. Therefore, employment is expected to grow rapidly as companies need more logisticians to move products efficiently, solve problems, and identify areas for improvement.

Governments and the military also rely on logisticians. Planning for and moving military supplies and personnel requires an enormous amount of logistical work. Employment of logisticians in government and contracting firms will continue to grow to meet the needs of the military.

Job Prospects. Job opportunities should be good for those with a bachelor's degree in business, industrial engineering, process engineering, supply chain management, or a related field.

Job prospects should be best for those with a college degree and work experience related to logistics, particularly previous experience using logistical software or doing logistical work for the military.

O*NET

➤ Logisticians (13-1081.00)
➤ Logistics Engineers (13-1081.01)
➤ Logistics Analysts (13-1081.02)

Contacts for More Information

For more information about logisticians, including certification, visit

➤ American Society of Transportation and Logistics (www.astl.org)
➤ International Society of Logistics (www.sole.org)

Similar Occupations   This table shows a list of occupations with job duties that are similar to those of logisticians.

Occupations	Entry-level Education	2012 Pay	Projected Job Growth	Average Annual Openings
Cost Estimators	Bachelor's degree	$58,860	26%	11,800
Industrial Engineering Technicians	Associate's degree	$50,980	-3%	1,410
Industrial Engineers	Bachelor's degree	$78,860	5%	7,540
Industrial Production Managers	Bachelor's degree	$89,190	-2%	3,140
Management Analysts	Bachelor's degree	$78,600	19%	24,520
Operations Research Analysts	Bachelor's degree	$72,100	27%	3,600
Quality Control Inspectors	High school diploma or equivalent	$34,460	6%	12,770

Management Analysts

- **2012 Median Pay** .... $78,600 per year
  $37.79 per hour

- **Entry-Level Education** .... Bachelor's degree

- **Work Experience in a Related Occupation** .... Less than 5 years

- **On-the-Job Training** .... None

- **Number of Jobs 2012** 718,700

- **Job Outlook, 2012–22** .... 19% (Faster than average)

- **Employment Change, 2012–22** 133,800

Management analysts collect and analyze information in order to make recommendations to managers.

What Management Analysts Do

Management analysts, often called management consultants, propose ways to improve an organization's efficiency. They advise managers on how to make organizations more profitable through reduced costs and increased revenues.

Duties. Management analysts typically do the following:

- Gather and organize information about the problem to be solved or the procedure to be improved

- Interview personnel and conduct on-site observations to determine the methods, equipment, and personnel that will be needed

- Analyze financial and other data, including revenue, expenditure, and employment reports

- Develop solutions or alternative practices

- Recommend new systems, procedures, or organizational changes

- Make recommendations to management through presentations or written reports

- Confer with managers to ensure that the changes are working

Although some management analysts work for the organization that they are analyzing, most work as consultants on a contractual basis.

Whether they are self-employed or part of a large consulting company, the work of a management analyst may vary from project to project. Some projects require a team of consultants, each specializing in one area. In other projects, consultants work independently with the client organization's managers.

Management analysts often specialize in certain areas, such as inventory management or reorganizing corporate structures to eliminate duplicate and nonessential jobs. Some consultants specialize in a specific industry, such as healthcare or telecommunications. In government, management analysts usually specialize by type of agency.

Organizations hire consultants to develop strategies for entering and remaining competitive in the electronic marketplace.

Management analysts who work on contract may write proposals and bid for jobs. Typically, an organization that needs the help of a management analyst solicits proposals from a number of consultants and consulting companies that specialize in the needed work. Those who want the work must then submit a proposal by the deadline that explains how they will do the work, who will do the work, why they are the best consultants to do the work, what the schedule will be, and how much it will cost. The organization that needs the consultants then selects the proposal that best meets its needs and budget.

Work Environment

Management analysts held about 718,700 jobs in 2012. They usually divide their time between their offices and the client's site. Because they must spend a significant amount of time with clients, analysts travel frequently. Analysts may experience stress when trying to meet a client's demands, often on a tight schedule.

In 2012, about 21 percent of management analysts were self-employed. Self-employed analysts can decide how much, when, and where to work. However, self-employed analysts often are under more pressure than those who are wage and salary employees, because their livelihood depends on their ability to maintain and expand their client base.

The industries that employed the most management analysts in 2012 were as follows:

Management, scientific, and technical consulting services 20%
Federal government, excluding postal service 9

Median Annual Wages, May 2012

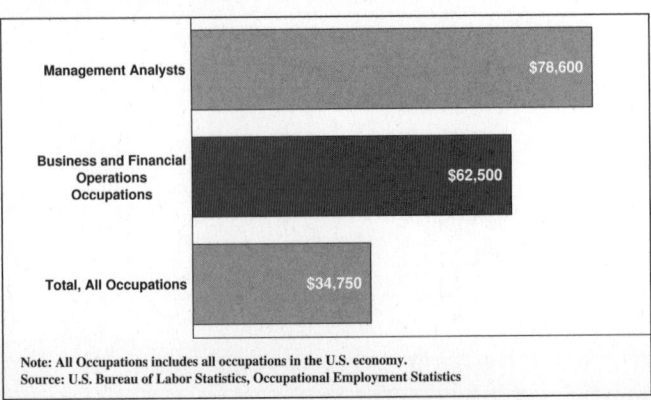

Management Analysts	$78,600
Business and Financial Operations Occupations	$62,500
Total, All Occupations	$34,750

Note: All Occupations includes all occupations in the U.S. economy.
Source: U.S. Bureau of Labor Statistics, Occupational Employment Statistics

Percent Change in Employment, Projected 2012–2022

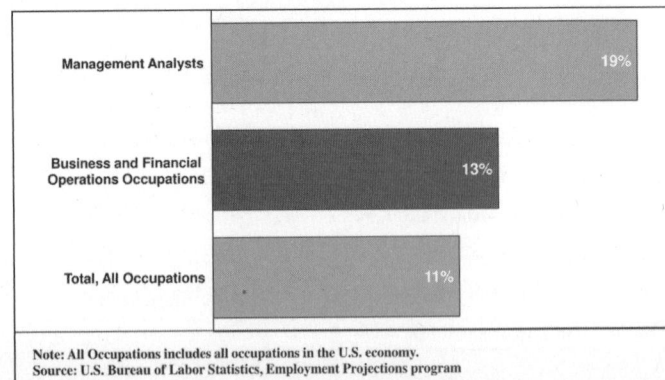

Management Analysts	19%
Business and Financial Operations Occupations	13%
Total, All Occupations	11%

Note: All Occupations includes all occupations in the U.S. economy.
Source: U.S. Bureau of Labor Statistics, Employment Projections program

Employment Projections Data for Management Analysts

Occupational title	SOC Code	Employment, 2012	Projected Employment, 2022	Change, 2012–2022	
				Percent	Numeric
Management analysts.. 13-1111		718,700	852,500	19	133,800

Source: U.S. Bureau of Labor Statistics, Employment Projections Program

Note: Data are rounded. Go to **Occupational Information Included in the OOH** *for a discussion of the data in this table.*

State and local government, excluding education
and hospitals..7
Insurance carriers 5
Management of companies and enterprises.............5

Work Schedules. Analysts work under tight deadlines, which often requires working long hours. In 2012, about 1 in 4 worked more than 40 hours per week.

How to Become One

Most management analysts have at least a bachelor's degree. The Certified Management Consultant (CMC) designation may improve job prospects.

Education. A bachelor's degree is the typical entry-level requirement for management analysts. However, some employers prefer to hire candidates who have a master's degree in business administration (MBA).

Few colleges and universities offer formal programs in management consulting. However, many fields of study provide a suitable education because of the range of areas that management analysts address. Common fields of study include business, management, economics, political science and government, accounting, finance, marketing, psychology, computer and information science, and English.

Analysts also routinely attend conferences to stay up to date on current developments in their field.

Licenses, Certifications, and Registrations. The Institute of Management Consultants USA (IMC USA) offers the Certified Management Consultant (CMC) designation to those who meet minimum levels of education and experience, submit client reviews, and pass an interview and exam covering the IMC USA's Code of Ethics. Management consultants with a CMC designation must be recertified every 3 years. Management analysts are not required to get certification, but it may give jobseekers a competitive advantage.

Work Experience in a Related Occupation. Many analysts enter the occupation with several years of work experience. Organizations that specialize in certain fields typically try to hire candidates who have experience in those areas. Typical work backgrounds include management, human resources, and information technology.

Advancement. As consultants gain experience, they often take on more responsibility. At the senior level, consultants may supervise teams working on more complex projects and become more involved in seeking out new business. Those with exceptional skills may eventually become partners in their consulting organization and focus on attracting new clients and bringing in revenue. Senior consultants who leave their consulting company often move to senior management positions at nonconsulting organizations.

Important Qualities

Analytical skills. Management analysts must be able to interpret a wide range of information and use their findings to make proposals.

Communication skills. Management analysts must be able to communicate clearly and precisely in both writing and speaking. Successful analysts also need good listening skills to understand the organization's problems and propose appropriate solutions.

Interpersonal skills. Management analysts must work with managers and other employees of the organizations where they provide consulting services. They should work as a team toward achieving the organization's goals.

Problem-solving skills. Management analysts must be able to think creatively to solve clients' problems. Although some aspects of different clients' problems may be similar, each situation is likely to present unique challenges for the analyst to solve.

Time-management skills. Management analysts often work under tight deadlines and must use their time efficiently to complete projects on time.

Similar Occupations   This table shows a list of occupations with job duties that are similar to those of management analysts.

Occupations	Entry-level Education	2012 Pay	Projected Job Growth	Average Annual Openings
Accountants and Auditors	Bachelor's degree	$63,550	13%	54,420
Administrative Services Managers	Bachelor's degree	$81,080	12%	7,990
Budget Analysts	Bachelor's degree	$69,280	6%	2,850
Cost Estimators	Bachelor's degree	$58,860	26%	11,800
Economists	Master's degree	$91,860	14%	740
Financial Analysts	Bachelor's degree	$76,950	16%	10,090
Financial Managers	Bachelor's degree	$109,740	9%	14,690
Market Research Analysts	Bachelor's degree	$60,300	32%	18,850
Operations Research Analysts	Bachelor's degree	$72,100	27%	3,600
Survey Researchers	Master's degree	$45,050	18%	560
Top Executives	Bachelor's degree	$104,073	11%	70,090

Pay

The median annual wage for management analysts was $78,600 in May 2012. The median wage is the wage at which half the workers in an occupation earned more than that amount and half earned less. The lowest 10 percent earned less than $44,370, and the top 10 percent earned more than $142,580.

In May 2012, the median annual wages for management analysts in the top five industries in which these analysts worked were as follows:

Federal government, excluding postal service	$84,530
Management, scientific, and technical consulting services	84,300
Management of companies and enterprises	78,030
Insurance carriers	73,370
State and local government, excluding education and hospitals	62,270

Job Outlook

Employment of management analysts is projected to grow 19 percent from 2012 to 2022, faster than the average for all occupations. Demand for consulting services is expected to grow as organizations seek ways to improve efficiency and control costs. As markets become more competitive, firms will need to use resources more efficiently.

Growth will be particularly strong in smaller consulting companies that specialize in specific industries or types of business function, such as information technology or human resources. Government agencies will also seek the services of management analysts as they look for ways to reduce spending and improve efficiency.

Growth of international business will also contribute to an expected increase in demand for management analysts. As U.S. organizations expand their business abroad, many will hire management analysts to help them form the right strategy for entering the foreign market.

Many firms are also expected to hire management analysts who specialize in areas such as lowering energy consumption or implementing "green" initiatives.

Job Prospects. Jobseekers may face strong competition for management analyst positions because the high earning potential in this occupation makes it attractive to many jobseekers. Job opportunities are expected to be best for those who have a graduate degree or a certification, specialized expertise, fluency in a foreign language, and a talent for sales and public relations.

O*NET

➤ Management Analysts (13-1111.00)

Contacts for More Information

For more information about management consulting, visit
➤ Association of Management Consulting Firms (http://amcf.org/)

For more information about the Certified Management Consultant designation, visit
➤ Institute of Management Consultants USA (www.imcusa.org/)

Market Research Analysts

- **2012 Median Pay** .... $60,300 per year
  $28.99 per hour
- **Entry-Level Education** .... Bachelor's degree
- **Work Experience in a Related Occupation** .... None
- **On-the-Job Training** .... None
- **Number of Jobs 2012** 415,700
- **Job Outlook, 2012–22** .... 32% (Much faster than average)
- **Employment Change, 2012–22** 131,500

What Market Research Analysts Do

Market research analysts study market conditions to examine potential sales of a product or service. They help companies understand what products people want, who will buy them, and at what price.

Duties. Market research analysts typically do the following:

- Monitor and forecast marketing and sales trends
- Measure the effectiveness of marketing programs and strategies
- Devise and evaluate methods for collecting data, such as surveys, questionnaires, and opinion polls
- Gather data about consumers, competitors, and market conditions
- Analyze data using statistical software
- Convert complex data and findings into understandable tables, graphs, and written reports
- Prepare reports and present results to clients and management

Market research analysts perform research and gather data to help a company market its products or services. They gather data on consumer demographics, preferences, needs, and buying habits. They collect data and information using a variety of methods, such as interviews, questionnaires, focus groups, market analysis surveys, public opinion polls, and literature reviews.

Analysts help determine a company's position in the marketplace by researching their competitors and analyzing their prices, sales, and marketing methods. Using this information, they may determine potential markets, product demand, and pricing. Their knowledge of the targeted consumer enables them to develop advertising brochures and commercials, sales plans, and product promotions.

Market research analysts may give presentations to clients.

Median Annual Wages, May 2012

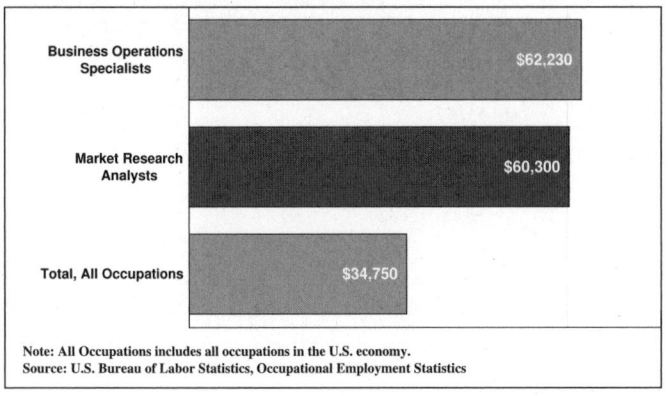

Note: All Occupations includes all occupations in the U.S. economy.
Source: U.S. Bureau of Labor Statistics, Occupational Employment Statistics

Percent Change in Employment, Projected 2012–2022

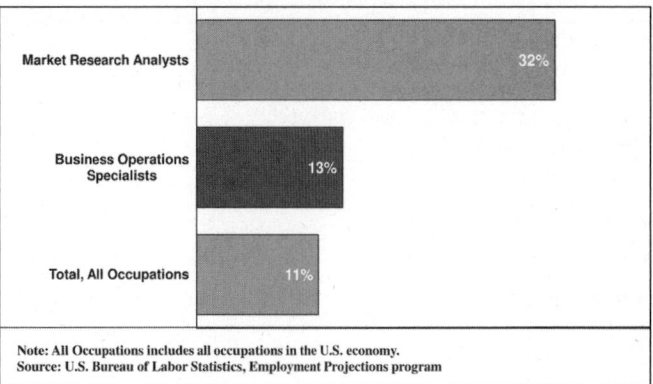

Note: All Occupations includes all occupations in the U.S. economy.
Source: U.S. Bureau of Labor Statistics, Employment Projections program

Market research analysts evaluate data using statistical techniques and software. They must interpret what the data means for their client, and they may forecast future trends. They often make charts, graphs, and other visual aids to present the results of their research.

Workers who design and conduct surveys are known as survey researchers.

Work Environment

Market research analysts held about 415,700 jobs in 2012. Because most industries use market research, these analysts are employed throughout the economy.

The industries employing the most market research analysts in 2012 were as follows:

Finance and insurance	10%
Management, scientific, and technical consulting services	10
Wholesale trade	9
Management of companies and enterprises	9
Manufacturing	8

Some market research analysts research trends for the company for which they work. Others work for consulting firms that do market research for many different clients.

Those who hold full-time jobs in government, business, or teaching also may consult on a part-time basis.

Market research analysts generally work alone at a computer, collecting and analyzing data and preparing reports. Some, however, work directly with the public to collect information and data.

Work Schedules. Most market research analysts work full time during regular business hours. Some, however, work under pressure of deadlines and tight schedules, which may require longer hours.

How to Become One

Most market research analysts need at least a bachelor's degree. Top research positions often require a master's degree. Strong math and analytical skills are essential.

Education. Market research analysts typically need a bachelor's degree in market research or a related field. Many have degrees in fields such as statistics, math, and computer science. Others have backgrounds in business administration, the social sciences, or communications.

Courses in statistics, research methods, and marketing are essential for these workers. Courses in communications and social sciences, such as economics, psychology, and sociology, are also important.

Some market research analyst jobs require a master's degree. Several schools offer graduate programs in marketing research, but many analysts complete degrees in other fields, such as statistics and marketing, and/or earn a Master of Business Administration (MBA). A master's degree is often required for leadership positions or positions that perform more technical research.

Other Experience. Most market research analysts can benefit from internships or work experience in business, marketing, or sales. Work experience in other positions that require analyzing data, writing reports, or surveying or collecting data can also be helpful in finding a market research position.

Licenses, Certifications, and Registrations. Certification is voluntary, but analysts may pursue certification to demonstrate a level of professional competency. The Marketing Research Association offers the Professional Researcher Certification (PRC) for market research analysts. Candidates qualify based on experience and knowledge; they must pass an exam, be a member of a professional organization, and have at least 3 years working in opinion and marketing research.

Important Qualities

Analytical skills. Market research analysts must be able to understand large amounts of data and information.

Communication skills. Market research analysts need strong communication skills when gathering information, interpreting data, and presenting results to clients.

Critical-thinking skills. Market research analysts must assess all available information to determine what marketing strategy would work best for a company.

Detail oriented. Market research analysts must be detail oriented because they often do precise data analysis.

Employment Projections Data for Market Research Analysts

Occupational title	SOC Code	Employment, 2012	Projected Employment, 2022	Change, 2012–2022 Percent	Change, 2012–2022 Numeric
Market research analysts and marketing specialists	13-1161	415,700	547,200	32	131,500

Source: U.S. Bureau of Labor Statistics, Employment Projections Program

Note: Data are rounded. Go to Occupational Information Included in the OOH *for a discussion of the data in this table.*

Similar Occupations   This table shows a list of occupations with job duties that are similar to those of market research analysts.

Occupations	Entry-level Education	2012 Pay	Projected Job Growth	Average Annual Openings
Advertising, Promotions, and Marketing Managers	Bachelor's degree	$115,087	12%	7,510
Cost Estimators	Bachelor's degree	$58,860	26%	11,800
Economists	Master's degree	$91,860	14%	740
Operations Research Analysts	Bachelor's degree	$72,100	27%	3,600
Public Relations Specialists	Bachelor's degree	$54,170	12%	5,880
Statisticians	Master's degree	$75,560	26%	1,610
Survey Researchers	Master's degree	$45,050	18%	560

Pay

The median annual wage for market research analysts was $60,300 in May 2012. The median wage is the wage at which half the workers in an occupation earned more than that amount and half earned less. The lowest 10 percent earned less than $33,280, and the top 10 percent earned more than $113,500.

In May 2012, the median annual wages for market research analysts in the top five industries in which these analysts worked were as follows:

Manufacturing... $67,550
Management of companies and enterprises......................... 67,330
Finance and insurance.. 64,490
Wholesale trade 60,200
Management, scientific, and technical consulting services... 56,760

Job Outlook

Employment of market research analysts is projected to grow 32 percent from 2012 to 2022, much faster than the average for all occupations.

Employment growth will be driven by an increased use of data and market research across all industries to understand the needs and wants of customers and to measure the effectiveness of marketing and business strategies.

Companies increasingly use research on consumer behavior to develop improved marketing strategies. By doing so, companies are better able to market directly to their target population. In addition, market research provides companies and organizations with an opportunity to cut costs.

Market research also lets companies monitor customer satisfaction and gather feedback about how to improve products or services, allowing companies to build an advantage over their competitors. They may use research to decide the location of stores, placement of products, and services offered. As more companies use research to develop marketing strategies, competing companies will likely engage in similar market research.

Job Prospects. Overall job prospects for market research analysts are expected to be good. Rapid employment growth in most industries means good job opportunities should be available.

Job prospects should be best for those with a master's degree in market research, marketing, statistics, or business administration. Candidates with a bachelor's degree are expected to face strong competition for jobs.

Those with a strong background in statistical and data analysis or related work experience will have better job opportunities than those without it.

O*NET

➤ Market Research Analysts and Marketing Specialists (13-1161.00)

Contacts for More Information

For more information about market research analysts, visit
➤ Council of American Survey Research Organizations (www.casro.org)
➤ Marketing Research Association (www.mra-net.org)

Meeting, Convention, and Event Planners

- **2012 Median Pay** .... $45,810 per year
  $22.02 per hour
- **Entry-Level Education** .... Bachelor's degree
- **Work Experience in a Related Occupation** .... None
- **On-the-Job Training** .... None
- **Number of Jobs 2012** 94,200
- **Job Outlook, 2012–22** .... 33% (Much faster than average)
- **Employment Change, 2012–22** 31,300

Meeting planners work with clients to determine the scope and purpose of a meeting.

Median Annual Wages, May 2012

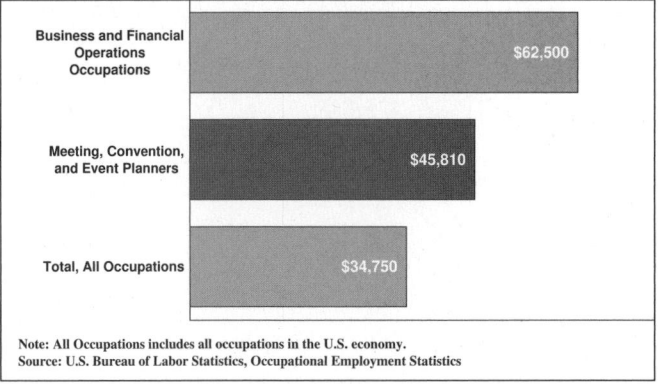

Note: All Occupations includes all occupations in the U.S. economy.
Source: U.S. Bureau of Labor Statistics, Occupational Employment Statistics

Percent Change in Employment, Projected 2012–2022

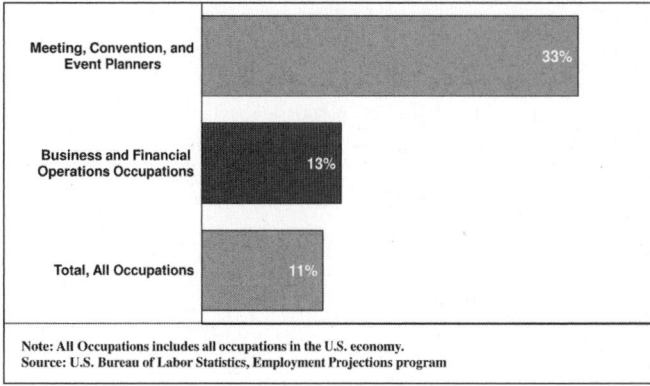

Note: All Occupations includes all occupations in the U.S. economy.
Source: U.S. Bureau of Labor Statistics, Employment Projections program

What Meeting, Convention, and Event Planners Do

Meeting, convention, and event planners coordinate all aspects of professional meetings and events. They choose meeting locations, arrange transportation, and coordinate other details.

Duties. Meeting, convention, and event planners typically do the following:

- Meet with clients to understand the purpose of the meeting or event
- Plan the scope of the event, including time, location, and cost
- Solicit bids from venues and service providers (for example, florists or photographers)
- Inspect venues to ensure that they meet the client's requirements
- Coordinate event services such as rooms, transportation, and food service
- Monitor event activities to ensure the client and event attendees are satisfied
- Review event bills and approve payment

Whether it is a wedding, educational conference, or business convention, meetings and events bring people together for a common purpose. Meeting, convention, and event planners work to ensure that this purpose is achieved efficiently and seamlessly. They coordinate every detail of events, from beginning to end. Before a meeting, for example, planners will meet with clients to estimate attendance and determine the meeting's purpose. During the meeting, they handle meeting logistics, such as registering guests and organizing audio/visual equipment for speakers. After the meeting, they may survey attendees to find out how the event was received.

Meeting, convention, and event planners also search for potential meeting sites, such as hotels and convention centers. They consider the lodging and services that the facility can provide, how easy it will be for people to get there, and the attractions that the surrounding area has to offer. More recently, planners also consider whether an online meeting can achieve the same objectives as a face-to-face meeting in certain cases.

Once a location is selected, planners arrange the meeting space and support services. For example, providing services such as wheelchair accessibility, interpreters, and other accommodations may be required. They may also negotiate contracts with suppliers to provide meals for attendees and coordinate plans with on-site staff. In addition, they organize speakers, entertainment, and activities. Meeting, convention, and event planners manage the finances of meetings and conventions within a budget set by their clients.

The following are examples of types of meeting, convention, and event planners:

Association planners organize annual conferences and trade shows for professional associations. Because member attendance is often voluntary, marketing the meeting's value is an important aspect of their work.

Corporate planners organize internal business meetings and meetings between businesses.

Government meeting planners organize meetings for government officials and agencies. Being familiar with government regulations, such as procedures for buying materials and booking hotels, is vital to their work.

Convention service managers help organize major events, as employees of hotels and convention centers. They act as liaisons between the meeting facility and the planners who work for associations, businesses, and governments. They present food service options to outside planners, coordinate special requests, and suggest hotel services depending on a planner's budget.

Event planners arrange the details of a variety of events, including weddings and large parties.

Non-profit event planners plan large events with the goal of raising donations for a charity or advocacy organization. Events may include banquets, charity races, and food drives.

Work Environment

Meeting, convention, and event planners held about 94,200 jobs in 2012. Most worked for private companies; about 1 in 6 were self-employed.

Meeting, convention, and event planners spend most of their time in offices. During meetings and events, they usually work on-site at hotels or convention centers. They travel regularly to attend the events they organize and to visit prospective meeting sites, sometimes in exotic locations around the world. Planners regularly collaborate with clients, hospitality workers, and meeting attendees.

The work of meeting, convention, and event planners can be fast-paced and demanding. Planners oversee many aspects of an event at the same time and face numerous deadlines.

Work Schedules. Most meeting, convention, and event planners work full time. In addition, many are required to work long, irregular hours in the time leading up to a major event. During meetings or conventions, planners may have very long work days. They sometimes work on weekends.

How to Become One

Applicants usually need a bachelor's degree and, increasingly, some experience related to event planning.

Employment Projections Data for Meeting, Convention, and Event Planners

Occupational title	SOC Code	Employment, 2012	Projected Employment, 2022	Change, 2012–2022	
				Percent	Numeric
Meeting, convention, and event planners	13-1121	94,200	125,400	33	31,300

Source: U.S. Bureau of Labor Statistics, Employment Projections Program

Note: Data are rounded. Go to **Occupational Information Included in the OOH** *for a discussion of the data in this table.*

Education. Many employers prefer applicants who have a bachelor's degree and some work experience in hotels or planning. The proportion of planners with a bachelor's degree is increasing because work responsibilities are becoming more complex and because there are more college degree programs related to hospitality or tourism management. If an applicant's degree is not related to these fields, employers are likely to require at least 1 to 2 years of related experience.

Meeting, convention, and event planners often come from a variety of academic disciplines. Some related undergraduate majors include marketing, public relations, communications, and business.

Planners who have studied hospitality management may start out with greater responsibilities than those from other academic disciplines. College students may also gain experience by planning meetings for a university club. In addition, some colleges offer continuing education courses in meeting and event planning.

Licenses, Certifications, and Registrations. The Convention Industry Council offers the Certified Meeting Professional (CMP) credential, a voluntary certification for meeting and convention planners. Although the CMP is not required, it is widely recognized in the industry and may help in career advancement. To qualify, candidates must have a minimum of 36 months of meeting management experience, recent employment in a meeting management job, and proof of continuing education credits. Those who qualify must then pass an exam that covers topics such as adult learning, financial management, facilities and services, logistics, and meeting programs.

The Society of Government Meeting Professionals (SGMP) offers the Certified Government Meeting Professional (CGMP) designation for meeting planners who work for, or contract with, federal, state, or local government. This certification is not required to work as a government meeting planner; however, it may be helpful for those who want to show that they know government buying policies and travel regulations. To qualify, candidates must have worked as a meeting planner for at least 1 year and have been a member of SGMP for 6 months. To become a certified planner, members must take a 3-day course and pass an exam.

Advancement. Entry-level planners tend to focus on meeting logistics, such as registering guests and organizing audio/visual equipment. Experienced planners manage interpersonal tasks, such as client relations and contract negotiations. With significant experience, meeting, convention, and event planners can become independent consultants.

Important Qualities

Communication skills. Meeting, convention, and event planners communicate with clients, suppliers, and event staff. They must have excellent written and oral communication skills and be able to convey the needs of their clients effectively.

Composure. Planners often work in a fast-paced environment and must be able to make quick decisions while remaining calm under pressure.

Customer-service skills. Planners must understand their clients' needs. They must act professionally in a variety of situations, know how to keep an audience engaged, and help participants network with peers.

Interpersonal skills. Planners must be good at establishing and maintaining positive relationships with clients and suppliers.

Negotiation skills. Planners must be able to negotiate service contracts to get good prices for their clients.

Organizational skills. To provide high quality meetings, planners must be detail-oriented and be able to multitask and meet tight deadlines. Many meetings are planned more than a year in advance, so long-term thinking ability is vital.

Problem-solving skills. When problems arise, planners must be able to come up with creative solutions that satisfy clients.

Pay

The median annual wage for meeting, convention, and event planners was $45,810 in May 2012. The median wage is the wage at which half the workers in an occupation earned more than that amount and half earned less. The lowest 10 percent earned less than $26,560, and the top 10 percent earned more than $79,270.

Job Outlook

Employment of meeting, convention, and event planners is projected to grow 33 percent from 2012 to 2022, much faster than the average for all occupations. As businesses and organizations become increasingly international, meetings and conventions are expected to become even more important.

For organizations with geographically separate offices and members, meetings are the only time they can bring everyone together.

Similar Occupations   This table shows a list of occupations with job duties that are similar to those of meeting, convention, and event planners.

Occupations	Entry-level Education	2012 Pay	Projected Job Growth	Average Annual Openings
Administrative Services Managers	Bachelor's degree	$81,080	12%	7,990
Food Service Managers	High school diploma or equivalent	$47,960	2%	6,240
Lodging Managers	High school diploma or equivalent	$46,810	1%	1,620
Travel Agents	High school diploma or equivalent	$34,600	-12%	1,110

Despite the spread of online communication, face-to-face interaction continues to be preferred by many people.

Job Prospects. Candidates with a bachelor's degree in hospitality or tourism management should have the best job opportunities. A Certified Meeting Professional (CMP) credential is also viewed favorably by potential employers. Those who have experience with virtual meeting software and social media outlets also should have an advantage.

Job opportunities for corporate planners fluctuate with economic activity. When the economy is in a downturn, companies often cut budgets for meetings. Planners who work for the healthcare industry are least likely to experience cutbacks during a recession because attendance at healthcare meetings and conventions is often required for medical professionals to maintain their license.

Event planners can expect strong competition for jobs. Those with related work experience should have the best job opportunities.

O*NET

➤ Meeting, Convention, and Event Planners (13-1121.00)

Contacts for More Information

For more information about meeting, convention, and event planners, including information about certification and industry trends, visit

➤ Convention Industry Council (www.conventionindustry.org/)
➤ Meeting Professionals International (www.mpiweb.org/)
➤ Professional Convention Management Association (www.pcma.org/)
➤ Society of Government Meeting Professionals (www.sgmp.org/)

Personal Financial Advisors

- **2012 Median Pay** .... $67,520 per year
  $32.46 per hour

- **Entry-Level Education** ....Bachelor's degree

- **Work Experience in a Related Occupation**............... None

- **On-the-Job Training** .... None

- **Number of Jobs 2012** 223,400

- **Job Outlook, 2012–22** .... 27% (Much faster than average)

- **Employment Change, 2012–22** 60,300

What Personal Financial Advisors Do

Personal financial advisors give financial advice to people. They help with investments, taxes, and insurance decisions.

Duties. Personal financial advisors typically do the following:

- Meet with clients in person to discuss their financial goals

- Explain the types of financial services they provide to potential clients

- Educate clients and answer questions about investment options and potential risks

- Recommend investments to clients or select investments on their behalf

- Help clients plan for specific circumstances, such as education expenses or retirement

- Monitor clients' accounts and determine if changes are needed to improve account performance or to accommodate life changes, such as getting married or having children

- Research investment opportunities

Personal financial advisors assess the financial needs of individuals and help them with decisions on investments (such as stocks and bonds), tax laws, and insurance. Advisors help clients plan for short-term and long-term goals, such as education expenses and retirement. They recommend investments to match the client's goals. They invest clients' money based on the clients' decisions. Many also provide tax advice or sell insurance.

Although most planners offer advice on a wide range of topics, some specialize in areas such as retirement or risk management (evaluating how willing the investor is to take chances and adjusting investments accordingly).

Many personal financial advisors spend a lot of time marketing their services, and they meet potential clients by giving seminars or through business and social networking. Networking is the process of meeting and exchanging information with people, or groups of people, who have similar interests.

After financial advisors have invested funds for a client, they and the client receive regular investment reports. They monitor the client's investments and usually meet with each client at least once a year to update the client on potential investments and to adjust the financial plan based on the client's circumstances or because investment options may have changed.

Many personal financial advisors are licensed to directly buy and sell financial products, such as stocks, bonds, annuities, and insurance. Depending on the agreement they have with their clients, personal financial advisors may have the client's permission to make decisions about buying and selling stocks and bonds.

Private bankers or *wealth managers* are personal financial advisors who work for people who have a lot of money to invest. These clients are similar to institutional investors (commonly companies or organizations), and they approach investing differently than the general public. Private bankers manage a collection of investments, called a portfolio, for these clients by using the resources of the bank, including teams of financial analysts, accountants, and other professionals.

Work Environment

Personal financial advisors held about 223,400 jobs in 2012.

Personal financial advisors mainly work for financial and insurance companies. In 2012, 20 percent of personal financial advi-

Personal financial advisors usually work with many clients and often must find their own customers.

Median Annual Wages, May 2012

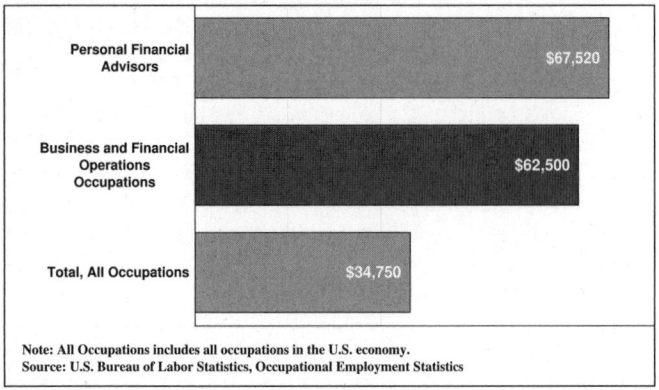

Note: All Occupations includes all occupations in the U.S. economy.
Source: U.S. Bureau of Labor Statistics, Occupational Employment Statistics

Percent Change in Employment, Projected 2012–2022

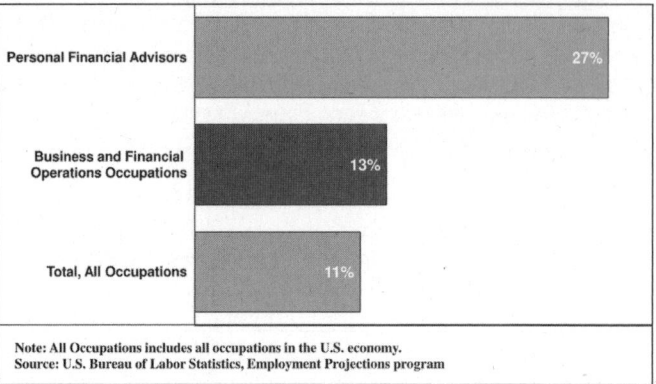

Note: All Occupations includes all occupations in the U.S. economy.
Source: U.S. Bureau of Labor Statistics, Employment Projections program

sors were self-employed. The industries that employed the most personal financial advisors in 2012 were as follows:

Other financial investment activities	27%
Credit intermediation and related activities	21
Securities and commodity contracts intermediation and brokerage	19
Insurance carriers and related activities	4
Professional, scientific, and technical services	3

Personal financial advisors typically work in offices. Some also travel to attend conferences or teach finance classes in the evening to bring in more clients. The work of personal financial advisors tends to be less stressful than other financial occupations.

Work Schedules. Most personal financial advisors work full time, and about 3 out of 10 worked more than 40 hours per week in 2012. They often go to meetings on evenings and weekends to meet with existing clients or to try to bring in new ones.

How to Become One

Personal financial advisors typically need a bachelor's degree. A master's degree and certification can improve chances for advancement in the occupation.

Education. Personal financial advisors typically need a bachelor's degree. Although employers usually do not require a specific field of study for personal financial advisors, a degree in finance, economics, accounting, business, mathematics, or law is good preparation for this occupation. Courses in investments, taxes, estate planning, and risk management are also helpful. Programs in financial planning are becoming more available in colleges and universities.

Licenses, Certifications, and Registrations. Personal financial advisors who directly buy or sell stocks, bonds, insurance policies, or specific investment advice need a combination of licenses that varies based on the products they sell. In addition to those licenses, smaller firms that manage clients' investments must be registered with state regulators, and larger firms must be registered with the Securities and Exchange Commission. Personal financial advisors

who choose to sell insurance need licenses issued by state boards. State licensing board information and requirements for registered investment advisors are available from the North American Securities Administrators Association.

Certifications can enhance a personal financial advisor's reputation and can help bring in new clients. The Certified Financial Planner Board of Standards offers the Certified Financial Planner (CFP) certification. For this certification, advisors must have a bachelor's degree, at least 3 years of relevant work experience, pass an exam, and agree to adhere to a code of ethics. The exam covers the financial planning process, insurance and risk management, employee benefits planning, taxes and retirement planning, investment and real estate planning, debt management, planning liability, emergency fund reserves, and statistical modeling.

Advancement. A master's degree in an area such as finance or business administration can improve a personal financial advisor's chances of moving into a management position and attracting new clients.

Important Qualities

Analytical skills. In determining an investment portfolio for a client, personal financial advisors must be able to take into account a range of information, including economic trends, regulatory changes, and the client's comfort with risky decisions.

Interpersonal skills. A major part of a personal financial advisor's job is making clients feel comfortable. They must establish trust with clients and respond well to their questions and concerns.

Math skills. Personal financial advisors should be good at mathematics because they constantly work with numbers. They determine the amount invested, how that amount has grown or decreased over time, and how a portfolio is distributed among different investments.

Sales skills. To expand their base of clients, personal financial advisors must be convincing and persistent in selling their services.

Speaking skills. Personal financial advisors interact with clients every day. They must explain complex financial concepts in understandable language.

Employment Projections Data for Personal Financial Advisors

Occupational title	SOC Code	Employment, 2012	Projected Employment, 2022	Change, 2012–2022	
				Percent	Numeric
Personal financial advisors	13-2052	223,400	283,700	27	60,300

Source: U.S. Bureau of Labor Statistics, Employment Projections Program

Note: Data are rounded. Go to **Occupational Information Included in the OOH** *for a discussion of the data in this table.*

Similar Occupations   This table shows a list of occupations with job duties that are similar to those of personal financial advisors.

Occupations	Entry-level Education	2012 Pay	Projected Job Growth	Average Annual Openings
Budget Analysts	Bachelor's degree	$69,280	6%	2,850
Financial Analysts	Bachelor's degree	$76,950	16%	10,090
Financial Managers	Bachelor's degree	$109,740	9%	14,690
Insurance Sales Agents	High school diploma or equivalent	$48,150	10%	15,020
Insurance Underwriters	Bachelor's degree	$62,870	-6%	2,890
Real Estate Brokers and Sales Agents	High school diploma or equivalent	$42,723	11%	8,630
Securities, Commodities, and Financial Services Sales Agents	Bachelor's degree	$71,720	11%	12,260

Pay

The median annual wage for personal financial advisors was $67,520 in May 2012. The median wage is the wage at which half the workers in an occupation earned more than that amount and half earned less. The lowest 10 percent earned less than $32,280, and the top 10 percent earned more than $187,200.

In May 2012, the median annual wages for personal financial advisors in the top five industries in which these advisors worked were as follows:

Other financial investment activities	$83,400
Professional, scientific, and technical services	82,360
Securities and commodity contracts intermediation and brokerage	72,630
Insurance carriers and related activities	63,500
Credit intermediation and related activities	47,780

Wages of self-employed advisors are not included in the earnings reported here.

Personal financial advisors who work for financial services firms are often paid a salary plus bonuses. Bonuses are not included in the wage data here.

Advisors who work for financial investment firms or planning firms, or who are self-employed, typically earn their money by charging a percentage of the clients' assets that they manage. They also may earn money by charging an hourly fee or by getting fees on stock and insurance purchases. In addition to their fees, advisors generally get commissions for financial products that they sell.

Job Outlook

Employment of personal financial advisors is projected to grow 27 percent from 2012 to 2022, much faster than the average for all occupations.

The primary driver of growth will be the aging population. As large numbers of baby boomers approach retirement, they will seek planning advice from personal financial advisors. In addition, longer life spans will lead to longer retirement periods, further increasing demand for financial planning services.

Decreased funds for corporate and state pensions also are expected to contribute to the trend of hiring personal financial advisors. Private corporations and state and local governments are facing shortfalls in their pension funds, which may lead to benefit reductions. This will require more financial planning from individuals and increase the demand for personal financial advisors.

Job Prospects. Job prospects for personal financial advisors should be relatively favorable compared with other financial sector occupations. Those who obtain certification will likely see the best prospects.

O*NET

➤ Personal Financial Advisors (13-2052.00)

Contacts for More Information

For more information about personal financial advisors, visit
➤ American Academy of Financial Management (www.aafm.us/)

For more information about regulation and licensure of personal financial advisors, visit
➤ Financial Industry Regulatory Authority (FINRA) (www.finra.org/)
➤ Securities Industry and Financial Markets Association (SIFMA) (www.sifma.org/)
➤ North American Securities Administrators Association (www.nasaa.org/)
➤ Securities and Exchange Commission (SEC) (www.sec.gov/)
➤ Certified Financial Planner Board of Standards (www.cfp.net/)

Purchasing Managers, Buyers, and Purchasing Agents

- **2012 Median Pay** .... $60,550 per year
  $29.11 per hour
- **Entry-Level Education** ....See "How to Become One"
- **Work Experience in a Related Occupation** .... See "How to Become One"
- **On-the-Job Training** ....See "How to Become One"
- **Number of Jobs 2012** 504,600
- **Job Outlook, 2012–22** .... 4% (Slower than average)
- **Employment Change, 2012–22** 19,700

What Purchasing Managers, Buyers, and Purchasing Agents Do

Purchasing managers, buyers, and purchasing agents buy products for organizations to use or resell. They evaluate suppliers, negotiate contracts, and review product quality.

Duties. Purchasing managers, buyers, and purchasing agents typically do the following:

- Evaluate suppliers based on price, quality, and delivery speed
- Interview vendors and visit suppliers' plants and distribution centers to examine and learn about products, services, and prices
- Attend meetings, trade shows, and conferences to learn about new industry trends and make contacts with suppliers

- Analyze price proposals, financial reports, and other information to determine reasonable prices

- Negotiate contracts on behalf of their organization

- Work out agreements with suppliers, such as when products will be delivered

- Meet with staff and vendors to discuss defective or unacceptable goods or services and determine corrective action

- Evaluate and monitor contracts to be sure that vendors and supplies comply with the terms and conditions of the contract and to determine the need for changes

- Maintain and review records of items bought, costs, deliveries, product performance, and inventories

Purchasing managers, buyers, and purchasing agents buy farm products, durable and nondurable goods, and services for organizations and institutions. They try to get the best deal for their organization–the highest quality goods and services at the lowest cost. They do this by studying sales records and inventory levels of current stock, identifying foreign and domestic suppliers, and keeping up to date with changes affecting both the supply of, and demand for, products and materials.

Purchasing agents and buyers consider price, quality, availability, reliability, and technical support when choosing suppliers and merchandise. To be effective, purchasing agents and buyers must have a working technical knowledge of the goods or services to be bought.

Evaluating suppliers is one of the most critical functions of a purchasing manager, buyer, or purchasing agent. Many organizations now run on a lean manufacturing schedule and use just-in-time inventories, so any delays in the supply chain can shut down production and potentially cause the organization to lose customers.

Purchasing managers, buyers, and purchasing agents use many resources to find out all they can about potential suppliers. They attend meetings, trade shows, and conferences to learn about new industry trends and make contacts with suppliers.

They often interview prospective suppliers and visit their plants and distribution centers to assess their capabilities. For example, they may discuss the design of products with design engineers, quality concerns with production supervisors, or shipping issues with managers in the receiving department.

Purchasing managers, buyers, and purchasing agents must make certain that the supplier can deliver the desired goods or services on time, in the correct quantities, and without sacrificing quality. Once they have gathered information on suppliers, they sign contracts with suppliers who meet the organization's needs, and they place orders.

Buyers who purchase items to resell to customers largely determine which products their organization will sell. They need to

Purchasing professionals use many resources to gather information about potential suppliers.

be able to predict what will appeal to their customers. If they are wrong, they could jeopardize the profits and reputation of their organization.

Wholesale and retail buyers purchase goods for resale to consumers. Examples of these goods are clothing and electronics. Purchasing specialists who buy finished goods for resale are commonly known as *buyers* or *merchandise managers*. Buyers who work for large organizations usually specialize in one or two lines of merchandise (for example, men's clothing or women's shoes or children's toys). Buyers who work for small stores may be responsible for buying everything the store sells.

Purchasing agents and buyers of farm products buy agricultural products for further processing or resale. Examples of these products include grain, cotton, and tobacco.

Purchasing agents, except wholesale, retail, and farm products buy items for the operation of an organization. Examples of these items include chemicals and industrial equipment needed for a manufacturing establishment, and office supplies.

Purchasing managers plan and coordinate the work of buyers and purchasing agents, and they usually handle purchases that are more complicated. Those employed by government agencies or manufacturing firms usually are called *purchasing directors*, *managers*, or *agents*; sometimes they are known as *contract specialists*. Some purchasing managers, called *contract, sourcing, or supply managers*, specialize in negotiating and supervising contracts for supplies.

Work Environment

Purchasing managers, buyers, and purchasing agents held about 504,600 jobs in 2012.

Median Annual Wages, May 2012

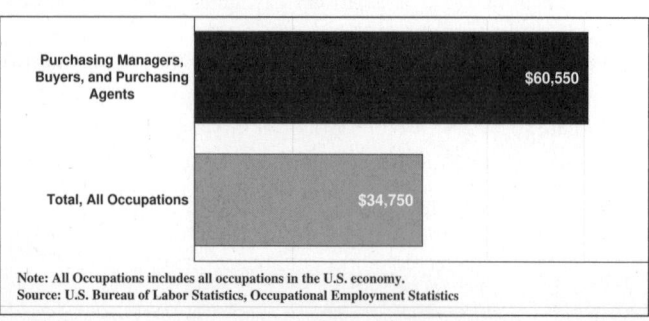

Purchasing Managers, Buyers, and Purchasing Agents	$60,550
Total, All Occupations	$34,750

Note: All Occupations includes all occupations in the U.S. economy.
Source: U.S. Bureau of Labor Statistics, Occupational Employment Statistics

Percent Change in Employment, Projected 2012–2022

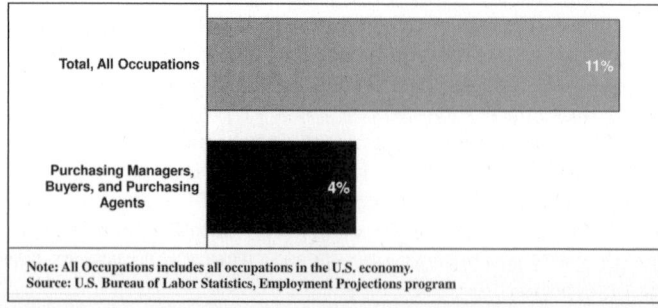

Total, All Occupations	11%
Purchasing Managers, Buyers, and Purchasing Agents	4%

Note: All Occupations includes all occupations in the U.S. economy.
Source: U.S. Bureau of Labor Statistics, Employment Projections program

Employment Projections Data for Purchasing Managers, Buyers, and Purchasing Agents

Occupational title	SOC Code	Employment, 2012	Projected Employment, 2022	Change, 2012–2022	
				Percent	Numeric
Purchasing managers, buyers, and purchasing agents............	—	504,600	524,300	4	19,700
Purchasing managers..	11-3061	71,900	73,400	2	1,500
Buyers and purchasing agents, farm products....................	13-1021	14,200	15,000	6	800
Wholesale and retail buyers, except farm products............	13-1022	124,600	133,500	7	8,900
Purchasing agents, except wholesale, retail, and farm products...	13-1023	294,000	302,400	3	8,400

Source: U.S. Bureau of Labor Statistics, Employment Projections Program

Note: Data are rounded. Go to **Occupational Information Included in the OOH** *for a discussion of the data in this table.*

The industries that employed the most purchasing managers, buyers, and purchasing agents in 2012 were as follows:

Manufacturing..	25%
Wholesale trade	15
Government..	12
Management of companies and enterprises...........................	10
Retail trade	8

Most purchasing managers, buyers, and purchasing agents work in comfortable offices. Travel is sometimes necessary, and purchasers for global organizations may need to travel outside the United States.

Work Schedules. Most purchasing managers, buyers, and purchasing agents work full time. Overtime is common in these occupations.

How to Become One

Although educational requirements for buyers and purchasing agents may vary by the size of the organization and the type of product, extensive on-the-job training is typically provided. Purchasing managers need a bachelor's degree and work experience as a buyer or purchasing agent.

Education. Educational requirements usually vary with the size of the organization. A high school diploma is enough at many organizations for entry into the purchasing agent occupation, although large stores and distributors may prefer applicants who have completed a bachelor's degree program and have taken some business or accounting classes. Many manufacturing firms put an even greater emphasis on formal training, preferring applicants who have a bachelor's or master's degree in engineering, business, economics, or one of the applied sciences.

Purchasing managers usually have at least a bachelor's degree and some work experience in the field. A master's degree may be required for advancement to some top-level purchasing manager jobs.

Training. Buyers and purchasing agents typically get on-the-job training for more than 1 year. During this time, they learn how to perform their basic duties, including monitoring inventory levels and negotiating with suppliers.

Licenses, Certifications, and Registrations. There are several recognized credentials for purchasing agents and purchasing managers. These certifications involve oral or written exams and have education and work experience requirements.

The Certified Professional in Supply Management (CPSM) credential, offered by the Institute for Supply Management, covers a wide scope of duties that purchasing professionals do. The exam requires applicants to either have a bachelor's degree and 3 years of supply management experience, or for those without a bachelor's degree, 5 years of supply management experience and the successful completion of three CPSM exams.

The American Purchasing Society offers two certifications: the Certified Purchasing Professional (CPP) and Certified Professional Purchasing Manager (CPPM). Candidates become eligible for these certifications through a combination of purchasing-related experience, education, and professional contributions (such as published articles or delivered speeches).

APICS offers the Certified Supply Chain Professional (CSCP) credential.

The Universal Public Procurement Certification Council offers two certifications for workers in federal, state, and local government: Certified Professional Public Buyer (CPPB) and Certified Public Purchasing Officer (CPPO). NIGP: The Institute for Public Procurement offers preparation courses for these certification exams.

Work Experience in a Related Occupation. Purchasing managers typically must have at least 5 years of experience as a buyer or purchasing agent. At the top levels, purchasing manager duties may overlap with other management functions, such as production, planning, logistics, and marketing.

Advancement. An experienced purchasing agent or buyer may become an assistant purchasing manager before advancing to purchasing manager, supply manager, or director of materials management.

Important Qualities

Analytical skills. When evaluating suppliers, purchasing managers and agents must analyze their options and choose a supplier with the best combination of price and quality.

Decision-making skills. Purchasing managers and agents must have the ability to make informed and timely decisions by choosing products that they think will sell.

Math skills. Purchasing managers and agents must possess basic math skills. They must be able to compare prices from different suppliers to ensure that their organization is getting the best deal.

Negotiating skills. Purchasing managers and agents often must negotiate the terms of a contract with a supplier. Interpersonal skills and self-confidence, in addition to knowledge of the product, can help lead to successful negotiation.

Pay

The median annual wage for purchasing managers, buyers, and purchasing agents was $60,550 in May 2012. The median wage is the wage at which half the workers in an occupation earned more than that amount and half earned less. The lowest 10 percent earned less than $34,990, and the top 10 percent earned more than $110,050.

The median annual wages for purchasing managers, buyers, and purchasing agents in May 2012 were as follows:

Purchasing managers	$100,170
Purchasing agents, except wholesale, retail, and farm products...	58,760

Similar Occupations This table shows a list of occupations with job duties that are similar to those of purchasing managers, buyers, and purchasing agents.

Occupations	Entry-level Education	2012 Pay	Projected Job Growth	Average Annual Openings
Advertising, Promotions, and Marketing Managers	Bachelor's degree	$115,087	12%	7,510
Bookkeeping, Accounting, and Auditing Clerks	High school diploma or equivalent	$35,170	11%	37,000
Financial Clerks	High school diploma or equivalent	$35,122	11%	43,930
Financial Managers	Bachelor's degree	$109,740	9%	14,690
Food Service Managers	High school diploma or equivalent	$47,960	2%	6,240
Lodging Managers	High school diploma or equivalent	$46,810	1%	1,620
Logisticians	Bachelor's degree	$72,780	22%	4,220
Wholesale and Manufacturing Sales Representatives	See "How to Become One"	$58,484	9%	53,250

Buyers and purchasing agents, farm products $55,720
Wholesale and retail buyers, except farm products 51,470

Job Outlook

Employment of purchasing managers, buyers, and purchasing agents is projected to grow 4 percent from 2012 to 2022, slower than the average for all occupations.

These workers will be needed to buy goods and services for business operations or for resale to customers. Growth will vary based on the type of purchasing agent or manager and the specific industry.

Employment of wholesale and retail buyers, except farm products, is projected to grow 7 percent from 2012 to 2022, slower than the average for all occupations. Growth will be driven largely by the performance of the wholesale and retail industries.

Employment of purchasing agents, farm products, is projected to grow 6 percent from 2012 to 2022, slower than the average for all occupations. Slower growth in the agricultural industry has led to slow growth in this occupation, and the trend is expected to continue.

Employment of purchasing agents, except wholesale, retail, and farm products, is projected to grow 3 percent from 2012 to 2022, slower than the average for all occupations. Continued employment decreases in manufacturing, as well as decreases in federal government, which includes defense purchasing, are expected. However, strong growth is expected for this occupation in health care and computer systems design and related services firms.

Employment of purchasing managers is projected to show little or no change from 2012 to 2022. The trends affecting growth for agents and buyers will also affect purchasing managers, although there will likely still be a need for purchasing managers to plan and direct buying activities for organizations and to supervise purchasing agents and buyers.

Job Prospects. Although a high school diploma is sufficient for some purchasing agent positions, jobseekers with a bachelor's degree are likely to have the best prospects. Candidates for positions as purchasing managers will improve their prospects by obtaining a master's degree in business or supply management.

O*NET

➤ Purchasing Managers (11-3061.00)
➤ Buyers and Purchasing Agents, Farm Products (13-1021.00)
➤ Wholesale and Retail Buyers, Except Farm Products (13-1022.00)
➤ Purchasing Agents, Except Wholesale, Retail, and Farm Products (13-1023.00)

Contacts for More Information

For more information about purchasing managers, buyers, and purchasing agents, including education, training, employment, and certification, visit

➤ American Purchasing Society (www.american-purchasing.com/)
➤ APICS (www.apics.org/)
➤ Institute for Supply Management (www.ism.ws/)
➤ NIGP: The Institute for Public Procurement (www.nigp.org/)
➤ Universal Public Procurement Certification Council (www.uppcc.org/)

Tax Examiners and Collectors, and Revenue Agents

- **2012 Median Pay** .... $50,440 per year
  $24.25 per hour
- **Entry-Level Education** .... Bachelor's degree
- **Work Experience in a Related Occupation** .... None
- **On-the-Job Training** .... Moderate-term on-the-job training
- **Number of Jobs 2012** 69,500
- **Job Outlook, 2012–22** .... -4% (Decline)
- **Employment Change, 2012–22** .... -2,700

What Tax Examiners and Collectors, and Revenue Agents Do

Tax examiners and collectors, and revenue agents ensure that federal, state, and local governments get their tax money from businesses and citizens. They review tax returns, conduct audits, identify taxes owed, and collect overdue tax payments.

Duties. Tax examiners and collectors, and revenue agents typically do the following:

- Review filed tax returns to determine whether tax credits and deductions claimed are allowed by law
- Contact taxpayers to address problems and to request supporting documentation
- Conduct field audits and investigations of income tax returns to verify information or to update tax liabilities

Tax examiners and collectors, and revenue agents work for federal, state, and local governments.

- Evaluate financial information, using their familiarity with accounting procedures and knowledge of changes to tax laws and regulations

- Keep records on each case they deal with, including contacts, telephone numbers, and actions taken

- Notify taxpayers of any overpayment or underpayment and either issue a refund or request additional payment

Tax examiners and collectors, and revenue agents are responsible for ensuring that individuals and businesses pay the taxes they owe. In addition to verifying that tax returns are filed properly, they follow up with taxpayers whose returns are questionable or who owe more money.

Different levels of government collect different types of taxes. The federal government deals primarily with personal and business income taxes. State governments collect income and sales taxes. Local governments collect sales and property taxes.

Because many states assess individual income taxes based on the taxpayer's reported federal income, tax examiners working for the federal government report to the states any adjustments or corrections they make. State tax examiners then determine whether the adjustments affect how much the taxpayer owes the state.

Tax examiners and collectors, and revenue agents have different duties and responsibilities:

Tax examiners usually deal with the simplest tax returns–those filed by individual taxpayers who claim few deductions and those filed by small businesses. At the entry level, many tax examiners do clerical tasks, such as reviewing tax returns and entering them into a computer system for processing. Tax examiners also may contact individual taxpayers in order to resolve any outstanding problems with their returns.

Much of a tax examiner's job involves making sure that tax credits and deductions claimed by taxpayers are lawful. If a taxpayer owes additional taxes, tax examiners adjust the total amount by assessing fees, interest, and penalties and then notify the taxpayer of the total amount owed.

Revenue agents specialize in tax-related accounting for the U.S. Internal Revenue Service (IRS) and for equivalent agencies in state and local governments. Like tax examiners, they review returns for accuracy. However, revenue agents handle complicated tax returns of large businesses and corporations.

Many experienced revenue agents specialize in a particular area. For example, they may focus exclusively on multinational businesses. Regardless of their specialty, revenue agents must keep up to date with changes in the lengthy and complex tax laws and regulations.

Collectors, also called *revenue officers* in the IRS, deal with overdue accounts. The process of collecting an overdue payment starts with the revenue agent or tax examiner sending a report to the taxpayer. If the taxpayer makes no effort to pay, the case is assigned to a collector.

When a collector takes a case, he or she first sends a notice to the taxpayer. The collector then works with the taxpayer to settle the debt. Settlement may involve setting up a plan in which the amount owed is paid back in small amounts over time.

When delinquent taxpayers claim that they cannot pay their taxes, collectors investigate and verify these claims. Collectors research information on taxpayer mortgages or financial statements and locate taxpayer-owned items of value through third parties, such as neighbors or local departments of motor vehicles. Ultimately, collectors must decide whether the IRS should take a lien–a claim on an asset such as a bank account, real estate, or an automobile–to settle a debt. Collectors also have the authority to garnish wages–that is, take a portion of earned wages–to collect taxes owed.

Work Environment

Tax examiners and collectors, and revenue agents held about 69,500 jobs in 2012.

Tax examiners and collectors, and revenue agents work for federal, state, and local governments. Many work primarily in an office environment; others spend most of their time conducting field audits in taxpayers' homes or places of business.

Median Annual Wages, May 2012

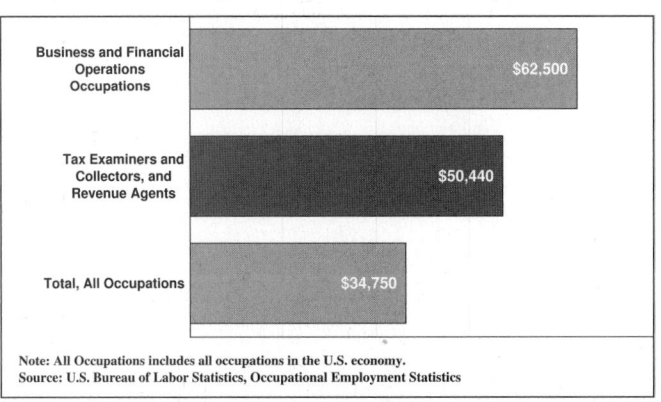

Note: All Occupations includes all occupations in the U.S. economy.
Source: U.S. Bureau of Labor Statistics, Occupational Employment Statistics

Percent Change in Employment, Projected 2012–2022

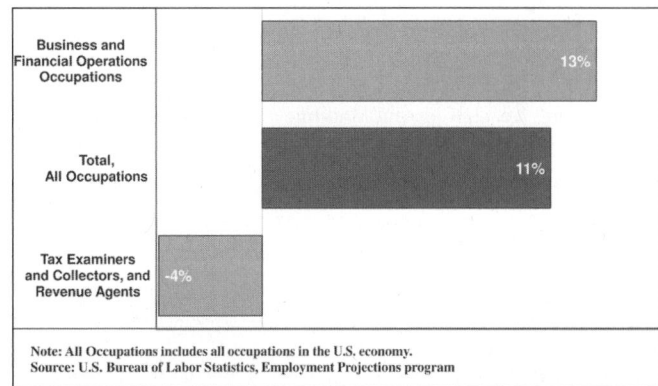

Note: All Occupations includes all occupations in the U.S. economy.
Source: U.S. Bureau of Labor Statistics, Employment Projections program

Employment Projections Data for Tax Examiners and Collectors, and Revenue Agents

Occupational title	SOC Code	Employment, 2012	Projected Employment, 2022	Change, 2012–2022	
				Percent	Numeric
Tax examiners and collectors, and revenue agents...............	17-2021	2,600	2,700	5	100

Source: U.S. Bureau of Labor Statistics, Employment Projections Program

Note: Data are rounded. Go to **Occupational Information Included in the OOH** *for a discussion of the data in this table.*

The industries that employed the most tax examiners and collectors, and revenue agents in 2012 were as follows:

Federal government, excluding postal service 46%
State government, excluding education and hospitals 35
Local government, excluding education and hospitals 19

Work Schedules. Most tax examiners and collectors, and revenue agents work full time.

How to Become One

Most tax examiners and collectors, and revenue agents need a bachelor's degree in accounting or a related field. However, the required level of education and experience varies by position and employer.

Education. Tax examiners need a bachelor's degree in accounting or a related field, or a combination of relevant education and specialized experience in accounting, auditing, or tax compliance work. Candidates for tax examiner positions at the Internal Revenue Service (IRS) must have a bachelor's degree or 1 year of full-time specialized experience.

Revenue agents need a bachelor's degree in accounting, business administration, economics, or a related discipline. A combination of relevant education and full-time experience in business administration, accounting, or auditing is also qualifying. Revenue agents with the IRS must have either a bachelor's degree or 30 semester hours of accounting coursework, along with specialized experience. Specialized experience includes work in accounting, bookkeeping, or tax analysis.

Collectors usually must have some combination of relevant college education and specialized experience. Specialized experience may include previous work as a loan officer or credit manager, or background in collections, management, customer service, or tax compliance. A bachelor's degree is needed for employment as a collector with the IRS; no additional experience is required, and experience may not be substituted for the degree. Degrees in business, finance, accounting, and criminal justice are desired by employers.

At the state and local levels, a bachelor's degree is not always required, although related work experience is desired.

Training. Newly hired tax examiners get some formal training, which typically lasts between 1 month and 1 year. All tax examiners must keep current with changes in the tax code and enforcement procedures.

Entry-level collectors get both formal training and on-the-job training under an instructor's guidance before working independently. Collectors also are encouraged to continue their professional education by attending meetings to exchange information about how modifications to tax laws affect collection methods.

Other Experience. Some state and local governments accept work experience as a substitute for education. In these cases, employers may hire tax examiners and revenue agents who have work experience in accounting, bookkeeping, or tax analysis. Employers may also hire collectors who have work experience in related areas, such as collections, customer service, or credit checking.

Advancement. Tax examiners, revenue agents, and collectors have different opportunities for career advancement. Tax examiners who review individual tax returns may advance to revenue agent positions, working on more complex business returns. Those with experience in supervisory or managerial roles may move to jobs that involve supervision of other examiners and revenue agents. Collectors who demonstrate leadership skills and a thorough knowledge of tax collection activities may advance to supervisory or managerial collector positions.

Important Qualities

Analytical skills. Tax examiners and revenue agents must be able to identify questionable claims for credits and deductions. Ultimately, they must be able to determine, on further review of financial documentation, if the credits or deductions are lawful.

Computer skills. Tax examiners and revenue agents must be comfortable using a variety of computer programs. These pro-

Similar Occupations   This table shows a list of occupations with job duties that are similar to those of tax examiners and collectors, and revenue agents.

Occupations	Entry-level Education	2012 Pay	Projected Job Growth	Average Annual Openings
Accountants and Auditors	Bachelor's degree	$63,550	13%	54,420
Bookkeeping, Accounting, and Auditing Clerks	High school diploma or equivalent	$35,170	11%	37,000
Budget Analysts	Bachelor's degree	$69,280	6%	2,850
Cost Estimators	Bachelor's degree	$58,860	26%	11,800
Financial Analysts	Bachelor's degree	$76,950	16%	10,090
Financial Managers	Bachelor's degree	$109,740	9%	14,690
Loan Officers	Bachelor's degree	$59,820	8%	7,720
Personal Financial Advisors	Bachelor's degree	$67,520	27%	9,640

grams include tax preparation and bookkeeping software used by individuals and businesses.

Detail oriented. Tax examiners and revenue agents verify the accuracy of each entry on the tax returns they review. Therefore, it is important that they pay attention to detail.

Interpersonal skills. Collectors must be comfortable dealing with people, including speaking with them during confrontational situations. When pursuing overdue accounts, collectors should be firm and composed.

Organizational skills. Tax examiners and revenue agents often work with multiple returns and a variety of financial documents. Keeping the various pieces of information organized is essential.

Pay

The median annual wage for tax examiners and collectors, and revenue agents was $50,440 in May 2012. The median wage is the wage at which half the workers in an occupation earned more than that amount and half earned less. The lowest 10 percent earned less than $30,350, and the top 10 percent earned more than $92,740.

In May 2012, the median annual wages for tax examiners and collectors, and revenue agents in federal, state, and local governments in May 2012 were as follows:

Federal government, excluding postal service $59,310
State government, excluding education and hospitals 46,790
Local government, excluding education and hospitals 40,140

Job Outlook

Employment of tax examiners and collectors, and revenue agents is projected to decline 4 percent from 2012 to 2022. Employment change will depend primarily on future changes to federal, state, and local government budgets. Budget reductions in recent years have resulted in decreased hiring for the agencies that employ these workers. Overall employment in federal government, excluding postal service is projected to decline 11 percent.

However, it is generally recognized that tax examiners and collectors, and revenue agents improve government budgets by increasing revenue. Therefore, job cuts in this occupation will be less severe than those in many other occupations concentrated in government.

O*NET

➤ Tax Examiners and Collectors, and Revenue Agents (13-2081.00)

Contacts for More Information

For information about tax examiner and collector, and revenue agent careers at the Internal Revenue Service (IRS), visit
➤ Internal Revenue Service (www.irs.gov)

Community and Social Service

Health Educators and Community Health Workers

- **2012 Median Pay** .... $41,830 per year
  $20.11 per hour
- **Entry-Level Education** ....See "How to Become One"
- **Work Experience in a Related Occupation**............... None
- **On-the-Job Training** ....See "How to Become One"
- **Number of Jobs 2012** 99,400
- **Job Outlook, 2012–22**............. 21% (Faster than average)
- **Employment Change, 2012–22** 21,400

What Health Educators and Community Health Workers Do

Health educators teach people about behaviors that promote wellness. They develop and implement strategies to improve the health of individuals and communities. Community health workers provide a link between the community and health educators and other healthcare workers and develop and implement strategies to improve the health of individuals and communities. They collect data and discuss health concerns with members of specific populations or communities. Although the two occupations often work together, responsibilities of health educators and community health workers are distinct.

Duties. Health educators typically do the following:

- Assess the needs of the people and communities they serve
- Develop programs and events to teach people about health topics
- Teach people how to cope with or manage existing health conditions
- Evaluate the effectiveness of programs and educational materials
- Help people find health services or information
- Provide training programs for other health professionals or community health workers
- Supervise staff who implement health education programs
- Collect and analyze data to learn about their audience and improve programs and services
- Advocate for improved health resources and policies that promote health

Community health workers do the following:

- Provide outreach and discuss health care concerns with community members
- Educate people about the importance and availability of health-care services, such as cancer screenings
- Collect data
- Report findings to health educators and other healthcare providers
- Provide informal counseling and social support
- Conduct outreach programs

Health educators attempt to prevent illnesses by informing and educating individuals and communities about health-related topics.

- Ensure that people have access to the healthcare services they need
- Advocate for individual and community needs

The duties of health educators, who are sometimes called health education specialists, vary with their work settings. Most work in health care facilities, colleges, public health departments, nonprofits, and private businesses. Health educators who teach health classes in middle and high schools are considered teachers. For more information, see the profiles on middle school teachers and high school teachers.

In *health care facilities*, health educators may work one-on-one with patients and their families. They teach patients about their diagnoses and about any necessary treatments or procedures. They may be called patient navigators because they help consumers find out about their health insurance options and direct people to outside resources, such as support groups and home health agencies. They lead hospital efforts in community health improvement. Health educators in health care facilities also help organize health screenings, such as blood pressure checks, and health classes on topics such as installing a car seat correctly. They also create programs to train medical staff to interact better with patients. For example, they may teach doctors how to explain complicated procedures to patients in simple language.

In *colleges*, health educators create programs and materials on topics that affect young adults, such as smoking and alcohol use. They may train students to be peer educators and supervise the students' delivery of health information in person or through social media. Health educators also advocate for campus wide policies to promote health.

In *public health departments*, health educators administer public health campaigns on topics such as emergency preparedness, immunizations, proper nutrition or stress management. They develop materials to be used by other public health officials. During emergencies, they may provide safety information to the public and the media. Some health educators work with other professionals to create public policies that support healthy behaviors and environments. They may also oversee grants and grant-funded programs to improve the health of the public. Some participate in statewide and local committees dealing with topics such as aging.

Median Annual Wages, May 2012

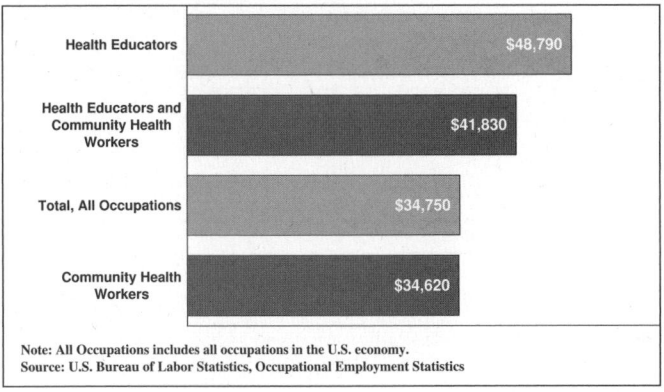

Note: All Occupations includes all occupations in the U.S. economy.
Source: U.S. Bureau of Labor Statistics, Occupational Employment Statistics

Percent Change in Employment, Projected 2012–2022

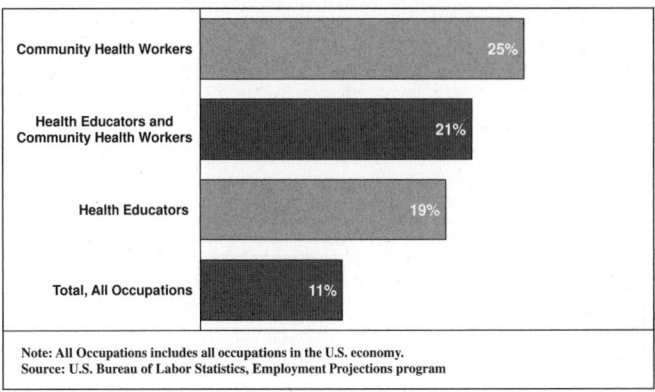

Note: All Occupations includes all occupations in the U.S. economy.
Source: U.S. Bureau of Labor Statistics, Employment Projections program

In *nonprofits* (including community health organizations), health educators create programs and materials about health issues for the community that their organization serves. They help organizations obtain funding and other resources. Many nonprofits focus on a particular disease or audience, so health educators in these organizations limit programs to that specific topic or audience. For example, a health educator may design a program to teach people with diabetes how to better manage their condition or a program for teen mothers on how to care for their newborns. In addition, health educators may educate policymakers about ways to improve public health and work on securing grant funding for programs to promote health and disease awareness.

In *private businesses*, health educators identify common health problems among employees and create programs to improve health. They work with management to develop incentives for employees to adopt healthy behaviors, such as losing weight or controlling cholesterol. Health educators recommend changes to the workplace, such as creating smoke-free areas, to improve employee health.

Community health workers have an in-depth knowledge of the communities they serve. They identify health-related issues that affect a community, they collect data, and they discuss health concerns with the people they serve. For example, they may help eligible residents of a neighborhood enroll in programs such as Medicaid or Medicare, explaining the benefits that these programs offer. Community health workers address any barriers to care and provide referrals for such needs as food, housing, education, and mental health services.

Community health workers report their findings to health educators and healthcare providers so that the educators can create new programs or adjust existing programs or events to better suit the demands of their audience. Community health workers also advocate for the health needs of community members. In addition, they conduct outreach to engage community residents, assist residents with health system navigation, and to improve care coordination.

Work Environment

Health educators held about 58,900 jobs in 2012. Community health workers held about 40,500 jobs in 2012.

The industries that employed the most health educators in 2012 were as follows:

Government 23%
Hospitals; state, local, and private 21
Ambulatory health care services 17
Religious, grantmaking, civic, professional, and similar
    organizations... 11
Social assistance.. 11

The industries that employed the most community health workers in 2012 were as follows:

Individual, family, community, and vocational rehabilitation
    services 25%
State and local government, excluding education
    and hospitals 18
Religious, grantmaking, civic, professional, and similar
    organizations... 12
Hospitals; state, local, and private 9
Outpatient, laboratory, and other ambulatory care services...... 7

Health educators and community health workers work in a variety of settings, including hospitals, nonprofit organizations, government, doctors' offices, private businesses, and colleges.

Although most health educators work in an office, they may spend a lot of time away from the office to carry out programs or attend meetings. Community health workers may spend much of their time in the field, communicating with community members and holding events.

Work Schedules. Most health educators and community health workers work full time. They may need to work nights and weekends to attend programs or meetings.

How to Become One

Health educators need a bachelor's degree. Some employers may require the Certified Health Education Specialist (CHES) credential. Community health workers typically have at least a high school diploma and must complete a brief period of on-the-job training. Some states have certification programs for community health workers.

Education. Entry-level health educator positions require a bachelor's degree in health education or health promotion. These programs teach students theories and methods of health education and help students gain the knowledge and skills they need to develop health education materials and programs. Most programs include an internship.

Some positions, such as those in the federal government or in state public health agencies, require a master's or doctoral degree. Graduate programs are commonly in community health education, school health education, public health education, or health promotion. Entering a master's degree program requires a bachelor's degree, but a variety of undergraduate majors may be acceptable.

Community health workers typically have a high school diploma, although some jobs may require postsecondary education. Education programs may lead to a 1-year certificate or a 2-year associate's degree and cover topics such as wellness, ethics, and cultural awareness, among others. Community health workers

Employment Projections Data for Health Educators and Community Health Workers

Occupational title	SOC Code	Employment, 2012	Projected Employment, 2022	Change, 2012–2022	
				Percent	Numeric
Health educators and community health workers	—	99,400	120,800	21	21,400
Health educators	21-1091	58,900	70,100	19	11,200
Community health workers	21-1094	40,500	50,700	25	10,200

Source: U.S. Bureau of Labor Statistics, Employment Projections Program

Note: Data are rounded. Go to **Occupational Information Included in the OOH** *for a discussion of the data in this table.*

typically have a shared language or life experience and an understanding of the community that they serve.

Training. Community health workers typically complete a brief period of on-the-job training. This training often covers core competencies such as communication or outreach skills as well as information about the specific health topics that they will be focusing on. For instance, community health workers who work with Alzheimer's patients may learn about how to communicate effectively with patients dealing with dementia.

Licenses, Certifications, and Registrations. Some employers require health educators to be a Certified Health Education Specialist (CHES). CHES certification, offered by the National Commission for Health Education Credentialing, Inc., is awarded after a candidate passes an exam. The exam is aimed at entry-level health educators who have completed a bachelor's degree or are within 3 months of completion. To maintain their certification, health educators must complete 75 hours of continuing education every 5 years. There is also a Master Certified Health Education Specialist (MCHES) credential for health educators with advanced education and experience.

Most states do not require community health workers to become certified, however voluntary certification exists or is being considered or developed in a number of states. Requirements vary but may include completing an approved training program. For more information, contact your state's board of health, nursing, or human services.

Important Qualities

Analytical skills. Health educators collect and analyze data and other information in order to evaluate programs and to determine the needs of the people they serve.

Instructional skills. Health educators and community health workers should be comfortable with public speaking so that they can lead programs, teach classes, and facilitate discussion with clients and families.

Interpersonal skills. Health educators and community health workers interact with many people from a variety of backgrounds. These workers must be good listeners and be culturally sensitive to respond to the needs of the people they serve.

Problem-solving skills. Health educators and community health workers must think creatively about how to improve the health of their audience through health education programs. In addition, health educators and community health workers may need to solve problems that arise in planning programs, such as changes to their budget or resistance from the community they are serving.

Writing skills. Health educators and community health workers develop written materials to convey health-related information. Health educators also write proposals to develop programs and apply for funding.

Other Experience. Community health workers usually have some knowledge of a specific community, population, medical condition, or disability. The ability to speak a foreign language may be helpful.

Pay

The median annual wage for health educators was $48,790 in May 2012. The median wage is the wage at which half the workers in an occupation earned more than that amount and half earned less. The lowest 10 percent earned less than $27,730, and the top 10 percent earned more than $86,810.

Similar Occupations   This table shows a list of occupations with job duties that are similar to those of health educators and community health workers.

Occupations	Entry-level Education	2012 Pay	Projected Job Growth	Average Annual Openings
Dietitians and Nutritionists	Bachelor's degree	$55,240	21%	2,230
Epidemiologists	Master's degree	$65,270	12%	160
High School Teachers	Bachelor's degree	$55,050	6%	31,260
Mental Health Counselors and Marriage and Family Therapists	Master's degree	$41,592	29%	8,360
Middle School Teachers	Bachelor's degree	$53,430	12%	21,120
Postsecondary Teachers	See "How to Become One"	$70,380	19%	42,690
School and Career Counselors	Master's degree	$53,610	12%	8,700
Social and Human Service Assistants	High school diploma or equivalent	$28,850	22%	17,870
Social Workers	See "How to Become One"	$44,541	19%	24,280
Substance Abuse and Behavioral Disorder Counselors	High school diploma or equivalent	$38,520	31%	4,720

In May 2012, the median annual wages for health educators in the top five industries in which these educators worked were as follows:

Hospitals; state, local, and private $60,360
Government 50,580
Ambulatory health care services 46,470
Religious, grantmaking, civic, professional, and similar
    organizations 45,090
Social assistance 36,500

The median annual wage for community health workers was $34,620 in May 2012. The lowest 10 percent earned less than $20,340, and the top 10 percent earned more than $58,650.

In May 2012, the median annual wages for community health workers in the top five industries in which they worked were as follows:

Hospitals; state, local, and private $42,610
State and local government, excluding education
    and hospitals 37,040
Religious, grantmaking, civic, professional, and similar
    organizations 35,760
Outpatient, laboratory, and other ambulatory
    care services 32,750
Individual, family, community, and vocational
    rehabilitation services 30,030

Job Outlook

Employment of health educators and community health workers is projected to grow 21 percent from 2012 to 2022, faster than the average for all occupations. Growth will be driven by efforts to improve health outcomes and to reduce healthcare costs by teaching people about healthy habits and behaviors and utilization of available health care services.

As healthcare costs continue to rise, insurance companies, employers, and governments are trying to find ways to both improve the quality of care and health outcomes, while curbing costs. One way is to employ health educators and community health workers, who teach people how to live healthy lives and how to avoid costly diseases and medical procedures. Lifestyle changes can reduce the probability of contracting a number of illnesses, such as lung cancer, HIV, heart disease, and skin cancer. If a person already has a disease such as asthma, health educators and community health workers help people understand how to manage their condition and avoid unnecessary trips to the emergency room. Health educators and community health workers help people understand how what they do affects their health.

For many illnesses, such as breast cancer and testicular cancer, finding the disease early greatly increases the likelihood that treatment will be successful. Therefore, it is important for people to know how to identify potential problems and when to seek medical help. The need to provide the public with this kind of information is expected to result in an increased demand for health educators and community health workers.

Federal health reform will increase access to medical care, such as preventative screenings. Health educators and community health workers will be needed to direct patients in obtaining access to healthcare services. In addition, a number of state and local programs designed to manage conditions such as diabetes and obesity include health educators and community health workers as part of intervention teams.

Job Prospects. Community health workers who have completed a formal education program and those who have experience working with a specific population may enjoy favorable job prospects. In addition, opportunities may be better for candidates who speak a foreign language.

O*NET

➤ Health Educators (21-1091.00)
➤ Community Health Workers (21-1094.00)

Contacts for More Information

For more information about health educators and community health workers, visit
➤ Society for Public Health Education (www.sophe.org/)
➤ American Public Health Association (www.apha.org/)
    For more information about the Certified Health Education Specialist (CHES) credential, visit
➤ National Commission for Health Education Credentialing, Inc. (www.nchec.org/)

Mental Health Counselors and Marriage and Family Therapists

- **2012 Median Pay** .... $41,500 per year
                                     $19.95 per hour
- **Entry-Level Education** ....Master's degree
- **Work Experience in a Related Occupation** .... None
- **On-the-Job Training** .... Internship/residency
- **Number of Jobs 2012** 166,300
- **Job Outlook, 2012–22** .... 29% (Much faster than average)
- **Employment Change, 2012–22** 48,200

What Mental Health Counselors and Marriage and Family Therapists Do

Mental health counselors and marriage and family therapists help people manage and overcome mental and emotional disorders and problems with their family and relationships. They listen to clients and ask questions, to help the clients understand their problems and develop strategies to improve their lives.

Duties. Mental health counselors and marriage and family therapists typically do the following:

- Diagnose and treat mental and emotional disorders, such as anxiety and depression
- Encourage clients to discuss their emotions and experiences

Counselors work in diverse community settings designed to provide a variety of counseling, rehabilitation, and support services.

Median Annual Wages, May 2012

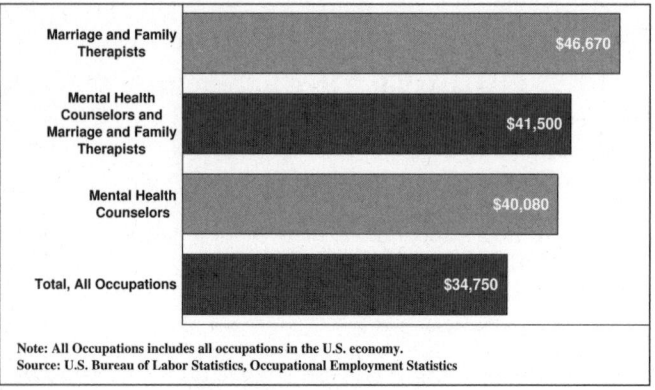

Note: All Occupations includes all occupations in the U.S. economy.
Source: U.S. Bureau of Labor Statistics, Occupational Employment Statistics

Percent Change in Employment, Projected 2012–2022

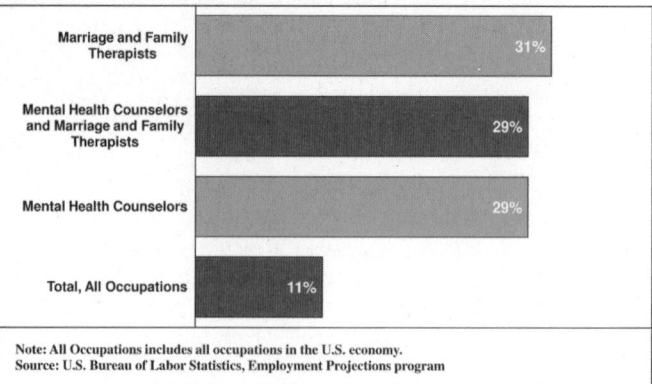

Note: All Occupations includes all occupations in the U.S. economy.
Source: U.S. Bureau of Labor Statistics, Employment Projections program

- Help clients process their reactions and adjust to changes in their life, such as divorce and layoffs

- Guide clients through the process of making decisions about their future

- Help clients develop strategies and skills to change their behavior and to cope with difficult situations

- Coordinate treatment with other professionals, such as psychiatrists and social workers

- Refer clients to other resources or services in the community, such as support groups or inpatient treatment facilities

Mental health counselors and marriage and family therapists use a variety of techniques and tools to help their clients. Many apply cognitive behavioral therapy, a goal-oriented approach that helps clients understand harmful thoughts, feelings, and beliefs and replace them with positive, life-enhancing ones. Furthermore, cognitive behavioral therapy teaches clients to eliminate unwanted and damaging behaviors and to replace them with more productive ones.

While some disorders can be overcome, others need to be managed. With the latter, mental health counselors and marriage and family therapists help the client develop strategies and skills to minimize the effects of their disorders or illnesses.

Some mental health counselors and marriage and family therapists work in private practice. They must spend time marketing their practice to prospective clients and working with insurance companies and clients to get payment for their services.

Mental health counselors provide treatment to individuals, families, couples, and groups. Some work with specific populations, such as the elderly, college students, or children. Mental health counselors deal with a variety of issues, including anxiety, depression, grief, low self-esteem, stress, and suicidal impulses. They also help with mental and emotional health issues and relationship problems.

Marriage and family therapists work with individuals, couples, and families. Unlike other types of mental health professionals, they bring a family-centered perspective to treatment, even when treating individuals. They evaluate family roles and development, to understand how clients' families affect their mental health. They treat the clients' relationships, not just the clients themselves. They address issues, such as low self-esteem, stress, addiction, and substance abuse.

Work Environment

Mental health counselors and marriage and family therapists held about 166,300 jobs in 2012.

Mental health counselors and marriage and family therapists work in variety of settings, such as mental health centers, sub-

stance abuse treatment centers, hospitals, and colleges. They also work in private practice and in Employee Assistance Programs (EAPs), which are mental health programs that some employers provide, to help employees deal with personal problems.

Mental health counselors held about 128,400 jobs in 2012. The industries that employed the most mental health counselors in 2012 were as follows:

Nursing and residential care facilities 18%
Outpatient care centers 18
Individual and family services.. 17
Hospitals; state, local, and private 12
Government.. 9

Marriage and family therapists held about 37,800 jobs in 2012. The industries that employed the most marriage and family therapists in 2012 were as follows:

Individual and family services.. 25%
Outpatient care centers 24
Government.. 22
Offices of health practitioners 8
Nursing and residential care facilities 5

Working with and assisting clients with a variety of emotional and mental problems may be stressful.

Mental health counselors and marriage and family therapists occasionally may travel to meet clients and patients.

Work Schedules. Mental health counselors and marriage and family therapists generally work full time. Because counseling sessions are scheduled to accommodate clients who may have job or family responsibilities, some counselors and therapists work evenings and weekends.

How to Become One

Mental health counselors and marriage and family therapists are typically required to have a master's degree and a license to practice.

Education. To become a mental health counselor or a marriage and family therapist, applicants typically need a master's degree in psychology, social work, counseling, marriage and family therapy, or a related mental health field. A bachelor's degree in most fields is acceptable to enter a master's-level program.

Counseling programs prepare students to recognize symptoms of mental and emotional disorders and to use effective counseling strategies. Marriage and family therapy programs teach students about how marriages, families, and relationships function and how they affect mental and emotional disorders.

Licenses. In most cases, both mental health counselors and marriage and family therapists must be licensed. Licensure requires a

Employment Projections Data for Mental Health Counselors and Marriage and Family Therapists

Occupational title	SOC Code	Employment, 2012	Projected Employment, 2022	Change, 2012–2022	
				Percent	Numeric
Mental health counselors and marriage and family therapists...	—	166,300	214,500	29	48,200
Marriage and family therapists...	21-1013	37,800	49,400	31	11,600
Mental health counselors..	21-1014	128,400	165,100	29	36,700

Source: U.S. Bureau of Labor Statistics, Employment Projections Program

Note: **Data are rounded. Go to Occupational Information Included in the OOH for a discussion of the data in this table.**

master's degree and 2,000 to 4,000 hours of post-degree supervised clinical experience. In addition, counselors and therapists must pass a state-recognized exam and complete annual continuing education classes.

Contact information for state boards regulating mental health counselors is available through the National Board for Certified Counselors.

Contact and licensing information for marriage and family therapists is available through the Association of Marital and Family Therapy Regulatory Boards.

Training. In most cases, both mental health counselors and marriage and family therapists must be licensed. Licensure requires a master's degree and 2,000 to 4,000 hours of post-degree supervised clinical experience. Students gain experience in providing family therapy, group therapy, psychotherapy and other therapeutic interventions, under the supervision of a licensed counselor.

Important Qualities

Compassion. Counselors and therapists often work with people who are dealing with stressful and difficult situations, so they must be compassionate and empathize with their clients.

Interpersonal skills. Being able to work with different types of people is essential for counselors and therapists, who spend most of their time working directly with clients and other professionals and must be able to encourage good relationships.

Listening skills. Good listening skills are essential for mental health counselors and marriage and family therapists, both of whom need to give their full attention to their clients to understand their problems and values.

Organizational skills. Good organizational skills are especially important for counselors and therapists in private practice, who must keep track of payments and work with insurance companies.

Speaking skills. Mental health counselors and marriage and family therapists need to be able to communicate with clients

effectively. They must express ideas and information in a way that clients can understand easily.

Pay

The median annual wage for mental health counselors was $40,080 in May 2012. The median wage is the wage at which half the workers in an occupation earned more than that amount and half earned less. The lowest 10 percent earned less than $25,430, and the top 10 percent earned more than $66,630.

In May 2012, the median annual wages for mental health counselors in the top five industries in which these counselors worked were as follows:

Government	$48,060
Hospitals; state, local, and private	43,190
Outpatient care centers	40,250
Individual and family services	40,200
Nursing and residential care facilities	32,530

The median annual wage for marriage and family therapists was $46,670 in May 2012. The lowest 10 percent earned less than $25,540, and the top 10 percent earned more than $75,120.

In May 2012, the median annual wages for marriage and family therapists in the top five industries in which these therapists worked were as follows:

Government	$61,230
Offices of health practitioners	45,090
Outpatient care centers	44,130
Individual and family services	41,960
Nursing and residential care facilities	37,450

Job Outlook

Employment of mental health counselors and marriage and family therapists is projected to grow 29 percent from 2012 to 2022, much faster than the average for all occupations. Growth is expected in

Similar Occupations   This table shows a list of occupations with job duties that are similar to those of mental health counselors and marriage and family therapists.

Occupations	Entry-level Education	2012 Pay	Projected Job Growth	Average Annual Openings
Physicians and Surgeons	Doctoral or professional degree	$182,294	18%	29,630
Psychologists	See "How to Become One"	$69,807	12%	6,230
Rehabilitation Counselors	Master's degree	$33,880	20%	4,840
School and Career Counselors	Master's degree	$53,610	12%	8,700
Social and Community Service Managers	Bachelor's degree	$59,970	21%	5,510
Social and Human Service Assistants	High school diploma or equivalent	$28,850	22%	17,870
Social Workers	See "How to Become One"	$44,541	19%	24,280
Substance Abuse and Behavioral Disorder Counselors	High school diploma or equivalent	$38,520	31%	4,720

both occupations as more people have mental health counseling services covered by their insurance policies.

Federal legislation mandating individual health coverage may increase the number of health insurance customers. In addition, the law requires insurance plans to cover treatment for mental health issues in the same way as other chronic diseases. These two factors will open up prevention and treatment services to more people who were previously uninsured, did not have these services covered, or found treatment to be cost-prohibitive. Mental health centers and other treatment and counseling facilities will need to hire more mental health counselors and marriage and family therapists, to meet this increased demand.

In addition, the number of military veterans needing and seeking mental health treatment is expected to increase over the next decade. The federal government, community clinics, and local hospitals will need to expand their mental health counseling staff, to provide timely and effective treatment for veterans and active duty personnel.

Furthermore, increasing numbers of people are expected to seek treatment for problems with mental and emotional problems than in earlier decades. As the population grows, the number of individuals entering therapy is expected to increase, as well. This trend will cause continued demand for counselors in mental health centers, hospitals, and colleges.

Job Prospects. Job prospects should be good for mental health counselors and marriage and family therapists, particularly in rural areas typically underserved by mental health practitioners.

O*NET

➤ Marriage and Family Therapists (21-1013.00)
➤ Mental Health Counselors (21-1014.00)

Contacts for More Information

For more information about mental health counselors, visit
➤ American Mental Health Counselors Association (www.amhca.org/)
For more information about marriage and family therapists, visit
➤ American Association for Marriage and Family Therapy (www.aamft.org/)
For general information about counseling and for information about counseling specialties, visit
➤ American Counseling Association (www.counseling.org/)
For information about contacting state regulating boards, visit
➤ National Board for Certified Counselors (www.nbcc.org/directory)

Probation Officers and Correctional Treatment Specialists

* **2012 Median Pay** .... $48,190 per year
  $23.17 per hour
* **Entry-Level Education** ....Bachelor's degree
* **Work Experience in a Related Occupation**............... None
* **On-the-Job Training** ....Short-term on-the-job training
* **Number of Jobs 2012** 90,300
* **Job Outlook, 2012–22** ....-1% (Little or no change)
* **Employment Change, 2012–22** .... -900

Probation and parole officers supervise offenders on probation or parole through personal contact with the offenders and their families.

What Probation Officers and Correctional Treatment Specialists Do

Probation officers and correctional treatment specialists work with and monitor offenders to prevent them from committing new crimes.

Duties. Probation officers and correctional treatment specialists typically do the following:

* Evaluate offenders to determine the best course of rehabilitation
* Provide offenders with resources, such as job training
* Test offenders for drugs and offer substance-abuse counseling
* Monitor offenders and help with their progress
* Conduct meetings with offenders and their family and friends
* Write reports on the progress of offenders

Probation officers and correctional treatment specialists work with offenders who are given probation instead of jail time, who are still in prison, or who have been released from prison.

The following are examples of types of probation officers and correctional treatment specialists:

Probation officers, who are called *community supervision officers* in some states, supervise people who have been placed on probation instead of being sent to prison. They work to ensure that the offender is not a danger to the community and to help in their rehabilitation. Probation officers write reports that detail each offender's treatment plan and their progress since being put on probation. Most work exclusively with either adults or juveniles.

Parole officers work with people who have been released from jail and are serving parole, to help them re-enter society. Parole officers monitor post-release offenders and provide them with information on various resources, such as substance-abuse counseling or job training, to aid in their rehabilitation. By doing so, the officers try to change the offenders' behavior and thus reduce the risk of that person committing another crime and having to return to prison.

Both probation and parole officers supervise offenders through personal contact with the offenders and their families. Probation and parole officers require regularly scheduled contact with offenders by telephone or through office visits, and they also may check on offenders at their homes or places of work. Probation and parole officers also oversee drug testing and electronic monitoring of offenders. In some states, officers do the jobs of both probation and parole officers.

Median Annual Wages, May 2012

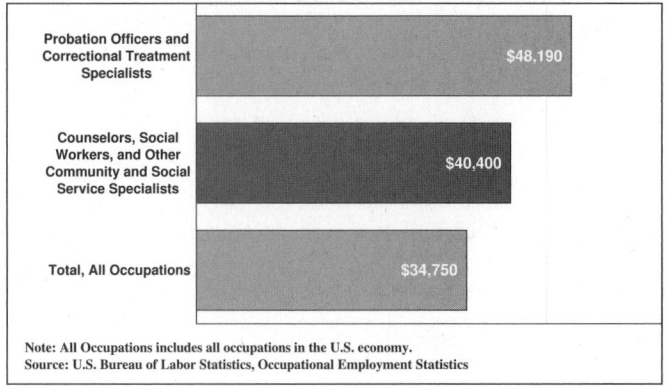

Probation Officers and Correctional Treatment Specialists — $48,190

Counselors, Social Workers, and Other Community and Social Service Specialists — $40,400

Total, All Occupations — $34,750

Note: All Occupations includes all occupations in the U.S. economy.
Source: U.S. Bureau of Labor Statistics, Occupational Employment Statistics

Percent Change in Employment, Projected 2012–2022

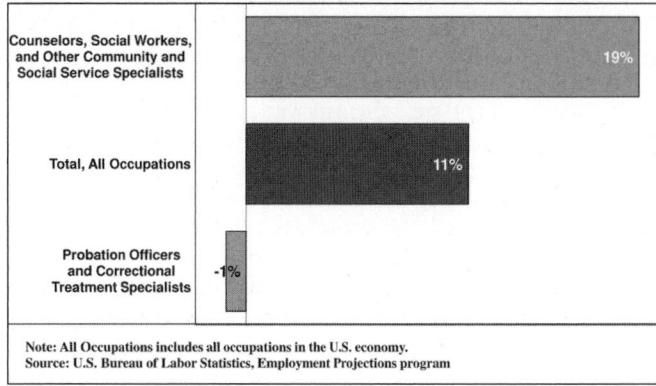

Counselors, Social Workers, and Other Community and Social Service Specialists — 19%

Total, All Occupations — 11%

Probation Officers and Correctional Treatment Specialists — -1%

Note: All Occupations includes all occupations in the U.S. economy.
Source: U.S. Bureau of Labor Statistics, Employment Projections program

Pretrial services officers investigate an offender's background to determine if the offender can be safely allowed back into the community before his or her trial date. Officers must assess the risk and make a recommendation to a judge who decides on the appropriate sentencing or bond amount. When offenders are allowed back into the community, pretrial officers supervise them to make sure that they stay within the terms of their release and appear at their trials.

Correctional treatment specialists, also known as *case managers* or *correctional counselors*, advise offenders and develop rehabilitation plans for them to follow when they are no longer in prison or on parole. They may evaluate inmates using questionnaires and psychological tests. They also work with inmates, probation officers, and staff of other agencies to develop parole and release plans. For example, they may plan education and training programs to improve offenders' job skills.

Correctional treatment specialists write case reports that cover the inmate's history and the likelihood that he or she will commit another crime. When offenders are eligible for release, the case reports are given to the appropriate parole board. The specialist may help set up counseling for the offenders and their families, find substance-abuse or mental health treatment options, aid in job placement, and find housing. Correctional treatment specialists also explain the terms and conditions of the prisoner's release and keep detailed written accounts of each offender's progress.

The number of cases a probation officer or correctional treatment specialist handles at one time depends on the needs of offenders and the risks associated with each individual. Higher-risk offenders usually command more of the officer's time and resources. Caseload size also varies by agency.

Technological advancements–such as improved tests for drug screening and electronic devices to monitor clients–help probation officers and correctional treatment specialists supervise and counsel offenders.

Work Environment

Probation officers and correctional treatment specialists held about 90,300 jobs in 2012. Nearly all worked for state or local governments.

Probation officers and correctional treatment specialists work with criminal offenders, some of whom may be dangerous. While supervising offenders, they may interact with others, such as family members and friends of their clients, who may be upset or difficult to work with. Workers may be assigned to fieldwork in high-crime areas or in institutions where there is a risk of violence or communicable disease.

Probation officers and correctional treatment specialists must meet many court-imposed deadlines, which contributes to heavy workloads and extensive paperwork. Many officers travel to

Employment Projections Data for Probation Officers and Correctional Treatment Specialists

Occupational title	SOC Code	Employment, 2012	Projected Employment, 2022	Change, 2012–2022	
				Percent	Numeric
Probation officers and correctional treatment specialists.......	21-1092	90,300	89,300	-1	-900

Source: U.S. Bureau of Labor Statistics, Employment Projections Program

Note: Data are rounded. Go to **Occupational Information Included in the OOH** *for a discussion of the data in this table.*

Similar Occupations   This table shows a list of occupations with job duties that are similar to those of probation officers and correctional treatment specialists.

Occupations	Entry-level Education	2012 Pay	Projected Job Growth	Average Annual Openings
Correctional Officers	High school diploma or equivalent	$38,961	5%	14,780
Police and Detectives	High school diploma or equivalent	$57,974	5%	27,500
Social and Human Service Assistants	High school diploma or equivalent	$28,850	22%	17,870
Social Workers	See "How to Become One"	$44,541	19%	24,280
Substance Abuse and Behavioral Disorder Counselors	High school diploma or equivalent	$38,520	31%	4,720

perform home and employment checks and property searches. Because of the hostile environments probation officers may encounter, some may carry a firearm or pepper spray for protection.

All of these factors, as well as the frustration some officers experience in dealing with offenders who violate the terms of their release, contribute to a stressful work environment. Although the high stress levels can make the job difficult at times, this work can also be rewarding. Many officers and specialists receive personal satisfaction from counseling members of their community and helping them become productive citizens.

Work Schedules. Although many officers and specialists work full time, the demands of the job often lead to working long hours. For example, many agencies rotate an on-call officer position. When these workers are on-call, they must respond to any issues with offenders or law enforcement 24 hours a day. Extensive travel and paperwork can also contribute to more hours of work.

How to Become One

Probation officers and correctional treatment specialists usually need a bachelor's degree. In addition, most employers require candidates to pass oral, written, and psychological exams.

Education. A bachelor's degree in social work, criminal justice, behavioral sciences, or a related field is usually required. Some employers require a master's degree in a related field.

Training. Most probation officers and correctional treatment specialists must complete a training program sponsored by their state government or the federal government, after which they may have to pass a certification test. In addition, they may be required to work as trainees for up to 1 year before being offered a permanent position.

Some probation officers specialize in a certain type of casework. For example, an officer may work only with domestic violence offenders or deal only with substance-abuse cases. Officers receive training specific to the group that they are working with so that they are better prepared to help that type of offender.

Licenses, Certifications, and Registrations. Most agencies require applicants to be at least 21 years old and, for federal employment, not older than 37 years of age. In addition, most departments require candidates to have a record free of felony convictions and to submit to drug testing.

A valid driver's license is often required.

Other Experience. Although job requirements vary, previous work experience in probation, pretrial services, parole, corrections, criminal investigations, substance abuse treatment, social work, or counseling can be helpful in the hiring process.

Previous experience working in court houses or with offenders in the criminal justice field can also be useful for some positions.

Advancement. Advancement to supervisory positions is primarily based on experience and performance. A master's degree in criminal justice, social work, or psychology may be required for advancement.

Important Qualities

Communication skills. Probation officers and correctional treatment specialists must be able to effectively interact with many different people.

Critical-thinking skills. Workers must be able to assess the needs of individual offenders before determining the best resources for helping them.

Decision-making skills. Probation officers and correctional treatment specialists must consider the relative costs and benefits of potential actions and be able to choose appropriately.

Emotional stability. Workers must cope with hostile individuals or otherwise upsetting circumstances on the job.

Organizational skills. Probation officers and correctional treatment specialists must be able to manage multiple cases at the same time.

Pay

The median annual wage for probation officers and correctional treatment specialists was $48,190 in May 2012. The median wage is the wage at which half the workers in an occupation earned more than that amount and half earned less. The lowest 10 percent earned less than $31,590, and the top 10 percent earned more than $83,410.

Union Membership. Compared with workers in all occupations, probation officers and correctional treatment specialists had a higher percentage of workers who belonged to a union in 2012.

Job Outlook

Employment of probation officers and correctional treatment specialists is projected to show little or no change from 2012 to 2022.

Employment growth depends primarily on the amount of state and local government funding for corrections, especially the amount allocated to probation and parole systems. Limited state and local government funding for corrections over the coming decade will stall employment growth.

However, as alternative forms of punishment, such as probation, continue to be used, some demand for probation officers and correctional treatment specialists should continue. Parole officers will be needed to supervise individuals who will be released from prison in the future.

Job Prospects. Many job openings will result from the need to replace those who leave the occupation each year. Competition for jobs should be lessened as heavy workloads and high job-related stress deter some from seeking this kind of work. For these reasons, job opportunities should be plentiful for those who qualify.

O*NET

➤ Probation Officers and Correctional Treatment Specialists (21-1092.00)

Contacts for More Information

For more information about probation officers and correctional treatment specialists, visit

➤ American Probation and Parole Association (www.appa-net.org/eweb/)

For more information about criminal justice job opportunities in your area, contact the departments of corrections, criminal justice, or probation for individual states.

Rehabilitation Counselors

- **2012 Median Pay** .... $33,880 per year
  $16.29 per hour
- **Entry-Level Education** ....Master's degree
- **Work Experience in a Related Occupation**............... None
- **On-the-Job Training** .... None
- **Number of Jobs 2012** 117,500
- **Job Outlook, 2012–22** .... 20% (Faster than average)
- **Employment Change, 2012–22** 23,400

Rehabilitation counselors evaluate clients' abilities, interests, experience, skills, health, and education.

What Rehabilitation Counselors Do

Rehabilitation counselors help people with emotional and physical disabilities live independently. They work with clients to overcome or manage the personal, social, and professional effects of disabilities on employment or independent living.

Duties. Rehabilitation counselors typically do the following:

- Provide individual and group counseling to help clients adjust to their disability

- Evaluate clients' abilities, interests, experience, skills, health, and education

- Develop a treatment plan in consultation with other professionals, such as doctors, therapists, and psychologists

- Create rehabilitation or treatment plans based on clients' values, strengths, limitations, and goals

- Arrange for clients to obtain services, such as medical care or career training

- Help employers understand the needs and abilities of people with disabilities, as well as laws and resources that impact people with disabilities

- Assist clients in creating strategies to develop their strengths and adjust to their limitations

- Locate resources, such as wheelchairs or computer programs, that help clients live and work more independently

- Monitor clients' progress and adjust the rehabilitation or treatment plan as necessary

- Advocate for the rights of people with disabilities to live in the community and work in the job of their choice

Rehabilitation counselors help people with physical, mental, emotional, or social disabilities at various stages in their lives. Some work with students to develop strategies to live with their disability and move from school to work. Others help veterans cope with the mental or physical effects of their military service. Still others help elderly people adapt to disabilities developed later in life from illness or injury. Some rehabilitation counselors deal specifically with employment issues. These counselors, sometimes called *vocational rehabilitation counselors*, typically work with older students and adults rather than young children.

Some rehabilitation counselors work in private practice. These counselors must spend time marketing their practice to prospective clients and working with insurance companies and clients to get paid for their services. Some may provide expert testimony or assessments during personal injury or workers' compensation cases.

Work Environment

Rehabilitation counselors held about 117,500 jobs in 2012.

They work in a variety of settings, such as colleges, elementary and secondary schools, prisons, insurance companies, and independent-living facilities. They also work in private practice and in state, private, and nonprofit rehabilitation agencies.

The industries that employed the most rehabilitation counselors in 2012 were as follows:

Social assistance... 46%
Health care 22
State government, excluding education and hospitals............. 15
Local government, excluding education and hospitals.............. 6

Work Schedules. Most rehabilitation counselors work full time.

How to Become One

Rehabilitation counselors typically need a master's degree in rehabilitation counseling or a related field. Some positions require certification or a license.

Education. Most employers require a master's degree in rehabilitation counseling or a related field. A bachelor's degree in most fields is acceptable to enter a master's-level program. Master's degree programs teach students the theories, skills, and techniques to provide effective mental health counseling. These programs also train students in evaluating clients' needs, formulating and implementing job placement strategies, and understanding the medical

Median Annual Wages, May 2012

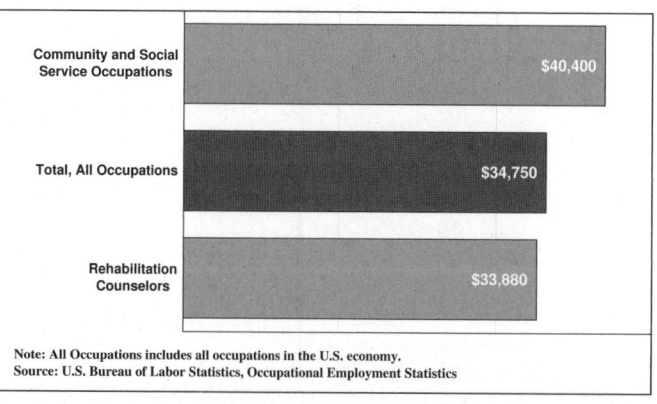

Community and Social Service Occupations — $40,400
Total, All Occupations — $34,750
Rehabilitation Counselors — $33,880

Note: All Occupations includes all occupations in the U.S. economy.
Source: U.S. Bureau of Labor Statistics, Occupational Employment Statistics

Percent Change in Employment, Projected 2012–2022

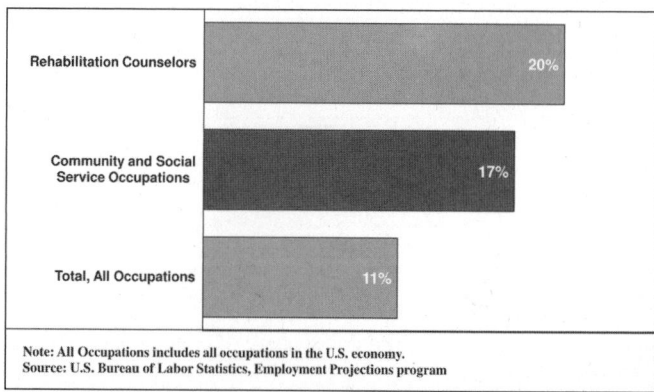

Rehabilitation Counselors — 20%
Community and Social Service Occupations — 17%
Total, All Occupations — 11%

Note: All Occupations includes all occupations in the U.S. economy.
Source: U.S. Bureau of Labor Statistics, Employment Projections program

Employment Projections Data for Rehabilitation Counselors

Occupational title	SOC Code	Employment, 2012	Projected Employment, 2022	Change, 2012–2022	
				Percent	Numeric
Rehabilitation counselors	21-1015	117,500	140,900	20	23,400

Source: U.S. Bureau of Labor Statistics, Employment Projections Program

Note: Data are rounded. Go to **Occupational Information Included in the OOH** *for a discussion of the data in this table.*

and psychological aspects of a disability. They typically require a period of supervised experience or training, such as an internship.

Although some employers hire workers with a bachelor's degree in rehabilitation and disability studies, these workers typically cannot offer the full range of services that a rehabilitation counselor with a master's degree can provide. Bachelor's degree programs teach students about issues that people with disabilities face and about the process of providing rehabilitation services.

Licenses. Licensing requirements for rehabilitation counselors differ by state and by type of services provided. Those providing counseling services to clients and patients must attain a license through their state licensing board. Other services provided by rehabilitation counselors, however, may be exempt from state licensing requirements. Rehabilitation counselors providing only vocational rehabilitation services or job placement assistance, for example, may not need a license.

Licensure requires a master's degree and 2,000 to 4,000 hours of supervised clinical experience. In addition, counselors must pass a state-recognized exam and complete annual continuing education credits. Applicants should contact the state licensing boards for information on what services or counseling positions require licensure. Contact information for these state licensing boards can be found through the Commission on Rehabilitation Counselor Certification website.

Certifications. Some employers prefer or require rehabilitation counselors to be Certified Rehabilitation Counselors (CRC). Applicants must meet advanced education, work experience, and clinical supervision requirements and pass a test. Counselors must complete continuing education requirements or pass a reexamination to renew their certification. For more information, contact the Commission on Rehabilitation Counselor Certification.

Important Qualities

Communication skills. Rehabilitation counselors need to be able to communicate with clients effectively, expressing ideas and information in a way that is easily understood.

Compassion. Counselors often work with people who are dealing with stressful and difficult situations, so they must be compassionate and empathize with their clients.

Interpersonal skills. Being able to work with different types of people is essential for rehabilitation counselors, who spend most of their time working directly with clients, families, employers, or other professionals. They must be able to develop and maintain a good working relationship.

Listening skills. Good listening skills are essential for rehabilitation counselors, who need to give their full attention to clients in order to understand their problems, concerns, and values.

Patience. To help people learn new skills and strategies, rehabilitation counselors must have patience as clients struggle to learn about and address the impact of their disabilities.

Pay

The median annual wage for rehabilitation counselors was $33,880 in May 2012. The median wage is the wage at which half the workers in an occupation earned more than that amount and half earned less. The lowest 10 percent earned less than $20,990 and the top 10 percent earned more than $59,330.

In May 2012, the median annual wages for rehabilitation counselors in the top four industries in which these counselors worked were as follows:

State government, excluding education and hospitals	$43,550
Local government, excluding education and hospitals	41,530
Health care	32,290
Social assistance	30,390

Job Outlook

Employment of rehabilitation counselors is projected to grow 20 percent from 2012 to 2022, faster than the average for all occupations. Demand for rehabilitation counselors is expected to grow with the increase in the elderly population and with the continued

Similar Occupations   This table shows a list of occupations with job duties that are similar to those of rehabilitation counselors.

Occupations	Entry-level Education	2012 Pay	Projected Job Growth	Average Annual Openings
Mental Health Counselors and Marriage and Family Therapists	Master's degree	$41,592	29%	8,360
Occupational Therapists	Master's degree	$75,400	29%	4,820
Occupational Therapy Assistants and Aides	See "How to Become One"	$47,638	41%	2,560
Psychologists	See "How to Become One"	$69,807	12%	6,230
School and Career Counselors	Master's degree	$53,610	12%	8,700
Social and Human Service Assistants	High school diploma or equivalent	$28,850	22%	17,870
Special Education Teachers	Bachelor's degree	$55,068	6%	10,220
Substance Abuse and Behavioral Disorder Counselors	High school diploma or equivalent	$38,520	31%	4,720

rehabilitation needs of other groups, such as veterans and people with disabilities.

Older adults are more likely than other age groups to become disabled or injured. They will need to learn to adapt to their disabilities and learn strategies to live independently. As a result, they will require the services of rehabilitation counselors. As the size of the elderly population grows, so will the need for rehabilitation counselors.

In addition, there will be a continued need for rehabilitation counselors to work with veterans who were disabled during their military service. They will also be needed to work with other groups, such as people who have learning disabilities, autism spectrum disorders, or substance abuse problems.

O*NET

➤ Rehabilitation Counselors (21-1015.00)

Contacts for More Information

For more information about counseling and information about counseling specialties, visit

➤ American Rehabilitation Counseling Association (www.arcaweb. org/)

For more information about the Certified Rehabilitation Counselors (CRC) certification and the state licensing regulating boards, visit

➤ Commission on Rehabilitation Counselor Certification (www.crc-certification.com/)

School and Career Counselors

- **2012 Median Pay** .... $53,610 per year
  $25.77 per hour
- **Entry-Level Education** ....Master's degree
- **Work Experience in a Related Occupation**............... None
- **On-the-Job Training** .... None
- **Number of Jobs 2012** 262,300
- **Job Outlook, 2012–22**................ 12% (As fast as average)
- **Employment Change, 2012–22** 31,200

School counselors work in private and public schools where they have private offices.

What School and Career Counselors Do

School counselors help students develop social skills and succeed in school. Career counselors assist people with the process of making career decisions, by helping them choose a career or educational program.

Duties. School counselors typically do the following:

- Help students understand and overcome social or behavioral problems through individual and group counseling
- Provide individual and small group counseling based on student needs
- Work with students to develop skills, such as organization, time management, and effective study habits
- Help students set realistic academic and career goals and develop a plan to achieve them
- Evaluate students' abilities and interests through aptitude assessments, interviews, and individual planning
- Collaborate with teachers, administrators, and parents to help students succeed
- Deliver classroom guidance lessons on topics, such as bullying, drug abuse, and planning for college or careers after graduation
- Identify and report possible cases of neglect or abuse
- Refer students and parents to resources outside the school for additional support

The specific duties of school counselors vary with the ages of the students they work with.

Elementary school counselors focus on helping students develop skills, such as decision-making and study skills, that they need to be successful in their social and academic lives. They meet with parents or guardians to discuss their child's strengths, weaknesses, and any possible special needs and behavioral issues. School counselors also work with teachers and administrators to ensure the curriculum addresses both the developmental and academic needs of students.

Middle school counselors work with students and parents to help students develop and achieve career and academic goals. They help students develop the skills and strategies necessary to succeed academically and socially.

High school counselors advise students in making academic and career plans. Many help students with personal problems that interfere with their education. They help students choose classes and plan for their lives after graduation. Counselors provide information about choosing and applying for colleges, training programs, financial aid, and apprenticeships. They may present career workshops to help students search and apply for jobs, write resumes, and improve interviewing skills.

Career counselors typically do the following:

- Use aptitude and achievement assessments, to help clients evaluate their interests, skills, and abilities
- Evaluate clients' background, education, and training, to help them develop realistic goals
- Guide clients through making decisions about their careers, such as choosing a new profession and the type of degree to pursue
- Help clients learn job search skills, such as interviewing and networking
- Assist clients in locating and applying for jobs, by teaching them strategies to find openings and how to write a resume
- Advise clients on how to resolve problems in the workplace, such as conflicts with bosses or coworkers

Median Annual Wages, May 2012

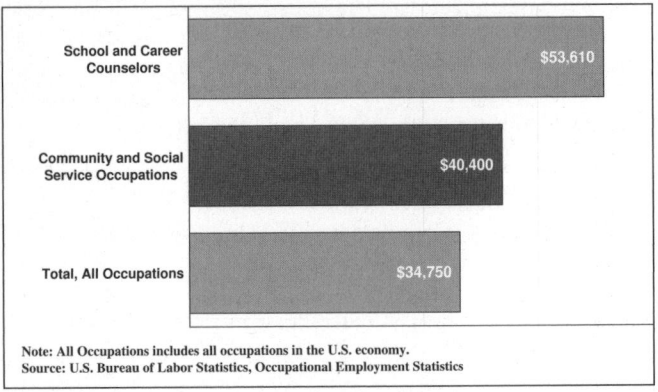

Note: All Occupations includes all occupations in the U.S. economy.
Source: U.S. Bureau of Labor Statistics, Occupational Employment Statistics

Percent Change in Employment, Projected 2012–2022

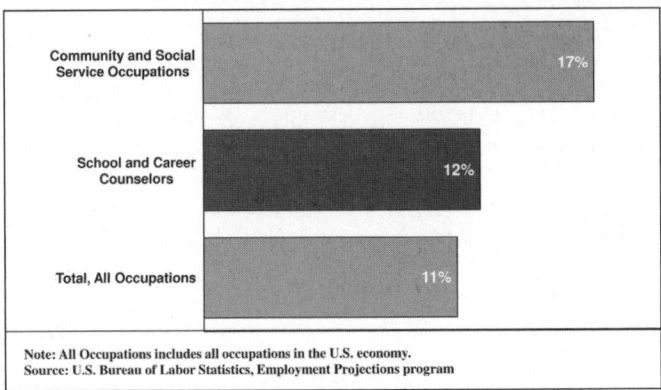

Note: All Occupations includes all occupations in the U.S. economy.
Source: U.S. Bureau of Labor Statistics, Employment Projections program

• Help clients select and apply for educational programs, to obtain the necessary degrees, credentials, and skills

Career counselors work with clients at various stages in their careers. Some work in colleges to help students choose a major. They also help students determine what jobs they are qualified for with their degrees. These counselors also work with people who have already entered the workforce. Career counselors develop plans to improve their client's current career and provide advice about entering a new profession. Some career counselors work in outplacement firms and assist laid-off workers with transitioning into new jobs or careers. Others work in corporate career centers to assist employees in making decisions about their career path within the company.

Some career counselors work in private practice. These counselors must spend time marketing their practice to prospective clients and working with clients to receive payments for their services.

Work Environment

School and career counselors held about 262,300 jobs in 2012. The industries that employed the most school and career counselors in 2012 were as follows:

Elementary and secondary schools; state, local,
  and private 47%
Junior colleges, colleges, universities, and
  professional schools; state, local, and private 31
Health care and social assistance 9
Government 4

School counselors work in private and public schools. They often have private offices so that they can have confidential conversations with students. Career counselors work in colleges, businesses, prisons, and state government career centers.

Work Schedules. Both school and career counselors generally work full time. Some school counselors have summers off when school is not in session.

How to Become One

Most school counselors must be credentialed, which most often requires a master's degree. Many employers prefer that career counselors have a master's degree. Career counselors who work in private practice may also need a license.

Education. Most states require school counselors to have a master's degree in school counseling or a related field. Programs in school counseling teach students about fostering academic development; conducting group and individual counseling; and working with parents, teachers, and other school staff. These

programs often require students to gain experience through an internship or practicum.

Most employers prefer that career counselors have a master's degree in counseling with a focus on career development. Career counseling programs prepare students to teach career development techniques and assess clients' skills and interests. Many programs require students to have a period of supervised experience, such as an internship.

Licenses, Certifications, and Registrations. Public school counselors must have a state-issued credential to practice. This credential can be called a certification, a license, or an endorsement, depending on the state. Licensure or certification typically requires a master's degree in school counseling and an internship or practicum completed under the supervision of a licensed professional school counselor.

Some states require applicants to have 1 to 2 years of classroom teaching experience or to hold a teaching license, prior to being certified. Other states allow full-time teaching experience to be substituted, in place of the internship requirement.

Most states require a criminal background check, as part of the credentialing process.

Information about requirements for each state is available from the American School Counselor Association.

Although some employers prefer to hire licensed career counselors, a license is not required in many settings. Career counselors in private practice, however, generally must be licensed. Licensure requires a master's degree and 2,000 to 3,000 hours of supervised clinical experience. In addition, counselors must pass a state-recognized exam and complete annual continuing education credits. Contact information for state regulating boards is available from the National Board for Certified Counselors.

Work Experience in a Related Occupation. Although most states do not require work experience in a related occupation, some states require school counselors to have 1 to 2 years of classroom teaching experience or to hold a teaching license, prior to being certified.

Important Qualities

Compassion. Counselors often work with people who are dealing with stressful and difficult situations, so they must be compassionate and empathize with their clients and students.

Interpersonal skills. Being able to work with different types of people is essential for counselors. They spend most of their time working directly with clients and students or other professionals and need good working relationships.

Listening skills. Good listening skills are essential for school and career counselors. They need to give their full attention to their students and clients to understand their problems.

Employment Projections Data for School and Career Counselors

Occupational title	SOC Code	Employment, 2012	Projected Employment, 2022	Change, 2012–2022	
				Percent	Numeric
Educational, guidance, school, and vocational counselors	21-1012	262,300	293,500	12	31,200

Source: U.S. Bureau of Labor Statistics, Employment Projections Program

Note: Data are rounded. Go to Occupational Information Included in the OOH *for a discussion of the data in this table.*

Speaking skills. School and career counselors must communicate effectively with clients and students. They should express ideas and information in a way that their clients and students understand easily.

Pay

The median annual wage for school and career counselors was $53,610 in May 2012. The median wage is the wage at which half the workers in an occupation earned more than that amount and half earned less. The bottom 10 percent earned less than $31,920, and the top 10 percent earned more than $86,680.

In May 2012, the median annual wages for school and career counselors in the top four industries in which these counselors worked were as follows:

Elementary and secondary schools; state, local, and private	$60,560
Government	50,710
Junior colleges, colleges, universities, and professional schools; state, local, and private	46,630
Health care and social assistance	35,590

Job Outlook

Employment of school and career counselors is projected to grow 12 percent from 2012 to 2022, about as fast as the average for all occupations. While overall employment growth is expected due to increasing school enrollments, hiring may be limited, due to slow growth–or decline–in education funding from state and local governments.

Rising student enrollments in elementary, middle, and high schools, as well as colleges and universities, are expected to increase demand for school counselors. As enrollments grow, schools will require more counselors to respond to the developmental and academic needs of their students. Colleges will need to hire additional counselors to meet the demand for career counseling services from their students.

Despite these projected increases in school enrollment, however, employment growth for school and career counselors will depend on state and local government budgets. When state and local governments experience budget deficits, they may lay off employees, including counselors. As a result, employment growth may be reduced by state and local government budget difficulties.

Demand for career counseling is projected to increase in vocational rehabilitation organizations and in private practice. Companies may expand their use of employment assistance programs and career counseling, to retain talent and increase the productivity and morale of their employees. Career counselors also will be needed to assist career changers and to help laid off workers find employment, as well as to help military personnel transition into the civilian job market.

O*NET

➤ Educational, Guidance, School, and Vocational Counselors (21-1012.00)

Contacts for More Information

For more information about counseling and information about counseling specialties, visit

➤ American Counseling Association (www.counseling.org/)

For more information about school counselors, visit

➤ American School Counselors Association (www.schoolcounselor.org/)

Similar Occupations   This table shows a list of occupations with job duties that are similar to those of school and career counselors.

Occupations	Entry-level Education	2012 Pay	Projected Job Growth	Average Annual Openings
High School Teachers	Bachelor's degree	$55,050	6%	31,260
Human Resources Specialists and Labor Relations Specialists	Bachelor's degree	$55,616	7%	12,370
Kindergarten and Elementary School Teachers	Bachelor's degree	$53,060	12%	53,250
Mental Health Counselors and Marriage and Family Therapists	Master's degree	$41,592	29%	8,360
Middle School Teachers	Bachelor's degree	$53,430	12%	21,120
Psychologists	See "How to Become One"	$69,807	12%	6,230
Rehabilitation Counselors	Master's degree	$33,880	20%	4,840
Social and Community Service Managers	Bachelor's degree	$59,970	21%	5,510
Social and Human Service Assistants	High school diploma or equivalent	$28,850	22%	17,870
Social Workers	See "How to Become One"	$44,541	19%	24,280
Substance Abuse and Behavioral Disorder Counselors	High school diploma or equivalent	$38,520	31%	4,720

For more information about career counselors, visit
➤ National Career Developers Association (www.ncda.org)
   For more information about state credentialing, visit
➤ National Board for Certified Counselors (www.nbcc.org/directory)

Social and Human Service Assistants

- **2012 Median Pay** .... $28,850 per year
  $13.87 per hour
- **Entry-Level Education** ... High school diploma or equivalent
- **Work Experience in a Related Occupation** .... None
- **On-the-Job Training** .... Short-term on-the-job training
- **Number of Jobs 2012** 372,700
- **Job Outlook, 2012–22** .... 22% (Much faster than average)
- **Employment Change, 2012–22** 81,200

What Social and Human Service Assistants Do

Social and human service assistants help people get through difficult times or get additional support. They help other workers, such as social workers, and they help clients find benefits or community services.

Duties. Social and human service assistants typically do the following:

- Work under the direction of social workers, psychologists, or others who have more education or experience
- Help determine what type of help their clients need
- Work with clients and other professionals, such as social workers, to develop a treatment plan
- Help clients get help with daily activities, such as eating and bathing
- Coordinate services provided to clients by their own or other organizations
- Research services available to their clients in their communities
- Determine clients' eligibility for services such as food stamps and Medicaid
- Help clients complete paperwork to apply for assistance programs
- Monitor clients to ensure that services are provided appropriately

Social and human service assistants have many job titles, including case work aide, clinical social work aide, family service assistant,

Social and human service assistants help social workers, healthcare workers, and other professionals to provide services to people.

social work assistant, addictions counselor assistant, and human service worker. Social and human service assistants help clients to identify and obtain benefits and services. In addition to initially connecting clients with benefits or services, social and human service assistants may follow up with clients to ensure that they are receiving the services and that the services are meeting their needs.

With *children and families,* social and human service assistants ensure that the children live in safe homes. They help parents get the resources, such as food stamps or childcare, they need to care for their children.

With the *elderly,* these workers help clients stay in their own homes and under their own care whenever possible. They coordinate meal deliveries or find personal care aides to help older people with their day-to-day needs, such as running errands or bathing. In some cases, human service workers help look for residential care facilities, such as nursing homes.

For *people with disabilities,* social and human service assistants help find rehabilitation services that aid their clients. They may work with employers to adapt the elements of a job to make it accessible to people with disabilities. Some workers find personal care services to help clients with daily living activities, such as bathing or making meals.

For *people with addictions,* human service assistants find rehabilitation centers that meet their clients' needs. They also find support groups or 12-step programs. They work with people who are dependent on alcohol, drugs, gambling, or other substances or behaviors.

Median Hourly Wages, May 2012

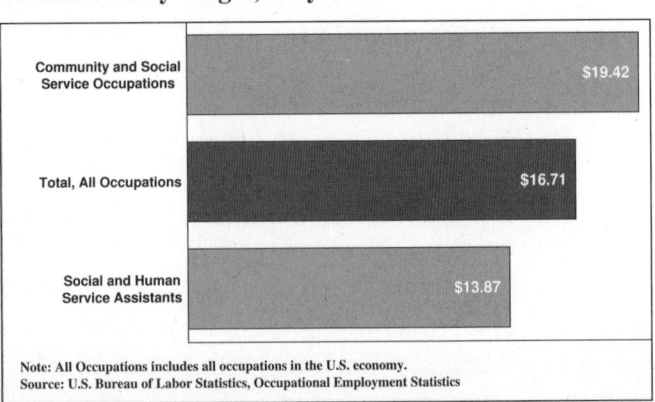

Community and Social Service Occupations — $19.42
Total, All Occupations — $16.71
Social and Human Service Assistants — $13.87

Note: All Occupations includes all occupations in the U.S. economy.
Source: U.S. Bureau of Labor Statistics, Occupational Employment Statistics

Percent Change in Employment, Projected 2012–2022

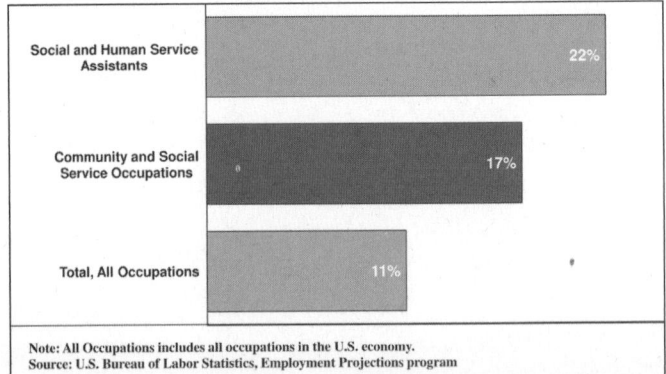

Social and Human Service Assistants — 22%
Community and Social Service Occupations — 17%
Total, All Occupations — 11%

Note: All Occupations includes all occupations in the U.S. economy.
Source: U.S. Bureau of Labor Statistics, Employment Projections program

Employment Projections Data for Social and Human Service Assistants

Occupational title	SOC Code	Employment, 2012	Projected Employment, 2022	Change, 2012–2022	
				Percent	Numeric
Social and human service assistants 21-1093		372,700	453,900	22	81,200

Source: U.S. Bureau of Labor Statistics, Employment Projections Program

Note: Data are rounded. Go to Occupational Information Included in the OOH *for a discussion of the data in this table.*

With *veterans*, assistants help people who have been discharged from the military adjust to civilian life. They help with practical needs, such as finding housing and applying skills gained in the military to civilian jobs. They also help with navigating the overwhelming number of services available to veterans.

For *people with mental illnesses,* social and human service assistants help clients find resources to cope with their illness. They find self-help and support groups to provide their clients with an assistance network. In addition, they may find personal care services or group housing to help those with more severe mental illnesses care for themselves.

With *immigrants,* workers help clients adjust to living in a new country. They help the clients locate jobs and housing. They also may help them find programs that teach English, or they may find legal assistance to help immigrants get their paperwork in order.

With *former prison inmates,* human service assistants find job training or placement programs to help clients reenter society. Human service assistants help former inmates find housing and connect with programs that help them make a new life for themselves.

With *homeless people,* assistants help clients meet their basic needs. They find temporary or permanent housing for their clients and locate places, such as soup kitchens, that provide meals. Human service assistants also help homeless people find facilities for other problems they may have, such as joblessness.

Work Environment

Social and human service assistants held about 372,700 jobs in 2012. They work for nonprofit organizations, private for-profit social service agencies, and state and local government. They may work in offices, clinics, hospitals, group homes, and shelters. Some travel around their communities to see clients.

The industries that employed the most social and human service assistants in 2012 were as follows:

Individual and family services	23%
State and local government	20
Residential care facilities	16
Community and vocational rehabilitation services	12
Religious, grantmaking, civic, professional, and similar organizations	10

Work Schedules. Most social and human service assistants work full time. Some work nights and weekends.

How to Become One

The minimum requirement is a high school diploma or the equivalent, but some employers prefer to hire workers who have additional education or experience. Without additional education, advancement opportunities are limited.

Education. A high school diploma is the minimum requirement, but some employers prefer to hire workers who have relevant work experience or education beyond high school. Certificates or associate's degrees in subjects such as human services, gerontology (working with older adults), or a social or behavioral science are common for workers entering this occupation.

Human services degree programs train students to observe and interview patients, carry out treatment plans, and handle people who are undergoing a crisis. Many programs include fieldwork to give students hands-on experience.

Similar Occupations   This table shows a list of occupations with job duties that are similar to those of social and human service assistants.

Occupations	Entry-level Education	2012 Pay	Projected Job Growth	Average Annual Openings
Childcare Workers	High school diploma or equivalent	$19,510	14%	57,000
Health Educators and Community Health Workers	See "How to Become One"	$43,015	22%	4,740
Home Health Aides	Less than high school	$20,820	48%	59,070
Mental Health Counselors and Marriage and Family Therapists	Master's degree	$41,592	29%	8,360
Personal Care Aides	Less than high school	$19,910	49%	66,600
Probation Officers and Correctional Treatment Specialists	Bachelor's degree	$48,190	-1%	2,360
Rehabilitation Counselors	Master's degree	$33,880	20%	4,840
School and Career Counselors	Master's degree	$53,610	12%	8,700
Social and Community Service Managers	Bachelor's degree	$59,970	21%	5,510
Social Workers	See "How to Become One"	$44,541	19%	24,280
Substance Abuse and Behavioral Disorder Counselors	High school diploma or equivalent	$38,520	31%	4,720

The level of education that social and human service assistants have completed often determines the responsibilities they are given. Those with a high school diploma are likely to do lower level work, such as helping clients fill out paperwork. However, assistants with some college education may coordinate program activities or manage a group home.

Training. Many social and human service assistants, particularly those without any postsecondary education, undergo a period of on-the-job training. Because such workers often are dealing with multiple clients from a wide variety of backgrounds, on-the-job training in case management helps them to respond to the different needs of their clients and to crises the clients sometimes undergo.

Advancement. For social and human service assistants, additional education is almost always necessary for advancement. In general, advancement to case management or social work jobs requires a bachelor's or master's degree in human services, counseling, rehabilitation, social work, or a related field.

Important Qualities

Communication skills. Social and human service assistants talk with clients about the challenges in their lives and assist them in getting help. These workers must be able listen to their clients and to communicate their needs to organizations that can help.

Compassion. Social and human service assistants often work with people who are in stressful and difficult situations. To develop strong relationships, they must have compassion and empathy for their clients.

Interpersonal skills. Social and human service assistants must make their clients feel comfortable discussing sensitive issues. Assistants also need to build relationships with other service providers to help themselves learn about all of the resources that are available in their communities.

Organizational skills. Social and human service assistants often must complete lots of paperwork and work with many different clients. They must be organized in order to ensure that the paperwork is filed properly and that clients are getting the help they need.

Problem-solving skills. Assistants help clients find solutions to their problems. They must be able to listen carefully to their clients' needs and offer multiple solutions.

Time-management skills. Social and human service assistants often work with many clients. They must learn to manage their time effectively to ensure that their clients are getting the attention they need.

Some employers require a criminal background check. In some settings, workers need a valid driver's license.

Pay

The median hourly wage for social and human service assistants was $13.87 in May 2012.The median wage is the wage at which half the workers in an occupation earned more than that amount and half earned less. The lowest 10 percent earned less than $9.34, and the top 10 percent earned more than $22.16.

In May 2012, the median hourly wages for social and human service assistants in the top five industries in which these assistants worked were as follows:

State and local government	$16.57
Religious, grantmaking, civic, professional, and similar organizations	14.77
Individual and family services	13.67
Community and vocational rehabilitation services	12.49
Residential care facilities	11.98

Job Outlook

Employment of social and human service assistants is projected to grow 22 percent from 2012 to 2022, much faster than the average for all occupations. Growth will be due to an increase in the elderly population and rising demand for health care and social services.

Much of the growth will be due to the needs of an aging population. An increase in number of older adults will cause growth in demand for social services. The elderly population often needs services such as delivery of meals and adult daycare. Social and human service assistants, who help find and provide these services, will be needed to meet this increased demand.

In addition, growth is expected as more people seek treatment for their addictions and more drug offenders are sent to treatment programs rather than to jail. The result will be an increase in demand for social and human service assistants who work in treatment programs or work with people with addictions.

There also will be continued demand for child and family social and human service assistants. These workers will be needed to help others, such as social workers, investigate child abuse cases, as well as place children in foster care and with adoptive families.

Job Prospects. Low pay and heavy workloads cause many workers to leave this occupation, creating opportunities for new workers entering the field.

O*NET

➤ Social and Human Service Assistants (21-1093.00)

Contacts for More Information

For more information about social and human service assistants, visit

➤ National Organization for Human Services (www.nationalhumanservices.org/)

Social Workers

- **2012 Median Pay** .... $44,200 per year
  $21.25 per hour
- **Entry-Level Education** ....See "How to Become One"
- **Work Experience in a Related Occupation**............... None
- **On-the-Job Training** .... None
- **Number of Jobs 2012** 607,300
- **Job Outlook, 2012–22** .... 19% (Faster than average)
- **Employment Change, 2012–22** 114,100

Social workers help people resolve issues in their lives.

Median Annual Wages, May 2012

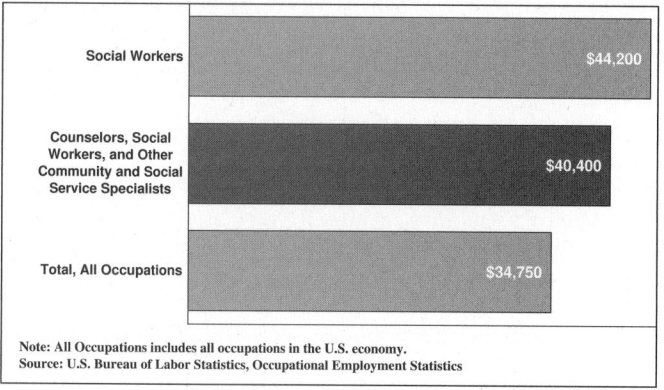

Note: All Occupations includes all occupations in the U.S. economy.
Source: U.S. Bureau of Labor Statistics, Occupational Employment Statistics

Percent Change in Employment, Projected 2012–2022

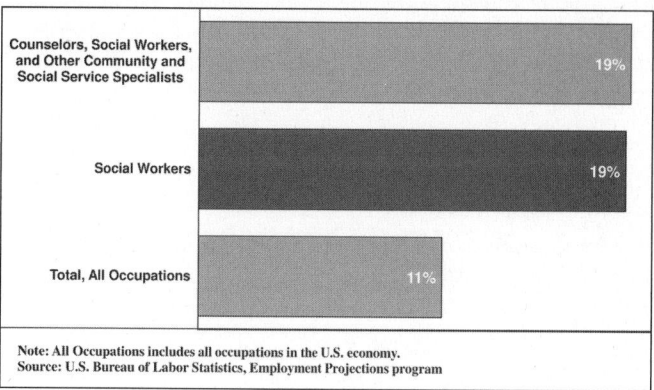

Note: All Occupations includes all occupations in the U.S. economy.
Source: U.S. Bureau of Labor Statistics, Employment Projections program

What Social Workers Do

Social workers help people solve and cope with problems in their everyday lives. Social workers in one specialization, clinical social workers, also diagnose and treat mental, behavioral, and emotional issues.

Duties. Social workers typically do the following:

- Identify people who need help
- Assess clients' needs, situations, strengths, and support networks to determine their goals
- Develop plans to improve their clients' well-being
- Help clients adjust to changes and challenges in their lives, such as illness, divorce, or unemployment
- Research and refer clients to community resources, such as food stamps, child care, and health care
- Help clients work with government agencies to apply for and receive benefits such as Medicare
- Respond to crisis situations such as child abuse
- Advocate for and help clients get resources that would improve their well-being
- Follow up with clients to ensure that their situations have improved
- Evaluate services provided to ensure that they are effective

Social workers help people cope with challenges in their lives. They help with a wide range of situations, such as adopting a child or being diagnosed with a terminal illness.

Social workers may work with children, people with disabilities, and people with serious illnesses and addictions. Their work varies based on the type of client they are working with.

The following are examples of types of social workers:

Child and family social workers protect vulnerable children and help families in need of assistance. They help parents find services, such as child care, or apply for benefits, such as food stamps. They intervene when children are in danger of neglect or abuse. Some help arrange adoptions, locate foster families, or work to get families back together. Clinical social workers provide mental health care to help children and families cope with changes in their lives, such as divorce or other family problems.

Clinical social workers–also called *licensed clinical social workers*–diagnose and treat mental, behavioral, and emotional disorders, including anxiety and depression. They provide individual, group, family, and couples therapy; they work with clients to develop strategies to change behavior or cope with difficult situations; and they refer clients to other resources or services, such as support groups or other mental health professionals. Clinical social workers can develop treatment plans with the client, doctors, and other healthcare professionals and may adjust the treatment plan if necessary based on their client's progress.

Many clinical social workers work in private practice. In these settings, clinical social workers have administrative and record-keeping tasks such as working with insurance companies to receive payment for their services. Some work in a group practice with other social workers or mental health professionals.

School social workers work with teachers, parents, and school administrators to develop plans and strategies to improve students' academic performance and social development. Students and their families are often referred to social workers to deal with problems such as aggressive behavior, bullying, or frequent absences from school.

Healthcare social workers help patients understand their diagnosis and make the necessary adjustments to their lifestyle, housing, or health care. For example, they may help people make the transition from the hospital back to their homes and communities. In addition, they may provide information on services, such as home healthcare or support groups, to help patients manage their illness or disease. Social workers help doctors and other healthcare professionals understand the effects that diseases and illnesses have on patients' mental and emotional health.

Some healthcare social workers specialize in geriatric social work, hospice and palliative care, or medical social work:

- *Geriatric social workers* help senior citizens and their families. They help clients find services, such as programs that provide older adults with meals or with home health care. In some cases, they provide information about assisted living facilities or nursing homes or work with older adults in those settings. They help clients and their families make plans for possible health complications or where clients will live if they can no longer care for themselves.

- *Hospice and palliative care social workers* help patients adjust to serious, chronic, or terminal illnesses. Palliative care focuses on relieving or preventing pain and other symptoms associated with serious illness. Hospice is a type of palliative care for people who are dying. Social workers in this setting provide and find services such as support groups or grief counselors to help patients and their families cope with the illness or disease.

- *Medical social workers* in hospitals help patients and their families by linking patients with resources in the hospital and in their own community. They may work with medical staff to create discharge plans, make referrals to community agencies, facilitate support groups, or conduct follow-up visits with patients once they have been discharged.

Mental health and substance abuse social workers help clients with mental illnesses or addictions. They provide information on services, such as support groups or 12-step programs, to help clients cope with their illness. Many clinical social workers function in these roles as well.

Work Environment

Social workers held about 607,300 jobs in 2012. They work in the following settings:

- Hospitals, primary care settings, and clinics, including veterans clinics
- Nursing homes
- Community mental health clinics
- Private practices
- State and local governments
- Schools
- Colleges and universities
- Substance abuse clinics
- Military bases and hospitals
- Correctional facilities
- Child welfare agencies

Although most social workers work in an office, they may spend time visiting clients. School social workers may be assigned to multiple schools and travel around the school district to see students. Understaffing and large caseloads may cause the work to be stressful.

The industries that employed the most child, family, and school social workers in 2012 were as follows:

State and local government, excluding education
and hospitals 41%
Health care and social assistance 36
Educational services; state, local, and private 15
Religious, grantmaking, civic, professional, and similar
organizations 5

The industries that employed the most healthcare social workers in 2012 were as follows:

Hospitals; state, local, and private 31%
Ambulatory health care services 21
Nursing and residential care facilities 15
Social assistance 13

The industries that employed the most mental health substance abuse social workers in 2012 were as follows:

Ambulatory health care services 27%
Social assistance 21

Nursing and residential care facilities 15
Hospitals; state, local, and private 15

Work Schedules. Social workers generally work full time. They sometimes work evenings, weekends, and holidays to see clients or attend meetings.

How to Become One

Although most social workers need a bachelor's degree in social work, clinical social workers must have a master's degree and two years of post-master experience in a supervised clinical setting. Clinical social workers must also be licensed in the state in which they practice.

Education. A bachelor's degree in social work (BSW) is the most common requirement for entry-level positions. However, some employers may hire workers who have a bachelor's degree in a related field, such as psychology or sociology.

A bachelor's degree in social work programs prepare students for direct-service positions such as caseworker or mental health assistant. These programs teach students about diverse populations, human behavior, and social welfare policy. All programs require students to complete supervised fieldwork or an internship.

Some positions, including those in schools and in health care, frequently require a master's degree in social work (MSW). For example, clinical social workers must have a master's degree in social work and two years of post-master experience in a supervised clinical setting.

A master's degree in social work generally takes 2 years to complete. However, some programs allow those with a bachelor's degree in social work to earn their master's degree in 1 year. Master's degree programs in social work prepare students for work in their chosen specialty by developing the skills to do clinical assessments, and take on supervisory duties. All programs require students to complete supervised practicum or an internship.

A bachelor's degree in social work is not required to enter a master's degree program in social work. A degree in almost any major is acceptable. However, courses in psychology, sociology, economics, and political science are recommended.

The Council on Social Work Education offers a Directory of Accredited Programs that lists all accredited bachelor's and master's degree programs.

Licenses, Certifications, and Registrations. All states have some type of licensure or certification requirement, which varies by state. All states require clinical social workers to be licensed. However, some states provide exemptions for clinical social workers who work in government agencies.

Becoming a licensed clinical social worker usually requires a master's degree in social work and a minimum of 2 years or 3,000 hours of supervised clinical experience after graduation. After

Employment Projections Data for Social Workers

Occupational title	SOC Code	Employment, 2012	Projected Employment, 2022	Change, 2012–2022	
				Percent	Numeric
Social workers	21-1020	607,300	721,500	19	114,100
Child, family, and school social workers	21-1021	285,700	328,800	15	43,100
Healthcare social workers	21-1022	146,200	185,500	27	39,200
Mental health and substance abuse social workers	21-1023	114,200	140,200	23	26,000
Social workers, all other	21-1029	61,200	67,000	9	5,800

Source: U.S. Bureau of Labor Statistics, Employment Projections Program

Note: Data are rounded. Go to Occupational Information Included in the OOH for a discussion of the data in this table.

Similar Occupations This table shows a list of occupations with job duties that are similar to those of social workers.

Occupations	Entry-level Education	2012 Pay	Projected Job Growth	Average Annual Openings
Health Educators and Community Health Workers	See "How to Become One"	$43,015	22%	4,740
Mental Health Counselors and Marriage and Family Therapists	Master's degree	$41,592	29%	8,360
Probation Officers and Correctional Treatment Specialists	Bachelor's degree	$48,190	-1%	2,360
Psychologists	See "How to Become One"	$69,807	12%	6,230
Rehabilitation Counselors	Master's degree	$33,880	20%	4,840
School and Career Counselors	Master's degree	$53,610	12%	8,700
Social and Community Service Managers	Bachelor's degree	$59,970	21%	5,510
Social and Human Service Assistants	High school diploma or equivalent	$28,850	22%	17,870
Substance Abuse and Behavioral Disorder Counselors	High school diploma or equivalent	$38,520	31%	4,720

completing their supervised experience, clinical social workers must pass a clinical exam to be licensed.

Because licensing requirements vary by state, those interested should contact their state board. Most states also have licenses for nonclinical social workers. For more information about regulatory licensure board by state, contact the Association of Social Work Boards.

Important Qualities

Compassion. Social workers often work with people who are in stressful and difficult situations. To develop strong relationships, they must have compassion and empathy for their clients.

Interpersonal skills. Being able to work with different groups of people is essential for social workers. They need strong people skills to foster healthy and productive relationships with their clients and colleagues.

Listening skills. Clients talk to social workers about challenges in their lives. To effectively help, social workers must be able to listen to and understand their clients' needs.

Organizational skills. Helping and managing multiple clients, often assisting with their paperwork or documenting their treatment, requires good organizational skills.

Problem-solving skills. Social workers need to develop practical and innovative solutions to their clients' problems.

Time-management skills. Social workers often have many clients. They must effectively manage their time to provide adequate service to all of their clients.

Pay

The median annual wage for social workers was $44,200 in May 2012. The median wage is the wage at which half the workers in an occupation earned more than that amount and half earned less. The lowest 10 percent earned less than $27,450, and the top 10 percent earned more than $72,980.

The median annual wages for social workers in May 2012 were as follows:

All other social workers $54,560
Healthcare social workers 49,830
Child, family, and school social workers 41,530
Mental health and substance abuse social workers 39,980

In May 2012, the median annual wages for child, family, and school social workers in the top four industries in which these professionals worked were as follows:

Educational services; state, local, and private $54,590
State and local government, excluding education
    and hospitals 44,370
Health care and social assistance 36,130
Religious, grantmaking, civic, professional, and similar
    organizations 35,910

In May 2012, the median annual wages for healthcare social workers in the top four industries in which these professionals worked were as follows:

Hospitals; state, local, and private $56,290
Ambulatory health care services 51,580
Nursing and residential care facilities 43,330
Social assistance... 38,920

In May 2012, the median annual wages for mental health and substance abuse social workers in the top four industries in which these professionals worked were as follows:

Hospitals; state, local, and private $47,880
Ambulatory health care services 39,840
Social assistance... 37,170
Nursing and residential care facilities 34,950

Job Outlook

Overall employment of social workers is projected to grow 19 percent from 2012 to 2022, faster than the average for all occupations. Employment growth will be driven by increased demand for health care and social services, but will vary by specialty.

Employment of child, family, and school social workers is projected to grow 15 percent from 2012 to 2022, faster than the average for all occupations. Child and family social workers will be needed to work with families to strengthen parenting skills, prevent child abuse, and identify alternative homes for children who are unable to live with their biological families. In schools, more social workers will be needed due to rising student enrollments.

However, growth of this specialty may be limited by budget constraints at all levels of government. Specifically, the availability of federal, state, and local funding will be a major factor in determining the employment growth in schools.

Employment of healthcare social workers is projected to grow 27 percent from 2012 to 2022, much faster than the average for all occupations. As baby boomers age, they and their families will require help from social workers to find care, increasing the need for healthcare social workers.

Employment of mental health and substance abuse social workers is projected to grow 23 percent from 2012 to 2022, much faster than the average for all occupations. Employment will grow as more people seek treatment for mental illness and substance use disorders. In addition, drug offenders are increasingly being sent to treatment programs rather than to jail. As a result, use of substance abuse treatment programs is expected to grow, increasing demand for these specialists.

O*NET

➤ Child, Family, and School Social Workers (21-1021.00)
➤ Healthcare Social Workers (21-1022.00)
➤ Mental Health and Substance Abuse Social Workers (21-1023.00)
➤ Social Workers, All Other (21-1029.00)

Contacts for More Information

For more information about social workers and clinical social workers, visit
➤ American Board of Examiners in Clinical Social Work (www. abecsw.org/)
➤ National Association of Social Workers (www.naswdc.org/)
    For more information about accredited baccalaureate and master's levels social work degree programs, visit
➤ Council on Social Work Education (www.cswe.org/)
    For more information about licensure requirements, visit
➤ Association of Social Work Boards (www.aswb.org/)

Substance Abuse and Behavioral Disorder Counselors

- **2012 Median Pay** .... $38,520 per year
                                                           $18.52 per hour
- **Entry-Level Education** ... High school diploma or equivalent
- **Work Experience in a Related Occupation** .... None
- **On-the-Job Training** .... Moderate-term on-the-job training
- **Number of Jobs 2012** 89,600
- **Job Outlook, 2012–22** .... 31% (Much faster than average)
- **Employment Change, 2012–22** 28,200

What Substance Abuse and Behavioral Disorder Counselors Do

Substance abuse and behavioral disorder counselors advise people who suffer from alcoholism, drug addiction, eating disorders, or other behavioral problems. They provide treatment and support to help the client recover from addiction or modify problem behaviors.

Duties. Substance abuse and behavioral disorder counselors typically do the following:

- Assess and evaluate clients' mental and physical health, addiction or problem behavior, and readiness to treatment
- Help clients develop treatment goals and plans
- Review and recommend treatment options with clients and their families

- Help clients develop skills and behaviors necessary to recover from their addiction or modify their behavior
- Work with clients to identify behaviors or situations that interfere with their recovery
- Teach families about addiction or behavior disorders and help them develop strategies to cope with those problems
- Refer clients to other resources and services, such as job placement services and support groups
- Conduct outreach programs to help people identify the signs of addiction and other destructive behavior, as well as steps to take to avoid such behavior

Substance abuse and behavioral disorder counselors, also called addiction counselors, work with clients individually and in group sessions. Many incorporate the principles of 12-step programs, such as Alcoholics Anonymous (AA) to guide their practice. They teach clients how to cope with stress and life's problems in ways that help them recover. Furthermore, they help clients rebuild professional relationships and, if necessary, reestablish their career. They also help clients improve their personal relationships and find ways to discuss their addiction or other problem with family and friends.

Some addiction counselors work in facilities that employ many types of healthcare and mental health professionals. Addiction counselors may work with psychiatrists, social workers, physicians, and registered nurses to develop treatment plans and coordinate care for patients.

Some counselors work with clients who have been ordered by a judge to receive treatment for addiction. Others work with specific populations, such as teenagers, veterans, or people with disabilities. Some specialize in crisis intervention; these counselors step in when someone is endangering his or her own life or the lives of others. Other counselors specialize in noncrisis interventions, which encourage a person with addictions or other issues to get help. Noncrisis interventions often are performed at the request of friends and family.

Some substance abuse and behavioral disorder counselors work in private practice, where they work alone or with a group of counselors or other professionals. These counselors manage their practice as a business. This includes working with clients and insurance companies to receive payment for their services. In addition, they market their practice to bring in new clients.

Substance abuse and behavioral disorder counselors work with clients both one-on-one and in group counseling sessions.

Median Annual Wages, May 2012

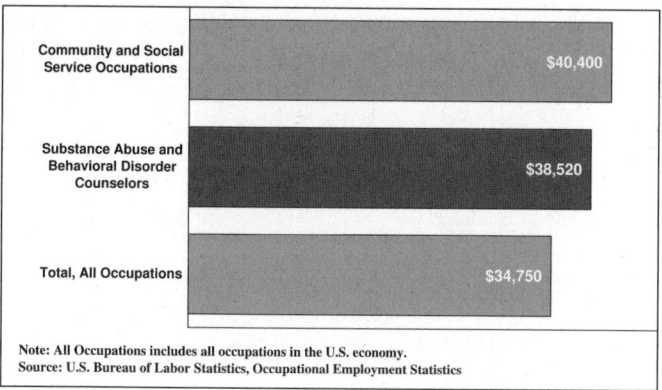

Note: All Occupations includes all occupations in the U.S. economy.
Source: U.S. Bureau of Labor Statistics, Occupational Employment Statistics

Percent Change in Employment, Projected 2012–2022

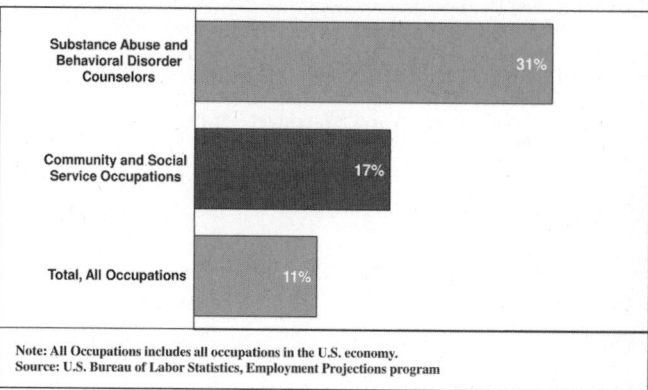

Note: All Occupations includes all occupations in the U.S. economy.
Source: U.S. Bureau of Labor Statistics, Employment Projections program

Work Environment

Substance abuse and behavioral disorder counselors held about 89,600 jobs in 2012. The industries that employed the most substance abuse and behavioral disorder counselors in 2012 were as follows:

Outpatient mental health and substance abuse centers	22%
Nursing and residential care facilities	22
Individual and family services	13
State and local government, excluding education and hospitals	11
Hospitals; state, local, and private	10

Substance abuse and behavioral disorder counselors work in a wide variety of settings, including mental health centers, prisons, probation or parole agencies, and juvenile detention facilities. They also work in halfway houses, detox centers, or in employee assistance programs (EAPs). EAPs are mental health programs provided by some employers to help employees deal with personal problems.

Some addiction counselors work in residential treatment centers, where clients live in the facility for a fixed period of time. Others work with clients in outpatient treatment centers. Some counselors work in private practice, where they may work alone or with a group of counselors or other professionals.

Although rewarding, the work of substance abuse and behavioral disorder counselors is often stressful. Many counselors have to deal with large workloads. They do not always have enough resources to meet the demand for their services. Also, they may have to intervene in crisis situations or work with agitated clients, which can be tense.

Work Schedules. Most substance abuse and behavioral disorder counselors work full time. In some settings, such as inpatient facilities, they may need to work evenings, nights, or weekends.

How to Become One

Educational requirements range from a high school diploma to a master's degree, depending on the setting, type of work, state regulations, and level of responsibility.

Education. Educational requirements range from a high school diploma and certification to a master's degree. Workers with more education are able to provide more services to their clients, such as private one-on-one counseling sessions, and they require less supervision than those with less education. Those interested should research their state's educational requirements.

Licenses, Certifications, and Registrations. Substance abuse and behavioral disorder counselors in private practice must be licensed. Licensing requirements vary by state, but all states require a master's degree and between 2,000 to 4,000 hours of supervised clinical experience. In addition, counselors must pass a state-recognized exam and complete continuing education every year. Contact information for your state's regulating board can be found through the National Board for Certified Counselors.

The licensure or certification criteria for substance abuse and behavioral disorder counselors outside of private practice vary from state to state. For example, not all states require a specific degree, but many require applicants to pass an exam. Contact information for your state's licensing board can found through the Addiction Technology Transfer Center.

Training. Workers with less education, such as a high school diploma, may be required to go through a period of on-the-job training. Training prepares counselors how to respond to a crisis situation and interact with people with addictions.

Important Qualities

Compassion. Counselors often work with people who are dealing with stressful and difficult situations, so they must be compassionate and empathize with their clients.

Interpersonal skills. Counselors must be able to work with different types of people. They spend most of their time working directly with clients or other professionals and must be able to develop and nurture good relationships.

Listening skills. Good listening skills are essential for substance abuse and behavioral disorder counselors. They need to give their full attention to a client to be able to understand that client's problems and values.

Employment Projections Data for Substance Abuse and Behavioral Disorder Counselors

Occupational title	SOC Code	Employment, 2012	Projected Employment, 2022	Change, 2012–2022	
				Percent	Numeric
Substance abuse and behavioral disorder counselors	21-1011	89,600	117,700	31	28,200

Source: U.S. Bureau of Labor Statistics, Employment Projections Program

Note: Data are rounded. Go to Occupational Information Included in the OOH for a discussion of the data in this table.

Similar Occupations   This table shows a list of occupations with job duties that are similar to those of substance abuse and behavioral disorder counselors.

Occupations	Entry-level Education	2012 Pay	Projected Job Growth	Average Annual Openings
Mental Health Counselors and Marriage and Family Therapists	Master's degree	$41,592	29%	8,360
Physicians and Surgeons	Doctoral or professional degree	$182,294	18%	29,630
Psychologists	See "How to Become One"	$69,807	12%	6,230
Registered Nurses	Associate's degree	$65,470	19%	105,260
Rehabilitation Counselors	Master's degree	$33,880	20%	4,840
School and Career Counselors	Master's degree	$53,610	12%	8,700
Social and Community Service Managers	Bachelor's degree	$59,970	21%	5,510
Social and Human Service Assistants	High school diploma or equivalent	$28,850	22%	17,870
Social Workers	See "How to Become One"	$44,541	19%	24,280

Patience. Substance abuse and behavioral disorder counselors must be able to remain calm when working with all types of clients, including those who may be distressed or angry.

Speaking skills. Substance abuse and behavioral disorder counselors need to be able to communicate with clients effectively. They must express ideas and information in a way that their clients easily understand.

Pay

The median annual wage for substance abuse and behavioral disorder counselors was $38,520 in May 2012. The median wage is the wage at which half the workers in an occupation earned more than that amount and half earned less. The lowest 10 percent earned less than $25,140 and the top 10 percent earned more than $60,000.

Job Outlook

Employment of substance abuse and behavioral disorder counselors is projected to grow 31 percent from 2012 to 2022, much faster than the average for all occupations. Growth is expected as addiction and mental health counseling services are increasingly covered by insurance policies.

Federal legislation mandating individual health coverage may increase the number of health insurance customers. In addition, the law requires insurance plans to cover treatment for mental health issues in the same way as other chronic diseases. These factors will open up prevention and treatment services to more people who were previously uninsured, did not have these services covered, or found treatment to be cost-prohibitive. Mental health centers and other treatment and counseling facilities will need to hire more mental health counselors and marriage and family therapists in order to meet this increased demand.

Demand for substance abuse and behavioral disorder counselors may also increase as states seek treatment and counseling services for drug offenders rather than jail time.

In recent years, the criminal justice system has recognized that drug and other substance abuse addicts are less likely to offend again if they get treatment for their addiction. As a result, sentences often require drug offenders to attend treatment and counseling programs. In addition, these programs are also typically believed to be more cost effective than incarceration and may be increasingly used by states to deal with both budget cuts and overcrowded prisons.

Job Prospects. Job prospects should be good for substance abuse and behavioral disorder counselors, particularly for those with specialized training or education. Employers often have difficulty recruiting workers with the proper educational requirements and experience in working with addiction. In addition, many workers leave the field after a few years and need to be replaced. As result, those interested in entering this field should find favorable prospects.

O*NET

➤ Substance Abuse and Behavioral Disorder Counselors (21-1011.00)

Contacts for More Information

For more information about addiction counselors, visit

➤ Addiction Technology Transfer Center Network (www.addiction-careers.org/)

For more information about counseling and counseling specialties, visit

➤ American Counseling Association (www.counseling.org/)

For contact information for State regulating boards, visit

➤ National Board for Certified Counselors (www.nbcc.org/directory)

Computer and Information Technology

Computer and Information Research Scientists

- **2012 Median Pay** .... $102,190 per year
$49.13 per hour
- **Entry-Level Education** ... Doctoral or professional degree
- **Work Experience in a Related Occupation**.............. None
- **On-the-Job Training** .... None
- **Number of Jobs 2012** 26,700
- **Job Outlook, 2012–22** .... 15% (Faster than average)
- **Employment Change, 2012–22** 4,100

What Computer and Information Research Scientists Do

Computer and information research scientists invent and design new approaches to computing technology and find innovative uses for existing technology. They study and solve complex problems in computing for business, science, medicine, and other fields.

Duties. Computer and information research scientists typically do the following:

- Explore fundamental issues in computing and develop theories and models to address those issues
- Help scientists and engineers solve complex computing problems
- Invent new computing languages, tools, and methods to improve the way in which people work with computers

Computer scientists develop theories that lead to technological innovation.

- Develop and improve the software systems that form the basis of the modern computing experience
- Design experiments to test the operation of these software systems
- Analyze the results of their experiments
- Publish their findings in academic journals

Computer and information research scientists create and improve computer algorithms, which are sets of instructions that tell a computer what to do. Some computer tasks are very difficult and require complex algorithms. Computer and information research scientists try to simplify these algorithms to make computer systems as efficient as possible. These algorithms allow advancements in many types of technology, such as machine learning systems and cloud computing.

The work of computer and information research scientists often leads to technological advancements and efficiencies, such as better networking technology, faster computing speeds, and improved information security. In general, computer and information research scientists work on a more theoretical level than do other computer professionals.

Many people with a computer and information research science background become postsecondary teachers. In general, researchers in an academic setting focus on computer theory, although those working for businesses or scientific organizations usually focus on projects that may produce profits.

Some computer scientists work with electrical engineers, computer hardware engineers, and other specialists on multidisciplinary projects. The following are examples of types of specialties for computer and information research scientists:

Data mining. Computer and information research scientists write algorithms that are used to detect and analyze patterns in very large datasets. They improve ways to sort, manage, and display data. Computer scientists build algorithms into software packages that make the data easier for analysts to use. For example, they may create an algorithm to analyze a very large set of medical data in order to find new ways to treat diseases. They may also look for patterns in traffic data to help clear accidents faster.

Robotics. Some computer and information research scientists study how to improve robots. Robotics explores how a machine can interact with the physical world. Computer and information research scientists create the programs that control the robots. They work closely with engineers who focus on the hardware design of robots. Together, these workers test how well the robots do the tasks they were created to do–such as assemble cars and collect data on other planets.

Programming. Computer and information research scientists design new programming languages that are used to write software. The new languages make software writing more efficient by improving an existing language, such as Java, or by making a specific aspect of programming, such as image processing, easier.

Work Environment

Computer and information research scientists held about 26,700 jobs in 2012.

The industries that employed the most computer and information research scientists in 2012 were as follows:

Median Annual Wages, May 2012

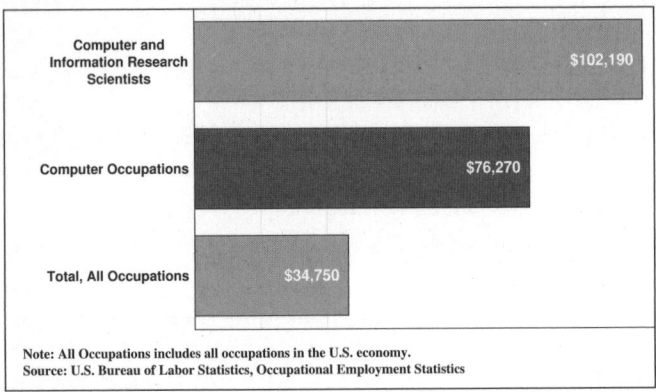

Note: All Occupations includes all occupations in the U.S. economy.
Source: U.S. Bureau of Labor Statistics, Occupational Employment Statistics

Percent Change in Employment, Projected 2012–2022

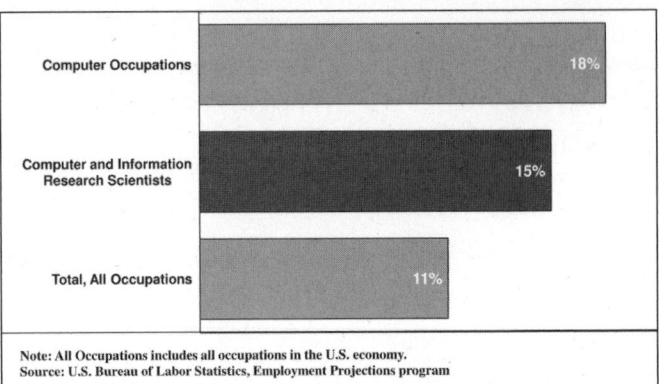

Note: All Occupations includes all occupations in the U.S. economy.
Source: U.S. Bureau of Labor Statistics, Employment Projections program

Federal government 26%
Computer systems design and related services 18
Colleges, universities, and professional schools; state,
    local, and private 13
Research and development in the physical, engineering,
    and life sciences 11
Software publishers 8

Most computer scientists employed by the federal government work for the Department of Defense.

Work Schedules. Most computer and information research scientists work full time. Those working on independent research may have flexible work schedules.

How to Become One

Most jobs for computer and information research scientists require a Ph.D. in computer science or a related field. In the federal government, a bachelor's degree may be sufficient for some jobs.

Education. Most computer and information research scientists need a Ph.D. in computer science or a related field, such as computer engineering. A Ph.D. usually requires 4 to 5 years of study after the bachelor's degree, typically in a computer-related field,

such as computer science or information systems. During their first 2 years in a Ph.D. program, students take a variety of computer science classes. They then choose a specialty and spend the remaining years doing research within that specialty.

Computer scientists who work in a specialized field may need knowledge of that field. For example, those working on biomedical applications may have to take some biology classes.

For some computer scientist positions in the federal government, a bachelor's degree in computer science is sufficient.

Advancement. Some computer scientists may become computer and information systems managers.

Important Qualities

Analytical skills. Computer and information research scientists must be organized in their thinking and analyze the results of their research to formulate conclusions.

Communication skills. Computer and information research scientists must communicate well with programmers and managers and be able to clearly explain their conclusions to people with no technical background. They often write for academic journals and similar publications.

Employment Projections Data for Computer and Information Research Scientists

Occupational title	SOC Code	Employment, 2012	Projected Employment, 2022	Change, 2012–2022	
				Percent	Numeric
Computer and information research scientists 15-1111		26,700	30,800	15	4,100

Source: U.S. Bureau of Labor Statistics, Employment Projections Program

Note: Data are rounded. Go to **Occupational Information Included in the OOH** *for a discussion of the data in this table.*

Similar Occupations   This table shows a list of occupations with job duties that are similar to those of computer and information research scientists.

Occupations	Entry-level Education	2012 Pay	Projected Job Growth	Average Annual Openings
Computer and Information Systems Managers	Bachelor's degree	$120,950	15%	9,710
Computer Hardware Engineers	Bachelor's degree	$100,920	7%	2,410
Computer Programmers	Bachelor's degree	$74,280	8%	11,810
Database Administrators	Bachelor's degree	$77,080	15%	4,030
Mechanical Engineers	Bachelor's degree	$80,580	4%	9,970
Postsecondary Teachers	See "How to Become One"	$70,380	19%	42,690
Software Developers	Bachelor's degree	$93,640	22%	35,320

Critical-thinking skills. Computer and information research scientists work on many complex problems.

Detail oriented. Computer and information research scientists must pay close attention to their work, because a small error can cause an entire project to fail.

Ingenuity. Computer and information research scientists must continually come up with innovative ways to solve problems, particularly when their ideas do not initially work as intended.

Logical thinking. Computer algorithms rely on logic. Computer and information research scientists must have a talent for reasoning.

Math skills. Computer and information research scientists must have knowledge of advanced math and other technical topics that are critical in computing.

Pay

The median annual wage for computer and information research scientists was $102,190 in May 2012. The median wage is the wage at which half the workers in an occupation earned more than that amount and half earned less. The lowest 10 percent earned less than $57,220, and the top 10 percent earned more than $151,900.

Job Outlook

Employment of computer and information research scientists is projected to grow 15 percent from 2012 to 2022, faster than the average for all occupations. Computer scientists are tasked with advancing all fields of computing. As demand for new and better technology grows, demand for computer scientists will grow as well.

Rapid growth in data collection by businesses may lead to an increased need for data mining services. Computer scientists will be needed to write algorithms that help businesses sort, manage, and display very large amounts of data. A growing emphasis on cybersecurity also should lead to new jobs, because computer scientists will be needed to find innovative ways to prevent cyberattacks or to track hackers.

In addition, job growth will be driven by advances in robotics, as more advanced robots are developed. Robots are already widely used in manufacturing, and their use is expected to expand in distribution centers and within the military. Computer scientists design the "brain system" of a robot and ensure that the robot does what it is supposed to do. In addition, an increase in software demand may increase the need for computer scientists who create new programming languages to make software writing more efficient.

Job Prospects. Computer and information research scientists are likely to enjoy excellent job prospects. There are a limited number of Ph.D. graduates each year. As a result, many companies report difficulties finding these highly skilled workers.

For applicants seeking employment in a specialized field, such as finance or biology, knowledge of that field, along with a computer science degree, may be helpful in getting a job.

O*NET

➤ Computer and Information Research Scientists (15-1111.00)

Contacts for More Information

For more information about computer and information research scientists, visit

➤ Association for Computing Machinery (www.acm.org)
➤ IEEE (www.computer.org)

For information about opportunities for women pursing information technology careers, visit

➤ National Center for Women and Information Technology (www.ncwit.org)

Computer Network Architects

- **2012 Median Pay** .... $91,000 per year
  $43.75 per hour
- **Entry-Level Education** ....Bachelor's degree
- **Work Experience in a Related Occupation** ... 5 years or more
- **On-the-Job Training** .... None
- **Number of Jobs 2012** 143,400
- **Job Outlook, 2012–22** .... 15% (Faster than average)
- **Employment Change, 2012–22** 20,900

What Computer Network Architects Do

Computer network architects design and build data communication networks, including local area networks (LANs), wide area networks (WANs), and intranets. These networks range from a small connection between two offices to a multinational series of globally distributed communications systems. Network architects must have extensive knowledge of an organization's business plan to design a network that can help the organization achieve its goals.

Duties. Computer network architects typically do the following:

- Create a plan and layout for a data communication network
- Present the plan to management and explain why it is in the organization's best interest to pursue it
- Consider information security when designing a network
- Decide what hardware, such as routers or adaptors, and software, such as network drivers, are needed to support the network
- Determine how cables will be laid out in the building and where other hardware will go
- Research new technology to determine what would best support their organization in the future

Computer network architects, or *network engineers*, also create models to predict future network needs. They look at current data traffic and estimate how growth will affect the network. They keep up to date on new hardware and software technology and test how it can improve network performance. Network architects also have to keep security in mind. When network vulnerabilities arise, they implement security patches or other countermeasures.

Architects often work with their organization's chief technology officer (CTO) to predict where the organization will most need new networks. They spend most of their time planning these new

Network architects design LANs, WANs, and intranets.

Median Annual Wages, May 2012

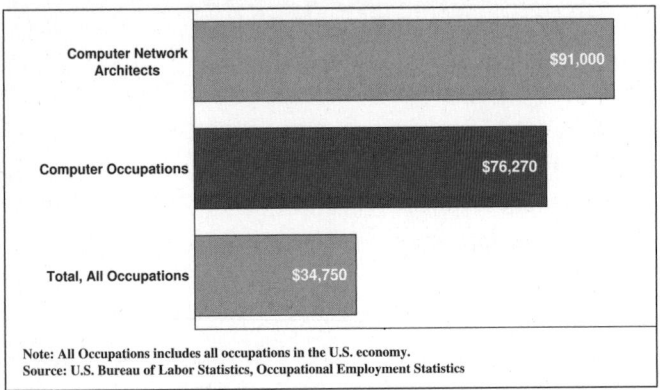

Note: All Occupations includes all occupations in the U.S. economy.
Source: U.S. Bureau of Labor Statistics, Occupational Employment Statistics

Percent Change in Employment, Projected 2012–2022

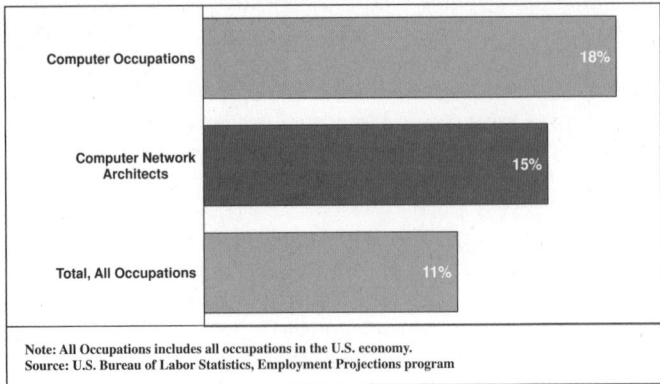

Note: All Occupations includes all occupations in the U.S. economy.
Source: U.S. Bureau of Labor Statistics, Employment Projections program

networks. Some network architects work in the field, supervising engineers and workers who build the networks a network architect has designed. Network architects are often experienced staff and have 5 to 10 years of experience working in network administration or with other information technology (IT) systems.

Work Environment

Computer network architects held about 143,400 jobs in 2012. The industries that employed the most computer network architects in 2012 were as follows:

Computer systems design and related services 27%
Telecommunications 12
Finance and insurance 9
Management of companies and enterprises 6

Work Schedules. Most computer network architects work full time. More than a quarter worked more than 40 hours per week in 2012.

How to Become One

Most computer network architects have a bachelor's degree in a computer-related field. They usually need experience in a related occupation also.

Education. Computer network architects usually need at least a bachelor's degree in computer science, information systems, engineering, or a related field. Employers of network architects sometimes prefer applicants to have a Master's of Business Administration (MBA) in information systems. MBA programs generally require 2 years of study beyond the undergraduate level and include both business and computer-related courses.

Employment Projections Data for Computer Network Architects

Occupational title	SOC Code	Employment, 2012	Projected Employment, 2022	Change, 2012–2022	
				Percent	Numeric
Computer network architects	15-1143	143,400	164,300	15	20,900

Source: U.S. Bureau of Labor Statistics, Employment Projections Program

Note: Data are rounded. Go to **Occupational Information Included in the OOH** *for a discussion of the data in this table.*

Similar Occupations   This table shows a list of occupations with job duties that are similar to those of computer network architects.

Occupations	Entry-level Education	2012 Pay	Projected Job Growth	Average Annual Openings
Computer and Information Research Scientists	Doctoral or professional degree	$102,190	15%	830
Computer and Information Systems Managers	Bachelor's degree	$120,950	15%	9,710
Computer Hardware Engineers	Bachelor's degree	$100,920	7%	2,410
Computer Programmers	Bachelor's degree	$74,280	8%	11,810
Computer Support Specialists	See "How to Become One"	$49,488	17%	23,650
Computer Systems Analysts	Bachelor's degree	$79,680	25%	20,960
Database Administrators	Bachelor's degree	$77,080	15%	4,030
Information Security Analysts	Bachelor's degree	$86,170	36%	3,920
Network and Computer Systems Administrators	Bachelor's degree	$72,560	12%	10,050
Software Developers	Bachelor's degree	$93,640	22%	35,320

Work Experience in a Related Occupation. Network architects generally need to have previous experience in a related occupation. They usually have at least 5 to 10 years of experience working with information technology (IT) systems. They often have experience as a network administrator but also may come from other computer-related occupations such as database administrator or computer systems analyst.

Advancement. Some network architects advance to become computer and information systems managers.

Important Qualities

Analytical skills. Computer network architects have to examine data networks and decide how to best connect the networks based on the needs and resources of the organization.

Detail oriented. Computer network architects create comprehensive plans of the networks they are creating with precise information describing how the network parts will work together.

Interpersonal skills. These workers must be able to work with different types of employees to accomplish their goals.

Leadership skills. Many computer network architects direct teams of engineers who build the networks they have designed.

Organizational skills. Computer network architects who work for large firms must coordinate many different types of communication networks and make sure they work well together.

Pay

The median annual wage for computer network architects was $91,000 in May 2012. The median wage is the wage at which half the workers in an occupation earned more than that amount and half earned less. The lowest 10 percent earned less than $52,580, and the top 10 percent earned more than $141,590.

Job Outlook

Employment of computer network architects is projected to grow 15 percent from 2012 to 2022, faster than the average for all occupations.

Demand for computer network architects will increase as firms continue to expand their use of wireless and mobile networks. Designing and building these new networks, as well as upgrading existing ones will create opportunities for computer network architects. The expansion of healthcare information technology will also contribute to employment growth.

Adoption of cloud computing, which allows users to access storage, software, and other computer services over the Internet, is likely to cause a decrease in the demand for computer network architects. Organizations will no longer have to design and build networks in-house; instead, firms that provide cloud services will do this. However, because architects at cloud providers can work on more than one organization's network, these providers will not have to employ as many architects as individual organizations do for the same amount of work.

Job Prospects. Prospects for computer network architects should be favorable, as many companies report difficulty finding network architects because of the considerable amount of education and work experience required for these highly skilled positions.

O*NET

➤ Computer Network Architects (15-1143.00)
➤ Telecommunications Engineering Specialists (15-1143.01)

Contacts for More Information

For more information about computer careers, visit
➤ Association for Computing Machinery (www.acm.org)
➤ IEEE (www.computer.org)

➤ Computing Research Association (www.cra.org)
➤ TechAmerica (www.techamerica.org)

For information about opportunities for women pursuing information technology careers, visit
➤ National Center for Women and Information Technology (www.ncwit.org)

Computer Programmers

- **2012 Median Pay** .... $74,280 per year
  $35.71 per hour
- **Entry-Level Education** ....Bachelor's degree
- **Work Experience in a Related Occupation**............... None
- **On-the-Job Training** .... None
- **Number of Jobs 2012** 343,700
- **Job Outlook, 2012–22** .... 8% (As fast as average)
- **Employment Change, 2012–22** 28,400

What Computer Programmers Do

Computer programmers write code to create software programs. They turn the program designs created by software developers and engineers into instructions that a computer can follow. Programmers must debug the programs–that is, test them to ensure that they produce the expected results. If a program does not work correctly, they check the code for mistakes and fix them.

Duties. Computer programmers typically do the following:

- Write programs in a variety of computer languages, such as C++ and Java
- Update and expand existing programs
- Debug programs by testing for and fixing errors
- Build and use computer-assisted software engineering (CASE) tools to automate the writing of some code

Programmers write instructions that a computer can follow, allowing it to perform specific tasks.

Median Annual Wages, May 2012

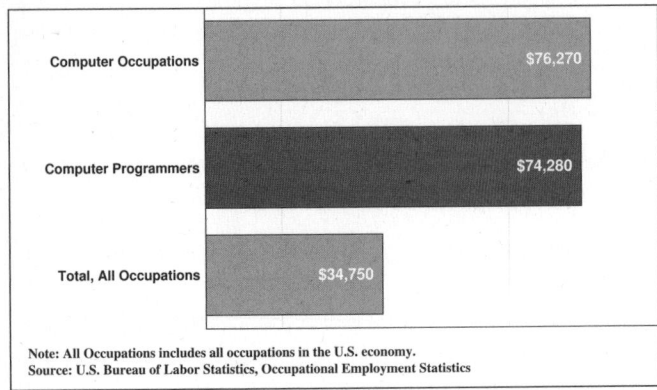

Note: All Occupations includes all occupations in the U.S. economy.
Source: U.S. Bureau of Labor Statistics, Occupational Employment Statistics

Percent Change in Employment, Projected 2012–2022

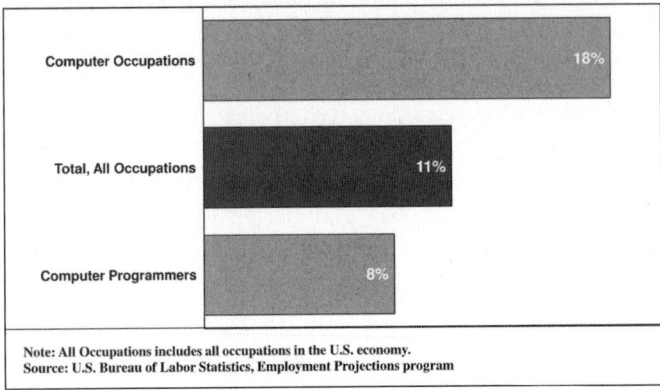

Note: All Occupations includes all occupations in the U.S. economy.
Source: U.S. Bureau of Labor Statistics, Employment Projections program

- Use code libraries, which are collections of independent lines of code, to simplify the writing

Programmers work closely with software developers, and in some businesses, their duties overlap. When this happens, programmers can do work that is typical of developers, such as designing the program. This entails initially planning the software, creating models and flowcharts detailing how the code is to be written, writing and debugging code, and designing an application or systems interface.

Some programs are relatively simple and usually take a few days to write, such as creating mobile applications for cell phones. Other programs, like computer operating systems, are more complex and can take a year or more to complete.

Software-as-a-service (SaaS), which consists of applications provided through the Internet, is a growing field. Although programmers typically need to rewrite their programs to work on different systems platforms such as Windows or OS X, applications created using SaaS work on all platforms. That is why programmers writing for software-as-a-service applications may not have to update as much code as other programmers and can instead spend more time writing new programs.

Work Environment

Computer programmers held about 343,700 jobs in 2012. They usually work in offices, most commonly in the computer systems design and related services industry.

Programmers normally work alone, but sometimes work with other computer specialists on large projects. Because writing code can be done anywhere, many programmers telecommute.

Work Schedules. Most computer programmers work full time.

How to Become One

Most computer programmers have a bachelor's degree in computer science or a related subject; however, some employers hire workers with an associate's degree. Most programmers specialize in a few programming languages.

Education. Most computer programmers have a bachelor's degree; however, some employers hire workers who have an associate's degree. Most programmers get a degree in computer science or a related subject. Programmers who work in specific fields, such as healthcare or accounting, may take classes in that field to supplement their degree in computer programming. In addition, employers value experience, which many students gain through internships.

Most programmers learn only a few computer languages while in school. However, a computer science degree gives students the skills needed to learn new computer languages easily. During their classes, students receive hands-on experience writing code, debugging programs, and doing many other tasks that they will perform on the job.

To keep up with changing technology, computer programmers may take continuing education and professional development seminars to learn new programming languages or about upgrades to programming languages they already know.

Licenses, Certifications, and Registrations. Programmers can become certified in specific programming languages or for vendor-specific programming products. Some companies may require their computer programmers to be certified in the products they use.

Other Experience. Many students gain experience in computer programming by completing an internship at a software company while in college.

Advancement. Programmers who have general business experience may become computer systems analysts. With experience, some programmers may become software developers. They may also be promoted to managerial positions. For more information, see the profiles on computer systems analysts, software developers, and computer and information systems managers.

Important Qualities

Analytical skills. Computer programmers must understand complex instructions in order to create computer code.

Concentration. Programmers must be able to work at a computer, writing lines of code for long periods of time.

Employment Projections Data for Computer Programmers

Occupational title	SOC Code	Employment, 2012	Projected Employment, 2022	Change, 2012–2022	
				Percent	Numeric
Computer programmers	15-1131	343,700	372,100	8	28,400

Source: U.S. Bureau of Labor Statistics, Employment Projections Program

Note: Data are rounded. Go to **Occupational Information Included in the OOH** *for a discussion of the data in this table.*

Similar Occupations This table shows a list of occupations with job duties that are similar to those of computer programmers.

Occupations	Entry-level Education	2012 Pay	Projected Job Growth	Average Annual Openings
Computer and Information Research Scientists	Doctoral or professional degree	$102,190	15%	830
Computer and Information Systems Managers	Bachelor's degree	$120,950	15%	9,710
Computer Hardware Engineers	Bachelor's degree	$100,920	7%	2,410
Computer Network Architects	Bachelor's degree	$91,000	15%	4,350
Computer Support Specialists	See "How to Become One"	$49,488	17%	23,650
Computer Systems Analysts	Bachelor's degree	$79,680	25%	20,960
Database Administrators	Bachelor's degree	$77,080	15%	4,030
Information Security Analysts	Bachelor's degree	$86,170	36%	3,920
Network and Computer Systems Administrators	Bachelor's degree	$72,560	12%	10,050
Software Developers	Bachelor's degree	$93,640	22%	35,320
Web Developers	Associate's degree	$62,500	20%	5,070

Detail oriented. Computer programmers must closely examine the code they write because a small mistake can affect the entire computer program.

Troubleshooting skills. An important part of a programmer's job is to check the code for errors and fix any they find.

Pay

The median annual wage for computer programmers was $74,280 in May 2012. The median wage is the wage at which half the workers in an occupation earned more than that amount and half earned less. The lowest 10 percent earned less than $42,850, and the top 10 percent earned more than $117,890.

Job Outlook

Employment of computer programmers is projected to grow 8 percent from 2012 to 2022, about as fast as the average for all occupations. Computer programming can be done from anywhere in the world, so companies sometimes hire programmers in countries where wages are lower. This ongoing trend is projected to limit growth for computer programmers in the United States. However, some companies are bringing programming jobs back to the United States. In addition, companies with small information technology operations may outsource computer programming to low-cost areas within the United States.

Many computer programmers work in computer system design and related services, an industry which is expected to grow as a result of an increasing demand for new computer software. This includes software offered over the Internet, which should lower costs for firms and allow for more customization for users. In addition, new applications will have to be developed for mobile technology and the healthcare industry. An increase in computer systems that are built into electronics and other non-computer products should result in some job growth for computer programmers and software developers.

Job Prospects. Job prospects will be best for programmers who have a bachelor's degree or higher and knowledge of a variety of programming languages. Keeping up to date with the newest programming tools will also improve job prospects.

O*NET

➤ Computer Programmers (15-1131.00)

Contacts for More Information

For more information about computer programmers, visit
➤ Association for Computing Machinery (www.acm.org/)
➤ IEEE (www.computer.org/)
➤ TechAmerica (www.techamerica.org)

For information about opportunities for women pursuing information technology careers, visit
➤ National Center for Women and Information Technology (www.ncwit.org/)

Computer Support Specialists

- **2012 Median Pay** .... $48,900 per year $23.51 per hour
- **Entry-Level Education** ....See "How to Become One"
- **Work Experience in a Related Occupation**............... None
- **On-the-Job Training** ....See "How to Become One"
- **Number of Jobs 2012** 722,400
- **Job Outlook, 2012–22** .... 17% (Faster than average)
- **Employment Change, 2012–22** 123,000

What Computer Support Specialists Do

Computer support specialists provide help and advice to people and organizations using computer software or equipment. Some, called computer network support specialists, support information technology (IT) employees within their organization. Others, called computer user support specialists, assist non-IT users who are having computer problems.

Duties. *Computer network support specialists* typically do the following:

- Test and evaluate existing network systems
- Perform regular maintenance to ensure that networks operate correctly
- Troubleshoot local area networks (LANs), wide area networks (WANs), and Internet systems

Computer network support specialists, also called technical support specialists, usually work in their organization's IT department. They help IT staff analyze, troubleshoot, and evaluate computer network problems. They play an important role in the daily upkeep of their organization's networks by finding solutions to problems as they occur. Solving an IT problem in a timely manner is important because organizations depend on their computer systems. Technical support specialists may provide assistance to the organization's computer users through phone, email, or in-person visits. They often work under network and computer systems administrators, who handle more complex tasks.

Computer user support specialists typically do the following:

- Pay attention to customers when they describe their computer problems
- Ask customers questions to properly diagnose the problem
- Walk customers through the recommended problem-solving steps
- Set up or repair computer equipment and related devices
- Train users to work with new computer hardware or software, such as printers, word-processing software, and email
- Assist users in installing software
- Provide others in the organization with information about what gives customers the most trouble and about other concerns customers have

Computer user support specialists, also called help-desk technicians, usually provide technical help to non-IT computer users. They respond to phone and email requests for help. Sometimes they make site visits so that they can solve a problem in person.

Help-desk technicians may solve a range of problems that vary with the industry and the particular firm. Some technicians work for large software companies or for support service firms and must give instructions to business customers on how to use complex programs. Sometimes they work with other technicians to resolve a problem.

Others work in call centers, answering simpler questions from consumers. Some technicians work for organizations and help non-IT workers with their computer problems.

Work Environment

Computer support specialists held about 722,400 jobs in 2012. They work in many different industries, including information technology (IT), education, finance, healthcare, and telecommunication. Many help-desk technicians work for outside support service firms on a contract basis and provide help to a range of businesses and consumers.

Computer support specialists work for a variety of industries.

The industries that employed the most computer network support specialists in 2012 were as follows:

Computer systems design and related services 20%
Telecommunications 10
Finance and insurance 8
Educational services; state, local, and private 8

The industries that employed the most computer user support specialists in 2012 were as follows:

Computer systems design and related services 19%
Educational services; state, local, and private 14
Information 11
Wholesale trade 8

Faster computer networks are making it possible for some support specialists, particularly help-desk technicians, to work from a home office. However, a few specialized help-desk technicians may have to travel to a client's location to solve a problem.

Median Annual Wages, May 2012

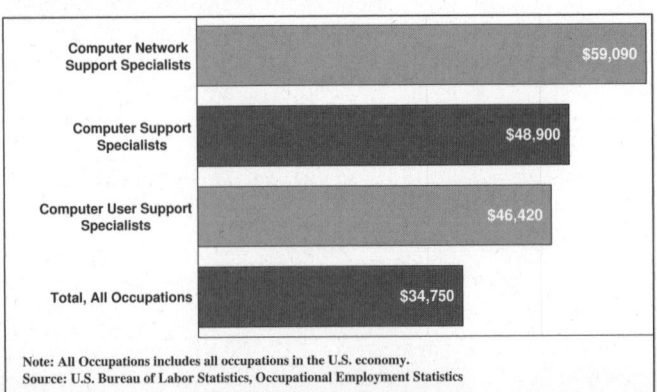

Note: All Occupations includes all occupations in the U.S. economy.
Source: U.S. Bureau of Labor Statistics, Occupational Employment Statistics

Percent Change in Employment, Projected 2012–2022

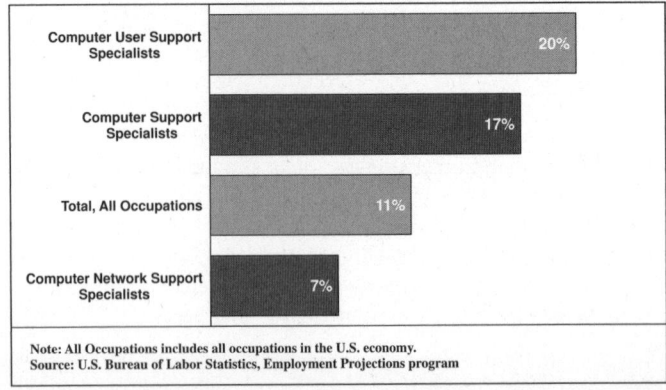

Note: All Occupations includes all occupations in the U.S. economy.
Source: U.S. Bureau of Labor Statistics, Employment Projections program

Employment Projections Data for Computer Support Specialists

Occupational title	SOC Code	Employment, 2012	Projected Employment, 2022	Change, 2012–2022	
				Percent	Numeric
Computer support specialists	—	722,400	845,300	17	123,000
Computer user support specialists	15-1151	547,700	658,500	20	110,800
Computer network support specialists	15-1152	174,600	186,800	7	12,100

Source: U.S. Bureau of Labor Statistics, Employment Projections Program

Note: Data are rounded. Go to Occupational Information Included in the OOH *for a discussion of the data in this table.*

Work Schedules. Most computer support specialists have full-time work schedules; however, many do not work typical 9-to-5 jobs. Because computer support is important for businesses, support specialists must be available 24 hours a day. As a result, many support specialists must work nights or weekends.

How to Become One

Because of the wide range of skills used in different computer support jobs, there are many paths into the occupation. A bachelor's degree is required for some computer support specialist positions, but an associate's degree or postsecondary classes may be enough for others.

Education. Education requirements for computer support specialists vary. Computer user support specialist jobs require some computer knowledge, but not necessarily a postsecondary degree. Applicants who have taken some computer-related classes are often qualified. For computer network support specialists, many employers accept applicants with an associate's degree, although some prefer applicants to have a bachelor's degree.

Large software companies that provide support to business users who buy their products or services often require a bachelor's degree. More technical positions are likely to require a degree in a field such as computer science, engineering, or information science, but for others, the applicant's field of study is less important.

To keep up with changes in technology, many computer support specialists continue their education throughout their careers.

Training. When they start out, computer user support specialists often work on simple problems. Over time, they learn more about the software or equipment they support and advance to positions that handle complex questions. Advancement can take anywhere

from several months to a year, depending on how complicated a position is and how fast the specialist learns.

Advancement. Many of these workers advance to other information technology positions, such as network and computer systems administrators and software developers. Some become managers in the computer support services department. Some organizations provide paths for support specialists to move into other parts of the organization, such as sales. For more information, see the profiles on network and computer systems administrators and software developers.

Important Qualities

Customer service skills. Computer support specialists must be patient and sympathetic. They must often help people who are frustrated with the software or hardware they are trying to use.

Listening skills. Support workers must be able to understand the problem that their customer is describing and know when to ask questions to clarify the situation.

Problem-solving skills. Support workers must identify both simple and complex computer problems, analyze them, and solve them.

Speaking skills. Support workers must describe the solution to a computer problem in a way that a nontechnical person can understand.

Writing skills. Strong writing skills are useful for preparing instructions and email responses for employees and customers, as well as real-time Web chat interactions.

Pay

The median annual wage for computer network support specialists was $59,090 in May 2012. The median wage is the wage at which half the workers in an occupation earned more than the

Similar Occupations   This table shows a list of occupations with job duties that are similar to those of computer support specialists.

Occupations	Entry-level Education	2012 Pay	Projected Job Growth	Average Annual Openings
Computer and Information Systems Managers	Bachelor's degree	$120,950	15%	9,710
Computer Network Architects	Bachelor's degree	$91,000	15%	4,350
Computer Programmers	Bachelor's degree	$74,280	8%	11,810
Computer Systems Analysts	Bachelor's degree	$79,680	25%	20,960
Customer Service Representatives	High school diploma or equivalent	$30,580	13%	94,160
Database Administrators	Bachelor's degree	$77,080	15%	4,030
Information Security Analysts	Bachelor's degree	$86,170	36%	3,920
Network and Computer Systems Administrators	Bachelor's degree	$72,560	12%	10,050
Software Developers	Bachelor's degree	$93,640	22%	35,320
Web Developers	Associate's degree	$62,500	20%	5,070

amount and half earned less. The lowest 10 percent earned less than $34,930, and the top 10 percent earned more than $96,850.

In May 2012, the median annual wages for computer network support specialists in the top four industries in which these specialists worked were as follows:

Telecommunications	$64,780
Finance and insurance	62,750
Computer systems design and related services	60,050
Educational services; state, local, and private	51,920

The median annual wage for computer user support specialists was $46,420 in May 2012. The lowest 10 percent earned less than $27,620, and the top 10 percent earned more than $77,430.

In May 2012, median annual wages for computer user support specialists in the top four industries in which these specialists worked were as follows:

Wholesale trade	$49,150
Information	47,950
Computer systems design and related services	46,690
Educational services; state, local, and private	43,620

Job Outlook

Employment of computer support specialists is projected to grow 17 percent from 2012 to 2022, faster than the average for all occupations. More support services will be needed as organizations upgrade their computer equipment and software. Computer support staff will be needed to respond to the installation and repair requirements of increasingly complex computer equipment and software. However, a rise in cloud computing could increase the productivity of computer support specialists, slowing their growth at many firms. Growth will be highest at firms that provide cloud-computing technology. Employment of support specialists in computer systems design and related firms is projected to grow 49 percent from 2012 to 2022.

Employment growth also should be strong in healthcare industries. This field is expected to greatly increase its use of information technology (IT), and support services will be crucial to keep everything running properly.

Some lower level tech support jobs, commonly found in call centers, may be sent to countries that have lower wage rates. However, a recent trend to move jobs to lower cost regions of the United States may offset some loss of jobs to other countries.

Job Prospects. Job prospects should be favorable. There are usually clear advancement possibilities for computer support specialists, creating new job openings. Applicants with a bachelor's degree and a strong technical background should have the best job opportunities.

O*NET

➤ Computer User Support Specialists (15-1151.00)
➤ Computer Network Support Specialists (15-1152.00)

Contacts for More Information

For more information about computer support specialists, visit
➤ Technology Services Industry Association (www.tsia.com/)
➤ Help Desk Institute (HDI) (www.thinkhdi.com/)
➤ Association of Support Professionals (http://asponline.com/)
  For more information about computer careers, visit
➤ Association for Computing Machinery (www.acm.org/)
➤ IEEE (www.computer.org/)
➤ Computing Research Association (www.cra.org/)
  For information about opportunities for women pursuing information technology careers, visit
➤ National Center for Women and Information Technology (www. ncwit.org/)

Computer Systems Analysts

- **2012 Median Pay** .... $79,680 per year
  $38.31 per hour
- **Entry-Level Education** .... Bachelor's degree
- **Work Experience in a Related Occupation** .... None
- **On-the-Job Training** .... None
- **Number of Jobs 2012** 520,600
- **Job Outlook, 2012–22** .... 25% (Much faster than average)
- **Employment Change, 2012–22** 127,700

What Computer Systems Analysts Do

Computer systems analysts study an organization's current computer systems and procedures and design information systems solutions to help the organization operate more efficiently and effectively. They bring business and information technology (IT) together by understanding the needs and limitations of both.

Duties. Computer systems analysts typically do the following:

- Consult with managers to determine the role of the IT system in an organization
- Research emerging technologies to decide if installing them can increase the organization's efficiency and effectiveness
- Prepare an analysis of costs and benefits so that management can decide if information systems and computing infrastructure upgrades are financially worthwhile
- Devise ways to add new functionality to existing computer systems
- Design and develop new systems by choosing and configuring hardware and software
- Oversee the installation and configuration of new systems to customize them for the organization
- Conduct testing to ensure that the systems work as expected
- Train the system's end users and write instruction manuals

Computer systems analysts use a variety of techniques to design computer systems such as data-modeling, which create rules for the computer to follow when presenting data, thereby allowing analysts to make faster decisions. Analysts conduct in-depth tests and analyze information and trends in the data to increase a system's performance and efficiency.

Computer systems analysts use information technology to help organizations operate more effectively.

Median Annual Wages, May 2012

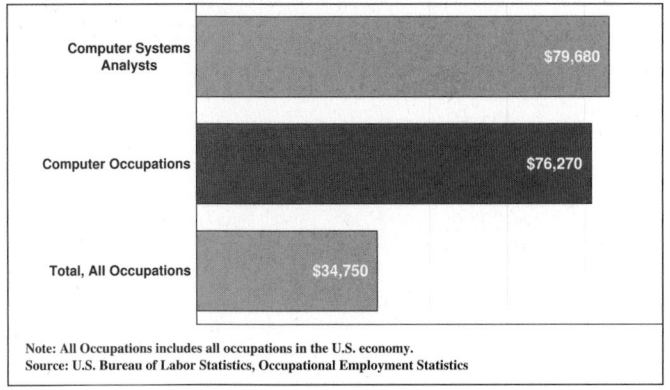

Note: All Occupations includes all occupations in the U.S. economy.
Source: U.S. Bureau of Labor Statistics, Occupational Employment Statistics

Percent Change in Employment, Projected 2012–2022

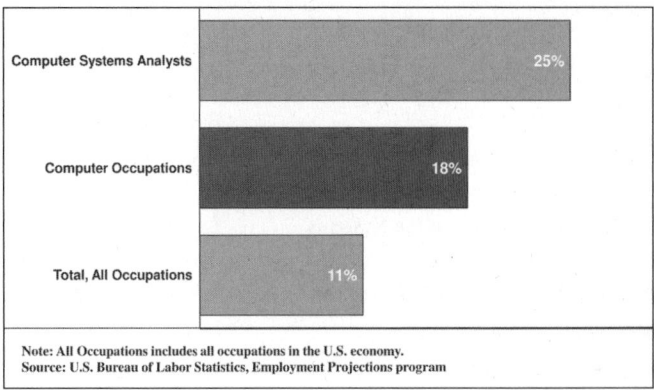

Note: All Occupations includes all occupations in the U.S. economy.
Source: U.S. Bureau of Labor Statistics, Employment Projections program

Analysts calculate requirements for how much memory and speed the computer system needs. They prepare flowcharts or other kinds of diagrams for programmers or engineers to use when building the system. Analysts also work with these people to solve problems that arise after the initial system is set up. Most analysts do some programming in the course of their work.

Most computer systems analysts specialize in certain types of computer systems that are specific to the organization they work with. For example, an analyst might work predominantly with financial computer systems or engineering systems.

Because systems analysts work closely with an organization's business leaders, they help the IT team understand how its computer systems can best serve the organization.

In some cases, analysts who supervise the initial installation or upgrade of IT systems from start to finish may be called IT project managers. They monitor a project's progress to ensure that deadlines, standards, and cost targets are met. IT project managers who plan and direct an organization's IT department or IT policies are included in the profile on computer and information systems managers.

Many computer systems analysts are general-purpose analysts who develop new systems or fine-tune existing ones; however, there are some specialized systems analysts. The following are examples of types of computer systems analysts:

Systems designers or *systems architects* specialize in helping organizations choose a specific type of hardware and software system. They translate the long-term business goals of an organization into technical solutions. Analysts develop a plan for the computer systems that will be able to reach those goals. They work with management to ensure that systems and the IT infrastructure are set up to best serve the organization's mission.

Software quality assurance (QA) analysts do in-depth testing of the systems they design. They run tests and diagnose problems in order to make sure that critical requirements are met. QA analysts write reports to management recommending ways to improve the system.

Programmer analysts design and update their system's software and create applications tailored to their organization's needs. They do more coding and debugging than other types of analysts, although they still work extensively with management and business analysts to determine what business needs the applications are meant to address. Other occupations that do programming are computer programmers and software developers.

Work Environment

Computer systems analysts held about 520,600 jobs in 2012.

Systems analysts work in many different industries.

The industries that employed the most systems analysts in 2012 were as follows:

Computer systems design and related services 27%
Finance and insurance 14
Management of companies and enterprises 8
Information 7
State and local government, excluding education
    and hospitals 7

Computer systems analysts can work directly for an organization or as consultants. Consultants usually work for an information technology firm. The projects that computer systems analysts work on usually require them to collaborate and coordinate with others.

Although technological advances have made telecommuting more common, many consultants still need to travel to see their clients. The length of an assignment can vary with the complexity of the job.

Work Schedules. Most systems analysts work full time. About a quarter worked more than 40 hours per week in 2012.

How to Become One

A bachelor's degree in a computer or information science field is common, although not always a requirement. Some firms hire analysts with business or liberal arts degrees who have skills in information technology or computer programming.

Employment Projections Data for Computer Systems Analysts

Occupational title	SOC Code	Employment, 2012	Projected Employment, 2022	Change, 2012–2022	
				Percent	Numeric
Computer systems analysts	15-1121	520,600	648,400	25	127,700

Source: U.S. Bureau of Labor Statistics, Employment Projections Program

Note: Data are rounded. Go to **Occupational Information Included in the OOH** *for a discussion of the data in this table.*

Similar Occupations   This table shows a list of occupations with job duties that are similar to those of computer systems analysts.

Occupations	Entry-level Education	2012 Pay	Projected Job Growth	Average Annual Openings
Actuaries	Bachelor's degree	$93,680	26%	1,320
Computer and Information Research Scientists	Doctoral or professional degree	$102,190	15%	830
Computer and Information Systems Managers	Bachelor's degree	$120,950	15%	9,710
Computer Network Architects	Bachelor's degree	$91,000	15%	4,350
Computer Programmers	Bachelor's degree	$74,280	8%	11,810
Database Administrators	Bachelor's degree	$77,080	15%	4,030
Information Security Analysts	Bachelor's degree	$86,170	36%	3,920
Management Analysts	Bachelor's degree	$78,600	19%	24,520
Network and Computer Systems Administrators	Bachelor's degree	$72,560	12%	10,050
Operations Research Analysts	Bachelor's degree	$72,100	27%	3,600
Software Developers	Bachelor's degree	$93,640	22%	35,320

Education. Most computer systems analysts have a bachelor's degree in a computer-related field. Because these analysts also are heavily involved in the business side of a company, it may be helpful to take business courses or major in management information systems.

Some employers prefer applicants who have a master of business administration (MBA) with a concentration in information systems. For more technically complex jobs, a master's degree in computer science may be more appropriate.

Although many computer systems analysts have technical degrees, such a degree is not always a requirement. Many analysts have liberal arts degrees and have gained programming or technical expertise elsewhere.

Many systems analysts continue to take classes throughout their careers so that they can learn about new and innovative technologies and keep their skills competitive. Technological advances come so rapidly in the computer field that continual study is necessary to remain competitive.

Systems analysts must understand the business field they are working in. For example, a hospital may want an analyst with a background or coursework in health management, and an analyst working for a bank may need to understand finance.

Advancement. With experience, systems analysts can advance to project manager and lead a team of analysts. Some can eventually become information technology (IT) directors or chief technology officers. For more information, see the profile on computer and information systems managers.

Important Qualities

Analytical skills. Analysts must interpret complex information from various sources and be able to decide the best way to move forward on a project. They must also be able to figure out how changes may affect the project.

Communication skills. Analysts work as a go-between with management and the IT department and must be able to explain complex issues in a way that both will understand.

Creativity. Because analysts are tasked with finding innovative solutions to computer problems, an ability to "think outside the box" is important.

Pay

The median annual wage for computer systems analysts was $79,680 in May 2012. The median wage is the wage at which half the workers in an occupation earned more than that amount and half earned less. The lowest 10 percent earned less than $49,950, and the top 10 percent earned more than $122,090.

Job Outlook

Employment of computer systems analysts is projected to grow 25 percent from 2012 to 2022, much faster than the average for all occupations.

As organizations across the economy increase their reliance on information technology (IT), analysts will be hired to design and install new computer systems. Growth in cloud-computing, wireless, and mobile networks will create a need for new systems that work well with these networks.

Additional job growth is expected in healthcare fields. A large increase is anticipated in electronic medical records, e-prescribing, and other forms of healthcare IT, and analysts will be needed to design computer systems to accommodate the increase.

Employment growth is expected in IT consulting firms, where many systems analysts work. These analysts, who will be hired by organizations to design computer systems in a variety of industries, will move on to another assignment when they are finished. As more small and medium-size firms demand advanced systems, the practice of analysts moving between businesses is expected to increase. Employment of systems analysts is projected to grow 35 percent in the computer systems design and related services industry from 2012 to 2022.

Job Prospects. Job applicants with a background in business may have better prospects because jobs for computer systems analysts often require knowledge of an organization's business needs. An understanding of the specific field an analyst is working in is also helpful. For example, a hospital may desire an analyst with a background or coursework in health management.

O*NET

➤ Computer Systems Analysts (15-1121.00)
➤ Informatics Nurse Specialists (15-1121.01)

Contacts for More Information

For more information about computer systems analysts, visit

➤ Association for Computing Machinery (www.acm.org/)
➤ IEEE (www.computer.org/)
➤ Computing Research Association (www.cra.org/)

For information about opportunities for women pursuing information technology careers, visit

➤ National Center for Women and Information Technology (www.ncwit.org/)

Database Administrators

- **2012 Median Pay** .... $77,080 per year
  $37.06 per hour
- **Entry-Level Education** ....Bachelor's degree
- **Work Experience in a Related Occupation**........ Less than 5 years
- **On-the-Job Training** .... None
- **Number of Jobs 2012** 118,700
- **Job Outlook, 2012–22**............. 15% (Faster than average)
- **Employment Change, 2012–22** 17,900

What Database Administrators Do

Database administrators use specialized software to store and organize data, such as financial information and customer shipping records. They make sure that data are available to users and are secure from unauthorized access.

Duties. Database administrators typically do the following:

- Identify user needs to create and administer databases
- Ensure that the database operates efficiently and without error
- Make and test modifications to the database structure when needed
- Maintain the database and update permissions
- Merge old databases into new ones
- Backup and restore data to prevent data loss
- Ensure that organizational data is secure

Database administrators usually require a bachelor's degree in a computer- or information-related subject.

Database administrators, often called DBAs, make sure that data analysts can easily use the database to find the information they need and that the system performs as it should. DBAs sometimes work with an organization's management to understand the company's data needs and to plan the goals of the database. Database administrators are responsible for backing up systems to prevent data loss in case of a power outage or other disaster. They also ensure the integrity of the database, guaranteeing that the data stored in it come from reliable sources.

Some DBAs oversee the development of new databases. They have to determine what the needs of the database are and who will be using it. Database administrators often plan security measures, making sure that data are secure from unauthorized access. Many databases contain personal or financial information, making security important.

Many database administrators are general-purpose DBAs and have all these duties. However, some DBAs specialize in certain tasks that vary with the organization and its needs. Two common specialties are as follows:

System DBAs are responsible for the physical and technical aspects of a database, such as installing upgrades and patches to fix program bugs. They typically have a background in system architecture and ensure that the firm's database management systems work properly.

Application DBAs support a database that has been designed for a specific application or a set of applications, such as customer service software. Using complex programming languages, they may write or debug programs and must be able to manage the aspects of the applications that work with the database. They also do all the tasks of a general DBA, but only for their particular application.

Work Environment

Database administrators (DBAs) held about 118,700 jobs in 2012. They were employed in many types of industries. The largest number work for computer systems design and related services firms, such as Internet service providers and data-processing firms. Other DBAs are employed by firms with large databases, such as insurance companies and banks, both of which keep track of vast amounts of personal and financial data for their clients. Some DBAs administer databases for retail companies that keep track of their buyers' credit card and shipping information; others work for healthcare firms and manage patients' medical records.

The industries that employed the most database administrators in 2012 were as follows:

Computer systems design and related services 16%
Finance and insurance 13
Information 11
Educational services; state, local, and private 10
Management of companies and enterprises.............................. 8

Work Schedules. Almost all database administrators work full time. About a quarter worked more than 40 hours per week in 2012.

How to Become One

Database administrators (DBAs) usually have a bachelor's degree in an information- or computer-related subject. Before becoming an administrator, these workers typically get work experience in a related field.

Education. Most database administrators have a bachelor's degree in management information systems (MIS) or a computer-related field. Firms with large databases may prefer applicants who

Median Annual Wages, May 2012

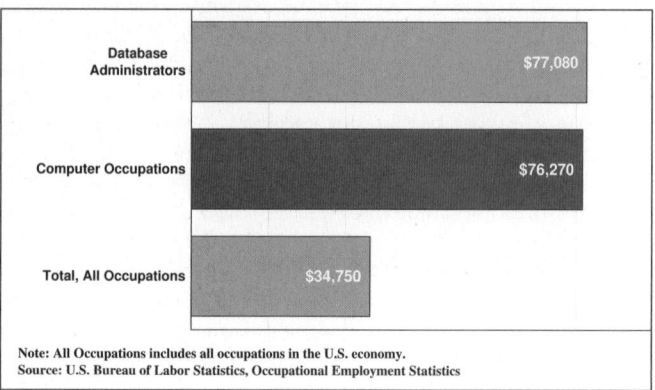

Note: All Occupations includes all occupations in the U.S. economy.
Source: U.S. Bureau of Labor Statistics, Occupational Employment Statistics

Percent Change in Employment, Projected 2012–2022

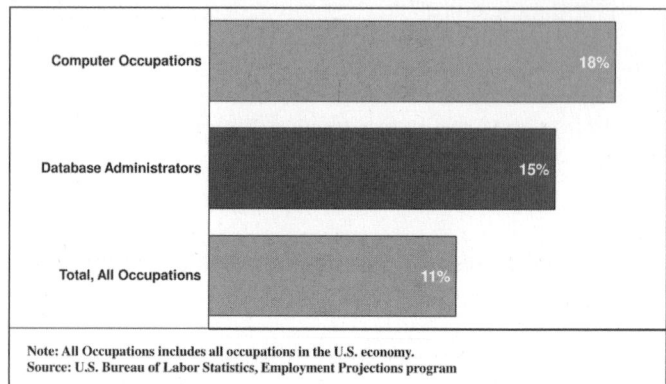

Note: All Occupations includes all occupations in the U.S. economy.
Source: U.S. Bureau of Labor Statistics, Employment Projections program

have a master's degree focusing on data or database management, typically either in computer science, information systems, or information technology.

Database administrators need an understanding of database languages, the most common of which is Structured Query Language, commonly called, SQL. Most database systems use some variation of SQL, and a DBA will need to become familiar with whichever programming language the firm uses.

Licenses, Certifications, and Registrations. Certification is a way to demonstrate competence and may provide a jobseeker with a competitive advantage. Certification programs are generally offered by product vendors or software firms. Some companies may require their database administrators to be certified in the product they use.

Work Experience in a Related Occupation. Most database administrators do not begin their careers in that occupation. Many first work as database developers or data analysts. A database developer is a type of software developer who specializes in creating databases. The job of a data analyst is to interpret the information stored in a database in a way the firm can use. Depending on their specialty, data analysts can have different job titles, including financial analyst, market research analyst, and operations research analyst. After mastering one of these fields, they may become a database administrator. For more information, see the profiles on software developers, financial analysts, market research analysts, and operations research analysts.

Advancement. Database administrators can advance to become computer and information systems managers.

Employment Projections Data for Database Administrators

Occupational title	SOC Code	Employment, 2012	Projected Employment, 2022	Change, 2012–2022	
				Percent	Numeric
Database administrators..	15-1141	118,700	136,600	15	17,900

Source: U.S. Bureau of Labor Statistics, Employment Projections Program

Note: Data are rounded. Go to **Occupational Information Included in the OOH** *for a discussion of the data in this table.*

Similar Occupations

This table shows a list of occupations with job duties that are similar to those of database administrators.

Occupations	Entry-level Education	2012 Pay	Projected Job Growth	Average Annual Openings
Computer and Information Systems Managers	Bachelor's degree	$120,950	15%	9,710
Computer Network Architects	Bachelor's degree	$91,000	15%	4,350
Computer Programmers	Bachelor's degree	$74,280	8%	11,810
Computer Support Specialists	See "How to Become One"	$49,488	17%	23,650
Computer Systems Analysts	Bachelor's degree	$79,680	25%	20,960
Financial Analysts	Bachelor's degree	$76,950	16%	10,090
Information Security Analysts	Bachelor's degree	$86,170	36%	3,920
Market Research Analysts	Bachelor's degree	$60,300	32%	18,850
Network and Computer Systems Administrators	Bachelor's degree	$72,560	12%	10,050
Operations Research Analysts	Bachelor's degree	$72,100	27%	3,600
Software Developers	Bachelor's degree	$93,640	22%	35,320
Web Developers	Associate's degree	$62,500	20%	5,070

Important Qualities

Analytical skills. DBAs must be able to monitor a database system's performance to determine when action is needed. They must be able to evaluate complex information that comes from a variety of sources.

Communication skills. Most database administrators work on teams and must be able to communicate effectively with developers, managers, and other workers.

Detail oriented. Working with databases requires an understanding of complex systems, in which a minor error can cause major problems. For example, mixing up customers' credit card information can cause someone to be charged for a purchase he or she didn't make.

Logical thinking. Database administrators use software to make sense of information and to arrange and organize it into meaningful patterns. The information is then stored in the databases that these workers manage, test, and maintain.

Problem-solving skills. When problems with a database arise, administrators must be able to diagnose and correct the problems.

Pay

The median annual wage for database administrators (DBAs) was $77,080 in May 2012. The median wage is the wage at which half the workers in an occupation earned more than that amount and half earned less. The lowest 10 percent earned less than $42,930, and the top 10 percent earned more than $118,720.

The wages for DBAs vary with the industry in which they work. In May 2012, the median annual wages for database administrators the top five industries in which these administrators worked were as follows:

Finance and insurance	$85,880
Computer systems design and related services	84,550
Management of companies and enterprises	82,290
Information	81,800
Educational services; state, local, and private	63,620

Job Outlook

Employment of database administrators (DBAs) is projected to grow 15 percent from 2012 to 2022, faster than the average for all occupations. Growth in this occupation will be driven by the increased data needs of companies in all sectors of the economy. Database administrators will be needed to organize and present data in a way that makes it easy for analysts and other stakeholders to understand. However employment growth may be slowed by new software tools that increase the productivity of DBAs.

The increasing popularity of database-as-a-service, which allows database administration to be done by a third party over the internet, could increase the employment of DBAs at cloud computing firms in the computer systems design and related services industry. Employment of DBAs is projected to grow 48 percent in this industry from 2012 to 2022.

Employment growth for database administrators is expected in healthcare industries because, as the use of electronic medical records increases, more databases will be needed to keep track of patient information. Employment of DBAs is projected to grow 43 percent in general medical and surgical hospitals from 2012 to 2022.

Job Prospects. Job prospects should be favorable. Database administrators are in high demand, and firms sometimes have difficulty finding qualified workers. Applicants who have experience with the latest technology should have the best prospects.

O*NET

➤ Database Administrators (15-1141.00)

Contacts for More Information

For more information about database administrators, visit

➤ Association for Computing Machinery (www.acm.org/)
➤ IEEE (www.computer.org/)
➤ Computing Research Association (www.cra.org/)

For information regarding opportunities for women pursuing information technology careers, visit

➤ National Center for Women and Information Technology (www.ncwit.org/)

Information Security Analysts

- **2012 Median Pay** .... $86,170 per year
  $41.43 per hour

- **Entry-Level Education** ....Bachelor's degree

- **Work Experience in a Related Occupation**.........Less than 5 years

- **On-the-Job Training** .... None

- **Number of Jobs 2012** 75,100

- **Job Outlook, 2012–22** .... 37% (Much faster than average)

- **Employment Change, 2012–22** 27,400

What Information Security Analysts Do

Information security analysts plan and carry out security measures to protect an organization's computer networks and systems. Their responsibilities are continually expanding as the number of cyberattacks increase.

Duties. Information security analysts typically do the following:

- Monitor their organization's networks for security breaches and investigate a violation when one occurs

- Install and use software, such as firewalls and data encryption programs, to protect sensitive information

- Prepare reports that document security breaches and the extent of the damage caused by the breaches

- Conduct penetration testing, which is when analysts simulate attacks to look for vulnerabilities in their systems before they can be exploited

- Research the latest information technology (IT) security trends

Information security analysts install and use software, such as firewalls and data encryption programs, to protect sensitive information.

Median Annual Wages, May 2012

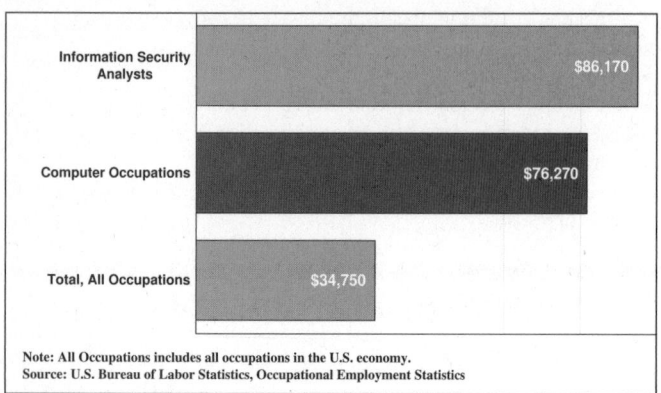

Note: All Occupations includes all occupations in the U.S. economy.
Source: U.S. Bureau of Labor Statistics, Occupational Employment Statistics

Percent Change in Employment, Projected 2012–2022

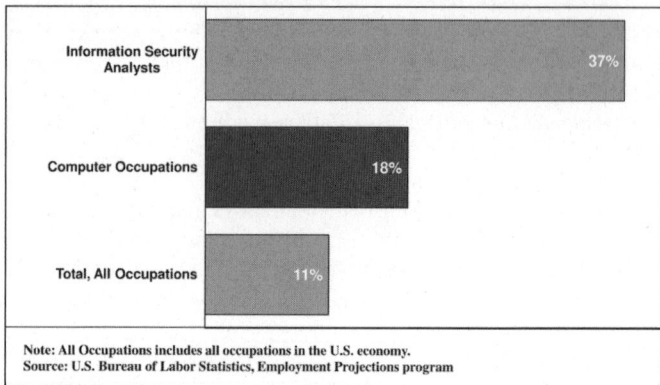

Note: All Occupations includes all occupations in the U.S. economy.
Source: U.S. Bureau of Labor Statistics, Employment Projections program

- Help plan and carry out an organization's way of handling security

- Develop security standards and best practices for their organization

- Recommend security enhancements to management or senior IT staff

- Help computer users when they need to install or learn about new security products and procedures

Information security analysts must continually adapt to stay a step ahead of cyberattackers. They must stay up to date on the latest methods attackers are using to infiltrate computer systems and on IT security. Analysts need to research new security technology to decide what will most effectively protect their organization. This may involve attending cybersecurity conferences to hear firsthand accounts of other professionals who have experienced new types of attacks.

IT security analysts are heavily involved with creating their organization's disaster recovery plan, a procedure that IT employees follow in case of emergency. The plan lets an organization's IT department continue functioning. It includes preventative measures such as regularly copying and transferring data to an offsite location. It also involves plans to restore proper IT functioning after a disaster. Analysts continually test the steps in their recovery plans.

Because information security is important, these workers usually report directly to upper management. Many information security analysts work with an organization's computer and information systems manager or Chief Technology Officer (CTO) to design security or disaster recovery systems.

Work Environment

Information security analysts held about 75,100 jobs in 2012. Most analysts work for computer companies, consulting firms, and business and financial companies. The industries that employed the most information security analysts in 2012 were as follows:

Computer systems design and related services 27%
Finance and insurance 19
Information 10
Management of companies and enterprises 8

Very few information security analysts are self-employed.

Many information security analysts work with other members of an information technology department, such as network administrators or computer systems analysts.

Work Schedules. Most information security analysts work full time. Information security analysts sometimes have to be on call outside of normal business hours in case of an emergency at their organization.

How to Become One

Most information security analysts have a bachelor's degree in a computer-related field. They also usually need experience in a related occupation.

Education. Information security analysts usually need at least a bachelor's degree in computer science, programming, or a related field. As information security continues to develop as a career field, many schools are responding with information security programs for prospective job seekers. These programs may become a common path for entry into the occupation. Currently, a well-rounded computer education is preferred.

Employers of information security analysts sometimes prefer applicants who have a Master's of Business Administration (MBA) in information systems. Programs offering the MBA in information systems generally require 2 years of study beyond the undergraduate level and include both business and computer-related courses.

Work Experience in a Related Occupation. Information security analysts generally need to have previous experience in a related occupation. Many analysts have experience in an information technology department, often as a network or systems administrator. Some employers look for people who have already worked in fields related to the one in which they are hiring. For example, if the job opening is in database security, they may look for a database

Employment Projections Data for Information Security Analysts

Occupational title	SOC Code	Employment, 2012	Projected Employment, 2022	Change, 2012–2022	
				Percent	Numeric
Information security analysts...	15-1122	75,100	102,500	37	27,400

Source: U.S. Bureau of Labor Statistics, Employment Projections Program

Note: Data are rounded. Go to **Occupational Information Included in the OOH** *for a discussion of the data in this table.*

Similar Occupations   This table shows a list of occupations with job duties that are similar to those of information security analysts.

Occupations	Entry-level Education	2012 Pay	Projected Job Growth	Average Annual Openings
Computer and Information Research Scientists	Doctoral or professional degree	$102,190	15%	830
Computer and Information Systems Managers	Bachelor's degree	$120,950	15%	9,710
Computer Network Architects	Bachelor's degree	$91,000	15%	4,350
Computer Programmers	Bachelor's degree	$74,280	8%	11,810
Computer Support Specialists	See "How to Become One"	$49,488	17%	23,650
Computer Systems Analysts	Bachelor's degree	$79,680	25%	20,960
Database Administrators	Bachelor's degree	$77,080	15%	4,030
Information Security Analysts	Bachelor's degree	$86,170	36%	3,920
Network and Computer Systems Administrators	Bachelor's degree	$72,560	12%	10,050
Software Developers	Bachelor's degree	$93,640	22%	35,320
Web Developers	Associate's degree	$62,500	20%	5,070

administrator. If they are hiring in systems security, a computer systems analyst may be an ideal candidate.

Licenses, Certifications, and Registrations. There are a number of information security certifications available and many employers prefer job candidates to have one. Some are general information security certificates, such as the Certified Information Systems Security Professional, while others have a narrow focus, such as penetration testing or systems auditing.

Advancement. Some information security analysts can advance to become a chief security officer or another type of computer and information systems manager.

Important Qualities

Analytical skills. Information security analysts must carefully study computer systems and networks and investigate any irregularities to determine if the networks have been compromised.

Detail oriented. Because cyberattacks can be difficult to detect, information security analysts pay careful attention to their computer systems and watch for minor changes in performance.

Ingenuity. Information security analysts try to outthink cybercriminals and invent new ways to protect their organization's computer systems and networks.

Problem-solving skills. Information security analysts uncover and fix flaws in computer systems and networks.

Pay

The median annual wage for information security analysts was $86,170 in May 2012. The median wage is the wage at which half the workers in an occupation earned more than that amount and half earned less. The lowest 10 percent earned less than $49,960, and the top 10 percent earned more than $135,600.

In May 2012, the median annual wages for information security analysts in the top four industries in which these analysts worked were as follows:

Finance and insurance	$92,080
Information	91,440
Computer systems design and related services	88,270
Management of companies and enterprises	81,130

Job Outlook

Employment of information security analysts is projected to grow 37 percent from 2012 to 2022, much faster than the average for all occupations.

Demand for information security analysts is expected to be very high. Cyberattacks have grown in frequency and sophistication over the last few years, and many organizations are behind in their ability to detect these attacks. Analysts will be needed to come up with innovative solutions to prevent hackers from stealing critical information or creating havoc on computer networks.

The federal government is expected to greatly increase its use of information security analysts to protect the nation's critical information technology (IT) systems. In addition, as the healthcare industry expands its use of electronic medical records, ensuring patients' privacy and protecting personal data are becoming more important. More information security analysts are likely to be needed to create the safeguards that will satisfy patients' concerns.

Job Prospects. Job prospects for information security analysts should be good. Information security analysts with related work experience will have the best opportunities. For example, an applicant with experience as a database administrator would have better prospects in database security than someone without that experience.

O*NET

➤ Information Security Analysts (15-1122.00)

Contacts for More Information

For more information about computer careers, visit

➤ Association for Computing Machinery (www.acm.org/)

➤ IEEE (www.computer.org/)

➤ Computing Research Association (www.cra.org/)

For information about opportunities for women pursuing information technology careers, visit

➤ National Center for Women and Information Technology (www.ncwit.org/)

Network and Computer Systems Administrators

- **2012 Median Pay** ....$72,560 per year
  $34.88 per hour
- **Entry-Level Education** ....Bachelor's degree
- **Work Experience in a Related Occupation**............... None
- **On-the-Job Training** .... None
- **Number of Jobs 2012** 366,400
- **Job Outlook, 2012–22**................. 12% (As fast as average)
- **Employment Change, 2012–22** 42,900

What Network and Computer Systems Administrators Do

Computer networks are critical parts of almost every organization. Network and computer systems administrators are responsible for the day-to-day operation of these networks. They organize, install, and support an organization's computer systems, including local area networks (LANs), wide area networks (WANs), network segments, intranets, and other data communication systems.

Duties. Network and computer systems administrators typically do the following:

- Determine what the organization needs in a network and computer system before it is set up
- Install all network hardware and software and make needed upgrades and repairs
- Maintain network and computer system security and ensure that all systems are operating correctly
- Collect data in order to evaluate the network's or system's performance and help make the system work better and faster
- Add users to a network and assign and update security permissions on the network
- Train users on the proper use of hardware and software
- Solve problems when a user or an automated monitoring system informs them that a problem exists

Administrators manage an organization's servers and desktop and mobile equipment. They ensure that email and data storage networks work properly. They also make sure that employees' workstations are working efficiently and stay connected to the central computer network. Some administrators manage telecommunication networks.

Administrators need strong computer skills.

In some cases, administrators help network architects design and analyze network models. They also participate in decisions about buying future hardware or software to upgrade their organization's network. Some administrators provide technical support to computer users, and they also may supervise computer support specialists who help solve users' problems.

Work Environment

Network and computer systems administrators held about 366,400 jobs in 2012. They work with the physical computer networks of a variety of organizations and therefore are employed in many industries.

The industries that employed the most network and computer systems administrators in 2012 were as follows:

Computer systems design and related services........................ 16%
Educational services; state, local, and private 11
Information 11
Finance and insurance... 9
Manufacturing 7

Network and computer systems administrators work with many types of workers, including computer network architects and computer and information systems managers as well as non information technology (IT) staff.

Work Schedules. In 2012, most network and computer systems administrators worked full time. Most organizations depend on their computer networks, so many administrators must work overtime to

Median Annual Wages, May 2012

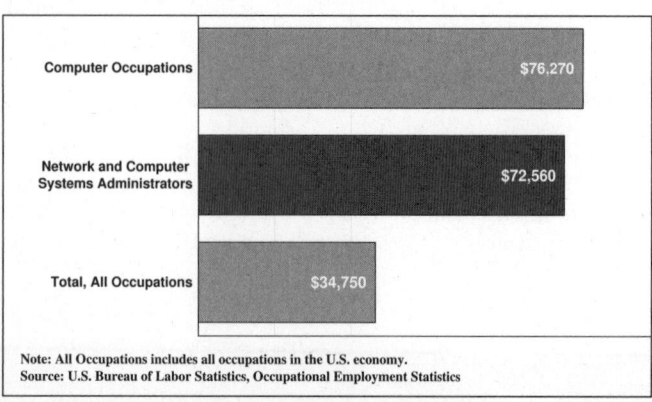

Note: All Occupations includes all occupations in the U.S. economy.
Source: U.S. Bureau of Labor Statistics, Occupational Employment Statistics

Percent Change in Employment, Projected 2012–2022

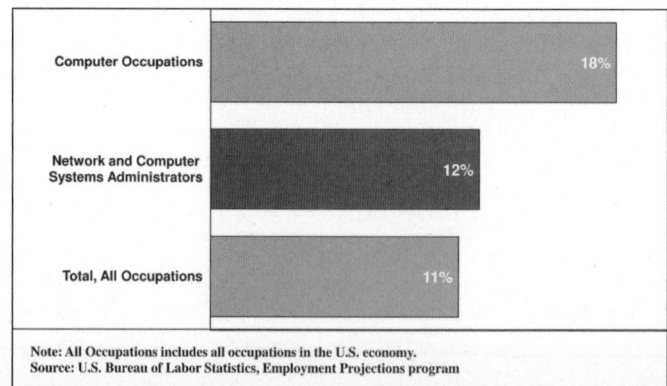

Note: All Occupations includes all occupations in the U.S. economy.
Source: U.S. Bureau of Labor Statistics, Employment Projections program

Employment Projections Data for Network and Computer Systems Administrators

Occupational title	SOC Code	Employment, 2012	Projected Employment, 2022	Change, 2012–2022	
				Percent	Numeric
Network and computer systems administrators 15-1142		366,400	409,400	12	42,900

Source: U.S. Bureau of Labor Statistics, Employment Projections Program

Note: Data are rounded. Go to **Occupational Information Included in the OOH** *for a discussion of the data in this table.*

ensure that the networks are operating properly. About a quarter of these administrators worked over 40 hours per week in 2012.

How to Become One

Although some employers require just a postsecondary certificate, most require a bachelor's degree in a field related to computer or information science.

Education. Although some employers require just a postsecondary certificate, most require a bachelor's degree in a field related to computer or information science. However, because administrators work with computer hardware and equipment, a degree in computer engineering or electrical engineering usually is acceptable as well. Such a degree usually entails classes in computer programming, networking, or systems design.

Because network technology is continually changing, administrators need to keep up with the latest developments. Many continue to take courses throughout their careers. Some businesses require that an administrator get a master's degree.

Licenses, Certifications, and Registrations. Certification is a way to show a level of competence and may provide a jobseeker with a competitive advantage. Certification programs generally are offered by product vendors or software firms. Companies may require their network and computer systems administrators to be certified in the product they use. Microsoft and Cisco offer some of the most common certifications.

Other Experience. To gain practical experience, many network administrators participate in an internship while in school.

Advancement. Network administrators can advance to become computer network architects. They can also advance to managerial jobs in information technology (IT) departments such as computer and information systems managers.

Important Qualities

Analytical skills. Administrators need analytical skills to evaluate network and system performance and determine how changes in the environment will affect it.

Communication skills. Administrators must be able to describe problems and their solutions to non-IT workers.

Computer skills. Administrators oversee the connections of many different types of computer equipment and must ensure that they all work together properly.

Multitasking skills. Administrators may have to work on many problems and tasks at the same time.

Problem-solving skills. Administrators must be able to quickly resolve any problems that arise with computer networks.

Pay

The median annual wage for network and computer systems administrators was $72,560 in May 2012. The median wage is the wage at which half the workers in an occupation earned more than that amount and half earned less. The lowest 10 percent earned less than $44,330, and the top 10 percent earned more than $115,180.

Network and computer systems administrators are employed in many different industries, and pay varies by industry. In May 2012, the median annual wages for network and computer systems administrators in the top five industries in which these administrators worked were as follows:

Finance and insurance	$77,370
Information	77,270
Computer systems design and related services	76,090
Manufacturing	70,250
Educational services; state, local, and private	61,830

Similar Occupations   This table shows a list of occupations with job duties that are similar to those of network and computer systems administrators.

Occupations	Entry-level Education	2012 Pay	Projected Job Growth	Average Annual Openings
Computer and Information Systems Managers	Bachelor's degree	$120,950	15%	9,710
Computer Hardware Engineers	Bachelor's degree	$100,920	7%	2,410
Computer Network Architects	Bachelor's degree	$91,000	15%	4,350
Computer Programmers	Bachelor's degree	$74,280	8%	11,810
Computer Support Specialists	See "How to Become One"	$49,488	17%	23,650
Computer Systems Analysts	Bachelor's degree	$79,680	25%	20,960
Database Administrators	Bachelor's degree	$77,080	15%	4,030
Electrical and Electronics Engineers	Bachelor's degree	$89,701	4%	7,940
Information Security Analysts	Bachelor's degree	$86,170	36%	3,920
Software Developers	Bachelor's degree	$93,640	22%	35,320
Web Developers	Associate's degree	$62,500	20%	5,070

Job Outlook

Employment of network and computer systems administrators is projected to grow 12 percent from 2012 to 2022, about as fast as the average for all occupations. Demand for information technology workers is high and should continue to grow as firms invest in newer, faster technology and mobile networks. However, an increase in cloud computing could raise the productivity of network administrators, slowing their growth across many industries. Growth will be highest at industries that provide cloud-computing technology. Employment of network administrators in the computer systems design and related services industry is projected to grow 35 percent from 2012 to 2022.

Growth is also expected in healthcare industries as their use of information technology increases. More administrators will be required to manage the growing systems and networks found at hospitals and other healthcare institutions.

Job Prospects. Job opportunities should be favorable for this occupation. Prospects should be best for applicants who have a bachelor's degree in computer science and who are up to date on the latest technology, especially cloud computing.

O*NET

➤ Network and Computer Systems Administrators (15-1142.00)

Contacts for More Information

For more information about computer careers, visit
➤ Association for Computing Machinery (www.acm.org/)
➤ IEEE (www.computer.org)
➤ Tech-America (www.techamerica.org/)

For more information about opportunities for women pursuing information technology careers, visit
➤ National Center for Women and Information Technology (www.ncwit.org/)

Software Developers

- **2012 Median Pay** .... $93,350 per year
  $44.88 per hour
- **Entry-Level Education** .... Bachelor's degree
- **Work Experience in a Related Occupation** .... None
- **On-the-Job Training** .... None
- **Number of Jobs 2012** 1,018,000
- **Job Outlook, 2012–22** .... 22% (Much faster than average)
- **Employment Change, 2012–22** 222,600

What Software Developers Do

Software developers are the creative minds behind computer programs. Some develop the applications that allow people to do specific tasks on a computer or other device. Others develop the underlying systems that run the devices or control networks.

Duties. Software developers typically do the following:

- Analyze users' needs, then design, test, and develop software to meet those needs
- Recommend software upgrades for customers' existing programs and systems
- Design each piece of the application or system and plan how the pieces will work together

- Create a variety of models and diagrams (such as flowcharts) that instruct programmers how to write the software code
- Ensure that the software continues to function normally through software maintenance and testing
- Document every aspect of the application or system as a reference for future maintenance and upgrades
- Collaborate with other computer specialists to create optimum software

Software developers are in charge of the entire development process for a software program. They begin by asking how the customer plans to use the software. They design the program and then give instructions to programmers, who write computer code and test it. If the program does not work as expected or people find it too difficult to use, software developers go back to the design process to fix the problems or improve the program. After the program is released to the customer, a developer may perform upgrades and maintenance.

Developers usually work closely with computer programmers. However, in some companies, developers write code themselves instead of giving instructions to computer programmers.

Developers who supervise a software project from the planning stages through implementation sometimes are called information technology (IT) project managers. These workers monitor the project's progress to ensure that it meets deadlines, standards, and cost targets. IT project managers who plan and direct an organization's IT department or IT policies are included in the profile on computer and information systems managers.

The following are types of software developers:

Applications software developers design computer applications, such as word processors and games, for consumers. They may create custom software for a specific customer or commercial software to be sold to the general public. Some applications software developers create complex databases for organizations. They also create programs that people use over the Internet and within a company's intranet.

Systems software developers create the systems that keep computers functioning properly. These could be operating systems that are part of computers the general public buys or systems built specifically for an organization. Often, systems software developers also build the system's interface, which is what allows users to interact with the computer. Systems software developers create the operating systems that control most of the consumer electronics in use today, including those in phones or cars.

Software developers design computer programs.

Median Annual Wages, May 2012

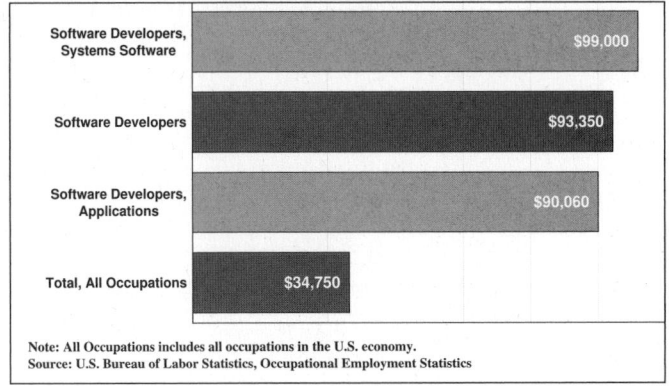

Note: All Occupations includes all occupations in the U.S. economy.
Source: U.S. Bureau of Labor Statistics, Occupational Employment Statistics

Percent Change in Employment, Projected 2012–2022

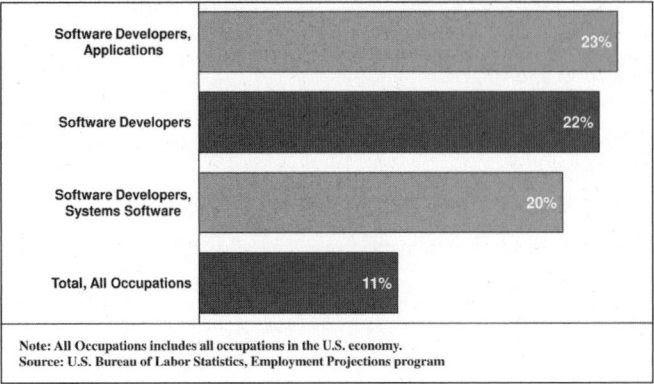

Note: All Occupations includes all occupations in the U.S. economy.
Source: U.S. Bureau of Labor Statistics, Employment Projections program

Work Environment

Software developers held about 1 million jobs in 2012.

Many software developers work for computer systems design and related services firms or software publishers. Some systems developers work in computer and electronic product manufacturing industries. Applications developers work in office environments, such as for insurance carriers or corporate headquarters.

In general, software development is a collaborative process and developers work on teams with others, who contribute to designing, developing, and programming successful software. However, some developers telecommute (work away from the office).

The industries that employed the most software developers in 2012 were as follows:

Computer systems design and related services 32%
Computer and electronic product manufacturing 9
Finance and insurance 8
Software publishers 7

Work Schedules. Most software developers work full time, and long hours are common. More than a quarter worked more than 40 hours per week in 2012.

How to Become One

Software developers usually have a bachelor's degree in computer science and strong computer programming skills.

Education. Software developers usually have a bachelor's degree, typically in computer science, software engineering, or a related field. A degree in mathematics is also acceptable. Computer science degree programs are the most common, because they tend to cover a broad range of topics. Students should focus on classes related to building software in order to better prepare themselves for work in the occupation. For some positions, employers may prefer a master's degree.

Although writing code is not their first priority, developers must have a strong background in computer programming. They usually gain this experience in school. Throughout their career, developers must keep up to date on new tools and computer languages.

Software developers also need skills related to the industry in which they work. Developers working in a bank, for example, should have knowledge of finance so that they can understand a bank's computing needs.

Other Experience. Many students gain experience in software development by completing an internship at a software company while in college.

Some software developers first work as computer programmers, and as they gain more experience they are given more responsibility and eventually become a developer.

Advancement. Software developers can advance to become information technology (IT) project managers, also called computer and information systems managers, and oversee the software development process.

Important Qualities

Analytical skills. Developers must analyze users' needs and then design software to meet those needs.

Communication skills. Developers must be able to give clear instructions to others working on a project.

Computer skills. Developers must understand computer capabilities and languages in order to design effective software.

Creativity. Developers are the creative minds behind new computer software.

Customer-service skills. Some developers must be able to explain to their customers how the software works and answer any questions that arise.

Detail oriented. Developers often work on many parts of an application or system at the same time and must be able to concentrate and pay attention to detail.

Interpersonal skills. Software developers must be able to work well with others who contribute to designing, developing, and programming successful software.

Problem-solving skills. Because developers are in charge of the software from beginning to end, they must be able to solve problems that arise throughout the design process.

Employment Projections Data for Software Developers

Occupational title	SOC Code	Employment, 2012	Projected Employment, 2022	Change, 2012–2022 Percent	Change, 2012–2022 Numeric
Software developers	—	1,018,000	1,240,600	22	222,600
Software developers, applications	15-1132	613,000	752,900	23	139,900
Software developers, systems software	15-1133	405,000	487,800	20	82,800

Source: U.S. Bureau of Labor Statistics, Employment Projections Program

Note: Data are rounded. Go to **Occupational Information Included in the OOH** *for a discussion of the data in this table.*

Similar Occupations   This table shows a list of occupations with job duties that are similar to those of software developers.

Occupations	Entry-level Education	2012 Pay	Projected Job Growth	Average Annual Openings
Computer and Information Research Scientists	Doctoral or professional degree	$102,190	15%	830
Computer and Information Systems Managers	Bachelor's degree	$120,950	15%	9,710
Computer Hardware Engineers	Bachelor's degree	$100,920	7%	2,410
Computer Network Architects	Bachelor's degree	$91,000	15%	4,350
Computer Programmers	Bachelor's degree	$74,280	8%	11,810
Computer Support Specialists	See "How to Become One"	$49,488	17%	23,650
Computer Systems Analysts	Bachelor's degree	$79,680	25%	20,960
Database Administrators	Bachelor's degree	$77,080	15%	4,030
Information Security Analysts	Bachelor's degree	$86,170	36%	3,920
Mathematicians	Master's degree	$101,360	23%	170
Postsecondary Teachers	See "How to Become One"	$70,380	19%	42,690
Web Developers	Associate's degree	$62,500	20%	5,070

Pay

The median annual wage for applications software developers was $90,060 in May 2012. The median wage is the wage at which half the workers in an occupation earned more than that amount and half earned less. The lowest 10 percent earned less than $55,190, and the top 10 percent earned more than $138,880.

The median annual wage for systems software developers was $99,000 in May 2012. The lowest 10 percent earned less than $62,800, and the top 10 percent earned more than $148,850.

In May 2012, the median annual wages for applications software developers in the top four industries in which these developers worked were as follows:

Computer and electronic product manufacturing $97,960
Software publishers 96,920
Finance and insurance 91,970
Computer systems design and related services 88,500

In May 2012, the median annual wages for systems software developers in the top four industries in which these developers worked were as follows:

Computer and electronic product manufacturing $105,030
Finance and insurance 99,940
Software publishers 99,750
Computer systems design and related services 98,500

Job Outlook

Employment of software developers is projected to grow 22 percent from 2012 to 2022, much faster than the average for all occupations. Employment of applications developers is projected to grow 23 percent, and employment of systems developers is projected to grow 20 percent.

The main reason for the rapid growth is a large increase in the demand for computer software. Mobile technology requires new applications. The healthcare industry is greatly increasing its use of computer systems and applications. Also, concerns over threats to computer security could result in more investment in security software to protect computer networks and electronic infrastructure.

Systems developers are likely to see new opportunities because of an increase in the number of products that use software. For example, computer systems are built into consumer electronics, such as cell phones, and into other products that are becoming computerized, such as appliances. In addition, an increase in software offered over the Internet should lower costs and allow more customization for businesses, also increasing demand for software developers.

Some outsourcing to foreign countries with lower wages may occur. However, because software developers should be close to their customers, the offshoring of this occupation is expected to be limited.

Job Prospects. Job prospects will be best for applicants with knowledge of the most up-to-date programming tools and languages.

O*NET

➤ Software Developers, Applications (15-1132.00)
➤ Software Developers, Systems Software (15-1133.00)

Contacts for More Information

For more information about software developers, visit
➤ Association for Computing Machinery (www.acm.org/)
➤ IEEE (www.ieee.org/index.html)
➤ Computing Research Association (www.cra.org)
➤ TechAmerica (www.techamerica.org/)

For information about opportunities for women pursuing information technology careers, visit
➤ National Center for Women and Information Technology (www.ncwit.org/)

Web Developers

- **2012 Median Pay** .... $62,500 per year
  $30.05 per hour
- **Entry-Level Education** .... Associate's degree
- **Work Experience in a Related Occupation** .... None
- **On-the-Job Training** .... None
- **Number of Jobs 2012** 141,400
- **Job Outlook, 2012–22** .... 20% (Faster than average)
- **Employment Change, 2012–22** 28,500

What Web Developers Do

Web developers design and create websites. They are responsible for the look of the site. They are also responsible for the site's technical aspects, such as performance and capacity, which are measures of a website's speed and how much traffic the site can handle. They also may create content for the site.

Duties. Web developers typically do the following:

- Meet with their clients or management to discuss the needs of the website and the expected needs of the website's audience and plan how it should look
- Create and debug applications for a website
- Write code for the site, using programming languages such as HTML or XML
- Work with other team members to determine what information the site will contain
- Work with graphics and other designers to determine the website's layout
- Integrate graphics, audio, and video into the website
- Monitor website traffic

When creating a website, developers have to make their client's vision a reality. They work with clients to make sure it fits in with the type of site it is supposed to be, such as ecommerce, news, or gaming. Different types of websites may require different applications to work right. For example, a gaming site should be able to handle advanced graphics while an ecommerce site needs a payment processing application. The developer decides which applications and designs will best fit the site.

Some developers handle all aspects of a website's construction, while others specialize in a certain aspect of it. The following are some types of specialized Web developers:

Web architects or programmers are responsible for the overall technical construction of the website. They create the basic framework of the site and ensure that it works as expected. Web architects also establish procedures for allowing others to add new pages to the website and meet with management to discuss major changes to the site.

Web designers are responsible for how a website looks. They create the site's layout and integrate graphics; applications, such as a retail checkout tool; and other content into the site. They also write Web-design programs in a variety of computer languages, such as HTML or JavaScript.

Webmasters maintain websites and keep them updated. They ensure that websites operate correctly and test for errors such as broken links. Many webmasters respond to user comments as well.

Web developers integrate graphics, audio, and video into websites.

Work Environment

Web developers held about 141,400 jobs in 2012. The industries that employed the most Web developers in 2012 were as follows:

Computer systems design and related services	16%
Data processing, hosting, related services, and other information services	8
Finance and insurance	5
Educational services; state, local, and private	5
Religious, grantmaking, civic, professional, and similar organizations	5

About a quarter of Web developers were self-employed in 2012.
Work Schedules. Most Web developers work full time.

How to Become One

The typical education needed to become a Web developer is an associate's degree in Web design or related field. Web developers need knowledge of both programming and graphic design.

Education. Educational requirements for Web developers vary with the setting they work in and the type of work they do. Requirements range from a high school diploma to a bachelor's degree. An associate's degree in Web design or related field is the most common requirement.

However, for Web architect or other, more technical, developer positions, some employers prefer workers who have at least a bachelor's degree in computer science, programming, or a related field.

Web developers need to have a thorough understanding of HTML. Many employers also want developers to understand other programming languages, such as JavaScript or SQL, as well

Median Annual Wages, May 2012

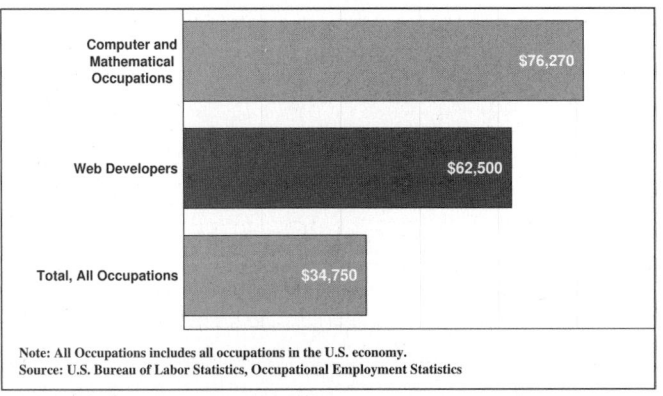

Computer and Mathematical Occupations: $76,270
Web Developers: $62,500
Total, All Occupations: $34,750

Note: All Occupations includes all occupations in the U.S. economy.
Source: U.S. Bureau of Labor Statistics, Occupational Employment Statistics

Percent Change in Employment, Projected 2012–2022

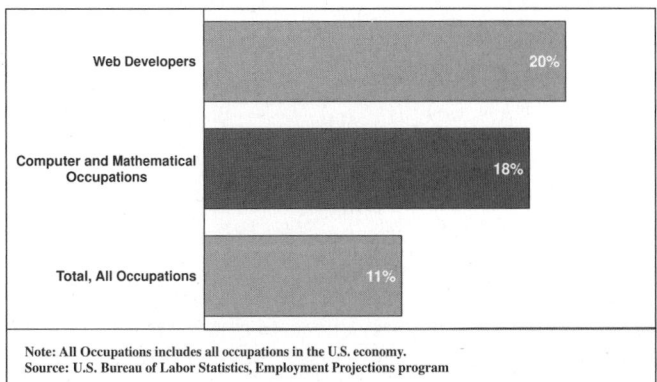

Web Developers: 20%
Computer and Mathematical Occupations: 18%
Total, All Occupations: 11%

Note: All Occupations includes all occupations in the U.S. economy.
Source: U.S. Bureau of Labor Statistics, Employment Projections program

Employment Projections Data for Web Developers

Occupational title	SOC Code	Employment, 2012	Projected Employment, 2022	Change, 2012–2022 Percent	Change, 2012–2022 Numeric
Web developers	15-1134	141,400	169,900	20	28,500

Source: U.S. Bureau of Labor Statistics, Employment Projections Program

Note: Data are rounded. Go to **Occupational Information Included in the OOH** *for a discussion of the data in this table.*

as have some knowledge of multimedia publishing tools, such as Flash. Throughout their career, Web developers must keep up to date on new tools and computer languages.

Some employers prefer Web developers who have both a computer degree and have taken classes in graphic design, especially when hiring developers who will be heavily involved in the website's visual appearance.

Advancement. Web developers who have a bachelor's degree can advance to become project managers. For more information, see the profile on computer and information systems managers.

Important Qualities

Concentration. Web developers must sit at a computer and write detailed code for long periods.

Creativity. Web developers are often involved in designing the appearance of a website and must make sure that it looks innovative and up to date.

Customer-service skills. Webmasters have to respond politely and correctly to user questions and requests.

Detail oriented. When Web developers write in HTML, a minor error could cause an entire webpage to stop working.

Pay

The median annual wage for Web developers was $62,500 in May 2012. The median wage is the wage at which half the workers in an occupation earned more than that amount and half earned less. The lowest 10 percent earned less than $33,550, and the top 10 percent earned more than $105,200.

Job Outlook

Employment of Web developers is projected to grow 20 percent from 2012 to 2022, faster than the average for all occupations.

Employment of Web developers is projected to grow as ecommerce continues to expand. Online purchasing is expected to grow faster than the overall retail industry. As retail firms expand their online offerings, demand for Web developers will increase. Additionally, an increase in the use of mobile devices to search the Web will also lead to an increase in employment of Web developers. Instead of designing a website for a desktop computer, developers will have to create sites that work on mobile devices with many different screen sizes, leading to more work.

Because websites can be built from anywhere in the world, some Web developer jobs may be moved to countries with lower wages, decreasing employment growth. However, this practice may decline because of a growing trend of firms hiring workers in low-cost areas of the United States instead of in foreign countries.

Job Prospects. Job opportunities for Web developers are expected to be good. Those with knowledge of multiple programming languages and digital multimedia tools, such as Flash and Photoshop, will have the best opportunities.

O*NET

➤ Web Developers (15-1134.00)

Contacts for More Information

For more information about Web developers, visit
➤ World Organization of Webmasters (http://webprofessionals.org/)
For more information about computer careers, visit
➤ Association for Computing Machinery (www.acm.org/)
➤ IEEE (www.computer.org)
➤ Computing Research Association (www.cra.org/)
For information about opportunities for women pursuing information technology careers, visit
➤ National Center for Women and Information Technology (www.ncwit.org/)

Similar Occupations This table shows a list of occupations with job duties that are similar to those of Web developers.

Occupations	Entry-level Education	2012 Pay	Projected Job Growth	Average Annual Openings
Computer and Information Systems Managers	Bachelor's degree	$120,950	15%	9,710
Computer Programmers	Bachelor's degree	$74,280	8%	11,810
Computer Support Specialists	See "How to Become One"	$49,488	17%	23,650
Computer Systems Analysts	Bachelor's degree	$79,680	25%	20,960
Database Administrators	Bachelor's degree	$77,080	15%	4,030
Graphic Designers	Bachelor's degree	$44,150	7%	8,600
Information Security Analysts	Bachelor's degree	$86,170	36%	3,920
Multimedia Artists and Animators	Bachelor's degree	$61,370	6%	2,060
Software Developers	Bachelor's degree	$93,640	22%	35,320

Boilermakers

- **2012 Median Pay** .... $56,560 per year
  $27.19 per hour
- **Entry-Level Education** ... High school diploma or equivalent
- **Work Experience in a Related Occupation** .... None
- **On-the-Job Training** .... Apprenticeship
- **Number of Jobs 2012** 18,000
- **Job Outlook, 2012–22** .... 4% (Slower than average)
- **Employment Change, 2012–22** 700

What Boilermakers Do

Boilermakers assemble, install, and repair boilers, closed vats, and other large vessels or containers that hold liquids and gases.

Duties. Boilermakers typically do the following:

- Use blueprints to determine locations, positions, or dimensions of parts
- Install small premade boilers into buildings and manufacturing facilities
- Lay out prefabricated parts of larger boilers before assembling them
- Assemble boiler tanks, often using robotic or automatic welders
- Test and inspect boiler systems for leaks or defects

Boilermakers weld sections of the boiler together.

- Clean vats using scrapers, wire brushes, and cleaning solvents
- Replace or repair broken valves, pipes, or joints, using hand and power tools, gas torches, and welding equipment

Boilers, tanks, and vats are used in many buildings, factories, and ships. Boilers heat water or other fluids under extreme pressure to generate electric power and to provide heat. Large tanks and vats are used to process and store chemicals, oil, beer, and hundreds of other products.

Boilers are made out of steel, iron, copper, or stainless steel. Manufacturers are increasingly automating the production of boilers to improve the quality of these vessels. However, boilermakers still use many tools to assemble or repair boilers. For example, they often use hand and power tools or flame cutting torches to cut pieces for a boiler. To bend the pieces into shape and accurately line them up, boilermakers use plumb bobs, levels, wedges, and turnbuckles.

If the plate sections are very large, cranes lift the parts into place. Once boilermakers have the parts lined up, they use metalworking machinery and other tools to remove irregular edges so the parts fit together properly. They then join the parts by bolting, welding, or riveting them together.

In addition to installing and maintaining boilers and other vessels, boilermakers help erect and repair air pollution equipment, blast furnaces, water treatment plants, storage and process tanks, and smokestacks. Boilermakers also install refractory brick and other heat-resistant materials in fireboxes or pressure vessels. Some install and maintain the huge pipes used in dams to send water to and from hydroelectric power generation turbines.

Because boilers last a long time–sometimes 50 years or more–boilermakers must regularly maintain them by upgrading parts. As a result, they frequently inspect fittings, feed pumps, safety and check valves, water and pressure gauges, and boiler controls.

Work Environment

Boilermakers held about 18,000 jobs in 2012. The industries that employed the most boilermakers in 2012 were as follows:

Building equipment contractors.. 26%
Nonresidential building construction....................................... 17
Utility system construction.. 12
Boiler, tank, and shipping container manufacturing............... 11

Boilermakers perform physically demanding and dangerous work. They often work outdoors in all types of weather, including in extreme heat and cold.

Because dams, boilers, storage tanks, and pressure vessels are large, boilermakers often work at great heights. When working on a dam, for example, they may be hundreds of feet above the ground.

Boilermakers also work in cramped quarters inside boilers, vats, or tanks that are often dark, damp, and poorly ventilated.

Injuries and Illnesses. Although boilermakers often use dangerous equipment, they have lower rates of injuries and illnesses than many other construction occupations. Still, common injuries include burns from acetylene torches, cuts from power grinders, muscle strains from lifting heavy parts and tools, and falls from ladders or large vessels.

To reduce the chance of injury, boilermakers often wear hardhats, harnesses, protective clothing, earplugs, and safety glasses. In addition, when working inside enclosed spaces, boilermakers often must wear a respirator.

Median Annual Wages, May 2012

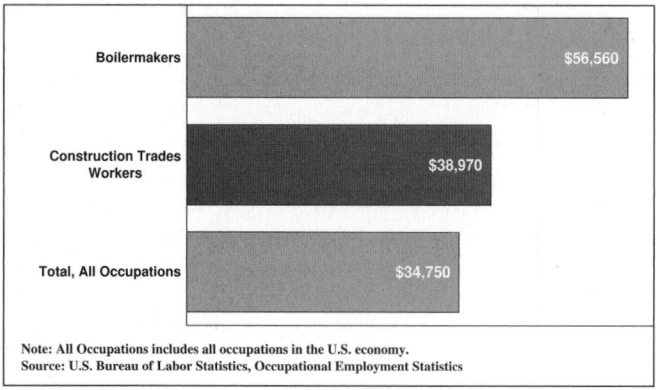

Note: All Occupations includes all occupations in the U.S. economy.
Source: U.S. Bureau of Labor Statistics, Occupational Employment Statistics

Percent Change in Employment, Projected 2012–2022

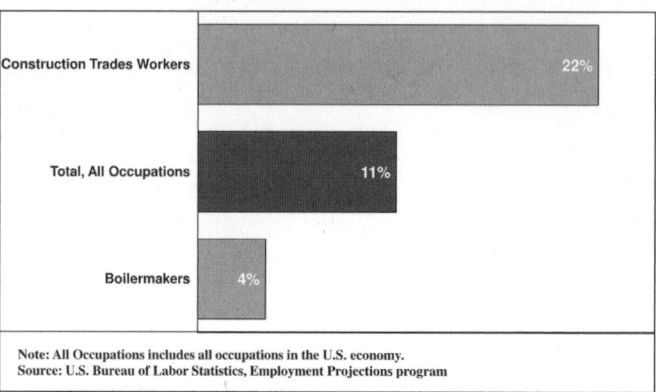

Note: All Occupations includes all occupations in the U.S. economy.
Source: U.S. Bureau of Labor Statistics, Employment Projections program

Work Schedules. Nearly all boilermakers work full time and may experience extended periods of overtime when equipment is shut down for maintenance. Overtime work also may be necessary to meet construction or production deadlines, especially during the spring and fall seasons. In contrast, because most field construction and repair work is contract work, there may be periods of unemployment when a contract is complete.

Many boilermakers must travel to worksites and live away from home for long periods.

How to Become One

Most boilermakers learn their trade through an apprenticeship program. Candidates are more likely to be accepted into training programs if they already have welding experience and certification.

Education. A high school diploma or GED is generally required. High school courses in math and welding are considered to be useful.

Training. Most boilermakers learn their trade through a 4- or 5-year apprenticeship. Each year, apprentices must have at least 144 hours of related technical training and 2,000 hours of paid on-the-job training. On the job, apprentices learn to use the tools and equipment of the trade. Those who already have welding experience complete training sooner than those without it. During technical training, apprentices learn about metals and installation techniques, as well as basic mathematics, blueprint reading and sketching, general construction techniques, safety practices, and first aid.

When they finish the apprenticeship program, boilermakers are considered to be journey workers, performing tasks under the guidance of experienced workers.

A few groups, including unions and contractor associations, sponsor apprenticeship programs. The basic qualifications to enter an apprenticeship program are as follows:

- Minimum age of 18
- High school education or equivalent
- Physically able to do the work

In addition to satisfying these qualifications, candidates with certification or documented welding experience usually have priority over applicants without experience.

Some boilermakers enter the trade through training in similar occupations, such as pipefitters, millwrights, sheet metal workers, or welders. Much of the core training of those occupations is similar to that of boilermakers.

Important Qualities

Physical stamina. Workers must have high endurance because they spend many hours on their feet while lifting heavy boiler components.

Physical strength. Workers must be strong enough to move heavy vat components into place.

Unafraid of confined spaces. Because workers often work inside boilers and vats, they cannot be claustrophobic.

Unafraid of heights. Some boilermakers must work at great heights. While installing water storage tanks, for example, workers may need to weld tanks several stories above the ground.

Pay

The median annual wage for boilermakers was $56,560 in May 2012. The median wage is the wage at which half the workers in an occupation earned more than that amount and half earned less. The lowest 10 percent earned less than $32,400, and the top 10 percent earned more than $79,970.

Apprentices usually start at 60 percent of the rate paid to fully trained boilermakers. They receive pay increases as they learn to do more tasks.

Union Membership. Compared with workers in all other occupations, boilermakers had a higher percentage of workers who belonged to a union in 2012. Although there is no single union that covers all boilermakers, the largest organizer of these workers is the International Brotherhood of Boilermakers, Iron Ship Builders, Blacksmiths, Forgers, and Helpers.

Employment Projections Data for Boilermakers

Occupational title	SOC Code	Employment, 2012	Projected Employment, 2022	Change, 2012–2022	
				Percent	Numeric
Boilermakers	47-2011	18,000	18,700	4	700

Source: U.S. Bureau of Labor Statistics, Employment Projections Program

Note: Data are rounded. Go to **Occupational Information Included in the OOH** *for a discussion of the data in this table.*

Similar Occupations   This table shows a list of occupations with job duties that are similar to those of boilermakers.

Occupations	Entry-level Education	2012 Pay	Projected Job Growth	Average Annual Openings
Assemblers and Fabricators	High school diploma or equivalent	$28,661	4%	37,140
Industrial Machinery Mechanics and Maintenance Workers and Millwrights	High school diploma or equivalent	$45,848	17%	18,700
Machinists and Tool and Die Makers	High school diploma or equivalent	$40,733	7%	13,060
Plumbers, Pipefitters, and Steamfitters	High school diploma or equivalent	$49,140	21%	13,050
Sheet Metal Workers	High school diploma or equivalent	$43,290	15%	4,890
Stationary Engineers and Boiler Operators	High school diploma or equivalent	$53,560	3%	1,270
Welders, Cutters, Solderers, and Brazers	High school diploma or equivalent	$36,300	6%	10,850

Job Outlook

Employment of boilermakers is projected to grow 4 percent from 2012 to 2022, slower than the average for all occupations.

Overall demand for boilermakers is linked to the relative cost of coal versus natural gas. Coal-fired power plants require more boilermakers for installation and maintenance. As a result, if natural gas prices remain low relative to the cost of coal as an input, fewer boilermakers will be needed. Conversely, if coal is the lower cost input, more boilermakers will be needed to meet federal Clean Air Act requirements by continuing to upgrade electrical generation plants' boiler and scrubbing systems.

The installation of new boilers and pressure vessels, air pollution equipment, water treatment plants, storage and process tanks, electric static precipitators, and stacks and liners will spur some demand for boilermakers, although to a lesser extent than repairs and upgrades will.

While boilers typically last more than 50 years, the need to replace parts, such as boiler tubes, heating elements, and ductwork, is an ongoing process that will require the work of boilermakers.

Job Prospects. Overall job prospects should be favorable because the work of a boilermaker remains hazardous and physically demanding, leading some qualified applicants to seek other types of work. Although employment growth will generate some job openings, the majority of positions will stem from the need to replace the large number of boilermakers expected to retire in the coming decade.

People who have welding training or a welding certificate should have the best opportunities to be selected for boilermaker apprenticeship programs. Those with general mechanical aptitude also will have better job opportunities.

As with many other construction workers, employment of boilermakers is sensitive to fluctuations of the economy. On the one hand, workers may experience periods of unemployment when the overall level of construction falls. On the other hand, shortages of workers may occur in some areas during peak periods of building activity.

Nonetheless, maintenance and repair of boilers must continue even during economic downturns, so boilermaker mechanics in manufacturing and other industries generally have more stable employment than those in construction.

O*NET

➤ Boilermakers (47-2011.00)

Contacts for More Information

For information about apprenticeships or job opportunities as a boilermaker, contact local boiler construction contractors, a local chapter of the International Brotherhood of Boilermakers, Iron Ship Builders, Blacksmiths, Forgers, and Helpers, a local joint union-management apprenticeship committee, or the nearest office of your state employment service or apprenticeship agency. Apprenticeship information is available from the U.S. Department of Labor's toll free help line, 1 (877) 872-5627, or the Employment and Training Administration (www.doleta.gov/OA/eta_default.cfm)

For apprenticeship information, visit
➤ International Brotherhood of Boilermakers, Iron Ship Builders, Blacksmiths, Forgers, and Helpers (www.boilermakers.org/)

For welding certification information, visit
➤ American Welding Society (www.aws.org/w/a/)

Brickmasons, Blockmasons, and Stonemasons

- **2012 Median Pay** .... $44,950 per year
  $21.61 per hour
- **Entry-Level Education** ... High school diploma or equivalent
- **Work Experience in a Related Occupation** .... None
- **On-the-Job Training** .... Apprenticeship
- **Number of Jobs 2012** 85,100
- **Job Outlook, 2012–22** .... 34% (Much faster than average)
- **Employment Change, 2012–22** 29,300

What Brickmasons, Blockmasons, and Stonemasons Do

Brickmasons, blockmasons, and stonemasons (or, simply, masons) use bricks, concrete blocks, and natural and man-made stones to build fences, walkways, walls, and other structures.

Duties. Masons typically do the following:

- Read blueprints or drawings to calculate materials needed
- Lay out patterns or foundations using a straightedge
- Break or cut bricks, stones, or blocks to their appropriate size
- Mix mortar or grout and spread it onto a slab or foundation
- Lay bricks, blocks, or stones according to plans
- Clean excess mortar with trowels and other hand tools
- Construct corners with a corner pole or by building a corner pyramid

A blockmason sets concrete blocks.

- Ensure that a structure is perfectly vertical and horizontal, using a plumb bob and level
- Clean and polish surfaces with hand or power tools
- Fill expansion joints with the appropriate caulking materials

The following are examples of types of masons:

Brickmasons and *blockmasons*–often called *bricklayers*–build and repair walls, floors, partitions, fireplaces, chimneys, and other structures with brick, precast masonry panels, concrete block, and other masonry materials.

Pointing, cleaning, and caulking workers repair brickwork, particularly on older structures on which mortar has come loose. Special care must be taken not to damage the structural integrity or the existing bricks.

Refractory masons are brickmasons who specialize in installing firebrick, gunite, castables, and refractory tile in high-temperature boilers, furnaces, cupolas, ladles, and soaking pits in industrial establishments. Most of these workers are employed in steel mills, where molten materials flow on refractory beds from furnaces to rolling machines. They also are employed at oil refineries, glass furnaces, incinerators, and other locations with manufacturing processes that require high temperatures.

Stonemasons build stone walls, as well as set stone exteriors and floors. They work with two types of stone: natural-cut stone, such as marble, granite, and limestone; and artificial stone, made from concrete, marble chips, or other masonry materials. Using a special hammer or a diamond-blade saw, workers cut stone to make various shapes and sizes. Some stonemasons specialize in setting marble, which is similar to setting large pieces of stone.

Work Environment

Brickmasons, blockmasons, and stonemasons (masons) held about 85,100 jobs in 2012, of which 54 percent were employed in the masonry contractors industry. About 20 percent were self-employed. Many self-employed contractors work on small jobs, such as residential patios, walkways, and fireplaces.

Although most masons work in residential construction, work in nonresidential construction is growing because most nonresidential buildings are now built with walls made of some combination of concrete block, brick veneer, stone, granite, marble, tile, and glass.

As with many other construction occupations, the work is physically demanding. Masons often lift heavy materials and stand, kneel, and bend for long periods.

Because they usually work outdoors, poor weather conditions may reduce work activity.

Injuries and Illnesses. Brickmasons and blockmasons have a higher rate of injuries and illnesses than the national average. Common injuries include muscle strains from lifting heavy materials, as well as cuts from tools and falls from scaffolds.

Work Schedules. Although most masons work full time, some work longer hours to meet construction deadlines. However, because they primarily work outdoors, masons may have to stop work in extreme cold or rainy weather. Nonetheless, processes and materials have been developed that allow masons to work in a greater variety of weather conditions than in the past.

Self-employed workers may be able to set their own schedule.

How to Become One

Although most brickmasons, blockmasons, and stonemasons (masons) learn through an apprenticeship, some learn their skills on the job. Others learn through 1- or 2-year mason programs at technical schools.

Median Annual Wages, May 2012

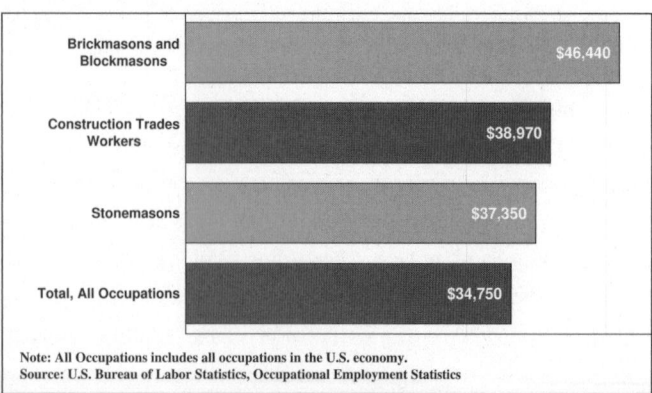

Brickmasons and Blockmasons	$46,440
Construction Trades Workers	$38,970
Stonemasons	$37,350
Total, All Occupations	$34,750

Note: All Occupations includes all occupations in the U.S. economy.
Source: U.S. Bureau of Labor Statistics, Occupational Employment Statistics

Percent Change in Employment, Projected 2012–2022

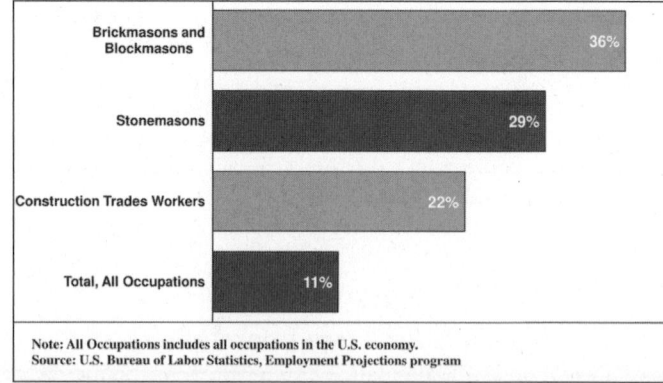

Brickmasons and Blockmasons	36%
Stonemasons	29%
Construction Trades Workers	22%
Total, All Occupations	11%

Note: All Occupations includes all occupations in the U.S. economy.
Source: U.S. Bureau of Labor Statistics, Employment Projections program

Employment Projections Data for Brickmasons, Blockmasons, and Stonemasons

Occupational title	SOC Code	Employment, 2012	Projected Employment, 2022	Change, 2012–2022	
				Percent	Numeric
Brickmasons, blockmasons, and stonemasons	—	85,100	114,400	34	29,300
Brickmasons and blockmasons...	47-2021	71,000	96,200	36	25,200
Stonemasons	47-2022	14,100	18,200	29	4,100

Source: U.S. Bureau of Labor Statistics, Employment Projections Program

Note: Data are rounded. Go to **Occupational Information Included in the OOH** for a discussion of the data in this table.

Education. A high school diploma or equivalent is required for all masons. High school courses in English, mathematics, mechanical drawing, and shop are considered useful.

Many technical schools offer 1-year programs in basic masonry. These programs operate both independently and in conjunction with apprenticeship training. The credits earned as part of an apprenticeship program usually count toward an associate's degree. Some people take courses before being hired, and some take them later as part of on-the-job training.

Training. A 3- to 4-year apprenticeship is how most masons learn the trade. For each year of the program, apprentices must complete at least 144 hours of related technical instruction and 2,000 hours of paid on-the-job training. Apprentices learn construction basics such as blueprint reading; mathematics, including measurement, volume, and mixing proportions; building code requirements; and safety and first-aid practices.

In the coming years, the focus of apprenticeships is likely to change from time served to proven competence. This may result in apprenticeships of shorter duration.

After completing an apprenticeship program, masons are considered journey workers and are able to perform tasks on their own.

Several groups, including unions and contractor associations, sponsor apprenticeship programs. The basic qualifications for entering an apprenticeship program are as follows:

- Minimum age of 18
- High school education or equivalent
- Physically able to do the work

Some contractors have their own training programs for masons. Although workers may enter apprenticeships directly, some masons start out as construction helpers.

Important Qualities

Hand-eye coordination. Workers must be able to apply smooth, even layers of mortar, set bricks, and remove any excess before the mortar hardens.

Math skills. Knowledge of math–including measurement, volume, and mixing proportions–is important in this trade.

Physical stamina. Brickmasons must keep a steady pace while setting bricks all day. Although no individual brick is extremely heavy, the constant lifting can be tiring.

Physical strength. Workers must be strong enough to lift blocks that sometimes weigh more than 40 pounds. They must also carry heavy tools, equipment, and other materials, such as bags of mortar and grout.

Visualization. Stonemasons must be able to see how stones fit together to build attractive and stable structures.

Pay

The median annual wage for brickmasons and blockmasons was $46,440 in May 2012. The median wage is the wage at which half the workers in an occupation earned more than that amount and half earned less. The lowest 10 percent earned less than $28,980, and the top 10 percent earned more than $77,950.

The median annual wage for stonemasons was $37,350 in May 2012. The lowest 10 percent earned less than $22,210, and the top 10 percent earned more than $63,330.

The starting pay for apprentices is usually about 50 percent of what fully trained workers make. They earn pay increases as they learn to do more.

About 20 percent of masons were self-employed in 2012.

Job Outlook

Employment of brickmasons, blockmasons, and stonemasons (masons) is projected to grow 34 percent from 2012 to 2022, much faster than the average for all occupations.

Population growth will result in the construction of more schools, hospitals, apartment buildings, and other structures, many of which are made of brick, block, or stone.

In addition, masons will be needed to restore a growing number of brick buildings. Although expensive, brick and stone exteriors should remain popular, reflecting a preference for low-maintenance, durable exterior materials.

Similar Occupations This table shows a list of occupations with job duties that are similar to those of brickmasons, blockmasons, and stonemasons.

Occupations	Entry-level Education	2012 Pay	Projected Job Growth	Average Annual Openings
Carpenters	High school diploma or equivalent	$39,940	24%	32,920
Cement Masons and Terrazzo Workers	See "How to Become One"	$35,856	29%	5,830
Construction Laborers and Helpers	See "How to Become One"	$29,277	25%	58,790
Drywall and Ceiling Tile Installers, and Tapers	Less than high school	$38,572	16%	2,880
Tile and Marble Setters	Less than high school	$37,040	15%	1,290

Building code requirements in hurricane-prone areas also will increase the demand for durable homes that use brick, block, or stone.

Job Prospects. Overall job prospects should continue to improve over the coming decade as construction activity rebounds from the recent recession. As with many other types of construction jobs, employment is sensitive to the fluctuations of the economy. On the one hand, workers may experience periods of unemployment when the overall level of construction falls. On the other hand, shortages of workers may occur in some areas during peak periods of building activity.

The current masonry workforce is growing older, and many workers are expected to retire over the next decade, which will create some job openings. However, job openings from employment growth are expected to be much greater.

Workers with a good job history and with experience in masonry and construction should have the best job opportunities.

O*NET

➤ Brickmasons and Blockmasons (47-2021.00)
➤ Stonemasons (47-2022.00)

Contacts for More Information

For details about apprenticeships or other work opportunities for brickmasons, blockmasons, and stonemasons, contact the offices of the state employment service, the state apprenticeship agency, local contractors or firms that employ masons, or local union-management apprenticeship committees. Information on apprenticeships is available from the U.S. Department of Labor's toll-free help line, 1 (877) 872-5627, or the Employment and Training Administration (www.doleta.gov/OA/eta_default.cfm).

For information about training for brickmasons, blockmasons, and stonemasons, visit

➤ International Masonry Institute National Training Center (www. imiweb.org)
➤ Mason Contractors Association of America (www.masoncontractors.org)
➤ National Association of Home Builders (www.nahb.org)

For information about training, including obtaining a credential in green construction, visit

➤ NCCER (www.nccer.org)

For general information about the work of bricklayers, visit

➤ Associated General Contractors of America (www.agc.org)

Carpenters

- **2012 Median Pay** .... $39,940 per year
  $19.20 per hour
- **Entry-Level Education** ... High school diploma or equivalent
- **Work Experience in a Related Occupation** .... None
- **On-the-Job Training** .... Apprenticeship
- **Number of Jobs 2012** 901,200
- **Job Outlook, 2012–22** .... 24% (Much faster than average)
- **Employment Change, 2012–22** 218,200

What Carpenters Do

Carpenters construct and repair building frameworks and structures–such as stairways, doorframes, partitions, and rafters–made from wood and other materials. They also may install kitchen cabinets, siding, and drywall.

Duties. Carpenters typically do the following:

- Follow blueprints and building plans to meet the needs of clients
- Install structures and fixtures, such as windows and molding
- Measure, cut, or shape wood, plastic, and other materials
- Construct building frameworks, including walls, floors, and doorframes
- Help erect, level, and install building framework with the aid of rigging hardware and cranes
- Inspect and replace damaged framework or other structures and fixtures
- Instruct and direct laborers and other construction helpers

Carpenters are one of the most versatile construction occupations, with workers usually doing many different tasks. For example, some carpenters insulate office buildings; others install drywall or kitchen cabinets in homes. Those who help construct tall buildings or bridges often install the wooden concrete forms for cement footings or pillars. Some carpenters erect shoring and scaffolding for buildings.

Carpenters use many different hand and power tools to cut and shape wood, plastic, fiberglass, or drywall. They commonly use hand tools, including squares, levels, and chisels, as well as many power tools, such as sanders, circular saws, nail guns, and welding machines. Carpenters fasten materials together with nails, screws, staples, and adhesives, and do a final check of their work to ensure accuracy. They use a tape measure on nearly every project because proper measuring increases productivity, reduces waste, and ensures that the pieces being cut are the proper size.

The following are examples of types of carpenters:

Residential carpenters typically specialize in new-home, town-home, and condominium building and remodeling. As part of a single job, they might build and set forms for footings, walls, and slabs, and frame and finish exterior walls, roofs, and decks. They also frame interior walls, build stairs, and install drywall, crown molding, doors, and cabinets. In addition, residential carpenters may tile floors and lay wood floors and carpet. Fully trained construction carpenters can easily switch from new-home building to remodeling.

Commercial carpenters typically remodel and help build commercial office buildings, hospitals, hotels, schools, and shopping malls. Some specialize in working with light-gauge and load-bearing steel framing for interior partitions, exterior framing, and curtain wall construction. Others specialize in working with

A carpenter uses a pneumatic gun for hammering nails.

Median Annual Wages, May 2012

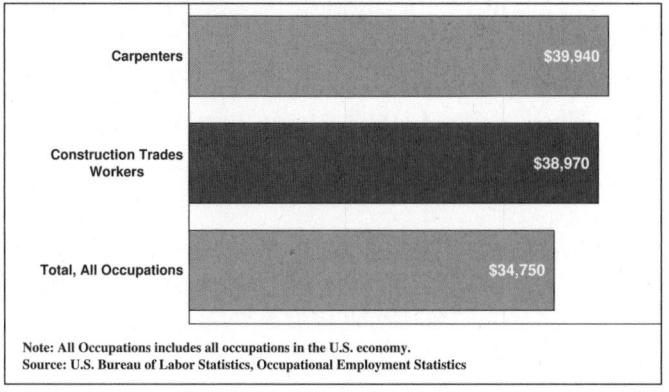

Note: All Occupations includes all occupations in the U.S. economy.
Source: U.S. Bureau of Labor Statistics, Occupational Employment Statistics

Percent Change in Employment, Projected 2012–2022

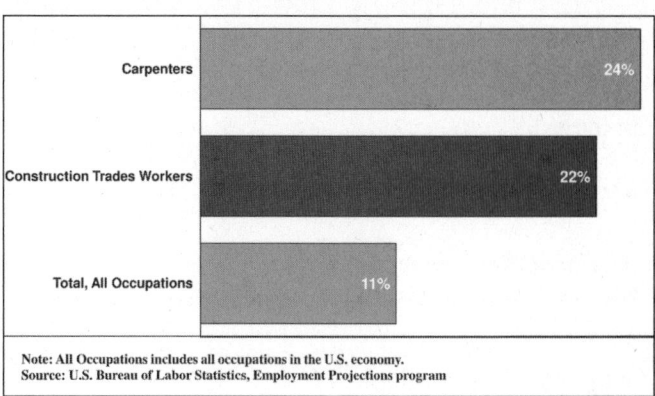

Note: All Occupations includes all occupations in the U.S. economy.
Source: U.S. Bureau of Labor Statistics, Employment Projections program

concrete forming systems and finishing interior and exterior walls, partitions, and ceilings. Most commercial carpenters perform many of the same tasks as residential carpenters.

Industrial carpenters typically work in civil and industrial settings, where they build scaffolding and create and set forms for pouring concrete. Some industrial carpenters build tunnel bracing or partitions in underground passageways and mines to control the circulation of air to worksites. Others build concrete forms for tunnels, bridges, dams, power plants, or sewer construction projects.

Work Environment

Carpenters held about 901,200 jobs in 2012. About 36 percent of carpenters were self-employed. Most carpenters work in the construction industry, where they account for the largest share of the building trades occupations. The industries that employed the most carpenters in 2012 were as follows:

Residential building construction 19%
Nonresidential building construction 12
Building finishing contractors 10
Foundation, structure, and building exterior contractors 7

Because carpenters are involved in many types of construction, from building highways and bridges to installing kitchen cabinets, they work both indoors and outdoors.

Carpenters may work in cramped spaces, and frequent lifting, standing, and kneeling can be tiring. Those who work outdoors are subject to variable weather conditions.

Injuries and Illnesses. Carpenters have a higher rate of injuries and illnesses than the national average. The most common injuries include muscle strains from lifting heavy materials, falls from ladders, and cuts from sharp objects and tools.

Work Schedules. Nearly all carpenters work full time, which may include working evenings and weekends. Overtime is common in order to meet deadlines.

About 36 percent of carpenters were self-employed in 2012. Self-employed workers often work in residential construction and may be able to set their own schedule.

How to Become One

Although most carpenters learn their trade through an apprenticeship, some learn on the job, starting as a helper.

Education. A high school diploma or equivalent is required. High school courses in English, mathematics, mechanical drawing, and shop are considered useful.

Training. Most carpenters learn their trade through a 3- or 4-year apprenticeship. For each year of the program, apprentices must complete at least 144 hours of technical training and 2,000 hours of paid on-the-job training. In the technical training, apprentices learn carpentry basics, blueprint reading, mathematics, building code requirements, and safety and first-aid practices. They also may receive specialized training in concrete, rigging, welding, scaffold building, fall protection, confined workspaces, and Occupational Safety and Health Administration (OSHA) 10- and 30-hour safety courses.

After finishing an apprenticeship, carpenters are considered to be journey workers and may perform tasks on their own.

Several groups, including unions and contractor associations, sponsor apprenticeship programs. The basic qualifications for a person to enter an apprenticeship program are as follows:

- Minimum age of 18
- High school education or equivalent
- Physically able to do the work
- U.S. citizen or proof of legal residency
- Pass substance abuse screening

Some contractors have their own carpenter training program. Although many workers enter apprenticeships directly, some carpenters start out as helpers.

Some apprenticeships offer special programs for veterans.

A number of 2-year technical schools offer carpentry degrees that are affiliated with unions or contractor organizations. Credits earned as part of an apprenticeship program usually count toward an associate's degree.

Advancement. Because they are exposed to the entire construction process, carpenters usually have more opportunities than other construction workers to become independent contractors or general construction supervisors.

Carpenters seeking advancement often take additional training provided by associations, unions, or employers. Also, it is increasingly important to be able to communicate in both English and Spanish to relay instructions to workers.

Important Qualities

Business skills. Self-employed carpenters must be able to bid new jobs, track inventory, and plan work assignments.

Detail oriented. Carpenters perform many tasks that are important in the overall building process. Making precise measurements, for example, may reduce gaps between windows and frames, limiting any leaks around the window.

Manual dexterity. Carpenters use many tools and need hand-eye coordination to avoid injury. Striking the head of a nail, for example, is crucial to not damaging wood.

Employment Projections Data for Carpenters

Occupational title	SOC Code	Employment, 2012	Projected Employment, 2022	Change, 2012–2022	
				Percent	Numeric
Carpenters..	47-2031	901,200	1,119,400	24	218,200

Source: U.S. Bureau of Labor Statistics, Employment Projections Program

Note: Data are rounded. Go to **Occupational Information Included in the OOH** *for a discussion of the data in this table.*

Math skills. Because carpenters use basic math skills every day, they need to be able to calculate volume and measure materials to be cut.

Physical stamina. Carpenters need physical endurance. They often lift heavy tools and materials while standing, climbing, or bending for long periods.

Physical strength. Many of the tools and materials that carpenters use are heavy. For example, plywood sheets can weigh 50 to 100 pounds.

Problem-solving skills. Because all construction jobs vary, carpenters must adjust project plans accordingly. For example, they may have to use wedges to level cabinets in homes that have settled and are sloping slightly.

Pay

The median annual wage for carpenters was $39,940 in May 2012. The median wage is the wage at which half the workers in an occupation earned more than that amount and half earned less. The lowest 10 percent earned less than $24,880, and the top 10 percent earned more than $72,580.

The starting pay for apprentices usually is between 30 percent and 50 percent of what fully trained carpenters make. As apprentices learn to do more, they receive pay increases.

Job Outlook

Employment of carpenters is projected to grow 24 percent from 2012 to 2022, much faster than the average for all occupations. Population growth should result in new-home construction–the largest segment employing carpenters–which will stimulate the need for many new workers. Home remodeling needs should also spur demand for carpenters.

In addition, the need to repair and replace roads and bridges should increase employment of carpenters. Much of this growth, however, depends on spending by federal and state governments as they attempt to upgrade existing infrastructure.

The construction of factories and power plants also may result in some new jobs.

However, will be the increasing use of modular and prefabricated components. Roof assemblies, walls, stairs, and complete bathrooms are just a few of the prefabricated components that can be manufactured in a separate facility and then assembled onsite by carpenters. Installing prefabricated components replaces the most labor-intensive and time-consuming onsite building activities.

Job Prospects. Overall job prospects for carpenters should improve over the coming decade as construction activity continues to rebound.

The number of job openings is expected to vary by geographic area. Because construction activity parallels the movement of people and businesses, areas of the country with the largest population increases will require the most carpenters.

Employment of carpenters, like that of many other construction workers, is sensitive to fluctuations in the economy. On the one hand, workers in these trades may experience periods of unemployment when the overall level of construction falls. On the other hand, peak periods of building activity may produce shortages of carpenters.

O*NET

➤ Carpenters (47-2031.00)
➤ Construction Carpenters (47-2031.01)
➤ Rough Carpenters (47-2031.02)

Contacts for More Information

For details about apprenticeships or other work opportunities in this trade, contact the offices of the state employment service, the state apprenticeship agency, local contractors or firms that employ carpenters, or local union-management carpenter apprenticeship committees. Apprenticeship information is available from the U.S. Department of Labor's toll-free help line, 1 (877) 872-5627, or the Employment and Training Administration (www.doleta.gov/OA/eta_default.cfm).

For more information about carpenters, including training opportunities, visit

➤ Associated Builders and Contractors (www.abc.org/)
➤ Associated General Contractors of America (www.agc.org/)
➤ National Association of Home Builders, Home Builders Institute (www.hbi.org)
➤ NCCER (www.nccer.org/carpentry?pID=105)
➤ United Brotherhood of Carpenters and Joiners of America, Carpenters Training Fund (www.carpenters.org/Home.aspx)

Similar Occupations   This table shows a list of occupations with job duties that are similar to those of carpenters.

Occupations	Entry-level Education	2012 Pay	Projected Job Growth	Average Annual Openings
Cement Masons and Terrazzo Workers	See "How to Become One"	$35,856	29%	5,830
Construction Laborers and Helpers	See "How to Become One"	$29,277	25%	58,790
Drywall and Ceiling Tile Installers, and Tapers	Less than high school	$38,572	16%	2,880
Industrial Machinery Mechanics and Maintenance Workers and Millwrights	High school diploma or equivalent	$45,848	17%	18,700
Tile and Marble Setters	Less than high school	$37,040	15%	1,290

Cement Masons and Terrazzo Workers

- **2012 Median Pay** .... $35,830 per year
  $17.23 per hour
- **Entry-Level Education** ....See "How to Become One"
- **Work Experience in a Related Occupation**.............. None
- **On-the-Job Training** ....See "How to Become One"
- **Number of Jobs 2012** 144,300
- **Job Outlook, 2012–22** .... 29% (Much faster than average)
- **Employment Change, 2012–22** 41,700

What Cement Masons and Terrazzo Workers Do

Cement masons pour, smooth, and finish concrete floors, sidewalks, roads, and curbs. Using a cement mixture, terrazzo workers create durable and decorative surfaces for floors and stairways.

Duties. Cement masons typically do the following:

- Set the forms that hold concrete in place
- Install reinforcing rebar or mesh wire to strengthen the concrete
- Signal truck drivers to facilitate the pouring of concrete
- Spread, level, and smooth concrete, using a trowel, float, or screed
- Mold expansion joints and edges
- Monitor curing (hardening) to ensure a durable, smooth, and uniform finish
- Apply sealants or waterproofing to protect concrete

Terrazzo workers typically do the following (in addition to what cement masons do):

- Measure ingredients for terrazzo
- Blend a marble chip mixture that may have colors in it
- Grind and polish surfaces for a smooth, lustrous look

Concrete is one of the most common and durable materials used in construction. Once set, concrete–a mixture of cement, sand, gravel, and water–becomes the foundation for everything from decorative patios and floors to huge dams or miles of roadways.

The following are examples of types of cement masons and terrazzo workers:

Cement masons and concrete finishers place and finish concrete. They may color concrete surfaces, expose aggregate (small stones) in walls and sidewalks, or make concrete beams, columns, and panels.

Throughout the process of pouring, leveling, and finishing concrete, cement masons must monitor how the wind, heat, or cold affects the curing of the concrete. They must have a thorough knowledge of the characteristics of concrete so that they can determine what is happening to the concrete and take measures to prevent defects.

Some small jobs may require the use of a supportive wire mesh called lath. On larger jobs, reinforcing iron and rebar workers install the reinforcing mesh.

Terrazzo workers and finishers create decorative walkways, floors, patios, and panels. Although much of the preliminary work in pouring, leveling, and finishing concrete is similar to that of cement masons, terrazzo workers create more decorative finishes by blending a fine marble chip into the epoxy or cement, which is often colored. Once the terrazzo is thoroughly set, workers correct any depressions or imperfections with a grinder to create a smooth, uniform finish. Terrazzo workers also install decorative toppings and/or polishing compounds to new or existing concrete.

Work Environment

Cement masons and terrazzo workers held about 144,300 jobs in 2012. About 90 percent were employed in the specialty trade contractors industry.

Concrete and terrazzo work is fast paced and strenuous. Because most of the work is done at floor level, workers often must bend and kneel. The work, either indoors or outdoors, may be in areas that are muddy, dusty, or dirty.

Injuries and Illnesses. Although the work is less dangerous than many other construction occupations, cement masons and terrazzo workers may experience chemical burns from uncured concrete, falls from scaffolding, and cuts from tools. To avoid injuries, workers wear protective gear, including kneepads, harnesses, and water-repellent boots.

Work Schedules. Most cement masons and terrazzo workers are employed full time.

About 5 percent were self-employed in 2012. Many of them can set their own schedule.

Because many cement and terrazzo jobs are outdoors, work generally stops in wet weather. Hours may also vary for other reasons, such as construction deadlines or coordination with other work activities.

How to Become One

Although most cement masons and terrazzo workers learn on the job, some learn their trade through an apprenticeship.

Education. Although there are no specific education requirements for cement masons and concrete finishers, terrazzo workers usually must have a high school diploma. High school courses in math, mechanical drawing, and blueprint reading are considered to be helpful.

Training. Most on-the-job training programs consist of experienced workers teaching helpers to use the tools, equipment, machines, and materials of the trade. Trainees begin with tasks such as edging, jointing, and using a straightedge on freshly placed concrete. As training progresses, assignments become more complex and trainees can usually perform finishing tasks more quickly.

Some cement masons and most terrazzo workers learn their trade through a 3-year apprenticeship. Each year, apprentices must have at least 144 hours of technical instruction and 2,000 hours of paid on-the-job training. Apprentices learn construction basics such as blueprint reading, mathematics, building code requirements, and safety and first-aid practices. Apprentices also learn

Concrete masons direct the concrete to a desired location.

Median Annual Wages, May 2012

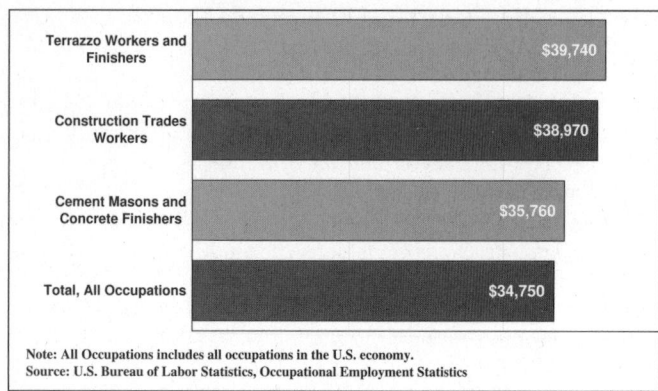

Note: All Occupations includes all occupations in the U.S. economy.
Source: U.S. Bureau of Labor Statistics, Occupational Employment Statistics

Percent Change in Employment, Projected 2012–2022

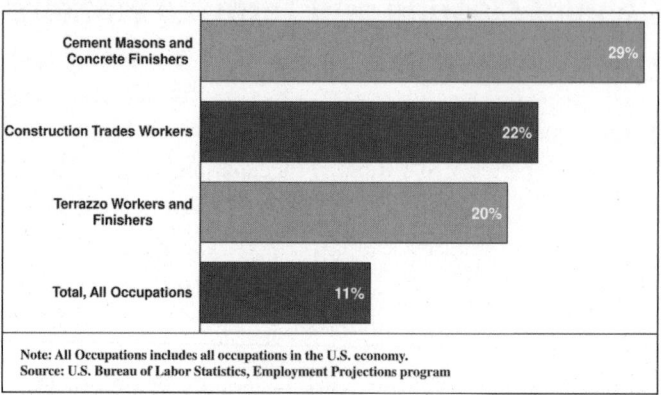

Note: All Occupations includes all occupations in the U.S. economy.
Source: U.S. Bureau of Labor Statistics, Employment Projections program

about the wide variety of materials and additives that can change color or allow concrete to cure in different conditions.

After completing an apprenticeship program, cement masons and terrazzo workers are considered to be journey workers, qualifying them to do tasks on their own.

Several groups, including unions and contractor associations, sponsor apprenticeship programs. The basic qualifications for entering an apprenticeship program are as follows:

• Minimum age of 18

• High school education or equivalent

• Physically able to do the work

Some contractors have their own cement masonry or terrazzo training programs. Although workers may enter apprenticeships directly, many start out as construction laborers and helpers.

Important Qualities

Color vision. Terrazzo workers must determine small color variances when setting terrazzo patterns. Because these patterns often include many different colors, terrazzo workers must be able to distinguish between colors for the best looking finish.

Physical stamina. Cement masons and terrazzo workers must be able to spend a lot of time kneeling, bending, and reaching.

Physical strength. Cement masons and terrazzo workers often must lift heavy materials. For example, many jobs require workers to be able to lift and carry 50-pound bags of gravel and sand.

Pay

The median annual wage for cement masons and concrete finishers was $35,760 in May 2012. The median wage is the wage at which half the workers in an occupation earned more than that amount and half earned less. The lowest 10 percent earned less than $23,380, and the top 10 percent earned more than $64,080.

The median annual wage for terrazzo workers and finishers was $39,740 in May 2012. The lowest 10 percent earned less than $23,050, and the top 10 percent earned more than $66,380.

The starting pay for apprentices usually is about 50 percent of what fully trained workers make. Apprentices receive pay increases as they learn to do more tasks.

Job Outlook

Employment of cement masons and terrazzo workers is projected to grow 29 percent from 2012 to 2022, much faster than the average for all occupations.

Employment Projections Data for Cement Masons and Terrazzo Workers

Occupational title	SOC Code	Employment, 2012	Projected Employment, 2022	Change, 2012–2022	
				Percent	Numeric
Cement masons and terrazzo workers	—	144,300	186,100	29	41,700
Cement masons and concrete finishers	47-2051	140,800	181,800	29	41,000
Terrazzo workers and finishers..	47-2053	3,500	4,200	20	700

Source: U.S. Bureau of Labor Statistics, Employment Projections Program

Note: Data are rounded. Go to **Occupational Information Included in the OOH** *for a discussion of the data in this table.*

Similar Occupations   This table shows a list of occupations with job duties that are similar to those of cement masons and terrazzo workers.

Occupations	Entry-level Education	2012 Pay	Projected Job Growth	Average Annual Openings
Brickmasons, Blockmasons, and Stonemasons	High school diploma or equivalent	$44,935	34%	3,840
Construction Laborers and Helpers	See "How to Become One"	$29,277	25%	58,790
Drywall and Ceiling Tile Installers, and Tapers	Less than high school	$38,572	16%	2,880
Tile and Marble Setters	Less than high school	$37,040	15%	1,290

Although employment growth will vary by specialty, both specialties' growth will depend on the number of commercial, public, and civil construction projects such as new roads, bridges, and buildings.

Employment of cement masons and concrete finishers is projected to grow 29 percent, much faster than the average for all occupations. More cement masons will be needed to build and renovate highways, bridges, factories, and residential structures to meet the demands of a growing population and aging infrastructure.

The use of concrete for buildings is increasing because its strength is an important asset in areas prone to severe weather. For example, residential construction projects in Florida are using more concrete as building requirements change in reaction to the increased frequency and intensity of hurricanes. The use of concrete is likely to expand into other hurricane-prone areas as the durability of Florida homes built with concrete becomes more established.

Employment of terrazzo workers and finishers is projected to grow 20 percent, faster than the average for all occupations. However, because it is a small occupation, the fast growth will result in only about 700 new jobs over the 10-year period. Terrazzo is a durable and attractive flooring option that is often used in schools, government buildings, and hospitals. The construction and renovation of such buildings will spur demand for these workers. However, because polished concrete is similar to terrazzo and usually less expensive, this may limit the need for terrazzo workers.

Job Prospects. Overall job opportunities for cement masons and terrazzo workers are expected to be good, particularly for those with more experience and skills. Applicants who take masonry-related courses at technical schools may have the best job opportunities. Employers also prefer candidates who are experienced in polished concrete.

As with many other construction workers, employment of cement masons and terrazzo workers is sensitive to the fluctuations of the economy. On the one hand, workers may experience periods of unemployment when the overall level of construction falls. On the other hand, shortages of workers may occur in some areas during peak periods of building activity.

O*NET

➤ Cement Masons and Concrete Finishers (47-2051.00)
➤ Terrazzo Workers and Finishers (47-2053.00)

Contacts for More Information

For information about apprenticeships or job opportunities as a cement mason or terrazzo worker, contact local cement or terrazzo contractors, a local joint union-management apprenticeship committee, or the nearest office of your state employment service or apprenticeship agency. Apprenticeship information is available from the U.S. Department of Labor's toll-free help line, 1 (877) 872-5627, or the Employment and Training Administration (www.doleta.gov/OA/eta_default.cfm).

For general information about cement masons and terrazzo workers, visit
➤ Associated Builders and Contractors (www.abc.org/)
➤ Associated General Contractors of America (www.agc.org)
➤ International Masonry Institute (www.imiweb.org)
➤ NCCER (www.nccer.org)
➤ National Terrazzo and Mosaic Association (www.ntma.com)
➤ Operative Plasterers' and Cement Masons' International Association (www.opcmia.org)
For more information about careers and training as a mason, visit
➤ Mason Contractors Association of America (www.masoncontractors.org)

Construction and Building Inspectors

- **2012 Median Pay** .... $53,450 per year
$25.70 per hour
- **Entry-Level Education** ... High school diploma or equivalent
- **Work Experience in a Related Occupation** ... 5 years or more
- **On-the-Job Training** ...Moderate-term on-the-job training
- **Number of Jobs 2012** 102,300
- **Job Outlook, 2012–22** .... 12% (As fast as average)
- **Employment Change, 2012–22** 12,500

What Construction and Building Inspectors Do

Construction and building inspectors ensure that construction meets local and national building codes and ordinances, zoning regulations, and contract specifications.

Duties. Construction and building inspectors typically do the following:

- Review plans to ensure they meet building codes, local ordinances, and zoning regulations
- Approve building plans that are satisfactory
- Monitor construction sites periodically to ensure overall compliance
- Use survey instruments, metering devices, and test equipment to perform inspections
- Inspect plumbing, electrical, and other systems to ensure that they meet code
- Verify alignment, level, and elevation of structures to ensure building compliance
- Issue violation notices and stop-work orders until building is compliant
- Keep daily logs, including photographs taken during inspection
- Provide written feedback related to the findings

Construction and building inspectors examine buildings, highways and streets, sewer and water systems, dams, bridges, and other structures. They also inspect electrical; heating, ventilation, air-conditioning, and refrigeration (HVACR); and plumbing systems. Although no two inspections are alike, inspectors perform an initial check during the first phase of construction and follow-up inspections throughout the construction project. When the project is finished, they do a final, comprehensive inspection and provide written or oral feedback related to their findings.

The following are examples of types of construction and building inspectors:

Building inspectors check the structural quality and general safety of buildings. Some specialize further in structural steel or reinforced-concrete structures, for example.

Coating inspectors examine the exterior paint and coating on bridges, pipelines, and large holding tanks. Inspectors perform checks at various stages of the painting process to ensure proper coating.

Electrical inspectors examine the installed electrical systems to ensure they function properly and comply with electrical codes and standards. The inspectors visit worksites to inspect new and existing sound and security systems, wiring, lighting, motors, and generating equipment. They also inspect the installed electrical wiring for HVACR systems and appliances.

Although inspections are primarily visual, inspectors may use tape measures, survey instruments, and metering devices.

Elevator inspectors examine lifting and conveying devices, such as elevators, escalators, moving sidewalks, lifts and hoists, inclined railways, ski lifts, and amusement rides. The inspections include both the mechanical and electrical control systems.

Home inspectors typically inspect newly built or previously owned homes, condominiums, townhomes, and other dwellings. Prospective home buyers often hire home inspectors to check and report on a home's structure and overall condition. Sometimes, homeowners hire a home inspector to evaluate their home's condition before placing it on the market.

In addition to examining structural quality, home inspectors examine all home systems and features, including roofing, exterior walls, attached garage or carport, foundation, interior, plumbing, electrical, and HVACR systems. They look for and report viola-

tions of building codes, but home inspectors do not have the power to enforce compliance with the codes.

Mechanical inspectors examine the installation of HVACR systems and equipment to ensure that they are installed and function properly. They also may inspect commercial kitchen equipment, gas-fired appliances, and boilers. Mechanical inspectors should not be confused with quality control inspectors who inspect goods at manufacturing plants.

Plan examiners determine whether the plans for a building or other structure comply with building codes. They also determine whether the structure is suited to the engineering and environmental demands of the building site.

Plumbing inspectors examine the installation of systems that ensure the safety and health of the drinking water system, piping for industrial uses, and the sanitary disposal of waste.

Public works inspectors ensure that the construction of federal, state, and local government water and sewer systems, highways, streets, bridges, and dams conform to detailed contract specifications. Workers inspect excavation and fill operations, the placement of forms for concrete, concrete mixing and pouring, asphalt paving, and grading operations. Public works inspectors may specialize in highways, structural steel, reinforced concrete, or ditches. Others may specialize in dredging operations required for bridges and dams or for harbors.

Specification inspectors ensure that construction work is performed according to design specifications. Specification inspectors represent the owner's interests, not those of the general public. Insurance companies and financial institutions also may use their services.

Some building inspectors are concerned with fire prevention safety. Fire inspectors and investigators ensure that buildings meet fire codes.

Work Environment

Construction and building inspectors held about 102,300 jobs in 2012. About 47 percent were employed in government, with most working in local government. An additional 26 percent were employed in the architectural, engineering, and related services industry. About 11 percent were self-employed.

Although construction and building inspectors spend most of their time inspecting worksites, they also spend time in a field office reviewing blueprints, writing reports, and scheduling inspections.

Some inspectors may have to climb ladders or crawl in tight spaces to complete their inspections.

Inspectors typically work alone. However, several inspectors may work as a team on large, complex projects, particularly because inspectors usually specialize in different areas of construction.

Median Annual Wages, May 2012

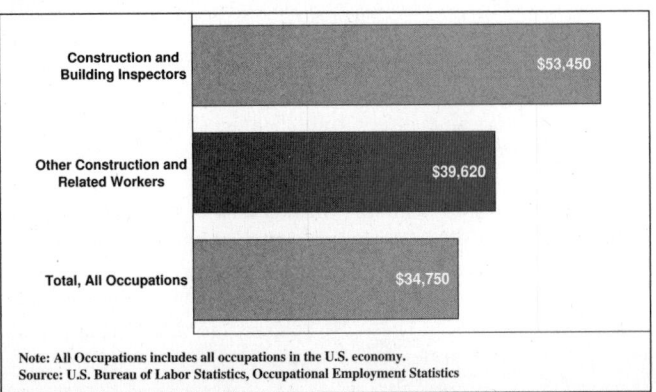

Note: All Occupations includes all occupations in the U.S. economy.
Source: U.S. Bureau of Labor Statistics, Occupational Employment Statistics

Percent Change in Employment, Projected 2012–2022

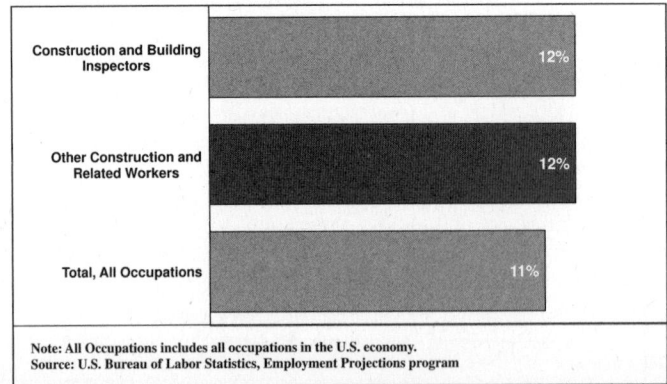

Note: All Occupations includes all occupations in the U.S. economy.
Source: U.S. Bureau of Labor Statistics, Employment Projections program

Employment Projections Data for Construction and Building Inspectors

Occupational title	SOC Code	Employment, 2012	Projected Employment, 2022	Change, 2012–2022	
				Percent	Numeric
Construction and building inspectors.................................... 47-4011		102,300	114,800	12	12,500

Source: U.S. Bureau of Labor Statistics, Employment Projections Program

Note: Data are rounded. Go to **Occupational Information Included in the OOH** *for a discussion of the data in this table.*

Work Schedules. Most inspectors work full time during regular business hours. However, some may work additional hours during periods of heavy construction activity. Also, if an accident occurs at a construction site, inspectors must respond immediately and may work additional hours to complete their report. Nongovernment inspectors–especially those who are self-employed–may have to work evenings and weekends. This is particularly true of home inspectors, who typically inspect homes during the day and write reports in the evening.

How to Become One

Most employers require inspectors to have at least a high school diploma and considerable knowledge of construction trades. Construction and building inspectors typically learn on the job. Many states and local jurisdictions require some type of license or certification.

Education. Most employers require workers to have at least a high school diploma, even for workers who have considerable related work experience.

Employers also seek candidates who have studied engineering or architecture or who have a certificate or an associate's degree that includes courses in building inspection, home inspection, construction technology, and drafting. Many community colleges offer programs in building inspection technology. Courses in blueprint reading, algebra, geometry, shop, and writing also are useful. Some courses in business management are helpful for those who plan to run their own inspecting business.

A growing number of construction and building inspectors are entering the occupation with a bachelor's degree, which often can substitute for related work experience.

Training. Training requirements vary by type of inspector, state, and local jurisdictions. In general, construction and building inspectors receive much of their training on the job, although they must learn building codes and standards on their own. Working with an experienced inspector, they learn about inspection techniques; codes, ordinances, and regulations; contract specifications; and recordkeeping and reporting duties. Supervised onsite inspections also may be a part of the training.

Work Experience in a Related Occupation. Because inspectors must possess the right mix of technical knowledge, work experience, and education, employers prefer applicants who have both training and experience in a construction trade. For example, many inspectors have experience working as carpenters, electricians, or plumbers. Specifically, many home inspectors combine knowledge of multiple specialties, so many of them enter the occupation having a combination of certifications and previous experience in various construction trades.

Licenses, Certifications, and Registrations. Many states and local jurisdictions require some type of license or certification. Typical requirements for licensure or certification include a certain amount of experience in the field; minimum education, such as a high school diploma; and passing a state-approved exam.

Some states have individual licensing programs for construction and building inspectors. Others may require certification by associations such as the International Code Council, International Association of Plumbing and Mechanical Officials, International

Similar Occupations   This table shows a list of occupations with job duties that are similar to those of construction and building inspectors.

Occupations	Entry-level Education	2012 Pay	Projected Job Growth	Average Annual Openings
Appraisers and Assessors of Real Estate	Bachelor's degree	$49,540	6%	1,210
Architects	Bachelor's degree	$73,090	17%	4,410
Carpenters	High school diploma or equivalent	$39,940	24%	32,920
Cartographers and Photogrammetrists	Bachelor's degree	$57,440	20%	490
Civil Engineers	Bachelor's degree	$79,340	20%	12,010
Construction Managers	Bachelor's degree	$82,790	16%	15,460
Cost Estimators	Bachelor's degree	$58,860	26%	11,800
Electrical and Electronics Engineering Technicians	Associate's degree	$57,850	0%	3,040
Electrical and Electronics Engineers	Bachelor's degree	$89,701	4%	7,940
Electricians	High school diploma or equivalent	$49,840	20%	22,460
Plumbers, Pipefitters, and Steamfitters	High school diploma or equivalent	$49,140	21%	13,050
Surveying and Mapping Technicians	High school diploma or equivalent	$39,670	14%	1,700
Surveyors	Bachelor's degree	$56,230	10%	1,340

Association of Electrical Inspectors, and National Fire Protection Association.

Similarly, most states require home inspectors to follow defined trade practices or obtain a state-issued license or certification. Currently, 35 states have policies regulating the conduct of home inspectors; a few states are considering adding licensure or certification requirements for home inspectors.

Home inspector license or certification requirements vary by state but may include the following:

- Minimum level of education
- Experience with inspections
- Maintain liability insurance
- Pass an exam

The exam is often based on the American Society of Home Inspectors and National Association of Home Inspectors exams. Most inspectors must renew their license every few years and take continuing education courses.

Inspectors must have a valid driver's license because they must travel to inspection sites.

Important Qualities

Communication skills. Home inspectors must have good communication skills in order to explain any problems they find and to help people understand what is needed to fix the problems.

Craft experience. Although not required, having experience in a related construction occupation provides inspectors with the necessary background that may help them to become certified to work in the field.

Detail oriented. Inspectors must thoroughly examine many different construction activities, often at the same time. Therefore, inspectors must pay close attention to detail so as to not overlook any items that need to be checked.

Mechanical knowledge. Inspectors use a variety of testing equipment as they check complex systems. In addition to using such equipment, they must also have detailed knowledge of how the systems operate.

Physical stamina. Inspectors are constantly on their feet and often must crawl through attics and other tight spaces. As a result, they should be somewhat physically fit.

Pay

The median annual wage for construction and building inspectors was $53,450 in May 2012. The median wage is the wage at which half the workers in an occupation earned more than that amount and half earned less. The lowest 10 percent earned less than $32,050, and the top 10 percent earned more than $83,760.

About 11 percent of construction and building inspectors were self-employed in 2012, which is similar to other construction occupations.

Job Outlook

Employment of construction and building inspectors is projected to grow 12 percent from 2012 to 2022, about as fast as the average for all occupations. Concern for public safety and a desire to improve the quality of construction should continue to increase demand for inspectors. Employment growth is expected to be strongest in government and in firms specializing in architectural, engineering, and related services.

Although employment of home inspectors should continue to grow, some states are increasingly limiting entry into the field to those with related work experience or to those who are certified. Increasingly, state and local budget constraints are forcing many

jurisdictions to only hire those who have certification in multiple specialties.

Job Prospects. Certified construction and building inspectors who can perform a variety of inspections should have the best job opportunities. Inspectors with construction-related work experience or training in engineering, architecture, construction technology, or related fields will likely also have better job prospects. In addition, inspectors with thorough knowledge of construction practices and skills, such as reading and evaluating blueprints and plans, should have better job opportunities.

Larger jurisdictions usually hire specialized inspectors with knowledge in a particular area of construction, such as electrical or plumbing. Conversely, for budgetary reasons, smaller jurisdictions typically prefer to hire combination inspectors with broad knowledge of multiple disciplines.

It was once the case that inspectors were less affected by the ups and downs of construction activity. However, significant staff cuts initiated during the recent construction downturn should result in strong competition for available jobs over the coming decade. Those who are self-employed, such as home inspectors, are more likely to be affected by economic downturns or fluctuations in the real estate market.

O*NET

➤ Construction and Building Inspectors (47-4011.00)

Contacts for More Information

For more information about building codes, certification, and a career as a construction or building inspector, visit

➤ International Code Council (www.iccsafe.org/)
➤ National Fire Protection Association (www.nfpa.org/)
  For more information about coating inspectors, visit
➤ NACE International (www.nace.org)
  For more information about construction inspectors, visit
➤ Association of Construction Inspectors (www.aci-assoc.org/)
  For more information about electrical inspectors, visit
➤ International Association of Electrical Inspectors (www.iaei.org/)
  For more information about elevator inspectors, visit
➤ National Association of Elevator Safety Authorities International (www.naesai.org/)
  For more information about education and training for mechanical and plumbing inspectors, visit
➤ International Association of Plumbing and Mechanical Officials (www.iapmo.org)
  For information about becoming a home inspector, visit
➤ American Society of Home Inspectors (www.ashi.org/)
➤ International Association of Certified Home Inspectors (InterNACHI) (www.nachi.org)
➤ National Association of Home Inspectors, Inc. (www.nahi.org/)

Construction Equipment Operators

- **2012 Median Pay** .... $40,980 per year
                                                                         $19.70 per hour
- **Entry-Level Education** ... High school diploma or equivalent
- **Work Experience in a Related Occupation** .... None
- **On-the-Job Training** .... Moderate-term on-the-job training
- **Number of Jobs 2012** 409,700
- **Job Outlook, 2012–22** .... 19% (Faster than average)
- **Employment Change, 2012–22** 78,200

What Construction Equipment Operators Do

Construction equipment operators drive, maneuver, or control the heavy machinery used to construct roads, bridges, buildings, and other structures.

Duties. Construction equipment operators typically do the following:

- Check to make sure that equipment functions properly
- Clean, maintain, and make basic repairs to equipment
- Report malfunctioning equipment to supervisors
- Move levers, push pedals, or turn valves to activate power equipment
- Drive and maneuver equipment
- Coordinate machine actions with crew members in response to hand or audio signals
- Ensure that safety standards are met

Construction equipment operators use machinery to move construction materials, earth, and other heavy materials at construction sites and mines. They operate equipment that clears and grades land to prepare it for construction of roads, bridges, and buildings, as well as airport runways, power generation facilities, dams, levees, and other structures.

The following are examples of types of construction equipment operators:

Operating engineers and other construction equipment operators work with one or several types of power construction equipment. They may operate excavation and loading machines equipped with scoops, shovels, or buckets that dig sand, gravel, earth, or similar materials. In addition to operating bulldozers, they operate trench excavators, road graders, and similar equipment. Sometimes, they may drive and control industrial trucks or tractors equipped with forklifts or booms for lifting materials. They may also operate and maintain air compressors, pumps, and other power equipment at construction sites.

Paving and surfacing equipment operators control the machines that spread and level asphalt or spread and smooth concrete for roadways or other structures. Paving and surfacing equipment operators may specialize further:

- *Asphalt spreader operators* turn valves to regulate the temperature of asphalt and the flow of asphalt onto the roadbed. They must ensure a constant flow of asphalt into the hopper and that the machine distributes the paving material evenly.
- *Concrete paving machine operators* control levers and turn handwheels to move attachments that spread, vibrate, and level wet

Construction equipment operators level the surface of a construction site.

concrete. They must watch the surface of the concrete carefully to identify low spots into which workers must add concrete.

- *Tamping equipment operators* use machines that compact earth and other fill materials for roadbeds or other construction sites. They also may operate machines with interchangeable hammers to cut or break up old pavement and drive guardrail posts into the ground.

Pile-driver operators use large machines mounted on skids, barges, or cranes to hammer piles into the ground. Piles are long heavy beams of concrete, wood, or steel driven into the ground to support retaining walls, bridges, piers, or building foundations. Some pile-driver operators work on offshore oil rigs.

Some workers, including material moving machine operators, use cranes to move construction materials.

Work Environment

Construction equipment operators held about 409,700 jobs in 2012. About 3 percent were self-employed. The employment levels of construction equipment operators were as follows:

Operating engineers and other construction
   equipment operators 351,200

Paving, surfacing, and tamping equipment operators 54,700
Pile-driver operators 3,800

Median Annual Wages, May 2012

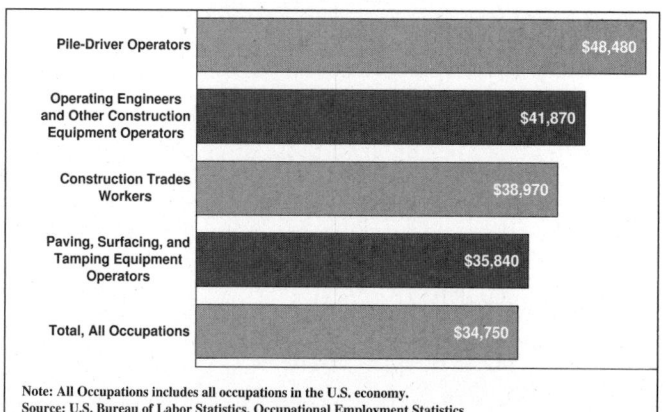

Pile-Driver Operators	$48,480
Operating Engineers and Other Construction Equipment Operators	$41,870
Construction Trades Workers	$38,970
Paving, Surfacing, and Tamping Equipment Operators	$35,840
Total, All Occupations	$34,750

Note: All Occupations includes all occupations in the U.S. economy.
Source: U.S. Bureau of Labor Statistics, Occupational Employment Statistics

Percent Change in Employment, Projected 2012–2022

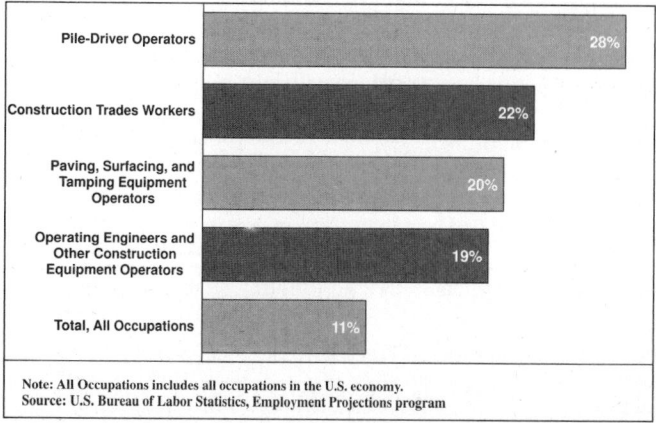

Pile-Driver Operators	28%
Construction Trades Workers	22%
Paving, Surfacing, and Tamping Equipment Operators	20%
Operating Engineers and Other Construction Equipment Operators	19%
Total, All Occupations	11%

Note: All Occupations includes all occupations in the U.S. economy.
Source: U.S. Bureau of Labor Statistics, Employment Projections program

Employment Projections Data for Construction Equipment Operators

Occupational title	SOC Code	Employment, 2012	Projected Employment, 2022	Change, 2012–2022	
				Percent	Numeric
Construction equipment operators..	—	409,700	487,900	19	78,200
Paving, surfacing, and tamping equipment operators.........	47-2071	54,700	65,500	20	10,800
Pile-driver operators..	47-2072	3,800	4,800	28	1,000
Operating engineers and other construction equipment operators..	47-2073	351,200	417,600	19	66,400

Source: U.S. Bureau of Labor Statistics, Employment Projections Program

Note: Data are rounded. Go to **Occupational Information Included in the OOH** *for a discussion of the data in this table.*

Construction equipment operators work in nearly every weather condition. Workers often get dirty, greasy, muddy, or dusty. Some operators work in remote locations on large construction projects, such as highways and dams, or in factories or mines.

Injuries and Illnesses. Operating engineers and other construction equipment operators have a higher rate of injuries and illnesses than the national average. Accidents generally can be avoided by observing proper operating procedures and safety practices, but some repetitive stress injuries do occur. In addition, bulldozers, scrapers, and especially pile-drivers, are noisy and shake or jolt the operator.

Work Schedule. Construction equipment operators may have irregular hours because work on some construction projects continues around the clock or must be done late at night. Extremely cold weather or rain can stop some types of construction. Nearly all operators work full time.

How to Become One

Many workers learn equipment operation on the job, while others learn through an apprenticeship or by attending private trade schools.

Education. A high school diploma or equivalent is required for most jobs. High school courses in English, math, and shop are useful. A course in auto mechanics can also be helpful because workers often perform maintenance on their machines.

Private vocational schools offer programs in certain types of construction equipment operation. Finishing one of these programs may help someone get a job. However, people considering this kind of training should check the school's reputation among employers in the area and find out if the school offers the opportunity to train on actual machines in realistic situations.

A lot of information can be learned through instruction; to become a skilled construction equipment operator, however, a worker needs to be able to physically perform the various tasks. Many training facilities incorporate sophisticated simulators into their training, allowing beginners to familiarize themselves with the equipment in a controlled environment.

Training. Many workers learn their jobs by operating light equipment under the guidance of an experienced operator. Later, they may operate heavier equipment, such as bulldozers. Techno-logically advanced construction equipment with computerized controls and improved hydraulics and electronics requires greater skill to operate. Operators of such equipment may need more training and some understanding of electronics.

Other workers learn their trade through a 3- or 4-year apprenticeship. For each year of the program, apprentices must have at least 144 hours of technical instruction and 2,000 hours of paid on-the-job training. On the job, apprentices learn to maintain equipment, operate machinery, and use special technology, such as a global positioning system (GPS). In the classroom, apprentices are taught map reading, operating procedures for special equipment, safety practices, and first aid. Because apprentices learn to operate a wider variety of machines than do other beginners, they usually have better job opportunities.

After completing an apprenticeship program, apprentices are considered journey workers, doing tasks with less guidance.

A few groups, including unions and contractor associations, sponsor apprenticeship programs. The basic qualifications for entering an apprenticeship program are as follows:

• Minimum age of 18

• High school education or equivalent

• Physically able to do the work

• Valid driver's license

Licenses, Certifications, and Registrations. Construction equipment operators often need a commercial driver's license to haul their equipment to various jobsites. State laws about commercial driver's licenses vary.

A few states have special operator's licenses for operators of backhoes, loaders, and bulldozers.

Currently, 18 states require pile-driver operators to have a crane license because these states classify pile-drivers as cranes. In addition, the cities of Chicago, New Orleans, New York, Omaha, Philadelphia, and Washington, DC require special crane licensure.

Some construction equipment operators choose to teach in training facilities. Other operators start their own contracting business, although doing so may be difficult because of high equipment startup costs.

Similar Occupations This table shows a list of occupations with job duties that are similar to those of construction equipment operators.

Occupations	Entry-level Education	2012 Pay	Projected Job Growth	Average Annual Openings
Farmers, Ranchers, and Other Agricultural Managers	High school diploma or equivalent	$69,300	-19%	15,020
Heavy and Tractor-trailer Truck Drivers	Postsecondary non-degree award	$38,200	11%	46,470
Material Moving Machine Operators	See "How to Become One"	$32,069	1%	16,560

Important Qualities

Hand-eye-foot coordination. Workers should have steady hands and feet to guide and control heavy machinery precisely, sometimes in tight spaces.

Mechanical skills. Construction equipment operators must perform basic maintenance on the equipment they operate. As a result, they should be familiar with hand and power tools and standard equipment care.

Unafraid of heights. A few equipment operators must work at great heights. For example, pile-driver operators may need to service the pulleys that are located on the roof of a building.

Pay

The median annual wage for construction equipment operators was $40,980 in May 2012. The median wage is the wage at which half the workers in an occupation earned more than that amount and half earned less. The lowest 10 percent earned less than $26,470, and the top 10 percent earned more than $72,440.

The median wages for construction equipment operators in May 2012 were as follows:

Pile-driver operators $48,480
Operating engineers and other construction
   equipment operators 41,870
Paving, surfacing, and tamping equipment operators 35,840

The starting pay for apprentices is usually between 60 percent and 70 percent of what fully trained operators make. They receive pay increases as they become more skilled.

Union Membership. Compared with workers in all occupations, construction equipment operators had a higher percentage of workers who belonged to a union in 2012. Although no single union covers all operators, the largest organizer of these workers is the International Union of Operating Engineers.

Job Outlook

Employment of construction equipment operators is projected to grow 19 percent from 2012 to 2022, faster than the average for all occupations.

The likelihood of increased spending on infrastructure to improve roads, bridges, water and sewer systems, and the electric power grid, many of which are in great need of repair across the country, is expected to result in numerous jobs. In addition, population growth increases the need for construction projects such as new roads and sewer lines, which are also expected to generate some jobs. However, without the extra spending on infrastructure by the federal government, employment growth may be tempered as states and localities struggle with budget shortfalls to pay for road and other improvements.

Job Prospects. Workers with the ability to operate multiple types of equipment should have the best job opportunities.

As with many other types of construction worker jobs, employment of construction equipment operators is sensitive to fluctuations of the economy. On the one hand, workers may experience periods of unemployment when the overall level of construction falls. On the other hand, shortages of workers may occur in some areas during peak periods of building activity.

Employment opportunities should be best in metropolitan areas, where most large commercial and residential buildings are constructed, and in states that undertake large transportation-related projects.

In addition, the need to replace workers who leave the occupation should result in some job opportunities.

O*NET

➤ Paving, Surfacing, and Tamping Equipment Operators (47-2071.00)
➤ Pile-Driver Operators (47-2072.00)
➤ Operating Engineers and Other Construction Equipment Operators (47-2073.00)

Contacts for More Information

For information about apprenticeships or job opportunities as a construction equipment operator, contact local cement or highway construction contractors, a local joint union-management apprenticeship committee, or the nearest office of your state employment service or apprenticeship agency. Information on apprenticeships is available from the U.S. Department of Labor's toll-free help line, 1 (877) 872-5627, or the Employment and Training Administration (www.doleta.gov/OA/eta_default.cfm).

For more information on construction equipment operators, visit
➤ Associated General Contractors of America (www3.agc.org/craft_programs/)
➤ Pile Driving Contractors Association (www.piledrivers.org/)

For information on training of construction equipment operators, visit
➤ International Union of Operating Engineers (www.iuoe.org/Training/tabid/116/Default.aspx)
➤ NCCER (www.nccer.org/heavy-equipment-operations?pID=105)

For information about crane certification and licensure, visit
➤ National Commission for the Certification of Crane Operators (www.nccco.org/)

Construction Laborers and Helpers

- **2012 Median Pay** .... $29,160 per year
  $14.02 per hour
- **Entry-Level Education** ....See "How to Become One"
- **Work Experience in a Related Occupation**............... None
- **On-the-Job Training** ....Short-term on-the-job training
- **Number of Jobs 2012** 1,284,600
- **Job Outlook, 2012–22** .... 25% (Much faster than average)
- **Employment Change, 2012–22** 325,200

What Construction Laborers and Helpers Do

Construction laborers and helpers perform many basic tasks that require physical labor on construction sites.

Duties. Construction laborers and helpers typically do the following:

- Clean and prepare construction sites by removing debris and possible hazards
- Load or unload building materials to be used in construction
- Build or take apart bracing, scaffolding, and temporary structures
- Dig trenches, backfill holes, or compact earth to prepare for construction
- Operate or tend equipment and machines used in construction
- Help craft workers with their duties
- Follow construction plans and instructions from supervisors or more experienced workers

Construction laborers and helpers work on almost all construction sites, performing a wide range of tasks from the very easy to the extremely difficult and hazardous. Although many of the tasks

Construction laborers often work building homes and businesses.

they do require some training and experience, most tasks usually require little skill and can be learned quickly.

Construction laborers perform a variety of construction-related activities during all phases of construction. However, the main task laborers perform is preparing and cleaning up construction sites. Although most laborers are generalists–such as those who install barricades, cones, and markers to control traffic patterns–many others specialize. For example, those who operate the machines and equipment that lay concrete or asphalt on roads are more likely to specialize in those areas.

Most construction laborers work in the following areas:

- Building homes and businesses
- Tearing down buildings
- Removing hazardous materials
- Building highways and roads
- Digging tunnels and mine shafts

Construction laborers use a variety of tools and equipment. Some tools are simple, such as brooms and shovels; other equipment is more sophisticated, such as pavement breakers, jackhammers, earth tampers, and surveying equipment.

With special training, laborers may help transport and use explosives or run hydraulic boring machines to dig out tunnels. They may learn to use laser beam equipment to place pipes and use computers to control robotic pipe cutters. They may become certified to remove asbestos, lead, or chemicals.

Helpers assist construction craft workers, such as electricians and carpenters, with a variety of basic tasks. They may carry tools and materials or help set up equipment. For example, many helpers work with cement masons to move and set forms (molds that determine the shape of concrete). Many other helpers assist with taking apart equipment, cleaning up sites, and disposing of waste, as well as helping with any other needs of craft workers.

Many construction trades have helpers who assist craft workers. The following are trades that have associated helpers:

- Brickmasons, blockmasons, and stonemasons
- Carpenters
- Electricians
- Painters, construction and maintenance
- Plumbers, pipefitters, and steamfitters
- Roofers
- Tile and marble setters

Work Environment

Construction laborers held about 1.1 million jobs in 2012, of which 60 percent were employed in the construction industry. About 23 percent of construction laborers were self-employed.

The employment levels of construction helper specialties were as follows:

Helpers—electricians	60,800
Helpers—pipelayers, plumbers, pipefitters, and steamfitters	47,400
Helpers—carpenters	36,400
Helpers—brickmasons, blockmasons, stonemasons, and tile and marble setters	24,400
Helpers, construction trades, all other	21,400
Helpers—roofers	12,000
Helpers—painters, paperhangers, plasterers, and stucco masons	11,100

Most construction laborers and helpers do physically demanding work. Some work at great heights or outdoors in all weather conditions; others may be required to work in tunnels. They must use earplugs around loud equipment and wear gloves, safety glasses, and other protective gear.

Injuries and Illnesses. Construction laborers have one of the highest rates of injuries and illnesses of all occupations. Workers may experience cuts from materials and tools, falls from ladders and scaffolding, and burns from chemicals or equipment. Some jobs expose workers to harmful materials, fumes, odors, or dangerous machinery. Workers also may experience muscle fatigue and

Median Annual Wages, May 2012

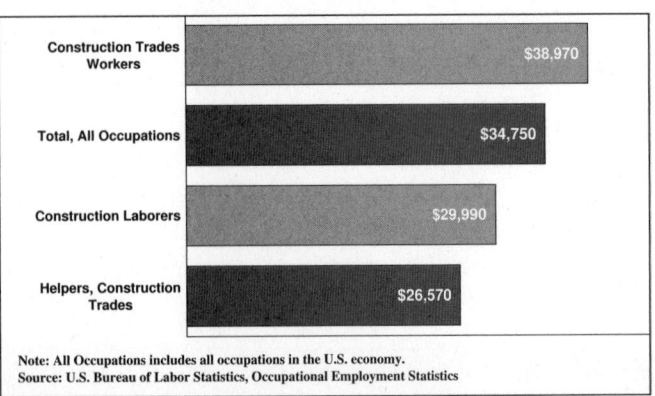

Percent Change in Employment, Projected 2012–2022

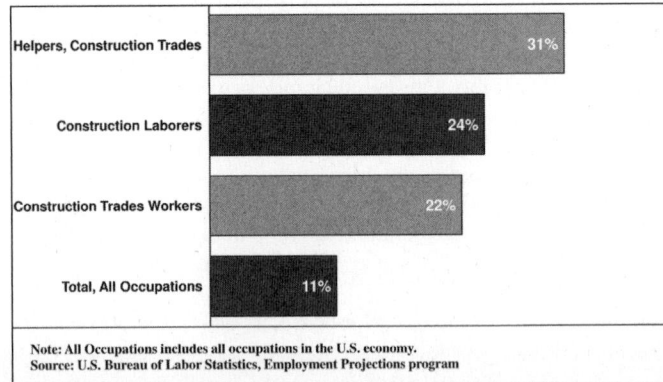

Employment Projections Data for Construction Laborers and Helpers

Occupational title	SOC Code	Employment, 2012	Projected Employment, 2022	Change, 2012–2022	
				Percent	Numeric
Construction laborers and helpers	—	1,284,600	1,609,700	25	325,200
Construction laborers	47-2061	1,071,100	1,331,000	24	259,800
Helpers—brickmasons, blockmasons, stonemasons, and tile and marble setters	47-3011	24,400	34,900	43	10,500
Helpers—carpenters	47-3012	36,400	47,100	30	10,800
Helpers—electricians...	47-3013	60,800	83,300	37	22,400
Helpers—painters, paperhangers, plasterers, and stucco masons	47-3014	11,100	12,200	10	1,100
Helpers—pipelayers, plumbers, pipefitters, and steamfitters	47-3015	47,400	60,600	28	13,200
Helpers—roofers	47-3016	12,000	14,000	17	2,100
Helpers, construction trades, all other...............................	47-3019	21,400	26,600	24	5,200

Source: U.S. Bureau of Labor Statistics, Employment Projections Program

Note: Data are rounded. Go to Occupational Information Included in the OOH *for a discussion of the data in this table.*

injuries related to lifting and carrying heavy materials. Although they face similar hazards, construction helpers generally experience a rate of injuries and illnesses that is close to the national average.

Work Schedules. Like many construction workers, most laborers and helpers work full time. Although they sometimes stop work because of bad weather, they often work overtime to meet deadlines. Laborers and helpers on highway and bridge projects may need to work overnight to avoid major disruptions to traffic. In some parts of the country, construction laborers and helpers may work only during certain seasons.

About 23 percent of construction laborers were self-employed in 2012. Self-employed workers may be able to set their own schedule. In contrast, very few helpers were self-employed.

How to Become One

Most construction laborers and helpers learn their trade through short-term on-the-job training.

Education. Although there are no specific education requirements, high school classes in English, mathematics, blueprint reading, welding, and shop can be helpful.

Some workers attend a trade or vocational school, an association training class, or community college to receive further training.

Training. Most construction laborers and helpers learn through short-term on-the-job training after being hired by a construction contractor or a temporary-help employment agency. Workers

typically gain experience by doing jobs under the guidance of experienced workers.

Although the majority of workers learn by assisting experienced workers, some opt for apprenticeship programs. Programs generally include 2 to 4 years of technical instruction and on-the-job training. The Laborers International Union of North America requires 160 hours of training before workers are allowed on site. Workers learn basic construction skills, such as communication, blueprint reading, proper tools and equipment use, and safety and health procedures. The remainder of the curriculum consists of specialized skills training in three of the largest segments of the construction industry: building construction, heavy and highway construction, and environmental remediation for removing such materials as lead or asbestos.

Several groups, including unions and contractor associations, sponsor apprenticeship programs. Apprenticeship programs usually have only a basic age qualification–age 18 or older–for entrance. A high school diploma or equivalent is preferred but not required.

Licenses, Certifications, and Registrations. Laborers who remove hazardous materials (hazmat) must have a federal hazmat license required for all hazardous materials removal workers.

Depending on the work they do, laborers may need specific certifications. Certification can help workers prove that they have the knowledge to perform more complex tasks.

Similar Occupations   This table shows a list of occupations with job duties that are similar to those of construction laborers and helpers.

Occupations	Entry-level Education	2012 Pay	Projected Job Growth	Average Annual Openings
Brickmasons, Blockmasons, and Stonemasons	High school diploma or equivalent	$44,935	34%	3,840
Carpenters	High school diploma or equivalent	$39,940	24%	32,920
Electricians	High school diploma or equivalent	$49,840	20%	22,460
Grounds Maintenance Workers	See "How to Become One"	$24,180	13%	46,350
Hazardous Materials Removal Workers	High school diploma or equivalent	$37,590	14%	1,340
Material Moving Machine Operators	See "How to Become One"	$32,069	1%	16,560
Painters, Construction and Maintenance	Less than high school	$35,190	20%	11,050
Plumbers, Pipefitters, and Steamfitters	High school diploma or equivalent	$49,140	21%	13,050
Tile and Marble Setters	Less than high school	$37,040	15%	1,290

The following are examples of areas which may require certification:

- Asbestos removal
- Energy auditing
- Lead abatement
- OSHA 10 and/or 30 hour Construction Safety Certification
- Pipeline operation
- Radiological work
- Rough terrain forklift operation
- Scaffold use and building
- Signaling
- Weatherization
- Welding
- Work zone safety

Advancement. Through experience and training, construction laborers can advance into positions that involve more complex tasks. For example, laborers may earn certifications in welding, scaffold erecting, or concrete finishing and then spend more time performing activities that require the specialized skill.

Through training and experience, helpers can potentially move into construction craft occupations. For example, experience as a helper may lead to becoming a tilesetter.

Important Qualities

Color vision. Laborers and helpers may need to be able to distinguish colors to do their job. For example, an electrician's helper must be able to distinguish different colors of wire to help the lead electrician.

Math skills. Laborers and some helpers need to perform basic math calculations to do their job. They often help with measuring on jobsites or they may be part of a surveying crew.

Mechanical skills. Laborers frequently are required to operate and maintain equipment, such as jackhammers.

Physical stamina. Laborers and helpers must have endurance to perform strenuous tasks throughout the day. Highway laborers, for example, spend hours on their feet–often in hot temperatures–with few breaks.

Physical strength. Laborers and helpers often must lift heavy materials or equipment. For example, cement mason helpers must move cinder blocks, which weigh more than 40 pounds each.

Pay

The median annual wage for construction laborers and helpers was $29,160 in May 2012. The median wage is the wage at which half the workers in an occupation earned more than that amount and half earned less. The lowest 10 percent earned less than $18,840, and the top 10 percent earned more than $55,750.

The median wages for construction laborers and helpers in May 2012 were as follows:

Construction laborers	$29,990
Brickmason, blockmason, stonemason, and tile and marble setter helpers	28,220
Electrician helpers	27,670
Pipelayer, plumber, pipefitter, and steamfitter helpers	26,670
Carpenter helpers	25,550
Painter, paperhanger, plasterer, and stucco mason helpers	24,290
Roofer helpers	23,300
All other construction helpers	25,610

The starting pay for apprentices is usually between 30 percent and 60 percent of what fully trained laborers make. As apprentices learn to do more, they receive pay increases.

Job Outlook

Overall employment of construction laborers and helpers is projected to grow 25 percent from 2012 to 2022, much faster than the average for all occupations.

Employment of construction laborers is projected to grow 24 percent from 2012 to 2022, much faster than the average for all occupations. Laborers work in all fields of construction, and demand for laborers will mirror the level of overall construction activity. Repairing and replacing the nation's infrastructure, such as roads, bridges, and water lines, should result in steady demand for laborers.

Although employment growth of specific types of helpers is expected to vary (see table below), overall demand for helpers will be driven by the construction of schools, office buildings, factories, and power plants. Population growth also is expected to result in construction of new homes, which will stimulate the need for many additional helpers. Remodeling needs will also result in some new jobs.

However, demand for helpers is also affected by economic downturns. In the construction slowdown following the 2007–09 recession, the number of jobs for helpers decreased faster than jobs for the craft workers they help. Contractors kept their more experienced workers and had them perform tasks that helpers would normally do. As construction returns to normal levels, helpers will be needed to perform their standard tasks again.

Job Prospects. Construction laborers with the most skills should have the best job opportunities. Job opportunities also will vary by occupation; for example, carpenters' helpers should have the best job prospects, while helpers for painters, paperhangers, plasterers, and stucco masons will likely find fewer job openings. Prospective employees with military service experience often have better opportunities when applying for a job.

Employment of construction laborers and helpers is especially sensitive to the fluctuations of the economy. On the one hand, workers in these trades may experience periods of unemployment when the overall level of construction falls. On the other hand, shortages of these workers may occur in some areas during peak periods of building activity.

O*NET

- Construction Laborers (47-2061.00)
- Helpers—Brickmasons, Blockmasons, Stonemasons, and Tile and Marble Setters (47-3011.00)
- Helpers—Carpenters (47-3012.00)
- Helpers—Electricians (47-3013.00)
- Helpers—Painters, Paperhangers, Plasterers, and Stucco Masons (47-3014.00)
- Helpers—Pipelayers, Plumbers, Pipefitters, and Steamfitters (47-3015.00)
- Helpers—Roofers (47-3016.00)
- Helpers, Construction Trades, All Other (47-3019.00)

Contacts for More Information

For details about apprenticeships or other work opportunities for construction laborers and helpers, contact the offices of the state employment service, the state apprenticeship agency, local construction contractors or firms that employ laborers, or local union-management apprenticeship committees. Apprenticeship information is available from the U.S. Department of Labor's toll-free help line, 1 (877) 872-5627, or the Employment and Training Administration (www.doleta.gov/OA/eta_default.cfm).

For information about education programs for laborers, visit

➤ Laborers' International Union of North America (www.liunatraining.org/)

➤ NCCER (www.nccer.org/construction-craft-laborer?pID=105)

Drywall and Ceiling Tile Installers, and Tapers

- **2012 Median Pay** .... $37,920 per year
  $18.23 per hour
- **Entry-Level Education** .... Less than high school
- **Work Experience in a Related Occupation** .... None
- **On-the-Job Training** .... Moderate-term on-the-job training
- **Number of Jobs 2012** 114,100
- **Job Outlook, 2012–22** .... 16% (Faster than average)
- **Employment Change, 2012–22** 17,900

What Drywall and Ceiling Tile Installers, and Tapers Do

Drywall and ceiling tile installers hang wallboards to walls and ceilings and install ceiling tile inside buildings. Tapers prepare the wallboards for painting, using tape and other materials. Many workers do both installing and taping.

Duties. *Drywall installers* typically do the following:

- Review design plans to minimize the number of cuts and waste of wallboard
- Measure the locations of electrical outlets, plumbing, and windows
- Cut drywall to the right size, using utility knives and power saws
- Fasten drywall panels to interior wall studs, using nails or screws
- Trim and smooth rough edges so that boards join evenly

Ceiling tile installers typically do the following:

- Measure ceiling tile to match blueprints or drawings
- Nail, screw, or clip in supports
- Put tiles or sheets of shock-absorbing materials on and into ceilings
- Keep the tile in place with cement adhesive, nails, screws, or clips

Tapers typically do the following:

- Prepare wall surfaces (wallboard) by patching nail holes
- Apply tape and use sealing compound to cover joints between wallboards
- Apply additional coats of sealing compound to create an even surface
- Sand all joints and holes to a smooth, seamless finish

Installers also are called *framers* or *hangers*. Tapers also are called *finishers*. Ceiling tile installers sometimes are called *acoustical carpenters* because they work with tiles that block sound. In addition to performing new installation, many installers and tapers do repair work by fixing damaged drywall and replacing ceiling tile.

Once wallboards are hung, workers use increasingly wider trowels to spread multiple coats of spackle over cracks, indentations, and any remaining imperfections. Some workers may use a mechanical applicator, a tool that spreads sealing compound on the wall joint while dispensing and setting tape at the same time.

To work on ceilings, installers and tapers may use mechanical lifts or stand on stilts, ladders, or scaffolds.

Work Environment

Drywall and ceiling tile installers and tapers held about 114,100 jobs in 2012, of which 63 percent worked in the drywall and insulation contractors industry. About 19 percent were self-employed.

Drywall and ceiling tile installers and tapers work indoors. As in many other construction trades, the work is physically demanding. Workers spend most of the day standing, bending, or stretching, and they often must lift and maneuver heavy, oversized wallboards. To work on ceilings, installers and tapers must stand on stilts, ladders, or scaffolds.

Because the work is dusty, irritating the skin, eyes, and lungs, workers must wear protective masks, goggles, and gloves. Common injuries include falls from ladders or stilts, cuts from sharp tools, and muscle strains from lifting heavy materials.

Work Schedules. Most drywall and ceiling tile installers and tapers work full time.

About 19 percent were self-employed. Self-employed installers and tapers may be able to set their own schedule.

How to Become One

Although most drywall and ceiling tile installers and tapers learn their trade on the job, some learn through an apprenticeship.

Education. Although there are no education requirements to become a drywaller, high school math and general shop courses are considered useful.

Training. Most drywall and ceiling tile installers and tapers learn their trade on the job by helping more experienced workers and gradually being given more duties. They start by carrying materi-

Drywall and ceiling tile installers and tapers learn their trade through informal training programs or through apprenticeships.

Median Annual Wages, May 2012

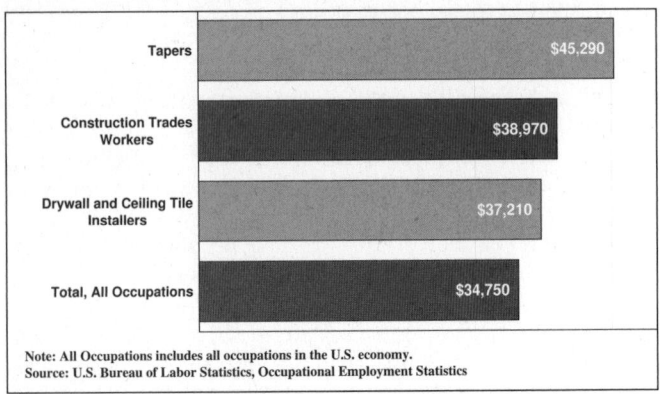

Note: All Occupations includes all occupations in the U.S. economy.
Source: U.S. Bureau of Labor Statistics, Occupational Employment Statistics

Percent Change in Employment, Projected 2012–2022

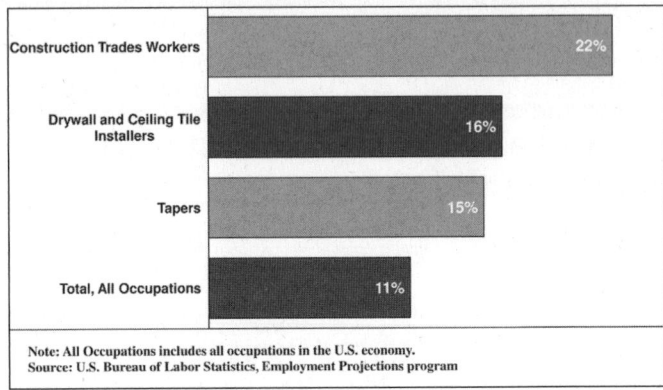

Note: All Occupations includes all occupations in the U.S. economy.
Source: U.S. Bureau of Labor Statistics, Employment Projections program

als and cleaning up, and then learn to use the tools of the trade. They also learn to measure, cut, and install or apply materials. Employers usually provide some on-the-job training, lasting up to 12 months.

A few drywall and ceiling tile installers and tapers learn their trade through a 3- or 4-year apprenticeship. For each year of the program, apprentices must have at least 144 hours of related technical work and 2,000 hours of paid on-the-job training. During training, apprentices learn construction basics related to blueprint reading, mathematics, building code requirements, and safety and first-aid practices.

After completing an apprenticeship program, installers and tapers are considered journey workers and may perform duties on their own.

A few groups, including unions and contractor associations, sponsor apprenticeship programs. The basic qualifications for entering such a program are as follows:

- Minimum age of 18
- High school education or equivalent
- Physically able to perform the work

Important Qualities

Math skills. Drywall and ceiling tile installers and tapers use basic math skills on every job. For example, they must be able to estimate the quantity of materials needed and measure accurately when cutting panels.

Physical stamina. Because installers and tapers constantly lift and move heavy materials into place, workers should be in good physical shape.

Physical strength. Standard drywall sheets can weigh 50 to 100 pounds. Drywall and ceiling tile installers often must lift heavy panels over their heads to secure onto the ceiling.

Pay

The median annual wage for drywall and ceiling tile installers was $37,210 in May 2012. The median wage is the wage at which half the workers in an occupation earned more than that amount and half earned less. The lowest 10 percent earned less than $24,720, and the top 10 percent earned more than $72,500.

The median annual wage for tapers was $45,290 in May 2012. The lowest 10 percent earned less than $27,340, and the top 10 percent earned more than $83,700.

Employment Projections Data for Drywall and Ceiling Tile Installers, and Tapers

Occupational title	SOC Code	Employment, 2012	Projected Employment, 2022	Change, 2012–2022	
				Percent	Numeric
Drywall installers, ceiling tile installers, and tapers	—	114,100	132,000	16	17,900
Drywall and ceiling tile installers	47-2081	94,800	109,900	16	15,100
Tapers	47-2082	19,200	22,100	15	2,900

Source: U.S. Bureau of Labor Statistics, Employment Projections Program

Note: Data are rounded. Go to **Occupational Information Included in the OOH** *for a discussion of the data in this table.*

Similar Occupations This table shows a list of occupations with job duties that are similar to those of drywall and ceiling tile installers, and tapers.

Occupations	Entry-level Education	2012 Pay	Projected Job Growth	Average Annual Openings
Brickmasons, Blockmasons, and Stonemasons	High school diploma or equivalent	$44,935	34%	3,840
Carpenters	High school diploma or equivalent	$39,940	24%	32,920
Construction Laborers and Helpers	See "How to Become One"	$29,277	25%	58,790
Painters, Construction and Maintenance	Less than high school	$35,190	20%	11,050
Tile and Marble Setters	Less than high school	$37,040	15%	1,290

The starting wage for apprentices is usually between 30 percent and 50 percent of what fully trained drywall and ceiling tile installers and tapers make. As apprentices learn to do more, they receive pay increases.

Job Outlook

Employment of drywall and ceiling tile installers and tapers is projected to grow 16 percent from 2012 to 2022, faster than the average for all occupations.

Drywall is, and will continue to be, the most common interior wall covering in nearly every building. As a result, new residential and commercial building construction will drive demand for workers. Home improvement and remodeling projects also are expected to create jobs, because existing homes and other buildings will require updating.

Job Prospects. Job prospects for drywall and ceiling tile installers and tapers may improve over the coming decade as construction activity rebounds from the recent recession. As with many other construction workers, employment is sensitive to fluctuations of the economy. On the one hand, they may experience periods of unemployment when the overall level of construction falls. On the other hand, shortages of workers may occur in some areas during peak periods of building activity.

Drywall and ceiling tile installers and tapers with a good work history and experience in the construction industry should have the best job opportunities.

O*NET

➤ Drywall and Ceiling Tile Installers (47-2081.00)
➤ Tapers (47-2082.00)

Contacts for More Information

For details about apprenticeships or other work opportunities in this trade, contact the offices of the state employment service; the state apprenticeship agency; local contractors or firms that employ drywall installers, ceiling tile installers, and tapers; or local union-management finishing trade apprenticeship committees. Apprenticeship information is available from the U.S. Department of Labor's toll-free help line, 1 (877) 872-5627, or the Employment and Training Administration (www.doleta.gov/OA/eta_default.cfm).

For more information about drywall and ceiling tile installers and tapers, visit
➤ Associated Builders and Contractors (www.abc.org/)
➤ Association of Wall and Ceiling Industries International (http://store.awci.org/cgi-bin/awci)
➤ Finishing Trades Institute (www.finishingtradesinstitute.org)
➤ National Association of Home Builders (www.nahb.org)
➤ NCCER (www.nccer.org/drywall)
➤ United Brotherhood of Carpenters (www.carpenters.org/Home.aspx)

Electricians

- **2012 Median Pay** .... $49,840 per year
  $23.96 per hour
- **Entry-Level Education** ... High school diploma or equivalent
- **Work Experience in a Related Occupation** .... None
- **On-the-Job Training** .... Apprenticeship
- **Number of Jobs 2012** 583,500
- **Job Outlook, 2012–22** .... 20% (Faster than average)
- **Employment Change, 2012–22** 114,700

An electrician prepares the wiring for an interior room.

What Electricians Do

Electricians install and maintain electrical power, communications, lighting, and control systems in homes, businesses, and factories.

Duties. Electricians typically do the following:

- Read blueprints or technical diagrams
- Install and maintain wiring, control, and lighting systems
- Inspect electrical components, such as transformers and circuit breakers
- Identify electrical problems with a variety of testing devices
- Repair or replace wiring, equipment, or fixtures using hand tools and power tools
- Follow state and local building regulations based on the National Electric Code
- Direct and train workers to install, maintain, or repair electrical wiring or equipment

Almost every building has an electrical power, communications, lighting, and control system that is installed during construction and maintained after that. These systems power the lights, appliances, and equipment that make people's lives and jobs easier and more comfortable.

Installing electrical systems in newly constructed buildings is less complicated than maintaining equipment in existing buildings. This is because electrical wiring is more easily accessible during construction. In addition, maintaining equipment and systems involves identifying problems and repairing broken equipment that is sometimes difficult to reach. Maintenance work may include fixing or replacing parts, light fixtures, control systems, motors, and other types of electrical equipment.

Electricians read blueprints, which are technical diagrams of electrical systems that show the location of circuits, outlets, and other equipment. They use different types of hand and power tools, such as conduit benders, to run and protect wiring. Other commonly used hand and power tools include screwdrivers, wire strippers, drills, and saws. While troubleshooting, electricians also may use ammeters, voltmeters, thermal scanners, and cable testers to find problems and ensure that components are working properly.

Many electricians work alone, but sometimes they collaborate with others. For example, experienced electricians may work with building engineers and architects to help design electrical systems for new construction. Some electricians may also consult with other construction specialists, such as elevator installers and heating and air conditioning workers, to help install or maintain electrical or power systems. At larger companies, electricians are more likely to work as part of a crew; they may direct helpers and apprentices to complete jobs.

The following are examples of types of electricians:

Inside electricians maintain and repair large motors, equipment, and control systems in businesses and factories. They use their knowledge of electrical systems to help these facilities run safely and efficiently. Some also install the wiring for businesses and factories that are being built. To minimize equipment failure, inside electricians often perform scheduled maintenance.

Residential electricians install wiring and troubleshoot electrical problems in peoples' homes. Those who work in new-home construction install outlets and provide access to power where needed. Those who work in maintenance and remodeling typically repair and replace faulty equipment. For example, if a circuit breaker repeatedly trips after being reset, electricians determine the reason and fix it.

Work Environment

Electricians held about 583,500 jobs in 2012, of which 61 percent were employed in the electrical contractors and other wiring installation contractors industry. About 9 percent were self-employed.

Electricians work indoors and outdoors, in homes, businesses, factories, and construction sites. Because electricians must travel to different worksites, local or long distance commuting is often required.

On the jobsite, they occasionally work in cramped spaces, and constant standing and kneeling can be tiring. Those who work in factories are often subject to noisy machinery. As a result, hearing protection must be worn to protect workers from excess noise.

Many electricians work alone, but sometimes they collaborate with others. At larger companies, electricians are more likely to work as part of a crew; they may direct helpers and apprentices to complete jobs.

Injuries and Illnesses. Electricians have a higher rate of injuries and illnesses than the national average. Although few accidents are potentially fatal, common injuries include electrical shocks,

falls, burns, and other minor injuries. Workers must therefore wear protective clothing and safety glasses to reduce these risks.

Work Schedules. Almost all electricians work full time, which may include evenings and weekends. However, work schedules may vary during times of inclement weather. During scheduled maintenance, or on construction sites, electricians can expect to work overtime.

About 9 percent of electricians were self-employed in 2012. Self-employed electricians often work in residential construction and may have the ability to set their own schedule.

How to Become One

Although most electricians learn through an apprenticeship, some start out by attending a technical school. Most states require electricians to be licensed. For more information, contact your local or state electrical licensing board.

Education. A high school diploma or equivalent is required.

Some electricians start out by attending a technical school. Many technical schools offer programs related to circuitry, safety practices, and basic electrical information. Graduates usually receive credit toward their apprenticeship.

After completing their initial training, electricians may be required to take continuing education courses. These courses are usually related to safety practices, changes to the electrical code, and training from manufacturers in specific products.

Training. Most electricians learn their trade in a 4- or 5-year apprenticeship program. For each year of the program, apprentices must complete at least 144 hours of technical training and 2,000 hours of paid on-the-job training. In the classroom, apprentices learn electrical theory, blueprint reading, mathematics, electrical code requirements, and safety and first-aid practices. They also may receive specialized training related to soldering, communications, fire alarm systems, and elevators.

After completing an apprenticeship program, electricians are considered to be journey workers and may perform duties on their own, subject to any local licensing requirements. Because of this comprehensive training, those who complete apprenticeship programs qualify to do both construction and maintenance work.

Several groups, including unions and contractor associations, sponsor apprenticeship programs. The basic qualifications to enter an apprenticeship program are as follows:

- Minimum age of 18
- High school education or equivalent
- One year of algebra
- Qualifying score on an aptitude test
- Pass substance abuse screening

Median Annual Wages, May 2012

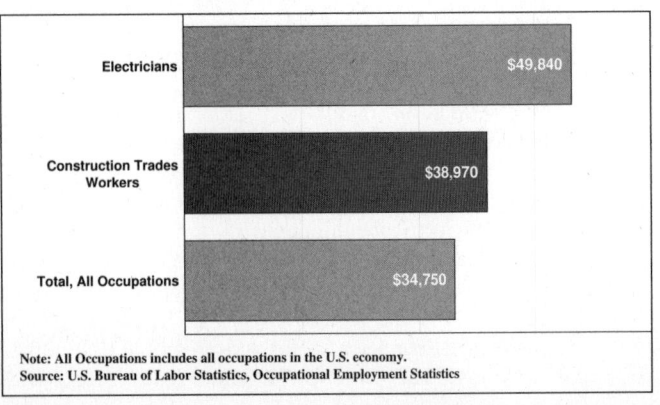

Note: All Occupations includes all occupations in the U.S. economy.
Source: U.S. Bureau of Labor Statistics, Occupational Employment Statistics

Percent Change in Employment, Projected 2012–2022

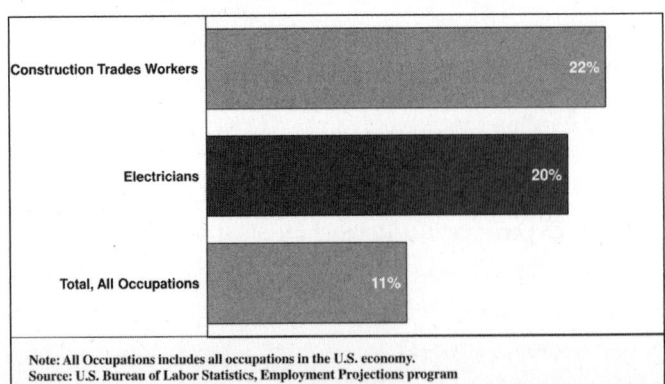

Note: All Occupations includes all occupations in the U.S. economy.
Source: U.S. Bureau of Labor Statistics, Employment Projections program

Employment Projections Data for Electricians

Occupational title	SOC Code	Employment, 2012	Projected Employment, 2022	Change, 2012–2022	
				Percent	Numeric
Electricians	47-2111	583,500	698,200	20	114,700

Source: U.S. Bureau of Labor Statistics, Employment Projections Program

Note: **Data are rounded.** Go to **Occupational Information Included in the OOH** *for a discussion of the data in this table.*

Some electrical contractors have their own training program. Although most workers enter apprenticeships directly, some electricians enter apprenticeship programs after working as a helper.

Licenses, Certifications, and Registrations. Most states require electricians to pass a test and be licensed. Requirements vary by state. For more information, contact your local or state electrical licensing board.

The tests have questions related to the National Electrical Code, state electrical codes, and local electrical codes.

Important Qualities

Business skills. Self-employed electricians must be able to bid on new jobs, track inventory, and plan payroll and work assignments.

Color vision. Electricians must identify electrical wires by color.

Critical-thinking skills. Electricians perform tests and use the results to diagnose problems. For example, when an outlet is not working, they may use a multimeter to check the voltage, amperage, or resistance to determine the best course of action.

Customer-service skills. Electricians work with people on a regular basis. As a result, they should be friendly and be able to address customers' questions.

Troubleshooting skills. Electricians find, diagnose, and repair problems. For example, if a motor stops working, they perform tests to determine the cause of its failure and then, depending on the results, fix or replace the motor.

Pay

The median annual wage for electricians was $49,840 in May 2012. The median wage is the wage at which half the workers in an occupation earned more than that amount and half earned less. The lowest 10 percent earned less than $30,420, and the top 10 percent earned more than $82,930.

The starting pay for apprentices is usually between 30 percent and 50 percent of what fully trained electricians make, receiving pay increases as they gain more skill.

Union Membership. Compared with workers in all occupations, electricians had a higher percentage of workers who belonged to a union in 2012. Although there is no single union, the largest organizer for electricians is the International Brotherhood of Electrical Workers.

Job Outlook

Employment of electricians is projected to grow 20 percent from 2012 to 2022, faster than the average for all occupations. As homes and businesses require more wiring, electricians will be needed to install the necessary components. Overall growth of the construction industry and the need to maintain older equipment in manufacturing plants also will require more electricians.

Alternative power generation, such as solar and wind, is an emerging field that should require more electricians for installation. Increasingly, electricians will be needed to link these alternative power sources to homes and power grids over the coming decade. Employment growth stemming from these sources, however, will largely be dependent on government policy.

With greater efficiency and reliability of newer manufacturing plants, demand for electricians in manufacturing should increase as more electricians are needed to install and maintain systems. However, this increase in demand will be partially offset by the closing of older facilities.

Job Prospects. Employment of electricians fluctuates with the overall economy. On the one hand, there is greater demand for

Similar Occupations   This table shows a list of occupations with job duties that are similar to those of electricians.

Occupations	Entry-level Education	2012 Pay	Projected Job Growth	Average Annual Openings
Computer, ATM, and Office Machine Repairers	Some college, no degree	$36,620	4%	3,280
Construction Laborers and Helpers	See "How to Become One"	$29,277	25%	58,790
Drafters	Associate's degree	$49,726	1%	3,220
Electrical and Electronics Engineering Technicians	Associate's degree	$57,850	0%	3,040
Electrical and Electronics Installers and Repairers	Postsecondary non-degree award	$51,081	1%	2,980
Elevator Installers and Repairers	High school diploma or equivalent	$76,650	24%	800
Heating, Air Conditioning, and Refrigeration Mechanics and Installers	Postsecondary non-degree award	$43,640	21%	12,370
Line Installers and Repairers	High school diploma or equivalent	$56,833	7%	9,110
Solar Photovoltaic Installers	High school diploma or equivalent	$37,900	23%	200
Wind Turbine Technicians	Some college, no degree	$45,970	25%	260

electricians during peak periods of construction building and maintenance. On the other hand, workers may experience periods of unemployment when the overall level of construction and maintenance falls.

Electricians in factories tend to have the most stable employment.

Electricians with the widest variety of skills should have the best job opportunities.

O*NET

➤ Electricians (47-2111.00)

Contacts for More Information

For details about apprenticeships or other work opportunities in this trade, contact the offices of the state employment service, the state apprenticeship agency, local electrical contractors, firms that employ maintenance electricians, or local union-management electrician apprenticeship committees. Apprenticeship information is available from the U.S. Department of Labor's toll-free help line, 1 (877) 872-5627, or the Employment and Training Administration (www.doleta.gov/OA/eta_default.cfm).

For information about apprenticeship and training programs for electricians, visit

➤ National Joint Apprenticeship Training Committee for the Electrical Industry sponsored by the International Brotherhood of Electrical Workers and the National Electrical Contractors Association (www.njatc.org/)
➤ Associated Builders and Contractors, Inc. (www.abc.org)
➤ Independent Electrical Contractors, Inc. (www.ieci.org/)
➤ National Association of Home Builders (www.nahb.org/)
➤ NCCER (www.nccer.org/electrical?pID=86)

Elevator Installers and Repairers

- **2012 Median Pay** .... $76,650 per year
  $36.85 per hour
- **Entry-Level Education** ... High school diploma or equivalent
- **Work Experience in a Related Occupation** .... None
- **On-the-Job Training** .... Apprenticeship
- **Number of Jobs 2012** 19,700
- **Job Outlook, 2012–22** .... 25% (Much faster than average)
- **Employment Change, 2012–22** 4,800

What Elevator Installers and Repairers Do

Elevator installers and repairers install, fix, and maintain elevators, escalators, moving walkways, and other lifts.

Duties. Elevator installers and repairers typically do the following:

- Read blueprints to determine the equipment needed for installation or repair
- Install or repair elevator doors, cables, motors, and control systems
- Locate malfunctions in brakes, motors, switches, and control systems
- Connect electrical wiring to control panels and electric motors
- Use test equipment, such as ammeters and voltmeters, to diagnose problems
- Adjust counterweights, door mechanisms, and safety controls

- Test newly installed equipment to ensure that it meets specifications
- Comply with safety regulations and building codes
- Keep service records of all maintenance and repair tasks

Elevator installers and repairers, also called *elevator constructors* or *elevator mechanics*, assemble, install, and replace elevators, escalators, chairlifts, moving walkways, and similar equipment in buildings.

Elevator installers and repairers usually specialize in installation, maintenance, or repair work. Maintenance and repair workers generally require greater knowledge of electronics, hydraulics, and electricity than do installers because a large part of maintenance and repair work is troubleshooting. In fact, most elevators today have computerized control systems, resulting in more complex systems and troubleshooting than in the past.

After an elevator is operating correctly, elevator installers and repairers must regularly maintain and service it to keep the elevator working. Workers generally perform preventive maintenance, such as oiling and greasing moving parts, replacing worn parts, and adjusting equipment for optimal performance. They also troubleshoot and may be called to perform emergency repairs. Unlike most elevator installers, people who specialize in elevator maintenance typically service many of the same elevators on multiple occasions over time.

A service crew usually handles major repairs–for example, replacing cables, elevator doors, or machine bearings. These tasks may require the use of cutting torches or rigging equipment–tools that an elevator repairer would not normally carry. Service crews also perform major modernization and alteration work, such as replacing electric motors, hydraulic pumps, and control panels.

The following are examples of types of elevator installers and repairers:

Adjusters specialize in fine-tuning all the equipment after installation. They ensure that an elevator operates according to specifications and stops correctly at each floor within a specified time. Adjusters need a thorough knowledge of electronics, electricity, and computers to ensure that newly installed elevators operate properly.

Assistant mechanics have completed a 4-year apprenticeship program. Although assistant mechanics are fully trained, they typically work under the guidance of a journeyman–a fully trained mechanic.

Employment of elevator installers and repairers is less affected by economic downturns and seasonality than employment in other construction trades.

Median Annual Wages, May 2012

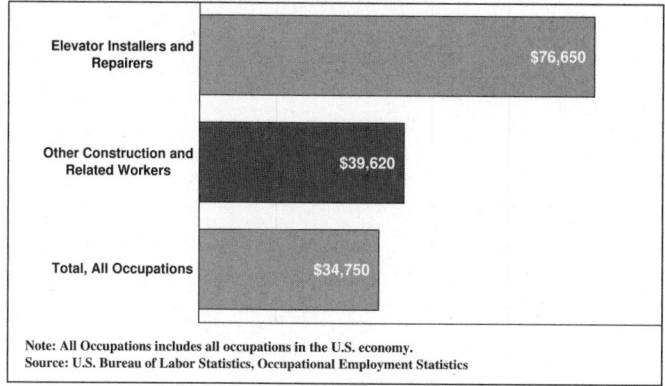

Elevator Installers and Repairers — $76,650
Other Construction and Related Workers — $39,620
Total, All Occupations — $34,750

Note: All Occupations includes all occupations in the U.S. economy.
Source: U.S. Bureau of Labor Statistics, Occupational Employment Statistics

Percent Change in Employment, Projected 2012–2022

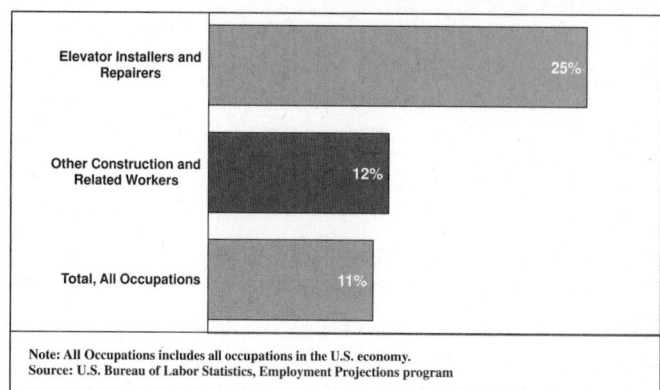

Elevator Installers and Repairers — 25%
Other Construction and Related Workers — 12%
Total, All Occupations — 11%

Note: All Occupations includes all occupations in the U.S. economy.
Source: U.S. Bureau of Labor Statistics, Employment Projections program

Work Environment

Elevator installers and repairers held about 19,700 jobs in 2012, of which 89 percent were employed in the building equipment contractors industry. In contrast to other construction trades, few elevator installers and repairers are self-employed.

Although installation and major repairs require mechanics to work in teams, workers often work alone when troubleshooting minor problems.

Injuries and Illnesses. Elevator installers and repairers may suffer falls from ladders, burns due to electrical shocks, and muscle strains from lifting and carrying heavy equipment. As a result, workers must take precaution and wear protective equipment such as hard hats, harnesses, and safety glasses.

Work Schedules. Almost all elevator installers and repairers work full time. They often work overtime when emergency repairs need to be made or construction deadlines need to be met. Some workers are on call 24 hours a day.

Because the vast majority of their work is indoors, elevator installers and repairers are less affected by weather conditions than workers in many other construction occupations.

How to Become One

Nearly all elevator installers and repairers learn through an apprenticeship. Currently, 35 states require workers to be licensed.

Education. A high school diploma or equivalent is required. High school classes in math, mechanical drawing, and shop may help applicants compete for apprenticeship openings.

Training. Elevator installers and repairers learn their trade through a 5-year apprenticeship. For each year of the program, apprentices must have at least 144 hours of related technical instruction and 2,000 hours of paid on-the-job training. During training, apprentices learn blueprint reading, electrical and electronic theory, mathematics, applied physics, and safety.

Unions and individual contractors offer apprenticeship programs. The basic qualifications to enter an apprenticeship program are the following:

• At least 18 years old

• High school diploma or equivalent

• Physically able to do the job

• Pass basic math, reading, and mechanical aptitude test

Licenses, Certifications, and Registrations. Currently, 35 states require elevator installers and repairers to be licensed. Check with your state's individual licensing agencies for specific requirements.

Some associations offer certification for workers. Although not required, certification can show competence and proficiency in the field. The National Association of Elevator Contractors offers two certification programs for elevator installers and repairers:

• Certified Elevator Technician

• Certified Accessibility and Private Residence Lift Technician

Advancement. Ongoing training is important for elevator installers and repairers in order to keep up with technological developments. Union elevator installers and repairers typically receive training throughout their careers. This training improves a worker's chances of keeping their job and getting promoted. Some installers may receive additional training in specialized areas and advance to be a mechanic-in-charge, adjustor, supervisor, or elevator inspector.

Important Qualities

Detail oriented. Elevator installers must keep accurate records of their service schedules. These records are used to schedule future maintenance, which often helps reduce breakdowns.

Mechanical skills. Elevator installers use a variety of power tools and handtools to install and repair lifts. Escalators, for example, run on tracks that must be installed using wrenches and screwdrivers.

Physical stamina. Elevators installers must be able to perform strenuous work for long periods.

Physical strength. Elevator installers often lift heavy equipment and parts, including escalator steps, conduit, and metal tracks. Some apprentices must be able to lift 100 pounds to participate in a program.

Employment Projections Data for Elevator Installers and Repairers

Occupational title	SOC Code	Employment, 2012	Projected Employment, 2022	Change, 2012–2022	
				Percent	Numeric
Elevator installers and repairers...	47-4021	19,700	24,500	25	4,800

Source: U.S. Bureau of Labor Statistics, Employment Projections Program

Note: Data are rounded. Go to **Occupational Information Included in the OOH** *for a discussion of the data in this table.*

Similar Occupations   This table shows a list of occupations with job duties that are similar to those of elevator installers and repairers.

Occupations	Entry-level Education	2012 Pay	Projected Job Growth	Average Annual Openings
Boilermakers	High school diploma or equivalent	$56,560	4%	880
Electrical and Electronics Installers and Repairers	Postsecondary non-degree award	$51,081	1%	2,980
Electricians	High school diploma or equivalent	$49,840	20%	22,460
Industrial Machinery Mechanics and Maintenance Workers and Millwrights	High school diploma or equivalent	$45,848	17%	18,700
Sheet Metal Workers	High school diploma or equivalent	$43,290	15%	4,890
Structural Iron and Steel Workers	High school diploma or equivalent	$46,140	22%	3,150

Troubleshooting skills. Elevator installers and repairers must be able to diagnose and repair problems. When an escalator stops moving, for example, mechanics determine why it stopped and make the necessary repairs.

Pay

The median annual wage for elevator installers and repairers was $76,650 in May 2012. The median wage is the wage at which half the workers in an occupation earned more than that amount and half earned less. The lowest 10 percent earned less than $39,540, and the top 10 percent earned more than $106,450.

The starting pay for apprentices is usually 50 percent of what fully trained elevator installers and repairers make. They earn pay increases as they learn to do more. Apprentices who are certified welders usually receive higher wages when welding. Assistant mechanics, by contract, receive 80 percent of the rate paid to journeyman elevator installers and repairers.

Union Membership. Most elevator installers and repairers belonged to a union in 2012. Although no single union covers all elevator installers and repairers, the largest organizer of these workers is the International Union of Elevator Constructors.

Job Outlook

Employment of elevator installers and repairers is projected to grow 25 percent from 2012 to 2022, much faster than the average for all occupations. However, because it is a small occupation, the fast growth will result in only about 4,800 new jobs over the 10-year period.

Demand for these workers will depend on growth of nonresidential construction, such as office buildings and stores that have elevators and escalators. This sector of the construction industry is expected to grow rapidly during the next decade as the economy rebounds from the recent recession.

In addition, the need to regularly maintain, update, and repair old equipment; provide access to the disabled; and install increasingly sophisticated equipment and controls should add to the demand for elevator installers and repairers.

Another factor driving demand for elevator installers and repairers is a growing number of elderly people who require stair lifts and elevators for easier access in their homes.

Job Prospects. Overall job opportunities for elevator installers and repairers should be good because the dangerous and physically challenging aspects of the work reduce the number of qualified applicants.

Job opportunities for entry-level workers should be best for those who have postsecondary education in electronics or who have experience in the military.

Elevators, escalators, lifts, moving walkways, and related equipment need to work year-round, so employment of elevator repairers is less affected by economic downturns and seasonality than employment in other construction occupations.

O*NET

➤ Elevator Installers and Repairers (47-4021.00)

Contacts for More Information

For information about apprenticeships or job opportunities as an elevator mechanic, contact local elevator contractors, a local chapter of the International Union of Elevator Constructors, a local joint union-management apprenticeship committee, or the nearest office of your state employment service or apprenticeship agency. Apprenticeship information is available from the U.S. Department of Labor's toll-free help line, 1 (877) 872-5627, or the Employment and Training Administration (www.doleta.gov/OA/eta_default.cfm).

For more information about elevator installers and repairers, visit

➤ International Union of Elevator Constructors (www.iuec.org)

For more information about the NAEC Apprenticeship Program, the Certified Elevator Technician program, or the Certified Accessibility and Private Residence Lift Technician program, visit

➤ National Association of Elevator Contractors (www.naec.org)

Glaziers

- **2012 Median Pay** .... $37,610 per year
  $18.08 per hour
- **Entry-Level Education** ... High school diploma or equivalent
- **Work Experience in a Related Occupation** .... None
- **On-the-Job Training** .... Apprenticeship
- **Number of Jobs 2012** 46,700
- **Job Outlook, 2012–22** .... 17% (Faster than average)
- **Employment Change, 2012–22** 8,000

What Glaziers Do

Glaziers install windows, skylights, and other glass products in storefronts and buildings.

Duties. Glaziers typically do the following:

- Follow blueprints or specifications
- Remove any old or broken glass before installing replacement glass

- Cut glass to the specified size and shape
- Make or install sashes or moldings for glass installation
- Fasten glass into sashes or frames with clips, moldings, or other types of fasteners
- Add weather seal or putty around pane edges to seal joints

Glass has many uses in modern life. For example, insulated and specially treated glass keeps in warm or cool air and controls sound and condensation. Tempered and laminated glass makes doors and windows more secure. The creative use of large windows, glass doors, skylights, and sunroom additions makes buildings bright, airy, and inviting. Glaziers specialize in installing these different glass products.

In homes, glaziers install or replace windows, mirrors, shower doors, and bathtub enclosures. They fit glass for tabletops and display cases. On commercial interior projects, glaziers install items such as heavy, often etched, decorative room dividers or security windows. Glazing projects also may involve replacing storefront windows for supermarkets, auto dealerships, banks, and many other establishments.

For most large-scale construction jobs, glass is pre-cut and mounted into frames at a factory or a contractor's shop. The finished glass arrives at the jobsite ready for glaziers to position and secure into place. Using cranes or hoists with suction cups, workers lift large, heavy pieces of glass for installation. In cases where the glass is not secure inside the frame, glaziers may attach steel and aluminum sashes or frames to the building, and then secure the glass with clips, moldings, or other types of fasteners.

Many windows are now being covered with laminates–a thin film or coating that covers glass. These coatings provide additional durability, security, and can add color or tint to interior and exterior glass. The laminate also prevents glass from shattering, making it ideal for commercial use in areas prone to high winds.

A few glaziers work with plastics, granite, marble, and other materials used as glass substitutes.

Workers who replace and repair glass in motor vehicles are covered in the automotive body and glass repairers profile.

Work Environment

Glaziers held about 46,700 jobs in 2012, of which 61 percent were employed in the foundation, structure, and building exterior contractors industry. Another 14 percent were employed in the building material and supplies dealers industry. About 8 percent of glaziers were self-employed.

As in many other construction trades, the work is physically demanding. Glaziers spend most of the day standing, bending, or stretching, and they often must lift and maneuver heavy, cumbersome materials, such as large glass plates.

Glaziers cut glass to lengths specified by the customer.

When installing glass plates on buildings, glaziers often lead a team of construction workers in guiding and installing the pieces into place.

Injuries and Illnesses. Typical injuries for glaziers include cuts from tools and glass, and falls from ladders and scaffolding.

Work Schedules. Most glaziers work full time. About 8 percent of glaziers were self-employed in 2012, many of whom can set their own schedule.

How to Become One

Glaziers typically enter the occupation with a high school diploma and learn their trade through an apprenticeship.

Education. Glaziers typically enter the occupation with a high school diploma or equivalent. High school courses in math are considered useful. Some prospective glaziers attend technical schools to earn a certificate.

Training. The typical training for glaziers is a 4-year apprenticeship. Each year, apprentices must have at least 144 hours of related technical training and 2,000 hours of paid on-the-job training. On the job, they learn to use the tools and equipment of the trade; handle, measure, cut, and install glass and metal framing; cut and fit moldings; and install and balance glass doors. Technical training includes installation techniques as well as basic mathematics, blueprint reading and sketching, general construction techniques, safety practices, and first aid.

After completing an apprenticeship program, glaziers are considered to be journey workers who may do tasks on their own.

Median Annual Wages, May 2012

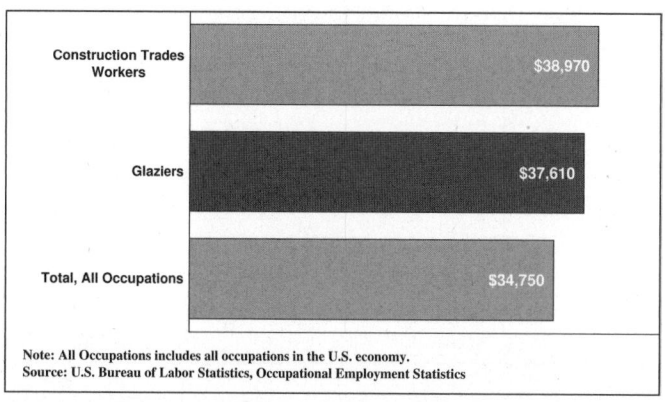

Construction Trades Workers	$38,970
Glaziers	$37,610
Total, All Occupations	$34,750

Note: All Occupations includes all occupations in the U.S. economy.
Source: U.S. Bureau of Labor Statistics, Occupational Employment Statistics

Percent Change in Employment, Projected 2012–2022

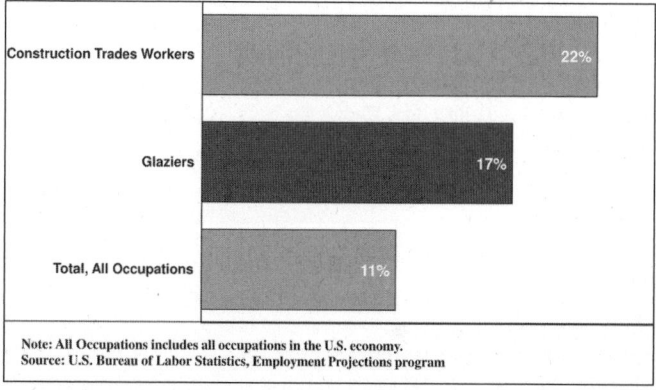

Construction Trades Workers	22%
Glaziers	17%
Total, All Occupations	11%

Note: All Occupations includes all occupations in the U.S. economy.
Source: U.S. Bureau of Labor Statistics, Employment Projections program

Employment Projections Data for Glaziers

Occupational title	SOC Code	Employment, 2012	Projected Employment, 2022	Change, 2012–2022 Percent	Change, 2012–2022 Numeric
Glaziers...	47-2121	46,700	54,700	17	8,000

Source: U.S. Bureau of Labor Statistics, Employment Projections Program

Note: Data are rounded. Go to **Occupational Information Included in the OOH** *for a discussion of the data in this table.*

A few groups sponsor apprenticeship programs, including several union and contractor associations. The basic qualifications to enter an apprenticeship program are as follows:

- Minimum age of 18
- High school education or equivalent
- Physically able to perform the work

Licenses, Certifications, and Registrations. Connecticut and Florida require glaziers to have a license. Licensure requirements include passing a test, completing an apprenticeship, and a combination of education and work experience.

The National Glass Association offers a series of written exams that certify an individual's competency to perform glazier work as a Certified Glass Installer Technician.

Important Qualities

Balance. To minimize the risk of falling, glaziers need a good sense of balance while working on ladders and scaffolding.

Hand-eye coordination. Glass must be precisely cut. As a result, a steady hand is needed to achieve a cut of the correct size and shape.

Physical stamina. Glaziers must be on their feet and move heavy pieces of glass most of the day. They need to be able to hold glass in place until it can be fully secured.

Physical strength. Glaziers must often lift heavy pieces of glass for hanging. Physical strength, therefore, is important for the occupation.

Pay

The median annual wage for glaziers was $37,610 in May 2012. The median wage is the wage at which half the workers in an occupation earned more than that amount and half earned less. The lowest 10 percent earned less than $24,170, and the top 10 percent earned more than $69,120.

The median annual wage for glaziers in the foundation, structure, and building exterior contractors industry was $39,080 in May 2012.

The median annual wage for glaziers in the building material and supplies dealers industry was $34,790 in May 2012.

The starting pay for apprentices is usually near 50 percent of what fully trained glaziers make, receiving pay increases as they learn to do more. Glaziers who work at great heights may be eligible for hazard-premium pay.

Job Outlook

Employment of glaziers is projected to grow 17 percent from 2012 to 2022, faster than the average for all occupations.

Employment growth is expected as commercial construction increasingly uses glass exteriors. As glass manufacturers continue to improve the energy efficiency of glass windows, architects are designing more buildings with glass exteriors, especially in the South.

In addition, the continuing need to modernize and repair existing structures, including many homes, often involves installing new windows. Furthermore, specialized laminated glass is increasingly being installed in homes and commercial and government buildings.

Nonetheless, the availability of prefabricated windows that carpenters and general contractors can install may limit overall employment growth of glaziers.

Job Prospects. Good job opportunities are expected from the need to replace glaziers who leave the occupation each year.

Because employers prefer workers who can do many different tasks, glaziers with a wide range of skills will have the best job opportunities. In addition, workers with military service experience are viewed favorably during initial hiring.

Like many other types of construction worker jobs, employment of glaziers is sensitive to the fluctuations of the economy. On the one hand, glaziers may experience periods of unemployment when the overall level of construction falls. On the other hand, shortages of workers may occur in some areas during peak periods of building activity.

Employment opportunities should be best in the South and in metropolitan areas, where most glazing contractors and glass shops are located.

O*NET

➤ Glaziers (47-2121.00)

Similar Occupations This table shows a list of occupations with job duties that are similar to those of glaziers.

Occupations	Entry-level Education	2012 Pay	Projected Job Growth	Average Annual Openings
Automotive Body and Glass Repairers	High school diploma or equivalent	$37,817	13%	5,700
Brickmasons, Blockmasons, and Stonemasons	High school diploma or equivalent	$44,935	34%	3,840
Carpenters	High school diploma or equivalent	$39,940	24%	32,920
Construction Laborers and Helpers	See "How to Become One"	$29,277	25%	58,790
Sheet Metal Workers	High school diploma or equivalent	$43,290	15%	4,890
Tile and Marble Setters	Less than high school	$37,040	15%	1,290

Contacts for More Information

For details about apprenticeships or other work opportunities in this trade, contact the offices of the state employment service, the state apprenticeship agency, local contractors or firms that employ glaziers, or local union-management finishing trade apprenticeship committees. Apprenticeship information is available from the U.S. Department of Labor's toll free help line: 1 (877) 872-5627 or the Employment and Training Administration (www.doleta.gov/OA/eta_default.cfm).

For more information about glaziers, visit

➤ Associated Builders and Contractors (www.abc.org/)
➤ Finishing Trades Institute (www.finishingtradesinstitute.org)
➤ International Union of Painters and Allied Trades (www.iupat.org/pages/start-a-career/glazing)
➤ National Glass Association (www.glass.org/)

Hazardous Materials Removal Workers

- **2012 Median Pay** .... $37,590 per year
  $18.07 per hour
- **Entry-Level Education** ... High school diploma or equivalent
- **Work Experience in a Related Occupation** .... None
- **On-the-Job Training** .... Moderate-term on-the-job training
- **Number of Jobs 2012** 37,500
- **Job Outlook, 2012–22** .... 14% (As fast as average)
- **Employment Change, 2012–22** 5,300

What Hazardous Materials Removal Workers Do

Hazardous materials (hazmat) removal workers identify and dispose of asbestos, radioactive and nuclear waste, arsenic, lead, and other hazardous materials. They also neutralize and clean up materials that are flammable, corrosive, reactive, or toxic.

Duties. Hazmat removal workers typically do the following:

- Follow safety procedures during cleanup
- Comply with state and federal laws regarding waste disposal
- Test hazardous materials to determine proper way to clean up
- Construct scaffolding or build containment areas before cleaning up
- Remove, neutralize, or clean up hazardous materials that are found or spilled
- Clean contaminated equipment for reuse
- Package, transport, or store hazardous and waste materials
- Keep records of cleanup activities

Hazmat removal workers clean up materials that are harmful to people and the environment. They usually work in teams and follow strict instructions and guidelines. The specific duties of hazmat removal workers depend on the substances and the cleanup location. For example, removing lead and asbestos is different from cleaning up radiation contamination and toxic spills, and cleaning up a fuel spill from a train derailment is more urgent than removing lead paint from a bridge.

The following are examples of types of hazmat removal workers:

Asbestos abatement workers and *lead abatement workers* remove asbestos and lead, respectively, from buildings and structures, particularly those that are being renovated or demolished. Most of this work is in older buildings that were originally built with asbestos insulation and lead-based paints–both of which are now banned.

Until the 1970s, asbestos was often used in buildings for fireproofing and insulation. However, asbestos particles can cause deadly lung diseases. Similarly, until the 1970s, lead was commonly used in paint, pipes, and plumbing fixtures. Inhaling lead dust or ingesting chips of lead-based paint may cause serious health problems, especially in children.

Lead abatement workers apply chemicals to walls in order to remove lead-based paint. Once applied, workers strip the walls, package the residue and paint chips, and place them in approved bags or containers for proper disposal. Some workers operate sandblasters, high-pressure water sprayers, and other tools to remove paint. Asbestos abatement workers also use scrapers or vacuums to remove asbestos from buildings.

Decommissioning and decontamination workers remove and treat radioactive materials generated by nuclear facilities and power plants. They break down contaminated items such as "gloveboxes," which are used to process radioactive materials. When a facility is being closed or decommissioned (taken out of service), these workers clean the facility and decontaminate it from radioactive materials.

Decontamination technicians perform tasks similar to those of janitors and cleaners, but the items and areas they clean are radioactive.

Emergency and disaster response workers clean up hazardous materials in response to natural or man-made disasters and accidents, such as those involving trains, trucks, or other vehicles transporting hazardous materials. Timely and thorough cleanups help to control and prevent more damage to accident or disaster sites.

Some hazardous materials removal workers specialize in radioactive substances.

Median Annual Wages, May 2012

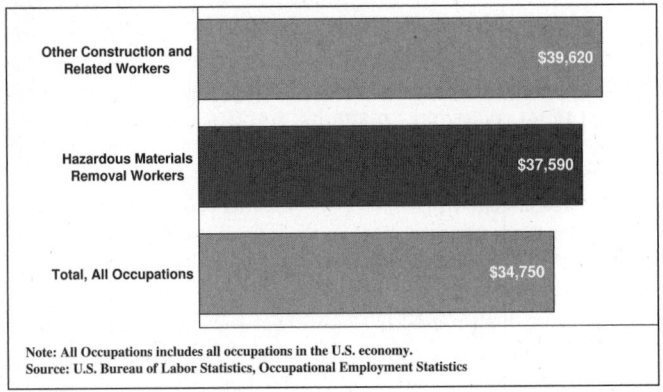

Note: All Occupations includes all occupations in the U.S. economy.
Source: U.S. Bureau of Labor Statistics, Occupational Employment Statistics

Percent Change in Employment, Projected 2012–2022

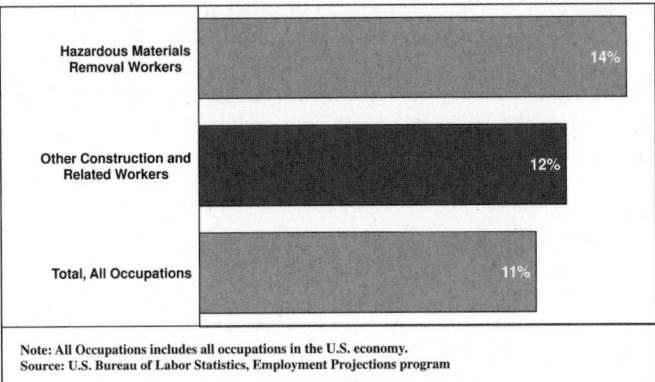

Note: All Occupations includes all occupations in the U.S. economy.
Source: U.S. Bureau of Labor Statistics, Employment Projections program

Radiation-protection technicians measure, record, and report radiation levels; operate high-pressure cleaning equipment for decontamination; and package radioactive materials for removal or storage.

Treatment, storage, and disposal workers prepare and transport hazardous materials for treatment, storage, or disposal. To ensure proper treatment of materials, workers must follow U.S. Environmental Protection Agency (EPA) or U.S. Occupational Safety and Health Administration (OSHA) regulations. They move materials from contaminated sites to incinerators, landfills, or storage facilities. They also organize and track the location of items in these facilities. Workers typically operate heavy machinery, such as forklifts, earthmoving machinery, and large trucks.

Mold remediation workers represent a small segment of hazardous materials removal. Although mold is not usually defined as a hazardous material, some mold–especially the types that cause allergic reactions–can affect a building to the extent that the mold must be removed. Workers typically use wet vacuums to remove water, dehumidifiers to reduce humidity levels, and fans to dry the affected areas. They sometimes must use chemicals to neutralize the mold or remove entire sections of drywall, insulation, or carpet.

Work Environment

Hazardous materials (hazmat) removal workers held about 37,500 jobs in 2012. About 77 percent were employed in the waste management and remediation services industry.

Working conditions differ depending on the hazardous material being cleaned. Nonetheless, workers usually must stand for long periods.

Asbestos and lead abatement workers typically work in office buildings, schools, or historic buildings that are being renovated. Completing projects often requires night and weekend work to meet deadlines.

Treatment, storage, and disposal workers are usually employed at facilities such as landfills, incinerators, and industrial furnaces.

Decommissioning and decontamination workers and technicians work at nuclear facilities and electric power plants.

Injuries and Illnesses. Because cleaning or removing hazardous materials is dangerous, workers must follow specific safety procedures to avoid injuries and illnesses. They usually work in teams and must follow careful instructions from a team leader or site supervisor. Each phase of an operation is planned in advance, and workers are trained to deal with hazardous situations. Crews and supervisors take every safety measure to ensure that the worksite is safe.

To reduce their exposure to harmful materials, workers wear coveralls, gloves, shoe covers, and safety glasses or goggles. Some must wear fully enclosed protective suits, which may be hot and uncomfortable, for several hours at a time. In extremely toxic cleanups, hazmat workers are required to wear respirators to protect themselves from airborne particles or noxious gases. Lead abatement workers wear a personal air monitor that measures the amount of lead exposure.

Work Schedules. Most hazmat removal workers are employed full time. Overtime and shift work are common, especially for emergency and disaster response workers.

Some hazmat removal workers travel to areas impacted by a disaster. During a cleanup, workers may be away from home until a project is complete, which may take several days or weeks.

Hazmat removal workers at nuclear facilities are busiest during refueling and may experience unemployment during other times.

How to Become One

Hazardous materials (hazmat) removal workers receive on-the-job training. They must complete up to 40 hours of training in accordance with Occupational Safety and Health Administration (OSHA) standards. There are no formal education requirements beyond a high school diploma. Some hazmat removal workers must be licensed. Positions in nuclear facilities require candidates to be U.S. citizens, pass a security background investigation, and pass drug and alcohol abuse screening.

Education. Hazmat removal workers need a high school diploma. Although not required, associate's degree programs related to radiation protection may help candidates seeking positions in nuclear facilities.

Training. Hazmat removal workers receive comprehensive training on the job. Training generally includes a combination of classroom instruction and field work. In the classroom, they learn safety procedures and the proper use of personal protective equipment. While on site, they learn about equipment and chemicals, and are supervised by an experienced worker.

As part of this training, workers must complete up to 40 hours of training in accordance with OSHA standards. The length of training depends on the type of hazardous material that workers handle. The training is given either in-house or in OSHA-approved training centers. It covers health hazards, personal protective equipment and clothing, site safety, recognizing and identifying hazards, and decontamination.

To work with a specific hazardous material, workers must complete training and work requirements set by state or federal agencies on handling that material. For example, employees who

Employment Projections Data for Hazardous Materials Removal Workers

Occupational title	SOC Code	Employment, 2012	Projected Employment, 2022	Change, 2012–2022	
				Percent	Numeric
Hazardous materials removal workers..................................	47-4041	37,500	42,900	14	5,300

Source: U.S. Bureau of Labor Statistics, Employment Projections Program

Note: Data are rounded. Go to Occupational Information Included in the OOH for a discussion of the data in this table.

only have a license for mold removal can only work on mold remediation.

Workers who treat asbestos or lead, the most common contaminants, must complete an employer-sponsored training program that meets OSHA standards. Employer-sponsored training is usually given in-house, and the employer is responsible for covering all technical and safety subjects outlined by OSHA.

Extensive training is required for decommissioning and decontamination workers employed at nuclear facilities. In addition to completing the hazardous waste removal training that meets OSHA standards, workers must take courses on nuclear materials and radiation safety as mandated by the Nuclear Regulatory Commission.

These courses add up to about 3 months of training, although most are not taken consecutively. Many agencies, organizations, and companies nationwide provide training programs that are approved by the U.S. Environmental Protection Agency, the U.S. Department of Energy, and other regulatory agencies.

Licenses, Certifications, and Registrations. In addition to completing the training required by OSHA, some states also have permit or license requirements, particularly for mold remediation and asbestos and lead removal. Workers who transport hazardous materials may need a state or federal permit.

License requirements vary by state, but candidates typically must meet the following criteria:

- Be at least 18 years old
- Complete training mandated by a state or federal agency
- Pass a written exam

To maintain their license, workers must take continuing education courses each year. For more information, check with the state's licensing agency.

Work Experience in a Related Occupation. Although previous work experience is not required, some employers prefer candidates with experience in the construction trades, such as construction laborers and helpers.

In addition, some employers at nuclear facilities prefer to hire workers with at least 2 years of related work experience. Experi-

ence in the U.S. Navy or experience working as a janitor at a nuclear facility may be helpful.

Important Qualities

Decision-making skills. Hazmat removal workers identify materials in a spill or leak and choose the proper method for cleaning up. For example, when a chemical tanker overturns, workers must decide if evacuation is needed, and clean up the site.

Detail oriented. Hazmat removal workers must follow safety procedures and keep records of their work. For example, workers must track the amount and type of waste disposed, equipment or chemicals used, and number of containers stored.

Math skills. Workers must be able to perform basic mathematical conversions and calculations when mixing solutions that neutralize contaminants.

Mechanical skills. Depending on the size and type of the cleanup, hazmat removal workers may use sandblasters, power washers, or earthmovers to clean contaminated sites.

Physical stamina. Hazmat cleanup work can be strenuous. For example, workers may have to stand and scrub equipment or surfaces for hours at a time to remove toxic materials.

Pay

The median annual wage for hazardous materials (hazmat) removal workers was $37,590 in May 2012. The median wage is the wage at which half the workers in an occupation earned more than that amount and half earned less. The lowest 10 percent earned less than $25,000, and the top 10 percent earned more than $66,730.

Job Outlook

Employment of hazardous materials (hazmat) removal workers is projected to grow 14 percent from 2012 to 2022, about as fast as the average for all occupations.

Employment growth will be driven by the need to safely remove and clean up abandoned hazmat sites recognized by the Environmental Protection Agency. Efforts to recycle waste on a larger scale should also contribute to some employment growth.

Similar Occupations   This table shows a list of occupations with job duties that are similar to those of hazardous materials removal workers.

Occupations	Entry-level Education	2012 Pay	Projected Job Growth	Average Annual Openings
Construction Laborers and Helpers	See "How to Become One"	$29,277	25%	58,790
Firefighters	Postsecondary non-degree award	$45,250	7%	10,400
Painters, Construction and Maintenance	Less than high school	$35,190	20%	11,050
Police and Detectives	High school diploma or equivalent	$57,974	5%	27,500
Power Plant Operators, Distributors, and Dispatchers	High school diploma or equivalent	$68,256	-8%	1,880
Water and Wastewater Treatment Plant and System Operators	High school diploma or equivalent	$42,760	8%	4,750

In addition, with a number of nuclear plants scheduled to close or decommission in the coming decade, hazmat removal workers will be needed to decontaminate equipment, store waste, and clean up these facilities for safe closure.

However, overall employment growth of hazmat removal workers will be limited by the amount of federal funding for many of these projects. Furthermore, with a declining number of structures containing asbestos and lead, demand for workers who remove these materials will be moderated.

Job Prospects. Many job openings are expected because of the need to replace workers who leave the occupation each year.

Applicants who have previous work experience with reactors in the U.S. Navy may have better job opportunities at nuclear facilities.

Lead and asbestos workers will have limited job opportunities as the pace of restoration of federal and historic buildings slows. Also, hazmat removal workers should continue to face competition from construction laborers and insulation workers who are trained to do hazmat removal or cleanups.

O*NET

➤ Hazardous Materials Removal Workers (47-4041.00)

Contacts for More Information

For more information about hazardous materials removal workers in the construction industry, including information on training, visit

➤ Laborers' International Union of North America (www.liunatraining.org/)

For more information about working in the nuclear industry, visit

➤ Nuclear Energy Institute (www.nei.org/)

For information about training and regulations mandated by federal agencies, visit

➤ Occupational Safety and Health Administration (www.osha.gov/index.html)
➤ U.S. Department of Energy (http://energy.gov/)
➤ U.S. Environmental Protection Agency (www.epa.gov/)
➤ U.S. Nuclear Regulatory Commission (www.nrc.gov/)

Insulation Workers

- **2012 Median Pay** .... $35,940 per year
  $17.28 per hour
- **Entry-Level Education** .... See "How to Become One"
- **Work Experience in a Related Occupation** .... None
- **On-the-Job Training** .... See "How to Become One"
- **Number of Jobs 2012** 52,100
- **Job Outlook, 2012–22** .... 38% (Much faster than average)
- **Employment Change, 2012–22** 19,600

What Insulation Workers Do

Insulation workers install and replace the materials used to insulate buildings and their mechanical systems to help control and maintain the temperatures in buildings. These workers are often referred to as *insulators*.

Duties. Insulation workers typically do the following:

- Remove old insulation and dispose of it properly
- Read blueprints and specifications to determine job requirements

- Determine the amount and type of insulation needed
- Measure and cut insulation to fit into walls and around pipes
- Fasten insulation in place with staples, tape, or screws
- Use compressors to spray insulation into some spaces
- Install plastic barriers to protect insulation from moisture
- Follow safety guidelines

Properly insulated buildings save energy by keeping heat in during the winter and out in the summer. Insulated vats, vessels, boilers, steam pipes, and hot water pipes also prevent the wasteful loss of heat or cold and prevent burns. Insulation also helps reduce noise that passes through walls and ceilings.

When renovating old buildings, insulators often must remove the old insulation. In the past, asbestos–now known to cause cancer–was used extensively to insulate walls, ceilings, pipes, and industrial equipment. Because of this danger, hazardous materials removal workers or specially trained insulators are required to remove asbestos before workers can begin installation.

Insulation workers use common hand tools, such as knives and scissors. They also may use a variety of power tools including power saws to cut insulating materials, welders to secure clamps, and staple guns to fasten insulation to walls. Some insulators use compressors to spray insulation.

Workers sometimes wrap a cover of aluminum, sheet metal, or vapor barrier (plastic sheeting) over the insulation. Doing so protects the insulation by keeping moisture out.

The following are examples of types of insulation workers:

Floor, ceiling, and wall insulators install insulation in attics, floors, and behind walls in homes and other buildings. Most of these workers unroll, cut, fit, and staple batts of fiberglass insulation between wall studs and ceiling joists. Some workers, however, spray foam insulation with a compressor hose into the space being filled.

Insulation workers should have excellent job opportunities.

Median Annual Wages, May 2012

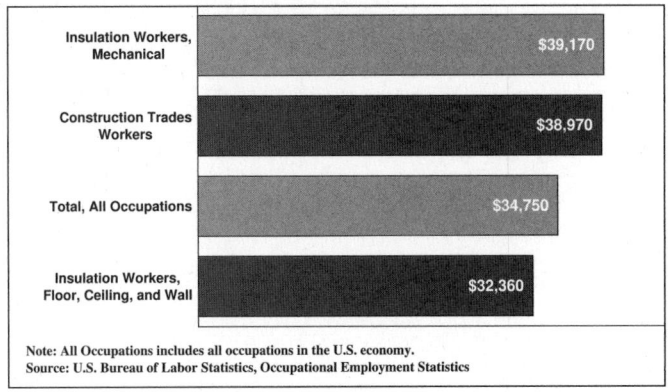

Note: All Occupations includes all occupations in the U.S. economy.
Source: U.S. Bureau of Labor Statistics, Occupational Employment Statistics

Percent Change in Employment, Projected 2012–2022

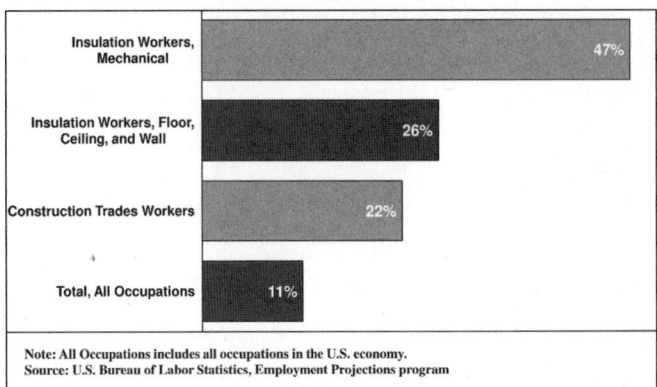

Note: All Occupations includes all occupations in the U.S. economy.
Source: U.S. Bureau of Labor Statistics, Employment Projections program

Mechanical insulators apply insulation to pipes or ductwork in businesses, factories, and many other types of buildings. When insulating a steam pipe, for example, the temperature, thickness, and diameter of the pipe are all factors that determine the type of insulation to be used.

Work Environment

Insulators held about 52,100 jobs in 2012. Employment was about split between mechanical insulators and floor, ceiling, and wall insulators.

Most floor, ceiling, and wall insulators were employed in the drywall and insulation contractors industry. The industries that employed the most mechanical insulators in 2012 were as follows:

Other building equipment contractors 38%
Drywall and insulation contractors 22
Plumbing, heating, and air-conditioning contractors 15

Insulation workers generally work indoors in residential and industrial settings. They spend most of their workday standing, bending, or kneeling in confined spaces.

Work Schedules. Most insulators work full time. Those who insulate gas and oil pipelines may have to stop work due to rain or very cold weather.

Injuries and Illnesses. Although insulation installation is not inherently dangerous, falls from ladders and cuts from knives are common hazards. In addition, small particles from insulation materials, especially when sprayed, can irritate the eyes, skin, and lungs. To protect themselves, insulators must keep the work area well ventilated. They must also wear personal protective equipment (PPE) which includes suits, masks, and respirators which protects against hazardous fumes or materials.

Mechanical insulators may get burns from the pipes they insulate.

How to Become One

Most floor, ceiling, and wall insulation workers learn their trade on the job. Most mechanical insulators complete an apprenticeship program.

Education. There are no specific education requirements for floor, ceiling, and wall insulation workers. Mechanical insulation workers should have a high school diploma. High school courses in English, math, woodworking, mechanical drawing, algebra, and general science are considered helpful for all insulation workers.

Training. Most mechanical insulation workers learn their trade through a 4-year apprenticeship. Some apprenticeships may last up to 5 years, depending on the program. For each year of the program, apprentices must have at least 1,700 to 2,000 hours of paid on-the-job training and a minimum of 144 hours of related technical instruction. The technical portion includes learning about installation techniques as well as basic mathematics, how to read and draw blueprints, general construction techniques, safety practices, and first aid.

Unions and individual businesses offer apprenticeship programs. Although most workers enter apprenticeships directly, some start out as helpers first. The basic qualifications to enter an apprenticeship program are as follows:

• Being 18 years old

• Physically able to do the work

Licenses, Certifications, and Registrations. Insulation workers who remove and handle asbestos must be trained through a program accredited by the U.S. Environmental Protection Agency.

Insulation contractor organizations offer voluntary certification to help workers prove their skills and knowledge of residential and industrial insulation.

The National Insulation Association also offers a certification for mechanical insulators in conducting energy appraisals to determine if and how insulation can benefit industrial customers.

Important Qualities

Dexterity. Insulation workers must be able to work in confined spaces while maintaining coordination and control of tools and materials. Also, insulators often must reach above their heads to fit and fasten insulation into place.

Employment Projections Data for Insulation Workers

Occupational title	SOC Code	Employment, 2012	Projected Employment, 2022	Change, 2012–2022	
				Percent	Numeric
Insulation workers	—	52,100	71,700	38	19,600
Insulation workers, floor, ceiling, and wall	47-2131	23,300	29,400	26	6,100
Insulation workers, mechanical	47-2132	28,900	42,400	47	13,500

Source: U.S. Bureau of Labor Statistics, Employment Projections Program

Note: Data are rounded. Go to **Occupational Information Included in the OOH** *for a discussion of the data in this table.*

Similar Occupations   This table shows a list of occupations with job duties that are similar to those of insulation workers.

Occupations	Entry-level Education	2012 Pay	Projected Job Growth	Average Annual Openings
Carpenters	High school diploma or equivalent	$39,940	24%	32,920
Construction Laborers and Helpers	See "How to Become One"	$29,277	25%	58,790
Drywall and Ceiling Tile Installers, and Tapers	Less than high school	$38,572	16%	2,880
Roofers	Less than high school	$35,290	11%	4,290
Sheet Metal Workers	High school diploma or equivalent	$43,290	15%	4,890

Mechanical skills. Insulation workers use a variety of hand and power tools to install insulation. Those who apply foam insulation, for example, must be able to operate a compressor and sprayer to spread the foam onto walls or across attics.

Physical stamina. Because insulators spend most of the day standing, stretching, and bending, workers should be able to stay physically active without getting tired.

Pay

The median annual wage for floor, ceiling, and wall insulation workers was $32,360 in May 2012. The median wage is the wage at which half the workers in an occupation earned more than that amount and half earned less. The lowest 10 percent earned less than $20,990, and the top 10 percent earned more than $59,440.

The median annual wage for mechanical insulation workers was $39,170 in May 2012. The lowest 10 percent earned less than $25,630, and the top 10 percent earned more than $75,390.

The starting pay for apprentices is usually near 50 percent of what fully trained insulators make. As they learn to do more, they receive pay increases.

Job Outlook

Overall employment of insulation workers is projected to grow 38 percent from 2012 to 2022, much faster than the average for all occupations. Growth rates, however, will vary by occupational specialty.

Employment of floor, ceiling, and wall insulators is projected to grow 26 percent from 2012 to 2022, much faster than the average for all occupations. However, because it is a small occupation, the fast growth will result in only about 6,100 new jobs over the 10-year period. Increases in home building will spur employment growth over the coming decade. In addition, insulation will continue to be added into existing buildings to save energy.

Employment of mechanical insulation workers is projected to grow 47 percent from 2012 to 2022, much faster than the average for all occupations. Demand for mechanical insulators will be spurred by the need to make existing buildings more energy efficient. In the past, mechanical insulation has been reduced or cut from building plans as a cost-saving method, but energy analyses show that improved insulation provides a greater return on investment. The anticipated construction of new power plants, which are big users of insulated pipes and equipment, should also result in greater employment demand.

Job Prospects. Floor, ceiling, and wall insulators are expected to face strong competition for jobs as they often compete with other construction trade workers and there are fewer entry requirements. Job openings will, nonetheless, continue to arise because the irritating nature of many insulation materials, combined with the often difficult working conditions, causes many residential insulation workers to leave the occupation each year.

Mechanical insulation workers who have completed training should have the best job opportunities. Overall opportunities for mechanical insulators should be very good as new construction opportunities continue to grow, as the increased focus on maintenance and retrofitting continues, and as government and private business strive for more energy efficiency.

Insulation workers in the construction industry may experience periods of unemployment because of the short duration of many construction projects and the cyclical nature of construction activity. Workers employed to do industrial plant maintenance generally have more stable employment because maintenance and repair must be done regularly.

O*NET

➤ Insulation Workers, Floor, Ceiling, and Wall (47-2131.00)
➤ Insulation Workers, Mechanical (47-2132.00)

Contacts for More Information

For details about apprenticeships or other opportunities for insulation workers, contact the offices of the state employment service, the state apprenticeship agency, local insulation contractors or firms that employ insulators, or local union-management apprenticeship committees. Apprenticeship information is available from the U.S. Department of Labor's toll free help line, 1 (877) 872-5627, or the Employment and Training Administration (www.doleta.gov/OA/eta_default.cfm).

For more information about apprenticeship or training for insulation workers, visit

➤ National Insulation Association (www.insulation.org)
➤ International Association of Heat and Frost Insulators and Allied Workers (www.insulators.org)

Painters, Construction and Maintenance

- **2012 Median Pay** .... $35,190 per year
  $16.92 per hour
- **Entry-Level Education** .... Less than high school
- **Work Experience in a Related Occupation** .... None
- **On-the-Job Training** .... Moderate-term on-the-job training
- **Number of Jobs 2012** 316,200
- **Job Outlook, 2012–22** .... 20% (Faster than average)
- **Employment Change, 2012–22** 62,600

What Painters, Construction and Maintenance Do

Painters apply paint, stain, and coatings to walls, buildings, bridges, and other structures.

Painters must stand for long periods, often working from scaffolding and ladders.

Duties. Painters typically do the following:

- Cover floors and furniture with dropcloths and tarps to protect surfaces
- Remove fixtures such as pictures, doorknobs, or electric switch covers
- Put up scaffolding and set up ladders
- Fill holes and cracks with putty, plaster, or other compounds
- Prepare surfaces by scraping, wire brushing, or sanding to a smooth finish
- Calculate the area to be painted and the amount of paint needed
- Apply primers or sealers so that the paint will adhere
- Choose paints and stains for desired color and appearance
- Apply paint or other finishes, using handbrushes, rollers, or sprayers

Applying paint to interior walls makes surfaces attractive and vibrant. In addition, paints and other sealers protect exterior surfaces from erosion caused by exposure to the weather.

Because there are several ways to apply paint, workers must be able to choose the proper tool for each job, such as the correct roller, power sprayer, or brush. Choosing the right tool typically depends on the surface to be covered and the characteristics of the finish.

A few painters–mainly industrial–use special safety equipment. For example, painting in confined spaces, such as the inside of a large storage tank, requires workers to wear self-contained suits to avoid inhaling toxic fumes. When painting bridges, ships, tall buildings, or oil rigs, painters may work from scaffolding, bosun's chairs, and harnesses in order to reach work areas.

The following are examples of types of painters:

Construction painters apply paints, stains, and coatings to interior and exterior walls, new buildings, and other structural surfaces.

Maintenance painters remove old finishes and apply paints, stains, and coatings later in a structure's life. Some painters specialize in painting or coating industrial structures, such as bridges and oil rigs, to prevent corrosion.

Artisan painters specialize in creating distinct finishes by using one of many decorative techniques. One such technique is adding glaze for increased depth and texture. Other common techniques are sponging, distressing, rag rolling, color blocking, and faux finishing.

Work Environment

Painters held about 316,200 jobs in 2012, of which 36 percent were employed in the painting and wall covering contractors industry. About 41 percent were self-employed.

Because painters apply finishes to a wide variety of structures–from bridges to the interiors and exteriors of buildings–they may work both indoors and outdoors.

Painting requires a lot of climbing, bending, kneeling, and stretching. Industrial painters typically work outdoors in dry, warm weather. Those who paint bridges or buildings may be exposed to extreme heights and uncomfortable positions; some painters are suspended by ropes or cables as they work.

Injuries and Illnesses. Painters have a higher rate of injuries and illnesses than the national average. Falls from ladders, muscle strains from lifting, and exposure to irritants such as drywall dust are common risks.

Work Schedules. Most painters work full time. About 41 percent were self-employed in 2012. Self-employed workers may be able to set their own schedule. Those who paint bridges, buildings, and other structures outside are not able to work when it rains.

Median Annual Wages, May 2012

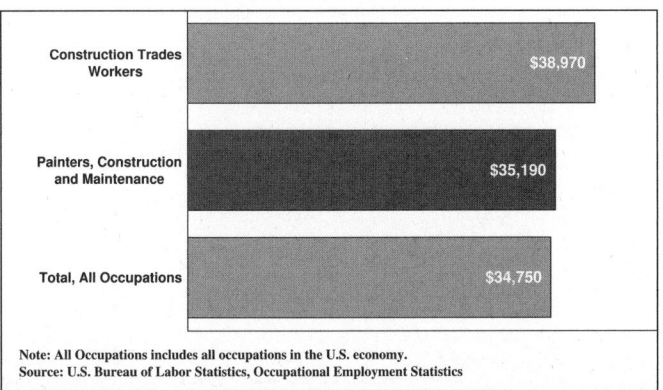

Construction Trades Workers	$38,970
Painters, Construction and Maintenance	$35,190
Total, All Occupations	$34,750

Note: All Occupations includes all occupations in the U.S. economy.
Source: U.S. Bureau of Labor Statistics, Occupational Employment Statistics

Percent Change in Employment, Projected 2012–2022

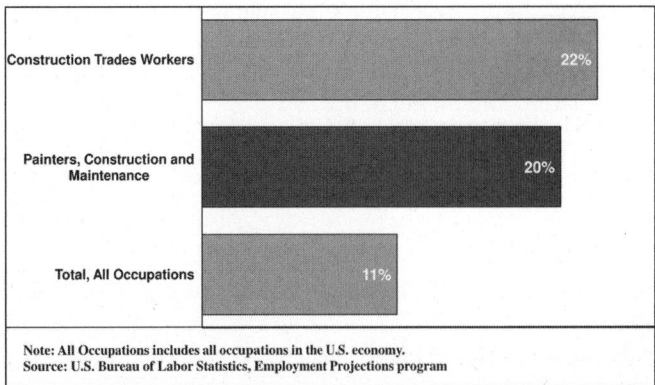

Construction Trades Workers	22%
Painters, Construction and Maintenance	20%
Total, All Occupations	11%

Note: All Occupations includes all occupations in the U.S. economy.
Source: U.S. Bureau of Labor Statistics, Employment Projections program

Employment Projections Data for Painters, Construction and Maintenance

Occupational title	SOC Code	Employment, 2012	Projected Employment, 2022	Change, 2012–2022	
				Percent	Numeric
Painters, construction and maintenance	47-2141	316,200	378,800	20	62,600

Source: U.S. Bureau of Labor Statistics, Employment Projections Program

Note: Data are rounded. Go to Occupational Information Included in the OOH *for a discussion of the data in this table.*

How to Become One

Although most painters learn their trade on the job, some learn through an apprenticeship.

Education. There are no specific education requirements to become a painter, but high school courses in English, mathematics, shop, and blueprint reading can be useful. Also, some 2-year technical schools offer courses affiliated with union and contractor organization apprenticeships. Credits earned as part of an apprenticeship program usually count toward an associate's degree.

Training. Some painters learn their trade through a 3- or 4-year apprenticeship, although a few local unions have additional time requirements. For each year of the program, apprentices must have at least 144 hours of technical instruction and 2,000 hours of paid on-the-job training. Through technical instruction, apprentices learn how to use and care for tools and equipment, how to prepare surfaces, mix and match paint, and read blueprints; application techniques; characteristics of different finishes; wood finishing; and safety practices.

After completing an apprenticeship program, painters are considered journey workers and may perform tasks on their own.

Unions and contractors sponsor apprenticeship programs. The basic qualifications to enter an apprenticeship program are as follows:

- Minimum age of 18
- High school diploma or equivalent
- Physically able to do the work

Although the vast majority of workers learn their trade on the job or through an apprenticeship, some contractors offer their own training program for new workers.

Licenses, Certifications, and Registrations. Those interested in industrial painting can earn several certifications from the National Association of Corrosion Engineers, also known as NACE International. The most common certification for construction painters is called Protective Coating Specialist. Courses range from 1 day to several weeks, depending on the certification program and specialty. Applicants also must meet work experience requirements.

Important Qualities

Color vision. Painters must be able to identify and differentiate between subtle differences in color of paints.

Customer-service skills. Workers who paint the inside and outside of residential homes often interact with clients. They must communicate with the client, listen to what the client wants, and select colors and application techniques that satisfy the client.

Detail oriented. Painters must be precise when creating or painting edges, because minor flaws can be noticeable.

Physical stamina. Painters should be able to stay physically active for many hours, because they spend most of the day standing with their arms extended.

Pay

The median annual wage for construction and maintenance painters was $35,190 in May 2012. The median wage is the wage at which half the workers in an occupation earned more than that amount and half earned less. The lowest 10 percent earned less than $22,980, and the top 10 percent earned more than $60,240.

The starting pay for apprentices is usually between 40 percent and 70 percent of what fully trained painters make. Apprentices receive pay increases as they learn to do more.

Workers who specialize in painting structures, such as bridges, tend to have higher wages.

Job Outlook

Employment of painters is projected to grow 20 percent from 2012 to 2022, faster than the average for all occupations.

The relatively short life of paint on homes, as well as changing trends in color and application, will continue to result in demand for painters. Investors who sell properties or rent them out also will require painters' services. Nonetheless, the ability of many homeowners to do the work themselves will temper employment growth somewhat.

Growing demand for industrial painting will be driven by the need to prevent the corrosion and deterioration of many industrial structures by painting or coating them. Applying a protective coating to the inside of a steel tank, for example, can add years to its life expectancy.

Job Prospects. Overall job prospects should be good because of the need to replace workers who leave the occupation each year. There are no formal education requirements for entry into these jobs, so many people with limited skills work as painters for a

Similar Occupations   This table shows a list of occupations with job duties that are similar to those of painters, construction and maintenance.

Occupations	Entry-level Education	2012 Pay	Projected Job Growth	Average Annual Openings
Carpenters	High school diploma or equivalent	$39,940	24%	32,920
Construction Laborers and Helpers	See "How to Become One"	$29,277	25%	58,790
Drywall and Ceiling Tile Installers, and Tapers	Less than high school	$38,572	16%	2,880
Painting and Coating Workers	See "How to Become One"	$33,161	4%	3,280

relatively short time and then move on to other types of work with higher pay or better working conditions.

Job opportunities for industrial painters should be excellent because the number of positions available should be greater than the pool of individuals qualified to fill them. Although industrial structures that require painting are located throughout the nation, the best employment opportunities will likely be in the Gulf Coast region, where strong demand and the largest concentration of workers exist.

New painters and those with limited experience should expect some periods of unemployment. In addition, many construction painting projects last only a short time.

Employment of painters, like that of many other construction workers, is sensitive to fluctuations in the economy. On the one hand, painters may experience periods of unemployment when the overall level of construction falls. On the other hand, peak periods of building activity may produce shortages of painters.

O*NET

➤ Painters, Construction and Maintenance (47-2141.00)

Contacts for More Information

For details about apprenticeships or other work opportunities for painters, contact the offices of the state employment service, the state apprenticeship agency, local contractors or firms that employ painters, or local union-management painter apprenticeship committees. Apprenticeship information is available from the U.S. Department of Labor's toll-free help line, 1 (877) 872-5627 or the Employment and Training Administration (www.doleta.gov/OA/eta_default.cfm).

For more information about painters and training opportunities, visit
➤ Associated Builders and Contractors (www.abc.org/)
➤ International Union of Painters and Allied Trades (www.iupat.org)
➤ NCCER (www.nccer.org/)
➤ Painting and Decorating Contractors of America (www.pdca.org/)

For general information about the work of industrial painters and about opportunities for training and certification as a protective coating specialist, visit
➤ NACE International (www.naceinstitute.org/Certification/)

Plumbers, Pipefitters, and Steamfitters

- **2012 Median Pay** .... $49,140 per year
  $23.62 per hour
- **Entry-Level Education** ... High school diploma or equivalent
- **Work Experience in a Related Occupation**.............. None
- **On-the-Job Training** .... Apprenticeship
- **Number of Jobs 2012** 386,900
- **Job Outlook, 2012–22** .... 21% (Faster than average)
- **Employment Change, 2012–22** 82,300

What Plumbers, Pipefitters, and Steamfitters Do

Plumbers, pipefitters, and steamfitters install and repair pipes that carry liquids or gases to and in businesses, homes, and factories.

Duties. Plumbers, pipefitters, and steamfitters typically do the following:

- Install pipes and fixtures

- Study blueprints and follow state and local building codes
- Determine the amount of material and type of equipment needed
- Inspect and test installed pipe systems and pipelines
- Troubleshoot systems that are not working
- Replace worn parts

Although plumbers, pipefitters, and steamfitters are three distinct specialties, their duties are often similar. For example, they all install pipes and fittings that carry water, steam, air, or other liquids or gases. They connect pipes, determine the necessary materials for a job, and perform pressure tests to ensure that a pipe system is airtight and watertight.

Plumbers, pipefitters, and steamfitters install, maintain, and repair many different types of pipe systems. Some of these systems carry water, dispose of waste, supply gas to ovens, or heat and cool buildings. Other systems, such as those in power plants, carry the steam that powers huge turbines. Pipes also are used in manufacturing plants to move acids, gases, and waste byproducts through the production process.

Master plumbers on construction jobs may be involved with developing blueprints that show where all the pipes and fixtures will go. Their input helps ensure that a structure's plumbing meets building codes, stays within budget, and works well with the location of other features, such as electric wires.

Plumbers, pipefitters, and steamfitters may use many different materials and construction techniques, depending on the type of project. Residential water systems, for example, use copper, steel, and plastic pipe that one or two plumbers can install. Power plant water systems, by contrast, are made of large steel pipes that usually take a crew of pipefitters to install. Some workers install stainless steel pipes on dairy farms and in factories, mainly to prevent contamination.

Plumbers and fitters sometimes cut holes in walls, ceilings, and floors. With some pipe systems, workers may hang steel supports from ceiling joists to hold the pipe in place. Because pipes are seldom manufactured to the exact length, plumbers and fitters measure and then cut and bend lengths of pipe as needed. Their tools often include saws and pipe cutters.

They then connect the pipes, using methods that vary by type of pipe. For example, copper pipe is joined with solder, whereas steel pipe is often screwed together.

Plumbers commonly solder copper pipes.

Median Annual Wages, May 2012

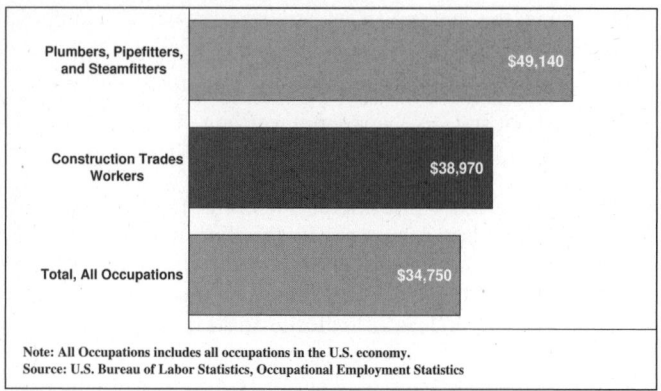

Note: All Occupations includes all occupations in the U.S. economy.
Source: U.S. Bureau of Labor Statistics, Occupational Employment Statistics

Percent Change in Employment, Projected 2012–2022

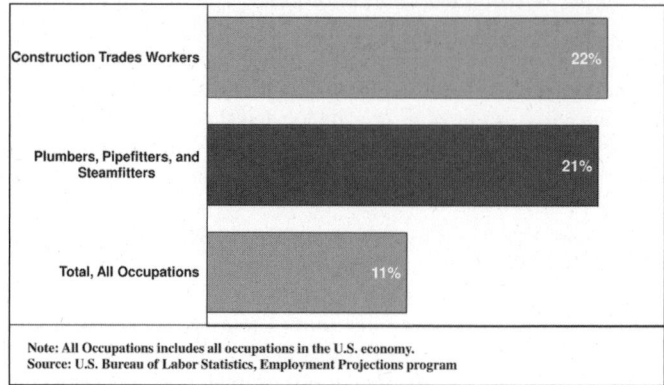

Note: All Occupations includes all occupations in the U.S. economy.
Source: U.S. Bureau of Labor Statistics, Employment Projections program

In addition to performing installation and repair work, journey- and master-level plumbers, pipefitters, and steamfitters often direct apprentices and helpers.

The following are examples of types of plumbers, pipefitters, and steamfitters:

Plumbers install and repair water, drainage, and gas pipes in homes, businesses, and factories. They install and repair large water lines, such as those which supply water to buildings, and smaller ones, including lines that supply water to refrigerators. Plumbers also install plumbing fixtures–bathtubs, showers, sinks, and toilets–and appliances such as dishwashers, garbage disposals, and water heaters. They also fix plumbing problems. For example, when a pipe is clogged or leaking, plumbers remove the clog or replace the pipe. Some plumbers maintain septic systems–the large, underground holding tanks that collect waste from houses not connected to a city or county's sewer system.

Pipefitters, sometimes referred to as just *fitters*, install and maintain pipes that carry chemicals, acids, and gases. These pipes are mostly in manufacturing, commercial, and industrial settings. Fitters often install and repair pipe systems in power plants, as well as heating and cooling systems in large office buildings. Some pipefitters specialize:

- *Gasfitters* install pipes that provide natural gas to heating and cooling systems and to stoves. They also install pipes that provide clean oxygen to patients in hospitals.

- *Sprinklerfitters* install and repair fire sprinkler systems in businesses, factories, and residential buildings.

- *Steamfitters* install pipe systems that move steam under high pressure. Most steamfitters work at college campuses and natural gas power plants where heat and electricity are generated, but others work in factories that use high-temperature steam pipes.

Work Environment

Plumbers, pipefitters, and steamfitters held about 386,900 jobs in 2012, of which 59 percent were employed in the plumbing, heating, and air-conditioning contractors industry. About 11 percent were self-employed.

Plumbers, pipefitters, and steamfitters work in factories, homes, businesses, and other places where there are pipes or septic systems.

Plumbers and fitters often must lift heavy materials, climb ladders, and work in tight spaces. Some plumbers travel to a variety of worksites every day. A few work outdoors, even in bad weather.

Injuries and Illnesses. Plumbers, pipefitters, and steamfitters have a higher rate of injuries and illnesses than the national average. Cuts from sharp tools, burns from hot pipes and soldering equipment, and falls from ladders are common injuries.

Work Schedules. Nearly all plumbers, pipefitters, and steamfitters work full time, including nights and weekends. They are often on call to handle emergencies, and overtime is common.

About 11 percent of plumbers, pipefitters, and steamfitters were self-employed in 2012. Although self-employed plumbers can set their own schedules, they are also more likely to deal with after-hours emergencies.

How to Become One

Although most plumbers, pipefitters, and steamfitters learn on the job through an apprenticeship, some start out by attending a technical school. Most states and localities require plumbers to be licensed.

Education. A high school diploma or equivalent is required.

Technical schools offer courses on pipe system design, safety, and tool use. They also offer welding courses that are considered necessary by some pipefitter and steamfitter apprenticeship training programs.

Training. Most plumbers, pipefitters, and steamfitters learn their trade through a 4- or 5-year apprenticeship. Each year, apprentices must have at least 1,700 to 2,000 hours of paid on-the-job training and a minimum of 246 hours of related technical education. Apprentices learn safety, local plumbing codes and regulations, and blueprint reading. They also study mathematics, applied physics, and chemistry.

After completing an apprenticeship program, plumbers, pipefitters, and steamfitters are considered to be journey workers, qualifying them to perform duties on their own.

With additional courses and several years of plumbing experience, plumbers are eligible to earn master status. Some states require a master plumber to get a plumbing contractor's license.

Apprenticeship programs are offered by unions and businesses. Although most workers enter apprenticeships directly, some start out as helpers. To enter an apprenticeship program, a trainee must meet the following requirements:

- Be at least 18 years old

- Have a high school diploma or equivalent

- Pass a basic math test

- Pass substance abuse screening

- Know how to use computers

Some plumbers, pipefitters, and steamfitters learn on the job through specific task-oriented training. Employers provide training that enables workers to complete a variety of tasks.

Licenses, Certifications, and Registrations. Most states and localities require plumbers to be licensed. Although licensing

Employment Projections Data for Plumbers, Pipefitters, and Steamfitters

Occupational title	SOC Code	Employment, 2012	Projected Employment, 2022	Change, 2012–2022	
				Percent	Numeric
Plumbers, pipefitters, and steamfitters.................................. 47-2152		386,900	469,200	21	82,300

Source: U.S. Bureau of Labor Statistics, Employment Projections Program

Note: Data are rounded. Go to Occupational Information Included in the OOH for a discussion of the data in this table.

requirements vary, most states and localities require workers to have 2 to 5 years of experience and to pass an exam that shows their knowledge of the trade and of local plumbing codes before they are permitted to work independently. Several states require a special license to work on gas lines. A few states require pipefitters to be licensed. Obtaining a license requires taking a test, gaining experience through work, or both. For more information, check with your state's licensing board.

Important Qualities

Business skills. Plumbers who own their own business must be able to direct workers, bid on jobs, and plan work schedules.

Customer-service skills. Plumbers work with customers on a regular basis, so they should be polite and courteous.

Mechanical skills. Plumbers, pipefitters, and steamfitters use a variety of tools to assemble and repair pipe systems. Choosing the right tool and successfully installing, repairing, or maintaining a system is crucial to their work.

Physical strength. Plumbers, pipefitters, and steamfitters must be strong enough to lift and move heavy pipe.

Troubleshooting skills. Plumbers, pipefitters, and steamfitters find, diagnose, and repair problems. For example, pipefitters must be able to perform pressure tests to pinpoint the location of a leak.

Pay

The median annual wage for plumbers, pipefitters, and steamfitters was $49,140 in May 2012. The median wage is the wage at which half the workers in an occupation earned more than that amount and half earned less. The lowest 10 percent earned less than $29,020, and the top 10 percent earned more than $84,440.

The starting pay for apprentices usually is between 30 percent and 50 percent of the rate paid to fully trained plumbers, pipefitters, and steamfitters. As they learn to do more, apprentices receive pay increases.

Union Membership. Compared with workers in all occupations, plumbers, pipefitters, and steamfitters had a higher percentage of workers who belonged to a union in 2012. The largest organizer

of these workers is the United Association of Journeymen and Apprentices of the Plumbing and Pipe Fitting Industry of the United States and Canada.

Job Outlook

Employment of plumbers, pipefitters, and steamfitters is projected to grow 21 percent from 2012 to 2022, faster than the average for all occupations.

Demand for plumbers will stem from new building construction and stricter water efficiency standards for plumbing systems, such as low-flow toilets and showerheads.

The construction of new power plants and factories should spur demand for pipefitters and steamfitters. Employment of sprinklerfitters and plumbers is expected to increase in states that adopt changes to the International Residential Code, which requires new single- and double-family homes to have fire sprinkler systems.

Job Prospects. Overall job opportunities are expected to be good as some employers continue to report difficulty finding qualified workers. In addition, many plumbers, pipefitters, and steamfitters are expected to retire over the next 10 years, resulting in more job openings. Workers with welding experience should have the best job opportunities.

As with other construction workers, employment of plumbers, pipefitters, and steamfitters is sensitive to fluctuations in the economy. On the one hand, workers may experience periods of unemployment when the overall level of construction falls. On the other hand, shortages of workers may occur in some areas during peak periods of building activity.

However, maintenance and repair of plumbing and pipe systems must continue even during economic downturns, so plumbers and fitters outside of construction, especially those in manufacturing, tend to have more stable employment.

O*NET

➤ Plumbers, Pipefitters, and Steamfitters (47-2152.00)
➤ Pipe Fitters and Steamfitters (47-2152.01)
➤ Plumbers (47-2152.02)

Similar Occupations This table shows a list of occupations with job duties that are similar to those of plumbers, pipefitters, and steamfitters.

Occupations	Entry-level Education	2012 Pay	Projected Job Growth	Average Annual Openings
Boilermakers	High school diploma or equivalent	$56,560	4%	880
Construction and Building Inspectors	High school diploma or equivalent	$53,450	12%	3,670
Construction Laborers and Helpers	See "How to Become One"	$29,277	25%	58,790
Construction Managers	Bachelor's degree	$82,790	16%	15,460
Electricians	High school diploma or equivalent	$49,840	20%	22,460
Heating, Air Conditioning, and Refrigeration Mechanics and Installers	Postsecondary non-degree award	$43,640	21%	12,370
Industrial Machinery Mechanics and Maintenance Workers and Millwrights	High school diploma or equivalent	$45,848	17%	18,700

Contacts for More Information

For details about apprenticeship or other opportunities in this trade, contact the offices of the state employment service; the state apprenticeship agency; local plumbing, heating, and cooling contractors or firms that employ fitters; or local union-management apprenticeship committees. Apprenticeship information is available from the U.S. Department of Labor's toll-free help line, 1 (877) 872-5627, or the Employment and Training Administration (www.doleta.gov/OA/eta_default.cfm).

For more information about apprenticeships for plumbers, pipefitters, and steamfitters, visit

➤ United Association of Journeymen and Apprentices of the Plumbing and Pipefitting Industry of the United States and Canada (http://ua.org/index.asp)

For more information about plumbers and pipefitters, visit

➤ Mechanical Contractors Association of America (www.mcaa.org/)
➤ NCCER (www.nccer.org/curriculum?mID=105)
➤ Plumbing-Heating-Cooling Contractors Association (www.phcc-web.org)

For general information about sprinklerfitters, visit

➤ American Fire Sprinkler Association (www.firesprinkler.org)
➤ National Fire Sprinkler Association (www.nfsa.org)

Roofers

- **2012 Median Pay** .... $35,290 per year
  $16.97 per hour
- **Entry-Level Education** .... Less than high school
- **Work Experience in a Related Occupation**............... None
- **On-the-Job Training** .... Moderate-term on-the-job training
- **Number of Jobs 2012** 132,700
- **Job Outlook, 2012–22** .... 11% (As fast as average)
- **Employment Change, 2012–22** 15,200

What Roofers Do

Roofers repair and install the roofs of buildings using a variety of materials, including shingles, asphalt, and metal.

Duties. Roofers typically do the following:

- Inspect problem roofs to determine the best way to repair them
- Measure roof to calculate the quantities of materials needed
- Replace damaged or rotting joists or plywood
- Install vapor barriers or layers of insulation
- Install shingles, asphalt, metal, or other materials to make the roof watertight
- Align roofing materials with edges of the roof
- Cut roofing materials to fit around walls or vents
- Cover exposed nail or screw heads with roofing cement or caulk to prevent leakage

Properly installed roofs keep water from leaking into buildings and damaging the interior, equipment, or furnishings. There are three basic types of roofs: low-slope, steep-slope, and sustainable. Roofers may specialize in the installation and replacement of one or more of these roof systems.

Low-slope roofs rise less than 3 inches per horizontal foot and are installed in layers. Low-slope roofs make up about two-thirds of all roofs, as most commercial, industrial, and apartment buildings use this type.

Many of today's low-slope roofs are covered with a single-ply membrane of waterproof rubber or thermoplastic compound. Most previously installed low-slope roofs, however, use several layers of roofing materials or felt membranes stuck together with hot bitumen (a tar-like substance).

Steep-slope roofs rise more than 3 inches per horizontal foot and use asphalt shingles, which often cost less than other coverings. Steep-slope roofs make up most of the remaining roofs, as most single-family homes use this type.

Although asphalt shingles are most commonly used, some roofers also install tile, solar shingles, fiberglass shingles, metal shingles, or shakes (rough wooden shingles).

Sustainable roofs are growing in popularity. A small but increasing number of buildings now have vegetative roofs that incorporate landscape materials into traditional roofing systems. A landscape roofing system typically begins with a single or multiple waterproof layers. After that layer is proven to be leak free, roofers put a root barrier over it, and, finally, layers of soil, in which vegetation is planted. Roofers must ensure that the roof is watertight and can endure the weight and water needs of the plants.

Solar is another sustainable roof that is becoming increasingly popular. These systems include solar reflective, which prevents the absorption of energy; solar thermal, which absorbs energy to heat water; and solar photovoltaic, which converts sunlight into electricity.

Work Environment

Roofers held about 132,700 jobs in 2012, of which 64 percent were employed in the roofing contractors industry. About 28 percent were self-employed.

Roofing work can be hot and physically demanding. It involves heavy lifting, as well as climbing, bending, and kneeling. Roofers work outdoors in all types of weather, particularly when making repairs. However, they rarely install roofs when it rains or when it is very cold.

Although some roofers work alone, many work as part of a crew.

Roofers need good physical condition, strength, and balance.

Median Annual Wages, May 2012

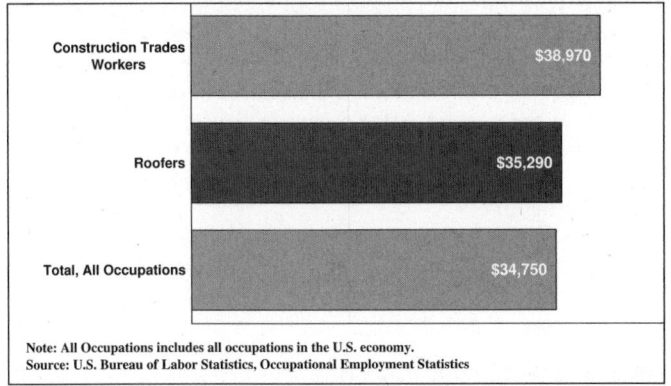

Note: All Occupations includes all occupations in the U.S. economy.
Source: U.S. Bureau of Labor Statistics, Occupational Employment Statistics

Percent Change in Employment, Projected 2012–2022

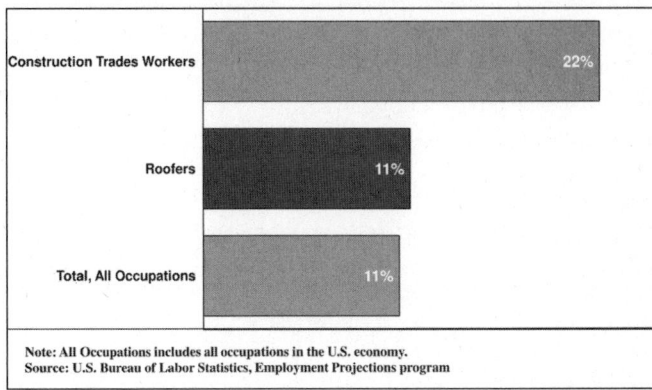

Note: All Occupations includes all occupations in the U.S. economy.
Source: U.S. Bureau of Labor Statistics, Employment Projections program

Injuries and Illnesses. Roofers have a higher rate of injuries and illnesses than the national average. Workers may slip or fall from scaffolds, ladders, or roofs. They may also be burned by hot bitumen. However, proper safety precautions can prevent most accidents.

Roofs can also become extremely hot during the summer, which can cause heat-related illnesses.

Work Schedules. Like many construction workers, most roofers work full time. In northern states, roofing work is limited during the winter months. During the summer, roofers may work overtime to complete jobs quickly, especially before rainfall.

About 28 percent of roofers were self-employed in 2012. Self-employed workers may be able to set their own schedules.

How to Become One

Although most roofers learn on the job, some learn their trade through an apprenticeship program. There are no specific education requirements for roofers.

Education. Although there are no specific education requirements for roofers, high school courses in math, shop, mechanical drawing, and blueprint reading are considered helpful. Technical

schools that offer courses related to roofing may be available in a few areas.

Training. Most on-the-job training programs consist of instruction in which experienced workers teach new workers how to use roofing tools, equipment, machines, and materials. Trainees begin with tasks such as carrying equipment and material and erecting scaffolds and hoists. Within 2 or 3 months, they are taught to measure, cut, and fit roofing materials and, later, to lay asphalt or fiberglass shingles. Because some roofing materials, such as solar tiles, are used infrequently, it can take several years to gain experience on all types of roofing. As training progresses, assignments become more complex.

Some roofers learn through a 3-year apprenticeship. For each year of the program, apprentices must have at least 144 hours of related technical training and 2,000 hours of paid on-the-job training. Apprentices learn about roofing and construction basics, such as blueprint reading, mathematics, building code requirements, and safety and first-aid practices.

After completing an apprenticeship program, roofers are considered journey workers who can perform tasks on their own.

Employment Projections Data for Roofers

Occupational title	SOC Code	Employment, 2012	Projected Employment, 2022	Change, 2012–2022	
				Percent	Numeric
Roofers..	47-2181	132,700	147,900	11	15,200

Source: U.S. Bureau of Labor Statistics, Employment Projections Program

Note: Data are rounded. Go to **Occupational Information Included in the OOH** *for a discussion of the data in this table.*

Similar Occupations   This table shows a list of occupations with job duties that are similar to those of roofers.

Occupations	Entry-level Education	2012 Pay	Projected Job Growth	Average Annual Openings
Carpenters	High school diploma or equivalent	$39,940	24%	32,920
Cement Masons and Terrazzo Workers	See "How to Become One"	$35,856	29%	5,830
Construction Laborers and Helpers	See "How to Become One"	$29,277	25%	58,790
Drywall and Ceiling Tile Installers, and Tapers	Less than high school	$38,572	16%	2,880
Sheet Metal Workers	High school diploma or equivalent	$43,290	15%	4,890
Solar Photovoltaic Installers	High school diploma or equivalent	$37,900	23%	200
Tile and Marble Setters	Less than high school	$37,040	15%	1,290

Several groups sponsor apprenticeship programs, including unions and contractor associations. The basic qualifications to enter an apprenticeship program are as follows:

• Minimum age of 18

• High school diploma or equivalent

• Physically able to do the work

Important Qualities

Balance. Roofing is often done on steep slopes at significant heights. Because of this, workers should have excellent balance to avoid falling.

Physical stamina. Roofers must have endurance to perform strenuous duties throughout the day. They may spend hours on their feet, bending and stooping–often in hot temperatures–with few breaks.

Physical strength. Roofers often lift and carry heavy materials. Some roofers, for example, must carry bundles of shingles that weigh 60 pounds or more.

Unafraid of heights. Because work is often done at significant heights, roofers must not fear working far above the ground.

Pay

The median annual wage for roofers was $35,290 in May 2012. The median wage is the wage at which half the workers in an occupation earned more than that amount and half earned less. The lowest 10 percent earned less than $22,350, and the top 10 percent earned more than $60,350.

The starting pay for apprentices is usually between 35 percent and 60 percent of what fully trained workers earn. They receive pay increases as they learn to do more.

Job Outlook

Employment of roofers is projected to grow 11 percent from 2012 to 2022, about as fast as the average for all occupations.

Roofs deteriorate more quickly than most other parts of buildings and, as a result, they need to be repaired or replaced more often. Results of a National Roofing Contractors Association survey indicate that about two-thirds of all roofing work is for repair and replacement. This factor should result in some new jobs over the coming decade.

In addition to repair and replacement work, the need to install roofs on new buildings should result in job growth. However, some roofing work may be done by other construction workers, and that may slow job growth for traditional roofing contractors.

Job Prospects. Job opportunities for roofers will occur primarily because of the need to replace workers who leave the occupation. The proportion of roofers who leave the occupation each year is higher than in most construction trades–roofing work is physically demanding and a considerable number of workers treat roofing as a temporary job until they find other work. Some roofers leave the occupation for other construction trades. Jobs are generally easier to find during spring and summer.

Demand for roofers is less vulnerable to downturns than for other construction trades because much roofing work consists of repair and reroofing, in addition to new construction. Still, workers may experience periods of unemployment when the overall level of new construction falls. However, shortages of workers may occur in some areas during peak periods of building activity.

O*NET

➤ Roofers (47-2181.00)

Contacts for More Information

For details about apprenticeships or other work opportunities for roofers, contact the offices of the state employment service, the state apprenticeship agency, local contractors or firms that employ roofers, or local union-management apprenticeship committees. Apprenticeship information is available from the U.S. Department of Labor's toll free help line, 1 (877) 872-5627, or the Employment and Training Administration (www.doleta.gov/OA/eta_default.cfm).

For information about the work of roofers, visit

➤ National Roofing Contractors Association (www.nrca.net/)

➤ United Union of Roofers, Waterproofers, and Allied Workers (www.unionroofers.com/)

Sheet Metal Workers

• **2012 Median Pay** .... $43,290 per year
$20.81 per hour

• **Entry-Level Education** ... High school diploma or equivalent

• **Work Experience in a Related Occupation**............... None

• **On-the-Job Training** .... Apprenticeship

• **Number of Jobs 2012** 142,300

• **Job Outlook, 2012–22** .... 15% (Faster than average)

• **Employment Change, 2012–22** 22,000

What Sheet Metal Workers Do

Sheet metal workers fabricate or install products that are made from thin metal sheets, such as ducts used for heating and air conditioning.

Duties. Sheet metal workers typically do the following:

• Select types of sheet metal or nonmetallic material

• Measure and mark dimensions and reference lines on metal sheets

• Drill holes in metal for screws, bolts, and rivets

• Install metal sheets with supportive frameworks

• Fabricate or alter parts at construction sites

• Maneuver large sheet metal parts to be installed, and anchor the parts

• Fasten seams or joints by welding, bolting, riveting, or soldering

Sheet metal workers fabricate, install, and maintain thin sheet metal products. Although sheet metal is used to make many products, such as rain gutters, outdoor signs, and siding, it is most commonly used to make ducts for heating and air conditioning.

Sheet metal workers study plans and specifications to determine the kind and quantity of materials they will need. Using computer-controlled saws, lasers, shears, and presses, they measure, cut, bend, and fasten pieces of sheet metal.

In shops without computerized equipment, sheet metal workers make the required calculations and use tapes and rulers to lay out the work. Then, they cut or stamp the parts with machine tools.

In manufacturing plants, sheet metal workers program and operate computerized metalworking equipment. For example, they may fabricate sheet metal parts for aircraft or industrial equipment. Sheet metal workers in those jobs may be responsible for programming the computer control systems of the equipment they operate. Additionally, they may make custom pieces and operate equipment that is manually controlled.

Sheet metal workers use a torch to heat a sheet of metal.

Before assembling pieces, sheet metal workers check each part for accurate measurements. If necessary, they use hand rotary or squaring shears and hacksaws to finish pieces.

After inspecting the metal pieces, workers fasten seams and joints with welds, bolts, rivets, solder, or other connecting devices. Then they take the parts constructed in the shop and further assemble the pieces as they install them.

Most fabrication work is done in shops with some final assembly done on the job. Some jobs are done completely at the jobsite. When installing a metal roof, for example, sheet metal workers usually measure and cut roofing panels onsite.

In addition to installing sheet metal, some workers install fiberglass and plastic board.

In some shops and factories, sheet metal workers maintain the equipment they use.

Sheet metal workers do both construction-related work and the mass production of sheet metal products in manufacturing. Sheet metal workers are often separated into four specialties: *fabrication, installation, maintenance,* and *testing and balancing.*

The following are examples of types of sheet metal workers:

Fabrication sheet metal workers, sometimes called *precision sheet metal workers,* make ducts, gutters, and other metal products. Most work in shops and factories, operating tools and equipment. Although some of the fabrication techniques used in large-scale manufacturing are similar to those used in smaller shops, the work may be highly automated and repetitive. Many fabrication shops have automated machinery, and workers use computer-aided drafting and design (CADD) and building information modeling (BIM) systems to make products.

Installation sheet metal workers install heating, ventilation, and air conditioning (HVAC) ducts. They also install other sheet metal products, such as metal roofs, siding, or gutters. They typically work on new construction and on renovation projects.

Maintenance sheet metal workers repair and clean ventilation systems so the systems use less energy. Workers remove dust and moisture and fix leaks or breaks in the sheet metal that makes up the ductwork.

Testing and balancing sheet metal specialists ensure that HVAC systems heat and cool rooms properly by making sure that air is transferred through sheet metal ducts efficiently. Information on workers who install or repair HVAC systems can be found in the profile on heating, air conditioning, and refrigeration mechanics and installers.

Work Environment

Sheet metal workers held about 142,300 jobs in 2012. About 59 percent worked in the construction industry and 27 percent worked in manufacturing.

Sheet metal fabricators usually work in small shops and manufacturing plants that are well ventilated. They often must lift heavy materials and stand for long periods.

Workers who install sheet metal at construction sites must bend, climb, and squat, sometimes in close quarters or in awkward positions.

Sheet metal installers who work outdoors are exposed to all kinds of weather.

Injuries and Illnesses. Sheet metal workers have a higher rate of injuries and illnesses than the national average. Common injuries include cuts from sharp metal, burns from soldering or welding, and falls from ladders or scaffolds.

Some sheet metal fabricators work around high-speed machines, which can be dangerous. Because of these hazards, workers often must wear safety glasses and must not wear jewelry or loose-fitting clothing that could easily get caught in a machine. To avoid

Median Annual Wages, May 2012

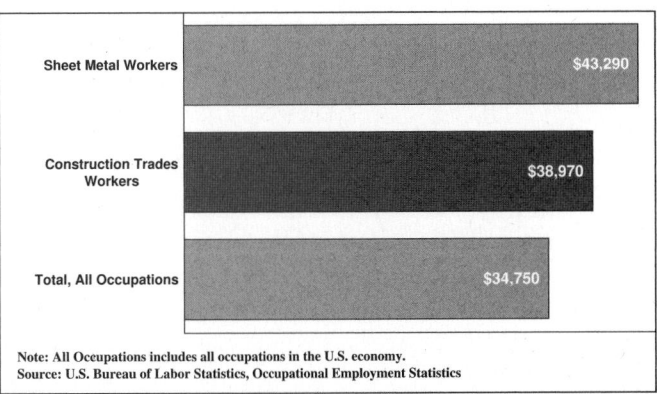

Note: All Occupations includes all occupations in the U.S. economy.
Source: U.S. Bureau of Labor Statistics, Occupational Employment Statistics

Percent Change in Employment, Projected 2012–2022

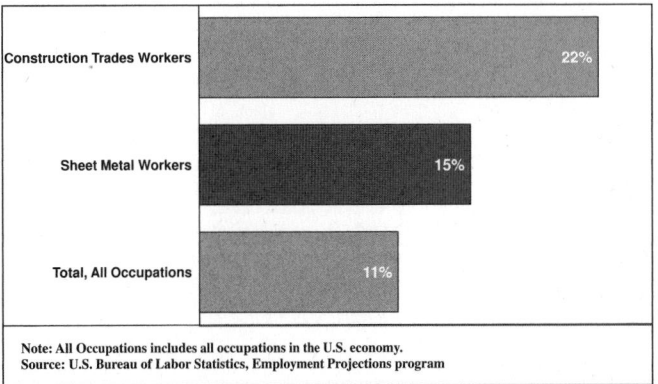

Note: All Occupations includes all occupations in the U.S. economy.
Source: U.S. Bureau of Labor Statistics, Employment Projections program

Employment Projections Data for Sheet Metal Workers

Occupational title	SOC Code	Employment, 2012	Projected Employment, 2022	Change, 2012–2022	
				Percent	Numeric
Sheet metal workers	47-2211	142,300	164,300	15	22,000

Source: U.S. Bureau of Labor Statistics, Employment Projections Program

Note: Data are rounded. Go to Occupational Information Included in the OOH *for a discussion of the data in this table.*

repetitive-type injuries, sheet metal workers may work at a variety of different production stations.

Work Schedules. Nearly all sheet metal workers are employed full time.

How to Become One

Although most sheet metal workers, particularly those in construction, learn their trade through an apprenticeship, those who work in manufacturing more often learn on the job or at a technical college.

Education. Those interested in becoming a sheet metal worker should take high school classes in English, algebra, geometry, physics, mechanical drawing and blueprint reading, and general shop.

Many technical colleges have programs that teach welding and metalworking. These programs help provide the basic knowledge that many sheet metal workers need to do their job.

Some manufacturers have partnerships with local technical schools to develop training programs specific to their factories.

Training. Most sheet metal workers learn their trade through 4- or 5-year apprenticeships. Each year, apprentices must have at least 1,700 to 2,000 hours of paid on-the-job training and a minimum of 246 hours of related technical instruction. Apprentices learn construction basics such as blueprint reading, mathematics, building code requirements, and safety and first-aid practices.

After completing an apprenticeship program, sheet metal workers are considered to be journey workers, qualifying them to do tasks on their own.

Apprenticeship programs are offered by unions and businesses. The basic qualifications for entering an apprenticeship program are reaching the age of 18 and having a high school diploma or the equivalent.

Although most workers enter apprenticeships directly after finishing high school or getting their GED, some start out with a job as a helper before entering an apprenticeship.

Licenses, Certifications, and Registrations. Although not required, sheet metal workers can earn certifications for several of the tasks that they perform. For example, some sheet metal workers can become certified in welding from the American Welding Society. In addition, the Sheet Metal Institute offers certification

in building information modeling (BIM), welding, testing and balancing, and other related skills.

Important Qualities

Computer skills. Designing and cutting sheet metal often requires the use of computer-aided drafting and design (CADD) programs and building information modeling (BIM) systems.

Customer-service skills. Because many sheet metal workers install ducts in customers' homes, workers should be polite and courteous.

Manual dexterity. Sheet metal workers need good hand-eye coordination to make precise cuts and bends in metal pieces.

Mechanical skills. Sheet metal workers use saws, lasers, shears, and presses to do their job. As a result, they should have good mechanical skills in order to help operate and maintain equipment.

Physical strength. Sheet metal workers must be able to lift and move ductwork that is often heavy and cumbersome. Some jobs require workers to be able to lift 50 pounds.

Spatial relationships. Airplane manufacturing requires the placement of structural metal pieces to be precise. Using hand-held tablets, for example, workers must be able to compare the installed sheet metal to the design specifications.

Pay

The median annual wage for sheet metal workers was $43,290 in May 2012. The median wage is the wage at which half the workers in an occupation earned more than that amount and half earned less. The lowest 10 percent earned less than $25,310, and the top 10 percent earned more than $74,740.

The starting pay for apprentices usually is between 40 percent and 50 percent of what fully trained sheet metal workers make. As they gain more skill, their pay increases.

Those who work in manufacturing are more likely to participate in profit sharing, work overtime, and receive output incentives to supplement their basic wages.

Union Membership. Compared with workers in all occupations, sheet metal workers had a higher percentage of workers who belonged to a union in 2012. Although there is no single union, the largest organizer for sheet metal workers is the International Association.

Similar Occupations   This table shows a list of occupations with job duties that are similar to those of sheet metal workers.

Occupations	Entry-level Education	2012 Pay	Projected Job Growth	Average Annual Openings
Assemblers and Fabricators	High school diploma or equivalent	$28,661	4%	37,140
Glaziers	High school diploma or equivalent	$37,610	17%	1,910
Heating, Air Conditioning, and Refrigeration Mechanics and Installers	Postsecondary non-degree award	$43,640	21%	12,370
Machinists and Tool and Die Makers	High school diploma or equivalent	$40,733	7%	13,060
Metal and Plastic Machine Workers	High school diploma or equivalent	$33,064	-6%	22,070
Roofers	Less than high school	$35,290	11%	4,290

Job Outlook

Employment of sheet metal workers is projected to grow 15 percent from 2012 to 2022, faster than the average for all occupations.

Employment growth reflects an expected increase in the number of industrial, commercial, and residential structures that will be built over the coming decade. It also reflects the need to install energy-efficient air conditioning, heating, and ventilation systems in older buildings and to maintain these systems.

Sheet metal workers in manufacturing are expected to experience faster-than-average employment growth as some work that was previously outsourced to other countries returns to the United States.

Job Prospects. Job opportunities should be particularly good for sheet metal workers who complete apprenticeship training or who are certified welders.

Some manufacturing companies report having difficulty finding qualified applicants. Workers who program equipment, possess multiple welding certifications, and show commitment to their work will have the best job opportunities.

In addition, workers at smaller firms are less likely to be laid off when demand for products slow down.

Employment of sheet metal workers, like that of many other construction workers, is sensitive to fluctuations in the economy. On the one hand, workers in these trades may experience periods of unemployment when the overall level of construction falls. On the other hand, peak periods of building activity may produce shortages of sheet metal workers.

O*NET

➤ Sheet Metal Workers (47-2211.00)

Contacts for More Information

For more information about apprenticeships or other work opportunities, contact local sheet metal contractors or heating, refrigeration, and air conditioning contractors; a local of the Sheet Metal Workers International Association; a local of the Sheet Metal and Air Conditioning Contractors' National Association; a local joint union-management apprenticeship committee; or the nearest office of your state employment service or apprenticeship agency. Apprenticeship information is available from the U.S. Department of Labor's toll-free help line, 1 (877) 872-5627, or the Employment and Training Administration (www.doleta.gov/OA/eta_default.cfm).

For general information about sheet metal workers, visit
➤ Fabricators and Manufacturers Association, International (www.fmanet.org)
➤ International Training Institute for the Sheet Metal and Air Conditioning Industry (www.sheetmetal-iti.org/index.asp)
➤ NCCER (www.nccer.org)
➤ Sheet Metal and Air Conditioning Contractors' National Association (www.smacna.org)
➤ Sheet Metal Workers International Association (www.smwia.org)
   For certification information, visit
➤ American Welding Society (www.aws.org/certification/)
➤ Sheet Metal Institute (www.sheetmetalinstitute.org/)

Solar Photovoltaic Installers

- **2012 Median Pay** .... $37,900 per year
  $18.22 per hour
- **Entry-Level Education** ... High school diploma or equivalent
- **Work Experience in a Related Occupation**.............. None
- **On-the-Job Training** .... Moderate-term on-the-job training
- **Number of Jobs 2012** 4,800
- **Job Outlook, 2012–22** .... 24% (Much faster than average)
- **Employment Change, 2012–22** 1,200

What Solar Photovoltaic Installers Do

Solar photovoltaic (PV) installers, often called *PV installers*, assemble, install, or maintain solar panel systems on roofs or other structures.

Duties. PV installers typically do the following:
- Plan PV system configuration based on customer needs, expectations, and site conditions
- Connect PV panels to the power grid
- Install solar modules, panels, or support structures in accordance with building codes and standards
- Apply weather sealing to equipment being installed
- Perform routine PV system maintenance
- Activate and test PV systems to verify performance

Sunlight is considered an environmentally safe source of energy. By way of solar panels, sunlight is transformed into electricity. Recent technological advances have sufficiently reduced the cost of solar panels, making it a viable source of electricity for businesses and homeowners alike. PV installers put these systems in place.

PV installers use a variety of hand and power tools to install photovoltaic panels. They often use wrenches, saws, and screwdrivers to connect panels to frames, wires, and support structures. This work is typically done on roofs, where the greatest amount of solar radiation–or sunlight–is captured.

Many new workers begin by performing basic tasks, such as installing support structures and placing PV panels or PV shingles on top of them. Once the panels are in place, more experienced installers usually perform more complex duties, such as evaluating sites, planning the layout of solar panels, and connecting electrical components.

Depending on the job, PV installers may connect the arrays to the electric grid, although electricians sometimes perform this duty. Once installed, workers check electrical systems for proper wiring, polarity, grounding, or integrity of terminations, and perform maintenance as needed.

Work Environment

Solar photovoltaic (PV) installers held about 4,800 jobs in 2012. The majority were employed in the construction industry.

The industries that employed the most solar photovoltaic installers in 2012 were as follows:

Plumbing, heating, and air-conditioning contractors.............. 34%
Electrical contractors and other wiring installation
   contractors 22
Power and communication line and related structures
   construction 12

Because solar panels typically weigh between 30 and 40 pounds, solar photovoltaic installers must do heavy lifting at times.

Although most PV installation is done outdoors, installers often work in attics and crawl spaces to connect panels to the electric grid. Those who work on rooftops must climb ladders.

PV installers may work alone or as part of a team. Installation of an array may require the help of roofers and electricians as well as solar photovoltaic installers.

Workers must travel to job sites.

Injuries and Illnesses. Solar photovoltaic installers risk falls from ladders and roofs, electrical shocks, and burns from hot equipment and materials while installing and maintaining PV systems.

Work Schedules. Nearly all solar photovoltaic installers work full time, which may include evenings and weekends. They often are required to be on call to handle emergencies.

How to Become One

Although some photovoltaic (PV) installers need only a high school diploma and receive on-the-job training lasting up to 1 year, most candidates receive training at a technical school or community college. These 2-year programs offer entry-level courses or may be part of an apprenticeship program.

Education. Most PV installers take courses at local community colleges and trade schools to learn about solar panel installation. Courses range from basic safety and PV knowledge to system design. Although course length varies by state and locality, most usually last a few days to several months.

Some candidates may enter the field by taking online training courses. This is particularly useful for candidates with prior construction experience, such as former electricians.

Training. Some PV installers learn their trade on the job by working with experienced installers. On-the-job training usually lasts between 1 month and 1 year, where workers learn about safety, tool use, and PV system installation techniques.

Solar PV system manufacturers may also provide specific training on a product. Such training usually includes a system overview and proper installation techniques of the manufacturer's products.

Some large construction contractors provide training to new employees on their own. Workers learn basic PV safety and are given increasingly complex tasks as they prove their abilities.

Although there are currently no apprenticeship programs for solar photovoltaic installers, a few workers learn PV installation through other occupational apprenticeship programs, such as electrician apprenticeships.

In most states, an electrician is fully qualified to connect PV systems to electric grids. They are also able to connect panels to battery sources.

Important Qualities

Customer-service skills. Residential panel installers must work in customers' homes. As a result, workers must maintain professionalism and perform the work in a timely manner.

Detail oriented. PV installers must carefully follow instructions during installation. If they fail to do so, the system may not work properly.

Mechanical skills. PV installers work with complex electrical and mechanical equipment. They must be able to build support structures that hold PV panels in place, and properly connect the panels to the electrical system.

Physical stamina. PV installers are often on their feet carrying panels and other heavy equipment. When installing rooftop panels, workers may need to climb ladders many times during the course of the day.

Physical strength. PV installers must often lift heavy equipment, parts, and tools. Workers should be strong enough to lift panels that weigh up to 40 pounds.

Work Experience in a Related Occupation. Prior experience in construction may shorten a new employees training time. For example, workers with prior experience as an electrician, roofer, carpenter, or laborer typically already understand and can perform basic construction duties.

In addition, those with knowledge of electrical work, such as electricians, are highly valued by contractors.

Licenses, Certifications, and Registrations. Although not mandatory, PV installers may obtain certification from the North American Board of Certified Energy Practitioners. Certification can demonstrate professionalism and basic PV knowledge to employers.

Median Annual Wages, May 2012

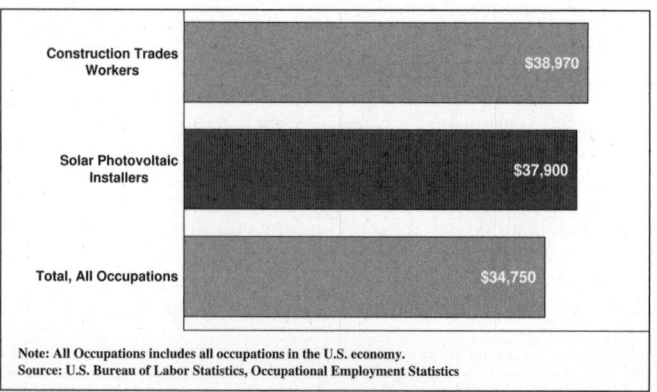

Construction Trades Workers — $38,970
Solar Photovoltaic Installers — $37,900
Total, All Occupations — $34,750

Note: All Occupations includes all occupations in the U.S. economy.
Source: U.S. Bureau of Labor Statistics, Occupational Employment Statistics

Percent Change in Employment, Projected 2012–2022

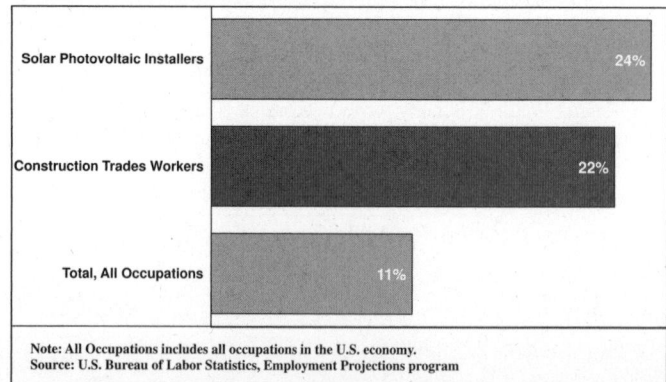

Solar Photovoltaic Installers — 24%
Construction Trades Workers — 22%
Total, All Occupations — 11%

Note: All Occupations includes all occupations in the U.S. economy.
Source: U.S. Bureau of Labor Statistics, Employment Projections program

Employment Projections Data for Solar Photovoltaic Installers

Occupational title	SOC Code	Employment, 2012	Projected Employment, 2022	Change, 2012–2022	
				Percent	Numeric
Solar photovoltaic installers...................................	47-2231	4,800	5,900	24	1,200

Source: U.S. Bureau of Labor Statistics, Employment Projections Program

Note: Data are rounded. Go to **Occupational Information Included in the OOH** *for a discussion of the data in this table.*

To qualify, candidates need at least 58 hours of advanced PV training by an accredited school or organization as well as complete a ten-hour construction safety course through OSHA.

The Electronics Technicians Association International also offers certification.

Pay

The median annual wage for solar photovoltaic installers was $37,900 in May 2012. The median wage is the wage at which half the workers in an occupation earned more than that amount and half earned less. The lowest 10 percent earned less than $26,250, and the top 10 percent earned more than $57,980.

In May 2012, the median annual wages for solar photovoltaic installers in the top three industries in which these installers worked were as follows:

Power and communication line and related structures
construction $41,250
Plumbing, heating, and air-conditioning contractors........... 39,520
Electrical contractors and other wiring installation
contractors 32,470

Job Outlook

Employment of solar photovoltaic (PV) installers is projected to grow 24 percent from 2012 to 2022, much faster than the average for all occupations. However, because it is a small occupation, the fast growth will result in only about 1,200 new jobs over the 10-year period.

The rapid expansion and adoption of solar panel installation is expected to create new jobs. As the cost of PV panels and shingles continue to fall, more residential households are expected to take advantage of these systems, resulting in greater demand for the workers who install them.

The long-term outlook, however, is heavily dependent on government incentives, cost, and the continuing efficiency of PV panels. States and localities that provide incentives to reduce the cost of PV systems should experience greater demand for workers.

Common incentives include tax rebates, direct subsidies, renewable energy purchase mandates, and net metering.

The development of solar leasing should create additional demand, as homeowners no longer must bear the upfront costs of installation.

Job Prospects. PV installers who complete training at a 2-year technical school will have the best job opportunities.

Those with apprenticeship or journey electrician experience will also have very good job opportunities. Workers with experience in construction occupations, such as laborers, roofers, and carpenters will have better job opportunities than those without construction experience.

Employment of PV installers fluctuates with the overall economy. On the one hand, there is great demand for PV installers during peak periods of building activity. On the other hand, workers may experience periods of unemployment when the overall level of construction falls.

There is less maintenance performed by many PV installers as compared to other construction occupations, so most work should be for installation and not maintenance.

O*NET

➤ Solar Photovoltaic Installers (47-2231.00)

Contacts for More Information

For details about apprenticeship or other training opportunities in this trade, contact the offices of the state employment service, technical colleges, the state apprenticeship agency, local photovoltaic contractors, firms that employ PV installers, or local union-management apprenticeship committees. Apprenticeship information is available from the U.S. Department of Labor's toll-free help line: 1 (877) 872-5627; or the Employment and Training Administration (www.doleta.gov/OA/eta_default.cfm).

For more information about apprenticeships for solar photovoltaic installers, visit

➤ International Brotherhood of Electrical Workers (www.ibew.org)

Similar Occupations This table shows a list of occupations with job duties that are similar to those of solar photovoltaic installers.

Occupations	Entry-level Education	2012 Pay	Projected Job Growth	Average Annual Openings
Cement Masons and Terrazzo Workers	See "How to Become One"	$35,856	29%	5,830
Construction Laborers and Helpers	See "How to Become One"	$29,277	25%	58,790
Electricians	High school diploma or equivalent	$49,840	20%	22,460
Glaziers	High school diploma or equivalent	$37,610	17%	1,910
Plumbers, Pipefitters, and Steamfitters	High school diploma or equivalent	$49,140	21%	13,050
Roofers	Less than high school	$35,290	11%	4,290
Sheet Metal Workers	High school diploma or equivalent	$43,290	15%	4,890
Structural Iron and Steel Workers	High school diploma or equivalent	$46,140	22%	3,150

For more information about accredited training programs, visit
➤ Interstate Renewable Energy Council, Inc. (www.irecusa.org/)
➤ North American Board of Certified Energy Practitioners (www.nabcep.org/)

An article related to solar careers was published by BLS in 2011 (www.bls.gov/green/solar_power/).

Structural Iron and Steel Workers

- **2012 Median Pay** .... $46,140 per year
$22.18 per hour
- **Entry-Level Education** ... High school diploma or equivalent
- **Work Experience in a Related Occupation** .... None
- **On-the-Job Training** .... Apprenticeship
- **Number of Jobs 2012** 58,100
- **Job Outlook, 2012–22** .... 22% (Much faster than average)
- **Employment Change, 2012–22** 12,700

What Structural Iron and Steel Workers Do

Structural iron and steel workers install iron or steel beams, girders, and columns to form buildings, bridges, and other structures. They are commonly referred to as ironworkers.

Duties. Ironworkers typically do the following:

- Unload and stack prefabricated steel so that it can be lifted easily with slings
- Use a crane to lift steel beams, girders, and columns into place
- Stand on beams or girders to help position pieces that are being lifted
- Signal crane operators for positioning of the structural steel
- Align beams and girders into position
- Verify vertical and horizontal alignment of the structural steel
- Connect columns, beams, and girders with bolts or by welding them into place
- Use metal shears, torches, and welding equipment to cut, bend, and weld the steel

Iron and steel are important parts of buildings, bridges, and other structures. Even though the primary metal involved in this work is steel, these workers often are known as *ironworkers* or *erectors*.

When building tall structures such as a skyscraper, ironworkers erect steel frames and assemble the cranes and derricks that move structural steel, reinforcing bars, buckets of concrete, lumber, and

Workers hammer large structural steel into the ground at a construction site.

other materials and equipment around the construction site. Workers also connect steel columns, beams, and girders according to blueprints and instructions from construction supervisors. A few also may install precast walls or work with wood or composite materials.

Although most of the work involves erecting new structures, some ironworkers also may help in the demolition, decommissioning, and rehabilitation of older buildings and bridges.

As they work, ironworkers use a variety of tools. They use rope (called a tag line) to guide the steel while it is being lifted; they use spud wrenches (long wrenches with a pointed handle) to put the steel in place; and they use driftpins or the handle of the spud wrench to line up the holes in the steel with the holes in the framework. To check for alignment, they may use plumb bobs, laser equipment, or levels.

Structural steel generally arrives at the construction site ready to be installed–cut to the proper size, with holes drilled for bolts and numbered for assembly.

Some ironworkers are assemblers and fabricators. They fabricate metal in shops, which are usually located away from the construction site.

Work Environment

Structural iron and steel workers held about 58,100 jobs in 2012. About 44 percent were employed in the foundation, structure, and building exterior contractors industry and about 23 percent were employed in nonresidential building construction.

Median Annual Wages, May 2012

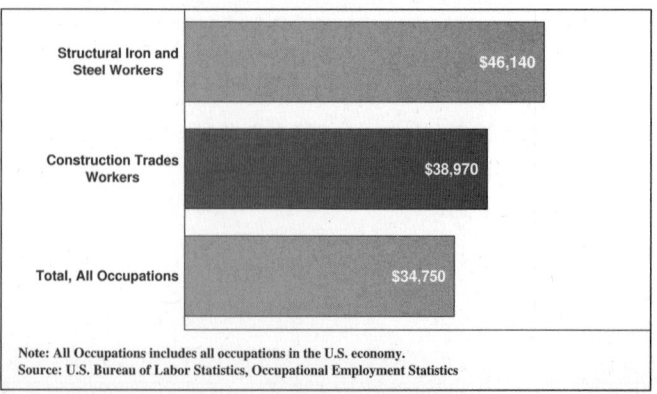

Structural Iron and Steel Workers	$46,140
Construction Trades Workers	$38,970
Total, All Occupations	$34,750

Note: All Occupations includes all occupations in the U.S. economy.
Source: U.S. Bureau of Labor Statistics, Occupational Employment Statistics

Percent Change in Employment, Projected 2012–2022

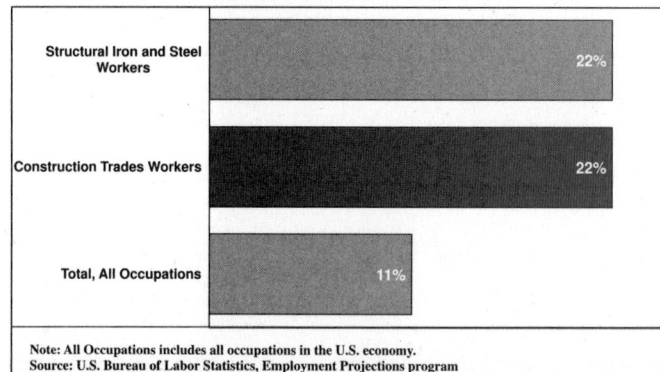

Structural Iron and Steel Workers	22%
Construction Trades Workers	22%
Total, All Occupations	11%

Note: All Occupations includes all occupations in the U.S. economy.
Source: U.S. Bureau of Labor Statistics, Employment Projections program

Employment Projections Data for Structural Iron and Steel Workers

Occupational title	SOC Code	Employment, 2012	Projected Employment, 2022	Change, 2012–2022	
				Percent	Numeric
Structural iron and steel workers	47-2221	58,100	70,800	22	12,700

Source: U.S. Bureau of Labor Statistics, Employment Projections Program

Note: Data are rounded. Go to **Occupational Information Included in the OOH** *for a discussion of the data in this table.*

Ironworkers help build the supporting structure for bridges and for industrial, commercial, and large residential buildings. In doing so, they perform physically demanding and dangerous work. For example, they usually work outside in most types of weather, and some must work at great heights. As a result, workers must wear safety devices, such as harnesses, to reduce the risk of falling.

Work Schedules. Nearly all ironworkers work full time. Those who work at great heights do not work during wet, icy, or extremely windy conditions.

Injuries and Illnesses. Ironworkers experience several work-related deaths each year due to falls. In addition to falls, workers may experience cuts from sharp metal edges and equipment, as well as muscle strains and other injuries from moving and guiding heavy structural steel.

How to Become One

Although most structural iron and steel workers learn through an apprenticeship, some learn on the job. Certifications in welding and rigging can be helpful.

Education. A high school diploma is generally required. Courses in math, shop, blueprint reading, and welding can be particularly useful.

Training. Most ironworkers learn their trade through a 3- or 4-year apprenticeship. For each year of the program, apprentices must have at least 144 hours of related technical training and 2,000 hours of paid on-the-job training. Nearly all apprenticeship programs teach both reinforcing and structural ironworking. On the job, apprentices learn to use the tools and equipment of the trade; handle, measure, cut, and lay rebar; and construct metal frameworks. In technical training, they are taught basic mathematics, blueprint reading and sketching, general construction techniques, safety practices, and first aid.

After completing an apprenticeship program, they are considered to be journeymen who perform tasks with less guidance.

A few groups, including unions and contractor associations, sponsor apprenticeship programs. The basic qualifications required for entering an apprenticeship program are as follows:

• Minimum age of 18

• High school diploma or equivalent

• Physical ability to perform the work

• Pass substance abuse screening

Licenses, Certifications, and Registrations. Many ironworkers become welders certified by the American Welding Society. Certifications in welding, rigging, and crane signaling may increase a worker's usefulness on the jobsite and result in higher pay.

Important Qualities

Balance. Because workers often walk on narrow beams, a good sense of balance is important to keep them from falling while doing their job.

Depth perception. Ironworkers must be able to envision the distance between objects and themselves to work safely. Ironworkers that misjudge the distance between girders, for example, may cause the girders to collide, which can be dangerous and costly.

Physical stamina. Ironworkers must have physical endurance because they spend many hours on their feet while connecting heavy and cumbersome beams.

Physical strength. Ironworkers must be strong enough to guide heavy beams into place and tighten bolts.

Unafraid of heights. Some ironworkers must not be afraid to work at great heights. For example, as they erect skyscrapers, workers must walk on narrow beams–sometimes over 50 stories high–while connecting girders.

Pay

The median annual wage for structural iron and steel workers was $46,140 in May 2012. The median wage is the wage at which half the workers in an occupation earned more than that amount and half earned less. The lowest 10 percent earned less than $26,970, and the top 10 percent earned more than $83,970.

The starting pay for apprentices is usually between 50 percent and 55 percent of what journeymen ironworkers make. They receive pay increases as they learn to do more.

Union Membership. Compared with workers in all occupations, structural iron and steel workers had a higher percentage of workers who belonged to a union in 2012. Although there is no single union that covers all ironworkers, the largest organizer of these

Similar Occupations This table shows a list of occupations with job duties that are similar to those of structural iron and steel workers.

Occupations	Entry-level Education	2012 Pay	Projected Job Growth	Average Annual Openings
Assemblers and Fabricators	High school diploma or equivalent	$28,661	4%	37,140
Boilermakers	High school diploma or equivalent	$56,560	4%	880
Carpenters	High school diploma or equivalent	$39,940	24%	32,920
Cement Masons and Terrazzo Workers	See "How to Become One"	$35,856	29%	5,830
Construction Laborers and Helpers	See "How to Become One"	$29,277	25%	58,790
Welders, Cutters, Solderers, and Brazers	High school diploma or equivalent	$36,300	6%	10,850

workers is the International Association of Bridge, Structural, Ornamental and Reinforcing Iron Workers.

Job Outlook

Employment of ironworkers is projected to grow 22 percent from 2012 to 2022, much faster than the average for all occupations.

The need to rehabilitate, maintain, or replace an increasing number of older highways and bridges is expected to drive employment growth, particularly because state and federal legislatures will likely fund these infrastructure projects.

In addition, steel is an important part of commercial and industrial buildings. Future construction of these structures should create additional demand for ironworkers.

Job Prospects. Those who are certified in welding, rigging, and crane signaling should have the best job opportunities. Those with prior military service experience are also viewed favorably during initial hiring.

Employment opportunities should be best in metropolitan areas, where most large commercial and industrial buildings are constructed.

As with many other construction workers, employment of ironworkers is sensitive to fluctuations of the economy. On the one hand, workers may experience periods of unemployment when the overall level of construction falls. On the other hand, shortages of workers may occur in some areas during peak periods of building activity.

O*NET

➤ Structural Iron and Steel Workers (47-2221.00)

Contacts for More Information

For information about apprenticeships or job opportunities as a structural iron and steel worker, contact local structural iron and steel construction contractors, a local joint union-management apprenticeship committee, or the nearest office of your state employment service or apprenticeship agency. Apprenticeship information is available from the U.S. Department of Labor's toll-free help line, 1 (877) 872-5627, or the Employment and Training Administration (www.doleta.gov/OA/eta_default.cfm).

For ironworker and apprenticeship information, visit
➤ International Association of Bridge, Structural, Ornamental and Reinforcing Iron Workers (www.ironworkers.org/)

For more information about ironworkers, visit
➤ Associated Builders and Contractors (www.abc.org/)
➤ Associated General Contractors of America (www.agc.org/)

Tile and Marble Setters

- **2012 Median Pay** .... $37,040 per year
                                                          $17.81 per hour
- **Entry-Level Education** .... Less than high school
- **Work Experience in a Related Occupation** .... None
- **On-the-Job Training** .... Long-term on-the-job training
- **Number of Jobs 2012** 39,200
- **Job Outlook, 2012–22** .... 15% (Faster than average)
- **Employment Change, 2012–22** 5,900

What Tile and Marble Setters Do

Tile and marble setters apply hard tile and marble to walls, floors, and other surfaces.

Duties. Tile and marble setters typically do the following:
- Clean and level the surface to be tiled
- Measure and cut tile and marble
- Arrange tiles according to design plans
- Prepare and apply mortar or other adhesives
- Install tile and marble in a planned area
- Apply grout with a rubber trowel
- Wipe off excess grout and apply necessary finishes, such as sealants

Tile and marble setters install materials on a variety of surfaces, such as floors, walls, ceilings, countertops, patios, and roof decks. Because tile and marble must be set on smooth, even surfaces, installers often must level the surface to be tiled with a layer of mortar or plywood. If the area to be tiled is unstable, workers must nail a support of metal mesh or tile backer board to create a stable surface.

The following are examples of types of tile and marble setters:

Marble setters cut marble to a specified size with a power wet saw. They then drill holes in the marble for the anchors that will hold it in place. After fastening the stone, marble setters polish the marble to a high luster, using power or hand sanders.

Tile finishers apply grout between tiles after the tiles are set, using a rubber trowel (called a float). When the grout dries, they must wipe the tiles for a clean, finished look.

Tile installers, sometimes called *tile setters,* cut and place tile. To cut tiles, workers use power wet saws, tile scribes, or hand-held tile cutters to create even edges. They use trowels of different sizes to spread mortar or a sticky paste, called mastic, evenly on the surface to be tiled. To minimize imperfections and keep rows even, they put spacers between tiles. The spacers keep tiles the same distance from each other until the mortar is dry.

Work Environment

Tile and marble setters held about 39,200 jobs in 2012, of which 52 percent were employed in the building finishing contractors industry. About 31 percent were self-employed.

Tile installers lay floor coverings in homes and other types of buildings.

Median Annual Wages, May 2012

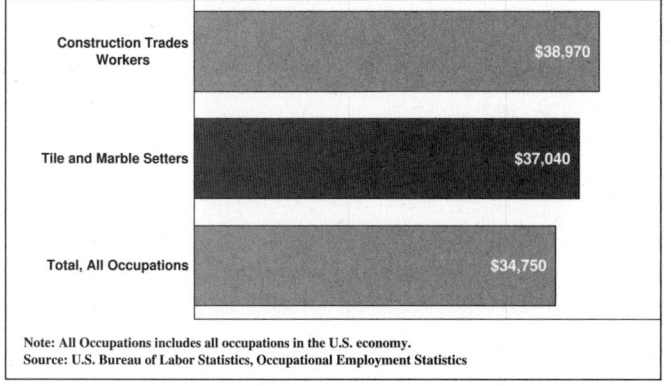

Note: All Occupations includes all occupations in the U.S. economy.
Source: U.S. Bureau of Labor Statistics, Occupational Employment Statistics

Percent Change in Employment, Projected 2012–2022

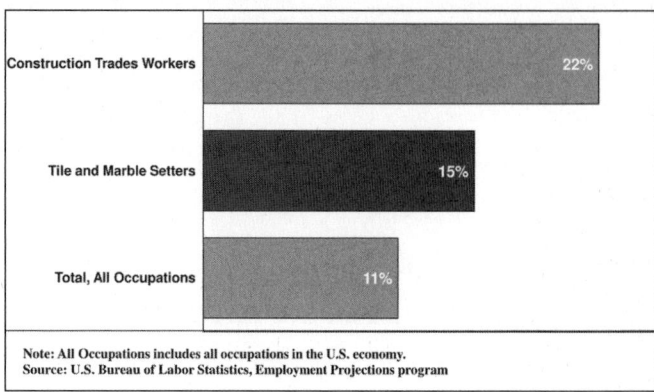

Note: All Occupations includes all occupations in the U.S. economy.
Source: U.S. Bureau of Labor Statistics, Employment Projections program

Tile and marble are usually installed after most of the construction has been completed, so the work area is typically clean and uncluttered. Still, mortar, adhesives, or grout may be sticky and messy.

Installing tile and marble is physically demanding, with workers spending much of their time bending and kneeling. As a result, workers typically wear kneepads for protection. Workers also wear safety goggles when using grinders, saws, and sanders.

Work Schedules. Most tile and marble setters work full time. In commercial settings, tile setters may work evenings and weekends, often for higher wages, to avoid disturbing regular business operations.

About 31 percent of tile and marble setters were self-employed in 2012. Self-employed workers may have the ability to set their own schedule.

How to Become One

Although some tile and marble setters learn their trade through an apprenticeship, most learn on the job, starting as a helper.

Education. There are no specific education requirements to become a tile and marble setter.

Some 2-year technical schools offer courses that are affiliated with unions and contractor organizations. The credits earned as part of an apprenticeship program usually count toward an associate's degree.

Training. Some contractors have their own training programs for tile and marble setters. New workers typically learn by working with experienced installers. Although workers may enter training directly, many first start out as helpers.

Helpers usually start by performing simple tasks, such as moving materials. As they gain experience, they are given more complex tasks, such as cutting tile. Some helpers become tile finishers.

Some tile and marble setters learn their trade through a 2- to 4-year apprenticeship. For each year of the program, apprentices must complete at least 144 hours of related technical training and 2,000 hours of paid on-the-job training. Tile and marble setters begin with 12 weeks of pre-apprenticeship instruction at a training center to learn construction basics. This may include mathematics, building code requirements, safety and first-aid practices, and blueprint reading.

After completing an apprenticeship program, tile and marble setters are considered to be journey workers and may perform duties on their own.

Several groups, including unions and contractor associations, sponsor apprenticeship programs. The basic qualifications for entering an apprenticeship program are as follows:

- Minimum age of 18

- High school education or equivalent

- Physically able to perform the work

Other Experience. Some manufacturers offer product-specific training for tile and marble setters. In addition, some installers attend conferences that offer training sessions.

Important Qualities

Color vision. Setting tile often involves determining small color variations. Because tile patterns may include many different colors, tile setters must be able to distinguish between colors and patterns for the best-looking finish.

Customer-service skills. Working in customers' homes is common. Therefore, tile and marble setters must be courteous and considerate of a customer's property while completing tasks.

Detail oriented. Some tile arrangements can be highly detailed and artistic, so workers must ensure that the patterns are properly and accurately arranged.

Math skills. Basic math skills are used on every job. Besides measuring the area to be tiled, installers must calculate the number of tiles needed to cover an area.

Physical stamina. Tile and marble setters must have the endurance to spend many hours on their feet. When setting tile or marble, installers also may be on their knees for hours at a time.

Physical strength. Some marble setters must be strong enough to carry and lift heavy marble countertops into position.

Employment Projections Data for Tile and Marble Setters

Occupational title	SOC Code	Employment, 2012	Projected Employment, 2022	Change, 2012–2022	
				Percent	Numeric
Tile and marble setters	47-2044	39,200	45,100	15	5,900

Source: U.S. Bureau of Labor Statistics, Employment Projections Program

Note: Data are rounded. Go to **Occupational Information Included in the OOH** *for a discussion of the data in this table.*

Similar Occupations   This table shows a list of occupations with job duties that are similar to those of tile and marble setters.

Occupations	Entry-level Education	2012 Pay	Projected Job Growth	Average Annual Openings
Carpenters	High school diploma or equivalent	$39,940	24%	32,920
Construction Laborers and Helpers	See "How to Become One"	$29,277	25%	58,790
Drywall and Ceiling Tile Installers, and Tapers	Less than high school	$38,572	16%	2,880
Painters, Construction and Maintenance	Less than high school	$35,190	20%	11,050
Roofers	Less than high school	$35,290	11%	4,290

Pay

The median annual wage for tile and marble setters was $37,040 in May 2012. The median wage is the wage at which half the workers in an occupation earned more than that amount and half earned less. The lowest 10 percent earned less than $21,450, and the top 10 percent earned more than $70,970.

The starting pay for apprentices usually is about 50 percent of what fully trained tile and marble setters make. As they gain more skill, they receive pay increases.

Job Outlook

Employment of tile and marble setters is projected to grow 15 percent from 2012 to 2022, faster than the average for all occupations.

Population growth and business growth, coupled with the continuing popularity of tile and marble, will be the major source of demand for workers. Tile and natural stone are used in many shopping malls, hospitals, schools, and restaurants, as well as other commercial and government buildings, and this trend is expected to continue. Tiles, including those made of glass, mosaic, and other high-end tiles and marble, are also becoming more popular, particularly in new and remodeled homes.

However, demand may be somewhat offset by the growing use and popularity of resilient flooring, such as vinyl or rubber, which can be installed by other construction workers.

Job Prospects. Overall job prospects should improve over the coming decade as construction activity continues to rebound. As with many other types of construction occupations, employment of tile and marble setters is sensitive to the fluctuations of the economy. On the one hand, workers may experience periods of unemployment when the overall level of construction falls. On the other hand, shortages of workers may occur in some areas during peak periods of building activity.

Experienced workers with a good job history and overall knowledge of construction will have the best employment opportunities.

O*NET

➤ Tile and Marble Setters (47-2044.00)

Contacts for More Information

For details about apprenticeships or other work opportunities in this trade, contact the offices of the state employment service, the state apprenticeship agency, local contractors or firms that employ tile and marble setters, or local union-management tile- and marble-setting apprenticeship committees. Apprenticeship information is available from the U.S. Department of Labor's toll-free help line, 1 (877) 872-5627, or the Employment and Training Administration (www.doleta.gov/OA/eta_default.cfm).

For more information about tile installers and finishers, visit

➤ International Masonry Institute National Training Center (http://imiweb.org/)
➤ Tile Contractors' Association of America (www.tcaainc.org/index.php)
➤ National Association of Home Builders, Home Builders Institute (www.hbi.org)

For more information about tile setting and tile training, visit

➤ International Certified Floorcovering Installers Association (www.cfiinstallers.com/)
➤ National Tile Contractors Association (www.tile-assn.com)
➤ Finishing Trades Institute International (www.finishingtradesinstitute.org/)

Education, Training, and Library

Adult Literacy and High School Equivalency Diploma Teachers

- **2012 Median Pay** .... $48,590 per year
  $23.36 per hour
- **Entry-Level Education** ....Bachelor's degree
- **Work Experience in a Related Occupation** .... None
- **On-the-Job Training** .... Internship/residency
- **Number of Jobs 2012** 77,400
- **Job Outlook, 2012–22** ....9% (As fast as average)
- **Employment Change, 2012–22** 6,700

What Adult Literacy and High School Equivalency Diploma Teachers Do

Adult literacy and high school equivalency diploma teachers instruct adults in basic skills, such as reading, writing, and speaking English. They also help students earn their high school diploma.

Duties. Adult literacy and high school equivalency diploma teachers typically do the following:

- Evaluate students' strengths and weaknesses
- Plan and teach lessons to help students gain the knowledge and skills needed to meet their goals, such as learning English or earning their high school diploma
- Emphasize skills that will help students find jobs, such as learning English words and common phrases used in the workplace
- Work with students individually to challenge them and overcome their weaknesses
- Assess students for possible learning disabilities
- Monitor students' progress toward their goals
- Help students develop study skills
- Connect students to other resources in their community, such as mental health services or job placement services

Adult literacy and GED teachers instruct adults in basic skills, such as reading, writing and speaking English.

Before students enter these education programs, their educational level and skills are assessed. Sometimes the teachers do this assessment, but in many cases another staff member does it. The teacher then uses information from the assessment and information about the student's goals to develop an individualized educational program.

Teachers must formally evaluate their students periodically to determine their progress and potential to go on to the next level. However, they informally evaluate their students' progress continually.

Adult literacy and high school equivalency diploma teachers often have students of various levels in their classes. As a result, teachers need to use teaching strategies and methods that meet all of their students' needs. In addition, teachers focus on helping students develop skills they need in the workplace. For example, they may teach students how to read a contract or how to estimate the cost of materials needed to remodel a kitchen. Teachers may also prepare adult learners for further education. Teachers may work with students in classes or tutor them one-on-one.

There are three basic types of education that adult literacy and high school equivalency diploma teachers provide:

Adult basic education classes teach students the basics of reading, writing, and math. Students often enter these classes at or below an eighth-grade level in these subjects. Students generally are 16 years or older and need to gain proficiency in these skills to improve their job situation.

High school equivalency and adult secondary education classes prepare students to take the test to earn the equivalent of a high school diploma. Sometimes these classes help students finish the credits necessary for them to earn a high school diploma. Some programs are combined with career preparation programs so that students can earn a high school diploma and a career-related credential at the same time.

Passing the a high school equivalency exam means passing five tests: reading, writing, mathematics, science, and social studies. In addition, adult literacy and high school equivalency diploma teachers help their students improve their skills in communicating, critical thinking, and problem solving–skills they will need for further education and successful careers.

English as a Second Language (ESL) classes teach students to read, write, and speak English. These classes are sometimes also called *English for speakers of other languages* (ESOL). People in these classes are immigrants to the United States and others whose native language is not English.

ESL teachers often focus on helping their students with practical vocabulary for jobs and daily living. They also may focus on preparing their students to take the citizenship exam.

In one class, an ESL teacher may have students from many different countries and cultures. Because the ESL teacher and the students may not share a common native language, ESL teachers must be creative in fostering communication in the classroom to achieve their education goals.

Work Environment

Adult literacy and high school equivalency diploma teachers held about 77,400 jobs in 2012.

Adult literacy and high school equivalency diploma teachers are often employed by community colleges, community-based organizations, and public schools. Some work in prisons.

Median Annual Wages, May 2012

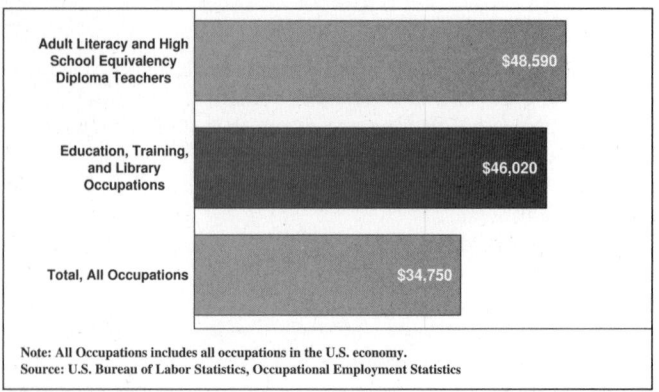

Note: All Occupations includes all occupations in the U.S. economy.
Source: U.S. Bureau of Labor Statistics, Occupational Employment Statistics

Percent Change in Employment, Projected 2012–2022

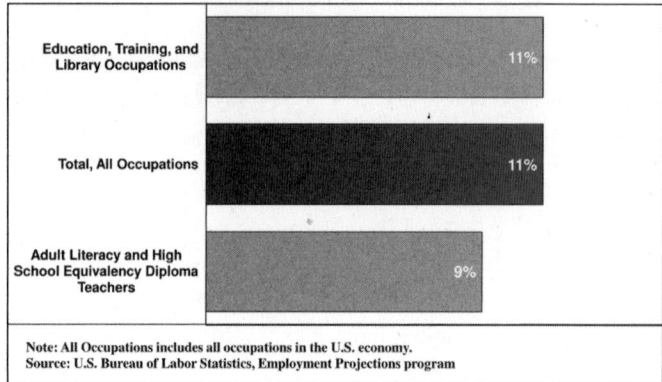

Note: All Occupations includes all occupations in the U.S. economy.
Source: U.S. Bureau of Labor Statistics, Employment Projections program

The industries that employed the most adult literacy and high school equivalency diploma teachers in 2012 were as follows:

Junior colleges; state, local, and private 29%
Elementary and secondary schools; state, local, and private... 28
Other schools and instruction; state, local, and private........... 11
Health care and social assistance 8
Colleges, universities, and professional schools;
    state, local, and private... 5

Students in adult literacy and high school equivalency programs attend classes by choice. As a result, they are often highly motivated, which can make teaching them rewarding and satisfying.

Work Schedules. Classes are held at times when students are not at work, so many teachers work in the mornings and evenings. Many adult education teachers work part time.

How to Become One

Most adult literacy and high school equivalency diploma teachers must have at least a bachelor's degree. Employers typically prefer workers who have some teaching experience, which they can get through teaching children or adults.

Education. Most states require adult literacy and high school equivalency diploma teachers to have at least a bachelor's degree. Although a bachelor's degree in any field is acceptable, some employers, such as community colleges, prefer to hire those with a master's degree or graduate coursework in adult education or English as a second language (ESL).

Master's degrees in adult education prepare prospective teachers to use effective teaching strategies for adult learners, to work with students from various backgrounds, and to develop adult education programs. Some programs allow these prospective teachers to specialize in adult basic education, secondary education, or ESL.

Some colleges and universities offer master's degrees or graduate certificates in teaching adult education or English for speakers of other languages (ESOL). Programs help prospective teachers learn how to teach adults, work with learners from a variety of cultures, and learn how to teach adults with learning disabilities.

Programs in English as a second language not only help these prospective teachers understand how adults learn languages, but also prepare them to teach communication skills. Prospective ESL teachers should take courses or training in linguistics and theories of how people learn second languages. Knowledge of a second language is not necessary to teach ESL, but it is helpful to understand what students are going through.

Many adult literacy and high school equivalency diploma teachers take professional development classes to ensure that they keep up with the latest research in teaching adults and improve their teaching skills.

Other Experience. Most employers require workers to have a few years of experience teaching. However, experience can be gained through teaching either children or adults.

Licenses, Certifications, and Registrations. Some states require adult literacy and high school equivalency diploma teachers to have a teaching certificate to work in government-run programs. Some states have certificates specifically for adult education. Other states require teachers to have a certificate in elementary or secondary education. To obtain a license, adult literacy and high school equivalency diploma teachers typically need a bachelor's degree and must have passed an approved teacher-training program. For more information, contact the state director of adult education. Contact information can be found from the U.S. Department of Education.

Training. In order to receive certification or licensure, teachers need to perform fieldwork, commonly referred to as student teaching. During student teaching, they work with a mentor teacher and get experience teaching students in a classroom setting. The amount of time required varies by state.

Important Qualities

Communication skills. Teachers must collaborate with other teachers and program administrators. In addition, they talk to students about their progress and goals, and must explain concepts in terms that students can understand.

Employment Projections Data for Adult Literacy and High School Equivalency Diploma Teachers

Occupational title	SOC Code	Employment, 2012	Projected Employment, 2022	Change, 2012–2022	
				Percent	Numeric
Adult basic and secondary education and literacy teachers and instructors	25-3011	77,400	84,200	9	6,700

Source: U.S. Bureau of Labor Statistics, Employment Projections Program

Note: Data are rounded. Go to **Occupational Information Included in the OOH** *for a discussion of the data in this table.*

Similar Occupations   This table shows a list of occupations with job duties that are similar to those of adult literacy and high school equivalency diploma teachers.

Occupations	Entry-level Education	2012 Pay	Projected Job Growth	Average Annual Openings
High School Teachers	Bachelor's degree	$55,050	6%	31,260
Instructional Coordinators	Master's degree	$60,050	13%	3,110
Kindergarten and Elementary School Teachers	Bachelor's degree	$53,060	12%	53,250
Librarians	Master's degree	$55,370	7%	4,440
Middle School Teachers	Bachelor's degree	$53,430	12%	21,120
Postsecondary Teachers	See "How to Become One"	$70,380	19%	42,690
School and Career Counselors	Master's degree	$53,610	12%	8,700
Social Workers	See "How to Become One"	$44,541	19%	24,280
Special Education Teachers	Bachelor's degree	$55,068	6%	10,220
Teacher Assistants	Some college, no degree	$23,640	9%	38,260

Cultural sensitivity. Adult literacy and high school equivalency diploma teachers must be able to work with students from a variety of cultural, educational, and economic backgrounds. They must be understanding and respectful of their students' backgrounds and be familiar with their concerns.

Patience. Working with students of different abilities and backgrounds can be difficult. Teachers must be patient when students struggle with material.

Resourcefulness. Adult literacy and high school equivalency diploma teachers need to be able to respond to difficult situations and think on their feet. For example, they need to be able to alter their teaching methods to meet the needs of each student they teach and find ways to keep students engaged in learning.

Pay

The median annual wage for adult literacy and high school equivalency diploma teachers was $48,590 in May 2012. The median wage is the wage at which half the workers in an occupation earned more than that amount and half earned less. The lowest 10 percent earned less than $27,460, and the top 10 percent earned more than $82,490.

Job Outlook

Employment of adult literacy and high school equivalency diploma teachers is projected to grow 9 percent from 2012 to 2022, about as fast as the average for all occupations. Employment growth is expected as a result of continued immigration to the United States and demand for adult education programs.

From 2012 to 2022, the number of Americans who need adult education is expected to continue to increase. Some adults leave high school before getting their high school diploma and seek their diploma or its equivalent through an adult education program.

In addition, traditional schooling does not always give some adults the literacy or other skills they need to find employment. These students often seek to improve their skills in adult education programs later in life. Adult literacy and high school equivalency diploma teachers will be needed to instruct them and to run adult education programs.

Some immigrants do not speak English and will want to improve their communications skills to find jobs in the United States. Adult literacy teachers who teach classes in English as a second language will be needed to help these students gain the required skills.

Job Prospects. Many positions for this occupation are part time, and full-time positions are uncommon and difficult to find. As a result, prospects will be best for workers who are willing and able to take a part-time position.

O*NET

➤ Adult Basic and Secondary Education and Literacy Teachers and Instructors (25-3011.00)

Contacts for More Information

For more information about adult education in your state, visit
➤ U.S. Department of Education (http://wdcrobcolp01.ed.gov/Programs/EROD/org_list.cfm?category_cd=DAE)

Archivists, Curators, and Museum Workers

- **2012 Median Pay** .... $44,410 per year
  $21.35 per hour
- **Entry-Level Education** ....See "How to Become One"
- **Work Experience in a Related Occupation**............... None
- **On-the-Job Training** .... None
- **Number of Jobs 2012** 29,300
- **Job Outlook, 2012–22** .... 11% (As fast as average)
- **Employment Change, 2012–22** 3,300

What Archivists, Curators, and Museum Workers Do

Archivists appraise, edit, and maintain permanent records and historically valuable documents. Curators oversee collections of artwork and historic items, and may conduct public service activities for an institution. Museum technicians and conservators prepare and restore objects and documents in museum collections and exhibits.

Duties. Archivists typically do the following:

- Authenticate and appraise historical documents and archival materials
- Preserve and maintain documents and objects
- Create and maintain computer archives and databases

- Organize and classify archival records to make them easy to search through
- Safeguard records by creating film and digital copies
- Direct workers who help arrange, exhibit, and maintain collections
- Set and administer policy guidelines concerning public access to materials
- Provide help to users
- Find and acquire new materials for their archives

Curators, museum technicians, and conservators typically do the following:

- Acquire, store, and exhibit collections
- Select the theme and design of exhibits
- Design, organize, and conduct tours and workshops for the public
- Attend meetings and civic events to promote their institution
- Clean objects such as ancient tools, coins, and statues
- Direct and supervise curatorial, technical, and student staff
- Plan and conduct special research projects

Archivists preserve many documents and records for their importance or historical significance. Most archivists coordinate educational and public outreach programs, such as tours, workshops, lectures, and classes. In addition, archivists may research topics and items relevant to their collections.

Some archivists specialize in an area of history, such as colonial history, so they can more accurately understand which records from that time period should become part of the archives.

Archivists work with specific forms of records, such as manuscripts, electronic records, websites, photographs, maps, motion pictures, and sound recordings.

Archives technicians help archivists organize, maintain, and provide access to historical documentary materials.

Curators manage museums, zoos, aquariums, botanical gardens, nature centers, and historic sites. The *museum director* often is a curator.

Curators direct the acquisition, storage, and exhibition of collections, including negotiating and authorizing the purchase, sale, exchange, and loan of collections. They also may authenticate, evaluate, and categorize the specimens in a collection.

Curators often oversee and help conduct the institution's research projects and related educational programs. Today, an

Museum technicians often prepare materials for display.

increasing part of a curator's duties involves fundraising and promotion, which may include writing and reviewing grant proposals, journal articles, and publicity materials. In addition, many curators attend meetings, conventions, and civic events.

Most curators specialize in a particular field, such as botany, art, or history. Those who work in large institutions may be highly specialized. A large natural history museum, for example, might employ separate curators for its collections of birds, fish, insects, and mammals.

Some curators focus primarily on taking care of their collections, some on researching items in their collections, and others spend most of their time performing administrative tasks. In small institutions with only one or a few curators, one curator may be responsible for a number of tasks, from taking care of collections to directing the affairs of the museum.

Museum technicians, commonly known as *registrars*, help curators by preparing and taking care of museum items. Registrars also may answer questions from the public and help curators and outside scholars use the collections.

Conservators manage, preserve, treat, and keep records of works of art, artifacts, and specimens–work that may require substantial historical, scientific, and archaeological research. They document their findings and treat items to minimize deterioration or to restore them to their original state. Conservators usually specialize in a particular material or group of objects, such as documents and books, paintings, decorative arts, textiles, metals, or architectural material. They use X-rays, chemical testing, microscopes, special

Median Annual Wages, May 2012

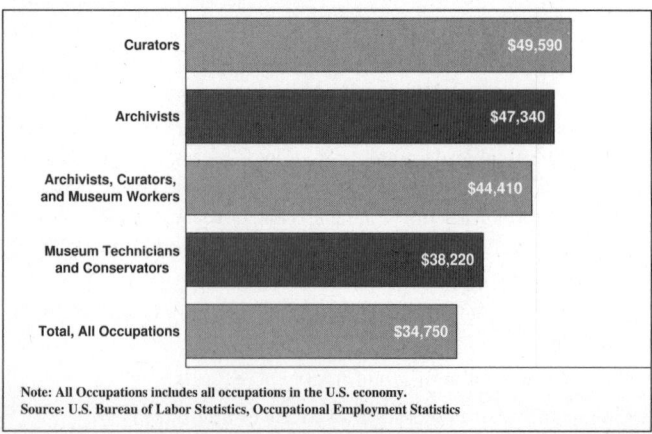

Curators	$49,590
Archivists	$47,340
Archivists, Curators, and Museum Workers	$44,410
Museum Technicians and Conservators	$38,220
Total, All Occupations	$34,750

Note: All Occupations includes all occupations in the U.S. economy.
Source: U.S. Bureau of Labor Statistics, Occupational Employment Statistics

Percent Change in Employment, Projected 2012–2022

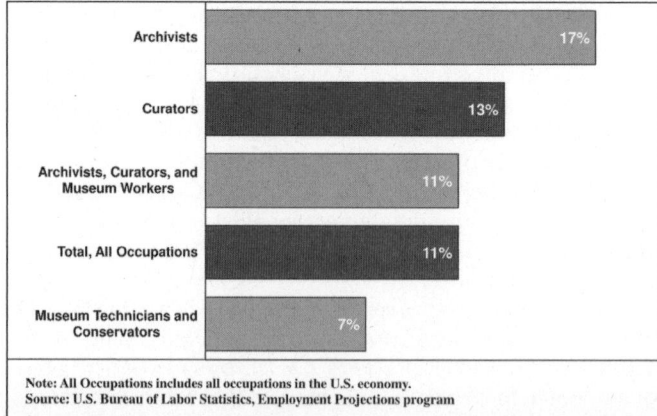

Archivists	17%
Curators	13%
Archivists, Curators, and Museum Workers	11%
Total, All Occupations	11%
Museum Technicians and Conservators	7%

Note: All Occupations includes all occupations in the U.S. economy.
Source: U.S. Bureau of Labor Statistics, Employment Projections program

Employment Projections Data for Archivists, Curators, and Museum Workers

Occupational title	SOC Code	Employment, 2012	Projected Employment, 2022	Change, 2012–2022	
				Percent	Numeric
Archivists, curators, and museum workers.............................	—	29,300	32,600	11	3,300
Archivists	25-4011	6,500	7,600	17	1,100
Curators..	25-4012	11,400	12,900	13	1,400
Museum technicians and conservators..............................	25-4013	11,300	12,100	7	800

Source: U.S. Bureau of Labor Statistics, Employment Projections Program

Note: Data are rounded. Go to Occupational Information Included in the OOH *for a discussion of the data in this table.*

lights, and other laboratory equipment and techniques to examine objects, determine their condition, and decide on the best way to preserve them.

In addition to their conservation work, conservators participate in outreach programs, research topics in their specialty, and write articles for scholarly journals. They may be employed by a museum or other institution that has objects needing conservation, or they may be self-employed and have several clients.

Work Environment

Archivists, curators, museum technicians, and conservators held about 29,300 jobs in 2012.

The industries that employed the most archivists, curators, museum technicians, and conservators in 2012 were as follows:

Museums, historical sites, and similar institutions.................. 38%
Government... 26
Educational services; state, local, and private 18

Archivists work in museums, government, colleges and universities, corporations, and other institutions that require experts to preserve important records.

Because most curators work at museums, zoos, aquariums, botanical gardens, nature centers, and historical sites, their working conditions vary. Some spend their time working with the public, providing reference assistance and educational services.

Those who restore and set up exhibits or work with bulky, heavy record containers may have to lift objects, climb ladders and scaffolding, and stretch to reach items.

Work Schedules. Archivists in government agencies and corporations generally work full time during regular business hours. Curators in large institutions may travel extensively to evaluate potential additions to the collection, organize exhibits, and conduct research. However, for curators in small institutions, travel may be rare.

Most archivists, curators, museum technicians, and conservators work full time.

How to Become One

Most archivist, curator, and conservator positions require a master's degree related to the field in which they work. People often gain experience by working or volunteering in archives and museums. Museum technicians must have a bachelor's degree.

Education. *Archivists.* Most employers prefer candidates to have a graduate degree in history, library science, archival science, or records management. Many colleges and universities offer courses or practical training in archival techniques in history, library science, and other similar programs. A few institutions offer master's degrees in archival studies. Some positions require candidates to have knowledge of the discipline related to a collection, such as computer science, business, or medicine. Many archives offer volunteer or internship opportunities where students can gain experience.

Curators. Most museums require curators to have a master's degree in an appropriate discipline of the museum's specialty–art, history, or archaeology–or in museum studies. Some employers prefer that curators have a doctoral degree, particularly for positions in natural history and science museums. Earning two graduate degrees–in museum studies (museology) and a specialized subject–may give candidates an advantage in a competitive job market.

In small museums, curator positions may be available to people with a bachelor's degree. Because curators–particularly those in small museums–may have administrative and managerial responsibilities, courses in business administration, public relations, marketing, and fundraising are recommended. For some positions, applicants need to have completed an internship of full-time museum work, as well as courses in museum practices.

Museum technicians (registrars). Registrars usually need a bachelor's degree related to the museum's specialty, training in museum studies, or previous experience working in museums, particularly in designing exhibits. Relatively few schools grant a bachelor's degree in museum studies; more common are undergraduate minors and tracks of study that are part of an undergraduate degree in a related field, such as art history, history, or archaeology. Students interested in further study might get a master's degree in museum studies offered in colleges and universities throughout the country. However, many employers feel that, although a degree in museum studies is helpful, a thorough knowledge of the museum's specialty and museum work experience are more important.

Conservators. When hiring conservators, employers look for a master's degree in conservation or in a closely related field, together with substantial experience. Only a few graduate programs in museum conservation techniques are offered in the United States. Competition for entry to these programs is very strong. To qualify, a student must have a background in chemistry, archaeology, studio art, and art history, as well as work experience. For some programs, knowledge of a foreign language is helpful. Completing a conservation internship as an undergraduate can enhance admission prospects. Graduate programs last 2 to 4 years, the latter years of which include internship training.

Licenses, Certifications, and Registrations. The Academy of Certified Archivists offers voluntary certification for archivists. Archivists with at least a master's degree and a year of professional archival experience can obtain the Certified Archivist credential by passing an exam. They must renew their certification periodically by retaking the exam or fulfilling continuing education credits. At this time, only a few employers require or prefer certification.

Other Experience. To gain marketable experience, candidates may have to work part time, as an intern, or even as a volunteer assistant curator or research associate during or after completing their education. Substantial experience in collection management,

Similar Occupations   This table shows a list of occupations with job duties that are similar to those of archivists, curators, and museum workers.

Occupations	Entry-level Education	2012 Pay	Projected Job Growth	Average Annual Openings
Anthropologists and Archeologists	Master's degree	$57,420	19%	260
Craft and Fine Artists	High school diploma or equivalent	$46,065	3%	1,360
Historians	Master's degree	$52,480	5%	80
Librarians	Master's degree	$55,370	7%	4,440

research, exhibit design, or restoration, as well as database management skills, is necessary for full-time positions.

Advancement. Continuing education is available through meetings, conferences, and workshops sponsored by archival, historical, and museum associations. Some large organizations, such as the U.S. National Archives and Records Administration in Washington, DC, offer in-house training.

Many archives, especially those maintained by one archivist, are small and have limited opportunities for promotion. Archivists typically advance by transferring to a larger archive that has supervisory positions. A doctorate in history, library science, or a related field may be needed for some advanced positions, such as director of a state archive.

In large museums, curators may advance through several levels of responsibility, eventually becoming museum directors. However, curators often start in small local and regional establishments at the beginning of their careers. As they gain experience, they may get the opportunity to work in larger facilities. The top museum positions are highly sought after and competitive. Performing unique research and producing published work are important for advancement in large institutions.

Important Qualities

Analytical skills. Archivists, curators, registrars, and conservators need excellent analytical skills to determine the origin, history, and importance of many of the objects they work with.

Computer skills. Archivists should have good computer skills because they use and develop complex databases related to the materials they store and access.

Customer-service skills. Archivists, curators, and registrars work with the general public on a regular basis. They must be courteous and friendly and be able to help users find materials.

Organizational skills. Archivists, curators, registrars, and conservators must be able to store and easily retrieve records and documents. They also must develop logical systems of storage for the public to use.

Technical skills. Many historical objects need to be analyzed and preserved. Conservators must use the appropriate chemicals and techniques to preserve the different objects they deal with. Examples of these objects are documents, paintings, fabrics, and pottery.

Pay

The median annual wage for archivists, curators, and museum workers was $44,410 in May 2012. The median wage is the wage at which half the workers in an occupation earned more than that amount and half earned less. The lowest 10 percent earned less than $25,570, and the top 10 percent earned more than $80,070.

In May 2012, median annual wages for archivists, curators, and museum workers were as follows:

Curators	$49,590
Archivists	47,340
Museum technicians and conservators	38,220

In May 2012, the median annual wages for archivists, curators, and museum workers in the top three industries in which these workers worked were as follows:

Government	$54,460
Educational services; state, local, and private	47,760
Museums, historical sites, and similar institutions	37,760

Job Outlook

Overall employment of archivists, curators, and museum workers is projected to grow 11 percent from 2012 to 2022, about as fast as the average for all occupations. Employment growth will vary by specialty.

Employment of archivists is projected to grow 17 percent from 2012 to 2022, faster than the average for all occupations. However, because it is a small occupation, the fast growth will result in only about 1,100 new jobs over the 10-year period. Jobs for archivists are expected to increase as public and private organizations require organization of, and access to, increasing volumes of records and information. The growing use of electronic records will cause demand for archivists who specialize in electronic records and records management to grow as well.

Employment of curators is projected to grow 13 percent from 2012 to 2022, about as fast as the average for all occupations. Museums receive millions of visitors every year and the number of visits has been increasing steadily. Continued public interest in these cultural centers will lead to demand for curators and the collections they manage.

Employment of museum technicians and conservators is projected to grow 7 percent from 2012 to 2022, slower than the average for all occupations. Public interest in science, art, history, and technology should spur some demand for museum technicians and conservators.

Job Prospects. Workers seeking jobs as archivists are likely to face very strong competition, because qualified applicants generally outnumber job openings.

Graduates with highly specialized training, such as a master's degree in library science or archival studies, with training in electronic records management and volunteer experience, should have the best job opportunities. However, archivist, curator, museum technician, and conservator jobs are attractive to many people, and many applicants have the necessary training and knowledge.

Job opportunities for those who have the computer skills to manage electronic records are expected to be better than for those who do not have those skills. Jobseekers with foreign language skills and the ability to relocate also could have better job opportunities.

Archives and museums can be subject to cuts in funding during recessions and periods of budget tightening, reducing demand for these workers. The need to replace workers who retire will create some job openings, but turnover is low for archivists, curators, museum technicians, and conservators.

O*NET

➤ Archivists (25-4011.00)
➤ Curators (25-4012.00)
➤ Museum Technicians and Conservators (25-4013.00)

Contacts for More Information

For information on archivists and on schools offering courses in archival studies, visit
➤ Society of American Archivists (www.archivists.org/)
   For information about archivists and archivist certification, visit
➤ Academy of Certified Archivists (www.certifiedarchivists.org/)
   For information about government archivists, visit
➤ Council of State Archivists (www.statearchivists.org/)
➤ National Association of Government Archives & Records Administrators (www.nagara.org/)
   For more information about museum careers, including schools offering courses in museum studies for curators and museum technicians, visit
➤ American Alliance of Museums (www.aam-us.org/)
   For more information about careers and education programs in conservation and preservation for conservators, visit
➤ American Institute for Conservation of Historic and Artistic Works (www.conservation-us.org/)
   For information on job openings as curators, museum technicians, and conservators with the federal government, visit
➤ USAJobs (www.usajobs.gov/)

Career and Technical Education Teachers

- **2012 Median Pay** .... $51,910 per year
  $24.96 per hour
- **Entry-Level Education** .... Bachelor's degree
- **Work Experience in a Related Occupation** .... Less than 5 years
- **On-the-Job Training** .... See "How to Become One"
- **Number of Jobs 2012** 239,800
- **Job Outlook, 2012–22** .... 9% (As fast as average)
- **Employment Change, 2012–22** 21,400

What Career and Technical Education Teachers Do

Career and technical education teachers instruct students in various technical and vocational subjects, such as auto repair, healthcare, and culinary arts. They teach academic and technical content to provide students with the skills and knowledge necessary to enter an occupation.

Duties. Career and technical education teachers typically do the following:

- Develop and plan lessons and assignments
- Instruct and demonstrate how to apply knowledge and to develop skills
- Demonstrate and supervise the safe and proper use of tools and equipment
- Monitor students' progress, assign tasks, and grade assignments
- Discuss students' progress with parents, students, and counselors
- Develop and enforce classroom rules and safety procedures

Career and technical education teachers help students explore and prepare to enter a specific occupation, such as ones in healthcare and information technology. They use a variety of teaching techniques to help students learn and develop skills related to a specific career or area of study. They demonstrate tasks, techniques, and tools used in an occupation. They may assign hands-on tasks, such as replacing brakes on cars, taking blood pressure, and recording vital signs to help students learn a specific skill. Teachers typically oversee these tasks in workshops and laboratories in the school.

Some teachers establish relationships with local businesses and nonprofit organizations to provide practical work experience for students.

The specific duties of career and technical education teachers vary by the grade and subject they teach. In middle schools and high schools, they teach in a classroom and through practical exercises in workshops and laboratories.

In postsecondary schools, they teach specific career skills that help students earn a certificate, diploma, or an associate degree, and prepare them for a specific job. For example, welding instructors teach students various welding techniques and essential safety practices. They also monitor the use of tools and equipment, and have students practice procedures until they meet the specific standards required by the trade.

In most states, teachers in middle and high schools instruct one subject within the 16 major career fields, also known as career clusters. For example, the career cluster known as *architecture and construction* includes instructions in designing, planning, managing, building, and maintaining structures.

Teachers instructing courses in *agricultural, food, and natural resources* teach topics, such as agricultural production; agriculture-related business; veterinary science; and plant, animal, and food systems. They have students plant and care for crops and tend to animals so that students can apply what they have learned in the classroom.

Career and technical education teachers in *hospitality and tourism* teach students in subjects such as nutrition, culinary art, or hotel lodging. For example, teachers may instruct and supervise students to create menus and prepare food.

Some teach the skills necessary to work as technicians and assistants, such as nursing and dental assistants in *health-related occupations.*

Career and technical education teachers assign students hands on tasks so that they can gain experience.

Median Annual Wages, May 2012

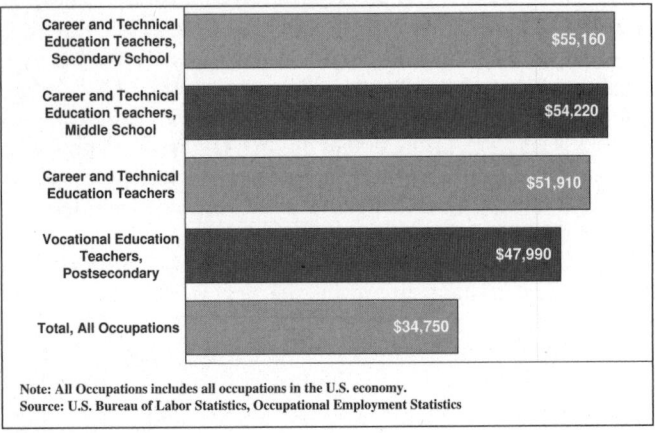

Note: All Occupations includes all occupations in the U.S. economy.
Source: U.S. Bureau of Labor Statistics, Occupational Employment Statistics

Percent Change in Employment, Projected 2012–2022

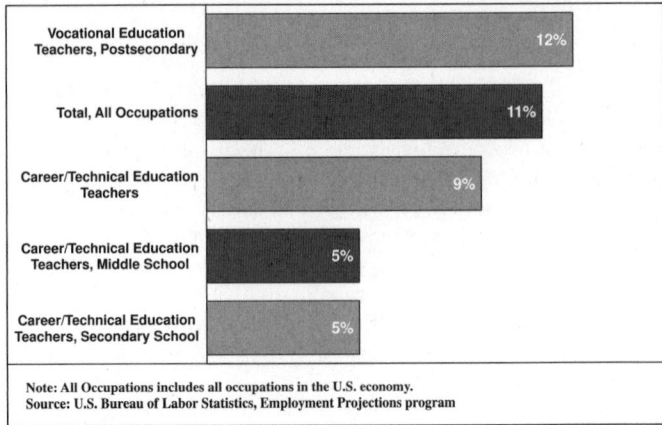

Note: All Occupations includes all occupations in the U.S. economy.
Source: U.S. Bureau of Labor Statistics, Employment Projections program

For information on all 16 major career clusters and programs in all other states, visit National Association of State Directors of Career Technical Education Consortium (www.careertech.org/career-clusters/).

Work Environment

Career and technical education teachers held about 239,800 jobs in 2012. Most work in public schools, including middle, high, and postsecondary schools, such as 2-year colleges. Others work in technical, trade, and business schools.

Work Schedules. Career and technical education teachers in middle and high schools generally work during school hours, between 8 a.m. and 3 p.m. They may meet with parents, students, and school staff before and after classes.

Some career and technical education teachers, especially those in postsecondary schools, instruct courses and develop lesson plans during evening hours and on weekends.

Teachers usually work the traditional 10-month school year with a 2-month break during the summer. Some teachers work for summer programs. Teachers in districts with a year-round schedule typically work 8 weeks in a row, are on break for 1 week, and have a 5-week midwinter break.

How to Become One

Although career and technical education teachers typically need a bachelor's degree, some enter the occupation with a high school diploma or an associate's degree. Career and technical education teachers also need work experience in the subject they teach. Some teachers, particularly those in public schools, may also be required to have a state-issued certification or license. Requirements for certification vary by state.

Education. Career and technical education teachers in public schools generally need a bachelor's degree in the field they teach, such as agriculture, engineering, or computer science.

Depending on the subject they teach, some enter the occupation with a high school diploma or an associate's degree after some years of related work experience. For example, teachers who instruct automotive mechanics need years of experience working as a mechanic. Some career and technical education teachers who have a high school diploma may be required to complete a degree while teaching to meet the full certification requirements.

Work Experience in a Related Occupation. Many career and technical education teachers need years of work experience in the field they teach. For example, automotive mechanics, chefs, and nurses typically spend years in their career before moving into teaching. Those who have a high school diploma as their highest

level of education may need several years of recent experience in a career field.

Training. Some states require prospective career and technical education teachers to complete a period of fieldwork, commonly referred to as student teaching. In some states, this program is a prerequisite for a license to teach in public schools. During student teaching, prospective teachers gain experience in preparing lessons and teaching students under the supervision and guidance of a mentor teacher. The amount of time required for these programs varies by state, but may last from 1 to 2 years.

Licenses, Certifications, and Registrations. States may require career and technical education teachers in public schools to be licensed or certified. Requirements for certification vary by state.

Certification typically involves completing a student teaching program and a bachelor's degree. States usually require candidates to pass a general teaching certification test. Most states require teachers to pass a background check.

Teachers may be required to complete annual professional development courses to maintain their license. For certification requirements in your state, visit Teach.org, previously known as Teacher Education and Compensation Helps.

Some states offer an alternative route to certification for prospective teachers who have a bachelor's degree or work experience in their field, but lack the education courses required for certification. Alternative programs typically cover teaching methods, development of lesson plans, and classroom management. For information about alternative certification programs, contact Teach-Now.

In addition to teaching certification, career and technical education teachers who prepare students for an occupation that requires a license or certification may need to have and maintain the same credential. For example, career and technical education teachers who instruct welding may need to have certification in welding.

Advancement. Experienced teachers can advance to become mentors and lead teachers helping less-experienced teachers to improve their teaching skills.

Teachers may become school counselors, instructional coordinators, and principals. These positions generally require additional education, an advanced degree, and certification. An advanced degree in education administration or leadership may be helpful.

Important Qualities

Communication skills. Career and technical education teachers must be able to explain technical concepts in terms that students can understand.

Employment Projections Data for Career and Technical Education Teachers

Occupational title	SOC Code	Employment, 2012	Projected Employment, 2022	Change, 2012–2022	
				Percent	Numeric
Career/technical education teachers	—	239,800	261,200	9	21,400
Vocational education teachers, postsecondary	25-1194	136,200	152,300	12	16,100
Career/technical education teachers, middle school	25-2023	18,200	19,100	5	900
Career/technical education teachers, secondary school	25-2032	85,400	89,700	5	4,300

Source: U.S. Bureau of Labor Statistics, Employment Projections Program

Note: Data are rounded. Go to **Occupational Information Included in the OOH** *for a discussion of the data in this table.*

Organizational skills. Teachers in middle and high schools have many students in different classes throughout the day. They must be able to organize their time and teaching materials.

Patience. Working with students of different abilities and backgrounds can be difficult. Teachers must be patient with each student in their classroom and develop a positive learning environment.

Resourcefulness. Teachers develop different ways to present information and to demonstrate a task so that students can learn.

Pay

The median annual wage for career and technical education teachers was $51,910 in May 2012. The median wage is the wage at which half the workers in an occupation earned more than that amount and half earned less. The lowest 10 percent earned less than $31,530, and the top 10 percent earned more than $83,180.

The median annual wages for career and technical education teachers by grade level in May 2012 were as follows:

Career/technical education teachers, secondary school $55,160
Career/technical education teachers, middle school 54,220
Vocational education teachers, postsecondary 47,990

Union Membership. Compared with workers in all occupations, career and technical education teachers had a higher percentage of workers who belonged to a union in 2012.

Job Outlook

Overall employment of career and technical education teachers is projected to grow 9 percent from 2012 to 2022, about as fast as the average for all occupations. Employment growth will vary by type. (See table below.)

Overall demand for career and technical education teachers will be driven by a continued need for programs that prepare students for technical careers.

Population growth will increase school enrollment, particularly in middle and high schools. However, students continue to take more academic and fewer career and technical classes. As a result, employment growth of career and education teachers in middle and high schools will be limited.

In addition, employment growth of teachers, particularly those in public schools, will depend on government funding. As federal and state governments reduce funds for career and technical education, fewer career and technical teachers may be hired.

Employment growth of career and technical education teachers at the postsecondary level, such as technical, trade, and business schools, often depends on the economy. As jobs become more limited, people seek additional technical skills to help them get a job. Also, changes in technology will drive the demand for people with technical skills. This will result in an increased demand for career and technical teachers at the postsecondary level.

Job Prospects. Most job opportunities will come from the need to replace teachers who leave the occupation. As a result, teachers with work experience in the subject they teach and certifications should have the best job prospects. Job opportunities may be better in some parts of the country–with higher enrollment rates–such as in the South, West, and rural areas.

Job opportunities also may be better in certain specialties, particularly at the postsecondary level. For example, those with experience in healthcare support occupations, such as teaching skills necessary to work as medical or dental assistants, may have better job opportunities.

O*NET

➤ Vocational Education Teachers, Postsecondary (25-1194.00)
➤ Career/Technical Education Teachers, Middle School (25-2023.00)
➤ Career/Technical Education Teachers, Secondary School (25-2032.00)

Similar Occupations This table shows a list of occupations with job duties that are similar to those of career and technical education teachers.

Occupations	Entry-level Education	2012 Pay	Projected Job Growth	Average Annual Openings
Elementary, Middle, and High School Principals	Master's degree	$87,760	6%	7,470
High School Teachers	Bachelor's degree	$55,050	6%	31,260
Instructional Coordinators	Master's degree	$60,050	13%	3,110
Middle School Teachers	Bachelor's degree	$53,430	12%	21,120
Postsecondary Teachers	See "How to Become One"	$70,380	19%	42,690
School and Career Counselors	Master's degree	$53,610	12%	8,700
Special Education Teachers	Bachelor's degree	$55,068	6%	10,220
Teacher Assistants	Some college, no degree	$23,640	9%	38,260

Contacts for More Information

For more information about career and technical education teachers, visit

➤ Association for Career and Technical Education (www.acteonline.org)

➤ National Association of State Directors of Career Technical Education Consortium (www.careertech.org/career-clusters/glance/career-clusters.html)

For information about teaching and becoming a teacher, visit

➤ Teach.org (www.teach.org)

For information about alternative certification programs, visit

➤ Teach-Now (http://teach-now.com/)

High School Teachers

- **2012 Median Pay** .... $55,050 per year
- **Entry-Level Education** .... Bachelor's degree
- **Work Experience in a Related Occupation** .... None
- **On-the-Job Training** .... Internship/residency
- **Number of Jobs 2012** 955,800
- **Job Outlook, 2012–22** .... 6% (Slower than average)
- **Employment Change, 2012–22** 52,900

What High School Teachers Do

High school teachers help prepare students for life after graduation. They teach academic lessons and various skills that students will need to attend college and to enter the job market.

Duties. High school teachers typically do the following:

- Plan lessons in the subjects they teach, such as biology or history

- Assess students to evaluate their abilities, strengths, and weaknesses

- Teach students as an entire class or in small groups

- Grade students' assignments to monitor progress

- Communicate with parents about students' progress

- Work with individual students to challenge them, to improve their abilities, and to work on their weaknesses

- Prepare students for standardized tests required by the state

- Develop and enforce classroom rules

- Supervise students outside of the classroom–for example, at lunchtime or during detention

High school teachers generally teach students from the 9th through 12th grades. They usually specialize in one subject area, such as math, science, or history. They may teach several different classes within that subject area. For example, a high school math teacher may teach courses in algebra, calculus, or geometry.

High school teachers may teach many grade levels throughout the day. For example, in one class they may have students from the 9th grade and then in the next class they may have students in 12th. In many schools, students are divided into classes based on their abilities, so teachers need to change their courses based on their students' capabilities.

High school teachers see several different classes of students throughout the day. They may teach the same material–for example, world history–to more than one class if the school has many students taking that subject.

Some high school teachers instruct special classes, such as art, music, and physical education.

When they do not have classes, teachers plan lessons, grade assignments, and meet with other teachers and staff.

In some schools, there are teachers of English as a second language (ESL) or teachers of English for speakers of other languages (ESOL) who work exclusively with students who are learning English. These students are often referred to as English language learners (ELLs). These teachers work with students individually or in groups to help them improve their English skills and help them with assignments for other classes.

Students with learning disabilities and emotional or behavioral disorders often are taught in traditional classes. Therefore, high school teachers may work with special education teachers to adapt lessons to these students' needs and to monitor the students' progress.

Some teachers maintain websites to communicate with parents about students' assignments, upcoming events, and grades. For students, teachers may create websites or discussion boards to present information and to expand a lesson taught in class.

Some high school teachers coach sports and advise student clubs and other groups, activities which frequently happen before or after school.

Work Environment

High school teachers held about 955,800 jobs in 2012.

Most high school teachers work in either public or private schools. Some teach in public magnet and charter schools. Others teach in private religious or secular schools.

Most states have tenure laws, which mean that after a certain number of years of teaching satisfactorily, teachers have some job security.

Seeing students develop new skills and gain an appreciation for knowledge and learning can be very rewarding. However, teaching may be stressful. Some schools have large classes and lack important teaching tools, such as computers and up-to-date textbooks. Most teachers are held accountable for their students' performance on standardized tests, which can be frustrating. Occasionally, teachers must cope with unmotivated or disrespectful students.

Work Schedules. High school teachers generally work school hours, which vary from school to school. However, they often spend time in the evenings and on weekends grading papers and preparing lessons. In addition, they may meet with parents, stu-

High school teachers generally specialize in a subject, such as English, math, or science.

Median Annual Wages, May 2012

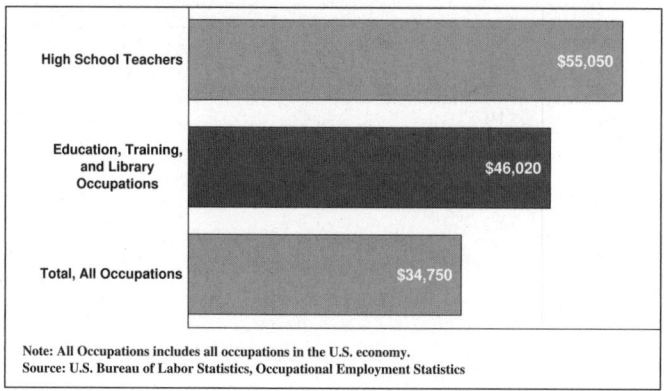

Note: All Occupations includes all occupations in the U.S. economy.
Source: U.S. Bureau of Labor Statistics, Occupational Employment Statistics

Percent Change in Employment, Projected 2012–2022

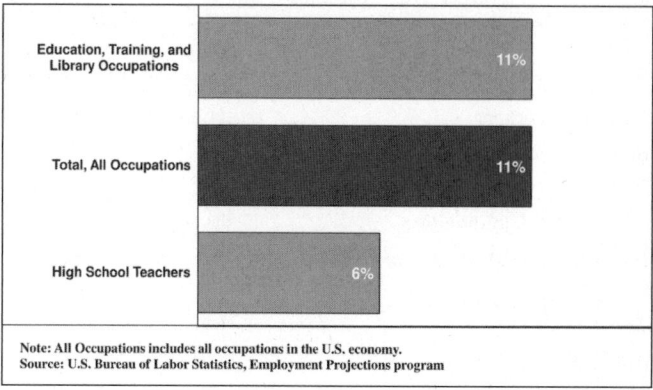

Note: All Occupations includes all occupations in the U.S. economy.
Source: U.S. Bureau of Labor Statistics, Employment Projections program

dents, and other teachers before and after school. Plus, teachers who coach sports or advise clubs generally do so before or after school.

Many work the traditional 10-month school year with a 2-month break during the summer. Although most do not teach during the summer, some teach in summer programs. Teachers in districts with a year-round schedule typically work 8 weeks in a row, are on break for 1 week, and have a 5-week midwinter break.

How to Become One

High school teachers must have a bachelor's degree. In addition, public school teachers must have a state-issued certification or license.

Education. All states require public high school teachers to have at least a bachelor's degree. Most states require high school teachers to have majored in a subject area, such as chemistry or history. While majoring in a subject area, future teachers typically enroll in their higher education's teacher preparation program and take classes in education and child psychology as well.

In teacher education programs, prospective high school teachers learn how to present information to students and how to work with students of varying abilities and backgrounds. Programs typically include fieldwork, such as student teaching. For information about teacher preparation programs in your state, visit Teach.org.

Some states require high school teachers to earn a master's degree after earning their teaching certification.

Teachers in private schools do not need to meet state requirements. However, private schools typically seek high school teachers who have a bachelor's degree and a major in a subject area.

Licenses, Certifications, and Registrations. All states require teachers in public schools to be licensed or certified. Those who teach in private schools are generally not required to be licensed.

High school teachers typically are awarded a secondary or high school certification. This allows them to teach the 7th through the 12th grades.

Requirements for certification vary by state. However, all states require that teachers have at least a bachelor's degree. States also require completing a teacher preparation program and supervised experience in teaching, typically gained through student teaching. Some states require a minimum grade point average. States typically require candidates to pass a general teaching certification test, as well as a test that demonstrates their knowledge in the subject they will teach. For information on certification requirements in your state, visit Teach.org.

Often, teachers are required to complete annual professional development classes to keep their license. Most states require teachers to pass a background check, and some states require teachers to complete a master's degree after receiving their certification.

All states offer an alternative route to certification for people who already have a bachelor's degree but lack the education courses required for certification. Some alternative certification programs allow candidates to begin teaching immediately under the supervision of an experienced teacher. These programs cover teaching methods and child development. After they complete the program, candidates are awarded full certification.

Other programs require students to take classes in education before they can teach. Students may be awarded a master's degree after completing either type of program. For more information about alternative certification programs, visit Teach-Now.

Training. In order to receive certification, teachers need to undergo a period of fieldwork, commonly referred to as student teaching. During student teaching, they work with a mentor teacher and gain experience teaching students in a classroom setting. The amount of time required varies by state.

Important Qualities

Communication skills. Teachers must collaborate with other teachers and special education teachers. In addition, teachers need to discuss students' needs with parents and administrators.

Employment Projections Data for High School Teachers

Occupational title	SOC Code	Employment, 2012	Projected Employment, 2022	Change, 2012–2022	
				Percent	Numeric
Secondary school teachers, except special and career/technical education 25-2031		955,800	1,008,700	6	52,900

Source: U.S. Bureau of Labor Statistics, Employment Projections Program

Note: Data are rounded. Go to **Occupational Information Included in the OOH** *for a discussion of the data in this table.*

Similar Occupations   This table shows a list of occupations with job duties that are similar to those of high school teachers.

Occupations	Entry-level Education	2012 Pay	Projected Job Growth	Average Annual Openings
Childcare Workers	High school diploma or equivalent	$19,510	14%	57,000
Elementary, Middle, and High School Principals	Master's degree	$87,760	6%	7,470
Instructional Coordinators	Master's degree	$60,050	13%	3,110
Kindergarten and Elementary School Teachers	Bachelor's degree	$53,060	12%	53,250
Librarians	Master's degree	$55,370	7%	4,440
Middle School Teachers	Bachelor's degree	$53,430	12%	21,120
Postsecondary Teachers	See "How to Become One"	$70,380	19%	42,690
Preschool Teachers	Associate's degree	$27,130	17%	19,940
School and Career Counselors	Master's degree	$53,610	12%	8,700
Social Workers	See "How to Become One"	$44,541	19%	24,280
Special Education Teachers	Bachelor's degree	$55,068	6%	10,220
Teacher Assistants	Some college, no degree	$23,640	9%	38,260

Patience. Working with students of different abilities and backgrounds can be difficult. High school teachers must be patient when students struggle with material.

Resourcefulness. High school teachers need to explain difficult concepts in terms students can understand. In addition, they must be able to engage students in learning and adapt lessons to each student's needs.

Advancement. Experienced teachers can advance to be mentors or lead teachers. In these positions, they often work with less-experienced teachers to help them improve their teaching skills.

With additional education or certification, teachers may become school counselors, school librarians, or instructional coordinators. Some become assistant principals or principals. Becoming a principal usually requires additional instruction in education administration or leadership. For more information, see the profiles on school and career counselors, librarians, instructional coordinators, and elementary, middle, and high school principals.

Pay

The median annual wage for high school teachers was $55,050 in May 2012. The median wage is the wage at which half the workers in an occupation earned more than that amount and half earned less. The lowest 10 percent earned less than $36,930, and the top 10 percent earned more than $85,690.

High school teachers generally work school hours, which vary from school to school. However, they often spend time in the evenings and on weekends grading papers and preparing lessons. In addition, they may meet with parents, students, and other teachers before and after school. Plus, teachers who coach sports or advise clubs generally do so before or after school.

Union Membership. Most high school teachers belonged to a union in 2012.

Job Outlook

Employment of high school teachers is projected to grow 6 percent from 2012 to 2022, slower than the average for all occupations. Overall growth is expected because of declines in student-to-teacher ratios and increases in enrollment. However, employment growth will vary by region.

From 2012 to 2022, the student-to-teacher ratio is expected to decline slightly. The student-to teacher ratio is the number of students for each teacher in school. When this ratio declines, each teacher is responsible for fewer students, so more teachers are required to instruct the same number of students. The expected decline in the student-to-teacher ratio will increase demand for high school teachers.

Over the projections period, the number of students in high schools is expected to increase, and the number of classes needed to accommodate these students will rise also. As a result, more teachers will be required to teach these additional classes of high school students.

However, enrollment growth in high school is expected to be slower than enrollment growth in other grades. Therefore, employment of high school teachers is expected to grow more slowly than that of other education occupations.

Although overall student enrollment is expected to grow, there will be variation by region. Enrollment is expected to grow fastest in the South and West. In the Midwest, enrollment is expected to hold steady, but the Northeast is projected to have declines. As a result, employment growth for high school teachers is expected to be faster in the South and West than in the Midwest and Northeast.

Despite expected increases in enrollment, however, employment growth for public high school teachers will depend on state and local government budgets. When state and local governments experience budget deficits, school boards may lay off employees, including teachers. As a result, employment growth of high school teachers may be reduced by state and local government budget deficits.

Job Prospects. From 2012 to 2022, a significant number of older teachers are expected to reach retirement age. These retirements will create job openings for new teachers.

In addition to overall openings, many schools report having difficulty filling teaching positions for certain subjects, including math, science (especially chemistry and physics), English as a second language, and special education. As a result, teachers with education or certifications to teach these specialties should have better job prospects. For more information about high school special education teachers, see the profile on special education teachers.

There is significant variation by region of the country and school setting. Opportunities are likely to be better in the South and West, where rapid enrollment growth is expected. Furthermore, opportunities should be better in urban and rural school districts than in suburban school districts.

O*NET

➤ Secondary School Teachers, Except Special and Career/Technical Education (25-2031.00)

Contacts for More Information

For more information about teaching and becoming a teacher, visit
➤ Teach.org (www.teach.org)
➤ American Federation of Teachers (www.aft.org/)
➤ National Education Association (www.nea.org/)

For more information about teacher preparation programs, visit
➤ Council for the Accreditation of Educator Preparation (www.caep-site.org/)

For more information about alternative certification programs, visit
➤ Teach-Now (www.teach-now.org/)

Instructional Coordinators

- **2012 Median Pay** .... $60,050 per year
  $28.87 per hour
- **Entry-Level Education** ....Master's degree
- **Work Experience in a Related Occupation** ... 5 years or more
- **On-the-Job Training** .... None
- **Number of Jobs 2012** 147,700
- **Job Outlook, 2012–22** .... 13% (As fast as average)
- **Employment Change, 2012–22** 18,500

What Instructional Coordinators Do

Instructional coordinators oversee school curriculums and teaching standards. They develop instructional material, coordinate its implementation with teachers and principals, and assess its effectiveness.

Duties. Instructional coordinators typically do the following:

- Develop and coordinate implementation of curriculum
- Plan, organize, and conduct teacher training conferences or workshops
- Observe and evaluate teachers' instruction and analyze student test data
- Assess and discuss implementation of education standards with school staff
- Review and recommend textbooks and other educational materials
- Recommend teaching techniques and the use of different or new technologies
- Develop procedures for teachers to implement curriculum
- Train teachers and other instructional staff in new content or programs
- Mentor or coach teachers to improve their skills

Instructional coordinators assess the effectiveness of curriculum and teaching techniques established by school boards, states, or federal regulations. For example, they may observe teachers in the classroom, review student test data, and interview school staff and principals about curriculum. Based on their research, they may recommend changes in curricula to school boards. They also may recommend that teachers use different teaching techniques that can help students learn.

Some instructional coordinators plan and conduct training for teachers related to teaching methods or the use of computers or tablets. For example, when a school district introduces new learning standards, coordinators explain the new standards to teachers and demonstrate effective teaching methods to achieve them.

Instructional coordinators, also known as *curriculum specialists*, *instructional coaches*, or *assistant superintendents of instruction*, may specialize in particular grade levels, such as elementary or high school, or specific subjects, such as language arts or math. Instructional coordinators in elementary and secondary schools may also focus on special education, English as a second language, or gifted-and-talented programs. Some coordinators provide educational support services, such as textbook or standardized test assessment and development.

Work Environment

Instructional coordinators held about 147,700 jobs in 2012.

The industries that employed the most instructional coordinators in 2012 were as follows:

Elementary and secondary schools; state, local, and private... 40%
Colleges, universities, and professional schools;
    state, local, and private.. 15
Government 9
Educational support services; state, local, and private 6

Most coordinators work out of an office in their school district, but they may also spend part of their time traveling to schools within the district to teach professional development classes and monitor the implementation of the curriculum.

Work Schedules. Instructional coordinators typically work year-round and do not have summer breaks, unlike teachers. Coordinators may meet with teachers and other administrators before and after classroom hours.

Instructional coordinators evaluate how well a school or training program's curriculum meets students' needs.

Median Annual Wages, May 2012

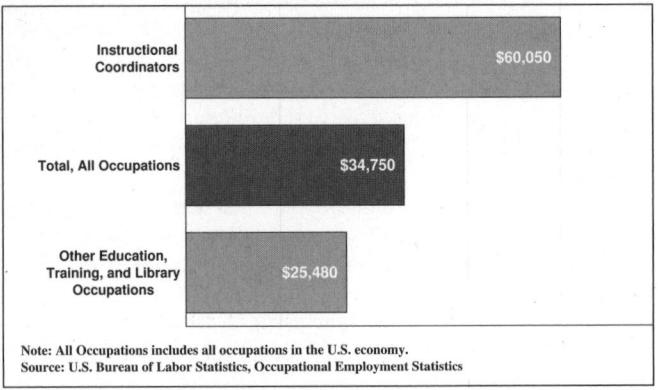

Note: All Occupations includes all occupations in the U.S. economy.
Source: U.S. Bureau of Labor Statistics, Occupational Employment Statistics

Percent Change in Employment, Projected 2012–2022

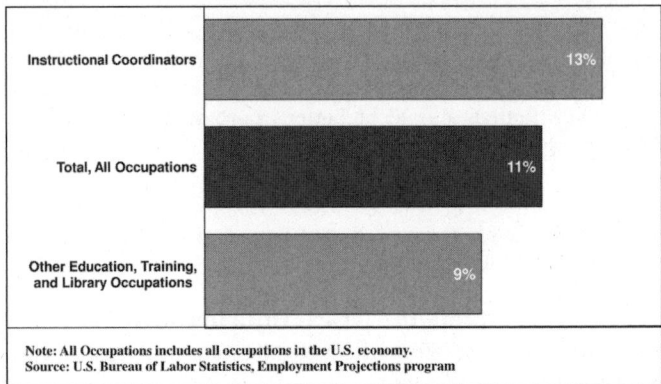

Note: All Occupations includes all occupations in the U.S. economy.
Source: U.S. Bureau of Labor Statistics, Employment Projections program

How to Become One

Instructional coordinators need a master's degree and related work experience. Coordinators in public schools may be required to be licensed teachers or licensed school administrators.

Education. Most employers, particularly public schools, require instructional coordinators to have a master's degree, typically in education or curriculum and instruction. Some instructional coordinators have a degree in the field they plan to specialize in, such as math or history.

Master's degree programs in curriculum and instruction teach about curriculum design, instructional theory, and collecting and analyzing data. To enter these programs, candidates usually need a bachelor's degree from a teacher education program.

Licenses, Certifications, and Registrations. Instructional coordinators in public schools may be required to have a license, such as a teaching license or an education administrator license. For

information about teaching licenses, see the profile on high school teachers. For information about education administrator licenses, see the profile on elementary, middle, and high school principals.

Work Experience in a Related Occupation. Most instructional coordinators need several years of related work experience. Depending on the position, experience working as a teacher or as a principal may be helpful. For some positions, experience teaching a specific subject or grade level may be required.

Important Qualities

Analytical skills. Instructional coordinators examine student test data and evaluate teaching strategies. They analyze the information to recommend improvements in curriculum and teaching.

Communication skills. Instructional coordinators need to explain changes in the curriculum and teaching standards to teachers, principals, and school staff.

Employment Projections Data for Instructional Coordinators

Occupational title	SOC Code	Employment, 2012	Projected Employment, 2022	Change, 2012–2022	
				Percent	Numeric
Instructional coordinators...	25-9031	147,700	166,200	13	18,500

Source: U.S. Bureau of Labor Statistics, Employment Projections Program

Note: Data are rounded. Go to **Occupational Information Included in the OOH** *for a discussion of the data in this table.*

Similar Occupations

This table shows a list of occupations with job duties that are similar to those of instructional coordinators.

Occupations	Entry-level Education	2012 Pay	Projected Job Growth	Average Annual Openings
Elementary, Middle, and High School Principals	Master's degree	$87,760	6%	7,470
High School Teachers	Bachelor's degree	$55,050	6%	31,260
Kindergarten and Elementary School Teachers	Bachelor's degree	$53,060	12%	53,250
Librarians	Master's degree	$55,370	7%	4,440
Middle School Teachers	Bachelor's degree	$53,430	12%	21,120
Postsecondary Teachers	See "How to Become One"	$70,380	19%	42,690
Preschool Teachers	Associate's degree	$27,130	17%	19,940
School and Career Counselors	Master's degree	$53,610	12%	8,700
Special Education Teachers	Bachelor's degree	$55,068	6%	10,220
Teacher Assistants	Some college, no degree	$23,640	9%	38,260

Decision-making skills. Instructional coordinators must be able to make sound decisions when recommending changes to curricula, teaching methods, and textbooks.

Interpersonal skills. Working with teachers, principals, and other administrators is an important part of instructional coordinators' jobs. They need to be able to establish and maintain positive working relationships with others.

Leadership skills. Instructional coordinators serve as mentors to teachers. They train teachers in developing useful and effective teaching techniques.

Pay

The median annual wage for instructional coordinators was $60,050 in May 2012. The median wage is the wage at which half the workers in an occupation earned more than that amount and half earned less. The lowest 10 percent earned less than $34,370, and the top 10 percent earned more than $93,500.

In May 2012, the medium annual wages for instructional coordinators in the top four industries employing these workers were as follows:

Government	$66,970
Elementary and secondary schools; state, local, and private	65,770
Educational support services; state, local, and private	60,100
Colleges, universities, and professional schools; state, local, and private	53,540

Job Outlook

Employment of instructional coordinators is projected to grow 13 percent from 2012 to 2022, about as fast as the average for all occupations.

Employment growth is expected as schools focus on evaluating and improving curriculums and teachers' effectiveness.

Many school districts and states are focusing on the teachers' role in improving students' learning. Some schools also provide training for teachers in curriculum changes or teaching techniques. In addition, there is an increased emphasis on holding teachers accountable for students' achievements. In fact, some states and school districts are using student attendance, test scores, and graduation rates to evaluate teachers.

With states and school districts using various accountability measures, coordinators will be needed to evaluate and improve curriculum and provide mentoring for teachers. As schools seek additional training for teachers, demand for instructional coordinators is expected to grow.

However, employment growth will depend on state and local government budgets.

O*NET

➤ Instructional Coordinators (25-9031.00)
➤ Instructional Designers and Technologists (25-9031.01)

Contacts for More Information

For more information about instructional coordinators, visit
➤ Learning Forward (www.learningforward.org)

Kindergarten and Elementary School Teachers

- **2012 Median Pay** .... $53,090 per year
- **Entry-Level Education** ....Bachelor's degree
- **Work Experience in a Related Occupation**............... None
- **On-the-Job Training** .... Internship/residency
- **Number of Jobs 2012** 1,519,700
- **Job Outlook, 2012–22** .... 12% (As fast as average)
- **Employment Change, 2012–22** 188,400

What Kindergarten and Elementary School Teachers Do

Kindergarten and elementary school teachers prepare younger students for future schooling by teaching them basic subjects such as math and reading.

Duties. Kindergarten and elementary school teachers typically do the following:

- Plan lessons that teach students subjects, such as reading and math, and skills, such as studying and communicating with others
- Assess students to evaluate their abilities, strengths, and weaknesses
- Teach lessons they have planned to an entire class of students or to smaller groups
- Grade students' assignments to monitor their progress
- Communicate with parents about their child's progress
- Work with students individually to help them overcome specific learning challenges
- Prepare students for standardized tests required by the state
- Develop and enforce classroom rules to teach children proper behavior
- Supervise children outside of the classroom–for example, during lunchtime or recess

Kindergarten and elementary school teachers help students learn and apply important concepts. Many teachers use a hands-on approach, such as the use of props, to help students understand abstract concepts, solve problems, and develop critical thinking skills.

For example, they may show students how to do a science experiment and then have the students do the experiment. They may have students work together to learn how to collaborate to solve problems.

Kindergarten and elementary school teachers generally teach kindergarten through fourth or fifth grade. However, in some schools, elementary school teachers may teach sixth, seventh, and eighth grade. They most often teach students many subjects, such as reading, science, and social studies, which students learn throughout the day.

Some teachers, particularly those who teach young students, may teach a multilevel class that includes children who would traditionally be in different grades. They may have the same group of students for several years.

Kindergarten and elementary school students spend most of their day in one classroom. Teachers may escort students to assemblies; to classes taught by other teachers, such as art or music; or to

Kindergarten and elementary school teachers use a variety of tools, such as computers, to present information to students.

recess. While students are away from the classroom, teachers plan lessons, grade assignments, or meet with other teachers and staff.

In some schools with older students, teachers work in teams. Each teacher often specializes in teaching one of two pairs of specialties, either English and social studies or math and science. Generally, students spend half their time with one teacher and half their time with the other.

Some kindergarten and elementary school teachers teach special classes, such as art, music, and physical education.

Some schools employ teachers of English as a second language (ESL) or English for speakers of other languages (ESOL). Both of these types of teachers work exclusively with students who are learning English, often referred to as English language learners (ELLs). The teachers work with students individually or in groups to help them improve their English skills and to help them with assignments they got in other classes.

Students with learning disabilities or emotional or behavioral disorders are often taught in traditional classes. Teachers work with special education teachers to adapt lessons to these students' needs and monitor the students' progress. In some cases, kindergarten and elementary school teachers may co-teach lessons with special education teachers.

Some teachers maintain websites to communicate with parents about students' assignments, upcoming events, and grades. For students in higher grades, teachers may create websites or dis-cussion boards to present information or to expand on a lesson taught in class.

Work Environment

Kindergarten and elementary school teachers held about 1.5 million jobs in 2012.

Kindergarten and elementary school teachers work in public and private schools. Some private early childhood education programs have preschool classes in addition to kindergarten.

Most states have tenure laws, which mean that after a certain number of years of teaching satisfactorily, teachers have some job security.

Seeing students develop new skills and learn information can be rewarding. At the same time, however, teaching also may be stressful. Some schools have large classes and lack important teaching tools, such as computers and up-to-date textbooks. Most teachers are held accountable for their students' performances on standardized tests, which can be frustrating.

Work Schedules. Kindergarten and elementary school teachers generally work during school hours when students are present. They may meet with parents, students, and other teachers before and after school. They often spend time in the evenings and on weekends grading papers and preparing lessons.

Many kindergarten and elementary school teachers work the traditional 10-month school year, with a 2-month break during the summer. Some teachers may teach summer programs. Teachers in districts with a year-round schedule typically work 8 weeks in a row, are on break for 1 week before starting a new schooling session, and also have a 5-week midwinter break.

How to Become One

Kindergarten and elementary school teachers must have a bachelor's degree. In addition, public school teachers must have a state-issued certification or license.

Education. All states require public kindergarten and elementary school teachers to have at least a bachelor's degree in elementary education. Some states also require kindergarten and elementary school teachers to major in a content area, such as math or science. They typically enroll in their university's teacher preparation program and also take classes in education and child psychology in addition to those required by their major.

In teacher education programs, future teachers learn how to present information to young students and how to work with young students of varying abilities and backgrounds. Programs typically include fieldwork, such as student teaching. For information about teacher preparation programs in your state, visit Teach.org.

Median Annual Wages, May 2012

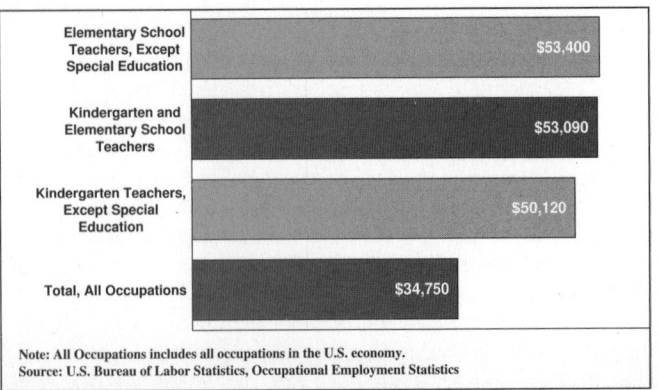

Elementary School Teachers, Except Special Education	$53,400
Kindergarten and Elementary School Teachers	$53,090
Kindergarten Teachers, Except Special Education	$50,120
Total, All Occupations	$34,750

Note: All Occupations includes all occupations in the U.S. economy.
Source: U.S. Bureau of Labor Statistics, Occupational Employment Statistics

Percent Change in Employment, Projected 2012–2022

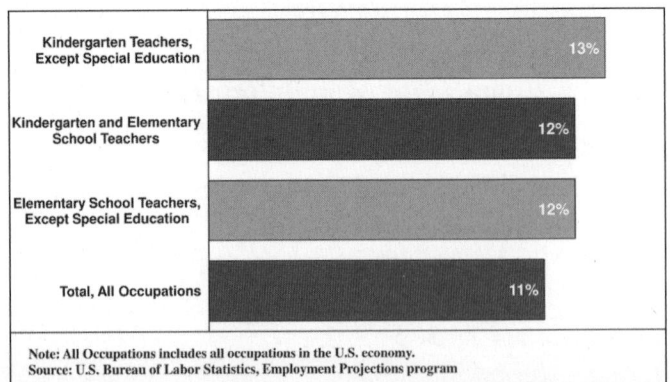

Kindergarten Teachers, Except Special Education	13%
Kindergarten and Elementary School Teachers	12%
Elementary School Teachers, Except Special Education	12%
Total, All Occupations	11%

Note: All Occupations includes all occupations in the U.S. economy.
Source: U.S. Bureau of Labor Statistics, Employment Projections program

Employment Projections Data for Kindergarten and Elementary School Teachers

Occupational title	SOC Code	Employment, 2012	Projected Employment, 2022	Change, 2012–2022	
				Percent	Numeric
Kindergarten and elementary school teachers........................	—	1,519,700	1,708,200	12	188,400
Kindergarten teachers, except special education................	25-2012	158,500	179,100	13	20,600
Elementary school teachers, except special education........	25-2021	1,361,200	1,529,100	12	167,900

Source: U.S. Bureau of Labor Statistics, Employment Projections Program

Note: Data are rounded. Go to Occupational Information Included in the OOH *for a discussion of the data in this table.*

Some states require all teachers to earn a master's degree after receiving their teaching certification.

Teachers in private schools do not need to meet state requirements, such as certifications or licenses. However, private schools typically seek kindergarten and elementary school teachers who have a bachelor's degree in elementary education.

Licenses, Certifications, and Registrations. All states require teachers in public schools to be licensed or certified. Those who teach in private schools are generally not required to be licensed.

Kindergarten and elementary school teachers are typically certified to teach early childhood grades, which are usually preschool through third grade, or elementary school grades, which are usually first through sixth grades or first through eighth grades.

Requirements for certification vary by state. However, all states require at least a bachelor's degree. They also require completing a teacher preparation program and supervised experience in teaching, typically gained through student teaching. Some states require a minimum grade point average. States often require candidates to pass a general teaching certification test, as well as a test that demonstrates their knowledge of the subject they will teach. Although kindergarten and elementary school teachers typically do not teach only a single subject, they may still be required to pass a content area test to earn their certification. For information on certification requirements in your state, visit Teach.org.

Teachers are frequently required to complete annual professional development classes to keep their license. Most states require teachers to pass a background check. Some states require teachers to complete a master's degree after receiving their certification.

All states offer an alternative route to certification for people who already have a bachelor's degree but lack the education courses required for certification.

Some alternative certification programs allow candidates to begin teaching immediately after graduation, under the supervision of an experienced teacher. These programs cover teaching methods and child development. After they complete the program, candidates are awarded full certification.

Other programs require students to take classes in education before they can teach.

Students may be awarded a master's degree after completing one of these programs. For information about alternative certification programs, contact Teach-Now.

Training. In order to receive certification, teachers need to undergo a period of fieldwork, commonly referred to as student teaching. During student teaching, they work with a mentor teacher and get experience teaching students in a classroom setting. The amount of time required varies by state.

Important Qualities

Communication skills. Teachers must collaborate with teacher assistants and special education teachers. In addition, they need to discuss students' needs with parents and administrators.

Creativity. Kindergarten and elementary school teachers must plan lessons that engage young students, adapting the lessons to different learning styles.

Patience. Working with students of different abilities and backgrounds can be difficult. Kindergarten and elementary school

Similar Occupations   This table shows a list of occupations with job duties that are similar to those of kindergarten and elementary school teachers.

Occupations	Entry-level Education	2012 Pay	Projected Job Growth	Average Annual Openings
Childcare Workers	High school diploma or equivalent	$19,510	14%	57,000
Elementary, Middle, and High School Principals	Master's degree	$87,760	6%	7,470
High School Teachers	Bachelor's degree	$55,050	6%	31,260
Instructional Coordinators	Master's degree	$60,050	13%	3,110
Librarians	Master's degree	$55,370	7%	4,440
Middle School Teachers	Bachelor's degree	$53,430	12%	21,120
Postsecondary Teachers	See "How to Become One"	$70,380	19%	42,690
Preschool Teachers	Associate's degree	$27,130	17%	19,940
School and Career Counselors	Master's degree	$53,610	12%	8,700
Social Workers	See "How to Become One"	$44,541	19%	24,280
Special Education Teachers	Bachelor's degree	$55,068	6%	10,220
Teacher Assistants	Some college, no degree	$23,640	9%	38,260

teachers must respond with patience when students struggle with material.

Resourcefulness. Kindergarten and elementary school teachers need to be able to explain difficult concepts in terms that young students can understand. In addition, they must be able to get students engaged in learning and adapt their lessons meet students' needs.

Advancement. Experienced teachers can advance to serve as mentors to newer teachers or to become lead teachers. In these roles, they help less experienced teachers to improve their teaching skills.

With additional education or certification, teachers may become school counselors, school librarians, or instructional coordinators. Some become assistant principals or principals, both of which generally require additional schooling in education administration or leadership.

Pay

The median annual wage for kindergarten teachers was $50,120 in May 2012. The median wage is the wage at which half the workers in an occupation earned more than that amount and half earned less. The lowest 10 percent earned less than $32,450, and the top 10 percent earned more than $78,230.

The median annual wage for elementary school teachers was $53,400. The lowest 10 percent earned less than $35,630, and the top 10 percent earned more than $83,160.

Union Membership. Compared with workers in all occupations, kindergarten and elementary school teachers had a higher percentage of workers who belonged to a union in 2012.

Job Outlook

Employment of kindergarten and elementary school teachers is projected to grow 12 percent from 2012 to 2022, about as fast as the average for all occupations. Growth is expected due to projected increases in enrollment as well as declines in student–teacher ratios. However, employment growth will vary by region.

From 2012 to 2022, the student–teacher ratio across schools is expected to decline slightly. This ratio is the number of students for each teacher in the school. A decline in the ratio means that each teacher is responsible for fewer students, and, consequently, more teachers are needed to teach the same number of students.

In addition, the number of students enrolling in kindergarten and elementary schools is expected to increase over the coming decade, and the number of classes needed to accommodate these students will also rise. As a result, more teachers will be required to teach these additional classes of kindergarten and elementary school students.

Although overall student enrollment is expected to grow, there will be some variation by region. Enrollment is expected to grow fastest in the South and West. In the Midwest, enrollment is expected to hold steady, and the Northeast is projected to have declines. As a result, employment growth for kindergarten and elementary school teachers is expected to be faster in the South and West than in the Midwest and Northeast.

However, despite expected increases in enrollment, employment growth for kindergarten and elementary school teachers will depend on state and local government budgets. When state and local governments experience budget deficits, they may lay off employees, including teachers. As a result, employment growth of kindergarten and elementary school teachers may be somewhat reduced by state and local government budget deficits.

Job Prospects. A significant number of older teachers are expected to reach retirement age between 2012 and 2022. Their retirement will create job openings for new teachers. However, many areas of the country already have a surplus of teachers who

are trained to teach kindergarten and elementary school, making it more difficult for new teachers to find jobs.

Teachers of English as a second language (ESL) and special education teachers are in short supply. Kindergarten and elementary school teachers with education or certifications to teach these specialties should have better job opportunities.

Opportunities will vary by region and school setting. Job prospects should be better in the South and West, which are expected to have rapid enrollment growth. Furthermore, opportunities will be better in urban and rural school districts than in suburban school districts.

O*NET

➤ Kindergarten Teachers, Except Special Education (25-2012.00)
➤ Elementary School Teachers, Except Special Education (25-2021.00)

Contacts for More Information

For more information about teaching and becoming a teacher, visit
➤ Teach.org (www.teach.org/)
➤ American Federation of Teachers (www.aft.org/)
➤ National Education Association (www.nea.org/)
  For more information about teacher preparation programs, visit
➤ Council for the Accreditation of Educator Preparation (www.caep-site.org/)
  For more information about alternative certification programs, visit
➤ Teach-Now (www.teach-now.org/)

Librarians

- **2012 Median Pay** .... $55,370 per year
  $26.62 per hour
- **Entry-Level Education** ....Master's degree
- **Work Experience in a Related Occupation**............... None
- **On-the-Job Training** .... None
- **Number of Jobs 2012** 148,400
- **Job Outlook, 2012–22** .... 7% (Slower than average)
- **Employment Change, 2012–22** 11,000

What Librarians Do

Librarians help people find information and conduct research for personal and professional use. Their job duties may change based on the type of library they work in, such as public, school, and medical libraries.

Duties. Librarians typically do the following:

- Help library patrons conduct research and find the information they need
- Teach classes about information resources and help users evaluate search results and reference materials
- Organize library materials so they are easy to find, and maintain collections
- Plan programs for different audiences, such as storytelling for young children
- Develop and index databases of library materials
- Research new books and materials by reading book reviews, publishers' announcements, and catalogs
- Choose new books, audio books, videos, and other materials for the library

- Research and buy new computers and other equipment as needed for the library
- Train and direct library technicians, assistants, other support staff, and volunteers
- Prepare library budgets

In small libraries, librarians are often responsible for many or all aspects of library operations. They may manage a staff of library assistants and technicians.

In larger libraries, librarians usually focus on one aspect of library work, including user services, technical services, or administrative services.

The following are examples of types of librarians:

User services librarians help patrons find the information they need. They listen to what patrons are looking for and help them conduct research using both electronic and print resources. These librarians also teach patrons how to use library resources to find information on their own. This may include familiarizing patrons with catalogs of print materials, helping them access and search digital libraries, or educating them on Internet search techniques. Some user services librarians work with a particular audience, such as children or young adults.

Technical services librarians obtain, prepare, and classify print and electronic library materials. They organize materials to make it easy for patrons to find information. These librarians are less likely to work directly with the public.

Administrative services librarians manage libraries. They hire and supervise staff, prepare budgets, and negotiate contracts for library materials and equipment. Some conduct public relations or fundraising for the library.

Librarians who work in different settings sometimes have different job duties.

Academic librarians assist students, faculty, and staff in colleges and universities. They help students research topics related to their coursework and teach students how to access information. They also assist faculty and staff in locating resources related to their research projects or studies. Some campuses have multiple libraries, and librarians may specialize in a particular subject.

Public librarians work in their communities to serve all members of the public. They help patrons find books to read for pleasure; conduct research for schoolwork, business, or personal interest; and learn how to access the library's resources. Many public librarians plan programs for users, such as story time for children, book clubs, or other educational activities.

School librarians, sometimes called school media specialists, work in elementary, middle, and high school libraries, and teach

Librarians help people find information and use it effectively for personal and professional purposes.

students how to use library resources. They also help teachers develop lesson plans and find materials for classroom instruction.

Special librarians work in settings other than school or public libraries. They are sometimes called information professionals. Law firms, hospitals, businesses, museums, government agencies, and many other groups have their own libraries that use special librarians. The main purpose of these libraries and information centers is to serve the information needs of the organization that houses the library. Therefore, special librarians collect and organize materials focused on those subjects. The following are examples of special librarians:

- *Corporate librarians* assist employees in private businesses in conducting research and finding information. They work for a wide range of businesses, including insurance companies, consulting firms, and publishers.

- *Government librarians* provide research services and access to information for government staff and the public.

- *Law librarians* help lawyers, law students, judges, and law clerks locate and organize legal resources. They often work in law firms and law school libraries.

- *Medical librarians*, also called health science librarians, help health professionals, patients, and researchers find health and science information. They may provide information about new clinical trials and medical treatments and procedures, teach medical students how to locate medical information, or answer consumers' health questions.

Median Annual Wages, May 2012

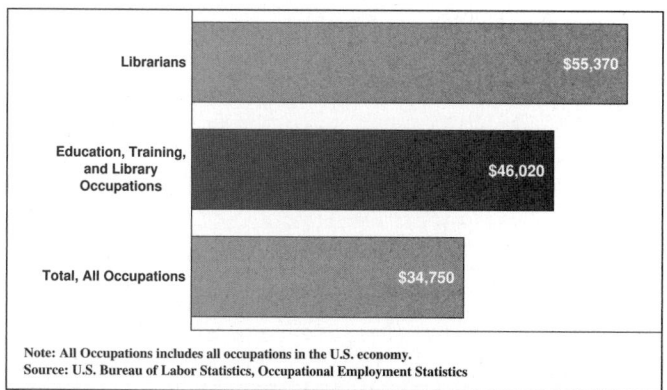

Librarians $55,370

Education, Training, and Library Occupations $46,020

Total, All Occupations $34,750

Note: All Occupations includes all occupations in the U.S. economy.
Source: U.S. Bureau of Labor Statistics, Occupational Employment Statistics

Percent Change in Employment, Projected 2012–2022

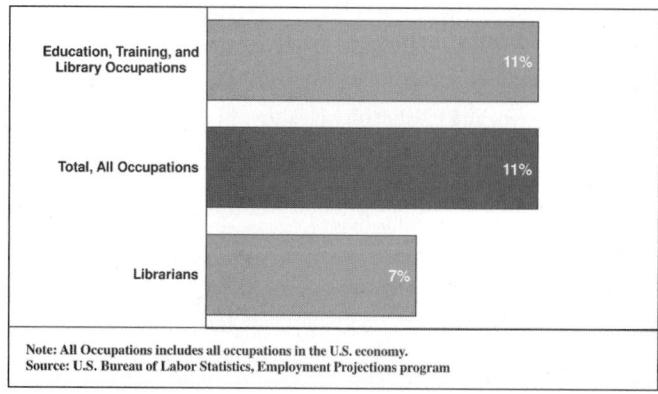

Education, Training, and Library Occupations 11%

Total, All Occupations 11%

Librarians 7%

Note: All Occupations includes all occupations in the U.S. economy.
Source: U.S. Bureau of Labor Statistics, Employment Projections program

Employment Projections Data for Librarians

Occupational title	SOC Code	Employment, 2012	Projected Employment, 2022	Change, 2012–2022	
				Percent	Numeric
Librarians..	25-4021	148,400	159,400	7	11,000

Source: U.S. Bureau of Labor Statistics, Employment Projections Program

Note: Data are rounded. Go to **Occupational Information Included in the OOH** *for a discussion of the data in this table.*

Work Environment

Librarians held about 148,400 jobs in 2012. The industries that employed the most librarians in 2012 were as follows:

Elementary and secondary schools; state, local, and private...	38%
Local government, excluding education and hospitals............	29
Colleges, universities, and professional schools; state, local, and private...	17
Information	5

Some librarians have private offices, but those in smaller libraries usually share work space with others.

Work Schedules. Most librarians work full time, although opportunities exist for part-time work. In 2012, about a quarter of librarians worked part time.

Public and academic librarians often work on weekends and evenings, and may work holidays. School librarians usually have the same work and vacation schedules as teachers, including summers off. Librarians in special libraries, such as law or corporate libraries, typically work normal business hours, but may need to work longer hours to help meet deadlines.

How to Become One

Most librarians need a master's degree in library science. Some positions have additional requirements, such as a teaching certificate or a degree in another field.

Education. Most employers require librarians to have a master's degree in library science (MLS). Students need a bachelor's degree to enter MLS programs, but any undergraduate major is accepted.

MLS programs usually take 1 to 2 years to complete. Coursework typically covers selecting library materials, organizing information, research methods and strategies, online reference systems, and Internet search methods.

A degree from an American Library Association accredited program may lead to better job opportunities. Some colleges and universities have other names for their library science programs, such as Master of Information Studies or Master of Library and Information Studies.

Librarians working in a special library, such as a law, medical, or corporate library, usually supplement a master's degree in library science with knowledge of their specialized field. Some employers require special librarians to have a master's degree, a professional degree, or a Ph.D. in that subject. For example, a law librarian may be required to have a law degree or a librarian in an academic library may need a Ph.D.

Licenses, Certifications, and Registrations. To work in public schools, school librarians often need to be certified. Certification typically requires librarians to hold a teacher's certification. For more information on teacher certifications, see the How to Become One section of the profile for high school teachers. Some states require librarians to pass a standardized test, such as the PRAXIS II Library Media Specialist test. A list of requirements by state and contact information for state regulating boards is available from School Library Monthly.

Some states also require certification for librarians in public libraries. Requirements vary by state. Contact your state's licensing board for specific requirements.

Important Qualities

Communication skills. Librarians need to be able to explain ideas and information in ways that patrons and users understand.

Computer skills. Librarians use computers to help patrons research topics. They also use computers to classify resources, create databases, and perform administrative duties.

Initiative. New information, technology, and resources constantly change the details of what librarians do. They must be able and willing to continually update their knowledge on these changes to be effective at their jobs in the varying circumstances.

Interpersonal skills. Librarians must be able to work both as part of a team and with the public or with researchers.

Similar Occupations   This table shows a list of occupations with job duties that are similar to those of librarians.

Occupations	Entry-level Education	2012 Pay	Projected Job Growth	Average Annual Openings
Adult Literacy and High School Equivalency Diploma Teachers	Bachelor's degree	$48,590	9%	1,990
Archivists, Curators, and Museum Workers	See "How to Become One"	$44,625	12%	970
Health Educators and Community Health Workers	See "How to Become One"	$43,015	22%	4,740
High School Teachers	Bachelor's degree	$55,050	6%	31,260
Kindergarten and Elementary School Teachers	Bachelor's degree	$53,060	12%	53,250
Library Technicians and Assistants	See "How to Become One"	$26,983	12%	13,070
Middle School Teachers	Bachelor's degree	$53,430	12%	21,120
Postsecondary Teachers	See "How to Become One"	$70,380	19%	42,690

Problem-solving skills. Librarians conduct and assist with research. This requires being able to identify a problem, figure out where to find information, and draw conclusions based on the information found.

Reading skills. Librarians must be excellent readers. Those working in special libraries are expected to continually read the latest literature in their field of specialization.

Pay

The median annual wage for librarians was $55,370 in May 2012. The median wage is the wage at which half of the workers in an occupation earned more than that amount and half earned less. The lowest 10 percent earned less than $33,380, and the top 10 percent earned more than $85,430.

In May 2012, the median annual wages for librarians in the top four industries in which these librarians worked were as follows:

Colleges, universities, and professional schools; state, local, and private	$58,700
Elementary and secondary schools; state, local, and private	57,310
Information	51,970
Local government, excluding education and hospitals	49,790

Union Membership. Compared with workers in all occupations, librarians had a higher percentage of workers who belonged to a union in 2012.

Job Outlook

Employment of librarians is projected to grow 7 percent from 2012 to 2022, slower than the average for all occupations.

There will continue to be a need for librarians to manage libraries and help patrons find information. As patrons and support staff become more comfortable using electronic resources, fewer librarians will be needed for assistance. However, the increased availability of electronic information is also expected to increase the demand for librarians in research and special libraries, where they will be needed to help sort through the large amount of available information.

Budget limitations, especially in local government and educational services, may slow demand for librarians. Some libraries may close, reduce the size of their staff, or focus on hiring library technicians and assistants, who can fulfill some librarian duties at a lower cost.

Job Prospects. Jobseekers may face strong competition for jobs, especially early in the decade, as many people with master's degrees in library science compete for a limited number of available positions. Later in the decade, prospects should be better, as older library workers retire and population growth generates openings.

Even though people with a master's degree in library science may have trouble finding a job as a librarian, their research and analytical skills can be valuable for jobs in a variety of other fields, such as market researchers or computer and information systems managers. A degree from an American Library Association accredited program may lead to better job opportunities.

O*NET

➤ Librarians (25-4021.00)

Contacts for More Information

For more information about librarians, including accredited library education programs, visit

➤ American Library Association (www.ala.org/)
    For more information about careers in libraries, visit

➤ Library Careers (http://librarycareers.drupalgardens.com/)
    For information about medical librarians, visit
➤ Medical Library Association (www.mlanet.org/)
    For information about law librarians, visit
➤ American Association of Law Libraries (www.aallnet.org/)
    For information about many different types of special librarians, visit
➤ Special Libraries Association (www.sla.org/)
    For more information about school librarians, visit
➤ School Library Monthly (www.schoollibrarymonthly.com/index.html)

Library Technicians and Assistants

- **2012 Median Pay** .... $26,800 per year
  $12.89 per hour
- **Entry-Level Education** ....See "How to Become One"
- **Work Experience in a Related Occupation**.............. None
- **On-the-Job Training** ....See "How to Become One"
- **Number of Jobs 2012** 216,600
- **Job Outlook, 2012–22** .... 12% (As fast as average)
- **Employment Change, 2012–22** 25,200

What Library Technicians and Assistants Do

Library technicians and assistants help librarians with all aspects of running a library. They assist patrons, organize library materials and information, and perform clerical and administrative tasks.

Duties. Library technicians and assistants typically do the following:

- Loan library materials to patrons and collect returned materials
- Sort and reshelve returned books, periodicals, and other materials
- Catalogue and maintain library materials
- Handle interlibrary loans
- Register new patrons and issue library cards
- Answer patrons' questions and help them find library resources
- Maintain computer databases used to locate library materials

Library technicians sort and reshelve returned books, periodicals, and other materials.

Median Hourly Wages, May 2012

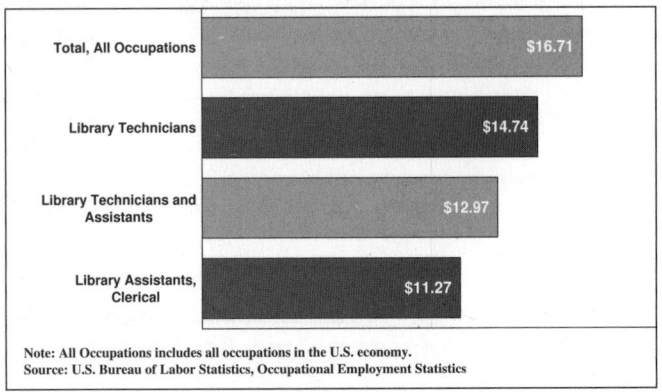

Note: All Occupations includes all occupations in the U.S. economy.
Source: U.S. Bureau of Labor Statistics, Occupational Employment Statistics

Percent Change in Employment, Projected 2012–2022

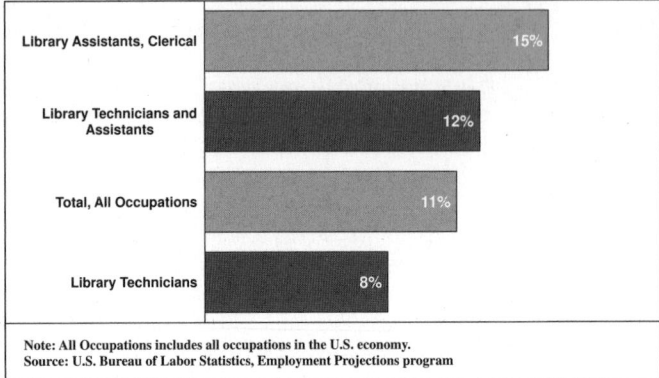

Note: All Occupations includes all occupations in the U.S. economy.
Source: U.S. Bureau of Labor Statistics, Employment Projections program

- Answer the phone, organize files, and perform other routine clerical tasks
- Help plan and participate in special programs, such as used-book sales, storytimes and outreach programs

Library technicians and assistants are usually supervised by a librarian. Library technicians typically have more responsibilities than library assistants, such as administering library programs and overseeing lower level staff.

Library technicians and assistants in smaller libraries have a broader range of duties. In larger libraries, they tend to specialize in a particular area, such as user services or technical services. Technicians and assistants in user services assist library patrons with locating resources and information. Those in technical services research and acquire, catalog, and process materials to be added to the library's collections.

The list that follows gives examples of types of library technicians and assistants based on the type of library they work in:

Academic library technicians and assistants assist students, faculties, and staff in colleges and universities. They help students, faculty, and staff access resources and information related to coursework or research projects. Some help teach students how to access and use library resources. They may work at service desks for reserve materials, special collections or computer labs.

Public library technicians and assistants work in their community libraries to serve all members of the public. They help patrons find books to read for pleasure; assist patrons with their research for schoolwork, business, or personal interest; and teach patrons how to access the library's resources. Some technicians in public libraries may help plan programs for users, such as story time for children, book clubs for teens or adults, or other educational or recreational activities.

School library technicians and assistants show students how to find and use library resources, maintain textbook collections and they help teachers develop curriculum materials.

Special library technicians and assistants work in libraries in government agencies, corporations, museums, law firms, and medical centers. They assist user, search library resources, compile bibliographies, and provide information on subjects of interest to the organization.

Work Environment

Library technicians and assistants held about 216,600 jobs in 2012. They work in local public libraries, corporate and specialty libraries, and school and university libraries.

The industries that employed the most library technicians and assistants in 2012 were as follows:

Local government, excluding education and hospitals............ 54%
Colleges, universities, and professional schools;
    state, local, and private.. 17
Elementary and secondary schools; state, local, and private... 16
Information 6

Library technicians and assistants generally work indoors. They spend much of their time at public service desks or computer terminals. Most also spend time in the library stacks while reshelving books, a task that may require bending or stretching to reach the shelves.

Work Schedules. More than half of clerical library assistants worked part time in 2012.

Library technicians and assistants in school libraries work during regular school hours. Those in public or college libraries often work weekends, evenings, and some holidays. In corporate libraries, library technicians and assistants work normal business hours but may be asked to work overtime.

How to Become One

Most library technicians need a postsecondary certificate or an associate's degree. Clerical library assistants usually learn through short-term on-the-job training.

Education. Most libraries prefer to hire library technicians who have a postsecondary certificate or an associate's degree. However,

Employment Projections Data for Library Technicians and Assistants

Occupational title	SOC Code	Employment, 2012	Projected Employment, 2022	Change, 2012–2022	
				Percent	Numeric
Library technicians and assistants..	—	216,600	241,800	12	25,200
Library technicians...	25-4031	106,200	115,200	8	9,000
Library assistants, clerical...	43-4121	110,400	126,600	15	16,300

Source: U.S. Bureau of Labor Statistics, Employment Projections Program

Note: Data are rounded. Go to Occupational Information Included in the OOH for a discussion of the data in this table.

Similar Occupations This table shows a list of occupations with job duties that are similar to those of library technicians and assistants.

Occupations	Entry-level Education	2012 Pay	Projected Job Growth	Average Annual Openings
Librarians	Master's degree	$55,370	7%	4,440
Medical Records and Health Information Technicians	Postsecondary non-degree award	$34,160	22%	9,040
Receptionists	High school diploma or equivalent	$25,990	13%	40,690
Teacher Assistants	Some college, no degree	$23,640	9%	38,260

some smaller libraries might hire prospective technicians with only a high school diploma.

To obtain an associate's degree or a certificate in library technology, candidates must take classes in acquisitions, cataloguing, circulation, reference, and automated library systems.

In some cases, library technicians who work in public schools must meet the same requirements as teacher assistants.

No formal education is required for clerical library assistants. Most libraries prefer to hire assistants who have earned a high school diploma or GED, but some will hire high school students.

Training. Clerical library assistants usually receive some short-term on-the-job training to learn about libraries and library resources.

Important Qualities

Communication skills. Library technicians need to listen to and understand patrons' needs, provide clear answers to questions, and teach patrons and students how to use library resources.

Computer skills. Library technicians and assistants use computers to help patrons research topics. Library technicians and assistants also use computers to maintain the library's database of collections.

Detail-oriented. Library technicians and assistants must pay close attention to ensure that library materials and information are organized correctly and according to the library's organizational system. Cataloging and processing library materials also require attention to detail.

Interpersonal skills. Library technicians and assistants provide customer service to library patrons and work on teams with librarians and, at times, teachers or researchers.

Advancement. Library technicians and assistants can advance as they assume additional responsibilities in other areas of the library. Some eventually become supervisors and oversee daily library operations. To become a librarian, technicians and assistants need to earn a master's degree in library science.

Pay

The median hourly wage for library technicians was $14.74 in May 2012. The median wage is the wage at which half the workers in an occupation earned more than that amount and half earned less. The lowest 10 percent earned less than $8.86, and the top 10 percent earned more than $23.33.

The median hourly wage for clerical library assistants was $11.27 in May 2012. The lowest 10 percent earned less than $8.21, and the top 10 percent earned more than $18.41.

In May 2012, the median hourly wages for library technicians and clerical library assistants in the top four industries in which these technicians and assistants worked were as follows:

Colleges, universities, and professional schools;
state, local, and private....................................$15.47
Elementary and secondary schools; state, local, and private...12.96
Local government, excluding education and hospitals...........12.08
Information 11.11

More than half of clerical library assistants worked part time in 2012.

Job Outlook

Employment of library technicians is projected to grow 8 percent from 2012 to 2022, about as fast as the average for all occupations.

Employment of clerical library assistants is projected to grow 15 percent from 2012 to 2022, faster than the average for all occupations.

Online databases and other electronic tools have simplified some tasks, allowing them to be performed by technicians and assistants rather than librarians. Library technicians and assistants earn less than librarians. As more libraries face budget constraints, technicians and assistants will be used increasingly as a lower cost method of providing library services.

O*NET

➤ Library Technicians (25-4031.00)
➤ Library Assistants, Clerical (43-4121.00)

Contacts for More Information

For more information about library technicians and assistants careers, visit
➤ American Library Association (www.ala.org/)
  For more information about careers in libraries, visit
➤ Library Careers (http://librarycareers.drupalgardens.com/)
  For information about medical libraries, visit
➤ Medical Library Association (www.mlanet.org/)
  For information about law libraries, visit
➤ American Association of Law Libraries (www.aallnet.org/)
  For information about many different types of special libraries, visit
➤ Special Libraries Association (www.sla.org/)

Middle School Teachers

- **2012 Median Pay** ....$53,430 per year
- **Entry-Level Education** ....Bachelor's degree
- **Work Experience in a Related Occupation**.............. None
- **On-the-Job Training** .... Internship/residency
- **Number of Jobs 2012** 614,400
- **Job Outlook, 2012–22**................ 12% (As fast as average)
- **Employment Change, 2012–22** 76,000

What Middle School Teachers Do

Middle school teachers educate students typically in sixth through eighth grade. Middle school teachers help students build on the fundamentals taught in elementary school and prepare students for the more difficult curriculum they will face in high school.

Duties. Middle school teachers typically do the following:

- Plan lessons that teach students a subject, such as biology and history

- Assess students to evaluate their abilities, strengths, and weaknesses

- Teach lessons they have planned to an entire class or to smaller groups

- Grade students' assignments to monitor their progress

- Communicate with parents about their child's progress

- Work with students individually to help them overcome specific learning challenges

- Prepare students for standardized tests required by the state

- Develop and enforce classroom rules

- Supervise students outside of the classroom–for example, at lunchtime or during detention

Middle school teachers generally teach students from sixth to eighth grades. However, in some school districts, they may teach students as early as fourth grade or as late as ninth grade.

In many schools, middle school teachers are responsible for only some of the subjects their students learn throughout the day. For example, one teacher may be responsible for teaching English and social studies while another is responsible for teaching math and science. Some middle school instructors teach specialized classes, such as art, music, or physical education.

Often, students change classrooms several times a day to attend lessons in different subjects. As a result, middle school teachers in these schools see several different classes of students throughout the day. In some schools, middle school teachers teach all the subjects for one class of students the entire day. In either type of school, teachers use time during the day when they do not have classes to plan lessons, grade assignments, or meet with other teachers and staff.

Some middle school teachers work in teams that teach the same group of students. These teachers meet to discuss students' progress and to plan future lessons.

In some schools, teachers of English as a second language (ESL) or English for speakers of other languages (ESOL) work exclusively with students who are learning English. These students are often referred to as English language learners (ELLs). ESL

Middle school teachers help students build on the fundamentals they learned in elementary schools to prepare them for the more difficult subjects and lessons in high school.

and ESOL teachers work with students individually or in groups to help them improve their English skills and to help the students with assignments for their other classes.

Middle school teachers also work with special education teachers to adapt lessons taught in traditional classes to the needs of students with learning disabilities and emotional or behavioral disorders. Middle school teachers also monitor the progress of these students. In some cases, middle school teachers may co-teach lessons with special education teachers.

Some teachers maintain websites to communicate with parents about students' assignments, upcoming events, and grades. For their students, teachers may create websites or discussion boards to present information or to expand a lesson taught in class.

Some middle school teachers coach sports teams and advise student clubs and groups, whose practices and meetings frequently take place before or after school.

Work Environment

Middle school teachers held about 614,400 jobs in 2012. The majority of middle school teachers work in public and private schools.

Most states have tenure laws, which mean that after a certain number of years of teaching satisfactorily, teachers have some job security.

Median Annual Wages, May 2012

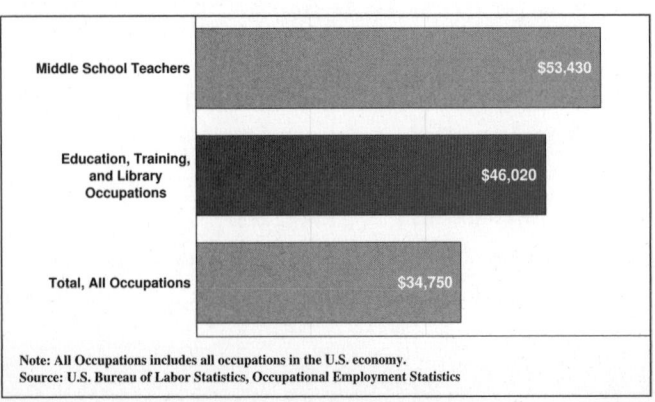

Middle School Teachers	$53,430
Education, Training, and Library Occupations	$46,020
Total, All Occupations	$34,750

Note: All Occupations includes all occupations in the U.S. economy.
Source: U.S. Bureau of Labor Statistics, Occupational Employment Statistics

Percent Change in Employment, Projected 2012–2022

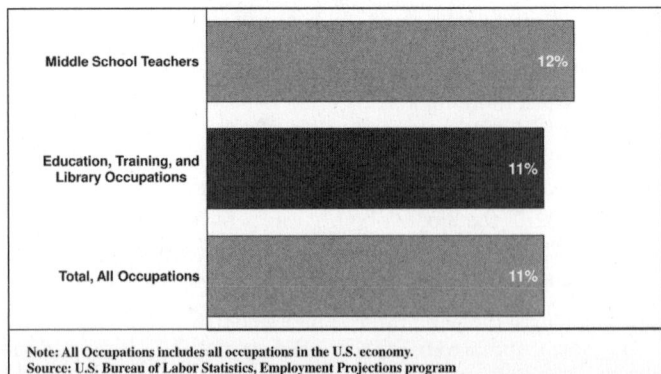

Middle School Teachers	12%
Education, Training, and Library Occupations	11%
Total, All Occupations	11%

Note: All Occupations includes all occupations in the U.S. economy.
Source: U.S. Bureau of Labor Statistics, Employment Projections program

Employment Projections Data for Middle School Teachers

Occupational title	SOC Code	Employment, 2012	Projected Employment, 2022	Change, 2012–2022	
				Percent	Numeric
Middle school teachers, except special and career/technical education 25-2022		614,400	690,400	12	76,000

Source: U.S. Bureau of Labor Statistics, Employment Projections Program

Note: Data are rounded. Go to **Occupational Information Included in the OOH** *for a discussion of the data in this table.*

Seeing students develop new skills and gain an appreciation for knowledge and learning can be very rewarding. However, teaching may be stressful. Some schools have large classes and lack important teaching tools, such as computers and current textbooks. Most teachers are held accountable for their students' performance on standardized tests, which can be frustrating. Occasionally, teachers must cope with unmotivated or disrespectful students.

Work Schedules. Middle school teachers generally work school hours when students are present. They may meet with parents, students, and other teachers before and after school. Teachers who coach sports or advise clubs generally do so before or after school. Teachers often spend time in the evenings and on weekends grading papers and preparing lessons.

Many work the traditional 10-month school year, with a 2-month break during the summer. Some teachers teach summer programs. Teachers in districts with a year-round schedule typically work 8 weeks in a row, are on break for 1 week before starting a new school session, and have a 5-week midwinter break.

How to Become One

Middle school teachers must have a bachelor's degree. In addition, public school teachers must have a state-issued certification or license.

Education. All states require public middle school teachers to have at least a bachelor's degree. Many states require middle school teachers to major in a content area, such as math or science. Other states require middle school teachers to major in elementary education. Those who major in a content area typically enroll in their university's teacher preparation program and take classes in education and child psychology in addition to the classes required by their major.

Teacher education programs teach prospective middle school teachers how to present information to students and how to work with students of varying abilities and backgrounds. Programs typically include fieldwork such as student teaching. For information about teacher preparation programs in your state, visit Teach.org.

Some states require middle school teachers to earn a master's degree after receiving their teaching certification.

Teachers in private schools do not need to meet state requirements. However, private schools typically seek middle school teachers who have a bachelor's degree and a major in elementary education or a content area.

Licenses, Certifications, and Registrations. All states require teachers in public schools to be licensed or certified. Those who teach in private schools are not usually required to be licensed.

Certification of middle school teachers varies considerably from state to state. In some states, they are certified to teach elementary school grades, which are typically first through sixth grades or first through eighth grades. In other states, they are certified to teach middle school grades, which include sixth through eighth grades. Still other states provide middle school teachers with a secondary school or high school certification, which often includes seventh through twelfth grades.

Requirements for certification also vary by state. However, all states require teachers to have at least a bachelor's degree. They also require completing a teacher preparation program and supervised experience in teaching, which is typically gained through student teaching. Some states require a minimum grade point average. States typically require candidates to pass a general teaching certification test, as well as a test that demonstrates their knowledge of the subject they will teach. For information on certification requirements in your state, visit Teach.org.

Similar Occupations   This table shows a list of occupations with job duties that are similar to those of middle school teachers.

Occupations	Entry-level Education	2012 Pay	Projected Job Growth	Average Annual Openings
Childcare Workers	High school diploma or equivalent	$19,510	14%	57,000
Elementary, Middle, and High School Principals	Master's degree	$87,760	6%	7,470
High School Teachers	Bachelor's degree	$55,050	6%	31,260
Instructional Coordinators	Master's degree	$60,050	13%	3,110
Librarians	Master's degree	$55,370	7%	4,440
Postsecondary Teachers	See "How to Become One"	$70,380	19%	42,690
Preschool Teachers	Associate's degree	$27,130	17%	19,940
School and Career Counselors	Master's degree	$53,610	12%	8,700
Social Workers	See "How to Become One"	$44,541	19%	24,280
Special Education Teachers	Bachelor's degree	$55,068	6%	10,220
Teacher Assistants	Some college, no degree	$23,640	9%	38,260

Teachers are often required to complete annual professional development classes to keep their license. Most states require teachers to pass a background check, and some states require teachers to complete a master's degree after receiving their certification.

All states offer an alternative route to certification for people who already have a bachelor's degree but lack the education courses required for certification. Some alternative certification programs allow candidates to begin teaching immediately after graduation, under the supervision of an experienced teacher. These programs cover teaching methods and child development. After they complete the program, candidates are awarded full certification.

Other programs require students to take classes in education before they can teach. Students may be awarded a master's degree after completing either of these programs. For more information about alternative certification programs, visit Teach-Now.

Training. In order to receive certification, teachers need to perform fieldwork, commonly referred to as student teaching. During student teaching, they work with a mentor teacher and get experience teaching students in a classroom setting. The amount of time required varies by state.

Important Qualities

Communication skills. Teachers must collaborate with other teachers and special education teachers. In addition, they need to discuss students' needs with parents and administrators.

Patience. Working with students of different abilities and backgrounds can be difficult. Middle school teachers must be patient when students struggle with material.

Resourcefulness. Middle school teachers need to be able to explain difficult concepts in terms that students can understand. In addition, they need to be able to get students engaged in learning and adapt lessons to each student's needs.

Advancement. Experienced teachers can advance to serve as mentors to newer teachers or to become lead teachers. In these positions, they help less experienced teachers to improve their teaching skills.

With additional education or certification, teachers may become school counselors, school librarians, or instructional coordinators. Some become assistant principals or principals, both of which generally require additional education in education administration or leadership. For more information, see the profiles on school and career counselors, librarians, instructional coordinators, and elementary, middle, and high school principals.

Pay

The median annual wage for middle school teachers was $53,430 in May 2012. The median wage is the wage at which half the workers in an occupation earned more than that amount and half earned less. The lowest 10 percent earned less than $36,740, and the top 10 percent earned more than $82,190.

Union Membership. Compared with workers in all occupations, middle school teachers had a higher percentage of workers who belonged to a union in 2012.

Job Outlook

Employment of middle school teachers is projected to grow 12 percent from 2012 to 2022, about as fast as the average for all occupations. Growth is projected due to expected increases in enrollment combined with declines in student–teacher ratios. However, employment growth will vary by region.

From 2012 to 2022, the student–teacher ratio across schools is expected to decline slightly. This ratio is the number of students for each teacher in the school. A decline in the ratio means that each teacher is responsible for fewer students, and, consequently, more teachers are needed to teach the same number of students.

In addition, the number of students in middle schools is expected to increase over the coming decade, and the number of classes needed to accommodate these students is projected to rise also. As a result, more teachers will be required to teach the additional classes of middle school students.

Although overall student enrollment is expected to grow, there will be some variation by region. Enrollment is expected to grow fastest in the South and West. In the Midwest, enrollment is projected to hold steady; the Northeast is projected to have declines. As a result, employment growth for middle school teachers is expected to be greater in the South and West than in the Midwest and Northeast.

Despite expected increases in enrollment, employment growth for middle school teachers will depend on state and local government budgets. When state and local governments experience budget deficits, they may lay off employees, including teachers. As a result, employment growth of middle school teachers may be somewhat reduced by state and local government budget difficulties.

Job Prospects. From 2012 to 2022, a significant number of older teachers are expected to reach retirement age. Their retirement will create job openings for new teachers. The short supply of teachers of English as a Second Language (ESL) and special education teachers will further result in job opportunities.

Middle school teachers with education or certifications to teach these specialties should have better job opportunities.

However, there is wide variation of job opportunities by region. Some regions of the country, such as the Northwest, are experiencing a surplus of teachers. Other regions, such as the Southeast, are experiencing a shortage. Furthermore, opportunities may be better in urban and rural school districts than in suburban school districts.

O*NET

➤ Middle School Teachers, Except Special and Career/Technical Education (25-2022.00)

Contacts for More Information

For more information about teaching and becoming a teacher, visit
➤ Teach.org (www.teach.org/)
➤ American Federation of Teachers (www.aft.org/)
➤ National Education Association (www.nea.org/)
    For more information about teacher preparation programs, visit
➤ Council for the Accreditation of Educator Preparation (www.caepsite.org/)
    For more information about alternative certification programs, visit
➤ Teach-Now (http://teach-now.com/)

Postsecondary Teachers

- **2012 Median Pay** .... $68,970 per year
- **Entry-Level Education** ....See "How to Become One"
- **Work Experience in a Related Occupation**.... See "How to Become One"
- **On-the-Job Training** .... None
- **Number of Jobs 2012** 1,267,700
- **Job Outlook, 2012–22** .... 19% (Faster than average)
- **Employment Change, 2012–22** 236,400

Professors and other postsecondary teachers instruct students in the theory and practice of a variety of subjects.

What Postsecondary Teachers Do

Postsecondary teachers instruct students in a wide variety of academic and vocational subjects beyond the high school level. They also conduct research and publish scholarly papers and books.

Duties. Postsecondary teachers typically do the following:

- Teach courses in their subject area
- Work with students who are studying for a degree or a certificate or certification or are taking classes to improve their knowledge or career skills
- Develop an instructional plan (known as a course outline or syllabus) for the course(s) they teach and ensure that it meets college and department standards
- Plan lessons and assignments
- Work with colleagues to develop or modify the curriculum for a degree or certificate program involving a series of courses
- Assess students' progress by grading papers, tests, and other work
- Advise students about which classes to take and how to achieve their goals
- Stay informed about changes and innovations in their field
- Conduct research and experiments to advance knowledge in their field
- Supervise graduate students who are working toward doctoral degrees

- Publish original research and analysis in books and academic journals
- Serve on academic and administrative committees that review and recommend policies, make budget decisions, or advise on hiring and promotions within their department

Professors and other postsecondary teachers specialize in any of a wide variety of subjects and fields. Some teach academic subjects, such as English or philosophy. Others focus on career-related subjects, such as law, nursing, or culinary arts.

Postsecondary teachers work for different types of institutions, and their job duties vary with the kind of organization they work for.

Some postsecondary teachers are professors who work for large universities. In this setting, they often spend a large portion of their time conducting research or experiments and applying for grants to fund their research. Frequently, they spend less time teaching. Classes may be taught by graduate teaching assistants, who are supervised by a professor.

At colleges and universities, professors (together called the "faculty" of the school) are organized into departments based on the subject matter of their specialty, such as English, physics, Spanish, or music. They may teach one or more courses within that department, such as a mathematics professor teaching calculus, statistics, and a graduate seminar in a very specific area of mathematics.

Professors may teach large classes of several hundred students (often with the help of graduate teaching assistants), smaller classes of about 40 to 50 students, seminars with just a few students, or laboratories where students practice the subject matter. They work with an increasingly varied student population as more part-time, older, and culturally diverse students are going to postsecondary schools.

Professors keep up with developments in their field by reading scholarly articles, talking with colleagues, and participating in professional conferences. To gain tenure (a guarantee that a professor cannot be fired without just cause), they must do original research, such as experiments, document analysis, or critical reviews, and publish their findings.

Other postsecondary teachers work in smaller colleges and universities or in community colleges. Postsecondary teachers in this setting often spend more time teaching classes and working with students. They may spend some time conducting research, but they are not given as much time to devote to it.

Some postsecondary teachers work for online universities or teach online classes. They use websites to present lessons and information and to assign and accept students' work. They communicate with students by email and by phone and may never meet their students in person.

Median Annual Wages, May 2012

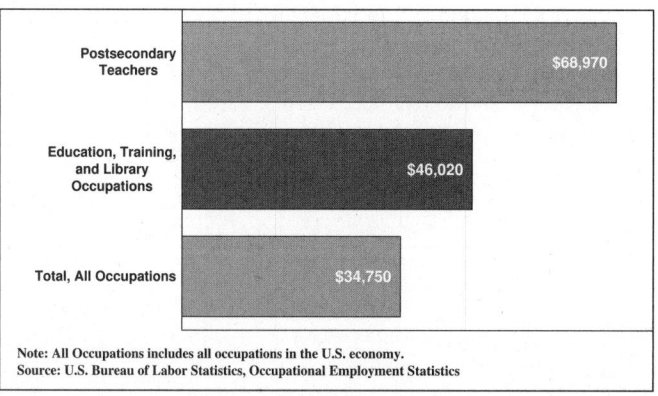

Note: All Occupations includes all occupations in the U.S. economy.
Source: U.S. Bureau of Labor Statistics, Occupational Employment Statistics

Percent Change in Employment, Projected 2012–2022

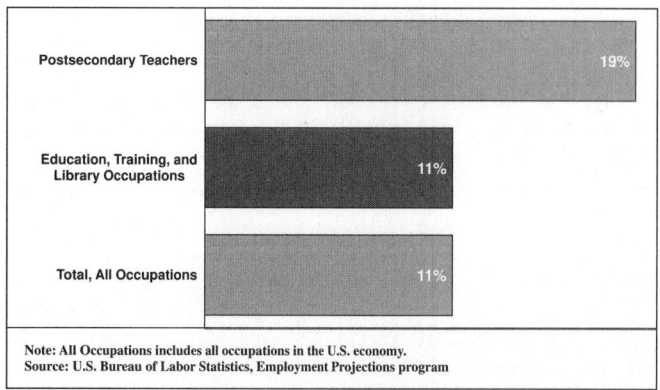

Note: All Occupations includes all occupations in the U.S. economy.
Source: U.S. Bureau of Labor Statistics, Employment Projections program

Employment Projections Data for Postsecondary Teachers

Occupational title	SOC Code	Employment, 2012	Projected Employment, 2022	Change, 2012–2022	
				Percent	Numeric
Postsecondary teachers...	—	1,267,700	1,504,200	19	236,400
Business teachers, postsecondary	25-1011	103,400	118,500	15	15,200
Computer science teachers, postsecondary	25-1021	41,700	47,000	13	5,300
Mathematical science teachers, postsecondary	25-1022	63,300	70,600	11	7,300
Architecture teachers, postsecondary	25-1031	9,100	10,400	14	1,300
Engineering teachers, postsecondary	25-1032	42,500	47,500	12	5,000
Agricultural sciences teachers, postsecondary	25-1041	12,800	13,900	8	1,000
Biological science teachers, postsecondary	25-1042	61,400	73,400	19	12,000
Forestry and conservation science teachers, postsecondary	25-1043	3,100	3,400	10	300
Atmospheric, earth, marine, and space sciences teachers, postsecondary	25-1051	13,200	14,700	11	1,500
Chemistry teachers, postsecondary	25-1052	25,300	28,800	14	3,500
Environmental science teachers, postsecondary	25-1053	6,300	7,100	13	800
Physics teachers, postsecondary..	25-1054	17,400	19,800	14	2,400
Anthropology and archeology teachers, postsecondary	25-1061	7,000	7,900	12	900
Area, ethnic, and cultural studies teachers, postsecondary ...	25-1062	12,400	14,300	16	1,900
Economics teachers, postsecondary....................................	25-1063	16,800	19,200	14	2,400
Geography teachers, postsecondary	25-1064	5,500	6,100	11	600
Political science teachers, postsecondary...........................	25-1065	21,100	24,100	15	3,100
Psychology teachers, postsecondary....................................	25-1066	47,500	54,200	14	6,800
Sociology teachers, postsecondary.....................................	25-1067	20,600	23,300	13	2,600
Social sciences teachers, postsecondary, all other	25-1069	12,400	14,100	13	1,700
Health specialties teachers, postsecondary	25-1071	190,000	258,600	36	68,600
Nursing instructors and teachers, postsecondary	25-1072	67,800	91,800	35	24,000
Education teachers, postsecondary....................................	25-1081	79,300	90,900	15	11,600
Library science teachers, postsecondary...........................	25-1082	5,500	6,100	11	600
Criminal justice and law enforcement teachers, postsecondary	25-1111	16,400	18,500	13	2,100
Law teachers, postsecondary	25-1112	20,000	23,500	18	3,500
Social work teachers, postsecondary	25-1113	12,400	14,000	13	1,600
Art, drama, and music teachers, postsecondary.................	25-1121	114,300	132,600	16	18,300
Communications teachers, postsecondary	25-1122	36,500	41,200	13	4,700
English language and literature teachers, postsecondary	25-1123	86,800	97,400	12	10,600
Foreign language and literature teachers, postsecondary	25-1124	35,800	41,200	15	5,500
History teachers, postsecondary	25-1125	29,200	33,100	14	4,000
Philosophy and religion teachers, postsecondary	25-1126	30,800	36,700	19	6,000

Source: U.S. Bureau of Labor Statistics, Employment Projections Program

Note: Data are rounded. Go to Occupational Information Included in the OOH *for a discussion of the data in this table.*

The amount of time postsecondary teachers spend teaching, serving on committees, and doing research also varies with their position in the university or college. Full-time professors, particularly those who have tenure, often are expected to spend more time on their research. They also may be expected to serve on more college and university committees. Part-time professors, often known as *adjunct professors*, spend most of their time teaching students.

Graduate teaching assistants, often referred to as *graduate TAs*, assist faculty by teaching or assisting with classes while earning a graduate degree as a student. Some teaching assistants have full responsibility for teaching a course. Others help faculty members by grading papers, monitoring exams and quizzes, holding help sessions for students, and conducting laboratory sessions. Graduate teaching assistants may work one-on-one with a faculty member, or, in large classes, they may be one of several assistants.

Work Environment

Postsecondary teachers held about 1.3 million jobs in 2012.

In 2012, about 75 percent of postsecondary teachers worked for colleges, universities, and professional schools and about 21 percent worked for junior colleges. Much smaller percentages of postsecondary teachers worked in industries such as technical and trade schools, business schools and computer and management training facilities, and hospitals.

Many postsecondary teachers find their jobs rewarding because they are surrounded by others who enjoy their subject. The opportunity to share their expertise with others also is appealing to many.

However, some postsecondary teachers must find a balance between teaching students and doing research and publishing their findings. This can be stressful, especially for beginning teachers seeking advancement in 4-year research universities. At the two-year college level, the balance is struck mainly between teaching students and administrative duties.

Similar to college and university professors, graduate teaching assistants usually have flexibility in their work schedules, but they also must devote time to their own academic coursework and studies. Work may be stressful, particularly when assistants have full responsibility for teaching a class.

Classes are generally held during the day, although some are offered in the evenings and weekends to accommodate students who have jobs or family obligations.

Similar Occupations   This table shows a list of occupations with job duties that are similar to those of postsecondary teachers.

Occupations	Entry-level Education	2012 Pay	Projected Job Growth	Average Annual Openings
Anthropologists and Archeologists	Master's degree	$57,420	19%	260
Biochemists and Biophysicists	Doctoral or professional degree	$81,480	18%	1,370
Chemists and Materials Scientists	Bachelor's degree	$73,247	6%	3,040
Economists	Master's degree	$91,860	14%	740
Geographers	Bachelor's degree	$74,760	29%	80
Historians	Master's degree	$52,480	5%	80
Microbiologists	Bachelor's degree	$66,260	7%	710
Political Scientists	Master's degree	$102,000	21%	250
Postsecondary Education Administrators	Master's degree	$86,490	15%	6,650
Sociologists	Master's degree	$74,960	15%	110
Zoologists and Wildlife Biologists	Bachelor's degree	$57,710	5%	670

Many postsecondary teachers do not teach classes in the summer; they often use that time to conduct research, involve themselves in professional development, or to travel. Other postsecondary teachers teach summer courses.

Work Schedules. Postsecondary teachers' schedules generally are flexible. Postsecondary teachers need to be on campus to teach classes and keep office hours. Otherwise, they are free to set their schedule and decide when and where they will prepare for class and will grade assignments. However, all postsecondary teachers typically spend some time, outside of their teaching and student advising duties, in carrying out administrative responsibilities such as serving on committees.

Many postsecondary teachers work part time. Some postsecondary teachers work part time at several colleges or universities.

Most graduate teaching assistants work part time while also studying for their degree. The number of hours they work may vary, depending on the institution and their particular assistantship.

How to Become One

Educational requirements vary with the subject taught and the type of educational institution. Most commonly, postsecondary teachers must have a Ph.D. However, a master's degree may be enough for some postsecondary teachers at community colleges. In technical and trade schools, work experience may be important for getting a postsecondary teaching job.

Education. Postsecondary teachers who work for 4-year colleges and universities are most often required to have a doctoral degree in their field. However, some schools may hire those who have a master's degree or those who are doctoral degree candidates for some specialties, such as fine arts, or for some part-time positions.

Doctoral programs generally take multiple years after the completion of a bachelor's degree program. Included is time spent completing a master's degree and then writing a doctoral dissertation, which is a paper presenting original research in the student's field of study. Candidates usually specialize in a subfield, such as organic chemistry or European history.

Two-year colleges or career and technical schools also may hire those with a master's degree. However, in some fields, there are more applicants than available positions. In these situations, institutions can be more selective, and they frequently choose applicants who have a Ph.D. over those with only a master's degree.

Postsecondary teachers who teach career and technical education courses, such as culinary arts or cosmetology, may not be required to have graduate-level education. At a minimum they must hold the degree of the program in which they are teaching e.g. having an associate degree if they teach a program that is at the associate degree level. In addition, work experience or certification may be just as important for getting a postsecondary teaching job at a technical and trade schools.

Other Experience. Although many prospective professors may have teaching or other work experience, in most cases this work experience is not required.

Some institutions may prefer to hire professors who have teaching or other work experience, but this is not a requirement for all fields or for all employers. For health specialties or art fields, hands-on work experience in the industry can be important. These professors often gain experience by working in an occupation related to their field of expertise.

In fields such as biological science, physics, and chemistry, some postsecondary teachers have postdoctoral research experience. These short-term jobs, sometimes called "post-docs," usually involve working for 2 to 3 years as a research associate or in a similar position, often at a college or university.

Some prospective professors gain teaching experience by working as graduate teaching assistants–students who are enrolled in a graduate program and teach classes in the institution where they are enrolled.

Some postsecondary teachers, especially adjunct professors, have jobs in other settings, such as government agencies, private businesses, or nonprofit organizations, in addition to teaching.

Licenses, Certifications, and Registrations. Postsecondary teachers who prepare students for an occupation that requires a license, certification, or registration, may need to have–or they may benefit from having–the same credential. Postsecondary nursing teachers, for example, might need a nursing license. And postsecondary education teachers might need a teaching license, often referred to as teacher certification.

Advancement. For postsecondary teachers, a major goal in the traditional academic career is attaining tenure–a guarantee that a professor cannot be fired without just cause. Tenure can take up to 7 years of moving up the ranks in tenure-track positions. The ranks are assistant professor, associate professor, and professor.

Tenure is granted through a review of the candidate's research, contribution to the institution, and teaching. However, institutions are relying more heavily on limited-term and part-time faculty contracts, so tenured positions and positions on a "tenure track" are declining.

Some tenured professors advance to administrative positions, such as dean or president. For information on deans and other administrative positions, see the profile on postsecondary education administrators. For more information about college and university presidents, see the profile on top executives.

Important Qualities

Communication skills. Postsecondary teachers need to write papers, give lectures, and serve on committees. To do so effectively, they need good communication skills.

Critical-thinking skills. To challenge established theories and beliefs, conduct original research, and design experiments, postsecondary teachers need good critical-thinking skills.

Resourcefulness. Postsecondary teachers need to be able to present information in a way that students will understand. They need to adapt to the different learning styles of their students and teach students who have little or no experience with the subject.

Writing skills. Most professors publish original research and analysis. Consequently, they need to be skilled writers.

Pay

The median annual wage for postsecondary teachers was $68,970 in May 2012. The median wage is the wage at which half the workers in an occupation earned more than that amount and half earned less. The lowest 10 percent earned less than $35,670, and the top 10 percent earned more than $142,270.

Median annual wages for postsecondary teachers in May 2012 were as follows:

law teachers, postsecondary $99,950
engineering teachers, postsecondary 92,670
economics teachers, postsecondary 87,950
atmospheric, earth, marine, and space sciences teachers,
    postsecondary 82,180
forestry and conservation science teachers,
    postsecondary 81,930
health specialties teachers, postsecondary 81,140
agricultural sciences teachers, postsecondary 80,490
physics teachers, postsecondary 78,540
environmental science teachers, postsecondary 77,320
anthropology and archeology teachers, postsecondary 76,020
biological science teachers, postsecondary 74,180
business teachers, postsecondary 73,660
computer science teachers, postsecondary 72,200
political science teachers, postsecondary 72,170
architecture teachers, postsecondary 71,610
chemistry teachers, postsecondary 71,140
social sciences teachers, postsecondary, all other 69,890
psychology teachers, postsecondary 68,020
geography teachers, postsecondary 67,820
area, ethnic, and cultural studies teachers, postsecondary 67,360
sociology teachers, postsecondary 66,150
history teachers, postsecondary 65,870
library science teachers, postsecondary 65,780
mathematical science teachers, postsecondary 64,990
philosophy and religion teachers, postsecondary 64,990
nursing instructors and teachers, postsecondary 64,850
social work teachers, postsecondary 63,250
communications teachers, postsecondary 62,180
art, drama, and music teachers, postsecondary 62,160
English language and literature teachers, postsecondary 60,040
education teachers, postsecondary 59,350
foreign language and literature teachers, postsecondary 58,670

criminal justice and law enforcement teachers,
    postsecondary 58,040

Wages can vary by institution type. Postsecondary teachers typically have higher wages in colleges, universities, and professional schools than they do in community colleges or other types of schools.

Job Outlook

Employment of postsecondary teachers is projected to grow 19 percent from 2012 to 2022, faster than the average for all occupations. Both part-time and full-time postsecondary teachers are included in this projection.

Growth is expected as enrollments at postsecondary institutions continue to rise, although at slower rates than they have in the past.

The number of people attending postsecondary institutions is projected to grow from 2012 to 2022. These students will seek higher education to gain the additional education and skills they need to meet their career goals. As more people enter colleges and universities, more postsecondary teachers will be needed to serve these additional students.

However, despite expected increases in enrollment, employment growth in public colleges and universities will depend in part on funding. If governments spend more on funding higher education and research, additional postsecondary teachers may be hired.

For-profit institutions are expected to have slower employment growth than they have in the past as enrollments slow and these types of schools face greater public scrutiny.

Although overall employment of postsecondary teachers is projected to increase, it will vary by field. Nursing instructors and teachers and health specialties teachers, for example, are projected to grow much faster than the average, while history teachers and sociology teachers are projected to grow about as fast as the average. As an aging population increasingly demands healthcare services, many additional postsecondary teachers are expected to be needed to help educate the workers who will provide these services.

In all fields, many of the new jobs will likely be for part-time or non-tenure-track faculty.

Job Prospects. Competition for tenure-track positions is expected to be high, as colleges and universities continue to move away from these positions and toward adjunct and part-time positions. Opportunities are expected to be good for part-time or adjunct professors.

Retirements of postsecondary teachers will create some opportunities for new workers entering the field. However, not all of these job openings will necessarily be full time or tenure–track positions.

Some fields, such as health specialties and nursing, will likely experience better job prospects than others, such as those in the humanities.

O*NET

➤ Business Teachers, Postsecondary (25-1011.00)
➤ Computer Science Teachers, Postsecondary (25-1021.00)
➤ Mathematical Science Teachers, Postsecondary (25-1022.00)
➤ Architecture Teachers, Postsecondary (25-1031.00)
➤ Engineering Teachers, Postsecondary (25-1032.00)
➤ Agricultural Sciences Teachers, Postsecondary (25-1041.00)
➤ Biological Science Teachers, Postsecondary (25-1042.00)
➤ Forestry and Conservation Science Teachers, Postsecondary (25-1043.00)
➤ Atmospheric, Earth, Marine, and Space Sciences Teachers, Postsecondary (25-1051.00)

- ➤ Chemistry Teachers, Postsecondary (25-1052.00)
- ➤ Environmental Science Teachers, Postsecondary (25-1053.00)
- ➤ Physics Teachers, Postsecondary (25-1054.00)
- ➤ Anthropology and Archeology Teachers, Postsecondary (25-1061.00)
- ➤ Area, Ethnic, and Cultural Studies Teachers, Postsecondary (25-1062.00)
- ➤ Economics Teachers, Postsecondary (25-1063.00)
- ➤ Geography Teachers, Postsecondary (25-1064.00)
- ➤ Political Science Teachers, Postsecondary (25-1065.00)
- ➤ Psychology Teachers, Postsecondary (25-1066.00)
- ➤ Sociology Teachers, Postsecondary (25-1067.00)
- ➤ Social Sciences Teachers, Postsecondary, All Other (25-1069.00)
- ➤ Health Specialties Teachers, Postsecondary (25-1071.00)
- ➤ Nursing Instructors and Teachers, Postsecondary (25-1072.00)
- ➤ Education Teachers, Postsecondary (25-1081.00)
- ➤ Library Science Teachers, Postsecondary (25-1082.00)
- ➤ Criminal Justice and Law Enforcement Teachers, Postsecondary (25-1111.00)
- ➤ Law Teachers, Postsecondary (25-1112.00)
- ➤ Social Work Teachers, Postsecondary (25-1113.00)
- ➤ Art, Drama, and Music Teachers, Postsecondary (25-1121.00)
- ➤ Communications Teachers, Postsecondary (25-1122.00)
- ➤ English Language and Literature Teachers, Postsecondary (25-1123.00)
- ➤ Foreign Language and Literature Teachers, Postsecondary (25-1124.00)
- ➤ History Teachers, Postsecondary (25-1125.00)
- ➤ Philosophy and Religion Teachers, Postsecondary (25-1126.00)

Contacts for More Information

For more information about postsecondary teachers, visit
- ➤ Council of Graduate Schools (www.cgsnet.org/)
- ➤ Association for Career and Technical Education (www.acteonline.org/)

Preschool Teachers

- **2012 Median Pay** .... $27,130 per year
  $13.04 per hour
- **Entry-Level Education** .... Associate's degree
- **Work Experience in a Related Occupation** .... None
- **On-the-Job Training** .... None
- **Number of Jobs 2012** 438,200
- **Job Outlook, 2012–22** .... 17% (Faster than average)
- **Employment Change, 2012–22** 76,400

What Preschool Teachers Do

Preschool teachers educate and care for children, usually ages 3 to 5, who have not yet entered kindergarten. They teach reading, writing, science, and other subjects in a way that young children can understand.

Duties. Preschool teachers typically do the following:

- Prepare children for kindergarten by introducing concepts they will explore further in kindergarten and elementary school
- Work with children in groups or one on one, depending on the needs of children and the subject matter
- Plan and carry out a curriculum that targets different areas of child development, such as language, motor, and social skills
- Organize activities so children can learn about the world, explore interests, and develop talents

- Develop schedules and routines to ensure children have enough physical activity, rest, and playtime
- Watch for signs of emotional or developmental problems in children and bring problems to the attention of parents
- Keep records of the students' progress, routines, and interests, and keep parents informed about their child's development

Young children learn from playing, problem solving, questioning, and experimenting. Preschool teachers use play and other instructional techniques to teach children about the world. For example, they use storytelling and rhyming games to teach language and vocabulary. They may help improve children's social skills by having them work together to build a neighborhood in a sandbox or teach math by having children count when building with blocks.

Preschool teachers work with children from different ethnic, racial, and religious backgrounds. Teachers include topics in their lessons to teach children to respect people of different backgrounds and cultures.

Work Environment

Preschool teachers held about 438,200 jobs in 2012.

Many preschool teachers work in public and private schools or in formal childcare centers that have preschool classrooms. Others work for charitable or religious organizations that have preschool programs or Head Start programs. Head Start programs receive federal funding for disadvantaged children between the ages of 3 and 5.

The industries that employed the most preschool teachers in 2012 were as follows:

Child day care services.. 54%
Religious, grantmaking, civic, professional, and similar
  organizations... 21
Elementary and secondary schools; state, local, and private... 16
Individual and family services.. 3

Seeing children develop new skills and gain an appreciation of knowledge and learning can be very rewarding. However, it can also be tiring to work with young, active children all day.

Work Schedules. Preschool teachers in public schools generally work during school hours. Many work the traditional 10-month school year, which includes a 2-month break during the summer. Some preschool teachers may teach in summer programs. Teachers

Preschool teachers use play to teach children about the world.

Median Annual Wages, May 2012

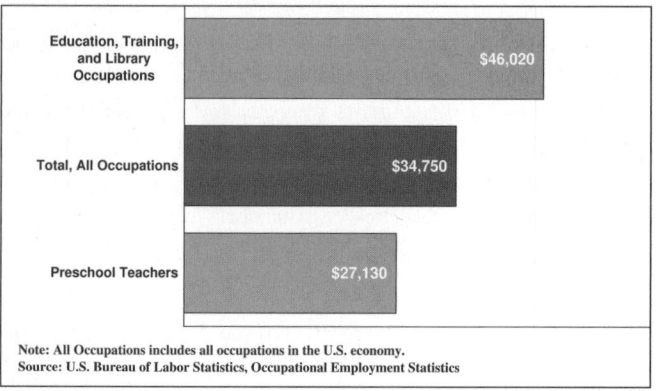

Note: All Occupations includes all occupations in the U.S. economy.
Source: U.S. Bureau of Labor Statistics, Occupational Employment Statistics

Percent Change in Employment, Projected 2012–2022

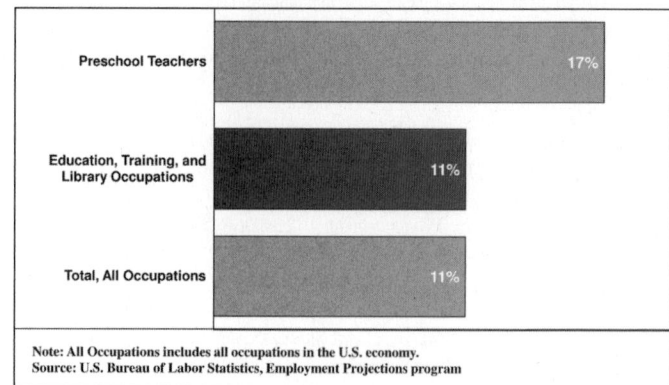

Note: All Occupations includes all occupations in the U.S. economy.
Source: U.S. Bureau of Labor Statistics, Employment Projections program

in districts with a year-round schedule typically work 8 weeks in a row then have a break for 1 week before starting a new school session. They also have a 5-week midwinter break. Those working in day care settings may work longer hours and often work the whole year.

How to Become One

Education and training requirements vary based on settings and state regulations. They range from a high school diploma and certification to a college degree.

Education. In childcare centers, preschool teachers generally are required to have a least a high school diploma and a certification in early childhood education. However, employers may prefer to hire workers with at least some postsecondary education in early childhood education.

Preschool teachers in Head Start programs are required to have at least an associate's degree. However, at least 50 percent of all preschool teachers in Head Start programs nationwide must have a bachelor's degree in early childhood education or a related field. Those with a degree in a related field must have experience teaching preschool-age children.

In public schools, preschool teachers are generally required to have at least a bachelor's degree in early childhood education or a related field. Bachelor's degree programs teach students about children's development, strategies to teach young children, and how to observe and document children's progress.

Licenses, Certifications, and Registrations. Many states require childcare centers, including those in private homes, to be licensed. To qualify for licensure, staff must pass a background check, have a complete record of immunizations, and meet a minimum training requirement. Some states require staff to have certifications in CPR and first aid.

Some states and employers require childcare workers to have a nationally recognized certification. Most often, states require the Child Development Associate (CDA) certification offered by the Council for Professional Recognition. Obtaining the CDA certification requires coursework, experience in the field, a written exam, and observation of the candidate working with children.

Some states recognize the Child Care Professional (CCP) designation offered by the National Early Childhood Program Accreditation. Candidates for the CCP must be 18 years old, have a high school diploma, experience in the field, take courses in early childhood education, and pass an exam.

In public schools, preschool teachers must be licensed to teach early childhood education, which covers preschool through third

Employment Projections Data for Preschool Teachers

Occupational title	SOC Code	Employment, 2012	Projected Employment, 2022	Change, 2012–2022 Percent	Change, 2012–2022 Numeric
Preschool teachers, except special education 25-2011		438,200	514,600	17	76,400

Source: U.S. Bureau of Labor Statistics, Employment Projections Program

Note: Data are rounded. Go to **Occupational Information Included in the OOH** *for a discussion of the data in this table.*

Similar Occupations   This table shows a list of occupations with job duties that are similar to those of preschool teachers.

Occupations	Entry-level Education	2012 Pay	Projected Job Growth	Average Annual Openings
Childcare Workers	High school diploma or equivalent	$19,510	14%	57,000
High School Teachers	Bachelor's degree	$55,050	6%	31,260
Kindergarten and Elementary School Teachers	Bachelor's degree	$53,060	12%	53,250
Middle School Teachers	Bachelor's degree	$53,430	12%	21,120
Preschool and Childcare Center Directors	Bachelor's degree	$43,950	17%	2,780
Special Education Teachers	Bachelor's degree	$55,068	6%	10,220
Teacher Assistants	Some college, no degree	$23,640	9%	38,260

grade. Requirements vary by state, but they generally require a bachelor's degree and passing an exam to demonstrate competency. Most states require teachers to complete continuing education credits to maintain their license.

Other Experience. A few states require preschool teachers to have some work experience in a childcare setting. The amount of experience necessary varies by state. In these cases, preschool teachers often start out as childcare workers or teacher assistants.

Important Qualities

Communication skills. Preschool teachers need good communication skills to tell parents and colleagues about students' progress. They need good writing and speaking skills to convey this information effectively. They must also be able to communicate well with small children.

Creativity. Preschool teachers must plan lessons that engage young students. In addition, they need to adapt their lessons to suit different learning styles.

Interpersonal skills. Preschool teachers must understand children's emotional needs and be able to develop good relationships with parents, children, and colleagues.

Organizational skills. Teachers need to be organized to plan lessons and keep records of their students.

Patience. Working with children can be frustrating, and preschool teachers should be able to respond calmly to overwhelming and difficult situations.

Physical stamina. Working with children can be physically taxing, so preschool teachers should have a lot of energy.

Advancement. Experienced preschool teachers can advance to become the director of a preschool or childcare center or a lead teacher, who may be responsible for the instruction of several classes. Those with a bachelor's degree in early childhood education frequently are qualified to teach kindergarten through grade 3, in addition to preschool. Teaching positions at these higher grades typically pay more. For more information, see the profiles on preschool and childcare center directors and kindergarten and elementary school teachers.

Pay

The median annual wage for preschool teachers was $27,130 in May 2012. The median wage is the wage at which half the workers in an occupation earned more than that amount and half earned less. The lowest 10 percent earned less than $18,090, and the top 10 percent earned more than $48,660.

In May 2012, the median annual wages for preschool teachers in the top four industries in which these teachers worked were as follows:

Elementary and secondary schools; state, local, and private	$41,520
Individual and family services	28,390
Religious, grantmaking, civic, professional, and similar organizations	27,390
Child day care services	24,410

Job Outlook

Employment of preschool teachers is projected to grow 17 percent from 2012 to 2022, faster than the average for all occupations.

Early childhood education is important for a child's intellectual and social development. As a result, there has been increasing demand for preschool programs, which is expected to create demand for preschool teachers.

In addition, the population of children ages 3 to 5 is expected to increase. Because children between these ages are typically enrolled in preschool, the demand for preschool teachers increases when this population increases.

Job Prospects. Workers who have postsecondary education, particularly those with a bachelor's degree, should have better job prospects than those with less education. In addition, workers with the Child Development Associate (CDA) or Child Care Professional (CCP) credential should have better prospects than those without these certifications.

O*NET

➤ Preschool Teachers, Except Special Education (25-2011.00)

Contacts for More Information

For more information about early childhood education, visit
➤ National Association for the Education of Young Children (www. naeyc.org)

For more information about professional credentials, visit
➤ Council for Professional Recognition (www.cdacouncil.org/)
➤ National Child Care Association (www.nccanet.org/)

Special Education Teachers

- **2012 Median Pay** .... $55,060 per year
- **Entry-Level Education** ....Bachelor's degree
- **Work Experience in a Related Occupation** .... None
- **On-the-Job Training** .... Internship/residency
- **Number of Jobs 2012** 442,800
- **Job Outlook, 2012–22** .... 6% (Slower than average)
- **Employment Change, 2012–22** 26,600

What Special Education Teachers Do

Special education teachers work with students who have a wide range of learning, mental, emotional, and physical disabilities. They adapt general education lessons and teach various subjects, such as reading, writing, and math, to students with mild and moderate disabilities. They also teach basic skills, such as literacy and communication techniques, to students with severe disabilities.

Duties. Special education teachers typically do the following:

- Assess students' skills to determine their needs and to develop teaching plans
- Adapt lessons to meet the needs of students
- Develop Individualized Education Programs (IEPs) for each student
- Plan, organize, and assign activities that are specific to each student's abilities
- Teach and mentor students as a class, in small groups, and one-on-one
- Implement IEPs, assess students' performance, and track their progress
- Update IEPs throughout the school year to reflect students' progress and goals
- Discuss student's progress with parents, teachers, counselors, and administrators
- Supervise and mentor teacher assistants who work with students with disabilities
- Prepare and help students transition from grade to grade and after graduation

Special education teachers work as part of a team that typically includes general education teachers, counselors, school superintendents, and parents. As a team, they develop individualized educational programs (IEPs) specific to each student's needs. IEPs outline goals and services for each student, such as sessions with the school psychologists, counselors, and special education teachers. Teachers also meet with parents, school administrators, and counselors to discuss updates and changes to the IEPs.

Special education teachers' duties vary by the type of setting they work in, student disabilities, and teacher specialty.

Some special education teachers work in classrooms or resource centers that only include students with disabilities. In these settings, teachers plan, adapt, and present lessons to meet each student's needs. They teach students in small groups or on a one-on-one basis.

Students with disabilities may attend classes with general education students, also known as inclusive classrooms. In these settings, special education teachers may spend a portion of the day teaching classes together with general education teachers. They help present the information in a manner that students with disabilities can more easily understand. They also assist general education teachers to adapt lessons that will meet the needs of the students with disabilities in their classes.

Special education teachers also collaborate with teacher assistants, psychologists, and social workers, to accommodate requirements of students with disabilities. For example, they may show a teacher assistant how to work with a student who needs particular attention.

Special education teachers work with students who have a wide variety of mental, emotional, physical, and learning disabilities. For example, some work with students who need assistance in subject areas, such as reading and math. Others help students develop study skills, such as using flashcards and text highlighting.

Some special education teachers work with students who have physical and sensory disabilities, such as blindness and deafness, and with students who are wheelchair-bound. They may also work with those who have autism spectrum disorders and emotional disorders, such as anxiety and depression.

Special education teachers work with students from preschool to high school. Some teachers work with students who have severe disabilities until the students are 21 years old.

Special education teachers help students with severe disabilities develop basic life skills, such as how to respond to questions and how to follow directions. Some teach students with moderate disabilities the skills necessary to live independently to find a job, such as managing money and time. For more information about other workers who help individuals with disabilities develop skills

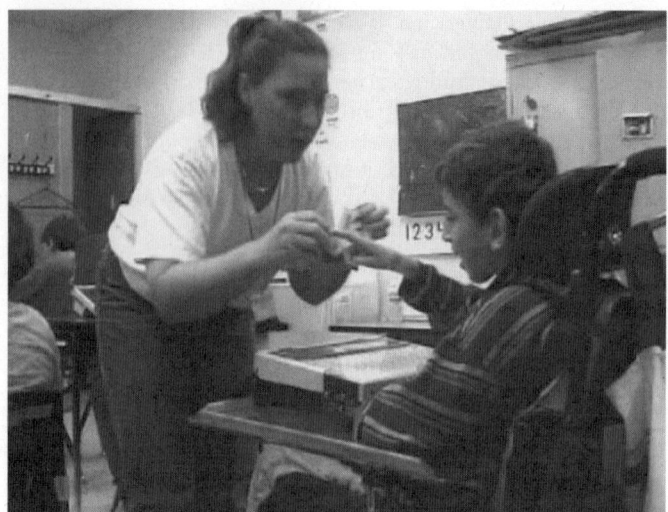

Special education teachers work with students who may have a wide range of learning, mental, emotional, and physical disabilities.

necessary to live independently, see the profiles on occupational therapists and occupational therapy assistants and aides.

Most special education teachers use computers to keep records of their students' performance, prepare lesson plans, and update IEPs. Some teachers also use various assistive technology aids, such as Braille writers and computer software that helps them communicate with students.

Work Environment

Special education teachers held about 442,800 jobs in 2012.

Most special education teachers work in public schools. Some teach in magnet, charter, and private schools. Some also work with young children in childcare centers.

A few work with students in residential facilities, hospitals, and students' homes. They may travel to these locations. Some teachers work with infants and toddlers at the child's home. They also teach the child's parents methods and ways to help the child develop skills.

Helping students with disabilities can be highly rewarding. It also can be quite stressful—emotionally demanding and physically draining.

Work Schedules. Special education teachers typically work during school hours. They also use that time to grade papers, update students' records, and prepare lessons. They may meet with parents, students, and other teachers before and after classes.

Median Annual Wages, May 2012

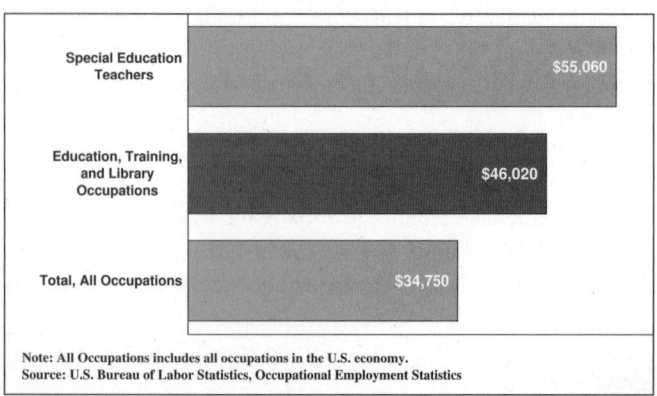

Special Education Teachers	$55,060
Education, Training, and Library Occupations	$46,020
Total, All Occupations	$34,750

Note: All Occupations includes all occupations in the U.S. economy.
Source: U.S. Bureau of Labor Statistics, Occupational Employment Statistics

Percent Change in Employment, Projected 2012–2022

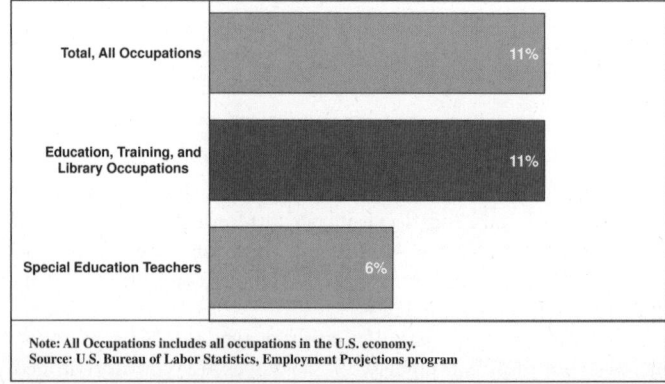

Total, All Occupations	11%
Education, Training, and Library Occupations	11%
Special Education Teachers	6%

Note: All Occupations includes all occupations in the U.S. economy.
Source: U.S. Bureau of Labor Statistics, Employment Projections program

Employment Projections Data for Special Education Teachers

Occupational title	SOC Code	Employment, 2012	Projected Employment, 2022	Change, 2012–2022	
				Percent	Numeric
Special education teachers	—	442,800	469,400	6	26,600
Special education teachers, preschool...............................	25-2051	22,300	25,900	16	3,600
Special education teachers, kindergarten and elementary school................................	25-2052	194,600	206,600	6	12,000
Special education teachers, middle school	25-2053	94,600	99,500	5	4,900
Special education teachers, secondary school	25-2054	131,300	137,400	5	6,100

Source: U.S. Bureau of Labor Statistics, Employment Projections Program

Note: Data are rounded. Go to Occupational Information Included in the OOH for a discussion of the data in this table.

Many work the traditional 10-month school year, with a 2-month break during the summer. Teachers in districts with a year-round schedule typically work 8 weeks in a row, are on break for 1 week, and have a 5-week midwinter break.

How to Become One

Special education teachers in public schools are required to have at least a bachelor's degree and a state-issued certification or license. Private schools typically require teachers to have a bachelor's degree, but teachers are not required to be licensed or certified. For information about teacher preparation programs and certification requirements, visit Teach.org–previously known as Teacher Education and Compensation Help, or contact your state's board of education.

Education. All states require special education teachers in public schools to have at least a bachelor's degree. Some of these teachers major in elementary education or a content area, such as math or chemistry, and minor in special education. Others complete a degree specifically in special education.

In a program leading to a bachelor's degree in special education, prospective teachers learn about the different types of disabilities and how to present information so that students will understand. These programs typically include fieldwork, such as student teaching. Some states require special education teachers to complete a master's degree in special education, to become fully certified.

Teachers in private schools do not need to meet state requirements. However, private schools may prefer to hire teachers who have at least a bachelor's degree in special education.

Licenses, Certifications, and Registrations. All states require teachers in public schools to be licensed. A license is frequently referred to as a certification. Those who teach in private schools are not required to be licensed.

Requirements for certification vary by state. However, all states require at least a bachelor's degree. They also require completing a teacher preparation program and supervised experience in teaching. Some states require a minimum grade point average. Most states require teachers to pass a background check. Teachers may be required to complete annual professional development classes or a master's degree to maintain their license.

Many states offer general licenses in special education that allow teachers to work with students with a variety of disabilities. Others offer licenses or endorsements based on a disability specific category, such as autism or behavior disorders.

Some states allow special education teachers to transfer their licenses from another state. Other states require even an experienced teacher to pass their state's licensing requirements.

All states offer an alternative route to certification for people who already have a bachelor's degree. Some alternative certification programs allow candidates to begin teaching immediately, under the close supervision of an experienced teacher.

Similar Occupations   This table shows a list of occupations with job duties that are similar to those of special education teachers.

Occupations	Entry-level Education	2012 Pay	Projected Job Growth	Average Annual Openings
Childcare Workers	High school diploma or equivalent	$19,510	14%	57,000
Elementary, Middle, and High School Principals	Master's degree	$87,760	6%	7,470
High School Teachers	Bachelor's degree	$55,050	6%	31,260
Instructional Coordinators	Master's degree	$60,050	13%	3,110
Kindergarten and Elementary School Teachers	Bachelor's degree	$53,060	12%	53,250
Middle School Teachers	Bachelor's degree	$53,430	12%	21,120
Occupational Therapists	Master's degree	$75,400	29%	4,820
Preschool Teachers	Associate's degree	$27,130	17%	19,940
Recreational Therapists	Bachelor's degree	$42,280	14%	670
Social Workers	See "How to Become One"	$44,541	19%	24,280
Teacher Assistants	Some college, no degree	$23,640	9%	38,260

These alternative programs cover teaching methods and child development. Candidates are awarded full certification after they complete the program. Other programs require prospective teachers to take classes in education before they can start to teach. They may be awarded a master's degree after completing either type of program. For more information about alternative certification programs, contact the Teach-Now.

Training. Some special education teachers need to complete a period of fieldwork, commonly referred to as student teaching, before they can work as a teacher. In some states, this program is a prerequisite for a license to teach in public schools. During student teaching, they gain experience in preparing lessons and teaching students in a classroom setting, under the supervision and guidance of a mentor teacher. The amount of time required for these programs varies by state, but may last from 1 to 2 years. Many universities offer student teaching programs as part of a degree in special education.

Advancement. Experienced teachers can advance to become mentor or lead teachers who help less experienced teachers improve their teaching skills.

Teachers may become school counselors, instructional coordinators, assistant principals, or principals. These positions generally require additional education, advanced degree, or certification. An advanced degree in education administration or leadership may be helpful.

Important Qualities

Communication skills. Special education teachers discuss student's needs and performances with general education teachers, parents, and administrators. They also explain difficult concepts in terms that students with learning disabilities can understand.

Critical-thinking skills. Special education teachers assess students' progress and use that information to adapt lessons to help them learn.

Interpersonal skills. Special education teachers regularly work with general education teachers, school counselors, administrators, and parents to develop Individualized Education Programs. As a result, they need to be able to build positive working relationships.

Patience. Working with students with special needs and different abilities can be difficult. Special education teachers should be patient with each student, as some may need the instruction given aloud, at a slower pace, or in writing.

Resourcefulness. Special education teachers must develop different ways to present information in a manner that meets the needs of their students. They also help general education teachers adapt their lessons to the needs of students with disabilities.

Pay

The median annual wage for special education teachers was $55,060 in May 2012. The median wage is the wage at which half the workers in an occupation earned more than that amount and half earned less. The lowest 10 percent earned less than $36,740, and the top 10 percent earned more than $87,390.

The median annual wages for special education teachers by grade level in May 2012 were as follows:

special education teachers, secondary school $56,830
special education teachers, middle school 55,780
special education teachers, kindergarten
   and elementary school 53,820
special education teachers, preschool................................. 52,480

Union Membership. Most special education teachers belonged to a union in 2012.

Job Outlook

Employment of special education teachers is projected to grow 6 percent from 2012 to 2022, slower than the average for all occupations. The employment growth of special education teachers will vary by type. (See table below.) However, overall demand will be driven by increasing enrollment and continued need for special education services.

Better screening and identification of various disabilities in children are expected to increase the demand for special education services. In addition, children with disabilities are being identified earlier and enrolled into special education programs, increasing the need for special education teachers in preschool and kindergarten grades.

Compliance with laws requiring free public education for students with disabilities should result in some jobs. As school districts continue to use inclusive classrooms, special education teachers will be needed to assist general education teachers to work with students who have disabilities.

However, overall employment growth of special education teachers will depend on government funding. When state and local governments experience budget deficits, school districts may close or consolidate some schools and lay off employees, including special education teachers. As a result, employment growth will likely be limited by tight government budgets.

Job Prospects. Many job opportunities will stem from the need to replace teachers who leave the occupation each year.

Because helping students with disabilities can be quite stressful–emotionally demanding and physically draining–many schools have difficulties recruiting and retaining special education teachers. As a result, special education teachers should have good job opportunities. Job opportunities may be even better in parts of the country with higher enrollment rates, such as in the South, West, and rural areas.

Job opportunities also may be better in certain specialties, such experience with early childhood intervention and skills in working with students who have multiple disabilities, severe disabilities, or autism spectrum disorders.

O*NET

➤ Special Education Teachers, Preschool (25-2051.00)
➤ Special Education Teachers, Kindergarten and Elementary School (25-2052.00)
➤ Special Education Teachers, Middle School (25-2053.00)
➤ Special Education Teachers, Secondary School (25-2054.00)

Contacts for More Information

For more information about special education teachers, visit
➤ Council for Exceptional Children (www.cec.sped.org)
➤ Personnel Improvement Center (www.personnelcenter.org)

For more information about teaching and becoming a teacher, visit
➤ Teach.org (www.teach.org)
➤ American Federation of Teachers (www.aft.org)
➤ National Education Association (www.nea.org)

For more information about alternative certification programs, visit
➤ Teach-Now (http://teach-now.com/)

Teacher Assistants

- **2012 Median Pay** .... $23,640 per year
- **Entry-Level Education** ....Some college, no degree
- **Work Experience in a Related Occupation**............... None
- **On-the-Job Training** .... None
- **Number of Jobs 2012** 1,223,400
- **Job Outlook, 2012–22** .... 9% (As fast as average)
- **Employment Change, 2012–22** 105,000

What Teacher Assistants Do

Teacher assistants work under a teacher's supervision to give students additional attention and instruction.

Duties. Teacher assistants typically do the following:

- Reinforce lessons presented by teachers by reviewing material with students one-on-one or in small groups
- Enforce school and class rules to help teach students proper behavior
- Help teachers with recordkeeping, such as tracking attendance and calculating grades
- Help teachers prepare for lessons by getting materials ready or setting up equipment, such as computers
- Help supervise students in class, between classes, during lunch and recess, and on field trips

Teacher assistants also are called teacher aides, instructional aides, paraprofessionals, education assistants and paraeducators.

Generally, teachers introduce new material to students, and teacher assistants help reinforce the lessons by working with individual students or small groups of students. For example, after the teacher presents a lesson, a teacher assistant may help a small group of students as they try to master the material.

Teachers may seek feedback from assistants to monitor students' progress. Some teachers and teacher assistants meet regularly to discuss lesson plans and student development. Teacher assistants sometimes help teachers by grading tests and checking homework.

Some teacher assistants work only with special education students. These students often attend regular classes, and teacher assistants help them understand the material and adapt the information to their learning style.

With students who have more severe disabilities, assistants may work with them in separate classes. Teacher assistants help these students with basic needs, such as eating or personal hygiene. With young adults, they may help students with disabilities learn skills necessary for them to find a job or live independently after graduation.

Some teacher assistants work in specific locations in the school. For example, some work in computer laboratories, teaching students how to use computers and helping them use software. Others work as recess or lunchroom attendants, supervising students during these times of the day.

Although most teacher assistants work in elementary, middle, and high schools, others work in preschools and childcare centers. Often, one or two assistants work with a lead teacher to provide the individual attention that young children need. They help with educational activities. They also supervise the children at play and help with feeding and other basic care.

Work Environment

Teacher assistants held about 1.2 million jobs in 2012. They work in both private and public elementary, middle, and high schools. They also work in preschools, childcare centers, community centers, and for religious organizations.

In 2012, about 76 percent of teacher assistants were employed by elementary and secondary schools and 9 percent were employed by child day care services.

Teacher assistants may spend some time outside, when students are at recess or getting on and off the bus. Those who work with special education students may need to lift the students at certain times.

Work Schedules. About 4 in 10 teacher assistants worked part time in 2012. Some ride the bus with students before and after school. Although many do not work during the summer, some work in year-round schools or help teachers in summer school.

How to Become One

Educational requirements, which vary by school district and position, range from a high school diploma to an associate's degree.

Education. Although some districts require applicants to have a high school diploma, most require at least 2 years of college or an associate's degree. Teacher assistants in schools that have Title 1 programs (a federal program for schools with a large proportion of students from low-income households) must have at least a 2-year degree, 2 years of college, or pass a state or local assessment.

Associate's degree programs for teacher assistants prepare the participants to develop educational materials, observe students, and understand the role of teachers and teaching assistants in the classroom.

Most states require instructional aides who work with special needs students to pass a skills-based test.

Teacher assistants support and assist children in learning class material, using the teacher's lesson plans.

Median Annual Wages, May 2012

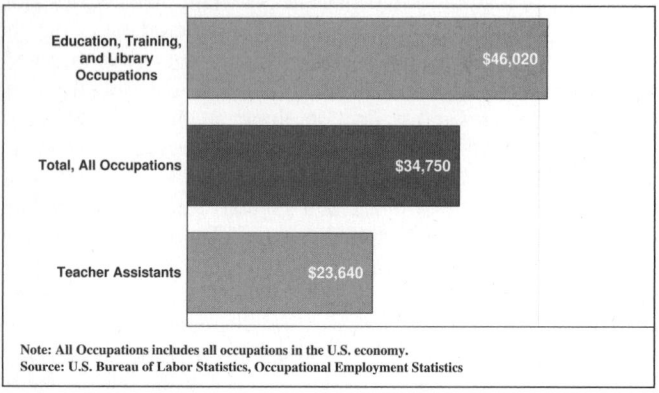

Note: All Occupations includes all occupations in the U.S. economy.
Source: U.S. Bureau of Labor Statistics, Occupational Employment Statistics

Percent Change in Employment, Projected 2012–2022

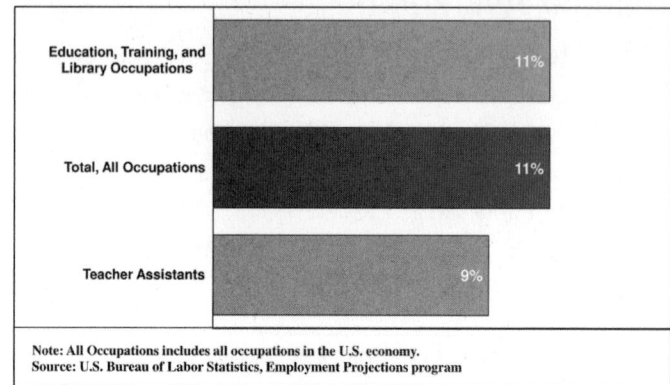

Note: All Occupations includes all occupations in the U.S. economy.
Source: U.S. Bureau of Labor Statistics, Employment Projections program

Important Qualities

Communication skills. Teacher assistants need to discuss students' progress with teachers, so they need to be able to communicate well.

Interpersonal skills. Teacher assistants interact with a variety of people, including teachers, students, parents, and administrators. They need to develop good working relationships with the people they work with.

Patience. Working with students of different abilities and backgrounds can be difficult. Teacher assistants must be patient with students who struggle with material.

Resourcefulness. To reinforce lessons, teacher assistants must explain information to students in a way that meets each student's learning style.

Pay

The median annual wage for teacher assistants was $23,640 in May 2012. The median wage is the wage at which half the workers in an occupation earned more than that amount and half earned less.

The lowest 10 percent earned less than $17,180, and the top 10 percent earned more than $36,680.

About 4 in 10 teacher assistants worked part time in 2012. Some ride the bus with students before and after school. Although many do not work during the summer, some work in year-round schools or assist teachers in summer school.

Union Membership. Compared with workers in all occupations, teacher assistants had a higher percentage of workers who belonged to a union in 2012.

Job Outlook

Employment of teacher assistants is projected to grow 9 percent from 2012 to 2022, about as fast as the average for all occupations. Growth is expected to result from increases in student enrollment, continued demand for special education services, and increases in childcare and preschool enrollment.

Student enrollment in public and private elementary and secondary schools is expected to increase from 2012 to 2022. Because teacher assistants work directly with students, the increase in the number of students will spur demand for teacher assistants. In

Employment Projections Data for Teacher Assistants

Occupational title	SOC Code	Employment, 2012	Projected Employment, 2022	Change, 2012–2022	
				Percent	Numeric
Teacher assistants...	25-9041	1,223,400	1,328,500	9	105,000

Source: U.S. Bureau of Labor Statistics, Employment Projections Program

Note: Data are rounded. Go to **Occupational Information Included in the OOH** *for a discussion of the data in this table.*

Similar Occupations   This table shows a list of occupations with job duties that are similar to those of teacher assistants.

Occupations	Entry-level Education	2012 Pay	Projected Job Growth	Average Annual Openings
Childcare Workers	High school diploma or equivalent	$19,510	14%	57,000
High School Teachers	Bachelor's degree	$55,050	6%	31,260
Kindergarten and Elementary School Teachers	Bachelor's degree	$53,060	12%	53,250
Library Technicians and Assistants	See "How to Become One"	$26,983	12%	13,070
Middle School Teachers	Bachelor's degree	$53,430	12%	21,120
Occupational Therapy Assistants and Aides	See "How to Become One"	$47,638	41%	2,560
Preschool Teachers	Associate's degree	$27,130	17%	19,940
Special Education Teachers	Bachelor's degree	$55,068	6%	10,220

addition, there will be continued demand for special education services and, in turn, demand for teacher assistants who work with these students.

Furthermore, enrollment is expected to increase in childcare services and preschool programs, both of which employ teacher assistants. Increases in enrollment will increase demand for teacher assistants in these settings.

Job Prospects. In addition to job openings from employment growth, numerous openings will arise as assistants leave the job and must be replaced. Because this occupation requires limited formal education and has low pay, many workers transfer to other occupations or leave the labor force to take care of family responsibilities, to return to school, or for other reasons.

Job opportunities for teacher assistants vary significantly by geography. Opportunities are likely to be better in the South and West, which are expected to have rapid increases in enrollment, and in urban schools, which often have difficulty recruiting and keeping teacher assistants.

O*NET

➤ Teacher Assistants (25-9041.00)

Contacts for More Information

For more information about teacher assistants, visit
➤ National Education Association (www.nea.org/)
➤ American Federation of Teachers (www.aft.org/)
➤ National Resource Center for Paraeducators (www.nrcpara.org/)

Training and Development Specialists

- **2012 Median Pay** .... $55,930 per year
  $26.89 per hour
- **Entry-Level Education** ....Bachelor's degree
- **Work Experience in a Related Occupation**.........Less than 5 years
- **On-the-Job Training** .... None
- **Number of Jobs 2012** 228,800
- **Job Outlook, 2012–22** .... 15% (Faster than average)
- **Employment Change, 2012–22** 35,400

Training and Development Specialists often develop visual aids to convey complex ideas.

What Training and Development Specialists Do

Training and development specialists help plan, conduct, and administer programs that train employees and improve their skills and knowledge.

Duties. Training and development specialists typically do the following:

- Assess training needs through surveys, interviews with employees, or consultations with managers or instructors
- Design and create training manuals, online learning modules, and course materials
- Review training materials from a variety of vendors and choose appropriate materials
- Deliver training to employees using a variety of instructional techniques
- Monitor and evaluate training programs to ensure they are current and effective
- Select and assign instructors or vendors to conduct training
- Perform administrative tasks such as monitoring costs, scheduling classes, setting up systems and equipment, and coordinating enrollment

Training and development specialists create, administer, and deliver training programs for businesses and organizations. To do this, they must first assess the needs of an organization. Once those needs are determined, specialists develop custom training programs that take place in a classroom, computer laboratory, or training facility.

Training and development specialists organize or offer training sessions using lectures, group discussions, team exercises, hands-on examples, and other training formats. Some training is in the form of a video, Web-based program, or self-guided instructional manual. Training also may be collaborative, which allows employees to connect informally with experts, mentors, and colleagues, often through the use of technology.

Training and development specialists also may monitor instructors, guide employees through media-based programs, or facilitate informal or collaborative learning programs.

Work Environment

Training and development specialists held about 228,800 jobs in 2012, and work in nearly every industry.

They spend much of their time working with people, giving presentations, and leading training activities.

Work Schedules. Most training and development specialists work full time during regular business hours.

How to Become One

Training and development specialists need a bachelor's degree, and most need related work experience.

Education. Training and development specialists need a bachelor's degree. Specialists can come from a variety of education backgrounds, but many have a bachelor's degree in training and development, human resources, education, or instructional design. Others may have a degree in business or the social sciences, such as educational or organizational psychology.

In addition, as technology continues to play a larger role in training and development, a growing number of organizations seek candidates who have a background in information technology or computer science.

Work Experience in a Related Occupation. Related work experience is important for most training and development specialists.

Median Annual Wages, May 2012

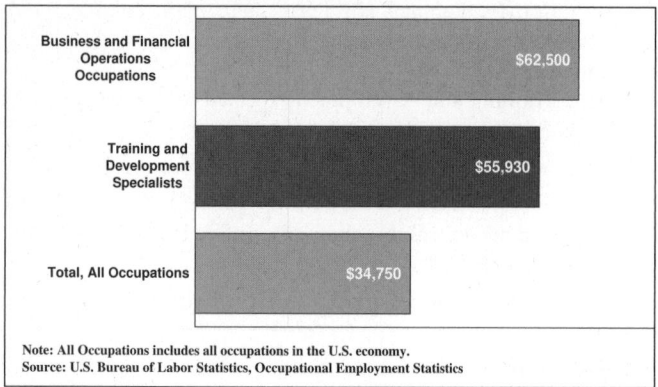

Note: All Occupations includes all occupations in the U.S. economy.
Source: U.S. Bureau of Labor Statistics, Occupational Employment Statistics

Percent Change in Employment, Projected 2012–2022

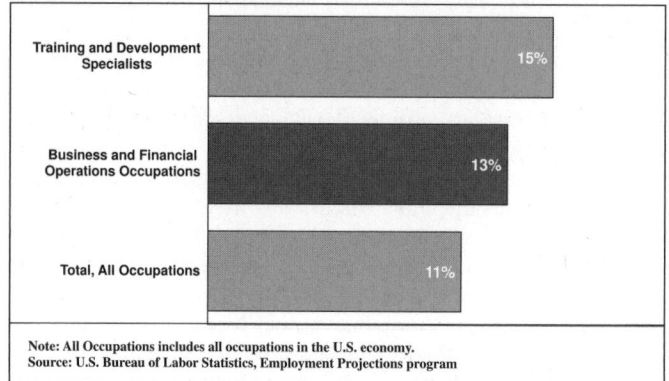

Note: All Occupations includes all occupations in the U.S. economy.
Source: U.S. Bureau of Labor Statistics, Employment Projections program

Many positions require work experience in training and development, instructional design, teaching, or related work. Some employers also prefer previous work experience in the industry in which the company operates. Increasingly, employers prefer candidates with experience in information technology, as organizations introduce more e-learning and technology-based tools.

Licenses, Certifications, and Registrations. Many professional associations for human resources professionals offer classes to enhance the skills of their members. Some associations, including the American Society for Training and Development and International Society for Performance Improvement, specialize in training and development and offer certification programs. Although not required, certification can show professional expertise and credibility. In fact, many employers prefer to hire certified candidates, and some positions may require certification.

Advancement. Training and development specialists may advance to training and development manager or human resources manager positions. Workers typically need several years of experience to advance.

Important Qualities

Analytical skills. Training and development specialists must evaluate training programs, methods, and materials, and choose those that best fit each situation.

Instructional skills. Training and development specialists often deliver training programs to employees. They use a variety of teaching techniques and sometimes must adapt their methods to meet the needs of particular groups.

Interpersonal skills. Training and development specialists need strong interpersonal skills because delivering training programs requires collaborating with instructors, trainees, and subject-matter experts. They also accomplish much of their work through teams.

Speaking skills. Speaking skills are essential for training and development specialists because they often give presentations. Specialists must communicate information clearly and facilitate learning by diverse audiences.

Pay

The median annual wage for training and development specialists was $55,930 in May 2012. The median wage is the wage at which half the workers in an occupation earned more than that amount and half earned less. The lowest 10 percent earned less than $31,910, and the top 10 percent earned more than $93,470.

In May 2012, the median annual wages for training and development specialists in the top five industries employing these specialists were as follows:

Professional, scientific, and technical services	$64,770
Educational services; state, local, and private	56,400
Finance and insurance	56,320
Health care and social assistance	50,360
Administrative and support services	47,600

Job Outlook

Employment of training and development specialists is projected to grow 15 percent from 2012 to 2022, faster than the average for all occupations.

In many fields, employees are required to take continuing education and skill development courses throughout their careers. In addition, innovations in training methods and learning technology should continue throughout the next decade. For example, organizations increasingly use social media, visual simulations, mobile learning, and social networks in their training programs. Training and development specialists will need to modify their programs to fit a new generation of workers for whom technology is a part of daily life and work.

Additionally, as baby boomers reach retirement age and begin to leave the workforce, organizations will need capable training and development staff to train their replacements. The need to replace a large workforce of highly skilled and knowledgeable employees should result in organizations increasing their training staff, or contracting out services, to sustain a workforce of high quality employees and maintain a competitive edge.

Across most industries, employment of training and development specialists is expected to grow as companies develop and

Employment Projections Data for Training and Development Specialists

Occupational title	SOC Code	Employment, 2012	Projected Employment, 2022	Change, 2012–2022 Percent	Change, 2012–2022 Numeric
Training and development specialists	13-1151	228,800	264,200	15	35,400

Source: U.S. Bureau of Labor Statistics, Employment Projections Program

Note: Data are rounded. Go to **Occupational Information Included in the OOH** *for a discussion of the data in this table.*

Similar Occupations   This table shows a list of occupations with job duties that are similar to those of training and development specialists.

Occupations	Entry-level Education	2012 Pay	Projected Job Growth	Average Annual Openings
Compensation and Benefits Managers	Bachelor's degree	$95,250	3%	610
Compensation, Benefits, and Job Analysis Specialists	Bachelor's degree	$59,090	6%	2,200
Human Resources Managers	Bachelor's degree	$99,720	13%	4,060
Human Resources Specialists and Labor Relations Specialists	Bachelor's degree	$55,616	7%	12,370
Instructional Coordinators	Master's degree	$60,050	13%	3,110
Psychologists	See "How to Become One"	$69,807	12%	6,230
School and Career Counselors	Master's degree	$53,610	12%	8,700
Training and Development Managers	Bachelor's degree	$95,400	11%	1,070

introduce new media and technology into their training programs. Training and development contracting firms are often better equipped with the technology and technical expertise to produce new training initiatives, so some organizations will likely contract out portions of their training or program development work to these companies.

Job Prospects. Job prospects should be best for those with a bachelor's degree in training and development, education, human resources, computer science, or instructional design, and with experience performing training and development work.

O*NET

➤ Training and Development Specialists (13-1151.00)

Contacts for More Information

For more information about training and development specialists, visit
➤ American Society for Training and Development (www.astd.org)
➤ International Society for Performance Improvement (www.ispi.org)
   For information about human resources management careers and certification, visit
➤ Society for Human Resource Management (www.shrm.org)

Entertainment and Sports

Actors

- **2012 Median Pay** .... $20.26 per hour
- **Entry-Level Education** ....Some college, no degree
- **Work Experience in a Related Occupation**.............. None
- **On-the-Job Training** .... Long-term on-the-job training
- **Number of Jobs 2012** 79,800
- **Job Outlook, 2012–22** .... 4% (Slower than average)
- **Employment Change, 2012–22** 3,300

What Actors Do

Actors express ideas and portray characters in theater, film, television, and other performing arts media. They also work at theme parks or other live events. They interpret a writer's script to entertain or inform an audience.

Duties. Actors typically do the following:

- Read scripts and meet with agents and other professionals before accepting a role
- Audition in front of directors and producers
- Research their character's personal traits and circumstances to portray them more authentically to an audience
- Memorize their lines
- Rehearse their lines and performance, including movement on stage or in front of the camera, with other actors
- Discuss their role with the director and other actors to improve the overall performance of the show
- Perform the role, following the director's directions

Most actors struggle to find steady work, and few achieve recognition as stars. Some work as "extras"–actors who appear on screen with no lines to deliver. Some do voiceover or narration work for animated features, audiobooks, or other electronic media.

In some stage or film productions, actors sing, dance, or play a musical instrument. For some roles, an actor must learn a new skill, such as horseback riding or stage fighting.

Actors spend a lot of time rehearsing their lines.

Most actors have long periods of unemployment between roles and often hold other jobs to make a living. Some actors teach acting classes as a second job.

Work Environment

Actors held about 79,800 jobs in 2012. Most work under pressure and are often under the stress of having to find their next job. Work assignments are usually short, ranging from 1 day to a few months, and actors often hold another job to make a living.

While working on location for a movie or television show and sometimes in a studio, actors may perform in unpleasant conditions, such as in bad weather or while wearing an uncomfortable costume.

Work Schedules. Work hours for actors are long and irregular. Evening, weekend, and holiday work is common. Few actors work full time, and many have variable schedules. Those who work in theater may travel with a touring show across the country. Film and television actors may also travel to work on location.

How to Become One

Many actors enhance their skills through formal dramatic education, and long-term training is common.

Education. Many actors enhance their skills through formal dramatic education. Many who specialize in theater have bachelor's degrees, although a degree is not required.

Although some people succeed in acting without getting a formal education, most actors acquire some formal preparation through an acting conservatory or a university drama or theater arts program. Students can take college classes in drama or filmmaking to prepare for a career as an actor. Classes in dance or music may help as well.

Actors who do not have a college degree may take acting or film classes to learn their craft. Community colleges, acting conservatories, and private film schools typically offer these classes. Many theater companies also have education programs. A bachelor's degree in theater is becoming more common among stage actors.

Important Qualities

Creativity. Actors interpret their characters' feelings and motives in order to portray the characters in the most compelling way.

Memorization skills. Actors memorize many lines before filming begins or a show opens. Television actors often appear on camera with little time to memorize scripts, and scripts frequently may be revised or written moments before filming.

Persistence. Actors may audition for many roles before getting a job. They must be able to accept rejection and keep going.

Physical stamina. Actors should be in good enough physical condition to endure heat from stage or studio lights and the weight of heavy costumes. They may work long hours, including acting in more than one performance a day, and they must do so without getting overly tired.

Reading skills. When looking for a new role, actors read many scripts and must be able to interpret how a writer has described their character.

Speaking skills. Actors–particularly stage actors–must be able to say their lines clearly, project their voice, and pronounce words so that audiences understand them.

Median Hourly Wages, May 2012

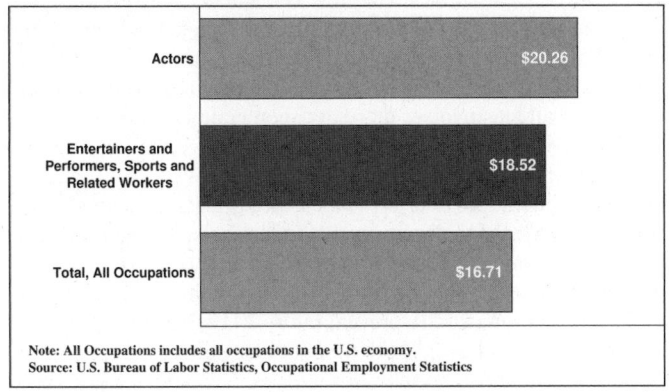

Note: All Occupations includes all occupations in the U.S. economy.
Source: U.S. Bureau of Labor Statistics, Occupational Employment Statistics

Percent Change in Employment, Projected 2012–2022

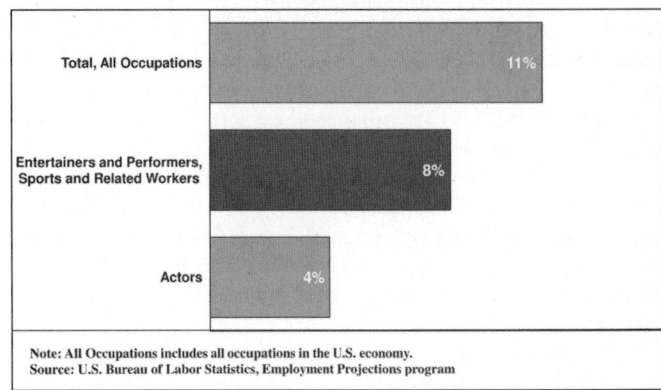

Note: All Occupations includes all occupations in the U.S. economy.
Source: U.S. Bureau of Labor Statistics, Employment Projections program

In addition to these qualities, actors usually must be physically coordinated to perform predetermined, sometimes complex movements with other actors to complete a scene.

Training. It takes many years of practice to develop the skills needed to be successful as an actor, and actors never truly finish training. They work to improve their acting skills throughout their career. Many actors continue to train through workshops or mentoring by a drama coach.

Every role is different, and an actor may need to learn something new for each one. For example, a role may require learning how to sing or dance, or an actor may have to learn to speak with an accent or to play a musical instrument or sport.

Many aspiring actors participate in high school, college, and local community plays. In television and film, actors usually start out in smaller roles or independent movies and work their way up to bigger productions.

Advancement. As an actor's reputation grows, he or she may work on bigger projects or in more prestigious venues. Some actors become producers and directors.

Pay

The median hourly wage for actors was $20.26 in May 2012. The median wage is the wage at which half the workers in an occupation earned more than that amount and half earned less. The lowest 10 percent earned less than $8.92, and the top 10 percent earned more than $90.00 in May 2012.

Union Membership. Compared with workers in all occupations, actors had a higher percentage of workers who belonged to a union in 2012. Many film and television actors join Screen Guild/ American Federation of Television and Radio Artists (SAG/ AFTRA), whereas many stage actors join the Actors' Equity Association. Union membership can help actors receive bigger parts for more money, although dues can be expensive for actors who are beginning their careers.

Job Outlook

Employment of actors is projected to grow 4 percent from 2012 to 2022, slower than the average for all occupations. Job growth in the motion picture industry will stem from continued strong demand

Employment Projections Data for Actors

Occupational title	SOC Code	Employment, 2012	Projected Employment, 2022	Change, 2012–2022	
				Percent	Numeric
Actors	27-2011	79,800	83,000	4	3,300

Source: U.S. Bureau of Labor Statistics, Employment Projections Program

Note: Data are rounded. Go to **Occupational Information Included in the OOH** *for a discussion of the data in this table.*

Similar Occupations
This table shows a list of occupations with job duties that are similar to those of actors.

Occupations	Entry-level Education	2012 Pay	Projected Job Growth	Average Annual Openings
Announcers	See "How to Become One"	$27,652	1%	1,160
Dancers and Choreographers	High school diploma or equivalent	The annual wage is not available.	13.2%	1,080
Film and Video Editors and Camera Operators	Bachelor's degree	$46,538	3%	510
Multimedia Artists and Animators	Bachelor's degree	$61,370	6%	2,060
Musicians and Singers	High school diploma or equivalent	The annual wage is not available.	5.2%	5,390
Producers and Directors	Bachelor's degree	$71,350	3%	3,790

for new movies and television shows. However, employment is not expected to keep pace with that demand.

Production companies are experimenting with new content delivery methods, such as video on demand and online television, which may lead to more work for actors in the future. However, these delivery methods are still in their early stages, and it remains to be seen how successful they will be.

Actors who work in performing arts companies are expected to see slower job growth than those in film. Many small and medium-size theaters have difficulty getting funding. As a result, the number of performances is expected to decline. Large theaters, with their more stable sources of funding, should provide more opportunities.

Job Prospects. Actors face intense competition for jobs. Most roles, no matter how minor, have many actors auditioning for them. For stage roles, actors with a bachelor's degree in theater may have a better chance than those without one.

O*NET

➤ Actors (27-2011.00)

Contacts for More Information

For more information about actors, visit
➤ Actors' Equity Association (www.actorsequity.org)
➤ National Endowment for the Arts (www.nea.gov)
➤ SAG/AFTRA (www.sag.org)

Athletes and Sports Competitors

- **2012 Median Pay** .... $40,060 per year
- **Entry-Level Education** ... High school diploma or equivalent
- **Work Experience in a Related Occupation** .... None
- **On-the-Job Training** .... Long-term on-the-job training
- **Number of Jobs 2012** 14,900
- **Job Outlook, 2012–22** .... 7% (Slower than average)
- **Employment Change, 2012–22** 1,000

What Athletes and Sports Competitors Do

Athletes and sports competitors participate in organized, officiated sporting events to entertain spectators.

Duties. Athletes and sports competitors typically do the following:

- Practice to develop and improve their skills
- Maintain the equipment they use in their sport in good condition
- Stay in the best physical condition by training, exercising, and following special diets
- Take instructions from coaches and other sports staff during games regarding strategy and tactics
- Obey the rules of the sport during competitions and games
- Assess how they did after each event and identify their strengths and weaknesses

Many people dream of becoming a paid professional athlete. Few people, however, beat the odds and make a full-time living from professional athletics. And when they do, professional athletes often have short careers with little job security.

When playing a game, athletes and sports competitors must understand the game strategies while obeying the rules and regula-

tions of the sport. The events in which athletes compete include team sports, such as baseball, softball, hockey, and soccer, and individual sports, such as golf, tennis, swimming, and skiing. The level of play varies greatly, where sometimes the best from around the world compete in events broadcast on international television.

Being an athlete involves more than competing in athletic events. Athletes spend many hours each day practicing skills and improving teamwork under the guidance of a coach or a sports instructor. They view videotapes to critique their own performances and techniques and to learn their opponents' tendencies and weaknesses so as to gain a competitive advantage.

Some athletes work regularly with strength trainers to gain muscle and stamina and to prevent injury. Many athletes push their bodies to the limit during both practice and play, so career-ending injury is always a risk; even minor injuries may put a player at risk of replacement.

Because competition at all levels is extremely intense and job security is always in question, many athletes train throughout the year to maintain excellent form and technique and remain in peak physical condition. Very little downtime from the sport exists at the professional level.

Work Environment

Athletes and sports competitors held about 14,900 jobs in 2012. More than half were employed in the spectator sports industry.

Athletes and sports competitors who participate in competitions that are held outdoors may be exposed to all weather conditions of the season in which they play their sport. Additionally, many athletes must travel to sporting events, which may include long bus rides or plane trips, and in some cases, international travel.

Work Schedules. Athletes and sports competitors often work irregular hours, including evenings, weekends, and holidays. They usually work more than 40 hours a week for several months during the sports season, if not most of the year.

Injuries and Illnesses. Athletes who play a contact sport, such as football or hockey, are highly susceptible to injuries. Because of this, many athletes wear pads, gloves, goggles, helmets, and other protective gear to protect against injury.

How to Become One

Athletes and sports competitors typically have at least a high school diploma or equivalent. They must have superior athletic

Athletes and sports competitors practice under the direction of coaches, sports instructors, or athletic trainers.

Median Annual Wages, May 2012

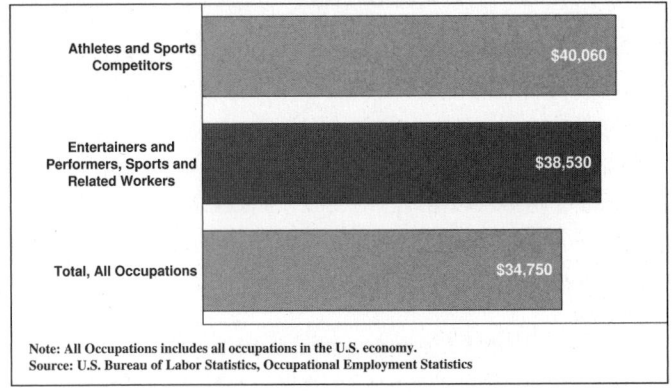

Note: All Occupations includes all occupations in the U.S. economy.
Source: U.S. Bureau of Labor Statistics, Occupational Employment Statistics

Percent Change in Employment, Projected 2012–2022

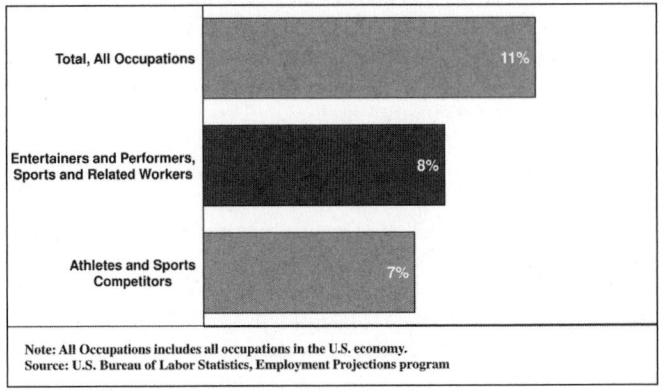

Note: All Occupations includes all occupations in the U.S. economy.
Source: U.S. Bureau of Labor Statistics, Employment Projections program

talent and immense knowledge of their sport, which they usually get through years of experience at lower levels of competition.

Education. Athletes and sports competitors typically have at least a high school diploma or equivalent. They must have extensive knowledge of the way the sport is played, especially its rules, regulations, and strategies.

Other Experience. Athletes typically learn the rules of the game and develop their skills by playing the sport at lower levels. They often learn by playing the sport in school or at a recreation center with the help of instructors or coaches. Some may attend camps that teach the fundamentals of the sport.

For most team sports, athletes compete in high school and collegiate athletics or on club teams. Other athletes may learn their sport by taking private or group lessons, such as in gymnastics or tennis.

Training. It typically takes many years of practice and experience to become an athlete or sports competitor.

Licenses, Certifications, and Registrations. Some sports and localities require athletes and sports competitors to be licensed or certified to practice. For example, in drag racing, drivers need to be licensed to compete in the various drag racing series. The governing body of the sport may revoke licenses and suspend participants who do not meet the required performance or training. In addition, athletes may have their licenses or certification suspended for inappropriate activity.

Advancement. For most aspiring athletes, turning professional is the biggest advancement. They often begin to compete immediately, although some may spend more time on the bench (as a reserve) to gain experience. In some sports, such as baseball, athletes may begin their professional career on a minor league team before moving up to the major leagues. Professional athletes generally advance in their sport by displaying superior performance, winning, and receiving accolades, and in turn they earn a higher salary.

Important Qualities

Athleticism. Nearly all athletes and sports competitors must possess superior athletic ability to be able to compete successfully against opponents.

Concentration. Athletes and sports competitors must be extremely focused when competing. The difference between winning and losing can often be a result of a momentary lapse in concentration.

Decision-making skills. Athletes and sports competitors often must make split-second decisions. Football quarterbacks, for example, usually only have seconds to decide whether to pass the football or run with it.

Dedication. Athletes and sports competitors must practice regularly to develop their skills and improve or maintain their physical conditioning. It often takes years to become successful, so athletes must be dedicated to their sport.

Employment Projections Data for Athletes and Sports Competitors

Occupational title	SOC Code	Employment, 2012	Projected Employment, 2022	Change, 2012–2022	
				Percent	Numeric
Athletes and sports competitors	27-2021	14,900	15,900	7	1,000

Source: U.S. Bureau of Labor Statistics, Employment Projections Program

Note: Data are rounded. Go to **Occupational Information Included in the OOH** *for a discussion of the data in this table.*

Similar Occupations   This table shows a list of occupations with job duties that are similar to those of athletes and sports competitors.

Occupations	Entry-level Education	2012 Pay	Projected Job Growth	Average Annual Openings
Coaches and Scouts	Bachelor's degree	$28,360	15%	10,850
Fitness Trainers and Instructors	High school diploma or equivalent	$31,720	13%	6,500
Recreation Workers	Bachelor's degree	$22,240	14%	8,970
Umpires, Referees, and Other Sports Officials	High school diploma or equivalent	$23,290	7%	650

Hand-eye coordination. For many sports, including tennis and baseball, the need to gauge and strike a fast-moving ball is highly dependent on the athlete's hand-eye coordination.

Stamina. Endurance can benefit athletes and sports competitors, particularly those athletes who participate in long-lasting sports competitions, such as marathons.

Teamwork. Because many athletes compete in a team sport, such as hockey or soccer, the ability to work with teammates as a cohesive unit is essential for success.

Many professional athletes are also required to pass drug tests.

Pay

The median annual wage for athletes and sports competitors was $40,060 in May 2012. The median wage is the wage at which half the workers in an occupation earned more than that amount and half earned less. The lowest 10 percent earned less than $18,040, and the top 10 percent earned more than $187,200.

Job Outlook

Employment of athletes and sports competitors is projected to grow 7 percent from 2012 to 2022, slower than the average for all occupations. Growth will be primarily due to population growth and increasing public interest in professional sports.

Growth and geographic shifts in population may lead to an increase in the number of professional sports teams. Some professional sports leagues may expand to new cities in the United States, creating new teams and new job opportunities for those looking to become professional athletes.

However, expansion is rare in professional sports leagues. Creating new teams is very costly and risky, requiring strong support from fans and both local and state government. When leagues do expand, they typically only create one or two teams at a time.

Instead, some teams simply relocate to another city that has a greater interest in the sport and a larger fan base. In this case no new jobs would be created. Some teams and sports leagues may disband altogether because of a lack of interest in the sport.

Job Prospects. Competition for professional athlete jobs will continue to be extremely intense. Very few high school or college athletes become professional athletes. In a major sport, such as basketball, only about 1 in 3,000 high school athletes make it to the professional level.

Most professional athletes' careers last only a few years because of debilitating injuries or retirements. Yearly replacement needs for these jobs is high and may create some job opportunities.

However, the talented young men and women who dream of becoming sports superstars greatly outnumber the number of openings.

O*NET

➤ Athletes and Sports Competitors (27-2021.00)

Contacts for More Information

For more information about team and individual sports, visit
➤ National Collegiate Athletic Association (www.ncaa.org/)
➤ National Council of Youth Sports (www.ncys.org/)
➤ National Federation of State High School Associations (www.nfhs.org)

For more information related to individual sports, refer to the organization that represents the sport.

Coaches and Scouts

- **2012 Median Pay** .... $28,360 per year
- **Entry-Level Education** .... Bachelor's degree
- **Work Experience in a Related Occupation** .... None
- **On-the-Job Training** .... None
- **Number of Jobs 2012** 243,900
- **Job Outlook, 2012–22** .... 15% (Faster than average)
- **Employment Change, 2012–22** 36,200

What Coaches and Scouts Do

Coaches teach amateur and professional athletes the skills they need to succeed at their sport. Scouts look for new players, evaluating their skills and likelihood for success at the college, amateur, or professional level. Many coaches are also involved in scouting.

Duties. Coaches typically do the following:

- Plan, organize, and conduct practice sessions
- Analyze the strengths and weaknesses of individual athletes and opposing teams
- Plan strategies and choose team members for each game
- Provide direction, encouragement, and motivation to prepare athletes for games
- Call plays and make decisions about strategy and player substitutions during games
- Plan and direct physical conditioning programs that enable athletes to achieve maximum performance
- Instruct athletes on proper techniques, game strategies, sportsmanship, and the rules of the sport
- Keep records of athletes' and opponents' performance
- Identify and recruit potential athletes
- Arrange for and offer incentives to prospective players

Scouts typically do the following:

- Read newspapers and other news sources to find athletes to consider
- Attend games, view videotapes of the athletes' performances, and study statistics about the athletes to determine talent and potential
- Talk to the athlete and the coaches to see if the athlete has what it takes to succeed
- Report to the coach, manager, or owner of the team for which he or she is scouting
- Arrange for and offer incentives to prospective players

Coaches teach professional and amateur athletes the fundamental skills of individual and team sports. They hold training and practice sessions to improve the athletes' form, technique, skills, and stamina. Along with refining athletes' individual skills, coaches are also responsible for instilling in their players the importance of good sportsmanship, a competitive spirit, and teamwork.

Many coaches evaluate their opponents to determine game strategies and to establish specific plays to practice. During competition, coaches call specific plays intended to surprise or overpower the opponent, and they may substitute players for optimum team chemistry and success.

Many high school coaches are primarily academic teachers who supplement their income by coaching part time.

Sports instructors differ from coaches in their approaches to athletes because of the focus of their work. For example, coaches manage the team during a game to optimize its chance for victory, but sports instructors are often not permitted to instruct their athletes during competition.

Like coaches, though, sports instructors hold practice sessions, assign specific drills, and correct athletes' techniques. They spend more of their time working one-on-one with athletes, designing customized training programs for each individual.

Sports instructors typically specialize in teaching athletes the skills of an individual sport, such as tennis, golf, or karate. Some sports instructors, such as pitching instructors in baseball, may teach individual athletes involved in team sports.

Scouts evaluate the skills of both amateur and professional athletes. Scouts seek out top athletic candidates for colleges or professional teams and evaluate their likelihood of success at a higher competitive level.

Work Environment

Coaches and scouts held about 243,900 jobs in 2012. About 11 percent were self-employed.

The industries that employed the most coaches and scouts in 2012 were as follows:

Elementary and secondary schools; state, local, and private... 25%
Colleges, universities, and professional schools;
   state, local, and private... 19
Other schools and instruction; state, local, and private........... 17
Amusement, gambling, and recreation industries 15
   Religious, grantmaking, civic, professional, and similar
   organizations... 5

Some scouts may work for organizations that work directly with high school athletes. These scouts collect information on the athlete and help promote him or her to potential colleges.

At the college level, scouts typically work for scouting organizations or as self-employed scouts to help colleges recruit the best high school athletes.

Scouts at the professional level are typically employed by the team or organization directly.

Those people who coach and scout for outdoor sports may be exposed to all weather conditions of the season. In addition, they must travel often to attend sporting events. This is particularly true for those in professional sports.

Work Schedules. Coaches and scouts often work irregular hours, including evenings, weekends, and holidays. They usually work more than 40 hours a week for several months during the sport's season, if not most of the year. Some high school coaches work part time, and they may coach more than one sport.

Coaches organize amateur and professional athletes and teach them the fundamental skills of individual and team sports.

How to Become One

Coaches and scouts typically need a bachelor's degree. They must also have extensive knowledge of the sport. Coaches typically gain this knowledge through their own experiences playing the sport at some level. Although previous playing experience may be beneficial, it is not required for most scouting jobs.

Education. High schools typically hire teachers at the school for most coaching jobs. If no suitable teacher is found, schools hire a qualified candidate from outside the school. For more information on education requirements for teachers, see the profile on high school teachers.

College and professional coaches must usually have a bachelor's degree. This degree can typically be in any subject. However, some coaches may decide to study exercise and sports science, physiology, kinesiology, nutrition and fitness, physical education, and sports medicine.

Scouts must also typically have a bachelor's degree. Some scouts decide to get a degree in business, marketing, sales, or sports management.

Other Experience. College and professional coaching jobs also typically require experience playing the sport at some level.

However, scouting jobs typically do not require experience playing a sport at the college or professional level. Employers look for applicants with a passion for sports and an ability to spot young players who have exceptional athletic ability and skills.

Licenses, Certifications, and Registrations. Most state high school athletic associations require coaches to be certified. Cer-

Median Annual Wages, May 2012

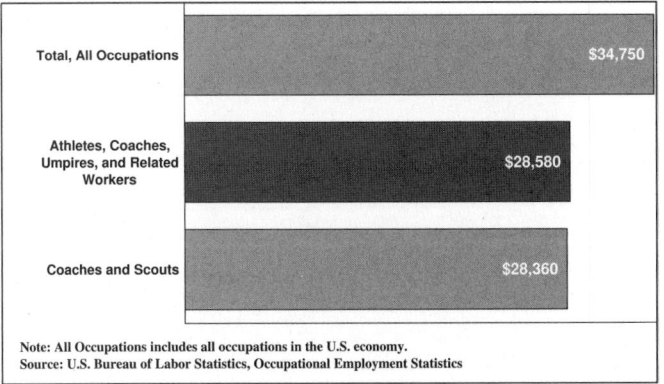

Note: All Occupations includes all occupations in the U.S. economy.
Source: U.S. Bureau of Labor Statistics, Occupational Employment Statistics

Percent Change in Employment, Projected 2012–2022

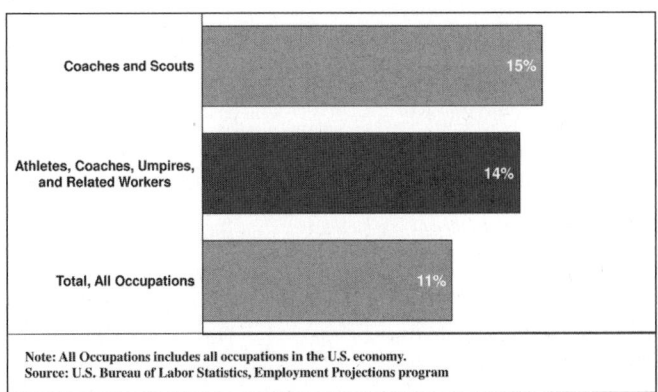

Note: All Occupations includes all occupations in the U.S. economy.
Source: U.S. Bureau of Labor Statistics, Employment Projections program

Employment Projections Data for Coaches and Scouts

Occupational title	SOC Code	Employment, 2012	Projected Employment, 2022	Change, 2012–2022	
				Percent	Numeric
Coaches and scouts...	27-2022	243,900	280,100	15	36,200

Source: U.S. Bureau of Labor Statistics, Employment Projections Program

Note: Data are rounded. Go to **Occupational Information Included in the OOH** *for a discussion of the data in this table.*

tification often requires coaches to be a minimum age (at least 18 years old) and be trained in cardiopulmonary resuscitation (CPR) and first-aid. Some states also require coaches to attend classes related to sports safety and coaching fundamentals prior to becoming certified.

Although most public high school coaches need to meet these state requirements in order to become a coach, certification may not be required for coaching and sports instructor jobs in private schools.

Certification requirements for college coaching positions also vary.

Additional certification may be highly desirable or even required in order to become an instructor in scuba diving, tennis, golf, karate, or other individual sports. There are many certifying organizations specific to the various sports, and their requirements vary.

Part-time workers and those in smaller facilities or youth leagues are less likely to need formal education or training and may not need certification.

Advancement. Many coaches begin their careers as assistant coaches to gain the knowledge and experience needed to become a head coach. Large schools and colleges that compete at the highest levels require a head coach with substantial experience at another school or as an assistant coach.

To reach the ranks of professional coaches, a candidate usually needs years of coaching experience and a winning record in the lower ranks or experience as an athlete in that sport.

Scouts may begin working as talent spotters in a particular area or region. They typically advance to become supervising scouts responsible for a whole territory or region.

Important Qualities

Communication skills. Because coaches instruct, organize, and motivate athletes, they must have excellent communication skills. They must effectively communicate proper techniques, strategies, and rules of the sport so every player on the team understands.

Decision-making skills. Coaches must choose the appropriate players to use at a given position at a given time during a game and find a strategy that yields the best chance for winning. Coaches and scouts also must be very selective when recruiting players from lower levels of athletics.

Dedication. Coaches must attend daily practices and assist their team and individual athletes in improving their skills and physical conditioning. Coaches must be dedicated to their sport, as it often takes years to become successful.

Interpersonal skills. Being able to relate to athletes helps coaches and scouts foster positive relationships with their current players and recruit potential players.

Leadership skills. Coaches must demonstrate good leadership skills to get the most out of athletes. They also must be able to motivate, develop, and direct young athletes.

Resourcefulness. Coaches must utilize the talent on a team to achieve the best chances for winning. For example, a coach may change players during the game to meet the defensive needs of the team.

Pay

The median annual wage for coaches and scouts was $28,360 in May 2012. The median wage is the wage at which half the workers in an occupation earned more than that amount, and half earned less. The lowest 10 percent earned less than $17,210, and the top 10 percent earned more than $65,910.

In May 2012, the median annual wages for coaches and scouts in the top five industries in which they worked were as follows:

Colleges, universities, and professional schools; state, local, and private	$39,960
Amusement, gambling, and recreation industries	30,320
Other schools and instruction; state, local, and private	26,090
Religious, grantmaking, civic, professional, and similar organizations	22,780
Elementary and secondary schools; state, local, and private	22,140

Similar Occupations   This table shows a list of occupations with job duties that are similar to those of coaches and scouts.

Occupations	Entry-level Education	2012 Pay	Projected Job Growth	Average Annual Openings
Athletes and Sports Competitors	High school diploma or equivalent	$40,060	7%	540
Athletic Trainers and Exercise Physiologists	Bachelor's degree	$42,676	19%	1,240
Dietitians and Nutritionists	Bachelor's degree	$55,240	21%	2,230
Fitness Trainers and Instructors	High school diploma or equivalent	$31,720	13%	6,500
High School Teachers	Bachelor's degree	$55,050	6%	31,260
Kindergarten and Elementary School Teachers	Bachelor's degree	$53,060	12%	53,250
Middle School Teachers	Bachelor's degree	$53,430	12%	21,120
Umpires, Referees, and Other Sports Officials	High school diploma or equivalent	$23,290	7%	650

Job Outlook

Employment of coaches and scouts is projected to grow 15 percent from 2012 to 2022, faster than the average for all occupations. Rising participation in high school and college sports could increase demand for coaches and scouts.

High school enrollment is projected to increase over the next decade, resulting in a rise in the number of student-athletes. As schools offer more athletic programs and more students participate in sports, the demand for coaches may increase.

Participation in college sports is also projected to increase over the next decade, particularly at smaller colleges and in women's sports. Many small, Division-III colleges are expanding their sports programs and adding new teams as a way to help promote the school and recruit potential students.

The growing interest in college and professional sports will also increase demand for scouts. Colleges must attract the best athletes to remain competitive. Successful teams help colleges enhance their reputation, recruit future students, and raise donations from alumni. Colleges, therefore, will increasingly rely on scouts to recruit the best possible high school athletes. In addition, as college tuition increases and scholarships become more competitive, high school athletes will hire scouts directly, in an effort to increase their chances of receiving a college scholarship.

However, funding for athletic programs at schools often is cut first when budgets become tight. For example, some high schools within the same school district may combine their sports programs in an effort to cut costs. Still, the popularity of team sports often enables shortfalls to be offset with help from fundraisers, booster clubs, and parents.

Job Prospects. Strong competition is expected for higher paying jobs at the college level and will be even greater for jobs in professional sports.

Job prospects at the high school level should be good, but coaching jobs typically go to those teaching in the school. Those who have a degree or are state-certified to teach academic subjects, therefore, should have the best prospects for getting coaching and instructor jobs at high schools. The need to replace the amount of high school coaches who change occupations or leave the labor force also will provide some jobs.

Coaches in girls' and women's sports may have better job opportunities and face less competition for positions.

Competition is likely to be strong also for jobs as scouts, particularly for professional teams.

O*NET

➤ Coaches and Scouts (27-2022.00)

Contacts for More Information

For more information about coaching and scouting for team and individual sports, visit
➤ National Collegiate Scouting Association (www.ncsasports.org)
➤ National High School Coaches Association (www.nhsca.com/)

For more information related to individual sports, refer to the organization that represents the sport.

Dancers and Choreographers

- **2012 Median Pay** .... $15.87 per hour
- **Entry-Level Education** ... High school diploma or equivalent
- **Work Experience in a Related Occupation** .... See "How to Become One"
- **On-the-Job Training** .... Long-term on-the-job training
- **Number of Jobs 2012** 25,800
- **Job Outlook, 2012–22** .... 13% (As fast as average)
- **Employment Change, 2012–22** 3,400

What Dancers and Choreographers Do

Dancers and choreographers express ideas and stories in performance, using dance. There are many types of dance, such as ballet, tango, modern dance, tap, and jazz.

Duties. Dancers typically do the following:

- Audition for a part in a show or for a job within a dance company
- Learn complex dance movements that entertain an audience
- Rehearse several hours each day to prepare for their performance
- Study new and emerging types of dance
- Work closely with instructors or other dancers to interpret or modify choreography
- Attend promotional events, such as photography sessions, for the production in which they are appearing

Dancers spend years learning dances and perfecting their skills. They usually perform as part of a group and in a variety of styles, including ballet, musical theater, and modern dance. Many perform on TV, in videos on the Internet, and in music videos, where they also may sing or act. Many dancers perform in shows at casinos, theme parks, and on cruise ships.

Choreographers typically do the following:

- Create dances or interpretations of existing dances
- Choose the music that will accompany a dance routine
- Audition dancers for a role in a show or within a dance company
- Assist with costume design, lighting, and other artistic aspects of a show

Most dancers begin formal training at an early age and many have their first professional audition by age 17 or 18.

Median Hourly Wages, May 2012

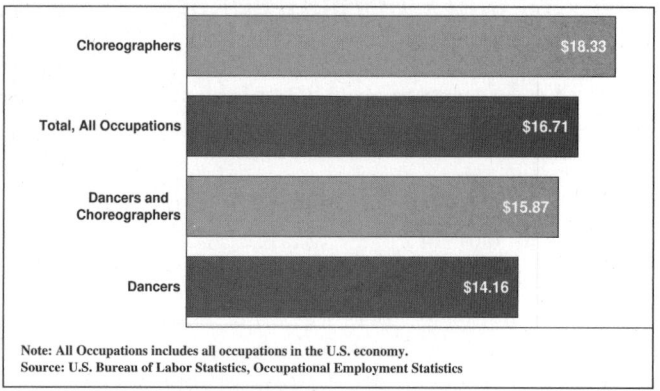

Note: All Occupations includes all occupations in the U.S. economy.
Source: U.S. Bureau of Labor Statistics, Occupational Employment Statistics

Percent Change in Employment, Projected 2012–2022

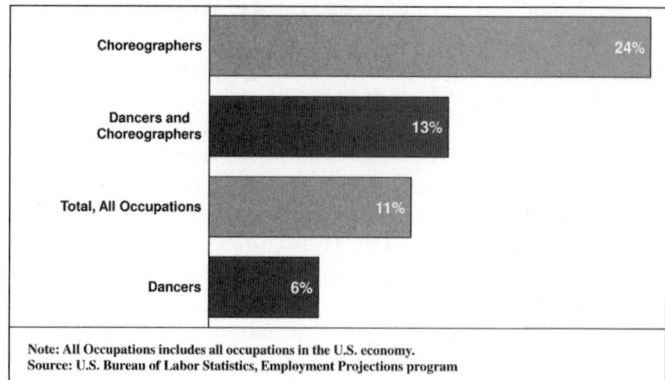

Note: All Occupations includes all occupations in the U.S. economy.
Source: U.S. Bureau of Labor Statistics, Employment Projections program

- Teach complex dance movements
- Study new and emerging types of dance to design more creative dance routines
- Help with the administrative duties of a dance company, such as budgeting

Choreographers create original dances and develop new interpretations of existing dances. They work in theaters, dance companies, and movie studios. During rehearsals, they typically demonstrate dance moves, to instruct dancers in the proper technique. Some choreographers work with performers other than dancers. For example, the complex martial arts scenes in movies are arranged by choreographers who specialize in martial arts.

Some people with dance backgrounds become dance teachers.

Work Environment

Dancers and choreographers held about 25,800 jobs in 2012. About 29 percent were self-employed.

About 30 percent of dancers work in performing arts companies, and about 57 work in private instruction.

Many dance companies tour for part of the year, and dancers and choreographers in those companies travel for months at a time.

Injuries and Illnesses. Dance takes a toll on a person's body, so on-the-job injuries for dancers are common. Many dancers stop performing by their late thirties because of the physical demands of their work. Nonperforming dancers may continue to work as choreographers, directors, or dance teachers.

Work Schedules. Schedules for dancers and choreographers vary, depending on where they work. During tours, dancers and choreographers spend most of the day in rehearsals and have performances at night, giving them long workdays. Some work part time at casinos, on cruise ships, and at theme parks. Although choreographers who work in dance schools may have a standard workweek when they are instructing students, they spend hours on their own creating new dance routines.

How to Become One

Education and training requirements vary with the type of dancer; however, all dancers need many years of formal training. Nearly all choreographers began their careers as dancers.

Education and Training. Many dancers begin training when they are young and continue to learn throughout their careers. Ballet dancers begin training the earliest, usually between the ages of 5 and 8 for girls and a few years later for boys. Their training becomes more serious as they enter their teens, and most ballet dancers begin their professional careers by the time they are 18.

Leading dance companies sometimes have summer training programs from which they sometimes select candidates for admission to their regular full-time training programs.

Modern dancers normally begin formal training while they are in high school. They attend after-school dance programs and summer training programs to prepare for their career or for a college dance program.

Some dancers and choreographers pursue postsecondary education. Many colleges and universities offer bachelor's and/or master's degrees in dance, typically through departments of theater or fine arts. The National Association of Schools of Dance accredits more than 70 dance programs. Most include coursework in a variety of dance styles, including modern, jazz, ballet, and hip-hop. Most entrants into college dance programs have previous formal training.

Some choreographers work as dance teachers. Teaching dance in college, high school, or elementary school requires a college degree. Some dance studios and conservatories prefer instructors who have a degree but may accept previous work, in lieu of a degree.

Work Experience in a Related Occupation. Nearly all choreographers began their careers as dancers. While working as dancers, they study different types of dance and learn how to choreograph routines.

Employment Projections Data for Dancers and Choreographers

Occupational title	SOC Code	Employment, 2012	Projected Employment, 2022	Change, 2012–2022 Percent	Change, 2012–2022 Numeric
Dancers and choreographers	27-2030	25,800	29,200	13	3,400
Dancers	27-2031	15,600	16,500	6	900
Choreographers	27-2032	10,200	12,700	24	2,500

Source: U.S. Bureau of Labor Statistics, Employment Projections Program

Note: Data are rounded. Go to **Occupational Information Included in the OOH** *for a discussion of the data in this table.*

Similar Occupations   This table shows a list of occupations with job duties that are similar to those of dancers and choreographers.

Occupations	Entry-level Education	2012 Pay	Projected Job Growth	Average Annual Openings
Actors	Some college, no degree	The annual wage is not available.	4.1%	2,890
Art Directors	Bachelor's degree	$80,880	3%	2,000
Music Directors and Composers	Bachelor's degree	$47,350	5%	2,440
Musicians and Singers	High school diploma or equivalent	The annual wage is not available.	5.2%	5,390
Postsecondary Teachers	See "How to Become One"	$70,380	19%	42,690
Producers and Directors	Bachelor's degree	$71,350	3%	3,790

Important Qualities

Athleticism. Successful dancers must have excellent balance, physical strength, and physical dexterity, so they can move their bodies without falling or losing their sense of rhythm.

Creativity. Dancers need artistic ability and creativity to express ideas through movement. Choreographers also must have artistic ability and innovative ideas, to create new and interesting dance routines.

Interpersonal skills. Dancers and choreographers may find job opportunities by networking within their communities.

Leadership skills. Choreographers must be able to direct a group of dancers to perform the routines that they have created.

Persistence. Dancers must commit to years of intense practice. They need to be able to accept rejection after an audition and to continue to practice for future spots. Choreographers must keep studying and creating new routines.

Physical stamina. Dancers are often physically active for long periods, so they must be able to rehearse for many hours without getting tired.

Teamwork. Most dance routines involve a group, so dancers must be able to work together to be successful.

Advancement. Some dancers take on more responsibility by becoming a dance captain in musical theater or a ballet master/ballet mistress in concert dance companies by leading rehearsals, or by working with less-experienced dancers when the choreographer is not present. Eventually, some dancers become choreographers.

Dancers and choreographers may also become producers and directors.

Pay

The median hourly wage for dancers was $14.16 in May 2012. The median wage is the wage at which half the workers in an occupation earned more than that amount and half earned less. The lowest 10 percent earned less than $8.50, and the top 10 percent earned more than $33.34.

The median hourly wage for choreographers was $18.33 in May 2012. The lowest 10 percent earned less than $9.41, and the top 10 percent earned more than $39.28.

Job Outlook

Employment of dancers is projected to grow 6 percent from 2012 to 2022, slower than the average for all occupations. Employment of choreographers is projected to grow 24 percent from 2012 to 2022, much faster than the average for all occupations. Dance companies are not expected to add many jobs over the decade. Generally, when one company disappears, a new one replaces it, without any change in the total number of companies. There may be better opportunities for dancers and choreographers in large cities, such as New York and Chicago, with many dance companies and performances.

A growing interest in dance in pop culture may provide opportunities in fields outside of dance companies, such as TV or movies, casinos, or theme parks. Many dancers and choreographers, nonetheless, struggle to find opportunities to express themselves creatively; newer dance companies rely on word-of-mouth, grants, and public funding. However, public funding and grants for dance performances can be highly competitive.

The growing interest in dance in pop culture is expected to lead more people to enroll in dance schools, and growing enrollment should create more jobs for choreographers.

Job Prospects. Dancers and choreographers face intense competition, and the number of applicants is expected to vastly exceed the number of job openings.

Dancers who attend schools or conservatories associated with a dance company may have a better chance of finding work at that company than others.

O*NET

➤ Dancers (27-2031.00)
➤ Choreographers (27-2032.00)

Contacts for More Information

For more information about dancers and choreographers, visit
➤ Dance USA (www.danceusa.org)
➤ Stage Directors and Choreographers Society (www.sdcweb.org)
➤ National Endowment for the Arts (www.nea.gov)
➤ National Association of Schools of Dance (http://nasd.arts-accredit.org)

Music Directors and Composers

- **2012 Median Pay** .... $47,350 per year
  $22.77 per hour
- **Entry-Level Education** .... Bachelor's degree
- **Work Experience in a Related Occupation** .... Less than 5 years
- **On-the-Job Training** .... None
- **Number of Jobs 2012** 77,600
- **Job Outlook, 2012–22** .... 5% (Slower than average)
- **Employment Change, 2012–22** 3,500

Composers write and arrange original music in a variety of musical styles.

What Music Directors and Composers Do

Music directors (also called conductors) lead orchestras and other musical groups during performances and recording sessions. Composers write and arrange original music in a variety of musical styles.

Duties. Music directors typically do the following:

- Select musical arrangements and compositions to be performed for live audiences or recordings
- Prepare for performances by reviewing and interpreting musical scores
- Direct rehearsals to prepare for performances and recordings
- Choose guest performers and soloists
- Audition new performers or assist section leaders with auditions
- Practice conducting to improve technique
- Meet with potential donors and attend fundraisers

Music directors lead orchestras and other musical groups. They ensure that the musicians play with one coherent sound, balancing the melody, timing, rhythm, and volume. They also give feedback to musicians and section leaders so that they can achieve the sound and style they want for the piece.

Music directors may work with a variety of orchestras and musical groups, including church choirs, youth orchestras, and high school or college bands, choirs, or orchestras. Some work with orchestras that accompany dance and opera companies.

Composers typically do the following:

- Write original music that orchestras, bands, and other musical groups perform
- Arrange existing music into new compositions
- Write lyrics for music or work with a lyricist
- Meet with companies, orchestras, or other musical groups that are interested in commissioning a piece of music
- Study and listen to music of various styles for inspiration
- Work with musicians to record their music

Composers write music for a variety of musical groups and users. Some work in a particular style of music, such as classical or jazz. They also may write for musicals, operas, or other types of theatrical productions.

Some composers write scores for movies or television; others write jingles for commercials. Many songwriters focus on composing music for audiences of popular music.

Some composers use instruments to help them as they write music. Others use software that allows them to hear a piece without musicians.

For more information about careers in music, see the profile on musicians and singers. Some music directors and composers give private music lessons to children and adults. Others work as music teachers in elementary, middle, or high schools. For more information, see the profiles on kindergarten and elementary school teachers, middle school teachers, and high school teachers.

Work Environment

Music directors and composers held about 77,600 jobs in 2012. About 23 percent were self-employed.

Jobs for music directors and composers are found all over the country. However, many jobs are located in cities in which entertainment activities are concentrated, such as New York, Los Angeles, and Chicago.

Many music directors work for religious organizations, frequently as choir directors. They also work in concert halls and recording studios. Music directors may spend a lot of time traveling to different performances.

Composers can work in offices, recording studios, or their own homes.

Work Schedules. Rehearsals and recording sessions are commonly held during business hours, but performances take place most often on nights and weekends. Because music writing is done primarily independently, composers may be able to set their own schedules.

Median Annual Wages, May 2012

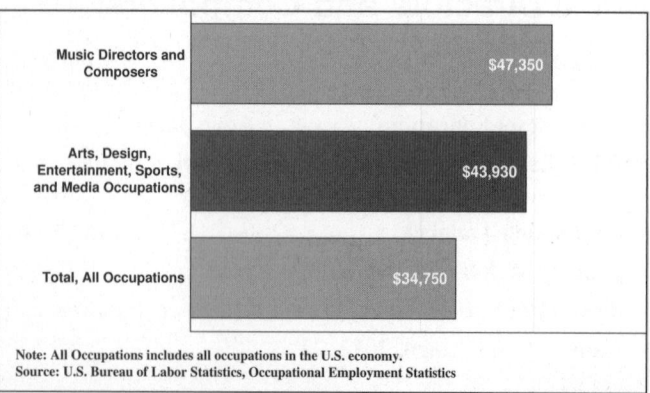

Note: All Occupations includes all occupations in the U.S. economy.
Source: U.S. Bureau of Labor Statistics, Occupational Employment Statistics

Percent Change in Employment, Projected 2012–2022

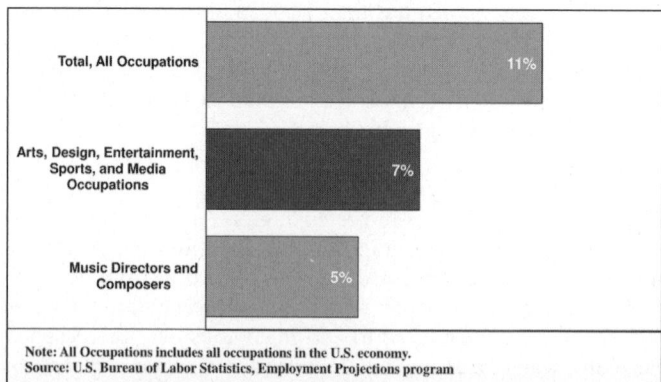

Note: All Occupations includes all occupations in the U.S. economy.
Source: U.S. Bureau of Labor Statistics, Employment Projections program

Employment Projections Data for Music Directors and Composers

Occupational title	SOC Code	Employment, 2012	Projected Employment, 2022	Change, 2012–2022	
				Percent	Numeric
Music directors and composers 27-2041		77,600	81,100	5	3,500

Source: U.S. Bureau of Labor Statistics, Employment Projections Program

Note: Data are rounded. Go to Occupational Information Included in the OOH for a discussion of the data in this table.

How to Become One

Educational and training requirements for music directors and composers vary. A conductor for a symphony orchestra typically needs a master's degree, but a choir director may need a bachelor's degree. There are no formal educational requirements for those interested in writing popular music. Music directors and composers typically begin their musical training at a young age by learning to play an instrument or singing.

Education. A degree in music theory, music composition, or conducting is generally preferred for those who want to work as a conductor or classical composer. To enter these programs, applicants are typically required to submit recordings, audition in person, or both.

These programs teach students about music history and styles, as well as composing and conducting techniques. Information on degree programs is available from the National Association of Schools of Music.

A bachelor's degree is typically required for those who want to work as a choir director.

There are no specific educational requirements for those interested in writing popular music. These composers usually find employment by submitting recordings of their compositions to bands, singers, and music and movie studios. Composers may promote themselves through personal websites or through online video or audio of their musical work.

Important Qualities

Discipline. Talent is not enough for most music directors and composers to find employment in this field. They must constantly practice and seek to improve their technique and style.

Interpersonal skills. Music directors and composers need to work with agents, musicians, and recording studios. Being friendly, respectful, open to criticism as well as praise, and enjoying being with others can help music directors and composers work well with a variety of people.

Leadership. Music directors and composers must guide musicians and singers by preparing musical arrangements and helping them achieve the best possible sound.

Musical talent. To become a music director or composer, one must have musical talent.

Perseverance. Attending auditions and submitting compositions can be frustrating because it may take many different auditions and submissions to find a job. Music directors and composers need determination and perseverance to continue attending auditions and submitting work after receiving many rejections.

Promotional skills. Music directors and composers need to promote their performances through local communities, word of mouth, and social media platforms. Good self-promotional skills are helpful in building a fan base and getting more work opportunities.

Training. Music directors and composers who are interested in classical music may seek additional training through music camps and fellowships. These programs provide participants with classes, lessons, and performance opportunities.

Work Experience in a Related Occupation. Often music directors and composers work as musicians or singers in a group, choir, or orchestra before they take on a leadership role. They use this time to master their instrument and gain an understanding of how the group functions.

Pay

The median annual wage for music directors and composers was $47,350 in May 2012. The median wage is the wage at which half the workers in an occupation earned more than that amount and

Similar Occupations This table shows a list of occupations with job duties that are similar to those of music directors and composers.

Occupations	Entry-level Education	2012 Pay	Projected Job Growth	Average Annual Openings
Actors	Some college, no degree	The annual wage is not available.	4.1%	2,890
Dancers and Choreographers	High school diploma or equivalent	The annual wage is not available.	13.2%	1,080
High School Teachers	Bachelor's degree	$55,050	6%	31,260
Kindergarten and Elementary School Teachers	Bachelor's degree	$53,060	12%	53,250
Middle School Teachers	Bachelor's degree	$53,430	12%	21,120
Musicians and Singers	High school diploma or equivalent	The annual wage is not available.	5.2%	5,390
Postsecondary Teachers	See "How to Become One"	$70,380	19%	42,690
Producers and Directors	Bachelor's degree	$71,350	3%	3,790
Writers and Authors	Bachelor's degree	$55,940	3%	3,180

half earned less. The lowest 10 percent earned less than $21,450, and the top 10 percent earned more than $86,110.

Job Outlook

Employment of music directors and composers is projected to grow 5 percent from 2012 to 2022, slower than the average for all occupations.

The number of people attending musical performances, such as symphonies and concerts, and theatrical performances, such as ballets and musical theater, is expected to increase moderately. Music directors will be needed to lead orchestras for concerts and musical theater performances. They will also conduct the music that accompanies ballet troupes and opera companies.

In addition, there will likely be a need for composers to write original music and arrange known works for performances. Composers are also expected to be needed to write film scores and music for television and commercials.

However, growth is expected to be limited because orchestras, opera companies, and other musical groups can have difficulty getting funds. Some music groups are nonprofit organizations that rely on donations and corporate sponsorships, in addition to ticket sales, to fund their work. These organizations often have difficulty finding enough money to cover their expenses. In addition, growth may be limited for music directors who work for public schools because state and local governments continue to struggle with school budgets.

Job Prospects. Despite expected growth, tough competition for jobs is anticipated because of the large number of people who are interested in entering this field. In particular, there will be considerable competition for full-time positions. Those with exceptional musical talent and dedication should have the best opportunities. Many music directors and composers experience periods of having no work; during these times, they may work in other occupations, attend auditions, or write music.

O*NET

➤ Music Directors and Composers (27-2041.00)
➤ Music Directors (27-2041.01)
➤ Music Composers and Arrangers (27-2041.04)

Contacts for More Information

For information about music degree programs, visit
➤ National Association of Schools of Music (http://nasm.arts-accredit.org/)

For more information about careers in music, visit
➤ Future of Music Coalition (http://futureofmusic.org/)

Musicians and Singers

- **2012 Median Pay** .... $23.50 per hour
- **Entry-Level Education** ... High school diploma or equivalent
- **Work Experience in a Related Occupation** .... None
- **On-the-Job Training** .... Long-term on-the-job training
- **Number of Jobs 2012** 167,400
- **Job Outlook, 2012–22** .... 5% (Slower than average)
- **Employment Change, 2012–22** 8,700

What Musicians and Singers Do

Musicians and singers play instruments or sing for live audiences and in recording studios. They perform in a variety of styles, such as classical, jazz, opera, hip-hop, or rock.

Duties. Musicians and singers typically do the following:

- Perform music for live audiences and recordings
- Audition for positions in orchestras, choruses, bands, and other types of music groups
- Practice playing instruments or singing to improve their technique
- Rehearse to prepare for performances
- Find locations for performances or concerts
- Travel, sometimes great distances, to performance venues
- Promote their careers by maintaining a website or social media presence or doing photo shoots and interviews

Musicians play one or more instruments. To make themselves more marketable, many musicians become proficient in multiple musical instruments or styles.

Musicians play in bands, orchestras, or small groups. Those in bands may play at weddings, private parties, clubs, or bars while they try to build enough fans to get a recording contract or representation by an agent. Some musicians work as a part of a large group of musicians who must work and practice together, such as an orchestra. A few musicians become section leaders, who may be responsible for assigning parts to other musicians or leading rehearsals.

Others musicians are "session" musicians, who specialize in playing backup for a singer or band leader during recording sessions and live performances.

Singers perform vocal music in a variety of styles. Some specialize in a particular vocal style, such as opera or jazz; others perform in a variety of musical genres. Singers, particularly those who specialize in opera or classical music, may perform in different languages, such as French or Italian. Opera singers act out a story by singing instead of speaking the dialogue.

Some singers become background singers, providing vocals to harmonize or support a lead singer.

Musicians interested in performing popular music typically find jobs by attending auditions or arranging their own performances. They may seek representation by an agent who will help them find jobs and performance opportunities.

Musicians face keen competition, especially for full-time jobs.

Median Hourly Wages, May 2012

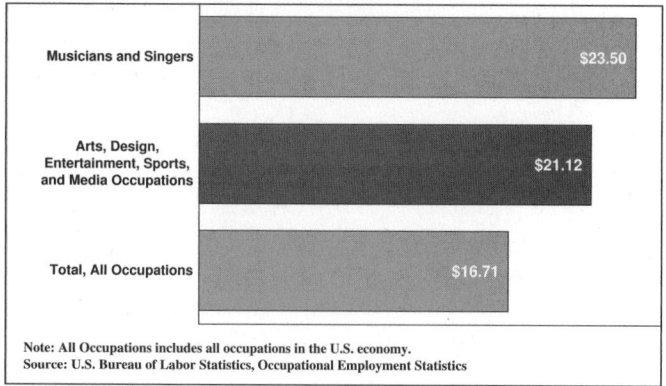

Note: All Occupations includes all occupations in the U.S. economy.
Source: U.S. Bureau of Labor Statistics, Occupational Employment Statistics

Percent Change in Employment, Projected 2012–2022

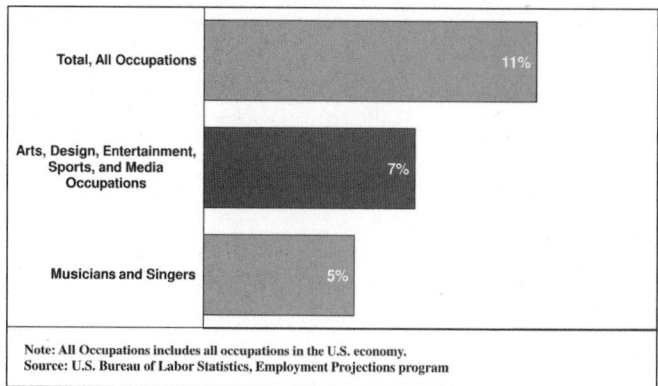

Note: All Occupations includes all occupations in the U.S. economy.
Source: U.S. Bureau of Labor Statistics, Employment Projections program

In some cases, musicians and singers write their own music to record and perform. For more information about careers in songwriting, see the profile on music directors and composers.

Some musicians and singers give private music lessons to children and adults.

Others with a background in music may teach music in public schools, but they typically need a bachelor's degree and a teaching license. See the profiles on kindergarten and elementary school teachers, middle school teachers, and high school teachers.

Work Environment

Musicians and singers held about 167,400 jobs in 2012. They perform in settings such as concert halls, arenas, and clubs. They often work for religious organizations and performing arts companies. In 2012, 36 percent of musicians and singers were self-employed.

Musicians and singers may spend a lot of time traveling between performances. Some spend time in recording studios. There are many jobs in cities that have a high concentration of entertainment activities, such as New York, Los Angeles, Chicago, and Nashville.

Musicians and singers who give recitals or perform in nightclubs travel frequently and may tour nationally or internationally.

Many musicians and singers find only part-time or intermittent work, however, and have long periods of unemployment between jobs. The stress of constantly looking for work leads many to accept permanent full-time jobs in other occupations while working part time as a musician or singer.

In 2012, the industries employing the most musicians and singers were as follows:

Religious, grantmaking, civic, professional, and similar
   organizations...45%
Performing arts companies 12
Educational services; state, local, and private 2

Work Schedules. Rehearsals and recording sessions are commonly held during business hours, but live performances are most often at night and on weekends.

How to Become One

There are no postsecondary education requirements for musicians or singers interested in performing popular music; however, many performers of classical music and opera have at least a bachelor's degree.

Education. There are no postsecondary education requirements for those interested in performing popular music. Many musicians and singers of classical music and opera have a bachelor's degree in music theory or performance. To be accepted into one of these programs, applicants are typically required to submit recordings or audition in person, and sometimes must do both. Undergraduate music programs teach students about music history and styles and teach methods for improving their instrumental and vocal technique and musical expression.

Some musicians and singers choose to continue their education by pursuing a master's degree in fine arts or music.

Important Qualities

Dedication. Auditioning for jobs can be a frustrating process because it may take many different auditions to get hired. Musicians and singers need determination and dedication to continue to audition after receiving many rejections.

Discipline. Talent is not enough for most musicians and singers to find employment in this field. They must constantly practice and rehearse to improve their technique, style, and performances.

Interpersonal skills. Musicians and singers need to work well with a variety of people, such as agents, music producers, conductors, and other musicians. Good people skills are helpful in building good working relationships.

Musical talent. Professional musicians or singers must have superior musical abilities.

Physical stamina. Musicians and singers who play in concerts or in nightclubs and those who tour must be able to endure frequent travel and irregular performance schedules.

Promotional skills. Musicians and singers need to promote their performances through local communities, word of mouth, and social media platforms. Good self-promotional skills are helpful in building a fan base.

Employment Projections Data for Musicians and Singers

Occupational title	SOC Code	Employment, 2012	Projected Employment, 2022	Change, 2012–2022	
				Percent	Numeric
Musicians and singers...	27-2042	167,400	176,200	5	8,700

Source: U.S. Bureau of Labor Statistics, Employment Projections Program

Note: Data are rounded. Go to **Occupational Information Included in the OOH** *for a discussion of the data in this table.*

Similar Occupations   This table shows a list of occupations with job duties that are similar to those of musicians and singers.

Occupations	Entry-level Education	2012 Pay	Projected Job Growth	Average Annual Openings
Actors	Some college, no degree	The annual wage is not available.	4.1%	2,890
Dancers and Choreographers	High school diploma or equivalent	The annual wage is not available.	13.2%	1,080
High School Teachers	Bachelor's degree	$55,050	6%	31,260
Kindergarten and Elementary School Teachers	Bachelor's degree	$53,060	12%	53,250
Middle School Teachers	Bachelor's degree	$53,430	12%	21,120
Music Directors and Composers	Bachelor's degree	$47,350	5%	2,440
Postsecondary Teachers	See "How to Become One"	$70,380	19%	42,690
Producers and Directors	Bachelor's degree	$71,350	3%	3,790

Training. Musicians and singers need extensive and prolonged learning and practice to acquire the skills and knowledge necessary to interpret music at a professional level. They typically begin singing or learning to play an instrument by taking lessons and classes when they are children. In addition, they must practice often to develop their talent and technique.

Musicians and singers interested in classical music may seek additional training through music camps and fellowships. These programs provide participants with classes, lessons, and performance opportunities. Sometimes these programs are associated with professional orchestras and may lead to a permanent spot in that orchestra.

Advancement. As with other occupations in which people perform, advancement for musicians and singers means becoming better known, finding work more easily, and earning more money for each performance. Successful musicians and singers often rely on agents or managers to find them jobs, negotiate contracts, and develop their careers.

Pay

The median hourly wage for musicians and singers was $23.50 in May 2012. The median wage is the wage at which half the workers in an occupation earned more than that amount and half earned less. The lowest 10 percent earned less than $8.81, and the top 10 percent earned more than $65.24.

In May 2012, the median hourly wages for musicians and singers in the top three industries in which these workers were employed were as follows:

Performing arts companies $26.72
Educational services; state, local, and private 20.46
Religious, grantmaking, civic, professional, and similar
organizations 19.43

Job Outlook

Employment of musicians and singers is projected to grow 5 percent from 2012 to 2022, slower than the average for all occupations. Growth will be due to increases in demand for musical performances.

Digital downloads and streaming platforms make it easier for fans to listen to recordings and view performances. Easier access to recordings gives musicians more publicity and grows interest in their work, and concertgoers may become interested in seeing them perform live.

There will be additional demand for musicians to serve as session musicians and backup artists for recordings and to go on tour. Singers will be needed to sing backup and to make recordings for commercials, films, and television.

However, employment growth will likely be limited in orchestras, opera companies, and other musical groups because they can have difficulty getting funding. Some musicians and singers work for nonprofit organizations that rely on donations, government funding, and corporate sponsorships in addition to ticket sales to fund their work. During economic downturns, these organizations may have trouble finding enough funding to cover their expenses.

Job Prospects. There will be tough competition for jobs because of the large number of workers who are interested in becoming musicians and singers. In particular, there will likely be considerable competition for full-time positions.

Musicians and singers with exceptional musical talent and dedication should have the best opportunities.

Many musicians and singers experience periods of unemployment.

O*NET

➤ Musicians and Singers (27-2042.00)
➤ Singers (27-2042.01)
➤ Musicians, Instrumental (27-2042.02)

Contacts for More Information

For more information about music degree programs, visit
➤ National Association of Schools of Music (http://nasm.arts-accredit.org/)

Producers and Directors

- **2012 Median Pay** .... $71,350 per year
  $34.31 per hour
- **Entry-Level Education** ....Bachelor's degree
- **Work Experience in a Related Occupation** ....Less than 5 years
- **On-the-Job Training** .... None
- **Number of Jobs 2012** 103,500
- **Job Outlook, 2012–22** .... 3% (Slower than average)
- **Employment Change, 2012–22** 2,900

Producers and directors often work long, irregular hours.

What Producers and Directors Do

Producers and directors create motion pictures, television shows, live theater, and other performing arts productions. They interpret a writer's script to entertain or inform an audience.

Duties. Producers and directors typically do the following:

- Select scripts
- Audition and select cast members and the film or stage crew
- Approve the design and financial aspects of a production
- Oversee the production process, including performances, lighting, and choreography
- Oversee the post-production process, including editing, special effects, music selection, and a performance's overall tone
- Ensure that a project stays on schedule and within budget
- Approve new developments in the production

Large productions often have associate, assistant, and line producers who share responsibilities. For example, on a large movie set an executive producer is in charge of the entire production, and a line producer runs the day-to-day operations. A TV show may employ sev-

eral assistant producers to whom the head or executive producer gives certain duties, such as supervising the costume and makeup team.

Similarly, large productions usually employ several assistant directors, who help the director with tasks such as making set changes or notifying the performers when it is their time to go onstage. The specific responsibilities of assistant producers or directors vary with the size and type of production they work on.

Producers make the business and financial decisions for a motion picture, TV show, or stage production. They raise money for the project and hire the director and crew. The crew may include set and costume designers, a musical director, a choreographer, and other workers. Some producers may assist in the selection of cast members. Producers set the budget and approve any major changes to the project. They make sure that the production is completed on time, and they are responsible for the way the finished project turns out.

Directors are responsible for the creative decisions of a production. They select cast members, conduct rehearsals, and direct the work of the cast and crew. During rehearsal, they work with the actors to help them more accurately portray their characters. They also work with cinematographers and other crew members to ensure the final product matches the overall vision.

Directors work with set designers, costume designers, location scouts, and art directors to build a project's set. During a film's postproduction phase, they work closely with film editors and music supervisors to make sure that the final product comes out the way the producer and director envisioned. Stage directors, unlike television or film directors who document their product with cameras, make sure the cast and crew give a consistently strong live performance.

Although directors are in charge of the creative aspects of a show, they ultimately answer to the executive producer.

Work Environment

Producers and directors held about 103,500 jobs in 2012. Producers and directors work under a lot of pressure, and many are under constant stress to finish their work on time. Work assignments are usually short, ranging from 1 day to a few months. They sometimes must work in unpleasant conditions, such as bad weather.

The industries that employed the most producers and directors in 2012 were as follows:

Motion picture and video industries 33%
Television broadcasting 14
Radio broadcasting 5
Performing arts companies 4
Cable and other subscription programming 3

About 15 percent of producers and directors were self-employed in 2012.

Median Annual Wages, May 2012

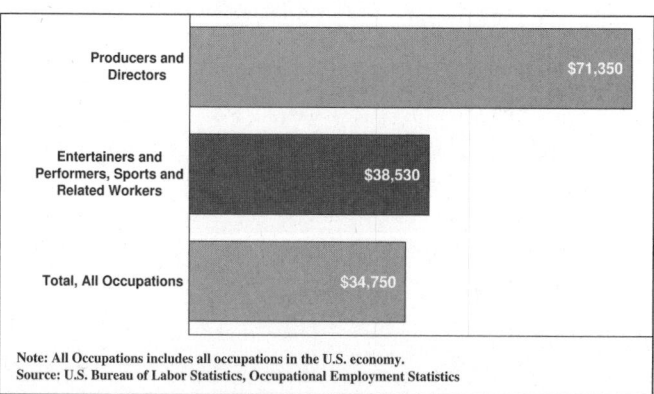

Note: All Occupations includes all occupations in the U.S. economy.
Source: U.S. Bureau of Labor Statistics, Occupational Employment Statistics

Percent Change in Employment, Projected 2012–2022

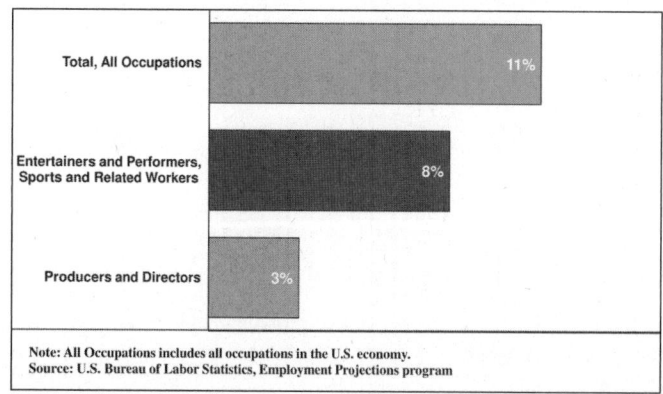

Note: All Occupations includes all occupations in the U.S. economy.
Source: U.S. Bureau of Labor Statistics, Employment Projections program

Employment Projections Data for Producers and Directors

Occupational title	SOC Code	Employment, 2012	Projected Employment, 2022	Change, 2012–2022	
				Percent	Numeric
Producers and directors	27-2012	103,500	106,400	3	2,900

Source: U.S. Bureau of Labor Statistics, Employment Projections Program

Note: Data are rounded. Go to **Occupational Information Included in the OOH** *for a discussion of the data in this table.*

Work Schedules. Work hours for producers and directors can be long and irregular. Evening, weekend, and holiday work is common. Many producers and directors do not work a standard workweek because they have variable schedules. Theater directors and producers may travel with a touring show across the country, while those in film and television may work on location (a site away from the studio where all or part of the filming occurs).

How to Become One

Most producers and directors have a bachelor's degree and several years of work experience in an occupation related to motion picture, TV, or theater production, such as an actor, film and video editor, or cinematographer.

Education. Producers and directors usually have a bachelor's degree. Many students study film or cinema at college and universities. In these programs, students learn about film history, editing, and lighting, and creating their own films. Others major in writing, acting, journalism, or communication. Some producers earn a degree in business, arts management, or nonprofit management.

Many stage directors complete a degree in theater and some go on to receive a Master of Fine Arts (MFA) degree. Classes may include directing, playwriting, and set design, as well as some acting classes. The National Association of Schools of Theater accredits more than 150 programs in theater arts.

Important Qualities

Communication skills. Producers and directors must coordinate the work of many different people to finish a production on time and within budget.

Creativity. Because a script can be interpreted in different ways, directors must decide how they want to interpret it and then how to represent the script's ideas on the screen or stage.

Leadership skills. A director instructs actors and helps them portray their characters in a believable manner. They also supervise the crew, who are responsible for the behind the scenes work.

Management skills. Producers must find and hire the best director and crew for the production and make sure that all involved do their jobs effectively and efficiently.

Work Experience in a Related Occupation. Producers and directors usually have several years of work experience in an occupation related to motion picture, TV, or theater production. Many directors begin as actors, writers, film or video editors, cinematographers, choreographers, or animators, and over time they learn about directing. For more information, see the profiles on actors, writers and authors, film and video editors and camera operators, dancers and choreographers, and multimedia artists and animators.

Directors may also begin their careers as assistants to successful directors on a film set. In nonprofit theaters, most aspiring directors begin as assistant directors, a position that is usually treated as an unpaid internship.

Producers might start out working in a theatrical management office as a business manager, or as an assistant or another low-profile job in a TV or movie studio. Some were directors or worked in another role behind the scenes of a show or movie.

Advancement. As a producer's or director's reputation grows, he or she may work on larger and higher profile projects.

Pay

The median annual wage for producers and directors was $71,350 in May 2012. The median wage is the wage at which half the workers in an occupation earned more than that amount and half earned less. The lowest 10 percent earned less than $32,080, and the top 10 percent earned more than $187,200 in May 2012.

Some producer's and director's income is earned as a percentage of ticket sales. A few of the most successful producers and directors have extraordinarily high earnings, but most do not.

Similar Occupations   This table shows a list of occupations with job duties that are similar to those of producers and directors.

Occupations	Entry-level Education	2012 Pay	Projected Job Growth	Average Annual Openings
Actors	Some college, no degree	The annual wage is not available.	4.1%	2,890
Announcers	See "How to Become One"	$27,652	1%	1,160
Art Directors	Bachelor's degree	$80,880	3%	2,000
Dancers and Choreographers	High school diploma or equivalent	The annual wage is not available.	13.2%	1,080
Film and Video Editors and Camera Operators	Bachelor's degree	$46,538	3%	510
Multimedia Artists and Animators	Bachelor's degree	$61,370	6%	2,060
Top Executives	Bachelor's degree	$104,073	11%	70,090
Writers and Authors	Bachelor's degree	$55,940	3%	3,180

In May 2012, the median annual wages for producers and directors in the top five industries in which they worked were as follows:

Motion picture and video industries $94,110
Cable and other subscription programming 83,220
Television broadcasting 56,950
Performing arts companies 49,690
Radio broadcasting 48,110

Job Outlook

Employment of producers and directors is projected to grow 3 percent from 2012 to 2022, slower than the average for all occupations.

Some job growth in the motion picture and video industry is expected to stem from strong demand from the public for more movies and television shows, as well as an increased demand from foreign audiences for U.S.-produced films. In addition, production companies are experimenting with new content delivery methods, such as mobile and online TV, which may lead to more work opportunities for producers and directors in the future. These delivery methods are still in their early stages, however, and their potential for success is not entirely known.

Theater producers and directors who work in small- and medium-sized theaters may see slower job growth because many of those theaters have difficulty finding funding as the number of performances decline. Large theaters in big cities, which usually have more stable sources of funding, should provide more opportunities.

Job Prospects. Producers and directors face intense competition for jobs because there are many more people who want to work in this field than there are jobs available. In film, directors who have experience on film sets should have the best job prospects. Producers who have good business skills will likely have the best prospects.

O*NET

➤ Producers and Directors (27-2012.00)
➤ Producers (27-2012.01)
➤ Directors—Stage, Motion Pictures, Television, and Radio (27-2012.02)
➤ Program Directors (27-2012.03)
➤ Talent Directors (27-2012.04)
➤ Technical Directors/Managers (27-2012.05)

Contacts for More Information

For more information about producers and directors, visit
➤ Directors Guild of America (www.dga.org)
➤ National Association of Schools of Theater (http://nast.arts-accredit.org)
➤ National Endowment for the Arts (www.nea.gov)
➤ Producers Guild of America (www.producersguild.org/)
➤ Stage Directors and Choreographers Society (www.sdcweb.org)

Umpires, Referees, and Other Sports Officials

- **2012 Median Pay** .... $23,290 per year
- **Entry-Level Education** ... High school diploma or equivalent
- **Work Experience in a Related Occupation** .... None
- **On-the-Job Training** .... Moderate-term on-the-job training
- **Number of Jobs 2012** 17,500
- **Job Outlook, 2012–22** .... 8% (As fast as average)
- **Employment Change, 2012–22** 1,300

What Umpires, Referees, and Other Sports Officials Do

Umpires, referees, and other sports officials preside over competitive athletic or sporting events to help maintain standards of play. They detect infractions and decide penalties according to the rules of the game.

Duties. Umpires, referees, and other sports officials typically do the following:

- Officiate sporting events, games, and competitions
- Judge performances in sporting competitions to determine a winner
- Inspect sports equipment and examine all participants to ensure safety
- Keep track of event times, starting or stopping play when necessary
- Signal participants and other officials when infractions occur or to regulate play or competition
- Settle claims of infractions or complaints by participants
- Enforce the rules of the game and assess penalties when necessary

While officiating at sporting events, umpires, referees, and sports officials must anticipate play and position themselves where they can best see the action, assess the situation, and determine any violations of the rules.

Sports officials typically rely on their judgment to call out infractions and penalties. Officials in some sports may use video replay to help make the correct call.

Some sports officials, such as boxing referees, may work independently. Others, such as baseball or softball umpires, work in group. Each official working in a group may have different responsibilities. For example, in baseball, one umpire is responsible for signaling balls and strikes while others are responsible for signaling fair and foul balls out in the field.

Regardless of the sport, the job is highly stressful because officials often must make split-second decisions. These decisions sometimes result in strong disagreement expressed by opposing team players, coaches, and spectators.

Many umpires, referees, and other sports officials are primarily employed in other occupations and supplement their income by officiating part time.

Work Environment

Umpires, referees, and other sports officials held about 17,500 jobs in 2012. About 9 percent were self-employed.

The industries that employed the most umpires, referees, and other sports officials in 2012 were as follows:

Local government, excluding education and hospitals 31%
Amusement, gambling, and recreation industries 18
Elementary and secondary schools; state, local, and private ... 14
Performing arts, spectator sports, and related industries 14
Religious, grantmaking, civic, professional, and similar
 organizations 10

Umpires, referees, and other sports officials work indoors and out, in all types of weather. Some workers must travel on long bus rides to sporting events. Others, especially officials in professional sports, travel by air.

Because sports officials must observe play and often make split-second decisions, the work can be filled with pressure. Strong disagreements and criticism from athletes, coaches, and fans can result in additional stress.

Work Schedules. Umpires, referees, and sports officials often work irregular hours, including evenings, weekends, and holidays.

How to Become One

Educational requirements vary by state and are sometimes determined by the local sports association. Although some states have no formal education requirements, other states require umpires, referees, and other sports officials to have a high school diploma. Training requirements also vary by state and the level and type of sport. All sports, however, require extensive knowledge of the rules of the game.

Education. Each state and sport association has its own education requirements for umpires, referees, and other sports officials. Some require no formal education, while others require sports officials to have a high school diploma.

For more information on educational requirements by state, refer to the specific state athletic or activity association.

Licenses, Certifications, and Registrations. To officiate at high school athletic events, umpires, referees, and other officials must register with the state or local agency that oversees high school athletics. They also typically need to pass an exam on the rules of the particular game. Some states and associations may require applicants to attend umpiring or refereeing classes before taking the exam or joining an association.

Some local associations may require officials to attend monthly association meetings.

Training. Umpires, referees, and other sports officials may be required to attend training sessions and seminars before, during, or after the season. These sessions allow officials to learn about rule changes, review and evaluate their own performances, and improve their officiating. Other associations require officials to attend annual training workshops before renewing their officiating license.

Advancement. Most new umpires, referees, and other sports officials begin by officiating youth or freshmen high school sports. After a few years, they may advance to the junior varsity or varsity levels. Those that wish to advance to the collegiate level must typically officiate at the varsity high school level for many years.

For some umpires, referees, and other sports officials, working in professional sports is the biggest advancement. Some officials may advance through the high school and collegiate levels to reach the professional level. Some sports, such as baseball, have their own professional training schools that prepare aspiring umpires and officials for a career at the minor and major league levels. In this system, umpires begin their professional career officiating in

Umpires and referees keep track of event times, starting or stopping play when necessary.

the minor leagues and typically need 7 to 10 years of experience before moving up into the major leagues.

Standards for umpires and other officials become more stringent as the level of competition advances.

Other Experience. Umpires, referees, and other sports official must have immense knowledge of the rules of the game they are officiating. Many officials gain the knowledge of the game by attending training sessions or camps that teach the important rules and regulations of the sport.

Some officials may also have gained this knowledge through years of playing the sport at some level. However, previous playing experience is not a requirement to become an umpire, referee, or other sports officials.

Important Qualities

Communication skills. Umpires, referees, and other sports officials must have good communication skills because they inform athletes on the rules of the game and settle disputes between competing players. Some sports officials also must communicate violations and infractions to opposing team players, coaches, and spectators.

Decision-making skills. Umpires, referees, and other sports officials must observe play, assess various situations, and often make split-second decisions.

Good vision. Umpires, referees, and other sports officials must have good vision to view infractions and determine any violations during play. In some sports, such as diving or gymnastics, sports

Median Annual Wages, May 2012

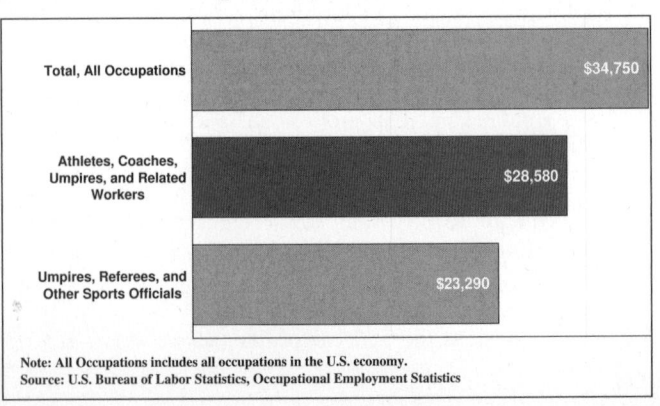

Total, All Occupations	$34,750
Athletes, Coaches, Umpires, and Related Workers	$28,580
Umpires, Referees, and Other Sports Officials	$23,290

Note: All Occupations includes all occupations in the U.S. economy.
Source: U.S. Bureau of Labor Statistics, Occupational Employment Statistics

Percent Change in Employment, Projected 2012–2022

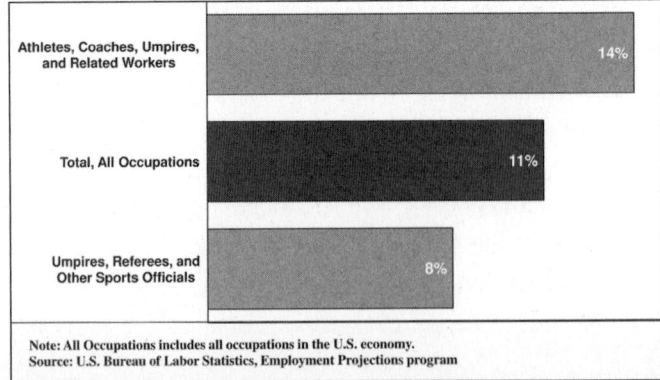

Athletes, Coaches, Umpires, and Related Workers	14%
Total, All Occupations	11%
Umpires, Referees, and Other Sports Officials	8%

Note: All Occupations includes all occupations in the U.S. economy.
Source: U.S. Bureau of Labor Statistics, Employment Projections program

Employment Projections Data for Umpires, Referees, and Other Sports Officials

Occupational title	SOC Code	Employment, 2012	Projected Employment, 2022	Change, 2012–2022	
				Percent	Numeric
Umpires, referees, and other sports officials............ 27-2023		17,500	18,800	8	1,300

Source: U.S. Bureau of Labor Statistics, Employment Projections Program

Note: Data are rounded. Go to Occupational Information Included in the OOH for a discussion of the data in this table.

Similar Occupations This table shows a list of occupations with job duties that are similar to those of umpires, referees, and other sports officials.

Occupations	Entry-level Education	2012 Pay	Projected Job Growth	Average Annual Openings
Athletes and Sports Competitors	High school diploma or equivalent	$40,060	7%	540
Coaches and Scouts	Bachelor's degree	$28,360	15%	10,850

officials must also be able to clearly observe an athlete's form for imperfections.

Stamina. Many umpires, referees, and sports officials are required to stand, walk, run, or squat for long periods during games and events.

Teamwork. Because many umpires, referees, and sports officials work in teams to officiate a game, the ability to cooperate and come to a mutual decision is essential.

Pay

The median annual wage for umpires, referees, and other sports officials was $23,290 in May 2012. The median wage is the wage at which half the workers in an occupation earned more than that amount and half earned less. The lowest 10 percent earned less than $17,040, and the top 10 percent earned more than $52,370.

In May 2012, the median annual wages for umpires, referees, and other sports officials in the top five industries in which these officials worked were as follows:

Local government, excluding education and hospitals.......	$25,140
Performing arts, spectator sports, and related industries......	23,970
Religious, grantmaking, civic, professional, and similar organizations..................................	23,400
Elementary and secondary schools; state, local, and private..................................	20,230
Amusement, gambling, and recreation industries................	19,610

Job Outlook

Employment of umpires, referees, and other sports officials is projected to grow 8 percent from 2012 to 2022, about as fast as the average for all occupations. Rising participation in high school and college sports may increase demand for these officials.

High school enrollment is projected to increase over the next decade, which could result in a rise in the number of student-athletes. As schools offer more athletic programs and more students participate in sports, the demand for umpires, referees, and other sports officials may increase.

However, funding for athletic programs often is cut first when budgets become tight. Still, the popularity of interscholastic sports often enables shortfalls to be offset with assistance from fundraisers, booster clubs, and parents.

Participation in college sports is also projected to increase over the next decade, particularly at smaller colleges and in women's sports. Many small, Division-III colleges are expanding their sports programs and adding new teams as a way to help promote the school and recruit potential students.

Demand for umpires, referees, and sports officials is also projected to grow as population growth increases the overall number of people participating in organized sports.

Job Prospects. Overall job prospects for umpires, referees, and sports officials are expected to be good at the youth and high school levels. Those with prior officiating experience will have the best job opportunities.

However, competition is expected to be strong for the college and professional levels. Many people are attracted to working in sports, and the collegiate and professional levels typically have few job openings and low turnover.

O*NET

➤ Umpires, Referees, and Other Sports Officials (27-2023.00)

Contacts for More Information

For more information about umpires, referees, and other sports officials, visit

➤ National Association of Sports Officials (www.naso.org/)

For more information on umpires, referees, and other sports officials, refer to the organization that represents the sport and the locality.

Farming, Fishing, and Forestry

Agricultural Workers

- **2012 Median Pay** .... $18,910 per year
  $9.09 per hour

- **Entry-Level Education** ....See "How to Become One"

- **Work Experience in
  a Related Occupation** ....See "How to Become One"

- **On-the-Job Training** ....Short-term on-the-job training

- **Number of Jobs 2012** 749,400

- **Job Outlook, 2012–22** .... -3% (Decline)

- **Employment Change, 2012–22** .... -25,000

What Agricultural Workers Do

Agricultural workers maintain the quality of farms, crops, and livestock by operating machinery and doing physical labor under the supervision of farmers, ranchers, and other agricultural managers.

Duties. Agricultural workers typically do the following:

- Harvest and inspect crops by hand

- Irrigate farm soil and maintain ditches or pipes and pumps

- Operate and service farm machinery

- Spray fertilizer or pesticide solutions to control insects, fungi, and weeds

- Move shrubs, plants, and trees with wheelbarrows or tractors

- Feed livestock and clean and disinfect their pens, cages, yards, and hutches

- Examine animals to detect symptoms of illness or injury

- Use brands, tags, or tattoos to mark livestock to identify ownership and grade

- Herd livestock to pastures for grazing or to scales, trucks, or other enclosures

- Administer vaccines to protect animals from diseases

The following are examples of types of agricultural workers:

Crop, nursery, and greenhouse farmworkers and laborers do numerous tasks related to growing and harvesting grains, fruits, vegetables, nuts, and other crops. They plant and seed, prune, irrigate, harvest, and pack and load crops for shipment.

Farmworkers also apply pesticides, herbicides, and fertilizers to crops. They repair fences and some farm equipment.

Nursery and greenhouse workers prepare land or greenhouse beds for growing horticultural products such as trees, plants, flowers, and sod. They also plant, water, prune, weed, and spray the plants. They may cut, roll, and stack sod; stake trees; tie, wrap, and pack plants to fill orders; and dig up or move field-grown shrubs and trees.

Farm and ranch animal farmworkers care for live animals, including cattle, sheep, pigs, goats, horses, poultry, finfish, or shellfish. These animals are usually raised to supply meat, fur, skins, feathers, eggs, milk, or honey.

These farmworkers may feed, herd, brand, weigh, and load animals. They also keep records on animals; examine animals to detect diseases and injuries; and administer medications, vaccinations, or insecticides.

Many workers clean and maintain animal housing areas every day. On dairy farms, animal farmworkers operate milking machines.

Agricultural equipment operators use a variety of farm equipment to plow and sow seeds, as well as maintain and harvest crops. They may use tractors, fertilizer spreaders, balers, combines, threshers, and trucks. These workers also operate machines such as conveyor belts, loading machines, separators, cleaners, and dryers. Workers may make adjustments and minor repairs to equipment.

Animal breeders use their knowledge of genetics and animal science to select and breed animals that will produce offspring with desired traits and characteristics. For example, they breed chickens that lay more eggs, pigs that produce leaner meat, and sheep with more desirable wool. Other animal breeders breed and raise cats, dogs, and other household pets.

To know which animals to breed and when to breed them, animal breeders keep detailed records. Breeders note animals' health, size and weight, and the amount and quality of the product they produce. Animal breeders also track the traits of animals' offspring.

Some animal breeders work as consultants for farmers, but others breed and raise their own animals for sale or future breeding. Breeders fix and clean animals' shelters, feed and water animals, and oversee animals' health.

A nursery worker waters flowers in a greenhouse.

Median Annual Wages, May 2012

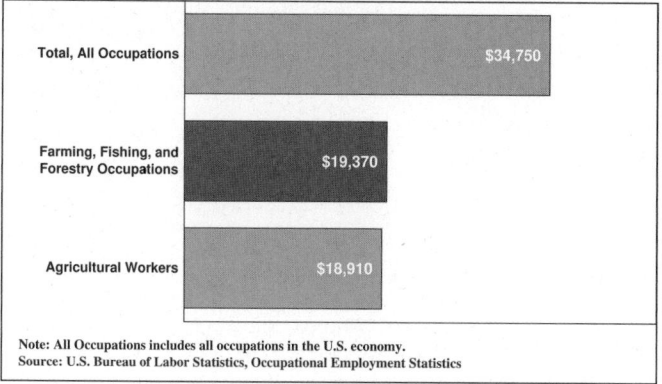

Total, All Occupations — $34,750

Farming, Fishing, and Forestry Occupations — $19,370

Agricultural Workers — $18,910

Note: All Occupations includes all occupations in the U.S. economy.
Source: U.S. Bureau of Labor Statistics, Occupational Employment Statistics

Percent Change in Employment, Projected 2012–2022

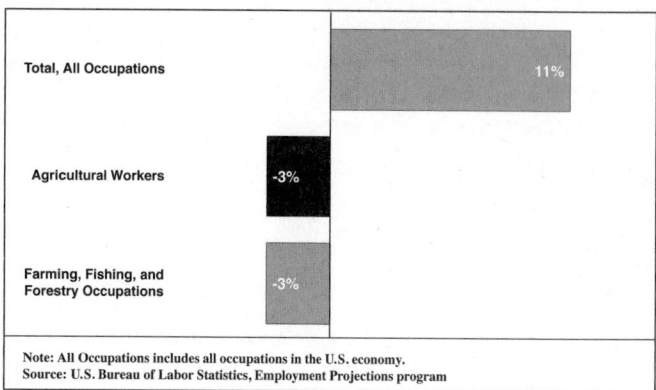

Total, All Occupations — 11%

Agricultural Workers — -3%

Farming, Fishing, and Forestry Occupations — -3%

Note: All Occupations includes all occupations in the U.S. economy.
Source: U.S. Bureau of Labor Statistics, Employment Projections program

Work Environment

Agricultural workers held about 749,400 jobs in 2012.

They usually work outdoors in all kinds of weather. Animal breeders may travel from farm to farm to consult with farmers, ranchers, and other agricultural managers about their livestock.

Agricultural workers' work can be difficult. To harvest fruits and vegetables by hand, workers frequently bend and crouch. They also lift and carry crops and tools.

Injuries and Illnesses. Agricultural workers risk exposure to pesticides sprayed on crops or plants. Exposure can be minimal, however, if workers follow the appropriate safety procedures. Tractors and other farm machinery can cause serious injury, so workers must be constantly alert. Agricultural workers who work directly with animals risk being bitten or kicked.

Work Schedules. Some agricultural workers, called migrant farmworkers, move from location to location as crops ripen. Their unsettled lifestyles and periods of unemployment between jobs can cause stress. Most agricultural workers are in Arizona, California, Colorado, Texas, and New Mexico.

Many agricultural workers have seasonal work schedules. Seasonal workers typically work longer hours during planting or harvesting times or when animals must be sheltered and fed. In 2012, nearly 1 in 3 worked part time.

How to Become One

Agricultural workers typically receive on-the-job training. Many do not need a high school diploma before they begin working, but animal breeders typically need a high school diploma and prior work experience.

Education and Training. Most agricultural workers do not need a high school diploma. They usually receive short-term on-the-job training.

Most animal breeders have a high school diploma, and typically have several years of experience in a related occupation.

Most agricultural workers receive some short-term on-the-job training. Employers instruct them on how to use simple farming tools, as well as more complex machinery. More experienced workers are also expected to perform routine maintenance on the tools they use.

Important Qualities

Dexterity. Agricultural workers need excellent hand-eye coordination to harvest crops and operate farm machinery.

Listening skills. Agricultural workers need to work well with others. Because they take instructions from farmers and other agricultural managers, effective listening is critical.

Physical stamina. Agricultural workers need to be able to perform laborious tasks repeatedly.

Physical strength. Agricultural workers must be strong enough to lift heavy objects, including tools and crops.

Mechanical skills. Agricultural workers must be able to operate complex farm machinery. They also occasionally do routine maintenance on the machinery.

Work Experience in a Related Occupation. Animal breeders typically have prior work experience before they begin interacting with livestock. Ranch workers may transition into animal breeding after they become more familiar with animals and learn how to handle them.

Advancement. Agricultural workers may advance to crew leader or other supervisory positions. The ability to speak both English and Spanish is helpful for agricultural supervisors.

Some agricultural workers aspire to become farmers, ranchers, or agricultural managers or to own their own farms and ranches. Knowledge of produce and livestock may provide an excellent background for becoming a purchasing agent or buyer of farm

Employment Projections Data for Agricultural Workers

Occupational title	SOC Code	Employment, 2012	Projected— Employment, 2022	Change, 2012–2022 Percent	Change, 2012–2022 Numeric
Agricultural workers	—	749,400	724,400	-3	-25,000
Animal breeders	45-2021	1,300	1,000	-23	-300
Agricultural equipment operators	45-2091	59,000	61,200	4	2,300
Farmworkers and laborers, crop, nursery, and greenhouse	45-2092	596,800	567,600	-5	-29,200
Farmworkers, farm, ranch, and aquacultural animals	45-2093	77,900	79,600	2	1,700
Agricultural workers, all other	45-2099	14,400	14,900	3	500

Source: U.S. Bureau of Labor Statistics, Employment Projections Program

Note: Data are rounded. Go to **Occupational Information Included in the OOH** *for a discussion of the data in this table.*

Similar Occupations   This table shows a list of occupations with job duties that are similar to those of agricultural workers.

Occupations	Entry-level Education	2012 Pay	Projected Job Growth	Average Annual Openings
Agricultural and Food Science Technicians	Associate's degree	$34,070	3%	1,010
Animal Care and Service Workers	See "How to Become One"	$20,076	15%	7,660
Farmers, Ranchers, and Other Agricultural Managers	High school diploma or equivalent	$69,300	-19%	15,020
Forest and Conservation Workers	High school diploma or equivalent	$24,340	5%	230
Grounds Maintenance Workers	See "How to Become One"	$24,180	13%	46,350

products. Those who earn a college degree in agricultural science could become agricultural or food scientists.

Pay

The median annual wage for agricultural workers was $18,910 in May 2012. The median wage is the wage at which half the workers in an occupation earned more than that amount and half earned less. The lowest 10 percent earned less than $17,050, and the top 10 percent earned more than $29,820.

Median annual wages for agricultural workers in 2012 were the following:

animal breeders.. $34,250
agricultural equipment operators......................... 25,860
agricultural workers, all other............................. 25,140
farmworkers, farm, ranch, and aquacultural animals.......... 22,060
farmworkers and laborers, crop, nursery, and greenhouse ... 18,670

Job Outlook

Employment of agricultural workers is projected to decline 3 percent from 2012 to 2022. However, agricultural workers should have good job prospects overall.

Despite increasing international demand for food and meat, fewer agricultural workers may be needed as agricultural and livestock establishments continue to consolidate.

Technological advancements in farm equipment raises output per farm worker, which could also affect employment for agricultural workers. On the other hand, nursery and greenhouse workers might experience some job growth, if the demand for landscaping plants continues.

Job Prospects. Job prospects for agricultural workers should be strong as workers frequently leave the occupation due to the intense, physical nature of the work. This is especially true for agricultural equipment operators and crop, greenhouse, and nursery farmworkers. Those who work with animals tend to have a more settled lifestyle because the work does not require them to follow crops for harvest. Prospects will be best for those who can speak English and Spanish.

O*NET

➤ Animal Breeders (45-2021.00)
➤ Agricultural Equipment Operators (45-2091.00)
➤ Farmworkers and Laborers, Crop, Nursery, and Greenhouse (45-2092.00)
➤ Nursery Workers (45-2092.01)
➤ Farmworkers and Laborers, Crop (45-2092.02)
➤ Farmworkers, Farm, Ranch, and Aquacultural Animals (45-2093.00)
➤ Agricultural Workers, All Other (45-2099.00)

Contacts for More Information

For more information about agricultural workers, visit

➤ The National Agricultural Workers Survey, U.S. Department of Labor (www.doleta.gov/agworker/naws.cfm)

For more information about agriculture policy and farm advocacy, visit

➤ Center for Rural Affairs (www.cfra.org/)

For more information about the Beginner Farmer and Rancher Competitive Grants Program, visit

➤ National Institute of Food and Agriculture, U.S. Department of Agriculture (www.csrees.usda.gov/)

For more general information about farming in the United States, visit

➤ Farm Service Agency, U.S. Department of Agriculture (www.fsa.usda.gov/FSA/)
➤ Association for Farmworker Opportunity Programs (www.afop.org)

Fishers and Related Fishing Workers

- **2012 Median Pay** .... $33,430 per year
  $16.07 per hour
- **Entry-Level Education** .... Less than high school
- **Work Experience in a Related Occupation** .... None
- **On-the-Job Training** .... Moderate-term on-the-job training
- **Number of Jobs 2012** 31,300
- **Job Outlook, 2012–22** .... -5% (Decline)
- **Employment Change, 2012–22** .... -1,600

What Fishers and Related Fishing Workers Do

Fishers and related fishing workers catch and trap various types of marine life. The fish they catch are for human food, animal feed, bait, and other uses.

Duties. Fishers and related fishing workers typically do the following:

- Locate fish using fish-finding equipment
- Direct fishing operations and supervise the crew of fishing vessels
- Steer vessels and operate navigational instruments
- Maintain engines, fishing gear, and other onboard equipment by doing minor repairs
- Sort, pack, and store the catch in holds with salt and ice
- Measure fish to ensure they comply with legal size
- Return undesirable or illegal catches to the water
- Guide nets, traps, and lines onto vessels by hand or using hoisting equipment
- Signal other workers to move, hoist, and position loads

To plot the ship's course, fishing boat captains use compasses, charts, and electronic navigational equipment, including global positioning systems (GPS). They also use radar and sonar to avoid obstacles above and below the water and to find fish.

Some fishers work in deep water on large fishing boats that are equipped for long stays at sea. Some process the fish they catch on board and prepare them for sale.

Other fishers work in shallow water on small boats that often have a crew of only one or two members. They might put nets across the mouths of rivers or inlets, or pots and traps for fish or shellfish such as lobsters and crabs, or they might use dredges to gather other shellfish, such as oysters and scallops.

A small portion of commercial fishing requires diving with diving suits or scuba gear. These divers use spears to catch fish and nets to gather shellfish, sea urchins, abalone, and sponges.

Some fishers harvest marine vegetation rather than fish. They use rakes and hoes to gather Irish moss and kelp.

Although most fishers work in commercial fishing, some in this occupation use their expertise in sport or recreational fishing.

Aquaculture–raising and harvesting fish and other aquatic life under controlled conditions in ponds or confined bodies of water–is a different field. For more information, see the profile on farmers, ranchers, and agricultural managers.

The *fishing boat captain* plans and oversees the fishing operation, the fish to be sought, location of the best fishing grounds, method of capture, duration of the trip, and sale of the catch. Captains direct the fishing operation and record daily activities in the ship's log. Increasingly, they use the Internet to bypass processors and sell their fish directly to consumers, grocery stores, and restaurants.

Fishers that specialize in catching certain species include *crabbers* and *lobster catchers*.

Work Environment

Fishers and related fishing workers held about 31,300 jobs in 2012. About 57 percent were self-employed. Fishing operations are conducted under various environmental conditions, depending on the region, body of water, and kinds of fish sought. Storms, fog, and wind may hamper fishing vessels or cause them to suspend fishing operations and return to port.

Although fishing gear has improved and operations have become more mechanized, netting and processing fish are nonetheless strenuous activities. Newer vessels have improved living quarters and amenities, but crews still experience the aggravations of confined quarters and the absence of family.

Injuries and Illnesses. Commercial fishing can be dangerous, and lead to workplace injuries or even fatalities. Fishers and

A fisher tends to his equipment on his fishing boat.

related fishing workers often work under hazardous conditions, and transportation to a hospital or doctor is often not readily available. Most fatalities for fishers and related fishing workers are from drowning. The crew must guard against the danger of injury from malfunctioning fishing gear, entanglement in fishing nets and gear, slippery decks, ice formation, or large waves washing over the deck. Malfunctioning navigation and communication equipment and other factors may lead to collisions or shipwrecks.

Work Schedules. Fishers and related fishing workers endure strenuous outdoor work and long hours. Commercial fishing trips may require workers to be away from their home port for several weeks or months.

Many fishers are seasonal workers, and those jobs are usually filled by students and by people from other occupations, such as teachers. For example, employment of fishers in Alaska more than doubles during the summer months, which is the salmon season.

How to Become One

Fishers and related fishing workers usually learn on the job. No formal education is required.

Education. Formal education is not required to be a fisher. However, by enrolling in 2-year vocational-technical programs offered by some high schools, fishers can improve their chances of getting a job. In addition, some community colleges and universities offer fishery technology and related programs that include courses in seamanship, vessel operations, marine safety, navigation, vessel repair, and fishing gear technology. Secondary and postsecond-

Median Annual Wages, May 2012

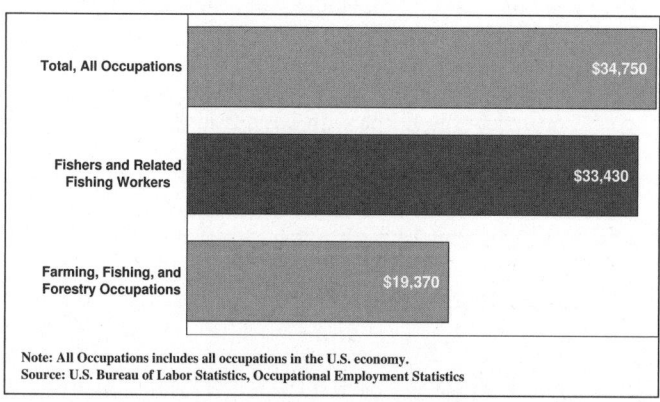

Total, All Occupations	$34,750
Fishers and Related Fishing Workers	$33,430
Farming, Fishing, and Forestry Occupations	$19,370

Note: All Occupations includes all occupations in the U.S. economy.
Source: U.S. Bureau of Labor Statistics, Occupational Employment Statistics

Percent Change in Employment, Projected 2012–2022

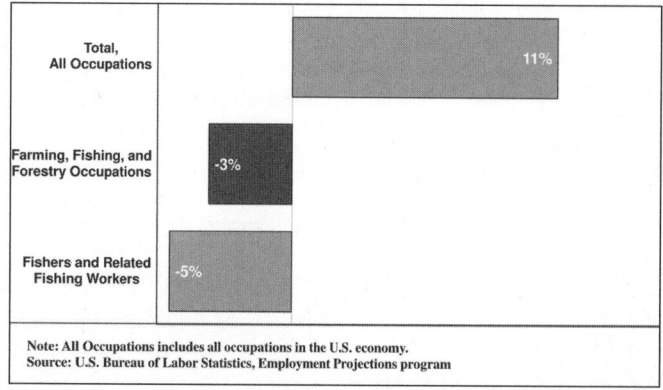

Total, All Occupations	11%
Farming, Fishing, and Forestry Occupations	-3%
Fishers and Related Fishing Workers	-5%

Note: All Occupations includes all occupations in the U.S. economy.
Source: U.S. Bureau of Labor Statistics, Employment Projections program

Employment Projections Data for Fishers and Related Fishing Workers

Occupational title	SOC Code	Employment, 2012	Projected— Employment, 2022	Change, 2012–2022	
				Percent	Numeric
Fishers and related fishing workers	45-3011	31,300	29,700	-5	-1,600

Source: U.S. Bureau of Labor Statistics, Employment Projections Program

Note: Data are rounded. Go to Occupational Information Included in the OOH *for a discussion of the data in this table.*

ary programs are typically located near coastal areas and include hands-on experience.

Training. Most fishers learn on the job. They start by finding work through family or friends, or simply by walking around the docks and asking for employment. Aspiring fishers can also look online for potential employment. Some larger trawlers and processing ships are run by larger companies, in which new workers can apply through the companies' human resources department. Operators of large commercial fishing vessels must complete a Coast Guard-approved training course.

Important Qualities

Analytical skills. Fishers and related fishing workers must measure the quality of their catch, which requires precision and accuracy.

Critical-thinking skills. Fishers and related fishing workers reach conclusions through sound reasoning and judgment. They determine how to improve the catch and must react appropriately to weather conditions.

Listening skills. Fishers and related fishing workers need to work well with others–they take instructions from captains and others–so effective listening is critical.

Machine operation skills. Fishers and related fishing workers must be able to operate complex fishing machinery competently and occasionally do routine maintenance.

Navigation skills. Fishers and related fishing workers must use complex tools to navigate boats to where the highest concentration of fish is located.

Physical stamina. Fishers and related fishing workers must be able to work long hours, often in strenuous conditions.

Physical strength. Fishers and related fishing workers must use physical strength along with hand dexterity and coordination to perform difficult tasks repeatedly.

Licenses, Certifications, and Registrations. Captains of fishing boats must be licensed.

Crew members on certain fish-processing vessels may need a merchant mariner's document. The U.S. Coast Guard issues these documents and licenses to people who meet the specific health, physical, and academic requirements.

States set licensing requirements for boats operating in state waters, defined as inland waters and waters within 3 miles of the coast.

Fishers need a permit to fish in almost any water. Permits are distributed by states for state waters and by regional fishing coun-

cils for federal waters. The permits specify the fishing season, the type and amount of fish that may be caught, and sometimes the type of permissible fishing gear.

Advancement. Experienced, reliable fishing boat deckhands can become boatswains, then second mates, first mates, and, finally, captains. Those who are interested in ship engineering may gain experience with maintaining and repairing ship engines to become licensed chief engineers on large commercial boats. This requires meeting the Coast Guard's licensing requirements. For more information, see the profile on water transportation occupations.

Almost all captains are self-employed, and most eventually own, or partially own, one or more fishing boats.

Pay

The median annual wage for fishers and related fishing workers was $33,430 in May 2012. The median wage is the wage at which half the workers in an occupation earned more than that amount and half earned less. The lowest 10 percent earned less than $24,130, and the top 10 percent earned more than $58,470.

Job Outlook

Employment of fishers and related fishing workers is projected to decline 5 percent from 2012 to 2022.

Fishers and related fishing workers depend on the natural ability of fish stocks to replenish themselves through growth and reproduction. They also depend on governmental regulation to promote replenishment of fisheries. In order to conserve the fish population in the coming years, the need for setting catch limits has risen. Additionally, improvements in fishing gear and vessel design have increased fish hauls.

Governmental efforts to replenish stocks are getting some positive results, which should increase fish stocks in the future. The U.S. government recently set catch limits for every species it manages.

Rising seafood imports and increasing competition from farm-raised fish are affecting fishing income and causing some fishers to leave the industry. However, because competition from farm-raised and imported seafood tends to be concentrated in specific species, some regions are more affected than others.

Job Prospects. Most job openings will result from the need to replace fishers and related fishing workers who leave the occupation. Many workers leave because of the strenuous and hazardous nature of the job and the lack of a steady year-round income. The best prospects should be with large fishing operations and

Similar Occupations

This table shows a list of occupations with job duties that are similar to those of fishers and related fishing workers.

Occupations	Entry-level Education	2012 Pay	Projected Job Growth	Average Annual Openings
Slaughterers, Meat Packers, and Meat, Poultry, and Fish Cutters and Trimmers	Less than high school	$23,331	3%	6,890
Water Transportation Occupations	See "How to Become One"	$54,020	13%	4,810

for seasonal employment. Opportunities with small independent fishers are expected to be limited.

O*NET

➤ Fishers and Related Fishing Workers (45-3011.00)

Contacts for More Information

For more information about licensing of fishing boat captains and about requirements for merchant mariner documentation, visit

➤ National Maritime Center, Coast Guard Headquarters (www.uscg. mil/nmc/)

For information about injuries and safety issues, visit

➤ Centers for Disease Control and Prevention (CDC) (www.cdc.gov/ niosh/topics/fishing/default.html)

➤ "Facts of the catch: occupational injuries, illnesses, and fatalities to fishing workers, 2003–2009," Beyond the Numbers, Bureau of Labor Statistics, August 2012 (www.bls.gov/opub/btn/volume-1/pdf/ facts-of-the-catch-occupational-inujuries-in-fishing-industries.pdf).

Forest and Conservation Workers

- **2012 Median Pay** .... $24,340 per year
  $11.70 per hour
- **Entry-Level Education** ... High school diploma or equivalent
- **Work Experience in a Related Occupation** .... None
- **On-the-Job Training** .... Moderate-term on-the-job training
- **Number of Jobs 2012** 10,500
- **Job Outlook, 2012–22** .... 4% (Slower than average)
- **Employment Change, 2012–22** 500

What Forest and Conservation Workers Do

Forest and conservation workers measure and improve the quality of forests. Under the supervision of foresters and forest and conservation technicians, they develop, maintain, and protect forests.

Duties. Forest and conservation workers typically do the following:

- Plant seedlings to reforest land
- Clear away brush and debris from camping trails, roadsides, and camping areas
- Count trees during tree-measuring efforts
- Select or cut trees according to markings, sizes, types, or grades
- Spray trees with insecticides and fungicides to kill insects and protect the trees from disease
- Identify and remove diseased or undesirable trees
- Inject vegetation with insecticides and herbicides
- Help prevent and suppress forest fires
- Check equipment to ensure that it is operating properly

Forest and conservation workers are supervised by foresters and forest and conservation technicians, who direct their work and evaluate their progress.

Forest and conservation workers do basic tasks to maintain and improve the quality of the forest. They use digging and planting tools to plant seedlings and power saws to cut down diseased trees.

Some forest workers work on tree farms, where they plant, cultivate, and harvest many different kinds of trees. Their duties vary with the type of farm and may include planting seedlings, spraying to control weed growth and insects, and harvesting trees.

Some forest and conservation workers work in forest nurseries, where they sort through tree seedlings, discarding the ones that do not meet standards. Others use handtools or their hands to gather woodland products, such as decorative greens, tree cones, bark, moss, and other wild plantlife. Some may tap trees to make syrup or chemicals.

Forest and conservation workers who are employed by or under contract with state and local governments may clear brush and debris from trails, roads, roadsides, and camping areas. They may clean kitchens and restrooms at recreational facilities and campgrounds.

Workers with a fire protection background help to suppress forest fires. For example, they may construct firebreaks, which are gaps in vegetation that can help slow down or stop the progress of a fire. In addition, they may work with technicians to study how quickly fires spread and how successful fire suppression activities were. For example, workers help count how many trees will be affected by a fire. They also sometimes respond to forest emergencies.

Work Environment

Forest and conservation workers held about 10,500 jobs in 2012. The industries that employed the most forest and conservation workers in 2012 were as follows:

State government, excluding education and hospitals 39%
Local government, excluding education and hospitals 20
Logging 4
Landscaping services 3

Forest and conversation workers typically work for state and local governments or on privately owned forest lands. Those employed by forest management services may work for the federal government on a contract basis.

Forest and conservation workers' jobs are concentrated in the western and southeastern areas of the United States, where there are many national and private forests and parks.

Forest and conversation workers work outdoors, sometimes in remote locations and in all types of weather. However, the increased use of machines has reduced some of the discomfort of working in bad weather and has made tasks much safer. Workers also use proper safety measures and equipment, such as hardhats, protective eyewear, and safety clothing.

Most of these jobs are physically demanding. Forest and conservation workers may have to walk long distances through densely wooded areas and carry their equipment with them.

Injuries and Illnesses. Forest and conversation workers whose primary duties involve fire suppression must take significant safety precautions because the work can be dangerous. Workers must follow prescribed safety procedures and wear proper safety gear.

Work Schedules. Most forest and conservation workers are employed full time and work regular hours. Seasonal employees may be expected to work longer hours and at night. Responding to an emergency may require workers to work longer hours and at any time of day.

How to Become One

Forest and conservation workers typically need a high school diploma before they begin working. Most workers get on-the-job training.

Education. Forest and conservation workers typically need a high school diploma before they begin working. Some vocational and technical schools and community colleges offer courses leading to a 2-year technical degree in forest management technology,

Forest and conservation workers strive to promote growth of individual trees and entire forests.

wildlife management, conservation, or forest harvesting. Programs that include field trips to watch and participate in forestry activities provide particularly good background knowledge.

Training. Entry-level forest and conservation workers generally get on-the-job training as they help more experienced workers. They do routine labor-intensive tasks, such as planting or thinning trees. When the opportunity arises, they learn from experienced technicians and foresters who do more complex tasks, such as gathering data.

Advancement. To advance their careers and become forest and conservation technicians or foresters, forest and conservation

workers usually need an associate's or bachelor's degree in forestry or a related field. For more information, see the profiles on forest and conservation technicians and conservation scientists and foresters.

Important Qualities

Communication skills. Forest and conservation workers must convey information effectively to technicians and other workers.

Decision-making skills. Forest and conservation workers must make quick, intelligent decisions, especially when they face dangerous conditions.

Detail oriented. Forest and conservation workers must watch gauges, dials, or other indicators to determine whether equipment and tools are working properly. Workers must follow safety procedures with precision.

Listening skills. Forest and conservation workers must give full attention to what their superiors are saying. They must understand the instructions they are given before performing tasks.

Physical stamina. Forest and conservation workers must plant trees and repeatedly perform a variety of physical tasks. They must also be able to walk long distances through densely wooded areas and carry heavy packs with them.

Pay

The median annual wage for forest and conservation workers was $24,340 in May 2012. The median wage is the wage at which half the workers in an occupation earned more than that amount and half earned less. The lowest 10 percent earned less than $16,690, and the top 10 percent earned more than $45,900.

In May 2012, median annual wages for forest and conservation workers in the top four industries employing these workers were as follows:

Logging $33,290
Local government, excluding education and hospitals 28,870
Landscaping services 22,300
State government, excluding education and hospitals 20,840

Job Outlook

Employment of forest and conservation workers is projected to grow 4 percent from 2012 to 2022, slower than the average for all occupations. Heightened demand for American timber and wood pellets will help increase demand for forest and conservation workers.

Jobs in private forests will grow with the increasing demand for timber and pellets, but ongoing fiscal crises may lessen the number of available positions in state and local governments. Wildfires caused by unpredictable climate conditions and overgrown vegeta-

Median Annual Wages, May 2012

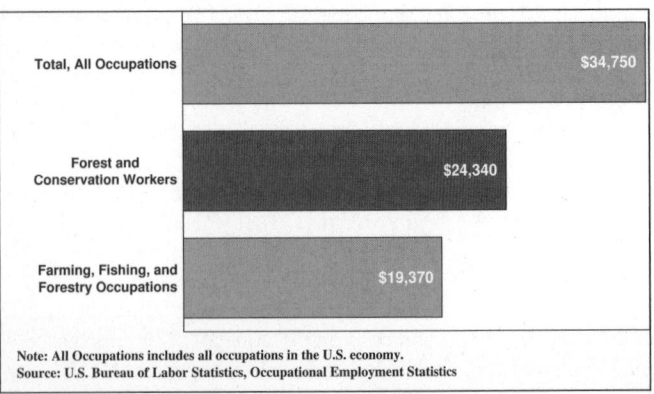

Note: All Occupations includes all occupations in the U.S. economy.
Source: U.S. Bureau of Labor Statistics, Occupational Employment Statistics

Percent Change in Employment, Projected 2012–2022

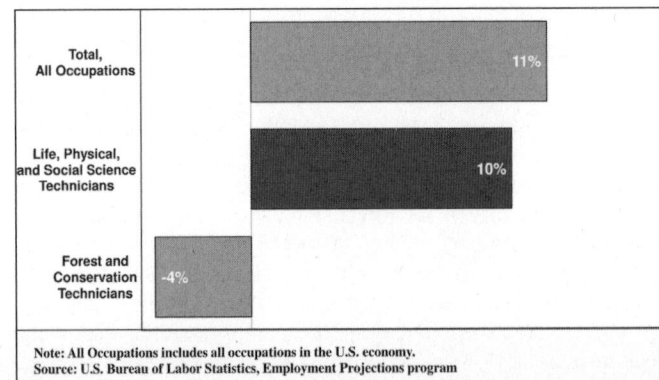

Note: All Occupations includes all occupations in the U.S. economy.
Source: U.S. Bureau of Labor Statistics, Employment Projections program

Employment Projections Data for Forest and Conservation Workers

Occupational title	SOC Code	Employment, 2012	Projected— Employment, 2022	Change, 2012–2022	
				Percent	Numeric
Forest and conservation workers	45-4011	10,500	11,000	4	500

Source: U.S. Bureau of Labor Statistics, Employment Projections Program

Note: Data are rounded. Go to Occupational Information Included in the OOH *for a discussion of the data in this table.*

Similar Occupations   This table shows a list of occupations with job duties that are similar to those of forest and conservation workers.

Occupations	Entry-level Education	2012 Pay	Projected Job Growth	Average Annual Openings
Agricultural Workers	See "How to Become One"	$19,703	-3%	23,190
Conservation Scientists and Foresters	Bachelor's degree	$59,354	3%	1,080
Firefighters	Postsecondary non-degree award	$45,250	7%	10,400
Forest and Conservation Technicians	Associate's degree	$33,920	-4%	1,340
Grounds Maintenance Workers	See "How to Become One"	$24,180	13%	46,350
Logging Workers	High school diploma or equivalent	$33,697	-8%	730

tion on forest lands will increase the fire suppression activities of forest and conservation workers.

Most employment growth for forest and conservation workers is expected to be in state-owned forest lands. Recent developments in western forests may result in the conversion of unused roads into forest land, thus creating some new jobs. In addition, increasing pressure on the U.S. Forest Service (part of the U.S. Department of Agriculture) to undertake major fire suppression duties may result in higher levels of employment.

Job Prospects. Job prospects will be best for workers who have a background in fire suppression activities. Workers who follow standard safety procedures, remain physically fit, and work well in teams will have the best opportunities.

Similar Occupations   This table shows a list of occupations with job duties that are similar to those of forest and conservation workers.

O*NET

➤ Forest and Conservation Workers (45-4011.00)

Contacts for More Information

For information about forestry careers and schools offering education in forestry, visit
➤ Society of American Foresters (www.safnet.org)

For information about careers in forestry, particularly conservation forestry and land management, visit
➤ Forest Guild (www.forestguild.org)

Logging Workers

- **2012 Median Pay** .... $33,630 per year
  $16.17 per hour
- **Entry-Level Education** ... High school diploma or equivalent
- **Work Experience in a Related Occupation** .... None
- **On-the-Job Training** .... Moderate-term on-the-job training
- **Number of Jobs 2012** 43,900
- **Job Outlook, 2012–22** .... -9% (Decline)
- **Employment Change, 2012–22** .... -3,800

What Logging Workers Do

Logging workers harvest thousands of acres of forests each year. The timber they harvest provides the raw material for countless consumer and industrial products.

Duties. Logging workers typically do the following:

- Cut down trees with hand-held power chainsaws or mobile felling machines
- Fasten cables around logs to be dragged by tractors
- Operate tractors that drag logs to the landing or deck area
- Separate logs by species and type of wood and load them onto trucks
- Drive and maneuver tractors and tree harvesters to shear trees and cut logs into desired lengths
- Grade logs according to characteristics such as knot size and straightness
- Inspect equipment for safety before using it and perform necessary basic maintenance tasks

Timber-cutting and logging are done by a logging crew. The following are examples of types of logging workers:

Fallers cut down trees with hand-held power chainsaws or mobile felling machines.

Buckers trim the tops and branches of felled trees and buck (cut) the logs into specific lengths.

Tree climbers use special equipment to scale tall trees and remove their limbs. They carry heavy tools and safety gear as they climb the trees, and are kept safe by a harness attached to a rope.

Choke setters fasten steel cables or chains, known as chokers, around logs to be skidded (dragged) by tractors or forwarded by the cable-yarding system to the landing or deck area, where the logs are separated by species and type of product, such as pulpwood, saw logs, or veneer logs, which are then loaded onto trucks.

Rigging slingers and chasers set up and dismantle the cables and guy wires of the yarding system.

Log sorters, markers, movers, and chippers sort, mark, and move logs based on species, size, and ownership. They also tend machines that chip up logs.

A logging worker cuts a log into smaller lengths.

Logging equipment operators use tree harvesters to fell trees, shear off tree limbs, and cut trees into desired lengths. They drive tractors and operate self-propelled machines called skidders or forwarders, which drag or transport logs to a loading area.

Log graders and scalers inspect logs for defects and measure the logs to determine their volume. They estimate the value of logs or pulpwood. These workers often use hand-held data collection devices to enter data on trees. The data are later downloaded to a computer.

A typical crew might consist of the following:

• One or two tree fallers or one or two logging equipment operators with a tree harvester to cut down trees

• One bucker to cut logs

• Two choker setters with tractors to drag cut trees to the loading deck

• One logging equipment operator to delimb, cut logs to length, and load the logs onto trucks

Work Environment
Logging workers held about 43,900 jobs in 2012.

Logging is physically demanding and can be dangerous. Workers spend all their time outdoors, sometimes in poor weather and often in isolated areas. The increased use of enclosed machines has decreased some of the discomforts caused by bad weather and has generally made logging much safer.

Most logging work involves lifting, climbing, and other strenuous activities, although machinery has eliminated some heavy labor. Falling branches, vines, and rough terrain are constant hazards, as are dangers associated with felling trees and handling logs.

Chainsaws and other power equipment can be dangerous; therefore, workers must be careful and must use proper safety measures and equipment, such as hard hats, safety clothing, hearing protection, and boots.

Injuries and Illnesses. Despite the strong emphasis on safety, logging workers have a high rate of fatal occupational injuries. Most fatal occupational injuries occur due to contact with a machine or an object.

Work Schedules. Workers sometimes commute long distances between their homes and logging sites. When workers are far away from their homes, they are given accommodations near logging sites. In more densely populated states, commuting distances are shorter. Logging work is often seasonal; workers can find more employment opportunities during the warmer months because snow and rain adversely affect working conditions.

How to Become One
Most logging workers have a high school diploma. They get on-the-job training to become familiar with forest environments and to learn how to operate logging machinery.

Education. A high school diploma is enough for most logging workers. Some vocational and technical schools and community colleges offer courses leading to a 2-year technical degree in forest harvesting. This degree may help workers get a job. Courses may include field trips to observe or participate in logging activities.

A few community colleges offer education programs for equipment operators.

Important Qualities
Communication skills. Logging workers must communicate within a crew so they can cut and delimb trees efficiently and safely.

Decision-making skills. Logging workers must make quick, intelligent decisions when hazards arise.

Detail oriented. Logging workers must watch gauges, dials, and other indicators to determine whether their equipment and tools are working properly.

Physical stamina. Logging workers need to be able to perform laborious tasks repeatedly.

Physical strength. Logging workers must be able to handle heavy equipment.

Training. Many states have training programs for loggers. Although specific coursework may vary by state, most programs usually include technical instruction or field training in a number of areas, including best management practices, environmental compliance, and reforestation.

Median Annual Wages, May 2012

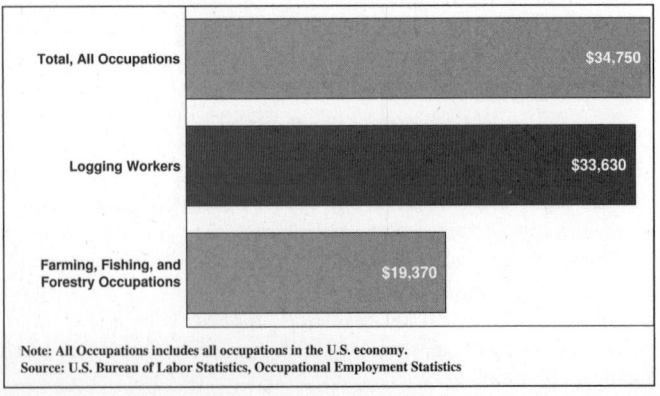

Total, All Occupations	$34,750
Logging Workers	$33,630
Farming, Fishing, and Forestry Occupations	$19,370

Note: All Occupations includes all occupations in the U.S. economy.
Source: U.S. Bureau of Labor Statistics, Occupational Employment Statistics

Percent Change in Employment, Projected 2012–2022

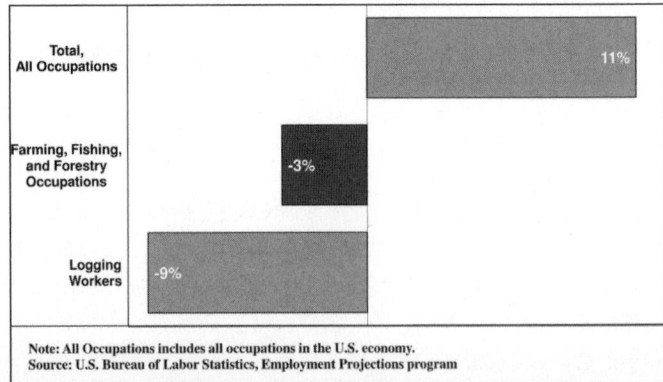

Total, All Occupations	11%
Farming, Fishing, and Forestry Occupations	-3%
Logging Workers	-9%

Note: All Occupations includes all occupations in the U.S. economy.
Source: U.S. Bureau of Labor Statistics, Employment Projections program

Safety training is a vital part of logging workers' instruction. Many state forestry or logging associations provide training sessions for logging equipment operators, whose jobs require more skill and experience than other logging positions. Sessions take place in the field, where trainees have the opportunity to practice various logging techniques.

Logging companies and trade associations offer training programs for workers who operate large, expensive machinery and equipment. The training program often culminates with a safety certification for the logging company.

Pay

The median annual wage for logging workers was $33,630 in May 2012. The median wage is the wage at which half the workers in an occupation earned more than that amount and half earned less. The lowest 10 percent earned less than $21,310, and the top 10 percent earned more than $49,950.

The median annual wages for logging worker occupations in May 2012 were as follows:

Fallers	$35,250
All other logging workers	34,260
Logging equipment operators	33,380
Log graders and scalers	32,880

Workers sometimes commute long distances between their homes and logging sites. When workers are far away from their homes, they are given accommodations near logging sites. In more densely populated states, commuting distances are shorter. Logging work is often seasonal; workers can find more employment opportunities during the warmer months since snow and rain adversely affect working conditions.

Job Outlook

Employment of logging workers is projected to decline 9 percent from 2012 to 2022. Logging workers may have good job prospects, particularly as more workers reach retirement age or leave the occupation permanently and need to be replaced.

In an effort to conserve federal forestlands, policies limit the logging industry's ability to cultivate raw forest material. However, federal legislation designed to prevent destructive wildfires by thinning susceptible forests may result in some additional jobs.

Domestic timber producers continue to face increasing competition from foreign producers.

Increased mechanization of logging operations and improvements in logging equipment will result in less demand for timber-cutting and logging workers who work by hand. Employment of logging equipment operators will be less affected and should rise, because they will be needed to operate logging equipment.

During prolonged periods of inactivity, some workers may stay on the job to maintain or repair logging machinery and equipment, while others take unemployment or seek work elsewhere.

Job Prospects. Job opportunities should be good because of the need to replace older workers who leave the occupation for retirement or other jobs that are less physically demanding.

Employment of logging workers can be unsteady because changes in the level of construction, particularly residential construction, can cause short-term slowdowns in logging activities.

O*NET

► Fallers (45-4021.00)
► Logging Equipment Operators (45-4022.00)
► Log Graders and Scalers (45-4023.00)
► Logging Workers, All Other (45-4029.00)

Contacts for More Information

For information about timber-cutting and logging careers and links to state associations, visit

► Forest Resources Association, Inc. (www.forestresources.org)

Employment Projections Data for Logging Workers

Occupational title	SOC Code	Employment, 2012	Projected— Employment, 2022	Change, 2012–2022 Percent	Numeric
Logging workers	45-4020	43,900	40,100	-9	-3,800
Fallers	45-4021	6,600	3,800	-43	-2,900
Logging equipment operators	45-4022	30,000	30,600	2	600
Log graders and scalers	45-4023	3,500	2,400	-32	-1,100
Logging workers, all other	45-4029	3,700	3,300	-12	-500

Source: U.S. Bureau of Labor Statistics, Employment Projections Program

Note: **Data are rounded. Go to** Occupational Information Included in the OOH *for a discussion of the data in this table.*

Similar Occupations   This table shows a list of occupations with job duties that are similar to those of logging workers.

Occupations	Entry-level Education	2012 Pay	Projected Job Growth	Average Annual Openings
Conservation Scientists and Foresters	Bachelor's degree	$59,354	3%	1,080
Construction Equipment Operators	High school diploma or equivalent	$41,099	19%	16,480
Forest and Conservation Technicians	Associate's degree	$33,920	-4%	1,340
Forest and Conservation Workers	High school diploma or equivalent	$24,340	5%	230

Food Preparation and Serving

Bartenders

- **2012 Median Pay** .... $18,900 per year
  $9.09 per hour
- **Entry-Level Education** .... Less than high school
- **Work Experience in a Related Occupation**.............. None
- **On-the-Job Training** ....Short-term on-the-job training
- **Number of Jobs 2012** 551,100
- **Job Outlook, 2012–22** .... 12% (As fast as average)
- **Employment Change, 2012–22** 65,600

What Bartenders Do

Bartenders mix drinks and serve them directly to customers or through wait staff.

Duties. Bartenders typically do the following:

- Greet customers, give them menus, and inform them about daily specials
- Take drink orders from customers
- Pour wine and serve draft and bottled beer and other drinks and beverages
- Mix drinks according to recipes
- Check identification of customers, to ensure that they are of legal drinking age
- Clean bars, tables, and work areas
- Operate cash registers, collect payments from customers, and return change
- Manage bar operation and order and maintain liquor and bar supplies

Bartenders spend most of their work time on their feet.

Bartenders fill drink orders either directly from customers at the bar or through waiters and waitresses who place drink orders for dining room customers. Bartenders must know a wide range of drink recipes and be able to mix drinks correctly, quickly, and without waste. They also must work well with waiters and waitresses and other kitchen staff to ensure that customers receive prompt service.

Some establishments, especially busy establishments with many customers, use equipment that automatically measures, pours, and mixes drinks at the push of a button. Bartenders who use this equipment, however, still must become familiar with the ingredients for special drink requests and be able to work quickly to handle numerous drink orders.

Bartenders in some establishments also use carbonated beverage dispensers, cocktail shakers and other accessories, commercial strainers, mist and trigger sprayers, and ice shaver machines.

In addition to mixing and serving drinks, bartenders stock and prepare garnishes for drinks and maintain an adequate supply of ice, glasses, and other bar supplies. They also may wash glassware and utensils and serve food to customers who eat at the bar. Bartenders are usually responsible for ordering and maintaining an inventory of liquor, mixers, and other bar supplies.

Some bartenders run their own bar or catering business. In addition to their standard bartending duties, they also are responsible for hiring, training, and supervising their staff, budgeting for and ordering supplies, and setting prices.

Work Environment

Bartenders held about 551,100 jobs in 2012.

The industries that employed the most bartenders in 2012 were as follows:

Restaurants and other eating places.......................................43%
Drinking places (alcoholic beverages)....................................29
Civic and social organizations 8
Traveler accommodation...7
Other amusement and recreation industries.............................5

Bartenders work at restaurants, bars, clubs, hotels, and other food service establishments. Although most bartenders work indoors, some work outdoors at pool or beach bars or when tending a bar at catered events.

During busy hours, bartenders are under pressure to serve customers quickly and efficiently, while ensuring that no alcohol is served to minors or overly intoxicated customers.

Bartenders perform repetitive tasks, and sometimes they lift heavy kegs of beer and cases of liquor. In addition, the work can be stressful, because they often deal with heavily intoxicated customers to whom they must deny service.

Because bartenders often are in the front line of customer service in bars and restaurants, a neat appearance is important. Those who work in upscale restaurants and bars may be required to wear uniforms, including ties or aprons, which are typically provided by their employers.

Work Schedules. Bartenders often work late evenings, weekends, and holidays. Nearly half worked part time in 2012.

Bartenders who run their own business often work long hours managing all aspects of the business to ensure bills and salaries are paid, supplies are ordered, and the business is profitable.

Median Hourly Wages, May 2012

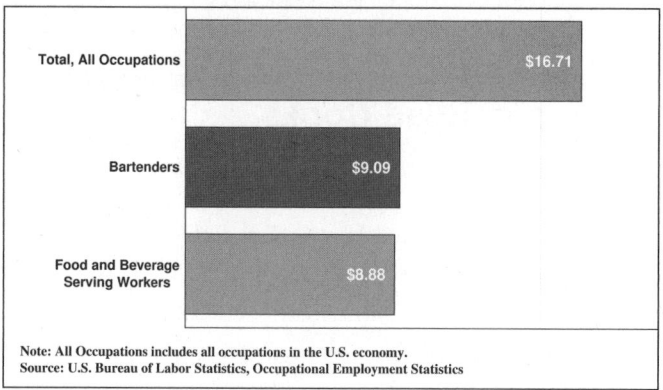

Note: All Occupations includes all occupations in the U.S. economy.
Source: U.S. Bureau of Labor Statistics, Occupational Employment Statistics

Percent Change in Employment, Projected 2012–2022

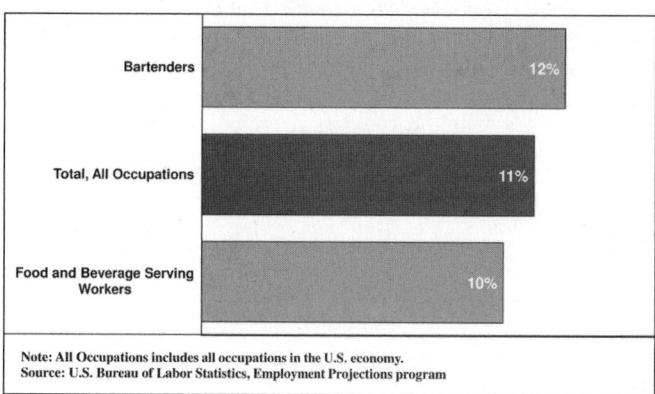

Note: All Occupations includes all occupations in the U.S. economy.
Source: U.S. Bureau of Labor Statistics, Employment Projections program

How to Become One

Most bartenders learn their skills through short-term on-the-job training. No formal education is required.

Many bartenders are promoted from other jobs at the establishments in which they work. Bartenders at upscale establishments usually have attended bartending classes or have previous work experience.

Although most states require workers who serve alcoholic beverages to be at least 18 years old, most bartenders are 25 or older. Bartenders must be familiar with state and local laws concerning the sale of alcoholic beverages.

Education. No formal education is required to become a bartender. However, some aspiring bartenders acquire their skills by attending a school for bartending or by attending bartending classes at a vocational or technical school. These programs often include instruction on state and local laws and regulations concerning the sale of alcohol, cocktail recipes, proper attire and conduct, and stocking a bar. The length of each program varies, but most courses last a few weeks. Some schools help their graduates find jobs.

Training. Most bartenders receive short-term on-the-job training, usually lasting a few weeks, under the guidance of an experienced bartender. Training focuses on cocktail recipes, bar-setup procedures, and customer service, which includes handling unruly customers and other unpleasant situations. In food service estab-

lishments where bartenders serve food, the training may cover teamwork and proper food-handling procedures.

Some employers teach bartending skills to new workers by providing self-study programs, online programs, audiovisual presentations, and instructional booklets that explain service skills. Such programs communicate the philosophy of the establishment, help new bartenders build rapports with other staff, and instill a desire to work as a team.

Other Experience. Some bartenders qualify through related work experience. They may start as bartender helpers and progress into full-fledged bartenders as they learn basic mixing procedures and recipes.

Advancement. Advancement for bartenders is usually limited to finding a job in a busier or more expensive restaurant or bar where prospects for earning tips are better. Some bartenders advance to supervisory jobs, such as dining room supervisor, maitre d', assistant manager, and restaurant general manager. A few bartenders open their own bars.

Important Qualities

Communication skills. Bartenders must listen carefully to their customers' orders, explain drink and food items, and make menu recommendations. They also should be able to converse with customers on a variety of subjects, to create a friendly and welcoming environment at a bar.

Employment Projections Data for Bartenders

Occupational title	SOC Code	Employment, 2012	Projected Employment, 2022	Change, 2012–2022	
				Percent	Numeric
Bartenders..	35-3011	551,100	616,700	12	65,600

Source: U.S. Bureau of Labor Statistics, Employment Projections Program

Note: Data are rounded. Go to Occupational Information Included in the OOH for a discussion of the data in this table.

Similar Occupations
This table shows a list of occupations with job duties that are similar to those of bartenders.

Occupations	Entry-level Education	2012 Pay	Projected Job Growth	Average Annual Openings
Cashiers	Less than high school	$18,970	3%	153,000
Flight Attendants	High school diploma or equivalent	$37,240	-7%	1,400
Food and Beverage Serving and Related Workers	Less than high school	$18,428	12%	245,590
Food Preparation Workers	Less than high school	$19,300	4%	26,050
Waiters and Waitresses	Less than high school	$18,540	6%	126,830

Customer-service skills. Because establishments that serve alcohol rely on retaining current customers and attracting new ones, bartenders should have good customer-service skills to ensure repeat business.

Decision-making skills. Because of the legal issues that come with serving alcohol, bartenders must be able to make good decisions. For example, they should be able to detect intoxicated customers and deny further service to those individuals.

Interpersonal skills. Bartenders should be friendly, tactful, and attentive when dealing with customers. For example, they should be able to tell a joke and laugh with a customer to build rapport.

Physical stamina. Bartenders spend hours on their feet preparing drinks, serving customers, and sometimes lifting and carrying heavy cases of liquor, beer, and other bar supplies.

Pay

The median hourly wage (including tips) for bartenders was $9.09 in May 2012. The median wage is the wage at which half the workers in an occupation earned more than that amount and half earned less. The lowest 10 percent earned less than $7.85 per hour, and the top 10 percent earned more than $15.49 per hour.

Bartenders' earnings often come from a combination of hourly wages and customers' tips. Earnings vary greatly, depending on the type of establishment. For example, in some popular and busy restaurants and bars, tips are higher than wages.

In some states, tipped employees are paid the federal minimum wage ($7.25 per hour as of July 24, 2009) in addition to tips. Others earn more per hour, because they work in states that set minimum wages higher than the federal minimum.

States may have exceptions to the minimum wage laws in specific circumstances for tipped employees. According to the Fair Labor Standards Act, tipped employees are those who regularly receive more than $30 a month in tips. The employer may consider tips as part of wages, but the employer must pay at least $2.13 an hour in direct wages. The Wage and Hour Division of the U.S. Department of Labor maintains a website with minimum wages for tipped employees, by state.

Job Outlook

Employment of bartenders is projected to grow 12 percent from 2012 to 2022, about as fast as the average for all occupations.

As the population grows, more people will dine out and drink at a variety of food and drinking places. In response, many new bars, taverns, clubs, and restaurants are expected to open to meet demand. However, the growing popularity of take-out food and the growing number and variety of places that offer self-service or carryout options, including many full-service restaurants, may moderate employment growth.

Job Prospects. Job opportunities are expected to be good because of the need to replace the many workers who leave the occupation each year.

Strong competition is expected for bartending jobs in popular restaurants and fine-dining establishments, where tips are highest. Those who have graduated from bartending school and those with previous work experience and excellent customer-service skills should have the best job prospects.

O*NET

➤ Bartenders (35-3011.00)

Contacts for More Information

For more information about bartenders, visit
➤ National Restaurant Association (www.restaurant.org/)

For more information about bartenders, including a list of bartending schools that offer courses and training programs, visit
➤ Bartender Magazine (www.bartender.com/bartending.htm)

Chefs and Head Cooks

- **2012 Median Pay** .... $42,480 per year
  $20.42 per hour
- **Entry-Level Education** ... High school diploma or equivalent
- **Work Experience in a Related Occupation** ...5 years or more
- **On-the-Job Training** .... None
- **Number of Jobs 2012** 115,400
- **Job Outlook, 2012–22** .... 5% (Slower than average)
- **Employment Change, 2012–22** 6,000

What Chefs and Head Cooks Do

Chefs and head cooks oversee the daily food preparation at restaurants and other places where food is served. They direct kitchen staff and handle any food-related concerns.

Duties. Chefs and head cooks typically do the following:

- Check freshness of food and ingredients
- Supervise and coordinate activities of cooks and other food preparation workers
- Develop recipes and determine how to present the food
- Plan menus and ensure uniform serving sizes and quality of meals
- Inspect supplies, equipment, and work areas for cleanliness and functionality
- Hire, train, and supervise cooks and other food preparation workers
- Order and maintain inventory of food and supplies
- Monitor sanitation practices and follow kitchen safety standards

Chefs, head cooks, and food preparation and serving supervisors work long hours preparing ingredients before cooking.

Median Annual Wages, May 2012

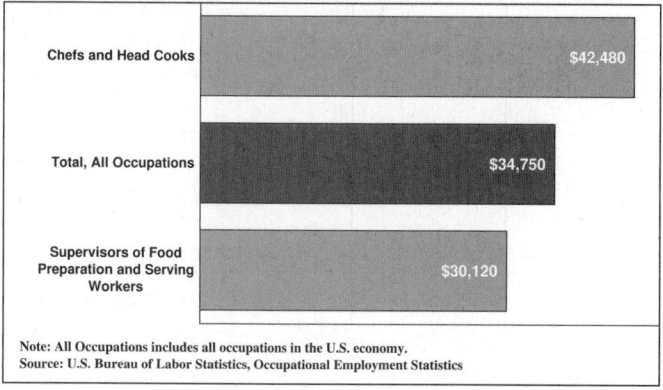

Note: All Occupations includes all occupations in the U.S. economy.
Source: U.S. Bureau of Labor Statistics, Occupational Employment Statistics

Percent Change in Employment, Projected 2012–2022

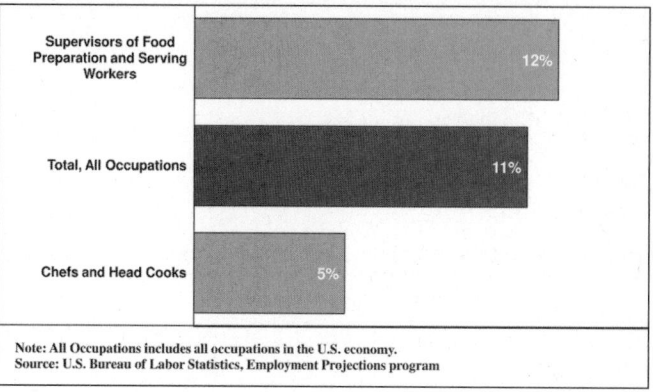

Note: All Occupations includes all occupations in the U.S. economy.
Source: U.S. Bureau of Labor Statistics, Employment Projections program

Chefs and head cooks use a variety of kitchen and cooking equipment, including step-in coolers, high-quality knives, meat slicers, and grinders. They also have access to large quantities of meats, spices, and produce. Some chefs use scheduling and purchasing software to help them in their administrative tasks.

Some chefs run their own restaurant or catering business. These chefs are often busy with kitchen and office work and have little time to interact with diners.

The following are examples of types of chefs and head cooks:

Executive chefs, head cooks, and chefs de cuisine are primarily responsible for overseeing the operation of a kitchen. They coordinate the work of sous chefs and other cooks, who prepare most of the meals. Executive chefs also have many duties beyond the kitchen. They design the menu, review food and beverage purchases, and often train cooks and other food preparation workers. Some executive chefs primarily handle administrative tasks and may spend less time in the kitchen.

Sous chefs are a kitchen's second-in-command. They supervise the restaurant's cooks, prepare meals, and report results to the head chefs. In the absence of the head chef, sous chefs run the kitchen.

Private household chefs typically work full time for one client, such as a corporate executive, university president, or diplomat, who regularly entertains as part of his or her official duties.

Work Environment

Chefs and head cooks held about 115,400 jobs in 2012. The industries that employed the most chefs and head cooks in 2012 were as follows:

Restaurants and other eating places.. 46%
Traveler accommodation.. 11
Special food services 10
Other amusement and recreation industries............................. 6

Chefs and head cooks work in restaurants, hotels, private households, and other food service facilities, all of which must be kept clean and sanitary. Chefs and head cooks usually stand for long periods and work in a fast-paced environment.

About 13 percent of chefs and head cooks were self-employed in 2012. Because some self-employed chefs run their own restaurant or catering business, their work can be additionally stressful. For example, outside the kitchen, they often spend long hours managing all aspects of the business, to ensure that bills and salaries are paid and that the business is profitable.

Injuries and Illnesses. Kitchens are usually crowded and filled with potential dangers, such as hot ovens and slippery floors. As a result, chefs and head cooks have a higher rate of injuries and illnesses than the national average. The most common hazards are slips, falls, cuts, and burns, but these injuries are seldom serious. To reduce these risks, workers often wear protective clothing, such as long-sleeve cotton shirts and non-slip shoes.

Work Schedules. Most chefs and head cooks work full time, including early mornings, late evenings, weekends, and holidays. Many executive chefs work 12-hour days, because they oversee the delivery of food supplies early in the day and use the afternoon to prepare special menu items.

How to Become One

Most chefs and head cooks learn their skills through work experience. Others receive training at a community college, technical school, culinary arts school, or a 4-year college. A small number learn through apprenticeship programs or in the armed forces.

Education. A growing number of chefs and head cooks receive formal training at community colleges, technical schools, culinary arts schools, and 4-year colleges.

Students in culinary programs spend most of their time in kitchens practicing their cooking skills. Programs cover all aspects of kitchen work, including menu planning, food sanitation procedures, and purchasing and inventory methods. Most training programs also require students to gain experience in a commercial kitchen through an internship or apprenticeship program.

Work Experience in a Related Occupation. Most chefs and head cooks start working in other positions, such as line cooks, learning cooking skills from the chefs they work for. Many spend years working in kitchens before learning enough to get promoted to chef or head cook positions.

Training. Some chefs and head cooks train on the job, where they learn the same skills as in a formal education program. Some train in mentorship programs, where they work under the direction of an experienced chef. Executive chefs, head cooks, and sous chefs who work in fine-dining restaurants often have many years of training and experience.

Some chefs and head cooks learn through apprenticeship programs sponsored by professional culinary institutes, industry associations, and trade unions in coordination with the U.S. Department of Labor. Apprenticeship programs generally last about 2 years and combine instructions and on-the-job training. Apprentices must complete at least 1,000 hours of both instructions and paid on-the-job training. Courses typically cover food sanitation and safety, basic knife skills, and equipment operation. Apprentices spend the rest of the training learning practical skills in a commercial kitchen under a chef's supervision.

The American Culinary Federation accredits more than 200 academic training programs at post-secondary schools and spon-

Employment Projections Data for Chefs and Head Cooks

Occupational title	SOC Code	Employment, 2012	Projected Employment, 2022	Change, 2012–2022	
				Percent	Numeric
Chefs and head cooks	35-1011	115,400	121,500	5	6,000

Source: U.S. Bureau of Labor Statistics, Employment Projections Program

Note: Data are rounded. Go to **Occupational Information Included in the OOH** *for a discussion of the data in this table.*

Similar Occupations   This table shows a list of occupations with job duties that are similar to those of chefs and head cooks.

Occupations	Entry-level Education	2012 Pay	Projected Job Growth	Average Annual Openings
Bakers	Less than high school	$23,140	6%	5,010
Cooks	See "How to Become One"	$21,144	10%	63,160
Food and Beverage Serving and Related Workers	Less than high school	$18,428	12%	245,590
Food Preparation Workers	Less than high school	$19,300	4%	26,050
Food Service Managers	High school diploma or equivalent	$47,960	2%	6,240

sors apprenticeships around the country. The basic qualifications to enter an apprenticeship program are as follows:

• Minimum age of 17

• High school education or equivalent

• Drug free

Some chefs and head cooks receive formal training in the armed forces or from individual hotel or restaurant chains.

Licenses, Certifications, and Registrations. Although not required, certification can show competence and lead to advancement and higher pay. The American Culinary Federation certifies personal chefs, in addition to various levels of chefs. Certification standards are based primarily on work-related experience and formal training. Minimum work experience for certification can range from 6 months to 5 years, depending on the level of certification.

Important Qualities

Business skills. Executive chefs and chefs who run their own restaurant should understand the restaurant business. They should be skilled at administrative tasks, such as accounting and personnel management, and be able to manage a restaurant efficiently and profitably.

Communication skills. Because the pace in the kitchen can be hectic during peak dining hours, chefs must be able to communicate their orders clearly and effectively to staff.

Creativity. Chefs and head cooks must be creative in order to develop and prepare interesting and innovative recipes. They should be able to use various ingredients to create appealing meals for their customers.

Dexterity. Chefs and head cooks need excellent manual dexterity, including proper knife techniques for cutting, chopping, and dicing.

Leadership skills. Chefs and head cooks must have the ability to motivate kitchen staff and develop constructive and cooperative working relationships with them.

Sense of taste and smell. Chefs and head cooks must have a keen sense of taste and smell, to inspect food quality and to design meals that their customers enjoy.

Time-management skills. Chefs and head cooks must efficiently manage their time and the time of their staff. They must ensure that meals are prepared and that customers are served on time, especially during busy hours.

Pay

The median annual wage for chefs and head cooks was $42,480 in May 2012. The median wage is the wage at which half the workers in an occupation earned more than that amount, and half earned less. The lowest 10 percent earned less than $24,530, and the top 10 percent earned more than $74,120.

In May 2012, the median annual wages for chefs and head cooks in the top four industries employing these workers were as follows:

Traveler accommodation.. $48,210
Other amusement and recreation industries......................... 47,490
Special food services 42,960
Restaurants and other eating places.................................... 9,790

The level of pay for chefs and head cooks varies greatly by region and employer. Pay is usually highest in upscale restaurants and hotels, where many executive chefs work, as well as in major metropolitan and resort areas.

Job Outlook

Employment of chefs and head cooks is projected to grow 5 percent from 2012 to 2022, slower than the average for all occupations.

Population and income growth are expected to result in greater demand for high-quality dishes at a variety of dining venues, including many upscale establishments.

However, employment growth should be limited, as many restaurants, in an effort to lower costs, choose to hire cooks or other food service workers to perform the work normally done by higher-paid chefs and head cooks.

Job Prospects. Job opportunities should be best for chefs and head cooks with several years of work experience. The majority of job openings will result from the need to replace workers who leave the occupation. The fast pace, long hours, and high energy levels required for these jobs often lead to a high rate of turnover.

There will be strong competition for jobs at upscale restaurants, hotels, and casinos, where the pay is typically highest. Workers with a combination of business skills, previous work experience, and creativity should have the best job prospects.

➤ Chefs and Head Cooks (35-1011.00)

Contacts for More Information

For career information about chefs, including a directory of 2-year and 4-year colleges that offer courses or training programs, visit
➤ American Culinary Federation (www.acfchefs.org/)
➤ National Restaurant Association (www.restaurant.org/)
  For information about becoming a private chef, visit
➤ American Personal & Private Chef Association (www.personalchef .com/)

Cooks

- **2012 Median Pay** .... $20,550 per year
  $9.88 per hour
- **Entry-Level Education** ....See "How to Become One"
- **Work Experience in a Related Occupation**.... See "How to Become One"
- **On-the-Job Training** ....See "How to Become One"
- **Number of Jobs 2012** 2,148,500
- **Job Outlook, 2012–22** .... 10% (As fast as average)
- **Employment Change, 2012–22** 205,300

What Cooks Do

Cooks prepare, season, and cook a wide range of foods. This may include soups, salads, entrees, and desserts.

Duties. Cooks typically do the following:

- Check the freshness of food and ingredients before cooking
- Weigh, measure, and mix ingredients according to recipes
- Bake, roast, grill, broil, or fry meats, fish, vegetables, and other foods

Cooks and food preparation workers must perform their duties quickly to keep up with food orders.

- Boil and steam meats, fish, vegetables, and other foods
- Garnish, arrange, and serve food
- Clean work areas, equipment, utensils, dishes, and silverware
- Cook, hold, and store food or food ingredients

Large restaurants and food service establishments often have varied menus and large kitchen staffs. Teams of restaurant cooks, sometimes called *assistant cooks* or *line cooks*, work at assigned stations equipped with the necessary types of stoves, grills, pans, and ingredients.

Job titles often reflect the principal ingredient cooks prepare or the type of cooking they do–*vegetable cook*, *fry cook*, or *grill cook*, for example. Cooks usually work under the direction of chefs, head cooks, or food service managers.

Cooks use a variety of kitchen equipment, including broilers, grills, slicers, grinders, and blenders.

The responsibilities of cooks vary with the place at which they work, the size of the facility, and the complexity and level of service offered.

The following are examples of types of cooks:

Institution and cafeteria cooks work in the kitchens of schools, cafeterias, businesses, hospitals, and other institutions. For each meal, they prepare a large quantity of a limited number of entrees, vegetables, and desserts, according to preset menus. Because meals are usually prepared in advance, cooks seldom take special orders.

Restaurant cooks prepare a wide selection of dishes and cook most orders individually. Some restaurant cooks may order supplies, set menu prices, and plan the daily menu.

Short-order cooks prepare foods in restaurants and coffee shops that emphasize fast service and quick food preparation. They usually prepare sandwiches, fry eggs, and cook french fries, often working on several orders at the same time.

Fast-food cooks prepare a limited selection of menu items in fast-food restaurants. They cook and package food, such as hamburgers and fried chicken, to be kept warm until served. For more information on workers who prepare and serve items in fast-food restaurants, see the profiles on food preparation workers and food and beverage serving and related workers.

Private household cooks and personal chefs plan and prepare meals in private homes, according to the client's tastes and dietary needs. They order groceries and supplies, clean the kitchen, and wash dishes and utensils. They also may cater parties, holiday meals, luncheons, and other social events. Private household cooks typically work for one full-time client. Some private household cooks and personal chefs are self-employed or employed by a private cooking company, regularly making meals for clients.

Work Environment

Cooks held about 2.1 million jobs in 2012. The industries that employed the most cooks in 2012 were as follows:

Restaurants and other eating places.. 68%
Health care and social assistance 8
Elementary and secondary schools 6

Cooks work in restaurants, schools, hospitals, hotels, and other establishments where food is served. Some work in private homes.

Cooks usually must stand for long periods and work under pressure in a fast-paced environment. Although most cooks work indoors in kitchens, some may work outdoors at food stands, at catered events, or in mobile food trucks.

Injuries and Illnesses. Kitchens are usually crowded and filled with dangerous things, such as hot ovens or slippery floors. As a

Median Hourly Wages, May 2012

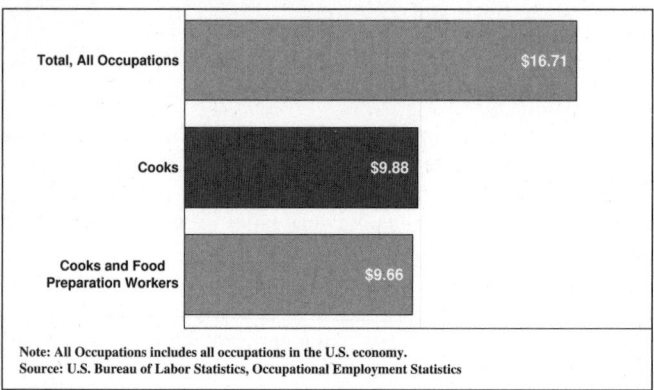

Note: All Occupations includes all occupations in the U.S. economy.
Source: U.S. Bureau of Labor Statistics, Occupational Employment Statistics

Percent Change in Employment, Projected 2012–2022

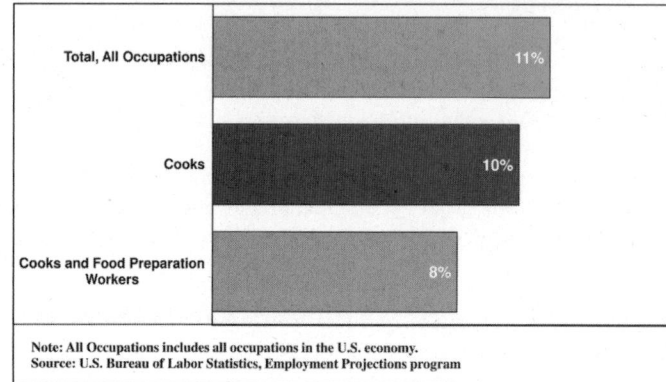

Note: All Occupations includes all occupations in the U.S. economy.
Source: U.S. Bureau of Labor Statistics, Employment Projections program

result, institution and cafeteria, restaurant, and short-order cooks have a higher rate of injuries and illnesses than the national average. The most common hazards are slips, falls, cuts, and burns, but the injuries are seldom serious. To reduce the risks, cooks wear protective coats, aprons, or nonslip shoes.

Work Schedules. Most cooks work full time. Work shifts often include early mornings, late evenings, weekends, and holidays. Schedules for cooks in school cafeterias and some institutional cafeterias usually are more regular. Cooks working in schools may work just during the school year, typically for 9 or 10 months. Similarly, some resort establishments offer seasonal employment only.

How to Become One

Short-term on-the-job training and work-related experience are the most common ways to become a cook. Although no formal education is required, some restaurant cooks and private household cooks attend culinary schools. Others attend vocational or apprenticeship programs.

Education. Independent and vocational cooking schools, professional culinary institutes, and college degree programs provide training for aspiring cooks. Programs generally last from a few months to 2 years. Some programs offer training in advanced cooking techniques, international cuisines, and cooking styles. To enter these programs, candidates may be required to have a high school diploma or equivalent. Depending on the type and length of the program, graduates generally qualify for entry-level positions as a restaurant cook.

Training. Most cooks learn their skills through short-term on-the-job training, usually lasting a few weeks. Training generally starts with learning kitchen basics and workplace safety and continues with handling and cooking food.

Some cooks learn through an apprenticeship program. Professional culinary institutes, industry associations, and trade unions sponsor such programs for cooks, in coordination with the U.S. Department of Labor. Typical apprenticeships last 1 year and combine technical training and work experience. Apprentices complete courses in food sanitation and safety, basic knife skills, and equipment operation. They also learn practical cooking skills under the supervision of an experienced chef. The American Culinary Federation accredits more than 200 academic training programs and sponsors apprenticeships through these programs around the country. The basic qualifications for entering an apprenticeship program are as follows:

- Minimum age of 17
- High school education or equivalent
- Pass substance abuse screening

Some hotels, a number of restaurants, and the Armed Forces have their own training programs.

Work Experience in a Related Occupation. Many cooks learn their skills through work-related experience. They typically start as a kitchen helper or food preparation worker learning basic cooking skills before they advance to assistant cook or line cook positions. Some learn by working under the guidance of a more experienced cook.

Advancement. The American Culinary Federation certifies chefs as proficient in different skill levels. For cooks seeking certification and advancement to higher level chef positions, certification can show accomplishment and lead to higher paying positions.

Advancement opportunities for cooks often depend on training, work experience, and the ability to prepare more complex dishes. Those who learn new cooking skills and who accept greater

Employment Projections Data for Cooks

Occupational title	SOC Code	Employment, 2012	Projected Employment, 2022	Change, 2012–2022 Percent	Change, 2012–2022 Numeric
Cooks...	35-2010	2,148,500	2,353,700	10	205,300
Cooks, fast food	35-2011	516,900	514,400	0	-2,500
Cooks, institution and cafeteria	35-2012	408,900	462,800	13	54,000
Cooks, private household	35-2013	7,000	6,900	-1	-100
Cooks, restaurant	35-2014	1,024,100	1,174,200	15	150,100
Cooks, short order...	35-2015	166,100	166,600	0	500
Cooks, all other	35-2019	25,500	28,700	13	3,200

Source: U.S. Bureau of Labor Statistics, Employment Projections Program

Note: Data are rounded. Go to **Occupational Information Included in the OOH** *for a discussion of the data in this table.*

Similar Occupations   This table shows a list of occupations with job duties that are similar to those of cooks.

Occupations	Entry-level Education	2012 Pay	Projected Job Growth	Average Annual Openings
Bakers	Less than high school	$23,140	6%	5,010
Chefs and Head Cooks	High school diploma or equivalent	$42,480	5%	2,470
Food and Beverage Serving and Related Workers	Less than high school	$18,428	12%	245,590
Food Preparation Workers	Less than high school	$19,300	4%	26,050
Food Service Managers	High school diploma or equivalent	$47,960	2%	6,240

responsibility often advance. Some cooks may train or supervise kitchen staff who have fewer cooking skills.

Some may become head cooks, chefs, or food service managers.

Important Qualities

Comprehension. Cooks must be able to understand customers' orders and follow recipes in order to prepare dishes correctly.

Customer-service skills. Restaurant and short-order cooks must be able to deal with customers' complaints and special requests.

Dexterity. Cooks should have excellent hand–eye coordination. For example, they need to know the proper knife techniques for cutting, chopping, and dicing.

Physical stamina. The work of a cook can be physically tiring because cooks spend a lot of time standing in one place, cooking food over hot stoves, and cleaning work areas.

Sense of taste and smell. Cooks must have a keen sense of taste and smell to prepare meals that customers enjoy.

Teamwork. Cooks often prepare only part of a dish. They must coordinate with other cooks and kitchen workers to complete meals on time.

Pay

The median hourly wage for cooks was $9.88 in May 2012. The median wage is the wage at which half the workers in an occupation earned more than that amount and half earned less. The lowest 10 percent earned less than $8.00 per hour, and the top 10 percent earned more than $14.68 per hour.

In May 2012, median hourly wages for cooks were as follows:

Cooks, private household $11.29
Cooks, institution and cafeteria 10.99
Cooks, restaurant..10.59
Cooks, short order 9.48
Cooks, fast food...8.85
Cooks, all other 11.18

Earnings of cooks vary greatly by region and type of employer. Earnings usually are highest in fine-dining restaurants and luxury hotels, which are often located in major metropolitan and resort areas.

Job Outlook

Overall employment of cooks is projected to grow 10 percent from 2012 to 2022, about as fast as the average for all occupations. Individual growth rates will vary by specialty.

People will continue to eat out, buy takeout meals, or have food delivered. In response, more restaurants will open and cafeterias, catering services, and nontraditional food-service operations, such as those found inside grocery stores, will serve more prepared food dishes. These circumstances will increase demand for cooks.

Employment growth for cooks also should increase as, in an effort to lower costs, many restaurants choose to hire cooks instead of chefs and head cooks, who often have higher wages.

Job Prospects. Overall job opportunities are expected to be good as a result of employment growth and the need to replace workers who leave the occupation. Cooks with training and related work experience will have the best job prospects.

Those who can prepare more complex dishes will have the best job opportunities at restaurant chains, upscale restaurants, and hotels. Candidates seeking full-time jobs at these restaurants will face strong competition because the number of job applicants often exceeds the number of job openings.

O*NET

➤ Cooks, Fast Food (35-2011.00)
➤ Cooks, Institution and Cafeteria (35-2012.00)
➤ Cooks, Private Household (35-2013.00)
➤ Cooks, Restaurant (35-2014.00)
➤ Cooks, Short Order (35-2015.00)
➤ Cooks, All Other (35-2019.00)

Contacts for More Information

For information about culinary apprenticeship programs registered with the U.S. Department of Labor, contact the local office of your state employment service agency, check the U.S. Department of Labor's toll-free help line, 1 (877) 872-5627, or the Employment and Training Administration (www.doleta.gov/OA/eta_default.cfm).

For more information about cooking careers, visit
➤ American Culinary Federation (www.acfchefs.org/)
➤ National Restaurant Association (www.restaurant.org/)
For information about becoming a personal chef, visit
➤ American Personal & Private Chef Association (www.personalchef.com/)

Food and Beverage Serving and Related Workers

- **2012 Median Pay** .... $18,400 per year
  $8.84 per hour

- **Entry-Level Education** .... Less than high school

- **Work Experience in a Related Occupation**.............. None

- **On-the-Job Training** ....See "How to Become One"

- **Number of Jobs 2012** 4,438,100

- **Job Outlook, 2012–22** .... 12% (As fast as average)

- **Employment Change, 2012–22** 523,200

Food and beverage serving workers assist diners at cafeterias.

What Food and Beverage Serving and Related Workers Do

Food and beverage serving and related workers perform a variety of customer service, food preparation, and cleaning duties in restaurants, cafeterias, and other eating and drinking establishments.

Duties. Food and beverage serving and related workers typically do the following:

- Greet customers and answer their questions about menu items and specials
- Take food or drink orders from customers
- Prepare food and drink orders, such as sandwiches, salads, and coffee
- Relay customers' orders to other kitchen staff
- Serve food and drinks to customers at a counter, at a stand, or in a hotel room
- Clean assigned work areas, dining tables, or serving counters
- Replenish and stock service stations, cabinets, and tables
- Set tables or prepare food trays for new customers

Food and beverage serving and related workers are the front line of customer service in restaurants, cafeterias, and other food service establishments. Depending on the establishment, they take customers' food and drink orders and serve food and beverages.

Most work as part of a team, helping coworkers to improve workflow and customer service.

The job titles of food and beverage serving and related workers vary with where they work and what they do.

The following are examples of types of food and beverage serving and related workers:

Combined food preparation and serving workers, including fast food, are employed primarily by fast-food restaurants. They take food and beverage orders, prepare or retrieve items when ready, fill cups with beverages, and accept customers' payments. They also heat food items and make salads and sandwiches.

Counter attendants take orders and serve food over a counter in snack bars, cafeterias, movie theaters, and coffee shops. They fill cups with coffee, soda, and other beverages, and may prepare fountain specialties, such as milkshakes and ice cream sundaes. Counter attendants take carryout orders from diners and wrap or place items in containers. They clean counters, prepare itemized bills, and accept customers' payments.

Food servers, nonrestaurant, serve food to customers outside of a restaurant environment. Many deliver room service meals in hotels or meals to hospital rooms. Some act as carhops, bringing orders to customers in parked cars.

Dining room and cafeteria attendants and bartender helpers– sometimes collectively referred to as bus staff–help waiters, waitresses, and bartenders by cleaning and setting tables, removing dirty dishes, and keeping serving areas stocked with supplies. They also may help waiters and waitresses by bringing meals out of the kitchen, distributing dishes to diners, filling water glasses, and delivering condiments. *Cafeteria attendants* stock serving tables with food trays, dishes, and silverware. They sometimes carry trays to dining tables for customers. *Bartender helpers* keep bar equipment clean and glasses washed.

Hosts and hostesses greet customers and manage reservation and waiting lists. They may direct customers to coatrooms, restrooms, or a waiting area until their table is ready. Hosts and hostesses assign guests to tables suitable for the size of their group, escort patrons to their seats, and provide menus. They also take reservations over the phone, arrange parties, and help with other customers' requests.

Work Environment

Food and beverage serving and related workers held about 4.4 million jobs in 2012. Nearly 3 in 4 worked in restaurants, including full-service and fast food restaurants.

Food and beverage serving and related workers are on their feet most of the time and often carry heavy trays of food, dishes, and glassware. During busy dining periods, they are required to serve customers quickly and efficiently.

Injuries and Illnesses. Food preparation and serving areas in restaurants often have potential safety hazards, such as hot ovens

Median Hourly Wages, May 2012

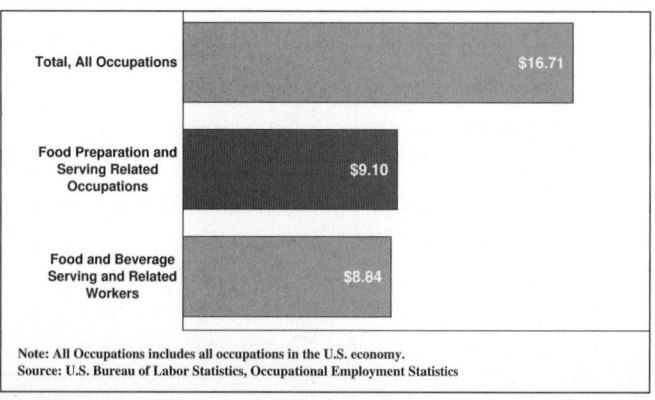

Total, All Occupations	$16.71
Food Preparation and Serving Related Occupations	$9.10
Food and Beverage Serving and Related Workers	$8.84

Note: All Occupations includes all occupations in the U.S. economy.
Source: U.S. Bureau of Labor Statistics, Occupational Employment Statistics

Percent Change in Employment, Projected 2012–2022

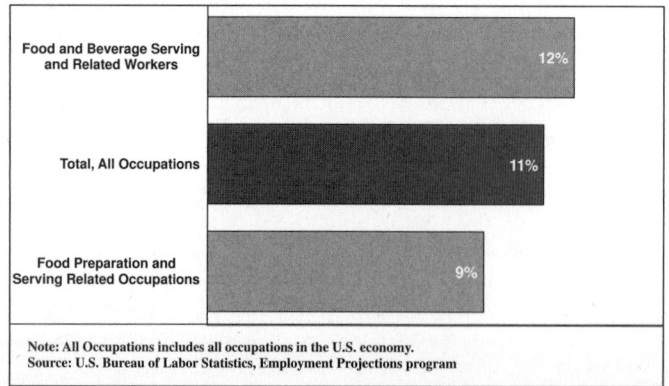

Food and Beverage Serving and Related Workers	12%
Total, All Occupations	11%
Food Preparation and Serving Related Occupations	9%

Note: All Occupations includes all occupations in the U.S. economy.
Source: U.S. Bureau of Labor Statistics, Employment Projections program

Employment Projections Data for Food and Beverage Serving and Related Workers

Occupational title	SOC Code	Employment, 2012	Projected Employment, 2022	Change, 2012–2022	
				Percent	Numeric
Food and beverage serving and related workers	—	4,438,100	4,961,300	12	523,200
Combined food preparation and serving workers, including fast food	35-3021	2,969,300	3,391,200	14	421,900
Counter attendants, cafeteria, food concession, and coffee shop	35-3022	439,200	436,900	-1	-2,300
Food servers, nonrestaurant	35-3041	241,300	289,900	20	48,600
Dining room and cafeteria attendants and bartender helpers ...	35-9011	403,200	435,400	8	32,100
Hosts and hostesses, restaurant, lounge, and coffee shop	35-9031	347,300	366,400	5	19,100
Food preparation and serving related workers, all other	35-9099	37,800	41,500	10	3,700

Source: U.S. Bureau of Labor Statistics, Employment Projections Program

Note: Data are rounded. Go to Occupational Information Included in the OOH for a discussion of the data in this table.

Similar Occupations   This table shows a list of occupations with job duties that are similar to those of food and beverage serving and related workers.

Occupations	Entry-level Education	2012 Pay	Projected Job Growth	Average Annual Openings
Bartenders	Less than high school	$18,900	12%	26,940
Cashiers	Less than high school	$18,970	3%	153,000
Cooks	See "How to Become One"	$21,144	10%	63,160
Flight Attendants	High school diploma or equivalent	$37,240	-7%	1,400
Food Preparation Workers	Less than high school	$19,300	4%	26,050
Retail Sales Workers	Less than high school	$21,514	10%	202,730
Waiters and Waitresses	Less than high school	$18,540	6%	126,830

and slippery floors. As a result, counter attendants, food servers, and dining room and cafeteria attendants and bartender helpers have a higher rate of injuries and illnesses than the national average. Common hazards include slips, cuts, and burns, but the injuries are seldom serious. To reduce these risks, workers often wear protective clothing, such as gloves, aprons, or nonslip shoes.

Work Schedules. About half of all food and beverage serving and related workers were employed part time in 2012. Because food service and drinking establishments typically have long dining hours, early morning, late evening, weekend, and holidays work is common. Those who work in school cafeterias may have more regular hours and work only during the school year, which is usually 9 to 10 months.

In addition, long business hours allow for flexible schedules that appeal to many teenagers, who can gain work experience. Compared with all other occupations, a much larger proportion of food and beverage serving and related workers were 16 to 19 years old in 2012.

How to Become One

Most food and beverage service jobs are entry-level jobs and do not require a high school diploma. The majority of workers receive short-term on-the-job training.

Most states require workers, such as nonrestaurant servers, who serve alcoholic beverages to be 18 years of age or older.

Education. There are no formal education requirements for becoming a food and beverage serving worker.

Training. Most workers learn their skills through short-term on-the-job training, usually lasting several weeks. Training includes basic customer service, kitchen safety, safe food-handling procedures, and good sanitation habits.

Some employers, particularly those in fast-food restaurants, teach new workers with the use of self-study programs, online programs, audiovisual presentations, or instructional booklets that explain food preparation and service procedures. However, most food and beverage serving and related workers learn their skills by watching and working with more experienced workers.

Some full-service restaurants provide new dining room employees with classroom training sessions that alternate with periods of on-the-job work experience. The training communicates the operating philosophy of the restaurant, helps new employees establish a personal rapport with other staff, teaches employees formal serving techniques, and instills a desire in the staff to work as a team.

Some nonrestaurant servers and bartender helpers who work in establishments where alcohol is served may need training on state and local laws concerning the sale of alcoholic beverages. Some states, counties, and cities mandate such training, which typically lasts a few hours and can be taken online or in-house.

Advancement. Advancement opportunities are limited to those who remain on the job for a long time. However, some dining room and cafeteria attendants and bartender helpers may advance to waiter, waitress, or bartender positions as they learn the basics of serving food or preparing drinks.

Important Qualities

Communication skills. Food and beverage serving and related workers must listen carefully to their customers' orders and relay them correctly to the kitchen staff so that the orders are prepared to the customers' request.

Customer-service skills. Food service establishments rely on good food and customer service to keep customers and succeed in a competitive industry. As a result, workers should be courteous and be able to attend to customers' requests.

Physical stamina. Food and beverage serving and related workers spend most of their worktime standing, carrying heavy trays, cleaning work areas, and attending to customers' needs.

Pay

The median hourly wage for food and beverage serving and related workers was $8.84 in May 2012. The median wage is the wage at which half the workers in an occupation earned more than that amount and half earned less. The lowest 10 percent earned less than $7.76 per hour, and the top 10 percent earned more than $11.63 per hour.

In May 2012, median hourly wages for food and beverage serving and related workers were as follows:

food servers, nonrestaurant...$9.44
hosts and hostesses, restaurant, lounge, and coffee shop 8.93
counter attendants, cafeteria, food concession,
   and coffee shop 8.92
dining room and cafeteria attendants and bartender helpers 8.89
combined food preparation and serving workers,
   including fast food 8.78
food preparation and serving related workers, all other...........9.76

Although some workers in this occupation earn tips, most get their earnings from hourly wages alone. Many entry-level or inexperienced workers earn the federal minimum wage ($7.25 per hour as of July 24, 2009). However, many others earn more per hour because they work in states that set minimum wages higher than the federal minimum.

Some food and beverage serving workers receive customers' tips. In some restaurants, workers contribute all or a portion of their tips to a tip pool, which is distributed among qualifying workers. Tip pools allow workers who do not usually receive tips directly from customers, such as dining room attendants, to be part of a team and to share in the rewards for good service.

Some states have exceptions to their minimum-wage laws for tipped employees in certain specific circumstances. According to the Fair Labor Standards Act, tipped employees are employees who regularly receive more than $30 a month in tips. The employer may consider tips as part of wages, but must pay at least $2.13 an hour in direct wages. The Wage and Hour Division of the U.S. Department of Labor maintains a website listing minimum wages for tipped employees by state.

Job Outlook

Overall employment of food and beverage serving and related workers is projected to grow 12 percent from 2012 to 2022, about as fast as the average for all occupations. Employment growth, however, will vary by specialty.

Employment of nonrestaurant servers, such as those who deliver food trays in hotels, in hospitals, in residential care facilities, and at catered events, is projected to grow 20 percent from 2012 to 2022, faster than the average for all occupations.

Employment of combined food preparation and serving workers, which includes fast-food workers, is projected to grow 14 percent from 2012 to 2022, about as fast as the average for all occupations.

Employment of dining room and cafeteria attendants, counter attendants, and hosts and hostesses is projected to grow 8 percent from 2012 to 2022, about as fast as the average for all occupations.

As a growing population continues to dine out, purchase carryout meals, or have food delivered, more restaurants, particularly

fast-food and casual dining restaurants, will open, increasing demand for food and beverage serving workers, including fast-food workers.

In addition, nontraditional food service operations, such as those found inside grocery stores and cafeterias in hospitals and residential care facilities, will serve more prepared meals. Because these workers are essential to the operation of a food-serving establishment, they will continue to be in demand.

Job Prospects. Job opportunities for food and beverage serving and related workers will be excellent, because many workers leave the occupation each year, resulting in a large number of job openings.

Workers with related work experience and excellent customer-service skills should have the best job opportunities at upscale restaurants. Still, those seeking positions at these establishments will face strong competition because the number of job applicants often exceeds the number of job openings because of higher tips.

O*NET

➤ Combined Food Preparation and Serving Workers, Including Fast Food (35-3021.00)
➤ Counter Attendants, Cafeteria, Food Concession, and Coffee Shop (35-3022.00)
➤ Baristas (35-3022.01)
➤ Food Servers, Nonrestaurant (35-3041.00)
➤ Dining Room and Cafeteria Attendants and Bartender Helpers (35-9011.00)
➤ Hosts and Hostesses, Restaurant, Lounge, and Coffee Shop (35-9031.00)
➤ Food Preparation and Serving Related Workers, All Other (35-9099.00)

Contacts for More Information

For more information on food and beverage serving careers, visit
➤ National Restaurant Association (www.restaurant.org/)

Food Preparation Workers

- **2012 Median Pay** .... $19,300 per year
                                                   $9.28 per hour
- **Entry-Level Education** .... Less than high school
- **Work Experience in a Related Occupation** .... None
- **On-the-Job Training** .... Short-term on-the-job training
- **Number of Jobs 2012** 807,800
- **Job Outlook, 2012–22** .... 4% (Slower than average)
- **Employment Change, 2012–22** 28,900

What Food Preparation Workers Do

Food preparation workers perform many routine tasks under the direction of cooks, chefs, or food service managers. Food preparation workers prepare cold foods, slice meat, peel and cut vegetables, brew coffee or tea, and perform many other food service tasks.

Duties. Food preparation workers typically do the following:

- Clean and sanitize work areas, equipment, utensils, and dishes
- Weigh or measure ingredients, such as meats and cheeses
- Prepare fresh condiments, including lettuce, tomatoes, and onions
- Cut or grind meats, poultry, and seafood in preparation for cooking them
- Mix ingredients for salads

- Store food in designated containers and storage areas to prevent spoilage
- Take and record the temperature of food and food storage areas
- Place food trays over food warmers for immediate service

Food preparation workers perform routine, repetitive tasks under the direction of cooks, chefs, or food service managers. To help cooks and other kitchen staff, they prepare ingredients for dishes by slicing and dicing vegetables and by making salads and cold food items.

Although most food preparation workers help prepare food, some also are responsible for retrieving cooking utensils, pots, and pans or for cleaning and storing other kitchen equipment. They also unload and store food supplies and retrieve them for cooks and chefs when needed. Other common duties include keeping salad bars and buffet tables stocked and clean.

Those who work at hotels or restaurants often use soda machines, coffeemakers, and espresso machines to prepare beverages for customers. In fast-food restaurants, food preparation workers may take customer orders and process payments with the use of cash registers.

In some kitchens, food preparation workers use a variety of commercial kitchen equipment, such as commercial dishwashers, blenders, slicers, or grinders.

Work Environment

Food preparation workers held about 807,800 jobs in 2012.

The industries that employed the most food preparation workers in 2012 were as follows:

Restaurants and other eating places.. 48%
Grocery stores 14
Special food services 6
Nursing and residential care facilities 6
Elementary and secondary schools 5

Food preparation workers are employed in restaurants, hotels, and other places where food is served, such as grocery stores, schools, hospitals, and cafeterias.

The work is often strenuous and tiring. Food preparation workers may stand or walk for hours at a time while cleaning or preparing ingredients. Some may be required to lift and carry heavy pots or unload heavy food supplies.

The fast-paced environment in kitchens can be hectic and stressful, especially during peak dining hours. Therefore, food preparation workers must work well with cooks and other kitchen staff to ensure that dishes are prepared properly and quickly.

Food preparation workers wash and cut up fresh ingredients.

Injuries and Illnesses. Food preparation areas in kitchens are often dangerous, containing hot ovens and slippery floors. As a result, food preparation workers have a higher rate of injuries and illnesses than the national average. The most common hazards include slips, falls, cuts, and burns, but these injuries are seldom serious. To reduce risks, workers often wear protective clothing, such as gloves, aprons, and nonslip shoes.

Work Schedules. Nearly half of all food preparation workers were employed part time in 2012. Because many restaurants are open extended hours, working early mornings, late evenings, weekends, or holidays is common. Those who work in school cafeterias may have more regular hours and work only during the school year, which is usually 9 or 10 months. Some resorts offer seasonal employment only.

How to Become One

Short-term on-the-job training is the most common way food preparation workers learn their skills. No formal education or previous work experience is required.

Education. There are no formal education requirements for becoming a food preparation worker.

Training. Most food preparation workers learn their skills through short-term on-the-job training, which usually lasts several weeks. Trainees typically start by working under the supervision of an experienced worker, who teaches them basic kitchen duties. Training may also include basic sanitation and workplace safety regulations, as well as instructions on how to handle and prepare food.

Median Hourly Wages, May 2012

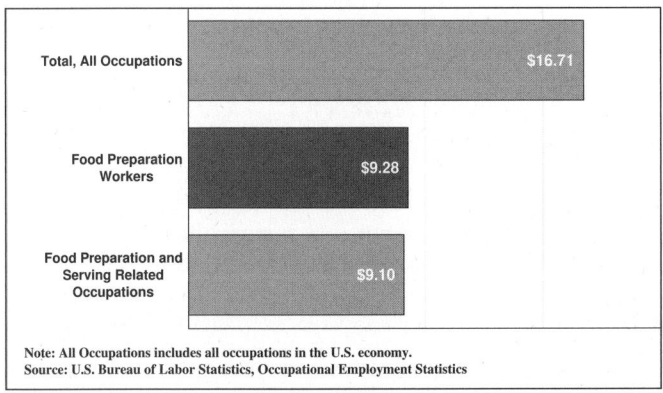

Total, All Occupations	$16.71
Food Preparation Workers	$9.28
Food Preparation and Serving Related Occupations	$9.10

Note: All Occupations includes all occupations in the U.S. economy.
Source: U.S. Bureau of Labor Statistics, Occupational Employment Statistics

Percent Change in Employment, Projected 2012–2022

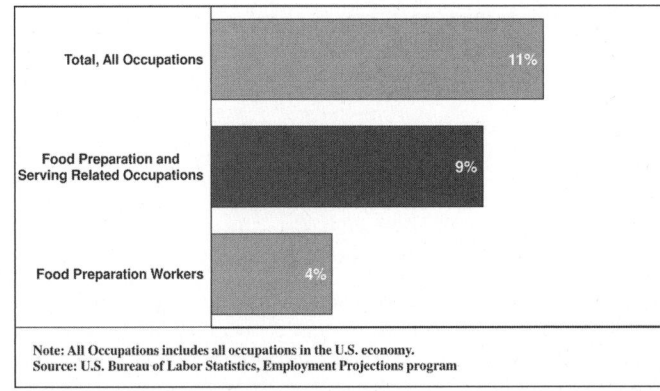

Total, All Occupations	11%
Food Preparation and Serving Related Occupations	9%
Food Preparation Workers	4%

Note: All Occupations includes all occupations in the U.S. economy.
Source: U.S. Bureau of Labor Statistics, Employment Projections program

Employment Projections Data for Food Preparation Workers

Occupational title	SOC Code	Employment, 2012	Projected Employment, 2022	Change, 2012–2022	
				Percent	Numeric
Food preparation workers	35-2021	807,800	836,700	4	28,900

Source: U.S. Bureau of Labor Statistics, Employment Projections Program

Note: **Data are rounded. Go to Occupational Information Included in the OOH** *for a discussion of the data in this table.*

Similar Occupations   This table shows a list of occupations with job duties that are similar to those of food preparation workers.

Occupations	Entry-level Education	2012 Pay	Projected Job Growth	Average Annual Openings
Bakers	Less than high school	$23,140	6%	5,010
Butchers and Meat Cutters	Less than high school	$28,490	5%	4,020
Chefs and Head Cooks	High school diploma or equivalent	$42,480	5%	2,470
Cooks	See "How to Become One"	$21,144	10%	63,160
Food and Beverage Serving and Related Workers	Less than high school	$18,428	12%	245,590
Slaughterers, Meat Packers, and Meat, Poultry, and Fish Cutters and Trimmers	Less than high school	$23,331	3%	6,890

Important Qualities

Dexterity. Because food preparation workers chop vegetables, cut meat, and perform many other tasks with sharp knives, they must have the ability to work quickly and safely with sharp objects.

Listening skills. Food preparation workers must understand customers' orders and follow directions from cooks, chefs, or food service managers.

Physical stamina. Food preparation workers stand on their feet for long periods while they prepare food, clean work areas, or lift heavy pots from the stove.

Physical strength. Food preparation workers should be strong enough to lift and carry heavy food supply boxes, which often can weigh up to 50 pounds.

Advancement. Advancement opportunities for food preparation workers depend on their training, work experience, and ability to cook. Many food preparation workers advance to assistant or line cook positions as they learn basic cooking skills.

Pay

The median hourly wage for food preparation workers was $9.28 in May 2012. The median wage is the wage at which half the workers in an occupation earned more than that amount and half earned less. The lowest 10 percent earned less than $7.92 per hour, and the top 10 percent earned more than $13.84 per hour.

In May 2012, the median hourly wages for food preparation workers in the top five industries employing these workers were as follows:

Elementary and secondary schools $11.01
Special food services 9.83
Grocery stores 9.66
Nursing and residential care facilities 9.37
Restaurants and other eating places......................... 9.07

Pay for food preparation workers varies by employer and region. Pay is usually highest for workers in elementary and secondary schools and in major metropolitan and resort areas.

Job Outlook

Employment of food preparation workers is projected to grow 4 percent from 2012 to 2022, slower than the average for all occupations.

People will continue to dine out, purchase carryout meals, or have food delivered to their homes or workplaces. In response, more restaurants will open and nontraditional food service operations, such as those found inside grocery stores, will serve more prepared meals.

In addition, because preparing fresh and made-from-scratch meals is labor intensive, many chefs at upscale restaurants will require the help of food preparation workers.

However, a growing number of fast-food restaurants and cafeterias are customizing their food orders from wholesalers and distributors in an effort to lower costs. As more food service establishments use these cost-saving strategies, fewer food preparation workers will be needed to wash, portion, and season ingredients.

Job Prospects. Job opportunities for food preparation workers should be very good because of the need to replace workers who leave the occupation each year.

Those with related work experience should find their best job opportunities at upscale restaurants. However, individuals seeking full-time positions at these restaurants will face strong competition because the number of job applicants often exceeds the number of job openings.

O*NET

➤ Food Preparation Workers (35-2021.00)

Contacts for More Information

For more information about job opportunities, contact local employers and local offices of the state employment service.

For more information about food preparation workers, visit

➤ National Restaurant Association (www.restaurant.org/)

Waiters and Waitresses

- **2012 Median Pay** .... $18,540 per year
  $8.92 per hour
- **Entry-Level Education** .... Less than high school
- **Work Experience in a Related Occupation**.............. None
- **On-the-Job Training** .... Short-term on-the-job training
- **Number of Jobs 2012** 2,362,200
- **Job Outlook, 2012–22** .... 6% (Slower than average)
- **Employment Change, 2012–22** 131,800

What Waiters and Waitresses Do

Waiters and waitresses take orders and serve food and beverages to customers in dining establishments.

Duties. Waiters and waitresses typically do the following:

- Greet customers, present menus, and explain daily specials to customers
- Answer questions related to menu items
- Take food and beverage orders from customers
- Relay food and beverage orders to the kitchen staff
- Prepare drinks and food garnishes
- Carry trays of food or drinks from the kitchen to the dining tables
- Remove dirty dishes and glasses, and clean tables after customers finish meals
- Prepare itemized checks and take payments from customers
- Clean and set up dining areas, refill condiments, roll silverware into napkins, and stock service areas

Waiters and waitresses, also called *servers*, are responsible for ensuring that customers have a satisfying dining experience. The specific duties of servers vary considerably with the establishment in which they work.

In casual-dining restaurants that offer simple fare, such as salads, soups, and sandwiches, servers are expected to provide fast, efficient, and courteous service. In fine-dining restaurants, where more complicated meals are prepared and are often served over several courses, waiters and waitresses provide more formal service. They emphasize personal, attentive treatment at a more leisurely pace.

Waiters and waitresses often meet with managers and chefs before each shift to discuss the menu or specials, review ingredients for potential food allergies, or talk about any food safety concerns. They also discuss coordination between the kitchen and the dining room and review any customer service issues from the previous day or shift.

In addition, waiters and waitresses usually check the identification of customers to ensure that they meet the minimum age requirement for the purchase of alcohol.

Work Environment

Waiters and waitresses held about 2.4 million jobs in 2012. About 77 percent worked in full-service restaurants–establishments that provide food service to customers who are served while seated and pay after eating.

Waiters and waitresses are on their feet most of the time and often carry heavy trays of food, dishes, and drinks. The work can be hectic and fast paced. During busy dining periods, they are under pressure to serve customers quickly and efficiently. They must be able to work well as a team with kitchen staff to ensure that customers receive prompt service.

Although the work is relatively safe, rushed servers can suffer injuries from slips and falls. To reduce these risks, waiters and waitresses are often required to wear non-slip shoes.

Because waiters and waitresses are the front line of customer service in food service and drinking establishments, a neat appearance is important. Those who work in fine-dining and upscale restaurants may be required to wear uniforms, including ties or aprons, which are typically provided by their employer.

Work Schedules. About half of all waiters and waitresses worked part time in 2012. Many work early mornings, late evenings, weekends, and holidays. This is especially true for those who work in full-service restaurants, which employed 77 percent of all waiters and waitresses in 2012.

In resorts that offer seasonal employment, waiters and waitresses may work for only a few months each year.

How to Become One

Most waiter and waitress jobs are at the entry level, and workers learn through short-term on-the-job training. No formal education or previous work experience is required to enter the occupation.

Most states require workers who serve alcoholic beverages to be at least 18 years of age, but some states require servers to be older. Waiters and waitresses who serve alcohol must be familiar with state and local laws concerning the sale of alcoholic beverages.

Education. No formal education is required to become a waiter or waitress.

Many entrants are in their late teens or early twenties and have less than a high school education. Waiter and waitress jobs are a major source of part-time employment for high school and college students, multiple jobholders, and those seeking supplemental incomes.

Some waiters and waitresses can acquire more skills by attending relevant classes offered by public or private vocational schools, restaurant associations, or large restaurant chains. However,

Waitresses bring food from the kitchen and sometimes refill customers' drinks.

Median Hourly Wages, May 2012

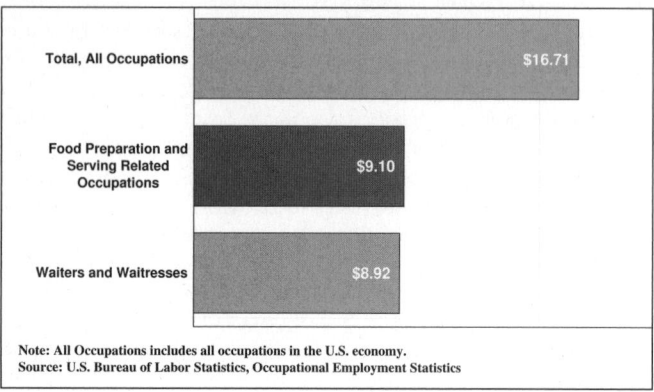

Note: All Occupations includes all occupations in the U.S. economy.
Source: U.S. Bureau of Labor Statistics, Occupational Employment Statistics

Percent Change in Employment, Projected 2012–2022

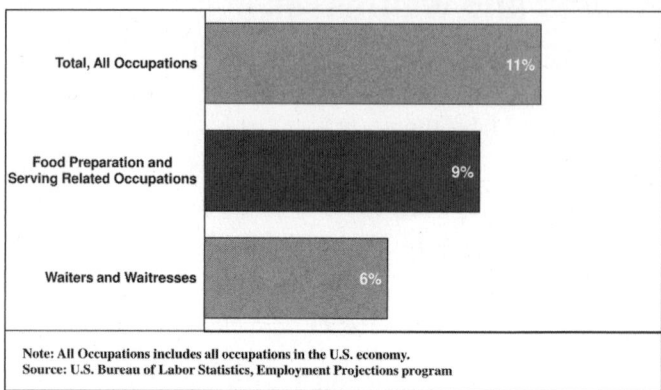

Note: All Occupations includes all occupations in the U.S. economy.
Source: U.S. Bureau of Labor Statistics, Employment Projections program

employers are more likely to hire and promote employees based on their people skills and personal qualities than on their education.

Training. Most waiters and waitresses learn their skills through short-term on-the-job-training, usually lasting a few weeks.

Some full-service restaurants provide new employees with some form of classroom training that alternates with periods of on-the-job work experience. These training programs communicate the operating philosophy of the restaurant, help new servers establish a rapport with other staff, teach formal serving techniques, and instill a desire to work as a team. They also discuss customer service situations and the proper ways to handle unpleasant circumstances or unruly customers.

Training for waiters and waitresses in establishments that serve alcohol typically involve learning state and local laws concerning the sale of alcoholic beverages. Some states, counties, and cities mandate the training, which typically lasts a few hours and can be taken online or in-house.

Important Qualities

Communication skills. Waiters and waitresses must listen carefully to customers' specific requests, ask any questions, and relay the information to the kitchen staff, so that orders are prepared to the customers' satisfaction.

Customer-service skills. Waiters and waitresses spend most of their work time serving customers. They should be friendly and polite and be able to develop a rapport with customers.

Detail oriented. Waiters and waitresses must keep customers' orders straight. They must be able to recall the details of each order and match the food or drink orders to customers.

Interpersonal skills. Waiters and waitresses must be courteous, tactful, and attentive as they deal with customers in all circumstances. For example, they must show an understanding of customers' complaints and help resolve any issues that arise.

Physical stamina. Waiters and waitresses spend hours on their feet carrying heavy trays, dishes, and drinks.

Pay

The median hourly wage (including tips) for waiters and waitresses was $8.92 in May 2012. The median wage is the wage at which half the workers in an occupation earned more than that amount and half earned less. The lowest 10 percent earned less than $7.79 per hour, and the top 10 percent earned more than $14.19 per hour.

Many waiters and waitresses get their earnings from a combination of hourly wages and customer tips. Earnings vary greatly with the type of establishment and region. For example, tips are generally much higher in upscale restaurants in major metropolitan areas and resorts.

In some states, tipped employees are paid the federal minimum wage ($7.25 per hour as of July 24, 2009) in addition to tips. Others earn more per hour because they work in states that set minimum wages higher than the federal minimum.

Employment Projections Data for Waiters and Waitresses

Occupational title	SOC Code	Employment, 2012	Projected Employment, 2022	Change, 2012–2022	
				Percent	Numeric
Waiters and waitresses...	35-3031	2,362,200	2,494,000	6	131,800

Source: U.S. Bureau of Labor Statistics, Employment Projections Program

Note: Data are rounded. Go to **Occupational Information Included in the OOH** *for a discussion of the data in this table.*

Similar Occupations   This table shows a list of occupations with job duties that are similar to those of waiters and waitresses.

Occupations	Entry-level Education	2012 Pay	Projected Job Growth	Average Annual Openings
Bartenders	Less than high school	$18,900	12%	26,940
Cashiers	Less than high school	$18,970	3%	153,000
Flight Attendants	High school diploma or equivalent	$37,240	-7%	1,400
Food and Beverage Serving and Related Workers	Less than high school	$18,428	12%	245,590
Retail Sales Workers	Less than high school	$21,514	10%	202,730

States may have exceptions to the minimum wage laws in specific circumstances for tipped employees. According to the Fair Labor Standards Act, tipped employees are those who regularly receive more than $30 a month in tips. The employer may consider tips as part of wages, but the employer must pay at least $2.13 an hour in direct wages. The Wage and Hour Division of the U.S. Department of Labor maintains a website with minimum wages for tipped employees, by state.

Many employers provide free meals and furnish uniforms, but some may deduct the cost from wages.

Job Outlook

Employment of waiters and waitresses is projected to grow 6 percent from 2012 to 2022, slower than the average for all occupations.

As the population grows and more people dine out, many new restaurants are expected to open. This will result in demand for waiters and waitresses, particularly at full-service restaurants.

However, consumers increasingly prefer take out, self-service, or food delivery from a growing number and variety of places. Establishments typically do not employ waiters and waitresses to handle these services, which reduces the need for servers.

In addition, technology-driven payment and ordering systems should limit employment growth of waiters and waitresses in many limited-service establishments, such as fast casual and cafeteria-style restaurants. In these places, waiters and waitresses may serve food or drinks only, because customers typically pay for food before eating. As a result, fewer waiters and waitresses will be needed to take orders and handle customers' payments.

Job Prospects. Job opportunities for waiters and waitresses are expected to be very good, primarily because of the large number of workers who leave the occupation each year.

Candidates with previous work experience and excellent customer-service skills will have the best job opportunities in fine-dining and upscale restaurants. Strong competition at these establishments is expected, as potential earnings from tips are greater than at other restaurants and the number of job applicants usually exceeds the number of job openings.

O*NET

➤ Waiters and Waitresses (35-3031.00)

Contacts for More Information

For more information on careers as a waiter or waitress, visit
➤ National Restaurant Association (www.restaurant.org/)

Health Care

Athletic Trainers and Exercise Physiologists

- **2012 Median Pay** .... $42,690 per year
  $20.52 per hour
- **Entry-Level Education** ....Bachelor's degree
- **Work Experience in a Related Occupation**.............. None
- **On-the-Job Training** .... None
- **Number of Jobs 2012** 28,900
- **Job Outlook, 2012–22**............. 19% (Faster than average)
- **Employment Change, 2012–22** 5,400

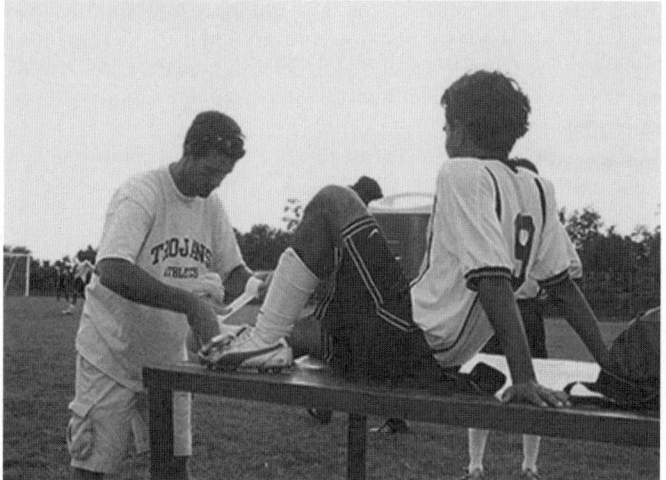

Athletic trainers apply protective devices such as tape, bandages, and braces.

What Athletic Trainers and Exercise Physiologists Do

Athletic trainers specialize in preventing, diagnosing, and treating muscle and bone injuries and illnesses. Exercise physiologists develop fitness and exercise programs that help patients recover from chronic diseases and improve cardiovascular function, body composition, and flexibility.

Duties. Athletic trainers (ATs) typically do the following:

- Apply protective or injury-preventive devices such as tape, bandages, and braces
- Recognize and evaluate injuries
- Provide first aid or emergency care
- Develop and carry out rehabilitation programs for injured athletes
- Plan and implement comprehensive programs to prevent injury and illness among athletes
- Perform administrative tasks such as keeping records and writing reports on injuries and treatment programs

Exercise physiologists (EPs) typically do the following:

- Analyze a patient's medical history to determine the best possible exercise and fitness regimen
- Perform fitness tests with medical equipment and analyze the subsequent patient data
- Measure body fat, blood pressure, oxygen usage, and other key patient health indicators
- Develop exercise programs to improve patient health
- Supervise clinical tests to ensure patient safety

Athletic trainers work with people of all ages and all skill levels, from young children to soldiers and professional athletes. Athletic trainers are usually one of the first healthcare providers on the scene when injuries occur. They work under the direction of a licensed physician and with other healthcare providers, and often discuss specific injuries and treatment options or evaluate and treat patients as directed by a physician. Some athletic trainers meet with a team physician or consulting physician regularly. An athletic trainer's administrative responsibilities may include regular meetings with an athletic director or other administrative officer to deal with budgets, purchasing, policy implementation, and other business-related issues.

Exercise physiologists work to improve overall patient health, and many of their patients suffer from health problems such as cardiovascular disease, or are obese. Exercise physiologists provide health education and exercise plans to improve key health indicators. Some physiologists work closely with primary physicians.

Athletic trainers and exercise physiologists should not be confused with fitness trainers and instructors, including personal trainers.

Work Environment

Athletic trainers held about 22,900 jobs in 2012. Exercise physiologists held about 6,000 jobs in 2012.

Many athletic trainers work in educational facilities, such as secondary schools or colleges. Others may work in physicians' offices or for professional sports teams. Some athletic trainers work in rehabilitation and therapy clinics, in the military, or with performing artists. They may spend their time working outdoors on sports fields, and in all types of weather.

The industries that employed the most athletic trainers in 2012 were as follows:

Colleges, universities, and professional schools;
state, local, and private.. 25%
Offices of other health practitioners 15
Hospitals; state, local, and private 13
Fitness and recreational sports centers 13

Exercise physiologists work in hospitals, outpatient clinics, and nursing and residential care facilities.

The industries that employed the most exercise physiologists in 2012 were as follows:

General medical and surgical hospitals;
state, local, and private.. 53%
Ambulatory health care services 21
Specialty (except psychiatric and substance abuse)
hospitals; state, local, and private... 6
Nursing and residential care facilities 4

Median Annual Wages, May 2012

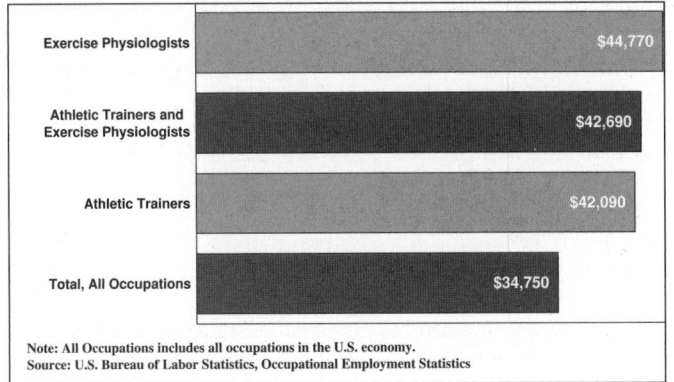

Note: All Occupations includes all occupations in the U.S. economy.
Source: U.S. Bureau of Labor Statistics, Occupational Employment Statistics

Percent Change in Employment, Projected 2012–2022

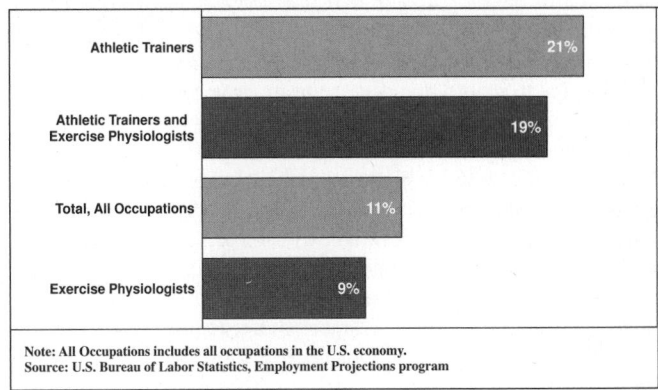

Note: All Occupations includes all occupations in the U.S. economy.
Source: U.S. Bureau of Labor Statistics, Employment Projections program

Work Schedules. Most athletic trainers and exercise physiologists work full time. Athletic trainers who work with teams during sporting events may work evenings or weekends and travel often. About 2 in 5 exercise physiologists worked part time.

How to Become One

Athletic trainers and exercise physiologists need at least a bachelor's degree. In most states, athletic trainers need a license or certification; requirements vary by state.

Education. Athletic trainers and exercise physiologists need at least a bachelor's degree from an accredited college or university. Master's degree programs are also common. Both degree programs have classroom and clinical components, including science and health-related courses, such as biology, anatomy, physiology, and nutrition.

The Commission on Accreditation of Athletic Training Education (CAATE) accredits athletic director programs, as well as post-professional and residency athletic trainer programs.

The Committee on Accreditation for the Exercise Sciences accredits exercise physiology programs.

High school students interested in postsecondary athletic training or exercise physiology programs should take courses in anatomy, physiology, and physics.

Important Qualities

Compassion. Athletic trainers and exercise physiologists work with athletes and patients who may be in considerable pain or discomfort. ATs and EPs must be sympathetic while providing treatments.

Employment Projections Data for Athletic Trainers and Exercise Physiologists

Occupational title	SOC Code	Employment, 2012	Projected Employment, 2022	Change, 2012–2022 Percent	Numeric
Athletic trainers and exercise physiologists............................	—	28,900	34,300	19	5,400
Athletic trainers..	29-9091	22,900	27,800	21	4,900
Exercise physiologists	29-1128	6,000	6,500	9	600

Source: U.S. Bureau of Labor Statistics, Employment Projections Program

Note: Data are rounded. Go to Occupational Information Included in the OOH for a discussion of the data in this table.

Similar Occupations   This table shows a list of occupations with job duties that are similar to those of athletic trainers and exercise physiologists.

Occupations	Entry-level Education	2012 Pay	Projected Job Growth	Average Annual Openings
Chiropractors	Doctoral or professional degree	$66,160	15%	1,520
EMTs and Paramedics	Postsecondary non-degree award	$31,020	23%	12,060
Licensed Practical and Licensed Vocational Nurses	Postsecondary non-degree award	$41,540	25%	36,310
Massage Therapists	Postsecondary non-degree award	$35,970	23%	4,410
Occupational Therapists	Master's degree	$75,400	29%	4,820
Physical Therapists	Doctoral or professional degree	$79,860	36%	12,370
Physician Assistants	Master's degree	$90,930	38%	4,890
Podiatrists	Doctoral or professional degree	$116,440	22%	460
Recreational Therapists	Bachelor's degree	$42,280	14%	670
Registered Nurses	Associate's degree	$65,470	19%	105,260
Respiratory Therapists	Associate's degree	$55,870	19%	4,010

Decision-making skills. Athletic trainers and exercise physiologists must be able to make informed clinical decisions that could affect the health or livelihood of patients.

Detail oriented. Athletic trainers and exercise physiologists must be able to record detailed, accurate progress and ensure that patients are receiving the appropriate treatments or practicing the correct fitness regimen.

Interpersonal skills. Athletic trainers and exercise physiologists must have strong interpersonal skills and be able to manage difficult situations. They must be able to communicate well with others, including physicians, patients, athletes, coaches, and parents.

Licenses, Certifications, and Registrations. Athletic trainers must be licensed or certified in most states; requirements vary by state. The independent Board of Certification, Inc. (BOC) offers the standard certification examination that most states use for licensing athletic trainers. Certification requires graduating from a CAATE-accredited program and completing the BOC exam. To maintain certification, athletic trainers must adhere to the BOC Standards of Practice and Disciplinary Process and take continuing education courses.

Requirements for an athletic trainer license typically include graduating from an accredited athletic training program and passing the BOC exam or a separate state exam. For specific information on requirements, contact the local state regulatory agency.

Just a few states require exercise physiologists to be licensed, although many states have pending legislation to create formal licensure requirements.

The American Society of Exercise Physiologists (ASEP) offers the Exercise Physiologist Certified (EPC) certification that physiologists can use to demonstrate their qualifications. Certification requires graduation with a relevant bachelor's degree and coursework, completing the ASEP exam, and taking continuing education courses every 5 years.

The American College of Sports Medicine (ACSM) also offers certifications for exercise physiologists. ACSM offers the Certified Clinical Exercise Specialist (CES) credential for candidates with bachelor's degrees and the Registered Clinical Exercise Physiologist (RCEP) for candidates with master's degrees.

Advancement. Assistant athletic trainers may become head athletic trainers, athletic directors, or physician, hospital, or clinic practice administrators, where they assume a management role. Some athletic trainers move into sales and marketing positions, using their expertise to sell medical and athletic equipment. Athletic trainers working in colleges and universities may pursue an advanced degree to increase their advancement opportunities.

Exercise physiologists with some business training have better opportunities to advance into management positions.

Pay

The median annual wage for athletic trainers was $42,090 in May 2012. The median wage is the wage at which half the workers in an occupation earned more than that amount and half earned less. The lowest 10 percent earned less than $25,960, and the top 10 percent earned more than $64,140.

The median annual wage for exercise physiologists was $44,770 in May 2012. The lowest 10 percent earned less than $31,000, and the top 10 percent earned more than $70,140.

Because some work with teams during sporting events, athletic trainers may be required to work evenings or weekends and travel often.

Job Outlook

Employment of athletic trainers is projected to grow 21 percent from 2012 to 2022, faster than the average for all occupations. However, because it is a small occupation, the fast growth will result in only about 4,900 new jobs over the 10-year period. As people become more aware of sports-related injuries at a young age, demand for athletic trainers is expected to increase, most significantly in colleges, universities, and youth leagues.

Recent research reveals that the effects of concussions are particularly severe and long lasting in child athletes. Although concussions are dangerous to athletes at any age, children's brains are still developing and are at risk for permanent complications. Parents and coaches are becoming educated about these greater risks through community health efforts. Because athletic trainers are usually onsite with athletes and are often the first responders when injuries occur, the demand for trainers should continue to increase.

Additionally, advances in injury prevention and detection and more sophisticated treatments are projected to increase the demand for athletic trainers. Growth in an increasingly active middle-aged and elderly population will likely lead to an increased incidence of athletic-related injuries, such as sprains. Sports programs at all ages and for all experience levels will continue to create demand for athletic trainers.

Insurance and workers' compensation costs have become a concern for many employers and insurance companies, especially in areas where employees are often injured on the job. For example, military bases hire athletic trainers to help train and rehabilitate injured military personnel. These trainers also create programs aimed at keeping injury rates down. Depending on the state, some insurance companies recognize athletic trainers as healthcare providers and reimburse the cost of an athletic trainer's services.

Employment of exercise physiologists is projected to grow 9 percent from 2012 to 2022, about as fast as the average for all occupations. This is a small occupation, and compared to athletic trainers, licensure for exercise physiologists is less common and therefore there are fewer recognized standards of practice for exercise physiologists. Demand may rise as hospitals emphasize exercise and preventive care as part of their treatment for chronic diseases and long-term rehabilitation. There are few available exercise physiologist positions, so competition for work remains high.

O*NET

➤ Exercise Physiologists (29-1128.00)
➤ Athletic Trainers (29-9091.00)

Contacts for More Information

For more information about athletic trainers, visit
➤ National Athletic Trainers' Association (www.nata.org/)

For more information about accredited athletic training programs, visit
➤ Commission on the Accreditation of Athletic Training Education (www.caate.net/)

For more information about certification and state regulatory requirements for athletic trainers, visit
➤ Board of Certification, Inc. (www.bocatc.org/)

For more information about exercise physiologists and certifications, visit
➤ The American Society of Exercise Physiologists (www.asep.org)
➤ The American College of Sports Medicine (www.acsm.org/)
➤ Committee on Accreditation for the Exercise Sciences (www.coaes.org/)

Audiologists

- **2012 Median Pay** .... $69,720 per year
  $33.52 per hour
- **Entry-Level Education** ... Doctoral or professional degree
- **Work Experience in a Related Occupation**.............. None
- **On-the-Job Training** .... None
- **Number of Jobs 2012** 13,000
- **Job Outlook, 2012–22** .... 34% (Much faster than average)
- **Employment Change, 2012–22** 4,300

What Audiologists Do

Audiologists diagnose and treat a patient's hearing and balance problems, using advanced technology and procedures.

Duties. Audiologists typically do the following:

- Examine patients who have hearing, balance, or related ear problems
- Assess the results of the examination and diagnose problems
- Determine and administer treatment
- Administer relief procedures for various forms of vertigo
- Fit and dispense hearing aids
- Counsel patients and their families on ways to listen and communicate, such as by lip reading or through American Sign Language
- See patients regularly to check on hearing and balance and to continue or change the treatment plan
- Keep records on the progress of patients
- Conduct research related to the causes and treatment of hearing and balance disorders

Audiologists use audiometers, computers, and other devices to test patients' hearing ability and balance. They work to determine the extent of hearing damage and identify the underlying cause. Audiologists measure the volume at which a person begins to hear sounds and the person's ability to distinguish between sounds.

Before determining treatment options, they evaluate psychological information to measure the impact of hearing loss on a patient.

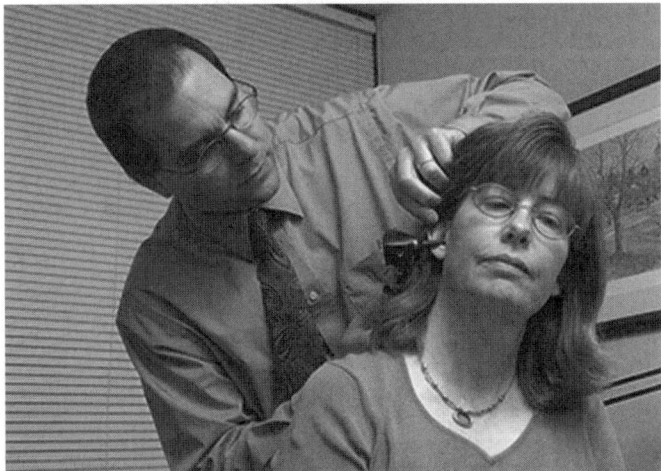

Audiologists examine individuals and identify symptoms of hearing loss and other auditory, balance, and related sensory and neural problems.

Treatment may include cleaning wax out of ear canals, fitting and checking hearing aids, or fitting the patient with cochlear implants to improve hearing. Cochlear implants are tiny devices that are placed under the skin near the ear in an operation. The implants deliver electrical impulses directly to the auditory nerve in the brain, so a person with certain types of deafness can hear.

Audiologists also counsel patients on other ways to cope with profound hearing loss, such as by learning to lip read or by using American Sign Language.

Audiologists can help a patient suffering from vertigo or dizziness. They work with patients and provide them with exercises involving head movement or positioning that might relieve some of their symptoms.

Some audiologists specialize in working with the elderly or with children. Others design products to help protect the hearing of workers on the job. Audiologists who are self-employed hire employees, keep records, order equipment and supplies, and complete other tasks related to running a business.

Work Environment

Audiologists held about 13,000 jobs in 2012. Most audiologists work in healthcare facilities, such as hospitals, physicians' offices, and audiology clinics. Some work in schools or for school districts and travel between facilities. Audiologists work closely with registered nurses, audiology assistants, and other healthcare professionals.

Work Schedules. Most audiologists work full time. Some work weekends and evenings to meet patients' needs. Those who work on a contract basis may spend a lot of time traveling between facilities. For example, an audiologist who is contracted by a school system may have to travel between different schools to provide services.

How to Become One

Audiologists need a doctoral degree and must be licensed in all states; requirements vary by state.

Education. The doctoral degree in audiology (Au.D.) is a graduate program typically lasting 4 years. A bachelor's degree in any field is needed to enter one of these programs.

Graduate coursework includes anatomy, physiology, physics, genetics, normal and abnormal communication development, diagnosis and treatment, pharmacology, and ethics. Graduate programs also include supervised clinical practice. Graduation from a program accredited by the Council on Academic Accreditation is required to get a license in most states.

Licenses, Certifications, and Registrations. Audiologists must be licensed in all states; requirements vary by state. For specific requirements, contact your state's licensing board for audiologists.

Audiologists can earn the Certificate of Clinical Competence in Audiology (CCC-A), offered by the American Speech-Language-Hearing Association. They also may be credentialed through the American Board of Audiology. Although it is not required in all cases, certification is required by some states or employers.

Important Qualities

Communication skills. Audiologists need to communicate test results, diagnoses, and proposed treatments, so patients clearly understand the situation and options. They also may need to work with other healthcare providers and education specialists regarding patient care.

Compassion. Audiologists work with people who are having problems with hearing or balance. They should be supportive of patients and their families.

Median Annual Wages, May 2012

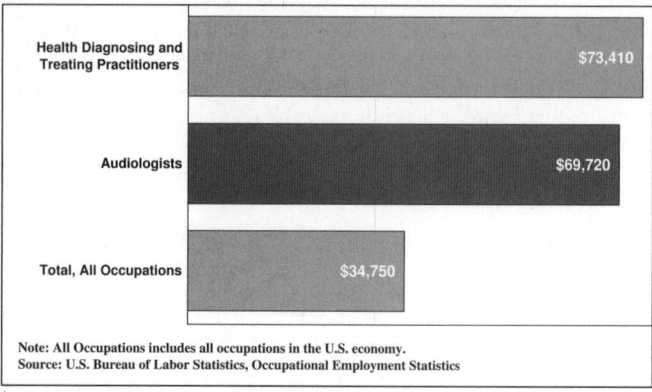

Note: All Occupations includes all occupations in the U.S. economy.
Source: U.S. Bureau of Labor Statistics, Occupational Employment Statistics

Percent Change in Employment, Projected 2012–2022

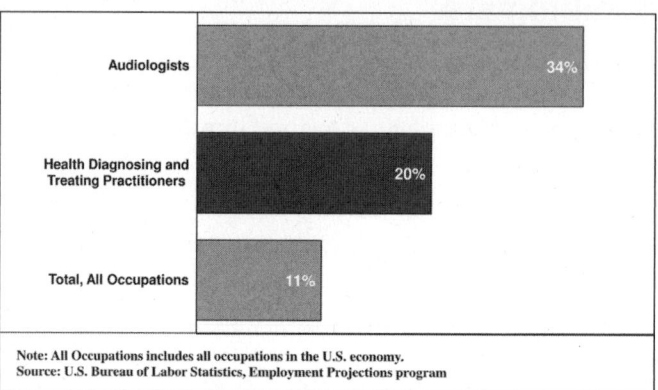

Note: All Occupations includes all occupations in the U.S. economy.
Source: U.S. Bureau of Labor Statistics, Employment Projections program

Critical-thinking skills. Audiologists must concentrate when testing a patient's hearing and be able to analyze each patient's situation, to offer the best treatment. They must also be able to provide alternative plans, when patients do not respond to initial treatment.

Patience. Audiologists must work with patients who may need a lot of time and special attention.

Problem-solving skills. Audiologists must figure out the causes of problems with hearing and balance and the appropriate treatment or treatments to address them.

Pay

The median annual wage for audiologists was $69,720 in May 2012. The median wage is the wage at which half the workers in an occupation earned more than that amount and half earned less. The lowest 10 percent earned less than $43,820, and the top 10 percent earned more than $101,130.

Job Outlook

Employment of audiologists is projected to grow 34 percent from 2012 to 2022, much faster than the average for all occupations. However, because it is a small occupation, the fast growth will result in only about 4,300 new jobs over the 10-year period.

An aging baby-boom population will continue to increase the demand for most healthcare services. Hearing loss increases as people age, so an aging population is likely to increase demand

for audiologists. The early identification and diagnosis of hearing disorders in infants also will spur employment growth. Advances in hearing aid design, such as smaller size and the reduction of feedback, may make such devices more appealing as a means to minimize hearing loss. This may lead to more demand for audiologists.

Job Prospects. Demand may be greater in areas with large numbers of retirees, so audiologists who are willing to relocate may have the best job prospects.

O*NET

➤ Audiologists (29-1181.00)

Contacts for More Information

For information on state-specific licensing requirements, contact the state's licensing board.

For more information about audiologists, including requirements for certification and state licensure, visit
➤ American Speech-Language-Hearing Association (www.asha.org/)
➤ American Board of Audiology (www.americanboardofaudiology.org/)

For information on doctoral programs in audiology, visit
➤ American Speech-Language-Hearing Association (www.asha.org/edfind/)

Employment Projections Data for Audiologists

Occupational title	SOC Code	Employment, 2012	Projected Employment, 2022	Change, 2012–2022	
				Percent	Numeric
Audiologists..	29-1181	13,000	17,300	34	4,300

Source: U.S. Bureau of Labor Statistics, Employment Projections Program

Note: Data are rounded. Go to **Occupational Information Included in the OOH** *for a discussion of the data in this table.*

Similar Occupations   This table shows a list of occupations with job duties that are similar to those of audiologists.

Occupations	Entry-level Education	2012 Pay	Projected Job Growth	Average Annual Openings
Optometrists	Doctoral or professional degree	$97,820	24%	1,770
Physical Therapists	Doctoral or professional degree	$79,860	36%	12,370
Physicians and Surgeons	Doctoral or professional degree	$182,294	18%	29,630
Psychologists	See "How to Become One"	$69,807	12%	6,230
Speech-Language Pathologists	Master's degree	$69,870	19%	4,620

Chiropractors

- **2012 Median Pay** .... $66,160 per year
  $31.81 per hour
- **Entry-Level Education** ... Doctoral or professional degree
- **Work Experience in a Related Occupation**............... None
- **On-the-Job Training** .... None
- **Number of Jobs 2012** 44,400
- **Job Outlook, 2012–22** .... 15% (Faster than average)
- **Employment Change, 2012–22** 6,500

What Chiropractors Do

Chiropractors care for patients with health problems of the neuromusculoskeletal system, which includes nerves, bones, muscles, ligaments, and tendons. They use spinal adjustments, manipulation, and other techniques to manage patients' health concerns, such as back and neck pain.

Duties. Chiropractors typically do the following:

- Assess a patient's medical condition by reviewing their medical history, listening to the patient's concerns, and performing a physical examination
- Analyze the patient's posture, spine, and reflexes
- Conduct tests, including evaluating a patient's posture and taking X-rays
- Identify health problems

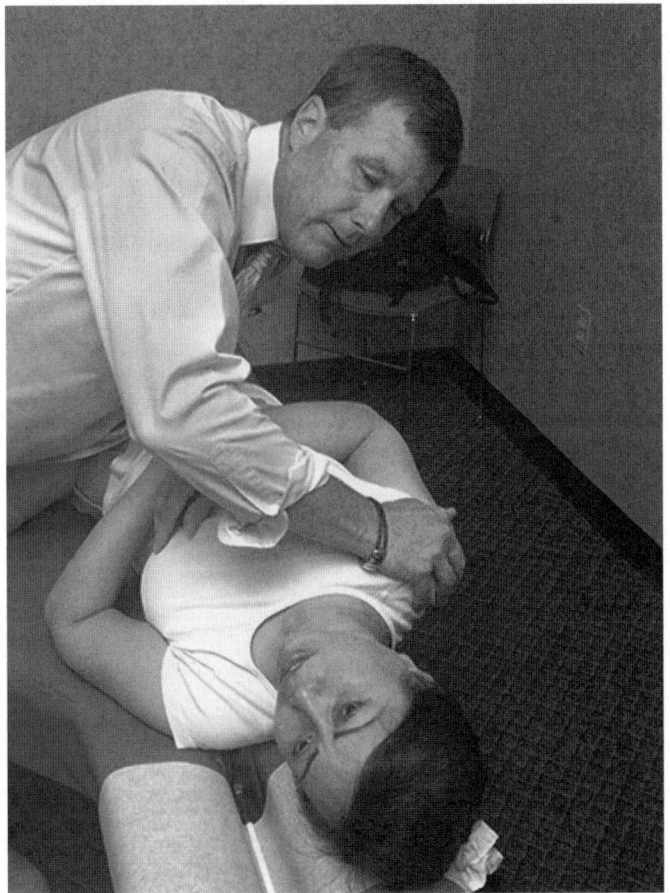

Chiropractors analyze the patient's posture and spine and may manually adjust the spinal column.

- Provide neuromusculoskeletal therapy, which involves adjusting a patient's spinal column and other joints by hand
- Give additional treatments, such as applying heat or cold to a patient's injured areas
- Advise patients on health and lifestyle issues, such as exercise, nutrition, and sleep habits
- Refer patients to other health care professionals, if needed

Chiropractors focus on patients' overall health. Chiropractors believe that misalignments of the spinal joints interfere with a person's neuromuscular system and can result in lower resistance to disease, as well as other conditions of poor health.

Some chiropractors use procedures such as massage therapy, rehabilitative exercise, and ultrasound in addition to spinal adjustments and manipulation. They also may apply supports, such as braces or shoe inserts, to treat patients and relieve pain.

In addition to operating a general chiropractic practice, some chiropractors concentrate in areas such as sports, neurology, orthopedics, pediatrics, or nutrition, among others. Chiropractors in private practice are responsible for marketing their businesses, hiring staff, and keeping records.

Work Environment

Chiropractors held about 44,400 jobs in 2012. Most chiropractors work in a solo or group practice. About 37 percent were self-employed in 2012. A small number work in hospitals or physicians' offices.

Chiropractors typically work in office settings that are clean and comfortable. They may be on their feet for long periods when examining and caring for patients.

Work Schedules. Although most chiropractors worked full time, about 1 out of 3 worked part time in 2012. Chiropractors may work in the evenings or on weekends, to accommodate working patients. Self-employed chiropractors set their own hours.

How to Become One

Chiropractors must earn a Doctor of Chiropractic (D.C.) degree and a state license. Doctor of Chiropractic programs typically take 4 years to complete and require at least 3 years of undergraduate college education for admission.

Education. Prospective chiropractors are required to have a Doctor of Chiropractic (D.C.) degree–a postgraduate professional degree that typically takes 4 years to complete. In 2012, there were 15 Doctor of Chiropractic programs on 18 campuses accredited by The Council on Chiropractic Education.

Admission to D.C. programs requires at least 90 semester hours of undergraduate education, with courses in the liberal arts and sciences, such as physics, chemistry, and biology. However, most students earn a bachelor's degree before going on to a chiropractic program.

Chiropractic education consists of classroom work in anatomy, physiology, biology, and similar subjects. Chiropractic students also get supervised clinical experience, in which they train in spinal assessment, spinal adjustment techniques, and diagnosis.

Following graduation, some chiropractors complete postgraduate programs leading to certification and diplomate credentials. These programs provide additional training in specialty areas, such as orthopedics and pediatrics. Others may choose to earn a master's degree in a related topic, such as nutrition or sports rehabilitation. Some D.C. programs offer a dual-degree option, in which students may earn a master's degree in a second topic, while completing their D.C.

Median Annual Wages, May 2012

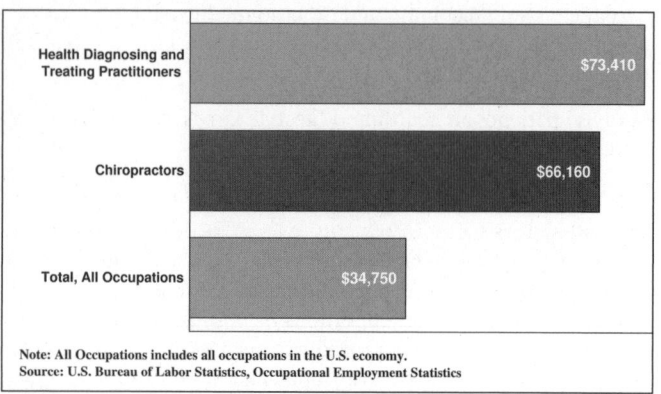

Note: All Occupations includes all occupations in the U.S. economy.
Source: U.S. Bureau of Labor Statistics, Occupational Employment Statistics

Percent Change in Employment, Projected 2012–2022

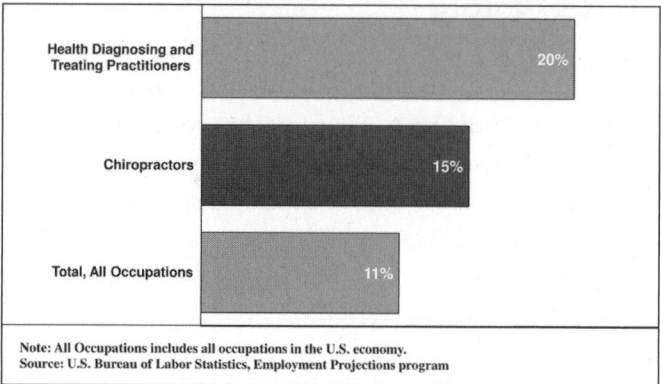

Note: All Occupations includes all occupations in the U.S. economy.
Source: U.S. Bureau of Labor Statistics, Employment Projections program

Licenses, Certifications, and Registrations. All states and the District of Columbia require chiropractors to be licensed. Although specific requirements vary by state, all jurisdictions require the completion of an accredited Doctor of Chiropractic (D.C.) program. Some states require chiropractors to have a bachelor's degree.

In addition, all jurisdictions require passing the National Board of Chiropractic Examiners exam, which include basic and clinical sciences, clinical case studies, and a practical exam. Many jurisdictions also require applicants to pass a state-specific law exam. All states require continuing education to keep the license. Check with your state's board of chiropractic examiners or health department for more specific information on licensure.

Important Qualities

Decision-making skills. Chiropractors must determine the best course of action when treating a patient. They must also decide when to refer patients to other health care professionals.

Detail oriented. Chiropractors must be observant and pay attention to details so that they can make proper diagnoses and avoid mistakes that could harm patients.

Dexterity. Because they use their hands to perform manual adjustments to the spine and other joints, chiropractors should be well-coordinated to perform therapy effectively.

Empathy. Chiropractors often care for people who are in pain. They must be understanding and sympathetic to their patients' problems and needs.

Interpersonal skills. Chiropractors must be personable to keep clients coming to them. Also, because chiropractors frequently touch patients in performing therapy, they should be able to put their patients at ease.

Pay

The median annual wage for chiropractors was $66,160 in May 2012. The median wage is the wage at which half the workers in an occupation earned more than that amount and half earned less. The lowest 10 percent earned less than $31,030, and the top 10 percent earned more than $142,950.

Chiropractors tend to earn significantly less early in their careers and then earn more as they build a client base and become owners of, or partners in, a practice.

Job Outlook

Employment of chiropractors is projected to grow 15 percent from 2012 to 2022, faster than the average for all occupations. People across all age groups are increasingly seeking chiropractic care, because most chiropractors treat patients without performing surgery or prescribing drugs.

Employment Projections Data for Chiropractors

Occupational title	SOC Code	Employment, 2012	Projected Employment, 2022	Change, 2012–2022	
				Percent	Numeric
Chiropractors	29-1011	44,400	50,900	15	6,500

Source: U.S. Bureau of Labor Statistics, Employment Projections Program

Note: Data are rounded. Go to **Occupational Information Included in the OOH** *for a discussion of the data in this table.*

Similar Occupations   This table shows a list of occupations with job duties that are similar to those of chiropractors.

Occupations	Entry-level Education	2012 Pay	Projected Job Growth	Average Annual Openings
Athletic Trainers and Exercise Physiologists	Bachelor's degree	$42,676	19%	1,240
Massage Therapists	Postsecondary non-degree award	$35,970	23%	4,410
Occupational Therapists	Master's degree	$75,400	29%	4,820
Physical Therapists	Doctoral or professional degree	$79,860	36%	12,370
Physicians and Surgeons	Doctoral or professional degree	$182,294	18%	29,630
Podiatrists	Doctoral or professional degree	$116,440	22%	460

Chiropractic treatment of the back, neck, limbs, and involved joints has become more accepted as a result of research and changing attitudes about additional approaches healthcare. As a result, chiropractors are increasingly working in hospitals and clinics as part of a team-based model of patient care.

The aging of the large baby-boom generation will lead to new opportunities for chiropractors. Older adults are more likely to have neuromusculoskeletal and joint problems and they are seeking treatment for these conditions more often as they lead longer, more active lives.

Demand for chiropractic treatment is related to the ability of patients to pay, either directly or through health insurance. Although most insurance plans now cover chiropractic services, the extent of such coverage varies among plans.

O*NET

➤ Chiropractors (29-1011.00)

Contacts for More Information

For information on a career as a chiropractor, visit
➤ American Chiropractic Association (www.acatoday.org/)
➤ International Chiropractors Association (www.chiropractic.org)

For a list of chiropractic programs and institutions, as well as for general information on chiropractic education, visit
➤ Association of Chiropractic Colleges (www.chirocolleges.org/)
➤ The Council on Chiropractic Education (www.cce-usa.org/)

For information on state education and licensure requirements, visit
➤ Federation of Chiropractic Licensing Boards (www.fclb.org/)

For information about licensing exams, visit
➤ National Board of Chiropractic Examiners (www.nbce.org/)

Dental Assistants

- **2012 Median Pay** .... $34,500 per year
  $16.59 per hour
- **Entry-Level Education** .... Postsecondary non-degree award
- **Work Experience in a Related Occupation** .... None
- **On-the-Job Training** .... None
- **Number of Jobs 2012** 303,200
- **Job Outlook, 2012–22** .... 25% (Much faster than average)
- **Employment Change, 2012–22** 74,400

Dental assistants sterilize and disinfect instruments and equipment.

What Dental Assistants Do

Dental assistants have many tasks, ranging from patient care and taking X-rays to recordkeeping and scheduling appointments. Their duties vary by state and by the dentists' offices where they work.

Duties. Dental assistants typically do the following:
- Work with patients to make them comfortable in the dental chair and to prepare them for treatments and procedures
- Sterilize dental instruments
- Prepare the work area for patient treatment by setting out instruments and materials
- Help dentists by handing them instruments during procedures
- Keep patients' mouths dry by using suction hoses and other equipment
- Instruct patients in proper dental hygiene
- Process X-rays and complete lab tasks, under the direction of a dentist
- Keep records of dental treatments
- Schedule patient appointments
- Work with patients on billing and payment

Assistants who perform lab tasks, such as making casts of a patient's teeth, work under the direction of a dentist. They may prepare materials for casts of teeth or to create temporary crowns.

All dental assistants complete tasks, such as helping dentists with procedures and keeping patient records, but there are four regulated tasks that assistants may perform, depending on the state where they work.
- Coronal polishing
- Sealant application
- Fluoride application
- Topical anesthetics application

Coronal polishing, which means removing soft deposits such as plaque, gives teeth a cleaner appearance. In sealant application, a dental assistant paints a thin, plastic substance over teeth that seals out food particles and acid-producing bacteria to keep teeth from developing cavities. Fluoride application, in which fluoride is put directly on the teeth, is another anti-cavity measure. Some dental assistants may be qualified to apply topical anesthetic to an area of a patient's mouth, temporarily numbing the area to help prepare a patient for procedures.

Not all states allow dental assistants to complete these tasks. Each state regulates the scope of practice for dental assistants and may require them to take specific exams or meet other requirements before allowing them to perform these procedures.

Work Environment

Dental assistants held about 303,200 jobs in 2012. Almost all dental assistants work in dentists' offices. Dental assistants work under the supervision of dentists and may work closely with dental hygienists in their day-to-day activities.

Dental assistants wear safety glasses, surgical masks, protective clothing, and gloves to protect themselves and patients from infectious diseases. They must also follow safety procedures to minimize risks associated with X-ray machines.

Work Schedules. Most dental assistants work full time. However, about 1 in 3 assistants worked part time in 2012. Some work evenings or weekends, depending on the office where they work.

Median Annual Wages, May 2012

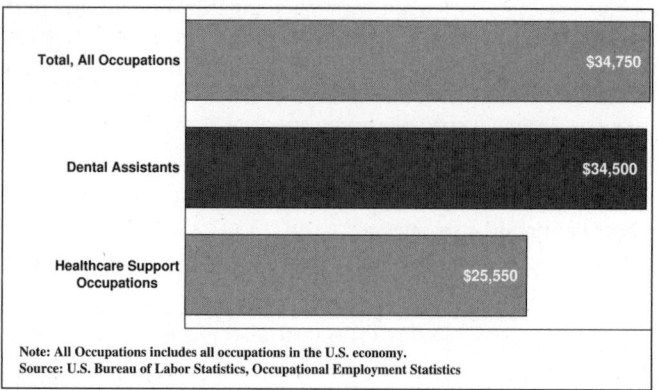

Note: All Occupations includes all occupations in the U.S. economy.
Source: U.S. Bureau of Labor Statistics, Occupational Employment Statistics

Percent Change in Employment, Projected 2012–2022

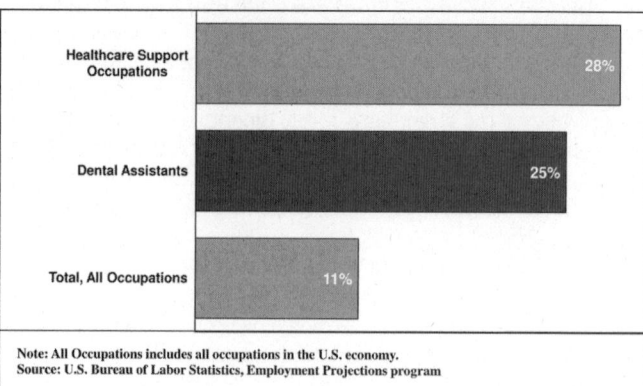

Note: All Occupations includes all occupations in the U.S. economy.
Source: U.S. Bureau of Labor Statistics, Employment Projections program

How to Become One

There are several possible paths to becoming a dental assistant. Some states require assistants to graduate from an accredited program and pass a state exam. In other states, there are no formal educational requirements.

Education. High school students interested in a career as a dental assistant should take courses in biology, chemistry, and anatomy. Some states require assistants to graduate from an accredited program and pass a state exam. Most programs are offered by community colleges, take about 1 year to complete, and lead to a certificate or diploma. Programs that last 2 years, also offered in community colleges, are less common and lead to an associate's degree. The Commission on Dental Accreditation (CODA), part of the American Dental Association, approved more than 250 dental-assisting training programs in 2013.

Accredited programs include classroom and laboratory work in which students learn about teeth, gums, jaws, and other areas that dentists work on and the instruments that dentists use. These programs also include supervised, practical experience.

Training. Dental assistants who do not have formal education in dental assisting may learn their duties through on-the-job training. A dental assistant or dentist in the office teaches the new assistant dental terminology, the names of the instruments, how to complete daily tasks, how to interact with patients, and other activities necessary to help keep the dental office running smoothly.

Important Qualities

Detail oriented. Dental assistants must follow specific rules and protocols to help dentists treat patients. Assistants must be aware of what practices they are allowed to complete in the state where they work.

Interpersonal skills. Dental assistants must work closely with dentists and patients. Sometimes, patients are in extreme pain and/or mental stress, so the assistant should be sensitive to their emotions.

Listening skills. Dental assistants should be able to listen to patients and other healthcare workers. They need to follow directions from a dentist or dental hygienist, so they can help treat patients and do tasks, such as taking an X-ray.

Organizational skills. Dental assistants should have excellent organizational skills. They should have the correct tools in place for a dentist or dental hygienist to use when treating a patient.

Licenses, Certifications, and Registrations. Some states require dental assistants to be certified; requirements vary by state. To obtain certification, dental assistants must pass the Certified Dental Assistant (CDA) exam from the Dental Assisting National Board (DANB). To take the exam, dental assistants must either have graduated from an accredited program or have a high school

Employment Projections Data for Dental Assistants

Occupational title	SOC Code	Employment, 2012	Projected Employment, 2022	Change, 2012–2022	
				Percent	Numeric
Dental assistants	31-9091	303,200	377,600	25	74,400

Source: U.S. Bureau of Labor Statistics, Employment Projections Program

Note: Data are rounded. Go to **Occupational Information Included in the OOH** *for a discussion of the data in this table.*

Similar Occupations   This table shows a list of occupations with job duties that are similar to those of dental assistants.

Occupations	Entry-level Education	2012 Pay	Projected Job Growth	Average Annual Openings
Dental Hygienists	Associate's degree	$70,210	33%	11,350
Medical Assistants	Postsecondary non-degree award	$29,370	29%	26,990
Occupational Therapy Assistants and Aides	See "How to Become One"	$47,638	41%	2,560
Pharmacy Technicians	High school diploma or equivalent	$29,320	20%	10,590
Physical Therapist Assistants and Aides	See "How to Become One"	$40,539	41%	7,630
Surgical Technologists	Postsecondary non-degree award	$41,790	30%	3,910

diploma, and complete the required amount of on-the-job training. Applicants must also have current certification in CPR (cardiopulmonary resuscitation).

Some states require that dental assistants be licensed or register with DANB to complete regulated tasks, such as coronal polishing, in a dentist's office; requirements vary by state. In other states, there are no formal educational requirements to become an entry-level dental assistant. Contact state boards of dentistry for specific requirements.

Pay

The median annual wage for dental assistants was $34,500 in May 2012. The median wage is the wage at which half the workers in an occupation earned more than that amount and half earned less. The lowest 10 percent earned less than $23,550, and the top 10 percent earned more than $47,580.

Job Outlook

Employment of dental assistants is projected to grow 25 percent from 2012 to 2022, much faster than the average for all occupations. Ongoing research linking oral health and general health will likely continue to increase the demand for preventive dental services. Dentists will continue to hire more dental assistants to complete routine tasks, allowing the dentist to see more patients in their practice and to spend their time on more complex procedures. As dental practices grow, more dental assistants will be needed.

As the large baby-boom population ages, and as people keep more of their original teeth than did previous generations, the need to maintain and treat teeth will continue to increase the need for dental care.

Federal health legislation is expected to expand the number of patients who have access to health insurance. People with new or expanded dental insurance coverage will be more likely to visit a dentist than in the past. This will increase the demand for all dental services, including those performed by dental assistants.

O*NET

➤ Dental Assistants (31-9091.00)

Contacts for More Information

For more information about becoming a dental assistant and for a list of accredited dental assistant programs, visit
➤ Commission on Dental Accreditation, American Dental Association (www.ada.org/117.aspx)

For more information about becoming a Certified Dental Assistant and for a list of state boards of dentistry, visit
➤ Dental Assisting National Board, Inc. (www.danb.org/)

Dental Hygienists

- **2012 Median Pay** .... $70,210 per year
  $33.75 per hour
- **Entry-Level Education** .... Associate's degree
- **Work Experience in a Related Occupation** .... None
- **On-the-Job Training** .... None
- **Number of Jobs 2012** 192,800
- **Job Outlook, 2012–22** .... 33% (Much faster than average)
- **Employment Change, 2012–22** 64,200

What Dental Hygienists Do

Dental hygienists clean teeth, examine patients for signs of oral diseases such as gingivitis, and provide other preventative dental care. They also educate patients on ways to improve and maintain good oral health.

Duties. Dental hygienists typically do the following:

- Remove tartar, stains, and plaque from teeth
- Apply sealants and fluorides to help protect teeth
- Take and develop dental X-rays
- Keep track of patient care and treatment plans
- Teach patients oral hygiene techniques, such as how to brush and floss correctly

Dental hygienists use many types of tools to do their job. They clean and polish teeth with hand, power, and ultrasonic tools. In some cases, they remove stains with an air-polishing device, which sprays a combination of air, water, and baking soda. They polish teeth with a powered tool that works like an automatic toothbrush. Hygienists use X-ray machines to take pictures to check for tooth or jaw problems.

Dental hygienists help patients develop and maintain good oral health. For example, they may explain the relationship between diet and oral health. They may also give advice to patients on how to select toothbrushes and other oral-care devices.

Other tasks hygienists may perform vary by state. Some states allow hygienists to place and carve filling materials, temporary fillings, and periodontal dressings.

Work Environment

Dental hygienists held about 192,800 jobs in 2012. Almost all dental hygienists work in dentists' offices. They work closely with dentists and dental assistants.

Dental hygienists wear safety glasses, surgical masks, and gloves to protect themselves and patients from infectious diseases. When taking X-rays, they follow strict procedures to protect themselves

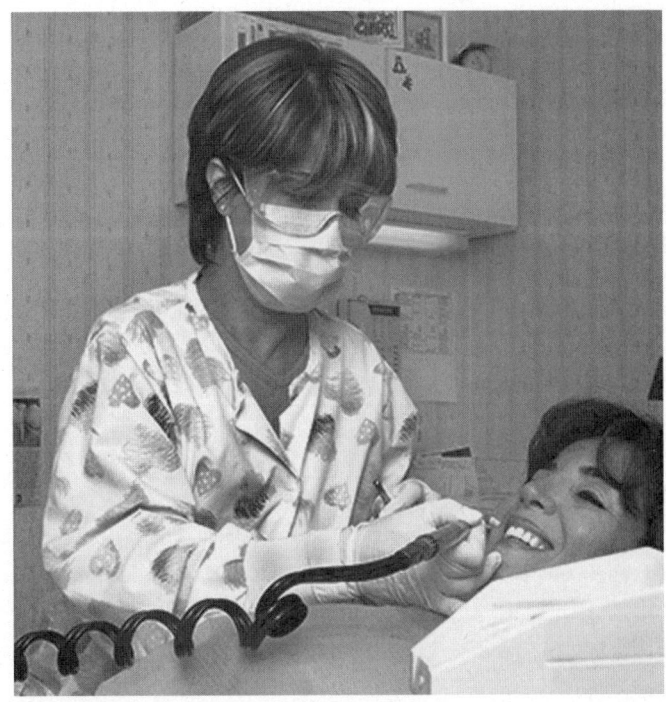

Dental hygienists remove soft and hard deposits from teeth and teach patients how to practice good oral hygiene.

Median Annual Wages, May 2012

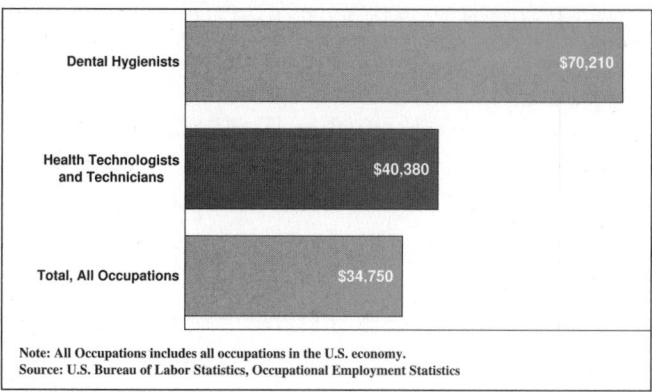

Note: All Occupations includes all occupations in the U.S. economy.
Source: U.S. Bureau of Labor Statistics, Occupational Employment Statistics

Percent Change in Employment, Projected 2012–2022

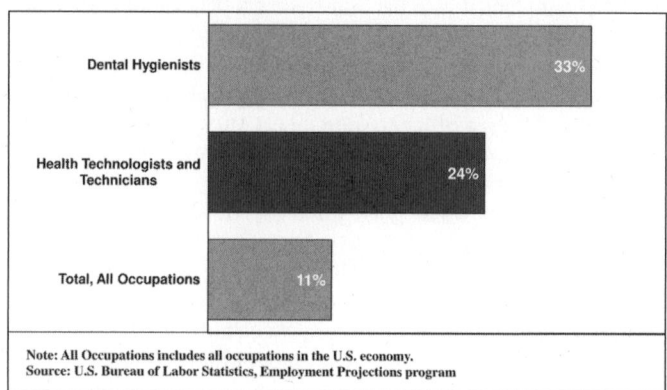

Note: All Occupations includes all occupations in the U.S. economy.
Source: U.S. Bureau of Labor Statistics, Employment Projections program

and patients. They may spend long periods bending over to work on patients.

Work Schedules. More than half of dental hygienists worked part time in 2012. Dentists often hire hygienists to work only a few days a week, so some hygienists work for more than one dentist.

How to Become One

Dental hygienists typically need an associate's degree in dental hygiene. All states require dental hygienists to be licensed; requirements vary by state.

Education. Dental hygienists typically need an associate's degree in dental hygiene. Bachelor's degrees in dental hygiene are also available, but are less common. A bachelor's or master's degree is usually required for research, teaching, or clinical practice in public or school health programs.

High school students interested in becoming dental hygienists should take courses in biology, chemistry, and mathematics. Some dental hygiene programs also require applicants to have completed at least 1 year of college. Specific entrance requirements vary by school.

Most schools offer laboratory, clinical, and classroom instruction. Hygienists study anatomy, physiology, nutrition, radiography, and periodontology, which is the study of gum disease.

Important Qualities

Compassion. Sometimes patients are in extreme pain or have fears about undergoing dental work, and the hygienist must be sensitive to their emotions.

Detail oriented. Dental hygienists must follow specific rules and protocols to help dentists diagnose and treat a patient. In rare cases, dental hygienists work without the direct supervision of a dentist.

Dexterity. Dental hygienists must be good at working with their hands. They generally work in tight quarters on a small part of the body, using very precise tools and instruments.

Interpersonal skills. Dental hygienists must work closely with dentists and patients.

Physical stamina. Dental hygienists should be comfortable performing physical tasks, such as bending over patients for a long time.

Licenses, Certifications, and Registrations. Every state requires dental hygienists to be licensed; requirements vary by state. In most states, a degree from an accredited dental hygiene program and passing grades on written and practical examinations are required for licensure. For specific application requirements, contact your state's medical or health board.

Employment Projections Data for Dental Hygienists

Occupational title	SOC Code	Employment, 2012	Projected Employment, 2022	Change, 2012–2022	
				Percent	Numeric
Dental hygienists	29-2021	192,800	256,900	33	64,200

Source: U.S. Bureau of Labor Statistics, Employment Projections Program

Note: Data are rounded. Go to **Occupational Information Included in the OOH** *for a discussion of the data in this table.*

Similar Occupations This table shows a list of occupations with job duties that are similar to those of dental hygienists.

Occupations	Entry-level Education	2012 Pay	Projected Job Growth	Average Annual Openings
Dental Assistants	Postsecondary non-degree award	$34,500	25%	13,720
Medical Assistants	Postsecondary non-degree award	$29,370	29%	26,990
Occupational Therapy Assistants and Aides	See "How to Become One"	$47,638	41%	2,560
Physical Therapist Assistants and Aides	See "How to Become One"	$40,539	41%	7,630
Physician Assistants	Master's degree	$90,930	38%	4,890
Radiation Therapists	Associate's degree	$77,560	24%	840
Registered Nurses	Associate's degree	$65,470	19%	105,260

Pay

The median annual wage for dental hygienists was $70,210 in May 2012. The median wage is the wage at which half the workers in an occupation earned more than that amount and half earned less. The lowest 10 percent earned less than $46,540, and the top 10 percent earned more than $96,280.

Some dental hygienists receive benefits, such as vacation, sick leave, and contributions to their retirement fund. However, benefits vary by employer and may be available only to full-time workers.

Job Outlook

Employment of dental hygienists is projected to grow 33 percent from 2012 to 2022, much faster than the average for all occupations. Ongoing research linking oral health and general health will continue to spur the demand for preventative dental services, which are often provided by dental hygienists.

As their practices expand, dentists will hire more hygienists to perform routine dental care, allowing the dentist to see more patients. In addition, as the large baby-boom population ages and people keep more of their original teeth than previous generations did, the need to maintain and treat these teeth will continue to drive demand for dental care.

Federal health legislation is expected to expand the number of patients who have access to health insurance. People with new or expanded dental insurance coverage will be more likely to visit a dentist than in the past. As a result, the demand for all dental services, including those performed by hygienists, will increase.

O*NET

➤ Dental Hygienists (29-2021.00)

Contacts for More Information

For information about educational requirements and available accredited programs for dental hygienists, visit
➤ American Dental Hygienists' Association (www.adha.org/)

For information about accredited programs and educational requirements, visit
➤ Commission on Dental Accreditation, American Dental Association (www.ada.org/117.aspx)

The State Board of Dental Examiners in each state can provide information on licensing requirements.

Dentists

- **2012 Median Pay** .... $149,310 per year
  $71.79 per hour
- **Entry-Level Education** ... Doctoral or professional degree
- **Work Experience in a Related Occupation**.............. None
- **On-the-Job Training** ....See "How to Become One"
- **Number of Jobs 2012** 146,800
- **Job Outlook, 2012–22**............. 16% (Faster than average)
- **Employment Change, 2012–22** 23,300

What Dentists Do

Dentists diagnose and treat problems with a patient's teeth, gums, and related parts of the mouth. They provide advice and instruction on taking care of teeth and gums and on diet choices that affect oral health.

Duties. Dentists typically do the following:

- Remove decay from teeth and fill cavities
- Repair cracked or fractured teeth and remove teeth
- Straighten teeth to correct bite issues
- Place sealants or whitening agents on teeth
- Administer anesthetics to keep patients from feeling pain during procedures
- Write prescriptions for antibiotics or other medications
- Examine X-rays of teeth, gums, the jaw, and nearby areas for problems
- Make models and measurements for dental appliances, such as dentures, to fit patients
- Teach patients about diet, flossing, use of fluoride, and other aspects of dental care

Dentists use a variety of equipment, including X-ray machines, drills, mouth mirrors, probes, forceps, brushes, and scalpels. They also use lasers, digital scanners, and other computer technologies.

Dentists in private practice also oversee a variety of administrative tasks, including bookkeeping and buying equipment and supplies. They employ and supervise dental hygienists, dental assistants, dental laboratory technicians, and receptionists.

Most dentists are general practitioners and handle a variety of dental needs. Other dentists practice in one of nine specialty areas:

Dental public health specialists promote good dental health and the prevention of dental diseases in specific communities.

Endodontists perform root-canal therapy, by which they remove the nerves and blood supply from injured or infected teeth.

Oral and maxillofacial radiologists diagnose diseases in the head and neck through the use of imaging technologies.

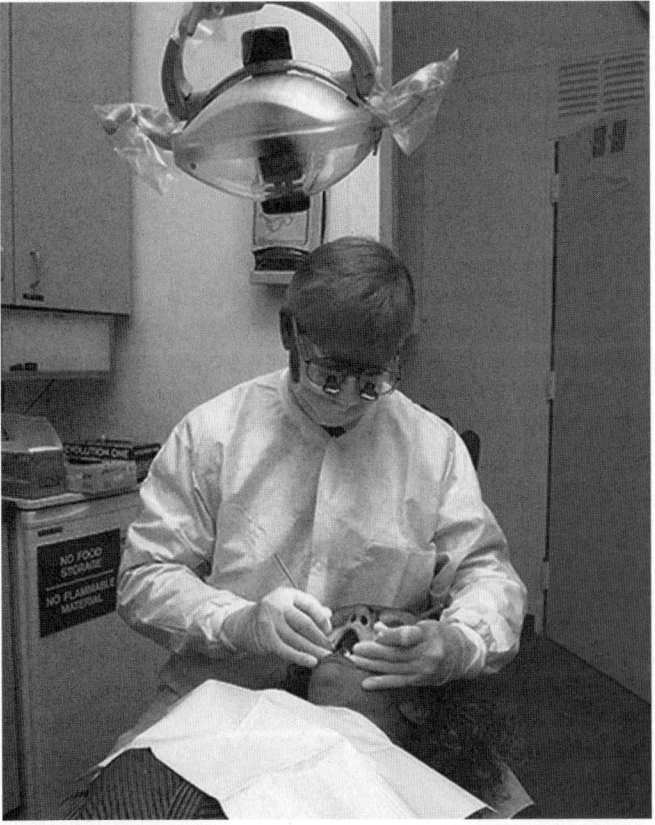

Dentists remove tooth decay, fill cavities, and repair fractured teeth.

Median Annual Wages, May 2012

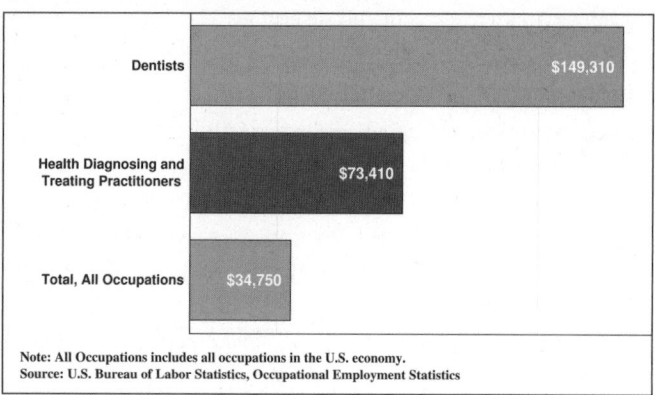

Note: All Occupations includes all occupations in the U.S. economy.
Source: U.S. Bureau of Labor Statistics, Occupational Employment Statistics

Percent Change in Employment, Projected 2012–2022

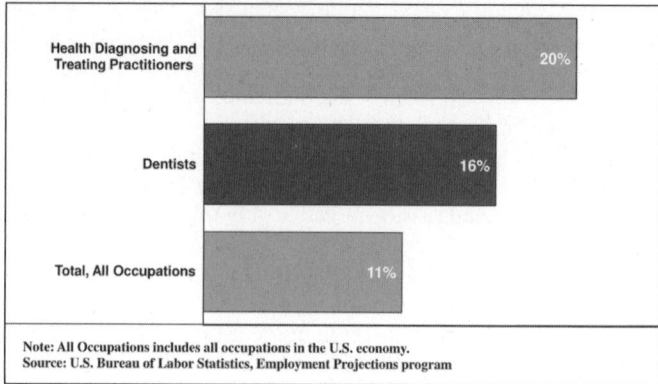

Note: All Occupations includes all occupations in the U.S. economy.
Source: U.S. Bureau of Labor Statistics, Employment Projections program

Oral and maxillofacial surgeons operate on the mouth, jaws, teeth, gums, neck, and head, including procedures such as surgically repairing a cleft lip and palate or removing impacted teeth.

Oral pathologists diagnose conditions in the mouth, such as bumps or ulcers, and oral diseases, such as cancer.

Orthodontists straighten teeth by applying pressure to the teeth with braces or other appliances.

Pediatric dentists focus on dentistry for children and special-needs patients.

Periodontists treat the gums and bone supporting the teeth.

Prosthodontists replace missing teeth with permanent fixtures, such as crowns and bridges, or with removable fixtures such as dentures.

Work Environment

Dentists held about 146,800 jobs in 2012. Some dentists own their own businesses and work alone or with a small staff. Other dentists have partners in their practice, and some work for more established dentists as associate dentists.

Dentists usually work in offices. They wear masks, gloves, and safety glasses to protect themselves and their patients from infectious diseases.

Work Schedules. Most dentists work full time. Some work evenings and weekends to meet their patients' needs. The number of hours worked varies greatly among dentists. It is common for dentists to continue in part-time practice well beyond the usual retirement age.

How to Become One

Dentists must be licensed in all states; requirements vary by state. To qualify for a license in most states, applicants must graduate from an accredited dental school and pass written and practical exams.

Education. Most dental students need at least a bachelor's degree before entering dental school; requirements vary by school. All dental schools require applicants to have completed certain required science courses, such as biology and chemistry. Majoring in a science, such as biology, might increase the chances of being accepted, but no specific major is required to enter most dental programs.

College undergraduates who plan on applying to dental school must usually take the Dental Acceptance Test (DAT) during their junior year. Admission to dental school can be competitive. Dental schools use these tests along with other factors, such as grade point average and recommendations, to admit students into their programs.

Dental schools require students to take classes in subjects such as local anesthesia, anatomy, periodontology (the study of oral disease and health), and radiology. All dental schools include practice where students work with patients in a clinical setting under the supervision of a licensed dentist.

High school students who want to become dentists should take courses in chemistry, physics, biology, anatomy, and mathematics.

Training. All nine dental specialties require dentists to complete additional training before practicing that specialty. They must usually complete a 1- or 2-year residency in a program related to their specialty. General dentists do not require any additional training after dental school.

Dentists who want to teach or to do research full time usually spend an additional 2 to 5 years in advanced dental training. Many practicing dentists also teach part time, including supervising students in dental school clinics.

Licenses, Certifications, and Registrations. All states require dentists to be licensed; requirements vary by state. Most states require a dentist to have a degree from an accredited dental school and to pass a written and practical exam.

In addition, a dentist who wants to practice in one of the nine specialties must have a license in that specialty. This usually requires 2 to 4 years of additional education after dental school and, in some cases, the completion of a special state exam. A postgraduate residency term also may be required, usually lasting up to 2 years.

Similar Occupations This table shows a list of occupations with job duties that are similar to those of dentists.

Occupations	Entry-level Education	2012 Pay	Projected Job Growth	Average Annual Openings
Chiropractors	Doctoral or professional degree	$66,160	15%	1,520
Optometrists	Doctoral or professional degree	$97,820	24%	1,770
Physicians and Surgeons	Doctoral or professional degree	$182,294	18%	29,630
Podiatrists	Doctoral or professional degree	$116,440	22%	460
Veterinarians	Doctoral or professional degree	$84,460	12%	3,100

Employment Projections Data for Dentists

Occupational title	SOC Code	Employment, 2012	Projected Employment, 2022	Change, 2012–2022	
				Percent	Numeric
Dentists..	29-1020	146,800	170,200	16	23,300
Dentists, general....................................	29-1021	125,800	146,400	16	20,600
Dentists, Oral and maxillofacial surgeons.........................	29-1022	6,700	7,800	16	1,100
Dentists, Orthodontists............................	29-1023	7,500	8,700	16	1,200
Dentists, Prosthodontists.........................	29-1024	400	500	15	100
Dentists, all other specialists.....................	29-1029	6,400	6,800	6	400

Source: U.S. Bureau of Labor Statistics, Employment Projections Program

Note: **Data are rounded. Go to Occupational Information Included in the OOH** *for a discussion of the data in this table.*

Important Qualities

Communication skills. Dentists must have excellent communication skills. They must be able to communicate effectively with patients, dental hygienists, dental assistants, and receptionists.

Detail oriented. Dentists must be detail oriented so patients receive appropriate treatments and medications. They must also pay attention to space, shape, and color of teeth. For example, they may need to closely match a false tooth with a patient's other teeth.

Dexterity. Dentists must be good at working with their hands. They work with tools in a limited area.

Leadership skills. Most dentists work in their own practice. This requires them to manage and lead a staff.

Organizational skills. Strong organizational skills, including keeping accurate records of patient care, are critical in both medical and business settings.

Patience. Dentists may work for long periods of time with patients who need special attention. Children and patients with a fear of dental work may require a lot of patience.

Physical stamina. Dentists should be comfortable performing physical tasks, such as bending over patients for long periods.

Problem-solving skills. Dentists need strong problem-solving skills. They must evaluate patients' symptoms and choose the appropriate treatments.

Pay

The median annual wage for dentists was $149,310 in May 2012. The median wage is the wage at which half the workers in an occupation earned more than that amount and half earned less. The lowest 10 percent earned less than $73,840, and the top 10 percent earned $187,200 or more. Earnings vary according to the number of years in practice, location, hours worked, and specialty.

The median annual wages for dentists in May 2012 were as follows:

Oral and maxillofacial
  surgeons ....equal to or greater than $187,200
Orthodontists............................equal to or greater than $187,200
Prosthodontists.. $169,130
Dentists, all other specialists... 154,990
General dentists.. 145,240

Job Outlook

Employment of dentists is projected to grow 16 percent from 2012 to 2022, faster than the average for all occupations.

Many members of the baby-boom generation will need complicated dental work. In addition, because each generation is more likely to keep their teeth than past generations, more dental care will be needed in the years to come. Dentists will continue to see an increase in public demand for their services as studies continue to link oral health to overall health.

Dentists are likely to hire more hygienists and dental assistants to handle routine services. Productivity increases from new technology should allow dentists to reduce the time needed to see each patient. These factors allow the dentist to see more patients when their practices expand.

Dentists will continue to provide care and instruction aimed at promoting good oral hygiene, rather than just providing treatments such as fillings.

Whether patients seek care is largely dependent on their insurance coverage. The number of individuals who have access to health insurance will increase as federal health insurance reform legislation is enacted. People with new or expanded dental insurance coverage will be more likely to visit a dentist than in the past.

Job Prospects. Employment of dentists is not expected to keep pace with the increased demand for dental services. There are still areas of the country where patients need dental care, but have little access to it. Cosmetic dental services, such as teeth-whitening treatments, will become increasingly popular. This trend is expected to continue as new technologies allow for less invasive, faster procedures.

In addition, many dentists are expected to retire in the next decade and replacement workers will be needed to fill those positions.

O*NET

➤ Dentists, General (29-1021.00)
➤ Oral and Maxillofacial Surgeons (29-1022.00)
➤ Orthodontists (29-1023.00)
➤ Prosthodontists (29-1024.00)
➤ Dentists, All Other Specialists (29-1029.00)

Contacts for More Information

For more information about dentists, including accredited dental schools and state boards of dental examiners, visit
➤ American Dental Association, Commission on Dental Accreditation (www.ada.org/117.aspx)
   For information on admission to dental schools, visit
➤ American Dental Education Association (www.adea.org/)
   For more information on general dentistry or on a specific dental specialty, visit
➤ Academy of General Dentistry (www.agd.org/)
➤ American Association of Orthodontists (www.mylifemysmile.org/)
➤ American Association of Oral and Maxillofacial Surgeons (www.aaoms.org/)
➤ American Academy of Pediatric Dentistry (www.aapd.org/)
➤ American Academy of Periodontology (www.perio.org/)
➤ American College of Prosthodontists (www.gotoapro.org/)
➤ American Association of Endodontists (www.aae.org/)
➤ American Academy of Oral and Maxillofacial Radiology (www.aaomr.org/)
➤ American Association of Public Health Dentistry (www.aaphd.org/)

Diagnostic Medical Sonographers and Cardiovascular Technologists and Technicians, Including Vascular Technologists

- **2012 Median Pay** .... $60,350 per year
  $29.02 per hour
- **Entry-Level Education** .... Associate's degree
- **Work Experience in a Related Occupation**.............. None
- **On-the-Job Training** .... None
- **Number of Jobs 2012** 110,400
- **Job Outlook, 2012–22** .... 39% (Much faster than average)
- **Employment Change, 2012–22** 42,700

What Diagnostic Medical Sonographers and Cardiovascular Technologists and Technicians, Including Vascular Technologists, Do

Diagnostic medical sonographers and cardiovascular technologists and technicians, including vascular technologists, operate special imaging equipment to create images or conduct tests. The images and test results that diagnostic imaging workers produce help physicians assess and diagnose medical conditions. Some technologists assist physicians and surgeons during surgical procedures.

Duties. Diagnostic medical sonographers and cardiovascular technologists and technicians, including vascular technologists, typically do the following:

- Prepare patients for procedures by taking a patient's history and answering any questions about the procedure
- Prepare and maintain diagnostic imaging equipment
- Operate equipment to obtain diagnostic images or conduct tests
- Analyze the images or test results to check for quality and adequate coverage of the areas needed for diagnoses
- Recognize the difference between normal and abnormal images and other diagnostic information
- Analyze diagnostic information to provide a summary of findings for physicians
- Record findings and keep track of patients' records

Diagnostic medical sonographers specialize in creating images of the body's organs and tissues. The images are known as sonograms (or ultrasounds). Sonograms are often the first imaging test performed when disease is suspected. Diagnostic medical sonographers may work closely with physicians or surgeons before, during, and after procedures. The following are examples of types of diagnostic medical sonographers:

- *Abdominal sonographers* specialize in imaging a patient's abdominal cavity and nearby organs, such as the kidney, liver, gallbladder, pancreas, or spleen. Abdominal sonographers may assist with biopsies or other examinations requiring ultrasound guidance.
- *Breast sonographers* specialize in imaging a patient's breast tissues. Sonography can confirm the presence of cysts and tumors that may have been detected by the patient, physician, or a mammogram. Breast sonographers work closely with physicians and assist with procedures that track tumors and help to pro-

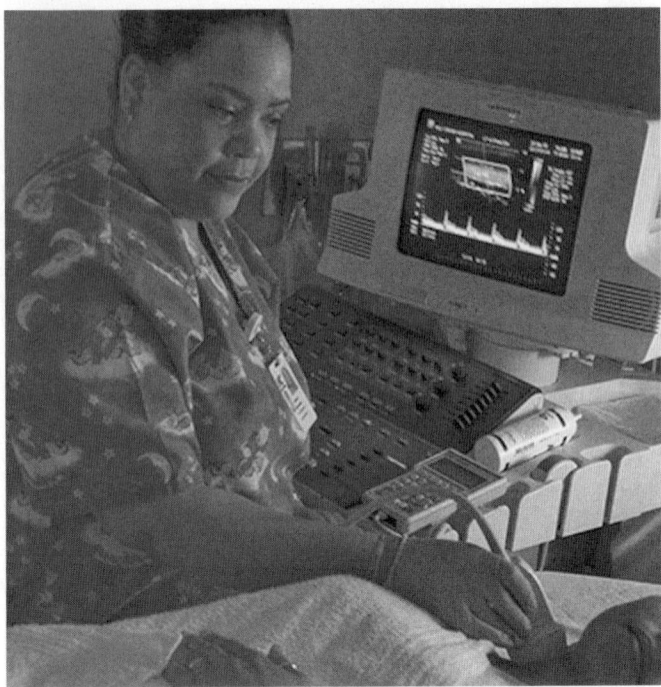

Diagnostic medical sonographers usually use diagnostic imaging machines in dark rooms, but may also perform procedures at a patient's bedside.

vide information for making decisions about the best treatment options for breast cancer patients.

- *Musculoskeletal sonographers* specialize in imaging muscles, ligaments, tendons, and joints. These sonographers may assist with ultrasound guidance for injections, or during surgical procedures, that deliver medication or treatment directly to affected tissues.
- *Neurosonographers* specialize in imaging a patient's nervous system, including the brain and spinal cord. Many diseases they image are associated with premature births or birth defects. They may work closely with pediatricians and other caregivers.
- *Obstetric and gynecologic sonographers* specialize in imaging the female reproductive system. Many pregnant women receive sonograms to track the baby's growth and health. Obstetrical sonographers work closely with physicians in detecting congenital birth defects.

Diagnostic sonography uses high-frequency sound waves to produce images of the inside of the body. The sonographer uses an instrument called an ultrasound transducer on the parts of the patient's body that are being examined. The transducer emits pulses of sound that bounce back, causing echoes. The echoes are then sent to the ultrasound machine, which processes them and displays them as images used by physicians for diagnosis.

Cardiovascular technologists and technicians create images, conduct tests, or assist with surgical procedures involving the heart. The following are examples of types of cardiovascular technologists and technicians:

- *Cardiac sonographers (echocardiographers)* specialize in imaging a patient's heart and use ultrasound equipment to examine the heart's chambers, valves, and vessels. The images are known as echocardiograms. The echocardiogram procedure may be done while the patient is either resting or after being physically active. Cardiac sonographers also may take echocardiograms of fetal hearts so that physicians can diagnose cardiac conditions during

Median Annual Wages, May 2012

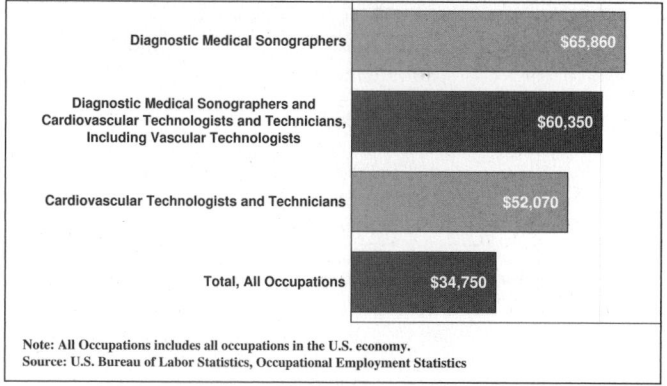

Diagnostic Medical Sonographers	$65,860
Diagnostic Medical Sonographers and Cardiovascular Technologists and Technicians, Including Vascular Technologists	$60,350
Cardiovascular Technologists and Technicians	$52,070
Total, All Occupations	$34,750

Note: All Occupations includes all occupations in the U.S. economy.
Source: U.S. Bureau of Labor Statistics, Occupational Employment Statistics

Percent Change in Employment, Projected 2012–2022

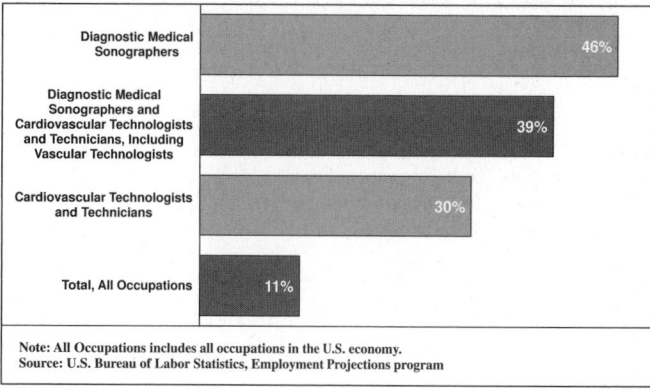

Diagnostic Medical Sonographers	46%
Diagnostic Medical Sonographers and Cardiovascular Technologists and Technicians, Including Vascular Technologists	39%
Cardiovascular Technologists and Technicians	30%
Total, All Occupations	11%

Note: All Occupations includes all occupations in the U.S. economy.
Source: U.S. Bureau of Labor Statistics, Employment Projections program

pregnancy. Cardiac sonographers work closely with physicians or surgeons before, during, and after procedures.

- *Cardiology technologists* monitor patients' heart rates and help physicians in diagnosing and treating problems with patients' hearts. They assist with cardiac catheterization, which involves threading a catheter through a patient's artery to the heart. Some cardiology technologists prepare and monitor patients during open-heart surgery and during the insertion of pacemakers and stents. Technologists prepare patients for these procedures by shaving and cleansing the area where the catheter will be inserted and administering topical anesthesia. During the procedure, they monitor the patient's blood pressure and heart rate.

- *Cardiovascular technicians* work closely with cardiovascular technologists. Technicians who specialize in electrocardiogram (EKG) testing are known as cardiographic or electrocardiogram (EKG) technicians. EKG machines monitor the heart's performance through electrodes attached to a patient's chest, arms, and legs. The tests can be done while the patient is at rest or while the patient is physically active. For a stress test, the patient walks on a treadmill and the technician gradually increases the speed to observe the effect of increased exertion.

Vascular technologists (vascular sonographers) are closely related to cardiovascular technologists and their duties are similar to those of diagnostic medical sonographers. Vascular technologists create images of blood vessels and collect data that help physicians diagnose disorders affecting blood flow. Vascular technologists often measure a patient's blood pressure and the volume of blood in their arms, legs, fingers, and toes to evaluate blood flow and identify blocked arteries. They complete noninvasive procedures using specialized ultrasound instruments or blood pressure cuffs to record information, such as the blood flow in arteries and veins, blood pressure (blood volume), oxygen saturation, and the presence of blood clots in the body. Vascular technologists may work closely with physicians or surgeons before, during, and after procedures.

Work Environment

Diagnostic medical sonographers held about 58,800 jobs in 2012. Cardiovascular technologists and technicians, including vascular technologists, held about 51,600 jobs in 2012. Most diagnostic imaging workers were employed in hospitals in 2012, while others worked in healthcare settings such as physician's offices and medical and diagnostic laboratories.

Diagnostic imaging workers complete most of their work at diagnostic imaging machines in dimly lit rooms, but they also

may perform procedures at patients' bedsides. They may be on their feet for long periods and may need to lift or turn patients who are disabled.

Work Schedules. Most diagnostic imaging workers work full time. Because they work in facilities that are always open, some may work evenings, weekends, or overnight.

How to Become One

Diagnostic medical sonographers and cardiovascular technologists and technicians, including vascular technologists, need formal education, such as an associate's degree or a postsecondary certificate. Many employers also require professional certification.

Education. Colleges and universities offer both associate's and bachelor's degree programs in sonography and in cardiovascular and vascular technology. One-year certificate programs also are available from colleges or in hospitals, although these are usually useful only to those who are already employed in related healthcare jobs, such as a radiation therapist. Employers typically prefer candidates with degrees or certificates from accredited institutes or hospital programs. Most programs also include a clinical component in which students earn credit while working under a more experienced technologist in a hospital, physician's office, or imaging laboratory.

Sonography, cardiovascular, and vascular education programs usually include courses in anatomy, medical terminology, and applied sciences. Most sonography programs are divided into the specialized fields that correspond to the relevant certification exams, such as abdominal sonography or breast sonography. Cardiovascular and vascular programs include coursework in either invasive or noninvasive cardiovascular or vascular technology procedures.

High school students who are interested in diagnostic medical sonography, cardiovascular technology, or vascular technology should take courses in anatomy, physiology, and mathematics.

Important Qualities

Detail oriented. Diagnostic imaging workers must follow precise instructions to obtain the images needed to diagnose and treat patients. They must also pay attention to the screen while scanning a patient's body because the cues that contrast healthy areas with unhealthy ones may be subtle.

Hand-eye coordination. To get quality images, diagnostic imaging workers must be able to accurately move equipment on the patient's body in response to what they see on the screen.

Interpersonal skills. Diagnostic imaging workers must work closely with patients. Sometimes patients are in extreme pain or

Employment Projections Data for Diagnostic Medical Sonographers and Cardiovascular Technologists and Technicians, Including Vascular Technologists

Occupational title	SOC Code	Employment, 2012	Projected Employment, 2022	Change, 2012–2022	
				Percent	Numeric
Diagnostic medical sonographers and cardiovascular technologists and technicians, including vascular technologists...................	—	110,400	153,200	39	42,700
Cardiovascular technologists and technicians	29-2031	51,600	67,300	30	15,700
Diagnostic medical sonographers	29-2032	58,800	85,900	46	27,000

Source: U.S. Bureau of Labor Statistics, Employment Projections Program

Note: Data are rounded. Go to **Occupational Information Included in the OOH** *for a discussion of the data in this table.*

mental stress, and they must get cooperation from the patient to create usable images.

Physical stamina. Diagnostic imaging workers are on their feet for long periods and must be able to lift and move patients who need assistance.

Technical skills. Diagnostic imaging workers must understand how to operate complex machinery and computerized instruments.

Training. Someone who works in a related occupation, such as a radiation therapist, could become a diagnostic medical sonographer or cardiovascular technologist or technician or vascular technologist after receiving on-the-job training from his or her employer.

Cardiovascular technicians who work as electrocardiogram (EKG) technicians are typically trained on the job by their employer. These programs usually take 4 to 6 weeks to complete.

Licenses, Certifications, and Registrations. Most employers prefer to hire diagnostic imaging workers with professional certification. Many insurance providers and Medicare pay for procedures only if a certified sonographer, technologist, or technician performed the work.

Diagnostic imaging workers can earn certification by graduating from an accredited program and passing an exam. Most exams relate to the specialty that the diagnostic imaging worker is most interested in–for example, a sonographer can take a specific exam to become certified in abdominal sonography. Most diagnostic imaging workers have at least one certification, but may earn various certifications. A few states require diagnostic medical sonographers to be licensed. Typically, professional certification is required for licensure; other requirements vary by state.

Pay

The median annual wage for diagnostic medical sonographers was $65,860 in May 2012. The median wage is the wage at which half the workers in an occupation earned more than that amount and half earned less. The lowest 10 percent earned less than $44,990, and the top 10 percent earned more than $91,070.

The median annual wage for cardiovascular technologists and technicians, including vascular technologists, was $52,070 in May

2012. The lowest 10 percent earned less than $27,830, and the top 10 percent earned more than $80,790.

Job Outlook

Employment of diagnostic medical sonographers is projected to grow 46 percent from 2012 to 2022, much faster than the average for all occupations. Employment of cardiovascular technologists and technicians, including vascular technologists, is projected to grow 30 percent from 2012 to 2022, much faster than the average for all occupations.

As imaging technology evolves, medical facilities will use it to replace more invasive, costly procedures. Technological advances and less expensive equipment now allow more procedures to be done outside of hospitals. Third-party payers encourage the use of these noninvasive measures over invasive ones.

Although hospitals remain the primary employer of diagnostic medical sonographers, cardiovascular technologists and technicians, and vascular technologists, employment is projected to grow more rapidly in physicians' offices and in medical and diagnostic laboratories. Employment in these healthcare settings is projected to increase because of a shift toward outpatient care whenever possible.

As the large baby-boom population ages and people remain active later in life, the need to diagnose medical conditions–such as blood clots and tumors–will likely increase, and imaging technology is a tool used in making these diagnoses. Additionally, federal health legislation will expand the number of patients who have access to health insurance, increasing patient access to medical care. Diagnostic imaging workers will continue to be needed to use and maintain the equipment needed for diagnosis and treatment.

Job Prospects. Diagnostic imaging personnel who are certified are expected to have the best job opportunities. Job opportunities increase when diagnostic imaging personnel are certified in more than one specialty.

O*NET

➤ Cardiovascular Technologists and Technicians (29-2031.00)
➤ Diagnostic Medical Sonographers (29-2032.00)

Similar Occupations This table shows a list of occupations with job duties that are similar to those of diagnostic medical sonographers and cardiovascular technologists and technicians, including vascular technologists.

Occupations	Entry-level Education	2012 Pay	Projected Job Growth	Average Annual Openings
Medical and Clinical Laboratory Technologists and Technicians	See "How to Become One"	$47,499	22%	15,600
Nuclear Medicine Technologists	Associate's degree	$70,180	20%	720
Radiologic and MRI Technologists	Associate's degree	$56,035	21%	8,090

Contacts for More Information

For more information about diagnostic medical sonographers, visit
➤ Society of Diagnostic Medical Sonography (www.sdms.org)

For more information about cardiovascular technologists and technicians, including vascular technologists, visit
➤ Alliance of Cardiovascular Professionals (www.acp-online.org)
➤ American Society of Echocardiography (www.asecho.org/)
➤ Society for Vascular Ultrasound (www.svunet.org)

For more information about registration and certification, visit
➤ American Registry of Radiologic Technologists (www.arrt.org)
➤ Cardiovascular Credentialing International (www.cci-online.org)
➤ American Registry for Diagnostic Medical Sonography (www.ardms.org)

For a current list of accredited education programs in diagnostic medical sonography and cardiovascular technology, including vascular technology, visit
➤ Joint Review Committee on Education in Diagnostic Medical Sonography (www.jrcdms.org)
➤ Joint Review Committee on Education in Cardiovascular Technology (www.jrccvt.org)
➤ Commission on Accreditation of Allied Health Education Programs (www.caahep.org)

Dietitians and Nutritionists

- **2012 Median Pay** .... $55,240 per year
  $26.56 per hour
- **Entry-Level Education** ....Bachelor's degree
- **Work Experience in a Related Occupation**............... None
- **On-the-Job Training** .... Internship/residency
- **Number of Jobs 2012** 67,400
- **Job Outlook, 2012–22** .... 21% (Faster than average)
- **Employment Change, 2012–22** 14,200

Dietitians counsel individuals and groups on nutritional practices designed to prevent disease and promote health.

What Dietitians and Nutritionists Do

Dietitians and nutritionists are experts in food and nutrition. They advise people on what to eat in order to lead a healthy lifestyle or achieve a specific health-related goal.

Duties. Dietitians and nutritionists typically do the following:

- Assess patients' and clients' health needs and diet
- Counsel patients on nutrition issues and healthy eating habits
- Develop meal plans, taking both cost and clients' preferences into account
- Evaluate the effects of meal plans and change the plans as needed
- Promote better nutrition by speaking to groups about diet, nutrition, and the relationship between good eating habits and preventing or managing specific diseases
- Keep up with the latest nutritional science research
- Write reports to document patient progress

Dietitians and nutritionists evaluate the health of their clients. Based on their findings, dietitians and nutritionists advise clients on which foods to eat–and those foods to avoid–to improve their health.

Some dietitians and nutritionists provide customized information for specific individuals. For example, a dietitian or nutritionist might teach a client with high blood pressure how to use less salt when preparing meals. Others work with groups of people who have similar needs. For example, a dietitian or nutritionist might plan a diet with limited fat and sugar to help patients lose weight. They may work with other healthcare professionals to coordinate patient care.

Dietitians and nutritionists who are self-employed may meet with patients, or they may work as consultants for a variety of organizations. They may need to spend time on marketing and other business-related tasks, such as scheduling appointments and preparing informational materials for clients.

Although many dietitians and nutritionists do similar tasks, there are several specialties within the occupations. The following are examples of types of dietitians and nutritionists:

Clinical dietitians and nutritionists provide medical nutrition therapy. They work in hospitals, long-term care facilities, clinics, private practice, and other institutions. They create nutritional programs based on the health needs of patients or residents and counsel patients on how to lead a healthier lifestyle. Clinical dietitians and nutritionists may further specialize, such as working only with patients with kidney diseases or those with diabetes.

Community dietitians and nutritionists develop programs and counsel the public on topics related to food and nutrition. They often work with specific groups of people, such as adolescents or the elderly. They work in public health clinics, government and nonprofit agencies, health maintenance organizations (HMOs), and other settings.

Management dietitians plan meal programs. They work in food service settings such as cafeterias, hospitals, prisons, and schools. They may be responsible for buying food and for carrying out other business-related tasks such as budgeting. Management dietitians may oversee kitchen staff or other dietitians.

Work Environment

Dietitians and nutritionists held about 67,400 jobs in 2012.

Dietitians and nutritionists work in hospitals, nursing homes, cafeterias, and schools. The industries that employed the most dietitians and nutritionists in 2012 were as follows:

Hospitals; state, local, and private 31%
Government.. 13

Median Annual Wages, May 2012

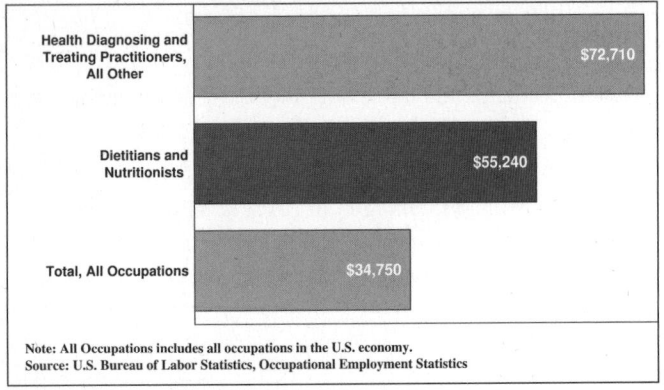

Note: All Occupations includes all occupations in the U.S. economy.
Source: U.S. Bureau of Labor Statistics, Occupational Employment Statistics

Percent Change in Employment, Projected 2012–2022

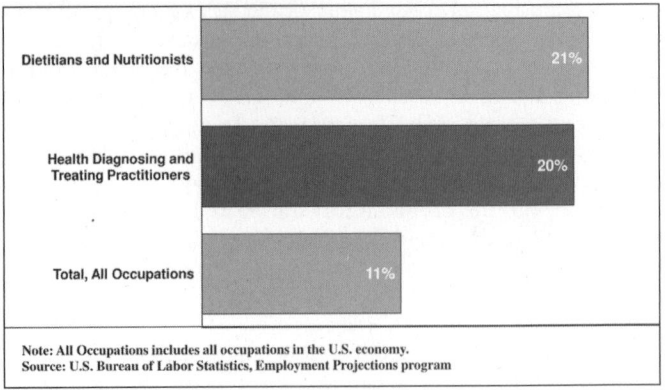

Note: All Occupations includes all occupations in the U.S. economy.
Source: U.S. Bureau of Labor Statistics, Employment Projections program

Nursing and residential care facilities 9
Offices of health practitioners 7
Outpatient care centers 7

About 11 percent of dietitians and nutritionists were self-employed in 2012. Self-employed dietitians and nutritionists work as consultants who provide advice to individual clients, or they work for healthcare establishments on a contract basis.

Work Schedules. Most dietitians and nutritionists worked full time in 2012, although about 1 out of 5 worked part time. Self-employed dietitians have more flexibility in setting their schedules. They may work evenings and weekends so that they can meet with clients.

How to Become One

Most dietitians and nutritionists have a bachelor's degree and receive supervised training through an internship or as a part of their coursework. Many states require dietitians and nutritionists to be licensed.

Education. Most dietitians and nutritionists have a bachelor's degree in dietetics, foods and nutrition, food service systems management, clinical nutrition, or a related area. Programs include courses in nutrition, psychology, chemistry, and biology.

Many dietitians and nutritionists also have advanced degrees.

Training. Dietitians and nutritionists typically receive several hundred hours of supervised training, usually in the form of an internship following graduation from college. Some dietetics schools offer Coordinated Programs in Dietetics that allow students to complete supervised training as part of their undergraduate or graduate-level coursework.

Licenses, Certifications, and Registrations. Most states require dietitians and nutritionists to be licensed. Other states require only state registration or certification, and a few states have no regulations for this occupation.

The requirements for state licensure and state certification vary by state, but most include having a bachelor's degree in food and nutrition or a related area, supervised practice, and passing an exam.

Many dietitians choose to earn the Registered Dietitian Nutritionist (RDN) credential. Although the RDN is not always required, the qualifications are often the same as those necessary to become a licensed dietitian in states that require a license. Many employers prefer or require the RDN, which is administered by the Commission on Dietetic Registration, the credentialing agency for the Academy of Nutrition and Dietetics.

The RDN requires dietitian nutritionists to complete a minimum of a bachelor's degree and a Dietetic Internship Program. Students may complete both criteria at once through a Coordinated Program, or they may finish coursework requirements before applying for an internship. These programs are accredited by the Accreditation Council for Education in Nutrition and Dietetics (ACEND). In order to maintain the RDN credential, Registered Dietitian Nutritionists must complete continuing professional education requirements.

Nutritionists may earn the Certified Nutrition Specialist (CNS) credential to show an advanced level of knowledge. The CNS credential is accepted in many states for licensure purposes. To qualify for the CNS exam, applicants must have a master's or doctoral degree and 1,000 hours of experience. The credential is administered by the Certification Board for Nutrition Specialists.

Dietitians and nutritionists may seek additional certifications in an area of specialty such as sports or pediatric nutrition.

Important Qualities

Analytical skills. Dietitians and nutritionists must keep up to date with the latest nutrition research. They should be able to interpret scientific studies and translate nutrition science into practical eating advice.

Compassion. Dietitians and nutritionists must be caring and empathetic when helping clients address dietary issues and any related emotions.

Listening skills. Dietitians and nutritionists must listen carefully to understand clients' goals and concerns. They may also work with other healthcare workers as part of team to improve the health of a patient and need to listen to team members when constructing eating plans.

Employment Projections Data for Dietitians and Nutritionists

Occupational title	SOC Code	Employment, 2012	Projected Employment, 2022	Change, 2012–2022	
				Percent	Numeric
Dietitians and nutritionists...	29-1031	67,400	81,600	21	14,200

Source: U.S. Bureau of Labor Statistics, Employment Projections Program

Note: Data are rounded. Go to **Occupational Information Included in the OOH** *for a discussion of the data in this table.*

Similar Occupations This table shows a list of occupations with job duties that are similar to those of dietitians and nutritionists.

Occupations	Entry-level Education	2012 Pay	Projected Job Growth	Average Annual Openings
Health Educators and Community Health Workers	See "How to Become One"	$43,015	22%	4,740
Registered Nurses	Associate's degree	$65,470	19%	105,260
Rehabilitation Counselors	Master's degree	$33,880	20%	4,840

Organizational skills. Because there are many aspects to the work of dietitians and nutritionists, they should have the ability to stay organized. Management dietitians, for example, must consider both the nutritional needs of their clients and the costs of meals. Self-employed dietitians and nutritionists may need to schedule their appointments and maintain patient files.

Problem-solving skills. They must evaluate the health status of patients and determine the most appropriate food choices for a client to improve overall health or manage a disease.

Speaking skills. Dietitians and nutritionists must explain complicated topics in a way that people with less technical knowledge can understand. They must be able to clearly explain eating plans to clients and to other healthcare professionals involved in a patient's care.

Pay

The median annual wage for dietitians and nutritionists was $55,240 in May 2012. The median wage is the wage at which half the workers in an occupation earned more than that amount and half earned less. The lowest 10 percent earned less than $34,500, and the top 10 percent earned more than $77,590.

According to the Academy of Nutrition and Dietetics, the median annual wage for Registered Dietitian Nutritionists (RDNs) was $60,000 in 2013.

Job Outlook

Employment of dietitians and nutritionists is projected to grow 21 percent from 2012 to 2022, faster than the average for all occupations. In recent years, interest in the role of food in promoting health and wellness has increased, particularly as a part of preventative healthcare in medical settings.

According to the Centers for Disease Control, more than one-third of U.S. adults are obese. Many diseases, such as diabetes and kidney disease, are associated with obesity. The importance of diet in preventing and treating illnesses is now well known. More dietitians and nutritionists will be needed to provide care for people with these conditions.

As the baby-boom generation grows older and looks for ways to stay healthy, there will be more demand for dietetic services. An aging population also will increase the need for dietitians and nutritionists in nursing homes and in home healthcare.

Job Prospects. Overall, job opportunities for dietitians and nutritionists are expected to be favorable. Dietitians and nutritionists who have earned advanced degrees or certification in a specialty area may enjoy better job prospects.

O*NET

➤ Dietitians and Nutritionists (29-1031.00)

Contacts for More Information

For a list of academic programs and other information about dietitians, visit
➤ Academy of Nutrition and Dietetics (www.eatright.org/)
  For information on the Registered Dietitian Nutritionist (RDN) exam and other specialty credentials, visit
➤ Commission on Dietetic Registration (www.cdrnet.org/)
  For information on the Certified Nutrition Specialist exam and credential, visit
➤ Certification Board for Nutrition Specialists (http://cbns.org/)

EMTs and Paramedics

- **2012 Median Pay** .... $31,020 per year
  $14.91 per hour
- **Entry-Level Education** .... Postsecondary non-degree award
- **Work Experience in a Related Occupation** .... None
- **On-the-Job Training** .... None
- **Number of Jobs 2012** 239,100
- **Job Outlook, 2012–22** .... 23% (Much faster than average)
- **Employment Change, 2012–22** 55,300

What EMTs and Paramedics Do

Emergency medical technicians (EMTs) and paramedics care for the sick or injured in emergency medical settings. People's lives often depend on their quick reaction and competent care. EMTs and paramedics respond to emergency calls, performing medical services and transporting patients to medical facilities.

A 911 operator sends EMTs and paramedics to the scene of an emergency, where they often work with police and firefighters.

Duties. EMTs and paramedics typically do the following:

- Respond to 911 calls for emergency medical assistance, such as cardiopulmonary resuscitation (CPR) or bandaging a wound
- Assess a patient's condition and determine a course of treatment
- Follow guidelines learned in training or received from physicians who oversee their work
- Use backboards and restraints to keep patients still and safe in an ambulance during transport
- Help transfer patients to the emergency department of a healthcare facility and report their observations and treatment to the staff
- Create a patient care report, documenting the medical care given to the patient
- Replace used supplies and check or clean equipment after use

When taking a patient to a hospital, one EMT or paramedic may drive the ambulance while another monitors the patient's vital signs and gives additional care. Some paramedics work as part of a helicopter's flight crew to transport critically ill or injured patients to a hospital.

EMTs and paramedics also transport patients from one medical facility to another. Some patients may need to be transferred to a hospital that specializes in treating their injury or illness or to a facility that provides long-term care, such as a nursing home.

If a patient has a contagious disease, EMTs and paramedics decontaminate the interior of the ambulance and may need to report the case to the proper authorities.

The specific responsibilities of EMTs and paramedics depend on whether they are an EMT or EMT-Basic, Advanced EMT, or paramedic; and the state they work in. The National Registry of Emergency Medical Technicians (NREMT) provides national certification of EMTs and paramedics at three levels: EMT/Basic, Advanced EMT or EMT-Intermediate, and Paramedic. Some states, however, have their own certification programs and use different titles.

An *EMT*, also known as an *EMT-Basic*, cares for patients at the scene of an incident and while taking patients by ambulance to a hospital. An EMT-Basic has the skills to assess a patient's condition and to manage respiratory, cardiac, and trauma emergencies.

An *Advanced EMT*, also known as an *EMT-Intermediate,* has completed the requirements for the EMT level, as well as instruction in more advanced medical procedures, such as administering intravenous fluids and some medications.

Paramedics provide more extensive prehospital care than do EMTs. In addition to being able to carry out the tasks of EMTs, paramedics can give medications orally and intravenously, interpret electrocardiograms (EKGs)–used to monitor heart function–and use other monitors and complex equipment.

The specific tasks or procedures EMTs and paramedics are allowed to perform at any level vary by state.

Work Environment

Emergency medical technicians (EMTs) and paramedics held about 239,100 jobs in 2012. They work both indoors and outdoors, in all types of weather. Their work is physically strenuous and can be stressful, sometimes involving life-or-death situations and patients who are suffering. Most paid EMTs and paramedics work in metropolitan areas. Volunteer EMTs and paramedics are more common in small cities, towns, and rural areas. These individuals volunteer for fire departments, providers of emergency medical services, or hospitals and may respond to only a few calls per month.

The industries that employed the most paid EMTs and paramedics in 2012 were as follows:

Ambulance services...48%
Government..30
Hospitals; state, local, and private 17

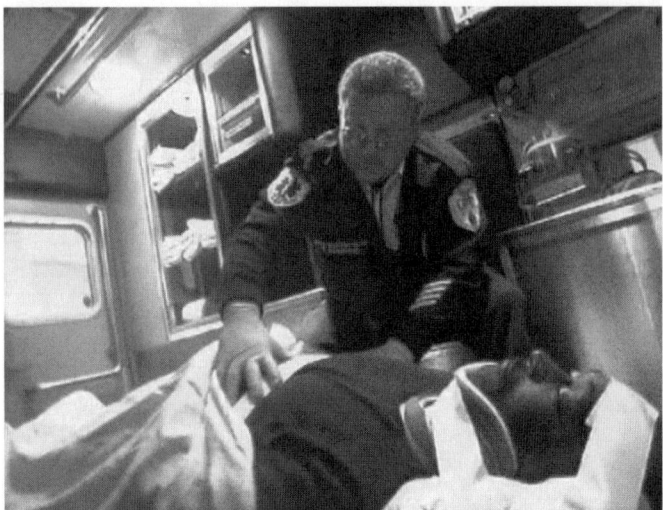

EMTs and paramedics use special equipment, including backboards and restraints, to immobilize patients and secure them in the ambulance for transport.

Injuries and Illnesses. EMTs and paramedics have a higher rate of injuries and illnesses than the national average. They are required to do considerable kneeling, bending, and lifting while caring for and moving patients. They may be exposed to contagious diseases, such as hepatitis B and AIDS. Sometimes they can be injured by mentally unstable or combative patients. These risks can be reduced by following proper safety procedures, such as waiting for police to clear an area in violent situations or wearing gloves while working with a patient.

Work Schedules. Most paid EMTs and paramedics work full time. About 1 in 3 worked more than 40 hours per week in 2012. Because EMTs and paramedics must be available to work in emergencies, they may work overnight and on weekends. Some EMTs and paramedics work shifts in 12- or 24-hour increments. Volunteer EMTs and paramedics have variable work schedules.

How to Become One

Emergency medical technicians (EMTs) and paramedics must complete a postsecondary educational program. All states require EMTs and paramedics to be licensed; requirements vary by state.

Education. Both a high school diploma or equivalent and cardiopulmonary resuscitation (CPR) certification are prerequisites for most postsecondary educational programs in emergency medical technology. Most of these programs are postsecondary non-degree award programs that can be completed in less than 1 year; others

Median Annual Wages, May 2012

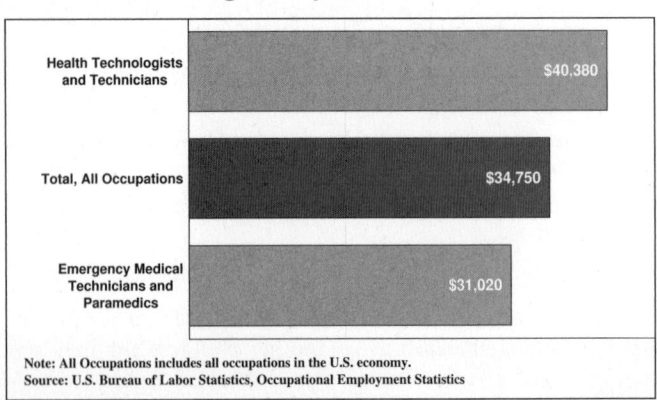

Health Technologists and Technicians	$40,380
Total, All Occupations	$34,750
Emergency Medical Technicians and Paramedics	$31,020

Note: All Occupations includes all occupations in the U.S. economy.
Source: U.S. Bureau of Labor Statistics, Occupational Employment Statistics

Percent Change in Employment, Projected 2012–2022

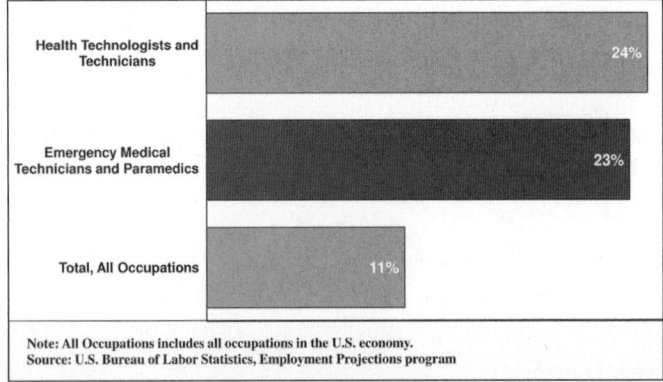

Health Technologists and Technicians	24%
Emergency Medical Technicians and Paramedics	23%
Total, All Occupations	11%

Note: All Occupations includes all occupations in the U.S. economy.
Source: U.S. Bureau of Labor Statistics, Employment Projections program

Employment Projections Data for EMTs and Paramedics

Occupational title	SOC Code	Employment, 2012	Projected Employment, 2022	Change, 2012–2022	
				Percent	Numeric
Emergency medical technicians and paramedics....................	29-2041	239,100	294,400	23	55,300

Source: U.S. Bureau of Labor Statistics, Employment Projections Program

Note: Data are rounded. Go to **Occupational Information Included in the OOH** *for a discussion of the data in this table.*

last up to 2 years. Paramedics, however, may need an associate's degree. Educational programs in emergency medical technology are offered by technical institutes, community colleges, and facilities that specialize in emergency care training. High school students interested in becoming EMTs or paramedics should take courses in anatomy and physiology.

Programs at the EMT level include instruction in assessing patients' conditions, dealing with trauma and cardiac emergencies, clearing obstructed airways, using field equipment, and handling emergencies. Formal courses include about 150 hours of specialized instruction, and some instruction may take place in a hospital or ambulance setting.

Programs at the Advanced EMT level typically requires about 300 hours of instruction based on the scope of practice. At this level, people must complete the requirements for the EMT level as well as more advanced ones, such as using complex airway devices, intravenous fluids, and some medications.

Paramedics have the most advanced level of education. They must complete EMT and Advanced EMT levels of instruction, along with courses in advanced medical skills. Community colleges and technical schools may offer these programs, which require about 1,200 hours of instruction and may lead to an associate's degree. Paramedics' broader scope of practice may include stitching wounds or administering intravenous medications.

Licenses, Certifications, and Registrations. The National Registry of Emergency Medical Technicians (NREMT) certifies EMTs and paramedics. All levels of NREMT certification require completing a certified education program and passing the national exam. The national exam has both written and practical parts.

All states require EMTs and paramedics to be licensed; requirements vary by state. In most states, an individual who has NREMT certification qualifies for licensure. In others, passing an equivalent state exam is required. Usually an applicant must be over the age of 18. Many states require background checks and may not give a license to an applicant who has a criminal history.

Although some emergency medical services hire separate drivers, most EMTs and paramedics take a course requiring about 8 hours of instruction before they can drive an ambulance.

Important Qualities

Compassion. EMTs and paramedics must be able to provide emotional support to patients in an emergency, especially patients who are in life-threatening situations or extreme mental distress.

Interpersonal skills. EMTs and paramedics usually work on teams and must be able to coordinate their activities closely with others in stressful situations.

Listening skills. EMTs and paramedics need to listen to patients to determine the extent of their injuries or illnesses.

Physical strength. EMTs and paramedics need to be physically fit. Their job requires a lot of bending, lifting, and kneeling.

Problem-solving skills. EMTs and paramedics need strong problem-solving skills. They must be able to evaluate patients' symptoms and administer the appropriate treatments.

Speaking skills. EMTs and paramedics need to be able explain procedures to patients, give orders, and relay information to others.

Pay

The median annual wage for emergency medical technicians (EMTs) and paramedics was $31,020 in May 2012. The median wage is the wage at which half the workers in an occupation earned more than that amount and half earned less. The lowest 10 percent earned less than $20,180, and the top 10 percent earned more than $53,550.

Union Membership. Compared with workers in all occupations, EMTs had a higher percentage of workers who belonged to a union in 2012.

Job Outlook

Employment of emergency medical technicians (EMTs) and paramedics is projected to grow 23 percent from 2012 to 2022, much faster than the average for all occupations. Emergencies, such as car crashes, natural disasters, or acts of violence, will continue to create demand for EMTs and paramedics. Demand for part-time, volunteer EMTs and paramedics in rural areas and smaller metropolitan areas will also continue.

Growth in the middle-aged and elderly population will lead to an increase in the number of age-related health emergencies, such as heart attacks or strokes. This, in turn, will create greater demand for EMTs and paramedic services. An increase in the number of specialized medical facilities will require more EMTs

Similar Occupations   This table shows a list of occupations with job duties that are similar to those of EMTs and paramedics.

Occupations	Entry-level Education	2012 Pay	Projected Job Growth	Average Annual Openings
Air Traffic Controllers	Associate's degree	$122,530	2%	1,140
Firefighters	Postsecondary non-degree award	$45,250	7%	10,400
Physician Assistants	Master's degree	$90,930	38%	4,890
Police and Detectives	High school diploma or equivalent	$57,974	5%	27,500
Registered Nurses	Associate's degree	$65,470	19%	105,260

and paramedics to transfer patients with specific conditions to these facilities for treatment.

O*NET

➤ Emergency Medical Technicians and Paramedics (29-2041.00)

Contacts for More Information

For more information about emergency medical technicians and paramedics, visit

➤ National Association of Emergency Medical Technicians (www. naemt.org/)

➤ National Highway Traffic Safety Administration, Office of Emergency Medical Services (www.ems.gov/)

➤ National Registry of Emergency Medical Technicians (www.nremt. org/)

Genetic Counselors

- **2012 Median Pay** .... $56,800 per year
  $27.31 per hour
- **Entry-Level Education** ....Master's degree
- **Work Experience in a Related Occupation**............... None
- **On-the-Job Training** .... None
- **Number of Jobs 2012** 2,100
- **Job Outlook, 2012–22** .... 41% (Much faster than average)
- **Employment Change, 2012–22** 900

What Genetic Counselors Do

Genetic counselors assess individual or family risk for a variety of inherited conditions, such as genetic disorders and birth defects. They provide information and advice to other healthcare providers, or to individuals and families concerned with the risk of inherited conditions.

Duties. Genetic counselors typically do the following:

- Analyze genetic information to identify patients or families at risk for specific disorders and syndromes

- Write detailed consultation reports to provide information on complex genetic concepts for patients or referring physicians

- Discuss testing options and the associated risks, benefits, and limitations with patients and families

- Interview patients to obtain comprehensive medical histories and document the findings

- Interpret laboratory results and communicate findings to patients or physicians

- Counsel patients and family members by providing information, education, or reassurance regarding genetic risks and inherited conditions

- Determine patient treatment plans by reviewing laboratory work, literature, and patient histories

- Participate in professional organizations or conferences to keep abreast of developments in genetics and genomics

Genetic counselors identify specific genetic disorders or syndromes through the study of genetics. A genetic disorder or syndrome is inherited. For parents who are expecting children, counselors use genetics to predict whether a baby is likely to have hereditary disorders, such as Down syndrome and cystic fibrosis, among others. Genetic counselors can also test whether an adult is likely to develop chronic disease, or cancer. Counselors identify these conditions by studying patients' genes through DNA testing. Counselors often perform the lab tests themselves, although sometimes they have medical laboratory technologists perform the tests, which they then interpret and use for counseling. They share this information with other health professionals, such as physicians, and with patients and their families. For more information, see the profiles on medical and clinical laboratory technologists and technicians and physicians and surgeons.

According to a 2012 survey from the National Society of Genetic Counselors, approximately two-thirds of genetic counselors work in traditional areas of genetic counseling: prenatal, cancer, and pediatric. The survey noted that the number of specialized fields for genetic counselors has increased. More genetic counselors are specializing in fields such as cardiovascular health, genomic medicine, neuropsychiatric genetics, and assisted reproductive technologies.

Work Environment

Genetic counselors held about 2,100 jobs in 2012. Genetic counselors work in university medical centers, private and public hospitals, physicians' offices, and diagnostic laboratories. They work with families, patients, and other medical professionals.

Work schedules

Most genetic counselors work full time and have a standard work schedule.

How to Become One

Genetic counselors typically need at least a master's degree in genetic counseling or genetics. Although most genetic counselors have a master's degree, some earn a Ph.D.

Education. Genetic counselors typically need at least a master's degree in genetic counseling or genetics, and some earn a Ph.D.

Coursework in genetic counseling includes public health, epidemiology, psychology, and developmental biology. Classes emphasize genetics, public health, and patient empathy. Advanced courses focus on clinical observations, review of previous genetic research, and health communication strategies.

Licenses, Certifications, and Registrations. The American Board of Genetic Counseling provides certification for genetic counselors. To become certified, a student must first complete a master's degree program that is certified by the board. There are currently 31 certified programs in the United States. Students then must pass

Genetic counselors explain the chances of a genetic condition occurring or recurring within a family.

Median Annual Wages, May 2012

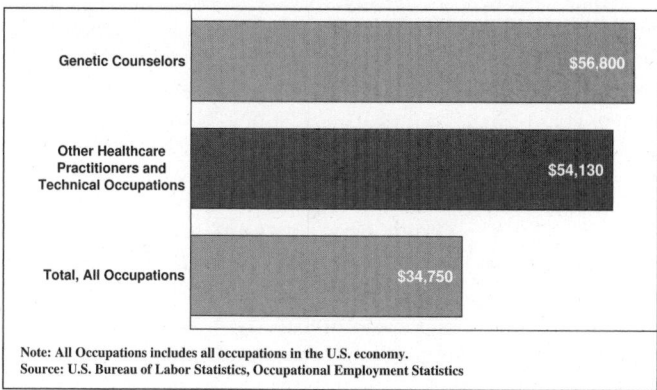

Note: All Occupations includes all occupations in the U.S. economy.
Source: U.S. Bureau of Labor Statistics, Occupational Employment Statistics

Percent Change in Employment, Projected 2012–2022

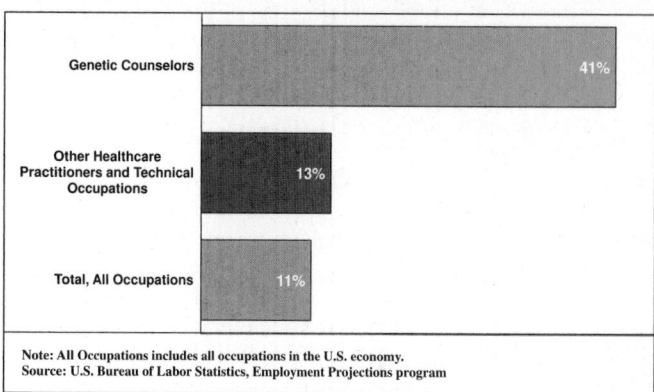

Note: All Occupations includes all occupations in the U.S. economy.
Source: U.S. Bureau of Labor Statistics, Employment Projections program

a comprehensive exam and continue to accrue continuing education units throughout their careers. Some states currently require a license in genetic counseling, and other states have pending legislation for licensure. Certification is typically needed to get a license.

Important Qualities

Compassion. Patients seek advice on family care or serious illness, so genetic counselors must be sensitive and compassionate when communicating their findings.

Critical-thinking skills. Genetic counselors analyze laboratory findings to determine how best to advise a patient or family. They use their applied knowledge of genetics to assess inherited risks properly.

Decision-making skills. Genetic counselors must use their expertise and experience to determine how to disseminate their findings properly to their patients.

Speaking skills. Genetic counselors must communicate complex findings so that their patients can understand the magnitude of a health problem.

Pay

The median annual wage for genetic counselors was $56,800 in May 2012. The median wage is the wage at which half the workers in an occupation earned more than that amount and half earned

less. The lowest 10 percent earned less than $25,540, and the top 10 percent earned more than $85,790.

In May 2012, the median annual wages for genetic counselors in the top four industries in which these counselors worked were as follows:

Specialty (except psychiatric and substance abuse)
  hospitals; private $67,480
General medical and surgical hospitals; local 63,590
Colleges, universities, and professional schools; state 63,240
Offices of physicians 47,790

Job Outlook

Employment of genetic counselors is projected to grow 41 percent from 2012 to 2022, much faster than the average for all occupations. However, because it is a small occupation, the fast growth will result in only about 900 new jobs over the 10-year period. Ongoing technological innovations, including lab tests and developments in genomics, are giving counselors the opportunities to conduct more types of analyses. Cancer genomics, for example, can determine a patient's risk for specific types of cancer. The number and types of tests that genetic counselors can administer and interpret has increased over the past few years.

Most growth over the next 10 years for genetic counselors is expected to be in hospitals.

Employment Projections Data for Genetic Counselors

Occupational title	SOC Code	Employment, 2012	Projected Employment, 2022	Change, 2012–2022	
				Percent	Numeric
Genetic counselors 29-9092		2,100	3,000	41	900

Source: U.S. Bureau of Labor Statistics, Employment Projections Program

Note: Data are rounded. Go to Occupational Information Included in the OOH *for a discussion of the data in this table.*

Similar Occupations   This table shows a list of occupations with job duties that are similar to those of genetic counselors.

Occupations	Entry-level Education	2012 Pay	Projected Job Growth	Average Annual Openings
Epidemiologists	Master's degree	$65,270	12%	160
Health Educators and Community Health Workers	See "How to Become One"	$43,015	22%	4,740
Medical Scientists	Doctoral or professional degree	$76,980	13%	3,550
Mental Health Counselors and Marriage and Family Therapists	Master's degree	$41,592	29%	8,360
Physicians and Surgeons	Doctoral or professional degree	$182,294	18%	29,630

Job Prospects. Genetic counselors can generally expect favorable job prospects. Ongoing innovations in genetic testing are likely to create demand for certified genetic counselors.

O*NET

➤ Genetic Counselors (29-9092.00)

Contacts for More Information

For information about genetic counselors, certification, and schools offering education in genetic counseling, visit
➤ American Board of Genetic Counseling (www.abgc.net/)

For more information about genetic counseling career requirements and developments in genetics, including licensure, visit
➤ National Society of Genetic Counselors (www.nsgc.org/)

For information about accreditation and schools offering education in genetic counseling, visit
➤ Accreditation Council for Genetic Counseling (http://gceducation. org/Pages/About%20ACGC.aspx)

Home Health Aides

- **2012 Median Pay** .... $20,820 per year
$10.01 per hour

- **Entry-Level Education** .... Less than high school

- **Work Experience in a Related Occupation**............... None

- **On-the-Job Training** ....Short-term on-the-job training

- **Number of Jobs 2012** 875,100

- **Job Outlook, 2012–22** .... 48% (Much faster than average)

- **Employment Change, 2012–22** 424,200

What Home Health Aides Do

Home health aides help people who are disabled, chronically ill, or cognitively impaired. They often help older adults who need assistance. In some states, home health aides may be able to give a client medication or check the client's vital signs under the direction of a nurse or other healthcare practitioner.

Duties. Home health aides typically do the following:

- Help clients in their daily personal tasks, such as bathing or dressing

- Provide basic health-related services according to a client's needs, such as checking vital signs or administering prescribed medication at scheduled times

- Do light housekeeping, such as laundry, washing dishes, and vacuuming in a client's home

- Organize a client's schedule and plan appointments

- Arrange transportation to doctors' offices or for other kinds of outings

- Shop for groceries and prepare meals to a client's dietary specifications

- Provide companionship

Home health aides, unlike personal care aides, typically work for certified home health or hospice agencies that receive government funding and therefore must comply with regulations. They work under the direct supervision of medical professionals, usually registered nurses. These aides keep records of services performed and of clients' conditions and progress. They report changes in clients' conditions to supervisors or case managers. Home health aides also work with therapists and other medical staff.

Depending on their clients' needs, home health aides may provide some basic health-related services, such as checking a client's pulse, temperature, and respiration rate. They may also help with simple prescribed exercises and with giving medications. Occasionally, they change bandages or dressings, give massages, care for skin, or help with braces and artificial limbs. With special training, experienced home health aides also may help with medical equipment such as ventilators, which help clients breathe.

Work Environment

Home health aides held about 875,100 jobs in 2012. They work in a variety of settings.

Most work in a client's home; others work in small group homes or larger care communities. Some home health aides go to the same home every day or week for months or even years. Some visit four or five clients in the same day, while others work only with one client all day. This may involve working with other aides in shifts so that the client always has an aide. They help people in hospices and day services programs, and also help people with disabilities go to work and stay engaged in their communities.

The industries that employed the most home health aides in 2012 were as follows:

Home health care services	37%
Residential care facilities	31
Individual, family, community, and vocational rehabilitation services	18

Work Schedules. Most home health aides worked full time in 2012.

Injuries and Illnesses. Home health aides have a higher rate of injuries and illnesses than the national average. Work as an aide can be physically and emotionally demanding. Aides must guard against back injury because they often move clients into and out of bed, or help them to stand or walk.

In addition, home health aides frequently work with clients who have cognitive impairments or mental health issues and who may display difficult or violent behaviors. Aides also face hazards from minor infections and exposure to communicable diseases, but can avoid infections by following proper procedures.

How to Become One

There is no formal education requirement for home health aides, but most aides have a high school diploma. Home health aides

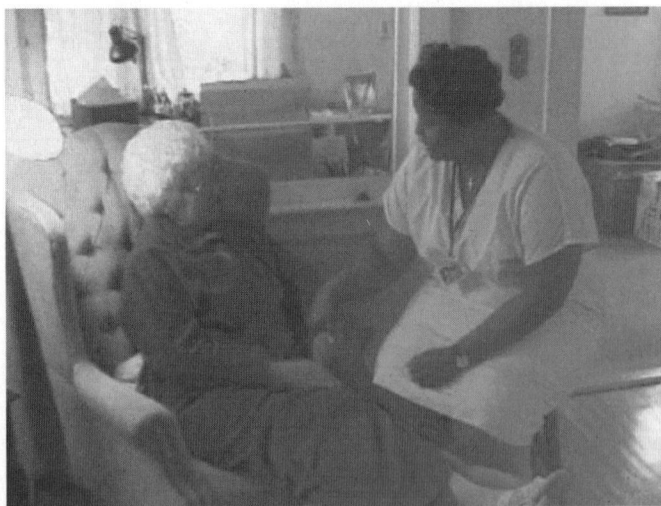

Home health and personal care aides help people in their own homes or in residential facilities.

Median Annual Wages, May 2012

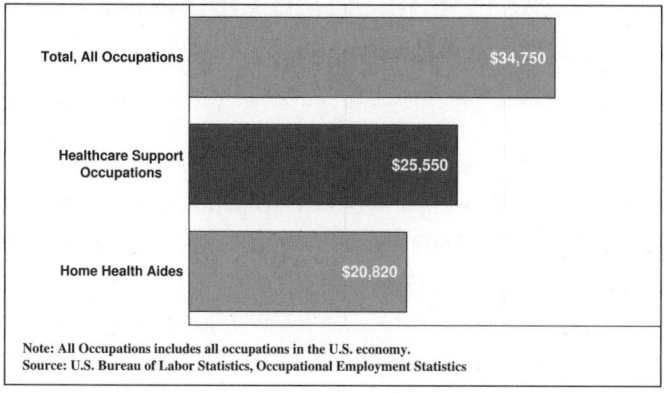

Note: All Occupations includes all occupations in the U.S. economy.
Source: U.S. Bureau of Labor Statistics, Occupational Employment Statistics

Percent Change in Employment, Projected 2012–2022

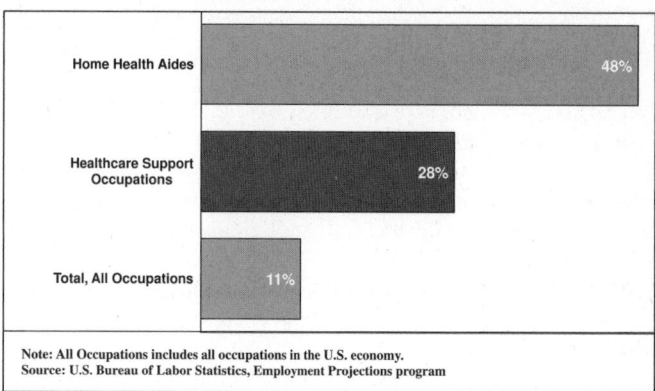

Note: All Occupations includes all occupations in the U.S. economy.
Source: U.S. Bureau of Labor Statistics, Employment Projections program

who work for certified home health or hospice agencies must get formal training and pass a standardized test.

Education. Although a high school diploma or equivalent is not generally required, most home health aides have one before entering the occupation. Some formal education programs may be available from community colleges or vocational schools.

Licenses, Certifications, and Registrations. Home health aides who work for agencies that receive reimbursement from Medicare or Medicaid must get a minimum level of training and pass a competency evaluation or receive state certification. Training includes learning about personal hygiene, reading and recording vital signs, infection control, and basic nutrition. Aides may take a competency exam to become certified without taking any training. These are the minimum requirements by law; additional requirements for certification vary by state.

In some states, the only requirement for employment is on-the-job training, which employers generally provide. Other states require formal training, which is available from community colleges, vocational

schools, elder care programs, and home health care agencies. In addition, states may conduct background checks on prospective aides.

Home health aides can be certified by the National Association for Home Care & Hospice (NAHC). Although certification is not always required, employers prefer to hire certified aides. Certification requires 75 hours of training, observation and documentation of 17 skills demonstrating competency, and passing a written exam.

Training. Home health aides may be trained in housekeeping tasks, such as cooking for clients who have special dietary needs. They learn basic safety techniques, including how to respond in an emergency. In addition, there may be specific training needed for certification if state certification is required.

A competency evaluation may be required to ensure that the home health aide can perform some certain tasks. Clients have their own preferences, and aides may need time to become comfortable working with them.

Employment Projections Data for Home Health Aides

Occupational title	SOC Code	Employment, 2012	Projected Employment, 2022	Change, 2012–2022	
				Percent	Numeric
Home health aides 31-1011		875,100	1,299,300	48	424,200

Source: U.S. Bureau of Labor Statistics, Employment Projections Program

Note: Data are rounded. Go to **Occupational Information Included in the OOH** *for a discussion of the data in this table.*

Similar Occupations   This table shows a list of occupations with job duties that are similar to those of home health aides.

Occupations	Entry-level Education	2012 Pay	Projected Job Growth	Average Annual Openings
Childcare Workers	High school diploma or equivalent	$19,510	14%	57,000
Licensed Practical and Licensed Vocational Nurses	Postsecondary non-degree award	$41,540	25%	36,310
Medical Assistants	Postsecondary non-degree award	$29,370	29%	26,990
Nursing Assistants and Orderlies	See "How to Become One"	$24,404	21%	61,300
Occupational Therapy Assistants and Aides	See "How to Become One"	$47,638	41%	2,560
Personal Care Aides	Less than high school	$19,910	49%	66,600
Physical Therapist Assistants and Aides	See "How to Become One"	$40,539	41%	7,630
Radiation Therapists	Associate's degree	$77,560	24%	840
Registered Nurses	Associate's degree	$65,470	19%	105,260
Social and Human Service Assistants	High school diploma or equivalent	$28,850	22%	17,870

Without additional training, advancement in this occupation is limited.

Important Qualities

Detail oriented. Home health aides must follow specific rules and protocols to help take care of clients.

Interpersonal skills. Home health aides must work closely with their clients. Sometimes, clients are in extreme pain or mental stress, and aides must be sensitive to their emotions. Aides must be cheerful, compassionate, and emotionally stable. They must enjoy helping people.

Physical stamina. Home health aides should be comfortable performing physical tasks. They might need to lift or turn clients who have a disability.

Time-management skills. Clients and their families rely on home health aides. Therefore, it is important that aides follow agreed-upon schedules and arrive at their clients' homes when they are expected.

Pay

The median annual wage for home health aides was $20,820 in May 2012. The median wage is the wage at which half the workers in an occupation earned more than that amount and half earned less. The lowest 10 percent earned less than $16,600, and the top 10 percent earned more than $29,250.

Job Outlook

Employment of home health aides is projected to grow 48 percent from 2012 to 2022, much faster than the average for all occupations.

As the baby-boom population ages and the elderly population grows, the demand for home health aides to provide assistance and companionship will continue to increase. The older population often has health problems and will need help with daily activities.

Elderly and disabled clients increasingly rely on home care as a less expensive alternative to nursing homes or hospitals. Clients who need help with everyday tasks and household chores, rather than medical care, can reduce their medical expenses by returning to their homes.

Another reason for home care is that most clients prefer to be cared for in their homes, where they are most comfortable. Studies have found that home treatment is often more effective than care in a nursing home or hospital.

Job Prospects. Job prospects for home health aides are excellent. This occupation is large and expected to grow very quickly, thus adding many jobs. In addition, the low pay and high emotional demands may cause many workers to leave this occupation, and they will have to be replaced.

O*NET

➤ Home Health Aides (31-1011.00)

Contacts for More Information

For information about voluntary credentials for aides, visit
➤ National Association for Home Care & Hospice (www.nahc.org/)

Licensed Practical and Licensed Vocational Nurses

- **2012 Median Pay** .... $41,540 per year
  $19.97 per hour
- **Entry-Level Education** .... Postsecondary non-degree award
- **Work Experience in a Related Occupation** .... None
- **On-the-Job Training** .... None
- **Number of Jobs 2012** 738,400
- **Job Outlook, 2012–22** .... 25% (Much faster than average)
- **Employment Change, 2012–22** 182,900

What Licensed Practical and Licensed Vocational Nurses Do

Licensed practical nurses (LPNs) and licensed vocational nurses (LVNs) provide basic medical care. They work under the direction of registered nurses and doctors.

Duties. Licensed practical and licensed vocational nurses typically do the following:

- Monitor patients' health–for example, by checking their blood pressure
- Administer basic patient care, including changing bandages and inserting catheters
- Provide for the basic comfort of patients, such as helping them bathe or dress
- Discuss the care they are providing with patients and listen to their concerns
- Report patients' status and concerns to registered nurses and doctors
- Keep records on patients' health

Duties of LPNs and LVNs vary, depending on their work setting and the state in which they work. For example, they may reinforce teaching done by registered nurses regarding how family members should care for a relative; help to deliver, care for, and feed infants; collect samples for testing and do routine laboratory tests; or feed patients who need help eating.

LPNs and LVNs may be limited to doing certain tasks, depending on their state. For example, in some states, LPNs with proper training can give medication or start intravenous (IV) drips, while in other states LPNs cannot perform these tasks. State regulations also govern the extent to which LPNs and LVNs must be directly supervised. For example, an LPN may provide certain forms of care only with instructions from a registered nurse.

In some states, experienced licensed practical and licensed vocational nurses oversee and direct other LPNs or LVNs and unlicensed medical staff.

Work Environment

Licensed practical and licensed vocational nurses (LPNs and LVNs) held about 738,400 jobs in 2012. The industries that employed the most licensed practical and licensed vocational nurses in 2012 were as follows:

Nursing care facilities (skilled nursing facilities) 29%
Hospitals; state, local, and private 20
Offices of physicians 12
Home health care services 11
Residential care facilities 8

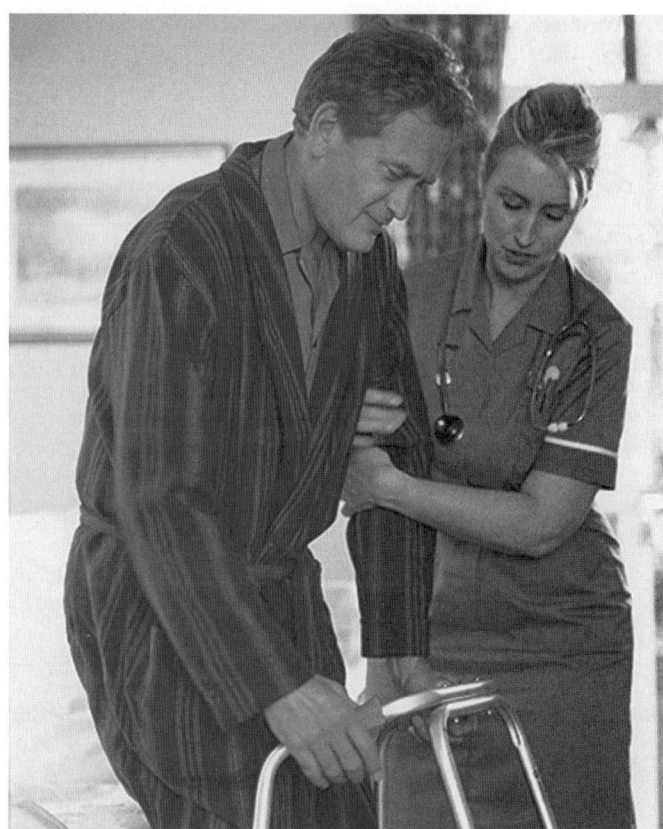

Licensed practical nurses may assist patients with bathing, dressing, standing, and walking.

Licensed practical and licensed vocational nurses work in nursing homes and extended care facilities, hospitals, physicians' offices, and private homes. LPNs and LVNs often wear scrubs, a type of medical clothing that usually consists of a shirt and drawstring pants.

Nurses must often be on their feet for much of the day and may have to lift patients who have trouble moving in bed, standing, or walking. These duties can be stressful, as can dealing with ill and injured people.

Work Schedules. Most licensed practical and licensed vocational nurses work full time, although about 1 in 5 worked part time in 2012. Many LPNs and LVNs work nights, weekends, and holidays, because medical care takes place at all hours. They may be required to work shifts of longer than 8 hours.

How to Become One

Becoming a licensed practical or licensed vocational nurse (LPN or LVN) requires completing an approved educational program. LPNs and LVNs must also have a license.

Education. LPNs and LVNs must complete an approved educational program. These programs award a certificate or diploma and typically take about 1 year to complete, but may take longer. They are commonly found in technical schools and community colleges, though some programs may be available in high schools and hospitals.

Practical nursing programs combine classroom learning in subjects, such as nursing, biology, and pharmacology. All programs also include supervised clinical experience.

Contact state boards of nursing for lists of approved programs.

Licenses, Certifications, and Registrations. After completing a state-approved educational program, prospective LPNs and LVNs can take the National Council Licensure Examination, or NCLEX-PN. In all states, they must pass the exam to get a license and work as an LPN or LVN.

LPNs and LVNs may choose to become certified through professional associations in areas such as gerontology and IV therapy, among others. Certifications show that an LPN or LVN has an advanced level of knowledge about a specific subject.

Important Qualities

Compassion. Licensed practical and licensed vocational nurses must be empathetic and caring toward the people they serve.

Detail oriented. LPNs and LVNs need to be responsible and detail-oriented, because they must make sure that patients get the correct care at the right time.

Interpersonal skills. Interacting with patients and other healthcare providers is a big part of their jobs, so LPNs and LVNs need good interpersonal skills.

Patience. Dealing with sick and injured people may be stressful. LPNs and LVNs should be patient, so they can cope with any stress that stems from providing healthcare to these patients.

Physical stamina. LPNs and LVNs should be comfortable performing physical tasks, such as bending over patients for a long time.

Speaking skills. It is important that LPNs and LVNs be able to communicate effectively. For example, they may need to relay information about a patient's current condition to a registered nurse.

Advancement. With experience, licensed practical and licensed vocational nurses may advance to supervisory positions. Some LPNs and LVNs advance to other healthcare occupations. For

Median Annual Wages, May 2012

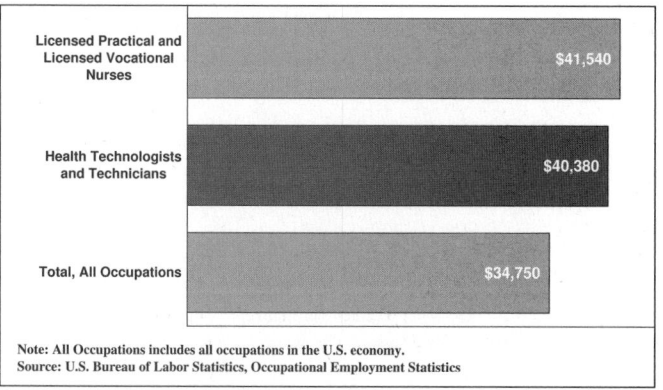

Licensed Practical and Licensed Vocational Nurses	$41,540
Health Technologists and Technicians	$40,380
Total, All Occupations	$34,750

Note: All Occupations includes all occupations in the U.S. economy.
Source: U.S. Bureau of Labor Statistics, Occupational Employment Statistics

Percent Change in Employment, Projected 2012–2022

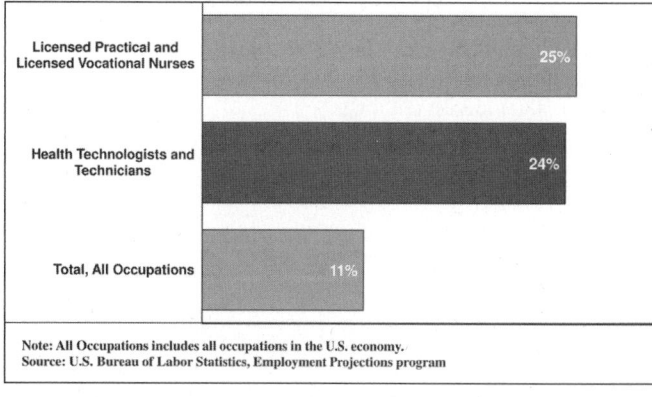

Licensed Practical and Licensed Vocational Nurses	25%
Health Technologists and Technicians	24%
Total, All Occupations	11%

Note: All Occupations includes all occupations in the U.S. economy.
Source: U.S. Bureau of Labor Statistics, Employment Projections program

Employment Projections Data for Licensed Practical and Licensed Vocational Nurses

Occupational title	SOC Code	Employment, 2012	Projected Employment, 2022	Change, 2012–2022	
				Percent	Numeric
Licensed practical and licensed vocational nurses................. 29-2061		738,400	921,300	25	182,900

Source: U.S. Bureau of Labor Statistics, Employment Projections Program

Note: Data are rounded. Go to **Occupational Information Included in the OOH** *for a discussion of the data in this table.*

Similar Occupations This table shows a list of occupations with job duties that are similar to those of licensed practical and licensed vocational nurses.

Occupations	Entry-level Education	2012 Pay	Projected Job Growth	Average Annual Openings
Nursing Assistants and Orderlies	See "How to Become One"	$24,404	21%	61,300
Occupational Therapy Assistants and Aides	See "How to Become One"	$47,638	41%	2,560
Physical Therapist Assistants and Aides	See "How to Become One"	$40,539	41%	7,630
Psychiatric Technicians and Aides	See "How to Become One"	$27,125	5%	3,030
Registered Nurses	Associate's degree	$65,470	19%	105,260
Surgical Technologists	Postsecondary non-degree award	$41,790	30%	3,910

example, an LPN may complete an LPN to RN education program to become a registered nurse.

Pay

The median annual wage for licensed practical and licensed vocational nurses was $41,540 in May 2012. The median wage is the wage at which half the workers in an occupation earned more than that amount and half earned less. The lowest 10 percent earned less than $30,970, and the top 10 percent earned more than $57,360.

Job Outlook

Employment of licensed practical and licensed vocational nurses is projected to grow 25 percent from 2012 to 2022, much faster than the average for all occupations.

As the baby-boom population ages, the overall need for health-care services is expected to increase. LPNs and LVNs will be needed in residential care facilities and in home health environments to care for geriatric patients.

Growing rates of chronic conditions, such as diabetes and obesity will lead to increased demand for LPNs and LVNs in skilled nursing and other extended care facilities. In addition, many procedures that once could be done only in hospitals are now being done outside of hospitals, creating demand in other settings, such as outpatient care centers.

Job Prospects. A large number of licensed practical and licensed vocational nurses are expected to retire over the coming decade, creating potential job openings. Job prospects should also be favorable for LPNs and LVNs, who are willing to work in rural and medically underserved areas.

O*NET

➤ Licensed Practical and Licensed Vocational Nurses (29-2061.00)

Contacts for More Information

For more information about licensed practical or licensed vocational nurses, visit

➤ National Association for Practical Nurse Education and Service (www.napnes.org)

➤ National Federation of Licensed Practical Nurses (www.nflpn.org)

Massage Therapists

- **2012 Median Pay** .... $35,970 per year
  $17.29 per hour
- **Entry-Level Education** .... Postsecondary non-degree award
- **Work Experience in a Related Occupation**............... None
- **On-the-Job Training** .... None
- **Number of Jobs 2012** 132,800
- **Job Outlook, 2012–22** .... 23% (Much faster than average)
- **Employment Change, 2012–22** 30,000

What Massage Therapists Do

Massage therapists treat clients by using touch to manipulate the soft-tissues of the body. With their touch, therapists relieve pain, help rehabilitate injuries, improve circulation, relieve stress, increase relaxation, and aid in the general wellness of clients.

Duties. Massage therapists typically do the following:

- Talk with clients about symptoms, medical history, and desired results
- Evaluate clients to locate painful or tense areas of the body
- Manipulate muscles or other soft tissues of the body
- Provide clients with guidance on stretching, strengthening, overall relaxation, and how to improve their posture
- Document client's condition and progress

Massage therapists use touch to treat clients' injuries and to promote general wellness. They use their hands, fingers, forearms, elbows, and sometimes feet to knead muscles and soft tissues of the body.

Massage therapists may use lotions and oils and massage tables or chairs, when treating a client. A massage can be as short as 5–10 minutes or could last more than an hour.

Therapists talk with clients about what they hope to achieve through massage. Some massage therapists suggest personalized treatment plans for their clients. They also may offer clients

Massage therapists apply pressure to relieve stress and promote health.

information about additional relaxation techniques to practice between sessions.

Massage therapists can specialize in many different types of massage, called modalities. Swedish massage, deep-tissue massage, and sports massage are just a few of the many modalities of massage therapy. Most massage therapists specialize in several modalities, which require different techniques.

Usually, the type of massage given depends on the client's needs and physical condition. For example, therapists may use a special technique for elderly clients that they would not use for athletes. Some forms of massage are given solely to one type of client; for example, prenatal massage is given to pregnant women.

Massage therapists who are self-employed may need to do business-related tasks such as marketing and maintaining financial records. They also may have to buy supplies and do laundry.

Work Environment

Massage therapists held about 132,800 jobs in 2012. About 46 percent of massage therapists were self-employed in 2012.

Massage therapists work in an array of settings, both private and public, such as private offices, spas, hospitals, and fitness centers. Some massage therapists also travel to clients' homes or offices to give a massage. Most massage therapists, especially those who are self-employed, provide their own table or chair, sheets, pillows, and body lotions or oils.

A massage therapist's working conditions depend heavily on the location and what the client wants. For example, a massage meant to help rehabilitate a client with an injury may be conducted in a

well-lit setting with several other clients receiving treatment in the same room. But when giving a massage to help clients relax, massage therapists generally work in dimly lit settings and use candles, incense, and calm, soothing music.

Injuries and Illnesses. Because massage is physically demanding, massage therapists can injure themselves if they do not use the proper techniques. Repetitive-motion problems and fatigue from standing for extended periods are most common.

Therapists can limit these risks by using good body mechanics, spacing sessions properly, exercising, and, in many cases, receiving a massage themselves regularly.

Work Schedules. Many massage therapists work part time; only about 1 out of 3 worked full time in 2012.

Because therapists work by appointment in most cases, their schedules and the number of hours worked each week vary considerably. In addition to giving massages, therapists, especially those who are self-employed, may spend time recording client notes, marketing, booking clients, washing linens, and conducting other general business tasks.

How to Become One

Massage therapists typically complete a postsecondary education program of 500 or more hours of study and experience, although standards and requirements vary greatly by state or other locality. Most states regulate massage therapy and require massage therapists to have a license or certification.

Education. Educational standards and requirements for massage therapists vary greatly by state or other locality. Education programs are typically found in private or public postsecondary institutions. Most programs require at least 500 hours of study to complete; some programs require 1,000 hours or more.

A high school diploma or equivalent degree is usually required for admission. Massage therapy programs generally include both classroom study and hands-on practice of massage techniques. Programs cover subjects such as anatomy; physiology, which is the study of organs and tissues; kinesiology, which is the study of motion and body mechanics; pathology, which is the study of disease; business management; and ethics.

Programs may concentrate on certain modalities, or specialties, of massage. Several programs also offer job placement and continuing education. Both full-time and part-time programs are available.

Licenses, Certifications, and Registrations. In 2012, 44 states and the District of Columbia regulated massage therapy. Although not all states license massage therapy, they may have regulations at the local level.

Median Annual Wages, May 2012

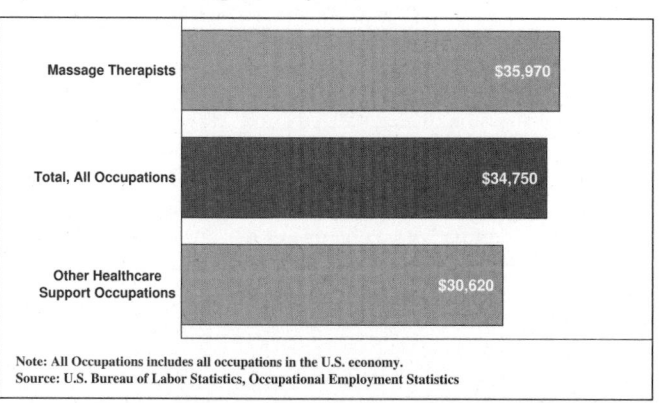

Note: All Occupations includes all occupations in the U.S. economy.
Source: U.S. Bureau of Labor Statistics, Occupational Employment Statistics

Percent Change in Employment, Projected 2012–2022

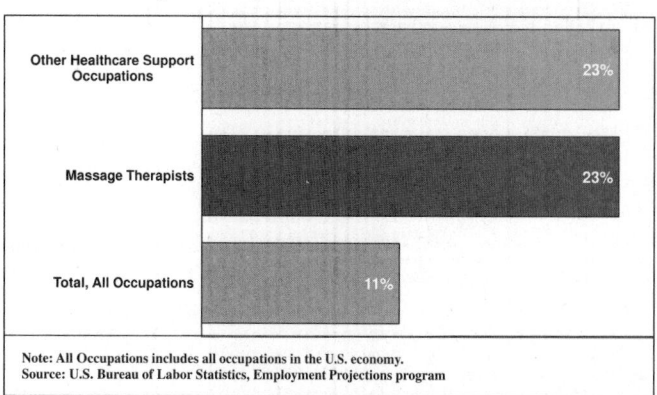

Note: All Occupations includes all occupations in the U.S. economy.
Source: U.S. Bureau of Labor Statistics, Employment Projections program

Employment Projections Data for Massage Therapists

Occupational title	SOC Code	Employment, 2012	Projected Employment, 2022	Change, 2012–2022	
				Percent	Numeric
Massage therapists	31-9011	132,800	162,800	23	30,000

Source: U.S. Bureau of Labor Statistics, Employment Projections Program

Note: Data are rounded. Go to **Occupational Information Included in the OOH** *for a discussion of the data in this table.*

Similar Occupations   This table shows a list of occupations with job duties that are similar to those of massage therapists.

Occupations	Entry-level Education	2012 Pay	Projected Job Growth	Average Annual Openings
Athletic Trainers and Exercise Physiologists	Bachelor's degree	$42,676	19%	1,240
Physical Therapist Assistants and Aides	See "How to Become One"	$40,539	41%	7,630
Physical Therapists	Doctoral or professional degree	$79,860	36%	12,370

In states with massage therapy regulations, workers must get a license or certification after graduating from an approved program and before practicing massage. Passing an exam is usually required for licensure.

The exam may be solely a state exam or one of two nationally recognized tests: the Massage and Bodywork Licensing Examination (MBLEx) and the National Certification Board for Therapeutic Massage & Bodywork (NCBTMB). Massage therapy licensure boards decide which certifications and tests to accept on a state-by-state basis.

Therapists also may need to pass a background check and be certified in cardiopulmonary resuscitation (CPR). Many states require massage therapists to complete continuing education credits and to renew their license periodically. Those wishing to practice massage therapy should look into legal requirements for the state and other locality in which they intend to practice.

Important Qualities

Communication skills. Massage therapists need to listen carefully to clients in order to understand what they want to achieve through massage sessions.

Decision-making skills. Massage therapists must evaluate each client's needs and recommend the best treatment on the basis of that person's needs.

Empathy. Massage therapists must give clients a positive experience, which requires building trust between therapist and client. Making clients feel comfortable is necessary for therapists to expand their client base.

Physical stamina. Massage therapists may give several treatments during a workday and have to stay on their feet throughout massage appointments.

Physical strength and dexterity. Massage therapists must be strong and able to exert pressure through a variety of movements of the arms and hands when manipulating a client's muscles.

Pay

The median annual wage for massage therapists was $35,970 in May 2012. The median wage is the wage at which half the workers in an occupation earned more than that amount and half earned less. The lowest 10 percent earned less than $18,420, and the top 10 percent earned more than $70,140.

Most massage therapists earn a combination of wages and tips.

Job Outlook

Employment of massage therapists is projected to grow 23 percent from 2012 to 2022, much faster than the average for all occupations. Continued growth in the demand for massage services will lead to new openings for massage therapists.

As an increasing number of states adopt licensing requirements and standards for therapists, the practice of massage is likely to be respected and accepted by more people as a way to treat pain and to improve overall wellness. Similarly, as more healthcare providers understand the benefits of massage, demand will increase as these services become part of treatment plans.

Massage also offers specific benefits to particular groups of people whose continued demand for massage services will lead to overall growth for the occupation. For example, some sports teams hire massage therapists to help give their athletes relief from pain and to rehabilitate clients with injuries.

Demand for massage services will grow as the baby-boom generation seeks these services as a way to help maintain their health as they age. Older people in nursing homes or assisted-living facilities also are finding benefits from massage, such as increased energy levels and reduced health problems. Demand for massage therapy should grow among older age groups because they increasingly are enjoying longer, more active lives.

In addition, the number of massage clinic franchises has increased in recent years. Many franchised clinics offer more affordable massages than those provided at spas and resorts, making massage services available to a wider range of customers.

However, demand for massage services may be limited by overall state of the economy. During tough economic times, both the number of people who seek massage therapy and the frequency of their massages may decline.

Job Prospects. In states that regulate massage therapy, opportunities should be available to those who complete formal programs and pass a professionally recognized exam. However, new massage therapists should expect to work only part time until they can build their own client base.

Because referrals are an important source of work for massage therapists, marketing and networking will increase the number of job opportunities. Joining a professional association also can help build strong contacts and further increase the likelihood of steady work.

It may also be helpful for massage therapists who are seeking to attract new clients to complete education programs in specific modalities.

O*NET

➤ Massage Therapists (31-9011.00)

Contacts for More Information

For more information about careers in massage therapy, visit

➤ Associated Bodywork & Massage Professionals (www.abmp.com/home/)
➤ American Massage Therapy Association (www.amtamassage.org)

For more information on national testing and national certification, visit

➤ Federation of State Massage Therapy Boards (www.fsmtb.org)
➤ National Certification Board for Therapeutic Massage & Bodywork (www.ncbtmb.org)

Medical and Clinical Laboratory Technologists and Technicians

- **2012 Median Pay** .... $47,820 per year
  $22.99 per hour
- **Entry-Level Education** ....See "How to Become One"
- **Work Experience in a Related Occupation**............... None
- **On-the-Job Training** .... None
- **Number of Jobs 2012** 325,800
- **Job Outlook, 2012–22** .... 22% (Much faster than average)
- **Employment Change, 2012–22** 70,600

What Medical and Clinical Laboratory Technologists and Technicians Do

Medical laboratory technologists (commonly known as medical laboratory scientists) and medical laboratory technicians collect samples and perform tests to analyze body fluids, tissue, and other substances. Medical laboratory technologists perform complex medical laboratory tests; medical laboratory technicians perform routine medical laboratory tests.

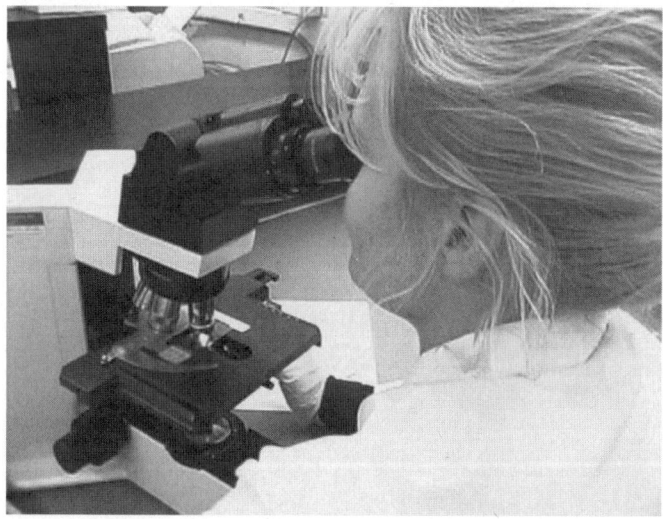

Clinical laboratory personnel examine and test body fluids and cells.

Duties. Medical laboratory technologists and technicians typically do the following:

- Analyze body fluids, such as blood, urine, and tissue samples, and record normal or abnormal findings
- Study blood samples for use in transfusions by identifying the number of cells, the cell morphology or the blood group, blood type, and compatibility with other blood types
- Operate sophisticated laboratory equipment, such as microscopes and cell counters
- Use automated equipment and computerized instruments capable of performing a number of tests at the same time
- Log data from medical tests and enter results into a patient's medical record
- Discuss results and findings of laboratory tests and procedures with physicians
- Supervise or train medical laboratory technicians

Both technicians and technologists perform tests and procedures that physicians and surgeons or other healthcare personnel order. However, technologists perform more complex tests and laboratory procedures than technicians do. For example, technologists may prepare specimens and perform manual tests that are based on detailed instructions, whereas technicians perform routine tests that may be more automated. Medical laboratory technicians usually work under the general supervision of medical laboratory technologists or laboratory managers.

Technologists in small laboratories perform many types of tests; in large laboratories, they generally specialize. The following are examples of types of specialized medical laboratory technologists:

Blood bank technologists, or *immunohematology technologists*, collect blood, classify it by type, and prepare blood and its components for transfusions.

Clinical chemistry technologists prepare specimens and analyze the chemical and hormonal contents of body fluids.

Cytotechnologists prepare slides of body cells and examine these cells with a microscope for abnormalities that may signal the beginning of a cancerous growth.

Immunology technologists examine elements of the human immune system and its response to foreign bodies.

Microbiology technologists examine and identify bacteria and other microorganisms.

Molecular biology technologists perform complex protein and nucleic acid tests on cell samples.

Like technologists, medical laboratory technicians may work in several areas of the laboratory or specialize in one particular area. For example, histotechnicians cut and stain tissue specimens for pathologists, who are doctors who study the cause and development of diseases at a microscopic level.

Technologists and technicians often specialize after they have worked in a particular area for a long time or have received advanced education or training in that area.

Work Environment

Medical laboratory technologists held about 164,300 jobs in 2012. Medical laboratory technicians held about 161,500 jobs in 2012.

The industries that employed the most medical laboratory technologists and technicians in 2012 were as follows:

General medical and surgical hospitals;
    state, local, and private.. 50%
Medical and diagnostic laboratories 17
Offices of physicians... 10

Median Annual Wages, May 2012

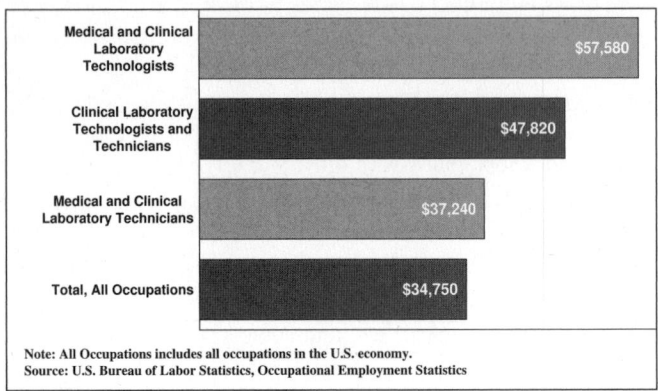

Note: All Occupations includes all occupations in the U.S. economy.
Source: U.S. Bureau of Labor Statistics, Occupational Employment Statistics

Percent Change in Employment, Projected 2012–2022

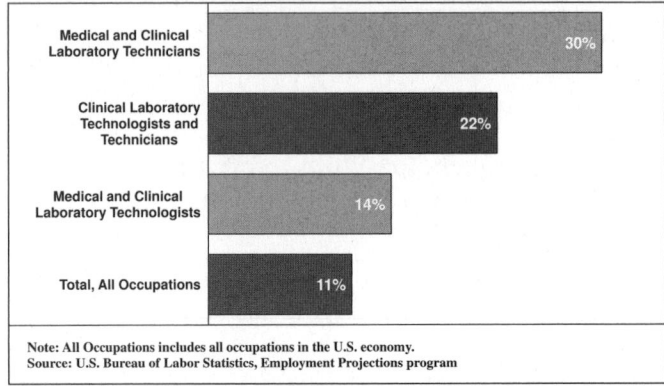

Note: All Occupations includes all occupations in the U.S. economy.
Source: U.S. Bureau of Labor Statistics, Employment Projections program

Colleges, universities, and professional schools;
state, local, and private..5

Work Schedules. Most medical laboratory technologists and technicians work full time. Technologists and technicians who work in facilities that operate around the clock, such as hospitals and some independent laboratories, may work evening, weekend, or overnight hours.

Medical laboratory personnel are trained to work with infectious specimens or with materials that produce fumes. When they follow proper methods to control infection and sterilize equipment, few hazards exist. They wear protective masks, gloves, and goggles for their safety and protection.

Technologists and technicians can be on their feet for long periods, and they may need to lift or turn disabled patients to collect samples.

How to Become One

Medical laboratory technologists typically need a bachelor's degree. Technicians usually need an associate's degree or a postsecondary certificate. Some states require technologists and technicians to be licensed.

Education. Universities and hospitals offer medical technology programs. An entry-level job for technologists usually requires a bachelor's degree in medical technology or life sciences.

A bachelor's degree program in medical laboratory technology includes courses in chemistry, biology, microbiology, mathematics, and statistics, as well as courses in clinical laboratory skills, management, and education. This degree often is known as a medical laboratory scientist degree.

The courses may be offered through a hospital-based program that students attend during their senior year of college. College graduates who major in other sciences and meet a program's prerequisites, such as having completed required courses in biology and chemistry, also may apply to a medical laboratory science program.

Medical laboratory technicians often complete an associate's degree program in clinical laboratory science. A limited number of 1-year certificate programs are available from hospitals for those who already have a degree in a related field, such as nursing. The Armed Forces and vocational or technical schools also may offer certificate programs for medical laboratory technicians. The technician coursework addresses the theoretical and practical aspects of each of the major laboratory disciplines.

High school students who are interested in pursuing a career in the medical laboratory sciences should take courses in chemistry, biology, and mathematics.

Licenses, Certifications, and Registrations. Some states require laboratory personnel to be licensed or registered. To be licensed, a technologist often needs a bachelor's degree and must pass an

Employment Projections Data for Medical and Clinical Laboratory Technologists and Technicians

Occupational title	SOC Code	Employment, 2012	Projected Employment, 2022	Change, 2012–2022 Percent	Change, 2012–2022 Numeric
Clinical laboratory technologists and technicians 29-2010		325,800	396,500	22	70,600
Medical and clinical laboratory technologists.................... 29-2011		164,300	187,100	14	22,700
Medical and clinical laboratory technicians 29-2012		161,500	209,400	30	47,900

Source: U.S. Bureau of Labor Statistics, Employment Projections Program

Note: Data are rounded. Go to **Occupational Information Included in the OOH** *for a discussion of the data in this table.*

Similar Occupations   This table shows a list of occupations with job duties that are similar to those of medical and clinical laboratory technologists and technicians.

Occupations	Entry-level Education	2012 Pay	Projected Job Growth	Average Annual Openings
Biological Technicians	Bachelor's degree	$39,750	10%	3,210
Chemical Technicians	Associate's degree	$42,920	9%	2,160
Chemists and Materials Scientists	Bachelor's degree	$73,247	6%	3,040
Veterinary Technologists and Technicians	Associate's degree	$30,290	29%	3,340

exam. However, requirements vary by state and specialty. For specific requirements, contact state departments of health or boards of occupational licensing.

Certification of medical laboratory technologists and technicians is required for licensure in some states and by some employers. Medical laboratory technologists and technicians can obtain a general certification as a medical laboratory technologist or technician, respectively, or a certification in a specialty, such as cytotechnology or medical biology. Most credentialing institutions require that technologists complete an accredited education program in order to qualify to sit for an examination. Although certification is not required to enter the occupation in all cases, employers typically prefer to hire certified technologists and technicians.

Important Qualities

Ability to use technology. Medical laboratory technologists and technicians must understand how to operate complex machinery.

Detail oriented. Medical laboratory technologists and technicians must follow exact instructions from physicians in order to perform correct tests or procedures.

Dexterity. Medical laboratory technologists and technicians require skill while working with their hands. They work closely with needles and precise laboratory instruments and must be able to handle these tools effectively.

Physical stamina. Medical laboratory technologists and technicians may work on their feet for long periods while collecting samples. They may need to lift or turn disabled patients to collect samples for testing.

Advancement. After additional education, work experience, or certification, technologists and technicians may specialize in one of many areas of laboratory science, such as immunology, histotechnology, or clinical chemistry.

Pay

The median annual wage for medical laboratory technologists was $57,580 in May 2012. The median wage is the wage at which half the workers in an occupation earned more than that amount and half earned less. The lowest 10 percent earned less than $39,580, and the highest 10 percent earned more than $78,900.

The median annual wage for medical laboratory technicians was $37,240 in May 2012. The lowest 10 percent earned less than $24,790, and the highest 10 percent earned more than $57,710.

Job Outlook

Employment of medical laboratory technologists is projected to grow 14 percent from 2012 to 2022, about as fast as the average for all occupations. Employment of medical laboratory technicians is projected to grow 30 percent from 2012 to 2022, much faster than the average for all occupations.

An increase in the aging population will lead to a greater need to diagnose medical conditions, such as cancer or type 2 diabetes, through laboratory procedures. Medical laboratory technologists and technicians will be in demand, to use and maintain the equipment needed for diagnosis and treatment.

Federal health legislation will increase the number of patients who have access to health insurance, increasing patient access to medical care. As a result, demand for the services of laboratory personnel will grow.

O*NET

➤ Medical and Clinical Laboratory Technologists (29-2011.00)
➤ Cytogenetic Technologists (29-2011.01)
➤ Cytotechnologists (29-2011.02)
➤ Histotechnologists and Histologic Technicians (29-2011.03)
➤ Medical and Clinical Laboratory Technicians (29-2012.00)

Contacts for More Information

For more information about medical laboratory technologists and technicians, visit

➤ American Society for Clinical Laboratory Science (www.ascls.org)
➤ American Society of Cytopathology (www.cytopathology.org)

For a list of accredited and approved educational programs for medical laboratory personnel, visit

➤ National Accrediting Agency for Clinical Laboratory Sciences (www.naacls.org)

For information on certification, visit

➤ American Association of Bioanalysts (www.aab.org)
➤ American Medical Technologists (www.amt1.com)
➤ American Society for Clinical Pathology (www.ascp.org)

Medical Assistants

- **2012 Median Pay** .... $29,370 per year
  $14.12 per hour
- **Entry-Level Education** .... Postsecondary non-degree award
- **Work Experience in a Related Occupation** .... None
- **On-the-Job Training** .... None
- **Number of Jobs 2012** 560,800
- **Job Outlook, 2012–22** .... 29% (Much faster than average)
- **Employment Change, 2012–22** 162,900

What Medical Assistants Do

Medical assistants complete administrative and clinical tasks in the offices of physicians, podiatrists, chiropractors, and other health practitioners. Their duties vary with the location, specialty, and size of the practice.

Duties. Medical assistants typically do the following:

- Take and record patient history and personal information
- Measure vital signs
- Help the physician with patient examinations
- Give patients injections as directed by the physician
- Schedule patient appointments
- Prepare blood for laboratory tests

Medical assistants take and record patients' personal information. They must be able to keep that information confidential and discuss it only with other medical personnel who are involved in treating the patient.

Electronic health records (EHRs) are changing medical assistants' jobs. More and more physicians are adopting EHRs, moving all their patient information online. Assistants need to learn the EHR software that their office uses.

Medical assistants should not be confused with physician assistants, who examine, diagnose, and treat patients under a physician's supervision.

In larger practices or hospitals, medical assistants may specialize in either administrative or clinical work.

Administrative medical assistants often fill out insurance forms or code patients' medical information. They often answer telephones and schedule patient appointments. Assistants may work closely with hospital administrators and laboratory services. Some assistants buy and store supplies and equipment for the office.

Clinical medical assistants have different duties, depending on the state where they work. They may do basic laboratory tests, dispose of contaminated supplies, and sterilize medical instruments. They may have additional responsibilities, such as instructing patients about medication or special diets, preparing patients for X-rays, removing stitches, drawing blood, or changing dressings.

Some medical assistants specialize according to the type of medical office where they work. The following are examples of specialized medical assistants:

Ophthalmic medical assistants and optometric assistants help ophthalmologists and optometrists, respectively, provide eye care. They show patients how to insert, remove, and care for contact lenses. Ophthalmic medical assistants also may help an ophthalmologist in surgery.

Podiatric medical assistants work closely with podiatrists (foot doctors). They may make castings of feet, expose and develop X-rays, and help podiatrists in surgery.

Work Environment

Medical assistants held about 560,800 jobs in 2012. Most of these assistants work in physicians' offices and other healthcare facilities. In 2012, more than half of all medical assistants worked in physicians' offices.

Work Schedules. Most medical assistants work full time. Some work evenings or weekends to cover shifts in medical facilities that are always open.

How to Become One

Most medical assistants have postsecondary education such as a certificate. Others enter the occupation with a high school diploma and learn through on-the-job training.

Education. High school students interested in a career as a medical assistant should take courses in biology, chemistry, and anatomy.

Medical assistants typically graduate from postsecondary education programs, and employers may prefer to hire assistants who have completed these programs. Programs for medical assisting are available from community colleges, vocational schools, technical schools, and universities and take about 1 year to complete. These programs usually lead to a certificate or diploma. Some community and junior colleges offer 2-year programs that lead to an associate's degree. All programs have classroom and laboratory portions that include lessons in anatomy and medical terminology.

Some medical assistants have a high school diploma or equivalent and learn their duties on the job.

There are no formal educational requirements for becoming a medical assistant in most states. Some states require assistants to

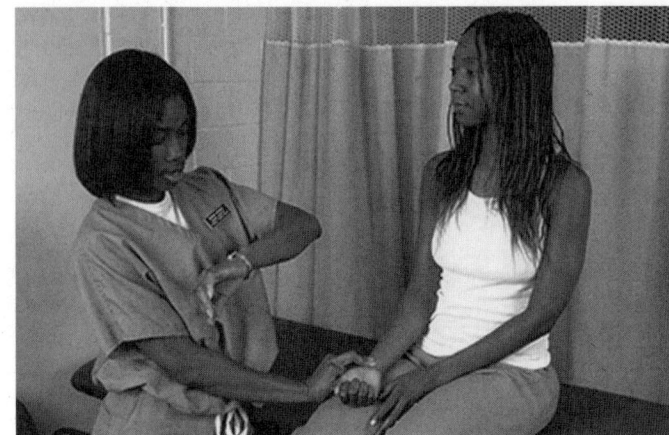

Medical assistants often take medical histories and record vital signs of patients.

graduate from an accredited program, pass an exam, or both to do advanced tasks, such as taking X-rays and giving injections.

Important Qualities

Analytical skills. Medical assistants must be able to understand and follow medical charts and diagnoses. They may be required to code a patient's medical records for billing purposes.

Detail oriented. Medical assistants need to be precise when taking vital signs or recording patient information. Physicians and insurance companies rely on accurate records.

Interpersonal skills. Medical assistants need to be able to discuss patient information with other medical personnel, such as physicians. They often interact with patients who may be in pain or in distress, so they need to be able to act in a calm and professional manner.

Technical skills. Medical assistants should be able to use basic clinical instruments so they can take a patient's vital signs, such as heart rate and blood pressure.

Training. Medical assistants who do not have postsecondary education learn their skills through on-the-job training. Physicians or other medical assistants may teach a new assistant medical terminology, the names of the instruments, how to do daily tasks, how to interact with patients, and other tasks that help keep an office running smoothly. Medical assistants also learn how to code both paper and electronic health records and how to record patient information. It can take several months for an assistant to complete training, depending on the facility.

Licenses, Certifications, and Registrations. Medical assistants are not required to be certified. However, employers prefer to hire certified assistants.

Median Annual Wages, May 2012

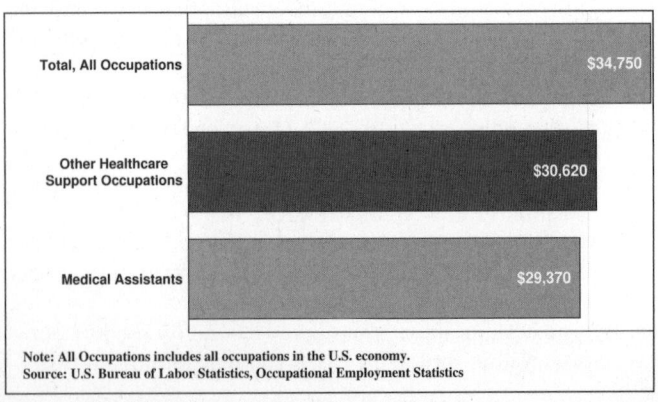

Total, All Occupations	$34,750
Other Healthcare Support Occupations	$30,620
Medical Assistants	$29,370

Note: All Occupations includes all occupations in the U.S. economy.
Source: U.S. Bureau of Labor Statistics, Occupational Employment Statistics

Percent Change in Employment, Projected 2012–2022

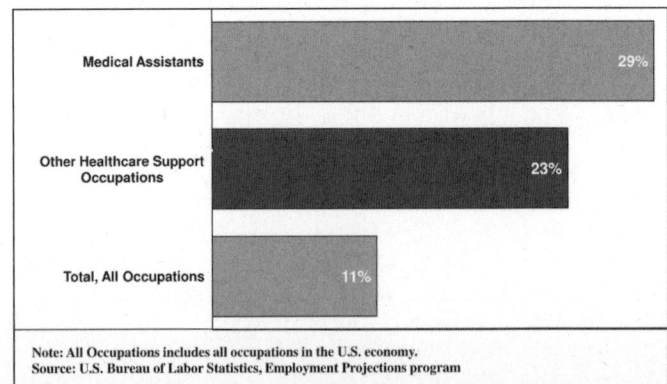

Medical Assistants	29%
Other Healthcare Support Occupations	23%
Total, All Occupations	11%

Note: All Occupations includes all occupations in the U.S. economy.
Source: U.S. Bureau of Labor Statistics, Employment Projections program

Employment Projections Data for Medical Assistants

Occupational title	SOC Code	Employment, 2012	Projected Employment, 2022	Change, 2012–2022	
				Percent	Numeric
Medical assistants	31-9092	560,800	723,700	29	162,900

Source: U.S. Bureau of Labor Statistics, Employment Projections Program

Note: Data are rounded. Go to Occupational Information Included in the OOH *for a discussion of the data in this table.*

Similar Occupations   This table shows a list of occupations with job duties that are similar to those of medical assistants.

Occupations	Entry-level Education	2012 Pay	Projected Job Growth	Average Annual Openings
Dental Assistants	Postsecondary non-degree award	$34,500	25%	13,720
Dental Hygienists	Associate's degree	$70,210	33%	11,350
Licensed Practical and Licensed Vocational Nurses	Postsecondary non-degree award	$41,540	25%	36,310
Medical Records and Health Information Technicians	Postsecondary non-degree award	$34,160	22%	9,040
Nursing Assistants and Orderlies	See "How to Become One"	$24,404	21%	61,300
Occupational Therapy Assistants and Aides	See "How to Become One"	$47,638	41%	2,560
Pharmacy Technicians	High school diploma or equivalent	$29,320	20%	10,590
Physical Therapist Assistants and Aides	See "How to Become One"	$40,539	41%	7,630
Psychiatric Technicians and Aides	See "How to Become One"	$27,125	5%	3,030

Several organizations offer certification. Some require the assistant to pass an exam, and others require graduation from an accredited program. In most cases, an applicant must be at least 18 years old before applying for certification.

The National Commission for Certifying Agencies, part of the Institute for Credentialing Excellence, accredits five certifications for medical assistants:

- Certified Medical Assistant (CMA) from the American Association of Medical Assistants (AAMA)

- Registered Medical Assistant (RMA) from American Medical Technologists

- National Certified Medical Assistant (NCMA) from the National Center for Competency Testing

- Certified Clinical Medical Assistant (CCMA) from the National Healthcareer Association

- Certified Medical Administrative Assistant (CMAA) from the National Healthcareer Association

Pay

The median annual wage for medical assistants was $29,370 in May 2012. The median wage is the wage at which half the workers in an occupation earned more than that amount and half earned less. The lowest 10 percent earned less than $21,080, and the top 10 percent earned more than $41,570.

Job Outlook

Employment of medical assistants is projected to grow 29 percent from 2012 to 2022, much faster than the average for all occupations. The growth of the aging baby-boom population will continue to spur demand for preventive medical services, which are often provided by physicians. As their practices expand, physicians will hire more assistants to perform routine administrative and clinical duties, allowing the physicians to see more patients.

An increasing number of group practices, clinics, and other healthcare facilities need support workers, particularly medical assistants, to do both administrative and clinical duties. Medical assistants work mostly in primary care, a steadily growing sector of the healthcare industry. In addition, federal health legislation will expand the number of patients who have access to health insurance, increasing patient access to medical care.

Additional demand also is expected because of new and changing tasks for medical assistants as part of the medical team. As more and more physicians' practices switch to electronic health records (EHRs), medical assistants' job responsibilities will continue to change. Assistants will need to become familiar with EHR computer software, including maintaining EHR security and analyzing electronic data, to improve healthcare information.

Job Prospects. Medical assistants who earn certification may have better job prospects.

O*NET

➤ Medical Assistants (31-9092.00)

Contacts for More Information

For more information about becoming a medical assistant, including information on certification, visit

➤ American Association of Medical Assistants (www.aama-ntl.org)
➤ American Medical Technologists (www.americanmedtech.org/default.aspx)
➤ National Center for Competency Testing (www.ncctinc.com/)
➤ National Healthcareer Association (www.nhanow.com)
➤ Institute for Credentialing Excellence (www.credentialingexcellence.org/)
➤ American Optometric Association (www.aoa.org)
➤ American Society of Podiatric Medical Assistants (www.aspma.org)

➤ Joint Commission on Allied Health Personnel in Ophthalmology (www.jcahpo.org)

For lists of accredited educational programs in medical assisting, visit

➤ Commission on Accreditation of Allied Health Education Programs (www.caahep.org)

➤ Accrediting Bureau of Health Education School (www.abhes.org)

Medical Records and Health Information Technicians

- **2012 Median Pay** .... $34,160 per year
$16.42 per hour
- **Entry-Level Education** .... Postsecondary non-degree award
- **Work Experience in a Related Occupation** .... None
- **On-the-Job Training** .... None
- **Number of Jobs 2012** 186,300
- **Job Outlook, 2012–22** .... 22% (Much faster than average)
- **Employment Change, 2012–22** 41,100

What Medical Records and Health Information Technicians Do

Medical records and health information technicians, commonly referred to as health information technicians, organize and manage health information data by ensuring its quality, accuracy, accessibility, and security in both paper and electronic systems. They use various classification systems to code and categorize patient information for insurance reimbursement purposes, for databases and registries, and to maintain patients' medical and treatment histories.

Duties. Health information technicians typically do the following:

- Review patient records for timeliness, completeness, accuracy, and appropriateness of data
- Organize and maintain data for clinical databases and registries
- Track patient outcomes for quality assessment
- Use classification software to assign clinical codes for reimbursement and data analysis
- Electronically record data for collection, storage, analysis, retrieval, and reporting
- Protect patients' health information for confidentiality, authorized access for treatment, and data security

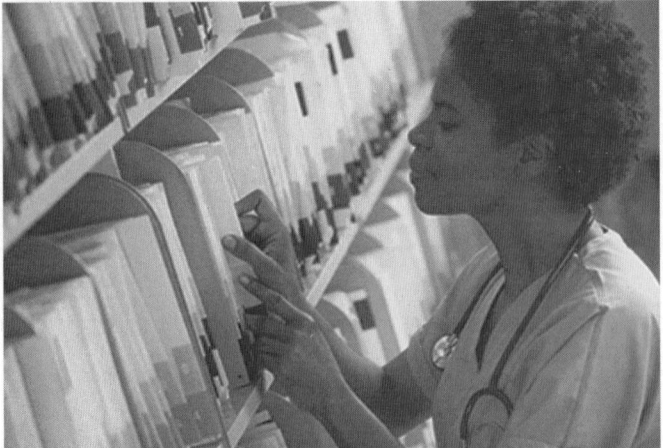

Some medical records and health information technicians specialize in coding medical information for insurance purposes.

All health information technicians document patients' health information, including their medical history, symptoms, examination and test results, treatments, and other information about healthcare services that are provided to patients. Their duties vary with the size of the facility in which they work.

Although health information technicians do not provide direct patient care, they work regularly with registered nurses and other healthcare professionals. They meet with these workers to clarify diagnoses or to get additional information to make sure that records are complete and accurate.

The increasing use of electronic health records (EHRs) will continue to change the job responsibilities of health information technicians. Federal legislation provides incentives for physicians' offices and hospitals to implement EHR systems into their practice. This will lead to continued adoption of this software in these facilities. Technicians will need to be familiar with, or be able to learn, EHR computer software, follow EHR security and privacy practices, and analyze electronic data to improve healthcare information as more healthcare providers and hospitals adopt EHR systems.

Health information technicians can specialize in many aspects of health information. Some work as medical coders, sometimes called coding specialists, or as cancer registrars.

Medical coders typically do the following:

- Review patient information for preexisting conditions such as diabetes
- Retrieve patient records for medical personnel

Median Annual Wages, May 2012

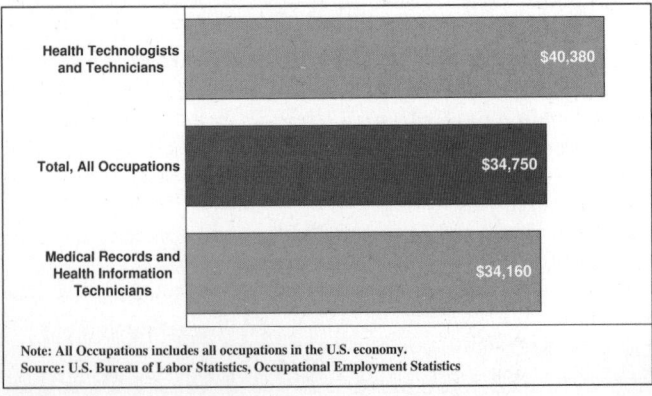

Health Technologists and Technicians	$40,380
Total, All Occupations	$34,750
Medical Records and Health Information Technicians	$34,160

Note: All Occupations includes all occupations in the U.S. economy.
Source: U.S. Bureau of Labor Statistics, Occupational Employment Statistics

Percent Change in Employment, Projected 2012–2022

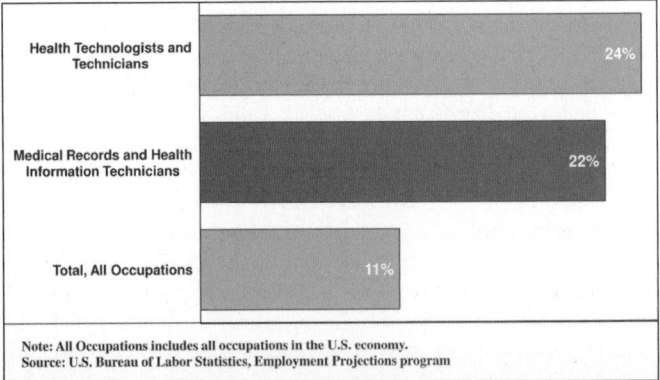

Health Technologists and Technicians	24%
Medical Records and Health Information Technicians	22%
Total, All Occupations	11%

Note: All Occupations includes all occupations in the U.S. economy.
Source: U.S. Bureau of Labor Statistics, Employment Projections program

Employment Projections Data for Medical Records and Health Information Technicians

Occupational title	SOC Code	Employment, 2012	Projected Employment, 2022	Change, 2012–2022	
				Percent	Numeric
Medical records and health information technicians	29-2071	186,300	227,500	22	41,100

Source: U.S. Bureau of Labor Statistics, Employment Projections Program

Note: Data are rounded. Go to **Occupational Information Included in the OOH** *for a discussion of the data in this table.*

- Work as a liaison between the health clinician and billing offices

Cancer registrars typically do the following:

- Review patient records and pathology reports for completeness and accuracy
- Assign classification codes to represent the diagnosis and treatment of cancers and benign tumors
- Conduct annual follow-ups to track treatment, survival, and recovery
- Analyze and compile cancer patient information for research purposes
- Maintain facility, regional, and national databases of cancer patients

Work Environment

Health information technicians held about 186,300 jobs in 2012. Most health information technicians work in hospitals or physicians' offices. Others work in nursing care facilities or for government entities. Technicians typically work at desks or in offices and may spend many hours in front of computer monitors.

The industries that employed the most health information technicians in 2012 were as follows:

General medical and surgical hospitals; state, local, and private...	37%
Offices of physicians..	22
Nursing and residential care facilities	9
Government..	5

Work Schedules. Most health information technicians work full time. In healthcare facilities that are always open, such as hospitals, technicians may work evening or overnight shifts.

How to Become One

Health information technicians typically need a postsecondary certificate to enter the occupation, although they may have an associate's degree. Many employers also require professional certification.

Education. Postsecondary certificate and associate's degree programs in health information technology typically include courses in medical terminology, anatomy and physiology, health data requirements and standards, classification and coding systems, healthcare reimbursement methods, healthcare statistics, and computer systems. Applicants to health information technology programs increase their chances of admission by taking high school courses in health, computer science, math, and biology.

Important Qualities

Analytical skills. Health information technicians must be able to understand and follow medical records and diagnoses, and then decide how best to code them in a patient's medical records.

Detail oriented. Health information technicians must be accurate when recording and coding patient information.

Integrity. Health information technicians work with patient data that are required, by law, to be kept confidential. They must exercise caution when working with this information in order to protect patient confidentiality.

Interpersonal skills. Health information technicians need to be able to discuss patient information, discrepancies, and data requirements with other professionals such as physicians and finance personnel.

Technical skills. Health information technicians must be able to use coding and classification software and the EHR system that their healthcare organization or physician practice has adopted.

Licenses, Certifications, and Registrations. Most employers prefer to hire health information technicians who have professional certification. A health information technician can earn certification from several organizations. Some organizations base certification on passing an exam. Others require graduation from an accredited program. Once certified, technicians typically must renew their certification regularly and take continuing education courses. Certifications include Registered Health Information Technician (RHIT) and Certified Tumor Registrar (CTR), among others. Many coding certifications require coding experience in a work setting.

Advancement. Health information technicians may advance to other health information positions by receiving additional education and certifications. Technicians can advance to a medical or health services manager after completing a bachelor's or master's degree program and taking the required certification courses. Requirements vary by facility.

Pay

The median annual wage for health information technicians was $34,160 in May 2012. The median wage is the wage at which half the workers in an occupation earned more than that amount and half earned less. The lowest 10 percent earned less than $22,250, and the top 10 percent earned more than $56,200.

Similar Occupations   This table shows a list of occupations with job duties that are similar to those of medical records and health information technicians.

Occupations	Entry-level Education	2012 Pay	Projected Job Growth	Average Annual Openings
Medical and Health Services Managers	Bachelor's degree	$88,580	23%	14,990
Medical Transcriptionists	Postsecondary non-degree award	$34,020	8%	2,240

Job Outlook

Employment of health information technicians is projected to grow 22 percent from 2012 to 2022, much faster than the average for all occupations. The demand for health services is expected to increase as the population ages. An aging population will need more medical tests, treatments, and procedures. This will mean more claims for reimbursement from insurance companies. Additional records, coupled with widespread use of electronic health records (EHRs) by all types of healthcare providers, could lead to an increased need for technicians to organize and manage the associated information in all areas of the healthcare industry.

Cancer registrars are expected to continue to be in high demand. As the population ages, there will likely be more types of special purpose registries because many illnesses are detected and treated later in life.

Job Prospects. Prospects will be best for those with a certification in health information, such as the RHIT or the CTR. As EHR systems continue to become more common, health information technicians with computer skills will be needed to use them.

O*NET

➤ Medical Records and Health Information Technicians (29-2071.00)

Contacts for More Information

For more information about health information technicians, including details about certification, visit

➤ American Health Information Management Association (www. ahima.org/)

➤ American Academy of Professional Coders (www.aapc.com/)

➤ Professional Association of Healthcare Coding Specialists (www. pahcs.org/)

➤ National Cancer Registrars Association (www.ncra-usa.org/i4a/ pages/index.cfm?pageid=1)

➤ National Healthcareer Association (www.nhanow.com/home.aspx)

For a list of accredited training programs, visit

➤ Commission on Accreditation for Health Informatics and Information Management Education (www.cahiim.org/)

Medical Transcriptionists

- **2012 Median Pay** .... $34,020 per year
  $16.36 per hour

- **Entry-Level Education** .... Postsecondary non-degree award

- **Work Experience in a Related Occupation** .... None

- **On-the-Job Training** .... None

- **Number of Jobs 2012** 84,100

- **Job Outlook, 2012–22** .... 8% (As fast as average)

- **Employment Change, 2012–22** 6,400

What Medical Transcriptionists Do

Medical transcriptionists listen to voice recordings that physicians and other healthcare professionals make and convert them into written reports. They may also review and edit medical documents created using speech recognition technology. Transcriptionists interpret medical terminology and abbreviations in preparing patients' medical histories, discharge summaries, and other documents.

Duties. Medical transcriptionists typically do the following:

- Listen to the recorded dictation of a doctor or other healthcare professional

- Transcribe and interpret the dictation into diagnostic test results, operative reports, referral letters, and other documents

- Review and edit drafts prepared by speech recognition software, making sure that the transcription is correct, complete, and has a consistent style

- Translate medical abbreviations and jargon into the appropriate long form

- Identify inconsistencies, errors, and missing information within a report that could compromise patient care

- Follow up with the healthcare provider to ensure the accuracy of the reports

- Submit health records for physicians to approve

- Follow patient confidentiality guidelines and legal documentation requirements

- Enter medical reports into electronic health records systems

- Perform quality improvement audits

Medical transcriptionists use audio playback equipment or software that is connected to their computer. This equipment often includes a headset and foot pedal, which are used to control the recording playback speed. They use word-processing and other specialized software, as well as medical reference materials, as needed.

Technological advances have changed the way some medical transcription is done. In the past, medical transcriptionists would listen to an entire dictation to produce a transcribed report. While many transcriptionists still perform these traditional transcription services, many are taking on additional roles. Today, many medical documents are prepared with the use of speech recognition technology, in which specialized software automatically prepares an initial draft of a report. The transcriptionist then reviews the draft for accuracy, identifying any errors, and editing the report, when necessary.

To do their work, medical transcriptionists must become familiar with medical terminology, anatomy and physiology, diagnostic procedures, pharmacology, and treatment assessments. Their

Transcriptionists receive dictation over the Internet and are able to quickly return transcribed documents to clients for approval.

Median Annual Wages, May 2012

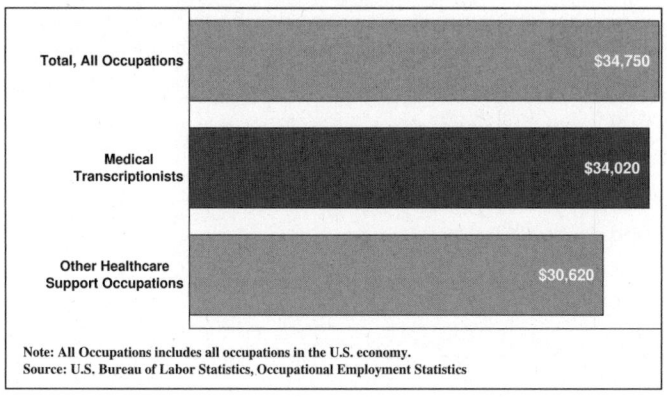

Note: All Occupations includes all occupations in the U.S. economy.
Source: U.S. Bureau of Labor Statistics, Occupational Employment Statistics

Percent Change in Employment, Projected 2012–2022

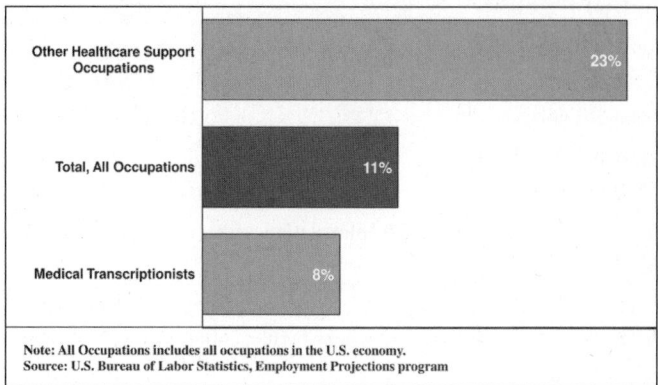

Note: All Occupations includes all occupations in the U.S. economy.
Source: U.S. Bureau of Labor Statistics, Employment Projections program

ability to understand what the health professional has recorded, correctly transcribe that information, and identify any inaccuracies in the transcript is critical to reducing the chance that patients will get ineffective or even harmful treatments. They are part of the team that ensures high-quality patient care.

Transcriptionists may need to be familiar with electronic health records (EHR) systems. They may need to enter reports, create templates, help develop documentation policies, and train physicians on how to use EHR systems.

Medical transcriptionists who work in doctors' offices may have other duties, such as answering phones and greeting patients.

Work Environment

Medical transcriptionists held about 84,100 jobs in 2012. The industries that employed the most medical transcriptionists in 2012 were as follows:

Hospitals; state, local, and private 34%
Offices of physicians 24
Administrative and support services 21

Most medical transcriptionists work for hospitals or in physicians' offices. Some work for companies that provide transcription services to healthcare establishments, and others are self-employed.

Many transcriptionists work from home offices, receiving dictation and submitting drafts electronically.

Work Schedules. Most medical transcriptionists work full time, although about one-third worked part time in 2012. Medical transcriptionists who work from home may work outside typical business hours or have some flexibility in determining their schedules.

How to Become One

Medical transcriptionists typically need postsecondary training. Prospective medical transcriptionists must have an understanding of medical terminology, anatomy and physiology, grammar, and word-processing software.

Education. Employers prefer to hire transcriptionists who have completed postsecondary training in medical transcription, which

is offered by many vocational schools, community colleges, and distance-learning programs.

A 1-year certificate program or 2-year associate's degree normally includes coursework in anatomy, medical terminology, risk management, legal issues relating to healthcare documentation, and English grammar and punctuation. Many of these programs include supervised on-the-job experience. Some transcriptionists, especially those already familiar with medical terminology from previous experience as a nurse or medical secretary, become proficient through refresher courses and training.

Licenses, Certifications, and Registrations. Although certification is not required, some medical transcriptionists choose to become certified. The Association for Healthcare Documentation Integrity offers the Registered Healthcare Documentation Specialist (RHDS) and the Certified Healthcare Documentation Specialist (CHDS) certifications.

The RHDS certification, formerly known as the Registered Medical Transcriptionist (RMT), is for recent graduates with less than 2 years of experience and who work in a single specialty environment, such as a clinic or a doctor's office.

The CHDS certification, formerly known as the Certified Medical Transcriptionist (CMT), is for transcriptionists who have at least 2 years of experience and those who handle dictation in several medical specialties.

Both certifications require passing an exam and periodic retesting or continuing education. While the RMT and the CMT exams are no longer offered, transcriptionists who hold those certifications may choose to maintain them or to complete a bridge course to earn the RHDS or the CHDS.

Important Qualities

Computer skills. Medical transcriptionists must be comfortable using computers and word-processing software, because those tools are an essential part of their jobs. Transcriptionists may also need to know how to operate electronic health records (EHR) systems.

Critical-thinking skills. Transcriptionists must be able to assess medical reports and spot any inaccuracies and inconsistencies in

Employment Projections Data for Medical Transcriptionists

Occupational title	SOC Code	Employment, 2012	Projected Employment, 2022	Change, 2012–2022 Percent	Change, 2012–2022 Numeric
Medical transcriptionists	31-9094	84,100	90,500	8	6,400

Source: U.S. Bureau of Labor Statistics, Employment Projections Program

Note: Data are rounded. Go to Occupational Information Included in the OOH *for a discussion of the data in this table.*

Similar Occupations This table shows a list of occupations with job duties that are similar to those of medical transcriptionists.

Occupations	Entry-level Education	2012 Pay	Projected Job Growth	Average Annual Openings
Court Reporters	Postsecondary non-degree award	$48,160	9%	550
Information Clerks	High school diploma or equivalent	$31,159	2%	47,000
Medical Assistants	Postsecondary non-degree award	$29,370	29%	26,990
Medical Records and Health Information Technicians	Postsecondary non-degree award	$34,160	22%	9,040
Receptionists	High school diploma or equivalent	$25,990	13%	40,690
Secretaries and Administrative Assistants	High school diploma or equivalent	$36,198	12%	97,210

finished drafts. They must also be able to think critically when doing research to find the information that they need and to ensure that sources are both accurate and reliable.

Listening skills. Transcriptionists must listen carefully to dictation from physicians. They must be able to hear and interpret the intended meaning of the medical report.

Time-management skills. Because dictation must be done quickly, medical transcriptionists must be comfortable working under short deadlines.

Writing skills. Medical transcriptionists need a good understanding of the English language and grammar.

Pay

The median annual wage for medical transcriptionists was $34,020 in May 2012. The median wage is the wage at which half the workers in an occupation earned more than that amount and half earned less. The lowest 10 percent earned less than $22,400, and the top 10 percent earned more than $47,250.

In May 2012, the median annual wages for medical transcriptionists in the top three industries in which these transcriptionists worked were as follows:

Hospitals; state, local, and private	$35,540
Offices of physicians	34,180
Administrative and support services	29,650

Some medical transcriptionists are paid based on the volume of transcription they produce. Others are paid an hourly rate or an annual salary.

Job Outlook

Employment of medical transcriptionists is projected to grow 8 percent from 2012 to 2022, about as fast as the average for all occupations.

Federal health legislation will expand the number of patients who have access to health insurance, increasing patient access to medical care. The increasing volume of healthcare services will result in a growing number of medical tests and procedures, all of which will require transcription.

At the same time, technological advances have changed the way medical transcription is done. Speech recognition software and other technological advances may make transcriptionists more productive and, therefore, limit employment growth.

In addition, as healthcare providers seek to cut costs, some have hired transcription services in other countries. However, concerns about patient confidentiality and data security suggest a continued need for transcriptionists within the United States.

Job Prospects. Prospects should be good for transcriptionists with formal education and for those with experience in electronic health records (EHR) management, training, and quality assessment. Job opportunities will stem from transcriptionists who retire over the next decade, creating opportunities for new transcriptionists.

O*NET

➤ Medical Transcriptionists (31-9094.00)

Contacts for More Information

For more information about medical transcriptionists and for a list of accredited medical transcription programs, visit

➤ Association for Healthcare Documentation Integrity (www.ahdionline.org/)

Nuclear Medicine Technologists

- **2012 Median Pay** .... $70,180 per year
  $33.74 per hour
- **Entry-Level Education** .... Associate's degree
- **Work Experience in a Related Occupation** .... None
- **On-the-Job Training** .... None
- **Number of Jobs 2012** 20,900
- **Job Outlook, 2012–22** .... 20% (Faster than average)
- **Employment Change, 2012–22** 4,200

What Nuclear Medicine Technologists Do

Nuclear medicine technologists use a scanner to create images of various areas of a patient's body. They prepare radioactive drugs and administer them to patients undergoing the scans. The radioactive drugs cause abnormal areas of the body to appear different from normal areas in the images.

Duties. Nuclear medicine technologists typically do the following:

- Explain imaging procedures to the patient and answer questions
- Follow safety procedures to protect themselves and the patient from unnecessary radiation exposure
- Examine machines to ensure that they are working properly
- Prepare radioactive drugs and administer them to the patient
- Monitor the patient to check for unusual reactions to the drugs
- Operate equipment that creates images of areas in the body, such as images of organs
- Keep detailed records of procedures

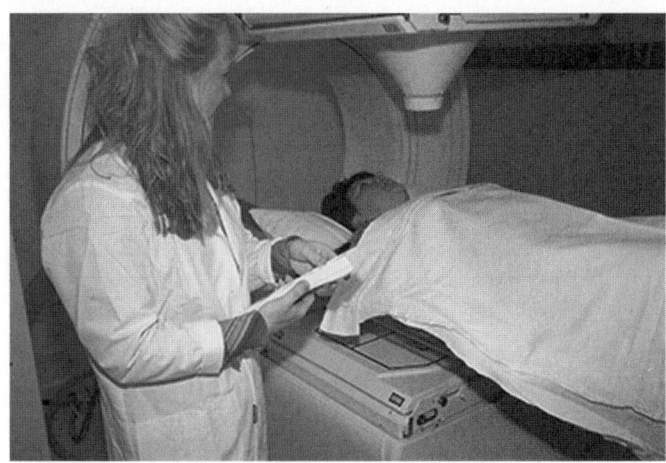

Nuclear medicine technologists operate complicated equipment that requires mechanical ability and manual dexterity.

Radioactive drugs, known as radiopharmaceuticals, give off radiation, allowing special scanners to monitor tissue and organ functions. Abnormal areas show higher-than-expected or lower-than-expected concentrations of radioactivity. Physicians and surgeons then interpret the images to help diagnose the patient's condition. For example, tumors can be seen in organs during a scan because of their concentration of the radioactive drugs.

After additional experience or training, a technologist can choose to specialize in positron emission tomography (PET) or nuclear cardiology (NCT). PET uses a machine that creates a three-dimensional image of a part of the body, such as the brain. NCT uses radioactive drugs to obtain images of the heart. Patients exercise during the imaging process while the technologist creates images of the heart and blood flow.

Work Environment

Nuclear medicine technologists held about 20,900 jobs in 2012. Technologists are on their feet for long periods and may need to lift or turn patients who are disabled.

The industries that employed the most nuclear medicine technologists in 2012 were as follows:

General medical and surgical hospitals; state, local, and private	65%
Offices of physicians	21
Medical and diagnostic laboratories	6
Outpatient care centers	2

Work Schedules. Most nuclear medicine technologists work full time. Because imaging is sometimes needed in emergencies, some nuclear medicine technologists work evenings, weekends, or on call.

Injuries and Illnesses. Although radiation hazards exist in this occupation, they are minimized by the use of gloves and other shielding devices. Nuclear medicine technologists wear badges that measure radiation levels in the radiation area. Instruments monitor their radiation exposure and detailed records are kept on how much radiation they get over their lifetime. When preparing radioactive drugs, technologists use safety procedures to minimize radiation exposure to patients, other healthcare workers, and themselves.

Like other healthcare workers, nuclear medicine technologists may be exposed to infectious diseases.

How to Become One

Nuclear medicine technologists typically need an associate's or a bachelor's degree in nuclear medicine technology. Technologists must be licensed in some states; requirements vary by state.

Education. Nuclear medicine technologists typically need an associate's degree in nuclear medicine technology. Bachelor's degrees are also common. Some technologists become qualified by completing an associate's or a bachelor's degree program in a related health field, such as radiologic technology or nursing, and then completing a 12-month certificate program in nuclear medicine technology. Generally, certificate programs are offered in hospitals, associate's degree programs are in community colleges, and bachelor's degrees are granted by colleges and universities.

Nuclear medicine technology programs include clinical experience–practice under the supervision of a certified nuclear medicine technologist and a physician or surgeon who specializes in nuclear medicine. In addition, these programs often include courses in human anatomy and physiology, physics, chemistry, radioactive drugs, and computer science.

Licenses, Certifications, and Registrations. Nuclear medicine technologists must be licensed in some states; requirements vary by state. For specifics, contact your state's health board.

Some nuclear medicine technologists become certified. Although certification is not required for a license, it fulfills most of the requirements for state licensure on its own.

Some employers require certification, regardless of state regulations. Certification usually involves completing required coursework and having the necessary hours of clinical experience, as well as graduating from an accredited nuclear medicine technology program. Certification is available from the American Registry of Radiologic Technologists (ARRT) and the Nuclear Medicine Technology Certification Board (NMTCB).

Median Annual Wages, May 2012

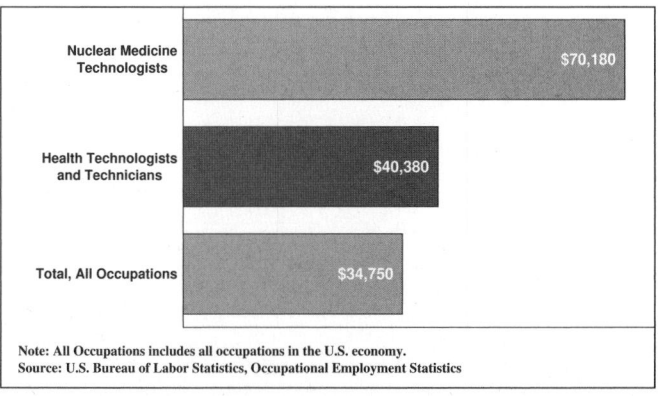

Nuclear Medicine Technologists	$70,180
Health Technologists and Technicians	$40,380
Total, All Occupations	$34,750

Note: All Occupations includes all occupations in the U.S. economy.
Source: U.S. Bureau of Labor Statistics, Occupational Employment Statistics

Percent Change in Employment, Projected 2012–2022

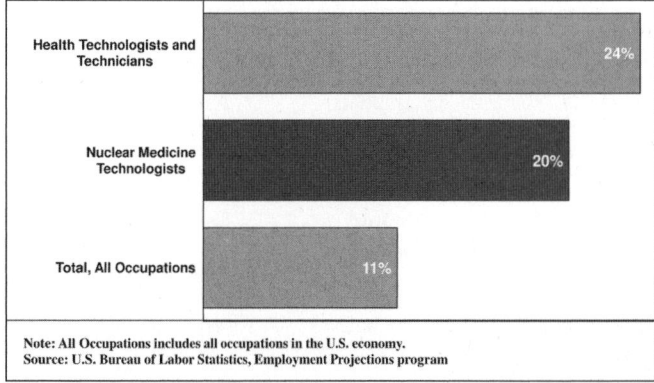

Health Technologists and Technicians	24%
Nuclear Medicine Technologists	20%
Total, All Occupations	11%

Note: All Occupations includes all occupations in the U.S. economy.
Source: U.S. Bureau of Labor Statistics, Employment Projections program

Employment Projections Data for Nuclear Medicine Technologists

Occupational title	SOC Code	Employment, 2012	Projected Employment, 2022	Change, 2012–2022	
				Percent	Numeric
Nuclear medicine technologists	29-2033	20,900	25,100	20	4,200

Source: U.S. Bureau of Labor Statistics, Employment Projections Program

Note: Data are rounded. Go to **Occupational Information Included in the OOH** *for a discussion of the data in this table.*

In addition to receiving general certification, technologists can earn specialty certifications that show their proficiency in specific procedures or on certain equipment. A technologist can earn certification in positron emission tomography (PET) or nuclear cardiology (NCT).

Both fields require the technologist to have a high level of knowledge about the specific procedures and technologies involved. The NMTCB offers NCT and PET certification exams.

Important Qualities

Ability to use technology. Nuclear medicine technologists work with computers and large pieces of technological equipment and must be comfortable operating them.

Analytical skills. Nuclear medicine technologists must understand anatomy, physiology, and other sciences and be able to calculate accurate dosages.

Compassion. Nuclear medicine technologists must be able to reassure and calm patients who are under physical and emotional stress.

Detail oriented. Nuclear medicine technologists must follow exact instructions to make sure that the correct dosage is given and that the patient is not overexposed to radiation.

Interpersonal skills. Nuclear medicine technologists interact with patients and often work as part of a team. They must be able to follow instructions from a supervising physician.

Physical stamina. Nuclear medicine technologists must stand for long periods and be able to lift and move patients who need help.

Pay

The median annual wage for nuclear medicine technologists was $70,180 in May 2012. The median wage is the wage at which half the workers in an occupation earned more than that amount and half earned less. The lowest 10 percent earned less than $50,560, and the top 10 percent earned more than $93,320.

Job Outlook

Employment of nuclear medicine technologists is projected to grow 20 percent from 2012 to 2022, faster than the average for all occupations. However, because it is a small occupation, the growth will result in only about 4,200 new jobs over the 10-year period.

Nuclear medicine technologists work mostly with adult patients, although procedures may be performed on children. A larger aging population should lead to the need to diagnose and treat medical conditions that require imaging, such as heart disease. Nuclear medicine technologists will be needed to administer radioactive drugs and maintain the imaging equipment required for diagnosis.

Federal health legislation will increase the number of patients who have access to health insurance, increasing patient access to medical care. This will increase the demand for medical imaging services, including those provided by nuclear medicine technologists.

Job Prospects. Nuclear medicine technologists can improve their job prospects by earning a specialty certification, such as in positron emission tomography (PET) or nuclear cardiology (NCT). The Nuclear Medicine Technology Certification Board (NMTCB) offers NCT and PET certification exams.

O*NET

➤ Nuclear Medicine Technologists (29-2033.00)

Contacts for More Information

For more information about nuclear medicine technologists, visit
➤ Society of Nuclear Medicine and Molecular Imaging (www.snm.org/)

For a list of accredited programs in nuclear medicine technology, visit
➤ Joint Review Committee on Educational Programs in Nuclear Medicine Technology (www.jrcnmt.org/)

For more information about certification for nuclear medicine technologists, visit
➤ Nuclear Medicine Technology Certification Board (www.nmtcb.org/root/default.php)
➤ American Registry of Radiologic Technologists (www.arrt.org/)

Similar Occupations   This table shows a list of occupations with job duties that are similar to those of nuclear medicine technologists.

Occupations	Entry-level Education	2012 Pay	Projected Job Growth	Average Annual Openings
Diagnostic Medical Sonographers and Cardiovascular Technologists and Technicians, Including Vascular Technologists	Associate's degree	$59,422	39%	5,830
Medical and Clinical Laboratory Technologists and Technicians	See "How to Become One"	$47,499	22%	15,600
Radiation Therapists	Associate's degree	$77,560	24%	840
Radiologic and MRI Technologists	Associate's degree	$56,035	21%	8,090

Nurse Anesthetists, Nurse Midwives, and Nurse Practitioners

- **2012 Median Pay** .... $96,460 per year
  $46.37 per hour
- **Entry-Level Education** .... Master's degree
- **Work Experience in a Related Occupation** .... None
- **On-the-Job Training** .... None
- **Number of Jobs 2012** 151,400
- **Job Outlook, 2012–22** .... 31% (Much faster than average)
- **Employment Change, 2012–22** 47,600

What Nurse Anesthetists, Nurse Midwives, and Nurse Practitioners Do

Nurse anesthetists, nurse midwives, and nurse practitioners, also referred to as advanced practice registered nurses (APRNs), coordinate patient care and they may provide primary and specialty health care. The scope of practice varies from state to state.

Duties. Advanced practice registered nurses typically do the following:

- Take and record patients' medical histories and symptoms and set up plans for patients' care or contribute to existing plans
- Perform physical exams
- Observe patients and diagnose various health problems
- Perform and order diagnostic tests and analyze results
- Give patients medicines and treatments
- Consult with doctors and other healthcare professionals as needed
- Operate and monitor medical equipment
- Provide counseling and teach patients and their families how to stay healthy or manage their illnesses or injuries
- Conduct research

APRNs work independently or in collaboration with physicians. In most states, they can prescribe medications, order medical tests, and diagnose health problems. They may provide primary and preventative care and may specialize in care for certain groups of people, such as children, pregnant women, or patients with mental health disorders.

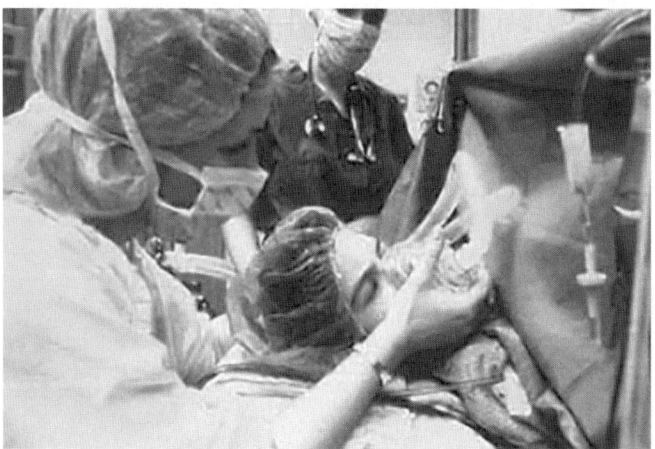

Nurse anesthetists administer every type of anesthetic, working in collaboration with other healthcare professionals.

APRNs who work with patients typically perform many of the same duties as registered nurses, gathering information about a patient's condition and taking action to treat or manage the patient's health. However, APRNs are also trained to perform many additional functions, including ordering and evaluating test results, referring patients to specialists, and diagnosing and treating ailments. APRNs focus on patient-centered care, which means understanding a patient's concerns and lifestyle before choosing a course of action.

APRNs may also conduct research or teach staff about new policies or procedures. Others may provide consultation services based on a specific field of knowledge, such as oncology, which is the study of cancer.

The following are examples of types of APRNs:

Nurse anesthetists provide anesthesia and related care before, during, and after surgical, therapeutic, diagnostic, and obstetrical procedures. They also provide pain management and some emergency services. Before a procedure begins, nurse anesthetists discuss with a patient any medications the patient is taking as well as any allergies or illnesses the patient may have, so that anesthesia can be safely administered. Nurse anesthetists then give a patient general anesthesia to put the patient to sleep or regional or local anesthesia to numb an area of the body. They remain with the patient throughout a procedure to monitor vital signs and adjust the anesthesia as necessary.

Nurse midwives provide care to women, including gynecological exams, family planning services, prenatal care, and attendance in labor and delivery. They may act as primary care providers for women and newborns. Many nurse midwives provide wellness care, educating their patients on how to lead healthy lives by discussing topics such as nutrition and disease prevention. Nurse midwives also provide care to their patients' partners for sexual or reproductive health issues.

Nurse practitioners (NPs) serve as primary and specialty care providers, providing advanced nursing services to patients and their families. NPs assess patients, determine the best way to improve or manage a patient's health, and discuss ways to integrate health promotion strategies into a patient's life. They typically care for a certain population of people. For instance, NPs may work in adult and geriatric health, pediatric health, or psychiatric and mental health.

Although the scope of their duties varies some by state, many nurse practitioners work independently, prescribe medications and order laboratory tests. All nurse practitioners consult with physicians and other health professionals when needed.

Clinical nurse specialists (CNSs) provide direct patient care to a certain population of people, such as pediatric patients, within one of many nursing specialties, such as orthopedic nursing or oncology nursing. CNSs also provide indirect care by working with other nurses, healthcare teams, and various other staff to improve the quality of care that patients receive. They also work at the system or organizational level to improve the quality of nursing care throughout a facility related to their specialty. Those with a research doctorate may conduct research.

Work Environment

Nurse anesthetists, nurse midwives, and nurse practitioners, also referred to as advanced practice registered nurses (APRNs), held about 151,400 jobs in 2012. The industries that employed the most APRNs in 2012 were as follows:

Offices of physicians 47%
Hospitals; state, local, and private 28
Outpatient care centers 6
Colleges, universities, and professional schools;
    state, local, and private....................................... 4
Offices of other health practitioners 3

Median Annual Wages, May 2012

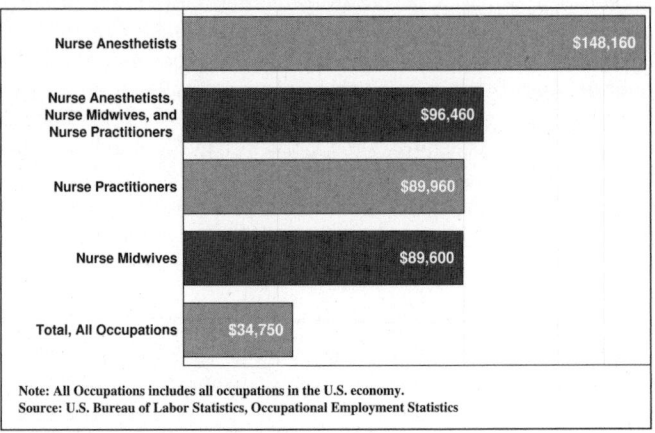

Note: All Occupations includes all occupations in the U.S. economy.
Source: U.S. Bureau of Labor Statistics, Occupational Employment Statistics

Percent Change in Employment, Projected 2012–2022

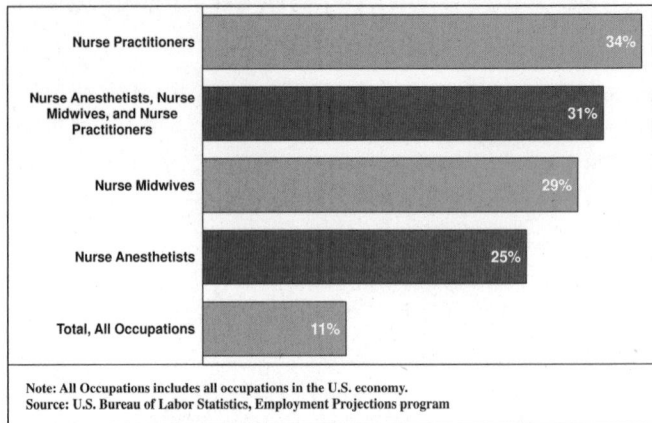

Note: All Occupations includes all occupations in the U.S. economy.
Source: U.S. Bureau of Labor Statistics, Employment Projections program

APRNs work in a variety of settings including physicians' offices, hospitals, nursing care facilities, schools, and clinics. Nurse midwives also work in birthing centers. Some APRNs may treat patients in their patients' homes.

APRNs may also travel long distances to help care for patients in places where there are not enough healthcare workers.

Injuries and Illnesses. APRN work can be both physically and emotionally demanding. Some APRNs spend much of their day on their feet. They are vulnerable to back injuries because they must lift and move patients. APRN work can also be stressful as critical decisions must be made.

Because of the environments in which they work, APRNs may come in close contact with infectious diseases and potentially harmful drugs. Therefore, they must follow strict, standardized guidelines to guard against diseases and other dangers, such as accidental needle sticks or patient outbursts.

Work Schedules. APRNs working in physicians' offices or schools typically work during normal business hours. Those working in hospitals and various other healthcare facilities may work in shifts to provide round-the-clock patient care. They may work nights, weekends, and holidays. Some APRNs, especially those who work in critical care or those who deliver babies, may also be on call.

How to Become One

Nurse anesthetists, nurse midwives, and nurse practitioners, also referred to as advanced practice registered nurses, must earn at least a master's degree in one of the specialty roles. APRNs must also be licensed registered nurses in their state and pass a national certification exam.

Education. Nurse anesthetists, nurse midwives, and nurse practitioners must earn a master's degree from an accredited program. These programs include both classroom education and clinical experience. Courses in anatomy, physiology, and pharmacology are common as well as coursework specific to the chosen APRN role.

An APRN must become a licensed registered nurse (RN) before pursuing education in one of the advanced practice roles. Many programs also require some period of clinical experience, and a strong background in science is helpful.

Most APRN programs prefer candidates who have a bachelor's degree in nursing. However, some schools offer bridge programs for registered nurses with an associate's degree or diploma in nursing. Graduate-level programs are also available for individuals who did not obtain a bachelor's degree in nursing but in a related health science field. These programs prepare the student for the RN licensure exam in addition to the APRN curriculum.

Although a master's degree is the most common form of entry-level education, many APRNs choose to earn a Doctor of Nursing Practice (DNP) or a Ph.D. The specific educational requirements and qualifications for each of the roles are available on professional organizations' websites.

Licenses, Certifications, and Registrations. Most states recognize all of the APRN roles. In states that recognize some or all of the roles, APRNs must have a registered nursing license, complete an approved graduate-level program, and pass a national certification exam. Each state's board of nursing can provide details.

The *Consensus Model for APRN Regulation*, a document developed by a wide variety of professional nursing organizations, including the National Council of State Boards of Nursing, aims to standardize APRN requirements. The model recommends all APRNs to complete a graduate degree from an accredited program, be a licensed registered nurse, pass a national certification exam, and earn a second license specific to one of the APRN roles and to a certain group of patients.

Certification is required in the vast majority of states to use an APRN title. Certification is used to show proficiency in an APRN role and is often a requirement for state licensure.

The National Board of Certification and Recertification for Nurse Anesthetists (NBCRNA) offers the National Certification Examination (NCE). Certified registered nurse anesthetists (CRNAs) must recertify every 2 years, which includes 40 hours of continuing education.

The American Midwifery Certification Board offers the Certified Nurse-Midwife and Certified Midwife designations. Individuals with these designations must recertify every 5 years.

There are a number of certification exams for nurse practitioners because of the large number of populations NPs may work with and the number of specialty areas in which they may practice. Certifications are available from a number of professional organizations, including the American Nurses Credentialing Center and the Pediatric Nursing Certification Board.

Important Qualities

Communication skills. Advanced practice registered nurses must be able to communicate with patients and other health care professionals to ensure that the appropriate course of action is understood.

Critical-thinking skills. ARPNs must be able to assess changes in a patient's health, quickly determining the most appropriate course of action and if a consultation with another health care professional is needed.

Employment Projections Data for Nurse Anesthetists, Nurse Midwives, and Nurse Practitioners

Occupational title	SOC Code	Employment, 2012	Projected Employment, 2022	Change, 2012–2022 Percent	Change, 2012–2022 Numeric
Nurse anesthetists, nurse midwives, and nurse practitioners	—	151,400	198,900	31	47,600
Nurse anesthetists..	29-1151	35,200	43,900	25	8,800
Nurse midwives...	29-1161	6,000	7,700	29	1,700
Nurse practitioners	29-1171	110,200	147,300	34	37,100

Source: U.S. Bureau of Labor Statistics, Employment Projections Program

Note: Data are rounded. Go to **Occupational Information Included in the OOH** *for a discussion of the data in this table.*

Compassion. Nurses should be caring and sympathetic when treating patients who are in pain or who are experiencing emotional distress.

Detail oriented. APRNs must be responsible and detail oriented because they provide various treatments and medications that affect the health of their patients. During an evaluation, they must pick up on even the smallest changes in a patient's condition.

Interpersonal skills. Advanced practice registered nurses must work with patients and families as well as with other health care providers and staff within the organizations where they provide care. They should work as part of a team to determine and execute the best possible healthcare options for the patients they treat.

Leadership skills. Advanced practice registered nurses often work in positions of seniority. They must effectively lead and sometimes manage other nurses on staff when providing patient care.

Resourcefulness. APRNs must know where to find the answers that they need in a timely fashion.

Advancement. Because the APRN designation is in itself an advancement of one's career, many APRNs choose to remain in this role for the duration of their career. Some APRNs may take on managerial or administrative roles, while others go into academia. APRNs who earn a doctoral degree may conduct independent research or work in an interprofessional research team.

Pay

The median annual wage for nurse anesthetists, nurse midwives, and nurse practitioners, was $96,460 in May 2012. The median wage is the wage at which half of the workers in an occupation earned more than that amount and half earned less. The lowest 10 percent earned less than $66,330, and the top 10 percent earned more than $161,030.

Median annual wages for APRNs in May 2012 were as follows:

Nurse anesthetists.. $148,160
Nurse practitioners 89,960
Nurse midwives.. 89,600

In May 2012, the median annual wages for advanced practice registered nurses in the top five industries in which APRNs worked were as follows:

Hospitals; state, local, and private $101,990
Offices of other health practitioners 98,260
Offices of physicians 97,600
Outpatient care centers 92,270
Colleges, universities, and professional schools;
    state, local, and private... 88,070

Many employers of APRNs offer flexible work schedules, childcare, and educational benefits.

Job Outlook

Employment of nurse anesthetists, nurse midwives, and nurse practitioners is expected to grow 31 percent from 2012 to 2022, much faster than the average for all occupations. Growth will occur because of an increase in the demand for healthcare services. Several factors, including healthcare legislation and the resulting newly insured, an increased emphasis on preventative care, and the large, aging baby-boom population will contribute to this demand.

The number of individuals who have access to health insurance will increase due to federal health insurance reform legislation. APRNs can perform many of the same services as physicians and may be needed to provide primary care services.

As states change their laws governing APRN practice authority, APRNs are being allowed to perform more services. They are also becoming more widely recognized by the public as a source for primary healthcare.

APRNs will also be needed to care for the aging baby-boom generation. As baby boomers age, they will experience ailments and complex conditions that require medical care. APRNs will be needed to keep these patients healthy and to treat the growing number of patients with chronic and acute conditions.

Job Prospects. Overall, job opportunities for advanced practice registered nurses are expected to be excellent. APRNs will be in high

Employment Projections Data for Nurse Anesthetists, Nurse Midwives, and Nurse Practitioners

Occupations	Entry-level Education	2012 Pay	Projected Job Growth	Average Annual Openings
Audiologists	Doctoral or professional degree	$69,720	33%	700
Occupational Therapists	Master's degree	$75,400	29%	4,820
Physical Therapists	Doctoral or professional degree	$79,860	36%	12,370
Physician Assistants	Master's degree	$90,930	38%	4,890
Physicians and Surgeons	Doctoral or professional degree	$182,294	18%	29,630
Registered Nurses	Associate's degree	$65,470	19%	105,260
Speech-Language Pathologists	Master's degree	$69,870	19%	4,620

demand, particularly in medically underserved areas such as inner cities and rural areas. Job opportunities may exist from attrition.

O*NET

➤ Nurse Anesthetists (29-1151.00)
➤ Nurse Midwives (29-1161.00)
➤ Nurse Practitioners (29-1171.00)

Contacts for More Information

For information about nurse anesthetists, including a list of accredited programs, visit
➤ American Association of Nurse Anesthetists (www.aana.com/Pages/default.aspx)
   For information about nurse midwives, including a list of accredited programs, visit
➤ American College of Nurse-Midwives (www.midwife.org/)
   For information about nurse practitioners, including a list of accredited programs, visit
➤ American Association of Nurse Practitioners (www.aanp.org/AANPCMS2)
   For more information about registered nurses, including credentialing, visit
➤ American Nurses Association (http://nursingworld.org/)
   For more information about nursing education and being a registered nurse, visit
➤ National League for Nursing (www.nln.org/)
   For information about undergraduate and graduate nursing education, nursing career options, and financial aid, visit
➤ American Association of Colleges of Nursing (www.aacn.nche.edu/)
   For information about the Consensus Model and for a list of the states' Boards of Nursing, visit
➤ National Council of State Boards of Nursing (www.ncsbn.org/index.htm)
   For information about certification, visit
➤ National Board of Certification and Recertification for Nurse Anesthetists (www.nbcrna.com/Pages/default.aspx)
➤ American Midwifery Certification Board (www.amcbmidwife.org/)
➤ American Nurses Credentialing Center (http://nursecredentialing.org/)
➤ Pediatric Nursing Certification Board (www.pncb.org/ptistore/control/exams/index)

Nursing Assistants and Orderlies

- **2012 Median Pay** .... $24,400 per year
                                                    $11.73 per hour
- **Entry-Level Education** ....See "How to Become One"
- **Work Experience in a Related Occupation**............... None
- **On-the-Job Training** ....See "How to Become One"
- **Number of Jobs 2012** 1,534,400
- **Job Outlook, 2012–22**............. 21% (Faster than average)
- **Employment Change, 2012–22** 321,200

What Nursing Assistants and Orderlies Do

Nursing assistants and orderlies help provide basic care for patients in hospitals and residents of long-term care facilities, such as nursing homes.

Duties. Nursing assistants, sometimes called nursing aides, provide basic care and help with activities of daily living. They typically do the following:

- Clean and bathe patients or residents
- Help patients use the toilet and dress
- Turn, reposition, and transfer patients between beds and wheelchairs
- Listen to and record patients' health concerns and report that information to nurses
- Measure patients' vital signs, such as blood pressure and temperature
- Serve meals and help patients eat

Some nursing assistants may also dispense medication, depending on their training level and the state in which they work.

In nursing homes, assistants are often the principal caregivers. They have more contact with residents than other members of the staff. Because some residents stay in a nursing home for months or years, assistants may develop close relationships with their patients.

Orderlies may do some of the same tasks as nursing assistants, although they do not usually provide healthcare services. They typically do the following:

- Transport patients, such as taking a hospital patient to an operating room
- Clean equipment and facilities

Nursing assistants and orderlies work as part of a healthcare team under the supervision of licensed practical or licensed vocational nurses and registered nurses.

Work Environment

Nursing assistants held about 1.5 million jobs in 2012. Orderlies held about 54,600 jobs in 2012. More than half of all nursing assistants work in nursing and residential care facilities. Most orderlies work in hospitals.

The industries that employed the most nursing assistants in 2012 were as follows:

Nursing care facilities (skilled nursing facilities).....................42%
Hospitals; state, local, and private 26
Residential care facilities...14
Home health care services..4
Government..4

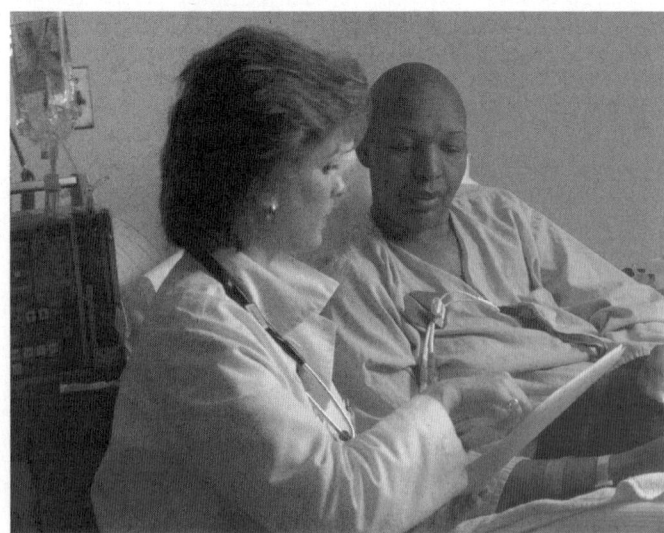

Nursing aides should be personable and enjoy helping people.

Median Annual Wages, May 2012

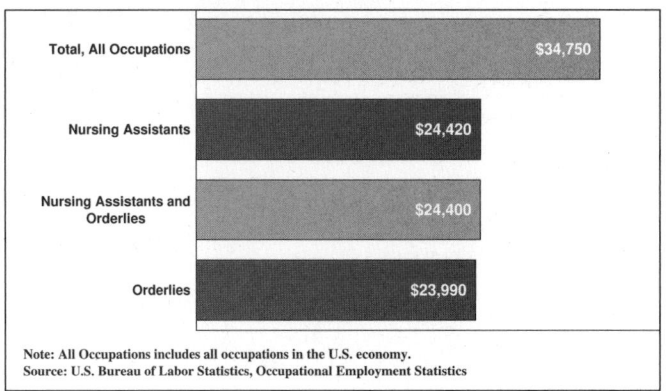

Note: All Occupations includes all occupations in the U.S. economy.
Source: U.S. Bureau of Labor Statistics, Occupational Employment Statistics

Percent Change in Employment, Projected 2012–2022

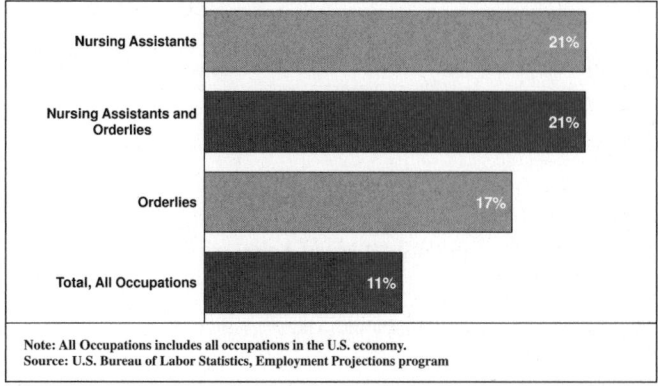

Note: All Occupations includes all occupations in the U.S. economy.
Source: U.S. Bureau of Labor Statistics, Employment Projections program

The industries that employed the most orderlies in 2012 were as follows:

Hospitals; state, local, and private 73%
Nursing care facilities (skilled nursing facilities) 13
Government 4
Ambulatory health care services 4
Residential care facilities 3

The work of nursing assistants and orderlies can be strenuous. They spend much of their time on their feet as they take care of many patients or residents.

They wear uniforms to protect their clothing and to promote cleanliness.

Injuries and Illnesses. Because they frequently lift people and do other physically demanding tasks, on-the-job injuries are more common for nursing assistants and orderlies than for most other occupations. They are typically trained in how to properly lift and move patients, which can reduce the risk of injury.

Work Schedules. Most nursing assistants and orderlies work full time. Because nursing homes and hospitals provide care at all hours, nursing assistants and orderlies may need to work nights, weekends, and holidays.

How to Become One

Nursing assistants must complete a state-approved education program and must pass their state's competency exam. Orderlies generally have at least a high school diploma.

Education and Training. Nursing assistants must complete a state-approved education program in which they learn the basic principles of nursing and complete supervised clinical work. These programs are found in high schools, community colleges, vocational and technical schools, hospitals, and nursing homes.

In addition, nursing assistants typically complete a brief period of on-the-job training to learn about their specific employer's policies and procedures.

Orderlies typically have at least a high school diploma and receive a short period of on-the-job training.

Licenses, Certifications, and Registrations. After completing a state-approved education program, nursing assistants take a competency exam. Passing this exam allows them to use state-specific titles. In some states, a nursing assistant or aide is called a Certified Nursing Assistant (CNA), but titles vary from state to state.

Nursing assistants who have passed the exam are placed on a state registry. Nursing assistants must be on the state registry to work in a nursing home.

Some states have other requirements, as well, such as continuing education and a criminal background check. Check with state boards of nursing or health for more information.

In some states, nursing assistants can earn additional credentials, such as becoming a Certified Medication Assistant (CMA). As a CMA, they can give medications. Nursing assistants may also choose to become certified in a specialty area, such as geriatrics.

Orderlies do not need a license, however, many jobs require a Basic Life Support certification which shows they are trained to provide CPR.

Important Qualities

Communication skills. Nursing assistants and orderlies must be able to communicate effectively to address patients' or residents' concerns. They also need to relay important information to other healthcare workers.

Compassion. Nursing assistants and orderlies provide care for the sick, injured, and elderly. Doing so requires a compassionate and empathetic attitude.

Patience. The routine tasks of cleaning, feeding, and bathing patients or residents can be stressful. Nursing assistants and orderlies must be patient to provide quality care.

Physical stamina. Nursing assistants and orderlies spend much of their time on their feet. They should be comfortable performing physical tasks, such as lifting or moving patients.

Employment Projections Data for Nursing Assistants and Orderlies

Occupational title	SOC Code	Employment, 2012	Projected Employment, 2022	Change, 2012–2022	
				Percent	Numeric
Nursing assistants and orderlies	—	1,534,400	1,855,600	21	321,200
Nursing assistants	31-1014	1,479,800	1,792,000	21	312,200
Orderlies	31-1015	54,600	63,600	17	9,100

Source: U.S. Bureau of Labor Statistics, Employment Projections Program

Note: Data are rounded. Go to **Occupational Information Included in the OOH** *for a discussion of the data in this table.*

Similar Occupations   This table shows a list of occupations with job duties that are similar to those of nursing assistants and orderlies.

Occupations	Entry-level Education	2012 Pay	Projected Job Growth	Average Annual Openings
Home Health Aides	Less than high school	$20,820	48%	59,070
Licensed Practical and Licensed Vocational Nurses	Postsecondary non-degree award	$41,540	25%	36,310
Medical Assistants	Postsecondary non-degree award	$29,370	29%	26,990
Occupational Therapy Assistants and Aides	See "How to Become One"	$47,638	41%	2,560
Personal Care Aides	Less than high school	$19,910	49%	66,600
Physical Therapist Assistants and Aides	See "How to Become One"	$40,539	41%	7,630
Psychiatric Technicians and Aides	See "How to Become One"	$27,125	5%	3,030
Registered Nurses	Associate's degree	$65,470	19%	105,260

Pay

The median annual wage for nursing assistants was $24,420 in May 2012. The median wage is the wage at which half the workers in an occupation earned more than that amount and half earned less. The lowest 10 percent earned less than $18,300, and the top 10 percent earned more than $35,330.

The median annual wage for orderlies was $23,990 in May 2012. The lowest 10 percent earned less than $17,730, and the top 10 percent earned more than $36,390.

Job Outlook

Employment of nursing assistants is projected to grow 21 percent from 2012 to 2022, faster than the average for all occupations. Employment of orderlies is projected to grow 17 percent from 2012 to 2022, faster than the average for all occupations.

As the baby-boom population ages, many nursing assistants and orderlies will be needed to care for elderly patients in long-term care facilities, such as nursing homes. In addition, growing rates of several chronic conditions and of dementia will lead to increased demand for patient care.

Demand for nursing assistants may be constrained by the fact that many nursing homes rely on government funding. Cuts to programs, such as Medicare and Medicaid, may affect patients' ability to pay for nursing home care. However, patient preferences and shifts in federal and state funding are increasing the demand for home and community-based long-term care, which should lead to increased opportunities for nursing assistants working in home health and community rehabilitation services.

Job Prospects. Job prospects for nursing assistants who have completed a state-approved education program and passed their state's competency exam should be good, particularly in home health care services and community-based care settings. Because of the emotional and physical demands of this occupation, many nursing assistants and orderlies choose to leave the profession to get more training or another job. This creates opportunities for jobseekers.

O*NET

➤ Nursing Assistants (31-1014.00)
➤ Orderlies (31-1015.00)

Contacts for More Information

For more information on nursing aides, orderlies, and attendants, visit

➤ National Association of Health Care Assistants (www.nahcacares. org)
➤ National Network of Career Nursing Assistants (www.cna-network. org)

Occupational Health and Safety Specialists

- **2012 Median Pay** .... $66,790 per year
  $32.11 per hour
- **Entry-Level Education** ....Bachelor's degree
- **Work Experience in a Related Occupation**............... None
- **On-the-Job Training** ....Short-term on-the-job training
- **Number of Jobs 2012** 62,900
- **Job Outlook, 2012–22** .... 7% (Slower than average)
- **Employment Change, 2012–22** 4,200

What Occupational Health and Safety Specialists Do

Occupational health and safety specialists analyze many types of work environments and work procedures. Specialists inspect workplaces for adherence to regulations on safety, health, and the environment. They also design programs to prevent disease or injury to workers and damage to the environment.

Duties. Occupational health and safety specialists typically do the following:

- Identify hazards in the workplace
- Collect samples of potentially toxic materials for analysis
- Inspect and evaluate workplace environments, equipment, and practices for compliance with corporate and government health and safety standards and regulations
- Design and implement workplace processes and procedures that help protect workers from potentially hazardous work conditions
- Investigate accidents and incidents to identify their causes and to determine how they might be prevented in the future
- Conduct training on a variety of topics such as emergency preparedness

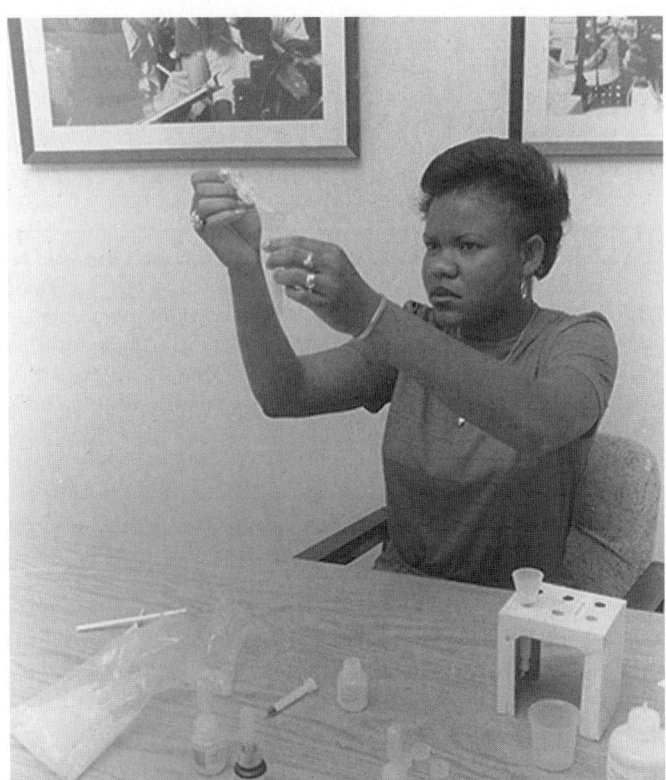

Occupational health and safety specialists may conduct inspections and inform an organization's managers of areas not in compliance with state and federal laws and employer policies.

Occupational health and safety specialists examine lighting, equipment, ventilation, and other conditions and materials in the workplace that could affect employee health, safety, comfort, and performance. Specialists seek to increase worker productivity by reducing absenteeism and equipment downtime. They also seek to save money by lowering insurance premiums and workers' compensation payments and by preventing government fines.

Some specialists develop and conduct employee safety and training programs. These programs cover a range of topics, such as how to use safety equipment correctly and how to respond in an emergency.

In addition to protecting workers, specialists also work to prevent harm to property, the environment, and the public by inspecting workplaces for chemical, physical, radiological, and biological hazards. Specialists who work for governments conduct safety inspections and can impose fines.

Occupational health and safety specialists work with engineers and physicians to control or fix potentially hazardous conditions or equipment. They also work closely with occupational health and safety technicians to collect and analyze data in the workplace.

The tasks of occupational health and safety specialists vary by industry, workplace, and types of hazards affecting employees. The following are examples of types of occupational health and safety specialists:

Ergonomists consider the design of industrial, office, and other equipment to maximize workers' comfort, safety, and productivity.

Health physicists work in locations that use radiation and radioactive material. They help to protect people and the environment from hazardous radiation exposure that may be caused by medical treatments or come from nuclear plants, among other sources.

Industrial or occupational hygienists identify workplace health hazards, such as lead, asbestos, noise, pesticides, and communicable diseases.

Work Environment

Occupational health and safety specialists held about 62,900 jobs in 2012. They work in a variety of settings, such as offices, factories, and mines. Their jobs often involve considerable fieldwork and travel.

About 32 percent of occupational health and safety specialists worked for federal, state, and local governments in 2012. In the federal government, specialists are employed by various agencies, including the National Institute for Occupational Safety and Health (NIOSH) and the Occupational Safety & Health Administration (OSHA). Most large government agencies employ specialists to protect agency employees. In addition to working for governments, occupational health and safety specialists worked in management, scientific, and technical consulting services; education services; hospitals; and manufacturing.

Occupational health and safety specialists may be exposed to strenuous, dangerous, or stressful conditions. Specialists use gloves, helmets, respirators, and other personal protective and safety equipment to minimize illness and injury.

Work Schedules. Most occupational health and safety specialists work full time. Some specialists may work weekends or irregular hours in emergency situations.

How to Become One

Occupational health and safety specialists typically need a bachelor's degree. Specialists usually receive on-the-job training in inspection procedures and regulations.

Education. Occupational health and safety specialists typically need a bachelor's degree in occupational health, safety, or a related

Median Annual Wages, May 2012

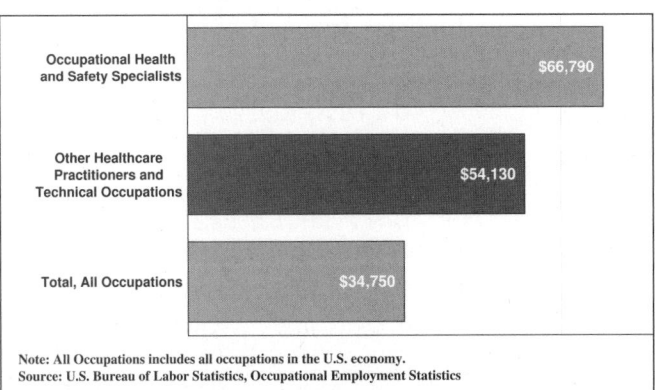

Occupational Health and Safety Specialists — $66,790
Other Healthcare Practitioners and Technical Occupations — $54,130
Total, All Occupations — $34,750

Note: All Occupations includes all occupations in the U.S. economy.
Source: U.S. Bureau of Labor Statistics, Occupational Employment Statistics

Percent Change in Employment, Projected 2012–2022

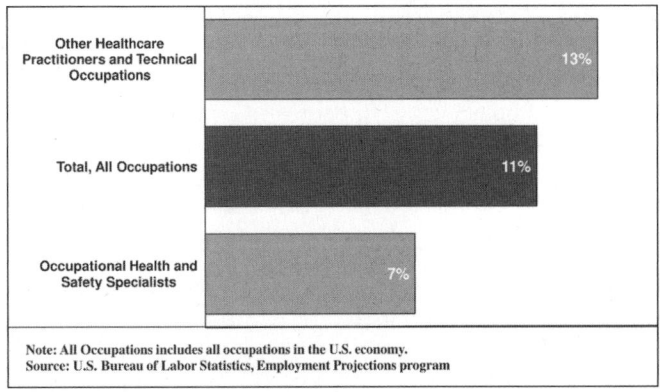

Other Healthcare Practitioners and Technical Occupations — 13%
Total, All Occupations — 11%
Occupational Health and Safety Specialists — 7%

Note: All Occupations includes all occupations in the U.S. economy.
Source: U.S. Bureau of Labor Statistics, Employment Projections program

Employment Projections Data for Occupational Health and Safety Specialists

Occupational title	SOC Code	Employment, 2012	Projected Employment, 2022	Change, 2012–2022	
				Percent	Numeric
Occupational health and safety specialists	29-9011	62,900	67,100	7	4,200

Source: U.S. Bureau of Labor Statistics, Employment Projections Program

Note: Data are rounded. Go to Occupational Information Included in the OOH *for a discussion of the data in this table.*

scientific or technical field, such as engineering, biology, or chemistry. For some positions, a master's degree is required in industrial hygiene, health physics, or a related subject.

Typical courses include radiation science, hazardous material management and control, risk communications, and respiratory protection. These courses may vary, depending on the specialty in which a student wants to work. For example, courses in health physics focus on topics that differ from those in industrial hygiene.

Internships are not required, but employers may prefer to hire candidates who have participated in one.

High school students interested in becoming occupational health and safety specialists should take courses in English, math, chemistry, biology, and physics.

Training. Although occupational health and safety specialists learn standard laws and procedures in their formal education, they also need some on-the-job training for specific work environments. For example, a specialist who will inspect offices needs different on-the-job training than a specialist inspecting factories.

Important Qualities

Ability to use technology. Occupational health and safety specialists must be able to use advanced technology. They often work with complex testing equipment.

Communication skills. Occupational health and safety specialists must be able to communicate safety instructions and concerns to employees and managers. They need to be able to work with technicians to collect and test samples of possible hazards, such as dust or vapors, in the workplace.

Detail oriented. Occupational health and safety specialists must pay attention to details. They need to recognize and adhere to specific safety standards and government regulations.

Physical stamina. Occupational health and safety specialists must be able to stand for long periods and be able to travel regularly. Some specialists work in environments that can be uncomfortable, such as tunnels or mines.

Problem-solving skills. Occupational health and safety specialists must be able to solve problems. They need to be able to find solutions to unsafe working conditions and environmental concerns in the workplace.

Licenses, Certifications, and Registrations. Although certification is voluntary, many employers encourage it. Certification is available through several organizations, depending on the field in which the specialists work. Specialists must have graduated from an accredited educational program and have work experience to be eligible to take most certification exams. To keep their certification, specialists are usually required to complete periodic continuing education.

Pay

The median annual wage for occupational health and safety specialists was $66,790 in May 2012. The median wage is the wage at which half the workers in an occupation earned more than that amount and half earned less. The lowest 10 percent earned less than $40,080, and the top 10 percent earned more than $97,380.

Job Outlook

Employment of occupational health and safety specialists is projected to grow 7 percent from 2012 to 2022, slower than the average for all occupations.

Specialists will be needed to work in a wide variety of industries to ensure that employers are adhering to both existing and new regulations. For example, technological advances that allow manufacturing workers to use new machinery will require specialists to create and enforce procedures to ensure safe use of the machinery.

The increased adoption of nuclear power as a source of energy may lead to job growth for specialists in that field. These specialists will be needed to maintain the safety of both the powerplant workers and the surrounding environment.

In addition, specialists will be necessary because insurance and workers' compensation costs have become a concern for many employers and insurance companies. An aging population is remaining in the workforce longer than past generations, and older workers usually have a greater proportion of workers' compensation claims.

Job Prospects. Despite slower than average employment growth, job opportunities for individuals with advanced degrees are expected to be good. Candidates with certification may enjoy more job opportunities. In addition, a large number of currently practic-

Similar Occupations   This table shows a list of occupations with job duties that are similar to those of occupational health and safety specialists.

Occupations	Entry-level Education	2012 Pay	Projected Job Growth	Average Annual Openings
Construction and Building Inspectors	High school diploma or equivalent	$53,450	12%	3,670
Environmental Scientists and Specialists	Bachelor's degree	$63,570	15%	3,970
Fire Inspectors and Investigators	High school diploma or equivalent	$53,990	7%	440
Health and Safety Engineers	Bachelor's degree	$76,830	11%	970
Occupational Health and Safety Technicians	High school diploma or equivalent	$47,440	10%	480

ing occupational health and safety specialists are expected to retire over the coming decade, creating opportunities for new specialists.

O*NET

➤ Occupational Health and Safety Specialists (29-9011.00)

Contacts for More Information

For more information about industrial hygienists, visit

➤ American Industrial Hygiene Association (www.aiha.org/Pages/default.aspx)

For more information about credentialing in industrial hygiene, visit

➤ American Board of Industrial Hygiene (www.abih.org/)

➤ AIHA Registry Programs (www.aiharegistries.org/Pages/default.aspx)

For more information about occupations in safety, a list of safety and related academic programs, and credentialing, visit

➤ Board of Certified Safety Professionals (www.bcsp.org/)

For more information about health physicists, visit

➤ Health Physics Society (www.hps.org/)

For more information about occupational health and safety, visit

➤ U.S. Department of Labor, Occupational Safety & Health Administration (OSHA) (www.osha.gov/)

➤ Centers for Disease Control and Prevention, National Institute for Occupational Safety and Health (NIOSH) (www.cdc.gov/niosh/)

For job vacancies within the federal government, visit

➤ USAJOBS (www.usajobs.gov/)

Occupational Health and Safety Technicians

- **2012 Median Pay** .... $47,440 per year
  $22.81 per hour
- **Entry-Level Education** ... High school diploma or equivalent
- **Work Experience in a Related Occupation** .... None
- **On-the-Job Training** .... Moderate-term on-the-job training
- **Number of Jobs 2012** 12,600
- **Job Outlook, 2012–22** .... 11% (As fast as average)
- **Employment Change, 2012–22** 1,400

What Occupational Health and Safety Technicians Do

Occupational health and safety technicians collect data on the safety and health conditions of the workplace. Technicians work with occupational health and safety specialists in conducting tests and measuring hazards to help prevent harm to workers, property, the environment, and the general public.

Duties. Occupational health and safety technicians typically do the following:

- Inspect, test, and evaluate workplace environments, equipment, and practices to ensure they follow safety standards and government regulations
- Collect samples of potentially toxic materials
- Work with occupational health and safety specialists to fix hazardous and potentially hazardous conditions or equipment
- Evaluate programs on workplace safety and health
- Educate employers and workers about workplace safety

- Demonstrate the correct use of safety equipment
- Investigate incidents and accidents to identify what caused them and how they might be prevented in the future

Technicians conduct tests and collect samples and measurements as part of workplace inspections. For example, they may collect and handle samples of dust, mold, gases, vapors, or other potentially hazardous materials. They conduct both routine and special inspections that an occupational health and safety specialist orders.

They test and identify work areas for potential health and safety hazards. Technicians may examine and test machinery and equipment such as scaffolding and lifting devices to be sure that they meet appropriate safety regulations. They may check that workers are using required protective gear, such as masks and hardhats. Technicians also check that hazardous materials are stored correctly.

In addition to working to maintain employee health and safety, technicians work with specialists to increase worker productivity by reducing the number of worker absences and equipment downtime. These actions save companies money by lowering insurance premiums and workers' compensation payments, preventing government fines, and improving productivity and product quality.

Although all occupational health and safety technicians work to maintain the health of workers and the environment, their responsibilities vary by industry, workplace, and types of hazards affecting employees. For example, a technician may test the levels of hazards at a waste processing plant or may inspect the lighting and ventilation in an office setting. Both of these inspections are focused on maintaining the health of the workers and the environment.

The following are examples of types of occupational health and safety technicians:

Health physics technicians work in places that use radiation and radioactive material. Their goal is to protect people and the environment from hazardous radiation exposure.

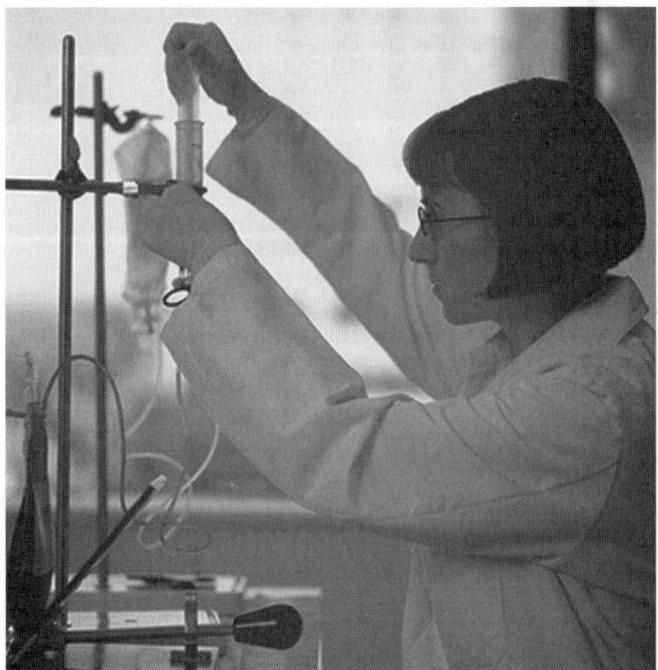

Occupational health and safety technicians prepare and calibrate scientific equipment.

Median Annual Wages, May 2012

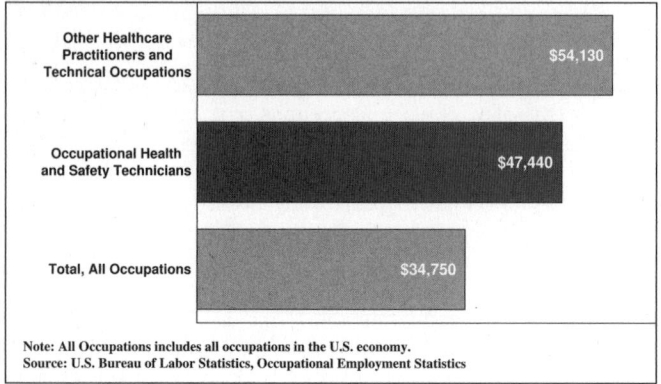

Note: All Occupations includes all occupations in the U.S. economy.
Source: U.S. Bureau of Labor Statistics, Occupational Employment Statistics

Percent Change in Employment, Projected 2012–2022

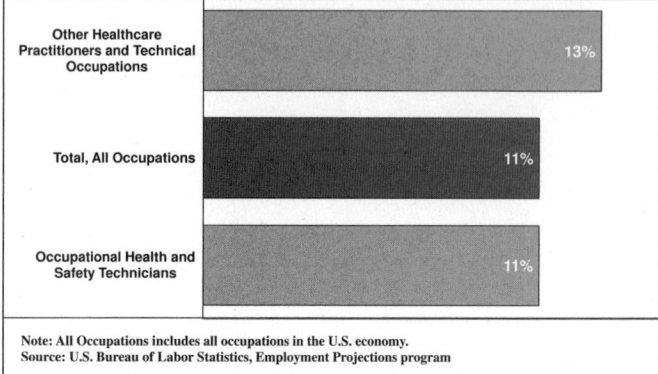

Note: All Occupations includes all occupations in the U.S. economy.
Source: U.S. Bureau of Labor Statistics, Employment Projections program

Industrial or occupational hygiene technicians examine the workplace for health hazards, such as exposure to lead, asbestos, pesticides, or contagious diseases.

Mine examiners inspect mines for proper air flow and potential health hazards such as the buildup of methane or other harmful gases.

Work Environment

Occupational health and safety technicians held about 12,600 jobs in 2012.

Occupational health and safety technicians work in a variety of settings, including offices, factories, and mines. About 19 percent worked for state and local governments in 2012. Others worked in hospitals; management, scientific and technical consulting services; and support activities for mining. Most private companies either employ their own occupational health and safety workers or contract with firms that provide such services.

Their jobs often involve considerable fieldwork and travel. In addition, occupational health and safety technicians may be exposed to strenuous, dangerous, or stressful conditions. Injuries are minimized by the use of gloves, helmets, and other safety equipment.

Work Schedules. Most occupational health and safety technicians work full time. Some technicians may work weekends or irregular hours in emergency situations.

How to Become One

Occupational health and safety technicians typically enter the occupation through one of two paths. Some technicians learn through on-the-job training; others enter with postsecondary education such as an associate's degree or certificate.

Education. Employers typically require technicians to have at least a high school diploma. High school students interested in this occupation should complete courses in English, mathematics, chemistry, biology, and physics.

Some employers may prefer to hire technicians who have earned an associate's degree or certificate from a community college or vocational school. These programs typically take 2 years or less. They include courses in respiratory protection, hazard communication, and material handling and storage procedures.

Postsecondary programs include instruction on standard laws and procedures; however, some on-the-job training is usually required to familiarize the technician with specific work environments.

Occupational health and safety technicians can become occupational health and safety specialists by earning a bachelor's or advanced degree.

Training. Technicians usually receive on-the-job training. They learn about specific laws, inspection procedures, conducting tests, and recognizing hazards. The length of training varies with the employee's level of experience, education, and the industry where they work.

Some technicians enter the occupation through a combination of related work experience and training. They may take on health and safety tasks at the company where they are employed at the time. For example, an employee may volunteer to complete annual workstation inspections for an office where they already work.

Licenses, Certifications, and Registrations. Certification is not required to become an occupational health and safety technician; however, many employers encourage it.

To apply for certification, technicians must have a high school diploma, related on-the-job experience, and pass a standardized health and safety exam. The Board of Certified Safety Professionals (BCSP) offers the following certifications at the technician level:

Construction Health and Safety Technician Certification (CHST) requires the applicant to have specific education or experience in construction safety. These technicians protect workers on construction sites from injury or illness.

Occupational Health and Safety Technologist Certification (OHST) is designed for workers who perform occupational health and safety tasks full- or part-time as part of their job duties.

Safety Trained Supervisor (STS) certification is geared toward first-line supervisors or managers. These workers are not safety practitioners but take on the certification in addition to their

Employment Projections Data for Occupational Health and Safety Technicians

Occupational title	SOC Code	Employment, 2012	Projected Employment, 2022	Change, 2012–2022	
				Percent	Numeric
Occupational health and safety technicians............................	29-9012	12,600	13,900	11	1,400

Source: U.S. Bureau of Labor Statistics, Employment Projections Program

Note: Data are rounded. Go to **Occupational Information Included in the OOH** *for a discussion of the data in this table.*

Similar Occupations This table shows a list of occupations with job duties that are similar to those of occupational health and safety technicians.

Occupations	Entry-level Education	2012 Pay	Projected Job Growth	Average Annual Openings
Construction and Building Inspectors	High school diploma or equivalent	$53,450	12%	3,670
Environmental Science and Protection Technicians	Associate's degree	$41,240	19%	1,900
Fire Inspectors and Investigators	High school diploma or equivalent	$53,990	7%	440
Occupational Health and Safety Specialists	Bachelor's degree	$66,790	7%	2,130

other job duties. This certification requires 1 year of supervisory experience.

Important Qualities

Ability to use technology. Occupational health and safety technicians often work with computers and complex testing equipment.

Communication skills. Occupational health and safety technicians must be able to work with specialists to collect and test samples of possible hazards, such as dust or vapors, in the workplace.

Detail oriented. Occupational health and safety technicians must be able to understand and adhere to specific safety standards and government regulations.

Physical stamina. Occupational health and safety technicians must be able to stay on their feet for long periods of time and to travel on a regular basis.

Problem-solving skills. Occupational health and safety technicians must be able to use their skills to find solutions to unsafe working conditions and environmental concerns in the workplace.

Pay

The median annual wage for occupational health and safety technicians was $47,440 in May 2012. The median wage is the wage at which half the workers in an occupation earned more than that amount and half earned less. The lowest 10 percent earned less than $28,920, and the top 10 percent earned more than $75,200.

Job Outlook

Employment of occupational health and safety technicians is projected to grow 11 percent from 2012 to 2022, about as fast as the average for all occupations. New environmental regulations and technological advances will require new or revised procedures in the workplace.

Increased adoption of nuclear power as a source of energy may lead to job growth as new regulations and precautions need to be enforced. Technicians will be needed to collect and test data to maintain the safety of both the workers and the environment.

Insurance and workers' compensation costs have become a concern for many employers and insurance companies. Because older workers usually have a greater incidence of workers' compensation claims, these costs can become larger with an aging population remaining in the workforce longer. Occupational health and safety technicians will be needed to work with occupational health and safety specialists in maintaining safety for all workers.

Although most occupational health and safety technicians work under the supervision of specialists, technicians can complete many routine tasks with little or no supervision. As a result, some employers may operate with more technicians because they are more cost effective than specialists.

Job Prospects. Occupational health and safety technicians with knowledge in more than one area of health and safety along with knowledge of general business functions will have the best prospects.

O*NET

➤ Occupational Health and Safety Technicians (29-9012.00)

Contacts for More Information

For more information about occupational health and safety technicians, visit

➤ Center for Disease Control and Prevention, National Institute for Occupational Safety and Health (NIOSH) (www.cdc.gov/niosh/)

➤ U.S. Department of Labor, Occupational Safety & Health Administration (OSHA) (www.osha.gov/)

For information on industrial or occupational hygiene, visit

➤ American Industrial Hygiene Association (AIHA) (www.aiha.org/Pages/default.aspx)

For information on credentials for industrial or occupational hygiene technicians and operators, visit

➤ AIHA Registry Programs (www.aiharegistries.org/Pages/default.aspx)

For information on health physics, visit

➤ Health Physics Society (www.hps.org/)

For more information on careers in safety and a list of safety and related academic programs, visit

➤ Board of Certified Safety Professionals (www.bcsp.org/)

Information about jobs in federal, state, and local governments and in private industry is available from state employment service offices.

Occupational Therapists

- **2012 Median Pay** .... $75,400 per year
  $36.25 per hour
- **Entry-Level Education** ....Master's degree
- **Work Experience in a Related Occupation**.............. None
- **On-the-Job Training** .... None
- **Number of Jobs 2012** 113,200
- **Job Outlook, 2012–22** .... 29% (Much faster than average)
- **Employment Change, 2012–22** 32,800

What Occupational Therapists Do

Occupational therapists treat injured, ill, or disabled patients through the therapeutic use of everyday activities. They help these patients develop, recover, and improve the skills needed for daily living and working.

Duties. Occupational therapists typically do the following:

- Observe patients doing tasks, ask them questions, and review their medical history

- Evaluate a patient's condition and needs

- Develop a treatment plan for patients, laying out the types of activities and specific goals to be accomplished

- Help people with various disabilities with different tasks, such as leading an autistic child in play activities

- Demonstrate exercises–for example, joint stretches for arthritis relief–that can help relieve pain for people with chronic conditions

- Evaluate a patient's home or workplace and, based on the patient's health needs, identify potential improvements, such as labeling kitchen cabinets for an older person with poor memory

- Educate a patient's family and employer about how to accommodate and care for the patient

- Recommend special equipment, such as wheelchairs and eating aids, and instruct patients on how to use that equipment

- Assess and record patients' activities and progress for patient evaluations, for billing, and for reporting to physicians and other healthcare providers

Patients with permanent disabilities, such as cerebral palsy, often need help performing daily tasks. Therapists show patients how to use appropriate adaptive equipment, such as leg braces, wheelchairs, and eating aids. These devices help patients perform a number of daily tasks, allowing them to function more independently.

Some occupational therapists work with children in educational settings. They evaluate disabled children's abilities, modify classroom equipment to accommodate children with certain disabilities, and help children participate in school activities.

Some therapists provide early intervention therapy to infants and toddlers who have, or are at risk of having, developmental delays.

Therapists who work with the elderly help their patients lead more independent and active lives. They assess patients' abilities and environment and make recommendations. For example, therapists may identify potential fall hazards in a patient's home and recommend their removal.

In some cases, occupational therapists help patients create functional work environments. They evaluate the work space, plan work activities, and meet with the patient's employer to collaborate on changes to the patient's work environment or schedule.

Occupational therapists also may work in mental health settings where they help patients who suffer from developmental disabili-

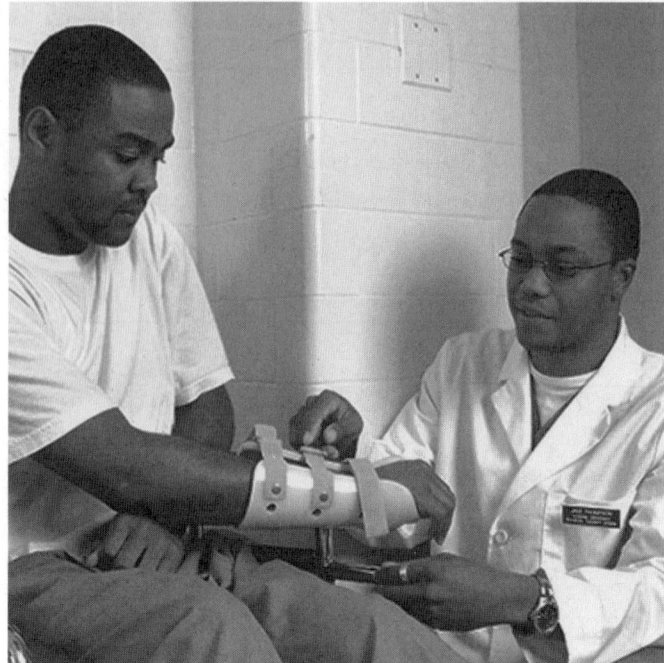

Occupational therapists help patients learn to perform all types of activities, from using a computer to caring for daily needs such as dressing, cooking, and eating.

ties, mental illness, or emotional problems. They help these patients cope with, and engage in, daily life by teaching skills such as time management, budgeting, using public transportation, and doing household chores. In addition, therapists may work with individuals who have problems with drug abuse, alcoholism, depression, or other disorders. They may also work with people who have been through a traumatic event.

Some occupational therapists, such as those employed in hospitals, work as part of a healthcare team along with doctors, registered nurses, and other types of therapists. They may work with patients with chronic conditions, such as diabetes, or help rehabilitate a patient recovering from a hip replacement surgery. Occupational therapists also oversee the work of occupational therapy assistants and aides.

Work Environment

Occupational therapists held about 113,200 jobs in 2012. The industries that employed the most occupational therapists in 2012 were as follows:

Median Annual Wages, May 2012

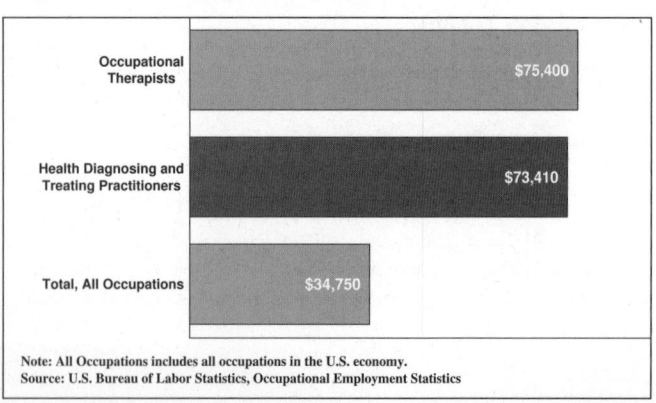

Occupational Therapists	$75,400
Health Diagnosing and Treating Practitioners	$73,410
Total, All Occupations	$34,750

Note: All Occupations includes all occupations in the U.S. economy.
Source: U.S. Bureau of Labor Statistics, Occupational Employment Statistics

Percent Change in Employment, Projected 2012–2022

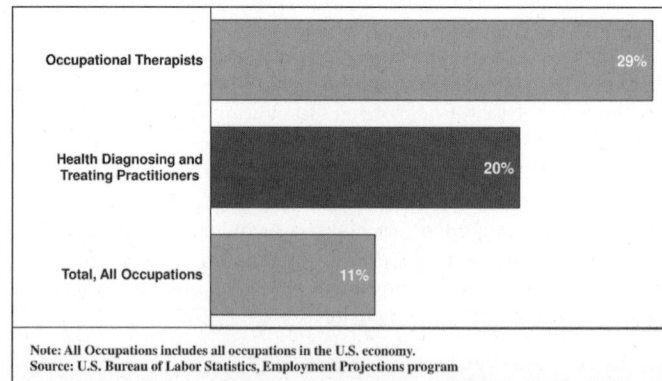

Occupational Therapists	29%
Health Diagnosing and Treating Practitioners	20%
Total, All Occupations	11%

Note: All Occupations includes all occupations in the U.S. economy.
Source: U.S. Bureau of Labor Statistics, Employment Projections program

Employment Projections Data for Occupational Therapists

Occupational title	SOC Code	Employment, 2012	Projected Employment, 2022	Change, 2012–2022	
				Percent	Numeric
Occupational therapists	29-1122	113,200	146,100	29	32,800

Source: U.S. Bureau of Labor Statistics, Employment Projections Program

Note: Data are rounded. Go to **Occupational Information Included in the OOH** *for a discussion of the data in this table.*

Hospitals; state, local, and private 28%
Offices of physical, occupational and speech therapists,
    and audiologists 22
Elementary and secondary schools; state, local, and private... 12
Nursing care facilities (skilled nursing facilities) 9
Home health care services... 9

Therapists spend a lot of time on their feet while working with patients. They also may be required to lift and move patients or heavy equipment. Many work in multiple facilities and have to travel from one job to another.

Work Schedules. Most occupational therapists worked full time in 2012. About 1 out of 4 worked part time. They may work nights or weekends, as needed, to accommodate patients' schedules.

How to Become One

Occupational therapists need at least a master's degree in occupational therapy; some therapists have a doctoral degree. Occupational therapists also must be licensed or registered.

Education. Most occupational therapists enter the occupation with a master's degree in occupational therapy. In March 2013, there were 149 occupational therapy programs accredited by the Accreditation Council for Occupational Therapy Education, part of the American Occupational Therapy Association; 145 are master's degree programs and the remaining 4 are doctoral degree programs.

Admission to graduate programs in occupational therapy generally requires a bachelor's degree and specific coursework, including biology and physiology. Many programs also require applicants to have volunteered or worked in an occupational therapy setting.

Master's programs generally take 2 to 3 years to complete; doctoral programs take about 3 years. Some schools offer a dual-degree program in which the student earns a bachelor's degree and a master's degree in 5 years. Part-time programs that offer courses on nights and weekends are also available.

Both master's and doctoral programs require at least 24 weeks of supervised fieldwork, in which prospective occupational therapists gain clinical work experience.

Licenses, Certifications, and Registrations. All states require occupational therapists to pass the national examination administered by the National Board for Certification in Occupational

Therapists (NBCOT). To sit for the NBCOT exam, candidates must have earned a degree from an accredited educational program and completed all fieldwork requirements.

Therapists must pass the NBCOT exam to use the title "Occupational Therapist Registered" (OTR). They must also take continuing education classes to maintain certification.

The American Occupational Therapy Association also offers a number of certifications for therapists who want to demonstrate their advanced level of knowledge in a specialty area, such as pediatrics, mental health, or low vision.

Important Qualities

Communication skills. Occupational therapists must be able to listen attentively to what patients tell them and be able to explain what they want their patients to do.

Compassion. Occupational therapists are usually drawn to the profession by a desire to help people and improve the daily lives of others.

Flexibility. Occupational therapists must be flexible when treating patients. Because not every type of therapy will work for each patient, therapists may need to be creative when determining the treatment plans and adaptive devices that best suit each patient's needs.

Interpersonal skills. Because occupational therapists spend their time teaching and explaining therapies to patients, they should be able to earn the trust and respect of their patients.

Patience. Dealing with injuries, illnesses, and disabilities is frustrating for many people. Occupational therapists should be patient in order to provide quality care to the people they serve.

Writing skills. When communicating in writing with other members of the patient's medical team, occupational therapists must be able to explain clearly the treatment plan for the patient and any progress made by the patient.

Pay

The median annual wage for occupational therapists was $75,400 in May 2012. The median wage is the wage at which half the workers in an occupation earned more than that amount and half earned less. The lowest 10 percent earned less than $50,500, and the top 10 percent earned more than $107,070.

Similar Occupations   This table shows a list of occupations with job duties that are similar to those of occupational therapists.

Occupations	Entry-level Education	2012 Pay	Projected Job Growth	Average Annual Openings
Athletic Trainers and Exercise Physiologists	Bachelor's degree	$42,676	19%	1,240
Occupational Therapy Assistants and Aides	See "How to Become One"	$47,638	41%	2,560
Physical Therapists	Doctoral or professional degree	$79,860	36%	12,370
Recreational Therapists	Bachelor's degree	$42,280	14%	670
Speech-Language Pathologists	Master's degree	$69,870	19%	4,620

In May 2012, the median annual wages for occupational therapists in the top five industries in which these therapists worked were as follows:

Nursing care facilities (skilled nursing facilities) $83,430
Home health care services 82,310
Offices of physical, occupational and speech
    therapists, and audiologists 77,430
Hospitals; state, local, and private 75,140
Elementary and secondary schools; state,
    local, and private 66,610

Job Outlook

Employment of occupational therapists is projected to grow 29 percent from 2012 to 2022, much faster than the average for all occupations. Occupational therapy will continue to be an important part of treatment for people with various illnesses and disabilities, such as Alzheimer's disease, cerebral palsy, autism, or the loss of a limb.

The need for occupational therapists is expected to increase as the large baby-boom generation ages and people remain active later in life. Occupational therapists can help senior citizens maintain their independence by recommending home modifications and strategies that make daily activities easier. Therapists also play a large role in the treatment of many conditions and ailments commonly associated with aging, such as arthritis and stroke. They will also be needed in a variety of healthcare settings to act as part of a healthcare team in treating patients with chronic conditions, such as diabetes. Patients will continue to seek noninvasive outpatient treatment for long-term disabilities and illnesses, either in their homes or in residential care environments.

In addition, medical advances now enable more patients with critical problems such as birth defects or limb amputations to survive. These patients may need occupational therapy to perform a variety of daily tasks.

Demand for occupational therapy services will also stem from patients with autism spectrum disorder. As an increasing number of states require insurance companies to cover autism-related services, more therapists will be needed in schools to assist children with autism in improving their social skills and accomplishing a variety of daily tasks.

Demand for occupational therapy services is related to the ability of patients to pay, either directly or through health insurance. The number of individuals who have access to occupational therapy services may increase because of federal health insurance reform. Both rehabilitation and habilitation services are listed among the essential health benefits that insurers will need to cover once reforms are implemented.

Job Prospects. Job opportunities should be good for licensed occupational therapists in all settings, particularly in acute hospital, rehabilitation, and orthopedic settings, because the elderly receive most of their treatment in these settings. Occupational therapists with specialized knowledge in a treatment area also will have better job prospects.

O*NET

➤ Occupational Therapists (29-1122.00)
➤ Low Vision Therapists, Orientation and Mobility Specialists, and Vision Rehabilitation Therapists (29-1122.01)

Contacts for More Information

For more information about occupational therapists, visit
➤ American Occupational Therapy Association, Inc. (www.aota.org/)

For more information about the Occupational Therapist Registered certification exam, visit
➤ National Board for Certification in Occupational Therapy (www.nbcot.org/)

For information regarding the requirements to practice as an occupational therapist in schools, contact state occupational therapy regulatory agencies.

Occupational Therapy Assistants and Aides

- **2012 Median Pay** .... $48,940 per year
    $23.53 per hour
- **Entry-Level Education** ....See "How to Become One"
- **Work Experience in a Related Occupation** .... None
- **On-the-Job Training** ....See "How to Become One"
- **Number of Jobs 2012** 38,600
- **Job Outlook, 2012–22** .... 41% (Much faster than average)
- **Employment Change, 2012–22** 15,900

What Occupational Therapy Assistants and Aides Do

Occupational therapy assistants and aides help patients develop, recover, and improve the skills needed for daily living and working. Occupational therapy assistants are directly involved in providing therapy to patients, while occupational therapy aides typically perform support activities. Both assistants and aides work under the direction of occupational therapists.

Duties. Occupational therapy assistants typically do the following:

- Help patients do therapeutic activities, such as stretches and other exercises
- Lead children who have developmental disabilities in play activities that promote coordination and socialization
- Teach patients how to use special equipment; for example, showing a patient with Parkinson's disease how to use devices that make eating easier
- Record patients' progress, report to occupational therapists, and do other administrative tasks

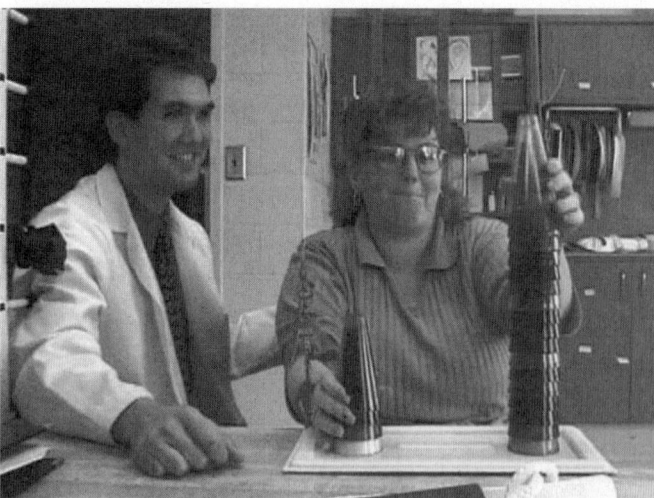

Occupational therapy assistants teach patients how to use special equipment, such as wheelchairs.

Median Annual Wages, May 2012

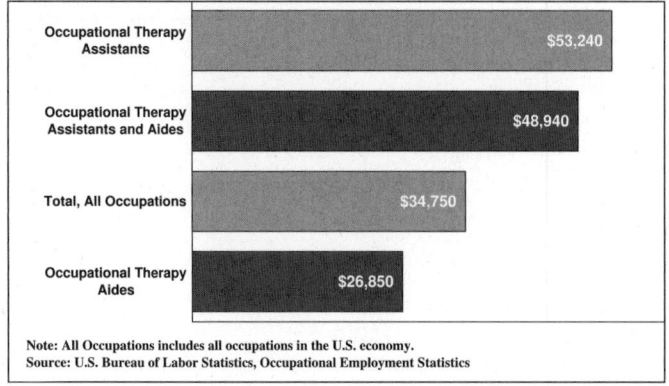

Note: All Occupations includes all occupations in the U.S. economy.
Source: U.S. Bureau of Labor Statistics, Occupational Employment Statistics

Percent Change in Employment, Projected 2012–2022

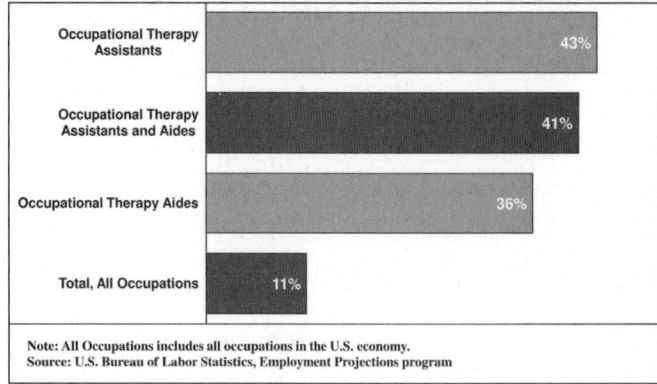

Note: All Occupations includes all occupations in the U.S. economy.
Source: U.S. Bureau of Labor Statistics, Employment Projections program

Occupational therapy aides typically do the following:

• Prepare treatment areas, such as setting up therapy equipment

• Transport patients

• Clean treatment areas and equipment

• Help patients with billing and insurance forms

• Perform clerical tasks, including scheduling appointments and answering telephones

Occupational therapy assistants collaborate with occupational therapists to develop and carry out a treatment plan for each patient. Activities in plans range from teaching the proper way for patients to move from a bed into a wheelchair to the best way to stretch their muscles. For example, an occupational therapy assistant might work with injured workers to help them get back into the workforce by teaching them how to work around lost motor skills. Occupational therapy assistants also may work with people with learning disabilities to teach them skills that allow them to be more independent.

Assistants monitor activities to make sure patients are doing them correctly. They also encourage the patients. They record the patient's progress so the therapist can change the treatment plan if the patient is not getting the desired results.

Occupational therapy aides typically prepare materials and assemble equipment used during treatment. They may assist patients with moving to and from treatment areas. After a therapy session, aides clean the treatment area and any communal equipment.

Occupational therapy aides also fill out insurance forms and other paperwork and are responsible for a range of clerical tasks, such as scheduling appointments, answering the telephone, and monitoring inventory levels.

Work Environment

Occupational therapy assistants held about 30,300 jobs in 2012. Occupational therapy aides held about 8,400 jobs in 2012. Occupational therapy assistants and aides work primarily in occupational therapists' offices, hospitals, and nursing care facilities.

The industries that employed the most occupational therapy assistants in 2012 were as follows:

Offices of physical, occupational and speech therapists,
   and audiologists 35%
Nursing and residential care facilities 22
Hospitals; state, local, and private 21
Educational services; state, local, and private 6
Home health care services... 4

The industries that employed the most occupational therapy aides in 2012 were as follows:

Offices of physical, occupational and speech therapists,
   and audiologists 33%
Hospitals; state, local, and private 32
Nursing and residential care facilities 13
Social assistance... 5
Educational services; state, local, and private 4

Occupational therapy assistants and aides spend much of their time on their feet setting up equipment and, in the case of assistants, working with patients. Constant kneeling and stooping are part of the job, as is the need to sometimes lift patients.

Work Schedules. Most occupational therapy assistants and aides work full time. Occupational therapy assistants and aides may work during evenings or on weekends to accommodate patients' schedules.

How to Become One

Occupational therapy assistants need an associate's degree from an accredited occupational therapy assistant program. They also must be licensed in most states. Occupational therapy aides typically have a high school diploma or equivalent.

Education and Training. People interested in becoming an occupational therapy assistant should take high school courses in biology and health. They can also increase their chances of getting into a community college or technical school program by doing vol-

Employment Projections Data for Occupational Therapy Assistants and Aides

Occupational title	SOC Code	Employment, 2012	Projected Employment, 2022	Change, 2012–2022	
				Percent	Numeric
Occupational therapy assistants and aides	31-2010	38,600	54,600	41	15,900
Occupational therapy assistants...	31-2011	30,300	43,200	43	12,900
Occupational therapy aides..	31-2012	8,400	11,400	36	3,000

Source: U.S. Bureau of Labor Statistics, Employment Projections Program

Note: Data are rounded. Go to Occupational Information Included in the OOH *for a discussion of the data in this table.*

Similar Occupations   This table shows a list of occupations with job duties that are similar to those of occupational therapy assistants and aides.

Occupations	Entry-level Education	2012 Pay	Projected Job Growth	Average Annual Openings
Dental Assistants	Postsecondary non-degree award	$34,500	25%	13,720
Medical Assistants	Postsecondary non-degree award	$29,370	29%	26,990
Occupational Therapists	Master's degree	$75,400	29%	4,820
Pharmacy Technicians	High school diploma or equivalent	$29,320	20%	10,590
Physical Therapist Assistants and Aides	See "How to Become One"	$40,539	41%	7,630

unteer work in a healthcare setting, such as a nursing care facility, an occupational therapist's office, or a physical therapist's office.

Occupational therapy assistants typically need an associate's degree from an accredited program. Occupational therapy assistant programs are commonly found in community colleges and technical schools. In March 2013, there were 162 occupational therapy assistant programs accredited by the Accreditation Council for Occupational Therapy Education, a branch of the American Occupational Therapy Association.

These programs generally require 2 years of full-time study. They include classroom instruction in subjects such as psychology, biology, and pediatric health. Occupational therapy assistants also must complete at least 16 weeks of fieldwork as part of their education to gain hands-on work experience.

Occupational therapy aides typically have a high school diploma or equivalent. They are trained on the job under the supervision of more experienced assistants or aides. Training can last from several weeks to a few months and covers a number of topics, including set up of therapy equipment and infection control procedures, among others. Prior work experience in healthcare as well as CPR and Basic Life Support (BLS) certifications may be helpful in getting a job.

Important Qualities

Compassion. Occupational therapy assistants and aides frequently work with patients who struggle with many of life's basic activities. As a result, they should be compassionate and caring and have the ability to encourage others.

Detail oriented. Occupational therapy assistants and aides must be able to quickly and accurately follow the instructions, both written and spoken, of an occupational therapist.

Flexibility. Assistants must be flexible when treating patients. Because not every type of therapy will work for each patient, assistants may need to be creative when working with occupational therapists to determine the best type of therapy to use for achieving a patient's goals.

Interpersonal skills. Occupational therapy assistants and aides spend much of their time interacting with patients. They should be friendly and courteous, and they should be able to communicate with patients to the extent of their ability and training.

Physical strength. Assistants and aides need to have a moderate degree of strength because of the physical exertion required to assist patients. Constant kneeling, stooping, and standing for long periods also are part of the job.

Licenses, Certifications, and Registrations. Most states require occupational therapy assistants to be licensed or registered. Licensure typically requires the completion of an accredited occupational therapy assistant education program, completion of all fieldwork requirements, and passing the National Board for Certification in Occupational Therapy (NBCOT) exam. Some states have additional requirements.

Occupational therapy assistants must pass the NBCOT exam to use the title "Certified Occupational Therapy Assistant" (COTA). They must also take continuing education classes to maintain certification.

Occupational therapy aides are not regulated.

Advancement. Some occupational therapy assistants and aides advance by gaining additional education to become occupational therapists. A small number of occupational therapist "bridge" education programs are designed for qualifying occupational therapy assistants to advance to therapists.

Pay

The median annual wage for occupational therapy assistants was $53,240 in May 2012. The median wage is the wage at which half the workers in an occupation earned more than that amount and half earned less. The lowest 10 percent earned less than $32,970, and the top 10 percent earned more than $73,120.

The median annual wage for occupational therapy aides was $26,850 in May 2012. The lowest 10 percent earned less than $18,030, and the top 10 percent earned more than $47,880.

In May 2012, the median annual wages for occupational therapy assistants in the top five industries in which they worked were as follows:

Home health care services	$57,840
Nursing and residential care facilities	57,260
Offices of physical, occupational and speech therapists, and audiologists	55,070
Hospitals; state, local, and private	49,460
Educational services; state, local, and private	43,330

In May 2012, the median annual wages for occupational therapy aides in the top five industries in which they worked were as follows:

Hospitals; state, local, and private	$29,370
Nursing and residential care facilities	28,380
Educational services; state, local, and private	27,970
Social assistance	25,890
Offices of physical, occupational and speech therapists, and audiologists	22,580

Job Outlook

Employment of occupational therapy assistants is projected to grow 43 percent from 2012 to 2022, much faster than the average for all occupations.

Employment of occupational therapy aides is projected to increase 36 percent from 2012 to 2022, much faster than the average for all occupations. However, because it is a small occupation, the fast growth will result in only about 3,000 new jobs over the 10-year period.

Demand for occupational therapy is expected to rise significantly over the coming decade in response to the health needs of the aging baby-boom generation and a growing elderly population. Older adults are more prone than younger people to conditions and ailments such as arthritis and stroke. These conditions can affect the ability to perform a variety of everyday activities. Occupational therapy assistants and aides will be needed to help occupational therapists in caring for these people. Occupational therapy will also continue to be used for treating children and young adults with developmental disabilities like autism.

Demand for occupational therapy assistants is also expected to stem from healthcare providers employing more assistants to reduce the cost of occupational therapy services. After the therapist has evaluated a patient and designed a treatment plan, the occupational therapy assistant can provide many aspects of the treatment that the therapist prescribed.

Demand for occupational therapy services is related to the ability of patients to pay, either directly or through health insurance. The number of individuals who have access to occupational therapy services may increase because of federal health insurance reform. Both rehabilitation and habilitation services are listed among the essential health benefits that insurers will need to cover once reforms are implemented. Occupational therapy assistants and aides will be needed to help therapists treat additional patients and to ensure that treatment facility operations run smoothly.

Job Prospects. Occupational therapy assistants and aides with experience working in an occupational therapy office or other healthcare setting should have the best job opportunities. In addition to overall employment growth, job openings will also result from the need to replace occupational therapy assistants and aides who leave the occupation.

O*NET

➤ Occupational Therapy Assistants (31-2011.00)
➤ Occupational Therapy Aides (31-2012.00)

Contacts for More Information

For more information about occupational therapy assistants or aides, visit
➤ American Occupational Therapy Association, Inc. (www.aota.org/)
    For more information about certification for occupational therapy assistants, visit
➤ National Board for Certification in Occupational Therapy (www.nbcot.org/)

Opticians, Dispensing

- **2012 Median Pay** .... $33,330 per year
    $16.03 per hour
- **Entry-Level Education** ... High school diploma or equivalent
- **Work Experience in a Related Occupation** .... None
- **On-the-Job Training** .... Long-term on-the-job training
- **Number of Jobs 2012** 67,600
- **Job Outlook, 2012–22** .... 23% (Much faster than average)
- **Employment Change, 2012–22** 15,800

What Opticians, Dispensing Do

Dispensing opticians help fit eyeglasses and contact lenses, following prescriptions from ophthalmologists and optometrists. They also help customers decide which eyeglass frames or contact lenses to buy.

Duties. Opticians typically do the following:

- Receive customers' prescriptions for eyeglasses or contact lenses

- Measure customers' eyes, such as the distance between their pupils
- Help customers choose eyeglass frames and lens treatments, such as eyewear for occupational use or sports, tints or anti-reflective coatings, based on their vision needs and style preferences
- Create work orders for ophthalmic laboratory technicians, providing information about the lenses needed
- Adjust eyewear to ensure a good fit
- Repair or replace broken eyeglass frames
- Educate customers about eyewear–for example, show them how to care for their contact lenses
- Perform business tasks, such as maintaining sales records, keeping track of customers' prescriptions, and ordering and maintaining inventory

Opticians who work in small shops or prepare custom orders may cut lenses and insert them into frames, tasks usually performed by ophthalmic laboratory technicians. For more information, see the profile on dental and ophthalmic laboratory technicians and medical appliance technicians.

Work Environment

Dispensing opticians held about 67,600 jobs in 2012.

The industries that employed the most dispensing opticians in 2012 were as follows:

Offices of optometrists 39%
Health and personal care stores... 32
General merchandise stores 11
Offices of physicians.. 11

Some opticians work in stores that sell eyeglasses, contact lenses, visual aids, and other optical goods. These stores may be stand-alone businesses or parts of larger retail establishments, such as department stores.

Other opticians work as part of a group optometry or medical practice where optometrists and ophthalmologists provide eye-related medical care to patients. For more information on ophthalmologists, see the profile on physicians and surgeons.

Work Schedules. Opticians who work in large retail establishments, such as department stores, may have to work evenings and weekends. Most opticians work full time, although part-time opportunities also are available.

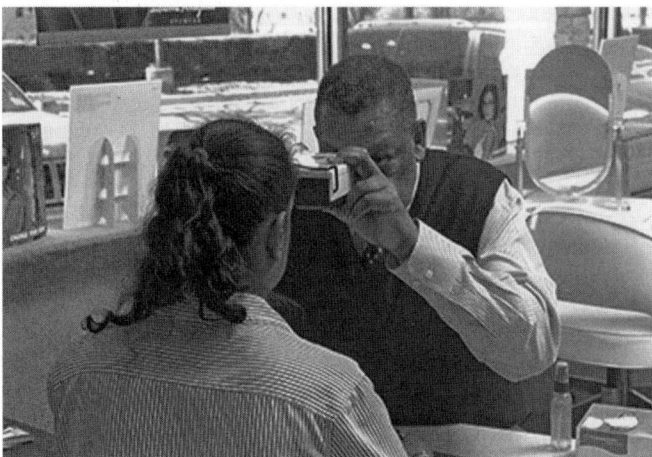

Dispensing opticians deal directly with the public, so they should be tactful, pleasant, and communicate well.

Median Annual Wages, May 2012

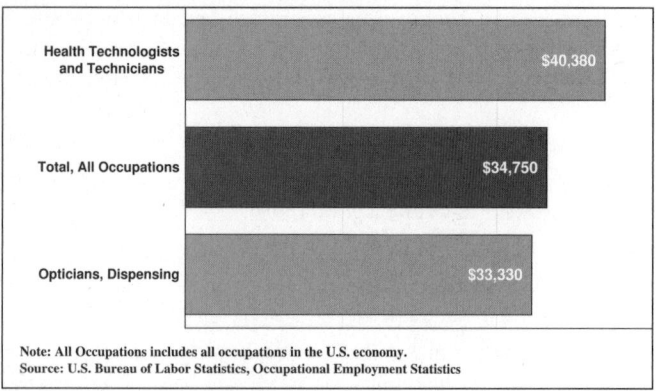

Note: All Occupations includes all occupations in the U.S. economy.
Source: U.S. Bureau of Labor Statistics, Occupational Employment Statistics

Percent Change in Employment, Projected 2012–2022

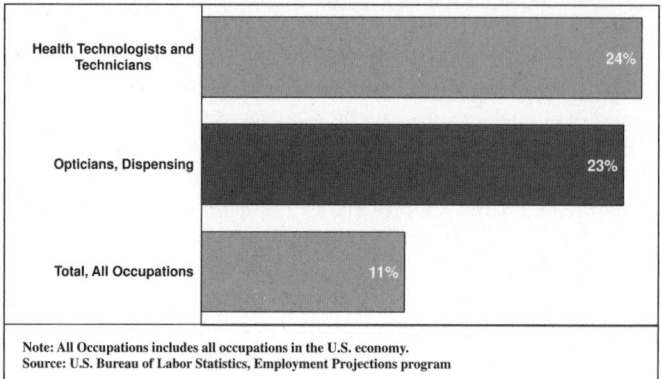

Note: All Occupations includes all occupations in the U.S. economy.
Source: U.S. Bureau of Labor Statistics, Employment Projections program

How to Become One

Opticians typically have a high school diploma or equivalent and receive some form of on-the-job training. Some opticians enter the occupation with an associate's degree or a certificate from a community college or technical school. Licensure is required in some states.

Education and Training. Opticians typically have a high school diploma or equivalent and learn job skills through on-the-job training. Training includes technical instruction in which, for example, a new optician measures a customer's eyes or adjusts frames under the supervision of an experienced optician. Trainees also learn sales and office management practices. Some opticians complete an apprenticeship, which typically takes at least 2 years.

Other opticians complete a postsecondary education program at a community college or technical school. These programs award a 2-year associate's degree or a 1-year certificate. As of 2012, the Commission on Opticianry Accreditation accredited 21 programs in 14 states.

Education programs typically include both classroom instruction and clinical experience. Coursework includes classes in optics, eye physiology, math, and business management, among other topics. Students also do supervised clinical work that gives them hands-on experience working as opticians and learning optical math, optical physics, and the use of precision measuring instruments. Some programs have distance-learning options.

The National Academy of Opticianry offers the Ophthalmic Career Progression Program (OCPP), a program designed for individuals who are already working in the field. The OCPP offers opticians another way to prepare for licensure exams or certifications.

Licenses, Certifications, and Registrations. About half of the states require opticians to be licensed. Licensure usually requires completing formal education through an approved program or completing an apprenticeship. In addition, opticians must pass one or more exams to be licensed. The opticianry licensing board in each state can supply information on licensing requirements.

Opticians may choose to become certified in eyeglass dispensing or contact lens dispensing or both. Certification requires passing exams from the American Board of Opticianry (ABO) and National Contact Lens Examiners (NCLE). Nearly all state licensing boards use the ABO and NCLE exams as the basis for state licensing. Some states also require opticians to pass state-specific exams.

In most states that require licensure, opticians must renew their license every 1 to 2 years and must complete continuing education requirements.

Important Qualities

Business skills. Opticians are often responsible for the business aspects of running an optical store. They should be comfortable making decisions and have some knowledge of sales and inventory management.

Communication skills. Opticians must be able to listen closely to what customers want. They must be able to clearly explain options and instructions for care in ways that customers understand.

Customer service skills. Because some opticians work in stores, they must answer questions and know about the products they sell. They interact with customers on a very personal level, fitting eyeglasses or contact lenses. To succeed, they must be friendly, courteous, patient, and helpful to customers.

Decision-making skills. Opticians must determine what adjustments need to be made to eyeglasses and contact lenses. They must decide which materials and styles are most appropriate for each customer on the basis of their preferences and lifestyle.

Dexterity. Opticians frequently use special tools to make final adjustments and repairs to eyeglasses. They must have good hand-eye coordination to do that work quickly and accurately.

Pay

The median annual wage for opticians was $33,330 in May 2012. The median wage is the wage at which half the workers in an occupation earned more than that amount and half earned less. The lowest 10 percent earned less than $21,030, and the top 10 percent earned more than $52,740.

In May 2012, the median annual wages for dispensing opticians in the top four industries in which they worked were as follows:

Employment Projections Data for Opticians, Dispensing

Occupational title	SOC Code	Employment, 2012	Projected Employment, 2022	Change, 2012–2022	
				Percent	Numeric
Opticians, dispensing	29-2081	67,600	83,500	23	15,800

Source: U.S. Bureau of Labor Statistics, Employment Projections Program

Note: Data are rounded. Go to **Occupational Information Included in the OOH** *for a discussion of the data in this table.*

Similar Occupations   This table shows a list of occupations with job duties that are similar to those of opticians, dispensing.

Occupations	Entry-level Education	2012 Pay	Projected Job Growth	Average Annual Openings
Dental and Ophthalmic Laboratory Technicians and Medical Appliance Technicians	High school diploma or equivalent	$33,281	7%	3,360
Jewelers and Precious Stone and Metal Workers	High school diploma or equivalent	$35,350	-10%	670
Optometrists	Doctoral or professional degree	$97,820	24%	1,770
Orthotists and Prosthetists	Master's degree	$62,670	35%	380

Health and personal care stores $35,990
Offices of physicians 34,680
Offices of optometrists 31,820
General merchandise stores 29,560

Job Outlook

Employment of opticians is projected to grow 23 percent from 2012 to 2022, much faster than the average for all occupations.

The growth in the older population is anticipated to lead to greater demand for eye care services. Because people usually have eye problems more frequently as they age, the need for opticians is expected to grow with the increase in the number of older people.

Increasing rates of chronic diseases such as diabetes may also increase demand for opticianry services because some chronic diseases cause vision problems. Additional opticians will be needed to fill prescriptions for corrective eyewear for individuals with conditions that damage their eyesight.

A growing proportion of opticians are expected to find employment in group medical practices. Optometrists and ophthalmologists are increasingly offering glasses and contact lenses to their patients as a way to expand their businesses, leading to a greater need for opticians in those settings.

However, employment growth is expected to be constrained by increases in productivity that will allow a given number of opticians to serve more customers.

Job Prospects. Having an associate's degree from an accredited program and ABO and NCLE certifications may improve an applicant's job prospects.

O*NET

➤ Opticians, Dispensing (29-2081.00)

Contacts for More Information

For more information about dispensing opticians, including certifications and a list of state licensing boards for opticians, visit
➤ American Board of Opticianry and National Contact Lens Examiners (www.abo-ncle.org/)
  For a list of accredited programs, visit
➤ Commission on Opticianry Accreditation (www.coaccreditation. com/)
  For more information about optician education, visit
➤ National Federation of Opticianry Schools (www.nfos.org/)
➤ National Academy of Opticianry (www.nao.org/)

Optometrists

- **2012 Median Pay** ....$97,820 per year
  $47.03 per hour
- **Entry-Level Education** ... Doctoral or professional degree
- **Work Experience in a Related Occupation**.............. None
- **On-the-Job Training** .... None
- **Number of Jobs 2012** 33,100
- **Job Outlook, 2012–22** .... 24% (Much faster than average)
- **Employment Change, 2012–22** 8,100

What Optometrists Do

Optometrists examine, diagnose, treat, and manage disorders of the visual system, eye diseases, and injuries. They prescribe eyeglasses or contact lenses as needed.

Duties. Optometrists typically do the following:

- Perform vision tests and analyze results
- Diagnose sight problems, such as nearsightedness or farsightedness and eye diseases, such as glaucoma
- Prescribe eyeglasses, contact lenses, and medications
- Provide treatments such as vision therapy or low-vision rehabilitation
- Provide pre- and postoperative care to patients undergoing eye surgery–for example, examining a patient's eyes the day after surgery
- Evaluate patients for the presence of diseases such as diabetes and refer patients to other healthcare providers as needed
- Promote eye health by counseling patients, including explaining how to clean and wear contact lenses

Some optometrists spend much of their time providing specialized care, particularly if they are working in a group practice with other optometrists or physicians. For example, some optometrists mostly treat patients with only partial sight, a condition known as low vision. Others may focus on treating infants and children.

Many optometrists own their practice and may spend more time on general business activities such as hiring employees, ordering supplies, and marketing their business.

Optometrists also may work as postsecondary teachers, do research in optometry colleges, or work as consultants in the eye care industry.

Optometrists should not be confused with ophthalmologists or dispensing opticians. Ophthalmologists are physicians who perform eye surgery and treat eye disease in addition to examining eyes and prescribing eyeglasses and contact lenses. For more information on ophthalmologists, see the physicians and surgeons profile. Dispensing opticians fit and adjust eyeglasses and, in some states, fill contact lens prescriptions that an optometrist or ophthalmologist has written.

Work Environment

Optometrists held about 33,100 jobs in 2012. About 53 percent of optometrists worked in stand-alone offices of optometry. Optometrists may also work in doctors' offices, retail stores, and outpatient clinics. About 11 percent of optometrists were self-employed in 2012.

The industries that employed the most optometrists in 2012 were as follows:

Offices of optometrists	53%
Offices of physicians	18
Health and personal care stores	11
Outpatient care centers	2
Educational services; state, local, and private	2

Work Schedules. Most optometrists work full time. Some work evenings and weekends to accommodate patients' needs.

How to Become One

Optometrists must complete a Doctor of Optometry (O.D.) degree program and obtain a license to practice in a particular state. Doctor of Optometry programs take 4 years to complete, and most students have a bachelor's degree before entering an O.D. program.

Education. Optometrists need a Doctor of Optometry (O.D.) degree. In 2012, there were 17 accredited Doctor of Optometry programs in the United States, one of which was in Puerto Rico. An additional 4 programs have received preliminary approval.

Applicants to O.D. programs must have completed at least 3 years of postsecondary education, including coursework in biology, chemistry, physics, English, and math. However, most students get a bachelor's degree before enrolling in a Doctor of Optometry program.

Applicants must also take the Optometry Admission Test (OAT) to apply to O.D. programs. The OAT is a computerized exam that tests applicants on four subject areas: science, reading comprehension, physics, and quantitative reasoning.

Doctor of Optometry programs take 4 years to complete. They combine classroom learning and supervised clinical experience. Coursework includes anatomy, physiology, biochemistry, optics, and visual science, and the diagnosis and treatment of diseases and disorders of the visual system.

After finishing an O.D. degree, some optometrists complete a 1-year residency program to get advanced clinical training in an area of emphasis. Areas of emphasis for residency programs

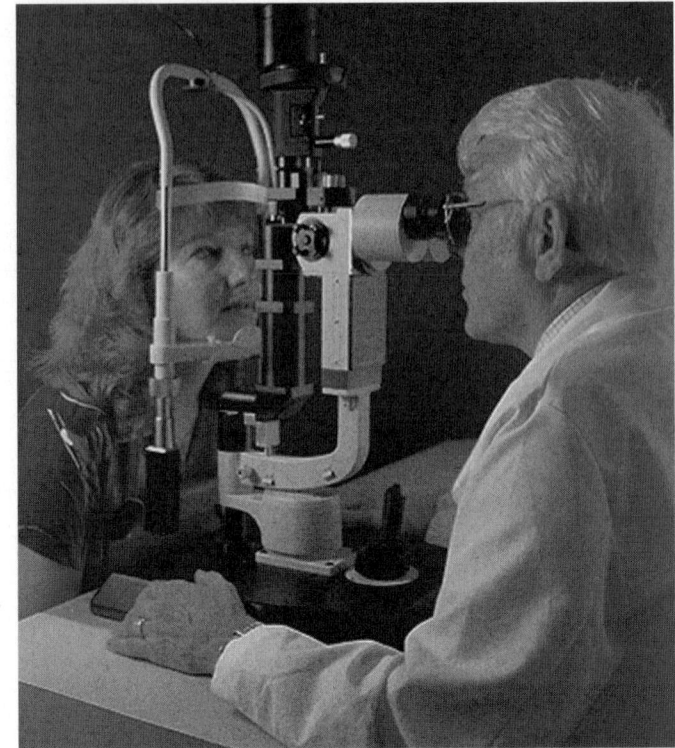

The Doctor of Optometry degree requires the completion of a 4-year program at an accredited optometry school.

include family practice, low vision care, pediatric or geriatric optometry, and ocular disease, among others.

Licenses, Certifications, and Registrations. All states require optometrists to be licensed. To get a license, a prospective optometrist must have an O.D. from an accredited optometry school and must complete all sections of the National Board of Examiners in Optometry.

Some states require individuals to pass an additional clinical exam or an exam on law. All states require optometrists to take continuing education and to renew their license periodically. The board of optometry in each state can provide information on licensing requirements.

Optometrists who wish to demonstrate an advanced level of knowledge may choose to become certified by the American Board of Optometry.

Important Qualities

Decision-making skills. Optometrists must be able to evaluate the results of a variety of diagnostic tests and decide on the best course of treatment for a patient.

Median Annual Wages, May 2012

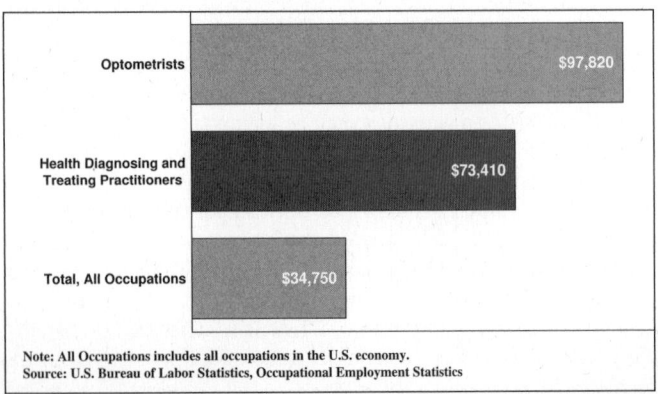

Optometrists $97,820

Health Diagnosing and Treating Practitioners $73,410

Total, All Occupations $34,750

Note: All Occupations includes all occupations in the U.S. economy.
Source: U.S. Bureau of Labor Statistics, Occupational Employment Statistics

Percent Change in Employment, Projected 2012–2022

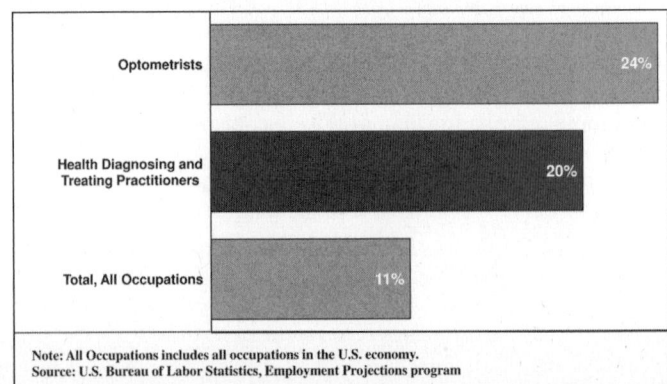

Optometrists 24%

Health Diagnosing and Treating Practitioners 20%

Total, All Occupations 11%

Note: All Occupations includes all occupations in the U.S. economy.
Source: U.S. Bureau of Labor Statistics, Employment Projections program

Employment Projections Data for Optometrists

Occupational title	SOC Code	Employment, 2012	Projected Employment, 2022	Change, 2012–2022	
				Percent	Numeric
Optometrists	29-1041	33,100	41,200	24	8,100

Source: U.S. Bureau of Labor Statistics, Employment Projections Program

Note: Data are rounded. Go to Occupational Information Included in the OOH *for a discussion of the data in this table.*

Similar Occupations This table shows a list of occupations with job duties that are similar to those of optometrists.

Occupations	Entry-level Education	2012 Pay	Projected Job Growth	Average Annual Openings
Chiropractors	Doctoral or professional degree	$66,160	15%	1,520
Dentists	Doctoral or professional degree	$149,795	16%	5,910
Opticians, Dispensing	High school diploma or equivalent	$33,330	24%	3,530
Physicians and Surgeons	Doctoral or professional degree	$182,294	18%	29,630
Podiatrists	Doctoral or professional degree	$116,440	22%	460
Veterinarians	Doctoral or professional degree	$84,460	12%	3,100

Interpersonal skills. Because they spend much of their time examining patients, optometrists must be able to help their patients feel at ease.

Speaking skills. Optometrists must be able to clearly explain eyecare instructions to their patients, as well as answer patients' questions.

Pay

The median annual wage for optometrists was $97,820 in May 2012. The median wage is the wage at which half the workers in an occupation earned more than that amount and half earned less. The lowest 10 percent earned less than $52,590, and the top 10 percent earned more than $184,530.

Job Outlook

Employment of optometrists is projected to grow 24 percent from 2012 to 2022, much faster than the average for all occupations. However, because it is a small occupation, the fast growth will result in only about 8,100 new jobs over the 10-year period.

Because vision problems tend to occur more frequently later in life, an aging population will require more optometrists. As people age, they become more susceptible to conditions that impair vision, such as cataracts and macular degeneration.

The number of people with chronic diseases, such as diabetes, has grown in recent years. Diabetes has been linked to increased rates of several eye conditions, including diabetic retinopathy, a condition that affects the blood vessels in the eye and may lead to vision loss. More optometrists will be needed to monitor, treat, and refer individuals with these chronic conditions.

In addition, an increasing number of insurance plans, including Medicare and Medicaid, provide some vision or eye care insurance coverage. Furthermore, the number of individuals, particularly children, who have vision or eye care insurance will increase as a result of federal health insurance reform legislation. More optometrists will be needed in order to provide services to more patients.

Job Prospects. Because the number of optometrists is limited by the number of accredited optometry schools, licensed optometrists should expect good job prospects. Like admission to professional degree programs in other fields, admission to optometry programs is highly competitive.

Students who choose to complete a residency program gain additional experience that may improve their job prospects. Certification from the American Board of Optometry may also be viewed favorably by employers.

In addition, a large number of currently practicing optometrists are expected to retire over the coming decade, creating opportunities for new optometrists.

O*NET

➤ Optometrists (29-1041.00)

Contacts for More Information

For more information about optometry, visit
➤ American Optometric Association (www.aoa.org/)

For more information about optometrists, including a list of accredited optometric programs, visit
➤ Association of Schools and Colleges of Optometry (www.opted. org/)

For information on specific admission requirements and sources of financial aid, contact the admissions officers of individual optometry schools.

For more information about the national board exam, visit
➤ National Boards of Examiners in Optometry (www.optometry.org/)

For more information about certification, visit
➤ American Board of Optometry (www.americanboardofoptometry.org/)

Orthotists and Prosthetists

- **2012 Median Pay** .... $62,670 per year
  $30.13 per hour
- **Entry-Level Education** ....Master's degree
- **Work Experience in a Related Occupation**............... None
- **On-the-Job Training** .... Internship/residency
- **Number of Jobs 2012** 8,500
- **Job Outlook, 2012–22** .... 36% (Much faster than average)
- **Employment Change, 2012–22** 3,000

What Orthotists and Prosthetists Do

Orthotists and prosthetists, also called O&P professionals, design medical supportive devices and measure and fit patients for them. These devices include artificial limbs (arms, hands, legs, and feet), braces, and other medical or surgical devices.

Duties. Orthotists and prosthetists typically do the following:

- Evaluate and interview patients to determine their needs
- Measure patients in order to design and fit medical devices
- Design orthopedic and prosthetic devices based on physicians' prescriptions
- Take a mold of the part of a patient's body that will be fitted with a brace or artificial limb
- Select materials to be used for the orthotic or prosthetic device
- Fit, test, and adjust devices on patients
- Instruct patients in how to use and care for their devices
- Repair or update prosthetic and orthotic devices
- Document care in patients' records

O&P professionals may work in both orthotics and prosthetics, or they may choose to specialize in one area. Orthotists are specifically trained to work with medical supportive devices, such as braces and inserts. Prosthetists are specifically trained to work with prostheses, such as artificial limbs and other body parts.

Some O&P professionals may construct devices for their patients. Others supervise the construction of the orthotic or prosthetic devices by medical appliance technicians. For more information, see the profile on dental and ophthalmic laboratory technicians and medical appliance technicians.

Work Environment

Orthotists and prosthetists held about 8,500 jobs in 2012. Most work in offices, where they meet with patients, and then design orthotic and prosthetic devices. They can work in small, private offices or in larger facilities, and they sometimes work in the shops where the orthotics and prosthetics are made.

The industries that employed the most orthotists and prosthetists in 2012 were as follows:

Medical equipment and supplies manufacturing....................... 30%
Health and personal care stores... 22
Offices of physicians... 11
Federal government, excluding postal service 7

General medical and surgical hospitals; state, local, and private 6

Injuries and Illnesses. O&P professionals who create orthotics and prosthetics may be exposed to health or safety hazards when

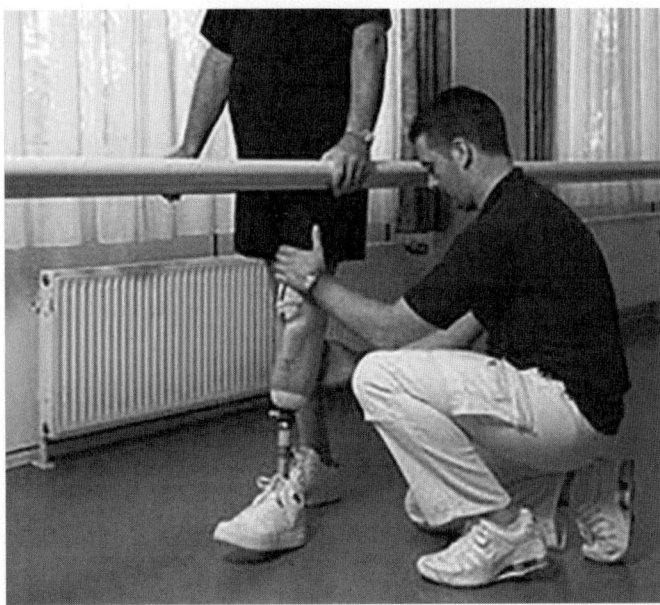

O&P professionals can work on both orthotics and prosthetics or may choose to specialize in one or the other.

handling certain materials, but there is little risk of injury if workers follow proper procedures, such as wearing goggles, gloves, and masks.

Work Schedules. Most orthotists and prosthetists work full time.

How to Become One

Orthotists and prosthetists need at least a master's degree and certification before entering the field. Both orthotists and prosthetists must complete a 1-year residency before they can be certified.

Education. All orthotists and prosthetists must complete a master's degree in orthotics and prosthetics. These programs include courses such as upper and lower extremity orthotics and prosthetics, spinal orthotics, and plastics and other materials.

All graduate degree programs have a clinical component in which the student works under the direction of an O&P professional. Most programs require at least 500 hours of clinical experience, split equally between orthotics and prosthetics.

Master's programs usually take 2 years to complete. Prospective students can have a bachelor's degree in any discipline if they have fulfilled prerequisite courses in science and mathematics; requirements vary by program.

Licenses, Certifications, and Registrations. Some states require O&P professionals to be licensed; requirements vary by state.

Median Annual Wages, May 2012

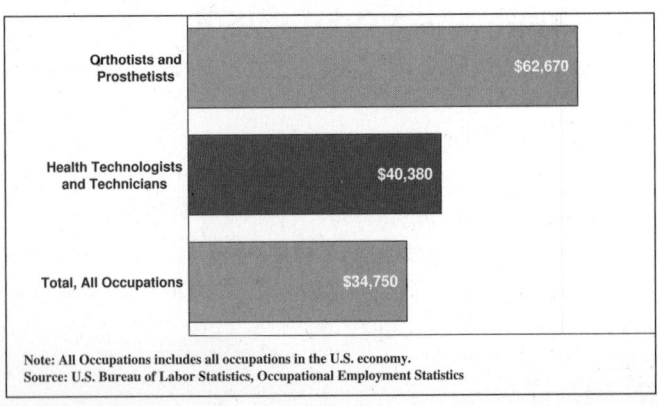

Orthotists and Prosthetists	$62,670
Health Technologists and Technicians	$40,380
Total, All Occupations	$34,750

Note: All Occupations includes all occupations in the U.S. economy.
Source: U.S. Bureau of Labor Statistics, Occupational Employment Statistics

Percent Change in Employment, Projected 2012–2022

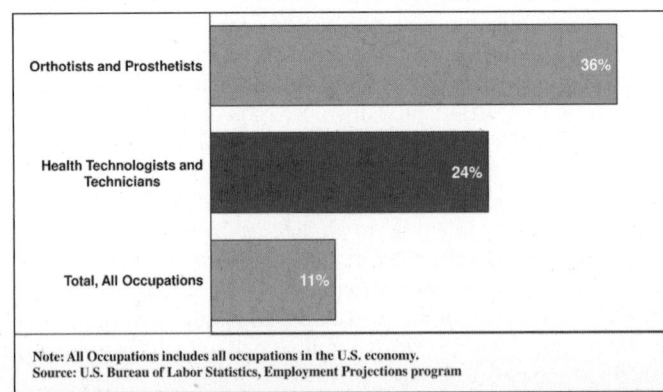

Orthotists and Prosthetists	36%
Health Technologists and Technicians	24%
Total, All Occupations	11%

Note: All Occupations includes all occupations in the U.S. economy.
Source: U.S. Bureau of Labor Statistics, Employment Projections program

Employment Projections Data for Orthotists and Prosthetists

Occupational title	SOC Code	Employment, 2012	Projected Employment, 2022	Change, 2012–2022	
				Percent	Numeric
Orthotists and prosthetists.. 29-2091		8,500	11,500	36	3,000

Source: U.S. Bureau of Labor Statistics, Employment Projections Program

Note: Data are rounded. Go to **Occupational Information Included in the OOH** *for a discussion of the data in this table.*

States that require licensure often require certification in order to practice. Most O&P professionals become certified by passing the exam administered by the American Board for Certification in Orthotics, Prosthetics & Pedorthics (ABC). To qualify for the exam, an O&P professional must complete a master's program in orthotics and prosthetics and a residency program. Many O&P professionals become certified regardless of state requirements.

Training. O&P professionals who wish to become certified must have a 1-year formal residency in orthotics or prosthetics before sitting for the certification exam. Professionals who want to be certified in both orthotics and prosthetics need to complete a year of residency for each specialty and pass both sets of exams.

Important Qualities

Communication skills. Orthotists and prosthetists must have excellent communication skills. They must be able to communicate effectively with the technicians who often create the medical devices. They must also be able to explain to patients how to use and care for the devices.

Detail oriented. Orthotists and prosthetists must be precise when recording measurements to ensure that devices are designed and fit properly.

Leadership skills. Orthotists and prosthetists who work in their own offices must be effective leaders. They must be able to manage a staff of other professionals in their office.

Organizational skills. Some orthotists and prosthetists own their practice or work in private offices. Strong organizational skills, including good recordkeeping, are critical in both medical and business settings.

Patience. Orthotists and prosthetists may work for long periods with patients who need special attention.

Physical dexterity. Orthotists and prosthetists must be good at working with their hands. They may design orthotics or prosthetics with intricate mechanical parts.

Physical stamina. Orthotists and prosthetists should be comfortable performing physical tasks, such as working with shop equipment and hand tools. They may spend a lot of time bending over or crouching to examine or measure patients.

Problem-solving skills. Orthotists and prosthetists must evaluate their patients' situations and often look for creative solutions to their rehabilitation needs.

Pay

The median annual wage for orthotists and prosthetists was $62,670 in May 2012. The median wage is the wage at which half the workers in an occupation earned more than that amount and half earned less. The lowest 10 percent earned less than $34,150, and the top 10 percent earned more than $111,030.

The wages for orthotists and prosthetists vary substantially depending on the industries they work in.

In May 2012, the median annual wages for orthotists and prosthetists in the top five industries employing these workers were as follows:

Medical equipment and supplies manufacturing	$68,680
Health and personal care stores	67,750
Federal government, excluding postal service	66,960
Offices of physicians	53,930
General medical and surgical hospitals; state, local, and private	51,950

Job Outlook

Employment of orthotists and prosthetists is projected to grow 36 percent from 2012 to 2022, much faster than the average for all occupations. However, because it is a small occupation, the fast growth will result in only about 3,000 new jobs over the 10-year period.

The large, aging baby-boom population will create a need for orthotists and prosthetists, since both diabetes and cardiovascular disease, which are the two leading causes of limb loss, are more common among older people. Advances in technology may spur demand for prostheses that allow for more natural movement.

In addition, older persons need other devices designed and fitted by O&P professionals, such as braces and orthopedic footwear.

Job Prospects. Job prospects should be best for orthotists and prosthetists with professional certification. Although it is not required in all states, certification shows a specific level of educational knowledge and training that employers may prefer.

O*NET

➤ Orthotists and Prosthetists (29-2091.00)

Similar Occupations   This table shows a list of occupations with job duties that are similar to those of orthotists and prosthetists.

Occupations	Entry-level Education	2012 Pay	Projected Job Growth	Average Annual Openings
Dental and Ophthalmic Laboratory Technicians and Medical Appliance Technicians	High school diploma or equivalent	$33,281	7%	3,360
Physical Therapists	Doctoral or professional degree	$79,860	36%	12,370
Physicians and Surgeons	Doctoral or professional degree	$182,294	18%	29,630
Respiratory Therapists	Associate's degree	$55,870	19%	4,010

Contacts for More Information

For more information about orthotists and prosthetists, visit

➤ American Academy of Orthotists & Prosthetists (www.opcareers.org/)

For a list of accredited programs for orthotists and prosthetists, visit

➤ National Commission on Orthotic & Prosthetic Education (www.ncope.org/)

For information about certification for orthotists and prosthetists, visit

➤ American Board for Certification in Orthotics, Prosthetics & Pedorthics (www.abcop.org/)

Personal Care Aides

- **2012 Median Pay** .... $19,910 per year
  $9.57 per hour
- **Entry-Level Education** .... Less than high school
- **Work Experience in a Related Occupation**............... None
- **On-the-Job Training** .... Short-term on-the-job training
- **Number of Jobs 2012** 1,190,600
- **Job Outlook, 2012–22** .... 49% (Much faster than average)
- **Employment Change, 2012–22** 580,800

What Personal Care Aides Do

Personal care aides help clients with self-care and everyday tasks, and provide companionship.

Duties. Personal care aides typically do the following:

- Care for and assist clients with cognitive impairments, such as Alzheimer's or mental illness
- Provide companionship by talking to, playing games with, or going for walks with clients
- Help clients with tasks related to hygiene, such as bathing, brushing teeth, and going to the bathroom
- Help transfer clients from a bed to a wheelchair or vice versa
- Complete housekeeping tasks, such as changing bed linens, washing dishes, and cleaning living areas
- Help prepare and plan meals

Personal care aides may prepare and serve meals for those who have difficulty doing so for themselves.

- Organize a client's schedule and plan appointments
- Arrange transportation to doctors' offices or to the store
- Help clients pay bills or manage money
- Shop for personal items and groceries

Personal care aides–also called homemakers, caregivers, companions, and personal attendants–provide clients with companionship and help with daily tasks. They often are hired in addition to healthcare or social workers who may visit a client's home, such as hospice workers. Personal care aides perform tasks that are similar to those of home health aides. However, personal care aides cannot provide any type of medical service, whereas home health aides may provide basic medical services.

Direct support professionals work with people who have developmental or intellectual disabilities. They may help create a behavior plan and teach self-care skills, such as doing laundry or cooking meals. They may also provide other personal assistance services.

Work Environment

Personal care aides held about 1.2 million jobs in 2012.

Most personal care aides work in clients' homes; others work in small group homes or larger care communities. Some are hired directly by the client or the client's family, but many are employed by organizations or agencies that provide in-home services or support.

Some aides work in many facilities or homes during the day, whereas others may work with a single client. Personal care aides may help people in hospice and day service programs or may help people with disabilities go to work and stay engaged in their communities.

The industries that employed the most personal care aides in 2012 were as follows:

Services for the elderly and persons with disabilities............... 30%
Home health care services... 25
Residential care facilities.. 13
Private households.. 9

About 6 percent of personal care aides were self-employed in 2012.

Work Schedules. About half of all personal care aides worked full time in 2012.

Injuries and Illnesses. Personal care aides have a higher rate of injuries and illnesses than the national average. Work as an aide can be physically and emotionally demanding. Aides may become injured when lifting or transferring clients in and out of beds or wheelchairs. Aides often work with clients who have mental health issues or cognitive impairments and may become difficult or violent at times. There are also dangers when working with clients who have communicable diseases or infections.

How to Become One

Most personal care aides are trained on the job. There are no formal education requirements for personal care aides, but most aides have a high school diploma.

Education. There are no formal education requirements for personal care aides, but most have a high school diploma.

Training. Aides may be trained on the job by registered nurses, other personal care aides, or their direct employer. They are trained in specific tasks, such as how to deal with a client who has a cognitive impairment and how to assist a client in preparing meals.

Some states require formal education or training programs available from community colleges, vocational schools, elder care programs, and home health care agencies. Some states and orga-

Median Annual Wages, May 2012

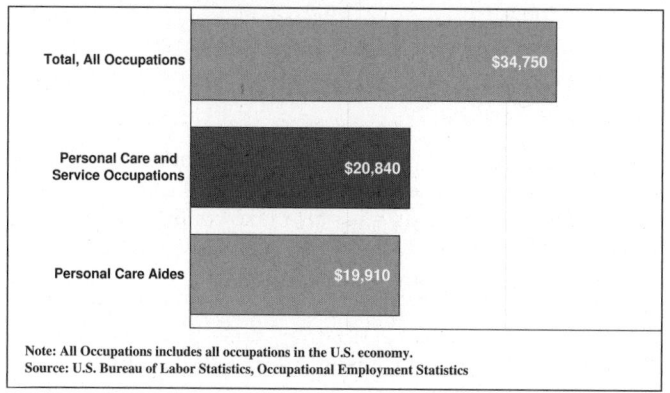

Note: All Occupations includes all occupations in the U.S. economy.
Source: U.S. Bureau of Labor Statistics, Occupational Employment Statistics

Percent Change in Employment, Projected 2012–2022

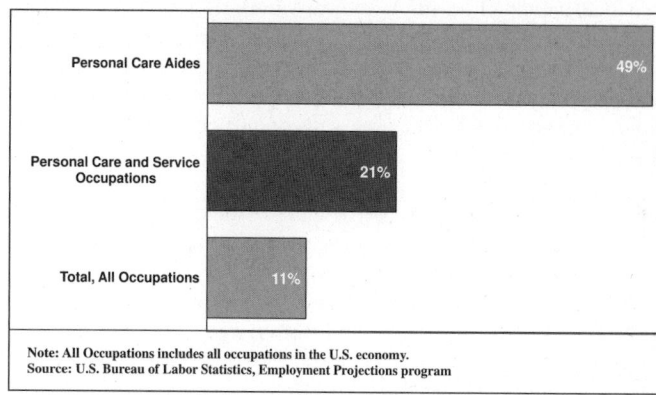

Note: All Occupations includes all occupations in the U.S. economy.
Source: U.S. Bureau of Labor Statistics, Employment Projections program

nizations may conduct background checks on prospective aides. A competency evaluation also may be required to ensure that the aide can perform some required tasks.

Most employers require aides to have training in first aid and cardiopulmonary resuscitation (CPR).

Important Qualities

Detail oriented. Personal care aides must follow specific rules and protocols to help take care of clients.

Interpersonal skills. Personal care aides must work closely with their clients. Sometimes clients are in extreme pain or mental stress, and aides must be sensitive to their emotions. Aides must be cheerful, compassionate, and emotionally stable. They must enjoy helping people.

Physical stamina. Personal care aides should be comfortable performing physical tasks. They often need to lift or turn clients who have a disability.

Time-management skills. Clients and their families rely on personal care aides. It is important that aides follow agreed-upon schedules and arrive on time.

Licenses, Certifications, and Registrations. A few states require aides to have specific training or certification. There are no federal training requirements for personal care aides.

Pay

The median annual wage for personal care aides was $19,910 in May 2012. The median wage is the wage at which half the workers in an occupation earned more than that amount and half earned less. The lowest 10 percent earned less than $16,330, and the top 10 percent earned more than $27,580.

Job Outlook

Employment of personal care aides is projected to grow 49 percent from 2012 to 2022, much faster than the average for all occupations.

As the baby-boom population ages, there will be an increase in the number of clients requiring assistance or companionship. As clients age, they often develop health or mobility problems and require assistance with daily tasks. The demand for the services that personal care aides provide will continue to rise.

Employment Projections Data for Personal Care Aides

Occupational title	SOC Code	Employment, 2012	Projected Employment, 2022	Change, 2012–2022	
				Percent	Numeric
Personal care aides	39-9021	1,190,600	1,771,400	49	580,800

Source: U.S. Bureau of Labor Statistics, Employment Projections Program

Note: Data are rounded. Go to **Occupational Information Included in the OOH** *for a discussion of the data in this table.*

Similar Occupations   This table shows a list of occupations with job duties that are similar to those of personal care aides.

Occupations	Entry-level Education	2012 Pay	Projected Job Growth	Average Annual Openings
Childcare Workers	High school diploma or equivalent	$19,510	14%	57,000
Home Health Aides	Less than high school	$20,820	48%	59,070
Licensed Practical and Licensed Vocational Nurses	Postsecondary non-degree award	$41,540	25%	36,310
Medical Assistants	Postsecondary non-degree award	$29,370	29%	26,990
Nursing Assistants and Orderlies	See "How to Become One"	$24,404	21%	61,300
Occupational Therapy Assistants and Aides	See "How to Become One"	$47,638	41%	2,560
Physical Therapist Assistants and Aides	See "How to Become One"	$40,539	41%	7,630
Radiation Therapists	Associate's degree	$77,560	24%	840
Social and Human Service Assistants	High school diploma or equivalent	$28,850	22%	17,870

Elderly and disabled clients who do not require medical care are increasingly choosing home care instead of entering nursing homes or hospitals. Home care is often a less expensive and more personal experience for the client. Because personal care aides do not provide any medical services, they are a less expensive option for families or clients who seek someone to perform light household chores or provide companionship.

Clients often prefer to be cared for in their own homes, rather than a home care facility or hospital. Studies have found that home treatment is frequently more effective than care in a nursing home or hospital.

Job Prospects. Job prospects for personal care aides are excellent. The occupation is large and expected to grow very quickly, thus adding many jobs. In addition, the low pay and high emotional demands cause many workers to leave the occupation, and they will have to be replaced.

O*NET

➤ Personal Care Aides (39-9021.00)

Contacts for More Information

For information about personal care aides, including state requirements, visit

➤ Paraprofessional Healthcare Institute (http://phinational.org/)

Pharmacists

- **2012 Median Pay** .... $116,670 per year
  $56.09 per hour
- **Entry-Level Education** ... Doctoral or professional degree
- **Work Experience in a Related Occupation**............... None
- **On-the-Job Training** .... None
- **Number of Jobs 2012** 286,400
- **Job Outlook, 2012–22** .... 14% (As fast as average)
- **Employment Change, 2012–22** 41,400

What Pharmacists Do

Pharmacists dispense prescription medications to patients and offer expertise in the safe use of prescriptions. They also may provide advice on how to lead a healthy lifestyle, conduct health and wellness screenings, provide immunizations, and oversee the medications given to patients.

Duties. Pharmacists typically do the following:

- Fill prescriptions, verifying instructions from physicians on the proper amounts of medication to give to patients
- Check whether the prescription will interact negatively with other drugs that a patient is taking or any medical conditions the patient has
- Instruct patients on how and when to take a prescribed medicine and inform them about potential side effects they may experience from taking the medicine
- Advise patients about general health topics, such as diet, exercise, and managing stress, and on other issues, such as what equipment or supplies would be best to treat a health problem
- Give flu shots and, in most states, other vaccinations
- Complete insurance forms and work with insurance companies to ensure that patients get the medicines they need

- Oversee the work of pharmacy technicians and pharmacists in training (interns)
- Keep records and do other administrative tasks
- Teach other healthcare practitioners about proper medication therapies for patients

Some pharmacists who own their pharmacy or manage a chain pharmacy spend time on business activities, such as inventory management. Pharmacists must also take continuing education courses throughout their career to keep up with the latest advances in pharmacological science.

With most drugs, pharmacists use standard dosages from pharmaceutical companies. However, some pharmacists create customized medications by mixing ingredients themselves, a process known as compounding.

The following are examples of types of pharmacists:

Community pharmacists work in retail stores such as chain drug stores or independently owned pharmacies. They dispense medications to patients and answer any questions that patients may have about prescriptions, over-the-counter medications, or any health concerns that the patient may have. They may also provide some primary care services such as giving flu shots.

Clinical pharmacists work in hospitals, clinics, and other healthcare settings. They spend little time dispensing prescriptions. Instead, they are involved in direct patient care. Clinical pharmacists may go on rounds in a hospital with a physician or healthcare team. They recommend medications to give to patients and oversee the dosage and timing of the delivery of those medications. They may also conduct some medical tests and offer advice to patients. For example, pharmacists working in a diabetes clinic may counsel patients on how and when to take medications, suggest healthy food choices, and monitor patients' blood sugar.

Consultant pharmacists advise healthcare facilities or insurance providers on patient medication use or improving pharmacy services. They also may give advice directly to patients, such as helping seniors manage their prescriptions.

Pharmaceutical industry pharmacists work in areas such as marketing, sales, or research and development. They may design or conduct clinical drug trials and help to develop new drugs. They also may help to establish safety regulations and ensure quality control for drugs.

Pharmacists provide prescription medications to patients in hospitals, grocery stores, and a variety of other settings.

Median Annual Wages, May 2012

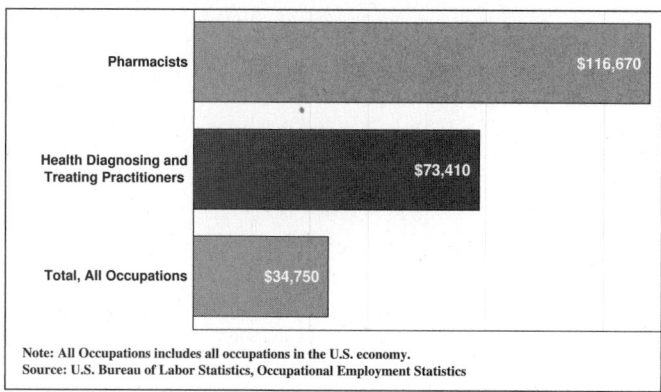

Pharmacists $116,670

Health Diagnosing and Treating Practitioners $73,410

Total, All Occupations $34,750

Note: All Occupations includes all occupations in the U.S. economy.
Source: U.S. Bureau of Labor Statistics, Occupational Employment Statistics

Percent Change in Employment, Projected 2012–2022

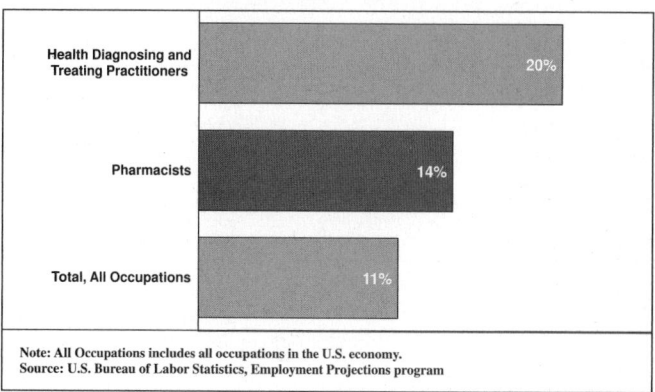

Health Diagnosing and Treating Practitioners 20%

Pharmacists 14%

Total, All Occupations 11%

Note: All Occupations includes all occupations in the U.S. economy.
Source: U.S. Bureau of Labor Statistics, Employment Projections program

Some pharmacists work as college professors. They may teach pharmacy students or conduct research. For more information, see the profile on postsecondary teachers.

Work Environment

Pharmacists held about 286,400 jobs in 2012. The industries that employed the most pharmacists in 2012 were as follows:

Pharmacies and drug stores 43%
Hospitals; state, local, and private 23
Grocery stores.. 8
Department stores 5
Other general merchandise stores 5

Pharmacists work in pharmacies, including those in grocery and drug stores. They also work in hospitals and clinics. Some pharmacists work for the government and the military. In most settings, they spend much of the workday on their feet.

Work Schedules. Most pharmacists work full time, although about 1 in 5 worked part time in 2012. Because many pharmacies are open at all hours, some pharmacists work nights and weekends.

How to Become One

Pharmacists must have a Doctor of Pharmacy (Pharm.D.) degree from an accredited pharmacy program. They also must be licensed, which requires passing licensure and law exams.

Education. Prospective pharmacists are required to have a Doctor of Pharmacy (Pharm.D.) degree, a postgraduate professional degree. In July 2012, there were 124 Doctor of Pharmacy programs fully accredited by the Accreditation Council for Pharmacy Education (ACPE).

Admissions requirements vary by program, however all Doctor of Pharmacy programs require applicants to take postsecondary courses such as chemistry, biology, and anatomy. Most programs require at least 2 years of undergraduate study, although some require a bachelor's degree. Most programs also require applicants to take the Pharmacy College Admissions Test (PCAT).

Pharm.D. programs usually take 4 years to finish, although some programs offer a 3-year option. Some schools admit high school graduates into a 6-year program. A Pharm.D. program includes courses in chemistry, pharmacology, and medical ethics. Students also complete supervised work experiences, sometimes referred to as internships, in different settings such as hospitals and retail pharmacies.

Some pharmacists who own their own pharmacy may choose to get a master's degree in business administration (MBA) in addition to their Doctor of Pharmacy degree. Others may get a degree in public health.

Training. Following graduation from a Pharm.D. program, pharmacists seeking an advanced position, such as a clinical pharmacy or research job, may need to complete a 1- to 2-year residency. Pharmacists who choose to complete the 2-year residency option receive additional training in a specialty area such as internal medicine or geriatric care.

Licenses, Certifications, and Registrations. All states license pharmacists. After they finish the Pharm.D. program, prospective pharmacists must pass two exams to get a license. The North American Pharmacist Licensure Exam (NAPLEX) tests pharmacy skills and knowledge. The Multistate Pharmacy Jurisprudence Exam (MPJE) or a state-specific test on pharmacy law is also required.

Pharmacists may also choose to earn a certification to show their advanced level of knowledge in a certain area. For instance, a pharmacist may become a Certified Diabetes Educator, a qualification offered by the National Certification Board for Diabetes Educators or earn certification in a specialty area, such as nutrition or oncology, from the Board of Pharmacy Specialties. Certifications from both organizations require varying degrees of work experience, as well as passing an exam and paying a fee.

Important Qualities

Analytical skills. Pharmacists must provide safe medications efficiently. To do this, they must be able to evaluate a patient's needs, evaluate the prescriber's orders, and have extensive knowledge about the effects and appropriate circumstances for giving out a specific medication.

Employment Projections Data for Pharmacists

Occupational title	SOC Code	Employment, 2012	Projected Employment, 2022	Change, 2012–2022	
				Percent	Numeric
Pharmacists..	29-1051	286,400	327,800	14	41,400

Source: U.S. Bureau of Labor Statistics, Employment Projections Program

Note: Data are rounded. Go to Occupational Information Included in the OOH *for a discussion of the data in this table.*

Similar Occupations   This table shows a list of occupations with job duties that are similar to those of pharmacists.

Occupations	Entry-level Education	2012 Pay	Projected Job Growth	Average Annual Openings
Biochemists and Biophysicists	Doctoral or professional degree	$81,480	18%	1,370
Medical Scientists	Doctoral or professional degree	$76,980	13%	3,550
Pharmacy Technicians	High school diploma or equivalent	$29,320	20%	10,590
Physicians and Surgeons	Doctoral or professional degree	$182,294	18%	29,630
Registered Nurses	Associate's degree	$65,470	19%	105,260

Communication skills. Pharmacists frequently offer advice to patients. They might need to explain how to take a medicine, for example, and what its side effects are. They also need to offer clear direction to pharmacy technicians and interns.

Computer skills. Pharmacists need computer skills to use any electronic health record (EHR) systems that their organization has adopted.

Detail oriented. Pharmacists are responsible for ensuring the accuracy of the prescriptions they fill, because improper use of medication can pose serious health risks. Pharmacists must be able to find the information that they need to make decisions about what medications are appropriate for each patient.

Managerial skills. Pharmacists–particularly those who run a retail pharmacy–must have good managerial skills, including managing inventory and overseeing a staff.

Pay

The median annual wage for pharmacists was $116,670 in May 2012. The median wage is the wage at which half the workers in an occupation earned more than that amount and half earned less. The lowest 10 percent earned less than $89,280, and the top 10 percent earned more than $145,910.

In May 2012, the median annual wages for pharmacists in the top five industries in which they worked were as follows:

Other general merchandise stores	$128,910
Department stores	120,540
Pharmacies and drug stores	117,850
Grocery stores	116,000
Hospitals; state, local, and private	114,100

Job Outlook

Employment of pharmacists is projected to grow 14 percent from 2012 to 2022, about as fast as the average for all occupations. Several factors are likely to contribute to this increase.

The population is aging, and older people typically use more prescription medicines than younger people. Higher rates of chronic diseases such as diabetes among all age groups will also lead to increased demand for prescription medications. In addition, scientific advances will lead to new drug products. As healthcare continues to become more complex and as more people take multiple medications, more pharmacists will be needed to dispense medications and to counsel patients on how to use their medications safely and effectively.

The number of individuals who have access to health insurance will increase as federal health insurance reform legislation is enacted. As more people have access to insurance coverage, more pharmacists will be needed to fill their prescriptions and to consult with patients about their medications.

Demand is also likely to increase for pharmacists in a variety of healthcare settings, including hospitals and clinics. These facilities will need more pharmacists to oversee the medications given to patients and to provide patient care, performing tasks such as testing a patient's blood sugar or cholesterol.

Job Prospects. The number of pharmacy schools has grown in recent years, creating more pharmacy school graduates and therefore more competition for jobs. Students who choose to complete a residency program gain additional experience that may improve their job prospects. Certification from the Board of Pharmacy Specialties or as a Certified Diabetes Educator may also be viewed favorably by employers.

O*NET

➤ Pharmacists (29-1051.00)

Contacts for More Information

For more information about pharmacists, visit

➤ American Society of Health-System Pharmacists (www.ashp.org/)
➤ National Association of Chain Drug Stores (www.nacds.org/)
➤ American Pharmacists Association (www.pharmacist.com/)
➤ American College of Clinical Pharmacy (www.accp.com/index.aspx)

For information on pharmacy as a career, preprofessional and professional requirements, programs offered by colleges of pharmacy, and student financial aid, visit

➤ American Association of Colleges of Pharmacy (www.aacp.org/Pages/Default.aspx)

For more information about accredited Doctor of Pharmacy programs, visit

➤ Accreditation Council for Pharmacy Education (www.acpe-accredit.org/)

For more information about certification options, visit

➤ Board of Pharmacy Specialties (www.bpsweb.org/)
➤ National Certification Board for Diabetes Educators (www.ncbde.org/certification_info/)

Pharmacy Technicians

- **2012 Median Pay** .... $29,320 per year
  $14.10 per hour
- **Entry-Level Education** ... High school diploma or equivalent
- **Work Experience in a Related Occupation** .... None
- **On-the-Job Training** .... Moderate-term on-the-job training
- **Number of Jobs 2012** 355,300
- **Job Outlook, 2012–22** .... 20% (Faster than average)
- **Employment Change, 2012–22** 70,700

What Pharmacy Technicians Do

Pharmacy technicians help licensed pharmacists dispense prescription medication to customers or health professionals. They work in retail pharmacies and hospitals.

Pharmacy technicians fill prescriptions and check inventory.

Duties. Pharmacy technicians typically do the following:

- Take the information needed to fill a prescription from customers or health professionals

- Measure amounts of medication for prescriptions

- Package and label prescriptions

- Organize inventory and alert pharmacists to any shortages of medications or supplies

- Accept payment for prescriptions and process insurance claims

- Enter customer or patient information, including any prescriptions taken, into a computer system

- Answer phone calls from customers

- Arrange for customers to speak with pharmacists if customers have questions about medications or health matters

Pharmacy technicians work under the supervision of pharmacists, who must review prescriptions before they are given to patients. In most states, technicians can compound or mix some medications and call physicians for prescription refill authorizations. Technicians also may need to operate automated dispensing equipment when filling prescription orders.

Pharmacy technicians working in hospitals and other medical facilities prepare a greater variety of medications, such as intravenous medications. They may make rounds in the hospital, giving medications to patients.

Work Environment

Pharmacy technicians held about 355,300 jobs in 2012. They worked primarily in pharmacies, including those found in grocery and drug stores. Some technicians work in hospitals or clinics. Pharmacy technicians spend most of the workday on their feet.

The industries that employed the most pharmacy technicians in 2012 were as follows:

Pharmacies and drug stores 53%
Hospitals; state, local, and private 17
General merchandise stores 12
Grocery stores.. 7
Ambulatory health care services 3

Work Schedules. Most pharmacy technicians work full time. Pharmacies may be open at all hours. Therefore, pharmacy technicians may have to work nights or weekends.

How to Become One

Becoming a pharmacy technician usually requires earning a high school diploma or the equivalent. Pharmacy technicians typically learn through on-the-job training, or they may complete a postsecondary education program. Most states regulate pharmacy technicians, which is a process that may require passing an exam or completing a formal education or training program.

Education and Training. Many pharmacy technicians learn how to perform their duties through on-the-job training. These programs vary in length and subject matter according to the employer's requirements.

Other pharmacy technicians enter the occupation after completing postsecondary education programs in pharmacy technology. These programs are usually offered by vocational schools or community colleges. Most programs award a certificate after 1 year or less, although some programs last longer and lead to an associate's degree. They cover a variety of subjects, such as arithmetic used in pharmacies, recordkeeping, ways of dispensing medications, and pharmacy law and ethics. Technicians also learn the names, uses, and doses of medications. Most programs also include clinical experience opportunities, in which students gain hands-on experience in a pharmacy.

The American Society of Health System Pharmacists (ASHP) accredits pharmacy technician programs that include at least 600 hours of instruction over a minimum of 15 weeks. In 2012, there were 213 fully accredited programs, including a few in retail drugstore chains.

Licenses, Certifications, and Registrations. Most states regulate pharmacy technicians in some way. Consult your state's Board of Pharmacy for its particular regulations. Requirements for phar-

Median Annual Wages, May 2012

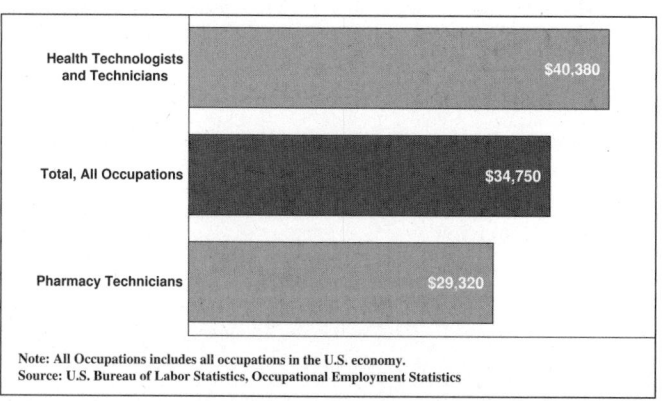

Note: All Occupations includes all occupations in the U.S. economy.
Source: U.S. Bureau of Labor Statistics, Occupational Employment Statistics

Percent Change in Employment, Projected 2012–2022

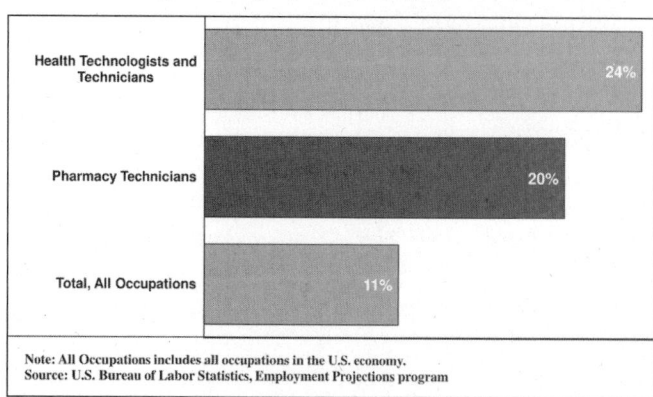

Note: All Occupations includes all occupations in the U.S. economy.
Source: U.S. Bureau of Labor Statistics, Employment Projections program

Employment Projections Data for Pharmacy Technicians

Occupational title	SOC Code	Employment, 2012	Projected Employment, 2022	Change, 2012–2022	
				Percent	Numeric
Pharmacy technicians..	29-2052	355,300	426,100	20	70,700

Source: U.S. Bureau of Labor Statistics, Employment Projections Program

Note: **Data are rounded.** Go to **Occupational Information Included in the OOH** *for a discussion of the data in this table.*

macy technicians in the states that regulate them typically include some or all of the following:

- High school diploma or GED
- Criminal background check
- Formal education or training program
- Exam
- Fees
- Continuing education

Some states and employers require pharmacy technicians to be certified. Even where it is not required, certification may make it easier to get a job. Many employers will pay for their pharmacy technicians to take the certification exam.

Two organizations offer certification. The Pharmacy Technician Certification Board (PTCB) certification requires a high school diploma and the passing of an exam. Applicants for the National Healthcareer Association (NHA) certification must be at least 18 years old, have a high school diploma, and have completed a training program or have 1 year of work experience. Technicians must recertify every 2 years by completing 20 hours of continuing education courses.

Important Qualities

Customer-service skills. Pharmacy technicians spend much of their time interacting with customers, so being helpful and polite are required of pharmacy technicians in a retail setting.

Detail oriented. Serious health problems can result from mistakes in filling prescriptions. Although the pharmacist is responsible for ensuring the safety of all medications dispensed, pharmacy technicians should be detail oriented so that complications are avoided.

Listening skills. Pharmacy technicians must communicate clearly with pharmacists and doctors when taking prescription orders. When speaking with customers, technicians must listen carefully to understand customers' needs and determine if they need to speak with a pharmacist.

Math skills. Pharmacy technicians need to have an understanding of the math concepts used in pharmacies when counting pills and compounding medications.

Organizational skills. Working as a pharmacy technician involves balancing a variety of responsibilities. Pharmacy technicians need good organizational skills to complete the work delegated by pharmacists while at the same time providing service to customers or patients.

Pay

The median annual wage for pharmacy technicians was $29,320 in May 2012. The median wage is the wage at which half the workers in an occupation earned more than that amount and half earned less. The lowest 10 percent earned less than $20,580, and the top 10 percent earned more than $42,400.

In May 2012, the median annual wages for pharmacy technicians in the top five industries in which these technicians worked were as follows:

Ambulatory health care services	$35,470
Hospitals; state, local, and private	33,550
Grocery stores..	28,760
Pharmacies and drug stores...	28,030
General merchandise stores	27,450

Job Outlook

Employment of pharmacy technicians is projected to grow 20 percent from 2012 to 2022, faster than the average for all occupations. Several factors will lead to increased demand for prescription medications.

The population is aging, and older people typically use more prescription medicines than younger people. Higher rates of chronic diseases such as diabetes among all age groups also will lead to increased demand for prescription medications. Advances in pharmaceutical research will allow for more prescription medications to be used to fight diseases.

The number of individuals who have health insurance will increase due to federal health insurance reform legislation. As more people have access to insurance coverage, more pharmacy technicians will be needed to handle their prescriptions.

In addition, pharmacy technicians may be needed to take on a greater role in pharmacy operations because pharmacists are increasingly performing more patient care activities such as giving flu shots. Technicians will need to perform tasks such as collecting patient

Similar Occupations   This table shows a list of occupations with job duties that are similar to those of pharmacy technicians.

Occupations	Entry-level Education	2012 Pay	Projected Job Growth	Average Annual Openings
Dental Assistants	Postsecondary non-degree award	$34,500	25%	13,720
Medical Assistants	Postsecondary non-degree award	$29,370	29%	26,990
Medical Records and Health Information Technicians	Postsecondary non-degree award	$34,160	22%	9,040
Medical Transcriptionists	Postsecondary non-degree award	$34,020	8%	2,240
Pharmacists	Doctoral or professional degree	$116,670	14%	10,980

information, preparing more types of medications, and verifying the work of other technicians, tasks formerly done by pharmacists.

Job Prospects. Job prospects should be good for pharmacy technicians, particularly those with formal training, certification, and those with experience in retail settings.

O*NET

➤ Pharmacy Technicians (29-2052.00)

Contacts for More Information

For information on becoming a pharmacy technician, visit
➤ National Pharmacy Technician Association (www.pharmacytechnician .org/)

For information about accredited pharmacy technician programs, visit
➤ American Society of Health System Pharmacists (www.ashp.org/)

For information about state licensure laws, contact individual state Boards of Pharmacy, or visit
➤ National Association of Boards of Pharmacy (www.nabp.net/)

For more information about certification, visit
➤ Pharmacy Technician Certification Board (www.ptcb.org/)
➤ National Healthcareer Association (www.nhanow.com/home.aspx)

Phlebotomists

- **2012 Median Pay** .... $29,730 per year
  $14.29 per hour
- **Entry-Level Education**.... Postsecondary non-degree award
- **Work Experience in a Related Occupation**............... None
- **On-the-Job Training** .... None
- **Number of Jobs 2012** 101,300
- **Job Outlook, 2012–22** .... 27% (Much faster than average)
- **Employment Change, 2012–22** 27,100

What Phlebotomists Do

Phlebotomists draw blood for tests, transfusions, research, or blood donations. Some of them explain their work to patients and provide assistance if patients have adverse reactions after their blood is drawn.

Duties. Phlebotomists typically do the following:

- Draw blood from patients and blood donors
- Talk with patients and donors so they are less nervous about having their blood drawn
- Verify a patient or donor's identity to ensure proper labeling
- Label the drawn blood for testing or processing
- Enter patient information into an onsite database
- Assemble and maintain medical instruments such as needles, test tubes, and blood vials

Phlebotomists primarily draw blood, which is then used for different kinds of medical laboratory testing. In medical and diagnostic laboratories, patient interaction is often only with the phlebotomist. Because all blood samples look the same, phlebotomists must identify and label the sample they have drawn and enter it into a database. Some phlebotomists draw blood for other purposes, such as at blood drives where people donate blood. In order to avoid causing infection or other complications, phlebotomists must keep their work area and instruments clean and sanitary.

Work Environment

Phlebotomists held about 101,300 jobs in 2012.

Phlebotomists work mainly in hospitals, medical and diagnostic laboratories, blood donor centers, and doctor's offices.

The industries that employed the most phlebotomists in 2012 were as follows:

General medical and surgical hospitals; state, local, and private	40%
Medical and diagnostic laboratories	26
Other ambulatory health care services	18
Offices of physicians	9

Work Schedules. Most phlebotomists work full time. Some phlebotomists, particularly those who work in hospitals and labs, are expected to work on nights, weekends, and holidays.

How to Become One

Phlebotomists typically enter the occupation with a postsecondary nondegree award from a phlebotomy program.

Education. Phlebotomists typically enter the occupation with a postsecondary non-degree award from a phlebotomy program. Programs for phlebotomy are available from community colleges, vocational schools, or technical schools. These programs usually take less than 1 year to complete and lead to a certificate or diploma. Programs have classroom and laboratory portions and include instruction in anatomy, physiology, and medical terminology.

Some phlebotomists may enter the occupation with a high school diploma and are trained to be a phlebotomist on the job.

Licenses, Certifications, and Registrations. Almost all employers prefer to hire phlebotomists who have earned professional certification.

Several organizations offer certifications for phlebotomists. The National Center for Competency Testing, the American Society for Clinical Pathology, and the American Medical Technologists (AMT) offer Phlebotomy Technician certifications.

Certification candidates typically need some classroom education, as well as some clinical experience. Certification testing usually includes an exam and may include practical components, such as drawing blood. Requirements vary by certifying organization. Phlebotomists must be certified in California, Louisiana, and Nevada.

Training. Phlebotomists usually get on-the-job training in their workplace to learn specific procedures on how their employers collect and track blood.

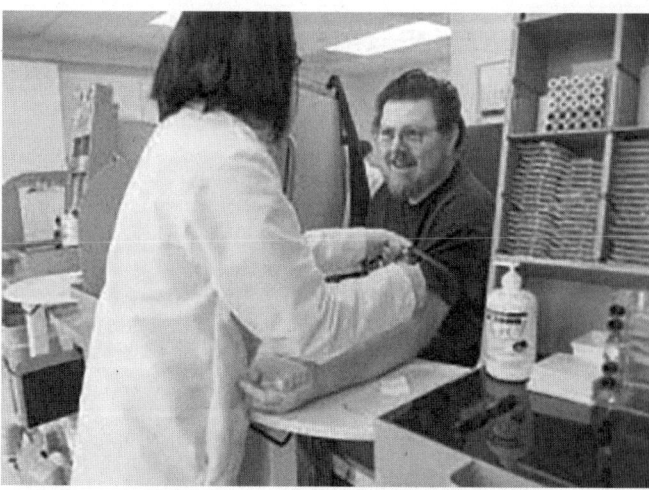

Phlebotomists draw blood for tests, transfusions, donations, or research.

Median Annual Wages, May 2012

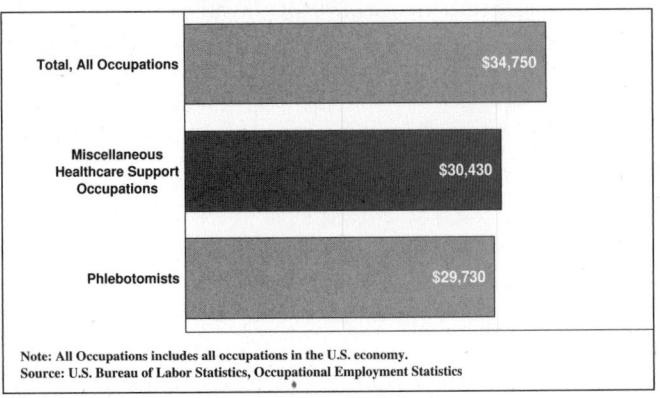

Note: All Occupations includes all occupations in the U.S. economy.
Source: U.S. Bureau of Labor Statistics, Occupational Employment Statistics

Percent Change in Employment, Projected 2012–2022

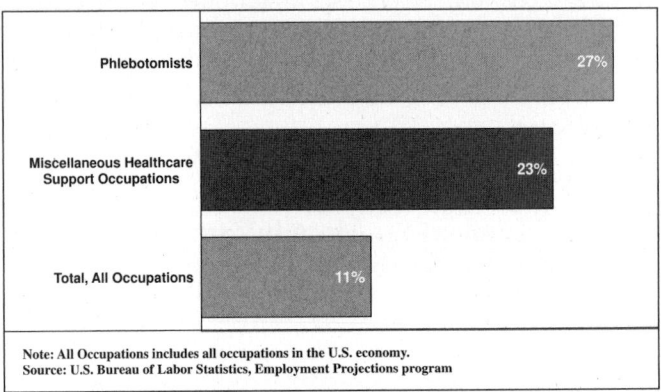

Note: All Occupations includes all occupations in the U.S. economy.
Source: U.S. Bureau of Labor Statistics, Employment Projections program

Those with just a high school diploma get some on-the-job training in how to be a phlebotomist.

Important Qualities

Compassion. Some patients or clients are afraid of having their blood drawn, so phlebotomists should show care when they perform their duties.

Detail oriented. Phlebotomists must draw the correct vials of blood for the tests ordered, track vials of blood, and enter data into a database. Attention to detail is necessary; otherwise, the specimens may be misplaced or lost, or a patient may be injured.

Dexterity. Phlebotomists work with their hands, and they must be able to use their equipment efficiently and properly.

Hand-eye coordination. Phlebotomists draw blood from many patients, and they must perform their duties on the first attempt, or their patients will experience discomfort.

Pay

The median annual wage for phlebotomists was $29,730 in May 2012. The median wage is the wage at which half the workers in an occupation earned more than that amount and half earned less. The lowest 10 percent earned less than $21,340, and the top 10 percent earned more than $42,600.

Job Outlook

Employment of phlebotomists is projected to grow 27 percent from 2012 to 2022, much faster than the average for all occupations. Hospitals, diagnostic laboratories, blood donor centers, and other locations will need phlebotomists to perform blood work.

Blood analysis remains an essential function in medical laboratories and hospitals. Demand for phlebotomists will remain high as doctors and other healthcare professionals require blood work for analysis and diagnoses.

However, federal health legislation will expand the number of patients who have access to health insurance, increasing patient access to medical care. As hospitals and medical laboratories evaluate their staffing needs, phlebotomists may be replaced by other more skilled healthcare workers.

Employment Projections Data for Phlebotomists

Occupational title	SOC Code	Employment, 2012	Projected Employment, 2022	Change, 2012–2022 Percent	Change, 2012–2022 Numeric
Phlebotomists..	31-9097	101,300	128,400	27	27,100

Source: U.S. Bureau of Labor Statistics, Employment Projections Program

Note: Data are rounded. Go to **Occupational Information Included in the OOH** *for a discussion of the data in this table.*

Similar Occupations   This table shows a list of occupations with job duties that are similar to those of phlebotomists.

Occupations	Entry-level Education	2012 Pay	Projected Job Growth	Average Annual Openings
Dental Assistants	Postsecondary non-degree award	$34,500	25%	13,720
Medical and Clinical Laboratory Technologists and Technicians	See "How to Become One"	$47,499	22%	15,600
Medical Assistants	Postsecondary non-degree award	$29,370	29%	26,990
Medical Records and Health Information Technicians	Postsecondary non-degree award	$34,160	22%	9,040
Medical Transcriptionists	Postsecondary non-degree award	$34,020	8%	2,240
Physician Assistants	Master's degree	$90,930	38%	4,890
Veterinary Assistants and Laboratory Animal Caretakers	High school diploma or equivalent	$23,130	10%	2,130
Veterinary Technologists and Technicians	Associate's degree	$30,290	29%	3,340

Job Prospects. Job prospects are best for phlebotomists who receive certification from one of several reputable organizations.

O*NET

➤ Phlebotomists (31-9097.00)

Contacts for More Information

For more information about phlebotomy and how to receive a phlebotomy certificate, visit

➤ Center for Phlebotomy Education (www.phlebotomy.com/)
➤ American Medical Technologists (AMT) (http://americanmedtech. org/Home.aspx)
➤ National Health Career Association (www.nhanow.com/home.aspx)

Physical Therapist Assistants and Aides

- **2012 Median Pay** .... $39,430 per year
  $18.96 per hour
- **Entry-Level Education** ....See "How to Become One"
- **Work Experience in a Related Occupation**............... None
- **On-the-Job Training** ....See "How to Become One"
- **Number of Jobs 2012** 121,400
- **Job Outlook, 2012–22** .... 41% (Much faster than average)
- **Employment Change, 2012–22** 49,400

What Physical Therapist Assistants and Aides Do

Physical therapist assistants (sometimes called PTAs) and physical therapist aides work under the direction and supervision of physical therapists. They help patients who are recovering from injuries and illnesses regain movement and manage pain. Physical therapist assistants are involved in the direct care of patients. Physical therapist aides often do tasks that are indirectly related to patient care, such as cleaning and setting up the treatment area, moving patients, and performing clerical duties.

Duties. Physical therapist assistants typically do the following:

- Observe patients before, during, and after therapy, noting their status and reporting to a physical therapist
- Help patients do specific exercises as part of the plan of care

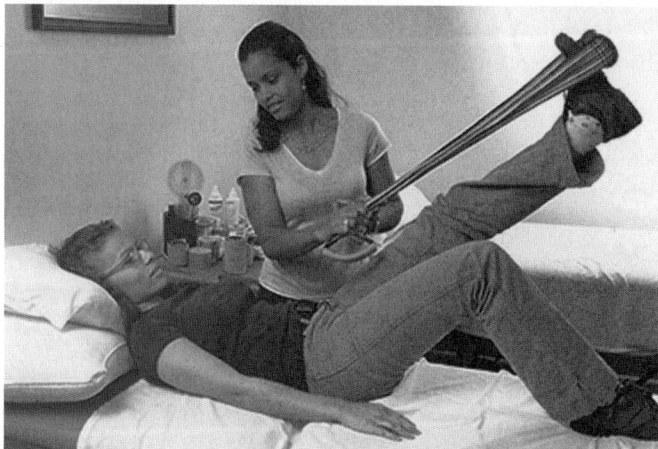

Physical therapist assistants and aides provide treatment that improves patient mobility, relieves pain, and prevents or lessens physical disabilities, under the direction of physical therapists.

- Use a variety of techniques, such as massage and stretching, to treat patients
- Use devices and equipment, such as walkers, to help patients
- Educate a patient and family members about what to do after treatment

Physical therapist aides typically do the following:

- Clean treatment areas and set up therapy equipment
- Wash linens
- Help patients move to or from a therapy area
- Do clerical tasks, such as answering phones and scheduling patients

Physical therapist assistants help physical therapists provide care to patients. Under the direction and supervision of physical therapists, they give therapy through exercise, massage, gait and balance training, and therapeutic modalities, such as electrical stimulation and ultrasound. Physical therapist assistants record patients' progress and report the results of each treatment to the physical therapist.

Physical therapist aides work under the direct supervision of a physical therapist or physical therapist assistant. They usually are responsible for keeping the treatment area clean and organized, and preparing for each patient's therapy. They also help patients who need assistance moving to or from a treatment area. In addition, aides do a variety of clerical tasks, such as ordering supplies, scheduling treatment sessions, and filling out insurance forms. The types of tasks that physical therapist aides are allowed to perform vary by state. Contact your state licensing board for more information.

Work Environment

Physical therapist assistants held about 71,400 jobs in 2012. Physical therapist aides held about 50,000 jobs in 2012.

The industries that employed the most physical therapist assistants in 2012 were as follows:

Offices of physical, occupational and speech therapists,
  and audiologists 40%
Hospitals; state, local, and private 27
Nursing care facilities (skilled nursing facilities) 11
Home health care services.. 8
Offices of physicians 5

The industries that employed the most physical therapist aides in 2012 were as follows:

Offices of physical, occupational and speech therapists,
  and audiologists 52%
Hospitals; state, local, and private 24
Nursing and residential care facilities 8
Offices of physicians 8
Government... 3

Physical therapist assistants and aides are frequently on their feet and moving as they set up equipment and help and treat patients. Because they must often lift and move patients, they are vulnerable to back injuries. Assistants and aides can limit these risks by using proper techniques when they assist patients.

Work Schedules. Most physical therapist assistants and aides work full time. Many physical therapy offices and clinics have evening and weekend hours to accommodate patients' schedules.

Median Annual Wages, May 2012

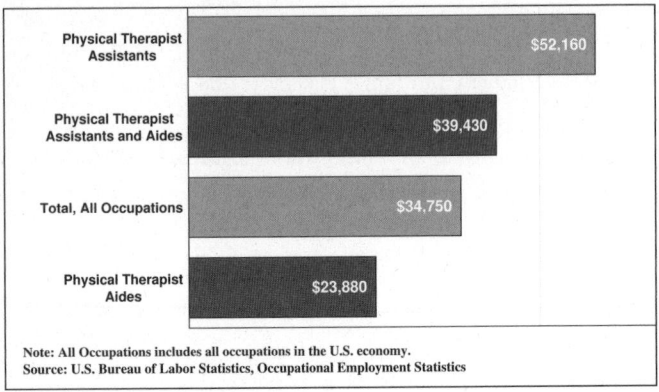

Note: All Occupations includes all occupations in the U.S. economy.
Source: U.S. Bureau of Labor Statistics, Occupational Employment Statistics

Percent Change in Employment, Projected 2012–2022

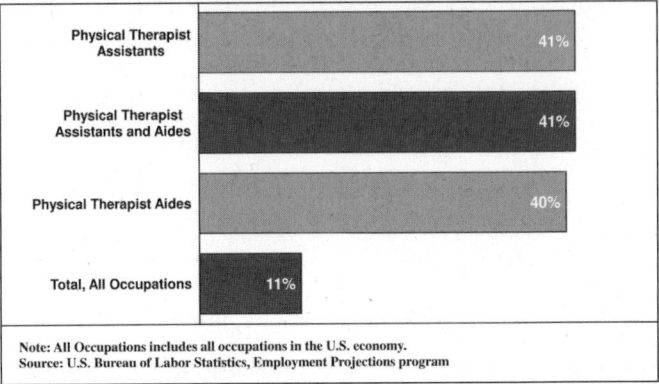

Note: All Occupations includes all occupations in the U.S. economy.
Source: U.S. Bureau of Labor Statistics, Employment Projections program

How to Become One

Most states require physical therapist assistants to have an associate's degree from an accredited physical therapist program. Physical therapist aides usually have a high school diploma and get on-the-job training.

Education and Training. Most states require physical therapist assistants to have an associate's degree from an accredited physical therapist assistant program. In 2012 the Commission on Accreditation in Physical Therapy Education accredited 298 associate's degree programs for physical therapist assistants.

Programs typically last about 2 years, and include both classroom study and clinical experience. PTA programs usually include courses in algebra, English, anatomy, physiology, and psychology. Assistants gain hands-on experience in treatment centers. They may also earn certifications in cardiopulmonary resuscitation (CPR) and other first-aid skills. Some programs offer evening classes.

Physical therapist aides typically have a high school diploma or the equivalent. They usually gain clinical experience through on-the-job training that can last from about a week to a few months. Employers may prefer to hire applicants with computer skills.

Some physical therapist assistants and aides continue their formal education to qualify for jobs in administration, management, and education.

Licenses, Certifications, and Registrations. All states except Hawaii require physical therapist assistants to be licensed or certified. Licensure typically requires graduation from an accredited physical therapist assistant program and passing the National Physical Therapy Exam administered by the Federation of State Boards of Physical Therapy. Some states require that applicants pass additional state-administered exams, undergo a criminal record check, and be at least 18 years old. Physical therapist assistants also may need to take continuing education courses to keep their license. Check with your state board for specific licensing requirements.

Physical therapist aides are not required to be licensed.

Important Qualities

Compassion. Physical therapist assistants and aides should enjoy helping people. They work with people who are in pain, and they must have empathy to help their patients.

Detail oriented. Like other healthcare professionals, physical therapist assistants and aides should be organized and have a keen eye for detail. They must keep accurate records and follow written and verbal instructions carefully to ensure quality care.

Dexterity. Physical therapist assistants should be comfortable using their hands to provide manual therapy and therapeutic exercises. Aides should also be comfortable working with their hands to set up equipment and prepare treatment areas.

Interpersonal skills. Physical therapist assistants and aides spend much of their time interacting with clients and therefore should be courteous and friendly.

Physical stamina. Physical therapist assistants and aides are frequently on their feet and moving as they work with their patients. They must often kneel, stoop, bend, and stand for long periods. They should enjoy physical activity.

Pay

The median annual wage for physical therapist assistants was $52,160 in May 2012. The median wage is the wage at which half the workers in an occupation earned more than that amount and half earned less. The lowest 10 percent earned less than $32,420, and the top 10 percent earned more than $72,720.

The median annual wage for physical therapist aides was $23,880 in May 2012. The lowest 10 percent earned less than $17,540, and the top 10 percent earned more than $35,420.

Job Outlook

Employment of physical therapist assistants is projected to grow 41 percent from 2012 to 2022, much faster than the average for all occupations. Employment of physical therapist aides is projected

Employment Projections Data for Physical Therapist Assistants and Aides

Occupational title	SOC Code	Employment, 2012	Projected Employment, 2022	Change, 2012–2022 Percent	Change, 2012–2022 Numeric
Physical therapist assistants and aides	31-2020	121,400	170,800	41	49,400
Physical therapist assistants	31-2021	71,400	100,700	41	29,300
Physical therapist aides	31-2022	50,000	70,100	40	20,100

Source: U.S. Bureau of Labor Statistics, Employment Projections Program

Note: Data are rounded. Go to Occupational Information Included in the OOH *for a discussion of the data in this table.*

Similar Occupations This table shows a list of occupations with job duties that are similar to those of physical therapist assistants and aides.

Occupations	Entry-level Education	2012 Pay	Projected Job Growth	Average Annual Openings
Dental Assistants	Postsecondary non-degree award	$34,500	25%	13,720
Medical Assistants	Postsecondary non-degree award	$29,370	29%	26,990
Nursing Assistants and Orderlies	See "How to Become One"	$24,404	21%	61,300
Occupational Therapy Assistants and Aides	See "How to Become One"	$47,638	41%	2,560
Pharmacy Technicians	High school diploma or equivalent	$29,320	20%	10,590
Physical Therapists	Doctoral or professional degree	$79,860	36%	12,370
Psychiatric Technicians and Aides	See "How to Become One"	$27,125	5%	3,030

to grow 40 percent from 2012 to 2022, much faster than the average for all occupations.

Demand for physical therapy services is expected to increase in response to the health needs of an aging population, particularly the large baby-boom generation. This group is staying more active later in life than previous generations. However, many baby boomers also are entering the prime age for heart attacks and strokes, increasing the demand for cardiac and physical rehabilitation. Older people are particularly vulnerable to a number of chronic and debilitating conditions that require therapeutic services. These patients often need additional help in their treatment, making the roles of physical therapist assistants and aides vital.

In addition, the incidence of chronic conditions such as diabetes and obesity is growing. More physical therapist assistants and aides will be needed to help patients maintain their mobility and manage the effects of such conditions.

Medical and technological developments should permit an increased percentage of trauma victims and newborns with birth defects to survive, creating added demand for therapy and rehabilitative services. In addition, federal health legislation will expand the number of patients who have access to health insurance, increasing patient access to physical therapy services.

Physical therapists are expected to increasingly use physical therapist assistants in order to reduce the cost of physical therapy services. Once the physical therapist has evaluated a patient and designed a plan of care, the assistant can provide many parts of the treatment, as directed by the therapist.

Job Prospects. Opportunities for physical therapist assistants are expected to be very good. Physical therapist assistants will be needed to help physical therapists care for and manage more patients. However, physical therapist aides may face strong competition from the large pool of qualified people.

Job opportunities should be particularly good in acute hospital, skilled nursing, and outpatient orthopedic settings, where the elderly are most often treated. Job prospects should be especially favorable in rural areas, as many physical therapists cluster in highly populated urban and suburban areas.

O*NET

➤ Physical Therapist Assistants (31-2021.00)
➤ Physical Therapist Aides (31-2022.00)

Contacts for More Information

For more information about physical therapist assistants, visit
➤ American Physical Therapy Association (www.apta.org/)
For a list of schools offering accredited programs, visit

➤ Commission on Accreditation in Physical Therapy Education (www.capteonline.org/home.aspx)

For more information about state licensing requirements and about the National Physical Therapy Exam, visit
➤ Federation of State Boards of Physical Therapy (www.fsbpt.org/)

Physical Therapists

- **2012 Median Pay** .... $79,860 per year
  $38.39 per hour
- **Entry-Level Education** ... Doctoral or professional degree
- **Work Experience in a Related Occupation** .... None
- **On-the-Job Training** .... None
- **Number of Jobs 2012** 204,200
- **Job Outlook, 2012–22** .... 36% (Much faster than average)
- **Employment Change, 2012–22** 73,500

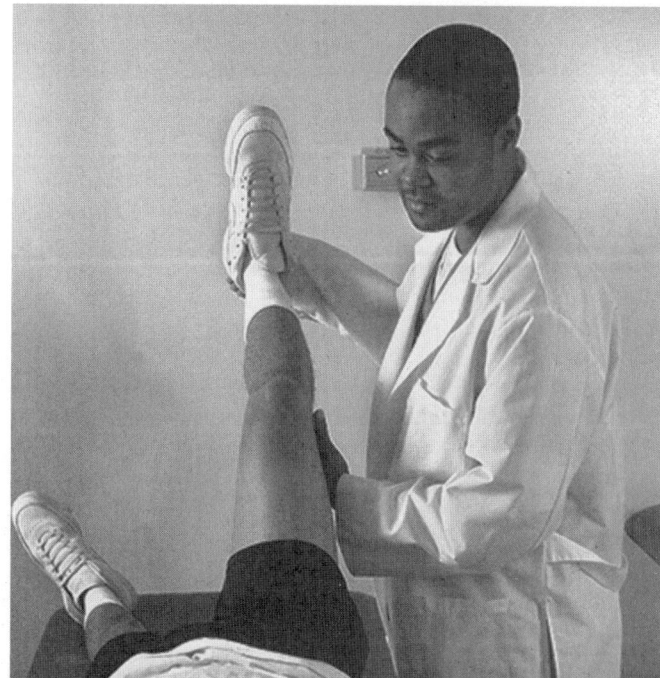

Physical therapists may practice in hospitals, clinics, private offices, private homes, or schools.

Median Annual Wages, May 2012

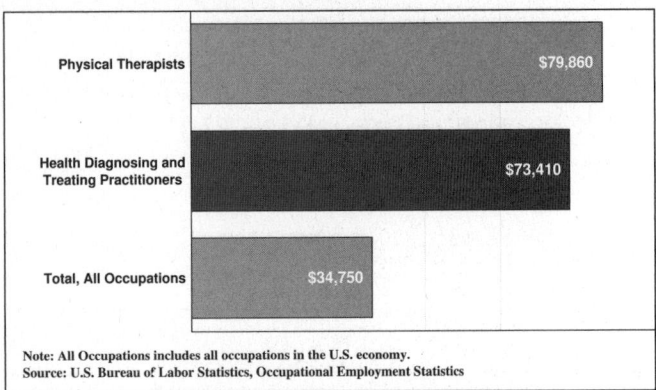

Note: All Occupations includes all occupations in the U.S. economy.
Source: U.S. Bureau of Labor Statistics, Occupational Employment Statistics

Percent Change in Employment, Projected 2012–2022

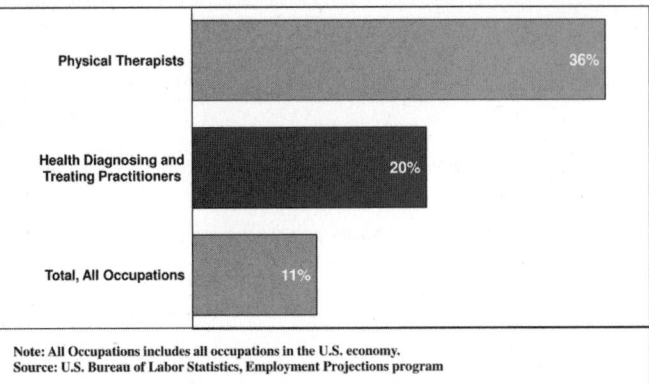

Note: All Occupations includes all occupations in the U.S. economy.
Source: U.S. Bureau of Labor Statistics, Employment Projections program

What Physical Therapists Do

Physical therapists, sometimes called PTs, help injured or ill people improve their movement and manage their pain. These therapists are often an important part of rehabilitation and treatment of patients with chronic conditions or injuries.

Duties. Physical therapists typically do the following:

- Review patients' medical history and any referrals or notes from doctors or surgeons

- Diagnose patients' dysfunctional movements by observing them stand or walk and by listening to their concerns, among other methods

- Set up a plan of care for patients, outlining the patient's goals and the expected outcome of the plan

- Use exercises, stretching maneuvers, hands-on therapy, and equipment to ease patients' pain, help them increase their mobility, prevent further pain or injury, and facilitate health and wellness.

- Evaluate a patient's progress, modifying a plan of care and trying new treatments as needed

- Educate patients and their families about what to expect from and how best to cope with the recovery process

Physical therapists provide care to people of all ages who have functional problems resulting from back and neck injuries; sprains, strains, and fractures; arthritis; amputations; neurological disorders, such as stroke or cerebral palsy; injuries related to work and sports; and other conditions.

Physical therapists are trained to use a variety of different techniques–sometimes called modalities–to care for their patients. These techniques include applying heat and cold and using assistive devices such as crutches, wheelchairs, and walkers and equipment, such as adhesive electrodes which apply electric stimulation to treat injuries and pain.

The work of physical therapists varies by type of patient. For example, a patient experiencing loss of mobility due to stroke needs different care from that given to an athlete recovering from an injury. Some physical therapists specialize in one type of care, such as orthopedics or geriatrics. Many physical therapists also work at preventing loss of mobility by developing fitness and wellness programs to encourage healthier and more active lifestyles.

Physical therapists work as part of a healthcare team, overseeing the work of physical therapist assistants and aides and consulting with physicians and surgeons and other specialists.

Work Environment

Physical therapists held about 204,200 jobs in 2012. Physical therapists typically work in private offices and clinics, hospitals, and nursing homes.

The industries that employed the most physical therapists in 2012 were as follows:

Offices of physical, occupational and speech therapists,
  and audiologists 33%
Hospitals; state, local, and private 28
Home health care services... 11
Nursing and residential care facilities 7
Offices of physicians 5

Physical therapists spend much of their time on their feet, working with patients. Because they must often lift and move patients, they are vulnerable to back injuries. Therapists can limit these risks by using proper body mechanics and lifting techniques when assisting patients.

Work Schedules. Most physical therapists work full time. About 1 in 4 worked part time in 2012. Although most therapists work during normal business hours, some may work evenings or weekends.

How to Become One

Physical therapists need a Doctor of Physical Therapy (DPT) degree. All states require physical therapists to be licensed.

Education. In 2013, there were 218 programs for physical therapists accredited by the Commission on Accreditation in Physical Therapy Education, all of which offered a Doctor of Physical Therapy (DPT) degree.

Employment Projections Data for Physical Therapists

Occupational title	SOC Code	Employment, 2012	Projected Employment, 2022	Change, 2012–2022 Percent	Change, 2012–2022 Numeric
Physical therapists..............................	29-1123	204,200	277,700	36	73,500

Source: U.S. Bureau of Labor Statistics, Employment Projections Program

Note: Data are rounded. Go to **Occupational Information Included in the OOH** *for a discussion of the data in this table.*

Similar Occupations This table shows a list of occupations with job duties that are similar to those of physical therapists.

Occupations	Entry-level Education	2012 Pay	Projected Job Growth	Average Annual Openings
Audiologists	Doctoral or professional degree	$69,720	33%	700
Chiropractors	Doctoral or professional degree	$66,160	15%	1,520
Occupational Therapists	Master's degree	$75,400	29%	4,820
Physical Therapist Assistants and Aides	See "How to Become One"	$40,539	41%	7,630
Recreational Therapists	Bachelor's degree	$42,280	14%	670
Speech-Language Pathologists	Master's degree	$69,870	19%	4,620

DPT programs typically last 3 years. Most programs require a bachelor's degree for admission as well as specific prerequisites, such as anatomy, physiology, biology, chemistry, and physics. Most DPT programs require applicants to apply through the Physical Therapist Centralized Application Service (PTCAS).

Physical therapist programs often include courses in biomechanics, anatomy, physiology, neuroscience, and pharmacology. Physical therapist students also complete clinical internships, during which they gain supervised experience in areas such as acute care and orthopedic care.

Physical therapists may apply to and complete a clinical residency program after graduation. Residencies typically last about 1 year and provide additional training and experience in specialty areas of care. Therapists who have completed a residency program may choose to specialize further by completing a fellowship in an advanced clinical area.

Licenses, Certifications, and Registrations. All states require physical therapists to be licensed. Licensing requirements vary by state but all include passing the National Physical Therapy Examination administered by the Federation of State Boards of Physical Therapy. Several states also require a law exam and a criminal background check. Continuing education is typically required for physical therapists to keep their license. Check with state boards for specific licensing requirements.

After gaining work experience, some physical therapists choose to become a board-certified specialist. The American Board of Physical Therapy Specialties offers certification in 8 clinical specialty areas, including orthopedics and geriatric physical therapy. Board specialist certification requires passing an exam and at least 2,000 hours of clinical work or completion of an APTA-accredited residency program in the specialty area.

Important Qualities

Compassion. Physical therapists are often drawn to the profession in part by a desire to help people. They work with people who are in pain and must have empathy for their patients.

Detail oriented. Like other healthcare providers, physical therapists should have strong analytic and observational skills to diagnose a patient's problem, evaluate treatments, and provide safe, effective care.

Dexterity. Physical therapists must use their hands to provide manual therapy and therapeutic exercises. They should feel comfortable massaging and otherwise physically assisting patients.

Interpersonal skills. Because physical therapists spend a lot of time interacting with patients, they should enjoy working with people. They must be able to explain treatment programs, motivate patients, and listen to patients' concerns to provide effective therapy.

Physical stamina. Physical therapists spend much of their time on their feet, moving as they work with patients. They should enjoy physical activity.

Resourcefulness. Physical therapists customize treatment plans for patients. They must be flexible and able to adapt plans of care to meet the needs of each patient.

Pay

The median annual wage for physical therapists was $79,860 in May 2012. The median wage is the wage at which half the workers in an occupation earned more than that amount and half earned less. The lowest 10 percent earned less than $55,620, and the top 10 percent earned more than $112,020.

Job Outlook

Employment of physical therapists is projected to grow 36 percent from 2012 to 2022, much faster than the average for all occupations.

Demand for physical therapy services will come from the aging baby boomers, who are staying more active later in life than their counterparts of previous generations. Older persons are more likely to experience heart attacks, strokes, and mobility-related injuries that require physical therapy for rehabilitation.

In addition, the incidence of patients with chronic conditions, such as diabetes and obesity, is growing. More physical therapists will be needed to help these patients maintain their mobility and manage the effects of chronic conditions.

Advances in medical technology have increased the use of outpatient surgery to treat a variety of injuries and illnesses. Medical and technological developments also are expected to permit a greater percentage of trauma victims and newborns with birth defects to survive, creating additional demand for rehabilitative care. Physical therapists will continue to play an important role in helping these patients recover more quickly from surgery.

Furthermore, the number of individuals who have access to physical therapy services may increase because of federal health insurance reform. Physical therapists will be needed to assist these patients with rehabilitation and treatment of any chronic conditions or injuries.

Job Prospects. Job opportunities will likely be good for licensed physical therapists in all settings. Job prospects should be particularly good in acute-care hospitals, skilled-nursing facilities, and orthopedic settings, where the elderly are most often treated. Job prospects should be especially favorable in rural areas, because many physical therapists live in highly populated urban and suburban areas.

O*NET

➤ Physical Therapists (29-1123.00)

Contacts for More Information

For more information about physical therapists, visit

➤ American Physical Therapy Association (www.apta.org/)

For more information about accredited physical therapy programs, visit

➤ Commission on Accreditation in Physical Therapy Education (www. capteonline.org/home.aspx)

For more information about state licensing requirements and about the National Physical Therapy Exam, visit

➤ Federation of State Boards of Physical Therapy (www.fsbpt.org/)

For more information about certification, visit

➤ American Board of Physical Therapy Specialties (www.abpts.org/ home.aspx)

For more information about how to apply to DPT programs, visit

➤ Physical Therapist Centralized Application Service (PTCAS) (www. ptcas.org/)

Physician Assistants

- **2012 Median Pay** .... $90,930 per year
  $43.72 per hour
- **Entry-Level Education** ....Master's degree
- **Work Experience in a Related Occupation**.............. None
- **On-the-Job Training** .... None
- **Number of Jobs 2012** 86,700
- **Job Outlook, 2012–22** .... 38% (Much faster than average)
- **Employment Change, 2012–22** 33,300

What Physician Assistants Do

Physician assistants, also known as PAs, practice medicine on a team under the supervision of physicians and surgeons. They are formally educated to examine patients, diagnose injuries and illnesses, and provide treatment.

Duties. Physician assistants typically do the following:

- Review patients' medical histories
- Conduct physical exams to check patients' health
- Order and interpret diagnostic tests, such as X-rays or blood tests
- Make diagnoses concerning a patient's injury or illness
- Give treatment, such as setting broken bones and immunizing patients
- Educate and counsel patients and their families–for example, answering questions about how to care for a child with asthma
- Prescribe medicine when needed
- Record a patient's progress
- Research the latest treatments to ensure the quality of patient care
- Conduct or participate in outreach programs; talking to groups about managing diseases and promoting wellness

Physician assistants work under the supervision of a physician or surgeon; however, their specific duties and the extent to which they must be supervised differ from state to state.

Physician assistants work in all areas of medicine, including primary care and family medicine, emergency medicine, and psychiatry. The work of physician assistants depends in large part on their specialty and what their supervising physician needs them to do. For example, a physician assistant working in surgery may close incisions and provide care before and after the operation. A physician assistant working in pediatrics may examine a child and give routine vaccinations.

In rural and medically underserved areas, physician assistants may be the primary care providers at clinics where a physician is present only 1 or 2 days per week. In these locations, physician assistants confer with the physician and other healthcare workers as needed and as required by law.

Some physician assistants make house calls or visit nursing homes to treat patients, reporting back to the physician afterward.

Physician assistants are different from medical assistants. Medical assistants do routine clinical and clerical tasks and they do not practice medicine.

Work Environment

Physician assistants held about 86,700 jobs in 2012. The industries that employed the most physician assistants in 2012 were as follows:

Offices of health practitioners 58%
Hospitals; state, local, and private 23
Outpatient care centers 7
Government 4
Educational services; state, local, and private 3

Physician assistant work can be both physically and emotionally demanding. Physician assistants spend much of their time on their feet, making rounds and evaluating patients. Physician assistants who work in operating rooms often stand for extended periods. Although the work can be stressful, helping patients can be rewarding.

Work Schedules. Most physician assistants work full time. In hospitals, physician assistants may work nights, weekends, or holidays. They may also be on call, meaning that they must be ready to respond to a work request with little notice.

How to Become One

Physician assistants typically need a master's degree from an accredited educational program. Earning that degree usually takes at least 2 years of full-time postgraduate study. Most applicants to physician assistant education programs already have a bachelor's degree and some healthcare-related work experience. All states require physician assistants to be licensed.

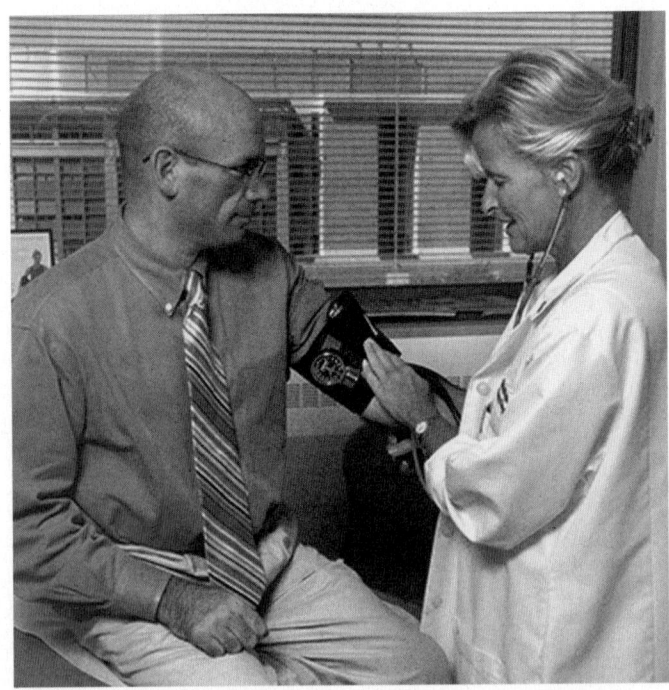

Physician assistants are formally trained to provide diagnostic, therapeutic, and preventive healthcare services, under the supervision of a physician.

Median Annual Wages, May 2012

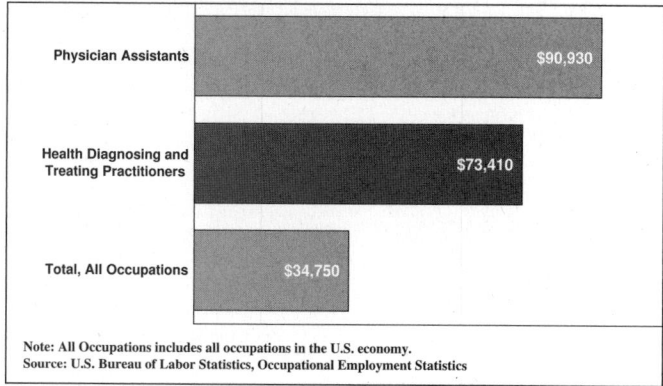

Note: All Occupations includes all occupations in the U.S. economy.
Source: U.S. Bureau of Labor Statistics, Occupational Employment Statistics

Percent Change in Employment, Projected 2012–2022

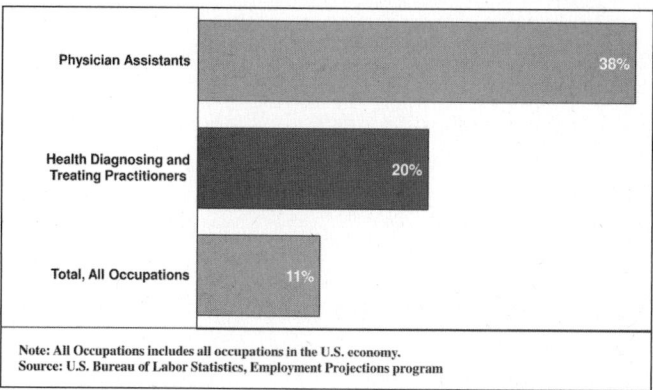

Note: All Occupations includes all occupations in the U.S. economy.
Source: U.S. Bureau of Labor Statistics, Employment Projections program

Education. Most applicants to physician assistant education programs already have a bachelor's degree and some healthcare-related work experience. While admissions requirements vary from program to program, most programs require two to four years of undergraduate coursework with a focus in science.

Many applicants already have experience as registered nurses or as EMTs and paramedics before they apply to a physician assistant program.

Physician assistant education programs usually take at least 2 years of full-time study. In 2012, the Accreditation Review Commission on Education for the Physician Assistant, Inc. (ARC-PA) accredited 170 education programs. Most of these accredited programs offer a master's degree.

Physician assistant education includes classroom and laboratory instruction in subjects such as pathology, human anatomy, physiology, clinical medicine, pharmacology, physical diagnosis, and medical ethics. The programs also include hundreds of hours of supervised clinical training in several areas, including family medicine, internal medicine, emergency medicine, and pediatrics.

Sometimes students serve in one or more of these areas under the supervision of a physician who is looking to hire a physician assistant. In this way, the rotation may lead to permanent employment.

Licenses, Certifications, and Registrations. All states and the District of Columbia require physician assistants to be licensed. To become licensed, they must pass the Physician Assistant National Certifying Examination (PANCE) from the National Commission on Certification of Physician Assistants (NCCPA). A physician assistant who passes the exam may use the credential "Physician Assistant-Certified (PA-C)."

To keep their certification, physician assistants must complete 100 hours of continuing education every 2 years. Beginning in 2014, the recertification exam will be required every 10 years.

Important Qualities

Communication skills. Physician assistants must explain complex medical issues in a way that patients can understand. They must also communicate with doctors and other healthcare workers to ensure that they provide the best possible patient care.

Compassion. Many physician assistants are drawn to the profession by a desire to help people. They should enjoy helping others.

Detail oriented. Physician assistants should be focused and observant to evaluate and treat patients properly.

Emotional stability. Physician assistants, particularly those working in surgery or emergency medicine, should be able to work well under pressure. They must remain calm in stressful situations in order to provide quality care.

Problem-solving skills. Physician assistants need to evaluate patients' symptoms and administer the appropriate treatments. They must be diligent when investigating complicated medical issues so that they can determine the best course of treatment for each patient.

Advancement. Some physician assistants pursue additional education in a specialty. Postgraduate educational programs are available in areas such as surgery, emergency medicine, and psychiatry. To enter one of these programs, a physician assistant must be a graduate of an accredited program and be certified by the NCCPA.

As they gain greater clinical knowledge and experience, physician assistants can earn new responsibilities and higher wages. For example, experienced physician assistants may supervise other staff and physician assistant students.

Pay

The median annual wage for physician assistants was $90,930 in May 2012. The median wage is the wage at which half the workers in an occupation earned more than that amount and half earned less. The lowest 10 percent earned less than $62,430, and the top 10 percent earned more than $124,770.

In May 2012, the median annual wages for physician assistants in the top five industries in which these assistants worked were as follows:

Hospitals; state, local, and private	$93,660
Outpatient care centers	93,520
Offices of health practitioners	90,150
Educational services; state, local, and private	88,890
Government	86,870

Employment Projections Data for Physician Assistants

Occupational title	SOC Code	Employment, 2012	Projected Employment, 2022	Change, 2012–2022 Percent	Change, 2012–2022 Numeric
Physician assistants	29-1071	86,700	120,000	38	33,300

Source: U.S. Bureau of Labor Statistics, Employment Projections Program

Note: Data are rounded. Go to **Occupational Information Included in the OOH** *for a discussion of the data in this table.*

Similar Occupations   This table shows a list of occupations with job duties that are similar to those of physician assistants.

Occupations	Entry-level Education	2012 Pay	Projected Job Growth	Average Annual Openings
Audiologists	Doctoral or professional degree	$69,720	33%	700
EMTs and Paramedics	Postsecondary non-degree award	$31,020	23%	12,060
Nurse Anesthetists, Nurse Midwives, and Nurse Practitioners	Master's degree	$103,602	31%	7,700
Occupational Therapists	Master's degree	$75,400	29%	4,820
Physical Therapists	Doctoral or professional degree	$79,860	36%	12,370
Physicians and Surgeons	Doctoral or professional degree	$182,294	18%	29,630
Registered Nurses	Associate's degree	$65,470	19%	105,260
Speech-Language Pathologists	Master's degree	$69,870	19%	4,620

Job Outlook

Employment of physician assistants is projected to grow 38 percent from 2012 to 2022, much faster than the average for all occupations.

Demand for healthcare services will increase because of the growing and aging population. More people means more need for healthcare specialists, and as the large baby-boom generation ages, it will require more healthcare. This, coupled with an increase in several chronic diseases such as diabetes, will drive the need for physician assistants to provide preventive care and treat those who are sick.

Physician assistants, who can perform many of the same services as doctors, are expected to have a larger role in giving routine care because they are more cost effective than physicians. As more physicians retire or enter specialty areas of medicine, more physician assistants are expected to take on the role of primary care provider. Furthermore, the number of individuals who have access to primary care services will increase as a result of federal health insurance reform.

The role of physician assistants is expected to expand as states continue to allow assistants to do more procedures and as insurance companies expand their coverage of physician assistant services.

Job Prospects. Good job prospects are expected, particularly for physician assistants working in rural and medically underserved areas, as well as physician assistants working in primary care.

O*NET

➤ Physician Assistants (29-1071.00)
➤ Anesthesiologist Assistants (29-1071.01)

Contacts for More Information

For more information on physician assistants, visit
➤ American Academy of Physician Assistants (www.aapa.org/)
  For a list of accredited physician assistant programs, visit
➤ Physician Assistant Education Association (www.paeaonline.org/)
➤ Accreditation Review Commission on Education for the Physician Assistant, Inc. (www.arc-pa.org/)
  For information about certification requirements, visit
➤ National Commission on Certification of Physician Assistants (www.nccpa.net/)

Physicians and Surgeons

- **2012 Median Pay** .... This wage is equal to or greater than $187,200 per year or $90.00 per hour.
- **Entry-Level Education** ... Doctoral or professional degree
- **Work Experience in a Related Occupation**............... None
- **On-the-Job Training** .... Internship/residency
- **Number of Jobs 2012** 691,400
- **Job Outlook, 2012–22** .... 18% (Faster than average)
- **Employment Change, 2012–22** 123,300

What Physicians and Surgeons Do

Physicians and surgeons diagnose and treat injuries or illnesses. Physicians examine patients; take medical histories; prescribe medications; and order, perform, and interpret diagnostic tests. They often counsel patients on diet, hygiene, and preventive healthcare. Surgeons operate on patients to treat injuries, such as broken bones; diseases, such as cancerous tumors; and deformities, such as cleft palates.

There are two types of physicians, with corresponding degrees: M.D. (Medical Doctor) and D.O. (Doctor of Osteopathic Medicine). Both use the same methods of treatment, including drugs and surgery, but D.O.s place additional emphasis on the body's musculoskeletal system, preventive medicine, and holistic (whole-

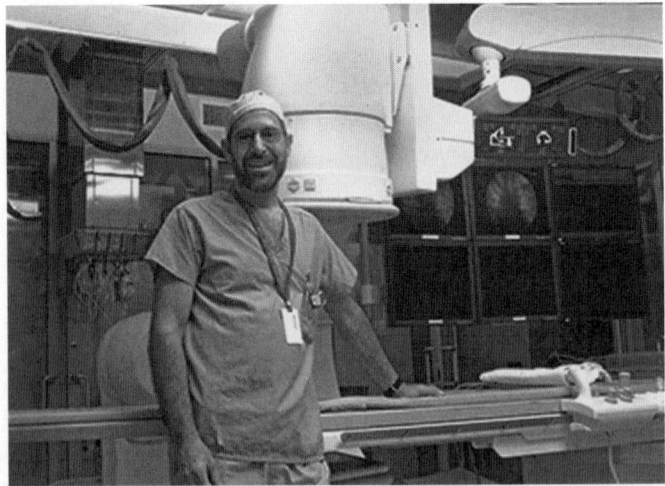

Physicians examine patients, obtain medical histories, and order, perform, and interpret diagnostic tests.

Median Annual Wages, May 2012

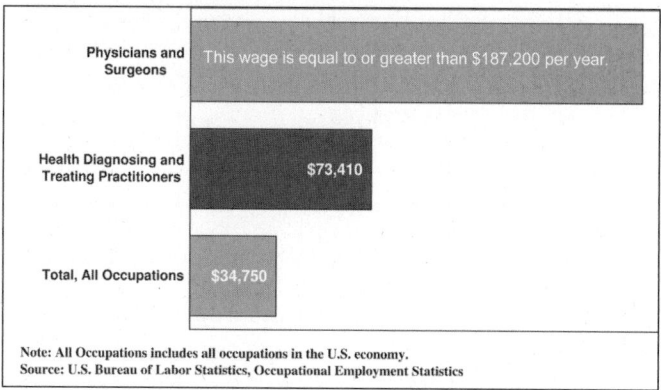

Physicians and Surgeons — This wage is equal to or greater than $187,200 per year.

Health Diagnosing and Treating Practitioners — $73,410

Total, All Occupations — $34,750

Note: All Occupations includes all occupations in the U.S. economy.
Source: U.S. Bureau of Labor Statistics, Occupational Employment Statistics

Percent Change in Employment, Projected 2012–2022

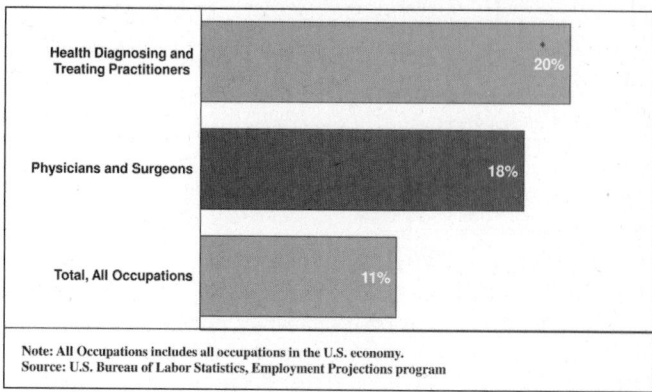

Health Diagnosing and Treating Practitioners — 20%

Physicians and Surgeons — 18%

Total, All Occupations — 11%

Note: All Occupations includes all occupations in the U.S. economy.
Source: U.S. Bureau of Labor Statistics, Employment Projections program

person) patient care. D.O.s are most likely to be primary care physicians, although they can be found in all specialties.

Duties. Physicians and surgeons typically do the following:

- Take a patient's medical history
- Update charts and patient information to show current findings and treatments
- Order tests for nurses or other healthcare staff to perform
- Review test results to identify any abnormal findings
- Recommend and design a plan of treatment
- Address concerns or answer questions that patients have about their health and well-being
- Help patients take care of their health by discussing topics such as proper nutrition and hygiene

In addition, surgeons operate on patients to treat injuries, diseases, or deformities.

Physicians and surgeons work in one or more of several specialties. The following are examples of types of physicians and surgeons:

Anesthesiologists focus on the care of surgical patients and on pain relief. They administer the drugs (anesthetics) that reduce or eliminate the sensation of pain during an operation or another medical procedure. During surgery, they are responsible for adjusting the amount of anesthetic as needed and monitoring the patient's heart rate, body temperature, blood pressure, and breathing. They also work outside of the operating room, providing pain relief in the intensive care unit, during labor and delivery, and for those who suffer from chronic pain. Anesthesiologists work with other physicians and surgeons to decide on treatments and procedures before, during, and after surgery.

Family and general physicians assess and treat a range of conditions that occur in everyday life. These conditions include anything from sinus and respiratory infections to broken bones. Family and general physicians typically have regular, long-term patients.

General internists diagnose and provide nonsurgical treatment for a range of problems that affect internal organ systems such as the stomach, kidneys, liver, and digestive tract. Internists use a variety of diagnostic techniques to treat patients through medication or hospitalization. They work mostly with adult patients.

General pediatricians provide care for infants, children, teenagers, and young adults. They specialize in diagnosing and treating problems specific to younger people. Most pediatricians treat common illnesses, minor injuries, and infectious diseases, and administer vaccinations. Some pediatricians specialize in pediatric surgery or serious medical conditions that commonly affect younger patients, such as autoimmune disorders or chronic ailments.

Obstetricians and gynecologists (OB/GYNs) provide care related to pregnancy, childbirth, and the female reproductive system. They treat and counsel women throughout their pregnancy and deliver babies. They also diagnose and treat health issues specific to women, such as breast cancer, cervical cancer, hormonal disorders, and symptoms related to menopause.

Psychiatrists are primary mental health physicians. They diagnose and treat mental illnesses through a combination of personal counseling (psychotherapy), psychoanalysis, hospitalization, and medication. Psychotherapy involves regular discussions with patients about their problems. The psychiatrist helps them find solutions through changes in their behavioral patterns, explorations of their past experiences, or group and family therapy sessions. Psychoanalysis involves long-term psychotherapy and counseling for patients. Psychiatrists may prescribe medications to correct chemical imbalances that cause some mental illnesses.

Surgeons specialize in treating injury, disease, and deformity through operations. Using a variety of instruments, a surgeon corrects physical deformities, repairs bone and tissue after injuries, or performs preventive surgeries on patients. Although a large number perform general surgery, many surgeons choose to specialize in a specific area. Specialties include orthopedic surgery (the treatment of the musculoskeletal system), neurological surgery (treatment of the brain and nervous system), cardiovascular surgery, and plastic or reconstructive surgery. Like other physicians, surgeons examine patients, perform and interpret diagnostic tests, and counsel patients on preventive healthcare. Some specialist physicians also perform surgery.

Physicians and surgeons may work in a number of other medical and surgical specialties and subspecialties. The following specialists are some of the most common examples:

- Allergists (specialists in diagnosing and treating hay fever and other allergies)
- Cardiologists (heart specialists)
- Dermatologists (skin specialists)
- Gastroenterologists (digestive system specialists)
- Ophthalmologists (eye specialists)
- Pathologists (specialists who study body tissue to see if it is normal or abnormal)
- Radiologists (specialists who review and interpret X-ray pictures and deliver radiation treatments for cancer and other illnesses)

Physicians work daily with other healthcare staff, such as registered nurses, other physicians, medical assistants, and medical records and health information technicians.

Employment Projections Data for Physicians and Surgeons

Occupational title	SOC Code	Employment, 2012	Projected Employment, 2022	Change, 2012–2022	
				Percent	Numeric
Physicians and surgeons	29-1060	691,400	814,700	18	123,300

Source: U.S. Bureau of Labor Statistics, Employment Projections Program

Note: *Data are rounded. Go to* **Occupational Information Included in the OOH** *for a discussion of the data in this table.*

Work Environment

Physicians and surgeons held about 691,400 jobs in 2012. Many physicians work in private offices or clinics, often with a small staff of nurses and administrative personnel. Some practice independently or with a small group of other doctors.

Increasingly, physicians are working in group practices, healthcare organizations, or hospitals, where they share a large number of patients with other doctors. The group setting allows them more time off and lets them coordinate care for their patients, but it gives them less independence than solo practitioners have.

Surgeons and anesthesiologists usually work in sterile environments while performing surgery and may stand for long periods.

Work Schedules. Most physicians and surgeons work full time. Many physicians and surgeons work long, irregular, and overnight hours. Physicians and surgeons may travel between their offices and hospitals to care for their patients. While on call, a physician may need to address a patient's concerns over the phone or make an emergency visit to a hospital or nursing home.

How to Become One

Physicians and surgeons have demanding education and training requirements. Almost all physicians complete at least 4 years of undergraduate school, 4 years of medical school, and, depending on their specialty, 3 to 8 years in internship and residency programs.

Education. Most applicants to medical school have at least a bachelor's degree, and many have advanced degrees. Although no specific major is required, all students must complete undergraduate work in biology, chemistry, physics, mathematics, and English. Students also take courses in the humanities and social sciences. Some students volunteer at local hospitals or clinics to gain experience in a healthcare setting.

Medical schools are highly competitive. Most applicants must submit transcripts, scores from the Medical College Admission Test (MCAT), and letters of recommendation. Schools also consider an applicant's personality, leadership qualities, and participation in extracurricular activities. Most schools require applicants to interview with members of the admissions committee.

A few medical schools offer combined undergraduate and medical school programs that last 6 or 7 years.

Students spend most of the first 2 years of medical school in laboratories and classrooms, taking courses such as anatomy, biochemistry, pharmacology, psychology, medical ethics, and the laws governing medicine. They also gain practical skills, learning to take medical histories, examine patients, and diagnose illnesses.

During their last 2 years, medical students work with patients under the supervision of experienced physicians in hospitals and clinics. Through rotations in internal medicine, family practice, obstetrics and gynecology, pediatrics, psychiatry, and surgery, they gain experience in diagnosing and treating illnesses in a variety of areas.

Important Qualities

Communication skills. Physicians and surgeons need to be excellent communicators. They must be able to communicate effectively with their patients and other healthcare support staff.

Compassion. Physicians and surgeons deal with patients who are sick or injured and may be in extreme pain or distress. Physicians and surgeons must be able to treat patients and their families with compassion and understanding.

Detail oriented. Physicians and surgeons must ensure that patients are receiving appropriate treatment and medications. They must also monitor and record various pieces of information related to patient care.

Dexterity. Physicians and surgeons must be good at working with their hands. They work with very precise and sometimes sharp tools, and mistakes can have serious consequences.

Leadership skills. Physicians who work in their own practice need to be effective leaders. They must be able to manage a staff of other professionals to run their practice.

Organizational skills. Some physicians own their own practice. Strong organizational skills, including good recordkeeping, are critical in both medical and business settings.

Patience. Physicians and surgeons may work for long periods with patients who need special attention. Children and adult patients who fear medical treatment may require more patience.

Physical stamina. Physicians and surgeons should be comfortable performing physical tasks, such as lifting or turning disabled patients. Surgeons may spend a great deal of time bending over patients during surgery.

Problem-solving skills. Physicians and surgeons need to evaluate patients' symptoms and administer the appropriate treatments. They often need to do this quickly in order to save a patient's life.

Training. After medical school, almost all graduates enter a residency program in their specialty of interest. A residency usually takes place in a hospital and varies in duration, generally lasting from 3 to 8 years, depending on the specialty.

Licenses, Certifications, and Registrations. All states require physicians and surgeons to be licensed; requirements vary by state. To qualify for a license, candidates must graduate from an accredited medical school, complete residency training in their specialty, and pass written and practical exams.

All physicians and surgeons must pass a standardized national licensure examination. M.D.s take the U.S. Medical Licensing Examination (USMLE). D.O.s take the Comprehensive Osteopathic Medical Licensing Examination (COMLEX-USA). For specific state information about licensing, contact your state's medical board.

Certification is not required for physicians and surgeons; however, it may increase their employment opportunities. M.D.s and D.O.s seeking board certification in a specialty may spend up to 7 years in residency training; the length of time varies with the specialty. An examination after residency is required for certification by the American Board of Medical Specialties (ABMS) or the American Osteopathic Association (AOA).

Pay

Wages for physicians and surgeons are among the highest of all occupations. According to the Medical Group Management

Similar Occupations   This table shows a list of occupations with job duties that are similar to those of physicians and surgeons.

Occupations	Entry-level Education	2012 Pay	Projected Job Growth	Average Annual Openings
Chiropractors	Doctoral or professional degree	$66,160	15%	1,520
Dentists	Doctoral or professional degree	$149,795	16%	5,910
Optometrists	Doctoral or professional degree	$97,820	24%	1,770
Physician Assistants	Master's degree	$90,930	38%	4,890
Podiatrists	Doctoral or professional degree	$116,440	22%	460
Registered Nurses	Associate's degree	$65,470	19%	105,260
Veterinarians	Doctoral or professional degree	$84,460	12%	3,100

Association's Physician Compensation and Production Survey, median total compensation for physicians varies with their type of practice. In 2012, physicians practicing primary care received total median annual compensation of $220,942 and physicians practicing in medical specialties received total median annual compensation of $396,233.

Median annual compensation for selected specialties in 2012, as reported by the Medical Group Management Association, was as follows:

Anesthesiology	$431,977
General surgery	367,885
Obstetrics/gynecology	301,737
Internal medicine	224,110
Psychiatry	220,252
Pediatrics/adolecent medicine	216,069
Family practice (without obstetrics)	207,117

Earnings vary with the physician's or surgeon's number of years in practice, geographic region of practice, hours worked, skill, personality, and professional reputation.

Job Outlook

Employment of physicians and surgeons is projected to grow 18 percent from 2012 to 2022, faster than the average for all occupations. Job growth will occur because of the continued expansion of healthcare-related industries. The growing and aging population is expected to drive overall growth in the demand for physician services as consumers continue to seek high levels of care that uses the latest technologies, diagnostic tests, and therapies. Some medical schools are increasing their enrollments on the basis of a perceived higher demand for physicians.

Although the demand for physicians and surgeons should continue, some factors will likely reduce growth. New technologies will allow physicians to treat more patients in the same amount of time, thereby reducing the number of physicians who would be needed to complete the same tasks. Physician assistants and nurse practitioners can do many of the routine duties of physicians and may be used to reduce costs at hospitals and outpatient care facilities.

Demand for physicians' services is sensitive to changes in healthcare reimbursement policies. Consumers may demand fewer physician services if changes to health coverage result in higher out-of-pocket costs for them. However, federal health legislation will expand the number of patients who have access to health insurance, increasing patient access to medical care. Such access will in turn increase demand for the services of physicians and surgeons.

Job Prospects. Job prospects should be good for physicians who are willing to practice in rural and low-income areas, because these areas tend to have difficulty attracting physicians. Job prospects also should be good for physicians in specialties dealing with health issues that largely affect aging baby boomers. For example, physicians specializing in cardiology and radiology will be needed because the risks for heart disease and cancer increase as people age.

O*NET

➤ Anesthesiologists (29-1061.00)
➤ Family and General Practitioners (29-1062.00)
➤ Internists, General (29-1063.00)
➤ Obstetricians and Gynecologists (29-1064.00)
➤ Pediatricians, General (29-1065.00)
➤ Psychiatrists (29-1066.00)
➤ Surgeons (29-1067.00)
➤ Physicians and Surgeons, All Other (29-1069.00)
➤ Allergists and Immunologists (29-1069.01)
➤ Dermatologists (29-1069.02)
➤ Hospitalists (29-1069.03)
➤ Neurologists (29-1069.04)
➤ Nuclear Medicine Physicians (29-1069.05)
➤ Ophthalmologists (29-1069.06)
➤ Pathologists (29-1069.07)
➤ Physical Medicine and Rehabilitation Physicians (29-1069.08)
➤ Preventive Medicine Physicians (29-1069.09)
➤ Radiologists (29-1069.10)
➤ Sports Medicine Physicians (29-1069.11)
➤ Urologists (29-1069.12)

Contacts for More Information

For more information about physicians and surgeons, visit
➤ American Medical Association (www.ama-assn.org/)
➤ American Osteopathic Association (www.osteopathic.org)
For information about various medical specialties, visit
➤ American Academy of Family Physicians (www.aafp.org/online/en/home.html)
➤ American Board of Medical Specialties (www.abms.org)
➤ American Congress of Obstetricians and Gynecologists (www.acog.org)
➤ American College of Surgeons (www.facs.org/)
For a list of medical schools and residency programs, as well as for general information on premedical education, financial aid, and medicine as a career, visit
➤ Association of American Medical Colleges (www.aamc.org)
➤ American Association of Colleges of Osteopathic Medicine (www.aacom.org/Pages/default.aspx)
For information about licensing, visit
➤ Federation of State Medical Boards (www.fsmb.org)

Podiatrists

- **2012 Median Pay** .... $116,440 per year
  $55.98 per hour
- **Entry-Level Education** ... Doctoral or professional degree
- **Work Experience in a Related Occupation**.............. None
- **On-the-Job Training** .... Internship/residency
- **Number of Jobs 2012** 10,700
- **Job Outlook, 2012–22** .... 23% (Much faster than average)
- **Employment Change, 2012–22** 2,400

What Podiatrists Do

Podiatrists provide medical and surgical care for people with foot, ankle, and lower leg problems. They diagnose illnesses, treat injuries, and perform surgery involving the lower extremities.

Duties. Podiatrists typically do the following:

- Assess the condition of a patient's feet, ankles, or lower legs by reviewing his or her medical history, listening to the patient's concerns, and performing a physical examination

- Diagnose foot, ankle, and lower-leg problems through physical exams, X-rays, medical laboratory tests, and other methods

- Provide treatment for foot, ankle, and lower leg ailments, such as prescribing special shoe inserts (orthotics) to improve a patient's mobility

- Perform foot and ankle surgeries, such as removing bone spurs and correcting foot and ankle deformities

- Give advice and instruction on foot and ankle care and on general wellness techniques

- Prescribe medications

- Refer patients to other physicians or specialists if they detect larger health problems, such as diabetes

- Read journals and attend conferences to keep up with advances in podiatric medicine

Podiatrists treat a variety of foot and ankle ailments, including calluses, ingrown toenails, heel spurs, and arch problems. They also treat foot and leg problems associated with diabetes and other diseases. Some podiatrists spend most of their time performing advanced surgeries, such as foot and ankle reconstruction. Others may choose a specialty such as sports medicine or pediatrics.

Podiatrists who own their practice may spend time on business-related activities, such as hiring employees and managing inventory.

Podiatrists diagnose and treat disorders, diseases, and injuries of the foot and lower leg.

Work Environment

Podiatrists held about 10,700 jobs in 2012.

Most podiatrists work in offices of podiatry, either on their own or with other podiatrists. Some work in group practices with other physicians or specialists. Others work in private and public hospitals and outpatient care centers.

About 14 percent of podiatrists were self-employed in 2012. Self-employed podiatrists either solely own or are partners in a medical practice.

Work Schedules. Most podiatrists work full time. Podiatrists' offices may be open in the evenings or on weekends to accommodate patients. In hospitals, podiatrists may have to work occasional nights or weekends, or may be on call.

Median Annual Wages, May 2012

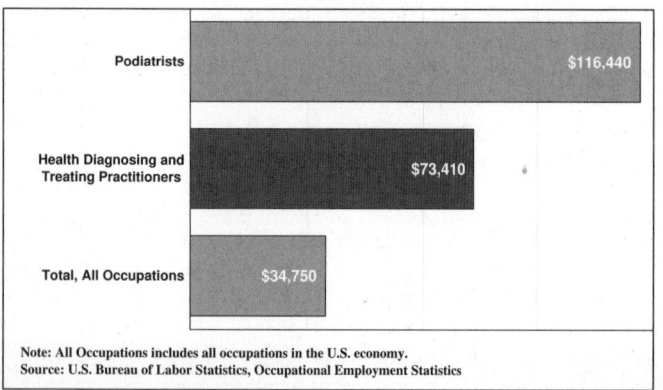

Podiatrists — $116,440

Health Diagnosing and Treating Practitioners — $73,410

Total, All Occupations — $34,750

Note: All Occupations includes all occupations in the U.S. economy.
Source: U.S. Bureau of Labor Statistics, Occupational Employment Statistics

Percent Change in Employment, Projected 2012–2022

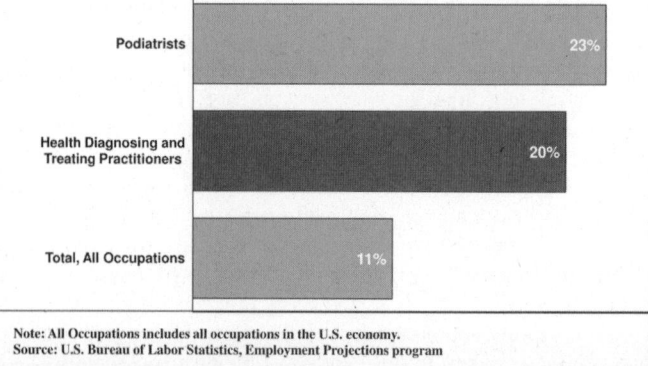

Podiatrists — 23%

Health Diagnosing and Treating Practitioners — 20%

Total, All Occupations — 11%

Note: All Occupations includes all occupations in the U.S. economy.
Source: U.S. Bureau of Labor Statistics, Employment Projections program

Employment Projections Data for Podiatrists

Occupational title	SOC Code	Employment, 2012	Projected Employment, 2022	Change, 2012–2022	
				Percent	Numeric
Podiatrists	29-1081	10,700	13,100	23	2,400

Source: U.S. Bureau of Labor Statistics, Employment Projections Program

Note: Data are rounded. Go to **Occupational Information Included in the OOH** for a discussion of the data in this table.

How to Become One

Podiatrists must earn a Doctor of Podiatric Medicine (DPM) degree and complete a 3-year residency program. Podiatrists must be licensed.

Education and Training. Podiatrists must have a Doctor of Podiatric Medicine (DPM) degree from an accredited college of podiatric medicine. A DPM degree program takes 4 years to complete. In 2012, there were 9 colleges of podiatric medicine accredited by the Council on Podiatric Medical Education.

Admission to podiatric medicine programs requires at least 3 years of undergraduate education, including specific courses in laboratory sciences such as biology, chemistry, and physics, as well as general coursework in subjects such as English. In practice, nearly all prospective podiatrists earn a bachelor's degree before attending a college of podiatric medicine. Admission to DPM programs usually requires taking the Medical College Admission Test (MCAT).

Courses for a Doctor of Podiatric Medicine degree are similar to those for other medical degrees. They include anatomy, physiology, pharmacology, and pathology among other subjects. During their last 2 years, podiatric medical students gain supervised experience by completing clinical rotations.

After earning a DPM, podiatrists must apply to and complete a podiatric medical and surgical residency (PMSR) program, which lasts 3 years. Residency programs take place in hospitals and provide both medical and surgical experience. They may do additional training in specific fellowship areas.

Licenses, Certifications, and Registrations. Podiatrists in every state must be licensed. Usually, Podiatrists must pay a fee and pass the American Podiatric Medical Licensing Exam (APMLE). Some states also require podiatrists to take a state-specific exam. Licenses must typically be renewed periodically, and podiatrists must take continuing medical education.

Many podiatrists choose to become board certified. The American Board of Podiatric Surgery is the certifying agency in podiatric surgery, and the American Board of Podiatric Medicine is the certifying agency in orthopedics and primary care podiatry. Certification requires a combination of work experience and passing scores on exams.

Important Qualities

Compassion. Podiatrists treat patients who may be in pain. They must be empathetic toward the people they serve.

Critical-thinking skills. Podiatrists must have a sharp, analytical mind to correctly diagnose a patient and determine the best course of treatment.

Detail oriented. To provide safe, effective healthcare, a podiatrist should be detail oriented. For example, a podiatrist must pay attention to a patient's medical history as well as current conditions when diagnosing a problem and deciding on a treatment.

Interpersonal skills. Because podiatrists spend much of their time interacting with patients, they should be able to listen well and communicate effectively. For example, they should be able to tell a patient who is slated to undergo surgery what to expect and calm his or her fears.

Pay

The median annual wage for podiatrists was $116,440 in May 2012. The median wage is the wage at which half the workers in an occupation earned more than that amount and half earned less. The lowest 10 percent earned less than $52,530, and the top 10 percent earned more than $187,200.

Self-employed podiatrists may earn more than salaried doctors, but they are also responsible for the costs of running a business, such as providing benefits for themselves and employees.

Job Outlook

Employment of podiatrists is projected to grow 23 percent from 2012 to 2022, much faster than the average for all occupations. However, because it is a small occupation, the fast growth will result in only about 2,400 new jobs over the 10-year period.

As the U.S. population both ages and increases, the number of people expected to have mobility and foot-related problems will rise. Growing rates of chronic conditions such as diabetes and obesity also may limit mobility of those with these conditions, and lead to problems such as poor circulation in the feet and lower extremities. More podiatrists will be needed to provide care for these patients.

In addition, podiatrists are increasingly working in group practices along with other healthcare professionals. Continued growth

Similar Occupations   This table shows a list of occupations with job duties that are similar to those of podiatrists.

Occupations	Entry-level Education	2012 Pay	Projected Job Growth	Average Annual Openings
Chiropractors	Doctoral or professional degree	$66,160	15%	1,520
Occupational Therapists	Master's degree	$75,400	29%	4,820
Optometrists	Doctoral or professional degree	$97,820	24%	1,770
Orthotists and Prosthetists	Master's degree	$62,670	35%	380
Physical Therapists	Doctoral or professional degree	$79,860	36%	12,370
Physicians and Surgeons	Doctoral or professional degree	$182,294	18%	29,630

in the use of outpatient surgery also will create new opportunities for podiatrists.

Job Prospects. Job prospects for trained podiatrists should be good given that there are a limited number of colleges of podiatry. In addition, the retirement of currently practicing podiatrists in the coming years is expected to increase the number of job openings for podiatrists.

O*NET

➤ Podiatrists (29-1081.00)

Contacts for More Information

For more information about podiatrists, visit
➤ American Podiatric Medical Association (www.apma.org/)

For information on colleges of podiatric medicine and their entrance requirements, curricula, and student financial aid, visit
➤ American Association of Colleges of Podiatric Medicine (www.aacpm.org/)

For a list of accredited podiatric programs and residency programs, visit
➤ Council on Podiatric Medical Education (www.cpme.org/)

For more information about the podiatric licensing exam, visit
➤ The National Board of Podiatric Medical Examiners (www.nbpme.com/)

For more information about board certification, visit
➤ American Board of Podiatric Surgery (www.abps.org/)
➤ American Board of Podiatric Medicine (www.abpmed.org/)

Psychiatric Technicians and Aides

- **2012 Median Pay** .... $27,440 per year
  $13.19 per hour
- **Entry-Level Education** ....See "How to Become One"
- **Work Experience in a Related Occupation**............... None
- **On-the-Job Training** ....Short-term on-the-job training
- **Number of Jobs 2012** 153,000
- **Job Outlook, 2012–22** .... 5% (Slower than average)
- **Employment Change, 2012–22** 7,600

What Psychiatric Technicians and Aides Do

Psychiatric technicians and aides care for people who have mental illness and developmental disabilities. Technicians typically provide therapeutic care. Aides help patients in their daily activities and ensure a safe, clean environment.

Duties. Psychiatric technicians, sometimes called mental health technicians, typically do the following:

- Observe patients' behavior, listen to their concerns, and record their condition

- Lead patients in therapeutic and recreational activities

- Give medications and other treatments to patients, following instructions from doctors and other medical professionals

- Help with admitting and discharging patients

- Monitor patients' vital signs, such as their blood pressure

- Help patients with activities of daily living, including eating and bathing

- Restrain patients who may become physically violent

Psychiatric aides typically do the following:

- Monitor patients' behavior and location in a mental healthcare facility

- Help patients with their daily living activities, such as bathing or dressing

- Serve meals and help patients eat

- Keep facilities clean by doing tasks such as changing bed linens

- Participate in group activities, such as playing sports or going on field trips

- Help transport patients within a hospital or residential care facility

- Restrain patients who may become physically violent

Many psychiatric technicians and aides work with patients who are severely developmentally disabled and need intensive care. Others work with patients undergoing rehabilitation for drug and alcohol addiction. The work of psychiatric technicians and aides varies depending on the types of patients they work with.

Psychiatric technicians and aides work as part of a medical team, under the direction of physicians and alongside other healthcare professionals, including psychiatrists, psychologists, psychiatric nurses, social workers, counselors, and therapists. For more information on the counselors and therapists they may work with, see the profiles on substance abuse and behavioral disorder counselors, rehabilitation counselors, and mental health counselors and marriage and family therapists.

Because they have such close contact with patients, psychiatric technicians and aides can have a great deal of influence on patients' outlook and treatment.

Work Environment

Psychiatric technicians held about 71,000 jobs in 2012. Psychiatric aides held about 82,000 jobs in 2012.

The industries that employed the most psychiatric technicians in 2012 were as follows:

Hospitals; state, local, and private	56%
State government, excluding education and hospitals	27
Residential care facilities	8
Outpatient care centers	3
Offices of health practitioners	2

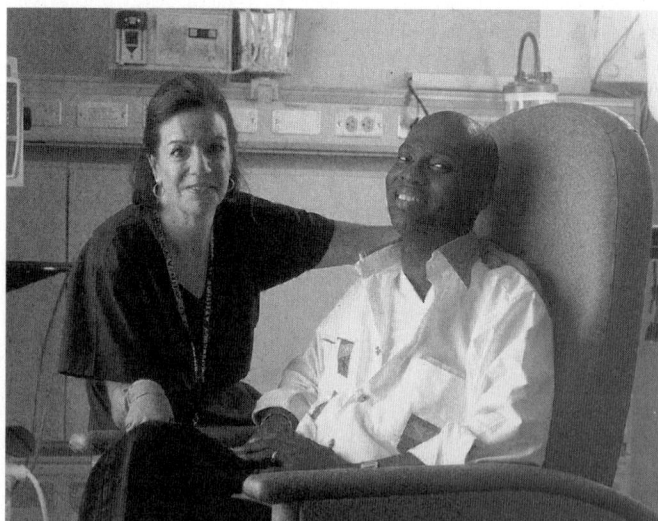

Psychiatric technicians and aides work in psychiatric hospitals, residential mental health facilities, and related healthcare settings, like drug or alcohol treatment centers.

Median Annual Wages, May 2012

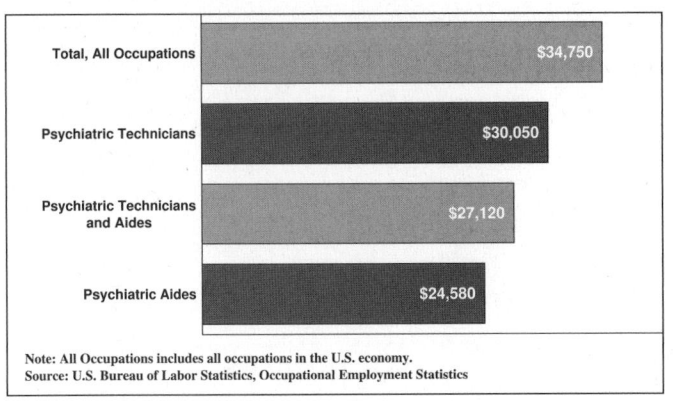

Note: All Occupations includes all occupations in the U.S. economy.
Source: U.S. Bureau of Labor Statistics, Occupational Employment Statistics

Percent Change in Employment, Projected 2012–2022

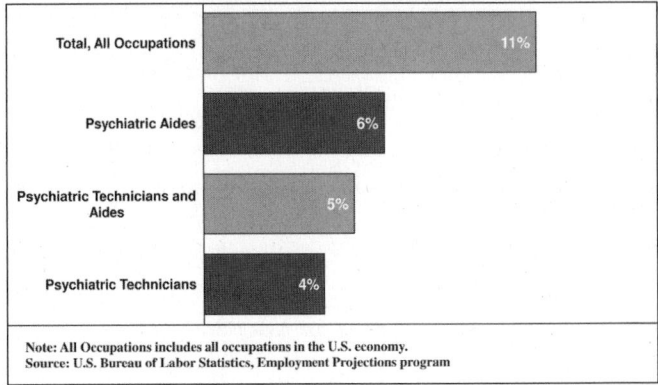

Note: All Occupations includes all occupations in the U.S. economy.
Source: U.S. Bureau of Labor Statistics, Employment Projections program

The industries that employed the most psychiatric aides in 2012 were as follows:

Hospitals; state, local, and private 42%
State government, excluding education and hospitals 26
Residential care facilities 21
Individual, family, community, and vocational
   rehabilitation services 4
Local government, excluding education and hospitals 2

Psychiatric technicians and aides may spend much of their shift on their feet. Some of the work that psychiatric aides do may be unpleasant. They may care for patients whose illnesses make them disoriented, uncooperative, or violent.

Injuries and Illnesses. Because their work requires many physically demanding tasks, such as lifting patients, psychiatric technicians and aides have high injury and illness rates.

Work Schedules. Psychiatric technicians and aides may work full time or part time. Because hospitals and residential facilities are open at all hours, many psychiatric technicians and aides work nights, weekends, and holidays.

How to Become One

Psychiatric technicians typically need postsecondary education, and aides need at least a high school diploma. Both technicians and aides receive on-the-job training.

Education. Psychiatric technicians typically enter the occupation with a postsecondary certificate. Programs in psychiatric or mental health technology are commonly offered by community colleges and technical schools.

Psychiatric technician programs include courses in biology, psychology, and counseling. The programs also may include supervised work experience or cooperative programs, in which students gain academic credit for structured work experience.

Programs for psychiatric technicians range in length from 1 semester to 2 years, and they may award a certificate or an associate's degree.

Psychiatric aides typically need a high school diploma or equivalent. Postsecondary courses in psychology or mental health technology may be helpful.

Training. Psychiatric technicians and aides typically participate in a short period of on-the-job training before they can work without direct supervision.

Training may include working with patients while under the close supervision of an experienced technician or aide. Technicians and aides may also attend workshops, lectures, or in-service training.

Important Qualities

Compassion. Because psychiatric technicians and aides spend much of their time interacting with patients, they should be caring and want to help people.

Interpersonal skills. Psychiatric technicians and aides often provide ongoing care for patients, so they should be able to develop a rapport with patients, making them better able to treat their patients and evaluate their condition.

Observational skills. Technicians must watch patients closely and be sensitive to any changes in behavior. For their safety and that of their patients, they must recognize signs of discomfort or trouble among patients.

Patience. Working with the mentally ill can be emotionally challenging. Psychiatric technicians and aides must be able to stay calm in stressful situations.

Physical stamina. Psychiatric technicians and aides must be able to lift, move, and sometimes restrain patients. They must also be able to spend much of their time on their feet.

Licenses, Certifications, and Registrations. In 2013, four states–Arkansas, California, Colorado, and Kansas–required licensure of psychiatric technicians. Although specific requirements vary, states

Employment Projections Data for Psychiatric Technicians and Aides

Occupational title	SOC Code	Employment, 2012	Projected Employment, 2022	Change, 2012–2022	
				Percent	Numeric
Psychiatric technicians and aides	—	153,000	160,600	5	7,600
Psychiatric technicians	29-2053	71,000	73,800	4	2,800
Psychiatric aides...	31-1013	82,000	86,800	6	4,900

Source: U.S. Bureau of Labor Statistics, Employment Projections Program

Note: Data are rounded. Go to **Occupational Information Included in the OOH** for a discussion of the data in this table.

Similar Occupations This table shows a list of occupations with job duties that are similar to those of psychiatric technicians and aides.

Occupations	Entry-level Education	2012 Pay	Projected Job Growth	Average Annual Openings
Childcare Workers	High school diploma or equivalent	$19,510	14%	57,000
Home Health Aides	Less than high school	$20,820	48%	59,070
Licensed Practical and Licensed Vocational Nurses	Postsecondary non-degree award	$41,540	25%	36,310
Medical Assistants	Postsecondary non-degree award	$29,370	29%	26,990
Nursing Assistants and Orderlies	See "How to Become One"	$24,404	21%	61,300
Occupational Therapy Assistants and Aides	See "How to Become One"	$47,638	41%	2,560
Personal Care Aides	Less than high school	$19,910	49%	66,600
Registered Nurses	Associate's degree	$65,470	19%	105,260
Social and Human Service Assistants	High school diploma or equivalent	$28,850	22%	17,870

usually require psychiatric technicians to complete an accredited education program, pass an exam, and pay a fee to be licensed.

Psychiatric aides are not required to be licensed.

The American Association of Psychiatric Technicians offers four levels of certification for psychiatric technicians. The certifications allow technicians to show a high level of professional competency. Requirements vary by certification.

Pay

The median annual wage for psychiatric technicians was $30,050 in May 2012. The median wage is the wage at which half the workers in an occupation earned more than that amount and half earned less. The lowest 10 percent earned less than $20,550, and the top 10 percent earned more than $52,980.

The median annual wage for psychiatric aides was $24,580 in May 2012. The lowest 10 percent earned less than $16,960, and the top 10 percent earned more than $40,430.

In May 2012, the median annual wages for psychiatric technicians in the top five industries in which these technicians worked were as follows:

State government, excluding education and hospitals........ $32,010
Offices of health practitioners 31,470
Hospitals; state, local, and private 30,830
Residential care facilities... 24,440
Outpatient care centers 23,560

In May 2012, the median annual wages for psychiatric aides in the top five industries in which these aides worked were as follows:

Hospitals; state, local, and private $28,340
Local government, excluding education and hospitals......... 25,580
Individual, family, community, and vocational
rehabilitation services... 25,040
Residential care facilities... 22,680
State government, excluding education and hospitals.......... 18,840

Job Outlook

Employment of psychiatric technicians is projected to grow 4 percent from 2012 to 2022, slower than the average for all occupations. Employment of psychiatric aides is projected to grow 6 percent from 2012 to 2022, slower than the average for all occupations.

As the nation's population ages and people live longer, there is likely to be an increase in the number of older men and women with cognitive mental diseases, such as Alzheimer's disease. Demand for psychiatric technicians and aides in residential facili-

ties are expected to rise as a result. In addition, the aging prison population has increased the need for psychiatric technicians and aides in correctional facilities.

More psychiatric technicians and aides will be needed in residential treatment facilities and in outpatient care centers for people with developmental disabilities, mental illness, and substance abuse problems. There is a long-term trend toward treating psychiatric patients in community-based settings rather than in hospitals. These settings allow patients greater independence, and they are often more cost-effective.

Federal health legislation will expand the number of patients who have access to health insurance, increasing patient access to medical care. Federal health insurance reform will expand coverage of mental health disorders to millions of people, and more technicians and aides will be needed to provide mental health services.

O*NET

➤ Psychiatric Technicians (29-2053.00)
➤ Psychiatric Aides (31-1013.00)

Contacts for More Information

For more information about psychiatric technicians and aides, visit
➤ American Association of Psychiatric Technicians (www.psychtechs. org/)

Radiation Therapists

- **2012 Median Pay** .... $77,560 per year
  $37.29 per hour
- **Entry-Level Education** .... Associate's degree
- **Work Experience in a Related Occupation** .... None
- **On-the-Job Training** .... None
- **Number of Jobs 2012** 19,100
- **Job Outlook, 2012–22** .... 24% (Much faster than average)
- **Employment Change, 2012–22** 4,500

What Radiation Therapists Do

Radiation therapists treat cancer and other diseases in patients by administering radiation treatments.

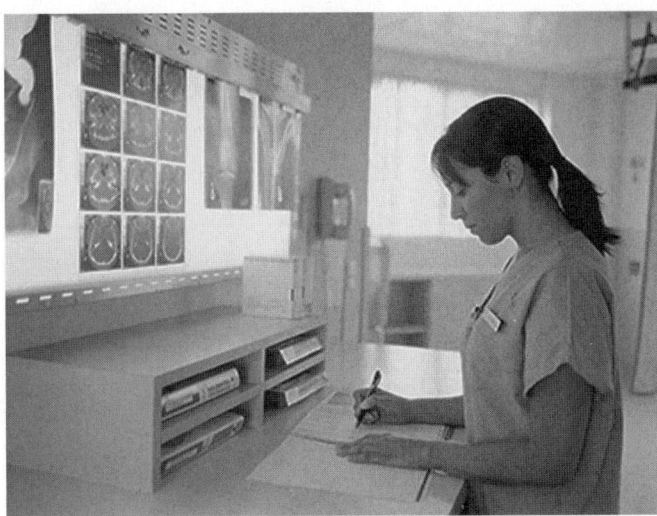

Radiation therapists have good Job Prospects.

Duties. Radiation therapists typically do the following:

- Explain treatment plans to the patient and answer questions about treatment
- Follow safety procedures to protect the patient and themselves from overexposure to radiation
- Examine machines to make sure they are safe and working properly
- X-ray the patient to determine the exact location of the area requiring treatment
- Check computer programs to make sure the machine will give the correct dose of radiation to the appropriate area of the patient's body
- Operate the machine to treat the patient with radiation
- Monitor the patient to check for unusual reactions to the treatment
- Keep detailed records of treatment

Machines called linear accelerators are used to deliver radiation therapy. These machines direct high-energy X-rays at specific cancer cells in a patient's body, shrinking or removing them.

Radiation therapists are part of the oncology team that treats patients with cancer. They often work with the following specialists:

- Radiation oncologists, physicians who specialize in radiation therapy

- Oncology nurses, registered nurses who specialize in caring for patients with cancer
- Radiation physicists, physicists who calibrate linear accelerators

Work Environment

Radiation therapists held about 19,100 jobs in 2012. Most therapists work in hospitals, offices of physicians, and outpatient centers.

Radiation therapists are on their feet for long periods and may need to lift or turn disabled patients. Because they work with radiation and radioactive material, radiation therapists must follow safety procedures to make sure that they are not exposed to a potentially harmful amount of radiation. These procedures usually require therapists to stand in a different room while the patient undergoes radiation procedures.

Work Schedules. Most radiation therapists work full time. Because radiation therapy procedures are usually planned in advance, radiation therapists keep a regular work schedule.

How to Become One

Most radiation therapists complete programs that lead to an associate's degree or bachelor's degree in radiation therapy. Radiation therapists must be licensed in most states; requirements vary by state.

Education. Although candidates may qualify by completing a 12-month certificate program, employers usually prefer to hire applicants who have an associate's degree or a bachelor's degree in radiation therapy.

Radiation therapy programs include courses in radiation therapy procedures and the scientific theories behind them. These programs often include courses in human anatomy and physiology, physics, algebra, computer science, and research methodology.

Important Qualities

Detail oriented. Radiation therapists must follow exact instructions and input exact measurements to make sure the patient is exposed to the correct amount of radiation.

Interpersonal skills. Radiation therapists work closely with patients. It is important that therapists be comfortable interacting with people who may be going through physical and emotional stress.

Physical stamina. Radiation therapists must be able to be on their feet for long periods and be able to lift and move patients who need assistance.

Technical skills. Radiation therapists work with computers and large pieces of technological equipment, so they must be comfortable operating those devices.

Median Annual Wages, May 2012

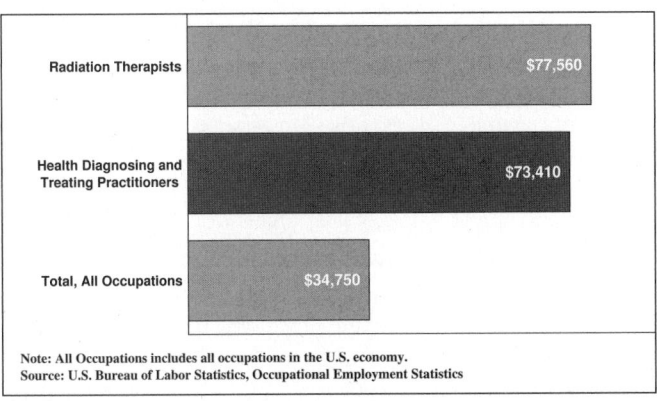

Radiation Therapists	$77,560
Health Diagnosing and Treating Practitioners	$73,410
Total, All Occupations	$34,750

Note: All Occupations includes all occupations in the U.S. economy.
Source: U.S. Bureau of Labor Statistics, Occupational Employment Statistics

Percent Change in Employment, Projected 2012–2022

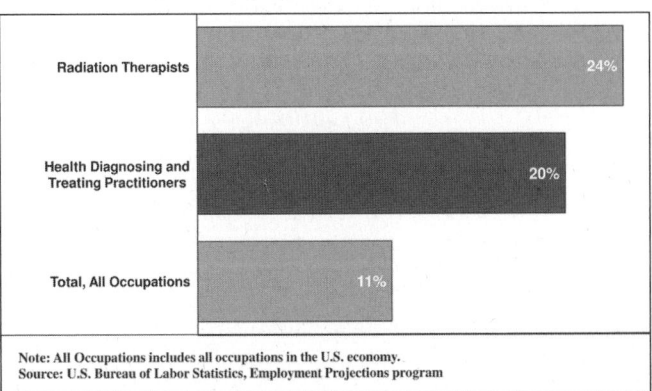

Radiation Therapists	24%
Health Diagnosing and Treating Practitioners	20%
Total, All Occupations	11%

Note: All Occupations includes all occupations in the U.S. economy.
Source: U.S. Bureau of Labor Statistics, Employment Projections program

Employment Projections Data for Radiation Therapists

Occupational title	SOC Code	Employment, 2012	Projected Employment, 2022	Change, 2012–2022 Percent	Change, 2012–2022 Numeric
Radiation therapists...	29-1124	19,100	23,600	24	4,500

Source: U.S. Bureau of Labor Statistics, Employment Projections Program

Note: Data are rounded. Go to **Occupational Information Included in the OOH** *for a discussion of the data in this table.*

Similar Occupations   This table shows a list of occupations with job duties that are similar to those of radiation therapists.

Occupations	Entry-level Education	2012 Pay	Projected Job Growth	Average Annual Openings
Dental Hygienists	Associate's degree	$70,210	33%	11,350
Diagnostic Medical Sonographers and Cardiovascular Technologists and Technicians, Including Vascular Technologists	Associate's degree	$59,422	39%	5,830
Nuclear Medicine Technologists	Associate's degree	$70,180	20%	720
Nursing Assistants and Orderlies	See "How to Become One"	$24,404	21%	61,300
Physical Therapist Assistants and Aides	See "How to Become One"	$40,539	41%	7,630
Radiologic and MRI Technologists	Associate's degree	$56,035	21%	8,090
Registered Nurses	Associate's degree	$65,470	19%	105,260

Licenses, Certifications, and Registrations. In most states, radiation therapists must be licensed; requirements vary by state. To be licensed, radiation therapists must graduate from an accredited radiation therapy program and be certified by the American Registry of Radiologic Technologists (ARRT). To become ARRT certified, an applicant must complete an accredited radiation therapy program, adhere to ARRT ethical standards, and pass the ARRT certification exam. The exam covers radiation protection and quality assurance, clinical concepts in radiation oncology, treatment planning, treatment delivery, and patient care and education.

Advancement. Experienced radiation therapists may advance to manage radiation therapy programs in hospitals or other healthcare facilities. Managers generally continue to treat patients while taking on managerial responsibilities. Other advancement opportunities include teaching, technical sales, and research. With additional training and certification, therapists can become dosimetrists. Dosimetrists are responsible for calculating the correct dose of radiation that is used in the treatment of cancer patients.

Pay

The median annual wage for radiation therapists was $77,560 in May 2012. The median wage is the wage at which half the workers in an occupation earned more than that amount and half earned less. The lowest 10 percent earned less than $51,720, and the top 10 percent earned more than $113,810.

Job Outlook

Employment of radiation therapists is projected to grow 24 percent from 2012 to 2022, much faster than the average for all occupations. However, because it is a small occupation, the fast growth will result in only about 4,500 new jobs over the 10-year period.

The risk of cancer increases as people age, so an aging population will increase demand for radiation therapists. Early diagnosis and the development of more sophisticated treatment techniques will also increase employment.

O*NET

➤ Radiation Therapists (29-1124.00)

Contacts for More Information

For information about radiation therapists, visit
➤ The American Registry of Radiologic Technologists (www.arrt.org/)
➤ American Society of Radiologic Technologists (www.asrt.org/)

Radiologic and MRI Technologists

- **2012 Median Pay** .... $55,910 per year
  $26.88 per hour
- **Entry-Level Education** ....Associate's degree
- **Work Experience in a Related Occupation** .... See "How to Become One"
- **On-the-Job Training** .... None
- **Number of Jobs 2012** 229,300
- **Job Outlook, 2012–22** .... 21% (Faster than average)
- **Employment Change, 2012–22** 48,600

What Radiologic and MRI Technologists Do

Radiologic technologists perform diagnostic imaging examinations, such as X-rays, on patients. MRI technologists operate magnetic resonance imaging (MRI) scanners to create diagnostic images.

Duties. Radiologic and MRI technologists typically do the following:

- Adjust and maintain imaging equipment
- Precisely follow orders from physicians on what areas of the body to image
- Prepare patients for procedures, including taking a medical history and answering questions about the procedure

magnetic fields in combination with the contrast agent to produce images that a physician can use to diagnose medical problems.

Healthcare professionals who specialize in other diagnostic equipment include nuclear medicine technologists, diagnostic medical sonographers, and cardiovascular technologists and technicians, including vascular technologists.

Work Environment

Radiologic technologists held about 199,200 jobs in 2012. MRI technologists held about 30,100 jobs in 2012. Radiologic and MRI technologists work in healthcare facilities. Like other healthcare workers, radiologic and MRI technologists may be exposed to infectious diseases. Technologists are often on their feet for long periods and may need to lift or turn patients who are disabled.

The industries that employed the most radiologic technologists in 2012 were as follows:

General medical and surgical hospitals; state, local,
    and private 59%
Offices of physicians 22
Medical and diagnostic laboratories 7
Outpatient care centers 4

The industries that employed the most MRI technologists in 2012 were as follows:

General medical and surgical hospitals;
    state, local, and private.. 55%
Medical and diagnostic laboratories 21
Offices of physicians 15
Specialty (except psychiatric and substance abuse)
    hospitals; state, local, and private.. 2

Injuries and Illnesses. Radiologic technologists wear badges measuring radiation levels in the radiation area, and detailed records are kept on their cumulative lifetime dose. Although radiation hazards exist in this occupation, they are minimized by the use of protective lead aprons, gloves, and other shielding devices, and by instruments that monitor exposure to radiation.

Work Schedules. Most radiologic and MRI technologists work full time. Because imaging is needed in emergency situations, some technologists work evenings, weekends, or on call.

How to Become One

An associate's degree is the most common educational path for radiologic and MRI technologists. Technologists must be licensed or certified in some states; requirements vary by state.

Education. There are postsecondary education programs in radiography and MRI that lead to graduate certificates, associate's degrees, or bachelor's degrees. Associate's degree programs are the most com-

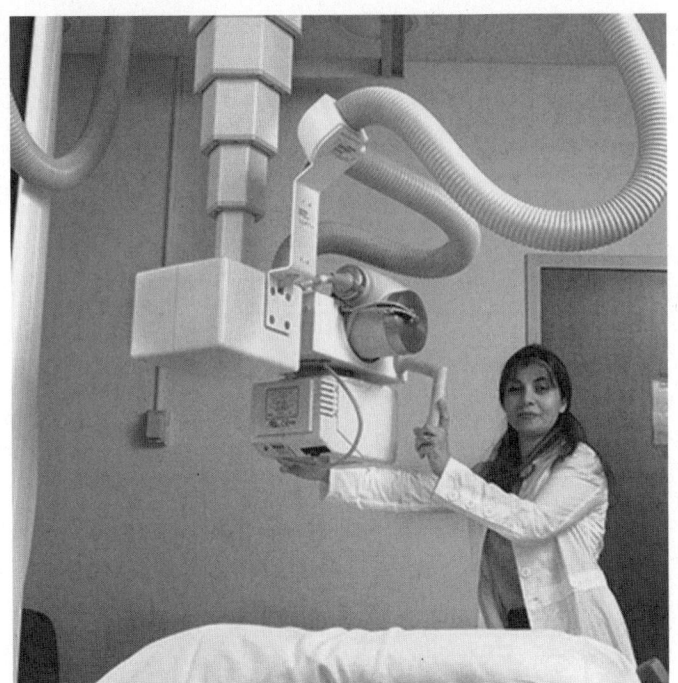

Radiologic technologists perform diagnostic imaging examinations on patients.

- Protect the patient by shielding exposed areas that do not need to be imaged
- Position the patient and the equipment in order to get the correct image
- Operate the computerized equipment to take the images
- Work with physicians to evaluate the images and to determine whether additional images need to be taken
- Keep detailed patient records

Healthcare professionals use many types of equipment to diagnose patients. Radiologic technologists specialize in X-ray, and computed tomography (CT) imaging. Some radiologic technologists prepare a mixture for the patient to drink that allows soft tissue to be viewed on the images that the radiologist reviews. Radiologic technologists might also specialize in mammography. Mammographers use low-dose X-ray systems to produce images of the breast. Technologists may be certified in multiple specialties.

MRI technologists specialize in magnetic resonance imaging scanners. MRI technologists inject patients with contrast dyes so that the images will show up on the scanner. The scanners use

Median Annual Wages, May 2012

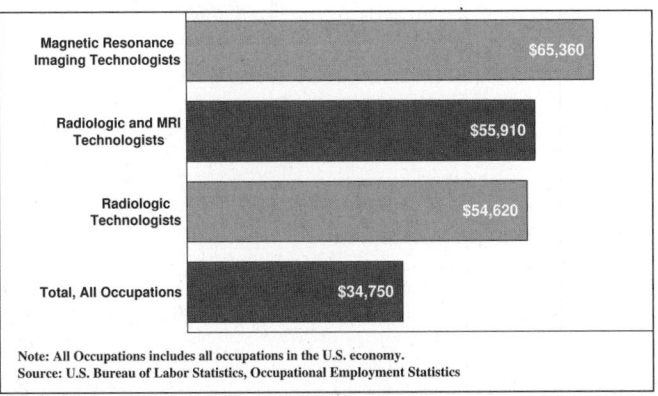

Note: All Occupations includes all occupations in the U.S. economy.
Source: U.S. Bureau of Labor Statistics, Occupational Employment Statistics

Percent Change in Employment, Projected 2012–2022

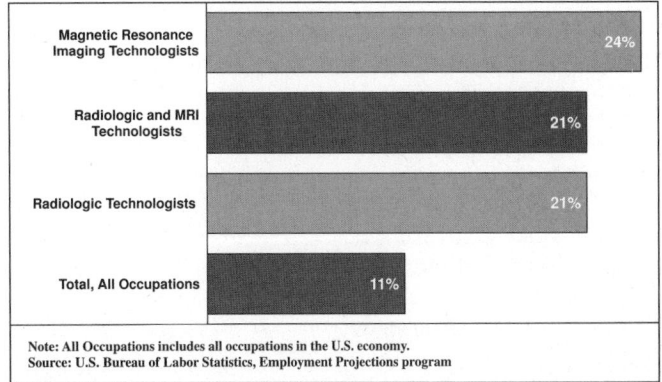

Note: All Occupations includes all occupations in the U.S. economy.
Source: U.S. Bureau of Labor Statistics, Employment Projections program

Employment Projections Data for Radiologic and MRI Technologists

Occupational title	SOC Code	Employment, 2012	Projected Employment, 2022	Change, 2012–2022	
				Percent	Numeric
Radiologic and MRI technologists.......................................	—	229,300	277,900	21	48,600
Radiologic technologists	29-2034	199,200	240,800	21	41,500
Magnetic resonance imaging technologists........................	29-2035	30,100	37,200	24	7,100

Source: U.S. Bureau of Labor Statistics, Employment Projections Program

Note: Data are rounded. Go to **Occupational Information Included in the OOH** *for a discussion of the data in this table.*

mon. Education programs typically include both classroom training and clinical training. Coursework includes anatomy, pathology, patient care, radiation physics and protection, and image evaluation.

The Joint Review Committee on Education in Radiologic Technology (JRCERT) accredits programs in radiography. Completing an accredited program is required for licensure in some states.

High school students who are interested in radiologic or MRI technology should take courses that focus on science and math. Suggested courses include anatomy, biology, chemistry, physiology, mathematics, and physics.

Work Experience in a Related Occupation. Many MRI technologists start out as radiologic technologists. After gaining experience in all of the areas of radiologic technology, they then begin to specialize in giving MRI examinations. After a few years, most technicians are considered to be experienced enough to sit for an MRI certification exam.

Other MRI technologists may be required to complete specific imaging examinations on patients and then have this information verified by a doctor before being considered an MRI technologist.

Licenses, Certifications, and Registrations. Radiologic and MRI technologists must be licensed or certified in some states; requirements vary by state. To become licensed, technologists must graduate from an accredited program and must pass a certification exam from the state or from the American Registry of Radiologic Technologists (ARRT).

Many MRI technologists are first licensed or certified radiologic technologists who have the required amount of work experience in magnetic resonance imaging to meet certification standards, which includes a set number of documented imaging examinations. Those who are not radiologic technologists need to complete a formal education program before taking the certification exam. MRI certification is available from the ARRT and is accepted by most states for licensure.

For specific state requirements, contact the state's health board.

Important Qualities

Detail oriented. Radiologic and MRI technologists must follow exact instructions to get the images needed to diagnose and treat the patient.

Interpersonal skills. Radiologic and MRI technologists work closely with patients who may be in extreme pain or mentally stressed. Technologists must be able to put the patient at ease to get usable images.

Math skills. Radiologic and MRI technologists may need to calculate and mix the right dose of chemicals used in imaging procedures.

Physical stamina. Radiologic and MRI technologists often work on their feet for long periods during the day and they must be able to lift and move patients who need assistance.

Technical skills. Radiologic and MRI technologists must understand how to operate complex machinery.

Pay

The median annual wage for radiologic technologists was $54,620 in May 2012. The median wage is the wage at which half the workers in an occupation earned more than that amount and half earned less. The lowest 10 percent earned less than $37,060, and the highest 10 percent earned more than $77,160.

The median annual wage for MRI technologists was $65,360 in May 2012. The lowest 10 percent earned less than $46,400, and the highest 10 percent earned more than $89,130.

Job Outlook

Employment of radiologic technologists is projected to grow 21 percent from 2012 to 2022, faster than the average for all occupations. Employment of MRI technologists is projected to grow 24 percent from 2012 to 2022, much faster than the average for all occupations.

As the population grows older, there will be an increase in medical conditions, such as breaks and fractures caused by osteoporosis, which can require imaging to diagnose them. Radiologic and MRI technologists will be needed to maintain and use the diagnostic equipment. In addition, federal health legislation will expand the number of patients who have access to health insurance, increasing patient access to medical care.

Although hospitals will remain the main employer of radiologic and MRI technologists, a number of new jobs will be in physicians' offices and in outpatient imaging centers. Employment in

Similar Occupations   This table shows a list of occupations with job duties that are similar to those of radiologic and MRI technologists.

Occupations	Entry-level Education	2012 Pay	Projected Job Growth	Average Annual Openings
Diagnostic Medical Sonographers and Cardiovascular Technologists and Technicians, Including Vascular Technologists	Associate's degree	$59,422	39%	5,830
Nuclear Medicine Technologists	Associate's degree	$70,180	20%	720
Radiation Therapists	Associate's degree	$77,560	24%	840

these healthcare settings is expected to increase because of the shift toward outpatient care whenever possible. Outpatient care is encouraged by third-party payers as a cost-saving measure and is made possible by technological advances, such as less expensive equipment, that allow for more procedures to be done outside of hospitals.

Job Prospects. Technologists with multiple certifications will have the best job prospects.

O*NET

➤ Radiologic Technologists (29-2034.00)
➤ Magnetic Resonance Imaging Technologists (29-2035.00)

Contacts for More Information

For information about radiologic and MRI technology, visit

➤ American Society of Radiologic Technologists (www.asrt.org/)
➤ Joint Review Committee on Education in Radiologic Technology (www.jrcert.org/)
➤ American Registry of Radiologic Technologists (www.arrt.org/)
➤ American Registry of Magnetic Resonance Imaging Technologists (www.armrit.org/index.shtml)

Recreational Therapists

- **2012 Median Pay** .... $42,280 per year
  $20.33 per hour
- **Entry-Level Education** .... Bachelor's degree
- **Work Experience in a Related Occupation** .... None
- **On-the-Job Training** .... None
- **Number of Jobs 2012** 19,800
- **Job Outlook, 2012–22** .... 13% (As fast as average)
- **Employment Change, 2012–22** 2,700

What Recreational Therapists Do

Recreational therapists plan, direct, and coordinate recreation-based treatment programs for people with disabilities, injuries, or illnesses. Recreational therapists use a variety of modalities, including arts and crafts, drama, music, dance, sports, games, and community reintegration field trips to help maintain or improve a patient's physical, social, and emotional well-being.

Duties. Recreational therapists typically do the following:

- Assess patients' needs through observations, medical records, tests, and talking with other healthcare professionals, patients' families, and patients
- Create treatment plans and programs that meet patients' needs and interests
- Plan and implement interventions to prevent harm to a patient
- Engage patients in therapeutic activities, such as games and field trips
- Help patients learn social skills needed to become or remain independent
- Teach patients about ways to cope with anxiety or depression
- Record and analyze a patient's progress
- Evaluate interventions for effectiveness

Recreational therapists help people reduce depression, stress, and anxiety; recover basic physical and mental abilities; build confidence; and socialize effectively. They help people with dis-

abilities integrate into the community by teaching them how to use community resources and recreational activities. For example, therapists may teach a patient who uses a wheelchair how to use public transportation.

Recreational therapists use activities, such as arts and crafts, dance, or sports, to help their patients. For instance, a recreational therapist can help a patient who is paralyzed on one side of their body by teaching them to adapt activities, like casting a fishing rod or playing a video game, to use their functional side.

Therapists may also provide interventions to patients who need help developing new social and coping skills. For example, a therapist may introduce a therapy dog to patients who need help managing their depression or anxiety.

Therapists may work with physicians or surgeons, registered nurses, psychologists, social workers, physical therapists, teachers, or occupational therapists. Recreational therapists are different from recreation workers, who organize recreational activities primarily for enjoyment.

Work Environment

Recreational therapists held about 19,800 jobs in 2012. The industries that employed the most recreational therapists in 2012 were as follows:

Hospitals; state, local, and private 35%
Nursing care facilities (skilled nursing facilities) 22
Government 19
Residential care facilities 10
Ambulatory health care services 6

Recreational therapists work in a variety of settings. Therapists often work in hospitals or nursing and residential care facilities. They also work in places such as substance abuse centers, rehabilitation centers, special education departments, and parks and recreation departments.

They may use offices for planning or other administrative activities, such as patient assessment, but may travel when working with patients. Therapists and their patients go to fields and parks for sports and other outdoor activities.

Recreational therapists observe and document a patient's participation, reaction, and progress.

Median Annual Wages, May 2012

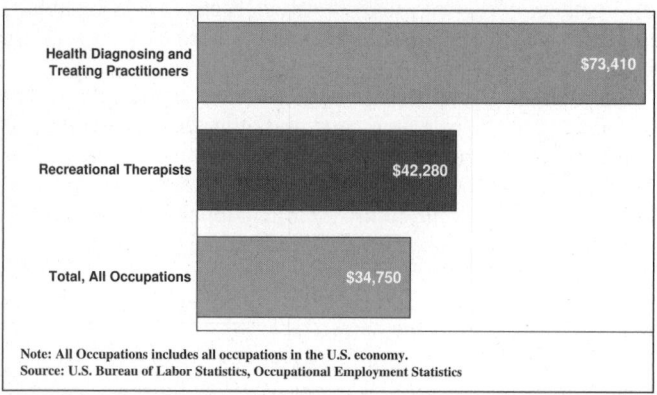

Note: All Occupations includes all occupations in the U.S. economy.
Source: U.S. Bureau of Labor Statistics, Occupational Employment Statistics

Percent Change in Employment, Projected 2012–2022

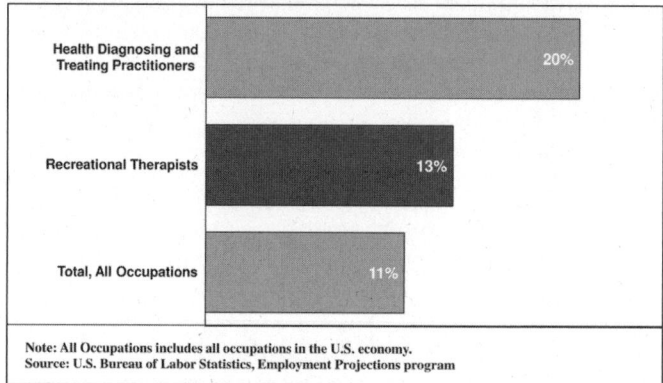

Note: All Occupations includes all occupations in the U.S. economy.
Source: U.S. Bureau of Labor Statistics, Employment Projections program

Some therapists may spend a lot of time on their feet actively working with patients. Recreational therapists also may need to physically assist patients or lift heavy objects such as wheelchairs.

Work Schedules. Most recreational therapists work full time, although about 1 in 5 worked part time in 2012. Some recreational therapists work evenings and weekends to meet the needs of their patients.

How to Become One

Recreational therapists typically need a bachelor's degree. Many employers require therapists to be certified by the National Council for Therapeutic Recreation Certification (NCTRC).

Education. Most recreational therapists need a bachelor's degree in recreational therapy or a related field. Though less common, associate's, master's, and doctoral degrees are also available.

Recreational therapy programs include courses in assessment, human anatomy, medical and psychiatric terminology, characteristics of illnesses and disabilities, and the use of assistive devices and technology. Bachelor's degree programs usually include an internship.

Licenses, Certifications, and Registrations. Most employers, particularly those in hospitals and other clinical settings, prefer to hire certified recreational therapists. The National Council for Therapeutic Recreation Certification (NCTRC) offers the Certified

Therapeutic Recreation Specialist (CTRS) credential. Certification requires a bachelor's degree, completion of a supervised internship (normally completed as part of their degree program) of at least 560 hours, and passing an exam. Although therapists typically need at least a bachelor's degree in recreational therapy, in some cases therapists may qualify for certification with an alternate combination of education, training, and experience. Therapists must also take continuing education classes to maintain certification.

NCTRC also offers specialty certification in five areas of practice: behavioral health, community inclusion services, developmental disabilities, geriatrics, and physical medicine/rehabilitation. Therapists may also earn certificates from other organizations to show proficiency in specific therapy techniques, such as aquatic therapy or aromatherapy.

As of 2012, only New Hampshire, North Carolina, Oklahoma, and Utah required recreational therapists to obtain a license. Requirements vary by state. For specific requirements, contact the state's medical board.

Important Qualities

Compassion. Recreational therapists should be kind, gentle, and sympathetic when providing support to patients and their families. They may deal with patients who are in pain or under emotional stress.

Employment Projections Data for Recreational Therapists

Occupational title	SOC Code	Employment, 2012	Projected Employment, 2022	Change, 2012–2022	
				Percent	Numeric
Recreational therapists	29-1125	19,800	22,500	13	2,700

Source: U.S. Bureau of Labor Statistics, Employment Projections Program

Note: Data are rounded. Go to **Occupational Information Included in the OOH** *for a discussion of the data in this table.*

Similar Occupations This table shows a list of occupations with job duties that are similar to those of recreational therapists.

Occupations	Entry-level Education	2012 Pay	Projected Job Growth	Average Annual Openings
Occupational Therapists	Master's degree	$75,400	29%	4,820
Physical Therapists	Doctoral or professional degree	$79,860	36%	12,370
Rehabilitation Counselors	Master's degree	$33,880	20%	4,840
School and Career Counselors	Master's degree	$53,610	12%	8,700
Special Education Teachers	Bachelor's degree	$55,068	6%	10,220
Speech-Language Pathologists	Master's degree	$69,870	19%	4,620

Critical-thinking skills. Recreational therapists should be able to quickly think of adaptations to activities when a patients' therapy plan requires adjustment.

Leadership skills. Recreational therapists must be able to plan, develop, and implement intervention programs in an effective manner. They must motivate patients to participate in a variety of therapeutic activities.

Listening skills. Recreational therapists must listen to a patient's problems and concerns. They can then determine an effective course of treatment or therapy program appropriate for that patient.

Patience. Recreational therapists may work with some patients who require more time and special attention than others.

Speaking skills. Recreational therapists need to communicate well with their patients. They need to be able to give clear directions during activities or instructions on healthy coping techniques.

Pay

The median annual wage for recreational therapists was $42,280 in May 2012. The median wage is the wage at which half the workers in an occupation earned more than that amount and half earned less. The lowest 10 percent earned less than $26,410, and the top 10 percent earned more than $67,280.

In May 2012, the median annual wages for recreational therapists in the top five industries in which they worked were as follows:

Government	$48,850
Hospitals; state, local, and private	46,160
Ambulatory health care services	39,770
Nursing care facilities (skilled nursing facilities)	36,900
Residential care facilities	36,430

Job Outlook

Employment of recreational therapists is projected to grow 13 percent from 2012 to 2022, about as fast as the average for all occupations.

As the large baby-boom generation ages, they will need recreational therapists to help treat age-related injuries and illnesses. Older persons are more likely to suffer from stroke, Alzheimer's disease, and mobility-related injuries that require recreational therapy. Continued growth is expected in nursing care facilities, adult daycare programs, and other settings that care for geriatric patients. Therapists will also be needed to help healthy seniors remain active in their communities and maintain their independence later in life.

In addition, the number of people with chronic conditions such as diabetes and obesity is growing. Recreational therapists will be needed to help patients maintain their mobility and to teach patients about managing their conditions. Therapists will also be needed to plan and lead programs designed to maintain overall wellness through participation in activities such as camps, day trips, and sports.

Legislation requiring federally funded services for students with disabilities will continue to shape the need for recreational therapists in education settings.

In addition, third party payers will continue to use therapists' services as a way to cut costs in patients' recoveries from injuries or illnesses, moving treatment to outpatient settings rather than more costly hospital settings.

Job Prospects. Job prospects will be best for recreational therapists with both a bachelor's degree and certification. Therapists who specialize in working with the elderly or who earn certification in geriatric therapy may have the best job prospects.

O*NET

➤ Recreational Therapists (29-1125.00)
➤ Art Therapists (29-1125.01)
➤ Music Therapists (29-1125.02)

Contacts for More Information

For information and materials on careers and academic programs in recreational therapy, visit
➤ American Therapeutic Recreation Association (www.atra-online.com/)
For information on certification, visit
➤ National Council for Therapeutic Recreation Certification (www.nctrc.org/)

Registered Nurses

- **2012 Median Pay** .... $65,470 per year
  $31.48 per hour
- **Entry-Level Education** .... Associate's degree
- **Work Experience in a Related Occupation** .... None
- **On-the-Job Training** .... None
- **Number of Jobs 2012** 2,711,500
- **Job Outlook, 2012–22** .... 19% (Faster than average)
- **Employment Change, 2012–22** 526,800

What Registered Nurses Do

Registered nurses (RNs) provide and coordinate patient care, educate patients and the public about various health conditions, and provide advice and emotional support to patients and their family members.

Duties. Registered nurses typically do the following:

- Record patients' medical histories and symptoms
- Administer patients' medicines and treatments
- Set up plans for patients' care or contribute to existing plans
- Observe patients and record observations
- Consult with doctors and other healthcare professionals
- Operate and monitor medical equipment
- Help perform diagnostic tests and analyze results
- Teach patients and their families how to manage illnesses or injuries
- Explain what to do at home after treatment

Most registered nurses work as part of a team with physicians and other healthcare specialists. Some registered nurses oversee licensed practical nurses, nursing assistants, and home health aides.

Registered nurses' duties and titles often depend on where they work and the patients they work with. They can focus in the following areas:

- A specific health condition, such as a diabetes management nurse who helps patients with diabetes or an oncology nurse who helps cancer patients
- A specific part of the body, such as a dermatology nurse working with patients who have skin problems
- A specific group of people, such as a geriatric nurse who works with the elderly or a pediatric nurse who works with children and teens
- A specific workplace, such as an emergency or trauma nurse who works in a hospital or stand-alone emergency department or a school nurse working in an elementary, middle, or high school

Some registered nurses combine one or more of these specific areas. For example, a pediatric oncology nurse works with children and teens who have cancer.

Many possibilities for working with specific patient groups exist. The following list includes just a few other examples:

Addiction nurses care for patients who need help to overcome addictions to alcohol, drugs, tobacco, and other substances.

Cardiovascular nurses care for patients with heart disease and people who have had heart surgery.

Critical care nurses work in intensive care units in hospitals, providing care to patients with serious, complex, and acute illnesses and injuries that need very close monitoring and treatment.

Genetics nurses provide screening, counseling, and treatment of patients with genetic disorders, such as cystic fibrosis.

Neonatology nurses take care of newborn babies.

Nephrology nurses care for patients who have kidney-related health issues stemming from diabetes, high blood pressure, substance abuse, or other causes.

Rehabilitation nurses care for patients with temporary or permanent disabilities.

Some nurses have jobs in which they do not work directly with patients, but they must still have an active registered nurse license. For example, they may work as nurse educators, healthcare consultants, public policy advisors, researchers, hospital administrators, salespeople for pharmaceutical and medical supply companies, or as medical writers and editors.

Registered nurses may work to promote general health, by educating the public on warning signs and symptoms of disease. They may also run general health screenings or immunization clinics, blood drives, or other outreach programs.

Clinical nurse specialists (CNSs) are a type of advanced practice registered nurse (APRN). They provide direct patient care in one of many nursing specialties, such as psychiatric-mental health or pediatrics. CNSs also provide indirect care, by working with other nurses and various other staff to improve the quality of care that patients receive. They often serve in leadership roles and may advise other nursing staff. CNSs also may conduct research and may advocate for certain policies.

Work Environment

As the largest healthcare occupation, registered nurses held about 2.7 million jobs in 2012. The industries that employed the most registered nurses in 2012 were as follows:

Hospitals; state, local, and private 61%
Nursing and residential care facilities 7
Offices of physicians 7
Home health care services... 6
Government 6

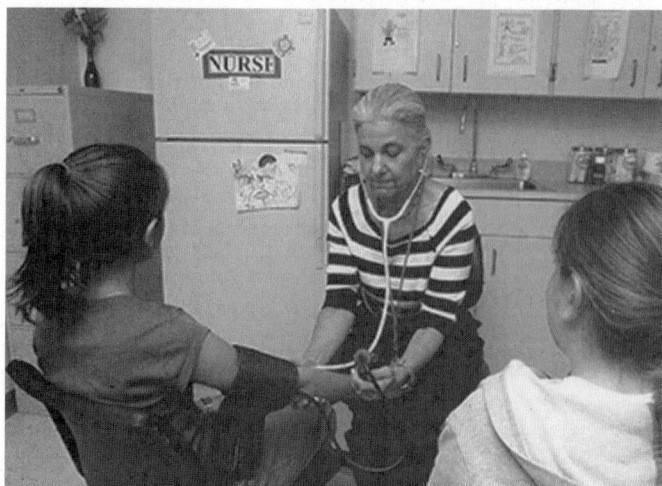

Registered nurses teach patients and their families how to manage their illness or injury.

Registered nurses work in hospitals, physicians' offices, home healthcare services, and nursing care facilities. Others work in correctional facilities, schools, clinics, or serve in the military.

Most registered nurses work in well-lit, comfortable healthcare facilities. Home health and public health nurses travel to patients' homes, schools, community centers, and other sites.

Some nurses move frequently, traveling in the United States and throughout the world to help care for patients in places where there are not enough healthcare workers.

Injuries and Illnesses. Registered nurses may spend a lot of time walking, bending, stretching, and standing. They are vulnerable to back injuries, because they must often lift and move patients.

In addition, the work of registered nurses may put them in close contact with people who have infectious diseases, and they often come in contact with potentially harmful and hazardous drugs and other substances. Therefore, registered nurses must follow strict, standardized guidelines to guard against diseases and other dangers, such as radiation, accidental needle sticks, or the chemicals used to create a sterile and clean environment.

Work Schedules. Because patients in hospitals and nursing care facilities need round-the-clock care, nurses in these settings usually work in rotating shifts, covering all 24 hours. They may work nights, weekends, and holidays. They may also be on call.

Nurses who work in offices, schools, and other places that do not provide 24-hour care are more likely to work regular business hours.

In 2012, about 1 out of 5 registered nurses worked part time.

Median Annual Wages, May 2012

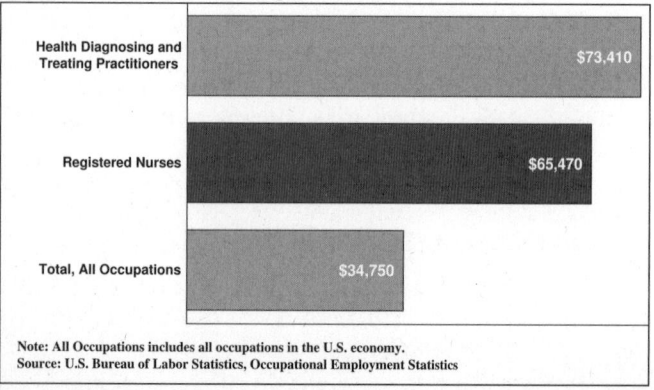

Health Diagnosing and Treating Practitioners	$73,410
Registered Nurses	$65,470
Total, All Occupations	$34,750

Note: All Occupations includes all occupations in the U.S. economy.
Source: U.S. Bureau of Labor Statistics, Occupational Employment Statistics

Percent Change in Employment, Projected 2012–2022

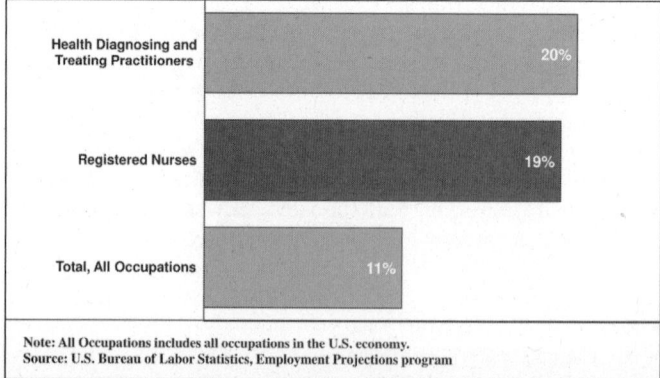

Health Diagnosing and Treating Practitioners	20%
Registered Nurses	19%
Total, All Occupations	11%

Note: All Occupations includes all occupations in the U.S. economy.
Source: U.S. Bureau of Labor Statistics, Employment Projections program

Employment Projections Data for Registered Nurses

Occupational title	SOC Code	Employment, 2012	Projected Employment, 2022	Change, 2012–2022	
				Percent	Numeric
Registered nurses..	29-1141	2,711,500	3,238,400	19	526,800

Source: U.S. Bureau of Labor Statistics, Employment Projections Program

Note: **Data are rounded. Go to Occupational Information Included in the OOH** *for a discussion of the data in this table.*

How to Become One

Registered nurses usually take one of three education paths: a bachelor's of science degree in nursing (BSN), an associate's degree in nursing (ADN), or a diploma from an approved nursing program. Registered nurses also must be licensed.

Education. In all nursing education programs, students take courses in anatomy, physiology, microbiology, chemistry, nutrition, psychology and other social and behavioral sciences, as well as in liberal arts. BSN programs typically take 4 years to complete; ADN and diploma programs usually take 2 to 3 years to complete. All programs also include supervised clinical experience.

Bachelor's degree programs usually include additional education in the physical and social sciences, communication, leadership, and critical thinking. These programs also offer more clinical experience in nonhospital settings. A bachelor's degree or higher is often necessary for administrative positions, research, consulting, and teaching.

Generally, licensed graduates of any of the three types of education programs (bachelor's, associate's, or diploma) qualify for entry-level positions as a staff nurse. However, some employers may require a bachelor's degree.

Many registered nurses with an ADN or diploma choose to go back to school to earn a bachelor's degree through an RN-to-BSN program. There are also master's degree programs in nursing, combined bachelor's and master's programs, and programs for those who wish to enter the nursing profession but hold a bachelor's degree in another field. Some employers offer tuition reimbursement.

Certified nurse specialists (CNSs) must earn a master's degree in nursing. CNSs who conduct research typically need a doctoral degree.

Licenses, Certifications, and Registrations. In all states, the District of Columbia, and U.S. territories, registered nurses must have a nursing license.

To become licensed, nurses must graduate from an approved nursing program and pass the National Council Licensure Examination, or NCLEX-RN.

Other requirements for licensing vary by state. Each state's board of nursing can give details. For more on the NCLEX-RN examination and a list of state boards of nursing visit the National Council of State Boards of Nursing.

Nurses may become certified through professional associations in specific areas, such as ambulatory care, gerontology, and pediatrics, among others. Although certification is usually voluntary, it demonstrates adherence to a higher standard, and some employers may require it.

CNSs must satisfy additional state licensing requirements. They may choose to earn certification in a specialty.

Important Qualities

Critical-thinking skills. Registered nurses must be able to assess changes in the health state of patients, including when to take corrective action and when to make referrals.

Compassion. Registered nurses should be caring and sympathetic, characteristics that are valuable when caring for patients.

Detail oriented. Registered nurses must be responsible and detail oriented because they must make sure that patients get the correct treatments and medicines at the right time.

Emotional stability. Registered nurses need emotional stability to cope with human suffering, emergencies, and other stresses.

Organizational skills. Nurses often work with multiple patients with various health needs. Organizational skills are critical to ensure that each patient is given proper care.

Physical stamina. Nurses should be comfortable performing physical tasks, such as helping to lift and to move patients. They may be on their feet for most of their shift.

Speaking skills. Registered nurses must be able to talk effectively with patients to assess their health conditions. Nurses need to explain how to take medication or to give other instructions. They must be able to work in teams with other health professionals and communicate the patients' needs.

Similar Occupations   This table shows a list of occupations with job duties that are similar to those of registered nurses.

Occupations	Entry-level Education	2012 Pay	Projected Job Growth	Average Annual Openings
Dental Hygienists	Associate's degree	$70,210	33%	11,350
Diagnostic Medical Sonographers and Cardiovascular Technologists and Technicians, Including Vascular Technologists	Associate's degree	$59,422	39%	5,830
EMTs and Paramedics	Postsecondary non-degree award	$31,020	23%	12,060
Licensed Practical and Licensed Vocational Nurses	Postsecondary non-degree award	$41,540	25%	36,310
Nurse Anesthetists, Nurse Midwives, and Nurse Practitioners	Master's degree	$103,602	31%	7,700
Physician Assistants	Master's degree	$90,930	38%	4,890

Advancement. Most registered nurses begin as staff nurses in hospitals or community health settings. With experience, good performance, and continuous education, they can move to other settings or be promoted to positions with more responsibility.

In management, nurses can advance from assistant unit manager or head nurse to more senior-level administrative roles, such as assistant director, director, vice president, and chief of nursing. Increasingly, management-level nursing positions require a graduate degree in nursing or health services administration. Administrative positions require leadership, communication skills, negotiation skills, and good judgment.

Some nurses move into the business side of healthcare. Their nursing expertise and experience on a healthcare team equip them to manage ambulatory, acute, home-based, and chronic care businesses.

Employers–including hospitals, insurance companies, pharmaceutical manufacturers, and managed care organizations, among others–need registered nurses for jobs in health planning and development, marketing, consulting, policy development, and quality assurance.

Some RNs choose to become nurse anesthetists, nurse midwives, or nurse practitioners, which, along with certified nurse specialists, are types of advanced practice registered nurses (APRNs). APRNs may provide primary and specialty care, and, in most states, they may prescribe medicines. For example, clinical nurse specialists provide direct patient care and expert consultations in one of many nursing specialties, such as psychiatric-mental health.

Other nurses work as postsecondary teachers in colleges and universities.

Pay

The median annual wage for registered nurses was $65,470 in May 2012. The median wage is the wage at which half of the workers in an occupation earned more than that amount and half earned less. The lowest 10 percent earned less than $45,040 and the top 10 percent earned more than $94,720.

In May 2012, the median annual wages for registered nurses in the top five industries in which they worked were as follows:

Government	$68,540
Hospitals; state, local, and private	67,210
Home health care services	62,090
Nursing and residential care facilities	58,830
Offices of physicians	58,420

Many employers offer flexible work schedules, childcare, educational benefits, and bonuses.

Job Outlook

Employment of registered nurses is projected to grow 19 percent from 2012 to 2022, faster than the average for all occupations. Growth will occur for a number of reasons.

Demand for healthcare services will increase because of the aging population, since older people typically have more medical problems than younger people. Nurses also will be needed to educate and to care for patients with various chronic conditions, such as arthritis, dementia, diabetes, and obesity. In addition, the number of individuals who have access to healthcare services will increase, as a result of federal health insurance reform. More nurses will be needed to care for these patients.

The financial pressure on hospitals to discharge patients as soon as possible may result in more people admitted to long-term care facilities, outpatient care centers, and greater need for home healthcare. Job growth is expected in facilities that provide long-term rehabilitation for stroke and head injury patients, as well as facilities that treat people with Alzheimer's disease. In addition, because many older people prefer to be treated at home or in residential care facilities, registered nurses will be in demand in those settings.

Growth is also expected to be faster than average in outpatient care centers where patients do not stay overnight, such as those that provide same-day chemotherapy, rehabilitation, and surgery. In addition, an increased number of procedures, as well as more sophisticated procedures previously done only in hospitals, are performed in ambulatory care settings and physicians' offices.

Job Prospects. Overall, job opportunities for registered nurses are expected to be good. Generally, registered nurses with at least a bachelor's degree in nursing (BSN) will have better job prospects than those without one. Employers may prefer candidates who have some related work experience.

Job opportunities should be good because of the need to replace workers who retire over the coming decade and because of the growing number of people with access to healthcare services.

O*NET

➤ Registered Nurses (29-1141.00)
➤ Acute Care Nurses (29-1141.01)
➤ Advanced Practice Psychiatric Nurses (29-1141.02)
➤ Critical Care Nurses (29-1141.03)
➤ Clinical Nurse Specialists (29-1141.04)

Contacts for More Information

For more information about registered nurses, including credentialing, visit
➤ American Nurses Association (www.nursingworld.org/)

For more information about nursing education and being a registered nurse, visit
➤ National League for Nursing (www.nln.org/)

For information about undergraduate and graduate nursing education, nursing career options, and financial aid, visit
➤ American Association of Colleges of Nursing (www.aacn.nche.edu/)

For information about the National Council Licensure Examination (NCLEX-RN) and a list of individual state boards of nursing, visit
➤ National Council of State Boards of Nursing (www.ncsbn.org/index.htm)

For information about clinical nurse specialists, including a list of accredited programs, visit
➤ National Association of Clinical Nurse Specialists (www.nacns.org/)

Respiratory Therapists

- **2012 Median Pay** .... $55,870 per year
  $26.86 per hour
- **Entry-Level Education** .... Associate's degree
- **Work Experience in a Related Occupation** .... None
- **On-the-Job Training** .... None
- **Number of Jobs 2012** 119,300
- **Job Outlook, 2012–22** .... 19% (Faster than average)
- **Employment Change, 2012–22** 22,700

What Respiratory Therapists Do

Respiratory therapists care for patients who have trouble breathing–for example, from a chronic respiratory disease, such as asthma or emphysema. Their patients range from premature infants with undeveloped lungs to elderly patients who have dis-

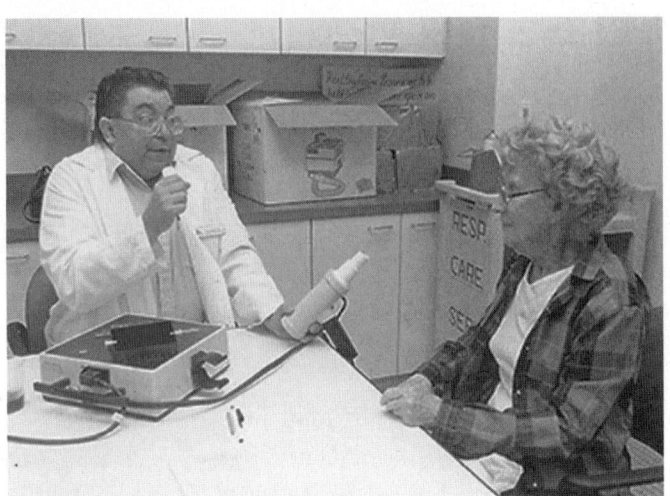

Respiratory therapists interview patients, perform limited physical examinations, and conduct diagnostic tests.

eased lungs. They also provide emergency care to patients suffering from heart attacks, drowning, or shock.

Duties. Respiratory therapists typically do the following:

- Interview and examine patients with breathing or cardiopulmonary disorders
- Consult with physicians to develop patient treatment plans
- Perform diagnostic tests such as measuring lung capacity
- Treat patients by using a variety of methods, including chest physiotherapy and aerosol medications
- Monitor and record the progress of treatment
- Supervise respiratory therapy technicians during tests and evaluate the findings of the tests
- Teach patients how to use treatments

Respiratory therapists use various tests to evaluate patients. For example, therapists test lung capacity by having patients breathe into an instrument that measures the volume and flow of oxygen when they inhale and exhale. Respiratory therapists also may take blood samples and use a blood gas analyzer to test oxygen and carbon dioxide levels.

Respiratory therapists perform chest physiotherapy on patients to remove mucus from their lungs and make it easier for them to breathe. Removing mucus is necessary for patients suffering from lung diseases, such as cystic fibrosis, and involves the therapist vibrating the patient's rib cage, often by tapping the patient's chest and encouraging him or her to cough.

Respiratory therapists may connect patients who cannot breathe on their own to ventilators that deliver oxygen to the lungs. Therapists insert a tube in the patient's windpipe (trachea) and connect the tube to ventilator equipment. They set up and monitor the equipment to ensure that the patient is receiving the correct amount of oxygen at the correct rate.

Respiratory therapists who work in home care teach patients and their families to use ventilators and other life-support systems in their homes. During these visits, they may inspect and clean equipment, check the home for environmental hazards, and ensure that patients know how to use their medications. Therapists also make emergency home visits when necessary.

In some hospitals, respiratory therapists are involved in related areas, such as diagnosing breathing problems for people with sleep apnea and counseling people on how to stop smoking.

Work Environment

Respiratory therapists held about 119,300 jobs in 2012. Most respiratory therapists work in hospitals. Others may work in nursing care facilities or travel to patients' homes. Respiratory therapists are on their feet for long periods and may need to lift or turn disabled patients.

Work Schedules. Most respiratory therapists work full time. Because they may work in medical facilities, such as hospitals that are always open, some may work evening, night, or weekend hours.

How to Become One

Respiratory therapists typically need an associate's degree, but some have bachelor's degrees. Respiratory therapists are licensed in all states except Alaska; requirements vary by state.

Education. Respiratory therapists need at least an associate's degree, but employers may prefer applicants who have a bachelor's degree. Many colleges and universities, vocational–technical institutes, and the Armed Forces offer education and training programs. Most programs award an associate's or bachelor's degree.

All programs have clinical components that allow therapists to earn course credit and gain supervised, practical experience treating patients.

Respiratory therapy programs include courses in human anatomy and physiology, chemistry, physics, microbiology, pharmacology, and mathematics. Other courses deal with therapeutic and diagnostic procedures and tests, equipment, patient assessment, and cardiopulmonary resuscitation (CPR).

High school students interested in applying to respiratory therapy programs should take courses in health, biology, mathematics, chemistry, and physics.

Median Annual Wages, May 2012

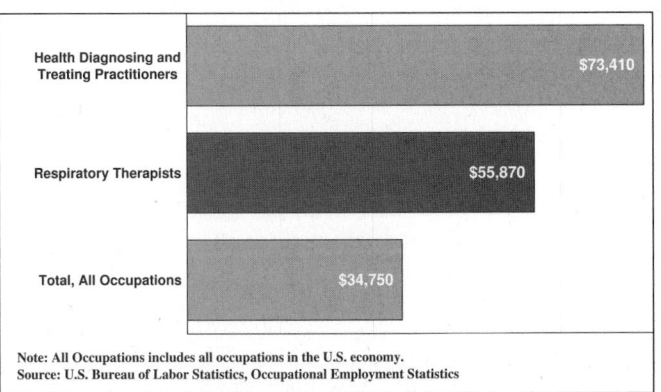

Note: All Occupations includes all occupations in the U.S. economy.
Source: U.S. Bureau of Labor Statistics, Occupational Employment Statistics

Percent Change in Employment, Projected 2012–2022

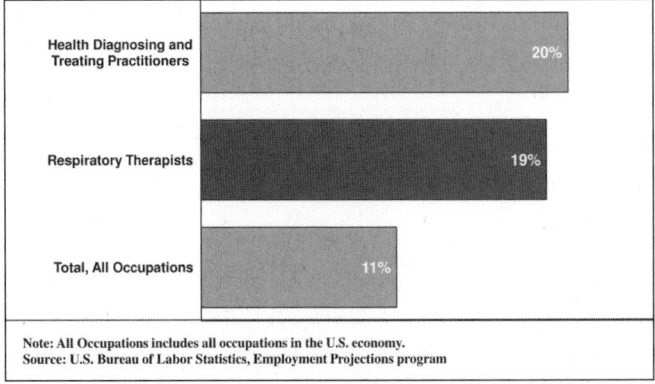

Note: All Occupations includes all occupations in the U.S. economy.
Source: U.S. Bureau of Labor Statistics, Employment Projections program

Employment Projections Data for Respiratory Therapists

Occupational title	SOC Code	Employment, 2012	Projected Employment, 2022	Change, 2012–2022	
				Percent	Numeric
Respiratory therapists...	29-1126	119,300	142,100	19	22,700

Source: U.S. Bureau of Labor Statistics, Employment Projections Program

Note: Data are rounded. Go to **Occupational Information Included in the OOH** *for a discussion of the data in this table.*

Licenses, Certifications, and Registrations. Respiratory therapists are licensed in all states except Alaska, although requirements vary by state. Licensure requirements in most states include completing a state or professional certification exam. For specific state requirements, contact the state's health board.

Many employers prefer to hire respiratory therapists who have certification. Certification is not always required, but it is widely respected throughout the occupation. Certification usually requires graduating from an accredited program and passing a certification exam and is often required in order to get a state license.

The National Board for Respiratory Care (NBRC) is the main certifying body for respiratory therapists. The Board offers two levels of certification: the Certified Respiratory Therapist (CRT) and the Registered Respiratory Therapist (RRT).

The CRT is the first-level certification. Applicants must have earned an associate's degree from an accredited respiratory therapy program, or completed the equivalent coursework in a bachelor's degree program, and pass an exam.

The second-level certification is the RRT certification. Applicants must have a CRT certification, meet other education or experience requirements, and pass an exam.

Important Qualities

Compassion. Respiratory therapists should be able to provide emotional support to patients undergoing treatment and be sympathetic to their needs.

Detail oriented. Respiratory therapists must be detail oriented to ensure that patients are receiving the appropriate treatments and medications in a timely manner. They must also monitor and record various pieces of information related to patient care.

Interpersonal skills. Respiratory therapists interact with patients and often work as part of a team. They must be able to follow instructions from a supervising physician.

Patience. Respiratory therapists may work for long periods with patients who need special attention.

Problem-solving skills. Respiratory therapists need strong problem-solving skills. They must evaluate patients' symptoms, consult with other healthcare professionals, and recommend and administer the appropriate treatments.

Science and math skills. Respiratory therapists must understand anatomy, physiology, and other sciences and be able to calculate the right dose of a patient's medicine.

Pay

The median annual wage for respiratory therapists was $55,870 in May 2012. The median wage is the wage at which half the workers in an occupation earned more than that amount and half earned less. The lowest 10 percent earned less than $40,980, and the top 10 percent earned more than $75,430.

Job Outlook

Employment of respiratory therapists is projected to grow 19 percent from 2012 to 2022, faster than the average for all occupations. Growth in the middle-aged and elderly population will lead to an increased incidence of respiratory conditions such as emphysema, chronic bronchitis, pneumonia, and other disorders that can permanently damage the lungs or restrict lung function. These factors will in turn lead to an increased demand for respiratory therapy services and treatments, mostly in hospitals and nursing homes. In addition, advances in preventing and detecting disease, improved medications, and more sophisticated treatments will increase the demand for respiratory therapists. Other conditions affecting the general population, such as smoking, air pollution, and respiratory emergencies, will continue to create demand for respiratory therapists.

Job Prospects. Job prospects will be best for therapists willing to travel to look for job opportunities. Some areas will be saturated with workers, while other areas (more often, rural areas) will be in need of respiratory therapists' services.

O*NET

➤ Respiratory Therapists (29-1126.00)

Contacts for More Information

For more information about respiratory therapists, visit
➤ American Association for Respiratory Care (www.aarc.org/)

Similar Occupations   This table shows a list of occupations with job duties that are similar to those of respiratory therapists.

Occupations	Entry-level Education	2012 Pay	Projected Job Growth	Average Annual Openings
Athletic Trainers and Exercise Physiologists	Bachelor's degree	$42,676	19%	1,240
Occupational Therapists	Master's degree	$75,400	29%	4,820
Physical Therapists	Doctoral or professional degree	$79,860	36%	12,370
Radiation Therapists	Associate's degree	$77,560	24%	840
Registered Nurses	Associate's degree	$65,470	19%	105,260
Speech-Language Pathologists	Master's degree	$69,870	19%	4,620

For a list of accredited educational programs for respiratory care practitioners, visit

➤ Commission on Accreditation for Respiratory Care (www.coarc.com/)

For a list of state licensing agencies, as well as information on gaining credentials in respiratory care, visit

➤ National Board for Respiratory Care, Inc. (www.nbrc.org/Pages/default.aspx)

Speech-Language Pathologists

- **2012 Median Pay** .... $69,870 per year
  $33.59 per hour
- **Entry-Level Education** ....Master's degree
- **Work Experience in a Related Occupation**............... None
- **On-the-Job Training** .... None
- **Number of Jobs 2012** 134,100
- **Job Outlook, 2012–22** .... 19% (Faster than average)
- **Employment Change, 2012–22** 26,000

What Speech-Language Pathologists Do

Speech-language pathologists (sometimes called speech therapists) assess, diagnose, treat, and help to prevent communication and swallowing disorders in patients. Speech, language, and swallowing disorders result from a variety of causes, such as a stroke, brain injury, hearing loss, developmental delay, a cleft palate, cerebral palsy, or emotional problems.

Duties. When diagnosing patients, speech-language pathologists typically do the following:

- Communicate with patients to evaluate their levels of speech or language difficulty
- Determine the extent of communication problems by having a patient complete basic reading and vocalizing tasks or by giving standardized tests
- Identify treatment options
- Create and carry out an individualized treatment plan

When treating patients, speech-language pathologists typically do the following:

- Teach patients how to make sounds and improve their voices
- Teach alternative communication methods, such as sign language, to patients with little or no speech capability
- Work with patients to improve their ability to read and write correctly
- Work with patients to develop and strengthen the muscles used to swallow
- Counsel patients and families on how to cope with communication disorders

Speech-language pathologists work with patients who have problems with speech. Their patients may be unable to speak at all or they may speak with difficulty or have rhythm and fluency problems, such as stuttering. They may work with those who are unable to understand language or with people who have voice disorders, such as inappropriate pitch or a harsh voice.

Speech-language pathologists must also complete administrative tasks, including keeping accurate records. They record their initial patient evaluations and diagnoses, treatment progress, any changes in a patient's condition or treatment plan, and, eventually, they complete a final evaluation when the patient finishes the therapy.

Some speech-language pathologists specialize in working with specific age groups, such as children or the elderly. Others focus on treatment programs for specific communication or swallowing problems, such as those resulting from strokes or cleft palate.

In medical facilities, speech-language pathologists work with physicians and surgeons, social workers, psychologists, and other healthcare workers. In schools, they work with teachers, other school personnel, and parents to develop and carry out individual or group programs, provide counseling, and support classroom activities. For more information on teachers, see the profiles on preschool teachers, kindergarten and elementary school teachers, middle school teachers, high school teachers, and special education teachers.

Work Environment

Speech-language pathologists held about 134,100 jobs in 2012. Almost half of all speech-language pathologists work in schools. Most others work in healthcare facilities, such as hospitals. Some work in patients' homes.

The industries that employed the most speech-language pathologists in 2012 were as follows:

Elementary and secondary schools; state, local,
  and private 41%
Offices of physical, occupational and
  speech therapists, and audiologists..................................... 17
Hospitals; state, local, and private 13
Nursing and residential care facilities 5

Work Schedules. Most speech-language pathologists work full time. About 1 out of 4 worked part time in 2012. Those who work on a contract basis may spend a lot of time traveling between facilities.

How to Become One

Speech-language pathologists typically need at least a master's degree. They must be licensed in most states; requirements vary by state.

Education. The standard level of education for speech-language pathologists is a master's degree. Although master's programs do not specify a particular undergraduate degree for admission, certain courses must be taken before entering the program. Required courses vary by institution. Graduate programs often include

Speech-language pathologists usually work at desks or tables in clean comfortable surroundings.

Median Annual Wages, May 2012

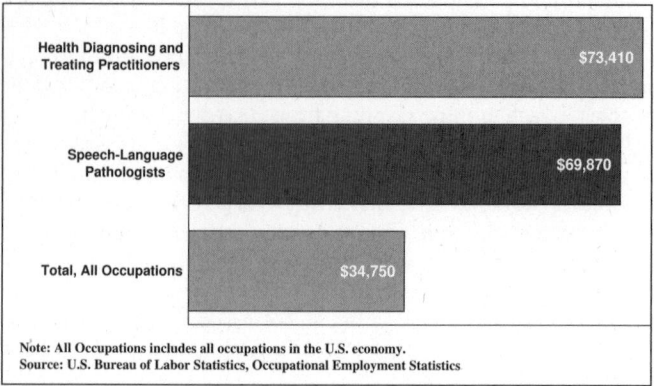

Note: All Occupations includes all occupations in the U.S. economy.
Source: U.S. Bureau of Labor Statistics, Occupational Employment Statistics

Percent Change in Employment, Projected 2012–2022

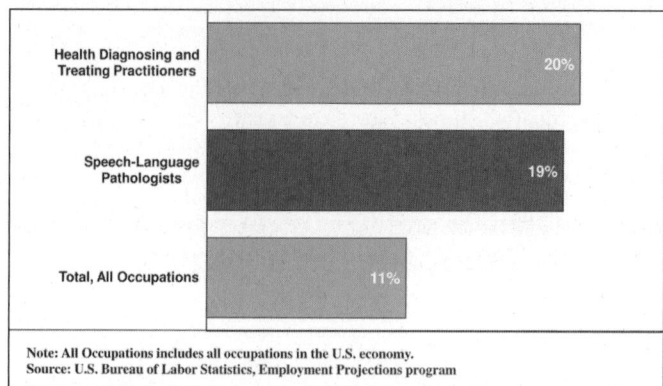

Note: All Occupations includes all occupations in the U.S. economy.
Source: U.S. Bureau of Labor Statistics, Employment Projections program

courses in age-specific speech disorders, alternative communication methods, and swallowing disorders. These programs also include supervised clinical practice in addition to coursework.

The Council on Academic Accreditation (CAA), part of the American Speech-Language-Hearing Association, accredits education programs in speech-language pathology. In 2012, the CAA accredited 253 master's degree programs in speech-language pathology.

Licenses, Certifications, and Registrations. Speech-language pathologists must be licensed in almost all states. A license requires at least a master's degree and supervised clinical experience. Some states require graduation from an accredited master's program to get a license. For specific requirements, contact your state's medical or health licensure board.

Speech-language pathologists can earn the Certificate of Clinical Competence in Speech-Language Pathology (CCC-SLP) offered by the American Speech-Language-Hearing Association. Certification satisfies some or all of the requirements for licensure and may be required by some employers.

Important Qualities

Communication skills. Speech-language pathologists need to communicate test results, diagnoses, and proposed treatments in a way that patients and their families can understand.

Compassion. Speech-language pathologists work with people who are often frustrated by their difficulties. Speech-language pathologists must be able to support emotionally demanding patients and their families.

Critical-thinking skills. Speech-language pathologists must be able to adjust their treatment plans as needed, finding alternative ways to help their patients.

Detail oriented. The work of speech-language pathologists requires intense concentration because they must closely listen to what patients are able to say and then help them improve their speech.

Listening skills. Speech-language pathologists must listen to a patient's symptoms and problems to decide on a course of treatment.

Patience. Speech-language pathologists may work with people who achieve goals slowly and need close attention.

Pay

The median annual wage for speech-language pathologists was $69,870 in May 2012. The median wage is the wage at which half the workers in an occupation earned more than that amount and half earned less. The lowest 10 percent earned less than $44,380 and the top 10 percent more than $107,650.

Union Membership. Compared with workers in all occupations, speech-language pathologists had a higher percentage of workers who belonged to a union in 2012.

Employment Projections Data for Speech-Language Pathologists

Occupational title	SOC Code	Employment, 2012	Projected Employment, 2022	Change, 2012–2022	
				Percent	Numeric
Speech-language pathologists	29-1127	134,100	160,100	19	26,000

Source: U.S. Bureau of Labor Statistics, Employment Projections Program

Note: Data are rounded. **Go to Occupational Information Included in the OOH** *for a discussion of the data in this table.*

Similar Occupations   This table shows a list of occupations with job duties that are similar to those of speech-language pathologists.

Occupations	Entry-level Education	2012 Pay	Projected Job Growth	Average Annual Openings
Audiologists	Doctoral or professional degree	$69,720	33%	700
Occupational Therapists	Master's degree	$75,400	29%	4,820
Physical Therapists	Doctoral or professional degree	$79,860	36%	12,370
Psychologists	See "How to Become One"	$69,807	12%	6,230
Recreational Therapists	Bachelor's degree	$42,280	14%	670

Job Outlook

Employment of speech-language pathologists is projected to grow 19 percent from 2012 to 2022, faster than the average for all occupations.

As the large baby-boom population grows older, there will be more instances of health conditions that cause speech or language impairments, such as strokes and hearing loss. More speech-language pathologists will be needed to treat the increased number of speech and language disorders in the older population.

Increased awareness of speech and language disorders, such as stuttering, in younger children should also lead to a need for more speech-language pathologists who specialize in treating that age group.

In addition, medical advances are improving the survival rate of premature infants and victims of trauma and strokes, many of whom need help from speech-language pathologists.

O*NET

➤ Speech-Language Pathologists (29-1127.00)

Contacts for More Information

For more information about speech-language pathologists, a description of the Certificate of Clinical Competence in Speech-Language Pathology (CCC-SLP) credential, and a listing of accredited graduate programs in speech-language pathology, visit
➤ American Speech-Language-Hearing Association (www.asha.org/)

State licensing boards have information about licensure requirements. State departments of education can provide information about certification requirements for those who want to work in public schools.

Surgical Technologists

- **2012 Median Pay** .... $41,790 per year
  $20.09 per hour
- **Entry-Level Education** .... Postsecondary non-degree award
- **Work Experience in a Related Occupation** .... None
- **On-the-Job Training** .... None
- **Number of Jobs 2012** 98,500
- **Job Outlook, 2012–22** .... 30% (Much faster than average)
- **Employment Change, 2012–22** 29,300

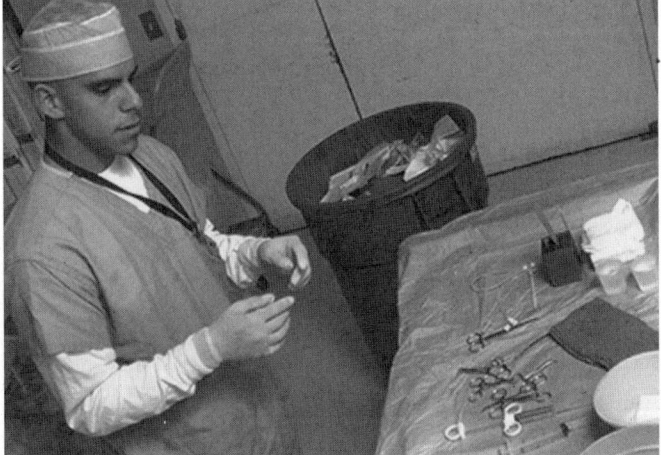

Before an operation, surgical technologists help prepare the operating room by setting up surgical instruments and equipment, sterile drapes, and sterile solutions.

What Surgical Technologists Do

Surgical technologists, also called operating room technicians, assist in surgical operations. They prepare operating rooms, arrange equipment, and help doctors during surgeries.

Duties. Surgical technologists typically do the following:

- Prepare operating rooms for surgery
- Sterilize equipment and make sure that there are adequate supplies for surgery
- Prepare patients for surgery, such as by washing and disinfecting incision sites
- Help surgeons during surgery by passing them instruments and other sterile supplies
- Count supplies such as sponges and instruments to maintain a sterile environment

Surgical technologists work as members of a healthcare team alongside physicians and surgeons, registered nurses, and other healthcare workers.

Before an operation, surgical technologists prepare the operating room by setting up surgical instruments and equipment. They also prepare patients for surgery by washing and disinfecting incision sites, positioning patients on the operating table, covering patients with sterile drapes, and taking patients to and from the operating room. Surgical technologists prepare sterile solutions and medications used in surgery and check that all surgical equipment is working properly. They help the surgical team put on sterile gowns and gloves.

During an operation, surgical technologists pass instruments and supplies to surgeons and first assistants. They also hold retractors and may hold internal organs in place during the procedure. Technologists also may handle specimens taken for laboratory analysis.

Once the operation is complete, surgical technologists may apply bandages and other dressings to the incision site. They may also help transfer patients to recovery rooms and restock operating rooms after a procedure.

Surgical first assistants have a hands-on role, directly assisting surgeons during a procedure. For instance, they may help to suction the incision site or suture a wound.

Work Environment

Surgical technologists held about 98,500 jobs in 2012. Most surgical technologists work in hospitals. Some work in outpatient care centers or in offices of physicians who perform outpatient surgery.

Surgical technologists wear scrubs (special sterile clothing) while they are in the operating room. Their work may be physically demanding, as they may be on their feet for long periods. Surgical technologists may also need to help move patients or lift heavy trays of medical supplies. At times, they may be exposed to communicable diseases and unpleasant sights, odors, and materials.

Work Schedules. Most surgical technologists work full time. Surgical technologists employed in hospitals may work or be on call during nights, weekends, and holidays. They may also be required to work shifts lasting longer than 8 hours.

How to Become One

Surgical technologists typically need a postsecondary certificate or an associate's degree. Certification can be beneficial in finding a job as a surgical technologist. A small number of states regulate surgical technologists.

Education. Surgical technologists typically need postsecondary education. Many community colleges and vocational schools, as

Median Annual Wages, May 2012

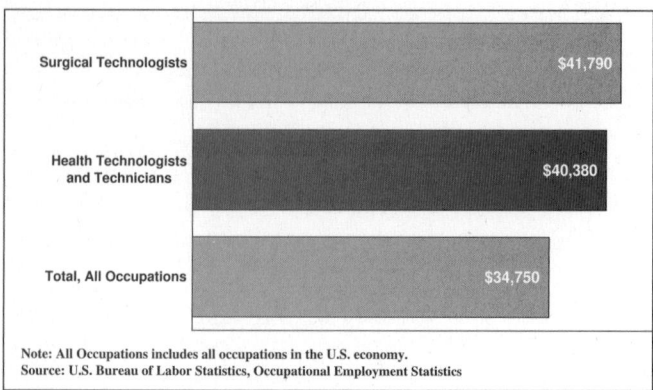

Note: All Occupations includes all occupations in the U.S. economy.
Source: U.S. Bureau of Labor Statistics, Occupational Employment Statistics

Percent Change in Employment, Projected 2012–2022

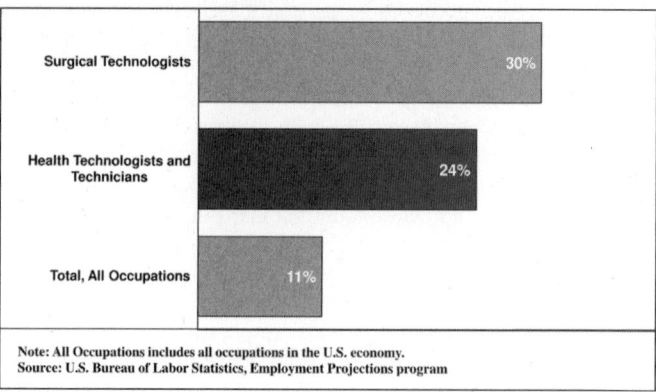

Note: All Occupations includes all occupations in the U.S. economy.
Source: U.S. Bureau of Labor Statistics, Employment Projections program

well as some universities and hospitals, have accredited programs in surgical technology. Programs range in length from several months to 2 years, and they grant a diploma, certificate, or associate's degree upon completion. Admission typically requires a high school diploma or GED.

Surgical technology education includes courses in anatomy, biology, medical terminology, pharmacology, and other topics. Surgical technologists are trained in the care and safety of patients, sterilization techniques, how to set up technical or robotic equipment, and preventing and controlling infections. In addition to classroom study, students also work in supervised clinical settings to gain hands-on experience.

In 2012, about 500 surgical technologist training programs were accredited by the Commission on Accreditation of Allied Health Education Programs (CAAHEP) and the Accrediting Bureau of Health Education Schools (ABHES).

First surgical assistants may complete a formal education program in surgical assisting. Others may work as a surgical technologist and receive additional on-the-job training before becoming a first assistant.

Important Qualities

Detail oriented. Surgical technologists must pay close attention to their work at all times. For example, they need to provide the correct sterile equipment for surgeons during an operation.

Dexterity. Surgical technologists should be comfortable working with their hands. They must be able to provide the needed equipment quickly.

Integrity. Surgical technologists must have integrity, as they are trusted to provide sterile supplies and quality patient care during surgical procedures.

Physical stamina. Surgical technologists should be comfortable standing for extended periods.

Stress-management skills. Working in an operating room can be stressful. Surgical technologists should be able to work well under pressure while providing a high level of care.

Licenses, Certifications, and Registrations. Certification can be beneficial in finding a job as a surgical technologist. Surgical technologists may earn certification through two credentialing organizations.

Certification through the National Board of Surgical Technology and Surgical Assisting allows the use of the title "Certified Surgical Technologist (CST)." Certification typically requires completing an accredited formal education program or military training program and passing an exam.

Certification through the National Center for Competency Testing allows the use of the title "Tech in Surgery-Certified (NCCT)." An applicant must pass an exam and have taken one of several

Employment Projections Data for Surgical Technologists

Occupational title	SOC Code	Employment, 2012	Projected Employment, 2022	Change, 2012–2022	
				Percent	Numeric
Surgical technologists	29-2055	98,500	127,800	30	29,300

Source: U.S. Bureau of Labor Statistics, Employment Projections Program

Note: Data are rounded. Go to **Occupational Information Included in the OOH** *for a discussion of the data in this table.*

Similar Occupations

This table shows a list of occupations with job duties that are similar to those of surgical technologists.

Occupations	Entry-level Education	2012 Pay	Projected Job Growth	Average Annual Openings
Dental Assistants	Postsecondary non-degree award	$34,500	25%	13,720
Licensed Practical and Licensed Vocational Nurses	Postsecondary non-degree award	$41,540	25%	36,310
Medical and Clinical Laboratory Technologists and Technicians	See "How to Become One"	$47,499	22%	15,600
Medical Assistants	Postsecondary non-degree award	$29,370	29%	26,990

routes to be eligible. These routes include formal education, military training, or work experience, among others.

Both certifications require surgical technologists to complete continuing education to maintain their certification.

A small number of states have regulations governing the work of surgical technologists. In these areas, surgical technologists must have graduated from an accredited education program and earned certification. Certification requirements vary by state.

The National Board of Surgical Technology and Surgical Assisting, the National Surgical Assistant Association, and the American Board of Surgical Assistants offer certification for surgical first assistants.

Advancement. Surgical technologists may choose to advance to other healthcare occupations, such as becoming a registered nurse. Technologists may also choose to become operating room managers or educators. For more information, see the profiles on medical and health services managers and postsecondary teachers.

Pay

The median annual wage for surgical technologists was $41,790 in May 2012. The median wage is the wage at which half the workers in an occupation earned more than that amount and half earned less. The lowest 10 percent earned less than $29,710, and the top 10 percent earned more than $60,240.

Job Outlook

Employment of surgical technologists is projected to grow 30 percent from 2012 to 2022, much faster than the average for all occupations. Several factors will lead to demand for surgical technologists.

Advances in medical technology have made surgery safer, and more operations are being done to treat a variety of illnesses and injuries. The aging of the large baby-boom generation also is expected to increase the need for surgical technologists because older people usually require more operations. Moreover, as these individuals age, they may be more willing than those in previous generations to seek medical treatment to improve their quality of life. For example, an individual may decide to have a knee replacement operation in order to maintain an active lifestyle.

Hospitals will continue to employ surgical technologists to work in operating rooms because they are more cost-effective than higher-paid registered nurses.

Job Prospects. Job prospects should be best for surgical technologists who have completed an accredited education program.

O*NET

➤ Surgical Technologists (29-2055.00)

Contacts for More Information

For more information about surgical technologists, visit
➤ Association of Surgical Technologists (www.ast.org/)
    For more information about accredited surgical technology programs, visit
➤ Commission on Accreditation of Allied Health Education Programs (www.caahep.org/)
➤ Accrediting Bureau of Health Education Schools (www.abhes.org/)
    For information about certification, visit
➤ National Board of Surgical Technology and Surgical Assisting (http://nbstsa.org/)
➤ National Center for Competency Testing (www.ncctinc.com/default.aspx)
➤ National Surgical Assistant Association (www.nsaa.net/)
➤ American Board of Surgical Assistants (www.absa.net/index.php)

Veterinarians

- **2012 Median Pay** .... $84,460 per year
  $40.61 per hour
- **Entry-Level Education** ... Doctoral or professional degree
- **Work Experience in a Related Occupation**............... None
- **On-the-Job Training** .... None
- **Number of Jobs 2012** 70,300
- **Job Outlook, 2012–22**................ 12% (As fast as average)
- **Employment Change, 2012–22** 8,400

What Veterinarians Do

Veterinarians care for the health of animals and work to improve public health. They diagnose, treat, and research medical conditions and diseases of pets, livestock, and other animals.

Duties. Veterinarians typically do the following:

- Examine animals to diagnose their health problems
- Diagnose and treat animals for medical conditions
- Treat and dress wounds
- Perform surgery on animals
- Test for and vaccinate against diseases
- Operate medical equipment, such as X-ray machines
- Advise animal owners about general care, medical conditions, and treatments
- Prescribe medication
- Euthanize animals

Veterinarians in private clinical practices treat the injuries and illnesses of pets and other animals with a variety of medical equipment, including surgical tools and X-ray and ultrasound machines. They provide treatment for animals that is similar to the services a physician provides to treat humans.

The following are examples of types of veterinarians:

Companion animal veterinarians treat pets and generally work in private clinics and hospitals. According to the American Veterinary Medical Association, more than 75 percent of veterinarians who work in private clinical practice treat pets. They most often care for cats and dogs, but also treat other pets, such as birds, ferrets, and rabbits. These veterinarians diagnose and provide treatment for animal health problems, consult with owners of animals about preventative health care, and carry out medical and surgical procedures, such as vaccinations, dental work, and setting fractures.

Equine veterinarians work with horses. In 2012, about 6 percent of private practice veterinarians diagnosed and treated horses.

Food animal veterinarians work with farm animals such as pigs, cattle, and sheep. In 2012, about 8 percent of private practice veterinarians treated food animals. They spend much of their time at farms and ranches treating illnesses and injuries and testing for and vaccinating against disease. They may advise owners or managers about feeding, housing, and general health practices.

Food safety and inspection veterinarians inspect and test livestock and animal products for major animal diseases, provide vaccines to treat animals, enhance animal welfare, conduct research to improve animal health, and enforce government food safety regulations. They design and administer animal and public health programs for the prevention and control of diseases transmissible among animals and between animals and people.

Research veterinarians work in laboratories, conducting clinical research on human and animal health problems. These veterinarians may perform tests on animals to identify the effects of drug therapies, or they may test new surgical techniques. They may also research how to prevent, control, and eliminate food- and animal-borne illnesses and diseases.

Some veterinarians become postsecondary teachers at colleges and universities.

Work Environment

Veterinarians held about 70,300 jobs in 2012, of which 74 percent were in the veterinary services industry. Others held positions at colleges or universities; in private industry, such as in medical and research laboratories; and in federal, state, or local government. About 18 percent of veterinarians were self-employed.

Although most veterinarians work in private clinics and hospitals, others travel to farms, work in laboratories or classrooms, or work for the government.

Veterinarians who treat horses or food animals must travel between their offices and farms and ranches. They work outdoors in all kinds of weather and may have to perform surgery, often under unsanitary conditions.

Veterinarians who work in food safety and inspection must travel to farms, slaughterhouses, and food-processing plants.

Veterinarians who conduct research work primarily in offices and laboratories and spend much of their time dealing with people, rather than animals.

Veterinarians' work can sometimes be emotionally stressful, as they deal with sick animals and the animals' anxious owners. Also, the workplace can be noisy, as animals make noise when sick or being handled. Working on farms and ranches, in slaughterhouses, or with wildlife can also be physically demanding.

Injuries and Illnesses. When working with animals that are frightened or in pain, veterinarians risk being bitten, kicked, and scratched. In addition, veterinarians working with diseased animals risk being infected by the disease.

Work Schedules. Veterinarians often work long hours. Some work nights or weekends, and they may have to respond to emergencies outside of scheduled work hours. About 1 in 3 veterinarians worked more than 50 hours per week in 2012.

How to Become One

Veterinarians must have a Doctor of Veterinary Medicine degree from an accredited veterinary college and a state license.

Education. Veterinarians must complete a Doctor of Veterinary Medicine (D.V.M. or V.M.D.) degree at an accredited college of veterinary medicine. There are currently 29 colleges with accred-

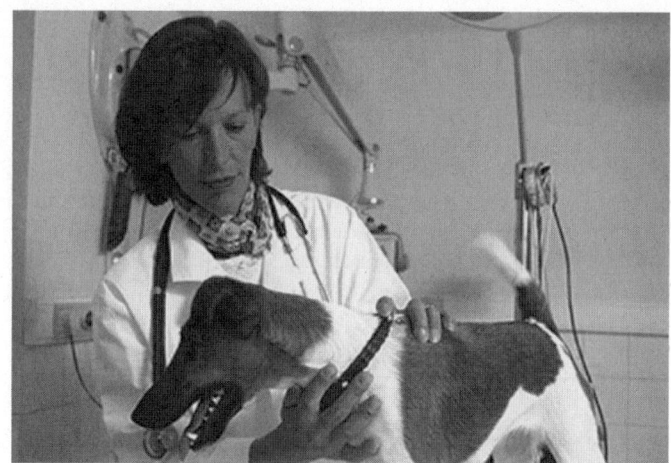

Employment opportunities for veterinarians are expected to be very good, but competition for admission to veterinary school is keen.

ited programs in the United States. A veterinary medicine program generally takes 4 years to complete and includes classroom, laboratory, and clinical components.

Although not required, most applicants to veterinary school have a bachelor's degree. Veterinary medical colleges typically require applicants to have taken many science classes, including biology, chemistry, anatomy, physiology, zoology, microbiology, and animal science. Most programs also require math and humanities and social science courses.

Admission to veterinary programs is very competitive, and fewer than half of all applicants were accepted in 2012.

In veterinary medicine programs, students take courses on normal animal anatomy and physiology, as well as disease prevention, diagnosis, and treatment. Most programs include 3 years of classroom, laboratory, and clinical work. Students typically spend the final year of the 4-year program doing clinical rotations in a veterinary medical center or hospital. In veterinary schools today, increasingly, courses include general business management and career development classes, to help new veterinarians learn how to effectively run a practice.

Licenses, Certifications, and Registrations. All states and the District of Columbia require veterinarians to have a license. Licensing requirements vary by state, but all states require prospective veterinarians to complete an accredited veterinary program and to pass the North American Veterinary Licensing Examination. Veterinarians working for the state or federal government may not be required to have a state license, because each agency has different requirements.

Median Annual Wages, May 2012

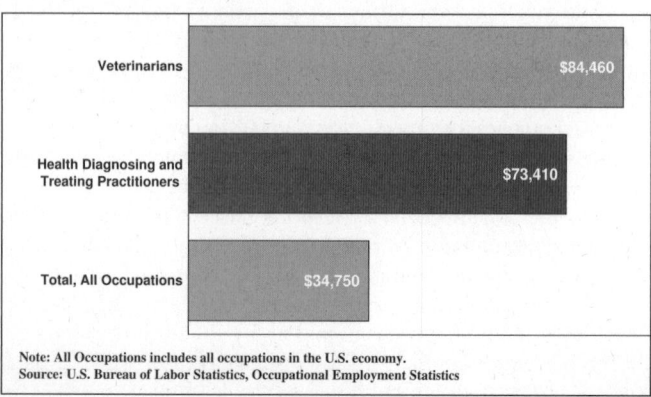

Veterinarians	$84,460
Health Diagnosing and Treating Practitioners	$73,410
Total, All Occupations	$34,750

Note: All Occupations includes all occupations in the U.S. economy.
Source: U.S. Bureau of Labor Statistics, Occupational Employment Statistics

Percent Change in Employment, Projected 2012–2022

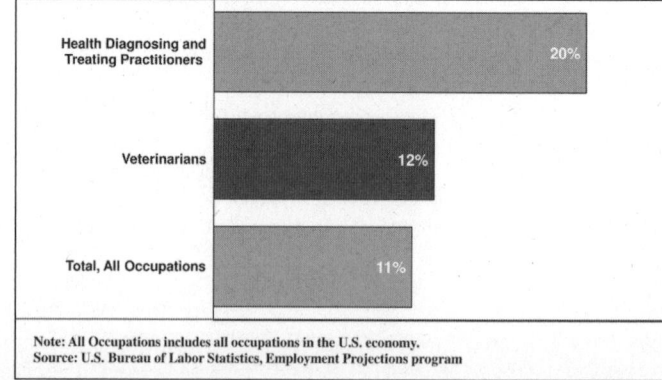

Health Diagnosing and Treating Practitioners	20%
Veterinarians	12%
Total, All Occupations	11%

Note: All Occupations includes all occupations in the U.S. economy.
Source: U.S. Bureau of Labor Statistics, Employment Projections program

Employment Projections Data for Veterinarians

Occupational title	SOC Code	Employment, 2012	Projected Employment, 2022	Change, 2012–2022	
				Percent	Numeric
Veterinarians	29-1131	70,300	78,700	12	8,400

Source: U.S. Bureau of Labor Statistics, Employment Projections Program

Note: Data are rounded. Go to **Occupational Information Included in the OOH** *for a discussion of the data in this table.*

Most states require not only the national exam but also have a state exam that covers state laws and regulations. Few states accept licenses from other states, so veterinarians who want to be licensed in another state usually must take that state's exam.

The American Veterinary Medical Association offers certification in 40 specialties, such as surgery, microbiology, and internal medicine. Although certification is not required for veterinarians, it can show exceptional skill and expertise in a particular field. To sit for the certification exam, veterinarians must have a certain number of years of experience in the field, complete additional education, and complete a residency program, typically lasting 3 to 4 years. Requirements vary by specialty.

Training. Although graduates of a veterinary program can begin practicing once they receive their license, some veterinarians pursue further education and training. Some new veterinary graduates enter 1-year internship programs to gain experience. Internships can be valuable experience for veterinarians who apply for competitive or better paying positions or in preparation for a certification program.

Other Experience. When deciding whom to admit, some veterinary medical colleges weigh experience heavily. Formal experience, such as work with veterinarians or scientists in clinics, agribusiness, research, or some area of health science, is particularly advantageous. Less formal experience, such as working with animals on a farm, at a stable, or in an animal shelter, can also be helpful.

Important Qualities

Compassion. Veterinarians must be compassionate when working with animals and their owners. They must treat animals with kindness and respect, and must be sensitive when dealing with the owners of sick pets.

Decision-making skills. Veterinarians must decide the correct method for treating the injuries and illnesses of animals. Deciding to euthanize a sick animal, for instance, can be difficult.

Interpersonal skills. Strong communication skills are essential for veterinarians, who must be able to discuss their recommendations and explain treatment options to animal owners and give instructions to their staff.

Management skills. Management skills are important for veterinarians who are in charge of running private clinics or laboratories, or directing teams of technicians or inspectors. In these settings, they are responsible for providing direction, delegating work, and overseeing daily operations.

Manual dexterity. Manual dexterity is important for veterinarians, because they must control their hand movements and be precise when treating injuries and performing surgery.

Problem-solving skills. Veterinarians need strong problem-solving skills because they must figure out what is ailing animals. Those who test animals to determine the effects of drug therapies also need excellent diagnostic skills.

Pay

The median annual wage for veterinarians was $84,460 in May 2012. The median wage is the wage at which half the workers in an occupation earned more than that amount and half earned less. The lowest 10 percent earned less than $51,530, and the top 10 percent earned more than $144,100.

The median annual wage for veterinarians in the federal government was $85,170 in May 2012.

Job Outlook

Employment of veterinarians is projected to grow 12 percent from 2012 to 2022, about as fast as the average for all occupations.

In private practice, demand for veterinarians will increase as more people are expected to take their pets for visits. Also, veterinary medicine has advanced considerably, and many of the veterinary services offered today are comparable to health care for humans, including cancer treatments and kidney transplants.

There also will be employment growth in fields related to food and animal safety, disease control, and public health. As the population grows, more veterinarians will be needed to inspect the food supply and to ensure animal and human health.

However, due to overall slowing growth of the veterinary services industry, employment gains of veterinarians will be slower than in the past.

Similar Occupations   This table shows a list of occupations with job duties that are similar to those of veterinarians.

Occupations	Entry-level Education	2012 Pay	Projected Job Growth	Average Annual Openings
Agricultural and Food Scientists	See "How to Become One"	$58,636	10%	1,640
Animal Care and Service Workers	See "How to Become One"	$20,076	15%	7,660
Medical Scientists	Doctoral or professional degree	$76,980	13%	3,550
Physicians and Surgeons	Doctoral or professional degree	$182,294	18%	29,630
Veterinary Assistants and Laboratory Animal Caretakers	High school diploma or equivalent	$23,130	10%	2,130
Veterinary Technologists and Technicians	Associate's degree	$30,290	29%	3,340
Zoologists and Wildlife Biologists	Bachelor's degree	$57,710	5%	670

Job Prospects. Candidates can expect very strong competition for most veterinarian positions. Job seekers with specializations and prior work experience should have the best job opportunities.

Although veterinary services are growing, the number of new graduates from veterinary schools has increased to roughly 3,000 per year, resulting in greater competition for jobs than in recent years. Additionally, most veterinary graduates are attracted to companion animal care, so there will be fewer job opportunities in that field, as overall growth of the veterinary services industry slows.

Job opportunities in farm animal care will be better, because fewer veterinarians compete to work on large animals. Also, there will be some job opportunities available in the federal government in food safety, animal health, and public health.

Given the training they receive from veterinary school, veterinarians are highly qualified for nontraditional industry positions in fields such as public health, disease control, corporate sales, and population studies. With potentially fewer opportunities in companion animal care, many graduating veterinarians will likely have better job prospects in these areas.

O*NET

➤ Veterinarians (29-1131.00)

Contacts for More Information

For more information on careers in veterinary medicine, a list of U.S. schools and colleges of veterinary medicine, and information on accreditation policies, visit

➤ American Veterinary Medical Association (www.avma.org/Pages/home.aspx)

For more information on veterinary education, visit

➤ Association of American Veterinary Medical Colleges (www.aavmc.org/)

For information on veterinarian positions with the federal government, visit

➤ USAJOBS (www.usajobs.gov/)

Veterinary Assistants and Laboratory Animal Caretakers

- **2012 Median Pay** .... $23,130 per year
  $11.12 per hour

- **Entry-Level Education** ... High school diploma or equivalent

- **Work Experience in a Related Occupation** .... None

- **On-the-Job Training** .... Short-term on-the-job training

- **Number of Jobs 2012** 74,600

- **Job Outlook, 2012–22** .... 10% (As fast as average)

- **Employment Change, 2012–22** 7,100

What Veterinary Assistants and Laboratory Animal Caretakers Do

Veterinary assistants and laboratory animal caretakers look after animals in laboratories, animal hospitals, and clinics. They care for the well-being of animals by performing routine tasks under the supervision of veterinarians, scientists, and veterinary technologists and technicians.

Duties. Veterinary assistants and laboratory animal caretakers typically do the following:

- Feed, bathe, and exercise animals

- Clean and disinfect cages, kennels, and examination and operation rooms

- Restrain animals during examination and laboratory procedures

- Maintain and sterilize surgical instruments and equipment

- Monitor and care for animals after surgery

- Help provide emergency first aid to sick and injured animals

- Give medication or immunizations that veterinarians prescribe

- Assist in the collection of blood, urine, and tissue samples

Veterinary assistants and laboratory animal caretakers are responsible for many daily tasks, such as feeding, weighing, and taking the temperature of animals. Other duties may include giving medication, cleaning cages, and providing nursing care before and after surgery and other medical procedures.

Veterinary assistants and laboratory animal caretakers play a large role in helping veterinarians and scientists with surgery and other minor procedures. They may prepare equipment and pass surgical instruments and materials to veterinarians during surgery. They also move animals and restrain them during testing and other procedures.

Veterinary assistants work mainly in clinics and animal hospitals, helping veterinarians and veterinary technicians and technologists treat injuries and illnesses of animals.

Laboratory animal caretakers work in laboratories under the supervision of a veterinarian, scientist, veterinary technician, or veterinary technologist. Their daily tasks include feeding animals, cleaning kennels, and monitoring the general well-being of laboratory animals.

Work Environment

Veterinary assistants and laboratory animal caretakers held about 74,600 jobs in 2012. About 82 percent were employed in the veterinary services industry, which includes private clinics and animal hospitals. Most others were employed in laboratories, colleges and universities, and research facilities.

The work of veterinary assistants and laboratory animal caretakers may be physically and emotionally demanding. Workers may witness abused animals and may assist in euthanizing sick, injured, and unwanted animals.

Injuries and Illnesses. Veterinary assistants and laboratory animal caretakers have a higher rate of injuries and illnesses than the

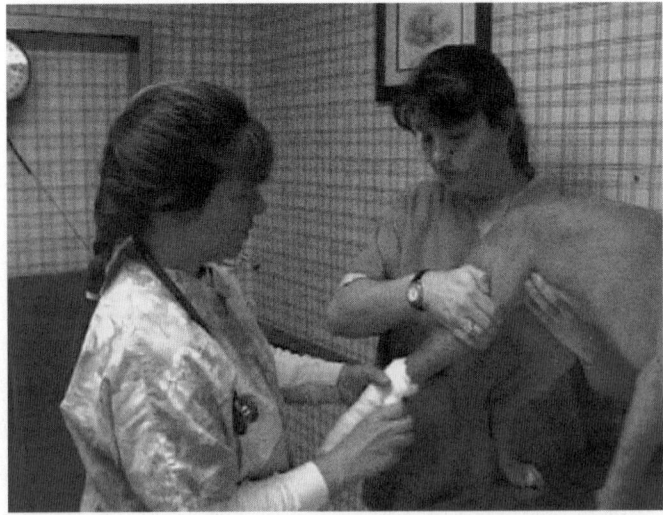

Veterinary technicians work under the supervision of a veterinarian.

Median Annual Wages, May 2012

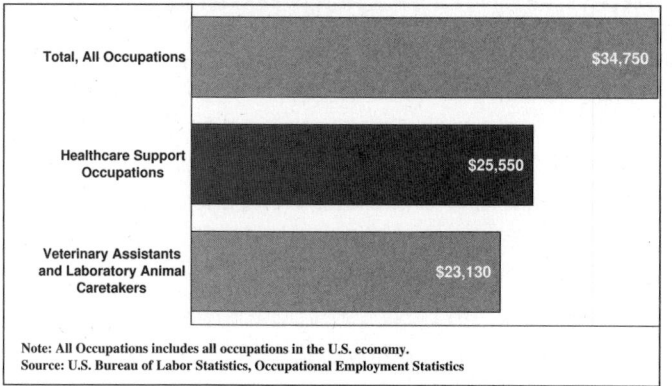

Note: All Occupations includes all occupations in the U.S. economy.
Source: U.S. Bureau of Labor Statistics, Occupational Employment Statistics

Percent Change in Employment, Projected 2012–2022

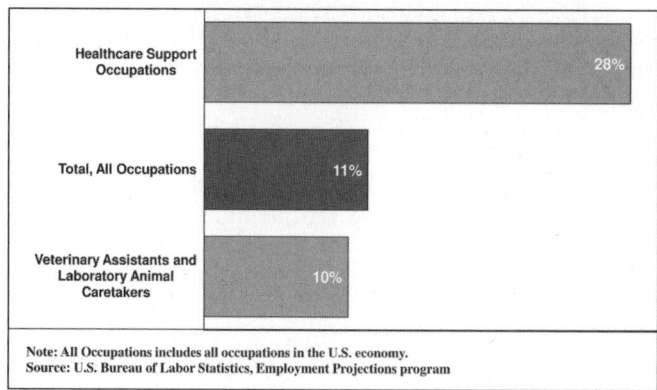

Note: All Occupations includes all occupations in the U.S. economy.
Source: U.S. Bureau of Labor Statistics, Employment Projections program

national average. When working with scared and aggressive animals, workers may be bitten, scratched, and kicked. A worker also may be injured while holding, bathing, or restraining an animal.

Work Schedules. Many clinics and laboratories operate 24 hours a day, so veterinary assistants and laboratory animal caretakers may be required to work nights, weekends, and holidays.

How to Become One

Most veterinary assistants and laboratory animal caretakers have a high school diploma and learn on the job. Experience working with animals can be helpful for jobseekers.

Education. Most workers entering the occupation have a high school diploma or its equivalent.

Training. Most veterinary assistants and laboratory animal caretakers are trained on the job, but some employers prefer candidates who already have experience working with animals.

Licenses, Certifications, and Registrations. Although not required by employers, veterinary assistants can become certified as an Approved Veterinary Assistant (AVA) through the National Association of Veterinary Technicians in America (NAVTA).

For laboratory animal caretakers seeking work in a research facility, the American Association for Laboratory Animal Science

(AALAS) offers three levels of certification: Assistant Laboratory Animal Technician (ALAT), Laboratory Animal Technician (LAT), and Laboratory Animal Technologist (LATG).

Although certification is not mandatory, it allows workers at each level to demonstrate competency in animal husbandry, health and welfare, and facility administration. To become certified, candidates must have work experience in a laboratory animal facility and pass the AALAS exam.

Important Qualities

Compassion. Veterinary assistants and laboratory animal caretakers must treat animals with kindness and be compassionate to both the animals and their owners.

Detail oriented. These workers must follow strict instructions. For example, workers must be precise when sterilizing surgical equipment, monitoring animals, and giving medication.

Dexterity. Veterinary assistants and laboratory animal caretakers must handle animals and use medical instruments and laboratory equipment with care.

Physical strength. Veterinary assistants and laboratory animal caretakers must be able to handle, move, and restrain animals.

Employment Projections Data for Veterinary Assistants and Laboratory Animal Caretakers

Occupational title	SOC Code	Employment, 2012	Projected Employment, 2022	Change, 2012–2022	
				Percent	Numeric
Veterinary assistants and laboratory animal caretakers.........	31-9096	74,600	81,700	10	7,100

Source: U.S. Bureau of Labor Statistics, Employment Projections Program

Note: Data are rounded. Go to **Occupational Information Included in the OOH** *for a discussion of the data in this table.*

Similar Occupations   This table shows a list of occupations with job duties that are similar to those of veterinary assistants and laboratory animal caretakers.

Occupations	Entry-level Education	2012 Pay	Projected Job Growth	Average Annual Openings
Animal Care and Service Workers	See "How to Become One"	$20,076	15%	7,660
Dental Assistants	Postsecondary non-degree award	$34,500	25%	13,720
Dental Hygienists	Associate's degree	$70,210	33%	11,350
Nursing Assistants and Orderlies	See "How to Become One"	$24,404	21%	61,300
Surgical Technologists	Postsecondary non-degree award	$41,790	30%	3,910
Veterinarians	Doctoral or professional degree	$84,460	12%	3,100
Veterinary Technologists and Technicians	Associate's degree	$30,290	29%	3,340

Pay

The median annual wage for veterinary assistants and laboratory animal caretakers was $23,130 in May 2012. The median wage is the wage at which half the workers in an occupation earned more than that amount and half earned less. The lowest 10 percent earned less than $17,150, and the top 10 percent earned more than $35,510.

Veterinary assistants and laboratory animal caretakers working in research positions often earn more than those in clinics and animal hospitals. In May 2012, the median annual wages for veterinary assistants and laboratory animal caretakers in the top three industries employing these workers were as follows:

Colleges, universities, and professional schools...................$30,760
Scientific research and development services 29,710
Veterinary services 22,450

Job Outlook

Employment of veterinary assistants and laboratory animal caretakers is projected to grow 10 percent from 2012 to 2022, about as fast as the average for all occupations.

Although veterinary assistants and laboratory animal caretakers will be needed to assist veterinarians and other veterinary care staff, many veterinary practices are expected to increasingly replace veterinary assistants with higher-skilled veterinary technicians and technologists, thus requiring fewer veterinary assistants.

However, there will be demand for laboratory animal caretakers in areas such as public health, food and animal safety, national disease control, and biomedical research on human health problems.

Job Prospects. Overall job opportunities for veterinary assistants and laboratory animal caretakers are expected to be good.

Although some establishments are replacing veterinary assistant positions with higher-skilled veterinary technicians and technologists, growth of the pet care industry means that the number of veterinary assistant positions should continue to increase.

Furthermore, veterinary assistants experience a high rate of job turnover, so many positions will become available from workers who leave the occupation each year.

O*NET

➤ Veterinary Assistants and Laboratory Animal Caretakers (31-9096.00)

Contacts for More Information

For more information about certification as a laboratory animal caretaker, visit
➤ American Association for Laboratory Animal Science (www.aalas.org/)
For more information about certification as a veterinary assistant, visit
➤ National Association of Veterinary Technicians in America (www.navta.net/)
For more information about becoming a veterinary assistant, including career opportunities, visit
➤ American Animal Hospital Association (www.aahanet.org/)

Veterinary Technologists and Technicians

- **2012 Median Pay** .... $30,290 per year
  $14.56 per hour
- **Entry-Level Education** ....Associate's degree
- **Work Experience in a Related Occupation**............... None
- **On-the-Job Training** .... None
- **Number of Jobs 2012** 84,800
- **Job Outlook, 2012–22**.... 30% (Much faster than average)
- **Employment Change, 2012–22** 25,000

What Veterinary Technologists and Technicians Do

Veterinary technologists and technicians perform medical tests under the supervision of a licensed veterinarian to help diagnose the illnesses and injuries of animals.

Duties. Veterinary technologists and technicians typically do the following:

- Observe the behavior and condition of animals
- Provide nursing care or emergency first aid to recovering or injured animals
- Administer anesthesia to animals and monitor their responses
- Collect laboratory samples, such as blood, urine, or tissue, for testing
- Perform laboratory tests, such as urinalyses and blood counts
- Take and develop X-rays
- Prepare animals and instruments for surgery
- Administer medications, vaccines, and treatments prescribed by a veterinarian
- Collect and record patients' case histories

In order to provide superior animal care, veterinarians rely on the skills of veterinary technologists and technicians. As such, many veterinary technologists and technicians work in private clinics, animal hospitals, and veterinary testing laboratories. They conduct a variety of clinical and laboratory procedures, including postoperative care, dental care, and specialized nursing care.

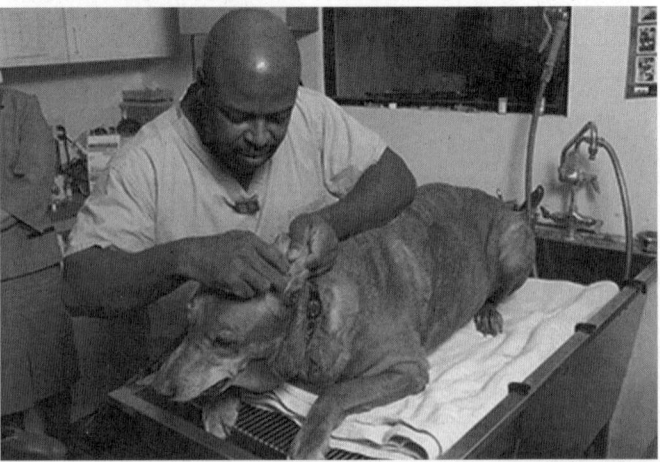

Veterinary technologists and technicians often assist veterinarians by conducting tests.

Median Annual Wages, May 2012

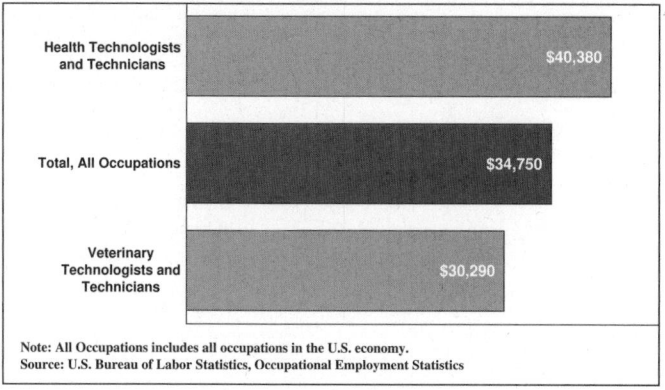

Note: All Occupations includes all occupations in the U.S. economy.
Source: U.S. Bureau of Labor Statistics, Occupational Employment Statistics

Percent Change in Employment, Projected 2012–2022

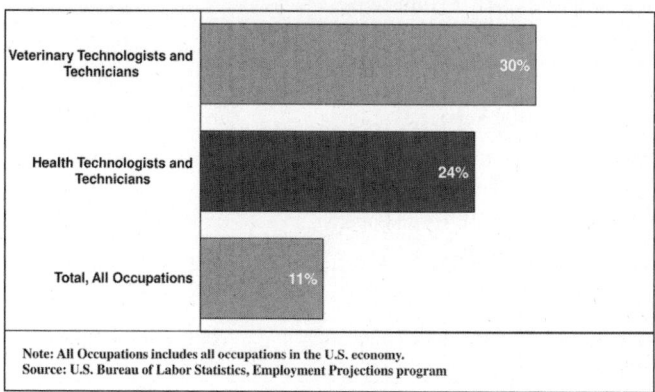

Note: All Occupations includes all occupations in the U.S. economy.
Source: U.S. Bureau of Labor Statistics, Employment Projections program

Veterinary technologists and technicians who work in research-related jobs do similar work. For example, they are responsible for making sure that animals are handled carefully and humanely. They commonly help veterinarians or scientists on research projects in areas such as biomedical research, disaster preparedness, and food safety.

Veterinary technologists and technicians most often work with small-animal practitioners who care for cats and dogs, but they also may do a variety of tasks involving mice, rats, sheep, pigs, cattle, and birds.

Veterinary technologists and technicians can specialize in a particular discipline. Specialties include dental technology, anesthesia, emergency and critical care, and zoological medicine.

The differences between technologists and technicians are the following:

Veterinary technologists usually have a 4-year bachelor's degree in veterinary technology. Although some technologists work in private clinical practices, many work in more advanced research-related jobs, usually under the guidance of a scientist and sometimes a veterinarian. Working primarily in a laboratory setting, they may administer medications; prepare tissue samples for examination; or record information on an animal's genealogy, weight, diet, and signs of pain.

Veterinary technicians usually have a 2-year associate's degree in a veterinary technology program. They generally work in private clinical practices under the guidance of a licensed veterinarian. Technicians may perform laboratory tests, such as a urinalysis, and help veterinarians conduct a variety of other diagnostic tests. Although some of their work is done in a laboratory setting, many technicians also talk with animal owners. For example, they explain a pet's condition or how to administer medication prescribed by a veterinarian.

Work Environment

Veterinary technologists and technicians held about 84,800 jobs in 2012, of which 92 percent were in the veterinary services industry.

Veterinary technologists and technicians typically work in private clinics, laboratories, and animal hospitals. They may also work in boarding kennels, animal shelters, rescue leagues, and zoos.

Their jobs may be physically or emotionally demanding. For example, they may witness abused animals or may need to help euthanize sick, injured, or unwanted animals.

Injuries and Illnesses. Veterinary technologists and technicians have a higher rate of injuries and illnesses than the national average. When working with scared or aggressive animals, they may be bitten, scratched, or kicked. Injuries may happen while the technologist or technician is holding, cleaning, or restraining an animal.

Work Schedules. Many clinics and laboratories are staffed 24 hours a day, so veterinary technologists and technicians may have to work evenings, weekends, or holidays. Many technicians have variable schedules, and some must work 7 days a week.

How to Become One

There are primarily two levels of education and training for entry into this occupation: a 4-year program for veterinary technologists and a 2-year program for veterinary technicians. Typically, both technologists and technicians must pass a credentialing exam and must become registered, licensed, or certified, depending on the state in which they work.

Education. Veterinary technologists and technicians must complete a postsecondary program in veterinary technology. In 2013, there were 217 veterinary technology programs accredited by the American Veterinary Medical Association (AVMA). Most of these programs offer a 2-year associate's degree for veterinary technicians. Twenty-two colleges offer a 4-year bachelor's degree in veterinary technology. Eight schools offer coursework through distance learning.

People interested in becoming a veterinary technologist or technician should take high school classes in biology and other sciences, as well as math.

Licenses, Certifications, and Registrations. Although each state regulates veterinary technologists and technicians differently, most

Employment Projections Data for Veterinary Technologists and Technicians

Occupational title	SOC Code	Employment, 2012	Projected Employment, 2022	Change, 2012–2022	
				Percent	Numeric
Veterinary technologists and technicians	29-2056	84,800	109,800	30	25,000

Source: U.S. Bureau of Labor Statistics, Employment Projections Program

Note: Data are rounded. Go to **Occupational Information Included in the OOH** *for a discussion of the data in this table.*

Similar Occupations   This table shows a list of occupations with job duties that are similar to those of veterinary technologists and technicians.

Occupations	Entry-level Education	2012 Pay	Projected Job Growth	Average Annual Openings
Animal Care and Service Workers	See "How to Become One"	$20,076	15%	7,660
Medical and Clinical Laboratory Technologists and Technicians	See "How to Become One"	$47,499	22%	15,600
Radiologic and MRI Technologists	Associate's degree	$56,035	21%	8,090
Surgical Technologists	Postsecondary non-degree award	$41,790	30%	3,910
Veterinarians	Doctoral or professional degree	$84,460	12%	3,100
Veterinary Assistants and Laboratory Animal Caretakers	High school diploma or equivalent	$23,130	10%	2,130

candidates must pass a credentialing exam. Most states require technologists and assistants to pass the Veterinary Technician National Examination.

For technologists seeking work in a research facility, American Association for Laboratory Animal Science (AALAS) offers three levels of certification: Assistant Laboratory Animal Technician (ALAT), Laboratory Animal Technician (LAT), and Laboratory Animal Technologist (LATG).

Although certification is not mandatory, workers at each level can show competency in animal husbandry, health and welfare, and facility administration and management to prospective employers. To become certified, candidates must have work experience in a laboratory animal facility and pass the AALAS examination.

Important Qualities

Communication skills. Veterinary technologists and technicians spend a substantial amount of their time communicating with supervisors, animal owners, and other staff. In addition, a growing number of technicians counsel pet owners on animal behavior and nutrition.

Compassion. Veterinary technologists and technicians must treat animals with kindness and must be sensitive when dealing with the owners of sick pets.

Detail oriented. Veterinary technologists and technicians must pay attention to details and be precise when recording information, performing diagnostic tests, and administering medication.

Manual dexterity. Veterinary technologists and technicians must handle animals, medical instruments, and laboratory equipment with care. They also do intricate tasks, such as dental work, giving anesthesia, and taking X-rays, which require a steady hand.

Problem-solving skills. Veterinary technologists and technicians need strong problem-solving skills in order to identify injuries and illnesses and offer the appropriate treatment.

Pay

The median annual wage for veterinary technologists and technicians was $30,290 in May 2012. The median wage is the wage at which half the workers in an occupation earned more than that amount and half earned less. The lowest 10 percent earned less than $21,030, and the top 10 percent earned more than $44,030.

In May 2012, the median annual wages for veterinary technologists and technicians in the top three industries employing these workers were as follows:

Colleges, universities, and professional schools; state $37,190
Research and development in the physical,
    engineering, and life sciences... 35,810
Veterinary services 29,920

Veterinary technologists and technicians working in research positions often earn more than those in other fields.

Job Outlook

Employment of veterinary technologists and technicians is projected to grow 30 percent from 2012 to 2022, much faster than the average for all occupations.

Because veterinarians perform specialized tasks, clinics and animal hospitals are increasingly using veterinary technologists and technicians to provide more general care and perform more laboratory work. Furthermore, veterinarians will continue to prefer higher skilled veterinary technologists and technicians over veterinary assistants for more complex work.

There will also be demand for veterinary technicians in areas such as public health, food and animal safety, national disease control, and biomedical research on human health problems.

Job Prospects. Overall job opportunities for veterinary technologists and technicians are expected to be good, particularly in rural areas.

However, the number of veterinary technology programs has been growing rapidly in recent years, so the number of new graduates vying for jobs over the coming decade should result in greater competition than in the past.

Workers who leave the occupation each year will also result in job openings.

O*NET

➤ Veterinary Technologists and Technicians (29-2056.00)

Contacts for More Information

For information on careers in veterinary medicine and a listing of AVMA-accredited veterinary technology programs, visit
➤ American Veterinary Medical Association (www.avma.org/Pages/home.aspx)

For more information on becoming a veterinary technician or technologist, visit
➤ National Association of Veterinary Technicians in America (www.navta.net/)

For information on certification as a laboratory animal technician or technologist, visit
➤ American Association for Laboratory Animal Science (www.aalas.org/)

For information on the Veterinary Technician National Examination, visit
➤ American Association of Veterinary State Boards (www.aavsb.org/)

Installation, Maintenance, and Repair

Aircraft and Avionics Equipment Mechanics and Technicians

- **2012 Median Pay** .... $55,230 per year
  $26.55 per hour
- **Entry-Level Education** ....See "How to Become One"
- **Work Experience in a Related Occupation**.............. None
- **On-the-Job Training** .... None
- **Number of Jobs 2012** 138,900
- **Job Outlook, 2012–22**.................2% (Little or no change)
- **Employment Change, 2012–22** 3,500

Avionics technicians are responsible for repairing an aircraft's electronics systems.

What Aircraft and Avionics Equipment Mechanics and Technicians Do

Aircraft and avionics equipment mechanics and technicians repair and perform scheduled maintenance on aircraft. They also perform aircraft inspections as required by the Federal Aviation Administration (FAA).

Duties. Aircraft mechanics typically do the following:

- Examine replacement aircraft parts for defects
- Diagnose mechanical or electrical problems
- Read maintenance manuals to identify repair procedures
- Repair wings, brakes, electrical systems, and other aircraft components
- Replace defective parts using hand tools or power tools
- Test aircraft parts with gauges and other diagnostic equipment
- Inspect completed work to ensure that it meets performance standards
- Keep records of maintenance and repair work

Avionics technicians typically do the following:

- Test electronic instruments, using circuit testers, oscilloscopes, and voltmeters
- Interpret flight test data to diagnose malfunctions and performance problems
- Assemble components, such as electrical controls and junction boxes, and install software
- Install instrument panels, using hand tools, power tools, and soldering irons
- Repair or replace malfunctioning components
- Keep records of maintenance and repair work

Today's airplanes are highly complex machines that require reliable parts and service to fly safely. To keep an airplane in peak operating condition, aircraft and avionics equipment mechanics and technicians perform scheduled maintenance, make repairs, and complete inspections. They must follow detailed federal regulations set by the FAA that dictate maintenance schedules for a variety of different operations.

Many mechanics are generalists and work on many different types of aircraft, such as jets, piston-driven airplanes, and helicopters. Others specialize in one section of a particular type of aircraft, such as the engine, hydraulics, or electrical system of a particular aircraft. In independent repair shops, mechanics usually inspect and repair many different types of aircraft.

Most mechanics who work on civilian aircraft have either one or both of the FAA's Airframe and Powerplant (A&P) certificates. Mechanics who have these certificates are authorized to work on most parts of the aircraft, excluding flight instruments and major work on propellers. Maintaining a plane's electronic flight instruments is typically the job of specialized avionics technicians.

The following are examples of types of aircraft and avionics equipment mechanics and technicians:

Airframe and Powerplant (A&P) mechanics are certified generalist mechanics who can independently perform many maintenance and alteration tasks on aircraft. A&P mechanics repair and maintain most parts of an aircraft, including the engines, landing gear, brakes, and air conditioning systems. Some specialized activities require additional experience and certification.

Maintenance schedules for aircraft may be based on hours flown, days since the last inspection, trips flown, or a combination of these factors. Maintenance also may need to be done to address specific issues recognized by manufacturers. To complete maintenance, mechanics use precision instruments to measure wear and identify defects. They may use X-rays, magnetic, or ultrasonic inspection equipment to discover cracks that cannot be seen on a plane's exterior. They check for corrosion, distortion, and cracks in the aircraft's main body, wings, and tail. They then repair the metal, fabric, wood, or composite materials that make up the airframe and skin.

After completing all repairs, mechanics must test the equipment to ensure that it works properly. Aircraft equipped with digital monitoring systems can provide mechanics with valuable diagnostic information from electronic consoles. Mechanics must also keep records of all maintenance that they do on an aircraft.

The A&P ratings are generally considered the initial and most basic ratings needed to be a professional mechanic. Many additional certifications and specializations can be pursued to expand the ability of a mechanic to perform additional duties. Some of these specializations are as follows:

Median Annual Wages, May 2012

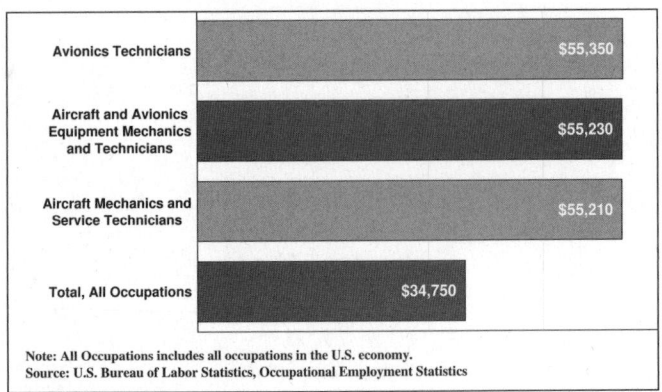

Note: All Occupations includes all occupations in the U.S. economy.
Source: U.S. Bureau of Labor Statistics, Occupational Employment Statistics

Percent Change in Employment, Projected 2012–2022

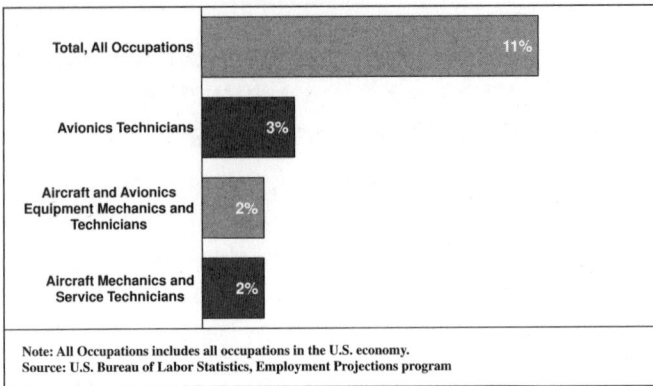

Note: All Occupations includes all occupations in the U.S. economy.
Source: U.S. Bureau of Labor Statistics, Employment Projections program

Avionics technicians are specialists who repair and maintain a plane's electronic instruments, such as radio communications, radar systems, and navigation aids. As the use of digital technology increases, more time is spent maintaining computer systems. The ability to repair and maintain many avionics and flight instrument systems is granted through the Airframe rating, but other licenses or certifications may be needed.

Designated airworthiness representatives (DARs) examine, inspect, and test aircraft for airworthiness. They issue airworthiness certificates, which aircraft must have to fly. There are two types of DARs, manufacturing DARs and maintenance DARs.

Inspection Authorized (IA) mechanics are mechanics who have both Airframe and Powerplant licenses and who may perform inspections on aircraft and return them to service. IA mechanics are able to do a wider variety of maintenance and alterations than any other type of maintenance personnel, such as comprehensive annual inspections or returning aircraft to service after a major repair.

Repairmen certificate holders may or may not have the A&P or other certificates. Repairmen certificates are issued by certified repair stations to aviation maintenance personnel and the certificates allow them to do very specific duties. Repairmen certificates are valid only while the mechanic works at the issuing repair center and are not transferable to other employers.

Work Environment

Aircraft mechanics and avionics technicians held about 138,900 jobs in 2012. Approximately 88 percent were aircraft mechanics and the rest were avionics technicians. The majority worked for private companies and about 14 percent worked for the federal government.

The industries that employed the most aircraft mechanics in 2012 were as follows:

Support activities for air transportation 26%
Scheduled air transportation.. 25
Aerospace product and parts manufacturing.......................... 16
Federal government, excluding postal service 15
Nonscheduled air transportation 4

The industries that employed the most avionics technicians in 2012 were as follows:

Aerospace product and parts manufacturing.......................... 30%
Support activities for air transportation 27
Federal government, excluding postal service 13
Scheduled air transportation.. 12
Professional, scientific, and technical services...................... 6

Mechanics and technicians work in hangars, in repair stations, or on airfields. They must meet strict deadlines while maintaining safety standards.

Most mechanics and technicians work near major airports. Mechanics may work outside, on the airfield, or in climate-controlled shops and hangars. Civilian mechanics employed by the U.S. Armed Forces work on military installations.

Injuries and Illnesses. Aircraft and avionics equipment mechanics and technicians experience rates of injuries and illnesses that are higher than the average across all occupations.

Mechanics and technicians often lift heavy objects, handle dangerous chemicals, or operate large power tools. They frequently stand, lie, or kneel on the ground and may work on scaffolds or ladders. Noise and vibrations are common, especially when engines are being tested, and they often endure hot and cold temperatures.

Work Schedules. Mechanics and technicians usually work full time on rotating 8-hour shifts. Overtime and weekend work is common. Day shifts are usually reserved for mechanics with the most seniority. General aviation mechanics and technicians typically have more flexible schedules than those working for airlines.

How to Become One

Most aircraft and avionics equipment mechanics and technicians learn their trade at an FAA-approved Aviation Maintenance Technician School. Others enter with a high school education or equivalent and are trained on the job. Some workers enter the occupation after getting training in the military. Aircraft mechanics and avionics technicians are typically certified by the FAA. See the Title 14 of the Code of Federal Regulations (14 CFR) part 65, subpart D and E, for the most current requirements for becoming a certified mechanic.

Education and Training. Aircraft mechanics and service technicians typically enter the occupation after attending a Part 147 FAA-approved Aviation Maintenance Technician School. These programs award a certificate of completion that the FAA recognizes as an alternate to the experience requirements stated in the regulations, and grants holders the ability to take the relevant FAA exams.

Some aircraft mechanics and service technicians enter the occupation with a high school diploma or equivalent and receive on-the-job training to learn their skills and to be able to pass the FAA exams. Some workers enter the occupation after getting training in the military. Aviation maintenance personnel who are not certified by the FAA work under supervision until they have enough experience and knowledge and become certified.

Avionics technicians typically earn an associate's degree before entering the occupation. Aircraft controls, systems, and flight

Employment Projections Data for Aircraft and Avionics Equipment Mechanics and Technicians

Occupational title	SOC Code	Employment, 2012	Projected Employment, 2022	Change, 2012–2022	
				Percent	Numeric
Aircraft and avionics equipment mechanics and technicians.....	—	138,900	142,300	2	3,500
Avionics technicians..	49-2091	17,100	17,600	3	500
Aircraft mechanics and service technicians........................	49-3011	121,700	124,700	2	3,000

Source: U.S. Bureau of Labor Statistics, Employment Projections Program

Note: Data are rounded. Go to **Occupational Information Included in the OOH** for a discussion of the data in this table.

instruments have become increasingly digital and computerized. Maintenance workers who have the proper background in aviation flight instruments or computer repair are needed to maintain these complex systems.

Licenses, Certifications, and Registrations. Although aircraft and avionics equipment mechanics and technicians are not required to get licenses or certifications, most do, as these credentials often improve a mechanic's wages and chances for employment. The FAA requires that aircraft maintenance either be done by or under the supervision of a certified mechanic with the appropriate ratings or authorizations.

The FAA offers separate certifications for body work (Airframe mechanics, or "A") and engine work (Powerplant mechanics, or "P"), but employers may prefer to hire mechanics who have both Airframe and Powerplant (A&P) ratings. The A&P ratings generally certify that aviation mechanics meet basic knowledge and ability standards.

Mechanics must be at least 18 years of age, be fluent in English, and have 30 months of experience to qualify for both the A and P ratings (A&P). If only one rating is sought by the mechanic, 18 months experience is required to take either the Airframe or the Powerplant exams. However, completion of a program at a Part 147 FAA-approved Aviation Maintenance Technician School can substitute for the experience requirement and shorten the time requirements to become eligible to take the FAA exams.

Applicants must pass written, oral, and practical exams that demonstrate the required skills. Candidates must pass all the tests within 2 years.

To keep their certification, mechanics must have completed relevant repair or maintenance work within the previous 24 months. To fulfill this requirement, mechanics may take classes from their employer, a school, or an aircraft manufacturer.

Avionics technicians are typically certified through a repair station for the specific work being done or hold the Airframe rating to work on an aircraft's electronic and flight instrument systems. An Aircraft Electronics Technician (AET) certification is available through the National Center for Aerospace and Transportation Technologies. It certifies that aviation mechanics have a basic level of knowledge in the subject area, but it is not required by the FAA for any specific tasks. Avionics technicians who work on communications equipment may need to have the proper radio-telephone operator certification issued by the Federal Communications Commission (FCC).

Other licenses and certifications are available to mechanics who wish to increase their skill set or advance their careers. The Inspection Authorization (IA) is available to mechanics who have had their A&P ratings for at least 3 years and meet other requirements. These mechanics are able to sign off on many major repairs and alterations. Mechanics can get many other certifications, such as Repairmen of light-sport aircraft, or Designated Airworthiness Representative (DAR).

Important Qualities

Agility. Mechanics and technicians need to climb on airplanes, balance, and reach without falling.

Detail oriented. Mechanics and technicians need to adjust airplane parts to exact specifications. For example, they often use precision tools to tighten wheel bolts to an exact tension.

Dexterity. Mechanics and technicians must possess dexterity to coordinate the movement of their fingers and hands to grasp, manipulate, or assemble parts.

Observational skills. Mechanics and technicians must recognize engine noises, read gauges, and otherwise collect information to determine whether an aircraft's systems are working properly.

Troubleshooting skills. Mechanics and technicians diagnose complex problems and they need to evaluate options to correct those problems.

Work Experience in a Related Occupation. Avionics technicians may begin their careers as aircraft mechanics and service technicians. As aircraft mechanics and service technicians gain experience, they may study independently, attend formal classes, or otherwise choose to pursue additional certifications that grant the privileges to work on specialized flight instruments. Eventually, they may become dedicated avionics technicians who work exclusively on flight instruments.

Advancement. As aircraft mechanics gain experience, they may advance to lead mechanic, lead inspector, or shop supervisor. Opportunities are best for those who have an aircraft inspector's authorization (IA). Many specialist certifications are available that allow mechanics to do a wider variety of repairs and alterations.

Mechanics with broad experience in maintenance and repair might become inspectors or examiners for the FAA.

Additional business and management training may help aircraft and avionics equipment mechanics and technicians open their own maintenance facility.

Pay

The median annual wage for aircraft mechanics and service technicians was $55,210 in May 2012. The median wage is the wage at which half the workers in an occupation earned more than that amount and half earned less. The lowest 10 percent of aircraft mechanics earned less than $35,190, and the top 10 percent earned more than $76,660.

In May 2012, the median annual wages for aircraft mechanics and service technicians in the top five industries in which these mechanics worked were as follows:

Scheduled air transportation..	$59,110
Federal government, excluding postal service......................	55,940
Aerospace product and parts manufacturing.......................	55,650
Nonscheduled air transportation	54,910
Support activities for air transportation	49,120

The median annual wage for avionics technicians was $55,350 in May 2012. The lowest 10 percent of avionics technicians

Similar Occupations   This table shows a list of occupations with job duties that are similar to those of aircraft and avionics equipment mechanics and technicians.

Occupations	Entry-level Education	2012 Pay	Projected Job Growth	Average Annual Openings
Aerospace Engineering and Operations Technicians	Associate's degree	$61,530	0%	210
Automotive Body and Glass Repairers	High school diploma or equivalent	$37,817	13%	5,700
Automotive Service Technicians and Mechanics	High school diploma or equivalent	$36,610	9%	23,760
Computer, ATM, and Office Machine Repairers	Some college, no degree	$36,620	4%	3,280
Electrical and Electronics Engineering Technicians	Associate's degree	$57,850	0%	3,040
Electrical and Electronics Installers and Repairers	Postsecondary non-degree award	$51,081	1%	2,980
Electricians	High school diploma or equivalent	$49,840	20%	22,460
Electro-mechanical Technicians	Associate's degree	$51,820	4%	430
Heavy Vehicle and Mobile Equipment Service Technicians	High school diploma or equivalent	$43,979	9%	6,710
Mechanical Engineering Technicians	Associate's degree	$51,980	5%	1,210
Network and Computer Systems Administrators	Bachelor's degree	$72,560	12%	10,050

earned less than $39,150, and the top 10 percent earned more than $73,770.

In May 2012, the median annual wages for avionics technicians in the top five industries in which these technicians worked were as follows:

Aerospace product and parts manufacturing	$60,780
Professional, scientific, and technical services	59,750
Scheduled air transportation	58,530
Federal government, excluding postal service	54,090
Support activities for air transportation	50,040

Union Membership. Compared with workers in all occupations, aircraft and avionics equipment mechanics and technicians had a higher percentage of workers who belonged to a union in 2012.

Job Outlook

Employment of aircraft and avionics equipment mechanics and technicians is projected to show little or no change from 2012 to 2022.

Air traffic is expected to gradually increase over the coming decade. However, new aircraft are generally expected to require less maintenance than older aircraft. Airlines may continue to outsource maintenance work to specialized maintenance and repair shops both domestically and abroad. Increased specialization will allow maintenance facilities to use their resources more efficiently and therefore limit growth in the number of aircraft and avionics equipment mechanics and technicians.

Job Prospects. Competition for aircraft and avionics equipment mechanic and technician jobs varies according to the type of job sought. In general, job opportunities will be best for mechanics who hold an A&P certificate and have knowledge about the most cutting edge technologies and composite materials. Familiarity with computers and digital systems will help provide the best opportunities.

Bachelor's degree holders typically have an advantage when trying to enter the occupation and may find it easier to advance.

O*NET

➤ Avionics Technicians (49-2091.00)
➤ Aircraft Mechanics and Service Technicians (49-3011.00)

Contacts for More Information

For more information about aircraft and avionics equipment mechanics and technicians, visit
➤ Federal Aviation Administration (www.faa.gov/)
➤ Professional Aviation Maintenance Association (http://pama.org/)
➤ Aviation Maintenance Magazine (www.avm-mag.com/)
➤ Aircraft Mechanics Fraternal Association (www.amfanational.org/)
➤ National Center for Aerospace & Transportation Technologies (www.ncatt.org/)

For additional career information about aircraft and avionics equipment mechanics and technicians, see the *Occupational Outlook Quarterly* article "Sky-high careers: jobs related to airlines." (www.bls.gov/opub/ooq/2007/summer/art01.pdf).

Automotive Body and Glass Repairers

- **2012 Median Pay** ... $37,680 per year
  $18.12 per hour
- **Entry-Level Education** ... High school diploma or equivalent
- **Work Experience in a Related Occupation** ... None
- **On-the-Job Training** ... Moderate-term on-the-job training
- **Number of Jobs 2012** ... 172,200
- **Job Outlook, 2012–22** ... 13% (As fast as average)
- **Employment Change, 2012–22** ... 22,900

What Automotive Body and Glass Repairers Do

Automotive body and glass repairers restore, refinish, and replace vehicle bodies and frames, windshields, and window glass.

Automotive body and glass repairers must carefully restore cars to given specifications following an accident.

Duties. Automotive body and glass repairers typically do the following:

• Review damage reports, prepare cost estimates, and plan work

• Inspect cars for structural damage

• Remove damaged body parts, including bumpers, fenders, hoods, grilles, and trim

• Realign car frames and chassis to repair structural damage

• Hammer out or patch dents, dimples, and other minor body damage

• Fit, attach, and weld replacement parts into place

• Install, repair, and weatherproof windows and windshields

• Grind, sand, buff, and prime refurbished and repaired surfaces

• Apply new finish to restored body parts

Automotive body and glass repairers can repair most damage from vehicle collisions and make vehicles look and drive like new. Damage may be minor, such as replacing a cracked windshield, or major, such as replacing an entire door panel. After a major collision, the underlying frame of a car can become bent out of shape. Repairers restore the structural integrity of car frames back to manufacturer specifications.

Repair technicians use many tools for their work. To remove damaged parts, such as bumpers and door panels, they use pneumatic tools, metal-cutting guns, and plasma cutters. For major structural repairs, such as aligning the body, they often use heavy-duty hydraulic jacks and hammers. For some work, they use common hand tools, such as metal files, pliers, wrenches, hammers, and screwdrivers.

In some cases, repair technicians do an entire job by themselves. In other cases, especially in large shops, they use an assembly line approach in which they work as a team with each repair technician specializing.

Although repair technicians sometimes prime and paint repaired parts, painting and coating workers generally perform these tasks.

The following are occupational specialties:

Automotive body and related repairers, or *collision repair technicians,* straighten metal panels, remove dents, and replace parts that cannot be fixed. Although they repair all types of vehicles, most work primarily on cars, sport utility vehicles, and small trucks.

Automotive glass installers and repairers remove, repair, and replace broken, cracked, or pitted windshields and window glass. They also weatherproof newly installed windows and windshields with chemical treatments.

Work Environment

Automotive body and glass repairers held about 172,200 jobs in 2012. About 65 percent worked in automotive repair and maintenance shops, 16 percent worked for automobile dealers, and another 12 percent were self-employed.

Collision repair technicians typically work indoors in body shops, which are often noisy. Most shops are well ventilated to disperse dust and paint fumes. Repair technicians sometimes work in awkward and cramped positions, and their work can be physically demanding. Automotive glass installers and repairers often travel to the customer's location to repair damaged windshields and window glass.

Injuries and Illnesses. Automotive body and related repairers have a higher rate of injuries and illnesses than the national average. Technicians commonly suffer minor injuries, such as cuts, burns, and scrapes. Following safety procedures, helps to avoid serious accidents.

Work Schedules. Most repair technicians work full time. When shops have to complete a backlog of work, overtime is common. This often includes repair technicians working evenings and weekends.

How to Become One

Most employers prefer to hire repair technicians who have completed a formal training program in automotive body repair or refinishing. Still, many new repair technicians begin work without formal training. Industry certification is increasingly important.

Education. High school, trade and technical school, and community college programs in collision repair combine hands-on practice

Median Annual Wages, May 2012

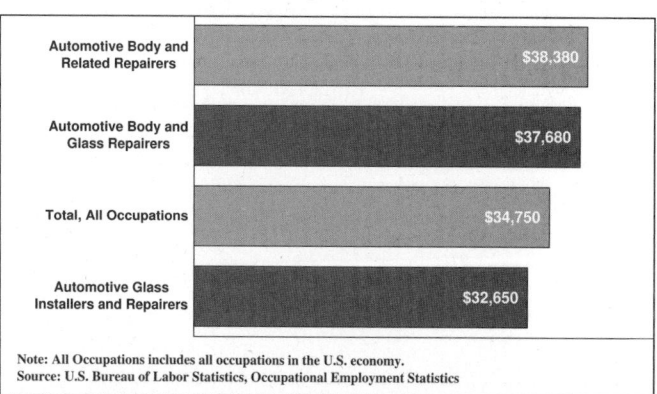

Automotive Body and Related Repairers	$38,380
Automotive Body and Glass Repairers	$37,680
Total, All Occupations	$34,750
Automotive Glass Installers and Repairers	$32,650

Note: All Occupations includes all occupations in the U.S. economy.
Source: U.S. Bureau of Labor Statistics, Occupational Employment Statistics

Percent Change in Employment, Projected 2012–2022

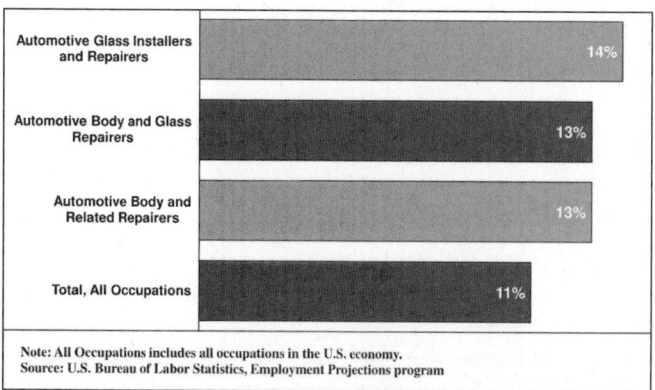

Automotive Glass Installers and Repairers	14%
Automotive Body and Glass Repairers	13%
Automotive Body and Related Repairers	13%
Total, All Occupations	11%

Note: All Occupations includes all occupations in the U.S. economy.
Source: U.S. Bureau of Labor Statistics, Employment Projections program

Employment Projections Data for Automotive Body and Glass Repairers

Occupational title	SOC Code	Employment, 2012	Projected Employment, 2022	Change, 2012–2022	
				Percent	Numeric
Automotive body and glass repairers	—	172,200	195,100	13	22,900
Automotive body and related repairers	49-3021	154,200	174,700	13	20,400
Automotive glass installers and repairers..........................	49-3022	18,000	20,500	14	2,400

Source: U.S. Bureau of Labor Statistics, Employment Projections Program

Note: Data are rounded. **Go to Occupational Information Included in the OOH** *for a discussion of the data in this table.*

and classroom instruction. Topics usually include electronics, physics, and mathematics, which provide a strong educational foundation for a career as a repair technician. Although not required, postsecondary education often provides the best preparation.

Trade and technical school programs typically award certificates after 6 months to 1 year of study. Some community colleges offer 2-year programs in collision repair. Many of these schools also offer certificates for individual courses, so students can take classes part time or as needed.

To keep up with rapidly changing automotive technology, repair technicians need to continue their education and training throughout their careers. Repair technicians are expected to develop their skills by reading technical manuals and by attending classes and seminars. Many employers regularly send workers to advanced training programs.

Licenses, Certifications, and Registrations. Although not required, certification is recommended because it shows competence and usually brings higher pay. In some instances, however, it is required for advancement beyond entry-level work.

Certification from the National Institute for Automotive Service Excellence is a standard credential for repair technicians. Many repair technicians get further certification through the Inter-Industry Conference on Auto Collision Repair.

In addition, many vehicle and paint manufacturers have product certification programs that train repair technicians in specific technologies and repair methods.

Important Qualities

Critical-thinking skills. Repair technicians must be able to evaluate vehicle damage and determine necessary repair strategies for each vehicle they work on. In some cases, they must decide if a vehicle is "totaled," or too damaged to justify the cost of repair.

Customer-service skills. Repair technicians must discuss auto body and glass problems, along with options to fix them, with customers. Because self-employed workers depend on repeat clients for business, they must be courteous, good listeners, and ready to answer customers' questions.

Detail oriented. Repair technicians must pay close attention to detail. Restoring a damaged auto body to its original state requires workers to have a keen eye for even the smallest imperfection.

Dexterity. Many repair technicians' tasks, such as removing door panels, hammering out dents, and using hand tools to install parts, require a steady hand and good hand–eye coordination.

Mechanical skills. Repair technicians must know which diagnostic, hydraulic, pneumatic, and other power equipment and tools are appropriate for certain procedures and repairs. They must be skilled with techniques and methods necessary to repair modern automobiles.

Time-management skills. Repair technicians must be timely in their repairs. For many people, their automobile is their primary mode of transportation.

Training. New workers typically begin their on-the-job training by helping an experienced repair technician with basic tasks. As they gain experience, they move on to more complex work. Some workers may become trained in as little as a 1 year, but generally, workers may need 2 years of hands-on training to become fully certified repair technicians.

Basic automotive glass installation and repair can be learned in as little as 6 months, but becoming fully qualified can take up to 1 year.

Formally educated workers often require significantly less on-the-job training and typically advance to independent work more quickly than those who do not have the same level of education.

Pay

The median annual wage for automotive body and related repairers was $38,380 in May 2012. The median wage is the wage at which half the workers in an occupation earned more than that amount and half earned less. The lowest 10 percent earned less than $22,530, and the top 10 percent earned more than $65,390.

The median annual wage for automotive glass installers and repairers was $32,650 in May 2012. The lowest 10 percent earned less than $20,590, and the top 10 percent earned more than $47,730.

Similar Occupations   This table shows a list of occupations with job duties that are similar to those of automotive body and glass repairers.

Occupations	Entry-level Education	2012 Pay	Projected Job Growth	Average Annual Openings
Automotive Service Technicians and Mechanics	High school diploma or equivalent	$36,610	9%	23,760
Diesel Service Technicians and Mechanics	High school diploma or equivalent	$42,320	9%	7,510
Glaziers	High school diploma or equivalent	$37,610	17%	1,910
Heavy Vehicle and Mobile Equipment Service Technicians	High school diploma or equivalent	$43,979	9%	6,710
Painting and Coating Workers	See "How to Become One"	$33,161	4%	3,280

The majority of repair shops and auto dealers pay repair technicians on an incentive basis. In addition to receiving a guaranteed base salary, employers pay workers a set amount for completing various tasks. Their earnings depend on both the amount of work assigned and how fast they complete it.

Trainees typically earn between 30 percent and 60 percent of skilled workers' pay. They are paid by the hour until they are competent enough to be paid on an incentive basis.

Job Outlook

Employment of automotive body and glass repairers is projected to grow 13 percent from 2012 to 2022, about as fast as the average for all occupations.

The growing number of vehicles in use should increase overall demand for collision repair services during the next decade. In some cases, demand may fluctuate throughout the year due to the seasonality of inclement weather in some regions. For example, the need for repair may be greater during the winter months in areas with snow and ice, because this may increase the chance of accidents. However, overall job growth will be limited because new repair technology allows fewer workers to do more work.

The increasing safety features in cars are likely to reduce demand for automotive body and glass repair work. For example, sensor technology, such as back up and parking assist, may decrease collisions. This, in turn, may lessen the need for replacing car bumpers that might otherwise have been damaged in a collision.

In addition, advances in automotive technology have raised the prices of new and replacement parts. This increases the likelihood that a damaged car is declared "totaled"–where repairing the car costs more than its overall value. This scenario will also likely reduce demand for repair work.

Job Prospects. Job opportunities are projected to be very good for jobseekers with industry certification and formal training in automotive body repair and refinishing and in collision repair. Those without any training or experience will face strong competition for jobs.

The need to replace experienced repair technicians who retire, change occupations, or stop working for other reasons also will provide some job opportunities.

O*NET

➤ Automotive Body and Related Repairers (49-3021.00)
➤ Automotive Glass Installers and Repairers (49-3022.00)

Contacts for More Information

For information about careers in automotive body and glass repair, visit

➤ Accrediting Commission of Career Schools and Colleges (www.accsc.org/)
➤ Automotive Service Association (http://asashop.org/)
➤ Inter-Industry Conference on Auto Collision Repair (www.i-car.com/)
➤ National Automotive Technicians Education Foundation (http://natef.org/)
➤ National Glass Association (www.glass.org)
➤ National Institute for Automotive Service Excellence (www.ase.com/Home.aspx)
➤ Society of Collision Repair Specialists (http://scrs.com/)

Automotive Service Technicians and Mechanics

- **2012 Median Pay** .... $36,610 per year
  $17.60 per hour
- **Entry-Level Education** ... High school diploma or equivalent
- **Work Experience in a Related Occupation**............... None
- **On-the-Job Training** .... Long-term on-the-job training
- **Number of Jobs 2012** 701,100
- **Job Outlook, 2012–22**..................9% (As fast as average)
- **Employment Change, 2012–22** 60,400

What Automotive Service Technicians and Mechanics Do

Automotive service technicians and mechanics, often called service technicians or service techs, inspect, maintain, and repair cars and light trucks.

Duties. Automotive service technicians and mechanics typically do the following:

- Identify mechanical problems, often by using computerized diagnostic equipment
- Test parts and systems to ensure that they are working properly
- Follow checklists to ensure that all critical parts are examined
- Perform basic care and maintenance, including changing oil, giving tuneups, checking fluid levels, and rotating tires
- Repair or replace worn parts, such as brake pads and wheel bearings
- Disassemble and reassemble parts
- Use testing equipment to ensure that repairs and maintenance are effective
- Explain to clients their automotive problems and the repairs done on their vehicles

Service technicians work on traditional mechanical components, such as engines, transmissions, and drive belts. However, they also must be familiar with a growing number of electronic systems. Braking, transmission, and steering systems, for example, are controlled primarily by computers and electronic components.

Other integrated electronic systems, such as accident-avoidance sensors, are becoming common as well. In addition, a growing number of technicians are required to work on vehicles that run on alternative fuels, such as ethanol and electricity.

Service technicians use many different tools, including computerized diagnostic tools and power tools such as pneumatic wrenches, lathes, welding torches, and jacks and hoists. These tools usually are owned by their employers.

Service technicians also use many common handtools, such as sockets and ratchets, wrenches, and pliers. These tools generally are owned by service technicians. In fact, experienced workers often have thousands of dollars invested in their personal tool collection. For example, some invest in their own set of pneumatic tools–tools, such as impact wrenches–powered by compressed air.

Service technicians sometimes specialize in a particular type of repair that may be subject to specific regulations or procedures. For instance, those focused on repairing air-conditioning system must follow federal and state regulations governing the handling, recycling, and disposal of refrigerants.

In some shops, technicians may specialize. The following are examples of types of service technicians:

Automotive air-conditioning repairers install and repair air conditioners and parts, such as compressors, condensers, and controls. They are trained in government regulations related to their work.

Brake repairers adjust brakes, replace brake rotors and pads, and make other repairs on brake systems. Some technicians specialize in both brake and front-end work.

Front-end mechanics align and balance wheels and repair steering mechanisms and suspension systems. They frequently use special alignment equipment and wheel-balancing machines.

Transmission technicians and rebuilders work on gear trains, couplings, hydraulic pumps, and other parts of transmissions. Extensive knowledge of computer controls, the ability to diagnose electrical and hydraulic problems, and other specialized skills are needed to work on these complex components.

Drivability technicians use their extensive knowledge of engine management, emission, fuel, electrical, and ignition systems to diagnose issues that prevent engines from performing efficiently. They often use the onboard diagnostic system of a car and electronic testing equipment such as a multimeter to find where the malfunction may be.

For information about technicians who work on large trucks and buses, see the profile on diesel service technicians and mechanics.

For information about technicians who work on farm equipment, construction vehicles, and railcars, see the profile on heavy vehicle and mobile equipment service technicians.

For information about technicians who repair and service motorcycles, motorboats, and small all-terrain vehicles, see the profile on small engine mechanics.

Work Environment

Automotive service technicians and mechanics held about 701,100 jobs in 2012. Most worked full time for private companies, and about 14 percent were self-employed.

The industries that employed the most automotive service technicians and mechanics in 2012 were as follows:

Automotive repair and maintenance	32%
Automobile dealers	29
Automotive parts, accessories, and tire stores	9
Government	4
Gasoline stations	3

Most service technicians work in well-ventilated and well-lit repair shops. Although automotive problems often can be identified and fixed with computers, technicians frequently work with greasy parts and tools, sometimes in uncomfortable positions.

Automotive service technicians and mechanics perform routine vehicle maintenance as well as major repairs.

Work Schedules. Most service technicians work full time, and many work evenings or weekends. Overtime is common.

Injuries and Illnesses. Automotive service technicians and mechanics have a higher rate of injuries and illnesses than the national average. Service technicians frequently must lift heavy parts and tools. As a result, minor workplace injuries, such as small cuts, sprains, and bruises, are common. However, the work is not generally dangerous if workers follow safety procedures and practices.

How to Become One

A high school diploma or the equivalent is typically the minimum requirement for someone to work as an automotive service technician or mechanic. Because automotive technology is becoming increasingly sophisticated, some employers prefer automotive service technicians and mechanics who have completed a formal training program in a postsecondary institution. Industry certification is usually required once the person is employed.

Education. A high school diploma or the equivalent is typically the minimum requirement for someone to work as an automotive

Median Annual Wages, May 2012

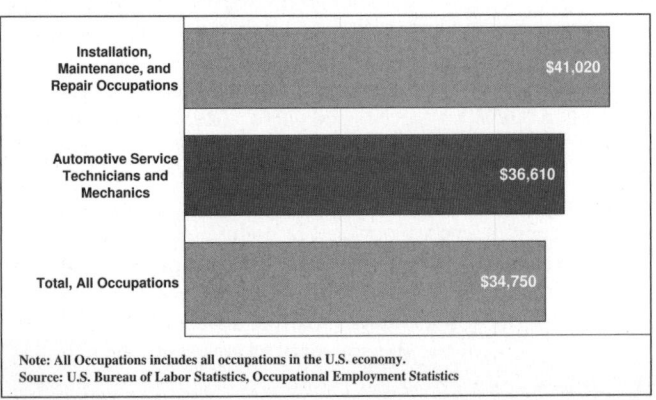

Note: All Occupations includes all occupations in the U.S. economy.
Source: U.S. Bureau of Labor Statistics, Occupational Employment Statistics

Percent Change in Employment, Projected 2012–2022

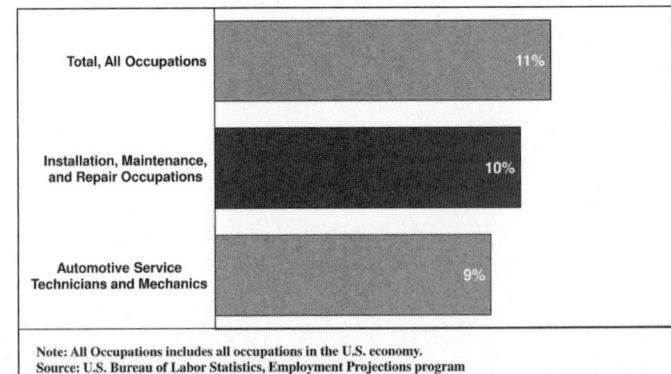

Note: All Occupations includes all occupations in the U.S. economy.
Source: U.S. Bureau of Labor Statistics, Employment Projections program

Employment Projections Data for Automotive Service Technicians and Mechanics

Occupational title	SOC Code	Employment, 2012	Projected Employment, 2022	Change, 2012–2022	
				Percent	Numeric
Automotive service technicians and mechanics........................	49-3023	701,100	761,500	9	60,400

Source: U.S. Bureau of Labor Statistics, Employment Projections Program

Note: Data are rounded. Go to **Occupational Information Included in the OOH** *for a discussion of the data in this table.*

service technician or mechanic. High school courses in automotive repair, electronics, computers, mathematics, and English provide a good background for prospective service technicians. However, high school graduates often need further training to become fully qualified.

Completing a vocational or other postsecondary training program in automotive service technology is considered the best preparation for entry-level positions. Programs usually last 6 months to a year and provide intensive career preparation through classroom instruction and hands-on practice. Short-term certificate programs in a particular skill are also available.

Some service technicians get an associate's degree. Courses usually include basic mathematics, computers, electronics, and automotive repair. Some programs add classes in customer service, English, and other necessary skills.

Various automobile manufacturers and dealers sponsor associate's degree programs. Students in these programs typically spend alternating periods attending classes full time and working full time in service shops under the guidance of an experienced technician.

Training. Most service technicians must complete on-the-job training.

How long it takes a new service technician to become fully qualified in the occupation depends on the person's educational background. A period of 2 to 5 years is typical. It then takes an additional 1 to 2 years of experience for service technicians to become familiar with all types of repairs.

New workers generally start as trainee technicians, technicians' helpers, or lubrication workers and gradually acquire and practice their skills by working with experienced mechanics and technicians.

Licenses, Certifications, and Registrations. The U.S. Environmental Protection Agency (EPA) requires all technicians who buy or work with refrigerants to be licensed in proper refrigerant handling. No formal test preparation is required, but many trade schools, unions, and employer associations offer training programs designed for the EPA exam.

Certification from the National Institute for Automotive Service Excellence is the standard credential for service technicians. Certification demonstrates competence and usually brings higher pay. Many employers require their service technicians to become certified.

Certification is available in eight different areas, including automatic transmission/transaxle, brakes, electrical/electronic systems, engine performance, engine repair, heating and air-conditioning, manual drive train and axles, and suspension and steering.

For each area, technicians must have at least 2 years of experience (or relevant schooling and 1 year of experience) and pass an exam. To become a Master Automobile Technician, technicians must pass all eight exams.

Important Qualities

Customer-service skills. Service technicians must discuss automotive problems–along with options to fix them–with their customers. Because workers may depend on repeat clients for business, they must be courteous, good listeners, and ready to answer customers' questions.

Detail oriented. Mechanical and electronic malfunctions are often due to misalignments or other easy-to-miss causes. Service mechanics must, therefore, account for such details when inspecting or repairing engines and components.

Dexterity. Many tasks that service technicians do, such as disassembling engine parts, connecting or attaching components, and using handtools, require a steady hand and good hand–eye coordination.

Mechanical skills. Service technicians must be familiar with engine components and systems and know how they interact with each other. They often must take apart major parts for repairs and be able to put them back together properly.

Troubleshooting skills. Service technicians must be able to use diagnostic equipment on engine systems and components in order to identify and fix problems in increasingly complicated mechanical and electronic systems. They must be familiar with electronic control systems and the appropriate tools needed to fix and maintain them.

Pay

The median annual wage for automotive service technicians and mechanics was $36,610 in May 2012. The median wage is the wage at which half the workers in an occupation earned more than that amount and half earned less. The lowest 10 percent earned less than $20,810, and the top 10 percent earned more than $60,070.

Similar Occupations   This table shows a list of occupations with job duties that are similar to those of automotive service technicians and mechanics.

Occupations	Entry-level Education	2012 Pay	Projected Job Growth	Average Annual Openings
Automotive Body and Glass Repairers	High school diploma or equivalent	$37,817	13%	5,700
Diesel Service Technicians and Mechanics	High school diploma or equivalent	$42,320	9%	7,510
Heavy Vehicle and Mobile Equipment Service Technicians	High school diploma or equivalent	$43,979	9%	6,710
Small Engine Mechanics	High school diploma or equivalent	$32,679	6%	1,820

In May 2012, the median annual wages for automotive service technicians in the top five industries employing these technicians were as follows:

Government	$47,240
Automobile dealers	41,360
Automotive repair and maintenance	33,230
Automotive parts, accessories, and tire stores	31,250
Gasoline stations	31,090

Many experienced technicians working for automobile dealers and independent repair shops receive a commission related to the labor cost charged to the customer. Under this system, weekly earnings depend on the amount of work completed. Some repair shops may pay technicians a fixed rate on an hourly basis instead.

Job Outlook

Employment of automotive service technicians and mechanics is projected to grow 9 percent from 2012 to 2022, about as fast as the average for all occupations.

As the number of vehicles in use continues to rise, more entry-level service technicians will be needed to do basic maintenance and repair, such as replacing brake pads and changing oil. The increasing lifespan of late-model cars and light trucks will further increase demand for qualified workers.

Job Prospects. With some employers reporting difficulty finding workers with the right skills and education, job opportunities for qualified applicants should be very good. Jobseekers who have completed formal postsecondary training programs–especially candidates with training in advanced automotive technology, such as hybrid fuel or computer systems–should enjoy the best job prospects.

Those without formal automotive training are likely to face strong competition for entry-level jobs.

More numerous openings will be in automobile dealerships and independent repair shops, where most service technicians currently work.

O*NET

➤ Automotive Service Technicians and Mechanics (49-3023.00)
➤ Automotive Master Mechanics (49-3023.01)
➤ Automotive Specialty Technicians (49-3023.02)

Contacts for More Information

For more details about work opportunities, contact local automobile dealers and repair shops or local offices of the state employment service. The state employment service also may have information about training programs.

For information about careers, education, and training programs, visit

➤ Accrediting Commission of Career Schools and Colleges (www. accsc.org/)
➤ Automotive Youth Educational Systems (www.ayes.org/)
➤ National Automotive Technicians Education Foundation (www. natef.org/)

For information about certification, visit

➤ National Institute for Automotive Service Excellence (www.ase. com/)

Computer, ATM, and Office Machine Repairers

- **2012 Median Pay** .... $36,620 per year
  $17.60 per hour
- **Entry-Level Education** ....Some college, no degree
- **Work Experience in a Related Occupation**.............. None
- **On-the-Job Training** .... None
- **Number of Jobs 2012** 133,100
- **Job Outlook, 2012–22** .... 4% (Slower than average)
- **Employment Change, 2012–22** 5,100

What Computer, ATM, and Office Machine Repairers Do

Computer, ATM, and office machine repairers install, fix, and maintain many of the machines that businesses, households, and other consumers use.

Duties. Computer, ATM, and office machine repairers typically do the following:

- Travel to customers' locations in response to service requests
- Communicate with customers to determine the source of a problem
- Perform administrative tasks, such as completing work order forms
- Use a variety of tools, such as a multimeter, to help diagnose problems
- Replace malfunctioning machine parts, such as video cards in desktop computers or keypads on ATM machines
- Install large equipment, such as mainframe computers or ATMs
- Test newly installed systems to make sure they work properly
- Explain the basic functions of machines and equipment to customers
- Provide preventive maintenance, such as cleaning the internal parts of machines

Computer, ATM, and office machine repairers replace malfunctioning machine parts, such as video cards in desktop computers or keypads on ATM machines.

Median Annual Wages, May 2012

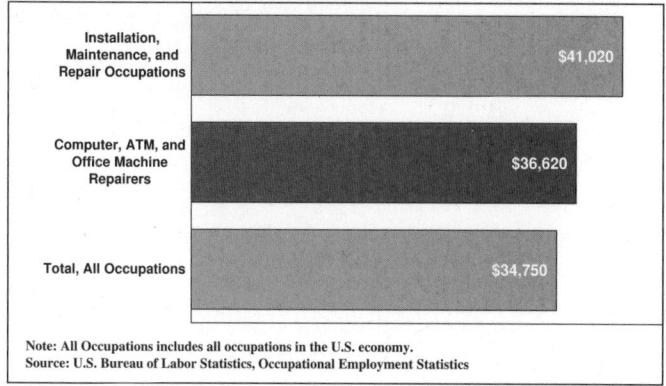

Note: All Occupations includes all occupations in the U.S. economy.
Source: U.S. Bureau of Labor Statistics, Occupational Employment Statistics

Percent Change in Employment, Projected 2012–2022

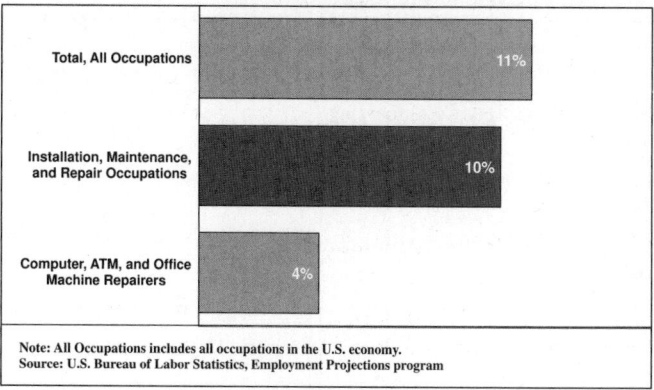

Note: All Occupations includes all occupations in the U.S. economy.
Source: U.S. Bureau of Labor Statistics, Employment Projections program

In most cases, machines do not break down entirely. Often just one broken part can keep a machine from working properly. Repairers fix machines by replacing these parts and other defective equipment because it is often less expensive than replacing the entire machine. They work with a number of advanced diagnostic tools and techniques, and use technology to test various processes and evaluate results. For example, they may remotely access a computer to run diagnostic tests.

Although the work of computer, ATM, and office machine repairers is very similar, the exact tasks differ depending on the type of equipment. For example, computer repairers replace desktop parts, such as a motherboard, in case of hardware failure. ATM repairers may replace a worn magnetic head on a card reader to allow an ATM to recognize customers' bank cards. Office machine repairers replace parts of office machines that break down from general wear and tear, such as the printheads of inkjet printers.

Some repairers have assigned areas where they do preventive maintenance on a regular basis.

Computer repairers service and repair computer parts, network connections, and computer equipment, such as an external hard drive or computer monitor. Computer repairers must be familiar with various operating systems and commonly used software packages. Some work from repair shops, while others travel to customers' locations.

ATM repairers install and repair automated teller machines and, increasingly, electronic kiosks. They generally work with a network of ATMs and travel to ATM locations when they are alerted to a malfunction.

Office machine repairers fix machinery at customers' workplaces because these machines are usually large and stationary, such as office printers or copiers. Office machines often need preventive maintenance, such as cleaning, or replacement of commonly used parts as they break down from general wear and tear.

Work Environment

Computer, ATM, and office machine repairers held about 133,100 jobs in 2012. They mostly worked for private businesses, but about 14 percent were self-employed.

Computer and office machine repairers work in air-conditioned and well-ventilated offices because computers and office machines are sensitive to extreme temperatures and humidity.

ATM repairers work in various environments depending on the location of an ATM. Some ATMs are outdoors, while others are indoors, such as in lobbies of buildings.

Some repairers, called *field technicians*, work onsite and have to travel to various locations to install, maintain, or repair a customer's equipment. Other repairers, called *bench technicians*, work in repair shops. In smaller companies, repairers may work both in repair shops and at customers' locations. Some companies provide only onsite repair and operate without a traditional shop.

In the course of fixing machinery, repairers often must lift equipment and work in a variety of postures, although it is not usually strenuous.

Work Schedules. Most computer, ATM, and office machine repairers work full time. Some occasionally work evenings, weekends, and holidays to maintain machines that may break down.

How to Become One

Knowledge of electronics is essential for computer, ATM, and office machine repairers. Most workers take some postsecondary classes, although some who can demonstrate knowledge may be hired with a high school diploma. Strong communication and customer-service skills are important because these workers often interact with customers to figure out what needs to be repaired.

Education. Most computer, ATM, and office machine repairers take some classes after high school. This is especially important for ATM repairers who work on complex machines. Prospective workers may take postsecondary classes in computers and electronics, network hardware configuration, electrical engineering, machine repair, or computer/digital technology.

Employment Projections Data for Computer, ATM, and Office Machine Repairers

Occupational title	SOC Code	Employment, 2012	Projected Employment, 2022	Change, 2012–2022	
				Percent	Numeric
Computer, automated teller, and office machine repairers	49-2011	133,100	138,200	4	5,100

Source: U.S. Bureau of Labor Statistics, Employment Projections Program

Note: *Data are rounded. Go to* **Occupational Information Included in the OOH** *for a discussion of the data in this table.*

Similar Occupations   This table shows a list of occupations with job duties that are similar to those of computer, ATM, and office machine repairers.

Occupations	Entry-level Education	2012 Pay	Projected Job Growth	Average Annual Openings
Broadcast and Sound Engineering Technicians	See "How to Become One"	$41,232	9%	3,250
Electrical and Electronics Engineering Technicians	Associate's degree	$57,850	0%	3,040
Electrical and Electronics Installers and Repairers	Postsecondary non-degree award	$51,081	1%	2,980
Electricians	High school diploma or equivalent	$49,840	20%	22,460
General Maintenance and Repair Workers	High school diploma or equivalent	$35,210	9%	37,970

In these classes students learn how to troubleshoot major issues, such as discovering which part is causing a machine to malfunction. A basic understanding of mechanical equipment is important because many of the parts that fail in office machines and ATMs, such as paper loaders, are mechanical. Those who do not take college classes may gain this knowledge though military training or high school vocational classes.

Training. Repairers typically have some experience with electronics before they are hired. However, because the tools they use vary by specialty, repairers usually get some company-specific training on the job to become familiar with diagnostic tools, such as proprietary software. As new tools and technology become available, repairers will typically attend classes that teach how to use and apply these tools.

In some cases, entry-level repairers with limited knowledge and experience will get on-the-job training from more experienced mentors. Newly hired repairers may work on problems that are less complex, such as doing preventive maintenance on machines. However, with experience, they can advance to positions where they maintain more sophisticated systems.

Licenses, Certifications, and Registrations. Various organizations offer certification for computer, ATM, and office machine repairers. For example, the Electronics Technicians Association International (ETA) offers more than 80 certification programs in numerous electronics specialties for varying levels of competence. Certification from equipment manufacturers is also available.

To become certified, applicants must meet several prerequisites and pass a comprehensive written or online exam. Certifications show a level of competency, and they can make an applicant more attractive to employers or increase an employee's opportunity for advancement.

Advancement. Over time, repairers become experts in their specialty and may train entry-level repairers. They may also move into management positions where they supervise other repairers.

Important Qualities

Analytical skills. Repairers often face problems with no standard solution. They must use logic, reasoning, and their experience to evaluate different possible solutions.

Communication skills. Repairers must be able to communicate effectively with customers because they work closely with customers to understand the problems with a machine.

Dexterity. Repairers must be able to make precise, coordinated movements with their fingers or hands to grasp, manipulate, or assemble objects.

Troubleshooting skills. Workers find, diagnose, and repair problems. They devise methods to run tests to determine the cause of problems. They solve the problem to repair the equipment.

Pay

The median annual wage for computer, ATM, and office machine repairers was $36,620 in May 2012. The median wage is the wage at which half the workers in an occupation earned more than that amount and half earned less. The lowest 10 percent earned less than $22,490, and the top 10 percent earned more than $57,960.

Job Outlook

Employment of computer, ATM, and office machine repairers is projected to grow 4 percent from 2012 to 2022, slower than the average for all occupations. Remote diagnostic software will result in repairers becoming more productive, limiting overall employment growth. For example, when repairers are able to diagnose and troubleshoot problems remotely, the need for on-site service calls decreases.

In some cases, replacing computers or other office equipment will be more cost-effective than having them repaired. However, office machine repairers will continue to see demand for their services as costly office equipment, such as high-volume printers, continue to break down and need preventive maintenance.

Computer repairers will see continued demand for their services as computer parts need replacing or organizations need hardware upgrades. As companies modernize and use advanced technology in their day-to-day operations, computer repairers will continue to see employment opportunities.

However, increasing use of electronic banking is causing a decline in the demand for new ATMs, which may result in a decreased need for ATM repairers.

Job Prospects. Job opportunities will be best for workers with training or experience in electronics.

O*NET

➤ Computer, Automated Teller, and Office Machine Repairers (49-2011.00)

Contacts for More Information

For more information about careers in computer repair, visit
➤ Association of Computer Repair Business Owners (www.acrbo.com/)

For more information about electronic careers and certification, visit
➤ Electronics Technician Association International (http://eta-i.org/)

Diesel Service Technicians and Mechanics

- **2012 Median Pay** .... $42,320 per year
  $20.35 per hour
- **Entry-Level Education** ... High school diploma or equivalent
- **Work Experience in a Related Occupation**............... None
- **On-the-Job Training** .... Long-term on-the-job training
- **Number of Jobs 2012** 250,800
- **Job Outlook, 2012–22** .... 9% (As fast as average)
- **Employment Change, 2012–22** 21,600

What Diesel Service Technicians and Mechanics Do

Diesel service technicians and mechanics inspect, repair, or overhaul buses, trucks, and anything else with a diesel engine.

Duties. Diesel service technicians and mechanics typically do the following:

- Follow a checklist of inspection procedures
- Test drive vehicles to diagnose malfunctions
- Read and interpret diagnostic test results from diagnostic equipment such as an oscilloscope, which is used to measure the voltage produced by electronic components
- Raise trucks, buses, and heavy parts or equipment by using hydraulic jacks or hoists
- Inspect brake systems, steering mechanisms, transmissions, engines, and other parts of vehicles
- Do routine maintenance, such as changing oil, checking batteries, and lubricating equipment and parts
- Adjust and align wheels, tighten bolts and screws, and attach system components
- Repair or replace malfunctioning components, parts, and other mechanical or electrical equipment
- Test-drive vehicles to ensure that they run smoothly

Because of their efficiency and durability, diesel engines have become the standard in powering our nation's trucks and buses. Other heavy vehicles and mobile equipment, including bulldozers and cranes, also are powered by diesel engines, as are many commercial boats, passenger vehicles, pickups, and other work trucks. Diesel service technicians who service and repair these engines are commonly known as *diesel mechanics*.

Diesel service technicians and mechanics repair large trucks to keep them running smoothly.

Diesel mechanics handle many kinds of repairs. They may work on a vehicle's electrical system, make major engine repairs, or retrofit exhaust systems with emission control systems to comply with pollution regulations.

Diesel engine maintenance and repair is becoming more complex as engines and other components use more electronic systems to control their operation. For example, fuel injection and engine timing systems rely heavily on microprocessors to maximize fuel efficiency and minimize harmful emissions. In most shops, workers often use hand-held or laptop computers to diagnose problems and adjust engine functions.

In addition to using computerized diagnostic equipment, diesel mechanics use a variety of power and machine tools, such as pneumatic wrenches, lathes, grinding machines, and welding equipment. Hand tools, including pliers, socket and ratchets, and screwdrivers, are commonly used.

Employers typically provide expensive power tools and computerized equipment, but workers generally acquire their own hand tools over time.

For information on technicians and mechanics who work primarily on automobiles, see the profile on automotive service technicians and mechanics.

For information on technicians and mechanics who work primarily on farm equipment, construction vehicles, and rail cars, see the profile on heavy vehicle and mobile equipment service technicians.

Median Annual Wages, May 2012

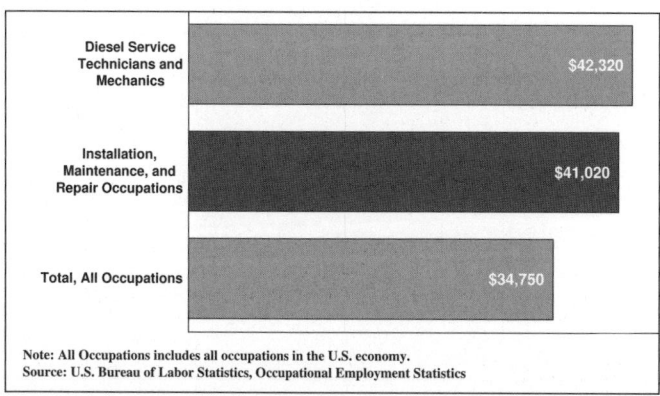

Diesel Service Technicians and Mechanics	$42,320
Installation, Maintenance, and Repair Occupations	$41,020
Total, All Occupations	$34,750

Note: All Occupations includes all occupations in the U.S. economy.
Source: U.S. Bureau of Labor Statistics, Occupational Employment Statistics

Percent Change in Employment, Projected 2012–2022

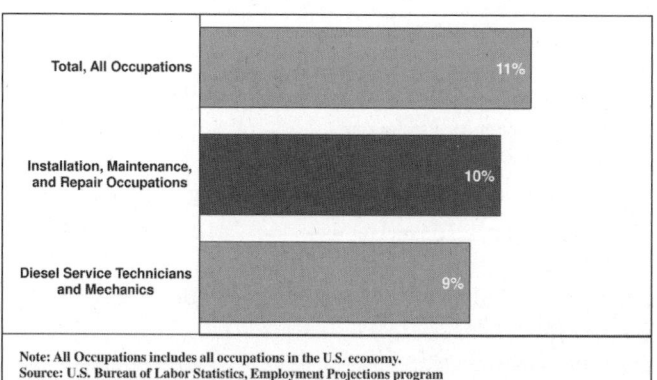

Total, All Occupations	11%
Installation, Maintenance, and Repair Occupations	10%
Diesel Service Technicians and Mechanics	9%

Note: All Occupations includes all occupations in the U.S. economy.
Source: U.S. Bureau of Labor Statistics, Employment Projections program

Employment Projections Data for Diesel Service Technicians and Mechanics

Occupational title	SOC Code	Employment, 2012	Projected Employment, 2022	Change, 2012–2022	
				Percent	Numeric
Bus and truck mechanics and diesel engine specialists 49-3031		250,800	272,500	9	21,600

Source: U.S. Bureau of Labor Statistics, Employment Projections Program

Note: Data are rounded. Go to **Occupational Information Included in the OOH** *for a discussion of the data in this table.*

For information on technicians and mechanics who work primarily on motorboats, motorcycles, and small all-terrain vehicles, see the profile on small engine mechanics.

Work Environment

Diesel service technicians and mechanics held about 250,800 jobs in 2012. The majority worked for private companies, but about 10 percent worked for the government.

The industries that employed the most diesel service technicians and mechanics in 2012 were as follows:

Truck transportation..18%
Government..10
Repair and maintenance 9
Motor vehicle and motor vehicle parts and supplies
    merchant wholesalers 8
Manufacturing...5

Diesel mechanics usually work in well-ventilated and sometimes noisy repair shops. They occasionally repair vehicles on roadsides or at worksites.

Injuries and Illnesses. Diesel service technicians and mechanics have a higher rate of injuries and illnesses than the national average. Diesel mechanics often lift heavy parts and tools, handle greasy or dirty equipment, and work in uncomfortable positions. Although cuts or burns are common, the work is generally not hazardous when workers follow basic safety precautions.

Work Schedules. Most diesel mechanics work full time. Overtime is common as many repair shops extend their service hours during evenings and weekends. In addition, some truck and bus repair shops provide 24-hour maintenance and repair services.

How to Become One

Many diesel mechanics learn informally on the job, but employers increasingly prefer applicants who have completed postsecondary training programs in diesel engine repair. Although not required, industry certification can be important for diesel mechanics.

Education. Most employers require a high school diploma or equivalent. High school or postsecondary courses in automotive repair, electronics, and mathematics provide a strong educational background for a career as a diesel mechanic.

Many employers look for workers with postsecondary training in diesel engine repair. A large number of community colleges and trade and vocational schools offer programs in diesel engine repair that may lead to a certificate of completion or an associate's degree.

Programs mix classroom instruction with hands-on training, including the basics of diesel technology, repair techniques and equipment, and practical exercises. Students also learn how to interpret technical manuals and electronic diagnostic reports.

Graduates usually advance to journeyworker status, where they may then work with minimal supervision.

Training. Some diesel mechanics begin working without postsecondary education and are trained on the job. Trainees are assigned basic tasks, such as cleaning parts, checking fuel and oil levels, and driving vehicles in and out of the shop.

After they learn routine maintenance and repair tasks and demonstrate competence, trainees move on to more complicated jobs. This process can last from 3 to 4 years, at which point a trainee is usually considered a journey-level diesel mechanic.

Over the course of their careers, diesel mechanics must learn new techniques and learn about new equipment. Employers often send experienced mechanics to special training classes conducted by manufacturers and vendors to learn about the latest diesel technology.

Licenses, Certifications, and Registrations. Certification from the National Institute for Automotive Service Excellence (ASE) is the recognized industry credential for diesel and other automotive service technicians and mechanics. Although not required, this certification represents a diesel mechanic's competence, experience, and value to potential employers and clients.

Diesel mechanics may be certified in specific repair areas, such as drive trains, electronic systems, or preventative maintenance and inspection. To earn certification, mechanics must have 2 years of work experience and pass one or more ASE exams. To remain certified, diesel mechanics must pass the test again every 5 years.

Some diesel mechanics may be required to have a commercial driver's license if their job duties include test-driving buses or large trucks.

Similar Occupations This table shows a list of occupations with job duties that are similar to those of diesel service technicians and mechanics.

Occupations	Entry-level Education	2012 Pay	Projected Job Growth	Average Annual Openings
Aircraft and Avionics Equipment Mechanics and Technicians	See "How to Become One"	$55,227	3%	3,960
Automotive Body and Glass Repairers	High school diploma or equivalent	$37,817	13%	5,700
Automotive Service Technicians and Mechanics	High school diploma or equivalent	$36,610	9%	23,760
Heavy Vehicle and Mobile Equipment Service Technicians	High school diploma or equivalent	$43,979	9%	6,710
Small Engine Mechanics	High school diploma or equivalent	$32,679	6%	1,820

Important Qualities

Customer-service skills. Diesel mechanics frequently talk to their customers about automotive problems and work that they have planned, started, or completed. They must be courteous, good listeners and ready to answer customers' questions.

Dexterity. Mechanics need a steady hand and good hand-eye coordination for many tasks, such as disassembling engine parts, connecting or attaching components, or using hand tools.

Mechanical skills. Diesel mechanics must be familiar with parts and components of engines, transmissions, braking mechanisms, and other complex systems. They must also be able to disassemble, work on, and reassemble parts and machinery.

Troubleshooting skills. Diesel mechanics must be able to identify mechanical and electronic problems, make repairs, and offer a proper maintenance strategy. They must be familiar with electronic control systems and the appropriate tools needed to fix and maintain them.

Pay

The median annual wage for diesel service technicians and mechanics was $42,320 in May 2012. The median wage is the wage at which half the workers in an occupation earned more than that amount and half earned less. The lowest 10 percent earned less than $26,820, and the top 10 percent earned more than $63,250.

In May 2012, the median annual wages for diesel service technicians and mechanics in the top five industries in which these technicians and mechanics worked were as follows:

Government... $49,130
Motor vehicle and motor vehicle parts and
   supplies merchant wholesalers 42,950
Manufacturing... 42,160
Repair and maintenance 38,880
Truck transportation... 38,250

Many diesel mechanics, especially those employed by truck fleet dealers and repair shops, receive a commission in addition to their base salary.

Job Outlook

Employment of diesel service technicians and mechanics is projected to grow 9 percent from 2012 to 2022, about as fast as the average for all occupations.

As more freight is shipped across the country, additional diesel-powered trucks will be needed. As a result, diesel mechanics will be needed to maintain and repair the nation's truck fleet. Demand for new workers in the freight trucking and automotive repair and maintenance industries is expected to drive overall diesel mechanic job growth.

Some older vehicles will need to be retrofitted and modernized to comply with environmental regulations, creating additional jobs for diesel mechanics.

Overall employment growth, however, may be dampened due to increasing durability of new truck and bus diesel engines. Also, continuing advances in repair technology, including computerized diagnostic equipment, will result in fewer mechanics doing the same amount of work, further reducing demand for mechanics.

Job Prospects. Job opportunities should be good for those who have completed formal postsecondary education and have strong technical skills, as employers sometimes report difficulty finding qualified workers.

Workers without formal training often require more supervision and on-the-job instruction than others–an expensive and time-consuming process for employers. Because of this, untrained candidates will face strong competition for jobs.

O*NET

➤ Bus and Truck Mechanics and Diesel Engine Specialists (49-3031.00)

Contacts for More Information

For more information about careers and education for diesel service technicians and mechanics, visit
➤ Association of Diesel Specialists (www.diesel.org/)
➤ National Automotive Technicians Education Foundation (www. natef.org/)
   For information about certification, visit
➤ National Institute for Automotive Service Excellence (www.ase. com/)

Electrical and Electronics Installers and Repairers

- **2012 Median Pay** .... $51,220 per year
  $24.63 per hour
- **Entry-Level Education** .... Postsecondary non-degree award
- **Work Experience in a Related Occupation**............... None
- **On-the-Job Training** ....See "How to Become One"
- **Number of Jobs 2012** 144,700
- **Job Outlook, 2012–22** .... 1% (Little or no change)
- **Employment Change, 2012–22** 900

What Electrical and Electronics Installers and Repairers Do

Electrical and electronics installers and repairers install, repair, or replace a variety of electrical equipment in telecommunications, transportation, utilities, and other industries.

Duties. Electrical and electronics installers and repairers typically do the following:

- Prepare cost estimates for clients
- Refer to service guides, schematics, and manufacturer specifications
- Repair or replace defective parts, such as motors, fuses, or gaskets
- Reassemble and test equipment after repairs
- Maintain records of parts used, labor time, and final charges

Electrical and electronics installers and repairers work on complex pieces of electronic equipment.

Because automated electronic control systems are becoming more complex, repairers use software programs and testing equipment to diagnose malfunctions. Among their diagnostic tools are multimeters–which measure voltage, current, and resistance–and advanced multimeters, which measure the capacitance, inductance, and current gain of transistors.

Repairers also use signal generators, which provide test signals, and oscilloscopes, which display signals graphically. In addition, repairers often use handtools such as pliers, screwdrivers, and wrenches to replace faulty parts and adjust equipment.

The following are examples of types of electrical and electronics installers and repairers:

Commercial and industrial equipment electrical and electronics repairers repair, test, adjust, or install electronic equipment, such as industrial controls, transmitters, and antennas.

Electrical and electronics installers and repairers of transportation equipment install, adjust, or maintain mobile communication equipment, including sound, sonar, security, navigation, and surveillance systems on trains, watercraft, or other vehicles.

Powerhouse, substation, and relay electrical and electronics repairers inspect, test, maintain, or repair electrical equipment used in generating stations, substations, and in-service relays. These workers also may be known as *powerhouse electricians, relay technicians,* or *power transformer repairers.*

Electric motor, power tool, and related repairers–such as *armature winders, generator mechanics,* and *electric golf cart repairers*–specialize in installing, maintaining, and repairing electric motors, wiring, or switches.

Electronic equipment installers and repairers of motor vehicles install, diagnose, and repair sound, security, and navigation equipment in motor vehicles. These installers and repairers work with a range of complex electronic equipment, including digital audio and video players, navigation systems, and passive and active security systems.

Electrical and electronics installers and repairers may also specialize, according to how and where they work:

Field technicians often travel to factories or a customer's site to repair broken down equipment. Because repairing components is a complex activity, workers in factories usually remove and replace defective units, such as circuit boards, instead of fixing them. Defective units are discarded or returned to the manufacturer or a specialized shop for repair.

Bench technicians work in repair shops in factories and service centers, fixing components that cannot be repaired on a factory floor. These workers also locate and repair circuit defects, such as poorly soldered joints, blown fuses, or malfunctioning transistors.

Work Environment

Electrical and electronics installers and repairers held about 144,700 jobs in 2012. Employment in the detailed occupations that make up this group was distributed as follows:

Electrical and electronics repairers, commercial
  and industrial equipment 69,000
Electrical and electronics repairers, powerhouse,
  substation, and relay 24,500
Electric motor, power tool, and related repairers 20,700
Electrical and electronics installers and repairers,
  transportation equipment................................. 15,900
Electronic equipment installers and repairers,
  motor vehicles 14,600

Many electrical and electronics installers and repairers work in factories, which can be noisy and sometimes warm. Bench technicians work primarily in repair shops, which are quiet and well lit. Motor vehicle electronic equipment installers and repairers normally work in repair shops.

Motor vehicle electronic equipment installers and repairers normally work indoors in well-ventilated and well-lighted repair shops.

Installers and repairers may have to lift heavy equipment and work in awkward positions.

Injuries and Illnesses. Electric motor, power tools, and related repairers and electrical and electronics installers and repairers of transportation equipment have a higher rate of injuries and illnesses than the national average.

As a result, workers must follow safety guidelines and wear protective goggles and hardhats. When working on ladders or on elevated equipment, repairers must wear harnesses to avoid falls.

Before repairing a piece of machinery, workers must follow procedures to ensure that others cannot start the equipment during the repair process. They must also take precautions against electric shock by locking off power to the unit under repair.

Work Schedules. Nearly all electrical and electronics installers and repairers work full time.

How to Become One

Most electrical and electronics installers and repairers obtain specialized training at a technical college. Gaining voluntary certification is common and can be useful in getting a job.

Education. Electrical and electronics installers and repairers must understand electrical equipment and electronics. As a result, employers often prefer applicants who have taken courses in electronics at a community college or technical school.

Median Annual Wages, May 2012

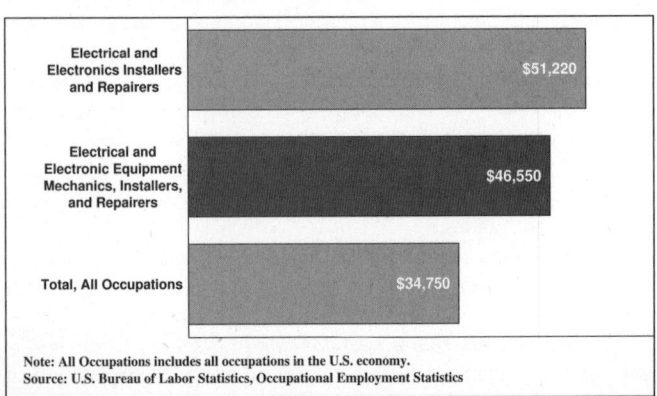

Electrical and Electronics Installers and Repairers	$51,220
Electrical and Electronic Equipment Mechanics, Installers, and Repairers	$46,550
Total, All Occupations	$34,750

Note: All Occupations includes all occupations in the U.S. economy.
Source: U.S. Bureau of Labor Statistics, Occupational Employment Statistics

Percent Change in Employment, Projected 2012–2022

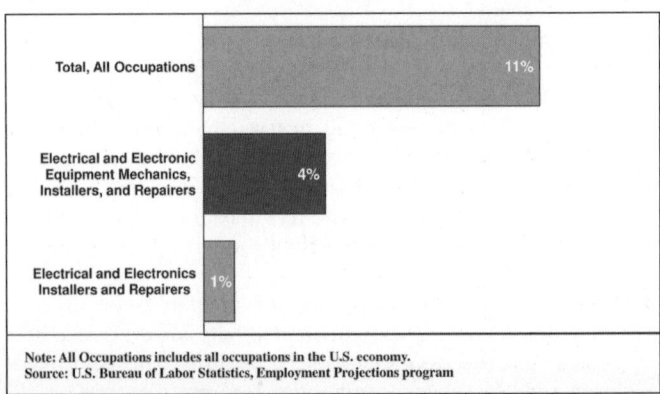

Total, All Occupations	11%
Electrical and Electronic Equipment Mechanics, Installers, and Repairers	4%
Electrical and Electronics Installers and Repairers	1%

Note: All Occupations includes all occupations in the U.S. economy.
Source: U.S. Bureau of Labor Statistics, Employment Projections program

Employment Projections Data for Electrical and Electronics Installers and Repairers

Occupational title	SOC Code	Employment, 2012	Projected Employment, 2022	Change, 2012–2022	
				Percent	Numeric
Electrical and electronics installers and repairers	—	144,700	145,600	1	900
Electric motor, power tool, and related repairers	49-2092	20,700	19,900	-4	-800
Electrical and electronics installers and repairers, transportation equipment	49-2093	15,900	16,200	2	400
Electrical and electronics repairers, commercial and industrial equipment	49-2094	69,000	71,300	3	2,300
Electrical and electronics repairers, powerhouse, substation, and relay	49-2095	24,500	24,500	0	-100
Electronic equipment installers and repairers, motor vehicles	49-2096	14,600	13,700	-6	-900

Source: U.S. Bureau of Labor Statistics, Employment Projections Program

Note: Data are rounded. Go to Occupational Information Included in the OOH for a discussion of the data in this table.

Training. In addition to technical education, workers usually receive training on specific types of equipment. This may entail manufacturer-specific training in order for repairers to perform warranty work.

Entry-level repairers usually begin by working with experienced technicians, who provide technical guidance, and work independently after developing their skills.

Licenses, Certifications, and Registrations. Various organizations offer certification. For example, the Electronics Technicians Association International (ETA) offers more than 50 certification programs in numerous electronics specialties for various levels of competence. The International Society of Certified Electronics Technicians (ISCET) also offers certification for several levels of competence. The ISCET focuses on a broad range of topics, including basic electronics, electronic systems, and appliance service. To become certified, applicants must meet prerequisites and pass a comprehensive exam.

Important Qualities

Color vision. Workers need to identify the color-coded components that are often used in electronic equipment.

Communication skills. Field technicians work closely with customers, so they must listen to and understand customers' problems and explain solutions in a simple, clear manner.

Technical skills. Workers use a variety of mechanical and diagnostic tools to install or repair equipment.

Troubleshooting skills. Electrical equipment and systems often involve intricate parts. Workers must be able to identify malfunctions and make the necessary repairs.

Pay

The median annual wage for electrical and electronics installers and repairers was $51,220 in May 2012. The median wage is the wage at which half the workers in an occupation earned more than that amount and half earned less. The lowest 10 percent earned less than $28,240, and the top 10 percent earned more than $75,740.

Median annual wages for electrical and electronics installers and repairers in May 2012 were as follows:

$68,810 for electrical and electronics repairers, powerhouse, substation, and relay

$52,650 for electrical and electronics repairers, commercial and industrial equipment

$51,240 for electrical and electronics installers and repairers, transportation equipment

$36,240 for electric motor, power tool, and related repairers

$31,340 for electronic equipment installers and repairers, motor vehicles

Union Membership. Compared with workers in all occupations, electrical and electronics installers and repairers had a higher percentage of workers who belonged to a union in 2012.

Job Outlook

Overall employment of electrical and electronics installers and repairers is projected to show little or no change from 2012 to 2022. Growth rates will vary by specialty.

Employment of electrical and electronics installers and repairers of commercial and industrial equipment is projected to grow 3 percent from 2012 to 2022, slower than the average for all occu-

Similar Occupations   This table shows a list of occupations with job duties that are similar to those of electrical and electronics installers and repairers.

Occupations	Entry-level Education	2012 Pay	Projected Job Growth	Average Annual Openings
Aircraft and Avionics Equipment Mechanics and Technicians	See "How to Become One"	$55,227	3%	3,960
Broadcast and Sound Engineering Technicians	See "How to Become One"	$41,232	9%	3,250
Computer, ATM, and Office Machine Repairers	Some college, no degree	$36,620	4%	3,280
Electricians	High school diploma or equivalent	$49,840	20%	22,460
Elevator Installers and Repairers	High school diploma or equivalent	$76,650	24%	800
General Maintenance and Repair Workers	High school diploma or equivalent	$35,210	9%	37,970

pations. As competition increases, businesses strive to lower costs by increasing and improving automation. Equipment that needs service and repair would generally increase the demand for electrical workers, but improved reliability of equipment is expected to temper employment growth.

Employment of motor vehicle electronic equipment installers and repairers is projected to decline 6 percent from 2012 to 2022. As motor vehicle manufacturers install more and better sound, security, entertainment, and navigation systems in new vehicles, and as newer electronic systems require progressively less maintenance, few aftermarket installers will be needed.

Employment of electric motor, power tool, and related repairers is projected to decline 4 percent from 2012 to 2022. Improvements in electrical and electronic equipment design, as well as the increased use of disposable tool parts, will result in declining employment.

Employment of electrical and electronics installers and repairers of transportation equipment is projected to show little or no change from 2012 to 2022. Declining employment in the rail transportation industry–the largest employing segment of these specialists–will dampen employment growth.

Employment of powerhouse, substation, and relay electrical and electronics installers and repairers is projected to show little or no change from 2012 to 2022. Although the installation of new, energy-efficient technologies will likely spur demand for workers, privatization in the utilities industries should improve productivity and offset any employment gains.

Job Prospects. Overall job opportunities should be excellent for qualified workers with an associate's degree in electronics along with certification.

O*NET

➤ Electric Motor, Power Tool, and Related Repairers (49-2092.00)
➤ Electrical and Electronics Installers and Repairers, Transportation Equipment (49-2093.00)
➤ Electrical and Electronics Repairers, Commercial and Industrial Equipment (49-2094.00)
➤ Electrical and Electronics Repairers, Powerhouse, Substation, and Relay (49-2095.00)
➤ Electronic Equipment Installers and Repairers, Motor Vehicles (49-2096.00)

Contacts for More Information

For information about electrical and electronics installers and repairers, including careers and certification, visit
➤ Electronics Technicians Association International (http://eta-i.org/)
➤ International Society of Certified Electronics Technicians (www.iscet.org)

General Maintenance and Repair Workers

- **2012 Median Pay** .... $35,210 per year
  $16.93 per hour
- **Entry-Level Education** ... High school diploma or equivalent
- **Work Experience in a Related Occupation** .... None
- **On-the-Job Training** .... Long-term on-the-job training
- **Number of Jobs 2012** 1,325,100
- **Job Outlook, 2012–22** .... 9% (As fast as average)
- **Employment Change, 2012–22** 125,200

What General Maintenance and Repair Workers Do

General maintenance and repair workers fix and maintain machines, mechanical equipment, and buildings. They work on plumbing, electrical, and air-conditioning and heating systems.

Duties. General maintenance and repair workers typically do the following:

- Maintain and repair machines, mechanical equipment, and buildings
- Troubleshoot and fix faulty electrical switches
- Inspect and diagnose problems and figure out the best way to correct them
- Do routine preventive maintenance to ensure that machines continue to run smoothly
- Assemble and set up machinery or equipment
- Plan repair work using blueprints or diagrams
- Do general cleaning and upkeep of buildings and properties
- Order supplies from catalogs and storerooms
- Meet with clients to estimate repairs and costs
- Keep detailed records of their work

General maintenance and repair workers are hired for maintenance and repair tasks that are not complex enough to need the specialized training of a licensed tradesperson, such as a plumber or electrician.

They are also responsible for recognizing when a job is above their skill level and requires the expertise of electricians; carpenters; heating, air-conditioning, and refrigeration mechanics and installers; and plumbers, pipefitters, and steamfitters.

Workers may fix plaster or drywall. They may fix or paint roofs, windows, doors, floors, woodwork, and other parts of buildings.

They also maintain and repair specialized equipment and machinery in cafeterias, laundries, hospitals, stores, offices, and factories.

They get supplies and repair parts from distributors or storerooms to fix problems. They use common hand and power tools such as screwdrivers, saws, drills, wrenches, and hammers to fix, replace, or repair equipment and parts of buildings.

General maintenance and repair workers often carry out many different tasks in a single day, at any number of locations.

Median Annual Wages, May 2012

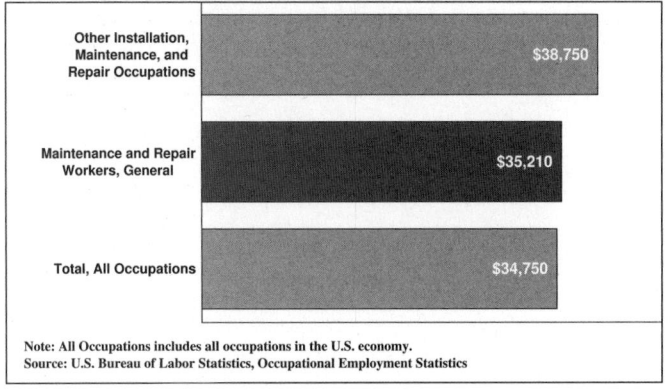

Note: All Occupations includes all occupations in the U.S. economy.
Source: U.S. Bureau of Labor Statistics, Occupational Employment Statistics

Percent Change in Employment, Projected 2012–2022

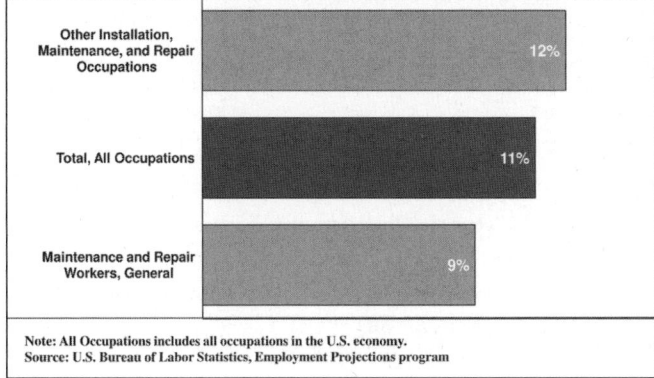

Note: All Occupations includes all occupations in the U.S. economy.
Source: U.S. Bureau of Labor Statistics, Employment Projections program

Work Environment

General maintenance and repair workers held about 1.3 million jobs in 2012. The industries that employed the most general maintenance and repair workers in 2012 were as follows:

Real estate and rental and leasing.. 19%
Manufacturing.. 15
State and local government, excluding education
   and hospitals... 10
Health care and social assistance 8
Educational services; state, local, and private 8

General maintenance and repair workers often carry out many different tasks in a single day, at any number of locations. They may work inside a single building, such as a hotel or hospital, or be responsible for the maintenance of many buildings, such as those in an apartment complex or college campus.

General maintenance and repair workers may have to stand for long periods or lift heavy objects. These workers may work in uncomfortably hot or cold environments, work in uncomfortable or cramped positions, or on ladders. The work involves a lot of walking, climbing, and reaching.

Injuries and Illnesses. Workers risk electrical shocks, falls, cuts, and bruises. As a result, general maintenance workers had a rate of injuries and illnesses that is much higher than the national average.

Work Schedules. Most general maintenance workers work full time, including evenings or weekends. Some are on call for emergency repairs.

How to Become One

Jobs in this field typically do not require any formal education beyond high school. General maintenance and repair workers often learn their skills on the job. They start by doing simple tasks and watching and learning from skilled maintenance workers.

Education. Many maintenance and repair workers may learn some basic skills in high school shop or technical education classes, postsecondary trade or vocational schools, or community colleges.

Courses in mechanical drawing, electricity, woodworking, blueprint reading, mathematics, and computers are useful. Maintenance and repair workers often do work that involves electrical, plumbing, heating, and air-conditioning systems or painting and roofing tasks. Workers need a good working knowledge of many repair and maintenance tasks.

Practical training, available at many adult education centers and community colleges, is another option for workers to learn tasks such as drywall repair and basic plumbing.

Training. General maintenance and repair workers usually start by watching and learning from skilled maintenance workers. They begin by doing simple tasks, such as fixing leaky faucets and replacing light bulbs. After gaining experience, general maintenance and repair workers move on to more difficult tasks, such as overhauling machinery or building walls.

Some learn their skills by working as helpers to other types of repair or construction workers, including machinery repairers, carpenters, or electricians.

Because a growing number of new buildings rely on computers to control their systems, general maintenance and repair workers may need to know basic computer skills, such as how to log onto a central computer system and navigate through a series of menus. Companies that install computer-controlled equipment usually give onsite training for general maintenance and repair workers.

Licenses, Certifications, and Registrations. Licensing requirements vary by state and locality. For more complex tasks, workers may need to be licensed in a particular specialty, such as electrical or plumbing work.

Advancement. Some maintenance and repair workers decide to train in one specific craft and become craft workers, such as electricians, heating and air-conditioning mechanics, or plumbers.

Other maintenance workers open their own repair or contracting business. However, those that want to become a project manager or own their own business may need some postsecondary education or a degree in construction management. For more information, see the profile on construction managers.

Within small organizations, promotion opportunities may be limited.

Employment Projections Data for General Maintenance and Repair Workers

Occupational title	SOC Code	Employment, 2012	Projected Employment, 2022	Change, 2012–2022	
				Percent	Numeric
Maintenance and repair workers, general............................. 49-9071		1,325,100	1,450,300	9	125,200

Source: U.S. Bureau of Labor Statistics, Employment Projections Program

*Note: Data are rounded. Go to **Occupational Information Included in the OOH** for a discussion of the data in this table.*

Similar Occupations   This table shows a list of occupations with job duties that are similar to those of general maintenance and repair workers.

Occupations	Entry-level Education	2012 Pay	Projected Job Growth	Average Annual Openings
Boilermakers	High school diploma or equivalent	$56,560	4%	880
Carpenters	High school diploma or equivalent	$39,940	24%	32,920
Construction Managers	Bachelor's degree	$82,790	16%	15,460
Electrical and Electronics Installers and Repairers	Postsecondary non-degree award	$51,081	1%	2,980
Electricians	High school diploma or equivalent	$49,840	20%	22,460
Heating, Air Conditioning, and Refrigeration Mechanics and Installers	Postsecondary non-degree award	$43,640	21%	12,370
Plumbers, Pipefitters, and Steamfitters	High school diploma or equivalent	$49,140	21%	13,050

Important Qualities

Customer-service skills. These workers interact with customers on a regular basis. They need to be friendly and able to address customers' questions.

Dexterity. Many technician tasks, such as repairing small devices, connecting or attaching components, and using hand tools, require a steady hand and good hand–eye coordination.

Troubleshooting skills. Workers find, diagnose, and repair problems. They do tests to figure out the cause of problems before fixing equipment.

Pay

The median annual wage for general maintenance and repair workers was $35,210 in May 2012. The median wage is the wage at which half the workers in an occupation earned more than that amount and half earned less. The lowest 10 percent earned less than $20,920, and the top 10 percent earned more than $57,260.

Job Outlook

Employment of general maintenance and repair workers is projected to grow 9 percent from 2012 to 2022, about as fast as the average for all occupations.

Employment will increase as the real estate market continues to improve. Increasing home sales may drive demand for remodeling and maintenance work. In addition, maintenance and repair workers will be needed to upgrade and renovate the large inventory of foreclosed and distressed properties caused by the recession.

Demographic changes may also affect the demand for general maintenance and repair workers. Because homeowners typically prefer to remain in their homes as they age, demand may increase for workers as the large baby-boom population nears retirement. These older homeowners will invest in projects and renovations to accommodate their future living needs and allow them to remain in their homes following retirement.

Because many general maintenance and repair workers are employed in industries related to real estate, employment opportunities may be sensitive to fluctuations in the economy. Some workers may experience periods of unemployment when the overall level of construction and real estate development falls. However, maintenance and repairs continue during economic downturns as people opt to repair rather than replace equipment.

Job Prospects. Employment growth and the need to replace workers who leave the occupation each year will likely result in good job prospects. Many job openings are expected as experienced workers retire. Those with experience in repair- or maintenance-related fields should continue to have the best job prospects.

O*NET

➤ Maintenance and Repair Workers, General (49-9071.00)

Contacts for More Information

For more information, visit
➤ Handyman Association of America (www.handymanaa.org/Home_Page.html)
➤ United Handyman Association (http://theuha.net/)

Heating, Air Conditioning, and Refrigeration Mechanics and Installers

- **2012 Median Pay** .... $43,640 per year
  $20.98 per hour
- **Entry-Level Education** .... Postsecondary non-degree award
- **Work Experience in a Related Occupation** .... None
- **On-the-Job Training** .... Long-term on-the-job training
- **Number of Jobs 2012** 267,600
- **Job Outlook, 2012–22** .... 21% (Faster than average)
- **Employment Change, 2012–22** 55,900

What Heating, Air Conditioning, and Refrigeration Mechanics and Installers Do

Heating, air conditioning, and refrigeration mechanics and installers–often called *HVACR technicians*–work on heating, ventilation, cooling, and refrigeration systems that control the temperature and air quality in buildings.

Duties. Heating, air conditioning, and refrigeration mechanics and installers typically do the following:

- Use blueprints or design specifications to install or repair HVACR systems
- Connect systems to fuel and water supply lines, air ducts, and other components
- Install electrical wiring and controls and test for proper operation
- Inspect and maintain customers' HVACR systems
- Test individual components to determine necessary repairs
- Repair or replace worn or defective parts

A heating, air conditioning, and refrigeration mechanic works on a thermostat for a heating and air-conditioning system.

- Determine HVACR systems' energy use and make recommendations to improve efficiency
- Travel to worksites

Heating and air conditioning systems control the temperature, humidity, and overall air quality in homes, businesses, and other buildings. By providing a climate-controlled environment, refrigeration systems make it possible to store and transport food, medicine, and other perishable items.

Although HVACR technicians are trained to both install and maintain heating, air conditioning, and refrigeration systems, many focus on either installation or maintenance. Some also may specialize in certain types of HVACR equipment, such as water-based heating systems, solar panels, or commercial refrigeration.

HVACR technicians use many different tools. For example, they often use screwdrivers, wrenches, pipe cutters, and other basic hand tools when installing systems. Technicians also use more sophisticated tools, such as carbon monoxide testers, voltmeters, combustion analyzers, and acetylene torches to test or install system components.

When working on air conditioning and refrigeration systems, technicians must follow government regulations regarding the conservation, recovery, and recycling of refrigerants. This includes the proper handling and disposal of fluids and pressurized gases.

Some HVACR technicians sell service contracts to their clients, providing regular maintenance of heating and cooling systems.

The service usually includes the cleaning of ducts, replacing filters, and checking refrigerant levels.

Other craft workers sometimes help install or repair cooling and heating systems. For example, on a large air conditioning installation job, especially one in which workers are covered by union contracts, duct work might be done by sheet metal workers and duct installers, electrical work by electricians, and pipe work by plumbers, pipefitters, and steamfitters. Boiler systems are often installed by a boilermaker. In addition, home appliance repairers usually service window air conditioners and household refrigerators.

Work Environment

Heating, air conditioning, and refrigeration mechanics and installers held about 267,600 jobs in 2012, of which 61 percent were employed in the plumbing, heating, and air-conditioning contractors industry. About 9 percent were self-employed.

HVACR technicians mostly work in residential homes, schools, stores, hospitals, office buildings, or factories. Some technicians are assigned to specific job sites at the beginning of each day. Others travel to several different locations making service calls.

Although most technicians work indoors, some may have to work on outdoor heat pumps, even in bad weather. Technicians often work in awkward or cramped spaces, and some work in buildings that are uncomfortable because the air conditioning or heating system is broken.

Work Schedules. The majority of HVACR technicians work full time, with occasional evening or weekend shifts. During peak heating and cooling seasons, they often work overtime or irregular hours. Although the majority of technicians work for construction contractors, about 9 percent are self-employed workers who have the ability to set their own schedules.

Technicians who service refrigeration, heating, and air conditioning equipment generally have stable employment throughout the year, particularly as a growing number of manufacturers and contractors now provide or even require year-round service contracts.

Injuries and Illnesses. HVACR technicians have a one of the highest rates of injuries and illnesses of all occupations. Potential hazards include electrical shock, burns, muscle strains, and other injuries from handling heavy equipment.

Appropriate safety equipment is necessary when handling refrigerants because they are hazardous, and contact can cause skin damage, frostbite, or blindness. When working in tight spaces, inhalation of refrigerants is also a risk. As of 2012, several newly introduced refrigerants are highly flammable, requiring additional care.

Median Annual Wages, May 2012

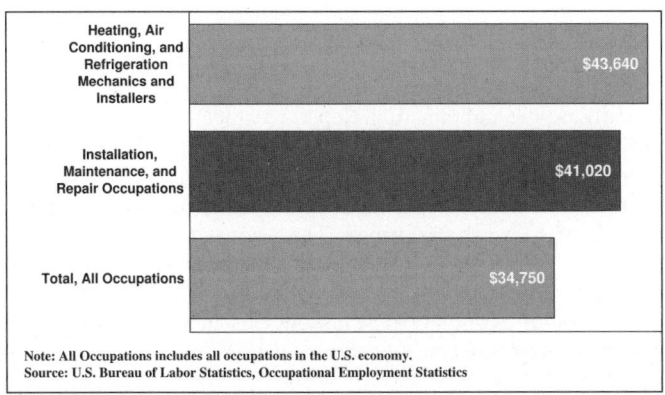

Note: All Occupations includes all occupations in the U.S. economy.
Source: U.S. Bureau of Labor Statistics, Occupational Employment Statistics

Percent Change in Employment, Projected 2012–2022

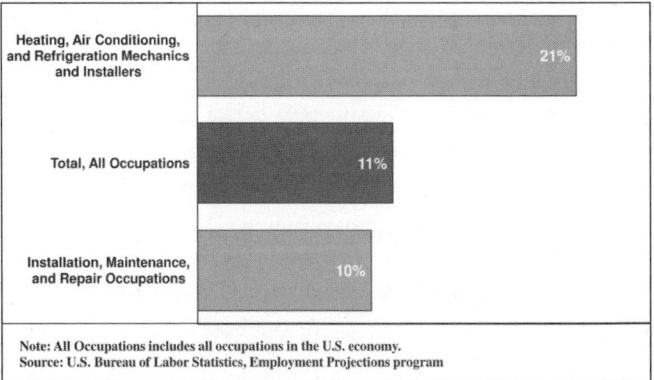

Note: All Occupations includes all occupations in the U.S. economy.
Source: U.S. Bureau of Labor Statistics, Employment Projections program

Employment Projections Data for Heating, Air Conditioning, and Refrigeration Mechanics and Installers

Occupational title	SOC Code	Employment, 2012	Projected Employment, 2022	Change, 2012–2022	
				Percent	Numeric
Heating, air conditioning, and refrigeration mechanics and installers..	49-9021	267,600	323,500	21	55,900

Source: U.S. Bureau of Labor Statistics, Employment Projections Program

Note: Data are rounded. Go to **Occupational Information Included in the OOH** *for a discussion of the data in this table.*

How to Become One

Because HVACR systems are increasingly complex, employers generally prefer applicants with postsecondary education or those who have completed an apprenticeship. Some states and localities require technicians to be licensed.

Education. A growing number of HVACR technicians receive postsecondary instruction from technical and trade schools or community colleges that offer programs in heating, air conditioning, and refrigeration. These programs generally last from 6 months to 2 years and lead to a certificate or an associate's degree.

High school students interested in becoming an HVACR technician should take courses in shop, math, and physics. Knowledge of plumbing or electrical work and a basic understanding of electronics is also helpful.

Training. Some HVACR technicians learn their trade on the job, although this is becoming much less common. Those who do usually begin by assisting experienced technicians with basic tasks, such as insulating refrigerant lines or cleaning furnaces. In time, they move on to more difficult tasks, including cutting and soldering pipes or checking electrical circuits.

Some technicians receive their training through an apprenticeship. Applicants for apprenticeships must have a high school diploma or general equivalency degree (GED). Math and reading skills are essential.

Apprenticeship programs usually last 3 to 5 years. Each year, apprentices must have at least 2,000 hours of on-the-job training and a minimum of 144 hours of related technical education. Over the course of the apprenticeship, technicians become familiar with subjects such as safety practices, blueprint reading, and how to use tools. They also learn about the numerous systems that heat and cool buildings. To enter an apprenticeship program, a trainee must meet the following requirements:

- Be at least 18 years old
- Have a high school diploma or equivalent
- Pass a basic math test
- Pass substance abuse screening
- Have a valid driver's license

Apprenticeship programs frequently are run by joint committees representing local chapters of various organizations, including the following:

- Air Conditioning Contractors of America
- Associated Builders and Contractors
- Mechanical Contractors Association of America
- National Association of Home Builders, Home Builders Institute
- Plumbing-Heating-Cooling Contractors Association
- Sheet Metal Workers' International Association

- United Association of Apprentice and Journeymen of the United States and Canada

Licenses, Certifications, and Registrations. Whether having learned the occupation through postsecondary education or through other means, HVACR technicians may take several different tests that measure their skills. These tests require different levels of experience. Technicians with relevant coursework and less than 2 years of experience may take the "entry-level" certification exams. These exams test basic competency in residential heating and cooling, light commercial heating and cooling, and commercial refrigeration. Technicians can take the exams at technical and trade schools.

HVACR technicians who have at least 1 year of installation experience and 2 years of maintenance and repair experience can take a number of specialized exams. These exams certify their competency in working with specific types of equipment, such as oil-burning furnaces or compressed-refrigerant cooling systems. Many organizations offer certifying exams. For example, the North American Technician Excellence offers the Industry Competency Exam; HVAC Excellence offers a Secondary Employment Ready Exam, a Secondary Heat exam, and a Heat Plus exam; the National Occupational Competency Testing Institute offers a secondary exam; and the Refrigeration Service Engineers Society offers two levels of certification.

Certifications can be helpful because they show that the technician has specific competencies. Some employers actively seek out industry-certified HVACR technicians.

Some states and localities require HVACR technicians to be licensed. Although specific licensing requirements vary, all candidates must pass an exam.

In addition, the U.S. Environmental Protection Agency (EPA) requires all technicians who buy or work with refrigerants to be certified in proper refrigerant handling. To become certified, technicians must pass a written exam specific to one of three specializations: Type I–servicing small appliances; Type II–high-pressure refrigerants; and Type III–low-pressure refrigerants. Many trade schools, unions, and employer associations offer training programs designed to prepare students for the EPA exam.

Important Qualities

Customer-service skills. HVACR technicians often work in customers' homes or business offices, so it is important that they are friendly, polite, and punctual. Repair technicians must sometimes deal with unhappy customers whose heating or air conditioning is not working.

Detail oriented. HVACR technicians must carefully maintain records of all work performed. The records must include what work was performed and the time it took, and list specific parts and equipment that were used.

Mechanical skills. HVACR technicians install and work on complicated climate-control systems. Workers must understand the

Similar Occupations   This table shows a list of occupations with job duties that are similar to those of heating, air conditioning, and refrigeration mechanics and installers.

Occupations	Entry-level Education	2012 Pay	Projected Job Growth	Average Annual Openings
Boilermakers	High school diploma or equivalent	$56,560	4%	880
Electricians	High school diploma or equivalent	$49,840	20%	22,460
Plumbers, Pipefitters, and Steamfitters	High school diploma or equivalent	$49,140	21%	13,050
Sheet Metal Workers	High school diploma or equivalent	$43,290	15%	4,890

HVAC components and be able to properly assemble, disassemble, and if needed, program them.

Physical strength. Workers may have to lift and support heavy equipment and components, often without help.

Time-management skills. HVACR technicians often have a set number of daily maintenance calls. They should be able to keep a schedule and complete all necessary repairs or tasks.

Troubleshooting skills. Heating, air conditioning, and refrigeration systems involve many intricate parts. To repair malfunctioning systems, technicians must be able to identify problems and then determine the best way to repair it.

Pay

The median annual wage for heating, air conditioning, and refrigeration mechanics and installers was $43,640 in May 2012. The median wage is the wage at which half the workers in an occupation earned more than that amount and half earned less. The lowest 10 percent earned less than $27,330, and the top 10 percent earned more than $68,990.

Apprentices usually earn about half of the wage paid to experienced workers. As they gain experience and improve their skills, apprentices receive periodic raises until they reach the wage of experienced workers.

Job Outlook

Employment of heating, air conditioning, and refrigeration mechanics and installers is projected to grow 21 percent from 2012 to 2022, faster than the average for all occupations.

Commercial and residential building construction will drive employment growth as the construction industry continues to recover from the recent recession. The growing number of sophisticated climate-control systems is also expected to increase demand for qualified HVACR technicians.

Climate-control systems generally need replacement after 10 to 15 years. As a result, many homes and commercial buildings that were constructed between 2002 and 2006 will need replacement climate-control systems, further spurring demand for technicians.

The growing emphasis on energy efficiency and pollution reduction will also require more HVACR technicians as climate-control systems are retrofitted, upgraded, or replaced entirely. In addition, regulations prohibiting the discharge and production of older types of refrigerant pollutants will result in the need to modify or replace many existing air conditioning systems.

Job Prospects. Job opportunities for HVACR technicians are expected to be excellent, particularly for those who have completed training at an accredited technical school or through an apprenticeship. Candidates familiar with computers and electronics, as well as those who have developed troubleshooting skills, will have the best job opportunities as employers continue to have difficulty finding qualified technicians to work on complex new systems.

Technicians who specialize in installation work may experience periods of unemployment when the level of new construction activity declines. Maintenance and repair work, however, usually remains relatively stable. Businesses and homeowners depend on their climate-control or refrigeration systems year round, and must keep them in good working order, regardless of economic conditions.

O*NET

➤ Heating, Air Conditioning, and Refrigeration Mechanics and Installers (49-9021.00)
➤ Heating and Air Conditioning Mechanics and Installers (49-9021.01)
➤ Refrigeration Mechanics and Installers (49-9021.02)

Contacts for More Information

For details about apprenticeships or other work opportunities, contact the offices of the state employment service, the state apprenticeship agency, local contractors, or local union-management HVACR apprenticeship committees. Apprenticeship information is available from the U.S. Department of Labor's toll-free help line, 1 (877) 872-5627, or the Employment and Training Administration (www.doleta.gov/OA/eta_default.cfm).

For information about career opportunities, training, and certification, visit

➤ Air Conditioning Contractors of America (www.acca.org/)
➤ Air-Conditioning, Heating, and Refrigeration Institute (www.ahrinet.org/)
➤ Associated Builders and Contractors (www.abc.org/)
➤ Carbon Monoxide Safety Association (http://cosafety.org/Default.aspx)
➤ Green Mechanical Council (www.greenmech.org/)
➤ HVAC Excellence (www.hvacexcellence.org/)
➤ Mechanical Contractors Association of America (www.mcaa.org/)
➤ National Association of Home Builders, Home Builders Institute (www.hbi.org/)
➤ National Occupational Competency Testing Institute (www.nocti.org/)
➤ NCCER (www.nccer.org/)
➤ North American Technician Excellence (www.natex.org/)
➤ Plumbing-Heating-Cooling Contractors Association (www.phccweb.org/)
➤ Radiant Professionals Alliance (www.radiantpanelassociation.org/)
➤ Refrigeration Service Engineers Society (www.rses.org/)
➤ Sheet Metal and Air Conditioning Contractors' National Association (www.smacna.org/)
➤ United Association of Journeymen and Apprentices of the Plumbing and Pipefitting Industry of the United States and Canada (http://ua.org/index.asp)

Heavy Vehicle and Mobile Equipment Service Technicians

- **2012 Median Pay** .... $43,820 per year
  $21.07 per hour
- **Entry-Level Education** ... High school diploma or equivalent
- **Work Experience in a Related Occupation** .... None
- **On-the-Job Training** .... Long-term on-the-job training
- **Number of Jobs 2012** 176,300
- **Job Outlook, 2012–22** .... 9% (As fast as average)
- **Employment Change, 2012–22** 16,200

Heavy vehicle and mobile equipment service technicians and mechanics often work on hydraulic equipment, performing needed repairs.

What Heavy Vehicle and Mobile Equipment Service Technicians Do

Heavy vehicle and mobile equipment service technicians, also called *mechanics*, inspect, maintain, and repair vehicles and machinery used in construction, farming, rail transportation, and other industries.

Duties. Heavy vehicle and mobile equipment service technicians typically do the following:

- Read and understand operating manuals, blueprints, and drawings
- Perform scheduled maintenance, such as cleaning and lubricating parts
- Diagnose and identify malfunctions, using computerized tools and equipment
- Inspect, repair, and replace defective or worn parts, such as bearings, pistons, and gears
- Overhaul and test major components, such as engines, hydraulics, and electrical systems
- Disassemble and reassemble heavy equipment and components
- Travel to worksites to repair large equipment, such as cranes

Heavy vehicles and mobile equipment are critical to many industrial activities, including construction and railroad transportation. Various types of equipment, such as tractors, cranes, and bulldozers, are used to haul materials, till land, lift beams, and dig earth to pave the way for development and construction.

Heavy vehicle and mobile equipment service technicians repair and maintain engines, hydraulic systems, transmissions, and electrical systems of agricultural, industrial, construction, and rail

equipment. They ensure the performance and safety of fuel lines, brakes, transmissions, and other systems.

Service technicians use diagnostic computers and equipment to identify problems and make adjustments or repairs. For example, technicians may use an oscilloscope to measure the voltage produced by electronic components. Technicians also use many different power and machine tools, including pneumatic wrenches, lathes, and welding equipment. A pneumatic tool such as an impact wrench is an air tool powered by compressed air.

Service technicians also use many different hand tools, such as screwdrivers, pliers, and wrenches, to work on small parts and in hard-to-reach areas. They generally purchase these tools over the course of their careers, often investing thousands of dollars in their collections.

After locating malfunctions, service technicians repair, replace, and recalibrate components such as hydraulic pumps or spark plugs. This may involve disassembling and reassembling major equipment or making adjustments through an onboard computer program.

The following are types of heavy vehicle and mobile equipment service technicians:

Farm equipment mechanics and service technicians service and repair farm equipment, such as tractors and harvesters. They also work on smaller consumer-grade lawn and garden tractors. Most work for dealer repair shops, where farmers increasingly send their equipment for maintenance.

Median Annual Wages, May 2012

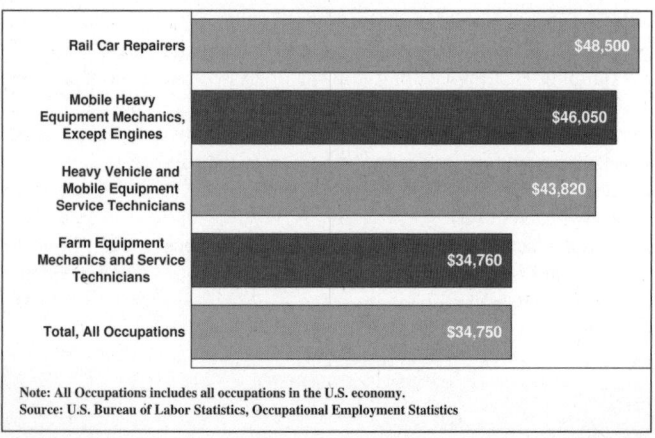

Rail Car Repairers	$48,500
Mobile Heavy Equipment Mechanics, Except Engines	$46,050
Heavy Vehicle and Mobile Equipment Service Technicians	$43,820
Farm Equipment Mechanics and Service Technicians	$34,760
Total, All Occupations	$34,750

Note: All Occupations includes all occupations in the U.S. economy.
Source: U.S. Bureau of Labor Statistics, Occupational Employment Statistics

Percent Change in Employment, Projected 2012–2022

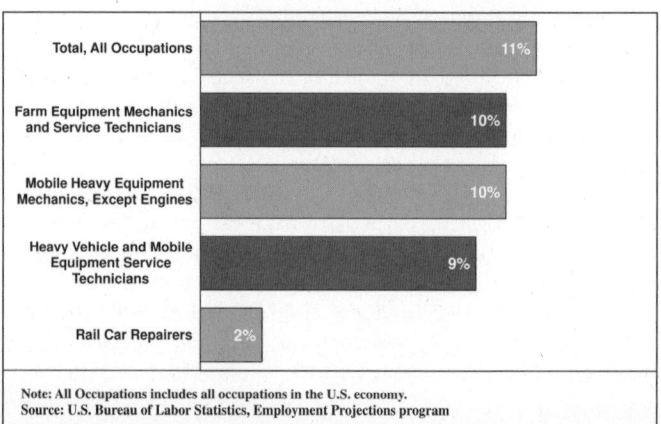

Total, All Occupations	11%
Farm Equipment Mechanics and Service Technicians	10%
Mobile Heavy Equipment Mechanics, Except Engines	10%
Heavy Vehicle and Mobile Equipment Service Technicians	9%
Rail Car Repairers	2%

Note: All Occupations includes all occupations in the U.S. economy.
Source: U.S. Bureau of Labor Statistics, Employment Projections program

Employment Projections Data for Heavy Vehicle and Mobile Equipment Service Technicians

Occupational title	SOC Code	Employment, 2012	Projected Employment, 2022	Change, 2012–2022	
				Percent	Numeric
Heavy vehicle and mobile equipment service technicians and mechanics	49-3040	176,300	192,500	9	16,200
Farm equipment mechanics and service technicians	49-3041	35,800	39,200	10	3,400
Mobile heavy equipment mechanics, except engines	49-3042	119,300	131,600	10	12,300
Rail car repairers	49-3043	21,200	21,700	2	500

Source: U.S. Bureau of Labor Statistics, Employment Projections Program

Note: **Data are rounded.** Go to **Occupational Information Included in the OOH** for a discussion of the data in this table.

Mobile heavy equipment mechanics repair and maintain construction and surface mining equipment, such as bulldozers, cranes, graders, and excavators. Many work for equipment wholesale and distribution shops and large construction and mining companies. Those working for the federal government may work on tanks and other military equipment.

Rail car repairers specialize in servicing railroad locomotives, subway cars, and other rolling stock. They usually work for railroad, public and private transit companies, and rail car manufacturers.

For information about technicians and mechanics who work primarily on automobiles, see the profile on automotive service technicians and mechanics.

For information about technicians and mechanics who work primarily on large trucks and buses, see the profile on diesel service technicians and mechanics.

For information about technicians and mechanics who primarily work on motorboats, motorcycles, and small all-terrain vehicles, see the profile on small engine mechanics.

Work Environment

Heavy vehicle and mobile equipment service technicians held about 176,300 jobs in 2012. Most technicians worked for private companies, but about 7 percent worked for state and local government. Industries employing the largest numbers of heavy vehicle and mobile equipment service technicians in 2012 were as follows:

Farm and garden machinery and equipment merchant
   wholesalers... 14%
Government... 11
Rail transportation 7
Mining, quarrying, and oil and gas extraction........... 6
Heavy and civil engineering construction 6

Service technicians usually work indoors in noisy repair shops. They often lift heavy parts and tools, handle greasy and dirty equipment, and stand or lie in awkward positions.

It is often too expensive to transport heavy or mobile equipment to a repair shop. As a result, some service technicians travel to worksites to make repairs, often driving long distances. Generally, more experienced service technicians specialize in field service. They drive trucks that are specially equipped with replacement parts and tools. These workers spend considerable time outdoors.

Work Schedules. Most heavy vehicle and mobile equipment service technicians work full time, and many work evenings or weekends. Overtime is common.

Farm equipment mechanics' work varies by time of the year. During busy planting and harvesting seasons, for example, mechanics often work six or seven 12-hour days per week. In the slower winter months, however, they may work less than full time.

How to Become One

Although a high school diploma is the typical education needed for entry, employers increasingly prefer to hire heavy vehicle and mobile equipment service technicians who have some postsecondary education. The majority of workers, however, still learn informally on the job.

Education. High school or postsecondary courses in automobile repair, mathematics, and physics provide a strong foundation for a service technician's career.

Postsecondary programs and degrees in diesel technology or heavy equipment mechanics provide the most comprehensive training for new service technicians. Offered by vocational schools and community colleges, these programs cover the basics of diagnostic techniques, electronics, and other related subjects.

Most programs last 1 to 2 years and lead to certificates of completion. Other programs, which lead to associate's degrees, generally take 2 years to complete.

Education significantly reduces the amount of on-the-job training new service technicians need.

Training. Entry-level workers with no formal background in heavy vehicle repair often receive a few months of on-the-job training before they begin doing routine service tasks and minor repairs. Trainees advance to more complex work as they show competence, and usually become fully qualified after 3 to 4 years of work.

Many employers send new technicians to training sessions conducted by equipment manufacturers. Training sessions may focus on particular components and technologies or types of equipment.

Licenses, Certifications, and Registrations. Some manufacturers offer certification in specific repair methods or equipment. Although not required, certification can demonstrate a mechanic's competence and usually brings higher pay.

Important Qualities

Dexterity. Many tasks, such as disassembling engine parts, connecting or attaching components, and using hand tools, require a steady hand and good hand-eye coordination.

Mechanical skills. Heavy vehicle and mobile equipment service technicians must be familiar with engine components and systems and know how they interact with each other. They must often disassemble major parts for repairs and be able to reassemble them.

Physical strength. Heavy vehicle and mobile equipment service technicians must be able to lift and move heavy equipment, tools, and parts without risking injury.

Troubleshooting skills. Heavy vehicle and mobile equipment service technicians must be familiar with diagnostic equipment, which can help find the source of malfunctions when they are difficult to identify.

Similar Occupations   This table shows a list of occupations with job duties that are similar to those of heavy vehicle and mobile equipment service technicians.

Occupations	Entry-level Education	2012 Pay	Projected Job Growth	Average Annual Openings
Aircraft and Avionics Equipment Mechanics and Technicians	See "How to Become One"	$55,227	3%	3,960
Automotive Service Technicians and Mechanics	High school diploma or equivalent	$36,610	9%	23,760
Diesel Service Technicians and Mechanics	High school diploma or equivalent	$42,320	9%	7,510
Industrial Machinery Mechanics and Maintenance Workers and Millwrights	High school diploma or equivalent	$45,848	17%	18,700
Small Engine Mechanics	High school diploma or equivalent	$32,679	6%	1,820

Pay

The median annual wage for heavy vehicle and mobile equipment service technicians was $43,820 in May 2012. The median wage is the wage at which half the workers in an occupation earned more than that amount and half earned less. The lowest 10 percent earned less than $27,730, and the top 10 percent earned more than $62,960.

In May 2012, median annual wages for heavy vehicle and mobile equipment service technician occupations were as follows:

Rail car repairers $48,500
Mobile heavy equipment mechanics 46,050
Farm equipment mechanics and service technicians 34,760

Union Membership. Compared with workers in all occupations, heavy vehicle and mobile equipment service technicians had a higher percentage of workers who belonged to a union in 2012.

Job Outlook

Employment of heavy vehicle and mobile equipment service technicians is projected to grow 9 percent from 2012 to 2022, about as fast as the average for all occupations.

As the stock of heavy vehicles and mobile equipment continues to increase, more service technicians will be needed to maintain them. In particular, demand for heavy equipment used in construction, mining, and energy exploration will result in employment growth for service technicians. Growth rates will vary by specialty.

Employment of farm equipment mechanics and service technicians is projected to grow 10 percent, about as fast as the average for all occupations. Demand for farm equipment repairers will be primarily driven by the need for agricultural products to feed a growing population. Demand for other products, such as biofuels, will also increase repairer employment.

Employment of mobile heavy equipment mechanics is projected to grow 10 percent, about as fast as the average for all occupations. Employment growth of mobile heavy equipment mechanics will be spurred by increased construction activity. Population and business growth will result in the construction of more houses, office buildings, roads, bridges, and other structures.

Employment of rail car repairers is projected to show little to no change. However, rail car repairers will continue to be needed to repair rail cars used for freight shipping and transportation.

Job Prospects. Most job opportunities will come from the need to replace workers who retire or leave the occupation. Those with certificates from vocational schools or 2-year degrees from community colleges should have very good job opportunities, as employers strongly prefer these candidates. Those without formal training will have difficulty finding jobs.

The majority of job openings are expected to be in sectors that sell, rent, or lease heavy vehicles and mobile equipment, where a large proportion of service technicians are employed.

The construction and mining industries, which use large numbers of heavy equipment, are sensitive to fluctuations in the economy. As a result, job opportunities for service technicians in these sectors will vary with overall economic conditions.

Job opportunities for farm equipment mechanics are seasonal, and are generally best during warmer months.

O*NET

➤ Farm Equipment Mechanics and Service Technicians (49-3041.00)
➤ Mobile Heavy Equipment Mechanics, Except Engines (49-3042.00)
➤ Rail Car Repairers (49-3043.00)

Contacts for More Information

For more details about job openings for heavy vehicle and mobile equipment service technicians, consult local heavy and mobile equipment dealers and distributors, construction contractors, and government agencies. Local offices of the state employment service also may have information on job openings and training programs.

For general information about careers and training programs, visit

➤ Associated Equipment Distributors (www.aedcareers.com/)
➤ National Automotive Technicians Education Foundation (www.natef.org/)
➤ National Institute for Automotive Service Excellence (www.ase.com/Home.aspx)

Industrial Machinery Mechanics and Maintenance Workers and Millwrights

- **2012 Median Pay** .... $45,840 per year
  $22.04 per hour
- **Entry-Level Education** ... High school diploma or equivalent
- **Work Experience in a Related Occupation** .... None
- **On-the-Job Training** .... See "How to Become One"
- **Number of Jobs 2012** 447,600
- **Job Outlook, 2012–22** .... 17% (Faster than average)
- **Employment Change, 2012–22** 77,400

Industrial machinery mechanics and maintenance workers adjust and calibrate equipment.

What Industrial Machinery Mechanics and Maintenance Workers and Millwrights Do

Industrial machinery mechanics and maintenance workers maintain and repair factory equipment and other industrial machinery, such as conveying systems, production machinery, and packaging equipment. Millwrights install, dismantle, repair, reassemble, and move machinery in factories, power plants, and construction sites.

Duties. Industrial machinery mechanics typically do the following:

- Read technical manuals to understand equipment and controls
- Disassemble machinery and equipment when there is a problem
- Repair or replace broken or malfunctioning components
- Perform tests and run initial batches to make sure that the machine is running smoothly
- Adjust and calibrate equipment and machinery to optimal specifications

Machinery maintenance workers typically do the following:

- Detect minor problems by performing basic diagnostic tests
- Clean and lubricate equipment or machinery
- Check the performance of machinery
- Test malfunctioning machinery to determine whether major repairs are needed

- Adjust equipment and reset or calibrate sensors and controls

Millwrights typically do the following:

- Install or repair machinery and equipment
- Adjust and align machine parts
- Replace defective parts of machinery as needed
- Take apart existing machinery to clear floor space for new machinery
- Move machinery and equipment

Industrial machinery mechanics and machinery maintenance workers maintain and repair complex machines, such as an automobile assembly line's conveyor belts, robotic welding arms, and hydraulic lifts.

Industrial machinery mechanics, also called *industrial machinery repairers* or *maintenance machinists*, keep machines in good working order. To do this, they must be able to detect and correct errors before the machine, or the products it produces, are damaged. Machinery mechanics use technical manuals, their understanding of industrial equipment, and careful observation to discover the cause of a problem. For example, after hearing a vibration from a machine, a mechanic must decide whether it is the result of worn belts, weak motor bearings, or some other problem. Mechanics often need years of training and experience to be able to diagnose all of the problems they find in their work. They may use computerized diagnostic systems and vibration analysis techniques to help figure out the source of problems.

After diagnosing a problem, the industrial machinery mechanic may take the equipment apart to repair or replace the necessary parts. Mechanics are expected to have electrical, electronics, and computer programming skills so they can repair sophisticated equipment. Once a repair is made, mechanics test a machine to ensure that it is running smoothly. Industrial machinery mechanics also do preventive maintenance.

In addition to handtools, mechanics commonly use lathes, grinders, or drill presses. Many also are required to weld.

Machinery maintenance workers do basic maintenance and repairs on machines. They are responsible for cleaning and lubricating machinery, performing basic diagnostic tests, checking performance, and testing damaged machine parts to determine whether major repairs are necessary.

Maintenance workers must follow machine specifications and adhere to maintenance schedules. They perform minor repairs, generally leaving major repairs to machinery mechanics.

Median Annual Wages, May 2012

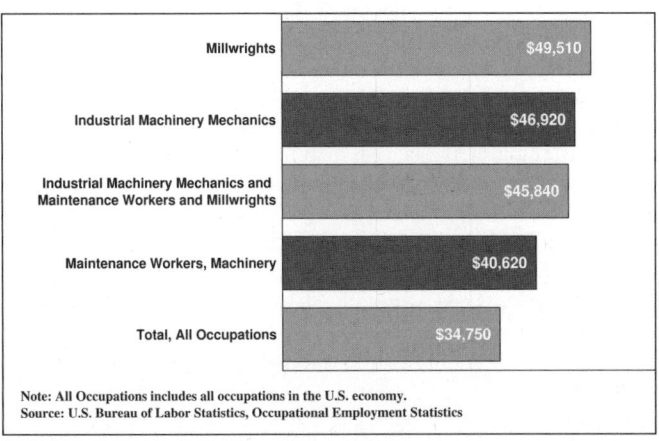

Millwrights	$49,510
Industrial Machinery Mechanics	$46,920
Industrial Machinery Mechanics and Maintenance Workers and Millwrights	$45,840
Maintenance Workers, Machinery	$40,620
Total, All Occupations	$34,750

Note: All Occupations includes all occupations in the U.S. economy.
Source: U.S. Bureau of Labor Statistics, Occupational Employment Statistics

Percent Change in Employment, Projected 2012–2022

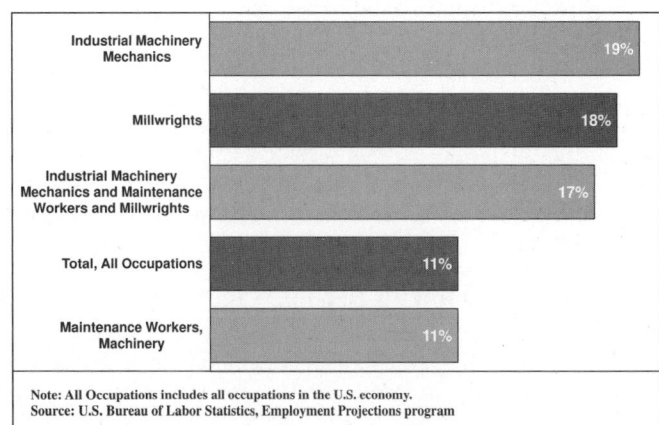

Industrial Machinery Mechanics	19%
Millwrights	18%
Industrial Machinery Mechanics and Maintenance Workers and Millwrights	17%
Total, All Occupations	11%
Maintenance Workers, Machinery	11%

Note: All Occupations includes all occupations in the U.S. economy.
Source: U.S. Bureau of Labor Statistics, Employment Projections program

Employment Projections Data for Industrial Machinery Mechanics and Maintenance Workers and Millwrights

Occupational title	SOC Code	Employment, 2012	Projected Employment, 2022	Change, 2012–2022	
				Percent	Numeric
Industrial machinery mechanics and maintenance					
workers and millwrights	—	447,600	525,100	17	77,400
Industrial machinery mechanics	49-9041	319,300	379,600	19	60,300
Maintenance workers, machinery	49-9043	89,000	98,900	11	9,900
Millwrights	49-9044	39,400	46,700	18	7,200

Source: U.S. Bureau of Labor Statistics, Employment Projections Program

Note: Data are rounded. Go to Occupational Information Included in the OOH *for a discussion of the data in this table.*

All maintenance workers use a variety of tools to do repairs and preventive maintenance. For example, they may use a screwdriver or socket wrenches to adjust a motor's alignment, or they might use a hoist to lift a heavy printing press off the ground.

Millwrights have a wide range of skills that aid in their work of installing, maintaining, and disassembling industrial machines. Putting together a machine can take a few days or several weeks.

Millwrights perform repairs that include replacing worn or defective parts of machines. Millwrights also may be involved in taking apart existing machines, a common situation when a manufacturing plant needs to clear floor space for new machinery. To do this, each part of the machine must be carefully taken apart, categorized, and packaged.

Millwrights use a variety of hand tools, such as hammers and levels, as well as equipment for welding, brazing, and cutting. They also use measuring tools, such as micrometers, measuring tapes, lasers, and other precision-measuring devices. On large projects, they commonly use cranes and trucks. When millwrights and managers determine the best place for a machine, millwrights bring the parts to the desired location using forklifts, hoists, winches, cranes, and other equipment.

Work Environment

Industrial machinery mechanics and maintenance workers and millwrights held about 447,600 jobs in 2012. Most worked in factories, power plants, or at construction sites.

Injuries and Illnesses. Industrial machinery mechanics and maintenance workers suffer common injuries, such as cuts, bruises, and strains. They also work in awkward positions, including on top of ladders or in cramped conditions under large machinery. To avoid injuries, workers must follow safety precautions and use protective equipment, such as hardhats, safety glasses, steel-toed shoes, and earplugs. Even so, industrial machinery mechanics and maintenance workers experience rates of injuries and illnesses that are much higher than the national average.

Work Schedules. Most industrial machinery mechanics and maintenance workers are employed full time during regular business hours. However, mechanics may be on call and work night or weekend shifts. Overtime is common, particularly for mechanics.

Millwrights typically are employed on a contract basis and can spend only a few days or weeks at a single site. As a result, workers often have variable schedules and may experience downtime between jobs.

How to Become One

Industrial machinery mechanics and maintenance workers and millwrights typically need a high school diploma. However, industrial machinery mechanics need a year or more of training

after high school, whereas maintenance workers typically receive on-the-job training that lasts a few months to a year.

Millwrights mostly go through an apprenticeship program that lasts about 4 years. Programs are usually a combination of technical instruction and on-the-job training. Others learn their trade through a 2-year associate's degree program in industrial maintenance. A high school diploma or equivalent is the typical education needed to become a millwright.

Education. Employers of industrial machinery mechanics and maintenance workers and millwrights generally require them to have at least a high school diploma or a General Educational Development (GED) certificate. However, employers increasingly prefer to hire workers with some education in industrial technology from a community or technical college. Employers also prefer to hire workers who have taken high school or postsecondary courses in mechanical drawing, mathematics, blueprint reading, computer programming, or electronics.

Industrial machinery mechanics usually need a year or more of education and training after high school to learn the necessary mechanical and technical skills. Although mechanics used to specialize in one area, such as hydraulics or electronics, many factories now require every mechanic to understand electricity, electronics, hydraulics, and computer programming. These skills allow mechanics to troubleshoot a much larger range of machine problems.

Some mechanics complete a 2-year associate's degree program in industrial maintenance. Others may start as helpers or in other factory jobs and learn the skills of the trade on the job or take courses offered through their employer.

Employers may offer onsite technical training or send workers to local technical schools in addition to on-the-job training. Classroom instruction focuses on subjects such as shop mathematics, blueprint reading, the use of hand tools, welding, electronics, and computer training. In addition to technical instruction, mechanics train on the specific machines that they will repair. They can get this training on the job, through dealers' or manufacturers' representatives, or in a classroom.

A high school diploma is the typical education needed to become a millwright. However, there are 2-year associate's degree programs in industrial maintenance that also provide good preparation for prospects. Employers may give workers classroom instruction in addition to on-the-job training.

Training. Most millwrights learn their trade through a 3- or 4-year apprenticeship. For each year of the program, apprentices must have at least 144 hours of related technical instruction and 2,000 hours of paid on-the-job training. On the job, apprentices learn to set up, clean, lubricate, repair, and start machinery. During technical instruction, they are taught welding, mathematics, how to read blueprints, how to use electronic devices, pneumatics (using

Similar Occupations   This table shows a list of occupations with job duties that are similar to those of industrial machinery mechanics and maintenance workers and millwrights.

Occupations	Entry-level Education	2012 Pay	Projected Job Growth	Average Annual Openings
Electrical and Electronics Engineers	Bachelor's degree	$89,701	4%	7,940
Electricians	High school diploma or equivalent	$49,840	20%	22,460
General Maintenance and Repair Workers	High school diploma or equivalent	$35,210	9%	37,970
Machinists and Tool and Die Makers	High school diploma or equivalent	$40,733	7%	13,060
Plumbers, Pipefitters, and Steamfitters	High school diploma or equivalent	$49,140	21%	13,050
Welders, Cutters, Solderers, and Brazers	High school diploma or equivalent	$36,300	6%	10,850

air pressure), and how to use grease and fluid properly. Many also receive computer training.

After completing an apprenticeship program, millwrights are considered fully qualified and can usually perform tasks with less guidance.

Apprenticeship programs are often sponsored by employers, local unions, contractor associations, and the state labor department. The basic qualifications for entering an apprenticeship program are as follows:

- Minimum age of 18
- High school diploma or equivalent
- Physically able to do the work

Machinery maintenance workers typically receive on-the-job training that lasts a few months to a year. They learn how to perform routine tasks, such as setting up, cleaning, lubricating, and starting machinery. This training may be offered on-the-job, by professional trainers hired by the employer, or by representatives of equipment manufacturers.

Important Qualities

Manual dexterity. When handling very small parts, workers must have a steady hand and good hand–eye coordination.

Mechanical skills. Workers must be able to reassemble large, complex machines after finishing a repair.

Technical skills. Industrial machinery mechanics and maintenance workers and millwrights use technical manuals and sophisticated diagnostic equipment to figure out why machines are not working.

Troubleshooting skills. Industrial machinery mechanics and maintenance workers and millwrights must observe and properly diagnose and fix problems that a machine may be having.

Pay

The median annual wage for industrial machinery mechanics and maintenance workers and millwrights was $45,840 in May 2012. The median wage is the wage at which half the workers in an occupation earned more than that amount and half earned less. The lowest 10 percent earned less than $29,020, and the top 10 percent earned more than $69,990.

In May 2012, median annual wages for industrial machinery mechanics and maintenance workers and millwrights were as follows:

Millwrights $49,510
Industrial machinery mechanics 46,920
Machinery maintenance workers 40,620

Union Membership. Compared with workers in all occupations, industrial machinery mechanics and maintenance workers and

millwrights had a higher percentage of workers who belonged to a union in 2012.

Job Outlook

Overall employment of industrial machinery mechanics and maintenance workers and millwrights is projected to grow 17 percent from 2012 to 2022, faster than the average for all occupations. Employment growth will vary by specialty.

Employment of industrial machinery mechanics is projected to grow 19 percent from 2012 to 2022, faster than the average for all occupations. Increased adoption of sophisticated manufacturing machinery will require more highly-skilled mechanics to keep machines in good working order.

Employment of machinery maintenance workers is projected to grow 11 percent from 2012 to 2022, about as fast as the average for all occupations. Increased automation, including the use of many new computer-controlled machines in factories and manufacturing plants, should spur demand for maintenance workers in order to keep machines operating well.

Employment of millwrights is projected to grow 18 percent from 2012 to 2022, faster than the average for all occupations. The use of machinery in manufacturing will require millwrights to install and disassemble this equipment, as well as perform some repair work.

Job Prospects. Overall, applicants with a broad range of skills in machine repair should have very good job prospects.

Faster-than-average employment growth and the need to replace many older workers who are expected to retire over the coming decade should result in numerous job openings.

Those that complete apprenticeships and educational programs designed for industrial machinery repair should have the best job prospects.

O*NET

➤ Industrial Machinery Mechanics (49-9041.00)
➤ Maintenance Workers, Machinery (49-9043.00)
➤ Millwrights (49-9044.00)

Contacts for More Information

For information about industrial machinery mechanics and maintenance workers, visit

➤ APICS (www.apics.org/home)
➤ Association for Maintenance Professionals (www.maintenance.org/home)
➤ National Association of Manufacturers (www.nam.org/)
➤ Society for Maintenance & Reliability Professionals (www.smrp.org/i4a/pages/index.cfm?pageid=1)

For information about millwrights and the precision machined products industry, training, and apprenticeships, visit

➤ Precision Machined Products Association (www.pmpa.org/)

➤ Employment and Training Administration. Apprenticeship information is available as well from the U.S. Department of Labor toll-free help line: (877) 872-5627.

For further information on apprenticeship programs, write to the Apprenticeship Council of your state's labor department or to local firms that employ machinery mechanics and repairers. You can also find information about registered apprenticeships, together with links to state apprenticeship programs, on the U.S. Department of Labor website (www.doleta.gov/OA/eta_default.cfm).

Line Installers and Repairers

- **2012 Median Pay** .... $58,210 per year
$27.99 per hour
- **Entry-Level Education** ... High school diploma or equivalent
- **Work Experience in a Related Occupation** .... None
- **On-the-Job Training** .... Long-term on-the-job training
- **Number of Jobs 2012** 249,400
- **Job Outlook, 2012–22** .... 7% (Slower than average)
- **Employment Change, 2012–22** 18,300

What Line Installers and Repairers Do

Line installers and repairers (also known as line workers) install or repair electrical power systems and telecommunications cables, including fiber optics.

Duties. Electrical power-line installers and repairers typically do the following:

- Drive work vehicles to job sites
- Install, maintain, or repair the power lines that move electricity
- Identify defective devices, voltage regulators, transformers, and switches
- Inspect and test power lines and auxiliary equipment
- String power lines between poles, towers, and buildings
- Climb poles and transmission towers and use truck-mounted buckets to get to equipment
- Operate power equipment when installing and repairing poles, towers, and lines
- Follow safety standards and procedures

Telecommunications line installers and repairers typically do the following:

- Drive work vehicles to job sites
- Install, maintain, or repair telecommunications equipment
- Inspect or test lines or cables
- Lay underground cable, including fiber optic lines, directly in trenches
- Install aerial cables, including under lakes or across rivers
- Operate power equipment when installing and repairing poles, towers, and lines
- Set up service for customers

Every time you turn on your lights, call someone on the phone, watch cable television, or access the Internet, you are connecting to complex networks of physical power lines and cables that provide you with electricity and connect you with the outside world. Line installers and repairers, also known as *line workers* or *linemen*, are the people who install and maintain these networks.

Line installers and repairers typically specialize, and the areas in which they specialize depend on the network and industry in which they work:

Electrical power-line installers and repairers install and maintain the power grid–the network of power lines that moves electricity from generating plants to customers. They routinely work with high-voltage electricity, which requires extreme caution. This can range from hundreds of thousands of volts for the long-distance transmission lines that make up the power grid to less than 10,000 volts for distribution lines that supply electricity to homes and businesses.

Line workers who maintain the interstate power grid work in crews that travel to locations throughout a large region to service transmission lines and towers. Workers employed by local utilities work mainly with lower voltage distribution lines, maintaining equipment such as transformers, voltage regulators, and switches. They also may work on traffic lights and street lights.

Telecommunications line installers and repairers install and maintain the lines and cables used by network communications companies. Depending on the service provided–local and long-distance telephone, cable television, or Internet–telecommunications companies use different types of cables, including fiber-optic cables. Unlike metallic cables that carry electricity, fiber-optic cables are made of glass or plastic and transmit signals using light. Working with fiber optics requires special skills, such as the ability to splice and finish off optical cables. Additionally, workers test and troubleshoot cables and networking equipment.

Because these systems are so complicated, many line workers also specialize by duty:

Line installers install new cable. They may work for construction contractors, utilities, or telecommunications companies. Workers generally start a new job by digging underground trenches or erecting utility poles and towers to carry the wires and cables. They use a variety of construction equipment, including digger derricks, which are trucks equipped with augers and cranes used to dig holes in the ground and set poles in place. Line installers also use trenchers, cable plows, and directional bore machines, which are used to cut openings in the earth to lay underground cables. Once the poles, towers, tunnels, or trenches are ready, line installers string cable along poles and towers or through tunnels and trenches.

Line repairers are employed by utilities and telecommunications companies that maintain existing power and telecommunications lines. Maintenance needs may be identified in a variety of ways, including remote monitoring, aerial inspections, and by customer reports of service outages. Line repairers often must replace aging or outdated equipment, so many of these workers have installation duties in addition to their repair duties.

Most line installers need several years of on-the-job training.

Median Annual Wages, May 2012

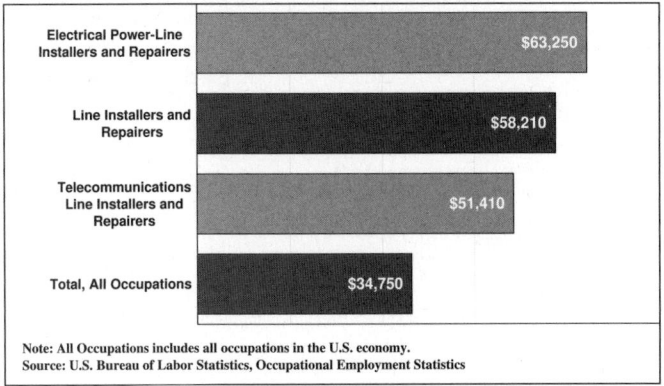

Note: All Occupations includes all occupations in the U.S. economy.
Source: U.S. Bureau of Labor Statistics, Occupational Employment Statistics

Percent Change in Employment, Projected 2012–2022

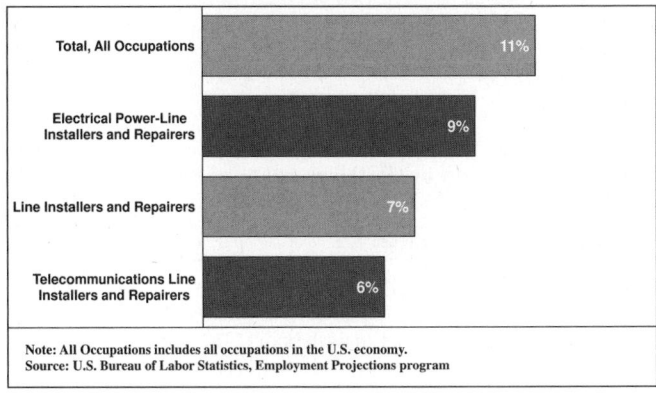

Note: All Occupations includes all occupations in the U.S. economy.
Source: U.S. Bureau of Labor Statistics, Employment Projections program

When a problem is reported, line repairers must identify the cause and fix it. This usually involves diagnostic testing and repair work. To work on poles, line installers usually use bucket trucks to raise themselves to the top of the structure, although all line workers must be adept at climbing poles and towers when necessary. Workers use special safety equipment to keep them from falling when climbing utility poles and towers.

Storms and other natural disasters can cause extensive damage to power lines. When power is lost, line repairers must work quickly to restore service to customers.

Work Environment

Line installers and repairers held about 249,400 jobs in 2012. Nearly two-thirds worked in the telecommunications and construction industries.

The industries that employed the most line installers and repairers in 2012 were as follows:

Wired telecommunications carriers 29%
Electric power generation, transmission and distribution 23
Utility system construction 18
Building equipment contractors... 11
Local government, excluding education and hospitals.............. 6

The work of line installers and repairers can be physically demanding. Line installers must be comfortable working at great heights and in confined spaces. Despite the help of bucket trucks, all line workers must be able to climb utility poles and transmission towers and balance while working on them.

Their work often requires that they drive utility vehicles, travel long distances, and work outdoors.

They often must work under challenging weather conditions, including in snow, wind, rain, and extreme heat and cold, in order to keep electricity flowing.

Injuries and Illnesses. Line workers encounter serious hazards on their jobs and must follow safety procedures to minimize danger. For example, workers must wear safety equipment when entering underground manholes and test for the presence of gas before going underground.

Specifically, electric power-line workers have hazardous jobs. A worker can be electrocuted if he or she comes in contact with a live cable on a high-voltage power line. When workers engage live wires, they use electrically insulated protective devices and tools to minimize their risk.

Power lines are typically higher than telephone lines, increasing the risk of severe injury from a fall. To prevent injuries, line installers use fall-protection equipment when working on poles or towers. Safety procedures and training have significantly reduced the danger for line workers. However, the occupation is still among the most dangerous. As a result, telecommunications and electrical line workers have a rate of injuries and illnesses that is higher than the national average.

Work Schedules. Although most work full time during regular business hours, some line installers and repairers must work evenings and weekends. In emergencies or after storms and other natural disasters, workers may have to work long hours for several days in a row.

How to Become One

To become proficient, most line installers and repairers require technical instruction and long-term on-the-job training. Apprenticeships are common.

Education. Most companies require line installers and repairers to have a high school diploma or equivalent. Employers prefer candidates with basic knowledge of algebra and trigonometry. In addition, technical knowledge of electricity or electronics obtained through military service, vocational programs, or community colleges can also be helpful.

Many community colleges offer programs in telecommunications, electronics, or electricity. Some programs work with local companies to offer 1-year certificates that emphasize hands-on field work.

More advanced 2-year associate's degree programs provide students with a broad knowledge of the technology used in telecommunications and electrical utilities. These programs offer courses in electricity, electronics, fiber optics, and microwave transmission.

Training. Electrical line installers and repairers often must complete apprenticeships or other employer training programs. These programs, which can last up to 5 years, combine on-the-job training with technical instruction and are sometimes administered jointly by the employer and the union representing the workers. For example, the National Joint Apprenticeship and Training Committee offers apprenticeship programs in four specialty areas. The basic qualifications to enter an apprenticeship program are as follows:

• Minimum age of 18

• High school education or equivalent

• One year of algebra

• Qualifying score on an aptitude test

• Pass substance abuse screening

Line installers and repairers who work for telecommunications companies typically receive several years of on-the-job training. They also may be encouraged to attend training from equipment manufacturers, schools, unions, or industry training organizations.

Employment Projections Data for Line Installers and Repairers

Occupational title	SOC Code	Employment, 2012	Projected Employment, 2022	Change, 2012–2022	
				Percent	Numeric
Line installers and repairers... 49-9050		249,400	267,700	7	18,300
Electrical power-line installers and repairers 49-9051		114,500	124,700	9	10,200
Telecommunications line installers and repairers 49-9052		134,900	143,000	6	8,100

Source: U.S. Bureau of Labor Statistics, Employment Projections Program

Note: Data are rounded. Go to **Occupational Information Included in the OOH** *for a discussion of the data in this table.*

Licenses, Certifications, and Registrations. Although not mandatory, certification for line installers and repairers is also available from several associations. For example, the National Joint Apprenticeship and Training Committee offers certification for line installers and repairers in several specialty areas.

In addition, The Fiber Optic Association (FOA) offers two levels of fiber optic certification for telecommunications line installers and repairers.

Workers who drive company vehicles usually need a commercial driver's license.

Advancement. Entry-level line workers generally begin with an apprenticeship, which includes both classroom training and hands-on work experience. As they learn additional skills from more experienced workers, they may advance to more complex tasks. In time, they advance to more sophisticated maintenance and repair positions in which they are responsible for increasingly large portions of the network.

After 3 to 5 years of working, qualified line workers reach the journey level. A journey-level line worker is no longer considered an apprentice and can perform most tasks without supervision. Journey-level line workers also may qualify for positions at other companies. Workers with many years of experience may become first-line supervisors or trainers.

Important Qualities

Color vision. Workers who handle electrical wires and cables must be able to distinguish colors because the wires and cables are often color coded.

Mechanical skills. Line installers and repairers must have the knowledge and skills to repair or replace complex electrical and telecommunications lines and equipment.

Physical stamina. Line installers and repairers often must climb poles and work at great heights with heavy tools and equipment. Therefore, installers and repairers should be able to work for long periods without tiring easily.

Physical strength. Line installers and repairers must be strong enough to lift heavy tools, cables, and equipment on a regular basis.

Teamwork. Because workers often rely on their fellow crew members for their safety, teamwork is critical.

Technical skills. Line installers use sophisticated diagnostic equipment on circuit breakers, switches, and transformers. They must be familiar with electrical systems and the appropriate tools needed to fix and maintain them.

Troubleshooting skills. Line installers and repairers must be able to diagnose problems in increasingly complex electrical systems and telecommunication lines.

Pay

The median annual wage for line installers and repairers was $58,210 in May 2012. The median wage is the wage at which half the workers in an occupation earned more than that amount and half earned less. The lowest 10 percent earned less than $30,340, and the top 10 percent earned more than $83,590.

The median annual wage for electrical power-line installers and repairers was $63,250 in May 2012. The lowest 10 percent earned less than $36,500, and the top 10 percent earned more than $89,020.

In May 2012, median annual wages for electrical power-line installers and repairers in the top five industries in which these installers and repairers worked were as follows:

Natural gas distribution..	$85,390
Electric power generation, transmission and distribution ...	65,690
Local government, excluding schools and hospitals	59,760
Utility system construction	55,930
Building equipment contractors	51,440

The median annual wage for telecommunications line installers and repairers was $51,410 in May 2012. The lowest 10 percent earned less than $27,620, and the top 10 percent earned more than $76,540.

In May 2012, median annual wages for telecommunications line installers and repairers in the top five industries in which these installers and repairers worked were as follows:

Other telecommunications	$65,160
Wired telecommunications carriers.....................................	61,860
Building equipment contractors	42,460
Cable and other subscription programming	37,800
Utility system construction	35,640

Union Membership. Compared with workers in all occupations, line installers and repairers had a higher percentage of workers who belonged to a union in 2012.

Similar Occupations   This table shows a list of occupations with job duties that are similar to those of line installers and repairers.

Occupations	Entry-level Education	2012 Pay	Projected Job Growth	Average Annual Openings
Electrical and Electronics Engineers	Bachelor's degree	$89,701	4%	7,940
Electricians	High school diploma or equivalent	$49,840	20%	22,460
Power Plant Operators, Distributors, and Dispatchers	High school diploma or equivalent	$68,256	-8%	1,880

Job Outlook

Employment of line installers and repairers is projected to grow 7 percent from 2012 to 2022, slower than the average for all occupations. Employment growth will vary by specialty.

Employment of telecommunications line installers and repairers is projected to grow 6 percent from 2012 to 2022, slower than the average for all occupations. As the population grows and customers increasingly demand enhanced connectivity, installers will continue to build out and provide newer and faster telephone, cable, and Internet services. In addition, the growth of the Internet will require more long-distance fiber-optic lines, including interstate and undersea cables.

Employment of electrical power-line installers and repairers is projected to grow 9 percent from 2012 to 2022, about as fast as the average for all occupations. Employment growth will be largely due to the growing population and expansion of cities. With each new housing development or office park, new electric power lines are installed and will require maintenance. In addition, the interstate power grid will continue to grow in complexity to ensure reliability.

Job Prospects. Good job opportunities are expected overall. Highly skilled workers with apprenticeship training or a 2-year associate's degree in telecommunications, electronics, or electricity should have the best job opportunities.

Employment opportunities should be particularly good for electrical power-line installers and repairers, as many workers in this field are expected to retire.

O*NET

➤ Electrical Power-Line Installers and Repairers (49-9051.00)
➤ Telecommunications Line Installers and Repairers (49-9052.00)

Contacts for More Information

For information about apprenticeships or job opportunities for line installers and repairers, contact local electrical contractors, a local chapter of the International Brotherhood of Electrical Workers, a local joint union-management apprenticeship committee, or the nearest office of your state employment service or apprenticeship agency. Apprenticeship information is available from the U.S. Department of Labor's toll-free help line, 1 (877) 872-5627 or the Employment and Training Administration (www.doleta.gov/OA/eta_default.cfm).

For more information about line installers and repairers, visit
➤ American Public Power Association (www.publicpower.org/)
➤ Center for Energy Workforce Development (www.cewd.org/)
➤ International Brotherhood of Electrical Workers (www.ibew.org/)
➤ Telecommunications Industry Association (www.tiaonline.org/)
    For information about certification, visit
➤ The Fiber Optic Association (www.thefoa.org/)
➤ National Joint Apprenticeship and Training Committee (www.njatc.org/home.aspx)

Medical Equipment Repairers

- **2012 Median Pay** .... $44,570 per year
  $21.43 per hour
- **Entry-Level Education** .... Associate's degree
- **Work Experience in a Related Occupation**............... None
- **On-the-Job Training** .... Moderate-term on-the-job training
- **Number of Jobs 2012** 42,300
- **Job Outlook, 2012–22** .... 30% (Much faster than average)
- **Employment Change, 2012–22** 12,800

What Medical Equipment Repairers Do

Medical equipment repairers install, maintain, and repair patient care equipment.

Duties. Medical equipment repairers typically do the following:

- Test and calibrate parts and equipment
- Repair and replace parts
- Perform preventive maintenance and service
- Keep records of maintenance and repairs
- Review technical manuals and regularly attend training sessions
- Explain and demonstrate how to operate medical equipment
- Manage replacement of medical equipment

Medical equipment repairers, also known as *biomedical equipment technicians (BMET)*, repair a wide range of electronic, electromechanical, and hydraulic equipment used in hospitals and health practitioners' offices. They may work on patient monitors, defibrillators, medical imaging equipment (X-rays, CAT scanners, and ultrasound equipment), voice-controlled operating tables, and electric wheelchairs, as well as work on medical equipment that dentists and eye doctors use.

If a machine has problems or is not functioning to its potential, the repairer may have to adjust the mechanical or hydraulic parts, or adjust the software in order to recalibrate the equipment.

To do their work, medical equipment repairers use a variety of tools. Most use hand tools, such as screwdrivers, wrenches, and soldering irons. Others use electronic tools, such as multimeters (an electronic measuring device that combines several measures) and computers, depending on the repair. Much of the equipment that they maintain and repair use specialized software, and repairers use that software to calibrate the machines.

Medical equipment repairers often test and calibrate equipment.

Median Annual Wages, May 2012

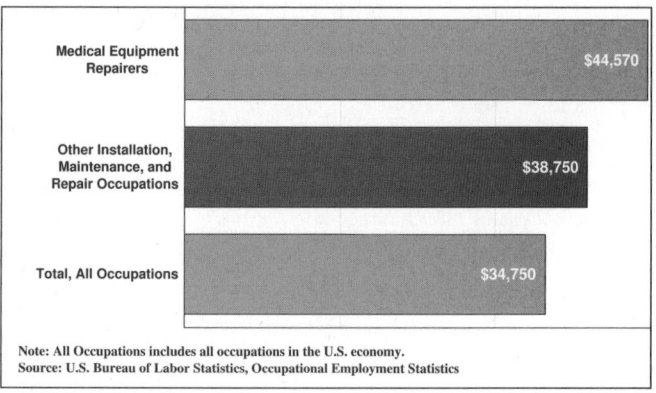

Note: All Occupations includes all occupations in the U.S. economy.
Source: U.S. Bureau of Labor Statistics, Occupational Employment Statistics

Percent Change in Employment, Projected 2012–2022

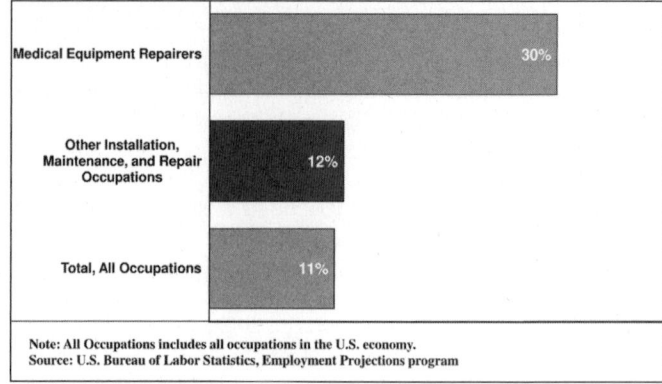

Note: All Occupations includes all occupations in the U.S. economy.
Source: U.S. Bureau of Labor Statistics, Employment Projections program

Many doctors, particularly specialty practitioners, rely on complex medical devices to run tests and diagnose patients, and they must be confident that the readings are accurate. Therefore, medical equipment repairers sometimes perform routine scheduled maintenance to ensure that sophisticated equipment, such as X-rays and CAT scanners, are in good working order. For less complicated equipment, such as electric hospital beds, workers make repairs as needed.

In a hospital setting, medical equipment repairers must be comfortable working around patients because repairs occasionally must take place while equipment is being used. When this is the case, the repairer must take great care to ensure that their work activities do not disturb patients.

Although some medical equipment repairers are trained to fix a variety of equipment, others specialize in repairing one or a small number of machines.

Work Environment

Medical equipment repairers held about 42,300 jobs in 2012. About 15 percent were self-employed.

The industries that employed the most medical equipment repairers in 2012 were as follows:

Professional and commercial equipment and supplies
merchant wholesalers 26%
Electronic and precision equipment repair and maintenance.... 15
Hospitals; state, local, and private 14
Ambulatory health care services 7
Health and personal care stores.............................. 6

Medical equipment repairers work for wholesale suppliers and at hospitals, electronic repair and maintenance shops, and health and personal care stores. Because repairing vital medical equipment is urgent, the work can be stressful.

Medical equipment repairers who work as contractors often have to travel–sometimes long distances–to perform needed repairs. Repairers often must work in a patient-caring environment, which has the potential to expose them to diseases and other health risks.

Work Schedules. Although medical equipment repairers usually work during the day, they are sometimes expected to be on call, including evenings and weekends. Most work full time, but some repairers have variable schedules.

How to Become One

Employers generally prefer candidates who have an associate's degree in biomedical technology or engineering. Depending on the area of specialization, repairers may need a bachelor's degree, especially for advancement.

Education. Education requirements for medical equipment repairers vary, depending on a worker's experience and area of specialization. However, the most common education is an associate's degree in biomedical equipment technology or engineering. Those who repair less-complicated equipment, such as hospital beds and electric wheelchairs, may learn entirely through on-the-job training, sometimes lasting up to 1 year. Others, particularly those who work on more sophisticated equipment, such as CAT scanners and defibrillators, may need a bachelor's degree.

Training. New workers generally start by observing and helping experienced repairers for 3 to 6 months. As they learn, workers tend to work more independently while still under supervision.

Each piece of equipment is different, so medical equipment repairers must learn each one separately. In some cases, this requires studying a machine's technical specifications and operating manual. Medical device manufacturers also may provide technical training.

Medical equipment technology is rapidly evolving, and new devices are frequently introduced. Repairers must continually update their skills and knowledge of new technologies and equipment through seminars and self-study.

Licenses, Certifications, and Registrations. Although not mandatory, certification can demonstrate competence and professionalism, making candidates more attractive to employers. It can also increase a repairer's opportunities for advancement. Most employers, particularly in hospitals, often pay for their in-house medical repairers to become certified.

Some associations offer certifications for medical equipment repairers. For example, the Association for the Advancement of

Employment Projections Data for Medical Equipment Repairers

Occupational title	SOC Code	Employment, 2012	Projected Employment, 2022	Change, 2012–2022	
				Percent	Numeric
Medical equipment repairers................................	49-9062	42,300	55,100	30	12,800

Source: U.S. Bureau of Labor Statistics, Employment Projections Program

Note: Data are rounded. Go to Occupational Information Included in the OOH *for a discussion of the data in this table.*

Similar Occupations This table shows a list of occupations with job duties that are similar to those of medical equipment repairers.

Occupations	Entry-level Education	2012 Pay	Projected Job Growth	Average Annual Openings
Computer, ATM, and Office Machine Repairers	Some college, no degree	$36,620	4%	3,280
Medical and Clinical Laboratory Technologists and Technicians	See "How to Become One"	$47,499	22%	15,600

Medical Instrumentation (AAMI) offers certification in three specialty areas–Certified Biomedical Equipment Technician (CBET), Certified Radiology Equipment Specialists (CRES), and Certified Laboratory Equipment Specialist (CLEB).

Important Qualities

Communication skills. Medical equipment repairers must effectively communicate technical information by telephone, in writing, and in person when speaking to clients, supervisors, and co-workers.

Dexterity. Many tasks, such as connecting or attaching parts and using hand tools require a steady hand and good hand–eye coordination.

Mechanical skills. Medical equipment repairers must be familiar with medical components and systems and how they interact. Often, repairers must disassemble and reassemble major parts for repair.

Physical stamina. Standing, crouching, and bending in awkward positions are common when making repairs to equipment. Therefore, workers should be physically fit enough as to not tire.

Technical skills. Technicians use sophisticated diagnostic tools when working on complex medical equipment. They must be familiar with both the equipments' internal parts and the appropriate tools needed to fix them.

Time-management skills. Because repairing vital medical equipment is urgent, workers must make good use of their time and perform repairs quickly.

Troubleshooting skills. As medical equipment becomes more intricate, problems become more difficult to identify. Therefore, repairers must be able to find and solve problems that are not immediately apparent.

Pay

The median annual wage for medical equipment repairers was $44,570 in May 2012. The median wage is the wage at which half the workers in an occupation earned more than that amount and half earned less. The lowest 10 percent earned less than $26,550, and the top 10 percent earned more than $72,080.

In May 2012, the median annual wages for medical equipment repairers in the top five industries in which these repairers worked were as follows:

Hospitals; state, local, and private	$48,870
Electronic and precision equipment repair and maintenance	46,610
Professional and commercial equipment and supplies merchant wholesalers	44,980
Ambulatory health care services	43,830
Health and personal care stores	35,050

Job Outlook

Employment of medical equipment repairers is projected to grow 30 percent from 2012 to 2022, much faster than the average for all occupations. Employment growth will stem from both greater demand for healthcare services and the increasing types and complexity of the equipment these workers maintain and repair.

A significant factor in the greater demand for healthcare services is the aging population. As people age, they usually need more medical care. With the expected increase in the number of older adults and with people living longer, health professionals are prescribing more medical tests that use new, complex equipment.

Changes in technology are bringing hospitals and health professionals more types of equipment and more complex equipment. Medical equipment repairers will be needed to maintain and repair CAT scans, electrocardiograms, magnetic resonance imaging, ultrasounds, X-ray machines, and other new equipment. They also will be needed to maintain and repair the sophisticated machines that private practitioners and technicians use to diagnose and treat problems with eyes, teeth, and other parts of the body. Some repairers will be needed to maintain and repair less complex health equipment, such as electric beds and wheelchairs.

Job Prospects. A combination of rapid employment growth and the need to replace workers who leave the occupation each year will result in excellent job opportunities over the coming decade.

Candidates who have an associate's degree in biomedical equipment technology or engineering should have the best job prospects. Job opportunities should be even better for those who are willing to relocate, because often there are relatively few qualified applicants in rural areas.

O*NET

➤ Medical Equipment Repairers (49-9062.00)

Contacts for More Information

For more information about medical equipment repairers, including a listing of schools offering related programs of study and information about certification, visit

➤ Association for the Advancement of Medical Instrumentation (www.aami.org/)
➤ Federation of Medical Equipment Support Associations (www.fmesa.org)
➤ Medical Equipment & Technology Association (www.mymeta.org/)

Small Engine Mechanics

- **2012 Median Pay** .... $32,640 per year
  $15.69 per hour
- **Entry-Level Education** ... High school diploma or equivalent
- **Work Experience in a Related Occupation** .... None
- **On-the-Job Training** ....See "How to Become One"
- **Number of Jobs 2012** 68,200
- **Job Outlook, 2012–22** .... 6% (Slower than average)
- **Employment Change, 2012–22** 3,800

What Small Engine Mechanics Do

Small engine mechanics inspect, service, and repair motorized power equipment. Mechanics often specialize in one type of equipment, such as motorcycles, motorboats, or outdoor power equipment.

Duties. Small engine mechanics typically do the following:

- Discuss equipment issues, maintenance plans, and work performed with customers
- Perform routine engine maintenance, such as lubricating parts and replacing spark plugs
- Test and inspect engines for malfunctioning parts
- Repair or replace worn, defective, or broken parts
- Reassemble and reinstall components and engines following repairs
- Keep records of inspections, test results, work performed, and parts used

Small engine mechanics regularly work on power equipment ranging from snowmobiles to chainsaws. When equipment breaks down, mechanics use many strategies to diagnose the source and the extent of the problem. Small engine mechanics determine mechanical, electrical, and fuel problems and make necessary repairs.

Mechanics' tasks vary in complexity and difficulty. Many jobs, such as maintenance inspections and repairs, involve minor adjustments or the replacement of a single part. Others, including piston calibration and spark plug replacement, may require taking an engine apart completely. Some highly skilled mechanics use computerized equipment for tasks, such as customizing and tuning racing motorcycles and motorboats.

Mechanics use a variety of hand tools, including screwdrivers, wrenches, and pliers, for many common tasks. Some mechanics also may regularly use compression gauges, ammeters, and voltmeters to test engine performance. For more complicated procedures, they commonly use pneumatic power tools or diagnostic equipment. A pneumatic tool such as an impact wrench is an air tool powered by compressed air.

Although employers usually provide the more expensive tools and testing equipment, mechanics are often expected to buy their own hand tools. Some mechanics have thousands of dollars invested in their tool collections.

The following are types of small engine mechanics:

Motorcycle mechanics specialize in working on motorcycles, scooters, mopeds, dirt bikes, and all-terrain vehicles. They service

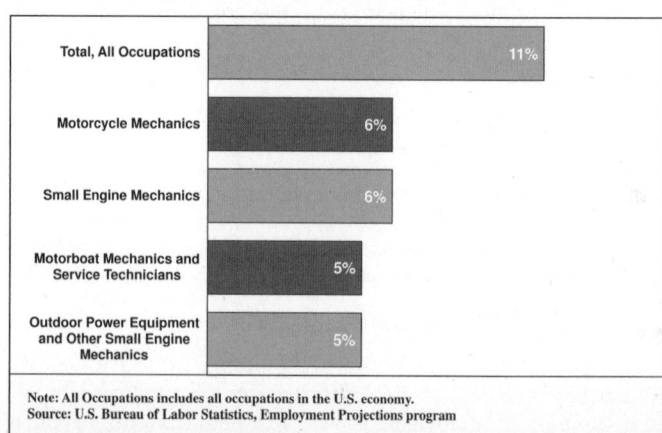

Motorcycle mechanics use hand tools to make needed adjustments and repairs.

engines, transmissions, brakes, and ignition systems and make minor body repairs, among other tasks. Most work is for individual dealers, servicing and repairing specific makes and models.

Motorboat mechanics and service technicians maintain and repair the mechanical and electrical components of boat engines. Most of their work, whether on small outboard engines or large diesel-powered inboard motors, is performed at docks and marinas where the repair shop is located. Motorboat mechanics also may work on propellers, steering mechanisms, marine plumbing, and other boat equipment.

Outdoor power equipment and other small engine mechanics service and repair outdoor power equipment, such as lawnmowers, edge trimmers, garden tractors, and portable generators. In certain parts of the country, mechanics may work on snowblowers and snowmobiles, but this work is both highly seasonal and regional.

For information about technicians and mechanics who work primarily on automobiles, see the profile on automotive service technicians and mechanics.

For information about technicians who work primarily on large trucks and buses, see the profile on diesel service technicians and mechanics.

For information about technicians and mechanics who work primarily on farm equipment, construction vehicles, and rail cars, see the profile on heavy vehicle and mobile equipment service technicians.

Median Annual Wages, May 2012

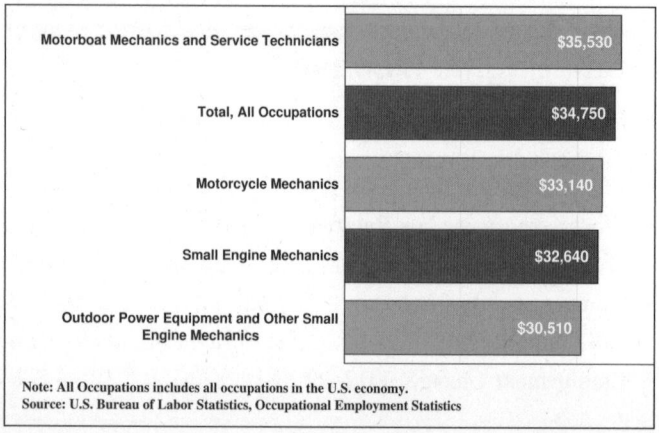

Motorboat Mechanics and Service Technicians	$35,530
Total, All Occupations	$34,750
Motorcycle Mechanics	$33,140
Small Engine Mechanics	$32,640
Outdoor Power Equipment and Other Small Engine Mechanics	$30,510

Note: All Occupations includes all occupations in the U.S. economy.
Source: U.S. Bureau of Labor Statistics, Occupational Employment Statistics

Percent Change in Employment, Projected 2012–2022

Total, All Occupations	11%
Motorcycle Mechanics	6%
Small Engine Mechanics	6%
Motorboat Mechanics and Service Technicians	5%
Outdoor Power Equipment and Other Small Engine Mechanics	5%

Note: All Occupations includes all occupations in the U.S. economy.
Source: U.S. Bureau of Labor Statistics, Employment Projections program

Employment Projections Data for Small Engine Mechanics

Occupational title	SOC Code	Employment, 2012	Projected Employment, 2022	Change, 2012–2022	
				Percent	Numeric
Small engine mechanics	—	68,200	72,000	6	3,800
Motorboat mechanics and service technicians	49-3051	20,800	22,000	5	1,100
Motorcycle mechanics	49-3052	16,800	17,800	6	1,000
Outdoor power equipment and other small engine mechanics	49-3053	30,500	32,200	5	1,700

Source: U.S. Bureau of Labor Statistics, Employment Projections Program

Note: Data are rounded. Go to **Occupational Information Included in the OOH** *for a discussion of the data in this table.*

Work Environment

Small engine mechanics held about 68,200 jobs in 2012. Although the majority worked for equipment dealers and repair shops, about 11 percent were self-employed.

Industries that employed the most small engine mechanics in 2012 were as follows:

Motor vehicle and parts dealers...	34%
Building material and garden equipment and supplies dealers	16
Amusement, gambling, and recreation industries	12
Personal and household goods repair and maintenance	10
Merchant wholesalers, durable goods	4

Small engine mechanics generally work in well-ventilated but noisy repair shops. They sometimes make onsite repair calls, which may require working in poor weather conditions. When repairing onboard engines, motorboat mechanics may work in cramped and uncomfortable positions.

Work Schedules. Most small engine mechanics work full time during regular business hours. However, seasonal work hours often fluctuate.

Most mechanics are busiest during the spring and summer, when demand for work on equipment from lawnmowers to boats is the highest. During the peak seasons, some mechanics work considerable overtime hours. In contrast, some mechanics are not busy during the winter, when demand for small engine work is low. As a result, during these months they work only part time.

Many employers schedule major repair work such as an engine rebuild to be performed during the off-season, to try to keep work consistent.

How to Become One

Small engine mechanics typically enter the occupation with a high school diploma and learn their trade through on-the-job training. As motorized power equipment becomes more sophisticated, employers increasingly prefer to hire mechanics who have completed postsecondary education programs.

Education. Small engine mechanics typically begin work with a high school diploma and learn on the job. Generally, employers look for candidates who have completed courses in small engine repair, automobile mechanics, and science. Some employers may hire applicants with less education if they have adequate reading, writing, and math skills.

Some motorcycle and marine equipment mechanics complete postsecondary education programs in small engine repair. Employers may prefer to hire these workers because they usually require significantly less on-the-job training. Because of the limited number of postsecondary programs, however, employers often have difficulty finding qualified workers.

Important Qualities

Customer-service skills. Mechanics must discuss equipment problems and repairs with their customers. They should be courteous, good listeners, and ready to answer customers' questions. In addition, self-employed workers frequently depend on repeat clients for business.

Detail oriented. Mechanical and electronic malfunctions often are due to misalignments or other easy-to-miss errors. Mechanics must account for those types of problems when inspecting or repairing engines and components.

Dexterity. Many tasks, such as disassembling engine parts, connecting or attaching components, and using hand tools, require a steady hand and good hand–eye coordination.

Mechanical skills. Mechanics must be familiar with engine components and systems and know how they interact with each other. They must frequently disassemble major parts for repairs and be able to reassemble them properly.

Troubleshooting skills. Mechanics, especially marine equipment and motorcycle specialists, must be able to identify problems in increasingly complicated mechanical and electronic systems using diagnostic equipment. They must be familiar with electronic control systems and the appropriate tools needed to fix and maintain them.

Training. Trainees work closely with experienced mechanics while learning basic tasks, such as replacing spark plugs or disassembling engine components. As they gain experience, trainees move on to more difficult tasks, such as advanced computerized diagnosis and engine overhauls. Achieving competency may

Similar Occupations This table shows a list of occupations with job duties that are similar to those of small engine mechanics.

Occupations	Entry-level Education	2012 Pay	Projected Job Growth	Average Annual Openings
Automotive Service Technicians and Mechanics	High school diploma or equivalent	$36,610	9%	23,760
Diesel Service Technicians and Mechanics	High school diploma or equivalent	$42,320	9%	7,510
Heavy Vehicle and Mobile Equipment Service Technicians	High school diploma or equivalent	$43,979	9%	6,710

take anywhere from several months to 3 years, depending on a mechanic's specialization and ability.

Because of the increased complexity of boat and motorcycle engines, motorcycle and marine equipment mechanics often need more on-the-job training than outdoor power equipment mechanics.

Employers frequently send mechanics to training courses run by motorcycle, motorboat, and outdoor power equipment manufacturers and dealers. Courses may last up to 2 weeks, teaching mechanics the most up-to-date technology and techniques. Often, these courses are a prerequisite for warranty and manufacturer-specific work.

Licenses, Certifications, and Registrations. Certification from the Equipment & Engine Training Council is the recognized industry credential for small engine mechanics. Some manufacturers offer certification in specific repair methods or equipment. Although not required, certification can demonstrate a mechanic's competence and usually brings higher pay.

Pay

The median annual wage for small engine mechanics was $32,640 in May 2012. The median wage is the wage at which half the workers in an occupation earned more than that amount and half earned less. The lowest 10 percent earned less than $20,490, and the top 10 percent earned more than $51,040.

Median annual wages for specialty occupations in May 2012 were as follows:

Motorboat mechanics and service technicians	$35,530
Motorcycle mechanics	33,140
Outdoor power equipment and other small engine mechanics	30,510

Mechanics employed in large shops often receive benefits, such as health insurance, sick leave, and paid vacation time. Conversely, those in small repair shops usually receive few benefits. Some employers pay for work-related training and help mechanics purchase new tools.

Job Outlook

Employment of small engine mechanics is projected to grow 6 percent from 2012 to 2022, slower than the average for all occupations.

Small engines have become more sophisticated and now release fewer pollutants into the atmosphere. Diagnostic equipment which mechanics use to troubleshoot issues with small engines can become too costly for self-employed businesses. Employment of self-employed small engine mechanics is projected to decline from 2012 to 2022, contributing to the slower-than-average growth for employment of small engine mechanics.

Since the number of registered motorcycles has increased steadily in recent years, there will continue to be a need for motorcycle repair services. Most new jobs will be in the motorcycle dealer industry, as service operations are an important aspect of business for many firms in this industry. In addition, as boat engines and engines and parts for outdoor power equipment have become more sophisticated and efficient, there will continue to be demand for repair services as people are less able to repair and service their own equipment.

Job Prospects. Job opportunities are expected to be better for candidates with postsecondary education. Those without postsecondary education can expect to face strong competition for jobs.

O*NET

➤ Motorboat Mechanics and Service Technicians (49-3051.00)
➤ Motorcycle Mechanics (49-3052.00)

➤ Outdoor Power Equipment and Other Small Engine Mechanics (49-3053.00)

Contacts for More Information

For more information on motorboat mechanics and training programs, visit
➤ Association of Marine Technicians (www.am-tech.org/)

For more information on outdoor power equipment and other small engine mechanics and training programs, visit
➤ Equipment & Engine Training Council (www.eetc.org/)

To learn about job opportunities for small engine mechanics, contact local motorcycle, motorboat, and lawn and garden equipment dealers; boatyards; and marinas. Local offices of the state employment service also may have information about employment and training opportunities.

Telecommunications Equipment Installers and Repairers Except Line Installers

- **2012 Median Pay** .... $54,530 per year
$26.22 per hour

- **Entry-Level Education**.... Postsecondary non-degree award

- **Work Experience in a Related Occupation**............... None

- **On-the-Job Training** .... Moderate-term on-the-job training

- **Number of Jobs 2012** 217,200

- **Job Outlook, 2012–22** .... 4% (Slower than average)

- **Employment Change, 2012–22** 8,400

What Telecommunications Equipment Installers and Repairers Except Line Installers Do

Telecommunications equipment installers and repairers, also known as *telecom technicians*, set up and maintain devices or equipment that carry communications signals, connect to telephone lines, or access the Internet.

Duties. Telecommunications equipment installers and repairers typically do the following:

- Install communications equipment in offices, private homes, and buildings that are under construction

- Set up, rearrange, or replace routing and dialing equipment

- Inspect and service equipment, wiring, and phone jacks

- Repair or replace faulty, damaged, or malfunctioning equipment

- Test repaired, newly installed, or updated equipment to ensure that it works properly

- Adjust or calibrate equipment settings to improve its performance

- Keep records of maintenance, repairs, and installations

- Demonstrate and explain the use of equipment to customers

Telephone, computer, and cable telecommunications systems rely on equipment to process and transmit vast amounts of data. Telecommunications equipment installers and repairers–often called *telecom technicians*–install and service this equipment.

Telecom technicians use many different tools to inspect equipment and diagnose problems. For instance, to locate distortions in signals, they may employ spectrum analyzers and polarity probes.

Telecommunications equipment installers and repairers often use computers to diagnose problems with telecommunications switching equipment.

They also commonly use hand tools, including screwdrivers and pliers, to take equipment apart and repair it.

Many technicians also work with computers, specialized hardware, and other diagnostic equipment. They follow manufacturer's instructions or technical manuals to install or update software and programs for devices.

Those who work at a client's location must track hours worked, parts used, and bills collected. Installers who set up and maintain lines outdoors are classified as line installers and repairers.

The specific tasks of telecom technicians vary depending on their specialization and where they work.

The following are examples of types of telecommunications equipment installers and repairers:

Central office technicians set up and maintain switches, routers, fiber optic cables, and other equipment at switching hubs, called central offices. These hubs send, process, and amplify data from thousands of telephone, Internet, and cable connections. Technicians receive alerts on equipment malfunctions from auto-monitoring switches and are able to correct the problems remotely.

Headend technicians perform similar work to central office installers and repairers, but work at distribution centers for cable and television companies, called headends.

PBX installers and repairers set up and service private branch exchange–or PBX–switchboards. This equipment relays incoming, outgoing, and interoffice telephone calls at a single location. Some systems use computers to run Internet access, network applica-

tions, and telephone communications, and support Voice over Internet Protocol–or VoIP–technology.

PBX installers connect telecom equipment to communications cables. They test the connections to ensure that adequate power is available and communication links work properly. They install frames, supports, power systems, alarms, and telephone sets. Because switches and switchboards are computerized, PBX installers also install software or program the equipment.

Station installers and repairers–sometimes known as home installers and repairers–set up and repair telecommunications equipment in customers' homes and businesses. For example, they set up modems to install telephone, Internet, or cable television services.

When customers have problems, station repairers test the customer's lines to determine if the problem is inside or outside. If the problem is inside, they try to repair it. If the problem is outside, they refer the problem to line repairers.

Work Environment

Telecommunications equipment installers and repairers held about 217,200 jobs in 2012.

The industries that employed the most telecommunications equipment installers and repairers in 2012 were as follows:

Wired telecommunications carriers	55%
Building equipment contractors	12
Other telecommunications	6
Cable and other subscription programming	5
Wireless telecommunications carriers (except satellite)	4

Central office technicians generally work in climate-controlled central offices or electronic service centers. PBX and station installers and repairers travel frequently to installation and repair sites, such as homes and offices. Equipment installation may require climbing on rooftops and into attics, and climbing ladders and telephone poles.

Telecom technicians occasionally work in cramped, awkward positions where they often stoop, crouch, crawl, or reach high to do their work. Sometimes they must lift or move heavy equipment and parts. They also may work on equipment while it is powered, so they need to take necessary precautions.

Injuries and Illnesses. Telecom technicians have a higher rate of injuries and illnesses than the national average. Although minor falls, burns, and electrical shocks are common, the work is generally not dangerous when safety precautions are taken.

To reduce risk of injury, workers wear hardhats and harnesses when working on ladders or on elevated equipment. To prevent electrical shocks, technicians also may lock off power to equipment under repair.

Median Annual Wages, May 2012

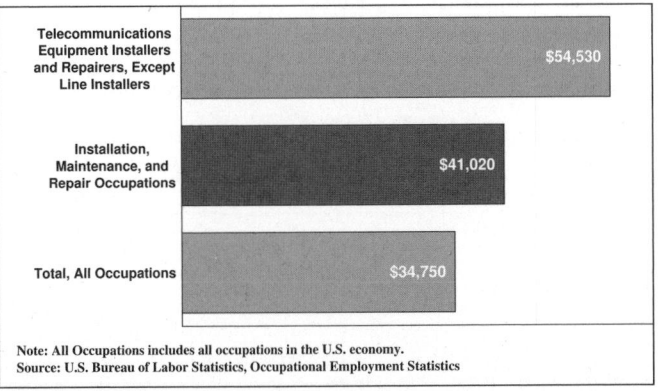

Note: All Occupations includes all occupations in the U.S. economy.
Source: U.S. Bureau of Labor Statistics, Occupational Employment Statistics

Percent Change in Employment, Projected 2012–2022

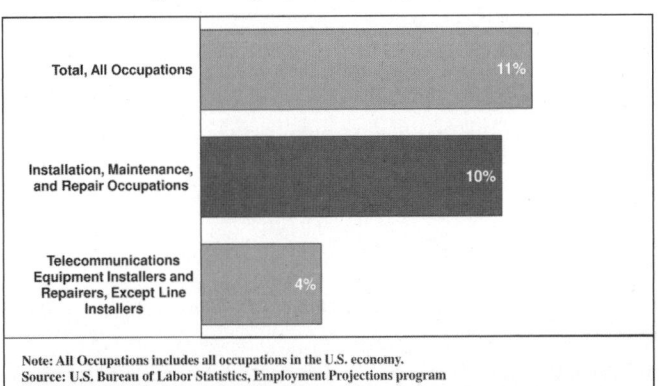

Note: All Occupations includes all occupations in the U.S. economy.
Source: U.S. Bureau of Labor Statistics, Employment Projections program

Employment Projections Data for Telecommunications Equipment Installers and Repairers Except Line Installers

Occupational title	SOC Code	Employment, 2012	Projected Employment, 2022	Change, 2012–2022	
				Percent	Numeric
Telecommunications equipment installers and repairers, except line installers....................................	49-2022	217,200	225,700	4	8,400

Source: U.S. Bureau of Labor Statistics, Employment Projections Program

Note: Data are rounded. Go to Occupational Information Included in the OOH *for a discussion of the data in this table.*

Work Schedules. Most telecom technicians work full time.

Some businesses offer 24-hour repair services. Telecom technicians in these companies work shifts, including evenings, holidays, and weekends. Some are on call around the clock in case of emergencies.

How to Become One

Telecom technicians typically need some postsecondary education in electronics, telecommunications, or computer technology and receive on-the-job training. Industry certification is required for some positions.

Education. Postsecondary education in electronics, telecommunications, or computers is typically needed for telecom technicians.

Technical programs with courses in basic electronics, telecommunications, and computer science offered in community colleges and technical schools may be particularly helpful. Most programs lead to a certificate or an associate's degree in electronics repair, computer science, or related subjects.

Some employers prefer to hire candidates with an associate's degree, particularly for positions such as central office technicians, headend technicians, and those working with commercial communications systems.

Training. Once hired, telecom technicians receive on-the-job training, typically lasting a few months. Training involves a combination of classroom instruction and hands-on work with an experienced technician. In these settings, workers learn the equipment's internal parts and the tools needed for repair. Technicians who have completed postsecondary education often require less on-the-job instruction than those who have not.

Large companies may send new employees to training sessions to learn about equipment, procedures, and technologies offered by equipment manufacturers or industry organizations.

Because technology in this field is rapidly evolving, telecom technicians must continue learning about new equipment over the course of their careers. They may attend manufacturers' training classes, study equipment manuals, or obtain hands-on experience with the latest equipment.

Licenses, Certifications, and Registrations. Some technicians must be certified to perform certain tasks or to work on specific equipment. Certification requirements vary by employer and specialization.

Organizations such as the Society of Cable Telecommunications Engineers and the Telecommunications Industry Association offer certifications for telecom technicians. Some manufacturers also provide certifications for working with specific equipment.

Advancement. Advancement opportunities often depend on previous work experience and training. Repairers with extensive knowledge of equipment may be qualified to become manufacturer's sales workers.

Important Qualities

Color vision. Installers and repairers must be able to distinguish different colors because the wires they work with are color-coded.

Customer-service skills. Because many telecom technicians work in customers' homes and offices, they should be friendly and polite. In addition, they often explain how to maintain and operate equipment to people who have little or no technical knowledge.

Dexterity. Many telecom technician tasks, such as repairing small devices, connecting components, and using hand tools, require a steady hand and good hand–eye coordination.

Mechanical skills. Telecom technicians must be familiar with the devices they install and repair, their internal parts, and the appropriate tools needed to use, install, or fix them. They must also be able to understand manufacturer's instructions when installing or repairing equipment.

Troubleshooting skills. When telecommunications equipment malfunctions, technicians troubleshoot and devise solutions to problems that are not immediately apparent.

Pay

The median annual wage for telecommunications equipment installers and repairers was $54,530 in May 2012. The median wage is the wage at which half the workers in an occupation earned more than that amount and half earned less. The lowest 10 percent earned less than $30,840, and the top 10 percent earned more than $75,040.

In May 2012, the median annual wages for telecommunications equipment installers and repairers in the top five industries employing these workers were as follows:

Other telecommunications	$65,540
Wireless telecommunications carriers (except satellite)	56,590
Wired telecommunications carriers	56,410

Similar Occupations   This table shows a list of occupations with job duties that are similar to those of telecommunications equipment installers and repairers except line installers.

Occupations	Entry-level Education	2012 Pay	Projected Job Growth	Average Annual Openings
Broadcast and Sound Engineering Technicians	See "How to Become One"	$41,232	9%	3,250
Computer, ATM, and Office Machine Repairers	Some college, no degree	$36,620	4%	3,280
Line Installers and Repairers	High school diploma or equivalent	$56,833	7%	9,110

Cable and other subscription programming........................49,270
Building equipment contractors..44,450

Union Membership. Compared with workers in all occupations, telecommunications equipment installers and repairers had a higher percentage of workers who belonged to a union in 2012.

Job Outlook

Employment of telecommunications equipment installers and repairers is projected to grow 4 percent from 2012 to 2022, slower than the average for all occupations.

Consumers, businesses, and governments will continue to demand Internet, cable, or wireless services that provide faster and better connections. Building, maintaining, and upgrading the networks and equipment that support them should create some jobs.

However, overall employment growth of telecom technicians may be offset by a decline in maintenance work. Modern equipment is more reliable, sturdier, easier to repair remotely, and more resistant to damage from the elements, limiting the need for telecom repair technicians.

Job Prospects. Although job opportunities will vary by specialty, those with postsecondary electronics or telecommunications education and strong customer-service and computer skills should have the best job prospects.

Technologies such as video on demand and broadband Internet require high data transfer rates in telecommunications systems. Central office, PBX installers, and headend technicians will be needed to service and upgrade switches and routers to handle increased usage and volume, resulting in very good job opportunities.

However, station installers and repairers can expect strong competition for most positions. Prewired buildings, the reliability of existing telephone lines, and increasing wireless technology usage may reduce the need for general installation and maintenance work.

O*NET

➤ Telecommunications Equipment Installers and Repairers, Except Line Installers (49-2022.00)

Contacts for More Information

For information on career, training, and certification opportunities for telecommunications equipment installers and repairers, visit
➤ Communications Workers of America (www.cwa-union.org)
➤ International Brotherhood of Electrical Workers (www.ibew.org/)
➤ National Coalition for Telecommunication Education and Learning (www.nactel.org/)
➤ Society of Cable Telecommunications Engineers (www.scte.org/default.aspx)
➤ Telecommunications Industry Association (www.tiaonline.org/)

Wind Turbine Technicians

- **2012 Median Pay** ....$45,970 per year
  $22.10 per hour
- **Entry-Level Education** ....Some college, no degree
- **Work Experience in a Related Occupation**.............. None
- **On-the-Job Training** .... Long-term on-the-job training
- **Number of Jobs 2012** 3,200
- **Job Outlook, 2012–22** .... 24% (Much faster than average)
- **Employment Change, 2012–22** 800

What Wind Turbine Technicians Do

Wind turbine service technicians, also known as *windtechs*, install, maintain, and repair wind turbines.

Duties. Wind turbine service technicians typically do the following:

- Inspect the exterior and physical integrity of towers
- Climb towers to inspect or repair turbine equipment
- Collect turbine data for testing or research and analysis
- Perform routine maintenance on wind turbines
- Test electrical components and systems, as well as mechanical and hydraulic systems
- Troubleshoot mechanical, hydraulic, or electrical malfunctions
- Service underground transmission systems, wind field substations, or fiber optic sensing and control systems
- Replace worn or malfunctioning components

Wind turbines are large mechanical devices that convert wind energy into electricity. They are located in areas where there is a lot of wind. The structure is made up of three major components: a tower, three blades, and a nacelle, which is composed of an outer case, brakes, generator, and gearbox. Wind turbine service technicians install and repair the various components of these structures.

Although some windtechs are involved in building new wind turbines, most of their work is maintaining them, particularly the nacelles, which contain the equipment that generates electricity.

Maintenance schedules are largely determined by hours of operation, but can also vary by manufacturer. Most manufacturers now recommend annual maintenance, which involves visual inspections of components and lubricating parts. For turbines that operate year round, typical maintenance may occur one to three times a year. Still, turbines are monitored electronically 24 hours a day from a central office. If a problem is detected, windtechs must travel to the worksite and perform as-needed service.

Windtechs use safety harnesses and a variety of hand and power tools to do their work. They also use computers to diagnose electrical malfunctions. Wind turbines integrate most monitoring equipment into the nacelle, which can be viewed on site.

Work Environment

Wind turbine service technicians (windtechs) held about 3,200 jobs in 2012.

The industries that employed the most wind turbine service technicians in 2012 were as follows:

Commercial and industrial machinery and equipment
 (except automotive and electronic) repair and maintenance... 29%
Electric power generation, transmission and distribution 29
Utility system construction 13

Windtechs generally work outdoors, often at great heights. When performing maintenance, working in confined spaces is common. In addition, workers must climb ladders–sometimes over 260 feet tall–in order to reach the equipment they are servicing, which is often located in confined areas. For example, when repairing blades, windtechs rappel–or descend by sliding down a rope– from the nacelle to the section of the blade that needs servicing.

For major service or repairs, additional windtechs and other specialists may be needed to complete the job.

Work Schedules. Windtechs generally work full time during regular business hours. However, they may be on call to handle emergencies during evenings and weekends.

When a wind turbine is not functioning, technicians must make the necessary repairs as quickly as possible. For those operating the turbine, lost power generation becomes lost revenue.

Windtechs often must travel to rural areas, where many wind farms are located.

How to Become One

Most wind turbine service technicians (windtechs) learn their trade by attending a technical school. After completing a 2-year technical program, employers usually provide on-the-job training, typically lasting over 12 months.

Education. Most windtechs learn their trade by attending technical schools. Associate's degree programs for wind turbine service technicians usually take 2 years and are offered at vocational–technical schools and community colleges.

Many technical schools have onsite wind turbines that students can work on as part of their studies. In addition to practical coursework, other areas of focus that reflect the various skill sets needed to do the job include the following:

- Safety/first aid/CPR training
- Electrical maintenance
- Hydraulic maintenance
- Braking systems
- Mechanical systems, including blade inspection and maintenance
- Computers and programmable logic control systems
- Physical fitness

Training. In addition to an associate's degree, windtechs typically receive over 12 months of on-the-job training related to the specific wind turbines they will maintain and service. Part of this training is manufacturer training. Other training may include an internship with a wind turbine servicing contractor.

Some windtechs are former electricians. Regardless of experience, all candidates must complete wind turbine training in addition to any other construction training they may already have. For example, the International Brotherhood of Electrical Workers offers intensive courses that provide wind turbine-related training specifically for journey electricians.

Other windtechs learn their trade through a windtech apprenticeship. For each year of the program, apprentices must have at least 144 hours of related technical instruction and 2,000 hours of paid on-the-job training. With prior experience or training, the time may be shortened to 1 year. Apprentice training focuses on safety, first aid, and CPR training; electrical, hydraulic, and mechanical systems maintenance; braking systems; and computers and programmable logic control systems.

Because they work at high elevations, wind turbine technicians must wear proper equipment to stay safe on the job.

Unions and individual contractors offer apprenticeship programs. The basic qualifications for workers to enter an apprenticeship program are the following:

- Minimum age of 18
- High school diploma or equivalent
- Physically and mentally able to do the job
- One year of high school or equivalent algebra with a grade of at least a "C"

Licenses, Certifications, and Registrations. Although not mandatory, certification can demonstrate a base level of knowledge and professionalism. The Electronics Technicians Association International (ETAI) offers certification for small wind tower installation. The ETAI will soon have certification for those interested in large commercial wind tower installation.

Important Qualities

Mechanical skills. Windtechs must understand and be able to maintain and repair all mechanical, hydraulic, braking, and electrical systems of a turbine.

Physical stamina. Service technicians must be able to climb high, often with tools and equipment, to reach the turbines. Some tower ladders may be 260 feet high or taller.

Physical strength. Windtechs must lift and climb with heavy equipment and parts and tools. Some weigh in excess of 45 pounds.

Troubleshooting skills. Windtechs must diagnose and repair problems. When a turbine stops generating electricity, technicians must determine the cause and then make the necessary repairs.

Median Annual Wages, May 2012

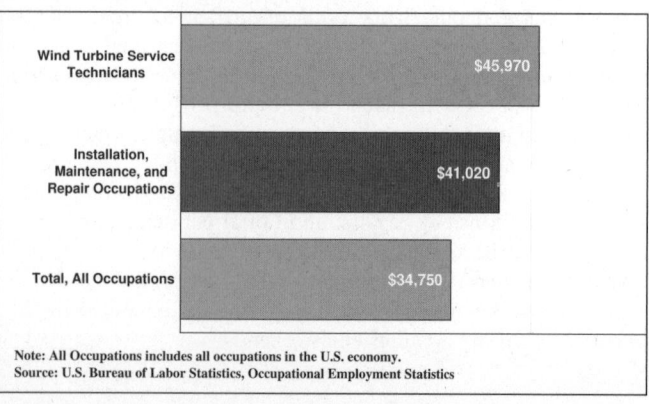

Wind Turbine Service Technicians — $45,970
Installation, Maintenance, and Repair Occupations — $41,020
Total, All Occupations — $34,750

Note: All Occupations includes all occupations in the U.S. economy.
Source: U.S. Bureau of Labor Statistics, Occupational Employment Statistics

Percent Change in Employment, Projected 2012–2022

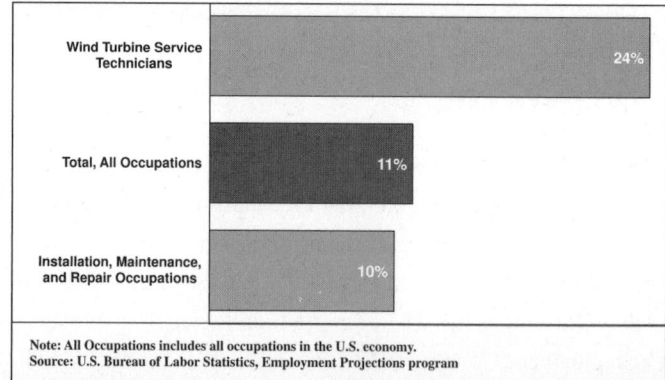

Wind Turbine Service Technicians — 24%
Total, All Occupations — 11%
Installation, Maintenance, and Repair Occupations — 10%

Note: All Occupations includes all occupations in the U.S. economy.
Source: U.S. Bureau of Labor Statistics, Employment Projections program

Employment Projections Data for Wind Turbine Technicians

Occupational title	SOC Code	Employment, 2012	Projected Employment, 2022	Change, 2012–2022	
				Percent	Numeric
Wind turbine service technicians 49-9081		3,200	4,000	24	800

Source: U.S. Bureau of Labor Statistics, Employment Projections Program

Note: Data are rounded. Go to **Occupational Information Included in the OOH** *for a discussion of the data in this table.*

Similar Occupations   This table shows a list of occupations with job duties that are similar to those of wind turbine technicians.

Occupations	Entry-level Education	2012 Pay	Projected Job Growth	Average Annual Openings
Electrical and Electronics Installers and Repairers	Postsecondary non-degree award	$51,081	1%	2,980
Electricians	High school diploma or equivalent	$49,840	20%	22,460
Elevator Installers and Repairers	High school diploma or equivalent	$76,650	24%	800
Heating, Air Conditioning, and Refrigeration Mechanics and Installers	Postsecondary non-degree award	$43,640	21%	12,370
Industrial Machinery Mechanics and Maintenance Workers and Millwrights	High school diploma or equivalent	$45,848	17%	18,700
Plumbers, Pipefitters, and Steamfitters	High school diploma or equivalent	$49,140	21%	13,050

Unafraid of heights and confined spaces. Service technicians often must repair turbines that are at least 260 feet high. In addition, technicians must work in confined spaces in order to access mechanical components of the turbine.

Pay

The median annual wage for wind turbine service technicians (windtechs) was $45,970 in May 2012. The median wage is the wage at which half the workers in an occupation earned more than that amount and half earned less. The lowest 10 percent earned less than $33,170, and the top 10 percent earned more than $66,960.

In May 2012, the median annual wages for wind turbine service technicians in the top three industries employing these technicians were as follows:

Electric power generation, transmission and distribution $48,720
Commercial and industrial machinery and equipment
   (except automotive and electronic) repair and
   maintenance 45,870
Utility system construction 44,130

The starting pay for apprentices is 60 percent of what fully trained windtechs earn. They receive pay increases as they learn to do more.

Job Outlook

Employment of wind turbine service technicians (windtechs) is projected to grow 24 percent from 2012 to 2022, much faster than the average for all occupations. However, because it is a small occupation, the fast growth will result in only about 800 new jobs over the 10-year period.

As wind electricity generation continues to grow, more windtechs will be needed to install and maintain new turbines.

Furthermore, development of taller towers with larger blades reduces the cost of wind power generation, making it more competitive with coal, natural gas, and other forms of power generation.

In addition, the Renewable Electricity Standard calls for 25 percent of U.S. electric power generation to come from renewable sources by 2025, which should further drive employment growth.

The most consistent winds are found offshore, and several offshore wind projects are currently being explored. If approved and developed, many more technicians will be needed. However, the high cost of building wind towers in the ocean may inhibit new offshore projects from being approved.

Job Prospects. Job prospects for qualified windtechs are expected to be excellent. The number of wind turbines being installed is increasing, which should result in consistent and growing demand for windtechs.

In fact, some areas have reported a shortage of qualified workers. Because many people prefer not to work in confined spaces or at great heights, competition for jobs is often light.

Job opportunities will vary by individual state's incentive programs and the prospects for consistent wind. For instance, coastal and Midwest states, where wind is generally more prevalent, are more likely to have wind farms and thus more job opportunities.

O*NET

➤ Wind Turbine Service Technicians (49-9081.00)

Contacts for More Information

For details about apprenticeships or other work opportunities in this trade, contact the offices of the state employment service, the state apprenticeship agency, local electrical contractors or firms that employ windtechs, or local union-management apprenticeship committees. Apprenticeship information is available from the U.S. Department of Labor's toll-free help line, 1 (877) 872-5627, or the Employment and Training Administration (www.doleta.gov/OA/eta_default.cfm).

For more information about union apprenticeship and training programs for electricians, visit
➤ International Brotherhood of Electrical Workers (www.ibew.org)

For more information about other educational opportunities, visit
➤ American Wind Energy Association (http://awea.org/)

Legal

Arbitrators, Mediators, and Conciliators

- **2012 Median Pay** .... $61,280 per year
$29.46 per hour
- **Entry-Level Education** ....Bachelor's degree
- **Work Experience in a Related Occupation**.........Less than 5 years
- **On-the-Job Training** .... Moderate-term on-the-job training
- **Number of Jobs 2012** 8,400
- **Job Outlook, 2012–22** .... 10% (As fast as average)
- **Employment Change, 2012–22** 900

Arbitrators, mediators, and conciliators resolve disputes and facilitate negotiations between parties.

What Arbitrators, Mediators, and Conciliators Do

Arbitrators, mediators, and conciliators help resolve conflicts outside of the court system by facilitating negotiation and dialogue between disputing parties.

Duties. Arbitrators, mediators, and conciliators typically do the following:

- Facilitate communication between disputants to guide parties toward mutual agreement
- Clarify issues, concerns, needs, and interests of all parties involved
- Conduct initial meetings with disputants to outline the arbitration process
- Settle procedural matters such as fees, or determine details such as witness numbers or time requirements
- Set up appointments for parties to meet for mediation or arbitration
- Interview claimants, agents, or witnesses to obtain information about disputed issues
- Prepare settlement agreements for disputants to sign
- Apply relevant laws, regulations, policies, or precedents to reach conclusions
- Evaluate information from documents such as claim applications, birth or death certificates, or physician or employer records

Arbitrators, mediators, or conciliators help opposing parties settle disputes outside of court. They hold private, confidential hearings, which are less formal than a court trial.

Arbitrators are usually attorneys or business people with expertise in a particular field. They hear and decide disputes between opposing parties as an impartial third party. Arbitrators may work alone or in a panel with other arbitrators. In some cases, arbitrators may decide procedural issues, such as what evidence may be submitted and when hearings will be held.

Arbitration may be mandatory and required by law for some claims and disputes. Other times, the parties in dispute voluntary agree to arbitration rather than proceed with litigation or a trial. In some cases, parties may appeal the arbitrator's decision.

Mediators are neutral parties who help people resolve their disputes. However, unlike arbitrators, they do not make decisions. Rather, mediators help facilitate discussion and guide the parties toward a mutually acceptable agreement. If the opposing sides cannot reach a settlement with the mediator's help, they are free to pursue other options.

Conciliators are similar to mediators. Their role is to help guide opposing sides to a settlement. However, they typically meet with the parties separately. The opposing sides must decide in advance

Median Annual Wages, May 2012

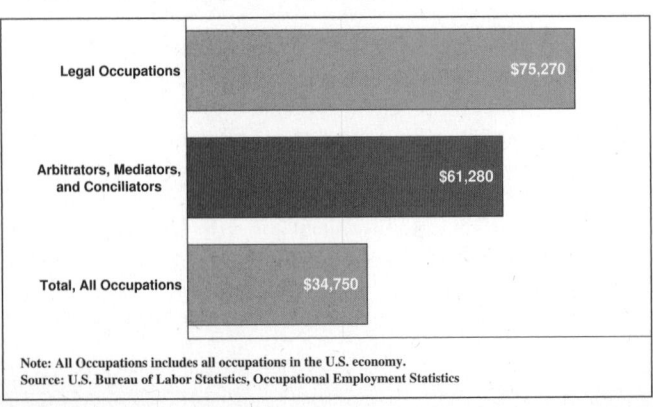

Note: All Occupations includes all occupations in the U.S. economy.
Source: U.S. Bureau of Labor Statistics, Occupational Employment Statistics

Percent Change in Employment, Projected 2012–2022

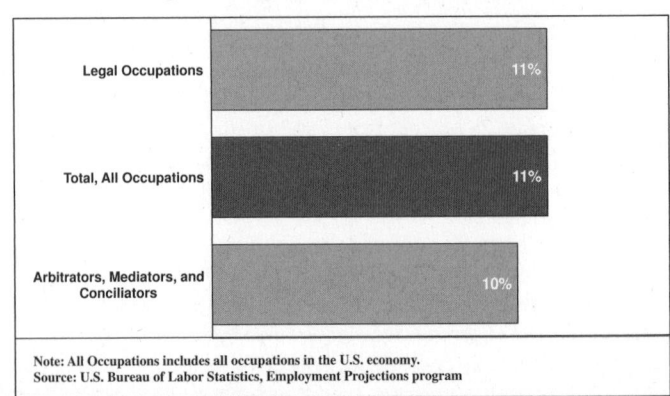

Note: All Occupations includes all occupations in the U.S. economy.
Source: U.S. Bureau of Labor Statistics, Employment Projections program

Employment Projections Data for Arbitrators, Mediators, and Conciliators

Occupational title	SOC Code	Employment, 2012	Projected Employment, 2022	Change, 2012–2022 Percent	Change, 2012–2022 Numeric
Arbitrators, mediators, and conciliators.............................. 23-1022		8,400	9,300	10	900

Source: U.S. Bureau of Labor Statistics, Employment Projections Program

Note: *Data are rounded. Go to* **Occupational Information Included in the OOH** *for a discussion of the data in this table.*

if they will be bound by the conciliator's recommendations. The conciliator typically has no authority to seek evidence or call witnesses. These workers typically do not write decisions or make awards.

Work Environment

Arbitrators, mediators, and conciliators held about 8,400 jobs in 2012. Many work for state or local governments or in the legal services industry.

The industries that employed the most arbitrators, mediators, and conciliators in 2012 were as follows:

State and local government, excluding education and hospitals	29%
Legal services	17
Religious, grantmaking, civic, professional, and similar organizations	10
Health care and social assistance	6
Finance and insurance	4

Arbitrators, mediators, and conciliators usually work in private offices or meeting rooms. They may travel to a neutral site chosen for negotiations.

Work Schedules. Some arbitrators, mediators, and conciliators work part time and may also have other occupations or careers.

How to Become One

Arbitrators, mediators, and conciliators learn their skills through a combination of education, training, and work experience.

Education. Education is one part to becoming an arbitrator, mediator, or conciliator. However, few receive a degree specific to the field of arbitration, mediation, or conflict resolution. Rather, many positions require an educational degree appropriate to the applicant's field of expertise, and a bachelor's degree is often sufficient. Many other positions, however, may require applicants to have a law degree, a master's in business administration, or other advanced degree.

Some colleges and universities offer a certificate program in conflict resolution or a 2-year master's degree in dispute resolution or conflict management, or a 4- or 5-year doctoral degree program. Applicants may use these programs to supplement their existing educational degree and work experience in other fields.

Work Experience in a Related Occupation. Arbitrators, mediators, and conciliators are usually lawyers, retired judges, or business professionals with expertise in a particular field, such as construction or insurance. They need to have knowledge of that industry and be able to relate well to people from different cultures and backgrounds.

Training. Although there are no state requirements for mediators working in private settings, mediators must typically meet specific training or experience standards to practice in state-funded or court-appointed mediation cases. Qualifications and standards vary by state or by court. However, most states require mediators to complete a 40-hour basic course in mediation and a 20-hour advanced or specialized training course.

Some states require mediators to work under the supervision of an experienced mediator for a certain amount of cases before becoming qualified.

Training for arbitrators, mediators, and conciliators is available through independent mediation programs, national and local mediation membership organizations, and postsecondary schools. Training is also available by volunteering at a community mediation center.

Licenses, Certifications, and Registrations. There is national license for arbitrators, mediators, and conciliators. State requirements vary widely. Some states require licenses appropriate to applicant's field of expertise. For example, some courts may require applicants to be licensed attorneys or certified public accountants.

Important Qualities

Critical-thinking skills. Arbitrators, mediators, and conciliators must apply rules of law. They must remain neutral and not let their own personal assumptions interfere with the proceedings.

Decision-making skills. Arbitrators, mediators, and conciliators must be able to weigh the facts, apply the law or rules, and make a decision relatively quickly.

Interpersonal skills. Arbitrators, mediators, and conciliators deal with disputing parties and must be able to facilitate discussion in a calm and respectful way.

Listening skills. Arbitrators, mediators, and conciliators must pay close attention to what is being said in order to evaluate information.

Similar Occupations This table shows a list of occupations with job duties that are similar to those of arbitrators, mediators, and conciliators.

Occupations	Entry-level Education	2012 Pay	Projected Job Growth	Average Annual Openings
Judges and Hearing Officers	Doctoral or professional degree	$106,005	1%	760
Lawyers	Doctoral or professional degree	$113,530	10%	19,650
Paralegals and Legal Assistants	Associate's degree	$46,990	17%	9,120
Private Detectives and Investigators	High school diploma or equivalent	$45,740	11%	1,180

Reading skills. Arbitrators, mediators, and conciliators must be able to evaluate and distinguish the important facts from large amounts of complex information.

Writing skills. Arbitrators, mediators, and conciliators write recommendations or decisions on appeals or disputes. They must be able to write their decisions clearly so that all sides understand the decision.

Pay

The median annual wage for arbitrators, mediators, and conciliators was $61,280 in May 2012. The median wage is the wage at which half the workers in an occupation earned more than that amount and half earned less. The lowest 10 percent earned less than $34,100, and the top 10 percent earned more than $137,350.

In May 2012, the median annual wages for arbitrators, mediators, and conciliators in the top five industries in which they worked were as follows:

Legal services	$109,470
Finance and insurance	59,730
Religious, grantmaking, civic, professional, and similar organizations	58,280
State and local government, excluding education and hospitals	57,370
Health care and social assistance	42,210

Many arbitrators, mediators, and conciliators work part time and may have other occupations or careers.

Job Outlook

Employment of arbitrators, mediators, and conciliators is projected to grow 10 percent from 2012 to 2022, about as fast as the average for all occupations.

Arbitration and other alternative dispute resolution methods are often seen as faster and less expensive than trials and litigation. In addition, many contracts, including employment, customer, and real estate contracts, may include clauses requiring complaints and disputes to be decided through mediation or arbitration.

However, employment growth of arbitrators, mediators, and conciliators is expected to be moderate. Because many arbitrators, mediators, and conciliators work for state or local government, budgetary constraints may limit employment growth. Also, in some cases or industries, litigation is either unavoidable or its benefits are still preferred over other types of conflict resolution.

Job Prospects. Because arbitrators, mediators, and conciliators deal extensively with legal issues and disputes, those with a law degree should have better job prospects. In addition, lawyers with expertise or experience in one or more particular legal areas, such as environmental, health, or corporate law, should also have the best job prospects.

O*NET

➤ Arbitrators, Mediators, and Conciliators (23-1022.00)

Contacts for More Information

For more information about arbitrators, mediators, and conciliators, visit

➤ American Arbitration Association (www.adr.org)

➤ Association for Conflict Resolution (www.acrnet.org/Page.aspx?id=532)

Court Reporters

- **2012 Median Pay** .... $48,160 per year
  $23.15 per hour
- **Entry-Level Education** .... Postsecondary non-degree award
- **Work Experience in a Related Occupation** .... None
- **On-the-Job Training** .... Short-term on-the-job training
- **Number of Jobs 2012** 21,200
- **Job Outlook, 2012–22** .... 10% (As fast as average)
- **Employment Change, 2012–22** 2,000

What Court Reporters Do

Court reporters create word-for-word transcriptions at trials, depositions, administrative hearings, and other legal proceedings. Some court reporters provide captioning for television and real-time translation for deaf or hard-of-hearing people at public events, at business meetings, and in classrooms.

Duties. Court reporters typically do the following:

- Attend depositions, hearings, proceedings, and other events that require written transcripts
- Capture spoken dialogue with specialized equipment, including stenography machines, video and audio recording devices, and covered microphones
- Read or play back all or a portion of the proceedings upon request from the judge
- Ask speakers to clarify inaudible or unclear statements or testimony
- Review notes for names of speakers and technical terminology
- Prepare transcripts for the record
- Edit transcripts for typographical errors

Voice writers record everything that is said by judges, witnesses, attorneys, and others in a court proceeding, and prepare written transcripts.

Median Annual Wages, May 2012

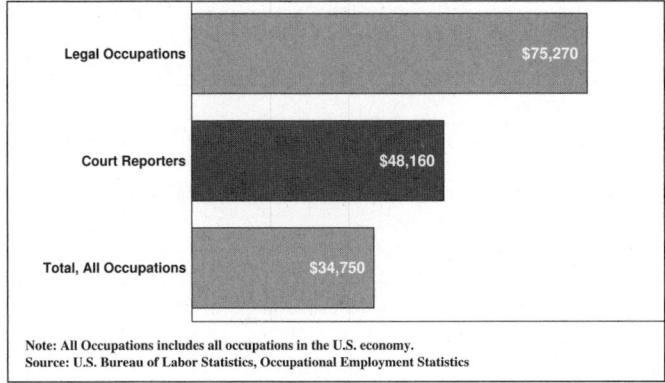

Legal Occupations	$75,270
Court Reporters	$48,160
Total, All Occupations	$34,750

Note: All Occupations includes all occupations in the U.S. economy.
Source: U.S. Bureau of Labor Statistics, Occupational Employment Statistics

Percent Change in Employment, Projected 2012–2022

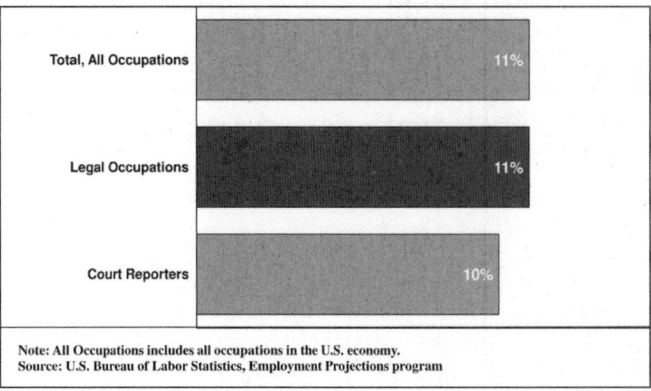

Total, All Occupations	11%
Legal Occupations	11%
Court Reporters	10%

Note: All Occupations includes all occupations in the U.S. economy.
Source: U.S. Bureau of Labor Statistics, Employment Projections program

- Provide copies of transcripts and recordings to the courts, counsels, and parties involved
- Transcribe television or movie dialogue onto screens to help deaf or hard-of-hearing viewers
- Provide real-time translation in classes and other public forums with deaf or hard-of-hearing students and individuals

Court reporters create word-for-word transcripts of speeches, conversations, legal proceedings, meetings, or other events.

Court reporters play a critical role in legal proceedings which require an exact record of what was said. They are responsible for producing a complete, accurate, and secure legal transcript of courtroom proceedings, witness testimonies, and depositions.

Court reporters in the legal setting also help judges and attorneys by capturing, organizing, and producing the official record. This allows users to efficiently search for important information contained in the transcript.

Some court reporters, however, do not work in the legal setting or in courtrooms. These reporters primarily serve people who are deaf or hard of hearing by transcribing speech to text as the speech occurs.

The following are examples of types of court reporters who do not work in the legal setting:

Broadcast captioners are court reporters who provide captions for television programs (called closed captions). These reporters transcribe dialogue onto television monitors to help deaf or hard-of-hearing viewers or others viewing television programs in public places. Some broadcast captioners may translate dialogue in real time during broadcasts; others may caption during postproduction of a program.

Communication Access Real-Time Translation (CART) providers are court reporters who work primarily with deaf or hard-of-hearing people in a variety of settings. They assist clients during board meetings, doctor's appointments, or any other events in which real-time translation is needed. For example, CART providers who use a stenograph machine may caption high school and college classes and provide an immediate transcript to students who are hard of hearing or learning English as a second language.

Although some court reporters may accompany their clients to events, many broadcast captioners and CART providers work remotely. An Internet or phone connection allows them to hear and type without having to be in the room.

Court reporters who work with deaf or hard-of-hearing people turn speech into text. For information on workers who help deaf or hard-of-hearing people through sign language, cued speech, or other spoken or gestural means, see the profile on interpreters and translators.

Court reporters may use different methods for recording speech, such as stenotype machine recording, steno mask recording, or digital recording.

Court reporters use stenotype machines to record dialogue as it is spoken. Stenotype machines work like keyboards, but create words through key combinations rather than single characters, allowing court reporters to keep up with fast-moving dialogue. Court reporters who use stenotype machines are known as stenographers.

Key combinations entered on a stenotype machine are recorded in a computer program. The program uses computer-assisted transcription (CAT) to translate the key combinations into the words and phrases they represent, creating real-time, readable text. The court reporter then reviews the text for accuracy and corrects spelling and grammar errors.

Court reporters also may use steno masks to transcribe speech. Court reporters who use steno masks speak directly into a covered microphone, recording dialogue and reporting gestures and actions. Because the microphone is covered, others cannot hear what the reporter is saying. The recording is sometimes converted by computerized voice-recognition software into a transcript that the court reporter reviews for accuracy, spelling, and grammar.

For both stenotype machine recording and steno mask recording, court reporters must create, maintain, and continuously update an online dictionary that the computer software uses to transcribe the key presses or voice recordings into text. For example, court reporters may put in the names of people involved in a court case or the specific words or specialized, technical jargon that are typically used in that type of legal proceeding.

Court reporters may also use digital recorders in their job. Digital recording creates an audio or video record rather than a written transcript. Court reporters who use digital recorders operate and monitor the recording equipment. They also take notes to identify the speakers and provide context. In some cases, court reporters use the audio recording to create a written transcript.

Work Environment

Court reporters held about 21,200 jobs in 2012. The industries that employed the most court reporters in 2012 were as follows:

Local government, excluding education and hospitals............ 31%
State government, excluding education and hospitals............. 30
Administrative and support services 27
Information 2

Most court reporters work for state or local governments in courts or legislatures. Some also work as freelance reporters for pretrial depositions and other events. Some broadcast caption-

Employment Projections Data for Court Reporters

Occupational title	SOC Code	Employment, 2012	Projected Employment, 2022	Change, 2012–2022	
				Percent	Numeric
Court reporters..	23-2091	21,200	23,200	10	2,000

Source: U.S. Bureau of Labor Statistics, Employment Projections Program

Note: Data are rounded. Go to **Occupational Information Included in the OOH** *for a discussion of the data in this table.*

ers and Communication Access Real-Time Translation (CART) providers work remotely from either their home or a central office.

Work Schedules. Court reporters who work in a court setting typically work full time, recording events and preparing transcripts. Freelance reporters have more flexibility in setting their work schedules.

How to Become One

Many community colleges and technical institutes offer postsecondary certificate programs for court reporters. Many states require court reporters who work in legal settings to be licensed.

Education. Many court reporters receive formal training at community colleges or technical institutes. There are different programs that lead to either a certificate or an associate's degree in court reporting. Either a certificate or an associate's degree will qualify applicants for many entry-level positions. Certification programs prepare students to pass the licensing exams successfully and typing speed tests required by most states and employers.

Most court reporting programs include courses in English grammar and phonetics, legal procedures, and legal terminology. Students also practice preparing transcripts to improve the speed and accuracy of their work.

Some schools also offer training in the use of different transcription machines, such as stenotype machines or steno masks.

Licenses, Certifications, and Registrations. Many states require court reporters who work in legal settings to be licensed or certified by a professional association. Licensing requirements vary by state and by method of court reporting.

The National Court Reporters Association (NCRA) offers certification for court reporters, broadcast captioners, and Communication Access Real-Time Translation (CART) providers. Certification as a Registered Professional Reporter (RPR) requires successful completion of a written test and a 3-part skills test in which applicants must type a minimum number of words per minute.

Currently, 22 states accept or use the RPR certification in place of a state certification or licensing exam. To maintain their certification with the NCRA, court reporters must complete continuing education classes and online training.

Digital and voice reporters also may obtain certification.

Specific state licensing and continuing education requirements can be found by visiting the state association's website.

Training. After completing their formal program, court reporters must complete short-term on-the-job training. This typically includes additional skills training as well as training on the more technical terminology that may be used during complex medical or legal proceedings.

Important Qualities

Concentration. Court reporters must be able to concentrate for long periods. They must remain focused on the dialogue they are recording even in the presence of auditory distractions.

Detail oriented. Court reporters must be able to produce error-free work, because they create transcripts that serve as legal records.

Listening skills. Court reporters must give their full attention to speakers and capture every word that is said.

Writing skills. Court reporters need a good command of grammar, vocabulary, and punctuation.

Pay

The median annual wage for court reporters was $48,160 in May 2012. The median wage is the wage at which half the workers in an occupation earned more than that amount and half earned less. The lowest 10 percent earned less than $24,790, and the top 10 percent earned more than $90,530.

Freelance court reporters are paid for their time, but can also sell their transcripts per page for an additional profit.

Job Outlook

Employment of court reporters is projected to grow 10 percent from 2012 to 2022, about as fast as the average for all occupations. Demand for court reporters will be influenced by new federal regulations requiring expanded use of captioning for television, the Internet, and other technologies.

Reporters will increasingly be needed for captioning outside of legal proceedings. All new television programming will continue to need closed captioning. Broadcasters are adding closed captioning to their online programming in order to comply with new federal regulations.

Growth of the elderly population also will increase demand for court reporters who are Communication Access Real-Time Translation (CART) providers or who can accompany their clients to doctor's appointments, townhall meetings, and religious services. In addition, movie theaters and sports stadiums will provide closed captioning for deaf or hard-of-hearing customers.

Employment growth may be negatively affected by the increased use of digital audio recording technology (DAR). Some states have already replaced court reporters with this technology; other states are currently assessing the reliability, accuracy, and costs associated with installing and maintaining the digital audio and video equipment and software.

Despite the cost savings that may be achieved with DAR, some state and federal courts may still prefer the quality provided by

Similar Occupations This table shows a list of occupations with job duties that are similar to those of court reporters.

Occupations	Entry-level Education	2012 Pay	Projected Job Growth	Average Annual Openings
Interpreters and Translators	Bachelor's degree	$45,430	46%	3,810
Medical Transcriptionists	Postsecondary non-degree award	$34,020	8%	2,240

highly trained court reporters. In addition, court reporters may still be needed to verify, check, and supervise the production of transcripts after proceedings have been digitally recorded.

Job Prospects. Job prospects for graduates of court reporting programs are expected to be very good. Court reporters with experience and training in CART and real-time captioning will have the best job prospects.

O*NET

➤ Court Reporters (23-2091.00)

Contacts for More Information

For more information on becoming a court reporter, including training programs and certification as a Register Professional Reporters, visit

➤ National Court Reporters Association (www.ncraonline.org)

For more information on certification and legal resources, as well as becoming an electronic/digital reporter, visit

➤ American Association of Electronic Reporters (www.aaert.org)

For more information on voice writing and certification, visit

➤ National Verbatim Reporters Association (www.nvra.org)

Judges and Hearing Officers

- **2012 Median Pay** .... $102,980 per year
  $49.51 per hour
- **Entry-Level Education** ... Doctoral or professional degree
- **Work Experience in a Related Occupation**.... See "How to Become One"
- **On-the-Job Training** ....Short-term on-the-job training
- **Number of Jobs 2012** 43,200
- **Job Outlook, 2012–22** .... 1% (Little or no change)
- **Employment Change, 2012–22** 400

Judges decide cases when the law does not require a jury trial or when the parties waive their right to a jury.

What Judges and Hearing Officers Do

Judges and hearing officers apply the law by overseeing the legal process in courts. They also conduct pretrial hearings, resolve administrative disputes, facilitate negotiations between opposing parties, and issue legal decisions.

Duties. Judges and hearing officers typically do the following:

- Research legal issues
- Read and evaluate information from documents, such as motions, claim applications, and records
- Preside over hearings and listen to and read arguments by opposing parties
- Determine if the information presented supports the charge, claim, or dispute
- Decide if the procedure is being conducted according to the rules and law
- Apply laws or precedents to reach judgments and to resolve disputes between parties
- Write opinions, decisions, and instructions regarding cases, claims, and disputes

Judges commonly preside over trials and hearings of cases regarding nearly every aspect of society, from individual traffic offenses to issues concerning the rights of large corporations. Judges listen to arguments and determine whether the evidence presented deserves a trial. In criminal cases, judges may decide that people charged with crimes should be held in jail until the trial, or they may set conditions for their release. They also approve search and arrest warrants.

Judges interpret the law to determine how a trial will proceed, which is particularly important when unusual circumstances arise for which standard procedures have not been established. They ensure that hearings and trials are conducted fairly and that the legal rights of all involved parties are protected.

In trials in which juries are selected to decide the case, judges instruct jurors on applicable laws and direct them to consider the facts from the evidence. For other trials, judges decide the case. A judge who determines guilt in criminal cases may impose a sentence or penalty on the guilty party. In civil cases, the judge may award relief, such as compensation for damages, to the parties who win lawsuits.

Judges use various forms of technology, such as electronic databases and software, to manage cases and to prepare for trials. In some cases, a judge may manage the court's administrative and clerical staff.

The following are examples of types of judges and hearing officers:

Judges, magistrate judges, and *magistrates* preside over trials and hearings. They typically work in local, state, and federal courts.

In local and state court systems, they have a variety of titles, such as *municipal court judge, county court judge, magistrate,* and *justice of the peace.* Traffic violations, misdemeanors, small-claims cases, and pretrial hearings make up the bulk of these judges' work.

In federal and state court systems, *district court judges* and *general trial court judges* have authority over any case in their system. *Appellate court judges* rule on a small number of cases, by reviewing decisions of the lower courts and lawyers' written and oral arguments.

Hearing officers, also known as *administrative law judges* or *adjudicators*, usually work for government agencies. They decide many issues, such as if a person is eligible for workers' compensation benefits, and if employment discrimination occurred.

Median Annual Wages, May 2012

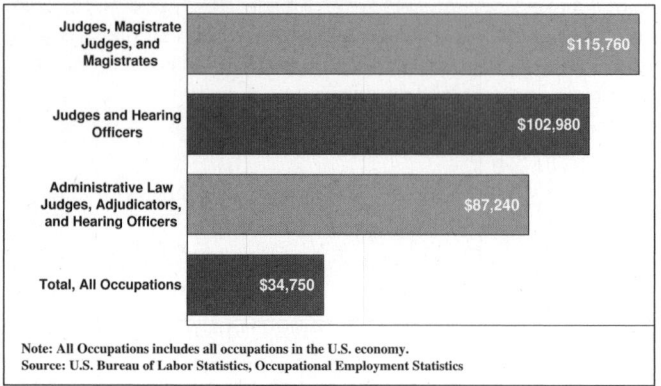

Note: All Occupations includes all occupations in the U.S. economy.
Source: U.S. Bureau of Labor Statistics, Occupational Employment Statistics

Percent Change in Employment, Projected 2012–2022

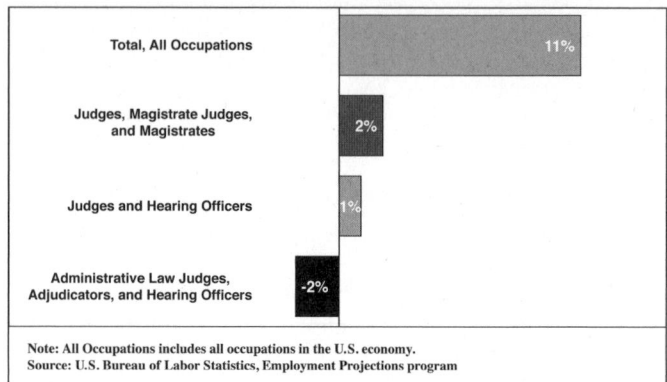

Note: All Occupations includes all occupations in the U.S. economy.
Source: U.S. Bureau of Labor Statistics, Employment Projections program

Work Environment

Judges and hearing officers held about 43,200 jobs in 2012. All were employed by federal, state, and local government.

Judges and hearing officers do most of their work in offices and courtrooms. Their jobs can be demanding, because they must sit in the same position in the court or hearing room for long periods and give undivided attention to the process.

Some judges and hearing officers may be required to travel to different counties and courthouses throughout their state.

Work Schedules. Most judges and hearing officers work full time, but many often work longer hours to prepare for hearings. Some judges and hearing officers work part time and divide their time between their judicial responsibilities and other careers.

Judges also have to be on-call during nights or weekends to issue emergency orders, such as search warrants and restraining orders.

How to Become One

Judges and hearing officers must typically have a law degree and work experience as a lawyer.

Education. A law degree is required for most jobs as a local, state, or federal judge or hearing officer.

In addition to a law degree, federal administrative law judges must also pass a competitive exam from the U.S. Office of Personnel Management.

Getting a law degree usually takes 7 years of full-time study after high school–4 years of undergraduate study, followed by 3 years of law school. Law degree programs include courses, such as constitutional law, contracts, property law, civil procedure, and legal writing. For more information on how to become a lawyer, see the profile on lawyers.

Most judges and magistrates must be appointed or elected into judge positions, a procedure that often takes political support. Many local and state judges are appointed to serve fixed renewable terms, ranging from 4 to 14 years. A few judges, such as appellate court judges, are appointed for life. Judicial nominating commissions screen candidates for judgeships in many states and for some federal judgeships. Some local and state judges are elected to a specific term, commonly 4 years, in an election process.

Work Experience in a Related Occupation. Most judges and hearing officers learn their skills through years of experience as practicing lawyers. Some states allow those who are not lawyers to hold limited-jurisdiction judgeships, but opportunities are better for those with law experience.

Training. All states have some type of orientation for newly elected or appointed judges. The Federal Judicial Center, American Bar Association, The National Judicial College, and the National Center for State Courts provide judicial education and training for judges and other judicial branch personnel.

More than half of all states, as well as Puerto Rico, require judges to take continuing education courses while serving on the bench. General and continuing education courses usually last from a few days to 3 weeks.

Licenses, Certifications, and Registrations. Judges who are lawyers already hold a license.

Federal administrative law judges must be licensed to practice law.

Advancement. Advancement for some judicial workers means moving to courts with a broader jurisdiction. Advancement for various hearing officers includes taking on more complex cases, starting businesses, practicing law, and becoming district court judges.

Important Qualities

Critical-thinking skills. Judges and hearing officers must apply rules of law. They cannot let their own personal assumptions interfere with the proceedings. For example, they must base their decisions on specific meanings of the law, when evaluating and deciding whether a person is a threat to others and must be sent to jail.

Employment Projections Data for Judges and Hearing Officers

Occupational title	SOC Code	Employment, 2012	Projected Employment, 2022	Change, 2012–2022	
				Percent	Numeric
Judges and hearing officers..	—	43,200	43,600	1	400
Administrative law judges, adjudicators,					
and hearing officers	23-1021	14,900	14,700	-2	-300
Judges, magistrate judges, and magistrates......................	23-1023	28,300	29,000	2	700

Source: U.S. Bureau of Labor Statistics, Employment Projections Program

Note: Data are rounded. Go to **Occupational Information Included in the OOH** *for a discussion of the data in this table.*

Similar Occupations   This table shows a list of occupations with job duties that are similar to those of judges and hearing officers.

Occupations	Entry-level Education	2012 Pay	Projected Job Growth	Average Annual Openings
Arbitrators, Mediators, and Conciliators	Bachelor's degree	$61,280	11%	220
Lawyers	Doctoral or professional degree	$113,530	10%	19,650
Paralegals and Legal Assistants	Associate's degree	$46,990	17%	9,120
Private Detectives and Investigators	High school diploma or equivalent	$45,740	11%	1,180

Decision-making skills. Judges and hearing officers must be able to weigh the facts, to apply the law and rules, and to make a decision relatively quickly.

Listening skills. Judges and hearing officers must pay close attention to what is being said, to evaluate information.

Reading skills. Judges and hearing officers must be able to evaluate and distinguish the important facts from large amounts of sometimes complex information.

Writing skills. Judges and hearing officers write recommendations and decisions on appeals and disputes. They must be able to write their decisions clearly so that all sides understand the decision.

Pay

The median annual wage for judges, magistrate judges and magistrates was $115,760 in May 2012. The median wage is the wage at which half the workers in an occupation earned more than that amount and half earned less. The lowest 10 percent earned less than $30,060, and the top 10 percent earned more than $166,880.

The median annual wage for administrative law judges, adjudicators and hearing officers was $87,240 in May 2012. The lowest 10 percent earned less than $40,330, and the top 10 percent earned more than $154,380.

Job Outlook

Employment of judges and hearing officers is projected to show little or no change from 2012 to 2022.

The number of federal and state judgeships is projected to remain steady because nearly every new position for a judge must be authorized and approved by legislature.

Budgetary constraints in federal, state, and local governments are expected to limit the employment growth of hearing officers and administrative law judges, despite the continued need for these workers to settle disputes.

Job Prospects. The prestige associated with becoming a judge will ensure continued competition for these positions. Most job openings will arise as a result of judges and hearing officers leaving the occupation because of retirement, to teach, or because it's the end of their elected term.

O*NET

➤ Administrative Law Judges, Adjudicators, and Hearing Officers (23-1021.00)
➤ Judges, Magistrate Judges, and Magistrates (23-1023.00)

Contacts for More Information

For more information about state courts and judgeships, visit
➤ National Center for State Courts (www.ncsc.org/)
For more information about federal judges, visit
➤ Administrative Office of the United States Courts (www.uscourts.gov/Home.aspx)

For more information about judicial education and training for judges and other judicial branch personnel, visit
➤ Federal Judicial Center (www.fjc.gov/)
➤ American Bar Association (www.americanbar.org)
➤ The National Judicial College (www.judges.org/)

Lawyers

- **2012 Median Pay** .... $113,530 per year
  $54.58 per hour
- **Entry-Level Education** ... Doctoral or professional degree
- **Work Experience in a Related Occupation**............... None
- **On-the-Job Training** .... None
- **Number of Jobs 2012** 759,800
- **Job Outlook, 2012–22** .... 10% (As fast as average)
- **Employment Change, 2012–22** 74,800

What Lawyers Do

Lawyers advise and represent individuals, businesses, and government agencies on legal issues and disputes.

Duties. Lawyers typically do the following:

- Advise and represent clients in courts, before government agencies, and in private legal matters
- Communicate with their clients and others
- Conduct research and analysis of legal problems
- Interpret laws, rulings, and regulations for individuals and businesses
- Present facts in writing and verbally to their clients or others and argue on their behalf
- Prepare and file legal documents, such as lawsuits, appeals, wills, contracts, and deeds

Lawyers, also called attorneys, act as both advocates and advisors.

As advocates, they represent one of the parties in criminal or civil trials by presenting evidence and arguing in support of their client.

As advisors, lawyers counsel their clients about their legal rights and obligations and suggest courses of action in business and personal matters. All attorneys research the intent of laws and judicial decisions and apply the laws to the specific circumstances that their clients face.

Lawyers often oversee the work of support staff, such as paralegals and legal assistants.

Lawyers may have different titles and different duties, depending on where they work.

Criminal law attorneys are also known as *prosecutors* and *defense attorneys.*

Prosecutors typically work for the government to file a lawsuit, or charge, against an individual or corporation accused of violating the law.

Defense attorneys work for either individuals or the government (as public defenders) to represent and defend the accused.

Government counsels commonly work in government agencies. They write and interpret laws and regulations and set up procedures to enforce them. Government counsels also write legal reviews on agencies' decisions. They argue civil and criminal cases on behalf of the government.

Corporate counsels, also called *in-house counsels*, are lawyers who work for corporations. They advise a corporation's executives about legal issues related to the corporation's business activities. These issues may involve patents, government regulations, contracts with other companies, property interests, taxes, or collective-bargaining agreements with unions.

Legal aid lawyers work for private, nonprofit organizations for disadvantaged people. They generally handle civil cases, such as those about leases, job discrimination, and wage disputes, rather than criminal cases.

Lawyers often specialize in a particular area. The following are some examples of types of lawyers:

Environmental lawyers deal with issues and regulations that are related to the environment. They may represent advocacy groups, waste disposal companies, and government agencies to make sure they comply with the relevant laws.

Tax lawyers handle a variety of tax-related issues for individuals and corporations. Tax lawyers may help clients navigate complex tax regulations, so that they pay the appropriate tax on items such as income, profits, or property. For example, they may advise a corporation on how much tax it needs to pay from profits made in different states to comply with the Internal Revenue Service (IRS) rules.

Intellectual property lawyers deal with the laws related to inventions, patents, trademarks, and creative works, such as music, books, and movies. An intellectual property lawyer may advise a client about whether it is okay to use published material in the client's forthcoming book.

Family lawyers handle a variety of legal issues that pertain to the family. They may advise clients regarding divorce, child custody, and adoption proceedings.

Securities lawyers work on legal issues arising from the buying and selling of stocks, ensuring that all disclosure requirements are met. They may advise corporations that are interested in listing in the stock exchange through an initial public offering (IPO) or buying shares in another corporation.

Trial lawyers spend most of their time outside the courtroom conducting research, interviewing clients and witnesses, and handling other details in preparation for a trial.

Litigation lawyers handle all lawsuits and disputes between parties. These could be contract disputes, personal injury disputes, and real estate and property disputes. Litigation lawyers may specialize in a certain area, such as personal injury law, or may be a general lawyer for all types of disputes and lawsuits.

Some attorneys become teachers in law schools. For more information on law school professors, see the profile on postsecondary teachers.

Work Environment

Lawyers held about 759,800 jobs in 2012. A majority of lawyers work in private or corporate legal offices. Some are employed in local, state and federal governments. About 22 percent of lawyers were self-employed in 2012.

Median Annual Wages, May 2012

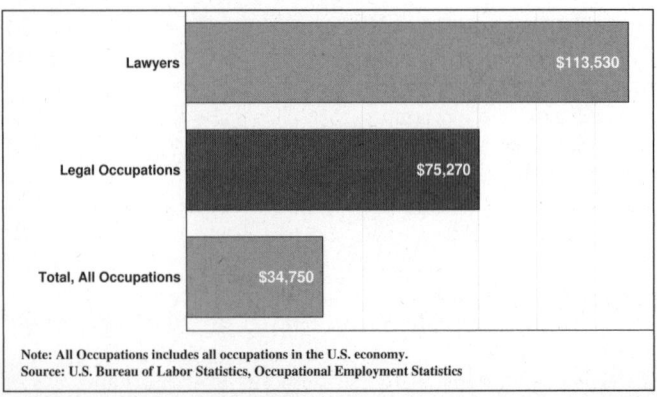

Lawyers — $113,530
Legal Occupations — $75,270
Total, All Occupations — $34,750

Note: All Occupations includes all occupations in the U.S. economy.
Source: U.S. Bureau of Labor Statistics, Occupational Employment Statistics

Percent Change in Employment, Projected 2012–2022

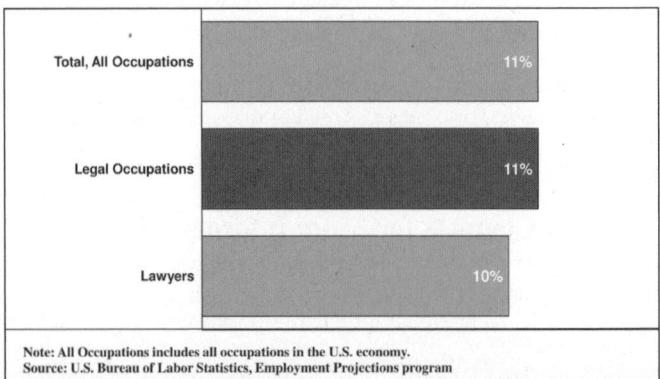

Total, All Occupations — 11%
Legal Occupations — 11%
Lawyers — 10%

Note: All Occupations includes all occupations in the U.S. economy.
Source: U.S. Bureau of Labor Statistics, Employment Projections program

Employment Projections Data for Lawyers

Occupational title	SOC Code	Employment, 2012	Projected Employment, 2022	Change, 2012–2022 Percent	Change, 2012–2022 Numeric
Lawyers..	23-1011	759,800	834,700	10	74,800

Source: U.S. Bureau of Labor Statistics, Employment Projections Program

Note: Data are rounded. Go to **Occupational Information Included in the OOH** *for a discussion of the data in this table.*

The industries that employed the most lawyers in 2012 were as follows:

Legal services.. 49%
Local government, excluding education and hospitals.............. 7
Federal government, excluding postal service 5
State government, excluding education and hospitals............... 5
Finance and insurance... 3

Lawyers work mostly in offices. However, some travel to attend meetings with clients at various locations, such as homes, hospitals, or prisons. Others travel to appear before courts. Lawyers who represent clients in court may face heavy pressure during trials.

Work Schedules. The majority of lawyers work full time, and many work long hours. Lawyers who are in private practice or those who work in large firms often work long hours, conducting research and preparing and reviewing documents.

How to Become One

All lawyers must have a law degree and must also typically pass a state's written bar examination.

Education. Becoming a lawyer usually takes 7 years of full-time study after high school–4 years of undergraduate study, followed by 3 years of law school. Most states and jurisdictions require lawyers to complete a juris doctor (J.D.) degree from a law school accredited by the American Bar Association (ABA). ABA accreditation signifies that the law school–particularly its curricula and faculty–meets certain standards.

A bachelor's degree is required for entry into most law schools, and courses in English, public speaking, government, history, economics, and mathematics are useful.

Almost all law schools, particularly those approved by the ABA, require applicants to take the Law School Admission Test (LSAT). This test measures applicants' aptitude for the study of law. As of August 2013, ABA had approved 203 law schools; others were approved by state authorities only. A J.D. degree program includes courses, such as constitutional law, contracts, property law, civil procedure, and legal writing. Law students may choose specialized courses in areas such as tax, labor, and corporate law.

Licenses. Becoming licensed as a lawyer is called being "admitted to the bar" and licensing exams are called "bar exams."

To practice law in any state, a person must be admitted to its bar under rules established by the jurisdiction's highest court. The requirements vary by individual states and jurisdictions. For more details on individual state and jurisdiction requirements, visit the National Conference of Bar Examiners.

Most states require that applicants graduate from an ABA-accredited law school, pass one or more written bar exams, and be found by an admitting board to have the character to represent and advise others. Lawyers who want to practice in more than one state often must take separate bar exams in each state.

After graduation, lawyers must keep informed about legal developments that affect their practices. Almost all states require lawyers to participate in continuing legal education either every year or every 3 years.

Many law schools and state and local bar associations provide continuing legal education courses that help lawyers stay current with recent developments. Courses vary by state and generally are related to the practice of law, such as legal ethics, taxes and tax fraud, and healthcare. Some states allow lawyers to take their continuing education credits through online courses.

Advancement. Newly hired attorneys usually start as associates and work with more experienced lawyers and judges. After several years, some lawyers may be admitted to partnership and become partial owners of the firm they work for. Some lawyers go into practice for themselves or move to the legal department of a large corporation.

A small number of experienced lawyers are nominated or elected to judgeships. Other lawyers may become full-time law school faculty and administrators. For more information about judges and law school faculty, see the profile on judges and hearing officers, and the profile on postsecondary teachers.

Other Experience. Law students often gain practical experience by participating in school-sponsored legal clinics, in a school's moot court competitions, in practice trials under the supervision of experienced lawyers and judges, and through research and writing on legal issues for a school's law journals.

Part-time or summer jobs in law firms, government agencies, and corporate legal departments also provide valuable experience. These experiences can help law students decide what kind of legal work they want to focus on in their careers. These experiences may also lead directly to a job after graduation.

Important Qualities

Analytical skills. Lawyers help their clients resolve problems and issues. As a result, they must be able to analyze large amounts of information, determine relevant facts, and propose viable solutions.

Similar Occupations   This table shows a list of occupations with job duties that are similar to those of lawyers.

Occupations	Entry-level Education	2012 Pay	Projected Job Growth	Average Annual Openings
Arbitrators, Mediators, and Conciliators	Bachelor's degree	$61,280	11%	220
Judges and Hearing Officers	Doctoral or professional degree	$106,005	1%	760
Paralegals and Legal Assistants	Associate's degree	$46,990	17%	9,120
Postsecondary Teachers	See "How to Become One"	$70,380	19%	42,690

Interpersonal skills. Lawyers must win the respect and confidence of their clients by building a trusting relationship, so that clients feel comfortable and share personal information related to their case.

Problem-solving skills. Lawyers must separate their emotions and prejudice from their clients' problems and objectively evaluate the matter. Therefore, good problem-solving skills are important for lawyers, to prepare the best defense and recommendation.

Research skills. Preparing legal advice or representation for a client commonly requires substantial research. All lawyers need to be able to find what applicable laws and regulations apply to a specific matter.

Speaking skills. Lawyers are hired by their clients to speak on their behalf. Lawyers must be able to clearly present and explain evidence to a judge and jury.

Writing skills. Lawyers need to be precise and specific when preparing documents, such as wills, trusts, and powers of attorney.

Pay

The median annual wage for lawyers was $113,530 in May 2012. The median wage is the wage at which half the workers in an occupation earned more than that amount and half earned less. The lowest 10 percent earned less than $54,310, and the top 10 percent earned more than $187,200.

In May 2012, the median annual wages for lawyers in the top five industries in which these lawyers worked were as follows:

Finance and insurance	$134,940
Federal government, excluding postal service	134,690
Legal services	116,630
Local government, excluding education and hospitals	87,140
State government, excluding education and hospitals	79,220

Salaries of experienced lawyers vary widely according to the type, size, and location of their employer. Lawyers who own their own practices usually earn less than those who are partners in law firms.

Job Outlook

Employment of lawyers is projected to grow 10 percent from 2012 to 2022, about as fast as the average for all occupations. Demand for legal work will continue as individuals, businesses, and all levels of government require legal services in many areas.

Despite this need for legal services, more price competition over the next decade may lead law firms to rethink their project staffing, to reduce costs to clients. As clients cut back on legal expenses, demand less expensive rates, and scrutinize invoices, work that was previously assigned to lawyers, such as document review, may now be given to paralegals and legal assistants. Some routine legal work may also be outsourced to other lower-cost legal providers located overseas.

While law firms will continue to be the largest employers of lawyers, many large corporations are increasing their in-house legal departments to cut costs. For many companies, the high cost of hiring outside counsel lawyers and their support staff makes it more economical to shift work to their in-house legal department. This will lead to an increase in the demand of lawyers in a variety of settings, such as financial and insurance firms, consulting firms, and healthcare providers.

Lawyers will continue to be needed in the federal government to prosecute or defend civil cases on behalf of the United States, prosecute criminal cases brought by the federal government, and collect money owed to the federal government. However, budget-ary constraints at all levels of government, especially federal, will moderate employment growth.

Demand is typically affected by cyclical swings in the economy. During recessions, demand declines for some discretionary legal services, such as planning estates, drafting wills, and handling real estate transactions. Also, corporations are less likely to litigate cases, when declining sales and profits restrict their budgets. Some corporations and law firms may cut staff to contain costs until business improves.

Job Prospects. Competition should continue to be strong, because more students are graduating from law school each year than there are jobs available. Some recent law school graduates who have been unable to find permanent positions are turning to the growing number of temporary staffing firms that place attorneys in short-term jobs. This service allows companies to hire lawyers "as-needed" and permits beginning lawyers to develop practical skills.

Because of the strong competition, a law graduate's willingness to relocate and his or her work experience are becoming more important. However, to be licensed in another state, a lawyer may have to take an additional state bar examination.

O*NET

➤ Lawyers (23-1011.00)

Contacts for More Information

For more information about law schools and a career in law, visit
➤ American Bar Association (www.americanbar.org)
➤ National Association for Law Placement (www.ncsc.org/)

For more information about the Law School Admission Test (LSAT) and the law school application process, visit
➤ Law School Admission Council (www.lsac.org)

For a list of state and jurisdiction admission bar offices, visit
➤ National Conference of Bar Examiners (www.ncbex.org)

The requirements for admission to the bar in a particular state or other jurisdiction may be obtained at the state capital, from the clerk of the Supreme Court, or from the administrator of the State Board of Bar Examiners.

Paralegals and Legal Assistants

- **2012 Median Pay** .... $46,990 per year
  $22.59 per hour
- **Entry-Level Education** .... Associate's degree
- **Work Experience in a Related Occupation** .... None
- **On-the-Job Training** .... None
- **Number of Jobs 2012** 277,000
- **Job Outlook, 2012–22** .... 17% (Faster than average)
- **Employment Change, 2012–22** 46,200

What Paralegals and Legal Assistants Do

Paralegals and legal assistants do a variety of tasks to support lawyers, including maintaining and organizing files, conducting legal research, and drafting documents.

Duties. Paralegals and legal assistants typically do the following:
- Investigate the facts of a case
- Conduct research on relevant laws, regulations, and legal articles
- Organize and maintain documents in a paper or electronic filing systems

In litigation involving many supporting documents, paralegals usually use computer databases to retrieve, organize, and index various materials.

- Gather and arrange evidence and other legal documents for attorney review and case preparation
- Write reports to help lawyers prepare for trials
- Draft correspondence and legal documents, such as contracts and mortgages
- Get affidavits and other formal statements that may be used as evidence in court
- Help lawyers during trials by handling exhibits, taking notes, or reviewing trial transcripts
- File exhibits, briefs, appeals and other legal documents with the court or opposing counsel
- Call clients, witnesses, lawyers, and outside vendors to schedule interviews, meetings, and depositions

Paralegals and legal assistants help lawyers prepare for hearings, trials, and corporate meetings. However, their specific duties may vary depending on the size of the firm and the area of law in which the paralegal works.

In small firms, paralegals duties tend to vary more. In addition to reviewing and organizing documents, paralegals may prepare written reports that help lawyers determine how to handle their cases. If lawyers decide to file lawsuits on behalf of clients, paralegals may help prepare the legal arguments and draft documents to be filed with the court.

In large organizations, paralegals may work on a particular phase of a case, rather than handling a case from beginning to end.

For example, a litigation paralegal may only review legal material for internal use, maintain reference files, conduct research for lawyers, or collect and organize evidence for hearings.

Litigation paralegals may assist attorneys in preparing for trial by organizing document binders, creating exhibit lists, or drafting settlement agreements. Some litigation paralegals may also help coordinate the logistics of attending the trial, including reserving office space, transporting exhibits and documents to the court-room, and setting up computers and other equipment.

Paralegals use technology and computer software for managing and organizing the increasing amount of documents and data collected during a case. Many paralegals use computer software to catalog documents, and to review documents for specific keywords or subjects. Because of these responsibilities, paralegals must be familiar with electronic database management and be up to date on the latest software used for electronic discovery. Electronic discovery refers to all electronic materials that are related to a trial, such as emails, data, documents, accounting databases, and websites.

Paralegals may specialize in areas such as litigation, personal injury, corporate law, criminal law, employee benefits, intellectual property, bankruptcy, immigration, family law, and real estate. In addition, experienced paralegals may assume supervisory responsibilities, such as overseeing team projects or delegating work to other paralegals.

Paralegals and legal assistants often work in teams with attorneys, fellow paralegals, and other legal support staff. They may also have frequent interactions with clients and third-party vendors.

The following are examples of types of paralegals:

Corporate paralegals often help lawyers prepare employee contracts, shareholder agreements, stock-option plans, and companies' annual financial reports. Corporate paralegals may monitor and review government regulations, to ensure that the corporation is aware of new legal requirements.

Litigation paralegals maintain documents received from clients, conduct research for lawyers, and retrieve and organize evidence for use at depositions and trials.

Work Environment

Paralegals and legal assistants held about 277,000 jobs in 2012. Paralegals are found in all types of organizations, but most work for law firms, corporations, and government agencies.

The industries that employed the most paralegals and legal assistants in 2012 were as follows:

Legal services 72%
Federal government, excluding postal service 5
Local government, excluding education and hospitals 5

Median Annual Wages, May 2012

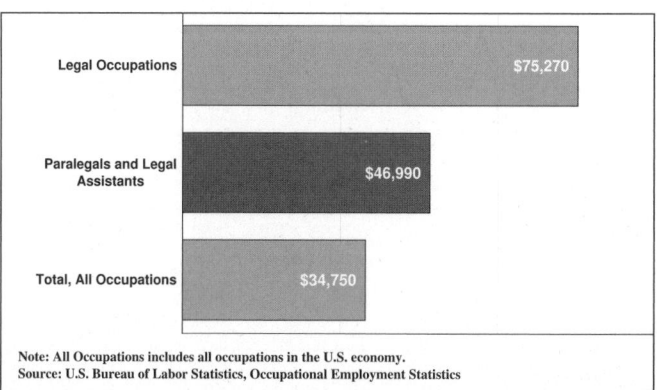

Note: All Occupations includes all occupations in the U.S. economy.
Source: U.S. Bureau of Labor Statistics, Occupational Employment Statistics

Percent Change in Employment, Projected 2012–2022

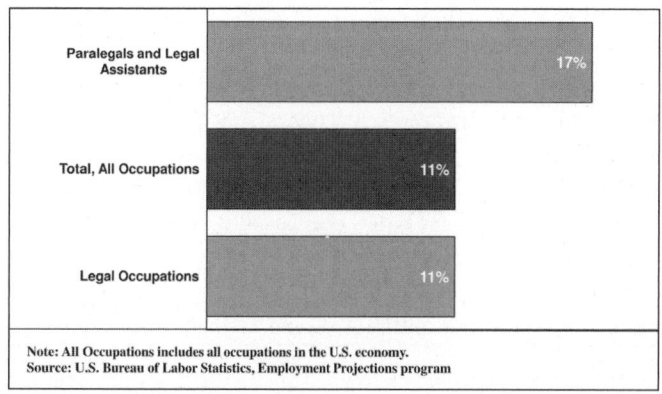

Note: All Occupations includes all occupations in the U.S. economy.
Source: U.S. Bureau of Labor Statistics, Employment Projections program

Employment Projections Data for Paralegals and Legal Assistants

Occupational title	SOC Code	Employment, 2012	Projected Employment, 2022	Change, 2012–2022	
				Percent	Numeric
Paralegals and legal assistants... 23-2011		277,000	323,300	17	46,200

Source: *U.S. Bureau of Labor Statistics, Employment Projections Program*

Note: *Data are rounded. Go to* Occupational Information Included in the OOH *for a discussion of the data in this table.*

State government, excluding education and hospitals............... 4
Finance and insurance... 3

Paralegals do most of their work in offices and law libraries. Occasionally, they travel to gather information and do other tasks.

Work Schedules. Most paralegals and legal assistants work full time.

How to Become One

Most paralegals and legal assistants have an associate's degree in paralegal studies, or a bachelor's degree in another field and a certificate in paralegal studies. In some cases, employers hire college graduates with a bachelor's degree with no legal experience or education and train them on the job.

Education. There are several paths to become a paralegal. Candidates can enroll in a community college paralegal program to earn an associate's degree. A small number of schools also offer bachelor's and master's degrees in paralegal studies. Those who already have a bachelor's degree in another subject can earn a certificate in paralegal studies. Finally, some employers hire entry-level paralegals without any experience or education in paralegal studies and train them on the job, though these jobs typically require a bachelor's degree.

Associate's and bachelor's degree programs in paralegal studies usually combine paralegal training, such as courses in legal research and the legal applications of computers, with other academic subjects. Most certificate programs provide intensive paralegal training for people who already hold college degrees. Some certificate programs only take a few months to complete.

Many paralegal training programs offer an internship, in which students gain practical experience by working for several months in a private law firm, the office of a public defender or attorney general, a corporate legal department, a legal aid organization, or a government agency. Internship experience helps students improve their technical skills and can enhance their employment prospects.

Employers sometimes hire college graduates with no legal experience or education and train them on the job. In these cases, the new employee may have experience in a technical field that is useful to law firms, such tax preparation, nursing, or criminal justice.

Other Experience. In many cases, employers prefer candidates who have at least one year of experience in a law firm or other office setting. In addition, a technical understanding of a specific legal specialty can be helpful. For example, a personal-injury law firm may desire a paralegal with a background in nursing or health administration.

Work experience in a law firm or other office setting is particularly important for people who do not have formal paralegal training.

Certifications. Although not required by most employers, earning voluntary certification may help applicants get a paralegal job. Many national and local paralegal organizations offer voluntary paralegal certifications to students able to pass an exam. Other organizations offer voluntary paralegal certifications for paralegals who meet certain experience and education criteria. For more information about paralegal certifications, see the Contacts for More Information section.

Advancement. Paralegals usually are given more responsibilities and require less supervision as they gain work experience. Experienced paralegals may supervise and delegate assignments to other paralegals and clerical staff.

Important Qualities

Communication skills. Paralegals must be able to document and present their research and related information to their supervising attorney.

Computer skills. Paralegals need to be familiar with using computers for legal research and litigation support. They also use computer programs for organizing and maintaining important documents.

Interpersonal skills. Paralegals spend most of their time working with clients and other professionals and must be able to develop good relationships. They must make clients feel comfortable sharing personal information related to their cases.

Organizational skills. Paralegals may be responsible for many cases at one time. They must adapt quickly to changing deadlines.

Research skills. Paralegals need good research and investigative skills to conduct legal research.

Similar Occupations   This table shows a list of occupations with job duties that are similar to those of paralegals and legal assistants.

Occupations	Entry-level Education	2012 Pay	Projected Job Growth	Average Annual Openings
Claims Adjusters, Appraisers, Examiners, and Investigators	See "How to Become One"	$59,902	3%	8,340
Lawyers	Doctoral or professional degree	$113,530	10%	19,650
Occupational Health and Safety Specialists	Bachelor's degree	$66,790	7%	2,130
Occupational Health and Safety Technicians	High school diploma or equivalent	$47,440	10%	480
Secretaries and Administrative Assistants	High school diploma or equivalent	$36,198	12%	97,210

Pay

The median annual wage for paralegals and legal assistants was $46,990 in May 2012. The median wage is the wage at which half the workers in an occupation earned more than that amount and half earned less. The lowest 10 percent earned less than $29,420, and the top 10 percent earned more than $75,410.

In May 2012, the median annual wages for paralegals and legal assistants in the top five industries in which these paralegals worked were as follows:

Federal government, excluding postal service	$62,400
Finance and insurance	54,670
Local government, excluding education and hospitals	47,000
Legal services	44,950
State government, excluding education and hospitals	42,050

In general, paralegals that work for large law firms or in large cities earn more than those who work for small firms or in smaller cities.

Job Outlook

Employment of paralegals and legal assistants is projected to grow 17 percent from 2012 to 2022, faster than the average for all occupations.

As law firms try to increase the efficiency of legal services and lower their expenses, they are expected to hire more paralegals and legal assistants. Some law firms are rethinking their project staffing and rebuilding their support staff by hiring paralegals, who may be given some of the administrative tasks previously assigned to legal secretaries.

Law firms also are attempting to reduce billing costs due to pressure from clients. Paralegals can be a less costly alternative to lawyers and can perform a wide variety of duties, including tasks once done by lawyers. This will cause an increase in demand for paralegals and legal assistants.

While law firms will continue to be the largest employers of paralegals, many large corporations are increasing their in-house legal departments to cut costs. For many companies, the high cost of lawyers and their support staff makes it more economical to have an in-house legal department, rather than to retain outside counsel. This will lead to an increase in the demand of legal workers in a variety of settings, such as finance and insurance firms, consulting firms, and healthcare providers.

However, demand for paralegals could be limited by law firms' workloads. When work is slow, lawyers may keep billable assignments for themselves and delegate less work to paralegals. This may make a firm less likely to keep some paralegals on staff or to hire new ones until the workload increases.

Job Prospects. This occupation attracts many applicants, and competition for jobs will be strong. Experienced, formally trained paralegals with strong computer and database management skills should have the best job prospects. In addition, many firms will prefer paralegals with experience and specialization in high-demand practice areas.

O*NET

➤ Paralegals and Legal Assistants (23-2011.00)

Contacts for More Information

For more information about paralegal careers, visit

➤ International Paralegal Management Association (www.paralegal-management.org/)

➤ Standing Committee on Paralegals, American Bar Association (www.americanbar.org/groups/paralegals.html)

➤ American Alliance of Paralegals (www.aapipara.org/)

For more information on the Certified Legal Assistant certification, schools that offer training programs in a specific State, and standards and guidelines for paralegals, visit

➤ NALA—The Association for Legal Assistants/Paralegals (www.nala.org)

For information on the Professional Paralegal certification, visit

➤ NALS—The Association for Legal Professionals (www.nals.org)

For information on the Paralegal Advanced Competency Exam, paralegal careers, and paralegal training programs visit

➤ National Federation of Paralegal Associations (www.paralegals.org)

Life, Physical, and Social Science

Agricultural and Food Science Technicians

- **2012 Median Pay** .... $34,070 per year
  $16.38 per hour
- **Entry-Level Education** ....Associate's degree
- **Work Experience in a Related Occupation**............... None
- **On-the-Job Training** .... Moderate-term on-the-job training
- **Number of Jobs 2012** 25,900
- **Job Outlook, 2012–22** .... 3% (Slower than average)
- **Employment Change, 2012–22** 800

What Agricultural and Food Science Technicians Do

Agricultural and food science technicians assist agricultural and food scientists by performing duties such as measuring and analyzing the quality of food and agricultural products. Duties range from typical agricultural labor with added record keeping duties to laboratory testing with significant amounts of office work, depending on the specific field the technician works in.

Duties. Specific duties of these technicians vary, depending on their specialty.

Agricultural science technicians typically do the following:

- Follow protocols to prepare, analyze, and properly store crop or animal samples

- Operate farm equipment and maintain agricultural production areas to conform to scientific testing parameters

- Examine animals and other specimens to determine the presence of diseases or other problems

- Measure ingredients used in testing of animal feed and for other purposes

- Compile and analyze test results that go into charts, presentations, and reports

- Prepare and operate complex equipment to perform laboratory tests

Food science technicians typically do the following:

- Collect and prepare samples following established procedures

- Test food, food additives, and food containers to ensure they comply with established safety standards

- Help food scientists with food research, development, and quality control

- Analyze chemical properties of food to determine ingredients and formulas

- Compile and analyze test results that go into charts, presentations, and reports

- Prepare and maintain quantities of chemicals needed to perform laboratory tests

- Keep a safe, sterile laboratory environment

Agricultural science technicians who work in private industry typically focus on increasing the productivity of crops and animals. These workers may keep detailed records, collect samples for analyses, ensure that samples meet proper safety and quality standards, and test crops and animals for disease or to otherwise confirm scientific experiment results.

Food science technicians who work in private industry typically inspect food and crops during processing to ensure products are fit for distribution or to investigate ways to improve efficiency. Many food science technicians spend time inspecting foodstuffs, chemicals, and additives to determine whether they are safe and have the proper combination of ingredients.

Agricultural and food science technicians often specialize by subject area. Some popular subjects include carbon management and sequestration, microbiology, and processing technology.

Agricultural and food science technicians who work for the federal government monitor regulatory compliance for the Food and Drug Administration (FDA), the Department of Agriculture, and other agencies. With the recent passage of the FDA Food Safety Modernization Act (FSMA), the frequency of food inspections is expected to increase, along with improvements in performance standards. The FSMA also requires more inspections of foreign food production facilities that export to the United States, so some agricultural and food science technicians may travel internationally.

Work Environment

Agricultural and food science technicians held about 25,900 jobs in 2012. The industries that employed the most agricultural and food science technicians in 2012 were as follows:

Food manufacturing 26%
Colleges, universities, and professional schools; state 19
Support activities for agriculture and forestry 17
Research and development in the physical,
  engineering, and life sciences.. 8
Animal production and aquaculture....................................... 7

Technicians work in a variety of settings including laboratories, processing plants, farms and ranches, and offices. Technicians who work in processing plants and agricultural work settings may face

Agricultural and food science technicians work in offices, laboratories, and processing plants.

Median Annual Wages, May 2012

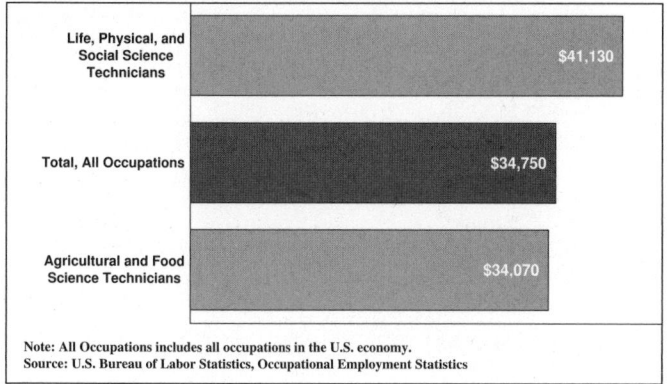

Note: All Occupations includes all occupations in the U.S. economy.
Source: U.S. Bureau of Labor Statistics, Occupational Employment Statistics

Percent Change in Employment, Projected 2012–2022

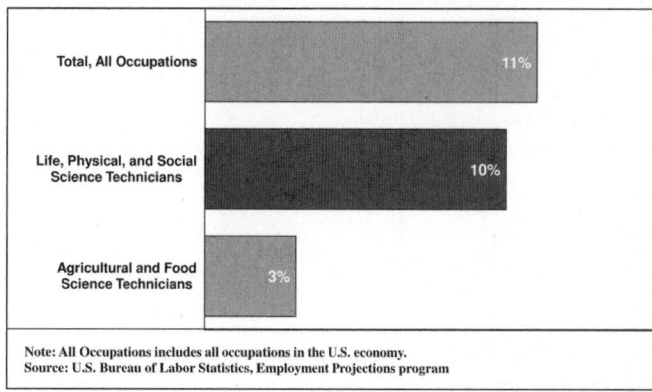

Note: All Occupations includes all occupations in the U.S. economy.
Source: U.S. Bureau of Labor Statistics, Employment Projections program

noise from processing and farming machinery, extreme temperatures, and odors from chemicals or animals.

Work Schedules. Agricultural and food science technicians typically work full time and have standard work schedules. Some of these technicians work more than standard full-time schedules, have variable schedules, or travel extensively.

How to Become One

Agricultural and food science technicians typically need an associate's degree in biology, animal science, or a related field. Some positions may require a bachelor's degree. For those positions that need only a high school diploma, technicians typically need to have previous work experience. Technicians typically need on-the-job training that may cover topics such as production techniques, personal hygiene, and sanitation procedures.

Education. Students interested in this occupation should take as many high school science and math classes as possible. A solid background in applied chemistry, biology, physics, math, and statistics is important. Knowledge of how to use spreadsheets and databases is also typically necessary.

Agricultural and food science technicians typically need an associate's degree in biology, animal science, or a related field from an accredited college or university. Some agricultural and food science technician positions require a bachelor's degree. While in college, prospective technicians learn through a combination of classroom and hands-on learning, such as internships.

Some agricultural and food science technicians successfully enter the occupation with a high school diploma but typically need related work experience and on-the-job training that may last a year or more.

A background in the biological sciences is important for agricultural and food science technicians. Students may find it helpful to take courses in biology, chemistry, animal science, and agricultural engineering as part of their programs. Many schools offer internships, cooperative-education, and other programs designed to provide hands-on experience and enhance employment prospects.

Training. Agricultural and food science technicians typically undergo on-the-job training. Various federal government regulations outline the types of training needed for technicians, and it varies according to the work environment and specific job requirements. Training may cover topics such as production techniques, personal hygiene, and sanitation procedures.

Important Qualities

Analytical skills. Agricultural and food science technicians must conduct a variety of observations and on-site measurements, all of which require precision and accuracy.

Communication skills. Agricultural and food science technicians must be able to understand and give clear instructions, keep detailed records, and occasionally may need to write reports.

Critical-thinking skills. Agricultural and food science technicians reach conclusions through sound reasoning and judgment. They determine how to improve food quality and must test products for a variety of safety standards.

Interpersonal skills. Agricultural and food science technicians need to work well with others. They may supervise agricultural and food science workers and receive instruction from scientists or specialists, so effective communication is critical.

Physical stamina. Agricultural and food science technicians who work in manufacturing or agricultural settings may need to stand for long periods, lift objects, and generally perform physical labor.

Work Experience in a Related Occupation. Workers who enter positions in the occupation with only a high school education often have years of experience in a related occupation during which they develop their scientific knowledge of agriculture or manufacturing.

Pay

The median annual wage for agricultural and food science technicians was $34,070 in May 2012. The median wage is the wage at which half the workers in an occupation earned more than that amount and half earned less. The lowest 10 percent earned less than $22,410, and the top 10 percent earned more than $53,460.

Employment Projections Data for Agricultural and Food Science Technicians

Occupational title	SOC Code	Employment, 2012	Projected Employment, 2022	Change, 2012–2022	
				Percent	Numeric
Agricultural and food science technicians 19-4011		25,900	26,700	3	800

Source: U.S. Bureau of Labor Statistics, Employment Projections Program

Note: Data are rounded. Go to Occupational Information Included in the OOH for a discussion of the data in this table.

Similar Occupations   This table shows a list of occupations with job duties that are similar to those of agricultural and food science technicians.

Occupations	Entry-level Education	2012 Pay	Projected Job Growth	Average Annual Openings
Agricultural and Food Scientists	See "How to Become One"	$58,636	10%	1,640
Agricultural Engineers	Bachelor's degree	$74,000	4%	80
Agricultural Workers	See "How to Become One"	$19,703	-3%	23,190
Animal Care and Service Workers	See "How to Become One"	$20,076	15%	7,660
Biochemists and Biophysicists	Doctoral or professional degree	$81,480	18%	1,370
Biological Technicians	Bachelor's degree	$39,750	10%	3,210
Chemical Technicians	Associate's degree	$42,920	9%	2,160
Conservation Scientists and Foresters	Bachelor's degree	$59,354	3%	1,080
Environmental Science and Protection Technicians	Associate's degree	$41,240	19%	1,900
Farmers, Ranchers, and Other Agricultural Managers	High school diploma or equivalent	$69,300	-19%	15,020
Microbiologists	Bachelor's degree	$66,260	7%	710
Occupational Health and Safety Technicians	High school diploma or equivalent	$47,440	10%	480
Zoologists and Wildlife Biologists	Bachelor's degree	$57,710	5%	670

Job Outlook

Employment of agricultural and food technicians is projected to grow 3 percent from 2012 to 2022, slower than the average for all occupations. More technology and scientific knowledge related to food production will allow greater control of the production and processing activities and in turn increase demand for these workers. Continued population growth will drive the need to increase efficiency of production and processing methods. More awareness and enforcement of food safety regulations will increase inspection requirements, which, in turn, will increase the need for agricultural and food science technicians.

O*NET

➤ Agricultural and Food Science Technicians (19-4011.00)
➤ Agricultural Technicians (19-4011.01)
➤ Food Science Technicians (19-4011.02)

Contacts for More Information

For more information about agricultural and soil science occupations, including certification, visit
➤ American Society of Agronomy (www.agronomy.org/)
➤ Soil Science Society of America (www.soils.org/)
   For more information about food and animal science occupations, including certifications, visit
➤ American Registry of Professional Animal Scientists (www.arpas.org/)
➤ American Society of Animal Science (www.asas.org)
➤ Institute of Food Technologists (www.ift.org/)
   For information from related governmental agencies, visit
➤ U.S. Department of Agriculture (www.usda.gov)
➤ Food and Drug Administration (www.fda.gov/)
➤ Smithsonian Institute (http://forces.si.edu/soils/index.html)

Agricultural and Food Scientists

- **2012 Median Pay** .... $58,610 per year
  $28.18 per hour
- **Entry-Level Education** ....See "How to Become One"
- **Work Experience in a Related Occupation**............... None
- **On-the-Job Training** .... None
- **Number of Jobs 2012** 38,500
- **Job Outlook, 2012–22** .... 9% (As fast as average)
- **Employment Change, 2012–22** 3,600

What Agricultural and Food Scientists Do

Agricultural and food scientists work to ensure that agricultural establishments are productive and food is safe.

Duties. Agricultural and food scientists typically do the following:

- Conduct research and experiments to improve the quantity and quality of field crops and farm animals
- Formulate new food products and develop new and better ways to process, package, and deliver them
- Study the composition of soil as it relates to plant growth
- Communicate research findings to the scientific community, food producers, and the public
- Travel between facilities to oversee the implementation of new projects

Agricultural and food scientists play an important role in maintaining and expanding the nation's food supply. Many work in basic or applied research and development. Basic research seeks to understand the biological and chemical processes by which crops and livestock grow. Applied research uses this knowledge to discover ways to improve the quality, quantity, and safety of agricultural products.

Some agricultural and food scientists conduct experiments on new varieties of crops.

Many agricultural and food scientists work with little supervision, forming their own hypotheses and developing research methods accordingly. In addition, they often lead teams of technicians or students who help in their research. Agricultural and food scientists who are employed in private industry may need to travel between different sites to perform various duties for their employers.

The following are types of agricultural and food scientists:

Animal scientists typically conduct research on domestic farm animals. With a focus on food production, they explore animal genetics, nutrition, reproduction, diseases, growth, and development. They work to develop efficient ways to produce and process meat, poultry, eggs, and milk. Animal scientists may crossbreed animals to get new combinations of desirable characteristics. They advise farmers on how to upgrade housing for animals, lower animal death rates, handle waste matter, and increase production.

Food scientists and technologists use chemistry and other sciences to study the underlying principles of food. They analyze nutritional content of food, discover new food sources, and research ways to make processed foods safe and healthy. Food technologists generally work in product development, applying findings from food science research to develop new or better ways of selecting, preserving, processing, packaging, and distributing food. Some food scientists use nanotechnology, problem solving techniques that work on the atomic scale, to develop sensors that can detect contaminants in food. Other food scientists enforce government regulations, inspecting food processing areas to ensure that they are sanitary and meet waste management standards.

Soil and plant scientists conduct research on soil, crops, and other agricultural products.

Soil scientists examine the scientific composition of soil as it relates to plant or crop growth, and investigate effects of alternative soil treatment practices on crop productivity. They develop methods of conserving and managing soil that farmers and forestry companies can use. Because soil science is closely related to environmental science, people trained in soil science also work to ensure environmental quality and effective land use.

Plant scientists work to improve crop yields and give advice to food and crop developers about techniques that could enhance production efforts. They develop ways to control pests and weeds.

Agricultural and food scientists in private industry commonly work for food production companies, farms, and processing plants. They typically improve inspection standards or overall food quality. They spend their time in a laboratory, where they do tests and experiments, or in the field, where they take samples or assess overall conditions. Other agricultural and food scientists work for pharmaceutical companies, where they use biotechnology processes to develop drugs or other medical products. Some look for ways to use agricultural products for fuels, such as ethanol produced from corn.

At universities, agricultural and food scientists do research and investigate new methods of improving animal or soil health, nutrition, and other facets of food quality. They also write grants to organizations such as the United States Department of Agriculture (USDA) or the National Institutes of Health (NIH) to get steady funding for their research. For more information on professors who teach agricultural and food science at universities, see the profile on postsecondary teachers.

In the federal government, agricultural and food scientists conduct research on animal safety and methods of improving food and crop production. They spend most of their time conducting clinical trials or developing experiments on animal and plant subjects. Agricultural and food scientists eventually present their findings in peer-reviewed journals or other publications.

Work Environment

Agricultural and food scientists held about 38,500 jobs in 2012. About 14 percent were self-employed. Most agricultural and food scientists work in research universities or private industry. Only 5 percent worked in the federal government. The work of agricultural and food scientists takes place in laboratories, offices, and in the field. They spend most of their time studying data and reports in a laboratory or office. Field work includes visits to farms or processing plants. When visiting a food or animal production facility, they must follow biosecurity measures, wear suitable clothing, and tolerate the environment associated with food production processes. This environment may include noise associated with large production machinery, cold temperatures associated with food production, and close proximity to animal byproducts.

The industries that employed the most animal scientists in 2012 were as follows:

Colleges, universities, and professional schools; state 33%
Research and development in the physical, engineering,
    and life sciences.. 16
Agriculture, forestry, fishing, and hunting 9
Management, scientific, and technical consulting services........ 8

The industries that employed the most food scientists and technologists in 2012 were as follows:

Food manufacturing 33%
Management of companies and enterprises............................. 9
Research and development in the physical, engineering,
    and life sciences.. 9

Colleges, universities, and professional schools; state 8
Crop production 7

The industries that employed the most soil and plant scientists in 2012 were as follows:

Research and development in the physical, engineering,
   and life sciences.. 17%
Colleges, universities, and professional schools; state 14
Federal government, excluding postal service 10
Merchant wholesalers, nondurable goods 10
Management, scientific, and technical consulting services........ 9

Work Schedules. Agricultural and food scientists typically work full time and have standard schedules. Some positions may require these workers to travel for a moderate portion of their work time.

How to Become One

Agricultural and food scientists need at least a bachelor's degree from an accredited postsecondary institution, although many obtain more advanced degrees. Food scientists and technologists and soil and plant scientists typically earn bachelor's degrees. Some scientists earn a Doctorate of Veterinary Medicine (DVM). Most animal scientists earn a doctoral or professional degree.

Education. Every state has at least one land-grant college that offers agricultural science degrees. Many other colleges and universities also offer agricultural science degrees or agricultural science courses. Degrees in related sciences, such as biology, chemistry, physics, or in a related engineering specialty also may qualify people for many agricultural science jobs.

Undergraduate coursework for food scientists and technologists and for soil and plant scientists typically includes biology, chemistry, botany, and plant conservation. Students preparing to be food scientists take courses such as food chemistry, food analysis, food microbiology, food engineering, and food processing operations. Students preparing to be soil and plant scientists take courses in plant pathology, soil chemistry, entomology (the study of insects), plant physiology, and biochemistry.

Undergraduate students in the agricultural and food sciences typically gain a strong foundation in their specialty, with an emphasis on teamwork through internships and research opportunities. Students are also encouraged to take humanities courses, which can help them develop good communication skills, and computer courses so that they may become familiar with common programs and databases.

Many people with bachelor's degrees in agricultural sciences find work in related jobs rather than becoming an agricultural or food scientist. For example, a bachelor's degree in agricultural science is a useful background for farming, ranching, agricultural inspection, farm credit institutions, or companies that make or sell feed, fertilizer, seed, and farm equipment. Combined with coursework in business, agricultural and food science could be a good background for managerial jobs in farm-related or ranch-related businesses. For more information, see the profile on farmers, ranchers, and other agricultural managers.

Graduate level study further develops an animal scientist's knowledge. Most students with bachelor's degrees in application-focused food sciences or agricultural sciences typically earn advanced degrees in applied topics such as nutrition or dietetics. Students who major in a more basic field, such as biology or chemistry, may be better suited for getting their Ph.D. and doing research within the agricultural and food sciences. During graduate school, there is additional emphasis on lab work and original research, where prospective animal scientists have the opportunity to do experiments and sometimes supervise undergraduates.

Advanced research topics include genetics, animal reproduction, and biotechnology, among others. Advanced coursework also emphasizes statistical analysis and experiment design, which are important as Ph.D. candidates begin their research.

Some agricultural and food scientists receive a Doctor of Veterinary Medicine before they begin their animal science training. Similar to Ph.D. candidates in animal science, a prospective veterinarian must first have a bachelor's degree before getting into veterinary school.

Important Qualities

Communication skills. Communication skills are critical for agricultural and food scientists. They must be able to explain their studies: what they were trying to learn, the methods they used, what they found, and what they think the implications are of their findings. They must also be able to communicate well when working with others, including technicians and student assistants.

Critical-thinking skills. Agricultural and food scientists must use their expertise to determine the best way to answer a specific research question.

Data-analysis skills. Agricultural and food scientists, like other researchers, collect data using a variety of methods, including quantitative surveys. They must then apply standard data analysis techniques to understand the data and get the answers to the questions they are studying.

Decision-making skills. Agricultural and food scientists must use their expertise and experience to determine whether their findings will have an impact on the food supply, farms, and other agricultural products.

Median Annual Wages, May 2012

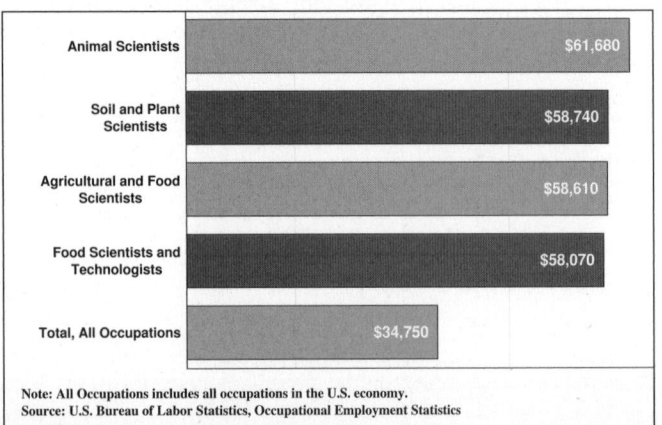

Note: All Occupations includes all occupations in the U.S. economy.
Source: U.S. Bureau of Labor Statistics, Occupational Employment Statistics

Percent Change in Employment, Projected 2012–2022

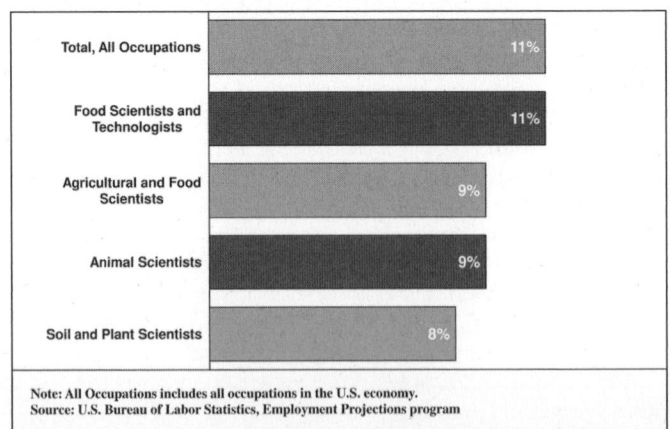

Note: All Occupations includes all occupations in the U.S. economy.
Source: U.S. Bureau of Labor Statistics, Employment Projections program

Employment Projections Data for Agricultural and Food Scientists

Occupational title	SOC Code	Employment, 2012	Projected Employment, 2022	Change, 2012–2022	
				Percent	Numeric
Agricultural and food scientists...	19-1010	38,500	42,000	9	3,600
Animal scientists	19-1011	2,700	3,000	9	200
Food scientists and technologists..	19-1012	19,400	21,500	11	2,100
Soil and plant scientists	19-1013	16,300	17,600	8	1,200

Source: U.S. Bureau of Labor Statistics, Employment Projections Program

Note: Data are rounded. Go to **Occupational Information Included in the OOH** *for a discussion of the data in this table.*

Math skills. Agricultural and food scientists, like many other scientists, must have a sound grasp of mathematical concepts.

Observation skills. Agricultural and food scientists conduct experiments that require precise observation of samples and other data. Any mistake could lead to inconclusive or inaccurate results.

Licenses, Certifications, and Registrations. Agricultural and food scientists can get certifications from organizations like the American Registry of Professional Animal Scientists (ARPAS), Institute of Food Technologists (IFT), or the Soil Science Society of America (SSSA). These certifications recognize expertise in agricultural and food science, and enhance the status of those who are certified.

According to the organizations, certification of professional expertise is broadly based on education, a comprehensive exam, and previous professional experience. Scientists may need to take continuing education courses every year to keep their certification, and they must follow the organization's code of ethics. Certifications are generally not required, but the agricultural and food science community recognize their importance. Some states require soil scientists to be licensed to practice. Licensing requirements vary by state, but generally include holding a bachelor's degree with a certain number of credit hours in soil science, a certain number of years working under a licensed scientist, and passage of an examination.

Other Experience. Internships are highly recommended for prospective food scientists and technologists. Many entry-level jobs in this occupation are related to food manufacturing, and hands-on experience is very important in that environment.

Pay

The median annual wage for agricultural and food scientists was $58,610 in May 2012. The median wage is the wage at which half the workers in an occupation earned more than that amount and half earned less. The lowest 10 percent earned less than $34,750, and the top 10 percent earned more than $104,840.

In May 2012, the median annual wages for animal scientists in the top three industries employing these scientists were as follows:

Management, scientific, and technical consulting services...	$82,720
Research and development in the physical, engineering, and life sciences..	72,050
Colleges, universities, and professional schools; state	49,930

In May 2012, the median annual wages for food scientists and technologists in the top four industries employing these workers were as follows:

Management of companies and enterprises.......................	$71,440
Research and development in the physical, engineering, and life sciences..	70,920
Food manufacturing	54,890
Colleges, universities, and professional schools; state	47,880

In May 2012, the median annual wages for soil and plant scientists in the top five industries employing these scientists were as follows:

Federal government, excluding postal service	$72,540
Merchant wholesalers, nondurable goods	63,280

Similar Occupations   This table shows a list of occupations with job duties that are similar to those of agricultural and food scientists.

Occupations	Entry-level Education	2012 Pay	Projected Job Growth	Average Annual Openings
Agricultural and Food Science Technicians	Associate's degree	$34,070	3%	1,010
Biochemists and Biophysicists	Doctoral or professional degree	$81,480	18%	1,370
Biological Technicians	Bachelor's degree	$39,750	10%	3,210
Chemical Technicians	Associate's degree	$42,920	9%	2,160
Conservation Scientists and Foresters	Bachelor's degree	$59,354	3%	1,080
Environmental Scientists and Specialists	Bachelor's degree	$63,570	15%	3,970
Farmers, Ranchers, and Other Agricultural Managers	High school diploma or equivalent	$69,300	-19%	15,020
Landscape Architects	Bachelor's degree	$64,180	14%	760
Microbiologists	Bachelor's degree	$66,260	7%	710
Veterinarians	Doctoral or professional degree	$84,460	12%	3,100
Zoologists and Wildlife Biologists	Bachelor's degree	$57,710	5%	670

Research and development in the physical, engineering, and life sciences...59,980
Management, scientific, and technical consulting services...56,550
Colleges, universities, and professional schools; state..........46,710

Job Outlook

Employment of agricultural and food scientists is projected to grow 9 percent from 2012 to 2022, about as fast as the average for all occupations.

Ongoing animal science research, as well as an increased reliance on food safety through biotechnology and nanotechnology, is expected to increase demand for agricultural and food scientists moderately. Agricultural scientists will also be needed to balance increased agricultural output with protecting and preserving soil, water, and ecosystems. They increasingly will help develop sustainable agricultural practices by creating and carrying out plans to manage pests, crops, soil fertility, erosion, and animal waste in ways that reduce the use of harmful chemicals and minimize damage to the natural environment. In addition, demand for biofuels–renewable energy sources from plants–is expected to increase.

Job growth for food scientists and technologists is expected to be driven by the demand for new food products and food safety measures. Food research is expected to increase because the public is more aware of nutrition, health, food safety. They will also continue research efforts that maintain and increase crop and herd health and productivity.

Most growth over the next 10 years for agricultural and food scientists will be in private industry. Private industry has increased its demand for agricultural and food scientists because their expertise is necessary for developing food, crops, and drugs, along with ensuring quality and safety.

Furthermore, research in genomics and agricultural sustainability also is expected to increase the number of available agricultural science positions. Findings from these scientists' studies may improve crop yields or have an impact on other fields, such as biofuels.

A number of job vacancies will arise as many scientists are expected to retire within the next 10 years.

O*NET

➤ Animal Scientists (19-1011.00)
➤ Food Scientists and Technologists (19-1012.00)
➤ Soil and Plant Scientists (19-1013.00)

Contacts for More Information

For more information about food and animal scientists, including certifications, visit
➤ American Society of Agronomy (www.agronomy.org/)
➤ American Society of Animal Science (www.asas.org)
➤ American Registry of Professional Animal Scientists (www.arpas.org/)
➤ Institute of Food Technologists (www.ift.org/cms/)
  For more information about agricultural and soil scientists, including certifications, visit
➤ Soil Science Society of America (www.soils.org/)
  For information from related governmental agencies, visit
➤ Food and Drug Administration (www.fda.gov/)
➤ Smithsonian Institute (http://forces.si.edu/soils/index.html)
➤ US Department of Agriculture (www.usda.gov)

Anthropologists and Archeologists

- **2012 Median Pay** ....$57,420 per year
  $27.61 per hour
- **Entry-Level Education** ....Master's degree
- **Work Experience in a Related Occupation**............... None
- **On-the-Job Training** .... None
- **Number of Jobs 2012** 7,200
- **Job Outlook, 2012–22**............. 19% (Faster than average)
- **Employment Change, 2012–22** 1,400

What Anthropologists and Archeologists Do

Anthropologists and archeologists study the origin, development, and behavior of humans. They examine the cultures, languages, archeological remains, and physical characteristics of people in various parts of the world.

Duties. Anthropologists and archeologists typically do the following:

- Plan research projects to answer questions and test hypotheses about the interaction between nature and culture
- Develop data collection methods tailored to a particular specialty or project
- Collect information from observations, interviews, and documents
- Record and manage records of observations taken in the field
- Analyze data, laboratory samples, and other sources of information to uncover patterns about human life, culture, and origins
- Prepare reports and present research findings
- Advise organizations on the cultural impact of policies, programs, and products

By drawing and building on knowledge from the humanities and the social, physical, and biological sciences, anthropologists and archeologists examine the ways of life, languages, archeological remains, and physical characteristics of people in various parts of the world. They also examine the customs, values, and social patterns of different cultures.

Archeologists mark archeological sites carefully so they can record exactly where they have found human artifacts.

Median Annual Wages, May 2012

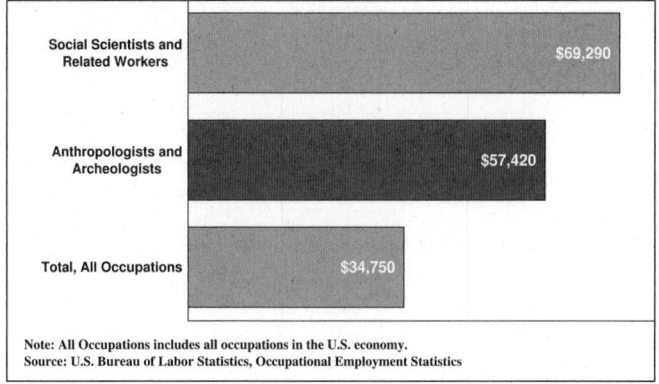

Note: All Occupations includes all occupations in the U.S. economy.
Source: U.S. Bureau of Labor Statistics, Occupational Employment Statistics

Percent Change in Employment, Projected 2012–2022

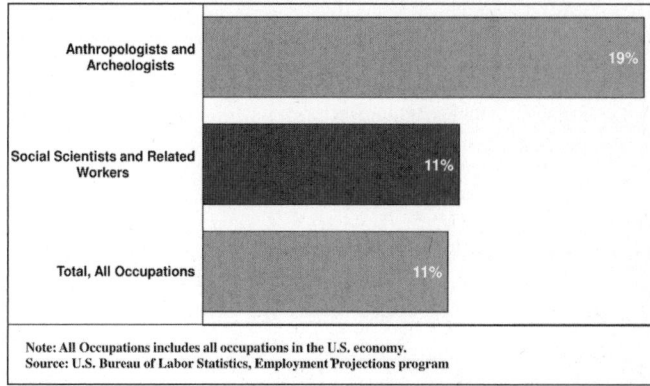

Note: All Occupations includes all occupations in the U.S. economy.
Source: U.S. Bureau of Labor Statistics, Employment Projections program

Many anthropologists and archeologists use sophisticated tools and technologies in their work. Although the equipment used varies by task and specialty, it often includes excavating tools, laboratory equipment, statistical and database software, geophysical tools and equipment, and geographic information systems.

Some anthropologists study the social and cultural consequences of current human issues, such as overpopulation, natural disasters, warfare, and poverty; others study the prehistory and the evolution of humans.

A growing number of anthropologists perform market research for businesses by studying the demand for products by a particular culture or social group. For example, using their anthropological background and a variety of techniques–including interviews, surveys, and observations–they may collect data on how a product is used by specific demographic groups.

Archeologists examine, recover, and preserve evidence and artifacts from past human cultures. They analyze skeletal remains and artifacts, such as tools, pottery, cave paintings, and ruins of buildings. They connect artifacts with information about past environments to learn about the history, customs, and living habits of people in earlier eras.

Archeologists also manage and protect archeological sites. Some work in national parks or at historical sites, providing site protection and educating the public. Others assess building sites to ensure that construction plans comply with federal regulations on site preservation. Archeologists often specialize in a particular geographic area, period, or objects of study, such as animal remains or underwater sites.

The following are examples of types of anthropologists:

Biological anthropologists, also known as *physical anthropologists*, research the evolution of the human species. They look for early evidence of human life, analyze genetics, study primates, and examine the biological variations in humans. They analyze how culture and biology influence each other. Some may examine human remains found at archeological sites to understand population demographics or to identify factors–such as nutrition and disease–that affected these populations. Others may work as forensic anthropologists in medical or legal settings, identifying and analyzing skeletal remains and genetic material.

Cultural anthropologists study the customs, cultures, and social lives of groups. They investigate social practices and processes in settings that range from remote, unindustrialized villages to modern urban centers. Cultural anthropologists often spend time living in the societies they study and collect information through observations, interviews, and surveys.

Linguistic anthropologists study how humans communicate and how language shapes social life. They investigate nonverbal communication, the structure and development of languages, and differences among languages. They also examine the role of language in different cultures, how social and cultural factors affect language, and how language affects a person's experiences. Most linguistic anthropologists study non-European languages, which they learn directly from native speakers.

Work Environment

Anthropologists and archeologists held about 7,200 jobs in 2012. They worked in research organizations, colleges and universities, museums, consulting firms, private corporations, and all levels of government.

The industries that employed the most anthropologists and archeologists in 2012 were as follows:

Research and development in the social sciences
and humanities.. 25%
Federal government, excluding postal service 21
Management, scientific, and technical consulting services 16

The work of anthropologists varies widely, depending on the specific job. Although most anthropologists work in an office, some analyze samples in laboratories or work in the field.

Archeologists often work for cultural resource management (CRM) firms. CRM firms identify, assess, and preserve archeological sites and ensure that developers and builders comply with regulations regarding archeological sites. Archeologists also work in museums, at historical sites, and for government agencies, such as the U.S. Department of the Interior's National Park Service.

Anthropologists and archeologists often do fieldwork, either in the United States or in foreign countries. Fieldwork may involve learning foreign languages, living in remote areas, and examining and excavating archeological sites.

Fieldwork for anthropologists and archeologists usually requires travel for extended periods–about 4 to 8 weeks, but sometimes longer. Field assignments also may require travel to remote areas or international locations, where anthropologists must live with the people they study to learn about their culture. The work may involve rugged living conditions and strenuous physical exertion. Anthropologists are expected to adapt to changing environments, integrate into new social circles, and often conduct research in a foreign language.

While in the field, anthropologists and archeologists often work long hours to meet research deadlines. In addition, many must deal with limited funding for their projects. As a result, fieldwork can be stressful.

Work Schedules. Many anthropologists and archeologists in government, research and consulting firms, museums, and businesses

Employment Projections Data for Anthropologists and Archeologists

Occupational title	SOC Code	Employment, 2012	Projected Employment, 2022	Change, 2012–2022	
				Percent	Numeric
Anthropologists and archeologists	19-3091	7,200	8,600	19	1,400

Source: U.S. Bureau of Labor Statistics, Employment Projections Program

Note: Data are rounded. Go to **Occupational Information Included in the OOH** *for a discussion of the data in this table.*

work full time during regular business hours. When doing field-work, however, anthropologists and archeologists may be required to travel and work long hours, including evenings and weekends.

How to Become One

Anthropologists and archeologists need a master's degree or Ph.D. in anthropology or archeology. Experience doing anthropological or archeological fieldwork is also important. Bachelor's degree holders may find work as assistants or fieldworkers.

Education. Anthropologists and archeologists may qualify for many positions with a master's degree in anthropology or archeology. Most master's degree programs are 2 years in duration and include field research.

Although a master's degree is enough for many positions, a Ph.D. may be needed for jobs that require leadership skills and advanced technical knowledge. To direct projects outside the United States, anthropologists and archeologists typically need a Ph.D. to comply with the requirements of foreign governments. A Ph.D. takes several years of study beyond a master's degree and completion of a doctoral dissertation. Ph.D. students typically spend between 12 and 30 months doing field research for their dissertation.

Those with a bachelor's degree in anthropology or archeology and work experience gained through an internship or field school can work as field or laboratory technicians or assistants. However, anthropologists and archeologists need a master's degree to advance beyond entry-level positions.

Many people with a Ph.D. in anthropology or archeology become professors or museum curators. For more information, see the profiles on postsecondary teachers and archivists, curators, and museum technicians.

Other Experience. In order to get a job, graduates of anthropology and archeology programs usually need work experience in these fields and training in a variety of research methods. Many candidates fulfill this requirement through field training or internships with museums, historical societies, or nonprofit organizations.

Anthropology and archeology students typically spend part of their graduate program conducting field research, often working abroad or in community-based research. Many students also attend archeological field schools, which teach students how to excavate historical and archeological sites and how to record and interpret their findings and data.

Important Qualities

Analytical skills. Anthropologists and archeologists need knowledge of scientific methods and data, which are often used in their research.

Critical-thinking skills. Anthropologists and archeologists must be able to draw logical conclusions from observations, laboratory experiments, and other methods of research.

Investigative skills. Anthropologists and archeologists must seek and explore all facts relevant to their research. They must be able to combine pieces of information to try to solve problems and to answer research questions.

Writing skills. Anthropologists and archeologists need strong writing skills because they often write reports detailing their research findings and publish results in scholarly journals and public interest publications.

Pay

The median annual wage for anthropologists and archeologists was $57,420 in May 2012. The median wage is the wage at which half the workers in an occupation earned more than that amount and half earned less. The lowest 10 percent earned less than $33,330, and the top 10 percent earned more than $91,140.

In May 2012, the median annual wages for anthropologists and archeologists in the top three industries employing these workers were as follows:

Federal government, excluding postal service $72,700
Research and development in the social sciences
   and humanities.. 52,090
Management, scientific, and technical consulting services... 51,470

Similar Occupations   This table shows a list of occupations with job duties that are similar to those of anthropologists and archeologists.

Occupations	Entry-level Education	2012 Pay	Projected Job Growth	Average Annual Openings
Archivists, Curators, and Museum Workers	See "How to Become One"	$44,625	12%	970
Economists	Master's degree	$91,860	14%	740
Geographers	Bachelor's degree	$74,760	29%	80
Historians	Master's degree	$52,480	5%	80
Postsecondary Teachers	See "How to Become One"	$70,380	19%	42,690
Psychologists	See "How to Become One"	$69,807	12%	6,230
Sociologists	Master's degree	$74,960	15%	110
Survey Researchers	Master's degree	$45,050	18%	560

Job Outlook

Employment of anthropologists and archeologists is projected to grow 19 percent from 2012 to 2022, faster than the average for all occupations. However, because it is a small occupation, the fast growth will result in only about 1,400 new jobs over the 10-year period.

Anthropologists and archeologists will be needed to study human life, history, and culture, and to apply that knowledge to current issues. Archeologists will also be needed to monitor construction projects, ensuring that builders comply with federal regulations on the preservation and handling of archeological and historical artifacts.

In addition, corporations will increasingly use anthropological research to gain a better understanding of consumer demand within specific cultures or social groups. Anthropologists and archeologists will also be needed to analyze markets, allowing businesses to serve their clients better or to target new customers or demographic groups.

Because anthropological and archeological research is highly dependent on the amount of research funding, federal budgetary decisions will affect the rate of employment growth in research.

Job Prospects. Overall job prospects will be best for candidates with a Ph.D. and extensive anthropological or archeological field-work experience.

Although job opportunities for anthropologists will continue to grow in businesses, consulting firms, and other non-traditional settings, workers will likely face very strong competition for jobs because of the small number of positions.

Archeologists should have the best job prospects in cultural resource management (CRM) firms. However, because of the large number of qualified graduates and relatively few positions available, jobseekers will likely face very strong competition. Candidates with experience in both qualitative and quantitative research methods who can communicate findings to a wide variety of audiences will be in greatest demand.

O*NET

➤ Anthropologists and Archeologists (19-3091.00)
➤ Anthropologists (19-3091.01)
➤ Archeologists (19-3091.02)

Contacts for More Information

For more information about careers in anthropology and archeology, visit
➤ American Anthropological Association (www.aaanet.org)
   For more information about careers in archeology, visit
➤ Archaeological Institute of America (www.archaeological.org/)
➤ Society for American Archaeology (www.saa.org/)
   For more information about physical anthropologists, visit
➤ American Association of Physical Anthropologists (http://physanth.org/)

Atmospheric Scientists, Including Meteorologists

- **2012 Median Pay** .... $89,260 per year
                                                        $42.91 per hour
- **Entry-Level Education** ....Bachelor's degree
- **Work Experience in a Related Occupation**.............. None
- **On-the-Job Training** .... None
- **Number of Jobs 2012** 11,100
- **Job Outlook, 2012–22**................. 10% (As fast as average)
- **Employment Change, 2012–22** 1,100

What Atmospheric Scientists, Including Meteorologists Do

Atmospheric scientists study the weather and climate and how it affects human activity and Earth in general. They may develop forecasts, collect and compile data from the field, assist in the development of new data collection instruments, or advise clients on risks or opportunities caused by weather events and climate change.

Duties. Atmospheric scientists typically do the following:

- Measure temperature, pressure, humidity, wind speed, dew point, and other properties of the atmosphere
- Use computer models that analyze data about the atmosphere (also called meteorological data)
- Write computer programs to support their modeling efforts
- Produce weather maps and graphics
- Report current weather conditions
- Prepare long- and short-term weather forecasts using sophisticated computers, mathematical models, satellites, radar, and local station data
- Plan, organize, and participate in outreach programs aimed at educating the public about weather
- Issue warnings to protect life and property when threatened by severe weather, such as hurricanes, tornadoes, and flash floods

Atmospheric scientists use highly developed instruments and computer programs to do their jobs. For example, they use weather balloons, radar systems, and satellites to monitor the weather and collect data. The data they collect and analyze are critical to understanding air pollution, drought, changes in the ozone layer, long-term changes in the climate, and other issues. Atmospheric scientists also use graphics software to illustrate their forecasts and reports to better advise their clients or the public.

Many atmospheric scientists work with other geoscientists or even social scientists to help solve problems in areas such as commerce, energy, transportation, agriculture, and the environment. For example, some atmospheric scientists work on teams with engineers and geologists to find the best locations for new wind farms, which are groups of wind turbines used to generate electricity. Others work closely with hydrologists and politicians to study the impact climate change may have on water supplies and to manage water resources.

The following are examples of types of atmospheric scientists:

Atmospheric chemists study atmospheric components, reactions, measurement techniques, and processes. They study climates and gases, chemical reactions that occur in clouds, and ultraviolet radiation.

Atmospheric physicists and dynamists study the physical movements and interactions that occur in the atmosphere. They may study how terrain affects weather and causes turbulence, how solar phenomena affect satellite communications and navigation, or they may study the causes and effects of lightning.

Broadcast meteorologists give forecasts to the general public through television, radio, and the Internet. They use graphics software to develop maps and charts that explain their forecasts. Not all weather broadcasters seen on television are meteorologists or atmospheric scientists. For more information on broadcasters who do not have specific training in meteorology, but present weather conditions and forecasts, see the profile on reporters, correspondents, and broadcast news analysts.

Climatologists study historical weather patterns to interpret and forecast long-term weather patterns or shifts in climate, such as expected precipitation levels years or decades in the future. Global climate change, past and future, is the main area of study for climatologists. Their studies can be used to design buildings, plan heating and cooling systems, and aid in efficient land use and agricultural production. Some climatologists work with specialists in other areas, such as economists or urban and regional planners, to help those experts assess the potential effects of projected climate changes. Paleoclimatology is a specialization within this field. Climatologists who specialize in paleoclimatology may take samples from icebergs and other sources to gather data on the atmosphere that covers very long periods of time.

Forensic meteorologists use historical weather data to reconstruct the weather conditions for a specific location and time. They investigate what role weather played in unusual events such as traffic accidents and fires. Forensic meteorologists may be called as experts to testify in court.

Research meteorologists develop new methods of data collection, observation, and forecasting. They also conduct studies to improve basic understandings of climate, weather, and other aspects of the atmosphere. For example, some research meteorologists study severe weather patterns, such as hurricanes and tornadoes, to understand why cyclones form and to develop better ways of predicting them. Others focus on environmental problems, such as air pollution. Research meteorologists often work with scientists in other fields. For example, they may work with computer scientists to develop new forecasting software or with oceanographers to study interactions between the ocean and the atmosphere. They may work with engineers to develop new instruments so that they can collect the data they need.

Weather forecasters use computer and mathematical models to produce weather reports and short-term forecasts that can range from a few minutes to more than a week. They develop forecasts for the general public and for specific customers such as airports, farmers, utilities, insurance companies, and other businesses. For example, they may provide forecasts to power suppliers so that the suppliers can plan for events, such as heat waves, which would cause a change in electricity demand. They also issue advanced warnings for potentially severe weather such as blizzards and hurricanes. Some forecasters prepare long-range outlooks, predicting whether temperatures and precipitation levels will be above or below average in a particular month or season. These workers become familiar with general weather patterns, atmospheric predictability, precipitation, and forecasting techniques.

Some people with an atmospheric science background may become professors or teachers. For more information, see the profile on postsecondary teachers.

Atmospheric scientists monitor current weather conditions and make weather forecasts.

Work Environment

Atmospheric scientists, including meteorologists held about 11,100 jobs in 2012. The industries that employed the most atmospheric scientists in 2012 were as follows:

Professional, scientific, and technical services.........................36%
Federal government, excluding postal service..........................29
Colleges, universities, and professional schools;
    state, local, and private...19
Radio and television broadcasting...8

In the federal government, most atmospheric scientists work as weather forecasters with the National Weather Service of the National Oceanic and Atmospheric Administration (NOAA) in weather stations throughout the United States –at airports, in or near cities, and in isolated and remote areas. In smaller stations, they often work alone; in larger ones, they work as part of a team. The U.S. Department of Defense employed several hundred atmospheric scientists in 2012. In addition, hundreds of members of the Armed Forces are involved in atmospheric science.

Atmospheric scientists involved in research often work in offices and laboratories. Some may travel frequently to collect data in the field and to observe weather events, such as tornadoes, up close. They watch actual weather conditions from the ground or from an aircraft.

Atmospheric scientists who work in private industry may have to travel to meet with clients or to gather information in the field. For example, forensic meteorologists may need to collect information from the scene of an accident as part of their investigation.

Median Annual Wages, May 2012

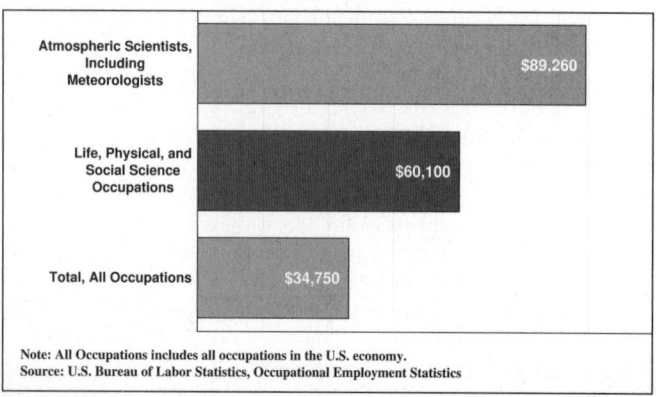

Atmospheric Scientists, Including Meteorologists	$89,260
Life, Physical, and Social Science Occupations	$60,100
Total, All Occupations	$34,750

Note: All Occupations includes all occupations in the U.S. economy.
Source: U.S. Bureau of Labor Statistics, Occupational Employment Statistics

Percent Change in Employment, Projected 2012–2022

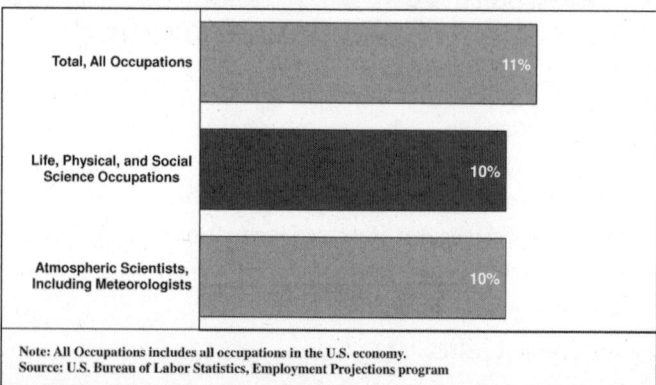

Total, All Occupations	11%
Life, Physical, and Social Science Occupations	10%
Atmospheric Scientists, Including Meteorologists	10%

Note: All Occupations includes all occupations in the U.S. economy.
Source: U.S. Bureau of Labor Statistics, Employment Projections program

Employment Projections Data for Atmospheric Scientists, Including Meteorologists

Occupational title	SOC Code	Employment, 2012	Projected Employment, 2022	Change, 2012–2022	
				Percent	Numeric
Atmospheric and space scientists	19-2021	11,100	12,200	10	1,100

Source: U.S. Bureau of Labor Statistics, Employment Projections Program

Note: Data are rounded. Go to **Occupational Information Included in the OOH** *for a discussion of the data in this table.*

Broadcast meteorologists give their reports to the general public from television and radio studios. They may also broadcast from outdoor locations to tell audiences about current weather conditions.

Work Schedules. Most atmospheric scientists work full time. Weather conditions can change quickly, so weather forecasters need to continuously monitor conditions. Many, especially entry-level staff at field stations, work rotating shifts to cover all 24 hours in a day, and they work on nights, weekends, and holidays to provide the most current weather information. In addition, they work extended hours during severe weather, such as hurricanes. Other atmospheric scientists have a standard workweek, although researchers may work nights and weekends on particular projects.

How to Become One

Atmospheric scientists need a bachelor's degree in meteorology or a closely related earth sciences field for most positions. For research positions, atmospheric scientists need a master's degree at minimum, but usually will need a Ph.D.

Education. Atmospheric scientists typically need a bachelor's degree, either in atmospheric science or a related scientific field that specifically studies atmospheric qualities and phenomena. A bachelor's degree in physics, chemistry, or geology may be adequate alternate majors for those who wish to enter the atmospheric sciences. Many schools offer atmospheric science courses through other departments, such as physics and geosciences. Prospective meteorologists usually take courses outside of the typical atmospheric sciences field.

Course requirements, in addition to courses in meteorology and atmospheric science, usually include advanced courses in physics and mathematics. Classes in computer programming are important because many atmospheric scientists have to write and edit the computer software programs that produce forecasts. Coursework in communications is also becoming important as organizations are becoming more focused on making their data useful and educating their communities and the nation.

Courses should be taken in subjects that are relevant to their desired area of specialization. For example, those who wish to become broadcast meteorologists for radio or television stations may take courses in speech, journalism, or related fields.

Atmospheric scientists who work in research must at least have a master's degree, but will usually need a Ph.D. in atmospheric science or a related field. Most graduate programs do not require prospective students to have a bachelor's degree in atmospheric science. A bachelor's degree in mathematics, physics, or engineering is excellent preparation for graduate study in atmospheric science. In addition to advanced meteorological coursework, graduate students take courses in other disciplines, such as oceanography and geophysics.

Important Qualities

Communication skills. Atmospheric scientists need to be able to write and speak clearly so that their knowledge about the weather can be used effectively by communities and individuals.

Critical-thinking skills. Atmospheric scientists need to be able to analyze the results of their computer models and forecasts to determine the most likely outcome.

Math skills. Atmospheric scientists use calculus, statistics, and other advanced topics in mathematics to develop models used to forecast the weather. They also use mathematical calculations to study the relationship between properties of the atmosphere, such as how changes in air pressure may affect air temperature.

Training. Atmospheric scientists and meteorologists who find employment in the National Weather Service will need to take 200 hours of on-the-job training per year for the first 2 years of employment.

Advancement. Although it is not necessary for entry, a master's degree in atmospheric science can greatly enhance employment opportunities, pay, and advancement potential for meteorologists in government and private industry. A master's degree in business administration (MBA) may be useful for meteorologists interested

Similar Occupations   This table shows a list of occupations with job duties that are similar to those of atmospheric scientists, including meteorologists.

Occupations	Entry-level Education	2012 Pay	Projected Job Growth	Average Annual Openings
Chemists and Materials Scientists	Bachelor's degree	$73,247	6%	3,040
Computer Programmers	Bachelor's degree	$74,280	8%	11,810
Environmental Engineers	Bachelor's degree	$80,890	15%	2,110
Environmental Scientists and Specialists	Bachelor's degree	$63,570	15%	3,970
Geoscientists	Bachelor's degree	$90,890	16%	1,730
Hydrologists	Master's degree	$75,530	9%	290
Mathematicians	Master's degree	$101,360	23%	170
Physicists and Astronomers	Doctoral or professional degree	$105,722	10%	810
Postsecondary Teachers	See "How to Become One"	$70,380	19%	42,690

in working in private industry as consultants who help firms make important business decisions on the basis of their forecasts.

Pay

The median annual wage for atmospheric scientists was $89,260 in May 2012. The median wage is the wage at which half the workers in an occupation earned more than that amount and half earned less. The lowest 10 percent earned less than $49,120, and the top 10 percent earned more than $134,730.

In May 2012, the median annual wages for atmospheric scientists, including meteorologists in the top four industries in which these scientists worked were as follows:

Federal government, excluding postal service $97,710
Colleges, universities, and professional schools;
    state, local, and private... 86,090
Radio and television broadcasting....................................... 82,360
Professional, scientific, and technical services...................... 82,310

Job Outlook

Employment of atmospheric scientists is projected to grow by 10 percent from 2010 to 2020, about as fast as the average for all occupations. New computer models have vastly improved the accuracy of forecasts and allow atmospheric scientists to tailor forecasts to specific purposes. This should increase the need for atmospheric scientists working in private industry as businesses demand more specialized weather information.

Job Prospects. Prospective atmospheric scientists should expect competition because the number of graduates from meteorology programs is expected to exceed the number of job openings. Workers with a graduate degree should enjoy better prospects than those whose highest level of education is a bachelor's degree.

Competition may be strong for research positions at colleges and universities because of the limited number of positions available. Few opportunities are expected in federal government because atmospheric scientists will be hired only to replace workers who retire or leave for other reasons. Budget constraints are also expected to limit hiring by federal agencies such as the National Weather Service. The best job prospects for meteorologists will be in private industry.

O*NET

➤ Atmospheric and Space Scientists (19-2021.00)

Contacts for More Information

For more information about atmospheric scientists, including a list of colleges and universities offering atmospheric science programs, visit
➤ American Meteorological Society (www.ametsoc.org/)

For a broad range of information concerning atmospheric scientists within the geosciences perspective, visit
➤ American Geosciences Institute (www.agiweb.org/)

For information about atmospheric science careers in research, visit
➤ University Corporation for Atmospheric Research (https://www2.ucar.edu/)

For information on federal government education requirements for atmospheric science positions, visit
➤ U.S. Office of Personnel Management (www.opm.gov/qualifications/standards/IORs/gs1300/1340.htm)

To find job openings for atmospheric scientists in the federal government, visit
➤ USAJOBS (www.usajobs.gov/)

For information about federal government atmospheric science careers in the National Weather Service and other agencies within the National Oceanic and Atmospheric Administration, visit
➤ National Oceanic and Atmospheric Administration (www.noaa.gov/)

Biochemists and Biophysicists

- **2012 Median Pay** .... $81,480 per year
                                                          $39.17 per hour
- **Entry-Level Education** ... Doctoral or professional degree
- **Work Experience in a Related Occupation**............... None
- **On-the-Job Training** .... None
- **Number of Jobs 2012** 29,200
- **Job Outlook, 2012–22** .... 19% (Faster than average)
- **Employment Change, 2012–22** 5,400

What Biochemists and Biophysicists Do

Biochemists and biophysicists study the chemical and physical principles of living things and of biological processes, such as cell development, growth, and heredity.

Duties. Biochemists and biophysicists typically do the following:

- Plan and conduct complex projects in basic and applied research
- Manage laboratory teams and monitor the quality of their work
- Isolate, analyze, and synthesize proteins, enzymes, DNA, and other molecules

Biochemists and biophysicists conduct research in college or university, private industry, and government laboratories.

Median Annual Wages, May 2012

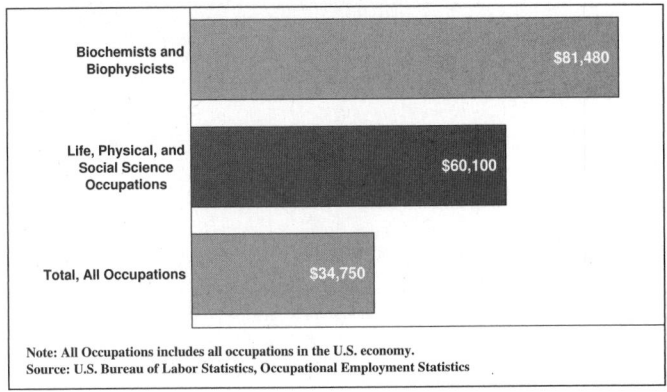

Note: All Occupations includes all occupations in the U.S. economy.
Source: U.S. Bureau of Labor Statistics, Occupational Employment Statistics

Percent Change in Employment, Projected 2012–2022

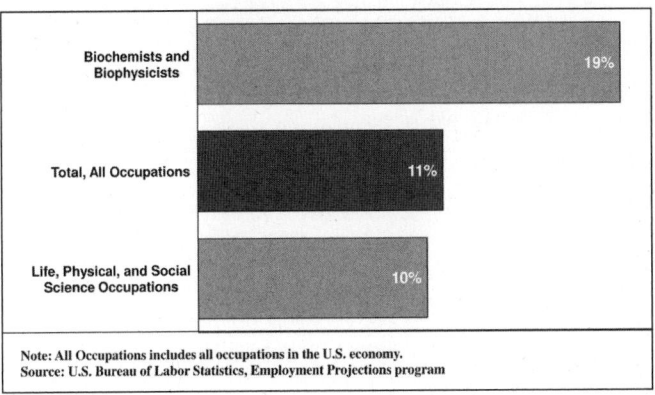

Note: All Occupations includes all occupations in the U.S. economy.
Source: U.S. Bureau of Labor Statistics, Employment Projections program

- Research the effects of substances, such as drugs, hormones, and food on tissues and biological processes
- Prepare technical reports, research papers, and recommendations based on their research
- Present research findings to scientists, engineers, and other colleagues

Biochemists and biophysicists use advanced technologies, such as electron microscopes and lasers to conduct scientific experiments and analysis. They also use computer modeling software to determine the three-dimensional structures of proteins and other molecules. Biochemists and biophysicists involved in biotechnology research use chemical enzymes to synthesize recombinant DNA.

Biochemists and biophysicists work in basic and applied research. Basic research is conducted without any immediately known application; the goal is to expand human knowledge. Applied research is directed toward solving a particular problem.

Biochemists involved in basic research may study the genetic mutations in organisms that lead to cancer and other diseases. Others study the evolution of plants and animals, to understand how genetic traits are carried through successive generations.

Biophysicists may conduct basic research to learn how nerve cells communicate or how proteins work. Biochemists and biophysicists who conduct basic research typically must submit written grant proposals to colleges and universities, private foundations, and the federal government, to get the money they need for their research.

Biochemists and biophysicists who conduct applied research attempt to develop products and processes that improve our lives. For example, in medicine, biochemists and biophysicists develop tests used to detect diseases, genetic disorders, and other illnesses. They also develop new drugs and medications, such as those used to treat cancer or Alzheimer's disease.

Applied research in biochemistry and biophysics has many uses outside of medicine. In agriculture, biochemists and biophysicists research ways to genetically engineer crops that are resistant to drought, disease, insects, and other afflictions. Biochemists and biophysicists also investigate alternative fuels, such as biofuels–renewable energy sources from plants. In addition, they develop ways to protect the environment and clean up pollution.

Large amounts of data are generated by biochemists, biophysicists, and others who work in biological research. Specialists called *bioinformaticians* use their knowledge of statistics, mathematics, and computer science to analyze these data. Bioinformaticians often work to create a theoretical framework intended to combine large amounts of data into meaningful theories. They mine large data sets for correlations that might suggest relationships or explain biological phenomena.

Many people with a biochemistry background become professors and teachers. For more information, see the profile on postsecondary teachers.

Work Environment

Biochemists and biophysicists held about 29,200 jobs in 2012. The industries employing the most biochemists and biophysicists in 2012 were as follows:

Research and development in the physical,
    engineering, and life sciences...47%
Colleges, universities, and professional schools;
    state, local, and private...17
Pharmaceutical and medicine manufacturing.........................14
Drugs and druggists' sundries merchant wholesalers...............2
Testing laboratories...2

Biochemists and biophysicists typically work in laboratories and offices, to conduct experiments and analyze the results. Those who work with dangerous organisms or toxic substances in the laboratory must follow safety procedures to avoid contamination.

Most biochemists and biophysicists work on teams. Research projects are often interdisciplinary; and biochemists and biophysicists frequently work with experts in other fields, such as physics, chemistry, computer science, and engineering.

Some biotech companies might need researchers to help sell their products. These technologies can be very complex, and having an expert explain them to potential customers might be necessary. This may be more common in smaller companies, where workers often fulfill multiple roles, such as working in research and in sales. Working in sales may require significant amounts of travel. For more information on sales representatives, see the profile on wholesale and manufacturing sales representatives.

Work Schedules. Most biochemists and biophysicists work full time and keep regular hours. Some positions may require longer hours.

How to Become One

Biochemists and biophysicists need a Ph.D. to work in independent research and development positions. Most Ph.D. holders begin their careers in temporary postdoctoral research positions. Bachelor's and master's degree holders are qualified for some entry-level positions in biochemistry and biophysics.

Education. Most Ph.D. holders in biochemistry and biophysics have bachelor's degrees in biochemistry or a related field, such as biology, chemistry, physics, or engineering. High school students can prepare for college by taking classes related to the natural and physical sciences.

Employment Projections Data for Biochemists and Biophysicists

Occupational title	SOC Code	Employment, 2012	Projected Employment, 2022	Change, 2012–2022	
				Percent	Numeric
Biochemists and biophysicists	19-1021	29,200	34,600	19	5,400

Source: U.S. Bureau of Labor Statistics, Employment Projections Program

Note: **Data are rounded. Go to Occupational Information Included in the OOH** *for a discussion of the data in this table.*

Students in bachelor's degree programs in biochemistry or a related field typically take courses in mathematics, physics, and computer science in addition to courses in the biological sciences. Courses in mathematics and computer science are important for biochemists and biophysicists, who must be able to do complex data analysis. Most bachelor's degree programs include required laboratory coursework. Additional laboratory coursework is excellent preparation for graduate school or for getting an entry-level position in industry. Students can gain valuable laboratory experience by working for a university's laboratories and occasionally through internships with prospective employers, such as pharmaceutical and medicine manufacturers.

Ph.D. programs typically include advanced coursework in topics such as toxicology, genetics, and proteomics (the study of proteins). Graduate students also spend a lot of time conducting laboratory research. Study at the master's level is generally considered good preparation for those interested in doing hands-on laboratory work. Ph.D. level studies provide additional training in research project planning and execution.

Training. Most biochemistry and biophysics Ph.D. holders begin their careers in temporary postdoctoral research positions. During their postdoctoral appointments, they work with experienced scientists, as they continue to learn about their specialties or develop a broader understanding of related areas of research.

Postdoctoral positions frequently offer the opportunity to publish research findings. A solid record of published research is essential to get a permanent position doing basic research, especially for those seeking a permanent college or university faculty position.

Important Qualities

Analytical skills. Biochemists and biophysicists must be able to conduct scientific experiments and analyses with accuracy and precision.

Communication skills. Biochemists and biophysicists have to write and publish reports and research papers, give presentations of their findings, and communicate with team members.

Critical-thinking skills. Biochemists and biophysicists draw conclusions from experimental results through sound reasoning and judgment.

Interpersonal skills. Biochemists and biophysicists typically work on research teams and need to work well with others toward a common goal. Many serve as team leaders and must be able to motivate and direct other team members.

Math skills. Biochemists and biophysicists regularly use complex equations and formulas in their work; and they need a broad understanding of mathematics, including calculus and statistics.

Perseverance. Biochemists and biophysicists need to be thorough in their research and in their approach to problems. Scientific research involves substantial trial and error, and biochemists and biophysicists must not become discouraged in their work.

Problem-solving skills. Biochemists and biophysicists use scientific experiments and analysis to find solutions to complex scientific problems.

Advancement. Some biochemists and biophysicists become natural sciences managers. Those who pursue management careers spend much of their time on administrative tasks, such as preparing budgets and schedules.

Pay

The median annual wage for biochemists and biophysicists was $81,480 in May 2012. The median wage is the wage at which half the workers in an occupation earned more than that amount and half earned less. The lowest 10 percent earned less than $41,430, and the top 10 percent earned more than $147,350.

In May 2012, the median annual wages for biochemists and biophysicists in the top five industries in which these scientists worked were as follows:

Drugs and druggists' sundries merchant wholesalers	$103,390
Research and development in the physical, engineering, and life sciences	86,530
Pharmaceutical and medicine manufacturing	82,490
Testing laboratories	74,230
Colleges, universities, and professional schools; state, local, and private	52,990

Job Outlook

Employment of biochemists and biophysicists is projected to grow 19 percent from 2012 to 2022, faster than the average for all occupations. However, because it is a small occupation, the fast growth will result in only about 5,400 new jobs over the 10-year period. More biochemists and biophysicists are expected to be needed to do basic research that increases scientific knowledge and to research and develop biological products and processes that improve our lives. However, budgetary concerns may limit the ability for researchers to find funding for basic research.

The aging baby-boom population and the demand for lifesaving new drugs and procedures to cure and to prevent disease likely will drive demand for biochemists and biophysicists involved in biomedical research. For example, biochemists will be needed to conduct genetic research and to develop new medicines and treatments that are used to fight genetic disorders and diseases such as cancer. They also will be needed to develop new tests used to detect diseases and other illnesses. Currently, there is a trend of smaller companies doing biomedical research, rather than the large pharmaceutical companies. This helps the larger companies avoid risks and costs.

Areas of research and development in biotechnology other than health are expected to provide employment growth for biochemists and biophysicists. Greater demand for clean energy should increase the need for biochemists that research and develop alternative energy sources, such as biofuels. A growing population and rising food prices are expected to fuel the development of genetically engineered crops and livestock that provide greater yields and require fewer resources. Efforts to discover new and improved ways to clean up and preserve the environment will increase demand for biochemists and biophysicists, as well.

Similar Occupations   This table shows a list of occupations with job duties that are similar to those of biochemists and biophysicists.

Occupations	Entry-level Education	2012 Pay	Projected Job Growth	Average Annual Openings
Agricultural and Food Scientists	See "How to Become One"	$58,636	10%	1,640
Biological Technicians	Bachelor's degree	$39,750	10%	3,210
Biomedical Engineers	Bachelor's degree	$86,960	27%	1,010
Chemists and Materials Scientists	Bachelor's degree	$73,247	6%	3,040
Epidemiologists	Master's degree	$65,270	12%	160
Medical Scientists	Doctoral or professional degree	$76,980	13%	3,550
Microbiologists	Bachelor's degree	$66,260	7%	710
Natural Sciences Managers	Bachelor's degree	$115,730	6%	1,370
Physicians and Surgeons	Doctoral or professional degree	$182,294	18%	29,630
Physicists and Astronomers	Doctoral or professional degree	$105,722	10%	810
Postsecondary Teachers	See "How to Become One"	$70,380	19%	42,690
Zoologists and Wildlife Biologists	Bachelor's degree	$57,710	5%	670

As the amount of biological data continues to grow and computer analytical techniques and software continue to become more sophisticated, the number of dedicated bioinformaticians should also continue to grow. This specialty is relatively new but is growing in importance and complexity.

Job Prospects. Biochemists and biophysicists involved in basic research should expect strong competition for permanent research and faculty positions at colleges and universities. Biochemists and biophysicists with postdoctoral experience who have had research articles published in scientific journals should have the best prospects for these positions. Many biochemists and biophysicists work through multiple postdoctoral appointments before getting a permanent position in academia.

A large portion of basic research in biochemistry and biophysics is dependent on funding from the federal government through the National Institutes of Health and the National Science Foundation. Therefore, federal budgetary decisions will have a large impact on job prospects in basic research from year to year. Typically, there is strong competition among biochemists and biophysicists for research funding.

Most applied research projects that involve biochemists and biophysicists require the expertise of scientists in multiple fields, such as microbiology, medicine, and chemistry. Biochemists and biophysicists who have a broad understanding of molecular biology and its relationship to other disciplines should have the best job opportunities.

Those who gain laboratory experience through coursework or employment during their undergraduate studies will be the best prepared and have the best chances to gain employment or to enter graduate level programs.

O*NET

➤ Biochemists and Biophysicists (19-1021.00)

Contacts for More Information

For more information about biochemists, visit
➤ American Chemical Society (www.acs.org/)
➤ American Society for Biochemistry and Molecular Biology (www. asbmb.org/)
For more information about biophysicists, visit
➤ Biophysical Society (www.biophysics.org/)

For general information about careers in biological sciences, visit
➤ American Institute of Biological Sciences (www.aibs.org)
➤ Federation of American Societies for Experimental Biology (www. faseb.org/)

Biological Technicians

- **2012 Median Pay** .... $39,750 per year
  $19.11 per hour
- **Entry-Level Education** .... Bachelor's degree
- **Work Experience in a Related Occupation** .... None
- **On-the-Job Training** .... None
- **Number of Jobs 2012** 80,200
- **Job Outlook, 2012–22** .... 10% (As fast as average)
- **Employment Change, 2012–22** 8,000

What Biological Technicians Do

Biological technicians help biological and medical scientists conduct laboratory tests and experiments.

Duties. Biological technicians typically do the following:

Set up, maintain, and clean laboratory instruments and equipment, such as microscopes, scales, and test tubes

- Gather and prepare biological samples, such as blood, food, or bacteria cultures, for laboratory analysis
- Conduct biological tests and experiments
- Document their work, including procedures, observations, and results
- Analyze experimental data and interpret results
- Write reports that summarize their findings

Most biological technicians work on teams. Biological technicians typically are responsible for doing scientific tests, experiments, and analyses under the supervision of biologists or other scientists who direct and evaluate their work. Biological technicians use traditional laboratory instruments, advanced robotics, and automated equipment to conduct experiments. They use specialized computer software to collect, analyze, and model experimental data. Some biological technicians will need to collect samples. To do this, they may need to have certain skills, such as handling a boat so they could collect water samples.

Biological technicians work in many research areas. They may assist medical researchers by helping to develop new medicines and treatments used to prevent, treat, or cure diseases.

Biological technicians working in a microbiological context, sometimes referred to as laboratory assistants, typically study living microbes and perform techniques specific to microbiology, such as growing cultures in Petri dishes or staining specimens to aid in identification.

Technicians working in biotechnology apply the knowledge and techniques they have gained from basic research to product development.

Biological technicians also may work in private industry and assist in the study of a wide range of topics concerning mining and industrial production. They may test samples in environmental impact studies, or monitor production processes to help ensure products are not contaminated.

Biological technicians working for the U.S. Department of the Interior or other government agencies may perform biological testing to support wildlife and resource management goals.

Work Environment

Biological technicians held about 80,200 jobs in 2012. The industries employing the most biological technicians in 2012 were as follows:

Colleges, universities, and professional schools;
   state, local, and private... 32%
Research and development in the physical,
   engineering, and life sciences... 23
Federal government, excluding postal service 15
Chemical manufacturing... 8
Hospitals; state, local, and private 8
Testing laboratories.. 4

Biological technicians typically work in laboratories and offices, where they conduct experiments and analyze the results under the supervision of biological scientists and medical scientists. Some biological technicians who do fieldwork may be exposed to weather events and wildlife, such as mosquitoes.

Biological technicians must follow strict procedures to avoid contaminating the experiment, themselves, or the environment. Some experiments may involve dangerous organisms or toxic substances.

Biological technicians work together on teams under the direction of biologists or other scientists.

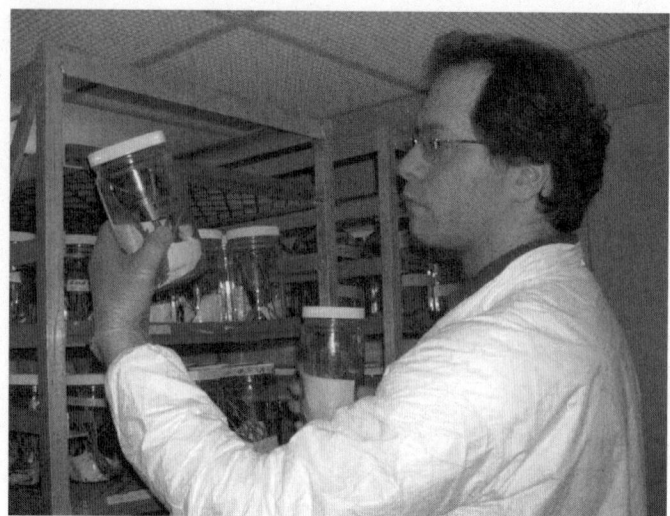

Most biological technicians work in laboratories.

Work Schedules. Most biological technicians work full time and keep regular hours. About 1 in 5 biological technicians worked part time in 2012.

How to Become One

Biological technicians typically need a bachelor's degree in biology or a closely related field. It is important for prospective biological technicians to gain laboratory experience while they are in school.

Education. Biological technicians typically need a bachelor's degree in biology or a closely related field. Most colleges and universities offer bachelor's degree programs in the biological sciences.

Biological science programs usually include courses in general biology, as well as in specific subfields such as ecology, microbiology, and physiology. In addition to taking courses in biology, students must study chemistry, mathematics, and physics. Computer science courses are helpful for learning how to model and simulate biological processes and for learning how to operate some laboratory equipment.

Laboratory experience is important for prospective biological technicians, and students should take biology courses that emphasize laboratory work.

Important Qualities

Analytical skills. Biological technicians need to be able to conduct scientific experiments and analyses with accuracy and precision.

Communication skills. Biological technicians must be able to understand and follow the instructions of their managing sci-

Median Annual Wages, May 2012

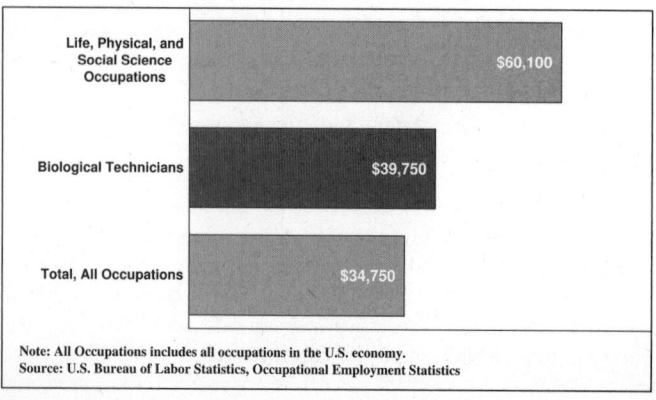

Life, Physical, and Social Science Occupations — $60,100
Biological Technicians — $39,750
Total, All Occupations — $34,750

Note: All Occupations includes all occupations in the U.S. economy.
Source: U.S. Bureau of Labor Statistics, Occupational Employment Statistics

Percent Change in Employment, Projected 2012–2022

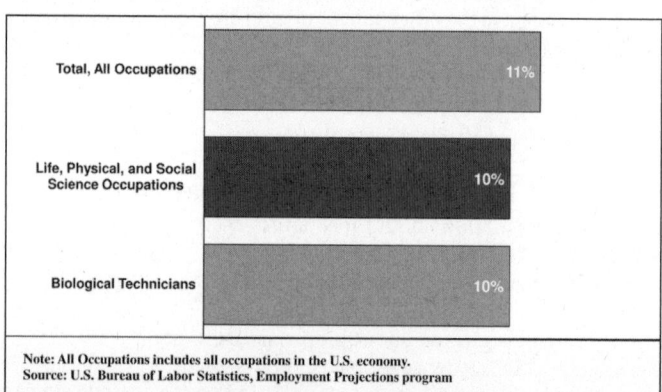

Total, All Occupations — 11%
Life, Physical, and Social Science Occupations — 10%
Biological Technicians — 10%

Note: All Occupations includes all occupations in the U.S. economy.
Source: U.S. Bureau of Labor Statistics, Employment Projections program

Employment Projections Data for Biological Technicians

Occupational title	SOC Code	Employment, 2012	Projected Employment, 2022	Change, 2012–2022 Percent	Change, 2012–2022 Numeric
Biological technicians	19-4021	80,200	88,300	10	8,000

Source: U.S. Bureau of Labor Statistics, Employment Projections Program

Note: Data are rounded. Go to Occupational Information Included in the OOH for a discussion of the data in this table.

entists. They also need to be able to clearly communicate their processes and findings in written reports.

Critical-thinking skills. Biological technicians draw conclusions from experimental results through sound reasoning and judgment.

Observational skills. Biological technicians must constantly monitor their experiments. They need to keep a complete, accurate record of their work, such as the conditions under which the experiment was carried out, the procedures they followed, and the results they obtained.

Technical skills. Biological technicians must be able to set up and operate sophisticated equipment and instruments. They also may need to adjust equipment to ensure that experiments are conducted properly.

Other Experience. Prospective biological technicians should have laboratory experience. In addition to coursework, laboratory experience may be gained during summer internships with prospective employers, such as pharmaceutical and medicine manufacturers, or in university laboratories.

Advancement. Biological technicians may advance to scientist positions, such as a microbiologist, after a few years of experience working as a technician or after earning a graduate degree. Gaining more experience and higher levels of education often allows biological technicians to move into positions such as natural sciences managers or postsecondary teachers.

Pay

The median annual wage for biological technicians was $39,750 in May 2012. The median wage is the wage at which half the workers in an occupation earned more than that amount and half earned less. The lowest 10 percent earned less than $25,280, and the top 10 percent earned more than $64,880.

In May 2012, median annual wages for biological technicians in the top six industries employing these technicians were as follows:

Chemical manufacturing..	$45,380
Research and development in the physical, engineering, and life sciences..	42,330
Colleges, universities, and professional schools; state, local, and private..	40,450
Hospitals; state, local, and private	38,450
Testing laboratories..	36,260
Federal government, excluding postal service	33,630

Job Outlook

Employment of biological technicians is projected to grow 10 percent from 2012 to 2022, about as fast as the average for all occupations. Greater demand for biotechnology research is expected to increase the need for these workers.

Biotechnology research plays a key role in scientific advancements that improve our quality of life. Biological technicians will be needed to help scientists develop new treatments for diseases, such as cancer and Alzheimer's disease.

In agriculture, biotechnology research will be used to create genetically engineered crops that provide greater yields and require less pesticide and fertilizer. Efforts to discover new and improved ways to clean and preserve the environment will also continue to add to job growth. In addition, biological technicians will be needed to help develop alternative sources of energy, such as biofuels and better sources of renewable biomass.

Job Prospects. Applicants who have laboratory experience, either through coursework or through previous work experience, should have the best opportunities.

Similar Occupations   This table shows a list of occupations with job duties that are similar to those of biological technicians.

Occupations	Entry-level Education	2012 Pay	Projected Job Growth	Average Annual Openings
Agricultural and Food Science Technicians	Associate's degree	$34,070	3%	1,010
Biochemists and Biophysicists	Doctoral or professional degree	$81,480	18%	1,370
Chemical Technicians	Associate's degree	$42,920	9%	2,160
Environmental Science and Protection Technicians	Associate's degree	$41,240	19%	1,900
Epidemiologists	Master's degree	$65,270	12%	160
Forensic Science Technicians	Bachelor's degree	$52,840	6%	580
Geoscientists	Bachelor's degree	$90,890	16%	1,730
Medical and Clinical Laboratory Technologists and Technicians	See "How to Become One"	$47,499	22%	15,600
Medical Scientists	Doctoral or professional degree	$76,980	13%	3,550
Microbiologists	Bachelor's degree	$66,260	7%	710
Zoologists and Wildlife Biologists	Bachelor's degree	$57,710	5%	670

O*NET

➤ Biological Technicians (19-4021.00)

Contacts for More Information

For more information on career opportunities in the biological sciences, visit

➤ American Institute for Biological Sciences (www.aibs.org)
➤ American Society for Cell Biology (www.ascb.org)
➤ American Society for Microbiology (www.asm.org)
➤ Federation of American Societies for Experimental Biology (www.faseb.org)

To find job openings for biological technician in the federal government, visit

➤ USAJOBS (www.usajobs.gov)

Chemical Technicians

- **2012 Median Pay** .... $42,920 per year
  $20.64 per hour
- **Entry-Level Education** .... Associate's degree
- **Work Experience in a Related Occupation** .... None
- **On-the-Job Training** .... Moderate-term on-the-job training
- **Number of Jobs 2012** 63,600
- **Job Outlook, 2012–22** .... 9% (As fast as average)
- **Employment Change, 2012–22** 6,000

What Chemical Technicians Do

Chemical technicians use special instruments and techniques to help chemists and chemical engineers research, develop, and produce chemical products and processes.

Duties. Chemical technicians typically do the following:

- Monitor chemical processes and test the quality of products to make sure that they meet standards and specifications
- Set up and maintain laboratory instruments and equipment
- Prepare chemical solutions
- Conduct chemical and physical experiments, tests, and analyses for a variety of purposes, including research and development
- Compile and interpret results of tests and analyses
- Prepare technical reports, graphs, and charts, and give presentations that summarize their results

Most chemical technicians work on teams. Typically, they are supervised by chemists or chemical engineers who direct their work and evaluate their results. For example, some chemical technicians help chemists and other scientists develop new medicines. Others help chemical engineers develop more efficient production processes.

Chemical technicians' duties and titles often depend on where they work. The following are the two main types of chemical technicians:

Laboratory technicians typically help scientists conduct experiments and analyses. Often, they prepare chemical solutions, test products for quality and performance, and analyze compounds produced through complex chemical processes. Chemical laboratory technicians may analyze samples of air and water to monitor pollution levels. Laboratory technicians usually set up and maintain laboratory equipment and instruments.

Processing technicians monitor the quality of products and processes at chemical manufacturing facilities. For example, they adjust processing equipment to improve production efficiency and output. They collect samples from production batches, which then are tested for impurities and other defects. Processing technicians also test product packaging to make sure it is well designed, will hold up well, and will have a limited impact on the environment.

Work Environment

Chemical technicians held about 63,600 jobs in 2012.

The industries that employed the most chemical technicians in 2012 were as follows:

Testing laboratories	22%
Research and development in the physical, engineering, and life sciences	13
Basic chemical manufacturing	8
Pharmaceutical and medicine manufacturing	7
Colleges, universities, and professional schools; state, local, and private	4

Chemical technicians typically work in laboratories or in industrial facilities such as chemical and pharmaceutical manufacturing plants. Some chemical technicians are exposed to health or safety hazards when handling certain chemicals, but there is little risk if they follow proper safety procedures.

Work Schedules. Most technicians work full time. Processing technicians often work longer and later shifts than laboratory technicians because many manufacturing facilities operate around the clock.

How to Become One

Chemical technicians need an associate's degree or 2 years of postsecondary education for most jobs. Most chemical technicians also receive on-the-job training.

Education. For most jobs, chemical technicians need an associate's degree in applied science or chemical technology or 2 years of postsecondary education.

Many technical and community colleges offer programs in applied sciences or chemical technology. Students typically take classes in mathematics, physics, and biology in addition to chemistry courses. Coursework in statistics and computer science is also useful because technicians routinely do data analysis and modeling.

One of the most important aspects of any degree program is laboratory time. Laboratory coursework provides students with hands-on experience in conducting experiments and using various instruments and techniques properly. Many schools also offer internships and cooperative-education programs that help students gain employment experience while attending school.

Science technicians monitor experiments and record the results.

Median Annual Wages, May 2012

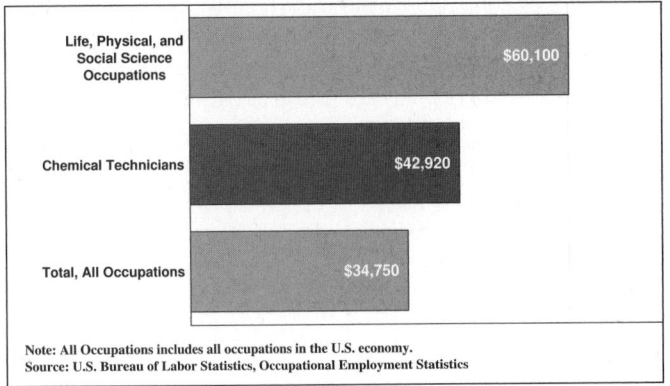

Note: All Occupations includes all occupations in the U.S. economy.
Source: U.S. Bureau of Labor Statistics, Occupational Employment Statistics

Percent Change in Employment, Projected 2012–2022

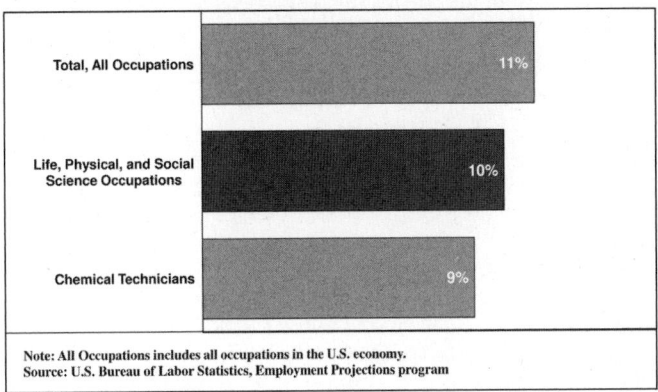

Note: All Occupations includes all occupations in the U.S. economy.
Source: U.S. Bureau of Labor Statistics, Employment Projections program

Important Qualities

Ability to use technology. Chemical technicians must be able to set up and operate sophisticated equipment and instruments. They also may need to adjust the equipment to ensure that experiments and processes are running properly and safely.

Analytical skills. Chemical technicians must be able to conduct scientific experiments with accuracy and precision.

Communication skills. Chemical technicians must explain their work to scientists, engineers, and to workers who may not have a technical background. They often write reports to communicate their results.

Critical-thinking skills. Chemical technicians reach their conclusions through sound reasoning and judgment.

Interpersonal skills. Chemical technicians must be able to work well with others as part of a team, because they often work with scientists, engineers, and other technicians.

Observation skills. Chemical technicians must carefully monitor chemical experiments and processes. They must keep complete records of their work, including conditions, procedures, and results.

Time-management skills. Chemical technicians often work on multiple tasks and projects at the same time and must be able to prioritize their assignments.

Training. Most chemical technicians receive on-the-job training. Typically, experienced technicians teach new employees proper methods and procedures for conducting experiments and operating equipment. Length of training varies with the new employee's level of experience and education and the industry the worker is employed in.

Advancement. Technicians who have a bachelor's degree may advance to positions as chemists or chemical engineers.

Pay

The median annual wage for chemical technicians was $42,920 in May 2012. The median wage is the wage at which half the workers in an occupation earned more than that amount and half earned less. The lowest 10 percent earned less than $26,220, and the top 10 percent earned more than $70,710.

Employment Projections Data for Chemical Technicians

Occupational title	SOC Code	Employment, 2012	Projected Employment, 2022	Change, 2012–2022 Percent	Numeric
Chemical technicians	19-4031	63,600	69,500	9	6,000

Source: U.S. Bureau of Labor Statistics, Employment Projections Program

Note: Data are rounded. Go to Occupational Information Included in the OOH *for a discussion of the data in this table.*

Similar Occupations

This table shows a list of occupations with job duties that are similar to those of chemical technicians.

Occupations	Entry-level Education	2012 Pay	Projected Job Growth	Average Annual Openings
Agricultural and Food Science Technicians	Associate's degree	$34,070	3%	1,010
Biological Technicians	Bachelor's degree	$39,750	10%	3,210
Chemical Engineers	Bachelor's degree	$94,350	5%	920
Chemists and Materials Scientists	Bachelor's degree	$73,247	6%	3,040
Environmental Science and Protection Technicians	Associate's degree	$41,240	19%	1,900
Forensic Science Technicians	Bachelor's degree	$52,840	6%	580
Geological and Petroleum Technicians	Associate's degree	$52,700	15%	810
Nuclear Technicians	Associate's degree	$69,060	15%	410

In May 2012, the median annual wages for chemical technicians in the top five industries in which these technicians worked were as follows:

Basic chemical manufacturing $50,710
Research and development in the physical,
    engineering, and life sciences.. 48,440
Pharmaceutical and medicine manufacturing...................... 43,390
Colleges, universities, and professional schools;
    state, local, and private... 41,590
Testing laboratories... 35,150

Job Outlook

Employment of chemical technicians is projected to grow 9 percent from 2012 to 2022, about as fast as the average for all occupations. Chemical technicians will continue to be in demand in scientific research and development (R&D) and to monitor the quality of chemical products and processes. Greater interest in environmental issues, such as pollution control, clean energy, and sustainability, are expected to increase the demand for chemistry research and development.

Declines in the employment of chemical technicians are projected in all chemical manufacturing industries, including pharmaceutical manufacturing. Many chemical and pharmaceutical manufacturers are expected to outsource their scientific R&D and testing operations to professional, scientific, and technical services firms that specialize in these services. However, due to the development of cheaper energy and raw materials sources such as shale gas, some chemical manufacturing is expected to return to the United States. This should generate more demand for these workers in the next decade.

Job Prospects. As the instrumentation and techniques used in research, development, and production become more complex, employers will seek job candidates with highly developed technical skills. Job opportunities are expected to be best for graduates of applied science technology programs who are well trained on equipment used in laboratories or production facilities.

O*NET

➤ Chemical Technicians (19-4031.00)

Contacts for More Information

For more information about chemical technicians, visit
➤ American Chemical Society (www.acs.org)
➤ American Chemistry Council (www.americanchemistry.com/)

Chemists and Materials Scientists

- **2012 Median Pay** .... $73,060 per year
                                                          $35.13 per hour
- **Entry-Level Education** .... Bachelor's degree
- **Work Experience in a Related Occupation**.............. None
- **On-the-Job Training** .... None
- **Number of Jobs 2012** 96,200
- **Job Outlook, 2012–22**.............. 6% (Slower than average)
- **Employment Change, 2012–22** 5,400

What Chemists and Materials Scientists Do

Chemists and materials scientists study substances at the atomic and molecular levels and the ways in which substances react with each other. They use their knowledge to develop new and improved products and to test the quality of manufactured goods.

Duties. Chemists and materials scientists typically do the following:

- Plan and carry out complex research projects, such as the development of new products and testing methods
- Direct technicians and other workers in testing and analyzing components and the physical properties of materials
- Instruct scientists and technicians on proper chemical processing and testing procedures, such as ingredients, mixing times, and operating temperatures
- Prepare solutions, compounds, and reagents used in laboratory procedures
- Analyze substances to determine their composition and concentration of elements
- Conduct tests on materials and other substances, to ensure that safety and quality standards are met
- Write technical reports that detail methods and findings
- Present research findings to scientists, engineers, and other colleagues

Many chemists and materials scientists work in basic and applied research. In basic research, chemists investigate the properties, composition, and structure of matter. They also experiment with combinations of elements and the ways in which they interact. In applied research, chemists investigate possible new products and ways to improve existing ones. Chemistry research has led to the discovery and development of new and improved drugs, plastics, cleaners, and thousands of other products.

Materials scientists study the structures and chemical properties of various materials, to develop new products or enhance existing ones. They determine ways to strengthen or combine materials or develop new materials for use in a variety of products. Applications of materials science include inventing or improving superconducting materials, ceramics, and metallic alloys.

Chemists and materials scientists develop new uses for substances and materials.

Median Annual Wages, May 2012

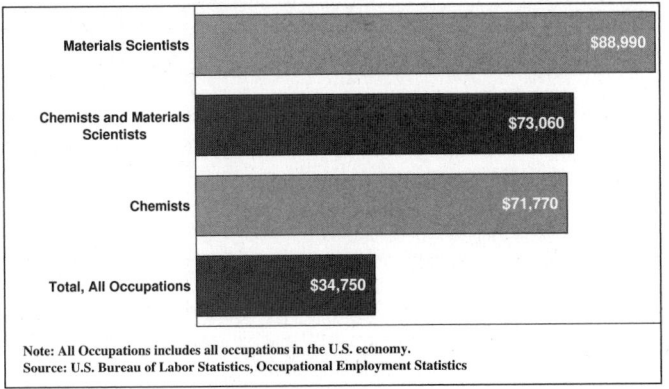

Note: All Occupations includes all occupations in the U.S. economy.
Source: U.S. Bureau of Labor Statistics, Occupational Employment Statistics

Percent Change in Employment, Projected 2012–2022

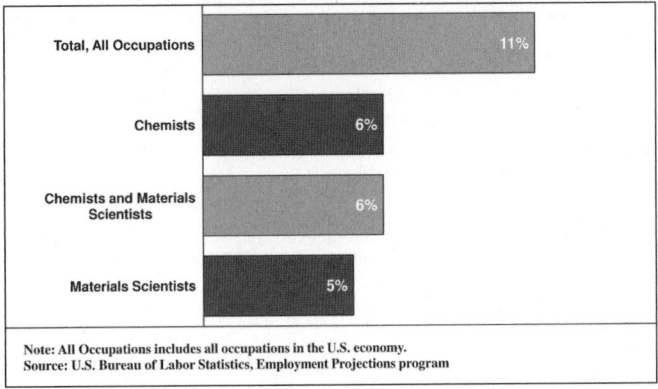

Note: All Occupations includes all occupations in the U.S. economy.
Source: U.S. Bureau of Labor Statistics, Employment Projections program

Chemists and materials scientists use computers and a wide variety of sophisticated laboratory instrumentation for modeling, simulation, and experimental analysis. For example, some chemists use three-dimensional (3D) computer modeling software to study the structure and other properties of complex molecules.

Most chemists and materials scientists work as part of a team. An increasing number of scientific research projects involve multiple disciplines, and it is common for chemists and materials scientists to work on teams with other scientists, such as biologists and physicists, computer specialists, and engineers. For example, in pharmaceutical research, chemists may work with biologists to develop new drugs and with engineers to design ways to mass produce the new drugs. For more information, see the profiles on biochemists and biophysicists, microbiologists, zoologists and wildlife biologists, physicists and astronomers, computer and information technology occupations, and engineers.

Chemists often specialize in a particular branch of the field. The following are examples of some types of chemists:

Analytical chemists determine the structure, composition, and nature of substances, by examining and identifying their various elements or compounds. They also study the relationships and interactions between the parts of compounds. Some analytical chemists specialize in developing new methods of analysis and new techniques for carrying out their work. Their research has a wide range of applications, including food safety, pharmaceuticals, and pollution control.

Inorganic chemists study the structure, properties, and reactions of molecules that do not contain carbon, such as metals. They work to understand the behavior and the characteristics of inorganic substances. Inorganic chemists figure out how these materials can be modified, separated, or used in products, such as ceramics and superconductors.

Medicinal chemists research and develop chemical compounds that can be used as pharmaceutical drugs. They work on teams with other scientists and engineers to create and test new drug products. They also help develop new and improved manufacturing processes to produce new drugs on a large scale effectively.

Organic chemists study the structure, properties, and reactions of molecules that contain carbon. They also design and make new organic substances that have unique properties and applications. These compounds have, in turn, been used to develop many commercial products, such as pharmaceutical drugs and plastics.

Physical chemists study the fundamental characteristics of how matter behaves on a molecular and atomic level and how chemical reactions occur. Based on their analyses, physical chemists may develop new theories, such as how complex structures are formed. Physical chemists often work closely with materials scientists, to research and develop potential uses for new materials.

Theoretical chemists investigate theoretical methods that can predict the outcomes of chemical experiments. Theoretical chemistry encompasses a variety of specializations itself, though most specializations incorporate advanced computation and programming. Some examples of theoretical chemists are computational chemists, mathematical chemists, and chemical informaticians.

Materials scientists tend to specialize by the material they work with most often. A few examples of materials in which these scientists specialize are ceramics, glass, semiconductors, and composite materials.

A growing numbers of chemists work in interdisciplinary fields, such as biochemistry and geochemistry. For more information, see the profile on geoscientists.

Many people with a chemistry background become professors or teachers. For more information, see the profiles on high school teachers and postsecondary teachers.

Work Environment

Chemists and material scientists held about 96,200 jobs in 2012. The industries that employed the most chemists in 2012 were as follows:

Research and development in the physical,
    engineering, and life sciences................................ 20%
Pharmaceutical and medicine manufacturing 17
Testing laboratories... 11
Federal government, excluding postal service 7
State and local government, excluding education
    and hospitals... 6

Most materials scientists work in manufacturing and scientific research and development. The industries that employed the most materials scientists in 2012 were as follows:

Research and development in the physical,
    engineering, and life sciences................................ 34%
Colleges, universities, and professional schools;
    state, local, and private.. 11
Pharmaceutical and medicine manufacturing 6
Computer and electronic product manufacturing 6
Basic chemical manufacturing 5

Chemists and materials scientists typically work in laboratories and offices, where they conduct experiments and analyze their results. In addition to laboratories, materials scientists work with engineers and processing specialists in industrial manufacturing facilities. Some chemists also work in these facilities and usually are responsible for monitoring the environmental conditions at the plant. Chemists and materials scientists, who work for manufactur-

Employment Projections Data for Chemists and Materials Scientists

Occupational title	SOC Code	Employment, 2012	Projected Employment, 2022	Change, 2012–2022	
				Percent	Numeric
Chemists and materials scientists...	—	96,200	101,600	6	5,400
Chemists	19-2031	87,900	92,900	6	5,000
Materials scientists..	19-2032	8,300	8,800	5	400

Source: *U.S. Bureau of Labor Statistics, Employment Projections Program*

Note: **Data are rounded. Go to** Occupational Information Included in the OOH *for a discussion of the data in this table.*

ing companies, may have to travel occasionally, especially if their company has multiple facilities.

Chemists and materials scientists typically work on research teams. They need to be able to work well with others towards a common goal. Many serve in a leadership capacity and need to be able to motivate and direct other team members.

Injuries and Illnesses. Chemists and materials scientists can be exposed to health or safety hazards when handling certain chemicals, but there is little risk if proper procedures are followed.

Work Schedules. Chemists and materials scientists typically work full time and keep regular hours.

How to Become One

Chemists and materials scientists need at least a bachelor's degree in chemistry or a related field. However, a master's degree or Ph.D. is needed for many research jobs.

Education. A bachelor's degree in chemistry or in a related field is needed for entry-level chemist jobs. Although some materials scientists hold a degree in materials science, these scientists commonly have a degree in chemistry, physics, or engineering. Many jobs require master's degrees or Ph.D.s and may also require significant levels of work experience. Chemists and materials scientists with Ph.D.s and postdoctoral experience typically lead basic and applied research teams.

Many colleges and universities offer degree programs in chemistry. There are few programs specifically in materials science, but the number of programs is gradually increasing. Some engineering schools offer degrees in the joint field of materials science and engineering.

Undergraduate chemistry majors typically are required to take courses in analytical, organic, inorganic, and physical chemistry. In addition to chemistry coursework, they also take classes in mathematics, biological sciences, and physics. Computer science courses are essential, because chemists and materials scientists need computer skills to perform modeling and simulation tasks, manage and manipulate databases, and to operate computerized laboratory equipment.

Laboratory experience, either at a college or university, or through internships, fellowships, or work-study programs in industry, is also useful.

Graduate students studying chemistry commonly specialize in a subfield, such as analytical chemistry or inorganic chemistry. For example, those interested in doing research in the pharmaceutical industry usually develop a strong background in medicinal or organic chemistry.

Important Qualities

Analytical skills. Chemists and materials scientists carry out scientific experiments and studies. They must be precise and accurate in their analyses, because errors could invalidate their research.

Communication skills. Chemists and materials scientists need to communicate with team members and other scientists. They must be able to read and write technical reports and give presentations.

Critical-thinking skills. Chemists and materials scientists carefully evaluate their own work and the work of others. They must determine if results and conclusions are based on sound science.

Mathematical skills. Chemists and materials scientists regularly use complex mathematical equations and formulas, and they need a broad understanding of mathematics, including calculus, algebra, and statistics.

Organizational skills. Chemists and materials scientists need to carefully document processes to conform to regulations and industry procedures. Disorganization in the workplace can lead to legal problems, damage to equipment, and chemical spills.

Problem-solving skills. Chemists and materials scientists research and develop new and improved chemical products, processes, and materials. This work requires a great deal of trial and error on the part of chemists and materials scientists before a unique solution is found.

Advancement. Chemists typically receive greater responsibility and independence in their work as they gain experience. Greater responsibility also is gained through further education. Ph.D. chemists usually lead research teams and have control over the direction and content of projects, but even Ph.D. holders have room to advance as they gain experience. They may take on larger, more complicated, and more expensive projects as they become more proficient in managing research projects.

Some chemists and materials scientists become natural sciences managers.

Pay

The median annual wage for chemists was $71,770 in May 2012. The median wage is the wage at which half the workers in an occupation earned more than that amount and half earned less. The lowest 10 percent earned less than $41,080, and the top 10 percent earned more than $120,600.

In May 2012, the median annual wages for chemists in the top five industries employing these scientists were as follows:

Federal government, excluding postal service..................	$100,920
Research and development in the physical, engineering, and life sciences..	79,140
Pharmaceutical and medicine manufacturing......................	70,480
State and local government, excluding education and hospitals...	57,190
Testing laboratories..	55,060

The median annual wage for materials scientists was $88,990 in May 2012. The lowest 10 percent earned less than $46,960, and the top 10 percent earned more than $134,130.

In May 2012, the median annual wages for materials scientists in the top five industries employing these scientists were as follows:

Basic chemical manufacturing	$106,770
Research and development in the physical, engineering, and life sciences..	96,630
Computer and electronic product manufacturing...............	96,620

Similar Occupations   This table shows a list of occupations with job duties that are similar to those of chemists and materials scientists.

Occupations	Entry-level Education	2012 Pay	Projected Job Growth	Average Annual Openings
Agricultural and Food Scientists	See "How to Become One"	$58,636	10%	1,640
Biochemists and Biophysicists	Doctoral or professional degree	$81,480	18%	1,370
Chemical Engineers	Bachelor's degree	$94,350	5%	920
Environmental Scientists and Specialists	Bachelor's degree	$63,570	15%	3,970
Geoscientists	Bachelor's degree	$90,890	16%	1,730
High School Teachers	Bachelor's degree	$55,050	6%	31,260
Materials Engineers	Bachelor's degree	$85,150	1%	750
Natural Sciences Managers	Bachelor's degree	$115,730	6%	1,370
Physicists and Astronomers	Doctoral or professional degree	$105,722	10%	810
Postsecondary Teachers	See "How to Become One"	$70,380	19%	42,690

Colleges, universities, and professional schools; state, local, and private..66,720
Pharmaceutical and medicine manufacturing......................66,230

Job Outlook

Employment of chemists and materials scientists is projected to grow 6 percent from 2012 to 2022, slower than the average for all occupations.

Employment of chemists is projected to grow 6 percent, as they will continue to be needed in scientific research and development and to monitor the quality of products and processes.

Employment of materials scientists is projected to grow 5 percent, owing to demand for cheaper, safer, and better quality materials for a variety of purposes, such as electronics, energy, and transportation.

Chemists research and solve a wide range of problems and are employed in a similarly wide range of industries. About a quarter of all chemists are employed in chemical manufacturing industries; but the remainder work at colleges and universities, in government, and for independent testing and research laboratories. Some chemical manufacturing industries, such as pharmaceutical manufacturing, increasingly may be outsourcing their research and development activities, rather than doing the research in-house. This is likely to cause faster growth in the employment of chemists in small, independent research and development firms than in the more traditional large manufacturers. However, as the economy improves and the expansion in domestic natural gas production lowers the cost of energy and raw inputs, manufacturers may have less of an incentive than they have in the past to outsource their research and development (R&D) activities.

Environmental research will offer many new opportunities for chemists and materials scientists. For example, chemical manufacturing industries will continue to develop technologies and processes that reduce pollution and improve energy efficiency at manufacturing facilities. Chemists also will continue to be needed to monitor pollution levels at manufacturing facilities and to ensure compliance with local, state, and federal environmental regulations.

Job Prospects. In addition to job openings resulting from employment growth, some job openings will result from the need to replace chemists and materials scientists who retire or otherwise leave the occupations.

Chemists and materials scientists with advanced degrees, particularly those with a Ph.D. and work experience, are expected to experience better opportunities. Large pharmaceutical and biotechnology firms provide openings for these workers at research laboratories, and many others work in colleges and universities. Furthermore, chemists with advanced degrees will continue to fill most senior research and upper-management positions.

O*NET

➤ Chemists (19-2031.00)
➤ Materials Scientists (19-2032.00)

Contacts for More Information

For information on career opportunities, earnings, and education for chemists and materials scientists, visit

➤ American Chemical Society (www.acs.org/)
➤ American Chemistry Council (www.americanchemistry.com/)
➤ ASM International (www.asminternational.org/)
➤ Materials Research Society (www.mrs.org/)

To find job openings for chemists in the federal government, visit

➤ USAJOBS (www.usajobs.gov/)

Conservation Scientists and Foresters

- **2012 Median Pay** ....$59,060 per year
$28.40 per hour
- **Entry-Level Education** ....Bachelor's degree
- **Work Experience in a Related Occupation**...............None
- **On-the-Job Training** ....None
- **Number of Jobs 2012** 34,200
- **Job Outlook, 2012–22** ....3% (Slower than average)
- **Employment Change, 2012–22** 900

What Conservation Scientists and Foresters Do

Conservation scientists and foresters manage overall land quality of forests, parks, rangelands, and other natural resources.

Duties. Conservation scientists typically do the following:

- Monitor forestry and conservation activities to assure compliance with government regulations and habitat protection

- Negotiate terms and conditions for forest harvesting and land-use contracts
- Establish plans for managing forest lands and resources
- Monitor forest-cleared lands to ensure that they are suitable for future use
- Work with private landowners, governments, farmers, and others to improve land for forestry purposes, while at the same time protecting the environment

Foresters typically do the following:

- Supervise activities of forest and conservation workers and technicians
- Choose and prepare sites for new trees using controlled burning, bulldozers, or herbicides to clear land
- Monitor the regeneration of forests
- Direct and participate in forest fire suppression
- Determine ways to remove timber with minimum environmental damage

Conservation scientists manage, improve, and protect the country's natural resources. They work with private landowners and federal, state, and local governments to find ways to use and improve the land while safeguarding the environment. Conservation scientists advise farmers, farm managers, and ranchers on how they can improve their land for agricultural purposes and to control erosion.

Foresters have a wide range of duties, and their responsibilities vary depending on their employer. Some primary duties of foresters include drawing up plans to regenerate forested lands, monitoring the progress of those lands, and supervising tree harvests. They also come up with plans to keep forests free from disease, harmful insects, and damaging wildfires.

Foresters may choose and direct the preparation of sites on which trees will be planted. They advise on the type, number, and placement of trees. When the trees reach a certain size, foresters decide which trees should be harvested and sold to sawmills.

Many foresters supervise forest and conservation workers and technicians, directing their work and evaluating their progress. For more information, see the profiles on forest and conservation workers and forest and conservation technicians.

Conservation scientists and foresters evaluate data on forest and soil quality, assessing damage to trees and forest lands caused by fires and logging activities. In addition, they lead activities such as fire suppression and planting seedlings. Fire suppression activities include measuring how quickly fires will spread and how successfully the planned suppression activities turn out.

Conservation scientists and foresters often work outdoors.

Conservation scientists and foresters use their skills to determine a fire's impact on a region's environment. Communication with firefighters and other forest workers is an important component of fire suppression and controlled burn activities because the information that conservation scientists and foresters provide can determine how firefighters work.

Conservation scientists and foresters use a number of tools to perform their jobs. They use clinometers to measure the heights of trees, diameter tapes to measure a tree's circumference, and increment borers and bark gauges to measure the growth of trees so that timber volumes can be computed and growth rates estimated.

In addition, conservation scientists and foresters often use remote sensing (aerial photographs and other imagery taken from airplanes and satellites) and geographic information systems (GIS) data to map large forest or range areas and to detect widespread trends of forest and land use. They make extensive use of hand-held computers and global positioning systems (GPS) to study these maps.

The following are examples of types of conservation scientists:

Conservation land managers work for land trusts or other conservation organization to protect the wildlife habitat, biodiversity, scenic value, and other unique attributes of preserves and conservation lands.

Range managers, also called range conservationists, protect rangelands to maximize their use without damaging the environment. Rangelands contain many natural resources and cover hundreds of millions of acres in the United States, mainly in the western states and Alaska.

Median Annual Wages, May 2012

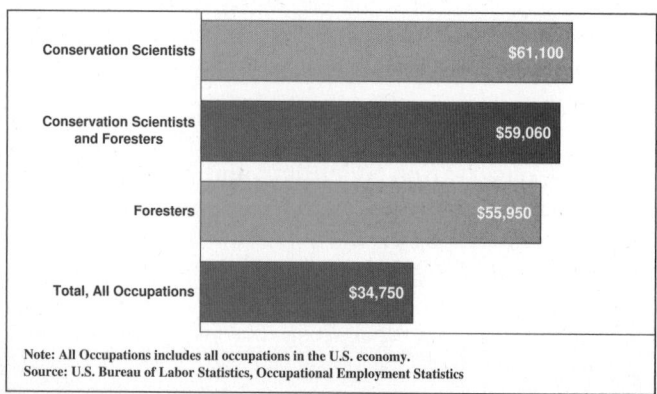

Conservation Scientists	$61,100
Conservation Scientists and Foresters	$59,060
Foresters	$55,950
Total, All Occupations	$34,750

Note: All Occupations includes all occupations in the U.S. economy.
Source: U.S. Bureau of Labor Statistics, Occupational Employment Statistics

Percent Change in Employment, Projected 2012–2022

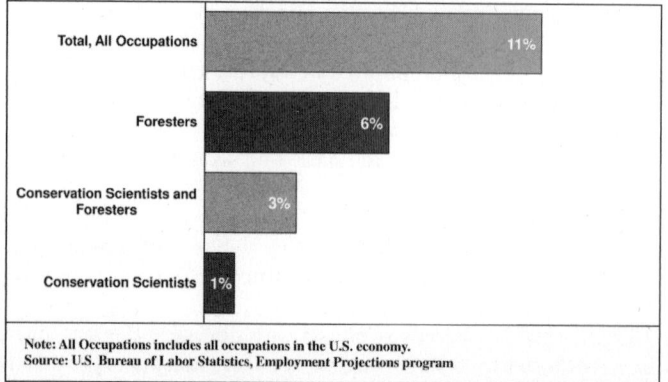

Total, All Occupations	11%
Foresters	6%
Conservation Scientists and Foresters	3%
Conservation Scientists	1%

Note: All Occupations includes all occupations in the U.S. economy.
Source: U.S. Bureau of Labor Statistics, Employment Projections program

Employment Projections Data for Conservation Scientists and Foresters

Occupational title	SOC Code	Employment, 2012	Projected Employment, 2022	Change, 2012–2022	
				Percent	Numeric
Conservation scientists and foresters	19-1030	34,200	35,000	3	900
Conservation scientists..	19-1031	22,100	22,300	1	100
Foresters	19-1032	12,000	12,800	6	700

Source: U.S. Bureau of Labor Statistics, Employment Projections Program

Note: Data are rounded. Go to Occupational Information Included in the OOH for a discussion of the data in this table.

Range managers may inventory soils, plants, and animals; develop resource management plans; help to restore degraded ecosystems; or help manage a ranch. They also maintain soil stability and vegetation for uses such as wildlife habitats and outdoor recreation. Like foresters, they work to prevent and reduce wildfires and invasive animal species.

Soil and water conservationists give technical help to people who are concerned with the conservation of soil, water, and related natural resources. For private landowners, they develop programs to make the most productive use of land without damaging it. They also help landowners with issues such as dealing with erosion. They help private landowners and governments by advising on water quality, preserving water supplies, preventing groundwater contamination, and conserving water.

The following are examples of types of foresters:

Procurement foresters buy timber by contacting local forest owners and negotiating a sale. This activity typically involves taking inventory on the type, amount, and location of all standing timber on the property. Procurement foresters then appraise the timber's worth, negotiate its purchase, and draw up a contract. The forester then subcontracts with loggers or pulpwood cutters to remove the trees and to help lay out roads to get to the timber.

Restoration planners study issues facing forests and related natural resources. They may study issues such as tree improvement and harvesting techniques, global climate change, improving wildlife habitats, and protecting forests from pests, diseases, and wildfires.

Urban foresters live and work in larger cities and manage urban trees. They are concerned with quality-of-life issues, including air quality, shade, and storm water runoff.

Conservation education foresters train teachers and students about issues facing forest lands.

Work Environment

Conservation scientists and foresters held about 34,200 jobs in 2012.

The industries that employed the most conservation scientists in 2012 were as follows:

Federal government, excluding postal service	34%
State government, excluding education and hospitals	21
Local government, excluding education and hospitals	14
Social advocacy organizations	9

The industries that employed the most foresters in 2012 were as follows:

State government, excluding education and hospitals	29%
Federal government, excluding postal service	13
Local government, excluding education and hospitals	11
Sawmills and wood preservation	5
Logging	4

Conservation scientists and foresters work for governments (federal, state, or local), on privately owned lands, or for social advocacy organizations. In the western and southwestern United States, they usually work for the federal government because of the number of national parks in that part of the country. In the eastern United States, they often work for private landowners. Social advocacy organizations work with lawmakers on behalf of sustainable land use and other issues facing forest land. They are concerned with the long-term impact of carbon emissions on forests worldwide.

Conservation scientists and foresters typically work in offices, in laboratories, and in the outdoors, sometimes doing fieldwork in remote locations. When visiting or working near logging operations or wood yards, they wear a hardhat.

The work can be physically demanding. Some conservation scientists and foresters work outdoors in all types of weather, occasionally in isolated areas. They may need to walk long distances through dense woods and underbrush to carry out their work. Insect bites, poisonous plants, and other natural hazards present some risk.

In an isolated location, a forester or conservation scientist may work alone, measuring tree densities, regeneration, or other outdoor activities. Other foresters work closely with the public, educating them about the forest or the proper use of recreational sites.

Fire suppression activities are an important aspect of their duties, which involve prevention as well as emergency response. Therefore, their work has occasional risk.

Work Schedules. Most conservation scientists and foresters work full time and have a standard work schedule. Responding to emergencies or fires may require conservation scientists and foresters to work longer hours.

How to Become One

Conservation scientists and foresters typically need a bachelor's degree in forestry or a related field. Employers seek applicants who have degrees from programs that are accredited by the Society of American Foresters (SAF) and other organizations.

Education. Conservation scientists and foresters typically need a bachelor's degree in forestry or a related field, such as agricultural science, rangeland management, or environmental science. Although graduate work is not generally required, some conservation scientists and foresters get a master's degree or Ph.D.

Most forest and conservation technology programs are accredited by the Society of American Foresters. There are accredited programs in every state.

Many colleges and universities offer degrees in forestry or a related field. Bachelor's degree programs are designed to prepare conservation scientists and foresters for their career or a graduate degree. Alongside practical skills, theory and education are important parts of these programs.

Courses for bachelor's and advanced degree programs in forestry and related fields typically include ecology, biology, and forest resource measurement. Scientists and foresters also typically have a

Similar Occupations   This table shows a list of occupations with job duties that are similar to those of conservation scientists and foresters.

Occupations	Entry-level Education	2012 Pay	Projected Job Growth	Average Annual Openings
Agricultural and Food Scientists	See "How to Become One"	$58,636	10%	1,640
Environmental Science and Protection Technicians	Associate's degree	$41,240	19%	1,900
Firefighters	Postsecondary non-degree award	$45,250	7%	10,400
Forest and Conservation Technicians	Associate's degree	$33,920	-4%	1,340
Forest and Conservation Workers	High school diploma or equivalent	$24,340	5%	230
Zoologists and Wildlife Biologists	Bachelor's degree	$57,710	5%	670

background in a geographic information systems (GIS) technology and other forms of computer modeling.

Important Qualities

Analytical skills. Conservation scientists and foresters must evaluate the results of a variety of field tests and experiments, all of which require precision and accuracy. They use sophisticated computer modeling to prepare their analysis.

Critical-thinking skills. Conservation scientists and foresters reach conclusions through sound reasoning and judgment. They determine how to improve forest conditions, and they must react appropriately to fires.

Decision-making skills. Conservation scientists and foresters must use their expertise and experience to determine whether their findings will have an impact on soil, forest lands, and the spread of fires.

Management skills. Conservation scientists and foresters need to work well with the forest and conservation workers and technicians they supervise, so effective communication is critical.

Physical stamina. Conservation scientists and foresters often walk long distances in steep and wooded areas. They work in all kinds of weather, including extreme heat and cold.

Speaking skills. Conservation scientists and foresters must give clear instructions to forest and conservation workers and technicians, who typically do the labor necessary for proper forest maintenance. They also need to communicate clearly with landowners and in some cases the general public.

Licenses, Certifications, and Registrations. Sixteen states sponsor some type of credentialing process for foresters. Alabama, California, Connecticut, Maine, Maryland, Massachusetts, and New Hampshire have licensing laws. Arkansas, Georgia, Mississippi, North Carolina, and South Carolina have laws requiring registration. Michigan, New Jersey, Oklahoma, and West Virginia have laws about voluntary registration.

Licensing and registration requirements both usually require a 4-year degree in forestry and several years of forestry work experience. Candidates who want a license also may be required to pass an exam.

The Society for Range Management offers a professional certification in rangeland management or as a range management consultant.

The Society of American Foresters certifies foresters who have at least a bachelor's degree from one of the 50 forestry or natural resources degree programs accredited by the society or from a forestry program that is substantially equivalent. The candidate also must have qualifying professional experience and pass an exam.

Advancement. Many conservation scientists and foresters advance to take on managerial duties. They also may conduct research or work on policy issues, often after getting an advanced

degree. Foresters in management usually leave fieldwork behind, spending more of their time in an office, working with teams to develop management plans and supervising others.

Soil conservationists usually begin working within one district and may advance to a state, regional, or national level. Soil conservationists also can transfer to occupations such as a farm or ranch management advisor or a land appraiser.

Pay

The median annual wage for conservation scientists was $61,100 in May 2012. The median wage is the wage at which half the workers in an occupation earned more than that amount and half earned less. The lowest 10 percent earned less than $38,350, and the top 10 percent earned more than $90,870.

The median annual wage for foresters was $55,950 in May 2012. The lowest 10 percent earned less than $36,380, and the top 10 percent earned more than $78,490.

In May 2012, the median annual wages for conservation scientists in the top four industries in which these scientists worked were as follows:

Federal government, excluding postal service	$71,110
State government, excluding education and hospitals	53,310
Social advocacy organizations	52,820
Local government, excluding education and hospitals	51,230

In May 2012, the median annual wages for foresters in the top five industries in which these foresters worked were as follows:

Logging	$64,180
Federal government, excluding postal service	61,680
Sawmills and wood preservation	56,430
Local government, excluding education and hospitals	54,290
State government, excluding education and hospitals	49,610

Job Outlook

Employment of conservation scientists and foresters is projected to grow 3 percent from 2012 to 2022, slower than the average for all occupations.

Heightened demand for American timber and wood pellets will help increase the overall job prospects for conservation scientists and foresters. Most growth from 2012 to 2022 for conservation scientists and foresters is expected to be in federal- and state-owned forest lands, particularly in the western United States. Jobs in private forests will grow alongside demand for timber and pellets, and governments are likely to hire more foresters as the number of forest fires increases and more people move into forest lands.

In recent years, preventing and suppressing wildfires has become the primary concern for government agencies managing forests and rangelands. The development of previously unused lands, in addition to changing weather conditions, has contributed to increasingly devastating and costly fires.

Job Prospects. Increases in funding, more retirees, and new programs should create opportunities for foresters and range managers. Restoring lands affected by fires also will be a major task, particularly in the southwestern and western states, where fires are most common. Job prospects are highest for conservation scientists and foresters who have a strong understanding of geographic information systems (GIS).

O*NET

➤ Conservation Scientists (19-1031.00)
➤ Soil and Water Conservationists (19-1031.01)
➤ Range Managers (19-1031.02)
➤ Park Naturalists (19-1031.03)
➤ Foresters (19-1032.00)

Contacts for More Information

For more information about conservation scientists and foresters, including schools offering education in forestry, visit

➤ Society of American Foresters (www.safnet.org)

For information about careers in forestry, particularly conservation forestry and land management, visit

➤ Forest Guild (www.forestguild.org)
➤ Society for Range Management (www.rangelands.org/)
➤ US Forest Service (www.fs.fed.us/)

Economists

- **2012 Median Pay** .... $91,860 per year
  $44.16 per hour
- **Entry-Level Education** ....Master's degree
- **Work Experience in a Related Occupation**............... None
- **On-the-Job Training** .... None
- **Number of Jobs 2012** 16,900
- **Job Outlook, 2012–22** .... 14% (As fast as average)
- **Employment Change, 2012–22** 2,300

What Economists Do

Economists study the production and distribution of resources, goods, and services by collecting and analyzing data, researching trends, and evaluating economic issues.

Duties. Economists typically do the following:

- Research and analyze economic issues
- Conduct surveys and collect data
- Analyze data using mathematical models and statistical techniques
- Prepare reports, tables, and charts that present research results
- Interpret and forecast market trends
- Advise businesses, governments, and individuals on economic topics
- Design policies or make recommendations for solving economic problems
- Write articles for publication in academic journals and other media sources

Economists apply economic analysis to issues within a variety of fields, such as education, health, development, and the environment. Some economists study the cost of products, healthcare, or energy. Others examine employment levels, business cycles, or exchange rates. Still, others analyze the effect of taxes, inflation, or interest rates.

Economists often study historical trends and use them to make forecasts. They research and analyze data using a variety of software programs, including spreadsheets, statistical analysis, and database management programs.

Nearly half of all economists work in federal, state, and local government. Federal government economists collect and analyze data about the U.S. economy, including employment, prices, productivity, and wages among other types of data. They also project spending needs and inform policymakers on the economic impact of laws and regulations.

Many economists work for corporations and help them understand how the economy will affect their business. Specifically, economists may analyze issues such as consumer demand and sales to help a company maximize its profits.

Economists also work for research firms and think tanks, where they study and analyze a variety of economic issues. Their analyses and forecasts are frequently published in newspapers and journal articles.

Some economists work for companies with major international operations and for international organizations such as the World Bank, International Monetary Fund, and United Nations.

Many people with an economics background become postsecondary teachers.

The following are examples of types of economists:

Econometricians develop models and use mathematical analyses to test economic relationships. They use techniques such as calculus, game theory, and regression analysis to explain economic facts or trends in all areas of economics.

Financial economists analyze savings, investments, and risk. They also study financial markets and financial institutions.

Industrial organization economists study how companies within an industry are organized and how they compete. They also examine how antitrust laws, which regulate attempts by companies to restrict competition, affect markets.

International economists study international trade and the impact of globalization. They also examine global financial markets and exchange rates.

Labor economists study the supply of workers and the demand for labor by employers. Specifically, they research employment levels and how wages are set. They also analyze the effects of labor-related policies, such as minimum wage laws, and institutions, such as unions.

Preparing reports on the results of economic research is an important part of an economist's job.

Median Annual Wages, May 2012

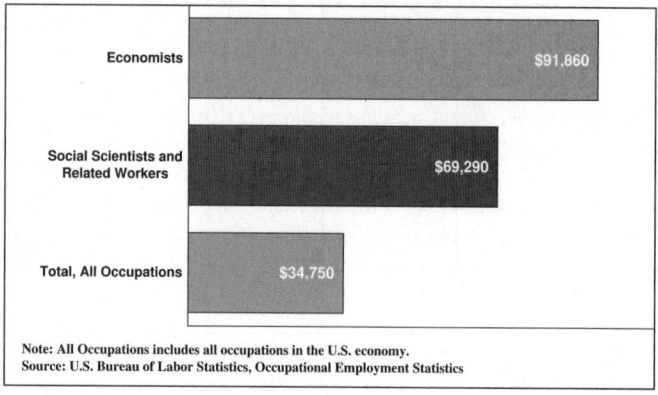

Note: All Occupations includes all occupations in the U.S. economy.
Source: U.S. Bureau of Labor Statistics, Occupational Employment Statistics

Percent Change in Employment, Projected 2012–2022

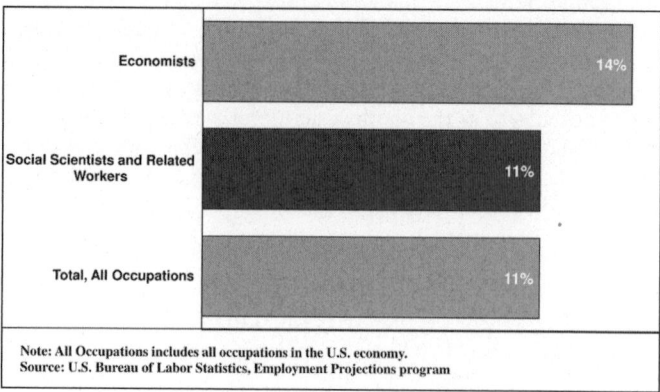

Note: All Occupations includes all occupations in the U.S. economy.
Source: U.S. Bureau of Labor Statistics, Employment Projections program

Macroeconomists and *monetary economists* examine the economy as a whole. They may research trends related to unemployment, inflation, and economic growth. They also study fiscal and monetary policies, which examine the effects of money supply and interest rates on the economy.

Microeconomists study supply and demand decisions of individuals and firms. For example, they may determine the quantity of products consumers will demand at a particular price.

Public finance economists study the role of government in the economy. Specifically, they may analyze the effects of tax cuts, budget deficits, and welfare policies.

Work Environment

Economists held about 16,900 jobs in 2012, of which 45 percent were in government. Another 19 percent worked in management, scientific, and professional consulting services.

The industries that employed the most economists in 2012 were as follows:

Federal government, excluding postal service 28%
Management, scientific, and technical consulting services 19
State and local government, excluding education
   and hospitals 17
Scientific research and development services 10
Finance and insurance 5

Economists typically work independently in an office. However, many economists collaborate with other economists and statisticians, sometimes working on teams. Some economists work from home, and others may be required to travel as part of their job or to attend conferences.

Some economists combine a full-time job in universities or business with part-time consulting work.

Work Schedules. Most economists work full time. Some work under pressure of deadlines and tight schedules that may require long hours.

How to Become One

Most economists need a master's degree or Ph.D. However, some entry-level jobs–primarily in government–are available for workers with a bachelor's degree.

Education. A master's degree or Ph.D. is required for most economist jobs. Positions in business, research, or international organizations often require a combination of graduate education and work experience.

Students can pursue an advanced degree in economics with a bachelor's degree in a number of fields, but a strong background in math is essential. A Ph.D. in economics requires several years of study after earning a bachelor's degree, including completion of detailed research in a specialty field.

Candidates with a bachelor's degree qualify for some entry-level economist positions, including jobs with the federal government. An advanced degree is sometimes required for advancement to higher level positions.

Most who complete a bachelor's degree in economics find jobs outside the economics profession as research assistants, financial analysts, market research analysts, and similar positions in business, finance, and consulting.

Other Experience. Aspiring economists can gain valuable experience from internships that involve gathering and analyzing data, researching economic issues and trends, and writing reports on their findings. In addition, related experience, such as working in business or finance, can be advantageous.

Important Qualities

Analytical skills. Economists must be able to review data, observe patterns, and draw logical conclusions. For example, some economists analyze historical employment trends to make future projections on jobs.

Communication skills. Economists must be able to explain their work to others. They may give presentations, explain reports, or advise clients on economic issues. They may collaborate with colleagues and sometimes must explain economic concepts to those without a background in economics.

Employment Projections Data for Economists

Occupational title	SOC Code	Employment, 2012	Projected Employment, 2022	Change, 2012–2022	
				Percent	Numeric
Economists	19-3011	16,900	19,200	14	2,300

Source: U.S. Bureau of Labor Statistics, Employment Projections Program

Note: Data are rounded. Go to **Occupational Information Included in the OOH** *for a discussion of the data in this table.*

Similar Occupations   This table shows a list of occupations with job duties that are similar to those of economists.

Occupations	Entry-level Education	2012 Pay	Projected Job Growth	Average Annual Openings
Actuaries	Bachelor's degree	$93,680	26%	1,320
Budget Analysts	Bachelor's degree	$69,280	6%	2,850
Financial Analysts	Bachelor's degree	$76,950	16%	10,090
Market Research Analysts	Bachelor's degree	$60,300	32%	18,850
Mathematicians	Master's degree	$101,360	23%	170
Operations Research Analysts	Bachelor's degree	$72,100	27%	3,600
Political Scientists	Master's degree	$102,000	21%	250
Postsecondary Teachers	See "How to Become One"	$70,380	19%	42,690
Statisticians	Master's degree	$75,560	26%	1,610
Survey Researchers	Master's degree	$45,050	18%	560

Critical-thinking skills. Economists must be able to use logic and reasoning to solve complex problems. For instance, they might identify how economic trends may affect an organization.

Detail oriented. Economists must pay attention to details. Precise data analysis is necessary to ensure accuracy in their findings.

Math skills. Economists use the principles of statistics, calculus, and other advanced topics in mathematics in their economic analyses.

Writing skills. Economists must be able to present their findings clearly. Many economists prepare reports for colleagues or clients; others write for publication in journals or for news media.

Pay

The median annual wage for economists was $91,860 in May 2012. The median wage is the wage at which half the workers in an occupation earned more than the amount and half earned less. The lowest 10 percent earned less than $51,410, and the top 10 percent earned more than $155,490.

In May 2012, the median annual wages for economists in the top five industries employing economists were as follows:

Finance and insurance $110,580
Federal government, excluding postal service 106,850
Scientific research and development services 94,630
Management, scientific, and technical consulting services ... 91,570
State and local government, excluding education
    and hospitals 63,880

Job Outlook

Employment of economists is projected to grow 14 percent from 2012 to 2022, about as fast as the average for all occupations.

Businesses and organizations across many industries are increasingly relying on economic analysis and quantitative methods to analyze and forecast business, sales, and other economic trends. Demand for economists should grow as a result of the increasing complexity of the global economy, additional financial regulations, and a more competitive business environment. As a result, demand for economists should be best in private industry, especially in management, scientific, and professional consulting services.

However, employment in the federal government–the largest employer of economists–is projected to decline. As a result, the need for economists in the federal government is likely to be limited.

Job Prospects. Job prospects should be best for those with a master's degree or Ph.D., strong quantitative and analytical skills, and related work experience. As companies contract out economics-related work, most job openings for economists will be in consulting services.

Applicants with a bachelor's degree should face very strong competition for jobs. Although there will be greater demand for workers with knowledge of economics, many bachelor's degree holders will likely find jobs outside the economist occupation, working instead as research assistants, financial analysts, market analysts, and in similar positions in business, finance, and consulting.

O*NET

➤ Economists (19-3011.00)
➤ Environmental Economists (19-3011.01)

Contacts for More Information

For more information about economists, visit
➤ American Economic Association (www.aeaweb.org)
    For information about careers in business economics, visit
➤ National Association for Business Economics (www.nabe.com)
    For information on federal government education requirements for economist positions, visit
➤ U.S. Office of Personnel Management (www.opm.gov/qualifications /Standards/IORs/gs0100/0110.htm)
    To find job openings for economists in the federal government, visit
➤ USAJOBS (www.usajobs.gov)

Environmental Science and Protection Technicians

- **2012 Median Pay** .... $41,240 per year
    $19.83 per hour
- **Entry-Level Education** .... Associate's degree
- **Work Experience in a Related Occupation** .... None
- **On-the-Job Training** .... None
- **Number of Jobs 2012** 32,800
- **Job Outlook, 2012–22** .... 19% (Faster than average)
- **Employment Change, 2012–22** 6,200

What Environmental Science and Protection Technicians Do

Environmental science and protection technicians monitor the environment and investigate sources of pollution and contamination, including those affecting health.

Duties. Environmental science and protection technicians typically do the following:

- Inspect establishments, including public places and businesses, to ensure that there are no environmental, health, or safety hazards

- Set up and maintain equipment used to monitor pollution levels, such as remote sensors that measure emissions from smokestacks

- Collect samples of air, soil, water, and other materials for laboratory analysis

- Clearly label, track, and ensure the integrity of samples being transported to the laboratory

- Perform scientific tests to identify and measure levels of pollutants in samples

- Prepare charts and reports that summarize test results

- Discuss test results and analyses with clients

Many environmental science and protection technicians work under the supervision of environmental scientists and specialists, who direct the technicians' work and evaluate their results. In addition, they often work on teams with scientists, engineers, and technicians in other fields to solve complex problems related to environmental degradation and public health. For example, they may work on teams with geoscientists and hydrologists to manage the cleanup of contaminated soils and ground water around an abandoned bomb manufacturing site.

Most environmental science and protection technicians work for state or local governments, testing laboratories, or consulting firms.

In **state and local governments**, environmental science and protection technicians spend a lot of time inspecting businesses and public places, and investigating complaints related to air quality, water quality, and food safety. Sometimes they may be involved with enforcement of environmental regulations. They may protect the environment and people's health by performing environmental impact studies of new construction or by evaluating the environmental health of sites that may contaminate the environment, such as abandoned industrial sites.

Environmental science and protection technicians work in testing laboratories collecting and tracking samples, and performing

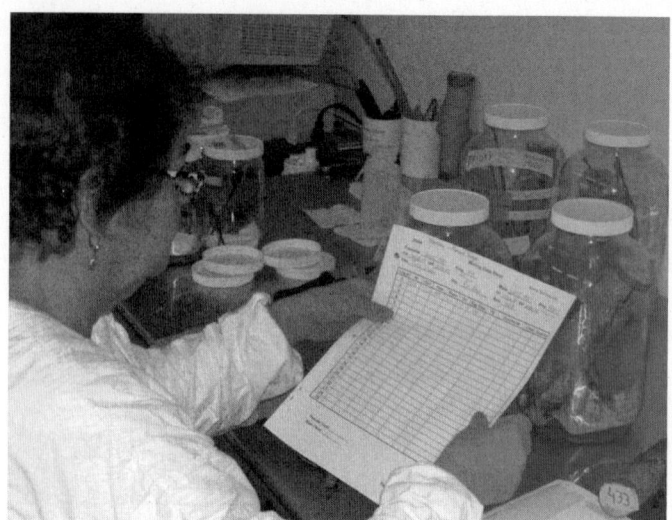

The work of environmental science and protection technicians is often divided between the outdoors and the laboratory.

tests that are often similar to what is done by chemical technicians, biological technicians, or microbiologists. However, the work done by environmental science and protection technicians focuses on topics that are directly related to the environment and how it affects human health.

In **consulting firms**, environmental science and protection technicians help clients monitor and manage the environment and comply with regulations. For example, they help businesses develop cleanup plans for contaminated sites, and they recommend ways to reduce, control, or eliminate pollution. Also, environmental science and protection technicians conduct feasibility studies for, and monitor the environmental impact of new construction projects.

Environmental science and protection technicians typically specialize in either laboratory testing or in fieldwork and sample collection. However, it is common for laboratory technicians to occasionally collect samples from the field, and for fieldworkers to do some work in a laboratory.

Work Environment

Environmental science and protection technicians held about 32,800 jobs in 2012. The industries that employed the most environmental science and protection technicians in 2012 were as follows:

Management, scientific, and technical consulting services...... 23%
Local government, excluding education and hospitals............ 19
Testing laboratories... 13

Median Annual Wages, May 2012

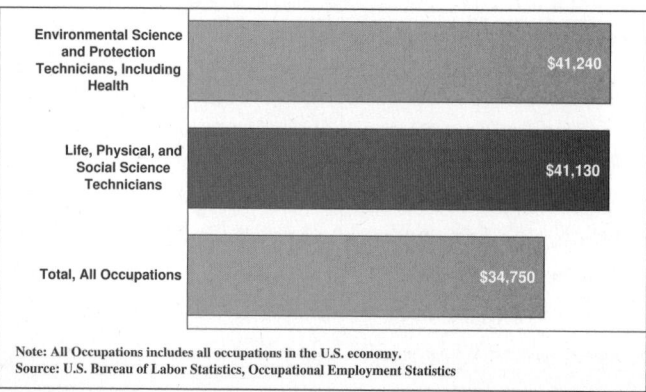

Environmental Science and Protection Technicians, Including Health — $41,240

Life, Physical, and Social Science Technicians — $41,130

Total, All Occupations — $34,750

Note: All Occupations includes all occupations in the U.S. economy.
Source: U.S. Bureau of Labor Statistics, Occupational Employment Statistics

Percent Change in Employment, Projected 2012–2022

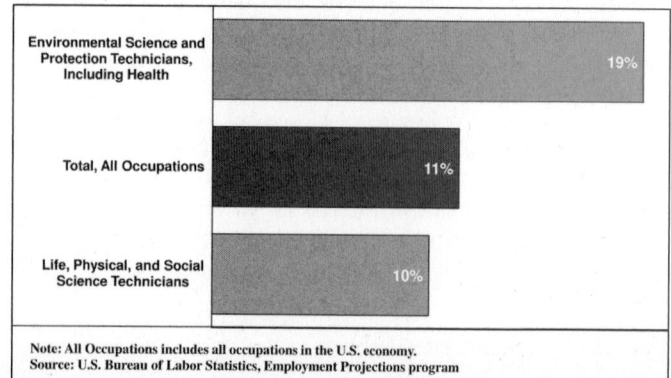

Environmental Science and Protection Technicians, Including Health — 19%

Total, All Occupations — 11%

Life, Physical, and Social Science Technicians — 10%

Note: All Occupations includes all occupations in the U.S. economy.
Source: U.S. Bureau of Labor Statistics, Employment Projections program

Employment Projections Data for Environmental Science and Protection Technicians

Occupational title	SOC Code	Employment, 2012	Projected Employment, 2022	Change, 2012–2022	
				Percent	Numeric
Environmental science and protection technicians, including health...	19-4091	32,800	38,900	19	6,200

Source: U.S. Bureau of Labor Statistics, Employment Projections Program

Note: Data are rounded. Go to Occupational Information Included in the OOH for a discussion of the data in this table.

State government, excluding education and hospitals............... 8
Engineering services... 7

Most environmental science and protection technicians work for state or local governments, testing laboratories, or consulting firms.

Environmental science and protection technicians work in laboratories, offices, and the field. Fieldwork offers a variety of settings. For example, a technician may investigate an abandoned manufacturing plant, or work outdoors testing the water quality of lakes and rivers. They may work around streams and rivers monitoring the levels of pollution caused by runoff from cities and landfills, or they may have to use the crawl spaces under a house to neutralize natural health risks such as radon. While working outdoors, they may be exposed to adverse weather conditions.

In the field, environmental science and protection technicians spend most of their time on their feet, which can be physically demanding. They also may need to carry and set up testing equipment, which can involve some heavy lifting and frequent bending and crouching.

Work Schedules. Environmental science and protection technicians typically work full time. In some cold climates, the ground may freeze, thus limiting the ability to take samples. This may cause some workers to work seasonally. They may also need to travel to meet with clients or to perform fieldwork. This may occasionally require technicians to work long or irregular hours.

How to Become One

Environmental science and protection technicians typically need an associate's degree or 2 years of postsecondary education, though some positions may require a bachelor's degree.

Education. Environmental science and protection technicians typically need an associate's degree in environmental science, environmental health, public health, or a related degree. Because of the wide range of tasks, environments, and industries in which these technicians work, there are jobs that do not require postsecondary education, and others that require a bachelor's degree.

A background in natural sciences is important for environmental science and protection technicians. Students should take courses in chemistry, biology, geology, and physics. Coursework in mathematics, statistics, and computer science also is useful because technicians routinely do data analysis and modeling.

Many schools offer internships and cooperative-education programs, which help students gain valuable experience while attending school. Internships and cooperative-education experience can enhance the students' employment prospects.

Many technical and community colleges offer programs in environmental studies or a related technology, such as remote sensing or geographic information systems (GIS). Associate's degree programs at community colleges traditionally are designed to provide easy transfer to bachelor's degree programs at colleges and universities.

Similar Occupations This table shows a list of occupations with job duties that are similar to those of environmental science and protection technicians.

Occupations	Entry-level Education	2012 Pay	Projected Job Growth	Average Annual Openings
Agricultural and Food Science Technicians	Associate's degree	$34,070	3%	1,010
Biological Technicians	Bachelor's degree	$39,750	10%	3,210
Chemical Technicians	Associate's degree	$42,920	9%	2,160
Environmental Engineering Technicians	Associate's degree	$45,350	18%	740
Environmental Engineers	Bachelor's degree	$80,890	15%	2,110
Environmental Scientists and Specialists	Bachelor's degree	$63,570	15%	3,970
Forensic Science Technicians	Bachelor's degree	$52,840	6%	580
Forest and Conservation Technicians	Associate's degree	$33,920	-4%	1,340
Geoscientists	Bachelor's degree	$90,890	16%	1,730
Hydrologists	Master's degree	$75,530	9%	290
Medical and Clinical Laboratory Technologists and Technicians	See "How to Become One"	$47,499	22%	15,600
Occupational Health and Safety Specialists	Bachelor's degree	$66,790	7%	2,130
Occupational Health and Safety Technicians	High school diploma or equivalent	$47,440	10%	480
Veterinary Technologists and Technicians	Associate's degree	$30,290	29%	3,340

Important Qualities

Analytical skills. Environmental science and protection technicians must be able to carry out a wide range of laboratory and field tests, and their results must be accurate and precise.

Communication skills. Environmental science and protection technicians must have good listening and writing skills, because they must follow precise directions for sample collection and communicate their results effectively in their written reports. They also may need to discuss their results with colleagues and clients.

Critical-thinking skills. Environmental science and protection technicians reach their conclusions through sound reasoning and judgment. They have to be able to determine the best way to address environmental hazards.

Interpersonal skills. Environmental science and protection technicians need to be able to work well and collaborate with others, because they often work with scientists and other technicians.

Licenses, Certifications, and Registrations. In some states, environmental science and protection technicians need a license to do certain types of environmental and health inspections. For example, some states require licensing for technicians who test buildings for radon. Licensure requirements vary by state but typically include minimum levels of education and experience and a passing score on an exam.

Pay

The median annual wage for environmental science and protection technicians was $41,240 in May 2012. The median wage is the wage at which half the workers in an occupation earned more than that amount and half earned less. The lowest 10 percent earned less than $26,330, and the top 10 percent earned more than $68,620.

In May 2012, the median annual wages for environmental science and protection technicians in the top five industries employing these technicians were as follows:

Local government, excluding education and hospitals....... $44,720
State government, excluding education and hospitals.......... 41,390
Management, scientific, and technical consulting services... 40,330
Engineering services... 39,040
Testing laboratories... 36,680

Job Outlook

Employment of environmental science and protection technicians is projected to grow 19 percent from 2012 to 2022, faster than the average for all occupations. Heightened public interest in the hazards facing the environment, as well as the increasing demands placed on the environment by population growth, is expected to spur demand for environmental science and protection technicians.

Most employment growth for environmental science and protection technicians is projected to be in consulting firms. More businesses and governments are expected to use these firms in the future to help them monitor and manage the environment and comply with regulations.

Job Prospects. Environmental science and protection technicians should have good opportunities for employment. In addition to openings due to growth, many job openings are expected to be created by those who retire or leave the occupation for other reasons. Job candidates with an associate's degree and laboratory experience should have the best opportunities.

O*NET

➤ Environmental Science and Protection Technicians, Including Health (19-4091.00)

Contacts for More Information

For more information about environmental health technicians and related occupations, visit

➤ National Environmental Health Association (www.neha.org/)

For more information specific to radon technicians, visit

➤ National Radon Safety Board (www.nrsb.org/)

Environmental Scientists and Specialists

- **2012 Median Pay** .... $63,570 per year
$30.56 per hour
- **Entry-Level Education** ....Bachelor's degree
- **Work Experience in a Related Occupation**.............. None
- **On-the-Job Training** .... None
- **Number of Jobs 2012** 90,000
- **Job Outlook, 2012–22** .... 15% (Faster than average)
- **Employment Change, 2012–22** 13,200

What Environmental Scientists and Specialists Do

Environmental scientists and specialists use their knowledge of the natural sciences to protect the environment and human health. They may clean up polluted areas, advise policy makers, or work with industry to reduce waste.

Duties. Environmental scientists and specialists typically do the following:

- Determine data collection methods for research projects, investigations, and surveys
- Collect and compile environmental data from samples of air, soil, water, food, and other materials for scientific analysis
- Analyze samples, surveys, and other information to identify and assess threats to the environment

Environmental scientists research methods to reduce hazards that affect the environment or public health.

Median Annual Wages, May 2012

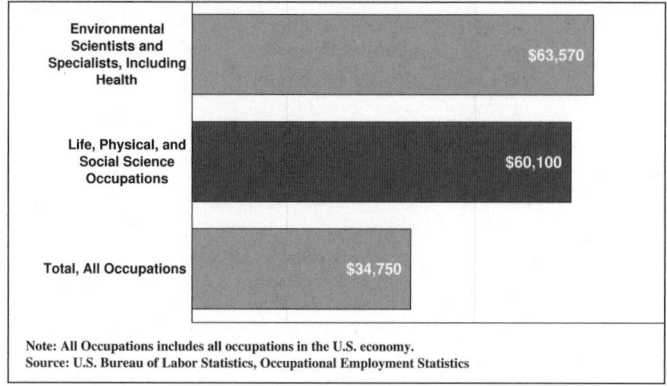

Environmental Scientists and Specialists, Including Health — $63,570

Life, Physical, and Social Science Occupations — $60,100

Total, All Occupations — $34,750

Note: All Occupations includes all occupations in the U.S. economy.
Source: U.S. Bureau of Labor Statistics, Occupational Employment Statistics

Percent Change in Employment, Projected 2012–2022

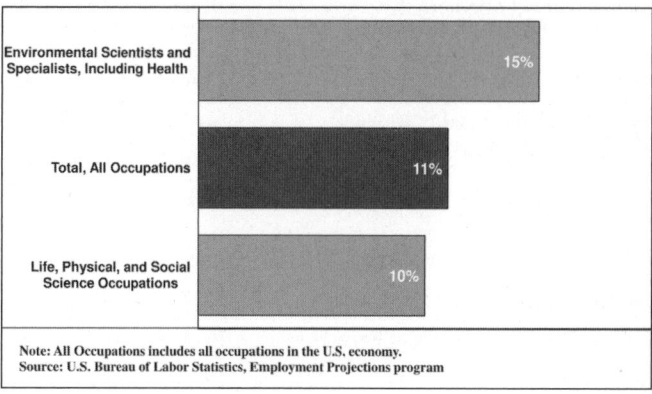

Environmental Scientists and Specialists, Including Health — 15%

Total, All Occupations — 11%

Life, Physical, and Social Science Occupations — 10%

Note: All Occupations includes all occupations in the U.S. economy.
Source: U.S. Bureau of Labor Statistics, Employment Projections program

- Develop plans to prevent, control, or fix environmental problems, such as land or water pollution
- Provide information and guidance to government officials, businesses, and the general public on possible environmental hazards and health risks
- Prepare technical reports and presentations that explain their research and findings

Environmental scientists and specialists analyze environmental problems and develop solutions. For example, many environmental scientists and specialists work to reclaim lands and waters that have been contaminated by pollution. Others assess the risks that new construction projects pose to the environment and make recommendations to governments and businesses on how to minimize the environmental impact of these projects. Environmental scientists and specialists may do research and provide advice on manufacturing practices, such as advising against the use of chemicals that are known to harm the environment.

The federal government and many state and local governments have regulations to ensure that there is clean air to breathe, safe water to drink, and no hazardous materials in the soil. The regulations also place limits on development, particularly near sensitive ecosystems such as wetlands. Many environmental scientists and specialists work for the government to ensure that these regulations are followed. Other environmental scientists and specialists work for consulting firms that help companies comply with regulations and policies.

Some environmental scientists and specialists focus on environmental regulations that are designed to protect people's health, while others focus on regulations designed to minimize society's impact on the ecosystem. The following are examples of types of specialists:

Climate change analysts study effects on ecosystems caused by the changing climate. They may do outreach education activities and grant writing typical of scientists.

Environmental health specialists study how environmental factors impact human health. They investigate potential environmental health risks. For example, they may investigate and address issues arising from soil and water contamination caused by nuclear weapons manufacturing. They also educate the public about potential health risks present in the environment.

Environmental restoration planners assess polluted sites and determine the cost and activities necessary to clean up the area.

Industrial ecologists work with industry to increase the efficiency of their operations and thereby limit the impacts these activities have on the environment. They analyze costs and benefits of various programs, as well as their impacts on ecosystems.

Other environmental scientists do work and receive training that is similar to that of other physical or life scientists, but they focus on environmental issues. Environmental chemists are an example.

Environmental chemists study the effects that various chemicals have on ecosystems. For example, they look at how acids affect plants, animals, and people. Some areas in which they work include waste management and the remediation of contaminated soils, water, and air.

Many people with backgrounds in environmental science become postsecondary teachers and high school teachers.

Work Environment

Environmental scientists and specialists held about 90,000 jobs in 2012. Most environmental scientists and specialists work for federal, state, or local governments or private consulting firms that may work with government or private industry.

The industries that employed the most environmental scientists and specialists in 2012 were as follows:

State government, excluding education and hospitals 22%
Management, scientific, and technical consulting services 21
Local government, excluding education and hospitals 14
Engineering services 10
Federal government, excluding postal service 7

Environmental scientists and specialists work in offices and laboratories. Some may spend time in the field gathering data and monitoring environmental conditions firsthand, but this work is much more likely to be done by environmental science and protection technicians. Fieldwork can be physically demanding, and

Employment Projections Data for Environmental Scientists and Specialists

Occupational title	SOC Code	Employment, 2012	Projected Employment, 2022	Change, 2012–2022	
				Percent	Numeric
Environmental scientists and specialists, including health	19-2041	90,000	103,200	15	13,200

Source: U.S. Bureau of Labor Statistics, Employment Projections Program

Note: Data are rounded. Go to **Occupational Information Included in the OOH** *for a discussion of the data in this table.*

Similar Occupations This table shows a list of occupations with job duties that are similar to those of environmental scientists and specialists.

Occupations	Entry-level Education	2012 Pay	Projected Job Growth	Average Annual Openings
Agricultural and Food Scientists	See "How to Become One"	$58,636	10%	1,640
Anthropologists and Archeologists	Master's degree	$57,420	19%	260
Atmospheric Scientists, Including Meteorologists	Bachelor's degree	$89,260	10%	380
Biochemists and Biophysicists	Doctoral or professional degree	$81,480	18%	1,370
Chemists and Materials Scientists	Bachelor's degree	$73,247	6%	3,040
Conservation Scientists and Foresters	Bachelor's degree	$59,354	3%	1,080
Environmental Engineers	Bachelor's degree	$80,890	15%	2,110
Environmental Science and Protection Technicians	Associate's degree	$41,240	19%	1,900
Epidemiologists	Master's degree	$65,270	12%	160
Geoscientists	Bachelor's degree	$90,890	16%	1,730
Hydrologists	Master's degree	$75,530	9%	290
Microbiologists	Bachelor's degree	$66,260	7%	710
Natural Sciences Managers	Bachelor's degree	$115,730	6%	1,370
Occupational Health and Safety Specialists	Bachelor's degree	$66,790	7%	2,130
Postsecondary Teachers	See "How to Become One"	$70,380	19%	42,690
Zoologists and Wildlife Biologists	Bachelor's degree	$57,710	5%	670

environmental scientists and specialists may work in all types of weather. Environmental scientists and specialists may have to travel to meet with clients or present research at conferences.

Most consulting firms fall into one of two categories: large multidisciplinary engineering companies that employ thousands of workers, or small specialty firms that employ only a few workers. Larger firms are more likely to engage in large-scale, long-term projects in which environmental scientists work with scientists and engineers in other disciplines. In smaller specialty firms, environmental scientists work directly with small businesses and clients in government and the private sector.

Work Schedules. Most environmental scientists and specialists work full time. They may have to work long or irregular hours when working in the field.

How to Become One

For most jobs, environmental scientists and specialists need at least a bachelor's degree in a natural science.

Education. For most entry-level jobs, environmental scientists and specialists must have a bachelor's degree in environmental science or a science-related field, such as biology, chemistry, physics, geosciences, or engineering. However, a master's degree may be needed for advancement. Environmental scientists and specialists who have a doctoral degree make up a small percentage of the occupation, and this level of training is typically needed only for the relatively few postsecondary teaching and basic research positions.

A bachelor's degree in environmental science offers a broad approach to the natural sciences. Students typically take courses in biology, chemistry, geology, and physics. Students often take specialized courses in hydrology, waste management, and fluid mechanics as part of their degree as well. Classes in environmental policy and regulation are also beneficial. Students who want to reach the Ph.D. level and have a career in academia or as an environmental scientist doing basic research may find it advantageous to major in a more specific natural science such as chemistry, biology, physics, or geology, rather than the broader environmental science degrees.

Students should look for opportunities, such as classes and internships, that allow for work with computer modeling, data analysis, and geographic information systems. Students with experience in these programs will be the best prepared to enter the job market.

Important Qualities

Analytical skills. Environmental scientists and specialists base their conclusions on careful analysis of scientific data. They must consider all possible methods and solutions in their analyses.

Communication skills. Environmental scientists and specialists may need to present and explain their findings and write technical reports.

Interpersonal skills. Environmental scientists and specialists typically work on teams with scientists, engineers, and technicians. Team members must be able to work together effectively to achieve their goals.

Problem-solving skills. Environmental scientists and specialists try to find the best possible solution to problems that affect the environment and people's health.

Self-discipline. Environmental scientists and specialists may spend a lot of time working alone. They need to be able to stay motivated and get their work done without supervision.

Advancement. Environmental scientists and specialists often begin their careers as field analysts, research assistants, or technicians in laboratories and offices. As they gain experience, they earn more responsibilities and autonomy and may supervise the work of technicians or other scientists. Eventually, they may be promoted to project leader, program manager, or other management or research position.

Other environmental scientists and specialists go on to work as researchers or faculty at colleges and universities.

Work Experience in a Related Occupation. Some environmental scientists and specialists begin their careers as scientists in related occupations, such as hydrology or engineering, and then move into the more interdisciplinary field of environmental science.

Pay

The median annual wage for environmental scientists and specialists was $63,570 in May 2012. The median wage is the wage at which half the workers in an occupation earned more than that amount and half earned less. The lowest 10 percent earned less than $38,570, and the top 10 percent earned more than $109,970.

Federal government, excluding postal service	$95,460
Engineering services	67,770
Management, scientific, and technical consulting services	64,940
Local government, excluding education and hospitals	60,280
State government, excluding education and hospitals	56,640

Job Outlook

Employment of environmental scientists and specialists is projected to grow 15 percent from 2012 to 2022, faster than the average for all occupations. Heightened public interest in the hazards facing the environment, as well as the increasing demands placed on the environment by population growth, is projected to spur demand for environmental scientists and specialists.

Most employment growth for environmental scientists and specialists is projected to be in private consulting firms that help clients monitor and manage environmental concerns and comply with regulations. However, most jobs will remain concentrated in the various levels of government and closely related industries, such as publicly funded universities, hospitals, and national research facilities.

More businesses are expected to consult with environmental scientists and specialists in the future to help them minimize the impact their operations have on the environment. For example, environmental consultants help businesses to develop practices that minimize waste, prevent pollution, and conserve resources. Other environmental scientists and specialists are expected to be needed to help planners develop and construct buildings, utilities, and transportation systems that protect natural resources and limit damage to the land.

Job Prospects. Environmental scientists and specialists should have good job opportunities. In addition to growth, many job openings will be created by scientists who retire, advance to management positions, or change careers.

O*NET

➤ Environmental Scientists and Specialists, Including Health (19-2041.00)
➤ Climate Change Analysts (19-2041.01)
➤ Environmental Restoration Planners (19-2041.02)
➤ Industrial Ecologists (19-2041.03)

Contacts for More Information

For more information about environmental scientists and specialists, including training, visit
➤ American Geosciences Institute (www.agiweb.org/)

For information about environmental health specialists and related occupations, visit
➤ National Environmental Health Association (www.neha.org/index.shtml)

Epidemiologists

- **2012 Median Pay** .... $65,270 per year
  $31.38 per hour
- **Entry-Level Education** ....Master's degree
- **Work Experience in a Related Occupation**............... None
- **On-the-Job Training** .... None
- **Number of Jobs 2012** 5,100
- **Job Outlook, 2012–22**................ 10% (As fast as average)
- **Employment Change, 2012–22** 500

What Epidemiologists Do

Epidemiologists are public health professionals who investigate patterns and causes of disease and injury in humans. They seek to reduce the risk and occurrence of negative health outcomes through community education and health policy.

Duties. Epidemiologists typically do the following:

- Plan and direct studies of public health problems to find ways to prevent and to treat the problems
- Collect and analyze data–including using observations, interviews, surveys, and samples of blood or other bodily fluids–to find the causes of diseases or other health problems
- Communicate their findings to health practitioners, policymakers, and the public
- Manage public health programs by planning programs, monitoring progress, analyzing data, and seeking ways to improve them, among other activities
- Supervise professional, technical, and clerical personnel

Epidemiologists collect and analyze data to investigate health issues. For example, an epidemiologist might collect and analyze demographic data to determine who is at the highest risk for a particular disease. They may also research and investigate the trends in populations of survivors of certain diseases, such as cancer, so that effective treatments can be identified and repeated across the population.

Epidemiologists typically work in applied public health or in research. Applied epidemiologists work for state and local governments, addressing public health problems directly. They are often involved with education outreach and survey efforts in communities. Research epidemiologists typically work for universities or in affiliation with federal agencies such as the Centers for Disease Control and Prevention (CDC) or the National Institutes of Health (NIH).

Epidemiologists who work in private industry commonly conduct research for health insurance companies or pharmaceutical companies. Those in nonprofit companies often do public health advocacy work. Epidemiologists involved in research are rarely advocates because scientific research is expected to be unbiased.

Epidemiologists typically specialize in one or more of the following public health areas:

- Infectious diseases
- Bioterrorism/emergency response
- Maternal and child health
- Chronic diseases
- Environmental health
- Injury

- Occupational health
- Substance abuse
- Oral health

For more information on occupations that concentrate on the biological workings of disease or the effects of disease on individuals, see the profiles for medical scientists, microbiologists, biochemists and biophysicists, and physicians and surgeons.

Work Environment

Epidemiologists held about 5,100 jobs in 2012. Work environments can vary widely because of the diverse nature of epidemiological specializations. Epidemiologists work in offices and laboratories usually at health departments for state and local governments, in hospitals, and at colleges and universities. They may work in the field.

Most research epidemiologists spend their time studying data and reports in an office setting. Work in laboratories and the field tends to be delegated to specialized scientists and other technical staff. In state and local government public health departments, epidemiologists may be more active in the community and may travel a significant amount to support community education efforts or to administer studies and surveys.

Modern science has greatly reduced the amount of infectious disease in developed countries. Infectious disease epidemiologists are more likely to travel to remote areas and developing nations in order to carry out their studies. Epidemiologists have minimal risk when they work in laboratories or in the field, because they take extensive precautions before interacting with samples or patients.

In 2012, 52 percent of epidemiologists worked for state and local governments, excluding education and hospitals. Other epidemiologists worked for hospitals; colleges and universities; life science research and development; management, scientific, and technical consulting services; and pharmaceutical companies.

Work Schedules. Most epidemiologists work full time and have a standard work schedule. Occasionally, epidemiologists may have to work long or irregular hours in order to complete fieldwork or tend to duties during public health emergencies.

How to Become One

Epidemiologists need at least a master's degree from an accredited postsecondary institution. Most have a master's degree in epidemiology or a related public health field. Some epidemiologists have a Ph.D.

Education. Epidemiologists need at least a master's degree from an accredited postsecondary institution. A master's degree in public health, with an emphasis in epidemiology is most common, but epidemiologists can earn degrees in a wide range of related fields

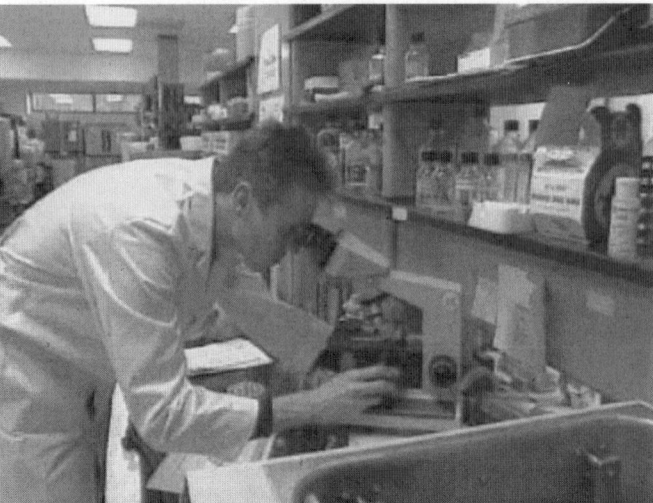

Epidemiologists need at least a master's degree from an accredited postsecondary institution.

and specializations. Epidemiologists who direct research projects–including those who work as postsecondary teachers in colleges and universities–have a Ph.D. in their chosen field.

Coursework in epidemiology includes public health, biological and physical sciences, and math and statistics. Classes emphasize statistical methods, causal analysis, and survey design. Advanced courses emphasize multiple regression, medical informatics, review of previous biomedical research, comparisons of healthcare systems, and practical applications of data.

Many Master's of Public Health programs and other programs that are specific to epidemiology require students to complete an internship or practicum that typically ranges from a semester to a year.

Some epidemiologists have a degree in epidemiology and a medical degree. These scientists often work in clinical capacities. In medical school, students spend most of the first 2 years in laboratories and classrooms, taking courses such as anatomy, biochemistry, physiology, pharmacology, psychology, microbiology, pathology, medical ethics, and laws governing medicine. They also learn to take medical histories, examine patients, and diagnose illnesses.

Important Qualities

Communication skills. Epidemiologists must use their speaking and writing skills to inform the public and community leaders of public health risks. Clear communication is also required to work effectively with other health professionals.

Median Annual Wages, May 2012

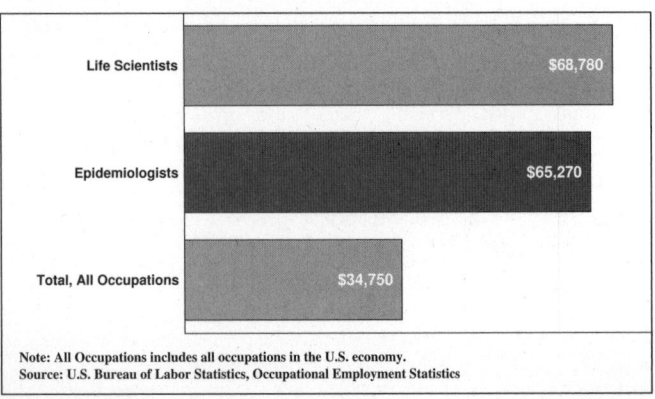

Life Scientists	$68,780
Epidemiologists	$65,270
Total, All Occupations	$34,750

Note: All Occupations includes all occupations in the U.S. economy.
Source: U.S. Bureau of Labor Statistics, Occupational Employment Statistics

Percent Change in Employment, Projected 2012–2022

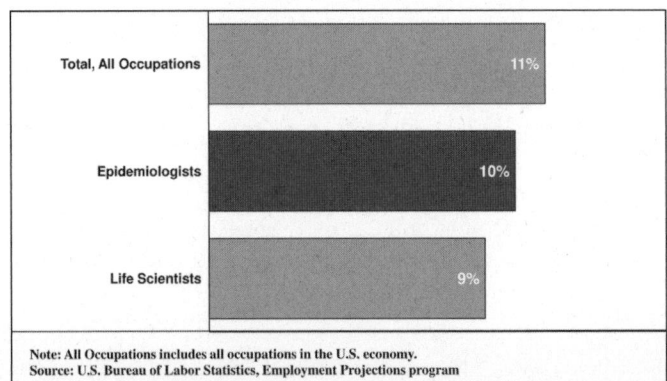

Total, All Occupations	11%
Epidemiologists	10%
Life Scientists	9%

Note: All Occupations includes all occupations in the U.S. economy.
Source: U.S. Bureau of Labor Statistics, Employment Projections program

Employment Projections Data for Epidemiologists

Occupational title	SOC Code	Employment, 2012	Projected Employment, 2022	Change, 2012–2022	
				Percent	Numeric
Epidemiologists 19-1041		5,100	5,700	10	500

Source: U.S. Bureau of Labor Statistics, Employment Projections Program

Note: Data are rounded. Go to **Occupational Information Included in the OOH** *for a discussion of the data in this table.*

Critical-thinking skills. Epidemiologists analyze data to determine how best to respond to a public health problem or an urgent health-related emergency.

Detail oriented. Epidemiologists must be precise and accurate in moving from observation and interview to conclusions.

Math and statistical skills. Epidemiologists may need advanced statistical skills when designing and administering studies and surveys. Skill in using large databases and statistical computer programs may also be important.

Teaching skills. Epidemiologists may be involved in community outreach activities that educate the public about health risks and healthy living.

Pay

The median annual wage for epidemiologists was $65,270 in May 2012. The median wage is the wage at which half the workers in an occupation earned more than that amount and half earned less. The lowest 10 percent earned less than $42,620, and the top 10 percent earned more than $108,320.

In May 2012, the median annual wages for epidemiologists in the top four industries employing these scientists were as follows:

Research and development in the physical, engineering, and life sciences...	$92,070
General medical and surgical hospitals; state, local, and private...	73,810
Colleges, universities, and professional schools; state, local, and private...	66,960
State and local government, excluding education and hospitals...	59,090

Job Outlook

Employment of epidemiologists is projected to grow 10 percent from 2012 to 2022, about as fast as the average for all occupations. Continued improvements in medical record-keeping will further improve epidemiologists' ability to track health outcomes, demographic data, and other useful data. Improvements in statistical and mapping software will improve analysis, make epidemiological data more useful, and increase demand for epidemiologists.

Demand for epidemiologists is expected to be strong in state and local governments over the next 10 years, but uncertain budgetary conditions are likely to moderate growth.

Job Prospects. There has been an increase in the interest of public health and epidemiology over the past decade. The number of master of public health programs specializing in epidemiology and the number of graduates from these programs has increased. Some entrants are finding strong competition for jobs, but applicants who are willing to work in any of the various specialties found in this occupation, rather than those tied to one specialty, rarely have trouble finding work. Because epidemiology is a diverse field, opportunities can generally be found if one takes a broad view.

O*NET

➤ Epidemiologists (19-1041.00)

Contacts for More Information

For more information about epidemiologists, including schools offering education in epidemiology, visit

➤ Council of State and Territorial Epidemiologists (www.cste.org/)

For more information about epidemiology careers in the federal government, visit

➤ Centers for Disease Control and Prevention (www.cdc.gov /employment/)
➤ National Institutes of Health (www.nih.gov/)

For public health related information, visit

➤ National Academy for State Health Policy (www.nashp.org/)
➤ American Public Health Association (www.apha.org/)
➤ Public Health Foundation (www.phf.org/)

Similar Occupations   This table shows a list of occupations with job duties that are similar to those of epidemiologists.

Occupations	Entry-level Education	2012 Pay	Projected Job Growth	Average Annual Openings
Anthropologists and Archeologists	Master's degree	$57,420	19%	260
Environmental Scientists and Specialists	Bachelor's degree	$63,570	15%	3,970
Geographers	Bachelor's degree	$74,760	29%	80
Health Educators and Community Health Workers	See "How to Become One"	$43,015	22%	4,740
Medical Scientists	Doctoral or professional degree	$76,980	13%	3,550
Microbiologists	Bachelor's degree	$66,260	7%	710
Physicians and Surgeons	Doctoral or professional degree	$182,294	18%	29,630
Political Scientists	Master's degree	$102,000	21%	250
Registered Nurses	Associate's degree	$65,470	19%	105,260
Survey Researchers	Master's degree	$45,050	18%	560

Forensic Science Technicians

- **2012 Median Pay** .... $52,840 per year
  $25.41 per hour
- **Entry-Level Education** ....Bachelor's degree
- **Work Experience in a Related Occupation**............... None
- **On-the-Job Training**.... Moderate-term on-the-job training
- **Number of Jobs 2012** 12,900
- **Job Outlook, 2012–22** .... 6% (Slower than average)
- **Employment Change, 2012–22** 700

What Forensic Science Technicians Do

Forensic science technicians help investigate crimes by collecting and analyzing physical evidence. Many technicians specialize in either crime scene investigation or laboratory analysis. Most forensic science technicians spend some time writing reports.

Duties. At crime scenes, forensic science technicians typically do the following:

- Analyze crime scenes to determine what and how evidence should be collected
- Take photographs of the crime scene and evidence
- Make sketches of the crime scene
- Record observations and findings, such as the location and position of evidence
- Collect physical evidence, including weapons, fingerprints, and bodily fluids
- Catalog and preserve evidence for transfer to crime labs

In laboratories, forensic science technicians typically do the following:

- Perform chemical, biological, and physical analysis on evidence taken from crime scenes
- Explore possible links between suspects and criminal activity using the results of scientific analyses
- Consult with experts in related or specialized fields, such as toxicology (the study of poisons and their effect on the body) and odontology (a branch of forensic medicine that concentrates on teeth)
- Reconstruct crime scenes

Forensic science technicians may either be generalists who perform all or many of the duties listed above, or they may specialize

Forensic science technicians work at crime scenes and in laboratories.

in certain techniques and sciences. Generalist forensic science technicians, sometimes called *criminalists*, perform the duties of *crime scene investigators* and laboratory analysts. They collect evidence at the scene of a crime and perform scientific and technical analysis in laboratories or offices.

Forensic science technicians who work primarily in laboratories may specialize in the natural sciences or engineering. Specialists typically apply their knowledge to the investigation of criminal cases rather than scientific enquiry. Those who work in laboratories, such as *forensic pathologists* and *latent print examiners*, typically use chemicals and laboratory equipment such as microscopes when analyzing evidence. They also may use computers to examine fingerprints, DNA, and other evidence collected at crime scenes. They often work to match evidence to people or other known elements, such as vehicles or weapons. Most forensic science technicians who perform laboratory analysis specialize in a specific type of evidence analysis, such as DNA or ballistics.

Median Annual Wages, May 2012

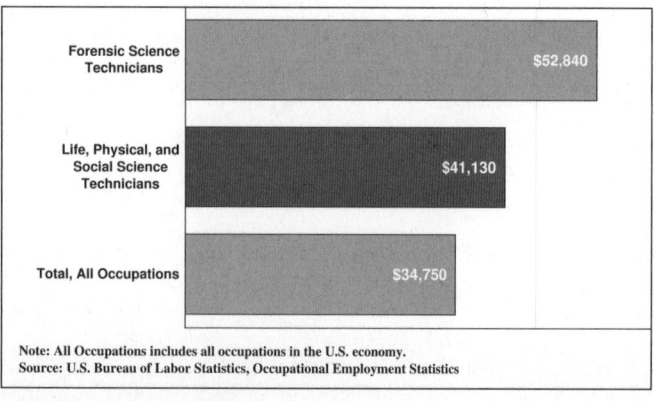

Forensic Science Technicians — $52,840
Life, Physical, and Social Science Technicians — $41,130
Total, All Occupations — $34,750

Note: All Occupations includes all occupations in the U.S. economy.
Source: U.S. Bureau of Labor Statistics, Occupational Employment Statistics

Percent Change in Employment, Projected 2012–2022

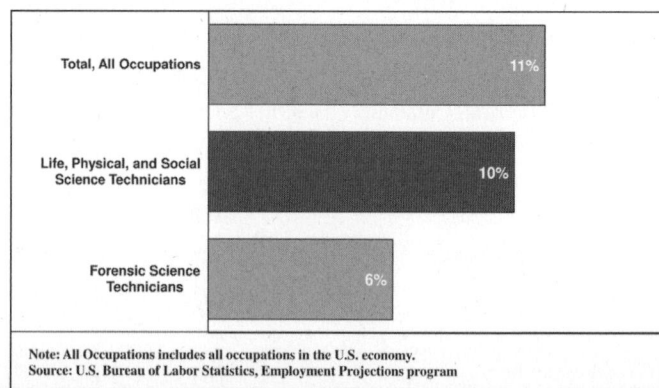

Total, All Occupations — 11%
Life, Physical, and Social Science Technicians — 10%
Forensic Science Technicians — 6%

Note: All Occupations includes all occupations in the U.S. economy.
Source: U.S. Bureau of Labor Statistics, Employment Projections program

Employment Projections Data for Forensic Science Technicians

Occupational title	SOC Code	Employment, 2012	Projected Employment, 2022	Change, 2012–2022	
				Percent	Numeric
Forensic science technicians 19-4092		12,900	13,700	6	700

Source: U.S. Bureau of Labor Statistics, Employment Projections Program

Note: Data are rounded. Go to **Occupational Information Included in the OOH** *for a discussion of the data in this table.*

Some forensic science technicians, called *forensic computer examiners* or *digital forensics analysts,* specialize in computer-based crimes. They collect data and analyze it to uncover and prosecute electronic fraud, scams, or identity theft. Because of the increased popularity of personal computing, digital data is often used to help solve non-cyber crimes. Computer forensics technicians must adhere to the same strict standards of evidence gathering found in general forensic science because the need to maintain evidence integrity is still critical.

All forensic science technicians prepare written reports that detail their findings and investigative methods. They must be able to explain their reports to lawyers, detectives, and other law enforcement officials. In addition, forensic science technicians may be called to testify in court about their findings and methods.

Work Environment

Forensic science technicians held about 12,900 jobs in 2012. About 9 in 10 forensic science technicians work in state and local government in the following workplaces:

- Police departments and offices
- Crime laboratories
- Morgues
- Medical examiner/coroner offices

Forensic science technicians may have to work outside in all types or weather, spend large quantities of time in laboratories and offices, or some combination of both. They often work in groups or teams with specialists and other law enforcement personnel. Many specialist forensic science technicians work only in laboratories.

Crime scene investigators travel all around their jurisdictions, which may be cities, counties, or states. Crimes can happen anywhere, so crime scene investigators and criminalists, especially at the state level, will experience a considerable amount of travel.

Crime scene investigators regularly see the results of violent crime.

Work Schedules. Crime scene investigators may work staggered day, evening, or night shifts and may have to work overtime because they must always be available to collect or analyze evidence. Technicians working in laboratories usually work a standard workweek, although they may have to be on call outside of normal business hours if they are needed to work immediately on a case. A number of high-level specialists work part time as forensic science experts. Small police departments may also have to rely on part-time forensic science technicians.

How to Become One

Forensic science technicians typically need at least a bachelor's degree in a natural science, such as chemistry or biology. On-the-job training is usually required for those who investigate crime scenes and for those who work in labs.

Education. Forensic science technicians typically need at least a bachelor's degree in the natural sciences, such as chemistry or biology. Students who major in forensic science should ensure that their program includes extensive course work in mathematics, chemistry, and biology. Students who attend more general natural science programs should make an effort to take classes related to forensic science. A list of schools that offer degrees in forensic science is available from the American Academy of Forensic Sciences. Many of those who seek to become forensic science technicians will have an undergraduate degree in the natural sciences and a master's degree in forensic science.

Many crime scene investigators are sworn police officers and have met educational requirements necessary for admittance into a police academy. Applicants for nonuniform crime scene investigator jobs should have a bachelor's degree in either forensic science, with a strong basic science background, or the natural sciences, but many rural agencies hire applicants with a high school diploma and years of related work experience. For more information on police officers, see the profile on police and detectives.

Important Qualities

Communication skills. Forensic science technicians write reports and testify in court. They often work with other law enforcement and specialists.

Composure. Crime scenes are often the results of acts of violence and destruction, but technicians have to maintain their professionalism and objectivity.

Critical-thinking skills. Forensic science technicians use their best judgment when matching physical evidence, such as fingerprints and DNA, to suspects.

Detail oriented. Forensic science technicians must be able to notice small changes in mundane objects to be good at collecting and analyzing evidence.

Math and science skills. Forensic science technicians need a solid understanding of statistics and natural sciences to be able to analyze crime scene evidence.

Problem-solving skills. Forensic science technicians use scientific tests and methods to help law enforcement officials solve crimes.

Training. Forensic science technicians receive on-the-job training before they are ready to work on cases independently.

Newly hired crime scene investigators typically assist experienced investigators. New investigators often learn proper procedures and methods for collecting and documenting evidence while working under supervision.

Forensic science technicians learn laboratory specialties on the job. The length of this training varies by specialty. Technicians may need to pass a proficiency exam or otherwise be approved by a laboratory or accrediting body before they may perform independent casework or testify in court.

Throughout their careers, forensic science technicians need to keep up with advances in technology and science that improve the collection or analysis of evidence.

Licenses, Certifications, and Registrations. A range of licenses and certifications are available to help credential and aid in the

Similar Occupations   This table shows a list of occupations with job duties that are similar to those of forensic science technicians.

Occupations	Entry-level Education	2012 Pay	Projected Job Growth	Average Annual Openings
Biochemists and Biophysicists	Doctoral or professional degree	$81,480	18%	1,370
Biological Technicians	Bachelor's degree	$39,750	10%	3,210
Chemical Technicians	Associate's degree	$42,920	9%	2,160
Chemists and Materials Scientists	Bachelor's degree	$73,247	6%	3,040
Environmental Science and Protection Technicians	Associate's degree	$41,240	19%	1,900
Epidemiologists	Master's degree	$65,270	12%	160
Fire Inspectors and Investigators	High school diploma or equivalent	$53,990	7%	440
Hazardous Materials Removal Workers	High school diploma or equivalent	$37,590	14%	1,340
Medical and Clinical Laboratory Technologists and Technicians	See "How to Become One"	$47,499	22%	15,600
Medical Scientists	Doctoral or professional degree	$76,980	13%	3,550
Police and Detectives	High school diploma or equivalent	$57,974	5%	27,500
Private Detectives and Investigators	High school diploma or equivalent	$45,740	11%	1,180

professional development of many types of forensic science technicians. Certifications and licenses are not typically necessary for entry into the occupation. Credentials can vary widely because standards and regulations vary considerably from one jurisdiction to another.

Pay

The median annual wage for forensic science technicians was $52,840 in May 2012. The median wage is the wage at which half the workers in an occupation earned more than that amount and half earned less. The lowest 10 percent earned less than $32,200, and the top 10 percent earned more than $85,210.

Job Outlook

Employment of forensic science technicians is projected to grow 6 percent from 2012 to 2022, slower than the average for all occupations. Scientific and technological advances are expected to increase the usefulness, availability, and reliability of objective forensic information used as evidence in trials. In addition, the use of forensic evidence in criminal proceedings is expected to expand. Popular media has increased the awareness of forensic evidence among potential jurors, and there is now an expectation that forensic evidence should contribute to many trials. More forensic science technicians will be needed to provide timely forensics information to law enforcement agencies and courts.

Job Prospects. Competition for jobs should be strong because of the substantial interest in forensic science and crime scene investigation that has been generated by popular media. Applicants who have both a bachelor's degree in a natural science and a master's degree in forensic science should have the best opportunities. Digital computer forensics and DNA specialties are expected to see the most growth and become the most dominant fields in forensic science.

Year to year, the number of job openings available will vary based on federal, state, and local law enforcement budgets.

O*NET

➤ Forensic Science Technicians (19-4092.00)

Contacts for More Information

For more information about forensic science technicians and related specialists, visit

➤ American Academy of Forensic Sciences (www.aafs.org/)
➤ American Board of Criminalistics (www.criminalistics.com/)
➤ American Board of Medicolegal Death Investigators (www.abmdi.org/)
➤ Association of Firearm and Tool Mark Examiners (www.afte.org/)
➤ International Crime Scene Investigators Association (www.icsia.org)

Forest and Conservation Technicians

- **2012 Median Pay** .... $33,920 per year
  $16.31 per hour
- **Entry-Level Education** ....Associate's degree
- **Work Experience in a Related Occupation**.............. None
- **On-the-Job Training** .... None
- **Number of Jobs 2012** 34,000
- **Job Outlook, 2012–22** .... -4% (Decline)
- **Employment Change, 2012–22** .... -1,200

What Forest and Conservation Technicians Do

Forest and conservation technicians measure and improve the quality of forests, rangeland, and other natural areas.

Duties. Forest and conservation technicians typically do the following:

- Gather data on water and soil quality, disease, insect damage to trees and other plants, and conditions that may pose a fire hazard
- Locate property lines and evaluate forested areas to determine the species, quality, and amount of standing timber
- Select and mark trees to be cut
- Track where wildlife goes, help build roads, and maintain trails, campsites, and other recreational facilities
- Train and lead seasonal workers who plant seedlings

Forest and conservation workers strive to promote growth of individual trees and entire forests.

- Monitor the activities of loggers and others who remove trees for sale as timber or for other reasons
- Patrol forest areas and enforce environmental protection regulations
- Communicate with foresters, scientists, and sometimes the public about ongoing forestry and conservation activities
- Suppress forest fires with fire control activities
- Train other forestry workers and coordinate detection programs

Forest and conservation technicians generally work under the supervision of foresters or conservation scientists and may themselves supervise forest and conservation workers.

Increasing numbers of forest and conservation technicians work in urban forestry–the study and management of trees and associated plants, individually or in groups within cities, suburbs, and towns–and other nontraditional specialties, rather than in forests or rural areas.

Work Environment

Forest and conservation technicians held about 34,000 jobs in 2012. The industries that employed the largest numbers of forest and conservation technicians in 2012 were as follows:

Federal government, excluding postal service 74%
State government, excluding education and hospitals 14
Local government, excluding education and hospitals 7

Most forest and conservation technicians work for federal, state, or local government or on privately owned forest lands. Most government technicians are employed by the federal government. Technicians in the eastern United States usually work on private forests. Because many national parks are in the West and Southwest, most technicians in these areas work for the federal government.

Forest and conservation technicians typically work outdoors, sometimes in remote locations and in all types of weather. The work can be physically difficult. They must walk long distances, sometimes on steep slopes and in heavily forested areas or wetlands.

When working near logging operations or in wood yards, technicians must wear a hardhat.

Other technicians work closely with the public, educating people about forest conservation or the proper use of recreational sites.

Work Schedules. Most forest and conservation technicians work full time and have a routine work schedule. Seasonal employees may work longer hours and at night. In addition, technicians may need to work longer hours to respond during emergencies.

How to Become One

Forest and conservation technicians typically need an associate's degree in forestry or a related field. Employers look for technicians who have a degree that is accredited by the Society of American Foresters (SAF).

Education. Forestry and conservation technicians typically need an associate's degree in a forestry technology or technician program or in a related field. Most forestry and conservation technology programs are accredited by SAF, and every state has accredited programs.

Many technical and community colleges offer programs in forestry technology or a related field. Associate's degree programs at community colleges are designed to provide easy transfer to bachelor's degree programs at colleges and universities. Training at technical institutes usually includes less theory and education than that in community colleges.

Coursework for an associate's degree in forestry technology or a related field includes ecology, biology, and forest resource measurement. Some technicians also have a background in a geographic information system (GIS) technology and other forms of computer modeling.

Important Qualities

Analytical skills. Forest and conservation technicians conduct a variety of field tests and onsite measurements, all of which require precision and accuracy.

Median Annual Wages, May 2012

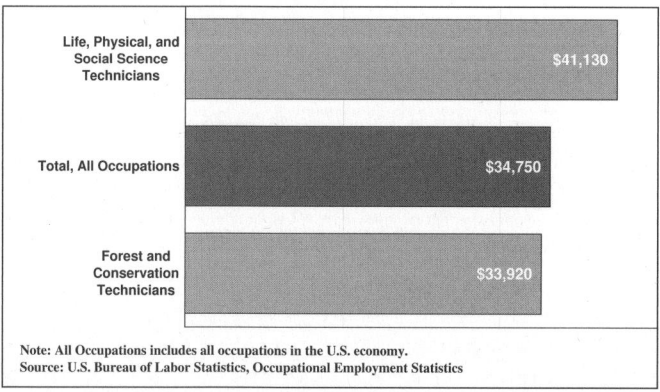

Note: All Occupations includes all occupations in the U.S. economy.
Source: U.S. Bureau of Labor Statistics, Occupational Employment Statistics

Percent Change in Employment, Projected 2012–2022

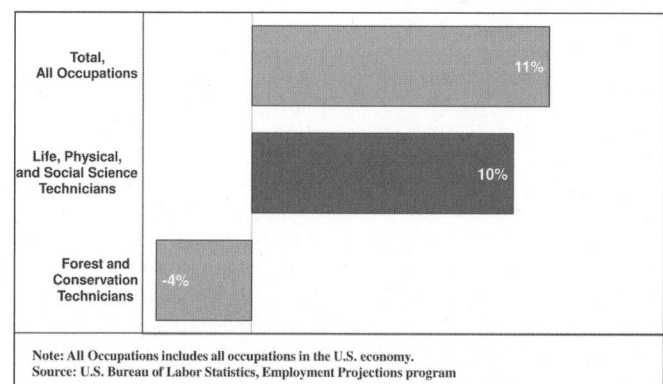

Note: All Occupations includes all occupations in the U.S. economy.
Source: U.S. Bureau of Labor Statistics, Employment Projections program

Employment Projections Data for Forest and Conservation Technicians

Occupational title	SOC Code	Employment, 2012	Projected Employment, 2022	Change, 2012–2022 Percent	Change, 2012–2022 Numeric
Forest and conservation technicians	19-4093	34,000	32,800	-4	-1,200

Source: *U.S. Bureau of Labor Statistics, Employment Projections Program*

Note: **Data are rounded. Go to Occupational Information Included in the OOH** *for a discussion of the data in this table.*

Similar Occupations   This table shows a list of occupations with job duties that are similar to those of forest and conservation technicians.

Occupations	Entry-level Education	2012 Pay	Projected Job Growth	Average Annual Openings
Agricultural and Food Scientists	See "How to Become One"	$58,636	10%	1,640
Biological Technicians	Bachelor's degree	$39,750	10%	3,210
Conservation Scientists and Foresters	Bachelor's degree	$59,354	3%	1,080
Firefighters	Postsecondary non-degree award	$45,250	7%	10,400
Forest and Conservation Workers	High school diploma or equivalent	$24,340	5%	230

Communication skills. Forest and conservation technicians must clearly instruct forest and conservation workers, who typically do the labor necessary to take care of the forest. Technicians must also follow instructions given to them by foresters and conservation scientists.

Critical-thinking skills. Forest and conservation technicians reach conclusions through sound reasoning and judgment. They determine how to improve forest conditions and must react appropriately to fires.

Physical stamina. Forest and conservation technicians often walk long distances in steep and wooded areas. They work in all kinds of weather, including extreme heat and cold.

Work Experience in a Related Occupation. Some forestry technician positions require related work experience. For example, technicians who work for The United States Forest Service in fire management positions typically need some previous experience in fighting wildfires or in wildfire suppression.

Pay

The median annual wage for forest and conservation technicians was $33,920 in May 2012. The median wage is the wage at which half the workers in an occupation earned more than that amount and half earned less. The lowest 10 percent earned less than $24,930, and the top 10 percent earned more than $53,780.

In May 2012, the median annual wages for forest and conservation technicians in the top three industries in which these technicians worked were as follows:

Local government, excluding education and hospitals................... $35,700
Federal government, excluding postal service 33,400
State government, excluding education and hospitals.......... 33,400

Job Outlook

Employment of forest and conservation technicians is projected to decline 4 percent from 2012 to 2022.

Heightened demand for American timber, wood pellets, and biomass will help overall job prospects for forest and conservation technicians. Most growth in employment over the next 10 years is expected to be in state owned forest lands. Because more people are living near federal and state forests, more technicians and other

forestry and conservation workers will be needed to combat fires and protect property.

O*NET

➤ Forest and Conservation Technicians (19-4093.00)

Contacts for More Information

For more information about forest and conservation technicians, visit
➤ Forest Guild (www.forestguild.org/)
   For more information about forestry careers and schools offering education in forestry, visit
➤ Society of American Foresters (www.safnet.org/)
   For more information about forest and conservation technicians in the federal government, visit
➤ The United States Forest Service (www.fs.fed.us/)

Geographers

- **2012 Median Pay** .... $74,760 per year
  $35.94 per hour
- **Entry-Level Education** .... Bachelor's degree
- **Work Experience in a Related Occupation**............... None
- **On-the-Job Training** .... None
- **Number of Jobs 2012** 1,700
- **Job Outlook, 2012–22** .... 29% (Much faster than average)
- **Employment Change, 2012–22** 500

What Geographers Do

Geographers study Earth and its land, features, and inhabitants. They also examine phenomena such as political or cultural structures as they relate to geography. They study the physical and human geographic characteristics of a region, ranging in scale from local to global.

Duties. Geographers typically do the following:

- Gather geographic data through field observations, maps, photographs, satellite imagery, and censuses

Geographers use maps and global positioning systems in their work.

- Use quantitative methods, such as statistical analysis, in their research
- Use qualitative methods, such as surveys, interviews, and focus groups, in their research
- Create and modify maps, graphs, diagrams, or other visual representations of geographic data
- Analyze the geographic distribution of physical and cultural characteristics and occurrences
- Use geographic information systems (GIS) to collect, analyze, and display geographic data
- Write reports and present research findings
- Assist, advise, or lead others in using GIS and geographic data
- Combine geographic data with data about a particular specialty, such as economics, the environment, health, or politics

Geographers use several technologies in their work, such as GIS, remote sensing, and global positioning systems (GPS). Geographers use GIS to find relationships and trends in geographic data. GIS allow geographers to present data visually as maps, reports, and charts. For example, geographers can overlay aerial or satellite images with GIS data, such as population density in a given region, and create computerized maps. They then use the results to advise governments, businesses, and the general public on a variety of issues, such as marketing strategies; planning homes, roads, and landfills; or disaster responses.

Many people who study geography and who use GIS in their work are employed as surveyors, cartographers and photogrammetrists, surveying and mapping technicians, urban and regional planners, and geoscientists.

The following are examples of types of geographers:

Physical geographers examine the physical aspects of a region and how those aspects relate to humans. They study features of the natural environment, such as land forms, climates, soils, natural hazards, water, and plants. For example, physical geographers may map where a natural resource occurs in a country and study the implications of that natural resource on the surrounding environment.

Human geographers analyze the organization of human activity and its relationships with the physical environment. Human geographers often combine issues from other disciplines into their research, which may include economic, social, or political topics. In their research, some human geographers rely primarily on statistical techniques, and others rely on non-statistical sources, such as field observations and interviews.

Human geographers are often further classified by their area of specialty:

- *Cultural geographers* examine the relationship between geography and culture, studying how features such as religion, language, or ethnicity relate to location.
- *Economic geographers* study economic activities and the distribution of resources. They may research subjects such as regional employment or the location of industries.
- *Environmental geographers* research the impact humans have on the environment and how human activities affect natural processes. They combine aspects of both physical and human geography and commonly study issues such as climate change, desertification, and deforestation.
- *Medical geographers* investigate the distribution of health issues, health care, and disease. For example, a medical geographer may examine the incidence of disease in a certain region.
- *Political geographers* study the relationship between geography and political structures and processes.
- *Regional geographers* focus on the geographic factors in a particular region, ranging in size from a neighborhood to an entire continent.
- *Urban geographers* study cities and metropolitan areas. For example, they may examine how certain geographic factors, such as climate, affect population density in cities.

Geographers often work on projects with people in related fields. For example, economic geographers may work with urban

Median Annual Wages, May 2012

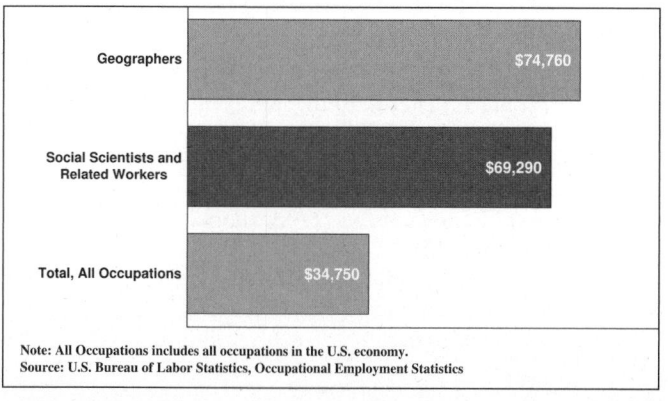

Note: All Occupations includes all occupations in the U.S. economy.
Source: U.S. Bureau of Labor Statistics, Occupational Employment Statistics

Percent Change in Employment, Projected 2012–2022

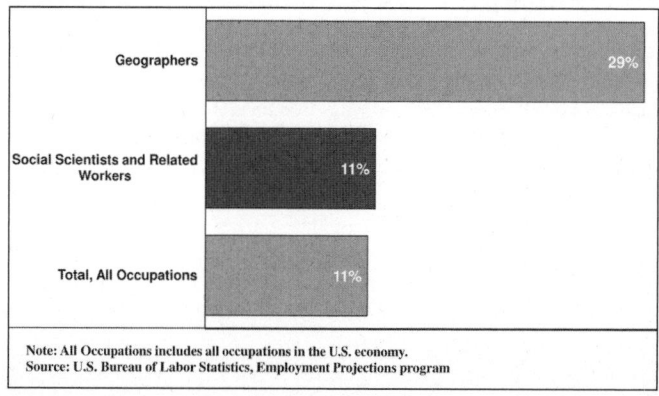

Note: All Occupations includes all occupations in the U.S. economy.
Source: U.S. Bureau of Labor Statistics, Employment Projections program

Employment Projections Data for Geographers

Occupational title	SOC Code	Employment, 2012	Projected Employment, 2022	Change, 2012–2022	
				Percent	Numeric
Geographers	19-3092	1,700	2,200	29	500

Source: U.S. Bureau of Labor Statistics, Employment Projections Program

Note: **Data are rounded. Go to Occupational Information Included in the OOH** *for a discussion of the data in this table.*

planners, civil engineers, legislators, and real estate professionals to determine the best location for new public transportation infrastructure.

Some people with a geography background become postsecondary teachers.

Work Environment

Geographers held about 1,700 jobs in 2012, of which 49 percent were in the federal government. Most others worked in architectural, engineering, and related services; colleges, universities, and professional schools; or were self-employed.

Many geographers do fieldwork to gather information and data. For example, geographers often make site visits to observe geographic features, such as the landscape and environment. Some geographers travel to the region they are studying, and sometimes that means working in foreign countries and remote locations.

Work Schedules. Most geographers work full time during regular business hours. Some do fieldwork that may include travel to foreign countries or remote locations.

How to Become One

Candidates with a bachelor's degree may qualify for some entry-level jobs, but these jobs often require previous geography experience or training in geographic information systems (GIS). Geographers need at least a master's degree for most positions outside of the federal government.

Education. Geographers outside of the federal government typically need a master's degree in geography. However, those with a bachelor's degree may qualify for some entry-level jobs in government or nonprofits. Some positions allow candidates to substitute work experience or GIS proficiency for an advanced degree. Top research positions usually require a Ph.D. or a master's degree and several years of relevant work experience.

Most geography programs include courses in both physical and human geography, statistics or mathematics, remote sensing, and GIS. In addition, courses in a specialized area of expertise are increasingly important because the geography field is broad and interdisciplinary. For example, business, economics, or real estate courses are increasingly important for geographers working in private industry.

Positions for geography professors require a Ph.D. For more information, see the profile on postsecondary teachers.

Other Experience. Students and new graduates often gain experience through internships or part-time jobs. These positions allow workers to develop new skills, explore their interests, and become familiar with the industry. Internships and part-time jobs can be useful for job seekers, because some employers prefer workers who have practical experience.

Licenses, Certifications, and Registrations. Most positions require geographers to be proficient in GIS. Geographers can become certified as a GIS professional (GISP) through the GIS Certification Institute. Although certification is not mandatory, it can demonstrate a level of professional expertise. Candidates

may qualify for certification through a combination of education, professional experience, and contributions to the profession, such as publications or conference participation. GISP certification can often help those without a master's degree or Ph.D. qualify for jobs.

Important Qualities

Analytical skills. Geographers commonly analyze information and spatial data from a variety of sources, such as maps, photographs, and censuses. They must then be able to draw conclusions from analysis of different sets of data.

Communication skills. Geographers often work closely with workers in related fields. They must be able to communicate with coworkers; present, explain, and defend their research; and work well on teams.

Computer skills. Geographers who use GIS technology need strong computer skills. They must be proficient in GIS programming and database management and should be comfortable creating and manipulating digital images in the software.

Critical-thinking skills. Geographers need critical-thinking skills when doing research because they must choose the appropriate data, methods, and scale of analysis for projects. For example, after reviewing a set of population data, they may determine the implications of a particular development plan.

Writing skills. Writing skills are important for geographers because they often write reports or articles detailing their research findings. Some geographers also must write proposals so that they can receive funding for their research or projects.

Pay

The median annual wage for geographers was $74,760 in May 2012. The median wage is the wage at which half the workers in an occupation earned more than that amount and half earned less. The lowest 10 percent earned less than $41,910, and the top 10 percent earned more than $103,870.

In May 2012, the median annual wages for geographers in the top three industries employing geographers were as follows:

Federal government $78,720
Professional, scientific, and technical services 65,150
Educational services; state, local, and private 53,150

Job Outlook

Employment of geographers is projected to grow 29 percent from 2012 to 2022, much faster than the average for all occupations. However, because it is a small occupation, the fast growth will result in only about 500 new jobs over the 10-year period.

More widespread use of geographic technologies, including geographic information systems (GIS), should drive job growth. These technologies allow government agencies, businesses, and nonprofits to use geographic data to make better business and planning decisions. Specifically, governments, businesses, and developers will need geographers to analyze information and offer

Similar Occupations   This table shows a list of occupations with job duties that are similar to those of geographers.

Occupations	Entry-level Education	2012 Pay	Projected Job Growth	Average Annual Openings
Anthropologists and Archeologists	Master's degree	$57,420	19%	260
Cartographers and Photogrammetrists	Bachelor's degree	$57,440	20%	490
Economists	Master's degree	$91,860	14%	740
Geoscientists	Bachelor's degree	$90,890	16%	1,730
Market Research Analysts	Bachelor's degree	$60,300	32%	18,850
Political Scientists	Master's degree	$102,000	21%	250
Postsecondary Teachers	See "How to Become One"	$70,380	19%	42,690
Sociologists	Master's degree	$74,960	15%	110
Surveying and Mapping Technicians	High school diploma or equivalent	$39,670	14%	1,700
Surveyors	Bachelor's degree	$56,230	10%	1,340
Urban and Regional Planners	Master's degree	$65,230	10%	2,140

advice on topics such as land use, building or infrastructure location, or environmental impact.

Due to greater focus on environmental and sustainable practices, geographers are increasingly needed to understand environmental changes and human impacts on the environment. Therefore, geographic analyses will be used to inform developers and policymakers of sustainable business practices and ensure adherence to increased regulations.

Governments and businesses also rely on geographers to research topics such as resource use, natural hazards, and climate change.

Job Prospects. Despite faster-than-average employment growth, the small size of the occupation will result in a limited number of positions–a scenario in which applicants can expect strong competition for jobs. Those with advanced degrees, specialized subject matter expertise, and experience working with geographic technologies, such as GIS, should have the best job prospects. Workers who have used geographic technologies to complete projects and solve problems within their specialized subfield should have better job opportunities.

Many workers with a background in geography find geography-related jobs, but most of these positions do not have the title of geographer. Some of these occupations include surveyors, cartographers and photogrammetrists, surveying and mapping technicians, urban and regional planners, and geoscientists.

O*NET

➤ Geographers (19-3092.00)

Contacts for More Information

For more information about geographers, visit
➤ Association of American Geographers (www.aag.org)

For more information about geographic information systems (GIS) certification, visit
➤ GIS Certification Institute (www.gisci.org/)

For information on federal government education requirements for geographer positions, visit
➤ U.S. Office of Personnel Management (www.opm.gov /qualifications/Standards/IORs/gs0100/0150.htm)

To find job openings for geographers in the federal government, visit
➤ USAJOBS (www.usajobs.gov)

Geological and Petroleum Technicians

- **2012 Median Pay** .... $52,700 per year
$25.34 per hour
- **Entry-Level Education** .... Associate's degree
- **Work Experience in a Related Occupation**............... None
- **On-the-Job Training** .... Moderate-term on-the-job training
- **Number of Jobs 2012** 15,800
- **Job Outlook, 2012–22** .... 15% (Faster than average)
- **Employment Change, 2012–22** 2,400

What Geological and Petroleum Technicians Do

Geological and petroleum technicians provide support to scientists and engineers in exploring and extracting natural resources, such as minerals, oil, and natural gas.

Duties. Geological and petroleum technicians typically do the following:

- Install and maintain laboratory and field equipment
- Gather samples such as rock, mud, and soil in the field and prepare samples for laboratory analysis
- Conduct scientific tests on samples to determine their content and characteristics
- Record data from tests and compile information from reports, computer databases, and other sources
- Prepare reports and maps that can be used to define geological characteristics of areas that may have valuable resources
- Monitor well exploration activities, and record data such as well temperatures and pressures
- Document their investigations and compare actual productivity with their estimates

Geological and petroleum technicians tend to specialize in either working in the field and in laboratories, or working in offices where they analyze data. However, many technicians have duties that overlap into multiple areas.

In the field, geological and petroleum technicians use sophisticated equipment such as seismic instruments and gravity-measuring devices to gather geological data. They also use tools to collect samples of rock and other materials for scientific analysis. In laboratories, these technicians analyze the samples for evidence of hydrocarbons, useful metals, or precious gemstones.

Geological and petroleum technicians use computers to analyze data from samples collected in the field and from previous research. They use Geographic Information Systems (GIS) software to map geological data; this creates a visual representation and makes the data easier to understand. The results of their analysis may explain a new site's potential for further exploration and development, or may focus on monitoring the current and future productivity of an existing site.

Geological and petroleum technicians work on geological prospecting and surveying teams under the supervision of scientists and engineers, who evaluate the work for accuracy and make final decisions about current and potential production sites. Geologic and petroleum technicians might work with scientists and technicians in other fields. For example, geological and petroleum technicians might work with environmental scientists and technicians to monitor the environmental impact of drilling and other activities.

Work Environment

Geological and petroleum technicians held about 15,800 jobs in 2012. The industries that employed the most geological and petroleum technicians in 2012 were as follows:

Support activities for mining 30%
Oil and gas extraction.. 19
Engineering services.. 11
Petroleum and coal products manufacturing 7
Chemical and allied products merchant wholesalers................. 5

In 2012, almost half of all technicians were employed in Texas because of the large amount of resource extraction activity.

Geological and petroleum technicians spend most of their time in the field and in laboratories, or analyzing data in offices. Fieldwork requires technicians to work outdoors, sometimes in remote locations, where they are exposed to all types of weather. In addition, technicians may need to stay on location in the field for days or weeks to collect data and monitor equipment. Geological and petroleum technicians who work in offices spend most of their time working on computers organizing and analyzing data, writing reports, and producing maps.

Work Schedules. Most geological and petroleum technicians work full time. Technicians generally work a standard schedule in laboratories and offices, but hours spent in the field may be long or irregular.

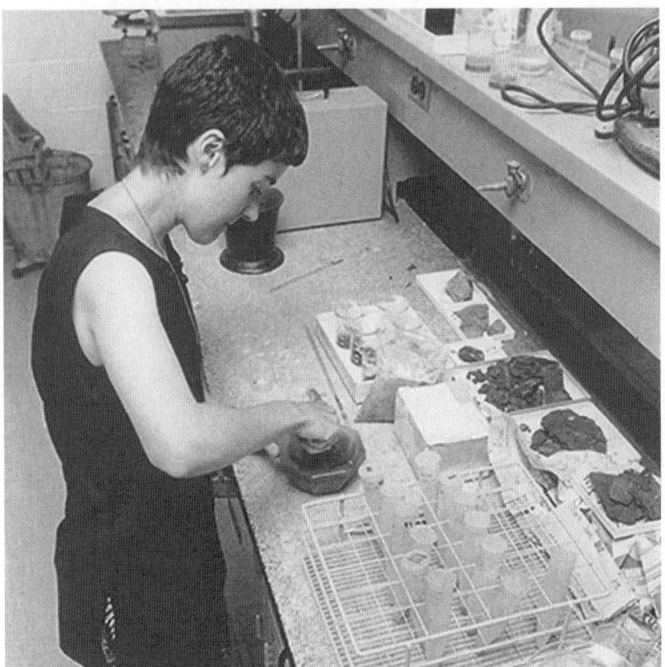

Geological and petroleum technicians help identify and map locations that are suitable for oil and gas wells.

How to Become One

Most employers prefer applicants who have an associate's degree or 2 years of postsecondary training in applied science or science-related technology. Geological and petroleum technicians also receive on-the-job training.

Education. Although some entry-level positions require only a high school diploma, most employers prefer applicants who have at least an associate's degree or 2 years of postsecondary training in applied science or a science-related technology. Geological and petroleum technician jobs that are data intensive or otherwise highly technical may require at least a bachelor's degree.

Many community colleges and technical institutes offer programs in geosciences, petroleum, mining, or a related technology such as geographic information systems (GIS). Community colleges offer associate's degree programs designed to provide an easy transition to bachelor's degree programs at colleges and universities; such programs can be useful for future career advancement.

Technical institutes typically offer 1-year certificate programs and 2-year associate's degree programs. Technical institutes offer technical training that usually includes less theory and offers fewer general education courses than community colleges.

Median Annual Wages, May 2012

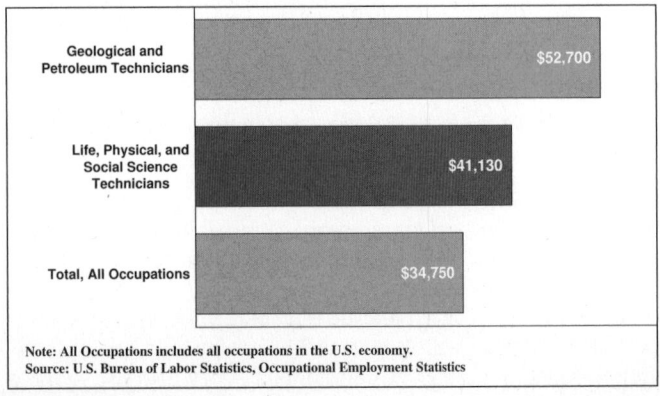

Geological and Petroleum Technicians — $52,700

Life, Physical, and Social Science Technicians — $41,130

Total, All Occupations — $34,750

Note: All Occupations includes all occupations in the U.S. economy.
Source: U.S. Bureau of Labor Statistics, Occupational Employment Statistics

Percent Change in Employment, Projected 2012–2022

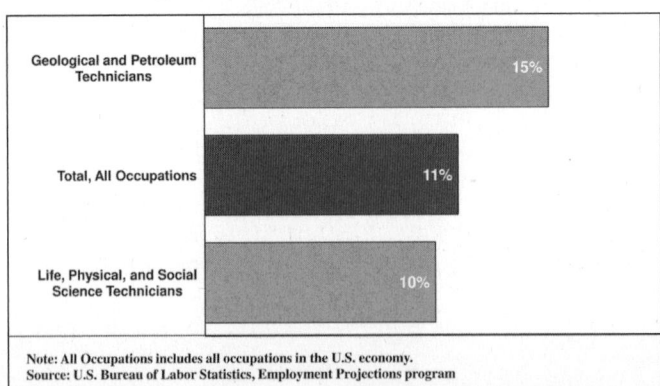

Geological and Petroleum Technicians — 15%

Total, All Occupations — 11%

Life, Physical, and Social Science Technicians — 10%

Note: All Occupations includes all occupations in the U.S. economy.
Source: U.S. Bureau of Labor Statistics, Employment Projections program

Employment Projections Data for Geological and Petroleum Technicians

Occupational title	SOC Code	Employment, 2012	Projected Employment, 2022	Change, 2012–2022	
				Percent	Numeric
Geological and petroleum technicians	19-4041	15,800	18,200	15	2,400

Source: U.S. Bureau of Labor Statistics, Employment Projections Program

Note: Data are rounded. Go to Occupational Information Included in the OOH *for a discussion of the data in this table.*

Regardless of the degree program, most students take classes in geology, mathematics, computer science, chemistry, and physics. Many schools also offer internships and cooperative-education programs that help students gain experience while attending school. Job-seekers who have this type of experience may have better prospects.

Important Qualities

Analytical skills. Geological and petroleum technicians examine data, using a variety of complex techniques, including laboratory experimentation and computer modeling.

Communication skills. Geological and petroleum technicians explain their methods and findings through oral and written reports to scientists, engineers, managers, and other technicians. Therefore, they must speak and write clearly.

Critical-thinking skills. Geological and petroleum technicians must use their best judgment when interpreting scientific data and determining what is relevant to their work.

Interpersonal skills. Geological and petroleum technicians need to be able to work well with others and as part of a team.

Physical stamina. To do fieldwork, geological and petroleum technicians need to be in good physical shape to hike to remote locations while carrying testing and sampling equipment.

Training. Most geological and petroleum technicians receive on-the-job training under the supervision of technicians who have more experience. During training, new technicians gain hands-on experience using field and laboratory equipment, as well as computer programs such as modeling and mapping software. The length of training can vary with the technician's previous experience, education, and specifics of the job.

Pay

The median annual wage for geological and petroleum technicians was $52,700 in May 2012. The median wage is the wage at which half the workers in an occupation earned more than that amount and half earned less. The lowest 10 percent earned less than $26,940, and the top 10 percent earned more than $99,300.

In May 2012, the median annual wages for geological and petroleum technicians in the top five industries employing these technicians were as follows:

Petroleum and coal products manufacturing	$85,110
Oil and gas extraction...	70,920
Chemical and allied products merchant wholesalers............	53,490
Support activities for mining	47,670
Engineering services..	45,040

Job Outlook

Employment of geological and petroleum technicians is projected to grow 15 percent from 2012 to 2022, faster than the average for all occupations. High prices for oil and strong demand for natural gas is expected to increase demand for geological exploration and extraction in the future.

Oil prices are likely to increase over time, as they have in the past. In addition, future demand for cheap energy will likely cause natural gas prices to increase before 2022. These expected price increases will support current and future exploration.

Since geological and petroleum technicians are sometimes involved in ongoing production processes, such as monitoring a well's productivity, more of these workers will be needed as production increases. Demand for exploration of resources such as coal, metals, and other mined goods is generally expected to continue as it has historically, or increase over the projection period. This growth will be due to growing world population and the growth of the middle class worldwide.

Job Prospects. The best job prospects will be for those technicians who have hands-on training, through an internship, and technical skills in computer programs such as Geographical Information Systems (GIS).

O*NET

➤ Geological and Petroleum Technicians (19-4041.00)
➤ Geophysical Data Technicians (19-4041.01)
➤ Geological Sample Test Technicians (19-4041.02)

Contacts for More Information

For more information about careers in geology, visit
➤ American Geosciences Institute (www.agiweb.org/)

Similar Occupations This table shows a list of occupations with job duties that are similar to those of geological and petroleum technicians.

Occupations	Entry-level Education	2012 Pay	Projected Job Growth	Average Annual Openings
Cartographers and Photogrammetrists	Bachelor's degree	$57,440	20%	490
Civil Engineering Technicians	Associate's degree	$47,560	1%	1,560
Civil Engineers	Bachelor's degree	$79,340	20%	12,010
Geoscientists	Bachelor's degree	$90,890	16%	1,730
Hydrologists	Master's degree	$75,530	9%	290
Petroleum Engineers	Bachelor's degree	$130,280	26%	1,960
Surveying and Mapping Technicians	High school diploma or equivalent	$39,670	14%	1,700

For more information about careers in oil and gas exploration, visit
➤ American Association of Petroleum Geologists (www.aapg.org/)
➤ Society of Petroleum Engineers (www.spe.org/index.php)

For more information about careers in coal and mineral extraction, visit
➤ National Mining Association (www.nma.org/)

Geoscientists

- **2012 Median Pay** .... $90,890 per year
  $43.70 per hour
- **Entry-Level Education** ....Bachelor's degree
- **Work Experience in a Related Occupation**............... None
- **On-the-Job Training** .... None
- **Number of Jobs 2012** 38,200
- **Job Outlook, 2012–22** .... 16% (Faster than average)
- **Employment Change, 2012–22** 6,000

What Geoscientists Do

Geoscientists study the physical aspects of Earth, such as its composition, structure, and processes, to learn about its past, present, and future.

Duties. Geoscientists typically do the following:

- Plan and conduct field studies, in which they visit locations to collect samples and conduct surveys
- Analyze aerial photographs, well logs (detailed records of geologic formations found during drilling), rock samples, and other data sources to locate natural resource deposits and estimate their size
- Conduct laboratory tests on samples collected in the field
- Make geologic maps and charts
- Prepare written scientific reports
- Present their findings to clients, colleagues, and other interested parties
- Review reports and research done by other scientists

Geoscientists use a wide variety of tools, both simple and complex. During a typical day in the field, they may use a hammer and chisel to collect rock samples and then use sophisticated ground-penetrating radar equipment to search for oil or minerals. In laboratories, they may use X-ray and electron microscopes to determine the chemical and physical composition of rock samples. They may also use remote sensing equipment to collect data and advanced geographic information systems (GIS) and modeling software to analyze data.

Geoscientists often supervise the work of technicians and coordinate work with other scientists, both in the field and in the lab.

Many geoscientists are involved in the search for and development of natural resources, such as petroleum. Others work in environmental protection and preservation, and are involved in projects to clean up and reclaim land. Some specialize in a particular aspect of Earth, such as its oceans.

The following are examples of types of geoscientists:

Engineering geologists apply geologic principles to civil and environmental engineering. They offer advice on major construction projects and help in other projects, such as environmental cleanup and reducing natural hazards.

Geologists study the materials, processes, and history of Earth. They investigate how rocks were formed and what has happened to them since their formation. There are sub-groups of geologists as well, such as stratigraphers, who study stratified rock, and mineralogists, who study the structure and composition of minerals.

Geochemists use physical and organic chemistry to study the composition of elements found in groundwater, such as water from wells or aquifers, and earth materials, such as rocks and sediment.

Geophysicists use the principles of physics to learn about Earth's surface and interior. They also study the properties of Earth's magnetic, electric, and gravitational fields.

Oceanographers study the motion and circulation of ocean waters; the physical and chemical properties of the oceans; and how these properties affect coastal areas, climate, and weather.

Paleontologists study fossils found in geological formations to trace the evolution of plant and animal life and the geologic history of Earth.

Petroleum geologists explore Earth for oil and gas deposits. They analyze geological information to identify sites that should be explored. They collect rock and sediment samples from sites through drilling and other methods and test them for the presence of oil and gas. They also estimate the size of oil and gas deposits and work to develop sites to extract oil and gas.

Seismologists study earthquakes and related phenomena like tsunamis. They use seismographs and other instruments to collect data on these events.

For a more extensive list of geoscientist specialties, visit the American Geosciences Institute.

People with a geosciences background may become professors or teachers. For more information, see the profile on postsecondary teachers.

Work Environment

Geoscientists held about 38,200 jobs in 2012. Industries employing the most geoscientists in 2012 were as follows:

Oil and gas extraction..26%
Engineering services..16
Management, scientific, and technical consulting services...... 12
State government, excluding education and hospitals...............7
Federal government, excluding postal service 7

Nearly a third of all geoscientists worked in the mining, quarrying, and oil and gas extraction industry in 2012. Also, about 3 out of 10 geoscientists were employed in Texas in 2012, because of the prominence of those activities in that state. Workers in

Geoscientists study Earth, often looking for natural resources.

Median Annual Wages, May 2012

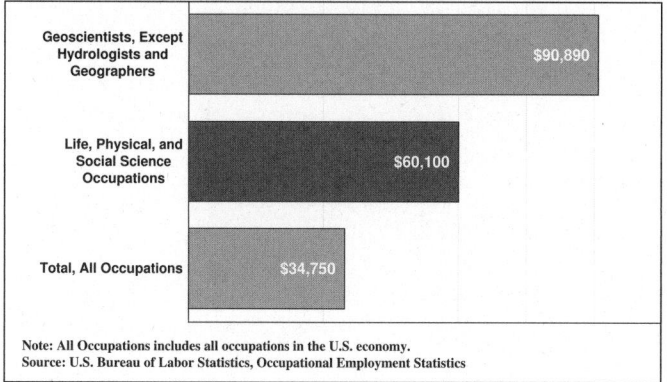

Note: All Occupations includes all occupations in the U.S. economy.
Source: U.S. Bureau of Labor Statistics, Occupational Employment Statistics

Percent Change in Employment, Projected 2012–2022

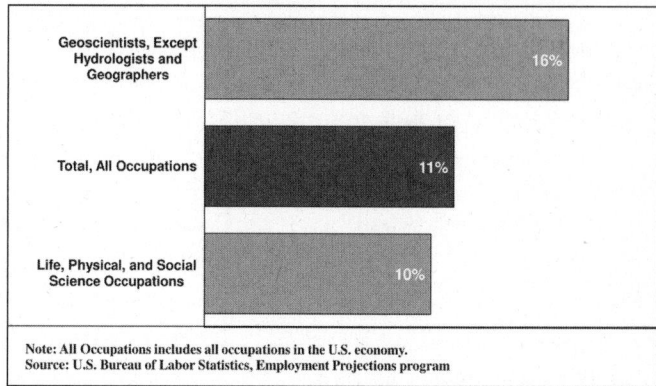

Note: All Occupations includes all occupations in the U.S. economy.
Source: U.S. Bureau of Labor Statistics, Employment Projections program

natural resource extraction fields usually work as part of a team, with other scientists and engineers. For example, they may work closely with petroleum engineers to find and develop new sources of oil and natural gas.

Most geoscientists split their time between working in the field, in laboratories, and in offices. Fieldwork can take geoscientists to remote locations all over the world and can be physically and possibly psychologically demanding. For example, oceanographers may spend months at sea on a research ship, and researchers studying advanced topics may need to collaborate with top scientists around the world.

The search for natural resources often takes geoscientists involved in exploration to remote areas and foreign countries. When in the field, geoscientists may work in both warm and cold climates, in all types of weather. They may have to travel by helicopter or four-wheel drive vehicles and cover large areas on foot. Having outdoor skills such as camping and boat-handling skills may be useful.

Work Schedules. Most geoscientists work full time. They may work long or irregular hours when doing fieldwork. Geoscientists travel frequently to meet with clients and to conduct fieldwork.

How to Become One

Geoscientists typically need at least a bachelor's degree for most entry-level positions. In several states, geoscientists may need a license to offer their services to the public.

Education. Geoscientists need at least a bachelor's degree for most entry-level positions. However, some workers begin their careers as geoscientists with a master's degree. A Ph.D. is necessary for most basic research and college teaching positions.

A degree in geosciences is preferred by employers, although degrees in physics, chemistry, biology, mathematics, engineering, or computer science are usually accepted if they include coursework in geology.

Most geosciences programs include geology courses in mineralogy, petrology, and structural geology, which are important for all geoscientists. In addition to classes in geology, most pro-

grams require students to take courses in other physical sciences, mathematics, engineering, and computer science. Some programs include training on specific software packages that will be useful to those seeking a career as a geoscientist.

Computer knowledge is essential for geoscientists. Students who have experience with computer modeling, data analysis, and digital mapping will be the most prepared to enter the job market.

Many employers seek applicants who have gained field and laboratory experience while pursuing a degree. Summer field camp programs offer students the opportunity to work closely with professors and apply their classroom knowledge in the field. Students can gain valuable experience in data collection and geologic mapping.

Important Qualities

Communication skills. Geoscientists write reports and research papers. They must be able to present their findings clearly to clients or professionals who do not have a background in geosciences.

Critical-thinking skills. Geoscientists base their findings on sound observation and careful evaluation of data.

Interpersonal skills. Most geoscientists work as part of a team with engineers, technicians, and other scientists.

Outdoor skills. Geoscientists may spend significant amounts of time outdoors. Familiarity with camping skills, general comfort being outside for long periods of time, and specific skills such as boat handling or even being able to pilot an aircraft could prove useful for geoscientists.

Physical stamina. Geoscientists may need to hike to remote locations while carrying testing and sampling equipment when they conduct fieldwork.

Problem-solving skills. Geoscientists work on complex projects filled with challenges. Geoscientists need to use and analyze complex sources of data. Evaluating statistical data and other forms of information to make judgments and inform the actions of other workers requires a special ability to perceive and address problems.

Licenses, Certifications, and Registrations. Geoscientists need a license to practice in some states. Requirements vary by state but

Employment Projections Data for Geoscientists

Occupational title	SOC Code	Employment, 2012	Projected Employment, 2022	Change, 2012–2022	
				Percent	Numeric
Geoscientists, except hydrologists and geographers	19-2042	38,200	44,200	16	6,000

Source: U.S. Bureau of Labor Statistics, Employment Projections Program

Note: **Data are rounded.** Go to **Occupational Information Included in the OOH** *for a discussion of the data in this table.*

Similar Occupations   This table shows a list of occupations with job duties that are similar to those of geoscientists.

Occupations	Entry-level Education	2012 Pay	Projected Job Growth	Average Annual Openings
Agricultural and Food Scientists	See "How to Become One"	$58,636	10%	1,640
Anthropologists and Archeologists	Master's degree	$57,420	19%	260
Atmospheric Scientists, Including Meteorologists	Bachelor's degree	$89,260	10%	380
Chemists and Materials Scientists	Bachelor's degree	$73,247	6%	3,040
Civil Engineers	Bachelor's degree	$79,340	20%	12,010
Environmental Engineers	Bachelor's degree	$80,890	15%	2,110
Environmental Scientists and Specialists	Bachelor's degree	$63,570	15%	3,970
Geological and Petroleum Technicians	Associate's degree	$52,700	15%	810
Hydrologists	Master's degree	$75,530	9%	290
Mining and Geological Engineers	Bachelor's degree	$84,320	13%	300
Natural Sciences Managers	Bachelor's degree	$115,730	6%	1,370
Petroleum Engineers	Bachelor's degree	$130,280	26%	1,960
Physicists and Astronomers	Doctoral or professional degree	$105,722	10%	810
Postsecondary Teachers	See "How to Become One"	$70,380	19%	42,690

typically include minimum education and experience requirements and a passing score on an exam.

Pay

The median annual wage for geoscientists was $90,890 in May 2012. The median wage is the wage at which half the workers in an occupation earned more than that amount and half earned less. The lowest 10 percent earned less than $48,270 and the top 10 percent more than $187,200.

In May 2012, the median annual wages for geoscientists in the top five industries employing these scientists were as follows:

Oil and gas extraction	$137,750
Federal government, excluding postal service	94,830
Engineering services	74,360
Management, scientific, and technical consulting services	74,020
State government, excluding education and hospitals	62,030

Job Outlook

Employment of geoscientists is projected to grow 16 percent from 2012 to 2022, faster than the average for all occupations. The need for energy, environmental protection, and responsible land and resource management is projected to spur demand for geoscientists in the future.

Horizontal drilling and hydraulic fracturing are examples of new technologies that are expected to increase demand for geoscientists. These technologies allow for the extraction of previously inaccessible oil and gas resources, and geoscientists will be needed to study effects they have on the surrounding areas. As oil prices remain high or increase into the future, even more technologies will likely be introduced that expand the ability to reach untapped oil reserves or introduce alternative ways to provide energy for the expanding population.

Geoscientists will be needed in planning for the construction of wind farms, geothermal power plants, and solar power plants. Alternative energies such as wind energy, geothermal energy, and solar power can use large areas of land and impact wildlife and other natural processes. In addition, only certain areas are suitable for harvesting these energies. For example, geothermal energy

plants must be located near sufficient hot groundwater, and one task for geoscientists would be studying maps and charts to decide if the site is suitable.

An expanding population and the corresponding increased use of space and resources may create a continued need for geoscientists.

Job Prospects. Job opportunities should be excellent for geoscientists, but particularly those who earn a master's degree. In addition to job growth, a number of job openings are expected as geoscientists leave the workforce due to retirement and other reasons.

Geoscientists with a doctoral degree will likely face competition for positions in academia and research.

Fewer opportunities are expected in state and federal governments than in the past. Budget constraints are likely to limit hiring by state governments and federal agencies such as the U.S. Geological Survey. In addition, more of the work traditionally done by government agencies is expected to be contracted out to consulting firms in the future. Most opportunities for geoscientists are expected to be related to resource extraction; in particular, gas and oil exploration and extraction operations.

O*NET

➤ Geoscientists, Except Hydrologists and Geographers (19-2042.00)

Contacts for More Information

For more information about geoscientists, visit
➤ American Geosciences Institute (www.agiweb.org/)
    For information about petroleum geologists, visit
➤ American Association of Petroleum Geologists (www.aapg.org/)
    To find job openings for geologists, geophysicists, or oceanographers in the federal government, visit
➤ USAJOBS (www.usajobs.gov/)
    For information on federal government education requirements for geoscience positions, visit
➤ U.S. Office of Personnel Management (www.opm.gov /qualifications/standards/indexes/num-ndx.asp)

Historians

- **2012 Median Pay** .... $52,480 per year
  $25.23 per hour
- **Entry-Level Education** ....Master's degree
- **Work Experience in a Related Occupation**.............. None
- **On-the-Job Training** .... None
- **Number of Jobs 2012** 3,800
- **Job Outlook, 2012–22** .... 6% (Slower than average)
- **Employment Change, 2012–22** 200

What Historians Do

Historians research, analyze, interpret, and present the past by studying a variety of historical documents and sources.

Duties. Historians typically do the following:

- Gather historical data from various sources, including archives, books, and artifacts
- Analyze and interpret historical information to determine its authenticity and significance
- Trace historical developments in a particular field
- Engage with the public through educational programs and presentations
- Archive or preserve materials and artifacts in museums, visitor centers, and historic sites
- Provide advice or guidance on historical topics and preservation issues
- Write reports, articles, and books on findings and theories

Historians conduct research and analysis for governments, businesses, nonprofits, historical associations, and other organizations. They use a variety of sources in their work, including government and institutional records, newspapers, photographs, interviews, films, and unpublished manuscripts (such as personal diaries and letters). They also may process, catalog, and archive these documents and artifacts.

Many historians present and interpret history in order to shape or build upon public knowledge of past events. They often trace and build a historical profile of a particular person, area, idea, organization, or event. Once their research is complete, they present their findings through articles, books, reports, exhibits, websites, and educational programs.

Historians may spend much of their time researching and writing reports.

In government, some historians conduct research to provide historical context for current policy issues. For example, they may research the history of Social Security as background for a new bill or upcoming funding debate. Many write about the history of a particular government agency, activity, or program, such as a military operation or the space program.

In historical associations, historians preserve artifacts and explain the historical significance of a wide variety of subjects, such as historic buildings, religious groups, and battlegrounds.

Historians who work for businesses may examine historical evidence for legal cases and regulatory matters.

Many people with an educational background in history become high school teachers or postsecondary teachers.

Work Environment

Historians held about 3,800 jobs in 2012, of which 58 percent were in government. Historians also worked in museums, archives, historical societies, research organizations, and nonprofits. Some worked as consultants for these organizations while being employed by consulting firms, and some worked as independent consultants.

The industries that employed the most historians in 2012 were as follows:

State and local government, excluding education
and hospitals... 36%
Federal government, excluding postal service 22
Professional, scientific, and technical services......................... 20

Median Annual Wages, May 2012

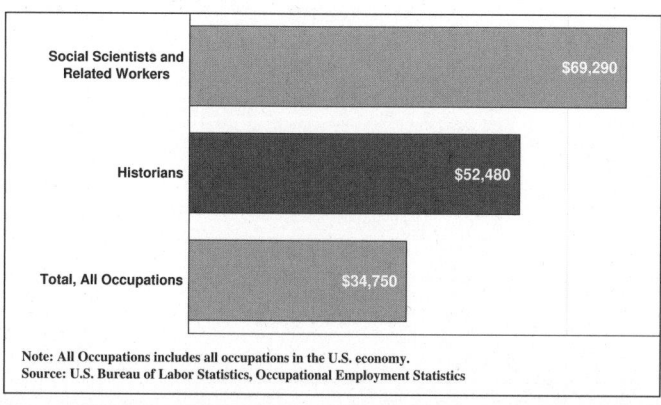

Social Scientists and Related Workers	$69,290
Historians	$52,480
Total, All Occupations	$34,750

Note: All Occupations includes all occupations in the U.S. economy.
Source: U.S. Bureau of Labor Statistics, Occupational Employment Statistics

Percent Change in Employment, Projected 2012–2022

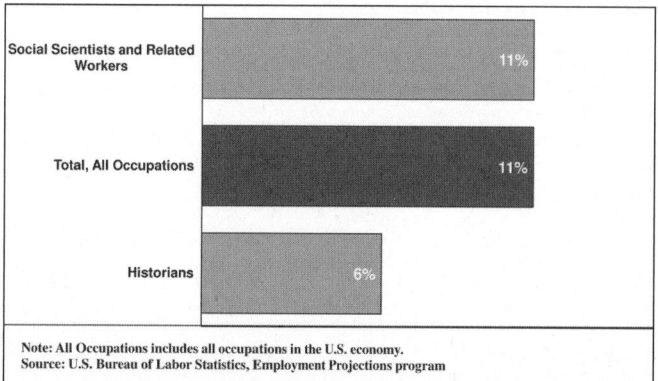

Social Scientists and Related Workers	11%
Total, All Occupations	11%
Historians	6%

Note: All Occupations includes all occupations in the U.S. economy.
Source: U.S. Bureau of Labor Statistics, Employment Projections program

Employment Projections Data for Historians

Occupational title	SOC Code	Employment, 2012	Projected Employment, 2022	Change, 2012–2022 Percent	Change, 2012–2022 Numeric
Historians	19-3093	3,800	4,000	6	200

Source: U.S. Bureau of Labor Statistics, Employment Projections Program

Note: Data are rounded. Go to Occupational Information Included in the OOH *for a discussion of the data in this table.*

Work Schedules. Most historians work full time during regular business hours. Some, including those who are self-employed, work independently and are able to set their own schedules. Historians who work in museums or other institutions open to the public may work evenings or weekends. Some historians travel to conduct practical work in different environments, which may involve collecting artifacts, going to sources, conducting interviews, or visiting an area to better understand its culture and environment.

How to Become One

Although most historian positions require a master's degree, some research positions require a doctoral degree. Candidates with a bachelor's degree may qualify for some entry-level positions, but most will not be traditional historian jobs.

Education. Historians need a master's degree or Ph.D. for most positions. Many historians have a master's degree in history or public history. Others complete degrees in related fields, such as museum studies, historical preservation, or archival management. Many programs require an internship or other onsite work experience as a part of the degree program.

Research positions, including many jobs within the federal government, typically require a Ph.D. Students in history Ph.D. programs usually concentrate in a specific area of history. Possible specializations include a particular country or region, period, or field, such as social, political, or cultural history.

Candidates with a bachelor's degree in history may qualify for entry-level positions at museums, historical associations, or other small organizations. However, most bachelor's degree holders usually work outside of traditional historian jobs–for example, jobs in education, communications, law, business, publishing, or journalism.

Many people with an educational background in history become high school teachers or postsecondary teachers.

Other Experience. Many historians benefit from previous history work, internships, or field experience when they look for positions outside of colleges and universities. Most master's programs in public history and similar fields require an internship as part of the curriculum. Internships offer an opportunity for students to learn practical skills, such as handling and preserving artifacts and creating exhibits. They also give students an opportunity to apply their academic knowledge in a hands-on setting.

Those without internship experience can benefit from volunteering or working in an entry-level position to gain similar practical experience. Positions are often available at local museums, historical societies, government agencies, or nonprofit and other organizations.

Important Qualities

Analytical skills. Historians must be able to examine the information and data in historical sources and draw logical conclusions from them, whether the sources are written documents, visual images, or material artifacts.

Communication skills. Communication skills are important for historians because many give presentations on their historical specialty to the public. Historians also need communication skills when they interview people to collect oral histories, consult with clients, or collaborate with colleagues in the workplace.

Problem-solving skills. Historians try to answer questions about the past. They may investigate something unknown about a past idea, event, or person; decipher historical information; or identify how the past has affected the present.

Research skills. Historians must be able to examine and process information from a large number of historical documents, texts, and other sources.

Writing skills. Writing skills are essential for historians as they often present their findings in reports, articles, and books.

Pay

The median annual wage for historians was $52,480 in May 2012. The median wage is the wage at which half the workers in an occupation earned more than that amount and half earned less. The

Similar Occupations   This table shows a list of occupations with job duties that are similar to those of historians.

Occupations	Entry-level Education	2012 Pay	Projected Job Growth	Average Annual Openings
Anthropologists and Archeologists	Master's degree	$57,420	19%	260
Archivists, Curators, and Museum Workers	See "How to Become One"	$44,625	12%	970
Economists	Master's degree	$91,860	14%	740
Editors	Bachelor's degree	$53,880	-2%	2,800
Geographers	Bachelor's degree	$74,760	29%	80
High School Teachers	Bachelor's degree	$55,050	6%	31,260
Political Scientists	Master's degree	$102,000	21%	250
Postsecondary Teachers	See "How to Become One"	$70,380	19%	42,690
Sociologists	Master's degree	$74,960	15%	110
Writers and Authors	Bachelor's degree	$55,940	3%	3,180

lowest 10 percent earned less than $27,020, and the top 10 percent earned more than $97,930.

In May 2012, the median annual wages for historians in the top three industries employing historians were as follows:

Federal government, excluding postal service $85,640
Professional, scientific, and technical services...................... 54,200
State and local government, excluding education
    and hospitals.. 37,540

Job Outlook

Employment of historians is projected to grow 6 percent from 2012 to 2022, slower than the average for all occupations.

Federal government, which employed nearly one-quarter of all historians in 2012, is expected decline 12 percent over the coming decade, which will limit overall employment growth for historians.

Historians will experience faster employment growth outside of the federal government in historical societies, research organizations, and historical consulting firms. However, many types of organizations that employ historians depend on donations or public funding. Thus, employment growth from 2012 to 2022 will depend largely on the amount of funding available.

Job Prospects. Historians should face very strong competition for most jobs. Because of the popularity of history degree programs, applicants are expected to outnumber positions available. Those with practical skills or hands-on work experience in a specialized field such as collections, fundraising, or exhibit design, should have the best job prospects.

Because historians have broad training and education in writing, analytical research, and critical thinking, they can apply their skills to many different occupations–for example, as writers and authors, editors, postsecondary teachers, high school teachers, or policy analysts.

Also, there are many history-related jobs that do not have the title of historian. Workers with a background in history often look for closely related jobs, working as archivists, curators, and museum workers, social science or humanities researchers, and cultural resource managers.

O*NET

➤ Historians (19-3093.00)

Contacts for More Information

For more information about historians, visit
➤ American Historical Association (www.historians.org)
➤ National Council on Public History (www.ncph.org)
➤ American Association for State and Local History (www.aaslh.org)

Hydrologists

- **2012 Median Pay** .... $75,530 per year
                                                     $36.31 per hour
- **Entry-Level Education** ....Master's degree
- **Work Experience in a Related Occupation**............... None
- **On-the-Job Training** .... None
- **Number of Jobs 2012** 7,400
- **Job Outlook, 2012–22** .... 10% (As fast as average)
- **Employment Change, 2012–22** 800

What Hydrologists Do

Hydrologists study how water moves across and through Earth's crust. They study how rain, snow, and other forms of precipita-

tion impact river flows or groundwater levels, and how surface water and groundwater evaporates back into the atmosphere or eventually reaches the oceans. Hydrologists analyze how water influences the surrounding environment and how changes to the environment influence the quality and quantity of water. They can use their expertise to solve problems concerning water quality and availability.

Duties. Hydrologists typically do the following:

- Measure the properties of bodies of water, such as volume and stream flow
- Collect water and soil samples to test for certain properties, such as the pH or pollution levels
- Analyze data on the environmental impacts of pollution, erosion, drought, and other problems
- Research ways to minimize the negative impacts of erosion, sedimentation, or pollution on the environment
- Use computer models to forecast future water supplies, the spread of pollution, floods, and other events
- Evaluate the feasibility of water-related projects, such as hydroelectric power plants, irrigation systems, and wastewater treatment facilities
- Prepare written reports and presentations of their findings

Hydrologists may use remote sensing equipment to collect data. They, or technicians whom they supervise, usually install and maintain this equipment. Hydrologists also use sophisticated computer programs to analyze the data collected. Computer models are often developed by hydrologists to help them understand complex datasets. Hydrologists also use geographic information systems (GIS) and global positioning system (GPS) equipment to do their jobs.

Hydrologists work closely with engineers, scientists, and public officials to study and manage the water supply. For example, they work with policymakers to develop water conservation plans and with biologists to monitor wildlife to allow for their water needs.

Most hydrologists specialize in a specific water source or a certain aspect of the water cycle, such as the evaporation of water from lakes and streams. The following are examples of types of hydrologists:

Groundwater hydrologists study the water below Earth's surface. Most groundwater hydrologists focus on the cleanup of ground-

Hydrologists often perform laboratory tests on water samples that were collected in the field.

Median Annual Wages, May 2012

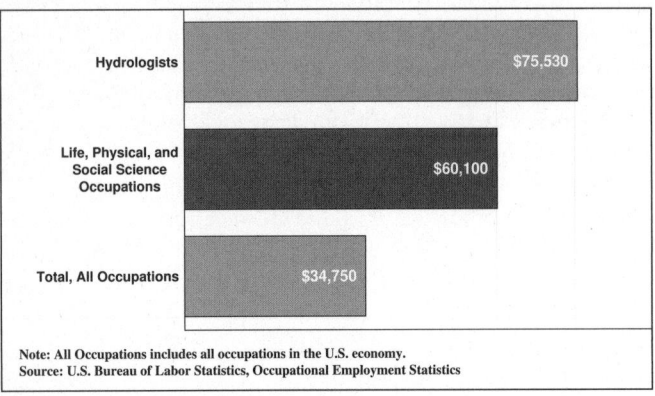

Note: All Occupations includes all occupations in the U.S. economy.
Source: U.S. Bureau of Labor Statistics, Occupational Employment Statistics

Percent Change in Employment, Projected 2012–2022

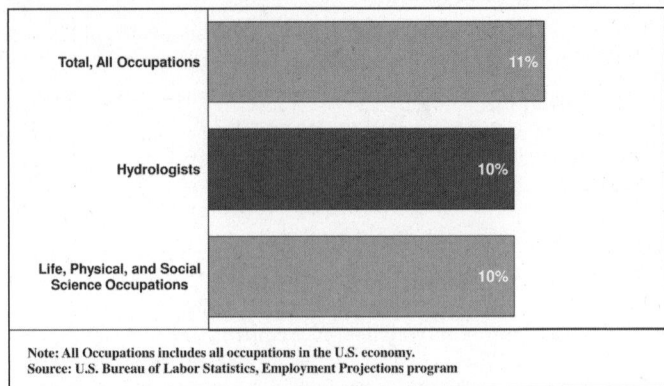

Note: All Occupations includes all occupations in the U.S. economy.
Source: U.S. Bureau of Labor Statistics, Employment Projections program

water contaminated by spilled chemicals at a factory, an airport or a gas station. Some groundwater hydrologists focus on water supply and decide the best locations for wells and the amount of water available for pumping. These hydrologists often give advice about the best places to build waste disposal sites to ensure that the waste does not contaminate the groundwater.

Surface water hydrologists study water from aboveground sources such as streams, lakes, and snow packs. They may predict future water levels by tracking usage and precipitation data to help reservoir managers decide when to release or store water. They also produce flood forecasts and help develop flood management plans.

Scientists with an education in hydrology who concentrate their efforts in the area of water quality are environmental scientists and specialists. Some people with a hydrology background become high school teachers or postsecondary teachers.

Work Environment

Hydrologists held about 7,400 jobs in 2012. The industries that employed the most hydrologists in 2012 were as follows:

Federal government, excluding postal service	29%
Management, scientific, and technical consulting services	20
Engineering services	18
State government, excluding education and hospitals	17
Local government, excluding education and hospitals	8

Hydrologists work in the field and in offices. In the field, hydrologists may have to wade into lakes and streams to collect samples or to read and inspect monitoring equipment. In the office, hydrologists spend much their time using computers to analyze data and model their findings. Hydrologists also need to write reports detailing the status of surface and ground water in specific regions. Many jobs require significant travel. Jobs in the private sector may require international travel.

Work Schedules. Most hydrologists work full time. However, the length of daily shifts may vary when hydrologists work in the field.

How to Become One

For most jobs, hydrologists need a master's degree with a focus in the natural sciences. Hydrologists may need a license in some states.

Education. Most hydrologists need a master's degree, but a bachelor's degree is adequate for some entry-level positions. Many hydrologists who enter the occupation at the bachelor's level have an education in a related subject that is not specific to hydrological issues, such as engineering. Applicants for advanced research and university faculty positions typically need a Ph.D.

Few universities offer undergraduate degrees in hydrology; instead, most universities offer hydrology concentrations in their geosciences, engineering, or earth science programs. Students interested in becoming hydrologists need extensive coursework in math, statistics, and physical, computer, and life sciences. Hydrologists may find it helpful to have a background in economics, environmental law, and other government policy related topics. Knowledge of these areas may help hydrologists communicate with and understand the goals of policy makers and other government workers.

Students who have experience with computer modeling, data analysis, and digital mapping will be the most prepared to enter the job market.

Important Qualities

Analytical skills. Hydrologists need to analyze data collected in the field and examine the results of laboratory tests.

Communication skills. Hydrologists prepare detailed reports that document their research methods and findings. They may have to present their findings to people who do not have a technical background, such as government officials or the general public.

Critical-thinking skills. Hydrologists assess the risks posed to the water supply by pollution, floods, droughts, and other threats. They develop water management plans to handle these threats.

Interpersonal skills. Most hydrologists work as part of a diverse team with engineers, technicians, and other scientists.

Physical stamina. When they are in the field, hydrologists may need to hike to remote locations while carrying testing and sampling equipment.

Employment Projections Data for Hydrologists

Occupational title	SOC Code	Employment, 2012	Projected Employment, 2022	Change, 2012–2022 Percent	Change, 2012–2022 Numeric
Hydrologists	19-2043	7,400	8,100	10	800

Source: U.S. Bureau of Labor Statistics, Employment Projections Program

Note: Data are rounded. Go to Occupational Information Included in the OOH *for a discussion of the data in this table.*

Similar Occupations This table shows a list of occupations with job duties that are similar to those of hydrologists.

Occupations	Entry-level Education	2012 Pay	Projected Job Growth	Average Annual Openings
Atmospheric Scientists, Including Meteorologists	Bachelor's degree	$89,260	10%	380
Civil Engineers	Bachelor's degree	$79,340	20%	12,010
Conservation Scientists and Foresters	Bachelor's degree	$59,354	3%	1,080
Environmental Engineers	Bachelor's degree	$80,890	15%	2,110
Environmental Science and Protection Technicians	Associate's degree	$41,240	19%	1,900
Environmental Scientists and Specialists	Bachelor's degree	$63,570	15%	3,970
Geoscientists	Bachelor's degree	$90,890	16%	1,730
Landscape Architects	Bachelor's degree	$64,180	14%	760
Postsecondary Teachers	See "How to Become One"	$70,380	19%	42,690
Surveyors	Bachelor's degree	$56,230	10%	1,340
Urban and Regional Planners	Master's degree	$65,230	10%	2,140

Pay

The median annual wage for hydrologists was $75,530 in May 2012. The median wage is the wage at which half the workers in an occupation earned more than that amount and half earned less. The lowest 10 percent earned less than $48,450 and the top 10 percent more than $112,840.

In May 2012, the median annual wages for hydrologists in the top five industries employing hydrologists were as follows:

Federal government, excluding postal service $84,540
Engineering services 80,310
Management, scientific, and technical consulting services ... 78,580
Local government, excluding education and hospitals 69,000
State government, excluding education and hospitals 63,450

Job Outlook

Employment of hydrologists is projected to grow 10 percent from 2012 to 2022, about as fast as the average for all occupations. Demand for the services of hydrologists will stem from increases in human activities such as mining, construction, and hydraulic fracturing. Environmental concerns, especially global climate change and the possibility of sea level rise in addition to local concerns such as flooding and drought, are likely to increase demand for hydrologists in the future.

Managing the nation's water resources will be critical as the population grows and increased human activity changes the natural water cycle. Population expansion into areas that were previously uninhabited may increase the risk of flooding, and new communities may encounter water availability issues. These issues will all need the understanding and knowledge that hydrologists have to find sustainable solutions.

More hydrologists will be necessary to assess the threats that global climate change poses to local, state, and national water supplies. For example, changes in climate affect the severity and frequency of droughts and floods. Hydrologists are critical to developing comprehensive water management plans that address these and other problems linked to climate change.

Job Prospects. Hydrologists with computer modeling experience will have the best opportunities in the future.

O*NET

➤ Hydrologists (19-2043.00)

Contacts for More Information

For more information about hydrology and the work of hydrologists in the federal government, visit
➤ United States Geological Survey (www.usgs.gov/)
   For more information about careers in hydrology, visit
➤ American Geosciences Institute (www.agiweb.org/)
➤ American Geophysical Union (http://sites.agu.org/)
➤ American Institute of Hydrology (www.aihydrology.org/)
➤ American Water Resources Association (www.awra.org/)

Medical Scientists

- **2012 Median Pay** .... $76,980 per year
  $37.01 per hour
- **Entry-Level Education** ... Doctoral or professional degree
- **Work Experience in a Related Occupation** .... None
- **On-the-Job Training** .... None
- **Number of Jobs 2012** 103,100
- **Job Outlook, 2012–22** .... 13% (As fast as average)
- **Employment Change, 2012–22** 13,700

What Medical Scientists Do

Medical scientists conduct research aimed at improving overall human health. They often use clinical trials and other investigative methods to reach their findings.

Duties. Medical scientists typically do the following:

- Conduct studies that investigate human diseases and methods of preventive care and treatment of diseases
- Develop instruments for medical applications
- Prepare and analyze medical samples and data to investigate causes and treatment of toxicity, pathogens, or chronic diseases
- Standardize drug potency, doses, and methods to allow for the mass manufacturing and distribution of drugs and medicinal compounds
- Work with health departments, industry personnel, and physicians to develop programs that improve health outcomes

- Apply for funding from government agencies and private funding sources, by writing research grant proposals
- Follow procedures to avoid contamination and maintain safety

Many medical scientists, especially in universities, work with little supervision, forming their own hypotheses and developing experiments, accordingly. They often lead teams of technicians, and sometimes students, who perform support tasks. For example, a medical scientist working in a university laboratory may have undergraduate assistants take measurements and make observations for the scientist's research.

Medical scientists study the causes of diseases and other health problems. For example, a medical scientist who does cancer research might put together a combination of drugs that could slow the cancer's progress. A clinical trial may be done to test the drugs. A medical scientist may work with licensed physicians, to test the new combination on patients who are willing to participate in the study.

In a clinical trial, patients agree to help determine if a particular drug, or combination of drugs, or other medical intervention works. Without knowing which group they are in, patients in a drug-related clinical trial either receive the trial drug or they receive a placebo, a pill or injection that looks like the trial drug but does not actually contain the drug.

Medical scientists analyze the data from all the patients in the clinical trial, to see how the trial drug performed. They compare the results to the control group that took the placebo and analyze the attributes of the participants. Publishing the findings is a very important final step in the process.

Medical scientists do research both to develop new treatments and to try to prevent health problems. For example, they may study the link between smoking and lung cancer or between diet and diabetes.

Medical scientists who work in private industry usually have to research the topics that benefit the company the most, rather than investigate their own interests. Although they may not have the pressure of writing grant proposals to get money for their research, they may have to explain their research plans to nonscientist managers or executives.

Medical scientists usually specialize in an area of research. The following are examples of types of medical scientists:

Cancer researchers research ways to prevent and cure cancers. They may specialize in one or more types of cancer.

Clinical and medical informaticians develop new ways to use large data sets. They look for explanations of health outcomes through the statistical analysis of existing data.

Clinical pharmacologists research, develop, and test existing and new drugs. They investigate the full effects drugs have on human

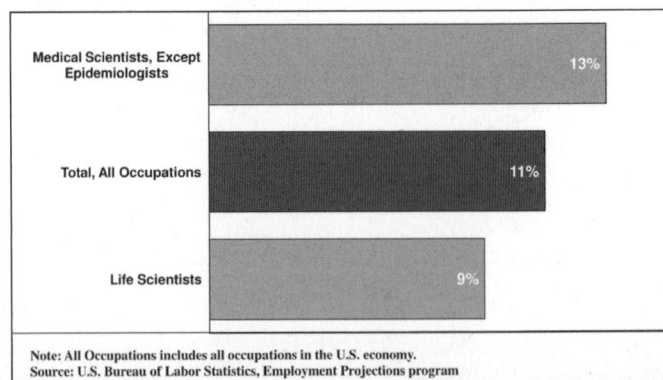

Medical scientists work in offices and laboratories.

health. Their interests may range from understanding specific molecules to the effects drugs have on large populations.

Gerontologists study the changes that people go through as they get older. Medical scientists who specialize in this field seek to understand the biology of aging and investigate ways to improve the quality of our later years.

Immunochemists investigate the reactions and effects various chemicals and drugs have on the human immune system.

Neuroscientists study the brain and nervous system.

Pharmacologists develop and research the effects of medicines.

Research histologists have a specific skill set that is used to research human tissue. They study how tissue grows, heals, and dies, and may investigate grafting techniques that can help people who have experienced serious injury.

Serologists research the serums, such as blood and saliva, found in the human body. Applied serologists often work in forensic sci-

Median Annual Wages, May 2012

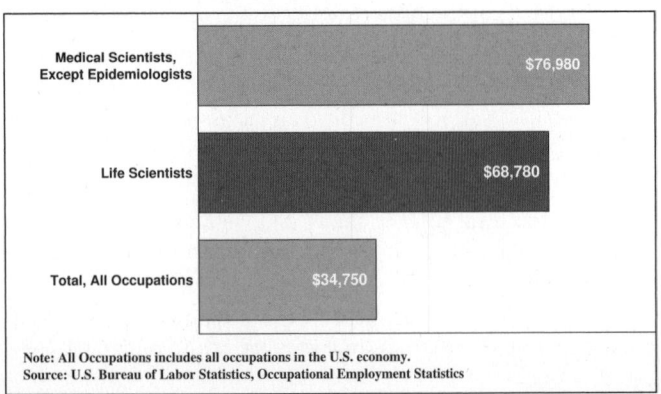

Medical Scientists, Except Epidemiologists	$76,980
Life Scientists	$68,780
Total, All Occupations	$34,750

Note: All Occupations includes all occupations in the U.S. economy.
Source: U.S. Bureau of Labor Statistics, Occupational Employment Statistics

Percent Change in Employment, Projected 2012–2022

Medical Scientists, Except Epidemiologists	13%
Total, All Occupations	11%
Life Scientists	9%

Note: All Occupations includes all occupations in the U.S. economy.
Source: U.S. Bureau of Labor Statistics, Employment Projections program

Employment Projections Data for Medical Scientists

Occupational title	SOC Code	Employment, 2012	Projected Employment, 2022	Change, 2012–2022 Percent	Change, 2012–2022 Numeric
Medical scientists, except epidemiologists 19-1042		103,100	116,800	13	13,700

Source: U.S. Bureau of Labor Statistics, Employment Projections Program

Note: Data are rounded. Go to **Occupational Information Included in the OOH** *for a discussion of the data in this table.*

ence. For more information on forensic science, see the profile on forensic science technicians.

Toxicologists research the harmful effects of drugs, household chemicals, and other potentially poisonous substances. They may ensure the safety of drugs by investigating safe dosage limits.

Work Environment

Medical scientists held about 103,100 jobs in 2012. The industries that employed the most medical scientists in 2012 were as follows:

Research and development in the physical, engineering, and life sciences	34%
Colleges, universities, and professional schools; state	21
General medical and surgical hospitals; private	10
Pharmaceutical and medicine manufacturing	8
Offices of physicians	4

Medical scientists usually work in offices and laboratories. They spend most of their time studying data and reports. Medical scientists sometimes work with dangerous biological samples and chemicals, but they take precautions that ensure a safe environment.

Work Schedules. Most medical scientists work full time.

How to Become One

Medical scientists typically need a Ph.D. from an accredited postsecondary institution. Some medical scientists get a medical degree instead of a Ph.D., but prefer doing research to practicing as a physician. It is helpful for medical scientists to have both a Ph.D. and a medical degree.

Education. Students planning careers as medical scientists typically pursue a bachelor's degree in biology, chemistry, or a related field. Undergraduate students benefit from taking a broad range of classes including life and physical sciences, mathematics, and disciplines that focus on developing communication skills. The importance of grant writing and publishing research findings makes writing skills essential.

After students have completed undergraduate studies, students typically enter Ph.D. programs. Dual degree programs are available that pair a Ph.D. with a range of specialized medical degrees. A few degree programs that are commonly paired with Ph.D. studies are Medical Doctor (M.D.), Doctor of Dental Surgery (D.D.S.), Doctor of Dental Medicine (D.M.D.), and Doctor of Osteopathic Medicine (D.O.). While Ph.D. studies focus on research methods, such as project design, students in dual degree programs learn both the clinical skills needed to be a physician and the research skills needed to be a scientist.

Graduate programs place additional emphasis on laboratory work and original research. These programs offer prospective medical scientists the opportunity to develop their experiments and, sometimes, to supervise undergraduates. Ph.D. programs culminate in a thesis that the candidate presents before a committee of professors. Students typically begin to specialize in one particular field, such as gerontology, neurology, or cancers, in this phase of their studies.

Those who go to medical school spend most of the first 2 years in labs and classrooms, taking courses such as anatomy, biochemistry, physiology, pharmacology, psychology, microbiology, pathology, medical ethics, and medical law. They also learn how to record medical histories, examine patients, and diagnose illnesses. They also may be required to participate in residency programs, as they will have to meet the same requirements that physicians and surgeons have to fulfill.

Medical scientists often continue their education with postdoctoral work. Postdoctoral work provides valuable lab experience, including experience in specific processes and techniques such as gene splicing, which is transferable to other research projects.

Licenses, Certifications, and Registrations. Medical scientists primarily conduct research and typically do not need licenses or certifications. However, those who administer drugs, gene therapy, or otherwise practice medicine on patients in clinical trials, or in a private practice, need a license to practice as a physician.

Similar Occupations   This table shows a list of occupations with job duties that are similar to those of medical scientists.

Occupations	Entry-level Education	2012 Pay	Projected Job Growth	Average Annual Openings
Agricultural and Food Scientists	See "How to Become One"	$58,636	10%	1,640
Biochemists and Biophysicists	Doctoral or professional degree	$81,480	18%	1,370
Epidemiologists	Master's degree	$65,270	12%	160
Health Educators and Community Health Workers	See "How to Become One"	$43,015	22%	4,740
Medical and Clinical Laboratory Technologists and Technicians	See "How to Become One"	$47,499	22%	15,600
Microbiologists	Bachelor's degree	$66,260	7%	710
Physicians and Surgeons	Doctoral or professional degree	$182,294	18%	29,630
Postsecondary Teachers	See "How to Become One"	$70,380	19%	42,690
Veterinarians	Doctoral or professional degree	$84,460	12%	3,100

Important Qualities

Communication skills. Communication is critical, because medical scientists must be able to explain their conclusions. In addition, medical scientists write grant proposals, which are often required to continue their research.

Critical-thinking skills. Medical scientists must use their expertise to determine the best method for solving a specific research question.

Data-analysis skills. Medical scientists use statistical techniques, so that they can properly quantify and analyze health research questions.

Decision-making skills. Medical scientists must use their expertise and experience to determine what research questions to ask, how best to investigate the questions, and what data will best answer the questions.

Observation skills. Medical scientists conduct experiments that require precise observation of samples and other health data. Any mistake could lead to inconclusive or misleading results.

Pay

The median annual wage for medical scientists was $76,980 in May 2012. The median wage is the wage at which half the workers in an occupation earned that amount and half earned less. The lowest 10 percent earned less than $41,340, and the top 10 percent earned more than $146,650.

In May 2012, the median annual wages for medical scientists in the top five industries employing these scientists were as follows:

Pharmaceutical and medicine manufacturing $92,940
Research and development in the physical,
  engineering, and life sciences 87,620
Offices of physicians 77,180
General medical and surgical hospitals; private 71,840
Colleges, universities, and professional schools; state 53,740

Job Outlook

Employment of medical scientists is projected to grow 13 percent between 2012 and 2022, about as fast as the average for all occupations.

An increased reliance on pharmaceuticals, greater affluence that allows for more spending on medicine–along with a larger and aging population, and a greater understanding of biological processes are all factors that are expected to increase demand for medical scientists. In addition, new discoveries should open frontiers in research that will require the services of medical scientists.

Employment of medical scientists should grow, as a result of expanded research related to illnesses such as AIDS, Alzheimer's disease, and cancer. Research into treatment problems, such as antibiotic resistance, also should spur growth. Moreover, higher population density and the increasing frequency of international travel will aid the spread of existing diseases and possibly give rise to new ones. Medical scientists will continue to be needed, because they contribute to the development of treatments and medicines that improve human health.

The federal government is a major source of funding for medical research. Large budget increases at the National Institutes of Health in the early part of the 2000s led to increases in federal basic research and development spending, with research grants growing in both number and dollar amount. However, increases in spending have slowed substantially in recent years. Going forward, the level of federal funding will continue to impact competition for winning and renewing research grants.

O*NET

➤ Medical Scientists, Except Epidemiologists (19-1042.00)

Contacts for More Information

For more information about some research specialties and opportunities within specialist fields for medical scientists, visit

➤ American Association for Cancer Research (www.aacr.org/)
➤ American Society for Biochemistry and Molecular Biology (www.asbmb.org/)
➤ American Society for Clinical Pharmacology and Therapeutics (www.ascpt.org/)
➤ Gerontological Society of America (www.geron.org/)
➤ Society for Neuroscience (www.sfn.org/)
➤ Society of Toxicology (www.toxicology.org/)

Microbiologists

- **2012 Median Pay** .... $66,260 per year
  $31.86 per hour
- **Entry-Level Education** .... Bachelor's degree
- **Work Experience in a Related Occupation** .... None
- **On-the-Job Training** .... None
- **Number of Jobs 2012** 20,100
- **Job Outlook, 2012–22** .... 7% (Slower than average)
- **Employment Change, 2012–22** 1,400

What Microbiologists Do

Microbiologists study microorganisms such as bacteria, viruses, algae, fungi, and some types of parasites. They try to understand how these organisms live, grow, and interact with their environments.

Duties. Microbiologists typically do the following:

- Plan and conduct complex research projects, such as developing new drugs to combat infectious diseases
- Supervise the work of biological technicians and other workers and evaluate the accuracy of their results
- Isolate and maintain cultures of bacteria or other microorganisms for study
- Identify and classify microorganisms found in specimens collected from humans, plants, animals, or the environment

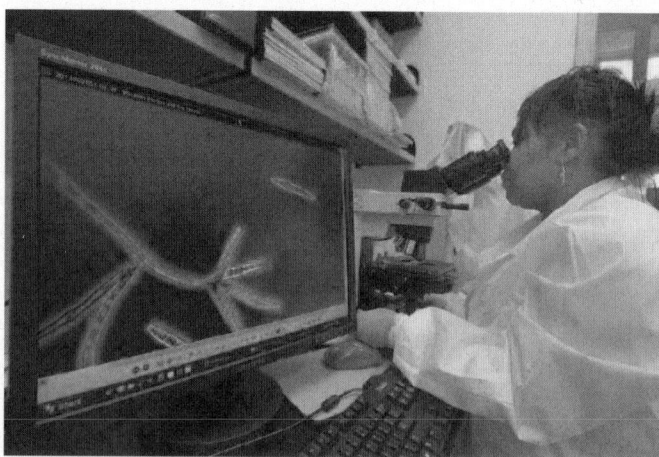

Research conducted by microbiologists has resulted in advanced treatments for many diseases.

Median Annual Wages, May 2012

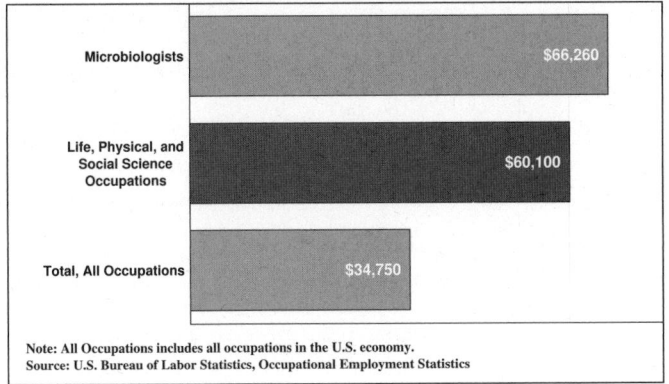

Note: All Occupations includes all occupations in the U.S. economy.
Source: U.S. Bureau of Labor Statistics, Occupational Employment Statistics

Percent Change in Employment, Projected 2012–2022

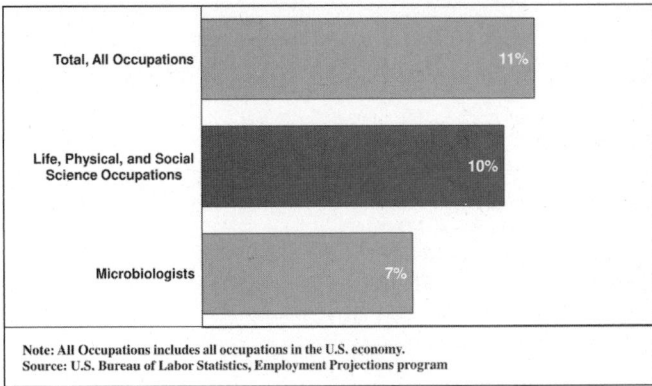

Note: All Occupations includes all occupations in the U.S. economy.
Source: U.S. Bureau of Labor Statistics, Employment Projections program

- Monitor the effect of microorganisms on plants, animals, other microorganisms, or the environment

- Keep up with current knowledge by reviewing the findings of other researchers and by attending conferences

- Prepare technical reports, publish research papers, and make recommendations based on their research findings

- Present research findings to scientists, non-scientist executives, engineers, other colleagues, and the public

Most microbiologists work in research and development. Many conduct basic research with the aim of increasing scientific knowledge. This may include growing strains of bacteria in various conditions to learn how they react to those conditions. Other microbiologists conduct applied research and develop new products or solve particular problems. Microbiologists who apply basic research to such problems may be developing genetically engineered crops or better biofuels.

Microbiologists use computers and a wide variety of sophisticated laboratory instruments to do their experiments. Electron microscopes are used to study bacteria and advanced computer software is used to analyze the growth of microorganisms found in samples.

It is increasingly common for microbiologists to work on teams with technicians and scientists in other fields, because many scientific research projects involve multiple disciplines. Microbiologists may work with medical scientists or biochemists while researching new drugs, or they may work in medical diagnostic laboratories alongside physicians and nurses to help prevent, treat, and cure diseases. For more information, see the profiles on biochemists and biophysicists, physicians and surgeons, and registered nurses.

The following are examples of types of microbiologists:

Bacteriologists study the growth, development, and other properties of bacteria, including the positive and negative effects that bacteria have on plants, animals, and humans.

Clinical microbiologists study how microorganisms live and interact with their environments so that they can later be used to cause, cure, or treat diseases in humans, plants, or animals. Clinical and medical microbiologists whose work is directly researching human health may be classified as medical scientists.

Environmental microbiologists study the ways in which microorganisms interact with the environment. They may study the use of microbes to clean up areas contaminated by heavy metals or study how microbes could aid crop growth.

Immunologists study how plant and animal immune systems react to and defend against pathogens or germs.

Industrial microbiologists work in industry and study and solve problems related to production. They may study microbial growth found in the pipes of a chemical factory, monitor the impact industrial waste has on the local ecosystem, or oversee the microbial activities used in cheese production.

Mycologists study the properties of fungi such as yeast and mold, as well as the ways fungi can be used (for example, in food or the environment) to benefit society.

Virologists study the structure, development, and other properties of viruses and any effects viruses have on infected organisms.

Many people with a microbiology background become high school teachers or professors. For more information, see the profiles on high school and postsecondary teachers.

Work Environment

Microbiologists held about 20,100 jobs in 2012. They typically work in laboratories and offices, where they conduct experiments and analyze the results. Microbiologists who work with dangerous organisms must follow strict safety procedures to avoid contamination. Some microbiologists collect samples from lakes, streams, and oceans, and spend some time outside as a result. Most microbiologists work full time and keep regular hours.

Basic researchers who work in academia usually choose the focus of their research and run their own laboratories. Applied researchers who work for companies study the products that the company will sell or suggest modifications to the production process so that it is more efficient. Basic researchers often need to fund their research by winning grants. These grants often put pressure on researchers to meet deadlines and other specifications. Research grants are generally awarded through a competitive selection process.

The industries that employed the most microbiologists in 2012 were as follows:

Pharmaceutical and medicine manufacturing 23%
Research and development in the physical,
    engineering, and life sciences 23
Federal government, excluding postal service 14
State and local government, excluding education
    and hospitals 11
Colleges, universities, and professional schools; state 9

Work Schedules. Most microbiologists work full time and keep regular hours.

How to Become One

A bachelor's degree in microbiology or a closely related field is needed for entry-level microbiologist jobs. A Ph.D. is needed to carry out independent research and to work in universities.

Employment Projections Data for Microbiologists

Occupational title	SOC Code	Employment, 2012	Projected Employment, 2022	Change, 2012–2022 Percent	Change, 2012–2022 Numeric
Microbiologists...	19-1022	20,100	21,600	7	1,400

Source: U.S. Bureau of Labor Statistics, Employment Projections Program

Note: Data are rounded. Go to **Occupational Information Included in the OOH** *for a discussion of the data in this table.*

Education. Microbiologists need at least a bachelor's degree in microbiology or a closely related field such as biochemistry or cell biology. Many colleges and universities offer degree programs in biological sciences, including microbiology.

Most microbiology majors take introductory courses in microbial genetics and microbial physiology before taking classes in more advanced topics such as environmental microbiology and virology. Students also must take classes in other sciences, such as biochemistry, chemistry, and physics, because it is important for microbiologists to have a broad understanding of the sciences. Courses in statistics, mathematics, and computer science are important for microbiologists because they must be able to do complex data analysis.

It is important for prospective microbiologists to have laboratory experience before entering the workforce. Most undergraduate microbiology programs include a mandatory laboratory requirement, but additional laboratory coursework is recommended. Students also can gain valuable laboratory experience through internships with prospective employers such as drug manufacturers.

Microbiologists typically need a Ph.D. to carry out independent research and work in colleges and universities. Graduate students studying microbiology commonly specialize in a subfield such as bacteriology or immunology. Ph.D. programs usually include class work, laboratory research, and completing a thesis or dissertation.

Training. Many microbiology Ph.D. holders begin their careers in temporary postdoctoral research positions. During their postdoctoral appointment, they work with experienced scientists as they continue to learn about their specialties or develop a broader understanding of related areas of research.

Postdoctoral positions typically offer the opportunity to publish research findings. A solid record of published research is essential to get a permanent position in basic research, especially a permanent faculty position at a college or university.

Important Qualities

Communication skills. Microbiologists should be able to effectively communicate their research processes and findings so that knowledge may be applied correctly.

Detail oriented. Microbiologists must be able to conduct scientific experiments and analyses with accuracy and precision.

Interpersonal skills. Microbiologists typically work on research teams and thus must work well with others toward a common goal. Many also lead research teams and must be able to motivate and direct other team members.

Logical-thinking skills. Microbiologists draw conclusions from experimental results through sound reasoning and judgment.

Math skills. Microbiologists regularly use complex mathematical equations and formulas in their work. Therefore, they need a broad understanding of mathematics, including calculus and statistics.

Observation skills. Microbiologists must constantly monitor their experiments. They need to keep a complete, accurate record of their work, noting conditions, procedures, and results.

Perseverance. Microbiological research involves substantial trial and error, and microbiologists must not become discouraged in their work.

Problem-solving skills. Microbiologists use scientific experiments and analysis to find solutions to complex scientific problems.

Advancement. Microbiologists typically receive greater responsibility and independence in their work as they gain experience. They also gain greater responsibility through more education. Ph.D. microbiologists usually lead research teams and control the direction and content of projects.

Some microbiologists move into managerial positions, often as natural sciences managers. Those who pursue management careers spend much of their time on administrative tasks such as preparing budgets and schedules.

Licenses, Certifications, and Registrations. Certifications are available for clinical microbiologists. They may help workers gain employment in the occupation or advance to new positions of responsibility. Certifications are not mandatory for the majority of work done by microbiologists.

Pay

The median annual wage for microbiologists was $66,260 in May 2012. The median wage is the wage at which half the workers in an occupation earned more than that amount and half earned less. The lowest 10 percent earned less than $39,720, and the top 10 percent earned more than $117,690.

In May 2012, the median annual wages for microbiologists in the top five industries in which these microbiologists worked were as follows:

Federal government, excluding postal service $96,520
Pharmaceutical and medicine manufacturing 67,070
Research and development in the physical, engineering, and life sciences 62,920
State and local government, excluding education and hospitals 54,640
Colleges, universities, and professional schools; state 52,790

Job Outlook

Employment of microbiologists is projected to grow 7 percent from 2012 to 2022, slower than the average for all occupations. More microbiologists will be needed to contribute to basic research, solve problems encountered in industrial production processes, and monitor environmental conditions to help ensure the public's health and safety.

The development of new medicines and treatments is expected to increase the demand for microbiologists in pharmaceutical and biotechnology research. Microbiologists will be needed to research and develop new medicines and treatments, such as vaccines and antibiotics that are used to fight infectious diseases. In addition, microbiologists will be needed to help pharmaceutical and biotechnology companies develop biological drugs that are produced with the aid of microorganisms.

Similar Occupations   This table shows a list of occupations with job duties that are similar to those of microbiologists.

Occupations	Entry-level Education	2012 Pay	Projected Job Growth	Average Annual Openings
Agricultural and Food Scientists	See "How to Become One"	$58,636	10%	1,640
Biochemists and Biophysicists	Doctoral or professional degree	$81,480	18%	1,370
Biological Technicians	Bachelor's degree	$39,750	10%	3,210
Chemical Technicians	Associate's degree	$42,920	9%	2,160
Epidemiologists	Master's degree	$65,270	12%	160
Medical and Clinical Laboratory Technologists and Technicians	See "How to Become One"	$47,499	22%	15,600
Medical Scientists	Doctoral or professional degree	$76,980	13%	3,550
Natural Sciences Managers	Bachelor's degree	$115,730	6%	1,370
Physicians and Surgeons	Doctoral or professional degree	$182,294	18%	29,630
Postsecondary Teachers	See "How to Become One"	$70,380	19%	42,690
Zoologists and Wildlife Biologists	Bachelor's degree	$57,710	5%	670

Aside from improving our health, other areas of research and development in biotechnology are expected to provide employment growth for microbiologists. Many companies, from food producers to chemical companies, will need microbiologists to ensure product quality and production efficiency. Increasing demand for clean energy should drive the need for microbiologists who research and develop alternative energy sources such as biofuels and biomass. In agriculture, more microbiologists will be needed to help develop genetically engineered crops that provide greater yields and require less pesticide and fertilizer. Finally, efforts to discover new and improved ways to preserve the environment and safeguard the public's health also will increase demand for microbiologists.

Job Prospects. Microbiology is a thriving field that should provide good prospects for qualified workers. Most of the applied research projects that microbiologists are involved in require the expertise of scientists in multiple fields such as biophysics, chemistry, and medicine. Microbiologists who have a solid understanding of microbiology and some familiarity with other disciplines should have the best opportunities.

Much of basic research depends on funding from the federal government through the National Institutes of Health, the National Science Foundation, and private venture capitalists. Federal budgetary decisions and venture capital availability will affect job prospects in basic research from year to year. There is strong competition among microbiologists for research funding. However, many opportunities for microbiologists should continue to be available.

O*NET

➤ Microbiologists (19-1022.00)

Contacts for More Information

For more information about microbiologists, visit
➤ American Society for Microbiology (www.asm.org/)
To find job openings for microbiologists in the federal government, visit
➤ USAJOBS (www.usajobs.gov/)
For general information about careers and specialties in biological sciences, visit
➤ American Institute of Biological Sciences (www.aibs.org)
➤ Federation of American Societies for Experimental Biology (www.faseb.org)

➤ Society for Industrial Microbiology and Biotechnology (www.simbhq.org/)
➤ American Society for Cell Biology (www.ascb.org/)
For information about microbiologists' tools and activities, visit
➤ The Virtual Urchin (http://virtualurchin.stanford.edu/)
For more information about microbiological topics, visit
➤ Microbiological Garden (www.pmbio.icbm.de/mikrobiologischer-garten/eng/index.php3)
➤ The Tree of Life Web Project (www.tolweb.org/tree/phylogeny.html)

Nuclear Technicians

- **2012 Median Pay** .... $69,060 per year
$33.20 per hour
- **Entry-Level Education** .... Associate's degree
- **Work Experience in a Related Occupation** .... None
- **On-the-Job Training** .... Moderate-term on-the-job training
- **Number of Jobs 2012** 8,100
- **Job Outlook, 2012–22** .... 15% (Faster than average)
- **Employment Change, 2012–22** 1,200

What Nuclear Technicians Do

Nuclear technicians typically work in nuclear power production or assist physicists, engineers, and other professionals in nuclear research. They operate special equipment used in these activities and monitor the levels of radiation that are produced.

Duties. Nuclear technicians typically do the following:

Monitor the performance of equipment used in nuclear experiments and power generation

- Measure the levels and types of radiation produced by nuclear experiments, power generation, and other activities
- Collect samples of air, water, and soil, and test for radioactive contamination
- Instruct personnel on radiation safety procedures and warn them when conditions are hazardous
- Maintain radiation monitoring and operating equipment

Job duties and titles of nuclear technicians often depend on where they work and what purpose the facility serves. Most nuclear technicians work in nuclear power plants, where they ensure that reactors and other equipment are operated safely and efficiently. The following are types of nuclear technicians who work in the power generation industry:

Operating technicians monitor the performance of systems in nuclear power plants. They measure levels of radiation and other contaminants in water systems that could indicate a leak or could decrease the efficiency of the turbines in the power plants. They measure efficiency and safety by making calculations based on factors such as temperature, pressure, and radiation intensity. Operating technicians must make adjustments and repairs to improve or maintain the performance of reactors and other equipment.

Radiation protection technicians monitor levels of contamination to protect personnel in nuclear power facilities and the local environment around a plant. They use radiation detectors to measure levels in and around facilities and dosimeters to measure the levels present in people and objects. They also monitor worker activity from a control room and alert personnel who may be entering a dangerous area or working in some other unsafe way. They use the data collected to map radiation levels throughout the plant and the surrounding environment. From their findings, they recommend radioactive decontamination plans and safety procedures for personnel.

Nuclear technicians also work in waste management and treatment facilities, where they monitor the disposal, recycling, and storage of nuclear waste. They perform duties similar to those of radiation protection technicians at nuclear power plants.

Other nuclear technicians work in laboratories. They help nuclear physicists, nuclear engineers, and other scientists conduct research and develop new types of nuclear reactors, fuels, medicines, and other technologies. They use equipment such as radiation detectors, spectrometers (used to measure gamma ray and X-ray radiation), and particle accelerators to conduct experiments and gather data. They also may use remote-controlled equipment to manipulate radioactive materials or materials exposed to radiation.

Work Environment

Nuclear technicians held about 8,100 jobs in 2012.

The industries that employed the most nuclear technicians in 2012 were as follows:

Electric power generation, transmission and distribution 50%
Engineering services.. 11
Research and development in the physical,
   engineering, and life sciences... 10
Management, scientific, and technical consulting services........ 9

In nuclear power plants, nuclear technicians typically work in offices and control rooms where they use computers and other

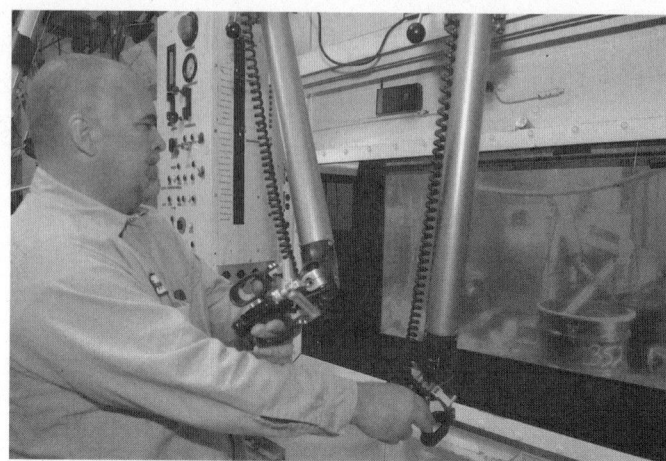

Nuclear technicians may use robotic arms and hands when working with nuclear materials.

equipment to monitor and help operate nuclear reactors. Nuclear technicians also need to measure radiation levels on-site, requiring them to visit several areas in and around the plant throughout the workday. This may require them to sometimes work outside, regardless of weather conditions. Working around nuclear reactors may involve exposure to high temperatures. Nuclear technicians who conduct scientific tests for scientists and engineers typically work in laboratories.

Nuclear technicians must take precautions when working with or around nuclear materials. They often have to wear protective gear and film badges that indicate if they have been exposed to radiation. Protective gear may include hard hats, hearing and eye protection, plastic suits, and respirators.

Work Schedules. Most nuclear technicians work full time. In power plants, which operate 24 hours a day, technicians may work variable schedules that include nights, holidays, and weekends. Occasionally plants stop operations for maintenance and upgrades. Workers may need to work overtime during these periods. In laboratories, technicians typically work during normal business hours.

How to Become One

Nuclear technicians typically enter the occupation with an associate's degree in nuclear science or a nuclear-related technology. Nuclear technicians also go through extensive on-the-job training. For safety and security reasons, nuclear technicians usually must undergo a background check and receive some type of security clearance after they are hired.

Median Annual Wages, May 2012

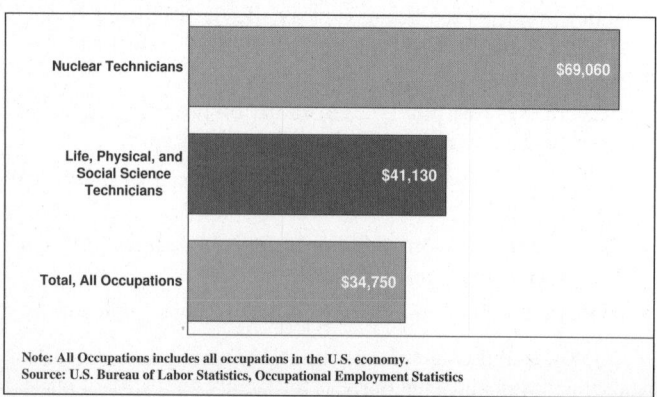

Nuclear Technicians — $69,060
Life, Physical, and Social Science Technicians — $41,130
Total, All Occupations — $34,750

Note: All Occupations includes all occupations in the U.S. economy.
Source: U.S. Bureau of Labor Statistics, Occupational Employment Statistics

Percent Change in Employment, Projected 2012–2022

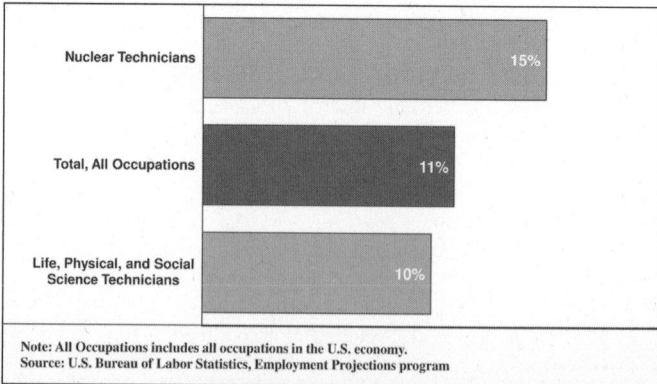

Nuclear Technicians — 15%
Total, All Occupations — 11%
Life, Physical, and Social Science Technicians — 10%

Note: All Occupations includes all occupations in the U.S. economy.
Source: U.S. Bureau of Labor Statistics, Employment Projections program

Employment Projections Data for Nuclear Technicians

Occupational title	SOC Code	Employment, 2012	Projected Employment, 2022	Change, 2012–2022 Percent	Change, 2012–2022 Numeric
Nuclear technicians 19-4051		8,100	9,300	15	1,200

Source: U.S. Bureau of Labor Statistics, Employment Projections Program

Note: Data are rounded. Go to **Occupational Information Included in the OOH** *for a discussion of the data in this table.*

Education. Nuclear technicians typically enter the occupation with an associate's degree, or after gaining equivalent experience in the Armed Forces, specifically the U.S. Navy. Many community colleges and technical institutes offer associate's degree programs in nuclear science, nuclear technology, or related fields. Students study nuclear energy, radiation, and the equipment and components used in nuclear power plants and laboratories. Other coursework includes mathematics, physics, and chemistry.

Training. In nuclear power plants, nuclear technicians start out as trainees under the supervision of more experienced technicians. During their training, they are taught the proper ways to use operating and monitoring equipment. They are also instructed on safety procedures, regulations, and plant policies. Workers who do not have the appropriate associate's degree or its equivalent usually have a significant period of on-site classroom training provided by their employer before they begin full duties and a normal training schedule.

Training varies with the technician's previous experience and education. Most training programs last between 6 months and 2 years. Nuclear technicians go through additional training and education throughout their careers to keep up with advances in nuclear science and technology.

Important Qualities

Communication skills. Nuclear technicians receive complex instructions from scientists and engineers that they must follow exactly. They have to be able to ask questions to clarify anything they do not understand. Nuclear technicians must be able to explain their work to scientists, engineers, and reactor operators. They must also instruct others on safety procedures and warn them when conditions are hazardous. Because of the risky nature of the work, many of the daily procedures and work processes must be thoroughly documented.

Computer skills. Nuclear technicians must be able to use computers for plant operations and for normal office work such as documenting their activities.

Critical-thinking skills. Nuclear technicians must carefully evaluate all available information before deciding on a course of action. For example, radiation protection technicians must evaluate data from radiation detectors to determine if areas are safe and develop decontamination plans if they are not safe.

Interpersonal skills. Nuclear technicians must be comfortable having open and honest discussions with supervisors because clear communication is very important to maintaining a high level of safety.

Math skills. Nuclear technicians use scientific and mathematical formulas to analyze experimental and production data such as reaction rates and radiation exposures.

Mechanical skills. Nuclear technicians need to have strong mechanical aptitude. Nuclear power facilities are complex, and workers need to understand how the facilities work in order to make adjustments and repairs to equipment and to maintain a safe working environment. Employers hiring nuclear technicians in nuclear power plants often conduct mechanical aptitude tests as part of the hiring process.

Monitoring skills. Nuclear technicians must be able to assess data from sensors, gauges, and other instruments to make sure that equipment and experiments are functioning properly and that radiation levels are controlled.

Advancement. With additional training and experience, technicians may become nuclear power reactor operators at nuclear power plants. Technicians can become nuclear engineers by earning a bachelor's degree in nuclear engineering. Nuclear physicists need a Ph.D. in physics. For more information, see the profiles on power plant operators, distributors, and dispatchers; nuclear engineers; and physicists and astronomers.

Pay

The median annual wage for nuclear technicians was $69,060 in May 2012. The median wage is the wage at which half the workers in an occupation earned more than that amount and half earned

Similar Occupations   This table shows a list of occupations with job duties that are similar to those of nuclear technicians.

Occupations	Entry-level Education	2012 Pay	Projected Job Growth	Average Annual Openings
Chemical Technicians	Associate's degree	$42,920	9%	2,160
Hazardous Materials Removal Workers	High school diploma or equivalent	$37,590	14%	1,340
Mechanical Engineering Technicians	Associate's degree	$51,980	5%	1,210
Nuclear Engineers	Bachelor's degree	$104,270	9%	710
Nuclear Medicine Technologists	Associate's degree	$70,180	20%	720
Occupational Health and Safety Technicians	High school diploma or equivalent	$47,440	10%	480
Physicists and Astronomers	Doctoral or professional degree	$105,722	10%	810
Power Plant Operators, Distributors, and Dispatchers	High school diploma or equivalent	$68,256	-8%	1,880

less. The lowest 10 percent earned less than $42,270, and the top 10 percent earned more than $97,300.

Job Outlook

Employment of nuclear technicians is projected to grow 15 percent from 2012 to 2022, faster than the average for all occupations. Most growth will be due to higher demand for nuclear energy, stemming from overall growth in energy demand and greater interest in energy sources that limit greenhouse gas emissions.

Greater interest in nuclear energy also is expected to increase demand for research in nuclear physics and nuclear engineering. Technicians will be needed to help scientists and engineers develop smaller and more efficient reactors, as well as fuels that are safer, last longer, and produce less waste.

Technicians are also expected to be in demand to develop nuclear medical technology, enforce waste management safety standards, and work in defense-related areas such as nuclear security.

Job Prospects. Nuclear technicians should have good job opportunities over the next decade. In the nuclear power industry, many openings should arise from technicians who retire or leave the occupation for other reasons.

O*NET

➤ Nuclear Technicians (19-4051.00)
➤ Nuclear Equipment Operation Technicians (19-4051.01)
➤ Nuclear Monitoring Technicians (19-4051.02)

Contacts for More Information

For more information about nuclear technicians, visit
➤ Center for Energy Workforce Development (www.cewd.org/)
➤ Get Into Energy (www.getintoenergy.com/)
➤ Nuclear Energy Institute (www.nei.org/)

Physicists and Astronomers

- **2012 Median Pay** .... $106,360 per year
  $51.14 per hour
- **Entry-Level Education** ... Doctoral or professional degree
- **Work Experience in a Related Occupation**.............. None
- **On-the-Job Training** .... None
- **Number of Jobs 2012** 23,300
- **Job Outlook, 2012–22** .... 10% (As fast as average)
- **Employment Change, 2012–22** 2,400

What Physicists and Astronomers Do

Physicists and astronomers study the ways in which various forms of matter and energy interact. Theoretical physicists and astronomers may study the nature of time or the origin of the universe. Physicists and astronomers in applied fields may develop new military technologies or new sources of energy, or monitor space debris that could endanger satellites.

Duties. Physicists and astronomers typically do the following:

- Develop scientific theories and models that attempt to explain the properties of the natural world, such as atom formation or the force of gravity
- Plan and conduct scientific experiments and studies to test theories and discover properties of matter and energy
- Write proposals and apply for research grants

- Do complex mathematical calculations to analyze physical and astronomical data, such as data that may indicate the existence of planets in distant solar systems
- Design new scientific equipment, such as telescopes and lasers
- Develop computer software to analyze and model data
- Write scientific papers that may be published in scholarly journals
- Present research findings at scientific conferences and lectures

Physicists explore the fundamental properties and laws that govern space, time, energy, and matter. Some physicists study theoretical areas, such as the fundamental properties of atoms and molecules and the evolution of the universe. Others design and perform experiments with sophisticated equipment such as particle accelerators, electron microscopes, and lasers. Through observation and analysis, they try to discover and formulate laws that explain the forces of nature, such as gravity, electromagnetism, and nuclear interactions. Others apply their knowledge of physics to practical areas, such as the development of advanced materials and medical equipment.

Astronomers study planets, stars, galaxies, and other celestial bodies. They use ground-based equipment, such as radio and optical telescopes, and space-based equipment, such as the Hubble Space Telescope. With these they make observations and collect data on the motions, compositions, and other properties of the objects they study. Some astronomers focus their research on objects in our own solar system, such as the sun or planets. Others study distant stars, galaxies, and phenomena such as neutron stars and black holes, and some monitor space debris that could interfere with satellite operations.

Many physicists and astronomers do basic research with the aim of increasing scientific knowledge. These researchers may attempt to develop theories that better explain what gravity is or how the universe works or was formed.

Other physicists and astronomers do applied research. They use the knowledge gained from basic research to develop new devices, processes, and other practical applications. Their work may lead to advances in areas such as energy, electronics, communications, navigation, and medical technology. Because of these workers, lasers can now be used in surgery and microwave ovens are in most kitchens.

Astronomers and physicists typically work on research teams with engineers, technicians, and other scientists. Some senior

Research jobs for physicists and astronomers usually require a Ph.D.

Median Annual Wages, May 2012

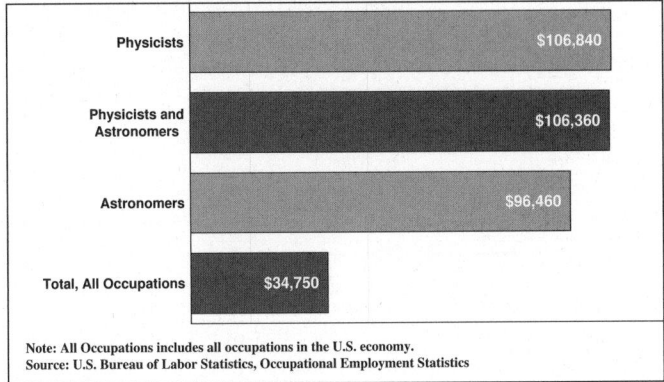

Note: All Occupations includes all occupations in the U.S. economy.
Source: U.S. Bureau of Labor Statistics, Occupational Employment Statistics

Percent Change in Employment, Projected 2012–2022

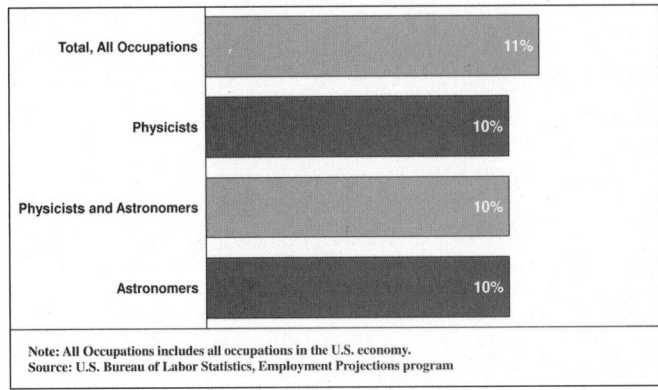

Note: All Occupations includes all occupations in the U.S. economy.
Source: U.S. Bureau of Labor Statistics, Employment Projections program

astronomers and physicists may be responsible for assigning tasks to other team members and monitoring their progress. They may also be responsible for finding funding for their projects and therefore may need to write applications for research grants.

Although all of physics involves the same fundamental principles, physicists generally specialize in one of many subfields. The following are examples of types of physicists:

Condensed matter physicists study the physical properties of condensed phases of matter, such as liquids and solids. They study phenomena ranging from superconductivity to liquid crystals.

Astrophysicists study the physics of the universe. Astrophysics is a term that is often used interchangeably with astronomy.

Particle and nuclear physicists study the properties of atomic and subatomic particles, such as quarks, electrons, and nuclei, and the forces that cause their interactions.

Medical physicists work in healthcare and use their knowledge of physics to develop new medical technologies and radiation-based treatments. For example, some develop better and safer radiation therapies for cancer patients. Others may develop more accurate imaging technologies that use various forms of radiant energy, such as magnetic resonance imaging (MRI) and ultrasound imaging.

Atomic, molecular, and optical physicists study atoms, simple molecules, electrons, and light, and their interactions. Some look for ways to control the states of individual atoms, which might allow for further miniaturization, or contribute toward the development of new materials or computer technology.

Plasma physicists study plasmas, which are considered a distinct state of matter and occur naturally in stars and interplanetary space and artificially in neon signs and plasma screen televisions. Many plasma physicists study ways to create possible fusion reactors that might be a future source of energy.

Unlike physicists, astronomers cannot do experiments on their subjects because they are so far away that they cannot be touched or interacted with. Therefore, astronomers generally make observations or work on theory. Observational astronomers observe and collect data. Theoretical astronomers analyze, model, and theorize about how systems work and evolve. Some astronomers specialize further into other subfields. The following are examples of types of astronomers who specialize by the objects and phenomena they study:

Planetary astronomers focus on the birth, evolution, and death of planets. They may try to discover planets outside our galaxy.

Stellar astronomers study stars, black holes, nebulae, white dwarfs, and supernovas.

Solar astronomers study the sun. They study the sun's many complex systems, such as its atmospheres, magnetic field, and they investigate new ways to study it.

Galactic astronomers study the Milky Way galaxy, the galaxy in which we live.

Cosmologists and *extragalactic astronomers* study the entire universe. They study the history, creation and evolution, and the possible futures of the universe and its galaxies. These scientists have recently developed several theories important to the study of physics and astronomy, including string, dark matter, and dark energy theories.

The following are examples of astronomers who specialize by how they study objects and phenomena:

High-energy astrophysicists study objects or phenomena by collecting and analyzing X-rays, gamma rays, and other forms of high-energy rays that can help locate and study black holes or neutron stars.

Optical astronomers use optical telescopes, which collect visible light, to study their subjects. Telescopes that collect visible light often have digital cameras that create an image on computer screens.

Radio astronomers analyze the radio spectrum for data about their subjects. These astronomers often study quasars, which are the high-energy nuclei of distant galaxies, and were the first to find compelling evidence for the Big Bang theory.

Theoretical astronomers generally do not collect data through observation, but analyze large data sets that others collect to create new theories or find new anomalies.

Growing numbers of physicists work in interdisciplinary fields, such as biophysics, chemical physics, and geophysics. For more information, see the profiles on biochemists and biophysicists and geoscientists.

Many people with a physics or astronomy background become professors or teachers. For more information, see the profiles on high school teachers and postsecondary teachers.

Work Environment

Physicists held about 20,600 jobs and astronomers held about 2,700 jobs in 2012. The industries that employed the most physicists in 2012 were as follows:

Research and development in the physical,
    engineering, and life sciences 29%
Colleges, universities, and professional schools;
    state, local, and private 19
Federal government, excluding postal service 16
Management, scientific, and technical consulting services 7
Hospitals; state, local, and private 5

Employment Projections Data for Physicists and Astronomers

Occupational title	SOC Code	Employment, 2012	Projected Employment, 2022	Change, 2012–2022	
				Percent	Numeric
Astronomers and physicists................................	—	23,300	25,700	10	2,400
Astronomers................................	19-2011	2,700	2,900	10	300
Physicists................................	19-2012	20,600	22,700	10	2,100

Source: *U.S. Bureau of Labor Statistics, Employment Projections Program*

Note: *Data are rounded. Go to* Occupational Information Included in the OOH *for a discussion of the data in this table.*

The industries that employed the most astronomers in 2012 were as follows:

Colleges, universities, and professional schools; state, local, and private................................	54%
Research and development in the physical, engineering, and life sciences................................	21
Federal government, excluding postal service................................	19

The National Aeronautics and Space Administration (NASA) and the U.S. Department of Defense are two of the largest employers of physicists and astronomers in the federal government. The scientific research-and-development industry includes both private and federally funded national laboratories, such as the Fermi National Accelerator Laboratory in Illinois and the Goddard Institute in Maryland.

Physics research is usually done in small- or medium-sized laboratories. However, experiments in some areas of physics, such as nuclear and high-energy physics, may require extremely large and expensive equipment, such as particle accelerators and nuclear reactors. Although physics research may require extensive experimentation in laboratories, physicists still spend much of their time in offices, planning, analyzing, fundraising, and reporting on research.

Most astronomers work in offices, and may visit observatories a few times a year. An observatory is a building that houses ground-based telescopes used to gather data and make observations. Some astronomers may work full time in observatories.

Increasingly, observations are done remotely via the Internet without the need for travel to an observatory. Observational astronomers rarely look through a telescope with their eyes, but rather use computers and sophisticated telescopes that can detect radiation other than visible light, such as gamma rays or radio waves. Rather than making direct observations, theoretical astronomers typically use the data from observational astronomers to develop their theories.

Some physicists and astronomers temporarily work away from home at national or international facilities that have unique equipment, such as particle accelerators and gamma ray telescopes. They also frequently travel to meetings to present research results, discuss ideas with colleagues, and learn more about new developments in their field.

Work Schedules. Most physicists and astronomers work full time. Astronomers may need to work at night, as radiation from the sun tends to interfere less with observations made during those hours. Most astronomers typically only visit observatories a few times per year and therefore keep normal office hours.

How to Become One

Physicists and astronomers need a Ph.D. for most jobs. After receiving a Ph.D. in physics or astronomy, many researchers seeking careers in academia begin in temporary postdoctoral research positions.

Education. A Ph.D. in physics, astronomy, or a related field is needed for most jobs, especially jobs that do basic research or for independent research positions in industry.

Graduate students usually concentrate in a subfield of physics or astronomy, such as condensed matter physics or cosmology. In addition to taking courses in physics or astronomy, Ph.D. students need to take courses in mathematics, such as calculus, linear algebra, and statistics. Computer science classes are also essential, because physicists and astronomers often develop specialized computer programs that are used to gather, analyze, and model data.

Those with a master's degree in physics may qualify for jobs in applied research and development for manufacturing and healthcare companies. Many master's degree programs specialize in preparing students for physics-related research-and-development positions that do not require a Ph.D.

Most physics and astronomy graduate students have bachelor's degrees in physics or a related field. Because astronomers need a strong background in physics, a bachelor's degree in physics is often considered good preparation for Ph.D. programs in astronomy, though an undergraduate degree in astronomy may be preferred by some universities. Undergraduate physics programs provide a broad background in the natural sciences and mathematics. Typical courses include classical and quantum mechanics, thermodynamics, optics, and electromagnetism.

Those with only a bachelor's degree in physics or astronomy typically are not qualified to fill research positions. However, they may be qualified to work as technicians and research assistants in related fields, such as engineering and computer science. Those with a bachelor's degree in astronomy may also qualify to work as an assistant at an observatory. Students who do not want to continue their studies to the doctorate level may want to take courses in instrument building and computer science.

Some master's degree and bachelor's degree holders may become science teachers in middle schools and high schools. For more information, see the profiles on middle school teachers and high school teachers.

Training. Many physics and astronomy Ph.D. holders who seek employment as full-time researchers begin their careers in a temporary postdoctoral research position, which typically lasts 2 to 3 years. During their postdoctoral appointment, they work with experienced scientists as they continue to learn about their specialties or develop a broader understanding of related areas of research. Their initial work may be carefully supervised by senior scientists, but as they gain experience, they usually do more complex tasks and have greater independence in their work.

Important Qualities

Analytical skills. Physicists and astronomers need to be able to think logically to carry out scientific experiments and studies. They must be precise and accurate in their analysis because errors could invalidate their research. They must also be able to find and use funding effectively.

Similar Occupations   This table shows a list of occupations with job duties that are similar to those of physicists and astronomers.

Occupations	Entry-level Education	2012 Pay	Projected Job Growth	Average Annual Openings
Aerospace Engineers	Bachelor's degree	$103,720	7%	2,540
Biochemists and Biophysicists	Doctoral or professional degree	$81,480	18%	1,370
Chemists and Materials Scientists	Bachelor's degree	$73,247	6%	3,040
Civil Engineers	Bachelor's degree	$79,340	20%	12,010
Computer and Information Research Scientists	Doctoral or professional degree	$102,190	15%	830
Computer Hardware Engineers	Bachelor's degree	$100,920	7%	2,410
Electrical and Electronics Engineers	Bachelor's degree	$89,701	4%	7,940
Geoscientists	Bachelor's degree	$90,890	16%	1,730
Mathematicians	Master's degree	$101,360	23%	170
Mechanical Engineers	Bachelor's degree	$80,580	4%	9,970
Nuclear Engineers	Bachelor's degree	$104,270	9%	710
Postsecondary Teachers	See "How to Become One"	$70,380	19%	42,690

Communication skills. Physicists and astronomers present their research at scientific conferences, to the public, or to government and business leaders. Physicists and astronomers write technical reports that may be published in scientific journals. They also write proposals for research funding.

Critical-thinking skills. Physicists and astronomers must carefully evaluate their own work and the work of others. They must determine whether results and conclusions are based on sound science.

Curiosity. Physicists and astronomers work in fields that are always on the cutting edge of technology. They must be very keen to learn continuously for their career. In-depth knowledge must be gained on a wide range of technical subjects, from computer programming to particle colliders.

Interpersonal skills. Physicists and astronomers must collaborate extensively with others–in both academic and industrial research contexts. They need to be able to work well with others toward a common goal. Interpersonal skills should also help researchers secure funding for their projects.

Math skills. Physicists and astronomers perform complex calculations involving calculus, geometry, algebra, and other areas of mathematics. They must be able to express their research in mathematical terms.

Problem-solving skills. Physicists and astronomers use scientific observation and analysis to solve complex scientific questions. Creative thinking may be needed to solve these complex scientific problems.

Self-discipline. Physicists and astronomers spend a lot of time working alone and need to be able to stay motivated as well as accurate in their work.

Licenses, Certifications, and Registrations. Some positions with the federal government, such as those involving nuclear energy and other sensitive research areas, may require applicants to be U.S. citizens and hold a security clearance.

Advancement. With experience, physicists and astronomers may gain greater independence in their work, larger research budgets, or tenure in university positions. Some physicists and astronomers move into managerial positions, typically as a natural sciences manager, and spend a large part of their time preparing budgets and schedules. Physicists and astronomers need a Ph.D. for most

management positions. For more information, see the profile on natural sciences managers.

Pay

The median annual wage for physicists was $106,840 in May 2012. The median wage is the wage at which half the workers in an occupation earned more than that amount and half earned less. The lowest 10 percent earned less than $57,640, and the top 10 percent earned at least $176,630.

In May 2012, the median annual wages for physicists in the top five industries in which these scientists worked were as follows:

Hospitals; state, local, and private $152,280
Management, scientific, and technical
    consulting services.. 130,980
Federal government, excluding postal service 111,020
Research and development in the physical,
    engineering, and life sciences....................................... 104,650
Colleges, universities, and professional schools;
    state, local, and private...................................... 81,180

The median annual wage for astronomers was $96,460 in May 2012. The lowest 10 percent earned less than $51,270, and the top 10 percent earned more than $165,300.

In May 2012, the median annual wages for astronomers in the top three industries in which these scientists worked were as follows:

Federal government, excluding postal service $139,140
Research and development in the physical,
    engineering, and life sciences... 93,870
Colleges, universities, and professional schools;
    state, local, and private...................................... 77,870

Pay for physicists or astronomers in postdoctoral positions is typically near the lower 10 percent values shown above.

Job Outlook

Employment of physicists and astronomers is expected to increase by 14 percent from 2010 to 2020, as fast as the average for all occupations.

Expected growth in federal government spending for physics and astronomy research should increase the need for physicists and astronomers, especially at colleges and universities and national laboratories.

Federal spending is the primary source of physics- and astronomy-related research funds, especially for basic research. Additional federal funding for energy and for advanced manufacturing research is expected to increase the need for physicists. Funding growth for astronomy research is expected to be smaller because of the limited applications of work in astronomy.

Declines in basic research are expected to be offset by growth in applied research in private industry. People with a physics background will continue to be in demand in medicine, information technology, communications technology, semiconductor technology, and other applied research-and-development fields.

Job Prospects. Competition for permanent research appointments, such as those at colleges and universities, is expected to be strong. Increasingly, those with a Ph.D. need to work through multiple postdoctoral appointments before finding a permanent position. In addition, the number of research proposals submitted for funding has been growing faster than the amount of funds available, causing more competition for research grants.

Despite competition for traditional research jobs, prospects should be good for physicists in applied research, development, and related technical fields. Graduates with any academic degree in physics or astronomy, from bachelor's degree to doctorate, will find their knowledge of science and mathematics useful for entry into many other occupations.

A large part of physics and astronomy research depends on federal funds, so federal budgets have a large impact on job prospects from year to year. This is especially true for astronomers, who are more likely than physicists to depend on federal funding for their work.

O*NET

➤ Astronomers (19-2011.00)
➤ Physicists (19-2012.00)

Contacts for More Information

For more information about astronomy careers and for a listing of colleges and universities offering astronomy programs, visit
➤ American Astronomical Society (http://aas.org/)

For more information about physics careers and education, visit
➤ American Institute of Physics (www.aip.org/)
➤ American Physical Society (www.aps.org/)

To find job openings for physicists and astronomers in the federal government, visit
➤ USAJOBS (www.usajobs.gov/)

Political Scientists

- **2012 Median Pay** .... $102,000 per year
  $49.04 per hour
- **Entry-Level Education** ....Master's degree
- **Work Experience in a Related Occupation**............... None
- **On-the-Job Training** .... None
- **Number of Jobs 2012** 6,600
- **Job Outlook, 2012–22** .... 21% (Faster than average)
- **Employment Change, 2012–22** 1,400

What Political Scientists Do

Political scientists study the origin, development, and operation of political systems. They research political ideas and analyze governments, policies, political trends, and related issues.

Duties. Political scientists typically do the following:

- Research political subjects, such as the U.S. political system, relations between the United States and foreign countries, and political ideologies
- Collect and analyze data from sources such as public opinion surveys and election results
- Use qualitative sources, such as historical documents, to develop theories
- Use quantitative methods, such as statistical analysis, to test theories
- Evaluate the effects of policies and laws on government, businesses, and people
- Monitor current events, policy decisions, and other issues relevant to their work
- Forecast political, economic, and social trends
- Present research results by writing reports, giving presentations, and publishing articles

Political scientists usually conduct research within one of four primary subfields: American politics, comparative politics, international relations, or political theory.

Often, political scientists use qualitative methods in their research, gathering information from numerous sources. For example, they may use historical documents to analyze past government structures and policies.

Political scientists also rely heavily on quantitative methods to develop and research theories. For example, they may analyze data to see whether a relationship exists between a certain political system and a particular outcome. In so doing, political scientists can study topics such as U.S. political parties, how political structures differ among countries, globalization, and the history of political thought.

Political scientists also work as policy analysts. In this position, they may work for a variety of organizations that have a stake in policy, such as government, labor, and political organizations. They also evaluate current policies and events using public opinion surveys, economic data, and election results. From these sources, they can learn the expected impact of new policies.

Political scientists sometimes work with teams of research assistants.

Median Annual Wages, May 2012

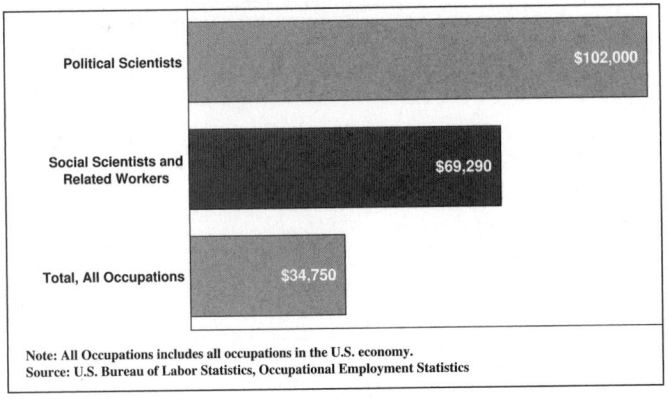

Note: All Occupations includes all occupations in the U.S. economy.
Source: U.S. Bureau of Labor Statistics, Occupational Employment Statistics

Percent Change in Employment, Projected 2012–2022

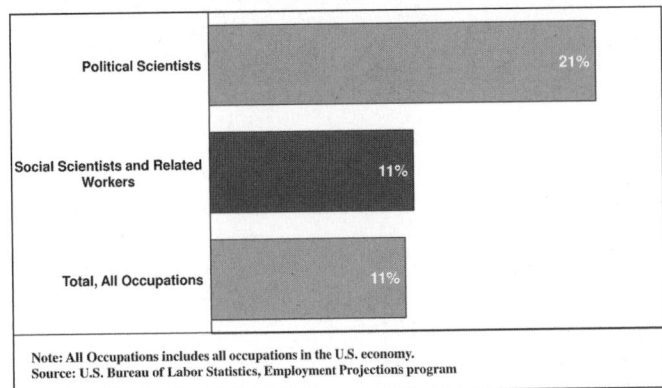

Note: All Occupations includes all occupations in the U.S. economy.
Source: U.S. Bureau of Labor Statistics, Employment Projections program

Political scientists often research the specific effects of government policies on a particular region or population, both domestically and internationally. In doing so, they can examine how a particular policy affects a social group, economy, or environment. They provide information and analysis that help in planning, developing, or carrying out policies.

Many people with a political science background become postsecondary teachers and high school teachers.

Work Environment

Political scientists held about 6,600 jobs in 2012. About half worked for the federal government. Others worked for think tanks, nonprofit organizations, colleges and universities, political lobbying groups, and labor organizations.

Work Schedules. Political scientists work full time in an office. They may work overtime to finish reports and meet deadlines.

How to Become One

Political scientists need a master's degree or Ph.D. in political science, public administration, or a related field.

Education. Jobseekers with a bachelor's degree in political science usually qualify for entry-level positions in many related fields. Some qualify for entry-level positions as research assistants for research organizations, political campaigns, nonprofit organizations, or government agencies. Many go into fields outside of politics and policymaking, such as business or law.

Most political scientists need to complete either a master's or Ph.D. program. To be admitted to a graduate program, applicants should complete undergraduate courses in political science, writing, and statistics. Applicants also benefit from having related work or internship experience. Working in an internship on a congressional staff or for a research organization will help applicants gain experience writing, researching, analyzing data, or working with policy issues.

Political scientists often complete a master of public administration (MPA), master of public policy (MPP), or master of public affairs degree. These programs usually combine several disciplines,

and students can choose to concentrate in a specific area of interest. Most offer core courses in research methods, policy formation, program evaluation, and statistics. Some colleges and universities also offer master's degrees in political science, international relations, or other applied political science specialties.

Political scientists can also complete a Ph.D. program, which requires several years of coursework followed by independent research for a dissertation. Most Ph.D. candidates choose to specialize in one of four primary subfields of political science: American politics, comparative politics, international relations, or political theory.

Political scientists who teach at colleges and universities need a Ph.D. Graduates with a master's degree in political science sometimes become postsecondary teachers and high school teachers.

Other Experience. Jobseekers who have earned a bachelor's degree can benefit from internships or volunteer work when looking for entry-level positions in political science or a related field. They give students a chance to apply their academic knowledge in a professional setting and develop skills needed for the field.

Important Qualities

Analytical skills. Political scientists often use qualitative and quantitative research methods. They rely on their analytical skills when they collect, evaluate, and interpret data.

Critical-thinking skills. Political scientists must be able to examine and process available information and draw logical conclusions from their findings.

Intellectual curiosity. Political scientists must continually explore new ideas and information to produce original papers and research. They must stay current on political subjects and come up with new ways to think about and address issues.

Writing skills. Writing skills are essential for those who write papers on political issues. They must be able to convey their research results clearly.

Pay

The median annual wage for political scientists was $102,000 in May 2012. The median wage is the wage at which half the workers

Employment Projections Data for Political Scientists

Occupational title	SOC Code	Employment, 2012	Projected Employment, 2022	Change, 2012–2022	
				Percent	Numeric
Political scientists...	19-3094	6,600	8,000	21	1,400

Source: U.S. Bureau of Labor Statistics, Employment Projections Program

Note: Data are rounded. Go to **Occupational Information Included in the OOH** *for a discussion of the data in this table.*

Similar Occupations This table shows a list of occupations with job duties that are similar to those of political scientists.

Occupations	Entry-level Education	2012 Pay	Projected Job Growth	Average Annual Openings
Anthropologists and Archeologists	Master's degree	$57,420	19%	260
Economists	Master's degree	$91,860	14%	740
Market Research Analysts	Bachelor's degree	$60,300	32%	18,850
Postsecondary Teachers	See "How to Become One"	$70,380	19%	42,690
Sociologists	Master's degree	$74,960	15%	110
Survey Researchers	Master's degree	$45,050	18%	560
Urban and Regional Planners	Master's degree	$65,230	10%	2,140

in an occupation earned more than that amount and half earned less. The lowest 10 percent earned less than $49,290, and the top 10 percent earned more than $155,490.

In May 2012, the median annual wages for political scientists in the top three industries employing political scientists were as follows:

Federal government, excluding postal service $115,740
Scientific research and development services 99,500
Colleges, universities, and professional schools;
   state, local, and private...................................... 65,030

Job Outlook

Employment of political scientists is projected to grow 21 percent from 2012 to 2022, faster than the average for all occupations. However, because it is a small occupation, the fast growth will result in only about 1,400 new jobs over the 10-year period.

Employment will increase in response to a growing interest in public policy and political issues. There will be demand for job-seekers with extensive knowledge of political systems, institutions, and policies.

Political organizations, lobbying firms, and many nonprofit, labor, and social organizations will rely on the knowledge of political scientists to manage complicated legal and regulatory issues and policies. Political scientists will also be needed at think- tanks to focus specifically on politics and political theory. Organizations that research or advocate for specific causes, such as immigration, healthcare, or the environment, will also need political scientists to analyze policies relating to their field.

The federal government employs about half of all political scientists, and political scientists will continue to be needed in the government to assess the impact of government policies, such as the efficiencies of public services, effects of departmental cuts, and advantages of proposed improvements.

Job Prospects. Political scientists should face strong competition for most jobs. The small number of positions, combined with the popularity of political science programs in colleges and universities, means that there will likely be many qualified candidates for relatively few positions.

Candidates with a graduate degree, strong writing and analytical skills, and experience researching or performing policy analysis should have the best job prospects. Candidates who have specialized knowledge or experience in their field of interest will also have better job opportunities.

Some candidates with a bachelor's degree in political science may find entry-level jobs as assistants and research assistants. Many will also find positions outside of politics and policy in fields such as business and law.

O*NET

➤ Political Scientists (19-3094.00)

Contacts for More Information

For more information about political scientists, visit
➤ American Political Science Association (www.apsanet.org)

For more information about college programs in public affairs and administration, visit
➤ National Association of Schools of Public Affairs and Administration (www.naspaa.org/)

Psychologists

- **2012 Median Pay** .... $69,280 per year
                                         $33.31 per hour
- **Entry-Level Education** ....See "How to Become One"
- **Work Experience in a Related Occupation**............... None
- **On-the-Job Training** .... Internship/residency
- **Number of Jobs 2012** 160,200
- **Job Outlook, 2012–22**................ 12% (As fast as average)
- **Employment Change, 2012–22** 18,700

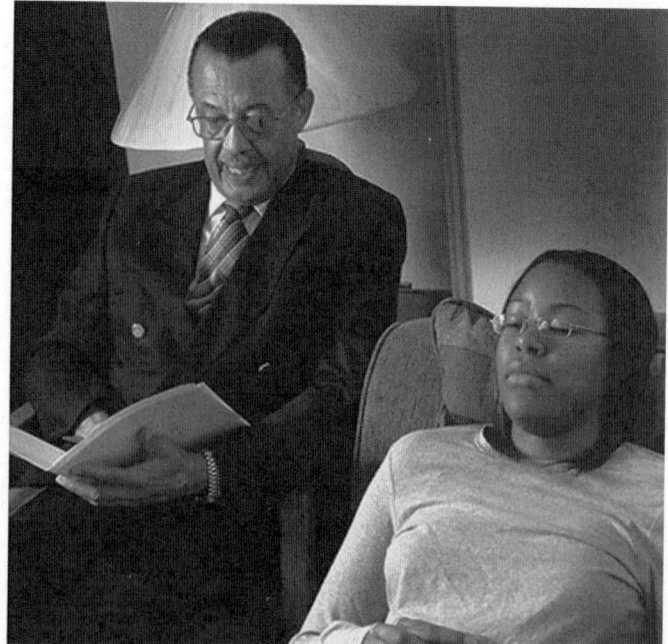

Psychologists who deal directly with patients must be emotionally stable, mature, sensitive, and have strong communication skills.

What Psychologists Do

Psychologists study cognitive, emotional, and social processes and human behavior by observing, interpreting, and recording how people relate to one another and their environments.

Duties. Psychologists typically do the following:

- Conduct scientific studies of behavior and brain function
- Collect information through observations, interviews, surveys, and other methods
- Research and identify behavioral or emotional patterns
- Test for patterns that will help them better understand and predict behavior
- Use their knowledge to increase understanding among individuals and groups

Psychology seeks to understand and explain thoughts, emotions, feelings, and behavior. Depending on the topic of study, psychologists use techniques such as observation, assessment, and experimentation to develop theories about the beliefs and feelings that influence a person's actions.

Psychologists often gather information and evaluate behavior through controlled laboratory experiments, psychoanalysis, or psychotherapy. They also may administer personality, performance, aptitude, or intelligence tests. They look for relationships or patterns of behavior between events, and use this information when testing theories in their research or treating patients.

The following are examples of types of psychologists:

Clinical psychologists assess, diagnose, and treat mental, emotional, and behavioral disorders. Clinical psychologists help people deal with problems ranging from short-term personal issues to severe, chronic conditions.

Clinical psychologists are trained to use a variety of approaches to help individuals. Although strategies generally differ by specialty, clinical psychologists often interview patients, give diagnostic tests, and provide individual, family, or group psychotherapy. They also design behavior modification programs and help patients implement their particular program.

Some clinical psychologists focus on certain populations, such as children or the elderly, or certain specialties, such as the following:

- *Health psychologists* study how psychological factors affect health and illness. They educate both patients and medical staff on psychological issues and promote healthy-living strategies. They also investigate health issues, such as substance abuse or teenage pregnancy, and develop programs to address the problems.

- *Neuropsychologists* study the relation between the brain and behavior. They typically work with patients who have sustained a brain injury.

Clinical psychologists often consult with other medical personnel regarding the best treatment for patients, especially treatment that includes medication. Two states, Louisiana and New Mexico, currently allow clinical psychologists to prescribe medication to patients. In most states, however, only psychiatrists and medical doctors may prescribe medication for treatment. See the profile on physicians and surgeons for more information.

Counseling psychologists advise people on how to deal with problems. They help patients understand problems, including issues at home, at the workplace, or in their community. Through counseling, they work with patients to identify their strengths or resources they can use to manage problems. For more information, see the profiles on mental health counselors and marriage and family therapists, substance abuse and behavioral disorder counselors, and social workers.

Developmental psychologists study the psychological progress and development that takes place throughout life. Many developmental psychologists focus on children and adolescents, but they also may study aging and problems facing the elderly.

Forensic psychologists use psychological principles in the legal and criminal justice system to help judges, attorneys, and other legal specialists understand the psychological aspects of a particular case. They often testify in court as expert witnesses. They typically specialize in family court, civil court, or criminal court.

Industrial-organizational psychologists apply psychology to the workplace by using psychological principles and research methods to solve problems and improve the quality of work life. They study issues such as workplace productivity, management or employee working styles, and employee morale. They also work with management on matters such as policy planning, employee screening or training, and organizational development.

School psychologists apply psychological principles and techniques to education-related and developmental issues. They may address student learning and behavioral problems; design, implement, and evaluate performances; and counsel students and families. They may also consult with other school-based professionals to suggest improvements to teaching, learning, and administrative strategies.

Social psychologists study how people's mindsets and behavior are shaped by social interactions. They examine both individual and group interactions and may investigate ways to improve negative interactions.

Some psychologists become postsecondary teachers or high school teachers.

Median Annual Wages, May 2012

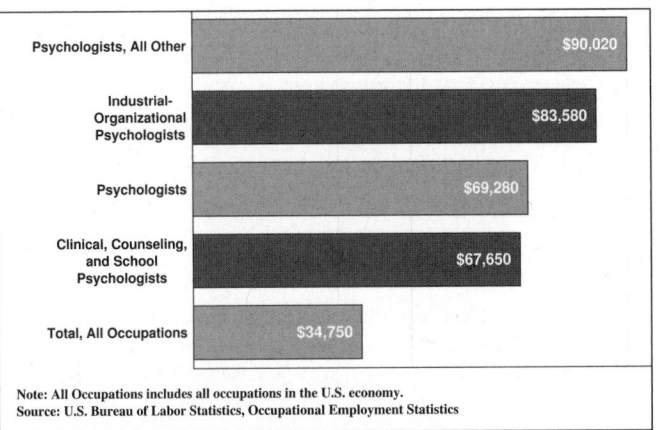

Note: All Occupations includes all occupations in the U.S. economy.
Source: U.S. Bureau of Labor Statistics, Occupational Employment Statistics

Percent Change in Employment, Projected 2012–2022

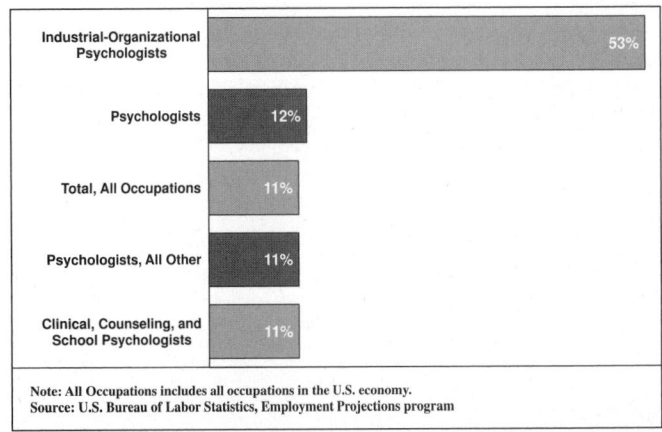

Note: All Occupations includes all occupations in the U.S. economy.
Source: U.S. Bureau of Labor Statistics, Employment Projections program

Employment Projections Data for Psychologists

Occupational title	SOC Code	Employment, 2012	Projected Employment, 2022	Change, 2012–2022	
				Percent	Numeric
Psychologists...	19-3030	160,200	178,900	12	18,700
Clinical, counseling, and school psychologists	19-3031	145,100	161,500	11	16,400
Industrial-organizational psychologists	19-3032	1,600	2,500	53	900
Psychologists, all other	19-3039	13,400	14,900	11	1,400

Source: U.S. Bureau of Labor Statistics, Employment Projections Program

Note: Data are rounded. Go to Occupational Information Included in the OOH *for a discussion of the data in this table.*

Work Environment

Psychologists held about 160,200 jobs in 2012. About 31 percent worked in educational services, and 29 percent worked in health-care and social assistance.

Nearly one-third of all psychologists were self-employed.

Some psychologists work alone, which may include independent research or patient counseling. Others work as part of a healthcare team, collaborating with physicians, social workers, and others to treat illness and promote overall wellness.

Many clinical and counseling psychologists in private practice have their own offices and can set their own schedules. Other typical workplaces include clinics, hospitals, rehabilitation facilities, and community and mental health centers.

Most research psychologists work in colleges and universities, government agencies, or private research organizations.

Most school psychologists work in public schools, ranging in level from nursery school through college. They also work in private schools, universities, hospitals and clinics, community treatment centers, and independent practice.

Work Schedules. Psychologists in private practice often set their own hours, and many work part time as independent consultants. They may offer evening or weekend hours to accommodate clients. Those employed in hospitals, nursing homes, or other healthcare facilities may also have evening or weekend shifts. Most psychologists in clinics, government, industry, or schools work full-time schedules during regular business hours.

How to Become One

Although psychologists typically need a doctoral degree or specialist degree in psychology, a master's degree is sufficient for some positions. Practicing psychologists also need a license or certification.

Education. Most clinical, counseling, and research psychologists need a doctoral degree. Psychologists can complete a Ph.D. in psychology or a Doctor of Psychology (Psy.D.) degree. A Ph.D. in psychology is a research degree that culminates in a comprehensive exam and a dissertation based on original research. In clinical, counseling, school, or health service settings, students usually complete a 1-year internship as part of the doctoral program. The Psy.D. is a clinical degree and is often based on practical work and examinations rather than a dissertation.

School psychologists need an advanced degree and certification or licensure to work. The advanced degree is most commonly the specialist degree (Ed.S. degree, which requires a minimum of 60 graduate semester hours and a 1,200-hour supervised internship), a doctoral degree in school psychology, or in some instances, a master's degree. School psychologists' training includes coursework in both education and psychology, because their work addresses education and mental health components of students' development.

Graduates with a master's degree in psychology can work as industrial-organizational psychologists. When working under the supervision of a doctoral psychologist, master's graduates can also work as psychological assistants in clinical, counseling, or research settings. Master's degree programs typically include courses in industrial-organizational psychology, statistics, and research design.

Most master's degree programs do not require an undergraduate major in psychology, but do require coursework in introductory psychology, experimental psychology, and statistics. Some doctoral degree programs require applicants to have a master's degree in psychology; others will accept applicants with a bachelor's degree and a major in psychology.

Most graduates with a bachelor's degree in psychology find work in other fields such as business administration, sales, or education.

Licenses, Certifications, and Registrations. In most states, practicing psychology or using the title of "psychologist" requires licensure or certification. In all states and the District of Columbia, psychologists who practice independently must be licensed. Licensing laws vary by state and type of position. Most clinical and counseling psychologists need a doctorate in psychology, an internship, at least 1 to 2 years of professional experience, and to pass the Examination for Professional Practice in Psychology. Information on specific requirements by state can be obtained from the Association of State and Provincial Licensing Boards. In many states, licensed psychologists must complete continuing education courses to keep their licenses.

The American Board of Professional Psychology awards specialty certification in 13 areas of psychology, such as clinical health, couple and family, psychoanalysis, or rehabilitation. Although board certification is not required for most psychologists, it can demonstrate professional expertise in a specialty area; however, some hospitals and clinics do require certification. In those cases, candidates must have a doctoral degree in psychology, state license or certification, and any additional criteria of the specialty field.

Training. To become licensed, psychologists must have completed one or more of the following:

• Pre-doctoral or post-doctoral supervised experience

• Internship

• Residency program

Important Qualities

Analytical skills. Psychologists must be able to examine the information they collect and draw logical conclusions from them.

Communication skills. Psychologists must have strong communication skills because they spend much of their time listening to and speaking with patients.

Similar Occupations   This table shows a list of occupations with job duties that are similar to those of psychologists.

Occupations	Entry-level Education	2012 Pay	Projected Job Growth	Average Annual Openings
Anthropologists and Archeologists	Master's degree	$57,420	19%	260
Market Research Analysts	Bachelor's degree	$60,300	32%	18,850
Mental Health Counselors and Marriage and Family Therapists	Master's degree	$41,592	29%	8,360
Physicians and Surgeons	Doctoral or professional degree	$182,294	18%	29,630
Postsecondary Teachers	See "How to Become One"	$70,380	19%	42,690
School and Career Counselors	Master's degree	$53,610	12%	8,700
Social Workers	See "How to Become One"	$44,541	19%	24,280
Sociologists	Master's degree	$74,960	15%	110
Special Education Teachers	Bachelor's degree	$55,068	6%	10,220
Substance Abuse and Behavioral Disorder Counselors	High school diploma or equivalent	$38,520	31%	4,720
Survey Researchers	Master's degree	$45,050	18%	560

Observational skills. Psychologists study attitude and behavior. They must be able to watch people and understand the possible meanings of people's facial expressions, body positions, actions, and interactions.

Patience. Psychologists must be able to demonstrate patience, because research or treatment of patients may take a long time. They must also be patient when dealing with people who have mental or behavioral disorders.

People skills. Psychologists study people and help people. They must be able to work well with clients, patients, and other medical professionals.

Problem-solving skills. Psychologists need problem-solving skills to find treatments or solutions for mental and behavioral problems.

Trustworthiness. Psychologists must keep patients' problems in confidence, and patients must be able to trust psychologists' expertise in treating sensitive problems.

Pay

The median annual wage for psychologists was $69,280 in May 2012. The median wage is the wage at which half the workers in an occupation earned more than that amount and half earned less. The lowest 10 percent earned less than $38,720, and the top 10 percent earned more than $110,880.

The median annual wages for psychologist occupations in May 2012 were as follows:

Industrial-organizational psychologists $83,580
Clinical, counseling, and school psychologists 67,650
Psychologists, all other 90,020

Job Outlook

Overall employment of psychologists is projected to grow 12 percent from 2012 to 2022, about as fast as the average for all occupations. Employment growth will vary by specialty.

Employment of clinical, counseling, and school psychologists is projected to grow 11 percent from 2012 to 2022, about as fast as the average for all occupations. Greater demand for psychological services in schools, hospitals, mental health centers, and social services agencies should drive employment growth.

Demand for clinical and counseling psychologists will increase as people continue to turn to psychologists to help solve or manage their problems. More psychologists will be needed to help people deal with issues such as depression and other mental disorders, marriage and family problems, job stress, and addiction. Psychologists will also be needed to provide services to an aging population, helping people deal with the mental and physical changes that happen as they grow older. Psychological services are also needed for veterans suffering from war trauma, for survivors of other trauma, and for individuals with autism.

Demand for psychologists in the healthcare industry is also expected to increase because their collaborative work with doctors, social workers, and other healthcare professionals provides patients with comprehensive, interdisciplinary treatments. In addition to treating mental and behavioral health issues, psychologists will be needed to work on teams to develop or administer prevention or wellness programs.

School psychologists will be needed to work with students, particularly those with special needs, learning disabilities, and behavioral issues. Schools also rely on school psychologists to assess and counsel students. In addition, school psychologists will be needed to study how both in-school and out-of-school factors affect learning, which teachers and administrators can use to improve education.

Employment of industrial-organizational psychologists is projected to grow 53 percent from 2012 to 2022, much faster than the average for all occupations. Organizations use industrial-organizational psychologists to help select and keep employees, increase productivity, and improve office morale. However, because it is a small occupation, the fast employment growth will result in only about 900 new jobs over the 10-year period.

Job Prospects. Competition for jobs for psychologists will vary by specialty. Overall, candidates with a doctoral or specialist degree and post-doctoral work experience will have the best job opportunities.

Job prospects should be best for those who have a specialist degree or doctoral degree in school psychology. Employment of school psychologists will continue to grow because of the raised awareness of the connection between mental health and learning and the need for mental health services in schools. Given the limited number of graduates in this specialty and the growing need of mental health services in schools, school psychologists are expected to have good job opportunities.

Candidates with a master's degree will face competition for most positions, and many of them will find jobs in a related field outside of psychology. Even industrial–organizational psychologists, despite much faster-than-average employment growth, are expected to face competition for positions due to the large number of qualified graduates. Industrial-organizational psychologists with extensive training in quantitative research methods and computer science may have a competitive edge.

Most graduates with a bachelor's degree in psychology find work in other fields such as business administration, sales, or education. However, they may be able to find work in the field of psychology as assistants.

O*NET

➤ Clinical, Counseling, and School Psychologists (19-3031.00)
➤ School Psychologists (19-3031.01)
➤ Clinical Psychologists (19-3031.02)
➤ Counseling Psychologists (19-3031.03)
➤ Industrial-Organizational Psychologists (19-3032.00)
➤ Psychologists, All Other (19-3039.00)
➤ Neuropsychologists and Clinical Neuropsychologists (19-3039.01)

Contacts for More Information

For more information on careers in all fields of psychology, visit
➤ American Psychological Association (www.apa.org/)
    For more information on careers for school psychologists, visit
➤ National Association of School Psychologists (www.nasponline.org)
    For more information on state licensing requirements, visit
➤ Association of State and Provincial Psychology Boards (www.asppb.net)
    For more information about psychology specialty certifications, visit
➤ American Board of Professional Psychology (www.abpp.org/)
    For more information about industrial-organizational psychologists, visit
➤ Society for Industrial & Organizational Psychology (www.siop.org/)
    For more information about careers and certification in neuropsychology, visit
➤ American Board of Professional Neuropsychology (http://abn-board.com/)

Sociologists

- **2012 Median Pay** .... $74,960 per year
                                                   $36.04 per hour
- **Entry-Level Education** ....Master's degree
- **Work Experience in a Related Occupation**............... None
- **On-the-Job Training** .... None
- **Number of Jobs 2012** 2,600
- **Job Outlook, 2012–22**............. 15% (Faster than average)
- **Employment Change, 2012–22** 400

What Sociologists Do

Sociologists study society and social behavior by examining the groups, cultures, organizations, social institutions, and processes that people develop.

Duties. Sociologists typically do the following:

- Design research projects to test theories about social issues
- Collect data through surveys, observations, interviews, and other sources
- Analyze and draw conclusions from data
- Prepare reports, articles, or presentations detailing their research findings

- Collaborate with other sociologists or social scientists
- Consult with and advise clients, policymakers, or other groups on research findings and sociological issues

Sociologists study human behavior, interaction, and organization within the context of larger social, political, and economic forces. They observe the activity of social, religious, political, and economic groups, organizations, and institutions. They examine the effect of social influences, including organizations and institutions, on different individuals and groups. They also trace the origin and growth of these groups and interactions.

Administrators, educators, lawmakers, and social workers use sociological research to solve social problems and formulate public policy. Sociologists specialize in a wide range of social topics, including the following:

- Health
- Crime
- Education
- Racial and ethnic relations
- Families
- Population
- Gender
- Poverty
- Aging

Many people with a sociology background become postsecondary teachers and high school teachers. Most others, particularly those with a bachelor's degree in sociology, often find work in related jobs outside the sociologist profession as policy analysts, demographers, survey researchers, and statisticians.

Work Environment

Sociologists held about 2,600 jobs in 2012.

The industries that employed the most sociologists in 2012 were as follows:

Colleges, universities, and professional schools; state, local, and private	36%
Research and development in the social sciences and humanities	30
Local government, excluding education and hospitals	9
Management, scientific, and technical consulting services	8

Sociologists often read and write research articles or reports.

Median Annual Wages, May 2012

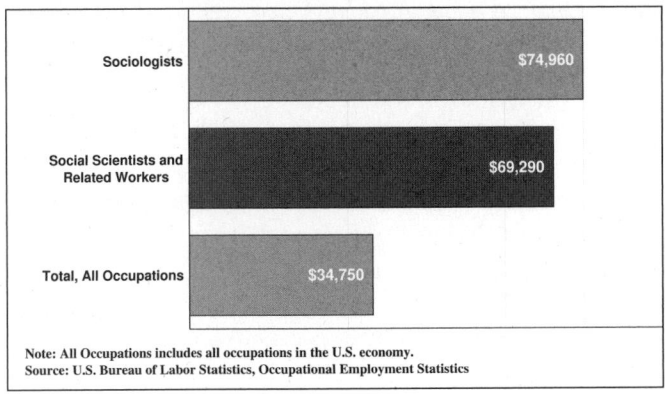

Sociologists — $74,960
Social Scientists and Related Workers — $69,290
Total, All Occupations — $34,750

Note: All Occupations includes all occupations in the U.S. economy.
Source: U.S. Bureau of Labor Statistics, Occupational Employment Statistics

Percent Change in Employment, Projected 2012–2022

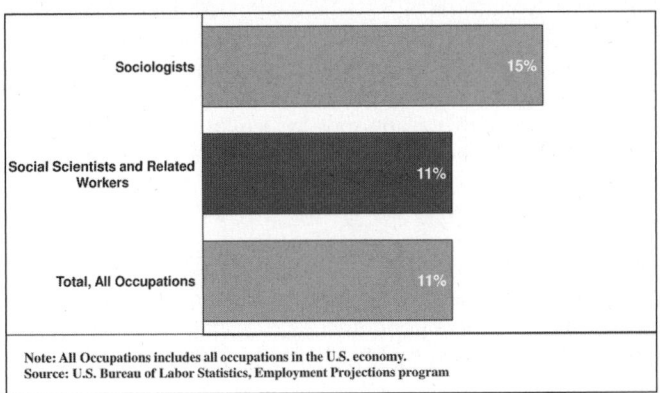

Sociologists — 15%
Social Scientists and Related Workers — 11%
Total, All Occupations — 11%

Note: All Occupations includes all occupations in the U.S. economy.
Source: U.S. Bureau of Labor Statistics, Employment Projections program

Sociologists typically work in an office. They occasionally may work outside the office to conduct research through interviews or observations or present research results.

Work Schedules. Most sociologists work full time during regular business hours.

How to Become One

Most sociology jobs require a master's degree or Ph.D. Many bachelor's degree holders find positions in related fields, such as social services, education, or public policy.

Education. Sociologists typically need a master's degree or Ph.D. There are two types of sociology master's degree programs: traditional programs and applied, clinical, and professional programs. Traditional programs prepare students to enter a Ph.D. program. Applied, clinical, and professional programs prepare students to enter the professional workplace, teaching them the necessary analytical skills to perform sociological research in a professional setting.

Many students who complete a Ph.D. in sociology become postsecondary teachers. Other Ph.D. graduates often become research sociologists for nonprofits, businesses, and governments.

Courses in research methods and statistics are important for both master's and Ph.D. candidates. Many programs also offer opportunities to gain experience through internships or by preparing reports for clients.

Although some graduates with a bachelor's degree find work as sociology research assistants, most find positions in other fields, such as social services, administration, management, or sales and marketing.

Other Experience. Bachelor's degree holders can benefit from internships or volunteer work when looking for entry-level positions in sociology or a related field. These types of opportunities give students a chance to apply their academic knowledge in a professional setting and develop skills needed for the field.

Important Qualities

Analytical skills. Sociologists must be able to carefully analyze data and other information, often utilizing statistical processes to test their theories.

Communication skills. Sociologists need strong communication skills when they conduct interviews, collaborate with colleagues, and present research results.

Employment Projections Data for Sociologists

Occupational title	SOC Code	Employment, 2012	Projected Employment, 2022	Change, 2012–2022	
				Percent	Numeric
Sociologists	19-3041	2,600	3,000	15	400

Source: U.S. Bureau of Labor Statistics, Employment Projections Program

Note: Data are rounded. Go to **Occupational Information Included in the OOH** *for a discussion of the data in this table.*

Similar Occupations   This table shows a list of occupations with job duties that are similar to those of sociologists.

Occupations	Entry-level Education	2012 Pay	Projected Job Growth	Average Annual Openings
Anthropologists and Archeologists	Master's degree	$57,420	19%	260
Economists	Master's degree	$91,860	14%	740
Political Scientists	Master's degree	$102,000	21%	250
Postsecondary Teachers	See "How to Become One"	$70,380	19%	42,690
Psychologists	See "How to Become One"	$69,807	12%	6,230
Social Workers	See "How to Become One"	$44,541	19%	24,280
Statisticians	Master's degree	$75,560	26%	1,610
Survey Researchers	Master's degree	$45,050	18%	560
Urban and Regional Planners	Master's degree	$65,230	10%	2,140

Critical-thinking skills. Sociologists must be able to think critically when doing research. They must design research projects and collect, process, and analyze information in order to draw logical conclusions about society and the groups it comprises.

Problem-solving skills. Sociologists' research typically is focused on identifying, studying, and solving sociological problems.

Writing skills. Sociologists frequently write reports detailing their findings.

Pay

The median annual wage for sociologists was $74,960 in May 2012. The median wage is the wage at which half the workers in an occupation earned more than that amount and half earned less. The lowest 10 percent earned less than $43,280, and the top 10 percent earned more than $129,760.

Job Outlook

Employment of sociologists is projected to grow 15 percent from 2012 to 2022, faster than the average for all occupations. However, because it is a small occupation, the fast growth will result in only about 400 new jobs over the 10-year period.

Employment of sociologists will be driven by the need for sociological research to further understand society and human social interactions. Social, political, and business organizations will continue to use sociologists to research, evaluate, and address many different social issues, programs, and problems.

Sociologists will be needed to apply sociological research to other disciplines as well. For example, sociologists may collaborate with researchers in other fields to study how social structures or groups influence policy decisions about health, education, politics, business, or economics.

Job Prospects. Holders of Ph.D. degrees can expect to face very strong competition for sociologist positions. Sociology is a popular field of study with a relatively small number of positions.

Many bachelor's and master's degree holders will find positions in related fields, such as social services, education, public policy, or other areas. Although these fields require the skills and concepts that sociologists learn as part of their education, workers should face less competition for positions not specifically labeled as "sociologists."

Candidates with an advanced degree, strong statistical and research skills, and a background in applied sociology will have the best job prospects.

O*NET

➤ Sociologists (19-3041.00)

Contacts for More Information

For more information about careers in sociology, visit
➤ American Sociological Association (www.asanet.org)

Survey Researchers

- **2012 Median Pay** .... $45,050 per year
  $21.66 per hour
- **Entry-Level Education** ....Master's degree
- **Work Experience in a Related Occupation**............... None
- **On-the-Job Training** .... None
- **Number of Jobs 2012** 18,000
- **Job Outlook, 2012–22** .... 18% (Faster than average)
- **Employment Change, 2012–22** 3,200

What Survey Researchers Do

Survey researchers design surveys and analyze data. Surveys are used to collect factual data, such as employment and salary information, or to ask questions in order to understand people's opinions, preferences, beliefs, or desires.

Duties. Survey researchers typically do the following:

- Conduct background research on survey topics
- Plan and design surveys and determine appropriate survey methods
- Test surveys to make sure that people will understand the questions
- Coordinate the work of survey interviewers and data collectors
- Account for and solve problems caused by non-respondents or other sampling issues
- Analyze data using statistical software and techniques
- Summarize survey data using tables, graphs, and fact sheets
- Evaluate surveys, methods, and performance to improve future surveys

Survey researchers design and conduct surveys for scientific, public opinion, and marketing research purposes. Surveys for scientific research cover various fields, including government, health, social sciences, and education. A survey researcher may, for example, try to accurately capture information such as prevalence of drug use or disease.

Some survey researchers design public opinion surveys, which are intended to gather information about the attitudes and opinions of society or of a certain group. Surveys cover a wide variety of topics, including political issues, social issues, culture, the economy, or health.

Other survey researchers design marketing surveys which examine products or services that consumers want, need, or prefer. Researchers who collect and analyze market research data are known as market research analysts.

Survey researchers design surveys and may conduct surveys in many different formats, such as interviews, questionnaires, and focus groups (in-person, small group sessions with a facilitator). They use different mediums to conduct surveys, including the Internet, mail, and telephone and in-person interviews.

Some surveys solicit the opinions of an entire population and others target a smaller group, such as residents of a particular state, a specific demographic group, or members of a political party. Researchers survey a sample of the population and use

Survey researchers use data from surveys to measure consumer preferences.

Median Annual Wages, May 2012

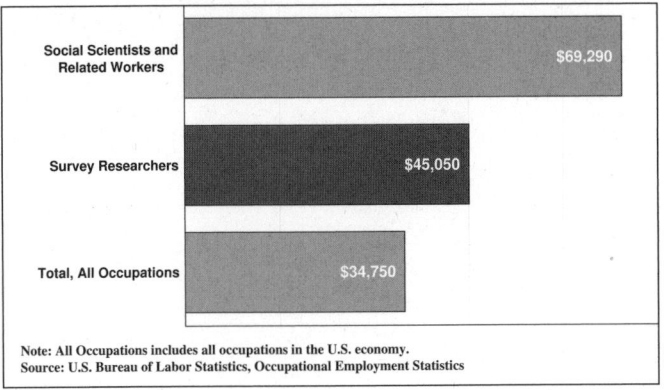

Note: All Occupations includes all occupations in the U.S. economy.
Source: U.S. Bureau of Labor Statistics, Occupational Employment Statistics

Percent Change in Employment, Projected 2012–2022

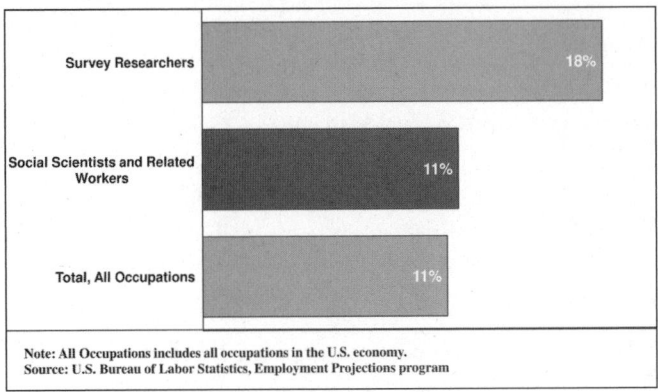

Note: All Occupations includes all occupations in the U.S. economy.
Source: U.S. Bureau of Labor Statistics, Employment Projections program

statistics to make sure the sample accurately represents the target population group. Researchers use a variety of statistical techniques and analytical software to plan surveys, adjust for errors in the data, and analyze the results.

Survey researchers sometimes supervise interviewers who collect the survey data through in-person or telephone interviews.

Work Environment

Survey researchers held about 18,000 jobs in 2012. They work in research firms, polling organizations, nonprofits, corporations, colleges and universities, and government agencies.

Survey researchers who conduct interviews have frequent contact with the public. Some occasionally work outside the office, traveling to meet with clients, or conduct in-person interviews and focus group sessions. When designing surveys and analyzing data, they usually work alone in a typical office setting, though some work on teams with other researchers.

Work Schedules. Most survey researchers work full time during regular business hours.

How to Become One

Although some survey researchers have a bachelor's degree, most technical research positions require a master's degree. In addition, employers generally prefer candidates who have previous experience performing research, using statistics, and analyzing data.

Education. Most technical research positions require a master's degree or Ph.D. Survey researchers can have a master's degree in a variety of fields, including marketing or survey research, statistics, and the social sciences.

A bachelor's degree is sufficient for a small number of entry-level positions. Students should take courses in research methods, survey methodology, and statistics. Many also may benefit from taking business courses, such as marketing and consumer behavior, and social science courses, such as psychology, sociology, and economics.

Other Experience. Prospective survey researchers can gain valuable experience through internships or fellowships. Many

businesses, research and polling firms, and marketing companies offer internships for college students or recent graduates who want to work in market and survey research.

Licenses, Certifications, and Registrations. The Marketing Research Association offers the Professional Researcher Certification (PRC) for survey researchers. Although not mandatory, certification can show a level of professional competence. Candidates qualify based on experience and knowledge, including at least 3 years working in opinion and marketing research, passing an exam, and acquiring membership in a professional organization. To keep their certification valid, researchers must take continuing education courses and apply for renewal every 2 years.

Important Qualities

Analytical skills. Survey researchers must be able to apply statistical techniques to large amounts of data and interpret the analysis correctly. They also should be proficient in statistical software to analyze data.

Communication skills. Survey researchers need strong communication skills when conducting surveys and interpreting and presenting results to clients.

Critical-thinking skills. Survey researchers must design or choose a survey and survey method that best captures the information needed. They must also be able to look at the data and analyses and understand what can be learned from the survey.

Detail oriented. Survey researchers must pay attention to details as they work because survey results depend on collecting, analyzing, and reporting the data accurately.

Problem-solving skills. Survey researchers need problem-solving skills when identifying survey design issues, adjusting data, and interpreting survey results.

Pay

The median annual wage for survey researchers was $45,050 in May 2012. The median wage is the wage at which half the workers in an occupation earned more than that amount and half earned less. The lowest 10 percent earned less than $19,640, and the top 10 percent earned more than $89,080.

Employment Projections Data for Survey Researchers

Occupational title	SOC Code	Employment, 2012	Projected Employment, 2022	Change, 2012–2022 Percent	Change, 2012–2022 Numeric
Survey researchers	19-3022	18,000	21,200	18	3,200

Source: U.S. Bureau of Labor Statistics, Employment Projections Program

Note: Data are rounded. Go to Occupational Information Included in the OOH *for a discussion of the data in this table.*

Similar Occupations This table shows a list of occupations with job duties that are similar to those of survey researchers.

Occupations	Entry-level Education	2012 Pay	Projected Job Growth	Average Annual Openings
Advertising Sales Agents	High school diploma or equivalent	$46,290	-1%	4,750
Advertising, Promotions, and Marketing Managers	Bachelor's degree	$115,087	12%	7,510
Economists	Master's degree	$91,860	14%	740
Market Research Analysts	Bachelor's degree	$60,300	32%	18,850
Operations Research Analysts	Bachelor's degree	$72,100	27%	3,600
Political Scientists	Master's degree	$102,000	21%	250
Psychologists	See "How to Become One"	$69,807	12%	6,230
Sociologists	Master's degree	$74,960	15%	110
Statisticians	Master's degree	$75,560	26%	1,610

In May 2012, the median annual wages for survey researchers in the top five industries employing these workers were as follows:

Scientific research and development services $60,260
Educational services; state, local, and private 56,540
Religious, grantmaking, civic, professional, and similar
organizations... 48,840
Management, scientific, and technical consulting services... 36,640
Other professional, scientific, and technical services............ 35,150

Job Outlook

Employment of survey researchers is projected to grow 18 percent from 2012 to 2022, faster than the average for all occupations. However, because it is a small occupation, the fast growth will result in only about 3,200 new jobs over the 10-year period.

Organizations throughout all industries are increasingly relying on data and information acquired through research, and survey researchers play an important role in the research process.

Governments, media, nonprofits, and other organizations will continue to use public opinion research to learn about citizens' thoughts and perspectives. They use this valuable information to understand groups of people; measure a program's effectiveness; or gauge support for people, policies, and actions. For example, public opinion research may help governments make decisions on transit systems, social programs, and numerous other issues.

Survey researchers also will be needed to design surveys for businesses and organizations. In an increasingly competitive economy, firms will continue to use market and consumer research surveys to help make business decisions, improve their products or services, and compete in the market. Many of these researcher jobs will be in consulting firms.

However, employment growth may be tempered by changing research methods. Research is an evolving field and companies occasionally adopt new research methods or adapt to new data sources. For example, collecting information from social media sites and data mining–finding trends in large sets of existing data–are expected to reduce the need for some traditional survey methods, such as telephone interviews.

Job Prospects. Job opportunities should be best for those with an advanced degree in market or survey research, statistics, or the social sciences. Jobseekers with strong statistical and analytical skills and research experience should have good job prospects. Due to the relatively small number of survey researcher positions, bachelor's degree holders will likely face strong competition from more qualified candidates.

O*NET

➤ Survey Researchers (19-3022.00)

Contacts for More Information

For information about careers in survey research, visit
➤ American Association for Public Opinion Research (www.aapor.org)
➤ Council of American Survey Research Organizations (www.casro.org)
➤ Marketing Research Association (www.marketingresearch.org/)

Urban and Regional Planners

• **2012 Median Pay** .... $65,230 per year
  $31.36 per hour

• **Entry-Level Education** ....Master's degree

• **Work Experience in a Related Occupation**............... None

• **On-the-Job Training** .... None

• **Number of Jobs 2012** 38,700

• **Job Outlook, 2012–22**............... 10% (As fast as average)

• **Employment Change, 2012–22** 4,000

What Urban and Regional Planners Do

Urban and regional planners develop plans and programs for the use of land. Their plans help create communities, accommodate population growth, and revitalize physical facilities in towns, cities, counties, and metropolitan areas.

Duties. Urban and regional planners typically do the following:

• Meet with public officials, developers, and the public regarding development plans and land use

• Gather and analyze economic and environmental studies, censuses, and market research data

• Conduct field investigations to analyze factors affecting land use

• Review site plans submitted by developers

• Assess the feasibility of proposals and identify needed changes

• Recommend whether proposals should be approved or denied

• Present projects to communities, planning officials, and planning commissions

• Stay current on zoning or building codes, environmental regulations, and other legal issues

Urban and regional planners develop plans to use land for the growth and revitalization of communities.

Urban and regional planners identify community needs and develop short- and long-term plans to create, grow, and revitalize communities and areas. For example, planners examine plans for proposed facilities, such as schools, to ensure that these facilities will meet the needs of a changing population.

As an area grows or changes otherwise, planners help communities manage the related economic, social, and environmental issues, such as planning a new park, sheltering the homeless, and making the region more attractive to businesses.

Some planners work on broad, community-wide plans; others focus on specific issues. Ultimately, planners advocate the best use of a community's land and resources for residential, commercial, educational, and recreational purposes.

When beginning a project, planners work with public officials, community members, and other groups to identify community issues and goals. Using research, data analysis, and collaboration with interest groups, planners formulate strategies to address issues and to meet goals.

They also may help carry out community plans, oversee projects, and organize the work of the groups involved. Projects may range from a policy recommendation for a specific initiative to a long-term, comprehensive area plan.

Planners use a variety of tools and technology in their work, including geographic information systems (GIS) that analyze and manipulate data. GIS is used to integrate data with electronic maps. For example, planners use GIS to overlay a land map with population density indicators. They also use statistical software, visualization and presentation programs, financial spreadsheets, and other database and software programs.

The following are examples of types of urban and regional planners:

Land use and code enforcement planners are concerned with the way land is used and whether development plans comply with codes, which are the standards and laws of a jurisdiction. These planners work to carry out effective planning and zoning policies and ordinances. For example, a planner may develop a policy to encourage development in an underutilized location and to discourage development in an environmentally sensitive area.

Transportation planners develop transportation plans and programs for an area. They identify transportation needs and issues, assess the impact of services or systems, and anticipate and address future transportation patterns. For example, as growth outside the city creates more jobs, the need for public transportation to get workers to those jobs increases. Transportation planners develop and model possible solutions and explain the possibilities to planning boards and the public.

Environmental and natural resources planners attempt to mitigate the harmful effects of development on the environment. They may focus on conserving resources, preventing destruction of ecosystems, or cleaning polluted areas.

Economic development planners focus on the economic activities of an area. They may work to expand or diversify commercial activity, attract businesses, create jobs, or build housing.

Urban design planners strive to make building architecture and public spaces look and function in accordance with an area's development and design goals. They combine planning with aspects of architecture and landscape architecture. Urban design planners focus on issues such as city layout, street design, and building and landscape patterns.

Work Environment

Urban and regional planners held about 38,700 jobs in 2012, a majority of which–about 65 percent–were in local government.

Most other planners worked for state and federal governments; real estate developers; nonprofit organizations; and consulting

Median Annual Wages, May 2012

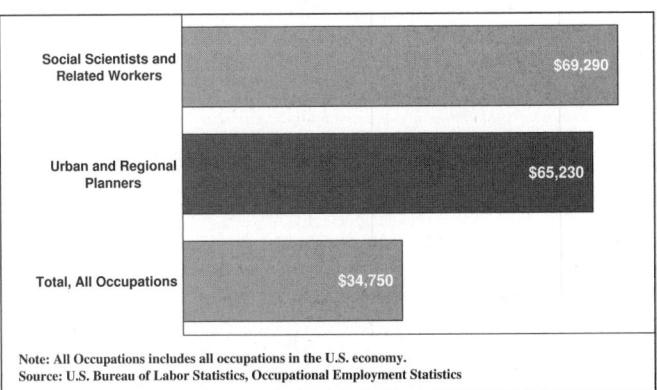

Note: All Occupations includes all occupations in the U.S. economy.
Source: U.S. Bureau of Labor Statistics, Occupational Employment Statistics

Percent Change in Employment, Projected 2012–2022

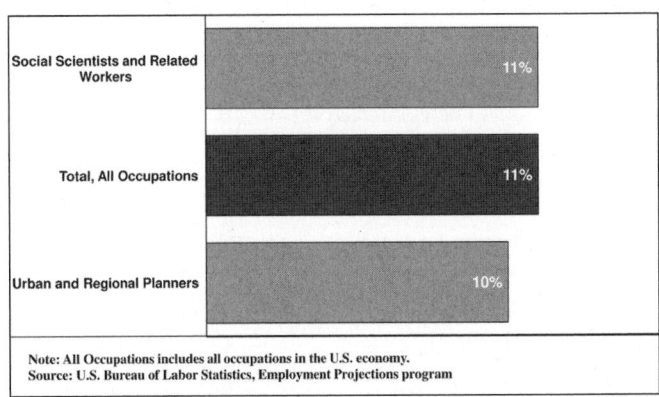

Note: All Occupations includes all occupations in the U.S. economy.
Source: U.S. Bureau of Labor Statistics, Employment Projections program

Employment Projections Data for Urban and Regional Planners

Occupational title	SOC Code	Employment, 2012	Projected Employment, 2022	Change, 2012–2022	
				Percent	Numeric
Urban and regional planners	19-3051	38,700	42,700	10	4,000

Source: U.S. Bureau of Labor Statistics, Employment Projections Program

Note: **Data are rounded. Go to Occupational Information Included in the OOH** *for a discussion of the data in this table.*

firms. Planners work throughout the country in all sizes of munici-pality, but most work in large metropolitan areas.

The industries that employed the most urban and regional plan-ners in 2012 were as follows:

Local government, excluding education and hospitals............ 65%
Architectural, engineering, and related services 14
State government, excluding education and hospitals............. 10
Management, scientific, and technical consulting services........ 7

Most planners work with others. They often collaborate with public officials, engineers, architects, lawyers, and developers and must give presentations, attend meetings, and manage projects.

Because planners must balance conflicting interests and negoti-ate deals, the work can be stressful. Planners face pressure from politicians, developers, and the public to design or recommend specific plans. They may also work against tight deadlines.

Urban and regional planners often travel to sites to inspect the land conditions and use. Those involved in inspecting development sites may spend much of their time in the field.

Work Schedules. Most planners work during normal business hours, but some also work evenings or weekends to attend meetings with officials, planning commissions, and neighborhood groups.

How to Become One

Urban and regional planners usually need a master's degree from an accredited planning program to qualify for professional positions.

Education. Most urban and regional planners have a master's degree from an accredited urban or regional planning program. In 2013, 72 universities offered an accredited master's degree program in planning.

Many master's programs accept students with a wide range of undergraduate backgrounds. However, many candidates who enter master's degree programs have a bachelor's degree in economics, geography, political science, or environmental design.

Most master's programs include considerable time in seminars, workshops, and laboratory courses, in which students learn to analyze and solve planning problems. Although most master's programs have a similar core curriculum, they often differ in the courses they offer and the issues on which they focus. For example, programs located in agricultural states may focus on rural plan-ning, and programs located in an area with high population density may focus on urban revitalization.

Some planners have a background in a related field, such as public administration, architecture, or landscape architecture.

Aspiring planners with a bachelor's degree can qualify for a small number of jobs as assistant or junior planners. There are currently 15 accredited bachelor's degree programs in planning. Candidates with a bachelor's degree typically need work experience in planning, public policy, or a related field.

Other Experience. Although not necessary for all positions, some entry-level positions require 1 to 2 years of work experience in a related field, such as architecture, public policy, or economic development. Many students gain experience through real-world planning projects or part-time internships while enrolled in a mas-ter's planning program. Often this includes summer internships. Others enroll in full-time internships after completing their degree.

Mid- and senior-level planner positions usually require several years of work experience in planning or in a specific planning specialty.

Licenses, Certifications, and Registrations. As of 2012, New Jersey was the only state that required planners to be licensed, although Michigan required registration to use the title "com-munity planner." More information can be requested from the regulatory boards of New Jersey and Michigan.

The American Institute of Certified Planners (AICP) offers the professional AICP Certification for planners. To become certified, candidates must meet certain education and experience require-ments and pass an exam. Certification must be maintained every 2 years. Although not required for all planning positions, some organizations prefer to hire certified planners.

Similar Occupations   This table shows a list of occupations with job duties that are similar to those of urban and regional planners.

Occupations	Entry-level Education	2012 Pay	Projected Job Growth	Average Annual Openings
Architects	Bachelor's degree	$73,090	17%	4,410
Cartographers and Photogrammetrists	Bachelor's degree	$57,440	20%	490
Civil Engineers	Bachelor's degree	$79,340	20%	12,010
Economists	Master's degree	$91,860	14%	740
Geographers	Bachelor's degree	$74,760	29%	80
Landscape Architects	Bachelor's degree	$64,180	14%	760
Market Research Analysts	Bachelor's degree	$60,300	32%	18,850
Survey Researchers	Master's degree	$45,050	18%	560
Surveyors	Bachelor's degree	$56,230	10%	1,340

Important Qualities

Analytical skills. Planners analyze information and data from a variety of sources, such as market research studies, censuses, and environmental impact studies. They use statistical techniques and technologies such as geographic information systems (GIS) in their analyses to determine the significance of the data.

Communication skills. Planners must be able to communicate clearly and effectively because they often give presentations and meet with a wide variety of audiences, including public officials, interest groups, and community members.

Decision-making skills. Planners must weigh all possible planning options and combine analysis, creativity, and realism to choose the appropriate action or plan.

Management skills. Planners must be able to manage projects, which may include overseeing tasks, planning assignments, and making decisions.

Writing skills. Planners need strong writing skills because they often prepare research reports, write grant proposals, and correspond with colleagues and stakeholders.

Pay

The median annual wage for urban and regional planners was $65,230 in May 2012. The median wage is the wage at which half the workers in an occupation earned more than that amount and half earned less. The lowest 10 percent earned less than $41,490, and the top 10 percent earned more than $97,630.

In May 2012, the median annual wages for urban and regional planners in the top four industries employing planners were as follows:

Architectural, engineering, and related services	$71,010
Management, scientific, and technical consulting services	67,390
State government, excluding education and hospitals	64,380
Local government, excluding education and hospitals	63,300

Job Outlook

Employment of urban and regional planners is projected to grow 10 percent from 2012 to 2022, about as fast as the average for all occupations. Population growth and environmental concerns will drive employment growth for planners in cities, suburbs, and other areas.

Planners will continue to be needed to make changes to plans, programs, or regulations to reflect demographic changes throughout the nation. Within cities, urban planners will be needed to develop revitalization projects and address problems associated with population growth, population diversity, environmental degradation, and resource scarcity. Similarly, suburban areas and municipalities will need planners to address the challenges associated with population changes, including housing needs and transportation systems.

Planners also will be important as new communities will require extensive development and infrastructure, including housing, roads, sewer systems, parks, and schools.

An increased focus on sustainable and environmentally conscious development also will increase demand for planners. Issues such as storm water management, environmental regulation, affordable housing, cultural proficiency, and historic preservation should drive employment growth.

Engineering and architecture firms are increasingly collaborating with planners for land use, development site design, and building design. In addition, many real estate developers and governments will continue to contract out various planning services to these consulting firms.

However, employment of planners in local or state government may suffer because many projects are canceled or deferred when municipalities have too little money for development. Expected tight budgets over the coming decade should slow planners' employment growth in government.

Job Prospects. Job opportunities for planners often depend on economic conditions. When municipalities and developers have funds for development projects, planners are in higher demand. However, planners often face strong competition for jobs in an economic downturn, when there is less funding for development work.

Although government funding issues will affect employment of planners in the short term, job prospects should improve over the coming decade. Planners will be needed to help plan, oversee, and carry out development projects that were deferred because of poor economic conditions. Combined with the increasing demands of a growing population, long-term prospects for qualified planners should be good.

Job prospects will be best for those with a master's degree from an accredited planning program and relevant work experience. Planners who are willing to relocate for work also will have more job opportunities.

O*NET

➤ Urban and Regional Planners (19-3051.00)

Contacts for More Information

For more information on careers in urban and regional planning, visit

➤ American Planning Association (www.planning.org)

For more information on certification in urban and regional planning, visit

➤ American Institute of Certified Planners (www.planning.org/aicp/)

For more information on New Jersey licensure in planning, visit

➤ New Jersey State Board of Professional Planners (www.njconsumer affairs.gov/plan/)

For information on accredited urban and regional planning programs, visit

➤ Planning Accreditation Board (www.planningaccreditationboard. org/)

Zoologists and Wildlife Biologists

- **2012 Median Pay** .... $57,710 per year
  $27.74 per hour
- **Entry-Level Education** ....Bachelor's degree
- **Work Experience in a Related Occupation**............... None
- **On-the-Job Training** .... None
- **Number of Jobs 2012** 20,100
- **Job Outlook, 2012–22** .... 5% (Slower than average)
- **Employment Change, 2012–22** 1,000

What Zoologists and Wildlife Biologists Do

Zoologists and wildlife biologists study animals and other wildlife, and how they interact with their ecosystems. They study the physical characteristics of animals, animal behaviors, and the impacts humans have on wildlife and natural habitats.

Duties. Zoologists and wildlife biologists typically do the following:

- Develop and conduct experimental studies with animals in controlled or natural surroundings

- Collect biological data and specimens for analysis
- Study the characteristics of animals, such as their interactions with other species, reproduction, population dynamics, diseases, and movement patterns
- Analyze the influence that human activity has on wildlife and their natural habitats
- Estimate, monitor, and manage wildlife populations and invasive plants and animals
- Write research papers, reports, and scholarly articles that explain their findings
- Give presentations on research findings to academics and the general public
- Develop conservation plans and make recommendations on wildlife conservation and management issues to policymakers and the general public

Zoologists and wildlife biologists perform a variety of scientific tests and experiments. For example, they take blood samples from animals to assess their levels of nutrition, check animals for disease and parasites, and tag animals in order to track them.

Zoologists and wildlife biologists use geographic information systems (GIS), modeling software, and other computer programs to estimate wildlife populations and track the movements of animals. They also use these computer programs to forecast the spread of invasive species, diseases, changes in the availability of habitat, and other potential threats to wildlife.

Zoologists and wildlife biologists conduct research for a variety of purposes. For example, many zoologists and wildlife biologists work to increase our knowledge and understanding of wildlife species. They also work closely with public officials to develop wildlife management and conservation plans that protect species from threats and help animal populations return to and remain at sustainable levels.

Most zoologists and wildlife biologists work on research teams with other scientists and technicians. For example, zoologists and wildlife biologists may work with environmental scientists and hydrologists to monitor the effects of water pollution on fish populations.

Many zoologists and wildlife biologists study specific species. The following are examples of those who specialize by species:

- *Cetologists* study marine mammals, such as whales and dolphins.
- *Entomologists* study insects, such as beetles and butterflies.
- *Herpetologists* study reptiles and amphibians, such as snakes and frogs.
- *Ichthyologists* study wild fish, such as sharks and lungfish.

Zoologists and wildlife biologists may study animals in the field or in captivity.

- *Mammalogists* study mammals, such as monkeys and bears.
- *Ornithologists* study birds, such as hawks and penguins.

Some wildlife biologists study animals based on where they live. The following are examples of those who specialize by habitat:

- *Limnologists* study organisms that live in freshwater.
- *Marine biologists* study organisms that live in saltwater
- *Terrestrial biologists* study organisms that live on land, including plants and microbes. Microbiologists study microbes exclusively.

Other zoologists and wildlife biologists are identified by the aspects of zoology and wildlife biology they study, such as evolution and animal behavior. The following are some examples:

- *Botanists* study plants, including their growth, diseases, and structures. Agronomy is the plant science concerning crop production. For more information on agronomists, see the profile on agricultural and food scientists.
- *Ecologists* study ecosystems, which include all relationships between organisms and with the surrounding environments.
- *Evolutionary biologists* study the origins of species and the changes in their inherited characteristics over generations.

Many people with a zoology and wildlife biology background become high school teachers or college or university professors. For more information, see the profiles on high school teachers and postsecondary teachers.

Median Annual Wages, May 2012

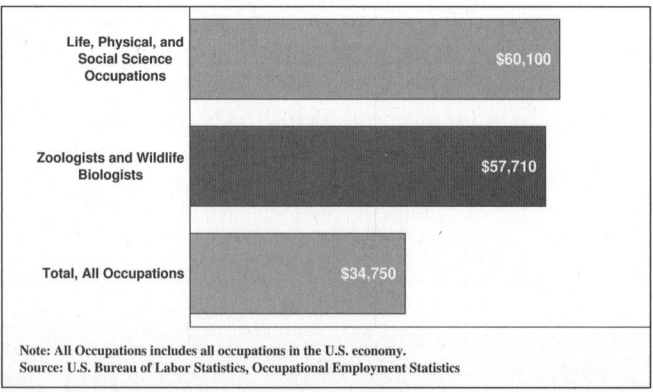

Life, Physical, and Social Science Occupations	$60,100
Zoologists and Wildlife Biologists	$57,710
Total, All Occupations	$34,750

Note: All Occupations includes all occupations in the U.S. economy.
Source: U.S. Bureau of Labor Statistics, Occupational Employment Statistics

Percent Change in Employment, Projected 2012–2022

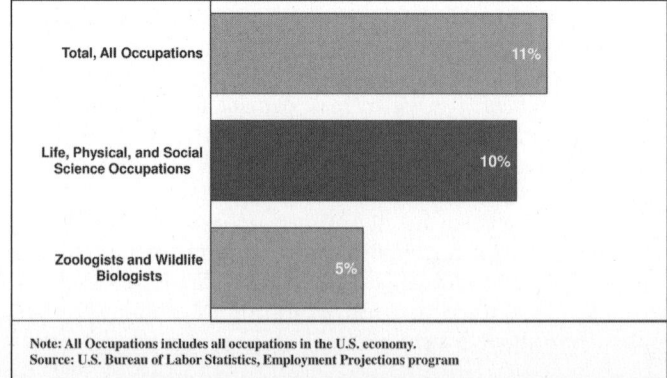

Total, All Occupations	11%
Life, Physical, and Social Science Occupations	10%
Zoologists and Wildlife Biologists	5%

Note: All Occupations includes all occupations in the U.S. economy.
Source: U.S. Bureau of Labor Statistics, Employment Projections program

Employment Projections Data for Zoologists and Wildlife Biologists

Occupational title	SOC Code	Employment, 2012	Projected Employment, 2022	Change, 2012–2022	
				Percent	Numeric
Zoologists and wildlife biologists	19-1023	20,100	21,100	5	1,000

Source: U.S. Bureau of Labor Statistics, Employment Projections Program

Note: Data are rounded. Go to **Occupational Information Included in the OOH** *for a discussion of the data in this table.*

Work Environment

Zoologists and wildlife biologists held about 20,100 jobs in 2012. They work in offices, laboratories, and outdoors. Depending on their position and interests, they may spend considerable time in the field gathering data and studying animals in their natural habitats.

Fieldwork can require zoologists and wildlife biologists to travel to remote locations anywhere in the world. For example, marine biologists may spend months at sea on a research ship. Other zoologists and wildlife biologists may spend significant amounts of time in deserts or remote mountainous and woodland regions. This ability to travel and study nature firsthand is often viewed as a benefit of working in this field, but there may be limited availability of modern amenities while traveling in remote areas.

Fieldwork can be physically demanding, and zoologists and wildlife biologists work in both warm and cold climates and in all types of weather. For example, marine biologists may need to spend significant amounts of time in cold water and on ships, which may cause seasickness. In all environments, working as a zoologist or wildlife biologist can be emotionally demanding since interpersonal contact may be limited.

The industries that employed the most zoologists and wildlife biologists in 2012 were as follows:

State government, excluding education and hospitals 34%
Federal government, excluding postal service 24
Research and development in the physical,
    engineering, and life sciences 10
Management, scientific, and technical consulting services 7
Colleges, universities, and professional schools; state 6
Local government, excluding education and hospitals 4

Work Schedules. Most zoologists and wildlife biologists work full time. They may work long or irregular hours when doing fieldwork. Zoologists and wildlife biologists who work with nocturnal animals may need to work a schedule which includes night hours.

How to Become One

Zoologists and wildlife biologists need a bachelor's degree for entry-level positions, but a master's degree is often needed for advancement. A Ph.D. is necessary for independent research and for university research positions.

Education. Zoologists and wildlife biologists need at least a bachelor's degree. Many schools offer bachelor's degree programs in zoology and wildlife biology or a closely related field such as ecology. An undergraduate degree in biology with coursework in zoology and wildlife biology is also good preparation for a career as a zoologist or wildlife biologist. Zoologists and wildlife biologists typically need at least a master's degree for higher-level positions. A Ph.D. is necessary for most independent research and for university research positions. Ph.D.-level researchers typically need familiarity with computer programming and statistical software.

Students typically take zoology and wildlife biology courses in ecology, anatomy, wildlife management, and cellular biology. They

also take courses that focus on a particular group of animals, such as herpetology (reptiles and amphibians) or ornithology (birds). Courses in botany, chemistry, and physics are important because zoologists and wildlife biologists must have a well-rounded scientific background. Wildlife biology programs may focus more on applied techniques in habitat analysis and conservation. Students should also take courses in mathematics and statistics because zoologists and wildlife biologists must be able to do complex data analysis.

Knowledge of computer science is important because zoologists and wildlife biologists frequently use advanced computer software, such as geographic information systems (GIS) and modeling software, to do their work.

Important Qualities

Communication skills. Zoologists and wildlife biologists write scientific papers and give talks to the public, policy makers, and academics.

Critical-thinking skills. Zoologists and wildlife biologists need sound reasoning and judgment to draw conclusions from experimental results and scientific observations.

Emotional stamina and stability. Zoologists and wildlife biologists may need to endure long periods of time with little human contact. As with other occupations that deal with animals, emotional stability is important when working with injured or sick animals.

Interpersonal skills. Zoologists and wildlife biologists typically work on teams. They must be able to work effectively with others to achieve their goals or negotiate conflicting goals.

Observation skills. Zoologists and wildlife biologists must be able to notice slight changes in an animal's characteristics, such as their behavior or appearance.

Outdoor skills. Zoologists and wildlife biologists may need to chop firewood, swim in cold water, navigate rough terrain in poor weather, or perform other activities associated with life in remote areas.

Problem-solving skills. Zoologists and wildlife biologists try to find the best possible solutions to threats that affect wildlife, such as disease and habitat loss.

Other Experience. Some zoologists and wildlife biologists may need to have well-rounded outdoors skills. They may need to be able to drive a tractor, use a generator, or provide for themselves in remote locations.

Advancement. Zoologists and wildlife biologists typically receive greater responsibility and independence in their work as they gain experience. More education can also lead to greater responsibility. Zoologists and wildlife biologists with a Ph.D. usually lead research teams and control the direction and content of projects. They may also be responsible for finding much of their own funding.

Pay

The median annual wage for zoologists and wildlife biologists was $57,710 in May 2012. The median wage is the wage at which half the workers in an occupation earned more than that amount and

Similar Occupations   This table shows a list of occupations with job duties that are similar to those of zoologists and wildlife biologists.

Occupations	Entry-level Education	2012 Pay	Projected Job Growth	Average Annual Openings
Agricultural and Food Scientists	See "How to Become One"	$58,636	10%	1,640
Biochemists and Biophysicists	Doctoral or professional degree	$81,480	18%	1,370
Biological Technicians	Bachelor's degree	$39,750	10%	3,210
Conservation Scientists and Foresters	Bachelor's degree	$59,354	3%	1,080
Environmental Scientists and Specialists	Bachelor's degree	$63,570	15%	3,970
Microbiologists	Bachelor's degree	$66,260	7%	710
Postsecondary Teachers	See "How to Become One"	$70,380	19%	42,690
Veterinarians	Doctoral or professional degree	$84,460	12%	3,100

half earned less. The lowest 10 percent earned less than $37,100, and the top 10 percent earned more than $95,430.

In May 2012, the median annual wages for zoologists and wildlife biologists in the top six industries in which these scientists worked were as follows:

Federal government, excluding postal service	$72,700
Research and development in the physical, engineering, and life sciences	59,670
Local government, excluding education and hospitals	57,110
Management, scientific, and technical consulting services	56,740
Colleges, universities, and professional schools; state	55,610
State government, excluding education and hospitals	51,780

Job Outlook

Employment of zoologists and wildlife biologists is projected to grow 5 percent from 2012 to 2022, slower than the average for all occupations. More zoologists and wildlife biologists will be needed to study the impact of population growth and development on wildlife and their habitats. However, demand for zoologists and wildlife biologists in local, state, and federal government agencies, such as the United States Fish and Wildlife Service, will vary based on the budgets for these agencies.

As the population grows and expands into new areas, it will expose wildlife to threats such as disease, invasive species, and habitat loss. Increased human activity causes problems, such as pollution and climate change, which endanger wildlife. Changes in climate patterns can be detrimental to the migration habits of animals, and increased sea levels can destroy wetlands. Therefore, zoologists and wildlife biologists will be needed to research, develop, and carry out wildlife management and conservation plans that combat these threats and protect our biological resources.

Job Prospects. Zoologists and wildlife biologists should have good job opportunities. In addition to job growth, many job openings will be created by zoologists and wildlife biologists who retire, advance to management positions, or change careers.

Year to year, the number of job openings available in local, state, and federal government agencies, such as the United States Fish and Wildlife Service, will vary based on the budgets for these agencies.

O*NET

➤ Zoologists and Wildlife Biologists (19-1023.00)

Contacts for More Information

For more information about zoologists and wildlife biologists, visit
➤ The Wildlife Society (www.wildlife.org)
➤ Association of Zoos and Aquariums (www.aza.org/)
➤ American Society of Mammalogists (www.mammalsociety.org/)
➤ American Society of Ichthyologists and Herpetologists (www.asih.org/)
➤ Ornithological Societies of North America (www.osnabirds.org/)
➤ Zoological Association of America (http://zaa.org/)

For more information about issues in zoology and wildlife biology, visit
➤ United States Geographical Survey (http://education.usgs.gov/index.html)
➤ National Park Service (www.nature.nps.gov/index.cfm)

For more information about careers in botany, visit
➤ Botanical Society of America (www.botany.org/bsa/careers/)

For more information about careers in ecology, visit
➤ Ecological Society of America (www.esa.org/)

For information on federal government education requirements for zoologists and wildlife biologists, visit
➤ U.S. Office of Personnel Management (www.opm.gov/qualifications/Standards/IORs/gs0400/0486.htm)

To find job openings for zoologists and wildlife biologists in the federal government, visit
➤ USAJOBS (www.usajobs.gov)

Management

Administrative Services Managers

- **2012 Median Pay** .... $81,080 per year
  $38.98 per hour
- **Entry-Level Education** .... Bachelor's degree
- **Work Experience in a Related Occupation** ...... Less than 5 years
- **On-the-Job Training** .... None
- **Number of Jobs 2012** 280,800
- **Job Outlook, 2012–22** .... 12% (As fast as average)
- **Employment Change, 2012–22** 34,200

What Administrative Services Managers Do

Administrative services managers plan, direct, and coordinate supportive services of an organization. Their specific responsibilities vary by the type of organization and may include keeping records, distributing mail, and planning and maintaining facilities. In a small organization, they may direct all support services and may be called the *business office manager*. Large organizations may have several layers of administrative managers who specialize in different areas.

Duties. Administrative services managers typically do the following:

- Buy, store, and distribute supplies
- Supervise clerical and administrative personnel
- Set goals and deadlines for the department
- Develop, manage, and monitor records
- Recommend changes to policies or procedures in order to improve operations, such as changing what supplies are kept or how to improve recordkeeping
- Plan budgets for contracts, equipment, and supplies
- Monitor the facility to ensure that it remains safe, secure, and well maintained
- Oversee the maintenance and repair of machinery, equipment, and electrical and mechanical systems
- Ensure that facilities meet environmental, health, and security standards and comply with government regulations

Administrative services managers review plans and contracts to ensure smooth implementation.

Administrative services managers plan, coordinate, and direct a broad range of services that allow organizations to operate efficiently. An organization may have several managers who oversee activities that meet the needs of multiple departments, such as mail, printing and copying, recordkeeping, security, building maintenance, and recycling.

The work of administrative services managers can make a difference in employees' productivity and satisfaction. For example, an administrative services manager might be responsible for making sure that the organization has the supplies and services it needs. In addition, an administrative services manager who is responsible for coordinating space allocation might take into account employee morale and available funds when determining the best way to arrange a given physical space.

Median Annual Wages, May 2012

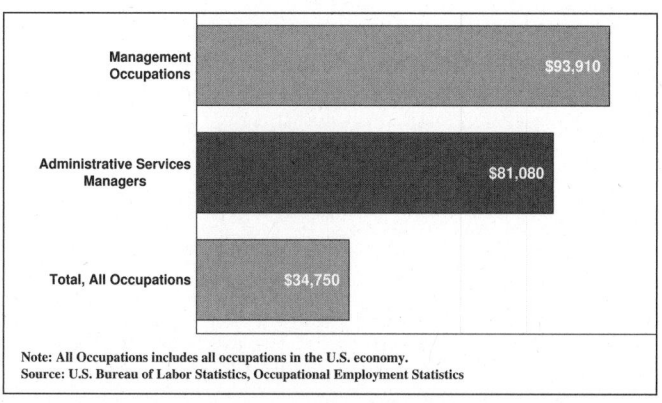

Management Occupations — $93,910
Administrative Services Managers — $81,080
Total, All Occupations — $34,750

Note: All Occupations includes all occupations in the U.S. economy.
Source: U.S. Bureau of Labor Statistics, Occupational Employment Statistics

Percent Change in Employment, Projected 2012–2022

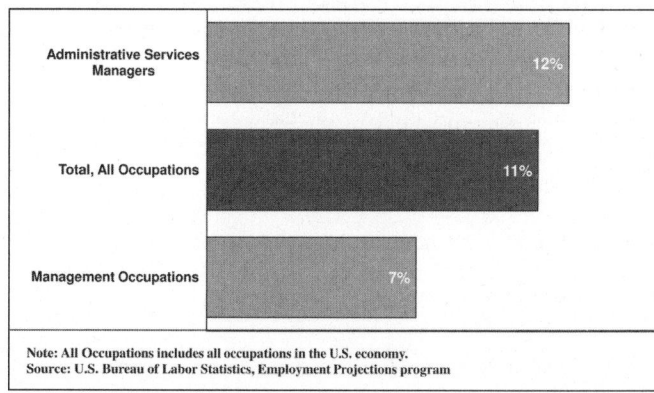

Administrative Services Managers — 12%
Total, All Occupations — 11%
Management Occupations — 7%

Note: All Occupations includes all occupations in the U.S. economy.
Source: U.S. Bureau of Labor Statistics, Employment Projections program

Employment Projections Data for Administrative Services Managers

Occupational title	SOC Code	Employment, 2012	Projected Employment, 2022	Change, 2012–2022	
				Percent	Numeric
Administrative services managers...	11-3011	280,800	315,000	12	34,200

Source: U.S. Bureau of Labor Statistics, Employment Projections Program

Note: Data are rounded. Go to **Occupational Information Included in the OOH** *for a discussion of the data in this table.*

Administrative services managers also ensure that the organization honors its contracts and follows government regulations and safety standards.

Administrative services managers may examine energy consumption patterns, technology usage, and office equipment. For example, managers may recommend buying new or different equipment or supplies in order to lower energy costs or improve indoor air quality.

Administrative services managers also plan for maintenance and the future replacement of equipment, such as computers. A timely replacement of equipment can help save money for the organization, because eventually the cost of upgrading and maintaining equipment becomes higher than the cost of buying new equipment.

The following are examples of types of administrative services managers:

Contract administrators handle buying, storing, and distributing equipment and supplies. They also oversee getting rid of surplus or unclaimed property.

Facility managers oversee buildings, grounds, equipment, and supplies. Their duties fall into several categories, including overseeing operations and maintenance, planning and managing projects, and dealing with environmental factors.

Facility managers may oversee renovation projects to improve efficiency or ensure that facilities meet government regulations and environmental, health, and security standards. For example, they may influence building renovation projects by recommending energy-saving alternatives or efficiencies that reduce waste. In addition, facility managers continually monitor the facility to ensure that it remains safe, secure, and well maintained. Facility managers also are responsible for directing staff, including maintenance, grounds, and custodial workers.

Records and information managers develop, monitor, and manage an organization's records. They provide information to executive management, and they ensure that employees throughout the organization follow information and records management guidelines.

Work Environment

Administrative services managers held about 280,800 jobs in 2012.

Administrative services managers spend much of their day in an office. They sometimes make site visits around the building, go outdoors to supervise groundskeeping activities, or inspect other facilities under their management.

The industries that employed the most administrative services managers in 2012 were as follows:

Educational services; state, local, and private	16%
Health care	13
State and local government, excluding education and hospitals	12
Professional, scientific, and technical services	9
Finance and insurance	8

Work Schedules. Most administrative services managers worked full time in 2012. About one-fourth worked more than 40 hours

per week. Facility managers often are on call to address a variety of problems that can arise in a facility during nonworking hours.

How to Become One

Educational requirements vary by the type of organization and the work they do. They must have related work experience.

Education. A high school diploma or a General Educational Development (GED) diploma is typically required for someone to become an administrative services manager. However, some administrative services managers need at least a bachelor's degree. Those with a bachelor's degree typically study business, engineering, or facility management.

Licenses, Certifications, and Registrations. The International Facility Management Association offers a competency-based professional certification program for administrative services managers. Completing this program may give prospective job candidates an advantage. The program has two levels: the Facilities Management Professional (FMP) certification and the Certified Facility Manager (CFM) certification. People entering the profession can get the FMP as a steppingstone to the CFM. For the CFM, applicants must meet certain educational and experience requirements.

Work Experience

Administrative services managers must have related work experience reflecting managerial and leadership abilities. For example, contract administrators need experience in purchasing and sales, as well as knowledge of the variety of supplies, machinery, and equipment that the organization uses. Managers who are concerned with supply, inventory, and distribution should be experienced in receiving, warehousing, packaging, shipping, transportation, and related operations.

Advancement. Advancement of facility managers is based on the practices and size of individual organizations. Some facility managers transfer among departments within an organization or work their way up from technical positions. Others advance through a progression of facility management positions that offer additional responsibilities. Advancement is easier in large organizations that employ several levels and types of administrative services managers.

A master's degree in business administration or a related field can enhance a manager's opportunities to advance to higher level positions, such as director of administrative services. Some experienced managers may join or establish a management consulting firm to provide administrative management services to other organizations on a contract basis.

Important Qualities

Analytical skills. Administrative services managers must be able to review an organization's procedures and find ways to improve efficiency.

Communication skills. Much of an administrative services manager's time is spent working with other people. Therefore, communication is a key quality.

Similar Occupations   This table shows a list of occupations with job duties that are similar to those of administrative services managers.

Occupations	Entry-level Education	2012 Pay	Projected Job Growth	Average Annual Openings
Cost Estimators	Bachelor's degree	$58,860	26%	11,800
Property, Real Estate, and Community Association Managers	High school diploma or equivalent	$52,610	12%	10,210
Purchasing Managers, Buyers, and Purchasing Agents	See "How to Become One"	$63,128	4%	12,230
Top Executives	Bachelor's degree	$104,073	11%	70,090

Detail oriented. Administrative services managers must pay attention to details. This quality is necessary across a range of tasks, from ensuring that the organization complies with building codes to managing the process of buying equipment.

Leadership skills. In managing workers and coordinating administrative duties, administrative services managers must be able to motivate employees and deal with issues that may arise.

Pay

The median annual wage for administrative services managers was $81,080 in May 2012. The median wage is the wage at which half the workers in an occupation earned more than that amount and half earned less. The lowest 10 percent earned less than $44,330, and the top 10 percent earned more than $143,070.

In May 2012, the median annual wages for administrative services managers in the top five industries in which these managers worked were as follows:

Finance and insurance $93,260
Professional, scientific, and technical services...................... 88,620
State and local government, excluding education
    and hospitals... 81,610
Health care 76,870
Educational services; state, local, and private 76,830

Job Outlook

Employment of administrative services managers is projected to grow 12 percent from 2012 to 2022, about as fast as the average for all occupations.

Administrative tasks, including facility management and records and information management, will remain important in a wide range of industries. Facility managers will be needed to plan for natural disasters, ensuring that any damage to a building will be minimal and that the organization can get back to work quickly.

In addition, facility managers will be in demand because there will be a greater focus on the environmental impact and energy efficiency of the buildings they manage. Improving energy efficiency can reduce costs and often is required by regulation. For example, building codes typically ensure that buildings meet environmental standards. Facility managers will be needed to oversee these improvements, in areas from heating and air systems to roofing.

Organizations also are expected to have more facility managers on staff, as opposed to using managers who manage several facilities on a contract basis. This will create demand for a larger total number of facility managers, leading to stronger growth for the occupation.

Contract administrators also are expected to be in demand as organizations contract out many services, such as food services, janitorial services, grounds maintenance, and equipment repair.

Job Prospects. Applicants will likely face strong competition for the limited number of higher level administrative services management jobs. Competition should be less severe for lower level

management jobs. Job prospects also are expected to be better for those who can manage a wide range of responsibilities than for those who specialize in particular functions.

O*NET

➤ Administrative Services Managers (11-3011.00)

Contacts for More Information

For more information about administrative services management, as well as the Certified Facility Manager designation, visit
➤ International Facility Management Association (http://ifma.org/)

Advertising, Promotions, and Marketing Managers

- **2012 Median Pay** .... $115,750 per year
                                                                 $55.65 per hour
- **Entry-Level Education** ....Bachelor's degree
- **Work Experience in a Related Occupation**.... See "How to Become One"
- **On-the-Job Training** .... None
- **Number of Jobs 2012** 216,000
- **Job Outlook, 2012–22** .... 12% (As fast as average)
- **Employment Change, 2012–22** 25,400

What Advertising, Promotions, and Marketing Managers Do

Advertising, promotions, and marketing managers plan programs to generate interest in a product or service. They work with art directors, sales agents, and financial staff members.

Duties. Advertising, promotions, and marketing managers typically do the following:

- Work with department heads or staff to discuss topics such as budgets and contracts, marketing plans, and the selection of advertising media
- Plan advertising and promotional campaigns
- Plan advertising, including which media to advertise in, such as radio, television, print, online media, and billboards
- Negotiate advertising contracts
- Evaluate the look and feel of websites used in campaigns or layouts, which are sketches or plans for an advertisement
- Initiate market research studies and analyze their findings to understand customer and market opportunities for businesses

- Develop pricing strategies for products or services marketed to the target customers of a firm

- Meet with clients to provide marketing or technical advice

- Direct the hiring of advertising, promotions, and marketing staff and oversee their daily activities

Advertising managers create interest among potential buyers of a product or service for a department, for an entire organization, or on a project basis (account). They work in advertising agencies that put together advertising campaigns for clients, in media firms that sell advertising space or time, and in organizations that advertise heavily.

Advertising managers work with sales staff and others to generate ideas for an advertising campaign. They oversee the staff that develops the advertising. They work with the finance department to prepare a budget and cost estimates for the advertising campaign.

Often, advertising managers serve as liaisons between the client requiring the advertising and an advertising or promotion agency that develops and places the ads. In larger organizations with an extensive advertising department, different advertising managers may oversee in-house accounts and creative and media services departments.

In addition, some advertising managers specialize in a particular field or type of advertising. For example, *media directors* determine the way in which an advertising campaign reaches customers. They can use any or all of various media, including radio, television, newspapers, magazines, the Internet, and outdoor signs.

Advertising managers known as *account executives* manage clients' accounts, but they are not responsible for developing or supervising the creation or presentation of the advertising. That task becomes the work of the creative services department.

Promotions managers direct programs that combine advertising with purchasing incentives to increase sales. Often, the programs use direct mail, inserts in newspapers, Internet advertisements, in-store displays, product endorsements, or special events to target customers. Purchasing incentives may include discounts, samples, gifts, rebates, coupons, sweepstakes, or contests.

Marketing managers estimate the demand for products and services that an organization and its competitors offer. They identify potential markets for the organization's products.

Marketing managers also develop pricing strategies to help organizations maximize their profits and market share while ensuring that the organizations' customers are satisfied. They work with sales, public relations, and product development staff.

For example, a marketing manager may monitor trends that indicate the need for a new product or service. Then they oversee the development of that product or service. For more information on sales or public relations, see the profiles on sales managers, pub-

Advertising, promotions, and marketing managers often serve as liaisons between the firm requiring the advertising and an advertising or promotion agency that develops and places the ads.

lic relations and fundraising managers, public relations specialists, and market research analysts.

Work Environment

Advertising and promotions managers held about 35,500 jobs in 2012. The industries that employed the most advertising and promotions managers in 2012 were as follows:

Advertising, public relations, and related services 24%
Management of companies and enterprises 8
Retail trade 7
Religious, grantmaking, civic, professional, and similar
   organizations 6
Information 6

Marketing managers held about 180,500 jobs in 2012. The industries that employed the most marketing managers in 2012 were as follows:

Professional, scientific, and technical services 19%
Management of companies and enterprises 16

Median Annual Wages, May 2012

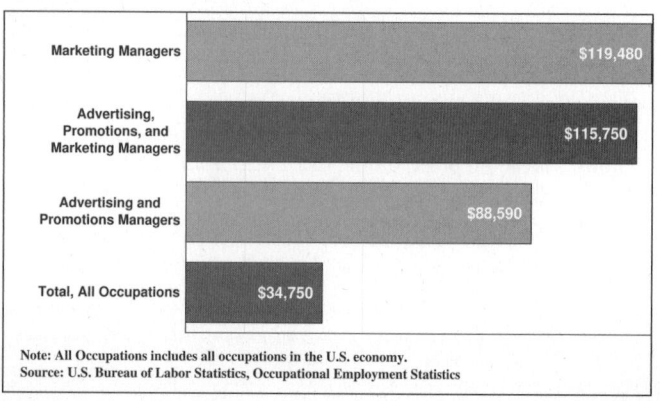

Note: All Occupations includes all occupations in the U.S. economy.
Source: U.S. Bureau of Labor Statistics, Occupational Employment Statistics

Percent Change in Employment, Projected 2012–2022

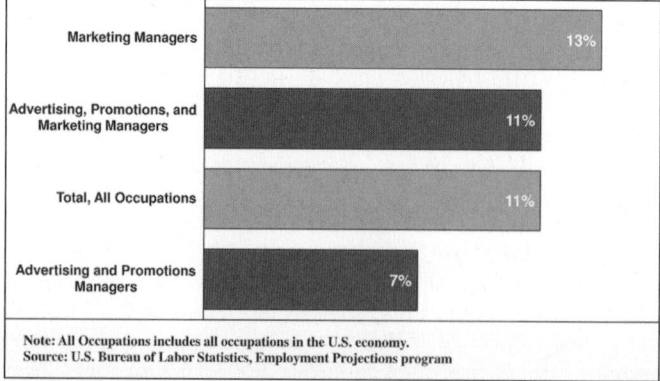

Note: All Occupations includes all occupations in the U.S. economy.
Source: U.S. Bureau of Labor Statistics, Employment Projections program

Employment Projections Data for Advertising, Promotions, and Marketing Managers

Occupational title	SOC Code	Employment, 2012	Projected Employment, 2022	Change, 2012–2022	
				Percent	Numeric
Advertising, promotions, and marketing managers	—	216,000	241,400	12	25,400
Advertising and promotions managers.............................	11-2011	35,500	38,000	7	2,400
Marketing managers	11-2021	180,500	203,400	13	22,900

Source: U.S. Bureau of Labor Statistics, Employment Projections Program

Note: Data are rounded. Go to Occupational Information Included in the OOH for a discussion of the data in this table.

Manufacturing...	12
Finance and insurance	12
Wholesale trade	9

Because the work of advertising, promotions, and marketing managers directly affects a firm's revenue, they typically work closely with top executives. The jobs of advertising, promotions, and marketing managers are usually stressful, particularly near deadlines. They may travel to meet with clients or representatives of communications media.

Work Schedules. Most advertising, promotions, and marketing managers work full time. About 2 in 5 advertising and promotions managers worked more than 40 hours per week in 2012.

How to Become One

A bachelor's degree is required for most advertising, promotions, and marketing management positions. These managers typically have work experience in advertising, marketing, promotions, or sales.

Education. A bachelor's degree is required for most advertising, promotions, and marketing management positions. For advertising management positions, some employers prefer a bachelor's degree in advertising or journalism. A relevant course of study might include classes in marketing, consumer behavior, market research, sales, communication methods and technology, visual arts, art history, and photography.

Most marketing managers have a bachelor's degree. Courses in business law, management, economics, finance, computer science, mathematics, and statistics are advantageous. For example, courses in computer science are helpful in developing an approach to maximize traffic through online search results, which is critical for digital advertisements and promotions. In addition, completing an internship while in school is highly recommended.

Work Experience in a Related Occupation. Advertising, promotional, and marketing managers typically have work experience in advertising, marketing, promotions, or sales. For example, many managers are former sales representatives; purchasing agents; buyers; or product, advertising, promotions, or public relations specialists.

Important Qualities

Analytical skills. Because the advertising industry changes with the rise of digital media, advertising, promotions, and marketing managers must be able to analyze industry trends to determine the most promising strategies for their organization.

Communication skills. Managers must be able to communicate effectively with a broad-based team made up of other managers or staff members during the advertising, promotions, and marketing process. They must also be able to communicate persuasively to the public.

Creativity. Advertising, promotions, and marketing managers must be able to generate new and imaginative ideas.

Decision-making skills. Managers often must choose between competing advertising and marketing strategies put forward by staff.

Interpersonal skills. These managers must deal with a range of people in different roles, both inside and outside the organization.

Organizational skills. Advertising, promotions, and marketing managers must manage their time and budget efficiently while directing and motivating staff members.

Pay

The median annual wage for advertising and promotions managers was $88,590 in May 2012. The median wage is the wage at which half the workers in an occupation earned more than that amount and half earned less. The lowest 10 percent earned less than $43,270, and the top 10 percent earned more than $187,200.

Similar Occupations   This table shows a list of occupations with job duties that are similar to those of advertising, promotions, and marketing managers.

Occupations	Entry-level Education	2012 Pay	Projected Job Growth	Average Annual Openings
Advertising Sales Agents	High school diploma or equivalent	$46,290	-1%	4,750
Art Directors	Bachelor's degree	$80,880	3%	2,000
Editors	Bachelor's degree	$53,880	-2%	2,800
Financial Managers	Bachelor's degree	$109,740	9%	14,690
Graphic Designers	Bachelor's degree	$44,150	7%	8,600
Market Research Analysts	Bachelor's degree	$60,300	32%	18,850
Public Relations and Fundraising Managers	Bachelor's degree	$95,450	13%	2,130
Public Relations Specialists	Bachelor's degree	$54,170	12%	5,880
Sales Managers	Bachelor's degree	$105,260	8%	10,690

The median annual wage for marketing managers was $119,480 in May 2012. The lowest 10 percent earned less than $62,650, and the top 10 percent earned more than $187,200.

Job Outlook

Employment of advertising and promotions managers is projected to grow 7 percent from 2012 to 2022, slower than the average for all occupations.

Employment of marketing managers is projected to grow 13 percent from 2012 to 2022, about as fast as the average for all occupations.

Advertising, promotional, and marketing campaigns will continue to be essential for organizations as they look to maintain and expand their share of the market.

Advertising and promotions managers will be needed to plan, direct, and coordinate advertising and promotional campaigns, as well as to introduce new products to the marketplace. They will also be needed to manage digital media campaigns, which often target customers through the use of websites, social media, or live chats.

Newspaper publishers, one of the top-employing industries of advertising and promotions managers, are projected to decline over the projection period. The continued rise of electronic media will result in decreasing demand for print newspapers. However, advertising and promotions managers are expected to see employment growth in other areas, in which they will be needed to plan the digital advertisements that replace print ads as consumers increasingly spend more time online.

Because marketing managers and their departments are important to an organization's revenue, marketing managers are less likely to be let go than other types of managers. Marketing managers will continue to be in demand as organizations seek to market their products to specific customers and localities.

Job Prospects. Advertising, promotions, and marketing manager positions are highly desirable and are often sought by other managers and experienced professionals. As a result, strong competition is expected. With Internet-based advertising becoming more important, advertising managers who can navigate the digital world should have the best prospects.

O*NET

➤ Advertising and Promotions Managers (11-2011.00)
➤ Green Marketers (11-2011.01)
➤ Marketing Managers (11-2021.00)

Contacts for More Information

For more information about advertising managers, visit
➤ American Association of Advertising Agencies (www.aaaa.org/)

Architectural and Engineering Managers

- **2012 Median Pay** .... $124,870 per year
  $60.03 per hour
- **Entry-Level Education** .... Bachelor's degree
- **Work Experience in a Related Occupation** ... 5 years or more
- **On-the-Job Training** .... None
- **Number of Jobs 2012** 193,800
- **Job Outlook, 2012–22** .... 7% (Slower than average)
- **Employment Change, 2012–22** 13,100

What Architectural and Engineering Managers Do

Architectural and engineering managers plan, coordinate, and direct activities in architectural and engineering companies.

Duties. Architectural and engineering managers typically do the following:

- Make detailed plans for the development of new products and designs
- Lead research and development teams that produce new products, processes, or designs
- Check the technical accuracy of their team's work
- Ensure the soundness of methods their staff uses
- Coordinate work with other teams and managers
- Propose budgets for projects and programs
- Determine staff, training, and equipment needs
- Hire, assign, and supervise staff

Architectural and engineering managers use their knowledge of architecture or engineering to oversee a variety of activities. They may direct and coordinate production, operations, quality assurance, testing, or maintenance at manufacturing sites, industrial plants, engineering services firms, and research-and-development laboratories.

Architectural and engineering managers are responsible for developing the overall concept of a new product or for solving technical problems preventing the completion of a project. To accomplish their aim, they must determine technical goals and produce detailed plans.

Architectural and engineering managers spend a great deal of time coordinating the activities of their unit with the activities of other units or organizations. They often confer with other managers, including financial, production, and marketing managers, and with contractors and equipment and materials suppliers.

In addition, architectural and engineering managers must know how to prepare budgets and hire and supervise employees. They propose budgets for projects and programs and determine staff, training, and equipment needs. These managers also must hire people and assign them to carry out specific parts of each project. Architectural and engineering managers supervise the work of their employees and set schedules and administrative procedures.

In addition to technical knowledge, architectural and engineering managers need administrative and communication skills.

Median Annual Wages, May 2012

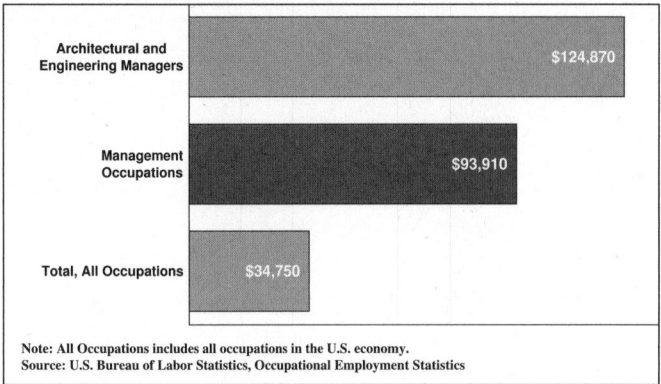

Architectural and Engineering Managers — $124,870

Management Occupations — $93,910

Total, All Occupations — $34,750

Note: All Occupations includes all occupations in the U.S. economy.
Source: U.S. Bureau of Labor Statistics, Occupational Employment Statistics

Percent Change in Employment, Projected 2012–2022

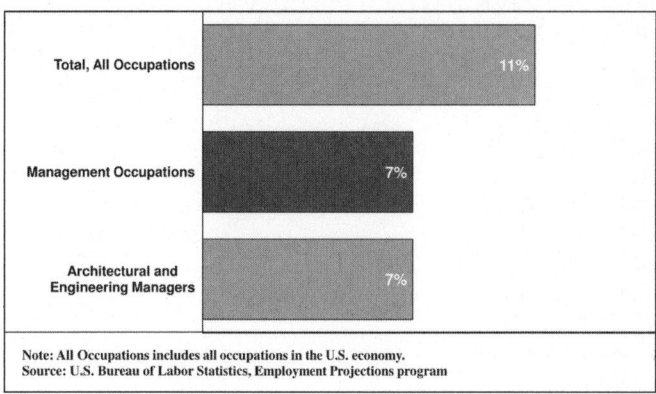

Total, All Occupations — 11%

Management Occupations — 7%

Architectural and Engineering Managers — 7%

Note: All Occupations includes all occupations in the U.S. economy.
Source: U.S. Bureau of Labor Statistics, Employment Projections program

Work Environment

Architectural and engineering managers held about 193,800 jobs in 2012.

Architectural and engineering managers spend most of their time working in offices. Some also may work in laboratories and industrial production plants or at construction sites.

The industries that employed the most architectural and engineering managers in 2012 were as follows:

Manufacturing 36%
Architectural, engineering, and related services 23
Government 9
Mining, quarrying, and oil and gas extraction 5
Scientific research and development services 5

Work Schedules. Although most managers work full time, about half worked more than 40 hours a week in 2012. As a result, workers often experience considerable pressure to meet deadlines and budgets.

How to Become One

Architectural and engineering managers typically need at least a bachelor's degree and considerable work experience as an architect or engineer.

Education. The vast majority of architectural and engineering managers have at least a bachelor's degree in an engineering specialty or a professional degree in architecture.

Many also gain business management skills by completing a master's degree in engineering management (MEM or MsEM) or technology management (MSTM) or a master's in business administration (MBA), either before or after advancing to management positions. Employers will sometimes pay for such education. Typically, those who prefer to manage in technical areas pursue an MsEM or MSTM and those interested in more general management skills earn an MBA.

Engineering management programs usually include classes in accounting, engineering economics, financial management, industrial and human resources management, and quality control.

Technology management programs typically provide instruction in production and operations management, project management, computer applications, quality control, safety and health issues, statistics, and general management principles.

Work Experience in a Related Occupation. Managers advance to their positions after years of employment as an architect or engineer. They usually have experience working on increasingly difficult projects, developing designs, solving problems, and making decisions. Before moving up to a management position, they also typically have experience leading engineering teams.

Important Qualities

Analytical skills. Architectural and engineering managers must evaluate information carefully and be able to solve complex problems.

Communication skills. Architectural and engineering managers oversee staff and confer with other levels of management. They must communicate orders effectively and be able to lead teams to meet goals.

Detail oriented. Architectural and engineering managers must pay attention to detail. Their duties require an understanding of complex systems, and a minor error can cause major problems.

Math skills. Architectural and engineering managers use calculus and other advanced mathematics to develop new products and processes.

Organizational skills. Architectural and engineering managers keep track of many workers, schedules, and budgets all at once.

Technical skills. Managers in these fields must thoroughly understand the specific area (architecture or a particular type of engineering) that they are managing.

Pay

The median annual wage for architectural and engineering managers was $124,870 in May 2012. The median wage is the wage at which half the workers in an occupation earned more than that amount and half earned less. The lowest 10 percent earned less than $80,300, and the top 10 percent earned more than $187,200.

Employment Projections Data for Architectural and Engineering Managers

Occupational title	SOC Code	Employment, 2012	Projected Employment, 2022	Change, 2012–2022 Percent	Change, 2012–2022 Numeric
Architectural and engineering managers	11-9041	193,800	206,900	7	13,100

Source: U.S. Bureau of Labor Statistics, Employment Projections Program

Note: Data are rounded. Go to **Occupational Information Included in the OOH** *for a discussion of the data in this table.*

Similar Occupations This table shows a list of occupations with job duties that are similar to those of architectural and engineering managers.

Occupations	Entry-level Education	2012 Pay	Projected Job Growth	Average Annual Openings
Architects	Bachelor's degree	$73,090	17%	4,410
Chemical Engineers	Bachelor's degree	$94,350	5%	920
Civil Engineers	Bachelor's degree	$79,340	20%	12,010
Construction Managers	Bachelor's degree	$82,790	16%	15,460
Electrical and Electronics Engineers	Bachelor's degree	$89,701	4%	7,940
Industrial Production Managers	Bachelor's degree	$89,190	-2%	3,140
Mechanical Engineers	Bachelor's degree	$80,580	4%	9,970
Natural Sciences Managers	Bachelor's degree	$115,730	6%	1,370

In May 2012, the median annual wages for architectural and engineering managers in the top five industries in which these managers worked were as follows:

Mining, quarrying, and oil and gas extraction................. $147,250
Scientific research and development services 142,310
Manufacturing... 124,000
Architectural, engineering, and related services................. 123,310
Government... 119,240

In addition, architectural and engineering managers, especially those at higher levels, often receive more benefits–such as expense accounts and bonuses–than nonmanagers.

Job Outlook

Employment of architectural and engineering managers is projected to grow 7 percent from 2012 to 2022, slower than the average for all occupations. Employment growth will largely reflect the growth of the industries in which these managers are employed.

For example, the engineering services industry is projected to grow 21 percent from 2012 to 2022, adding the most new architectural and engineering manager jobs. Engineering services is composed of consulting firms that provide services to many different industries. Civil engineering services related to the construction of large buildings, roads, and other infrastructure projects are the most common services provided by this industry. Demand for these services is expected to be high as the nation's aging infrastructure needs repair and expansion. Mechanical and electrical engineering services are also commonly provided by this industry and will continue to be used on many different projects.

However, employment in manufacturing–the largest industry employing architectural and engineering managers–is projected to decline by 6 percent from 2012 to 2022, impeding overall growth of the occupation.

Job Prospects. Because these jobs are highly desirable, candidates can expect very strong competition for openings.

Those with technical knowledge, strong communication skills, and years of related work experience will likely be in the best position to become managers.

In addition, because architectural and engineering managers are involved in the financial, production, and marketing activities of their firm, business management skills can be beneficial for those seeking management positions.

O*NET

➤ Architectural and Engineering Managers (11-9041.00)
➤ Biofuels/Biodiesel Technology and Product Development Managers (11-9041.01)

Contacts for More Information

For information on architecture and engineering management programs, visit
➤ American Institute of Architects (www.aia.org)
➤ ABET (www.abet.org)
➤ Association of Technology, Management, and Applied Engineering (http://atmae.org/)

Compensation and Benefits Managers

- **2012 Median Pay** .... $95,250 per year
  $45.79 per hour
- **Entry-Level Education** ....Bachelor's degree
- **Work Experience in a Related Occupation** ... 5 years or more
- **On-the-Job Training** .... None
- **Number of Jobs 2012** 20,700
- **Job Outlook, 2012–22** .... 3% (Slower than average)
- **Employment Change, 2012–22** 600

What Compensation and Benefits Managers Do

Compensation managers plan, direct, and coordinate how much an organization pays its employees and how employees are paid. Benefits managers plan, direct, and coordinate retirement plans, health insurance, and other benefits that an organization offers its employees.

Duties. Compensation and benefits managers typically do the following:

- Set the organization's pay structure and benefits offerings
- Determine competitive wage rates and develop or modify compensation plans
- Evaluate employee benefits policies to assess whether they are current, competitive, and legal
- Choose and manage outside partners such as benefits vendors and investment brokers
- Coordinate and supervise the work activities of specialists and support staff
- Oversee the distribution of pay and benefits information to the organization's employees
- Ensure that pay and benefits plans comply with federal and state regulations
- Prepare a program budget and keep operations within budget

Compensation and benefits managers explain company procedures and benefits to new employees.

Although some managers administer both the compensation and benefits programs in an organization, other managers–particularly at large organizations–often specialize and oversee one or the other. All managers, however, routinely meet with senior staff, managers of other human resources departments, and the financial officers of their organization. They provide expertise and make recommendations on compensation and benefits policies, programs, and plans.

In addition to their administrative responsibilities, compensation and benefits managers also have several technical and analytical duties. For example, they may perform complex data analysis to determine the best pay and benefits plans for an organization. They may also monitor trends affecting pay and benefits and assess how their organization can improve its practices or policies. Using a variety of analytical, database, and presentation software, managers draw conclusions, present their findings, and make recommendations to other managers in the organization.

Compensation managers are responsible for managing an organization's pay structure. They monitor market conditions and government regulations to ensure their pay rates are current and competitive. They may analyze data on wages and salaries, and they evaluate how their organization's pay structure compares with that of other companies. Compensation managers then use this information to maintain or develop pay scales for an organization.

Some also design pay-for-performance plans, which include guidelines for bonuses and incentive pay. They may help to determine commission rates and other incentives for sales staff.

Benefits managers administer a company's employee benefits program, which includes retirement plans, leave policies, wellness programs, and insurance policies such as health, life, and disability. They select benefits vendors and oversee the enrollment, renewal, and distribution processes for an organization's employees. They must frequently monitor government regulations and market trends to ensure that their programs are legal, current, and competitive.

Work Environment

Compensation and benefits managers held about 20,700 jobs in 2012 and worked in nearly every industry. Compensation and benefits managers typically work in offices.

Work Schedules. Most compensation and benefits managers work full time and may work long hours.

How to Become One

Candidates need a combination of education and related work experience to become a compensation and benefits manager.

Education. Compensation and benefits managers need at least a bachelor's degree for most positions, and some jobs require a master's degree. Because not all undergraduate programs offer a degree in human resources, managers often have a bachelor's degree in business administration, business management, finance, or a related field.

Many employers prefer to hire managers who have a master's degree, particularly one with a concentration in human resources management, finance, or business administration (MBA).

Work Experience in a Related Occupation. Related work experience is essential for compensation and benefits managers. Compensation managers usually need experience in compensation or another job where they performed complex financial analysis. For example, compensation and benefits managers often start out as compensation, benefits, and job analysis specialists.

In addition to experience working with benefits plans, most benefits managers must have strong knowledge of benefits practices and government regulations. Work experience in other human resource fields, finance, or management is also helpful for getting a job as a benefits manager.

Licenses, Certifications, and Registrations. Many professional associations for human resources workers offer classes to enhance the skills and credibility of their members. Some associations, including the International Foundation of Employee Benefit Plans and WorldatWork, offer certification programs that specialize in compensation and benefits. Others, including the HR Certification Institute, offer general human resources credentials.

Median Annual Wages, May 2012

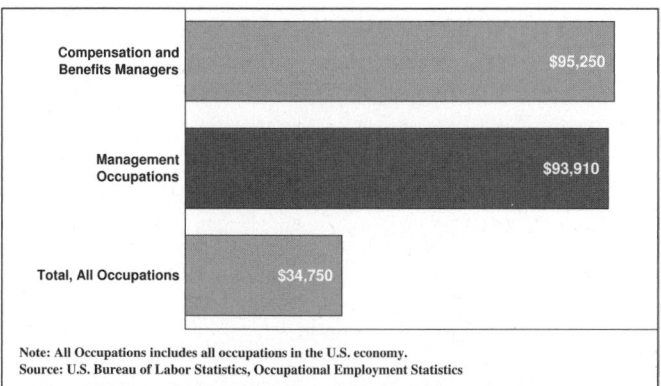

Note: All Occupations includes all occupations in the U.S. economy.
Source: U.S. Bureau of Labor Statistics, Occupational Employment Statistics

Percent Change in Employment, Projected 2012–2022

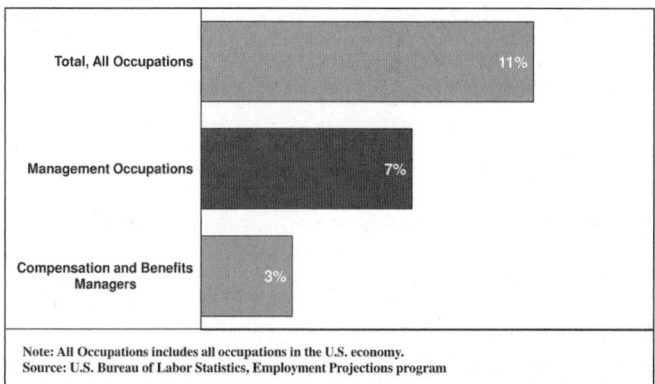

Note: All Occupations includes all occupations in the U.S. economy.
Source: U.S. Bureau of Labor Statistics, Employment Projections program

Employment Projections Data for Compensation and Benefits Managers

Occupational title	SOC Code	Employment, 2012	Projected Employment, 2022	Change, 2012–2022	
				Percent	Numeric
Compensation and benefits managers....................................	11-3111	20,700	21,400	3	600

Source: U.S. Bureau of Labor Statistics, Employment Projections Program

Note: Data are rounded. Go to **Occupational Information Included in the OOH** *for a discussion of the data in this table.*

Although not required, certification can show expertise and credibility. In fact, many employers prefer to hire certified candidates, and some positions may require certification. Certification programs for management positions often require several years of related work experience to qualify for the credential.

Important Qualities

Analytical skills. Analytical skills are essential for compensation and benefits managers. In addition to analyzing data on salaries and the cost of benefits, they must assess and devise programs that best fit an organization and its employees.

Business acumen. Compensation and benefits managers must manage a budget, build a case for their recommendations, and understand how compensation and benefits plans affect the company's finances.

Communication skills. Compensation and benefits managers use their communication skills when directing their staff, giving presentations, and working with colleagues. For example, they may present the advantages of a certain pay scale to management and address any concerns.

Decision-making skills. Compensation and benefits managers need strong decision-making skills. They must weigh the strengths and weaknesses of different pay structures and benefits plans and choose the best options for an organization.

Leadership skills. Compensation and benefits managers must coordinate the work activities of their staff and properly administer compensation and benefits programs, ensuring work is completed accurately and on schedule.

Writing skills. Compensation and benefits managers need strong writing skills to prepare informational materials on compensation and benefits plans for an organization's employees. They also must clearly convey recommendations in written reports.

Pay

The median annual wage for compensation and benefits managers was $95,250 in May 2012. The median wage is the wage at which half the workers in an occupation earned more than that amount and half earned less. The lowest 10 percent earned less than $54,060, and the top 10 percent earned more than $172,450.

Job Outlook

Employment of compensation and benefits managers is projected to grow 3 percent from 2012 to 2022, slower than the average for all occupations.

Due to healthcare reform and rising healthcare costs, organizations will need the expertise of benefits managers when choosing, updating, and administering their benefits policies. Similarly, compensation managers will be needed to analyze compensation policies and design competitive compensation packages.

As organizations focus on reducing compensation and benefits costs, many have established increasingly complex plans, such as pay-for-performance strategies and health and wellness programs. Organizations will need managers to evaluate and direct these compensation and benefits policies and plans.

However, many organizations increasingly contract out a portion of their compensation and benefits functions to human resources consulting firms in order to reduce costs and gain access to technical expertise. For example, to reduce administrative costs, organizations commonly use an outside vendor for processing payroll and insurance claims. These consulting firms are able to automate tasks and operate overseas call centers, thereby reducing the need for compensation and benefits managers.

Job Prospects. Jobseekers can expect strong competition for available jobs because the slow projected growth will result in only about 600 new positions over the 10-year period. Compensation

Similar Occupations This table shows a list of occupations with job duties that are similar to those of compensation and benefits managers.

Occupations	Entry-level Education	2012 Pay	Projected Job Growth	Average Annual Openings
Administrative Services Managers	Bachelor's degree	$81,080	12%	7,990
Compensation, Benefits, and Job Analysis Specialists	Bachelor's degree	$59,090	6%	2,200
Financial Managers	Bachelor's degree	$109,740	9%	14,690
Human Resources Managers	Bachelor's degree	$99,720	13%	4,060
Human Resources Specialists and Labor Relations Specialists	Bachelor's degree	$55,616	7%	12,370
Purchasing Managers, Buyers, and Purchasing Agents	See "How to Become One"	$63,128	4%	12,230
Top Executives	Bachelor's degree	$104,073	11%	70,090
Training and Development Managers	Bachelor's degree	$95,400	11%	1,070
Training and Development Specialists	Bachelor's degree	$55,930	15%	7,720

and benefits manager positions typically offer high pay, and job openings often attract many qualified applicants. Those who have a master's degree, certification, and extensive experience working with compensation or benefits plans should have the best job opportunities.

O*NET

➤ Compensation and Benefits Managers (11-3111.00)

Contacts for More Information

For more information about compensation and benefits managers, including certification, visit

➤ International Foundation of Employee Benefit Plans (www.ifebp.org)

➤ WorldatWork (www.worldatwork.org)

For information about human resources management careers and certification, visit

➤ HR Certification Institute (www.hrci.org/)

➤ Society for Human Resource Management (www.shrm.org)

Computer and Information Systems Managers

- **2012 Median Pay** .... $120,950 per year
  $58.15 per hour
- **Entry-Level Education** ....Bachelor's degree
- **Work Experience in a Related Occupation** ... 5 years or more
- **On-the-Job Training** .... None
- **Number of Jobs 2012** 332,700
- **Job Outlook, 2012–22** .... 15% (Faster than average)
- **Employment Change, 2012–22** 50,900

What Computer and Information Systems Managers Do

Computer and information systems managers, often called information technology (IT) managers, or IT project managers, plan, coordinate, and direct computer-related activities in an organization. They help determine the information technology goals of

Computer and information systems managers oversee a variety of workers, including systems analysts, support specialists, and software engineers.

an organization and are responsible for implementing computer systems to meet those goals.

Duties. Computer and information systems managers typically do the following:

- Analyze their organization's computer needs and recommend possible upgrades to top executives

- Plan and direct installing and upgrading computer hardware and software

- Ensure the security of an organization's network and electronic documents

- Assess the costs and benefits of a new project and justify spending on the project to top executives

- Learn about new technology and look for ways to upgrade their organization's computer systems

- Determine short- and long-term personnel needs for their department

- Plan and direct the work of other IT professionals, including computer systems analysts, software developers, information security analysts, and computer support specialists

- Negotiate with vendors to get the highest level of service for their organization's technology

Few managers carry out all of these duties. There are various types of computer and information systems managers, and the specific duties of each are determined by the size and structure of the firm. Smaller firms may not employ every type of manager.

The following are types of computer and information systems managers:

Chief information officers (CIOs) are responsible for the overall technology strategy of their organizations. They help determine the technology or information goals of an organization and then oversee planning to implement technology to meet those goals.

CIOs may focus on a specific area, such as electronic data processing or information systems, but they differ from chief technology officers (CTOs; see next) in that the CIO is more focused on long-term, or "big picture," issues. At small organizations a CIO has more direct control over the IT department, while at larger organizations other mangers under the CIO may handle the day-to-day activities of the IT department.

CIOs who do not have technical expertise and who focus solely on the business aspects of creating an overall company vision are included in a separate profile on top executives.

Chief technology officers (CTOs) evaluate new technology and determine how it can help their organization. When both CIOs and CTOs are present, the CTO usually has more technical expertise.

The CTO is responsible for designing and recommending the appropriate technology solutions to support the policies and directives issued by the CIO. CTOs also work with different departments to implement the organization's technology plans.

The CTO usually reports directly to the CIO and also may be responsible for overseeing the development of new technologies or other research-and-development activities. When a company does not have a CIO, the CTO determines the overall technology strategy for the firm and presents it to top executives.

IT directors, including management information systems (MIS) directors, are in charge of their organizations' information technology (IT) departments, and they directly supervise other employees. IT directors help to determine the business requirements for IT systems, and they implement the policies that have been chosen by top executives. IT directors often have a direct role in hiring members of the IT department. It is their job to ensure the avail-

Median Annual Wages, May 2012

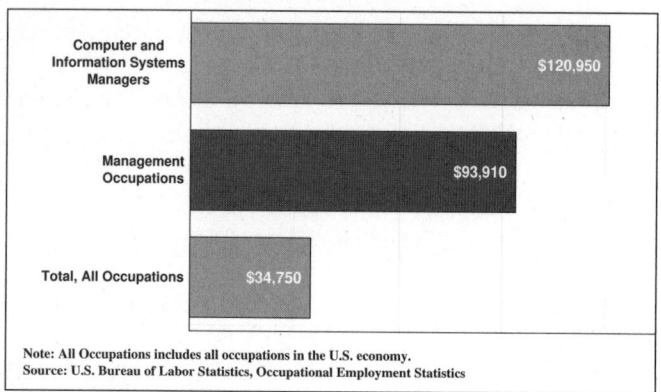

Computer and Information Systems Managers — $120,950
Management Occupations — $93,910
Total, All Occupations — $34,750

Note: All Occupations includes all occupations in the U.S. economy.
Source: U.S. Bureau of Labor Statistics, Occupational Employment Statistics

Percent Change in Employment, Projected 2012–2022

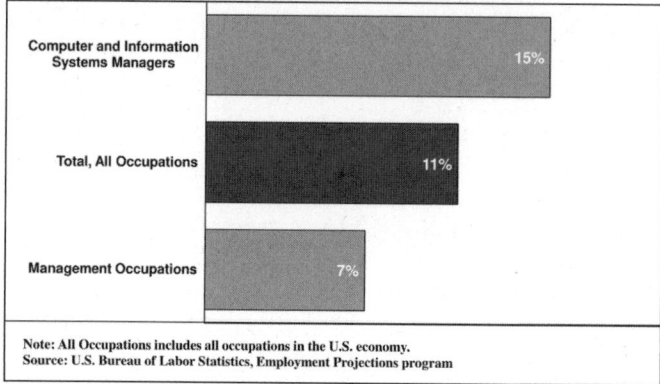

Computer and Information Systems Managers — 15%
Total, All Occupations — 11%
Management Occupations — 7%

Note: All Occupations includes all occupations in the U.S. economy.
Source: U.S. Bureau of Labor Statistics, Employment Projections program

ability of data and network services by coordinating IT activities. IT directors also oversee the financial aspects of their department, such as budgeting.

IT security managers oversee their organizations' network and data security. They work with top executives to plan security policies and promote a culture of information security throughout the organization. They develop programs to keep employees aware of security threats. These managers must keep up to date on IT security measures. They also supervise investigations if there is a security violation.

Work Environment

Computer and information systems managers held about 332,700 jobs in 2012.

The industries that employed the most computer and information systems managers in 2012 were as follows:

Computer systems design and related services 19%
Finance and insurance 12
Information 11
Management of companies and enterprises 9
Government 7

As network speeds increase, telecommuting is becoming more common. Although few managers can work remotely, many have to supervise employees who work from home.

Work Schedules. Most computer and information systems managers work full time. Many of them must work overtime to solve problems. In 2012, about one third worked more than 40 hours per week.

How to Become One

Typically, a bachelor's degree in computer or information science, plus related work experience, is required. Many computer and information systems managers also have a graduate degree.

Education. Computer and information systems managers normally must have a bachelor's degree in a computer- or information science–related field. Such a degree usually takes 4 years to complete and includes courses in computer programming, soft-

ware development, and mathematics. Management information systems (MIS) programs usually include business classes as well as computer-related ones.

Many organizations require their computer and information systems managers to have a graduate degree as well. A master of business administration (MBA) is common and takes 2 years beyond the undergraduate level to complete. Many people pursuing an MBA take classes while working, an option that can increase the time required to complete that degree.

Work Experience in a Related Occupation. Most jobs for computer and information systems managers require several years of experience in a related information technology (IT) job. Lower level management positions may require only a few years of experience. Directors are more likely to need 5 to 10 years of related work experience. A chief technology officer (CTO), who oversees the technology plan for a large organization, may need more than 15 years of experience in the IT field before being considered for a job.

The number of years of experience required varies with the organization. Generally, smaller companies do not require as much experience as larger, more established ones.

Computer systems are used throughout the economy, and IT employees may gain experience in a variety of industries. However, an applicant's work experience should be related to the industry the applicant plans to manage. For example, an IT security manager should have previously worked in information security. A hospital IT director should have experience in the healthcare field.

Advancement. Most computer and information systems managers start out as lower level managers and advance to higher positions within the IT department. IT directors or project managers can advance to become CTOs. A CTO or other manager who is especially business minded can advance to become a chief information officer (CIO), the person in charge of all IT-related decisions in an organization. CIOs can advance to become top executives in an organization.

Important Qualities

Analytical skills. IT managers must be able to analyze a problem, consider ways to solve the problem, and select the best way.

Employment Projections Data for Computer and Information Systems Managers

Occupational title	SOC Code	Employment, 2012	Projected Employment, 2022	Change, 2012–2022	
				Percent	Numeric
Computer and information systems managers	11-3021	332,700	383,600	15	50,900

Source: U.S. Bureau of Labor Statistics, Employment Projections Program

Note: Data are rounded. Go to Occupational Information Included in the OOH for a discussion of the data in this table.

Similar Occupations   This table shows a list of occupations with job duties that are similar to those of computer and information systems managers.

Occupations	Entry-level Education	2012 Pay	Projected Job Growth	Average Annual Openings
Computer and Information Research Scientists	Doctoral or professional degree	$102,190	15%	830
Computer Hardware Engineers	Bachelor's degree	$100,920	7%	2,410
Computer Network Architects	Bachelor's degree	$91,000	15%	4,350
Computer Programmers	Bachelor's degree	$74,280	8%	11,810
Computer Systems Analysts	Bachelor's degree	$79,680	25%	20,960
Database Administrators	Bachelor's degree	$77,080	15%	4,030
Information Security Analysts	Bachelor's degree	$86,170	36%	3,920
Network and Computer Systems Administrators	Bachelor's degree	$72,560	12%	10,050
Software Developers	Bachelor's degree	$93,640	22%	35,320
Top Executives	Bachelor's degree	$104,073	11%	70,090
Web Developers	Associate's degree	$62,500	20%	5,070

Communication skills. IT managers must be able to explain their work to top executives and give clear instructions to their subordinates.

Decision-making skills. Some IT managers must make important decisions about how to allocate their organizations' resources in order to reach their goals.

Leadership skills. IT managers must be able to lead and motivate IT teams or departments so that workers are efficient and effective.

Organizational skills. Some IT managers must coordinate the work of several different IT departments to make the organization run efficiently.

Pay

The median annual wage for computer and information systems managers was $120,950 in May 2012. The median wage is the wage at which half the workers in an occupation earned more than that amount and half earned less. The lowest 10 percent earned less than $74,940, and the top 10 percent earned more than $187,200.

In May 2012, the median annual wages for computer and information systems managers in the five industries in which most of these managers worked were as follows:

Information	$133,120
Computer systems design and related services	128,830
Finance and insurance	126,680
Management of companies and enterprises	124,260
Government	101,690

Job Outlook

Employment of computer and information systems managers is projected to grow 15 percent from 2012 to 2022, faster than the average for all occupations.

Demand for computer and information systems managers will increase as firms continue to expand their use of wireless and mobile networks. A rapid increase in demand for computer software will also increase the need for employees at all levels of management.

Additional employment growth will likely result from the need to bolster cybersecurity in information technology (IT) departments. More attention is being directed at cyber threats, a trend that is expected to increase over the next decade.

A number of jobs in this occupation are expected to be created in the healthcare industry, which is aggressively implementing information technology. This industry is expected to increase IT use greatly, resulting in job growth. In general medical and surgical hospitals, employment of IT managers is projected to grow 42 percent.

An increase in cloud computing may shift some IT services from non-computer industries, such as financial firms or schools, to firms engaged in computer systems design and related services, resulting in a concentration of jobs in the latter industry. The reason is that firms will increasingly be outsourcing services from on-premise IT departments to cloud- computing companies.

A number of IT jobs are at risk of being sent to other countries with lower wages, dampening some employment growth. However, this risk may be reduced by a recent trend of firms moving jobs to lower cost regions of the United States instead of to other countries.

Job Prospects. Prospects should be favorable for this occupation. Many companies note that it is difficult to find qualified applicants for positions.

Because innovation is fast paced in IT, opportunities should be best for those who have extensive work experience and knowledge of the newest technology.

O*NET

➤ Computer and Information Systems Managers (11-3021.00)

Contacts for More Information

For more information about computer careers, visit

➤ Association for Computing Machinery (www.acm.org/)

➤ IEEE (www.computer.org/)

➤ Computing Research Association (www.cra.org/)

➤ Tech America (www.techamerica.org/)

For more information about opportunities for women pursuing information technology careers, visit

➤ National Center for Women and Information Technology (www.ncwit.org/)

Construction Managers

- **2012 Median Pay** .... $82,790 per year
  $39.80 per hour
- **Entry-Level Education** ....Bachelor's degree
- **Work Experience in a Related Occupation**.............. None
- **On-the-Job Training**.... Moderate-term on-the-job training
- **Number of Jobs 2012** 485,000
- **Job Outlook, 2012–22**............. 16% (Faster than average)
- **Employment Change, 2012–22** 78,200

What Construction Managers Do

Construction managers plan, coordinate, budget, and supervise construction projects from development to completion.

Duties. Construction managers typically do the following:

- Prepare cost estimates, budgets, and work timetables
- Interpret and explain contracts and technical information to other professionals
- Report work progress and budget matters to clients
- Collaborate with architects, engineers, and other construction specialists
- Select, schedule, and coordinate subcontractor activities
- Respond to work delays, emergencies, and other problems
- Comply with legal requirements, building and safety codes, and other regulations

Construction managers, often called *general contractors* or *project managers*, coordinate and supervise a wide variety of projects, including the building of all types of public, residential, commercial, and industrial structures, as well as roads, memorials, and bridges. Although most managers oversee construction projects from start to finish, some consult with developers and builders on construction related issues.

Construction managers oversee specialized contractors and other personnel. They schedule and coordinate all construction processes so that projects meet design specifications. They ensure that projects are completed on time and within budget. Some managers may be responsible for several projects at once–for example, the construction of multiple apartment buildings.

Construction managers work closely with other building specialists, such as architects, civil engineers, and a variety of trade workers, including stonemasons, electricians, and carpenters.

Construction managers direct and monitor the progress of construction activities, occasionally through construction supervisors or other construction managers.

Projects may require specialists in everything from structural steel and painting to landscaping, paving roads, and excavating sites. Depending on the project, construction managers may interact with lawyers and local government officials. For example, when working on city-owned property or municipal buildings, managers sometimes confer with city inspectors to ensure that all regulations are met.

For projects too large to be managed by one person, such as office buildings and industrial complexes, a top-level construction manager hires other construction managers to be in charge of different aspects of the project. For example, each construction manager would oversee a specific phase of the project, such as structural foundation, plumbing, or electrical work, and choose subcontractors to complete it. The top-level construction manager would then collaborate and coordinate with the other construction managers.

To maximize efficiency and productivity, construction managers often perform the tasks of a cost estimator. They use specialized

Median Annual Wages, May 2012

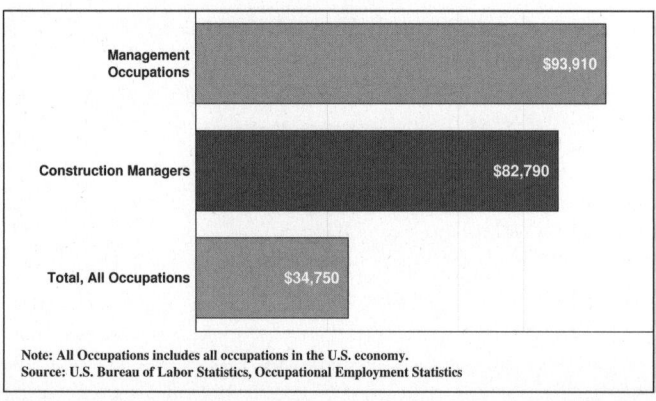

Management Occupations — $93,910
Construction Managers — $82,790
Total, All Occupations — $34,750

Note: All Occupations includes all occupations in the U.S. economy.
Source: U.S. Bureau of Labor Statistics, Occupational Employment Statistics

Percent Change in Employment, Projected 2012–2022

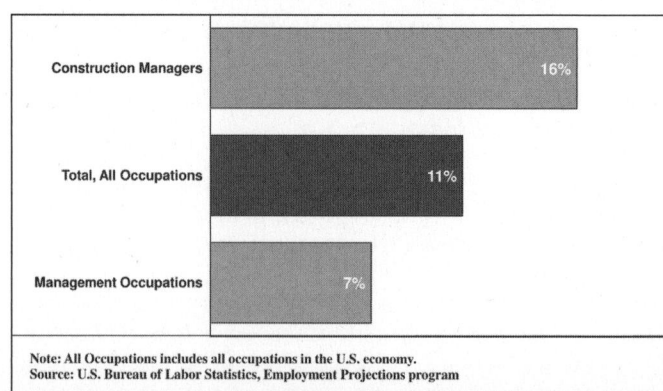

Construction Managers — 16%
Total, All Occupations — 11%
Management Occupations — 7%

Note: All Occupations includes all occupations in the U.S. economy.
Source: U.S. Bureau of Labor Statistics, Employment Projections program

Employment Projections Data for Construction Managers

Occupational title	SOC Code	Employment, 2012	Projected Employment, 2022	Change, 2012–2022	
				Percent	Numeric
Construction managers	11-9021	485,000	563,200	16	78,200

Source: U.S. Bureau of Labor Statistics, Employment Projections Program

Note: Data are rounded. Go to Occupational Information Included in the OOH for a discussion of the data in this table.

cost-estimating and planning software to allocate time and money in order to complete their projects. Many managers also use software to plan the best way to get materials to the building site.

Work Environment

Construction managers held about 485,000 jobs in 2012. Approximately 57 percent were self-employed.

The industries that employed the most construction managers in 2012 were as follows:

Construction of buildings 17%
Specialty trade contractors 13
Heavy and civil engineering construction 5

Many construction managers work from a main office, but most work out of a field office at the construction site, where they monitor the project and make daily decisions about construction activities. For those managing multiple projects, frequent travel between sites is required.

Injuries and Illnesses. Construction managers have a lower rate of injuries and illnesses than the national average.

Work Schedules. Most construction managers work full time. However, the need to meet deadlines and to respond to delays and emergencies often requires long hours. Many managers also may be on call 24 hours a day.

How to Become One

Large construction firms increasingly prefer candidates with both construction experience and a bachelor's degree in a construction-related field. However, some managers may qualify with a high school diploma and by working many years in a construction trade, although most will qualify primarily as self-employed general contractors.

Education. It is increasingly important for construction managers to have a bachelor's degree in construction science, construction management, architecture, or engineering. As construction processes become more complex, employers are placing greater importance on specialized education.

More than 100 colleges and universities offer accredited bachelor's degree programs in construction science, building science, or construction engineering. These programs include courses in project control and management, design, construction methods and materials, cost estimation, building codes and standards, and contract administration. Courses in mathematics and statistics are also relevant.

A number of 2-year colleges offer construction management or construction technology programs. An associate's degree combined with work experience is typical for managers who supervise smaller projects.

A few universities offer master's degree programs in construction management.

Those with a high school diploma and several years of relevant work experience may qualify to become a construction manager, although most will do so primarily as self-employed general contractors.

Training. All new construction managers are initially hired as assistants and work under the guidance of an experienced manager. This training period may last several months to several years, depending on the firm.

Work Experience

Practical construction experience is important when entering the occupation, because it reduces the need for initial on-the-job training. Internships, cooperative education programs, and previous work in the construction industry can provide that experience. Some construction managers become qualified solely through extensive construction experience, spending many years in carpentry, masonry, or other construction specialties.

Licenses, Certifications, and Registrations. Although not required, certification is becoming increasingly important for construction managers. Certification is valuable because it can demonstrate knowledge and experience.

The Construction Management Association of America awards the Certified Construction Manager (CCM) designation to workers who have the required experience and who pass a technical exam. It is recommended that applicants for this certification complete a self-study course that covers the professional role of a construction manager, legal issues, the allocation of risk, and other topics related to construction management.

The American Institute of Constructors awards the Associate Constructor (AC) and Certified Professional Constructor (CPC) designations to candidates who meet its requirements and pass the appropriate construction exams.

Some states require licensure for construction managers overseeing a public project. For more information, contact your state licensing board.

Important Qualities

Analytical skills. Most managers plan a project strategy, handle unexpected issues and delays, and solve problems that arise over the course of the project. In addition, many managers use cost-estimating and planning software to determine how much materials are needed and the time and cost required to complete projects.

Business skills. Construction managers address budget matters and coordinate and supervise workers. Choosing competent staff and establishing good working relationships with them is critical.

Customer-service skills. Construction managers are in constant contact with owners, inspectors, and the public. They must communicate work plans clearly, and explain work stoppages when they occur.

Decision-making skills. Construction managers choose personnel and subcontractors for specific tasks and jobs. Often, these decisions must be made quickly to meet deadlines and budgets.

Initiative. Self-employed construction managers generate their own business opportunities and must be proactive in finding new clients. They often market their services, bid on jobs, and must

Similar Occupations   This table shows a list of occupations with job duties that are similar to those of construction managers.

Occupations	Entry-level Education	2012 Pay	Projected Job Growth	Average Annual Openings
Architects	Bachelor's degree	$73,090	17%	4,410
Architectural and Engineering Managers	Bachelor's degree	$124,870	7%	6,060
Civil Engineers	Bachelor's degree	$79,340	20%	12,010
Cost Estimators	Bachelor's degree	$58,860	26%	11,800
Landscape Architects	Bachelor's degree	$64,180	14%	760

learn to perform special home improvement projects such as installing mosaic glass tiles, sanding wood floors, and insulating homes.

Leadership skills. Managers must effectively delegate tasks to construction workers, subcontractors, and other lower level managers.

Speaking skills. Managers must give clear orders, explain complex information to construction workers and clients, and discuss technical details with other building specialists, such as architects. Self-employed construction managers must get their own projects, so the need to sell their services to potential clients is critical.

Technical skills. Managers must know construction methods and technologies, and must be able to interpret contracts and technical drawings.

Time-management skills. Construction managers must meet deadlines. They ensure that construction phases are completed on time so that the next phase can begin as scheduled. For instance, a building's foundation cannot be constructed until the land is completely excavated.

Writing skills. Construction managers must write proposals, plans, and budgets, as well as document the progress of the work for clients and others involved in the building process.

Pay

The median annual wage for construction managers was $82,790 in May 2012. The median wage is the wage at which half the workers in an occupation earned more than that amount and half earned less. The lowest 10 percent earned less than $49,680, and the highest 10 percent earned more than $144,520.

In May 2012, the median annual wages for construction managers in the top three industries employing these managers were as follows:

Heavy and civil engineering construction $85,130
Construction of buildings.. 81,830
Specialty trade contractors 79,470

Salaried construction managers also may earn bonuses and overtime pay. About 57 percent of construction managers were self-employed in 2012. Their earnings are highly dependent on the amount of business they generate.

Job Outlook

Employment of construction managers is projected to grow 16 percent from 2012 to 2022, faster than the average for all occupations.

Construction managers will be needed as overall construction activity expands. Population and business growth will result in the construction of many new residences, office buildings, retail outlets, hospitals, schools, restaurants, and other structures over the coming decade. Also, the need to improve portions of the national

infrastructure will spur employment growth as roads, bridges, and sewer pipe systems are upgraded or replaced.

In addition, a growing emphasis on retrofitting buildings to make them more energy efficient should create jobs for general contractors, who are more likely to manage the renovation and upgrading of buildings than oversee new large-scale construction projects.

To ensure that projects are completed on time and under budget, firms are increasingly focusing on hiring construction managers. Furthermore, construction processes and building technology are becoming more complex, requiring greater oversight and spurring demand for specialized management personnel. Sophisticated technology, worker safety, environmental protection, and new regulations setting standards for building and construction material also will drive employment growth.

Job Prospects. Job opportunities for qualified construction managers are expected to be good. Specifically, those with a bachelor's degree in construction science, construction management, or civil engineering, coupled with construction experience, will have the best job prospects.

Although employment growth will provide many new jobs, a substantial number of construction managers are expected to retire over the next decade, resulting in additional job openings.

Employment of construction managers, like that of many other construction workers, is sensitive to fluctuations in the economy. On the one hand, workers in the construction industry may experience periods of unemployment when the overall level of construction falls. On the other hand, peak periods of building activity may produce abundant job opportunities for construction managers.

O*NET

➤ Construction Managers (11-9021.00)

Contacts for More Information

For information about construction manager certification, visit
➤ American Institute of Constructors (www.aicnet.org)

For information about construction management and construction manager certification, visit
➤ Construction Management Association of America (www.cmaanet.org)

For information on accredited construction science and management educational programs, visit
➤ ABET (www.abet.org/accreditation/)
➤ American Council for Construction Education (www.acce-hq.org)
➤ NCCER (www.nccer.org)

Elementary, Middle, and High School Principals

- **2012 Median Pay** .... $87,760 per year
- **Entry-Level Education** ....Master's degree
- **Work Experience in a Related Occupation** ... 5 years or more
- **On-the-Job Training** .... None
- **Number of Jobs 2012** 231,500
- **Job Outlook, 2012–22** .... 6% (Slower than average)
- **Employment Change, 2012–22** 13,100

What Elementary, Middle, and High School Principals Do

Elementary, middle, and high school principals are responsible for managing all school operations. They manage daily school activities, coordinate curricula, and oversee teachers and other school staff to provide a safe and productive learning environment for students.

Duties. Elementary, middle, and high school principals typically do the following:

- Manage school activities and staff, including teachers and support personnel
- Establish and oversee class schedules
- Counsel and discipline students
- Mentor teachers in managing students' behavior
- Evaluate teachers' performance
- Meet with parents and teachers to discuss students' progress and behavior
- Assess and prepare reports on test scores and other student achievement data
- Organize professional development programs and workshops for staff
- Manage the school's budget, order school supplies, and schedule maintenance
- Establish and coordinate security procedures for students, staff, and visitors

Elementary, middle, and high school principals manage the overall operation of schools, including building maintenance and cafeteria services. They set and oversee academic goals and ensure that teachers have the equipment and resources necessary to meet

Elementary, middle, and high school principals provide leadership to teachers and other members of school staff and manage the day-to-day operations of schools.

these goals. In public schools, principals also implement standards and programs set by a school district, state, or federal regulations. They evaluate and prepare reports on their school performance based on these standards by assessing student achievement and teacher performance. Principals may establish and oversee additional programs in their school, such as counseling, special education programs, and before- and after-school child care programs.

Principals serve as the public face of their school. They meet with superintendents, legislators, and members of the community to request or explain funding for their schools. They also address the concerns of parents and members of the community.

The duties of principals vary by the size of the school and district. In larger schools and districts, principals have additional resources and staff to help them achieve goals. For example, large school districts often have instructional coordinators who help with data analysis and with teachers' professional development. Principals in small school districts may need to assume these and other duties themselves. In addition, they may be required to oversee the hiring process of all staff in their school, including teachers, custodians, and cafeteria workers. In larger districts, staff may perform some of these duties.

Many schools have assistant principals that help principals with school administration. Principals typically assign specific administrative duties to their assistants. In some school districts, assistant principals are hired to handle a specific subject area, such as literacy or math. Assistant principals may be assigned to handle student safety and discipline. They provide student academic counseling and

Median Annual Wages, May 2012

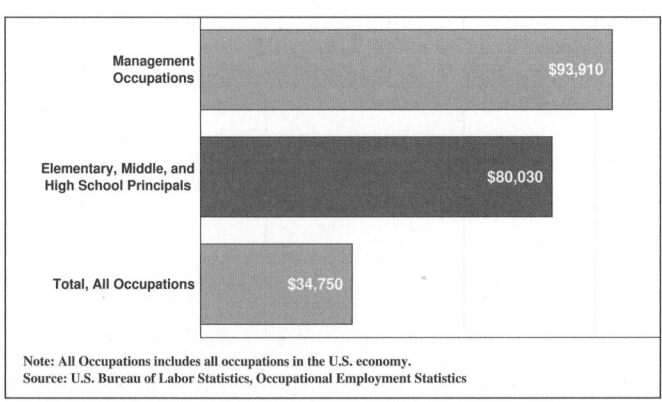

Note: All Occupations includes all occupations in the U.S. economy.
Source: U.S. Bureau of Labor Statistics, Occupational Employment Statistics

Percent Change in Employment, Projected 2012–2022

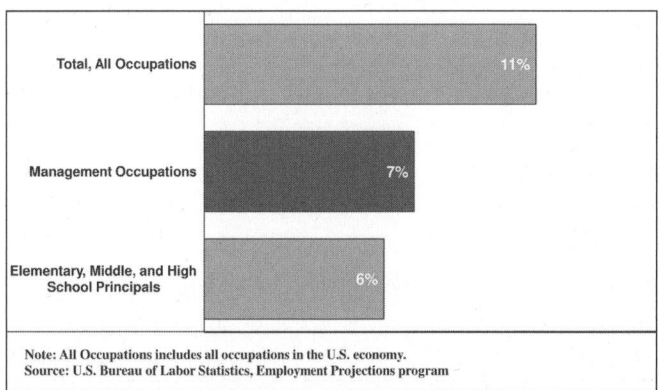

Note: All Occupations includes all occupations in the U.S. economy.
Source: U.S. Bureau of Labor Statistics, Employment Projections program

Employment Projections Data for Elementary, Middle, and High School Principals

Occupational title	SOC Code	Employment, 2012	Projected Employment, 2022	Change, 2012–2022	
				Percent	Numeric
Education administrators, elementary and secondary school....	11-9032	231,500	244,700	6	13,100

Source: U.S. Bureau of Labor Statistics, Employment Projections Program

Note: Data are rounded. Go to **Occupational Information Included in the OOH** *for a discussion of the data in this table.*

enforce disciplinary or attendance rules. Assistant principals may also coordinate buses or supervise building and grounds maintenance.

Work Environment

Elementary, middle, and high school principals held about 231,500 jobs in 2012.

Principals work in public or private elementary, middle, and high schools. Some work in public magnet and charter schools. Others work in private religious and secular schools.

Elementary, middle, and high school principals hold leadership positions with significant responsibility. Working with students may be rewarding. However, coordinating and interacting with faculty, parents, students, community members, and state and local policymakers can be demanding. Principals' work can sometimes be stressful because they are accountable for schools meeting state and federal standards for student performance and teacher qualification.

Work Schedules. Principals typically work full time. They may work in the evening to meet parents and other members of the community and to attend school functions, such as concerts and athletic events.

Many principals work year-round and do not have summers off, even if students are not in school. During the summer, principals prepare for the upcoming school year, schedule building maintenance, order school supplies, or hire teachers and staff.

How to Become One

Most schools require elementary, middle, and high school principals to have a master's degree in education administration or leadership. Most principals also have work experience as teachers.

Education. Principals typically need a master's degree in education leadership or education administration. These master's degree programs prepare future principals to manage teachers and staff, prepare and manage budgets, set goals, and work with parents and the community.

To enter these programs, candidates typically need a bachelor's degree in education, school counseling, or a related field.

Work Experience in a Related Occupation. Candidates for the position of principal usually need work experience as a teacher. For more information on how to become a teacher, see the profiles on kindergarten and elementary school teachers, middle school teachers, and high school teachers.

Licenses, Certifications, and Registrations. Most states require public school principals to be licensed as school administrators. Licensure requirements vary from state to state, but most require a master's degree. In addition, some require candidates to pass a test and take continuing education classes to maintain their license. Working with a mentor may be required, as well. Some states have alternative programs for candidates who do not have a degree in education administration or leadership. Most states require principals to pass a background check as part of their certification.

Principals in private schools are not required to have a state-issued license.

Advancement. An assistant principal can advance to become a principal. Some principals advance to become superintendents, which may require completion of additional education. Others become instructional coordinators.

Important Qualities

Communication skills. Principals must communicate effectively with students, teachers, and parents. For example, when dealing

Similar Occupations   This table shows a list of occupations with job duties that are similar to those of elementary, middle, and high school principals.

Occupations	Entry-level Education	2012 Pay	Projected Job Growth	Average Annual Openings
High School Teachers	Bachelor's degree	$55,050	6%	31,260
Instructional Coordinators	Master's degree	$60,050	13%	3,110
Kindergarten and Elementary School Teachers	Bachelor's degree	$53,060	12%	53,250
Librarians	Master's degree	$55,370	7%	4,440
Middle School Teachers	Bachelor's degree	$53,430	12%	21,120
Postsecondary Education Administrators	Master's degree	$86,490	15%	6,650
Postsecondary Teachers	See "How to Become One"	$70,380	19%	42,690
Preschool and Childcare Center Directors	Bachelor's degree	$43,950	17%	2,780
Preschool Teachers	Associate's degree	$27,130	17%	19,940
School and Career Counselors	Master's degree	$53,610	12%	8,700
Special Education Teachers	Bachelor's degree	$55,068	6%	10,220
Teacher Assistants	Some college, no degree	$23,640	9%	38,260

with student disciplinary or academic issues, they consult with and listen to parents and teachers to understand the problem.

Critical-thinking skills. Principals analyze student test results and testing procedures to determine any improvements to help students achieve better results.

Decision-making skills. Because principals are responsible for students, staff members, and the overall operation of the school, they consider many factors when making decisions. For example, they consider the safety of students and staff when making a recommendation to close a school before a snowstorm.

Interpersonal skills. Because principals work with teachers, parents, and superintendants, they must be able to develop positive working relationships with them.

Leadership skills. Principals set educational goals and establish policies and procedures for the school. They need to be able to motivate teachers and other staff to achieve set goals.

Problem-solving skills. Teachers, students, and other staff members report problems to the principal. Principals need to be able to analyze problems, and develop and implement solutions.

Pay

The median annual wage for elementary, middle, and high school principals was $87,760 in May 2012. The median wage is the wage at which half the workers in an occupation earned more than that amount and half earned less. The lowest 10 percent earned less than $58,530, and the top 10 percent earned more than $130,810.

Job Outlook

Employment of elementary, middle, and high school principals is projected to grow 6 percent from 2012 to 2022, slower than the average for all occupations. Employment growth will be driven by increases in school enrollments.

From 2012 to 2022, the number of students enrolled in schools is projected to increase. Some additional schools may open to accommodate these students, resulting in a need for assistant principals and principals.

However, despite expected increases in enrollment, employment growth of school principals will depend on state and local budgets. Budget deficits may delay the building or opening of new schools. In addition, some school districts plan to consolidate and close some schools within their districts, thereby limiting employment growth.

Job Prospects. Job opportunities will vary by region of the country. Because population and student enrollments are projected to grow faster in the South and West, job opportunities for principals may be better in those parts of the country. In the Midwest, enrollment is expected to remain steady, and enrollment in the Northeast is expected to decline.

O*NET

➤ Education Administrators, Elementary and Secondary School (11-9032.00)

Contacts for More Information

For more information on elementary, middle, and high school principals, visit

➤ National Association of Elementary School Principals (http://naesp.org/)

➤ National Association of Secondary School Principals (www.nassp.org/)

Emergency Management Directors

- **2012 Median Pay** .... $59,770 per year
  $28.73 per hour
- **Entry-Level Education** .... Bachelor's degree
- **Work Experience in a Related Occupation** ... 5 years or more
- **On-the-Job Training** .... None
- **Number of Jobs 2012** 9,900
- **Job Outlook, 2012–22** .... 8% (As fast as average)
- **Employment Change, 2012–22** 800

What Emergency Management Directors Do

Emergency management directors prepare plans and procedures for responding to natural disasters or other emergencies. They also lead the response during and after emergencies, often in coordination with fire and law enforcement officials, elected officials, nonprofit organizations, and government agencies.

Duties. Emergency management directors typically do the following:

- Plan responses to emergencies and disasters in order to minimize risk to people and property
- Meet with law enforcement officials, private companies, and the general public to get recommendations regarding emergency response plans
- Organize emergency response training programs for staff, volunteers, and other first responders
- Coordinate the use and sharing of resources and equipment within the community to assist in emergency response
- Prepare and analyze damage assessments following disasters or emergencies
- Review emergency plans of individual organizations, such as medical facilities, to ensure their adequacy
- Apply for federal funding for emergency management responses and report on the progress of such grants
- Revise and review local emergency operations plans

Emergency management directors are responsible for planning and leading the responses to natural disasters and other emergencies. Directors work with government agencies, nonprofits, private companies, and the general public to develop effective plans that

Emergency Management Directors sometimes need to coordinate their activities with federal authorities.

Median Annual Wages, May 2012

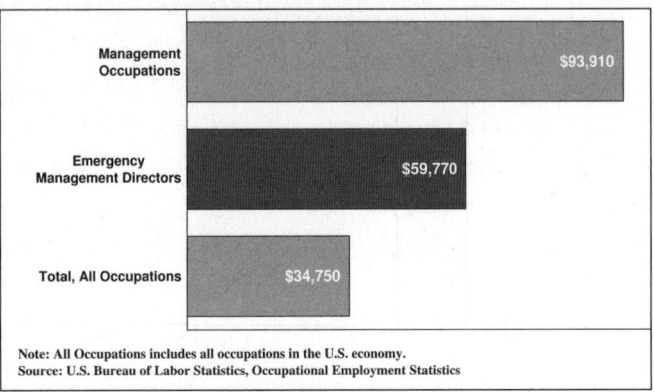

Note: All Occupations includes all occupations in the U.S. economy.
Source: U.S. Bureau of Labor Statistics, Occupational Employment Statistics

Percent Change in Employment, Projected 2012–2022

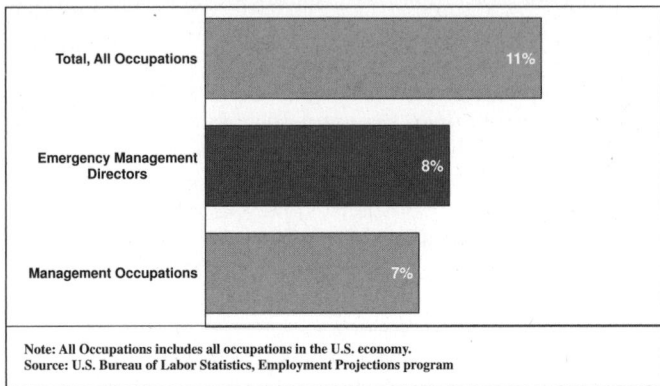

Note: All Occupations includes all occupations in the U.S. economy.
Source: U.S. Bureau of Labor Statistics, Employment Projections program

minimize damage and disruptions during an emergency. Directors must prepare plans and objectives that meet local, state, and federal regulations.

To develop emergency response plans, directors typically research "best practices" from around the country and from other emergency management agencies.

Directors must analyze the resources, equipment, and staff available to respond to emergencies. If resources or equipment is lacking, directors must either revise their plans or obtain the needed resources from another county or state. Many directors coordinate with fire, emergency medical service, and police departments in other counties to locate and share equipment during an emergency. Directors must be in contact with other agencies to collect and share data.

After plans are developed, emergency management directors typically ensure that individuals and groups become familiar with the emergency procedures.

Emergency management directors run training courses or disaster exercises for staff, volunteers, and local agencies to ensure an effective and coordinated response to an emergency. Directors also may visit schools, hospitals, or other community groups to update everyone on the emergency plans.

During an emergency, directors lead the response, making adjustments to or prioritizing certain actions if necessary. These actions may include ordering evacuations, conducting rescue missions, or opening up public shelters for those displaced by the disaster. Emergency management directors may also need to conduct press conferences or other outreach activities to keep the public informed about the emergency.

Following an emergency, directors must assess the damage to their community and coordinate getting assistance and supplies into the community. Directors may need to apply for state or federal assistance to help execute their emergency response plan. Directors also revise their plans and procedures when necessary, in order to prepare for future emergencies or disasters.

Emergency management directors working for hospitals, universities, or private companies may be called *business continuity managers*. Similar to their counterparts in local and state government, business continuity managers prepare plans and procedures to help businesses maintain operations and minimize losses during and after an emergency.

Work Environment

Emergency management directors held about 9,900 jobs in 2012. Most work for state or local governments. However, some may work for private companies, hospitals, universities, or nonprofit institutions.

The industries that employed the most emergency management directors in 2012 were as follows:

Local government, excluding education and hospitals............ 54%
Health care and social assistance.. 17
State government, excluding education and hospitals............. 12
Professional, scientific, and technical services......................... 4
Educational services; state, local, and private 3

Although most emergency management directors work in an office, they typically travel to meet with various agency or company personnel or community groups. Many directors work in stressful situations during disasters or emergencies.

Work Schedules. Most emergency management directors work full time. However, most are on call at all times and may need to work overtime to respond to emergencies and to support emergency management operations. Others may work evenings and weekends to meet with various community groups in preparing their emergency response plans.

How to Become One

Emergency management directors typically need a bachelor's degree, as well as multiple years of work experience in emergency response, disaster planning, or public administration.

Education. Emergency management directors typically need a bachelor's degree. Many emergency management directors get their degree in business or public administration, fire science, or emergency management.

Employment Projections Data for Emergency Management Directors

Occupational title	SOC Code	Employment, 2012	Projected Employment, 2022	Change, 2012–2022	
				Percent	Numeric
Emergency management directors...	11-9161	9,900	10,700	8	800

Source: U.S. Bureau of Labor Statistics, Employment Projections Program

Note: Data are rounded. Go to **Occupational Information Included in the OOH** *for a discussion of the data in this table.*

Similar Occupations   This table shows a list of occupations with job duties that are similar to those of emergency management directors.

Occupations	Entry-level Education	2012 Pay	Projected Job Growth	Average Annual Openings
Budget Analysts	Bachelor's degree	$69,280	6%	2,850
EMTs and Paramedics	Postsecondary non-degree award	$31,020	23%	12,060
Firefighters	Postsecondary non-degree award	$45,250	7%	10,400
Management Analysts	Bachelor's degree	$78,600	19%	24,520
Police and Detectives	High school diploma or equivalent	$57,974	5%	27,500
Top Executives	Bachelor's degree	$104,073	11%	70,090

Although some smaller municipalities or local governments may hire applicants with a high school degree, these applicants usually need more extensive work experience in emergency management.

Work Experience in a Related Occupation. Applicants typically need years of work experience, often in law enforcement, fire safety, or another emergency management field, before they can be hired as an emergency management director. Previous work experience in these fields enables applicants to make difficult decisions in often stressful and time-sensitive situations. Such experience also prepares one to work with various agencies to ensure that proper resources are used to respond to emergencies.

For more information, see the profiles on police and detectives, firefighters, police and fire dispatchers, and EMTs and paramedics.

Licenses, Certifications, and Registrations. Many agencies and states offer voluntary certificate programs to help emergency management directors obtain additional skills. Some states require directors to obtain certification within a certain timeframe after being hired in the position.

Important Qualities

Communication skills. Emergency management directors must write out and communicate their emergency preparedness plans to all levels of government, as well as to the public.

Critical-thinking skills. Emergency management directors must anticipate hazards and problems that may arise from an emergency in order to respond effectively.

Decision-making skills. Emergency management directors must make timely decisions, often in stressful situations. They must also identify the strengths and weaknesses of all solutions and approaches, and the costs and benefits of each action.

Interpersonal skills. Emergency management directors must work with other government agencies, law enforcement officials, and the general public to coordinate emergency responses.

Leadership skills. To ensure effective responses to emergencies, emergency management directors need to organize and train a variety of people.

Pay

The median annual wage for emergency management directors was $59,770 in May 2012. The median wage is the wage at which half the workers in an occupation earned more than that amount and half earned less. The lowest 10 percent earned less than $30,760, and the top 10 percent earned more than $107,810.

Job Outlook

Employment of emergency management directors is projected to grow 8 percent from 2012 to 2022, about as fast as the average for all occupations. Despite increased hiring in the private sector,

overall employment growth is expected to be restrained by local and state budget cuts.

Changes in weather patterns may make more areas vulnerable to flooding, droughts, powerful hurricanes, and other weather-related emergencies. In addition, growing urbanization and a population shift toward coastal regions may increase the number of people living in these high-risk areas. Emergency directors will be needed to develop response plans to protect more people, and property, and to limit the damage from emergencies and disasters.

Emergency management directors will be needed to help businesses and organizations continue providing essential products and services during and after emergencies. Employment of emergency management directors is expected to grow the fastest in hospitals, schools, and private companies. For example, employment of emergency management directors is projected to grow 18 percent in health care and social assistance and 22 percent in the professional, scientific, and technical services industries from 2012 to 2022.

Some local and state governments, however, may need to limit emergency management services and hiring because of budgetary constraints. In addition, some local and state governments are increasingly relying on federal financial assistance to fund their emergency management agencies. Yet federal budgetary problems may lead to continued cutbacks in funding and grants to local and state agencies, further limiting the hiring of emergency management personnel. Some smaller counties may not hire full-time, stand-alone emergency management directors, choosing instead to shift the job responsibilities to the fire chief, police chief, or other government employees.

Job Prospects. Competition for jobs is expected to be strong. Emergency management directors are a relatively small occupation, and decreased funding means that new openings at the local or county level are unlikely.

However, retirements over the next decade may provide some opportunities for those interested in entering the occupation.

O*NET

➤ Emergency Management Directors (11-9161.00)

Contacts for More Information

For more information on emergency management directors, visit
➤ National Emergency Management Association (www.nemaweb.org/)
➤ International Association of Emergency Managers (www.iaem.com/home.cfm)

Farmers, Ranchers, and Other Agricultural Managers

- **2012 Median Pay** .... $69,300 per year
  $33.32 per hour
- **Entry-Level Education** ... High school diploma or equivalent
- **Work Experience in a Related Occupation** ... 5 years or more
- **On-the-Job Training** .... None
- **Number of Jobs 2012** 930,600
- **Job Outlook, 2012–22** ....-19% (Decline)
- **Employment Change, 2012–22** ....-179,900

Some farmers work primarily with crops, whereas other farmers and ranchers handle livestock.

What Farmers, Ranchers, and Other Agricultural Managers Do

Farmers, ranchers, and other agricultural managers run establishments that produce crops, livestock, and dairy products.

Duties. Farmers, ranchers, and other agricultural managers typically do the following:

- Supervise all steps of the crop production and ranging process, including planting, fertilizing, harvesting, and herding
- Determine how to raise crops or livestock according to factors such as market conditions, federal program availability, and soil conditions
- Select and purchase supplies, such as seed, fertilizers, and farm machinery
- Repair farm machinery so it cultivates, harvests, and hauls crops
- Adapt their duties to the seasons, weather conditions, or a crop's growing cycle
- Maintain farm facilities, such as water pipes, hoses, fences, and animal shelters
- Serve as the sales agent for livestock and crops
- Keep financial, tax, production, and employee records

American farmers, ranchers, and other agricultural managers produce enough crops and livestock to meet the needs of the United States and for export. However, farm output and income are strongly influenced by weather, disease, fluctuations in prices, and federal farm programs.

Farmers, ranchers, and other agricultural managers monitor the constantly changing prices for their product. They use different strategies to protect themselves from unpredictable changes in the markets.

Many farmers carefully plan the combination of crops that they grow, so if the price of one crop drops, they will have enough income from another crop to make up the loss. When farmers and ranchers plan ahead, they may be able to store their crops or keep their livestock to take advantage of higher prices later in the year.

Most farm output goes to food-processing companies. However, some farmers now choose to sell their goods directly to consumers through farmer's markets or use cooperatives to reduce their financial risk and to gain a larger share of the final price of their goods. In community-supported agriculture, cooperatives sell shares of a harvest to consumers before the planting season to ensure a market for the farm's produce.

Farmers, ranchers, and other agricultural managers also negotiate with banks and other credit lenders to get financing, because they must buy seed, livestock, and equipment before they have products to sell.

Farmers and ranchers own and operate mainly family-owned farms. They also may lease land from a landowner and operate it as a working farm.

The size of the farm or range determines which tasks farmers and ranchers handle. Those who operate small farms or ranges usually do all tasks. In addition to growing crops and raising animals, they keep records, service machinery, and maintain buildings.

Farmers and ranchers who operate large farms, however, have employees–including agricultural workers–who help with physical work. Some employees of large farms are in nonfarm occupations,

Median Annual Wages, May 2012

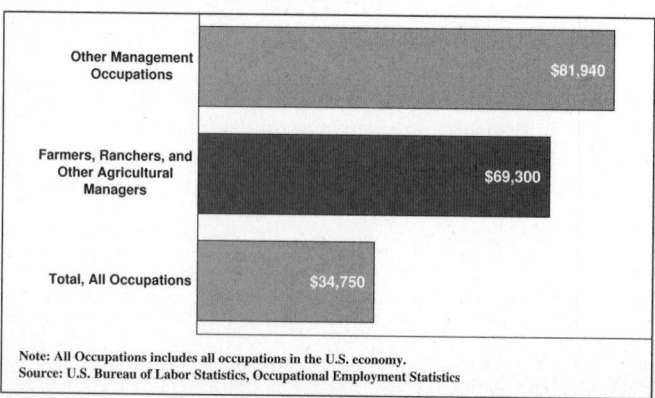

Note: All Occupations includes all occupations in the U.S. economy.
Source: U.S. Bureau of Labor Statistics, Occupational Employment Statistics

Percent Change in Employment, Projected 2012–2022

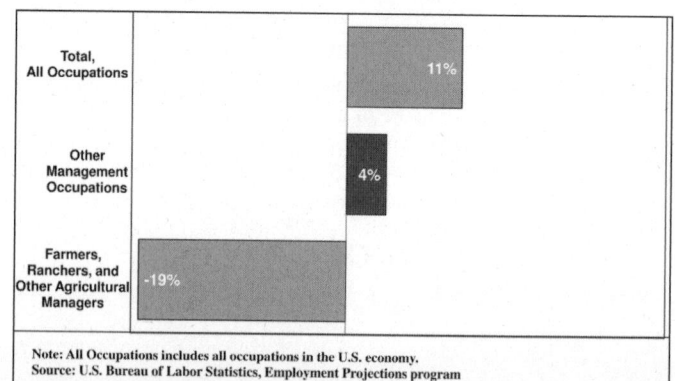

Note: All Occupations includes all occupations in the U.S. economy.
Source: U.S. Bureau of Labor Statistics, Employment Projections program

Employment Projections Data for Farmers, Ranchers, and Other Agricultural Managers

Occupational title	SOC Code	Employment, 2012	Projected Employment, 2022	Change, 2012–2022	
				Percent	Numeric
Farmers, ranchers, and other agricultural managers............. 11-9013		930,600	750,700	-19	-179,900

Source: U.S. Bureau of Labor Statistics, Employment Projections Program

Note: Data are rounded. Go to **Occupational Information Included in the OOH** *for a discussion of the data in this table.*

working as truck drivers, sales representatives, bookkeepers, and IT specialists.

Both farmers and ranchers monitor the operation of machinery and maintain their equipment and facilities. They track technological improvements in animal breeding and seeds, choosing new products that might improve output. Many livestock and dairy farmers monitor and attend to the health of their herds, which may include assisting in births.

Agricultural managers take care of the day-to-day operation of one or more farms, ranches, nurseries, timber tracts, greenhouses, and other agricultural establishments for corporations, farmers, and owners who do not live and work on their farm or ranch.

Agricultural managers usually do not do production activities themselves. Instead, they hire and supervise farm and livestock workers to do most daily production tasks.

Managers may determine budgets. They may decide how to store and transport crops. They oversee proper maintenance of equipment and property.

The following are examples of types of farmers, ranchers, and other agricultural managers:

Crop farmers and managers–those who grow grain, fruits and vegetables, and other crops–are responsible for all steps of plant growth. After a harvest, they make sure that the crops are properly packaged and stored.

Livestock, dairy, and poultry farmers, ranchers, and managers feed and care for animals. They keep livestock in barns, pens, and other well-maintained farm buildings. These workers also oversee breeding and marketing.

Horticultural specialty farmers and managers oversee the production of fruits, vegetables, flowers, and plants (including turf) used for landscaping. They also grow grapes, berries, and nuts used in making wine.

Aquaculture farmers and managers raise fish and shellfish in ponds, floating net pens, raceways, and recirculating systems. They stock, feed, protect, and maintain aquatic life used for food and for recreational fishing.

Work Environment

Farmers, ranchers, and other agricultural managers held about 930,600 jobs in 2012. About 73 percent were self-employed. The rest were wage and salary agricultural managers.

Farmers, ranchers, and other agricultural managers typically work outdoors and may spend some time in offices. They sometimes do strenuous physical work.

Some farmers work primarily with crops and vegetables. Other farmers and ranchers handle livestock.

Injuries and Illnesses. The work environment for farmers, ranchers, and other agricultural managers can be hazardous. Tractors and other farm machinery can cause serious injury, so workers must be alert on the job. They must operate equipment and handle chemicals properly to avoid accidents and safeguard the surrounding environment.

Work Schedules. Most farmers, ranchers, and other agricultural managers work full time. Farmers and farm managers on crop farms usually work from sunrise to sunset during the planting and harvesting seasons. During the rest of the year, they plan the next season's crops, market their output, and repair and maintain machinery.

On livestock-producing farms and ranches, work goes on throughout the year. Animals require care every day.

On very large farms, farmers and farm managers spend time meeting with farm supervisors. Managers who oversee several farms may divide their time between traveling to meet farmers and landowners and planning the farm operations in their offices.

How to Become One

Traditionally, experience growing up on or working on a family farm or ranch is the way farmers and ranchers learn their trade.

Education. Farmers, ranchers, and other agricultural managers typically gain skills through work experience and usually have at least a high school diploma. Traditionally, experience growing up on or working on a family farm or ranch was the way farmers and ranchers learn their trade.

However, as farm and land management has grown more complex, more farmers, ranchers, and other agricultural managers now have a bachelor's degree in agriculture or a related field. Completing a degree at a college of agriculture is becoming important for workers who want to make a living from this occupation. There are a number of government programs that help new farmers get training.

All state university systems have at least one land-grant college or university with a school of agriculture. Common programs of study include business with a concentration in agriculture, plant breeding, farm management, agronomy, dairy science, and agricultural economics.

At an agricultural college, students learn about crops, growing conditions, and plant diseases. Prospective ranchers and dairy farmers, on the other hand, learn basics of veterinary science, including how pesticides can affect livestock.

Important Qualities

Analytical skills. Farmers, ranchers, and other agricultural managers must monitor and assess the quality of their land or livestock. These tasks require precision and accuracy.

Critical-thinking skills. Farmers, ranchers, and other agricultural managers make tough decisions through sound reasoning and judgment. They determine how to improve their harvest and livestock, reacting appropriately to external factors.

Interpersonal skills. Farmers, ranchers, and other agricultural managers supervise laborers and other workers, so effective communication is critical.

Mechanical skills. Farmers, ranchers, and other agricultural managers–particularly those working on smaller farms–must be able to operate complex machinery and occasionally perform routine maintenance.

Training. Those without postsecondary education take a longer time to learn the more complex aspects of farming. A small num-

Similar Occupations This table shows a list of occupations with job duties that are similar to those of farmers, ranchers, and other agricultural managers.

Occupations	Entry-level Education	2012 Pay	Projected Job Growth	Average Annual Openings
Agricultural and Food Science Technicians	Associate's degree	$34,070	3%	1,010
Agricultural and Food Scientists	See "How to Become One"	$58,636	10%	1,640
Agricultural Workers	See "How to Become One"	$19,703	-3%	23,190
Purchasing Managers, Buyers, and Purchasing Agents	See "How to Become One"	$63,128	4%	12,230

ber of farms offer formal apprenticeships to help young people learn the practical skills of farming and ranching. Government projects, such as the Beginner Farmer and Rancher Competitive Grants Program, provide a way for people without any farm training to be paired with experienced farmers, learning through internships or apprentice programs.

Work Experience in a Related Occupation. Prospective farmers, ranchers, and agricultural managers typically work and gain experience under more experienced farmers. Universities and forms of government assistance give prospective farmers alternatives to the traditional training method of being raised on a family farm.

Licenses, Certifications, and Registrations. To show competency in farm management, agricultural managers may choose to become certified. The American Society of Farm Managers and Rural Appraisers (ASFMR) offers a farm manager accreditation to ASFMR members who have 4 years of work experience and a bachelor's degree. A complete list of requirements, including consultant course work and exams, is available from ASFMR.

Pay

The median annual wage for farmers, ranchers, and other agricultural managers was $69,300 in May 2012. The median wage is the wage at which half the workers in an occupation earned more than that amount and half earned less. The lowest 10 percent earned less than $31,700, and the top 10 percent earned more than $124,160.

Incomes of farmers and ranchers vary from year to year because prices of farm products fluctuate with weather conditions and other factors. In addition to income from their farm business, farmers can receive government subsidies or other payments that add to their income and reduce some of the risk of farming.

Also, increasingly more farmers, especially operators of small farms, are relying on off-farm sources of income such as Community Supported Agriculture (CSA) programs.

Job Outlook

Employment of farmers, ranchers, and other agricultural managers is projected to decline 19 percent from 2012 to 2022.

The continuing ability of the agricultural sector to produce more with fewer workers will cause some farmers to go out of business.

As land, machinery, seed, and chemicals become more expensive, only well-capitalized farmers and corporations will be able to buy many of the farms that become available. These larger, more productive farms are better able to withstand the adverse effects of climate and price fluctuations on farm output and income.

Still, several new programs such as the Beginning Farmers and Ranchers Development Program are designed to help beginning farmers and ranchers acquire land and operating capital may offset these market pressures.

In contrast, agricultural managers should have more opportunities. Owners of large tracts of land, who often do not live on the property they own, increasingly will seek the expertise of agricultural managers, to run their farms and ranches as businesses.

Despite the expected continued consolidation of farmland and the projected decline in overall employment of this occupation, an increasing number of small-scale farmers have developed successful market niches that involve personalized, direct contact with their customers. Many are finding opportunities in horticulture and organic food production, which are among the fastest growing segments of agriculture. Others use farmer's markets that cater directly to urban and suburban consumers, allowing the farmers to capture a greater share of consumers' food dollars.

Some small-scale farmers belong to collectively owned marketing cooperatives that process and sell their products. Other farmers participate in community-supported agriculture (CSA) cooperatives that allow consumers to buy a share of the farmer's harvest directly.

O*NET

- ➤ Farmers, Ranchers, and Other Agricultural Managers (11-9013.00)
- ➤ Nursery and Greenhouse Managers (11-9013.01)
- ➤ Farm and Ranch Managers (11-9013.02)
- ➤ Aquacultural Managers (11-9013.03)

Contacts for More Information

For more information about agriculture policy and farm advocacy, visit
- ➤ Center for Rural Affairs (www.cfra.org)

For more information about the Beginner Farmer and Rancher Competitive Grants Program, visit
- ➤ National Institute of Food and Agriculture (www.nifa.usda.gov/funding/bfrdp/bfrdp.html)

For more general information about farming in the United States, visit
- ➤ Farm Service Agency (www.fsa.usda.gov/)

For more information on farm manager certification, visit
- ➤ American Society of Farm Managers and Rural Appraisers (www.asfmra.org/)

Financial Managers

- **2012 Median Pay** .... $109,740 per year
  $52.76 per hour
- **Entry-Level Education** ....Bachelor's degree
- **Work Experience in a Related Occupation** ... 5 years or more
- **On-the-Job Training** .... None
- **Number of Jobs 2012** 532,100
- **Job Outlook, 2012–22** .... 9% (As fast as average)
- **Employment Change, 2012–22** 47,100

- Analyze market trends to find opportunities for expansion or for acquiring other companies
- Help management make financial decisions

The role of the financial manager, particularly in business, is changing in response to technological advances that have substantially reduced the amount of time it takes to produce financial reports. Financial managers' main responsibility used to be monitoring a company's finances, but they now do more data analysis and advise senior managers on ideas as to how to maximize profits. They often work on teams, acting as business advisors to top executives.

Financial managers also do tasks that are specific to their organization or industry. For example, government financial managers must be experts on government appropriations and budgeting processes, and healthcare financial managers must know about issues in healthcare finance. Moreover, financial managers must be aware of special tax laws and regulations that affect their industry. For more information on chief financial officers, see the profile on top executives.

The following are examples of types of financial managers:

Controllers direct the preparation of financial reports that summarize and forecast the organization's financial position, such as income statements, balance sheets, and analyses of future earnings or expenses. Controllers also are in charge of preparing special reports required by governmental agencies that regulate businesses. Often, controllers oversee the accounting, audit, and budget departments of their organization.

Treasurers and *finance officers* direct their organization's budgets to meet its financial goals. They oversee the investment of funds and carry out strategies to raise capital (such as issuing stocks or bonds) to support the firm's expansion. They also develop financial plans for mergers (two companies joining together) and acquisitions (one company buying another).

Credit managers oversee their firm's credit business. They set credit-rating criteria, determine credit ceilings, and monitor the collections of past-due accounts.

Cash managers monitor and control the flow of cash that comes in and goes out of the company to meet the company's business and investment needs. For example, they must project cash flow (amounts coming in and going out) to determine whether the company will not have enough cash and will need a loan or will have more cash than needed and so can invest some of its money.

Risk managers control financial risk by using hedging and other strategies to limit or offset the probability of a financial loss or a company's exposure to financial uncertainty. Among the risks they try to limit are those due to currency or commodity price changes.

Financial managers oversee the preparation of financial reports and investment activities.

What Financial Managers Do

Financial managers are responsible for the financial health of an organization. They produce financial reports, direct investment activities, and develop strategies and plans for the long-term financial goals of their organization.

Duties. Financial managers typically do the following:

- Prepare financial statements, business activity reports, and forecasts
- Monitor financial details to ensure that legal requirements are met
- Supervise employees who do financial reporting and budgeting
- Review company financial reports and seek ways to reduce costs

Median Annual Wages, May 2012

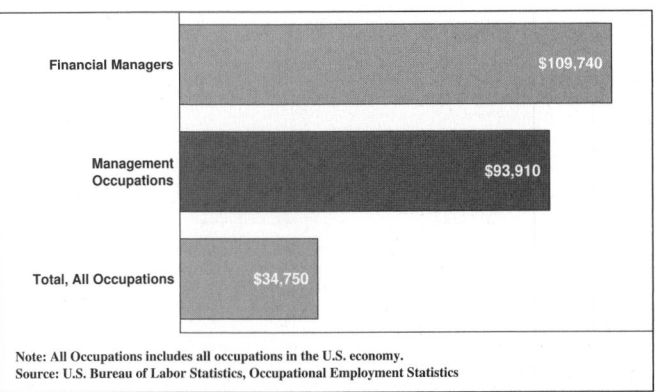

Financial Managers $109,740
Management Occupations $93,910
Total, All Occupations $34,750

Note: All Occupations includes all occupations in the U.S. economy.
Source: U.S. Bureau of Labor Statistics, Occupational Employment Statistics

Percent Change in Employment, Projected 2012–2022

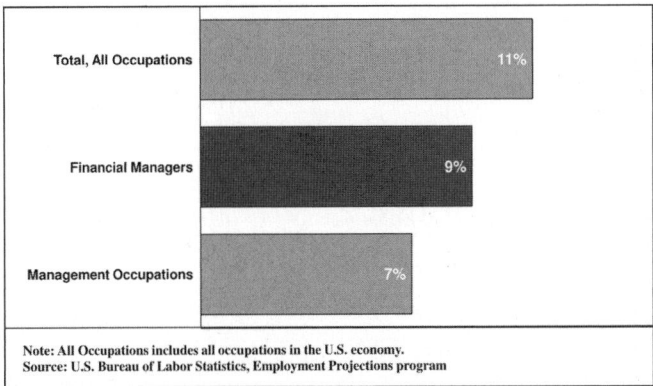

Total, All Occupations 11%
Financial Managers 9%
Management Occupations 7%

Note: All Occupations includes all occupations in the U.S. economy.
Source: U.S. Bureau of Labor Statistics, Employment Projections program

Employment Projections Data for Financial Managers

Occupational title	SOC Code	Employment, 2012	Projected Employment, 2022	Change, 2012–2022	
				Percent	Numeric
Financial managers..	11-3031	532,100	579,200	9	47,100

Source: U.S. Bureau of Labor Statistics, Employment Projections Program

Note: **Data are rounded. Go to Occupational Information Included in the OOH** *for a discussion of the data in this table.*

Insurance managers decide how best to limit a company's losses by obtaining insurance against risks such as the need to make disability payments for an employee who gets hurt on the job and costs imposed by a lawsuit against the company.

Work Environment

Financial managers held about 532,100 jobs in 2012. They work in many industries, including banks and insurance companies. They work closely with top executives and with departments that develop the data financial managers need.

The industries that employed the most financial managers in 2012 were as follows:

Finance and insurance	28%
Management of companies and enterprises	10
Professional, scientific, and technical services	10
Manufacturing	8
Government	8

Work Schedules. Most financial managers work full time, and many work long hours.

How to Become One

Financial managers typically have a bachelor's degree and 5 years or more of experience in another business or financial occupation, such as loan officer, accountant, auditor, securities sales agent, or financial analyst.

Education. A bachelor's degree in finance, accounting, economics, or business administration is often the minimum education needed for financial managers. However, many employers now seek candidates with a master's degree, preferably in business administration, finance, or economics. These academic programs help students develop analytical skills and learn financial analysis methods and software.

Licenses, Certifications, and Registrations. Professional certification is not required, but some financial managers still get it to demonstrate a level of competence. The CFA Institute confers the Chartered Financial Analyst (CFA) certification to investment professionals who possess at least a bachelor's degree, have 4 years of work experience, and pass three exams. The Association for Financial Professionals confers the Certified Treasury Professional credential to those who pass an exam and have a minimum of 2 years of relevant experience.

Work Experience in a Related Occupation. Financial managers usually have experience in another business or financial occupation, such as loan officer, accountant or auditor, securities sales agent, or financial analyst.

In some cases, companies provide formal management training programs to help prepare highly motivated and skilled financial workers to become financial managers.

Important Qualities

Analytical skills. Financial managers increasingly are assisting executives in making decisions that affect their organization, a task for which these managers need analytical ability.

Communication skills. Excellent communication skills are essential because financial managers must explain and justify complex financial transactions.

Detail oriented. In preparing and analyzing reports such as balance sheets and income statements, financial managers must pay attention to detail.

Math skills. Financial managers must be skilled in math, including algebra. An understanding of international finance and complex financial documents also is important.

Organizational skills. Financial managers deal with a range of information and documents and so must stay organized to do their jobs effectively.

Similar Occupations   This table shows a list of occupations with job duties that are similar to those of financial managers.

Occupations	Entry-level Education	2012 Pay	Projected Job Growth	Average Annual Openings
Accountants and Auditors	Bachelor's degree	$63,550	13%	54,420
Budget Analysts	Bachelor's degree	$69,280	6%	2,850
Financial Analysts	Bachelor's degree	$76,950	16%	10,090
Insurance Sales Agents	High school diploma or equivalent	$48,150	10%	15,020
Insurance Underwriters	Bachelor's degree	$62,870	-6%	2,890
Loan Officers	Bachelor's degree	$59,820	8%	7,720
Personal Financial Advisors	Bachelor's degree	$67,520	27%	9,640
Real Estate Brokers and Sales Agents	High school diploma or equivalent	$42,723	11%	8,630
Securities, Commodities, and Financial Services Sales Agents	Bachelor's degree	$71,720	11%	12,260
Top Executives	Bachelor's degree	$104,073	11%	70,090

Pay

The median annual wage for financial managers was $109,740 in May 2012. The median wage is the wage at which half the workers in an occupation earned more than that amount and half earned less. The lowest 10 percent earned less than $59,630, and the top 10 percent earned more than $187,200.

In May 2012, the median annual wages for financial managers in the top five industries in which these managers worked were as follows:

Professional, scientific, and technical services	$130,120
Management of companies and enterprises	124,840
Finance and insurance	108,690
Manufacturing	107,730
Government	102,270

Job Outlook

Employment of financial managers is projected to grow 9 percent from 2012 to 2022, about as fast as the average for all occupations. However, growth will vary by industry.

Services provided by financial managers, such as planning, directing, and coordinating investments, will continue to be in demand as the economy grows. The United States remains an international financial center, meaning that the economic growth of countries around the world will likely contribute to employment growth in the U.S. financial industry. In recent years, companies have been accumulating more cash on their balance sheets. This will lead to demand for financial managers, as companies will be in need of cash management expertise.

Overall growth of employment for financial managers will be limited by slower expected growth in depository credit intermediation. This industry includes commercial banking and savings institutions, and employs a large percentage of these managers. From 2012 to 2022, employment of financial managers is projected to grow 5 percent in the depository credit intermediation industry.

Job Prospects. As with other managerial occupations, jobseekers are likely to face competition because the number of job openings is expected to be fewer than the number of applicants. Candidates with expertise in accounting and finance–particularly those with a master's degree or certification–should enjoy the best job prospects. An understanding of international finance and complex financial documents is important.

O*NET

➤ Financial Managers (11-3031.00)
➤ Treasurers and Controllers (11-3031.01)
➤ Financial Managers, Branch or Department (11-3031.02)

Contacts for More Information

For more information about financial managers, including certification, visit
➤ Financial Management Association International (www.fma.org/)

For information about careers in financial and treasury management and the Certified Treasury Professional program, visit
➤ Association for Financial Professionals (www.afponline.org/)

For information about the Chartered Financial Analyst program, visit
➤ CFA Institute (www.cfainstitute.org)

Food Service Managers

- **2012 Median Pay** .... $47,960 per year
  $23.06 per hour
- **Entry-Level Education** ... High school diploma or equivalent
- **Work Experience in a Related Occupation** ...... Less than 5 years
- **On-the-Job Training** .... None
- **Number of Jobs 2012** 321,400
- **Job Outlook, 2012–22** .... 2% (Little or no change)
- **Employment Change, 2012–22** 5,000

What Food Service Managers Do

Food service managers are responsible for the daily operation of restaurants and other establishments that prepare and serve food and beverages. They direct staff to ensure that customers are satisfied with their dining experience and the business is profitable.

Duties. Food service managers typically do the following:

- Interview, hire, train, oversee, and sometimes fire employees
- Manage the inventory and order food and beverages, equipment, and supplies
- Oversee food preparation, portion sizes, and the overall presentation of food
- Inspect supplies, equipment, and work areas
- Ensure employees comply with health and food safety standards and regulations
- Investigate and resolve complaints regarding food quality or service
- Schedule staff hours and assign duties
- Maintain budgets and payroll records and review financial transactions
- Establish standards for personnel performance and customer service

Besides coordinating activities of the kitchen and dining room staff, managers ensure that customers are served properly and in a timely manner. They monitor orders in the kitchen and, if needed, they work with the chef to remedy any delays in service.

Some food service managers, including those who manage their own business, deal with suppliers and arrange for delivery of food and beverages and other supplies. Some also plan or approve menus and set prices for food and beverage items.

Food service managers are responsible for all functions of the business, related to employees. For example, most managers interview, hire, train, and sometimes fire employees. Managers also schedule work hours, making sure that enough workers are present to cover each shift. During busy periods, they may expedite the service by helping to serve customers, cashiering, or cleaning tables.

Food service managers also plan and arrange for cleaning and maintenance services of the equipment and facility. For example, they arrange for linen service, heavy cleaning when the dining room and kitchen are not in use, trash removal, and pest control when needed.

In addition, managers perform many administrative tasks, such as keeping employee records; preparing the payroll; and completing paperwork to comply with licensing, tax and wage, unemployment compensation, and Social Security laws. Although they sometimes assign these tasks to an assistant manager or bookkeeper, most managers are responsible for the accuracy of business records.

Full-service restaurants (those with table service) may have a management team that includes a general manager, one or more assistant managers, and an executive chef. Managers add up the cash and charge slips and secure them in a safe place. Many managers also lock up the establishment; check that ovens, grills, and lights are off; and switch on the alarm system.

Work Environment

Food service managers held about 321,400 jobs in 2012. About 40 percent were self-employed.

Food service managers typically work in restaurants, including fine-dining and fast-food chains and franchises. Others work in hotels, catering, and other establishments, such as cafeterias in schools, hospitals, factories, or offices.

Many food service managers work long hours, and the job is often hectic. Dealing with unhappy customers can sometimes be stressful.

Work Schedules. Most food service managers work full time. Managers at fine-dining and fast-food restaurants often work long hours. Managers of institutional food service facilities in schools, factories, or office buildings usually work traditional business hours. Those who oversee multiple locations of a chain or franchise may be called in on short notice, including evenings, weekends, and holidays.

How to Become One

Most applicants qualify with a high school diploma and long-term work experience in the food service industry as a cook, waiter or waitress, or counter attendant. However, some receive training at a community college, technical or vocational school, culinary school, or at a 4-year college.

Education. Although a bachelor's degree is not required, some postsecondary education is increasingly preferred for many manager positions, especially at upscale restaurants and hotels. Some food service companies and national or regional restaurant chains recruit management trainees from college hospitality or food service management programs, which require internships and real-life experience to graduate.

Many colleges and universities offer bachelor's degree programs in restaurant and hospitality management or institutional food service management. In addition, numerous community and junior colleges, technical institutes, and other institutions offer programs in the field leading to an associate's degree. Some culinary schools offer programs in restaurant management with courses designed for those who want to start and run their own restaurant.

Food service managers ensure that food is in adequate supply and stored at the appropriate temperature.

Regardless of length, nearly all programs provide instruction in nutrition, sanitation, and food planning and preparation, as well as courses in accounting, business law, and management. Some programs combine classroom and practical study with internships.

Work Experience in a Related Occupation. Most food service managers start working in industry-related jobs, such as cooks, waiters and waitresses, or dining room attendants. They often spend years working under the direction of an experienced worker, learning the necessary skills before they are promoted to manager positions.

Training. Managers who work for restaurant chains and food service management companies may undergo programs that combine classroom instruction and on-the-job training. Topics may include food preparation, nutrition, sanitation, security, company

Median Annual Wages, May 2012

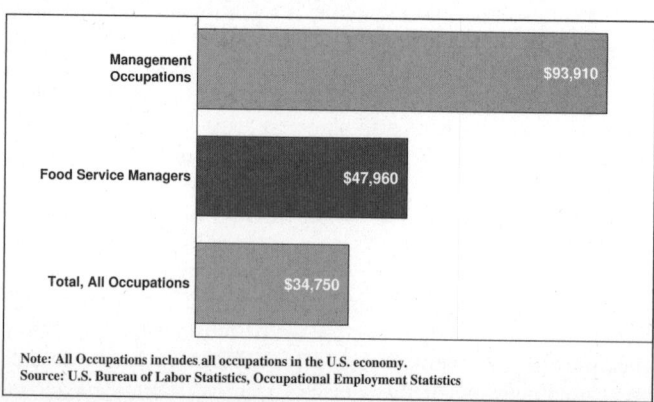

Management Occupations — $93,910

Food Service Managers — $47,960

Total, All Occupations — $34,750

Note: All Occupations includes all occupations in the U.S. economy.
Source: U.S. Bureau of Labor Statistics, Occupational Employment Statistics

Percent Change in Employment, Projected 2012–2022

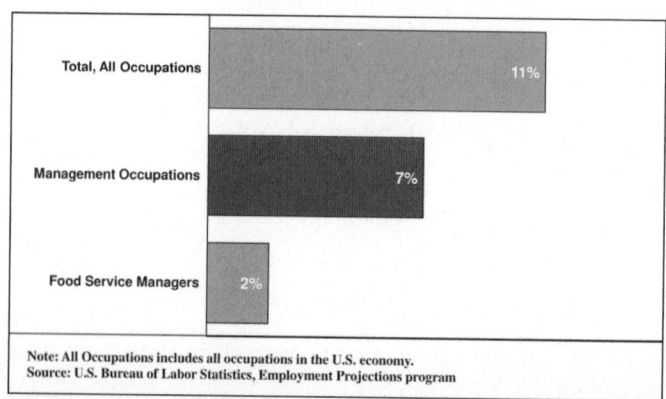

Total, All Occupations — 11%

Management Occupations — 7%

Food Service Managers — 2%

Note: All Occupations includes all occupations in the U.S. economy.
Source: U.S. Bureau of Labor Statistics, Employment Projections program

Employment Projections Data for Food Service Managers

Occupational title	SOC Code	Employment, 2012	Projected Employment, 2022	Change, 2012–2022	
				Percent	Numeric
Food service managers..	11-9051	321,400	326,500	2	5,000

Source: U.S. Bureau of Labor Statistics, Employment Projections Program

Note: Data are rounded. Go to Occupational Information Included in the OOH for a discussion of the data in this table.

policies, personnel management, and recordkeeping. Some include training on the use of the restaurant's computer system.

Licenses, Certifications, and Registrations. Although not required, voluntary certification shows professional competence, particularly for managers who learned their skills on the job. The National Restaurant Association Educational Foundation awards the Foodservice Management Professional designation to managers who meet several criteria, including passing a written exam, completing coursework, and meeting experience requirements.

Important Qualities

Business skills. Food service managers, especially those who run their own restaurant, must understand all aspects of the restaurant business. They should know how to budget for supplies, set prices, and manage workers to ensure that the restaurant is profitable.

Customer-service skills. Food service managers must be courteous and attentive when dealing with patrons. Satisfying customers' dining needs is critical for success and ensures customer loyalty.

Detail oriented. Managers deal with many different types of activities. They interact with suppliers, workers, and customers; they make sure there is enough food to serve to customers; they take care of financial records; and they ensure health and food safety.

Leadership skills. Managers must establish good working relationships to ensure a productive work environment. This may involve motivating workers, resolving conflicts, or actively listening to complaints or criticism from customers.

Organizational skills. Food service managers keep track of many different schedules, budgets, and people. This becomes more complex as the size of the restaurant or food service facility increases.

Physical stamina. Food service managers, especially managers working in small establishments or those who run their own business, often work long hours and sometimes spend entire evenings on their feet helping to serve customers.

Problem-solving skills. The ability to resolve personnel issues and customer-related problems is imperative to the work of managers.

Speaking skills. Food service managers must give clear orders to staff and be able to explain information to employees and customers.

Pay

The median annual wage for food service managers was $47,960 in May 2012. The median wage is the wage at which half the workers in an occupation earned more than that amount and half earned less. The lowest 10 percent earned less than $30,820, and the top 10 percent earned more than $81,030.

In May 2012, median annual wages for food service managers in the top five industries employing these managers were as follows:

Traveler accommodation	$54,850
Special food services	54,210
Nursing care facilities	49,650
Elementary and secondary schools	49,440
Restaurants and other eating places	46,360

Job Outlook

Employment of food service managers is projected to show little or no change from 2012 to 2022.

Population and income growth are expected to result in greater demand for food at a variety of dining establishments. People will continue to dine out, purchase take-out meals, or have food delivered to their homes or workplaces. In response, more restaurants will open, and cafeterias, catering services, and nontraditional food services, such as those found inside grocery or retail stores, will serve more prepared dishes.

However, employment growth should be limited as companies that operate restaurants and other food service establishments continue to consolidate managerial functions and use first-line supervisors to perform the work normally done by managers.

Job Prospects. Job opportunities should be best for food service managers with several years of work experience in a restaurant or food service establishment. Most job openings will result from the need to replace managers who retire or transfer to other occupations.

Jobseekers with a combination of work experience in food service and a bachelor's degree in hospitality, restaurant, or food service management should have an edge when competing for jobs at upscale restaurants.

O*NET

➤ Food Service Managers (11-9051.00)

Similar Occupations This table shows a list of occupations with job duties that are similar to those of food service managers.

Occupations	Entry-level Education	2012 Pay	Projected Job Growth	Average Annual Openings
Bartenders	Less than high school	$18,900	12%	26,940
Chefs and Head Cooks	High school diploma or equivalent	$42,480	5%	2,470
Cooks	See "How to Become One"	$21,144	10%	63,160
Lodging Managers	High school diploma or equivalent	$46,810	1%	1,620
Sales Managers	Bachelor's degree	$105,260	8%	10,690
Waiters and Waitresses	Less than high school	$18,540	6%	126,830

Contacts for More Information

For more information about food service managers, including a directory of college programs in food service, visit

➤ National Restaurant Association (www.restaurant. org/?wwparam=1326903377)

For more information about food service managers and certification as a Foodservice Management Professional, visit

➤ National Restaurant Association Educational Foundation (www. nraef.org/)

For general information about food service managers, visit

➤ Society for Foodservice Management (www.sfm-online.org/)

Human Resources Managers

- **2012 Median Pay** .... $99,720 per year
  $47.94 per hour

- **Entry-Level Education** .... Bachelor's degree

- **Work Experience in a Related Occupation** ... 5 years or more

- **On-the-Job Training** .... None

- **Number of Jobs 2012** 102,700

- **Job Outlook, 2012–22** .... 13% (As fast as average)

- **Employment Change, 2012–22** 13,600

What Human Resources Managers Do

Human resources managers plan, direct, and coordinate the administrative functions of an organization. They oversee the recruiting, interviewing, and hiring of new staff; consult with top executives on strategic planning; and serve as a link between an organization's management and its employees.

Duties. Human resources managers typically do the following:

- Plan and coordinate an organization's workforce to best use employees' talents

- Link an organization's management with its employees

- Administer employee services

- Advise managers on organizational policies, such as equal employment opportunity and sexual harassment

- Coordinate and supervise the work of specialists and support staff

- Oversee an organization's recruitment, interview, selection, and hiring processes

- Handle staffing issues, such as mediating disputes and directing disciplinary procedures

Every organization wants to attract, motivate, and keep qualified employees and match them to jobs for which they are well suited. Human resources managers accomplish this by directing the administrative functions of human resource departments. Their work involves overseeing employee relations, regulatory compliance, and employee-related services such as payroll, training, and benefits. They supervise the department's specialists and support staff and ensure that tasks are completed accurately and on time.

Human resources managers also consult with top executives regarding the organization's strategic planning. They identify ways to maximize the value of the organization's employees and ensure that they are used as efficiently as possible. For example, they might assess worker productivity and recommend changes to the organization's structure to help it meet budgetary goals.

Some human resources managers oversee all aspects of an organization's human resources department, including the compensa-

tion and benefits or training and development programs. In many larger organizations, these programs are directed by specialized managers, such as compensation and benefits managers and training and development managers.

The following are examples of types of human resources managers:

Labor relations managers, also called *employee relations managers*, oversee employment policies in union and non-union settings. They draw up, negotiate, and administer labor contracts that cover issues such as grievances, wages, benefits, and union and management practices. They also handle labor complaints between employees and management and coordinate grievance procedures.

Payroll managers supervise the operations of an organization's payroll department. They ensure that all aspects of payroll are processed correctly and on time. They administer payroll procedures, prepare reports for the accounting department, and resolve any payroll problems or discrepancies.

Recruiting managers, sometimes called *staffing managers*, oversee the recruiting and hiring responsibilities of the human resources department. They often supervise a team of recruiters, and some take on recruiting duties when trying to fill high-level positions. They must develop a recruiting strategy that helps them meet the staffing needs of their organization and effectively compete for the best employees.

Work Environment

Human resources managers held about 102,700 jobs in 2012 and were employed in nearly every industry.

The industries that employed the most human resources managers in 2012 were as follows:

Management of companies and enterprises	14%
Manufacturing	14
Government	12
Professional, scientific, and technical services	10
Health care and social assistance	10

Human resources managers work in offices. Some managers, especially those working for organizations that have offices nationwide, must travel to visit other branches as well as to attend professional meetings or to recruit employees.

Work Schedules. Most human resources managers work full time during regular business hours.

About one-third worked more than 40 hours a week in 2012.

Human resources managers oversee an organization's recruitment, interview, selection, and hiring processes.

Median Annual Wages, May 2012

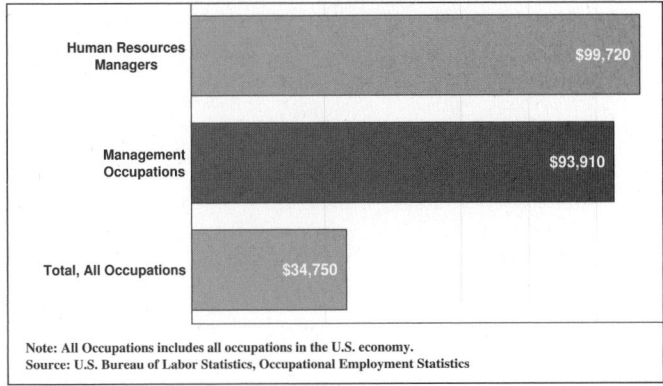

Note: All Occupations includes all occupations in the U.S. economy.
Source: U.S. Bureau of Labor Statistics, Occupational Employment Statistics

Percent Change in Employment, Projected 2012–2022

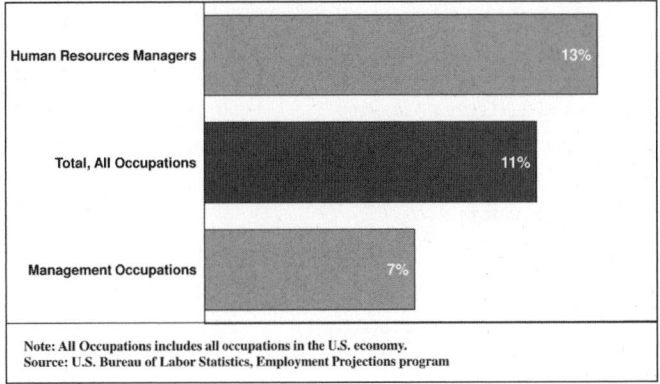

Note: All Occupations includes all occupations in the U.S. economy.
Source: U.S. Bureau of Labor Statistics, Employment Projections program

How to Become One

Candidates need a combination of education and several years of related work experience to become a human resources manager. Although a bachelor's degree is sufficient for most positions, some jobs require a master's degree. Candidates should have strong interpersonal skills.

Education. Human resources managers usually need a bachelor's degree in human resources or business administration. Alternatively, candidates can complete a bachelor's degree in another field and take courses in human resources subjects, such as labor or industrial relations, organizational development, or industrial psychology. Some positions are also filled by experienced individuals with other backgrounds, including finance, business management, education, and information technology.

Some higher-level jobs require a master's degree in human resources, labor relations, or a Master of Business Administration (MBA) degree.

Work Experience in a Related Occupation. To demonstrate an ability to organize, manage, and lead others, related work experience is essential for human resources managers. Some employers accept management experience in a variety of fields. However, many positions require experience working with human resources programs, such as compensation and benefits plans or with a Human Resources Information System (HRIS), and require a solid understanding of federal, state, and local employment laws.

Others start out as human resources specialists or labor relations specialists.

Licenses, Certifications, and Registrations. Although certification is voluntary, it can show professional expertise and credibility and may enhance advancement opportunities. Many employers prefer to hire certified candidates, and some positions may require certification. The Society for Human Resource Management and the International Foundation of Employee Benefit Plans are among many professional associations that offer a variety of certification programs.

Important Qualities

Decision-making skills. Human resources managers must be able to balance the strengths and weaknesses of different options and decide the best course of action. Many of their decisions have a significant impact on workers or operations, such as deciding whether to fire an employee.

Interpersonal skills. Human resources managers need strong interpersonal skills because they regularly interact with people. They often collaborate on teams and must develop positive working relationships with their colleagues.

Leadership skills. Human resources managers must be able to direct a staff and oversee the operations of their department. They must coordinate work activities and ensure that workers in the department complete their duties and fulfill their responsibilities.

Organizational skills. Organizational skills are essential for human resources managers. They must be able to manage several projects at once and prioritize tasks.

Speaking skills. Human resources managers rely on speaking skills to give presentations and direct their staff. They must clearly communicate information and instructions to their staff and other employees.

Pay

The median annual wage for human resources managers was $99,720 in May 2012. The median wage is the wage at which half the workers in an occupation earned more than that amount and half earned less. The lowest 10 percent earned less than $59,020, and the top 10 percent earned more than $173,140.

In May 2012, the median annual wages for human resources managers in the top five industries employing these managers were as follows:

Management of companies and enterprises $112,550
Professional, scientific, and technical services 112,210
Manufacturing 97,930
Government 92,020
Health care and social assistance 85,870

Employment Projections Data for Human Resources Managers

Occupational title	SOC Code	Employment, 2012	Projected Employment, 2022	Change, 2012–2022	
				Percent	Numeric
Human resources managers	11-3121	102,700	116,300	13	13,600

Source: U.S. Bureau of Labor Statistics, Employment Projections Program

Note: Data are rounded. Go to **Occupational Information Included in the OOH** *for a discussion of the data in this table.*

Similar Occupations   This table shows a list of occupations with job duties that are similar to those of human resources managers.

Occupations	Entry-level Education	2012 Pay	Projected Job Growth	Average Annual Openings
Administrative Services Managers	Bachelor's degree	$81,080	12%	7,990
Compensation and Benefits Managers	Bachelor's degree	$95,250	3%	610
Human Resources Specialists and Labor Relations Specialists	Bachelor's degree	$55,616	7%	12,370
Top Executives	Bachelor's degree	$104,073	11%	70,090
Training and Development Managers	Bachelor's degree	$95,400	11%	1,070
Training and Development Specialists	Bachelor's degree	$55,930	15%	7,720

Job Outlook

Employment of human resources managers is projected to grow 13 percent from 2012 to 2022, about as fast as the average for all occupations.

Employment growth largely depends on the performance and growth of individual companies. However, as new companies form and organizations expand their operations, they will need more human resources managers to oversee and administer their programs.

Managers will also be needed to ensure that firms adhere to changing, complex employment laws regarding occupational safety and health, equal employment opportunity, healthcare, wages, and retirement plans. For example, adoption of the Affordable Care Act may spur the need to hire more managers to help implement this program.

Job Prospects. Although job opportunities are expected to vary based on the staffing needs of individual companies, very strong competition can be expected for most positions.

Job opportunities should be best in the management of companies and enterprises industry as organizations continue to use outside firms to assist with some of their human resources functions.

Candidates with certification or a master's degree–particularly those with a concentration in human resources management–should have the best job prospects.

Those with a solid background in human resources programs, policies, and employment law should also have better job opportunities.

O*NET

➤ Human Resources Managers (11-3121.00)

Contacts for More Information

For more information about human resources managers, including certification, visit

➤ Society for Human Resource Management (www.shrm.org/Pages/default.aspx)

For information about careers and certification in employee compensation and benefits, visit

➤ International Foundation of Employee Benefit Plans (www.ifebp.org/)

➤ WorldatWork (www.worldatwork.org/waw/home/html/home.jsp)

For information about careers in employee training and development and certification, visit

➤ American Society for Training and Development (www.astd.org/)

➤ International Society for Performance Improvement (www.ispi.org/)

Industrial Production Managers

- **2012 Median Pay** .... $89,190 per year
  $42.88 per hour
- **Entry-Level Education** ....Bachelor's degree
- **Work Experience in a Related Occupation** ... 5 years or more
- **On-the-Job Training** .... None
- **Number of Jobs 2012** 172,700
- **Job Outlook, 2012–22** ....-2% (Little or no change)
- **Employment Change, 2012–22** .... -4,100

What Industrial Production Managers Do

Industrial production managers oversee the daily operations of manufacturing and related plants. They coordinate, plan, and direct the activities used to create a wide range of goods, such as cars, computer equipment, or paper products.

Duties. Industrial production managers typically do the following:

- Decide how best to use a plant's workers and equipment to meet production goals
- Ensure that production stays on schedule and within budget
- Hire, train, and evaluate workers
- Analyze production data
- Write production reports
- Monitor a plant's workers to ensure they meet performance and safety requirements
- Create ways to make the production process more efficient
- Determine whether new machines are needed or whether overtime work is necessary
- Fix any production problems

Depending on the size of the manufacturing plant, industrial production managers (also referred to as *plant managers*) may oversee the entire plant or a specific area of production.

Industrial production managers are responsible for carrying out quality control programs to make sure the finished product meets a specific level of quality. Often called *quality control systems managers*, these managers use programs to help identify defects in products, identify the cause of the defect, and solve the problem creating it. For example, a manager may determine that a defect is being caused by parts from an outside supplier. The manager can then work with the supplier to improve the quality of the parts.

Industrial production managers oversee all stages of the production process.

Industrial production managers work closely with managers from other departments as well. For example, the procurement (buying) department orders the supplies that the production department uses. A breakdown in communication between these two departments can cause production slowdowns. Industrial production managers also communicate with other managers and departments, such as sales, warehousing, and research and design.

Work Environment

Industrial production managers held about 172,700 jobs in 2012. About 75 percent of industrial production managers work in various manufacturing industries.

The manufacturing industries that employed the most industrial production managers in 2012 were as follows:

Fabricated metal product manufacturing 10%
Transportation equipment manufacturing 9
Chemical manufacturing 7
Machinery manufacturing 7
Food manufacturing 7

Industrial production managers split their time between the production area and a nearby office. When they are working in the production area, they may need to wear protective equipment such as a helmet or safety goggles.

Work Schedules. Most industrial production managers work full time and almost half worked more than 40 hours per week in 2012. In some facilities, managers work night or weekend shifts and must be on call to deal with emergencies at any time.

How to Become One

Industrial production managers typically need a bachelor's degree and 1 to 5 years of related work experience.

Education. Employers prefer managers have at least a bachelor's degree. While the degree may be in any field, many industrial production managers have a bachelor's degree in business administration or industrial engineering. Sometimes, production workers with many years of experience take management classes and become a production manager. At large plants, where managers have more oversight responsibilities, employers may look for managers who have a Master of Business Administration (MBA) or a graduate degree in industrial management.

Work Experience in a Related Occupation. Many industrial production managers begin as production workers and move up through the ranks. They usually advance to a first-line supervisory position before eventually being selected for management. Most earn a college degree in business management or take company-sponsored classes to increase their chances of a promotion.

Production managers who join a firm immediately after graduating from college sometimes work as first-line supervisors before beginning their jobs as production managers.

Some managers begin working at a company directly after college or graduate school. They spend their first few months in training programs, becoming familiar with the production process, company policies, and safety regulations. In large companies, many also spend short periods of time working in other departments, such as purchasing or accounting, to learn more about the company.

Median Annual Wages, May 2012

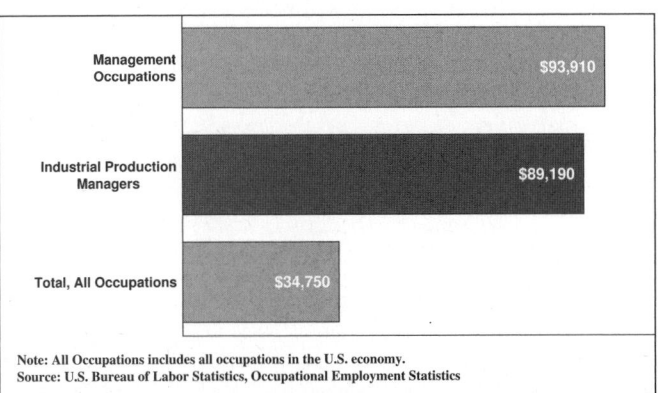

Note: All Occupations includes all occupations in the U.S. economy.
Source: U.S. Bureau of Labor Statistics, Occupational Employment Statistics

Percent Change in Employment, Projected 2012–2022

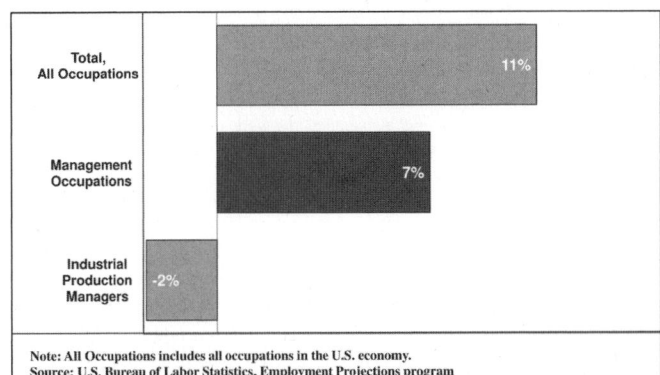

Note: All Occupations includes all occupations in the U.S. economy.
Source: U.S. Bureau of Labor Statistics, Employment Projections program

Employment Projections Data for Industrial Production Managers

Occupational title	SOC Code	Employment, 2012	Projected Employment, 2022	Change, 2012–2022	
				Percent	Numeric
Industrial production managers...	11-3051	172,700	168,600	-2	-4,100

Source: U.S. Bureau of Labor Statistics, Employment Projections Program

Note: Data are rounded. Go to **Occupational Information Included in the OOH** *for a discussion of the data in this table.*

Important Qualities

Interpersonal skills. Industrial production must have excellent communication skills so they can work with managers from other departments, as well as with the company's senior-level management.

Leadership skills. To keep the production process running smoothly, industrial production managers must motivate and direct the employees they manage.

Problem-solving skills. Production managers must be able to identify problems immediately and solve them. For example, if a product has a defect, the manager determines whether it is a onetime problem or the result of the production process.

Time-management skills. To meet production deadlines, managers must carefully manage their employees' time as well as their own.

Licenses, Certifications, and Registrations. While not required, industrial production managers can earn certifications that show a higher level of competency in quality or management systems. The Association for Operations Management offers a Certified in Production and Inventory Management (CPIM) credential. The American Society for Quality offers credentials in quality control. Both certifications require specific amounts of work experience before applying for the credential, so they are generally not earned before entering the occupation.

Pay

The median annual wage for industrial production managers was $89,190 in May 2012. The median wage is the wage at which half the workers in the occupation earned more than the amount and half earned less. The lowest 10 percent earned less than $54,250, and the top 10 percent earned more than $150,020.

In May 2012, the median annual wages for industrial production managers in the top five manufacturing industries where these managers worked were as follows:

Chemical manufacturing...$99,250
Transportation equipment manufacturing............................91,870
Machinery manufacturing 87,270
Fabricated metal product manufacturing............................82,730
Food manufacturing 80,430

Job Outlook

Employment of industrial production managers is projected to show little or no change from 2012 to 2022. Most of these managers are employed in various manufacturing industries, which are expected to see a decrease in overall employment as a result of increased productivity. In the past, employment of industrial production managers was less affected by productivity gains, since these managers were responsible for coordinating work activities with the goal of increased productivity. However, as facilities adapt to this new, leaner production model, employment of workers and managers should be equally affected by productivity increases.

Some manufacturing jobs are at risk of being sent to other countries with lower wages, dampening some employment growth. However, this risk may be reduced by recent trends of "reshoring," where previously outsourced personnel and services are being brought back to the United States, and "domestic sourcing," where firms move jobs to lower cost regions of the United States instead of to other countries.

Job Prospects. Applicants who have a bachelor's degree in industrial management or business administration should have the best prospects.

O*NET

➤ Industrial Production Managers (11-3051.00)
➤ Quality Control Systems Managers (11-3051.01)
➤ Geothermal Production Managers (11-3051.02)
➤ Biofuels Production Managers (11-3051.03)
➤ Biomass Power Plant Managers (11-3051.04)
➤ Methane/Landfill Gas Collection System Operators (11-3051.05)
➤ Hydroelectric Production Managers (11-3051.06)

Similar Occupations   This table shows a list of occupations with job duties that are similar to those of industrial production managers.

Occupations	Entry-level Education	2012 Pay	Projected Job Growth	Average Annual Openings
Advertising, Promotions, and Marketing Managers	Bachelor's degree	$115,087	12%	7,510
Construction Managers	Bachelor's degree	$82,790	16%	15,460
Health and Safety Engineers	Bachelor's degree	$76,830	11%	970
Industrial Engineers	Bachelor's degree	$78,860	5%	7,540
Management Analysts	Bachelor's degree	$78,600	19%	24,520
Mechanical Engineers	Bachelor's degree	$80,580	4%	9,970
Operations Research Analysts	Bachelor's degree	$72,100	27%	3,600
Sales Managers	Bachelor's degree	$105,260	8%	10,690
Top Executives	Bachelor's degree	$104,073	11%	70,090

Contacts for More Information

For more information about careers in production management and certification, visit

➤ Association for Operations Management (APICS) (www.apics.org/)

For more information about quality management and certification, visit

➤ American Society for Quality (http://asq.org/index.aspx)

For general information about manufacturing careers, visit

➤ National Association of Manufacturers (www.nam.org/)

Lodging Managers

- **2012 Median Pay** .... $46,810 per year
  $22.50 per hour

- **Entry-Level Education** ... High school diploma or equivalent

- **Work Experience in a Related Occupation** .... Less than 5 years

- **On-the-Job Training** .... None

- **Number of Jobs 2012** 50,400

- **Job Outlook, 2012–22** ....1% (Little or no change)

- **Employment Change, 2012–22** 700

What Lodging Managers Do

Lodging managers ensure that guests on vacation or business travel have a pleasant experience at a hotel, motel, or other types of establishment with accommodations. They also ensure that the establishment is run efficiently and profitably.

Duties. Lodging managers typically do the following:

- Inspect guest rooms, public areas, and grounds for cleanliness and appearance

- Greet and register guests

- Ensure that company standards for guest services, décor, and housekeeping are met

- Answer questions from guests about hotel policies and services

- Keep track of how much money the hotel or lodging facility is making

- Interview, hire, train, and sometimes fire staff members

- Monitor staff performance to ensure that guests are happy and that the hotel is well run

Lodging managers may oversee individual departments, such as housekeeping.

- Coordinate office activities of hotels or motels and resolve problems

- Set room rates and budgets, approve expenditures, and allocate funds to various departments

A comfortable room, good food, and a helpful staff can make being away from home an enjoyable experience for guests on vacation or business travel. Lodging managers try to make sure that guests have that good experience.

Lodging establishments vary in size, from independently owned bed and breakfasts to motels with just a few rooms or to hotels that can hold more than 1,000 guests. Services can vary from providing a room to granting access to a swimming pool; from offering a free breakfast to having a full-service restaurant; from having a lobby to operating a casino and hosting conventions.

Though specific duties vary by size and type of establishment, increasingly, many lodging managers use online social media for marketing purposes.

The following are examples of types of lodging managers:

General managers oversee all lodging operations at a property. At large hotels with several departments and multiple layers of management, the general manager and several assistant managers coordinate the activities of separate departments. These departments may include housekeeping, personnel, office administration, marketing and sales, purchasing, security, maintenance, recreational facilities, and other activities. For more information, see the profiles on human resources managers; public relations and fundraising managers; financial managers; advertising, promotions, and marketing managers; and food service managers.

Revenue managers work in financial management, monitoring room sales and reservations, overseeing accounting and cash-flow matters at the hotel, projecting occupancy levels, and deciding which rooms to discount and when to offer special rates.

Front-office managers coordinate reservations and room assignments and train and direct the hotel's front-desk staff. They ensure that guests are treated courteously, that complaints and problems are resolved, and that requests for special services are carried out. Most front-office managers also are responsible for handling adjustment to bills.

Convention service managers coordinate the activities of various departments, to accommodate meetings, conventions, and special events. They meet with representatives of groups to plan the number of conference rooms to be reserved, design the configuration of the meeting space, and determine what other services the groups will need, such as catering or audiovisual requirements. During a meeting or event, they resolve unexpected problems and ensure that hotel operations meet a group's expectations.

Work Environment

Lodging managers held about 50,400 jobs in 2012. More than half were employed in the traveler accommodation industry, which includes hotels and motels.

Most of the remainder worked in other lodging establishments, such as recreational vehicle (RV) and recreational camps, youth hostels, inns, boardinghouses, bed-and-breakfasts, and resorts. About 39 percent were self-employed.

The pressures of coordinating a wide range of activities, turning a profit for investors, and dealing with dissatisfied guests can be stressful.

Work Schedules. Most lodging managers are employed full time. Because hotels are open around the clock, working evenings, weekends, and holidays is common. Some managers must be on call 24 hours a day, particularly if they reside at the lodging establishment.

Median Annual Wages, May 2012

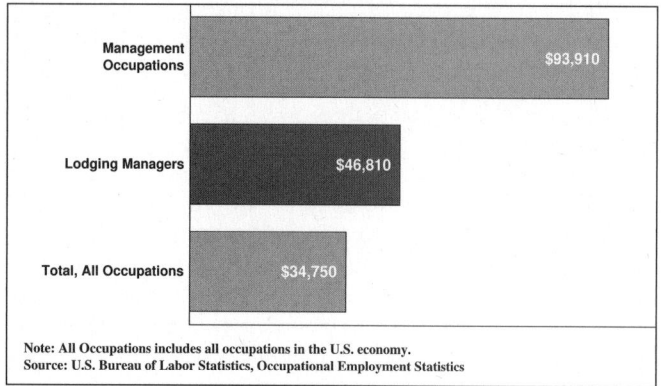

Note: All Occupations includes all occupations in the U.S. economy.
Source: U.S. Bureau of Labor Statistics, Occupational Employment Statistics

Percent Change in Employment, Projected 2012–2022

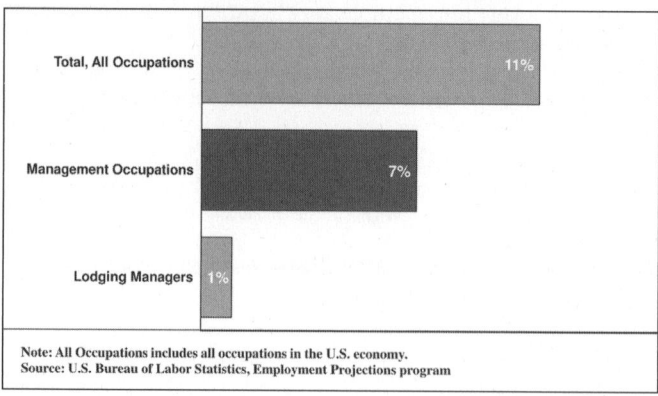

Note: All Occupations includes all occupations in the U.S. economy.
Source: U.S. Bureau of Labor Statistics, Employment Projections program

How to Become One

Many applicants can qualify as a lodging manager by having a high school diploma and several years of experience working in a hotel. However, most large, full-service hotels require applicants to have a bachelor's degree. Hotels that provide fewer services generally accept applicants who have an associate's degree or certificate in hotel management or operations.

Education. Currently, 26 states plus the District of Columbia offer high school academic training for prospective lodging managers.

Most full-service hotel chains hire candidates with a bachelor's degree in hospitality or hotel management. Hotel management programs typically include instruction in hotel administration, accounting, marketing, housekeeping, food service management and catering, and hotel maintenance and engineering. Computer training is also an integral part of many degree programs, because hotels use hospitality-specific software in reservations, billing, and housekeeping management. The Accreditation Commission for Programs in Hospitality Administration accredits about 60 hospitality management programs.

At hotels that provide few services, candidates with an associate's degree or certificate in hotel, restaurant, or hospitality management may qualify for a job as a lodging manager.

Also, many technical institutes and vocational and trade schools offer courses that are recognized by the hospitality industry that may help in getting a job.

Work Experience in a Related Occupation. Hotel employees who do not have hospitality management training, but who show leadership potential and have several years of related work experience, may qualify for assistant manager positions.

Licenses, Certifications, and Registrations. Aspiring high school students can enroll in the Hospitality and Tourism Management Program (HTMP) created by the American Hotel & Lodging Educational Institute. The HTMP is a 2-year program that teaches management principles and leads to professional certification: Certified Hospitality & Tourism Management Professional

(CHTMP). Currently, 26 states plus the District of Columbia offer the program.

Advancement. Large hotel chains may offer better opportunities than small, independently owned hotels for advancing from assistant manager to manager or from managing one hotel to being a regional manager. However, these opportunities usually involve relocating to another city or state.

Important Qualities

Business skills. Lodging managers address budget matters and coordinate and supervise workers. Operating a profitable hotel is important–as is the need to motivate and direct the work of employees.

Customer-service skills. Lodging managers must have good customer-service skills when dealing with guests. Satisfying guests' needs is critical to a hotel's success and helps to ensure customer loyalty.

Interpersonal skills. Lodging managers need strong interpersonal skills because they interact regularly with many different people. They must be effective communicators and must have positive interactions with guests and hotel staff, even in stressful situations.

Leadership skills. Lodging managers must establish good working relationships to ensure a productive work environment. This objective may involve motivating personnel, resolving conflicts, and listening to complaints or criticism from guests.

Listening skills. Lodging managers should have excellent listening skills. Listening to the needs of guests allows managers to take the appropriate course of action, ensuring guests' satisfaction. Listening to the needs of workers helps managers keep good working relationships with the staff.

Organizational skills. Lodging managers keep track of many different schedules, budgets, and people at once. This task becomes more complex as the size of the hotel increases.

Problem-solving skills. The ability to resolve personnel issues and guest-related dissatisfaction is critical to the work of lodging managers. As a result, they should be creative and practical when confronted with problems.

Employment Projections Data for Lodging Managers

Occupational title	SOC Code	Employment, 2012	Projected Employment, 2022	Change, 2012–2022	
				Percent	Numeric
Lodging managers	11-9081	50,400	51,100	1	700

Source: U.S. Bureau of Labor Statistics, Employment Projections Program

Note: Data are rounded. Go to Occupational Information Included in the OOH *for a discussion of the data in this table.*

Similar Occupations This table shows a list of occupations with job duties that are similar to those of lodging managers.

Occupations	Entry-level Education	2012 Pay	Projected Job Growth	Average Annual Openings
Food Service Managers	High school diploma or equivalent	$47,960	2%	6,240
Gaming Services Occupations	High school diploma or equivalent	$25,951	10%	5,110
Human Resources Managers	Bachelor's degree	$99,720	13%	4,060
Property, Real Estate, and Community Association Managers	High school diploma or equivalent	$52,610	12%	10,210
Sales Managers	Bachelor's degree	$105,260	8%	10,690

Pay

The median annual wage for lodging managers was $46,810 in May 2012. The median wage is the wage at which half the workers in an occupation earned more than that amount and half earned less. The lowest 10 percent earned less than $29,290, and the top 10 percent earned more than $89,530.

In May 2012, median annual wages for lodging managers in the top four industries in which they worked were as follows:

Administrative and support services $58,670
RV (recreational vehicle) parks and recreational camps 48,460
Traveler accommodation 46,260
Religious, grantmaking, civic, professional, and similar
   organizations 45,830

Job Outlook

Employment of lodging managers is projected to show little or no change from 2012 to 2022.

Despite expected growth in tourism and travel, fewer managers will be needed as the lodging industry shifts to building more limited-service hotels and fewer full-service properties that have separate departments to manage.

In addition, some lodging places are streamlining operations to cut expenses, by either eliminating some managers or scaling back the total number. Chain hotels, for instance, are increasingly assigning a single manager to oversee multiple properties within a region. Still, some large full-service hotels, including casinos, resorts, and convention hotels that provide a wide range of services to a larger customer base, will continue to generate jobs for experienced managers.

Job Prospects. Those seeking jobs at hotels with the highest level of guest services are expected to face strong competition, as these positions are highly sought after by people trained in hospitality management or administration.

Applicants with a bachelor's degree in hospitality or hotel management are expected to have the best job opportunities, particularly at upscale and luxury hotels.

O*NET

➤ Lodging Managers (11-9081.00)

Contacts for More Information

For information about the lodging industry, visit
➤ American Hotel & Lodging Association (www.ahla.com/)
   For information about careers, professional development and training programs, visit
➤ American Hotel & Lodging Educational Institute (www.ahlei.org/)
   For information about schools and educational programs in hotel and restaurant management, including correspondence courses, visit

➤ Accreditation Commission for Programs in Hospitality Administration (www.chrie.org/about/accreditation/acpha-accredited-institutions/index.aspx)
➤ International Council on Hotel, Restaurant, and Institutional Education (www.chrie.org/)
   For information about lodging news operations, visit
➤ Hotel News Now (www.hotelnewsnow.com/)
➤ Lodging Magazine (www.lodgingmagazine.com/Main/Home.aspx)

Medical and Health Services Managers

- **2012 Median Pay** .... $88,580 per year
  $42.59 per hour
- **Entry-Level Education** .... Bachelor's degree
- **Work Experience in a Related Occupation** .... None
- **On-the-Job Training** .... None
- **Number of Jobs 2012** 315,500
- **Job Outlook, 2012–22** .... 23% (Much faster than average)
- **Employment Change, 2012–22** 73,300

What Medical and Health Services Managers Do

Medical and health services managers, also called *healthcare executives* or *healthcare administrators*, plan, direct, and coordinate medical and health services. They might manage an entire facility or specialize in managing a specific clinical area or department, or manage a medical practice for a group of physicians. Medical and health services managers must be able to adapt to changes in healthcare laws, regulations, and technology.

Duties. Medical and health services managers typically do the following:

- Work to improve efficiency and quality in delivering healthcare services
- Keep up to date on new laws and regulations so that the facility in which they work complies with them
- Supervise assistant administrators in facilities that are large enough to need them
- Manage the finances of the facility, such as patient fees and billing
- Create work schedules
- Represent the facility at investor meetings or on governing boards
- Keep and organize records of the facility's services, such as the number of inpatient beds used
- Communicate with members of the medical staff and department heads

In group medical practices, managers work closely physicians and surgeons, registered nurses, medical and clinical laboratory technologists and technicians and other healthcare workers.

Medical and health services managers' titles depend on the facility or area of expertise in which they work. The following are some examples of types of medical and health services managers:

Nursing home administrators manage staff, admissions, finances, and care of the building, as well as care of the residents in nursing homes. All states require them to be licensed; licensing requirements vary by state.

Clinical managers oversee a specific department, such as nursing, surgery, or physical therapy, and have responsibilities based on that specialty. Clinical managers set and carry out policies, goals, and procedures for their departments; evaluate the quality of the staff's work; and develop reports and budgets.

Health information managers are responsible for the maintenance and security of all patient records. They must stay up to date with evolving information technology and current or proposed laws about health information systems. Health information managers must ensure that databases are complete, accurate, and accessible only to authorized personnel.

Assistant administrators work under the top administrator in larger facilities and often handle daily decisions. Assistants might direct activities in clinical areas, such as nursing, surgery, therapy, medical records, or health information.

Work Environment

Medical and health services managers held about 315,500 jobs in 2012. Most medical and health services managers work in offices in healthcare facilities, including hospitals and nursing homes, and group medical practices.

The industries that employed the most medical and health services managers in 2012 were as follows:

Hospitals; state, local, and private	39%
Ambulatory health care services	26
Nursing and residential care facilities	11
Government	8

Work Schedules. Most medical and health services managers work full time. Because their services are sometimes needed in emergencies or at facilities that are always open, some work may be required during evenings, on weekends, or overnight.

How to Become One

Most medical and health services managers have at least a bachelor's degree before entering the field; however, master's degrees also are common. Requirements vary by facility.

Large healthcare facilities usually have several assistant administrators who aid the top administrator and handle daily decisions.

Education. Medical and health services managers typically need at least a bachelor's degree to enter the occupation. However, master's degrees in health services, long-term care administration, public health, public administration, or business administration also are common.

Prospective medical and health services managers should have a bachelor's degree in health administration. These programs prepare students for higher level management jobs than programs that graduate students with other degrees. Courses needed for a degree in health administration often include hospital organization and management, accounting and budgeting, human resources administration, strategic planning, law and ethics, health economics, and health information systems. Some programs allow students to specialize in a particular type of facility, such as a hospital, a nursing care home, a mental health facility, or a group medical practice. Graduate programs often last between 2 and 3 years and may include up to 1 year of supervised administrative experience.

Important Qualities

Analytical skills. Medical and health services managers must be able to understand and follow current regulations and be able to adapt to new laws.

Communication skills. These managers must be able to communicate effectively with other health professionals.

Detail oriented. Medical and health services managers must pay attention to detail. They might be required to organize and maintain scheduling and billing information for very large facilities, such as hospitals.

Median Annual Wages, May 2012

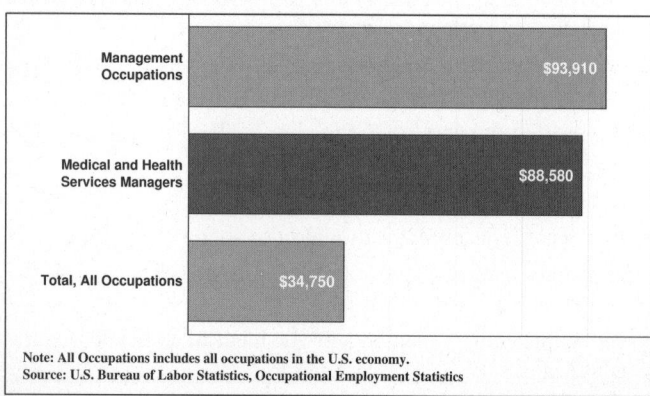

Management Occupations	$93,910
Medical and Health Services Managers	$88,580
Total, All Occupations	$34,750

Note: All Occupations includes all occupations in the U.S. economy.
Source: U.S. Bureau of Labor Statistics, Occupational Employment Statistics

Percent Change in Employment, Projected 2012–2022

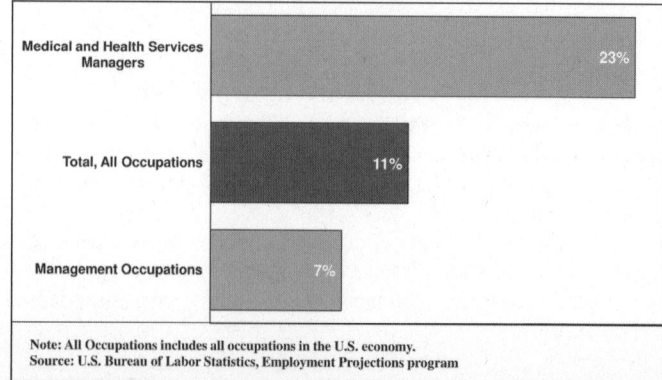

Medical and Health Services Managers	23%
Total, All Occupations	11%
Management Occupations	7%

Note: All Occupations includes all occupations in the U.S. economy.
Source: U.S. Bureau of Labor Statistics, Employment Projections program

Employment Projections Data for Medical and Health Services Managers

Occupational title	SOC Code	Employment, 2012	Projected Employment, 2022	Change, 2012–2022	
				Percent	Numeric
Medical and health services managers.................................	11-9111	315,500	388,800	23	73,300

Source: U.S. Bureau of Labor Statistics, Employment Projections Program

Note: Data are rounded. Go to **Occupational Information Included in the OOH** *for a discussion of the data in this table.*

Interpersonal skills. Medical and health services managers need to be able to discuss staffing problems and patient information with other professionals, such as physicians and health insurance representatives. They must be able to motivate and lead staff.

Problem-solving skills. These managers are often responsible for finding creative solutions to staffing or other administrative problems.

Technical skills. Medical and health services managers must be able to follow advances in healthcare technology. For example, they may need to use coding and classification software and electronic health record (EHR) systems as their facility adopts these technologies.

Work Experience in a Related Occupation. Some facilities may hire those with specialized experience in a healthcare occupation in addition to administrative experience. For example, nursing service administrators usually are supervisory registered nurses with administrative experience and graduate degrees in nursing or health administration.

Licenses, Certifications, and Registrations. All states require nursing care facility administrators to be licensed; requirements vary by state. In most states, these administrators must have a bachelor's degree, pass a licensing exam, and complete a state-approved training program. Some states also require administrators in assisted-living facilities to be licensed. A license is not required in other areas of medical and health services management.

Although certification is not required, some managers choose to become certified. Certification is available in many areas of practice. For example, the Professional Association of Health Care Office Management offers certification in health information management or medical management, while the American College of Health Care Administrators offers the Certified Nursing Home Administrator and Certified Assisted Living Administrator distinctions.

Advancement. Medical and health services managers advance by moving into more responsible and higher paying positions. In large hospitals, graduates of health administration programs usually begin as administrative assistants or assistant department heads. In small hospitals or nursing care facilities, they may begin as department heads or assistant administrators. Some experienced managers also may become consultants or professors of healthcare management. The level of the starting position varies with the experience of the applicant and the size of the organization.

Pay

The median annual wage for medical and health services managers was $88,580 in May 2012. The median wage is the wage at which half the workers in an occupation earned more than that amount and half earned less. The lowest 10 percent earned less than $53,940, and the top 10 percent earned more than $150,560.

Earnings of medical and health services managers vary by type and size of the facility and by level of responsibility. For example, the Medical Group Management Association reported that, in 2012, median compensation for administrators was $87,862 in practices with 6 or fewer physicians; $126,478 in practices with 7 to 25 physicians; and $148,604 in practices with 26 or more physicians.

Job Outlook

Employment of medical and health services managers is projected to grow 23 percent from 2012 to 2022, much faster than the average for all occupations. As the large baby-boom population ages and people remain active later in life, the healthcare industry as a whole will see an increase in the demand for medical services. This demand will in turn result in an increase in the number of physicians, patients, and procedures, as well as in the number of facilities. Managers will be needed to organize and manage medical information and staffs in the healthcare industry. There will likely be increased demand for nursing care facility administrators as baby boomers age.

Employment is projected to grow in offices of health practitioners. Many services previously provided in hospitals will shift to these settings, especially as medical technologies improve. Demand in medical group practice management is expected to grow as medical group practices become larger and more complex.

O*NET

➤ Medical and Health Services Managers (11-9111.00)

Contacts for More Information

For information about medical and healthcare management, visit
➤ Professional Association of Health Care Office Management (www. pahcom.com/)
➤ American Health Information Management Association (www. ahima.org/)
➤ American College of Health Care Administrators (www.achca.org/)

Similar Occupations   This table shows a list of occupations with job duties that are similar to those of medical and health services managers.

Occupations	Entry-level Education	2012 Pay	Projected Job Growth	Average Annual Openings
Human Resources Managers	Bachelor's degree	$99,720	13%	4,060
Insurance Underwriters	Bachelor's degree	$62,870	-6%	2,890
Social and Community Service Managers	Bachelor's degree	$59,970	21%	5,510

For more information about academic programs in this field, visit

➤ Association of University Programs in Health Administration (www.aupha.org/)

➤ Commission on Accreditation of Healthcare Management Education (www.cahme.org/)

For information about career opportunities in healthcare management, visit

➤ American College of Healthcare Executives (www.ache.org/)

For information about career opportunities in medical group practices and ambulatory care management, visit

➤ Medical Group Management Association (www.mgma.com/)

Natural Sciences Managers

- **2012 Median Pay** .... $115,730 per year
  $55.64 per hour
- **Entry-Level Education** ....Bachelor's degree
- **Work Experience in a Related Occupation** ... 5 years or more
- **On-the-Job Training** .... None
- **Number of Jobs 2012** 51,600
- **Job Outlook, 2012–22** .... 6% (Slower than average)
- **Employment Change, 2012–22** 2,900

What Natural Sciences Managers Do

Natural sciences managers supervise the work of scientists, including chemists, physicists, and biologists. They direct activities related to research and development, and coordinate activities such as testing, quality control, and production.

Duties. Natural sciences managers typically do the following:

- Work with top executives to develop goals and strategies for researchers and developers
- Make budgets for projects and programs by determining staffing, training, and equipment needs
- Hire, supervise, and evaluate scientists, technicians, and other staff members
- Review the methods used in their staff's work and the accuracy of the work produced
- Ensure that laboratories are stocked with equipment and supplies
- Monitor the progress of projects, review research, and draft operational reports
- Provide technical assistance to scientists, technicians, and support staff

Natural sciences managers prepare budgets for projects and programs and determine staff, training, and equipment needs.

- Establish and follow administrative procedures, policies, and standards
- Communicate project proposals, research findings, and the status of projects to clients and top management

Natural sciences managers direct scientific research activities and direct and coordinate product development projects and production activities. Research projects are aimed at improving manufacturing processes, advancing basic scientific knowledge, or developing new products.

Some natural sciences managers are former scientists and, after becoming managers, may continue to conduct their own research in addition to overseeing the work of others. These managers are sometimes called *working managers* and usually have smaller staffs, allowing them to do research in addition to carrying out their administrative duties.

Managers who are responsible for larger staffs may not have time to contribute to research and may spend all their time performing administrative duties.

Laboratory managers need to ensure that laboratories are fully supplied so that scientists and students can run their tests and experiments.

During all stages of a project, natural sciences managers coordinate the activities of their unit with those of other units or organizations. They work with higher levels of management; with

Median Annual Wages, May 2012

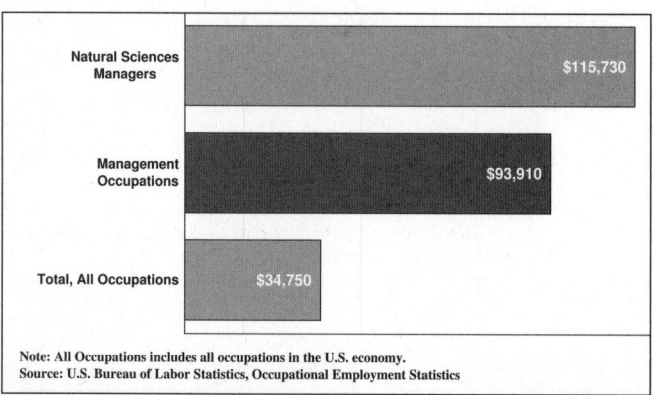

Natural Sciences Managers — $115,730
Management Occupations — $93,910
Total, All Occupations — $34,750

Note: All Occupations includes all occupations in the U.S. economy.
Source: U.S. Bureau of Labor Statistics, Occupational Employment Statistics

Percent Change in Employment, Projected 2012–2022

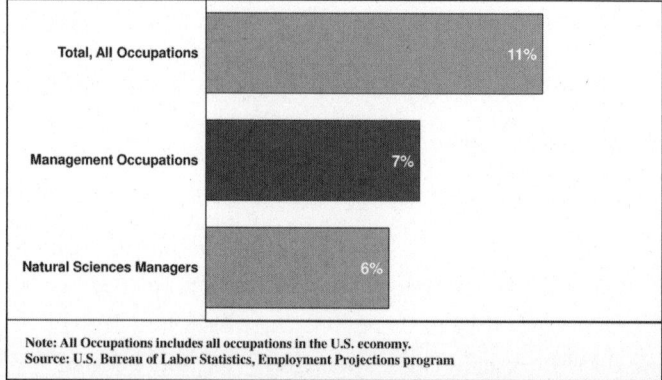

Total, All Occupations — 11%
Management Occupations — 7%
Natural Sciences Managers — 6%

Note: All Occupations includes all occupations in the U.S. economy.
Source: U.S. Bureau of Labor Statistics, Employment Projections program

Employment Projections Data for Natural Sciences Managers

Occupational title	SOC Code	Employment, 2012	Projected Employment, 2022	Change, 2012–2022	
				Percent	Numeric
Natural sciences managers..	11-9121	51,600	54,500	6	2,900

Source: U.S. Bureau of Labor Statistics, Employment Projections Program

Note: Data are rounded. Go to **Occupational Information Included in the OOH** *for a discussion of the data in this table.*

financial, production, and marketing specialists; and with suppliers of equipment and materials.

Work Environment

Natural sciences managers held about 51,600 jobs in 2012. Most of the time, they work in offices, but they also may spend time in laboratories. Like managers in other fields, natural sciences managers may spend a large portion of their time using computers and talking to other members of their organization.

Natural sciences managers have different requirements, based on the size of their staff. Working managers who have research responsibilities and smaller staffs may need to work in laboratories or in the field. Managers with larger staffs spend their time primarily in an administrative role and little time doing research or working in the field or in laboratories. Field and laboratory work may require traveling, sometimes to remote locations.

Although natural sciences managers work in many industries, about 1 in 3 natural sciences managers was employed by federal, state, or local government in 2012. Many others worked in industries and businesses that rely on public funding through research grants or on other types of public and private funding.

The industries that employed the most natural sciences managers in 2012 were as follows:

Research and development in the physical,
    engineering, and life sciences.. 24%
Federal government, excluding postal service 21
Pharmaceutical and medicine manufacturing 9
Colleges, universities, and professional schools;
    state, local, and private.. 8
State government, excluding education and hospitals............... 7

Work Schedules. Almost all natural sciences managers work full time. Natural sciences managers may need to work longer hours to meet technical or scientific goals on a short deadline or within a tight budget.

How to Become One

Natural sciences managers usually advance to management positions after years of employment as scientists. Natural sciences managers typically have a bachelor's degree, master's degree, or Ph.D. in a scientific discipline or a related field, such as engineering. Some managers may find it advantageous to have an advanced management degree–for example, a Master of Business Administration (MBA) or a Master of Public Administration (MPA).

Education. Natural sciences managers typically begin their careers as scientists; therefore, most have a bachelor's degree, master's degree, or Ph.D. in a scientific discipline or a closely related field, such as engineering. Scientific and technical knowledge is essential for managers because they must be able to understand the work of their subordinates and be able to provide technical assistance when needed.

Natural sciences managers who are interested in acquiring postsecondary education in management should be able to find master's degree or Ph.D. programs in a natural science that incorporate business management courses. Those interested in acquiring general management skills may pursue a Master of Business Administration (MBA) or a Master of Public Administration (MPA).

Sciences managers must continually upgrade their knowledge because of the rapid growth of scientific developments.

Work Experience in a Related Occupation. Natural sciences managers usually advance to management positions after years of employment as scientists. While employed as scientists, they typically are given more responsibility and independence in their work as they gain experience. Eventually, they may lead research teams and have control over the direction and content of projects before being promoted to an administrative position.

Important Qualities

Communication skills. Natural sciences managers need to be able communicate clearly to a variety of audiences, such as scientists,

Similar Occupations   This table shows a list of occupations with job duties that are similar to those of natural sciences managers.

Occupations	Entry-level Education	2012 Pay	Projected Job Growth	Average Annual Openings
Agricultural and Food Scientists	See "How to Become One"	$58,636	10%	1,640
Architectural and Engineering Managers	Bachelor's degree	$124,870	7%	6,060
Biochemists and Biophysicists	Doctoral or professional degree	$81,480	18%	1,370
Chemists and Materials Scientists	Bachelor's degree	$73,247	6%	3,040
Environmental Scientists and Specialists	Bachelor's degree	$63,570	15%	3,970
Geoscientists	Bachelor's degree	$90,890	16%	1,730
Medical Scientists	Doctoral or professional degree	$76,980	13%	3,550
Physicists and Astronomers	Doctoral or professional degree	$105,722	10%	810
Postsecondary Teachers	See "How to Become One"	$70,380	19%	42,690

policymakers, and the public. Both written and oral communication are important.

Critical-thinking skills. Natural sciences managers must carefully evaluate the work of others. They must determine if their staff's methods and results are based on sound science.

Interpersonal skills. Natural sciences managers lead research teams and therefore need to be able to work well with others in order to reach common goals. Managers routinely deal with conflict, which they must be able to turn into positive outcomes for their organization.

Leadership skills. Natural sciences managers must be able to organize, direct, and motivate others. They need to identify the strengths and weaknesses of their workers and create an environment in which workers can succeed.

Problem-solving skills. Natural sciences managers use scientific observation and analysis to find solutions to complex technical questions.

Time-management skills. Natural sciences managers must be able to do multiple administrative, supervisory, and technical tasks while ensuring that projects remain on schedule.

Pay

The median annual wage for natural sciences managers was $115,730 in May 2012. The median wage is the wage at which half the workers in an occupation earned more than that amount and half earned less. The lowest 10 percent earned less than $65,040, and the top 10 percent earned more than $187,200.

In May 2012, the median annual wages for natural sciences managers in the top five industries in which these managers worked were as follows:

Research and development in the physical, engineering, and life sciences	$155,560
Pharmaceutical and medicine manufacturing	116,800
Federal government, excluding postal service	107,210
Colleges, universities, and professional schools; state, local, and private	81,340
State government, excluding education and hospitals	73,080

Job Outlook

Employment of natural sciences managers is projected to grow 6 percent from 2012 to 2022, slower than the average for all occupations. Employment growth should be affected by many of the same factors that affect employment growth for the scientists whom these managers supervise. However, job growth for managers is expected to be somewhat slower than that for scientists, because managers tend to be flexible in the number of workers they are able to manage. In addition, research-and-development activities are increasingly being outsourced to specialized scientific research services firms. This outsourcing will lead to some consolidation of management.

Job Prospects. In addition to job openings resulting from employment growth, openings will arise from the need to replace managers who retire or move into other occupations.

Competition for job openings in this occupation is expected to be strong because of its typically higher salaries, greater control over some types of projects, and better access to resources. Experiences can vary widely with the variety of industries and organizations these managers work in. Private industry, government, and colleges and universities will have different goals. Prospective managers should take these differences into consideration when applying for positions.

O*NET

➤ Natural Sciences Managers (11-9121.00)
➤ Clinical Research Coordinators (11-9121.01)
➤ Water Resource Specialists (11-9121.02)

Contacts for More Information

To find job openings for natural science managers in the federal government, visit

➤ USAJOBS (www.usajobs.gov)

Postsecondary Education Administrators

- **2012 Median Pay** .... $86,490 per year
  $41.58 per hour
- **Entry-Level Education** ....Master's degree
- **Work Experience in a Related Occupation** ... 5 years or more
- **On-the-Job Training** .... None
- **Number of Jobs 2012** 161,800
- **Job Outlook, 2012–22** .... 15% (Faster than average)
- **Employment Change, 2012–22** 23,500

What Postsecondary Education Administrators Do

Postsecondary education administrators oversee student services, academics, and faculty research at colleges and universities. Their job duties vary depending on the area of the college they manage, such as admissions, the office of the registrar, or student affairs.

Duties. Postsecondary education administrators who work in *admissions* decide whether potential students should be admitted to the school. They typically do the following:

- Determine how many students to admit to fill the available spaces
- Prepare promotional materials about the school
- Meet with prospective students and encourage them to apply
- Review applications to determine if each potential student should be admitted
- Analyze data about applicants and admitted students

Postsecondary education administrators need to build good relationships with colleagues, students, and parents.

Median Annual Wages, May 2012

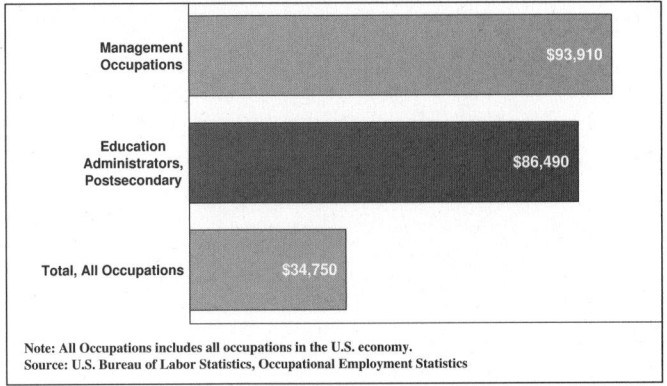

Note: All Occupations includes all occupations in the U.S. economy.
Source: U.S. Bureau of Labor Statistics, Occupational Employment Statistics

Percent Change in Employment, Projected 2012–2022

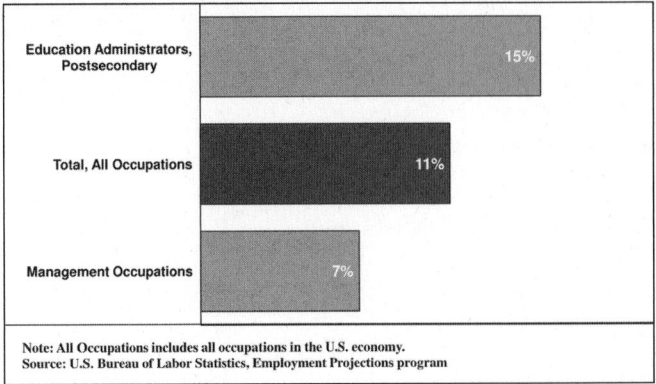

Note: All Occupations includes all occupations in the U.S. economy.
Source: U.S. Bureau of Labor Statistics, Employment Projections program

Many admissions counselors are assigned a region of the country and travel to that region to speak to high school counselors and students.

In addition, admissions officers often work with the financial aid department, which helps students determine if they are able to afford tuition and creates packages of federal and institutional financial aid if necessary.

Postsecondary education administrators who work in the *registrar's office* maintain student and course records. They typically do the following:

- Schedule and register students for classes
- Schedule space and times for classes
- Ensure that students meet graduation requirements
- Plan commencement ceremonies
- Prepare transcripts and diplomas for students
- Produce data about students and classes
- Maintain the academic records of the institution

How registrars spend their time varies depending on the time of year. Before students register for classes, registrars must prepare schedules and course offerings. Then during registration and for the first few weeks of the semester, they help students sign up for, drop, and add courses. Toward the end of the semester, they plan graduation and ensure that students meet the requirements to graduate. Workers in a registrar's office need advanced computer skills to create and maintain databases.

Postsecondary education administrators who work in *student affairs* are responsible for a variety of co-curricular school functions, such as student athletics and activities. They typically do the following:

- Advise students on topics such as housing issues, personal problems, or academics
- Communicate with parents and families
- Create, support, and assess nonacademic programs for students
- Schedule programs and services, such as athletic events or recreational activities

Postsecondary education administrators in student affairs can specialize in student activities, housing and residential life, or multicultural affairs. In student activities, education administrators plan events and advise student clubs and organizations. In housing and residential life, education administrators assign students rooms and roommates, ensure that residential facilities are well maintained, and train student workers, such as residential advisers. Education administrators who specialize in multicultural affairs plan events to celebrate different cultures and diverse backgrounds. Sometimes, they manage multicultural centers on campus.

Other postsecondary education administrators are *provosts* or *academic deans*. Provosts, also sometimes called chief academic officers, help college presidents develop academic policies, participate in making faculty appointments and tenure decisions, and manage budgets. Academic deans direct and coordinate the activities of the individual colleges or schools. For example, in a large university, there may be a dean who oversees the law school.

Education administrators have varying duties depending on the size of their college or university. Small schools often have smaller staffs who take on many different responsibilities, but larger schools may have different offices for each of these functions. For example, at a small college, the Office of Student Life may oversee student athletics and other activities, whereas a large university may have an Athletics Department.

Work Environment

Postsecondary education administrators held about 161,800 jobs in 2012.

Postsecondary education administrators work in colleges, universities, community colleges, and technical and trade schools. Some work for public schools, and others work for private schools.

In 2012, about 74 percent of postsecondary education administrators worked for colleges, universities, and professional schools and about 16 percent worked for junior colleges.

Work Schedules. Postsecondary education administrators generally work full time. Most work year-round, but some administrators may reduce their hours during the summer.

Employment Projections Data for Postsecondary Education Administrators

Occupational title	SOC Code	Employment, 2012	Projected Employment, 2022	Change, 2012–2022	
				Percent	Numeric
Education administrators, postsecondary	11-9033	161,800	185,300	15	23,500

Source: U.S. Bureau of Labor Statistics, Employment Projections Program

Note: Data are rounded. Go to Occupational Information Included in the OOH *for a discussion of the data in this table.*

Similar Occupations This table shows a list of occupations with job duties that are similar to those of postsecondary education administrators.

Occupations	Entry-level Education	2012 Pay	Projected Job Growth	Average Annual Openings
Administrative Services Managers	Bachelor's degree	$81,080	12%	7,990
Human Resources Managers	Bachelor's degree	$99,720	13%	4,060
Postsecondary Teachers	See "How to Become One"	$70,380	19%	42,690
Public Relations and Fundraising Managers	Bachelor's degree	$95,450	13%	2,130
Public Relations Specialists	Bachelor's degree	$54,170	12%	5,880
School and Career Counselors	Master's degree	$53,610	12%	8,700
Top Executives	Bachelor's degree	$104,073	11%	70,090
Training and Development Managers	Bachelor's degree	$95,400	11%	1,070

How to Become One

Although a bachelor's degree may be acceptable for some entry-level positions, a master's or higher degree is often required. Employers often want candidates who have experience working in the field, particularly for such occupations as registrars and academic deans.

Education. Educational requirements vary for different positions. For entry-level positions, a bachelor's degree may be sufficient. Degrees can be in a variety of disciplines, such as social work, accounting, or marketing.

For higher level positions, a master's degree or Ph.D. is generally required. Provosts and deans often must have a Ph.D. Some provosts and deans begin their career as professors and later move into administration. These administrators have doctorates in the field in which they taught, such as English or chemistry. Other provosts and deans have a Ph.D. in higher education or a related field.

Work Experience in a Related Occupation. Employers often want candidates who have experience working in the field, particularly for such occupations as registrars and academic deans. For example, some postsecondary education administrators work in the registrar's office or as a resident assistant while in college to gain the necessary experience. For other positions, such as those in admissions and student affairs, experience may or may not be necessary depending on the position.

Other Experience. Many postsecondary education administrators, particularly those working in student affairs, were involved in student activities while they were attending college. For example, they may lead student organizations or participate in student government to gain the experience necessary to work in student affairs after graduating.

Important Qualities

Computer skills. Registrars often need to be adept at working with computers so they can create and maintain databases and computer programs to manage student and school records.

Interpersonal skills. Postsecondary education administrators need to build good relationships with colleagues, students, and parents. Those in admissions and student affairs need to be outgoing so they can encourage prospective students to apply to the school and existing students to participate in co-curricular activities.

Organizational skills. Regardless of their field, administrators need to be organized so they can manage records, prioritize tasks, and coordinate the activities of their staff.

Problem-solving skills. Administrators often need to respond to difficult situations, develop creative solutions to problems, and react calmly when problems arise.

Advancement. Education administrators with advanced degrees can be promoted to higher level positions within their department or the college. Some become college presidents, which is discussed in the profile on top executives.

Pay

The median annual wage for postsecondary education administrators was $86,490 in May 2012. The median wage is the wage at which half the workers in an occupation earned more than that amount and half earned less. The lowest 10 percent earned less than $48,920, and the top 10 percent earned more than $168,330.

In May 2012, the median annual wage in colleges, universities, and professional schools, the industry that employed the most postsecondary education administrators, was $89,200. The median annual wage in junior colleges, the second largest industry, was $82,070.

As part of their employee benefits plan, many colleges and universities allow full-time employees to attend classes for a discount or for free.

Job Outlook

Employment of postsecondary education administrators is projected to grow 15 percent from 2012 to 2022, faster than the average for all occupations. Expected growth is due to increases in enrollments.

The number of people attending postsecondary school will increase as individuals seek additional education and skills to accomplish their career goals. As more people enter colleges and universities, more postsecondary education administrators will be needed to serve the needs of these additional students.

Additional admissions officers will be needed to process students' applications. More registrars will be needed to register students for classes and ensure that they meet graduation requirements. More student affairs workers will be needed to make housing assignments and plan events for students.

In particular, significant increases in enrollment are expected in online colleges and universities. As a result, there will be more demand for postsecondary education administrators in these types of schools.

However, despite expected increases in enrollment, employment growth in public colleges and universities will depend on state and local government budgets. When state and local governments have budget deficits, they may lay off employees, including administrators. As a result, employment growth may be somewhat slowed by state and local government budget deficits.

O*NET

➤ Education Administrators, Postsecondary (11-9033.00)

Contacts for More Information

For more information on registrars or admissions counselors, visit
➤ American Association of Collegiate Registrars and Admissions Officers (www.aacrao.org)

For more information about education administrators specializing in student affairs, visit
➤ NASPA: Student Affairs Administrators in Higher Education (http://naspa.org/)

Preschool and Childcare Center Directors

- **2012 Median Pay** .... $43,950 per year
                                                      $21.13 per hour
- **Entry-Level Education** ....Bachelor's degree
- **Work Experience in a Related Occupation** .... Less than 5 years
- **On-the-Job Training** .... None
- **Number of Jobs 2012** 63,800
- **Job Outlook, 2012–22** .... 17% (Faster than average)
- **Employment Change, 2012–22** 10,900

What Preschool and Childcare Center Directors Do

Preschool and childcare center directors direct and lead staffs, oversee daily activities, and prepare plans and budgets. They are responsible for all aspects of their program.

Duties. Preschool and childcare center directors typically do the following:

- Supervise preschool teachers and childcare workers
- Hire and train new staff members
- Provide training and professional development opportunities for staff
- Establish policies and communicate them to staff and parents
- Develop educational programs and set educational standards
- Help staff resolve conflicts between children
- Assist staff in communicating with parents
- Meet with parents and staff to discuss students' progress
- Establish budgets and set fees for programs
- Ensure facilities are maintained and cleaned according to state regulations

Some preschools and childcare centers are independently owned and operated. In these facilities, directors must follow the instructions and guidelines of the owner. Sometimes, directors own the facilities, so they decide how to operate the facilities.

Other preschools and childcare centers are part of a national chain or franchise. The director of a chain or franchise must also ensure that the facility meets its parent organization's standards and regulations.

In addition, some preschools and childcare centers, such as Head Start programs, receive state and federal funding. Directors of these schools and centers must ensure that their programs, staff, and facilities meet state and federal guidelines. For example, they must ensure that the staff meets the educational requirements set by the Department of Health and Human Services.

Work Environment

Preschool and childcare center directors held about 63,800 jobs in 2012.

The industries that employed the most preschool and childcare center directors in 2012 were as follows:

Child day care services... 54%
Religious, grantmaking, civic, professional, and similar organizations....................................... 17
Elementary and secondary schools; state, local, and private 12
Individual and family services.................................... 4

Although preschool and childcare center directors work in schools and childcare centers, they spend most of their day in an office. They also visit classrooms to check on students or speak to preschool teachers or childcare workers.

Many preschool and childcare center directors find working in an early childhood educational environment rewarding, but they also have significant responsibilities. Coordinating and interacting with staff, parents, and children can be fast paced and stimulating, but also can be stressful.

Work Schedules. Preschool and childcare center directors generally work full time. When childcare centers are open, a director must always be on staff, so directors and assistant directors stagger their schedules to ensure someone is always available.

How to Become One

Education requirements range from a high school diploma to a college degree. Most states require these directors to have experience in early childhood education. Some states or employers require preschool and childcare center directors to have a nation-

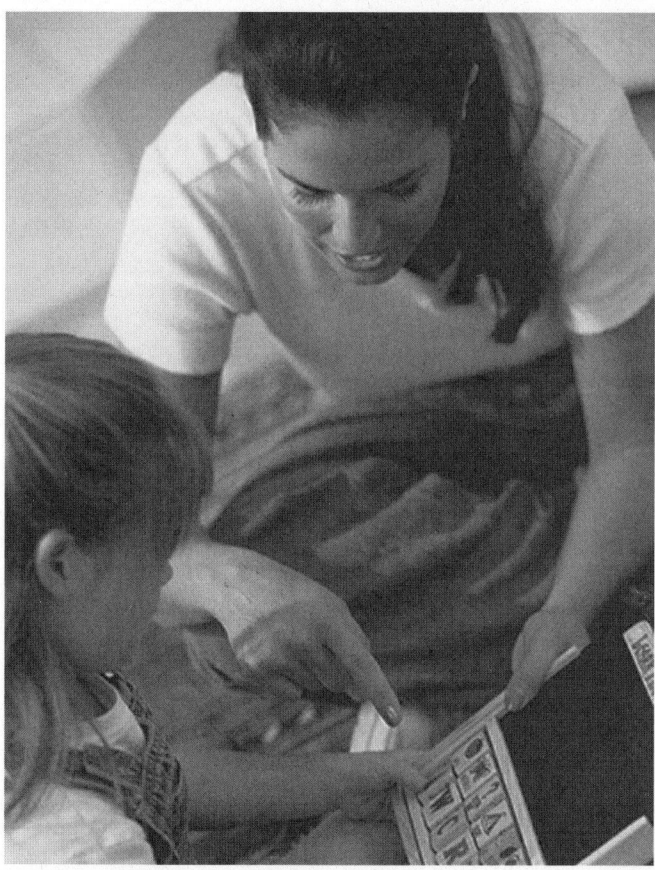

Preschool and childcare center directors assist staff with caring for and teaching children.

Median Annual Wages, May 2012

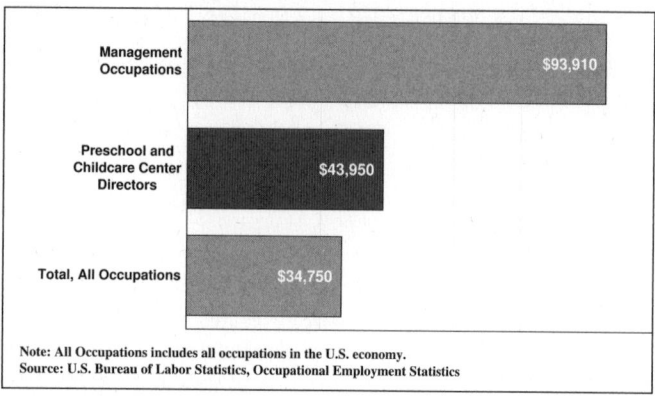

Note: All Occupations includes all occupations in the U.S. economy.
Source: U.S. Bureau of Labor Statistics, Occupational Employment Statistics

Percent Change in Employment, Projected 2012–2022

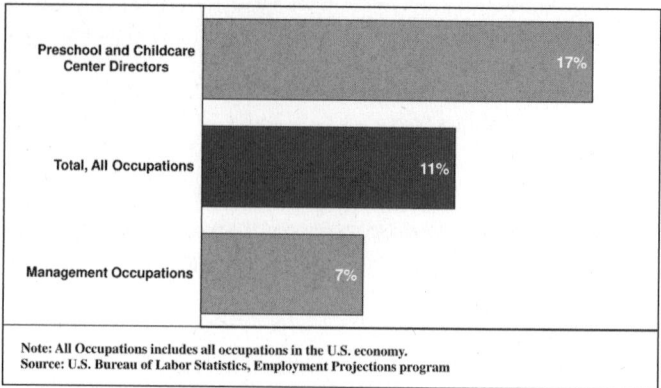

Note: All Occupations includes all occupations in the U.S. economy.
Source: U.S. Bureau of Labor Statistics, Employment Projections program

ally recognized certification such as the Child Development Associate (CDA) certification.

Education. Most states require preschool and childcare center directors to have at least a high school diploma, but some require an associate's or bachelor's degree in early childhood education. These degree programs teach students about child development, strategies to teach young children, and how to observe and document children's progress. Employers may prefer candidates who have a degree in early childhood education, or at least some postsecondary education in early childhood education.

Work Experience in a Related Occupation. Most states require preschool and childcare center directors to have experience in early childhood education. The amount of necessary experience varies by state.

Licenses, Certifications, and Registrations. Many states require childcare centers, including those in private homes, to be licensed. To qualify for licensure, staff must pass a background check, have a complete record of immunizations, and meet a minimum training requirement. Some states require staff to have certifications in CPR and First Aid.

Some states and employers require preschool and childcare center directors to have a nationally recognized certification. Most often, states require the Child Development Associate (CDA) certification offered by the Council for Professional Recognition. Obtaining the CDA certification requires coursework, experience in the field, and being observed while working with children.

Some states recognize the Child Care Professional (CCP) designation offered by the National Early Childhood Program Accreditation. Candidates for the CCP must be at least 18 years old, have a high school diploma, have experience in the field, take courses in early childhood education, and pass an exam.

Important Qualities

Business skills. Many preschool and childcare center directors own childcare centers and need to be able to manage their business effectively.

Communication skills. Preschool and childcare center directors need to inform parents and colleagues about the progress of the children. They need good writing and speaking skills to convey this information effectively.

Interpersonal skills. Preschool and childcare center directors must be able to develop good relationships with parents, children, and co-workers.

Leadership skills. Preschool and childcare center directors supervise staff, so they need good leadership skills to inspire staff to work diligently. They also must enforce rules and regulations.

Organizational skills. Directors need to maintain clear records about students and staff. In addition, they must be able to multitask when multiple people or situations require their attention.

Pay

The median annual wage for preschool and childcare center directors was $43,950 in May 2012. The median wage is the wage at which half the workers in an occupation earned more than that amount and half earned less. The lowest 10 percent earned less than $27,930, and the top 10 percent earned more than $84,340.

In May 2012, the median annual wages for preschool and childcare center directors in the top four industries in which these directors worked were as follows:

Elementary and secondary schools; state, local, and private	$68,410
Individual and family services	47,500
Religious, grantmaking, civic, professional, and similar organizations	43,240
Child day care services	40,880

Job Outlook

Employment of preschool and childcare center directors is projected to grow 17 percent from 2012 to 2022, faster than the average for all occupations.

Working parents will continue to need help caring for their children. The number of children who are of preschool age is increasing, leading to a greater need for childcare and increasing the demand for preschool and childcare center directors.

Employment Projections Data for Preschool and Childcare Center Directors

Occupational title	SOC Code	Employment, 2012	Projected Employment, 2022	Change, 2012–2022 Percent	Change, 2012–2022 Numeric
Education administrators, preschool and childcare center/program	11-9031	63,800	74,700	17	10,900

Source: U.S. Bureau of Labor Statistics, Employment Projections Program

Note: Data are rounded. Go to **Occupational Information Included in the OOH** *for a discussion of the data in this table.*

Similar Occupations   This table shows a list of occupations with job duties that are similar to those of preschool and childcare center directors.

Occupations	Entry-level Education	2012 Pay	Projected Job Growth	Average Annual Openings
Childcare Workers	High school diploma or equivalent	$19,510	14%	57,000
High School Teachers	Bachelor's degree	$55,050	6%	31,260
Kindergarten and Elementary School Teachers	Bachelor's degree	$53,060	12%	53,250
Middle School Teachers	Bachelor's degree	$53,430	12%	21,120
Preschool Teachers	Associate's degree	$27,130	17%	19,940
Special Education Teachers	Bachelor's degree	$55,068	6%	10,220
Teacher Assistants	Some college, no degree	$23,640	9%	38,260

In addition, there is a continued focus on the importance of early childhood education, specifically preschool. Early childhood education is widely recognized as important for a child's intellectual and emotional development. As the number of preschool programs grows, the need for preschool and childcare center directors will increase as well.

Job Prospects. Workers with formal postsecondary education, such as an associate's or bachelor's degree, should have better job prospects than those with a high school diploma. Those with a bachelor's degree should have the best prospects.

O*NET

➤ Education Administrators, Preschool and Childcare Center/Program (11-9031.00)

Contacts for More Information

For more information on childcare centers, visit
➤ Child Care Aware (http://childcareaware.org/)
    For information about early childhood education, visit
➤ National Association for the Education of Young Children (www.naeyc.org)
    For more information about professional credentials, visit
➤ Council for Professional Recognition (www.cdacouncil.org)
➤ National Early Childhood Program Accreditation (www.necpa.net/)

Property, Real Estate, and Community Association Managers

- **2012 Median Pay** .... $52,610 per year
                                                                       $25.29 per hour
- **Entry-Level Education** .... High school diploma or equivalent
- **Work Experience in a Related Occupation** .... Less than 5 years
- **On-the-Job Training** .... None
- **Number of Jobs 2012** 297,000
- **Job Outlook, 2012–22** .... 12% (As fast as average)
- **Employment Change, 2012–22** 35,000

What Property, Real Estate, and Community Association Managers Do

Property, real estate, and community association managers take care of the many aspects of residential, commercial, or industrial properties. They make sure the property is well maintained, has a nice appearance, operates smoothly, and preserves its resale value.

Duties. Property, real estate, and community association managers typically do the following:

- Meet with prospective renters and show them properties
- Discuss the lease and explain the terms of occupancy or ownership
- Collect monthly fees from tenants or individual owners
- Inspect all building facilities, including the grounds and equipment
- Arrange for new equipment or repairs as needed
- Pay bills or delegate bill payment for such expenditures as taxes, insurance, payroll, and maintenance
- Contract for trash removal, swimming pool maintenance, landscaping, security, and other services
- Investigate and settle complaints, disturbances, and violations
- Keep records of rental activity and owner requests
- Prepare budgets and financial reports
- Avoid discrimination when renting or advertising by knowing and complying with relevant laws, such as the Americans with Disabilities Act, the Federal Fair Housing Amendment Act, and local fair housing laws

When owners of homes, apartments, office buildings, or retail or industrial properties lack the time or expertise needed for the day-to-day management of their real estate properties, they often hire a property or real estate manager or a community association manager. Managers are employed either directly by the owner or indirectly through a contract with a property management firm.

The following are examples of types of property, real estate, and community association managers:

Property and real estate managers oversee the operation of income-producing commercial or residential properties and ensure that real estate investments achieve their expected revenues. They handle the financial operations of the property, making certain that rent is collected and that mortgages, taxes, insurance premiums, payroll, and maintenance bills are paid on time. They may oversee financial statements, and periodically report to the owners on the status of the property, occupancy rates, expiration dates of leases, and other matters. When vacancies occur, property managers may advertise the property or hire a leasing agent to find a tenant. They may also suggest to the owners what rent to charge.

Community association managers work on behalf of homeowner or community associations to manage the communal property and services of condominiums, cooperatives, and planned communities. Usually hired by a volunteer board of directors of the association, they manage the daily affairs and supervise the maintenance of property and facilities that the homeowners use jointly through the association. Like property managers, community association managers collect monthly fees, prepare financial statements and budgets, negotiate with contractors, and help to resolve complaints. Community association managers also help the board and owners comply with association rules and regulations.

Onsite property managers are responsible for the day-to-day operation of a single property, such as an apartment complex, an office building, or a shopping center. To ensure that the property is well maintained, onsite managers routinely inspect the grounds, facilities, and equipment to determine whether maintenance or repairs are needed. They meet with current tenants to handle requests for repairs or to resolve complaints. They also meet with prospective tenants to show vacant apartments or office space. In addition, onsite managers enforce the terms of rental or lease contracts along with an association's governing rules. They make sure that tenants pay their rent on time, follow restrictions on parking or pets, and follow the correct procedures when the lease is up. Other important duties of onsite managers include keeping accurate, up-to-date records of income and expenditures from property operations and submitting regular expense reports to the senior-level property manager or the owner(s).

Real estate asset managers plan and direct the purchase, sale, and development of real estate properties on behalf of businesses and investors. They focus on long-term strategic financial planning, rather than on the day-to-day operations of the property. In deciding to acquire property, real estate asset managers consider several factors, such as property values, taxes, zoning, population growth, transportation, and traffic volume and patterns. Once a site is selected, they negotiate contracts to buy or lease the property on the most favorable terms. Real estate asset managers review their company's real estate holdings periodically and identify properties that are no longer financially profitable. They then negotiate the sale of the properties or arrange for the end of leases.

Work Environment

Property, real estate, and community association managers held about 297,000 jobs in 2012. About half were self-employed.

The industries that employed the most property, real estate, and community association managers in 2012 were as follows:

Activities related to real estate	21%
Lessors of real estate	16
Offices of real estate agents and brokers	3
Civic, social, professional, and similar organizations	3
Local government, excluding education and hospitals	2

When vacancies occur, property, real estate, and community association managers may advertise the property or hire a leasing agent to find a tenant.

Most property, real estate, and community association managers work out of an office. However, many managers spend much of their time away from their desks. Onsite managers, in particular, may spend a large part of their workday visiting the building engineer, showing apartments, dealing with owners and board members, checking on the janitorial and maintenance staff, or investigating problems reported by residents. Real estate asset managers may spend time away from home while traveling to company real estate holdings or searching for properties to buy.

Managing properties or community associations, or selling and leasing real estate can sometimes be stressful.

Work Schedules. Property, real estate, and community association managers often must attend evening meetings with residents, property owners, community association board members, or civic groups. As a result, long hours are common. Some apartment managers are required to live in the apartment complexes where they work, so that they are available to respond to emergencies even when they are off duty.

Median Annual Wages, May 2012

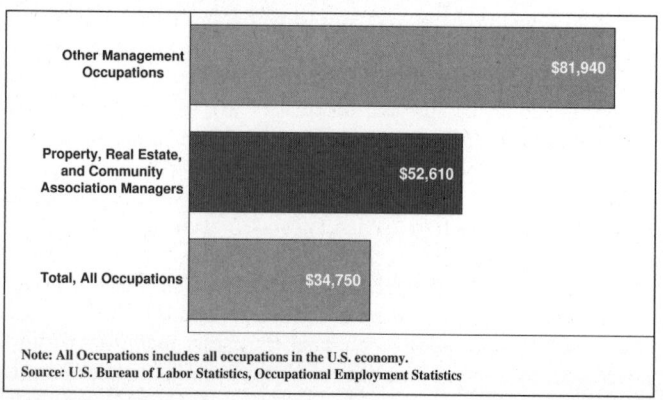

Note: All Occupations includes all occupations in the U.S. economy.
Source: U.S. Bureau of Labor Statistics, Occupational Employment Statistics

Percent Change in Employment, Projected 2012–2022

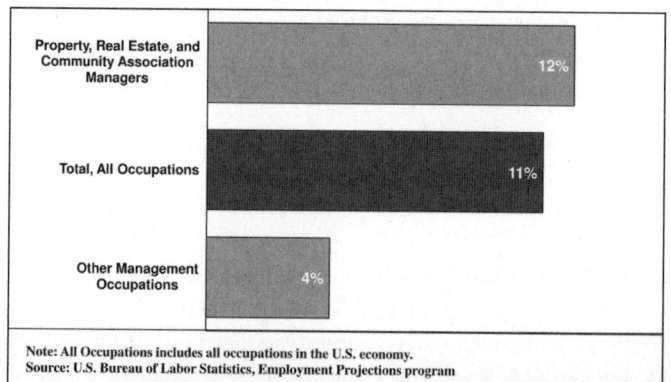

Note: All Occupations includes all occupations in the U.S. economy.
Source: U.S. Bureau of Labor Statistics, Employment Projections program

Employment Projections Data for Property, Real Estate, and Community Association Managers

Occupational title	SOC Code	Employment, 2012	Projected Employment, 2022	Change, 2012–2022	
				Percent	Numeric
Property, real estate, and community association managers	11-9141	297,000	332,000	12	35,000

Source: U.S. Bureau of Labor Statistics, Employment Projections Program

Note: **Data are rounded. Go to Occupational Information Included in the OOH** *for a discussion of the data in this table.*

Most property, real estate, and community association managers work full time. Many apartment managers get time off during the week so that they can show apartments to prospective renters on weekends, the most popular time for such showings.

How to Become One

Although many employers prefer to hire college graduates, a high school diploma or equivalent is enough for some jobs. Some managers receive vocational training. Other managers must have a real estate license.

Education. Many employers prefer to hire college graduates for property management positions, particularly for offsite positions dealing with a property's finances or contract management. Employers also prefer to hire college graduates to manage residential and commercial properties. A bachelor's or master's degree in business administration, accounting, finance, real estate, or public administration is preferred for commercial management positions. Managers of commercial properties and those dealing with a property's finances and contract management increasingly are finding that they need a bachelor's or master's degree in business administration, accounting, finance, or real estate management, especially if they do not have much practical experience.

Work Experience in a Related Occupation. Experience in real estate sales is a good background for onsite managers because real estate salespeople also show commercial properties to prospective tenants or buyers.

Licenses, Certifications, and Registrations. Real estate managers who buy or sell property must have a real estate license in the state in which they practice. In a few states, property and community association managers must also have a real estate license. Managers of public housing subsidized by the federal government must hold certifications.

Many property, real estate, and community association managers obtain professional certification showing competence and professionalism. For example, the BOMI International, the Community Associations Institute, the Institute of Real Estate Management, the National Association of Residential Property Managers, and the Community Association Managers International Certification Board all offer various designations, certifications, and professional development courses.

Often, employers require managers to attend formal training programs from various professional and trade real estate associations. Employers send managers to these programs to develop their management skills and expand their knowledge of specialized fields, such as how to operate and maintain mechanical systems in buildings, how to improve property values, insurance and risk management, personnel management, business and real estate law, community association risks and liabilities, tenant relations, communications, accounting and financial concepts, and reserve funding. Managers also participate in these programs to prepare themselves for positions of greater responsibility in property management. With related job experience, completing these programs and receiving a satisfactory score on a written exam can lead to certification or the formal award of a professional designation by the sponsoring association.

Obtaining these certifications also can help in getting a job.

Advancement. Many people begin property management careers as assistant managers, working closely with a property manager. In time, many assistants advance to property manager positions.

Some people start as onsite managers of apartment buildings, office complexes, or community associations. As they gain experience, they may advance to positions of greater responsibility. Those who excel as onsite managers often transfer to assistant offsite property manager positions, in which they gain experience handling a broad range of property management responsibilities.

The responsibilities and pay of property, real estate, and community association managers increase as these workers manage more and larger properties. Property managers are often responsible for several properties at a time. Some experienced managers open their own property management firms.

Important Qualities

Customer-service skills. Property, real estate, and community association managers must provide excellent customer service to keep existing clients and expand their business with new ones.

Interpersonal skills. Because property, real estate, and community association managers interact with people every day, they must have excellent interpersonal skills.

Listening skills. Property, real estate, and community association managers must listen to and understand residents and property owners in order to meet their needs.

Organizational skills. Property, real estate, and community association managers must be able to plan, coordinate, and direct multiple contractors at the same time, often for multiple properties.

Similar Occupations   This table shows a list of occupations with job duties that are similar to those of property, real estate, and community association managers.

Occupations	Entry-level Education	2012 Pay	Projected Job Growth	Average Annual Openings
Administrative Services Managers	Bachelor's degree	$81,080	12%	7,990
Food Service Managers	High school diploma or equivalent	$47,960	2%	6,240
Lodging Managers	High school diploma or equivalent	$46,810	1%	1,620

Problem-solving skills. Property, real estate, and community association managers must be able to mediate disputes or legal issues between residents, homeowners, or board members.

Speaking skills. Property, real estate, and community association managers must understand leasing or rental contracts and must be able to clearly explain the materials and answer questions raised by a resident or group of board members.

Pay

The median annual wage for property, real estate, and community association managers was $52,610 in May 2012. The median wage is the wage at which half the workers in an occupation earned more than that amount and half earned less. The lowest 10 percent earned less than $26,600, and the top 10 percent earned more than $113,400.

In May 2012, the median annual wages for property, real estate, and community association managers in the top five industries in which these managers worked were as follows:

Local government, excluding education and hospitals....... $61,320
Offices of real estate agents and brokers............................ 53,600
Activities related to real estate 50,700
Lessors of real estate 48,430
Civic, social, professional, and similar organizations........... 43,990

Job Outlook

Employment of property, real estate, and community association managers is projected to grow 12 percent from 2012 to 2022, about as fast as the average for all occupations.

Employment will grow because more people will live in the buildings that property management companies operate, such as apartment buildings, condominiums, cooperatives, planned communities, and senior housing. Increasingly, new developments provide community services and have jointly owned common areas that are professionally managed by community or homeowner associations.

In addition, property owners are becoming increasingly aware that property management firms help make properties more profitable and improve the resale value of homes and commercial property.

Job Prospects. Job opportunities should be best for those with a bachelor's degree in business administration, real estate, or a related field and for those with professional certification.

Because of the projected increase in the elderly population, particularly good job opportunities are expected for those with experience managing housing for older people and with experience managing healthcare facilities.

O*NET

➤ Property, Real Estate, and Community Association Managers (11-9141.00)

Contacts for More Information

For information about professional designation and certification programs for property, real estate, and community association managers, visit

➤ BOMI International (www.bomi.org/)
➤ Community Associations Institute (www.caionline.org/)
➤ Community Association Managers International Certification Board (www.nbccam.org/)
➤ Institute of Real Estate Management (www.irem.org/)
➤ National Association of Residential Property Managers (www.narpm.org/)

Public Relations and Fundraising Managers

- **2012 Median Pay** .... $95,450 per year
  $45.89 per hour
- **Entry-Level Education** ....Bachelor's degree
- **Work Experience in a Related Occupation** ... 5 years or more
- **On-the-Job Training** .... None
- **Number of Jobs 2012** 62,100
- **Job Outlook, 2012–22**................ 13% (As fast as average)
- **Employment Change, 2012–22** 8,000

What Public Relations and Fundraising Managers Do

Public relations managers plan and direct the creation of material that will maintain or enhance the public image of their employer or client. Fundraising managers coordinate campaigns that bring in donations for their organization.

Duties. Public relations managers typically do the following:

- Write press releases and prepare information for the media
- Identify main client groups and audiences and determine the best way to reach them
- Designate an appropriate spokesperson or information source for media inquiries
- Help clients communicate effectively with the public
- Develop their organization's or client's corporate image and identity
- Assist and inform an organization's executives and spokespeople
- Devise advertising and promotion programs
- Assign, supervise, and review the activities of staff

Fundraising managers typically do the following:

- Manage progress towards achieving an organization's fundraising goals
- Develop and carry out fundraising strategies
- Identify and contact potential donors

Public relations managers and specialists work in fairly high-stress environments, often managing and organizing several events at the same time.

Median Annual Wages, May 2012

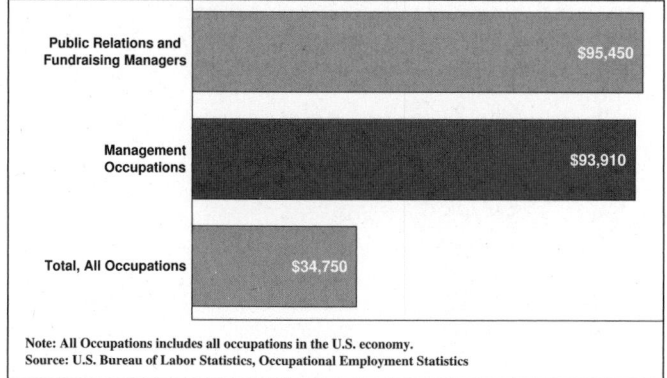

Public Relations and Fundraising Managers $95,450
Management Occupations $93,910
Total, All Occupations $34,750

Note: All Occupations includes all occupations in the U.S. economy.
Source: U.S. Bureau of Labor Statistics, Occupational Employment Statistics

Percent Change in Employment, Projected 2012–2022

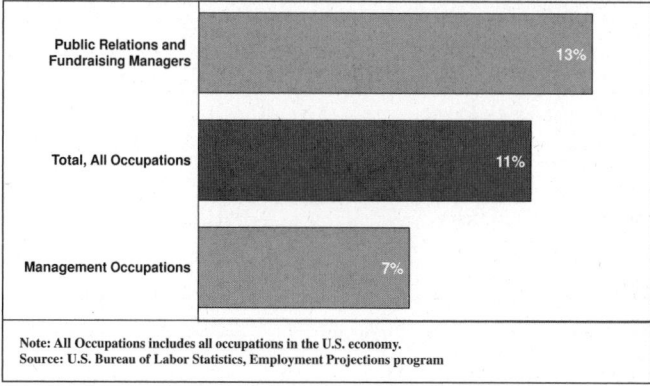

Public Relations and Fundraising Managers   13%
Total, All Occupations   11%
Management Occupations   7%

Note: All Occupations includes all occupations in the U.S. economy.
Source: U.S. Bureau of Labor Statistics, Employment Projections program

- Create and plan different events that can generate donations
- Meet face-to-face with highly important donors
- Apply for grants
- Assign, supervise, and review the activities of staff

Public relations managers review press releases and sponsor corporate events to help maintain and improve the image of their organization or client.

Public relations managers help to clarify their organization's point of view to its main audience through media releases and interviews. They observe social, economic, and political trends that might ultimately affect their organization, and they recommend ways to enhance the firm's image based on those trends. For example, in response to a growing concern about the environment, the public relations manager for an oil company may create a campaign to publicize its efforts to develop cleaner fuels.

In large organizations, public relations managers often supervise a staff of public relations specialists. They also work with advertising, promotions, and marketing managers to ensure that advertising campaigns are compatible with the image the company or client is trying to portray. For example, if a firm decides to emphasize its appeal to a certain group, such as young people, the public relations manager needs to make sure that current advertisements are well received by that group.

In addition, public relations managers may handle internal communications, such as company newsletters, and may help financial managers produce an organization's reports. They may also help the organization's top executives by drafting speeches, arranging interviews, and maintaining other forms of public contact.

Public relations managers must be able to work well with many types of specialists to report the facts accurately. In some cases, the information they write has legal consequences. As a result, they must work with the company's or client's lawyers to be sure that the information they release is both legally accurate and clear to the public.

Fundraising managers oversee campaigns and events intended to bring in donations for their organization. Many organizations that employ fundraisers rely heavily on the donations they gather in order to run their operations.

Fundraising managers usually decide which fundraising techniques are necessary in a certain situation. Common techniques may include annual campaigns, capital campaigns, planned giving, or major gifts.

Those who work on annual campaigns focus heavily on contacting donors who have given in the past, and request that they give again. Finding new contacts for future donations is also a component of a successful annual campaign.

Capital campaigns are different; they are generally used to raise money over a shorter time period and for a specific project, such as the construction of a new building at a university.

Fundraisers who spend most of their time on planned giving must have specialized training in taxes regarding gifts of stocks, bonds, charitable annuities, and real estate bequests in a will.

Major gifts are a feature of many different campaigns and are generally requested personally given the large value of the potential donation.

Work Environment

Public relations and fundraising managers held about 62,100 jobs in 2012.

The industries that employed the most public relations and fundraising managers in 2012 were as follows:

Religious, grantmaking, civic, professional, and similar organizations 24%
Educational services; state, local, and private 17
Health care and social assistance 9
Advertising, public relations, and related services 8
Management of companies and enterprises 8

Public relations and fundraising managers usually work in offices during regular business hours. However, many must travel to deliver speeches and attend meetings and community activities.

They work in high-stress environments, often managing and organizing several events at the same time.

Employment Projections Data for Public Relations and Fundraising Managers

Occupational title	SOC Code	Employment, 2012	Projected Employment, 2022	Change, 2012–2022	
				Percent	Numeric
Public relations and fundraising managers 11-2031		62,100	70,100	13	8,000

Source: U.S. Bureau of Labor Statistics, Employment Projections Program

Note: Data are rounded. Go to Occupational Information Included in the OOH for a discussion of the data in this table.

Similar Occupations   This table shows a list of occupations with job duties that are similar to those of public relations and fundraising managers.

Occupations	Entry-level Education	2012 Pay	Projected Job Growth	Average Annual Openings
Advertising Sales Agents	High school diploma or equivalent	$46,290	-1%	4,750
Advertising, Promotions, and Marketing Managers	Bachelor's degree	$115,087	12%	7,510
Craft and Fine Artists	High school diploma or equivalent	$46,065	3%	1,360
Fundraisers	Bachelor's degree	$50,680	17%	2,430
Market Research Analysts	Bachelor's degree	$60,300	32%	18,850
Multimedia Artists and Animators	Bachelor's degree	$61,370	6%	2,060
Public Relations Specialists	Bachelor's degree	$54,170	12%	5,880

Work Schedules. Most public relations and fundraising managers work full time, which often includes long hours. About 2 in 5 managers worked more than 40 hours per week in 2012.

How to Become One

Public relations and fundraising managers need at least a bachelor's degree and some positions may require a master's degree. Many years of related work experience are also necessary.

Education. For public relations and fundraising management positions, a bachelor's degree in public relations, communications, English, fundraising, or journalism is generally required. However, some employers prefer a master's degree, particularly in public relations, journalism, fundraising, or nonprofit management.

Courses in advertising, business administration, public affairs, public speaking, and creative and technical writing can be helpful.

Licenses, Certifications, and Registrations. Although not mandatory, public relations managers can get certified through the Public Relations Society of America. Candidates qualify based on years of experience and must pass an exam to become certified.

The Accredited Business Communicator credential is also available from the International Association of Business Communicators.

The Certified Fund Raising Executive program, offered by CFRE International, is voluntary, but fundraisers who pursue certification demonstrate a level of professional competency to prospective employers. To qualify, candidates are required to have 5 years of work experience in fundraising and have 80 hours of continuing education through conference attendance and classroom instruction. To keep their certification valid, fundraisers must apply for renewal every 3 years.

Work Experience in a Related Occupation. Public relations and fundraising managers must have several years of experience in a related or entry-level position, such public relations specialist or fundraiser.

Lower level management positions may require only a few years of experience, whereas directors are more likely to need 5 to 10 years of related work experience.

Important Qualities

Communication skills. Managers deal with the public regularly; therefore, they must be friendly enough to build rapport and receive cooperation from their media contacts and donors.

Leadership skills. Public relations and fundraising managers often lead large teams of specialists or fundraisers and must be able to guide their activities.

Organizational skills. Public relations and fundraising managers are often in charge of running several events at the same time, requiring superior organizational skills.

Problem-solving skills. Managers sometimes must explain how the company or client is handling sensitive issues. They must use good judgment in what they report and how they report it.

Speaking skills. Public relations and fundraising managers regularly speak on behalf of their organization. When doing so, they must be able to explain the organization's position clearly.

Writing skills. Managers must be able to write well-organized and clear press releases and speeches. They must be able to grasp the key messages they want to get across and write them succinctly in order to keep the attention of busy readers or listeners.

Pay

The median annual wage for public relations and fundraising managers was $95,450 in May 2012. The median wage is the wage at which half the workers in an occupation earned more than that amount and half earned less. The lowest 10 percent earned less than $51,630, and the top 10 percent earned more than $180,480.

In May 2012, the median annual wages for public relations and fundraising managers in the top five industries in which these managers worked were as follows:

Advertising, public relations, and related services	$119,500
Management of companies and enterprises	111,030
Religious, grantmaking, civic, professional, and similar organizations	93,580
Educational services; state, local, and private	87,730
Health care and social assistance	78,590

Job Outlook

Employment of public relations and fundraising managers is projected to grow 13 percent from 2012 to 2022, about as fast as the average for all occupations.

As online social media increase the speed at which news travels, public relations managers will be needed to address good and bad news for their organization or client.

Organizations continue to emphasize community outreach and customer relations as a way to enhance their reputation and visibility. Public opinion can change quickly, particularly as news spreads rapidly through the Internet. Consequently, managers will be needed to coordinate and help respond to news developments in order to maintain their organization's reputation.

Fundraising managers are expected to become increasingly important for organizations (such as colleges and universities) that depend heavily on donations, as state funding for these institutions has fallen. More nonprofit organizations are focusing on cultivating an online presence and are increasingly using social media for fundraising activities.

Social media have created a new avenue for fundraising managers to connect with potential donors and to spread their organization's message.

Job Prospects. Competition for public relations and fundraising manager jobs is expected to be very strong.

Competition for jobs for public relations managers should be toughest at businesses that have large media exposure and also at the most prestigious public relations firms.

Job prospects for fundraising managers should be best for those with a master's degree in philanthropic studies or fundraising. These degree programs lead to experience in the industry, giving graduates an advantage over those who do not have such experience.

O*NET

➤ Public Relations and Fundraising Managers (11-2031.00)

Contacts for More Information

For more information about public relations and fundraising managers, including professional certification in public relations, visit

➤ CFRE International (www.cfre.org/)
➤ Public Relations Society of America (www.prsa.org/)
➤ International Association of Business Communicators (www.iabc.com/)

Sales Managers

- **2012 Median Pay** .... $105,260 per year
  $50.60 per hour
- **Entry-Level Education** .... Bachelor's degree
- **Work Experience in a Related Occupation**...... Less than 5 years
- **On-the-Job Training** .... None
- **Number of Jobs 2012** 359,300
- **Job Outlook, 2012–22** .... 8% (As fast as average)
- **Employment Change, 2012–22** 29,800

What Sales Managers Do

Sales managers direct organizations' sales teams. They set sales goals, analyze data, and develop training programs for organizations' sales representatives.

Duties. Sales managers typically do the following:

- Resolve customer complaints regarding sales and service
- Prepare budgets and approve expenditures
- Monitor customer preferences to determine the focus of sales efforts
- Analyze sales statistics
- Project sales and determine the profitability of products and services
- Determine discount rates or special pricing plans
- Develop plans to acquire new customers or clients, through direct sales techniques, cold calling, and business-to-business marketing visits
- Assign sales territories and set sales quotas
- Plan and coordinate training programs for sales staff

Sales managers' responsibilities vary with the size of the organization they work for. However, most sales managers direct the distribution of goods and services by assigning sales territories,

setting sales goals, and establishing training programs for the organization's sales representatives.

Some sales managers recruit, hire, and train new members of the sales staff. For more information about salesworkers, see the profiles on retail sales workers and wholesale and manufacturing sales representatives.

Sales managers advise sales representatives on ways to improve their sales performance. In large multiproduct organizations, they oversee regional and local sales managers and their staffs.

Sales managers also stay in contact with dealers and distributors. They analyze sales statistics that their staff gathers, both to determine the sales potential and inventory requirements of products and stores and to monitor customers' preferences.

Sales managers work closely with managers from other departments. For example, the marketing department identifies new customers that the sales department can target. The relationship between these two departments is critical to helping an organization expand its client base. Because sales managers monitor customers' preferences and stores' and organizations' inventory needs, they work closely with research and design departments and warehousing departments.

Work Environment

Sales managers held about 359,300 jobs in 2012.

The industries that employed the most sales managers in 2012 were as follows:

Retail trade	20%
Wholesale trade	20
Manufacturing	13
Finance and insurance	10
Management of companies and enterprises	8

Sales managers have a lot of responsibility, and the position can be stressful. Many sales managers travel to national, regional, and local offices and to dealers' and distributors' offices.

Work Schedules. Most sales managers work full time. Long hours, including evenings and weekends, are common.

How to Become One

Most sales managers have a bachelor's degree and work experience as a sales representative.

Education. Most sales managers have a bachelor's degree: some have a master's degree. Educational requirements are less strict

Most sales managers have a bachelor's degree and previous work experience as a sales representative.

Median Annual Wages, May 2012

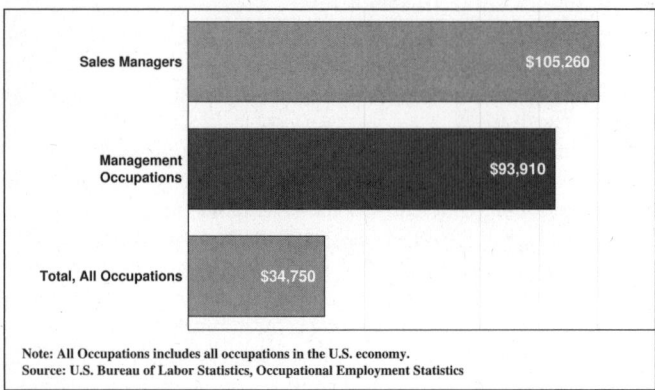

Note: All Occupations includes all occupations in the U.S. economy.
Source: U.S. Bureau of Labor Statistics, Occupational Employment Statistics

Percent Change in Employment, Projected 2012–2022

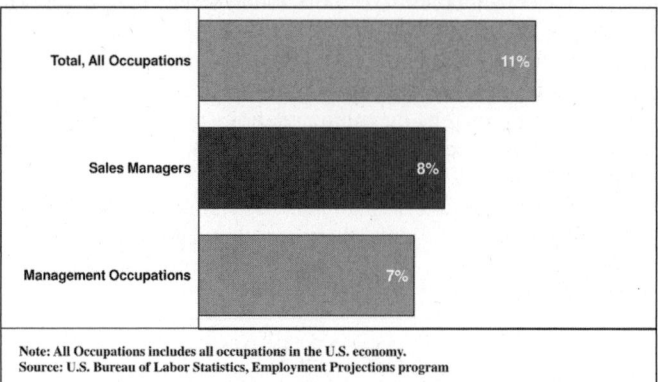

Note: All Occupations includes all occupations in the U.S. economy.
Source: U.S. Bureau of Labor Statistics, Employment Projections program

for job candidates who have significant experience as a sales representative. Courses in business law, management, economics, accounting, finance, mathematics, marketing, and statistics are advantageous.

Work Experience in a Related Occupation. Work experience is typically required for someone to become a sales manager. The preferred duration varies, but employers usually seek candidates who have at least 1 to 5 years of experience.

Sales managers typically enter the occupation from other sales and related occupations, such as sales representatives or purchasing agents. In small organizations, the number of sales manager positions often is limited, so advancement for salesworkers usually comes slowly. In large organizations, promotion may occur more quickly.

Important Qualities

Analytical skills. Sales managers must collect and interpret complex data to target the most promising geographic areas and/

or demographic groups, and determine the most effective sales strategies.

Communication skills. Sales managers need to work with people in other departments and with customers, so they must be able to communicate clearly.

Customer-service skills. When helping to make a sale, sales managers must listen and respond to the customer's needs.

Leadership skills. Sales managers must be able to evaluate how their sales staff performs and must develop strategies for meeting sales goals.

Pay

The median annual wage for sales managers was $105,260 in May 2012. The median wage is the wage at which half the workers in an occupation earned more than that amount and half earned less. The lowest 10 percent earned less than $52,950, and the top 10 percent earned more than $187,200.

Employment Projections Data for Sales Managers

Occupational title	SOC Code	Employment, 2012	Projected Employment, 2022	Change, 2012–2022	
				Percent	Numeric
Sales managers..	11-2022	359,300	389,000	8	29,800

Source: U.S. Bureau of Labor Statistics, Employment Projections Program

Note: Data are rounded. Go to Occupational Information Included in the OOH *for a discussion of the data in this table.*

Similar Occupations   This table shows a list of occupations with job duties that are similar to those of sales managers.

Occupations	Entry-level Education	2012 Pay	Projected Job Growth	Average Annual Openings
Advertising Sales Agents	High school diploma or equivalent	$46,290	-1%	4,750
Advertising, Promotions, and Marketing Managers	Bachelor's degree	$115,087	12%	7,510
Market Research Analysts	Bachelor's degree	$60,300	32%	18,850
Public Relations and Fundraising Managers	Bachelor's degree	$95,450	13%	2,130
Public Relations Specialists	Bachelor's degree	$54,170	12%	5,880
Purchasing Managers, Buyers, and Purchasing Agents	See "How to Become One"	$63,128	4%	12,230
Retail Sales Workers	Less than high school	$21,514	10%	202,730
Sales Engineers	Bachelor's degree	$91,830	9%	1,740
Wholesale and Manufacturing Sales Representatives	See "How to Become One"	$58,484	9%	53,250

In May 2012, the median annual wages for sales managers in the top five industries in which they worked were as follows:

Finance and insurance	$132,070
Management of companies and enterprises	115,000
Wholesale trade	114,180
Manufacturing	109,550
Retail trade	74,870

Compensation methods for sales managers vary significantly with the type of organization and the product sold. Most employers use a combination of salary and commissions or salary plus bonuses. Commissions usually are based on the value of sales, whereas bonuses may depend on individual performance, on the performance of all salesworkers in the group or district, or on the organization's performance.

Job Outlook

Employment of sales managers is projected to grow 8 percent from 2012 to 2022, about as fast as the average for all occupations. Employment growth of these managers will depend primarily on growth or contraction in the industries that employ them.

An effective sales team remains crucial for profitability. As the economy grows, organizations will focus on generating new sales and will look to their sales strategy as a way to increase competitiveness.

Growth is expected to be stronger for sales managers involved in business-to-business sales than in business-to-consumer sales, because the rise of online shopping will reduce the need for sales calls to individual consumers.

Sales managers and their departments are some of the most important personnel in an organization. Therefore, they are less likely to be let go or to have their jobs contracted out than are other types of managers, except in the case of organizations that are merging and consolidating.

Offshoring of these workers is also unlikely. Although domestic companies may hire some sales managers in foreign countries, those workers will function largely to support expansion into foreign markets rather than to replace domestic sales managers.

Job Prospects. Strong competition is expected because other managers and highly experienced professionals often seek these jobs.

O*NET

➤ Sales Managers (11-2022.00)

Contacts for More Information

For more information about sales managers, visit
➤ Sales Management Association (http://salesmanagement.org/)

Social and Community Service Managers

- **2012 Median Pay** .... $59,970 per year
  $28.83 per hour
- **Entry-Level Education** .... Bachelor's degree
- **Work Experience in a Related Occupation** ... 5 years or more
- **On-the-Job Training** .... None
- **Number of Jobs 2012** 132,900
- **Job Outlook, 2012–22** .... 21% (Faster than average)
- **Employment Change, 2012–22** 27,700

What Social and Community Service Managers Do

Social and community service managers coordinate and supervise social service programs and community organizations. They direct and lead staff who provide social services to the public.

Duties. Social and community service managers typically do the following:

- Work with members of the community and other stakeholders to identify the types of programs and services that are needed
- Design and oversee programs to meet the needs of the target audience or community
- Establish methods to gather information about the impact of their programs
- Supervise staff, such as social workers, who provide services to clients
- Analyze data to determine the effectiveness of programs
- Suggest and implement improvements to programs and services
- Develop and manage budgets for programs and organizations
- Plan and manage community outreach efforts to advocate for increased awareness of programs
- Write proposals for social services funding

Social and community service managers work for a variety of social and human service organizations. The organizations may focus on working with a particular demographic, such as children, people who are homeless, older adults, or veterans. Other organizations may focus on helping people with particular challenges, such as mental health needs, chronic hunger, or long-term unemployment.

Social and community service managers are often expected to show that their programs and services are effective. To do so, they collect statistics and other information to evaluate the impact that programs have in their community or on their target audience. They are usually required to report this information to administrators or funders. They may also use evaluations to identify areas that need improvement for programs to be more effective, such as providing mentorship and assessments for their staff.

Although specific job duties of social and community service managers vary based on the size of the organization, most managers must recruit, hire, and train new staff members.

Social and community service managers meet with members of the community and funders to discuss their programs.

Median Annual Wages, May 2012

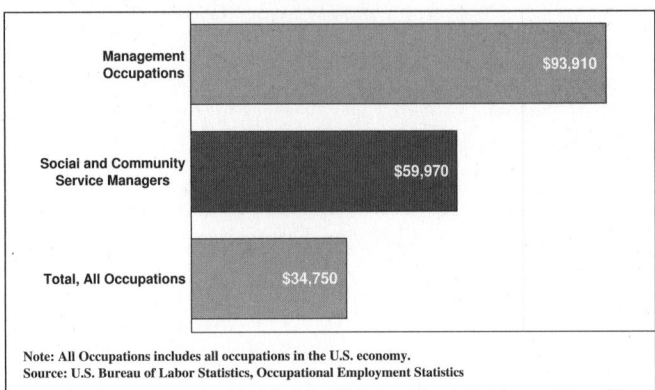

Note: All Occupations includes all occupations in the U.S. economy.
Source: U.S. Bureau of Labor Statistics, Occupational Employment Statistics

Percent Change in Employment, Projected 2012–2022

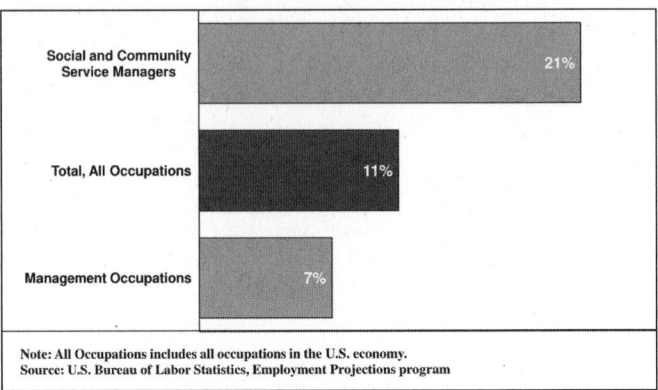

Note: All Occupations includes all occupations in the U.S. economy.
Source: U.S. Bureau of Labor Statistics, Employment Projections program

In large agencies, managers tend to have specialized duties. Depending on their position, they may be responsible for running only one program in an organization and reporting to the agency's upper management. They usually do not design programs. Instead, they supervise and implement programs set up by administrators, elected officials, or other stakeholders.

In small organizations, social and community managers often have many roles. They represent the organization to the public through speaking engagements or in community-wide committees; they oversee, and execute program implementations; they spend time on administrative tasks, such as managing budgets; and they also help with raising funds and meeting with potential donors.

Work Environment

Social and community service managers held about 132,900 jobs in 2012. They work for nonprofit organizations, private for-profit social service companies, and government agencies. Social and community service managers work in a variety of settings, including offices, clinics, hospitals, and shelters.

Some social and community service managers focus on working with a particular demographic, such as children, homeless or elderly people, or veterans; others focus on helping people with particular challenges, such as hunger or joblessness.

The industries that employed the most social and community service managers in 2012 were as follows:

Individual and family services...	23%
State and local government, excluding education and hospitals...	19
Religious, grantmaking, civic, professional, and similar organizations...	15
Community and vocational rehabilitation services	10
Nursing and residential care facilities	10

Some aspects of the work, such as fundraising or balancing budgets, may be stressful, particularly during economic downturns.

Work Schedules. Social and community service managers typically work full time.

How to Become One

Social and community service managers need at least a bachelor's degree and some work experience. However, many employers prefer candidates who have a master's degree.

Education. A bachelor's degree in social work, urban studies, public administration, or a related field is the minimum requirement. Employers usually require those with a bachelor's degree to have some work experience as well.

Many employers prefer workers with a master's degree in social work, public or business administration, public health, or a related field. Coursework in statistics, program management, and policy analysis is considered helpful.

Work Experience

Work experience is often needed to become a social and community service manager and is essential for those wishing to enter the occupation with a bachelor's degree. Workers must demonstrate an ability to lead other workers and manage services and programs. They can get this experience by working as a social worker or in a similar occupation. Lower-level management positions may require only a few years of experience; directors typically have much more experience.

Important Qualities

Analytical skills. Managers need to understand and evaluate data to provide strategic guidance to their organization. They must be able to monitor and evaluate current programs as well as determine new initiatives.

Communication skills. Working with the community and employees requires effective communication. Managers must be able to speak and write clearly so others can understand them. Public speaking experience is also helpful because they often participate in community outreach.

Interpersonal skills. Social and community service managers should have good interpersonal skills. When speaking with members of their staff or members of the community, they must be tactful and able to explain and discuss all matters related to services that are needed.

Employment Projections Data for Social and Community Service Managers

Occupational title	SOC Code	Employment, 2012	Projected Employment, 2022	Change, 2012–2022 Percent	Change, 2012–2022 Numeric
Social and community service managers................................ 11-9151		132,900	160,600	21	27,700

Source: U.S. Bureau of Labor Statistics, Employment Projections Program

Note: Data are rounded. Go to **Occupational Information Included in the OOH** *for a discussion of the data in this table.*

Similar Occupations This table shows a list of occupations with job duties that are similar to those of social and community service managers.

Occupations	Entry-level Education	2012 Pay	Projected Job Growth	Average Annual Openings
Health Educators and Community Health Workers	See "How to Become One"	$43,015	22%	4,740
Mental Health Counselors and Marriage and Family Therapists	Master's degree	$41,592	29%	8,360
Probation Officers and Correctional Treatment Specialists	Bachelor's degree	$48,190	-1%	2,360
Rehabilitation Counselors	Master's degree	$33,880	20%	4,840
School and Career Counselors	Master's degree	$53,610	12%	8,700
Social and Human Service Assistants	High school diploma or equivalent	$28,850	22%	17,870
Social Workers	See "How to Become One"	$44,541	19%	24,280
Substance Abuse and Behavioral Disorder Counselors	High school diploma or equivalent	$38,520	31%	4,720

Leadership skills. Social and community service managers must motivate and lead their employees and set the overall direction of the program.

Managerial skills. Social and community service managers spend much of their time administering budgets and responding to a variety of issues.

Problem-solving skills. Managers must be able to effectively address client, staff, and agency related issues as they occur.

Time-management skills. Social and community service managers must be able to prioritize and handle numerous tasks for multiple customers, often in a short timeframe.

Pay

The median annual wage for social and community service managers was $59,970 in May 2012. The median wage is the wage at which half the workers in an occupation earned more than that amount and half earned less. The lowest 10 percent earned less than $36,250, and the top 10 percent earned more than $99,150.

In May 2012, the median annual wages for social and community service managers in the top five industries in which these managers worked were as follows:

State and local government, excluding education and hospitals	$69,490
Religious, grantmaking, civic, professional, and similar organizations	61,500
Individual and family services	55,810
Community and vocational rehabilitation services	54,120
Nursing and residential care facilities	53,090

Job Outlook

Employment of social and community service managers is projected to grow 21 percent from 2012 to 2022, faster than the average for all occupations.

Much of the job growth in this occupation is the result of meeting the needs of an aging population. An increase in the number of older adults will result in a need for more social services. Elderly people often need services, such as adult day care and meal delivery. Social and community service managers, who administer programs that provide these services, will likely be needed to meet this increased demand. As a result, employment of social and community service managers is expected to grow fastest in industries serving the elderly, such as home health care services and services for the elderly and persons with disabilities.

In addition, employment growth is projected as more people seek treatment for their addictions and as illegal drug offenders are increasingly sent to treatment programs rather than to jail. As a result, managers who direct treatment programs will be needed.

Although this occupation is projected to have rapid employment growth, gains could be limited by budget cuts in state and local governments. Social and human services rely heavily on government funding, and if funding decreases, services may not grow fast enough to meet demand.

O*NET

➤ Social and Community Service Managers (11-9151.00)

Contacts for More Information

For more information about social and community service managers, visit

➤ Council on Social Work Education (www.cswe.org/)
➤ National Association of Social Workers (www.naswdc.org/)
➤ Network for Social Work Management (https://socialworkmanager. org/)

Top Executives

- **2012 Median Pay** .... $101,650 per year
  $48.87 per hour
- **Entry-Level Education** .... Bachelor's degree
- **Work Experience in a Related Occupation**.... See "How to Become One"
- **On-the-Job Training** .... None
- **Number of Jobs 2012** 2,303,200
- **Job Outlook, 2012–22** .... 11% (As fast as average)
- **Employment Change, 2012–22** 261,500

What Top Executives Do

Top executives devise strategies and policies to ensure that an organization meets its goals. They plan, direct, and coordinate operational activities of companies and organizations.

Duties. Top executives typically do the following:

- Establish and carry out departmental or organizational goals, policies, and procedures

- Direct and oversee an organization's financial and budgetary activities
- Manage general activities related to making products and providing services
- Consult with other executives, staff, and board members about general operations
- Negotiate or approve contracts and agreements
- Appoint department heads and managers
- Analyze financial statements, sales reports, and other performance indicators
- Identify places to cut costs and to improve performance, policies, and programs

The responsibilities of top executives largely depend on an organization's size. For example, an owner or manager of a small organization, such as an independent retail store, often is responsible for purchasing, hiring, training, quality control, and day-to-day supervisory duties. In large organizations, however, top executives typically focus more on formulating policies and strategic planning, while general and operations managers direct day-to-day operations.

The following are examples of types of top executives:

Chief executive officers (CEOs), who are also known by titles such as *executive director, president*, and *vice president*, provide overall direction for companies and organizations. CEOs manage company operations, formulate policies, and ensure goals are met. They collaborate with and direct the work of other top executives and typically report to a board of directors.

Companies may also have chief officers who lead various departments or focus on specific areas of work:

- *Chief financial officers (CFOs)* are accountable for the accuracy of a company's or organization's financial reporting, especially among publicly traded companies. They direct the organization's financial goals, objectives, and budgets. For example, they may oversee the investment of funds and manage associated risks.

- *Chief information officers (CIOs)* are responsible for the overall technological direction of an organization, which includes managing information technology and computer systems. They organize and supervise information-technology-related workers, projects, and policies.

- *Chief operating officers (COOs)* oversee other executives who direct the activities of various departments, such as human resources and sales. They also carry out the organization's guidelines on a day-to-day basis.

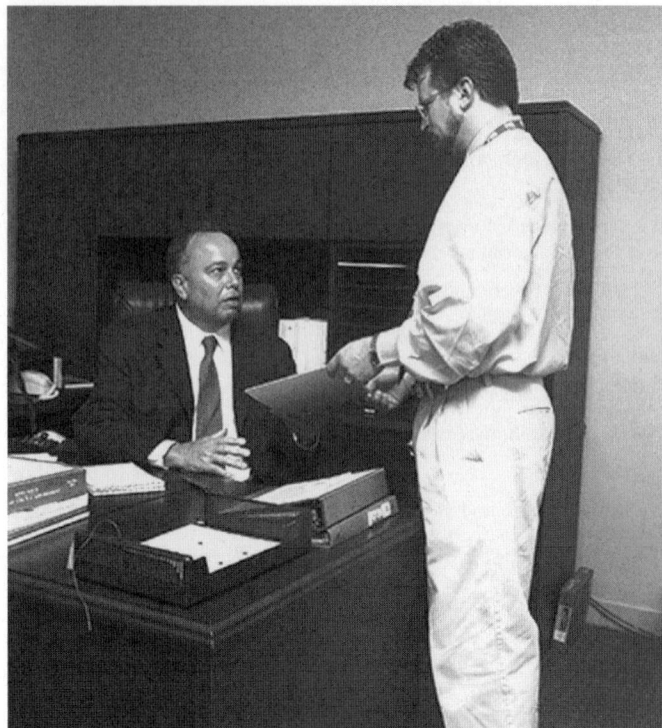

Top executives need highly developed management skills and the ability to communicate clearly and persuasively.

- *Chief sustainability officers* oversee a corporation's environmental programs. For instance, they may manage programs and policies to ensure that the organization complies with environmental or other government regulations.

Mayors, along with *governors*, *city managers*, and *county administrators*, are chief executive officers of governments. They typically oversee budgets, programs, and the use of resources. Mayors and governors must be elected to office, whereas managers and administrators are typically appointed.

School superintendents and *college* or *university presidents* are chief executive officers of school districts and postsecondary schools. They manage issues such as student achievement, budgets and resources, general operations, and relations with government agencies and other stakeholders.

General and operations managers oversee operations that are too diverse and general to be classified into one area of management or administration. Responsibilities may include formulating policies, managing daily operations, and planning the use of materials

Median Annual Wages, May 2012

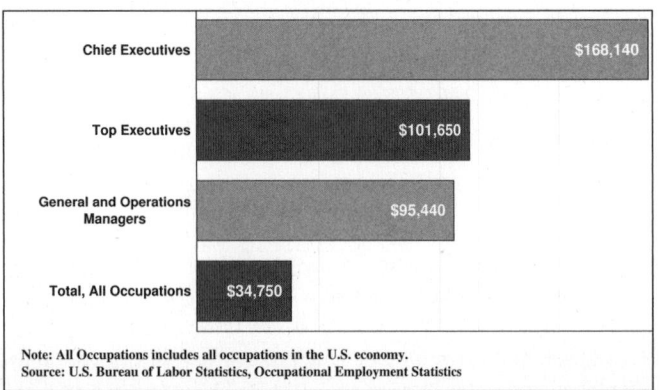

Chief Executives	$168,140
Top Executives	$101,650
General and Operations Managers	$95,440
Total, All Occupations	$34,750

Note: All Occupations includes all occupations in the U.S. economy.
Source: U.S. Bureau of Labor Statistics, Occupational Employment Statistics

Percent Change in Employment, Projected 2012–2022

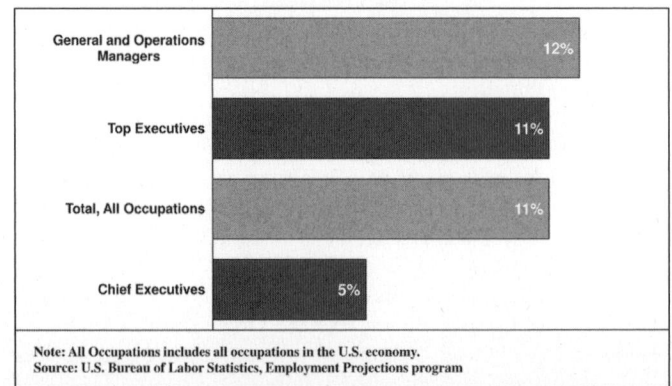

General and Operations Managers	12%
Top Executives	11%
Total, All Occupations	11%
Chief Executives	5%

Note: All Occupations includes all occupations in the U.S. economy.
Source: U.S. Bureau of Labor Statistics, Employment Projections program

Employment Projections Data for Top Executives

Occupational title	SOC Code	Employment, 2012	Projected Employment, 2022	Change, 2012–2022	
				Percent	Numeric
Top executives	—	2,303,200	2,564,700	11	261,500
Chief executives.......................................	11-1011	330,500	347,900	5	17,400
General and operations managers	11-1021	1,972,700	2,216,800	12	244,100

Source: U.S. Bureau of Labor Statistics, Employment Projections Program

Note: Data are rounded. Go to **Occupational Information Included in the OOH** *for a discussion of the data in this table.*

and human resources. They make staff schedules, assign work, and ensure that projects are completed. In some organizations, the tasks of chief executive officers may overlap with those of general and operations managers.

Work Environment

Top executives held about 2.3 million jobs in 2012. About 86 percent of those jobs were held by general and operations managers and 14 percent were held by chief executives.

Top executives work in nearly every industry. They work for both large and small businesses, ranging from one-person companies to firms with thousands of employees.

Top executives of large organizations typically have large offices and numerous support staff. However, the work of top executives is often stressful because they are under intense pressure to succeed. Executives in charge of poorly performing organizations or departments may find their jobs in jeopardy.

Work Schedules. Top executives frequently travel to attend meetings and conferences or to visit their company's local, regional, national, and international offices. In large organizations, executives may occasionally transfer jobs, moving between local offices or subsidiaries.

Top executives often work long hours, including evenings and weekends. In 2012, about half worked more than 40 hours per week.

How to Become One

Although education and training requirements vary widely by position and industry, many top executives have at least a bachelor's degree and a considerable amount of work experience.

Education. Many top executives have a bachelor's or master's degree in business administration or in an area related to their field of work. Top executives in the public sector often have a degree in business administration, public administration, law, or the liberal arts. Top executives of large corporations often have a master of business administration (MBA). College presidents and school superintendents typically have a doctoral degree in the field in which they originally taught or in education administration.

Work Experience in a Related Occupation. Many top executives advance within their own firm, moving up from lower level managerial or supervisory positions. However, other companies may prefer to hire qualified candidates from outside their organization. Top executives that are promoted from lower level positions may be able to substitute experience for education to move up in the company. For example, in industries such as retail trade or transportation, workers without a college degree may work their way up to higher levels within the company to become executives or general managers.

Chief executives typically need extensive managerial experience. Executives are also expected to have experience in the organization's area of specialty. Most general and operations managers

hired from outside an organization need lower level supervisory or management experience in a related field.

Some general managers advance to higher level managerial or executive positions. Company training programs, executive development programs, and certification can often benefit managers or executives hoping to advance. Chief executive officers often become a member of the board of directors.

Licenses, Certifications, and Registrations. Top executives may complete a certification program through the Institute of Certified Professional Managers to earn the Certified Manager (CM) credential. To become a CM, candidates must meet education and experience requirements and pass three exams.

Although not mandatory, certification can show management competency and potential leadership skills. Certification can also help those seeking advancement or can give jobseekers a competitive edge.

Important Qualities

Communication skills. Top executives must be able to communicate clearly and persuasively. They must effectively discuss issues and negotiate with others, direct subordinates, and explain their policies and decisions to those within and outside the organization.

Decision-making skills. Top executives need decision-making skills when setting policies and managing an organization. They must assess different options and choose the best course of action, often daily.

Leadership skills. Top executives must be able to lead an organization successfully by coordinating policies, people, and resources.

Management skills. Top executives must organize and direct the operations of an organization. For example, they must manage business plans, employees, and budgets.

Problem-solving skills. Top executives need problem-solving skills after identifying issues within an organization. They must be able to recognize shortcomings and effectively carry out solutions.

Time-management skills. Top executives must be able to do many tasks at the same time, typically under their own direction, to ensure that their work gets done and that they meet their goals.

Pay

The median annual wage for chief executives was $168,140 in May 2012. The median wage is the wage at which half the workers in an occupation earned more than that amount and half earned less. The lowest 10 percent earned less than $76,220, and the top 10 percent earned more than $187,200.

The median annual wage for general and operations managers was $95,440 in May 2012. The lowest 10 percent earned less than $46,890, and the top 10 percent earned more than $187,200.

Because the responsibilities of general and operations managers vary significantly among industries, earnings also tend to vary considerably.

Top executives are among the highest paid workers in the United States. However, salary levels vary substantially, depending on

Similar Occupations   This table shows a list of occupations with job duties that are similar to those of top executives.

Occupations	Entry-level Education	2012 Pay	Projected Job Growth	Average Annual Openings
Administrative Services Managers	Bachelor's degree	$81,080	12%	7,990
Advertising, Promotions, and Marketing Managers	Bachelor's degree	$115,087	12%	7,510
Architectural and Engineering Managers	Bachelor's degree	$124,870	7%	6,060
Computer and Information Systems Managers	Bachelor's degree	$120,950	15%	9,710
Construction Managers	Bachelor's degree	$82,790	16%	15,460
Financial Managers	Bachelor's degree	$109,740	9%	14,690
Human Resources Managers	Bachelor's degree	$99,720	13%	4,060
Industrial Production Managers	Bachelor's degree	$89,190	-2%	3,140
Medical and Health Services Managers	Bachelor's degree	$88,580	23%	14,990
Sales Managers	Bachelor's degree	$105,260	8%	10,690

executives' responsibilities and lengths of service and the types, sizes, and locations of the firms, organizations, or government agencies for which they work. For example, a top manager in a large corporation can earn significantly more than the mayor of a small town.

In addition to salaries, total compensation for corporate executives often includes stock options and other performance bonuses. Workers also may enjoy benefits, such as access to expense allowances, use of company-owned aircraft and cars, club memberships, and company-paid insurance premiums. Nonprofit and government executives usually receive fewer benefits.

Job Outlook

Employment of top executives is projected to grow 11 percent from 2012 to 2022, about as fast as the average for all occupations. Employment growth will vary widely by industry and is largely dependent on the rate of industry growth.

Generally, employment growth will be driven by the formation of new organizations and expansion of existing ones, which will require more managers and executives to direct these operations.

In addition, top executives are essential for running companies and organizations and their work is central to the success of a company.

Job Prospects. Top executives are expected to face very strong competition for jobs. The high pay and prestige associated with these positions attract many qualified applicants.

For chief executives, those with an advanced degree and extensive managerial experience will have the best job prospects.

For general and operations managers, education requirements vary by industry, but candidates who can demonstrate strong leadership abilities and experience getting positive results will have better job opportunities.

O*NET

➤ Chief Executives (11-1011.00)
➤ Chief Sustainability Officers (11-1011.03)
➤ General and Operations Managers (11-1021.00)

Contacts for More Information

For more information about top executives, including educational programs, visit
➤ American Management Association (www.amanet.org)
➤ National Management Association (NMA) (www.nma1.org)

For more information about executive financial management careers, visit
➤ Financial Executives International (www.financialexecutives.org)
➤ Financial Management Association International (www.fma.org)

For information about management skills development, including the Certified Manager (CM) credential, visit
➤ Institute of Certified Professional Managers (www.icpm.biz)

Training and Development Managers

- **2012 Median Pay** .... $95,400 per year
  $45.86 per hour
- **Entry-Level Education** .... Bachelor's degree
- **Work Experience in a Related Occupation** ... 5 years or more
- **On-the-Job Training** .... None
- **Number of Jobs 2012** 28,600
- **Job Outlook, 2012–22** .... 11% (As fast as average)
- **Employment Change, 2012–22** 3,200

What Training and Development Managers Do

Training and development managers plan, direct, and coordinate programs to enhance the knowledge and skills of an organization's employees. They also oversee a staff of training and development specialists.

Duties. Training and development managers typically do the following:

- Assess employees' needs for training
- Align training with the organization's strategic goals
- Create a training budget and keep operations within budget
- Develop training programs that make the best use of available resources
- Update training programs to ensure that they are current
- Oversee the creation of online learning modules and other educational materials for employees
- Review training materials from a variety of vendors and select materials with appropriate content
- Teach training methods and skills to instructors and supervisors
- Evaluate the effectiveness of training programs and instructors

Training and development managers often give presentations.

Executives increasingly realize that developing the skills of their organization's workforce is essential to staying competitive in business. Providing opportunity for development is a selling point for recruiting high-quality employees, and it helps in retaining employees who can contribute to business growth. Training and development managers work to align training and development with an organization's goals.

Training and development managers oversee training programs, staff, and budgets. They are responsible for organizing training programs, including creating or selecting course content and materials. Often, training takes place in a classroom, computer laboratory, or training facility. Some training is in the form of a video, Web-based program, or self-guided instructional manual. Training may also be collaborative, which allows employees to informally connect with experts, mentors, and colleagues, often through social media or other online mediums. Regardless of how it is conducted, managers must ensure that training content, software, systems, and equipment are appropriate and meaningful.

Training and development managers typically supervise a staff of training and development specialists, such as instructional designers, program developers, and instructors. Managers teach training methods to specialists who, in turn, instruct the organization's employees–both new and experienced. Managers direct the daily activities of specialists and evaluate their effectiveness. Although most managers primarily oversee specialists and training and development program operations, some–particularly those in smaller companies–also may direct training courses.

To enhance employees' skills and an organization's overall quality of work, training and development managers often confer with managers of each department to identify its training needs. They may work with top executives and financial officers to identify and match training priorities with overall business goals. They also prepare training budgets and ensure that expenses stay within budget.

Work Environment

Training and development managers held about 28,600 jobs in 2012 and worked in nearly every industry. Some also work for organizations and in government.

Training and development managers typically work in offices. Some travel between a main office and regional offices or training facilities. They spend much of their time working with people, giving presentations, and leading training activities.

Work Schedules. Most training and development managers work full time during regular business hours, and some must travel for work.

How to Become One

Candidates need a combination of education and related work experience to become a training and development manager.

Education. Although managers need a bachelor's degree for many positions, some jobs require a master's degree. Managers can have a variety of educational backgrounds, but they often have a bachelor's degree in human resources, business administration, or a related field.

Some employers prefer or require that managers have a master's degree, usually with a concentration in training and development, human resources management, organizational development, or business administration.

Training and development managers also may benefit from studying instructional design, behavioral psychology, or educational psychology. In addition, as technology continues to play a larger role in training and development, a growing number of organizations seek candidates who have a background in information technology or computer science.

Work Experience in a Related Occupation. Related work experience is essential for training and development managers. Many positions require work experience in training and development or another human resources field, management, or teaching. For example, many training and development managers start out as training and development specialists. Some employers also prefer experience in the industry in which the company operates. Increasingly, employers look for workers with experience in information technology as organizations introduce more e-learning and technology-based tools.

Median Annual Wages, May 2012

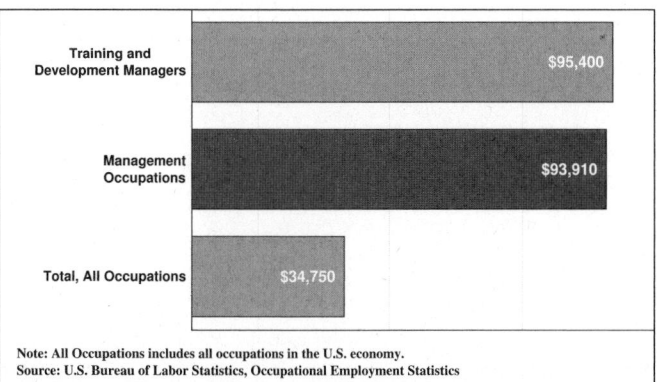

Note: All Occupations includes all occupations in the U.S. economy.
Source: U.S. Bureau of Labor Statistics, Occupational Employment Statistics

Percent Change in Employment, Projected 2012–2022

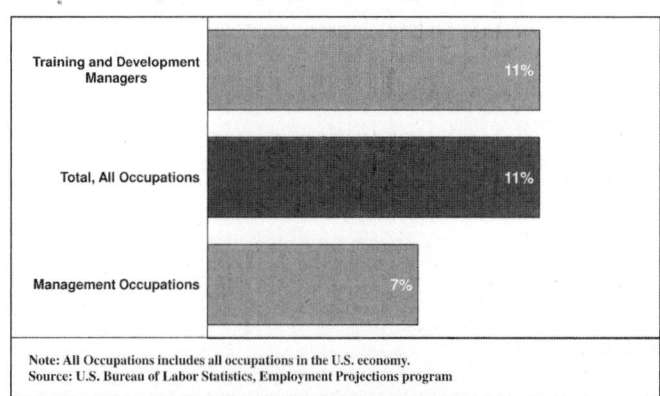

Note: All Occupations includes all occupations in the U.S. economy.
Source: U.S. Bureau of Labor Statistics, Employment Projections program

Employment Projections Data for Training and Development Managers

Occupational title	SOC Code	Employment, 2012	Projected Employment, 2022	Change, 2012–2022	
				Percent	Numeric
Training and development managers	11-3131	28,600	31,800	11	3,200

Source: U.S. Bureau of Labor Statistics, Employment Projections Program

Note: Data are rounded. Go to **Occupational Information Included in the OOH** *for a discussion of the data in this table.*

Licenses, Certifications, and Registrations. Many professional associations for human resources professionals offer classes to enhance the skills of their members. Some associations, including the American Society for Training and Development and International Society for Performance Improvement, specialize in training and development and offer certification programs. Although not required, certification can show professional expertise and credibility. In fact, many employers prefer to hire certified candidates, and some positions may require certification.

Important Qualities

Communication skills. Communication skills are essential for training and development managers because they often give presentations. Workers must communicate information clearly and facilitate learning by diverse audiences. They also must be able to effectively convey instructions to their staff.

Critical-thinking skills. Training and development managers use critical-thinking skills when assessing classes, materials, and programs. They must identify the training needs of an organization and recognize where changes and improvements can be made.

Decision-making skills. Training and development managers must decide the best training programs to meet the needs of the organization. For example, they must review available training methods and materials and choose those that best fit each program.

Interpersonal skills. Training and development managers need strong interpersonal skills because delivering training programs requires collaborating with staff, trainees, subject matter experts, and the organization's leaders. They also accomplish much of their work through teams.

Leadership skills. Leadership skills are important for training and development managers, who are often in charge of a staff and are responsible for many programs. Managers must be able to organize, motivate, and instruct those working under them.

Pay

The median annual wage for training and development managers was $95,400 in May 2012. The median wage is the wage at which half the workers in an occupation earned more than that amount and half earned less. The lowest 10 percent earned less than $54,070, and the top 10 percent earned more than $164,640.

In May 2012, the median annual wages for training and development managers in the top five industries employing these workers were as follows:

Professional, scientific, and technical services.................. $109,090
Management of companies and enterprises....................... 102,350
Finance and insurance 100,360
Health care and social assistance 90,140
Educational services; state, local, and private 86,620

Job Outlook

Employment of training and development managers is projected to grow 11 percent from 2012 to 2022, about as fast as the average for all occupations.

In many fields, employees are required to take continuing education and skill development courses throughout their careers. In addition, innovations in training methods and learning technology are expected to continue throughout the next decade. For example, organizations increasingly use social media, visual simulations, mobile learning, and social networks in their training programs. Training and development managers will need to modify their programs to fit a new generation of workers for whom technology is a part of daily life and work.

Similar Occupations This table shows a list of occupations with job duties that are similar to those of training and development managers.

Occupations	Entry-level Education	2012 Pay	Projected Job Growth	Average Annual Openings
Compensation and Benefits Managers	Bachelor's degree	$95,250	3%	610
Compensation, Benefits, and Job Analysis Specialists	Bachelor's degree	$59,090	6%	2,200
Human Resources Managers	Bachelor's degree	$99,720	13%	4,060
Human Resources Specialists and Labor Relations Specialists	Bachelor's degree	$55,616	7%	12,370
Instructional Coordinators	Master's degree	$60,050	13%	3,110
Postsecondary Education Administrators	Master's degree	$86,490	15%	6,650
Psychologists	See "How to Become One"	$69,807	12%	6,230
School and Career Counselors	Master's degree	$53,610	12%	8,700
Top Executives	Bachelor's degree	$104,073	11%	70,090
Training and Development Specialists	Bachelor's degree	$55,930	15%	7,720

As social media and collaborative learning become more common, training and development managers will need to modify training programs, allocate budgets, and integrate these features into training programs and curricula.

In addition, as companies seek to reduce costs, training and development managers will be required to structure programs to enlist available experts, take advantage of existing resources, and facilitate positive relationships among staff. Training and development managers will use informal collaborative learning and social media to engage and train employees in the most cost effective way.

Job Prospects. Those who have a master's degree, certification, or work experience in training and development should have the best job prospects.

O*NET

➤ Training and Development Managers (11-3131.00)

Contacts for More Information

For more information about training and development managers, visit

➤ American Society for Training and Development (www.astd.org)
➤ International Society for Performance Improvement (www.ispi.org)

For information about human resources management careers and certification, visit

➤ Society for Human Resource Management (www.shrm.org)

Math

Actuaries

- **2012 Median Pay** .... $93,680 per year
  $45.04 per hour
- **Entry-Level Education** ....Bachelor's degree
- **Work Experience in a Related Occupation**.............. None
- **On-the-Job Training** .... Long-term on-the-job training
- **Number of Jobs 2012** 24,300
- **Job Outlook, 2012–22** .... 26% (Much faster than average)
- **Employment Change, 2012–22** 6,300

What Actuaries Do

Actuaries analyze the financial costs of risk and uncertainty. They use mathematics, statistics, and financial theory to assess the risk that an event will occur and help businesses and clients develop policies that minimize the cost of that risk. Actuaries' work is essential to the insurance industry.

Duties. Actuaries typically do the following:

- Compile statistical data and other information for further analysis
- Estimate the probability and likely economic cost of an event such as death, sickness, an accident, or a natural disaster
- Design, test, and administer insurance policies, investments, pension plans, and other business strategies to minimize risk and maximize profitability
- Produce charts, tables, and reports that explain calculations and proposals
- Explain their findings and proposals to company executives, government officials, shareholders, and clients

Most actuarial work is done with computers. Actuaries use database software to compile information. They use advanced statistics and modeling software to forecast the cost and probability of an event.

Actuaries typically work on teams that often include managers and professionals in other fields, such as accounting, underwriting, and finance. For example, some actuaries work with accountants and financial analysts to set the price for security offerings or with market research analysts to forecast demand for new products.

Actuaries need a strong background in mathematics.

With experience, actuaries are often given supervisory roles. They are responsible for delegating tasks and providing advice to senior management. They also may be called on to testify before public agencies on proposed laws that affect their business, such as state laws placing caps on auto insurance prices.

Most actuaries work at insurance companies, where they help design policies and determine the premiums that should be charged for each policy. They must ensure that the premiums are profitable, yet competitive with other insurance companies.

Actuaries in the insurance industry typically specialize in a specific field of insurance, such as one of the following:

Health insurance actuaries help develop long-term care and health insurance policies by predicting expected costs of providing care under the terms of an insurance contract. Their predictions are based on numerous factors, including family history, geographic location, and occupation.

Life insurance actuaries help develop annuity and life insurance policies for individuals and groups by estimating, on the basis of risk factors such as age, gender, and tobacco use, how long someone is expected to live.

Property and casualty insurance actuaries help develop insurance policies that insure policyholders against property loss and liability resulting from accidents, natural disasters, fires, and other events. They calculate the expected number of claims resulting from automobile accidents, which varies depending on the insured person's age, sex, driving history, type of car, and other factors.

Some actuaries apply their expertise to financial matters outside of the insurance industry. For example, they develop investment strategies that manage risks and maximize returns for companies or individuals. Some actuaries help companies develop broad policies and strategies that assess risks across all areas of business, a practice known as enterprise risk management.

Pension and retirement benefits actuaries design, test, and evaluate company pension plans to determine if the expected funds available in the future will be enough to ensure payment of future benefits. They must report the results of their evaluations to the federal government. Pension actuaries also help businesses develop other types of retirement plans, such as 401(k)s, and healthcare plans for retirees. In addition, they provide retirement planning advice to individuals.

Some people with an actuarial science background may become postsecondary teachers.

Work Environment

Actuaries held about 24,300 jobs in 2012. Actuaries typically work in an office setting. However, actuaries who work for consulting firms may need to travel frequently to meet with clients. Actuaries typically work on teams that often include managers and professionals in other fields, such as accounting, underwriting, and finance.

The industries that employed the most actuaries in 2012 were as follows:

Insurance carriers and related activities 69%
Professional, scientific, and technical services.......................... 17
Management of companies and enterprises............................. 6
Funds, trusts, and other financial vehicles 3
Government.. 3

Some actuaries are considered consultants and provide advice to clients on a contract basis. Many consulting actuaries audit

Median Annual Wages, May 2012

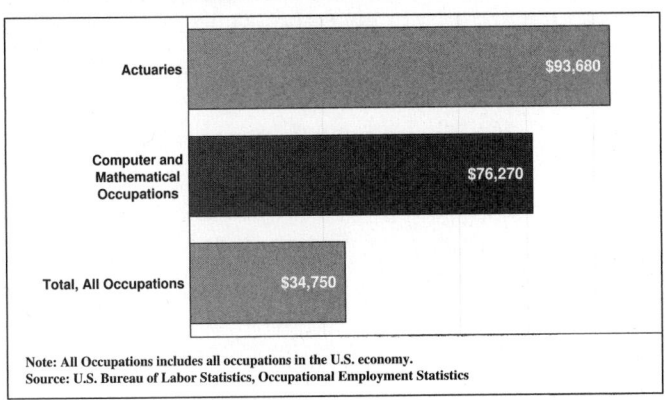

Note: All Occupations includes all occupations in the U.S. economy.
Source: U.S. Bureau of Labor Statistics, Occupational Employment Statistics

Percent Change in Employment, Projected 2012–2022

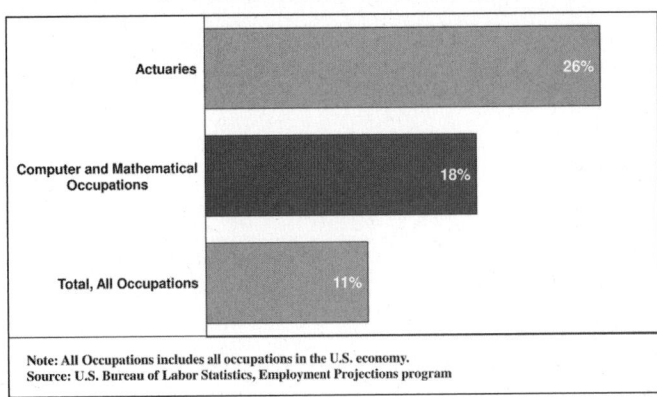

Note: All Occupations includes all occupations in the U.S. economy.
Source: U.S. Bureau of Labor Statistics, Employment Projections program

the work of internal actuaries at insurance companies or handle actuarial duties for insurance companies that are not large enough to keep their own actuaries on staff. Other consulting actuaries work for employee benefits firms. These firms design, analyze, and manage employee benefit programs such as employer-sponsored healthcare and retirement plans for companies.

Work Schedules. Most actuaries worked full time, and about 3 out of 10 worked more than 40 hours per week in 2012.

How to Become One

Actuaries need a bachelor's degree, typically in mathematics, actuarial science, statistics, or other analytical field. Students must complete coursework in economics, applied statistics, and corporate finance, and pass a series of exams to become certified professionals.

Education. Actuaries must have a strong background in mathematics, statistics, and business. Typically, an actuary has an undergraduate degree in mathematics, actuarial science, statistics, or other analytical field. Coursework in calculus and business, such as accounting and management, is essential for students as well.

To become certified professionals, students must complete coursework in economics, applied statistics, and corporate finance.

Students should also take classes outside of mathematics and business to prepare them for a career as an actuary. Coursework in computer science, especially programming languages, and the ability to use and develop spreadsheets, databases, and statistical analysis tools, are valuable. Classes in writing and public speaking will improve students' ability to communicate in the business world.

Many students gain experience through internships. In some cases, employers offer their interns permanent jobs after they graduate.

Many employers expect students to have passed at least one of the initial actuary exams needed for professional certification (as described in the Certifications section) before graduation.

Certifications. Two professional societies–the Casualty Actuarial Society (CAS) and the Society of Actuaries (SOA)–sponsor programs leading to full professional status. The CAS and SOA offer two levels of certification: associate and fellowship.

The CAS certifies actuaries who work in the property and casualty field, which includes automobile, homeowners', medical malpractice, and workers' compensation insurance.

The SOA certifies actuaries who work in life insurance, health insurance, retirement benefits, investments, and finance. Most actuaries in the United States are certified by the SOA.

The main requirement for associate certification in each society is the successful completion of exams. The SOA requires that candidates pass five exams for associate (ASA) certification. The CAS requires that candidates pass seven exams for associate (ACAS) certification. In addition, both CAS and SOA require that candidates take seminars on professionalism. Both societies have mandatory e-learning courses for candidates.

It typically takes 4 to 6 years for an actuary to get an ACAS or an ASA certification because each exam requires hundreds of hours of study and months of preparation.

After becoming associates, actuaries typically take another 2 to 3 years to earn fellowship status.

The SOA offers fellowship certification in five separate tracks: life and annuities, group and health benefits, retirement benefits, investments, and finance/enterprise risk management. Unlike the SOA, the CAS does not offer specialized study tracks for fellowship certification.

Both the CAS and the SOA have continuing education requirements. Most actuaries meet this requirement by attending training seminars that are sponsored by their employers or the societies.

Training. Most entry-level actuaries start out as trainees. They are typically on teams with more experienced actuaries who serve as mentors. At first, they perform basic tasks such as compiling data, but as they gain more experience, they may conduct research and write reports. Beginning actuaries may spend time working in other departments, such as marketing, underwriting, and product development, to learn all aspects of the company's work and how actuarial work applies to them.

Most employers support their actuaries throughout the certification process. For example, employers typically pay the cost of exams and study materials. Many firms provide paid time to study

Employment Projections Data for Actuaries

Occupational title	SOC Code	Employment, 2012	Projected Employment, 2022	Change, 2012–2022 Percent	Numeric
Actuaries..	15-2011	24,300	30,600	26	6,300

Source: U.S. Bureau of Labor Statistics, Employment Projections Program

Note: Data are rounded. Go to **Occupational Information Included in the OOH** for a discussion of the data in this table.

Similar Occupations   This table shows a list of occupations with job duties that are similar to those of actuaries.

Occupations	Entry-level Education	2012 Pay	Projected Job Growth	Average Annual Openings
Accountants and Auditors	Bachelor's degree	$63,550	13%	54,420
Budget Analysts	Bachelor's degree	$69,280	6%	2,850
Cost Estimators	Bachelor's degree	$58,860	26%	11,800
Economists	Master's degree	$91,860	14%	740
Financial Analysts	Bachelor's degree	$76,950	16%	10,090
Insurance Underwriters	Bachelor's degree	$62,870	-6%	2,890
Mathematicians	Master's degree	$101,360	23%	170
Personal Financial Advisors	Bachelor's degree	$67,520	27%	9,640
Postsecondary Teachers	See "How to Become One"	$70,380	19%	42,690
Statisticians	Master's degree	$75,560	26%	1,610

and encourage their employees to set up study groups. Employees usually receive raises or bonuses for each exam that they pass.

Licenses. Pension actuaries must be enrolled by the U.S. Department of Labor and U.S. Department of the Treasury's Joint Board for the Enrollment of Actuaries. Applicants must meet certain experience requirements and pass two exams administered through the SOA to qualify for enrollment.

Advancement. Advancement depends largely on job performance and the number of actuarial exams passed. For example, actuaries who achieve fellowship status often supervise the work of other actuaries and provide advice to senior management. Actuaries with a broad knowledge of risk management and how it applies to business can rise to executive positions in their companies, such as chief risk officer or chief financial officer.

Important Qualities

Analytical skills. Actuaries use analytical skills to identify patterns and trends in complex sets of data to determine the factors that have an effect on certain types of events.

Communication skills. Actuaries must be able to explain complex technical matters to those without an actuarial background. They must also communicate clearly through the reports and memos that describe their work and recommendations.

Computer skills. Actuaries must know programming languages and be able to use and develop spreadsheets, databases, and statistical analysis tools.

Interpersonal skills. Actuaries serve as leaders and members of teams, so they must be able to listen to other people's opinions and suggestions before reaching a conclusion.

Math skills. Actuaries quantify risk by using the principles of calculus, statistics, and probability.

Problem-solving skills. Actuaries identify risks and develop ways for businesses to manage those risks.

Pay

The median annual wage for actuaries was $93,680 in May 2012. The median wage is the wage at which half the workers in an occupation earned more than that amount and half earned less. The lowest 10 percent earned less than $55,780, and the top 10 percent earned more than $175,330.

Job Outlook

Employment of actuaries is projected to grow 26 percent from 2012 to 2022, much faster than the average for all occupations. However, because it is a small occupation, the fast growth will result in only about 6,300 new jobs over the 10-year period. Actu-

aries will be needed to develop, price, and evaluate a variety of insurance products and calculate the costs of new risks.

In the health insurance industry, more actuaries will be needed to evaluate the effects that new healthcare laws, such as changes in coverage and expansion of customer pools, pose to insurance companies and to develop new products in response. Changes in healthcare laws will also boost demand for consulting actuaries who evaluate healthcare plans for companies.

More actuaries will be needed in property and casualty insurance to evaluate the risks to properties and communities vulnerable to more frequent and powerful storms. These actuaries will be needed not only to predict the likelihood of such storms, but also to calculate the costs of insuring these properties and help insurance companies create specialized policies and products.

More actuaries will also be needed to help companies manage their own risk, a practice known as enterprise risk management. Actuaries will help companies avoid, manage, and respond to any potential financial risks across all areas of their business operations. This analysis helps companies adjust their business or investment strategies to achieve economic returns and respond to new financial regulations and requirements.

Job Prospects. Actuaries should expect strong competition for jobs. Actuaries make up a small occupation, and the relatively high pay and comfortable working conditions make being an actuary a desirable career. Students who have passed at least two actuarial exams and have had an internship while in college should have the best job prospects for entry-level positions.

O*NET

➤ Actuaries (15-2011.00)

Contacts for More Information

For more information about actuaries, visit
➤ American Academy of Actuaries (www.actuary.org)

For more information about actuaries in property and casualty insurance, visit
➤ Casualty Actuarial Society (www.casact.org)

For more information about actuaries in life and health insurance, retirement benefits, investments, and finance/enterprise risk management, visit
➤ Society of Actuaries (www.soa.org)

For more information about how to become an actuary, visit
➤ Be an Actuary (www.BeAnActuary.org)

For more information about pension actuaries, visit
➤ American Society of Pension Professionals and Actuaries (www. asppa.org)

Mathematicians

- **2012 Median Pay** .... $101,360 per year
  $48.73 per hour
- **Entry-Level Education** ....Master's degree
- **Work Experience in a Related Occupation**.............. None
- **On-the-Job Training** .... None
- **Number of Jobs 2012** 3,500
- **Job Outlook, 2012–22** .... 23% (Much faster than average)
- **Employment Change, 2012–22** 800

Applied mathematicians use math to solve practical problems.

What Mathematicians Do

Mathematicians use advanced mathematics to develop and understand mathematical principles, analyze data, and solve real-world problems.

Duties. Mathematicians typically do the following:

- Expand knowledge in mathematical areas, such as algebra or geometry, by developing new rules, theories, and concepts
- Use mathematical formulas and models to prove or disprove theories
- Apply mathematical theories and techniques to solve practical problems in business, engineering, the sciences, or other fields
- Develop mathematical or statistical models to analyze data
- Interpret data and report conclusions from their analyses
- Use data analysis to support and improve business decisions
- Read professional journals, talk with other mathematicians, and attend professional conferences to maintain knowledge of current trends

The following are examples of types of mathematicians:

Applied mathematicians use theories and techniques, such as mathematical modeling, to solve practical problems. These mathematicians typically work with individuals in other occupations to solve these problems. For example, they may work with chemists and materials scientists and chemical engineers to analyze the effectiveness of new drugs. Other applied mathematicians may work with industrial designers to study the aerodynamic characteristics of new automobiles.

Theoretical mathematicians do research to identify unexplained issues in mathematics and resolve them. They are primarily concerned with exploring new areas and relationships of mathematical theories to increase knowledge and understanding about the field. Although some may not consider the practical use of their findings, the knowledge they develop can be an important part of many scientific and engineering achievements.

Despite the differences, these areas of mathematics frequently overlap. Many mathematicians will use both applied and theoretical knowledge in their job duties.

However, most people with a degree in mathematics or who develop mathematical theories and models are not formally known as mathematicians. Instead, they work in related fields and professions. In the computer systems design and related services industries, they may be known as computer programmers or systems analysts. In finance, they may be known as quantitative analysts, financial analysts, or statisticians.

Computer and information research scientists, physicists and astronomers, economists, actuaries, operations research analysts, and many other occupations also use mathematics extensively.

Some people with a mathematics background become middle school or high school math teachers.

Many people with a Ph.D. in mathematics, particularly theoretical mathematics, work as postsecondary teachers in education institutions. They usually have a mix of teaching and research responsibilities. Some may do individual research or collaborate with other professors or mathematicians. Collaborators may work together at the same institution or from different locations.

Work Environment

Mathematicians held about 3,500 jobs in 2012. Most mathematicians work for the federal government or for private scientific and engineering research and development companies.

Median Annual Wages, May 2012

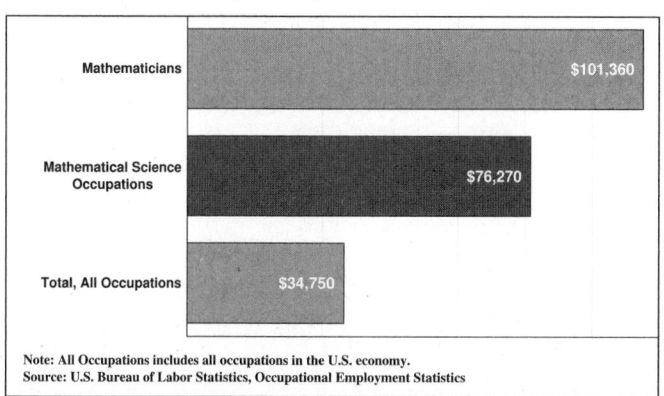

Note: All Occupations includes all occupations in the U.S. economy.
Source: U.S. Bureau of Labor Statistics, Occupational Employment Statistics

Percent Change in Employment, Projected 2012–2022

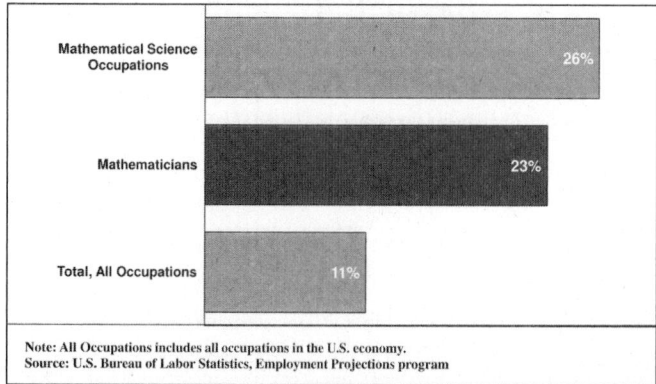

Note: All Occupations includes all occupations in the U.S. economy.
Source: U.S. Bureau of Labor Statistics, Employment Projections program

Employment Projections Data for Mathematicians

Occupational title	SOC Code	Employment, 2012	Projected Employment, 2022	Change, 2012–2022	
				Percent	Numeric
Mathematicians...	15-2021	3,500	4,300	23	800

Source: U.S. Bureau of Labor Statistics, Employment Projections Program

Note: Data are rounded. Go to **Occupational Information Included in the OOH** *for a discussion of the data in this table.*

The industries that employed the most mathematicians in 2012 were as follows:

Federal government 30%
Scientific research and development services 20
Educational services; state, local, and private 18
Management of companies and enterprises............................. 7
Manufacturing.. 3

Mathematicians typically work in comfortable offices. They also may work on teams with engineers, scientists, and other professionals.

Work Schedules. Most mathematicians work full time. Deadlines and last-minute requests for data or analysis may require overtime. In addition, mathematicians may have to travel to attend seminars and conferences.

How to Become One

Mathematicians typically need a master's degree in mathematics. However, there are some positions available for those with a bachelor's degree.

Education. In private industry, mathematicians typically need an advanced degree, either a master's degree or a doctorate. For jobs with the federal government, candidates need at least a bachelor's degree in mathematics or significant coursework in mathematics.

Most colleges and universities offer a bachelor's degree in mathematics. Courses usually include calculus, differential equations, and linear and abstract algebra. Many colleges and universities advise or require mathematics students to take courses in a related field, such as computer science, engineering, physics, or statistics. Candidates who have a double major in mathematics and a related discipline are particularly desirable to many employers.

Many universities offer master's and doctoral degrees in theoretical or applied mathematics. Many students who get a doctoral degree work as professors of mathematics in a college or university, rather than work in government or private industry.

Also, holders of bachelor's degrees who meet state certification requirements may become middle or high school mathematics teachers.

Students who are interested in becoming mathematicians should take as many math courses as possible in high school.

Important Qualities

Analytical skills. Mathematicians use mathematical techniques and models to analyze large amounts of data. They must be precise and accurate in their analysis.

Communication skills. Mathematicians must interact with and propose solutions to people who may not have extensive knowledge of mathematics.

Math skills. Mathematicians use statistics, calculus, and linear algebra to develop their models and analyses.

Problem-solving skills. Mathematicians must devise new solutions to problems encountered by scientists or engineers.

Pay

The median annual wage for mathematicians was $101,360 in May 2012. The median wage is the wage at which half the workers in an occupation earned more than that amount and half earned less. The lowest 10 percent earned less than $56,040, and the top 10 percent earned more than $152,950.

In May 2012, the median annual wages for mathematicians in the top five industries in which these mathematicians worked were as follows:

Scientific research and development services $118,030
Manufacturing... 116,860
Federal government 106,360
Management of companies and enterprises......................... 74,980
Educational services; state, local, and private 66,590

Similar Occupations   This table shows a list of occupations with job duties that are similar to those of mathematicians.

Occupations	Entry-level Education	2012 Pay	Projected Job Growth	Average Annual Openings
Actuaries	Bachelor's degree	$93,680	26%	1,320
Computer Programmers	Bachelor's degree	$74,280	8%	11,810
Computer Systems Analysts	Bachelor's degree	$79,680	25%	20,960
Database Administrators	Bachelor's degree	$77,080	15%	4,030
Financial Analysts	Bachelor's degree	$76,950	16%	10,090
Market Research Analysts	Bachelor's degree	$60,300	32%	18,850
Nuclear Engineers	Bachelor's degree	$104,270	9%	710
Operations Research Analysts	Bachelor's degree	$72,100	27%	3,600
Physicists and Astronomers	Doctoral or professional degree	$105,722	10%	810
Postsecondary Teachers	See "How to Become One"	$70,380	19%	42,690
Statisticians	Master's degree	$75,560	26%	1,610
Survey Researchers	Master's degree	$45,050	18%	560

Job Outlook

Employment of mathematicians is projected to grow 23 percent from 2012 to 2022, much faster than the average for all occupations. However, because it is a small occupation, the fast growth will result in only about 800 new jobs over the 10-year period.

The amount of digitally stored data will increase over the next decade as more people and companies conduct business online and use social media, smartphones, and other mobile devices. As a result, businesses will increasingly need mathematicians to analyze the large amount of information and data collected. Analyses will help companies improve their business processes, design and develop new products, and even advertise products to potential customers.

Mathematicians will also be needed to help information security analysts create data-security systems to protect the confidentiality and personal information of individuals.

Job Prospects. Because the occupation is small and there are relatively few mathematician positions, strong competition for jobs is expected. Despite the strong competition for mathematician positions, many candidates with a background in advanced mathematical techniques and modeling will find positions in other closely related fields.

Those with a graduate degree in math, very strong quantitative and data analysis skills, and a background in a related discipline, such as business, computer science, or statistics, should have the best job prospects. Computer programming skills are also important to many employers.

O*NET

➤ Mathematicians (15-2021.00)

Contacts for More Information

For more information about mathematicians, including training, especially for doctoral-level employment, visit

➤ American Mathematical Society (www.ams.org)

For specific information on careers in applied mathematics, visit

➤ Society for Industrial and Applied Mathematics (www.siam.org)

For information on job openings as a mathematician with the federal government, visit

➤ USAJOBS (www.usajobs.gov)

Operations Research Analysts

- **2012 Median Pay** .... $72,100 per year
  $34.66 per hour
- **Entry-Level Education** .... Bachelor's degree
- **Work Experience in a Related Occupation**............... None
- **On-the-Job Training** .... None
- **Number of Jobs 2012** 73,200
- **Job Outlook, 2012–22** .... 27% (Much faster than average)
- **Employment Change, 2012–22** 19,500

What Operations Research Analysts Do

Operations research analysts use advanced mathematical and analytical methods to help organizations solve problems and make better decisions.

Duties. Operations research analysts typically do the following:

- Identify and define business problems, such as those in production, logistics, or sales

- Collect and organize information from a variety of sources, such as computer databases
- Gather input from workers involved in all aspects of the problem or from others who have specialized knowledge, so that they can help solve the problem
- Examine information to figure out what is relevant to the problem and what methods should be used to analyze it
- Use statistical analysis or simulations to analyze information and develop practical solutions to business problems
- Advise managers and other decision makers on the impacts of various courses of action to take in order to address a problem
- Write memos, reports, and other documents, outlining their findings and recommendations for managers, executives, and other officials

Operations research analysts are involved in all aspects of an organization. They help managers decide how to allocate resources, develop production schedules, manage the supply chain, and set prices. For example, they may help decide how to organize products in supermarkets or help companies figure out the most effective way to ship and distribute products.

Analysts must first identify and understand the problem to be solved or the processes to be improved. Analysts typically collect relevant data from the field and interview clients or managers involved in the business processes. Analysts show the implications of pursuing different actions and may assist in achieving a consensus on how to proceed.

Operations research analysts use sophisticated computer software, such as databases and statistical programs, and modeling packages, to analyze and solve problems. Analysts break down problems into their various parts and analyze the effect that different changes and circumstances would have on each of these parts. For example, to help an airline schedule flights and decide what to charge for tickets, analysts may take into account the cities that have to be connected, the amount of fuel required to fly those routes, the expected number of passengers, pilots' schedules, maintenance costs, and fuel prices.

There is no one way to solve a problem, and analysts must weigh the costs and benefits of alternative solutions or approaches in their recommendations to managers.

Because problems are complex and often require expertise from many disciplines, most analysts work on teams. Once a manager

Operations research analysts can advance by becoming technical specialists or supervisors on more complicated projects.

Median Annual Wages, May 2012

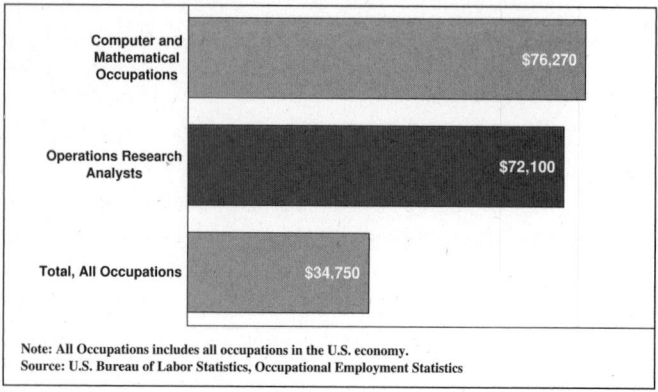

Note: All Occupations includes all occupations in the U.S. economy.
Source: U.S. Bureau of Labor Statistics, Occupational Employment Statistics

Percent Change in Employment, Projected 2012–2022

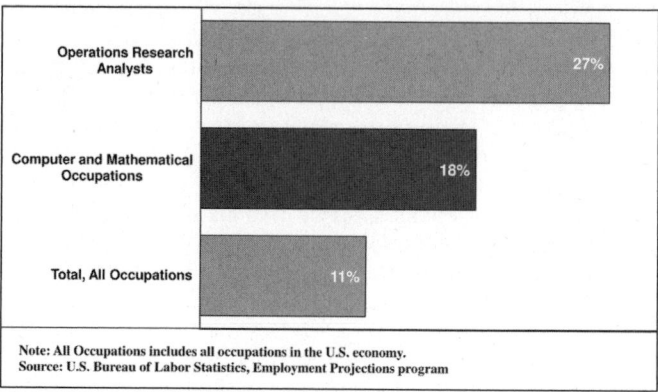

Note: All Occupations includes all occupations in the U.S. economy.
Source: U.S. Bureau of Labor Statistics, Employment Projections program

reaches a final decision, these teams may work with others in the organization to ensure that the plan is successful.

Work Environment

Operations research analysts held about 73,200 jobs in 2012. The industries that employed the most operations research analysts in 2012 were as follows:

Finance and insurance	25%
Computer systems design and related services	10
Manufacturing	8
State and local government, excluding education and hospitals	8
Management of companies and enterprises	8

Most operations research analysts in the federal government work for the Department of Defense, which also employs a large number of analysts through private consulting firms.

Operations research analysts spend most of their time in offices. Many also spend some time in the field, gathering information and analyzing processes through direct observation. Analysts may travel to work with clients and company executives and to attend conferences.

Because problems are complex and often require expertise from many disciplines, most analysts work on teams. Once a manager reaches a final decision, these teams may work with others in the organization to ensure that the plan is successful. Because they work on projects that are of immediate interest to top managers, operations research analysts often are under pressure to meet deadlines.

Work Schedules. Almost all operations research analysts work full time. About 1 in 5 worked more than 40 hours per week in 2012.

How to Become One

Applicants need a master's degree for most operations research positions, but a bachelor's degree is enough for many entry-level positions. Since few schools offer bachelor's and advanced degree programs in operations research, analysts typically have degrees in other related fields.

Education. Although some employers prefer to hire applicants with a master's degree, many entry-level positions are available for those with a bachelor's degree. Although some schools offer bachelor's and advanced degree programs in operations research, many analysts typically have degrees in other technical or quantitative fields, such as engineering, computer science, mathematics, or physics.

Because operations research is based on quantitative analysis, students need extensive coursework in mathematics. Courses include statistics, calculus, and linear algebra. Coursework in computer science is important because analysts rely on advanced statistical and database software to analyze and model data. Courses in other areas, such as engineering, economics, and political science, are useful because operations research is a multidisciplinary field with a wide variety of applications.

Continuing education is important for operations research analysts. Keeping up with advances in technology, software tools, and improved analytical methods is vital.

Other Experience. Many operations research analysts who work with the military are veterans of the U.S. Armed Forces.

Important Qualities

Analytical skills. Operations research analysts use a wide range of methods, such as forecasting, data mining, and statistical analysis, to examine and interpret data.

Communication skills. Operations research analysts need to be able to gather information, which includes interviewing people and listening carefully to the answers. They also need to communicate technical information to people who do not have a technical background.

Critical-thinking skills. Operations research analysts must be able to figure out what information is relevant to their work. They also must be able to evaluate the costs and benefits of alternative solutions before making a recommendation.

Ingenuity. Solutions to operations problems are not usually obvious, and analysts need to be able to think creatively to solve problems.

Employment Projections Data for Operations Research Analysts

Occupational title	SOC Code	Employment, 2012	Projected Employment, 2022	Change, 2012–2022	
				Percent	Numeric
Operations research analysts	15-2031	73,200	92,700	27	19,500

Source: U.S. Bureau of Labor Statistics, Employment Projections Program

Note: Data are rounded. Go to **Occupational Information Included in the OOH** *for a discussion of the data in this table.*

Similar Occupations   This table shows a list of occupations with job duties that are similar to those of operations research analysts.

Occupations	Entry-level Education	2012 Pay	Projected Job Growth	Average Annual Openings
Economists	Master's degree	$91,860	14%	740
Industrial Engineers	Bachelor's degree	$78,860	5%	7,540
Logisticians	Bachelor's degree	$72,780	22%	4,220
Management Analysts	Bachelor's degree	$78,600	19%	24,520
Market Research Analysts	Bachelor's degree	$60,300	32%	18,850
Mathematicians	Master's degree	$101,360	23%	170
Software Developers	Bachelor's degree	$93,640	22%	35,320
Statisticians	Master's degree	$75,560	26%	1,610

Interpersonal skills. Operations research analysts typically work on teams. They also need to be able to convince managers and top executives to accept their recommendations.

Math skills. The models and methods used by operations research analysts are rooted in statistics, calculus, linear algebra, and other advanced mathematical disciplines.

Problem-solving skills. Operations research analysts need to be able to diagnose problems on the basis of information given to them by others. They then analyze relevant information to solve the problems.

Writing skills. Operations research analysts write memos, reports, and other documents outlining their findings and recommendations for managers, executives, and other officials.

Pay

The median annual wage for operations research analysts was $72,100 in May 2012. The median wage is the wage at which half of the workers in an occupation earned more than that amount and half earned less. The lowest 10 percent earned less than $40,550, and the top 10 percent earned more than $129,490.

In May 2012, the median annual wages for operations research analysts in the top five industries in which these analysts worked were as follows:

Manufacturing	$79,630
Computer systems design and related services	74,490
Management of companies and enterprises	72,630
Finance and insurance	67,480
State and local government, excluding education and hospitals	56,670

Job Outlook

Employment of operations research analysts is projected to grow 27 percent from 2012 to 2022, much faster than the average for all occupations. As technology advances and companies seek efficiency and cost savings, demand for operations research analysis should continue to grow.

Operations research analysts will continue to be needed to provide support for the Armed Forces and to assist in the development and implementation of policies and programs in other areas of government.

Technological advances have made it faster and easier for organizations to get data. In addition, improvements in analytical software have made operations research more affordable and more applicable to a wider range of areas. More companies are expected to use operations research analysts to help them turn data into valuable information that managers can use in order to make better decisions in all aspects of their business. For example, operations research analysts will be needed to help businesses improve their manufacturing operations and logistics.

Job Prospects. Opportunities should be better for those who have a master's or Ph.D. degree in operations research, management science, or a related field.

O*NET

➤ Operations Research Analysts (15-2031.00)

Contacts for More Information

For more information about operations research analysts, visit

➤ Institute for Operations Research and the Management Sciences (www.informs.org)

➤ Military Operations Research Society (www.mors.org)

Statisticians

- **2012 Median Pay** .... $75,560 per year
  $36.33 per hour
- **Entry-Level Education** ....Master's degree
- **Work Experience in a Related Occupation**............... None
- **On-the-Job Training** .... None
- **Number of Jobs 2012** 27,600
- **Job Outlook, 2012–22** .... 27% (Much faster than average)
- **Employment Change, 2012–22** 7,400

What Statisticians Do

Statisticians use statistical methods to collect and analyze data and help solve real-world problems in business, engineering, the sciences, or other fields.

Duties. Statisticians typically do the following:

- Apply statistical theories and methods to solve practical problems in business, engineering, the sciences, or other fields
- Decide what data are needed to answer specific questions or problems
- Determine methods for finding or collecting data
- Design surveys or experiments or opinion polls to collect data
- Collect data or train others to do so
- Analyze and interpret data
- Report conclusions from their analyses

Statisticians design surveys, questionnaires, experiments, and opinion polls to collect the data they need. They may also write instructions for other workers on how to collect and arrange the data. Surveys may be mailed, conducted over the phone, collected online, or gathered through some other means.

Some surveys, such as the U.S. census, include data from nearly everyone. For most surveys and opinion polls, however, statisticians use sampling to collect data from some people in a particular group. Statisticians determine the type and size of the sample to be surveyed or polled.

Statisticians use computers with specialized statistical software to analyze data. In their analyses, statisticians identify trends and relationships within the data. They also conduct tests to find out the data's reliability and validity. Some statisticians may help create new statistical software packages to analyze data more accurately and efficiently.

Statisticians present the findings from their analyses and discuss the data's limitations to prevent inaccurate conclusions from being drawn. They may present written reports, tables, charts, and graphs to other team members and to clients. Statisticians also recommend how to improve the design of future surveys or experiments.

Statisticians work in many fields, such as education, marketing, psychology, sports, or any other field that requires collection and analysis of data. In particular, government, healthcare, and research and development companies employ many statisticians.

Government. Nearly every agency in the federal government employs statisticians. These workers develop advanced statistical models for several purposes, such as filling in gaps from nonresponses to surveys. Some statisticians hired by the federal government are known as mathematical statisticians.

Some government statisticians develop and analyze surveys that measure unemployment, wages, or other estimates of jobs and workers. Other statisticians help to figure out the average level of pesticides in drinking water, the number of endangered species living in a particular area, or the number of people who have a certain disease. At national defense agencies, statisticians use computer programs to test the likely outcomes of different defense strategies.

Healthcare. Statisticians known as biostatisticians or biometricians work in pharmaceutical companies, public health agencies, or hospitals. They may design studies to test whether drugs successfully treat diseases or conditions. They may also work for hospitals or public health agencies to help identify the sources of outbreaks of illnesses in humans and animals.

Research and development. Statisticians design experiments for product testing and development. For instance, they may help design experiments to see how car engines perform when exposed to extreme weather conditions. Statisticians may also help develop marketing strategies and prices for consumer goods.

Some people with a degree in statistics or who collect and analyze statistical data, however, may not be formally known as statisticians. Instead, they may work in related fields and professions. In some industries, for example, they may be known as quantitative analysts, financial analysts, data analysts, or data scientists.

Work Environment

Statisticians held about 27,600 jobs in 2012. About a quarter of statisticians worked for government, mostly at the federal level.

The industries that employed the most statisticians in 2012 were as follows:

Federal government 17%
Finance and insurance 12
Educational services; state, local, and private 11

Advanced computer programs have led to jobs for statisticians in many industries.

State and local government, excluding education
    and hospitals 9
Health care and social assistance 8

Federal statisticians are commonly employed at the Census Bureau, the Bureau of Economic Analysis, the National Agricultural Statistics Service, or the Bureau of Labor Statistics.

Statisticians who work for private businesses often work in teams with other professionals. For example, in pharmaceutical companies, statisticians may work with scientists to test drugs for government approval. In insurance companies, they may work with actuaries to calculate the risks of insuring different events.

Statisticians may travel occasionally to meet with team members, set up surveys and research projects, or oversee the collection of data.

Work Schedules. Statisticians typically work full time.

How to Become One

Statisticians typically need a master's degree in statistics, mathematics, or survey methodology. However, a bachelor's degree is sufficient for some entry-level jobs. Research and academic jobs generally require a Ph.D.

Education. Many colleges and universities offer undergraduate and graduate degree programs in statistics. A bachelor's degree in statistics is not needed to enter a graduate program. However, significant coursework in statistics or mathematics is essential. Required subjects for a bachelor's degree in statistics include differential and integral calculus, statistical methods, mathematical modeling, and probability theory.

Many colleges and universities advise or require students to take courses in a related field, such as computer science, engineering,

Median Annual Wages, May 2012

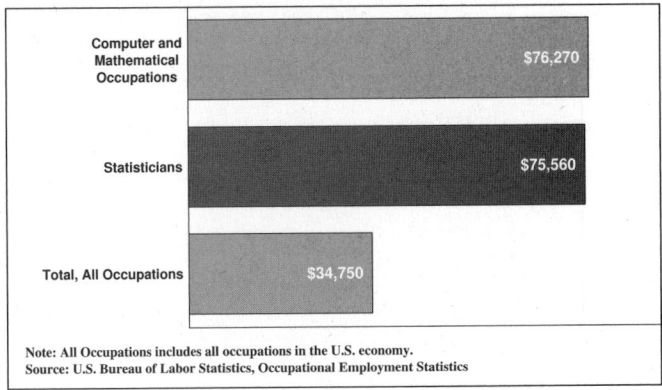

Note: All Occupations includes all occupations in the U.S. economy.
Source: U.S. Bureau of Labor Statistics, Occupational Employment Statistics

Percent Change in Employment, Projected 2012–2022

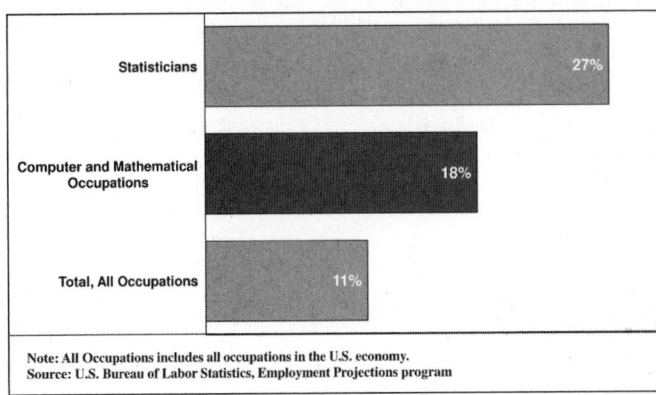

Note: All Occupations includes all occupations in the U.S. economy.
Source: U.S. Bureau of Labor Statistics, Employment Projections program

physics, or mathematics. Candidates with experience in a related discipline are particularly desirable to many employers.

For example, training in engineering or physical science is useful for statisticians working in manufacturing on quality or productivity improvement. A background in biology, chemistry, or health sciences is useful for work testing pharmaceutical or agricultural products.

Because statisticians use and write computer programs for many calculations, a strong background in computer science is also helpful.

Advancement. Opportunities for promotion are greater for people with master's degrees or Ph.D.s. Statisticians with a master's degree or a Ph.D. usually can design their own work. They may develop new statistical methods or become independent consultants.

Important Qualities

Critical-thinking skills. Statisticians use logic and reasoning to identify the strengths and weaknesses of alternative solutions, conclusions, or approaches to problems.

Math skills. Statisticians use statistics, calculus and linear algebra to develop their models and analyses.

Problem-solving skills. Statisticians must develop techniques to overcome problems in data collection and analysis, such as high nonresponse rates, so that they can draw meaningful conclusions.

Speaking skills. Because statisticians often work in teams, they must be able to present statistical information and ideas so that others will understand.

Writing skills. Good writing skills are important for statisticians because they write reports explaining technical matters to persons without their level of statistical expertise.

Pay

The median annual wage for statisticians was $75,560 in May 2012. The median wage is the wage at which half the workers in an occupation earned more than that amount and half earned less. The lowest 10 percent earned less than $42,220 and the top 10 percent earned more than $121,890.

In May 2012, the median annual wages for statisticians in the top five industries in which statisticians worked were as follows:

Federal government	$97,250
Finance and insurance	69,850
Educational services; state, local, and private	66,210
Health care and social assistance	63,420
State and local government, excluding education and hospitals	50,860

Job Outlook

Employment of statisticians is projected to grow 27 percent from 2012 to 2022, much faster than the average for all occupations. Growth is expected to result from more widespread use of statistical analysis to make informed business, healthcare, and policy decisions. In addition, the large increase in available data from the Internet will open up new areas for analysis.

A large amount of data is generated from Internet searching and the use of social media, smartphones, and other mobile devices. Businesses will increasingly need statisticians to organize, analyze, and sort through the data for commercial reasons. Analyses will help companies improve their business processes, design and develop new products, and advertise products to potential customers.

Statisticians will increasingly be needed in the pharmaceutical industry. An aging U.S. population will encourage pharmaceutical companies to develop new treatments and medical technologies. Biostatisticians will be needed to conduct the research and clinical trials necessary for companies to obtain approval for their products from the Food and Drug Administration.

Government agencies will also employ more statisticians to improve the quality of the data available for policy analysis. This occupation will also see growth in research and development in the physical, engineering, and life sciences, where statisticians' skills in designing tests and assessing results are highly useful.

Job Prospects. Job prospects for statisticians are projected to be very good. An increasing number of jobs over the next decade will require high levels of statistical knowledge. Job opportunities are

Employment Projections Data for Statisticians

Occupational title	SOC Code	Employment, 2012	Projected Employment, 2022	Change, 2012–2022	
				Percent	Numeric
Statisticians	15-2041	27,600	34,900	27	7,400

Source: U.S. Bureau of Labor Statistics, Employment Projections Program

Note: Data are rounded. Go to **Occupational Information Included in the OOH** *for a discussion of the data in this table.*

Similar Occupations   This table shows a list of occupations with job duties that are similar to those of statisticians.

Occupations	Entry-level Education	2012 Pay	Projected Job Growth	Average Annual Openings
Actuaries	Bachelor's degree	$93,680	26%	1,320
Computer Systems Analysts	Bachelor's degree	$79,680	25%	20,960
Economists	Master's degree	$91,860	14%	740
Financial Analysts	Bachelor's degree	$76,950	16%	10,090
Market Research Analysts	Bachelor's degree	$60,300	32%	18,850
Mathematicians	Master's degree	$101,360	23%	170
Operations Research Analysts	Bachelor's degree	$72,100	27%	3,600
Survey Researchers	Master's degree	$45,050	18%	560

expected to be favorable for those with very strong quantitative and data analysis skills.

Graduates with a master's degree in statistics and a strong background in a related discipline, such as finance, biology, engineering, or computer science, are projected have the best prospects of finding jobs in their field of study.

O*NET

➤ Statisticians (15-2041.00)
➤ Biostatisticians (15-2041.01)
➤ Clinical Data Managers (15-2041.02)

Contacts for More Information

For more information about statisticians, visit
➤ American Statistical Association (www.amstat.org)

For more information on doctoral-level careers and training in mathematics, a field closely related to statistics, visit
➤ American Mathematical Society (www.ams.org)

For information on job openings for statisticians or mathematical statisticians in the federal government, visit
➤ USAJOBS (www.usajobs.gov)

Media and Communication

Announcers

- **2012 Median Pay** .... $27,750 per year
  $13.34 per hour
- **Entry-Level Education** ....See "How to Become One"
- **Work Experience in a Related Occupation**............... None
- **On-the-Job Training** ....See "How to Become One"
- **Number of Jobs 2012** 52,000
- **Job Outlook, 2012–22** ....2% (Little or no change)
- **Employment Change, 2012–22** 800

What Announcers Do

Announcers present music, news, and sports and may provide commentary or interview guests about these topics or other important events. Some act as masters of ceremonies (emcees) or disc jockeys (DJs) at weddings, parties, or clubs.

Duties. Radio and television announcers typically do the following:

- Present music, news, sports, the weather, the time, and commercials
- Interview guests and moderate panels or discussions on their shows
- Announce station programming information, such as program schedules and station breaks for commercials, or public service information
- Research topics for comment and discussion during shows
- Read prepared scripts on radio or television shows
- Comment on important news stories

Radio announcers who broadcast music often are called disc jockeys, or DJs.

- Provide commentary for the audience during sporting events, at parades, and on other occasions
- Select program content
- Make promotional appearances at public or private events

Radio and television announcers present music or the news and comment on important current events. Announcers are expected to be up to date with current events or a specific field, such as politics or sports, so that they can comment on these issues during their programs. They may research and prepare information on current topics before appearing on air. In addition, announcers schedule guests on their shows and work with producers to develop other creative content.

Radio and television announcers also may be responsible for other aspects of television or radio broadcasting. They may operate studio equipment, sell commercial time to advertisers, or produce advertisements and other recorded material. At many radio stations, announcers do much of the work traditionally done by editors and broadcast technicians, such as broadcasting program schedules, commercials, and public service announcements.

Many radio and television announcers increasingly maintain a presence on social media networking sites. Establishing a presence allows them to promote their stations and better engage with their audiences through listener feedback, music requests, or program contests.

Many radio stations now require DJs to update station websites with show schedules, interviews, or photos.

Public address system and other announcers typically do the following:

- Meet with event directors to review schedules and obtain other event details
- Present information or announcements, such as train schedules or security precautions
- Introduce upcoming acts and guide the audience through the entertainment
- Provide commentary for a live audience during sporting events
- Make promotional appearances at public or private events

The duties of public address system announcers vary greatly depending on where these announcers work. For example, a ringmaster at a circus directs the audience's attention to the appropriate act. A public address system announcer's role is to enhance the performance and entertain and inform the audience. They may prepare their own scripts or improvise lines in their speeches.

Train announcers are responsible for reading prepared scripts containing details and data related to train schedules and safety procedures. Their job is to provide information rather than entertainment.

Public address system announcers for a sports team may have to present starting lineups (official lists of players who will participate in an event), read advertisements, and announce players as they enter and exit a game.

The following are examples of types of announcers:

DJs broadcast music for radio stations. They typically specialize in one kind of music genre and announce selections as they air them. While on air, DJs comment on the music being broadcast as well as on weather and traffic conditions. They may take requests from listeners, interview guests, or manage listener contests.

Median Annual Wages, May 2012

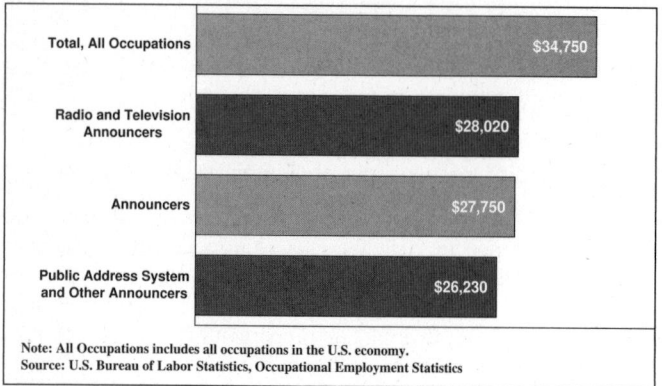

Note: All Occupations includes all occupations in the U.S. economy.
Source: U.S. Bureau of Labor Statistics, Occupational Employment Statistics

Percent Change in Employment, Projected 2012–2022

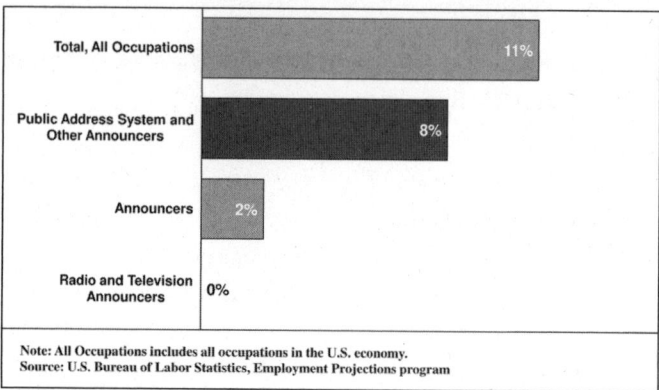

Note: All Occupations includes all occupations in the U.S. economy.
Source: U.S. Bureau of Labor Statistics, Employment Projections program

Talk show hosts may work in radio or television and specialize in a certain area of interest, such as politics, personal finance, sports, or health. They contribute to the preparation of program content, interview guests, and discuss issues with viewers, listeners, or the studio or radio audience.

Public address system announcers provide information to the audience at sporting, performing arts, and other events.

Party DJs are hired to provide music and commentary at an event, such as a wedding, a birthday party, or a corporate party. Many DJs use digital files or portable media devices.

Emcees host planned events. They introduce speakers or performers to the audience. They may tell jokes or provide commentary to transition from one speaker to the next.

Work Environment

Radio and television announcers held about 41,300 jobs in 2012. About 70 percent were employed in the radio and television broadcasting industry, and about 24 percent were self-employed. These self-employed workers can record their shows at home and sell them to networks, individual stations, advertising agencies, or other independent producers.

Public address system and other announcers held about 10,700 jobs in 2012. About 32 percent worked in the arts, entertainment, and recreation industry, and about 25 percent were self-employed.

Radio and television announcers usually work in well-lit, air-conditioned, soundproof studios.

The pressure of deadlines and tight work schedules can be stressful.

Work Schedules. Although most announcers work full time, many work part time.

Many radio and television stations are on air 24 hours a day. Some announcers present early morning shows, when most people are getting ready for work or commuting. Others do late-night programs.

The shifts, however, are not as varied as in the past. Technology has allowed stations to eliminate most of the overnight hours,

because shows that air during the night can now be recorded earlier in the day.

How to Become One

Educational requirements for announcers vary. Radio and television announcers typically have a bachelor's degree in journalism, broadcasting, or communications, along with work experience gained from working at their college radio or television station. Public address announcers typically need a high school diploma, along with short-term on-the-job training.

Education. Although public address announcers do not need any formal education beyond a high school diploma, radio announcers should have a bachelor's degree to be competitive for entry-level positions. Television announcers typically need a bachelor's degree in programs such as communications, broadcasting, or journalism.

College broadcasting programs offer courses, such as voice and diction, to help students improve their vocal qualities. In addition, these programs prepare students to work with the computer equipment and software used at radio and television studios.

Training. Public address system and other announcers typically need short-term on-the-job training upon being hired. This training allows these announcers to become familiar with the equipment they will be using during sporting and entertainment events. For sports public address announcers, training also may go over basic rules and information for the sports they are covering.

Radio and television announcers may also need some short-term on-the-job training to learn to operate the station's equipment. Many employers, however, expect applicants to have some basic skills prior to employment. Applicants typically gain these skills from their college degree program, work on the college radio or television station, or previous internships.

Advancement. Because radio and television stations in smaller markets have smaller staff, advancement within the same small-

Employment Projections Data for Announcers

Occupational title	SOC Code	Employment, 2012	Projected Employment, 2022	Change, 2012–2022	
				Percent	Numeric
Announcers..........	27-3010	52,000	52,700	2	800
Radio and television announcers	27-3011	41,300	41,200	0	0
Public address system and other announcers	27-3012	10,700	11,500	8	800

Source: U.S. Bureau of Labor Statistics, Employment Projections Program

Note: Data are rounded. Go to Occupational Information Included in the OOH *for a discussion of the data in this table.*

Similar Occupations   This table shows a list of occupations with job duties that are similar to those of announcers.

Occupations	Entry-level Education	2012 Pay	Projected Job Growth	Average Annual Openings
Actors	Some college, no degree	The annual wage is not available.	4.1%	2,890
Broadcast and Sound Engineering Technicians	See "How to Become One"	$41,232	9%	3,250
Musicians and Singers	High school diploma or equivalent	The annual wage is not available.	5.2%	5,390
Producers and Directors	Bachelor's degree	$71,350	3%	3,790
Reporters, Correspondents, and Broadcast News Analysts	Bachelor's degree	$37,858	-12%	1,960
Writers and Authors	Bachelor's degree	$55,940	3%	3,180

market station is unlikely. Rather, many radio and television announcers advance by relocating to a station in a larger market.

Announcers typically need a few years at a small-market station to work out the "kinks" of their on-air personalities. During that time, they learn to sound more comfortable and credible as an on-air talent and become more conversational with their audiences and guests. Therefore, time and experience allow applicants to advance to positions in larger markets, which offer higher pay and more responsibility and challenges.

When making hiring decisions, large-market stations rely on announcers' personalities and past performance. Radio and television announcers need to have proven that they can attract, engage, and keep a sizeable audience. Therefore, ratings for an announcer's show in the smaller market can effect advancement opportunities.

Large-market stations also rely on radio and television announcers to do other tasks, such as creating and updating a social media presence on social networking sites, making promotional appearances on behalf of the station, or even selling commercial time to advertisers. Therefore, an applicant needs to have demonstrated versatility and flexibility at the smaller market station.

Important Qualities

Computer skills. Announcers, especially those seeking careers in radio, should have good computer skills and be able to use computers, editing equipment, and other broadcast-related devices.

Interpersonal skills. Radio and television announcers must be able to interview guests and answer phone calls on air. Party disc jockeys (DJs) and emcees should be comfortable working with clients to plan entertainment options.

Persistence. Entry into this occupation is very competitive, and many auditions may be needed for an opportunity to work on the air. Many entry-level announcers must be willing to work for a small station and be flexible to move to a small market to secure their first job.

Research skills. Announcers must research the important topics of the day in order to be knowledgeable enough to comment on them during their program.

Speaking skills. Announcers must have a pleasant and well-controlled voice, good timing, and excellent pronunciation.

Writing skills. Announcers need strong writing skills, because they normally write their own material.

Pay

The median annual wage for radio and television announcers was $28,020 in May 2012. The median wage is the wage at which half the workers in an occupation earned more than that amount and half earned less. The lowest 10 percent earned less than $17,270, and the top 10 percent earned more than $78,630.

The median annual wage for public address system and other announcers was $26,230 in May 2012. The lowest 10 percent earned less than $17,370, and the top 10 percent earned more than $70,890.

In general, announcers working in larger markets earn more than those working in smaller markets.

Job Outlook

Employment of announcers is projected to show little or no change from 2012 to 2022.

Employment of radio and television announcers is projected to show little or no change from 2012 to 2022. Employment of public address system and other announcers is projected to grow 8 percent from 2012 to 2022, about as fast as the average for all occupations.

Improving technology and consolidation of radio and television stations will limit the employment growth for radio and television announcers. Many stations are able to do more tasks with less staff. Advancements in digital technology continue to increase the productivity of radio and television announcers and reduce the time required to edit and distribute material or do other off-air technical and production work.

In addition, radio stations use voice tracking, also called "cyber jockeying," which allows radio announcers to prerecord their segments rather than air them live. A radio announcer can record many segments for use at a later date or even on another radio station.

This technique allows stations to use fewer employees, while still appearing to air live shows. It has eliminated most late-night shifts and allowed multiple stations to use material from the same announcer.

Consolidation among broadcasting companies also may contribute to increasing use of syndicated programming and programs originating outside a station's viewing or listening area.

Despite these limiting factors, the growing number of national news and satellite stations may increase the demand for local radio and television programs. Listeners want local programs with news and information that are more relevant to their communities. Therefore, to distinguish themselves from other stations or other media formats, stations are adding a local element to their broadcasts.

In addition, Internet radio may positively influence employment growth. Startup costs for Internet radio stations are relatively lower than the costs for land-based radio. These stations can cheaply target a specific demographic or listening audience and create new opportunities for announcers.

Demand for public address system announcers will remain stable. These announcers will continue to present important information to customers or provide entertainment for special events.

Job Prospects. Strong competition is expected for jobs as a radio or television announcer. Many of the openings will be due to people leaving jobs and the need to replace workers who move out of smaller markets or out of the radio or television field entirely.

Consolidation of stations has decreased the demand for radio and television announcers and pushed experienced announcers into medium and smaller market stations. Therefore, an entry-level announcer may be competing with an on-air announcer who already has years of experience.

Applicants need to be persistent and flexible because many entry-level positions will require moving to a smaller market city. Small radio and television stations are more inclined to hire beginners, but the pay is low.

Those with a formal education in journalism, broadcasting, or mass communications and with hands-on work experience at a radio or television network will have the best job prospects.

In addition, because announcers may be responsible for gathering video or audio for their programs or for updating and maintaining the station's website, multimedia and computer skills are beneficial.

O*NET

➤ Radio and Television Announcers (27-3011.00)
➤ Public Address System and Other Announcers (27-3012.00)

Contacts for More Information

For more information about the broadcasting industry, in which many announcers are employed, visit
➤ National Association of Broadcasters (www.nab.org)
  For more information on sports public address announcers, visit
➤ National Association of Sports Public Address Announcers (www.naspaa.net/)

Broadcast and Sound Engineering Technicians

- **2012 Median Pay** .... $41,200 per year
                                                    $19.81 per hour
- **Entry-Level Education** ....See "How to Become One"
- **Work Experience in a Related Occupation**............... None
- **On-the-Job Training** ....Short-term on-the-job training
- **Number of Jobs 2012** 121,400
- **Job Outlook, 2012–22** ....9% (As fast as average)
- **Employment Change, 2012–22** 10,600

What Broadcast and Sound Engineering Technicians Do

Broadcast and sound engineering technicians set up, operate, and maintain the electrical equipment for radio and television broadcasts, concerts, sound recordings, and movies and in office and school buildings.

Duties. Broadcast and sound engineering technicians typically do the following:

- Operate, monitor, and adjust audio and video equipment to regulate the volume and ensure quality in radio and television broadcasts, concerts, and other performances
- Set up and tear down equipment for events and live performances

- Record speech, music, and other sounds on recording equipment or computers, sometimes using complex software
- Synchronize sounds and dialogue with action taking place on television or in movie productions
- Convert video and audio records to digital formats for editing on computers
- Install audio, video, and sometimes lighting equipment in hotels, offices, and schools
- Report and repair complex equipment problems
- Keep records of recordings and equipment used

These workers may be called broadcast or sound engineering technicians, operators, or engineers. At smaller radio and television stations, broadcast and sound technicians may do many jobs. At larger stations, they are likely to do more specialized work, although their job assignments may vary day to day. They set up and operate audio and video equipment, and the kind of equipment they use may depend on the particular type of technician or industry.

Duties of broadcast and sound engineering technicians vary by specific focus, but they share many of the same responsibilities.

Audio and video equipment technicians set up and operate audio and video equipment. They also connect wires and cables and set up and operate sound and mixing boards and related electronic equipment.

Audio and video equipment technicians work with microphones, speakers, video screens, projectors, video monitors, and recording equipment. The equipment they operate is used for meetings, concerts, sports events, conventions, and news conferences. They also operate equipment at conferences and at presentations for businesses and universities.

Audio and video equipment technicians may also set up and operate custom lighting systems. They frequently work directly with clients and must provide solutions to problems in a simple, clear manner.

Broadcast technicians set up, operate, and maintain equipment that regulates the signal strength, clarity, and ranges of sounds and

Broadcast technicians set up, operate, and maintain electrical equipment.

Median Annual Wages, May 2012

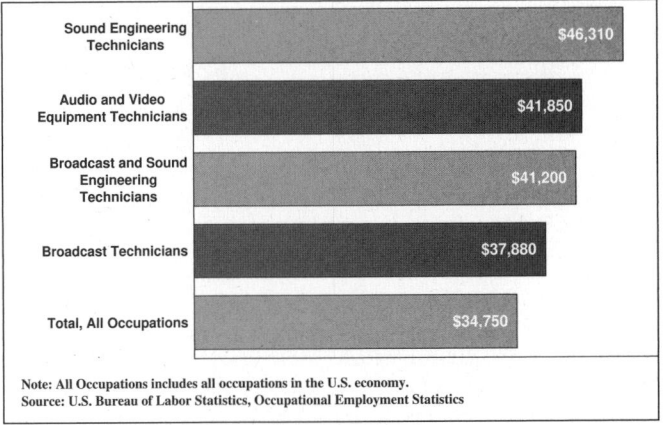

Note: All Occupations includes all occupations in the U.S. economy.
Source: U.S. Bureau of Labor Statistics, Occupational Employment Statistics

Percent Change in Employment, Projected 2012–2022

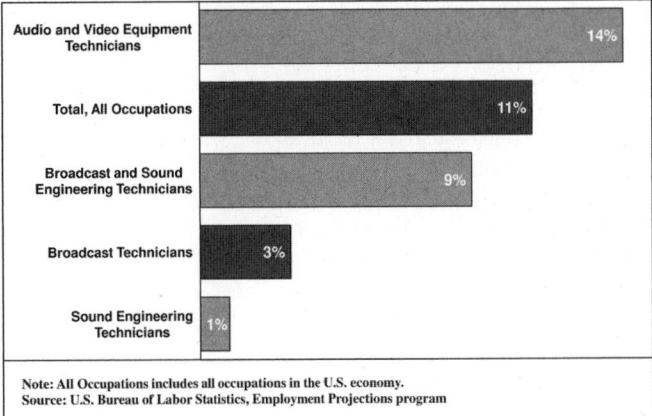

Note: All Occupations includes all occupations in the U.S. economy.
Source: U.S. Bureau of Labor Statistics, Employment Projections program

colors for radio or television broadcasts. They operate transmitters to broadcast radio or television programs and use computer programs to edit audio and video recordings.

Sound engineering technicians operate computers and equipment that record, synchronize, mix, or reproduce music, voices, or sound effects in recording studios, sporting arenas, theater productions, or movie and video productions. They record audio performances or events and may combine tracks that were recorded separately to create a multilayered final product. Sound engineering technicians operate transmitters to broadcast radio or television programs and use computers to program the equipment and edit audio recordings.

(Information on foley artists, a type of sound engineering technician, can be accessed from the *Occupational Outlook Quarterly*—www.bls.gov/ooq/2011/spring/yawhat.htm.)

The following are examples of types of broadcast and sound engineering technicians:

Recording engineers operate and maintain video and sound recording equipment. These engineers work with computers, computer networks, and software to produce special effects for radio, television, or movies.

Sound mixers, or *rerecording mixers,* produce soundtracks for movies or television programs. After filming or recording is complete, these workers often dub the final product by adding or removing sounds.

Field technicians set up and operate portable equipment outside the studio—for example, for television news coverage. Because this coverage requires so much electronic equipment and the technology is changing so rapidly, many technicians are assigned exclusively to news coverage teams.

Chief engineers, transmission engineers, and *broadcast field supervisors* oversee other technicians and maintain broadcasting equipment.

Work Environment

Broadcast and sound engineering technicians held about 121,400 jobs in 2012. Their employment was distributed among the detailed occupations as follows:

Audio and video equipment technicians 67,700
Broadcast technicians 36,700
Sound engineering technicians 17,000

Broadcast and sound engineering technicians typically work indoors in radio, television, movie, or recording studios. However, some work outdoors in all types of conditions to broadcast news and other programming on location. Audio and video technicians

also set up systems in offices, schools, government agencies, hospitals, and homes.

The industries that employed the most broadcast and sound engineering technicians in 2012 were as follows:

Radio and television broadcasting 24%
Television broadcasting.. 17
Motion picture and video industries..................................... 10
Colleges, universities, and professional schools;
  state, local, and private.. 6

Technicians doing maintenance may climb poles or antenna towers, and those setting up equipment do heavy lifting.

Work Schedules. Technicians typically work full time. Some may occasionally work overtime to meet broadcast deadlines or set up for live events. Evening, weekend, and holiday work is common because most stations are on the air 24 hours a day.

Technicians who work on motion pictures may be on a tight schedule and may work long hours to meet contract deadlines with movie studios.

How to Become One

Broadcast and sound engineering technicians typically need postsecondary education, but depending on the work they do, it could be a postsecondary non-degree award or an associate's degree.

Education. Audio and video equipment technicians, as well as sound engineering technicians, typically need a postsecondary non-degree award or certificate, whereas broadcast technicians typically need an associate's degree. However, in some cases they may only need a high school diploma to be eligible for entry-level positions.

Postsecondary non-degree programs for audio and video equipment technicians and sound engineering technicians may take several months to a year to complete. The programs include hands-on experience with the equipment used in many entry-level positions.

Broadcast technicians typically need an associate's degree. In addition to courses in math and science, coursework for prospective broadcast technicians should emphasize practical skills such as video editing and production management.

Prospective broadcast and sound engineering technicians should complete high school courses in math, physics, and electronics. They must have excellent computer skills to be successful.

Important Qualities

Communication skills. Technicians need to communicate with supervisors and coworkers to ensure that clients' needs are met

Employment Projections Data for Broadcast and Sound Engineering Technicians

Occupational title	SOC Code	Employment, 2012	Projected Employment, 2022	Change, 2012–2022	
				Percent	Numeric
Broadcast and sound engineering technicians	—	121,400	131,900	9	10,600
Audio and video equipment technicians	27-4011	67,700	76,900	14	9,300
Broadcast technicians	27-4012	36,700	37,900	3	1,200
Sound engineering technicians	27-4014	17,000	17,100	1	100

Source: U.S. Bureau of Labor Statistics, Employment Projections Program

Note: Data are rounded. Go to Occupational Information Included in the OOH *for a discussion of the data in this table.*

and that equipment is set up properly before broadcasts, live performances, and presentations.

Computer skills. Technicians need computer skills since they use computer systems to program equipment and edit audio and video recordings.

Manual dexterity. Technicians set up audio and visual equipment and cables, which requires a steady hand and good hand-eye coordination. Others adjust small knobs, dials, and sliders during radio and television broadcasts and live performances.

Problem-solving skills. Technicians need to recognize equipment problems and propose possible solutions to them. Employers typically desire applicants with a variety of skills, who are able to set up equipment, maintain the equipment, and troubleshoot and solve any problems.

Training. Because technology is constantly improving, technicians often enroll in continuing education and receive on-the-job training to become skilled in new equipment and hardware. On-the-job training takes less than 6 months and includes topics such as setting up cables or automation systems, testing electrical equipment, learning the codes and standards of the industry, and following safety procedures.

Training for new hires can be accomplished in a variety of ways, depending on the types of products and services the employer provides. Although some formal apprenticeship programs do exist, more frequently a new technician will accompany a more experienced technician to get the training and skills necessary for advancement.

Other Experience. Practical experience working in a high school or college audiovisual department can also help prepare someone to be an audio and video equipment technician.

Licenses, Certifications, and Registrations. Although not required by most employers, earning voluntary certification will offer advantages in getting a job as a broadcast or sound engineering technician. Certification tells employers that the technician meets certain industry standards and has kept up to date with new technologies.

For example, the Society of Broadcast Engineers offers eight broadcast engineering certifications, two operator certifications, and a broadcast networking certification, each of which requires passing an exam. Similarly, InfoComm International offers an audiovisual Certified Technology Specialist credential.

Advancement. Although many broadcast and sound engineering technicians work first in small markets or with small stations in big markets, after they gain the necessary experience and skills they often transfer to larger, better paying radio or television stations. Few large stations hire someone without previous experience, and they value more specialized skills.

Experienced workers with strong technical skills can become supervisory technicians or chief engineers. To become chief engineer at large television stations, technicians typically need a bachelor's degree in engineering or computer science.

Pay

The median annual wage for broadcast and sound engineering technicians was $41,200 in May 2012. The median wage is the wage at which half the workers in an occupation earned more than that amount and half earned less. The lowest 10 percent earned less than $20,680, and the top 10 percent earned more than $79,170.

Median annual wages for broadcast and sound engineering technicians in May 2012 were as follows:

Sound engineering technicians..	$46,310
Audio and video equipment technicians	41,850
Broadcast technicians	37,880

Technicians working in major cities typically earn more than those working in smaller locations.

Job Outlook

Employment of broadcast and sound engineering technicians is projected to grow 9 percent from 2012 to 2022, about as fast as the average for all occupations. Growth is expected to stem from businesses, schools, and radio and television stations seeking new equipment to improve their audio and video capabilities.

Similar Occupations   This table shows a list of occupations with job duties that are similar to those of broadcast and sound engineering technicians.

Occupations	Entry-level Education	2012 Pay	Projected Job Growth	Average Annual Openings
Computer Support Specialists	See "How to Become One"	$49,488	17%	23,650
Electrical and Electronics Engineering Technicians	Associate's degree	$57,850	0%	3,040
Electrical and Electronics Installers and Repairers	Postsecondary non-degree award	$51,081	1%	2,980
Film and Video Editors and Camera Operators	Bachelor's degree	$46,538	3%	510

Employment of audio and visual equipment technicians is projected to grow 14 percent from 2012 to 2022, about as fast as the average for all occupations. Audio and video equipment is in demand in many buildings, where technicians set up new equipment or upgrade and maintain old, complex systems. More companies are increasing their video budgets so they can use video conferencing to reduce travel costs and communicate worldwide with other offices and clients.

An increase in the use of digital signage for schools, hospitals, and hotels also will lead to higher demand for audio and video equipment technicians.

Schools and universities are seeking to improve their audio and video capabilities to attract and keep the best students. They are building classrooms with interactive whiteboards and video equipment so teachers can give more interactive multimedia presentations and record lectures.

Employment of broadcast technicians is projected to grow 3 percent from 2012 to 2022, slower than the average for all occupations. Employment of sound engineering technicians is projected to show little or no change from 2012 to 2022. The television and motion picture industry will continue to need technicians to improve the picture quality of shows and movies. The industry is installing the latest technologies, such as digital or 3D screens, in movie and home theaters and is converting existing theaters to new formats.

Job Prospects. Competition for jobs will be strong. This occupation attracts many applicants who are interested in working with the latest technology and electronic equipment. Many applicants also are attracted to working in the radio and television industry.

Those looking for work in this industry will have the most job opportunities in smaller markets or stations. Those with hands-on experience with complex electronics and software, or with work experience at a radio or television station, will have the best job prospects. In addition, technicians should be versatile since they set up, operate, and maintain equipment, whereas previously technicians typically specialized in one area.

An associate's or bachelor's degree in broadcast technology, broadcast production, computer networking, or a related field will also improve job prospects for applicants.

O*NET

➤ Audio and Video Equipment Technicians (27-4011.00)
➤ Broadcast Technicians (27-4012.00)
➤ Sound Engineering Technicians (27-4014.00)

Contacts for More Information

For more career information and links to employment resources, visit

➤ National Association of Broadcasters (www.nab.org/)

For more information on certification and links to employment information, visit

➤ Society of Broadcast Engineers (www.sbe.org/)

For more information on certification and career information for audio and video equipment technicians, visit

➤ InfoComm International (www.infocomm.org/cps/rde/xchg /infocomm/hs.xsl/index.htm)
➤ National Systems Contractors Association (www.nsca.org/)

Editors

- **2012 Median Pay** .... $53,880 per year
  $25.90 per hour
- **Entry-Level Education** ....Bachelor's degree
- **Work Experience in a Related Occupation**...... Less than 5 years
- **On-the-Job Training** .... None
- **Number of Jobs 2012** 115,300
- **Job Outlook, 2012–22** ....-2% (Little or no change)
- **Employment Change, 2012–22** .... -2,800

What Editors Do

Editors plan, review, and revise content for publication.
Duties. Editors typically do the following:

• Read content and correct for errors in spelling, punctuation, and grammar
• Rewrite copy to make it easier for readers to understand
• Verify facts using standard reference sources
• Evaluate submissions from writers to decide what to publish
• Work with writers to help their ideas and stories succeed
• Plan the content of digital media and publications according to the publication's style and editorial policy
• Develop story and content ideas while being mindful of the audience
• Allocate space for the text, photos, and illustrations that make up a story
• Approve final versions submitted by staff

Editors plan, coordinate, and revise material for publication in books, newspapers, magazines, or websites. Editors review story ideas and decide what material will appeal most to readers. They also review and edit digital media and drafts of books and articles,

Editors check a writer's sources and facts for accuracy.

Median Annual Wages, May 2012

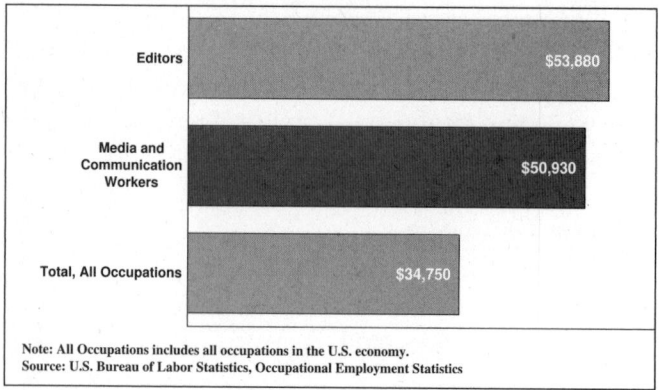

Note: All Occupations includes all occupations in the U.S. economy.
Source: U.S. Bureau of Labor Statistics, Occupational Employment Statistics

Percent Change in Employment, Projected 2012–2022

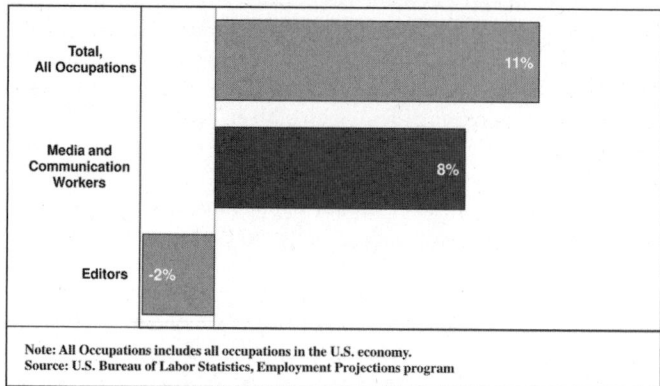

Note: All Occupations includes all occupations in the U.S. economy.
Source: U.S. Bureau of Labor Statistics, Employment Projections program

offer comments to improve the product, and suggest titles and headlines. In smaller organizations, a single editor may perform all of the editorial duties or share them with only a few other people.

The following are examples of types of editors:

Copy editors review copy for errors in grammar, punctuation, and spelling and check the copy for readability, style, and agreement with editorial policy. They suggest revisions, such as changing words and rearranging sentences and paragraphs to improve clarity or accuracy. They also may carry out research, confirm sources for writers, and verify facts, dates, and statistics. In addition, they may arrange page layouts of articles, photographs, and advertising.

Publication assistants who work for book-publishing houses may read and evaluate manuscripts submitted by freelance writers, proofread uncorrected proofs, and answer questions about published material. Assistants on small newspapers or in smaller media markets may compile articles available from wire services or the Internet, answer phones, and proofread articles.

Executive editors oversee assistant editors and generally have the final say about what stories are published and how they are covered. Executive editors typically hire writers, reporters, and other employees. They also plan budgets and negotiate contracts with freelance writers, who are sometimes called "stringers" in the news industry. Although many executive editors work for newspaper publishers, some work for television broadcasters, magazines, or advertising and public relations firms.

Assistant editors are responsible for a particular subject, such as local news, international news, feature stories, or sports. Most assistant editors work for newspaper publishers, television broadcasters, magazines, book publishers, or advertising and public relations firms.

Managing editors typically work for magazines, newspaper publishers, and television broadcasters, and are responsible for the daily operation of a news department.

Work Environment

Editors held about 115,300 jobs in 2012. The industries that employed the most editors in 2012 were as follows:

Newspaper, periodical, book, and directory publishers	48%
Religious, grantmaking, civic, professional, and similar organizations	8
Professional, scientific, and technical services	7
Educational services state, local, and private	5

Although most editors work in offices, a growing number work remotely from home. They often use desktop or electronic publishing software, scanners, and other electronic communications equipment to produce their material.

Jobs are somewhat concentrated in major media and entertainment markets–Boston, Chicago, Los Angeles, New York, and Washington, DC–but improved communications and Internet capabilities allow editors to work from a greater variety of locations.

Work Schedules. Editors' schedules generally are determined by the production schedule and the type of editorial position. Most editors work in busy offices much of the time and have to deal with production deadline pressures and the stresses of ensuring that the information they publish is accurate. As a result, editors often work long hours, especially at those times leading up to a publication deadline, which can be daily or even more frequently when an editor is working on digital material for the Internet or for a live broadcast.

Overseeing and coordinating multiple writing projects simultaneously is common among editors and may lead to stress, fatigue, or other chronic problems.

Freelance editors face the added pressures of finding work on an ongoing basis and continually adjusting to new work environments.

Most editors work full time.

How to Become One

Proficiency with computers and a bachelor's degree in communications, journalism, or English are typically required to be an editor.

Employment Projections Data for Editors

Occupational title	SOC Code	Employment, 2012	Projected Employment, 2022	Change, 2012–2022	
				Percent	Numeric
Editors	27-3041	115,300	112,500	-2	-2,800

Source: U.S. Bureau of Labor Statistics, Employment Projections Program

Note: Data are rounded. Go to **Occupational Information Included in the OOH** *for a discussion of the data in this table.*

Similar Occupations This table shows a list of occupations with job duties that are similar to those of editors.

Occupations	Entry-level Education	2012 Pay	Projected Job Growth	Average Annual Openings
Announcers	See "How to Become One"	$27,652	1%	1,160
Reporters, Correspondents, and Broadcast News Analysts	Bachelor's degree	$37,858	-12%	1,960
Technical Writers	Bachelor's degree	$65,500	15%	2,260
Writers and Authors	Bachelor's degree	$55,940	3%	3,180

Education. Employers generally prefer candidates with a bachelor's degree in communications, journalism, or English. They also prefer candidates with mass- or cross-media experience.

Those with other backgrounds who can show strong writing skills also may find jobs as editors. Editors who deal with specific subject matter may need previous work experience related to that field. Fashion editors, for example, may need expertise in fashion that they gain through formal training or work experience.

Training. The ability to use computers and communications equipment is necessary for editors to stay in touch with writers and other editors and to work on the increasingly important digital media or online side of a publication. Familiarity with electronic publishing, graphics, Web design, and multimedia production is important as well, because more and more material is being read online.

Work Experience in a Related Occupation. Many editors start off as editorial assistants, writers, or reporters.

Those who are particularly skilled at identifying good stories, recognizing writing talent, and interacting with writers may be interested in editing jobs.

Other Experience. Editors can also gain experience by working on their high school and college newspapers, for magazines, radio and television stations, advertising and publishing companies, or for nonprofit organizations. Magazines and newspapers also have internships for students. For example, the American Society of Magazine Editors offers a Magazine Internship Program to qualified full-time students in their junior or senior year of college. Interns may write stories, conduct research and interviews, and gain general publishing experience.

Advancement. Except for copy editors, most editors hold management positions and must make decisions related to running a business. For them, advancement generally means moving up to publications with larger circulation or greater prestige. Copy editors may move into original writing or substantive editing positions, or become freelancers.

Important Qualities

Creativity. Editors must be creative, curious, and knowledgeable in a broad range of topics. Some editors must regularly come up with interesting story ideas and attention-grabbing headlines.

Detail oriented. One of an editor's main tasks is to make sure that material is error-free and matches the style of a publication.

Good judgment. Editors must decide if certain stories are ethical or if there is enough evidence to report them.

Interpersonal skills. In working with writers, editors must have tact and the ability to guide and encourage them in their work.

Language skills. Editors must ensure that all written content has correct grammar, punctuation, and syntax. As a result, strong language skills are essential for an editor.

Writing skills. Editors should enjoy writing and must be excellent writers overall. They must have good knowledge of grammar and punctuation rules and be able to express ideas clearly and logically.

Pay

The median annual wage for editors was $53,880 in May 2012. The median wage is the wage at which half the workers in an occupation earned more than that amount and half earned less. The lowest 10 percent earned less than $29,340, and the highest 10 percent earned more than $104,660.

Job Outlook

Employment of editors is projected to show little or no change from 2012 to 2022, as print media continue to face strong pressure from online publications.

Despite some job growth for editors in online media, the number of traditional editing jobs in print newspapers and magazines is declining and will temper overall employment growth.

Job Prospects. Competition for jobs with established newspapers and magazines will be particularly strong because the publishing industry is projected to decline in employment. Editors who have adapted to online media and are comfortable writing for and working with a variety of electronic and digital tools should have an advantage in finding work. Although the way in which people consume media is changing, editors will continue to add value by reviewing and revising drafts and keeping the style and voice of a publication consistent.

O*NET

➤ Editors (27-3041.00)

Contacts for More Information

For more information about editors, visit
➤ American Copy Editors Society (www.copydesk.org/?homepage=1)
➤ American Society of Magazine Editors (www.magazine.org/asme)
➤ Association of Alternative Newsmedia (www.altweeklies.com)
➤ Radio and Television Digital News Association (www.rtdna.org/)

Film and Video Editors and Camera Operators

- **2012 Median Pay** .... $46,280 per year $22.25 per hour
- **Entry-Level Education** .... Bachelor's degree
- **Work Experience in a Related Occupation** .... None
- **On-the-Job Training** .... None
- **Number of Jobs 2012** 49,500
- **Job Outlook, 2012–22** .... 3% (Slower than average)
- **Employment Change, 2012–22** 1,400

What Film and Video Editors and Camera Operators Do

Film and video editors and camera operators manipulate images that entertain or inform an audience. Camera operators capture a wide range of material for TV shows, motion pictures, music videos, documentaries, or news and sporting events. Editors organize the final productions from the many different images that camera operators capture. They collaborate with producers and directors to create the final production.

Duties. Film and video editors and camera operators typically do the following:

- Shoot and record television programs, motion pictures, music videos, documentaries, or news and sporting events
- Organize raw film footage into a continuous whole
- Collaborate with a director to determine the overall vision of the production
- Discuss filming and editing techniques with a director to improve a scene
- Select the appropriate equipment, from the type of lens to the appropriate lighting
- Shoot or edit a scene based on the director's vision

Most camera operators have one or more assistants working under their supervision. The assistants set up the camera equipment and may be responsible for its storage and care. They also help the operator determine the best shooting angle and make sure that the camera stays in focus.

Likewise, editors usually have one or more assistants. The assistants support the editor by keeping track of each shot in a database or loading raw film into an editing bay. Assistants also may do some of the editing tasks.

The increased use of digital filming has changed the work of a large number of editors and camera operators. Many camera operators prefer using digital cameras because these inexpensive instruments give the operator more flexibility in shooting angles. Digital cameras also have changed the job of some camera assistants: instead of loading film or choosing lenses, they download digital images or choose a type of software program to use with the camera.

Nearly all editing work is done on a computer, and editors often are trained in a specific type of editing software.

The following are examples of types of camera operators:

Studio camera operators work in a broadcast studio and videotape their subjects from a fixed position. There may be one or several cameras in use at a time. Operators normally follow directions that give the order of the shots. They often have time to practice

Most video editing is done digitally.

camera movements before shooting begins. If they are shooting a live event, they must be able to make adjustments at a moment's notice and follow the instructions of the show's director.

Cinematographers film motion pictures. They usually have a team of camera operators and assistants working under them. They determine the angles and types of equipment that will best capture a shot. They also adjust a light in a shot, because that is an important part of how the image looks.

Cinematographers may use stationary cameras that shoot whatever passes in front of them, or they may use a camera mounted on a track and move around the action. Some cinematographers sit on cranes and follow the action. Others carry the camera on their shoulder while they move around the action.

Some cinematographers specialize in filming cartoons or special effects.

Videographers film or videotape private ceremonies or special events, such as weddings. They also may work with companies and make corporate documentaries on a variety of topics. Some videographers post on video-sharing websites for businesses. Most videographers edit their own material.

Many videographers run their own business or do freelance work. They may submit bids, write contracts, and get permission to shoot on locations that may not be open to the public. They also get copyright protection for their work and keep financial records.

Many editors and camera operators, particularly videographers, put their creative work online. If it becomes popular, they gain more recognition, which can lead to future employment or freelance work.

Median Annual Wages, May 2012

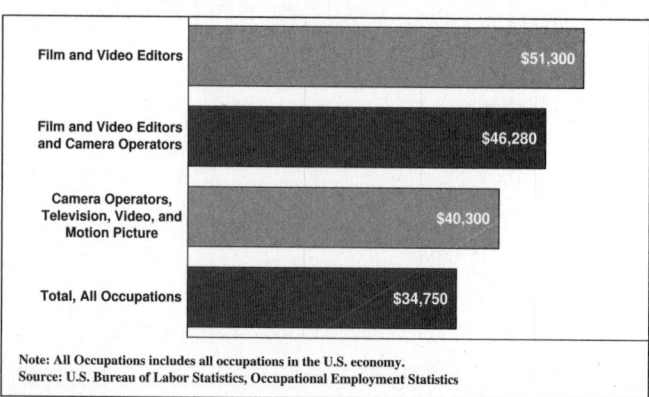

Note: All Occupations includes all occupations in the U.S. economy.
Source: U.S. Bureau of Labor Statistics, Occupational Employment Statistics

Percent Change in Employment, Projected 2012–2022

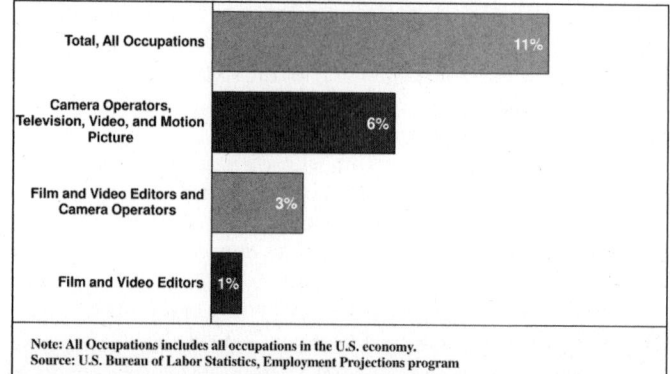

Note: All Occupations includes all occupations in the U.S. economy.
Source: U.S. Bureau of Labor Statistics, Employment Projections program

Employment Projections Data for Film and Video Editors and Camera Operators

Occupational title	SOC Code	Employment, 2012	Projected Employment, 2022	Change, 2012–2022	
				Percent	Numeric
Television, video, and motion picture					
camera operators and editors	27-4030	49,500	50,900	3	1,400
Camera operators, television, video, and motion picture	27-4031	21,400	22,600	6	1,200
Film and video editors	27-4032	28,100	28,300	1	200

Source: U.S. Bureau of Labor Statistics, Employment Projections Program

Note: Data are rounded. Go to **Occupational Information Included in the OOH** *for a discussion of the data in this table.*

Work Environment

Film and video editors and camera operators typically work in studios or in office settings. Camera operators and videographers often shoot raw footage on location.

Film and video editors held about 28,100 jobs in 2012. About 47 percent were employed by motion picture and video industries and 10 percent worked in television broadcasting. About 24 percent of editors were self-employed in 2012.

Camera operators held about 21,400 jobs in 2012. About 28 percent worked in radio and television broadcasting, and another 28 percent worked in motion picture and video industries, and about 22 percent of camera operators were self-employed in 2012.

Film and video editors work in editing rooms by themselves for many hours at a time. Cinematographers and operators who film movies or TV shows may film on location and be away from home for months at a time. Operators who travel usually carry heavy equipment.

Some camera operators work in uncomfortable or even dangerous conditions, such as severe weather, military conflicts, and natural disasters. They may have to stand for long periods waiting for an event to take place. They may carry heavy equipment.

Work Schedules. Work hours vary with the type of operator or editor, although most work full time. Those who work in broadcasting may put in long hours to meet a deadline. Those who work in the motion picture industry may have long, irregular hours while filming, but go through a period of unemployment after their work on the film is complete and before they are hired for their next job.

How to Become One

Film and video editors and camera operators typically need a bachelor's degree in a field related to film or broadcasting.

Education. Most editor and camera operator positions require a bachelor's degree in a field related to film or broadcasting. Many colleges offer courses in camera operation or video-editing software. Coursework involves a mix of film theory with practical training.

Camera operators must have an understanding of digital cameras and editing software because both are now used on film sets. Most editors eventually specialize in one type of software, but beginners should be familiar with as many as possible.

Important Qualities

Communication skills. Film and video editors and camera operators must communicate with other members of a production team, including the director, to ensure that the project goes smoothly.

Computer skills. Film and video editors must use sophisticated editing software.

Creativity. Film and video editors and camera operators should be able to imagine what the result of their filming or editing will look like to an audience.

Detail oriented. Editors look at every frame of film and decide what should be kept and what should be cut to make the best content.

Hand–eye coordination. Camera operators need to be able to move about the action while holding a camera steady.

Visual skills. Camera operators must be able to see clearly what they are filming.

Pay

The median annual wage for film and video editors was $51,300 in May 2012. The median wage is the wage at which half the workers in an occupation earned more than that amount and half earned less. The lowest 10 percent earned less than $25,660, and the top 10 percent earned more than $119,250.

The median annual wage for camera operators was $40,300 in May 2012. The lowest 10 percent earned less than $19,610, and the top 10 percent earned more than $86,000.

Similar Occupations   This table shows a list of occupations with job duties that are similar to those of film and video editors and camera operators.

Occupations	Entry-level Education	2012 Pay	Projected Job Growth	Average Annual Openings
Broadcast and Sound Engineering Technicians	See "How to Become One"	$41,232	9%	3,250
Editors	Bachelor's degree	$53,880	-2%	2,800
Multimedia Artists and Animators	Bachelor's degree	$61,370	6%	2,060
Photographers	High school diploma or equivalent	$28,490	4%	2,030
Producers and Directors	Bachelor's degree	$71,350	3%	3,790
Reporters, Correspondents, and Broadcast News Analysts	Bachelor's degree	$37,858	-12%	1,960

Job Outlook

Employment of film and video editors and camera operators is projected to grow 3 percent from 2012 to 2022, slower than the average for all occupations.

Job growth is expected to be slow in broadcasting because automatic camera systems reduce the need for camera operators at many TV stations. Because of the public's continued strong demand for new movies and TV shows, companies are hiring more people as the motion picture industry becomes more productive.

Production companies and video freelancers are working within new content delivery methods, such as mobile and online TV, which has led to more work for operators and editors. These delivery methods are still in their early stages, yet they provide an opportunity for operators and editors to showcase their work.

In broadcasting, the consolidation of roles, such as field reporters who edit their own work, may lead to fewer jobs for editors at TV stations. However, more editors are expected to be needed in the motion picture industry because of an increase in special effects and content.

Job Prospects. Job openings are projected to be in entertainment hubs such as New York and Los Angeles because specialized editing jobs are needed there. Still, film and video editors and camera operators will face strong competition for jobs. Those with more experience at a TV station or on a film set should have the best prospects.

O*NET

➤ Camera Operators, Television, Video, and Motion Picture (27-4031.00)
➤ Film and Video Editors (27-4032.00)

Contacts for More Information

For more information about film and video editors and camera operators, visit
➤ Motion Picture Editors Guild (www.editorsguild.com)

Interpreters and Translators

- **2012 Median Pay** .... $45,430 per year
  $21.84 per hour
- **Entry-Level Education** ....Bachelor's degree
- **Work Experience in a Related Occupation**............... None
- **On-the-Job Training** ....Short-term on-the-job training
- **Number of Jobs 2012** 63,600
- **Job Outlook, 2012–22** .... 46% (Much faster than average)
- **Employment Change, 2012–22** 29,300

What Interpreters and Translators Do

Interpreters and translators convert information from one language into another language. Interpreters work in spoken or sign language; translators work in written language.

Duties. Interpreters and translators typically do the following:

- Convert concepts in the source language to equivalent concepts in the target language
- Compile information, such as technical terms used in legal settings, into glossaries and terminology databases to be used in translations
- Speak, read, and write fluently in at least two languages, including English and one or more others
- Relay the style and tone of the original language
- Manage work schedules to meet deadlines
- Render spoken messages accurately, quickly, and clearly

Interpreters and translators aid communication by converting message or text from one language into another language. Although some people do both, interpreting and translating are different professions: interpreters work with spoken communication, and translators work with written communication.

Interpreters convert information from one spoken language into another–or, in the case of sign language interpreters, between spoken language and sign language. The goal of an interpreter is to have people hear the interpretation as if it were the original. Interpreters must usually be fluent speakers or signers of both languages, because they communicate back and forth among the people who do not share a common language.

There are three common modes of interpreting: simultaneous, consecutive, and whispered.

Simultaneous interpreters cannot begin interpreting until the general meaning of the sentence is understood. Simultaneous interpreting requires interpreters to listen or watch and speak or sign at the same time someone is speaking or signing. It requires a high level of concentration. For that reason, simultaneous interpreters usually work in pairs, each interpreting for about 20 to 30 minutes and then resting while the other interprets. Simultaneous interpreters are often familiar with the subject matter, so they can anticipate the end of the speaker's sentences.

Consecutive interpreting begins only after the speaker has said or signed a group of words or sentences. Consecutive interpreters may take notes while listening to or watching the speakers before presenting their interpretation. Note taking is an essential part of consecutive interpreting.

Interpreters in *whispered* mode sit very close to the listeners and provide a simultaneous interpretation in a quiet voice. At least two interpreters take turns.

Translators convert written materials from one language into another language. The goal of a translator is to have people read the translation as if it were the original. To do that, the translator must be able to write sentences that maintain or duplicate the structure and style of the original meaning while keeping the ideas and facts of the original meaning accurate. Translators must properly transmit any cultural references, including slang, and other expressions that do not translate literally.

Interpreters and translators must have a thorough understanding of various languages.

Median Annual Wages, May 2012

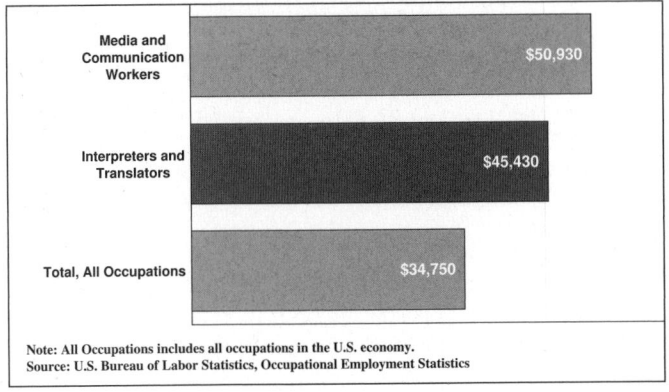

Note: All Occupations includes all occupations in the U.S. economy.
Source: U.S. Bureau of Labor Statistics, Occupational Employment Statistics

Percent Change in Employment, Projected 2012–2022

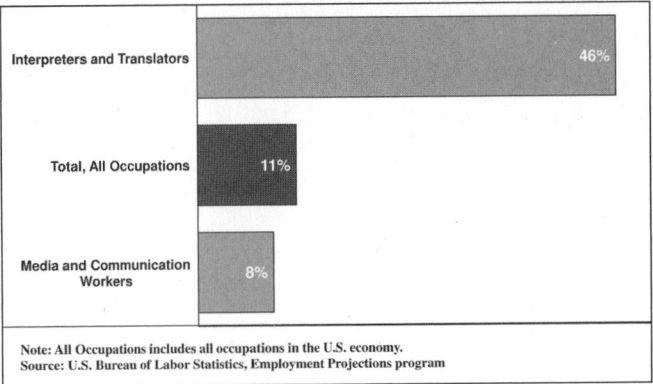

Note: All Occupations includes all occupations in the U.S. economy.
Source: U.S. Bureau of Labor Statistics, Employment Projections program

Translators must read the original language fluently. They usually translate only into their native language.

Nearly all translation work is done on a computer, and translators receive and submit most assignments electronically. Translations often go through several revisions before becoming final.

Translation is usually done with computer-assisted translation (CAT) tools, in which a computer database of previously translated sentences or segments (Translation Memories) may be used to translate new text. CAT tools allow translators to work more efficiently and consistently.

Interpretation and translation services are needed in virtually all subject areas. Although some interpreters and translators do not to specialize in any particular field or industry, many focus on one or several areas of expertise.

The following are examples of types of interpreters and translators:

Conference interpreters work at conferences that have non-English-speaking attendees. The work is often in the field of international business or diplomacy, although conference interpreters can interpret for any organization that works with speakers of foreign languages. Employers generally prefer more experienced interpreters who have the ability to convert from at least two languages into one native language–for example, the ability to interpret from Spanish and French into English. For some positions, such as those with the United Nations, this qualification is required.

Conference interpreters often do simultaneous interpreting. Attendees at a conference who do not understand the language of the speaker wear earphones tuned to the interpreter who speaks the language they want to hear. The interpreter listens to a bit of the speaker's talk and then translates that bit. Simultaneous interpreters must be able to listen to the next bit the speaker is saying while converting the previous bit of what the speaker said.

Guide or escort interpreters accompany either U.S. visitors abroad or foreign visitors in the United States to ensure that they are able to communicate during their stay. These specialists interpret in both formal and informal settings. Frequent travel is common for these workers.

Health or medical interpreters and translators typically work in healthcare settings and help patients communicate with doctors, nurses, technicians, and other medical staff. Interpreters and translators must have knowledge of medical terminology and the common words for medical terms in both languages.

Health or medical interpreters must be sensitive to patients' personal circumstances, as well as maintain confidentiality and ethics.

Health or medical translators often do not have the same level of personal interaction with patients and providers that interpreters do. They primarily convert information brochures, materials that patients must read and sign, website information, and patient records from one language into another language. Interpretation may be provided remotely, by video relay, or over-the-phone.

Legal or judiciary interpreters and translators typically work in courts and other legal settings. At hearings, arraignments, depositions, and trials, they help people who have limited English proficiency. As a result, they must understand legal terminology. Many court interpreters must sometimes read documents aloud in a language other than that in which they were written, a task known as sight translation. Both interpreters and translators must have strong understanding of legal terminology in both languages.

Literary translators convert journal articles, books, poetry, and short stories from one language into another language. They work to keep the tone, style, and meaning of the author's work. Whenever possible, literary translators work closely with authors to capture the intended meaning as well as the literary and cultural characteristics of the original.

Localizers adapt text for a product or service from one language into another, a task known as localization. Localization specialists work to make it appear as though the product originated in the country where it will be sold. They must know not only both languages, but they must also understand the technical information they are working with and the culture of the people who will be using the product or service.

Localization may include adapting websites, software, marketing materials, user documentation, and various other publications. Usually, these adaptations are related to products and services in manufacturing and other business sectors.

Localization may be helped by computer-assisted translation, in which a computer program develops an early draft of a translation for the localization translator. Also, translators may use computers to compare previous translations with specific terminology.

Sign language interpreters facilitate communication between people who are deaf or hard of hearing and people who can hear. Sign language interpreters must be fluent in English and in American Sign Language (ASL), which combines signing, finger spelling, and specific body language. ASL is a separate language from English and has its own grammar.

Some interpreters specialize in other forms of interpreting for people who are deaf or hard of hearing.

Some people who are deaf or hard of hearing lip-read English instead of signing in ASL. Interpreters who work with these people do "oral interpretation," mouthing speech silently and very carefully so that their lips can be read easily. They also may use facial expressions and gestures to help the lip-reader understand.

Other modes of interpreting include cued speech, which uses hand shapes placed near the mouth to give lip-readers more

Employment Projections Data for Interpreters and Translators

Occupational title	SOC Code	Employment, 2012	Projected Employment, 2022	Change, 2012–2022	
				Percent	Numeric
Interpreters and translators...................................	27-3091	63,600	92,900	46	29,300

Source: U.S. Bureau of Labor Statistics, Employment Projections Program

Note: Data are rounded. Go to **Occupational Information Included in the OOH** *for a discussion of the data in this table.*

information; signing exact English; and tactile signing, which is interpreting for people who are blind as well as deaf by making hand signs into the deaf–blind person's hand.

Trilingual interpreters facilitate communication among an English speaker, a speaker of another language, and an ASL user. They must have the versatility, adaptability, and cultural understanding necessary to interpret in all three languages without changing the fundamental meaning of the message.

Work Environment

Interpreters and translators held about 63,600 jobs in 2012. About 1 in 5 were self-employed.

The industries that employed the most interpreters and translators in 2012 were as follows:

Professional, scientific, and technical services.......................... 30%
Educational services; state, local, and private 25
Health care and social assistance... 13
Government... 7

Interpreters work in settings such as schools, hospitals, courtrooms, and conference centers. They must sometimes travel to conferences. Simultaneous interpreting can be stressful, as the interpreter must keep up with the speaker who may not know to slow down when an interpreter is present.

Translators typically work from home. They receive and submit their work electronically. They must sometimes deal with the pressure of deadlines and tight schedules.

Work Schedules. Self-employed interpreters and translators often have variable work schedules, which may include periods of limited work and periods of long, irregular hours. Most interpreters and translators work full time during regular business hours.

How to Become One

Although interpreters and translators typically need at least a bachelor's degree, the most important requirements are that they be fluent in two languages (English and at least one other language). Many complete job-specific training programs. It is not necessary for interpreters and translators to have been raised in two languages to succeed in these jobs, but many grew up communicating in the languages in which they work.

Education. The educational backgrounds of interpreters and translators vary widely, but it is essential that they be fluent in English and at least one other language.

High school students interested in becoming an interpreter or translator should take a broad range of courses that focus on English writing and comprehension, foreign languages, and computer proficiency. Other helpful pursuits for prospects include spending time in a foreign country, engaging in direct contact with foreign cultures, and reading extensively on a variety of subjects in English and at least one other language. Through community organizations, students interested in sign language interpreting may take introductory classes in American Sign Language (ASL) and seek out volunteer opportunities to work with people who are deaf or hard of hearing.

Beyond high school, people interested in becoming interpreters or translators have many educational options. Although many jobs require a bachelor's degree, majoring in a language is not always necessary. Rather, an educational background in a particular field of study can provide a natural area of subject-matter expertise.

Training. Interpreters and translators generally need specialized training on how to do their work. Formal programs in interpreting and translating are available at colleges and universities nationwide and through nonuniversity training programs, conferences, and courses.

Many people who work as interpreters or translators in more technical areas–such as software localization, engineering, or finance–have a master's degree. Those working in the community as court or medical interpreters or translators are more likely to complete job-specific training programs.

Licenses, Certifications, and Registrations. There is currently no universal certification required of interpreters and translators beyond passing the required court interpreting exams offered by most states. However, workers can take a variety of tests that show proficiency. For example, the American Translators Association provides certification in 26 language combinations involving English.

Federal courts provide judiciary certification for Spanish, Navajo, and Haitian Creole interpreters, and many states offer their own certification or licensing. The National Association of Judiciary Interpreters and Translators also offers certification for court interpreting.

The National Association of the Deaf and the Registry of Interpreters for the Deaf jointly offer certification for general sign language interpreters. In addition, the registry offers specialty tests in legal interpreting, speech reading, and deaf-to-deaf interpreting–which includes interpreting among deaf speakers with different native languages and from ASL to tactile signing.

The U.S. Department of State has a three-test series for prospective interpreters–one test in simple consecutive interpreting (for escort work), another in simultaneous interpreting (for court work), and a third in conference-level interpreting (for international conferences)–as well as a test for prospective translators. These tests are not considered a credential, but their completion indicates that a person has significant skill in the occupation.

The International Association of Conference Interpreters offers information for conference interpreters.

The Certification Commission for Healthcare Interpreters offers two types of certifications for healthcare interpreters: one for Associate Healthcare Interpreter (for interpreters of languages other than Spanish, Arabic, and Mandarin), and the other for Certified Healthcare Interpreter (for interpreters of Spanish, Arabic, and Mandarin).

The National Board of Certification for Medical Interpreters offers certification for medical interpreters of Spanish.

Similar Occupations   This table shows a list of occupations with job duties that are similar to those of interpreters and translators.

Occupations	Entry-level Education	2012 Pay	Projected Job Growth	Average Annual Openings
Adult Literacy and High School Equivalency Diploma Teachers	Bachelor's degree	$48,590	9%	1,990
Court Reporters	Postsecondary non-degree award	$48,160	9%	550
High School Teachers	Bachelor's degree	$55,050	6%	31,260
Kindergarten and Elementary School Teachers	Bachelor's degree	$53,060	12%	53,250
Medical Transcriptionists	Postsecondary non-degree award	$34,020	8%	2,240
Middle School Teachers	Bachelor's degree	$53,430	12%	21,120
Postsecondary Teachers	See "How to Become One"	$70,380	19%	42,690
Special Education Teachers	Bachelor's degree	$55,068	6%	10,220
Technical Writers	Bachelor's degree	$65,500	15%	2,260
Writers and Authors	Bachelor's degree	$55,940	3%	3,180

Work Experience in a Related Occupation. Work experience is essential. In fact, some companies hire only interpreters or translators who have related work experience.

A good way for translators to learn firsthand about the occupation is to start working in-house for a translation company. Doing informal or volunteer work is an excellent way for people seeking interpreter or translator jobs to gain experience.

Volunteer opportunities for interpreters are available through community organizations, hospitals, and sporting events, such as marathons, that involve international competitors.

Paid or unpaid internships are other ways that interpreters and translators can gain experience. Escort interpreting may offer an opportunity for inexperienced candidates to work alongside a more experienced interpreter. Interpreters may also find it easier to begin working in industries with particularly high demand for language services, such as court or medical interpreting.

Whatever path of entry new interpreters and translators pursue, they should develop relationships with experienced workers in the field to build their skills, confidence, and network. Mentoring may be formal, such as that through a professional association, or informal, such as with a coworker or an acquaintance that has experience as an interpreter or translator. Both the American Translators Association and the Registry of Interpreters for the Deaf offer formal mentoring programs.

Advancement. After interpreters and translators have enough experience, they can move up to more difficult assignments, seek certification, and obtain editorial responsibility. They can also manage or start their own business.

Many self-employed interpreters and translators start their own business by first establishing themselves in their field. They may submit resumes and samples to different translation and interpreting companies and work for companies that match their skills with a job. Many then get work based on their reputation or through referrals from existing clients.

Important Qualities

Business skills. Self-employed and freelance interpreters and translators need general business skills to manage their finances and careers successfully. They must set prices for their work, bill customers, keep records, and market their services to build their client base.

Concentration. Interpreters and translators must have the ability to concentrate while others are speaking or moving around them.

Cultural sensitivity. Interpreters and translators must be sensitive to cultural differences and expectations among the people whom they are helping to communicate. Successful interpreting and translating is not only a matter of knowing the words in different languages but also of understanding people's cultures.

Dexterity. Sign language interpreters must be able to make quick and coordinated hand, finger, and arm movements when interpreting.

Interpersonal skills. Interpreters and translators, particularly those who are self-employed, must be able to get along with those who hire or use their services in order to retain clients and attract new business.

Listening skills. Interpreters and translators must listen carefully when interpreting for audiences to ensure that they hear and interpret correctly.

Speaking skills. Interpreters and translators must speak clearly in the languages they are conveying.

Writing skills. Interpreters and translators must be able to write clearly and effectively in the languages they translate.

Pay

The median annual wage for interpreters and translators was $45,430 in May 2012. The median wage is the wage at which half the workers in an occupation earned more than the amount and half earned less. The lowest 10 percent earned less than $23,570, and the top 10 percent earned more than $91,800.

In May 2012, the median annual wages in the top four industries in which interpreters and translators worked were as follows:

Professional, scientific, and technical services $54,110
Government 52,740
Educational services; state, local, and private 43,260
Health care and social assistance 40,130

Wages depend on the language, specialty, skill, experience, education, and certification of the interpreter or translator, as well as on the type of employer. Wages of interpreters and translators vary widely. Interpreters and translators who know languages that are in high demand or that relatively few people can translate often earn higher wages. Those who perform services requiring a high level of skill, such as conference interpreters, also receive higher pay.

Self-employed interpreters usually charge an hourly rate. Self-employed translators typically charge a rate per word or per hour.

Job Outlook

Employment of interpreters and translators is projected to grow 46 percent from 2012 to 2022, much faster than the average for all occupations. Employment growth reflects increasing globalization and a more diverse U.S. population, which is expected to require more interpreters and translators.

Demand will likely remain strong for translators of frequently translated languages, such as French, German, Portuguese, Russian, and Spanish. Demand also should be strong for translators of Arabic and other Middle Eastern languages and for the principal Asian languages: Chinese, Japanese, Hindi, and Korean.

Demand for American Sign Language interpreters is expected to grow rapidly, driven by the increasing use of video relay services, which allow people to conduct online video calls and use a sign language interpreter.

In addition, growing international trade and broadening global ties should require more interpreters and translators. The need for military interpreters and translators should result in more jobs as well. Emerging markets in Asia and Africa are expected to increase the need for translation and interpreting in those languages.

Computers have made the work of translators and localization specialists more efficient. However, these jobs cannot be entirely automated. Computers cannot yet produce work comparable to the work that human translators do in most cases.

Job Prospects. Job prospects should be best for those who have at least a bachelor's degree and for those who have professional certification. Those with a master's degree in interpreting and/or translation should also have an advantage.

In addition, urban areas–especially Washington DC, New York, San Francisco, and Los Angeles–should continue to provide the largest numbers of jobs, especially for interpreters.

Job prospects for interpreters and translators should also vary by specialty and language. For example, interpreters and translators of Spanish should have good job prospects because of expected increases in the population of Spanish-speakers in the United States. In particular, job opportunities should be plentiful for interpreters and translators specializing in healthcare and law, because of the critical need for all parties to fully understand the information communicated in these fields.

In addition, there should be many job opportunities for specialists in localization, driven by the globalization of business and the expansion of the Internet.

Interpreters for the deaf will continue to have favorable employment prospects because there are relatively few people with the needed skills.

O*NET

➤ Interpreters and Translators (27-3091.00)

Contacts for More Information

For more information about interpreters, visit
➤ Discover Interpreting (www.discoverinterpreting.com/)

For more information about interpreter and literary translator specialties, including professional certification, visit
➤ American Literary Translators Association (www.utdallas.edu/alta/)
➤ American Translators Association (www.atanet.org/)
➤ Certification Commission for Healthcare Interpreters (www.health careinterpretercertification.org/)
➤ International Association of Conference Interpreters (http://aiic. net/)

➤ National Association of Judiciary Interpreters and Translators (www.najit.org/)
➤ National Board of Certification for Medical Interpreters (www. certifiedmedicalinterpreters.org/)
➤ National Council on Interpreting in Health Care (www.ncihc.org/)
➤ Registry of Interpreters for the Deaf (www.rid.org/)

For more information about testing to become a federal contract interpreter or translator, visit
➤ U.S. State Department (http://languageservices.state.gov/)

Photographers

- **2012 Median Pay** .... $28,490 per year
  $13.70 per hour
- **Entry-Level Education** ... High school diploma or equivalent
- **Work Experience in a Related Occupation** .... None
- **On-the-Job Training** .... Long-term on-the-job training
- **Number of Jobs 2012** 136,300
- **Job Outlook, 2012–22** .... 4% (Slower than average)
- **Employment Change, 2012–22** 5,900

What Photographers Do

Photographers use their technical expertise, creativity, and composition skills to produce and preserve images that visually tell a story or record an event.

Duties. Photographers typically do the following:

- Market and advertise services to attract clients
- Analyze and decide how to compose a subject
- Use various photographic techniques and equipment

Portrait photographers take pictures of individuals or groups of people and often work out of their own studios.

Median Hourly Wages, May 2012

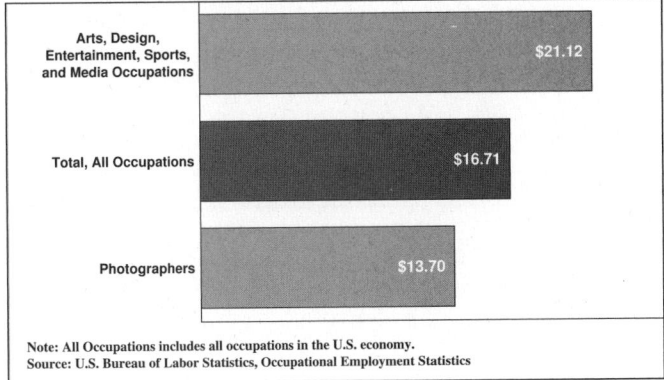

Note: All Occupations includes all occupations in the U.S. economy.
Source: U.S. Bureau of Labor Statistics, Occupational Employment Statistics

Percent Change in Employment, Projected 2012–2022

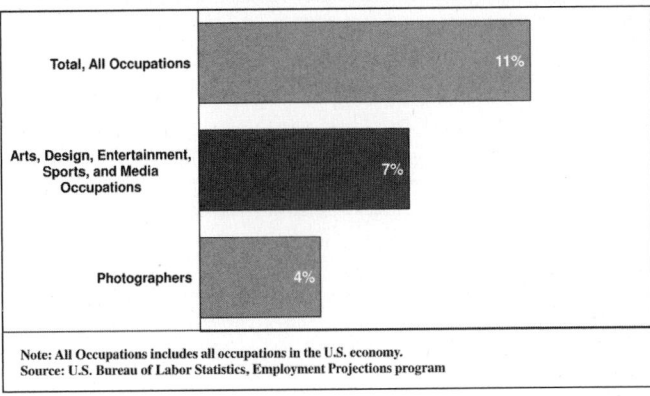

Note: All Occupations includes all occupations in the U.S. economy.
Source: U.S. Bureau of Labor Statistics, Employment Projections program

- Capture subjects in commercial-quality photographs
- Enhance the subject's appearance with natural or artificial light
- Use photo enhancing software
- Maintain a digital portfolio, often on a website, to demonstrate work

Today, most photographers use digital cameras instead of the traditional silver-halide film cameras. Digital cameras capture images electronically, so the photographer can edit the image on a computer. Images can be stored on portable memory devices, such as compact disks, memory cards, and flash drives. Once the raw image has been transferred to a computer, photographers can use processing software to crop or modify the image and enhance it through color correction and other specialized effects. Photographers who edit their own pictures use computers, high-quality printers, and editing software. For information on workers who specialize in developing and processing photographic images from film or digital media, see photographic process workers and processing machine operators included in occupations not covered in detail.

Photographers who work for commercial clients will often present finalized photographs in a digital format to the client. However, wedding and portrait photographers, who primarily serve noncommercial clients, often also provide framing services and present the photographs they capture in albums.

Many wedding and portrait photographers are self-employed. Photographers who own and operate their own business have additional responsibilities. They must advertise, schedule appointments, set and adjust equipment, purchase supplies, keep records, bill customers, pay bills, and–if they have employees–hire, train, and direct their workers.

In addition, some photographers teach photography classes or conduct workshops in schools or in their own studios.

The following are examples of types of photographers:

Portrait photographers take pictures of individuals or groups of people and usually work in their own studios. Photographers who specialize in weddings, religious ceremonies, or school photographs may work on location.

Commercial and industrial photographers take pictures of various subjects, such as buildings, models, merchandise, artifacts, and landscapes. These photographs are used for a variety of purposes, including magazine covers and images to supplement analysis of engineering projects. These photographs are frequently taken on location.

Aerial photographers use planes or helicopters to capture photographs of buildings and landscapes. They often use gyrostabilizers to counteract the movement of the aircraft and ensure high-quality images.

Scientific photographers focus on the accurate visual representation of subjects and limit the use of image manipulation software for clarifying an image. Scientific photographs record scientific or medical data or phenomena. Scientific photographers typically use microscopes to photograph subjects.

News photographers, also called *photojournalists*, photograph people, places, and events for newspapers, journals, magazines, or television. In addition to taking still photos, photojournalists often work with digital video.

Fine arts photographers sell their photographs as artwork. In addition to technical knowledge, such as lighting and use of lenses, fine arts photographers need artistic talent and creativity. Most use traditional silver-halide film instead of digital cameras.

University photographers serve as general photographers for academic institutions. They may be required to take portraits, document an event, or take photographs for press releases. University photographers are found primarily in larger academic institutions, because smaller institutions often contract with freelancers to do their photography work.

Work Environment

Photographers held about 136,300 jobs in 2012.

The industries that employed the most photographers in 2012 were as follows:

Photographic services	27%
Newspaper, periodical, book, and directory publishers	3
Television broadcasting	3
Arts, entertainment, and recreation	2
Junior colleges, colleges, universities, and professional schools; state, local, and private	1

In 2012, about 60 percent of photographers were self-employed.

The work environment for photographers can vary considerably, depending on their specialty.

Portrait photographers may work in studios, but they also often travel to take photographs at a client's location, such as a school, a company office, or a private home.

News and commercial photographers may travel locally or internationally. News photographers often work long, irregular hours in uncomfortable or even dangerous surroundings and must be available to work on short notice. For example, a news photographer may be sent to a war zone to capture images.

Aerial photographers often work in planes or helicopters.

Most photographers stand or walk for long periods while carrying heavy equipment.

Work Schedules. About 1 in 3 photographers worked part time in 2012. Hours often are flexible so they can meet with current and

Employment Projections Data for Photographers

Occupational title	SOC Code	Employment, 2012	Projected Employment, 2022	Change, 2012–2022	
				Percent	Numeric
Photographers	27-4021	136,300	142,200	4	5,900

Source: U.S. Bureau of Labor Statistics, Employment Projections Program

Note: Data are rounded. Go to **Occupational Information Included in the OOH** *for a discussion of the data in this table.*

potential clients or visit the sites where they will work. Demand for certain types of photographers may fluctuate with the season. For example, the demand for wedding photographers typically increases in the spring and summer.

How to Become One

Although postsecondary education is not required for portrait photographers, many take classes since employers usually seek applicants with a "good eye" and creativity, as well as a good technical understanding of photography. Photojournalists and industrial and scientific photographers often need a bachelor's degree.

Education. Although postsecondary education is not required for most photographers, many take classes or earn a bachelor's degree in a related field, which can improve their skills and employment prospects.

Many universities, community and junior colleges, vocational–technical institutes, and private trade and technical schools offer classes in photography. Basic courses in photography cover equipment, processes, and techniques. Art schools may offer useful training in photographic design and composition.

Entry-level positions in photojournalism or in industrial or scientific photography generally require a college degree in photography or in a field related to the industry in which the photographer seeks employment. For example, classes in biology, medicine, or chemistry may be useful for scientific photographers.

Business, marketing, and accounting classes can be helpful for self-employed photographers.

Training. Photographers have a talent or natural ability for taking good photos and this talent is typically cultivated over years of practice. For many artists, including photographers, developing a portfolio–a collection of an artist's work that demonstrates his or her styles and abilities–is essential. This portfolio is necessary because art directors, clients, and others look at an artist's portfolio when deciding whether to hire or contract with the photographer.

Photographers often start working as an assistant to a professional photographer. This work provides an opportunity to gain experience, build their portfolio, and gain exposure to prospective clients.

Important Qualities

Artistic ability. Photographers capture their subjects in images, and they must be able to evaluate the artistic quality of a photograph. Photographers need "a good eye"–the ability to use colors, shadows, shades, light, and distance to compose good photographs.

Business skills. Photographers must be able to plan marketing strategies, reach out to prospective clients, and anticipate seasonal employment.

Computer skills. Most photographers do their own postproduction work and must be familiar with photo editing software. They also use computers to keep a digital portfolio and communicate with clients.

Customer-service skills. Photographers must be able to understand the needs of their clients and propose solutions.

Detail oriented. Photographers who do their own postproduction work must be careful not to overlook details and must be thorough when editing photographs. In addition, photographers accumulate many photographs and must maintain them in an orderly fashion.

Interpersonal skills. Photographers often photograph people. They must communicate effectively to achieve a certain composition in a photograph.

Pay

The median hourly wage for photographers was $13.70 in May 2012. The median wage is the wage at which half the workers in an occupation earned more than that amount and half earned less. The lowest 10 percent earned less than $8.42, and the top 10 percent earned more than $32.21.

Photographers in the District of Columbia earned the highest hourly median wage, earning $33.15 in May 2012.

Similar Occupations   This table shows a list of occupations with job duties that are similar to those of photographers.

Occupations	Entry-level Education	2012 Pay	Projected Job Growth	Average Annual Openings
Architects	Bachelor's degree	$73,090	17%	4,410
Craft and Fine Artists	High school diploma or equivalent	$46,065	3%	1,360
Desktop Publishers	Associate's degree	$37,040	-5%	300
Fashion Designers	Bachelor's degree	$62,860	-3%	590
Film and Video Editors and Camera Operators	Bachelor's degree	$46,538	3%	510
Graphic Designers	Bachelor's degree	$44,150	7%	8,600
Industrial Designers	Bachelor's degree	$59,610	4%	1,210
Printing Workers	See "How to Become One"	$34,110	-5%	5,190
Reporters, Correspondents, and Broadcast News Analysts	Bachelor's degree	$37,858	-12%	1,960

Job Outlook

Employment of photographers is projected to grow 4 percent from 2012 to 2022, slower than the average for all occupations. Overall growth will be limited because of the decreasing cost of digital cameras and the increasing number of amateur photographers and hobbyists. Improvements in digital technology reduce barriers of entry into this profession and allow more individual consumers and businesses to produce, store, and access photographic images on their own.

Employment of self-employed photographers is projected to grow 4 percent from 2012 to 2022. Demand for portrait photographers will continue as people continue to need new portraits. In addition, corporations will continue to require the services of commercial photographers to develop compelling advertisements to sell products.

Declines in the newspaper industry will reduce demand for news photographers to provide still images for print. Employment of photographers in newspaper publishing is projected to decline 36 percent from 2012 to 2022.

Job Prospects. Photographers will face strong competition for most jobs. Because of reduced barriers to entry, there will be many qualified candidates for relatively few positions.

In addition, salaried jobs may be more difficult to obtain as companies increasingly contract with freelancers rather than hire their own photographers. Job prospects will be best for candidates who are multitalented and possess related skills such as picture editing and capturing digital video.

O*NET

➤ Photographers (27-4021.00)

Contacts for More Information

For more information about careers in photography, visit
➤ American Society of Media Photographers (http://asmp.org/)
    For more information about university photographers, visit
➤ University Photographers' Association of America (www.upaa.org/)

Public Relations Specialists

- **2012 Median Pay** .... $54,170 per year
                                                    $26.04 per hour
- **Entry-Level Education** .... Bachelor's degree
- **Work Experience in a Related Occupation** .... None
- **On-the-Job Training** .... None
- **Number of Jobs 2012** 229,100
- **Job Outlook, 2012–22** .... 12% (As fast as average)
- **Employment Change, 2012–22** 27,400

What Public Relations Specialists Do

Public relations specialists create and maintain a favorable public image for the organization they represent. They design media releases to shape public perception of their organization and to increase awareness of its work and goals.

Duties. Public relations specialists typically do the following:

- Write press releases and prepare information for the media
- Respond to information requests from the media
- Help clients communicate effectively with the public
- Help maintain their organization's corporate image and identity

- Draft speeches and arrange interviews for an organization's top executives
- Evaluate advertising and promotion programs to determine whether they are compatible with their organization's public relations efforts

Public relations specialists, also called *communications specialists* and *media specialists*, handle an organization's communication with the public, including consumers, investors, reporters, and other media specialists. In government, public relations specialists may be called *press secretaries*. In this setting, workers keep the public informed about the activities of government officials and agencies.

Public relations specialists draft press releases and contact people in the media who might print or broadcast their material. Many radio or television special reports, newspaper stories, and magazine articles start at the desks of public relations specialists. For example, a press release might describe a public issue, such as health, energy, or the environment, and what an organization does with regard to that issue.

In addition to publication through traditional media outlets, press releases are increasingly being sent through the Internet and social media.

Public relations specialists are different from advertisers in that they get their stories covered by media instead of purchasing ad space in publications and on television.

Work Environment

Public relations specialists held about 229,100 jobs in 2012.

The industries that employed the most public relations specialists in 2012 were as follows:

Religious, grantmaking, civic, professional, and similar
    organizations 20%
Advertising, public relations, and related services 14
Educational services; state, local, and private 12
Government 9
Health care and social assistance 8

Public relations specialists usually work in offices, but they also deliver speeches, attend meetings and community activities, and occasionally travel.

Public relations specialists handle an organization's communication with the public, including consumers, investors, and media outlets.

Median Annual Wages, May 2012

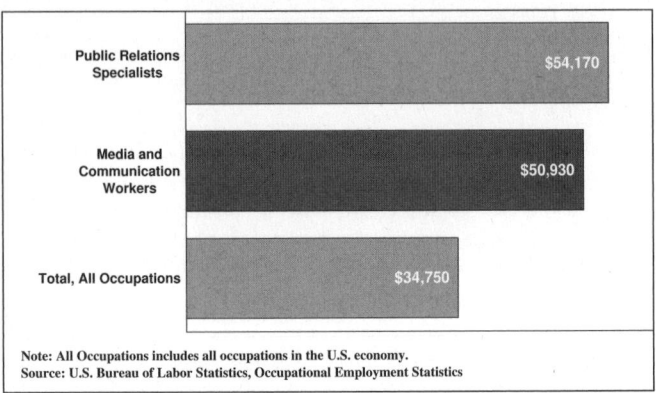

Note: All Occupations includes all occupations in the U.S. economy.
Source: U.S. Bureau of Labor Statistics, Occupational Employment Statistics

Percent Change in Employment, Projected 2012–2022

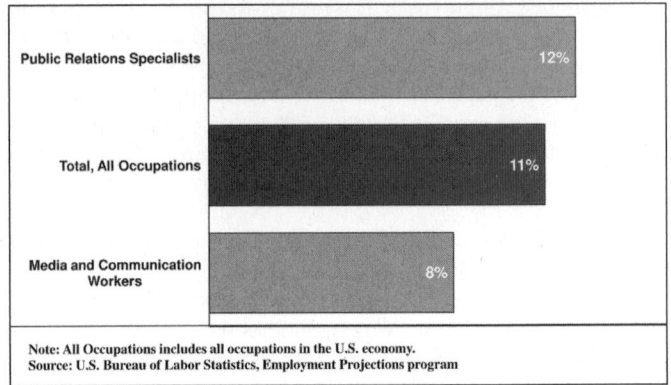

Note: All Occupations includes all occupations in the U.S. economy.
Source: U.S. Bureau of Labor Statistics, Employment Projections program

Work Schedules. Most public relations specialists work full time during regular business hours. Long workdays are common, as is overtime.

How to Become One

Public relations specialists typically need a bachelor's degree. Employers prefer candidates who have studied public relations, journalism, communications, English, or business.

Education. Public relations specialists typically need a bachelor's degree in public relations, journalism, communications, English, or business. Through such programs, students produce a portfolio of work that demonstrates their ability to prospective employers.

Training. Entry-level workers typically begin by maintaining files of material about an organization's activities, skimming and retaining relevant media articles, and assembling information for speeches and pamphlets. After gaining experience, public relations specialists begin to write news releases, speeches, articles for publication, or carry out public relations programs.

Other Experience. Internships at public relations firms or in the public relations departments of other businesses can be helpful in getting a job as a public relations specialist.

Some employers prefer candidates that have experience communicating with others through a school newspaper or a leadership position in school or in their community.

Important Qualities

Interpersonal skills. Public relations specialists deal with the public and the media regularly; therefore, they must be open and friendly to maintain a favorable image for their organization.

Organizational skills. Public relations specialists are often in charge of managing several events at the same time, requiring superior organizational skills.

Problem-solving skills. Public relations specialists sometimes must explain how a company or client is handling sensitive issues.

Employment Projections Data for Public Relations Specialists

Occupational title	SOC Code	Employment, 2012	Projected Employment, 2022	Change, 2012–2022	
				Percent	Numeric
Public relations specialists	27-3031	229,100	256,500	12	27,400

Source: U.S. Bureau of Labor Statistics, Employment Projections Program

Note: Data are rounded. Go to **Occupational Information Included in the OOH** *for a discussion of the data in this table.*

Similar Occupations   This table shows a list of occupations with job duties that are similar to those of public relations specialists.

Occupations	Entry-level Education	2012 Pay	Projected Job Growth	Average Annual Openings
Advertising Sales Agents	High school diploma or equivalent	$46,290	-1%	4,750
Advertising, Promotions, and Marketing Managers	Bachelor's degree	$115,087	12%	7,510
Editors	Bachelor's degree	$53,880	-2%	2,800
Market Research Analysts	Bachelor's degree	$60,300	32%	18,850
Meeting, Convention, and Event Planners	Bachelor's degree	$45,810	33%	4,420
Multimedia Artists and Animators	Bachelor's degree	$61,370	6%	2,060
Public Relations and Fundraising Managers	Bachelor's degree	$95,450	13%	2,130
Wholesale and Manufacturing Sales Representatives	See "How to Become One"	$58,484	9%	53,250
Writers and Authors	Bachelor's degree	$55,940	3%	3,180

They must use good judgment in what they report and how they report it.

Speaking skills. Public relations specialists regularly speak on behalf of their organization. When doing so, they must be able to clearly explain the organization's position.

Writing skills. Public relations specialists must be able to write well-organized and clear press releases and speeches. They must be able to grasp the key messages they want to get across and write them in a short, succinct way to get the attention of busy readers or listeners.

Pay

The median annual wage for public relations specialists was $54,170 in May 2012. The median wage is the wage at which half the workers in an occupation earned more than that amount and half earned less. The lowest 10 percent earned less than $30,760, and the top 10 percent earned more than $101,030.

Job Outlook

Employment of public relations specialists is projected to grow 12 percent from 2012 to 2022, about as fast as the average for all occupations.

Organizations will continue to emphasize community outreach and customer relations as a way to maintain and enhance their reputation and visibility. Public opinion can change quickly, particularly because both good and bad news spreads rapidly through the Internet. Consequently, public relations specialists will be needed to respond to news developments and maintain their organization's reputation.

Increased use of social media also is expected to increase employment for public relations specialists. These media outlets will create more work for public relations specialists as they try to appeal to consumers and the general public in new ways. Public relations specialists will be needed to help their clients use these new types of social media effectively.

Job Prospects. Because many college graduates apply for the limited amount of public relations positions each year, candidates can expect strong competition for jobs.

Candidates can expect particularly strong competition at advertising firms, organizations with large media exposure, and at prestigious public relations firms.

O*NET

➤ Public Relations Specialists (27-3031.00)

Contacts for More Information

For more information about public relations managers, including professional certification in public relations, visit
➤ Public Relations Society of America (www.prsa.org/)
➤ Public Relations Student Society of America (http://prssa.org/)
➤ International Association of Business Communicators (www.iabc.com/)

Reporters, Correspondents, and Broadcast News Analysts

- **2012 Median Pay** .... $37,090 per year
  $17.83 per hour
- **Entry-Level Education** .... Bachelor's degree
- **Work Experience in a Related Occupation** .... None
- **On-the-Job Training** .... None
- **Number of Jobs 2012** 57,600
- **Job Outlook, 2012–22** .... -13% (Decline)
- **Employment Change, 2012–22** .... -7,200

What Reporters, Correspondents, and Broadcast News Analysts Do

Reporters, correspondents, and broadcast news analysts inform the public about news and events happening internationally, nationally, and locally. They report the news for newspapers, magazines, websites, television, and radio.

Duties. Reporters, correspondents, and broadcast news analysts typically do the following:

- Research topics and stories that an editor or news director has assigned to them
- Interview people who have information, analysis, or opinions about a story or article
- Write articles for newspapers, blogs, and magazines and write scripts to be read on television or radio
- Review articles for accuracy and proper style and grammar
- Develop relationships with experts and contacts who provide tips and leads on stories
- Analyze and interpret information to increase their audiences' understanding of the news
- Update stories as new information becomes available

Reporters and correspondents, also called journalists, often work for a particular type of media organization, such as a television or radio station, newspaper, or website.

Those who work in television and radio set up and conduct interviews, which can be broadcast live or recorded for future broadcasts. These workers are often responsible for editing interviews and other recordings to create a cohesive story and for writing and recording voiceovers that provide the audience with the facts of the story. They may create multiple versions of the same story for different broadcasts or different media platforms.

Television reporters often compose stories and report "live" from the scene.

Median Annual Wages, May 2012

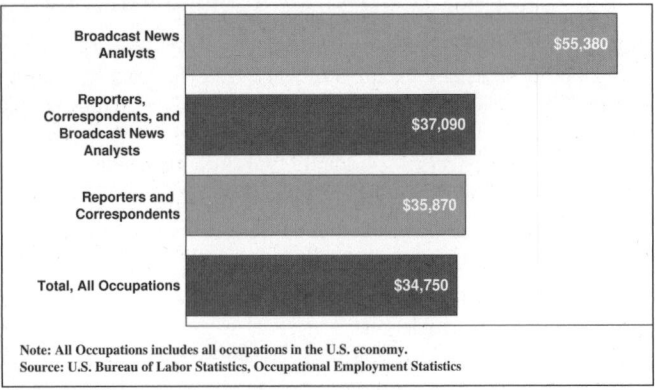

Note: All Occupations includes all occupations in the U.S. economy.
Source: U.S. Bureau of Labor Statistics, Occupational Employment Statistics

Percent Change in Employment, Projected 2012–2022

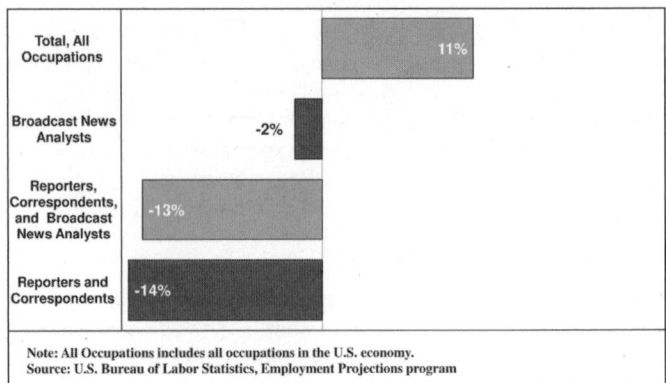

Note: All Occupations includes all occupations in the U.S. economy.
Source: U.S. Bureau of Labor Statistics, Employment Projections program

Most television and radio shows have hosts, also called anchors, who report the news and introduce stories from reporters.

Journalists for print media conduct interviews and write articles to be used in newspapers, magazines, and online publications. Because most newspapers and magazines have both print and online versions, reporters typically produce content for both versions. Doing so often requires staying up to date with new developments of a story, so that the online editions can be updated with the most current information.

Some journalists also may convey stories through both broadcast and print media and help manage the organization's Web content. For example, television stations often have a website, and a reporter may produce a blog post or an article for the website. Similarly, a reporter working for newspapers or magazines may create videos or podcasts that people access online. Depending on the employer, these workers may be known as multimedia producers, social media producers, or Web content managers rather than as reporters or correspondents.

Stations are increasingly relying on multimedia journalists to publish content on a variety of platforms, including radio and television stations, websites, and mobile devices. Multimedia journalists typically shoot, report, write, and edit their own stories. They also gather the audio, video, or graphics that accompany their stories.

Reporters, correspondents, and broadcast news analysts may need to maintain a presence on social media networking sites. Many may use social media to cover live events, provide additional information for readers and viewers, promote their stations and newscasts, and better engage with their audiences.

Some journalists cover a particular topic, such as sports, medicine, or politics. Others cover a wide range of issues.

Journalists working in large cities or for large news organizations are more likely to specialize. Journalists who work in small cities, towns, or organizations may need to cover a wider range of subjects.

Some reporters live in other countries and cover international news. Some journalists, called commentators or columnists, interpret the news or offer opinions to readers, viewers, or listeners.

Although some broadcast news analysts present weather reports, broadcast meteorologists are a type of atmospheric scientist. Many other broadcast news analysts come from fields outside of journalism, for example politics or medicine, and are hired on a contract basis to provide analyses of the subjects being discussed.

Some reporters–particularly those who work for print news–are self-employed and take freelance assignments from news organizations. Freelance assignments are given to writers on an as-needed basis. Because freelance reporters are paid for the individual story, they work with many organizations and often spend some of their time marketing their stories and looking for their next assignment.

Some people with a background as a reporter, correspondent, or broadcast news analyst work as postsecondary teachers and teach journalism or communications at colleges and universities.

Work Environment

Reporters, correspondents, and broadcast news analysts held about 57,600 jobs in 2012. The industries that employed the most reporters, correspondents, and broadcast news analysts in 2012 were as follows:

Newspaper publishers 44%
Television broadcasting 20
Data processing, hosting, related services,
    and other information services 8
Radio broadcasting 5

Reporters, correspondents, and broadcast news analysts spend a lot of time in the field, conducting interviews and investigating stories. Many reporters spend little to no time in an office. They travel to be on location for events or to meet contacts and file stories remotely.

Reporters, correspondents, and broadcast news analysts covering international news often live in other countries. Working on

Employment Projections Data for Reporters, Correspondents, and Broadcast News Analysts

Occupational title	SOC Code	Employment, 2012	Projected Employment, 2022	Change, 2012–2022	
				Percent	Numeric
News analysts, reporters and correspondents	27-3020	57,600	50,400	-13	-7,200
Broadcast news analysts	27-3021	5,900	5,800	-2	-100
Reporters and correspondents	27-3022	51,700	44,600	-14	-7,100

Source: U.S. Bureau of Labor Statistics, Employment Projections Program

Note: Data are rounded. Go to Occupational Information Included in the OOH *for a discussion of the data in this table.*

Similar Occupations This table shows a list of occupations with job duties that are similar to those of reporters, correspondents, and broadcast news analysts.

Occupations	Entry-level Education	2012 Pay	Projected Job Growth	Average Annual Openings
Announcers	See "How to Become One"	$27,652	1%	1,160
Atmospheric Scientists, Including Meteorologists	Bachelor's degree	$89,260	10%	380
Broadcast and Sound Engineering Technicians	See "How to Become One"	$41,232	9%	3,250
Editors	Bachelor's degree	$53,880	-2%	2,800
Film and Video Editors and Camera Operators	Bachelor's degree	$46,538	3%	510
Photographers	High school diploma or equivalent	$28,490	4%	2,030
Postsecondary Teachers	See "How to Become One"	$70,380	19%	42,690
Public Relations and Fundraising Managers	Bachelor's degree	$95,450	13%	2,130
Public Relations Specialists	Bachelor's degree	$54,170	12%	5,880
Technical Writers	Bachelor's degree	$65,500	15%	2,260
Writers and Authors	Bachelor's degree	$55,940	3%	3,180

stories about natural disasters or wars can put reporters in dangerous situations.

Work Schedules. Most reporters, correspondents, and broadcast news analysts work full time. The work is often fast paced, with constant demands to meet deadlines and to be the first reporter to publish a news story on a subject. Reporters may need to work long hours or change their work schedule in order to follow breaking news. Because news can happen at any time of the day, journalists may need to work nights and weekends.

How to Become One

Employers generally prefer workers who have a bachelor's degree in journalism or communications along with an internship or work experience from a college radio or television station or a newspaper.

Education. Most employers prefer workers who have a bachelor's degree in journalism or communications. However, some employers may hire applicants who have a degree in a related subject, such as English or political science, and relevant work experience.

Bachelor's degree programs in journalism and communications include classes in journalistic ethics and techniques for researching stories and conducting interviews. Many programs require students to take liberal arts classes, such as English, history, economics, and political science, so that students are prepared to cover stories on a wide range of subjects.

Some journalism students may benefit from classes in multimedia design, coding, and programming. Because content is increasingly delivered on television, websites, and mobile devices, reporters need to know how to develop stories with video, audio, data, and graphics.

Some schools offer graduate programs in journalism and communications. These programs prepare students who have a bachelor's degree in another field to become journalists.

Other Experience. Employers generally require workers to have experience gained through internships or by working on school newspapers. While attending college, many students seek multiple internships with different news organizations.

Advancement. After gaining more work experience, reporters and correspondents can advance by moving from news organiza-

tions in small cities or towns to news organizations in large cities. Larger markets offer job opportunities with higher pay and more responsibility and challenges. Reporters and correspondents also may become editors or news directors.

Important Qualities

Communication skills. Journalists must be able to report the news both verbally and in writing. Strong writing skills are important for journalists in all kinds of media.

Computer skills. Journalists should be able to use editing equipment and other broadcast-related devices.

Interpersonal skills. To develop contacts and conduct interviews, reporters need to build good relationships with many people. They also need to work well with other journalists, editors, and news directors.

Objectivity. Journalists need to report the facts of the news without inserting their opinion or bias into the story.

Persistence. Sometimes, getting the facts of a story is difficult, particularly when those involved refuse to be interviewed or provide comment. Journalists need to be persistent in their pursuit of the story.

Stamina. The work of journalists is often fast paced, with long and exhausting hours. Reporters must be able to keep up with the long hours.

Pay

The median annual wage for reporters and correspondents was $35,870 in May 2012. The median wage is the wage at which half the workers in an occupation earned more than that amount and half earned less. The lowest 10 percent earned less than $20,770, and the top 10 percent earned more than $78,530.

The median annual wage for broadcast news analysts was $55,380 in May 2012. The lowest 10 percent earned less than $27,450, and the top 10 percent earned more than $170,400.

Job Outlook

Employment of reporters, correspondents, and broadcast news analysts is projected to decline 13 percent from 2012 to 2022. Employment of reporters and correspondents is projected to decline 14 percent while employment of broadcast news analysts is projected to show little or no change. Declining advertising revenue in radio, newspapers, and television will negatively impact the employment growth for these occupations.

Readership and circulation of newspapers are expected to continue to decline over the next decade. In addition, television and radio stations are increasingly publishing content online and on mobile devices. As a result, news organizations may have more difficulty selling traditional forms of advertising, which is often their primary source of revenue.

Declining revenue will force news organizations to downsize and employ fewer journalists. Increasing demand for online news and podcasts (audio or video digital media files that can often be downloaded from a website) may offset some of the downsizing. However, because online and mobile ad revenue is typically less than print revenue, the growth in digital advertising may not offset the decline in print advertising, circulation, and readership.

News organizations also continue to consolidate and increasingly share resources, staff, and content with other media outlets. Reporters are able to gather and report on news for multiple media stations owned by the same corporation, while television stations reuse news and material already gathered by other stations and reporters. As consolidations, mergers, and news sharing continue, the demand for journalists may decrease.

Following a merger or content-sharing agreements, some news agencies may reduce the number of reporters and correspondents on staff. However, in some instances, consolidations may help limit the loss of jobs. Mergers may allow financially troubled newspapers, radio stations, and television stations to keep staff because of increased funding and resources from the larger organization.

Job Prospects. Reporters, correspondents, and broadcast news analysts are expected to face strong competition for jobs, because of both the number of workers who are interested in entering the field and the projected employment declines of both occupations. Those with experience in the field–experience often gained through internships or by working for school newspapers, television stations, or radio stations–should have the best job prospects.

Multimedia journalism experience, including shooting and editing pieces, should also improve job prospects. Because stations are increasingly publishing content on multiple media platforms, particularly on the web, employers may prefer applicants who have experience in website design and coding.

In addition, opportunities will likely be better in small local newspapers or television and radio stations.

Competition will be particularly strong in large metropolitan areas, at national newspapers with higher circulation figures, and at network television stations.

O*NET

➤ Broadcast News Analysts (27-3021.00)
➤ Reporters and Correspondents (27-3022.00)

Contacts for More Information

For more information about broadcast news analysts, visit
➤ National Association of Broadcasters (www.nab.org)
➤ Radio Television Digital News Association (www.rtdna.org/)

For more information about careers in journalism and about internships, visit
➤ Dow Jones News Fund (www.newsfund.org/)
➤ Society of Professional Journalists (www.spj.org/)

Technical Writers

- **2012 Median Pay** .... $65,500 per year
$31.49 per hour
- **Entry-Level Education** ....Bachelor's degree
- **Work Experience in a Related Occupation**...... Less than 5 years
- **On-the-Job Training** ....Short-term on-the-job training
- **Number of Jobs 2012** 49,500
- **Job Outlook, 2012–22** .... 15% (Faster than average)
- **Employment Change, 2012–22** 7,400

What Technical Writers Do

Technical writers, also called *technical communicators*, prepare instruction manuals, journal articles, and other supporting documents to communicate complex and technical information more easily. They also develop, gather, and disseminate technical information among customers, designers, and manufacturers.

Duties. Technical writers typically do the following:

- Determine the needs of end users of technical documentation
- Study product samples and talk with product designers and developers
- Work with technical staff to make products easier to use and thus need fewer instructions
- Organize and write supporting documents for products
- Use photographs, drawings, diagrams, animation, and charts that increase users' understanding
- Select appropriate medium for message or audience, such as manuals or online videos
- Standardize content across platforms and media
- Gather usability feedback from customers, designers, and manufacturers
- Revise documents as new issues arise

Technical writers create operating instructions, how-to manuals, assembly instructions, and "frequently asked questions" pages to help technical support staff, consumers, and other users within a company or an industry. After a product is released, technical writers also may

Technical writers use computer and communications technologies extensively, which allows them to work from home or wherever their work takes them.

Median Annual Wages, May 2012

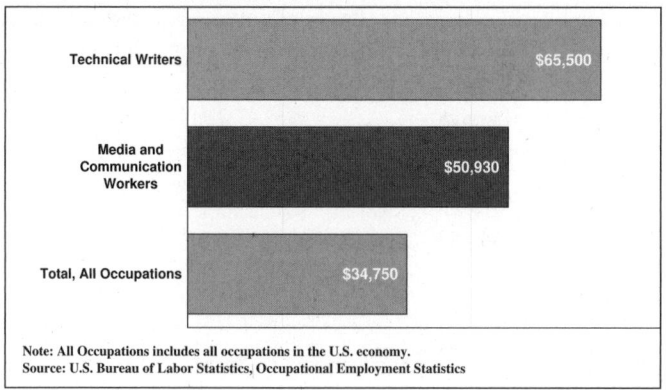

Note: All Occupations includes all occupations in the U.S. economy.
Source: U.S. Bureau of Labor Statistics, Occupational Employment Statistics

Percent Change in Employment, Projected 2012–2022

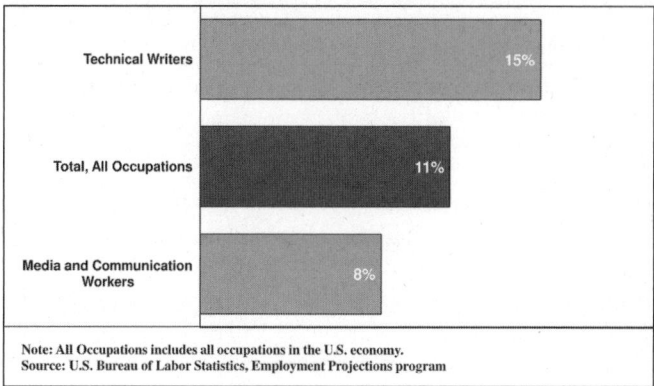

Note: All Occupations includes all occupations in the U.S. economy.
Source: U.S. Bureau of Labor Statistics, Employment Projections program

work with product liability specialists and customer service managers to improve the end-user experience through product design changes.

Technical writers often work with computer hardware engineers, scientists, computer support specialists, and software developers to manage the flow of information among project workgroups during development and testing. Therefore, technical writers must be able to understand complex information and communicate the information to people with diverse professional backgrounds.

Applying their knowledge of the user of the product, technical writers may serve as part of a team conducting usability studies to help improve the design of a product that is in the prototype stage. Technical writers may conduct research on their topics through personal observation, library and Internet research, and discussions with technical specialists.

Some technical writers help write grant proposals for research scientists and institutions.

Increasingly, technical information is being delivered online, and technical writers are using the interactive technologies of the Web to blend text, graphics, multidimensional images, sound, and video.

Work Environment

Technical writers held about 49,500 jobs in 2012. The industries employing the most technical writers in 2012 were as follows:

Professional, scientific, and technical services......................... 38%
Manufacturing... 17
Information 12
Administrative and support and waste management
   and remediation services 6

Most technical writers work in offices. They routinely work with engineers and other technology experts to manage the flow of information throughout an organization.

Although most technical writers are employed directly by the companies that use their services, some work on a freelance basis and are paid per assignment. Either they are self-employed, or they work for a technical consulting firm and are given specific short-term or recurring assignments, such as writing about a new

product or coordinating the work and communication among different offices to keep a project on track.

Technical writing jobs are usually concentrated in locations with information technology or scientific and technical research companies, such as California and Texas.

Work Schedules. Technical writers may be expected to work evenings and weekends to coordinate with those in other time zones or to meet deadlines. Most work full time.

How to Become One

A college degree is usually required for a position as a technical writer. In addition, experience with a technical subject, such as computer science, Web design, or engineering, is important.

Education. Employers generally prefer candidates with a bachelor's degree in journalism, English, or communications. Many technical writing jobs require both a degree and knowledge in a specialized field, such as engineering, computer science, or medicine. Web design experience also is helpful because of the growing use of online technical documentation.

Work Experience

Some technical writers begin their careers not as writers, but as specialists or research assistants in a technical field. By developing technical communication skills, they eventually assume primary responsibilities for technical writing. In small firms, beginning technical writers may work on projects right away; in larger companies with more standard procedures, beginners may observe experienced technical writers and interact with specialists before being assigned projects.

Training. Many technical writers need short-term on-the-job training to adapt to a different style of writing.

Licenses, Certifications, and Registrations. Some associations, including the Society for Technical Communication, offers certification for technical writers. In addition, the American Medical Writers Association offers extensive continuing education programs and certificates in medical writing. These certificates are available to professionals in the medical and allied scientific communication fields.

Employment Projections Data for Technical Writers

Occupational title	SOC Code	Employment, 2012	Projected Employment, 2022	Change, 2012–2022 Percent	Change, 2012–2022 Numeric
Technical writers	27-3042	49,500	56,900	15	7,400

Source: U.S. Bureau of Labor Statistics, Employment Projections Program

Note: Data are rounded. Go to Occupational Information Included in the OOH for a discussion of the data in this table.

Similar Occupations   This table shows a list of occupations with job duties that are similar to those of technical writers.

Occupations	Entry-level Education	2012 Pay	Projected Job Growth	Average Annual Openings
Computer Hardware Engineers	Bachelor's degree	$100,920	7%	2,410
Computer Programmers	Bachelor's degree	$74,280	8%	11,810
Editors	Bachelor's degree	$53,880	-2%	2,800
Interpreters and Translators	Bachelor's degree	$45,430	46%	3,810
Public Relations and Fundraising Managers	Bachelor's degree	$95,450	13%	2,130
Public Relations Specialists	Bachelor's degree	$54,170	12%	5,880
Writers and Authors	Bachelor's degree	$55,940	3%	3,180

Although not mandatory, certification can demonstrate competence and professionalism, making candidates more attractive to employers. It can also increase a technical writer's opportunities for advancement.

Advancement. Prospects for advancement generally include working on more complex projects and leading or training junior staff. Some technical writers become self-employed and produce work on a freelance basis.

Important Qualities

Communication skills. Technical writers must be able to take complex, technical information and translate it for colleagues and consumers who have nontechnical backgrounds.

Detail oriented. Technical writers create detailed instructions for others to follow. As a result, they must be detailed and precise at every step so that the instructions can be useful.

Imagination. Technical writers must be able to think about a procedure or product in the way that a person without technical experience would think about it.

Teamwork. Technical writers must be able to work well with others. They are almost always part of a team: with other writers; with designers, editors, and illustrators; and with the technical people whose information they are explaining.

Technical skills. Technical writers must be able to understand and then explain highly technical information. Many technical writers need a background in engineering or computer science in order to do this.

Writing skills. Technical communicators must have excellent writing skills to be able to explain technical information clearly.

Pay

The median annual wage for technical writers was $65,500 in May 2012. The median wage is the wage at which half the workers in an occupation earned more than that amount and half earned less. The lowest 10 percent earned less than $38,700 and the highest 10 percent earned more than $101,660.

In May 2012, the median annual wages for technical writers in the top four industries in which these writers worked were as follows:

Information	$70,460
Administrative and support and waste management and remediation services	67,140
Professional, scientific, and technical services	66,440
Manufacturing	64,170

Job Outlook

Employment of technical writers is projected to grow 15 percent from 2012 to 2022, faster than the average for all occupations.

Employment growth will be driven by the continuing expansion of scientific and technical products and by growth in Web-based product support. Growth and change in the high-technology and electronics industries will result in a greater need for those who can write instruction manuals and communicate information clearly to users.

Professional, scientific, and technical services firms will continue to grow rapidly and should be a good source of new jobs even as the occupation finds acceptance in a broader range of industries, including data processing, hosting, and related services.

Job Prospects. Job opportunities, especially for applicants with technical skills, are expected to be good. The growing reliance on technologically sophisticated products in the home and the workplace and the increasing complexity of medical and scientific information needed for daily living will create many new job opportunities for technical writers.

In addition, the need to replace workers who retire over the coming decade will result in some job openings. However, there will be competition among freelance technical writers.

O*NET

➤ Technical Writers (27-3042.00)

Contacts for More Information

For more information about technical writers, visit
➤ American Medical Writers Association (www.amwa.org/)
➤ National Association of Science Writers (www.nasw.org/)
➤ Society for Technical Communication (www.stc.org/)

Writers and Authors

- **2012 Median Pay** .... $55,940 per year
  $26.89 per hour
- **Entry-Level Education** ....Bachelor's degree
- **Work Experience in a Related Occupation**............... None
- **On-the-Job Training** .... Moderate-term on-the-job training
- **Number of Jobs 2012** 129,100
- **Job Outlook, 2012–22** .... 3% (Slower than average)
- **Employment Change, 2012–22** 3,800

What Writers and Authors Do

Writers and authors develop written content for advertisements, books, magazines, movie and television scripts, songs, and online publications.

Duties. Writers and authors typically do the following:

- Choose subject matter that interests readers
- Write fiction or nonfiction through scripts, novels, and biographies

Writers and authors work in an office or wherever they have a computer.

- Conduct research to obtain factual information and authentic detail
- Write advertising copy for use by newspapers, magazines, broadcasts, and the Internet
- Present drafts to editors and clients for feedback
- Work with editors and clients to shape the material so it can be published

Writers and authors develop written material, namely, stories and advertisements, for books, magazines, and online publications.

Writers must establish their credibility with editors and readers through strong research and the use of appropriate sources and citations. Writers and authors select the material they want to use and then convey the information to readers. With help from editors, they may revise or rewrite sections, searching for the best organization and the most appropriate phrasing.

An increasing number of writers are *freelance writers*–that is, they are self-employed and earn their living by selling their written content to book and magazine publishers; news organizations; advertising agencies; and movie, theater, and television producers. Many freelance writers are hired to complete specific short-term or recurring assignments, such as writing a newspaper column, contributing to a series of articles in a magazine, or producing an organization's newsletter.

An increasing number of writers are producing material that is published directly online in videos and on blogs.

The following are examples of types of writers and authors:

Copywriters prepare advertisements to promote the sale of a good or service. They often work with a client to produce advertising themes, jingles, and slogans.

Biographers write a thorough account of a person's life. They gather information from interviews and research about the person to accurately portray important events in that person's life.

Generalists write about any topic of interest, unlike writers who usually specialize in a given field.

Novelists write books of fiction, creating characters and plots that may be imaginary or based on real events.

Songwriters compose music and lyrics for songs. They may write and perform their own songs or sell their work to a music publisher. They sometimes work with a client to produce advertising themes, jingles, and slogans, and they may be involved in marketing the product or service.

Playwrights write scripts for theatrical productions. They produce lines for actors to say, stage direction for actors to follow, and ideas for theatrical set design.

Screenwriters create scripts for movies and television. They may produce original stories, characters, and dialogue, or turn a book into a movie or television script. Some may produce content for radio broadcasts and other types of performance.

Journalists write reports on current events. For more information, see the profile on reporters, correspondents, and broadcast news analysts.

Work Environment

Writers and authors held about 129,100 jobs in 2012. About two-thirds were self-employed.

The industries that employed the most writers and authors in 2012 were as follows:

Information	12%
Professional, scientific, and technical services	7
Other services (except public administration)	5
Arts, entertainment, and recreation	3
Educational services; state, local, and private	2

Writers and authors work in an office, at home, or wherever else they have access to a computer.

Jobs are somewhat concentrated in major media and entertainment markets–Boston, Chicago, Los Angeles, New York, and Washington, DC–but improved communications and Internet capabilities allow writers and authors to work from almost anywhere. Many prefer to work outside these cities and travel regularly to meet with publishers and clients and to perform research or conduct in-person interviews.

Work Schedules. About 1 in 4 writers and authors worked part time in 2012. Some writers keep regular office hours, either to stay in contact with sources and editors or to set up a writing routine, but many writers set their own hours.

Freelance writers are paid per assignment; therefore, they work any number of hours necessary to meet a deadline. As a result, they must be willing to work evenings and weekends to produce something acceptable to an editor or client. Although many freelance writers enjoy running their own business and working flexible hours, most routinely face the pressures of juggling multiple projects or continually looking for new work.

How to Become One

A college degree is generally required for a salaried position as a writer or author. Proficiency with computers is necessary for staying in touch with sources, editors, and other writers while working on assignments. Excellent writing skills are essential.

Education. A bachelor's degree is typically needed for a full-time job as a writer. Because writing skills are essential in this occupation, many employers prefer candidates with a degree in English, journalism, or communications.

Other Work Experience. Writers can obtain job experience by working for high school and college newspapers, magazines, radio and television stations, advertising and publishing companies, or not-for-profit organizations. College theater and music programs offer playwrights and songwriters an opportunity to have their work performed. Many magazines and newspapers also have internships for students. Interns may write stories, conduct research and interviews, and gain general publishing experience.

In addition, Internet blogs can provide writing experience to anyone with online access. Some of this writing may lead to paid assignments regardless of education, because the quality of writ-

Median Annual Wages, May 2012

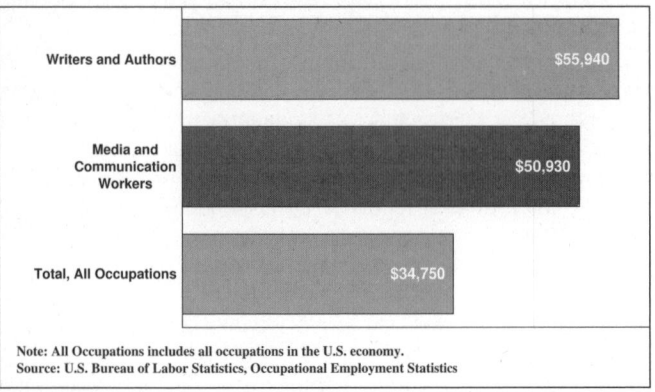

Note: All Occupations includes all occupations in the U.S. economy.
Source: U.S. Bureau of Labor Statistics, Occupational Employment Statistics

Percent Change in Employment, Projected 2012–2022

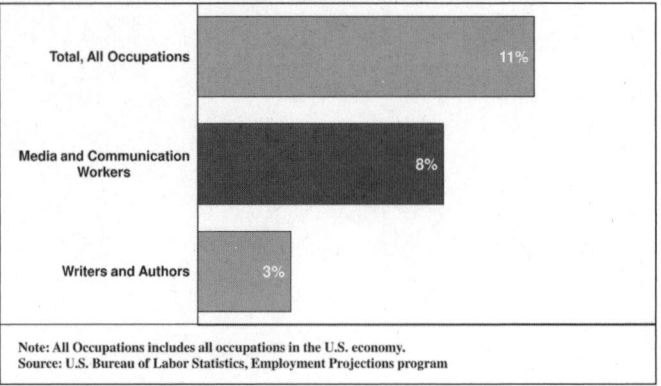

Note: All Occupations includes all occupations in the U.S. economy.
Source: U.S. Bureau of Labor Statistics, Employment Projections program

ing, the unique perspective, and the size of the potential audience are the greatest determinants of success for a piece of writing. Online publications require knowledge of computer software and editing tools that are used to combine text with graphics, audio, video, and animation.

Those with other backgrounds who demonstrate strong writing skills also may find jobs as writers.

Training. Writers and authors often need years of writing experience through on-the-job training before their work is ready for publication.

Writers who want to write about a particular topic may need formal training or experience related to that topic.

Because many writers today prepare material directly for the Internet, knowing graphic design, page layout, and multimedia software can be advantageous.

Licenses, Certifications, and Registrations. Some associations offer certifications for writers and authors. Certification can demonstrate competence and professionalism, making candidates more attractive to employers. For example, the American Grant Writers' Association (AGWA) offers the Certified Grant Writer® credential.

Certification can also increase opportunities for advancement.

Advancement. Writers and authors generally advance by building a reputation, taking on more complex writing assignments, and getting published in more prestigious markets and publications. Having published work that has been well received and maintaining a track record of meeting deadlines are important for advancement. Writing for smaller businesses, local newspapers, advertising agencies, and not-for-profit organizations allows beginning writers and authors to start taking credit for their work immediately.

However, opportunities for advancement within these organizations may be limited because they usually do not have enough regular work.

Many editors begin work as writers. Those who are particularly skilled at identifying stories, correcting writing style, and interacting with writers may be interested in editing jobs.

Important Qualities

Adaptability. Writers and authors need to be able to adapt to newer software platforms and programs, including various *Content Management Systems* (CMS).

Creativity. Writers and authors must be able to develop new and interesting plots, characters, or ideas so they can come up with new stories.

Critical-thinking skills. Writers and authors must have dual expertise in thinking through or understanding new concepts, and conveying it through written word.

Determination. Writers and authors sometimes work on projects that take years to complete. Freelance writers who are paid per assignment must demonstrate perseverance and personal drive.

Persuasion. Writers, especially those in advertising, must be able to persuade others to feel a certain way about a good or service.

Social perceptiveness. Writers and authors must understand how readers react to certain ideas in order to connect with their audience.

Writing skills. Writers and authors must be able to write effectively in order to convey feeling and emotion and communicate with readers.

Pay

The median annual wage for writers and authors was $55,940 in May 2012. The median wage is the wage at which half the workers in an occupation earned more than that amount and half earned less. The lowest 10 percent earned less than $27,770, and the top 10 percent earned more than $117,860.

In May 2012, the median annual wages in the top five industries in which writers and authors worked were as follows:

Professional, scientific, and technical services	$61,630
Arts, entertainment, and recreation	59,290
Other services (except public administration)	54,410
Educational services; state, local, and private	52,340
Information	51,940

Freelance writers earn income from their articles, books, and, less commonly, television and movie scripts. Although most

Employment Projections Data for Writers and Authors

Occupational title	SOC Code	Employment, 2012	Projected Employment, 2022	Change, 2012–2022 Percent	Change, 2012–2022 Numeric
Writers and authors	27-3043	129,100	132,900	3	3,800

Source: U.S. Bureau of Labor Statistics, Employment Projections Program

Note: Data are rounded. Go to Occupational Information Included in the OOH for a discussion of the data in this table.

Similar Occupations   This table shows a list of occupations with job duties that are similar to those of writers and authors.

Occupations	Entry-level Education	2012 Pay	Projected Job Growth	Average Annual Openings
Announcers	See "How to Become One"	$27,652	1%	1,160
Editors	Bachelor's degree	$53,880	-2%	2,800
Public Relations and Fundraising Managers	Bachelor's degree	$95,450	13%	2,130
Public Relations Specialists	Bachelor's degree	$54,170	12%	5,880
Reporters, Correspondents, and Broadcast News Analysts	Bachelor's degree	$37,858	-12%	1,960
Technical Writers	Bachelor's degree	$65,500	15%	2,260

freelance writers work on an individual project basis for multiple publishers, many support themselves with income derived from other sources. Freelancers generally have to provide for their own health insurance and pension, unless they receive coverage from another job.

Job Outlook

Employment of writers and authors is projected to grow 3 percent from 2012 to 2022, slower than the average for all occupations.

Despite slower-than-average employment growth, online publications and services are growing in number and sophistication, spurring demand for writers and authors with Web and multimedia experience.

Some experienced writers should find work in the public relations departments of corporations and not-for-profit organizations. Others will likely find freelance work for newspaper, magazine, or journal publishers, and some will write books.

Job Prospects. Strong competition is expected for most job openings, given that many people are attracted to this occupation. Competition for jobs with established newspapers and magazines will be particularly strong because employment in the publishing industry is projected to decline.

Writers and authors who have adapted to online media and are comfortable writing for and working with a variety of electronic and digital tools should have an advantage in finding work. The declining costs of self-publishing, the growing popularity of electronic books, and the increasing number of readers of electronic books will allow many freelance writers to have their work published.

O*NET

➤ Writers and Authors (27-3043.00)
➤ Copy Writers (27-3043.04)
➤ Poets, Lyricists and Creative Writers (27-3043.05)

Contacts for More Information

For more information about writers and authors, visit
➤ American Grant Writers' Association (www.agwa.us/)
➤ American Society of Journalists and Authors (www.asja.org/)
➤ Association of Writers & Writing Programs (www.awpwriter.org/)
➤ National Association of Science Writers (www.nasw.org/)
➤ Society of Professional Journalists (www.spj.org/)
➤ Writers Guild of America, East (www.wgaeast.org/)

Military Careers

What Military Servicemembers Do

Members of the U.S. military service train for and perform a variety of tasks in order to maintain the U.S. national defense. Servicemembers work in occupations specific to the military, such as fighter pilots or infantrymen. Many other members work in occupations that are equivalent to civilian occupations, such as nurses, doctors, and lawyers. Members serve in the Army, Navy, Air Force, Marine Corps, Coast Guard, or in the Reserve components of these branches, and in the Air National Guard and Army National Guard. (The Coast Guard, which is included in this profile, is part of the Department of Homeland Security.)

Duties. Members of the U.S. military service train for and perform a variety of tasks in order to maintain the U.S. national defense. Servicemembers work in occupations specific to the military, such as fighter pilots or infantrymen. Many other members work in occupations that are equivalent to civilian occupations, such as nurses, doctors, and lawyers. Members serve in the Army, Navy, Air Force, Marine Corps, Coast Guard, or in the Reserve components of these branches, and in the Air National Guard and Army National Guard. (The Coast Guard, which is included in this profile, is part of the Department of Homeland Security.)

Enlisted personnel typically do the following:

- Participate in, or support, combat and other military operations, such as humanitarian or disaster relief

- Operate, maintain, and repair equipment

- Perform technical and support activities

- Supervise junior enlisted personnel

Officers typically do the following:

- Plan, organize, and lead troops and activities in military operations

- Manage enlisted personnel

- Operate and command aircraft, ships, or armored vehicles

- Provide military personnel with professional services in medical, legal, engineering, and other fields

Types of Enlisted Personnel. The following are examples of types of occupations for enlisted personnel:

Administrative personnel maintain data and files on personnel, equipment, funds, and other military-related activities. They work in a support area, such as finance, accounting, legal affairs, maintenance, supply, or transportation.

Combat specialty personnel train and work as members of combat units, such as the infantry, artillery, or Special Forces. For example, infantry specialists conduct ground combat operations; armored vehicle specialists operate battle tanks; and seamanship specialists maintain ships. Combat specialty personnel may maneuver against enemy forces and positions and fire artillery, guns, mortars, or missiles to destroy those positions. They may also operate various types of combat vehicles, such as amphibious assault vehicles, tanks, or small boats. Members of elite Special Operations teams are trained to perform specialized missions anywhere in the world on a moment's notice.

Construction personnel in the military build or repair buildings, airfields, bridges, and other structures. They also may operate heavy equipment, such as bulldozers or cranes. They work with engineers and other building specialists as part of military construction teams. Some construction personnel specialize in areas such as plumbing, electrical wiring, or water purification.

Electronic and electrical equipment repair personnel maintain and repair electronic equipment used by the military. Repairers specialize in an area, such as aircraft electrical systems, computers, optical equipment, communications, or weapons systems. For example, weapons electronic maintenance technicians maintain and repair electronic components and systems that help locate targets and help aim and fire weapons.

Engineering, science, and technical personnel perform a variety of tasks, such as operating technical equipment, solving problems, and collecting and interpreting information. They typically perform technical tasks in information technology, environmental health and safety, or intelligence:

- *Environmental health and safety specialists* inspect military facilities and food supplies to ensure that they are safe for use.

- *Information technology specialists* manage and maintain computer and network systems.

- *Intelligence specialists* gather information and prepare reports for military planning and operations.

Healthcare personnel provide medical services to military personnel and their family members. They may work as part of a patient-service team with doctors, nurses, or other healthcare professionals. Some specialize in providing emergency medical treatment in combat or remote areas. Others specialize in laboratory testing of tissue and blood samples; maintaining pharmacy supplies or patients' records; assisting with dental procedures; operating diagnostic tools, such as X-ray and ultrasound machines; or other healthcare tasks.

Human resources development personnel recruit qualified people into the military, place them in suitable occupations, and provide training programs:

- *Personnel specialists* maintain information about military personnel and their training, job assignments, promotions, and health.

- *Recruiting specialists* provide information about military careers; explain pay, benefits, and service life; and recruit individuals into the military.

- *Training specialists and instructors* teach military personnel how to perform their jobs.

Machine operator and production personnel operate industrial equipment and machinery to fabricate and repair parts for a variety of equipment and structures. They may operate engines, nuclear reactors, or water pumps, usually performing a specific job. Welders and metalworkers, for example, work with various types of metals to repair or form the structural parts of ships, buildings, or other equipment. Survival equipment specialists inspect, maintain, and repair survival equipment, such as parachutes and aircraft life support equipment.

Media and public affairs personnel prepare and present information about military activities to the military and the public. They take photographs, make video programs, present news and music programs, or conduct interviews.

Protective service personnel enforce military laws and regulations and provide emergency responses to disasters:

- *Firefighters* prevent and extinguish fires in buildings, on aircraft, and aboard ships.

Active Duty Enlisted personnel by broad occupational group and branch of military, and Coast Guard, June 2013

Occupational Group – Enlisted	Army	Air Force	Coast Guard	Marine Corps	Navy	Total enlisted personnel in each occupation group
Administrative occupations	6,042	14,946	1,546	12,268	19,147	53,949
Combat Specialty occupations	122,254	581	636	43,707	8,219	175,397
Construction occupations	18,144	5,647	—	6,102	4,410	34,303
Electronic and Electrical Equipment Repair occupations	35,203	32,359	4,633	17,561	46,387	136,143
Engineering, Science, and Technical occupations	44,873	49,557	1,272	28,472	38,923	163,097
Health Care occupations	32,199	16,638	730	—	26,253	75,820
Human Resource Development occupations	16,608	8,292	1	2,284	3,956	31,141
Machine Operator and Production occupations	4,615	6,609	1,886	2,711	8,353	24,174
Media and Public Affairs occupations	7,643	6,870	141	2,561	1,882	19,097
Protective Service occupations	25,167	35,695	2,828	6,359	11,378	81,427
Support Service occupations	11,086	5,744	1,239	2,441	7,901	28,411
Transportation and Material Handling occupations	53,833	31,935	10,284	24,396	37,246	157,694
Vehicle and Machinery Mechanic occupations	49,237	44,634	5,641	21,806	46,551	167,869
Non-occupation or unspecified coded personnel	2,984	4,722	1,531	2,100	2,966	14,303
Total enlisted personnel for each military branch and Coast Guard	429,888	264,229	32,368	172,768	263,572	1,162,825

Source: U.S. Department of Defense, Defense Manpower Data Center

- *Military police* responsibilities include controlling traffic, preventing crime, and responding to emergencies.
- *Other law enforcement and security specialists* investigate crimes committed on military property and guard inmates in military correctional facilities.

Support service personnel provide services that support the morale and well-being of military personnel and their families:

- *Food service specialists* prepare food in dining halls, hospitals, and ships.
- *Religious program specialists* assist chaplains with religious services, religious education programs, and related administrative duties.

Transportation and material-handling personnel transport military personnel and cargo. Most personnel within this occupational group are classified according to the mode of transportation, such as aircraft, motor vehicle, or ship:

- *Aircrew members* operate equipment on aircraft.
- *Cargo specialists* load and unload military supplies, using forklifts and cranes.
- *Quartermasters and boat operators* navigate and pilot many types of small watercraft, including tugboats, gunboats, and barges.
- *Vehicle drivers* operate various military vehicles, including fuel or water tank trucks.

Vehicle and machinery mechanical personnel conduct preventive and corrective maintenance on aircraft, automotive and heavy equipment, and powerhouse station equipment. These workers typically specialize by the type of equipment that they maintain:

- *Aircraft mechanics* inspect and service various types of aircraft.
- *Automotive and heavy equipment mechanics* maintain and repair vehicles, such as Humvees, trucks, tanks, and other combat vehicles. They also repair bulldozers and other construction equipment.
- *Heating and cooling mechanics* install and repair air-conditioning, refrigeration, and heating equipment.
- *Marine engine mechanics* repair and maintain engines on ships, boats, and other watercraft.

- *Powerhouse mechanics* install, maintain, and repair electrical and mechanical equipment in power-generating stations.

Types of Officers. The following are examples of types of officers:

Combat specialty officers plan and direct military operations, oversee combat activities, and serve as combat leaders. They may be in charge of tanks and other armored assault vehicles, artillery systems, special operations, or infantry units. This group also includes naval surface warfare and submarine warfare officers, combat pilots, and aircrews.

Engineering, science, and technical officers' responsibilities depend on their area of expertise. They work in scientific and professional occupations, such as atmospheric scientists, meteorologists, physical scientists, biological scientists, social scientists, attorneys, and other types of scientists or professionals. For example, meteorologists in the military may study the weather to assist in planning flight paths for aircraft.

Executive, administrative, and managerial officers manage administrative functions in the Armed Forces, such as human resources management, training, personnel, information, police, or other support services. Officers who oversee military bands are included in this category.

Healthcare officers provide medical services to military personnel in order to maintain or improve their health and physical readiness. Officers such as physicians, physician assistants, nurses, and dentists examine, diagnose, and treat patients. Other healthcare officers provide therapy, rehabilitative treatment, and additional healthcare for patients:

- *Dentists* treat diseases, disorders, and injuries of the mouth.
- *Nurses* provide and coordinate patient care in military hospitals and clinics.
- *Optometrists* treat vision problems and prescribe glasses, contact lenses, or medications.
- *Pharmacists* purchase, store, and dispense drugs and medicines.
- *Physical and occupational therapists* plan and administer therapy to help patients adjust to injuries, regain independence, and return to work.
- *Physicians, surgeons,* and *physician assistants* furnish the majority of medical services to the military and their families.

Active Duty Officer personnel by broad occupational group and branch of military (excluding Coast Guard), June 2013

Occupational Group – Officer	Army	Air Force	Coast Guard	Marine Corps	Navy	Total officer personnel in each occupation group
Combat Specialty occupations	23,312	3,870	—	4,649	5,845	37,676
Engineering, Science, and Technical occupations	25,343	16,238	—	4,375	9,720	55,676
Executive, Administrative, and Managerial occupations	14,716	7,275	—	3,025	6,942	31,958
Health Care occupations	12,192	9,286	—		6,382	27,860
Human Resource Development occupations	3,172	1,940	—	271	3,189	8,572
Media and Public Affairs occupations	388	327	—	206	256	1,177
Protective Service occupations	3,145	1,146	—	414	991	5,696
Support Service occupations	1,782	716	—	41	939	3,478
Transportation occupations	13,055	19,782	—	6,484	11,025	50,346
Non-occupation or unspecified coded personnel	2,686	4,523	—	2,575	8,967	18,751
Total officer personnel for each military branch and Coast Guard	99,791	65,103	8,659	22,040	54,256	249,849

Source: U.S. Department of Defense, Defense Manpower Data Center

- *Psychologists* provide mental healthcare and also may conduct research on behavior and emotions.

For more information, see the profiles on dentists, occupational therapists, optometrists, nurse practitioners, pharmacists, physical therapists, physician assistants, physicians and surgeons, registered nurses, and psychologists.

Human resource development officers manage recruitment, placement, and training programs in the military:

- *Personnel managers* direct and oversee military personnel functions, such as job assignments, staff promotions, and career counseling.

- *Recruiting managers* direct and oversee recruiting personnel and recruiting activities.

- *Training and education directors* identify training needs and develop and manage educational programs.

Media and public affairs officers oversee the development, production, and presentation of information or events for the military and the public. They may produce and direct videos and television and radio broadcasts that are used for training, news, and entertainment. Some plan, develop, and direct the activities of military bands. Public affairs officers respond to public inquiries about military activities and prepare news releases.

Protective service officers are responsible for the safety and protection of individuals and property on military bases and vessels. Emergency management officers plan and prepare for all types of disasters. They develop warning, evacuation, and response procedures in the event of a disaster. Law enforcement and security officers enforce all applicable laws on military bases and oversee investigations of crimes.

Support services officers manage military activities in key functional areas, such as logistics, transportation, and supply. They may oversee the transportation and distribution of materials by ground vehicles, aircraft, or ships. They also direct food service facilities and other support activities. Purchasing and contracting managers negotiate and monitor contracts for the purchase of equipment, supplies, and services that the military buys from private industry.

Transportation officers manage and perform activities related to the safe transport of military personnel and equipment by air and water. They operate and command an aircraft or a ship:

- *Navigators* use radar, radio, and other navigation equipment to determine their position and plan their route of travel.

- *Pilots* in the military fly various types of military airplanes and helicopters to carry troops and equipment.

- *Ships' engineers* direct engineering departments, including engine operations, maintenance, and power generation, aboard ships.

Work Environment

New enlisted members of the Armed Forces undergo initial-entry training, better known as basic training or boot camp.

In June 2013, more than 2.7 million people served in the Armed Forces. More than 1.4 million were on active duty, including about 529,679 in the Army, 329,332 in the Air Force, 317,828 in the Navy, and 194,808 in the Marines. In addition, about 1.3 million people served in the Reserve components of the branches and in the Air National Guard and Army National Guard, and about 41,027 people served in the Coast Guard, which is part of the Department of Homeland Security.

The specific work environments and conditions for military occupations depend on occupational specialty, unit, branch of service, and other factors. Most active-duty military personnel live and work on or near military bases and facilities throughout the United States and the world. These bases and facilities usually offer comfortable housing and amenities, such as stores and recreation centers. Service members move regularly for training or job assignments, with most rotations lasting 2 to 4 years. Some are deployed internationally to defend national interests.

Skills learned in military training often can be carried over to civilian jobs.

Military members must be physically fit, mentally stable, and ready to participate in or support combat missions that may be difficult and dangerous and involve long periods of time away from family; however, some personnel are rarely deployed near combat areas.

The table below shows officers, warrant officers, and enlisted ranks by grade and branch of service who served on active duty in June 2013.

Injuries. Members of the military are often placed in dangerous situations with the risk of serious injury or death. Members deployed to combat zones or those who work in dangerous areas,

Military rank and employment for Activity Duty Personnel, June 2013

Grade	Army	Navy	Air Force	Marine Corps	Coast Guard	Active Duty Personnel (including Coast Guard)
Commissioned Officers:						
O-10	General	Admiral	General	General	Admiral	36
O-9	Lieutenant General	Vice Admiral	Lieutenant General	Lieutenant General	Vice Admiral	165
O-8	Major General	Rear Admiral (Upper Half)	Major General	Major General	Rear Admiral (Upper Half)	328
O-7	Brigadier General	Rear Admiral (Lower Half)	Brigadier General	Brigadier General	Rear Admiral (Lower Half)	450
O-6	Colonel	Captain	Colonel	Colonel	Captain	12,478
O-5	Lieutenant Colonel	Commander	Lieutenant Colonel	Lieutenant Colonel	Commander	29,939
O-4	Major	Lieutenant Commander	Major	Major	Lieutenant Commander	47,788
O-3	Captain	Lieutenant	Captain	Captain	Lieutenant	80,808
O-2	1st Lieutenant	Lieutenant Junior Grade	1st Lieutenant	1st Lieutenant	Lieutenant Junior Grade	32,238
O-1	2nd Lieutenant	Ensign	2nd Lieutenant	2nd Lieutenant	Ensign	24,439
Warrant Officers:						
W-5	Chief Warrant Officer 5	Chief Warrant Officer 5	—	Chief Warrant Officer 5		844
W-4	Chief Warrant Officer 4	Chief Warrant Officer 4	—	Chief Warrant Officer 4	Chief Warrant Officer 4	3,494
W-3	Chief Warrant Officer 3	Chief Warrant Officer 3	—	Chief Warrant Officer 3	Chief Warrant Officer 3	5,660
W-2	Chief Warrant Officer 2	Chief Warrant Officer 2	—	Chief Warrant Officer 2	Chief Warrant Officer 2	8,778
W-1	Warrant Officer 1		—	Warrant Officer 1		2,404
Enlisted Personnel:						
E-9	Sergeant Major	Master Chief Petty Officer	Chief Master Sergeant	Sergeant Major/ Master Gunnery Sergeant	Master Chief Petty Officer	10,780
E-8	First Sergeant/ Master Sergeant	Senior Chief Petty Officer	Senior Master Sergeant	First Sergeant/ Master Sergeant	Senior Chief Petty Officer	28,417
E-7	Sergeant First Class	Chief Petty Officer	Master Sergeant	Gunnery Sergeant	Chief Petty Officer	99,368
E-6	Staff Sergeant	Petty Officer First Class	Technical Sergeant	Staff Sergeant	Petty Officer First Class	176,817
E-5	Sergeant	Petty Officer Second Class	Staff Sergeant	Sergeant	Petty Officer Second Class	245,938
E-4	Corporal/Specialist	Petty Officer Third Class	Senior Airman	Corporal	Petty Officer Third Class	280,501
E-3	Private First Class	Seaman	Airman First Class	Lance Corporal	Seaman	205,967
E-2	Private	Seaman Apprentice	Airman	Private First Class	Seaman Apprentice	66,987
E-1	Private	Seaman Recruit	Airman Basic	Private	Seaman Recruit	48,050

Source: U.S. Department of Defense, Defense Manpower Data Center

such as the flight deck of an aircraft carrier, face a higher rate of injury and death.

Work Schedules. In many circumstances, military personnel work standard full time. However, hours vary significantly, depending on occupational specialty, rank, branch of service, and the needs of the military. In all cases, personnel must be prepared to work long hours to fulfill missions.

How to Become One

Educational requirements will continue to rise as military jobs become more technical and complex.

To join the military, applicants must meet age, education, aptitude, physical, and character requirements. These requirements vary by branch of service and for officers and enlisted members. Members are assigned an occupational specialty based on their aptitude, former training, and the needs of their branch of service. All service members must sign a contract and commit to a minimum term of service.

Those considering joining the military should learn as much as they can about military life before making a decision. Potential applicants should speak to people with military experience and weigh the pros and cons of a career in the military.

Applicants should talk to a recruiter, who can determine whether they qualify for enlistment or as an officer, explain the various enlistment options, and describe the military occupational specialties.

Prospective recruits who wish to enlist must take a placement exam called the Armed Forces Vocational Aptitude Battery (ASVAB), which is used to determine an applicant's suitability for military occupational specialties.

The recruiter can schedule applicants to take the ASVAB without any obligation to join. Many high schools offer the exam as a way for students to explore the possibility of a military career. Selection for a certain job specialty is based on ASVAB test results, whether the candidate possesses the physical requirements for the job, and the needs of the service.

Applicants who decide to join the military must pass the physical examination before signing an enlistment contract. Negotiating the contract involves choosing, qualifying for, and agreeing on a number of enlistment options, such as the length of active-duty or reserve-duty time, job training, and bonuses. Most active-duty programs have first-term enlistments of 4 years, although there are some 2-, 3-, and 6-year programs.

All branches of the Armed Services offer a delayed-entry program allowing candidates to postpone entry to active duty for up to 14 months after enlisting. High school students can enlist during their senior year and enter service after graduation. Others may select this kind of program because the job training they desire will be available within the coming year or because they need time to arrange their personal affairs.

To become an officer, candidates typically need to have at least a bachelor's degree, be a U.S. citizen, pass a background check, and meet physical and age requirements. Candidates for officer positions do not need to take the ASVAB. Some enter officer candidacy by completing a degree and training through the federal service academies (Military, Naval, Air Force, Coast Guard, and Merchant Marine) or the Reserve Officer Training Corps (ROTC) programs offered at many colleges and universities.

Education. All branches of the Armed Forces require their members to be high school graduates or have equivalent credentials, such as a General Educational Development (GED) certificate. Officers usually need a bachelor's degree. Some officers entering the service may need to have education beyond the bachelor's

degree. For example, officers entering as military lawyers need a law degree.

Those who want to become an officer have several routes, including the aforementioned federal service academies, (Military, Naval, Air Force, Coast Guard, and Merchant Marine); the Reserve Officer Training Corps (ROTC) programs, Officer Candidate School (OCS), and other programs.

Important Qualities

Mental preparedness. Members of the Armed Forces must be mentally stable and able to handle stressful situations that can occur during military operations.

Physical fitness. Military members must be physically fit to participate in or support combat missions that may be difficult or dangerous.

Readiness. Members of the Armed Forces must be ready and able to report for military assignments on short notice.

Entry requirements for each service vary, but certain qualifications for enlistment are common to all branches. The following are typical enlistment requirements:

• Minimum of 17 years of age

• U.S. citizenship or permanent resident status

• Pass a background investigation

• Never convicted of a felony

• Able to pass a drug test

Applicants who are 17 years old must have the consent of a parent or legal guardian before entering the military. To enter service in the Army, the maximum age is 41; for the Navy, 34; for the Marine Corps, 29; and for the Air Force and Coast Guard, 27. Each branch may have different maximum age requirements for entry into active-duty service. All applicants must meet certain minimum physical standards for height, weight, vision, and overall health. Officers must be U.S. citizens. Officers and some enlisted members must be able to pass a security clearance.

Women are eligible to enter most military specialties; for example, they may become mechanics, missile maintenance technicians, heavy-equipment operators, and fighter pilots, or they may enter into medical care, administrative support, and intelligence specialties. Generally, women are excluded only from occupations involving direct exposure to combat. However, all services have plans to integrate and open these occupations to women in the near future.

Training. *Training for enlisted personnel.* Newly enlisted members of the Armed Forces undergo initial-entry training, better known as basic training or boot camp. Basic training includes courses in military skills and protocols and typically lasts 8 to 13 weeks, including a week of orientation and introduction to military life. Basic training also includes weapons training, team building, and rigorous physical exercise designed to improve strength and endurance.

Following basic training, military members attend additional training at technical schools that prepare them for a particular military occupational specialty. This formal training period generally lasts from 10 to 20 weeks. Training for certain occupations—nuclear power plant operator, for example—may take as long as a year. In addition to getting classroom instructions, military members receive on-the-job training at their first duty assignment.

Training for warrant officers. Warrant officers are technical and tactical experts in a specific area; for example, Army aviators make up one group of warrant officers. About 1 percent of all military personnel are warrant officers. All services except the U.S. Air Force have warrant officer programs. Selection to attend Warrant

Officer Candidate School is highly competitive and is restricted to those who meet rank and length-of-service requirements. Courses typically include additional leadership and management training. Depending on the branch of service, training may last several weeks. The only exception is the selection process for Army aviator warrant officer, which has no requirement of previous military service.

Training for officers. Officer training in the Armed Forces is provided through the federal service academies (Military, Naval, Air Force, Coast Guard, and Merchant Marine); the Reserve Officers' Training Corps (ROTC) program; Officer Candidate School (OCS) or Officer Training School (OTS); the National Guard (State Officer Candidate School programs); and the Uniformed Services University of Health Sciences.

Candidates interested in the federal service academies must be unmarried and without dependents, while those seeking training through OCS, OTS, or ROTC may be married.

The federal service academies provide a 4-year academic program leading to a Bachelor of Science (B.S.) degree. Midshipmen and cadets receive free room and board, free tuition, free medical and dental care, and a monthly allowance. Graduates receive regular or reserve commissions and have a 5-year active-duty obligation, which may be longer if they are entering flight training.

Candidates for appointment as a cadet or midshipman in one of the service academies must be nominated by an authorized source, usually a member of Congress. However, they do not need to know the member of Congress personally in order to request a nomination. In addition, nominees must submit their academic record, college aptitude test scores, and recommendations from teachers or other school officials. They also must pass a medical examination. Academies make appointments from the list of eligible nominees. Appointments to the Coast Guard Academy, however, are based on merit and do not require a nomination.

Participants in ROTC programs take regular college courses along with 3 to 5 hours of military instruction per week. After graduation, they may serve as officers on active duty for a specific period. Some may serve their obligation in the Reserves or National Guard. In the last 2 years of an ROTC program, students typically receive a monthly allowance while attending school, as well as additional pay for summer training. ROTC scholarships for 2, 3, and 4 years of school are available on a competitive basis. All scholarships pay for tuition and have allowances for textbooks, supplies, and other costs.

College graduates can earn a commission in the Armed Forces through OCS or OTS training programs in the Army, Navy, Air Force, Marine Corps, Coast Guard, and National Guard. These programs consist of several weeks of intensive academic, physical, and leadership training. Those who complete the programs as officers generally must serve their obligation on active duty.

Personnel with training in certain health occupations may qualify for direct appointment as officers. For those studying health professions, financial assistance and internship opportunities are available from the military in return for specified periods of military service. Prospective medical students can apply to the Uniformed Services University of Health Sciences, which offers a salary and free tuition in a program leading to a Doctor of Medicine (M.D.) degree. In return, graduates must serve for 7 years in either the military or the U.S. Public Health Service.

Direct appointments also are available for those qualified to serve in other specialty areas, such as the Judge Advocate General's Corps for those in the legal field or the Chaplain Corps for those in religious ministry. Flight training is available to commissioned officers in each branch of the Armed Forces. In addition, the Army has a direct enlistment option for those who wish to become a warrant officer aviator. All prospective officers who enter the service through a direct appointment attend several weeks of military-related training that typically includes military orientation, academic, and officer leadership and tactics courses. Depending on the branch of service, this program usually lasts a few months.

Licenses, Certifications, and Registrations. Depending on the occupational specialty, members of the military may need to have and maintain civilian licenses or certifications. For example, officers serving as lawyers, also known as Judge Advocates, may need to have and maintain their state bar licenses to enter and remain in the U.S. military. Air traffic controllers, dental assistants, medical laboratory technicians, and many others also need to have civilian occupation equivalent licenses or certifications.

Advancement. Each branch of the military has different criteria for determining the promotion of personnel. Criteria for promotion may include time in service and in grade, job performance, a fitness report, and passing scores on written exams. Enlisted personnel can be promoted to higher ranks, which may include serving in a supervisory position and being in charge of junior enlisted members.

Each military service may have other advancement opportunities for its enlisted personnel. For example, enlisted personnel may become warrant officers if they complete a bachelor's degree, have several years of experience in higher enlisted positions, and meet age and physical requirements. The Army offers a direct enlistment option to become a warrant officer aviator.

Pay

Basic pay is based on rank and time in service. The pay structure for military personnel is shown in the table on the next page. Pay bands are the same for all branches of service. Members of the Armed Forces may receive additional pay based on their job assignment or qualifications. For example, they receive additional pay for foreign, hazardous, submarine, or flight duty, or for being medical or dental officers. Retirement pay is generally available after 20 years of service.

In addition to receiving basic pay, members of the military are housed free of charge on base or receive a housing allowance.

Members who serve for a certain number of years may receive additional benefits. These benefits may include educational benefits through the Montgomery GI Bill, which pays for a portion of educational costs at accredited institutions; medical care at military or the U.S. Department of Veterans Affairs hospitals; and guaranteed home loans.

Job Outlook

The United States spends a significant amount of its overall budget on national defense. The total number of active-duty and reserve personnel serving in the Armed Forces is expected to remain roughly the same through 2022. The drawdown from recent conflicts is expected to result in some reductions of active-duty personnel.

In addition, the current goal of the Armed Forces is to maintain a force sufficient to deter, fight, and overcome various threats or conflicts in multiple regions at the same time. Emerging conflicts and threatening global events, however, could lead to a significant restructuring and a demand for an increase in force, resulting in the need for military personnel. In response to this contingency, the nation is expected to maintain adequate personnel in the Reserve, National Guard, and Air National Guard.

Job Prospects. Opportunities should be good for qualified individuals in all branches of the Armed Forces through 2022. All

Monthly Pay by Military Rank, January 2013

Pay Grade					Years of Service							
	2 or less	Over 2	Over 3	Over 4	Over 6	Over 8	Over 10	Over 12	Over 14	Over 16	Over 20	
O-10											$15,913.20	
O-9											13,917.60	
O-8	$9,847.80	$10,170.30	$10,384.50	$10,444.20	$10,711.50	$11,157.60	$11,261.40	$11,685.00	$11,806.50	$12,171.60	13,187.10	
O-7	8,182.50	8,562.90	8,738.70	8,878.50	9,131.70	9,381.90	9,671.10	9,959.40	10,248.60	11,157.60	11,924.70	
O-6	6,064.80	6,663.00	7,100.10	7,100.10	7,127.10	7,432.80	7,473.00	7,473.00	7,897.80	8,648.70	9,529.80	
O-5	5,055.90	5,695.50	6,089.70	6,164.10	6,410.10	6,557.10	6,880.80	7,118.40	7,425.30	7,895.10	8,338.80	
O-4	4,362.30	5,049.90	5,386.80	5,461.80	5,774.70	6,109.80	6,527.70	6,852.90	7,078.80	7,208.70	7,283.70	
O-3	3,835.50	4,347.90	4,692.90	5,116.50	5,361.60	5,630.70	5,804.70	6,090.60	6,240.00	6,240.00	6,240.00	
O-2	3,314.10	3,774.30	4,347.00	4,493.70	4,586.40	4,586.40	4,586.40	4,586.40	4,586.40	4,586.40	4,586.40	
O-1	2,876.40	2,994.00	3,619.20	3,619.20	3,619.20	3,619.20	3,619.20	3,619.20	3,619.20	3,619.20	3,619.20	
W-5											7,047.90	
W-4	3,963.90	4,263.90	4,386.00	4,506.60	4,713.90	4,919.10	5,126.70	5,439.60	5,713.50	5,974.20	6,395.40	
W-3	3,619.50	3,770.40	3,925.20	3,975.90	4,138.20	4,457.10	4,789.20	4,945.50	5,126.40	5,313.00	5,874.30	
W-2	3,202.80	3,505.80	3,599.40	3,663.30	3,871.20	4,194.00	4,353.90	4,511.40	4,704.00	4,854.30	5,153.70	
W-1	2,811.60	3,114.00	3,195.30	3,367.50	3,570.90	3,870.60	4,010.40	4,205.70	4,398.30	4,549.80	4,858.20	
E-9							4,788.90	4,897.50	5,034.30	5,194.80	5,617.50	
E-8						3,920.10	4,093.50	4,200.90	4,329.60	4,469.10	4,847.70	
E-7	2,725.20	2,974.50	3,088.20	3,239.10	3,357.00	3,559.20	3,673.20	3,875.70	4,043.70	4,158.60	4,328.40	
E-6	2,357.10	2,593.80	2,708.10	2,819.40	2,935.50	3,196.50	3,298.50	3,495.30	3,555.60	3,599.70	3,650.70	
E-5	2,159.40	2,304.30	2,415.90	2,529.90	2,707.50	2,893.50	3,045.60	3,064.20	3,064.20	3,064.20	3,064.20	
E-4	1,979.70	2,081.10	2,193.90	2,304.90	2,403.30	2,403.30	2,403.30	2,403.30	2,403.30	2,403.30	2,403.30	
E-3	1,787.40	1,899.90	2,014.80	2,014.80	2,014.80	2,014.80	2,014.80	2,014.80	2,014.80	2,014.80	2,014.80	
E-2	1,699.80	1,699.80	1,699.80	1,699.80	1,699.80	1,699.80	1,699.80	1,699.80	1,699.80	1,699.80	1,699.80	
E-1	1,516.20											

Source: U.S. Department of Defense, Defense Finance and Accounting Services

services have needs to fill entry-level and professional positions as members of the Armed Forces move up through the ranks, leave the service, or retire.

About 155,000 personnel must be recruited each year to replace those who complete their commitment or retire. Since the end of the draft in 1973, the military has met its personnel requirements with volunteers.

When the economy is thriving and civilian employment opportunities generally are more favorable, it is more difficult for the military to meet its recruitment quotas. It is also more difficult to meet these goals during times of war, when recruitment goals typically rise. During economic downturns, candidates for military service may face competition.

Similar Occupations

The military employs people in numerous occupational specialties, many of which are similar to civilian occupations. To match military occupations with similar civilian occupations, O*Net OnLine offers the Military Crosswalk Search tool (www.onetonline.org/crosswalk/MOC/).

Contacts for More Information

Each of the military services publishes handbooks, fact sheets, and pamphlets describing its entrance requirements, its training opportunities, and other aspects of military careers. These publications are available at all recruiting stations; at most state employment service offices; and in high schools, colleges, and public libraries.

For more information on the individual services, visit
➤ U.S. Air Force (www.airforce.com/)
➤ Air National Guard (www.ang.af.mil/)
➤ U.S. Army (www.goarmy.com/)
➤ Army National Guard (www.arng.army.mil/Pages/Default.aspx)
➤ U.S. Coast Guard (www.uscg.mil/)
➤ U.S. Marine Corps (www.marines.com/)
➤ U.S. Navy (www.navy.com/)

In addition, the Defense Manpower Data Center, an agency of the Department of Defense, maintains the website providing information and resource for parents, educators, and young adults curious about joining military service. To see the information, visit Today's Military (www.todaysmilitary.com/).

For more information about military testing, visit
➤ ASVAB (http://official-asvab.com/index.htm)

Office and Administrative Support

Bill and Account Collectors

- **2012 Median Pay** .... $32,480 per year
  $15.61 per hour
- **Entry-Level Education** ... High school diploma or equivalent
- **Work Experience in a Related Occupation** .... None
- **On-the-Job Training** .... Moderate-term on-the-job training
- **Number of Jobs 2012** 397,400
- **Job Outlook, 2012–22** .... 15% (Faster than average)
- **Employment Change, 2012–22** 58,200

What Bill and Account Collectors Do

Bill and account collectors, sometimes called collectors, try to recover payment on overdue bills. They negotiate repayment plans with debtors and help them find solutions to make paying their overdue bills easier.

Duties. Bill and account collectors typically do the following:

- Find consumers and businesses who have overdue bills
- Track down consumers who have an out-of-date address by using the Internet, post office, credit bureaus, or neighbors–a process called "skip tracing"
- Inform debtors that they have an overdue bill and try to negotiate a payment
- Explain the terms of sale or contract with the debtor, when necessary
- Learn the reasons for the overdue bills, which can help with the negotiations
- Offer credit advice or refer a consumer to a debt counselor, when appropriate

Bill and account collectors generally contact debtors by phone, although sometimes they do so by mail. They use computer systems to update contact information and record past collection attempts with a particular debtor. Keeping these records can help collectors with future negotiations.

The main job of bill and account collectors is finding a solution that is acceptable to the debtor and maximizes payment to the

Bill and account collectors must have good communication and people skills as their work requires daily interactions with customers.

creditor. Listening to the debtor and paying attention to his or her concerns can help the collector negotiate a solution.

After the collector and debtor agree on a repayment plan, the collector continually checks to ensure that the debtor pays on time. If the debtor does not pay, the collector submits a statement to the creditor, who can take legal action. In extreme cases, this legal action may include taking back goods or disconnecting service.

Collectors must follow federal and state laws that govern debt collection. These laws require that a collector make sure they are talking with the debtor before announcing that the purpose of the call is to collect a debt. A collector also must give a statement, called "mini-Miranda," which informs the account holder that they are speaking with a bill or debt collector.

Although many collectors work for third-party collection agencies, some work in-house for the original creditor, such as a credit-card company or a health care provider. The day-to-day activities of in-house collectors are generally the same as those of other collectors.

Collectors usually have goals they are expected to meet. Typically, these include calls per hour and success rates.

Median Annual Wages, May 2012

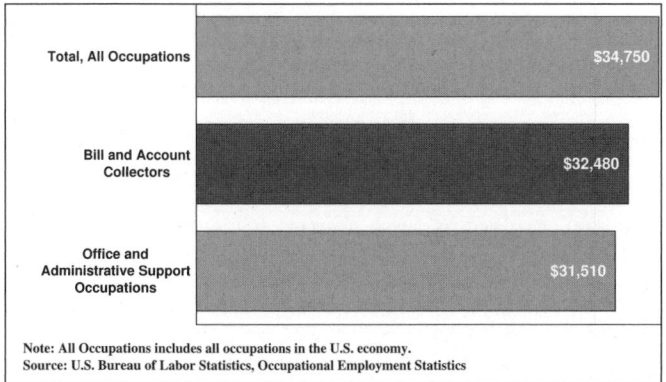

Total, All Occupations — $34,750
Bill and Account Collectors — $32,480
Office and Administrative Support Occupations — $31,510

Note: All Occupations includes all occupations in the U.S. economy.
Source: U.S. Bureau of Labor Statistics, Occupational Employment Statistics

Percent Change in Employment, Projected 2012–2022

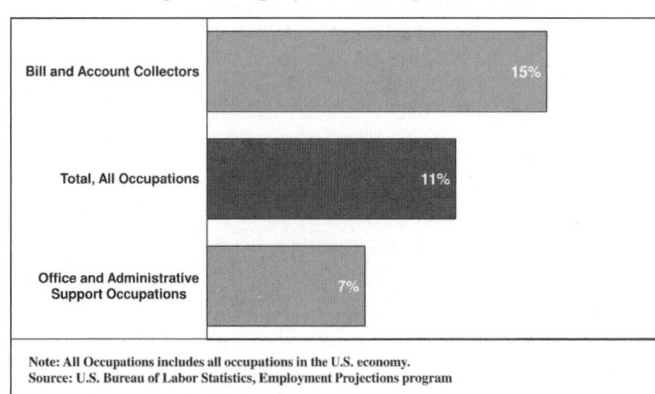

Bill and Account Collectors — 15%
Total, All Occupations — 11%
Office and Administrative Support Occupations — 7%

Note: All Occupations includes all occupations in the U.S. economy.
Source: U.S. Bureau of Labor Statistics, Employment Projections program

733

Employment Projections Data for Bill and Account Collectors

Occupational title	SOC Code	Employment, 2012	Projected Employment, 2022	Change, 2012–2022	
				Percent	Numeric
Bill and account collectors	43-3011	397,400	455,600	15	58,200

Source: U.S. Bureau of Labor Statistics, Employment Projections Program

Note: Data are rounded. Go to Occupational Information Included in the OOH for a discussion of the data in this table.

Work Environment

Bill and account collectors held about 397,400 jobs in 2012. Many work in a call center for a third-party collection agency rather than the original creditor.

The industries that employed the most bill and account collectors in 2012 were as follows:

Business support services... 26%
Credit intermediation and related activities 21
Health care 15
Professional, scientific, and technical services........................... 6
Management of companies and enterprises............................... 5

Whichever industry the collectors work in, most of their time is spent on the phone tracking down or negotiating with debtors. They also spend time on the computer, updating information and recording the results of their calls.

Collectors' work can be stressful because many people become angry and confrontational when pressed about their debts. Collectors often face resistance while trying to do their job tasks. Successful collectors must face regular rejection and still be ready to make the next call in a polite and positive voice. Fortunately, some consumers appreciate help in resolving their outstanding debts and can be quite grateful.

Work Schedules. Most bill and account collectors work full time. Some collectors work flexible schedules, often calling people on weekends or during the evenings as they learn the best times to call.

How to Become One

Collectors usually must have a high school diploma. A few months of on-the-job training is common.

Education. Most bill and account collectors are required to have a high school diploma, although some employers prefer applicants who have taken some college courses. Communication, accounting, and basic computer courses are examples of classes that are helpful for entering this occupation.

Training. Collectors usually get 1 to 3 months of on-the-job training after being hired. Training includes learning the company's policies and computer software and learning the laws for debt collection in the Fair Debt Collection Practices Act, as well as their

state's debt collection regulations. If they do not have experience, collectors also may be trained in negotiation techniques.

Important Qualities

Listening skills. Collectors must pay attention to what debtors say when trying to negotiate a repayment plan. Learning the particular situation of the debtors and how they fell into debt can help collectors suggest solutions.

Negotiating skills. The main aspects of a collector's job are reconciling the differences between two parties (the debtor and the creditor) and offering a solution that is acceptable to both parties.

Speaking skills. Collectors must be able to speak to debtors to explain their choices and ensure that they fully understand what is being said.

Pay

The median annual wage for bill and account collectors was $32,480 in May 2012. The median wage is the wage at which half the workers in an occupation earned more than that amount and half earned less. The lowest 10 percent earned less than $21,850, and the top 10 percent earned more than $48,640. These wage data include money earned from commissions. Collectors earn more when their collection rate is high.

In May 2012, median annual wages for bill and account collectors in the top five industries in which these collectors worked were as follows:

Management of companies and enterprises....................... $34,950
Professional, scientific, and technical services..................... 34,560
Credit intermediation and related activities 33,780
Health care 33,670
Business support services.. 28,130

Job Outlook

Employment of bill and account collectors is projected to grow 15 percent from 2012 to 2022, faster than the average for all occupations.

Fast job growth is expected for collectors in medical industries. As the cost of healthcare increases, the amount of medical debt that people incur is likely to rise as well. Employment of bill and

Similar Occupations   This table shows a list of occupations with job duties that are similar to those of bill and account collectors.

Occupations	Entry-level Education	2012 Pay	Projected Job Growth	Average Annual Openings
Bookkeeping, Accounting, and Auditing Clerks	High school diploma or equivalent	$35,170	11%	37,000
Customer Service Representatives	High school diploma or equivalent	$30,580	13%	94,160
Financial Clerks	High school diploma or equivalent	$35,122	11%	43,930
Information Clerks	High school diploma or equivalent	$31,159	2%	47,000
Loan Officers	Bachelor's degree	$59,820	8%	7,720

account collectors is projected to grow 30 percent in offices of health practitioners from 2012 to 2022.

In addition, credit card companies are more commonly selling their debts to third-party agencies, likely also increasing job growth in the collections industry. From 2012 to 2022, employment of bill and account collectors is projected to grow 20 percent in business support services, which includes collection agencies.

However, the increasing efficiency of collectors is expected to slow employment growth for this occupation. New software and automated calling systems should increase productivity and allow collectors to handle more accounts.

Although some collection jobs will likely be sent to other countries where wages are lower, creditors will continue to hire collectors in the United States because workers in this country tend to have greater success in negotiating with debtors.

Job Prospects. Job prospects are likely to be excellent for this occupation. Workers frequently leave the occupation, which leads to numerous job openings.

Unlike many other occupations, collections jobs usually remain stable during economic downturns. When the economy weakens, many consumers and businesses fall behind on their financial obligations, increasing the amount of debt to be collected. However, the success rate of collectors decreases because fewer people can afford to pay their debts.

O*NET

➤ Bill and Account Collectors (43-3011.00)

Contacts for More Information

For more information about bill and account collectors, visit
➤ ACA International, The Association of Credit and Collections Professionals (www.acainternational.org/)

Bookkeeping, Accounting, and Auditing Clerks

- **2012 Median Pay** .... $35,170 per year
  $16.91 per hour
- **Entry-Level Education** ... High school diploma or equivalent
- **Work Experience in a Related Occupation** .... None
- **On-the-Job Training** .... Moderate-term on-the-job training
- **Number of Jobs 2012** 1,799,800
- **Job Outlook, 2012–22** .... 11% (As fast as average)
- **Employment Change, 2012–22** 204,600

What Bookkeeping, Accounting, and Auditing Clerks Do

Bookkeeping, accounting, and auditing clerks produce financial records for organizations. They record financial transactions, update statements, and check financial records for accuracy.

Duties. Bookkeeping, accounting, and auditing clerks typically do the following:

- Use bookkeeping software, online spreadsheets, and databases
- Enter (post) financial transactions into the appropriate computer software
- Receive and record cash, checks, and vouchers
- Put costs (debits) and income (credits) into the software, assigning each to an appropriate account

- Produce reports, such as balance sheets (costs compared with income), income statements, and totals by account
- Check for accuracy in figures, postings, and reports
- Reconcile or note and report any differences they find in the records

The records that bookkeeping, accounting, and auditing clerks work with include expenditures (money spent), receipts (money that comes in), accounts payable (bills to be paid), accounts receivable (invoices, or what other people owe the organization), and profit and loss (a report that shows the organization's financial health).

Workers in this occupation have a wide range of tasks. Some in this occupation are full-charge bookkeeping clerks who maintain an entire organization's books. Others are accounting clerks who handle specific tasks.

These clerks use basic mathematics (adding, subtracting) throughout the day.

As organizations continue to computerize their financial records, many bookkeeping, accounting, and auditing clerks use specialized accounting software, spreadsheets, and databases. Most clerks now enter information from receipts or bills into computers, and the information is then stored electronically. They must be comfortable using computers to record and calculate data.

The widespread use of computers also has enabled bookkeeping, accounting, and auditing clerks to take on additional responsibilities, such as payroll, billing, purchasing (buying), and keeping track of overdue bills. Many of these functions require clerks to communicate with clients.

Bookkeeping clerks, also known as *bookkeepers*, often are responsible for some or all of an organization's accounts, known as the general ledger. They record all transactions and post debits (costs) and credits (income).

They also produce financial statements and other reports for supervisors and managers. Bookkeepers prepare bank deposits by compiling data from cashiers, verifying receipts, and sending cash, checks, or other forms of payment to the bank.

In addition, they may handle payroll, make purchases, prepare invoices, and keep track of overdue accounts.

Accounting clerks typically work for larger companies and have more specialized tasks. Their titles, such as accounts payable clerk or accounts receivable clerk, often reflect the type of accounting they do.

Bookkeeping, accounting, and auditing clerks handle financial records for many small businesses.

Median Annual Wages, May 2012

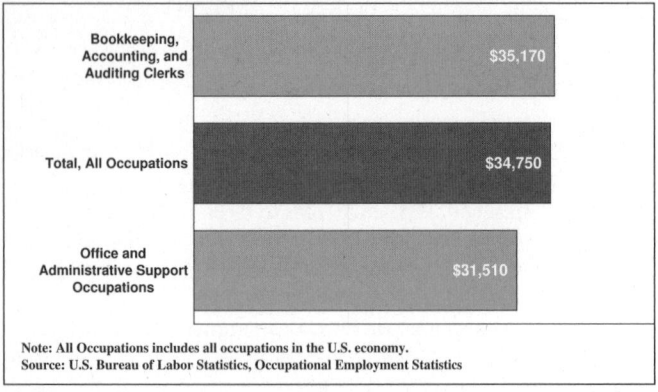

Note: All Occupations includes all occupations in the U.S. economy.
Source: U.S. Bureau of Labor Statistics, Occupational Employment Statistics

Percent Change in Employment, Projected 2012–2022

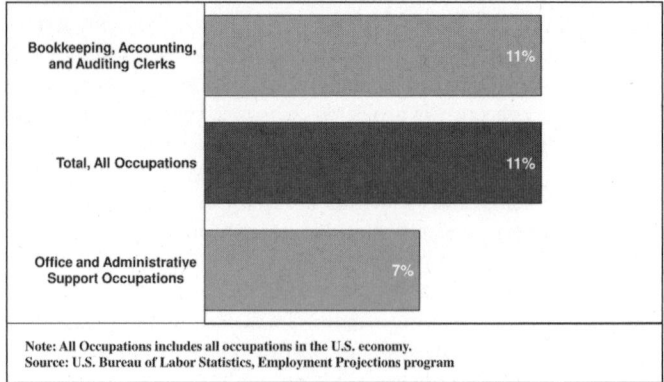

Note: All Occupations includes all occupations in the U.S. economy.
Source: U.S. Bureau of Labor Statistics, Employment Projections program

Often, their responsibilities vary by level of experience. Entry-level accounting clerks may enter (post) details of transactions (including date, type, and amount), add up accounts, and determine interest charges. They also may monitor loans and accounts to ensure that payments are up to date.

More advanced accounting clerks may add and balance billing vouchers, ensure that account data is complete and accurate, and code documents according to an organization's procedures.

Auditing clerks check figures, postings, and documents to ensure that they are mathematically accurate and properly coded. They also correct or note errors for accountants or other workers to fix.

Work Environment

Bookkeeping, accounting, and auditing clerks held about 1.8 million jobs in 2012.

The industries that employed the most bookkeeping, accounting, and auditing clerks in 2012 were as follows:

Professional, scientific, and technical services.......................... 12%
Retail trade 9
Wholesale trade 7
Health care and social assistance 7
Finance and insurance 7

The professional, scientific, and technical services industry includes the accounting, tax preparation, bookkeeping, and payroll services sub-industry.

Bookkeeping, accounting, and auditing clerks work in offices. Bookkeepers who work for multiple firms may do site visits to their clients' places of business. They often work alone, but sometimes they collaborate with accountants and managers, and depending on the size of the organization, they may work with bookkeeping, accounting, and auditing clerks from other departments.

Work Schedules. Many bookkeeping, accounting, and auditing clerks work full time. About 1 in 4 worked part time in 2012. They may work longer hours to meet deadlines at the end of the fiscal year, during tax time, or when monthly or yearly accounting audits are done. Those who work in hotels, restaurants, and stores may put in overtime during peak holiday and vacation seasons.

How to Become One

Most bookkeeping, accounting, and auditing clerks need a high school diploma, and they usually learn some of their skills on the job. They must have basic math and computer skills, including knowledge of spreadsheets and bookkeeping software.

Education. Most bookkeeping, accounting, and auditing clerks need a high school diploma. However, some employers prefer candidates who have some postsecondary education, particularly coursework in accounting.

Training. Bookkeeping, accounting, and auditing clerks usually get on-the-job training. Under the guidance of a supervisor or another experienced employee, new clerks learn how to do their tasks, including double-entry bookkeeping. (Double-entry bookkeeping means that each transaction is entered twice, once as a debit (cost) and once as a credit (income) to ensure that all accounts are balanced.)

Some formal classroom training also may be necessary, such as training in specialized computer software. This on-the-job training typically takes around 6 months.

Licenses, Certifications, and Registrations. Some bookkeeping, accounting, and auditing clerks become certified. The Certified Bookkeeper (CB) designation, awarded by the American Institute of Professional Bookkeepers, shows that people have the skills and knowledge needed to carry out all bookkeeping tasks, including overseeing payroll and balancing accounts, according to accepted accounting procedures.

For certification, candidates must have at least 2 years of full-time bookkeeping experience or equivalent part-time work, pass a four-part exam, and adhere to a code of ethics.

The National Association of Certified Public Bookkeepers also offers certification. The Uniform Bookkeeper Certification Examination is an online test with 50 multiple-choice questions. Test takers must answer 80 percent of the questions correctly to pass the exam.

Advancement. With appropriate experience and education, some bookkeeping, accounting, and auditing clerks may become accountants or auditors.

Employment Projections Data for Bookkeeping, Accounting, and Auditing Clerks

Occupational title	SOC Code	Employment, 2012	Projected Employment, 2022	Change, 2012–2022	
				Percent	Numeric
Bookkeeping, accounting, and auditing clerks	43-3031	1,799,800	2,004,500	11	204,600

Source: U.S. Bureau of Labor Statistics, Employment Projections Program

Note: Data are rounded. Go to Occupational Information Included in the OOH *for a discussion of the data in this table.*

Similar Occupations This table shows a list of occupations with job duties that are similar to those of bookkeeping, accounting, and auditing clerks.

Occupations	Entry-level Education	2012 Pay	Projected Job Growth	Average Annual Openings
Accountants and Auditors	Bachelor's degree	$63,550	13%	54,420
Budget Analysts	Bachelor's degree	$69,280	6%	2,850
Cost Estimators	Bachelor's degree	$58,860	26%	11,800
Financial Clerks	High school diploma or equivalent	$35,122	11%	43,930
Loan Officers	Bachelor's degree	$59,820	8%	7,720
Tax Examiners and Collectors, and Revenue Agents	Bachelor's degree	$50,440	-4%	2,390

Important Qualities

Computer skills. Bookkeeping, accounting, and auditing clerks need basic computer skills. They should be comfortable using spreadsheets and bookkeeping software.

Detail oriented. These clerks are responsible for producing accurate financial records. They must pay attention to detail to avoid making errors and to recognize errors that others have made.

Integrity. Bookkeeping, accounting, and auditing clerks have control of an organization's financial documentation, which they must use properly and keep confidential. It is vital that they keep records transparent and guard against misappropriating an organization's funds.

Math skills. Bookkeeping, accounting, and auditing clerks deal with numbers daily and should be comfortable with basic arithmetic.

Pay

The median annual wage for bookkeeping, accounting, and auditing clerks was $35,170 in May 2012. The median wage is the wage at which half the workers in an occupation earned more than that amount and half earned less. The lowest 10 percent earned less than $21,610, and the top 10 percent earned more than $54,310.

In May 2012, the median annual wages for bookkeeping, accounting and auditing clerks in the top five industries in which these clerks worked were as follows:

Professional, scientific, and technical services	$36,600
Finance and insurance	35,750
Wholesale trade	35,490
Health care and social assistance	34,960
Retail trade	30,770

Job Outlook

Employment of bookkeeping, accounting, and auditing clerks is projected to grow 11 percent from 2012 to 2022, about as fast as the average for all occupations.

Job growth for these workers is largely driven by overall economic growth. As the number of organizations increases, more bookkeepers will be needed to keep these organizations' books. In addition, in response to the recent financial crisis, investors will pay increased attention to the accuracy of corporate books. Stricter regulation in the financial sector will create demand for accounting services, creating opportunities for accounting clerks.

Some tasks that these clerks do have been affected by technological changes. For example, electronic banking and bookkeeping software has reduced the need for bookkeepers and clerks to send and receive checks. However, when checks are sent or received, these workers are still needed to update statements and check for accuracy. Rather than reduce the need for these workers, these technological changes are expected to help bookkeeping, accounting, and auditing clerks do their jobs.

Job Prospects. Because bookkeeping, accounting, and auditing clerks is a large occupation, there will be a large number of job openings from workers leaving the occupation. This means that opportunities to enter the occupation should be plentiful.

O*NET

➤ Bookkeeping, Accounting, and Auditing Clerks (43-3031.00)

Contacts for More Information

For more information about bookkeeping, accounting, and auditing clerks, visit

➤ American Institute of Professional Bookkeepers (www.aipb.org/)
➤ National Association of Certified Public Bookkeepers (www.nacpb.org)

Customer Service Representatives

- **2012 Median Pay** .... $30,580 per year
  $14.70 per hour
- **Entry-Level Education** ... High school diploma or equivalent
- **Work Experience in a Related Occupation** .... None
- **On-the-Job Training** .... Short-term on-the-job training
- **Number of Jobs 2012** 2,362,800
- **Job Outlook, 2012–22** .... 13% (As fast as average)
- **Employment Change, 2012–22** 298,700

What Customer Service Representatives Do

Customer service representatives handle customer complaints, process orders, and provide information about an organization's products and services.

Duties. Customer service representatives typically do the following:

- Listen to customers' questions and concerns, and provide answers or responses
- Provide information about products and services
- Take orders, calculate charges, and process billing or payments
- Review or make changes to customer accounts
- Handle returns or complaints
- Record details of customer contacts and actions taken
- Review and select standard responses for answers or solutions
- Refer customers to supervisors or more experienced employees

Customer service representatives answer questions or requests from customers or the public. They typically answer incoming phone calls, but some also interact with customers face to face, by email, or live chat.

The specific duties of customer service representatives vary depending on what kind of company they work for. For example, representatives who work in banks may answer customers' questions about their accounts. Representatives who work for utility and communication companies may help customers with service problems, such as outages. Those who work in retail stores often handle returns, process cash refunds, and help customers locate items. Some representatives make changes to customers' accounts, such as updating addresses or canceling orders. Although selling is not their main job, some representatives may help to generate sales leads while providing information about a product or service.

Customer service representatives typically use a telephone, computer, and other office equipment. Those employed in retail stores may occasionally use cash registers to process returns or orders.

Work Environment

Customer service representatives held about 2.4 million jobs in 2012 and were employed in nearly every industry. Many work in telephone call centers, credit and insurance agencies, banks, and retail stores.

The industries that employed the most customer service representatives in 2012 were as follows:

Administrative and support services 16%
Insurance carriers and related activities 12
Credit intermediation and related activities 9
Professional, scientific, and technical services 6

Representatives usually work in an office setting, sharing a large room with other employees. As a result, the work area can be crowded and noisy. Some workers may be under pressure to answer a designated number of calls while supervisors monitor them for quality assurance. In addition, the work can sometimes be stressful when they have to interact with difficult or irate customers.

In retail stores, representatives may spend hours on their feet assisting customers in person.

Work Schedules. Most customer service representatives work full time. About 1 in 5 worked part time in 2012.

Because many call centers are open around the clock, these positions may require early morning or late night shifts. Weekend or holiday work is also common.

In retail stores, customer service representatives are often needed to work during busy times, such as evenings, weekends, and holi-

Good communication and problem-solving skills are essential for customer service representatives.

days. Some companies hire additional workers during the holiday season when more customers are expected.

How to Become One

Customer service representatives typically need a high school diploma and receive on-the-job training to learn the specific skills needed for the job. They should be good at communicating and interacting with people and have basic computer skills.

Education. Customer service representatives typically need a high school diploma.

Training. Customer service representatives usually receive short-term on-the-job training, lasting 2 to 3 weeks. Those who work in finance and insurance may need several months of training to learn more complicated financial regulations.

General customer service training may focus on procedures for answering questions, information about a company's products and services, and computer and telephone use. Trainees often work under the guidance of an experienced worker for the first few weeks of employment.

Median Hourly Wages, May 2012

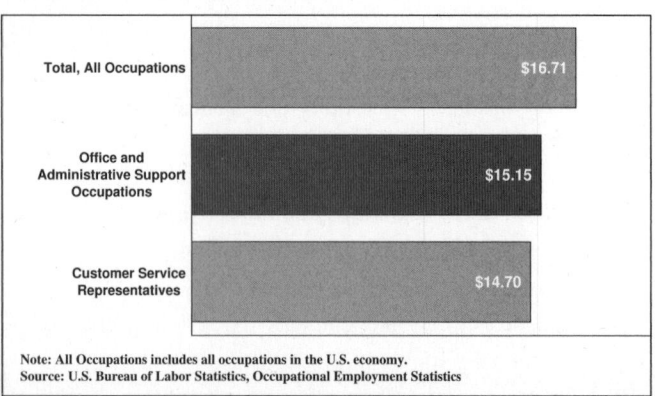

Total, All Occupations	$16.71
Office and Administrative Support Occupations	$15.15
Customer Service Representatives	$14.70

Note: All Occupations includes all occupations in the U.S. economy.
Source: U.S. Bureau of Labor Statistics, Occupational Employment Statistics

Percent Change in Employment, Projected 2012–2022

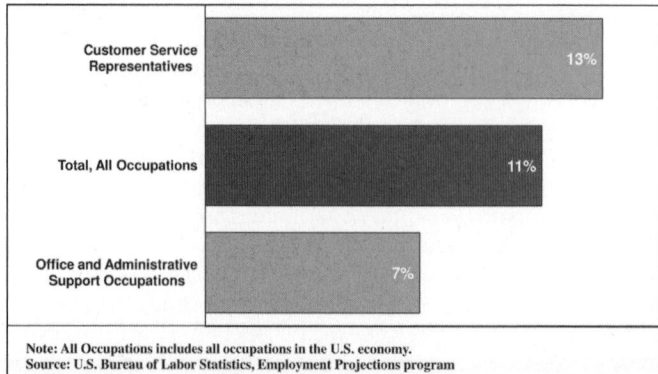

Customer Service Representatives	13%
Total, All Occupations	11%
Office and Administrative Support Occupations	7%

Note: All Occupations includes all occupations in the U.S. economy.
Source: U.S. Bureau of Labor Statistics, Employment Projections program

Employment Projections Data for Customer Service Representatives

Occupational title	SOC Code	Employment, 2012	Projected Employment, 2022	Change, 2012–2022	
				Percent	Numeric
Customer service representatives..	43-4051	2,362,800	2,661,400	13	298,700

Source: U.S. Bureau of Labor Statistics, Employment Projections Program

Note: Data are rounded. Go to **Occupational Information Included in the OOH** *for a discussion of the data in this table.*

In certain industries, such as finance and insurance, customer service representatives must keep up-to-date with changing regulations.

Licenses, Certifications, and Registrations. Customer service representatives who provide information about finance and insurance may need a state license. Although licensing requirements vary by state, they usually include passing a written exam. Some employers may provide training for these exams.

Important Qualities

Communication skills. Customer service representatives need strong communication skills to answer customers clearly. They must understand and communicate information effectively in writing, by phone, or in person.

Customer-service skills. Companies rely on representatives to help retain customers by answering customer questions and complaints in a helpful and professional manner.

Interpersonal skills. Creating positive interactions with customers is an essential part of a representative's job.

Listening skills. Representatives must listen carefully and understand a customer's situation in order to help them.

Patience. Workers should be patient and polite, especially when interacting with difficult or irate customers.

Problem-solving skills. Representatives must determine solutions to a customer's problem. By resolving issues effectively, representatives contribute to customer loyalty and retention.

Pay

The median hourly wage for customer service representatives was $14.70 in May 2012. The median wage is the wage at which half the workers in an occupation earned more than that amount and half earned less. The lowest 10 percent earned less than $9.38 per hour, and the top 10 percent earned more than $24.00 per hour.

In May 2012, the median hourly wages for customer service representatives in the top four industries employing these workers were as follows:

Insurance carriers and related activities...............................$16.44
Professional, scientific, and technical services........................16.01
Credit intermediation and related activities...........................14.96
Administrative and support services.....................................12.71

Job Outlook

Employment of customer service representatives is projected to grow 13 percent from 2012 to 2022, about as fast as the average for all occupations.

Overall employment growth should result from growing industries that specialize in handling customer service. Specifically, telephone call centers, also known as customer contact centers, are expected to add the most new jobs for customer service representatives. Employment of representatives in these centers is projected to grow 38 percent from 2012 to 2022, much faster than the average for all occupations. Some businesses are increasingly contracting out their customer service operations to telephone call centers as they provide consolidated sales and customer service functions.

Employment growth of customer service representatives in all other industries will be driven by growth of those industries, as well as consumers' demand for products and services that require customer support. Some companies will continue to use in-house service centers to differentiate themselves from competitors, particularly for inquiries that are more complex, such as refunding accounts or confirming insurance coverage.

However, some companies are increasingly using Internet self-service or interactive voice-response systems that enable customers to resolve simple problems, such as changing addresses or reviewing account billing, without speaking to a representative.

Similar Occupations   This table shows a list of occupations with job duties that are similar to those of customer service representatives.

Occupations	Entry-level Education	2012 Pay	Projected Job Growth	Average Annual Openings
Cashiers	Less than high school	$18,970	3%	153,000
Computer Support Specialists	See "How to Become One"	$49,488	17%	23,650
Financial Clerks	High school diploma or equivalent	$35,122	11%	43,930
Information Clerks	High school diploma or equivalent	$31,159	2%	47,000
Insurance Sales Agents	High school diploma or equivalent	$48,150	10%	15,020
Receptionists	High school diploma or equivalent	$25,990	13%	40,690
Retail Sales Workers	Less than high school	$21,514	10%	202,730
Securities, Commodities, and Financial Services Sales Agents	Bachelor's degree	$71,720	11%	12,260
Tellers	High school diploma or equivalent	$24,940	1%	25,980
Wholesale and Manufacturing Sales Representatives	See "How to Become One"	$58,484	9%	53,250

In addition, some businesses are expected to move customer service functions to other countries in order to cut costs, a practice known as offshoring. However, demand for customer service representatives in the United States should continue as companies adjust to consumers' preference for U.S.-based customer support.

Job Prospects. Job prospects for customer service representatives are expected to be good due to employment growth and the need to replace workers who leave the occupation each year. Job opportunities should be best in telephone call centers.

There will be greater competition for in-house customer service jobs in the insurance and finance sectors–which often have higher pay–than for jobs in the telephone call center industry.

Candidates with good customer service and computer skills should have the best job prospects.

O*NET

➤ Customer Service Representatives (43-4051.00)
➤ Patient Representatives (43-4051.03)

Contacts for More Information

For more information about customer service representatives, visit
➤ International Customer Management Institute (www.icmi.com/)

Desktop Publishers

- **2012 Median Pay** .... $37,040 per year
  $17.81 per hour
- **Entry-Level Education** ....Associate's degree
- **Work Experience in a Related Occupation**............... None
- **On-the-Job Training** ....Short-term on-the-job training
- **Number of Jobs 2012** 16,400
- **Job Outlook, 2012–22** .... -5% (Decline)
- **Employment Change, 2012–22** .... -900

What Desktop Publishers Do

Desktop publishers use computer software to design page layouts for newspapers, books, brochures, and other items that are printed or put online. They collect the text, graphics, and other materials they will need and format them into a finished product.

Duties. Desktop publishers typically do the following:

- Gather existing materials or work with designers and writers to create new artwork or text
- Find and edit graphics, such as photographs or illustrations
- Use scanners to turn drawings and other materials into digital images
- Import text and graphics into desktop publishing software programs
- Position artwork and text on the page layout
- Select formatting properties, such as text size, column width, and spacing
- Check proofs, or preliminary layouts, for errors and make corrections
- Finalize formatted documents for printing or electronic publication
- Send final files to a commercial printer or print the documents on a high-resolution printer

Desktop publishers use publishing software to create page layouts for print or electronic publication. In addition to designing pages, desktop publishers may edit or write text. Some desktop publishers might be responsible for correcting spelling, punctuation, and grammar or for writing original content themselves.

Desktop publishers' responsibilities may vary widely from project to project and employer to employer. Smaller firms typically use desktop publishers to perform a wide range of tasks, while desktop publishers at larger firms may specialize in one part of the publishing process.

Desktop publishers work with other design and media professionals, such as writers, editors, and graphic designers. For example, they work with graphic designers to come up with images that complement the text and fit the available space.

Work Environment

Desktop publishers held about 16,400 jobs in 2012. About one-third of them worked in publishing industries. Most of the rest worked for companies in other industries that produce their own printed materials, including advertising and public relations industries which are included in professional, scientific, and technical services.

The industries that employed the most desktop publishers in 2012 were as follows:

Newspaper, periodical, book, and directory publishers 31%
Printing and related support activities 16
Professional, scientific, and technical services........................ 12
Administrative and support services 8

Work Schedules. Many desktop publishers work full time. They may need to work long hours to meet publication deadlines.

How to Become One

Desktop publishers have a variety of educational backgrounds, but most have earned some form of postsecondary degree or award, such as an associate's degree.

Education. Desktop publishers have various educational backgrounds, but postsecondary education, such as an associate's degree, is typical. Workers usually learn some of their skills on the job. Computer skills, including knowledge of desktop publishing software, are important.

Although many desktop publishers have earned associate's degrees, others have earned postsecondary nondegree awards. These usually take less than 2 years to complete, or they sometimes earn bachelor's degrees. Experience in a related field can sometimes substitute for education.

Desktop publishers format text, data, photographs, and other graphics into documents that are to be printed.

Median Annual Wages, May 2012

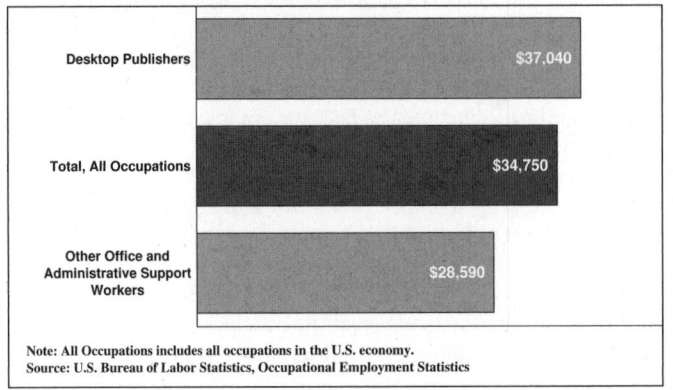

Note: All Occupations includes all occupations in the U.S. economy.
Source: U.S. Bureau of Labor Statistics, Occupational Employment Statistics

Percent Change in Employment, Projected 2012–2022

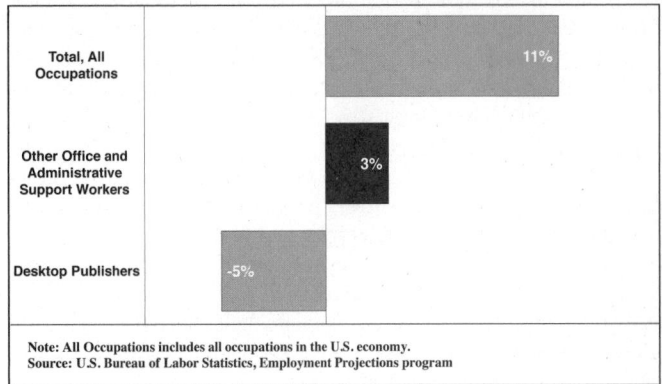

Note: All Occupations includes all occupations in the U.S. economy.
Source: U.S. Bureau of Labor Statistics, Employment Projections program

Those who earn degrees usually study fields such as graphic design, graphic arts, or graphic communications. Community colleges and trade and technical schools also may offer desktop publishing courses. These classes teach students about desktop publishing software used to format pages and how to import text and graphics into electronic page layouts.

Training. Desktop publishers learn some of their skills on the job. They learn by observing more experienced workers or by taking classes that teach them how to use desktop publishing software. Ongoing training is often necessary, as technologies and desktop publishing software change.

Important Qualities

Artistic ability. Desktop publishers must have a good eye for how graphics and text will look to create pages that are visually appealing, legible, and easy to read.

Communication skills. Desktop publishers talk through different concepts for a page layout with writers, editors, and graphic designers. They listen to ideas and explain their own.

Computer skills. Many desktop publishers use computer software exclusively when creating page layouts and formatting text and graphics.

Detail oriented. When designing and reviewing page layouts, desktop publishers must pay careful attention to details such as

margins, font sizes, and the overall appearance and accuracy of their work.

Organizational skills. Desktop publishers often work under strict deadlines and must be good at scheduling and prioritizing tasks in order to have a document ready on time for publication.

Work Experience in a Related Occupation. Many employers prefer to hire workers who have experience in preparing layouts. This experience can sometimes substitute for formal education, such as a degree in graphic design.

Pay

The median annual wage for desktop publishers was $37,040 in May 2012. The median wage is the wage at which half the workers in an occupation earned more than that amount and half earned less. The lowest 10 percent earned less than $19,740, and the top 10 percent earned more than $60,470.

Job Outlook

Employment of desktop publishers is projected to decline 5 percent from 2012 to 2022. Companies are expected to hire fewer desktop publishers, as other types of workers–such as graphic designers, Web designers, and copy editors–increasingly take on desktop publishing tasks.

Employment Projections Data for Desktop Publishers

Occupational title	SOC Code	Employment, 2012	Projected Employment, 2022	Change, 2012–2022	
				Percent	Numeric
Desktop publishers	43-9031	16,400	15,500	-5	-900

Source: U.S. Bureau of Labor Statistics, Employment Projections Program

Note: Data are rounded. Go to **Occupational Information Included in the OOH** *for a discussion of the data in this table.*

Similar Occupations   This table shows a list of occupations with job duties that are similar to those of desktop publishers.

Occupations	Entry-level Education	2012 Pay	Projected Job Growth	Average Annual Openings
Editors	Bachelor's degree	$53,880	-2%	2,800
Film and Video Editors and Camera Operators	Bachelor's degree	$46,538	3%	510
Graphic Designers	Bachelor's degree	$44,150	7%	8,600
Multimedia Artists and Animators	Bachelor's degree	$61,370	6%	2,060
Printing Workers	See "How to Become One"	$34,110	-5%	5,190
Technical Writers	Bachelor's degree	$65,500	15%	2,260

Desktop publishing is commonly used to design printed materials, such as advertisements, brochures, newsletters, and forms. However, increased computer-processing capacity and the widespread availability of more elaborate desktop publishing software make it easier and more affordable for nonprinting professionals to create their own materials. As a result, there will be less need for people to specialize in desktop publishing.

Some of the tasks that desktop publishers do, such as creating initial page layouts or converting pages to PDF files, can now be automated, further reducing employment.

Overall declines in the printing and publishing industries–those most likely to employ desktop publishers–will also restrict growth. As organizations increasingly publish their materials electronically instead of in print to save on printing and distribution costs, employment of desktop publishers may decline further.

Job Prospects. Prospects will be better for those with a degree in graphic design or a related field, or for those with experience in desktop publishing. Expertise in electronic and Web-publishing is increasingly in demand. Workers with a diverse range of skills, such as graphic design, Web design, writing, and editing may have better prospects.

O*NET

➤ Desktop Publishers (43-9031.00)

Contacts for More Information

For more information about the printing industry, visit
➤ Printing Industries of America (www.printing.org/)
➤ Society for Technical Communication (www.stc.org)

Financial Clerks

- **2012 Median Pay** .... $34,960 per year
  $16.81 per hour
- **Entry-Level Education** ... High school diploma or equivalent
- **Work Experience in a Related Occupation** .... None
- **On-the-Job Training** ....See "How to Become One"
- **Number of Jobs 2012** 1,404,000
- **Job Outlook, 2012–22** .... 11% (As fast as average)
- **Employment Change, 2012–22** 154,200

What Financial Clerks Do

Financial clerks do administrative work for many types of organizations. They keep records, help customers, and carry out financial transactions.

Duties. Financial clerks typically do the following:

- Keep and update financial records
- Compute bills and charges
- Offer customer assistance
- Carry out financial transactions

Financial clerks give administrative and clerical support in financial settings. Their specific job duties vary by specialty and by setting.

Billing and posting clerks calculate charges, develop bills, and prepare them to be mailed to customers. They review documents such as purchase orders, sales tickets, charge slips, and hospital records to compute fees or charges due. They also contact customers to get or give account information.

Gaming cage workers work in casinos and other gaming establishments. The "cage" in which they work is the central depository

for money and gaming chips. Gaming cage workers sell gambling chips, tokens, or tickets to patrons. They count funds and reconcile daily summaries of transactions to balance books.

Payroll and timekeeping clerks compile and post employee time and payroll data. They verify and record attendance, hours worked, and pay adjustments. They ensure that employees are paid on time and that their paychecks are accurate.

Procurement clerks compile requests for materials, prepare purchase orders, keep track of purchases and supplies, and handle questions about orders. They respond to questions from customers and suppliers about the status of orders. They handle requests to change or cancel orders. They make sure that purchases arrive on schedule and that the items meet the purchaser's specifications.

Brokerage clerks help with tasks about securities such as stocks, bonds, commodities, and other kinds of investments. Their duties include writing orders for stock purchases and sales, computing transfer taxes, verifying stock transactions, accepting and delivering securities, distributing dividends, and keeping records of daily transactions and holdings.

Credit authorizers, checkers, and clerks review the credit history and get the information needed to determine the creditworthiness of individuals or businesses applying for credit. Credit authorizers evaluate customers' computerized credit records and payment histories to decide, based on predetermined standards, whether to approve new credit. Credit checkers call or write credit departments of business and service establishments to get information about applicants' credit standing.

Loan interviewers, also called *loan processors* or *loan clerks*, interview applicants and others to get and verify personal and financial information needed to complete loan applications. They also prepare the documents that go to the appraiser and are issued at the closing of a loan.

New accounts clerks interview people who want to open accounts in financial institutions. They explain the account services available to prospective customers and help them fill out applications. They also investigate and correct errors in accounts.

Insurance claims and policy processing clerks process applications for insurance policies. They also handle customers' requests to

Gaming cage workers exchange tickets and chips for money.

Median Annual Wages, May 2012

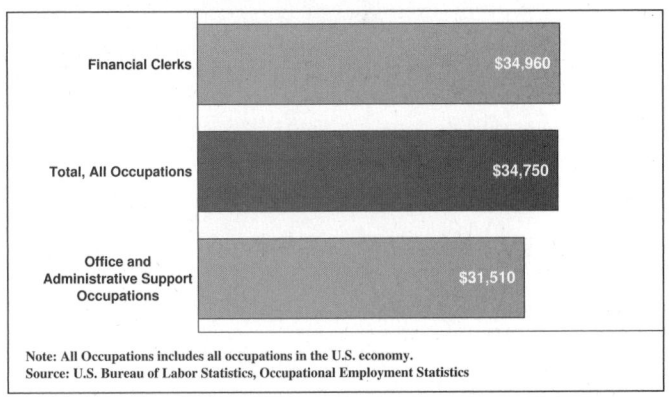

Note: All Occupations includes all occupations in the U.S. economy.
Source: U.S. Bureau of Labor Statistics, Occupational Employment Statistics

Percent Change in Employment, Projected 2012–2022

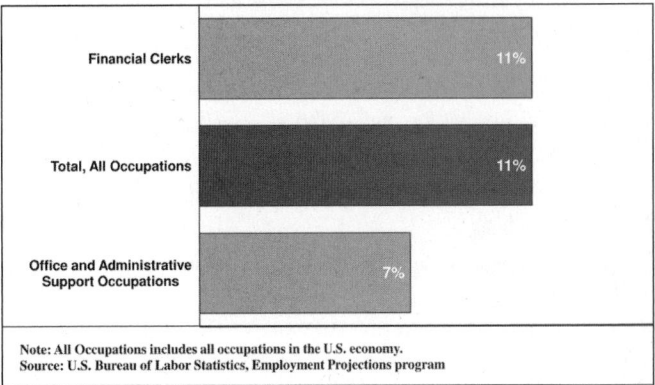

Note: All Occupations includes all occupations in the U.S. economy.
Source: U.S. Bureau of Labor Statistics, Employment Projections program

change or cancel their existing policies. Their duties include interviewing clients and reviewing insurance applications to ensure that all questions have been answered. They also notify insurance agents and accounting departments of policy cancellations or changes.

Work Environment

Financial clerks held about 1.4 million jobs in 2012.

Financial clerks work in a variety of office settings, including bank branches, medical offices, and government agencies. The industries that employed the most financial clerks in 2012 were as follows:

Credit intermediation and related activities 18%
Insurance carriers and related activities 18
Health care 17
Professional, scientific, and technical services........................... 7

Work Schedules. Most financial clerks work full time. About 1 in 3 procurement clerks worked more than 40 hours per week in 2012, as did about 1 in 3 brokerage clerks.

How to Become One

A high school diploma or equivalent is enough for most jobs as a financial clerk. These workers usually learn their duties through on-the-job training.

Education. Financial clerks typically need a high school diploma or equivalent to enter the occupation. Employers of brokerage clerks may prefer candidates who have taken some college courses in business or economics, and in some cases require a 2- or 4-year college degree.

Training. Most financial clerks learn how to do their job duties through on-the-job training. Some formal technical training also

may be necessary; for example, gaming cage workers may need training in specific gaming regulations and procedures.

Advancement. Financial clerks can advance to related occupations in finance. For example, a loan interviewer or clerk can become a loan officer, while a brokerage clerk can become a securities, commodities, or financial services sales agent, after obtaining the required education and license.

Important Qualities

Communication skills. Financial clerks should have good communication skills so that they can explain policies and procedures to colleagues and customers.

Math skills. The job duties of financial clerks, including calculating charges and checking credit scores, require basic math skills.

Organizational skills. Strong organizational skills are important for financial clerks because they must be able to find files quickly and efficiently.

Pay

The median annual wage for financial clerks was $34,960 in May 2012. The median wage is the wage at which half the workers in an occupation earned more than that amount and half earned less. The lowest 10 percent earned less than $23,840, and the top 10 percent earned more than $51,440.

The median annual wages for financial clerks in May 2012 were as follows:

Brokerage clerks...$42,440
Procurement clerks 38,220
Payroll and timekeeping clerks... 37,690

Employment Projections Data for Financial Clerks

Occupational title	SOC Code	Employment, 2012	Projected Employment, 2022	Change, 2012–2022 Percent	Change, 2012–2022 Numeric
Financial clerks	—	1,404,000	1,558,200	11	154,200
Billing and posting clerks................................	43-3021	513,800	607,000	18	93,200
Gaming cage workers	43-3041	18,400	19,800	7	1,300
Payroll and timekeeping clerks	43-3051	179,500	202,000	13	22,500
Procurement clerks..	43-3061	72,200	73,600	2	1,400
Brokerage clerks..	43-4011	61,900	64,300	4	2,400
Credit authorizers, checkers, and clerks...........................	43-4041	52,100	50,500	-3	-1,700
Loan interviewers and clerks............................	43-4131	195,900	213,000	9	17,100
New accounts clerks...	43-4141	55,700	53,000	-5	-2,700
Insurance claims and policy processing clerks	43-9041	254,400	275,000	8	20,600

Source: U.S. Bureau of Labor Statistics, Employment Projections Program

Note: Data are rounded. Go to Occupational Information Included in the OOH for a discussion of the data in this table.

Similar Occupations   This table shows a list of occupations with job duties that are similar to those of financial clerks.

Occupations	Entry-level Education	2012 Pay	Projected Job Growth	Average Annual Openings
Bill and Account Collectors	High school diploma or equivalent	$32,480	15%	17,000
Bookkeeping, Accounting, and Auditing Clerks	High school diploma or equivalent	$35,170	11%	37,000
Gaming Services Occupations	High school diploma or equivalent	$25,951	10%	5,110
Information Clerks	High school diploma or equivalent	$31,159	2%	47,000
Medical Records and Health Information Technicians	Postsecondary non-degree award	$34,160	22%	9,040
Secretaries and Administrative Assistants	High school diploma or equivalent	$36,198	12%	97,210
Tellers	High school diploma or equivalent	$24,940	1%	25,980

Insurance claims and policy processing clerks $35,700
Loan interviewers and clerks 35,310
Credit authorizers, checkers, and clerks 33,600
Billing and posting clerks 33,450
New accounts clerks 31,720
Gaming cage workers 24,610

Job Outlook

Employment of financial clerks is projected to grow 11 percent from 2012 to 2022, about as fast as the average for all occupations. Projected employment change will vary by specialty as follows:

- Employment of billing and posting clerks is projected to grow 18 percent. Job growth will be particularly strong for those in medical billing because increased demand for healthcare services will require more of these workers.

- Employment of payroll and timekeeping clerks is projected to grow 13 percent. Although payroll and timekeeping functions continue to be important for companies, the automation of this work and the use of computer software that allows employees to update and record their own payroll and timekeeping information will limit the growth of this occupation.

- Employment of insurance claims and policy processing clerks is projected to grow 8 percent. These workers are heavily concentrated in the insurance industry; therefore, their job growth will be determined mainly by the performance of the insurance industry as a whole.

- Employment of procurement clerks is projected to show little or no change. The need for procurement clerks will be limited because of the increasing use of the Internet to place orders, which means that fewer procurement clerks are required to handle the same amount of orders.

- Employment of brokerage clerks is projected to grow 4 percent. The automation of securities transactions will lead to slower growth for these workers.

- Employment of credit authorizers, checkers, and clerks is projected to decline 3 percent. The availability of online credit reports will reduce the need for these workers.

- Employment of new accounts clerks is projected to decline 5 percent. There is less of a need for these workers since many customers can open accounts online.

- Employment of loan interviewers and clerks is projected to grow 9 percent. Tighter lending standards and regulations will create demand for workers whose job is to verify the accuracy of loan applications. However, the use of online loan applications will somewhat reduce the need for these workers to conduct in-person interviews.

- Employment of gaming cage workers is projected to grow 7 percent. Employment will grow as more state-owned casinos open and the private gaming industry expands.

Job Prospects. Job prospects for financial clerks are likely to be favorable, because many workers are expected to leave this occupation. Employers will need to hire new workers to replace those leaving the occupation.

O*NET

- ➤ Billing and Posting Clerks (43-3021.00)
- ➤ Statement Clerks (43-3021.01)
- ➤ Billing, Cost, and Rate Clerks (43-3021.02)
- ➤ Gaming Cage Workers (43-3041.00)
- ➤ Payroll and Timekeeping Clerks (43-3051.00)
- ➤ Procurement Clerks (43-3061.00)
- ➤ Brokerage Clerks (43-4011.00)
- ➤ Credit Authorizers, Checkers, and Clerks (43-4041.00)
- ➤ Credit Authorizers (43-4041.01)
- ➤ Credit Checkers (43-4041.02)
- ➤ Loan Interviewers and Clerks (43-4131.00)
- ➤ New Accounts Clerks (43-4141.00)
- ➤ Insurance Claims and Policy Processing Clerks (43-9041.00)
- ➤ Insurance Claims Clerks (43-9041.01)
- ➤ Insurance Policy Processing Clerks (43-9041.02)

Contacts for More Information

For more information about financial clerks, visit

- ➤ American Bankers Association (www.aba.com)
- ➤ Insurance Information Institute (www.iii.org)
- ➤ Mortgage Bankers Association (www.mbaa.org)

General Office Clerks

- **2012 Median Pay** .... $27,470 per year
  $13.21 per hour
- **Entry-Level Education** ... High school diploma or equivalent
- **Work Experience in a Related Occupation** .... None
- **On-the-Job Training** .... Short-term on-the-job training
- **Number of Jobs 2012** 2,983,500
- **Job Outlook, 2012–22** .... 6% (Slower than average)
- **Employment Change, 2012–22** 184,100

General office clerks operate photocopiers, fax machines, and other office equipment.

Rather than performing a single specialized task, general office clerks have responsibilities that often change daily with the needs of the specific job and the employer.

Some clerks spend their time filing documents or answering phones; others enter data into computers. Because organizations often keep files and records on computers, office clerks use computer software applications. They also frequently use photocopiers, fax machines, and other office equipment.

The specific duties assigned to clerks can vary significantly, depending on the type of office in which they work. For example, a general office clerk at a college or university may process application materials or answer questions from prospective students. A clerk at a hospital may file and retrieve medical records.

Clerks' duties also vary by level of experience. Inexperienced employees may sort mail and take phone messages. Experienced clerks usually have additional responsibilities. For example, they may be required to maintain financial records, set up spreadsheets, or check statistical reports for accuracy.

Some senior office clerks may supervise and direct the work of other clerks.

Work Environment

General office clerks held about 3 million jobs in 2012 and were employed in nearly every industry.

The industries that employed the most general office clerks in 2012 were as follows:

Educational services; state, local, and private	12%
Health care and social assistance	12
Administrative and support and waste management and remediation services	10
Government	9

General office clerks usually work in comfortable office settings.

Work Schedules. Most general office clerks work full time. About 1 in 4 clerks worked part time in 2012.

How to Become One

General office clerks typically need a high school diploma or equivalent and learn their skills on the job.

Education. General office clerks typically need a high school diploma or equivalent.

Business education programs offered in community colleges and postsecondary vocational schools can help candidates prepare for an entry-level job. Courses in office practices, word processing, and other common computer applications are particularly helpful.

Training. General office clerks usually learn their skills on the job. On-the-job training typically lasts up to 1 month and may include instructions on office procedures and the use of office equipment.

What General Office Clerks Do

General office clerks perform a variety of administrative tasks, including answering telephones, typing or word processing, making copies of documents, and maintaining records.

Duties. General office clerks typically do the following:

- Answer telephone calls, take messages, or transfer calls to staff
- Sort and deliver incoming mail and send outgoing mail
- Schedule appointments and receive customers or visitors
- Provide general information to staff, clients, or the public
- Type, format, or edit routine memos or other reports
- Copy, file, and maintain paper or electronic documents and records
- Prepare and process travel vouchers, billing, or other office documents
- Obtain information, send correspondence, or perform data entry

Median Hourly Wages, May 2012

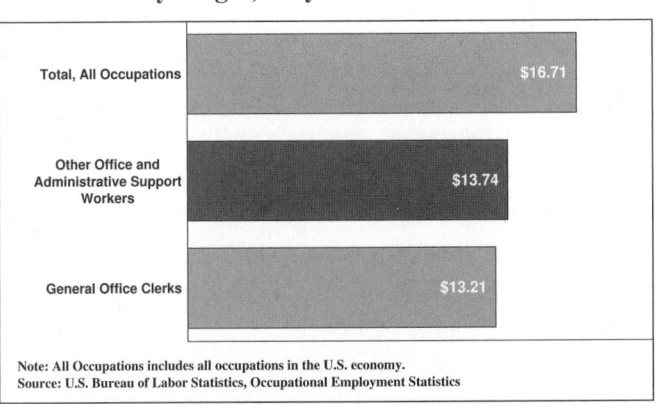

Note: All Occupations includes all occupations in the U.S. economy.
Source: U.S. Bureau of Labor Statistics, Occupational Employment Statistics

Percent Change in Employment, Projected 2012–2022

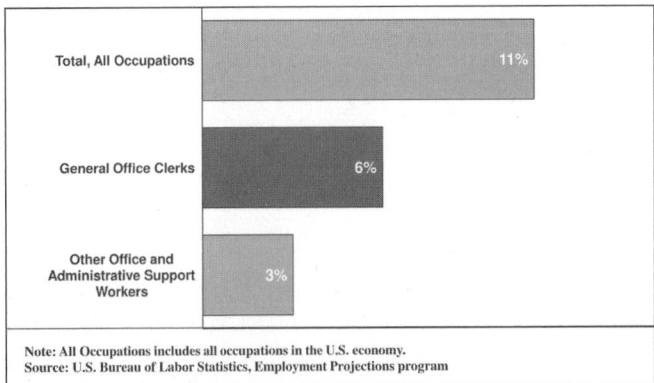

Note: All Occupations includes all occupations in the U.S. economy.
Source: U.S. Bureau of Labor Statistics, Employment Projections program

Employment Projections Data for General Office Clerks

Occupational title	SOC Code	Employment, 2012	Projected Employment, 2022	Change, 2012–2022	
				Percent	Numeric
Office clerks, general..	43-9061	2,983,500	3,167,600	6	184,100

Source: *U.S. Bureau of Labor Statistics, Employment Projections Program*

Note: Data are rounded. Go to **Occupational Information Included in the OOH** *for a discussion of the data in this table.*

Similar Occupations   This table shows a list of occupations with job duties that are similar to those of general office clerks.

Occupations	Entry-level Education	2012 Pay	Projected Job Growth	Average Annual Openings
Bookkeeping, Accounting, and Auditing Clerks	High school diploma or equivalent	$35,170	11%	37,000
Customer Service Representatives	High school diploma or equivalent	$30,580	13%	94,160
Information Clerks	High school diploma or equivalent	$31,159	2%	47,000
Material Recording Clerks	See "How to Become One"	$26,007	1%	84,000
Receptionists	High school diploma or equivalent	$25,990	13%	40,690
Secretaries and Administrative Assistants	High school diploma or equivalent	$36,198	12%	97,210
Tellers	High school diploma or equivalent	$24,940	1%	25,980

Advancement. General office clerks may advance to other administrative positions with more responsibility, such as executive secretaries and executive administrative assistants.

Advancement opportunities often depend on work experience, work habits, and computer software skills.

Important Qualities

Customer-service skills. Clerks often provide general information to company staff, customers, or the public. As a result, they should be courteous and prompt with their response.

Detail oriented. Many administrative tasks, such as proofreading documents and arranging schedules, require excellent attention to detail.

Organizational skills. Being organized helps office clerks retrieve files and other important information quickly and efficiently.

Pay

The median hourly wage for general office clerks was $13.21 in May 2012. The median wage is the wage at which half the workers in an occupation earned more than that amount and half earned less. The lowest 10 percent earned less than $8.59 per hour, and the top 10 percent earned more than $21.21 per hour.

In May 2012, median hourly wages for general office clerks in the top four industries employing these clerks were as follows:

Government..	$15.24
Health care and social assistance...	13.23
Educational services; state, local, and private.......................	13.08
Administrative and support and waste management and remediation services	12.25

Job Outlook

Employment of general office clerks is projected to grow 6 percent from 2012 to 2022, slower than the average for all occupations. Employment growth will vary by industry.

For example, healthcare facilities are expected to require more workers to handle various administrative tasks related to billing and insurance processing as more people have access to health insurance

and medical services. Conversely, employment of general office clerks in the federal government is projected to decline as other workers are increasingly performing tasks that general office clerks used to do.

Overall, employment growth of office clerks should moderate as technology makes them more productive. For example, many organizations maintain electronic documents or use automated phone systems, reducing the need for general office clerks.

Job Prospects. Job prospects are expected to be good due to employment growth and the need to replace workers who leave the occupation. Job opportunities in healthcare facilities should be best, while opportunities in schools and government are expected to be less favorable.

Candidates who have a combination of work experience and computer software skills should have the best job prospects.

O*NET

➤ Office Clerks, General (43-9061.00)

Contacts for More Information

For more information about administrative occupations, visit
➤ International Association of Administrative Professionals (www.iaap-hq.org)

Information Clerks

- **2012 Median Pay** .... $30,650 per year
$14.74 per hour
- **Entry-Level Education** ... High school diploma or equivalent
- **Work Experience in a Related Occupation**............... None
- **On-the-Job Training** ....See "How to Become One"
- **Number of Jobs 2012** 1,567,100
- **Job Outlook, 2012–22**...............2% (Little or no change)
- **Employment Change, 2012–22** 32,800

Hotel, motel and resort desk clerks provide customer service to hotel guests and other customers often at the hotel's front desk.

What Information Clerks Do

Information clerks perform routine clerical duties such as maintaining records, collecting data, and providing information to customers.

Duties. Information clerks typically do the following:

- Prepare routine office correspondence, reports, claims, bills, or orders
- Collect and record data from customers, staff, and the public
- Answer questions from customers and the public about products or services
- File and maintain paper or electronic records and information

Information clerks perform routine office support functions in an organization, business, or government. They use telephones, computers, and other office equipment such as scanners and fax machines.

The following are examples of types of information clerks:

Correspondence clerks respond to inquiries from the public or customers. They prepare standard responses to requests for merchandise, damage claims, delinquent accounts, incorrect billings, or unsatisfactory services. They also may review the organization's records and type response letters for their supervisor's signature.

Court clerks organize and maintain court records. They prepare the calendar of cases, also known as a docket, and inform attorneys and witnesses about court appearances. Court clerks also put together materials for court and receive, file, and forward court documents.

Eligibility interviewers conduct interviews both in person and over the phone to determine if applicants qualify for government assistance and benefits. They answer applicants' questions about programs and may refer them to other agencies for assistance.

File clerks maintain electronic or paper records, enter and retrieve data, organize records, and file documents. In organizations with electronic filing systems, file clerks scan and upload documents.

Hotel, motel, and resort desk clerks, also called *front desk clerks*, provide customer service to guests at the establishment's front desk. They check guests in and out, assign rooms, and process payments. They also keep occupancy records; take, confirm, or change room reservations; and provide information on the hotel's policies and services. In addition, front desk clerks answer phone calls, take and deliver messages for guests, and handle guests' requests or complaints. For example, when guests report a problem in their rooms, clerks must coordinate with maintenance staff to resolve the issue.

Human resources assistants provide administrative support to human resources managers. They maintain personnel records on employees, including their addresses, employment history, and performance evaluations. They may post information about job openings and review candidates' resumes for qualifications.

Interviewers conduct interviews over the phone, in person, through mail, or electronically. They use the information to complete forms, applications, or questionnaires for market research surveys, census forms, and medical histories. Interviewers typically follow set procedures and questionnaires to obtain specific information.

License clerks process applications for licenses and permits, administer tests, and collect application fees. They determine if applicants are qualified to receive the particular license or if additional documentation needs to be submitted. They also maintain records of applications received and licenses issued.

Municipal clerks provide administrative support for town or city governments by maintaining their records. They record, maintain, and distribute minutes of town and city council meetings to local officials and staff and help prepare for elections. They also may answer requests for information from local, state, and federal officials and the public.

Order clerks receive orders from customers and process payments. For example, they may enter information about customers, such as their address and method of payment, into the order entry system. They also answer questions about prices and shipping.

Reservation and transportation ticket agents and travel clerks take and confirm passengers' reservations for hotels and transporta-

Median Annual Wages, May 2012

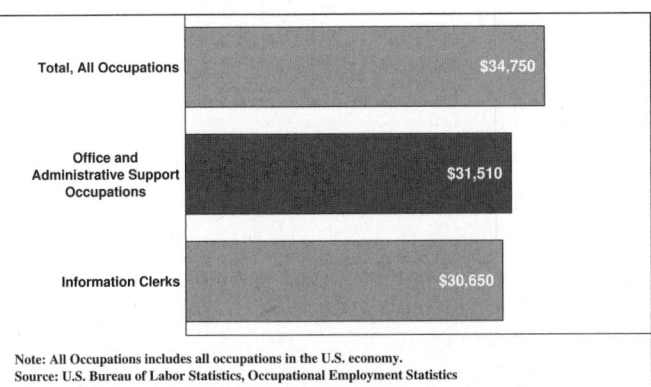

Total, All Occupations	$34,750
Office and Administrative Support Occupations	$31,510
Information Clerks	$30,650

Note: All Occupations includes all occupations in the U.S. economy.
Source: U.S. Bureau of Labor Statistics, Occupational Employment Statistics

Percent Change in Employment, Projected 2012–2022

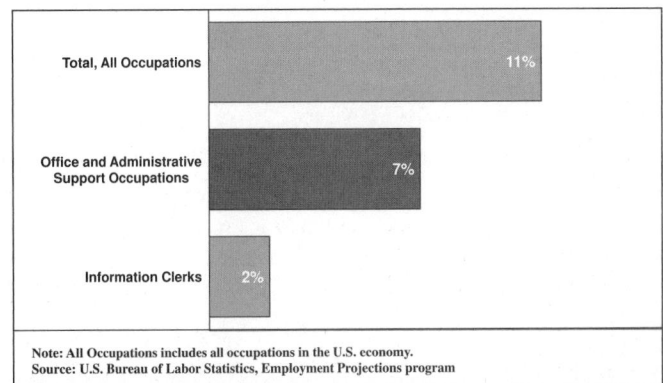

Total, All Occupations	11%
Office and Administrative Support Occupations	7%
Information Clerks	2%

Note: All Occupations includes all occupations in the U.S. economy.
Source: U.S. Bureau of Labor Statistics, Employment Projections program

Employment Projections Data for Information Clerks

Occupational title	SOC Code	Employment, 2012	Projected Employment, 2022	Change, 2012–2022	
				Percent	Numeric
Information clerks	—	1,567,100	1,599,900	2	32,800
Correspondence clerks	43-4021	11,100	11,500	4	500
Court, municipal, and license clerks	43-4031	130,000	143,800	11	13,800
Eligibility interviewers, government programs	43-4061	138,100	152,000	10	13,900
File clerks	43-4071	164,200	158,800	-3	-5,300
Hotel, motel, and resort desk clerks	43-4081	231,600	263,400	14	31,800
Interviewers, except eligibility and loan	43-4111	204,500	225,800	10	21,300
Order clerks	43-4151	212,700	207,400	-2	-5,300
Human resources assistants, except payroll and timekeeping	43-4161	146,900	145,300	-1	-1,600
Reservation and transportation ticket agents and travel clerks	43-4181	139,100	119,600	-14	-19,500
Information and record clerks, all other	43-4199	188,900	172,200	-9	-16,700

Source: U.S. Bureau of Labor Statistics, Employment Projections Program

Note: Data are rounded. Go to **Occupational Information Included in the OOH** *for a discussion of the data in this table.*

tion. They also sell and issue tickets and answer questions about itineraries, rates, and package tours. Ticket agents who work at airports also check bags and issue boarding passes to passengers.

Work Environment

Information clerks held about 1.6 million jobs in 2012 and were employed in nearly every industry. However, employment was mostly concentrated in government agencies, hotels, and healthcare facilities.

Although most clerks work in an office setting, interviewers may travel to applicants' locations to conduct interviews.

The work of information clerks who provide customer service can be stressful, particularly when dealing with difficult or irate customers.

Reservation and transportation agents at airports or shipping counters may need to lift or maneuver heavy luggage or packages, sometimes weighing up to 100 pounds.

Work Schedules. Most information clerks work full time. However, part-time work is common for hotel clerks, file clerks, and interviewers.

Clerks in lodging and transportation establishments that are open around the clock or extended hours may work evenings, holidays, and weekends.

Injuries and Illnesses. Although the work of most clerks is not dangerous, reservation and transportation agents have one of the highest rates of injuries and illnesses of all occupations. The most common injury is muscle strains from lifting heavy suitcases.

How to Become One

Information clerks typically need a high school diploma and learn their skills on the job. Employers may prefer to hire candidates with some college education, depending on the specialty.

Education. Candidates typically need a high school diploma for most positions. However, employers may prefer to hire candidates with some college education or an associate's degree. This is particularly true for eligibility interviewer and municipal clerk positions. Courses in social and behavioral science and computer software are particularly helpful.

Training. Most information clerks receive short-term on-the-job training, usually lasting a few weeks. Training typically covers office procedures and computer use. Those employed in government receive training that may last several months and include instructions on government programs and regulations.

Important Qualities

Communication skills. Information clerks must be able to clearly explain policies and procedures to customers and the public.

Integrity. Information clerks, particularly human resources assistants, have access to confidential information, and they must be trusted to keep this information private.

Similar Occupations   This table shows a list of occupations with job duties that are similar to those of information clerks.

Occupations	Entry-level Education	2012 Pay	Projected Job Growth	Average Annual Openings
Bookkeeping, Accounting, and Auditing Clerks	High school diploma or equivalent	$35,170	11%	37,000
Compensation and Benefits Managers	Bachelor's degree	$95,250	3%	610
Financial Clerks	High school diploma or equivalent	$35,122	11%	43,930
General Office Clerks	High school diploma or equivalent	$27,470	6%	81,090
Human Resources Specialists and Labor Relations Specialists	Bachelor's degree	$55,616	7%	12,370
Lodging Managers	High school diploma or equivalent	$46,810	1%	1,620
Material Recording Clerks	See "How to Become One"	$26,007	1%	84,000
Receptionists	High school diploma or equivalent	$25,990	13%	40,690

Interpersonal skills. Good people skills are important because information clerks deal with the public. They must understand and communicate information effectively to establish positive relationships.

Organizational skills. Being organized helps information clerks retrieve files and other important information quickly and efficiently.

Pay

The median annual wage for information clerks was $30,650 in May 2012. The median wage is the wage at which half the workers in an occupation earned more than that amount and half earned less. The lowest 10 percent earned less than $18,600, and the top 10 percent earned more than $48,510.

In May 2012, the median annual wages for information clerks were as follows:

Eligibility interviewers, government programs	$40,530
Human resources assistants, except payroll and timekeeping	37,510
Correspondence clerks	36,140
Court, municipal, and license clerks	34,830
Reservation and transportation ticket agents and travel clerks	32,400
Interviewers, except eligibility and loan	29,910
Order clerks	29,480
File clerks	26,190
Hotel, motel, and resort desk clerks	20,340
Information and record clerks, all other	37,240

Job Outlook

Employment of information clerks is projected to show little or no change from 2012 to 2022. Although employment growth of information clerks will vary by specialty (see table below), a growing population's need for travel-related services, government services, and healthcare will drive overall demand.

Increased travel is expected to result in the demand for new hotels and other lodging establishments. Because customer service and personal services are not easily automated, hotels will continue to use clerks to provide guests services.

Also, as more baby boomers become eligible for Social Security and Medicare, demand for clerical support to handle eligibility requests will increase. In addition, the number of individuals who have access to health insurance will increase due to federal health insurance reform legislation, resulting in a greater need for office staff in healthcare facilities.

However, overall employment growth of information clerks is expected to be limited as organizations and businesses automate and consolidate their administrative functions. For example, many businesses increasingly use online applications for benefits and employment, thereby streamlining the process.

Furthermore, increased use of online ordering and reservations systems and self-service ticketing kiosks will result in the need for fewer clerks to process orders and maintain files. In some businesses, including medical offices, receptionists and other workers are increasingly performing the tasks that clerks used to do.

Job Prospects. Despite little or no change in employment, overall job prospects should be good because of the need to replace workers who leave the occupation each year. Job opportunities should be best in hotels and other lodging establishments.

Clerks with some college education and good computer software skills should have the best job prospects.

O*NET

➤ Correspondence Clerks (43-4021.00)

➤ Court, Municipal, and License Clerks (43-4031.00)
➤ Court Clerks (43-4031.01)
➤ Municipal Clerks (43-4031.02)
➤ License Clerks (43-4031.03)
➤ Eligibility Interviewers, Government Programs (43-4061.00)
➤ File Clerks (43-4071.00)
➤ Hotel, Motel, and Resort Desk Clerks (43-4081.00)
➤ Interviewers, Except Eligibility and Loan (43-4111.00)
➤ Order Clerks (43-4151.00)
➤ Human Resources Assistants, Except Payroll and Timekeeping (43-4161.00)
➤ Reservation and Transportation Ticket Agents and Travel Clerks (43-4181.00)
➤ Information and Record Clerks, All Other (43-4199.00)

Contacts for More Information

For more information about hotel, motel and resort desk clerks, visit
➤ American Hotel & Lodging Association (www.ahla.com)

For more information about human resources assistants, visit
➤ Society for Human Resource Management (www.shrm.org)

Material Recording Clerks

- **2012 Median Pay** .... $24,810 per year
  $11.93 per hour
- **Entry-Level Education** ....See "How to Become One"
- **Work Experience in a Related Occupation**............... None
- **On-the-Job Training** ....See "How to Become One"
- **Number of Jobs 2012** 2,859,500
- **Job Outlook, 2012–22** .... 1% (Little or no change)
- **Employment Change, 2012–22** 18,300

What Material Recording Clerks Do

Material recording clerks keep track of information in order to keep businesses and supply chains on schedule. They ensure proper scheduling, recordkeeping, and inventory control.

Duties. Material recording clerks typically do the following:

- Keep records of items shipped, received, or transferred to another location
- Compile reports on various aspects of changes in production or inventory

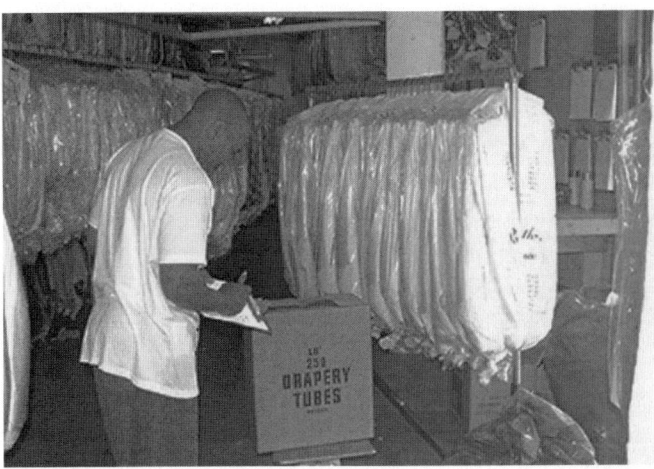

Shipping clerks weigh orders for shipment.

Median Annual Wages, May 2012

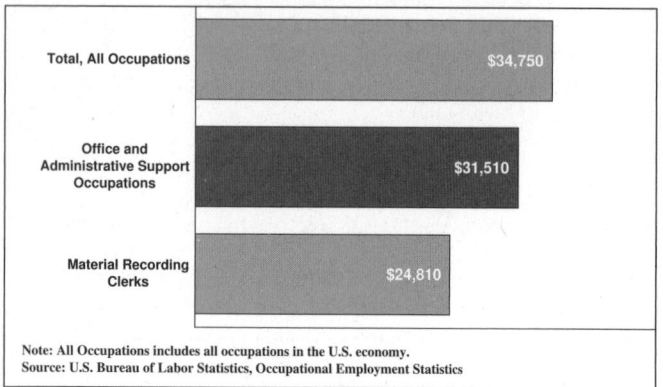

Note: All Occupations includes all occupations in the U.S. economy.
Source: U.S. Bureau of Labor Statistics, Occupational Employment Statistics

Percent Change in Employment, Projected 2012–2022

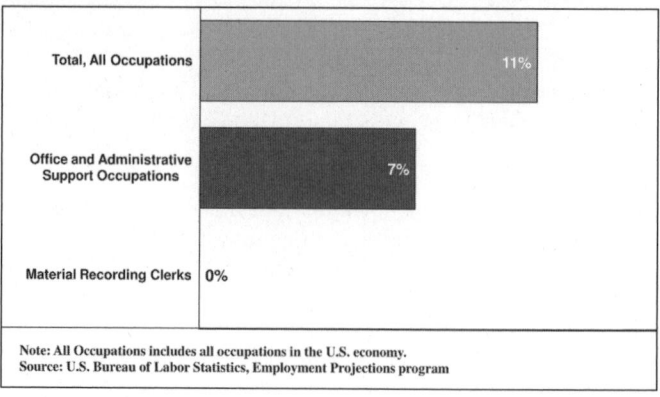

Note: All Occupations includes all occupations in the U.S. economy.
Source: U.S. Bureau of Labor Statistics, Employment Projections program

- Find, sort, or move goods between different parts of the business

- Check inventory records for accuracy

As warehouses increase their use of automation and computers, clerks will become more adept at using technology. Many clerks use tablets or hand-held computers to keep track of inventory. New sensors and tags enable these computers to automatically detect when and where products are moved, making clerks' jobs more efficient.

Production, planning, and expediting clerks ease the flow of information, work, and materials within or among offices in a business. They compile reports on the progress of work and on any production problems that arise. These clerks set workers' schedules, estimate costs, keep track of materials, and write special orders for new materials. They perform general office tasks, such as distributing mail, sending faxes, or entering data. Expediting clerks maintain contact with vendors to ensure that supplies and equipment are shipped on time. They also may inspect the quality of products.

Shipping, receiving, and traffic clerks keep track of and record all outgoing and incoming shipments and ensure that they have been filled correctly. Many of these clerks scan barcodes with hand-held devices or use radiofrequency identification (RFID) scanners to keep track of inventory. They may ensure that orders were correctly processed in their company's computer system. They also compute freight costs and prepare invoices for other parts of the organization. Some of these clerks move goods from the warehouse to the loading dock.

Stock clerks and order fillers receive, unpack, and track merchandise. Stock clerks move products from a warehouse to shelves in stores. They keep a record of all items that enter or leave the stockroom and inspect for damaged goods. These clerks also use hand-held scanners to keep track of merchandise. Order fillers retrieve customer orders and ready them to be shipped.

Material and product inspectors weigh, measure, check, sample, and keep accurate records on materials, supplies, and other equipment that enters a warehouse. They verify the quantity and quality of items they are assigned, checking for defects and recording what they find. To gather information, they use scales, counting devices, and calculators. Some inspectors decide what to do about a defective product, such as to scrap it or send it back to the factory to be repaired. Some clerks also prepare reports on warehouse inventory levels.

Work Environment

Material recording clerks held about 2.9 million jobs in 2012. They work in a variety of industries.

Stock clerks and order fillers held about 1.8 million jobs in 2012. The industries that employed the most stock clerks and order fillers in 2012 were as follows:

General merchandise stores 29%
Food and beverage stores 24
Wholesale trade 10

Shipping, receiving, and traffic clerks held about 695,500 jobs in 2012. The industries that employed the most shipping, receiving, and traffic clerks in 2012 were as follows:

Manufacturing 27%
Wholesale trade 23
Retail trade 21
Transportation and warehousing 12

Production, planning, and expediting clerks held about 284,700 jobs in 2012. The industries that employed the most production, planning, and expediting clerks in 2012 were as follows:

Manufacturing 36%
Professional, scientific, and technical services 9
Wholesale trade 8
Information 7
Administrative and support and waste management
and remediation services 7

Material and product inspectors held about 72,200 jobs in 2012. The industries that employed the most material and product inspectors in 2012 were as follows:

Administrative and support services 19%
Manufacturing 18
Wholesale trade 17
Retail trade 14
Transportation and warehousing 10

Most material recording clerks spend significant time in warehouses.

Shipping, receiving, and traffic clerks; production, planning, and expediting clerks; and material inspectors usually work in an office inside a warehouse or manufacturing plant.

Production clerks spend more of their time in their office, on the computer or telephone, setting up schedules or writing production reports.

Although shipping clerks and material inspectors prepare reports in an office, too, they also spend time in the warehouse, where they sometimes handle packages or automatic equipment such as conveyor systems.

Stock clerks and order fillers usually work in retail settings and sometimes help customers. They move items from the back room

Employment Projections Data for Material Recording Clerks

Occupational title	SOC Code	Employment, 2012	Projected Employment, 2022	Change, 2012–2022	
				Percent	Numeric
Material recording clerks	—	2,859,500	2,877,900	1	18,300
Production, planning, and expediting clerks......................	43-5061	284,700	294,800	4	10,100
Shipping, receiving, and traffic clerks	43-5071	695,500	702,300	1	6,800
Stock clerks and order fillers...	43-5081	1,807,200	1,801,200	0	-6,000
Weighers, measurers, checkers, and samplers, recordkeeping	43-5111	72,200	79,600	10	7,300

Source: U.S. Bureau of Labor Statistics, Employment Projections Program

Note: Data are rounded. Go to **Occupational Information Included in the OOH** for a discussion of the data in this table.

to the store's shelves, a job that can involve frequent bending and lifting. However, automated devices usually transport heavy items.

Work Schedules. Production, planning, and expediting clerks; shipping, receiving, and traffic clerks; and material inspectors usually work full time. Many have standard Monday-through-Friday shifts, although some work nights and weekends or holidays when large shipments arrive.

About one third of stock clerks and order fillers worked part-time in 2012. Evening and weekend work is common because these clerks work when retail stores are open. They sometimes work overnight shifts when large shipments arrive or it is time to take inventory.

How to Become One

Most workers must have a high school diploma and are trained on the job in under 6 moths.

Education. Most material recording clerks must have a high school diploma or the equivalent. Production, planning, and expediting clerks need to have some basic computer skills. Candidates who have taken some business classes may be given preference over those who have not.

Stock clerks and order fillers generally are not required to have a high school diploma.

Training. Material recording clerks usually learn their work on the job. Training for stock clerks, shipping clerks, and material inspectors may last less than a month. The more complex the automatic equipment and sensors used in warehouses, the longer on-the-job training can take. For production clerks, training can take up to 6 months.

Typically, a supervisor or more experienced worker trains new clerks.

Clerks first learn to count stock and mark inventory and then move onto more difficult tasks, such as recordkeeping. Production clerks need to learn how their company operates before they can write production and work schedules.

Advancement. With additional training or education, material recording clerks can advance to other, similar positions within their firm, such as purchasing agent. For more information, see the profile on purchasing managers, buyers, and purchasing agents. Clerks in retail establishments can move into the sales department.

Important Qualities

Clerical skills. Typing, filing, and recordkeeping are common tasks for most material recording clerks.

Communication skills. Production, planning, and expediting clerks are frequently in contact with suppliers, vendors, and production managers and need to be able to communicate the firm's scheduling needs effectively..

Customer-service skills. Stock clerks sometimes interact with customers in retail stores and may have to get the item the customer is looking for from the storeroom.

Detail oriented. Material inspectors check items for defects, some of which are small and difficult to spot.

Math skills. Some types of material recording clerks are required to have basic math skills. For example, they might use math to calculate shipping costs or take measurements.

Pay

The median annual wage for material recording clerks was $24,810 in May 2012. The median wage is the wage at which half the workers in an occupation earned more than that amount and half earned less. The lowest 10 percent earned less than $17,340 and the top 10 percent earned more than $44,850.

Median wages for material recording clerk occupations in May 2012 were as follows:

Production, planning, and expediting clerks...................... $43,740
Shipping, receiving, and traffic clerks 29,010
Material and product inspectors... 27,920
Stock clerks and order fillers 22,050

Similar Occupations This table shows a list of occupations with job duties that are similar to those of material recording clerks.

Occupations	Entry-level Education	2012 Pay	Projected Job Growth	Average Annual Openings
Delivery Truck Drivers and Driver/Sales Workers	High school diploma or equivalent	$27,113	5%	27,250
General Office Clerks	High school diploma or equivalent	$27,470	6%	81,090
Hand Laborers and Material Movers	Less than high school	$23,155	10%	133,630
Heavy and Tractor-trailer Truck Drivers	Postsecondary non-degree award	$38,200	11%	46,470
Information Clerks	High school diploma or equivalent	$31,159	2%	47,000
Material Moving Machine Operators	See "How to Become One"	$32,069	1%	16,560

Job Outlook

Employment of shipping, receiving, and traffic clerks and employment of stock clerks and order fillers are both projected to show little or no change from 2012 to 2022.

An expected increase in the use of radiofrequency identification (RFID) tags will enhance the productivity of these two occupations. RFID tags allow stock clerks to locate an item or count inventory much faster than they previously could. In warehouses, both RFID tags and increased automation will affect shipping, receiving, and traffic clerks because each of these technologies will make it easier to keep track of material. The resulting increases in productivity will allow fewer clerks to do the same amount of work.

Employment of material and product inspectors is projected to grow 10 percent from 2012 to 2022, about as fast as the average for all occupations. RFID tags are expected to increase accuracy in shipping, reducing the number of times a product needs to be weighed, checked, or measured and, in turn, reducing the demand for material inspectors; however, these workers will be less affected than shipping or stock clerks. In addition, certain types of automation may do some of the job functions of material and product inspectors.

Employment of production, planning, and expediting clerks is projected to grow 4 percent from 2012 to 2022, slower than the average for all occupations. These clerks are less likely to be affected by RFID or automation because they spend more time doing office work than shipping or stock clerks do. However, production clerks are employed mostly by slow-growing or declining manufacturing industries, a factor that will limit their growth.

Job Prospects. There should be favorable job opportunities for material recording clerks because of the need to replace workers who leave these occupations. The increase in RFID and other sensors will enable clerks who are more comfortable with computers to have better job prospects.

O*NET

➤ Production, Planning, and Expediting Clerks (43-5061.00)
➤ Shipping, Receiving, and Traffic Clerks (43-5071.00)
➤ Stock Clerks and Order Fillers (43-5081.00)
➤ Stock Clerks, Sales Floor (43-5081.01)
➤ Marking Clerks (43-5081.02)
➤ Stock Clerks- Stockroom, Warehouse, or Storage Yard (43-5081.03)
➤ Order Fillers, Wholesale and Retail Sales (43-5081.04)
➤ Weighers, Measurers, Checkers, and Samplers, Recordkeeping (43-5111.00)

Contacts for More Information

For more information about material recording clerks, visit
➤ MHI (www.mhi.org)
➤ The Warehousing Education and Research Council (www.werc.org)

Police, Fire, and Ambulance Dispatchers

- **2012 Median Pay** .... $36,300 per year
  $17.45 per hour
- **Entry-Level Education** ... High school diploma or equivalent
- **Work Experience in a Related Occupation** .... None
- **On-the-Job Training** .... Moderate-term on-the-job training
- **Number of Jobs 2012** 98,500
- **Job Outlook, 2012–22** .... 8% (As fast as average)
- **Employment Change, 2012–22** 7,600

What Police, Fire, and Ambulance Dispatchers Do

Police, fire, and ambulance dispatchers, also called *911 operators* or *public safety telecommunicators*, answer emergency and nonemergency calls.

Duties. Police, fire, and ambulance dispatchers typically do the following:

- Answer 911 telephone calls
- Determine the type of emergency and its location
- Decide the appropriate response based on agency procedures
- Relay information to the appropriate first responder agency
- Coordinate the dispatch of emergency response personnel to accident scenes
- Give over-the-phone medical instructions before emergency personnel arrive
- Monitor and track the status of police, fire, and ambulance units
- Synchronize responses with other area communication centers
- Keep detailed records about calls

Dispatchers answer calls when someone needs help from police, fire fighters, emergency services, or a combination of the three. They take both emergency and nonemergency calls.

Dispatchers must stay calm while collecting vital information from callers to determine the severity of a situation and the location of those who need help. They then give the appropriate first-responder agencies information about the call.

Some dispatchers only take calls. Others use radios to send appropriate personnel. Many dispatchers do both.

Dispatchers keep detailed records about the calls that they take. They use computers to log important facts, such as the nature of the incident and the name and location of the caller. Some location data is automatically entered into the system from GPS in cell phones and physical addresses of landline phones.

Some dispatchers also use crime databases, maps, and weather reports when helping emergency response teams. Other dispatchers monitor alarm systems, alerting law enforcement or fire personnel

Police, fire, and ambulance dispatchers work in a communication center, often called a Public Safety Answering Point (PSAP).

Median Annual Wages, May 2012

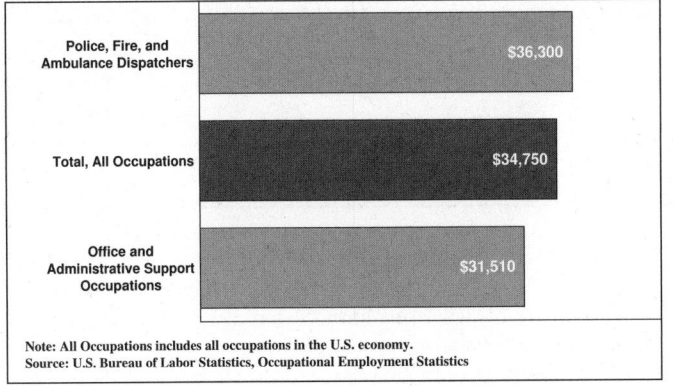

Note: All Occupations includes all occupations in the U.S. economy.
Source: U.S. Bureau of Labor Statistics, Occupational Employment Statistics

Percent Change in Employment, Projected 2012–2022

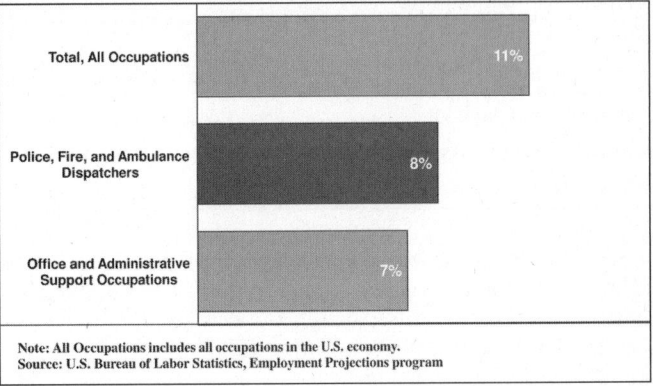

Note: All Occupations includes all occupations in the U.S. economy.
Source: U.S. Bureau of Labor Statistics, Employment Projections program

when a crime or fire occurs. In some situations, dispatchers must work with people in other jurisdictions to share information and transfer calls.

Dispatchers must often instruct callers on what to do before responders arrive. Many dispatchers are trained to offer medical help over the phone. For example, they might help the person on the line to provide first aid at the scene until emergency medical services arrive.

Work Environment

Police, fire, and ambulance dispatchers held about 98,500 jobs in 2012.

Dispatchers work in communication centers, often called Public Safety Answering Points (PSAP).

About 82 percent of dispatchers worked for local governments in 2012–the majority employed by law enforcement agencies and fire departments. Some dispatchers work for state governments or for private companies.

Work as a dispatcher can be stressful. They often work long hours, take many calls, and deal with troubling situations. Some calls require assisting people who are in life-threatening situations, and the pressure to respond quickly and calmly can be demanding.

Work Schedules. Most dispatchers work 8- to 12-hour shifts, but some agencies may use 24-hour shifts. Overtime is common in this occupation.

Because emergency calls can happen any time, dispatchers are required to work some shifts during evenings, weekends, and holidays.

How to Become One

Most police, fire, and ambulance dispatchers have a high school diploma. Many states require dispatchers to have certification.

Education. Most dispatchers are required to have a high school diploma. In addition, candidates must pass a written exam and a typing test. In some instances, applicants may need to pass a background check, lie detector and drug tests, as well as tests for hearing and vision.

Most states require dispatchers to be U.S. citizens, and some jobs require a driver's license. Both computer skills and customer-service skills can be helpful. The ability to speak Spanish is desirable in this occupation as well.

Training. Training requirements vary by state. The Association of Public-Safety Communications Officials (APCO) can provide information on which states require training and certification.

Some states require 40 hours or more of initial training and some require continuing education every 2 to 3 years. Other states do not mandate any specific training, leaving individual localities and agencies to conduct their own courses.

Some agencies have their own programs for certifying dispatchers; others use training from a professional association. The Association of Public-Safety Communications Officials (APCO), the National Emergency Number Association (NENA), and the International Academies of Emergency Dispatch (IAED) have established a number of recommended standards and best practices that agencies often use as a guideline for their own training programs.

Training is usually conducted in both a classroom and on the job, and is often followed by a probationary period of about 1 year. However, this may vary by agency as there is no national standard of how training is conducted or the length of probation.

Training covers a wide variety of topics, such as local geography, agency protocols, and standard procedures. Dispatchers are also taught how to use specialized equipment, such as a 2-way radio and computer-aided dispatch (CAD) software. Computer systems that dispatchers use consist of several monitors that display call information, location mapping, relevant criminal history, and video depending on the location of the incident. They often receive specialized training to prepare for high-risk incidents, such as a child abduction or a suicidal caller.

Licenses, Certifications, and Registrations. Many states require dispatchers to be certified. The Association of Public-Safety Communications Officials (APCO) has information on which states require training and certification. One commonly required certification is the Emergency Medical Dispatcher (EMD) certification, which enables dispatchers to give medical assistance over the phone.

Employment Projections Data for Police, Fire, and Ambulance Dispatchers

Occupational title	SOC Code	Employment, 2012	Projected Employment, 2022	Change, 2012–2022	
				Percent	Numeric
Police, fire, and ambulance dispatchers	43-5031	98,500	106,200	8	7,600

Source: U.S. Bureau of Labor Statistics, Employment Projections Program

Note: Data are rounded. Go to Occupational Information Included in the OOH for a discussion of the data in this table.

Similar Occupations   This table shows a list of occupations with job duties that are similar to those of police, fire, and ambulance dispatchers.

Occupations	Entry-level Education	2012 Pay	Projected Job Growth	Average Annual Openings
Air Traffic Controllers	Associate's degree	$122,530	2%	1,140
Customer Service Representatives	High school diploma or equivalent	$30,580	13%	94,160
EMTs and Paramedics	Postsecondary non-degree award	$31,020	23%	12,060

Dispatchers may choose to pursue additional certifications, such as the National Emergency Number Association's Emergency Number Professional (ENP) or APCO's Registered Public-Safety Leader (RPL) certifications to prove their leadership skills and knowledge of the profession.

Advancement. Dispatchers can become senior dispatchers or supervisors before advancing to administrative positions, in which they may focus on a specific area, such as training or policy and procedures.

Additional education and related work experience may be helpful in advancing to management-level positions.

Important Qualities

Ability to multitask. Responding to an emergency over the phone can be stressful. Dispatchers must stay calm to simultaneously answer calls, collect vital information, coordinate responders, use mapping software and camera feeds, and assist callers.

Communication skills. Dispatchers work with law enforcement, emergency response teams, and civilians. They must be able to effectively communicate the nature of an emergency and coordinate the appropriate response.

Decision-making skills. Dispatchers must be able to choose wisely between tasks that are competing for their attention. They must be able to quickly determine the appropriate action when people call for help.

Empathy. People who call 911 are often in distress. Dispatchers must be willing and able to help callers with a wide range of needs. They must be calm, polite, and sympathetic, while also quickly getting information.

Listening skills. When answering an emergency call or handling radio communications, a dispatcher must listen carefully. Some callers might have trouble speaking because of anxiety or stress.

Pay

The median annual wage for police, fire, and ambulance dispatchers was $36,300 in May 2012. The median wage is the wage at which half the workers in an occupation earned more than that amount, and half earned less. The lowest 10 percent earned less than $23,190, and the top 10 percent earned more than $56,580. Overtime pay is common.

Job Outlook

Employment of police, fire, and ambulance dispatchers is projected to grow 8 percent from 2012 to 2022, about as fast as the average for all occupations.

The prevalence of cellular phones has increased the number of calls that dispatchers receive, and this trend is expected to continue. A growing elderly population should also result in more emergency calls, requiring more dispatchers.

It is expected that Next Generation 911—a service that allows people to communicate through text and video messages with emergency dispatchers—will be implemented in the coming years. This development should also increase demand for dispatchers as emergency call centers will take in more information.

However, most police, fire, and ambulance dispatchers are employed by local and state governments. Therefore, any future budget constraints will likely limit the number of dispatchers hired in the coming decade.

Job Prospects. Overall job prospects should be favorable because the work of a dispatcher remains stressful and demanding, leading some applicants to seek other types of work.

Although employment growth will generate some job openings, the majority of positions will come from the need to replace the large number of dispatchers expected to transfer to other occupations or leave the labor force.

Those with good communication and computer skills should have the best job prospects.

O*NET

➤ Police, Fire, and Ambulance Dispatchers (43-5031.00)

Contacts for More Information

For more information about police, fire, and ambulance dispatcher training and certification, visit

➤ Association of Public-Safety Communications Officials (www. apco911.org/)
➤ International Academies of Emergency Dispatch (www.emergency dispatch.org/)
➤ National Emergency Number Association (www.nena.org/)
➤ National 911 Program (U.S. Department of Transportation's http://911.gov/)

Postal Service Workers

- **2012 Median Pay** .... $53,100 per year
  $25.53 per hour
- **Entry-Level Education** ... High school diploma or equivalent
- **Work Experience in a Related Occupation**............... None
- **On-the-Job Training** ....Short-term on-the-job training
- **Number of Jobs 2012** 491,600
- **Job Outlook, 2012–22**...............................-28% (Decline)
- **Employment Change, 2012–22** ....-139,100

What Postal Service Workers Do

Postal Service workers sell postal products and collect, sort, and deliver mail.

Duties. Postal Service workers typically do the following:

- Collect letters and parcels
- Sort incoming letters and parcels
- Sell stamps and other postal products
- Get customer signatures for registered, certified, and insured mail
- Operate various types of postal equipment

and collect postage, and answer questions about other postal matters.

Postal Service mail sorters, processors, and processing machine operators prepare incoming and outgoing mail for distribution at post offices and mail processing centers. They load and unload postal trucks and move mail around mail processing centers. They also operate and adjust mail processing and sorting machinery.

Work Environment

Postal Service workers held about 491,600 jobs in 2012. They all worked in the federal government.

Employment in the detailed occupations that make up Postal Service workers was distributed as follows:

Postal Service mail carriers 295,100
Postal Service mail sorters, processors, and
    processing machine operators 129,600
Postal Service clerks... 66,900

Postal Service clerks and mail sorters, processors, and processing machine operators work indoors, typically in a post office. Mail carriers mostly work outdoors, delivering mail in all kinds of weather. Although carriers face many natural hazards, such as extreme temperatures and wet and icy roads and sidewalks, the work is not especially dangerous. However, repetitive stress injuries from lifting and bending may occur.

Work Schedules. Most Postal Service workers are employed full time. However, overtime is sometimes required, particularly during the holiday season. Because mail is delivered 6 days a week, many Postal Service workers must work on Saturdays.

How to Become One

Although there is no specific postsecondary education requirement to become a Postal Service worker, all applicants for these jobs must take a written exam.

Education. Although there is no specific postsecondary education requirement to become a Postal Service worker, all applicants must have a good command of English.

Postal Service mail carriers must be at least 18 years old. They must be U.S. citizens or have permanent resident-alien status. Males must have registered with the Selective Service when they reached age 18.

All applicants must pass a written exam that measures speed and accuracy at checking names and numbers and the ability to memorize mail distribution procedures. Jobseekers should contact the post office or mail processing center where they want to work to find out when exams are given.

When accepted, applicants must undergo a criminal background check and pass a physical exam and a drug test. Applicants also may be asked to show that they can lift and handle heavy mail

Postal Service mail carriers receive good benefits.

- Distribute incoming mail from postal trucks

Postal Service workers receive and process mail for delivery to homes, businesses, and post office boxes. Workers are classified based on the type of work they perform.

The following are examples of types of Postal Service workers:

Postal Service mail carriers deliver mail to homes and businesses in cities, towns, and rural areas. Most travel established routes, delivering and collecting mail. Carriers cover their routes by foot, vehicle, or a combination of both. Some mail carriers collect money for postage due. Others, particularly in rural areas, sell postal products, such as stamps and money orders. All carriers must be able to answer customers' questions about postal regulations and services and, upon request, provide change-of-address cards and other postal forms.

Postal Service clerks sell stamps, money orders, postal stationary, mailing envelopes, and boxes in post offices throughout the country. These workers register, certify, and insure mail, calculate

Median Annual Wages, May 2012

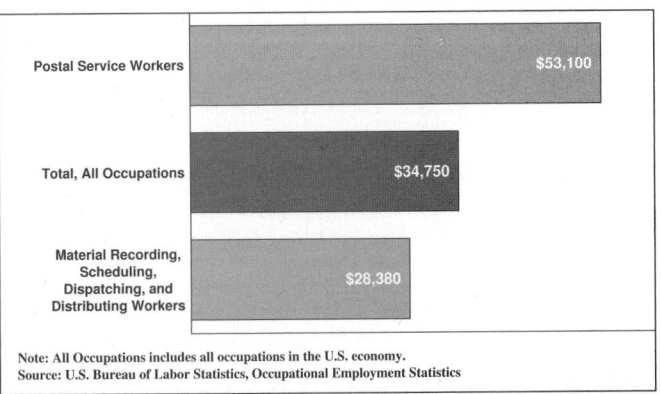

Note: All Occupations includes all occupations in the U.S. economy.
Source: U.S. Bureau of Labor Statistics, Occupational Employment Statistics

Percent Change in Employment, Projected 2012–2022

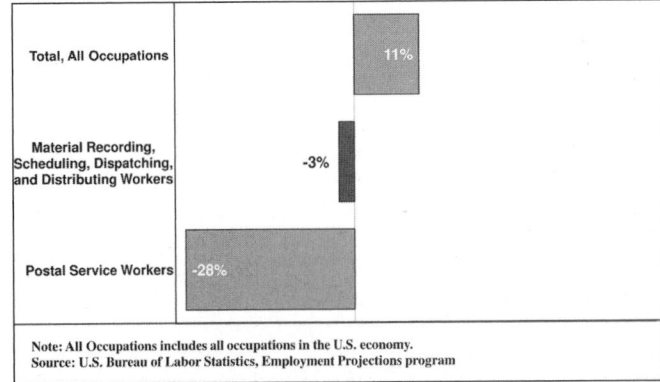

Note: All Occupations includes all occupations in the U.S. economy.
Source: U.S. Bureau of Labor Statistics, Employment Projections program

Employment Projections Data for Postal Service Workers

Occupational title	SOC Code	Employment, 2012	Projected Employment, 2022	Change, 2012–2022	
				Percent	Numeric
Postal service workers.....................................	43-5050	491,600	352,600	-28	-139,100
Postal service clerks	43-5051	66,900	45,700	-32	-21,300
Postal service mail carriers...........................	43-5052	295,100	215,800	-27	-79,200
Postal service mail sorters, processors, and processing machine operators	43-5053	129,600	91,000	-30	-38,600

Source: *U.S. Bureau of Labor Statistics, Employment Projections Program*

Note: *Data are rounded. Go to* Occupational Information Included in the OOH *for a discussion of the data in this table.*

sacks. Mail carriers who drive at work must have a safe driving record, and applicants must receive a passing grade on a road test.

Training. Newly hired Postal Service workers receive short-term on-the-job training, usually lasting less than one month. Those who have a mail route may initially work alongside an experienced carrier.

Important Qualities

Customer-service skills. Postal Service workers, particularly clerks, regularly interact with customers. As a result, they must be courteous and tactful and provide good client service.

Physical stamina. Postal Service workers, particularly carriers, must be able to stand or walk for long periods.

Physical strength. Postal Service workers must be able to lift heavy mail bags and parcels without injuring themselves.

Pay

The median annual wage for Postal Service workers was $53,100 in May 2012. The median wage is the wage at which half the workers in an occupation earned more than that amount and half earned less. The lowest 10 percent earned less than $40,460, and the top 10 percent earned more than $56,510.

Median annual wages for Postal Service occupations in May 2012 were as follows:

Postal Service mail carriers $56,490
Postal Service clerks.. 53,090
Postal Service mail sorters, processors, and processing machine operators 53,090

Union Membership. Most Postal Service workers belonged to a union in 2012.

Job Outlook

Overall employment of Postal Service workers is projected to decline 28 percent from 2012 to 2022. Automated sorting systems, cluster mailboxes, and tight budgets will adversely affect employment. Employment declines, however, will vary by specialty.

Employment of Postal Service clerks is projected to decline 32 percent from 2012 to 2022. Employment will be adversely affected by the decline in first-class mail volume due to increasing use of automated bill pay and email.

Employment of Postal Service mail carriers is projected to decline 27 percent from 2012 to 2022. Employment will be adversely affected by the use of automated "delivery point sequencing" systems that sort letter mail directly. This reduces the amount of time that carriers spend sorting, allowing them to spend more time on the streets delivering mail.

The amount of time carriers save on sorting letter mail and flat mail will allow them to increase the size of their routes, which should reduce the need to hire more carriers. In addition, the Postal Service is moving toward more centralized mail delivery, such as the use of cluster mailboxes, to cut down on the number of door-to-door deliveries.

Employment of Postal Service mail sorters, processors, and processing machine operators is projected to decline 30 percent from 2012 to 2022. The Postal Services will likely need fewer workers because new mail sorting technology can read text and automatically sort, forward, and process mail. The greater use of online services to pay bills and the increased use of email should also reduce the need for sorting and processing workers.

Job Prospects. Despite declining employment, the need to replace workers who retire will result in some job openings. However, very strong competition can be expected as the number of applicants typically exceeds the number of available positions.

O*NET

➤ Postal Service Clerks (43-5051.00)
➤ Postal Service Mail Carriers (43-5052.00)
➤ Postal Service Mail Sorters, Processors, and Processing Machine Operators (43-5053.00)

Contacts for More Information

For more information about Postal Service workers, including job requirements, entrance examinations, and employment opportunities, visit

➤ United States Postal Service (http://about.usps.com/careers /welcome.htm)
➤ U.S. Postal Regulatory Commission (www.prc.gov)
➤ National Association of Letter Carriers (www.nalc.org/)
  For information about national Postal Service unions, visit
➤ American Postal Workers Union (www.apwu.org/)
➤ National Postal Mail Handlers Union (www.npmhu.org/)

Similar Occupations   This table shows a list of occupations with job duties that are similar to those of postal service workers.

Occupations	Entry-level Education	2012 Pay	Projected Job Growth	Average Annual Openings
Delivery Truck Drivers and Driver/Sales Workers	High school diploma or equivalent	$27,113	5%	27,250
Retail Sales Workers	Less than high school	$21,514	10%	202,730

Receptionists

- **2012 Median Pay** .... $25,990 per year
  $12.49 per hour
- **Entry-Level Education** ... High school diploma or equivalent
- **Work Experience in a Related Occupation**.............. None
- **On-the-Job Training** ....Short-term on-the-job training
- **Number of Jobs 2012** 1,006,700
- **Job Outlook, 2012–22** .... 14% (As fast as average)
- **Employment Change, 2012–22** 135,900

Receptionists answer telephones, route and screen calls, greet visitors, respond to inquiries from the public, and provide information about the organization.

What Receptionists Do

Receptionists perform administrative tasks, such as answering phones, receiving visitors, and providing general information about their organization to the public and customers.

Duties. Receptionists typically do the following:

- Answer telephone calls and take messages or forward calls
- Schedule and confirm appointments and maintain event calendars
- Greet and welcome customers, clients, and other visitors
- Check visitors in and direct or escort them to specific destinations
- Inform other employees of visitors' arrivals or cancellations
- Enter customer data and send correspondence
- Copy, file, and maintain paper or electronic documents and records
- Handle incoming and outgoing mail

Receptionists are often the first employee of an organization to have contact with a customer or client. They are responsible for making a good first impression for the organization, which can affect the organization's success.

The specific responsibilities of receptionists vary depending on where they work.

For example, receptionists in hospitals and doctors' offices may gather patients' personal information and direct patients to the waiting room. Some may handle billing and insurance payments.

In beauty or hair salons, they schedule appointments, direct clients to the hairstylist, and may serve as cashiers.

In factories, large corporations, and government offices, receptionists may also provide a security function. For example, they control access, provide visitor passes, and arrange to take visitors to the proper office.

When they are not busy with callers or visitors, receptionists perform other office tasks, such as processing documents or entering data.

Receptionists use telephones, computers, and other office equipment such as scanners and fax machines.

Work Environment

Receptionists held about 1 million jobs in 2012 and were employed in nearly every industry.

The industries that employed the most receptionists in 2012 were as follows:

Offices of physicians 19%
Offices of dentists 7
Offices of other health practitioners 5
Personal care services... 5

Receptionists usually work in an area that is visible, such as a front desk of an office lobby or a waiting room, and easily accessible to the public and other employees.

The work that some receptionists do may be stressful, as they answer numerous phone calls and sometimes deal with difficult or irate callers.

Work Schedules. Although most receptionists work during regular business hours, about 1 in 3 worked part time in 2012. Some receptionists, including those who work in hospitals and nursing homes, may work evenings and weekends.

Median Hourly Wages, May 2012

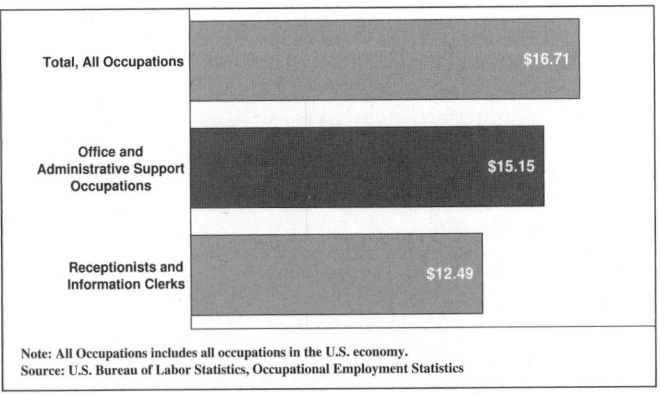

Total, All Occupations	$16.71
Office and Administrative Support Occupations	$15.15
Receptionists and Information Clerks	$12.49

Note: All Occupations includes all occupations in the U.S. economy.
Source: U.S. Bureau of Labor Statistics, Occupational Employment Statistics

Percent Change in Employment, Projected 2012–2022

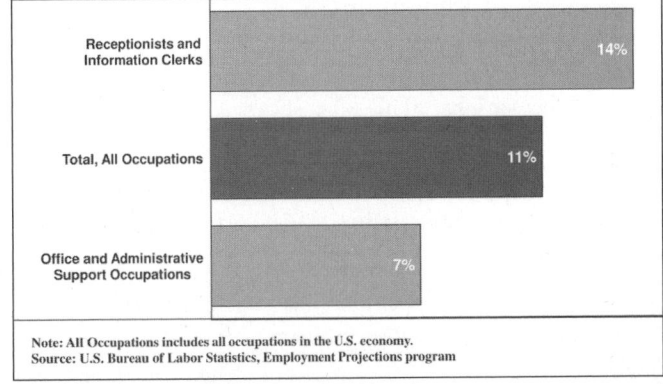

Receptionists and Information Clerks	14%
Total, All Occupations	11%
Office and Administrative Support Occupations	7%

Note: All Occupations includes all occupations in the U.S. economy.
Source: U.S. Bureau of Labor Statistics, Employment Projections program

Employment Projections Data for Receptionists

Occupational title	SOC Code	Employment, 2012	Projected Employment, 2022	Change, 2012–2022	
				Percent	Numeric
Receptionists and information clerks.................................... 43-4171		1,006,700	1,142,600	14	135,900

Source: *U.S. Bureau of Labor Statistics, Employment Projections Program*

Note: *Data are rounded. Go to* Occupational Information Included in the OOH *for a discussion of the data in this table.*

How to Become One

Although hiring requirements vary by industry and employer, receptionists typically need a high school diploma and good communication skills.

Education. Receptionists typically need a high school diploma or its equivalent, and some employers may prefer to hire candidates who also possess basic computer skills. Courses in word processing and spreadsheet application at community colleges and vocational schools can be particularly helpful.

Training. Most receptionists receive short-term on-the-job training, usually lasting a few days to a week. Training typically covers procedures for visitors and telephone and computer use. Medical and legal offices also may instruct new employees on privacy rules related to patient and client information.

Advancement. Receptionists may advance to other administrative positions with more responsibilities, such as secretaries and administrative assistants. Advancement opportunities often depend on the employees' computer skills, work habits, and work experience.

Important Qualities

Communication skills. The ability to communicate clearly is essential for receptionists because much of their job involves conveying information by phone or in person.

Customer-service skills. Receptionists represent an organization. As a result, they should be courteous, professional, and helpful toward the public and customers.

Integrity. In medical and legal offices, receptionists handle client and patient data. As a result, they must be trustworthy and protect the privacy of their clients.

Interpersonal skills. Good people skills are important because receptionists deal with the public. They should be comfortable when interacting with people, even in stressful situations.

Organizational skills. Because receptionists take messages, schedule appointments, and maintain employee files, they should have good organizational skills.

Pay

The median hourly wage for receptionists was $12.49 in May 2012. The median wage is the wage at which half the workers in an occupation earned more than that amount and half earned less. The lowest 10 percent earned less than $8.71 per hour, and the top 10 percent earned more than $18.16 per hour.

In May 2012, the median hourly wages for receptionists in the top four industries employing receptionists were as follows:

Offices of dentists	$14.67
Offices of physicians	13.09
Offices of other health practitioners	11.86
Personal care services..	9.65

Job Outlook

Employment of receptionists is projected to grow 14 percent from 2012 to 2022, about as fast as the average for all occupations.

Employment growth will result mainly from a growing healthcare industry. Specifically, offices of physicians and dentists are expected to add the most receptionist jobs as an aging population will demand more medical services. In addition, the number of individuals who have health insurance is expected to increase due to federal health insurance reform legislation, resulting in a greater need for office staff in healthcare facilities. Some receptionists' tasks, such as checking patients in and coordinating patient care, are not easily automated.

Employment growth of receptionists in most other industries should be slower than the average for all occupations as organizations continue to automate or consolidate administrative functions, such as using computer software to interact with the public or customers.

In addition, technology will continue to make organizations more productive with the use of automated phone systems, further reducing the need for receptionists.

Job Prospects. Overall job prospects should be good, with the best job opportunities in the healthcare industry.

Many job openings will stem from the need to replace workers who leave the occupation. Those with related work experience and good computer skills should have the best job prospects.

O*NET

➤ Receptionists and Information Clerks (43-4171.00)

Contacts for More Information

For information about administrative professionals, visit

➤ American Society of Administrative Professionals (www.asaporg.com/)

➤ Association of Executive and Administrative Professionals (www.theaeap.com/)

➤ International Association of Administrative Professionals (www.iaap-hq.org/)

Similar Occupations   This table shows a list of occupations with job duties that are similar to those of receptionists.

Occupations	Entry-level Education	2012 Pay	Projected Job Growth	Average Annual Openings
Customer Service Representatives	High school diploma or equivalent	$30,580	13%	94,160
General Office Clerks	High school diploma or equivalent	$27,470	6%	81,090
Information Clerks	High school diploma or equivalent	$31,159	2%	47,000
Secretaries and Administrative Assistants	High school diploma or equivalent	$36,198	12%	97,210
Tellers	High school diploma or equivalent	$24,940	1%	25,980

Secretaries and Administrative Assistants

- **2012 Median Pay** .... $35,330 per year
  $16.99 per hour
- **Entry-Level Education** ... High school diploma or equivalent
- **Work Experience in a Related Occupation**.... See "How to Become One"
- **On-the-Job Training** ....See "How to Become One"
- **Number of Jobs 2012** 3,947,100
- **Job Outlook, 2012–22**................. 12% (As fast as average)
- **Employment Change, 2012–22** 479,500

What Secretaries and Administrative Assistants Do

Secretaries and administrative assistants perform routine clerical and administrative duties. They organize files, draft messages, schedule appointments, and support other staff.

Duties. Secretaries and administrative assistants typically do the following:

- Answer telephones and take messages or transfer calls
- Schedule appointments and update event calendars
- Arrange staff meetings
- Handle incoming and outgoing mail and faxes
- Draft routine memos, billing, or other reports
- Edit company correspondence and ensure document accuracy
- Maintain databases and filing systems, whether electronic or paper
- Perform basic bookkeeping

Secretaries and administrative assistants perform a variety of clerical and administrative duties that are necessary to run an organization efficiently. They use computer software to create spreadsheets, manage databases, and prepare presentations, reports, and documents. They also may negotiate with vendors, buy supplies, and manage stockrooms or corporate libraries. Secretaries and

Secretaries and administrative assistants often use computers to create spreadsheets, compose correspondence, manage databases, and create presentations and reports.

administrative assistants also operate videoconferencing, fax, and other office equipment. Specific job duties vary by experience, job title, and specialty.

The following are examples of types of secretaries and administrative assistants:

Executive secretaries and executive administrative assistants provide high-level administrative support for an office and for top executives of an organization. They often handle more complex responsibilities, such as reviewing incoming documents, conducting research, and preparing reports. Some also supervise clerical staff.

Legal secretaries perform work requiring knowledge of legal terminology and procedures. They prepare messages and legal papers, such as summonses, complaints, motions, and subpoenas under the supervision of an attorney or a paralegal. They also review legal journals and help with legal research–for example, by verifying quotes and citations in legal briefs.

Medical secretaries transcribe dictation and prepare reports or articles for physicians or medical scientists. They also take simple medical histories of patients, arrange for patients to be hospitalized, or process insurance payments. Medical secretaries need to be familiar with medical terminology, medical records, and hospital or laboratory procedures.

Secretaries and administrative assistants, except legal, medical, and executive is the largest subcategory of secretaries and administrative assistants. They handle an office's administrative activities in almost every sector of the economy, including schools, government, and private corporations. For example, secretaries in schools are often responsible for handling most of the communications among parents, students, the community, teachers, and school administrators. They schedule appointments, receive visitors, and keep track of students' records.

Virtual assistants work from a home office, providing support to one or more clients on a contract basis. They use the Internet, email, and fax machines to communicate with clients. Although their assignments often vary from short term to long term, their typical duties are similar to those of other secretaries and administrative assistants. Working from a remote location allows virtual assistants to support multiple clients in different industries.

Work Environment

Secretaries and administrative assistants held about 3.9 million jobs in 2012 and worked in nearly every industry.

The industries that employed the most secretaries and administrative assistants in 2012 were as follows:

Health care and social assistance... 21%
Educational services; state, local, and private 14
Professional, scientific, and technical services......................... 14
Government... 8

Most secretaries and administrative assistants work in office settings. Virtual assistants typically work from a home office.

Work Schedules. Most secretaries and administrative assistants work full time. Virtual assistants may have more flexible schedules because they work from home.

How to Become One

High school graduates who have basic office and computer skills usually qualify for entry-level positions. Although most secretaries learn their job in several weeks, many legal and medical secretaries require several months of training to learn industry-specific terminology. Executive secretaries usually need several years of related work experience.

Median Annual Wages, May 2012

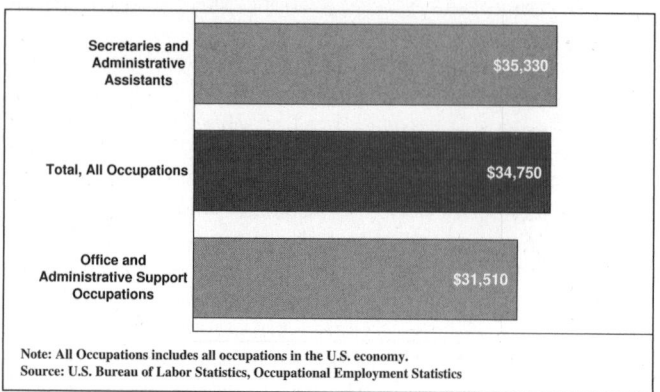

Note: All Occupations includes all occupations in the U.S. economy.
Source: U.S. Bureau of Labor Statistics, Occupational Employment Statistics

Percent Change in Employment, Projected 2012–2022

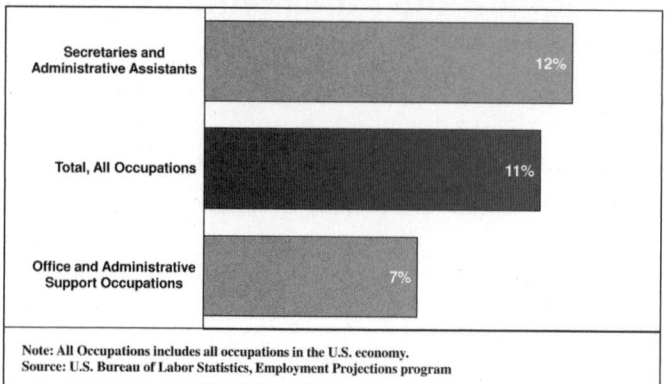

Note: All Occupations includes all occupations in the U.S. economy.
Source: U.S. Bureau of Labor Statistics, Employment Projections program

Education. High school graduates can obtain basic office, computer, and English grammar skills at technical schools or community colleges. Some temporary placement agencies also provide formal training in computer and office skills.

Some medical and legal secretaries learn industry-specific terminology and practices by attending courses offered at community colleges or technical schools. For executive secretary positions, employers increasingly prefer to hire those who have taken some college courses or have a bachelor's degree.

Training. Secretaries and administrative assistants typically learn their skills through short-term on-the-job training, usually lasting a few weeks. During this time they learn about office procedures, computer programs, and how to prepare office documents. However, employers of more specialized positions, including medical and legal secretaries, often have training that may last several months. Training typically covers industry-specific terminology and practices.

Work Experience in a Related Occupation. Executive secretaries can gain experience by working in administrative positions that have less complicated responsibilities. Many secretaries and administrative assistants advance to higher-level administrative positions.

Licenses, Certifications, and Registrations. Although not required, certification can demonstrate competency to employers.

The International Association of Administrative Professionals offers the Certified Administrative Professional (CAP) certification. Candidates must have a minimum of 2 to 4 years of administrative work experience, depending on their level of education, and pass an examination.

Legal secretaries have several certification options. For example, those with 1 year of general office experience, or who have completed an approved training course, can acquire the Accredited Legal Professional (ALP) designation through a testing process administered by NALS (previously known as National Association of Legal Secretaries). NALS offers two additional designations: the Professional Legal Secretary (PLS), considered to be an advanced certification for legal support professionals, and the Professional Paralegal (PP), a designation to show proficiency as a paralegal.

The Certified Legal Secretary Specialist (CLSS) designation is conferred by Legal Secretaries International in areas such as intellectual property, criminal law, civil litigation, probate, and business law. Candidates must have 5 years of legal experience and pass an examination to become certified. In some instances, certain requirements may be waived.

Advancement. Secretaries and administrative assistants generally advance to other administrative positions with more responsibilities, such as office supervisor, office manager, or executive secretary.

With additional training, many legal secretaries become paralegals or legal assistants.

Important Qualities

Integrity. Secretaries may have access to sensitive or private information that they must keep confidential. For example, medical secretaries collect patient data that are required, by law, to be kept confidential. They should be trusted to handle this information in order to protect patient privacy.

Interpersonal skills. Secretaries and administrative assistants often interact with clients, customers, or staff. They should communicate effectively and be courteous when interacting with others to create a positive work environment and client experience.

Organizational skills. Secretaries and administrative assistants keep files, folders, and schedules in proper order so an office can run efficiently.

Employment Projections Data for Secretaries and Administrative Assistants

Occupational title	SOC Code	Employment, 2012	Projected Employment, 2022	Change, 2012–2022	
				Percent	Numeric
Secretaries and administrative assistants.............................	43-6000	3,947,100	4,426,600	12	479,500
Executive secretaries and executive administrative assistants..	43-6011	873,900	863,400	-1	-10,500
Legal secretaries..	43-6012	223,100	216,100	-3	-7,000
Medical secretaries..	43-6013	525,600	714,900	36	189,200
Secretaries and administrative assistants, except legal, medical, and executive...	43-6014	2,324,400	2,632,300	13	307,800

Source: U.S. Bureau of Labor Statistics, Employment Projections Program

Note: Data are rounded. Go to **Occupational Information Included in the OOH** *for a discussion of the data in this table.*

Similar Occupations This table shows a list of occupations with job duties that are similar to those of secretaries and administrative assistants.

Occupations	Entry-level Education	2012 Pay	Projected Job Growth	Average Annual Openings
Bookkeeping, Accounting, and Auditing Clerks	High school diploma or equivalent	$35,170	11%	37,000
Court Reporters	Postsecondary non-degree award	$48,160	9%	550
General Office Clerks	High school diploma or equivalent	$27,470	6%	81,090
Information Clerks	High school diploma or equivalent	$31,159	2%	47,000
Medical Records and Health Information Technicians	Postsecondary non-degree award	$34,160	22%	9,040
Medical Transcriptionists	Postsecondary non-degree award	$34,020	8%	2,240
Paralegals and Legal Assistants	Associate's degree	$46,990	17%	9,120
Receptionists	High school diploma or equivalent	$25,990	13%	40,690

Writing skills. Secretaries and administrative assistants often write memos and emails when communicating with managers, employees, and customers. Therefore, they must have good grammar, ensure accuracy, and maintain a professional tone.

Pay

The median annual wage for secretaries and administrative assistants was $35,330 in May 2012. The median wage is the wage at which half the workers in an occupation earned more than that amount and half earned less. The lowest 10 percent earned less than $21,910, and the top 10 percent earned more than $57,750.

Median annual wages for secretaries and administrative assistants in May 2012 were as follows:

Executive secretaries and executive
   administrative assistants.. $47,500
Legal secretaries.. 42,170
Medical secretaries.. 31,350
Secretaries, except legal, medical, and executive 32,410

Job Outlook

Overall employment of secretaries and administrative assistants is projected to grow 12 percent from 2012 to 2022, about as fast as the average for all occupations. Employment growth, however, will vary by occupational specialty.

Employment of executive secretaries and administrative assistants is projected to show little or no change from 2012 to 2022. This is largely because companies are replacing executive secretaries with lower-cost administrative assistants. Many administrative assistants can also support more than one manager in an organization.

In addition, many managers now perform work that was previously done by their executive secretaries. For example, they often type their own correspondence or schedule their own travel and meetings.

Employment of medical secretaries is projected to grow 36 percent from 2012 to 2022, much faster than the average for all occupations. Federal health legislation will expand the number of patients who have access to health insurance, increasing patient access to medical care. In addition, the aging population will have increased demand for medical services. As a result, medical secretaries will be needed to handle administrative tasks related to billing and insurance processing.

Employment of legal secretaries is projected to decline 3 percent from 2012 to 2022. In order to cut costs, a growing number of legal firms are having paralegals and legal assistants perform work normally done by legal secretaries.

Employment of secretaries, except legal, medical, and executive, is projected to grow 13 percent from 2012 to 2022, about as fast as the average for all occupations. Many secretarial and administrative duties are of a personal, interactive nature. Because technology cannot substitute for interpersonal skills, secretaries and administrative assistants will continue to play a role in most organizations.

Job Prospects. Many job openings are expected to come from the need to replace secretaries and administrative assistants who leave the occupation.

Those with a combination of related work experience and computer skills should have the best job prospects.

O*NET

➤ Executive Secretaries and Executive Administrative Assistants (43-6011.00)
➤ Legal Secretaries (43-6012.00)
➤ Medical Secretaries (43-6013.00)
➤ Secretaries and Administrative Assistants, Except Legal, Medical, and Executive (43-6014.00)

Contacts for More Information

For more information on careers in secretarial and administrative work, visit
➤ Association of Executive and Administrative Professionals (www.theaeap.com)
➤ International Association of Administrative Professionals (www.iaap-hq.org)

For more information on legal secretaries and administrative assistants, visit
➤ Legal Secretaries International Inc (www.legalsecretaries.org)
➤ NALS (www.nals.org)

For more information on virtual assistants, visit
➤ International Virtual Assistants Association (www.ivaa.org)

Tellers

- **2012 Median Pay** .... $24,940 per year
  $11.99 per hour
- **Entry-Level Education** ... High school diploma or equivalent
- **Work Experience in a Related Occupation** .... None
- **On-the-Job Training** .... Short-term on-the-job training
- **Number of Jobs 2012** 545,300
- **Job Outlook, 2012–22** .... 1% (Little or no change)
- **Employment Change, 2012–22** 5,600

What Tellers Do

Tellers are responsible for accurately processing routine transactions at a bank. These transactions include cashing checks, depositing money, and collecting loan payments.

Duties. Tellers typically do the following:

- Count the cash in their drawer at the start of their shift
- Accept checks, cash, and other forms of payment from customers
- Answer questions from customers about their accounts
- Prepare specialized types of funds, such as traveler's checks, savings bonds, and money orders
- Exchange dollars for foreign currency
- Order bank cards and checks for customers
- Record all transactions electronically throughout their shift
- Count the cash in their drawer at the end of their shift and make sure the amounts balance

Tellers are responsible for the safe and accurate handling of the money they process. When cashing a check, they must verify the customer's identity and make sure that the account has enough money to cover the transaction. When counting cash, tellers must be careful not to make errors. If a customer is interested in financial products or services, such as certificates of deposits (CDs) and loans, tellers explain the products and services offered by the bank and refer the customer to the appropriate personnel.

In most banks, tellers record account changes using computers that give them easy access to the customer's financial information. Tellers also can use this information when recommending a new product or service.

Head tellers manage teller operations. Besides doing the same tasks as those done by other tellers, they perform some managerial

Tellers work in bank branches and assist customers with simple financial transactions.

duties, such as setting work schedules or helping less experienced tellers. Because of their experience, head tellers may deal with difficult customer problems, such as errors in customer accounts. Head tellers also go to the vault (where larger amounts of money are kept) and ensure that other tellers have enough cash to cover their shift.

Work Environment

Tellers held about 545,300 jobs in 2012. About 91 percent worked in the depository credit intermediation industry, which includes commercial bank branches.

Work Schedules. Although most tellers worked full time, about 1 in 3 worked part time in 2012.

How to Become One

Most tellers have a high school diploma and receive about 1 month of on-the-job training. Some banks do background checks before hiring a new teller.

Education. Tellers usually need a high school diploma or equivalent. Some tellers may take some college courses, but a degree is rarely required for a job applicant to be hired.

Training. New tellers usually receive brief on-the-job training, typically lasting about 1 month. Normally, a head teller or another experienced teller trains them. During this training, tellers learn how to balance cash drawers and verify signatures. They also

Median Annual Wages, May 2012

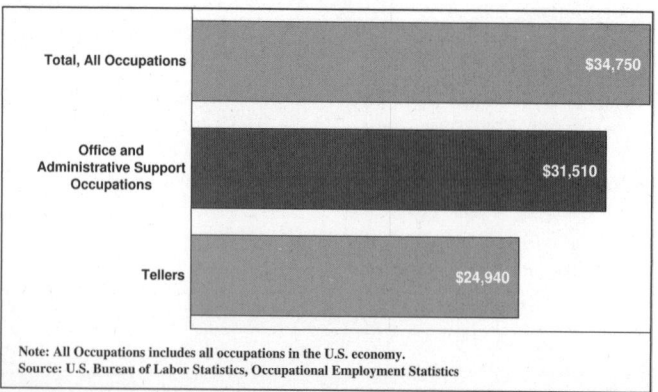

Total, All Occupations — $34,750
Office and Administrative Support Occupations — $31,510
Tellers — $24,940

Note: All Occupations includes all occupations in the U.S. economy.
Source: U.S. Bureau of Labor Statistics, Occupational Employment Statistics

Percent Change in Employment, Projected 2012–2022

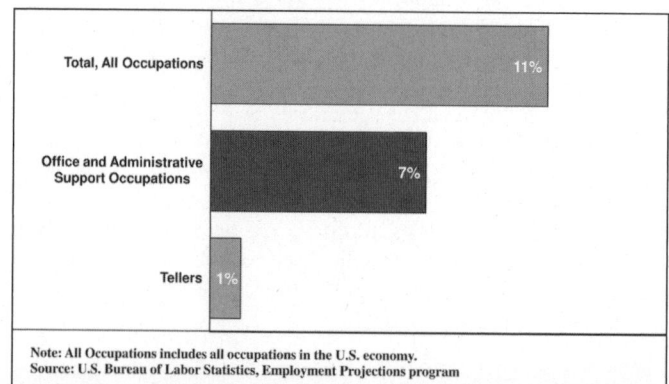

Total, All Occupations — 11%
Office and Administrative Support Occupations — 7%
Tellers — 1%

Note: All Occupations includes all occupations in the U.S. economy.
Source: U.S. Bureau of Labor Statistics, Employment Projections program

Employment Projections Data for Tellers

Occupational title	SOC Code	Employment, 2012	Projected Employment, 2022	Change, 2012–2022	
				Percent	Numeric
Tellers	43-3071	545,300	551,000	1	5,600

Source: U.S. Bureau of Labor Statistics, Employment Projections Program

Note: Data are rounded. Go to Occupational Information Included in the OOH *for a discussion of the data in this table.*

Similar Occupations   This table shows a list of occupations with job duties that are similar to those of tellers.

Occupations	Entry-level Education	2012 Pay	Projected Job Growth	Average Annual Openings
Bookkeeping, Accounting, and Auditing Clerks	High school diploma or equivalent	$35,170	11%	37,000
Cashiers	Less than high school	$18,970	3%	153,000
Customer Service Representatives	High school diploma or equivalent	$30,580	13%	94,160
Information Clerks	High school diploma or equivalent	$31,159	2%	47,000
Loan Officers	Bachelor's degree	$59,820	8%	7,720
Receptionists	High school diploma or equivalent	$25,990	13%	40,690

learn the computer software that their bank uses and the financial products and services the bank offers.

Advancement. Experienced tellers can advance within their bank. They can become head tellers or move to other supervisory positions. Some tellers can advance to other occupations, such as loan officer. They can also move to sales positions.

Important Qualities

Customer-service skills. Tellers spend their day interacting with bank customers. They must be friendly, helpful, and patient. They must be able to understand customer needs and explain service options to their customers.

Detail oriented. Tellers must be sure not to make errors when dealing with customers' money.

Math skills. Because they count and handle large amounts of money, tellers must be good at arithmetic.

Pay

The median annual wage for tellers was $24,940 in May 2012. The median wage is the wage at which half the workers in an occupation earned more than that amount and half earned less. The lowest 10 percent earned less than $19,630, and the top 10 percent earned more than $34,320.

Job Outlook

Employment of tellers is projected to show little or no change from 2012 to 2022.

Past job growth for tellers was driven by a rapid expansion of bank branches, where most tellers work. However, the growth of bank branches is expected to slow because of both changes to the industry and the abundance of banks in certain areas.

In addition, online and mobile banking allows customers to handle many transactions traditionally handled by tellers. As more people use online banking, fewer bank customers will visit the teller window. This will result in decreased demand for tellers. Some banks also are developing systems that allow customers to interact with tellers through webcams at ATMs. This technology will allow tellers to service a greater number of customers from one location, reducing the number of tellers needed for each bank.

Job Prospects. Job prospects for tellers should be excellent because many workers leave this occupation.

O*NET

➤ Tellers (43-3071.00)

Contacts for More Information

For general information about the banking industry, visit
➤ American Bankers Association (www.aba.com/)

Personal Care and Service

Animal Care and Service Workers

- **2012 Median Pay** .... $19,970 per year
  $9.60 per hour
- **Entry-Level Education** ....See "How to Become One"
- **Work Experience in a Related Occupation**............... None
- **On-the-Job Training** ....See "How to Become One"
- **Number of Jobs 2012** 232,100
- **Job Outlook, 2012–22**............. 15% (Faster than average)
- **Employment Change, 2012–22** 35,400

What Animal Care and Service Workers Do

Animal care and service workers provide care for animals. They feed, water, groom, bathe, and exercise pets and other nonfarm animals. Job tasks vary by position and place of work.

Duties. Animal care and service workers typically do the following:

- Give food and water to animals
- Clean equipment and the living spaces of animals
- Monitor animals and record details of their diet, physical condition, and behavior
- Examine animals for signs of illness or injury
- Exercise animals
- Bathe animals, trim nails, clip hair, and attend to other grooming needs
- Train animals to obey or to behave in a specific manner

Animal care and service workers train, feed, groom, and exercise animals. They also clean, disinfect, and repair animal cages. They play with the animals, provide companionship, and observe behavioral changes that could indicate illness or injury.

Boarding kennels, pet stores, animal shelters, rescue leagues, veterinary hospitals and clinics, stables, aquariums and natural aquatic habitats, zoological parks, and many laboratories house animals and employ animal care and service workers.

The following are examples of types of animal care and service workers:

Nonfarm animal caretakers typically work with cats and dogs in animal shelters or rescue leagues. All caretakers attend to the

Animal caretakers who specialize in grooming or maintaining a pet's appearance are called groomers.

basic needs of animals, but experienced caretakers may have more responsibilities, such as helping to vaccinate or euthanize animals under the direction of a veterinarian. Caretakers also may have administrative duties, such as keeping records, answering questions from the public, educating visitors about pet health, or screening people who want to adopt an animal.

Animal trainers train animals for riding, security, performance, obedience, or assisting people with disabilities. They familiarize animals with human voices and contact, and they teach animals to respond to commands. Most animal trainers work with dogs and horses, but some work with marine mammals, such as dolphins. Trainers teach a variety of skills. For example, some may train dogs to guide people with disabilities; others teach animals to cooperate with veterinarians or train animals for a competition or show.

Groomers specialize in maintaining a pet's appearance. Groomers may operate their own business, work in a grooming salon,

Median Annual Wages, May 2012

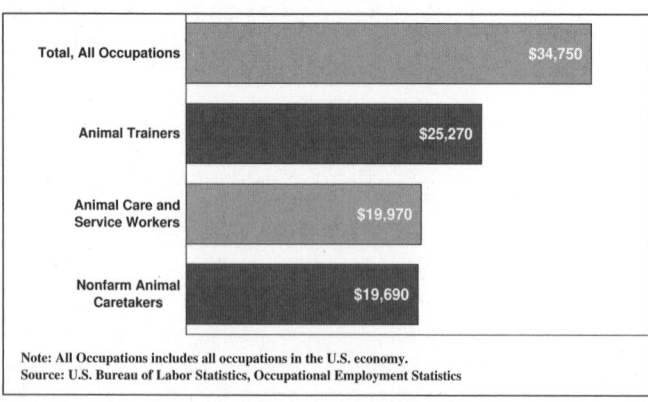

Total, All Occupations	$34,750
Animal Trainers	$25,270
Animal Care and Service Workers	$19,970
Nonfarm Animal Caretakers	$19,690

Note: All Occupations includes all occupations in the U.S. economy.
Source: U.S. Bureau of Labor Statistics, Occupational Employment Statistics

Percent Change in Employment, Projected 2012–2022

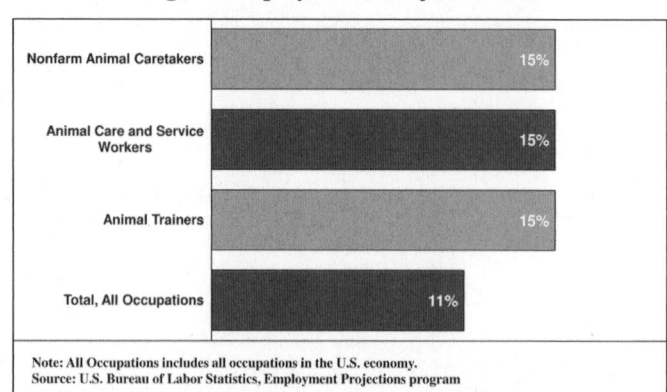

Nonfarm Animal Caretakers	15%
Animal Care and Service Workers	15%
Animal Trainers	15%
Total, All Occupations	11%

Note: All Occupations includes all occupations in the U.S. economy.
Source: U.S. Bureau of Labor Statistics, Employment Projections program

Employment Projections Data for Animal Care and Service Workers

Occupational title	SOC Code	Employment, 2012	Projected Employment, 2022	Change, 2012–2022	
				Percent	Numeric
Animal care and service workers...........................	—	232,100	267,500	15	35,400
Animal trainers................................	39-2011	41,600	47,700	15	6,100
Nonfarm animal caretakers	39-2021	190,600	219,800	15	29,200

Source: U.S. Bureau of Labor Statistics, Employment Projections Program

Note: Data are rounded. Go to **Occupational Information Included in the OOH** *for a discussion of the data in this table.*

or run their own mobile grooming service that travels to clients' homes. Demand for mobile grooming services is growing because these services are convenient for pet owners, allowing the pet to stay in its familiar environment.

Kennels, veterinary clinics, or pet supply stores employ groomers, where they groom mostly dogs, but some cats, too. In addition to cutting, trimming, and styling the pet's fur, groomers clip nails, clean ears, and bathe pets. Groomers also schedule appointments, sell products to pet owners, and identify problems that may require veterinary attention.

Grooms care for horses. Grooms work at stables and are responsible for feeding, grooming, and exercising horses. They saddle and unsaddle horses, give them rubdowns, and cool them off after a ride. In addition, grooms clean stalls, polish saddles, and organize the tack room where they keep harnesses, saddles, and bridles. They also take care of food and supplies for the horses. Experienced grooms sometimes help train horses.

Keepers care for animals in zoos. They plan diets, feed, and monitor the eating patterns of animals. They also clean the animals' enclosures, monitor their behavior, and watch for signs of illness or injury. Depending on the size of the zoo, they may work with one species or multiple species of animals. Keepers may help raise young animals, and they often spend time answering questions from the public.

Kennel attendants care for pets while their owners are working or traveling. Basic attendant duties include cleaning cages and dog runs, and feeding, exercising, and playing with animals. Experienced attendants also may provide basic health care, bathe animals, and attend to other basic grooming needs.

Pet sitters look after animals while their owner is away. They go to the pet owner's home, allowing the pet to stay in its familiar surroundings and follow its routine. Most pet sitters feed, walk, and play with pets daily. More experienced pet sitters also may bathe, groom, or train pets. Pet sitters typically watch over dogs, but some also take care of cats.

Work Environment

Animal care and service workers held about 232,100 jobs in 2012. About 82 percent of these workers were nonfarm animal caretakers, and 18 percent were animal trainers.

Animal care and service workers are employed in a variety of settings. Although many work at kennels, others work at zoos, stables, animal shelters, pet stores, veterinary clinics, and aquariums. Mobile groomers and pet sitters typically travel to customers' homes. Caretakers of show and sports animals must travel to competitions.

Although most animal care and service workers consider the work enjoyable and rewarding, the work may be unpleasant and emotionally distressing at times. For example, those who work in shelters may see abused, injured, or sick animals. Some caretakers may have to help euthanize injured or unwanted animals. In addition, most of the work involves physical tasks, such as moving and cleaning cages, lifting bags of food, and exercising animals.

Injuries and Illnesses. Animal care and service workers have a higher rate of injuries and illnesses than the national average. When working with scared or aggressive animals, caretakers may be bitten, scratched, or kicked. Also, injuries may happen while the caretaker is holding, cleaning, or restraining an animal.

Work Schedules. Animals need care around the clock, so many facilities, such as kennels, zoos, animal shelters, and stables operate 24 hours a day. Therefore, caretakers often work irregular hours including evenings, weekends, and holidays. About one-third of animal caretakers worked part time in 2012.

About 25 percent of animal care and service workers were self-employed in 2012. Many of these workers can set their own schedule.

How to Become One

Most animal care and service workers learn on the job. Still, many employers prefer to hire people who have experience with animals. Zookeeper and marine mammal trainer positions require formal education.

Education. Most animal care and service worker positions do not require formal education, but many animal care facilities require at least a high school diploma or the equivalent.

Although pet groomers typically learn by working under the guidance of an experienced groomer, they can also attend one of 50 state-licensed grooming schools. The length of each program varies with the school and the number of advanced skills taught.

Most zoos require keepers to have a bachelor's degree in biology, animal science, or a related field.

Animal trainers usually need a high school diploma or the equivalent, although some positions may require a bachelor's degree. For example, marine mammal trainers usually need a bachelor's degree in marine biology, animal science, biology, or a related field.

Dog trainers and horse trainers typically qualify by taking courses at community colleges or vocational and private training schools.

Training. Most animal care and service workers learn through short-term on-the-job training. They begin by performing basic tasks and work up to positions that require more responsibility and experience.

Some animal care and service workers may receive training before they enter their position. For example, caretakers in shelters can attend training programs through the Humane Society of the United States and the American Humane Association. Pet groomers often learn their trade by training under the guidance of an experienced groomer.

Licenses, Certifications, and Registrations. Although not required, certifications available in many of these occupations may help workers establish their credentials and enhance their skills. For example, several professional associations and hundreds of

Similar Occupations   This table shows a list of occupations with job duties that are similar to those of animal care and service workers.

Occupations	Entry-level Education	2012 Pay	Projected Job Growth	Average Annual Openings
Agricultural Workers	See "How to Become One"	$19,703	-3%	23,190
Farmers, Ranchers, and Other Agricultural Managers	High school diploma or equivalent	$69,300	-19%	15,020
Veterinarians	Doctoral or professional degree	$84,460	12%	3,100
Veterinary Assistants and Laboratory Animal Caretakers	High school diploma or equivalent	$23,130	10%	2,130
Veterinary Technologists and Technicians	Associate's degree	$30,290	29%	3,340

private vocational and state-approved trade schools offer certification for dog trainers. The National Dog Groomers Association of America offers certification for master status as a groomer. Both the National Association of Professional Pet Sitters and Pet Sitters International offer a home-study certification program for pet sitters. Marine mammal trainers should be certified in SCUBA.

Other Experience. For many caretaker positions, it helps to have experience working with animals. Nearly all animal trainer and zookeeper positions require candidates to have experience with animals. Volunteering and internships at zoos and aquariums are excellent ways to gain experience in working with animals.

Important Qualities

Compassion. Workers must be compassionate when dealing with animals and their owners. They should like animals and must treat them with kindness.

Customer-service skills. Animal care and service workers should understand pet owners' needs so they can provide services that leave the owners satisfied. Some animal care and service workers may need to deal with distraught pet owners; for example, caretakers working in animal shelters may need to reassure owners looking for a lost pet.

Detail oriented. Workers must be detail oriented because they are often responsible for keeping animals on a strict diet, maintaining records, and monitoring changes in animals' behavior.

Patience. Animal caretakers and all animal trainers need to be patient when training or working with animals that do not respond to commands.

Physical stamina. Stamina is important for animal care and service workers because their work often involves kneeling, crawling, bending, and occasionally lifting heavy supplies, such as bags of food.

Problem-solving skills. Animal trainers must be able to assess whether the animals are responding to teaching methods and identify which methods are most successful.

Pay

The median annual wage for nonfarm animal caretakers was $19,690 in May 2012. The median wage is the wage at which half the workers in an occupation earned more than that amount and half earned less. The lowest 10 percent earned less than $16,490, and the top 10 percent earned more than $32,500.

The median annual wage for animal trainers was $25,270 in May 2012. The lowest 10 percent earned less than $17,580, and the top 10 percent earned more than $49,840.

Job Outlook

Overall employment of animal care and service workers is projected to grow 15 percent from 2012 to 2022, faster than the average for all occupations. Employment growth coupled with high job turnover should result in very good job opportunities for candidates for most positions.

Animal care and service workers will continue to be needed as the variety and number of pet services increases. Employment in kennels, grooming shops, and pet stores is projected to increase to keep up with the growing demand for animal care.

Demand for zookeepers, marine mammal trainers, and horse trainers is projected to grow slowly. Many trainers work at zoos and amusement and recreation establishments, which are not expected to add as many positions as other traditional pet care facilities.

Furthermore, the cost of owning and riding horses is too high for many people, so employment of horse trainers is not expected to grow as fast as employment of those who train companion pets, such as dogs.

Job Prospects. Job opportunities should be very good for most positions. Employment growth and high job turnover are expected to result in many openings for dog trainers, groomers, pet sitters, kennel attendants, and caretakers in shelters and rescue leagues.

As the number of pet services increase, more workers will be needed. In addition, entry requirements are low for most animal care occupations, so positions should continue to be available for workers looking to enter the field.

However, candidates will face very strong competition for positions as marine mammal trainers, horse trainers, and zookeepers. The relatively few positions and the popularity of the occupations should result in far more applicants than available positions.

O*NET

➤ Animal Trainers (39-2011.00)
➤ Nonfarm Animal Caretakers (39-2021.00)

Contacts for More Information

For more information about pet groomers, visit
➤ National Dog Groomers Association of America (www.nationaldoggroomers.com/)
➤ Petgroomer.com (http://petgroomer.com/)

For more information about pet sitters, including certification information, visit
➤ National Association of Professional Pet Sitters (www.petsitters.org/)
➤ Pet Sitters International (www.petsit.com/)

For more information about animal trainers, visit
➤ Association of Professional Dog Trainers (www.apdt.com/)
➤ International Marine Animal Trainers' Association (www.imata.org/)

For more information about keepers, visit
➤ Association of Zoos and Aquariums (www.aza.org/)
➤ American Association of Zoo Keepers (http://aazk.org/)

Barbers, Hairdressers, and Cosmetologists

- **2012 Median Pay** .... $22,770 per year
$10.95 per hour
- **Entry-Level Education**.... Postsecondary non-degree award
- **Work Experience in a Related Occupation**............... None
- **On-the-Job Training** .... None
- **Number of Jobs 2012** 663,300
- **Job Outlook, 2012–22**................ 13% (As fast as average)
- **Employment Change, 2012–22** 83,300

What Barbers, Hairdressers, and Cosmetologists Do

Barbers, hairdressers, and cosmetologists provide hairstyling and beauty services.

Duties. Barbers, hairdressers, and cosmetologists typically do the following:

- Inspect hair, face, and scalp, to recommend treatment
- Discuss hair-style options
- Wash, color, and condition hair
- Cut, dry, and style hair
- Receive payments from clients
- Clean and sanitize all tools and work areas

Barbers, hairdressers, and cosmetologists provide hair and beauty services to enhance clients' appearance. Those who operate their own barbershop or salon have managerial duties that may include hiring, supervising, and firing workers, as well as keeping business and inventory records, ordering supplies, and arranging for advertising.

Barbers cut, trim, shampoo, and style hair, mostly for male clients. They also may fit hairpieces and offer facial shaving. Depending on the state in which they work, some barbers are licensed to color, bleach, and highlight hair and to offer permanent-wave services. Common tools include combs, scissors, and clippers.

Hairdressers, or *hairstylists*, offer a wide range of hair services, such as shampooing, cutting, coloring, and styling. They often advise clients, both male and female, on how to care for their hair at home. They also keep records of products and services provided to clients, such as hair color, shampoo, conditioner, and hair treat-

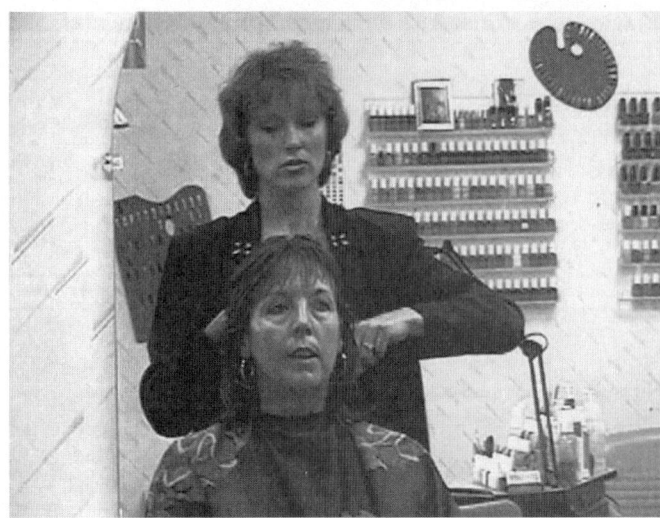

Barbers, hairdressers, and cosmetologists wash, color, and dry hair.

ment used. Tools include hairbrushes, scissors, blow dryers, and curling irons.

Cosmetologists provide scalp and facial treatments and makeup analysis. Some also clean and style wigs and hairpieces. In addition, most cosmetologists actively sell skin care products.

Work Environment

Barbers, hairdressers, and cosmetologists held about 663,300 jobs in 2012. Nearly half were self-employed.

Employment in the detailed occupations that make up barbers, hairdressers, and cosmetologists was distributed as follows:

Hairdressers, hairstylists, and cosmetologists..................... 611,200
Barbers 52,100

Barbers, hairdressers, and cosmetologists work mostly in a barbershop or salon, although some work in a spa, hotel, or resort. Some lease booth space in other people's salons. A good number manage salons or open their own shop after several years of experience.

Barbers, hairdressers, and cosmetologists usually work in pleasant surroundings with good lighting. Physical stamina is important, because they are on their feet for most of their shift. Prolonged exposure to some chemicals may cause skin irritation, so they often wear protective clothing, such as disposable gloves or aprons.

Work Schedules. Many barbers, hairdressers, and cosmetologists work part time. However, some self-employed workers may

Median Hourly Wages, May 2012

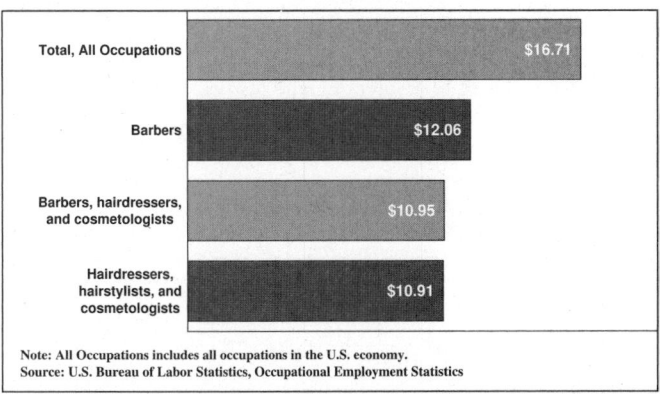

Total, All Occupations	$16.71
Barbers	$12.06
Barbers, hairdressers, and cosmetologists	$10.95
Hairdressers, hairstylists, and cosmetologists	$10.91

Note: All Occupations includes all occupations in the U.S. economy.
Source: U.S. Bureau of Labor Statistics, Occupational Employment Statistics

Percent Change in Employment, Projected 2012–2022

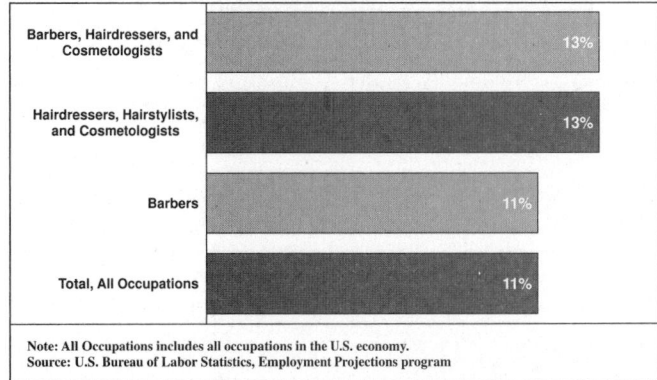

Barbers, Hairdressers, and Cosmetologists	13%
Hairdressers, Hairstylists, and Cosmetologists	13%
Barbers	11%
Total, All Occupations	11%

Note: All Occupations includes all occupations in the U.S. economy.
Source: U.S. Bureau of Labor Statistics, Employment Projections program

Employment Projections Data for Barbers, Hairdressers, and Cosmetologists

Occupational title	SOC Code	Employment, 2012	Projected Employment, 2022	Change, 2012–2022	
				Percent	Numeric
Barbers, hairdressers, hairstylists and cosmetologists............	39-5010	663,300	746,600	13	83,300
Barbers	39-5011	52,100	57,900	11	5,800
Hairdressers, hairstylists, and cosmetologists....................	39-5012	611,200	688,700	13	77,600

Source: U.S. Bureau of Labor Statistics, Employment Projections Program

Note: Data are rounded. Go to Occupational Information Included in the OOH *for a discussion of the data in this table.*

have long hours. Work schedules often include evenings and weekends—the times when barbershops and beauty salons are busiest. Those who are self-employed usually determine their own schedules.

How to Become One

All states require barbers, hairdressers, and cosmetologists to be licensed. To qualify for a license, candidates are required to graduate from a state-approved cosmetology program.

Education. A high school diploma or equivalent is required for some positions. In addition, every state requires that barbers, hairdressers, and cosmetologists complete a program in a state-licensed barber or cosmetology school. Programs in hairstyling, skin care, and other personal appearance services are available in postsecondary vocational schools.

Full-time programs in barbering and cosmetology usually last at least 9 months and may lead to an associate's degree. Most of these workers take advanced courses in hairstyling or in other personal appearance services to keep up with the latest trends. Those who want to open their own business also may take courses in sales and marketing.

Licenses, Certifications, and Registrations. All states require barbers, hairdressers, and cosmetologists to be licensed. Qualifications for a license vary by state, but generally, a person must fulfill the following:

• Minimum age of 16

• High school diploma or equivalent

• Graduated from a state-licensed barber or cosmetology school

After graduating from a state-approved training program, students take a state licensing exam that includes a written test and, in some cases, a practical test of styling skills or an oral exam.

In many states, cosmetology training may be credited toward a barbering license and vice versa, and a few states combine the two licenses. A fee usually is required to apply for a license, and periodic renewals may be necessary.

Some states have reciprocity agreements that allow licensed barbers and cosmetologists to get a license in another state without needing additional formal training, but such agreements are not common. Consequently, people who want to work in a particular state should review the laws of that state before entering a training program.

Important Qualities

Creativity. Barbers, hairdressers, and cosmetologists must keep up with the latest trends and be ready to try new hairstyles for their clients.

Customer-service skills. Workers must be pleasant, friendly, and able to interact with customers in order to retain clients.

Listening skills. Barbers, hairdressers, and cosmetologists should be good listeners. They must listen carefully to what the client wants in order to make sure that the client is happy with the result.

Physical stamina. Barbers, hairdressers, and cosmetologists must be able to stand on their feet for long periods.

Tidiness. Workers must keep a neat personal appearance and keep their work area clean and sanitary. This requirement is necessary for the health and safety of their clients, as well as to make the clients comfortable enough to want to return.

Time-management skills. Time-management skills are important in scheduling appointments and providing services. For example, routine haircuts do not require the precise timing of some other services, such as applying neutralizer after a permanent wave. Clients who receive timely hair care are more likely to return.

Pay

The median hourly wage for barbers, hairdressers, and cosmetologists was $10.95 in May 2012. The median wage is the wage at which half the workers in an occupation earned more than that amount and half earned less. The lowest 10 percent earned less than $8.11, and the top10 percent earned more than $20.39.

The median hourly wages for occupational specialties for barbers, hairdressers, and cosmetologists in May 2012 were as follows:

Barbers $12.06
Hairdressers, hairstylists and cosmetologists 10.91

Job Outlook

Overall employment of barbers, hairdressers, and cosmetologists is projected to grow 13 percent from 2012 to 2022, about as fast as the average for all occupations. Growth rates will vary by specialty.

Employment of barbers is projected to grow 11 percent from 2012 to 2022, about as fast as the average for all occupations. The need for barbers will stem primarily from an increasing population, which will lead to greater demand for basic hair-care services.

Employment of hairdressers, hairstylists, and cosmetologists is projected to grow 13 percent from 2012 to 2022, about as fast as

Similar Occupations   This table shows a list of occupations with job duties that are similar to those of barbers, hairdressers, and cosmetologists.

Occupations	Entry-level Education	2012 Pay	Projected Job Growth	Average Annual Openings
Manicurists and Pedicurists	Postsecondary non-degree award	$19,220	16%	2,070
Skincare Specialists	Postsecondary non-degree award	$28,640	40%	2,130

the average for all occupations. Demand for hair coloring, hair straightening, and other advanced hair treatments has risen in recent years, a trend that is expected to continue over the coming decade.

Job Prospects. Overall job opportunities are expected to be good. A large number of job openings will stem from the need to replace workers who transfer to other occupations, retire, or leave the occupation for other reasons. However, workers should expect strong competition for jobs and clients at higher paying salons, of which there are relatively few and for which applicants must compete with a large pool of experienced hairdressers and cosmetologists.

O*NET

➤ Barbers (39-5011.00)
➤ Hairdressers, Hairstylists, and Cosmetologists (39-5012.00)

Contacts for More Information

For more information about barbers, hairdressers, and cosmetologists, including training, visit

➤ American Association of Cosmetology Schools (www.beautyschools .org/)
➤ National Association of Barber Boards of America (www.national barberboards.com/index.html)

For information about state licensing, practice exams, and other professional links, visit

➤ National-Interstate Council of State Boards of Cosmetology (www. nictesting.org/index.asp)
➤ Professional Beauty Association (www.probeauty.org/)

Childcare Workers

- **2012 Median Pay** .... $19,510 per year
  $9.38 per hour
- **Entry-Level Education** ... High school diploma or equivalent
- **Work Experience in a Related Occupation**.............. None
- **On-the-Job Training** .... Short-term on-the-job training
- **Number of Jobs 2012** 1,312,700
- **Job Outlook, 2012–22**................ 14% (As fast as average)
- **Employment Change, 2012–22** 184,100

What Childcare Workers Do

Childcare workers care for children when parents and other family members are unavailable. They care for children's basic needs, such as bathing and feeding. In addition, some help children prepare for kindergarten or help older children with homework.

Duties. Childcare workers typically do the following:

- Supervise and monitor the safety of children in their care
- Prepare meals and organize mealtimes and snacks for children
- Help children keep good hygiene
- Change the diapers of infants and toddlers
- Organize activities or implement a curriculum that allow children to learn about the world and explore interests
- Develop schedules and routines to ensure that children have enough physical activity, rest, and playtime
- Watch for signs of emotional or developmental problems in children and bring the problems to the attention of parents
- Keep records of children's progress, routines, and interest

Childcare workers introduce babies and toddlers to basic concepts, such as manners, by reading to them and playing with them. For example, they teach young children how to share and take turns by playing games with other children.

Childcare workers often help preschool-age children prepare for kindergarten. Young children learn from playing, solving problems, questioning, and experimenting. Childcare workers use play and other instructional techniques to help children's development. For example, they use storytelling and rhyming games to teach language and vocabulary. They may help improve children's social skills by having them work together to build something in a sandbox or teach math by having children count when building with blocks. They may involve the children in creative activities, such as art, dance, and music.

Childcare workers also often watch school-age children before and after school. They help these children with homework and take them to afterschool activities, such as sports practices and club meetings.

During the summer, when children are out of school, childcare workers may watch older children as well as younger ones for the entire day while the parents are at work.

The following are examples of types of childcare workers:

Childcare center workers work in teams in childcare centers, including Head Start and Early Head Start programs. They often work with preschool teachers and teacher assistants to teach children through a structured curriculum. They prepare daily and long-term schedules of activities to stimulate and educate the children in their care. They also monitor and keep records of children's progress.

Family childcare providers care for children in the provider's own home during traditional working hours. They need to ensure that their homes and all staff they employ meet the regulations for family childcare providers.

In addition, family childcare providers perform tasks related to running their business. For example, they write contracts that outline rates of pay, when payment can be expected, and the number of hours children can be in care. Furthermore, they establish policies about issues, such as if sick children can be in their care, who can pick children up, and how behavioral issues will be dealt with. Family childcare providers frequently spend some of their time marketing their services to prospective families.

Childcare workers nurture, teach, and care for children who have not yet entered kindergarten and older children before and after school.

Median Hourly Wages, May 2012

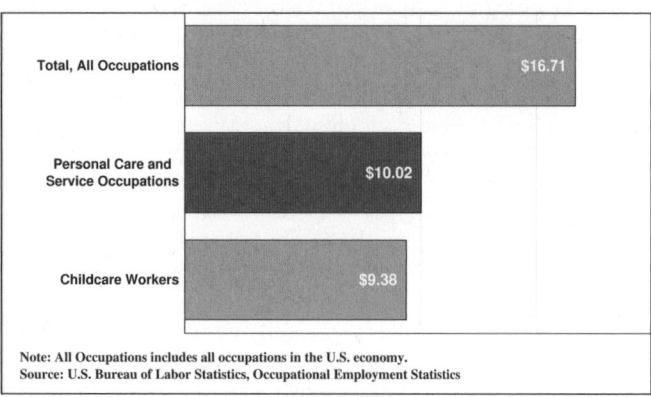

Note: All Occupations includes all occupations in the U.S. economy.
Source: U.S. Bureau of Labor Statistics, Occupational Employment Statistics

Percent Change in Employment, Projected 2012–2022

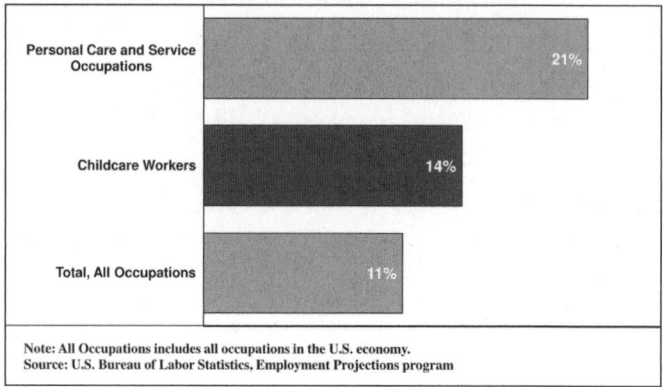

Note: All Occupations includes all occupations in the U.S. economy.
Source: U.S. Bureau of Labor Statistics, Employment Projections program

Nannies work in the homes of the children they care for and the parents that employ them. Most often, they work full time for one family. They may be responsible for driving children to school, appointments, or afterschool activities. Some live in the homes of the families that employ them.

Babysitters, like nannies, work in the homes of the children in their care. However, they work for many families instead of just one. In addition, they generally do not work full time, but rather take care of the children on occasional nights and weekends when parents have other obligations.

Work Environment

Childcare workers held about 1.3 million jobs in 2012. They are employed in childcare centers, preschools, public schools, and private homes.

The industries that employed the most childcare workers in 2012 were as follows:

Child day care services.. 24%
Elementary and secondary schools; state, local, and private... 11
Religious, grantmaking, civic, professional,
    and similar organizations...................................... 8

Family childcare workers work in their own homes. They may convert a portion of their living space into a dedicated space for the children. Nannies and babysitters usually work in their employers' homes. About 29 percent of childcare workers were self-employed in 2012.

Many states limit the number of children that each staff member is responsible for by regulating the ratio of staff to children. The ratios vary with the age of the children. With babies and toddlers, childcare workers are responsible for relatively few children. As the children get older, workers can be responsible for more.

Work Schedules. Although many childcare workers work full time, more than a third worked part time in 2012.

Childcare workers' schedules vary widely. Childcare centers usually are open year round, with long hours so that parents can drop off and pick up their children before and after work. Some centers employ full-time and part-time staff with staggered shifts to cover the entire day.

Family childcare providers may work long or unusual hours to fit parents' work schedules. In some cases, these childcare providers may offer evening and overnight care to meet the needs of families. After the children go home, childcare providers often have more responsibilities, such as shopping for food or supplies, doing accounting, keeping records, and cleaning.

Nannies may work either full or part time. Full-time nannies may work more than 40 hours a week to give parents enough time to commute to and from work.

How to Become One

Education and training requirements vary by setting, state, and employer. They range from less than a high school diploma to a certification in early childhood education.

Education. Childcare workers must meet education and training requirements, which vary by state regulations. Some states require these workers to have a high school diploma, but many states do not have any education requirements for entry-level occupations. However, workers with postsecondary education or an early childhood education credential may be qualified for higher-level positions.

Employers often prefer to hire workers with at least a high school diploma and, in some cases, some postsecondary education in early childhood education.

Workers in Head Start programs must at least be enrolled in a program in which they will earn a postsecondary degree in early childhood education or a child development credential.

States do not regulate educational requirements for nannies. However, some employers may prefer to hire workers with at least some formal instruction in childhood education or a related field, particularly when they will be hired as full-time nannies.

Licenses, Certifications, and Registrations. Many states require childcare centers, including those in private homes, to be licensed. To qualify for licensure, staff must pass a background check, have a complete record of immunizations, and meet a minimum training requirement. Some states require staff to have certifications in CPR and first aid.

Some states and employers require childcare workers to have a nationally recognized certification. Most often, states require the Child Development Associate (CDA) certification offered by the Council for Professional Recognition. Obtaining the CDA certification requires coursework, experience in the field, and a period during which the applicant is observed while working with children.

Some states recognize the Child Care Professional (CCP) designation offered by the National Early Childhood Program Accreditation. Candidates for the CCP must be at least 18 years old, have a high school diploma, have experience in the field, take courses in early childhood education, and pass an exam.

The National Association for Family Child Care (NAFCC) offers a nationally recognized accreditation for family child care providers. This accreditation requires training and experience in the field as well as a period during which the applicant is observed while working with children.

Training. Many states and employers require providers to complete some training before beginning work. Also, many states require staff in childcare centers to complete a minimum number

Employment Projections Data for Childcare Workers

Occupational title	SOC Code	Employment, 2012	Projected Employment, 2022	Change, 2012–2022	
				Percent	Numeric
Childcare workers..	39-9011	1,312,700	1,496,800	14	184,100

Source: U.S. Bureau of Labor Statistics, Employment Projections Program

Note: Data are rounded. Go to Occupational Information Included in the OOH *for a discussion of the data in this table.*

of hours of training annually. Training may include information about basic care of babies, such as how to warm a bottle, and customer-service skills.

Important Qualities

Communication skills. Childcare workers must be able to talk with parents and colleagues about the progress of the children in their care. They need both good speaking skills to provide this information effectively and good listening skills to understand parents' instructions.

Decision-making skills. Good judgment is necessary for childcare workers so they can respond to emergencies or difficult situations.

Instructional skills. Childcare workers need to be able to explain things in terms young children can understand.

Interpersonal skills. Childcare workers need to work well with people to develop good relationships with parents, children, and colleagues.

Patience. Working with children can be frustrating, so childcare workers need to be able to respond to overwhelming and difficult situations calmly.

Physical stamina. Working with children can be physically taxing, so childcare workers should have a lot of energy.

Pay

The median hourly wage for childcare workers was $9.38 in May 2012. The median wage is the wage at which half the workers in an occupation earned more than that amount and half earned less. The lowest 10 percent earned less than $7.85, and the top 10 percent earned more than $14.19.

Pay varies with the worker's education and work setting. Those in formal childcare settings and those with more education usually earn higher wages. Pay for self-employed workers is based on the number of hours they work and the number and ages of the children in their care.

In May 2012, the median hourly wages for childcare workers in the top three industries in which these childcare workers worked were as follows:

Elementary and secondary schools; state, local,
and private $10.98

Religious, grantmaking, civic, professional, and similar
organizations..9.11
Child day care services...9.04

Job Outlook

Employment of childcare workers is projected to grow 14 percent from 2012 to 2022, about as fast as the average for all occupations. Parents will increasingly need assistance during working hours to care for their children. Because the number of children requiring childcare is expected to grow, demand for childcare workers is expected to grow as well.

In the past decade, early childhood education has become widely recognized as important for children's development. Childcare workers often work alongside preschool teachers as assistants. This continued focus on the importance of early childhood education will spur demand for preschool programs and thus for childcare workers.

Job Prospects. Workers with formal education should have the best job prospects. However, even those without formal education who are interested in the occupation should have little trouble finding employment because of the need to replace workers who leave the occupation.

O*NET

➤ Childcare Workers (39-9011.00)
➤ Nannies (39-9011.01)

Contacts for More Information

For more information about becoming a childcare provider, visit
➤ Child Care Aware (http://childcareaware.org/)
For more information about working as a nanny, visit
➤ International Nanny Association (www.nanny.org/)
For more information about family childcare providers, visit
➤ National Association for Family Child Care (www.nafcc.org)
For more information about early childhood education, visit
➤ National Association for the Education of Young Children (www.naeyc.org/)
For more information about professional credentials, visit
➤ Council for Professional Recognition (www.cdacouncil.org/)
➤ National Early Childhood Program Accreditation (www.necpa.net/)

Similar Occupations   This table shows a list of occupations with job duties that are similar to those of childcare workers.

Occupations	Entry-level Education	2012 Pay	Projected Job Growth	Average Annual Openings
Kindergarten and Elementary School Teachers	Bachelor's degree	$53,060	12%	53,250
Preschool and Childcare Center Directors	Bachelor's degree	$43,950	17%	2,780
Preschool Teachers	Associate's degree	$27,130	17%	19,940
Special Education Teachers	Bachelor's degree	$55,068	6%	10,220
Teacher Assistants	Some college, no degree	$23,640	9%	38,260

Fitness Trainers and Instructors

- **2012 Median Pay** .... $31,720 per year
  $15.25 per hour
- **Entry-Level Education** ... High school diploma or equivalent
- **Work Experience in a Related Occupation**............... None
- **On-the-Job Training** ....Short-term on-the-job training
- **Number of Jobs 2012** 267,000
- **Job Outlook, 2012–22** .... 13% (As fast as average)
- **Employment Change, 2012–22** 33,500

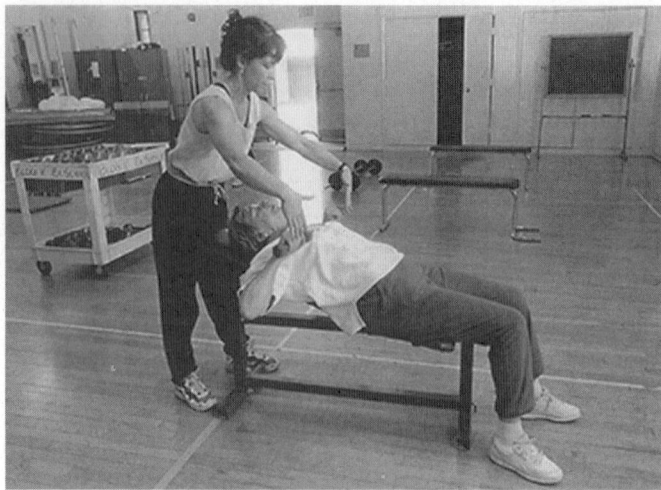

Personal trainers work one-on-one or with two or three clients, either in a gym or in the client's home.

What Fitness Trainers and Instructors Do

Fitness trainers and instructors lead, instruct, and motivate individuals or groups in exercise activities, including cardiovascular exercise (exercises for the heart and blood system), strength training, and stretching. They work with people of all ages and skill levels.

Duties. Fitness trainers and instructors typically do the following:

- Demonstrate how to carry out various exercises and routines
- Watch clients do exercises and show or tell them correct techniques to minimize injury and improve fitness
- Give alternative exercises during workouts or classes for different levels of fitness and skill
- Monitor clients' progress and adapt programs as needed
- Explain and enforce safety rules and regulations on sports, recreational activities, and the use of exercise equipment
- Give clients information or resources about nutrition, weight control, and lifestyle issues
- Give emergency first aid if needed

Both group and specialized fitness instructors often plan or choreograph their own classes. They choose music that is appropriate for their exercise class and create a routine or a set of moves for a class to follow. Some may teach pre-choreographed routines that were originally created by fitness companies or other organizations.

Personal fitness trainers design and carry out workout routines specific to the needs of their clients. In larger facilities, personal trainers must often sell their training sessions to members. They start by evaluating their clients' current fitness level, personal goals, and skills. Then, they develop personalized training programs for their clients to follow, and they monitor the clients' progress.

Fitness trainers and instructors in smaller facilities often do a variety of tasks in addition to their fitness duties, such as tending the front desk, signing up new members, giving tours of the fitness center, writing newsletter articles, creating posters and flyers, and supervising the weight-training and cardiovascular equipment areas.

In some facilities, a single trainer or instructor may provide individual sessions and teach group classes.

Gyms and other types of health clubs offer many different activities for clients. However, trainers and instructors often specialize in only a few areas. The following are some types of fitness trainers and instructors:

Personal fitness trainers work with a single client or a small group. They may train in a gym or in the clients' homes. Personal fitness trainers assess the clients' level of physical fitness and help them set and reach their fitness goals.

Group fitness instructors organize and lead group exercise sessions, which can include aerobic exercise, stretching, muscle conditioning, or meditation. Some classes are set to music. In these classes, instructors may select the music and choreograph an exercise sequence.

Specialized fitness instructors teach popular conditioning methods such as Pilates or yoga. In these classes, instructors show the different moves and positions of the particular method. They also watch students and correct those who are doing the exercises improperly.

Fitness directors oversee the fitness-related aspects of a gym or other type of health club. They often handle administrative duties, such as scheduling personal training sessions for clients or creating

Median Annual Wages, May 2012

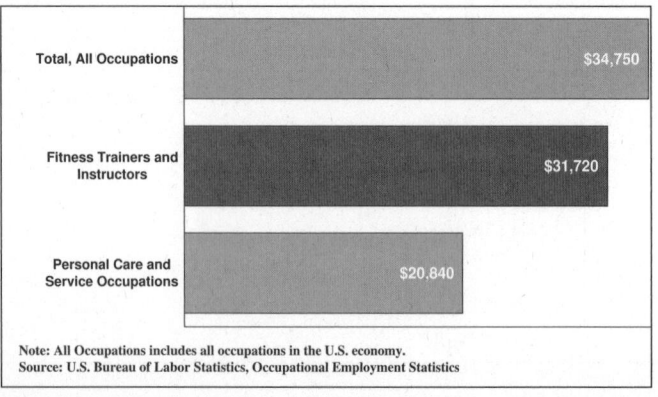

Note: All Occupations includes all occupations in the U.S. economy.
Source: U.S. Bureau of Labor Statistics, Occupational Employment Statistics

Percent Change in Employment, Projected 2012–2022

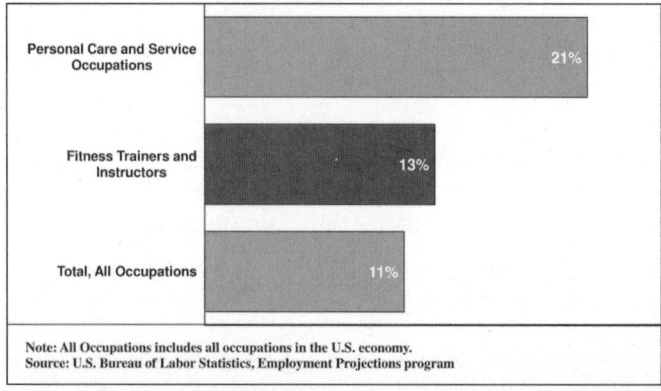

Note: All Occupations includes all occupations in the U.S. economy.
Source: U.S. Bureau of Labor Statistics, Employment Projections program

Employment Projections Data for Fitness Trainers and Instructors

Occupational title	SOC Code	Employment, 2012	Projected Employment, 2022	Change, 2012–2022	
				Percent	Numeric
Fitness trainers and aerobics instructors.................................	39-9031	267,000	300,500	13	33,500

Source: U.S. Bureau of Labor Statistics, Employment Projections Program

Note: Data are rounded. Go to **Occupational Information Included in the OOH** *for a discussion of the data in this table.*

workout incentive programs. They often select and order fitness equipment for their facility.

Work Environment

Fitness trainers and instructors held about 267,000 jobs in 2012.

Fitness trainers and instructors work in health clubs, fitness or recreation centers, gyms, country clubs, hospitals, universities, yoga and Pilates studios, resorts, and clients' homes. Some fitness trainers and instructors also work in offices, where they organize and direct health and fitness programs for employees.

The industries that employed the most fitness trainers and instructors in 2012 were as follows:

Fitness and recreational sports centers 58%
Civic and social organizations 13
Health care and social assistance 4
Other schools and instruction; state, local, and private............. 4

About 1 out of 10 fitness trainers and instructors were self-employed in 2012.

Work Schedules. Some group fitness instructors and personal fitness trainers work other full-time jobs and teach fitness classes or offer personal training sessions during the week or on the weekend. Fitness trainers and instructors may work nights, weekends, or holidays. Some travel to different gyms or to clients' homes to teach classes or offer personal training sessions.

How to Become One

The education and training required for fitness trainers and instructors varies by type of specialty, and employers often hire those with certification. Personal fitness trainers, group fitness instructors, and specialized fitness instructors each need different preparation. Requirements vary by facility.

Education. Almost all trainers and instructors have at least a high school diploma before entering the occupation. An increasing number of employers require fitness workers to have an associate's or bachelor's degree related to a health or fitness field, such as exercise science, kinesiology, or physical education. Programs often include courses in nutrition, exercise techniques, and group fitness.

Personal fitness trainers often start out by taking classes to become certified. Then they work alongside an experienced trainer before they are allowed to train clients alone.

Important Qualities

Customer-service skills. Many fitness trainers and instructors must sell their services, motivating clients to hire them as personal trainers or to sign up for the classes they lead. Fitness trainers and instructors must therefore be polite, friendly, and encouraging to maintain relationships with their clients.

Listening skills. Fitness trainers and instructors must be able to listen carefully to what clients tell them to determine the client's fitness levels and desired fitness goals.

Motivational skills. Getting fit and staying fit takes a lot of work for many clients. To keep clients coming back for more classes or

to continue personal training, fitness trainers and instructors must keep their clients motivated.

Physical fitness. Fitness trainers and instructors need to be physically fit because their job requires a considerable amount of exercise. Group instructors often participate in classes, and personal trainers often need to show exercises to their clients.

Problem-solving skills. Fitness trainers and instructors must evaluate each client's level of fitness and create an appropriate fitness plan to meet the client's individual needs.

Speaking skills. Fitness trainers and instructors must be able to communicate well because they need to be able to explain exercises and movements to clients, as well as motivate them verbally during exercises.

Training. Training for specialized fitness instructors can vary greatly. For example, the duration of programs for yoga instructors can range from a few days to more than 2 years. The Yoga Alliance has training standards requiring at least 200 hours with a specified number of hours in techniques, teaching methods, anatomy, physiology, philosophy, and other areas.

Many group fitness instructors often take training and become certified, and then they must audition for instructor positions. If they succeed at the audition, they may begin teaching classes.

Licenses, Certifications, and Registrations. Employers prefer to hire fitness trainers and instructors who are certified. Many personal trainers must be certified before they begin working with clients or with members of a gym or other type of health club. Group fitness instructors can begin work without certification, but employers often encourage or require them to become certified.

Most trainers or instructors need certification in cardiopulmonary resuscitation (CPR) before applying for certification in physical fitness.

Many organizations offer certification. The National Commission for Certifying Agencies (NCCA), part of the Institute for Credentialing Excellence, lists certifying organizations that are accredited.

All certification exams have a written part, and some also have a practical part. The exams measure the candidate's knowledge of human physiology, understanding of proper exercise techniques, assessment of clients' fitness levels, and development of appropriate exercise programs.

No specific education or training is required for certification. Many certifying organizations offer study materials, including books, CDs, other audio and visual materials, and exam preparation workshops and seminars.

Advanced certification requires an associate's or bachelor's degree in an exercise-related subject that presents more specialized instruction, such as training athletes, working with people who are injured or ill, or advising clients on general health.

Advancement. Fitness trainers and instructors who are interested in management positions should get a bachelor's degree in exercise science, physical education, kinesiology, or a related subject. Experience is often required to advance to management positions in a

Similar Occupations　This table shows a list of occupations with job duties that are similar to those of fitness trainers and instructors.

Occupations	Entry-level Education	2012 Pay	Projected Job Growth	Average Annual Openings
Athletic Trainers and Exercise Physiologists	Bachelor's degree	$42,676	19%	1,240
Physical Therapist Assistants and Aides	See "How to Become One"	$40,539	41%	7,630
Physical Therapists	Doctoral or professional degree	$79,860	36%	12,370
Recreation Workers	Bachelor's degree	$22,240	14%	8,970
Recreational Therapists	Bachelor's degree	$42,280	14%	670

health club or fitness center. Some organizations require a master's degree for certain positions.

Personal trainers may eventually advance to a head trainer position and become responsible for hiring and overseeing the personal training staff or for bringing in new personal training clients. Some fitness trainers and instructors go into business for themselves and open their own fitness centers. Group fitness instructors may be promoted to group exercise director, a position responsible for hiring instructors and coordinating exercise classes. Trainers and instructors may eventually become a fitness director or general manager.

Pay

The median annual wage for fitness trainers and instructors was $31,720 in May 2012. The median wage is the wage at which half the workers in an occupation earned more than that amount and half earned less. The lowest 10 percent earned less than $17,630, and the top 10 percent earned more than $66,530.

Job Outlook

Employment of fitness trainers and instructors is projected to grow 13 percent from 2012 to 2022, about as fast as the average for all occupations.

As businesses, government, and insurance organizations continue to recognize the benefits of health and fitness programs for their employees, incentives to join gyms or other types of health clubs is expected to increase the need for fitness trainers and instructors. Some businesses may even decide to open their own onsite facility to decrease the need for their employees to travel for exercise.

As baby boomers age, many remain active to help prevent injuries and illnesses associated with aging. With the increasing number of older residents in nursing homes or residential care facilities and communities, jobs for fitness trainers and instructors are expected to rise in the fitness centers in these locations.

Other employment growth will come from the continuing emphasis on exercise for young people to combat obesity and encourage healthier lifestyles. More young people and families are likely to join fitness institutions or commit to personal training programs.

Participation in yoga and Pilates is expected to continue to increase, driven partly by older adults who want low-impact forms of exercise and relief from arthritis and other ailments.

Job Prospects. Job prospects should be best for workers with professional certification or increased levels of formal education in health or fitness.

O*NET

➤ Fitness Trainers and Aerobics Instructors (39-9031.00)

Contacts for More Information

For more information about fitness careers and about health and fitness programs in universities and other institutions, visit

➤ American College of Sports Medicine (www.acsm.org)
➤ National Strength and Conditioning Association (www.nsca-lift. org)

For information about certifications for personal trainers and group fitness instructors, visit

➤ American Council on Exercise (www.acefitness.org)
➤ National Academy of Sports Medicine (www.nasm.org)
➤ National Federation of Professional Trainers (www.NFPT.com)

For information about health clubs and sports clubs, visit

➤ International Health, Racquet, & Sportsclub Association (www. ihrsa.org/)

For information about yoga teacher certification and a list of registered schools, visit

➤ Yoga Alliance (www.yogaalliance.org)

Funeral Service Occupations

- **2012 Median Pay** .... $51,600 per year
  $24.81 per hour
- **Entry-Level Education** .... Associate's degree
- **Work Experience in a Related Occupation** .... See "How to Become One"
- **On-the-Job Training** .... See "How to Become One"
- **Number of Jobs 2012** 32,800
- **Job Outlook, 2012–22** .... 12% (As fast as average)
- **Employment Change, 2012–22** 4,000

What Funeral Service Occupations Do

Funeral service workers organize and manage the details of a funeral.

Duties. Funeral service workers typically do the following:

- Provide emotional support to the bereaved
- Arrange for removal of the deceased's body
- Prepare the remains (body)
- File death certificate and other legal documents
- Train junior staff

Together with the family, funeral service workers establish the locations, dates, and times of the visitations (wakes), funerals or memorial services, burials, and cremations. They handle other details as well, such as determining whether the body should be buried, entombed, or cremated. This decision is critical because funeral practices vary among cultures and religions.

Funeral directors, also called morticians and undertakers, arrange the details of funerals, taking into account the wishes of the deceased and family members.

Most funeral service workers deal with paperwork pertaining to the person's death, including submitting papers to state officials to receive a death certificate. Some help resolve insurance claims or apply for veterans' funeral benefits on behalf of the family. They also may notify the Social Security Administration of the death.

A growing number of funeral service workers collaborate with clients who wish to plan their own funerals in advance to ensure that their needs are met.

Increasingly, funeral service workers also help individuals adapt to changes in their lives following a death with support groups.

The following are examples of types of funeral service workers:

Funeral service managers oversee the general operations of a funeral home business. In this position, they perform a wide variety of duties, such as allocating the resources of the funeral home, managing staff, and handling the marketing and public relations.

Morticians, undertakers, and funeral directors plan the details of a funeral. They often prepare obituary notices and arrange for pallbearers and clergy. If a burial is chosen, they schedule the opening and closing of a grave with a representative of the cemetery. If cremation is chosen, they coordinate the process with the crematory. They also decorate and prepare the sites of all services, and provide transportation for the deceased and mourners. They also direct the preparation and shipment of bodies' out-of-state or out-of-country for final disposition.

Morticians, undertakers, and funeral directors also handle administrative duties. For example, they often must apply for the transfer of any pensions, insurance policies, or annuities on behalf of survivors.

Most morticians, undertakers, and funeral directors embalm bodies. Embalming is a cosmetic and temporary preservative process through which the body is prepared for a viewing of visitation by family and friends of the deceased.

Work Environment

Funeral service workers held about 32,800 jobs in 2012. Approximately 97 percent worked in the death care services industry.

Funeral services typically take place in a home, house of worship, funeral home, or at the gravesite or crematory.

Funeral service managers work mostly in a funeral home office.

Morticians, undertakers, and funeral directors work mostly in funeral homes that have a merchandise selection room, and sometimes a chapel. Some may also operate a crematory or cemetery, which may be on the premises. The mood can be quiet and somber, and the work often is stressful, because workers must arrange the many details of a funeral within 24 to 72 hours of death. They also may be responsible for multiple funerals on the same day.

Although workers sometimes may come into contact with bodies that have contagious diseases, the work is not inherently dangerous if proper safety and health regulations are followed. Those working in crematories are exposed to high temperatures and must wear protective clothing.

Work Schedules. Most funeral service workers are employed full time. They often are on call and work long hours, including evenings and weekends.

How to Become One

An associate's degree in mortuary science is the minimum education requirement for morticians, undertakers, funeral directors, and funeral service managers. With the exception of funeral managers, funeral directors and embalmers must be licensed in Washington D.C. and every state in which they work, except Colorado.

Education. An associate's degree in mortuary science is the minimum education requirement for all funeral service workers. Courses typically include ethics, grief counseling, funeral service, and business law. All accredited programs also include courses in embalming and restorative techniques. States have their own education requirements, and state licensing laws vary. Most employers require applicants to be 21 years old; have two years of formal education; serve a 1-year apprenticeship before, during, or after Mortuary College; and pass a state licensing exam after graduation.

In some states, licensure for funeral directors and embalmers are separate.

Median Annual Wages, May 2012

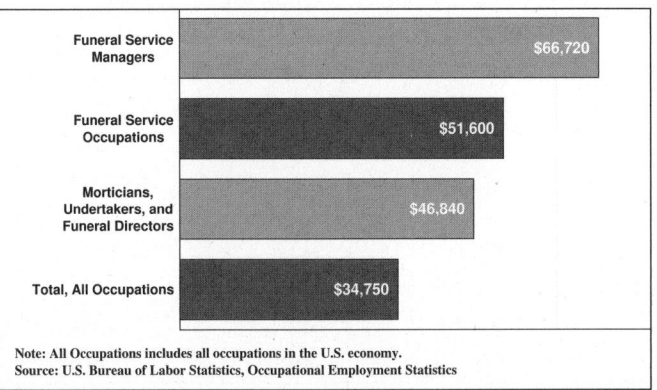

Note: All Occupations includes all occupations in the U.S. economy.
Source: U.S. Bureau of Labor Statistics, Occupational Employment Statistics

Percent Change in Employment, Projected 2012–2022

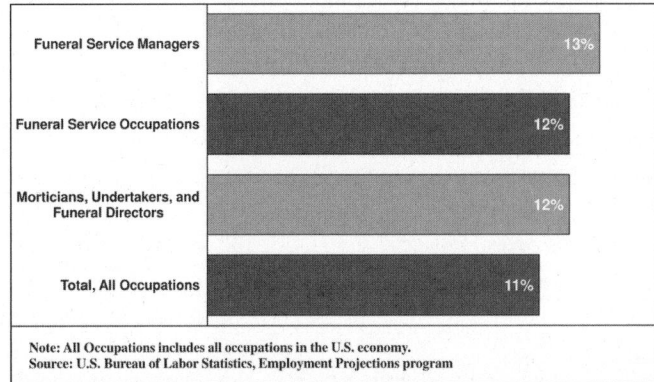

Note: All Occupations includes all occupations in the U.S. economy.
Source: U.S. Bureau of Labor Statistics, Employment Projections program

Employment Projections Data for Funeral Service Occupations

Occupational title	SOC Code	Employment, 2012	Projected Employment, 2022	Change, 2012–2022	
				Percent	Numeric
Funeral service occupations...	—	32,800	36,800	12	4,000
Funeral service managers...	11-9061	9,300	10,500	13	1,200
Morticians, undertakers, and funeral directors..................	39-4031	23,500	26,300	12	2,800

Source: U.S. Bureau of Labor Statistics, Employment Projections Program

Note: *Data are rounded. Go to* Occupational Information Included in the OOH *for a discussion of the data in this table.*

The American Board of Funeral Service Education (ABFSE) accredits 57 mortuary science programs, most of which are 2-year associate's degree programs offered at community colleges. About 7 programs offer a bachelor's degree.

Although an associate's degree is usually adequate, some employers prefer applicants to have a bachelor's degree.

High school students can prepare to become a funeral service worker by taking courses in biology, chemistry, and business, and by participating in public speaking.

Part-time or summer jobs in funeral homes also are good experience.

Training. Morticians, undertakers, and funeral directors must complete hands-on training, usually lasting 1 to 3 years, under the direction of a licensed funeral director or manager. The apprenticeship may be completed before, during, or after completing a 2-year mortuary program. Apprenticeships provide practical experience in all aspects of the funeral service.

Licenses, Certifications, and Registrations. With the exception of funeral service managers, funeral directors and embalmers are required to be licensed in Washington DC and every state, except Colorado. Although licensing laws and examinations vary by state, most applicants should meet the following:

- Be 21 years old
- Complete 2 years in an ABFSE mortuary science program
- Serve an apprenticeship lasting 1 to 3 years

Applicants must then pass a qualifying exam. Working in multiple states may require multiple licenses. For specific requirements, applicants should contact their state licensing board.

Most states require morticians, undertakers, and funeral directors to receive continuing education credits annually to keep their licenses.

Work Experience

Workers increasingly should have some office management experience, particularly for funeral service managers who run their own funeral home business.

Important Qualities

Business skills. Knowledge of financial statements and the ability to run a funeral home efficiently and profitably are important for funeral directors and managers.

Compassion. Death is a delicate and emotional matter. Funeral service workers must be able to treat clients with care and sympathy in their time of loss.

Interpersonal skills. Funeral service workers should have good interpersonal skills. When speaking with families, for instance, they must be tactful and able to explain and discuss all matters about services provided.

Time-management skills. Funeral service workers must be able to handle numerous tasks for multiple customers, often in a short time frame.

Pay

The median annual wage for funeral service occupations was $51,600 in May 2012. The median wage is the wage at which half the workers in an occupation earned more than that amount and half earned less. The lowest 10 percent earned less than $28,100, and the top 10 percent earned more than $94,860.

The median annual wage for funeral service managers was $66,720 in May 2012. The lowest 10 percent earned less than $38,420, and the top 10 percent earned more than $140,740.

The median annual wage for morticians, undertakers, and funeral directors was $46,840 in May 2012. The lowest 10 percent earned less than $26,580, and the top 10 percent earned more than $80,900.

Job Outlook

Employment of funeral service workers is projected to grow 12 percent from 2012 to 2022, about as fast as the average for all occupations.

Employment growth reflects an increase in the number of expected deaths among the largest segment of the population, aging baby boomers.

In addition, a growing number of older people are expected to prearrange their end-of-life services, increasing the need for funeral

Similar Occupations   This table shows a list of occupations with job duties that are similar to those of funeral service occupations.

Occupations	Entry-level Education	2012 Pay	Projected Job Growth	Average Annual Openings
Administrative Services Managers	Bachelor's degree	$81,080	12%	7,990
Advertising, Promotions, and Marketing Managers	Bachelor's degree	$115,087	12%	7,510
Human Resources Managers	Bachelor's degree	$99,720	13%	4,060
Physicians and Surgeons	Doctoral or professional degree	$182,294	18%	29,630
Psychologists	See "How to Become One"	$69,807	12%	6,230
Social Workers	See "How to Become One"	$44,541	19%	24,280

service workers. This service offers people a stress-free understanding that their final wishes will be met.

Job Prospects. Job prospects for funeral service workers are expected to be good overall and more favorable for those who are licensed as both a funeral director and an embalmer and are willing to relocate.

Some job openings should result from the need to replace workers who leave the occupation each year.

O*NET

➤ Funeral Service Managers (11-9061.00)
➤ Morticians, Undertakers, and Funeral Directors (39-4031.00)

Contacts for More Information

For more information about funeral service occupations, including accredited mortuary science programs, visit
➤ National Funeral Directors Association (www.nfda.org/)
For scholarships and educational programs in funeral service and mortuary science, visit
➤ American Board of Funeral Service Education (www.abfse.org/)
➤ National Funeral Directors & Morticians Association, Inc. (www.nfdma.com/main.htm)
For information about crematories, visit
➤ Cremation Association of North America (www.cremation association.org/)
➤ International Cemetery, Cremation and Funeral Association (www.iccfa.com/)
Candidates should contact their state board for specific licensing requirements.

Gaming Services Occupations

* **2012 Median Pay** .... $20,210 per year
$9.71 per hour
* **Entry-Level Education** ... High school diploma or equivalent
* **Work Experience in a Related Occupation**.... See "How to Become One"
* **On-the-Job Training** ....See "How to Become One"
* **Number of Jobs 2012** 182,200
* **Job Outlook, 2012–22** .... 10% (As fast as average)
* **Employment Change, 2012–22** 17,900

What Gaming Services Occupations Do

Gaming services workers serve customers in gambling establishments, such as casinos or racetracks. Some workers tend slot machines or deal cards. Others take bets or pay out winnings. Still others supervise or manage gaming workers and operations.

Duties. Gaming services workers typically do the following:

* Interact with customers and ensure that they have a pleasant experience
* Monitor customers for violations of gaming regulations or casino policies
* Inform their supervisor or a security employee of any irregularities they observe
* Enforce safety rules and report hazards

Gaming managers and supervisors direct and oversee the gaming operations and personnel in their assigned area. Supervisors circulate among the tables to make sure that everything is running smoothly and that all areas are properly staffed. Gaming managers and supervisors typically do the following:

* Keep an eye on customers and employees to ensure compliance with all gaming and casino rules
* Communicate with other departments if security or customer-service issues arise
* Address customers' complaints about service
* Explain house operating rules, such as betting limits, if customers do not understand them
* Schedule when and where employees in their section will work
* Interview, hire, and train new employees

Slot supervisors oversee the activities of the slot department. The job duties of this occupation have changed significantly, as slot machines have become more automated. Because most casinos use video slot machines that give out tickets instead of cash and thus require very little oversight, workers in this occupation spend most of their time providing customer service to slot players. Slot supervisors typically do the following:

* Watch over the slot section and ensure that players are satisfied with the games
* Refill machines with tickets or money when they run out
* Reset cash slot machines after a payout
* Respond to and resolve customer complaints
* Interview, hire, and train new employees

Gaming dealers operate table games such as craps, blackjack, and roulette. They stand or sit behind tables while serving customers. Dealers control the pace and action of the game. They announce each player's move to the rest of the table and let players know when it is their turn. Most dealers can work with at least two games, usually blackjack or craps. Gaming dealers typically do the following:

* Give out cards and provide dice or other equipment to customers
* Determine winners, calculate and pay off winning bets, and collect on losing bets
* Continually inspect cards or dice
* Inform players of the rules of the game
* Keep track of the amount of money that customers have already bet
* Exchange paper money for gaming chips

Gaming service employees must have excellent customer service skills.

Median Annual Wages, May 2012

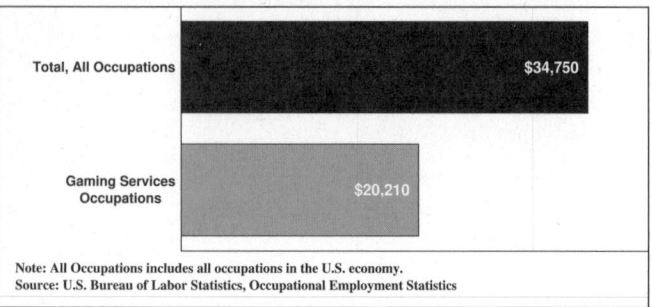

Note: All Occupations includes all occupations in the U.S. economy.
Source: U.S. Bureau of Labor Statistics, Occupational Employment Statistics

Percent Change in Employment, Projected 2012–2022

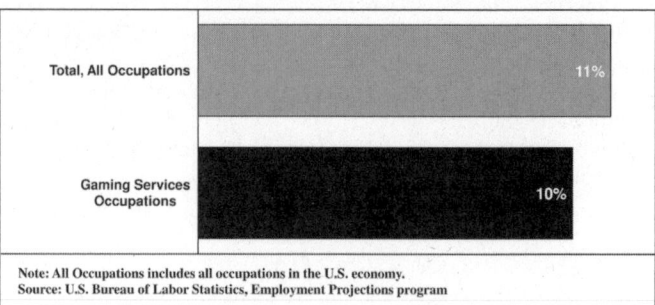

Note: All Occupations includes all occupations in the U.S. economy.
Source: U.S. Bureau of Labor Statistics, Employment Projections program

Gaming and sports book writers and runners handle bets on sporting events and take and record bets for customers. Sports book writers and runners also verify tickets and pay out winning tickets. In addition, they help run games such as bingo and keno. Some gaming runners collect winning tickets from customers in a casino. Gaming and sports book writers and runners typically do the following:

- Scan tickets and calculate winnings
- Operate the equipment that randomly selects bingo or keno numbers
- Announce bingo or keno numbers when they are selected
- Are responsible for the cash that comes in (on bets) and goes out (on winnings) during their shift

Work Environment

Workers in gaming services occupations held about 182,200 jobs in 2012. Many of the jobs were in commercial casinos, riverboat casinos, casino hotels, Native American casinos, and racetracks with casinos. However, these establishments are not legal in every state.

Some gaming services occupations are physically demanding. Gaming dealers spend most of their shift standing behind a table. Managers and supervisors are constantly walking up and down the casino floor.

A casino atmosphere may also expose gaming services workers to hazards such as secondhand smoke from cigarettes, cigars, and pipes. Noise from slot machines, gaming tables, and loud customers may be distracting to some, although workers wear protective headgear in areas where machinery is used to count money.

Work Schedules. Most casinos are open 24 hours a day, 7 days a week. Employees work nights, weekends, and holidays. Most managers and supervisors have full-time work schedules. Most gaming dealers, sports book writers, and other gaming services workers also work full time.

How to Become One

Most gaming jobs require a high school diploma or equivalent. Some casinos may require gaming managers to have a college degree. In addition, all gaming services workers must have excellent customer-service skills.

Education. Gaming dealers, gaming supervisors, sports book writers and runners, and slot supervisors typically need a high school diploma or a equivalent. Educational requirements for gaming managers, however, differ by casino. Although some casinos may only require a high school diploma or equivalent, others require gaming managers to have a college degree. Those who choose to pursue a degree may study hotel management, hospitality, or accounting in addition to taking formal management classes.

Training. Individual casinos or other gaming establishments have their own training requirements. Usually, new gaming dealers are sent to gaming school for a few weeks to learn a casino game, such as blackjack or craps. These schools teach the rules and procedures of the game, as well as state and local laws and regulations related to the game.

Although gaming school is primarily for new employees, some experienced dealers have to go to gaming school if they want to be trained in a new casino game.

Gaming and sports book writers and runners usually do not have to go to gaming school. They can be trained by the casino in less than 1 month. The casino teaches them state and local laws and regulations related to the game, as well the particulars of their job, such as keno calling.

Completing gaming school before being hired may increase a prospective dealer's chances of being hired, but it does not guarantee a job. Casinos usually audition prospective dealers for open positions to assess their personal qualities.

Licenses, Certifications, and Registrations. Gaming services workers must be licensed by a state regulatory agency, such as a state casino control board or gaming commission. Licensing requirements for supervisory or managerial positions may differ from those for gaming dealers, gaming and sports book writers and runners, and all other gaming workers. However, all applicants for a license must provide photo identification and pay a fee. They must also typically pass a background check and drug test.

Age requirements also vary by state. For specific licensing requirements, visit the state's gaming commission website.

Work Experience in a Related Occupation. Gaming and slot supervisors and gaming managers usually have several years of experience working in a casino. Gaming supervisors often have experience as a dealer or in the customer outreach department of the casino. Slot supervisors usually have experience as a slot technician or slot attendant. Some also may have worked in entry-level marketing or customer-service positions.

Advancement. Gaming managers are often promoted from positions as slot or gaming supervisors. They also may be moved from a management job in another part of the resort, such as hospitality, after learning about casino operations through an internship or on-the-job training.

Gaming dealers can advance to gaming supervisors and eventually managers. A slot supervisor can also advance to gaming manager.

Important Qualities

Communication skills. Gaming services workers must be able to explain the rules of the game to customers and answer any questions they have. Simple misunderstandings can cost a customer a lot of money and damage the reputation of the casino.

Employment Projections Data for Gaming Services Occupations

Occupational title	SOC Code	Employment, 2012	Projected Employment, 2022	Change, 2012–2022	
				Percent	Numeric
Gaming services occupations.................................	—	182,200	200,100	10	17,900
Gaming managers.................................	11-9071	4,800	5,200	7	400
Gaming supervisors	39-1011	38,500	41,600	8	3,100
Slot supervisors	39-1012	10,700	11,400	6	600
Gaming dealers	39-3011	100,300	111,700	11	11,400
Gaming and sports book writers and runners	39-3012	14,700	15,800	8	1,100
Gaming service workers, all other......................................	39-3019	13,200	14,400	9	1,200

Source: U.S. Bureau of Labor Statistics, Employment Projections Program

Note: Data are rounded. Go to **Occupational Information Included in the OOH** *for a discussion of the data in this table.*

Customer-service skills. All gaming jobs involve a lot of interaction with customers. The success or failure of a casino depends on how customers view the casino, making customer service important for all gaming services occupations.

Leadership skills. Gaming managers and supervisors oversee other gaming services workers and must be able to guide them in doing their jobs and developing their skills.

Math skills. Because they deal with large amounts of money, many casino workers must be good at math.

Organizational skills. Gaming managers and supervisors must be well organized to handle administrative and other tasks required in overseeing gaming services workers.

Patience. All gaming services workers have to be able to keep their composure when they handle a customer who becomes upset or breaks a rule. They must also be patient in dealing with equipment failure of malfunction.

Pay

The median annual wage for workers in gaming services occupations was $20,210 in May 2012. The median wage is the wage at which half the workers in an occupation earned more than that amount and half earned less. The lowest 10 percent earned less than $16,530, and the top 10 percent earned more than $54,830.

The median annual wages for gaming services occupations in May 2012 were as follows:

Gaming managers..	$65,220
Gaming supervisors	49,290
Slot supervisors...	32,390
All other gaming services workers	23,490
Gaming and sports book writers and runners	21,810
Gaming dealers..	18,630

Job Outlook

Employment in gaming services occupations is projected to grow 10 percent from 2012 to 2022, about as fast as the average for all occupations. Employment growth of gaming managers and supervisors is projected to be 7 and 8 percent, respectively. Employment of gaming and sports book writers and runners is projected to grow 8 percent.

These occupations will be driven by the increasing popularity of gambling establishments such as Native American casinos and regional casinos. Because states benefit from some casinos in the form of tax revenues, additional states may expand the number of gambling establishments over the next decade.

Increased demand for table games will drive growth for gaming dealers, whose employment is projected to grow 11 percent from 2012 to 2022. Many jurisdictions that currently allow only slot machines are expected to begin allowing table games for the additional money they bring. However, new electronic table games, which eliminate the need for a dealer, may moderate employment growth.

Employment of slot supervisors is projected to grow 6 percent from 2012 to 2022, which is slower than that of other gaming services occupations. Almost all slot machines now use tickets instead of coins, reducing the need for workers to pay out jackpots, fill hoppers, and reset machines. In addition, advancements in technology allow slot machines to be linked to a network and adjusted from a central computer, rather than one at a time on the floor.

Some casinos may be at risk due to potential oversaturation. As more states approve the expansion in the number of gaming establishments, the competition for customers will increase. Those establishments that fail to keep or attract customers may be forced to close.

Similar Occupations   This table shows a list of occupations with job duties that are similar to those of gaming services occupations.

Occupations	Entry-level Education	2012 Pay	Projected Job Growth	Average Annual Openings
Customer Service Representatives	High school diploma or equivalent	$30,580	13%	94,160
Lodging Managers	High school diploma or equivalent	$46,810	1%	1,620
Public Relations and Fundraising Managers	Bachelor's degree	$95,450	13%	2,130
Public Relations Specialists	Bachelor's degree	$54,170	12%	5,880
Retail Sales Workers	Less than high school	$21,514	10%	202,730
Sales Managers	Bachelor's degree	$105,260	8%	10,690
Security Guards and Gaming Surveillance Officers	High school diploma or equivalent	$24,019	12%	29,630

In addition, new state taxes on casinos may make some casinos unprofitable and lead to closings or hesitancy among investors to invest in new gaming establishments.

Job Prospects. Although job openings will occur due to workers leaving the occupation, strong competition is expected for jobs at casinos. Those with work experience in customer service at a hotel or resort should have better job prospects because of the importance of customer service in casinos.

O*NET

➤ Gaming Managers (11-9071.00)
➤ Gaming Supervisors (39-1011.00)
➤ Slot Supervisors (39-1012.00)
➤ Gaming Dealers (39-3011.00)
➤ Gaming and Sports Book Writers and Runners (39-3012.00)
➤ Gaming Service Workers, All Other (39-3019.00)

Contacts for More Information

For more information about gaming services occupations, visit
➤ American Gaming Association (www.americangaming.org/)
➤ Casino Careers (www.casinocareers.com/)

Manicurists and Pedicurists

- **2012 Median Pay** .... $19,220 per year
  $9.24 per hour
- **Entry-Level Education** .... Postsecondary non-degree award
- **Work Experience in a Related Occupation** .... None
- **On-the-Job Training** .... None
- **Number of Jobs 2012** 86,900
- **Job Outlook, 2012–22** .... 16% (Faster than average)
- **Employment Change, 2012–22** 13,500

What Manicurists and Pedicurists Do

Manicurists and pedicurists clean, shape, and beautify fingernails and toenails.

Duties. Manicurists and pedicurists typically do the following:

- Discuss nail treatments and services available
- Remove nail polish and rough skin
- Clean, trim, and file nails
- Massage and moisturize hands (for a manicure) and feet (for a pedicure)
- Polish or buff nails
- Advise clients about nail and skin care for hands and feet
- Promote and sell nail and skin care products
- Clean and disinfect their work area and tools

Manicurists and pedicurists work exclusively on the hands and feet, providing treatments to groom fingernails and toenails. A typical treatment involves soaking the clients' hands or feet to soften the skin in order to remove dead skin cells. Manicurists and pedicurists apply lotion to the hands and feet to moisturize the skin. They may also shape and apply polish to artificial fingernails.

Manicurists and pedicurists use a variety of tools, including nail clippers, nail files, and specialized cuticle tools. They must be focused while they perform their duties, because most of the tools they use are sharp. Keeping their tools clean and sanitary is important.

Some manicurists and pedicurists operate their own nail salon business. They manage the daily decision-making tasks, such as keeping inventory records and ordering supplies. They also hire and supervise workers and sell nail care products, such as nail polish and hand or foot cream, to clients. A small, but growing, number of workers make house calls. Their mobile manicure and pedicure services are popular because clients consider them convenient.

Work Environment

Manicurists and pedicurists held about 86,900 jobs in 2012, of which 69 percent were in the personal care services industry. About 27 percent were self-employed, many running their own nail salon business.

Manicurists and pedicurists usually work in a nail salon, spa, or hair salon. The job involves a lot of sitting. Those who own a mobile grooming company must travel to their clients' homes.

Manicurists and pedicurists use chemicals when working on fingernails and toenails, so they often wear protective clothing, including protective gloves and masks.

Work Schedules. Although most manicurists and pedicurists work full time, many have variable schedules and work part time. Their schedules are often determined by the type of establishment. For example, a full-service salon may require manicurists and pedicurists to work an 8-hour day. A boutique hair salon, however, may require shorter work hours on a part-time basis. Longer hours are not unusual for self-employed workers. Weekends and evenings tend to be the busiest times for manicurists and pedicurists.

How to Become One

Manicurists and pedicurists must complete a state-approved cosmetology or nail technician program and then pass a state exam for licensure, which all states except Connecticut require.

Education. Manicurists and pedicurists must complete a state-approved cosmetology or nail technician program. Currently, there are hundreds of programs nationwide.

Licenses, Certifications, and Registrations. State licensing requirements vary. However, applicants need to be at least 16 years old and have a high school diploma or the equivalent. After completing a state-approved cosmetology or nail technician program, manicurists and pedicurists must take a written exam and a practical exam to get a license through their state board.

The National-Interstate Council of State Boards of Cosmetology (NIC) provides information on state examinations for licensing, with sample questions. The Professional Beauty Association

Nail technicians work in salons and provide various services including manicures.

Median Hourly Wages, May 2012

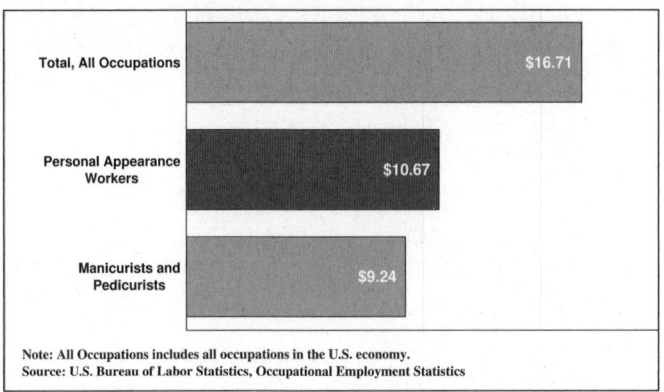

Note: All Occupations includes all occupations in the U.S. economy.
Source: U.S. Bureau of Labor Statistics, Occupational Employment Statistics

Percent Change in Employment, Projected 2012–2022

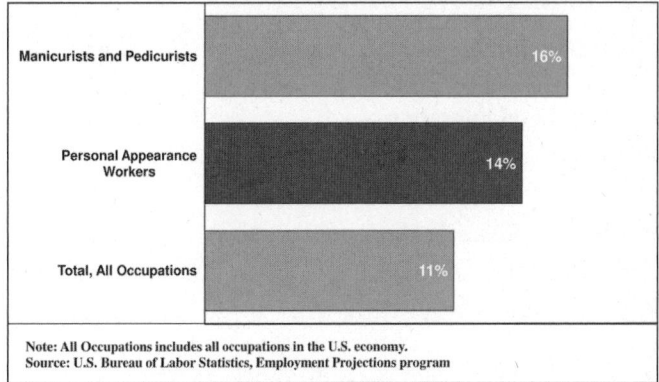

Note: All Occupations includes all occupations in the U.S. economy.
Source: U.S. Bureau of Labor Statistics, Employment Projections program

(PBA) and the American Association of Cosmetology Schools (AACS) also provide information on state examinations, as well as offering other professional links.

Important Qualities

Business skills. Manicurists and pedicurist who run their own nail salon must understand general business principles. For example, they should be skilled at administrative tasks, such as accounting and personnel management, and be able to manage a salon efficiently and profitably.

Creativity. The ability to neatly finish small, intricate designs is important, as is the ability to suggest and match nail designs to individual tastes.

Customer-service skills. Good listening and interpersonal skills are important in working with clients. Also, meeting the needs of clients, including interacting with them while doing a manicure or pedicure, encourages repeat business.

Dexterity. A steady hand is essential in achieving a creative and precise nail design. Also, because manicurists and pedicurists often use sharp tools, they must have good finger dexterity.

Pay

The median hourly wage for manicurists and pedicurists was $9.24 in May 2012. The median wage is the wage at which half the workers in an occupation earned more than that amount and half earned less. The lowest 10 percent earned less than $8.00 per hour, and the top 10 percent earned more than $14.21 per hour.

Job Outlook

Employment of manicurists and pedicurists is projected to grow 16 percent from 2012 to 2022, faster than the average for all occupations.

The increase in employment reflects demand for new nail services being offered, such as minisessions (quick manicures at a low cost) and mobile manicures and pedicures (house calls).

The desire among young women and a growing number of men to lead a healthier lifestyle through better grooming and wellness should also result in higher employment for manicurists and pedicurists.

Considered a low-cost luxury service, manicures and pedicures will continue to be in demand by individuals at all income levels.

Job Prospects. Job opportunities should be very good overall. The growing number of nail salons and the need to replace workers who leave the occupation each year will result in many job openings.

O*NET

➤ Manicurists and Pedicurists (39-5092.00)

Contacts for More Information

For information about training and cosmetology schools, visit
➤ American Association of Cosmetology Schools (www.beautyschools.org/)
➤ International Pedicure Association (www.pedicureassociation.org/)
For information about state licensing, practice exams and other professional links, visit
➤ National-Interstate Council of State Boards of Cosmetology (www.nictesting.org/index.asp)
➤ Professional Beauty Association (www.probeauty.org/links/)

Employment Projections Data for Manicurists and Pedicurists

Occupational title	SOC Code	Employment, 2012	Projected Employment, 2022	Change, 2012–2022 Percent	Change, 2012–2022 Numeric
Manicurists and pedicurists 39-5092		86,900	100,400	16	13,500

Source: U.S. Bureau of Labor Statistics, Employment Projections Program

Note: Data are rounded. Go to **Occupational Information Included in the OOH** *for a discussion of the data in this table.*

Similar Occupations   This table shows a list of occupations with job duties that are similar to those of manicurists and pedicurists.

Occupations	Entry-level Education	2012 Pay	Projected Job Growth	Average Annual Openings
Barbers, Hairdressers, and Cosmetologists	Postsecondary non-degree award	$22,782	13%	23,990
Skincare Specialists	Postsecondary non-degree award	$28,640	40%	2,130

Recreation Workers

- **2012 Median Pay** .... $22,240 per year
  $10.69 per hour
- **Entry-Level Education** ....Bachelor's degree
- **Work Experience in a Related Occupation**.............. None
- **On-the-Job Training** .... None
- **Number of Jobs 2012** 345,400
- **Job Outlook, 2012–22**................ 14% (As fast as average)
- **Employment Change, 2012–22** 49,000

What Recreation Workers Do

Recreation workers design and lead leisure activities for groups in volunteer agencies or recreation facilities, such as playgrounds, parks, camps, aquatic centers, and senior centers. They may lead activities such as arts and crafts, sports, adventure programs, music, and camping.

Duties. Recreation workers typically do the following:

- Plan, organize, and lead activities for groups or recreation centers
- Explain the rules of the activities and instruct participants at a variety of skill levels
- Enforce safety rules to prevent injury
- Modify activities to suit the needs of specific groups, such as seniors
- Administer basic first aid if needed
- Organize and set up the equipment that is used in recreational activities
- Teach activity participants about the local environment, such as area wildlife

The specific responsibilities of recreation workers vary greatly with their job title, their level of training, and the state they work in. The following are examples of types of recreation workers:

Camp counselors work directly with youth in residential (overnight) or day camps. They often lead and instruct children and teenagers in a variety of outdoor activities, such as swimming, hiking, horseback riding, or nature study. Counselors also provide guidance and supervise daily living and socialization. Some counselors may specialize in a specific activity, such as archery, boating, music, drama, or gymnastics.

Camp directors typically supervise camp counselors, plan camp activities or programs, and do the administrative tasks that keep

Many recreation workers spend most of their time outdoors in various weather conditions.

the camp running. Directors may also be involved in fund-raising, public relations, and community engagement.

Activity specialists provide instruction and coaching primarily in one activity, such as dance, swimming, or tennis. These workers may work in camps, aquatic centers, or anywhere else where there is interest in a single activity.

Recreation leaders are responsible for a recreation program's daily operation. They primarily organize and direct participants, schedule the use of facilities, set up and keep records of equipment use, and ensure that recreation facilities and equipment are used and maintained properly. They may lead classes and provide instruction in a recreational activity, such as kayaking or golf.

Median Annual Wages, May 2012

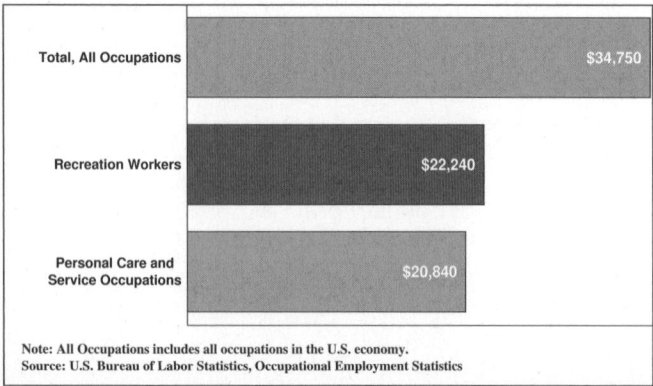

Total, All Occupations	$34,750
Recreation Workers	$22,240
Personal Care and Service Occupations	$20,840

Note: All Occupations includes all occupations in the U.S. economy.
Source: U.S. Bureau of Labor Statistics, Occupational Employment Statistics

Percent Change in Employment, Projected 2012–2022

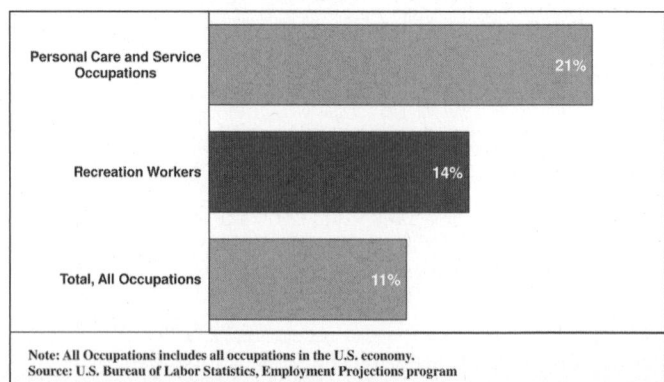

Personal Care and Service Occupations	21%
Recreation Workers	14%
Total, All Occupations	11%

Note: All Occupations includes all occupations in the U.S. economy.
Source: U.S. Bureau of Labor Statistics, Employment Projections program

Employment Projections Data for Recreation Workers

Occupational title	SOC Code	Employment, 2012	Projected Employment, 2022	Change, 2012–2022	
				Percent	Numeric
Recreation workers	39-9032	345,400	394,400	14	49,000

Source: U.S. Bureau of Labor Statistics, Employment Projections Program

Note: Data are rounded. Go to **Occupational Information Included in the OOH** *for a discussion of the data in this table.*

Recreation supervisors oversee recreation leaders. They often serve as a point of contact between the director of a park or recreation center and the recreation leaders. Some supervisors also may direct special activities or events or oversee a major activity, such as aquatics, gymnastics, or one or more performing arts.

Directors of recreation and parks develop and manage comprehensive recreation programs in parks, playgrounds, and other settings. Directors usually serve as technical advisors to state and local recreation and park commissions and may be responsible for recreation and park budgets.

Work Environment

Recreation workers held about 345,400 jobs in 2012. The industries that employed the most recreation workers in 2012 were as follows:

Local government, excluding education and hospitals............ 33%
Nursing and residential care facilities 16
Religious, grantmaking, civic, professional, and similar
    organizations.. 12
Arts, entertainment, and recreation 10
Social assistance.. 8

Recreation workers are employed in a variety of settings, including summer camps, recreation centers, parks, resorts, and cruise ships. They may also work in nursing and residential care facilities as well as in community and vocational rehabilitation services. Many workers spend much of their time outdoors. Recreation directors and supervisors, however, typically spend most of their time in an office, planning programs and special events.

All recreation workers may risk injury while participating in physical activities.

Work Schedules. In 2012, about half of all recreation workers worked full time. Some recreation workers, such as camp counselors, may work weekends or irregular hours or may be seasonally employed.

How to Become One

The education and training requirements for recreation workers vary with the type of job, but workers typically need at least a bachelor's degree.

Education and Training. Recreation workers who work full time typically need at least a bachelor's degree. Though less common, associate's, master's, and doctoral degrees are also available.

In 2012, the Council on Accreditation of Parks, Recreation, Tourism, and Related Professions, a branch of the National Recreation and Park Association, accredited 81 bachelor's degree programs in recreation or leisure studies.

Programs typically include courses in management, human development, community organization, supervision, and administration. Students also take courses in developing programs for populations with specific needs, such as the elderly or people with special needs. Students may specialize in areas such as park management, outdoor recreation, industrial or commercial recreation, and camp management.

A bachelor's degree in other subjects, such as liberal arts or public administration, may also qualify applicants for some positions.

Supervisory positions may require at least a master's degree in parks and recreation, business administration, or public administration.

A seasonal or part-time worker may not need postsecondary education. They typically learn to do their jobs through a short period of on-the-job training.

Important Qualities

Communication skills. Recreation workers must be able to communicate well. They often work with large groups of people and need to give clear instructions, motivate participants, and maintain order and safety.

Flexibility. Recreation workers must be flexible when planning activities. They must be able to adapt plans to suit changing environmental conditions and each client's needs.

Similar Occupations This table shows a list of occupations with job duties that are similar to those of recreation workers.

Occupations	Entry-level Education	2012 Pay	Projected Job Growth	Average Annual Openings
Athletic Trainers and Exercise Physiologists	Bachelor's degree	$42,676	19%	1,240
Fitness Trainers and Instructors	High school diploma or equivalent	$31,720	13%	6,500
Meeting, Convention, and Event Planners	Bachelor's degree	$45,810	33%	4,420
Probation Officers and Correctional Treatment Specialists	Bachelor's degree	$48,190	-1%	2,360
Psychologists	See "How to Become One"	$69,807	12%	6,230
Recreational Therapists	Bachelor's degree	$42,280	14%	670
Rehabilitation Counselors	Master's degree	$33,880	20%	4,840
School and Career Counselors	Master's degree	$53,610	12%	8,700
Social Workers	See "How to Become One"	$44,541	19%	24,280

Leadership skills. Recreation workers should be able to lead both large and small groups. They often lead activities for people of all ages and abilities.

Physical strength. Recreation workers need to be physically fit. Their job may require a considerable amount of movement because they often demonstrate activities while explaining them.

Problem-solving skills. Recreation workers need strong problem-solving skills. They must be able to create and reinvent activities and programs for all types of participants.

For recreation workers who generally work part time, such as camp counselors and activity specialists, certain qualities may be more important than postsecondary education. These qualities include a worker's experience leading activities, the ability to work well with children or the elderly, and the ability to ensure the safety of participants.

Licenses, Certifications, and Registrations. The National Recreation and Park Association (NRPA) offers four certifications for recreation workers. Applicants may qualify for certification with different combinations of education and work experience. They must also take continuing education classes to maintain certification.

The American Camp Association also offers four certificates for various levels of camp staff. Individuals who complete online courses may show their advanced level of knowledge of core competencies.

Some recreation jobs require certification. For example, a lifesaving certificate is often required for teaching or coaching water-related activities. These certifications are available from organizations such as the YMCA or the Red Cross. Specific requirements vary by job and employer.

Advancement. As workers gain experience, they may be promoted to positions with greater responsibilities. Recreation workers with experience and managerial skills may advance to supervisory or managerial positions. Eventually, they may become directors of a recreation department or may start their own recreation company.

Pay

The median annual wage for recreation workers was $22,240 in May 2012. The median wage is the wage at which half the workers in an occupation earned more than that amount and half earned less. The lowest 10 percent earned less than $16,900, and the top 10 percent earned more than $38,750.

In May 2012, the median annual wages for recreation workers in the top five industries in which they worked were as follows:

Nursing and residential care facilities	$24,210
Social assistance	22,640
Local government, excluding education and hospitals	22,160
Religious, grantmaking, civic, professional, and similar organizations	20,310
Arts, entertainment, and recreation	19,320

Job Outlook

Employment of recreation workers is projected to grow 14 percent from 2012 to 2022, about as fast as the average for all occupations. In response to growing rates of childhood obesity, a number of federal, state, and local campaigns have been established to encourage young people to be physically active. As more emphasis is placed on the importance of exercise, more recreation workers will be needed to work in fitness centers, sports centers, and camps specializing in younger participants.

In addition, as the baby-boom generation grows older, there will be more demand for recreation workers to work with older clients

in social assistance organizations and in nursing and residential care facilities.

Job Prospects. Job prospects will be best for those seeking part-time, seasonal, or temporary recreation jobs. Because workers in these jobs tend to be students or young people, they must be replaced when they leave for school or jobs in other occupations, thus creating many job openings.

Workers with higher levels of formal education related to recreation should have better prospects at getting full-time positions. Volunteer experience, part-time work during school, and a summer job also are viewed favorably for both full- and part-time positions.

O*NET

➤ Recreation Workers (39-9032.00)

Contacts for More Information

For information on careers, certification, and academic programs in parks and recreation, visit
➤ National Recreation and Park Association (www.nrpa.org/)
 For information about a career as a camp counselor, visit
➤ American Camp Association (www.acacamps.org/)

Skincare Specialists

- **2012 Median Pay** .... $28,640 per year
  $13.77 per hour
- **Entry-Level Education** .... Postsecondary non-degree award
- **Work Experience in a Related Occupation** .... None
- **On-the-Job Training** .... None
- **Number of Jobs 2012** 44,400
- **Job Outlook, 2012–22** .... 40% (Much faster than average)
- **Employment Change, 2012–22** 17,700

What Skincare Specialists Do

Skincare specialists cleanse and beautify the face and body to enhance a person's appearance.

Duties. Skincare specialists typically do the following:

- Evaluate clients' skin condition and appearance
- Discuss available treatments and determine which products will improve clients' skin quality

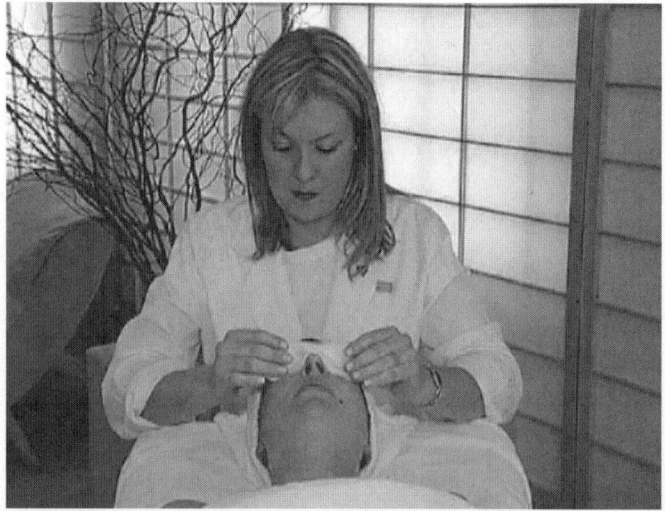

Skincare specialists cleanse and beautify a client's face and body.

Median Hourly Wages, May 2012

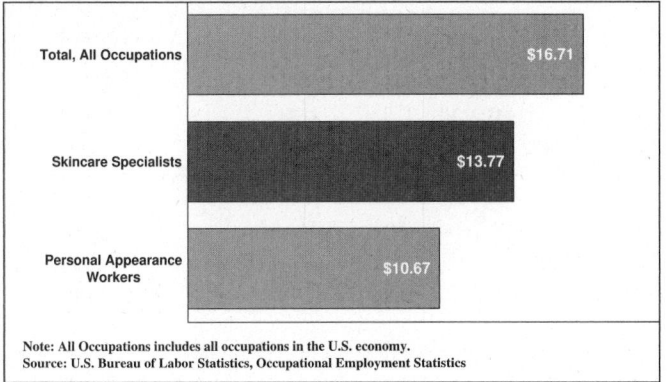

Note: All Occupations includes all occupations in the U.S. economy.
Source: U.S. Bureau of Labor Statistics, Occupational Employment Statistics

Percent Change in Employment, Projected 2012–2022

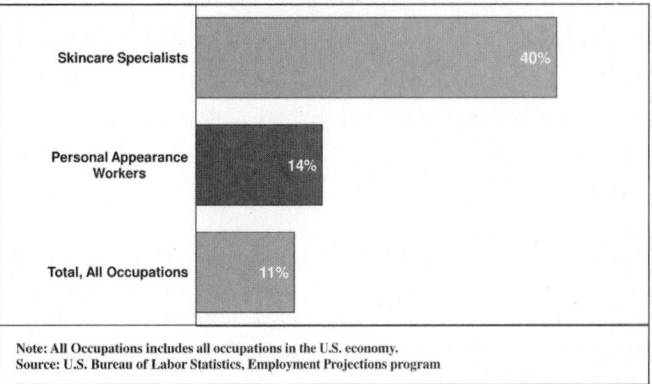

Note: All Occupations includes all occupations in the U.S. economy.
Source: U.S. Bureau of Labor Statistics, Employment Projections program

- Remove unwanted hair, using wax, laser, or other approved treatments
- Clean the skin before applying makeup
- Recommend skin care products, such as cleansers, lotions, or creams
- Teach and advise clients on how to apply makeup and how to take care of their skin
- Refer clients to another skincare specialist, such as a dermatologist, for serious skin problems
- Disinfect equipment and clean work areas

Skincare specialists provide facials, full-body treatments, and head and neck massages to improve the health and appearance of the skin. Some may provide other skin care treatments, such as peels, masks, or scrubs, to remove dead or dry skin.

In addition to working with clients, skincare specialists create daily skin care routines based on skin analysis and help clients understand which skin care products will work best for them. A growing number of specialists actively sell skin care products, such as cleansers, lotions, and creams.

Those who operate their own salons have managerial duties that include hiring, firing, and supervising workers, as well as keeping business and inventory records, ordering supplies, and arranging for advertising.

Work Environment

Skincare specialists held about 44,400 jobs in 2012, of which 51 percent were in the personal care services industry. About 27 percent of skincare specialists were self-employed.

Skincare specialists usually work in salons, health and beauty spas, or, less frequently, medical offices. The job may involve a lot of standing.

Because skincare specialists must evaluate the condition of the skin, good lighting and clean surroundings are important. Protective clothing and good ventilation also may be necessary, because skincare specialists often use chemicals on the face and body.

Work Schedules. Skincare specialists typically work full time, with many working evenings and weekends. Long hours are common, especially for self-employed workers.

How to Become One

Skincare specialists must complete a state-approved cosmetology or esthetician program and then pass a state exam for licensure, which all states except Connecticut require.

Education. Skincare specialists usually take a state-approved cosmetology or esthetician program. Although some high schools offer vocational training, most people receive their training from a postsecondary vocational school. The Associated Skin Care Professionals, the largest organization devoted to these workers, offers a State Regulation Guide, which includes the number of prerequisite hours required to complete a cosmetology program.

Training. Newly hired specialists sometimes receive on-the-job training, especially when working with chemicals. Those who are employed in a medical environment also may receive on-the-job training, often working alongside an experienced skincare specialist.

Licenses, Certifications, and Registrations. After completing an approved cosmetology or esthetician program, skincare specialists take a written and practical exam to get a state license. Licensing requirements vary by state, so those interested should contact their state board.

The National-Interstate Council of State Boards of Cosmetology (NIC) provides contact information on state examinations for licensing, with sample exam questions. The Professional Beauty Association (PBA) and the American Association of Cosmetology Schools (AACS) also provides information on state examinations, as well as offering other professional links.

Many states offer continuing education seminars and programs designed to keep skincare specialists current on new techniques and products. Post-licensing training is also available through manufacturers, associations, and at trade shows.

Employment Projections Data for Skincare Specialists

Occupational title	SOC Code	Employment, 2012	Projected Employment, 2022	Change, 2012–2022	
				Percent	Numeric
Skincare specialists...	39-5094	44,400	62,000	40	17,700

Source: U.S. Bureau of Labor Statistics, Employment Projections Program

Note: Data are rounded. Go to **Occupational Information Included in the OOH** *for a discussion of the data in this table.*

Similar Occupations   This table shows a list of occupations with job duties that are similar to those of skincare specialists.

Occupations	Entry-level Education	2012 Pay	Projected Job Growth	Average Annual Openings
Barbers, Hairdressers, and Cosmetologists	Postsecondary non-degree award	$22,782	13%	23,990
Manicurists and Pedicurists	Postsecondary non-degree award	$19,220	16%	2,070
Massage Therapists	Postsecondary non-degree award	$35,970	23%	4,410

Important Qualities

Business skills. Skincare specialists who run their own salon must understand general business principles. For example, they should be skilled at administrative tasks, such as accounting and personnel management, and be able to manage a salon efficiently and profitably.

Customer-service skills. Skincare specialists should be friendly and courteous when dealing with clients. Repeat business is important, particularly for self-employed workers.

Initiative. Self-employed skincare specialists generate their own business opportunities and must be proactive in finding new clients.

Physical stamina. Skincare specialists must be able to spend most of their day standing and massaging clients' faces and bodies.

Tidiness. Workers must keep a neat personal appearance and keep their work area clean and sanitary. This requirement is necessary for the health and safety of their clients, as well as to make the clients comfortable enough to want to return.

Time-management skills. Time-management skills are important in scheduling appointments and providing services.

Pay

The median hourly wage for skincare specialists was $13.77 in May 2012. The median wage is the wage at which half the workers in an occupation earned more than that amount and half earned less. The lowest 10 percent of skincare specialists earned less than $8.39 per hour, and the top 10 percent earned more than $24.95 per hour.

In May 2012, median hourly wages for skincare specialists in the top five industries in which these specialists worked were as follows:

Ambulatory health care services	$17.87
Other amusement and recreation industries	14.12
Health and personal care stores	13.31
Personal care services	12.91
Traveler accommodation	11.25

Job Outlook

Employment of skincare specialists is projected to grow 40 percent from 2012 to 2022, much faster than the average for all occupations.

The increase in employment reflects demand for new services being offered, such as minisessions (quick facials at a lower cost) and mobile facials (making house calls). In addition, the desire among women and a growing number of men to reduce the effects of aging and to lead a healthier lifestyle through better grooming, including skin treatments for relaxation and well-being, should result in employment growth.

Job Prospects. Job opportunities should be good because of the growing number of beauty salons and spas. Those with related work experience should have the best job opportunities.

O*NET

➤ Skincare Specialists (39-5094.00)

Contacts for More Information

For more information about skincare specialists, visit

➤ Aesthetics International Association (www.aestheticsassociation.com/)

➤ Associated Skin Care Professionals (www.ascpskincare.com/)

For information about cosmetology schools, visit

➤ American Association of Cosmetology Schools (www.beautyschools.org/)

For information about the spa industry, visit

➤ International Spa Association (www.experienceispa.com/)

For information about state licensing, practice exams and other professional links, visit

➤ National-Interstate Council of State Boards of Cosmetology (www.nictesting.org/index.asp)

➤ Professional Beauty Association (www.probeauty.org/links/)

Production

Assemblers and Fabricators

- **2012 Median Pay** .... $28,580 per year
  $13.74 per hour
- **Entry-Level Education** ... High school diploma or equivalent
- **Work Experience in a Related Occupation** .... None
- **On-the-Job Training** .... See "How to Become One"
- **Number of Jobs 2012** 1,755,200
- **Job Outlook, 2012–22** .... 4% (Slower than average)
- **Employment Change, 2012–22** 64,200

What Assemblers and Fabricators Do

Assemblers and fabricators assemble finished products and the parts that go into them. They use tools, machines, and their hands to make engines, computers, aircraft, ships, boats, toys, electronic devices, control panels, and more.

Duties. Assemblers and fabricators typically do the following:

- Read and understand schematics and blueprints
- Use hand tools or machines to assemble parts
- Conduct quality control checks
- Work closely with designers and engineers in product development

Assemblers test circuits in electronic devices.

Assemblers and fabricators have an important role in the manufacturing process. They assemble both finished products and the pieces that go into them. The products encompass a full range of manufactured products, including aircraft, toys, household appliances, automobiles, computers, and electronic devices.

Changes in technology have transformed the manufacturing and assembly process. Modern manufacturing systems use robots, computers, programmable motion-control devices, and various sensing technologies. These systems change the way in which goods are made and affect the jobs of those who make them. Advanced assemblers must be able to work with these new technologies and use them to manufacture goods.

The job of an assembler or fabricator requires a range of knowledge and skills. Skilled assemblers putting together complex machines, for example, read detailed schematics that show how to assemble the machine. After determining how parts should connect, they use hand or power tools to trim, shim, cut, and make other adjustments to fit components together. Once the parts are properly aligned, they connect them with bolts and screws or weld or solder pieces together.

Quality control is important throughout the assembly process, so assemblers look for faulty components and mistakes in the assembly process. They attempt to help fix problems before defective products are made.

Manufacturing techniques are moving away from traditional assembly line systems toward lean manufacturing systems, which use teams of workers to produce entire products or components. Lean manufacturing has changed the nature of the assemblers' duties.

It has become more common to involve assemblers and fabricators in product development. Designers and engineers consult manufacturing workers during the design stage to improve product reliability and manufacturing efficiency. Some experienced assemblers work with designers and engineers to build prototypes or test products.

Although most assemblers and fabricators are classified as team assemblers, others specialize in producing one type of product or perform the same or similar tasks throughout the assembly process.

The following are examples of types of assemblers and fabricators:

Aircraft structure, surfaces, rigging, and systems assemblers fit, fasten, and install parts of airplanes, space vehicles, or missiles, such as wings, fuselage, landing gear, rigging and control equipment, or heating and ventilating systems.

Coil winders, tapers, and finishers wind wire coils of electrical components used in a variety of electric and electronic products, including resistors, transformers, generators, and electric motors.

Electrical and electronic equipment assemblers build products such as electric motors, computers, electronic control devices, and sensing equipment. Automated systems have been put in place because many small electronic parts are too small or fragile for human assembly. Much of the remaining work of electrical and electronic assemblers is done by hand during the small-scale production of electronic devices used in all types of aircraft, military systems, and medical equipment. Production by hand requires these workers to use devices such as soldering irons.

Electromechanical equipment assemblers assemble and modify electromechanical devices such as household appliances, computer tomography scanners, or vending machines. The workers use a variety of tools, such as rulers, rivet guns, and soldering irons.

Median Annual Wages, May 2012

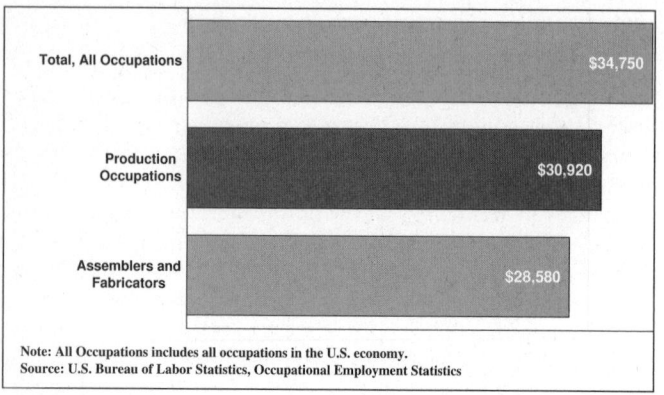

Note: All Occupations includes all occupations in the U.S. economy.
Source: U.S. Bureau of Labor Statistics, Occupational Employment Statistics

Percent Change in Employment, Projected 2012–2022

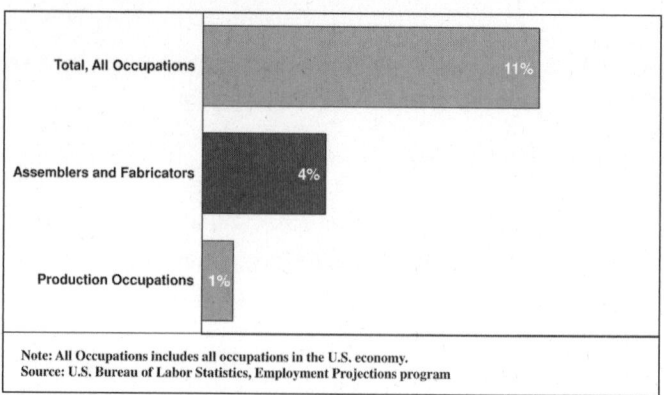

Note: All Occupations includes all occupations in the U.S. economy.
Source: U.S. Bureau of Labor Statistics, Employment Projections program

Engine and machine assemblers construct, assemble, or rebuild engines, turbines, and machines used in automobiles, construction and mining equipment, and power generators.

Structural metal fabricators and fitters cut, align, and fit together structural metal parts and may help weld or rivet the parts together.

Fiberglass laminators and fabricators laminate layers of fiberglass on molds to form boat decks and hulls, bodies for golf carts, automobiles, or other products.

Team assemblers work on an assembly line, but they rotate through different tasks, rather than specializing in a single task. The team may decide how the work is assigned and how different tasks are done. Some aspects of lean production, such as rotating tasks and seeking worker input on improving the assembly process, are common to all assembly and fabrication occupations.

Timing device assemblers, adjusters, and calibrators do precision assembling or adjusting of timing devices within very narrow tolerances.

Work Environment

Assemblers and fabricators held about 1.8 million jobs in 2012; most of these jobs were in manufacturing industries.

Employment in the detailed occupations that make up assemblers and fabricators was distributed as follows:

Team assemblers 1,031,800
Assemblers and fabricators, all other 277,700
Electrical and electronic equipment assemblers 198,300
Structural metal fabricators and fitters 79,700

Electromechanical equipment assemblers 50,500
Engine and other machine assemblers 42,000
Aircraft structure, surfaces, rigging, and
  systems assemblers 41,500
Fiberglass laminators and fabricators 18,200
Coil winders, tapers, and finishers 14,400
Timing device assemblers and adjusters 1,200

Most assemblers and fabricators work in manufacturing plants, and working conditions vary by plant and by industry. Many physically difficult tasks have been automated or made easier through the use of power tools, such as tightening massive bolts or moving heavy parts into position. Assembly work, however, may still involve long periods of standing, sitting, or working on ladders, such as in the shipbuilding industry.

Injuries and Illnesses. Some assemblers may come into contact with potentially harmful chemicals or fumes, but ventilation systems normally minimize any harmful effects. Other assemblers may come in contact with oil and grease, and their work areas may be noisy. Fiberglass laminators and fabricators are exposed to fiberglass, which may irritate the skin. Therefore, fiberglass workers must wear gloves and long sleeves and must use respirators for safety.

Work Schedules. Most assemblers and fabricators are employed full time, sometimes working evenings and weekends.

How to Become One

The education level and qualifications needed to enter these jobs vary depending on the industry and employer. Although a high

Employment Projections Data for Assemblers and Fabricators

Occupational title	SOC Code	Employment, 2012	Projected Employment, 2022	Change, 2012–2022	
				Percent	Numeric
Assemblers and fabricators	51-2000	1,755,200	1,819,400	4	64,200
Aircraft structure, surfaces, rigging,					
and systems assemblers	51-2011	41,500	44,000	6	2,400
Coil winders, tapers, and finishers	51-2021	14,400	12,900	-10	-1,500
Electrical and electronic equipment assemblers	51-2022	198,300	184,900	-7	-13,500
Electromechanical equipment assemblers	51-2023	50,500	46,900	-7	-3,600
Engine and other machine assemblers	51-2031	42,000	41,400	-1	-600
Structural metal fabricators and fitters	51-2041	79,700	85,900	8	6,200
Fiberglass laminators and fabricators	51-2091	18,200	17,400	-4	-700
Team assemblers	51-2092	1,031,800	1,081,300	5	49,500
Timing device assemblers and adjusters	51-2093	1,200	1,100	-3	0
Assemblers and fabricators, all other	51-2099	277,700	303,700	9	26,000

Source: U.S. Bureau of Labor Statistics, Employment Projections Program

Note: Data are rounded. Go to **Occupational Information Included in the OOH** *for a discussion of the data in this table.*

Similar Occupations   This table shows a list of occupations with job duties that are similar to those of assemblers and fabricators.

Occupations	Entry-level Education	2012 Pay	Projected Job Growth	Average Annual Openings
Industrial Machinery Mechanics and Maintenance Workers and Millwrights	High school diploma or equivalent	$45,848	17%	18,700
Metal and Plastic Machine Workers	High school diploma or equivalent	$33,064	-6%	22,070
Welders, Cutters, Solderers, and Brazers	High school diploma or equivalent	$36,300	6%	10,850

school diploma is enough for most jobs, experience and additional training is needed for more advanced assembly work.

Education. Most employers require a high school diploma or the equivalent for assembler and fabricator positions.

Training. Workers usually receive on-the-job training, sometimes including employer-sponsored technical instruction.

Some employers may require specialized training or an associate's degree for the most skilled assembly and fabrication jobs. For example, jobs with electrical, electronic, and aircraft and motor vehicle products manufacturers typically require more formal education through technical schools. Apprenticeship programs are also available.

Licenses, Certifications, and Registrations. The Fabricators & Manufacturers Association International (FMA) offers the Precision Sheet Metal Operator Certification (PSMO) and the Precision Press Brake Certification (PPB). Although not required, becoming certified can demonstrate competence and professionalism. It also may help a candidate advance in the profession.

In addition, many employers that hire electrical and electronic assembly workers, especially those in the aerospace and defense industries, require certifications in soldering, such as those offered by the Association Connecting Electronics Industries.

Important Qualities

Color vision. Assemblers and fabricators who make electrical and electronic products must be able to distinguish different colors because the wires they work with often are color coded.

Dexterity. Assemblers and fabricators should have a steady hand and good hand-eye coordination, as they must grasp, manipulate, or assemble parts and components that are often very small.

Math skills. Assemblers and fabricators must know basic math and must be able to use computers, as the manufacturing process continues to advance technologically.

Mechanical skills. Modern production systems require assemblers and fabricators to be able to use programmable motion-control devices, computers, and robots on the factory floor.

Physical stamina. Assemblers and fabricators must be able to stand for long periods and perform repetitive work.

Physical strength. Assemblers and fabricators must be strong enough to lift heavy components or pieces of machinery. Some assemblers, such as those in the aerospace industry, must frequently bend or climb ladders when assembling parts.

Technical skills. Assemblers and fabricators must be able to understand technical manuals, blue prints, and schematics for a wide range of products and machines to properly manufacture the final product.

Pay

The median annual wage for assemblers and fabricators was $28,580 in May 2012. The median wage is the wage at which half the workers in an occupation earned more than that amount, and half earned less. The lowest 10 percent earned less than $18,400, and the top 10 percent earned more than $48,110.

In May 2012, the median annual wages for assemblers and fabricators were as follows:

Aircraft structure, surfaces, rigging, and systems assemblers	$45,950
Engine and other machine assemblers	36,110
Structural metal fabricators and fitters	35,750
Electromechanical equipment assemblers	31,460
Coil winders, tapers, and finishers	30,840
Fiberglass laminators and fabricators	28,830
Electrical and electronic equipment assemblers	28,810
Team assemblers	27,640
Timing device assemblers and adjusters	25,600
Assemblers and fabricators, all other	25,920

Wages vary by industry, geographic region, skill, education level, and complexity of the machinery operated.

Job Outlook

Employment of assemblers and fabricators is projected to grow 4 percent from 2012 to 2022, slower than the average for all occupations.

Within the manufacturing sector, employment of assemblers and fabricators will be determined largely by the growth or decline in the production of certain manufactured goods. In general, overall employment is not expected to grow as fast as all other occupations because many manufacturing sectors are expected to become more efficient and able to produce more with fewer workers.

However, some individual industries are projected to have more jobs than others. The aircraft products and parts manufacturing industry is projected to gain jobs over the decade as demand for new commercial planes grow significantly. Thus, the need for assemblers for aircraft structures, surfaces, rigging, and systems is expected to grow.

In most other manufacturing industries, improved processes, tools, and, in some cases, automation will reduce job growth. Automation will replace workers in operations with a large volume of simple, repetitive work.

However, automation is not expected to have a large effect on the assembly of products that are low in volume or very complicated. Intricate product manufacturing and complicated techniques often cannot be automated.

The use of team production techniques has been one factor in the continuing success of the manufacturing sector, boosting productivity and improving the quality of goods. Thus, while the number of assemblers overall is expected to decline in manufacturing, the number of team assemblers should grow as more manufacturing plants convert to team production techniques.

Some manufacturers have sent their assembly functions to countries where labor costs are lower. Decisions by U.S. corporations to move manufacturing to other nations may limit employment growth for assemblers in some industries.

The largest increase in the number of assemblers and fabricators is projected to be in the employment services industry, which supplies temporary workers to various industries. Temporary workers are gaining importance in the manufacturing sector and other sectors, as companies facing cost pressures strive for a more flexible workforce to meet fluctuations in the market.

Job Prospects. Qualified applicants, including those with technical vocational training and certification, are likely to have the best job opportunities in the manufacturing sector, particularly in growing, high-technology industries, such as aerospace and electro-medical devices.

Some employers report difficulty finding qualified applicants looking for manufacturing employment. Many job openings are expected to result from the need to replace workers who leave or retire from this large occupation.

O*NET

➤ Aircraft Structure, Surfaces, Rigging, and Systems Assemblers (51-2011.00)
➤ Coil Winders, Tapers, and Finishers (51-2021.00)
➤ Electrical and Electronic Equipment Assemblers (51-2022.00)
➤ Electromechanical Equipment Assemblers (51-2023.00)
➤ Engine and Other Machine Assemblers (51-2031.00)
➤ Structural Metal Fabricators and Fitters (51-2041.00)
➤ Fiberglass Laminators and Fabricators (51-2091.00)
➤ Team Assemblers (51-2092.00)
➤ Timing Device Assemblers and Adjusters (51-2093.00)
➤ Assemblers and Fabricators, All Other (51-2099.00)

Contacts for More Information

For more information about assemblers and fabricators, including certification, training, and professional development, visit
➤ Fabricators & Manufacturers Association International (http://fmanet.org/)
  For information about careers in manufacturing, visit
➤ Nuts, Bolts & Thingamajigs (www.nutsandboltsfoundation.org/)
  For information about unions, visit
➤ International Association of Machinists & Aerospace Workers (www.iamdl19.org/)
➤ International Brotherhood of Electrical Workers (www.ibew.org)
➤ United Automobile, Aerospace and Agricultural Implement Workers of America (www.uaw.org/)
➤ United Steelworkers of America (www.usw.org/)
  For information about certifications in electronics soldering, visit:
➤ Association Connecting Electronics Industries (www.ipc.org/)

Bakers

- **2012 Median Pay** .... $23,140 per year
                                                     $11.13 per hour
- **Entry-Level Education** .... Less than high school
- **Work Experience in a Related Occupation** .... None
- **On-the-Job Training** .... Long-term on-the-job training
- **Number of Jobs 2012** 167,600
- **Job Outlook, 2012–22** .... 6% (Slower than average)
- **Employment Change, 2012–22** 9,400

What Bakers Do

Bakers mix ingredients according to recipes to make breads, pastries, and other baked goods.

Duties. Bakers typically do the following:

- Check the quality of baking ingredients
- Prepare equipment for baking
- Measure and weigh flour and other ingredients
- Combine measured ingredients in mixers or blenders
- Knead, roll, cut, and shape dough
- Place dough in pans, molds, or on sheets
- Set oven temperatures
- Place and bake items in hot ovens or on grills
- Observe color and state of products being baked
- Apply glazes, icings, or other toppings

Bakers produce various types and quantities of breads, pastries, and other baked goods sold by grocers, wholesalers, restaurants, and institutional food services. Some bakers create new recipes.

The following are examples of types of bakers:

Commercial bakers commonly work in manufacturing facilities that produce breads and pastries at high speeds. In these facilities, bakers use high-volume mixing machines, ovens, and other equipment to mass-produce standardized baked goods. Commercial bakers often operate large, automated machines, such as commercial mixers, ovens, and conveyors. They must carefully follow instructions for production schedules and recipes.

Retail bakers work primarily in grocery stores and specialty shops, including bakeries. In these settings, they produce smaller quantities of baked goods for people to eat in the shop or for sale as specialty baked goods. Retail bakers may take orders from customers, prepare goods to order, and occasionally serve customers. Although the quantities prepared and sold in these stores are often small, they usually come in a wide variety of flavors and sizes.

Some retail bakers own bakery shops or other types of businesses where they make and sell breads, pastries, pies, cupcakes, and other baked goods. In addition to preparing the baked goods and overseeing the entire baking process, they are also responsible for hiring, training, and supervising their staff. They must budget for and order supplies, set prices, and know how much to produce each day. Most retail bakers are also responsible for cleaning their work area and equipment and unloading supplies.

Work Environment

Bakers held about 167,600 jobs in 2012. About 6 percent were self-employed.

The industries that employed the most bakers in 2012 were as follows:

Bakeries and tortilla manufacturing 29%
Grocery stores... 26

Bakers prepare various types of baked goods and apply icing.

Median Annual Wages, May 2012

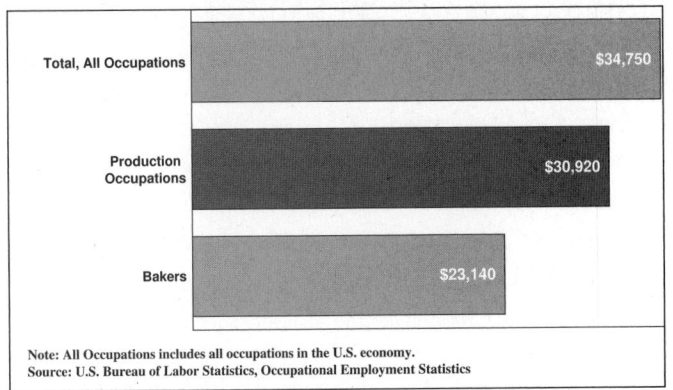

Note: All Occupations includes all occupations in the U.S. economy.
Source: U.S. Bureau of Labor Statistics, Occupational Employment Statistics

Percent Change in Employment, Projected 2012–2022

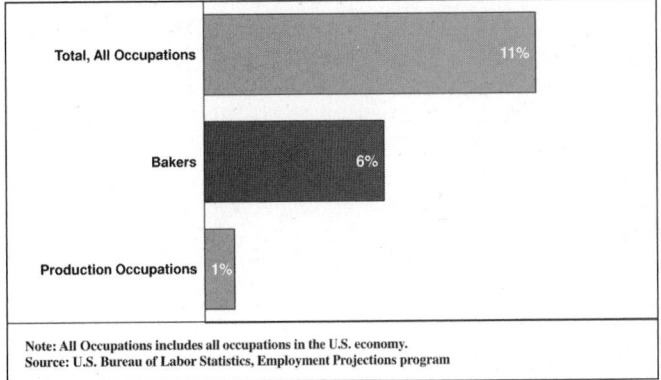

Note: All Occupations includes all occupations in the U.S. economy.
Source: U.S. Bureau of Labor Statistics, Employment Projections program

Restaurants and other eating places.. 15
Other general merchandise stores 11
Specialty food stores 3

The work can be stressful because bakers often work under strict deadlines and critical, time-sensitive baking requirements.

Bakers who run their own businesses often spend long hours managing all aspects of the business to ensure bills and salaries are paid, supplies are ordered, and the business is profitable.

Injuries and Illnesses. Bakeries, especially large manufacturing facilities, are filled with potential dangers such as hot ovens, mixing machines, and dough cutters. As a result, bakers have a higher rate of injuries and illnesses than the national average.

Although their work is generally safe, bakers may endure back strains caused by repetitive lifting or moving heavy bags of flour or other packages. Other common hazards include cuts, scrapes, and burns. To reduce these risks, bakers often wear protective clothing, such as aprons and gloves.

Work Schedules. Nearly 1 in 3 bakers worked part time in 2012.

Grocery stores and restaurants, which employ more than half of all bakers, sell freshly baked goods throughout the day. As a result, bakers are often scheduled to work shifts during early mornings, late evenings, weekends, and holidays.

Bakers who work in commercial bakeries that bake continuously may have to work late evenings and weekends.

How to Become One

Long-term on-the-job training is the most common path to gain the skills necessary to become a baker. Some bakers start their careers through an apprenticeship program or by attending a technical or culinary school. No formal education is required.

Education. Although no formal education is required to become a baker, some candidates attend a technical or culinary school. Programs generally last from 1 to 2 years and cover nutrition, food safety, and basic math. To enter these programs, candidates may be required to have a high school diploma or equivalent.

Training. Most bakers learn their skills through long-term on-the-job training, lasting 1 to 3 years. Some employers may provide apprenticeship programs for aspiring bakers. Bakers in specialty bakery shops and grocery stores often start as apprentices or trainees and learn the basics of baking, icing, and decorating. They usually study topics such as nutrition, sanitation procedures, and basic baking. Some participate in correspondence study and may work toward a certificate in baking.

In manufacturing facilities, commercial bakers learn how to operate and maintain the industrial mixing and blending machines that are used to produce baked goods. They also learn how to combine ingredients and the ways in which certain ingredients are affected by heat.

Other Experience. Some bakers learn their skills through work experience related to baking. For example, they may start as a baker's assistant and progress into a full-fledged baker as they learn baking techniques.

Licenses, Certifications, and Registrations. Although not required, certification can show that a baker has the skills and knowledge to work at a retail baking establishment.

Employment Projections Data for Bakers

Occupational title	SOC Code	Employment, 2012	Projected Employment, 2022	Change, 2012–2022 Percent	Change, 2012–2022 Numeric
Bakers.................	51-3011	167,600	177,000	6	9,400

Source: U.S. Bureau of Labor Statistics, Employment Projections Program

Note: Data are rounded. Go to **Occupational Information Included in the OOH** *for a discussion of the data in this table.*

Similar Occupations   This table shows a list of occupations with job duties that are similar to those of bakers.

Occupations	Entry-level Education	2012 Pay	Projected Job Growth	Average Annual Openings
Chefs and Head Cooks	High school diploma or equivalent	$42,480	5%	2,470
Cooks	See "How to Become One"	$21,144	10%	63,160
Food Preparation Workers	Less than high school	$19,300	4%	26,050

The Retail Bakers of America offers certification in four levels of competence, with a focus on several specialties, including baking sanitation, management, retail sales, and staff training. Those who wish to become certified must satisfy a combination of education and experience requirements before taking an exam.

The education and experience requirements vary by the level of certification desired. For example, a *certified journey baker* requires no formal education but must have at least 1 year of work experience. A *certified baker* must have 4 years of work experience, and a *certified master baker* must have 8 years of work experience, 30 hours of sanitation course work, and 30 hours of professional development training.

Important Qualities

Detail oriented. Bakers must closely monitor their products in the oven to keep from burning the goods. They also should have an eye for detail because many pastries and cakes require intricate decorations.

Math skills. Bakers must possess basic math skills, especially knowledge of fractions, in order to precisely mix recipes, weigh ingredients, or adjust the mixes.

Physical stamina. Bakers must stand on their feet for long periods while they prepare dough, monitor baking, or package baked goods.

Physical strength. Bakers must be able to lift and carry heavy bags of flour and other ingredients, which often can weigh up to 50 pounds.

Pay

The median annual wage for bakers was $23,140 in May 2012. The median wage is the wage at which half the workers in an occupation earned more than that amount and half earned less. The lowest 10 percent earned less than $17,200, and the top 10 percent earned more than $36,980.

In May 2012, the median annual wages for bakers in the top five industries employing these workers were as follows:

Bakeries and tortilla manufacturing	$23,870
Grocery stores	23,510
Other general merchandise stores	22,920
Specialty food stores	21,710
Restaurants and other eating places	21,190

Job Outlook

Employment of bakers is projected to grow 6 percent from 2012 to 2022, slower than the average for all occupations.

Population and income growth are expected to result in greater demand for specialty baked goods, such as cupcakes, pies, and cakes, from grocery stores, bakeries, and restaurants.

However, employment growth of bakers will be limited as manufacturing facilities increasingly use more automated machines and equipment to mass-produce baked goods.

Job Prospects. Highly skilled bakers with years of experience should have the best job opportunities.

O*NET

➤ Bakers (51-3011.00)

Contacts for More Information

For information about job opportunities, contact local employers and local offices of the state employment service.

For information on certification or training programs, visit
➤ AIB International (www.aibonline.org/)
➤ Retail Bakers of America (www.retailbakersofamerica.org/)

Butchers and Meat Cutters

- **2012 Median Pay** .... $28,490 per year
  $13.70 per hour
- **Entry-Level Education** .... Less than high school
- **Work Experience in a Related Occupation** .... None
- **On-the-Job Training** .... Long-term on-the-job training
- **Number of Jobs 2012** 136,700
- **Job Outlook, 2012–22** .... 5% (Slower than average)
- **Employment Change, 2012–22** 6,500

What Butchers and Meat Cutters Do

Butchers and meat cutters cut, trim, and package meat for retail sale.
Duties. Butchers and meat cutters typically do the following:

- Sharpen and adjust cutting equipment
- Receive, inspect, and store meat upon delivery
- Cut, bone, or grind pieces of meat
- Weigh, wrap, and display cuts of meat
- Cut or prepare meats to specification or customer's orders
- Store meats in refrigerators or freezers at the required temperature
- Keep inventory of meat sales and order meat supplies
- Clean equipment and work areas to maintain health and sanitation standards

Butchers and meat cutters cut and trim meat from larger, wholesale portions into steaks, chops, roasts, and other cuts. They then prepare meat for sale by performing various duties, such as weighing meat, wrapping it, and putting it out for display. In retail stores, they also may wait on customers and prepare special cuts of meat upon request.

Butchers and meat cutters in meat processing plants may have a more limited range of duties than those working in a grocery store or specialty meat shop. Because they typically work on an assembly line, those in processing plants usually perform one specific function–a single cut–during their shift.

Butchers and meat cutters use sharp tools such as knives, grinders, or meat saws. They must follow sanitation standards when cleaning equipment, counter tops, and working areas in order to prevent meat contamination.

Butchers cut steaks and chops and shape and tie roasts.

Median Annual Wages, May 2012

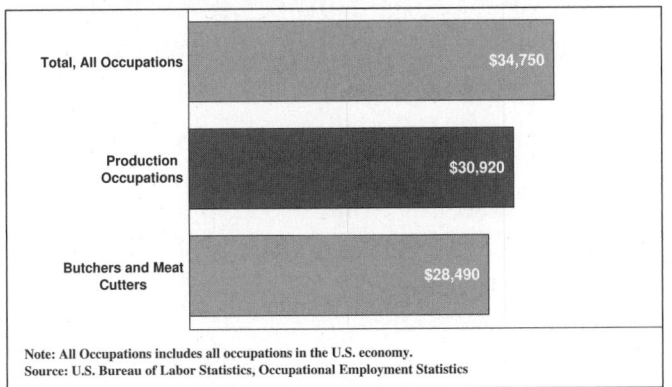

Note: All Occupations includes all occupations in the U.S. economy.
Source: U.S. Bureau of Labor Statistics, Occupational Employment Statistics

Percent Change in Employment, Projected 2012–2022

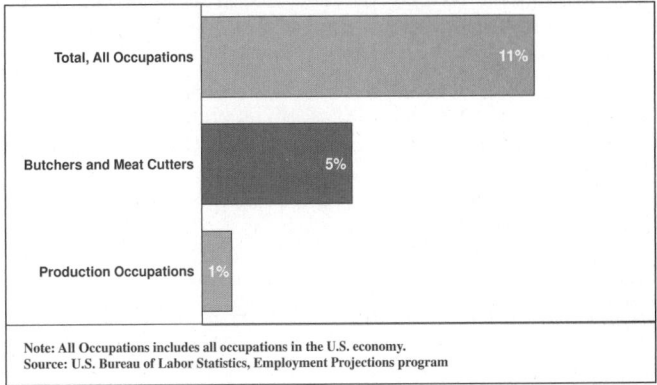

Note: All Occupations includes all occupations in the U.S. economy.
Source: U.S. Bureau of Labor Statistics, Employment Projections program

Some butchers run their own retail store. In these settings, they usually track inventory, order supplies, and perform other recordkeeping duties.

Work Environment

Butchers and meat cutters held about 136,700 jobs in 2012. About 73 percent worked in grocery stores, and another 6 percent worked in animal slaughtering and processing plants in 2012.

The work can be physically demanding, particularly for those who make repetitive cuts in processing plants. In addition, butchers and meat cutters typically stand all day, and workers often must lift and move heavy carcasses or boxes of meat supplies.

Because meat must be kept at certain temperatures, working in cold rooms–below 40 degrees Fahrenheit–for extended periods is common.

Butchers and meat cutters, especially those who fill customer's orders in grocery or specialty stores, must keep their hands and working areas clean to prevent meat contamination and to be presentable for customers.

Injuries and Illnesses. Butchers and meat cutters use sharp knives and meat saws, resulting in a rate of injuries and illnesses that is higher than the national average. To reduce the risk of cuts and falls, workers wear protective clothing, such as cut-resistant gloves, heavy aprons, and nonslip footwear.

Work Schedules. Most butchers and meat cutters work full time. Butchers who work in grocery or retail stores may work early mornings, late evenings, weekends, and holidays. Meat cutters who work in animal slaughtering and processing facilities may work shifts that start in the early morning or in the afternoon or evening.

Butchers who run their own meat shops often work long hours.

How to Become One

Most butchers and meat cutters learn their skills through long-term on-the-job training. No formal education is required.

Education. There are no formal education requirements to become a butcher or meat cutter.

Training. Butchers and meat cutters typically learn their skills on the job and the length of training varies considerably. Training for simple cutting may take only a few days. However, more complicated cutting tasks generally require several months of training. The training period for butchers at the retail level may last 1 to 2 years.

Training for entry-level workers often begins by learning less difficult tasks, such as making simple cuts, removing bones, or dividing wholesale cuts into retail portions. Under the guidance of more experienced workers, trainees learn the proper use and care of tools and equipment.

Trainees also may learn how to shape, roll, and tie roasts, prepare sausage, and cure meat. Those employed in retail stores are

Employment Projections Data for Butchers and Meat Cutters

Occupational title	SOC Code	Employment, 2012	Projected Employment, 2022	Change, 2012–2022	
				Percent	Numeric
Butchers and meat cutters...	51-3021	136,700	143,200	5	6,500

Source: U.S. Bureau of Labor Statistics, Employment Projections Program

Note: Data are rounded. Go to **Occupational Information Included in the OOH** for a discussion of the data in this table.

Similar Occupations This table shows a list of occupations with job duties that are similar to those of butchers and meat cutters.

Occupations	Entry-level Education	2012 Pay	Projected Job Growth	Average Annual Openings
Chefs and Head Cooks	High school diploma or equivalent	$42,480	5%	2,470
Fishers and Related Fishing Workers	Less than high school	$33,430	-5%	630
Food and Tobacco Processing Workers	See "How to Become One"	$26,047	0%	6,190
Slaughterers, Meat Packers, and Meat, Poultry, and Fish Cutters and Trimmers	Less than high school	$23,331	3%	6,890

usually taught basic business operations, such as inventory control, meat buying, and recordkeeping. Because of the growing concern about foodborne pathogens in meats, employees also receive training in food safety.

Butchers who follow religious guidelines for food preparation may be required to undergo a lengthy apprenticeship, certification process, or both, before becoming completely qualified and endorsed by an organization to prepare meat.

Important Qualities

Concentration. Butchers and meat cutters must pay close attention to what they are doing to avoid injury and waste of product.

Customer-service skills. Those who work in retail stores should be courteous, be able to answer customers' questions, and fill orders to the customers' satisfaction.

Manual dexterity. Butchers and meat cutters use sharp knives and meat cutting equipment as part of their duties. Therefore, they must have good hand control in order to make proper cuts of meat that are the right size.

Physical stamina. Butchers and meat cutters spend hours on their feet while cutting, packaging, or storing meat.

Physical strength. Butchers and meat cutters should be strong enough to lift and carry heavy boxes of meat, which often weigh up to 50 pounds.

Pay

The median annual wage for butchers and meat cutters was $28,490 in May 2012. The median wage is the wage at which half the workers in an occupation earned more than that amount and half earned less. The lowest 10 percent earned less than $18,150, and the top 10 percent earned more than $45,300.

Job Outlook

Employment of butchers and meat cutters is projected to grow 5 percent from 2012 to 2022, slower than the average for all occupations.

As more people demand pre-cut, partially prepared, and easy-to-cook meat products, butchers and meat cutters will be needed to prepare them. The popularity of various meat products such as sausages, cured meats, or specialty cuts is expected to result in demand for butchers and meat cutters in grocery and specialty stores.

However, meat processing plants continue to consolidate animal slaughtering and meat processing by preparing and packaging meat products simultaneously. As a result, employment growth should be limited as fewer workers will be needed to pre-cut, trim, or package meats.

Job Prospects. Many meat cutter jobs, particularly those in processing plants, are physically demanding with difficult working conditions. As a result, job opportunities are expected to be good because of the need to replace workers who leave the occupation each year.

Meat cutters with several years of work experience, including training in various meat cutting techniques, should have the best job prospects as retail butchers.

O*NET

➤ Butchers and Meat Cutters (51-3021.00)

Contacts for More Information

For information about the meat processing industry and related trends, visit

➤ American Meat Institute (www.meatami.com/)

Dental and Ophthalmic Laboratory Technicians and Medical Appliance Technicians

- **2012 Median Pay** .... $33,070 per year
  $15.90 per hour
- **Entry-Level Education** ... High school diploma or equivalent
- **Work Experience in a Related Occupation** .... None
- **On-the-Job Training** ....See "How to Become One"
- **Number of Jobs 2012** 82,900
- **Job Outlook, 2012–22** .... 7% (Slower than average)
- **Employment Change, 2012–22** 5,600

What Dental and Ophthalmic Laboratory Technicians and Medical Appliance Technicians Do

Dental and ophthalmic laboratory technicians and medical appliance technicians construct, fit, or repair devices that increase function in the lives of patients. These devices include dentures, eyeglasses, and prosthetics.

Duties. Dental and ophthalmic laboratory technicians and medical appliance technicians typically do the following:

- Follow detailed work orders and prescriptions
- Decide which materials and tools will be needed
- Bend, form, and shape fabric or material
- Use hand or power tools to polish and shape the devices
- Adjust devices to allow for a more natural look or to improve function
- Inspect the final product for quality and accuracy
- Repair appliances that may be cracked or damaged

In small laboratories and offices, technicians may handle every phase of production. In larger ones, technicians may be responsible for only one phase of production, such as polishing, measuring, or testing.

Dental laboratory technicians use impressions, or molds, of a patient's teeth to create crowns, bridges, dentures, and other den-

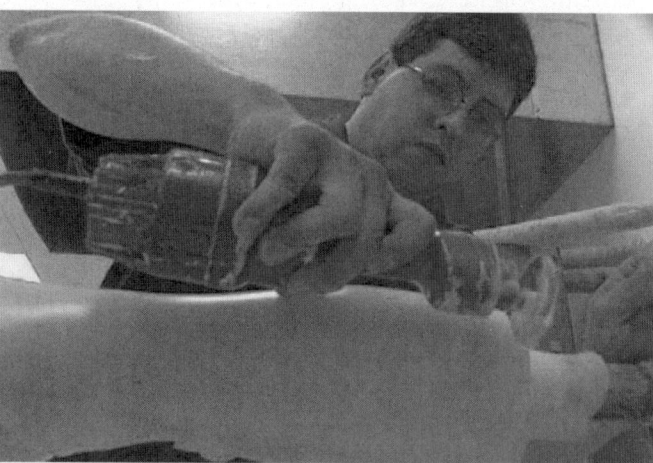

Technicians take prescriptions from orthotists, prosthetists, and other medical professionals to create medical appliances.

Median Annual Wages, May 2012

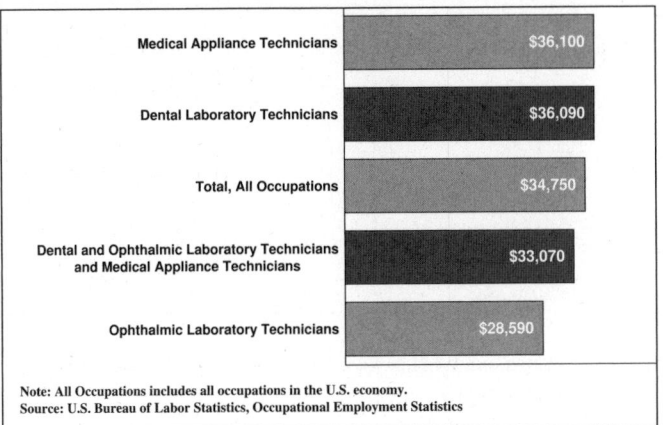

Note: All Occupations includes all occupations in the U.S. economy.
Source: U.S. Bureau of Labor Statistics, Occupational Employment Statistics

Percent Change in Employment, Projected 2012–2022

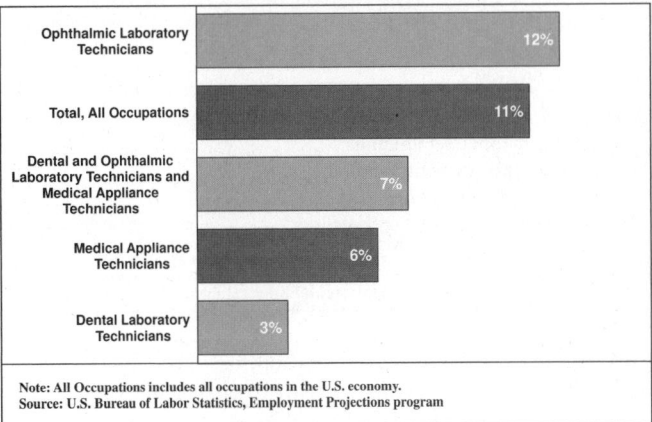

Note: All Occupations includes all occupations in the U.S. economy.
Source: U.S. Bureau of Labor Statistics, Employment Projections program

tal appliances. They work closely with dentists, but have limited contact with patients.

Dental laboratory technicians work with small hand tools, such as files and polishers. They work with many different materials to make prosthetic appliances, including wax, plastic, and porcelain. In some cases, technicians use computer programs to create appliances or to get impressions sent from a dentist's office.

Dental laboratory technicians can specialize in one of six areas: orthodontic appliances, crowns and bridges, complete dentures, partial dentures, implants, or ceramics. Technicians may have different job titles, depending on their specialty. For example, technicians who make porcelain and acrylic restorations, such as veneers and bridges, are called dental ceramists.

Ophthalmic laboratory technicians make prescription eyeglasses and contact lenses. They are also commonly known as manufacturing opticians, optical mechanics, or optical goods workers.

Although they make some lenses by hand, ophthalmic laboratory technicians often use automated equipment. Some technicians manufacture lenses for optical instruments, such as telescopes and binoculars. Ophthalmic laboratory technicians should not be confused with dispensing opticians, who work with customers to select eyeware and may prepare work orders for ophthalmic laboratory technicians.

Medical appliance technicians construct, fit, and repair medical supportive devices, including arch supports, facial parts, and foot and leg braces.

Medical appliance technicians use many different types of materials, such as metal, plastic, and leather, to create a variety of medical devices for patients who need them because of a birth defect, an accident, disease, amputation, or the effects of aging. For example, some medical appliance technicians make hearing aids.

Orthotic and prosthetic technicians are medical appliance technicians who create orthoses (braces, supports, and other devices) and prostheses (replacement limbs and facial parts). These technicians work closely with orthotists and prosthetists.

Work Environment

Dental and ophthalmic laboratory technicians and medical appliance technicians held about 82,900 jobs in 2012.

Dental and ophthalmic laboratory technicians and medical appliance technicians typically work in clean, well-lit, and well-ventilated laboratories. Most laboratories are small and employ only a few workers. Some laboratories, however, have as many as several hundred employees. Other technicians work in health and personal care stores. Technicians usually have limited contact with the public.

Injuries and illness

Technicians may be exposed to health and safety hazards when they handle certain materials, but there is little risk if they follow proper procedures, such as wearing goggles, gloves, or masks. They may spend a great deal of time standing or bending.

Work Schedules. Most dental and ophthalmic laboratory technicians and medical appliance technicians work full time.

How to Become One

There are no specific educational requirements to become a dental or ophthalmic laboratory technician or medical appliance technician. Most technicians learn their skills on the job.

Education. Although there are no formal educational requirements to become a dental or ophthalmic laboratory technician or medical appliance technician, most technicians have at least a high school diploma. Some community colleges and technical or vocational schools have formal education programs, but such programs are not common. High school students interested in becoming dental or ophthalmic laboratory technicians or medical appliance technicians should take courses in science, mathematics, computer programming, and art.

Training. Most dental and ophthalmic laboratory technicians and medical appliance technicians learn through on-the-job training. They usually begin as helpers in a laboratory and learn more advanced skills as they gain experience. For example, dental laboratory technicians may begin by pouring plaster into an impression to make a model. As they become more experienced, they may progress to more complex tasks, such as making porcelain crowns and bridges. Because all laboratories are different, the length of training varies.

Important Qualities

Analytical skills. Because dental and ophthalmic laboratory technicians and medical appliance technicians must construct medical devices with accuracy and precision, they need to have an in-depth knowledge of how different tools and materials work.

Detail oriented. Dental and ophthalmic laboratory technicians and medical appliance technicians must pay attention to detail. They need to be able to recognize and correct any imperfections in the devices.

Dexterity. Dental and ophthalmic laboratory technicians and medical appliance technicians must work well with their hands because they use precise laboratory instruments.

Interpersonal skills. Dental and ophthalmic laboratory technicians and medical appliance technicians need to be able to get along with others because they may be part of a team of technicians

Employment Projections Data for Dental and Ophthalmic Laboratory Technicians and Medical Appliance Technicians

Occupational title	SOC Code	Employment, 2012	Projected Employment, 2022	Change, 2012–2022	
				Percent	Numeric
Dental and ophthalmic laboratory technicians and medical appliance technicians..	—	82,900	88,500	7	5,600
Dental laboratory technicians	51-9081	39,000	40,000	3	1,000
Medical appliance technicians	51-9082	12,900	13,800	6	800
Ophthalmic laboratory technicians	51-9083	31,000	34,700	12	3,700

Source: *U.S. Bureau of Labor Statistics, Employment Projections Program*

Note: **Data are rounded. Go to** Occupational Information Included in the OOH *for a discussion of the data in this table.*

working on a single project. In addition, they need good communication to ensure safety when they work with hazardous materials.

Technical skills. Dental and ophthalmic laboratory technicians and medical appliance technicians must understand how to operate complex machinery. Some procedures are automated, so technicians must know how to operate and change the programs that run the machinery.

Licenses, Certifications, and Registrations. Certification is not required for dental and ophthalmic laboratory technicians or medical appliance technicians. However, several organizations offer certifications for these technicians to indicate they have a certain level of professional skill.

The National Board for Certification in Dental Laboratory Technology (NBC) offers certification as a Certified Dental Technician (CDT). Certification is available in six specialty areas: orthodontic appliances, crowns and bridges, complete dentures, partial dentures, implants, and ceramics.

To qualify for the CDT, technicians must have at least 5 years of on-the-job training or experience in dental technology, or have graduated from an accredited dental laboratory technician program, and pass three exams.

The NBC also provides a modularization program that leads to a Certificate of Competency. Dental technicians can also get a Certificate of Competency in each specific skill through a written and practical exam on that skill.

The American Board for Certification in Orthotics, Prosthetics & Pedorthics (ABC) offers certification for medical appliance technicians. Technicians are eligible for the certification exam after completing an accredited program or if they have 2 years of experience as a technician under the direct supervision of a certified medical appliance technician.

Advancement. In large laboratories, dental and ophthalmic laboratory technicians and medical appliance technicians may work their way up to a supervisory level and may train new technicians. Some may go on to own their own laboratory.

Medical appliance technicians can advance to become orthotists or prosthetists after completing additional formal education.

These practitioners work with patients who need braces, prostheses, or related devices.

Pay

The median annual wage for dental and ophthalmic laboratory technicians and medical appliance technicians was $33,070 in May 2012. The median wage is the wage at which half the workers in an occupation earned more than that amount and half earned less. The lowest 10 percent earned more than $20,160, and the top 10 percent earned more than $55,270.

Median annual wages for dental and ophthalmic laboratory technicians and medical appliance technicians in May 2012 were as follows:

Dental laboratory technicians...$36,090
Medical appliance technicians 36,100
Ophthalmic laboratory technicians....................................28,590

Job Outlook

Employment of dental and ophthalmic laboratory technicians and medical appliance technicians is projected to grow 7 percent from 2012 to 2022, slower than the average for all occupations.

As cosmetic prosthetics, such as veneers and crowns, become less expensive, there should be an increase in demand for these appliances. Accidents and poor oral health, which can cause damage and loss of teeth, will continue to create a need for dental laboratory technician services. Dental technician services will be in demand, as dentists work to improve the aesthetics and function of patients' teeth.

On the other hand, baby boomers and their children are more likely to retain their teeth than previous generations. This is due to increased visits to dentists, increased use of fluoride, and more dental health education. These factors will likely lead to a decrease in the number of full and partial dentures and other prosthetics used to replace missing teeth and will temper demand for the technicians that make them.

Similar Occupations   This table shows a list of occupations with job duties that are similar to those of dental and ophthalmic laboratory technicians and medical appliance technicians.

Occupations	Entry-level Education	2012 Pay	Projected Job Growth	Average Annual Openings
Dentists	Doctoral or professional degree	$149,795	16%	5,910
Medical Equipment Repairers	Associate's degree	$44,570	30%	2,460
Opticians, Dispensing	High school diploma or equivalent	$33,330	24%	3,530
Optometrists	Doctoral or professional degree	$97,820	24%	1,770
Orthotists and Prosthetists	Master's degree	$62,670	35%	380

An aging baby-boomer population will create a need for medical appliance technicians because diabetes and cardiovascular disease, the two leading causes of limb loss, are more likely to occur as people age. The demand for orthotic devices, such as braces and orthopedic footwear, will increase because older people tend to need these supportive devices. In addition, advances in technology may spur demand for prostheses that allow for more natural movement.

Most people need vision correction at some point in their lives. As the population continues to grow, people will need more vision aids, such as glasses and contact lenses, and this will cause demand for ophthalmic laboratory technicians.

As laser vision correction becomes less expensive, there will be an increase in the demand for that service and a decrease in the demand for eyeglasses. However, this decrease will be tempered, as even with laser correction, almost all adults need reading glasses or corrective eyewear later in their lives. This is caused by retinal hardening, which happens naturally as people age, making it harder for the eye to focus.

O*NET

➤ Dental Laboratory Technicians (51-9081.00)
➤ Medical Appliance Technicians (51-9082.00)
➤ Ophthalmic Laboratory Technicians (51-9083.00)

Contacts for More Information

For a list of accredited programs in dental laboratory technology, visit

➤ Commission on Dental Accreditation, American Dental Association (www.ada.org/117.aspx)

For information on requirements for certification of dental laboratory technicians, visit

➤ National Board for Certification in Dental Laboratory Technology (www.nbccert.org)

For information on career opportunities in commercial dental laboratories, visit

➤ National Association of Dental Laboratories (www.nadl.org)

For a list of ophthalmic laboratories, visit

➤ The Vision Council (http://ola.networkats.com/members_online/members/directory.asp)

For a list of accredited programs for medical appliance technicians, visit

➤ American Academy of Orthotists & Prosthetists (www.opcareers.org)
➤ National Commission on Orthotic & Prosthetic Education (www.ncope.org)

For information on requirements for certification of medical appliance technicians, visit

➤ American Board for Certification in Orthotics, Prosthetics & Pedorthics (www.abcop.org/)

Food and Tobacco Processing Workers

- **2012 Median Pay** .... $25,780 per year
  $12.39 per hour
- **Entry-Level Education** ....See "How to Become One"
- **Work Experience in a Related Occupation**............... None
- **On-the-Job Training** .... Moderate-term on-the-job training
- **Number of Jobs 2012** 198,300
- **Job Outlook, 2012–22** ....0% (Little or no change)
- **Employment Change, 2012–22** 500

What Food and Tobacco Processing Workers Do

Food and tobacco processing workers operate equipment that mixes, cooks, or processes ingredients used in the manufacturing of food or tobacco products.

Duties. Food and tobacco processing workers typically do the following:

- Set up, start, and load food or tobacco processing equipment
- Check, weigh, and mix ingredients according to recipes
- Set and control temperatures, flow rates, and pressures of machinery
- Monitor and adjust ingredient mixes during production process
- Observe and regulate equipment gauges and sensors
- Report equipment malfunctions to team leaders or maintenance staff
- Clean workspaces and equipment to meet health and safety standards
- Check final products to ensure quality

Depending on what type of food and tobacco is being processed or made, these workers often have different duties.

The following are examples of types of food and tobacco processing workers:

Food and tobacco roasting, baking, and drying machine operators and tenders operate machines that produce roasted, baked, or dried food or tobacco products. The following are examples of types of these workers:

- *Coffee roasters* follow recipes to produce standard or specialty coffees.
- *Tobacco roasters* tend machines that cure tobacco for wholesale distribution to cigarette manufacturers and other makers of tobacco products.
- *Dryers of fruits and vegetables* operate machines that produce raisins, prunes, or other dehydrated foods.

Food processing workers cut meat into smaller sizes and wrap them for sale.

Median Annual Wages, May 2012

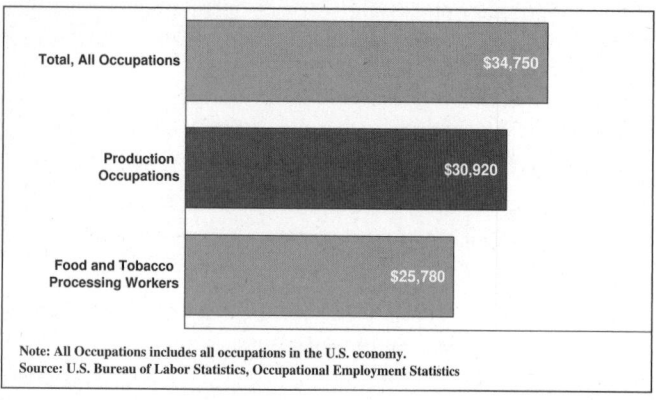

Note: All Occupations includes all occupations in the U.S. economy.
Source: U.S. Bureau of Labor Statistics, Occupational Employment Statistics

Percent Change in Employment, Projected 2012–2022

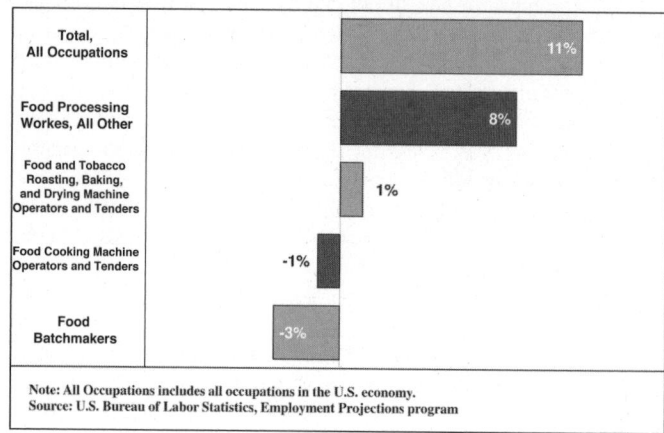

Note: All Occupations includes all occupations in the U.S. economy.
Source: U.S. Bureau of Labor Statistics, Employment Projections program

Food batchmakers typically work in facilities that produce baked goods, pasta, and tortillas. Workers mix ingredients to make dough, load and unload ovens, operate noodle extruders, and perform tasks specific to large-scale commercial baking.

Food cooking machine operators and tenders operate or tend cooking equipment to prepare food products. For example, workers who preserve and can fruits and vegetables usually operate equipment to cook and preserve their products.

Potato and corn chip manufacturers employ workers who operate frying machines and work around hot oil. Sugar and confectionary manufacturers have equipment that blends, heats, coats, and packages candies, chocolates, doughnuts, or other sweets.

Other workers may operate equipment that mixes spices for meat products, mills grains, or extracts oil from seeds.

Work Environment

Food and tobacco processing workers held about 198,300 jobs in 2012 and mostly worked in food manufacturing facilities.

The industries that employed the most food and tobacco processing workers in 2012 were as follows:

Bakeries and tortilla manufacturing 16%
Animal slaughtering and processing 15
Fruit and vegetable preserving and specialty
food manufacturing.. 11
Other food manufacturing... 11
Dairy product manufacturing.. 9

Food manufacturing facilities are typically large, open floor areas, and filled with noisy machinery. Workers also are frequently exposed to high temperatures when working around cooking machinery. Some work in cold environments for long periods with goods that need to be refrigerated or frozen.

Workers usually stand for the majority of their shifts while tending machines or observing the production process. Their equipment is often large, and loading, unloading, or cleaning it may require heavy lifting, bending, and reaching.

Because the work is typically on assembly lines, workers must be able to keep up with the line speed while maintaining product quality.

Injuries and Illnesses. Working around hot liquids or machinery that cuts or presses can be dangerous. The most common hazards are slips, falls, or cuts. To reduce these risks, workers are required to wear protective clothing and nonslip shoes.

Work Schedules. Most food and tobacco processing workers are employed full time. Because of production schedules, working early morning, evening, or night shifts is common in many manufacturing facilities.

Some food processing facilities offer only seasonal jobs.

How to Become One

Although no formal education is required for some food and tobacco processing workers, food batchmakers and food cooking machine operators typically need a high school diploma or equivalent. Food and tobacco processing workers learn their skills through on-the-job training.

Education. Although no formal education is required for some food and tobacco processing workers, food batchmakers and food cooking machine operators typically need a high school diploma or equivalent.

Because workers often adjust the quantity of ingredients that go into a mix, basic math and reading skills are considered helpful.

Training. Food and tobacco processing workers learn on the job. Training may last from several weeks to a few months. During

Employment Projections Data for Food and Tobacco Processing Workers

Occupational title	SOC Code	Employment, 2012	Projected Employment, 2022	Change, 2012–2022	
				Percent	Numeric
Food and tobacco processing workers.....................................	—	198,300	198,800	0	500
Food and tobacco roasting, baking, and drying machine operators and tenders..	51-3091	20,000	20,200	1	200
Food batchmakers	51-3092	105,200	102,500	-3	-2,700
Food cooking machine operators and tenders....................	51-3093	33,400	33,200	-1	-200
Food processing workers, all other	51-3099	39,700	42,900	8	3,200

Source: U.S. Bureau of Labor Statistics, Employment Projections Program

Note: Data are rounded. Go to Occupational Information Included in the OOH *for a discussion of the data in this table.*

Similar Occupations   This table shows a list of occupations with job duties that are similar to those of food and tobacco processing workers.

Occupations	Entry-level Education	2012 Pay	Projected Job Growth	Average Annual Openings
Bakers	Less than high school	$23,140	6%	5,010
Chefs and Head Cooks	High school diploma or equivalent	$42,480	5%	2,470
Construction Equipment Operators	High school diploma or equivalent	$41,099	19%	16,480
Construction Laborers and Helpers	See "How to Become One"	$29,277	25%	58,790
Metal and Plastic Machine Workers	High school diploma or equivalent	$33,064	-6%	22,070
Slaughterers, Meat Packers, and Meat, Poultry, and Fish Cutters and Trimmers	Less than high school	$23,331	3%	6,890
Stationary Engineers and Boiler Operators	High school diploma or equivalent	$53,560	3%	1,270

training, they learn health and safety rules related to the type of food or tobacco that is processed. Training also involves learning how to operate specific equipment, follow safety procedures, and report equipment malfunction.

Experienced workers typically show trainees how to properly use and care for equipment.

Important Qualities

Concentration. Workers must pay close attention to what they are doing to avoid injury.

Coordination. Food and tobacco processing workers must be quick and have good hand-eye coordination to keep up with the assembly line.

Detail oriented. Workers must be able to detect small changes in quality or quantity of food products. They must also closely follow health and safety standards to avoid any food contamination.

Physical stamina. Workers stand on their feet for long periods as they tend machines and monitor the production process.

Physical strength. Food and tobacco processing workers should be strong enough to lift or move heavy boxes of fruit or vegetables, which often can weigh up to 50 pounds.

Pay

The median annual wage for food and tobacco processing workers was $25,780 in May 2012. The median wage is the wage at which half the workers in an occupation earned more than that amount and half earned less. The lowest 10 percent earned less than $17,780, and the top 10 percent earned more than $41,930.

The median annual wages for food and tobacco processing workers in May 2012 were as follows:

Food and tobacco roasting, baking, and drying machine
    operators and tenders..$28,430
Food batchmakers 26,550
Food cooking machines operators and tenders....................26,350
Food processing workers, all other.......................................23,140

Job Outlook

Employment of food and tobacco processing workers is projected to show little or no change from 2012 to 2022.

Population growth and consumer preference for convenience foods and tobacco will maintain demand for these workers.

However, food manufacturing companies increasingly use automation to raise productivity. As these companies further consolidate their facilities and streamline production processes, fewer workers will be needed to operate machines.

Job Prospects. The need to replace food and tobacco processing workers who leave the occupation will result in many job openings

each year. Those with related work experience in manufacturing will have the best job opportunities.

The food processing industry continues to consolidate. As a result, job prospects should be best in rural areas or near smaller cities where many large food processing facilities are located.

O*NET

➤ Food and Tobacco Roasting, Baking, and Drying Machine Operators and Tenders (51-3091.00)
➤ Food Batchmakers (51-3092.00)
➤ Food Cooking Machine Operators and Tenders (51-3093.00)
➤ Food Processing Workers, All Other (51-3099.00)

Contacts for More Information

For more information about line workers and food safety, visit
➤ U.S. Department of Agriculture Food Safety and Inspection Service (www.fsis.usda.gov/)
➤ U.S. Food and Drug Administration (www.fda.gov/)
    For more information about the food industry, visit
➤ Food Engineering (www.foodengineeringmag.com/)
➤ Grocery Manufacturers Association (www.gmaonline.org/)

Jewelers and Precious Stone and Metal Workers

- **2012 Median Pay** ....$35,350 per year
    $16.99 per hour
- **Entry-Level Education** ... High school diploma or equivalent
- **Work Experience in a Related Occupation**.............. None
- **On-the-Job Training** .... Long-term on-the-job training
- **Number of Jobs 2012** 32,700
- **Job Outlook, 2012–22** ....-10% (Decline)
- **Employment Change, 2012–22** .... -3,200

What Jewelers and Precious Stone and Metal Workers Do

Jewelers and precious stone and metal workers design, manufacture, and sell jewelry. They also adjust, repair, and appraise gems and jewelry.

Duties. Jewelers and precious stone and metal workers typically do the following:

- Examine and grade diamonds and other gems
- Create jewelry from gold, silver, and precious gemstones

Jewelers need a high degree of skill and must pay attention to detail.

- Shape metal to hold the gems when making individual pieces
- Make a model with carved wax or with computer-aided design, and then cast pieces with the model
- Solder pieces together and insert stones
- Smooth joints and rough spots and polish smoothed areas
- Clean and polish jewelry using polishing wheels and chemical baths
- Repair jewelry by replacing broken clasps, altering ring sizes, or resetting stones
- Compute the costs of labor and material for new pieces and repairs

Technology is helping to produce high-quality jewelry at a reduced cost and in less time. For example, lasers are often used for cutting and improving the quality of stones, for intricate engraving or design work, and for inscribing personal messages on jewelry. Jewelers also use lasers to weld metals together without seams or blemishes, improving the quality and appearance of jewelry.

Some manufacturing firms use computer-aided design and manufacturing (CAD/CAM) to make product design easier and to automate some steps. With CAD, jewelers can create a model of a piece of jewelry on the computer and then see the effect of changing different aspects–the design, the stone, the setting–before cutting a stone or taking other costly steps. With CAM, they can then create a mold of the piece, which makes producing many copies easy.

Some jewelers also use CAD software to design custom jewelry. They let the customer review the design on the computer and see the effect of changes, so that the customer is satisfied before committing to the expense of a customized piece of jewelry.

The following are examples of types of jewelers and precious stone and metal workers:

Precious metal workers expertly manipulate gold, silver, and other metals. They use pliers and other hand tools to shape and manipulate metal. Some may mix alloy ingredients according to chemical properties.

Gemologists analyze, describe, and certify the quality and characteristics of gemstones. After using microscopes, computerized tools, and other grading instruments to examine gemstones or finished pieces of jewelry, they write reports certifying that the items are of a particular quality. Most gemologists have completed the Graduate Gemologist program through the Gemological Institute of America.

Jewelry appraisers carefully examine jewelry to determine its value and then write appraisal documents. They determine value by researching the jewelry market and by using reference books, auction catalogs, price lists, and the Internet. They may work for jewelry stores, appraisal firms, auction houses, pawnbrokers, or insurance companies. Many gemologists also become appraisers.

Bench jewelers usually work for jewelry retailers, doing tasks from simple jewelry cleaning and repair to making molds and pieces from scratch.

Work Environment

Jewelers and precious stone and metal workers held about 32,700 jobs in 2012. About one-third were self-employed. Many work from home and sell their products at trade and craft shows on weekends.

Most wage and salary workers in this occupation are employed in jewelry stores, repair shops, and manufacturing plants.

The industries that employed the most jewelers and precious stone and metal workers in 2012 were as follows:

Jewelry, luggage, and leather goods stores	33%
Jewelry and silverware manufacturing	21
Merchant wholesalers, durable goods	7
Personal and household goods repair and maintenance	2

Median Hourly Wages, May 2012

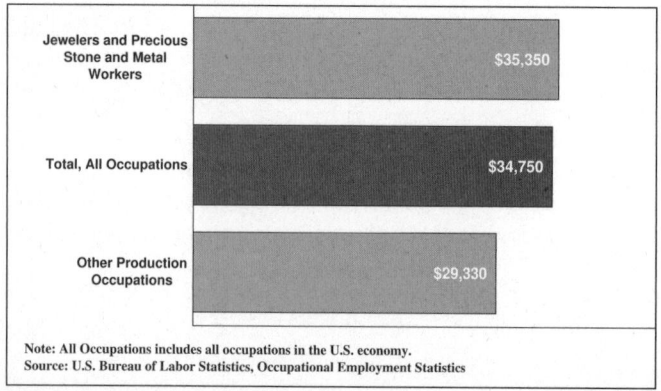

Jewelers and Precious Stone and Metal Workers — $35,350
Total, All Occupations — $34,750
Other Production Occupations — $29,330

Note: All Occupations includes all occupations in the U.S. economy.
Source: U.S. Bureau of Labor Statistics, Occupational Employment Statistics

Percent Change in Employment, Projected 2012–2022

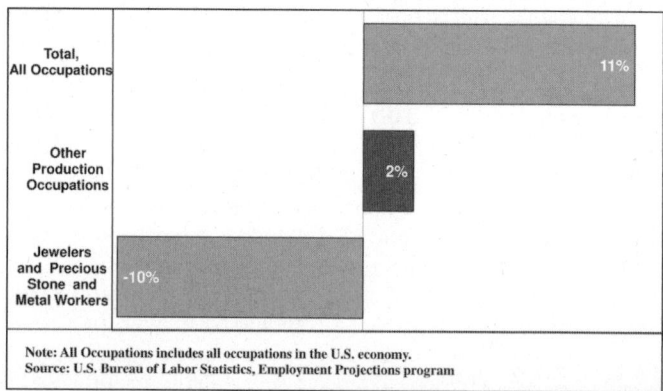

Total, All Occupations — 11%
Other Production Occupations — 2%
Jewelers and Precious Stone and Metal Workers — -10%

Note: All Occupations includes all occupations in the U.S. economy.
Source: U.S. Bureau of Labor Statistics, Employment Projections program

Employment Projections Data for Jewelers and Precious Stone and Metal Workers

Occupational title	SOC Code	Employment, 2012	Projected Employment, 2022	Change, 2012–2022	
				Percent	Numeric
Jewelers and precious stone and metal workers......................	51-9071	32,700	29,500	-10	-3,200

Source: U.S. Bureau of Labor Statistics, Employment Projections Program

Note: Data are rounded. Go to **Occupational Information Included in the OOH** *for a discussion of the data in this table.*

Jewelers and precious stone and metal workers spend much of their time at a workbench, using different tools and chemicals. Computers are also becoming an increasingly important tool in the jewelry industry as computer-aided design (CAD) can save workers time and resources. Many tools, such as jeweler's torches and lasers, must be handled carefully to avoid injury. Polishing processes such as chemical baths must also be performed with safety in mind. Sharp or pointed tools also may pose hazards.

In repair shops, jewelers usually work alone with little supervision. In retail stores, they may talk with customers about repairs, do custom design work, and even do some selling. Because many of their materials are valuable, jewelers must follow security procedures, including making use of burglar alarms and, in larger jewelry stores, working in the presence of security guards.

Work Schedules. Jewelers and precious stone and metal workers have varied work schedules. Self-employed workers often decide their own hours. Many work weekends, showing and selling their products at trade and craft shows. Retail store workers might also work nonstandard hours because they must be available when consumers are not working, such as on holidays and weekends. About 1 in 5 worked part time in 2012.

How to Become One

Jewelers and precious stone and metal workers have traditionally learned their trade through long-term on-the-job training. This method is still common, particularly in jewelry manufacturing, but a growing number of workers now learn their skills at trade schools.

Education. Many trade schools offer training for jewelers and precious stone and metal workers. Course topics can include introduction to gems and metals, resizing, repair, and computer-aided design (CAD). Programs vary from 6 months to 1 year, and many teach students how to design, cast, set, and polish jewelry and gems, as well as how to use and care for a jeweler's tools and equipment. Graduates of these programs may be more attractive to employers because they require less on-the-job training. Many gemologists graduate from the Gemological Institute of America.

In jewelry manufacturing plants, workers develop their skills through on-the-job training. The length of training required to become proficient depends on the difficulty of the specialty. Train-

ing usually focuses on casting, setting stones, making models, or engraving.

Other Experience. Some workers gain their skills through related work experience. This may include working alongside a bench jeweler or gemologist while performing the duties of a sales person in a retail jewelry store. Time spent in a store with a bench jeweler or gemologist can provide valuable experience.

Advancement. In manufacturing, some jewelers advance to supervisory jobs, such as master jeweler or head jeweler. Jewelers who work in jewelry stores or repair shops may become managers; some open their own business.

Jewelers and precious stone and metal workers who want to open their own store should first establish themselves and build a reputation for their work within the jewelry trade. After they achieve sufficient sales, they can acquire the necessary inventory for a store from a jewelry wholesaler. Also, because the jewelry business is highly competitive, jewelers who plan to open their own store should have sales experience and knowledge of marketing and business management.

Important Qualities

Artistic ability. Jewelers must have the ability to create designs that are unique and beautiful.

Detail oriented. Creating designs requires concentration and patience. Jewelers and precious stone and metal workers must give attention to large and small details on the pieces they make.

Fashion sense. Jewelry designers must know what is stylish and attractive because that is what people are likely to buy.

Finger dexterity. Jewelers and precious stone and metal workers must precisely move their fingers in order to grasp, manipulate, and assemble very small objects.

Interpersonal skills. Whether selling products in stores or at craft shows, jewelers and precious stone and metal workers interact with customers.

Visualization skills. Jewelers and precious stone and metal workers must imagine how something might look after its shape is altered or when its parts are rearranged.

Similar Occupations   This table shows a list of occupations with job duties that are similar to those of jewelers and precious stone and metal workers.

Occupations	Entry-level Education	2012 Pay	Projected Job Growth	Average Annual Openings
Craft and Fine Artists	High school diploma or equivalent	$46,065	3%	1,360
Fashion Designers	Bachelor's degree	$62,860	-3%	590
Industrial Designers	Bachelor's degree	$59,610	4%	1,210
Retail Sales Workers	Less than high school	$21,514	10%	202,730
Welders, Cutters, Solderers, and Brazers	High school diploma or equivalent	$36,300	6%	10,850
Woodworkers	High school diploma or equivalent	$28,576	8%	3,940

Pay

The median annual wage for jewelers and precious stone and metal workers was $35,350 in May 2012. The median wage is the wage at which half the workers in an occupation earned more than that amount and half earned less. The lowest 10 percent earned less than $19,600, and the highest 10 percent earned more than $61,940.

Job Outlook

Employment of jewelers and precious stone and metal workers is projected to decline 10 percent from 2012 to 2022. Employment of these workers will decline because most jewelry manufacturing is now done outside of the country.

Traditional jewelry stores may continue to lose some of their customers to nontraditional sellers, such as department stores, but they will still maintain a large customer base. In addition, new jewelry sold by nontraditional retailers should create some demand for skilled jewelers who can size, clean, and repair jewelry. Custom jewelry has become more popular and may be a source of demand for jewelers over the coming decade.

Job Prospects. Job opportunities should be available for bench jewelers who are skilled at design or repair. New jewelers will be needed to replace those who retire or who leave the occupation for other reasons. As master jewelers retire, shops lose expertise and knowledge that is difficult and costly to replace.

Job opportunities in jewelry stores and repair shops should be best for those who have graduated from a trade school or training program and have related work experience.

Strong competition is expected for lower skilled manufacturing jobs that are susceptible to automation. Jewelry designers who wish to create their own jewelry lines should expect intense competition. Although demand for customized and boutique jewelry is strong, it is difficult for independent designers to establish themselves. Experience with computer-aided design (CAD) makes creating custom pieces of jewelry easier.

During economic downturns, demand for jewelry products and for jewelers usually decreases. However, demand for repair workers should remain strong even during economic slowdowns because maintaining and repairing jewelry is cheaper than buying new jewelry.

O*NET

➤ Jewelers and Precious Stone and Metal Workers (51-9071.00)
➤ Jewelers (51-9071.01)
➤ Gem and Diamond Workers (51-9071.06)
➤ Precious Metal Workers (51-9071.07)

Contacts for More Information

For more information about jewelers, precious stone and metal workers, and gemologists, including job opportunities and training programs, visit
➤ Gemological Institute of America Inc. (www.gia.edu)
➤ Jewelers of America (www.jewelers.org/)
➤ Manufacturing Jewelers & Suppliers of America (www.mjsa.org/)

Laundry and Dry-cleaning Workers

- **2012 Median Pay** .... $19,930 per year
  $9.58 per hour
- **Entry-Level Education** .... Less than high school
- **Work Experience in a Related Occupation**............... None
- **On-the-Job Training** ....Short-term on-the-job training
- **Number of Jobs 2012** 210,700
- **Job Outlook, 2012–22** .... 10% (As fast as average)
- **Employment Change, 2012–22** 20,500

What Laundry and Dry-cleaning Workers Do

Laundry and dry-cleaning workers clean clothing, linens, drapes, and other articles, using washing, drying, and dry-cleaning machines. They also may clean leather, suede, furs, and rugs. Items made of a combination of fabrics frequently need special attention to avoid damaging items during the cleaning process.

Duties. Laundry and dry-cleaning workers typically do the following:

- Receive items from customers and mark them with codes or names
- Inspect articles for stains and fabrics that require special care
- Sort articles to be cleaned by fabric type, color, and cleaning technique
- Load clothing into laundry and dry-cleaning machines
- Add detergent, bleach, and other chemicals to laundry and dry-cleaning machines
- Remove, sort, and hang clothing and other articles after they are removed from the machines
- Clean and maintain laundry and dry-cleaning machines

Laundry and dry-cleaning workers ensure proper cleaning of clothing, linens, and other articles. They adjust machine settings for a given fabric or article, as determined by the cleaning instructions on each item of clothing. Workers add the proper type and amount of cleaning detergent or liquid solvents to washing machines, which agitate clothes similar to washing machines in most homes.

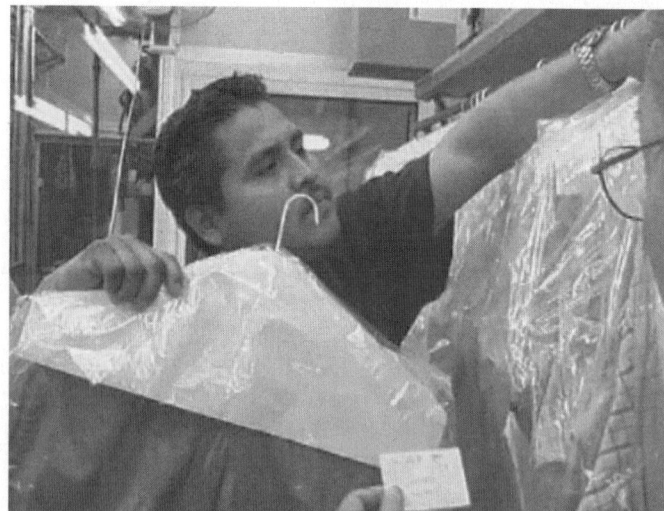

Laundry and dry-cleaning workers remove, sort, and hang clothing and other articles from the machines.

Employment Projections Data for Laundry and Dry-cleaning Workers

Occupational title	SOC Code	Employment, 2012	Projected Employment, 2022	Change, 2012–2022	
				Percent	Numeric
Laundry and dry-cleaning workers...	51-6011	210,700	231,200	10	20,500

Source: U.S. Bureau of Labor Statistics, Employment Projections Program

*Note: **Data are rounded.** Go to **Occupational Information Included in the OOH** for a discussion of the data in this table.*

Similar Occupations   This table shows a list of occupations with job duties that are similar to those of laundry and dry-cleaning workers.

Occupations	Entry-level Education	2012 Pay	Projected Job Growth	Average Annual Openings
Fashion Designers	Bachelor's degree	$62,860	-3%	590

When necessary, workers treat spots and stains on articles before washing or dry-cleaning. They monitor machines during the cleaning process and ensure that items are not lost or placed with items of another customer.

Often laundry and dry-cleaning workers interact with customers. They take the receipts, find the customer's clothing, take payment, make change, and do the cash register work that retail sales people do.

Some dry-cleaners offer alteration services. Often, sewers and tailors do these tasks, but some laundry and dry-cleaning workers do them as well.

Work Environment

Laundry and dry-cleaning workers held about 210,700 jobs in 2012.

The industries that employed the most laundry and dry-cleaning workers in 2012 were as follows:

Drycleaning and laundry services	50%
Nursing care facilities (skilled nursing facilities)	14
Traveler accommodation..	13
General medical and surgical hospitals; private	4
Administrative and support services	3

Laundry and dry-cleaning machines can make the work environment warm and noisy. Workers may also be exposed to harsh chemicals, although newer environmentally friendly and less-toxic cleaning synthetic solvents and detergents are improving their work environment.

In addition, laundry and dry-cleaning workers spend many hours standing.

Work Schedules. Most workers are employed full time. However, about 1 in 5 worked part time in 2012. Workers may need to begin work early in the day to have customers' cleaning done on time.

How to Become One

There are no formal education requirements to become a laundry or dry-cleaning worker. Most workers are trained on the job.

Education. There are no formal education requirements. Most laundry and dry-cleaning workers have a high school diploma or less. Some take classes on how to operate dry-cleaning machines or how to remove certain stains such as from inks or grease from clothing, but most employers do not require this.

Training. Laundry and dry-cleaning workers generally receive short-term on-the-job training. This training includes proper cleaning techniques, how to clean different fabrics, and how to treat stains.

Important Qualities

Customer-service skills. Laundry and dry-cleaning workers interact with customers who drop off and pick up their clothes. Workers may need to respond to customers who are unsatisfied with the quality of the cleaning.

Detail oriented. Many fabrics are delicate and require special care in cleaning. In addition to looking for spots and stains, laundry and dry-cleaning workers must pay attention to the type of fabric to ensure that the item is cleaned properly.

Stamina. Laundry and dry-cleaning workers often spend many hours standing in a warm environment.

Median Annual Wages, May 2012

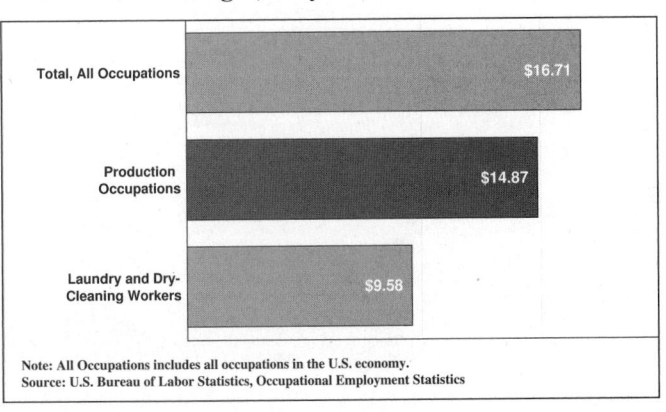

Note: All Occupations includes all occupations in the U.S. economy.
Source: U.S. Bureau of Labor Statistics, Occupational Employment Statistics

Percent Change in Employment, Projected 2012–2022

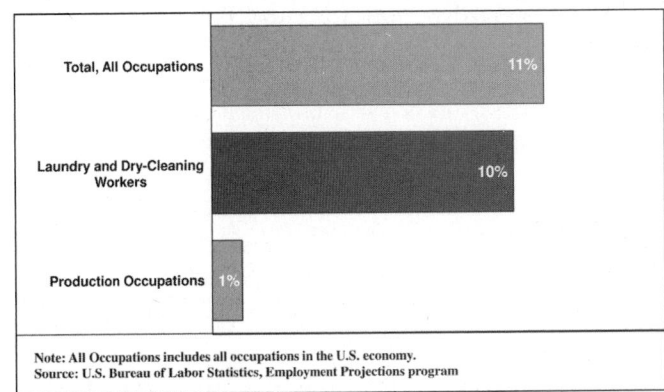

Note: All Occupations includes all occupations in the U.S. economy.
Source: U.S. Bureau of Labor Statistics, Employment Projections program

Pay

The median hourly wage for laundry and dry-cleaning workers was $9.58 in May 2012. The median wage is the wage at which half the workers in an occupation earned more than that amount and half earned less. The lowest 10 percent earned less than $7.95, and the top 10 percent earned more than $14.25.

Job Outlook

Employment of laundry and dry-cleaning workers is projected to grow 10 percent from 2012 to 2022, about as fast as the average for all occupations.

A growing population will continue to demand laundry and dry-cleaning services, particularly the dry-cleaning of professional attire and work uniforms and apparel.

However, employment growth may be slowed as consumers purchase clothing and other articles that can be cleaned at home. Concern over the effects of liquid solvents such as perchloroethylene on the environment and people's health, will continue the trend towards the use of environmentally friendly and less-toxic cleaning synthetic solvents and detergents.

Job Prospects. Job prospects are expected to be good. Because this occupation requires limited formal education and has low pay, many workers transfer to other occupations or leave the labor force because of family responsibilities, to return to school, or for other reasons.

O*NET

➤ Laundry and Dry-Cleaning Workers (51-6011.00)

Contacts for More Information

For more information about laundry and dry-cleaning workers, visit
➤ The Drycleaning and Laundry Institute (www.ifi.org/)
➤ National Cleaners Association (www.nca-i.com/)

Machinists and Tool and Die Makers

- **2012 Median Pay** .... $40,910 per year
  $19.67 per hour
- **Entry-Level Education** ... High school diploma or equivalent
- **Work Experience in a Related Occupation**............... None
- **On-the-Job Training** .... Long-term on-the-job training
- **Number of Jobs 2012** 476,200
- **Job Outlook, 2012–22**.............. 7% (Slower than average)
- **Employment Change, 2012–22** 33,700

What Machinists and Tool and Die Makers Do

Machinists and tool and die makers set up and operate a variety of computer-controlled and mechanically-controlled machine tools to produce precision metal parts, instruments, and tools.

Duties. Machinists typically do the following:

- Work from blueprints, sketches or computer-aided design (CAD), and computer-aided manufacturing (CAM) files
- Set up, operate, and disassemble manual, automatic, and computer-numeric controlled (CNC) machine tools
- Align, secure, and adjust cutting tools and workpieces
- Monitor the feed and speed of machines
- Turn, mill, drill, shape, and grind machine parts to specifications

- Measure, examine, and test completed products for defects
- Smooth the surfaces of parts or products
- Present finished workpieces to customers and make modifications if needed

Tool and die makers typically do the following:

- Read blueprints, sketches, specifications, or CAD and CAM files for making tools and dies
- Compute and verify dimensions, sizes, shapes, and tolerances of workpieces
- Set up, operate, and disassemble conventional, manual, and computer-numeric controlled (CNC) machine tools
- File, grind, and adjust parts so that they fit together properly
- Test completed tools and dies to ensure that they meet specifications
- Smooth and polish the surfaces of tools and dies

Machinists use machine tools, such as lathes, milling machines, and grinders, to produce precision metal parts. These tools are either manually controlled or computer-numerically controlled (CNC). CNC machines control the cutting tool speed and do all necessary cuts to create a part. The machinist determines the cutting path, the speed of the cut, and the feed rate by programming instructions into the CNC machine. Many machinists must be able to use both manual and computer-controlled machinery in their jobs.

Although workers may produce large quantities of one part, precision machinists often produce small batches or one-of-a-kind items. The parts that machinists make range from simple bolts of steel to titanium bone screws for orthopedic implants. Hydraulic parts, anti-lock brakes, and automobile pistons are other widely known products that machinists make.

Some machinists repair or make new parts for existing machinery. After an industrial machinery mechanic discovers a broken part in a machine, a machinist would need to remanufacture the broken part. The machinist refers to blueprints and performs the same machining operations that were used to create the original part in order to create the replacement.

Because the technology of machining is changing rapidly, workers must learn to operate a wide range of machines. Some newer manufacturing processes use lasers, water jets, electrical discharge machines (EDM), and electrified wires to cut the workpiece.

Machinists remove and replace worn-out machine tools.

Employment Projections Data for Machinists and Tool and Die Makers

Occupational title	SOC Code	Employment, 2012	Projected Employment, 2022	Change, 2012–2022	
				Percent	Numeric
Machinists and tool and die makers	—	476,200	509,900	7	33,700
Machinists...	51-4041	397,500	432,400	9	34,800
Tool and die makers	51-4111	78,600	77,500	-1	-1,100

Source: U.S. Bureau of Labor Statistics, Employment Projections Program

Note: Data are rounded. Go to Occupational Information Included in the OOH *for a discussion of the data in this table.*

Although some of the computer controls are similar to those of other machine tools, machinists must understand the unique capabilities of different machines. As engineers create new types of machine tools, machinists constantly must learn new machining properties and techniques.

Toolmakers craft precision tools that are used to cut, shape, and form metal and other materials. They also produce jigs and fixtures–devices that hold metal while it is bored, stamped, or drilled–and gauges and other measuring devices.

Die makers construct metal forms, called dies, that are used to shape metal in stamping and forging operations. They also make metal molds for die casting and for molding plastics, ceramics, and composite materials.

Many tool and die makers use computer-aided design (CAD) to develop products and parts. Designs are entered into computer programs that electronically develop blueprints for the required tools and dies. Computer-numeric control programmers, found in the metal and plastic machine workers profile, convert computer-aided designs into computer-aided manufacturing (CAM) programs that contain instructions for a sequence of cutting tool operations. Once these programs are developed, CNC machines follow the set of instructions contained in the program to produce the part. Machinists normally operate CNC machines, but tool and die makers often are trained to both operate CNC machines and write CNC programs; they may do either task.

Work Environment

Machinists and tool and die makers held about 476,200 jobs in 2012. The vast majority worked in manufacturing. The industries that employed the most machinists and tool and die makers in 2012 were as follows:

Machinery manufacturing	20%
Machine shops..	19
Transportation equipment manufacturing	15

Machinists and tool and die makers work in machine shops, tool rooms, and factories, where work areas are usually well ventilated.

Work Schedules. Most machinists and tool and die makers work full time during regular business hours. However, overtime is somewhat common. Because many manufacturers run machinery for long hours, evening and weekend work is also common.

Injuries and Illnesses. Although the work of machinists and tool and die makers is not inherently dangerous, working around machine tools presents hazards, and workers must follow precautions. For example, workers must wear protective equipment, such as safety glasses, to shield against bits of flying metal, and earplugs to dampen the noise produced by machinery.

How to Become One

There are many different ways to become a machinist or tool and die maker. Machinists train in apprenticeship programs, vocational schools, or community or technical colleges, or on the job. To become a fully trained tool and die maker takes several years of technical instruction, as well as on-the-job training. Good math, problem-solving, and computer skills are important. A high school diploma is necessary.

Education. Machinists and tool and die makers must have a high school diploma or equivalent. In high school, students should take math courses, especially trigonometry and geometry. They also should take courses in blueprint reading, metalworking, and drafting, if available.

Some advanced positions, such as those in the aircraft manufacturing industry, require the use of advanced applied calculus and physics. The increasing use of computer-controlled machinery requires machinists and tool and die makers to have basic computer skills before entering a training program.

Some community colleges and technical schools have 2-year programs that train students to become machinists. These programs usually teach design and blueprint reading, how to use a variety of welding and cutting tools, and the programming and function of computer-numerically controlled (CNC) machines.

Training. Apprenticeship programs, typically sponsored by a manufacturer, are an excellent way to become a machinist or tool and die maker, but they are often hard to get into. Apprentices usually must have a high school diploma or equivalent, and most have taken algebra and trigonometry classes.

Apprenticeship programs consist of paid shop training and related technical instruction lasting several years. Apprenticeship classes often are taught in cooperation with local community colleges and vocational–technical schools.

Similar Occupations   This table shows a list of occupations with job duties that are similar to those of machinists and tool and die makers.

Occupations	Entry-level Education	2012 Pay	Projected Job Growth	Average Annual Openings
Industrial Machinery Mechanics and Maintenance Workers and Millwrights	High school diploma or equivalent	$45,848	17%	18,700
Metal and Plastic Machine Workers	High school diploma or equivalent	$33,064	-6%	22,070
Welders, Cutters, Solderers, and Brazers	High school diploma or equivalent	$36,300	6%	10,850

A growing number of machinists and tool and die makers receive their technical training from community and technical colleges. In this setting, employees learn while employed by a manufacturer that supports the employee's training goals and provides the needed on-the-job training.

Apprentices usually work 40 hours per week and receive technical instruction during evenings. Trainees often begin as machine operators and gradually take on more difficult assignments. Machinists and tool and die makers must have good computer skills to work with CAD/CAM technology, CNC machine tools, and computerized measuring machines. Some machinists become tool and die makers.

Even after completing a formal training program, tool and die makers still need years of experience to become highly skilled.

Licenses, Certifications, and Registrations. To boost the skill level of machinists and tool and die makers and to create a more uniform standard of competency, a number of training facilities, state apprenticeship boards, and colleges offer certification programs. The Right Skills Now initiative, for example, is an industry-driven program that aims to align education pathways with career pathways.

Completing a recognized certification program provides machinists and tool and die makers with better job opportunities and helps employers judge the abilities of new hires.

Journey-level certification is available from state apprenticeship boards after completing an apprenticeship. Many employers recognize this certification, and it often leads to better job opportunities.

Important Qualities

Analytical skills. Machinists and tool and die makers must understand highly technical electronic and written blueprints, models, and specifications, so they can craft precision tools and metal parts.

Manual dexterity. The work of machinists and tool and die makers must be highly accurate. For example, machining parts may demand accuracy of .0001 inch, which requires workers' precision, concentration, and dexterity.

Math and computer skills. Workers must have good math and computer skills to work with CAD/CAM technology, CNC machine tools, and computerized measuring machines.

Mechanical skills. Machinists and tool and die makers must be mechanically inclined. They operate milling machines, lathes, grinders, laser and water cutting machines, wire electrical discharge machines, and other machine tools. They also may use a variety of hand tools and power tools.

Physical stamina. The ability to endure long periods of standing and performing repetitive movements is important for machinists and tool and die makers.

Technical skills. Machinists and tool and die makers must understand computerized measuring machines and metalworking processes, such as stock removal, chip control, and heat treating and plating.

Pay

The median hourly wage for machinists was $18.99 in May 2012. The median wage is the wage at which half the workers in an occupation earned more than that amount and half earned less. The lowest 10 percent earned less than $11.70 per hour, and the top 10 percent earned more than $28.75 per hour.

The median hourly wage for tool and die makers was $22.60 in May 2012. The lowest 10 percent earned less than $15.16 per hour, and the top 10 percent earned more than $33.44 per hour.

The pay of apprentices is tied to their skill level. As they gain more skills and reach specific levels of performance and experience, their pay increases.

Job Outlook

Overall employment of machinists and tool and die makers is projected to grow 7 percent from 2012 to 2022, slower than the average for all occupations. Employment growth will vary by specialty.

Employment of machinists is projected to grow 9 percent from 2012 to 2022, about as fast as the average for all occupations. Despite improvements in technologies, such as computer-numerically controlled (CNC) machine tools, autoloaders, high-speed machining, and lights-out manufacturing, machinists will still be required to set up, monitor, and maintain these automated systems.

In addition, employers will continue to need machinists, who have a wide range of skills and are capable of performing modern production techniques, in a machine shop. Manufacturers will continue to rely heavily on skilled machinists, as they invest in new equipment, modify production techniques, and implement product design changes more rapidly.

Employment of tool and die makers is projected to show little or no change from 2012 to 2022.

Although foreign competition in manufacturing and advances in automation, including CNC machine tools and computer-aided design, should improve worker productivity, tool and die makers will still be needed to program CNC machines. There also will be a need for tool and die makers to manufacture small production orders and special order parts.

Job Prospects. Job opportunities for machinists and tool and die makers should be excellent, as employers continue to value

Median Hourly Wages, May 2012

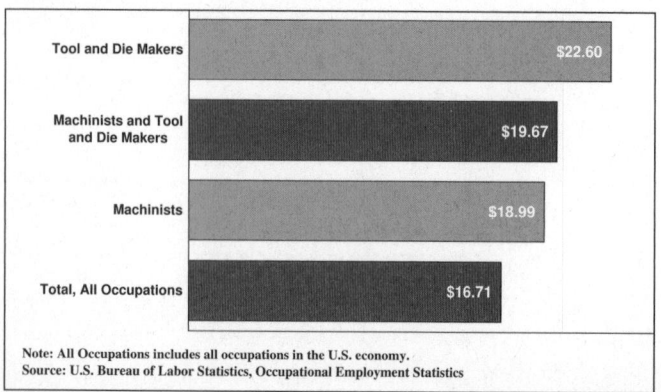

Note: All Occupations includes all occupations in the U.S. economy.
Source: U.S. Bureau of Labor Statistics, Occupational Employment Statistics

Percent Change in Employment, Projected 2012–2022

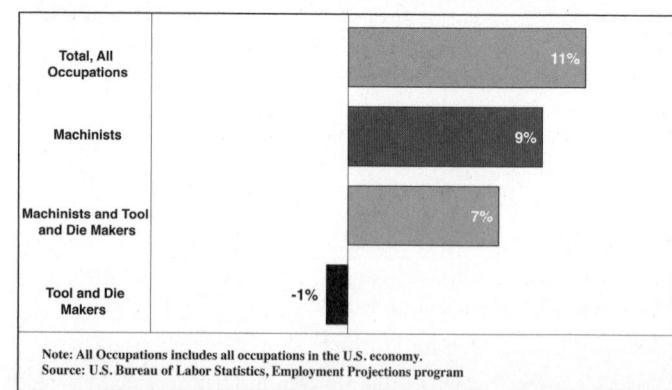

Note: All Occupations includes all occupations in the U.S. economy.
Source: U.S. Bureau of Labor Statistics, Employment Projections program

the wide-ranging skills of these workers. Also, many young people with the right education and personal qualifications needed to become machinists and tool and die makers prefer to attend college or may not wish to enter production occupations. Therefore, the number of workers learning to be machinists and tool and die makers is expected to be smaller than the number of job openings arising each year from the need to replace experienced machinists who retire or leave the occupation for other reasons.

O*NET

➤ Machinists (51-4041.00)
➤ Tool and Die Makers (51-4111.00)

Contacts for More Information

For more information about machinists and tool and die makers, including training and certification, visit

➤ Fabricators & Manufacturers Association, International (FMA) (www.fmanet.org/)
➤ National Institute for Metalworking Skills (NIMS) (www.nims-skills.org/)

For general information about manufacturing careers, including machinery and tool and die makers, visit

➤ American Mold Builders Association (AMBA) (www.amba.org/)
➤ Association for Manufacturing Technology (AMT) (www.amtonline.org/)
➤ National Tooling and Machining Association (NTMA) (www.ntma.org/)
➤ Precision Machined Products Association (PMPA) (www.pmpa.org/)
➤ Precision Metalforming Association (PMA) (www.pma.org/home/)

Metal and Plastic Machine Workers

- **2012 Median Pay** .... $32,950 per year
  $15.84 per hour
- **Entry-Level Education** ... High school diploma or equivalent
- **Work Experience in a Related Occupation** .... None
- **On-the-Job Training** .... See "How to Become One"
- **Number of Jobs 2012** 1,013,200
- **Job Outlook, 2012–22** .... -6% (Decline)
- **Employment Change, 2012–22** .... -59,100

What Metal and Plastic Machine Workers Do

Metal and plastic machine workers set up and operate machines that cut, shape, and form metal and plastic materials or pieces.

Duties. Metal and plastic machine workers typically do the following:

- Set up machines according to blueprints
- Monitor machines for unusual sound or vibration
- Insert material into machines, manually or with a hoist
- Operate metal or plastic molding, casting, or coremaking machines
- Adjust machine settings for temperature, speed and feed rates, and cycle times
- Remove finished products and smooth rough edges and imperfections
- Test and compare finished workpieces to specifications
- Remove and replace dull cutting tools
- Document production numbers in a computer database

Consumer products are made with many metal and plastic parts. These parts are produced by machines that are operated by metal and plastic machine workers. In general, these workers are separated into two groups: those who set up machines for operation and those who operate machines during production.

Although many workers both set up and operate machines, some specialize in one of the following job types:

Machine setters, or setup workers, prepare the machines before production, perform test runs, and, if necessary, adjust and make minor repairs to the machinery before and during operation.

If, for example, the cutting tool inside a machine becomes dull after extended use, it is common for a setter to remove the tool, use a grinder or file to sharpen it, and reinstall it into the machine. New tools are produced by tool and die makers.

After installing the tools into a machine, setup workers often produce the initial batch of goods, inspect the products, and turn the machine over to an operator.

Machine operators and tenders monitor the machinery during operation.

After a setter prepares a machine for production, an operator observes the machine and the products it makes. Operators may have to load the machine with materials for production or adjust the machine's speeds during production. They must periodically inspect the parts a machine produces. If they detect a minor problem, operators may fix it themselves. If the repair is more serious, they may have an industrial machinery mechanic fix it.

Setters, operators, and tenders are usually identified by the type of machine they work with. Job duties generally vary with the size of the manufacturer and the type of machine being operated. Although some workers specialize in one or two types of machinery, many are trained to set up or operate a variety of machines. Increasing automation allows machine operators to control multiple machines at the same time.

In addition, new production techniques, such as team-oriented "lean" manufacturing, require machine operators to rotate between different machines. Rotating assignments results in more varied work but also requires workers to have a wide range of skills.

Machine operators stop production when faulty parts are produced.

Median Hourly Wages, May 2012

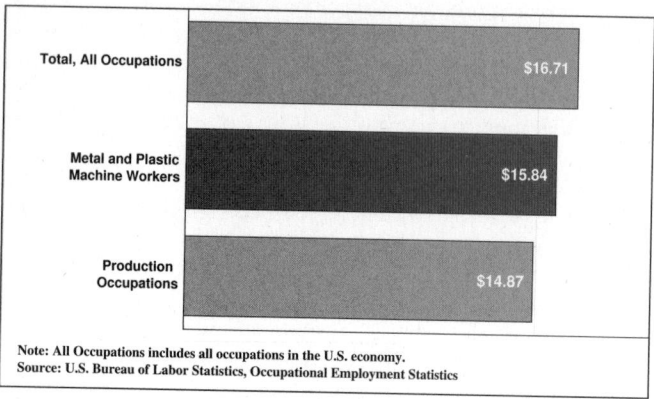

Total, All Occupations	$16.71
Metal and Plastic Machine Workers	$15.84
Production Occupations	$14.87

Note: All Occupations includes all occupations in the U.S. economy.
Source: U.S. Bureau of Labor Statistics, Occupational Employment Statistics

Percent Change in Employment, Projected 2012–2022

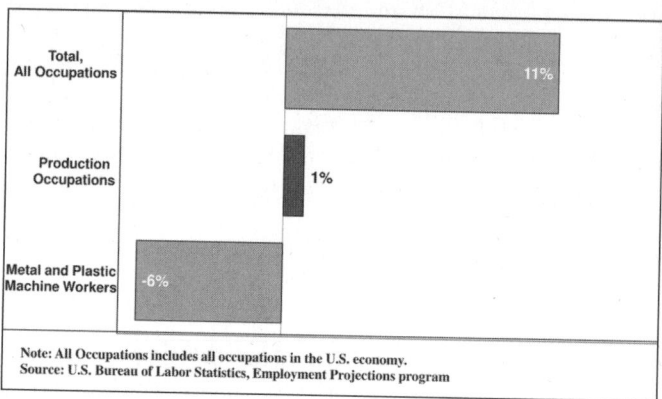

Total, All Occupations	11%
Production Occupations	1%
Metal and Plastic Machine Workers	-6%

Note: All Occupations includes all occupations in the U.S. economy.
Source: U.S. Bureau of Labor Statistics, Employment Projections program

The following are examples of types of metal and plastic machine workers:

Computer-controlled machine tool operators operate computer-controlled machines or robots to perform functions on metal or plastic workpieces.

Computer numerically controlled machine tool programmers develop computer programs to control the machining or processing of metal or plastic parts by automatic machine tools, equipment, or systems.

Extruding and drawing machine setters, operators, and tenders set up or operate machines to extrude (pull out) thermoplastic or metal materials in the form of tubes, rods, hoses, wire, bars, or structural shapes.

Forging machine setters, operators, and tenders set up or operate machines that shape or form metal or plastic parts.

Rolling machine setters, operators, and tenders set up or operate machines to roll steel or plastic or to flatten, temper, or reduce the thickness of materials.

Cutting, punching, and press machine setters, operators, and tenders set up or operate machines to saw, cut, shear, notch, bend, or straighten metal or plastic materials.

Drilling and boring machine tool setters, operators, and tenders set up or operate drilling machines to drill, bore, mill, or countersink metal or plastic workpieces.

Grinding, lapping, polishing, and buffing machine tool setters, operators, and tenders set up or operate grinding and related tools that remove excess material from surfaces, sharpen edges or corners, or buff or polish metal or plastic workpieces.

Lathe and turning machine tool setters, operators, and tenders set up or operate lathe and turning machines to turn, bore, thread, or form metal or plastic materials, such as wire or rod.

Milling and planing machine setters, operators, and tenders set up or operate milling or planing machines to shape, groove, or profile metal or plastic workpieces.

Metal-refining furnace operators and tenders operate or tend furnaces, such as gas, oil, coal, electric-arc or electric induction, open-hearth or oxygen furnaces to melt and refine metal before casting or to produce specified types of steel.

Pourers and casters operate hand-controlled mechanisms to pour and regulate the flow of molten metal into molds to produce castings or ingots.

Model makers set up and operate machines, such as milling and engraving machines to make working models of metal or plastic objects.

Patternmakers lay out, machine, fit, and assemble castings and parts to metal or plastic foundry patterns and core molds.

Foundry mold and coremakers make or form wax or sand cores or molds used in the production of metal castings in foundries.

Molding, coremaking, and casting machine setters, operators, and tenders set up or operate metal or plastic molding, casting, or coremaking machines to mold or cast metal or thermoplastic parts or products.

Multiple machine tool setters, operators, and tenders set up or operate more than one type of cutting or forming machine tool or robot.

Welding, soldering, and brazing machine setters, operators, and tenders (including workers who operate laser cutters or laser-beam machines) set up or operate welding, soldering, or brazing machines or robots that weld, braze, solder, or heat treat metal products, components, or assemblies.

Heat treating equipment setters, operators, and tenders set up or operate heating equipment, such as heat treating furnaces, flame-hardening machines, induction machines, soaking pits, or vacuum equipment, to temper, harden, anneal, or heat treat metal or plastic objects.

Plating and coating machine setters, operators, and tenders set up or operate plating or coating machines to coat metal or plastic products with zinc, copper, nickel, or some other metal to protect or decorate surfaces (includes electrolytic processes).

Work Environment

Metal and plastic machine workers held about 1 million jobs in 2012. Nearly all worked in manufacturing industries.

Employment in the detailed occupations that make up this group was distributed as follows:

Cutting, punching, and press machine setters, operators, and tenders, metal and plastic 184,700
Computer-controlled machine tool operators, metal and plastic 140,300
Molding, coremaking, and casting machine setters, operators, and tenders, metal and plastic 125,000
Multiple machine tool setters, operators, and tenders, metal and plastic 85,900
Extruding and drawing machine setters, operators, and tenders, metal and plastic 74,900
Grinding, lapping, polishing, and buffing machine tool setters, operators, and tenders, metal and plastic 71,500
Welding, soldering, and brazing machine setters, operators, and tenders 53,500
Lathe and turning machine tool setters, operators, and tenders, metal and plastic 38,600
Rolling machine setters, operators, and tenders, metal and plastic 36,400
Plating and coating machine setters, operators,

Employment Projections Data for Metal and Plastic Machine Workers

Occupational title	SOC Code	Employment, 2012	Projected Employment, 2022	Change, 2012–2022	
				Percent	Numeric
Metal and plastic machine workers......................................	—	1,013,200	954,100	-6	-59,100
Computer-controlled machine tool operators, metal and plastic..	51-4011	140,300	160,700	15	20,400
Computer numerically controlled machine tool programmers, metal and plastic	51-4012	24,300	31,000	28	6,700
Extruding and drawing machine setters, operators, and tenders, metal and plastic	51-4021	74,900	63,000	-16	-11,900
Forging machine setters, operators, and tenders, metal and plastic..	51-4022	22,600	19,700	-13	-2,900
Rolling machine setters, operators, and tenders, metal and plastic..	51-4023	36,400	32,800	-10	-3,600
Cutting, punching, and press machine setters, operators, and tenders, metal and plastic.......................	51-4031	184,700	168,200	-9	-16,400
Drilling and boring machine tool setters, operators, and tenders, metal and plastic	51-4032	20,900	16,200	-22	-4,700
Grinding, lapping, polishing, and buffing machine tool setters, operators, and tenders, metal and plastic....	51-4033	71,500	62,500	-13	-9,000
Lathe and turning machine tool setters, operators, and tenders, metal and plastic	51-4034	38,600	33,200	-14	-5,400
Milling and planing machine setters, operators, and tenders, metal and plastic	51-4035	23,100	20,200	-13	-2,900
Metal-refining furnace operators and tenders....................	51-4051	20,800	18,500	-11	-2,300
Pourers and casters, metal..	51-4052	10,700	8,700	-19	-2,000
Model makers, metal and plastic	51-4061	6,100	6,300	2	100
Patternmakers, metal and plastic......................................	51-4062	4,400	4,700	6	300
Foundry mold and coremakers	51-4071	12,400	10,400	-16	-2,000
Molding, coremaking, and casting machine setters, operators, and tenders, metal and plastic.................	51-4072	125,000	105,800	-15	-19,200
Multiple machine tool setters, operators, and tenders, metal and plastic..	51-4081	85,900	74,500	-13	-11,400
Welding, soldering, and brazing machine setters, operators, and tenders..	51-4122	53,500	64,100	20	10,600
Heat treating equipment setters, operators, and tenders, metal and plastic	51-4191	22,000	21,600	-2	-400
Plating and coating machine setters, operators, and tenders, metal and plastic	51-4193	35,000	31,900	-9	-3,000

Source: U.S. Bureau of Labor Statistics, Employment Projections Program

Note: Data are rounded. Go to **Occupational Information Included in the OOH** *for a discussion of the data in this table.*

and tenders, metal and plastic.. 35,000
Computer numerically controlled machine tool programmers, metal and plastic................................. 24,300
Milling and planing machine setters, operators, and tenders, metal and plastic....................................... 23,100
Forging machine setters, operators, and tenders, metal and plastic.. 22,600
Heat treating equipment setters, operators, and tenders, metal and plastic....................................... 22,000
Drilling and boring machine tool setters, operators, and tenders, metal and plastic 20,900
Metal-refining furnace operators and tenders...................... 20,800
Foundry mold and coremakers 12,400
Pourers and casters, metal... 10,700
Model makers, metal and plastic 6,100
Patternmakers, metal and plastic 4,400

Metal and plastic machine workers are employed mostly in factories.

These workers often operate powerful, high-speed machines that can be dangerous, so they must observe safety rules. Operators usually wear protective equipment, such as safety glasses, to protect them from flying particles of metal or plastic, earplugs to guard against noise from the machines, and steel-toed boots, to shield their feet from heavy objects that are dropped.

Other required safety equipment varies by work setting and machine. For example, respirators are common for those in the plastics industry who work near materials that emit dangerous fumes or dust.

Work Schedules. Most metal and plastic machine workers are employed full time and work during regular business hours. Overtime is common, and because many manufacturers run their machinery for many hours a day, evening and weekend work also is common.

How to Become One

A few months of on-the-job training is enough for most workers to learn basic machine operations, but 1 year or more is required to become highly skilled. Computer-controlled machine workers may need more training. Although not always required, employers prefer to hire workers who have a high school diploma.

Education. For jobs as machine setters, operators, and tenders, employers generally prefer workers who have a high school diploma. Those interested in this occupation can improve their

Similar Occupations   This table shows a list of occupations with job duties that are similar to those of metal and plastic machine workers.

Occupations	Entry-level Education	2012 Pay	Projected Job Growth	Average Annual Openings
Assemblers and Fabricators	High school diploma or equivalent	$28,661	4%	37,140
Computer Programmers	Bachelor's degree	$74,280	8%	11,810
Industrial Machinery Mechanics and Maintenance Workers and Millwrights	High school diploma or equivalent	$45,848	17%	18,700
Machinists and Tool and Die Makers	High school diploma or equivalent	$40,733	7%	13,060
Painting and Coating Workers	See "How to Become One"	$33,161	4%	3,280

employment opportunities by completing high school courses in computer programming, shop and blueprint reading, and by gaining a working knowledge of the properties of metals and plastics. A solid math background, including courses in algebra, geometry, trigonometry, and basic statistics is useful.

Some community colleges and other schools offer courses and certificate programs in operating metal and plastics machines.

Training. Machine operator trainees usually begin by watching and helping experienced workers on the job. Under supervision, they may start by supplying materials, starting and stopping the machines, or removing finished products from it. Then they advance to more difficult tasks that operators perform, such as adjusting feed speeds, changing cutting tools, or inspecting a finished product for defects. Eventually, some develop the skills and experience to set up machines and help newer operators.

The complexity of the equipment usually determines the time required to become an operator. Some operators and tenders learn basic machine operations and functions in a few weeks; but other workers, such as computer-controlled machine tool operators, may need a year or more to become skilled or to advance to the more highly skilled job of setter.

In addition to providing on-the-job training, employers may pay for some machine operators to attend classes. Other employers prefer to hire workers who have completed or are enrolled in a training program.

As the manufacturing process continues to advance with computerized machinery, knowledge of computer-aided design (CAD), computer-aided manufacturing (CAM), and computer numerically-controlled (CNC) machines can be helpful.

Licenses, Certifications, and Registrations. Although certification is not required, a growing number of employers prefer that applicants become certified. Certification can show competence and professionalism and can be helpful for advancement. The National Institute for Metalworking Skills (NIMS) has developed skills standards in 24 operational areas.

Advancement. Advancement usually includes higher pay and more responsibilities. With experience and expertise, workers can become trainees for more highly skilled positions. It is common for machine operators to move into setup or machinery maintenance positions. Setup workers may become industrial machinery mechanics and maintenance workers, machinists, or tool and die makers.

Skilled workers with good communication and analytical skills may move into supervisory positions.

Important Qualities

Computer skills. Employers who have modern technology systems require that metal and plastic machine workers be able to use programmable devices, computers, and robots on the factory floor.

Dexterity. Precise hand movements are necessary in order to produce workpieces that meet exact specifications. Those who

work in metal and plastic machined goods manufacturing must have good manual dexterity in order to make the necessary shapes, cuts, and edges that designs require.

Mechanical skills. Although modern technology has brought a lot of computer-based systems to this occupation, workers still set up and operate machinery. They must be comfortable working with machines and have a good understanding of how the machines and all their parts work.

Physical stamina. Metal and plastic machine workers must be able to stand for long periods and perform repetitive work.

Physical strength. Although most material handling is done using automated systems, some metal and plastic machine workers must be strong enough to guide and load heavy and bulky parts and materials into machines.

Pay

The median hourly wage for metal and plastic machine workers was $15.84 in May 2012. The median wage is the wage at which half the workers in an occupation earned more than that amount and half earned less. The lowest 10 percent earned less than $10.09 per hour, and the top 10 percent earned more than $24.17 per hour.

Wages vary by the size of the company, union status, industry, skill level, and experience of the operator.

In May 2012, the median hourly wages for metal and plastic machine workers were as follows:

Computer numerically controlled machine tool programmers, metal and plastic	$22.08
Model makers, metal and plastic	22.04
Patternmakers, metal and plastic	20.40
Metal-refining furnace operators and tenders	18.70
Rolling machine setters, operators, and tenders, metal and plastic	17.98
Lathe and turning machine tool setters, operators, and tenders, metal and plastic	17.57
Milling and planing machine setters, operators, and tenders, metal and plastic	17.22
Computer-controlled machine tool operators, metal and plastic	17.10
Welding, soldering, and brazing machine setters, operators, and tenders	16.69
Forging machine setters, operators, and tenders, metal and plastic	16.37
Pourers and casters, metal	16.37
Heat treating equipment setters, operators, and tenders, metal and plastic	16.35
Multiple machine tool setters, operators, and tenders, metal and plastic	16.33
Drilling and boring machine tool setters, operators, and tenders, metal and plastic	16.32
Extruding and drawing machine setters, operators, and tenders, metal and plastic	15.54

Grinding, lapping, polishing, and buffing machine tool
setters, operators, and tenders, metal and plastic 15.20
Foundry mold and coremakers 14.68
Plating and coating machine setters, operators,
and tenders, metal and plastic 14.29
Cutting, punching, and press machine setters,
operators, and tenders, metal and plastic 14.27
Molding, coremaking, and casting machine setters,
operators, and tenders, metal and plastic 13.77

Job Outlook

Employment of metal and plastic machine workers is projected to decline 6 percent from 2012 to 2022. Employment declines stem from advances in technology, foreign competition, and changing demand for the goods these workers produce.

One of the most important factors influencing employment growth in these occupations is the use of labor-saving machinery. Many firms are adopting new technologies, such as computer numerically-controlled (CNC) machine tools and robots, to improve quality and lower production costs. The switch to CNC machinery requires computer programmers instead of machine setters, operators, and tenders. Therefore, demand for lower skilled manual machine tool operator and tender jobs are more likely to be reduced by these new technologies, because CNC machinery does the work more effectively. Conversely, demand for CNC machine programmers is expected to be strong. Demand for welding machine operators is also expected to be high because the skill required makes it harder to automate than other metal and plastic machine work.

The demand for metal and plastic machine workers also is affected by the demand for the parts they produce. Both the plastic and metal manufacturing industries face stiff foreign competition that is limiting the orders for parts produced in this country. Some U.S. manufacturers have sent their production to foreign countries, reducing jobs for machine setters and operators. However, some companies are bringing jobs back to the United States from overseas. This is expected to continue over the coming decade.

Job Prospects. Workers that are able to operate computer-numerically controlled machines are expected to have the best job prospects.

Despite declining employment, a number of these jobs are expected to become available for highly skilled workers, because of an expected increase in retirements in the coming years.

Workers who have an extensive background in machine operations, certifications from industry associations, and good knowledge of the properties of metals and plastics should have the best job opportunities.

O*NET

➤ Computer-Controlled Machine Tool Operators, Metal and Plastic (51-4011.00)
➤ Computer Numerically Controlled Machine Tool Programmers, Metal and Plastic (51-4012.00)
➤ Extruding and Drawing Machine Setters, Operators, and Tenders, Metal and Plastic (51-4021.00)
➤ Forging Machine Setters, Operators, and Tenders, Metal and Plastic (51-4022.00)
➤ Rolling Machine Setters, Operators, and Tenders, Metal and Plastic (51-4023.00)
➤ Cutting, Punching, and Press Machine Setters, Operators, and Tenders, Metal and Plastic (51-4031.00)
➤ Drilling and Boring Machine Tool Setters, Operators, and Tenders, Metal and Plastic (51-4032.00)
➤ Grinding, Lapping, Polishing, and Buffing Machine Tool Setters, Operators, and Tenders, Metal and Plastic (51-4033.00)

➤ Lathe and Turning Machine Tool Setters, Operators, and Tenders, Metal and Plastic (51-4034.00)
➤ Milling and Planing Machine Setters, Operators, and Tenders, Metal and Plastic (51-4035.00)
➤ Metal-Refining Furnace Operators and Tenders (51-4051.00)
➤ Pourers and Casters, Metal (51-4052.00)
➤ Model Makers, Metal and Plastic (51-4061.00)
➤ Patternmakers, Metal and Plastic (51-4062.00)
➤ Foundry Mold and Coremakers (51-4071.00)
➤ Molding, Coremaking, and Casting Machine Setters, Operators, and Tenders, Metal and Plastic (51-4072.00)
➤ Multiple Machine Tool Setters, Operators, and Tenders, Metal and Plastic (51-4081.00)
➤ Welding, Soldering, and Brazing Machine Setters, Operators, and Tenders (51-4122.00)
➤ Heat Treating Equipment Setters, Operators, and Tenders, Metal and Plastic (51-4191.00)
➤ Plating and Coating Machine Setters, Operators, and Tenders, Metal and Plastic (51-4193.00)

Contacts for More Information

For more information about metal and plastic machine workers, including training and certification, visit
➤ Fabricators & Manufacturers Association, International (FMA) (www.fmanet.org/)
➤ National Institute for Metalworking Skills (NIMS) (www.nims-skills.org/)

For general information about manufacturing careers, machinery, and equipment, visit
➤ Association for Manufacturing Technology (AMT) (www.amtonline.org/)
➤ National Tooling and Machining Association (NTMA) (www.ntma.org/)
➤ Precision Machined Products Association (PMPA) (www.pmpa.org/)
➤ Precision Metalforming Association (PMA) (www.pma.org/home/)

Painting and Coating Workers

- **2012 Median Pay** .... $32,850 per year
  $15.79 per hour
- **Entry-Level Education** ....See "How to Become One"
- **Work Experience in a Related Occupation** .... None
- **On-the-Job Training** .... Moderate-term on-the-job training
- **Number of Jobs 2012** 149,700
- **Job Outlook, 2012–22** .... 4% (Slower than average)
- **Employment Change, 2012–22** 5,500

What Painting and Coating Workers Do

Painting and coating workers paint and coat a wide range of products, including cars, jewelry, and ceramics.

Duties. Painting and coating workers typically do the following:
- Set up and operate machines that paint or coat products
- Select the paint or coating needed for the job
- Clean and prepare products to be painted or coated
- Determine the required flow of paint and the quality of the coating
- Clean and maintain tools, equipment, and work area

Millions of items ranging from cars to furniture are covered by paint, plastic, varnish, or other types of coating. Painting or coating is used to make a product more attractive or protect it from the elements. The paint finish on an automobile, for example, makes the vehicle more attractive and provides protection from corrosion.

Before workers begin to apply the paint or other coating, they often need to prepare the surface by sanding or cleaning it carefully to prevent dust from becoming trapped under the paint. Sometimes, masking is required, which involves carefully covering portions of the product with tape and paper.

After the product is prepared, workers may use a number of techniques to apply the paint or coating. The most straightforward technique is dipping an item in a large vat of paint or some other coating. Spraying products with a solution of paint or another coating is also common. Many factories use automated painting systems.

The following are examples of types of painting and coating workers:

Dippers use power hoists to immerse products in vats of paint, liquid plastic, or other solutions. This technique is commonly used for small parts in electronic equipment, such as cell phones.

Spray machine operators use spray guns to coat metal, wood, ceramic, fabric, and paper products with paint and other coating solutions.

Coating, painting, and spraying machine setters, operators, and tenders position the spray guns, set the nozzles, and synchronize the action of the guns with the speed of the conveyor carrying products through the machine and through drying ovens. During the process, these workers tend the equipment, watch gauges on the control panel, and check products to ensure that they are being painted evenly. The operator may use a manual spray gun to touch up flaws.

Painting, coating, and decorating workers paint, coat, or decorate products such as furniture, glass, pottery, toys, and books. Paper is often coated to give it its gloss. Silver, tin, and copper solutions are frequently sprayed on glass to make mirrors.

Transportation equipment painters are the best-known group of painting and coating workers. There are three major specialties:

• Transportation equipment workers who refinish old or damaged cars, trucks, and buses in automotive body repair and paint shops normally apply paint by hand with a controlled spray gun. Those who work in repair shops are among the most highly-skilled manual spray operators: they perform intricate, detailed work and mix paints to match the original color, a task that is

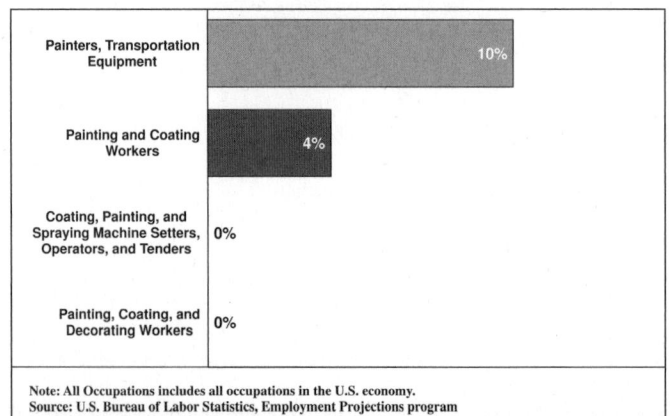

Automotive painters wear ventilators to ensure safety.

especially difficult if the color has faded. Preparing an old car is similar to painting other metal objects.

• Transportation equipment painters who work on new cars oversee several automated steps. A modern car is first dipped in an anticorrosion bath, coated with colored paint, and then painted in several coats of clear paint to prevent damage to the colored paint.

• Other transportation equipment painters either paint equipment too large to paint automatically–such as ships or giant construction equipment–or do touchup work to fix flaws in the paint caused by damage either during assembly or during the automated painting process.

Work Environment

Painting and coating workers held about 149,700 jobs in 2012. Employment in the detailed occupations that make up painting and coating worker was distributed as follows:

Coating, painting, and spraying machine setters,
   operators, and tenders...83,800

Median Annual Wages, May 2012

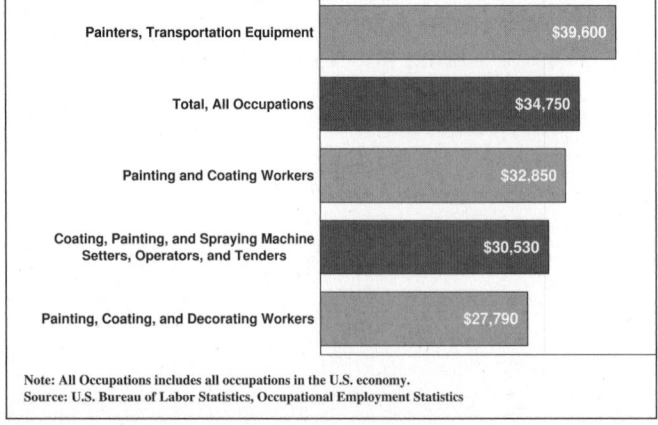

Painters, Transportation Equipment	$39,600
Total, All Occupations	$34,750
Painting and Coating Workers	$32,850
Coating, Painting, and Spraying Machine Setters, Operators, and Tenders	$30,530
Painting, Coating, and Decorating Workers	$27,790

Note: All Occupations includes all occupations in the U.S. economy.
Source: U.S. Bureau of Labor Statistics, Occupational Employment Statistics

Percent Change in Employment, Projected 2012–2022

Painters, Transportation Equipment	10%
Painting and Coating Workers	4%
Coating, Painting, and Spraying Machine Setters, Operators, and Tenders	0%
Painting, Coating, and Decorating Workers	0%

Note: All Occupations includes all occupations in the U.S. economy.
Source: U.S. Bureau of Labor Statistics, Employment Projections program

Employment Projections Data for Painting and Coating Workers

Occupational title	SOC Code	Employment, 2012	Projected Employment, 2022	Change, 2012–2022	
				Percent	Numeric
Painting and coating workers...	—	149,700	155,200	4	5,500
Coating, painting, and spraying machine setters,					
operators, and tenders...	51-9121	83,800	84,200	0	400
Painters, transportation equipment	51-9122	48,900	54,000	10	5,100
Painting, coating, and decorating workers........................	51-9123	17,000	17,000	0	0

Source: U.S. Bureau of Labor Statistics, Employment Projections Program

Note: Data are rounded. Go to Occupational Information Included in the OOH *for a discussion of the data in this table.*

Painters, transportation equipment......................................48,900
Painting, coating, and decorating workers............................17,000

Painting, coating, and decorating are usually done in special ventilated areas. Nonetheless, workers still must wear masks or respirators that cover their nose and mouth.

Coating workers often stand for long periods. When using a spray gun, they may have to bend, stoop, or crouch in uncomfortable positions to reach different parts of the products.

Injuries and Illnesses. Painting, coating, and decorating workers have a higher rate of injuries and illnesses than the national average. Common hazards include muscle strains and exposure to toxic materials. More sophisticated paint booths and fresh-air systems are increasingly being used to provide a safer work environment.

Work Schedules. Most painting and coating workers are employed full time. Automotive painters in repair shops often work overtime, depending on the number of vehicles that need repainting.

How to Become One

Most painting and coating workers learn on the job. Although training for most new workers usually lasts from a few days to several months, those who paint automobiles generally need 1 to 2 years of training.

Education. Painting and coating workers in the manufacturing sector usually must have a high school diploma or equivalent. Employers outside of manufacturing sometimes hire workers without a high school diploma.

High school courses in automotive painting are recommended.

Automobile repair painters often attend a technical or vocational school where they receive hands-on training and learn the intricacies of mixing and applying different types of paint.

Training. Most entry-level workers receive on-the-job training that may last from a few days to a few months.

Workers who modify the operation of computer-controlled equipment may require additional training in computer operations and programming.

Transportation equipment painters typically learn to paint on the job.

Licenses, Certifications, and Registrations. Voluntary certification by the National Institute for Automotive Service Excellence (ASE) is recognized as the standard of achievement for automotive painters. To obtain certification, painters must pass a written exam and have at least 2 years of experience in the field. Recertification is required every 5 years. Few painting and coating workers other than automobile painters obtain certification.

ASE-approved training in automotive refinishing taken while in high school, a trade or vocational school, or community college may substitute for up to 1 year of work experience. To keep the certification, painters must retake the exam at least every 5 years.

Important Qualities

Artistic ability. Some workers make elaborate or decorative designs. For example, some automotive painters specialize in making custom designs for vehicles.

Color vision. Workers must be able to blend new paint colors properly in order to match existing colors on a surface.

Mechanical skills. Because workers must operate and maintain sprayers that apply paints and coatings, they should have good mechanical skills.

Pay

The median annual wage for painting and coating workers was $32,850 in May 2012. The median wage is the wage at which half the workers in an occupation earned more than that amount and half earned less. The lowest 10 percent earned less than $20,870, and the top 10 percent earned more than $54,600.

In May 2012, median annual wages for painting and coating occupations were as follows:

Transportation equipment painters.....................................$39,600
Coating, painting, and spraying machine setters,
operators, and tenders..30,530
Painting, coating, and decorating workers...........................27,790

Many automotive painters who work for motor vehicle dealers and independent automotive repair shops get a commission. Employers frequently guarantee commissioned painters a minimum weekly salary.

Similar Occupations   This table shows a list of occupations with job duties that are similar to those of painting and coating workers.

Occupations	Entry-level Education	2012 Pay	Projected Job Growth	Average Annual Openings
Automotive Body and Glass Repairers	High school diploma or equivalent	$37,817	13%	5,700
Metal and Plastic Machine Workers	High school diploma or equivalent	$33,064	-6%	22,070
Painters, Construction and Maintenance	Less than high school	$35,190	20%	11,050

Helpers and trainees usually get an hourly rate until they become skilled enough to work on commission.

Trucking companies, bus lines, and other organizations that repair and refinish their own vehicles generally pay by the hour.

Job Outlook

Overall employment of painting and coating workers is projected to grow 4 percent from 2012 to 2022, slower than the average for all occupations. Employment growth will vary by specialty and industry.

Employment of coating, painting, and spraying machine setters, operators, and tenders is projected to show little or no change from 2012 to 2022. Despite little or no employment growth, the many consumer, commercial, and industrial products that require painting or coating will provide opportunities for these workers. However, productivity gains are expected to offset any employment growth.

Employment of transportation equipment painters is projected to grow 10 percent from 2012 to 2022, about as fast as the average for all occupations. The vast majority of all new jobs will be driven by the need for painters in auto repair shops.

Employment of painting, coating, and decorating workers is projected to show little or no change from 2012 to 2022. Increased automation in most manufacturing facilities will reduce the need for these workers.

Job Prospects. As with many skilled manufacturing jobs, employers often report difficulty finding qualified workers. Therefore, job opportunities should be very good for those with painting experience.

Many job openings should result from the need to replace workers who leave the occupation and from increased specialization in manufacturing. Although higher education requirements would normally reduce competition for automotive painters in repair shops, the large number of people who enjoy working on cars should offset that reduction.

O*NET

➤ Coating, Painting, and Spraying Machine Setters, Operators, and Tenders (51-9121.00)
➤ Painters, Transportation Equipment (51-9122.00)
➤ Painting, Coating, and Decorating Workers (51-9123.00)

Contacts for More Information

For more information about job opportunities for painting and coating workers, visit
➤ Local manufacturers
➤ Automotive body repair shops
➤ Motor vehicle dealers
➤ Vocational schools
➤ Local unions representing painting and coating workers
➤ Local offices of state employment services
For a directory of certified automotive painting programs, visit
➤ National Automotive Technician Education Foundation (www. natef.org/)
➤ National Institute for Automotive Service Excellence (www.ase.com)

Power Plant Operators, Distributors, and Dispatchers

- **2012 Median Pay** .... $68,230 per year
  $32.80 per hour
- **Entry-Level Education** ... High school diploma or equivalent
- **Work Experience in a Related Occupation**............... None
- **On-the-Job Training** .... Long-term on-the-job training
- **Number of Jobs 2012** 60,700
- **Job Outlook, 2012–22** .... -8% (Decline)
- **Employment Change, 2012–22** .... -4,600

What Power Plant Operators, Distributors, and Dispatchers Do

Power plant operators, dispatchers, and distributors control the systems that generate and distribute electric power.

Duties. Power plant operators, distributors, and dispatchers typically do the following:

- Control power-generating equipment which may use any one type of fuel, such as coal, nuclear fuel, or natural gas
- Read charts, meters, and gauges to monitor voltage and electricity flows
- Check equipment and indicators to detect evidence of operating problems
- Adjust controls to regulate the flow of power
- Start or stop generators, turbines, and other equipment as necessary

Electricity is one of our nation's most vital resources. Power plant operators, distributors, and dispatchers control power plants and the flow of electricity from plants to substations, which distribute electricity to businesses, homes, and factories. Electricity is generated from many sources, including coal, gas, nuclear energy, hydroelectric energy (from water sources), and wind and solar power.

Nuclear power reactor operators control nuclear reactors. They adjust control rods, which affect how much electricity a reactor generates. They monitor reactors, turbines, generators, and cooling

Power plant operators use computers to report unusual incidents, malfunctioning equipment, or maintenance performed during their shifts.

Median Annual Wages, May 2012

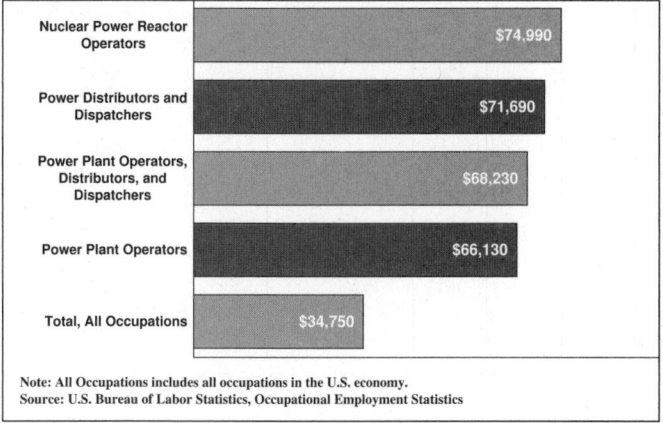

Note: All Occupations includes all occupations in the U.S. economy.
Source: U.S. Bureau of Labor Statistics, Occupational Employment Statistics

Percent Change in Employment, Projected 2012–2022

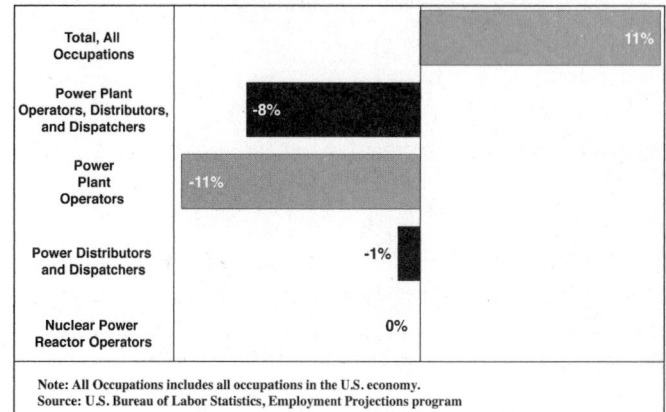

Note: All Occupations includes all occupations in the U.S. economy.
Source: U.S. Bureau of Labor Statistics, Employment Projections program

systems, adjusting controls as necessary. Operators also start and stop equipment and record the data. They may need to respond to abnormalities, determine the cause, and take corrective action.

Power distributors and dispatchers, also known as *systems operators*, control the flow of electricity as it travels from generating stations to substations and users by monitoring and operating current converters, voltage transformers, and circuit breakers over a network of transmission and distribution lines. They prepare and issue switching orders to route electrical currents around areas that need maintenance or repair. They must detect and respond to emergencies, such as transformer or transmission line failures which can cause cascading power outages over the network of transmission and distribution lines they control.

Power plant operators control, operate, and maintain machinery to generate electricity. They use control boards to distribute power among generators and regulate the output from several generators. They monitor instruments to maintain voltage and electricity flows from the plant to meet consumer demand for electricity, which fluctuates throughout the day.

Work Environment

Power plant operators, distributors, and dispatchers held about 60,700 jobs in 2012. About 69 percent were power plant operators, 19 percent were power distributors and dispatchers, and 12 percent were nuclear power reactor operators.

About 70 percent of power plant operators, distributors, and dispatchers worked in the electric power generation, transmission, and distribution industry in 2012. State and local governments employed 13 percent of power plant operators, distributors, and dispatchers.

Operators, distributors, and dispatchers who work in control rooms generally sit or stand at a control station. The work is not physically strenuous, but it does require constant attention. Workers also may do rounds, checking equipment and doing other work

outside the control room. Transmission stations and substations where distributors and dispatchers work are typically in separate locations from the generating station where power plant operators work.

Because power transmission is both vitally important and sensitive to attack, security is a major concern for utility companies. Nuclear power plants and transmission stations have especially high security, and employees work in secure environments.

Work Schedules. Because electricity is provided around the clock, operators, distributors, and dispatchers usually work rotating 8- or 12-hour shifts. As a result, all operators share the less desirable shifts. Work on rotating shifts can be stressful and tiring because of the constant changes in living and sleeping patterns.

How to Become One

Power plant operators, dispatchers, and distributors need extensive on-the-job training which may include a combination of classroom and hands-on training. Nuclear power reactor operators also need a license. Many jobs require a background check, and workers are subject to drug and alcohol screenings.

Many companies require potential workers to take the Power Plant Maintenance (MASS) and Plant Operator (POSS) exams from the Edison Electrical Institute to see if they have the right aptitudes for this work. These tests measure reading comprehension, understanding of mechanical concepts, spatial ability, and mathematical ability.

Education. Power plant operators, distributors, and dispatchers need at least a high school diploma. However, employers may prefer workers with college or vocational school degrees.

Employers generally look for people with strong math and science backgrounds for these highly technical jobs. Understanding electricity and math, especially algebra and trigonometry, is important.

Employment Projections Data for Power Plant Operators, Distributors, and Dispatchers

Occupational title	SOC Code	Employment, 2012	Projected Employment, 2022	Change, 2012–2022	
				Percent	Numeric
Power plant operators, distributors, and dispatchers..............	—	60,700	56,000	-8	-4,600
Nuclear power reactor operators.......................................	51-8011	7,200	7,200	0	0
Power distributors and dispatchers....................................	51-8012	11,700	11,600	-1	-100
Power plant operators...	51-8013	41,800	37,200	-11	-4,500

Source: U.S. Bureau of Labor Statistics, Employment Projections Program

Note: Data are rounded. Go to **Occupational Information Included in the OOH** for a discussion of the data in this table.

Similar Occupations   This table shows a list of occupations with job duties that are similar to those of power plant operators, distributors, and dispatchers.

Occupations	Entry-level Education	2012 Pay	Projected Job Growth	Average Annual Openings
Construction Equipment Operators	High school diploma or equivalent	$41,099	19%	16,480
Electrical and Electronics Installers and Repairers	Postsecondary non-degree award	$51,081	1%	2,980
Electricians	High school diploma or equivalent	$49,840	20%	22,460
Line Installers and Repairers	High school diploma or equivalent	$56,833	7%	9,110
Stationary Engineers and Boiler Operators	High school diploma or equivalent	$53,560	3%	1,270
Water and Wastewater Treatment Plant and System Operators	High school diploma or equivalent	$42,760	8%	4,750

Training. Power plant operators and dispatchers undergo rigorous, long-term on-the-job training and technical instruction. Several years of onsite training and experience are necessary to become fully qualified. Even fully qualified operators and dispatchers must take regular training courses to keep their skills up to date.

Nuclear power reactor operators usually start working as equipment operators or auxiliary operators, helping more experienced workers operate and maintain the equipment while learning the basics of how to operate the power plant.

Along with this extensive on-the-job training, nuclear power plant operators typically receive formal technical training to prepare for the license exam from the U.S. Nuclear Regulatory Commission (NRC). Once licensed, operators are authorized to control equipment that affects the power of the reactor in a nuclear power plant. Operators continue frequent onsite training which familiarizes them with new monitoring systems that provide operators better real time information on situations regarding the plant.

Licenses, Certifications, and Registrations. Nuclear power reactor operators must be licensed through the NRC. To become licensed, operators must meet training and experience requirements, pass a medical exam, and pass the NRC licensing exam. To keep their license, operators must pass a plant-operating exam each year, pass a medical exam every 2 years, and apply for license renewal every 6 years. Licenses cannot be transferred between plants, so an operator must get a new license to operate in another facility.

Power plant operators who do not work at a nuclear power reactor may be licensed as engineers or fire fighters by state licensing boards. Requirements vary by state and depend on the specific job functions that the operator performs.

Power distributors and dispatchers who are in positions in which they could affect the power grid must be certified through the North American Electric Reliability Corporation's (NERC) System Operator Certification Program. NERC offers four types of certification, and each qualifies a worker to handle a different job function. A dispatcher's certification is valid for 3 years, and a worker must fulfill continuing education requirements to renew the credential.

Other Experience. Previous related work experience can be helpful. Many employers prefer experience in electricity generation, transmission, and distribution, or in other occupations in the utilities industry, such as line worker or helper, or laborer in a power plant.

Some nuclear power reactor operators gain experience working with nuclear reactors in the U.S. Navy.

Advancement. After finishing work in the classroom, most entry-level workers start as helpers or laborers and advance to more responsible positions as they become comfortable in the plant. Workers are generally classified into levels on the basis of their experience. For each level, there are training requirements, mandatory waiting times, and exams. With sufficient training and experience, workers can become shift supervisors, trainers, or consultants.

Nuclear power plant operators begin working in nuclear power plants, typically as non-licensed operators. After in-plant training and passing the NRC licensing exam, they become licensed reactor operators. Licensed operators can advance to senior reactor operators, who supervise the operation of all controls in the control room. Senior reactor operators may also become plant managers or licensed operator instructors.

Important Qualities

Concentration skills. Power plant operators, distributors, and dispatchers must be careful, attentive, and persistent. They must be able to concentrate on a task, such as monitoring the temperature of reactors over a period of time without being distracted.

Detail oriented. Power plant operators, distributors, and dispatchers must monitor complex controls and intricate machinery to ensure that everything is operating properly.

Dexterity. Power plant operators, distributors, and dispatchers must use precise and repeated motions when working in a control room.

Mechanical skills. Power plant operators, distributors, and dispatchers must know how to work with machines and use tools. They must be familiar with how to operate, repair, and maintain equipment.

Problem-solving skills. Power plant operators, distributors, and dispatchers must find and quickly solve problems that arise with equipment or controls.

Pay

The median annual wage for power plant operators, distributors, and dispatchers was $68,230 in May 2012. The median wage is the wage at which half the workers in an occupation earned more than that amount and half earned less. The lowest 10 percent earned less than $44,110, and the top 10 percent earned more than $92,570.

Median annual wages for power plant operators, distributors, and dispatchers in May 2012 were as follows:

Nuclear power reactor operators $74,990
Power distributors and dispatchers 71,690
Power plant operators 66,130

Because electricity is provided around the clock, operators, distributors, and dispatchers usually work rotating 8- or 12-hour shifts. As a result, all operators share the less desirable shifts. Work on rotating shifts can be stressful and tiring because of the constant changes in living and sleeping patterns.

Union Membership. Compared with workers in all occupations, power plant operators, distributors, and dispatchers had a higher percentage of workers who belonged to a union in 2012.

Job Outlook

Employment of power plant operators, distributors, and dispatchers is projected to decline 8 percent from 2012 to 2022. Although electricity usage is expected to grow, advances in technology and increased energy efficiency will contribute to decreases in employment for the occupation. Employment growth will vary by specialty.

Employment of power plant operators in nonnuclear power plants is projected to decline 11 percent from 2012 to 2022. Energy companies are increasingly promoting energy efficiency to cut costs and comply with environmental regulations. Consequently, the demand for electricity is expected to grow much more slowly than in the past, resulting in fewer new job opportunities for workers.

In addition, as old power plants close, they will be replaced with new plants that produce electricity more efficiently and, in many cases, have higher capacities. These new plants will have modernized control rooms which are more automated and provide workers with more information. As a result, fewer workers will be needed to produce the same amount of electricity in these new plants.

Employment of power distributors and dispatchers is projected to show little to no change from 2012 to 2022. Although some distributors and dispatchers will be needed to manage an increasingly complex electrical grid, employment growth will be tempered by advances in technology and smart grid projects that automate some of the work of dispatchers.

Employment of nuclear power reactor operators is projected to show little to no change from 2012 to 2022. Although no new plants have opened since the 1990s, new sites have applied for construction and operating licenses, and they will need to be staffed before the end of the next decade.

Job Prospects. Job prospects should be better for those with related training and good mechanical skills. Many people will seek these high-paying jobs, so job prospects will be best for those with strong technical and mechanical skills.

O*NET

➤ Nuclear Power Reactor Operators (51-8011.00)
➤ Power Distributors and Dispatchers (51-8012.00)
➤ Power Plant Operators (51-8013.00)

Contacts for More Information

For more information about power plant operators, nuclear power reactor operators, and power plant distributors and dispatchers, visit
➤ American Public Power Association (www.publicpower.org/)
➤ Center for Energy Workforce Development (www.cewd.org/)
➤ International Brotherhood of Electrical Workers (www.ibew.org/)

For more information on nuclear power reactor operators, including licensing, visit
➤ U.S. Nuclear Regulatory Commission (www.nrc.gov/)
➤ Nuclear Energy Institute (www.nei.org/)

For information on certification for power distributors and dispatchers, visit
➤ North American Electric Reliability Corporation (www.nerc.com/)

Printing Workers

- **2012 Median Pay** .... $34,100 per year
  $16.40 per hour
- **Entry-Level Education** .... See "How to Become One"
- **Work Experience in a Related Occupation**............... None
- **On-the-Job Training** ....See "How to Become One"
- **Number of Jobs 2012** 276,000
- **Job Outlook, 2012–22** .... -5% (Decline)
- **Employment Change, 2012–22** .... -14,500

What Printing Workers Do

Printing workers produce print material in three stages: prepress, press, and binding and finishing. They review specifications, calibrate color settings on printers, identify and fix problems with printing equipment, and assemble pages.

Duties. Printing workers typically do the following:

- Review job orders to determine quantities to be printed, paper specifications, colors, and special printing instructions
- Arrange pages so that materials can be printed
- Operate laser plate-making equipment that converts electronic data to plates
- Feed paper through press cylinders and adjust equipment controls
- Collect and inspect random samples during print runs to identify any needed adjustments
- Cut material to specified dimensions, fitting and gluing material to binder boards by hand or machine
- Compress sewed or glued sets of pages, which are called signatures, using hand presses or smashing machines
- Bind new books, using hand tools such as bone folders, knives, hammers, or brass binding tools

The printing process has three stages: prepress, press, and binding or finishing. In small print shops, the same person may take care of all three stages. However, in most print shops, workers

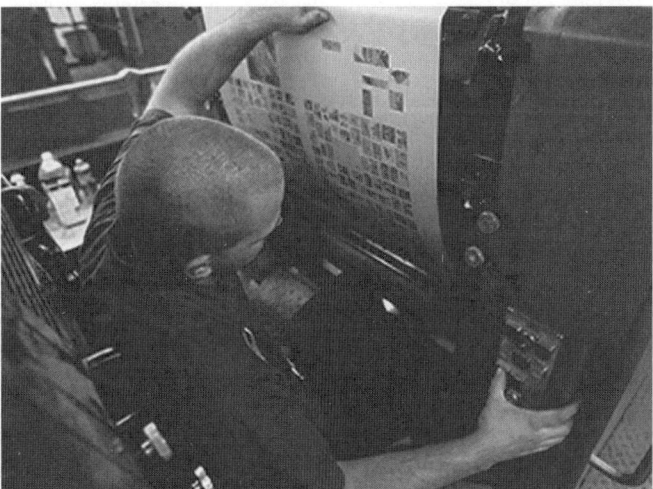

Prepress technicians and workers ensure that printing presses are set correctly and that images and colors are correct before the full job order is printed.

Median Annual Wages, May 2012

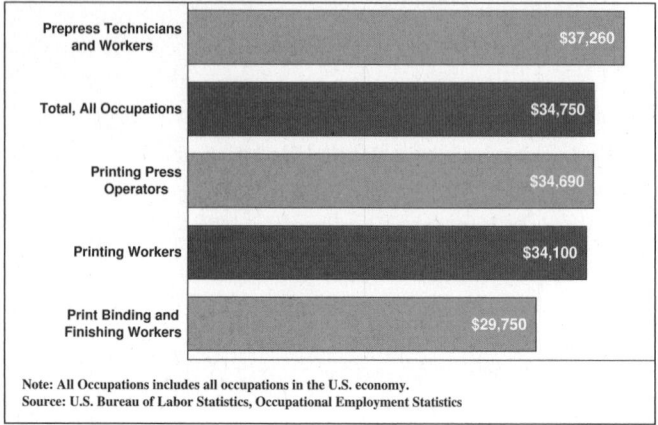

Note: All Occupations includes all occupations in the U.S. economy.
Source: U.S. Bureau of Labor Statistics, Occupational Employment Statistics

Percent Change in Employment, Projected 2012–2022

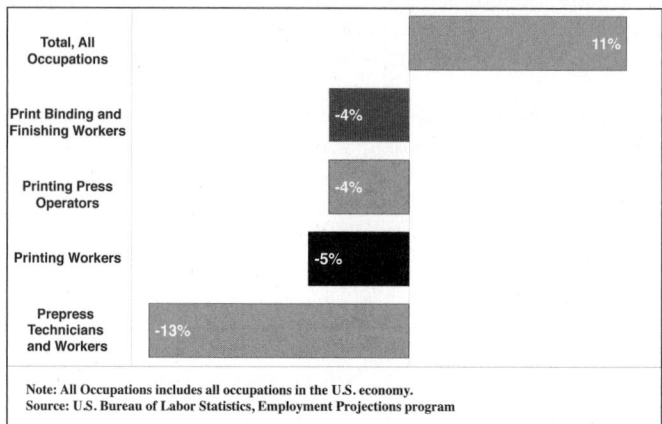

Note: All Occupations includes all occupations in the U.S. economy.
Source: U.S. Bureau of Labor Statistics, Employment Projections program

specialize in an occupation that focuses on one step in the printing process:

Prepress technicians and workers prepare print jobs. They do a variety of tasks to help turn text and pictures into finished pages and prepare the pages for print. Some prepress technicians, known as preflight technicians, take images from graphic designers or customers and check them for completeness. They review job specifications and designs from submitted sketches or clients' electronic files to ensure that everything is correct and all files and photos are included.

Some prepress workers use a photographic process also known as "cold-type" technology to make offset printing plates (sheets of metal that carry the final image to be printed). This is a complex process, involving ultraviolet light and chemical exposure, through which the text and images of a print job harden on a metal plate and become water repellent. These hard, water-repellent portions of the metal plate are in the form of the text and images that will be printed.

More recently, however, the printing industry has moved to technology known as direct-to-plate. Many prepress technicians now send the data directly to a plating system, bypassing the need for the photographic technique. The direct-to-plate technique is an example of how digital imaging technology has largely replaced cold-type print technology.

Printing press operators prepare, run, and maintain printing presses. Their duties vary according to the type of press they operate. Traditional printing methods, such as offset lithography, gravure, flexography, and letterpress, use a plate or roller that carries the final image that is to be printed and then copies the image to paper.

In addition to the traditional printing processes, plateless or nonimpact processes are becoming more common. Plateless processes–including digital, electrostatic, and ink-jet printing–are used for copying, duplicating, and document and specialty printing, usually in quick-printing shops and smaller printing shops.

Commercial printers are increasingly using digital presses with longer-run capabilities for short-run or customized printing jobs. Digital presses also allow printers to transfer files, blend colors, and proof images electronically, thus avoiding the costly and time-consuming steps of making printing plates that are common in offset printing.

Print binding and finishing workers combine printed sheets into a finished product, such as a book, magazine, or catalog. Their duties depend on what they are binding. Some types of binding and finishing jobs take only one step. Preparing leaflets or newspaper inserts, for example, requires only folding and trimming.

Binding books and magazines, however, takes several steps. Bindery workers first assemble the books and magazines from large, flat, printed sheets of paper. They then operate machines that fold printed sheets into signatures, which are groups of pages arranged sequentially. They assemble the signatures in the right order and join them by saddle stitching (stapling them through the middle of the binding) or perfect binding (using glue, not stitches or staples).

Some bookbinders repair rare books by sewing, stitching, or gluing the covers or the pages.

Work Environment

Printing workers held about 276,000 jobs in 2012. Prepress technicians usually work in quiet areas. Printing press operators and print binding and finishing workers work in noisy settings. Press operators' jobs may require considerable lifting, standing, and carrying. Binding often resembles an assembly line on which workers do tedious, repetitive tasks, such as folding and trimming leaflets or newspaper inserts.

The industries that employed the most printing workers in 2012 were as follows:

Printing and related support activities 61%
Newspaper, periodical, book, and directory publishers 9
Paper manufacturing 7
Administrative and support services 3
Advertising, public relations, and related services 3

Work Schedules. Most printing workers work full time. Weekend and holiday hours may be necessary to meet production schedules. For example, newspaper printing may need to take place at night.

How to Become One

Prepress technicians typically need an associate's degree or postsecondary non-degree award. Printing press operators and print binding and finishing workers need a high school diploma and on-the-job training.

Education. Most prepress technicians receive some formal postsecondary classroom instruction before entering the occupation. They typically get either a postsecondary non-degree award or an associate's degree from a technical school, junior college, or community college. Workers with experience in other printing techniques can take a few college-level graphic communications or prepress-related courses to upgrade their skills and qualify for prepress jobs.

For printing press operators and print binding and finishing workers, a high school diploma is sufficient to enter the occupa-

Employment Projections Data for Printing Workers

Occupational title	SOC Code	Employment, 2012	Projected Employment, 2022	Change, 2012–2022 Percent	Change, 2012–2022 Numeric
Printing workers...	—	276,000	261,500	-5	-14,500
Prepress technicians and workers........................	51-5111	42,700	37,200	-13	-5,500
Printing press operators...................................	51-5112	178,400	171,400	-4	-7,000
Print binding and finishing workers..................	51-5113	54,900	52,900	-4	-2,000

Source: U.S. Bureau of Labor Statistics, Employment Projections Program

Note: Data are rounded. Go to Occupational Information Included in the OOH *for a discussion of the data in this table.*

tion. Postsecondary coursework is offered through community colleges and vocational schools, although most workers learn the required skills through on-the-job training.

There are also bachelor's degree programs in graphic design aimed primarily at students who plan to move into management positions in printing or design.

Training. Beginning press operators load, unload, and clean presses. With time and training, they become fully qualified to operate a particular type of press. Operators can gain experience on more than one kind of printing press during the course of their career.

Experienced operators periodically get retraining to update their skills. For example, printing plants that change from sheet-fed offset presses to digital presses have to retrain the entire press crew because skill requirements for the two types of presses are different.

Most bookbinders and bindery workers learn through on-the-job training. Inexperienced workers may start out as helpers who do simple tasks, such as moving paper from cutting machines to folding machines, or catching stock as it comes off machines.

They learn basic binding skills, including the characteristics of paper and how to cut large sheets of paper into different sizes with the least amount of waste. Usually, it takes about 1 month to learn to operate simpler machines, but it can take up to 1 year to become completely familiar with more complex equipment, such as computerized binding machines.

As workers gain experience, they learn to operate more types of equipment. To keep pace with changing technology, retraining is increasingly important for bindery workers.

Important Qualities

Communication skills. Prepress workers in particular need good communication skills because they must confer with clients about the details of a printing order.

Computer skills. The printing process is computer-based, requiring printing workers to have basic computer skills. Most prepress technicians must be familiar with publishing software.

Detail oriented. Printing workers must pay attention to detail to identify and fix problems with print jobs.

Math skills. Printing workers use basic math when computing percentages, weights, and measures and when calculating the amount of ink and paper needed to do a job.

Mechanical skills. Printing press operators must be comfortable with printing equipment and be prepared to make adjustments if a printing error occurs. Mechanical aptitude is also important for print binding and finishing workers, who use automated binding machines.

Pay

The median annual wage for printing workers was $34,100 in May 2012. The median wage is the wage at which half the workers in an occupation earned more than that amount and half earned less. The lowest 10 percent earned less than $20,390, and the top 10 percent earned more than $53,990.

The median wages for printing occupations in May 2012 were as follows:

Prepress technicians and workers.. $37,260
Printing press operators... 34,690
Print binding and finishing workers..................................... 29,750

Job Outlook

Employment of printing workers is projected to decline 5 percent from 2012 to 2022. Newspapers and magazines have seen substantial declines in print volume in recent years, as these media have increasingly moved to digital formats. With a declining volume of printed material in these areas, demand for print workers has decreased.

This trend is expected to continue, and it is expected to result in further employment declines in the printing industry. Employment declines for printing workers should be moderated by other segments of the industry that will likely experience steady demand, including print logistics (labels, wrappers, and packaging) and print marketing (catalogs and direct mail).

Employment of prepress technicians and workers is projected to decline 13 percent from 2012 to 2022. Computer software now allows office workers to specify text typeface and style and to format pages. This development shifts traditional prepress func-

Similar Occupations This table shows a list of occupations with job duties that are similar to those of printing workers.

Occupations	Entry-level Education	2012 Pay	Projected Job Growth	Average Annual Openings
Desktop Publishers	Associate's degree	$37,040	-5%	300
Graphic Designers	Bachelor's degree	$44,150	7%	8,600
Metal and Plastic Machine Workers	High school diploma or equivalent	$33,064	-6%	22,070
Multimedia Artists and Animators	Bachelor's degree	$61,370	6%	2,060

tions away from printing plants and toward advertising and public relations agencies, graphic design firms, and large corporations. In addition, new technologies are increasing the amount of automation in printing companies, so that it takes fewer prepress workers to accomplish the same amount of work.

The employment of printing press operators is projected to decline 4 percent from 2012 to 2022, driven by trends in the printing industry. Their employment is not expected to decline as rapidly as that of prepress technicians, however, because printing press operators are less susceptible to automation.

Employment of print binding and finishing workers is projected to decline 4 percent from 2012 to 2022. The growth of electronic books should reduce demand for print books, which will limit employment of these workers. Demand for quick turnaround for commercial printing, however, will provide some employment opportunities.

O*NET

➤ Prepress Technicians and Workers (51-5111.00)
➤ Printing Press Operators (51-5112.00)
➤ Print Binding and Finishing Workers (51-5113.00)

Contacts for More Information

For more information about printing workers, visit
➤ Printing Industries of America (www.printing.org/)
➤ National Association for Printing Leadership (NAPL) (www.napl.org/)
➤ The Association for Suppliers of Printing, Publishing and Converting Technologies (NPES) (www.npes.org/)
  For more information on accredited print technologies courses, visit
➤ Graphic Arts Education and Research Foundation (GAERF) (www.gaerf.org/)

Quality Control Inspectors

* **2012 Median Pay** .... $34,460 per year
  $16.57 per hour
* **Entry-Level Education** ... High school diploma or equivalent
* **Work Experience in a Related Occupation** .... None
* **On-the-Job Training** .... Moderate-term on-the-job training
* **Number of Jobs 2012** 464,300
* **Job Outlook, 2012–22** .... 6% (Slower than average)
* **Employment Change, 2012–22** 25,700

What Quality Control Inspectors Do

Quality control inspectors examine products and materials for defects or deviations from specifications.

Duties. Quality control inspectors typically do the following:

* Read blueprints and specifications
* Monitor operations to ensure that they meet production standards
* Recommend adjustments to the assembly or production process
* Inspect, test, or measure materials or products being produced
* Measure products with rulers, calipers, gauges, or micrometers
* Accept or reject finished items
* Remove all products and materials that fail to meet specifications
* Discuss inspection results with those responsible for products

* Report inspection and test data

Quality control inspectors, for example, ensure that the food or medicine you take will not make you sick, that your car will run properly, and that your pants will not split the first time you wear them. These workers monitor quality standards for nearly all manufactured products, including foods, textiles, clothing, glassware, motor vehicles, electronic components, computers, and structural steel. Specific job duties vary across the wide range of industries in which these inspectors work.

Quality control workers rely on a number of tools to do their jobs. Although some still use hand-held measurement devices, such as calipers and alignment gauges, workers more commonly operate electronic inspection equipment, such as coordinate-measuring machines (CMMs). Inspectors testing electrical devices may use voltmeters, ammeters, and ohmmeters to test potential difference, current flow, and resistance, respectively.

Quality control workers record the results of their inspections through test reports. When they find defects, inspectors notify supervisors and help to analyze and correct production problems.

In some firms, the inspection process is completely automated, with advanced vision inspection systems installed at one or several points in the production process. Inspectors in these firms monitor the equipment, review output, and conduct random product checks.

The following are examples of types of quality control inspectors:

Inspectors mark, tag, or note problems. They may reject defective items outright, send them for repair, or fix minor problems themselves. If the product is acceptable, the inspector certifies it. Inspectors may further specialize:

* *Materials inspectors* check products by sight, sound, or feel to locate imperfections such as cuts, scratches, missing pieces, or crooked seams.
* *Mechanical inspectors* generally verify that parts fit, move correctly, and are properly lubricated. They may check the pressure of gases and the level of liquids, test the flow of electricity, and conduct test runs to ensure that machines run properly.

Samplers test or inspect a sample for malfunctions or defects during a batch or production run.

Sorters separate goods according to length, size, fabric type, or color.

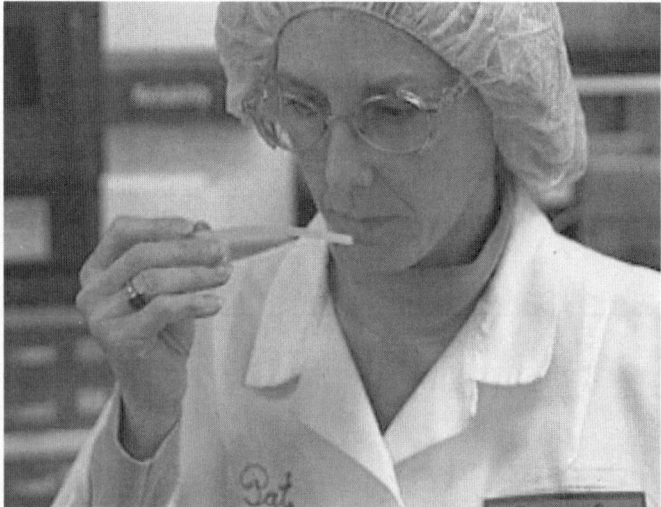

Quality control inspectors inspect, test, or measure materials or products being produced.

Median Hourly Wages, May 2012

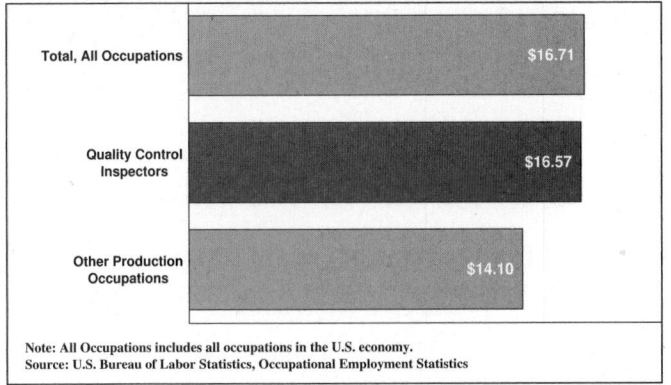

Note: All Occupations includes all occupations in the U.S. economy.
Source: U.S. Bureau of Labor Statistics, Occupational Employment Statistics

Percent Change in Employment, Projected 2012–2022

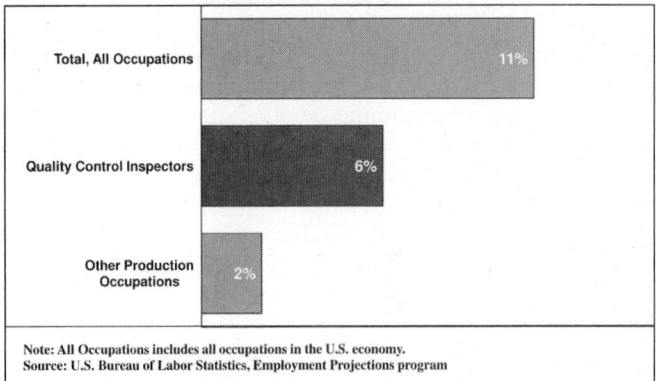

Note: All Occupations includes all occupations in the U.S. economy.
Source: U.S. Bureau of Labor Statistics, Employment Projections program

Testers repeatedly test existing products or prototypes under real-world conditions. Through these tests, manufacturers determine how long a product will last, what parts will break down first, and how to improve durability.

Weighers weigh quantities of materials for use in production.

Work Environment

Quality control inspectors held about 464,300 jobs in 2012. About two-thirds worked in manufacturing industries.

Work environments vary by industry and establishment size; some inspectors examine similar products for an entire shift, while others examine a variety of items.

In manufacturing, it is common for most inspectors to remain at a single workstation. Inspectors in some industries may be on their feet all day and may have to lift heavy items. In other industries, workers may sit during their shift and read electronic printouts of data.

Workers in heavy-manufacturing plants may be exposed to the noise and grime of machinery. In other plants, inspectors work in clean, air-conditioned environments suitable for testing products.

Injuries and Illnesses. Some quality control inspectors may be exposed to airborne particles, which may irritate the eyes and skin. As a result, workers typically wear protective eyewear, ear plugs, and appropriate clothing.

Work Schedules. Although most quality control inspectors work full time during regular business hours, some inspectors work evenings or weekends. Shift assignments generally are based on seniority. Overtime may be required to meet production deadlines.

How to Become One

Although a high school diploma is enough for the basic testing of products, complex precision-inspecting positions are typically filled by more experienced workers.

Education. Candidates for inspector jobs can improve their chances of finding work by studying industrial trades in high school or in a postsecondary vocational program. Laboratory work in the natural or biological sciences also may improve analytical skills and increase the chances of finding work in medical or pharmaceutical labs, where many of these workers are employed.

Training. Education and training requirements vary with the responsibilities of the quality control worker. However, workers usually receive on-the-job training that typically lasts as little as 1 month or up to 1 year.

For inspectors who do simple pass/fail tests of products, a high school diploma and some in-house training are generally enough.

Training for new inspectors may cover the use of special meters, gauges, computers, and other instruments; quality control techniques such as Six Sigma; blueprint reading; safety; and reporting requirements. Some postsecondary training programs exist, but many employers prefer to train inspectors on the job.

As manufacturers use more automated techniques that require less inspection by hand, workers in this occupation increasingly must know how to operate and program more sophisticated equipment and utilize software applications. Because these operations require additional skills, higher education may be necessary. To address this need, some colleges are offering associate's degrees in fields such as quality control management.

Employment Projections Data for Quality Control Inspectors

Occupational title	SOC Code	Employment, 2012	Projected Employment, 2022	Change, 2012–2022 Percent	Change, 2012–2022 Numeric
Inspectors, testers, sorters, samplers, and weighers 51-9061		464,300	490,000	6	25,700

Source: U.S. Bureau of Labor Statistics, Employment Projections Program

Note: Data are rounded. Go to **Occupational Information Included in the OOH** *for a discussion of the data in this table.*

Similar Occupations   This table shows a list of occupations with job duties that are similar to those of quality control inspectors.

Occupations	Entry-level Education	2012 Pay	Projected Job Growth	Average Annual Openings
Construction and Building Inspectors	High school diploma or equivalent	$53,450	12%	3,670
Fire Inspectors and Investigators	High school diploma or equivalent	$53,990	7%	440

Licenses, Certifications, and Registrations. The American Society for Quality (ASQ) offers various certifications, including a designation for Certified Quality Inspector (CQI), and numerous sources of information and various levels of certification for Lean Six Sigma. Certification can demonstrate competence and professionalism, making candidates more attractive to employers. It can also increase opportunities for advancement. Requirements for certification generally include a certain number of years of experience in the field and passing an exam.

Important Qualities

Dexterity. Quality control inspectors should be able to quickly remove sample parts or products during the manufacturing process.

Math skills. Knowledge of basic math and computer skills are important because measuring, calibrating, and calculating specifications are major parts of quality control testing.

Mechanical skills. Quality control inspectors must be able to use specialized tools and machinery when testing products.

Physical stamina. Quality control inspectors must be able to stand for long periods on the job.

Physical strength. Because workers sometimes lift heavy objects, inspectors should be in good physical condition.

Technical skills. Quality control inspectors must understand blueprints, technical documents, and manuals, ensuring that products and parts meet quality standards.

Pay

The median hourly wage for quality control inspectors was $16.57 in May 2012. The median wage is the wage at which half the workers in an occupation earned more than that amount and half earned less. The lowest 10 percent earned less than $9.84 per hour, and the top 10 percent earned more than $28.29 per hour.

Job Outlook

Employment of quality control inspectors is projected to grow 6 percent from 2012 to 2022, slower than the average for all occupations. Employment growth reflects the continuing need to have quality assurance testing in a variety of manufacturing industries, particularly in pharmaceuticals and medical equipment and supplies.

Despite technological advances in quality control in many industries, automation is not always a substitute for inspecting by hand. Automation will likely become more important for inspecting elements related to size, such as length, width, or thickness. But inspections will continue to be done by workers for products that require testing taste, smell, texture, appearance, complexity of fabric, or performance of the product.

Nonetheless, many manufacturers have invested in automated inspection equipment to improve quality and productivity. Continued improvements in technology allow manufacturers to automate inspection tasks, increasing workers productivity and reducing the demand for inspectors.

Manufacturers increasingly are integrating quality control into the production process. Many inspection duties are being reassigned from specialized inspectors to fabrication and assembly workers, who monitor quality at every stage of production. In addition, the growing use of statistical process control results in smarter inspections. Using this system, manufacturers survey the sources and incidence of defects so that they can focus their efforts on reducing the number of defective products. These factors are expected to result in less demand for quality control inspectors.

Job Prospects. Numerous jobs in the manufacturing industry are expected to arise over the coming decade as workers retire or leave the occupation for other reasons.

Those with advanced skills, such as improvement certifications for Lean and Six Sigma, and related work experience should qualify for many of these positions.

O*NET

➤ Inspectors, Testers, Sorters, Samplers, and Weighers (51-9061.00)

Contacts for More Information

For more information about quality control inspectors, including certification, visit

➤ American Society for Quality (ASQ) (http://asq.org/index.aspx)

For more information about quality control training, visit

➤ International Society of Automation (ISA) (www.isa.org/)
➤ Quality Assurance Association (QAA) (www.qualityassuranceassociation.org/)
➤ Society of Quality Assurance (SQA) (www.sqa.org/)

Semiconductor Processors

- **2012 Median Pay** .... $33,020 per year
  $15.88 per hour
- **Entry-Level Education** .... Associate's degree
- **Work Experience in a Related Occupation**.............. None
- **On-the-Job Training** .... Moderate-term on-the-job training
- **Number of Jobs 2012** 21,300
- **Job Outlook, 2012–22** ....-27% (Decline)
- **Employment Change, 2012–22** .... -5,800

What Semiconductor Processors Do

Semiconductor processors oversee the manufacturing of electronic semiconductors, which are commonly known as integrated circuits or microchips. These microchips are found in all electronic devices–including cell phones, cars, and laptops–and are an important part of modern life.

Duties. Semiconductor processors typically do the following:

- Look over work orders, instructions, and processing charts to determine a work schedule

Semiconductor processors troubleshoot problems in the production of microchips and make equipment adjustments and repairs.

Median Annual Wages, May 2012

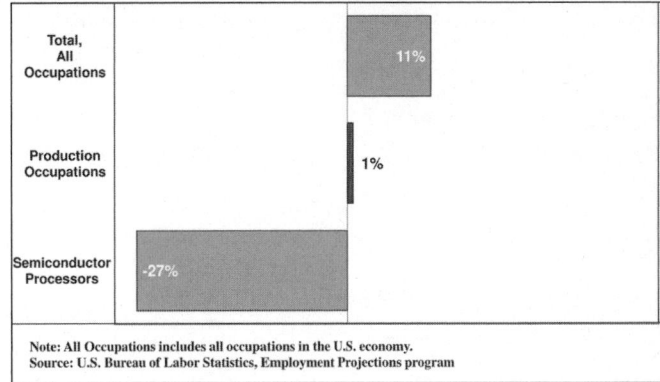

Note: All Occupations includes all occupations in the U.S. economy.
Source: U.S. Bureau of Labor Statistics, Occupational Employment Statistics

Percent Change in Employment, Projected 2012–2022

Note: All Occupations includes all occupations in the U.S. economy.
Source: U.S. Bureau of Labor Statistics, Employment Projections program

- Monitor machines that slice silicon crystals into wafers for processing
- Use robots to clean and polish the silicon wafers
- Load wafers into the equipment that creates patterns and forms the electronic circuitry
- Set and adjust controls to regulate the manufacturing equipment's power level, temperature, and other process parameters
- Adjust the process equipment and repair as needed during the manufacturing process
- Test completed microchips to ensure they work properly
- Review the manufacturing process and suggest improvements

Semiconductor processors, also known as process technicians, are largely responsible for quality control in the manufacturing process. They check equipment regularly for problems and test completed chips to make sure they work properly. If a problem with a chip does arise, they determine if it is due to contamination of that particular wafer or if it was caused by a flaw in the manufacturing process.

Work Environment

Semiconductor processors held about 21,300 jobs in 2012. About 90 percent worked in the semiconductor and other electronic component manufacturing industry.

Microchips must be kept completely clean and free of impurities because the microchips are so small that they can be damaged by a particle of dust. Therefore, semiconductor processors work in clean rooms that are filtered to have as little as one particle of dust in a cubic foot of air.

In addition, they wear special lightweight garments, called "bunny suits," over their clothes to keep lint or other particles from contaminating the clean room. Managers closely monitor workers going into and out of the clean room, and workers must put on a new bunny suit each time they go in.

The work pace in clean rooms is deliberately slow. Because the machinery sets the operators' rate of work, workers keep a relaxed pace. Limiting movement in the clean room is important to keep the air as dust-free as possible.

The temperature in the clean rooms is generally comfortable for workers. Although bunny suits cover almost the entire body, the lightweight fabric keeps the temperature inside fairly comfortable.

Work Schedules. Most employees work full time. Because semiconductor factories, also known as fabricating plants, run around the clock, night and weekend work is common for these workers. Although some plants schedule workers for the standard 40-hour week (8-hour shifts, 5 days a week), others schedule workers in 12-hour shifts.

How to Become One

Many employers prefer that semiconductor processors have an associate's degree in a field such as microelectronics.

Education. Many semiconductor processors have an associate's degree in a field such as microelectronics. These programs are usually offered at community colleges. Students should take science and engineering courses, such as chemistry, physics, and classes in electronic circuits.

There is an emerging trend of employers preferring semiconductor processors to have a bachelor's degree in engineering or a physical science because of the increasing complexity of the manufacturing plants.

Training. New semiconductor processors need on-the-job training from 1 month to 1 year. During this training, a processor learns how to operate equipment and test new chips. Manufacturing microchips is a complex process, and it takes months of supervised work to become fully proficient.

Workers with more education may have learned some techniques in school and need less on-the-job training. Because the technology used in manufacturing microchips is always evolving, processors must continue to be trained on new techniques and methods throughout their careers.

Employment Projections Data for Semiconductor Processors

Occupational title	SOC Code	Employment, 2012	Projected Employment, 2022	Change, 2012–2022	
				Percent	Numeric
Semiconductor processors..	51-9141	21,300	15,500	-27	-5,800

Source: U.S. Bureau of Labor Statistics, Employment Projections Program

Note: Data are rounded. Go to Occupational Information Included in the OOH for a discussion of the data in this table.

Similar Occupations This table shows a list of occupations with job duties that are similar to those of semiconductor processors.

Occupations	Entry-level Education	2012 Pay	Projected Job Growth	Average Annual Openings
Assemblers and Fabricators	High school diploma or equivalent	$28,661	4%	37,140
Chemical Engineers	Bachelor's degree	$94,350	5%	920
Computer Hardware Engineers	Bachelor's degree	$100,920	7%	2,410
Electrical and Electronics Engineering Technicians	Associate's degree	$57,850	0%	3,040
Electrical and Electronics Engineers	Bachelor's degree	$89,701	4%	7,940
Machinists and Tool and Die Makers	High school diploma or equivalent	$40,733	7%	13,060
Quality Control Inspectors	High school diploma or equivalent	$34,460	6%	12,770

Important Qualities

Communication skills. Semiconductor processors must clearly communicate their recommendations on how to improve the manufacturing process to engineers and other workers.

Computer skills. Much of the equipment that these workers use is programmable–that is, a computer language determines how the equipment operates. Semiconductor processors must modify the specifications in programs to adjust for a change in the manufacturing process, such as a change in robot sensing requirements.

Critical-thinking skills. Semiconductor processors use logic and reasoning to uncover problems and determine solutions during the manufacturing process.

Detail oriented. Because a minor error or impurity can ruin a chip, processors must be able to spot tiny imperfections.

Dexterity. Semiconductor processors must be able to use tools and operate equipment to make precise cuts and measurements.

Science skills. Processors must understand the chemical composition and properties of certain substances that they may use in manufacturing semiconductors. They need to know a lot about electronics and about the manufacturing process, which involves the application of ideas from chemistry and physics.

Pay

The median annual wage for semiconductor processors was $33,020 in May 2012. The median wage is the wage at which half the workers in an occupation earned more than that amount and half earned less. The lowest 10 percent earned less than $22,820, and the top 10 percent earned more than $48,340.

Processors employed in the semiconductor and other electronic component manufacturing industry earned $32,940 in May 2012.

Job Outlook

Employment of semiconductor processors is projected to decline 27 percent from 2012 to 2022. Although there is a strong demand for semiconductors in many products, automation at fabricating plants is expected to grow, meaning that plants will need fewer workers. Because during the manufacturing process semiconductors are highly sensitive to impurities, it is more effective to use robots to do many of the simple tasks that processors once did. In addition, the increasing complexity of chips, combined with their reduced size, makes it difficult for people to work on them.

The semiconductor manufacturing industry, where most processors work, is also expected to decline, leading to more job losses. Operating a plant in the United States is more expensive than operating one in another country where manufacturing costs are often lower. This leads to companies sending the manufacturing

of chips abroad, even though designing the chips will continue to take place in the United States.

Job Prospects. Competition for semiconductor processor jobs is expected to be tough because of the projected decline in employment. Prospects should be best for those who have a bachelor's degree or experience in other high-tech manufacturing jobs. Employment opportunities are not available in all states because semiconductor plants are expensive to construct, due to the high-tech manufacturing process that semiconductors must undergo. Employment opportunities for semiconductor processors are therefore concentrated in states where there are existing semiconductor plants.

O*NET

➤ Semiconductor Processors (51-9141.00)

Contacts for More Information

For more information about semiconductor processors, visit
➤ Maricopa Advanced Technology Education Center (www.matec.org/)
➤ SEMI (www.semi.org/)
➤ Semiconductor Industry Association (www.sia-online.org)

Slaughterers, Meat Packers, and Meat, Poultry, and Fish Cutters and Trimmers

- **2012 Median Pay** .... $23,320 per year
  $11.21 per hour
- **Entry-Level Education** .... Less than high school
- **Work Experience in a Related Occupation** .... None
- **On-the-Job Training** .... Short-term on-the-job training
- **Number of Jobs 2012** 244,100
- **Job Outlook, 2012–22** .... 3% (Slower than average)
- **Employment Change, 2012–22** 6,700

What Slaughterers, Meat Packers, and Meat, Poultry, and Fish Cutters and Trimmers Do

Slaughterers, meat packers, and meat, poultry, and fish cutters and trimmers kill, clean, or prepare animals for sale or further processing. They also cut, prepare, or package meats for wholesale or retail sale.

Meat trimmers and packers divide carcasses into saleable sections.

Duties. Slaughterers, meat packers, and meat, poultry, and fish cutters and trimmers typically do the following:

- Slaughter animals, cut meat into smaller portions, or package meat
- Use tools, such as stun guns, saws, or knives, to cut meat
- Clean, trim, and cut carcasses to prepare them for further processing
- Lift carcasses onto conveyors and inspect meat for defects
- Grind, chop, or cut meat into retail sizes and package it for shipping
- Sharpen knives or blades on cutting equipment
- Clean and sanitize workspaces and equipment according to industry health standards
- Weigh and label meat products or packages for processing or sale

Slaughterers, meat packers, and meat, poultry, and fish cutters and trimmers perform various tasks in animal slaughtering and meat processing. They typically work in either slaughtering yards or processing facilities. Workers may rotate through stations, doing different tasks.

Slaughterers may use stun guns or other federally approved means of slaughtering cattle, hogs, or sheep. They skin animals or wash carcasses with hot water to get the meat ready for further processing.

Workers also use power saws for cutting carcasses into manageable pieces of meat, known as boxed meat or case-ready meat, suitable for sale to wholesalers or retailers. Workers may be assigned to do routine cuts on meat as it moves along production lines.

Some workers prepare ready-to-eat, partially cooked, or display-ready packages of meat products for sale in retail stores. This preparation often involves filleting meat, poultry, or fish; cutting it into retail-size pieces; and adding vegetables, flavorings, or breading.

In processing plants, workers may produce hamburger meat, sausages, luncheon meats, or other fabricated meat products.

Fish cutters and trimmers remove inedible parts of the fish, cut the fish into steaks or fillets, and package fish.

Depending on the type of cut or task they are assigned on the production line, workers use knives for deboning, grinders for grinding meat, or handsaws to cut meat. They also may operate wrapping machines to package the meat.

The following are examples of types of slaughterers, meat packers, meat, poultry, and fish cutters and trimmers:

Poultry eviscerators clean birds so that the meat can be used for various products.

Fish filleters use sharp knives and precise cuts to separate fillets of fish from the bones.

Oyster shuckers and *shrimp pickers* separate the flesh of oysters and shrimp from the shells for packaging and wholesale or retail sale.

Some types of slaughterers follow religious specifications. For example, *halal and kosher slaughterers* follow strict guidelines during the slaughtering process in order to make sure that the product can qualify for religious specifications of what is permissible to eat.

Work Environment

In 2012, slaughterers and meat packers held about 80,700 jobs, and meat, poultry, and fish cutters and trimmers held about 163,400 jobs. Most workers were employed in animal slaughtering and processing facilities.

The working conditions in most processing facilities are physically demanding and often very difficult.

Workers are usually exposed to hot or cold temperatures. For example, the slaughtering rooms can be very hot and humid, as workers use steam or hot water–often at least 180 degrees Fahrenheit–for cleaning equipment used in slaughtering. Also, meat-packing areas are kept at lower temperatures–often below 40 degrees Fahrenheit for safe meat handling.

Meat, poultry, and fish cutters and trimmers in the meat-processing industry may work on an assembly line and do one specific

Median Annual Wages, May 2012

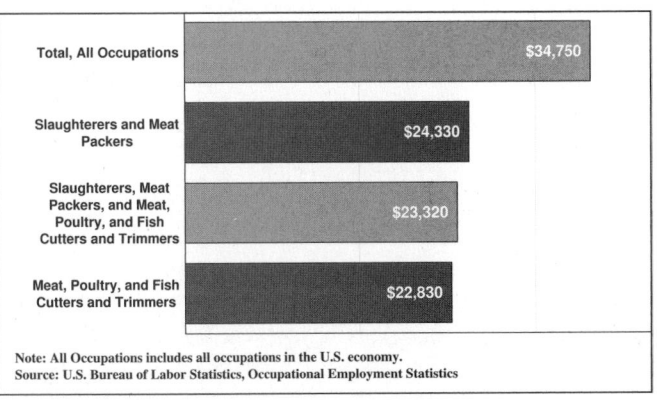

Total, All Occupations	$34,750
Slaughterers and Meat Packers	$24,330
Slaughterers, Meat Packers, and Meat, Poultry, and Fish Cutters and Trimmers	$23,320
Meat, Poultry, and Fish Cutters and Trimmers	$22,830

Note: All Occupations includes all occupations in the U.S. economy.
Source: U.S. Bureau of Labor Statistics, Occupational Employment Statistics

Percent Change in Employment, Projected 2012–2022

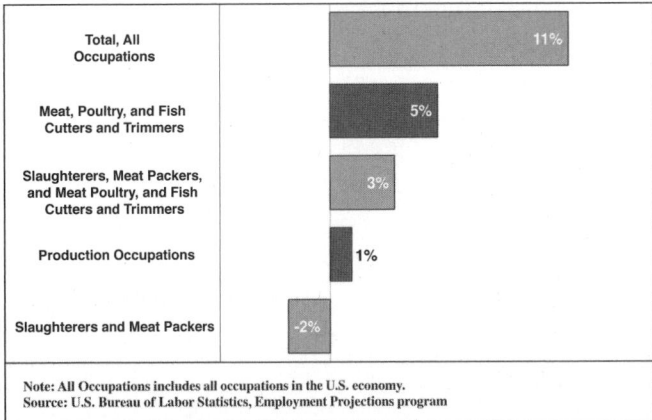

Total, All Occupations	11%
Meat, Poultry, and Fish Cutters and Trimmers	5%
Slaughterers, Meat Packers, and Meat Poultry, and Fish Cutters and Trimmers	3%
Production Occupations	1%
Slaughterers and Meat Packers	-2%

Note: All Occupations includes all occupations in the U.S. economy.
Source: U.S. Bureau of Labor Statistics, Employment Projections program

Employment Projections Data for Slaughterers, Meat Packers, and Meat, Poultry, and Fish Cutters and Trimmers

Occupational title	SOC Code	Employment, 2012	Projected Employment, 2022	Change, 2012–2022	
				Percent	Numeric
Slaughterers, meat packers, and meat, poultry, and fish cutters and trimmers..............................	—	244,100	250,800	3	6,700
Slaughterers and meat packers	51-3023	80,700	78,800	-2	-2,000
Meat, poultry, and fish cutters and trimmers.....................	51-3022	163,400	172,000	5	8,600

Source: *U.S. Bureau of Labor Statistics, Employment Projections Program*

Note: *Data are rounded. Go to* Occupational Information Included in the OOH *for a discussion of the data in this table.*

function–a single repetitive cut– during their shift. However, they often rotate between stations.

Slaughterers may work on mobile slaughtering trucks that travel to where the livestock are, such as on farms or ranches. There, they slaughter the animals on site.

Some fish processing is done aboard ships, where workers process, package, and flash freeze fish to preserve their freshness.

Injuries and Illnesses. Slaughterers, meat packers, and meat, poultry, and fish cutters and trimmers use dangerous equipment, such as saws and knives, and are commonly exposed to animal waste.

In addition, processing plant floors are often slippery, causing workers to fall. To reduce risks, workers must wear protective clothing, such as cut-resistant gloves, hardhats, face shields, and nonslip footwear.

Work Schedules. Most slaughterers, meat packers, and meat, poultry, and fish cutters and trimmers work full time. Shift work is common in processing facilities, with assignments based on seniority. Shifts may include early morning, late evening, or night hours.

How to Become One

Workers learn their skills through short-term on-the-job training. No formal education is required.

Education. There are no formal education requirements for someone to become a slaughterer, meat packer, or meat, poultry, and fish cutter and trimmer.

Training. Most slaughterers, meat packers, and meat, poultry, and fish cutters and trimmers learn their skills through short-term on-the-job training, which usually lasts a few weeks. Training typically includes basic sanitation and workplace safety regulations. Trainees usually start by working under the supervision of an experienced worker and learn basic duties such as knife skills. They also receive instructions on safe meat handling and on the use and maintenance of their equipment.

Advancement. Advancement opportunities for slaughterers, meat packers, and meat, poultry, and fish cutters and trimmers depend on their training and work experience. However, some workers

may advance to become butchers after they spend years working in meat processing, learning various cutting techniques.

Important Qualities

Concentration. Workers must pay close attention when using sharp knives or cutting equipment in order to avoid injuries.

Coordination. Good hand–eye coordination is important for workers as they must quickly cut or package meat in order to keep up with the conveyor line.

Detail oriented. Workers must be able to see and cut small portions of fat, bone, or cartilage according to specifications.

Dexterity. Workers need good manual dexterity, including proper knife techniques for trimming the inedible parts of meat and for filleting the meat.

Physical stamina. Workers stay on their feet for long periods doing repetitive cutting, stretching their arms to cut meat on a conveyor, or moving packages of meat.

Physical strength. Workers should be strong enough to lift or move heavy carcasses or boxes of packaged meat, which often can weigh up to 50 pounds.

Pay

The median annual wage for slaughterers and meat packers was $24,330 in May 2012. The median wage is the wage at which half the workers in an occupation earned more than that amount and half earned less. The lowest 10 percent earned less than $18,210, and the top 10 percent earned more than $32,670.

The median annual wage for meat, poultry, and fish cutters and trimmers was $22,830 in May 2012. The lowest 10 percent earned less than $17,380, and the top 10 percent earned more than $30,690.

Job Outlook

Overall employment of slaughterers, meat packers, and meat, poultry, and fish cutters and trimmers is projected to grow 3 percent from 2012 to 2022, slower than the average for all occupations. Employment growth will vary by specialty.

Similar Occupations This table shows a list of occupations with job duties that are similar to those of slaughterers, meat packers, and meat, poultry, and fish cutters and trimmers.

Occupations	Entry-level Education	2012 Pay	Projected Job Growth	Average Annual Openings
Bakers	Less than high school	$23,140	6%	5,010
Butchers and Meat Cutters	Less than high school	$28,490	5%	4,020
Chefs and Head Cooks	High school diploma or equivalent	$42,480	5%	2,470
Fishers and Related Fishing Workers	Less than high school	$33,430	-5%	630
Food and Tobacco Processing Workers	See "How to Become One"	$26,047	0%	6,190

Employment of slaughterers and meat packers is projected to show little or no change from 2012 to 2022. Slaughtering and processing companies continue to consolidate their facilities and streamline production processes, which will limit the need for slaughterers and meat packers.

Employment of meat, poultry, and fish cutters and trimmers is projected to grow 5 percent from 2012 to 2022, slower than the average for all occupations. As more people buy case-ready, prepared, or partially prepared meat products, there should be a need for these workers.

Although processing facilities increasingly are using automation to raise productivity and efficiency, workers will continue to be needed to perform some functions of slaughtering, skinning, or cutting that is otherwise difficult to automate.

Job Prospects. Despite slow employment growth, job opportunities for slaughterers, meat packers, and meat, poultry, and fish cutters and trimmers should be very good because of the need to replace the large number of workers who leave the occupation each year. Working conditions in most processing facilities are physically demanding and often very difficult and unpleasant, resulting in high job turnover.

As the animal slaughtering and processing industry continues to consolidate, most jobs are in areas where there are large processing facilities. The majority of large meat-packing plants are located in the Midwestern and High Plains regions of the country. The five states with the largest number of slaughterers and meat packers are Texas, North Carolina, Minnesota, Nebraska, and Iowa. Processing facilities often are located in rural areas or near smaller cities.

O*NET

➤ Meat, Poultry, and Fish Cutters and Trimmers (51-3022.00)
➤ Slaughterers and Meat Packers (51-3023.00)

Contacts for More Information

For training information regarding line workers and food safety, visit
➤ U.S. Department of Agriculture Food Safety and Inspection Service (www.fsis.usda.gov)

For information about the meat-processing industry and related trends, visit
➤ American Meat Institute (www.meatami.com)

Stationary Engineers and Boiler Operators

- **2012 Median Pay** .... $53,560 per year
  $25.75 per hour
- **Entry-Level Education** ... High school diploma or equivalent
- **Work Experience in a Related Occupation** .... None
- **On-the-Job Training** .... Long-term on-the-job training
- **Number of Jobs 2012** 37,900
- **Job Outlook, 2012–22** .... 3% (Slower than average)
- **Employment Change, 2012–22** 1,200

What Stationary Engineers and Boiler Operators Do

Stationary engineers and boiler operators control stationary engines, boilers, or other mechanical equipment to provide utilities for buildings or for industrial purposes.

Duties. Stationary engineers and boiler operators typically do the following:

- Operate engines, boilers, and auxiliary equipment
- Read gauges, meters, and charts to track boiler operations
- Monitor boiler water, chemical, and fuel levels
- Activate valves to change the amount of water, air, and fuel in boilers
- Fire coal furnaces or feed boilers, using gas feeds or oil pumps
- Inspect equipment to ensure that it is operating efficiently
- Check safety devices routinely
- Record data and keep logs of operation, maintenance, and safety activity

Most large office buildings, malls, warehouses, and other commercial facilities have extensive heating, ventilation, and air-conditioning systems that maintain comfortable temperatures all year long. Industrial plants often have additional facilities to provide electrical power, steam, or other services. Stationary engineers and boiler operators control and maintain these systems, which include boilers, air-conditioning and refrigeration equipment, turbines, generators, pumps, and compressors.

Stationary engineers and boiler operators start up, regulate, repair, and shut down equipment. They monitor meters, gauges, and computerized controls to ensure that equipment operates safely and within established limits. They use sophisticated electrical and electronic test equipment when servicing, troubleshooting, repairing, and monitoring heating, cooling, and ventilation systems.

Stationary engineers and boiler operators also regularly perform routine maintenance. They may do a complete overhaul or replace defective valves, gaskets, or bearings. In addition, stationary engineers and boiler operators lubricate moving parts, replace filters, and remove soot and corrosion that can make a boiler less efficient.

Work Environment

Stationary engineers and boiler operators held about 37,900 jobs in 2012.

They were employed in a variety of industries. Because most stationary engineers and boiler operators work in large commercial or industrial buildings, the majority of jobs were in manufacturing, government, educational services, and hospitals.

The industries employing the largest numbers of stationary engineers and boiler operators in 2012 were as follows:

Manufacturing	26%
Government	19
Hospitals; state, local, and private	16
Junior colleges, colleges, universities, and professional schools; state, local, and private	13
Electric power generation, transmission and distribution	5

In a large building or industrial plant, a senior stationary engineer or boiler operator may be in charge of all mechanical systems in the building and may supervise a team of assistant stationary engineers, assistant boiler tenders, and other operators or mechanics.

In small buildings, there may be only one stationary engineer or boiler operator who operates and maintains all of the systems.

Some stationary engineers and boiler operators are exposed to high temperatures, dust, dirt, and loud noise from the equipment. Maintenance duties also may require contact with oil, grease, and smoke.

Median Annual Wages, May 2012

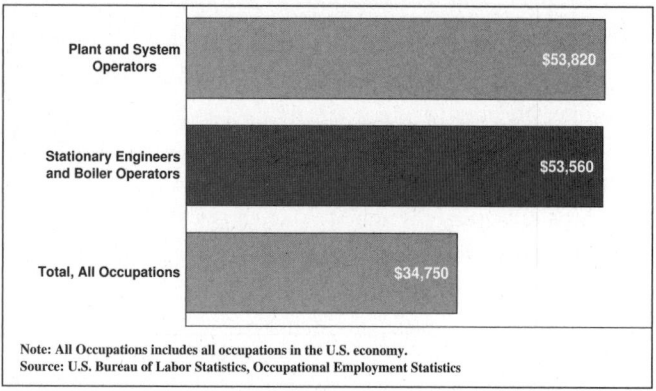

Note: All Occupations includes all occupations in the U.S. economy.
Source: U.S. Bureau of Labor Statistics, Occupational Employment Statistics

Percent Change in Employment, Projected 2012–2022

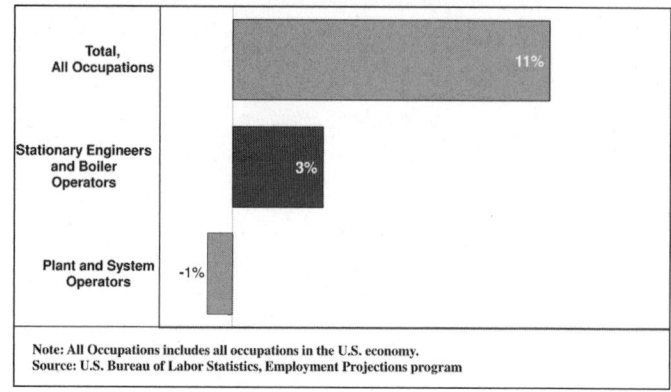

Note: All Occupations includes all occupations in the U.S. economy.
Source: U.S. Bureau of Labor Statistics, Employment Projections program

Workers spend much of their time on their feet. They also may have to crawl inside boilers and work while crouched, or kneel to inspect, clean, or repair equipment.

Injuries and Illnesses. Stationary engineers and boiler operators work around hazardous machinery. They must follow procedures to guard against burns, electric shock, noise, dangerous moving parts, and exposure to hazardous materials.

Work Schedules. Most stationary engineers and boiler operators work full time during regular business hours. In facilities that operate around the clock, engineers and operators usually work one of three 8-hour shifts on a rotating basis. Because buildings such as hospitals are open 365 days a year and depend on the steam generated by boilers and other machines, many must work weekends and holidays.

How to Become One

Stationary engineers and boiler operators need at least a high school diploma and are trained on the job by more experienced engineers. Many employers require stationary engineers and boiler operators to demonstrate competency through licenses or company-specific exams before they are able to operate equipment without supervision.

Education. Stationary engineers and boiler operators need at least a high school diploma. Students should take courses in math, science, and mechanical and technical subjects.

With the growing complexity of the work, vocational school or college courses may benefit workers trying to advance in the occupation.

Training. Stationary engineers and boiler operators typically learn their work through long-term on-the-job training under the supervision of an experienced engineer. Trainees are assigned basic tasks, such as monitoring the temperatures and pressure in the heating and cooling systems and low-pressure boilers. After they demonstrate competence in basic tasks, trainees move on to more complicated tasks, such as the repair of cracks or ruptured tubes for high-pressure boilers.

Some stationary engineers and boiler operators complete apprenticeship programs sponsored by the International Union of Operating Engineers. Apprenticeships usually last 4 years, include 8,000 hours of on-the-job training, and require 600 hours of technical instruction. Apprentices learn about the operation and maintenance of equipment; controls and balancing of heating, ventilation, and air conditioning (HVAC) systems; safety; electricity; and air quality. Employers may prefer to hire these workers because they usually require significantly less on-the-job training. However, because of the limited number of apprenticeship pro-

grams, employers often have difficulty finding workers who have completed an apprenticeship program.

Experienced stationary engineers and boiler operators update their skills regularly through training, especially when new equipment is introduced or when regulations change.

Licenses, Certifications, and Registrations. Some state and local governments require licensure for stationary engineers and boiler operators. These governments typically have several classes of stationary engineer and boiler operator licenses. Each class specifies the type and size of equipment the engineer is permitted to operate without supervision. Many employers require stationary engineers and boiler operators to demonstrate competency through licenses or company-specific exams before they are able to operate the equipment without supervision.

A top-level engineer or operator is qualified to run a large facility, supervise others, and operate equipment of all types and capacities. Engineers and operators with licenses below this level are limited in the types or capacities of equipment they may operate without supervision.

Applicants for licensure usually must be at least 18 years of age, meet experience requirements, and pass a written exam. In some cases, employers may require that workers be licensed before starting the job. A stationary engineer or boiler operator who moves from one state or city to another may have to pass an examination for a new license because of regional differences in licensing requirements.

Advancement. Generally, stationary engineers and boiler operators can advance as they become qualified to operate larger, more

Stationary engineers and boiler operators control and maintain equipment that is used to generate heat or electricity.

Employment Projections Data for Stationary Engineers and Boiler Operators

Occupational title	SOC Code	Employment, 2012	Projected Employment, 2022	Change, 2012–2022	
				Percent	Numeric
Stationary engineers and boiler operators	51-8021	37,900	39,000	3	1,200

Source: U.S. Bureau of Labor Statistics, Employment Projections Program

Note: Data are rounded. Go to Occupational Information Included in the OOH *for a discussion of the data in this table.*

Similar Occupations   This table shows a list of occupations with job duties that are similar to those of stationary engineers and boiler operators.

Occupations	Entry-level Education	2012 Pay	Projected Job Growth	Average Annual Openings
Boilermakers	High school diploma or equivalent	$56,560	4%	880
General Maintenance and Repair Workers	High school diploma or equivalent	$35,210	9%	37,970
Heating, Air Conditioning, and Refrigeration Mechanics and Installers	Postsecondary non-degree award	$43,640	21%	12,370
Industrial Machinery Mechanics and Maintenance Workers and Millwrights	High school diploma or equivalent	$45,848	17%	18,700
Power Plant Operators, Distributors, and Dispatchers	High school diploma or equivalent	$68,256	-8%	1,880
Water and Wastewater Treatment Plant and System Operators	High school diploma or equivalent	$42,760	8%	4,750

powerful, and more varied equipment by obtaining higher-class licenses. In jurisdictions where licenses are not required, workers usually advance by taking company-administered exams, which ensures a level of knowledge needed to safely operate different types of boilers among stationary engineers and boiler operators.

Important Qualities

Detail oriented. Stationary engineers and boiler operators monitor intricate machinery, gauges, and meters to ensure that everything is operating properly.

Dexterity. Stationary engineers and boiler operators must use precise motions to control or repair machines. They grasp tools and use their hands to perform many tasks.

Mechanical skills. Stationary engineers and boiler operators must know how to use tools and work with machines. They must be able to repair, maintain, and operate equipment.

Problem-solving skills. Stationary engineers and boiler operators must figure out how things work and quickly solve problems that arise with equipment or controls.

Pay

The median annual wage for stationary engineers and boiler operators was $53,560 in May 2012. The median wage is the wage at which half the workers in an occupation earned more than that amount and half earned less. The lowest 10 percent earned less than $33,600, and the top 10 percent earned more than $78,050.

Union Membership. Compared with workers in all occupations, stationary engineers and boiler operators had a higher percentage of workers who belonged to a union in 2012.

Job Outlook

Employment of stationary engineers and boiler operators is projected to grow 3 percent from 2012 to 2022, slower than the average for all occupations. Employment in the manufacturing industry is projected to experience a slight decline over the projection period contributing to the slower than the average growth for stationary engineers.

Although employment is spread across many industries, it is concentrated in those that require large commercial and industrial buildings. As a result, most employment gains will come from growth in these industries.

Faster employment growth is expected in educational services and in healthcare facilities as more buildings are built to accommodate a growing population in need of these services. Stationary engineers and boiler operators are especially important in buildings that operate around the clock and need precise temperature control, such as hospitals.

Job Prospects. Job opportunities should be best for those with apprenticeship training. Although apprenticeship programs have a competitive application process, they are the most reliable path into the occupation. In addition, workers who are licensed before they seek employment will have better job opportunities.

O*NET

➤ Stationary Engineers and Boiler Operators (51-8021.00)

Contacts for More Information

For information about apprenticeships, vocational training, and job opportunities, visit

➤ State employment service offices
➤ Local chapters of the International Union of Operating Engineers (www.iuoe.org/)
➤ Vocational schools
➤ State and local licensing agencies

Information about apprenticeships is also available from the U.S. Department of Labor's toll-free help line: (877) 872-5627 or the Employment and Training Administration (www.doleta.gov/OA/eta_default.cfm).

For more information about training or becoming a stationary engineer or boiler operator, visit

➤ National Association of Power Engineers (www.powerengineers.com/)

Water and Wastewater Treatment Plant and System Operators

- **2012 Median Pay** .... $42,760 per year
  $20.56 per hour
- **Entry-Level Education** ... High school diploma or equivalent
- **Work Experience in a Related Occupation** .... None
- **On-the-Job Training** .... Long-term on-the-job training
- **Number of Jobs 2012** 111,000
- **Job Outlook, 2012–22** .... 8% (As fast as average)
- **Employment Change, 2012–22** 8,600

Water and wastewater treatment plant and system operators read meters and gauges to make sure that plant equipment is working properly.

What Water and Wastewater Treatment Plant and System Operators Do

Water and wastewater treatment plant and system operators manage a system of machines, often through the use of control boards, to transfer or treat water or wastewater.

Duties. Water and wastewater treatment plant and system operators typically do the following:

- Add chemicals, such as ammonia or chlorine, to disinfect water or other liquids
- Inspect equipment on a regular basis
- Monitor operating conditions, meters, and gauges
- Collect and test water and sewage samples
- Record meter and gauge readings and operational data
- Operate equipment to purify and clarify water or to process or dispose of sewage
- Clean and maintain equipment, tanks, filter beds, and other work areas
- Follow U.S. Environmental Protection Agency regulations
- Ensure safety standards are met

It takes a lot of work to get water from natural sources–reservoirs, streams, and groundwater–into our taps. Similarly, it is a complicated process to convert the wastewater in our drains and sewers into a form that is safe to release into the environment.

The specific duties of plant operators depend on the type and size of the plant. In a small plant, one operator may be responsible for maintaining all of the systems. In large plants, multiple operators work the same shifts and are more specialized in their duties, often relying on computerized systems to help them monitor plant processes.

Occasionally, operators must work during emergencies. For example, weather conditions may cause large amounts of storm water or wastewater to flow into sewers, exceeding a plant's capacity. Emergencies also may be caused by malfunctions within a plant, such as chemical leaks or oxygen deficiencies. Operators are trained in emergency management procedures and use safety equipment to protect their health, as well as that of the public.

Water treatment plant and system operators work in water treatment plants. Fresh water is pumped from wells, rivers, streams, or reservoirs to water treatment plants, where it is treated and distributed to customers. Water treatment plant and system operators run the equipment, control the processes, and monitor the plants that treat water to make it safe to drink.

Wastewater treatment plant and system operators do similar work to remove pollutants from domestic and industrial waste. Used water, also known as wastewater, travels through sewage pipes to treatment plants where it is treated and either returned to streams, rivers, and oceans, or used for irrigation.

Work Environment

Water and wastewater treatment plant and system operators held about 111,000 jobs in 2012, of which 78 percent were in local government. About 11 percent worked for water, sewage, and other systems utilities.

Median Annual Wages, May 2012

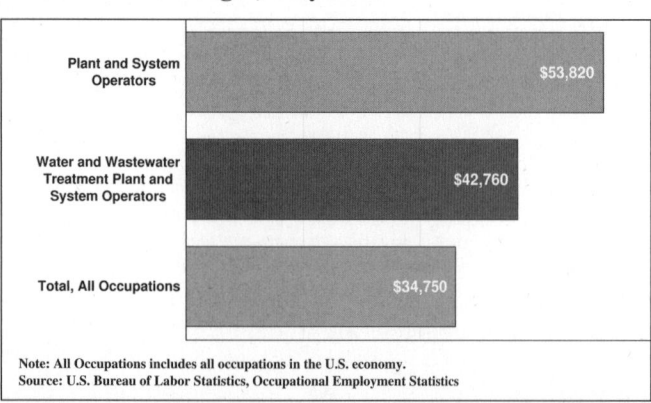

Note: All Occupations includes all occupations in the U.S. economy.
Source: U.S. Bureau of Labor Statistics, Occupational Employment Statistics

Percent Change in Employment, Projected 2012–2022

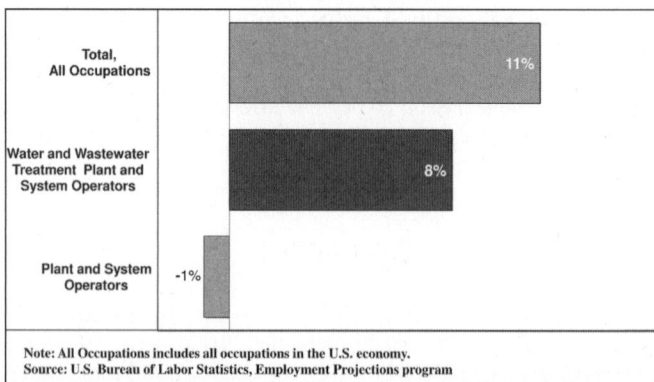

Note: All Occupations includes all occupations in the U.S. economy.
Source: U.S. Bureau of Labor Statistics, Employment Projections program

Employment Projections Data for Water and Wastewater Treatment Plant and System Operators

Occupational title	SOC Code	Employment, 2012	Projected Employment, 2022	Change, 2012–2022	
				Percent	Numeric
Water and wastewater treatment plant and system operators..	51-8031	111,000	119,600	8	8,600

Source: U.S. Bureau of Labor Statistics, Employment Projections Program

Note: Data are rounded. Go to **Occupational Information Included in the OOH** *for a discussion of the data in this table.*

Injuries and Illnesses. Water and wastewater treatment plant and system operators work both indoors and outdoors. They may be exposed to noise from machinery and are often exposed to unpleasant odors. Operators' work is physically demanding and usually is performed in locations that are unclean or difficult to access.

They must pay close attention to safety procedures because of hazardous conditions, such as slippery walkways, the presence of dangerous gases, and malfunctioning equipment. As a result, workers experience an occupational injury and illness rate that is much higher than the average for all occupations.

Work Schedules. Plants operate 24 hours a day, 7 days a week. In small plants, operators are likely to work during the day and be on call nights and weekends. In medium- and large-size plants that require constant monitoring, operators work in shifts to control the plant at all hours. During severe weather conditions and natural disasters, operators are more likely to be on call and may have to work overtime, weekends, or holidays.

How to Become One

Water and wastewater treatment plant and system operators typically need a high school diploma and a license to work. They also typically undergo on-the-job training.

Education. Water and wastewater treatment plant and system operators need a high school diploma or equivalent to become operators. Employers may prefer applicants who have completed a certificate or an associate's degree program in water quality management or wastewater treatment technology, because the education minimizes the training a worker will need. Community colleges, technical schools, and trade associations offer these certificate or associate's degree programs.

Training. Water and wastewater treatment plant and system operators need long-term on-the-job training to become fully qualified. Trainees usually start as attendants or operators-in-training and learn their skills on the job under the direction of an experienced operator. The trainees learn by observing and doing routine tasks, such as recording meter readings, taking samples of wastewater and sludge, and doing simple maintenance and repair work on plant equipment.

Larger treatment plants generally combine this on-the-job training with formal classroom or self-paced study programs. As plants get larger and more complicated, operators need more skills before they are allowed to work without supervision.

Licenses, Certifications, and Registrations. Water and wastewater treatment plant and system operators must be licensed by the state in which they work. Requirements and standards vary widely depending on the state.

States licenses typically have four levels, which indicate the operator's experience and training. Although some states will honor licenses from other states, operators who move from one state to another may need to take a new set of exams to become licensed in their new state.

Advancement. Most states have four levels of licenses for water and wastewater treatment plant and system operators. Each increase in license level allows the operator to control a larger plant and more complicated processes without supervision.

At the largest plants, operators who have the highest license level work as shift supervisors and may be in charge of large teams of operators.

Important Qualities

Analytical skills. Water and wastewater treatment plant and system operators must conduct tests and inspections on water or wastewater and evaluate the results.

Detail oriented. Water and wastewater treatment plant and system operators must monitor machinery, gauges, dials, and controls to ensure everything is operating properly. Because tap water and wastewater are highly regulated by the U.S. Environmental Protection Agency, operators must be careful and thorough in completing these tasks.

Math skills. Water and wastewater treatment plant and system operators must have the ability to apply data to formulas that determine treatment requirements, flow levels, and concentration levels.

Mechanical skills. Water and wastewater treatment plant and system operators must know how to work with machines and use tools. They must be familiar with how to operate, repair, and maintain equipment.

Similar Occupations This table shows a list of occupations with job duties that are similar to those of water and wastewater treatment plant and system operators.

Occupations	Entry-level Education	2012 Pay	Projected Job Growth	Average Annual Openings
Construction Equipment Operators	High school diploma or equivalent	$41,099	19%	16,480
General Maintenance and Repair Workers	High school diploma or equivalent	$35,210	9%	37,970
Hydrologists	Master's degree	$75,530	9%	290
Power Plant Operators, Distributors, and Dispatchers	High school diploma or equivalent	$68,256	-8%	1,880
Stationary Engineers and Boiler Operators	High school diploma or equivalent	$53,560	3%	1,270

Pay

The median annual wage for water and wastewater treatment plant and system operators was $42,760 in May 2012. The median wage is the wage at which half the workers in an occupation earned more than that amount and half earned less. The lowest 10 percent earned less than $25,850, and the top 10 percent earned more than $67,810.

Union Membership. Compared with workers in all occupations, water and wastewater treatment plant and system operators had a higher percentage of workers who belonged to a union in 2012.

Job Outlook

Employment of water and wastewater treatment plant and system operators is projected to grow 8 percent from 2012 to 2022, about as fast as the average for all occupations.

A growing population and increased demand for water and wastewater treatment services will drive employment growth. Population growth, particularly in suburban areas, will require new plants or increased capacity at current plants. As existing plants expand and new plants are built to meet this demand, new operator jobs will be created.

Plants will also need more operators to ensure compliance with increased environmental and safety regulations. New regulations often require that plants install new systems or features that operators need to control. Although some work can be automated, plants will need skilled workers to operate increasingly complex controls and water and wastewater systems.

Job Prospects. Job prospects for water and wastewater treatment plant and system operators should be excellent. New jobs will be created when existing plants expand and new plants are built. The number of applicants for these positions is normally low, because of the physically demanding and unappealing nature of some of the work. Job prospects will be best for those with training or education in water or wastewater systems and good mechanical skills.

O*NET

➤ Water and Wastewater Treatment Plant and System Operators (51-8031.00)

Contacts for More Information

For information on employment opportunities, contact state or local water pollution control agencies, state water and wastewater operator associations, state environmental training centers, or local offices of the state employment service.

For information related to a career as a water or wastewater treatment plant and system operator, visit
➤ American Water Works Association (www.awwa.org/)
➤ The National Rural Water Association (www.nrwa.org/)
➤ Water Environment Federation (www.wef.org/)
➤ Work for Water (www.workforwater.org/)

Welders, Cutters, Solderers, and Brazers

- **2012 Median Pay** .... $36,300 per year
  $17.45 per hour

- **Entry-Level Education** ... High school diploma or equivalent

- **Work Experience in a Related Occupation** .... None

- **On-the-Job Training** .... Moderate-term on-the-job training

- **Number of Jobs 2012** 357,400

- **Job Outlook, 2012–22** .... 6% (Slower than average)
- **Employment Change, 2012–22** 20,800

What Welders, Cutters, Solderers, and Brazers Do

Welders, cutters, solderers, and brazers weld or join metal parts. They also fill holes, indentions, or seams of metal products, using hand-held metal joining equipment.

Duties. Welders, cutters, solderers, and brazers typically do the following:

- Study blueprints, sketches, or specifications
- Calculate dimensions to be welded
- Inspect structures or materials to be welded
- Ignite torches or start power supplies
- Monitor the welding process to avoid overheating
- Maintain equipment and machinery

Welding is the most common way of permanently joining metal parts. In this process, heat is applied to metal pieces, melting and fusing them to form a permanent bond. Because of its strength, welding is used in shipbuilding, automobile manufacturing and repair, aerospace applications, and thousands of other manufacturing activities. Welding also is used to join steel beams in the construction of buildings, bridges, and other structures and to join pipes in pipelines, powerplants, and refineries.

Welders work in a wide variety of industries, from car racing to manufacturing. The work that welders do and the equipment they use vary with the industry. Arc welding, the most common type of welding today, uses electrical currents to create heat and bond metals together—but there are more than 100 different processes

Welders inspect the placement of parts before bonding metals.

Median Annual Wages, May 2012

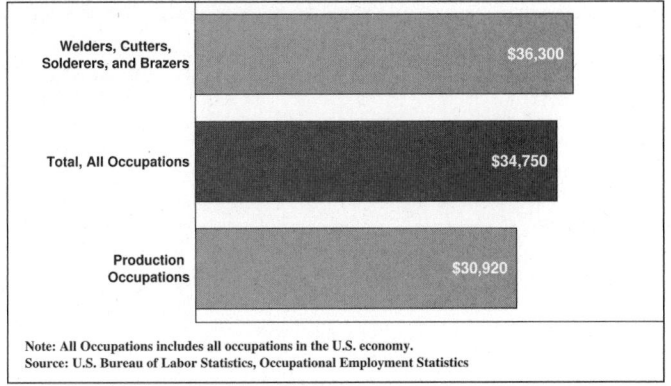

Welders, Cutters, Solderers, and Brazers — $36,300
Total, All Occupations — $34,750
Production Occupations — $30,920

Note: All Occupations includes all occupations in the U.S. economy.
Source: U.S. Bureau of Labor Statistics, Occupational Employment Statistics

Percent Change in Employment, Projected 2012–2022

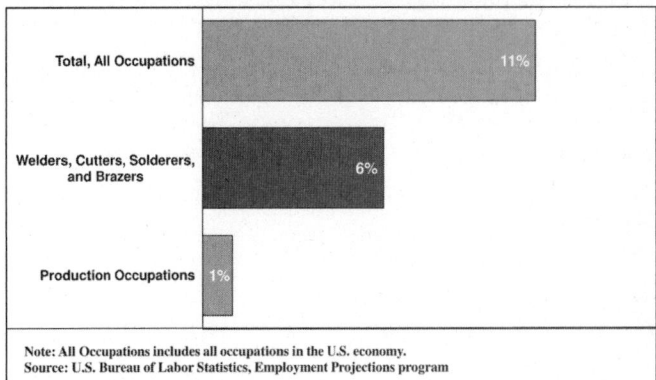

Total, All Occupations — 11%
Welders, Cutters, Solderers, and Brazers — 6%
Production Occupations — 1%

Note: All Occupations includes all occupations in the U.S. economy.
Source: U.S. Bureau of Labor Statistics, Employment Projections program

that a welder can use. The type of weld normally is determined by the types of metals being joined and the conditions under which the welding is to take place.

Cutters use heat to cut and trim metal objects to specific dimensions. The work of *arc, plasma,* and *oxy–gas cutters* is closely related to that of welders. However, instead of joining metals, cutters use the heat from an electric arc, a stream of ionized gas called plasma, or burning gases to cut and trim metal objects to specific dimensions. Cutters also dismantle large objects, such as ships, railroad cars, automobiles, buildings, and aircraft. Some operate and monitor cutting machines similar to those used by welding machine operators.

Solderers and *brazers* also use heat to join two or more metal objects together. Soldering and brazing are similar, except that the temperature used to melt the filler metal is lower in soldering. Soldering uses metals with a melting point below 840 degrees Fahrenheit. Brazing uses metals with a higher melting point.

Soldering and brazing workers use molten metal to join two pieces of metal. However, the metal added during the soldering or brazing process has a melting point lower than that of the piece, so only the added metal is melted, not the piece. Therefore, these processes normally do not create distortions or weaknesses in the piece, as can occur with welding.

Soldering commonly is used to make electrical and electronic circuit boards, such as computer chips. Soldering workers tend to work with small pieces that must be positioned precisely.

Brazing often is used to connect cast iron and thinner metals that the higher temperatures of welding would warp. Brazing also can be used to apply coatings to parts in order to reduce wear and protect against corrosion.

Work Environment

Welders, cutters, solderers, and brazers held about 357,400 jobs in 2012. The industries employing the most welders, cutters, solderers, and brazers in 2012 were as follows:

Manufacturing.. 61%
Construction... 11

Other services (except public administration) 5
Wholesale trade 5

Welders and cutters may work outdoors, often in inclement weather, or indoors, sometimes in a confined area designed to contain sparks and glare. When working outdoors, they may work on a scaffold or platform high off the ground.

In addition, they may have to lift heavy objects and work in awkward positions while bending, stooping, or standing to work overhead.

Injuries and Illnesses. Welders, cutters, solderers, and brazers are often exposed to a number of hazards, including very hot materials and the intense light created by the arc. They wear safety shoes, heat-resistant gloves, goggles, masks with protective lenses, and other equipment to prevent burns and eye injuries and to protect them from falling objects.

The Occupational Safety & Health Administration requires that welders work in safely ventilated areas in order to avoid danger from inhaling gases and fine particles that can result from welding processes. Because of these hazards, welding, cutting, soldering, and brazing workers have a rate of injuries and illnesses that is higher than the national average. However, they can minimize injuries if they follow safety procedures.

Work Schedules. Most welders, cutters, solderers, and brazers work full time, and overtime is common. Many manufacturing firms have two or three 8- to 12-hour shifts each day, allowing the firm to continue production around the clock if needed. As a result, welders, cutters, solderers, and brazers may work evenings and weekends.

How to Become One

Training ranges from a few weeks of technical school or on-the-job training to several years of combined technical school and on-the-job training.

Education. Formal training is available in high school technical education courses and in postsecondary institutions, such as vocational–technical institutes, community colleges, and private welding, soldering, and brazing schools.

Employment Projections Data for Welders, Cutters, Solderers, and Brazers

Occupational title	SOC Code	Employment, 2012	Projected Employment, 2022	Change, 2012–2022	
				Percent	Numeric
Welders, cutters, solderers, and brazers................................ 51-4121		357,400	378,200	6	20,800

Source: U.S. Bureau of Labor Statistics, Employment Projections Program

Note: Data are rounded. Go to Occupational Information Included in the OOH for a discussion of the data in this table.

Similar Occupations   This table shows a list of occupations with job duties that are similar to those of welders, cutters, solderers, and brazers.

Occupations	Entry-level Education	2012 Pay	Projected Job Growth	Average Annual Openings
Assemblers and Fabricators	High school diploma or equivalent	$28,661	4%	37,140
Boilermakers	High school diploma or equivalent	$56,560	4%	880
Jewelers and Precious Stone and Metal Workers	High school diploma or equivalent	$35,350	-10%	670
Machinists and Tool and Die Makers	High school diploma or equivalent	$40,733	7%	13,060
Metal and Plastic Machine Workers	High school diploma or equivalent	$33,064	-6%	22,070
Plumbers, Pipefitters, and Steamfitters	High school diploma or equivalent	$49,140	21%	13,050
Sheet Metal Workers	High school diploma or equivalent	$43,290	15%	4,890

Courses in blueprint reading, shop mathematics, mechanical drawing, physics, chemistry, and metallurgy are helpful.

An understanding of electricity also is helpful, and knowledge of computers is gaining importance as welding, soldering, and brazing machine operators become more responsible for programming robots and other computer-controlled machines.

In addition, the U.S. Armed Forces operate welding and soldering schools.

Training. Although numerous employers are willing to hire inexperienced entry-level workers and train them on the job, many prefer to hire workers who have been through training or credentialing programs.

Because understanding the welding process and inspecting welds is important for both welders and welding machine operators, companies hiring machine operators prefer workers with a background in welding.

Licenses, Certifications, and Registrations. Courses leading to certification are offered at many welding schools. For example, the American Welding Society offers the Certified Welder and Certified Welding Fabricator designations.

Some welding positions require general certification in welding or certification in specific skills, such as Certified Welding Inspector or Certified Robotic Arc Welding.

The Institute for Printed Circuits offers certification and training in soldering. In industries such as aerospace and defense, which need highly skilled workers, many employers require these certifications. Certification can show mastery of lead-free soldering techniques, which are important to many employers.

Some employers pay the cost of training and testing for employees.

Important Qualities

Detail oriented. Welders, cutters, solderers, and brazers perform precision work, often with straight edges and minimal flaws. The ability to see details and characteristics of the joint and detect changes in molten metal flows requires good eyesight and attention to detail.

Manual dexterity. Welders, cutters, solderers, and brazers must have a steady hand to hold a torch in one place. Workers must also have good hand-eye coordination.

Physical stamina. The ability to endure long periods of standing or repetitive movements is important for welders, cutters, solderers, and brazers.

Physical strength. Welders, cutters, solderers, and brazers must be in good physical condition. They often must lift heavy pieces of metal and move welding or cutting equipment, and sometimes bend, stoop, or reach while working.

Spatial-orientation skills. Welders, cutters, solderers, and brazers must be able to read, understand, and interpret two- and three-dimensional diagrams in order to fit metal products correctly.

Technical skills. Welders, cutters, solderers, and brazers must be able to operate manual or semiautomatic welding equipment to fuse metal segments.

Pay

The median annual wage for welders, cutters, solderers and brazers was $36,300 in May 2012. The median wage is the wage at which half the workers in an occupation earned more than that amount and half earned less. The lowest 10 percent earned less than $24,720, and the top 10 percent earned more than $56,130.

Wages for welders, cutters, solderers, and brazers vary with the worker's experience and skill level, the industry, and the size of the company.

Job Outlook

Employment of welders, cutters, solderers, and brazers is projected to grow 6 percent from 2012 to 2022, slower than the average for all occupations.

Employment growth reflects the need for welders in manufacturing because of the importance and versatility of welding as a manufacturing process. The basic skills of welding are similar across industries, so welders can easily shift from one industry to another, depending on where they are needed most. For example, welders laid off in the automotive manufacturing industry may be able to find work in the oil and gas industry.

The nation's aging infrastructure will require the expertise of welders, cutters, solderers, and brazers to help rebuild bridges, highways, and buildings. The construction of new power generation facilities and, specifically, pipelines transporting natural gas and oil will also result in new jobs.

Job Prospects. Overall job prospects will vary with the worker's skill level. Job prospects should be good for welders trained in the latest technologies. Welding schools report that graduates have little difficulty finding work, and many employers report difficulty finding properly skilled welders. However, welders who do not have up-to-date training may face strong competition for jobs.

For all welders, job prospects should be better for those willing to relocate.

O*NET

➤ Welders, Cutters, Solderers, and Brazers (51-4121.00)
➤ Welders, Cutters, and Welder Fitters (51-4121.06)
➤ Solderers and Brazers (51-4121.07)

Contacts for More Information

For more information about welders, cutters, solderers, and brazers, visit

➤ American Welding Society (www.aws.org)
➤ Fabricators & Manufacturers Association, International (http://fmanet.org/)
➤ Institute for Printed Circuits (www.ipc.org)
➤ Precision Machined Products Association (www.pmpa.org/)

Woodworkers

- **2012 Median Pay** .... $28,440 per year
$13.67 per hour
- **Entry-Level Education** ... High school diploma or equivalent
- **Work Experience in a Related Occupation** .... None
- **On-the-Job Training** ....See "How to Become One"
- **Number of Jobs 2012** 202,700
- **Job Outlook, 2012–22** .... 8% (As fast as average)
- **Employment Change, 2012–22** 15,700

What Woodworkers Do

Woodworkers manufacture a variety of products such as cabinets and furniture, using wood, veneers, and laminates. They often combine and incorporate different materials into wood.

Duties. Woodworkers typically do the following:

- Understand detailed architectural drawings, schematics, shop drawings, and blueprints
- Prepare and set up machines and tooling for woodwork manufacturing
- Lift wood pieces onto machines, either by hand or with hoists
- Operate woodworking machines, including saws and milling and sanding machines
- Listen for unusual sounds or detect excessive vibration in machinery
- Ensure that products meet industry standards and project specifications, making adjustments as necessary
- Select and adjust the proper cutting, milling, boring, and sanding tools for completing a job
- Use hand tools to trim pieces or assemble products

Despite the abundance of plastics, metals, and other materials, wood products continue to be an important part of our daily lives.

Woodworkers make wood products from lumber and synthetic wood materials. Many of these products, including most furniture, kitchen cabinets, and musical instruments, are mass produced. Other products are custom made from architectural designs and drawings.

Although the term "woodworker" may evoke the image of a craftsman who uses handtools to build ornate furniture, the modern woodworking trade is highly technical and relies on advanced equipment and highly skilled operators. Workers use automated machinery, such as computerized numerical control (CNC) machines, to do much of the work with great accuracy.

Even specialized artisans generally use CNC machines and a variety of power tools in their work. Much of the work is done in a high-production assembly line facility, but there is also some work that is customized and does not lend itself to being made on an assembly line.

Woodworkers set up, operate, and tend all types of woodworking machines, such as saws, milling machines, drill presses, lathes, shapers, routers, sanders, planers, and wood-fastening machines. Operators set up the equipment, cut and shape wooden parts, and verify dimensions, using a template, caliper, and rule. After the parts are machined, woodworkers add fasteners and adhesives and connect the parts to form an assembled unit. They also install hardware, such as pulls and drawer slides, and fit specialty products for glass, metal trims, electrical components, and stone. Finally, workers then sand, stain, and, if necessary, coat the wood product with a sealer or topcoats, such as a lacquer or varnish.

Many of these tasks are handled by different workers with specialized training.

The following are examples of types of woodworkers:

Cabinetmakers and *bench carpenters* cut, shape, assemble, and make parts for wood products. They often design and create sets of cabinets that are customized for particular spaces. In some cases, their duties begin with designing a set of cabinets to specifications and end with installing the cabinets.

Furniture finishers shape, finish, and refinish damaged and worn furniture. They may work with antiques and must judge how to preserve and repair them. They also do the staining, sealing, and top coating at the end of the process of making wooden products.

Wood sawing machine setters, operators, and tenders specialize in operating specific pieces of woodworking machinery. They often operate CNC machines.

Woodworking machine setters, operators, and tenders, except sawing, operate woodworking machines, such as drill presses, lathes, routers, sanders, and planers.

Median Hourly Wages, May 2012

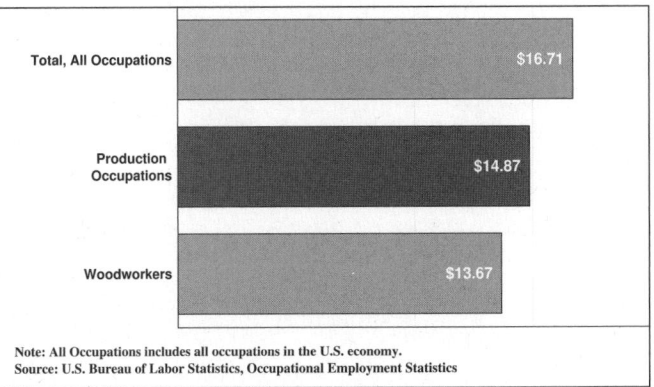

Note: All Occupations includes all occupations in the U.S. economy.
Source: U.S. Bureau of Labor Statistics, Occupational Employment Statistics

Percent Change in Employment, Projected 2012–2022

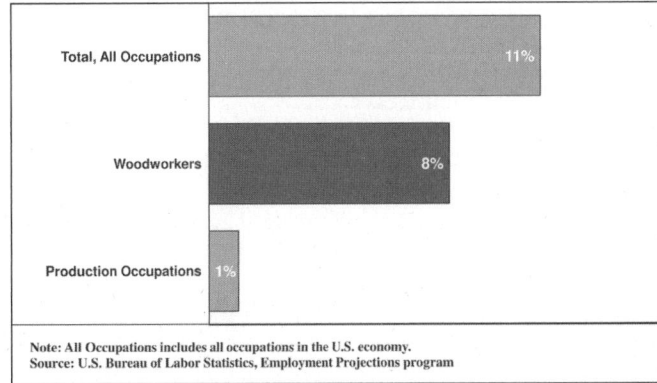

Note: All Occupations includes all occupations in the U.S. economy.
Source: U.S. Bureau of Labor Statistics, Employment Projections program

Employment Projections Data for Woodworkers

Occupational title	SOC Code	Employment, 2012	Projected Employment, 2022	Change, 2012–2022	
				Percent	Numeric
Woodworkers..	—	202,700	218,400	8	15,700
Cabinetmakers and bench carpenters	51-7011	86,200	89,700	4	3,500
Furniture finishers	51-7021	14,800	15,300	3	500
Sawing machine setters, operators, and tenders, wood.......	51-7041	40,200	45,700	13	5,400
Woodworking machine setters, operators, and tenders, except sawing	51-7042	61,500	67,700	10	6,300

Source: U.S. Bureau of Labor Statistics, Employment Projections Program

Note: **Data are rounded. Go to Occupational Information Included in the OOH** *for a discussion of the data in this table.*

Similar Occupations   This table shows a list of occupations with job duties that are similar to those of woodworkers.

Occupations	Entry-level Education	2012 Pay	Projected Job Growth	Average Annual Openings
Carpenters	High school diploma or equivalent	$39,940	24%	32,920
Computer Programmers	Bachelor's degree	$74,280	8%	11,810
Machinists and Tool and Die Makers	High school diploma or equivalent	$40,733	7%	13,060
Sheet Metal Workers	High school diploma or equivalent	$43,290	15%	4,890
Structural Iron and Steel Workers	High school diploma or equivalent	$46,140	22%	3,150

Work Environment

Woodworkers held about 202,700 jobs in 2012. About 83 percent worked in manufacturing industries.

The industries that employed the most woodworkers in 2012 were as follows:

Cabinetmakers and bench carpenters 86,200
Woodworking machine setters, operators, and tenders, except
   sawing 61,500
Sawing machine setters, operators, and tenders, wood......... 40,200
Furniture finishers 14,800

Although many smaller shops employ a few workers, production factories can have as many as 2,000 employees.

Working conditions vary with the specific job duties. At times, workers have to handle heavy, bulky materials and may encounter noise and dust. As a result, they regularly wear hearing protection devices, goggles, and respirators or masks.

Injuries and Illnesses. Woodworkers are exposed to hazards such as harmful dust, chemicals, or fumes. Others may be exposed to excessive noise and must wear hearing protection devices.

Specifically, cabinet makers and bench carpenters have a higher rate of injuries and illnesses than the national average.

Most injuries involve sprains, back pain, carpal tunnel syndrome, and hernia. These injuries or illnesses come from excessive amounts of awkward bending, reaching, twisting, and overexertion or repetition.

Work Schedules. Most woodworkers are employed full time and work during regular business hours.

How to Become One

Although some entry-level jobs can be learned in less than 1 year, becoming fully proficient generally takes at least 3 years of on-the-job training. The ability to use computer-controlled machinery is becoming increasingly important.

Education. Because of the growing sophistication of machinery, many employers are seeking applicants who have a high school diploma or the equivalent. People seeking woodworking jobs can enhance their employment prospects by completing high school and getting training in computer applications and math.

Some woodworkers obtain their skills by taking courses at technical schools or community colleges. Others attend universities that offer training in wood technology, furniture manufacturing, wood engineering, and production management. These programs prepare students for jobs in production, supervision, engineering, and management, and are becoming increasingly important as woodworking technology advances.

Training. Education is helpful, but woodworkers are trained primarily on the job, where they learn skills from experienced

Woodworkers set up equipment, verify dimensions, and cut and shape wooden parts.

workers. Beginning workers are given basic tasks, such as placing a piece of wood through a machine and grabbing the finished product at the end of the process.

As they gain experience, new woodworkers perform more complex tasks with less supervision. In about 1 year, they learn basic machine operations and job tasks. Becoming a skilled woodworker often takes 3 or more years. Skilled workers can read blueprints, set up machines, and plan work sequences.

Licenses, Certifications, and Registrations. Although not required, becoming certified can demonstrate competence and professionalism. It also may help a candidate advance in the profession. The Architectural Woodwork Institute (AWI) offers a national certificate program, which adds a level of credibility to the work of woodworkers. The Woodwork Career Alliance of North America also offers five progressive credentials.

Important Qualities

Detail oriented. Woodworkers must pay attention to details in order to meet specifications and to keep themselves safe.

Dexterity. Woodworkers must make precise cuts with a variety of hand tools and power tools, so they need a steady hand and good hand-eye coordination.

Math skills. Knowledge of basic math and computer skills are important, particularly for those who work in manufacturing, in which technology continues to advance. Woodworkers need to understand basic geometry to visualize how the wood pieces will fit together to fabricate a three-dimensional object, such as a cabinet or piece of furniture.

Mechanical skills. Modern technology systems require woodworkers to be able to use robots, computers, and other programmable devices.

Physical stamina. The ability to endure long periods of standing and repetitious movements is crucial for woodworkers, who often stand all day performing many of the same functions.

Physical strength. Woodworkers must be strong enough to lift bulky and heavy pieces of wood, such as plywood.

Technical skills. Woodworkers must be able to understand and interpret design drawings and technical manuals for a range of products and machines.

Pay

The median hourly wage for woodworkers was $13.67 in May 2012. The median wage is the wage at which half the workers in an occupation earned more than that amount and half earned less. The lowest 10 percent earned less than $9.03 per hour, and the highest 10 percent earned more than $21.31 per hour.

Median hourly wages for woodworker occupations in May 2012 were as follows:

Cabinetmakers and bench carpenters $14.90
Furniture finishers 13.70

Woodworking machine setters, operators,
and tenders, except sawing 13.00
Sawing machine setters, operators, and tenders, wood 12.59

Job Outlook

Employment of woodworkers is projected to grow 8 percent from 2012 to 2022, about as fast as the average for all occupations.

Employment growth will stem from greater demand for domestic wood products. In particular, the continuing need to repair and renovate residential and commercial properties will likely require more woodworkers.

Employment growth should be good for woodworkers who specialize in items used in renovation, such as moldings, cabinets, stairs, and windows. Firms that focus on custom woodwork should be able to compete against imports without the need to outsource jobs to other countries.

The increasing use of automated systems is expected to require more workers to operate and maintain the newer equipment in manufacturing facilities.

Woodworkers who know how to create and carry out custom designs on a computer will likely be in strong demand.

Job Prospects. Those with advanced skills, including advanced math and the ability to interpret design drawings, should have the best job opportunities in manufacturing industries.

Those who can demonstrate leadership and problem-solving skills should also have the best job prospects.

Some job openings will result from the need to replace those who retire or leave the occupation for another job.

Although overall job opportunities should be good, employment in all woodworking specialties is highly sensitive to economic cycles. During economic downturns, woodworkers are subject to layoffs or reductions in hours.

O*NET

➤ Cabinetmakers and Bench Carpenters (51-7011.00)
➤ Furniture Finishers (51-7021.00)
➤ Sawing Machine Setters, Operators, and Tenders, Wood (51-7041.00)
➤ Woodworking Machine Setters, Operators, and Tenders, Except Sawing (51-7042.00)

Contacts for More Information

For more information about woodworkers, visit

➤ Architectural Woodwork Institute (http://awinet.org/)
➤ Association for Manufacturing Technology (www.amtonline.org/)
➤ Fabricators & Manufacturers Association, International (http://fmanet.org/)
➤ National Tooling and Machining Association (www.ntma.org/)
➤ Wood Machinery Manufacturers of America (www.wmma.org/)
➤ Woodwork Career Alliance of North America (www.woodworkcareer.org)
➤ Woodworking Machinery Industry Association (www.wmia.org/)

Protective Service

Correctional Officers

- **2012 Median Pay** .... $38,970 per year
  $18.74 per hour
- **Entry-Level Education** ... High school diploma or equivalent
- **Work Experience in a Related Occupation** .... None
- **On-the-Job Training** .... Moderate-term on-the-job training
- **Number of Jobs 2012** 469,500
- **Job Outlook, 2012–22** .... 5% (Slower than average)
- **Employment Change, 2012–22** 23,000

What Correctional Officers Do

Correctional officers are responsible for overseeing individuals who have been arrested and are awaiting trial or who have been sentenced to serve time in a jail or prison.

Duties. Correctional officers typically do the following:

- Enforce rules and keep order within jails or prisons
- Supervise activities of inmates
- Aid in rehabilitation and counseling of offenders
- Inspect facilities to ensure that they meet standards
- Search inmates for contraband items
- Report on inmate conduct

Inside the prison or jail, correctional officers enforce rules and regulations. They maintain security by preventing disturbances, assaults, and escapes. Correctional officers supervise the daily activities of inmates, ensuring that inmates obey the rules. They must also ensure the whereabouts of all inmates at all times.

On any given day, officers search inmates for contraband, such as weapons and drugs, settle disputes between inmates, and enforce discipline. Officers enforce regulations through effective communication and the use of progressive sanctions, which involve punishments, such as loss of privileges. Sanctions are progressive in that they start out small for a lesser offense but become more severe for more serious offenses. In addition, officers may aid inmates in their rehabilitation by scheduling work assignments, counseling, and educational opportunities.

Correctional officers inspect mail and visitors for prohibited items.

Correctional officers periodically inspect facilities. They check cells and other areas for unsanitary conditions, contraband, signs of a security breach (such as tampering with window bars and doors), and any other evidence of violations of the rules. Officers also inspect mail and visitors for prohibited items. They write reports and fill out daily logs detailing inmate behavior and anything else of note that occurred during their shift.

Correctional officers may have to restrain inmates in handcuffs and leg irons to escort them safely to and from cells and to see authorized visitors. Officers also escort prisoners between the institution and courtrooms, medical facilities, and other destinations.

Correctional officers must report any inmate who violates the rules. If a crime is committed within their institution or an inmate escapes, they help law enforcement authorities investigate and search for the escapee.

Correctional officers have no responsibilities for law enforcement outside their place of work. Probation officers and correctional treatment specialists work with counseling offenders outside of prison.

Bailiffs, also known as *marshals* or *court officers*, are law enforcement officers who maintain safety and order in courtrooms. Their duties, which vary by location, include enforcing courtroom rules, assisting judges, guarding juries, delivering court documents, and providing general security for courthouses.

Median Annual Wages, May 2012

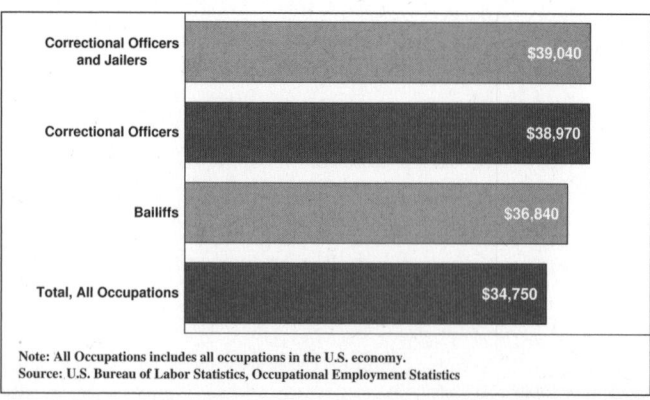

Correctional Officers and Jailers — $39,040
Correctional Officers — $38,970
Bailiffs — $36,840
Total, All Occupations — $34,750

Note: All Occupations includes all occupations in the U.S. economy.
Source: U.S. Bureau of Labor Statistics, Occupational Employment Statistics

Percent Change in Employment, Projected 2012–2022

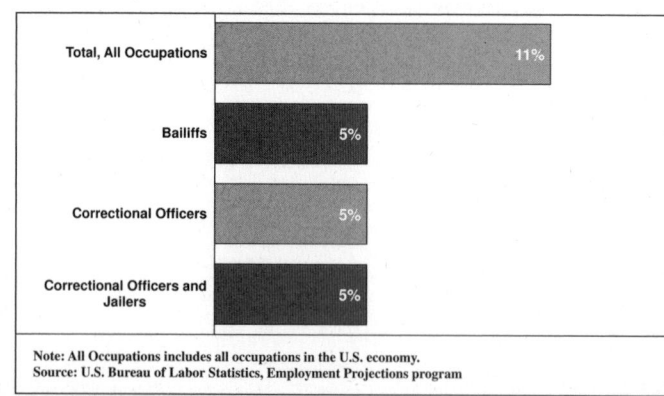

Total, All Occupations — 11%
Bailiffs — 5%
Correctional Officers — 5%
Correctional Officers and Jailers — 5%

Note: All Occupations includes all occupations in the U.S. economy.
Source: U.S. Bureau of Labor Statistics, Employment Projections program

Employment Projections Data for Correctional Officers

Occupational title	SOC Code	Employment, 2012	Projected Employment, 2022	Change, 2012–2022	
				Percent	Numeric
Bailiffs, correctional officers, and jailers	33-3010	469,500	492,600	5	23,000
Bailiffs	33-3011	16,800	17,700	5	900
Correctional officers and jailers	33-3012	452,800	474,900	5	22,100

Source: U.S. Bureau of Labor Statistics, Employment Projections Program

Note: Data are rounded. Go to Occupational Information Included in the OOH for a discussion of the data in this table.

Work Environment

Correctional officers held about 469,500 jobs in 2012. Almost all worked for federal, state, and local governments. The remainder were employed by private companies that provide correctional services to prisons and jails.

Correctional officers may work indoors or outdoors. Some correctional institutions are temperature controlled and ventilated; but others are old, overcrowded, hot, and noisy.

Correctional officers may be required to stand for long periods of time. Bailiffs generally work in courtrooms.

Work Schedules. Correctional officers usually work 8 hours per day, 5 days per week, on rotating shifts. Because jail and prison security must be provided around the clock, officers work all hours of the day and night, weekends, and holidays. Some correctional facilities have longer shifts and more days off between scheduled workweeks. Many officers are required to work overtime.

Injuries and Illnesses. Working in a correctional institution can be stressful and dangerous. Every year, correctional officers are injured in confrontations with inmates, and some are exposed to contagious diseases. As a result, correctional officers have one of the highest rates of injuries and illnesses of all occupations.

The job demands that officers be alert and ready to react throughout their entire shift. As a result, some officers experience anxiety.

Because offenders typically stay longer in state and federal prisons than in county jails, correctional officers in prisons come to know the people with whom they are dealing. Officers know what offenders need in terms of security and being taken care of.

How to Become One

Correctional officers go through a training academy and then are assigned to a facility for on-the-job training. Although qualifications vary by state and agency, all agencies require a high school diploma. Some federal agencies also require some college education or previous work experience.

Correctional officers usually must be at least 18 to 21 years of age, must be a U.S. citizen or permanent resident, and must have no felony convictions. New applicants for federal corrections positions must be appointed before they are 37 years old.

Education. Correctional officers must have at least a high school diploma or equivalent. Some state and local corrections agencies require some college credits. Law enforcement or military experience may be substituted for this requirement.

For employment in federal prisons, the Federal Bureau of Prisons requires entry-level correctional officers to have at least a bachelor's degree; 3 years of full-time experience in a field providing counseling, assistance, or supervision to individuals; or a combination of the two.

Training. Federal, state, and some local departments of corrections, as well as some private corrections companies, provide training for correctional officers based on guidelines established by the American Correctional Association (ACA). Some states have regional training academies that are available to local agencies. Academy trainees receive instruction in a number of subjects, including self-defense, institutional policies, regulations, operations, and custody and security procedures. Although most correctional officers do not carry firearms when on duty, they may receive training in the use of firearms.

After formal academy instruction, state and local correctional agencies provide on-the-job training, including training on legal restrictions and interpersonal relations. Trainees typically receive several weeks or months of training under the supervision of an experienced officer. However, on-the-job training varies widely from agency to agency.

New federal correctional officers must undergo 200 hours of formal training within the first year of employment, including 120 hours of specialized training at the Federal Bureau of Prisons residential training center. Experienced officers receive annual in-service training to keep up on new developments and procedures.

Correctional officers who are members of prison tactical response teams are trained to respond to disturbances, riots, hostage situations, and other potentially dangerous confrontations. Team members practice disarming prisoners, wielding weapons, and using other tactics to maintain the safety of inmates and officers alike.

Similar Occupations This table shows a list of occupations with job duties that are similar to those of correctional officers.

Occupations	Entry-level Education	2012 Pay	Projected Job Growth	Average Annual Openings
Police and Detectives	High school diploma or equivalent	$57,974	5%	27,500
Probation Officers and Correctional Treatment Specialists	Bachelor's degree	$48,190	-1%	2,360
Security Guards and Gaming Surveillance Officers	High school diploma or equivalent	$24,019	12%	29,630

Advancement. Qualified officers may advance to the position of correctional sergeant. Sergeants are responsible for maintaining security and directing the activities of other officers. Qualified officers also can be promoted to supervisory or administrative positions, including warden. Officers sometimes transfer to related jobs, such as probation officer, parole officer, and correctional treatment specialist.

Important Qualities

Good judgment. Officers must use both their training and common sense to quickly determine the best course of action and to take necessary steps to achieve a desired outcome.

Interpersonal skills. Correctional officers must be able to interact and effectively communicate with inmates and others to maintain order in correctional facilities and courtrooms.

Negotiating skills. Officers must be able to assist others in resolving differences to avoid conflict.

Physical strength. Correctional officers must have the strength to physically subdue inmates.

Resourcefulness. Correctional officers often encounter dangerous and unpredictable situations that require a quick response. They must determine the best practical approach to solving a problem and follow through with it.

Self discipline. Correctional officers must control their emotions when confronted with hostile situations.

Pay

The median annual wage for correctional officers and jailers was $39,040 in May 2012. The median wage is the wage at which half the workers in an occupation earned more than that amount and half earned less. The lowest 10 percent earned less than $27,000, and the top 10 percent earned more than $69,610.

The median annual wage for bailiffs was $36,840 in May 2012. The lowest 10 percent earned less than $18,700, and the top 10 percent earned more than $66,860.

In addition to receiving typical benefits, correctional officers employed in the public sector usually are provided with uniforms or with a clothing allowance to buy their own uniforms. Many departments offer retirement benefits, although benefits vary.

Union Membership. Compared with workers in all occupations, correctional officers had a higher percentage of workers who belonged to a union in 2012.

Job Outlook

Employment of correctional officers is projected to grow 5 percent from 2012 to 2022, slower than the average for all occupations.

Although some demand for correctional officers will occur over the coming decade, anticipated budget constraints and a general downward trend in crime rates in recent years will likely mitigate employment growth.

Faced with growing costs for keeping people in prison, many state governments have moved toward laws requiring shorter prison terms and alternatives to prison. Community-based programs designed to rehabilitate offenders and limit their risk of repeated offenses, while keeping the public safe, may also reduce prison rates.

Job Prospects. Job prospects should be good in the private sector as public authorities contract with private companies to provide and staff corrections facilities. A growing number of state and federal corrections agencies are using private prison services.

Some local and state corrections agencies experience high job turnover because of job-related stress and shift work. The need to replace correctional officers who transfer to other occupations,

retire, or leave the labor force–coupled with rising employment demand–should also generate some job openings.

O*NET

➤ Bailiffs (33-3011.00)
➤ Correctional Officers and Jailers (33-3012.00)

Contacts for More Information

For more information about correctional officers, visit
➤ American Correctional Association (www.aca.org)
➤ American Jail Association (www.aja.org)

For information about career opportunities for correctional officers at the federal level, visit
➤ Federal Bureau of Prisons (www.bop.gov)

Form information on obtaining a position as a correctional officer with the federal government, visit
➤ USAJOBS (www.usajobs.gov)

Firefighters

- **2012 Median Pay** .... $45,250 per year
$21.75 per hour
- **Entry-Level Education** .... Postsecondary non-degree award
- **Work Experience in a Related Occupation** .... None
- **On-the-Job Training** .... Long-term on-the-job training
- **Number of Jobs 2012** 307,000
- **Job Outlook, 2012–22** .... 7% (Slower than average)
- **Employment Change, 2012–22** 20,300

What Firefighters Do

Firefighters control fires and respond to other emergencies, including medical emergencies.

Duties. Firefighters typically do the following:

- Drive fire trucks and other emergency vehicles
- Put out fires using water hoses, fire extinguishers, and pumps
- Find and rescue victims in burning buildings or in other emergency situations
- Treat sick or injured people
- Prepare written reports on emergency incidents
- Clean and maintain equipment
- Conduct drills and physical fitness training
- Provide public education on fire safety

When responding to an emergency, firefighters are responsible for connecting hoses to hydrants, operating pumps to power the hoses, climbing ladders, and using other tools to break through debris. Firefighters may also be required to enter burning buildings to extinguish a fire and rescue individuals. Other firefighters are responsible for providing medical attention, particularly as 2 out of 3 calls firefighters respond to are medical emergencies–not fires, according to the National Fire Protection Association.

Firefighters' duties may change several times while they are at the scene of an emergency. In some cases, they remain at disaster scenes for days, rescuing trapped survivors and assisting with medical treatment.

When firefighters are not responding to an emergency, they are on-call at a fire station. During this time, they regularly inspect

Firefighters help protect the public by responding to fires and a variety of other emergencies.

equipment and perform practice drills. They also eat and sleep and remain on call, as their shifts usually last 24 hours.

The following is an example of a type of firefighter:

Forest firefighters use heavy equipment and water hoses to control forest fires. They also frequently create fire lines–a swathe of cut-down trees and dug-up grass in the path of a fire–to deprive a fire of fuel. Some forest firefighters, known as *smoke jumpers*, parachute from airplanes to reach otherwise inaccessible areas.

Some firefighters also work in hazardous materials units and are specially trained to control, prevent, and clean up hazardous materials, such as oil spills and chemical accidents. They work with hazardous materials removal workers in these cases.

Work Environment

Firefighters held about 307,000 jobs in 2012. The vast majority–about 91 percent– worked for local governments. Most of the remainder worked for federal and state governments. A few worked at airports, chemical plants, and other industrial sites.

These employment numbers exclude volunteer firefighters. There are approximately twice as many volunteer firefighters as there are paid career firefighters.

Volunteer firefighters' share the same duties as paid firefighters and account for the majority of firefighters in many areas. According to the National Fire Protection Association, about 69 percent of fire departments were staffed entirely by volunteer firefighters in 2012.

When not on the scene of an emergency, firefighters work at fire stations, where they sleep, eat, and remain on call. When an alarm sounds, firefighters respond, regardless of the weather or time of day.

Work Schedules. Firefighters typically work long and varied hours. Most firefighters work 24-hour shifts on duty and are off the following 48 or 72 hours. Some firefighters work 10/14 shifts which means 10 hours working and 14 hours off. When combating forest fires, firefighters may work for extended periods without time off.

Injuries and Illnesses. Firefighters have one of the highest rates of injuries and illnesses of all occupations. They often encounter dangerous situations, including collapsing floors and walls, traffic accidents, and overexposure to flames and smoke. As a result, workers must wear protective gear to help lower these risks. Often, the protective gear can be very heavy and hot.

How to Become One

Firefighters typically need a high school diploma and training in emergency medical services. Most firefighters also must pass a written and physical test, complete a series of interviews, and hold an emergency medical technician (EMT) certification. All firefighters receive extensive training after being hired.

Applicants for firefighter jobs typically must be at least 18 years old and have a valid driver's license. They must also pass a medical exam and drug screening to be hired. After being hired, firefighters may be subject to random drug tests.

Education. The entry-level education needed to become a firefighter is a high school diploma or equivalent. However, some class work beyond high school usually is needed to obtain the emergency medical technician (EMT) basic certification. EMT requirements vary by city and state.

Training. Entry-level firefighters receive several weeks of training at fire academies run by the fire department or by the state. Through classroom instruction and practical training, recruits study fire-fighting and fire-prevention techniques, local building codes, and emergency medical procedures. They also learn how to fight fires with standard equipment, including axes, chain saws, fire extinguishers, and ladders.

Some fire departments have accredited apprenticeship programs that last up to 4 years. These programs combine classroom instruction with on-the-job-training under the supervision of experienced firefighters.

In addition to participating in training programs conducted by local or state fire departments and agencies, some firefighters attend federal training sessions sponsored by the National Fire Academy. These training sessions cover topics including execu-

Median Annual Wages, May 2012

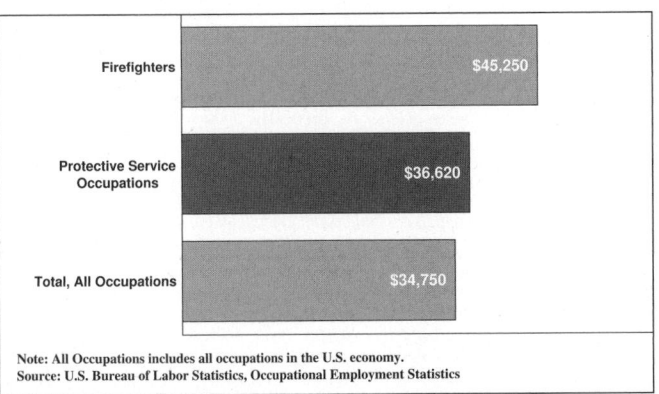

Firefighters	$45,250
Protective Service Occupations	$36,620
Total, All Occupations	$34,750

Note: All Occupations includes all occupations in the U.S. economy.
Source: U.S. Bureau of Labor Statistics, Occupational Employment Statistics

Percent Change in Employment, Projected 2012–2022

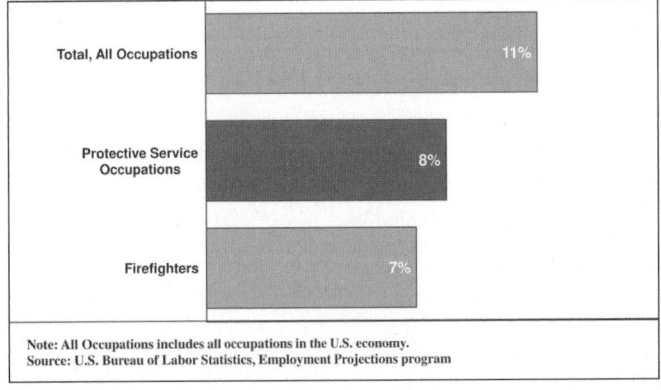

Total, All Occupations	11%
Protective Service Occupations	8%
Firefighters	7%

Note: All Occupations includes all occupations in the U.S. economy.
Source: U.S. Bureau of Labor Statistics, Employment Projections program

Employment Projections Data for Firefighters

Occupational title	SOC Code	Employment, 2012	Projected Employment, 2022	Change, 2012–2022	
				Percent	Numeric
Firefighters...	33-2011	307,000	327,300	7	20,300

Source: U.S. Bureau of Labor Statistics, Employment Projections Program

Note: Data are rounded. Go to Occupational Information Included in the OOH *for a discussion of the data in this table.*

tive development, anti-arson techniques, disaster preparedness, hazardous materials control, and public fire safety and education.

Licenses, Certifications, and Registrations. Firefighters must usually be certified as emergency medical technicians at the EMT-Basic level. In addition, some fire departments require firefighters to be certified as an EMT-Paramedic. The National Registry of Emergency Medical Technicians (NREMT) certifies EMTs and paramedics. All levels of NREMT certification require completing a training or education program and passing the national exam. The national exam has both a written part and a practical part. In some departments, it is possible to earn these certifications after being hired. EMTs and paramedics may work with firefighters at the scenes of accidents.

Some states have mandatory or voluntary firefighter training and certification programs.

Other Experience. Working as a volunteer firefighter may help in getting a job as a career firefighter.

Advancement. Firefighters can be promoted to engineer, then lieutenant, captain, battalion chief, assistant chief, deputy chief, and finally, chief. For promotion to positions beyond battalion chief, many fire departments now require applicants to have a bachelor's degree, preferably in fire science, public administration, or a related field. Some firefighters eventually become fire inspectors or investigators after gaining enough experience.

The National Fire Academy also offers a certification as Executive Fire Officer. To be eligible for certification, firefighters must have a bachelor's degree.

Important Qualities

Communication skills. Firefighters must be able to communicate conditions at an emergency scene to other firefighters and to emergency-response crews.

Courage. Firefighters are confronted with dangerous situations, such as entering a burning building, while doing their jobs.

Decision-making skills. Firefighters must be able to make quick and smart decisions in an emergency. The ability to make good decisions under pressure could potentially save someone's life.

Physical stamina. Firefighters may have to stay at disaster scenes for long periods of time to rescue and treat victims. They must also be ready to respond to emergencies at any hour of the day.

Physical strength. Firefighters must be strong enough to carry heavy equipment and move debris at an emergency site. They must also be able to carry victims who are injured or cannot walk.

Pay

The median annual wage for firefighters was $45,250 in May 2012. The median wage is the wage at which half the workers in an occupation earned more than that amount and half earned less. The lowest 10 percent earned less than $22,030, and the top 10 percent earned more than $79,150.

Union Membership. Most firefighters belonged to a union in 2012. The largest organizer for firefighters is the International Association of Fire Fighters.

Job Outlook

Employment of firefighters is projected to grow 7 percent from 2012 to 2022, slower than the average for all occupations.

The aging of the population will lead to an increased demand for emergency responders as the elderly tend to use more emergency medical services. Currently, about 2 of out 3 situations that firefighters respond to are medical–rather than fire–emergencies.

In addition, jobs will be created as volunteer firefighters are converted to paid positions in areas where population growth creates the need for a full-time workforce. An increase in urban populations, where full-time firefighters are more common, also is expected to increase the demand for firefighters.

Job Prospects. Prospective firefighters will likely face strong competition for jobs. Many people are attracted to the job's challenge, opportunity for public service, and relatively low formal education requirements. As a result, a department may receive hundreds of applicants for a single position.

Physically-fit applicants with high test scores, some post-secondary firefighter education, and paramedic training should have the best job prospects.

O*NET

➤ Firefighters (33-2011.00)
➤ Municipal Firefighters (33-2011.01)
➤ Forest Firefighters (33-2011.02)

Similar Occupations
This table shows a list of occupations with job duties that are similar to those of firefighters.

Occupations	Entry-level Education	2012 Pay	Projected Job Growth	Average Annual Openings
Correctional Officers	High school diploma or equivalent	$38,961	5%	14,780
EMTs and Paramedics	Postsecondary non-degree award	$31,020	23%	12,060
Fire Inspectors and Investigators	High school diploma or equivalent	$53,990	7%	440
Police and Detectives	High school diploma or equivalent	$57,974	5%	27,500
Security Guards and Gaming Surveillance Officers	High school diploma or equivalent	$24,019	12%	29,630

Contacts for More Information

For information about a career as a firefighter, contact your local fire department or visit

➤ International Association of Fire Fighters (www.iaff.org/)
➤ International Association of Women in Fire & Emergency Services (www.i-women.org/)
➤ U.S. Fire Administration (www.usfa.fema.gov/)
➤ National Fire Protection Association (www.nfpa.org/)

For information about professional qualifications and a list of colleges and universities offering 2- or 4-year degree programs in fire science and fire prevention, visit

➤ National Fire Academy, U.S. Fire Administration (www.usfa.fema.gov/nfa)

Fire Inspectors and Investigators

- **2012 Median Pay** .... $53,990 per year
  $25.96 per hour
- **Entry-Level Education** ... High school diploma or equivalent
- **Work Experience in a Related Occupation** ...5 years or more
- **On-the-Job Training** .... Moderate-term on-the-job training
- **Number of Jobs 2012** 12,200
- **Job Outlook, 2012–22** .... 6% (Slower than average)
- **Employment Change, 2012–22** 800

What Fire Inspectors and Investigators Do

Fire inspectors examine buildings to detect fire hazards and ensure that federal, state, and local fire codes are met. Fire investigators determine the origin and cause of fires and explosions.

Duties. Fire inspectors typically do the following:

- Search for fire hazards
- Ensure that buildings comply with fire codes
- Test fire alarms, sprinklers, and other fire protection equipment
- Inspect gasoline storage tanks and air compressors
- Review emergency evacuation plans
- Conduct follow-up visits when an infraction is found
- Review building plans with developers
- Conduct fire and safety education programs
- Keep detailed records that may be used in a court of law

Fire investigators typically do the following:

- Collect and analyze evidence from scenes of fires and explosions
- Interview witnesses
- Reconstruct the scene of a fire or arson
- Send evidence to laboratories to be tested for fingerprints or an accelerant
- Analyze information with chemists, engineers, and attorneys
- Document evidence by taking photographs and creating diagrams
- Determine the origin and cause of a fire
- Keep detailed records and protect evidence for use in a court of law
- Testify in civil and criminal legal proceedings
- Exercise police powers, such as the power of arrest, and carry a weapon

The following is an example of one type of fire inspector:

Forest fire inspectors and prevention specialists assess fire hazards in both public and residential areas. They look for infractions and conditions that pose a wildfire risk and recommend ways to reduce the fire hazard. During patrols, they enforce fire regulations and report fire conditions to central command.

Work Environment

Fire inspectors and investigators held about 12,200 jobs in 2012. The vast majority worked for state and local fire departments. A few also worked for insurance companies or attorney's offices.

Fire inspectors and investigators work in both offices and in the field. In the field, inspectors examine public buildings, such as museums, and multifamily residential buildings, such as high-rise condominiums. They may also visit and inspect other structures, such as arenas and industrial plants.

Investigators must visit the scene where a fire has occurred.

Work Schedules. Most fire inspectors typically work during regular business hours. Because investigators must be ready to respond when a fire happens, they often work evenings, weekends, and holidays.

Injuries and Illnesses. Fire inspectors and investigators have a higher rate of injuries and illnesses than the national average. For example, it can be very dangerous to walk on structures that are unstable because they were damaged in a fire. Inhaling fumes from a fire can also result in health issues.

When working in the field, inspectors and investigators often must wear protective clothing, such as boots, gloves, and a helmet.

How to Become One

Most fire inspectors and investigators have a high school diploma and previous work experience in a fire or police department. They attend training academies and receive on-the-job training in inspection and investigation.

Fire inspectors and investigators usually must pass a background check, which may include a drug test. Most employers also require inspectors to be U.S. citizens and have a valid driver's license.

Work Experience in a Related Occupation. Most fire inspectors and investigators are required to have work experience in a related occupation, such as firefighters or police officers. Some fire departments or law enforcement agencies require investigators to have a certain number of years within the organization or to be a certain

Fire inspectors ensure that buildings comply with fire codes.

Median Annual Wages, May 2012

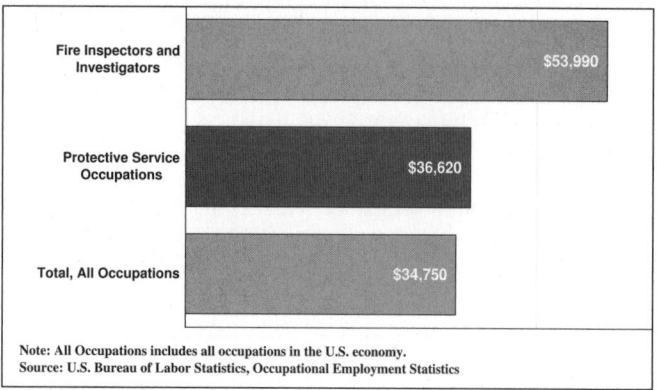

Note: All Occupations includes all occupations in the U.S. economy.
Source: U.S. Bureau of Labor Statistics, Occupational Employment Statistics

Percent Change in Employment, Projected 2012–2022

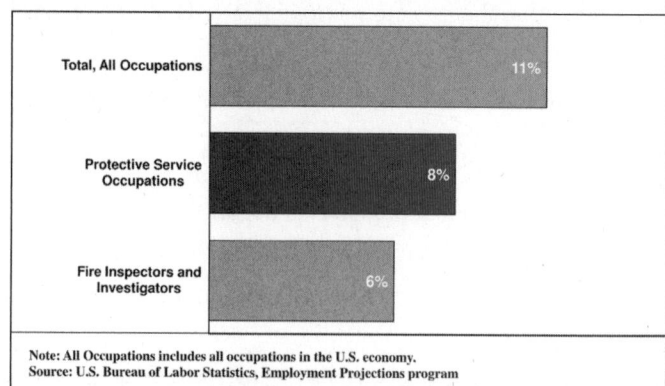

Note: All Occupations includes all occupations in the U.S. economy.
Source: U.S. Bureau of Labor Statistics, Employment Projections program

rank, such as lieutenant or captain, before they are eligible for promotion to an inspector or investigator position.

Education. Most fire inspector and investigator jobs require a high school diploma. However, some employers prefer candidates with a 2- or 4-year degree in fire science, engineering, or chemistry.

Training. Training requirements vary by state, but programs usually include instruction in a classroom setting in addition to on-the-job training.

Classroom training often takes place at a fire or police academy over the course of several months. A variety of topics are covered, including guidelines for conducting an inspection or investigation, legal codes, courtroom procedures, protocols for handling hazardous materials and bombs, and the proper use of equipment.

In most agencies, after inspectors and investigators have finished their classroom training, they also receive on-the-job training, during which they work with a more experienced officer.

Licenses, Certifications, and Registrations. Many states have certification exams that cover information on standards established by the National Fire Protection Association. To maintain registration, many agencies require additional training for inspectors and investigators each year.

The National Fire Protection Association also offers several certifications for fire inspectors. Some jobs in the private sector require that job candidates already have these certifications.

Fire investigators may also choose to pursue certification from a nationally recognized professional association, such as the International Association of Arson Investigators (IAAI) - Certified Fire

Investigator (CFI) or the National Association of Fire Investigators (NAFI) - Certified Fire and Explosion Investigator (CFEI). The Bureau of Alcohol, Tobacco, Firearms and Explosives (ATF) also offers a CFI certification. However, this program is available only to ATF employees.

Fire investigators who work for private companies may have to obtain a private investigation license from their state.

Important Qualities

Communication skills. Inspectors must clearly explain fire code violations to building and property managers. Investigators must carefully interview witnesses as part of their fact-finding mission.

Critical-thinking skills. Inspectors must be able to recognize code violations and recommend a way to fix the problem. Investigators must be able to analyze evidence from a fire and determine a reasonable conclusion.

Detail oriented. Fire inspectors and investigators must notice details when inspecting a site for code violations or investigating the cause of a fire.

Integrity. Inspectors must be consistent in the methods they use to enforce fire codes. Investigators must be unbiased when conducting their research and when testifying as an expert witness in court.

Pay

The median annual wage for fire inspectors and investigators was $53,990 in May 2012. The median wage is the wage at which half the workers in an occupation earned more than that amount and

Employment Projections Data for Fire Inspectors and Investigators

Occupational title	SOC Code	Employment, 2012	Projected Employment, 2022	Change, 2012–2022	
				Percent	Numeric
Fire inspectors and investigators 33-2021		12,200	13,000	6	800

Source: U.S. Bureau of Labor Statistics, Employment Projections Program

Note: **Data are rounded. Go to Occupational Information Included in the OOH** *for a discussion of the data in this table.*

Similar Occupations This table shows a list of occupations with job duties that are similar to those of fire inspectors and investigators.

Occupations	Entry-level Education	2012 Pay	Projected Job Growth	Average Annual Openings
Firefighters	Postsecondary non-degree award	$45,250	7%	10,400
Police and Detectives	High school diploma or equivalent	$57,974	5%	27,500
Private Detectives and Investigators	High school diploma or equivalent	$45,740	11%	1,180

half earned less. The lowest 10 percent earned less than $33,920, and the top 10 percent earned more than $87,400.

Job Outlook

Employment of fire inspectors and investigators is projected to grow 6 percent from 2012 to 2022, slower than the average for all occupations.

Because local government employs about 75 percent of all fire inspectors and investigators, employment growth will be tempered as this sector is projected to grow slower than average from 2012 to 2022.

However, fire inspectors will still be needed to assess potential fire hazards in newly constructed residential, commercial, public, and other buildings in the coming decade. Fire inspectors will also be needed to ensure that existing buildings meet updated and revised federal, state, and local fire codes each year.

Although the number of fires occurring across the country has been falling for some time, fire investigators will still be needed to determine the cause of fires and explosions.

Job Prospects. Jobseekers should expect strong competition for the limited number of available positions.

Those who have previous work experience in fire suppression, have completed some fire science education, or have training related to criminal investigation should have an advantage over candidates who do not.

O*NET

➤ Fire Inspectors and Investigators (33-2021.00)
➤ Fire Inspectors (33-2021.01)
➤ Fire Investigators (33-2021.02)

Contacts for More Information

For more information about federal fire investigator jobs, visit
➤ Bureau of Alcohol, Tobacco, Firearms and Explosives (www.atf.gov/)

For more information about fire inspectors and investigators training, visit
➤ National Fire Academy (www.usfa.dhs.gov/nfa)

For information about standards for fire inspectors and investigators, visit
➤ National Fire Protection Association (www.nfpa.org)

For information about certifications, visit
➤ International Association of Arson Investigators (www.firearson.com)
➤ National Association of Fire Investigators (www.nafi.org)

Police and Detectives

- **2012 Median Pay** .... $56,980 per year
  $27.40 per hour

- **Entry-Level Education** ... High school diploma or equivalent

- **Work Experience in a Related Occupation** .... See "How to Become One"

- **On-the-Job Training** .... See "How to Become One"

- **Number of Jobs 2012** 780,000

- **Job Outlook, 2012–22** .... 5% (Slower than average)

- **Employment Change, 2012–22** 41,400

What Police and Detectives Do

Police officers protect lives and property. Detectives and criminal investigators, who are sometimes called *agents* or *special agents*, gather facts and collect evidence of possible crimes.

Duties. Uniformed police officers typically do the following:

- Enforce laws
- Respond to emergency and non-emergency calls
- Patrol assigned areas
- Conduct traffic stops and issue citations
- Obtain warrants and arrest suspects
- Write detailed reports and fill out forms
- Prepare cases and testify in court

Detectives and criminal investigators typically do the following:

- Investigate crimes
- Collect and secure evidence from crime scenes
- Conduct interviews with suspects and witnesses
- Observe the activities of suspects
- Obtain warrants and arrest suspects
- Write detailed reports and fill out forms
- Prepare cases and testify in court

Police officers pursue and apprehend people who break the law. They then warn, cite, or arrest them. Most police officers patrol their jurisdictions and investigate suspicious activity. They also respond to calls, issue traffic tickets, and give first aid to accident victims.

Detectives perform investigative duties, such as gathering facts and collecting evidence.

The daily activities of police and detectives vary with their occupational specialty, such as canine units and special weapons and tactics (SWAT). Whether they work at a local, state, or federal agency also determines job duties; and duties differ among federal agencies, because they enforce different aspects of the law. Regardless of job duties or location, police officers and detectives at all levels must write reports and keep detailed records that will be needed if they testify in court. Most carry law enforcement tools, such as radios, handcuffs, and guns.

The following are examples of types of police and detectives who work in state and local law enforcement and in federal law enforcement:

The daily activities of police and detectives vary with their occupational specialty.

Median Annual Wages, May 2012

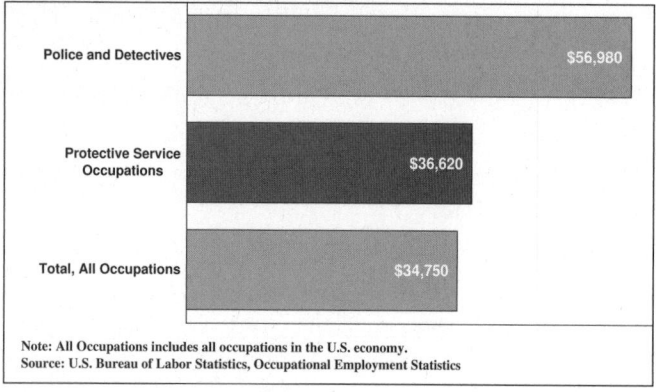

Police and Detectives — $56,980
Protective Service Occupations — $36,620
Total, All Occupations — $34,750

Note: All Occupations includes all occupations in the U.S. economy.
Source: U.S. Bureau of Labor Statistics, Occupational Employment Statistics

Percent Change in Employment, Projected 2012–2022

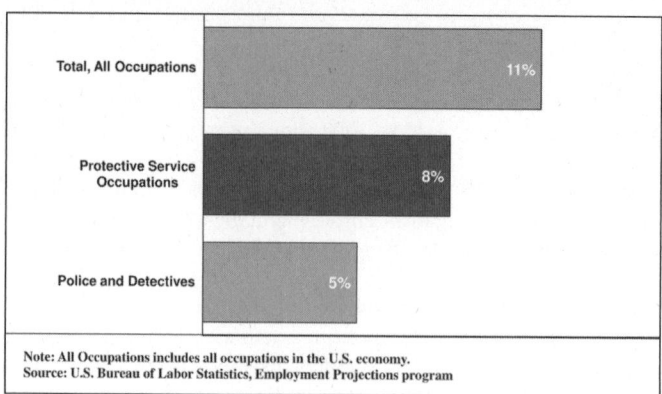

Total, All Occupations — 11%
Protective Service Occupations — 8%
Police and Detectives — 5%

Note: All Occupations includes all occupations in the U.S. economy.
Source: U.S. Bureau of Labor Statistics, Employment Projections program

State and Local Law Enforcement

Uniformed police officers have general law enforcement duties. They wear uniforms that allow the public to easily recognize them as police officers. They have regular patrols and also respond to emergency and non-emergency calls.

Police agencies are usually organized into geographic districts, with uniformed officers assigned to patrol a specific area. Officers in large agencies often patrol with a partner. During patrols, officers look for any signs of criminal activity and may conduct searches and arrest suspected criminals. They may also respond to emergency calls, investigate complaints, and enforce traffic laws.

Some police officers work only on a specific type of crime, such as narcotics. Officers, especially those working in large departments, may work in special units, such as horseback, motorcycle, canine corps, and special weapons and tactics (SWAT) teams. Typically, officers must work as patrol officers for a certain number of years before they may be appointed to one of these units.

Some city police agencies are involved in community policing, a philosophy of bringing police and members of the community together to prevent crime. A neighborhood watch program is one type of community policing.

Some agencies have special geographic and enforcement responsibilities. Examples include public college and university police forces, public school police, and transit police. Most law enforcement workers in special agencies are uniformed officers.

State police officers, sometimes called *state troopers* or *highway patrol officers*, have many of the same duties as other police officers, but they may spend more time enforcing traffic laws and issuing traffic citations. State police officers have authority to work anywhere in the state and are frequently called on to help other law enforcement agencies, especially those in rural areas or small towns.

Transit and railroad police patrol railroad yards and transit stations. They protect property, employees, and passengers from crimes such as thefts and robberies. They remove trespassers from railroad and transit properties and check IDs of people who try to enter secure areas.

Sheriffs and deputy sheriffs enforce the law on the county level. Sheriffs' departments tend to be relatively small. Sheriffs usually are elected by the public and do the same work as a local or county police chief. Some sheriffs' departments do the same work as officers in urban police departments. Others mainly operate the county jails and provide services in local courts. Police and sheriffs' deputies who provide security in city and county courts are sometimes called bailiffs.

Detectives and criminal investigators are uniformed or plain-clothes investigators who gather facts and collect evidence for criminal cases. They conduct interviews, examine records, observe the activities of suspects, and participate in raids and arrests. Detectives usually specialize in investigating one type of crime, such as homicide or fraud. Detectives are typically assigned cases on a rotating basis and work on them until an arrest and trial are completed or until the case is dropped.

Fish and game wardens enforce fishing, hunting, and boating laws. They patrol hunting and fishing areas, conduct search and rescue operations, investigate complaints and accidents, and educate the public about laws pertaining to the outdoors.

Federal Law Enforcement

Federal law enforcement officials carry out many of the same duties that other police officers do; however, they have jurisdiction over the entire country. Many federal agents are highly specialized. The following are examples of federal agencies in which officers and agents enforce particular types of laws.

- Federal Bureau of Investigation (FBI) agents are the federal government's principal investigators, responsible for enforcing more than 300 federal statutes and conducting sensitive national security investigations.

- Drug Enforcement Administration (DEA) agents enforce laws and regulations relating to illegal drugs.

- United States Secret Service uniformed officers protect the President, the Vice President, their immediate families, and other public officials. Other Secret Service agents investigate financial crimes.

- Federal Air Marshals provide air security by guarding against attacks targeting U.S. aircraft, passengers, and crews.

- U.S. Border Patrol agents protect international land and water boundaries.

See the Contacts for More Information section for additional information about federal law enforcement agencies.

Work Environment

Police and detectives held about 780,000 jobs in 2012. Most police and detectives work for local governments and some work for state governments or the federal government.

Police and detective work can be physically demanding, stressful, and dangerous.

The jobs of some federal agents, such as U.S. Secret Service and DEA special agents, require extensive travel, often on short notice. These agents may relocate a number of times over the course of their careers. Some special agents, such as those in the U.S. Border Protection, may work outdoors in rugged terrain and in all kinds of weather.

Employment Projections Data for Police and Detectives

Occupational title	SOC Code	Employment, 2012	Projected Employment, 2022	Change, 2012–2022	
				Percent	Numeric
Police and detectives...	—	780,000	821,300	5	41,400
Detectives and criminal investigators	33-3021	115,200	117,500	2	2,300
Fish and game wardens..	33-3031	6,600	6,700	1	100
Police and sheriff's patrol officers....................................	33-3051	653,800	692,700	6	38,800
Transit and railroad police...	33-3052	4,300	4,400	3	100

Source: U.S. Bureau of Labor Statistics, Employment Projections Program

Note: Data are rounded. Go to Occupational Information Included in the OOH for a discussion of the data in this table.

Injuries and Illnesses. Police and sheriff's patrol officers have one of the highest rates of injuries and illnesses of all occupations. They may face physical injury when conflicts with criminals occur, during motor-vehicle pursuits, when exposure to communicable diseases occurs, or through many other high-risk situations.

Police work can be both physically and mentally demanding, as officers must be alert and ready to react throughout their entire shift. Officers regularly work at crime and accident scenes and deal with the death and suffering that they encounter there. Although a career in law enforcement may be stressful, many officers find it rewarding to help members of their communities.

Work Schedules. Uniformed officers, detectives, agents, and inspectors usually are scheduled to work full time. Paid overtime is common. Shift work is necessary because protection of the public must be provided around the clock. Because more experienced employees typically receive preference, junior officers frequently work weekends, holidays, and nights.

How to Become One

Education requirements range from a high school diploma to a college, or higher, degree. Most police and detectives must graduate from their agency's training academy before completing a period of on-the-job training. Candidates must be U.S. citizens, usually at least 21 years old, and meet rigorous physical and personal qualifications.

Education. Police and detective applicants must have at least a high school education or GED and be a graduate of their agency's training academy. Many agencies and some police departments require some college coursework or a college degree. Knowledge of a foreign language is an asset in many federal agencies and in certain geographical regions.

Candidates must be U.S. citizens, usually be at least 21 years old, have a driver's license, and meet specific physical qualifications. Applicants may have to pass physical exams of vision, hearing, strength, and agility, as well as competitive written exams. Previous work or military experience is often seen as a plus. Candidates typically go through a series of interviews and may be asked to take lie detector and drug tests. A felony conviction may disqualify a candidate.

Training. Applicants usually have training as a recruit before becoming an officer. In state and large local police departments, recruits get training in their agency's police academy. In small agencies, recruits often attend a regional or state academy. Training includes classroom instruction in constitutional law, civil rights, state laws and local ordinances, and police ethics. Recruits also receive training and supervised experience in areas such as patrol, traffic control, use of firearms, self-defense, first aid, and emergency response.

Detectives normally begin their career as police officers before being promoted to detective.

State and local agencies encourage applicants to continue their education after high school, by taking courses and training related to law enforcement. Many applicants for entry-level police jobs have taken some college classes, and a significant number are college graduates. Many junior colleges, colleges, and universities offer programs in law enforcement and criminal justice. Many agencies offer financial assistance to officers who pursue these, or related, degrees.

Fish and game wardens also must meet specific requirements; however, these vary. Candidates applying for federal jobs with the U.S. Fish & Wildlife Service typically need a college degree; and those applying to work for state departments often need a high school diploma or some college study in a related field, such as biology or natural resources management. Military or police experience may be considered an advantage. Once hired, fish and game wardens attend a training academy and sometimes get additional training in the field.

Although similar to state and local requirements, requirements for federal law enforcement agencies, such as the FBI and Secret Service, are generally stricter. Federal agencies require a bachelor's degree, related work experience, or a combination of the two. For example, FBI special agent applicants typically must be college graduates with at least 3 years of professional work experience. Also required are lie detector tests, as well as interviews with the applicant's references. Jobs that require security clearances have additional requirements.

Federal law enforcement agents undergo extensive training, usually at the U.S. Marine Corps base in Quantico, Virginia, or at the Federal Law Enforcement Training Centers in Glynco, Georgia. Furthermore, some federal positions have a maximum age for applicants. Specific education requirements, qualifications, and training information for a particular federal agency are available on its website. See the Contacts for More Information section for links to various federal agencies.

Other Experience. Some police departments have cadet programs for people interested in a career in law enforcement who do not yet meet age requirements for becoming an officer. These cadets do clerical work and attend classes until they reach the minimum age requirement and can apply for a position with the regular force.

Advancement. Police officers usually become eligible for promotion after a probationary period. Promotions to corporal, sergeant, lieutenant, and captain usually are made according to a candidate's position on a promotion list, as determined by scores on a written examination and on-the-job performance. In large departments, promotion may enable an officer to become a detective or to specialize in one type of police work, such as working with juveniles.

Similar Occupations　This table shows a list of occupations with job duties that are similar to those of police and detectives.

Occupations	Entry-level Education	2012 Pay	Projected Job Growth	Average Annual Openings
Correctional Officers	High school diploma or equivalent	$38,961	5%	14,780
EMTs and Paramedics	Postsecondary non-degree award	$31,020	23%	12,060
Firefighters	Postsecondary non-degree award	$45,250	7%	10,400
Private Detectives and Investigators	High school diploma or equivalent	$45,740	11%	1,180
Probation Officers and Correctional Treatment Specialists	Bachelor's degree	$48,190	-1%	2,360
Security Guards and Gaming Surveillance Officers	High school diploma or equivalent	$24,019	12%	29,630

Important Qualities

Communication skills. Police and detectives must be able to speak with people when gathering facts about a crime and to express details about a given incident in writing.

Empathy. Police officers need to understand the perspectives of a wide variety of people in their jurisdiction and have a willingness to help the public.

Good judgment. Police and detectives must be able to determine the best way to solve a wide array of problems quickly.

Leadership skills. Police officers must be comfortable with being a highly visible member of their community, as the public looks to them for assistance in emergency situations.

Perceptiveness. Officers must be able to anticipate another person's reactions and understand why people act a certain way.

Physical stamina. Officers and detectives must be in good physical shape, both to pass required tests for entry into the field, and to keep up with the daily rigors of the job.

Physical strength. Police officers must be strong enough to physically apprehend offenders.

Pay

The median annual wage for police and detectives was $56,980 in May 2012. The median wage is the wage at which half the workers in an occupation earned more than that amount and half earned less. The lowest 10 percent earned less than $33,060, and the top 10 percent earned more than $93,450.

The median wages for police and detective occupations in May 2012 were as follows:

$74,300 for detectives and criminal investigators
$55,270 for police and sheriff's patrol officers
$55,210 for transit and railroad police
$48,070 for fish and game wardens

Many agencies provide officers with an allowance for uniforms, as well as extensive benefits and the option to retire at an age that is younger than typical retirement age.

Union Membership. Compared with workers in all occupations, police and detectives had a higher percentage of workers who belonged to a union in 2012.

Job Outlook

Employment of police and detectives is projected to grow 5 percent from 2012 to 2022, slower than the average for all occupations.

Continued desire for public safety will result in a need for more officers. However, demand for employment is expected to vary depending on location, driven largely by local and state budgets. Even with crime rates falling in the last few years, there will be continued demand for police services to maintain and improve public safety.

Job Prospects. Applicants with a bachelor's degree and law enforcement or military experience, especially investigative experience, as well as those who speak more than one language, should have the best job opportunities.

The level of government spending determines the level of employment for police and detectives. The number of job opportunities, therefore, can vary from year to year and from place to place. Job prospects should be best for trained officers with related work experience.

O*NET

➤ Detectives and Criminal Investigators (33-3021.00)
➤ Police Detectives (33-3021.01)
➤ Police Identification and Records Officers (33-3021.02)
➤ Criminal Investigators and Special Agents (33-3021.03)
➤ Immigration and Customs Inspectors (33-3021.05)
➤ Intelligence Analysts (33-3021.06)
➤ Fish and Game Wardens (33-3031.00)
➤ Police and Sheriff's Patrol Officers (33-3051.00)
➤ Police Patrol Officers (33-3051.01)
➤ Sheriffs and Deputy Sheriffs (33-3051.03)
➤ Transit and Railroad Police (33-3052.00)

Contacts for More Information

For general information about sheriffs, visit
➤ National Sheriffs' Association (www.sheriffs.org/)
For information about chiefs of police, visit
➤ International Association of Chiefs of Police (IACP) (www.theiacp.org/)
For more information about careers in state and local law enforcement, visit
➤ Bureau of Justice Assistance and www.theiacp.org/IACP websites (The www.bja.gov/)
For more information about federal law enforcement, visit
➤ Bureau of Alcohol, Tobacco, Firearms and Explosives (www.atf.gov/)
➤ Drug Enforcement Administration (www.usdoj.gov/dea)
➤ Federal Bureau of Investigation (www.fbi.gov/)
➤ U.S. Customs and Border Protection (www.cbp.gov/)
➤ U.S. Department of Homeland Security (www.dhs.gov/)
➤ U.S. Marshals Service (www.usmarshals.gov/)
➤ United States Secret Service (www.secretservice.gov/)
➤ U.S. Fish & Wildlife Service (www.fws.gov/)

Private Detectives and Investigators

- **2012 Median Pay** .... $45,740 per year
  $21.99 per hour

- **Entry-Level Education** ... High school diploma or equivalent

- **Work Experience in a Related Occupation** .... Less than
  5 years

- **On-the-Job Training** .... Moderate-term on-the-job training

- **Number of Jobs 2012** 30,000

- **Job Outlook, 2012–22** .... 11% (As fast as average)

- **Employment Change, 2012–22** 3,300

What Private Detectives and Investigators Do

Private detectives and investigators find facts and analyze information about legal, financial, and personal matters. They offer many services, including verifying people's backgrounds, finding missing persons, and investigating computer crimes.

Duties. Private detectives and investigators typically do the following:

- Interview people to gather information
- Search records to uncover clues
- Conduct surveillance
- Collect evidence to present in court
- Verify employment, income, and other facts about a person
- Investigate computer crimes and information theft

Private detectives and investigators offer many services for individuals, attorneys, and businesses. They may perform background checks or look into charges that someone has been stealing money from a company. They might be hired to prove or disprove infidelity in a divorce case.

Private detectives and investigators use a variety of tools when researching the facts in a case. Much of their work is done with a computer, allowing them to obtain information, such as telephone numbers, social networking-site details, and records of a person's prior arrests. They make phone calls to verify facts and interview people when conducting a background investigation.

Investigators may go undercover to observe suspects and to obtain information.

Detectives also conduct surveillance when investigating a case. They may watch locations, such as a person's home or office, often from an inconspicuous position. Using various hand-held devices, video cameras, binoculars, and GPS tracking, detectives gather information on persons of interest.

Detectives and investigators must be mindful of the law when conducting investigations. Because they lack police powers, their work must be done with the same authority as a private citizen.

Private detectives and investigators may use many methods to determine the facts in a case.

As a result, they must have a good understanding of federal, state, and local laws, such as privacy laws, and other legal issues affecting their work. Otherwise, evidence they collect may not be useable in court.

The following are examples of types of private detectives and investigators:

Computer forensic investigators specialize in recovering, analyzing, and presenting information from computers to be used as evidence. Many focus on recovering deleted emails and documents.

Legal investigators help prepare criminal defenses, verify facts in civil law suits, locate witnesses, and serve legal documents. They often work for lawyers and law firms.

Corporate investigators conduct internal and external investigations for corporations. Internally, they may investigate drug use in the workplace or ensure that expense accounts are not abused. Externally, they may try to identify and stop criminal schemes, such as fraudulent billing by a supplier.

Financial investigators may be hired to collect financial information on individuals and companies attempting to do large financial transactions. These investigators often are certified public

Median Annual Wages, May 2012

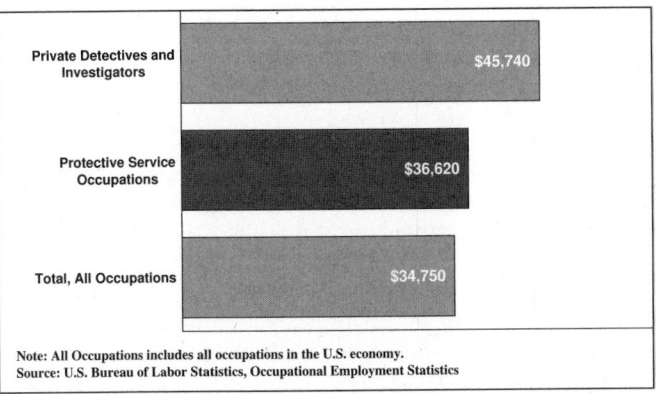

Note: All Occupations includes all occupations in the U.S. economy.
Source: U.S. Bureau of Labor Statistics, Occupational Employment Statistics

Percent Change in Employment, Projected 2012–2022

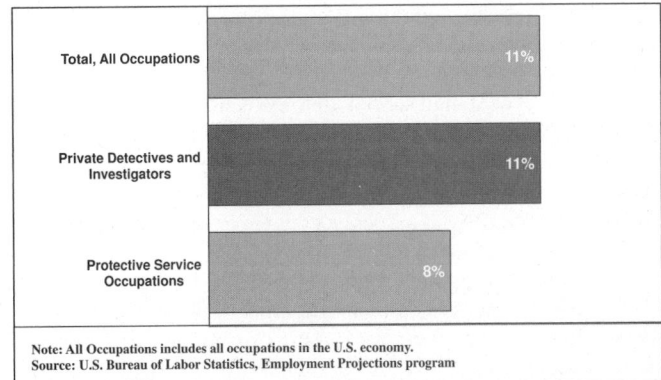

Note: All Occupations includes all occupations in the U.S. economy.
Source: U.S. Bureau of Labor Statistics, Employment Projections program

Employment Projections Data for Private Detectives and Investigators

Occupational title	SOC Code	Employment, 2012	Projected Employment, 2022	Change, 2012–2022	
				Percent	Numeric
Private detectives and investigators 33-9021		30,000	33,300	11	3,300

Source: U.S. Bureau of Labor Statistics, Employment Projections Program

Note: Data are rounded. Go to Occupational Information Included in the OOH *for a discussion of the data in this table.*

accountants (CPAs) who work closely with investment bankers and other accountants. Investigators might search for assets to recover damages awarded by a court in fraud and theft cases.

Store detectives, also known as *loss prevention agents*, catch people who try to steal merchandise or destroy store property.

Work Environment

Private detectives and investigators held about 30,000 jobs in 2012. About 1 in 5 were self-employed.

The industries that employed the most private detectives and investigators in 2012 were as follows:

Investigation, guard, and armored car services	37%
Finance and insurance	8
Government	8
Legal services	4

Private detectives and investigators work in many places, depending on the case. Some spend more time in offices doing computer searches and making phone calls. Others spend more time in the field, conducting interviews or performing surveillance.

Although investigators often work alone, some work with others while conducting surveillance or working on a large and complicated assignment.

Some of the work can involve confrontation. Some situations, such as certain bodyguard assignments, call for the investigator to be armed. In most cases, however, a weapon is not necessary because private detectives and investigators' purpose is information gathering and not law enforcement or criminal apprehension.

Private detectives and investigators may have to work with demanding and, sometimes, distraught clients.

Work Schedules. Private detectives and investigators often work irregular hours because they conduct surveillance and contact people outside of normal work hours.

In addition, they may have to work outdoors or from a vehicle, in all kinds of weather, depending on what the subject of investigation is doing.

How to Become One

Private detectives and investigators mostly need several years of work experience in law enforcement. Workers must also have a high school diploma, and the vast majority of states require private detectives and investigators to have a license.

Education. Education requirements vary greatly depending on the job. However, a high school diploma is usually required.

Some jobs may require a 2- or 4 year degree. Although previous work experience is usually the most important requirement, candidates sometimes enter the occupation directly after graduating from college with an associate's degree or bachelor's degree in criminal justice or police science.

Corporate investigators typically need a bachelor's degree. Coursework in finance, accounting, and business is often preferred. Because many financial investigators have an accountant's

background, they typically have a bachelor's degree in accounting or a related field and may be Certified Public Accountants (CPAs).

Computer forensics investigators often need a bachelor's degree in computer science or criminal justice. Many colleges and universities now offer certificate programs in computer forensics, and others offer a bachelor's or a master's degree.

Training. Most private detectives and investigators learn through on-the-job experience, often lasting several years.

Although new investigators must learn how to gather information, additional training depends on the type of firm that hires them. For instance, at an insurance company, a new investigator will learn to recognize insurance fraud on the job. And corporate investigators hired by large companies may receive formal training in business practices, management structure, and various finance-related topics.

Because computer forensics specialists need both computer skills and investigative skills, extensive training may be required. Many learn their trade while working for a law enforcement agency for several years where they are taught how to gather evidence and spot computer-related crimes.

Continuing education is important in this area because computer forensic investigators work with changing technologies. Investigators must learn the latest methods of fraud detection and new software programs. Many accomplish this by attending conferences and courses offered by software vendors and professional associations.

Work Experience in a Related Occupation. Private detectives and investigators typically must have previous work experience, usually in law enforcement, the military, or federal intelligence jobs.

Some have worked for insurance or collections companies, as paralegals, in finance, or in accounting. Many of these people, who retire after 25 years of work, often become private detectives or investigators as a second career.

Licenses, Certifications, and Registrations. The vast majority of states require private detectives and investigators to have a license. Requirements vary, depending on the state. Professional Investigator Magazine has links to each state's licensing requirements. Because laws often change, jobseekers should verify the licensing laws related to private investigators with the state and locality in which they want to work.

In most states, detectives and investigators who carry handguns must meet additional requirements.

Some states require an additional license to work as a bodyguard.

Although there are no license requirements for computer forensic investigators, some states require them to be licensed private investigators. Even in states and localities where licensure is not required, having a private investigator license is useful, because it allows computer forensic investigators to perform related investigative work.

Candidates also can obtain certification. Although not required, becoming certified through professional organizations can demon-

Similar Occupations   This table shows a list of occupations with job duties that are similar to those of private detectives and investigators.

Occupations	Entry-level Education	2012 Pay	Projected Job Growth	Average Annual Openings
Accountants and Auditors	Bachelor's degree	$63,550	13%	54,420
Bill and Account Collectors	High school diploma or equivalent	$32,480	15%	17,000
Claims Adjusters, Appraisers, Examiners, and Investigators	See "How to Become One"	$59,902	3%	8,340
Financial Analysts	Bachelor's degree	$76,950	16%	10,090
Financial Examiners	Bachelor's degree	$75,800	7%	920
Personal Financial Advisors	Bachelor's degree	$67,520	27%	9,640
Police and Detectives	High school diploma or equivalent	$57,974	5%	27,500
Security Guards and Gaming Surveillance Officers	High school diploma or equivalent	$24,019	12%	29,630

strate competence. In addition, certification may help candidates advance in their careers.

For investigators who specialize in negligence or criminal defense investigation, the National Association of Legal Investigators offers the Certified Legal Investigator certification. For investigators who specialize in security, ASIS International offers the Professional Certified Investigator certification.

Important Qualities

Communication skills. Detectives and investigators must listen carefully and ask appropriate questions when interviewing a person of interest.

Decision-making skills. Detectives and investigators must be able to think on their feet and make quick decisions, based on the information that they have at a given time.

Inquisitiveness. Private detectives and investigators must want to ask questions and search for the truth.

Patience. Private detectives and investigators may have to spend long periods on surveillance, while waiting for an event to occur. Investigations may take a long time and they may not provide a resolution quickly–or at all.

Resourcefulness. Detectives and investigators must work persistently with whatever leads they have, no matter how limited, to determine the next step toward their goal. They sometimes need to anticipate what a person of interest will do next.

Pay

The median annual wage for private detectives and investigators was $45,740 in May 2012. The median wage is the wage at which half the workers in an occupation earned more than that amount and half earned less. The lowest 10 percent earned less than $27,670, and the top 10 percent earned more than $79,790.

In May 2012, the median annual wages for private detectives and investigators in the top four industries in which these law enforcement agents worked were as follows:

Finance and insurance	$55,660
Legal services	47,080
Government	46,690
Investigation, guard, and armored car services	43,640

Job Outlook

Employment of private detectives and investigators is projected to grow 11 percent from 2012 to 2022, about as fast as the average for all occupations.

Increased demand for private detectives and investigators will stem from heightened security concerns and the need to protect property and confidential information.

Technological advances have led to an increase in cybercrimes, such as identity theft and spamming. Internet scams, as well as other types of financial and insurance fraud, create demand for investigative services, particularly by the legal services industry.

Background checks will continue to be a source of work for many investigators, as both employers and personal contacts wish to verify a person's credibility.

Job Prospects. Strong competition for jobs can be expected because private detective and investigator careers attract many qualified people, including relatively young retirees from law enforcement and the military.

The best job opportunities will be for entry-level positions in detective agencies. Candidates with related work experience, as well as those with interviewing and strong computer skills, may find more job opportunities than others.

O*NET

➤ Private Detectives and Investigators (33-9021.00)

Contacts for More Information

For more information about private detectives and investigators, including certification information, visit

➤ National Association of Legal Investigators (www.nalionline.org/)
➤ ASIS International (www.asisonline.org/)
➤ Professional Investigator Magazine (www.pimagazine.com/)

Security Guards and Gaming Surveillance Officers

- **2012 Median Pay** .... $24,020 per year
  $11.55 per hour
- **Entry-Level Education** ... High school diploma or equivalent
- **Work Experience in a Related Occupation** .... None
- **On-the-Job Training** .... Short-term on-the-job training
- **Number of Jobs 2012** 1,083,600
- **Job Outlook, 2012–22** .... 12% (As fast as average)
- **Employment Change, 2012–22** 130,200

What Security Guards and Gaming Surveillance Officers Do

Security guards and gaming surveillance officers patrol and protect property against theft, vandalism, terrorism, and illegal activity.

Duties. Security guards and gaming surveillance officers typically do the following:

- Protect and enforce laws on an employer's property
- Monitor alarms and closed-circuit TV cameras
- Control access for employees and visitors
- Conduct security checks over a specified area
- Write reports on what they observed while on patrol
- Interview witnesses for court testimony
- Detain violators

Guards must remain alert, looking out for anything unusual. In an emergency, they are required to call for assistance from police, fire, or ambulance services. Some security guards are armed.

A security guard's responsibilities vary from one employer to another. In retail stores, guards protect people, records, merchandise, money, and equipment. They may work with undercover store detectives to prevent theft by customers and employees, detain shoplifting suspects until the police arrive, and patrol parking lots.

In office buildings, banks, hotels, and hospitals, guards maintain order and protect the organization's customers, staff, and property.

Guards who work in museums and art galleries protect paintings and exhibits by watching people and inspecting the contents of personal handbags that patrons carry.

In factories, government buildings, and military bases, security guards protect workers and equipment and check the credentials of people and vehicles entering and leaving the premises.

Guards working in parks and at sports stadiums control crowds, supervise parking and seating, and direct traffic.

Security guards stationed at the entrance to bars and nightclubs keep underage people from entering, collect cover charges, and maintain order among customers.

Security guards working in schools and universities patrol the buildings and grounds, looking for suspicious activity.

The following are examples of types of security guards and gaming surveillance officers:

Security guards, also called *security officers,* protect property, enforce rules on the property, and deter criminal activity. Some guards are assigned a stationary position from which they monitor alarms or surveillance cameras. Other guards are assigned a patrol area where they conduct security checks.

Guards assigned to static security positions usually stay at one location for a specified length of time.

Armored car guards protect money and valuables during transit. They pick up money and other valuables from businesses and transport them to another location. These guards usually wear bulletproof vests and carry firearms, because transporting money between the truck and the business is potentially dangerous.

Gaming surveillance officers, also known as *surveillance agents* and *gaming investigators,* act as security agents for casinos. Using audio and video equipment in an observation room, they watch casino operations for suspicious activities, such as cheating and theft, and monitor compliance with rules, regulations, and laws. They maintain and organize recordings from security cameras, which are sometimes used as evidence in police investigations.

Work Environment

Security guards and gaming surveillance officers held about 1.1 million jobs in 2012.

Security guards work in a wide variety of places, including public buildings, retail stores, and office buildings. Gaming surveillance officers and investigators mostly work in the gaming industry

Median Annual Wages, May 2012

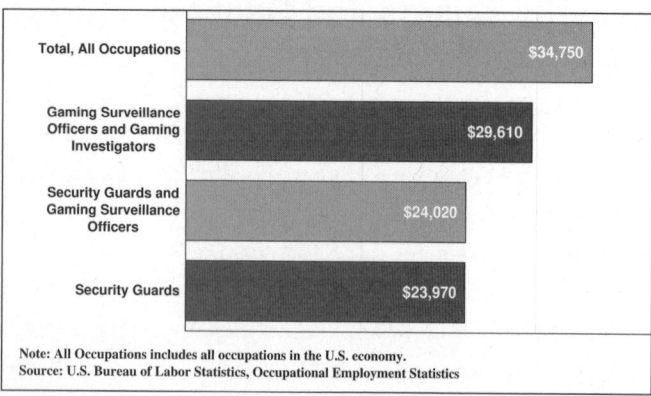

Note: All Occupations includes all occupations in the U.S. economy.
Source: U.S. Bureau of Labor Statistics, Occupational Employment Statistics

Percent Change in Employment, Projected 2012–2022

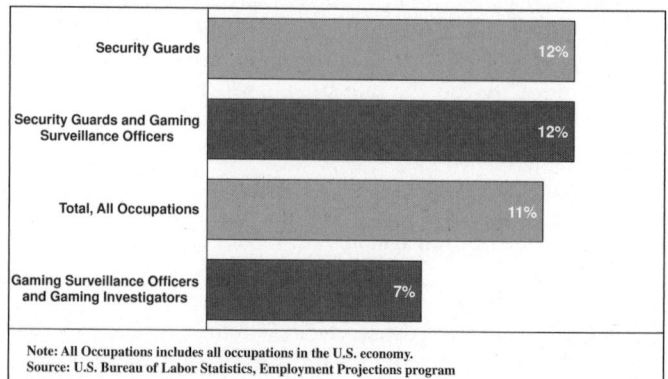

Note: All Occupations includes all occupations in the U.S. economy.
Source: U.S. Bureau of Labor Statistics, Employment Projections program

Employment Projections Data for Security Guards and Gaming Surveillance Officers

Occupational title	SOC Code	Employment, 2012	Projected Employment, 2022	Change, 2012–2022	
				Percent	Numeric
Security guards and gaming surveillance officers...................	—	1,083,600	1,213,800	12	130,200
Gaming surveillance officers and gaming investigators	33-9031	9,300	10,000	7	600
Security guards	33-9032	1,074,300	1,203,900	12	129,600

Source: U.S. Bureau of Labor Statistics, Employment Projections Program

Note: Data are rounded. Go to Occupational Information Included in the OOH *for a discussion of the data in this table.*

and at casino hotels. They are employed only in those states, and on those Indian reservations, where gambling is legal.

The industries that employed the most security guards and gaming surveillance officers in 2012 were as follows:

Investigation, guard, and armored car services.......................	56%
Educational services; state, local, and private	6
Health care and social assistance	6
Accommodation and food services	6
Government..	5

Most security guards spend considerable time on their feet, either at a single post or patrolling buildings and grounds. Some may sit for long periods behind a counter or in a guardhouse at the entrance to a gated facility or community.

Guards who work during the day may have a great deal of contact with other employees and the public.

Although the work can be routine, it can be hazardous, particularly when an altercation occurs.

Most gaming surveillance officers sit behind a desk observing gamers on video surveillance equipment.

Injuries and Illnesses. Security guards have a higher rate of injuries and illnesses than the national average. Although the work is mostly routine, there can be potential dangers. As a result, guards must always be alert for threats to themselves and the people and property they are protecting.

Work Schedules. Security guards and gaming surveillance officers usually work in shifts of 8 hours, or longer, with rotating schedules.

How to Become One

Most security guard jobs require a high school diploma. Gaming surveillance officers sometimes need additional experience with security and video surveillance. Most states require guards to be registered with the state, especially if they carry a firearm.

Education. Security guards generally need a high school diploma or GED, although some jobs may not have any education requirements. Some employers, however, prefer to hire security guards with higher education, such as a 2- or 4-year degree in police science or criminal justice.

Training. Although most employers provide instruction for newly hired guards, the amount of training they receive varies. Most, however, learn their job in a few weeks. During those few weeks, training typically covers emergency procedures, detention of suspected criminals, and proper communication.

Many states recommend that security guards receive approximately 8 hours of pre-assignment training, 8–16 hours of on-the-job training, and 8 hours of annual training. This may include training in protection, public relations, report writing, deterring crises, first aid, and specialized training related to the guard's assignment.

Training is more rigorous for armed guards because they require weapons training. Armed guards may periodically be tested in the use of firearms.

For gaming surveillance officers and investigators, some employers prefer candidates with previous work experience in casinos or individuals with a background in law enforcement. Technical skills and computer skills can also be helpful in using surveillance systems and software.

Drug testing may be required.

Licenses, Certifications, and Registrations. Most states require that guards be registered with the state in which they work. Although registration requirements vary by state, basic qualifications for candidates are as follows:

- Be at least 18 years old
- Pass a background check
- Complete training

An increasing number of states are making ongoing training a legal requirement for staying registered.

Guards who carry weapons must be registered by the appropriate government authority. Armed guard positions have more stringent background checks and entry requirements than those of unarmed guards. Rigorous hiring and screening programs, including background, criminal record, and fingerprint checks, are typical for armed guards.

Some jobs may also require a driver's license.

Advancement. Some guards advance to supervisory or security manager positions. Those with postsecondary education or with industry certifications should have an advantage. Armed security guards have a greater potential for advancement and enjoy higher earnings.

Some guards with management skills open their own security guard business. Guards also can move to an organization that needs higher levels of security, which may result in more prestige or higher pay.

Important Qualities

Decision-making skills. Guards must be able to quickly determine the best course of action when a dangerous situation arises.

Patience. Security guards may need to spend long periods standing and observing their environment without distractions.

Observation skills. Guards must be alert and aware of their surroundings, and be able to quickly recognize anything out of the ordinary.

Physical strength. Guards must be strong enough to apprehend offenders and to handle emergency situations.

Pay

The median annual wage for security guards and gaming surveillance officers was $24,020 in May 2012. The median wage is the wage at which half the workers in an occupation earned more than

Similar Occupations   This table shows a list of occupations with job duties that are similar to those of security guards and gaming surveillance officers.

Occupations	Entry-level Education	2012 Pay	Projected Job Growth	Average Annual Openings
Correctional Officers	High school diploma or equivalent	$38,961	5%	14,780
Gaming Services Occupations	High school diploma or equivalent	$25,951	10%	5,110
Police and Detectives	High school diploma or equivalent	$57,974	5%	27,500
Private Detectives and Investigators	High school diploma or equivalent	$45,740	11%	1,180

that amount and half earned less. The lowest 10 percent earned $17,400, and the top 10 percent earned more than $42,560.

The median annual wages for security guard and gaming surveillance officer occupations in May 2012 were as follows:

Gaming surveillance officers and gaming investigators...... $29,610
Security guards 23,970

Job Outlook

Overall employment of security guards and gaming surveillance officers is projected to grow 12 percent from 2012 to 2022, about as fast as the average for all occupations. Employment growth will vary by specialty.

Employment of security guards is projected to grow 12 percent, about as fast as the average for all occupations. Security guards will continue to be needed to protect both people and property. Concern about crime, vandalism, and terrorism will result in the need for security. Demand should be strong in the private sector as private security firms take over some of the work police officers used to do.

Employment of gaming surveillance officers and investigators is projected to grow 7 percent, slower than the average for all occupations. As gambling continues to be legalized in more states and casinos grow in number, demand for gaming surveillance officers and investigators will also grow.

Job Prospects. Overall job opportunities should be excellent, especially for security guards. The large size of the occupation will result in many job openings as workers leave the occupation each year. However, there will be more competition for higher paying positions that require more training and experience.

Candidates who have experience with video surveillance equipment should have the best job prospects in the gaming industry. Also, those with a background in law enforcement will have an advantage.

O*NET

➤ Gaming Surveillance Officers and Gaming Investigators (33-9031.00)
➤ Security Guards (33-9032.00)

Contacts for More Information

The *OOH* does not have contacts for more information for this occupation.

Sales

Advertising Sales Agents

- **2012 Median Pay** .... $46,290 per year
  $22.26 per hour
- **Entry-Level Education** .... High school diploma
  or equivalent
- **Work Experience in a Related Occupation** .... None
- **On-the-Job Training** .... Moderate-term on-the-job training
- **Number of Jobs 2012** 154,600
- **Job Outlook, 2012–22** .... -1% (Little or no change)
- **Employment Change, 2012–22** .... -1,000

What Advertising Sales Agents Do

Advertising sales agents, also called *advertising sales representatives*, sell advertising space to businesses and individuals. They contact potential clients, make sales presentations, and maintain client accounts.

Duties. Advertising sales agents typically do the following:

- Locate and contact potential clients to offer their firm's advertising services
- Explain to clients how specific types of advertising will help promote their products or services in the most effective way possible
- Provide clients with estimates of the costs of advertising products or services
- Process all correspondence and paperwork related to accounts
- Prepare and deliver sales presentations to new and existing clients
- Inform clients of available options for advertising art, formats, or features and provide samples of previous work for other clients
- Deliver advertising or illustration proofs to clients for approval
- Prepare promotional plans, sales literature, media kits, and sales contracts
- Recommend appropriate sizes and formats for advertising

Bringing in new clients is an important part of an advertising sales agent's job.

Most advertising sales agents work outside the office occasionally, meeting with clients and prospective clients at their places of business. Some may make telephone sales calls as well–calling prospects, attempting to sell the media firm's advertising space or time, and arranging follow-up appointments with interested prospects.

A critical part of building relationships with clients is learning about their needs. Before the first meeting with a client, a sales agent gathers background information on the client's products, current clients, prospective clients, and the geographic area of the target market.

The sales agent then meets with the client to explain how specific types of advertising will help promote the client's products or services most effectively. If a client wishes to proceed, the advertising sales agent prepares and presents an advertising proposal to the client. The proposal may include an overview of the advertising medium to be used, sample advertisements, and cost estimates for the project.

Because of consolidation among media industries, agents increasingly sell several types of ads in one package. For example,

Median Annual Wages, May 2012

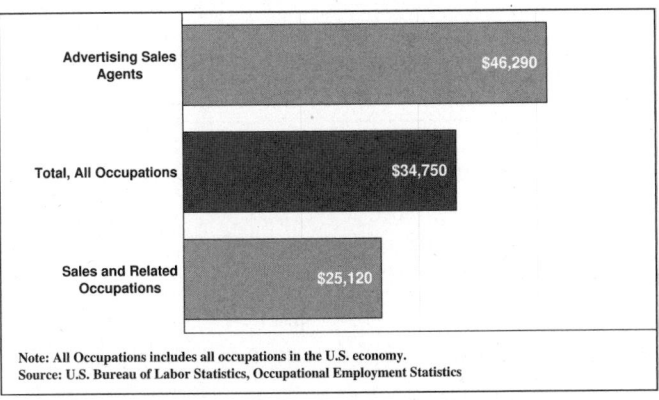

Note: All Occupations includes all occupations in the U.S. economy.
Source: U.S. Bureau of Labor Statistics, Occupational Employment Statistics

Percent Change in Employment, Projected 2012–2022

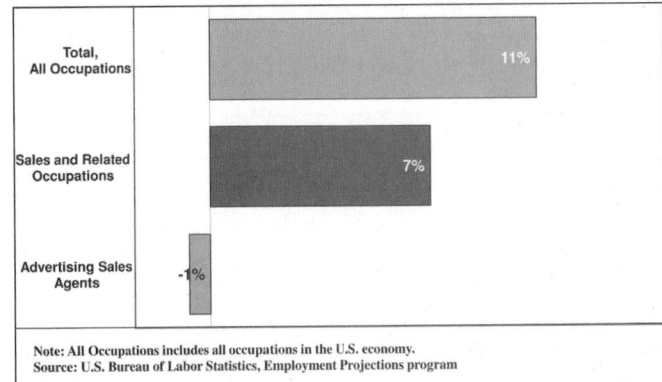

Note: All Occupations includes all occupations in the U.S. economy.
Source: U.S. Bureau of Labor Statistics, Employment Projections program

855

Employment Projections Data for Advertising Sales Agents

Occupational title	SOC Code	Employment, 2012	Projected Employment, 2022	Change, 2012–2022	
				Percent	Numeric
Advertising sales agents	41-3011	154,600	153,600	-1	-1,000

Source: U.S. Bureau of Labor Statistics, Employment Projections Program

Note: **Data are rounded. Go to Occupational Information Included in the OOH** *for a discussion of the data in this table.*

agents may sell ads that would be found in print editions as well as online editions for a particular publication such as a newspaper.

In addition to maintaining sales and overseeing their accounts, advertising sales agents' other duties include analyzing sales statistics and preparing reports about clients' accounts. They keep up to date on industry trends by reading about new and existing products, and they monitor the sales, prices, and products of their competitors.

In many firms, the advertising sales agent drafts contracts, which specify the cost and the advertising work to be done. Agents also may continue to help the client, answering questions or addressing problems the client may have with the proposal.

Sales agents may also be responsible for developing sales tools, promotional plans, and media kits, which they use to help make a sale. In other cases, firms may have a marketing team that sales agents work with to develop these sales tools.

Work Environment

Advertising sales agents held about 154,600 jobs in 2012.

Selling can be stressful because income and job security depend directly on agents' ability to keep and expand their client base. Companies generally set monthly sales quotas and place considerable pressure on advertising sales agents to meet those quotas.

Getting new accounts is an important part of the job, and agents may spend much of their time traveling to and visiting prospective advertisers and maintaining relationships with current clients. Sales agents also may work in their employer's offices and handle sales for walk-in clients or for those who call or email the firm to ask about advertising.

The industries that employed the most advertising sales agents in 2012 were as follows:

Advertising, public relations, and related services...................	35%
Newspaper, periodical, book, and directory publishers	28
Radio broadcasting..	11
Television broadcasting...	6
Other information services...	3

Work Schedules. Most advertising sales agents work full time. About 1 in 5 advertising sales agents worked more than 40 hours

a week in 2012. They frequently work irregular hours and on weekends and holidays.

How to Become One

Although a high school diploma is typically enough education for an entry-level advertising sales position, some employers prefer applicants with a bachelor's degree. Proven sales success and communication skills are essential. Most training for advertising sales agents takes place on the job.

Education. Although a high school diploma is typically the minimum education requirement for an entry-level advertising sales position, some employers prefer applicants with a college degree. Publishing companies with large circulations or broadcasting stations with a large audience may prefer workers with at least a college degree. Courses in marketing, communications, business, and advertising are helpful. For those who have a proven record of successfully selling other products, educational requirements are not likely to be strict.

Training. Most training takes place on the job and can be either formal or informal. In most cases, an experienced sales manager instructs a newly hired advertising sales agent who lacks sales experience. In this one-on-one environment, supervisors typically coach new hires and observe them as they make sales calls and contact clients. Supervisors then advise the new hires on ways to improve their interaction with clients. Employers may bring in consultants to lead formal training sessions when agents sell to a specialized market segment, such as automotive dealers or real estate professionals.

Advancement. Agents with proven leadership ability and a strong sales record may advance to supervisory and managerial positions, such as sales manager, account executive, or vice president of sales. Successful advertising sales agents may also advance to positions in other industries, such as corporate sales.

Important Qualities

Communication skills. Advertising sales agents must be persuasive during sales calls. In addition, they should listen to the client's desires and concerns, and recommend an appropriate advertising package.

Similar Occupations　This table shows a list of occupations with job duties that are similar to those of advertising sales agents.

Occupations	Entry-level Education	2012 Pay	Projected Job Growth	Average Annual Openings
Advertising, Promotions, and Marketing Managers	Bachelor's degree	$115,087	12%	7,510
Insurance Sales Agents	High school diploma or equivalent	$48,150	10%	15,020
Sales Managers	Bachelor's degree	$105,260	8%	10,690
Wholesale and Manufacturing Sales Representatives	See "How to Become One"	$58,484	9%	53,250

Initiative. Advertising sales agents must actively seek new clients, keep in touch with current clients, and expand their client base, in order to meet sales quotas.

Organizational skills. Agents work with many clients, each of whom may be at a different stage in the sales process. Agents must be well-organized to keep track of their clients or potential clients.

Self-confidence. Advertising sales agents should be confident when calling potential clients (cold calls). Because potential clients are often unwilling to commit on a first call, agents often must continue making sales calls, even if rejected at first.

Pay

The median annual wage for advertising sales agents was $46,290 in May 2012. The median wage is the wage at which half the workers in an occupation earned more than that amount and half earned less. The lowest 10 percent earned less than $22,930, and the top 10 percent earned more than $103,170.

Performance-based pay, including bonuses and commissions, can make up a large portion of an advertising sales agent's earnings. Most employers pay some combination of salaries, commissions, and bonuses. Commissions are usually based on individual sales numbers. Bonuses may depend on individual performance, the performance of all sales workers in a group, or the performance of the entire firm.

Job Outlook

Employment of advertising sales agents is projected to show little or no change from 2012 to 2022.

Media companies will continue to rely on advertising revenue for profitability, driving growth in the advertising industry as a whole. Employment growth of advertising sales agents will largely follow broader industry trends. For example, although newspaper print advertising is expected to decline, some of this decline will be offset by the sale of ad space on newspaper websites. Therefore, although employment of advertising sales agents is projected to decline in the newspaper publishers industry, it is not projected to decline as fast as other occupations in that industry.

However, an increasing amount of advertising is expected to be concentrated in digital media, including digital ads intended for cell phones, tablet-style computers, and online radio stations. Digital advertising allows companies to directly target potential consumers because websites are usually associated with the types of products that possible customers would like to buy. Digital advertising can be done without an advertising sales agent. For example, in some cases it can be done through a software application or search engine program. Therefore, an increase in digital advertising expenditures will not necessarily result in increased demand for advertising sales agents.

Job Prospects. Competition is expected to be strong for advertising sales agents. Applicants with experience in sales or a bachelor's degree should have the best opportunities.

O*NET

➤ Advertising Sales Agents (41-3011.00)

Contacts for More Information

For information about advertising sales in the newspaper industry, visit

➤ Newspaper Association of America (www.naa.org/)
    For information about the radio advertising industry, visit
➤ Radio Advertising Bureau (www.rab.com/)

Cashiers

- **2012 Median Pay** .... $18,970 per year
  $9.12 per hour
- **Entry-Level Education** .... Less than high school
- **Work Experience in a Related Occupation**.............. None
- **On-the-Job Training** ....Short-term on-the-job training
- **Number of Jobs 2012** 3,338,900
- **Job Outlook, 2012–22** .... 3% (Slower than average)
- **Employment Change, 2012–22** 86,500

What Cashiers Do

Cashiers handle payments from customers purchasing goods and services.

Duties. Cashiers typically do the following:

- Greet customers
- Ring up items purchased by customers on scanners, cash registers, and calculators
- Accept payments from customers and give change and receipts
- Bag or wrap customers' purchases
- Process returns and exchanges of merchandise, which includes inspecting whether the items are in good condition and using the right procedure for cash, credit cards, or other types of payment
- Answer customer questions and provide information about the store's procedures and policies
- Help customers to sign up for store rewards programs and to apply for store credit cards
- Count how much money is in their register at the beginning and end of their shift

In some establishments, cashiers have to check the age of their customers when selling age-restricted products, such as alcohol and tobacco. Some cashiers may have duties not directly related to sales and customer service, such as mopping floors, taking out the trash, and other custodial tasks. Others may stock shelves or mark prices on items.

Cashiers must be friendly and courteous when interacting with customers.

Median Hourly Wages, May 2012

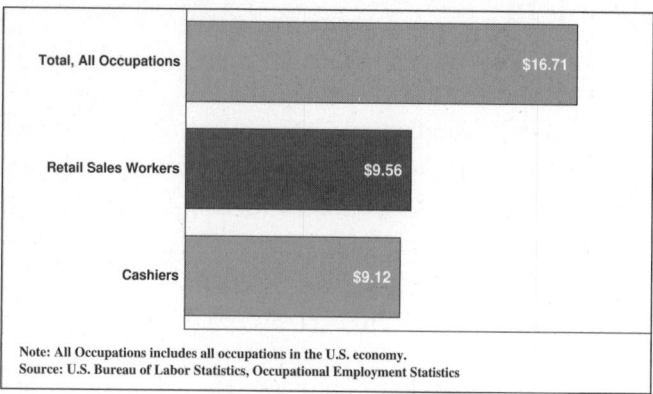

Note: All Occupations includes all occupations in the U.S. economy.
Source: U.S. Bureau of Labor Statistics, Occupational Employment Statistics

Percent Change in Employment, Projected 2012–2022

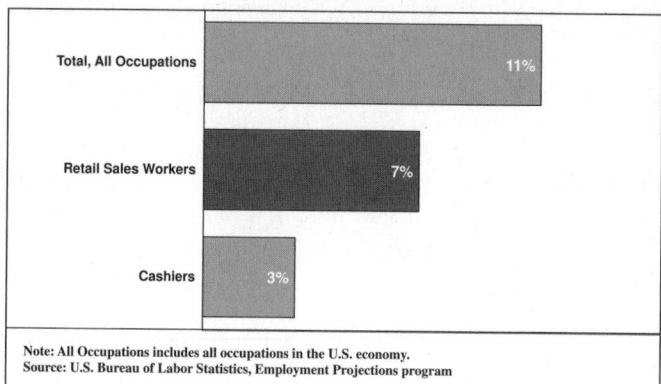

Note: All Occupations includes all occupations in the U.S. economy.
Source: U.S. Bureau of Labor Statistics, Employment Projections program

Work Environment

Cashiers held about 3.3 million jobs in 2012. Most cashiers work indoors, usually in retail establishments such as supermarkets, department stores, and restaurants.

The industries that employed the most cashiers in 2012 were as follows:

Grocery stores	25%
Gasoline stations	17
Other general merchandise stores	11
Restaurants and other eating places	7
Department stores	6

The work is often repetitive, and cashiers spend most of their time standing behind counters or checkout stands.

Injuries and Illnesses. Working as a cashier can sometimes be dangerous; the risk from robberies and homicides is higher for cashiers than for most other workers. However, more safety precautions, such as limited access to cash and security cameras, help deter criminals.

Work Schedules. Work hours vary by employer, but cashiers typically must work nights, weekends, and holidays. Employers may restrict the use of vacation from Thanksgiving through early January because that is the busiest time of year for most retailers.

How to Become One

Cashiers are usually trained on the job. There are typically no formal educational requirements.

Education. Many jobs for cashiers have no specific educational requirements, although some employers prefer applicants with at least a high school diploma or equivalent. Cashiers should have a basic knowledge of mathematics, because they need to be able to make change and count the money in their registers.

Training. Cashiers go through a brief training period when they are hired. In small firms, an experienced worker typically trains beginners. In larger businesses, trainees spend time in training classes before being placed at cash registers. During training, new cashiers learn store policies and procedures and how to operate equipment such as cash registers.

Important Qualities

Customer-service skills. Cashiers must be courteous and friendly when helping customers.

Dexterity. Cashiers use their hands to operate registers and scan purchases.

Listening skills. Cashiers must pay attention to customer questions, instructions, and complaints.

Patience. Cashiers must be able to remain calm when interacting with customers who are upset or angry.

Physical stamina. Cashiers must be able to stand for long periods.

Advancement. Working as a cashier is often a steppingstone to other careers in retail. For example, with experience, cashiers may become customer service representatives, retail sales workers, or sales managers. Cashiers with at least a high school diploma or equivalent typically have the best chances for promotion.

Employment Projections Data for Cashiers

Occupational title	SOC Code	Employment, 2012	Projected Employment, 2022	Change, 2012–2022	
				Percent	Numeric
Cashiers	41-2011	3,338,900	3,425,400	3	86,500

Source: U.S. Bureau of Labor Statistics, Employment Projections Program

Note: Data are rounded. Go to **Occupational Information Included in the OOH** *for a discussion of the data in this table.*

Similar Occupations   This table shows a list of occupations with job duties that are similar to those of cashiers.

Occupations	Entry-level Education	2012 Pay	Projected Job Growth	Average Annual Openings
Customer Service Representatives	High school diploma or equivalent	$30,580	13%	94,160
Retail Sales Workers	Less than high school	$21,514	10%	202,730
Tellers	High school diploma or equivalent	$24,940	1%	25,980
Waiters and Waitresses	Less than high school	$18,540	6%	126,830

Pay

The median hourly wage for cashiers was $9.12 in May 2012. The median wage is the wage at which half the workers in an occupation earned more than that amount and half earned less. The lowest 10 percent earned less than $7.89, and the top 10 percent earned more than $13.20.

Many cashiers start at the federal minimum wage, which is $7.25 an hour. Some states set the minimum wage above $7.25 an hour.

Job Outlook

Employment of cashiers is projected to grow 3 percent from 2012 to 2022, slower than the average for all occupations. Retail sales are expected to grow, leading to increased need for cashiers over the projections decade. However, employment growth will be limited by advances in technology, such as a rise in the number of self-service checkout stands in retail stores and increasing online sales, which decrease the need for cashiers.

Job opportunities should be good because of the need to replace the large number of workers who leave the occupation for a variety of reasons each year.

Historically, workers under the age of 25 have filled many of the openings for cashiers. In 2012, about half of all cashiers were 24 years old or younger.

O*NET

➤ Cashiers (41-2011.00)

Contacts for More Information

The *OOH* does not have contacts for more information for this occupation.

Insurance Sales Agents

- **2012 Median Pay** .... $48,150 per year
  $23.15 per hour
- **Entry-Level Education** ... High school diploma or equivalent
- **Work Experience in a Related Occupation**............... None
- **On-the-Job Training** .... Moderate-term on-the-job training
- **Number of Jobs 2012** 443,400
- **Job Outlook, 2012–22** .... 10% (As fast as average)
- **Employment Change, 2012–22** 45,900

What Insurance Sales Agents Do

Insurance sales agents help insurance companies generate new business by contacting potential customers and selling one or more types of insurance. Insurance sales agents explain various insurance policies and help clients choose plans that suit them.

Duties. Insurance sales agents typically do the following:

- Call potential clients to expand their customer base
- Interview prospective clients to get data about their financial resources and discuss existing coverage
- Explain the features of various policies
- Analyze clients' current insurance policies and suggest additions or changes
- Customize insurance programs to suit individual clients
- Handle policy renewals
- Maintain electronic and paper records
- Help policyholders settle claims

Insurance sales agents commonly sell one or more types of insurance, such as property and casualty, life, and health and long-term care insurance.

Property and casualty insurance agents sell policies that protect people and businesses from financial loss resulting from automobile accidents, fire, theft, and other events that can damage property. For businesses, property and casualty insurance also covers injured workers' compensation, product liability claims, or medical malpractice claims.

Life insurance agents specialize in selling policies that pay beneficiaries when a policyholder dies. Life insurance agents also sell annuities that promise a retirement income.

Health and long-term care insurance agents sell policies that cover the costs of medical care and assisted-living services in old age. They also may sell dental insurance and short-term and long-term disability insurance.

Agents may specialize in any one of these products or function as generalists providing multiple products.

An increasing number of insurance sales agents offer their clients comprehensive financial planning services, especially for clients approaching retirement. These services include retirement planning, estate planning, and help in setting up pension plans for businesses. In addition to offering insurance, these agents may become licensed to sell mutual funds, variable annuities, and other securities. This practice is most common with life insurance agents who already sell annuities, but many property and casualty agents also sell financial products. For more information on agents who sell financial products, see the profile on securities, commodities, and financial services sales agents.

Many agents spend a lot of time marketing their services and creating their own base of clients. They do this in a variety of ways, including making "cold" sales calls to people who are not current clients.

Clients often learn about policies by themselves, by comparison shopping online and getting information from the insurance companies. They then contact the company directly to buy a policy, so the client comes to the agent ready to buy.

Insurance agents also find new clients through referrals by current clients. Keeping clients happy so they recommend the agent to others is a key to success for insurance sales agents.

Insurance agents may work for a single insurance company or an insurance brokerage.

Captive agents are insurance sales agents who work exclusively for one insurance company. They can only sell policies provided by the company that employs them.

Independent insurance agents work for insurance brokerages, selling the policies of several companies. They match insurance policies for their clients with the company that offers the best rate and coverage.

Work Environment

Insurance sales agents held about 443,400 jobs in 2012. In 2012, about 78 percent of insurance sales agents worked in the insurance carriers and related activities industry, and about 19 percent were self-employed. Although most insurance sales agents, 53 percent, worked for insurance agencies and brokerages, which sell the policies of several companies, others worked directly for a single insurance carrier.

Most insurance sales agents work in offices, although some may spend much of their time traveling to meet with clients. Their work environment may vary depending on the type of company that employs them. Because some companies are small, agents may work alone or with only a few others.

Work Schedules. Insurance sales agents usually determine their own hours of work and often schedule evening and weekend appointments for the convenience of clients. Some sales agents meet with clients during business hours and then spend evenings doing paperwork and preparing presentations to prospective clients. Most agents work full time, and about 1 in 5 worked more than 40 hours per week in 2012.

How to Become One

Most employers require agents to have a high school diploma. Agents must be licensed in the states where they work.

Education. A high school diploma is the typical requirement for insurance sales agents, although a bachelor's degree can improve job prospects. Public speaking classes can be useful in improving sales techniques, and often agents will have taken courses in business, finance, or economics. Business knowledge is also helpful for sales agents hoping to advance to a managerial position.

Training. Insurance sales agents learn many of their job duties on the job from other agents. Many employers have new agents shadow an experienced agent. This allows the new agent to learn how to conduct the company's business and how the agency interacts with clients.

Employers also are increasingly placing greater emphasis on continuing professional education as the variety of financial products sold by insurance sales agents increases. Changes in tax laws, government benefits programs, and other state and federal regulations can affect the insurance needs of clients and the way in which agents conduct business. Agents can enhance their selling skills and broaden their knowledge of insurance and other financial services by taking courses at colleges and universities or by attending conferences and seminars sponsored by insurance organizations.

Licenses, Certifications, and Registrations. Insurance sales agents must have a license in the states where they work. Separate licenses are required for agents to sell life and health insurance and property and casualty insurance. In most states, licenses are issued only to applicants who complete specified courses and who pass state exams covering insurance fundamentals and state insurance laws. Most state licensing authorities also require agents to take continuing education courses focusing on insurance laws, consumer protection, ethics, and the technical details of various insurance policies.

As the demand for financial products and financial planning services increases, many agents also choose to get licensed and certified to sell securities and other financial products. Doing so, however, requires substantial study and passing an additional exam–either the Series 6 or Series 7 licensing exam, both of which are administered by the Financial Industry Regulatory Authority (FINRA). The Series 6 exam is for people who want to sell only

An increasing number of insurance sales agents offer comprehensive financial planning services to their clients.

mutual funds and variable annuities. The Series 7 exam is the main FINRA series license that qualifies agents as general securities sales representatives.

A number of organizations offer certifications that show an agent's expertise in insurance specialties. These certifications are not required for employment, but they can give job candidates an advantage over other applicants. Certifications can also be a source of continuing education credit. For details on specific designations, contact The Institutes and The American College of Financial Services.

Important Qualities

Analytical skills. Insurance sales agents must evaluate the characteristics of each client to determine the appropriate insurance policy.

Median Annual Wages, May 2012

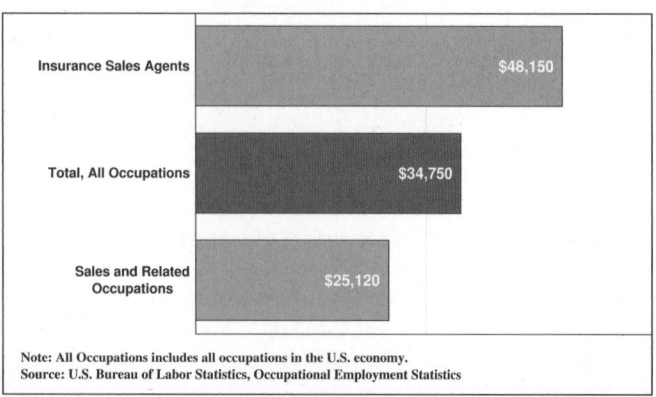

Insurance Sales Agents	$48,150
Total, All Occupations	$34,750
Sales and Related Occupations	$25,120

Note: All Occupations includes all occupations in the U.S. economy.
Source: U.S. Bureau of Labor Statistics, Occupational Employment Statistics

Percent Change in Employment, Projected 2012–2022

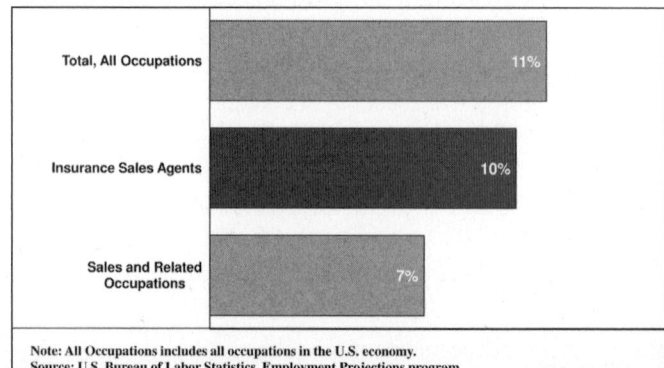

Total, All Occupations	11%
Insurance Sales Agents	10%
Sales and Related Occupations	7%

Note: All Occupations includes all occupations in the U.S. economy.
Source: U.S. Bureau of Labor Statistics, Employment Projections program

Employment Projections Data for Insurance Sales Agents

Occupational title	SOC Code	Employment, 2012	Projected Employment, 2022	Change, 2012–2022	
				Percent	Numeric
Insurance sales agents...	41-3021	443,400	489,300	10	45,900

Source: U.S. Bureau of Labor Statistics, Employment Projections Program

Note: Data are rounded. Go to **Occupational Information Included in the OOH** *for a discussion of the data in this table.*

Communication skills. Insurance sales agents must be able to communicate effectively with customers by listening to their requests and suggesting suitable policies.

Initiative. Insurance sales agents need to actively seek out new customers to maintain a flow of commissions.

Self-confidence. Insurance sales agents should be confident when making "cold" calls (calls to prospective customers who have not been contacted before). They must speak clearly and persuasively and maintain their composure if rejected.

Pay

The median annual wage for insurance sales agents was $48,150 in May 2012. The median wage is the wage at which half the workers in an occupation earned more than that amount and half earned less. The lowest 10 percent earned less than $26,120 and the top 10 percent earned more than $116,940.

Many independent agents are paid by commission only. Sales workers who are employees of an agency or an insurance carrier may be paid in one of three ways: salary only, salary plus commission, or salary plus bonus.

In general, commissions are the most common form of compensation, especially for experienced agents. The amount of the commission depends on the type and amount of insurance sold, and whether the transaction is a new policy or a renewal. When agents meet their sales goals or when an agency meets its profit goals, agents usually get bonuses. Some agents involved with financial planning receive a fee for their services rather than a commission.

Job Outlook

Employment of insurance sales agents is projected to grow 10 percent from 2012 to 2022, about as fast as the average for all occupations.

The insurance industry generally grows with the economy as a whole. Overall economic growth will continue to create demand for insurance policies. Direct online purchases of insurance are not expected to negatively affect employment of traditional sales agents, because they will continue to have a critical role in the insurance industry. Because the profitability of insurance companies depends on a steady stream of new customers, the demand for insurance sales agents is expected to continue. Employment growth will likely be strongest for independent sales agents, as insurance companies rely more on brokerages and less on captive agents as a way to control costs.

Many clients do their own Internet research and purchase insurance online. This somewhat reduces demand for insurance sales agents, as many purchases can be made without their services. Agents are still needed to interact with clients regarding more complicated policies, however. Also, many people lack the time or expertise to study the different types of insurance to decide what they need. These clients will continue to rely on the advice from insurance sales agents.

Employment growth should be stronger for agents selling health and long-term care insurance. As the population ages over the next decade, demand will likely increase for packages that cover long-term care. The number of individuals who have access to health insurance will increase due to federal health insurance reform legislation. Insurance companies will rely on sales agents to enroll people from this new customer base.

Job Prospects. College graduates who have sales ability, excellent customer-service skills, and expertise in a range of insurance and financial services products are likely to have the best prospects. Multilingual agents may have an advantage, because they can serve a wider customer base. In addition, insurance terminology is often technical, so agents who have a firm understanding of the relevant technical and legal terms should also be desirable to employers.

Many beginning agents fail to earn enough from commissions to meet their income goals and eventually transfer to other careers. Many job openings are likely to result from the need to replace agents who leave the occupation or retire.

Agents may face some competition from traditional securities brokers and bankers who also sell insurance policies. Insurance sales agents will need to expand the products and services they

Similar Occupations   This table shows a list of occupations with job duties that are similar to those of insurance sales agents.

Occupations	Entry-level Education	2012 Pay	Projected Job Growth	Average Annual Openings
Advertising Sales Agents	High school diploma or equivalent	$46,290	-1%	4,750
Insurance Underwriters	Bachelor's degree	$62,870	-6%	2,890
Personal Financial Advisors	Bachelor's degree	$67,520	27%	9,640
Real Estate Brokers and Sales Agents	High school diploma or equivalent	$42,723	11%	8,630
Sales Managers	Bachelor's degree	$105,260	8%	10,690
Securities, Commodities, and Financial Services Sales Agents	Bachelor's degree	$71,720	11%	12,260
Wholesale and Manufacturing Sales Representatives	See "How to Become One"	$58,484	9%	53,250

offer as consolidation increases among insurance companies, banks, and brokerage firms and as demand increases from clients for more comprehensive financial planning.

O*NET

➤ Insurance Sales Agents (41-3021.00)

Contacts for More Information

For more information about insurance sales agents, visit

➤ National Association of Professional Insurance Agents (www. pianet.org/)

➤ Insurance Information Institute (www.iii.org)

For information about insurance sales agents in the healthcare industry, visit

➤ National Association of Health Underwriters (www.nahu.org/)

For more information about certifications, visit

➤ The Institutes (www.theinstitutes.org/)

➤ The American College of Financial Services (www.theamerican college.edu/)

For more information about securities licensure, visit

➤ Financial Industry Regulatory Authority (FINRA) (www.finra.org/)

Information about insurance sales agent licensure is available from state insurance department websites.

Models

- **2012 Median Pay** .... $18,750 per year
  $9.02 per hour

- **Entry-Level Education** .... Less than high school

- **Work Experience in a Related Occupation**............... None

- **On-the-Job Training** .... None

- **Number of Jobs 2012** 4,800

- **Job Outlook, 2012–22**............. 15% (Faster than average)

- **Employment Change, 2012–22** 700

What Models Do

Models pose for artists, photographers, or customers to help advertise a variety of products, including clothing, cosmetics, food, and appliances.

Duties. Models typically do the following:

- Display clothing and merchandise in print and online advertisements

- Promote products and services in television commercials

- Wear designers' clothing for runway fashion shows

- Model accessories, such as handbags, shoes, and jewelry, and promote beauty products, including fragrances and cosmetics

- Pose for workers taking photos or creating paintings or sculptures

- Work closely with photographers, hair and clothing stylists, makeup artists, and clients to produce a desired look

- Create and maintain a portfolio of their work

- Travel to meet and interview with potential clients

- Conduct research on the product being promoted–for example, the designer or type of fabric of a particular article of clothing

Models appear in different types of media to promote a product or service. Models advertise products and merchandise in magazine or newspaper advertisements, department store catalogs, or television commercials. Increasingly, models are appearing in online ads or on retail websites.

Other models may appear on fashion magazine covers or in photographs accompanying magazine articles. These models typically participate in photo shoots and pose for photographers to show off the features of clothing and other products. Models change their posture and facial expressions to capture the look the client wants. The photographer usually takes many pictures of the model in different poses and expressions during the photo shoot.

Models often display clothes and merchandise live in different situations. At fashion shows, models stand, turn, and walk to show off clothing to an audience of photographers, journalists, designers, and garment buyers. Other clients may require models to interact directly with customers. In retail establishments and department stores, models display clothing directly to shoppers and describe the features and prices of the merchandise. At trade shows or conventions, models show off a business' products and provide information to consumers. These models may work alongside demonstrators and product promoters to help advertise and sell merchandise.

Other models pose for sketch artists, painters, and sculptors.

Almost all models work with agents, who provide a link between the models and clients. Clients prefer to work with agents, making it very difficult for a model to pursue a freelance career. Agents recruit new models, advise and train models, and promote them to clients in return for a portion of the model's earnings. Models must do research before signing with an agency to make sure it has a good reputation in the modeling industry. For information on agencies, models should contact a local consumer affairs organization, such as the Better Business Bureau.

Models often prepare for photo shoots or fashion shows by having their hair and makeup done by professionals in those industries. The hair stylists and makeup artists may touch up the model's hair and makeup and change the model's look throughout the event. However, models might sometimes be responsible for applying their own makeup and bringing their own clothing.

Models spend a considerable amount of time trying to book jobs with potential clients. Models put together and maintain portfolios, print composite cards, and travel to meet prospective clients. A portfolio is a collection of a model's previous work and is carried to all client meetings and bookings. A composite card contains the best photographs from a model's portfolio, along with his or her measurements.

Models appear in printed publications, at live modeling events, and on television to advertise and promote products and services.

Median Hourly Wages, May 2012

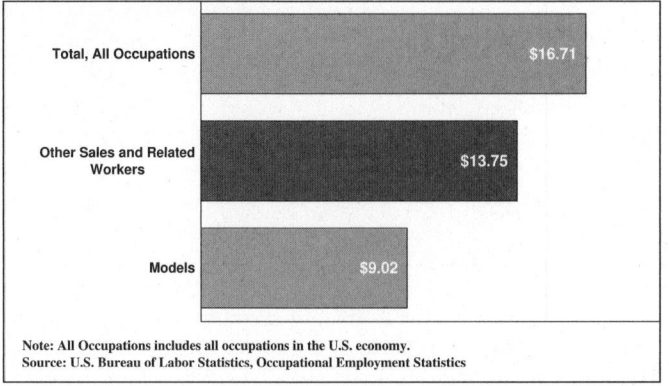

Note: All Occupations includes all occupations in the U.S. economy.
Source: U.S. Bureau of Labor Statistics, Occupational Employment Statistics

Percent Change in Employment, Projected 2012–2022

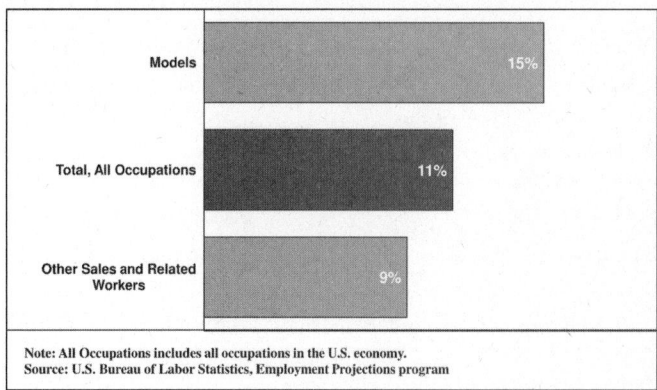

Note: All Occupations includes all occupations in the U.S. economy.
Source: U.S. Bureau of Labor Statistics, Employment Projections program

Because advertisers often need to target specific segments of the population, models may specialize in a certain area. For example, petite and plus-size fashions are modeled by women whose sizes are, respectively, smaller and larger than that worn by the typical model. Models who are disabled may be used to model fashions or products for consumers with disabilities. "Parts" models have a body part, such as a hand or foot, particularly well suited to model products such as nail polish or shoes.

Work Environment

Models held about 4,800 jobs in May 2012. Most models work for clothing stores. Other models work for educational services, including modeling schools, or for employment placement services, such as casting and modeling agencies.

Models work in a variety of conditions, from comfortable studios and runway fashion shows to outdoors in all weather conditions.

Work Schedules. Many models work part time and have unpredictable work schedules. Models must be ready on short notice to work for a show or a photo shoot, and the number of hours worked will vary depending on the job. Many models experience periods of unemployment.

Schedules can be demanding and stressful, although some models may enjoy the frequent travel to meet clients in different cities.

How to Become One

No formal education is required and training is limited. Specific requirements depend on the client, with different jobs requiring different physical characteristics. However, most models must be within certain ranges for height, weight, and clothing size to meet the needs of fashion designers, photographers, and advertisers.

Education. Although there are no formal education requirements, some aspiring models attend modeling schools that provide training in posing, walking, applying makeup, and other basic tasks. Attending such schools, however, does not necessarily lead to more job opportunities.

Although some models are discovered when agents scout for "fresh faces" at modeling schools, most agencies allow applicants to email photos directly to the agency. Models who are well liked are then invited to be interviewed and seen in person by an agent. Some agencies also have "open calls" where aspiring models can walk into an agency during a specified time and meet directly with agents and clients.

Advancement. Models advance by working more regularly and being selected for assignments that have higher pay. They may appear in magazines, print campaigns, commercials, or runway shows that have higher profiles and provide more widespread exposure.

Because advancement depends on a model's previous work, maintaining a good portfolio of high-quality, up-to-date photographs is important for getting assignments.

A model's selection of an agency is also important for advancement: the better the reputation and skill of the agency, the more assignments a model is likely to get.

Important Qualities

Specific requirements depend on the client, but most models must be within certain ranges for height, weight, and clothing size to meet the needs of fashion designers, photographers, and advertisers. Requirements may change slightly from time to time, as the perceptions of physical beauty change.

Courteous. Models must interact with a large number of people, such as agents, photographers, and customers. It is important to be polite, professional, prompt, and respectful.

Discipline. A model's career depends on the maintenance of his or her physical characteristics. Models must control their diet, exercise regularly, and get enough sleep to stay healthy and photogenic. Haircuts, pedicures, and manicures are necessary work-related expenses.

Listening skills. Models must be able to take direction from photographers and clients during photo shoots and commercials.

Organizational skills. Models must be able to manage their portfolios and their work and travel schedules.

Persistence. Competition for jobs is strong and most clients have specific needs for each job, so patience and persistence are essential.

Employment Projections Data for Models

Occupational title	SOC Code	Employment, 2012	Projected Employment, 2022	Change, 2012–2022	
				Percent	Numeric
Models	41-9012	4,800	5,500	15	700

Source: U.S. Bureau of Labor Statistics, Employment Projections Program

Note: Data are rounded. Go to **Occupational Information Included in the OOH** *for a discussion of the data in this table.*

Similar Occupations This table shows a list of occupations with job duties that are similar to those of models.

Occupations	Entry-level Education	2012 Pay	Projected Job Growth	Average Annual Openings
Actors	Some college, no degree	The annual wage is not available.	4.1%	2,890
Barbers, Hairdressers, and Cosmetologists	Postsecondary non-degree award	$22,782	13%	23,990
Fashion Designers	Bachelor's degree	$62,860	-3%	590
Photographers	High school diploma or equivalent	$28,490	4%	2,030

Photogenic. Models spend most of their time being photographed. They must be comfortable in front of a camera for photographers to capture the desired look.

Style. Models must have a basic knowledge of hair styling, makeup, and clothing. For photographic and runway work, models must be able to move gracefully and confidently.

Pay

The median hourly wage for models was $9.02 in May 2012. The median wage is the wage at which half the workers in an occupation earned more than that amount and half earned less. The lowest 10 percent earned less than $7.81, and the top 10 percent earned more than $20.91.

Job Outlook

Employment of models is projected to grow 15 percent from 2012 to 2022, faster than the average for all occupations. However, because it is a small occupation, the fast growth will result in only about 700 new jobs over the 10-year period.

Demand for models is expected to increase as the economy continues to grow. Increasing consumer confidence and spending will encourage the expansion of retail clothing stores, the industry employing the largest number of models.

In addition, efforts to increase sales and the growing competition from online retailers will likely force stores to create a better overall shopping experience for customers. Stores will rely in part on models to create a more inviting, customer-service oriented experience for shoppers. By interacting directly with consumers, models increase awareness of a store's merchandise and create more positive impressions and interest among customers.

Rising consumer confidence and spending will also encourage businesses to increase their advertising and marketing budgets to reach out to potential customers. Businesses may also introduce new advertising campaigns and product launches. These will require models to promote and market products in stores, television commercials, and fashion shows.

Models may increasingly appear in online publications, digital advertisements, and websites. Spending on online and mobile advertisements will likely increase in response to the continuing growth in online shopping and consumer use of smartphones and tablets. Although models will still be needed to promote products in print advertisements and catalogs, businesses may begin to shift away from this traditional form of advertising.

In addition, businesses may cut back on their advertising budgets during economic downturns, making them less likely to develop new advertising campaigns or hire models.

Job Prospects. Many people are drawn to this occupation because of its glamour and potential for fame. Some enjoy traveling and modeling for famous designers. In addition, there are no education or training requirements for entering this occupation. Therefore, many applicants will be competing for very few job openings.

Although there may be more jobs available in large cities like New York and Los Angeles, competition for these jobs is expected to be very strong. Aspiring models may have the best job opportunities in smaller cities working for smaller modeling agencies and local clients and businesses.

Modeling careers are typically short, and many agencies and clients are always looking for new, young models. Therefore, younger models with a solid portfolio will have the best opportunities for jobs. However, age, weight, and height requirements are typically less rigid for models appearing in commercials and advertisements than for those looking to become a runway or fashion model. As the U.S. population becomes increasingly diverse and businesses become more globalized, demand for racially and ethnically diverse models may increase.

O*NET

➤ Models (41-9012.00)

Contacts for More Information

For information about modeling schools and agencies in your area, contact a local consumer affairs organization, such as the Better Business Bureau (www.bbb.org/).

Real Estate Brokers and Sales Agents

- **2012 Median Pay** .... $41,990 per year
  $20.19 per hour
- **Entry-Level Education** ... High school diploma or equivalent
- **Work Experience in a Related Occupation** .... See "How to Become One"
- **On-the-Job Training** ....See "How to Become One"
- **Number of Jobs 2012** 422,000
- **Job Outlook, 2012–22** .... 11% (As fast as average)
- **Employment Change, 2012–22** 46,600

What Real Estate Brokers and Sales Agents Do

Real estate brokers and sales agents help clients buy, sell, and rent properties. Although brokers and agents do similar work, brokers are licensed to manage their own real estate businesses. Sales agents must work with a real estate broker.

Duties. Real estate brokers and sales agents typically do the following:

- Solicit potential clients to buy, sell, and rent properties
- Advise clients on prices, mortgages, market conditions, and other related information
- Compare properties to determine a competitive market price

Most real estate brokers and sales agents sell residential property.

- Generate lists of properties for sale, including details such as location and features
- Promote properties through advertisements, open houses, and listing services
- Take prospective buyers or renters to see properties
- Present purchase offers to sellers for consideration
- Mediate negotiations between the buyer and seller
- Ensure all terms of purchase contracts are met
- Prepare documents, such as loyalty contracts, purchase agreements, and deeds

Because of the complexity of buying or selling a home or commercial property, people often seek help from real estate brokers and sales agents.

Most real estate brokers and sales agents sell residential property. Others sell commercial property, and a small number sell industrial, agricultural, or other types of real estate.

Brokers and agents can represent either the buyer or the seller in a transaction. Buyers' brokers and agents meet with clients to understand what they are looking for and how much they can afford. Sellers' brokers and agents meet with clients to help them decide how much to ask for and to convince them that the agent or broker can find them a qualified buyer.

Real estate brokers and sales agents must be knowledgeable about the real estate market in their area. To match properties to clients' needs, they should be familiar with local communities, including knowledge of the crime rate and the proximity to schools and shopping. Brokers and agents also must stay current on financing options; government programs; types of available mortgages; and real estate, zoning, and fair housing laws.

Real estate brokers are licensed to manage their own businesses. Brokers, as independent businesspeople, often sell real estate owned by others. In addition to helping clients buy and sell properties, they may help rent or manage properties for a fee. Many operate a real estate office, handling business details and overseeing the work of sales agents.

Real estate sales agents must work with a broker. Sales agents often work for brokers on a contract basis, earning a portion of the commission from each property they sell.

Work Environment

Real estate brokers and sales agents held about 422,000 jobs in 2012. About 52 percent were self-employed.

Most of the remainder worked in the real estate industry in brokerage offices, leasing offices, and other real estate establishments. Workplace size can range from a one-person business to a large firm with numerous branch offices. Many brokers have franchise agreements with national or regional real estate companies. Under this arrangement, the broker pays a fee to be affiliated with a widely known real estate organization.

While some real estate brokers and sales agents work in a typical office environment, others are able to telecommute and work out of their homes. In both cases, however, real estate workers spend much of their time away from their desks showing properties to customers, traveling to see properties for sale, and meeting with prospective clients.

Work Schedules. Many real estate brokers and sales agents work more than 40 hours per week. They often work evenings and weekends to accommodate clients' schedules. Many brokers and sales agents may spend a significant amount of time networking and attending community events to meet potential clients. Although they frequently work long or irregular hours, many can set their own schedules.

Some brokers and sales agents work part time and may combine their real estate activities with other careers.

How to Become One

Real estate brokers and sales agents need at least a high school diploma. Both brokers and sales agents must be licensed. To become licensed, candidates must complete a number of real estate courses and pass a licensing exam.

Licenses, Certifications, and Registrations. In all states and the District of Columbia, real estate brokers and sales agents must be licensed. Licensing requirements vary by state, but most have similar basic requirements for candidates:

Median Annual Wages, May 2012

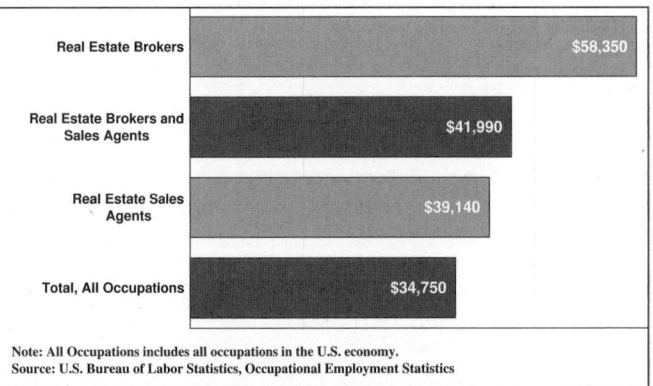

Real Estate Brokers	$58,350
Real Estate Brokers and Sales Agents	$41,990
Real Estate Sales Agents	$39,140
Total, All Occupations	$34,750

Note: All Occupations includes all occupations in the U.S. economy.
Source: U.S. Bureau of Labor Statistics, Occupational Employment Statistics

Percent Change in Employment, Projected 2012–2022

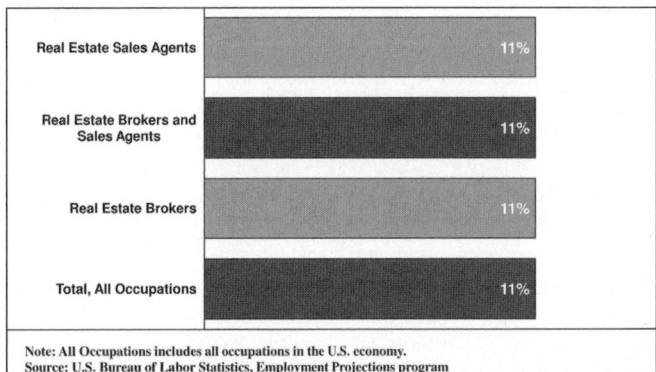

Real Estate Sales Agents	11%
Real Estate Brokers and Sales Agents	11%
Real Estate Brokers	11%
Total, All Occupations	11%

Note: All Occupations includes all occupations in the U.S. economy.
Source: U.S. Bureau of Labor Statistics, Employment Projections program

Employment Projections Data for Real Estate Brokers and Sales Agents

Occupational title	SOC Code	Employment, 2012	Projected Employment, 2022	Change, 2012–2022	
				Percent	Numeric
Real estate brokers and sales agents....................................	41-9020	422,000	468,600	11	46,600
Real estate brokers	41-9021	79,600	88,300	11	8,600
Real estate sales agents	41-9022	342,400	380,300	11	38,000

Source: U.S. Bureau of Labor Statistics, Employment Projections Program

Note: Data are rounded. Go to **Occupational Information Included in the OOH** *for a discussion of the data in this table.*

- Be 18 years old
- Complete a number of real estate courses
- Pass an exam

Some states have additional requirements, such as passing a background check. Licenses are typically not transferrable among states. However, some states have reciprocity agreements and will accept licenses issued by some other states.

To obtain a broker's license, individuals typically need 1 to 3 years of experience as a licensed sales agent. They also must take additional formal classroom training. In some states, a bachelor's degree may be substituted in place of some experience or training requirements.

State licenses typically must be renewed every 2 to 4 years. In most states, brokers and agents must complete continuing education courses to renew their license. To verify exact licensing requirements, prospective brokers and agents should contact the real estate licensing commission of the state in which they wish to work.

Education. Real estate brokers and sales agents must have at least a high school diploma or equivalent. Although most brokers and agents must take state-accredited prelicensing courses to become licensed, some states may waive this requirement if the candidate has taken college courses in real estate.

As the real estate market becomes more competitive and complex, some employers prefer to hire candidates with college courses or a college degree. Some community colleges, colleges, and universities offer courses in real estate. Some offer associate's and bachelor's degree programs in real estate, and many others offer certificate programs. Courses in finance, business administration, economics, and law also can be useful.

Brokers intending to open their own company often take business courses, such as marketing and accounting.

In addition to offering prelicensing courses, many real estate associations have courses and professional development programs for both beginners and experienced agents. These courses cover a variety of topics, such as real estate fundamentals, real estate law, and mortgage financing.

Work Experience in a Related Occupation. To get a broker's license in most states, real estate brokers must have experience working as a licensed real estate sales agent. Requirements vary by state, but most require 1 to 3 years of experience.

Training. Real estate sales agents improve their skills though practice and repetition. Because of the sales environment and the complexity of real estate deals, new agents typically observe and work closely with more senior agents. For example, new agents in some real estate firms may work with mentors and split commission on their first few homes sold. In addition, some of the larger real estate companies provide formal classroom training for new agents as a way to gain knowledge and experience.

Advancement. In larger firms, experienced agents can advance to sales manager or general manager. Sales agents who earn their broker's license may open their own offices.

Important Qualities

Business skills. Because most brokers are self-employed, they must manage every aspect of their business. This includes reaching out to prospective clients, handling their finances, and advertising their services.

Interpersonal skills. Strong interpersonal skills are essential for real estate brokers and sales agents, because they spend much of their time interacting with clients and customers. To attract and keep clients, they must be pleasant, enthusiastic, and trustworthy.

Organizational skills. Real estate brokers and sales agents must be able to work independently, managing their own time and organizing, planning, and prioritizing their work.

Problem-solving skills. Real estate brokers and sales agents need to be able to quickly (sometimes immediately) address concerns clients or potential customers may have with a property. They also mediate negotiations between the seller and buyer.

Pay

The median hourly wage for real estate brokers was $28.05 in May 2012. The median wage is the wage at which half the workers in an occupation earned more than that amount and half earned less. The lowest 10 percent earned less than $12.32, and the top 10 percent earned more than $85.07.

The median hourly wage for real estate sales agents was $18.82 in May 2012. The lowest 10 percent earned less than $9.95, and the top 10 percent earned more than $45.93.

Brokers and sales agents earn most of their income from commissions on sales. The commission varies by the type of property and its value. Commissions are often divided among the buying agent, selling agent, brokers, and firms.

An agent's income, therefore, often depends on economic conditions, the agent's individual motivation, and the types of property available. Income usually increases as agents become better and more experienced at sales. Earnings can be irregular, especially for beginners, and agents sometimes go weeks or months without a sale. Some agents become active in community organizations and local real estate organizations to broaden their contacts and increase their sales.

Job Outlook

Employment of real estate brokers and sales agents is projected to grow 11 percent from 2012 to 2022, about as fast as the average for all occupations.

Because people increasingly use real estate brokers and sales agents when purchasing homes, employment will grow as the real estate market improves.

Similar Occupations   This table shows a list of occupations with job duties that are similar to those of real estate brokers and sales agents.

Occupations	Entry-level Education	2012 Pay	Projected Job Growth	Average Annual Openings
Advertising Sales Agents	High school diploma or equivalent	$46,290	-1%	4,750
Appraisers and Assessors of Real Estate	Bachelor's degree	$49,540	6%	1,210
Insurance Sales Agents	High school diploma or equivalent	$48,150	10%	15,020
Loan Officers	Bachelor's degree	$59,820	8%	7,720
Property, Real Estate, and Community Association Managers	High school diploma or equivalent	$52,610	12%	10,210
Sales Engineers	Bachelor's degree	$91,830	9%	1,740
Securities, Commodities, and Financial Services Sales Agents	Bachelor's degree	$71,720	11%	12,260
Wholesale and Manufacturing Sales Representatives	See "How to Become One"	$58,484	9%	53,250

Both financial and nonfinancial factors spur demand for home sales. Real estate is perceived as a good long-term investment, and many people want to own their homes.

Population growth and mobility also will continue to stimulate the need for new brokers and agents. In addition to first-time home buyers, people will need brokers and agents when looking for a larger home, relocating for a new job, and other reasons.

In addition, an improving job market and rising consumer spending will drive demand for brokers and agents to handle commercial, retail, and industrial real estate transactions.

The real estate market is sensitive to fluctuations in the economy, and employment of real estate brokers and agents will vary accordingly. In periods of economic growth or stability, employment will grow to accommodate people looking to buy homes and businesses looking to expand office or retail space. Alternatively, during periods of declining economic activity or rising interest rates, the amount of work for brokers and agents will slow and employment may decline.

Job Prospects. It is relatively easy to enter the occupation, but getting listings as a broker or agents depends on the real estate market and overall economic conditions. As the economy expands and more people look to buy homes, job competition may increase as more people attain their real estate license. Although the real estate market declines in an economic downturn, there also tend to be fewer active and licensed real estate agents.

New agents will face competition from well-established, more experienced brokers and agents. Because income is dependent on sales, beginners may have trouble sustaining themselves in the occupation during periods of slower activity.

Brokers should fare better because they generally have a large client base from years of experience as sales agents. Those with strong sales ability and extensive social and business connections in their communities should have the best chances for success.

O*NET

➤ Real Estate Brokers (41-9021.00)
➤ Real Estate Sales Agents (41-9022.00)

Contacts for More Information

Information on licensing requirements for real estate brokers and sales agents is available from most local real estate organizations and from the state real estate commission or board.

For more information about opportunities in real estate, visit
➤ National Association of Realtors (www.realtor.org/)

Retail Sales Workers

- **2012 Median Pay** .... $21,410 per year
  $10.29 per hour
- **Entry-Level Education** .... Less than high school
- **Work Experience in a Related Occupation**.............. None
- **On-the-Job Training** ....See "How to Become One"
- **Number of Jobs 2012** 4,668,300
- **Job Outlook, 2012–22** .... 10% (As fast as average)
- **Employment Change, 2012–22** 450,200

What Retail Sales Workers Do

Retail sales workers include both those who sell retail merchandise, such as clothing, furniture, and cars, (called retail salespersons) and those who sell spare and replacement parts and equipment, especially car parts (called parts salespersons). Both types of workers help customers find the products they want and process customers' payments.

Duties. Retail sales workers typically do the following:

- Greet customers and determine what each customer wants or needs
- Recommend merchandise based on customers' wants and needs
- Explain the use and benefit of merchandise to customers
- Answer customers' questions
- Show how merchandise works, if applicable
- Add up customers' total purchases and accept payment
- Know about current sales and promotions, policies about payments and exchanges, and security practices

The following are examples of types of retail sales workers:

Retail salespersons work in stores where they sell goods, such as books, cars, clothing, cosmetics, electronics, furniture, lumber, plants, shoes, and many other types of merchandise.

In addition to helping customers find and select items to buy, many retail salespersons process the payment for the sale. This typically involves operating cash registers.

After taking payment for the purchases, retail salespersons may bag or package the purchases.

Depending on the hours they work, retail salespersons may have to open or close cash registers. This includes counting the money in the register and separating charge slips, coupons, and exchange vouchers. They may also make deposits at a cash office.

For information about other workers who receive and disburse money, see the profile on cashiers.

In addition, retail salespersons may help stock shelves or racks, arrange for mailing or delivery of purchases, mark price tags, take inventory, and prepare displays.

For some retail sales jobs, particularly those involving expensive and complex items, retail sales workers need special knowledge or skills. For example, those who sell cars must be able to explain the features of various models, the manufacturers' specifications, the types of options on the car and financing available, and the details of associated warranties.

In addition, retail sales workers must recognize security risks and thefts and understand their organization's procedures for handling thefts–procedures that may include notifying security guards or calling police.

Parts salespersons sell spare and replacement parts and equipment. Most deal with car parts, by working in either automotive parts stores or automobile dealerships. They take customers' orders, inform customers of part availability and price, and take inventory.

Work Environment

Retail sales workers held about 4.7 million jobs in 2012. Retail salespersons held about 4.4 million of these jobs, while parts salespersons held about 221,300 jobs.

The industries that employed the most retail sales workers in 2012 were as follows:

Clothing and clothing accessories stores..................................21%
General merchandise stores 19
Motor vehicle and parts dealers...11
Building material and garden equipment
    and supplies dealers 9
Sporting goods, hobby, book, and music stores.........................7

Most retail sales workers work in clean, comfortable, well-lit stores. However, they often stand for long periods and may need permission from a supervisor to leave the sales floor. If they sell items such as cars, plants, or lumberyard materials, they may work outdoors.

Work Schedules. Many sales workers work evenings and weekends, particularly during holidays and other peak sales periods. Because the end-of-year holiday season is often the busiest time, many employers limit retail sales workers' use of vacation time between November and the beginning of January.

About 1 in 3 retail salespersons worked part time in 2012.

Retail salespersons work in various settings, including clothing stores, automobile dealers, and electronics and appliance stores.

How to Become One

Typically, retail sales workers do not need a formal education. However, some employers prefer applicants who have a high school diploma or its equivalent.

Education. Although retail or parts sales positions usually have no formal education requirements, some employers prefer applicants who have a high school diploma or equivalent, especially those who sell technical products or "big-ticket" items, such as electronics or cars.

Training. Most retail sales workers receive on-the-job training, which usually lasts a few days to a few months. In small stores, newly hired workers often are trained by an experienced employee. In large stores, training programs are more formal and generally are conducted over several days.

Topics often include customer service, security, the store's policies and procedures, and how to operate the cash register.

Depending on the type of product they are selling, employees may be given additional specialized training. For example, salespersons working in cosmetics get instruction on the types of products the store offers and for whom the cosmetics would be most beneficial. Likewise, those who sell computers may be instructed on the technical differences between computer products.

Because providing exceptional service to customers is a priority for many employers, employees often get periodic training to update and refine their skills.

Advancement. Retail sales workers typically have opportunities to advance to supervisory or managerial positions. Some employ-

Median Hourly Wages, May 2012

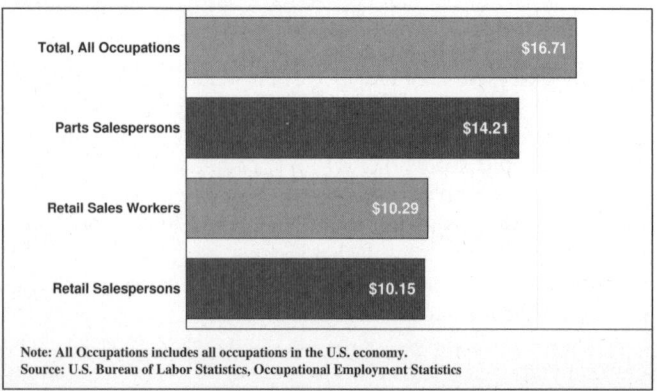

Total, All Occupations	$16.71
Parts Salespersons	$14.21
Retail Sales Workers	$10.29
Retail Salespersons	$10.15

Note: All Occupations includes all occupations in the U.S. economy.
Source: U.S. Bureau of Labor Statistics, Occupational Employment Statistics

Percent Change in Employment, Projected 2012–2022

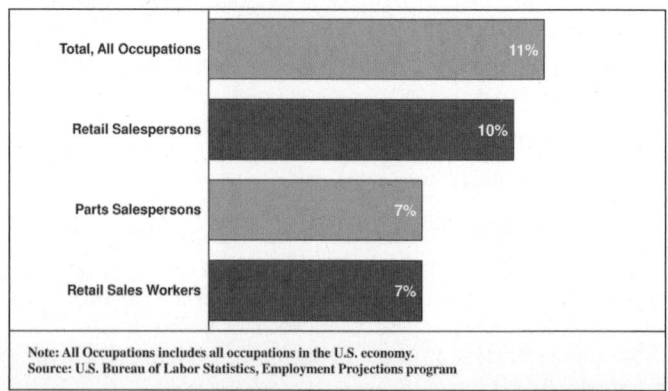

Total, All Occupations	11%
Retail Salespersons	10%
Parts Salespersons	7%
Retail Sales Workers	7%

Note: All Occupations includes all occupations in the U.S. economy.
Source: U.S. Bureau of Labor Statistics, Employment Projections program

Employment Projections Data for Retail Sales Workers

Occupational title	SOC Code	Employment, 2012	Projected Employment, 2022	Change, 2012–2022	
				Percent	Numeric
Retail sales workers...	—	4,668,300	5,118,500	10	450,200
Parts salespersons	41-2022	221,300	236,800	7	15,500
Retail salespersons...	41-2031	4,447,000	4,881,700	10	434,700

Source: U.S. Bureau of Labor Statistics, Employment Projections Program

Note: Data are rounded. Go to Occupational Information Included in the OOH *for a discussion of the data in this table.*

ers want candidates for managerial positions to have a college degree.

As sales workers gain experience and seniority, they often move into positions that have greater responsibility and may be given their choice of departments in which to work. This opportunity often means moving to positions with higher potential earnings and commissions. The highest earnings potential usually lies in selling "big-ticket" items–such as cars, jewelry, furniture, and electronics. These positions often require workers with extensive knowledge of the product and an excellent talent for persuasion.

Important Qualities

Customer-service skills. Retail sales workers must be responsive to the wants and needs of customers. They should explain the product options available to customers and make appropriate recommendations.

Interpersonal skills. A friendly and outgoing personality is important for these workers because the job requires almost constant interaction with people.

Persistence. A large number of attempted sales may not be successful, so sales workers should not be discouraged easily. They must start each new sales attempt with a positive attitude.

Selling skills. Retail sales workers must be persuasive when interacting with customers. They must clearly and effectively explain the benefits of merchandise.

Pay

The median hourly wage for retail salespersons was $10.15 in May 2012. The median wage is the wage at which half of the workers in an occupation earned more than that amount and half earned less. The lowest 10 percent earned less than $8.09, and the top 10 percent earned more than $18.73.

The median hourly wage for parts salespersons was $14.21 in May 2012. The lowest 10 percent earned less than $8.96, and the top 10 percent earned more than $23.93.

In May 2012, the median hourly wages for retail sales workers in the top five industries in which they worked were as follows:

Motor vehicle and parts dealers..	$14.73
Building material and garden equipment and supplies dealers	12.21
General merchandise stores	9.73
Sporting goods, hobby, book, and music stores.......................	9.46
Clothing and clothing accessories stores..................................	9.24

Compensation systems vary by type of establishment and merchandise sold. Retail sales workers get hourly wages, commissions, or a combination of the two. Under a commission system, they get a percentage of the sales they make. This system offers sales workers the opportunity to increase their earnings considerably, but they may find that their earnings depend strongly on their ability to sell their product and on the ups and downs of the economy.

Job Outlook

Employment of retail sales workers is projected to grow 10 percent from 2012 to 2022, about as fast as the average for all occupations.

Employment of retail salespersons is projected to grow 10 percent from 2012 to 2022, about as fast as the average for all occupations. Employment of retail salespersons has traditionally grown with the overall economy, and this trend is expected to continue. Population growth will increase retail sales and demand for these workers.

Online sales have had a detrimental effect on certain in-store retailers, primarily book and media stores. However, other retail segments, such as automobile dealers and clothing stores, have seen much less of an impact. In general, although consumers are increasing their online retail shopping, they will continue to do the vast majority of their retail shopping in stores. Retail salespersons will be needed in stores to help customers and complete sales.

Among the various retail industries, other general merchandise stores, which include warehouse clubs and supercenters, are

Similar Occupations This table shows a list of occupations with job duties that are similar to those of retail sales workers.

Occupations	Entry-level Education	2012 Pay	Projected Job Growth	Average Annual Openings
Cashiers	Less than high school	$18,970	3%	153,000
Customer Service Representatives	High school diploma or equivalent	$30,580	13%	94,160
Information Clerks	High school diploma or equivalent	$31,159	2%	47,000
Insurance Sales Agents	High school diploma or equivalent	$48,150	10%	15,020
Real Estate Brokers and Sales Agents	High school diploma or equivalent	$42,723	11%	8,630
Sales Engineers	Bachelor's degree	$91,830	9%	1,740
Securities, Commodities, and Financial Services Sales Agents	Bachelor's degree	$71,720	11%	12,260
Wholesale and Manufacturing Sales Representatives	See "How to Become One"	$58,484	9%	53,250

expected to see strong job growth. These large stores sell a wide range of goods from a single location. Thus, employment of retail salespersons in this industry is projected to grow 28 percent during the next decade. However, employment of these workers in department stores is projected to grow only 5 percent.

Employment of parts salespersons is projected to grow 7 percent from 2012 to 2022, slower than the average for all occupations. People are keeping their cars longer and are buying new cars less often. Older cars need to be serviced more frequently, creating demand for car parts and parts salespersons. However, growth will be slowed by the motor vehicle and motor vehicle parts and supplies merchant wholesalers industry, in which employment of parts salespersons is projected to decline 7 percent from 2012 to 2022.

Job Prospects. Many workers leave this occupation, which means there will be a large number of job openings. This should result in many employment opportunities for qualified workers.

O*NET

➤ Parts Salespersons (41-2022.00)
➤ Retail Salespersons (41-2031.00)

Contacts for More Information

For information about the retail industry, visit
➤ National Retail Federation (www.nrf.com)

For information about training for a career in automobile sales, visit
➤ National Automobile Dealers Association (www.nada.org/)

Sales Engineers

- **2012 Median Pay** .... $91,830 per year
  $44.15 per hour
- **Entry-Level Education** ....Bachelor's degree
- **Work Experience in a Related Occupation**............... None
- **On-the-Job Training**.... Moderate-term on-the-job training
- **Number of Jobs 2012** 66,000
- **Job Outlook, 2012–22** .... 9% (As fast as average)
- **Employment Change, 2012–22** 5,900

What Sales Engineers Do

Sales engineers sell complex scientific and technological products or services to businesses. They must have extensive knowledge of the products' parts and functions and must understand the scientific processes that make these products work.

Duties. Sales engineers typically do the following:

- Prepare and deliver technical presentations explaining products or services to customers and prospective customers
- Confer with customers and engineers to assess equipment needs and to determine system requirements
- Collaborate with sales teams to understand customer requirements and provide sales support
- Secure and renew orders and arrange delivery
- Plan and modify products to meet customer needs
- Help clients solve problems with installed equipment
- Recommend improved materials or machinery to customers, showing how changes will lower costs or increase production
- Help in researching and developing new products

Sales engineers specialize in technologically and scientifically advanced products. They use their technical skills to explain the benefits of their products or services to potential customers and to show how their products or services are better than their competitors' products. Some sales engineers work for the companies that design and build technical products. Others work for independent sales firms.

Many of the duties of sales engineers are similar to those of other salespersons. They must interest the client in buying their products or services, negotiate a price, and complete the sale. To do this, sales engineers give technical presentations during which they explain the technical aspects of the product and how it will solve a specific customer problem.

Some sales engineers, however, team with salespersons who concentrate on marketing and selling the product, which lets the sales engineer concentrate on the technical aspects of the job. By working as part of a sales team, each member is able to focus on his or her strengths and expertise. For more information on other sales occupations, see the profile on wholesale and manufacturing sales representatives.

In addition to giving technical presentations, sales engineers are increasingly doing other tasks related to sales, such as market research. They also may ask for technical requirements from customers and modify and adjust products to meet customers' specific needs. Some sales engineers work with research and development (R&D) departments to help identify and develop new products.

Work Environment

Sales engineers held about 66,000 jobs in 2012. Sales engineers encounter stress because their income and job security often depend directly on their success in sales and customer service. Some sales engineers have large territories and travel extensively. Because sales regions may cover several states, sales engineers may be away from home for several days or even weeks at a time. Other sales engineers cover a smaller region and spend only a few nights away from home. International travel to secure contracts with foreign clients is becoming more common.

The industries that employed the most sales engineers in 2012 were as follows:

Merchant wholesalers, durable goods	24%
Manufacturing	23
Computer systems design and related services	17
Wholesale electronic markets and agents and brokers	11
Telecommunications	9

Sales engineers use scientific knowledge to help their customers choose the right technical products.

Median Annual Wages, May 2012

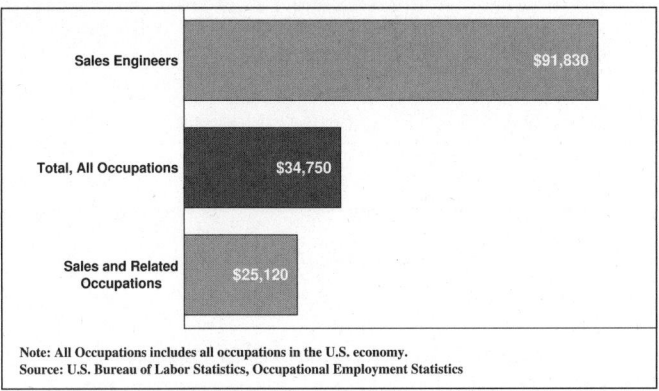

Note: All Occupations includes all occupations in the U.S. economy.
Source: U.S. Bureau of Labor Statistics, Occupational Employment Statistics

Percent Change in Employment, Projected 2012–2022

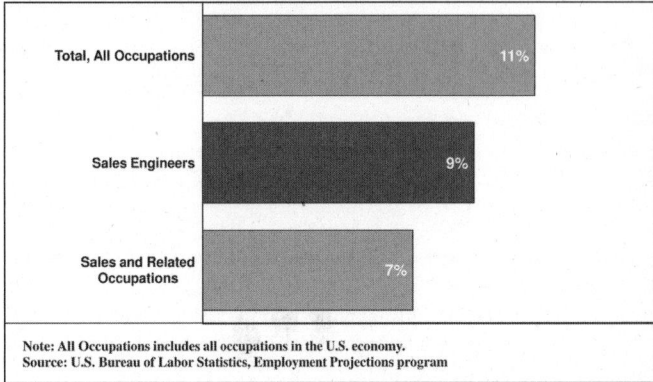

Note: All Occupations includes all occupations in the U.S. economy.
Source: U.S. Bureau of Labor Statistics, Employment Projections program

Work Schedules. Most sales engineers work full time, and about 6 in 10 worked more than 40 hours per week in 2012. Some may work long and irregular hours to meet sales goals and client needs. However, many sales engineers can decide their own schedules.

How to Become One

A bachelor's degree is typically required to become a sales engineer. Successful sales engineers combine technical knowledge of the products or services they are selling with strong interpersonal skills.

Education. Sales engineers typically need a bachelor's degree in engineering or a related field. However, a worker without a degree, but with previous sales experience as well as technical experience or training, sometimes holds the title of sales engineer. Workers who have a degree in a science, such as chemistry, or in business with little or no previous sales experience, also may be called sales engineers.

University engineering programs generally require 4 years of study. They vary in content, but all programs include courses in math and the physical sciences. In addition, most programs require developing strong computer skills.

Some programs offer a general engineering curriculum; students then specialize on the job or in graduate school. Most programs, however, require students to choose an area of specialization. The most common majors are electrical, mechanical, or civil engineering, but some programs offer additional majors, such as chemical, biomedical, or computer hardware engineering.

Training. New graduates with engineering degrees typically need sales experience and training before they can work independently as sales engineers. Training covers general sales techniques and may involve teaming with a sales mentor who is familiar with the employer's business practices, customers, procedures, and company culture. After the training period, sales engineers may continue to partner with someone who lacks technical skills yet excels in the art of sales.

It is important for sales engineers to continue their engineering and sales education throughout their careers. Much of their value to their employers depends on their knowledge of, and ability to sell, the latest technologies. Sales engineers in high-technology fields, such as information technology and advanced electronics, may find that their technical knowledge rapidly becomes obsolete, requiring frequent retraining.

Advancement. Promotions may include a higher commission rate, a larger sales territory, or elevation to the position of supervisor or marketing manager.

Important Qualities

Interpersonal skills. Strong interpersonal skills are a valuable characteristic for sales engineers, both for building relationships with clients and effectively communicating with other members of the sales team.

Problem-solving skills. Sales engineers must be able to listen to the customer's desires and concerns, and then recommend solutions, possibly including customizing a product.

Similar Occupations   This table shows a list of occupations with job duties that are similar to those of sales engineers.

Occupations	Entry-level Education	2012 Pay	Projected Job Growth	Average Annual Openings
Aerospace Engineers	Bachelor's degree	$103,720	7%	2,540
Computer Hardware Engineers	Bachelor's degree	$100,920	7%	2,410
Electrical and Electronics Engineers	Bachelor's degree	$89,701	4%	7,940
Industrial Engineers	Bachelor's degree	$78,860	5%	7,540
Insurance Sales Agents	High school diploma or equivalent	$48,150	10%	15,020
Mechanical Engineers	Bachelor's degree	$80,580	4%	9,970
Purchasing Managers, Buyers, and Purchasing Agents	See "How to Become One"	$63,128	4%	12,230
Securities, Commodities, and Financial Services Sales Agents	Bachelor's degree	$71,720	11%	12,260
Wholesale and Manufacturing Sales Representatives	See "How to Become One"	$58,484	9%	53,250

Employment Projections Data for Sales Engineers

Occupational title	SOC Code	Employment, 2012	Projected Employment, 2022	Change, 2012–2022	
				Percent	Numeric
Sales engineers	41-9031	66,000	71,800	9	5,900

Source: U.S. Bureau of Labor Statistics, Employment Projections Program

Note: Data are rounded. Go to **Occupational Information Included in the OOH** *for a discussion of the data in this table.*

Self-confidence. Sales engineers should be confident and persuasive when making sales presentations.

Technological skills. Sales engineers must have extensive knowledge of the technologically sophisticated products they sell in order to explain their advantages and answer questions.

Pay

The median annual wage for sales engineers was $91,830 in May 2012. The median wage is the wage at which half the workers in an occupation earned more than that amount and half earned less. The lowest 10 percent earned less than $55,660 and the top 10 percent earned more than $150,970.

In May 2012, the median annual wages for sales engineers in the top five industries in which these engineers worked were as follows:

Computer systems design and related services	$106,440
Telecommunications	97,130
Wholesale electronic markets and agents and brokers	95,500
Merchant wholesalers, durable goods	85,020
Manufacturing	82,240

How much a sales engineer earns varies significantly by the type of firm and the product sold. Most employers offer a combination of salary and commission payments or salary plus a bonus. Some sales engineers who work for independent sales companies earn only commissions. Commissions are usually based on the value of sales. Bonuses may depend on individual performance, on the performance of all workers in the group or district, or on the company's performance. Earnings from commissions and bonuses may vary from year to year depending on sales ability, the demand for the company's products or services, and the overall economy. In addition to their earnings, sales engineers who work for manufacturers usually are reimbursed for expenses such as transportation, meals, hotels, and customer entertainment.

Job Outlook

Employment of sales engineers is projected to grow 9 percent from 2012 to 2022, about as fast as the average for all occupations. As a wider range of technologically sophisticated products comes on the market, sales engineers will be in demand to help sell products or services related to these products.

Employment growth is expected to be strong in independent sales agencies (companies that sell on behalf of manufacturers without taking title to the goods being sold). As manufacturing companies outsource their sales staff as a way to control costs, employment in these independent agencies is expected to increase. Growth is also likely to be strong for sales engineers selling computer software and hardware. Employment of sales engineers in computer systems design and related services is projected to grow 35 percent from 2012 to 2022.

Job Prospects. Successful sales engineers must have strong technical knowledge of the products they are selling, in addition to having interpersonal skills and the ability to persuade. Job prospects should be good for candidates with these abilities.

O*NET

➤ Sales Engineers (41-9031.00)

Contacts for More Information

For more information about careers in sales occupations, visit

➤ Manufacturers' Agents National Association (MANA) (www.manaonline.org/)

➤ Manufacturers' Representatives Educational Research Foundation (MRERF) (www.mrerf.org/)

Securities, Commodities, and Financial Services Sales Agents

- **2012 Median Pay** .... $71,720 per year $34.48 per hour
- **Entry-Level Education** .... Bachelor's degree
- **Work Experience in a Related Occupation** .... None
- **On-the-Job Training** .... Moderate-term on-the-job training
- **Number of Jobs 2012** 354,600
- **Job Outlook, 2012–22** .... 11% (As fast as average)
- **Employment Change, 2012–22** 39,700

What Securities, Commodities, and Financial Services Sales Agents Do

Securities, commodities, and financial services sales agents connect buyers and sellers in financial markets. They sell securities to individuals, advise companies in search of investors, and conduct trades.

Duties. Securities, commodities, and financial services sales agents typically do the following:

- Contact prospective clients to present information and explain available services
- Offer advice on the purchase or sale of particular securities
- Buy and sell securities, such as stocks and bonds
- Buy and sell commodities, such as corn, oil, and gold
- Monitor financial markets and the performance of individual securities
- Analyze company finances to provide recommendations for public offerings, mergers, and acquisitions
- Evaluate cost and revenue of agreements

Securities, commodities, and financial services sales agents deal with a wide range of products and clients. Agents spend much of the day interacting with people, whether selling stock to an individual or discussing the status of a merger deal with a company executive. The work is usually stressful because agents deal with large amounts of money and have time constraints.

People increasingly seek the advice and services of securities, commodities, and financial services sales agents to realize their financial goals.

A security or commodity can be traded in two ways: electronically or in an auction-style setting on the floor of an exchange market. Markets such as the National Association of Securities Dealers Automated Quotation system (NASDAQ) use vast computer networks rather than human traders to match buyers and sellers. Others, such as the New York Stock Exchange (NYSE), rely on floor brokers to complete transactions.

The following are examples of types of securities, commodities, and financial services sales agents:

Brokers sell securities and commodities directly to individual clients. They advise people on appropriate investments based on the client's needs and financial ability. The people they advise may have very different levels of expertise in financial matters.

Finding clients is a large part of a broker's job. They must create their own client base by calling from a list of potential clients. Some agents network by joining social groups, and others may rely on referrals from satisfied clients.

Investment bankers connect businesses that need money to finance their operations or expansion plans with investors who are interested in providing that funding. This process is called underwriting, and it is the main function of investment banks. The banks first sell their advisory services to help companies issue new stocks or bonds, and then the banks sell the issued securities to investors.

Some of the most important services that investment bankers provide are initial public offerings (IPOs), and mergers and acquisitions. An IPO is the process by which a company becomes open for public investment by issuing its first stock. Investment bankers must estimate how much the company is worth and ensure that it meets the legal requirements to become publicly traded.

Investment bankers also connect companies in mergers (when two companies join together) and acquisitions (when one company buys another). Investment bankers provide advice throughout the process to ensure that the transaction goes smoothly.

Investment banking sales agents and traders carry out buy-and-sell orders for stocks, bonds, and commodities from clients and make trades on behalf of the firm itself. These workers are primarily employed by investment banks, although some work for commercial banks, hedge funds, and private equity groups. Because markets fluctuate so much, trading is a split-second decision-making process. Slight changes in the price of a trade can greatly affect its profitability, making the trader's decision extremely important.

Floor brokers work directly on the floor–a large room where trading is done–of a securities or commodities exchange. After a trader places an order for a security, floor brokers negotiate the price, make the sale, and forward the purchase price to the trader.

Financial services sales agents consult on a wide variety of banking, securities, insurance, and related services to individuals and businesses, often catering the services to meet the client's financial needs. They contact potential clients to explain their services, which may include the handling of checking accounts, loans, certificates of deposit, individual retirement accounts, credit cards, and estate and retirement planning.

Work Environment

Securities, commodities, and financial services sales agents held about 354,600 jobs in 2012.

The industries that employed the most securities, commodities, and financial services sales agents in 2012 were as follows:

Securities and commodity contracts intermediation
 and brokerage 39%
Depository credit intermediation 29
Other financial investment activities 11
Nondepository credit intermediation 5

Most securities, commodities, and financial services sales agents work long hours under stressful conditions. The pace of work

Median Annual Wages, May 2012

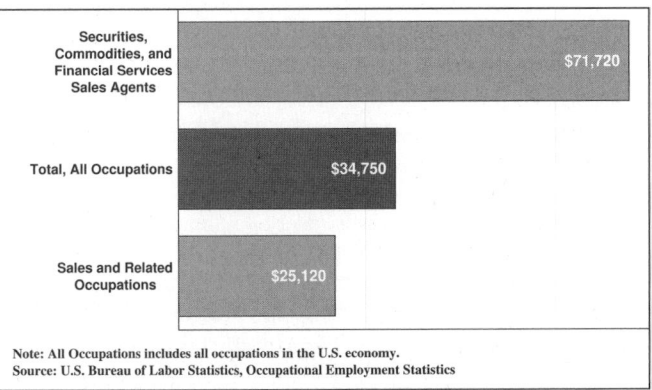

Securities, Commodities, and Financial Services Sales Agents	$71,720
Total, All Occupations	$34,750
Sales and Related Occupations	$25,120

Note: All Occupations includes all occupations in the U.S. economy.
Source: U.S. Bureau of Labor Statistics, Occupational Employment Statistics

Percent Change in Employment, Projected 2012–2022

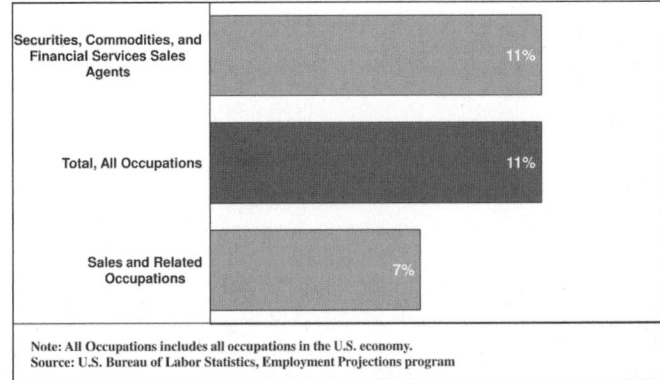

Securities, Commodities, and Financial Services Sales Agents	11%
Total, All Occupations	11%
Sales and Related Occupations	7%

Note: All Occupations includes all occupations in the U.S. economy.
Source: U.S. Bureau of Labor Statistics, Employment Projections program

Employment Projections Data for Securities, Commodities, and Financial Services Sales Agents

Occupational title	SOC Code	Employment, 2012	Projected Employment, 2022	Change, 2012–2022	
				Percent	Numeric
Securities, commodities, and financial services sales agents...	41-3031	354,600	394,300	11	39,700

Source: U.S. Bureau of Labor Statistics, Employment Projections Program

Note: Data are rounded. Go to Occupational Information Included in the OOH *for a discussion of the data in this table.*

is fast, and managers are usually demanding of their workers, because both commissions and advancements are tied to sales.

Investment bankers travel extensively because they frequently work with companies in other countries.

Because computers can conduct trades faster than people can, electronic trading is quickly replacing verbal auction-style trades on exchange floors. The environment of the stock exchange is changing as a result, with more traders carrying out orders behind a desk and fewer working on the exchange floor.

A growing number of securities sales agents, employed mostly by discount or online brokerage firms, work in call-center environments. In these centers, hundreds of agents spend much of the day on the telephone taking orders from clients or offering help and information on their accounts.

Since most of the major investment banks are located in New York City, employment of securities, commodities, and financial services sales agents is concentrated in this metropolitan area.

Work Schedules. Securities, commodities, and financial services sales agents usually work full time and more than 1 in 3 worked more than 40 hours per week in 2012. In addition, they may work evenings and weekends because many of their clients work during the day. Call centers often operate 24 hours a day, requiring agents to work in shifts.

How to Become One

A bachelor's degree is required for entry-level jobs, and a master's degree in business administration (MBA) is useful for advancement.

Education. Securities, commodities, and financial services sales agents generally must have a bachelor's degree to get an entry-level job. Studies in business, finance, accounting, or economics are important, especially for larger firms. Many firms hire summer interns before their last year of college, and those who are most successful are offered full-time jobs after they graduate.

Numerous agents eventually get a master's degree in business administration (MBA), which is often a requirement for high-level positions in the securities industry. Because the MBA exposes students to real-world business practices, it can be a major asset for jobseekers. Employers often reward MBA holders with higher level positions, better compensation, and large signing bonuses.

Training. Most employers provide intensive on-the-job training, teaching employees the specifics of the job, such as the products and services offered. Trainees in large firms may receive technical instruction in securities analysis and selling strategies. Firms often rotate their trainees among various departments to give them a broad understanding of the securities business.

Securities, commodities, and financial services sales agents must keep up with new products and services and other developments. They attend conferences and training seminars regularly.

Licenses, Certifications, and Registrations. Brokers and investment bankers must register as representatives of their firm with the Financial Industry Regulatory Authority (FINRA). To obtain the license, potential agents must pass a series of exams.

Many other licenses are available, each of which gives the holder the right to sell different investment products and services. Traders and some other sales representatives also need licenses, although these vary by firm and specialization. Financial services sales agents may need to be licensed, especially if they sell securities or insurance. Most firms offer training to help their employees pass the licensing exams.

Agents who are registered with FINRA must attend continuing education classes to keep their licenses. Courses consist of computer-based training on legal requirements or new financial products or services.

Although not always required, certification enhances professional standing and is recommended by employers. Brokers, investment bankers, and financial services sales agents can earn the Chartered Financial Analyst (CFA) certification, sponsored by the CFA Institute. To qualify for this certification, applicants need a bachelor's degree or 4 years of related work experience and must pass three exams, which require several hundred hours of independent study. Applicants also must have an international passport. Exams cover subjects in accounting, economics, securities analysis, financial markets and instruments, corporate finance, asset valuation, and portfolio management. Applicants can take the exams while they are getting the required work experience.

Advancement. Securities, commodities, and financial services sales agents usually advance to senior positions in a firm by accumulating a greater number of accounts. Although beginners often service the accounts of individual investors, they may eventually service large institutional accounts, such as those of banks and retirement funds.

After taking a series of tests, some brokers become portfolio managers and have greater authority to make investment decisions regarding an account. For more information on portfolio managers, see the profile on financial analysts.

Some experienced sales agents become branch office managers and supervise other sales agents while continuing to provide services for their own clients. A few agents advance to top management positions or become partners in their firms.

Many investment banks use an "up or out" policy, in which entry-level investment bankers are either promoted or terminated after 2 or 3 years. Investment banks use this policy to ensure that entry-level positions are not occupied long term, allowing the bank to bring in new workers.

Important Qualities

Customer-service skills. Securities, commodities, and financial services sales agents must be persuasive and make clients feel comfortable with the agent's recommendations.

Decision-making skills. Investment banking traders must make split-second decisions, with large sums of money at stake.

Detail oriented. Investment bankers must pay close attention to the details of initial public offerings and mergers and acquisitions because small changes can have large consequences.

Initiative. Securities, commodities, and financial services sales agents must create their own client base by making "cold" sales

Similar Occupations   This table shows a list of occupations with job duties that are similar to those of securities, commodities, and financial services sales agents.

Occupations	Entry-level Education	2012 Pay	Projected Job Growth	Average Annual Openings
Financial Analysts	Bachelor's degree	$76,950	16%	10,090
Financial Managers	Bachelor's degree	$109,740	9%	14,690
Insurance Sales Agents	High school diploma or equivalent	$48,150	10%	15,020
Personal Financial Advisors	Bachelor's degree	$67,520	27%	9,640
Real Estate Brokers and Sales Agents	High school diploma or equivalent	$42,723	11%	8,630

calls to people to whom they have not been referred and to people not expecting the call.

Math skills. To judge the profitability of potential deals, securities, commodities, and financial services sales agents must have strong math skills.

Pay

The median annual wage for securities, commodities, and financial services sales agents was $71,720 in May 2012. The median wage is the wage at which half the workers in an occupation earned more than that amount and half earned less. The lowest 10 percent earned less than $32,030, and the top 10 percent earned more than $187,200.

In May 2012, the median annual wages for securities, commodities, and financial services sales agents in the top four industries in which these agents worked were as follows:

Other financial investment activities $108,250
Securities and commodity contracts intermediation
   and brokerage 99,940
Nondepository credit intermediation 58,080
Depository credit intermediation 42,960

Many securities and commodities brokers earn a commission based on the monetary value of the products they sell. Most firms pay brokers a minimum salary in addition to commissions.

Trainee brokers usually earn a salary until they develop a client base. The salary gradually decreases in favor of commissions as the broker gains clients.

Investment bankers in corporate finance and mergers and acquisitions generally earn a base salary with the opportunity to earn a substantial bonus. At higher levels, bonuses far exceed base salary.

Job Outlook

Employment of securities, commodities, and financial services sales agents is projected to grow 11 percent from 2012 to 2022, about as fast as the average for all occupations.

The financial services industry has experienced some consolidation in recent years, which has slowed employment growth for these workers. Overall employment in the finance and insurance industry is projected to grow 9 percent from 2012 to 2022.

Financial regulation, including restrictions on proprietary trading, may create a shift of employment among traders from investment banks to hedge funds; however, overall employment growth for the occupation should not be affected by this shift.

Services that investment bankers provide, such as helping with initial public offerings and mergers and acquisitions, will continue to be in demand as the economy grows. The United States remains an international financial center, meaning that the economic growth of countries around the world will contribute to employment growth in the American financial industry.

In addition, employment growth will likely be stronger for commodities brokers and traders than other financial services sales agents. Trading in commodities markets has increased substantially in recent years, driven by large group investors, such as retirement funds, entering the market. As the number of transactions grows in commodities trading, such as in oil futures, employment of commodities sales agents is expected to increase to meet this demand.

Job Prospects. The high pay associated with securities, commodities, and financial services sales agents draws many more applicants than there are openings. Therefore, competition for jobs is intense.

Certification and a graduate degree, such as a Chartered Financial Analyst (CFA) certification and a master's degree in business administration (MBA), can improve an applicant's prospects. For entry-level jobs, having an excellent grade-point average (GPA) in college is important.

O*NET

➤ Securities, Commodities, and Financial Services Sales Agents (41-3031.00)
➤ Sales Agents, Securities and Commodities (41-3031.01)
➤ Sales Agents, Financial Services (41-3031.02)
➤ Securities and Commodities Traders (41-3031.03)

Contacts for More Information

For more information about securities, commodities, and financial services sales agents, visit

➤ American Academy of Financial Management (www.aafm.us/)
➤ Securities Industry and Financial Markets Association (SIFMA) (www.sifma.org/)

For more information about licensing of securities, commodities, and financial services sales agents, visit

➤ Financial Industry Regulatory Authority (FINRA) (www.finra.org)

For more information about certification for securities, commodities, and financial services sales agents, visit

➤ CFA Institute (www.cfainstitute.org/)

Travel Agents

- **2012 Median Pay** .... $34,600 per year
   $16.64 per hour
- **Entry-Level Education** ... High school diploma or equivalent
- **Work Experience in a Related Occupation** .... None
- **On-the-Job Training** .... Moderate-term on-the-job training
- **Number of Jobs 2012** 73,300
- **Job Outlook, 2012–22** .... -12% (Decline)
- **Employment Change, 2012–22** .... -8,900

What Travel Agents Do

Travel agents sell transportation, lodging, and admission to entertainment activities to individuals and groups planning trips. They offer advice on destinations, plan trip itineraries, and make travel arrangements for clients.

Duties. Travel agents typically do the following:

- Arrange travel for business and vacation customers
- Determine customers' needs and preferences, such as schedules and costs
- Plan and arrange tour packages, excursions, and day trips
- Find fare and schedule information
- Calculate total travel costs
- Book reservations for travel, hotels, rental cars, and special events, such as tours and excursions
- Tell clients about what their trip will be like, including giving details on required documents, such as passports or visas
- Give advice about local weather conditions, customs, and attractions
- Make alternative booking arrangements if changes arise before or during the trip

Travel agents help travelers by sorting through vast amounts of information to find the best possible travel arrangements. In addition, resorts and specialty travel groups use travel agents to promote travel packages to their clients.

Travel agents also may visit destinations to get firsthand experience so that they can make recommendations to clients or colleagues. They may visit hotels, resorts, and restaurants to evaluate the comfort, cleanliness, and quality of the establishment. However, most of their time is spent talking with clients, promoting tours, and contacting airlines and hotels to make travel arrangements. Travel agents use a reservation system called a Global Distribution System (GDS) to access travel information and make reservations with travel suppliers such as airlines or hotels.

Travel agents increasingly are focusing on a specific type of travel, such as adventure tours. Some may cater to a specific group of people, such as senior citizens or single people. Other travel agents primarily make corporate travel arrangements for employee business travel. Some work for tour operators and are responsible for selling the company's tours and services.

Work Environment

Travel agents held about 73,300 jobs in 2012. Travel agents work in offices, where they spend much of their time on the phone and on the computer. In some cases, busy offices or call centers may be

Travel agents help clients plan personal and business trips.

noisy and crowded. Agents may face stress during travel emergencies or unanticipated schedule changes.

In 2012, 83 percent of all travel agents worked for the travel arrangement and reservation services industry, which includes those who work for travel agencies. In addition, 12 percent of travel agents were self-employed.

Work Schedules. Most travel agents work full time. Some work longer hours during peak travel times or when they must accommodate customers' schedule changes and last-minute needs.

How to Become One

A high school diploma typically is required for someone to become a travel agent. However, many employers prefer additional formal training as well. Good communication and computer skills are essential.

Education. Employers may prefer candidates who have taken classes related to the travel industry. Many community colleges,

Median Annual Wages, May 2012

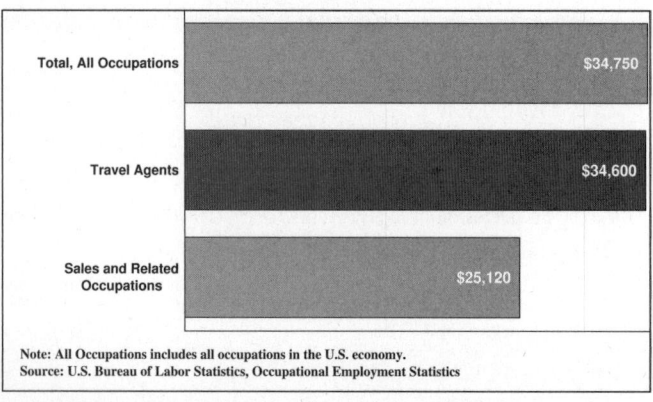

Total, All Occupations	$34,750
Travel Agents	$34,600
Sales and Related Occupations	$25,120

Note: All Occupations includes all occupations in the U.S. economy.
Source: U.S. Bureau of Labor Statistics, Occupational Employment Statistics

Percent Change in Employment, Projected 2012–2022

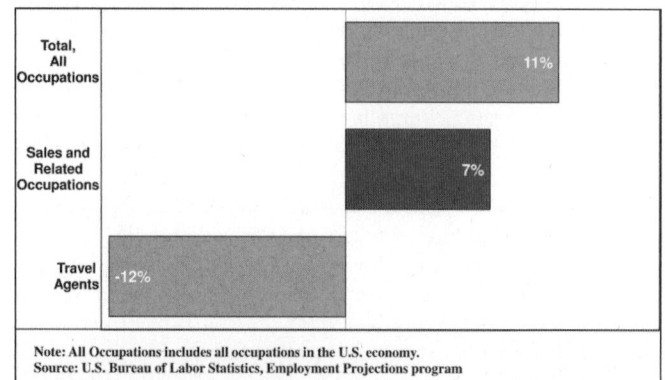

Total, All Occupations	11%
Sales and Related Occupations	7%
Travel Agents	-12%

Note: All Occupations includes all occupations in the U.S. economy.
Source: U.S. Bureau of Labor Statistics, Employment Projections program

Employment Projections Data for Travel Agents

Occupational title	SOC Code	Employment, 2012	Projected Employment, 2022	Change, 2012–2022	
				Percent	Numeric
Travel agents	41-3041	73,300	64,400	-12	-8,900

Source: U.S. Bureau of Labor Statistics, Employment Projections Program

Note: Data are rounded. Go to **Occupational Information Included in the OOH** for a discussion of the data in this table.

vocational schools, and industry associations offer technical training or continuing education classes in professional travel planning. Classes usually focus on reservations systems, regulations regarding international travel, and marketing. In addition, a few colleges offer degrees in travel and tourism.

Training. Employers in the travel industry always provide some on-the-job training on the computer systems used in the industry. For example, a travel agent could be trained to work with a reservation system used by several airlines.

Licenses, Certifications, and Registrations. Some associations offer certifications that may help travel agents once they are on the job. The Travel Institute, for example, provides training and professional development opportunities for experienced travel agents. Examinations for different levels of certification are offered, depending on a travel agent's experience. Certification for airlines or cruise lines is available from associations such as the International Airline Transport Association's Training and Development Institute and the Cruise Lines International Association.

Some states require agents to have a business license to sell travel services. Requirements among states vary greatly. Contact individual state licensing agencies for more information.

Other Experience. Some agencies prefer travel agents with firsthand experience visiting a country. These agencies especially prefer travel agents who specialize in specific destinations or particular types of travelers, such as groups with a special interest or corporate travelers.

Important Qualities

Adventurousness. Travel agencies that specialize in exotic destinations or particular types of travel, such as adventure travel or ecotourism, may prefer to hire travel agents who share these interests.

Communication skills. Travel agents must listen to customers, understand their travel needs, and offer appropriate travel advice and information.

Customer-service skills. When customers need to make last-minute changes in their travel arrangements, travel agents must be able to respond to questions and complaints in a friendly and professional manner.

Detail oriented. Travel agents must pay attention to details in order to ensure that the reservations they make match travelers' needs. They must make reservations at the correct dates, times, and locations to meet travelers' schedules.

Organizational skills. Travel agents should have strong organizational skills because they often work on itineraries for many customers at once. Keeping client information in order and ensuring that bills and receipts are processed in a timely manner is essential.

Sales skills. Travel agents must be able to persuade clients to buy transportation, lodging, or tours. Sometimes they might need to persuade tour operators, airline staff, or others to take care of their clients' special needs. Earnings for many travel agents depend on commissions and service fees.

Pay

The median annual wage for travel agents was $34,600 in May 2012. The median wage is the wage at which half the workers in an occupation earned more than that amount and half earned less. The lowest 10 percent earned less than $19,930, and the top 10 percent earned more than $57,400. These wage data include money earned from commissions.

Job Outlook

Employment of travel agents is projected to decline 12 percent from 2012 to 2022.

Clients who want customized travel experiences, such as adventure tours, will continue to require the expertise of agents. However, the ability of travelers to use the Internet to research vacations and book their own trips is expected to continue to suppress demand for travel agents.

Job Prospects. Job prospects should be best for travel agents who specialize in specific destinations or particular types of travelers, such as groups with a special interest or corporate travelers.

O*NET

➤ Travel Agents (41-3041.00)

Contacts for More Information

For more information about training opportunities, visit
➤ American Society of Travel Agents (www.asta.org/)

For more information about voluntary certification opportunities, visit
➤ The Travel Institute (http://thetravelinstitute.com/)

Similar Occupations   This table shows a list of occupations with job duties that are similar to those of travel agents.

Occupations	Entry-level Education	2012 Pay	Projected Job Growth	Average Annual Openings
Information Clerks	High school diploma or equivalent	$31,159	2%	47,000
Meeting, Convention, and Event Planners	Bachelor's degree	$45,810	33%	4,420
Secretaries and Administrative Assistants	High school diploma or equivalent	$36,198	12%	97,210

Wholesale and Manufacturing Sales Representatives

- **2012 Median Pay** .... $57,870 per year
  $27.82 per hour
- **Entry-Level Education** ....See "How to Become One"
- **Work Experience in a Related Occupation**............... None
- **On-the-Job Training**.... Moderate-term on-the-job training
- **Number of Jobs 2012** 1,863,000
- **Job Outlook, 2012–22**.................. 9% (As fast as average)
- **Employment Change, 2012–22** 169,300

What Wholesale and Manufacturing Sales Representatives Do

Wholesale and manufacturing sales representatives sell goods for wholesalers or manufacturers to businesses, government agencies, and other organizations. They contact customers, explain product features, answer any questions that their customers may have, and negotiate prices.

Duties. Wholesale and manufacturing sales representatives typically do the following:

- Identify prospective customers by using business directories, follow leads from existing clients, and attend trade shows and conferences
- Contact new and existing customers to discuss their needs and to explain how specific products and services can meet these needs
- Help customers select products based on the customers' needs, product specifications, and regulations
- Emphasize product features based on analyses of customers' needs and on technical knowledge of product capabilities and limitations
- Answer customers' questions about prices, availability, and product uses
- Negotiate prices and terms of sale and service agreements
- Prepare sales contracts and submit orders for processing
- Collaborate with colleagues to exchange information, such as selling strategies and marketing information
- Follow up with customers to make sure they are satisfied with their purchases and to answer any questions or concerns

Wholesale and manufacturing sales representatives–sometimes called manufacturers' representatives or manufacturers' agents–generally work for manufacturers or wholesalers. Some work for a single organization, while others represent several companies and sell a range of products.

Rather than selling goods directly to consumers, wholesale and manufacturing sales representatives deal with businesses, government agencies, and other organizations. For more information about people who sell directly to consumers, see the profile on

Sales representatives may travel extensively to meet with clients.

retail sales workers. For more information about people who specialize in sales of technical products and services, see the profile on sales engineers.

Some wholesale and manufacturing sales representatives specialize in technical and scientific products, ranging from agricultural and mechanical equipment to computer and pharmaceutical goods. Other representatives deal with nonscientific products such as food, office supplies, and clothing.

Wholesale and manufacturing sales representatives who lack expertise about a given product frequently team with a technical expert. In this arrangement, the technical expert–sometimes a sales engineer–attends the sales presentation to explain the product and answer questions or concerns. The sales representative makes the initial contact with customers, introduces the company's product, and obtains final agreement from the potential buyer.

By working with a technical expert, the representative is able to spend more time maintaining and soliciting accounts and less time needing to gain technical knowledge.

After the sale, representatives may make follow-up visits to ensure that equipment is functioning properly and may even help train customers' employees to operate and maintain new equipment.

Median Annual Wages, May 2012

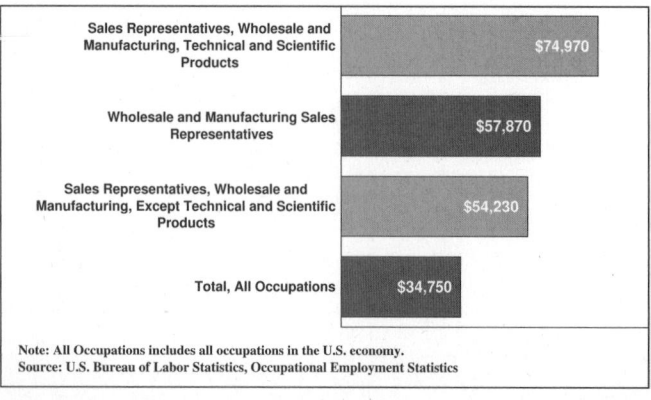

Sales Representatives, Wholesale and Manufacturing, Technical and Scientific Products	$74,970
Wholesale and Manufacturing Sales Representatives	$57,870
Sales Representatives, Wholesale and Manufacturing, Except Technical and Scientific Products	$54,230
Total, All Occupations	$34,750

Note: All Occupations includes all occupations in the U.S. economy.
Source: U.S. Bureau of Labor Statistics, Occupational Employment Statistics

Percent Change in Employment, Projected 2012–2022

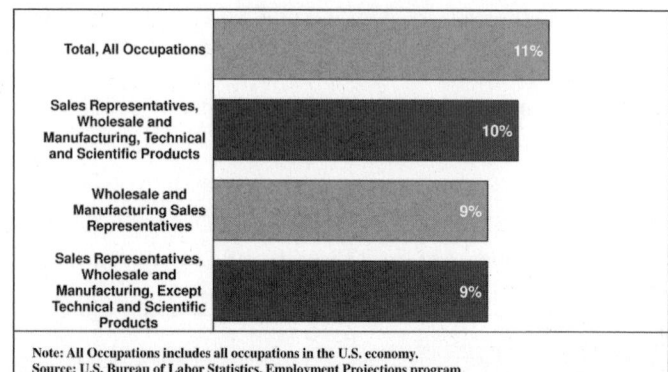

Total, All Occupations	11%
Sales Representatives, Wholesale and Manufacturing, Technical and Scientific Products	10%
Wholesale and Manufacturing Sales Representatives	9%
Sales Representatives, Wholesale and Manufacturing, Except Technical and Scientific Products	9%

Note: All Occupations includes all occupations in the U.S. economy.
Source: U.S. Bureau of Labor Statistics, Employment Projections program

Employment Projections Data for Wholesale and Manufacturing Sales Representatives

Occupational title	SOC Code	Employment, 2012	Projected Employment, 2022	Change, 2012–2022	
				Percent	Numeric
Sales representatives, wholesale and manufacturing...............	41-4000	1,863,000	2,032,300	9	169,300
Sales representatives, wholesale and manufacturing, technical and scientific products....................................	41-4011	382,300	419,500	10	37,200
Sales representatives, wholesale and manufacturing, except technical and scientific products	41-4012	1,480,700	1,612,800	9	132,000

Source: U.S. Bureau of Labor Statistics, Employment Projections Program

Note: Data are rounded. Go to Occupational Information Included in the OOH *for a discussion of the data in this table.*

Those selling consumer goods often suggest how and where merchandise should be displayed. When working with retailers, they may help arrange promotional programs, store displays, and advertising.

In addition to selling products, wholesale and manufacturing sales representatives analyze sales statistics, prepare reports, and handle administrative duties such as filing expense accounts, scheduling appointments, and making travel plans.

Staying up-to-date on new products and the changing needs of their customers is important. Sales representatives accomplish this in a variety of ways, including attending trade shows at which new products and technologies are showcased. They attend conferences and conventions to meet other sales representatives and clients and to discuss new product developments. They also read about new and existing products and monitor the sales, prices, and products of their competitors.

The following are examples of types of wholesale and manufacturing sales representatives:

Inside sales representatives work mostly in offices while making sales. Frequently, they are responsible for getting new clients by "cold calling" various organizations–calling potential customers to establish an initial contact. They also take incoming calls from customers who are interested in their product, and process paperwork to complete the sale.

Outside sales representatives spend much of their time traveling to and visiting with current clients and prospective buyers. During a sales call, they discuss the client's needs and suggest how their merchandise or services can meet those needs. They may show samples or catalogs that describe items their company provides, and they may inform customers about prices, availability, and ways in which their products can save money and boost productivity. Because many sales representatives sell several complementary products made by different manufacturers, they may take a broad approach to their customers' businesses. For example, sales representatives may help install new equipment and train employees in its use.

Work Environment

Wholesale and manufacturing sales representatives held about 1.9 million jobs in 2012.

The industries that employed the most wholesale and manufacturing sales representatives in 2012 were as follows:

Wholesale electronic markets and agents and brokers	17%
Manufacturing..	14
Machinery, equipment, and supplies merchant wholesalers......	7
Professional and commercial equipment and supplies merchant wholesalers...	6
Grocery and related product wholesalers.................................	5

Some wholesale and manufacturing sales representatives have large territories and travel considerably. Because a sales region may cover several states, representatives may be away from home for several days or weeks at a time. Others cover a smaller region, spending few nights away from home.

Inside wholesale and manufacturing sales representatives spend a lot of their time on the phone, selling goods, taking orders, and resolving problems or complaints about the merchandise. They also use Web technology, including chat, email, and video conferencing, to contact clients.

Workers in this occupation can be under considerable stress because their income and job security often depend directly on the amount of merchandise they sell, and their companies usually set goals or quotas that they are expected to meet.

Work Schedules. Most wholesale and manufacturing sales representatives work full time. Since sales calls take place during regular working hours, many do much of the planning and paperwork involved with sales in the evening and on weekends. Although the hours are often irregular, many sales representatives may determine their own schedules.

How to Become One

Educational requirements vary, depending on the type of product sold. If the products are not scientific or technical, a high school diploma is generally enough for entry into the occupation. If the products are scientific or technical, sales representatives typically need at least a bachelor's degree.

Education. A high school diploma is sufficient for many positions, primarily for selling nontechnical or scientific products. However, those selling scientific and technical products typically must have a bachelor's degree. Scientific and technical products include pharmaceuticals, medical instruments, and industrial equipment. A degree in a field related to the product sold, such as chemistry, biology, or engineering, is often required.

Many sales representatives attend seminars in sales techniques or take courses in marketing, economics, communication, or even a foreign language to improve their ability to make sales.

Training. Many companies have formal training programs for beginning wholesale and manufacturing sales representatives that last up to 1 year. In some programs, trainees rotate among jobs in plants and offices to learn all phases of producing, installing, and distributing the product. In others, trainees receive formal technical instruction at the plant, followed by on-the-job training under the supervision of a field sales manager.

Regardless of where they work, new employees may be trained by going along with experienced workers on their sales calls. As they gain familiarity with the firm's products and clients, the new workers gain more responsibility until they eventually get their own territory.

Similar Occupations   This table shows a list of occupations with job duties that are similar to those of wholesale and manufacturing sales representatives.

Occupations	Entry-level Education	2012 Pay	Projected Job Growth	Average Annual Openings
Advertising Sales Agents	High school diploma or equivalent	$46,290	-1%	4,750
Insurance Sales Agents	High school diploma or equivalent	$48,150	10%	15,020
Purchasing Managers, Buyers, and Purchasing Agents	See "How to Become One"	$63,128	4%	12,230
Real Estate Brokers and Sales Agents	High school diploma or equivalent	$42,723	11%	8,630
Retail Sales Workers	Less than high school	$21,514	10%	202,730
Sales Engineers	Bachelor's degree	$91,830	9%	1,740
Securities, Commodities, and Financial Services Sales Agents	Bachelor's degree	$71,720	11%	12,260

Licenses, Certifications, and Registrations. Many in this occupation have either the Certified Professional Manufacturers' Representative (CPMR) certification or the Certified Sales Professional (CSP) certification, both offered by the Manufacturers' Representatives Educational Research Foundation (MRERF). Certification typically involves completing formal technical training and passing an exam.

Other Experience. Although not required, sales experience can be helpful, particularly for nontechnical positions.

Advancement. Frequently, promotion takes the form of an assignment to a larger account or territory, where commissions are likely to be greater. Those who have good sales records and leadership ability may advance to higher level positions, such as sales supervisor, district manager, or vice president of sales. For more information on these positions, see the profile on sales managers.

Important Qualities

Customer-service skills. Sales representatives must be able to listen to the customer's needs and concerns before and after the sale.

Interpersonal skills. Sales representatives must be able to work well with many types of people. They must be able to build good relationships with clients and with other members of the sales team.

Self-confidence. Sales representatives must be confident and persuasive when making sales presentations. In addition, making a call to a potential customer who is not expecting to be contacted, or "cold calling," requires confidence and composure.

Stamina. Sales representatives are often on their feet for long periods of time and may carry heavy sample products.

Pay

The median annual wage for wholesale and manufacturing sales representatives, technical and scientific products was $74,970 in May 2012. The median wage is the wage at which half of the workers in an occupation earned more than that amount and half earned less. The lowest 10 percent earned less than $37,270, and the top 10 percent earned more than $147,320.

The median annual wage for wholesale and manufacturing sales representatives, except technical and scientific products was $54,230 in May 2012. The lowest 10 percent earned less than $27,340, and the top 10 percent earned more than $112,650.

Compensation methods for representatives vary significantly by the type of firm and the product sold. Most employers use a combination of salary and commissions or salary plus bonuses. Commissions are usually based on the value of sales. Bonuses may depend on individual performance, on the performance of all sales workers in the group or district, or on the company's performance.

Job Outlook

Employment of wholesale and manufacturing sales representatives is projected to grow 9 percent from 2012 to 2022, about as fast as the average for all occupations.

Employment growth for wholesale and manufacturing sales representatives will largely follow growth of the overall economy.

In addition to the total volume of sales, a wider range of products and technologies will lead to increased demand for sales representatives.

Because the work of sales representatives requires a lot of face-to-face interaction with potential buyers, this type of work is not likely to be sent to other countries.

Employment growth is expected to be strongest for sales representatives working at independent sales agencies. Companies are increasingly giving their sales activities to independent companies as a way to cut costs and boost revenue. These independent companies do not buy and hold the products they are selling. Instead, they operate on a fee or commission basis in representing the product manufacturer. Employment of sales representatives in this industry–wholesale electronic markets and agents and brokers–is projected to grow 30 percent from 2012 to 2022.

Job Prospects. Job opportunities should be best for those with previous sales experience. Though the large size of the occupation creates many job openings, the relatively high pay will also likely attract a large number of applicants.

O*NET

➤ Sales Representatives, Wholesale and Manufacturing, Technical and Scientific Products (41-4011.00)
➤ Solar Sales Representatives and Assessors (41-4011.07)
➤ Sales Representatives, Wholesale and Manufacturing, Except Technical and Scientific Products (41-4012.00)

Contacts for More Information

For more information about wholesale sales representatives, visit
➤ Manufacturers' Agents National Association (MANA) (www.manaonline.org)
For more information about certification, visit
➤ Manufacturers' Representatives Educational Research Foundation (MRERF) (www.mrerf.org)

Transportation and Material Moving

Air Traffic Controllers

- **2012 Median Pay** .... $122,530 per year
  $58.91 per hour
- **Entry-Level Education** ....Associate's degree
- **Work Experience in a Related Occupation**............... None
- **On-the-Job Training** .... Long-term on-the-job training
- **Number of Jobs 2012** 25,000
- **Job Outlook, 2012–22** ....1% (Little or no change)
- **Employment Change, 2012–22** 400

What Air Traffic Controllers Do

Air traffic controllers coordinate the movement of air traffic, to ensure that aircraft stay safe distances apart.

Duties. Air traffic controllers typically do the following:

- Issue landing and takeoff instructions to pilots
- Monitor and direct the movement of aircraft on the ground and in the air, using radar, computers, or visual references
- Control all ground traffic at airports, including baggage vehicles and airport workers
- Manage communications by transferring control of departing flights to traffic control centers and accepting control of arriving flights
- Provide information to pilots, such as weather updates, runway closures, and other critical information
- Alert airport response staff, in the event of an aircraft emergency

Air traffic controllers' primary concern is safety, but they also must direct aircraft efficiently to minimize delays. They manage the flow of aircraft into and out of the airport airspace, guide pilots during takeoff and landing, and monitor aircraft, as they travel through the skies.

Controllers usually manage multiple aircraft at the same time and must make quick decisions to ensure the safety of the aircraft. For example, a controller might direct one aircraft on its landing approach, while providing another aircraft with weather information.

The following are examples of types of air traffic controllers:

Tower controllers direct the movement of vehicles on runways and taxiways. They check flight plans, give pilots clearance for takeoff or landing, and direct the movement of aircraft and other traffic on the runways and other parts of the airport. Most work from control towers, as they generally must be able to see the traffic they control.

Approach and departure controllers ensure that aircraft traveling within an airport's airspace maintain minimum separation for safety. They give clearances to enter controlled airspace and hand off control of aircraft to en route controllers. They use radar equipment to monitor flight paths and work in buildings known as Terminal Radar Approach Control Centers (TRACONs). They also provide information to pilots, such as weather conditions and other critical notices.

En route controllers monitor aircraft once they leave an airport's airspace. They work at air route traffic control centers located throughout the country, which typically are not located at airports.

Each center is assigned an airspace based on the geography and altitude of the area in which it is located. As an airplane approaches and flies through a center's airspace, en route controllers guide the airplane along its route. They may adjust the flight path of aircraft for safety and collision avoidance.

As an airplane goes along its route, en route controllers hand the plane off to the next center, approach control, or tower along the path, as needed. En route controllers pay special attention to aircraft as they descend and get closer to the busier airspace around an airport. En route controllers turn the aircraft over to the airport's approach controllers when the aircraft is about 50 miles from the airport.

Some air traffic controllers work at the Air Traffic Control Systems Command Center. These controllers monitor traffic patterns within the entire national airspace that could create bottlenecks in the system. When they find a bottleneck, they provide instructions to other controllers that help to prevent traffic jams. Their objective is to keep traffic levels manageable for the airport and for en route controllers.

Work Environment

Air traffic controllers held about 25,000 jobs in 2012. The majority of controllers worked for the Federal Aviation Administration (FAA).

Air traffic controllers work in control towers, approach control facilities, or en-route centers. Many tower and approach/departure controllers work near large airports. En route controllers work in secure office buildings located across the country, which typically are not located at airports.

Approach/departure controllers often work in semi dark rooms. The aircraft they control appear as points of light moving across their radar screens, and a well-lit room would make it difficult to see the screen properly.

Controllers must work rapidly and efficiently, while maintaining total concentration. The mental stress of being responsible for the

Competition for air traffic controller jobs is expected to remain high.

safety of aircraft and their passengers can be taxing. As a result, controllers tend to retire earlier than most workers: those with 20 years of experience are eligible to retire at age 50. Controllers are required to retire at age 56.

Work Schedules. Most air traffic controllers work full time, and some work additional hours. Controllers may rotate shifts between day, evening, and night, because major control centers operate continuously. Controllers also work weekend and holiday shifts. Less busy airports may have towers that only operate part time. Controllers at these airports have more normal work schedules.

How to Become One

To become an air traffic controller, a person must be a U.S. citizen, pass medical and background checks, achieve a qualifying score on the Federal Aviation Administration (FAA) pre-employment test, and complete a training course at the FAA Academy.

Controllers also must pass a physical exam each year and a job performance exam twice per year. In addition, they must pass periodic drug screenings.

Most applicants must take and pass the Air Traffic Standardized Aptitude Test (AT-SAT). It is an 8-hour, computer-based exam. Some of the characteristics tested include arithmetic, prioritization, planning, tolerance for high intensity, decisiveness, visualization, problem solving, and movement detection.

Education. The FAA sets guidelines for schools to offer specific programs called the Air Traffic Collegiate Training Initiative, or the AT-CTI program. AT-CTI schools offer 2- or 4-year degrees that are designed to prepare students for a career in air traffic control. The curriculum is not standardized, but courses focus on subjects that are fundamental to aviation. Topics include aviation weather, airspace, clearances, reading maps, federal regulations, and other related topics.

Candidates who have a recommendation letter from their AT-CTI school are eligible to take the AT-SAT. Students typically take the exam before graduation but must have met their school's specific requirements to get their recommendation. Once they pass the exam they are able to apply for air traffic controller vacancies through special vacancy announcements specifically for AT-CTI graduates. Applicants who pass the test and accept a job offer are then eligible to enroll in an intensive training course at the FAA Academy.

Air traffic controllers may also apply for positions through vacancy announcements made to the general public, when available. These vacancy announcements allow the public, with no special experience or education, to apply to become air traffic controllers. These applicants generally must have completed a 4-year degree, have equivalent progressive work experience, or have some combination of the two. Applicants from the general public should try to educate themselves along the lines of the AT-CTI and AT-SAT standards, to improve their chances of passing the exam.

Although general public vacancy announcements have contributed substantially to the numbers of new hires in the past, this path is expected to decline rapidly as a source of new candidates, according to the FAA.

Work Experience in a Related Occupation. Applicants who have only a high school education will need to have years of progressive work experience or a combination of experience and education. Work experience includes work as a commercial pilot, navigator, or flight dispatcher. Other work experience that requires knowledge of aviation topics, such as weather and flight regulations, may be accepted.

Candidates with previous air traffic control experience are automatically eligible to apply for air traffic controller positions. They do not need to take the FAA pre-employment test. There can be specific job postings for those who already have experience working as an air traffic controller, such as through the military.

Training. All newly hired air traffic controllers are trained at the FAA Academy. The FAA academy is located in Oklahoma City, Oklahoma. The training usually lasts between 2 and 5 months, depending on the position and the applicant's background.

After graduating from the Academy, trainees are assigned to an air traffic control facility as *developmental controllers*, until they complete all requirements for becoming a certified air traffic controller. Developmental controllers begin their careers by supplying pilots with basic flight data and airport information. They then advance to positions within the control room that have more responsibility.

As the developmental controllers master various duties, they earn increases in pay and advance in their training. Generally, it takes new controllers 2 to 4 years to complete the on-the-job training that leads to full certification. Those with previous controller experience may take less time to become fully certified.

Trainees who fail to complete the Academy or their on-the-job training within a specified time limit are usually dismissed.

There are few opportunities for a controller to switch from an en route position to an airport position. However, within these categories, controllers can transfer to jobs at different locations or advance to supervisory positions.

Licenses, Certifications, and Registrations. All air traffic controllers must hold an Air Traffic Control Tower Operator Certificate or be appropriately qualified and supervised as stated in Title 14 of the Code of Federal Regulations part 65. They must be at least 18 years old, fluent in English, and comply with all knowledge and skill requirements.

Median Annual Wages, May 2012

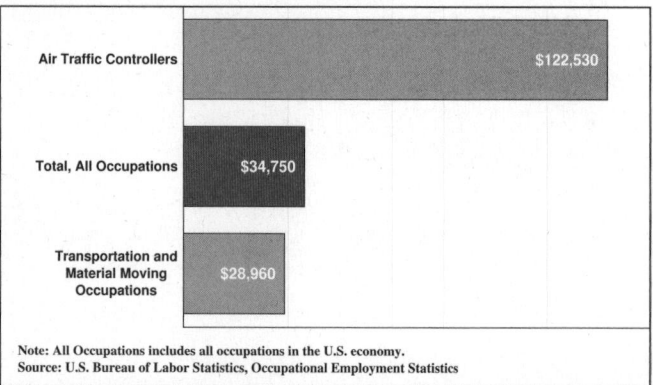

Note: All Occupations includes all occupations in the U.S. economy.
Source: U.S. Bureau of Labor Statistics, Occupational Employment Statistics

Percent Change in Employment, Projected 2012–2022

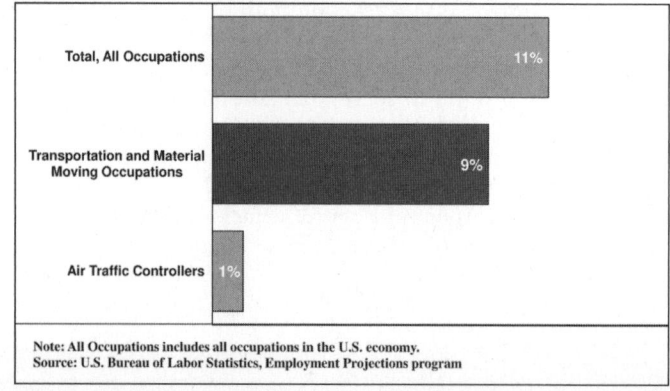

Note: All Occupations includes all occupations in the U.S. economy.
Source: U.S. Bureau of Labor Statistics, Employment Projections program

Employment Projections Data for Air Traffic Controllers

Occupational title	SOC Code	Employment, 2012	Projected Employment, 2022	Change, 2012–2022	
				Percent	Numeric
Air traffic controllers...	53-2021	25,000	25,400	1	400

Source: U.S. Bureau of Labor Statistics, Employment Projections Program

Note: Data are rounded. Go to **Occupational Information Included in the OOH** *for a discussion of the data in this table.*

Similar Occupations   This table shows a list of occupations with job duties that are similar to those of air traffic controllers.

Occupations	Entry-level Education	2012 Pay	Projected Job Growth	Average Annual Openings
Aircraft and Avionics Equipment Mechanics and Technicians	See "How to Become One"	$55,227	3%	3,960
Airline and Commercial Pilots	See "How to Become One"	$100,060	-1%	3,360
Cartographers and Photogrammetrists	Bachelor's degree	$57,440	20%	490
Police, Fire, and Ambulance Dispatchers	High school diploma or equivalent	$36,300	8%	3,600

Important Qualities

Communication skills. Air traffic controllers must be able to give clear, concise instructions, listen carefully to pilot's requests, and respond by speaking clearly.

Concentration skills. Controllers must be able to concentrate in a room where multiple conversations occur at once. For example, in a large airport tower, several controllers may be speaking with several pilots at the same time.

Decision-making skills. Controllers must make quick decisions. For example, when a pilot requests a change of altitude or heading to avoid poor weather, the controller must respond quickly, so that the plane can operate safely.

Math skills. Controllers must be able to do arithmetic accurately and quickly. They often need to compute speed, time, and distance problems, and recommend heading and altitude changes.

Organizational skills. Controllers must be able to coordinate the actions of multiple flights. Controllers need to be able to prioritize tasks, as they may be required to guide several pilots at the same time.

Problem-solving skills. Controllers must be able to understand complex situations, such as the impact of changing weather patterns on a plane's flight path. Controllers must be able to review important information and provide pilots with an appropriate solution.

To be employed by the FAA, air traffic controllers who do not have prior experience must begin their careers before they reach their 31st birthday. Private air traffic controllers must hold an appropriate medical certificate. Air traffic controllers may have to undergo background checks and drug screenings.

Pay

The median annual wage for air traffic controllers was $122,530 in May 2012. The median wage is the wage at which half the workers in an occupation earned more than that amount and half earned less. The lowest 10 percent earned less than $64,930, and the top 10 percent earned more than $171,340.

According to the Federal Aviation Administration (FAA), the starting salary for new controllers undergoing training was $17,803 in 2012. Controllers' salaries increase as they complete each new training phase. According to the FAA, controllers who have completed on-the-job training and had been placed at a facility had a starting annual salary of $37,070 in 2012. A full explanation of current starting wages can be found on the Federal Aviation Administration (FAA) jobs & careers page.

Union Membership. Most air traffic controllers belonged to a union in 2012.

Job Outlook

Employment of air traffic controllers is projected to show little or no change from 2012 to 2022. Most employment opportunities will result from the need to replace workers who retire.

The Federal Aviation Administration (FAA) has not, and does not expect to reduce the overall number of controllers, although total air traffic has fallen since 2000. Even though air traffic is expected to increase, employment growth will not keep pace, because the FAA already has enough personnel capacity. In addition, federal budget constraints should limit the hiring of new controllers. In the long term, the NextGen satellite-based system is expected to allow individual controllers to handle more air traffic.

Job Prospects. Job opportunities will be best for individuals with prior experience or those who are in their early 20s and have completed an AT-CTI study program. Competition for air traffic controller jobs is expected to be very strong, as many people will apply to a relatively few number of jobs. Those who are willing to live anywhere in the country will have an advantage.

O*NET

➤ Air Traffic Controllers (53-2021.00)

Contacts for More Information

For more information about air traffic controllers, visit
➤ Federal Aviation Administration (www.faa.gov/)
➤ National Air Traffic Controllers Association (www.natca.org/)

For additional career information about air traffic controllers, see the *Occupational Outlook Quarterly* article "Sky-high careers: jobs related to airlines." (www.bls.gov/opub/ooq/2007/summer /art01.pdf).

Airline and Commercial Pilots

- **2012 Median Pay** .... $98,410 per year

- **Entry-Level Education** ....See "How to Become One"
- **Work Experience in a Related Occupation**.... See "How to Become One"
- **On-the-Job Training**.... Moderate-term on-the-job training
- **Number of Jobs 2012** 104,100
- **Job Outlook, 2012–22** ....-1% (Little or no change)
- **Employment Change, 2012–22** .... -800

What Airline and Commercial Pilots Do

Airline and commercial pilots fly and navigate airplanes, helicopters, and other aircraft. Airline pilots fly for airlines that transport people and cargo on a fixed schedule. Commercial pilots fly aircraft for other reasons, such as charter flights, rescue operations, firefighting, aerial photography, and aerial application of agricultural materials.

Duties. Pilots typically do the following:

- Check the overall condition of the aircraft before and after every flight
- Ensure that the aircraft is balanced and below its weight limit
- Ensure fuel supply is adequate, weather conditions are acceptable, and submit flight plans to air traffic control
- Communicate with air traffic control over the aircraft's radio system
- Operate and control aircraft along planned routes, and during takeoffs, and landings
- Monitor engines, fuel consumption, and other aircraft systems during flight and respond to any changes in weather or other events, such as engine failure
- Navigate the aircraft by using cockpit instruments and visual references

Many aircraft used for hire use two pilots. The most experienced pilot, the captain or pilot in command, supervises all other crew members and has primary responsibility for the flight. The copilot, often called the first officer or second in command, shares flight duties with the captain. Some older planes require a third pilot known as a flight engineer, who monitors instruments and operates controls. New technology has automated many of these tasks, and new aircraft do not require flight engineers.

Pilots must have good teamwork skills because they must work closely with other pilots on the flight deck, as well as with air traffic controllers and flight dispatchers. They need to be able to coordinate actions and provide clear and honest feedback.

Pilots plan their flights carefully by making sure the aircraft is operable and safe, that the cargo has been loaded correctly, and that the weather conditions are acceptable. They file flight plans with air traffic control that they may modify in flight because of weather conditions or other factors.

Takeoffs and landings can be the most difficult parts of the flight and require close coordination between the pilot, copilot, and flight engineer, if present. Once in the air, the captain and first officer usually alternate flying activities so each can rest. After landing, pilots must fill out records that document their flight and the status of the aircraft.

Many pilots will have some contact with passengers and customers. Charter and corporate pilots will often need to greet their passengers before embarking. Some airline pilots may have to help handle customer complaints.

Commercial pilots employed by charter companies usually have many more nonflight duties than airline pilots have. Commercial pilots may have to schedule flights, arrange for maintenance of the plane, and load luggage themselves.

With proper training, airline pilots may also be deputized as federal law enforcement officers and be issued firearms to protect the cockpit.

Pilots who routinely fly at low levels must constantly look for trees, bridges, power lines, transmission towers, and other dangerous obstacles. This is a common danger to agricultural pilots and air ambulance helicopter pilots, who frequently land on or near highways and accident sites that do not have improved landing sites.

The following are examples of types of pilots:

Airline pilots are commercial pilots who primarily work for airlines that transport passengers and cargo on a fixed schedule.

Commercial pilots are involved in unscheduled flight activities, such as aerial application, charter flights, aerial photography, and aerial tours.

Flight instructors are commercial pilots who use simulators and dual-controlled aircraft to teach students how to fly.

Work Environment

Pilots held about 104,100 jobs in 2012. About 64 percent worked as airline pilots, copilots, and flight engineers. The remainder worked as commercial pilots.

In 2012, most airline pilots, copilots, and flight engineers–about 87 percent–worked for scheduled air transportation providers, mainly the airlines.

The industries that employed the most commercial pilots in 2012 were as follows:

Nonscheduled air transportation 35%
Technical and trade schools; private 12
Scenic and sightseeing transportation and support activities.... 9
Ambulance services.. 7

About 4 percent of commercial pilots were self-employed in 2012.

Pilots must learn to cope with several work-related hazards. For example, airline pilots assigned to long-distance routes may experience fatigue and jetlag. Weather and the condition of the aircraft

Before every flight, pilots inspect the aircraft.

Median Annual Wages, May 2012

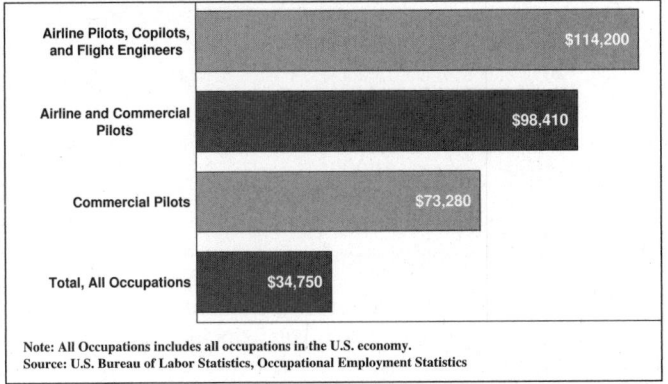

Airline Pilots, Copilots, and Flight Engineers: $114,200
Airline and Commercial Pilots: $98,410
Commercial Pilots: $73,280
Total, All Occupations: $34,750

Note: All Occupations includes all occupations in the U.S. economy.
Source: U.S. Bureau of Labor Statistics, Occupational Employment Statistics

Percent Change in Employment, Projected 2012–2022

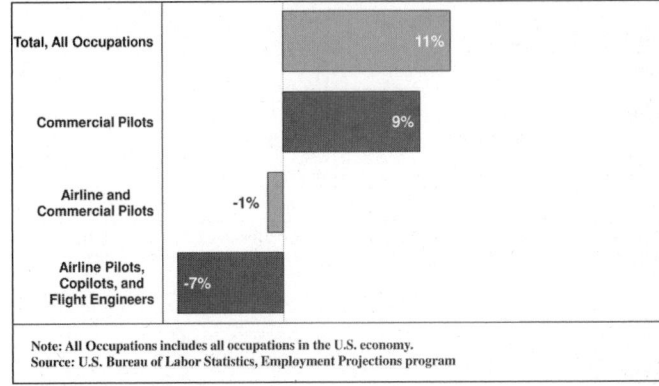

Total, All Occupations: 11%
Commercial Pilots: 9%
Airline and Commercial Pilots: -1%
Airline Pilots, Copilots, and Flight Engineers: -7%

Note: All Occupations includes all occupations in the U.S. economy.
Source: U.S. Bureau of Labor Statistics, Employment Projections program

can also pose unique hazards. In addition, flights can be long and flight decks are often sealed, so pilots must be able to work in small teams for long periods in close proximity to one another.

Commercial pilots face other types of job hazards. Aerial applicators, also known as crop dusters, may be exposed to toxic chemicals, typically use unimproved landing strips, and are at a higher risk of collision with power lines and birds than many other pilots. Helicopter pilots involved in rescue operations regularly fly at low levels during bad weather or at night. These pilots also often land in areas surrounded by power lines and other obstacles, such as highways. Pilots also face the risk of hearing loss resulting from prolonged exposure to engine noise.

Although flying may not involve unusually high levels of physical effort, the high-level of concentration required to fly an aircraft and the mental stress of being responsible for the safety of passengers can be fatiguing. Pilots must be alert and quick to react if something goes wrong, particularly during takeoff and landing. As a result, federal law requires pilots to retire at age 65.

Pilots work all over the country, but most are based near large airports.

Work Schedules. For most pilots, federal regulations set maximum work hours and minimum requirements for rest between flights. Airline pilots fly an average of 75 hours per month and work an additional 150 hours per month performing other duties. Pilots have variable work schedules that may include some days of intense work followed by some days off. Flight assignments are based on seniority. In general, that means that pilots who have worked at a company for a long time get preferred routes and schedules.

Airline pilots spend a considerable amount of time away from home because flight assignments often involve overnight layovers—sometimes up to 3 nights a week. When pilots are away from home, the airlines typically provide hotel accommodations, transportation to the airport, and an allowance for meals and other expenses.

Commercial pilots also have irregular schedules. They typically fly between 30 hours and 90 hours each month. Commercial pilots may have less free time than airline pilots because they frequently have more nonflight responsibilities than airline pilots. Although most commercial pilots remain near their home overnight, they may still work nonstandard hours.

How to Become One

Most airline pilots begin their careers as commercial pilots. Commercial pilots typically need a high school diploma or equivalent. Airline pilots typically need a bachelor's degree. All pilots who are paid to fly must have at least a commercial pilot's license from the Federal Aviation Administration (FAA). Additionally, airline pilots must have the Airline Transport Pilot (ATP) certificate. Rat-

ings such as the ATP, instrument, or multi-engine ratings, expand the privileges granted by the commercial pilot's license and may be required by certain employers.

Most pilots begin their flight training with independent instructors or through flight schools. Fixed base operators (FBO) usually provide a wide range of general aviation services, such as aircraft fueling, maintenance, and on-demand air transportation services, and they may also offer flight training. An FBO may call itself a school or call their training department a school. Some flight schools are parts of 2 and 4-year colleges and universities.

Education and Training. Airline pilots typically need a bachelor's degree in any subject, along with a commercial pilot's license and an Airline Transport Pilot (ATP) certificate from the FAA. Airline pilots typically start their careers in flying as commercial pilots. Pilots usually accrue thousands of hours of flight experience to get a job with regional or major airlines.

The military has traditionally been an important source of experienced pilots because of the extensive training provided. However, increased duty requirements have reduced the incentives for these pilots to transfer out of military aviation and into civilian aviation. Most military pilots who transfer to civilian aviation are able to transfer directly into the airlines rather than working in commercial aviation.

Commercial pilots must have a commercial pilot's license and typically need a high school diploma or the equivalent. Some employers will have additional requirements. For example, agricultural pilots will need to have an understanding of common agricultural practices, fertilizers, fungicides, herbicides, and pesticides. Flight instructors will have to have special FAA-issued ratings, such as the Certified Flight Instructor (CFI), CFI-Instrument (CFII), Multi-Engine Instructor (MEI), MEI-Instrument (MEII), and possibly others. Many other requirements exist for other specialties. They range from glider and banner towing to helicopter and airship qualifications.

Commercial pilots typically begin their flight training with independent FAA-certified flight instructors or at schools that offer flight training. The FAA certifies hundreds of civilian flight schools, which range from small FBOs to large state universities. Some colleges and universities offer pilot training as part of a 2- or 4-year aviation degree. Regardless of whether pilots attend flight schools or learn from independent instructors, all pilots need the FAA's commercial pilot license before they can be paid to fly. Additionally, most commercial pilots need an instrument rating. Instrument ratings are typically needed to fly through clouds or other conditions that limit visibility. An instrument rating is required to carry paying passengers over 50 miles from the point of origin or at night.

Employment Projections Data for Airline and Commercial Pilots

Occupational title	SOC Code	Employment, 2012	Projected Employment, 2022	Change, 2012–2022	
				Percent	Numeric
Airline and commercial pilots...............................	—	104,100	103,300	-1	-800
Airline pilots, copilots, and flight engineers......................	53-2011	66,400	62,100	-7	-4,400
Commercial pilots	53-2012	37,600	41,200	9	3,600

Source: U.S. Bureau of Labor Statistics, Employment Projections Program

Note: **Data are rounded. Go to** Occupational Information Included in the OOH *for a discussion of the data in this table.*

Interviews for positions with major and regional airlines often reflect the FAA exams for pilot licenses, certificates, and instrument ratings, and can be intense. Airlines will often conduct their own psychological and aptitude tests in order to make sure that their pilots are of good moral character and can make good decisions under pressure.

Airline and commercial pilots who are newly hired by airlines or on-demand air services companies must undergo moderate-term on-the-job training in accordance with the Federal Aviation Regulations (FARs). This training usually includes 6-8 weeks of ground school and 25 hours of flight time. Additionally, commercial pilots may need specific training based on the type of flying they are doing. For example, those who work in aerial application need training in agricultural practices and fertilizers, pesticides, and other substances that can be applied to crops by air to increase yield or production efficiency. Additionally, various type ratings for specific aircraft, such as the Boeing 737 or Cessna Citation, are typically acquired through employer-based training and are generally earned by pilots who have at least the commercial license.

In addition to initial training and licensing requirements, all pilots must maintain recency of experience in performing certain maneuvers. This means that pilots must perform specific maneuvers and procedures a given number of times within a specified amount of time. In addition, pilots must undergo periodic training and medical examinations, generally every year or every other year.

Work Experience in a Related Occupation. Airline pilots typically begin their careers as commercial pilots. Pilots usually accrue thousands of hours of flight experience as commercial pilots or in the military to get a job with regional or major airlines.

Licenses, Certifications, and Registrations. Those who are seeking a career as a professional pilot typically get their licenses and ratings in the following order:

- Student Pilot Certificate
- Private Pilot License
- Instrument Rating
- Commercial Pilot License
- Multi-Engine Rating
- Airline Transport Pilot Certificate

Each certificate and rating requires that pilots pass a written exam on the ground and a practical flying exam, usually called a check ride, in an appropriate aircraft. In addition to these licenses, many pilots get Certified Flight Instructor (CFI) ratings after they get their commercial certificate, which helps them build flight time and experience more quickly and at less personal expense. Current licensing regulations can be found in FARs.

Commercial pilot's license. To qualify for a commercial pilot license, applicants must be at least 18 years old and meet certain hour requirements. When pilots first begin their training, student pilots need to get a logbook and keep detailed records of their flight time. They may also need to log their ground instruction time as well, depending on their school. This logbook must be endorsed by the flight instructor for the student to be able to take the FAA knowledge and practical exams. For specific requirements, including details on types and quantities of flight experience and knowledge requirements, see the FARs. Title 14 of the code of federal regulations (14 CFR), Federal Aviation Regulations part 61, covers the basic rules for the certification of pilots. Flight schools can train pilots in accordance with part 61 rules or the rules found in 14 CFR part 141 (www.ecfr.gov/cgi-bin/text-idx?c=ecfr&tpl=/ecfrbrowse/Title14/14cfr141_main_02.tpl).

In addition, applicants must pass the appropriate medical exam, meet all of the detailed flight experience and knowledge requirements, and pass a written exam and a practical flight exam in order to become commercially licensed. The physical exam confirms that the pilot's vision is correctable to 20/20 and that no physical handicaps exist that could impair their performance.

Commercial pilots must hold an instrument rating if they want to carry passengers for pay over 50 miles from the point of origin or at night.

Instrument rating. Earning their instrument rating enables pilots to fly during periods of low visibility, also known as instrument meteorological conditions or IMC. They may qualify for this rating by having at least 40 hours of instrument flight experience, 50 hours of cross-country flight time as pilot in command, and by meeting other requirements detailed in the FARs.

Airline transport pilot (ATP) certification. Beginning in 2013, all pilot crew of a scheduled commercial airliner must have ATP certificates. To earn the ATP certificate, applicants must be at least 23 years old, have a minimum of 1,500 hours of flight time, and pass written and practical flight exams. Furthermore, airline pilots usually maintain one or more aircraft-type ratings, which allow pilots to fly aircraft that require specific training, depending on the requirements of their particular airline. Some exceptions and alternate requirements are detailed in the FARs.

Pilots must pass periodic physical and practical flight examinations to be able to perform the duties granted by their certificate.

Other Experience. Minimum time requirements to get a certificate or rating may not be enough to get some jobs. To make up the gap between paying for training and flying for the major airlines, many commercial pilots begin their careers as flight instructors and on-demand charter pilots. These positions typically require less experience than airline jobs require. When pilots have built enough flying hours, they can then apply to the airlines. Newly hired pilots at regional airlines typically have about 2,000 hours of flight experience. Newly hired pilots at major airlines typically have about 4,000 hours of flight experience.

Important Qualities

Communication skills. Pilots must speak clearly when conveying information to air traffic controllers. They must also listen carefully for instructions.

Similar Occupations This table shows a list of occupations with job duties that are similar to those of airline and commercial pilots.

Occupations	Entry-level Education	2012 Pay	Projected Job Growth	Average Annual Openings
Air Traffic Controllers	Associate's degree	$122,530	2%	1,140
Aircraft and Avionics Equipment Mechanics and Technicians	See "How to Become One"	$55,227	3%	3,960
Bus Drivers	High school diploma or equivalent	$30,206	9%	17,800
Construction Equipment Operators	High school diploma or equivalent	$41,099	19%	16,480
Delivery Truck Drivers and Driver /Sales Workers	High school diploma or equivalent	$27,113	5%	27,250
Flight Attendants	High school diploma or equivalent	$37,240	-7%	1,400
Heavy and Tractor-trailer Truck Drivers	Postsecondary non-degree award	$38,200	11%	46,470
Material Moving Machine Operators	See "How to Become One"	$32,069	1%	16,560
Railroad Occupations	High school diploma or equivalent	$52,386	-4%	3,450
Taxi Drivers and Chauffeurs	Less than high school	$22,820	15%	6,370
Water Transportation Occupations	See "How to Become One"	$54,020	13%	4,810

Observational skills. Pilots must regularly watch over screens, gauges, and dials to make sure that all systems are in working order. They also need to maintain situational awareness by looking for other aircraft or obstacles. Pilots must be able to see clearly and judge the distance between objects, and possess good color vision.

Problem-solving skills. Pilots must be able to identify complex problems and figure out appropriate solutions. When a plane encounters turbulence, for example, pilots may assess the weather conditions and request a route or altitude change from air traffic control.

Quick reaction time. Pilots must be able to respond quickly and with good judgment to any impending danger, because warning signals can appear with no notice.

Advancement. For airline pilots, advancement depends on a system of seniority outlined in collective bargaining contracts. Typically, after 1 to 5 years, flight engineers may advance to first officer positions and, after 5 to 15 years, first officers can become captains. In large companies, a captain could become a chief pilot or director of aviation.

Pay

The median annual wage for airline pilots, copilots, and flight engineers was $114,200 in May 2012. The median wage is the wage at which half the workers in an occupation earned more than that amount and half earned less. The lowest 10 percent earned less than $66,970, and the top 10 percent earned more than $187,200.

According to the Air Line Pilots Association, International, most airline pilots begin their careers earning about $20,000 per year. Wages increase each year until the pilot accumulates the experience and seniority needed to become a captain. The average captain at a regional airline earns about $55,000 per year, while the average captain at a major airline earns about $135,000 per year.

In addition, airline pilots receive an expense allowance, or "per diem," for every hour they are away from home, and they may earn extra pay for international flights. Airline pilots also are eligible for health insurance and retirement benefits, and their immediate families usually are entitled to free or reduced-fare flights.

The median annual wage for commercial pilots was $73,280 in May 2012. The lowest 10 percent earned less than $38,520, and the top 10 percent earned more than $134,990.

In May 2012, the median annual wages for commercial pilots in the top four industries employing these pilots were as follows:

Nonscheduled air transportation $73,660
Ambulance services 69,700
Technical and trade schools; private 69,500
Scenic and sightseeing transportation
    and support activities 66,550

Union Membership. Most airline and commercial pilots belonged to a union in 2012.

Job Outlook

Employment of airline pilots, copilots, and flight engineers is projected to decline 7 percent from 2012 to 2022. It is likely that scheduled airlines will attempt to increase profitability over the next decade by increasing the average number of passengers in all aircraft. This will probably be done by eliminating routes with low demand and reducing the number of flights per day along more heavily used routes. These practices will ultimately lower the overall number of flights and lower the total number of pilot jobs.

Employment of commercial pilots is projected to grow 9 percent from 2012 to 2022, about as fast as the average for all occupations. Commercial pilots are projected to add jobs in various industries, including ambulance services and support activities for air transportation.

Job Prospects. Most job opportunities will arise from the need to replace pilots who leave the workforce. From 2012 to 2022, many pilots are expected to retire as they reach the required retirement age of 65.

Job prospects should be best with regional airlines, low-cost carriers, or with nonscheduled aviation services as entry-level requirements are lower for regional and commercial jobs. There is typically less competition among applicants in these sectors than there is for major airlines.

Pilots seeking jobs at the major airlines will face strong competition because those firms tend to attract many more applicants than the number of job openings. Applicants also will have to compete with furloughed pilots for available jobs.

Pilots with the greatest number of flight and instrument hours usually have some advantage, but the type of time also matters a great deal. For example, pilots with significant amounts of time in turbine engine-powered aircraft often have an advantage over those who do not. For this reason, military and experienced pilots will have an advantage over applicants whose flight time only consists of small piston-driven aircraft.

O*NET

➤ Airline Pilots, Copilots, and Flight Engineers (53-2011.00)
➤ Commercial Pilots (53-2012.00)

Contacts for More Information

For specific information about licensing requirements and other federal regulations regarding pilots and operators, visit

➤ Regulations concerning the certification of airmen and general flight rules (www.ecfr.gov/cgi-bin/text-idx?SID=78f6bbb41989ae81f749ed19fb0b00cc&c=ecfr&tpl=/ecfrbrowse/Title14/14cfrv2_02.tpl)
➤ Regulations concerning air carriers and operators for compensation or hire, and flight schools (www.ecfr.gov/cgi-bin/text-idx?SID=78f6bbb41989ae81f749ed19fb0b00cc&c=ecfr&tpl=/ecfrbrowse/Title14/14cfrv3_02.tpl)

For more information about pilots, visit

➤ Aircraft Owners and Pilots Association (www.aopa.org/)
➤ Air Line Pilots Association, International (www.clearedtodream.org/)
➤ Coalition of Airline Pilots Associations (www.capapilots.org/)
➤ Federal Aviation Administration (www.faa.gov/)
➤ Helicopter Association International (www.rotor.com/)
➤ National Agricultural Aviation Association (www.agaviation.org/)

For additional career information about pilots, see the *Occupational Outlook Quarterly* article "Sky-high careers: jobs related to airlines." (www.bls.gov/opub/ooq/2007/summer/art01.pdf).

Bus Drivers

- **2012 Median Pay** .... $29,550 per year
  $14.21 per hour
- **Entry-Level Education** ... High school diploma or equivalent
- **Work Experience in a Related Occupation** .... None
- **On-the-Job Training** ....See "How to Become One"
- **Number of Jobs 2012** 654,300
- **Job Outlook, 2012–22** .... 9% (As fast as average)
- **Employment Change, 2012–22** 57,900

What Bus Drivers Do

Bus drivers transport people between various places–including, work, school, shopping malls–and across state and national borders. Some drive regular routes, and others transport passengers on chartered trips or sightseeing tours. They drive a range of vehicles, from 15-passenger buses to 60-foot articulated buses (with two connected sections) that can carry more than 100 passengers.

Duties. Bus drivers typically do the following:

- Check the bus tires, lights, and oil and do other basic maintenance
- Keep the bus clean and presentable to the public
- Pick up and drop off passengers at designated locations
- Follow a planned route according to a time schedule
- Help disabled passengers get on and off the bus
- Obey traffic laws and state and federal transit regulations
- Follow procedures to make sure they and all passengers are safe
- Keep passengers informed of possible delays

Local transit bus drivers follow a daily schedule while transporting people on regular routes along city or suburban streets. They usually stop frequently, often every few blocks and when a passenger requests a stop. Some large transit agencies may require bus drivers to submit traffic data for analysis. Local transit drivers typically do the following:

- Collect bus fares, sometimes making change for passengers
- Answer questions about schedules, routes, and transfer points
- Report accidents or other traffic disruptions to a central dispatcher, and follow directions when using an alternate route

Intercity bus drivers transport passengers between cities or towns, sometimes crossing state lines. They may travel between distant cities or between towns only a few miles apart. They usually pick up and drop off passengers at bus stations. Increasingly, intercity buses are using curbside locations in downtown urban areas instead of stations. Intercity drivers typically do the following:

- Ensure all passengers have a valid ticket to ride the bus
- May sell tickets to passengers when there are unsold seats available
- Keep track of when and at what stops passengers get on or off the bus
- Follow a central dispatcher's instruction when taking an alternate route
- Help passengers load or unload baggage

Charter bus drivers, sometimes called *motor coach drivers* transport passengers on chartered trips or sightseeing tours. Their schedule and route are generally arranged by a trip planner for the convenience of the passengers, who often are on vacation. Motor coach drivers are occasionally away for long periods of time because they usually stay with vacationers for the length of the trip. Motor coach drivers typically do the following:

- Listen to and sometimes address passenger complaints
- Ensure the tour stays on schedule
- Help passengers load or unload baggage
- Account for all passengers before leaving a location
- Sometimes act as tour guides for passengers

School bus drivers transport students to and from school and other activities. On school days, drivers pick up students in the morning and return them home or to the designated bus stop in the afternoon. School bus drivers also drive students on field trips and to sporting events and other activities. Some drivers work at schools in other occupations, such as janitors, cafeteria workers, or mechanics, between morning and afternoon trips. School bus drivers typically do the following:

- Watch traffic and people carefully to ensure the safety of children getting on and off the bus
- Take care of the needs of children with disabilities
- Keep order and safety on the school bus
- Understand and enforce the school system's rules regarding student conduct
- Report disciplinary problems to the school district or parents

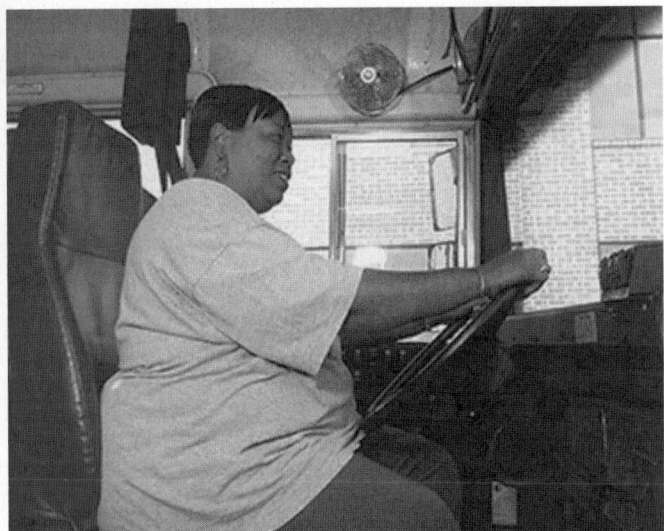

Bus drivers must be alert, especially in heavy traffic or in bad weather, to prevent accidents.

Work Environment

Bus drivers held about 654,300 jobs in 2012. Of those, about 74 percent were school bus drivers or special-client bus drivers.

Most transit bus drivers worked for local governments or urban transit systems, which are private companies that contract with a city or town to provide bus service. Most charter-bus drivers worked in the charter-bus industry and intercity bus drivers typically work in the interurban and rural bus transportation industry.

The industries that employed the most transit and intercity bus drivers in 2012 were as follows:

Local government, excluding education and hospitals............ 46%
Urban transit systems.. 15
Charter bus industry.. 11
Interurban and rural bus transportation............................ 6
Other transit and ground passenger transportation................. 6

School bus drivers or special-client bus drivers are usually employed by a school district or private transportation company that contracts with a district to provide bus service. Some school bus service is provided by a local government.

The industries that employed the most school bus drivers in 2012 were as follows:

Elementary and secondary schools; local........................... 43%
School and employee bus transportation............................ 30
Local government, excluding education and hospitals............... 11

Other transit and ground passenger transportation.................. 6

Driving through heavy traffic or bad weather and dealing with unruly passengers can be stressful for bus drivers.

Injuries and Illnesses. Bus drivers, especially transit and intercity drivers, had a higher rate of work-related injuries and illness in 2012 than the national average. Most injuries to bus drivers were due to highway accidents.

Work Schedules. About half of all bus drivers worked full time in 2012. The rest either worked part time or had variable schedules. School bus drivers work only when school is in session. Some make multiple runs if schools in their district each open and close at different times. Others make only two runs, one in the morning and one in the afternoon, so their work hours are limited.

Transit drivers may work weekends, late nights, and early mornings.

Motor coach drivers travel with their vacationing passengers. Driver hours are dictated by a tour schedule, and drivers may work all hours of the day, as well as weekends and holidays. Some intercity bus drivers have long-distance routes, so they spend some nights away. Other intercity bus drivers make a round trip and go home at the end of each shift.

How to Become One

Bus drivers must have a commercial driver's license (CDL) and complete a training program. A bus driver must also meet hearing and vision requirements. In addition, bus drivers often need a high school diploma or the equivalent.

Education. Most employers prefer drivers to have a high school diploma or equivalent.

Training. Bus drivers typically go through 1 to 3 months of training. Part of the training is spent on a driving course, where drivers practice various maneuvers with a bus. They then begin to drive in light traffic and eventually make practice runs on the type of route that they expect to drive. New drivers make regularly scheduled trips with passengers and are accompanied by an experienced driver who gives helpful tips, answers questions, and evaluates the new driver's performance.

Some drivers' training is also spent in the classroom. They learn their company's rules and regulations, state and municipal traffic laws, and safe driving practices. Drivers also learn about schedules and bus routes, fares, and how to interact with passengers.

Licenses, Certifications, and Registrations. All bus drivers must have a commercial driver's license (CDL). The qualifications for getting one vary by state but generally include passing both knowledge and driving tests. States have the right to not issue a license to someone who has had a CDL suspended by another state.

Median Annual Wages, May 2012

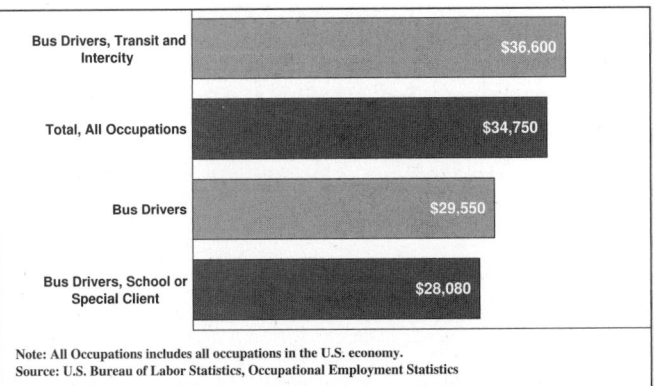

Bus Drivers, Transit and Intercity	$36,600
Total, All Occupations	$34,750
Bus Drivers	$29,550
Bus Drivers, School or Special Client	$28,080

Note: All Occupations includes all occupations in the U.S. economy.
Source: U.S. Bureau of Labor Statistics, Occupational Employment Statistics

Percent Change in Employment, Projected 2012–2022

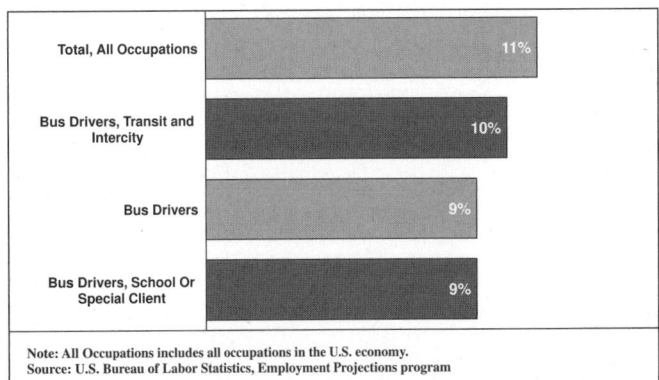

Total, All Occupations	11%
Bus Drivers, Transit and Intercity	10%
Bus Drivers	9%
Bus Drivers, School Or Special Client	9%

Note: All Occupations includes all occupations in the U.S. economy.
Source: U.S. Bureau of Labor Statistics, Employment Projections program

Employment Projections Data for Bus Drivers

Occupational title	SOC Code	Employment, 2012	Projected Employment, 2022	Change, 2012–2022	
				Percent	Numeric
Bus drivers...	—	654,300	712,200	9	57,900
Bus drivers, transit and intercity	53-3021	170,600	187,400	10	16,800
Bus drivers, school or special client	53-3022	483,600	524,800	9	41,100

Source: U.S. Bureau of Labor Statistics, Employment Projections Program

Note: Data are rounded. Go to **Occupational Information Included in the OOH** *for a discussion of the data in this table.*

Drivers can get endorsements to a CDL that reflect their ability to drive a special type of vehicle. All bus drivers must have a passenger (P) endorsement, and school bus drivers must also have a school bus (S) endorsement. Getting the P and S endorsements requires additional knowledge and driving tests administered by a certified examiner.

Many states require all bus drivers to be 18 years of age or older and those who drive across state lines to be at least 21 years old.

Federal regulations require random testing of bus drivers for drug or alcohol abuse while on duty. In addition, bus drivers can have their CDL suspended if they are convicted of a felony involving the use of a motor vehicle or of driving under the influence of alcohol or drugs. Other actions also can result in a suspension after multiple violations. A list of violations is available from the U.S. Federal Motor Carrier Safety Administration.

Advancement. Opportunities for promotion are generally limited, but experienced drivers may become supervisors or dispatchers. Some veteran bus drivers become instructors of new bus drivers. Other bus drivers get a job as a light truck or delivery driver or truck driver.

Important Qualities

Customer-service skills. Bus drivers regularly interact with passengers and must be courteous and helpful.

Hand-eye coordination. Driving a bus requires the controlled use of multiple limbs on the basis of what a person observes. Federal regulations require drivers to have normal use of their arms and legs.

Hearing ability. Bus drivers need good hearing. Federal regulations require the ability to hear a forced whisper in one ear at five feet (with or without the use of a hearing aid).

Patience. Because of possible traffic congestion and sometimes unruly passengers, bus drivers are put in stressful situations and must be able to continue to calmly operate their bus.

Physical health. Federal regulations do not allow people to become bus drivers if they have a medical condition that may interfere with their operation of a bus, such as high blood pressure or epilepsy. A full list of medical reasons that keep someone from becoming a licensed bus driver is available from the U.S Federal Motor Carrier Safety Administration.

Visual ability. Bus drivers must be able to pass vision tests. Federal regulations require at least 20/40 vision with a 70-degree field of vision in each eye and the ability to distinguish colors on a traffic light.

Pay

The median annual wage for transit and intercity bus drivers, which includes charter-bus drivers, was $36,600 in May 2012. The median wage is the wage at which half the workers in an occupation earned more than that amount and half earned less. The lowest 10 percent earned less than $21,320, and the top 10 percent earned more than $59,480.

In May 2012, the median annual wages for transit and intercity bus drivers in the top five industries in which these drivers worked were as follows:

Local government, excluding education and hospitals......	$45,390
Interurban and rural bus transportation..............................	34,640
Urban transit systems...	33,370
Other transit and ground passenger transportation.............	27,690
Charter bus industry...	27,610

The median annual wage of school or special client bus drivers was $28,080 in May 2012. The lowest 10 percent of school or special-client bus drivers earned less than $17,610, and the top 10 percent earned more than $43,560.

In May 2012, the median annual wages for school or special client bus drivers in the top four industries in which these drivers worked were as follows:

Local government, excluding education and hospitals......	$31,620
School and employee bus transportation.............................	30,000
Elementary and secondary schools; local............................	26,860
Other transit and ground passenger transportation.............	26,480

Union Membership. Compared with workers in all occupations, bus drivers had a higher percentage of workers who belonged to a union in 2012.

Job Outlook

Employment of bus drivers is projected to grow 9 percent from 2012 to 2022, about as fast as the average for all occupations.

Similar Occupations This table shows a list of occupations with job duties that are similar to those of bus drivers.

Occupations	Entry-level Education	2012 Pay	Projected Job Growth	Average Annual Openings
Delivery Truck Drivers and Driver/Sales Workers	High school diploma or equivalent	$27,113	5%	27,250
Heavy and Tractor-trailer Truck Drivers	Postsecondary non-degree award	$38,200	11%	46,470
Railroad Occupations	High school diploma or equivalent	$52,386	-4%	3,450
Taxi Drivers and Chauffeurs	Less than high school	$22,820	15%	6,370
Water Transportation Occupations	See "How to Become One"	$54,020	13%	4,810

Employment of transit and intercity drivers (including charter buses) is projected to grow 10 percent. Demand for buses is expected to remain relatively flat over the next decade. An increase in gas prices could lead more people to choose the bus; however, trains are often preferred when available. Employment in the charter bus industry is expected to experience little or no change, limiting opportunities for charter bus drivers.

Recently, intercity bus travel that picks up passengers from curbside locations in urban downtowns has grown rapidly. This form of travel is expected to continue to grow, leading to more jobs for intercity bus drivers.

For local transit, a new type of bus service has gotten a lot of attention lately: bus rapid transit (BRT). BRT creates routes in cities where buses can travel quickly with only a few stops. Because it is less expensive than light rail, some cities are considering BRT lines instead of rail lines; this could create more jobs for bus drivers.

Employment of school or special client bus drivers is projected to grow 9 percent, largely due to an increase in the number of school-age children. However, growth will be tempered as budget limitations lead school districts to focus on increasing efficiency. They do this by using computer programs to determine more efficient bus routes, allowing some routes (and drivers) to be cut.

Job Prospects. Job opportunities for bus drivers should be favorable, especially for school bus drivers, as many drivers are expected to leave the occupation. Those willing to work part time or irregular shifts should have the best prospects. Prospects for motor coach drivers will depend on tourism, which fluctuates with the economy.

O*NET

➤ Bus Drivers, Transit and Intercity (53-3021.00)
➤ Bus Drivers, School or Special Client (53-3022.00)

Contacts for More Information

For more information about school bus drivers, visit
➤ National School Transportation Association (www.yellowbuses. org/)
➤ National Association of State Directors of Pupil Transportation Services (www.nasdpts.org/)
   For more information about transit bus drivers, visit
➤ American Public Transportation Association (www.apta.com/Pages/default.aspx)
   For more information about motor coach drivers, visit
➤ United Motor Coach Association (www.uma.org/)
   For more information on federal regulations for commercial vehicle drivers, visit
➤ US Federal Motor Carrier Safety Administration (www.fmcsa.dot. gov/)

Delivery Truck Drivers and Driver/Sales Workers

- **2012 Median Pay** .... $27,530 per year
   $13.23 per hour
- **Entry-Level Education** ... High school diploma or equivalent
- **Work Experience in a Related Occupation** .... None
- **On-the-Job Training** .... Short-term on-the-job training
- **Number of Jobs 2012** 1,273,600
- **Job Outlook, 2012–22** .... 5% (Slower than average)
- **Employment Change, 2012–22** 68,800

Delivery drivers and driver/sales workers transport goods around an urban area or small region.

What Delivery Truck Drivers and Driver/Sales Workers Do

Delivery truck drivers and driver/sales workers pick up, transport, and drop off packages and small shipments within a local region or urban area. They drive trucks with a 26,000-pound gross vehicle weight (GVW) capacity or less. Most of the time, they transport merchandise from a distribution center to businesses and households.

Duties. Delivery truck drivers and driver/sales workers typically do the following:

- Load and unload their cargo
- Report any incidents they encounter on the road to a dispatcher
- Follow all applicable traffic laws
- Report serious mechanical problems to the appropriate personnel
- Keep their truck and associated equipment clean and in good working order
- Accept payments for the shipment
- Handle paperwork, such as receipts or delivery confirmation notices

Most drivers plan their routes. Some have a regular daily or weekly delivery schedule. Others have different routes each day.

These drivers generally receive instructions to go to a delivery location at a particular time, and it is up to them to determine the best route. They must have a thorough understanding of an area's street grid and know which roads allow trucks and which do not.

Light truck drivers, often called *pick-up and delivery* or *P&D drivers,* are the most common type of delivery driver. They drive small trucks or vans from distribution centers to delivery locations. Drivers make deliveries based on a set schedule. Some drivers stop at the distribution center once only, in the morning, and make many stops throughout the day. Others make multiple trips between the distribution center and delivery locations. Some drivers make deliveries from a retail location to customers.

Driver/sales workers are delivery drivers who additionally have sales responsibilities. They recommend new products to businesses and solicit new customers. These drivers may have a regular delivery route and be responsible for adding new clients located along their route. For example, they may make regular deliveries to a hardware store and encourage the store's manager to offer a new

Median Annual Wages, May 2012

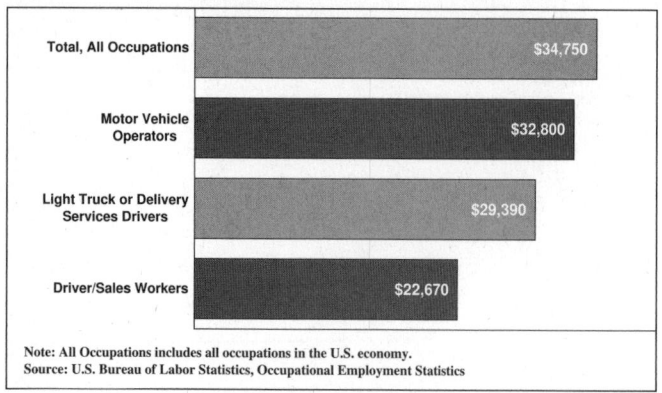

Note: All Occupations includes all occupations in the U.S. economy.
Source: U.S. Bureau of Labor Statistics, Occupational Employment Statistics

Percent Change in Employment, Projected 2012–2022

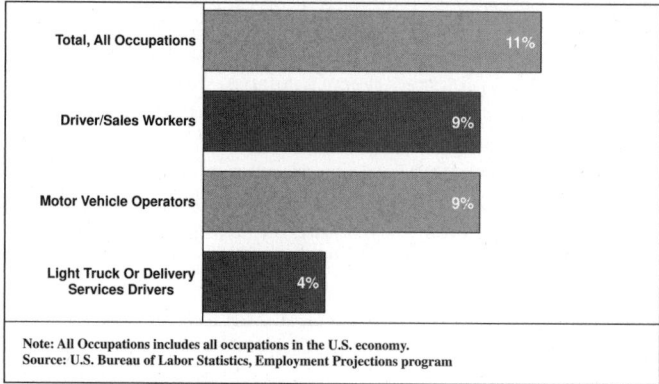

Note: All Occupations includes all occupations in the U.S. economy.
Source: U.S. Bureau of Labor Statistics, Employment Projections program

type of product. Driver/sales workers also deliver goods, such as take-out food to consumers, and accept payment for those goods.

Work Environment

Light truck drivers or delivery services drivers held about 841,600 jobs in 2012.

The industries that employed the most light truck or delivery service drivers in 2012 were as follows:

Retail trade 20%
Couriers and messengers.. 20
Wholesale trade 17

Driver/sales workers held about 432,000 jobs in 2012.

The industries that employed the most driver/sales workers in 2012 were as follows:

Restaurants and other eating places....................................... 32%
Wholesale trade 29
Retail trade 13

Delivery truck drivers and driver/sales workers have physically demanding jobs. Driving a truck for long periods of time can be tiring. When loading and unloading cargo, drivers do a lot of lifting, carrying, and walking.

Injuries and Illnesses. Given the nature of their jobs, these workers are at risk of being involved in motor vehicle accidents and have a higher risk of injuries due to lifting and moving heavy objects than workers in most other occupations.

Work Schedules. Most drivers work full time, and many work additional hours. Those who work on regular routes sometimes must begin work very early in the morning or work late at night. For example, a driver who delivers bread to a deli every day must be there before the deli opens. Drivers often work weekends and holidays.

How to Become One

Delivery truck drivers and driver/sales workers typically enter their occupations with a high school diploma or equivalent. They undergo 1 month or less of on-the-job training. They must have a driver's license from the state in which they work.

Education. Delivery truck drivers and driver/sales workers typically enter their occupations with a high school diploma or equivalent.

Training. Companies train new delivery truck drivers and driver/sales workers on the job. This may include driving training from a driver-mentor who rides along with a new employee to ensure that a new driver is able to operate a truck safely on crowded streets.

New drivers also have training to learn company policies about package dropoffs, returns, taking payment, and what to do with damaged goods.

Driver/sales workers must learn detailed information about the products they offer. Their company also may teach them proper sales techniques, such as how to approach potential new customers.

Licenses, Certifications, and Registrations. All delivery drivers need a driver's license.

Other Experience. Some delivery drivers begin as package loaders at warehouse facilities, especially if the driver works for a large company. For more information on package loaders, see the profile on hand laborers and material movers.

Important Qualities

Customer-service skills. When completing deliveries, drivers often interact with customers and should make a good impression to ensure repeat business.

Hand-eye coordination. When driving, delivery drivers need to observe their surroundings while simultaneously operating a complex machine.

Math skills. Because delivery truck drivers and driver/sales workers sometimes take payment, they must be able to count cash and make change quickly and accurately.

Patience. When driving through heavy traffic congestion, delivery drivers must remain calm and composed.

Sales skills. Driver/sales workers are expected to convince customers to purchase new or different products from them.

Speaking ability. Drivers must comprehend English well enough to read road signs, prepare written reports, and communicate verbally with the public and law enforcement officials.

Visual ability. To have a driver's license, delivery truck drivers and driver/sales workers must be able to pass a state vision test.

Pay

The median annual wage for driver/sales workers was $22,670 in May 2012. The median wage is the wage at which half the workers in an occupation earned more than that amount and half earned less. The lowest 10 percent earned less than $16,780, and the top 10 percent earned more than $46,240.

In May 2012, the median annual wages for driver/sales workers in the top three industries in which these drivers worked were as follows:

Wholesale trade $30,170
Retail trade 25,490
Restaurants and other eating places..................................... 18,330

Employment Projections Data for Delivery Truck Drivers and Driver/Sales Workers

Occupational title	SOC Code	Employment, 2012	Projected Employment, 2022	Change, 2012–2022	
				Percent	Numeric
Delivery truck drivers and driver/sales workers......................	—	1,273,600	1,342,400	5	68,800
Driver/sales workers	53-3031	432,000	468,800	9	36,800
Light truck or delivery services drivers..................................	53-3033	841,600	873,600	4	32,000

Source: U.S. Bureau of Labor Statistics, Employment Projections Program

Note: Data are rounded. Go to Occupational Information Included in the OOH *for a discussion of the data in this table.*

Similar Occupations   This table shows a list of occupations with job duties that are similar to those of delivery truck drivers and driver/sales workers.

Occupations	Entry-level Education	2012 Pay	Projected Job Growth	Average Annual Openings
Bus Drivers	High school diploma or equivalent	$30,206	9%	17,800
Hand Laborers and Material Movers	Less than high school	$23,155	10%	133,630
Heavy and Tractor-trailer Truck Drivers	Postsecondary non-degree award	$38,200	11%	46,470
Material Recording Clerks	See "How to Become One"	$26,007	1%	84,000
Postal Service Workers	High school diploma or equivalent	$55,130	-28%	12,230
Taxi Drivers and Chauffeurs	Less than high school	$22,820	15%	6,370
Water Transportation Occupations	See "How to Become One"	$54,020	13%	4,810

The median annual wage for light truck or delivery services drivers was $29,390 in May 2012. The lowest 10 percent earned less than $18,190 and the top 10 percent earned more than $62,520.

In May 2012, the median annual wages for light truck or delivery services drivers in the top 3 industries in which these drivers worked were as follows:

Couriers and messengers......................................	$55,130
Wholesale trade	27,750
Retail trade	23,060

Job Outlook

Employment of light truck or delivery services drivers is projected to grow 4 percent from 2012 to 2022, slower than the average for all occupations.

Employment of driver/sales workers is projected to grow 9 percent over the same period, about as fast as the average for all occupations.

Improved routing through GPS technology can make existing truck drivers more productive, which may limit the demand for additional drivers. With improved routing, drivers can be more efficient, navigating better in traffic and spending less time idling at each stop.

Additionally, higher diesel prices could cause companies to limit their hiring of new drivers and increase the company's focus on technological solutions. The limits on hiring will be especially true for drivers at large shipping companies.

However, as the economy grows, the need for more deliveries is expected to increase. From the distribution of warehouse goods to the delivery of packages to households, nearly all goods are brought to their final destination by delivery drivers.

Job Prospects. Job opportunities for delivery truck driver and driver/sales worker are expected to be competitive. Because these drivers do not have to spend long periods away from home, these jobs tend to be more desirable than long-haul trucking jobs. Job applicants with experience, a clean driving record, or who work for the company in another occupation should have the best job prospects.

O*NET

➤ Driver/Sales Workers (53-3031.00)
➤ Light Truck or Delivery Services Drivers (53-3033.00)

Contacts for More Information

For more information about truck drivers, including delivery truck drivers and driver/sales workers, visit

➤ American Trucking Associations (www.trucking.org)
➤ Professional Truck Driver Institute (www.ptdi.org)

Flight Attendants

- **2012 Median Pay** .... $37,240 per year
- **Entry-Level Education** ... High school diploma or equivalent
- **Work Experience in a Related Occupation**......... Less than 5 years
- **On-the-Job Training** .... Moderate-term on-the-job training
- **Number of Jobs 2012** 84,800
- **Job Outlook, 2012–22** .... -7% (Decline)
- **Employment Change, 2012–22** .... -5,500

What Flight Attendants Do

Flight attendants provide personal services to ensure the safety and comfort of airline passengers.

Duties. Flight attendants typically do the following:

- Attend preflight briefings on details of the flight
- Ensure that adequate supplies of refreshments and emergency equipment are on board
- Assist in cleaning the cabin between flights
- Demonstrate the use of safety and emergency equipment

- Ensure all passengers have seatbelts fastened and ensure other safety requirements are met
- Serve, and sometimes sell, beverages, meals, or snacks
- Take care of passengers' needs, particularly those with special needs
- Reassure passengers during flight, such as when the aircraft hits turbulence
- Administer first aid to passengers or coordinate first aid efforts, when needed
- Direct passengers in case of emergency

Airlines are required by law to provide flight attendants for the safety and security of passengers. The primary job of flight attendants is to keep passengers safe and to ensure that everyone follows security regulations. Flight attendants also try to make flights comfortable and enjoyable for passengers.

About 1 hour before takeoff, the captain (pilot) informs attendants about evacuation procedures, the length of the flight, and weather conditions. Flight attendants must ensure that emergency equipment is working, the cabin is clean, and there is an adequate supply of food and beverages on board. Flight attendants greet passengers as they board the aircraft and direct them to their seats, assisting as needed.

Before the plane takes off, flight attendants instruct all passengers on the use of safety equipment, either by playing a video recording or demonstrating its use in person. They also ensure that seatbelts are fastened, seats are locked in the upright position, and all carry-on items are properly stowed in accordance with federal law and company policy.

A flight attendant's most important responsibility, however, is to help passengers in the event of an emergency. This responsibility ranges from dealing with unruly passengers to performing first aid, fighting fires, and directing evacuations. Flight attendants also answer questions about the flight, attend to passengers with special needs, help anyone else needing assistance, and generally assist all passengers as needed.

Before the plane lands, flight attendants once again ensure that seatbelts are fastened, seats are locked in the upright position, and all carry-on items are properly stowed.

Before they leave the plane, flight attendants take inventory of headsets, alcoholic beverages, and payments. They also submit reports to the airline company on the condition of the cabin, as well as on any medical problems that may have occurred during the flight.

Flight attendants spend a great deal of time away from home.

Work Environment

Flight attendants held about 84,800 jobs in 2012. Although most worked for scheduled airlines, a small number worked for corporations or chartered flight companies.

Flight attendants work primarily in the cabin of passenger aircraft. Dealing directly with the public and standing for long periods can be stressful and tiring. Occasionally, flight attendants must deal with turbulence, which can make providing service more difficult and causes anxiety in some passengers. Although rare, dealing with emergency situations and unruly customers can also be difficult and cause stress.

Flight attendants spend many nights away from home and often sleep in hotels or apartments shared by a group of flight attendants.

Injuries and Illnesses. Injuries may occur when opening overhead compartments, during turbulence, pushing carts, or during aircraft emergencies. In addition, medical problems can arise from irregular sleep patterns, the stress of frequent travel, and exposure to ill passengers. As a result, flight attendants experience some work-related injuries and illnesses.

Median Annual Wages, May 2012

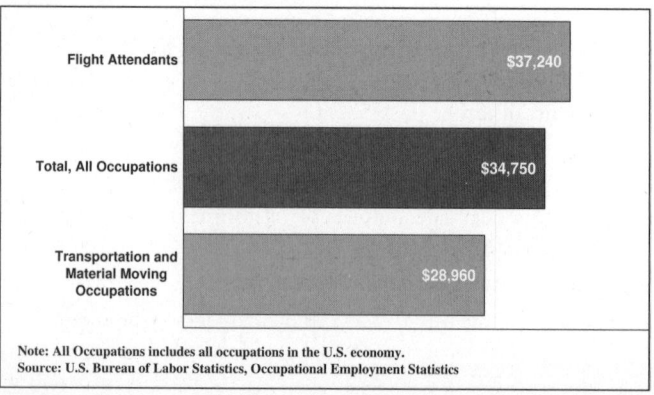

Flight Attendants	$37,240
Total, All Occupations	$34,750
Transportation and Material Moving Occupations	$28,960

Note: All Occupations includes all occupations in the U.S. economy.
Source: U.S. Bureau of Labor Statistics, Occupational Employment Statistics

Percent Change in Employment, Projected 2012–2022

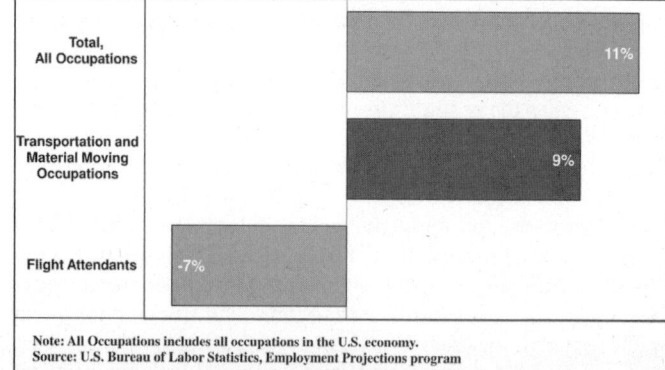

Total, All Occupations	11%
Transportation and Material Moving Occupations	9%
Flight Attendants	-7%

Note: All Occupations includes all occupations in the U.S. economy.
Source: U.S. Bureau of Labor Statistics, Employment Projections program

Employment Projections Data for Flight Attendants

Occupational title	SOC Code	Employment, 2012	Projected Employment, 2022	Change, 2012–2022 Percent	Change, 2012–2022 Numeric
Flight attendants	53-2031	84,800	79,200	-7	-5,500

Source: U.S. Bureau of Labor Statistics, Employment Projections Program

Note: Data are rounded. Go to **Occupational Information Included in the OOH** *for a discussion of the data in this table.*

Work Schedules. Most flight attendants work full time, but they usually have variable schedules. Flight attendants often work nights, weekends, and holidays because airlines operate every day and have overnight flights. In most cases, a contract between the airline and the flight attendant union determines the total daily and monthly workable hours. A typical on-duty shift is usually about 12 to 14 hours per day. However, duty time can be increased for international flights. The Federal Aviation Administration (FAA) requires that flight attendants receive 9 consecutive hours of rest following any duty period before starting their next duty period.

Attendants usually fly 75 to 90 hours a month and generally spend another 50 hours a month on the ground, preparing flights, writing reports, and waiting for aircraft to arrive. On average, they spend about two to three nights a week away from home. During this time, employers typically arrange hotel accommodations and a meal allowance.

An attendant's assignments of home base and route are based on seniority. New flight attendants must be flexible with their schedule and location. Almost all flight attendants start out working on call, also known as reserve status. Flight attendants on reserve usually live near their home airport, because they have to report to work on short notice.

As they earn more seniority, attendants gain more control over their schedules. For example, some senior flight attendants may choose to live outside their home base and commute to work. Others may choose to work only on regional flights. On small corporate airlines, flight attendants often work on an as-needed basis and must be able to adapt to changing schedules. About a quarter of all flight attendants work part time.

How to Become One

Flight attendants receive training from their employer and must be certified by the Federal Aviation Administration (FAA). Although flight attendants must have at least a high school diploma or the equivalent, some airlines prefer to hire applicants who have some college. Prospective flight attendants typically need previous work experience in customer service. Applicants must be at least 18 years old, eligible to work in the United States, have a valid passport, and pass a background check.

Education. A high school diploma is typically the minimum educational requirement for becoming a flight attendant. However, some airlines prefer to hire applicants who have taken some college courses.

Many employers prefer applicants with a degree in hospitality and tourism, public relations, business, social science, or communications. Those who work on international flights may have to be fluent in a foreign language. Some flight attendants attend special flight attendant academies.

Work Experience in a Related Occupation. Flight attendants typically have 1 or 2 years of work experience in a service occupation before getting their first job as a flight attendant. This experience may include customer service positions in restaurants, hotels, or resorts. Experience in sales or in other positions that require close contact with the public and focus on service to the customers may also help develop the skills needed to be a successful flight attendant.

Training. Once a flight attendant is hired, airlines provide their initial training, ranging from 3 to 6 weeks. The training usually takes place at the airline's flight training center and is required for FAA certification.

Trainees learn emergency procedures such as evacuating aircraft, operating emergency equipment, and administering first aid. They also receive specific instruction on flight regulations, company operations, and job duties.

Toward the end of the training, students go on practice flights. They must successfully complete the training to keep a job with the airline. Once they have passed initial training, new flight attendants receive the FAA Certificate of Demonstrated Proficiency. To maintain their certification, flight attendants must take periodic retraining throughout their career.

Licenses, Certifications, and Registrations. All flight attendants must be certified by the FAA. To become certified, flight attendants must complete their employer's initial training program and pass a proficiency check. Flight attendants are certified for specific types of aircraft and must take new training for each type of aircraft on which they are to work, in addition to recurrent training every year if they are to maintain their certification.

Similar Occupations   This table shows a list of occupations with job duties that are similar to those of flight attendants.

Occupations	Entry-level Education	2012 Pay	Projected Job Growth	Average Annual Openings
Bartenders	Less than high school	$18,900	12%	26,940
Customer Service Representatives	High school diploma or equivalent	$30,580	13%	94,160
EMTs and Paramedics	Postsecondary non-degree award	$31,020	23%	12,060
Food and Beverage Serving and Related Workers	Less than high school	$18,428	12%	245,590
Retail Sales Workers	Less than high school	$21,514	10%	202,730
Waiters and Waitresses	Less than high school	$18,540	6%	126,830

Advancement. After completing initial training, new flight attendants are placed on call, also known as reserve status. While on reserve status, attendants must be able to report to the airport on short notice to staff extra flights or fill in for absent crewmembers.

New attendants usually remain on reserve status for at least 1 year, but in some cities attendants may be on reserve for several years. After a few years in this reserve period, flight attendants gain enough seniority to bid on monthly assignments. Assignments are based on seniority and the most preferred routes go to the most experienced attendants.

Career advancement is based on seniority. Senior flight attendants exercise the most control over route assignments and schedules; therefore, they can often choose how much time to spend away from home. On international flights, senior attendants often oversee the work of other attendants. Senior attendants may be promoted to management positions in which they are responsible for recruiting, instructing, and scheduling.

Important Qualities

Attentiveness. Flight attendants must be aware of passengers' needs to ensure a pleasant travel experience. They must also be aware of any security or safety risks.

Communication skills. Flight attendants should speak clearly, listen attentively, and interact comfortably with passengers and other crew members.

Customer-service skills. Flight attendants should have poise, tact, and resourcefulness to handle stressful situations and meet passengers' needs.

Decision-making skills. Flight attendants must be able to act decisively in emergency situations.

Physical stamina. Flight attendants may need to lift baggage and stand and walk for long periods. They often need to conform to height and weight requirements and have vision that is correctable to at least 20/40. Flight attendants may have to pass a medical evaluation.

Flight attendants should present a professional appearance and not have visible tattoos, body piercings, or an unusual hairstyle or makeup.

Pay

The median annual wage for flight attendants was $37,240 in May 2012. The median wage is the wage at which half the workers in an occupation earned more than that amount and half earned less. The lowest 10 percent earned less than $27,240, and the top 10 percent earned more than $66,460.

Flight attendants receive an allowance for meals and accommodations while working away from home. Although they are required to purchase an initial set of uniforms and luggage, the airlines usually pay for replacements and upkeep. Flight attendants are usually eligible for discounts on airfare through their airline. Attendants often receive health and retirement benefits and some airlines offer incentive pay for working holidays, nights, and weekends.

Union Membership. Most flight attendants belonged to a union in 2012.

Job Outlook

Employment of flight attendants is projected to decline 7 percent from 2012 to 2022. Despite modest growth in air travel, continued economic difficulties and union contracts may prevent airlines from hiring new flight attendants.

Job Prospects. Economic difficulties and other issues have caused many flight attendants to be furloughed. Union contracts generally stipulate that furloughed flight attendants must be rehired before new

employees are found. Competition for jobs will remain strong because the occupation typically attracts many more applicants than there are job openings. When entry-level positions do become available, job prospects should be best for applicants with a college degree. Job opportunities may be slightly better at regional or low-cost airlines.

Most current job opportunities will come from the need to replace attendants who leave the workforce. Over the next decade, a number of flight attendants are expected to retire. However, if airlines decide to reduce their workforce or rehire furloughed attendants, the number of job openings for entry-level candidates may be reduced.

O*NET

➤ Flight Attendants (53-2031.00)

Contacts for More Information

For more information about flight attendants, visit the career webpage of any airline company, contact its personnel department, or visit

➤ Association of Flight Attendants–CWA (www.afanet.org/)
➤ Association of Professional Flight Attendants (www.apfa.org/)

For additional career information about pilots, see the *Occupational Outlook Quarterly* article "Sky-high careers: jobs related to airlines." (www.bls.gov/opub/ooq/2007/summer/art01.pdf).

Hand Laborers and Material Movers

- **2012 Median Pay** .... $22,970 per year
  $11.04 per hour
- **Entry-Level Education** .... Less than high school
- **Work Experience in a Related Occupation**.............. None
- **On-the-Job Training** ....Short-term on-the-job training
- **Number of Jobs 2012** 3,428,800
- **Job Outlook, 2012–22** .... 10% (As fast as average)
- **Employment Change, 2012–22** 341,700

What Hand Laborers and Material Movers Do

Hand laborers and material movers transport objects without using machines. Some workers move freight, stock, or other materials around in storage facilities; others clean vehicles; some pick up unwanted household goods; and still others pack materials for moving.

Duties. Hand laborers and material movers typically do the following:

- Manually move material from one place to another
- Pack or wrap material by hand
- Keep a record of the material they move
- Use signals, when necessary, to assist machine operators who are moving larger pieces of material
- Ensure a clean and orderly workplace

In warehouses and wholesale and retail operations, hand material movers work closely with material moving machine operators and material recording clerks. Automatic sensors and tags are increasingly being used to track items that allow hand material movers to work faster. Some workers are employed in manufacturing industries in which they load material onto conveyor belts or other machines.

Laborers and hand freight, stock, and material movers move materials to and from storage and production areas, loading docks,

Many vehicle cleaners work at car washes, but others work where commerical vehicles are serviced.

delivery trucks, ships, and containers. Most of these movers, often called *pickers*, work in warehouses, although their specific duties vary. Some workers find products in storage and transport them to the loading area. Other workers load and unload cargo from a truck. When moving a package, pickers keep track of the package number, sometimes with a hand-held scanner, to ensure proper delivery. Sometimes they open containers and sort the material.

Hand packers and packagers package a variety of materials by hand. They may label cartons, inspect items for defects, and record items packed. Some of these workers pack materials for shipment and transport them to a loading dock. Others work in retail as gift wrappers. Many hand packers are employed by grocery stores, where they bag groceries for customers at checkout.

Machine feeders and offbearers process materials by feeding them into equipment or by removing them from equipment. The equipment generally is operated by other workers, such as material-moving machine operators. Machine feeders and offbearers might help the operator if the machine becomes jammed or needs minor repairs. Machine feeders track the amount of material they process during a shift.

Cleaners of vehicles and equipment clean automobiles and other vehicles, as well as storage tanks, pipelines, and related machinery. They use cleaning products, vacuums, hoses, and brushes. Most of these workers clean cars at a carwash, an automobile dealership, or a rental agency. Some clean industrial equipment at manufacturing firms. Some–for example, those who work at a carwash–may have to interact with customers.

Refuse and recyclable material collectors gather garbage and recyclables from homes and businesses to transport to a dump, landfill, or recycling center. Many collectors lift garbage cans by hand and empty them into their truck. Some collectors drive the garbage or recycling truck along a scheduled route. When collecting materials from a dumpster, drivers use a hydraulic lift to empty the contents of the dumpster into their truck.

Work Environment

Hand laborers and material movers held about 3.4 million jobs in 2012. They work in a variety of industries.

Laborers and hand, freight, stock, and material movers held about 2.2 million jobs in 2012. The industries that employed the most laborers and hand, freight, stock, and material movers in 2012 were as follows:

Employment services 18%
Merchant wholesalers, nondurable goods 8
Warehousing and storage................................. 8
Merchant wholesalers, durable goods 8

Hand packers and packagers held about 666,900 jobs in 2012. The industries that employed the most hand packers and packagers in 2012 were as follows:

Grocery stores.. 23%
Employment services 16
Food manufacturing 10
Merchant wholesalers, nondurable goods 8
Warehousing and storage.............................. 7

Cleaners of vehicles and equipment held about 325,200 jobs in 2012. The industries that employed the most cleaners of vehicles and equipment in 2012 were as follows:

Other automotive repair and maintenance 34%
Automobile dealers.................................... 22
Food manufacturing 6

Refuse and recyclable material collectors held about 133,200 jobs in 2012. The industries that employed the most refuse and recyclable material collectors in 2012 were as follows:

Waste collection.. 40%
Local government, excluding education and hospitals............ 34
Waste treatment and disposal and waste management
   services... 11

Machine feeders and offbearers held about 106,100 jobs in 2012. The industries that employed the most machine feeders and offbearers in 2012 were as follows:

Food manufacturing 12%
Wood product manufacturing.................................. 10
Paper manufacturing 8
Plastics and rubber products manufacturing............................. 7

The work of hand laborers and material movers is usually repetitive and physically demanding. Workers may lift and carry heavy objects. They bend, kneel, crouch, or crawl in awkward positions.

Injuries and Illnesses. Some material-moving jobs can be dangerous. Hand laborers and freight, stock, and material movers, as well as refuse and recyclable material collectors, have some of the highest rates of injuries and illnesses of all occupations. When hand laborers and freight, stock, and material movers move heavy objects around a warehouse or onto trucks, injury-causing accidents can happen. Similarly, because refuse and recyclable material collectors drive so much to complete their rounds, they are vulnerable to traffic accidents. They also lift heavy objects, a practice that can lead to accidents.

Work Schedules. Most people in these occupations work full time. Almost a quarter of laborers and hand, freight, stock, and material movers and packers and packagers worked part time in 2012, a somewhat higher percentage than that of many other occupations. In addition, most workers have 8-hour shifts, although longer shifts and overtime are common. Because materials are shipped around the clock, some workers, especially those in warehousing, work overnight shifts.

How to Become One

Generally, hand laborers and material movers need no work experience or minimum level of education. Employers require only that applicants be physically able to do the work.

Median Annual Wages, May 2012

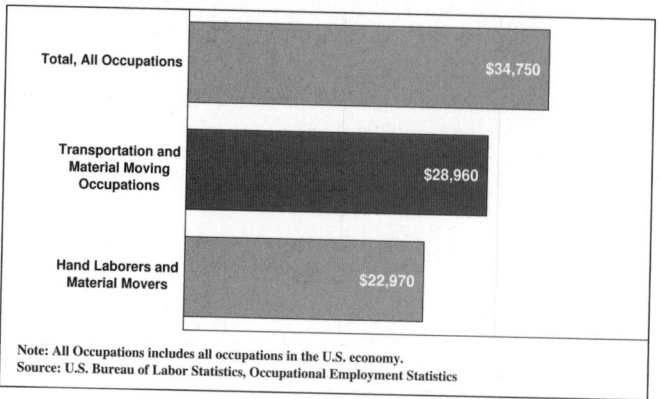

Note: All Occupations includes all occupations in the U.S. economy.
Source: U.S. Bureau of Labor Statistics, Occupational Employment Statistics

Percent Change in Employment, Projected 2012–2022

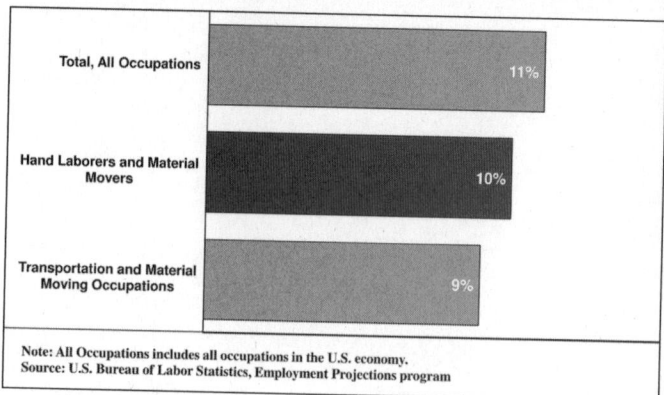

Note: All Occupations includes all occupations in the U.S. economy.
Source: U.S. Bureau of Labor Statistics, Employment Projections program

Education. Some employers may prefer to hire workers who have a high school diploma, although it is generally not required for these jobs.

Training. Most of these positions require less than 1 month of on-the-job training. Some workers need only a few days of training. Certain hand freight, stock, and material movers and refuse and recyclable material collectors have up to 3 months of training. Most training is done by a supervisor or a more experienced worker who decides when trainees are ready to work on their own.

Workers learn safety rules as part of their training. Many of these rules are standardized through the Occupational Safety and Health Administration (OSHA). Workers who handle hazardous materials receive additional training.

Licenses, Certifications, and Registrations. Refuse and recyclable material collectors who drive a truck that surpasses a certain size have to have a commercial driver's license (CDL). Getting a CDL requires passing written, skills, and vision tests.

Advancement. Many of these workers advance to other jobs. Some become material moving machine operators or material recording clerks; others become construction laborers or production workers. In warehousing or retail, experienced workers can move to other parts of the company, such as sales.

Important Qualities

Customer-service skills. Laborers and material handlers who work with the public, such as grocery baggers or carwash attendants, must be pleasant and courteous to customers.

Hand-eye coordination. Most laborers and material handlers have to be able to use their arms and hands to manipulate objects or move objects into specific positions.

Listening skills. Laborers and material movers often need to follow instructions that a supervisor gives them.

Physical strength. Some workers must be able to lift heavy objects throughout the day.

Pay

The median annual wage for hand laborers and material movers was $22,970 in May 2012. The median wage is the wage at which half the workers in an occupation earned more than that amount and half earned less. The lowest 10 percent earned less than $17,100, and the top 10 percent earned more than $38,410.

Median wages for hand laborers and material moving occupations in May 2012 were as follows:

$32,930 for refuse and recyclable material collectors
$27,120 for machine feeders and offbearers
$23,890 for laborers and hand freight, stock, and material movers
$19,910 for hand packers and packagers
$19,850 for cleaners of vehicles and equipment

Job Outlook

Overall employment of hand laborers and material movers is projected to grow 10 percent from 2012 to 2022, about as fast as the average of all occupations.

Projected employment changes for specific groups of workers within this occupation are as follows:

• Employment of refuse and recyclable material collectors is projected to grow 16 percent from 2012 to 2022. Trash collection will continue to grow as population and income grow, and collectors will be needed to remove trash. An increase in recycling collection is expected to drive the rapid growth of this occupation.

• Employment of cleaners of vehicles and equipment is projected to grow 11 percent from 2012 to 2022. Growth in automobile dealers, an industry in which many of these workers are employed, is expected to drive employment growth of cleaners

Employment Projections Data for Hand Laborers and Material Movers

Occupational title	SOC Code	Employment, 2012	Projected Employment, 2022	Change, 2012–2022	
				Percent	Numeric
Hand laborers and material movers....................................	—	3,428,800	3,770,400	10	341,700
Cleaners of vehicles and equipment..................................	53-7061	325,200	361,200	11	35,900
Laborers and freight, stock, and material movers, hand	53-7062	2,197,300	2,439,200	11	241,900
Machine feeders and offbearers	53-7063	106,100	108,200	2	2,100
Packers and packagers, hand...	53-7064	666,900	707,000	6	40,100
Refuse and recyclable material collectors	53-7081	133,200	154,900	16	21,600

Source: U.S. Bureau of Labor Statistics, Employment Projections Program

Note: Data are rounded. Go to **Occupational Information Included in the OOH** *for a discussion of the data in this table.*

Similar Occupations This table shows a list of occupations with job duties that are similar to those of hand laborers and material movers.

Occupations	Entry-level Education	2012 Pay	Projected Job Growth	Average Annual Openings
Construction Laborers and Helpers	See "How to Become One"	$29,277	25%	58,790
Delivery Truck Drivers and Driver/Sales Workers	High school diploma or equivalent	$27,113	5%	27,250
Heavy and Tractor-trailer Truck Drivers	Postsecondary non-degree award	$38,200	11%	46,470
Material Moving Machine Operators	See "How to Become One"	$32,069	1%	16,560
Material Recording Clerks	See "How to Become One"	$26,007	1%	84,000
Water Transportation Occupations	See "How to Become One"	$54,020	13%	4,810

of vehicles and equipment. However, a decline in the use of full-service carwashes in favor of automatic conveyors may limit job growth somewhat.

- Employment of laborers and hand, freight, stock, and material movers is projected to grow 11 percent from 2012 to 2022. The need for warehouses is expected to grow as consumer spending increases. However, greater automation will increase the efficiency of hand material movers. Most warehouses are installing equipment, such as high-speed conveyors and sorting systems and robotic pickers, that will decrease the number of workers needed.

- Employment of hand packers and packagers is projected to grow 6 percent from 2012 to 2022. A decline in the use of baggers in grocery stores, where many hand packers and packagers are employed, is expected to dampen growth in this occupation. The growing number of cashiers who also bag groceries is contributing to the decline in baggers. However, those employed in warehouses are expected to see some employment growth as the industry grows.

- Employment of machine feeders and offbearers is projected to show little or no change from 2012 to 2022. These workers are heavily employed in declining manufacturing industries in which automation is further decreasing the need for them. In addition, other workers who operate the machines are increasingly doing the tasks of machine feeders and offbearers.

Job Prospects. Job prospects for hand laborers and material movers are likely to be favorable. The need to replace workers who leave the occupations should create a large number of job openings. As automation increases, the technology used by workers in some of these occupations will become more complex. Employers will likely prefer workers who are comfortable using technology such as tablet computers and hand-held scanners.

O*NET

➤ Cleaners of Vehicles and Equipment (53-7061.00)
➤ Laborers and Freight, Stock, and Material Movers, Hand (53-7062.00)
➤ Machine Feeders and Offbearers (53-7063.00)
➤ Packers and Packagers, Hand (53-7064.00)
➤ Refuse and Recyclable Material Collectors (53-7081.00)

Contacts for More Information

For more information about hand laborers and material movers, visit
➤ MHI (www.mhi.org/)
➤ The Warehousing Education and Research Council (www.werc.org/)

Heavy and Tractor-trailer Truck Drivers

- **2012 Median Pay** .... $38,200 per year
  $18.37 per hour
- **Entry-Level Education** ...Postsecondary non-degree award
- **Work Experience in a Related Occupation**............... None
- **On-the-Job Training** ....Short-term on-the-job training
- **Number of Jobs 2012** 1,701,500
- **Job Outlook, 2012–22**............... 11% (As fast as average)
- **Employment Change, 2012–22** 192,600

What Heavy and Tractor-trailer Truck Drivers Do

Heavy and tractor-trailer truck drivers transport goods from one location to another. Most tractor-trailer drivers are long-haul drivers and operate trucks with a gross vehicle weight (GVW) capacity of more than 26,000 pounds. These drivers deliver goods over intercity routes, sometimes spanning several states.

Duties. Heavy and tractor-trailer truck drivers typically do the following:

- Drive long distances
- Report to a dispatcher any incidents encountered on the road
- Follow all applicable traffic laws
- Inspect their trailer before and after the trip, and record any defects they find
- Keep a log of their activities
- Report serious mechanical problems to the appropriate personnel
- Keep their truck and associated equipment clean and in good working order

Most heavy and tractor-trailer truck drivers plan their own routes. They may use satellite tracking to help them plan.

Before leaving, a driver usually is told a delivery location and time, but it is up to the driver to determine how to get the cargo there.

A driver must know which roads allow trucks and which do not. Drivers also must plan legally required rest periods into their trip. Some drivers have one or two routes that they drive regularly, and others drivers take many different routes throughout the country. Also, some drivers have routes that include Mexico or Canada.

Companies sometimes use two drivers, known as teams, on long runs to minimize downtime. On these team runs, one driver sleeps in a berth behind the cab while the other drives.

Some heavy truck drivers transport hazardous materials, such as chemical waste, and so have to take special precautions when driving. Also, these drivers normally carry specialized safety equipment in case of an accident. Other drivers, such as those carrying liquids, oversized loads, or cars, must follow rules that apply specifically to them.

Some long-haul truck drivers, called *owner-operators*, buy or lease trucks and go into business for themselves. They then have business tasks, including finding and keeping clients and doing administrative work such as accounting, in addition to their driving tasks.

Work Environment

Heavy and tractor-trailer truck drivers held about 1.7 million jobs in 2012.

Many heavy and tractor-trailer truck drivers are employed in general freight trucking. The industries that employed the most truck drivers in 2012 were as follows:

General freight trucking 34%
Specialized freight trucking 13
Merchant wholesalers, nondurable goods 8

Working as a long-haul truck driver is a major lifestyle choice because these drivers can be away from home for days or weeks at a time. They spend much of this time alone. Truck driving can be a physically demanding job as well. Driving for many hours in a row can be tiring, and some drivers must load and unload cargo.

Injuries and Illnesses. Because of the potential for traffic accidents, heavy and tractor-trailer truck drivers have one of the highest rates of injury and illnesses of all occupations.

Work Schedules. The Federal Motor Carrier Safety Administration regulates the hours that a long-haul truck driver may work. Drivers may not work more than 14 straight hours comprising up to 11 hours spent driving and the remaining time spent doing other work, such as unloading cargo. Between working periods, drivers must have at least 10 hours off duty. Drivers also are limited to driving no more than 60 hours within 7 days or 70 hours within 8 days; then drivers must take 34 hours off before starting another 7- or 8-day run. Drivers must record their hours in a logbook. Truck drivers often work nights, weekends, and holidays.

How to Become One

Heavy and tractor-trailer truck drivers usually have a high school diploma and attend a professional truck driving school. They must have a commercial driver's license (CDL).

Education. Most companies require their truck drivers to have a high school diploma or equivalent.

Many companies require drivers to attend professional truck-driving schools, where they take training courses to learn how to maneuver large vehicles on highways or through crowded streets.

Heavy truck and tractor-trailer drivers are often responsible for planning their own routes to their shipment destinations.

During these classes, drivers also learn the federal laws and regulations governing interstate truck driving. Students attend either a private truck-driving school or a program at a community college that lasts between 3 and 6 months.

Upon finishing these classes, drivers receive a certificate of completion.

The U.S. Department of Transportation is considering requiring all newly hired interstate truck drivers to take a truck-driving course.

The Professional Truck Driver Institute (PTDI) certifies a small percentage of driver-training courses at truck-driver training schools that meet both the industry standards and the U.S. Department of Transportation guidelines for training tractor-trailer drivers.

Licenses, Certifications, and Registrations. All long-haul truck drivers must have a commercial driver's license (CDL). Qualifications for obtaining a CDL vary by state but generally include passing both a knowledge test and a driving test. States have the right to refuse to issue a CDL to anyone who has had a CDL suspended by another state.

Drivers can get endorsements to their CDL that show their ability to drive a specialized type of vehicle. Truck drivers transporting

Median Annual Wages, May 2012

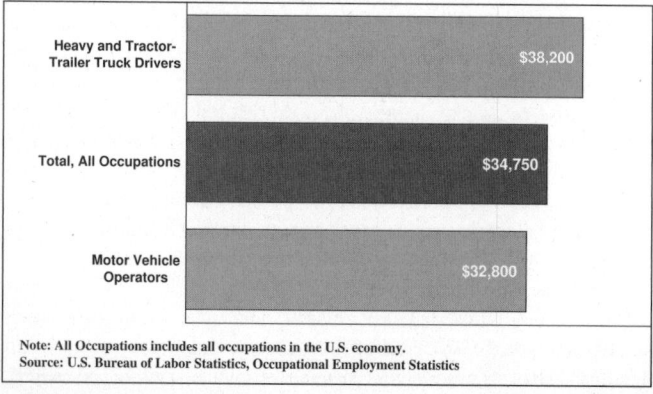

Heavy and Tractor-Trailer Truck Drivers	$38,200
Total, All Occupations	$34,750
Motor Vehicle Operators	$32,800

Note: All Occupations includes all occupations in the U.S. economy.
Source: U.S. Bureau of Labor Statistics, Occupational Employment Statistics

Percent Change in Employment, Projected 2012–2022

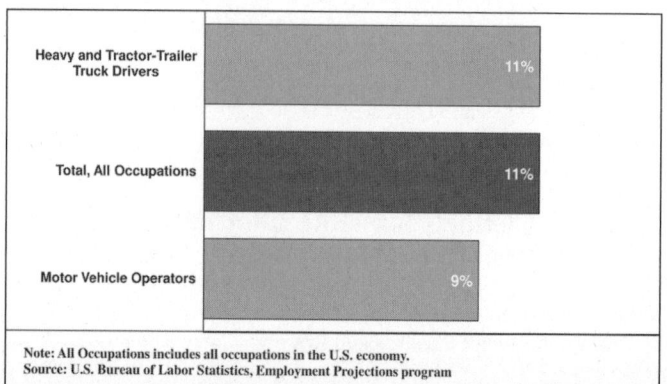

Heavy and Tractor-Trailer Truck Drivers	11%
Total, All Occupations	11%
Motor Vehicle Operators	9%

Note: All Occupations includes all occupations in the U.S. economy.
Source: U.S. Bureau of Labor Statistics, Employment Projections program

Employment Projections Data for Heavy and Tractor-trailer Truck Drivers

Occupational title	SOC Code	Employment, 2012	Projected Employment, 2022	Change, 2012–2022	
				Percent	Numeric
Heavy and tractor-trailer truck drivers..................................	53-3032	1,701,500	1,894,100	11	192,600

Source: U.S. Bureau of Labor Statistics, Employment Projections Program

Note: Data are rounded. Go to **Occupational Information Included in the OOH** *for a discussion of the data in this table.*

hazardous materials (HAZMAT) must have a hazardous materials endorsement (H). Getting this endorsement requires an additional knowledge test and a background check.

Federal regulations require random testing of on-duty truck drivers for drug or alcohol abuse. In addition, truck drivers can have their CDL suspended if they are convicted of driving under the influence of alcohol or drugs or are convicted of a felony involving the use of a motor vehicle.

Other actions can result in a suspension after multiple violations. The Federal Motor Carrier Safety Administration website has a list of these violations. Additionally, some companies have stricter standards than what federal regulations require.

Training. After completing truck driving school and being hired by a company, drivers normally receive between 1 and 3 months of on-the-job training. During this time, they drive a truck with a more experienced mentor-driver in the passenger seat. This period of on-the-job training is to learn more about the specific type of truck they will drive and material they will be transporting.

Important Qualities

Hand-eye coordination. Drivers of heavy trucks and tractor-trailers must be able to coordinate their legs, hands, and eyes simultaneously so that the driver reacts appropriately to the situation around them and drives the vehicle safely.

Hearing ability. Truck drivers need good hearing. Federal regulations require that a driver be able to hear a forced whisper in one ear at 5 feet (with or without the use of a hearing aid).

Physical health. Federal regulations do not allow people to become truck drivers if they have a medical condition that may interfere with their ability to operate a truck, such as high blood pressure or epilepsy. The Federal Motor Carrier Safety Administration website has a full list of medical conditions that disqualify someone from driving a long-haul truck.

Visual ability. Truck drivers must be able to pass vision tests. Federal regulations require a driver to have at least 20/40 vision with a 70-degree field of vision in each eye and the ability to distinguish the colors on a traffic light.

Pay

The median annual wage for heavy and tractor-trailer truck drivers was $38,200 in May 2012. The median wage is the wage at which half the workers in an occupation earned more than the amount and half earned less. The lowest 10 percent earned less than $25,110, and the top 10 percent earned more than $58,910.

In May 2012, the median annual wages for heavy and tractor-trailer drivers in the top three industries in which these drivers worked were as follows:

General freight trucking $40,360
Specialized freight trucking 37,710
Merchant wholesalers, nondurable goods 39,630

Drivers of heavy trucks and tractor-trailers are usually paid by how many miles they have driven, plus bonuses. The per-mile rate varies from employer to employer and may depend on the type of cargo and the experience of the driver. Some long-distance drivers, especially owner-operators, are paid a share of the revenue from shipping.

Job Outlook

Employment of heavy and tractor-trailer truck drivers is projected to grow 11 percent from 2012 to 2022, about as fast as the average of all occupations.

As the economy grows, the demand for goods will increase, and more truck drivers will be needed to keep supply chains moving. Trucks transport most of the freight in the United States, so as households and businesses increase their spending, the trucking industry will grow.

As fuel prices rise, some companies may switch their shipping to rail to lower costs. However, rail is unlikely to take much market share away from trucks, because even with high diesel prices for truck fuel, trucks are more efficient for short distances. Additionally, many products need to be delivered within the short time frame that only trucks can operate in.

Demand for truck drivers is expected to increase in oil and gas industries as more drivers become needed to transport materials to and from mining sites.

Similar Occupations   This table shows a list of occupations with job duties that are similar to those of heavy and tractor-trailer truck drivers.

Occupations	Entry-level Education	2012 Pay	Projected Job Growth	Average Annual Openings
Bus Drivers	High school diploma or equivalent	$30,206	9%	17,800
Delivery Truck Drivers and Driver/Sales Workers	High school diploma or equivalent	$27,113	5%	27,250
Hand Laborers and Material Movers	Less than high school	$23,155	10%	133,630
Material Recording Clerks	See "How to Become One"	$26,007	1%	84,000
Railroad Occupations	High school diploma or equivalent	$52,386	-4%	3,450
Taxi Drivers and Chauffeurs	Less than high school	$22,820	15%	6,370
Water Transportation Occupations	See "How to Become One"	$54,020	13%	4,810

Job Prospects. Job prospects for heavy and tractor-trailer truck drivers with the proper training are projected to be favorable. Because of truck drivers' difficult lifestyle and time spent away from home, many companies have trouble finding and retaining qualified long-haul drivers.

O*NET

➤ Heavy and Tractor-Trailer Truck Drivers (53-3032.00)

Contacts for More Information

For more information about truck drivers, visit
➤ American Trucking Association (www.trucking.org/)
➤ Federal Motor Carrier Safety Administration (www.fmcsa.dot.gov/)
    For more information about truck driving schools and programs, visit
➤ Commercial Vehicle Training Association (http://cvta.org/)
➤ National Association of Publicly Funded Truck Driving Schools (http://napftds.org/)
➤ Professional Truck Driver Institute (www.ptdi.org)

Material Moving Machine Operators

- **2012 Median Pay** ....$31,530 per year
    $15.16 per hour

- **Entry-Level Education** ....See "How to Become One"

- **Work Experience in a Related Occupation**.... See "How to Become One"

- **On-the-Job Training** ....See "How to Become One"

- **Number of Jobs 2012** 650,600

- **Job Outlook, 2012–22**.................1% (Little or no change)

- **Employment Change, 2012–22** 3,600

What Material Moving Machine Operators Do

Material moving machine operators use machinery to transport various objects. Some operators move construction materials around building sites or the land around a mine. Others move goods around a warehouse or onto container ships.

Duties. Material moving machine operators typically do the following:

- Control equipment with levers, wheels, or foot pedals

- Move material according to a plan or schedule they receive from their superiors

- Set up and inspect material moving equipment

- Make minor repairs to their equipment

- Record the material they have moved and where they moved it from and to

In warehouse environments, most material moving machine operators use forklifts and conveyor belts. Automated sensors and tags are increasingly used to keep track of merchandise, allowing operators to work faster. Some operators also check items for damage.

In warehouses, operators usually work closely with hand material movers. For more information, see the profile on hand laborers and material movers.

Many operators work for underground and surface mining companies. They help to dig or expose the mine, remove the earth and rock, and extract the ore and other mined materials.

In construction, material movers remove earth to clear space for buildings. Some work on a building site for the entire length of the construction project. For example, material moving machine operators often help to construct high-rise buildings by transporting materials to workers far above ground level.

All material moving machine operators are responsible for the safe operation of their equipment or vehicle.

Industrial truck and tractor operators drive trucks and tractors that move materials around warehouses, storage yards, or worksites. These trucks, often called forklifts, have a lifting mechanism and forks, which makes them useful for moving heavy and large objects. Some industrial truck and tractor operators drive tractors that pull trailers loaded with material around factories or storage areas.

Excavating and loading machine and dragline operators use machines equipped with scoops or shovels. They dig sand, earth, or other materials and load them onto conveyors or into trucks for transport elsewhere. They also may move material within a confined area, such as a construction site. Operators typically receive instructions from workers on the ground through hand signals or radios. Most of these operators work in construction or mining industries.

Dredge operators excavate waterways. They operate equipment on the water to remove sand, gravel, or rock from harbors or lakes to help prevent erosion and improve trade. Removing these materials helps maintain navigable waterways and allows larger ships to use more ports. Operators also measure the water depth, as well as how much they will be excavating. Dredging is also used to help restore wetlands and maintain beaches.

Underground mining loading machine operators load coal, ore, and other rocks onto shuttles, mine cars, or conveyors for transport from a mine to the surface. These workers generally work underground in mines. They may use power shovels, hoisting engines equipped with scrapers or scoops, and automatic gathering arms that move materials onto a conveyor. Operators also drive their machines further into the mine in order to gather more material.

Crane and tower operators use tower and cable equipment to lift and move materials, machinery, or other heavy objects. Operators extend and retract horizontal arms and lower and raise hooks attached to cables at the end of their crane or tower. Operators are usually guided by other workers on the ground using hand signals or a radio. Most crane and tower operators work at construction

Material movers often work in the construction industry.

sites or major ports, where they load and unload cargo. Some also work in iron and steel mills.

Hoist and winch operators, also called *derrick operators* or *hydraulic boom operators*, control the movement of platforms, cables, and cages that transport workers or materials for industrial operations, such as constructing a high-rise building. Many of these operators raise platforms far above the ground. Operators regulate the speed of the equipment based on the needs of the workers. Most work in manufacturing or construction industries.

Conveyor operators and tenders control conveyor systems that move materials on an automatic belt. They move materials to and from places such as building sites, storage areas, and vehicles. They monitor sensors on the conveyor to regulate the speed with which the conveyor belt moves. Operators may determine the route materials take along a conveyor based on shipping orders.

Work Environment

Material moving machine operators held about 650,600 jobs in 2012. They worked in a variety of industries. The tables that follow show the distribution of the different kinds of material moving machine operators.

Industrial truck and tractor operators held about 508,600 jobs in 2012. The industries that employed the most industrial truck and tractor operators in 2012 were as follows:

Warehousing and storage... 15%
Employment services 8
Merchant wholesalers, nondurable goods 8

Excavating and loading machine and dragline operators held about 50,700 jobs in 2012. The industries that employed the most excavating and loading machine and dragline operators in 2012 were as follows:

Mining (except oil and gas).. 24%
Specialty trade contractors 22
Heavy and civil engineering construction 13

Crane and tower operators held about 43,800 jobs in 2012. The industries that employed the most crane and tower operators in 2012 were as follows:

Specialty trade contractors 23%
Primary metal manufacturing.. 15
Support activities for mining 10
Heavy and civil engineering construction 8
Support activities for transportation... 8

Conveyor operators and tenders held about 39,100 jobs in 2012. The industries that employed the most conveyor operators and tenders in 2012 were as follows:

Couriers and messengers.. 22%
Merchant wholesalers, nondurable goods 21
Food manufacturing... 13
Warehousing and storage... 8
Merchant wholesalers, durable goods 8

Underground mining loading machine operators held about 3,300 jobs in 2012. The industries that employed the most underground mining loading machine operators in 2012 were as follows:

Coal mining... 62%
Metal ore mining 13
Nonmetallic mineral mining and quarrying.............................. 7

Hoist and winch operators held about 3,100 jobs in 2012. The industries that employed the most hoist and winch operators in 2012 were as follows:

Support activities for water transportation 17%
State and local government, excluding education
    and hospitals.. 9
Support activities for mining 7

Dredge operators held about 2,000 jobs in 2012. The industries that employed the most dredge operators in 2012 were as follows:

Nonmetallic mineral mining and quarrying............................ 48%
Heavy and civil engineering construction 29
State and local government, excluding education
    and hospitals.. 5

Injuries and Illnesses. Some material moving machine operator jobs can be dangerous. For example, crane operators and hoist and winch operators work outdoors at great heights in all types of weather.

Operators in some industries might be exposed to harmful chemicals or dangerous machinery. However, these jobs have become far less dangerous as safety equipment and regulations have improved. Many workers wear gloves, hardhats, or respirators.

Work Schedules. Most material moving machine operators work full time and have 8-hour shifts, although longer shifts and overtime are common. Because materials are shipped around the clock, some operators–especially those in warehousing–work overnight shifts.

How to Become One

Education and training requirements vary by the type of job. Crane operators and excavating machine operators usually have several years of experience in related occupations.

Median Annual Wages, May 2012

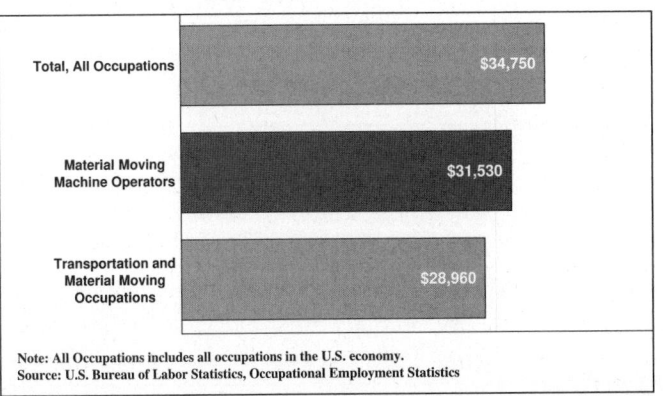

Note: All Occupations includes all occupations in the U.S. economy.
Source: U.S. Bureau of Labor Statistics, Occupational Employment Statistics

Percent Change in Employment, Projected 2012–2022

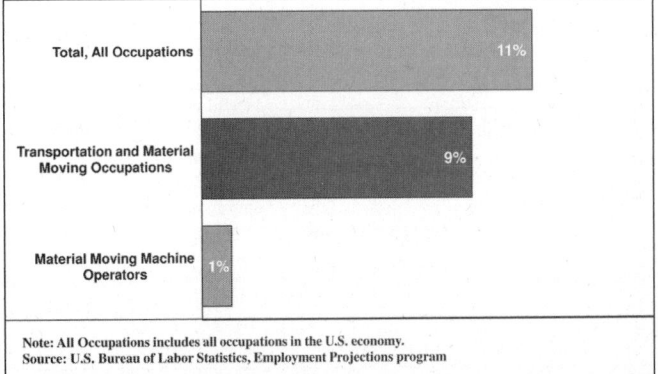

Note: All Occupations includes all occupations in the U.S. economy.
Source: U.S. Bureau of Labor Statistics, Employment Projections program

Employment Projections Data for Material Moving Machine Operators

Occupational title	SOC Code	Employment, 2012	Projected Employment, 2022	Change, 2012–2022	
				Percent	Numeric
Material moving machine operators.....................................	—	650,600	654,200	1	3,600
Conveyor operators and tenders....................................	53-7011	39,100	40,500	3	1,300
Crane and tower operators..	53-7021	43,800	51,200	17	7,400
Dredge operators	53-7031	2,000	2,200	13	300
Excavating and loading machine and dragline operators........	53-7032	50,700	58,900	16	8,200
Loading machine operators, underground mining	53-7033	3,300	3,300	-1	0
Hoist and winch operators	53-7041	3,100	3,200	3	100
Industrial truck and tractor operators.............................	53-7051	508,600	495,000	-3	-13,600

Source: U.S. Bureau of Labor Statistics, Employment Projections Program

Note: Data are rounded. Go to **Occupational Information Included in the OOH** *for a discussion of the data in this table.*

Education. Although it is usually not required, some companies prefer material moving machine operators to have a high school diploma.

Crane operators and excavating machine operators are normally required to have a high school diploma or equivalent.

Training. Most material moving machine operators are trained on the job in less than a month. Some machines are more complex than others, so the amount of time spent in training will vary with the type of machine the operator is using. Training time also can vary by industry. Most workers are trained by a supervisor or another experienced employee, who decides when the workers are ready to work on their own.

The International Union of Operating Engineers offers apprenticeship programs for heavy equipment operators, such as excavating machine operators or crane operators. Apprenticeships combine paid on-the-job training with technical instruction.

During their training, machine operators learn a number of safety rules, many of which are standardized through the Occupational Safety and Health Administration (OSHA) and the Mine Safety and Health Administration (MSHA). Employers must certify that each operator has received the proper training. Operators who work with hazardous materials receive further specialized training.

Licenses, Certifications, and Registrations. A number of states and several cities require crane operators to be licensed. To get a license, operators typically must complete a skills test in which they show that they can control a crane. They also usually must pass a written exam that tests their knowledge of safety rules and procedures.

Work Experience in a Related Occupation. Crane operators and excavating machine operators usually have several years of experience in related occupations. They may start as construction laborers and helpers and work as construction equipment operators or hoist and winch operators.

Advancement. Some material moving machine operators become construction equipment operators. Others find work as a production or mining worker. In warehousing or retail environments, experienced workers can move to other parts of the company, such as the sales department, or become a material recording clerk.

Important Qualities

Alertness. Machine operators must stay aware of their surroundings while operating machinery.

Dexterity. Operators sometimes have to maneuver their machines through tight spaces, around large objects, and on uneven surfaces.

Mechanical skills. Operators make minor adjustments to their machines when necessary.

Visual ability. When operating their machines, operators must be able to see clearly where they are driving or what they are moving. They must also watch for nearby workers, who may unknowingly be in their path.

Pay

The median annual wage for material moving machine operators was $31,530 in May 2012. The median wage is the wage at which half the workers in an occupation earned more than that amount and half earned less. The lowest 10 percent earned less than $20,800, and the top 10 percent earned more than $51,110.

The median wages for material moving machine operator occupations in May 2012 were the following:

Underground mining loading machine operators $48,420
Crane and tower operators 47,290
Hoist and winch operators... 39,960

Similar Occupations   This table shows a list of occupations with job duties that are similar to those of material moving machine operators.

Occupations	Entry-level Education	2012 Pay	Projected Job Growth	Average Annual Openings
Construction Equipment Operators	High school diploma or equivalent	$41,099	19%	16,480
Delivery Truck Drivers and Driver/Sales Workers	High school diploma or equivalent	$27,113	5%	27,250
Hand Laborers and Material Movers	Less than high school	$23,155	10%	133,630
Heavy and Tractor-trailer Truck Drivers	Postsecondary non-degree award	$38,200	11%	46,470
Material Recording Clerks	See "How to Become One"	$26,007	1%	84,000
Water Transportation Occupations	See "How to Become One"	$54,020	13%	4,810

Excavating and loading machine and dragline operators... $38,290
Dredge operators 37,170
Industrial truck and tractor operators 30,220
Conveyor operators and tenders 29,610

Union Membership. Compared with workers in all occupations, material moving machine operators had a higher percentage of workers who belonged to a union in 2012.

Job Outlook

Employment of material moving machine operators is projected to show little or no change from 2012 to 2022.

Employment of conveyor operators and tenders is projected to grow 3 percent and employment of industrial truck and tractor operators is projected to decline 3 percent. Both of these occupations are heavily concentrated in warehouse environments. The need for warehouses will grow as consumer spending increases.

However, employment growth will be limited as automation becomes more commonplace. Most warehouses are installing equipment such as high-speed conveyors, high-speed sorting systems, and robotic pickers. This equipment increases the efficiency of material movers, allowing warehouses to trim the number of workers they employ.

Employment of crane and tower operators is projected to grow 17 percent from 2012 to 2022. As global shipping increases, more of these operators will be needed at ports to load and unload large cargo ships. However, increasing automation at ports may moderate growth. Employment growth also will be driven by the recovery of the construction industry, in which many of these workers are employed. Employment of crane operators is projected to grow 40 percent in construction.

Employment of hoist and winch operators is projected to grow 3 percent from 2012 to 2022. Like crane and tower operators, they will be needed at ports to help load and unload cargo, but may see growth reduced by port automation. Employment of hoist and winch operators is projected to decline 15 percent in support activities for water transportation. They are also heavily concentrated in declining manufacturing industries, which will contribute to slower growth.

Employment of excavating and loading machine and dragline operators is projected to grow 16 percent from 2012 to 2022. Many of these operators work in the construction industry, whose projected fast growth will drive job growth in this occupation.

Employment of dredge operators is projected to grow 13 percent from 2012 to 2022 as the need for more dredging in the Great Lakes and in other large ports increases. However, environmental concerns are expected to hold up some dredging projects, limiting the growth of this occupation.

Employment of underground mining loading machine operators is projected to experience little or no change from 2012 to 2022, largely due to an expected decline in coal mining, where many of these workers are employed. This will be caused by technology gains that boost worker productivity. Employment of these operators is projected to decline 4 percent in coal mining.

Job Prospects. Job prospects should be favorable. A high number of job openings should be created by the need to replace workers who leave these occupations.

As automation increases, the technology used by these occupations will become more complex. Employers will prefer workers who are comfortable using technology such as tablet computers and hand-held scanners.

O*NET

➤ Conveyor Operators and Tenders (53-7011.00)
➤ Crane and Tower Operators (53-7021.00)
➤ Dredge Operators (53-7031.00)
➤ Excavating and Loading Machine and Dragline Operators (53-7032.00)
➤ Loading Machine Operators, Underground Mining (53-7033.00)
➤ Hoist and Winch Operators (53-7041.00)
➤ Industrial Truck and Tractor Operators (53-7051.00)

Contacts for More Information

For more information about careers as a material moving machine operator, visit
➤ MHI (www.mhi.org)
➤ The Warehousing Education and Research Council (www.werc.org)
➤ International Union of Operating Engineers (www.iuoe.org)
➤ National Commission for the Certification of Crane Operators (www.nccco.org)

Railroad Occupations

- **2012 Median Pay** .... $52,400 per year
$25.19 per hour
- **Entry-Level Education** ... High school diploma or equivalent
- **Work Experience in a Related Occupation** .... See "How to Become One"
- **On-the-Job Training** .... Moderate-term on-the-job training
- **Number of Jobs 2012** 113,800
- **Job Outlook, 2012–22** .... -3% (Decline)
- **Employment Change, 2012–22** .... -4,000

What Railroad Occupations Do

Workers in railroad occupations ensure that passenger and freight trains run on time and travel safely. Some workers drive trains, some coordinate the activities of the trains, while others operate signals and switches in the rail yard.

Duties. Railroad occupations typically do the following:
- Check the mechanical condition of locomotives and make adjustments when necessary
- Document issues with a train that require further inspection
- Operate locomotive engines within or between stations

Freight trains move billions of tons of goods around the country to ports where they are shipped around the world. Passenger trains transport millions of passengers and commuters to destinations around the country. These railroad occupations are essential to keeping freight and passenger trains running properly.

All workers in railroad occupations work together closely. Locomotive engineers travel with conductors and, sometimes, brake operators. Locomotive engineers and conductors are in constant contact and keep each other informed of any changes in the condition of the train.

Signal and switch operators communicate with both locomotive and rail yard engineers to make sure that trains end up at the correct destination. All occupations are in contact with dispatchers, who give them directions on where to go and what to do.

Locomotive engineers drive freight or passenger trains between stations. They drive long-distance trains and commuter trains, but not subway trains. Most locomotive engineers drive diesel-electric engines, although some drive locomotives powered by battery or electricity.

Engineers must be aware of the goods their train is carrying because different types of freight require different types of driving, based on the conditions of the rails. For example, a train carrying hazardous material though a snowstorm is driven differently than a train carrying coal though a mountain region.

Locomotive engineers typically do the following:

- Monitor speed, air pressure, battery use, and other instruments to ensure that the locomotive runs smoothly

- Use a variety of controls, such as throttles and airbrakes, to operate the train

- Communicate with dispatchers over radios to get information about delays or changes in the schedule

Conductors travel on both freight and passenger trains. They coordinate activities of the train crew. On passenger trains, they ensure safety and comfort and make announcements to keep passengers informed. On freight trains, they oversee, and are ultimately responsible for, the loading and unloading of cargo.

Conductors typically do the following:

- Check passengers' tickets

- Take payments from passengers who did not buy tickets in advance

- Announce stations and give other announcements as needed

- Help passengers to safety when needed

- Deal with unruly passengers when needed

- Oversee loading and unloading of cargo

Yardmasters do work similar to that of conductors, except that they do not travel on trains. They oversee and coordinate the activities of workers in the rail yard. They tell yard engineers where to move cars to fit the planned configuration or to load freight. Yardmasters ensure that trains are carrying the correct material before leaving the yard. Not all rail yards use yardmasters. In rail yards that do not have yardmasters, a conductor performs the duties of a yardmaster.

Yardmasters typically do the following:

- Review schedules, switching orders, and shipping records of freight trains

- Operate freight cars within rail yards that use remote locomotive technology

- Arrange for defective cars to be removed from a train for repairs

- Switch train traffic to a certain section of the line to allow other inbound and outbound trains to get around

- Break up or put together train cars according to a schedule

Rail yard engineers operate train engines within the rail yard. They move locomotives between tracks to keep the trains organized and on schedule. Some operate small locomotives called dinkeys. Sometimes, rail yard engineers are called *hostlers* and drive locomotives to and from maintenance shops or prepare them for the locomotive engineer.

Locomotive firers are part of a train crew and typically monitor tracks and train instruments. They look for equipment that is dragging, obstacles on the tracks, and other potential safety problems.

Firers also monitor oil, temperature, and pressure gauges on train dashboards to determine if engines are operating safely and efficiently. Firers relay traffic signals from yard workers to engineers in a railroad yard.

Conductors are the head of the train's crew.

Few trains still use firers, because their work has been automated or is now done by a locomotive engineer or conductor.

Railroad brake, signal, or switch operators control equipment that keeps the trains running safely.

Brake operators help couple and decouple train cars. Some travel with the train as part of the crew.

Signal operators install and maintain the signals along tracks and in the rail yard. Signals are important in preventing accidents because they allow increased communication between trains and yards.

Switch operators control the track switches in rail yards. These switches allow trains to move between tracks and ensure trains are heading in the right direction.

Work Environment

Workers in railroad occupations held about 113,800 jobs in 2012.

Nearly all locomotive engineers; conductors and yardmasters; and brake, signal, and switch operators work in the rail transportation industry. Rail yard engineers work in rail transportation and support activities for rail transportation.

Rail yard engineers spend most of their time working outside, regardless of weather conditions.

Conductors on passenger trains generally work in cleaner, more comfortable conditions than conductors on freight trains. However, conductors on passenger trains sometimes must respond to upset or unruly passengers when a train is delayed.

Injuries and Illnesses. Rail yard engineers and conductors and yardmasters have higher rates of work-related injuries than most occupations. Rail yard workers must move heavy equipment around and climb up and down equipment, which can be dangerous.

Work Schedules. Trains are scheduled to operate 24 hours a day, 7 days a week, meaning that many railroad workers sometimes work nights, weekends, and holidays. Most rail employees work full time. Federal regulations require a minimum number of rest hours for train operators.

Locomotive engineers and conductors whose trains travel long routes can be away from home for long periods of time. Those

Median Annual Wages, May 2012

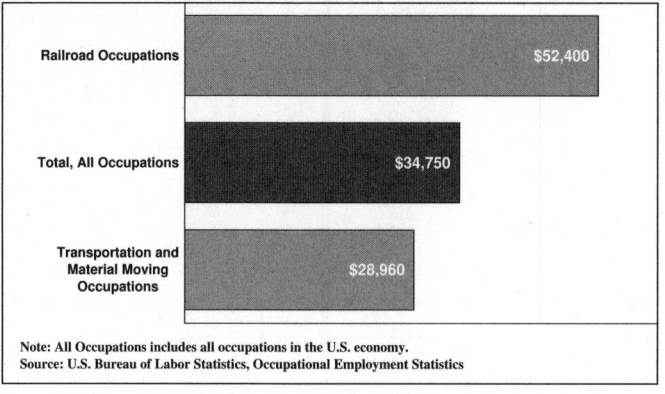

Note: All Occupations includes all occupations in the U.S. economy.
Source: U.S. Bureau of Labor Statistics, Occupational Employment Statistics

Percent Change in Employment, Projected 2012–2022

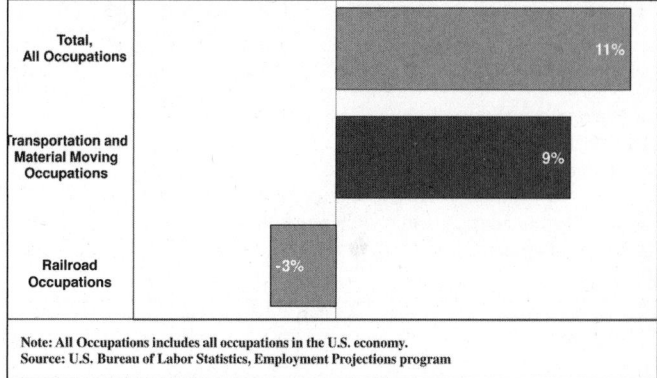

Note: All Occupations includes all occupations in the U.S. economy.
Source: U.S. Bureau of Labor Statistics, Employment Projections program

who work on passenger trains with short routes generally have a more predictable schedule. Workers on some freight trains have irregular schedules.

For engineers, seniority (the number of years on the job) usually dictates who receives the most desired shifts. Some engineers, called "extra board," are hired on a temporary basis and get an assignment only when a railroad needs an extra or substitute worker on a certain route.

How to Become One

Workers in railroad occupations generally need a high school diploma and several months of on-the-job training.

Education. Some rail companies require a high school diploma or equivalent, especially for locomotive engineers and conductors. Other positions may not have any formal education requirements.

Training. Locomotive engineers generally receive 2 to 3 months of on-the-job training before they can operate a train on their own. Typically, this training involves riding with an experienced engineer who teaches them the nuances of that particular train route.

During training, an engineer learns the track length, where the switches are, and any unusual features of the track. An experienced engineer who switches to a new route also has to spend a few months in training to learn the route with an engineer who is familiar with it. In addition, railroad companies provide continuing education so that engineers can maintain their skills.

Most railroad companies have 1 to 3 months of on-the-job training for conductors and yardmasters. Amtrak (the passenger train company) and some of the larger freight railroad companies operate their own training programs. Smaller and regional railroads may send conductors to a central training facility or a community college.

Yardmasters may be sent to training programs or may be trained by an experienced yardmaster. They learn how to operate remote locomotive technology and how to manage railcars in the yard.

Conductors and yardmasters working for freight railroads also learn the proper procedures for loading and unloading different types of cargo. Conductors on passenger trains learn ticketing procedures and how to handle passengers.

Rail yard engineers and signal and switch operators also receive on the job training, generally through a company training program. This program may last a few weeks to a few months, depending on the company and the complexity of the job. The program may include some time in a classroom and some hands-on experience under the direction of an experienced employee.

Work Experience in a Related Occupation. Most locomotive engineers first work as conductors for several years.

Licenses, Certifications, and Registrations. Locomotive engineers must be certified by the Federal Railroad Administration (FRA). The certification, conducted by the railroad that employs them, involves a written knowledge test, a skills test, and a supervisor determining that the engineer understands all physical aspects of the particular route on which he or she will be operating.

An experienced engineer who changes routes must be recertified for the new route. Even engineers who do not switch routes must be recertified every few years.

At the end of the certification process, the engineer must pass a vision and hearing test.

Recent legislation will soon require conductors who operate on national, regional, or commuter railroads to become certified. New conductors will have to pass a test that has been designed and administered by the railroad and approved by the FRA. Existing conductors will be granted automatic certification.

Advancement. Rail yard engineers, switch operators, and signal operators can advance to become conductors or yardmasters. Some conductors or yardmasters advance to become locomotive engineers.

Important Qualities

Communication skills. All rail employees have to be able to communicate effectively with each other to avoid accidents and keep the trains on schedule.

Customer-service skills. Conductors on passenger trains ensure customers' comfort, make announcements, and answer any questions a passenger has. They must be courteous and patient. They may have to deal with unruly or upset passengers.

Decision-making skills. When operating a locomotive, engineers must be able to make fast decisions to avoid accidents.

Hand-eye coordination. Locomotive engineers have to operate various controls while staying aware of their surroundings.

Hearing ability. To show that they can hear warning signals and communicate with other employees, locomotive engineers have to pass a hearing test conducted by their rail company.

Leadership skills. On some trains, a conductor directs a crew. Yardmasters oversee other rail yard workers.

Mechanical skills. All rail employees work with complex machines. Most have to be able to adjust equipment when it does not work properly. Some rail yard engineers spend most of their time fixing broken equipment.

Physical strength. Some rail yard engineers have to lift heavy equipment.

Speaking skills. Conductors on passenger trains announce stations and make other announcements. They must be able to speak clearly so passengers understand what they are saying.

Employment Projections Data for Railroad Occupations

Occupational title	SOC Code	Employment, 2012	Projected Employment, 2022	Change, 2012–2022	
				Percent	Numeric
Railroad occupations	—	113,800	109,800	-3	-4,000
Locomotive engineers	53-4011	38,000	36,500	-4	-1,500
Locomotive firers..	53-4012	1,600	900	-42	-700
Rail yard engineers, dinkey operators, and hostlers	53-4013	5,300	5,400	2	100
Railroad brake, signal, and switch operators	53-4021	25,000	24,400	-3	-700
Railroad conductors and yardmasters..................................	53-4031	43,800	42,500	-3	-1,300

Source: U.S. Bureau of Labor Statistics, Employment Projections Program

Note: Data are rounded. Go to **Occupational Information Included in the OOH** *for a discussion of the data in this table.*

Visual ability. To drive a train, locomotive engineers have to pass a vision test conducted by their rail company. Eyesight, peripheral vision, and color vision may be tested.

In addition, locomotive operators must be at least 21 years of age and pass a background test. They must also pass random drug and alcohol screenings over the course of their employment.

Pay

The median annual wage for all railroad occupations was $52,400 in May 2012. The median wage is the wage at which half the workers in an occupation earned more than that amount and half earned less. The lowest 10 percent earned less than $35,400, and the top 10 percent earned more than $76,220.

Median wages for specific railroad occupations in May 2012 were as follows:

Conductors and yardmasters	$54,700
Locomotive engineers	52,280
Brake, signal, and switch operators......................................	51,340
Locomotive firers..	44,920
Rail yard engineers, dinkey operators, and hostlers	41,230

Union Membership. Most railroad workers belonged to a union in 2012.

Job Outlook

Employment of railroad occupations is projected to decline 3 percent from 2012 to 2022.

Employment of locomotive engineers is projected to decline 4 percent. Employment of conductors and yardmasters is projected to decline 3 percent. Employment of rail yard engineers, dinkey operators, and hostlers is projected to experience little or no change. Employment of brake, signal, and switch operators is projected to decline 3 percent.

Employment growth in these occupations will depend on demand for rail transportation. Demand for rail is driven by population growth and an increase in global trade. Although demand for rail transportation may grow, an increase in productivity may hold back employment growth in rail occupations. Because building new tracks is expensive, freight companies have found other ways to increase capacity, such as double-stacking (stacking one railcar on top of another) or running longer trains. With both of these approaches, passenger rail can also add more cars to existing trains to increase capacity without increasing either the number of locomotives or the number of conductors on these trains.

Some employment growth may occur as rising gas prices may lead some travelers to use passenger rail and some shipping companies to use freight rail. In addition, an increase in intermodal freight–the shipment of goods through multiple transportation modes–may shift some goods from trucks to freight rail.

Employment of locomotive firers is projected to decline 42 percent from 2012 to 2022. Most railroads are phasing out this occupation, as their duties are typically preformed by locomotive engineers and conductors.

Job Prospects. Job opportunities should be favorable for railroad occupations. Although growth is projected to be slower than other occupations, more railroad workers are nearing retirement than are workers in most occupations. When these workers begin to retire, many jobs should open up, except for locomotive firers, as railroad companies will continue to phase them out of the workforce.

O*NET

➤ Locomotive Engineers (53-4011.00)
➤ Locomotive Firers (53-4012.00)
➤ Rail Yard Engineers, Dinkey Operators, and Hostlers (53-4013.00)
➤ Railroad Brake, Signal, and Switch Operators (53-4021.00)
➤ Railroad Conductors and Yardmasters (53-4031.00)

Similar Occupations   This table shows a list of occupations with job duties that are similar to those of railroad occupations.

Occupations	Entry-level Education	2012 Pay	Projected Job Growth	Average Annual Openings
Bus Drivers	High school diploma or equivalent	$30,206	9%	17,800
Delivery Truck Drivers and Driver/Sales Workers	High school diploma or equivalent	$27,113	5%	27,250
Flight Attendants	High school diploma or equivalent	$37,240	-7%	1,400
Heavy and Tractor-trailer Truck Drivers	Postsecondary non-degree award	$38,200	11%	46,470
Material Moving Machine Operators	See "How to Become One"	$32,069	1%	16,560
Taxi Drivers and Chauffeurs	Less than high school	$22,820	15%	6,370
Water Transportation Occupations	See "How to Become One"	$54,020	13%	4,810

Contacts for More Information

For more information about commuter rail, visit

➤ American Public Transportation Association (www.apta.com)

For more information about training programs and job opportunities in passenger rail, visit

➤ National Railroad Passenger Corporation (Amtrak) (www.amtrak.com)

For information about railroad occupation career opportunities, visit

➤ Brotherhood of Locomotive Engineers and Trainmen (www.ble.org)
➤ United Transportation Union (www.utu.org)

Taxi Drivers and Chauffeurs

- **2012 Median Pay** .... $22,820 per year
  $10.97 per hour
- **Entry-Level Education** .... Less than high school
- **Work Experience in a Related Occupation** .... None
- **On-the-Job Training** .... Short-term on-the-job training
- **Number of Jobs 2012** 233,000
- **Job Outlook, 2012–22** .... 16% (Faster than average)
- **Employment Change, 2012–22** 36,200

What Taxi Drivers and Chauffeurs Do

Taxi drivers and chauffeurs drive people to and from the places they need to go, such as homes, workplaces, airports, and shopping centers. They must know their way around a city in order to take both residents and visitors to their destinations.

Duties. Taxi drivers and chauffeurs typically do the following:

- Check their car for problems and do basic maintenance
- Keep both the inside and outside of their car clean
- Refuel their car when necessary
- Pick up passengers and listen to where they want to go
- Operate wheelchair lifts when needed
- Help passengers load and unload their luggage
- Drive to passengers' destinations
- Obey all traffic laws
- Collect fares, including allowed extra charges
- Provide a receipt if the passenger requests one
- Keep a record of miles traveled

Taxi drivers and chauffeurs must stay alert and monitor the conditions of the road. They have to take precautions to ensure their passengers safety, especially in heavy traffic or bad weather. They must also follow all vehicle-for-hire or livery regulations, such as where they can pick up passengers and how much they can charge.

Good drivers are familiar with the streets in the areas they serve. They choose the most efficient routes, considering the traffic at that time of day. They know where the most frequently requested destinations are, such as airports, train stations, convention centers, hotels, and other points of interest. They also know where to find fire and police stations and hospitals in case of an emergency.

Taxi drivers, also called cabbies, generally use a meter to determine the fare when a passenger requests a destination. The most common way for cabbies to provide their services is when a customer calls a central dispatcher to request a cab and the central dispatcher tells the taxi driver where to go to pick up the customer.

Another way some drivers pick up passengers is when customers are waiting in lines at cabstands or in the taxi line at airports, train stations, and hotels. In some large cities, cabbies drive around the streets looking for passengers, although this is not legal in all cities.

Chauffeurs take passengers on prearranged trips. They operate limousines, vans, or private cars. They may work for hire for single trips or they may work for a person (in general), a private business, or for a government agency. Customer service is important for chauffeurs, especially luxury car drivers. Some do the duties of executive assistants, acting as driver, secretary, and itinerary planner. Other chauffeurs drive large vans between airports or train stations and hotels.

Paratransit drivers transport people with special needs, such as the elderly or those with disabilities. They operate specially equipped vehicles designed to help people with a variety of needs in nonemergency situations. For example, their vehicles may be equipped with wheelchair lifts, and the driver helps a passenger with boarding.

Work Environment

Taxi drivers and chauffeurs held about 233,000 jobs in 2012. About a quarter of taxi drivers and chauffeurs were self-employed. Self-employed drivers may own their own car and contract with a company. The company refers passengers and allows the driver to use their facilities for a fee. Some drivers use a company's car as part of the fee. Drivers keep all their fares and pay their own expenses.

Other taxi drivers and chauffeurs are directly employed by an organization that provides them with a car. The industries that employed the most taxi drivers and chauffeurs in 2012 were as follows:

Taxi and limousine service 21%
Health care and social assistance 13
Other transit and ground passenger transportation 10

Driving for long periods, especially in heavy traffic, can be stressful for taxi drivers and chauffeurs. In addition, they often have to pick up heavy luggage and packages.

Injuries and Illnesses. Taxi drivers and chauffeurs have one of the highest rates of injuries and illnesses of all occupations. This is largely due to car accidents.

Work Schedules. Work hours for taxi drivers and chauffeurs vary. About a quarter worked part time in 2012 and about one in

Job opportunities for taxi drivers and chauffeurs should be plentiful.

Median Annual Wages, May 2012

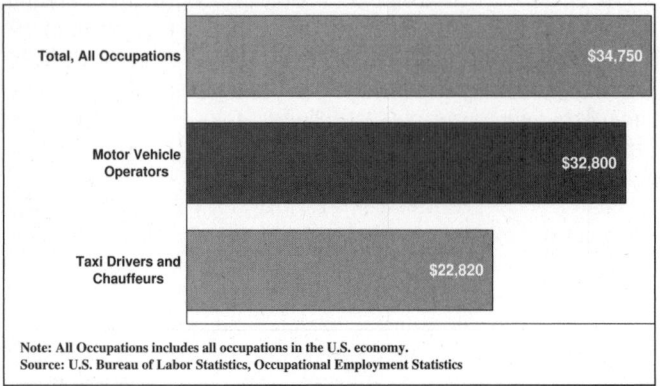

Note: All Occupations includes all occupations in the U.S. economy.
Source: U.S. Bureau of Labor Statistics, Occupational Employment Statistics

Percent Change in Employment, Projected 2012–2022

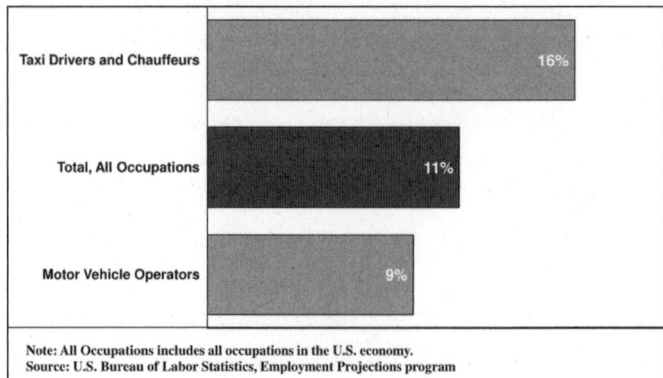

Note: All Occupations includes all occupations in the U.S. economy.
Source: U.S. Bureau of Labor Statistics, Employment Projections program

seven had variable schedules. Evening and weekend work is common. Some drivers work very late at night or early in the morning.

Taxi drivers work with little or no supervision, and their work schedules are flexible. They can break for a meal or rest whenever they do not have a passenger.

Chauffeurs' work schedules are much more structured. The hours they work are based on the needs of their clients. Some chauffeurs are on call while they are not at work.

How to Become One

Most taxi drivers and chauffeurs go through brief training. Many states and local municipalities require them to get a taxi or limousine license. Although a high school diploma is not required, many taxi drivers and chauffeurs have one.

Education. Many drivers have a high school diploma or equivalent; but, generally, it is not required.

Training. Most taxi and limousine companies provide their new drivers with a short period of on-the-job training. This training usually takes from 1 day to 2 weeks, depending on the company and the location. Some municipalities require training by law.

Training typically covers local traffic laws, driver safety, and the local street layout. Taxi drivers also get training in operating the taximeter and communications equipment. Taxi drivers are trained in accordance with local regulations; in contrast, limousine chauffeurs usually are trained by their company, and customer service is emphasized. Paratransit drivers receive special training in how to handle wheelchair lifts and other mechanical devices.

Licenses, Certifications, and Registrations. All taxi drivers and chauffeurs must have a regular automobile driver's license. States and local municipalities set other requirements; many require drivers to get a taxi or chauffeur's license, commonly referred to as a "hack" license. This normally requires passing a written test, with information such as local geography and regulations and a drug test.

The Federal Motor Carrier Safety Administration requires that limousine drivers who transport at least 16 passengers at a time (including the driver) have a commercial driver's license (CDL)

with a passenger (P) endorsement. To get these, a driver has to pass knowledge and driving skills tests.

Advancement. Taxi drivers and chauffeurs have limited advancement opportunities. However some may find managerial positions. For chauffeurs, advancement usually takes the form of driving more important clients and different types of cars. Some taxi drivers and chauffeurs can become a "lead driver," which means they train new drivers in addition to continuing to drive their own clients.

Important Qualities

Customer-service skills. Taxi drivers and chauffeurs regularly interact with their customers and have to represent their company positively and make sure passengers are satisfied with their ride.

Dependability. Customers rely on taxi drivers and chauffeurs to pick them up at the agreed-upon time so they get to their destinations when they need to be there.

Hand-eye coordination. Taxi drivers and chauffeurs have to be able to observe their surroundings and steer away from obstacles and dangerous drivers while operating a vehicle.

Map-reading skills. Although many cabs and limousines have GPS systems, it is still important for taxi drivers and chauffeurs to be able to understand directions and read maps.

Math skills. Taxi drivers count cash when a customer pays a fare and have to be able to make change quickly.

Patience. Drivers must be calm and composed when driving through heavy traffic, congestion, or dealing with rude passengers.

Professionalism. Chauffeurs are the face of their company and are expected to dress, speak, and act in a professional manner when they are with a customer.

Visual ability. Taxi drivers and chauffeurs must be able to pass a state-issued vision test in order to hold a driver's license.

Taxi drivers and chauffeurs usually work with little or no supervision, so they must be self-motivated and able to take initiative to earn a living.

Employment Projections Data for Taxi Drivers and Chauffeurs

Occupational title	SOC Code	Employment, 2012	Projected Employment, 2022	Change, 2012–2022	
				Percent	Numeric
Taxi drivers and chauffeurs..	53-3041	233,000	269,100	16	36,200

Source: U.S. Bureau of Labor Statistics, Employment Projections Program

Note: Data are rounded. Go to **Occupational Information Included in the OOH** *for a discussion of the data in this table.*

Similar Occupations This table shows a list of occupations with job duties that are similar to those of taxi drivers and chauffeurs.

Occupations	Entry-level Education	2012 Pay	Projected Job Growth	Average Annual Openings
Automotive Service Technicians and Mechanics	High school diploma or equivalent	$36,610	9%	23,760
Bus Drivers	High school diploma or equivalent	$30,206	9%	17,800
Delivery Truck Drivers and Driver/Sales Workers	High school diploma or equivalent	$27,113	5%	27,250
Heavy and Tractor-trailer Truck Drivers	Postsecondary non-degree award	$38,200	11%	46,470
Railroad Occupations	High school diploma or equivalent	$52,386	-4%	3,450
Water Transportation Occupations	See "How to Become One"	$54,020	13%	4,810

Pay

The median annual wage for taxi drivers and chauffeurs was $22,820 in May 2012. The median wage is the point at which half the workers in an occupation earned more than that amount and half earned less. The lowest 10 percent earned less than $17,050, and the top 10 percent earned more than $37,200. These wage data include money earned from tips. The better the service taxi drivers and chauffeurs provide their customers, the more likely they are to make a good tip on each fare.

Taxi drivers and chauffeurs who lease their car from a company may pay a fee for the use of the car. This fee covers storage, insurance, and maintenance costs. Drivers who own their cars can contract with a company that allows the drivers to use their facilities for a fee. In addition, drivers usually pay their own fuel costs, so those who use hybrid taxis will have lower expenses.

Job Outlook

Employment of taxi drivers and chauffeurs is projected to grow 16 percent from 2012 to 2022, faster than the average for all occupations.

Job growth is expected to be affected by an increase in demand for taxi drivers. Taxis generally complement public transit systems because people who regularly take a train or bus are more likely to use a taxi than would people who drive their own car. Therefore, as public transport systems grow, the demand for taxis should grow.

Paratransit is expected to grow rapidly. The growing number of elderly people who wish to remain independent might increase their use of these types of services to get around. Some growth will occur at nursing homes and assisted living facilities as these institutions try to increase mobility and quality of life for their residents. Growth may also occur due to federal legislation that requires transit agencies to offer paratransit services for the elderly and people with disabilities.

Some employment growth for chauffeurs is expected due to an increasing amount of corporate travel. To be successful, most chauffeurs depend on clients who travel for business.

Job Prospects. Job prospects for taxi drivers and chauffeurs will likely be excellent. The occupation has low barriers to entry and high turnover. Applicants with a clean driving record and flexible schedules should have the best chance of being hired. Most taxi drivers and chauffeurs work in metropolitan areas, and those areas that are experiencing fast economic growth should offer the most job opportunities.

O*NET

➤ Taxi Drivers and Chauffeurs (53-3041.00)

Contacts for More Information

For more information about taxi drivers, chauffeurs, and paratransit drivers, visit

➤ Taxicab, Limousine, and Paratransit Association (www.tlpa.org/)

For more information about limousine drivers, visit

➤ National Limousine Association (www.limo.org/)

Water Transportation Occupations

- **2012 Median Pay** .... $48,980 per year $23.55 per hour
- **Entry-Level Education** ....See "How to Become One"
- **Work Experience in a Related Occupation**............... None
- **On-the-Job Training** ....See "How to Become One"
- **Number of Jobs 2012** 81,600
- **Job Outlook, 2012–22** .... 13% (As fast as average)
- **Employment Change, 2012–22** 10,900

What Water Transportation Occupations Do

Workers in water transportation occupations operate and maintain vessels that take cargo and people over water. These vessels travel to and from foreign ports across the ocean, to domestic ports along the coasts, across the Great Lakes, and along the country's many inland waterways.

Duties. Water transportation workers typically do the following:

- Operate and maintain non-military vessels
- Follow their vessel's strict chain of command
- Ensure the safety of all people and cargo on board

These workers, sometimes called *merchant mariners*, work on a variety of ships.

Some operate large deep-sea container ships to transport manufactured goods around the world.

Others work on bulk carriers that move heavy commodities, such as coal or iron ore, across the oceans and over the Great Lakes.

Still others work on both large and small tankers that carry oil and other liquid products around the country and the world. Others work on supply ships that transport equipment and supplies to offshore oil and gas platforms.

Workers on tugboats help barges and other boats maneuver in small harbors and at sea.

Salvage vessels that offer emergency services also employ merchant mariners.

Cruise ships employ a large number of water transportation workers, and some merchant mariners work on ferries to transport passengers along shorter distances.

A typical deep sea merchant ship, large coastal ship, or Great Lakes merchant ship employs a captain and chief engineer, along with three mates, three assistant engineers, and a number of sailors and marine oilers. Smaller vessels that operate in harbors or rivers may have a smaller. The specific compliment of mariners is dependent on US Coast Guard regulations.

Also, there are other workers on ships, such as cooks, electricians, and mechanics. For more information, see the profiles on cooks, electricians, and general maintenance and repair workers.

Captains, sometimes called *masters*, have overall command of a vessel. They have the final responsibility for the safety of the crew, cargo, and passengers. Captains typically do the following:

- Supervise the work of other officers and the crew

- Ensure that proper safety procedures are followed

- Prepare a maintenance and repair budget

- Oversee the loading and unloading of cargo or passengers

- Keep logs and other records that track the ship's movements and activities

- Interact with passengers on cruise ships

Mates, or *deck officers*, direct the operation of a vessel while the captain is off duty. Large ships have three officers, called first, second, and third mates. The first mate has the highest authority and takes command of the ship if the captain is incapacitated. Usually, the first mate is in charge of the cargo and/or passengers, the second mate is in charge of navigation, and the third mate is in charge of safety. On smaller vessels, there may be only one mate who handles all of the responsibilities. Deck officers typically do the following:

- Alternate watches with the captain and other officers

- Supervise and coordinate the activities of the deck crew

- Assist with docking the ship

- Monitor the ship's position, using charts and other navigational aides

- Determine the speed and direction of the vessel

- Inspect the cargo hold during loading, to ensure that the cargo is stowed according to specifications

- Make announcements to passengers, when needed

Pilots guide ships in harbors, on rivers, and on other confined waterways. They are not part of a ship's crew but go aboard a ship to guide it through a particular waterway that they are familiar with. They work in places where a high degree of familiarity with local tides, currents, and hazards is needed. Some, called *harbor pilots*, work for ports and help many ships coming into the harbor during the day. When coming into a commercial port, a captain will often have to turn control of the vessel over to a pilot, who can safely guide it into the harbor. Pilots typically do the following:

- Board an unfamiliar ship from a small boat in the open water, often using a ladder

- Confer with a ship's captain about the vessel's destination and any special requirements it has

- Establish a positive working relationship with a vessel's captain and deck officers

- Receive mooring instructions from shore dispatchers

Work schedules for water transportation workers vary based upon the type of ship and length of voyage.

Sailors, or *deckhands*, operate and maintain the vessel and deck equipment. They make up the deck crew and keep all parts of a ship, other than areas related to the engine and motor, in good working order. New deckhands are called *ordinary seamen* and do the least-complicated tasks. Experienced deckhands are called *able seamen* and usually make up most of a crew. Some large ships have a *boatswain,* who is the chief of the deck crew. Sailors typically do the following:

- Stand watch, looking for other vessels or obstructions in their ship's path, and for navigational aids, such as buoys and lighthouses

- Steer the ship and measure water depth in shallow water

- Do routine maintenance, such as painting the deck and chipping away rust

- Keep the inside of the ship clean

- Handle lines when docking or departing

- Tie barges together when they are being towed

- Load and unload cargo

- Help passengers, when needed

Ship engineers operate and maintain a vessel's propulsion system. This includes the engine, boilers, generators, pumps, and other machinery. Large vessels usually carry a *chief engineer*, who has command of the engine room and its crew, and a first, second, and third assistant engineer. The assistant engineer oversees the engine and related machinery when the chief engineer is off duty. Small ships may only have one engineer. Engineers typically do the following:

- Maintain the electrical, refrigeration, and ventilation systems of a ship

- Start the engine and regulate the vessel's speed, based on the captain's orders

- Record information in an engineering log

- Keep an inventory of mechanical parts and supplies

- Do routine maintenance checks throughout the day

- Calculate refueling requirements

Marine oilers work in the engine room, helping the engineers keep the propulsion system in working order. They are the engine room equivalent of sailors. New oilers are usually called *wipers,* or *pumpmen,* on vessels handling liquid cargo. With experience, a

Median Annual Wages, May 2012

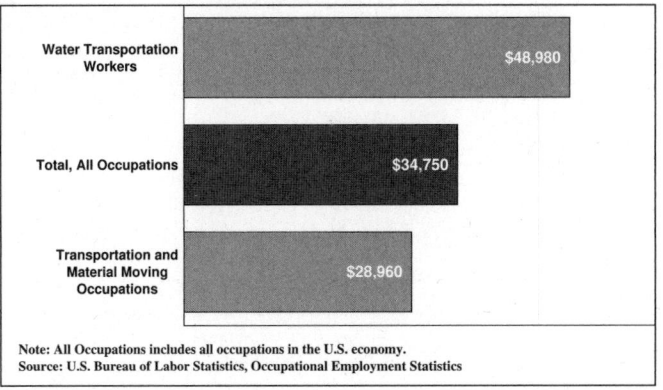

Note: All Occupations includes all occupations in the U.S. economy.
Source: U.S. Bureau of Labor Statistics, Occupational Employment Statistics

Percent Change in Employment, Projected 2012–2022

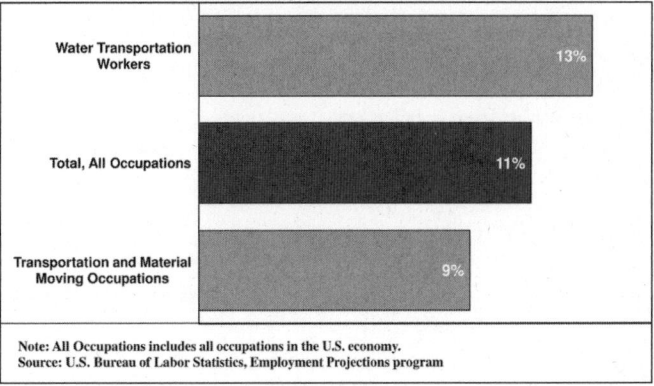

Note: All Occupations includes all occupations in the U.S. economy.
Source: U.S. Bureau of Labor Statistics, Employment Projections program

wiper can become a Qualified Member of the Engine Department (QMED). Marine oilers typically do the following:

- Lubricate gears, shafts, bearings, and other parts of the engine or motor
- Read pressure and temperature gauges and record data
- Help engineers with repairs to machinery
- Connect hoses, operate pumps, and clean tanks
- May assist the deck crew with loading or unloading of cargo

Motorboat operators run small, motor-driven boats that only carry a few passengers. They work for a variety of services, such as fishing charters, tours, and harbor patrols. Motorboat operators typically do the following:

- Check and change the oil and other fluids on their boat
- Pick up passengers and help them board the boat
- May act as a tour guide

Work Environment

Workers in water transportation occupations held about 81,600 jobs in 2012.

The industries that employed the most water transportation workers in 2012 were as follows:

Deep sea, coastal, and great lakes water transportation 24%
Inland water transportation 21
Support activities for water transportation 19
Government 12
Scenic and sightseeing transportation, water 6

Workers in water transportation occupations usually work for long periods on small and cramped ships, which can be uncomfortable. Many people decide life at sea is not for them because of difficult conditions onboard ships and long periods away from home.

However, companies try to provide a pleasant living condition aboard their vessels. Most vessels are now air-conditioned and include comfortable living quarters. Many also include entertainment systems with satellite TV and Internet connections. Large ships usually have one or two full-time cook as well.

Injuries and Illnesses. Sailors' and marine oilers' jobs can be more dangerous than most jobs. Crew members work outside in storms and other bad weather, which increases the risk of injury.

Workers can also be hurt working with certain machinery, heavy equipment, and cargo. However, modern safety procedures and communication systems have greatly improved safety for mariners.

Work Schedules. Workers on deep sea ships can spend months at a time away from home.

Workers on supply ships have shorter trips, usually lasting for a few hours to a month.

Tugboats and barges travel along the coasts and on inland waterways and are usually away for 2 to 3 weeks at a time.

Those who work on the Great Lakes have longer trips, around 2 months, but often do not work in the winter when the lakes freeze.

Crews on all vessels often work long hours, 7 days a week, while aboard.

Ferry workers and motorboat operators usually are away only for a few hours at a time and return home each night. Many ferry and motorboat operators service ships for vacation destinations and have seasonal schedules.

How to Become One

Education and training requirements vary by the type of job. Officers and engineers usually must have a bachelor's degree. Most water transportation jobs require the Transportation Worker Identification Credential (TWIC) from the U.S. Department of Homeland Security and a Merchant Marine Credential (MMC).

Education. Most deck officers, engineers, and pilots have a bachelor's degree from a merchant marine academy. The academy programs offer a bachelor's degree and a Merchant Marine Credential (MMC) with an endorsement as a third mate or third assistant engineer. Graduates of these programs can also choose to receive a commission as an ensign in the U.S. Naval Reserve, Merchant Marine Reserve, or U.S. Coast Guard Reserve.

Non-officers, such as sailors or marine oilers, usually do not need a degree.

Training. Ordinary seamen, wipers, and other entry-level mariners get on-the-job training for 6 months to a year. Length of training depends on the size and type of ship and waterway they work on. For example, workers on deep sea vessels need more complex training than those whose ships travel on a river.

Licenses, Certifications, and Registrations. All mariners working on ships with U.S. flags must have a Transportation Worker Identification Credential (TWIC) from the Transportation Security Administration. This credential states that a person is a U.S. citizen or permanent resident and has passed a security screening.

Most mariners must also have a Merchant Marine Credential (MMC). They can apply for an MMC at a U.S. Coast Guard regional examination center. Entry-level employees, such as ordinary seamen or wipers, do not have to pass a written exam. However, some have to pass physical, hearing, and vision tests, and all must undergo a drug screening, to get their MMC. They also have to take a class on shipboard safety.

Crew members can apply for endorsements to their MMC that allow them to move into more advanced positions.

Employment Projections Data for Water Transportation Occupations

Occupational title	SOC Code	Employment, 2012	Projected Employment, 2022	Change, 2012–2022	
				Percent	Numeric
Water transportation occupations	—	81,600	92,400	13	10,900
Sailors and marine oilers	53-5011	31,900	36,900	16	5,000
Captains, mates, and pilots of water vessels.....................	53-5021	35,400	40,200	14	4,900
Motorboat operators	53-5022	3,400	3,600	6	200
Ship engineers	53-5031	10,800	11,700	8	800

Source: U.S. Bureau of Labor Statistics, Employment Projections Program

Note: Data are rounded. Go to Occupational Information Included in the OOH *for a discussion of the data in this table.*

Wipers can get an endorsement to become a Qualified Member of the Engine Department (QMED) after 6 months of experience by passing a written test.

Ordinary seamen can get an able seamen endorsement after 6 months to 1 year of experience, depending on the type of ship they work on, by passing a written test.

Able seamen can complete a number of training and testing requirements, after at least 3 years of experience in the deck department, to get an endorsement as a third mate. Experience and testing requirements increase with the size and complexity of the ship.

Officers who graduate from a maritime academy receive an MMC with a third mate or third assistant engineer endorsement, depending on which department they are trained in.

To move up each step of the occupation ladder, from third mate/third assistant engineer to second to first and then to captain or chief engineer, requires 365 days of experience at the previous level. A second mate or second assistant engineer who wants to move to first mate/first assistant engineer also must complete a 12-week training course and pass an exam.

Pilots are licensed by the state in which they work. The U.S. Coast Guard licenses pilots on the Great Lakes. The requirements for these licenses vary, depending on where a pilot works.

More information on MMCs and endorsements is available from the U.S. Coast Guard National Maritime Center.

Other Experience. Instead of attending a maritime academy, captains and mates can attain their position after at least 3 to 4 years of experience as a member of a deck crew. This experience must be on a ship similar to the type they hope to serve on as an officer. They also must take several training courses and pass written and on-board exams. The difficulty of these requirements increases with the complexity and size of the vessel. Most officers who take this career path work on the great lakes or inland waterways rather than on deep-sea ships.

Many pilots have years of experience as a mate on a ship. The ship should be of the type they expect to pilot. For example, if they work at a deep-sea port, they should have experience on an ocean-going vessel.

Although there are no license requirements for motorboat operators, some employers prefer applicants who have several years of boating experience.

Important Qualities

Customer-service skills. Many motorboat operators interact with passengers and must ensure that passengers have a pleasant experience.

Hand-eye coordination. Officers and pilots who steer ships have to operate various controls while staying aware of their surroundings.

Hearing ability. Mariners must pass a hearing test to get an MMC.

Manual dexterity. Crew members need good balance to maneuver through tight spaces and on wet or uneven surfaces.

Mechanical skills. Members of the engine department keep complex machines working properly.

Physical strength. Sailors on freight ships load and unload cargo. While away at sea, most workers have to do some heavy lifting.

Visual ability. Mariners must pass a vision test to get an MMC.

Pay

The median annual wage for water transportation occupations was $48,980 in May 2012. The median wage is the wage at which half the workers in an occupation earned more than that amount and half earned less. The lowest 10 percent earned less than $24,920, and the top 10 percent earned more than $105,440.

Median annual wages for water transportation occupations in May 2012 were as follows:

Ship engineers..	$70,890
Captains, mates, and pilots of water vessels.........................	66,150
Sailors and marine oilers	38,190
Motorboat operators	35,190

In May 2012, the median annual wages for water transportation workers in the top five industries in which these workers worked were as follows:

Support activities for water transportation	$59,290
Deep sea, coastal, and great lakes water transportation	50,230
Government..	47,600
Inland water transportation...	46,780
Scenic and sightseeing transportation, water	35,190

Job Outlook

Employment of water transportation occupations is projected to grow 13 percent from 2012 to 2022, about as fast as the average for all occupations.

Employment of captains, mates, and pilots of water vessels is projected to grow 14 percent. Employment of ship engineers is projected to grow 8 percent. Employment of sailors and marine oilers is projected to grow 16 percent from 2012 to 2022.

As the economy recovers, the demand for waterway freight shipping will grow, increasing the need for these workers. Job growth is likely to be concentrated on inland rivers and the Great Lakes. This will be driven by the demand for commodities such as iron ore, grain, and petroleum. In addition, the need to supply offshore oil platforms will drive growth of supply ships.

However, growth in domestic waterways freight may be limited by an increase in intermodal shipping. Intermodal shipping means that shippers use more than one method to transport a good. An increase in intermodal shipping may send some freight from barges

Similar Occupations   This table shows a list of occupations with job duties that are similar to those of water transportation occupations.

Occupations	Entry-level Education	2012 Pay	Projected Job Growth	Average Annual Openings
Electrical and Electronics Installers and Repairers	Postsecondary non-degree award	$51,081	1%	2,980
Fishers and Related Fishing Workers	Less than high school	$33,430	-5%	630
Heavy and Tractor-trailer Truck Drivers	Postsecondary non-degree award	$38,200	11%	46,470
Heavy Vehicle and Mobile Equipment Service Technicians	High school diploma or equivalent	$43,979	9%	6,710
Material Moving Machine Operators	See "How to Become One"	$32,069	1%	16,560
Plumbers, Pipefitters, and Steamfitters	High school diploma or equivalent	$49,140	21%	13,050
Railroad Occupations	High school diploma or equivalent	$52,386	-4%	3,450
Stationary Engineers and Boiler Operators	High school diploma or equivalent	$53,560	3%	1,270

to trains. For some products, rail is a more direct route from the Midwest to a coastal port, which saves time and money.

Jobs in coastal shipping will likely continue to decline, as more companies use foreign vessels to transport goods internationally. However, there is a limit to the decline because federal laws and subsidies ensure that there will always be a fleet of merchant ships with U.S. flags. Keeping a fleet of merchant ships is considered important for the nation's defense.

The popularity of river cruises as a type of vacation is growing. This trend may lead to more opportunities for workers on inland rivers such as the Mississippi or Ohio River. However, most ocean-going cruise ships go to international destinations, and these ships generally do not employ U.S. workers.

Employment of motorboat operators is projected to grow 6 percent from 2012 to 2022. Demand for these workers will be driven by growth in tourism and recreational activities, where they are primarily employed.

Job Prospects. Job prospects should be favorable for most water transportation occupations. Many workers leave these occupations, especially sailors and marine oilers, because recently hired workers often decide they do not enjoy spending a lot of time away at sea.

In addition, a number of officers and engineers are approaching retirement, creating job openings. The number of applicants for all types of jobs may be limited by high regulatory and security requirements.

O*NET

➤ Sailors and Marine Oilers (53-5011.00)
➤ Captains, Mates, and Pilots of Water Vessels (53-5021.00)
➤ Ship and Boat Captains (53-5021.01)
➤ Mates- Ship, Boat, and Barge (53-5021.02)
➤ Pilots, Ship (53-5021.03)
➤ Motorboat Operators (53-5022.00)
➤ Ship Engineers (53-5031.00)

Contacts for More Information

For more information about water transportation occupations, including employment and training information, visit
➤ Maritime Administration, U.S. Department of Transportation (www.marad.dot.gov/)
   For more information about licensing requirements, visit
➤ The U.S. Coast Guard (www.uscg.mil/)
   For information about jobs on inland and coastal waterways on barges, tugboats, and towboats, visit
➤ The American Waterways Operators (www.americanwaterways.com/)
➤ Lake Carriers' Association (www.lcaships.com/)
➤ Passenger Vessel Association (www.passengervessel.com/mypva.aspx)

Data for Occupations Not Covered in Detail

Although hundreds of occupations are covered in detail in the *Occupational Outlook Handbook*, this chapter presents summary data on additional occupations for which employment projections are prepared but detailed occupational information is not developed. For each occupation, the Occupational Information Network (O*NET) code, the occupational definition, 2012 employment, the May 2012 median annual wage, the projected employment change and growth rate from 2012 to 2022, and education and training categories are presented.

Arts and Design Occupations

Merchandise Displayers and Window Trimmers

(O*NET 27-1026.00)

Plan and erect commercial displays, such as those in windows and interiors of retail stores and at trade exhibitions.

- **2012 employment:** 98,700

- **May 2012 median annual wage:** $26,410

- **Projected employment change, 2012-22:**
  - **Number of new jobs:** 10,000
  - **Growth rate:** 10 percent (about as fast as average)

- **Education and training:**
  - **Typical entry-level education:** High school diploma or equivalent
  - **Work experience in a related occupation:** None
  - **Typical on-the-job-training:** Moderate-term on-the-job training

Set and Exhibit Designers

(O*NET 27-1027.00)

Design special exhibits and movie, television, and theater sets. May study scripts, confer with directors, and conduct research to determine appropriate architectural styles.

- **2012 employment:** 11,400

- **May 2012 median annual wage:** $50,300

- **Projected employment change, 2012-22:**
  - **Number of new jobs:** 700
  - **Growth rate:** 6 percent (slower than average)

- **Education and training:**
  - **Typical entry-level education:** Bachelor's degree
  - **Work experience in a related occupation:** None
  - **Typical on-the-job-training:** None

Building and Grounds Cleaning Occupations

First-Line Supervisors of Housekeeping and Janitorial Workers

(O*NET 37-1011.00)

Directly supervise and coordinate work activities of cleaning personnel in hotels, hospitals, offices, and other establishments.

- **2012 employment:** 249,500

- **May 2012 median annual wage:** $35,310

- **Projected employment change, 2012-22:**
  - **Number of new jobs:** 32,000
  - **Growth rate:** 13 percent (about as fast as average)

- **Education and training:**
  - **Typical entry-level education:** High school diploma or equivalent
  - **Work experience in a related occupation:** Less than 5 years
  - **Typical on-the-job-training:** None

First-Line Supervisors of Landscaping, Lawn Service, and Groundskeeping Workers

(O*NET 37-1012.00)

Directly supervise and coordinate activities of workers engaged in landscaping or groundskeeping activities. Work may involve reviewing contracts to determine service, machine, and workforce requirements; answering inquiries from potential customers regarding methods, materials, and price ranges; and preparing estimates according to labor, material, and machine costs.

- **2012 employment:** 207,300

- **May 2012 median annual wage:** $42,160

- **Projected employment change, 2012-22:**
  - **Number of new jobs:** 26,300
  - **Growth rate:** 13 percent (about as fast as average)

- **Education and training:**
  - **Typical entry-level education:** High school diploma or equivalent
  - **Work experience in a related occupation:** Less than 5 years
  - **Typical on-the-job-training:** None

Business and Financial Occupations

Agents and Business Managers of Artists, Performers, and Athletes

(O*NET 13-1011.00)

Represent and promote artists, performers, and athletes in dealings with current or prospective employers. May handle contract negotiations and other business matters for clients.

- **2012 employment:** 18,300

- **May 2012 median annual wage:** $63,370

- **Projected employment change, 2012-22:**
  - **Number of new jobs:** 1,800
  - **Growth rate:** 10 percent (about as fast as average)

- **Education and training:**
  - **Typical entry-level education:** Bachelor's degree
  - **Work experience in a related occupation:** Less than 5 years
  - **Typical on-the-job-training:** None

Compliance Officers

(O*NET 13-1041.00, 13-1041.01, 13-1041.02, 13-1041.03, 13-1041.04, 13-1041.06, and 13-1041.07)

Examine, evaluate, and investigate eligibility for or conformity with laws and regulations governing contract compliance of licenses and permits. Perform other compliance and enforcement inspection and analysis activities not classified elsewhere. Excludes

"Financial Examiners" (13-2061), "Tax Examiners and Collectors, and Revenue Agents" (13-2081), "Occupational Health and Safety Specialists" (29-9011), "Occupational Health and Safety Technicians" (29-9012), "Transportation Security Screeners" (33-9093), "Agricultural Inspectors" (45-2011), "Construction and Building Inspectors" (47-4011), and "Transportation Inspectors" (53-6051).

- **2012 employment:** 239,800

- **May 2012 median annual wage:** $62,020

- **Projected employment change, 2012-22:**
  - **Number of new jobs:** 11,000
  - **Growth rate:** 5 percent (slower than average)

- **Education and training:**
  - **Typical entry-level education:** Bachelor's degree
  - **Work experience in a related occupation:** None
  - **Typical on-the-job-training:** Moderate-term on-the-job training

Credit Analysts

(O*NET 13-2041.00)

Analyze credit data and financial statements of individuals or firms to determine the degree of risk involved in extending credit or lending money. Prepare reports with credit information for use in decision-making.

- **2012 employment:** 61,800

- **May 2012 median annual wage:** $61,080

- **Projected employment change, 2012-22:**
  - **Number of new jobs:** 6,400
  - **Growth rate:** 10 percent (about as fast as average)

- **Education and training:**
  - **Typical entry-level education:** Bachelor's degree
  - **Work experience in a related occupation:** None
  - **Typical on-the-job-training:** None

Credit Counselors

(O*NET 13-2071.00 and 13-2071.01)

Advise and educate individuals or organizations on acquiring and managing debt. May provide guidance in determining the best type of loan and may explain loan requirements or restrictions. May help develop debt management plans, advise on credit issues, or provide budget, mortgage, and bankruptcy counseling.

- **2012 employment:** 30,900

- **May 2012 median annual wage:** $39,420

- **Projected employment change, 2012-22:**
  - **Number of new jobs:** 6,400
  - **Growth rate:** 21 percent (faster than average)

- **Education and training:**
  - **Typical entry-level education:** Bachelor's degree
  - **Work experience in a related occupation:** None
  - **Typical on-the-job-training:** Moderate-term on-the-job training

Tax Preparers

(O*NET 13-2082.00)

Prepare tax returns for individuals or small businesses. Excludes "Accountants and Auditors" (13-2011).

- **2012 employment:** 87,600

- **May 2012 median annual wage:** $33,730

- **Projected employment change, 2012-22:**

- **Number of new jobs:** 8,700
- **Growth rate:** 10 percent (about as fast as average)

- **Education and training:**
  - **Typical entry-level education:** High school diploma or equivalent
  - **Work experience in a related occupation:** None
  - **Typical on-the-job-training:** Moderate-term on-the-job training

Community and Social Service Occupations

Clergy

(O*NET 21-2011.00)

Conduct religious worship and perform other spiritual functions associated with beliefs and practices of religious faiths or denominations. Provide spiritual and moral guidance and assistance to members.

- **2012 employment:** 239,600

- **May 2012 median annual wage:** $44,060

- **Projected employment change, 2012-22:**
  - **Number of new jobs:** 23,600
  - **Growth rate:** 10 percent (about as fast as average)

- **Education and training:**
  - **Typical entry-level education:** Bachelor's degree
  - **Work experience in a related occupation:** None
  - **Typical on-the-job-training:** Moderate-term on-the-job training

Directors, Religious Activities and Education

(O*NET 21-2021.00)

Plan, direct, or coordinate programs designed to promote the religious education or activities of a denominational group. May provide counseling and guidance for marital, health, financial, and religious problems.

- **2012 employment:** 134,200

- **May 2012 median annual wage:** $37,280

- **Projected employment change, 2012-22:**
  - **Number of new jobs:** 11,300
  - **Growth rate:** 8 percent (about as fast as average)

- **Education and training:**
  - **Typical entry-level education:** Bachelor's degree
  - **Work experience in a related occupation:** Less than 5 years
  - **Typical on-the-job-training:** None

Construction and Extraction Occupations

First-Line Supervisors of Construction Trades and Extraction Workers

(O*NET 47-1011.00 and 47-1011.03)

Directly supervise and coordinate activities of construction or extraction workers.

- **2012 employment:** 545,500

- **May 2012 median annual wage:** $59,700

- **Projected employment change, 2012-22:**
  - **Number of new jobs:** 128,300

- **Growth rate:** 24 percent (much faster than average)

- **Education and training:**
  - **Typical entry-level education:** High school diploma or equivalent
  - **Work experience in a related occupation:** 5 years or more
  - **Typical on-the-job-training:** None

Carpet Installers

(O*NET 47-2041.00)

Lay and install carpet from rolls or blocks onto floors. Install padding and trim flooring materials. Excludes "Floor Layers, Except Carpet, Wood, and Hard Tiles" (47-2042).

- **2012 employment:** 36,700

- **May 2012 median annual wage:** $36,740

- **Projected employment change, 2012-22:**
  - **Number of new jobs:** 3,200
  - **Growth rate:** 9 percent (about as fast as average)

- **Education and training:**
  - **Typical entry-level education:** Less than high school
  - **Work experience in a related occupation:** None
  - **Typical on-the-job-training:** Short-term on-the-job training

Floor Layers, Except Carpet, Wood, and Hard Tiles

(O*NET 47-2042.00)

Apply blocks, strips, or sheets of shock-absorbing, sound-deadening, or decorative coverings to floors.

- **2012 employment:** 14,500

- **May 2012 median annual wage:** $35,510

- **Projected employment change, 2012-22:**
  - **Number of new jobs:** 1,900
  - **Growth rate:** 13 percent (about as fast as average)

- **Education and training:**
  - **Typical entry-level education:** High school diploma or equivalent
  - **Work experience in a related occupation:** None
  - **Typical on-the-job-training:** Moderate-term on-the-job training

Floor Sanders and Finishers

(O*NET 47-2043.00)

Scrape and sand wooden floors to smooth surfaces, using floor scrapers and floor-sanding machines. May also apply coats of finish.

- **2012 employment:** 6,000

- **May 2012 median annual wage:** $33,240

- **Projected employment change, 2012-22:**
  - **Number of new jobs:** 900
  - **Growth rate:** 15 percent (faster than average)

- **Education and training:**
  - **Typical entry-level education:** High school diploma or equivalent
  - **Work experience in a related occupation:** None
  - **Typical on-the-job-training:** Moderate-term on-the-job training

Paperhangers

(O*NET 47-2142.00)

Cover interior walls or ceilings of rooms with decorative wallpaper or fabric, or attach advertising posters on surfaces such as walls and billboards. May remove old materials or prepare surfaces to be papered.

- **2012 employment:** 3,500

- **May 2012 median annual wage:** $34,600

- **Projected employment change, 2012-22:**
  - **Number of new jobs:** 0
  - **Growth rate:** 0 percent (little or no change)

- **Education and training:**
  - **Typical entry-level education:** High school diploma or equivalent
  - **Work experience in a related occupation:** None
  - **Typical on-the-job-training:** Moderate-term on-the-job training

Pipelayers

(O*NET 47-2151.00)

Lay pipe for storm or sanitation sewers, drains, and water mains. Perform any combination of the following tasks: grade trenches or culverts, position pipes, and seal joints. Excludes "Welders, Cutters, Solderers, and Brazers" (51-4121).

- **2012 employment:** 48,500

- **May 2012 median annual wage:** $36,180

- **Projected employment change, 2012-22:**
  - **Number of new jobs:** 10,100
  - **Growth rate:** 21 percent (faster than average)

- **Education and training:**
  - **Typical entry-level education:** Less than high school
  - **Work experience in a related occupation:** None
  - **Typical on-the-job-training:** Short-term on-the-job training

Plasterers and Stucco Masons

(O*NET 47-2161.00)

Apply interior or exterior plaster, cement, stucco, or similar materials. May also set ornamental plaster.

- **2012 employment:** 22,800

- **May 2012 median annual wage:** $37,130

- **Projected employment change, 2012-22:**
  - **Number of new jobs:** 3,400
  - **Growth rate:** 15 percent (faster than average)

- **Education and training:**
  - **Typical entry-level education:** Less than high school
  - **Work experience in a related occupation:** None
  - **Typical on-the-job-training:** Long-term on-the-job training

Reinforcing Iron and Rebar Workers

(O*NET 47-2171.00)

Position and secure steel bars or mesh in concrete forms in order to reinforce concrete. Use a variety of fasteners, rod-bending machines, blowtorches, and hand tools. Includes rod busters.

- **2012 employment:** 15,500

- **May 2012 median annual wage:** $45,910

- **Projected employment change, 2012-22:**
  - **Number of new jobs:** 3,600
  - **Growth rate:** 23 percent (much faster than average)

- **Education and training:**
  - **Typical entry-level education:** High school diploma or equivalent
  - **Work experience in a related occupation:** None
  - **Typical on-the-job-training:** Apprenticeship

Fence Erectors

(O*NET 47-4031.00)

Erect and repair fences, including gates, using hand and power tools.

- **2012 employment:** 24,900

- **May 2012 median annual wage:** $30,190

- **Projected employment change, 2012-22:**
  - **Number of new jobs:** 7,500
  - **Growth rate:** 30 percent (much faster than average)

- **Education and training:**
  - **Typical entry-level education:** High school diploma or equivalent
  - **Work experience in a related occupation:** None
  - **Typical on-the-job-training:** Moderate-term on-the-job training

Highway Maintenance Workers

(O*NET 47-4051.00)

Maintain highways, municipal and rural roads, airport runways, and rights-of-way. Duties include patching broken or eroded pavement and repairing guard rails, highway markers, and snow fences. Also may mow or clear brush from along roads or plow snow from roadways. Excludes "Tree Trimmers and Pruners" (37-3013).

- **2012 employment:** 147,600

- **May 2012 median annual wage:** $35,260

- **Projected employment change, 2012-22:**
  - **Number of new jobs:** 8,400
  - **Growth rate:** 6 percent (slower than average)

- **Education and training:**
  - **Typical entry-level education:** High school diploma or equivalent
  - **Work experience in a related occupation:** None
  - **Typical on-the-job-training:** Moderate-term on-the-job training

Rail-Track Laying and Maintenance Equipment Operators

(O*NET 47-4061.00)

Lay, repair, and maintain track for standard or narrow-gauge railroad equipment used in regular railroad service or in plant yards, quarries, sand and gravel pits, and mines. Includes ballast cleaning machine operators and railroad bed tamping machine operators.

- **2012 employment:** 17,300

- **May 2012 median annual wage:** $45,920

- **Projected employment change, 2012-22:**
  - **Number of new jobs:** 900
  - **Growth rate:** 5 percent (slower than average)

- **Education and training:**
  - **Typical entry-level education:** High school diploma or equivalent
  - **Work experience in a related occupation:** None
  - **Typical on-the-job-training:** Moderate-term on-the-job training

Septic Tank Servicers and Sewer Pipe Cleaners

(O*NET 47-4071.00)

Clean and repair septic tanks, sewer lines, or drains. May patch walls and partitions of tanks, replace damaged drain tiles, or repair breaks in underground piping.

- **2012 employment:** 25,400

- **May 2012 median annual wage:** $34,020

- **Projected employment change, 2012-22:**
  - **Number of new jobs:** 6,600
  - **Growth rate:** 26 percent (much faster than average)

- **Education and training:**
  - **Typical entry-level education:** Less than high school
  - **Work experience in a related occupation:** None
  - **Typical on-the-job-training:** Moderate-term on-the-job training

Segmental Pavers

(O*NET 47-4091.00)

Lay out, cut, and place segmental paving units. Includes installers of bedding and restraining materials for the paving units.

- **2012 employment:** 1,800

- **May 2012 median annual wage:** $33,720

- **Projected employment change, 2012-22:**
  - **Number of new jobs:** 700
  - **Growth rate:** 38 percent (much faster than average)

- **Education and training:**
  - **Typical entry-level education:** High school diploma or equivalent
  - **Work experience in a related occupation:** None
  - **Typical on-the-job-training:** Moderate-term on-the-job training

Derrick Operators, Oil and Gas

(O*NET 47-5011.00)

Rig derrick equipment and operate pumps to circulate mud through drill hole.

- **2012 employment:** 22,800

- **May 2012 median annual wage:** $46,900

- **Projected employment change, 2012-22:**
  - **Number of new jobs:** 4,300
  - **Growth rate:** 19 percent (faster than average)

- **Education and training:**
  - **Typical entry-level education:** Less than high school
  - **Work experience in a related occupation:** None
  - **Typical on-the-job-training:** Short-term on-the-job training

Rotary Drill Operators, Oil and Gas

(O*NET 47-5012.00)

Set up or operate a variety of drills to remove underground oil and gas, or remove core samples for testing during oil and gas exploration. Excludes "Earth Drillers, Except Oil and Gas" (47-5021).

- **2012 employment:** 26,000

- **May 2012 median annual wage:** $49,220

- **Projected employment change, 2012-22:**
  - **Number of new jobs:** 4,800
  - **Growth rate:** 19 percent (faster than average)

- **Education and training:**
  - **Typical entry-level education:** Less than high school
  - **Work experience in a related occupation:** None
  - **Typical on-the-job-training:** Moderate-term on-the-job training

Service Unit Operators, Oil, Gas, and Mining

(O*NET 47-5013.00)

Operate equipment to increase oil flow from producing wells or to remove stuck pipe, casing, tools, or other obstructions from drilling wells. May also perform similar services in mining exploration operations.

- **2012 employment:** 59,300

- **May 2012 median annual wage:** $41,970

- **Projected employment change, 2012-22:**
  - **Number of new jobs:** 12,400
  - **Growth rate:** 21 percent (faster than average)

- **Education and training:**
  - **Typical entry-level education:** Less than high school
  - **Work experience in a related occupation:** None
  - **Typical on-the-job-training:** Moderate-term on-the-job training

Earth Drillers, Except Oil and Gas

(O*NET 47-5021.00)

Operate a variety of drills, such as rotary, churn, and pneumatic drills, to tap subsurface water and salt deposits, to remove core samples during mineral exploration or soil testing, and to facilitate the use of explosives in mining or construction. May use explosives. Includes horizontal and earth boring machine operators.

- **2012 employment:** 19,700

- **May 2012 median annual wage:** $40,790

- **Projected employment change, 2012-22:**
  - **Number of new jobs:** 3,800
  - **Growth rate:** 19 percent (faster than average)

- **Education and training:**
  - **Typical entry-level education:** High school diploma or equivalent
  - **Work experience in a related occupation:** None
  - **Typical on-the-job-training:** Moderate-term on-the-job training

Explosives Workers, Ordnance Handling Experts, and Blasters

(O*NET 47-5031.00)

Place and detonate explosives to demolish structures or to loosen, remove, or displace earth, rock, or other materials. May perform specialized handling, storage, and accounting procedures. Includes seismograph shooters. Excludes "Earth Drillers, Except Oil and Gas" (47-5021) who also may work with explosives.

- **2012 employment:** 6,500

- **May 2012 median annual wage:** $48,620

- **Projected employment change, 2012-22:**
  - **Number of new jobs:** 300
  - **Growth rate:** 5 percent (slower than average)

- **Education and training:**
  - **Typical entry-level education:** High school diploma or equivalent
  - **Work experience in a related occupation:** Less than 5 years
  - **Typical on-the-job-training:** Long-term on-the-job training

Continuous Mining Machine Operators

(O*NET 47-5041.00)

Operate self-propelled mining machines that rip coal, metal and nonmetal ores, rock, stone, or sand from the mine face and load it onto conveyors or into shuttle cars in a continuous operation.

- **2012 employment:** 14,300

- **May 2012 median annual wage:** $51,950

- **Projected employment change, 2012-22:**
  - **Number of new jobs:** –100

- **Growth rate:** –1 percent (little or no change)

- **Education and training:**
  - **Typical entry-level education:** High school diploma or equivalent
  - **Work experience in a related occupation:** None
  - **Typical on-the-job-training:** Moderate-term on-the-job training

Mine Cutting and Channeling Machine Operators

(O*NET 47-5042.00)

Operate machinery such as longwall shears, plows, and cutting machines to cut or channel along the faces or seams of coal mines, stone quarries, or other mining surfaces in order to facilitate blasting, separating, or removing minerals or materials from mines or the Earth's surface. Includes shale planers.

- **2012 employment:** 7,100

- **May 2012 median annual wage:** $47,950

- **Projected employment change, 2012-22:**
  - **Number of new jobs:** 200
  - **Growth rate:** 3 percent (slower than average)

- **Education and training:**
  - **Typical entry-level education:** High school diploma or equivalent
  - **Work experience in a related occupation:** None
  - **Typical on-the-job-training:** Moderate-term on-the-job training

Rock Splitters, Quarry

(O*NET 47-5051.00)

Separate blocks of rough-dimension stone from quarry mass, using a jackhammer and wedges.

- **2012 employment:** 4,600

- **May 2012 median annual wage:** $32,280

- **Projected employment change, 2012-22:**
  - **Number of new jobs:** 800
  - **Growth rate:** 17 percent (faster than average)

- **Education and training:**
  - **Typical entry-level education:** High school diploma or equivalent
  - **Work experience in a related occupation:** None
  - **Typical on-the-job-training:** Short-term on-the-job training

Roof Bolters, Mining

(O*NET 47-5061.00)

Operate machinery to install roof support bolts in underground mines.

- **2012 employment:** 6,700

- **May 2012 median annual wage:** $54,320

- **Projected employment change, 2012-22:**
  - **Number of new jobs:** -300
  - **Growth rate:** -4 percent (decline)

- **Education and training:**
  - **Typical entry-level education:** High school diploma or equivalent
  - **Work experience in a related occupation:** None
  - **Typical on-the-job-training:** Moderate-term on-the-job training

Roustabouts, Oil and Gas

(O*NET 47-5071.00)

Assemble or repair oil field equipment using hand and power tools. Perform other tasks as needed.

- **2012 employment:** 61,100

- **May 2012 median annual wage:** $34,130

- **Projected employment change, 2012-22:**
  - **Number of new jobs:** 11,700
  - **Growth rate:** 19 percent (faster than average)

- **Education and training:**
  - **Typical entry-level education:** Less than high school
  - **Work experience in a related occupation:** None
  - **Typical on-the-job-training:** Moderate-term on-the-job training

Helpers—Extraction Workers

(O*NET 47-5081.00)

Help extraction craftworkers, such as earth drillers, blasters and explosives workers, derrick operators, and mining machine operators, by performing duties requiring less skill. Duties include supplying equipment or cleaning work areas. Apprentices are classified with the appropriate skilled construction trade occupation (47-2011 through 47-2231).

- **2012 employment:** 26,400

- **May 2012 median annual wage:** $31,460

- **Projected employment change, 2012-22:**
  - **Number of new jobs:** 4,400
  - **Growth rate:** 17 percent (faster than average)

- **Education and training:**
  - **Typical entry-level education:** High school diploma or equivalent
  - **Work experience in a related occupation:** None
  - **Typical on-the-job-training:** Moderate-term on-the-job training

Education Occupations

Graduate Teaching Assistants

(O*NET 25-1191.00)

Assist faculty or other instructional staff in postsecondary institutions by performing teaching or teaching-related duties, such as teaching lower level courses, developing teaching materials, preparing and giving examinations, and grading examinations or papers. Excludes "Teacher Assistants" (25-9041).

- **2012 employment:** 150,300

- **May 2012 median annual wage:** $31,270

- **Projected employment change, 2012-22:**
  - **Number of new jobs:** 15,500
  - **Growth rate:** 10 percent (about as fast as average)

- **Education and training:**
  - **Typical entry-level education:** Bachelor's degree
  - **Work experience in a related occupation:** None
  - **Typical on-the-job-training:** None

Home Economics Teachers, Postsecondary

(O*NET 25-1192.00)

Teach courses in childcare, family relations, finance, nutrition, and related subjects pertaining to home management. Includes both teachers engaged primarily in teaching and those who do a combination of teaching and research.

- **2012 employment:** 5,600

- **May 2012 median annual wage:** $64,040

- **Projected employment change, 2012-22:**
  - **Number of new jobs:** 500

- **Growth rate:** 10 percent (about as fast as average)

- **Education and training:**
  - **Typical entry-level education:** Master's degree
  - **Work experience in a related occupation:** None
  - **Typical on-the-job-training:** None

Recreation and Fitness Studies Teachers, Postsecondary

(O*NET 25-1193.00)

Teach courses pertaining to recreation, leisure, and fitness studies, including exercise physiology and facilities management. Includes both teachers engaged primarily in teaching and those who do a combination of teaching and research.

- **2012 employment:** 23,000

- **May 2012 median annual wage:** $57,920

- **Projected employment change, 2012-22:**
  - **Number of new jobs:** 2,800
  - **Growth rate:** 12 percent (about as fast as average)

- **Education and training:**
  - **Typical entry-level education:** Doctoral or professional degree
  - **Work experience in a related occupation:** None
  - **Typical on-the-job-training:** None

Self-Enrichment Education Teachers

(O*NET 25-3021.00)

Teach or instruct courses other than those which normally lead to an occupational objective or degree. Courses may include self-improvement, nonvocational, and nonacademic subjects. Teaching may or may not take place in a traditional educational institution. Excludes "Fitness Trainers and Aerobics Instructors" (39-9031). Flight instructors are included with "Aircraft Pilots and Flight Engineers" (53-2010).

- **2012 employment:** 316,200

- **May 2012 median annual wage:** $35,320

- **Projected employment change, 2012-22:**
  - **Number of new jobs:** 43,900
  - **Growth rate:** 14 percent (about as fast as average)

- **Education and training:**
  - **Typical entry-level education:** High school diploma or equivalent
  - **Work experience in a related occupation:** Less than 5 years
  - **Typical on-the-job-training:** None

Audio Visual and Multimedia Collections Specialists

(O*NET 25-9011.00)

Prepare, plan, and operate multimedia teaching aids for use in education. May record, catalog, and file materials.

- **2012 employment:** 9,700

- **May 2012 median annual wage:** $43,350

- **Projected employment change, 2012-22:**
  - **Number of new jobs:** –100
  - **Growth rate:** –1 percent (little or no change)

- **Education and training:**
  - **Typical entry-level education:** Bachelor's degree
  - **Work experience in a related occupation:** Less than 5 years
  - **Typical on-the-job-training:** None

Farm and Home Management Advisors

(O*NET 25-9021.00)

Advise, instruct, and assist individuals and families engaged in agriculture, agriculture-related processes, or home economics activities. Demonstrate procedures and apply research findings to solve problems; and instruct and train in product development, sales, and the use of machinery and equipment to promote general welfare. Includes county agricultural agents, feed and farm management advisors, home economists, and extension service advisors.

- **2012 employment:** 13,700

- **May 2012 median annual wage:** $46,760

- **Projected employment change, 2012-22:**
  - **Number of new jobs:** 1,300
  - **Growth rate:** 10 percent (about as fast as average)

- **Education and training:**
  - **Typical entry-level education:** Master's degree
  - **Work experience in a related occupation:** None
  - **Typical on-the-job-training:** None

Farming, Fishing, and Forestry Occupations

First-Line Supervisors of Farming, Fishing, and Forestry Workers

(O*NET 45-1011.00, 45-1011.05, 45-1011.06, 45-1011.07, and 45-1011.08)

Directly supervise and coordinate the activities of agricultural, forestry, aquacultural, and related workers. Excludes "First-Line Supervisors of Landscaping, Lawn Service, and Groundskeeping Workers" (37-1012).

- **2012 employment:** 45,900

- **May 2012 median annual wage:** $43,660

- **Projected employment change, 2012-22:**
  - **Number of new jobs:** –1,100
  - **Growth rate:** –2 percent (little or no change)

- **Education and training:**
  - **Typical entry-level education:** High school diploma or equivalent
  - **Work experience in a related occupation:** Less than 5 years
  - **Typical on-the-job-training:** None

Agricultural Inspectors

(O*NET 45-2011.00)

Inspect agricultural commodities, processing equipment and facilities, and fish and logging operations in order to ensure compliance with regulations and laws governing health, quality, and safety.

- **2012 employment:** 17,000

- **May 2012 median annual wage:** $42,160

- **Projected employment change, 2012-22:**
  - **Number of new jobs:** –200
  - **Growth rate:** –1 percent (little or no change)

- **Education and training:**
  - **Typical entry-level education:** Bachelor's degree
  - **Work experience in a related occupation:** None
  - **Typical on-the-job-training:** Moderate-term on-the-job training

Graders and Sorters, Agricultural Products

(O*NET 45-2041.00)

Grade, sort, or classify unprocessed food and other agricultural products by size, weight, color, or condition. Excludes "Agricultural Inspectors" (45-2011).

- **2012 employment:** 49,200

- **May 2012 median annual wage:** $19,150

- **Projected employment change, 2012-22:**
  - **Number of new jobs:** –1,000
  - **Growth rate:** –2 percent (little or no change)

- **Education and training:**
  - **Typical entry-level education:** Less than high school
  - **Work experience in a related occupation:** None
  - **Typical on-the-job-training:** Short-term on-the-job training

Food Preparation and Serving Occupations

First-Line Supervisors of Food Preparation and Serving Workers

(O*NET 35-1012.00)

Directly supervise and coordinate activities of workers who prepare and serve food.

- **2012 employment:** 848,500

- **May 2012 median annual wage:** $29,270

- **Projected employment change, 2012-22:**
  - **Number of new jobs:** 109,400
  - **Growth rate:** 13 percent (about as fast as average)

- **Education and training:**
  - **Typical entry-level education:** High school diploma or equivalent
  - **Work experience in a related occupation:** Less than 5 years
  - **Typical on-the-job-training:** None

Dishwashers

(O*NET 35-9021.00)

Clean dishes, utensils, kitchens, and food preparation equipment.

- **2012 employment:** 508,500

- **May 2012 median annual wage:** $18,460

- **Projected employment change, 2012-22:**
  - **Number of new jobs:** 31,700
  - **Growth rate:** 6 percent (slower than average)

- **Education and training:**
  - **Typical entry-level education:** Less than high school
  - **Work experience in a related occupation:** None
  - **Typical on-the-job-training:** Short-term on-the-job training

Healthcare Occupations

Dietetic Technicians

(O*NET 29-2051.00)

Assist in the provision of food service and nutritional programs under the supervision of a dietitian. May plan and produce meals based on established guidelines, teach principles of food and nutrition, or counsel individuals.

- **2012 employment:** 25,100
- **May 2012 median annual wage:** $26,260
- **Projected employment change, 2012-22:**
  - **Number of new jobs:** 4,500
  - **Growth rate:** 18 percent (faster than average)
- **Education and training:**
  - **Typical entry-level education:** Associate's degree
  - **Work experience in a related occupation:** None
  - **Typical on-the-job-training:** None

Respiratory Therapy Technicians

(O*NET 29-2054.00)

Provide respiratory care under the direction of respiratory therapists and physicians.

- **2012 employment:** 13,600
- **May 2012 median annual wage:** $46,760
- **Projected employment change, 2012-22:**
  - **Number of new jobs:** 2,300
  - **Growth rate:** 17 percent (faster than average)
- **Education and training:**
  - **Typical entry-level education:** Associate's degree
  - **Work experience in a related occupation:** None
  - **Typical on-the-job-training:** Moderate-term on-the-job training

Ophthalmic Medical Technicians

(O*NET 29-2057.00)

Assist ophthalmologists by performing ophthalmic clinical functions. May administer eye exams, administer eye medications, and instruct the patient in the care and use of corrective lenses.

- **2012 employment:** 29,600
- **May 2012 median annual wage:** $34,240
- **Projected employment change, 2012-22:**
  - **Number of new jobs:** 8,800
  - **Growth rate:** 30 percent (much faster than average)
- **Education and training:**
  - **Typical entry-level education:** Postsecondary nondegree award
  - **Work experience in a related occupation:** None
  - **Typical on-the-job-training:** None

Hearing Aid Specialists

(O*NET 29-2092.00)

Select and fit hearing aids for customers. Administer and interpret tests of hearing. Assess hearing instrument efficacy. Take ear impressions and prepare, design, and modify ear molds. Excludes "Audiologists" (29-1181).

- **2012 employment:** 5,300
- **May 2012 median annual wage:** $41,430
- **Projected employment change, 2012-22:**
  - **Number of new jobs:** 1,300
  - **Growth rate:** 25 percent (much faster than average)
- **Education and training:**
  - **Typical entry-level education:** High school diploma or equivalent
  - **Work experience in a related occupation:** None
  - **Typical on-the-job-training:** None

Medical Equipment Preparers

(O*NET 31-9093.00)

Prepare, sterilize, install, or clean laboratory or healthcare equipment. May perform routine laboratory tasks and operate or inspect equipment.

- **2012 employment:** 51,600
- **May 2012 median annual wage:** $30,820
- **Projected employment change, 2012-22:**
  - **Number of new jobs:** 10,400
  - **Growth rate:** 20 percent (faster than average)
- **Education and training:**
  - **Typical entry-level education:** High school diploma or equivalent
  - **Work experience in a related occupation:** None
  - **Typical on-the-job-training:** Moderate-term on-the-job training

Pharmacy Aides

(O*NET 31-9095.00)

Record drugs delivered to the pharmacy, store incoming merchandise, and inform the supervisor of stock needs. May operate the cash register and accept prescriptions for filling.

- **2012 employment:** 42,900
- **May 2012 median annual wage:** $21,860
- **Projected employment change, 2012-22:**
  - **Number of new jobs:** 4,800
  - **Growth rate:** 11 percent (about as fast as average)
- **Education and training:**
  - **Typical entry-level education:** High school diploma or equivalent
  - **Work experience in a related occupation:** None
  - **Typical on-the-job-training:** Short-term on-the-job training

Installation, Maintenance, and Repair Occupations

First-Line Supervisors of Mechanics, Installers, and Repairers

(O*NET 49-1011.00)

Directly supervise and coordinate the activities of mechanics, installers, and repairers. Excludes team or work leaders.

- **2012 employment:** 436,400
- **May 2012 median annual wage:** $60,250
- **Projected employment change, 2012-22:**
  - **Number of new jobs:** 33,900
  - **Growth rate:** 8 percent (about as fast as average)
- **Education and training:**
  - **Typical entry-level education:** High school diploma or equivalent
  - **Work experience in a related occupation:** Less than 5 years
  - **Typical on-the-job-training:** None

Radio, Cellular, and Tower Equipment Installers and Repairs

(O*NET 49-2021.00 and 49-2021.01)

Repair, install, or maintain mobile or stationary radio transmitting, broadcasting, and receiving equipment; two-way radio communications systems used in cellular telecommunications, mobile broadband, ship-to-shore, and aircraft-to-ground communications; and radio equipment in service and emergency vehicles. May test and analyze network coverage.

- **2012 employment:** 16,400

- **May 2012 median annual wage:** $43,900

- **Projected employment change, 2012-22:**
  - **Number of new jobs:** 1,100
  - **Growth rate:** 7 percent (slower than average)

- **Education and training:**
  - **Typical entry-level education:** Associate's degree
  - **Work experience in a related occupation:** None
  - **Typical on-the-job-training:** Moderate-term on-the-job training

Electronic Home Entertainment Equipment Installers and Repairers

(O*NET 49-2097.00)

Repair, adjust, or install audio or television receivers, stereo systems, camcorders, video systems, or other electronic home entertainment equipment.

- **2012 employment:** 31,300

- **May 2012 median annual wage:** $35,060

- **Projected employment change, 2012-22:**
  - **Number of new jobs:** 400
  - **Growth rate:** 1 percent (little or no change)

- **Education and training:**
  - **Typical entry-level education:** Postsecondary nondegree award
  - **Work experience in a related occupation:** None
  - **Typical on-the-job-training:** None

Security and Fire Alarm Systems Installers

(O*NET 49-2098.00)

Install, program, maintain, and repair security and fire alarm wiring and equipment. Ensure that work is in accordance with relevant codes. Excludes "Electricians" (47-2111) who do a broad range of electrical wiring.

- **2012 employment:** 58,000

- **May 2012 median annual wage:** $41,030

- **Projected employment change, 2012-22:**
  - **Number of new jobs:** 9,200
  - **Growth rate:** 16 percent (faster than average)

- **Education and training:**
  - **Typical entry-level education:** High school diploma or equivalent
  - **Work experience in a related occupation:** None
  - **Typical on-the-job-training:** Moderate-term on-the-job training

Bicycle Repairers

(O*NET 49-3091.00)

Repair and service bicycles.

- **2012 employment:** 10,600

- **May 2012 median annual wage:** $24,150

- **Projected employment change, 2012-22:**
  - **Number of new jobs:** 2,700
  - **Growth rate:** 25 percent (much faster than average)

- **Education and training:**
  - **Typical entry-level education:** High school diploma or equivalent

- **Work experience in a related occupation:** None
- **Typical on-the-job-training:** Moderate-term on-the-job training

Recreational Vehicle Service Technicians

(O*NET 49-3092.00)

Diagnose, inspect, adjust, repair, or overhaul recreational vehicles, including travel trailers. May specialize in maintaining gas, electrical, hydraulic, plumbing, or chassis/towing systems, as well as in repairing generators, appliances, and interior components. Includes workers who perform customized van conversions. Excludes "Automotive Service Technicians and Mechanics" (49-3023) and "Bus and Truck Mechanics and Diesel Engine Specialists" (49-3031), who also work on recreation vehicles.

- **2012 employment:** 11,100

- **May 2012 median annual wage:** $34,540

- **Projected employment change, 2012-22:**
  - **Number of new jobs:** 1,000
  - **Growth rate:** 9 percent (about as fast as average)

- **Education and training:**
  - **Typical entry-level education:** High school diploma or equivalent
  - **Work experience in a related occupation:** None
  - **Typical on-the-job-training:** Long-term on-the-job training

Tire Repairers and Changers

(O*NET 49-3093.00)

Repair and replace tires.

- **2012 employment:** 98,400

- **May 2012 median annual wage:** $23,410

- **Projected employment change, 2012-22:**
  - **Number of new jobs:** 8,600
  - **Growth rate:** 9 percent (about as fast as average)

- **Education and training:**
  - **Typical entry-level education:** High school diploma or equivalent
  - **Work experience in a related occupation:** None
  - **Typical on-the-job-training:** Short-term on-the-job training

Mechanical Door Repairers

(O*NET 49-9011.00)

Install, service, or repair automatic door mechanisms and hydraulic doors. Includes garage door mechanics.

- **2012 employment:** 15,800

- **May 2012 median annual wage:** $36,110

- **Projected employment change, 2012-22:**
  - **Number of new jobs:** 3,800
  - **Growth rate:** 24 percent (much faster than average)

- **Education and training:**
  - **Typical entry-level education:** High school diploma or equivalent
  - **Work experience in a related occupation:** None
  - **Typical on-the-job-training:** Moderate-term on-the-job training

Control and Valve Installers and Repairers, Except Mechanical Door

(O*NET 49-9012.00)

Install, repair, and maintain mechanical regulating and controlling devices, such as electric meters, gas regulators, thermostats, safety and flow valves, and other mechanical governors.

- **2012 employment:** 41,000
- **May 2012 median annual wage:** $50,960
- **Projected employment change, 2012-22:**
  - **Number of new jobs:** -200
  - **Growth rate:** 0 percent (little or no change)
- **Education and training:**
  - **Typical entry-level education:** High school diploma or equivalent
  - **Work experience in a related occupation:** None
  - **Typical on-the-job-training:** Moderate-term on-the-job training

Home Appliance Repairers

(O*NET 49-9031.00)

Repair, adjust, or install all types of electric or gas household appliances, such as refrigerators, washers, dryers, and ovens.

- **2012 employment:** 43,700
- **May 2012 median annual wage:** $35,170
- **Projected employment change, 2012-22:**
  - **Number of new jobs:** 300
  - **Growth rate:** 1 percent (little or no change)
- **Education and training:**
  - **Typical entry-level education:** High school diploma or equivalent
  - **Work experience in a related occupation:** None
  - **Typical on-the-job-training:** Moderate-term on-the-job training

Refractory Materials Repairers, Except Brickmasons

(O*NET 49-9045.00)

Build or repair equipment, such as furnaces, kilns, cupolas, boilers, converters, ladles, soaking pits, and ovens, using refractory materials.

- **2012 employment:** 2,100
- **May 2012 median annual wage:** $41,370
- **Projected employment change, 2012-22:**
  - **Number of new jobs:** 0
  - **Growth rate:** 0 percent (little or no change)
- **Education and training:**
  - **Typical entry-level education:** High school diploma or equivalent
  - **Work experience in a related occupation:** None
  - **Typical on-the-job-training:** Moderate-term on-the-job training

Camera and Photographic Equipment Repairers

(O*NET 49-9061.00)

Repair and adjust cameras and photographic equipment, including commercial video and motion picture camera equipment.

- **2012 employment:** 3,100
- **May 2012 median annual wage:** $37,980
- **Projected employment change, 2012-22:**
  - **Number of new jobs:** 100
  - **Growth rate:** 3 percent (slower than average)
- **Education and training:**
  - **Typical entry-level education:** Associate's degree
  - **Work experience in a related occupation:** None
  - **Typical on-the-job-training:** Long-term on-the-job training

Musical Instrument Repairers and Tuners

(O*NET 49-9063.00)

Repair percussion, stringed, reed, or wind instruments. May specialize in one area, such as piano tuning. Excludes "Electronic Home Entertainment Equipment Installers and Repairers" (49-2097), who repair electrical and electronic musical instruments.

- **2012 employment:** 8,200
- **May 2012 median annual wage:** $30,630
- **Projected employment change, 2012-22:**
  - **Number of new jobs:** 500
  - **Growth rate:** 6 percent (slower than average)
- **Education and training:**
  - **Typical entry-level education:** High school diploma or equivalent
  - **Work experience in a related occupation:** None
  - **Typical on-the-job-training:** Apprenticeship

Watch Repairers

(O*NET 49-9064.00)

Repair, clean, and adjust mechanisms of timing instruments, such as watches and clocks. Includes watchmakers, watch technicians, and mechanical timepiece repairers.

- **2012 employment:** 3,200
- **May 2012 median annual wage:** $37,650
- **Projected employment change, 2012-22:**
  - **Number of new jobs:** 100
  - **Growth rate:** 2 percent (little or no change)
- **Education and training:**
  - **Typical entry-level education:** High school diploma or equivalent
  - **Work experience in a related occupation:** None
  - **Typical on-the-job-training:** Long-term on-the-job training

Coin, Vending, and Amusement Machine Servicers and Repairers

(O*NET 49-9091.00)

Install, service, adjust, or repair coin, vending, or amusement machines, including video games, jukeboxes, pinball machines, or slot machines.

- **2012 employment:** 40,900
- **May 2012 median annual wage:** $31,150
- **Projected employment change, 2012-22:**
  - **Number of new jobs:** -900
  - **Growth rate:** -2 percent (little or no change)
- **Education and training:**
  - **Typical entry-level education:** High school diploma or equivalent
  - **Work experience in a related occupation:** None
  - **Typical on-the-job-training:** Short-term on-the-job training

Commercial Divers

(O*NET 49-9092.00)

Work below the surface of waters, using scuba gear to inspect, repair, remove, or install equipment and structures. May use a variety of power and hand tools, such as drills, sledge hammers, torches, and welding equipment. May conduct tests or experiments, rig explosives, or photograph structures or marine life. Excludes "Fishers and Related Fishing Workers" (45-3011), "Athletes and Sports Competitors" (27-2021), and "Police and Sheriff's Patrol Officers" (33-3051).

- **2012 employment:** 3,600

- **May 2012 median annual wage:** $46,880

- **Projected employment change, 2012-22:**
  - **Number of new jobs:** 1,100
  - **Growth rate:** 29 percent (much faster than average)

- **Education and training:**
  - **Typical entry-level education:** Postsecondary nondegree award
  - **Work experience in a related occupation:** None
  - **Typical on-the-job-training:** Moderate-term on-the-job training

Fabric Menders, Except Garment

(O*NET 49-9093.00)

Repair tears, holes, and other defects in fabrics, such as draperies, linens, parachutes, and tents.

- **2012 employment:** 1,000

- **May 2012 median annual wage:** $27,020

- **Projected employment change, 2012-22:**
  - **Number of new jobs:** –100
  - **Growth rate:** –10 percent (decline)

- **Education and training:**
  - **Typical entry-level education:** Less than high school
  - **Work experience in a related occupation:** None
  - **Typical on-the-job-training:** Long-term on-the-job training

Locksmiths and Safe Repairers

(O*NET 49-9094.00)

Repair and open locks, make keys, change locks and safe combinations, and install and repair safes.

- **2012 employment:** 22,300

- **May 2012 median annual wage:** $37,560

- **Projected employment change, 2012-22:**
  - **Number of new jobs:** 1,600
  - **Growth rate:** 7 percent (slower than average)

- **Education and training:**
  - **Typical entry-level education:** High school diploma or equivalent
  - **Work experience in a related occupation:** None
  - **Typical on-the-job-training:** Long-term on-the-job training

Manufactured Building and Mobile Home Installers

(O*NET 49-9095.00)

Move or install mobile homes or prefabricated buildings.

- **2012 employment:** 5,300

- **May 2012 median annual wage:** $28,080

- **Projected employment change, 2012-22:**
  - **Number of new jobs:** -800
  - **Growth rate:** –15 percent (decline)

- **Education and training:**
  - **Typical entry-level education:** High school diploma or equivalent
  - **Work experience in a related occupation:** None
  - **Typical on-the-job-training:** Moderate-term on-the-job training

Riggers

(O*NET 49-9096.00)

Set up or repair rigging for construction projects, manufacturing plants, logging yards, ships and shipyards, or the entertainment industry.

- **2012 employment:** 15,200

- **May 2012 median annual wage:** $42,660

- **Projected employment change, 2012-22:**
  - **Number of new jobs:** 3,500
  - **Growth rate:** 23 percent (much faster than average)

- **Education and training:**
  - **Typical entry-level education:** High school diploma or equivalent
  - **Work experience in a related occupation:** None
  - **Typical on-the-job-training:** Short-term on-the-job training

Signal and Track Switch Repairers

(O*NET 49-9097.00)

Install, inspect, test, maintain, or repair electric gate crossings, signals, signal equipment, track switches, section lines, or intercommunications systems within a railroad system.

- **2012 employment:** 8,800

- **May 2012 median annual wage:** $55,450

- **Projected employment change, 2012-22:**
  - **Number of new jobs:** –100
  - **Growth rate:** –1 percent (little or no change)

- **Education and training:**
  - **Typical entry-level education:** High school diploma or equivalent
  - **Work experience in a related occupation:** None
  - **Typical on-the-job-training:** Moderate-term on-the-job training

Helpers—Installation, Maintenance, and Repair Workers

(O*NET 49-9098.00)

Help installation, maintenance, and repair workers replace parts and maintain and repair vehicles, industrial machinery, and electrical and electronic equipment. Perform duties such as furnishing tools, materials, and supplies to other workers; cleaning work areas, machines, and tools; and holding materials or tools for other workers.

- **2012 employment:** 127,500

- **May 2012 median annual wage:** $24,210

- **Projected employment change, 2012-22:**
  - **Number of new jobs:** 17,500
  - **Growth rate:** 14 percent (about as fast as average)

- **Education and training:**
  - **Typical entry-level education:** High school diploma or equivalent
  - **Work experience in a related occupation:** None
  - **Typical on-the-job-training:** Moderate-term on-the-job training

Legal Occupations

Judicial Law Clerks

(O*NET 23-1012.00)

Assist judges in court or by conducting research or preparing legal documents. Excludes "Lawyers" (23-1011) and "Paralegals and Legal Assistants" (23-2011).

- **2012 employment:** 12,100

- **May 2012 median annual wage:** $47,120

- **Projected employment change, 2012-22:**
  - **Number of new jobs:** 500

- **Growth rate:** 4 percent (slower than average)
- **Education and training:**
  - **Typical entry-level education:** Doctoral or professional degree
  - **Work experience in a related occupation:** None
  - **Typical on-the-job-training:** None

Title Examiners, Abstractors, and Searchers

(O*NET 23-2093.00)

Search real estate records, examine titles, or summarize pertinent legal or insurance documents. May compile lists of mortgages, contracts, and other instruments pertaining to titles by searching public and private records for law firms, real estate agencies, or title insurance companies.

- **2012 employment:** 67,900
- **May 2012 median annual wage:** $41,970
- **Projected employment change, 2012-22:**
  - **Number of new jobs:** 6,200
  - **Growth rate:** 9 percent (about as fast as average)
- **Education and training:**
  - **Typical entry-level education:** High school diploma or equivalent
  - **Work experience in a related occupation:** None
  - **Typical on-the-job-training:** Short-term on-the-job training

Life, Physical, and Social Science Occupations

Social Science Research Assistants

(O*NET 19-4061.00 and 19-4061.01)

Assist social scientists in laboratory, survey, and other research. May help prepare findings for publication and assist in laboratory analysis, quality control, or data management. Excludes "Graduate Teaching Assistants" (25-1191).

- **2012 employment:** 29,600
- **May 2012 median annual wage:** $37,140
- **Projected employment change, 2012-22:**
  - **Number of new jobs:** 4,400
  - **Growth rate:** 15 percent (faster than average)
- **Education and training:**
  - **Typical entry-level education:** Associate's degree
  - **Work experience in a related occupation:** None
  - **Typical on-the-job-training:** None

Management Occupations

Legislators

(O*NET 11-1031.00)

Develop, introduce, or enact laws and statutes at the local, tribal, state, or federal level. Includes only workers in elected positions.

- **2012 employment:** 58,400
- **May 2012 median annual wage:** $19,780
- **Projected employment change, 2012-22:**
  - **Number of new jobs:** 3,700
  - **Growth rate:** 6 percent (slower than average)
- **Education and training:**
  - **Typical entry-level education:** Bachelor's degree

- **Work experience in a related occupation:** Less than 5 years
- **Typical on-the-job-training:** None

Transportation, Storage, and Distribution Managers

(O*NET 11-3071.00, 11-3071.01, 11-3071.02, and 11-3071.03)

Plan, direct, or coordinate transportation, storage, or distribution activities in accordance with organizational policies and applicable government laws or regulations. Includes logistics managers.

- **2012 employment:** 105,200
- **May 2012 median annual wage:** $81,830
- **Projected employment change, 2012-22:**
  - **Number of new jobs:** 5,100
  - **Growth rate:** 5 percent (slower than average)
- **Education and training:**
  - **Typical entry-level education:** High school diploma or equivalent
  - **Work experience in a related occupation:** 5 years or more
  - **Typical on-the-job-training:** None

Postmasters and Mail Superintendents

(O*NET 11-9131.00)

Plan, direct, or coordinate operational, administrative, management, and supportive services of a U.S. post office. Also coordinate activities of workers engaged in postal and related work in assigned post office.

- **2012 employment:** 23,000
- **May 2012 median annual wage:** $63,050
- **Projected employment change, 2012-22:**
  - **Number of new jobs:** –5,600
  - **Growth rate:** –24 percent (decline)
- **Education and training:**
  - **Typical entry-level education:** High school diploma or equivalent
  - **Work experience in a related occupation:** Less than 5 years
  - **Typical on-the-job-training:** Moderate-term on-the-job training

Math Occupations

Mathematical Technicians

(O*NET 15-2091.00)

Apply standardized mathematical formulas, principles, and methodology to technological problems in engineering and physical sciences in relation to specific industrial and research objectives, processes, equipment, and products.

- **2012 employment:** 1,900
- **May 2012 median annual wage:** $56,820
- **Projected employment change, 2012-22:**
  - **Number of new jobs:** 200
  - **Growth rate:** 13 percent (about as fast as average)
- **Education and training:**
  - **Typical entry-level education:** Bachelor's degree
  - **Work experience in a related occupation:** None
  - **Typical on-the-job-training:** None

Media and Communication Occupations

Radio Operators

(O*NET 27-4013.00)

Receive and transmit communications, using radiotelephone equipment in accordance with government regulations. May repair equipment. Excludes "Radio, Cellular, and Tower Equipment Installers and Repairers" (49-2021).

- **2012 employment:** 1,400
- **May 2012 median annual wage:** $42,080
- **Projected employment change, 2012-22:**
  - **Number of new jobs:** 0
  - **Growth rate:** 1 percent (little or no change)
- **Education and training:**
  - **Typical entry-level education:** High school diploma or equivalent
  - **Work experience in a related occupation:** None
  - **Typical on-the-job-training:** Short-term on-the-job training

Office and Administrative Support Occupations

First-Line Supervisors of Office and Administrative Support Workers

(O*NET 43-1011.00)

Directly supervise and coordinate the activities of clerical and administrative support workers.

- **2012 employment:** 1,418,100
- **May 2012 median annual wage:** $49,330
- **Projected employment change, 2012-22:**
  - **Number of new jobs:** 171,500
  - **Growth rate:** 12 percent (about as fast as average)
- **Education and training:**
  - **Typical entry-level education:** High school diploma or equivalent
  - **Work experience in a related occupation:** Less than 5 years
  - **Typical on-the-job-training:** None

Switchboard Operators, Including Answering Service

(O*NET 43-2011.00)

Operate telephone business systems equipment or switchboards to relay incoming, outgoing, and interoffice calls. May supply information to callers and record messages.

- **2012 employment:** 131,000
- **May 2012 median annual wage:** $25,370
- **Projected employment change, 2012-22:**
  - **Number of new jobs:** –17,300
  - **Growth rate:** –13 percent (decline)
- **Education and training:**
  - **Typical entry-level education:** High school diploma or equivalent
  - **Work experience in a related occupation:** None
  - **Typical on-the-job-training:** Short-term on-the-job training

Telephone Operators

(O*NET 43-2021.00)

Provide information by accessing alphabetical, geographical, or other directories. Assist customers with special billing requests, such as charges to a third party and credits or refunds for incorrectly dialed numbers or bad connections. May handle emergency calls and assist children or people who have physical disabilities with making telephone calls.

- **2012 employment:** 11,100
- **May 2012 median annual wage:** $32,850
- **Projected employment change, 2012-22:**
  - **Number of new jobs:** –1,400
  - **Growth rate:** –13 percent (decline)
- **Education and training:**
  - **Typical entry-level education:** High school diploma or equivalent
  - **Work experience in a related occupation:** None
  - **Typical on-the-job-training:** Short-term on-the-job training

Cargo and Freight Agents

(O*NET 43-5011.00)

Expedite and route movement of incoming and outgoing cargo and freight shipments in airline, train, and trucking terminals and shipping docks. Take orders from customers and arrange pickup of freight and cargo for delivery to loading platform. Prepare and examine bills of lading to determine shipping charges and tariffs.

- **2012 employment:** 79,500
- **May 2012 median annual wage:** $39,720
- **Projected employment change, 2012-22:**
  - **Number of new jobs:** 11,500
  - **Growth rate:** 14 percent (about as fast as average)
- **Education and training:**
  - **Typical entry-level education:** High school diploma or equivalent
  - **Work experience in a related occupation:** None
  - **Typical on-the-job-training:** Short-term on-the-job training

Couriers and Messengers

(O*NET 43-5021.00)

Pick up and deliver messages, documents, packages, and other items between offices or departments within an establishment or directly to other business concerns, traveling by foot, bicycle, motorcycle, automobile, or public conveyance. Excludes "Light Truck or Delivery Services Drivers" (53-3033).

- **2012 employment:** 98,200
- **May 2012 median annual wage:** $25,440
- **Projected employment change, 2012-22:**
  - **Number of new jobs:** –10,900
  - **Growth rate:** –11 percent (decline)
- **Education and training:**
  - **Typical entry-level education:** High school diploma or equivalent
  - **Work experience in a related occupation:** None
  - **Typical on-the-job-training:** Short-term on-the-job training

Dispatchers, Except Police, Fire, and Ambulance

(O*NET 43-5032.00)

Schedule and dispatch workers, work crews, equipment, or service vehicles for the conveyance of materials, freight, or passengers or for normal installation, service, or emergency repairs rendered outside the place of business. Duties may include using a radio, telephone, or computer to transmit assignments and compiling statistics and reports on work progress.

- **2012 employment:** 190,900

- **May 2012 median annual wage:** $35,690

- **Projected employment change, 2012-22:**
  - **Number of new jobs:** 21,400
  - **Growth rate:** 11 percent (about as fast as average)

- **Education and training:**
  - **Typical entry-level education:** High school diploma or equivalent
  - **Work experience in a related occupation:** None
  - **Typical on-the-job-training:** Moderate-term on-the-job training

Meter Readers, Utilities

(O*NET 43-5041.00)

Read meters and record the consumption of electricity, gas, water, or steam.

- **2012 employment:** 40,200

- **May 2012 median annual wage:** $35,940

- **Projected employment change, 2012-22:**
  - **Number of new jobs:** –7,700
  - **Growth rate:** –19 percent (decline)

- **Education and training:**
  - **Typical entry-level education:** High school diploma or equivalent
  - **Work experience in a related occupation:** None
  - **Typical on-the-job-training:** Short-term on-the-job training

Computer Operators

(O*NET 43-9011.00)

Monitor and control electronic computer and peripheral electronic data-processing equipment to process business, scientific, engineering, and other data according to operating instructions. Monitor and respond to operating and error messages. May enter commands at a computer terminal and set controls on the computer and peripheral devices. Excludes "Computer Occupations" (15-1100) and "Data Entry Keyers" (43-9021).

- **2012 employment:** 74,600

- **May 2012 median annual wage:** $38,390

- **Projected employment change, 2012-22:**
  - **Number of new jobs:** –12,700
  - **Growth rate:** –17 percent (decline)

- **Education and training:**
  - **Typical entry-level education:** High school diploma or equivalent
  - **Work experience in a related occupation:** None
  - **Typical on-the-job-training:** Moderate-term on-the-job training

Data Entry Keyers

(O*NET 43-9021.00)

Operate a data entry device, such as a keyboard or photocomposing perforator. Duties may include verifying data and preparing materials for printing. Excludes "Word Processors and Typists" (43-9022).

- **2012 employment:** 220,300

- **May 2012 median annual wage:** $28,010

- **Projected employment change, 2012-22:**
  - **Number of new jobs:** –54,200

- **Growth rate:** –25 percent (decline)

- **Education and training:**
  - **Typical entry-level education:** High school diploma or equivalent
  - **Work experience in a related occupation:** None
  - **Typical on-the-job-training:** Moderate-term on-the-job training

Word Processors and Typists

(O*NET 43-9022.00)

Use a word processor, computer, or typewriter to type letters, reports, forms, or other material from rough draft, corrected copy, or voice recordings. May perform other clerical duties as assigned. Excludes "Data Entry Keyers" (43-9021), "Secretaries and Administrative Assistants" (43-6011 through 43-6014), "Court Reporters" (23-2091), and "Medical Transcriptionists" (31-9094).

- **2012 employment:** 104,400

- **May 2012 median annual wage:** $35,270

- **Projected employment change, 2012-22:**
  - **Number of new jobs:** –26,200
  - **Growth rate:** –25 percent (decline)

- **Education and training:**
  - **Typical entry-level education:** High school diploma or equivalent
  - **Work experience in a related occupation:** None
  - **Typical on-the-job-training:** Short-term on-the-job training

Mail Clerks and Mail Machine Operators, Except Postal Service

(O*NET 43-9051.00)

Prepare incoming and outgoing mail for distribution. Use hand or mail-handling machines to time-stamp, open, read, sort, and route incoming mail; address, seal, stamp, fold, stuff, and affix postage to outgoing mail or packages. Duties also may include storing, filing, or archiving necessary records and completed forms.

- **2012 employment:** 108,500

- **May 2012 median annual wage:** $26,900

- **Projected employment change, 2012-22:**
  - **Number of new jobs:** –9,600
  - **Growth rate:** –9 percent (decline)

- **Education and training:**
  - **Typical entry-level education:** High school diploma or equivalent
  - **Work experience in a related occupation:** None
  - **Typical on-the-job-training:** Short-term on-the-job training

Office Machine Operators, Except Computer

(O*NET 43-9071.00)

Operate one or more of a variety of office machines, such as photocopying, photographic, and duplicating machines. Excludes "Computer Operators" (43-9011), "Mail Clerks and Mail Machine Operators, Except Postal Service" (43-9051), and "Billing and Posting Clerks" (43-3021).

- **2012 employment:** 68,800

- **May 2012 median annual wage:** $27,950

- **Projected employment change, 2012-22:**
  - **Number of new jobs:** –7,000
  - **Growth rate:** –10 percent (decline)

- **Education and training:**
  - **Typical entry-level education:** High school diploma or equivalent

- **Work experience in a related occupation:** None
- **Typical on-the-job-training:** Short-term on-the-job training

Proofreaders and Copy Markers

(O*NET 43-9081.00)

Read transcripts or proof type to detect and correct any grammatical, typographical, or compositional errors. Excludes workers whose primary duty is editing copy. Includes proofreaders of Braille.

- **2012 employment:** 13,200
- **May 2012 median annual wage:** $32,780
- **Projected employment change, 2012-22:**
  - **Number of new jobs:** –200
  - **Growth rate:** –1 percent (little or no change)
- **Education and training:**
  - **Typical entry-level education:** Bachelor's degree
  - **Work experience in a related occupation:** None
  - **Typical on-the-job-training:** None

Statistical Assistants

(O*NET 43-9111.00 and 43-9111.01)

Compile and compute data according to statistical formulas for use in statistical studies. May perform actuarial computations and compile charts and graphs for actuaries. Includes actuarial clerks.

- **2012 employment:** 17,200
- **May 2012 median annual wage:** $39,840
- **Projected employment change, 2012-22:**
  - **Number of new jobs:** 1,600
  - **Growth rate:** 9 percent (about as fast as average)
- **Education and training:**
  - **Typical entry-level education:** Bachelor's degree
  - **Work experience in a related occupation:** None
  - **Typical on-the-job-training:** None

Personal Care and Service Occupations

First-Line Supervisors of Personal Service Workers

(O*NET 39-1021.00 and 39-1021.01)

Directly supervise and coordinate activities of personal service workers, such as flight attendants, hairdressers, or caddies.

- **2012 employment:** 251,500
- **May 2012 median annual wage:** $35,150
- **Projected employment change, 2012-22:**
  - **Number of new jobs:** 28,000
  - **Growth rate:** 11 percent (about as fast as average)
- **Education and training:**
  - **Typical entry-level education:** High school diploma or equivalent
  - **Work experience in a related occupation:** Less than 5 years
  - **Typical on-the-job-training:** None

Motion Picture Projectionists

(O*NET 39-3021.00)

Set up and operate motion picture projection and related sound reproduction equipment.

- **2012 employment:** 8,000
- **May 2012 median annual wage:** $19,830
- **Projected employment change, 2012-22:**
  - **Number of new jobs:** -2,100
  - **Growth rate:** -26 percent (decline)
- **Education and training:**
  - **Typical entry-level education:** Less than high school
  - **Work experience in a related occupation:** None
  - **Typical on-the-job-training:** Short-term on-the-job training

Ushers, Lobby Attendants, and Ticket Takers

(O*NET 39-3031.00)

Assist patrons at entertainment events by collecting admission tickets and passes from patrons, assisting in finding seats, searching for lost articles, and locating rest rooms and telephones.

- **2012 employment:** 108,800
- **May 2012 median annual wage:** $18,730
- **Projected employment change, 2012-22:**
  - **Number of new jobs:** 1,900
  - **Growth rate:** 2 percent (little or no change)
- **Education and training:**
  - **Typical entry-level education:** Less than high school
  - **Work experience in a related occupation:** None
  - **Typical on-the-job-training:** Short-term on-the-job training

Amusement and Recreation Attendants

(O*NET 39-3091.00)

Perform a variety of duties at amusement or recreation facilities. May schedule the use of recreation facilities, maintain and provide equipment to participants in sporting events or recreational pursuits, or operate amusement concessions and rides.

- **2012 employment:** 267,100
- **May 2012 median annual wage:** $18,710
- **Projected employment change, 2012-22:**
  - **Number of new jobs:** 30,300
  - **Growth rate:** 11 percent (about as fast as average)
- **Education and training:**
  - **Typical entry-level education:** Less than high school
  - **Work experience in a related occupation:** None
  - **Typical on-the-job-training:** Short-term on-the-job training

Costume Attendants

(O*NET 39-3092.00)

Select, fit, and take care of costumes for cast members, and aid entertainers. May assist with multiple costume changes during performances.

- **2012 employment:** 5,600
- **May 2012 median annual wage:** $36,760
- **Projected employment change, 2012-22:**
  - **Number of new jobs:** 400
  - **Growth rate:** 7 percent (slower than average)
- **Education and training:**
  - **Typical entry-level education:** High school diploma or equivalent
  - **Work experience in a related occupation:** None
  - **Typical on-the-job-training:** Short-term on-the-job training

Locker Room, Coatroom, and Dressing Room Attendants

(O*NET 39-3093.00)

Provide personal items to patrons or customers in locker rooms, dressing rooms, or coatrooms.

- **2012 employment:** 19,600

- **May 2012 median annual wage:** $19,160

- **Projected employment change, 2012-22:**
  - **Number of new jobs:** 2,000
  - **Growth rate:** 10 percent (about as fast as average)

- **Education and training:**
  - **Typical entry-level education:** High school diploma or equivalent
  - **Work experience in a related occupation:** None
  - **Typical on-the-job-training:** Short-term on-the-job training

Embalmers

(O*NET 39-4011.00)

Prepare dead bodies for interment in conformity with legal requirements.

- **2012 employment:** 5,100

- **May 2012 median annual wage:** $42,240

- **Projected employment change, 2012-22:**
  - **Number of new jobs:** -800
  - **Growth rate:** –15 percent (decline)

- **Education and training:**
  - **Typical entry-level education:** Postsecondary nondegree award
  - **Work experience in a related occupation:** None
  - **Typical on-the-job-training:** Short-term on-the-job training

Funeral Attendants

(O*NET 39-4021.00)

Perform a variety of tasks during funerals, such as placing caskets in the parlor or chapel prior to services, arranging floral offerings or lights around caskets, directing or escorting mourners, closing caskets, and issuing and storing funeral equipment.

- **2012 employment:** 32,400

- **May 2012 median annual wage:** $22,610

- **Projected employment change, 2012-22:**
  - **Number of new jobs:** 500
  - **Growth rate:** 1 percent (little or no change)

- **Education and training:**
  - **Typical entry-level education:** High school diploma or equivalent
  - **Work experience in a related occupation:** None
  - **Typical on-the-job-training:** Short-term on-the-job training

Makeup Artists, Theatrical and Performance

(O*NET 39-5091.00)

Apply makeup to performers to reflect the period, setting, and situation of their roles.

- **2012 employment:** 2,700

- **May 2012 median annual wage:** $64,450

- **Projected employment change, 2012-22:**
  - **Number of new jobs:** 100
  - **Growth rate:** 3 percent (slower than average)

- **Education and training:**
  - **Typical entry-level education:** Postsecondary nondegree award
  - **Work experience in a related occupation:** None
  - **Typical on-the-job-training:** None

Shampooers

(O*NET 39-5093.00)

Shampoo and rinse customers' hair.

- **2012 employment:** 18,900

- **May 2012 median annual wage:** $18,310

- **Projected employment change, 2012-22:**
  - **Number of new jobs:** –300
  - **Growth rate:** –2 percent (little or no change)

- **Education and training:**
  - **Typical entry-level education:** Less than high school
  - **Work experience in a related occupation:** None
  - **Typical on-the-job-training:** Short-term on-the-job training

Baggage Porters and Bellhops

(O*NET 39-6011.00)

Handle baggage for travelers at transportation terminals or for guests at hotels or similar establishments.

- **2012 employment:** 41,000

- **May 2012 median annual wage:** $20,050

- **Projected employment change, 2012-22:**
  - **Number of new jobs:** 5,000
  - **Growth rate:** 12 percent (about as fast as average)

- **Education and training:**
  - **Typical entry-level education:** High school diploma or equivalent
  - **Work experience in a related occupation:** None
  - **Typical on-the-job-training:** Short-term on-the-job training

Concierges

(O*NET 39-6012.00)

Offer personal services to assist patrons at hotels, apartments, or office buildings. May take messages; arrange or give advice on transportation, business services, or entertainment; or monitor guests' requests for housekeeping and maintenance.

- **2012 employment:** 26,300

- **May 2012 median annual wage:** $27,250

- **Projected employment change, 2012-22:**
  - **Number of new jobs:** 6,100
  - **Growth rate:** 23 percent (much faster than average)

- **Education and training:**
  - **Typical entry-level education:** High school diploma or equivalent
  - **Work experience in a related occupation:** None
  - **Typical on-the-job-training:** Moderate-term on-the-job training

Tour Guides and Escorts

(O*NET 39-7011.00)

Escort individuals or groups on sightseeing tours or through places of interest, such as industrial establishments, public buildings, and art galleries.

- **2012 employment:** 41,400

- **May 2012 median annual wage:** $23,940

- **Projected employment change, 2012-22:**
  - **Number of new jobs:** 3,400
  - **Growth rate:** 8 percent (about as fast as average)

- **Education and training:**
  - **Typical entry-level education:** High school diploma or equivalent
  - **Work experience in a related occupation:** None
  - **Typical on-the-job-training:** Moderate-term on-the-job training

Travel Guides

(O*NET 39-7012.00)

Plan, organize, and conduct long-distance travel, tours, and expeditions for individuals and groups.

- **2012 employment:** 5,700

- **May 2012 median annual wage:** $30,780

- **Projected employment change, 2012-22:**
  - **Number of new jobs:** 200
  - **Growth rate:** 4 percent (slower than average)

- **Education and training:**
  - **Typical entry-level education:** High school diploma or equivalent
  - **Work experience in a related occupation:** None
  - **Typical on-the-job-training:** Moderate-term on-the-job training

Residential Advisors

(O*NET 39-9041.00)

Coordinate activities in residential facilities in secondary school and college dormitories, group homes, or similar establishments. Order supplies and determine necessary maintenance, repairs, and furnishings. May maintain household records and assign rooms. May help residents solve problems or refer residents to counseling resources.

- **2012 employment:** 89,700

- **May 2012 median annual wage:** $24,520

- **Projected employment change, 2012-22:**
  - **Number of new jobs:** 18,500
  - **Growth rate:** 21 percent (faster than average)

- **Education and training:**
  - **Typical entry-level education:** High school diploma or equivalent
  - **Work experience in a related occupation:** None
  - **Typical on-the-job-training:** Short-term on-the-job training

Production Occupations

First-Line Supervisors of Production and Operating Workers

(O*NET 51-1011.00)

Directly supervise and coordinate the activities of production and operating workers, such as inspectors, precision workers, machine setters and operators, assemblers, fabricators, and plant and system operators. Excludes team or work leaders.

- **2012 employment:** 594,700

- **May 2012 median annual wage:** $54,040

- **Projected employment change, 2012-22:**
  - **Number of new jobs:** –10,500
  - **Growth rate:** –2 percent (little or no change)

- **Education and training:**
  - **Typical entry-level education:** Postsecondary nondegree award

- **Work experience in a related occupation:** Less than 5 years
- **Typical on-the-job-training:** None

Layout Workers, Metal and Plastic

(O*NET 51-4192.00)

Lay out reference points and dimensions on metal or plastic stock or workpieces, such as sheets, plates, tubes, structural shapes, castings, or machine parts, for further processing. Includes shipfitters.

- **2012 employment:** 12,700

- **May 2012 median annual wage:** $42,050

- **Projected employment change, 2012-22:**
  - **Number of new jobs:** -400
  - **Growth rate:** –3 percent (decline)

- **Education and training:**
  - **Typical entry-level education:** High school diploma or equivalent
  - **Work experience in a related occupation:** None
  - **Typical on-the-job-training:** Moderate-term on-the-job training

Tool Grinders, Filers, and Sharpeners

(O*NET 51-4194.00)

Perform precision smoothing, sharpening, polishing, or grinding of metal objects.

- **2012 employment:** 12,600

- **May 2012 median annual wage:** $34,300

- **Projected employment change, 2012-22:**
  - **Number of new jobs:** 100
  - **Growth rate:** 0 percent (little or no change)

- **Education and training:**
  - **Typical entry-level education:** High school diploma or equivalent
  - **Work experience in a related occupation:** None
  - **Typical on-the-job-training:** Moderate-term on-the-job training

Pressers, Textile, Garment, and Related Materials

(O*NET 51-6021.00)

Press or shape articles by hand or machine.

- **2012 employment:** 54,300

- **May 2012 median annual wage:** $19,670

- **Projected employment change, 2012-22:**
  - **Number of new jobs:** 1,400
  - **Growth rate:** 3 percent (slower than average)

- **Education and training:**
  - **Typical entry-level education:** Less than high school
  - **Work experience in a related occupation:** None
  - **Typical on-the-job-training:** Short-term on-the-job training

Sewing Machine Operators

(O*NET 51-6031.00)

Operate or tend sewing machines to join, reinforce, decorate, or perform related sewing operations in the manufacture of garments or nongarment products.

- **2012 employment:** 161,400

- **May 2012 median annual wage:** $21,270

- **Projected employment change, 2012-22:**
  - **Number of new jobs:** –41,700
  - **Growth rate:** –26 percent (decline)

- **Education and training:**
  - **Typical entry-level education:** Less than high school
  - **Work experience in a related occupation:** None
  - **Typical on-the-job-training:** Short-term on-the-job training

Shoe and Leather Workers and Repairers

(O*NET 51-6041.00)

Construct, decorate, or repair leather and leather-like products, such as luggage, shoes, and saddles.

- **2012 employment:** 8,700

- **May 2012 median annual wage:** $23,950

- **Projected employment change, 2012-22:**
  - **Number of new jobs:** –1,200
  - **Growth rate:** –14 percent (decline)

- **Education and training:**
  - **Typical entry-level education:** High school diploma or equivalent
  - **Work experience in a related occupation:** None
  - **Typical on-the-job-training:** Moderate-term on-the-job training

Shoe Machine Operators and Tenders

(O*NET 51-6042.00)

Operate or tend a variety of machines to join, decorate, reinforce, or finish shoes and shoe parts.

- **2012 employment:** 3,500

- **May 2012 median annual wage:** $24,310

- **Projected employment change, 2012-22:**
  - **Number of new jobs:** –1,200
  - **Growth rate:** –35 percent (decline)

- **Education and training:**
  - **Typical entry-level education:** High school diploma or equivalent
  - **Work experience in a related occupation:** None
  - **Typical on-the-job-training:** Short-term on-the-job training

Sewers, Hand

(O*NET 51-6051.00)

Sew, join, reinforce, or finish, usually with needle and thread, a variety of manufactured items. Includes weavers and stitchers. Excludes "Fabric Menders, Except Garment" (49-9093).

- **2012 employment:** 11,100

- **May 2012 median annual wage:** $22,820

- **Projected employment change, 2012-22:**
  - **Number of new jobs:** –1,000
  - **Growth rate:** –9 percent (decline)

- **Education and training:**
  - **Typical entry-level education:** Less than high school
  - **Work experience in a related occupation:** None
  - **Typical on-the-job-training:** Moderate-term on-the-job training

Tailors, Dressmakers, and Custom Sewers

(O*NET 51-6052.00)

Design, make, alter, repair, or fit garments.

- **2012 employment:** 49,900

- **May 2012 median annual wage:** $26,280

- **Projected employment change, 2012-22:**
  - **Number of new jobs:** -900
  - **Growth rate:** –2 percent (little or no change)

- **Education and training:**
  - **Typical entry-level education:** Less than high school
  - **Work experience in a related occupation:** None
  - **Typical on-the-job-training:** Moderate-term on-the-job training

Textile Bleaching and Dyeing Machine Operators and Tenders

(O*NET 51-6061.00)

Operate or tend machines that bleach, shrink, wash, dye, or finish textiles or synthetic or glass fibers.

- **2012 employment:** 11,400

- **May 2012 median annual wage:** $24,210

- **Projected employment change, 2012-22:**
  - **Number of new jobs:** –2,700
  - **Growth rate:** –24 percent (decline)

- **Education and training:**
  - **Typical entry-level education:** High school diploma or equivalent
  - **Work experience in a related occupation:** None
  - **Typical on-the-job-training:** Short-term on-the-job training

Textile Cutting Machine Setters, Operators, and Tenders

(O*NET 51-6062.00)

Set up, operate, or tend machines that cut textiles.

- **2012 employment:** 15,500

- **May 2012 median annual wage:** $24,050

- **Projected employment change, 2012-22:**
  - **Number of new jobs:** –4,200
  - **Growth rate:** –27 percent (decline)

- **Education and training:**
  - **Typical entry-level education:** High school diploma or equivalent
  - **Work experience in a related occupation:** None
  - **Typical on-the-job-training:** Moderate-term on-the-job training

Textile Knitting and Weaving Machine Setters, Operators, and Tenders

(O*NET 51-6063.00)

Set up, operate, or tend machines that knit, loop, weave, or draw in textiles. Excludes "Sewing Machine Operators" (51-6031).

- **2012 employment:** 21,900

- **May 2012 median annual wage:** $26,540

- **Projected employment change, 2012-22:**
  - **Number of new jobs:** –5,400
  - **Growth rate:** –25 percent (decline)

- **Education and training:**
  - **Typical entry-level education:** High school diploma or equivalent
  - **Work experience in a related occupation:** None
  - **Typical on-the-job-training:** Moderate-term on-the-job training

Textile Winding, Twisting, and Drawing Out Machine Setters, Operators, and Tenders

(O*NET 51-6064.00)

Set up, operate, or tend machines that wind or twist textiles; or draw out and combine sliver, such as wool, hemp, or synthetic fibers. Includes slubber machine and drawing frame operators.

- **2012 employment:** 27,500

- **May 2012 median annual wage:** $25,850

- **Projected employment change, 2012-22:**
  - **Number of new jobs:** –5,600
  - **Growth rate:** –21 percent (decline)

- **Education and training:**
  - **Typical entry-level education:** High school diploma or equivalent
  - **Work experience in a related occupation:** None
  - **Typical on-the-job-training:** Moderate-term on-the-job training

Extruding and Forming Machine Setters, Operators, and Tenders, Synthetic and Glass Fibers

(O*NET 51-6091.00)

Set up, operate, or tend machines that extrude and form continuous filaments from synthetic materials, such as liquid polymer, rayon, and fiberglass.

- **2012 employment:** 18,000

- **May 2012 median annual wage:** $32,430

- **Projected employment change, 2012-22:**
  - **Number of new jobs:** -2,200
  - **Growth rate:** –12 percent (decline)

- **Education and training:**
  - **Typical entry-level education:** High school diploma or equivalent
  - **Work experience in a related occupation:** None
  - **Typical on-the-job-training:** Moderate-term on-the-job training

Fabric and Apparel Patternmakers

(O*NET 51-6092.00)

Draw and construct sets of precision master fabric patterns or layouts. Also may mark and cut fabrics and apparel.

- **2012 employment:** 6,500

- **May 2012 median annual wage:** $38,650

- **Projected employment change, 2012-22:**
  - **Number of new jobs:** –1,600
  - **Growth rate:** –25 percent (decline)

- **Education and training:**
  - **Typical entry-level education:** High school diploma or equivalent
  - **Work experience in a related occupation:** None
  - **Typical on-the-job-training:** Moderate-term on-the-job training

Upholsterers

(O*NET 51-6093.00)

Make, repair, or replace upholstery for household furniture or transportation vehicles.

- **2012 employment:** 40,900

- **May 2012 median annual wage:** $29,930

- **Projected employment change, 2012-22:**
  - **Number of new jobs:** 300
  - **Growth rate:** 1 percent (little or no change)

- **Education and training:**
  - **Typical entry-level education:** High school diploma or equivalent
  - **Work experience in a related occupation:** None
  - **Typical on-the-job-training:** Moderate-term on-the-job training

Model Makers, Wood

(O*NET 51-7031.00)

Construct full-size and scale wooden precision models of products. Includes wood jig builders and loft workers.

- **2012 employment:** 1,300

- **May 2012 median annual wage:** $28,800

- **Projected employment change, 2012-22:**
  - **Number of new jobs:** 100
  - **Growth rate:** 6 percent (slower than average)

- **Education and training:**
  - **Typical entry-level education:** High school diploma or equivalent
  - **Work experience in a related occupation:** None
  - **Typical on-the-job-training:** Moderate-term on-the-job training

Patternmakers, Wood

(O*NET 51-7032.00)

Plan, lay out, and construct wooden unit or sectional patterns used in forming sand molds for castings.

- **2012 employment:** 800

- **May 2012 median annual wage:** $39,840

- **Projected employment change, 2012-22:**
  - **Number of new jobs:** 0
  - **Growth rate:** 0 percent (little or no change)

- **Education and training:**
  - **Typical entry-level education:** High school diploma or equivalent
  - **Work experience in a related occupation:** None
  - **Typical on-the-job-training:** Moderate-term on-the-job training

Chemical Plant and System Operators

(O*NET 51-8091.00)

Control or operate entire chemical processes or systems through the use of machines.

- **2012 employment:** 38,300

- **May 2012 median annual wage:** $54,390

- **Projected employment change, 2012-22:**
  - **Number of new jobs:** –4,400
  - **Growth rate:** –11 percent (decline)

- **Education and training:**
  - **Typical entry-level education:** High school diploma or equivalent
  - **Work experience in a related occupation:** None
  - **Typical on-the-job-training:** Long-term on-the-job training

Gas Plant Operators

(O*NET 51-8092.00)

Distribute or process gas for utility companies and others by controlling compressors to maintain specified pressures on main pipelines.

- **2012 employment:** 12,500

- **May 2012 median annual wage:** $61,140

- **Projected employment change, 2012-22:**
  - **Number of new jobs:** –1,100
  - **Growth rate:** –9 percent (decline)

- **Education and training:**
  - **Typical entry-level education:** High school diploma or equivalent
  - **Work experience in a related occupation:** None
  - **Typical on-the-job-training:** Long-term on-the-job training

Petroleum Pump System Operators, Refinery Operators, and Gaugers

(O*NET 51-8093.00)

Operate or control petroleum-refining or petroleum-processing units. May specialize in controlling manifold and pumping systems, gauging or testing oil in storage tanks, or regulating the flow of oil into pipelines.

- **2012 employment:** 41,900
- **May 2012 median annual wage:** $61,850
- **Projected employment change, 2012-22:**
  - **Number of new jobs:** –2,100
  - **Growth rate:** –5 percent (decline)
- **Education and training:**
  - **Typical entry-level education:** High school diploma or equivalent
  - **Work experience in a related occupation:** None
  - **Typical on-the-job-training:** Long-term on-the-job training

Chemical Equipment Operators and Tenders

(O*NET 51-9011.00)

Operate or tend equipment that controls chemical changes or reactions in the processing of industrial or consumer products. Equipment used includes devulcanizers, steam-jacketed kettles, and reactor vessels. Excludes "Chemical Plant and System Operators" (51-8091).

- **2012 employment:** 56,400
- **May 2012 median annual wage:** $47,100
- **Projected employment change, 2012-22:**
  - **Number of new jobs:** –4,700
  - **Growth rate:** –8 percent (decline)
- **Education and training:**
  - **Typical entry-level education:** High school diploma or equivalent
  - **Work experience in a related occupation:** None
  - **Typical on-the-job-training:** Moderate-term on-the-job training

Separating, Filtering, Clarifying, Precipitating, and Still Machine Setters, Operators, and Tenders

(O*NET 51-9012.00)

Set up, operate, or tend continuous-flow or vat-type equipment; filter presses; shaker screens; centrifuges; condenser tubes; precipitating, fermenting, or evaporating tanks; scrubbing towers; or batch stills. These machines extract, sort, or separate liquids, gases, or solids from other materials in order to recover a refined product. Includes dairy processing equipment operators. Excludes "Chemical Equipment Operators and Tenders" (51-9011).

- **2012 employment:** 41,300
- **May 2012 median annual wage:** $38,570
- **Projected employment change, 2012-22:**
  - **Number of new jobs:** –1,200
  - **Growth rate:** –3 percent (decline)
- **Education and training:**
  - **Typical entry-level education:** High school diploma or equivalent
  - **Work experience in a related occupation:** None
  - **Typical on-the-job-training:** Moderate-term on-the-job training

Crushing, Grinding, and Polishing Machine Setters, Operators, and Tenders

(O*NET 51-9021.00)

Set up, operate, or tend machines to crush, grind, or polish materials, such as coal, glass, grain, stone, food, or rubber.

- **2012 employment:** 30,200
- **May 2012 median annual wage:** $31,830
- **Projected employment change, 2012-22:**
  - **Number of new jobs:** –700
  - **Growth rate:** –2 percent (little or no change)
- **Education and training:**
  - **Typical entry-level education:** High school diploma or equivalent
  - **Work experience in a related occupation:** None
  - **Typical on-the-job-training:** Moderate-term on-the-job training

Grinding and Polishing Workers, Hand

(O*NET 51-9022.00)

Grind, sand, or polish, using hand tools or hand-held power tools, a variety of metal, wood, stone, clay, plastic, or glass objects. Includes chippers, buffers, and finishers.

- **2012 employment:** 31,500
- **May 2012 median annual wage:** $27,890
- **Projected employment change, 2012-22:**
  - **Number of new jobs:** –500
  - **Growth rate:** –2 percent (little or no change)
- **Education and training:**
  - **Typical entry-level education:** Less than high school
  - **Work experience in a related occupation:** None
  - **Typical on-the-job-training:** Moderate-term on-the-job training

Mixing and Blending Machine Setters, Operators, and Tenders

(O*NET 51-9023.00)

Set up, operate, or tend machines that mix or blend materials, such as chemicals, tobacco, liquids, color pigments, or explosive ingredients. Excludes "Food Batchmakers" (51-3092).

- **2012 employment:** 120,100
- **May 2012 median annual wage:** $33,840
- **Projected employment change, 2012-22:**
  - **Number of new jobs:** –3,700
  - **Growth rate:** –3 percent (decline)
- **Education and training:**
  - **Typical entry-level education:** High school diploma or equivalent
  - **Work experience in a related occupation:** None
  - **Typical on-the-job-training:** Moderate-term on-the-job training

Cutters and Trimmers, Hand

(O*NET 51-9031.00)

Use hand tools or hand-held power tools to cut and trim a variety of manufactured items, such as carpet, fabric, stone, glass, or rubber.

- **2012 employment:** 14,200
- **May 2012 median annual wage:** $24,530
- **Projected employment change, 2012-22:**
  - **Number of new jobs:** –2,200

- **Growth rate:** –15 percent (decline)
- **Education and training:**
  - **Typical entry-level education:** Less than high school
  - **Work experience in a related occupation:** None
  - **Typical on-the-job-training:** Short-term on-the-job training

Cutting and Slicing Machine Setters, Operators, and Tenders

(O*NET 51-9032.00)

Set up, operate, or tend machines that cut or slice materials, such as glass, stone, cork, rubber, tobacco, food, paper, or insulating material. Excludes "Woodworking Machine Setters, Operators, and Tenders" (51-7040), "Cutting, Punching, and Press Machine Setters, Operators, and Tenders, Metal and Plastic" (51-4031), and "Textile Cutting Machine Setters, Operators, and Tenders" (51-6062).

- **2012 employment:** 58,300
- **May 2012 median annual wage:** $31,430
- **Projected employment change, 2012-22:**
  - **Number of new jobs:** –4,900
  - **Growth rate:** –8 percent (decline)
- **Education and training:**
  - **Typical entry-level education:** High school diploma or equivalent
  - **Work experience in a related occupation:** None
  - **Typical on-the-job-training:** Short-term on-the-job training

Extruding, Forming, Pressing, and Compacting Machine Setters, Operators, and Tenders

(O*NET 51-9041.00)

Set up, operate, or tend machines, such as glass-forming machines, plodder machines, and tuber machines, to shape and form products, such as glassware, food, rubber, soap, brick, tile, clay, wax, tobacco, or cosmetics. Excludes "Paper Goods Machine Setters, Operators, and Tenders" (51-9196) and "Shoe Machine Operators and Tenders" (51-6042).

- **2012 employment:** 70,600
- **May 2012 median annual wage:** $31,310
- **Projected employment change, 2012-22:**
  - **Number of new jobs:** –2,200
  - **Growth rate:** –3 percent (decline)
- **Education and training:**
  - **Typical entry-level education:** High school diploma or equivalent
  - **Work experience in a related occupation:** None
  - **Typical on-the-job-training:** Moderate-term on-the-job training

Furnace, Kiln, Oven, Drier, and Kettle Operators and Tenders

(O*NET 51-9051.00)

Operate or tend heating equipment other than basic metal-, plastic-, or food-processing equipment. Includes activities such as annealing glass, drying lumber, curing rubber, removing moisture from materials, and boiling soap.

- **2012 employment:** 20,500
- **May 2012 median annual wage:** $35,530
- **Projected employment change, 2012-22:**
  - **Number of new jobs:** –900
  - **Growth rate:** –4 percent (decline)

- **Education and training:**
  - **Typical entry-level education:** High school diploma or equivalent
  - **Work experience in a related occupation:** None
  - **Typical on-the-job-training:** Moderate-term on-the-job training

Packaging and Filling Machine Operators and Tenders

(O*NET 51-9111.00)

Operate or tend machines that prepare industrial or consumer products for storage or shipment. Includes cannery workers who pack food products.

- **2012 employment:** 369,200
- **May 2012 median annual wage:** $25,860
- **Projected employment change, 2012-22:**
  - **Number of new jobs:** 2,300
  - **Growth rate:** 1 percent (little or no change)
- **Education and training:**
  - **Typical entry-level education:** High school diploma or equivalent
  - **Work experience in a related occupation:** None
  - **Typical on-the-job-training:** Moderate-term on-the-job training

Photographic Process Workers and Processing Machine Operators

(O*NET 51-9151.00)

Perform work to develop and process photographic images from film or from digital media. May perform precision tasks, such as editing photographic negatives and prints.

- **2012 employment:** 47,100
- **May 2012 median annual wage:** $23,120
- **Projected employment change, 2012-22:**
  - **Number of new jobs:** 100
  - **Growth rate:** 0 percent (little or no change)
- **Education and training:**
  - **Typical entry-level education:** High school diploma or equivalent
  - **Work experience in a related occupation:** None
  - **Typical on-the-job-training:** Short-term on-the-job training

Adhesive Bonding Machine Operators and Tenders

(O*NET 51-9191.00)

Operate or tend bonding machines that use adhesives to join items for further processing or to form a completed product. Processes include joining veneer sheets into plywood; gluing paper; and joining rubber and rubberized fabric parts, plastic, simulated leather, or other materials. Excludes "Shoe Machine Operators and Tenders" (51-6042).

- **2012 employment:** 16,800
- **May 2012 median annual wage:** $29,830
- **Projected employment change, 2012-22:**
  - **Number of new jobs:** 100
  - **Growth rate:** 1 percent (little or no change)
- **Education and training:**
  - **Typical entry-level education:** High school diploma or equivalent
  - **Work experience in a related occupation:** None
  - **Typical on-the-job-training:** Moderate-term on-the-job training

Cleaning, Washing, and Metal Pickling Equipment Operators and Tenders

(O*NET 51-9192.00)

Operate or tend machines that wash or clean products, such as barrels or kegs, glass items, tin plates, food, pulp, coal, plastic, or rubber, to remove impurities.

- **2012 employment:** 16,000
- **May 2012 median annual wage:** $26,210
- **Projected employment change, 2012-22:**
  - **Number of new jobs:** –100
  - **Growth rate:** –1 percent (little or no change)
- **Education and training:**
  - **Typical entry-level education:** Less than high school
  - **Work experience in a related occupation:** None
  - **Typical on-the-job-training:** Moderate-term on-the-job training

Cooling and Freezing Equipment Operators and Tenders

(O*NET 51-9193.00)

Operate or tend equipment, such as cooling and freezing units, refrigerators, batch freezers, and freezing tunnels, that cools or freezes products, food, blood plasma, and chemicals.

- **2012 employment:** 8,300
- **May 2012 median annual wage:** $28,200
- **Projected employment change, 2012-22:**
  - **Number of new jobs:** 100
  - **Growth rate:** 1 percent (little or no change)
- **Education and training:**
  - **Typical entry-level education:** High school diploma or equivalent
  - **Work experience in a related occupation:** None
  - **Typical on-the-job-training:** Moderate-term on-the-job training

Etchers and Engravers

(O*NET 51-9194.00)

Engrave or etch metal, wood, rubber, or other materials. Includes such workers as etcher-circuit processors, pantograph engravers, and silk-screen etchers. Photoengravers are included in "Prepress Technicians and Workers" (51-5111).

- **2012 employment:** 9,700
- **May 2012 median annual wage:** $28,390
- **Projected employment change, 2012-22:**
  - **Number of new jobs:** –400
  - **Growth rate:** –4 percent (decline)
- **Education and training:**
  - **Typical entry-level education:** High school diploma or equivalent
  - **Work experience in a related occupation:** None
  - **Typical on-the-job-training:** Moderate-term on-the-job training

Molders, Shapers, and Casters, except Metal and Plastic

(O*NET 51-9195.00, 51-9195.03, 51-9195.04, 51-9195.05, and 51-9195.07)

Mold, shape, form, cast, or carve products, such as food products, figurines, tile, pipes, and candles, consisting of clay, glass, plaster, concrete, stone, or combinations of materials.

- **2012 employment:** 42,000
- **May 2012 median annual wage:** $29,300
- **Projected employment change, 2012-22:**
  - **Number of new jobs:** 3,100
  - **Growth rate:** 7 percent (slower than average)
- **Education and training:**
  - **Typical entry-level education:** High school diploma or equivalent
  - **Work experience in a related occupation:** None
  - **Typical on-the-job-training:** Long-term on-the-job training

Paper Goods Machine Setters, Operators, and Tenders

(O*NET 51-9196.00)

Set up, operate, or tend paper goods machines that perform a variety of functions, such as converting, sawing, corrugating, banding, wrapping, boxing, stitching, forming, or sealing paper or paperboard sheets into products.

- **2012 employment:** 95,000
- **May 2012 median annual wage:** $34,690
- **Projected employment change, 2012-22:**
  - **Number of new jobs:** –7600
  - **Growth rate:** –8 percent (decline)
- **Education and training:**
  - **Typical entry-level education:** High school diploma or equivalent
  - **Work experience in a related occupation:** None
  - **Typical on-the-job-training:** Moderate-term on-the-job training

Tire Builders

(O*NET 51-9197.00)

Operate machines that build tires.

- **2012 employment:** 17,400
- **May 2012 median annual wage:** $41,210
- **Projected employment change, 2012-22:**
  - **Number of new jobs:** –1,500
  - **Growth rate:** –9 percent (decline)
- **Education and training:**
  - **Typical entry-level education:** High school diploma or equivalent
  - **Work experience in a related occupation:** None
  - **Typical on-the-job-training:** Moderate-term on-the-job training

Helpers—Production Workers

(O*NET 51-9198.00)

Help production workers by performing duties requiring less skill. Duties include supplying or holding materials or tools and cleaning work areas and equipment. Apprentices are classified in the appropriate production occupations (51-0000).

- **2012 employment:** 419,900
- **May 2012 median annual wage:** $22,810
- **Projected employment change, 2012-22:**
  - **Number of new jobs:** 29,800
  - **Growth rate:** 7 percent (slower than average)
- **Education and training:**
  - **Typical entry-level education:** Less than high school
  - **Work experience in a related occupation:** None
  - **Typical on-the-job-training:** Short-term on-the-job training

Protective Service Occupations

First-Line Supervisors of Correctional Officers

(O*NET 33-1011.00)

Directly supervise and coordinate activities of correctional officers and jailers.

- **2012 employment:** 46,700

- **May 2012 median annual wage:** $57,840

- **Projected employment change, 2012-22:**
  - **Number of new jobs:** 1,900
  - **Growth rate:** 4 percent (slower than average)

- **Education and training:**
  - **Typical entry-level education:** High school diploma or equivalent
  - **Work experience in a related occupation:** Less than 5 years
  - **Typical on-the-job-training:** Moderate-term on-the-job training

First-Line Supervisors of Police and Detectives

(O*NET 33-1012.00)

Directly supervise and coordinate activities of members of the police force.

- **2012 employment:** 103,700

- **May 2012 median annual wage:** $78,270

- **Projected employment change, 2012-22:**
  - **Number of new jobs:** 5,000
  - **Growth rate:** 5 percent (slower than average)

- **Education and training:**
  - **Typical entry-level education:** High school diploma or equivalent
  - **Work experience in a related occupation:** Less than 5 years
  - **Typical on-the-job-training:** Moderate-term on-the-job training

First-Line Supervisors of Fire Fighting and Prevention Workers

(O*NET 33-1021.00, 33-1021.01, and 33-1021.02)

Directly supervise and coordinate activities of workers engaged in firefighting and fire prevention and control.

- **2012 employment:** 62,300

- **May 2012 median annual wage:** $68,210

- **Projected employment change, 2012-22:**
  - **Number of new jobs:** 3,900
  - **Growth rate:** 6 percent (slower than average)

- **Education and training:**
  - **Typical entry-level education:** Postsecondary nondegree award
  - **Work experience in a related occupation:** Less than 5 years
  - **Typical on-the-job-training:** Moderate-term on-the-job training

Forest Fire Inspectors and Prevention Specialists

(O*NET 33-2022.00)

Enforce fire regulations, inspect forests for fire hazards, and recommend forest fire prevention or control measures. May report forest fires and weather conditions.

- **2012 employment:** 1,900

- **May 2012 median annual wage:** $35,780

- **Projected employment change, 2012-22:**
  - **Number of new jobs:** 100
  - **Growth rate:** 3 percent (slower than average)

- **Education and training:**
  - **Typical entry-level education:** High school diploma or equivalent
  - **Work experience in a related occupation:** Less than 5 years
  - **Typical on-the-job-training:** Moderate-term on-the-job training

Parking Enforcement Workers

(O*NET 33-3041.00)

Patrol assigned area, such as public parking lots or city streets, to issue tickets to overtime parking violators and illegally parked vehicles.

- **2012 employment:** 9,700

- **May 2012 median annual wage:** $35,690

- **Projected employment change, 2012-22:**
  - **Number of new jobs:** 0
  - **Growth rate:** 0 percent (little or no change)

- **Education and training:**
  - **Typical entry-level education:** High school diploma or equivalent
  - **Work experience in a related occupation:** None
  - **Typical on-the-job-training:** Short-term on-the-job training

Animal Control Workers

(O*NET 33-9011.00)

Handle animals to investigate possible mistreatment; control abandoned, dangerous, or unattended animals.

- **2012 employment:** 14,600

- **May 2012 median annual wage:** $31,680

- **Projected employment change, 2012-22:**
  - **Number of new jobs:** 1,100
  - **Growth rate:** 8 percent (about as fast as average)

- **Education and training:**
  - **Typical entry-level education:** High school diploma or equivalent
  - **Work experience in a related occupation:** None
  - **Typical on-the-job-training:** Moderate-term on-the-job training

Crossing Guards

(O*NET 33-9091.00)

Guide or control vehicular or pedestrian traffic at places such as streets, schools, railroad crossings, or construction sites.

- **2012 employment:** 71,400

- **May 2012 median annual wage:** $23,910

- **Projected employment change, 2012-22:**
  - **Number of new jobs:** 3,100
  - **Growth rate:** 4 percent (slower than average)

- **Education and training:**
  - **Typical entry-level education:** High school diploma or equivalent
  - **Work experience in a related occupation:** None
  - **Typical on-the-job-training:** Short-term on-the-job training

Lifeguards, Ski Patrol, and Other Recreational Protective Service Workers

(O*NET 33-9092.00)

Monitor recreational areas, such as pools, beaches, or ski slopes, to provide assistance and protection to participants.

- **2012 employment:** 130,100

- **May 2012 median annual wage:** $18,950

- **Projected employment change, 2012-22:**
  - **Number of new jobs:** 13,300
  - **Growth rate:** 10 percent (about as fast as average)
- **Education and training:**
  - **Typical entry-level education:** High school diploma or equivalent
  - **Work experience in a related occupation:** None
  - **Typical on-the-job-training:** Short-term on-the-job training

Transportation Security Screeners

(O*NET 33-9093.00)

Conduct screening of passengers, baggage, or cargo to ensure compliance with Transportation Security Administration (TSA) regulations. May operate basic security equipment, such as x-ray machines and hand wands, at screening checkpoints.

- **2012 employment:** 50,800
- **May 2012 median annual wage:** $36,850
- **Projected employment change, 2012-22:**
  - **Number of new jobs:** 3,000
  - **Growth rate:** 6 percent (slower than average)
- **Education and training:**
  - **Typical entry-level education:** High school diploma or equivalent
  - **Work experience in a related occupation:** None
  - **Typical on-the-job-training:** Short-term on-the-job training

Sales Occupations

First-Line Supervisors of Retail Sales Workers

(O*NET 41-1011.00)

Directly supervise and coordinate activities of retail sales workers in an establishment or a department. Duties also may include management functions, such as purchasing, budgeting, accounting, and personnel work.

- **2012 employment:** 1,603,300
- **May 2012 median annual wage:** $36,820
- **Projected employment change, 2012-22:**
  - **Number of new jobs:** 70,900
  - **Growth rate:** 4 percent (slower than average)
- **Education and training:**
  - **Typical entry-level education:** High school diploma or equivalent
  - **Work experience in a related occupation:** Less than 5 years
  - **Typical on-the-job-training:** None

First-Line Supervisors of Nonretail Sales Workers

(O*NET 41-1012.00)

Directly supervise and coordinate activities of sales workers other than retail sales workers. Duties also may include budgeting, accounting, and personnel work.

- **2012 employment:** 394,400
- **May 2012 median annual wage:** $70,060
- **Projected employment change, 2012-22:**
  - **Number of new jobs:** –3,200
  - **Growth rate:** –1 percent (little or no change)
- **Education and training:**
  - **Typical entry-level education:** High school diploma or equivalent
  - **Work experience in a related occupation:** Less than 5 years
  - **Typical on-the-job-training:** None

Gaming Change Persons and Booth Cashiers

(O*NET 41-2012.00)

Exchange coins, tokens, and chips for patrons' money. May issue payoffs and obtain customer's signature on receipt. May operate a booth in the slot machine area and count and audit money in drawers. Excludes "Cashiers" (41-2011).

- **2012 employment:** 22,300
- **May 2012 median annual wage:** $24,690
- **Projected employment change, 2012-22:**
  - **Number of new jobs:** 0
  - **Growth rate:** 0 percent (little or no change)
- **Education and training:**
  - **Typical entry-level education:** High school diploma or equivalent
  - **Work experience in a related occupation:** None
  - **Typical on-the-job-training:** Short-term on-the-job training

Counter and Rental Clerks

(O*NET 41-2021.00)

Receive orders, generally in person, for repairs, rentals, and services. May describe available options, compute costs, and accept payment. Excludes "Counter Attendants, Cafeteria, Food Concession, and Coffee Shop" (35-3022), "Hotel, Motel, and Resort Desk Clerks" (43-4081), "Order Clerks" (43-4151), and "Reservation and Transportation Ticket Agents and Travel Clerks" (43-4181).

- **2012 employment:** 437,800
- **May 2012 median annual wage:** $23,130
- **Projected employment change, 2012-22:**
  - **Number of new jobs:** 46,600
  - **Growth rate:** 11 percent (about as fast as average)
- **Education and training:**
  - **Typical entry-level education:** Less than high school
  - **Work experience in a related occupation:** None
  - **Typical on-the-job-training:** Short-term on-the-job training

Demonstrators and Product Promoters

(O*NET 41-9011.00)

Demonstrate merchandise and answer questions for the purpose of creating public interest in buying the product. May sell merchandise demonstrated.

- **2012 employment:** 78,100
- **May 2012 median annual wage:** $23,860
- **Projected employment change, 2012-22:**
  - **Number of new jobs:** 12,600
  - **Growth rate:** 16 percent (faster than average)
- **Education and training:**
  - **Typical entry-level education:** High school diploma or equivalent
  - **Work experience in a related occupation:** None
  - **Typical on-the-job-training:** Short-term on-the-job training

Telemarketers

(O*NET 41-9041.00)

Solicit donations or orders for goods or services over the telephone.

- **2012 employment:** 250,100
- **May 2012 median annual wage:** $22,330
- **Projected employment change, 2012-22:**

- **Number of new jobs:** 19,200
- **Growth rate:** 8 percent (about as fast as average)

- **Education and training:**
  - **Typical entry-level education:** Less than high school
  - **Work experience in a related occupation:** None
  - **Typical on-the-job-training:** Short-term on-the-job training

Door-to-Door Sales Workers, News and Street Vendors, and Related Workers

(O*NET 41-9091.00)

Sell goods or services door to door or on the street.

- **2012 employment:** 92,700

- **May 2012 median annual wage:** $21,470

- **Projected employment change, 2012-22:**
  - **Number of new jobs:** –14,200
  - **Growth rate:** –15 percent (decline)

- **Education and training:**
  - **Typical entry-level education:** High school diploma or equivalent
  - **Work experience in a related occupation:** None
  - **Typical on-the-job-training:** Short-term on-the-job training

Transportation and Material Moving Occupations

Aircraft Cargo Handling Supervisors

(O*NET 53-1011.00)

Supervise and coordinate the activities of ground crews in the loading, unloading, securing, and staging of aircraft cargo or baggage. May determine the quantity and orientation of cargo and compute aircraft center of gravity. May accompany flight crew in aircraft, monitor and handle cargo in flight, and assist and brief passengers on safety and emergency procedures. Includes loadmasters.

- **2012 employment:** 6,800

- **May 2012 median annual wage:** $47,930

- **Projected employment change, 2012-22:**
  - **Number of new jobs:** 0
  - **Growth rate:** 1 percent (little or no change)

- **Education and training:**
  - **Typical entry-level education:** High school diploma or equivalent
  - **Work experience in a related occupation:** Less than 5 years
  - **Typical on-the-job-training:** None

First-Line Supervisors of Helpers, Laborers, and Material Movers, Hand

(O*NET 53-1021.00 and 53-1021.01)

Directly supervise and coordinate the activities of helpers, laborers, or material movers.

- **2012 employment:** 171,600

- **May 2012 median annual wage:** $45,180

- **Projected employment change, 2012-22:**
  - **Number of new jobs:** 14,700
  - **Growth rate:** 9 percent (about as fast as average)

- **Education and training:**
  - **Typical entry-level education:** High school diploma or equivalent
  - **Work experience in a related occupation:** Less than 5 years
  - **Typical on-the-job-training:** None

First-Line Supervisors of Transportation and Material-Moving Machine and Vehicle Operators

(O*NET 53-1031.00)

Directly supervise and coordinate activities of transportation and material-moving machine and vehicle operators and helpers.

- **2012 employment:** 201,000

- **May 2012 median annual wage:** $53,240

- **Projected employment change, 2012-22:**
  - **Number of new jobs:** 17,300
  - **Growth rate:** 9 percent (about as fast as average)

- **Education and training:**
  - **Typical entry-level education:** High school diploma or equivalent
  - **Work experience in a related occupation:** Less than 5 years
  - **Typical on-the-job-training:** None

Airfield Operations Specialists

(O*NET 53-2022.00)

Ensure the safe takeoff and landing of commercial and military aircraft. Duties include coordinating between air-traffic control and maintenance personnel, dispatching, using airfield landing and navigational aids, implementing airfield safety procedures, monitoring and maintaining flight records, and applying knowledge of weather information.

- **2012 employment:** 7,100

- **May 2012 median annual wage:** $48,080

- **Projected employment change, 2012-22:**
  - **Number of new jobs:** 400
  - **Growth rate:** 5 percent (slower than average)

- **Education and training:**
  - **Typical entry-level education:** High school diploma or equivalent
  - **Work experience in a related occupation:** None
  - **Typical on-the-job-training:** Long-term on-the-job training

Ambulance Drivers and Attendants, Except Emergency Medical Technicians

(O*NET 53-3011.00)

Drive ambulance or assist ambulance driver in transporting sick, injured, or convalescent persons. Assist in lifting patients.

- **2012 employment:** 18,900

- **May 2012 median annual wage:** $23,440

- **Projected employment change, 2012-22:**
  - **Number of new jobs:** 5,900
  - **Growth rate:** 31 percent (much faster than average)

- **Education and training:**
  - **Typical entry-level education:** High school diploma or equivalent
  - **Work experience in a related occupation:** None
  - **Typical on-the-job-training:** Moderate-term on-the-job training

Subway and Streetcar Operators

(O*NET 53-4041.00)

Operate and tend bridges, canal locks, and lighthouses to permit marine passage on inland waterways, near shores, and at danger points in waterway passages. May supervise such operations. Includes drawbridge operators, lock operators, and slip bridge operators.

- **2012 employment:** 9,000

- **May 2012 median annual wage:** $62,730

- **Projected employment change, 2012-22:**
  - **Number of new jobs:** 600
  - **Growth rate:** 6 percent (slower than average)

- **Education and training:**
  - **Typical entry-level education:** High school diploma or equivalent
  - **Work experience in a related occupation:** None
  - **Typical on-the-job-training:** Moderate-term on-the-job training

Bridge and Lock Tenders

(O*NET 53-6011.00)

Operate and tend bridges, canal locks, and lighthouses to permit marine passage on inland waterways, near shores, and at danger points in waterway passages. May supervise such operations. Includes drawbridge operators, lock operators, and slip bridge operators.

- **2012 employment:** 3,600

- **May 2012 median annual wage:** $45,940

- **Projected employment change, 2012-22:**
  - **Number of new jobs:** –100
  - **Growth rate:** –2 percent (little or no change)

- **Education and training:**
  - **Typical entry-level education:** High school diploma or equivalent
  - **Work experience in a related occupation:** None
  - **Typical on-the-job-training:** Short-term on-the-job training

Parking Lot Attendants

(O*NET 53-6021.00)

Park vehicles or issue tickets for customers in a parking lot or garage. May collect fee.

- **2012 employment:** 128,300

- **May 2012 median annual wage:** $19,540

- **Projected employment change, 2012-22:**
  - **Number of new jobs:** 9,300
  - **Growth rate:** 7 percent (slower than average)

- **Education and training:**
  - **Typical entry-level education:** Less than high school
  - **Work experience in a related occupation:** None
  - **Typical on-the-job-training:** Short-term on-the-job training

Automotive and Watercraft Service Attendants

(O*NET 53-6031.00)

Service automobiles, buses, trucks, boats, and other automotive or marine vehicles with fuel, lubricants, and accessories. Collect payment for services and supplies. May lubricate vehicle, change motor oil, install antifreeze, or replace lights or other accessories, such as windshield wiper blades or fan belts. May repair or replace tires.

- **2012 employment:** 109,500

- **May 2012 median annual wage:** $20,140

- **Projected employment change, 2012-22:**
  - **Number of new jobs:** 19,800
  - **Growth rate:** 18 percent (faster than average)

- **Education and training:**
  - **Typical entry-level education:** Less than high school
  - **Work experience in a related occupation:** None
  - **Typical on-the-job-training:** Short-term on-the-job training

Traffic Technicians

(O*NET 53-6041.00)

Work under the direction of a traffic engineer to conduct field studies determining volume and speed of traffic, effectiveness of signals, adequacy of lighting, and other factors that influence traffic conditions.

- **2012 employment:** 6,600

- **May 2012 median annual wage:** $38,380

- **Projected employment change, 2012-22:**
  - **Number of new jobs:** 800
  - **Growth rate:** 12 percent (about as fast as average)

- **Education and training:**
  - **Typical entry-level education:** High school diploma or equivalent
  - **Work experience in a related occupation:** None
  - **Typical on-the-job-training:** Moderate-term on-the-job training

Transportation Inspectors

(O*NET 53-6051.00, 53-6051.01, 53-6051.07, and 53-6051.08)

Inspect equipment or goods in connection with the safe transport of cargo or people. Includes rail transportation inspectors, such as freight inspectors; rail inspectors; and other inspectors of transportation vehicles, not elsewhere classified. Excludes "Transportation Security Screeners" (33-9093).

- **2012 employment:** 26,200

- **May 2012 median annual wage:** $63,680

- **Projected employment change, 2012-22:**
  - **Number of new jobs:** 2,900
  - **Growth rate:** 11 percent (about as fast as average)

- **Education and training:**
  - **Typical entry-level education:** High school diploma or equivalent
  - **Work experience in a related occupation:** None
  - **Typical on-the-job-training:** Moderate-term on-the-job training

Transportation Attendants, Except Flight Attendants

(O*NET 53-6061.00)

Provide services to ensure the safety and comfort of passengers aboard ships, buses, and trains or within the station or terminal. Perform duties such as greeting passengers, explaining the use of safety equipment, serving meals or beverages, and answering questions related to travel. Excludes "Baggage Porters and Bellhops" (39-6011).

- **2012 employment:** 23,300

- **May 2012 median annual wage:** $21,490

- **Projected employment change, 2012-22:**
  - **Number of new jobs:** 2,600
  - **Growth rate:** 11 percent (about as fast as average)

- **Education and training:**
  - **Typical entry-level education:** High school diploma or equivalent
  - **Work experience in a related occupation:** None
  - **Typical on-the-job-training:** Short-term on-the-job training

Gas Compressor and Gas Pumping Station Operators

(O*NET 53-7071.00)

Operate steam, gas, electric motor, or internal combustion engine-driven compressors. Transmit, compress, or recover gases, such as butane, nitrogen, hydrogen, and natural gas.

- **2012 employment:** 4,800

- **May 2012 median annual wage:** $51,150

- **Projected employment change, 2012-22:**
  - **Number of new jobs:** –100
  - **Growth rate:** –3 percent (decline)

- **Education and training:**
  - **Typical entry-level education:** Less than high school
  - **Work experience in a related occupation:** None
  - **Typical on-the-job-training:** Moderate-term on-the-job training

Pump Operators, Except Wellhead Pumpers

(O*NET 53-7072.00)

Tend, control, or operate power-driven, stationary, or portable pumps and manifold systems to transfer gases, oil, other liquids, slurries, or powdered materials to and from various vessels and processes.

- **2012 employment:** 13,200

- **May 2012 median annual wage:** $44,610

- **Projected employment change, 2012-22:**
  - **Number of new jobs:** 1,400
  - **Growth rate:** 11 percent (about as fast as average)

- **Education and training:**
  - **Typical entry-level education:** Less than high school
  - **Work experience in a related occupation:** None
  - **Typical on-the-job-training:** Moderate-term on-the-job training

Wellhead Pumpers

(O*NET 53-7073.00)

Operate power pumps and auxiliary equipment to produce and maintain the flow of oil or gas from wells in oilfields.

- **2012 employment:** 16,200

- **May 2012 median annual wage:** $45,690

- **Projected employment change, 2012-22:**
  - **Number of new jobs:** 2,400
  - **Growth rate:** 15 percent (faster than average)

- **Education and training:**
  - **Typical entry-level education:** Less than high school
  - **Work experience in a related occupation:** Less than 5 years
  - **Typical on-the-job-training:** Moderate-term on-the-job training

Mine Shuttle Car Operators

(O*NET 53-7111.00)

Operate diesel or electric-powered shuttle cars in underground mines to transport materials from the working face to mine cars or conveyors.

- **2012 employment:** 3,000

- **May 2012 median annual wage:** $52,110

- **Projected employment change, 2012-22:**
  - **Number of new jobs:** –100
  - **Growth rate:** –4 percent (decline)

- **Education and training:**
  - **Typical entry-level education:** Less than high school
  - **Work experience in a related occupation:** None
  - **Typical on-the-job-training:** Short-term on-the-job training

Tank Car, Truck, and Ship Loaders

(O*NET 53-7121.00)

Use material-moving equipment to load and unload chemicals and bulk solids, such as coal, sand, and grain, into or from tank cars, trucks, or ships. May perform a variety of other tasks relating to the shipment of products. May gauge or sample shipping tanks and test them for leaks.

- **2012 employment:** 12,500

- **May 2012 median annual wage:** $44,100

- **Projected employment change, 2012-22:**
  - **Number of new jobs:** 300
  - **Growth rate:** 3 percent (slower than average)

- **Education and training:**
  - **Typical entry-level education:** Less than high school
  - **Work experience in a related occupation:** None
  - **Typical on-the-job-training:** Short-term on-the-job training

Employment Projections Methodology

Bureau of Labor Statistics projections of industry and occupational employment are developed in a series of six interrelated steps, each of which is based on a different procedure or model and assumptions: labor force, aggregate economy, final demand (GDP) by consuming sector and product, industry output, industry employment, and employment and openings by occupation. The results produced by each step are key inputs to following steps, and the sequence may be repeated multiple times to allow feedback and to ensure consistency. Further detail is presented in Chapter 13 of the BLS Handbook of Methods (http://www.bls.gov/opub/hom/).

Labor Force

Labor force projections are based on expectations of the future size and composition of the population, as well as on the trends in labor force participation rates of different age, gender, race, and ethnic groups, a total of 136 separate categories.

The U.S. Census Bureau prepares projections of the resident population. The size and composition of the population are affected by the interaction of three variables: births, deaths, and net immigration. More information about population projections is available on the Census Bureau web site. BLS converts these population projections to the civilian noninstitutional population concept, a basis for labor force projections. BLS develops participation rate projections using data from the Current Population Survey (CPS) conducted for BLS by the Census Bureau.

For this latest round of projections, the Census Bureau's 2012 population projections based on Census 2010 population weights were used as the base for the labor force projections. The size and composition of the population affect not only the labor force projections, but the projected composition of GDP and the demand for workers in various industries and occupations.

BLS currently disaggregates the various race and ethnic categories into 5-year age groups by gender. Participation rates for these groups are smoothed, using a robust-resistant nonlinear filter and then transformed into logits. The logits of the participation rates are then extrapolated linearly by regressing against time and then extending the fitted series to or beyond the target year. When the series are transformed back into participation rates, the projected path is nonlinear.

After the labor force participation rates have been projected, they are reviewed from the perspectives of the time path, the cross section in the target year, and cohort patterns of participation. The projected participation rate for each age, gender, race, and ethnicity group is multiplied by the corresponding projection of the civilian noninstitutional population to obtain the labor force projection for that group. The groups are then summed to obtain the total civilian labor force. The labor force outlook plays a critical role in long run macroeconomic trends and is therefore the most important exogenous data within the BLS macroeconomic projections.

Aggregate Economy

BLS' macroeconomic projections are produced using the MA/US model, licensed from Macroeconomic Advisers, LLC (MA). The 2012—2022 projections are the first to employ the new model, which was introduced in late 2012; previously the Bureau relied on MA's Washington University Macro Model (WUMM). MA/US has the same foundations as WUMM: consumption follows a life-cycle model and investment is based on a neoclassical model. Foreign sector estimates rely on forecasts from Oxford Economics. However, many improvements were made; most notably, the model is explicitly designed to reach a full-employment solution in the target years. Within MA/US, a sub-model calculates an estimate of potential output from the nonfarm business sector, based upon full-employment estimates of the sector's hours worked and output per hour. Error correction models are embedded into MA/US to align the model's solution with the full-employment submodel.

Certain critical variables set the parameters for the nation's economic growth and determine in large part the trend that GDP will follow. In developing the macroeconomic projections, BLS elects to determine these critical variables through research and modeling, and then supplies them to the MA/US model as exogenous variables. The in-house labor force projections, described above, are of particular importance, as they are the primary constraint on future economic growth. Other fundamental exogenous variables in the model include energy prices and assumptions about fiscal and monetary policy. For the 2022 projections, initial estimates of key economic variables, as well as the underlying exogenous assumptions, were reviewed by a panel of Federal economists. The final solution was evaluated for consistency with the detailed output and employment projections. The specific assumptions and target variables for the 2022 projections are presented in the December 2013 *Monthly Labor Review*.

Final Demand

Demand is the key determinant in explaining future jobs. Therefore, underlying the projections of employment by industries and occupations, BLS publishes a projected final demand matrix consisting of roughly 120 demand categories by 200 commodity groups. Aggregate gross domestic product (GDP) as well as some underlying subcomponent categories are determined by the MA/US model and serve as constraints to BLS' more detailed projections of GDP. Solutions supplied by MA/US include the aggregates projections of: personal consumption expenditures (PCE), private investment in equipment and software (PIES), residential and nonresidential construction, change in private inventories (CIPI), exports and imports of goods and services, as well as consumption and investment of federal defense, nondefense, and State & Local government. BLS uses several behavioral models as well as distributional trends and/or assumptions in breaking out these twelve categories of GDP supplied by the macro model to the detailed matrix of final demand data.

Personal consumption expenditures (PCE) and Private Investment in Equipment and Software (PIES) are projected using the Houthakker-Taylor model[1] and the Modified Neoclassical Model of Investment. Projections are made for 76 PCE product categories and 28 PIES asset groups consistent with the national income and product account (NIPA) data published by the Bureau of Economic Analysis (BEA).

These column totals for PCE and PIES are adjusted as necessary to ensure consistency between the aggregate projection from the MA/US solution and the detailed estimates based on the Houthakker-Taylor and Modified Neoclassical models. Column totals for the remaining components of final demand are output directly from the MA/US software. Although net exports is equivalent, adjustments are made to the MA/US projections of trade goods and services to account for re-exports and re-imports, effectively transforming the data from a NIPA based estimate to an I-O framework.

Bridge tables are developed based on the most recent Benchmark and annual Input-Output Accounts published by BEA. For some columns the bridge table is held constant from the last historical year while other components forecast the bridge table based on trends over the historical series. The bridge tables are used to distribute projected column controls out to the roughly 200 commodity groups or rows within the final demand matrix. The only exception to the use of bridge tables occurs in the column of Change in Private Inventories (CIPI). Business inventories by detailed commodities are projected based on a two stage least squares model where inventories are regressed on lagged values of both inventories and commodity output. Results are aggregated and adjusted to conform to the projection of CIPI from the macro model.

As a last step, data are converted from purchaser value to producer value. Margin columns are projected for each component of final demand. Summing across the rows of a particular component (ie. PCE) with its related margin columns (consisting of transportation costs as well as wholesale and retail markups), results in a vector of producer value data by detailed commodity. For example, in buying a sweater, the margin column would subtract the retail markup by the vendor from the textile commodity row and move that value to the retail trade commodity row. In estimating employment, it is helpful to know the producer value of the data as it helps separate employment in the wholesale, retail, and transportation industries from the remaining economy.

Adjustments to the initial estimates of the final demand matrix are made based on research and analysis by industry experts including information pertaining to energy forecasts, existing and expected shares of the domestic output, known changes to trade agreements, expected government political and policy changes, and so forth.

Industry Output

Industry output is derived using a set of projected input-output tables consisting of two basic matrices for each year, a "use" and a "make" table. The use table consists of final demand, from the preceding step, together with intermediate demand and value added. The use table shows the use of commodities by each industry as inputs into its production process. The make table allocates commodity output to the industry in which it is the primary commodity output and to those industries in which it is secondary. In percentage form, the use table provides the direct requirements table and the make table becomes a market share table. These two tables are then used to create total requirements tables which yield the projected levels of industry and commodity output required to satisfy projected final demand.

Industry Employment

The next step is to project the industry employment necessary to produce the projected output. To do so, projected output is used in regression analysis to estimate hours worked by industry. The regression model utilizes industry output, industry wage rate relative to industry output price, and time. Additionally, average weekly hours are derived as a time trend for each industry. From these hours' data, projected wage and salary employment by industry is derived.

For each industry, the share of self-employed and unpaid family workers is extrapolated using historical data. These data are derived from the ratio of self-employed and unpaid family workers to total employment and extrapolated based on time and the unemployment rate. The ratio, along with the projected level of wage and salary employment is then used to derive the projected number of self-employed and unpaid family workers and total employment by industry. Projected average weekly hours and total hours for self-employed and unpaid family workers also are derived from these data.

Implied output per hour (labor productivity) is calculated for each industry for both the total and for wage and salary employees. These data are used to evaluate the projected output and employment.

Factors Affecting Industry Employment

Many assumptions underlie the BLS projections of the aggregate economy and of industry output, productivity, and employment. Often, these assumptions bear specifically on econometric factors, such as the aggregate unemployment rate, the anticipated time path of labor productivity, and expectations regarding the Federal budget surplus or deficit. Other assumptions deal with factors that affect industry-specific measures of economic activity.

Detailed industry employment projections are based largely on econometric models, which, by their very nature, project future economic behavior on the basis of a continuation of economic relationships that held in the past. For the most part, the determinants of industry employment are expressed both in the structure of the models' equations and as adjustments imposed on the specific equations to ensure that the models are indeed making a smooth transition from actual historical data to projected results. However, one of the most important steps associated with the preparation of the BLS projections is a detailed review of the results by analysts who have studied recent economic trends in specific industries. In some cases, the results of the aggregate and industry models are modified because of the analysts' judgment that historical relationships need to be redefined in some manner.

Table 2.7 **Employment and Output by Industry** (http://www.bls.gov/emp/ep_table_207.htm) presents historical and projected information about employment and output for aggregate and detailed industries. Industry sector employment projections prepared in the Division of Industry Employment Projections (DIEP) used comprehensive modeling techniques that estimate output as well as employment.

Occupational Employment

To allocate projected industry employment to occupations, a set of industry-occupation matrices are developed. These include a base-year employment matrix for 2012 and a projected-year employment matrix for 2022. These matrices, referred to collectively as the National Employment Matrix, constitute a comprehensive employment database. For each occupation, the Matrix provides a detailed breakdown of employment by industry and class of worker. Similarly, for each industry and class of worker, the Matrix provides a detailed breakdown of occupational employment.

Base-year employment data for wage and salary workers, self-employed workers, and unpaid family workers come from a variety of sources, and measure total employment as a count of jobs, not a count of individual workers. This concept is different from that used by another measure familiar to many readers, the Current Population Survey's total employment as a count of the number of workers. The Matrix's total employment concept is also different from the BLS Current Employment Statistics (CES) total employment measure. Although the CES measure is also a count of jobs, it covers nonfarm payroll jobs, whereas the Matrix includes all jobs.

The Matrix does not include employment estimates for every industry which employs an occupation, or every occupation employed within an industry. Some data are not released due to confidentiality and/or quality reasons[2]. Employment data in the National Employment Matrix are presented in thousands. Detailed data may not sum to totals because of rounding or because some data are not released.

2012 Base-Year Employment

For most industries, the Occupational Employment Statistics (OES) survey provides data for the occupational staffing patterns—the distribution of wage and salary employment by occupation in each industry—and Current Employment Statistics (CES) data provide information on total wage and salary employment in each nonfarm industry. Estimates of occupational employment for each industry are derived by multiplying each occupation's proportion–or ratio– of employment in each industry, based on OES survey data, by CES industry employment.

BLS staff obtains industry and occupational employment data for workers in all agricultural industries except logging[3], workers in private households, self-employed workers, and unpaid family workers from the Current Population Survey. Data are used for workers' primary job only. CPS data are coded using the 2010 Census occupation classification system. Although the Census system is based on the Standard Occupational Classification (SOC) system used by OES, it does not provide the same level of detail. CPS employment data were proportionally distributed to detailed SOC occupations using the employment distribution from the OES data.

Total base-year employment for an occupation is the sum of employment across all industries and class-of-worker categories— the combination of wage and salary, self-employed, and unpaid family workers. Occupational employment within each industry, divided by total wage and salary employment in each industry, yields the occupational distribution ratios used to project occupational employment. These ratios are referred to as staffing patterns.

2022 Projected-Year Employment

Projected-year employment data for industries and class-of-worker categories are first developed at a higher level of aggregation, and then distributed to corresponding detailed Matrix industries and by class of worker.

To derive projected-year staffing patterns, BLS economists place base-year staffing patterns under an iterative process of qualitative and quantitative analyses. They examine historical staffing pattern data and conduct research on factors that may affect demand for occupations within given industries during the projection decade. Such factors include shifts in product mix, and changes in technology or business practices. Once these factors are identified, change factors are developed which give the proportional change in an occupation's share of industry employment over the 10-year projection period. These change factors are applied to the 2012 occupational staffing patterns to derive projected staffing patterns. An occupation's projected share of an industry may increase, decrease, or remain the same, depending on the change factors and underlying rationales.

For each industry, the projected-year employment is multiplied by the projected-year occupational ratio to yield projected-year wage and salary occupational employment for the industry. Occupational employment data for self-employed and unpaid family workers are projected separately. Total projected-year occupational employment is the sum of the projected employment figures for wage and salary, self-employed, and unpaid family workers.

Factors Affecting Demand for Occupations within Industries

BLS projections of wage and salary employment are developed within the framework of an industry-occupation matrix, which shows the occupational distribution in each industry—the proportion of each industry's employment which each occupation comprises. Historical data indicate that the occupational distribution within industries shifts over time as the demand for some occupations changes relative to that of other occupations.

Among the various factors that can affect the demand for workers in an occupation in particular industries are technology, business practices, the mix of goods and services produced, the size of business establishments, and offshore outsourcing. BLS staff analyzes each occupation in the matrix to identify the factors that are likely to cause an increase or decrease in demand for that occupation within particular industries. Their analyses incorporate judgments about new trends that may influence occupational demand, such as the use of the Internet and electronic commerce.

Estimating Replacement Needs

Projections of job growth provide valuable insight into future employment opportunities because each new job created is an opening for a worker entering an occupation. However, opportunities also result when workers leave their occupations and need to be replaced. In most occupations, these replacement needs provide more job openings than employment growth does. Further detail is presented in Estimating Occupational Replacement Needs technical documentation (http://www.bls.gov/emp/ep_replacements.htm).

Measures of Education and Training

BLS provides information about education and training requirements for hundreds of occupations. In the BLS education and training system, each of the occupations for which the office publishes projections data is assigned separate categories for education, work experience, and on-the-job training. Occupations can be grouped in order to create estimates of the education and training needs for the labor force as a whole and estimates of the outlook for occupations with various types of education or training needs. In addition, educational attainment data for each occupation are presented to show the level of education achieved by current workers. Further detail is presented in Measures of Education and Training technical documentation (http://www.bls.gov/emp/ep_education_tech.htm).

[1]Houthakker, H. S. and Lester D. Taylor, "Consumer Demand in the United States: Analyses and Projections", 1970 Harvard University Press, Cambridge, MA.
[2]As discussed in the section on the 2012 base-year employment, Occupational Employment Statistics (OES) survey data are an input to the Matrix. For information on why OES estimates may be withheld from publication, see http://www.bls.gov/oes/oes_ques.htm#other.
[3]Staffing pattern data for the Logging industry come from the OES and industry employment data come from the CES.

Occupational Information Network Coverage

The Occupational Information Network (O*NET), which replaced the Dictionary of Occupational Titles, is used by public employment service offices to classify and place jobseekers. The O*NET was developed by job analysts. The information on job duties, knowledge and skills, education and training, and other occupational characteristics comes directly from workers and employers. Information on O*NET is available from O*NET Project, U.S. Department of Labor/ETA, 200 Constitution Ave. NW, Room N-5637, Washington, DC 20210-0001. (202) 693-3660. www.doleta.gov/programs/onet.

The O*NET reflects the 2010 Standard Occupational Classification (SOC) system. Presently with 845 detailed occupations, the SOC represents the federal government's most recent effort to analyze the occupational structure in the United States and to provide a universal occupational classification system. All federal agencies that collect occupational data adhere to the SOC. Information on the SOC, including its occupational structure, is available on the Internet: www.bls.gov/soc.

Occupational profiles in this 2014–2015 edition of the *OOH* list the SOC codes that relate to, or match the definitions used in, the Bureau's Occupational Employment Statistics (OES) survey—the principal source of occupational employment data in the *OOH*. The SOC codes are listed in each profile in one column of the Employment Projections data table. All related O*NET-SOC occupations also appear in the table below. The table is arranged by the O*NET-SOC code, followed by the O*NET-SOC title. The O*NET-SOC title provides a page reference to the corresponding *OOH* profile or listing in the section called "Occupations Not Covered in Detail."

Index

C

G

H

I

N

O

P

Q

R

W